CW00959746
ESSO
DANKA
NEC

The PFA Premier & Football League Players' Records 1946 – 1998

The PFA Premier & Football League Players' Records 1946 – 1998

Edited And Compiled By Barry J. Hugman

Assistant editors

Alan Platt and Michael Featherstone

Queen Anne Press

Queen Anne Press
is a division of Lennard Associates
Mackerye End, Harpenden
Hertfordshire, AL5 5DR

First published in Great Britain in 1998

A CIP catalogue record for this book
is available from the British Library

ISBN 1 85291 585 4

Cover design by Design2Print
Typesetting and internal design by Typecast (Artwork & Design)
8 Mudford Road, Yeovil BA21 4AA

Printed and bound in Great Britain by
Butler & Tanner, London and Frome

CONTENTS

FOREWORD

The idea of compiling a list of every footballer to have played in the Football League since the Second World War would be enough to drive most journalists into an early grave, or a football statistician into Seventh Heaven! So, where exactly do you start on such a project? How many years of research are needed to complete the job? On the face of it, the task would seem an impossible one!

However, Barry Hugman and his team of enthusiasts, have, without question, given us the definitive record of all our professional (and a few amateur) players who have graced the Football and Premier Leagues.

To be good enough to be selected for a Premier or Football League club's first team is proof enough of a players ability. You only have to ask all those who didn't make the grade! So, here then is the official list of all those who actually wore their club colours in League battle. And, of course, this book also shows the transfers, plus the career records of every single player. All of these men have belonged to the Professional Footballers' Association and we at the PFA are proud to see such a magnificently produced record of the careers of so many members, past and present.

In my opinion, this book will give hours and hours of pleasure to ex-players reminiscing, present-day players comparing records, plus supporters of all ages, who can check on players they saw years and years ago, or even only last season. The statistics, and those long lost names from the distant past provide a remarkable cast list.

We are delighted to be involved with this publication and anticipate referring to it time and time again, and our thanks go to Barry and his team for all their dedicated hard work.

Gordon Taylor
Chief Executive
Professional Footballers' Association

INTRODUCTION
by Barry J. Hugman
(Editor & Compiler)

This is the fifth edition of this now well-established work of reference on post-war footballers. Since the first edition appeared in 1980, published by Rothmans, I have striven to improve its accuracy, not only by updating the statistics and listing new entries for players who made their Football League debuts since the last edition, but also correcting, where necessary, the details of players long since retired.

When I first started this compendium in the mid-1970s, the only source of data were the hardy football perennials – the *News of the World* and *News Chronicle (later Playfair) Football Annuals* – which listed each player's appearances and goals for the previous season. During the 1980s, a number of football statisticians began to chronicle the detailed history of their favourite clubs, match by match, with reference to Football League archives and local newspapers. Much of their research has since come to fruition in the shape of club histories, which include line-ups for every match played, and, at the time of going to press, there are at least 80 such books in circulation. A big thank you should also be given to the Association of Football Statisticians, who, through Tony Brown, are now publishing the definitive histories of clubs yet to be dealt with.

All their researches have been cross-referenced with the data contained in previous editions of this book and many discrepancies in appearances and goals have been noted. In most cases the discrepancies were trival, a question of one or two appearances or goals difference. In a few cases they were significant, usually when players with the same (or similar) surname played in the same season for the same club. If the FLPR team are satisfied that the research has been done correctly and that the statistics continued in these books are more reliable than the figures in by-gone football annuals, we have corrected our records accordingly.

It should be noted, however, that while an appearance in a particular match is a matter of fact, goalscorers are often a matter of opinions. In a goalmouth scramble, a goal may be credited to one player by the assembled journalists sitting 100 yards from the action and reported as such by the press the following day, whilst the club, following a post-mortem, credits the goal to another of its players. In such cases we accept the opinion of the club rather than the press. However, there are other cases where the club is anxious to credit a goal to one of its own players when it is quite manifestly an own goal. For example, the misjudged back pass, the misdirected shot deflected into goal by an opposing defender, or the goalkeeper stepping over the line after safely catching a high ball. Such examples we consider as "own goals" and not credited to any player. As a result of these differences of interpretation, there are inevitably some small discrepancies between the goalscoring figures of some players in this book and those logged by other sources.

Players Names: As far as is humanly possible, we have listed players in alphabetic order, firstly by surname and then by christian names. However, in cases where players are better known by their second or third christian name, we have listed them under their commonly used name. For example Mark Hughes of Manchester United was christened "Leslie Mark" but will be found under "Mark". Philip Lee Jones of Liverpool will be found under "Lee". To do otherwise could cause confusion to the reader searching for the entry of a player with a very common surname. Other players are not recorded under the family surname. For example, the Brazilian, Mirandinha, of Newcastle United, is in fact "Francisco da Silva", but is listed under his adopted moniker rather than his family name. In the case of double-barrelled surnames we have taken a pragmatic view, according to the name most commonly used by themselves or the media. Thus, Ian

Storey-Moore and Forbes Phillipson-Masters will be found under their full names while the Martin-Chambers brothers, Derek and Philip, will be found under "Chambers" and Jeffrey Thompson-Minton, under "Minton". In many cases players were known by a corruption of their christian names or by a totally different nickname, such as the Brentford goalkeeper, "Sonny" Feehan, christened Ignatius. In these cases, players are listed under their christened name with their familiar moniker shown in brackets afterwards.

Birthplaces: The purpose of showing birthplaces is to indicate the area of the British Isles a player originates from. However, this is frequently misleading. Many players were born overseas, either as sons of fathers serving in the armed forces stationed in West Germany, or in further flung former colonies. Their birthplace does not, however, indicate their nationality, which is conferred on them by their parentage. A player may be born in one area, but grow up in another. In such cases the place of education is more meaningful than place of birth. Some players were born while their parents were on holiday, such as the Kimble brothers, Alan and Garry, in Poole (Dorset). In their particular case, as it was known to us, the birthplace is shown as the family home of Dagenham. Birthplaces are taken from birth certificates, copies of which are deposited with the Football League when the player is registered by a club. However, birth certificates may only indicate an area of the county, such as a county or the birth registration district with an antiquated name, often not stating the town or village of birth. All persons born in the counties of Gloucestershire and Worcestershire are registered as born in the county town. Those born in County Durham are shown by obscure registration districts such as "Central South-East" and "North-West", which do not indicate the town of origin. Most players shown with their birthplace as "Ormskirk" were almost certainly born in the neighbouring new town of Skelmersdale. Some players were born in maternity hospitals located in different administrative areas from the parential home, such as Rochford (for Southend) and Orsett (for Grays and Thurrock). In cases where the actual birthplace is known to the authors, the original information as shown in earlier editions has been corrected. In some cases where the birthplace was an obscure country village, or suburb of a large city, the name of the nearest market town or city has been substituted. However, in the case of mining villages which produced many fine players, we have taken care to preserve their identity. For players born outside the British Isles and Ireland, only the name of the country is given. Irishmen born outside of Dublin and Belfast are indicated by (Ire) and (NI), respectively, while players from the numerous Caribbean islands are indicated by (WI) for the West Indies. In some cases the following code is used to determine the county of origin: (Cam) Cambridgeshire; (Dm) Durham; (Dst) Dorset; (Dy) Derbyshire; (Ex) Essex; (Kt) Kent; (Lei) Leicestershire; (Lk) Lanarkshire; (Nd) Northumberland; (Nk) Norfolk; (Nts) Nottinghamshire; (Sf) Suffolk; (Sx) Sussex; (IoW) Isle of Wight.

Birthdate: Since these are taken from the Premiership and Football League's records, which copy the birth certificate of every professional, this evidence is regarded as incontrovertible, although some discrepancies with club histories have been noted, mainly in the year of birth. However, when we are satisfied that a transcribing error has occurred we have corrected the original birthdate.

League Clubs: Self explanatory.

Source (or Previous Club): This column indicates a player's origins, whether from outside the P/FL or within the ranks of the Leagues. For the latter the following code is used:

Jnrs = Junior players signed from school/college, without serving an apprenticeship or trainee period.
App = Apprentice signing prior to 1986.
YT = Trainee. This rank was introduced in 1986 and includes players sponsored by the Government's Youth Training Scheme.
Tr = Transfers (including free transfers).
L = Loan signing, or temporary transfer, shown only when the player made an appearance.

For players signed from overseas clubs, the following code for countries is employed:
(Arg) Argentina; (Aus) Australia; (Aut) Austria; (Bar) Barbados; (Bel) Belgium; (Ber) Bermuda; (Bol) Bolivia; (Br) Brazil; (Can) Canada; (Col) Colombia; (CR) Costa Rica; (Cro) Croatia; (Cyp) Cyprus; (Cz); Czechoslovakia; (Den) Denmark; (Est) Estonia; (Fin) Finland; (Fr) France; (Ger) Germany; (Gre) Greece; (HK) Hong Kong; (Hun) Hungary; (Ice) Iceland; (Ind) India; (Isr) Israel; (It) Italy; (Jap) Japan; (Mal) Malaysia; (Neth) Netherlands; (NZ) New Zealand; (Nor) Norway; (Pol) Poland; (Por) Portugal; (Rom) Romania; (Rus) Russia; (St V) St Vincent; (SA) South Africa; (Sp) Spain; (Swe) Sweden; (Swi) Switzerland; (Tu) Turkey; (Ur) Uruguay; (Yug) Yugoslavia; (Zim) Zimbabwe.

Date Signed: The date given by month/year is when the player signed professional forms, or as in the case of non-contract players and amateurs, the date of signing is that of the status indicated, while trainees who made an appearance, but did not sign professional forms, are shown by the use of •. For players first signed on loan, before a permanent transfer was arranged, the date of signing is that of the loan transfer, except when the player returned to his former club and made further appearances. Non-League (N/L) is only shown where the compilers have not been able to find the necessary date in question.

Seasons Played: The year shown is the first year of the season played. Thus, 1997 indicates the season 1997-98, "1979-85" means that the player made his debut in 1979-80 and his last appearance in 1985-86, but does not necessarily mean that he played in every intervening season.

Appearances, Subs and Goals: The statistics shown are for Premiership and Football League matches only. Cup games and end of season play-offs are not included, nor are appearances made for League clubs before they entered the League or in temporary absence (e.g. Lincoln City 1987-88 and Darlington 1989-90). Whilst other sources have aggregated full and substitute appearances into a single total, we consider it important to maintain the distinction. Most substitutions occur in the final quarter of the game and we feel that one full appearance, plus 17 substitute appearances, is not the same as 18 full appearances.

Positions:

(G)	Goalkeeper	(D)	Defender – general
(RB)	Right Back	(LB)	Left Back
(RWB)	Right Wing Back	(LWB)	Left Wing Back
(FB)	Both Full-Back positions	(CD)	Central Defender
(HB)	Half Back – wing and centre	(CH)	Centre Half
(RH)	Right Half	(LH)	Left Half
(WH)	Wing Half – left or right	(M)	Midfield – central
(RM)	Right-sided Midfielder	(LM)	Left-sided Midfielder
(OR)	Outside Right	(OL)	Outside Left
(RW)	Right Winger	(LW)	Left Winger
(W)	Winger – either flank	(IF)	Inside Forward
(CF)	Centre Forward	(F)	Forward – general

The position shown for each player is that in which he played most frequently, or is most commonly associated. However, today, many players frequently switch between defence and midfield, or between defence and attack. In such cases their two most common positions are shown e.g. (FB/M), (CD/F), (M/F). The nomenclature of playing positions has changed considerably since the last war. From 1946 to the early 1960s it was widely assumed that teams played a 2-3-5 formation with two full backs, three half backs and five forwards. In fact, the true formation was 3-3-4, since the change in the off-side law in the 1930s when the centre half was converted to centre back and one inside forward was withdrawn into a deeper position.

Despite all the changes, the term "centre half" still persists up to the present day, whilst, until the invention of the term "midfield" in the mid 1960s, inside forwards could be either deep lying schemers such as Johnny Haynes (Fulham), or lethal goalscorers such as Ted Phillips (Ipswich Town). In 1958 Brazil introduced 4-2-4 to the world, when winning the World Cup in Sweden. Under this system, one wing half was converted to twin centre back, while the other wing half, plus an inside forward, patrolled the middle of the park. Although this system was copied by many English clubs, it was not entirely successful since it required two talented and hard-working players in the central positions. After Alf Ramsey won the 1966 World Cup for England with a 4-3-3 system, with one winger withdrawn to augment the midfield, most English clubs adopted the same system and when Ramsey dispensed with wingers altogether with a 4-4-2 system for the 1970 World Cup in Mexico, the orthodox attacking winger disappeared for several years from the English game, to be replaced by workaholic midfielders. By 1970 the terms "centre half", "wing half", "inside forward" and "centre forward", "outside right" and "outside left" were virtually obsolescent, to be replaced by "centre backs" (or defenders), "midfielders", "twin strikers" and, occasionally, "wingers". Happily, the orthodox winger returned to favour in the 1980s with a corresponding increase in the goal rate, as some clubs reverted to 4-3-3 instead of 4-4-2. Since the late 1980s many teams have played with three central defenders, with one deployed behind the other two as a "sweeper" and the two full backs pushed forward into midfield as auxiliary wingers. The result has been the emergence of a 3-5-2 formation, with overcrowded midfield areas, or a more fluid 3-4-3 system with one winger deployed as an auxiliary forward.

Since the first edition we have implemented several changes, including that of listing the complete career record of all players who played in the Football League prior to the last war. This takes into account famous players like Sir Stanley Matthews, who played for eight seasons before the outbreak of war and for nearly 20 after, and also many other stars whose careers ran parallel with a man such as Stan Cullis. These are the players who had lost the best years of their football life because of hostilities and retired early into the post-war period. Previous editions showed Cullis as having played only 37 games for "Wolves", whereas, in fact, he played 152 times between 1934-35 and 1946-47. This time round, we are introducing full christian names for the first time, along with many additional notifications of players who have unfortunately deceased, provided by Michael Featherstone, and will continue to bring on board relevant information as and when it becomes available.

As we have stated in previous editions, one thing is for sure . . . if they have played in the post-war Football League and Premiership, they are included within the pages of this book and somebody, somewhere, sometime, will look them up. *Premier & Football League Players' Records* is a testament to all of the men who have donned the colours of their specific side since 1946-47 and to the Professional Footballers' Association who have magnificently supported their members throughout that period.

Finally, we have tried without success to trace birth and birthplace details for the following:-
John A. Charlton (Gateshead), Joe Cini (Q.P.R.), Len Davies (Southend), William E. Davies (Crewe), David Ellis (Bury, Halifax and Barrow), James Grant (Brighton), Michael Gray (Aldershot and Watford), William Johnston (Barrow), Arthur Jones (Rochdale), James M. Jones (Hull), John Jones (Bradford City), Stan J. Jones (Crewe), James J. Kelly (Barrow), Michael J. Kelly (Wolves and Crewe), Eryk Kubicki (York), William McClean (New Brighton), Alf Morris (Accrington), John Peat (Workington), Joe Riley (Darlington), Alex Shaw (Crewe), Alan Smith (Hull), Alf Smith (Walsall), George T. Smith (Walsall), Jim Smith (Burnley and Leyton Orient), John Smith (Ipswich), Tommy Teasdale (Hull), Adam Wasilewski (Rochdale), Ken Williams (Watford), and Robert Wilson (Workington).
If anyone can help with details, additonal to what we already have within the pages of this book, please write to Michael Featherstone, c/o 6a River Court, Ickleford, Herts. SG5 3UD.

ACKNOWLEDGEMENTS

With *Football League Players' Records* now in its fifth edition, I would once again like to thank the many experts without whose help this book would not have been updated as effectively.

The assistant editor, Alan Platt, is by profession a freelance transport planner whose most recent assignments have been abroad. He first introduced himself to me as long ago as 1981, following the release of the first edition. His help on the ever continuing project has been invaluable, especially in the area of current players, which he researches diligently. Unlike many schoolboys he did not take an interest in soccer until reaching the age of 14, but from that moment he was hooked. From 1960 onwards he has kept detailed records on all Football League clubs and their players. During 1985 to 1986 he contributed to the Chesterfield match programme, but more recently he has thrown himself wholeheartedly into the tremendous amount of research that is required to make FLPRs the "Bible" that it has hopefully become.

Another important member of the production team, and also an assistant editor, is Michael Featherstone. Michael was a willing helper when I first perceived the idea for such a book way back in 1975. His speciality is in researching births and deaths, something he also does for the various cricketing societies and the new wave of soccer histories that have begun to be produced over the last 20 years or so, with Tony Matthews and Anton Rippon of Breedon Books, leading the way. He started out by collecting both cricket and football information, often topping up with visits to the Colindale National Newspaper Library. Eventually, he joined Ray Spiller's Association of Football Statisticians after being introduced by his good friend, the late Morley Farror. He has also contributed to the *British Boxing Yearbook, The Olympic Games: Complete Track & Field Results 1896-1988, A Who's Who of Cricketers, The Official Football League Yearbook, PFA Footballers' Factfile*, and many other publications.

More recently, I have received invaluable help from Jim Creasy and Mike Davage, the editor of *Canary Citizens, The Official History of Norwich City FC*. They have been involved in football for a good many years now and are currently compiling a Football League Players' Records covering the period between the two wars. With their vast pre-war expertise, I asked them for help when it came to producing complete career records for men who had played prior to 1946. Both men responded brilliantly, so much so, that after much research between us, I have managed to include these records in FLPRs. At the same time, I would like to think that we have helped them in no little way, proving the point that without a great deal of teamwork a major football publication, such as this, would just not be possible.

Also, I would like to place on record my thanks to all the editors of the various club histories that have been published since the first edition of *Premier and Football League Players' Records*. My gratitude is also extended to all the contributors of the *PFA Footballers' Factfile*, an annual work which went much of the way in updating this edition. Recently, Gareth Davies, who is co-editing the forthcoming Wrexham who's who, aptly named Robins of the Racecourse, advised me that after all these years he had discovered a new player. It transpired that Derek Hughes, an amateur who played one game for Wrexham in 1961-62, had long been confused with David, who later played for Tranmere. This then is one of the delights of such a work and something that makes it so rewarding.

Once again I would like to show my appreciation for the support given by Gordon Taylor, the chief executive, and Brendon Batson of the Professional Footballers' Association, who have always recognised that this book is a testament to their members, both past and present. My thanks also go to the other sponsors of the book – Windsor, the game's leading insurance brokers, and Nationwide, who sponsor the Football League. To produce such an epic, one has to have a good working relationship with the controlling bodies and I am exceedingly grateful to all those at the Football League, such as Sheila Andrew, Debbie Birch, and Jonathan Hargreaves, and Mike Foster, Adrian Cook and Mike Kelleher at the Premiership, for their help in establishing good, solid, and reliable information.

Finally, I must thank Adrian Stephenson, the publisher, for his faith in FLPRs; Jean Bastin, the typesetter, for her many months of patient and time consuming work which would drive the average person into the ground; and Jennifer Hugman, my wife, for reading and correcting many hours worth of galleys.

Barry J. Hugman

League Club	Source	Date Signed	Seasons Played	Apps	Subs	Gls
AAS Einar Jan						
Norway, 12 October, 1955 Norwegian Int						(CD)
Nottingham F.	Bayem Munich (Ger)	03.81	80-81	20	1	1
ABBISS Keith Douglas						
Hatfield, 26 April, 1932						(LH)
Brighton & H.A.	Hitchin T.	10.57	59-60	19	-	3
ABBLEY Stephen George						
Liverpool, 19 March, 1957						(W)
Swindon T.	Parks	10.79	79-81	14	9	0
ABBOTT Gregory Stephen						
Coventry, 14 December, 1963						(M)
Coventry C.	App	01.82				
Bradford C.	Tr	09.82	82-90	256	25	38
Halifax T.	Tr	07.91	91	24	4	1
Hull C.	Guiseley	12.92	92-95	120	4	16
ABBOTT John						
Winsford, 25 May, 1943						(CH)
Crewe Alex.	Winsford U.	06.61	61-64	4	-	0
ABBOTT Peter Ashley						
Rotherham, 1 October, 1953						(F)
Manchester U.	App	10.70				
Swansea C.	Tr	02.74	73-75	34	7	3
Crewe Alex.	Hartford (USA)	08.76	76	27	4	8
Southend U.	Tr	07.77	77-78	26	1	4
ABBOTT Ronald Frederick						
Lambeth, 2 August, 1953						(CD)
Queens Park R.	App	07.71	73-78	32	14	4
ABBOTTS John						
Stoke, 10 October, 1924						(CH)
Port Vale	Ravenscliffe	05.49	50	3	-	0
ABEL Graham						
Runcorn, 17 September, 1960						(CD)
Chester C.	Northwich Vic.	10.85	85-92	287	9	30
Crewe Alex.	Tr	08.93	93	18	2	1
ABLETT Gary Ian						
Liverpool, 19 November, 1965 Eu21-1/E 'B'						(D)
Liverpool	App	11.83	86-91	103	6	1
Derby Co.	L	01.85	84	3	3	0
Hull C.	L	09.86	86	5	0	0
Everton	Tr	01.92	91-95	128	0	5
Sheffield U.	L	03.96	95	12	0	0
Birmingham C.	Tr	06.96	96-97	73	5	1
ABOU Samassi						
Ivory Coast, 4 August, 1973						(F)
West Ham U.	Cannes (Fr)	11.97	97	12	7	5
ABRAHAM Gareth John						
Merthyr Tydfil, 13 February, 1969						(CD)
Cardiff C.	YT	07.87	87-91	82	5	4
Hereford U.	Tr	01.93	92-93	48	1	2
ABRAHAMS Lawrence Adam Michael						
Stepney, 3 April, 1953						(F)
Charlton Ath.	Barking	05.77	77	12	4	2
ABRAHAMS Paul						
Colchester, 31 October, 1973						(F)
Colchester U.	YT	08.92	92-94	30	25	8
Brentford	Tr	03.95	94-96	26	9	8
Colchester U.	L	12.95	95	8	0	2
Colchester U.	Tr	10.96	96-97	43	11	14
ABREY Brian Anthony						
Hendon, 25 April, 1939						(CH)
Chelsea	Jnrs	10.56				
Colchester U.	Tr	05.61	61	38	-	2
ABRUZZESE David John						
Aberdare, 8 October, 1969 W Yth						(D)
Newport Co.	YT	08.86	86-87	24	1	0
ABTHORPE John						
Nottingham, 19 January, 1933						(CF)
Notts Co. (Am)	Wolverhampton W. (Am)	09.55	55	5	-	3
ACHAMPONG Kenneth						
Kilburn, 26 June, 1966						(W)
Fulham	App	06.84	84-87	68	13	15
Charlton Ath.	Tr	08.89	89	2	8	0
Leyton Orient	Tr	08.90	90-92	64	19	7
ACKERLEY Ernest Nicol						
Dunfermline, 23 September, 1943						(CF)
Manchester U.	Jnrs	10.60				
Barrow	Tr	04.63	62-63	53	-	12
ACKERLEY Stanley						
Manchester, 12 July, 1942						(FB)
Manchester U.	Jnrs	11.59				
Oldham Ath.	Tr	06.61	61	2	-	0
ACKERMAN Alfred Arthur Eric						
South Africa, 5 January, 1929 Died 1988						(CF)
Hull C.	Clyde	07.50	50	34	-	21
Norwich C.	Tr	08.51	51-53	66	-	31
Hull C.	Tr	10.53	53-54	58	-	28
Derby Co.	Tr	03.55	54-56	36	-	21
Carlisle U.	Tr	11.56	56-58	97	-	61
Millwall	Tr	01.59	58-60	81	-	35
ACKERMAN Charles George **Anthony**						
Islington, 20 February, 1948						(CH)
Leyton Orient	West Ham U. (Am)	10.66	66-67	4	0	0
ACLAND Michael Edward						
Sidcup, 4 June, 1935						(IF)
Gillingham	Harland Social	08.55	56	2	-	0
A'COURT Alan						
Rainhill, 30 September, 1934 Eu23-7/EF Lge/E-5						(OL)
Liverpool	Prescot Cables	09.52	52-62	355	-	61
Tranmere Rov.	Tr	10.64	64-65	50	0	11
ACRES Basil Derek John						
Samford, 27 October, 1926						(FB)
Ipswich T.	Brantham	09.50	51-59	217	-	6
ACTON Alec Edward						
Billesdon, 12 November, 1938 Died 1994						(LH)
Stoke C.	Leicester C. (Am)	01.56				
Stockport Co.	Brush Sports	08.58	58-59	9	-	0
ADAM Charles						
Glasgow, 22 March, 1919 Died 1996						(W)
Leicester C.	Strathclyde	09.38	46-50	158	-	22
Mansfield T.	Tr	07.52	52-54	93	-	6
ADAM James						
Blantyre, 13 May, 1931						(OL)
Aldershot (Am)	Blantyre Celtic	08.50	50	1	-	0
Luton T.	Spennymoor U.	07.53	53-58	137	-	22
Aston Villa	Tr	08.59	59-60	24	-	3
Stoke C.	Tr	07.61	61	22	-	7
ADAM James						
Paisley, 22 April, 1931						(IF)
Leeds U.	Penilee U.	06.51				
Mansfield T.	Tr	08.54	54	39	-	10
ADAMS Brian Thomas						
Tottenham, 18 May, 1947						(WH)
Millwall	Chelsea (App)	08.64	64-65	15	0	0
ADAMS Christopher James						
Romford, 6 September, 1927						(OL)
Tottenham H.	Romford	11.48	51-52	6	-	1
Norwich C.	Tr	12.52	52-54	29	-	3
Watford	Tr	03.54	53-55	75	-	5
ADAMS Craig John						
Northampton, 9 November, 1974						(CD)
Northampton T.	YT	●	91	0	1	0
ADAMS Darren Steven						
Newham, 12 January, 1974						(F)
Cardiff C.	Danson Furness	01.94	93-95	21	13	4
ADAMS Derek Watt						
Aberdeen, 25 June, 1975						(M)
Burnley	Aberdeen	01.95	95	0	2	0

ADAMS Donald Frederick
Northampton, 15 February, 1931 Died 1993 (CF)

League Club	Source	Date Signed	Seasons Played	Apps	Subs	Gls
Northampton T.		05.51	51-55	23	-	7

ADAMS, Ernest Robert
Hackney, 17 January, 1948 (G)

League Club	Source	Date Signed	Seasons Played	Apps	Subs	Gls
Arsenal	App	01.65				
Colchester U.	Tr	07.67	67-68	48	0	0
Crewe Alex.	Tr	07.69	69-71	112	0	0
Darlington	Tr	07.72	72	25	0	0

ADAMS Ernest William
Willesden, 3 April, 1922 (W)

League Club	Source	Date Signed	Seasons Played	Apps	Subs	Gls
Preston N.E.		01.45				
Queens Park R.	Tr	09.47	47-49	5	-	0

ADAMS Francis Nicholas
Liverpool, 8 February, 1933 (G)

League Club	Source	Date Signed	Seasons Played	Apps	Subs	Gls
Bury	Bury Amats	01.56	56-61	169	-	0
Chester C.	Tr	07.63	63	8	-	0
Tranmere Rov.	Tr	02.64				

ADAMS George
Falkirk, 16 October, 1926 (W)

League Club	Source	Date Signed	Seasons Played	Apps	Subs	Gls
Leyton Orient	Chelmsford C.	05.49	49	4	-	0

ADAMS George Robert
Shoreditch, 28 September, 1947 (WH)

League Club	Source	Date Signed	Seasons Played	Apps	Subs	Gls
Chelsea	Jnrs	09.65				
Peterborough U.	Tr	07.66	66-67	13	3	2

ADAMS Graham Wallace
Torrington, 1 March, 1933 (FB)

League Club	Source	Date Signed	Seasons Played	Apps	Subs	Gls
Plymouth Arg.		01.58	57	1	-	0

ADAMS James Arthur
Stoke, 2 August, 1937 (FB)

League Club	Source	Date Signed	Seasons Played	Apps	Subs	Gls
Port Vale		06.56	57	1	-	0

ADAMS Keiran Charles
Cambridge, 20 October, 1977 (M)

League Club	Source	Date Signed	Seasons Played	Apps	Subs	Gls
Barnet	YT	07.96	94-96	8	11	1

ADAMS Laurence Edward
Barnet, 14 February, 1931 (IF)

League Club	Source	Date Signed	Seasons Played	Apps	Subs	Gls
Watford (Am)		01.52	51	1	-	0

ADAMS Michael Alan
Banwell (Avon), 20 February, 1965 (M)

League Club	Source	Date Signed	Seasons Played	Apps	Subs	Gls
Bristol Rov.	App	02.83	82	0	1	0

ADAMS Michael Richard
Sheffield, 8 November, 1961 E Yth (LB)

League Club	Source	Date Signed	Seasons Played	Apps	Subs	Gls
Gillingham	App	11.79	79-82	85	7	5
Coventry C.	Tr	07.83	83-86	85	5	9
Leeds U.	Tr	01.87	86-88	72	1	2
Southampton	Tr	03.89	88-93	141	3	7
Stoke C.	Tr	03.94	93	10	0	3
Fulham	Tr	07.94	94-96	25	4	8

ADAMS Neil James
Stoke, 23 November, 1965 Eu21-1 (W)

League Club	Source	Date Signed	Seasons Played	Apps	Subs	Gls
Stoke C.	Queens Park R. (Jnrs)	07.85	85	31	1	4
Everton	Tr	07.86	86-87	17	3	0
Oldham Ath.	L	01.89	88	9	0	0
Oldham Ath.	Tr	06.89	89-93	93	36	23
Norwich C.	Tr	02.94	93-97	149	15	22

ADAMS Rex Malcolm
Oxford, 13 February, 1928 (OR)

League Club	Source	Date Signed	Seasons Played	Apps	Subs	Gls
Blackpool	Oxford C.	06.48	48-50	16	-	0
Oldham Ath.	Worcester C.	06.53	53	23	-	1

ADAMS Rodney Leslie
Bath, 15 September, 1945 (W)

League Club	Source	Date Signed	Seasons Played	Apps	Subs	Gls
Bournemouth	Frome T.	06.66	66-68	15	2	4

ADAMS Stephen
Sheffield, 7 September, 1959 (W)

League Club	Source	Date Signed	Seasons Played	Apps	Subs	Gls
Scarborough	Worksop T.	09.87	87-88	25	23	5
Doncaster Rov.	Tr	10.89	89-90	25	10	2

ADAMS Stephen Thomas
Windsor, 18 June, 1958 (M)

League Club	Source	Date Signed	Seasons Played	Apps	Subs	Gls
Queens Park R.	App	07.75				
Millwall	Tr	07.77	77	1	0	0
Cambridge U.	Windsor & Eton	03.78	77-78	1	2	0

ADAMS Tony Alexander
Romford, 10 October, 1966 E Yth/Eu21-5/E'B'/E-55 (CD)

League Club	Source	Date Signed	Seasons Played	Apps	Subs	Gls
Arsenal	App	01.84	83-97	417	4	30

ADAMS Vincent
Chesterfield, 16 October, 1946 E Sch (WH)

League Club	Source	Date Signed	Seasons Played	Apps	Subs	Gls
Arsenal	App	10.63				
Chesterfield	Tr	11.65	65-66	15	2	1

ADAMS William Henry
Arlecdon, 8 January, 1919 Died 1989 (RB)

League Club	Source	Date Signed	Seasons Played	Apps	Subs	Gls
Tottenham H.	Hartlepool U. (Am)	05.39				
Carlisle U.	Tr	06.46	46	33	-	1
Workington	Cheltenham T.	(N/L)	51	3	-	0

ADAMS William Victor
Plymouth, 10 May, 1921 (FB)

League Club	Source	Date Signed	Seasons Played	Apps	Subs	Gls
Plymouth Arg.	Plymouth U.	04.45	46	1	-	0

ADAMSON Christopher
Ashington, 4 November, 1978 (G)

League Club	Source	Date Signed	Seasons Played	Apps	Subs	Gls
West Bromwich A.	YT	07.97	97	3	0	0

ADAMSON David Henry
Chester-le-Street, 7 May, 1951 E Semi Pro (FB)

League Club	Source	Date Signed	Seasons Played	Apps	Subs	Gls
Doncaster Rov.	Durham C.	07.70	70-71	28	0	0

ADAMSON Henry
Kelty, 27 June, 1924 Died 1997 (WH)

League Club	Source	Date Signed	Seasons Played	Apps	Subs	Gls
Notts Co.	Jeanfield Swifts	08.46	47-55	233	-	5

ADAMSON James
Ashington, 4 April, 1929 EF Lge (WH)

League Club	Source	Date Signed	Seasons Played	Apps	Subs	Gls
Burnley	Ashington	01.47	50-63	426	-	17

ADAMSON Keith Brian
Houghton-le-Spring, 3 July, 1945 (F)

League Club	Source	Date Signed	Seasons Played	Apps	Subs	Gls
Barnsley	Tow Law T.	03.66	65-66	7	0	0

ADAMSON Terence
Houghton-le-Spring, 15 October, 1948 (FB)

League Club	Source	Date Signed	Seasons Played	Apps	Subs	Gls
Sunderland	App	11.65				
Luton T.	Tr	07.66	66	2	0	0
Hartlepool U.	Tr	07.67	67	1	0	0

ADCOCK Anthony Charles
Bethnal Green, 27 March, 1963 (F)

League Club	Source	Date Signed	Seasons Played	Apps	Subs	Gls
Colchester U.	App	03.81	80-86	192	18	98
Manchester C.	Tr	06.87	87	12	3	5
Northampton T.	Tr	01.88	87-89	72	0	30
Bradford C.	Tr	10.89	89-90	33	5	6
Northampton T.	Tr	01.91	90-91	34	1	10
Peterborough U.	Tr	12.91	91-93	107	4	35
Luton T.	Tr	08.94	94	0	2	0
Colchester U.	Tr	08.95	95-97	86	16	28

ADCOCK Paul Malcolm
Ilminster, 2 May, 1972 (F)

League Club	Source	Date Signed	Seasons Played	Apps	Subs	Gls
Plymouth Arg.	YT	08.90	90-92	11	10	2
Torquay U.	Bath C.	08.96	96	0	1	0

ADDINALL Albert William
Paddington, 30 January, 1921 (CF)

League Club	Source	Date Signed	Seasons Played	Apps	Subs	Gls
Queens Park R.	British Oxygen	04.45	46-52	150	-	59
Brighton & H.A.	Tr	01.53	52-53	60	-	31
Crystal Palace	Tr	07.54	54	12	-	2

ADDISON Colin
Taunton, 18 May, 1940 (IF)

League Club	Source	Date Signed	Seasons Played	Apps	Subs	Gls
York C.	Jnrs	05.57	57-60	87	-	28
Nottingham F.	Tr	01.61	60-66	160	0	62
Arsenal	Tr	09.66	66-67	27	1	9
Sheffield U.	Tr	12.67	67-70	93	1	22
Hereford U.	Tr	10.71	72-73	23	0	1

ADDY Michael
Knottingley, 20 February, 1943 (WH)

League Club	Source	Date Signed	Seasons Played	Apps	Subs	Gls
Leeds U.	Jnrs	05.62	62	2	-	0
Barnsley	Tr	06.64	64-66	50	1	5

ADEBOLA Bamberdele (Dele)
Nigeria, 23 June, 1975 (F)

League Club	Source	Date Signed	Seasons Played	Apps	Subs	Gls
Crewe Alex.	YT	06.93	92-97	98	26	39
Birmingham C.	Tr	02.98	97	16	1	7

ADEKOLA David Adeolu
Liverpool, 19 May, 1968 Nigerian Int (F)

League Club	Source	Date Signed	Seasons Played	Apps	Subs	Gls
Bury	Cannes (Fr)	01.93	92-93	21	14	12
Exeter C.	L	02.94	93	1	2	1

League Club	Source	Date Signed	Seasons Played	Career Record Apps	Subs	Gls
Wigan Ath. (N/C)	Bournemouth (N/C)	10.94	94	1	3	0
Cambridge U. (N/C)	Bath C.	08.95	95	1	4	1
Brighton & H.A. (N/C)	Preussen Munster (Ger)	10.96	96	1	0	0

ADEY Arthur Lewis
Glasgow, 1 March, 1930 (CF)

League Club	Source	Date Signed	Seasons Played	Apps	Subs	Gls
Doncaster Rov	Bishop Auckland	09.50	50-53	48	-	10
Gillingham	Tr	07.54	54	7	-	1
Bradford P.A.	Tr	10.54	54	13	-	4

ADKINS Nigel Howard
Birkenhead, 11 March, 1965 E Sch (G)

League Club	Source	Date Signed	Seasons Played	Apps	Subs	Gls
Tranmere Rov.	App	03.83	82-85	86	0	0
Wigan Ath.	Tr	08.86	86-92	155	0	0

ADLINGTON Terence
Blackwell, 21 November, 1935 Died 1994 (G)

League Club	Source	Date Signed	Seasons Played	Apps	Subs	Gls
Derby Co.	Blackwell Colly	12.55	56-61	36	-	0
Torquay U.	Tr	06.62	62-65	148	0	0

AFFOR Louis Kofi Jeffrey
Ghana, 29 August, 1972 (W)

League Club	Source	Date Signed	Seasons Played	Apps	Subs	Gls
Barnet		08.93	93	0	3	0

AGANA Patrick **Anthony** Olozinka
Bromley, 2 October, 1963 E Semi Pro (F)

League Club	Source	Date Signed	Seasons Played	Apps	Subs	Gls
Watford	Weymouth	08.87	87	12	3	1
Sheffield U.	Tr	02.88	87-91	105	13	42
Notts Co.	Tr	11.91	91-96	114	31	15
Leeds U.	L	02.92	91	1	1	0
Hereford U.	Tr	03.97	96	3	2	2

AGAR Roy
Islington, 1 April, 1936 E Amat (IF)

League Club	Source	Date Signed	Seasons Played	Apps	Subs	Gls
Swindon T. (Am)	Barnet	12.55	55-56	12	-	0

AGBOOLA Reuben Omajola Folasanje
Camden, 30 May, 1962 (LB)

League Club	Source	Date Signed	Seasons Played	Apps	Subs	Gls
Southampton	App	04.80	80-84	89	1	0
Sunderland	Tr	01.85	84-91	129	11	0
Charlton Ath.	L	10.86	86	1	0	0
Port Vale	L	11.90	90	9	0	0
Swansea C.	Tr	11.91	91-92	26	2	0

AGNEW David
Belfast, 31 March, 1925 NI Amat (G)

League Club	Source	Date Signed	Seasons Played	Apps	Subs	Gls
Sunderland	Crusaders	01.50	50	1	-	0

AGNEW David Young
Kilwinning, 4 August, 1939 (FB)

League Club	Source	Date Signed	Seasons Played	Apps	Subs	Gls
Leicester C.	Jnrs	08.58				
Scunthorpe U.	Tr	06.61	61	1	-	0
Notts Co.	Tr	06.62	62-66	85	0	1

AGNEW John Terence
Stockton, 27 June, 1935 (OL)

League Club	Source	Date Signed	Seasons Played	Apps	Subs	Gls
Sheffield Wed.		11.53				
Darlington	Tr	08.54	54-55	24	-	4

AGNEW Paul
Lisburn (NI), 15 August, 1965 NI Sch/NI Yth/NIu23-1 (LB)

League Club	Source	Date Signed	Seasons Played	Apps	Subs	Gls
Grimsby T.	Cliftonville	02.84	83-94	219	23	3
West Bromwich A.	Tr	02.95	94-96	38	1	1
Swansea C. (N/C)	Tr	09.97	97	7	0	0

AGNEW Stephen Mark
Shipley, 9 November, 1965 (M)

League Club	Source	Date Signed	Seasons Played	Apps	Subs	Gls
Barnsley	App	11.83	83-90	186	8	29
Blackburn Rov.	Tr	06.91	91	2	0	0
Portsmouth	L	11.92	92	3	2	0
Leicester C.	Tr	02.93	92-94	52	4	4
Sunderland	Tr	01.95	94-97	56	7	9

AGOGO Manuel
Accra, Ghana, 1 August, 1979 (F)

League Club	Source	Date Signed	Seasons Played	Apps	Subs	Gls
Sheffield Wed.	Willesden Constontaine	10.96	97	0	1	0

AGOSTINO Paul
Australia, 9 June, 1975 Australian Int (F)

League Club	Source	Date Signed	Seasons Played	Apps	Subs	Gls
Bristol C.	Young Boys Berne (Swit)	07.95	95-96	63	21	19

AHERNE Thomas
Limerick (Ire), 26 January, 1919 NI-4/IR-16 (FB)

League Club	Source	Date Signed	Seasons Played	Apps	Subs	Gls
Luton T.	Belfast Celtic	03.49	48-56	267	-	0

AIKEN Thomas
Ballymena (NI), 18 March, 1946 NI Amat (OR)

League Club	Source	Date Signed	Seasons Played	Apps	Subs	Gls
Doncaster Rov.	Ballymena	11.67	67-68	12	1	1

AIMSON Paul Edward
Macclesfield, 3 August, 1943 (CF)

League Club	Source	Date Signed	Seasons Played	Apps	Subs	Gls
Manchester C.	Jnrs	08.60	61-63	16	-	4
York C.	Tr	07.64	64-65	77	0	43
Bury	Tr	03.66	65-66	30	1	11
Bradford C.	Tr	09.67	67	23	0	11
Huddersfield T.	Tr	03.68	67-68	34	4	13
York C.	Tr	08.69	69-72	133	9	55
Bournemouth	Tr	03.73	72	7	2	2
Colchester U.	Tr	08.73	73	3	1	2

AINDOW Roger Allan
Liverpool, 23 October, 1946 (D)

League Club	Source	Date Signed	Seasons Played	Apps	Subs	Gls
Southport	Blackpool (Am)	10.67	68-70	52	6	4

AINGE Ronald Percy
Pontardawe, 5 August, 1920 (W)

League Club	Source	Date Signed	Seasons Played	Apps	Subs	Gls
Newport Co.	Llanelli	10.46	46	5	-	0

AINSCOUGH John
Adlington, 26 March, 1926 (CH)

League Club	Source	Date Signed	Seasons Played	Apps	Subs	Gls
Blackpool	Astley Bridge	08.49	50-53	7	-	0

AINSCOW Alan
Bolton, 15 July, 1953 E Yth (M)

League Club	Source	Date Signed	Seasons Played	Apps	Subs	Gls
Blackpool	App	07.71	71-77	178	14	28
Birmingham C.	Tr	07.78	78-80	104	4	16
Everton	Tr	08.81	81-82	24	4	3
Barnsley	L	11.82	82	2	0	0
Wolverhampton W.	Eastern (HK)	08.84	84-85	56	2	5
Blackburn Rov.	Tr	12.85	85-88	42	23	5
Rochdale	Tr	07.89	89	19	1	0

AINSCOW Andrew Paul
Orrell, 1 October, 1968 E Yth (F)

League Club	Source	Date Signed	Seasons Played	Apps	Subs	Gls
Wigan Ath.	App	10.86	87-88	14	8	4
Rotherham U.	Tr	08.89	89	0	1	0

AINSLEY George Edward
South Shields, 15 April, 1915 Died 1985 (CF)

League Club	Source	Date Signed	Seasons Played	Apps	Subs	Gls
Sunderland	South Shields St A.	04.32	32-33	4	-	0
Bolton W.	Tr	08.36	36	7	-	0
Leeds U.	Tr	12.36	36-47	89	-	30
Bradford P.A.	Tr	11.47	47-48	44	-	29

AINSLEY Jason
Stockton, 13 July, 1970 (M)

League Club	Source	Date Signed	Seasons Played	Apps	Subs	Gls
Hartlepool U.	Spennymoor	07.94	94	14	1	1

AINSWORTH Alphonso
Manchester, 31 July, 1913 Died 1975 (IF)

League Club	Source	Date Signed	Seasons Played	Apps	Subs	Gls
Manchester U.	Ashton U.	02.34	33	2	-	0
New Brighton	Tr	09.35	35-47	178	-	48

AINSWORTH David
Bolton, 28 January, 1958 (F)

League Club	Source	Date Signed	Seasons Played	Apps	Subs	Gls
Rochdale	App	01.76	75	0	2	0

AINSWORTH Gareth
Blackburn, 10 May, 1973 (W)

League Club	Source	Date Signed	Seasons Played	Apps	Subs	Gls
Preston N.E.	Blackburn Rov. (YT)	08.91	91	2	3	0
Cambridge U.	Tr	08.92	92	1	3	1
Preston N.E.	Tr	12.92	92-95	76	6	12
Lincoln C.	Tr	10.95	95-97	83	0	37
Port Vale	Tr	09.97	97	38	2	5

AINSWORTH John
Birkenhead, 20 September, 1922 Died 1981 (CF)

League Club	Source	Date Signed	Seasons Played	Apps	Subs	Gls
New Brighton (Am)		03.47	46-47	14	-	3

AIRD John (Jock) Rae
Glencraig (Fife), 18 February, 1926 S-4 (FB)

League Club	Source	Date Signed	Seasons Played	Apps	Subs	Gls
Burnley	Jeanfield Swifts	08.48	49-54	132	-	0

AIREY Carl
Wakefield, 6 February, 1965 (F)

League Club	Source	Date Signed	Seasons Played	Apps	Subs	Gls
Barnsley	App	02.83	82-83	30	8	5
Bradford C.	L	10.83	83	4	1	0
Darlington	Tr	08.84	84-85	72	3	28
Chesterfield (L)	Charleroi (Bel)	12.86	86	24	2	4
Rotherham U.	Tr	08.87	87	25	7	11
Torquay U.	Charleroi (Bel)	01.89	88-89	21	8	11

AIREY John (Jack)
Bedford, 28 November, 1937 (W)

League Club	Source	Date Signed	Seasons Played	Apps	Subs	Gls
Blackburn Rov.		01.59	58-59	3	-	1

AISTON Samuel James
Newcastle, 21 November, 1976 E Sch (LM)

League Club	Source	Date Signed	Seasons Played	Apps	Subs	Gls
Sunderland	Newcastle U. (YT)	07.95	95-96	5	14	0
Chester C.	L	02.97	96-97	14	0	0

AITCHISON Barrie George
Colchester, 15 November, 1937 (W)

League Club	Source	Date Signed	Seasons Played	Apps	Subs	Gls
Tottenham H.	Jnrs	01.55				
Colchester U.	Tr	08.64	64-65	49	1	6

AITCHISON Peter Munro
Harlow, 19 September, 1931 (W)

League Club	Source	Date Signed	Seasons Played	Apps	Subs	Gls
Colchester U.		10.51	51-54	18	-	2

AITKEN Andrew Fox Scott
Edinburgh, 21 August, 1934 (W)

League Club	Source	Date Signed	Seasons Played	Apps	Subs	Gls
West Bromwich A.	Hibernian	09.59	59-60	22	-	2

AITKEN Charles Alexander
Edinburgh, 1 May, 1942 Su23-3 (LB)

League Club	Source	Date Signed	Seasons Played	Apps	Subs	Gls
Aston Villa	Edinburgh Thistle	08.59	60-75	559	2	14

AITKEN George Bruce
Dalkeith, 13 August, 1928 (CH)

League Club	Source	Date Signed	Seasons Played	Apps	Subs	Gls
Middlesbrough	Edinburgh Thistle	06.46	51-52	17	-	0
Workington	Tr	07.53	53-59	262	-	3

AITKEN George Graham
Lochgelly, 28 May, 1925 S-8 (WH)

League Club	Source	Date Signed	Seasons Played	Apps	Subs	Gls
Sunderland	Third Lanark	11.51	51-58	245	-	3
Gateshead	Tr	03.59	58-59	58	-	0

AITKEN Glenn Leslie
Woolwich, 30 September, 1952 E Yth (FB)

League Club	Source	Date Signed	Seasons Played	Apps	Subs	Gls
Gillingham	Chelsea (Am)	12.72	72-74	19	4	0
Wimbledon	Tr	09.74	77	11	0	1

AITKEN Peter Gerald
Penarth, 30 June, 1954 (D)

League Club	Source	Date Signed	Seasons Played	Apps	Subs	Gls
Bristol Rov.	App	07.72	72-79	230	4	3
Bristol C.	Tr	11.80	80-81	41	0	1
York C.	Tr	02.82	81	18	0	2
Bournemouth (N/C)	Hong Kong	11.82	82	1	0	0

AITKEN Robert (Roy) Sime
Irvine, 24 November, 1958 S Sch/Su21-16/S-57 (M)

League Club	Source	Date Signed	Seasons Played	Apps	Subs	Gls
Newcastle U.	Glasgow Celtic	01.90	89-90	54	0	1

AITKEN William Robert Crawford
Dumfries, 11 January, 1951 (IF)

League Club	Source	Date Signed	Seasons Played	Apps	Subs	Gls
Oldham Ath.	App	01.68	68	1	0	0

AIZLEWOOD Mark
Newport, 1 October, 1959 W Sch/Wu21-2/W-39 (CD)

League Club	Source	Date Signed	Seasons Played	Apps	Subs	Gls
Newport Co.	App	10.77	75-77	35	3	3
Luton T.	Tr	04.78	78-81	90	8	3
Charlton Ath.	Tr	11.82	82-86	152	0	9
Leeds U.	Tr	02.87	86-88	65	5	3
Bradford C.	Tr	08.89	89	39	0	1
Bristol C.	Tr	08.90	90-93	99	2	3
Cardiff C.	Tr	10.93	93-94	39	0	3

AIZLEWOOD Steven
Newport, 9 October, 1952 W Sch (CD)

League Club	Source	Date Signed	Seasons Played	Apps	Subs	Gls
Newport Co.	Jnrs	01.70	68-75	191	6	18
Swindon T.	Tr	03.76	75-78	111	1	10
Portsmouth	Tr	07.79	79-83	175	0	13

AKERS Victor David
Islington, 24 August, 1946 (FB)

League Club	Source	Date Signed	Seasons Played	Apps	Subs	Gls
Cambridge U.	Bexley U.	07.71	71-74	122	7	5
Watford	Tooting & Mitcham	07.75	75	22	0	0

AKINBIYI Adeola (Ade) Peter
Hackney, 10 October, 1974 (F)

League Club	Source	Date Signed	Seasons Played	Apps	Subs	Gls
Norwich C.	YT	02.93	93-96	22	27	3
Hereford U.	L	01.94	93	3	1	2
Brighton & H.A.	L	11.94	94	7	0	4
Gillingham	Tr	01.97	96-97	63	0	28

ALBERRY William Edward
Doncaster, 21 July, 1922 Died 1978 (CH)

League Club	Source	Date Signed	Seasons Played	Apps	Subs	Gls
Leeds U.	Doncaster Rov. (Am)	05.46				
Hull C.	Tr	04.47	46	1	-	0

ALBERT Philippe
Belgium, 10 August, 1967 Belgian Int (CD)

League Club	Source	Date Signed	Seasons Played	Apps	Subs	Gls
Newcastle U.	Anderlecht (Bel)	08.94	94-97	84	6	8

ALBESON Brian
Oldham, 14 December, 1946 E Yth (CD)

League Club	Source	Date Signed	Seasons Played	Apps	Subs	Gls
Bury	Jnrs	05.65	65	0	1	0
Darlington	Tr	07.67	67-70	135	2	2
Southend U.	Tr	07.71	71-73	109	1	9
Stockport Co.	Tr	03.74	73-74	54	0	1

ALBISTON Arthur Richard
Edinburgh, 14 July, 1957 S Sch/Su21-5/S-14 (LB)

League Club	Source	Date Signed	Seasons Played	Apps	Subs	Gls
Manchester U.	App	07.74	74-87	364	15	6
West Bromwich A.	Tr	08.88	88	43	0	2
Chesterfield (L)	Dundee	11.90	90	3	0	1
Chester C.	Tr	08.91	91	44	0	0
Chester C.	Molde (Nor)	11.92	92	23	1	0

ALBURY William Frederick
Portsmouth, 10 August, 1933 (WH)

League Club	Source	Date Signed	Seasons Played	Apps	Subs	Gls
Portsmouth	Jnrs	10.51	56-57	23	-	0
Gillingham	Tr	07.59	59	38	-	12

ALCIDE Colin James
Huddersfield, 14 April, 1972 (LM)

League Club	Source	Date Signed	Seasons Played	Apps	Subs	Gls
Lincoln C.	Emley	12.95	95-97	85	13	26

ALCOCK Terence
Hanley, 9 December, 1946 (D)

League Club	Source	Date Signed	Seasons Played	Apps	Subs	Gls
Port Vale	App	09.64	63-66	112	0	0
Blackpool	Tr	08.67	67-75	190	6	21
Bury	L	02.72	71	6	0	1
Blackburn Rov.	L	12.76	76	3	0	1
Port Vale	Tr	02.77	76-77	4	0	0
Halifax T.	Portland (USA)	09.77	77	14	0	2

ALDECOA Emilio
Spain, 30 November, 1922 Spanish Int (W)

League Club	Source	Date Signed	Seasons Played	Apps	Subs	Gls
Wolverhampton W.		12.43				
Coventry C.	Tr	12.45	46	29	-	0

ALDERSON Brian Roderick
Dundee, 5 May, 1950 Died 1997 Su23-1 (W)

League Club	Source	Date Signed	Seasons Played	Apps	Subs	Gls
Coventry C.	Lochee Harp	07.70	70-74	116	11	29
Leicester C.	Tr	07.75	75-77	87	3	9

ALDERSON Kevin
Shildon, 21 August, 1953 (W)

League Club	Source	Date Signed	Seasons Played	Apps	Subs	Gls
Darlington	App	•	70	1	0	0

ALDERSON Richard
Durham, 27 January, 1975 (RW)

League Club	Source	Date Signed	Seasons Played	Apps	Subs	Gls
York C.	Spennymoor U.	12.97	97	0	1	0

ALDERSON Stuart
Bishop Auckland, 15 August, 1948 (OR)

League Club	Source	Date Signed	Seasons Played	Apps	Subs	Gls
Newcastle U.	Evenwood T.	08.65	66	3	0	0
York C.	Tr	06.67	67	17	2	5

ALDERTON James Harris
Wingate, 6 December, 1924 (WH)

League Club	Source	Date Signed	Seasons Played	Apps	Subs	Gls
Wolverhampton W.	Jnrs	12.41	46	11	-	0
Coventry C.	Tr	10.47	47-51	62	-	0

ALDIS Peter Basil
Kings Norton, 11 April, 1927 (FB)

League Club	Source	Date Signed	Seasons Played	Apps	Subs	Gls
Aston Villa	Hay Green	05.49	50-58	262	-	1

ALDOUS Stanley Elvey Reginald
Northfleet, 10 February, 1923 Died 1995 (CH)

League Club	Source	Date Signed	Seasons Played	Apps	Subs	Gls
Leyton Orient	Gravesend & Nft	07.50	50-57	302	-	3

ALDREAD Paul
Mansfield, 6 November, 1946 (CF)

League Club	Source	Date Signed	Seasons Played	Apps	Subs	Gls
Mansfield T.	Jnrs	12.63	65-66	11	1	3

ALDRED Arthur
Atherton, 27 August, 1919 (W)

League Club	Source	Date Signed	Seasons Played	Apps	Subs	Gls
Aston Villa	Hereford U.	07.46				
Walsall	Tr	05.48	48	11	-	1

ALDRED Graeme
Ferryhill, 11 September, 1966 Died 1987 (D)

League Club	Source	Date Signed	Seasons Played	Apps	Subs	Gls
Darlington	Newcastle U. (YT)	09.84	84-85	31	13	1

ALDRIDGE John William
Liverpool, 18 September, 1958 IR-69 (F)

League Club	Source	Date Signed	Seasons Played	Apps	Subs	Gls
Newport Co.	South Liverpool	05.79	79-83	159	11	69
Oxford U.	Tr	03.84	83-86	111	3	72
Liverpool	Tr	01.87	86-89	69	14	50
Tranmere Rov.	Real Sociedad (Sp)	07.91	91-97	221	21	138

ALDRIDGE Martin James
Northampton, 6 December, 1974 (F)

League Club	Source	Date Signed	Seasons Played	Apps	Subs	Gls
Northampton T.	YT	08.93	91-95	50	20	17
Oxford U.	Tr	12.95	95-97	46	26	19
Southend U.	L	02.98	97	7	4	1

League Club	Source	Date Signed	Seasons Played	Career Record Apps	Subs	Gls
ALDRIDGE Neil Robert						
Manchester, 10 January, 1966 E Yth						(LB)
Manchester C.	App	11.83				
Crewe Alex.	Tr	07.84	84	12	3	0
ALDRIDGE Norman Hubert						
Foleshill, 23 February, 1921						(FB)
West Bromwich A.	Foxford	05.46	46	1	-	0
Northampton T.	Tr	06.48	48	2	-	0
ALDRIDGE Stephen Paul						
Armthorpe, 2 November, 1957						(F)
Sheffield U.	App	12.75				
Doncaster Rov. (N/C)		02.81	80	1	0	0
ALEKSIC Milija Antony						
Newcastle-u-Lyme, 14 April, 1951						(G)
Plymouth Arg.	Stafford R.	02.73	73-75	32	0	0
Luton T.	Tr	12.76	76-78	77	0	0
Tottenham H.	Tr	12.78	78-81	25	0	0
Luton T.	L	11.81	81	4	0	0
ALESINOYE Martin						
Middlesbrough, 1 October, 1955						(M)
Doncaster Rov.	Barnsley (Am)	10.75	75	13	1	1
ALEXANDER Alan						
Cumbernauld, 1 November, 1941						(G)
Bradford P.A.		07.59	61	5	-	0
ALEXANDER Alexander						
Glasgow, 28 September, 1924						(OL)
Tranmere Rov.	New Brighton (Am)	10.47	46-48	23	-	3
ALEXANDER Angus (Gus) Charles						
Arbroath, 10 January, 1934						(IF)
Burnley	Jnrs	01.51				
Southport	Tr	07.57	57	14	-	1
Workington	Tr	02.58	57-58	49	-	4
York C.	Tr	06.59	59	7	-	0
ALEXANDER Anthony Alan						
Reading, 8 February, 1935						(F)
Reading	Jnrs	08.52	52-55	11	-	2
ALEXANDER Dennis Leslie						
Nottingham, 19 February, 1935						(IF)
Nottingham F.	Jnrs	06.55	55-56	20	-	4
Brighton & H.A.	Tr	03.58				
Gateshead	Tr	10.58	58	18	-	1
ALEXANDER Graham						
Coventry, 10 October, 1971						(RM)
Scunthorpe U.	YT	03.90	90-94	149	10	18
Luton T.	Tr	07.95	95-97	118	3	11
ALEXANDER Ian						
Glasgow, 26 January, 1963						(RB)
Rotherham U.	Leicester Juveniles	10.81	81-82	5	6	0
Bristol Rov.	Pezoporikos Larnaca (Cyp)	08.86	86-93	284	7	6
ALEXANDER John Eric						
Liverpool, 5 October, 1955						(F)
Millwall	Ulysses	07.77	76-77	10	5	2
Reading	Tr	10.78	78-80	22	3	9
Northampton T.	Tr	08.81	81	21	1	4
ALEXANDER Keith						
Nottingham, 14 November, 1958 St Lucian Int						(W/F)
Grimsby T.	Barnet	07.88	88-90	64	19	26
Stockport Co.	Tr	09.90	90	9	2	0
Lincoln C.	Tr	12.90	90-92	26	19	4
Mansfield T. (N/C)	Tr	08.94	94-95	0	3	0
ALEXANDER Philip James						
Slough, 4 September, 1962						(D)
Norwich C.	Wokingham T.	08.81	82	0	1	0
ALEXANDER Rowan Samuel						
Ayr, 28 January, 1961						(F)
Brentford	St Mirren	09.84	84-85	41	6	6
ALEXANDER Timothy Mark						
Chertsey, 29 March, 1974						(CD)
Barnet	Wimbledon (YT)	08.92	93-94	29	7	0
ALEXANDERSSON Niclas						
Halmstad, Sweden, 29 December, 1971 Swedish Int						(RM)
Sheffield Wed.	Gothenburg (Swe)	12.97	97	5	1	0
ALFORD Carl Peter						
Manchester, 11 February, 1972						(F)
Rochdale	YT	●	88	0	4	0
ALISON James						
Peebles, 11 October, 1923						(WH)
Manchester C.	Falkirk	12.49	49-50	19	-	0
Aldershot	Tr	07.52	52-56	171	-	8
ALJOFREE Hasney						
Manchester, 11 July, 1978						(LWB)
Bolton W.	YT	07.96	97	2	0	0
ALLAN Alexander (Sandy) Begg						
Forfar, 29 October, 1947						(CF)
Cardiff C.	Rhyl	03.67	67-69	8	0	1
Bristol Rov.	Tr	03.70	69-72	52	7	18
Swansea C.	L	03.73	72	6	2	1
ALLAN Derek Thomas						
Irvine, 24 December, 1974 S Yth						(CD)
Southampton	Ayr U.	03.93	92	0	1	0
Brighton & H.A.	Tr	03.96	95-97	56	2	1
ALLAN James						
Inverness, 10 November, 1953						(G)
Swindon T.	App	07.71	71-83	371	0	0
ALLAN John						
Stirling, 22 March, 1931						(CF)
Bradford P.A.	Third Lanark	02.59	58-60	70	-	51
Halifax T.	Tr	03.61	60	10	-	1
ALLAN John						
Amble, 26 September, 1931						(G)
Barnsley	Amble W.	01.49	51-52	11	-	0
ALLANSON Gary Ernest						
Hull, 6 March, 1965						(RB)
Doncaster Rov.	App	03.83	81-82	11	2	0
ALLARDYCE Craig Samuel						
Bolton, 9 June, 1975						(CD)
Preston N.E.	YT	07.93	92	0	1	0
Blackpool	Northwich Vic.	09.94	95	0	1	0
Chesterfield (N/C)	Chorley	03.98	97	0	1	0
ALLARDYCE Samuel						
Dudley, 19 October, 1954						(CD)
Bolton W.	App	11.71	73-79	180	4	21
Sunderland	Tr	07.80	80	24	1	2
Millwall	Tr	09.81	81-82	63	0	2
Coventry C.	Tampa Bay (USA)	09.83	83	28	0	1
Huddersfield T.	Tr	07.84	84	37	0	0
Bolton W.	Tr	07.85	85	14	0	0
Preston N.E.	Tr	08.86	86-88	88	2	2
West Bromwich A.	Tr	06.89	89	0	1	0
Preston N.E. (N/C)	(Retired)	08.92	92	1	2	0
ALLATT Vernon						
Cannock, 28 May, 1959						(F)
Halifax T.	Hednesford T.	11.79	79-82	93	5	14
Rochdale	Tr	08.83	83	40	0	8
Crewe Alex.	Tr	06.84	84-85	36	3	8
Preston N.E.	Tr	11.85	85	17	2	3
Stockport Co.	Tr	10.86	86	23	1	10
Crewe Alex. (N/C)	Hednesford T.	12.87	87	4	1	2
ALLAWAY James Frederick						
Bristol, 23 April, 1922 Died 1991						(IF)
Bristol Rov.		12.46	46	4	-	0
Bristol C.	Tr	09.47				
ALLCHURCH Ivor John						
Swansea, 16 December, 1929 Died 1997 W-68						(IF)
Swansea C.	Plasmarl	05.47	49-58	330	-	124
Newcastle U.	Tr	10.58	58-61	143	-	46
Cardiff C.	Tr	08.62	62-64	103	-	39
Swansea C.	Tr	07.65	65-67	116	2	42
ALLCHURCH Leonard						
Swansea, 12 September, 1933 W Sch/W-11						(OR)
Swansea C.	Jnrs	10.50	51-60	272	-	49
Sheffield U.	Tr	03.61	60-64	123	-	32
Stockport Co.	Tr	09.65	65-68	131	0	16
Swansea C.	Tr	07.69	69-70	70	3	11

League Club	Source	Date Signed	Seasons Played	Career Record Apps	Subs	Gls
ALLCOCK Frank Edward						
Beeston, 7 September, 1925						(FB)
Nottingham F.	Beeston B.C.	03.45				
Aston Villa	Tr	08.46				
Bristol Rov.	Cheltenham T.	06.52	53-55	59	-	0
ALLCOCK Kenneth						
Kirkby-in-Ashfield, 24 April, 1921 Died 1996						(CF)
Mansfield T.	Notts Co. (Am)	04.47	47	1	-	0
ALLCOCK Terence						
Leeds, 10 December, 1935						(IF)
Bolton W.	Jnrs	12.52	53-57	31	-	9
Norwich C.	Tr	03.58	57-68	334	5	106
ALLDER Douglas Stewart						
Hammersmith, 30 December, 1951 E Yth						(M)
Millwall	App	10.69	69-74	191	11	10
Leyton Orient	Tr	07.75	75-76	34	7	0
Watford (N/C)	Torquay U. (N/C)	09.77	77	1	0	0
Brentford	Tr	10.77	77-79	68	20	2
ALLDIS Gilbert John						
Birkenhead, 26 January, 1920						(WH)
Tranmere Rov.		10.38	38-48	74	-	4
New Brighton	Tr	07.50	50	12	-	0
ALLEN Adrian						
Preston , 23 March, 1934						(OR)
Southport (Am)	Preston N.E. (Am)	05.54	54	6	-	0
ALLEN Andrew						
Liverpool, 4 September, 1974						(W)
Chester C.	YT	●	91	0	1	0
ALLEN Anthony						
Stoke, 27 November, 1939 E Yth/Eu23-7/EF Lge/E-3						(LB)
Stoke C.	Jnrs	11.56	57-69	414	3	2
Bury	Tr	10.70	70-71	29	0	0
ALLEN Herbert **Anthony (Tanner)**						
Nottingham, 27 October, 1924						(FB)
Nottingham F.	Beeston B.C.	01.46	47	1	-	0
Notts Co.	Tr	08.49	51-53	30	-	0
ALLEN Bradley James						
Romford, 13 September, 1971 E Yth/Eu21-8						(F)
Queens Park R.	Jnrs	09.88	88-95	56	25	27
Charlton Ath.	Tr	03.96	95-97	30	10	9
ALLEN Brynley William						
Gilfach Goch, 23 March, 1921 W-2						(IF)
Swansea C.	Gilfach Welfare	03.39				
Cardiff C.	Tr	12.45	46-47	41	-	18
Newport Co.	Tr	10.47	47	26	-	7
Cardiff C.	Tr	08.48	48	17	-	4
Reading	Tr	05.49	49	26	-	12
Coventry C.	Tr	02.50	49-52	88	-	26
ALLEN Christopher Anthony						
Oxford, 18 November, 1972 E U21-2						(LW)
Oxford U.	YT	05.91	91-95	110	40	12
Nottingham F.	L	02.96	95	1	2	1
Nottingham F.	Tr	07.96	96-97	17	8	0
Luton T.	L	11.97	97	14	0	1
ALLEN Clive Darren						
Stepney, 20 May, 1961 E Sch/E Yth/Eu21-3/EF Lge/E-5						(F)
Queens Park R.	App	09.78	78-79	43	6	32
Arsenal	Tr	06.80				
Crystal Palace	Tr	08.80	80	25	0	9
Queens Park R.	Tr	06.81	81-83	83	4	40
Tottenham H.	Tr	08.84	84-87	97	8	60
Manchester C.	Bordeaux (Fr)	08.89	89-91	31	22	16
Chelsea	Tr	12.91	91	15	1	7
West Ham U.	Tr	03.92	91-93	36	2	17
Millwall	Tr	03.94	93-94	11	1	0
Carlisle U. (N/C)	Tr	09.95	95	3	0	0
ALLEN Dennis James						
Romford, 2 March, 1939 Died 1995						(IF)
Charlton Ath.	Jnrs	08.56	57-60	5	-	1
Reading	Tr	06.61	61-69	332	4	85
Bournemouth	Tr	08.70	70	17	0	3
ALLEN Derrick						
Wombwell, 14 July, 1946						(HB)
Rotherham U.	Jnrs	11.65	65	1	0	0
ALLEN Derrick Sydney						
Luton, 18 April, 1930 Died 1978						(F)
Luton T.	Alton T.	01.52	54	1	-	0
Watford	Tr	06.56	56	6	-	1
ALLEN Frank						
Shirebrook, 28 June, 1927						(FB)
Chesterfield	Langwith Imps	03.51	51-52	3	-	0
Mansfield T.	Tr	07.53	53-54	6	-	0
ALLEN Geoffrey Barry						
Newcastle, 10 November, 1946 E Yth						(OL)
Newcastle U.	Jnrs	02.64	63-68	22	0	1
ALLEN George Henry						
Birmingham, 23 January, 1932						(FB)
Birmingham C.	Coventry C. (Am)	11.52	53-61	135	-	0
Torquay U.	Tr	01.62	61-64	133	-	0
ALLEN Graham						
Bolton, 8 April, 1977 E Yth						(FB)
Everton	YT	12.94	96-97	2	4	0
ALLEN Graham Frederick						
Walsall, 30 August, 1932						(F)
Walsall (Am)		04.54	53	2	-	1
ALLEN Gregory Frank						
West Ham, 18 October, 1967						(M)
Arsenal	App	07.85				
Cambridge U. (N/C)	Dagenham	08.88	88	4	0	0
ALLEN John						
Chester, 14 November, 1964 W Sch/W Yth						(M)
Chester C.	App	11.81	81-83	67	12	5
Mansfield T.	Tr	08.84	84	1	1	0
ALLEN John						
Coventry, 24 April, 1955						(F)
Leicester C.	Hinckley Ath.	08.78				
Port Vale	Tr	06.80	80	18	0	4
ALLEN John (Ian) Craig						
Elderslie, 27 January, 1932						(F)
Queens Park R.	Beith Jnrs	09.52	53	1	-	0
Bournemouth	Tr	07.54	54-55	52	-	11
ALLEN Keith						
Ryde (IOW), 9 November, 1943						(IF)
Portsmouth	Ryde	12.62				
Grimsby T.	Tr	05.64	64	6	-	1
Stockport Co.	Tr	06.65	65-66	49	0	15
Luton T.	Tr	03.67	66-69	128	9	36
Plymouth Arg.	Tr	07.70	70-72	74	5	10
ALLEN Kenneth Richard						
Thornaby, 12 January, 1952						(G)
Hartlepool U. (Am)	Jnrs	08.68	68	7	0	0
West Bromwich A.	Hellenic (SA)	12.72				
Bournemouth	Bath C.	08.78	78-82	152	0	0
Peterborough U. (N/C)	Bury (N/C)	12.83				
Torquay U.	Tr	03.84	83-85	58	0	0
Swindon T.	Tr	09.85	85-86	45	0	0
Torquay U.	Tr	12.86	86-87	74	0	0
Torquay U.	Salisbury	03.89				
ALLEN Kevin						
Ryde (IOW), 22 March, 1961						(FB)
Bournemouth	Jnrs	08.79	79	1	0	0
ALLEN Leighton Gary						
Brighton, 22 November, 1973						(F)
Wimbledon	YT	07.92				
Colchester U.	Tr	08.94	94	0	2	0
ALLEN Leslie William						
Romford, 4 September, 1937 Eu23-1/EF Lge						(CF)
Chelsea	Briggs Sports	09.54	56-59	44	-	11
Tottenham H.	Tr	12.59	59-64	119	-	47
Queens Park R.	Tr	07.65	65-68	123	5	55
ALLEN Malcolm						
Caernarfon, 21 March, 1967 W Yth/W 'B'/W-14						(F)
Watford	App	03.85	85-87	27	12	5
Aston Villa	L	09.87	87	4	0	0
Norwich C.	Tr	08.88	88-89	24	11	8
Millwall	Tr	03.90	89-92	64	17	24
Newcastle U.	Tr	08.93	93-94	9	1	5

League Club	Source	Date Signed	Seasons Played	Career Record Apps	Subs	Gls
ALLEN Mark Stephen						
Newcastle, 18 December, 1963						(F)
Burnley	App	12.81	81	0	2	1
Tranmere Rov.	Tr	08.83	83	6	4	0
ALLEN Martin James						
Reading, 14 August, 1965 E Yth/Eu21-2						(M)
Queens Park R.	App	05.83	84-89	128	8	16
West Ham U.	Tr	08.89	89-95	163	27	26
Portsmouth	L	09.95	95	15	0	3
Portsmouth	Tr	02.96	95-97	19	11	1
Southend U.	L	09.97	97	5	0	0
ALLEN Michael						
South Shields, 30 March, 1949						(D)
Middlesbrough	App	05.66	67-71	32	2	0
Brentford	Tr	10.71	71-78	223	10	11
ALLEN Paul Kevin						
Aveley, 28 August, 1962 E Yth/Eu21-3						(RM)
West Ham U.	App	08.79	79-84	149	3	6
Tottenham H.	Tr	06.85	85-93	276	16	23
Southampton	Tr	09.93	93-95	40	3	1
Luton T.	L	12.94	94	4	0	0
Stoke C.	L	01.95	94	17	0	1
Swindon T.	Tr	10.95	95-96	30	7	1
Bristol C.	Tr	01.97	96	13	1	0
Millwall	Tr	08.97	97	21	7	0
ALLEN Paul Michael						
Doncaster, 30 July, 1967						(G)
Doncaster Rov. (N/C)	Bradford C. (YT)	10.84	84-85	4	0	0
ALLEN Paul Robert						
Radcliffe, 13 March, 1968						(M)
Bolton W.	YT	07.86	86	0	1	0
ALLEN Peter Charles						
Hove, 1 November, 1946						(M)
Leyton Orient	Tottenham H. (Am)	07.65	65-77	424	8	27
Millwall	Tr	03.78	77-78	16	2	0
ALLEN Peter Michael						
Bristol, 8 October, 1934						(CH)
Bristol C.		07.53	54	1	-	0
ALLEN Arthur **Reginald**						
Marylebone, 3 May, 1919 EF Lge						(G)
Queens Park R.	Corona	05.38	38-49	183	-	0
Manchester U.	Tr	06.50	50-52	75	-	0
ALLEN Robert						
Belfast, 16 January, 1939						(WH)
Wolverhampton W.	Denbigh T.	09.57				
Coventry C.	Tr	06.59	60-61	25	-	2
ALLEN Robert Howard Allen						
Shepton Mallet, 5 December, 1916						(FB)
Notts Co.		02.45	46	1	-	0
Bristol C.	Tr	11.46	46	1	-	0
ALLEN Albert **Robert**						
Bromley, 11 October, 1916 Died 1992 E Sch						(FB)
Leyton Orient (Am)	Tottenham H. (Am)	12.33	33	1	-	0
Fulham	Leytonstone	05.34	34-36	11	-	0
Doncaster Rov.	Tr	06.37	37	31	-	6
Brentford	Tr	06.38				
Northampton T.	Tr	09.45	46	5	-	0
Colchester U.	Tr	(N/L)	50	29	-	1
ALLEN Ronald						
Fenton, 15 January, 1929 EF Lge/E'B'/E-5						(CF)
Port Vale	Jnrs	04.46	46-49	123	-	34
West Bromwich A.	Tr	03.50	49-60	415	-	208
Crystal Palace	Tr	05.61	61-64	100	-	34
ALLEN Ronald Leslie						
Birmingham, 22 April, 1935						(RB)
Birmingham C.	Jnrs	05.53				
Lincoln C.	Tr	07.58	58-60	60	-	1
ALLEN Rory William						
Beckenham, 17 October, 1977 Eu21-3						(F)
Tottenham H.	YT	03.96	96-97	10	6	2
Luton T.	L	03.98	97	8	0	6
ALLEN Russell Philip						
Smethwick, 9 January, 1954						(F)
West Bromwich A.	Arsenal (App)	05.71				
Tranmere Rov.	Tr	07.73	73-77	137	19	44
Mansfield T.	Tr	07.78	78-80	99	17	18
ALLEN William						
Newburn, 22 October, 1917 Died 1981						(IF)
Chesterfield		11.37	38	2	-	0
York C.	Tr	05.39	46-49	129	-	23
Scunthorpe U.	Tr	06.50	50-51	64	-	1
ALLEYNE Andrew McArthur						
Barbados (WI), 19 May, 1951						(FB)
Reading	Newbury T.	11.72	72-75	46	2	2
ALLEYNE Robert Anthony						
Birmingham, 27 September, 1968						(F)
Leicester C.	Jnrs	01.87	86	1	2	0
Wrexham	L	10.87	87	7	3	2
Chesterfield	Tr	03.88	87-88	32	8	5
ALLINSON Ian James Robert						
Hitchin, 1 October, 1957						(W)
Colchester U.	App	10.75	74-82	291	17	69
Arsenal	Tr	08.83	83-86	60	23	16
Stoke C.	Tr	06.87	87	6	3	0
Luton T.	Tr	10.87	87-88	24	8	3
Colchester U.	Tr	12.88	88-89	36	2	10
ALLINSON Jamie						
Stockton, 15 June, 1978						(CD)
Hartlepool U.	YT	●	95	3	1	0
ALLISON John						
Stannington (Nd), 31 July, 1922 Died 1985						(OL)
Chesterfield	West Sleekburn	04.47				
Reading	Blyth Spartans	01.49	48-49	29	-	4
Walsall	Tr	06.50	50-51	47	-	1
ALLISON John Alfred						
Cramlington, 9 August, 1932						(CH)
Chesterfield	Blyth Spartans	05.55	57-60	32	-	0
ALLISON John Joseph						
Consett, 17 November, 1913 Died 1971						(WH)
Barnsley	Workington	05.39				
Hartlepool U.	Tr	09.46	46	13	-	0
ALLISON Kenneth						
Edinburgh, 6 January, 1937						(IF)
Darlington	Cowdenbeath	07.63	63-65	75	0	39
Lincoln C.	Tr	02.66	65-66	41	1	12
ALLISON Malcolm Alexander						
Dartford, 5 September, 1927						(CH)
Charlton Ath.	Erith & Belvedere	12.45	49	2	-	0
West Ham U.	Tr	02.51	50-57	238	-	10
ALLISON Michael						
Bolton, 17 March, 1966						(G)
Chesterfield	Horwich R.M.I.	07.89	90	16	0	0
ALLISON Neil James						
Hull, 20 October, 1973						(CD)
Hull C.	YT	07.90	90-96	95	11	3
Swindon T.	Tr	11.96				
Chesterfield (N/C)	N. Ferriby U.	03.97	96	0	2	0
ALLISON Thomas						
Fencehouses (Dm), 20 February, 1921						(IF)
Darlington	South Hetton	09.46	46	6	-	0
ALLISON Wayne Anthony						
Huddersfield, 16 October, 1968						(F)
Halifax T.	YT	07.87	86-88	74	10	21
Watford	Tr	07.89	89	6	1	0
Bristol C.	Tr	08.90	90-94	149	46	48
Swindon T.	Tr	07.95	95-97	98	3	31
Huddersfield T.	Tr	11.97	97	27	0	6
ALLISTER John Grandison						
Edinburgh, 30 June, 1927						(IF)
Chelsea	Tranent Jnrs	07.49	51-52	4	-	1
Chesterfield	Aberdeen	06.58				
ALLMAN George						
Stockport, 23 July, 1930						(F)
Stockport Co.		05.50	50-51	7	-	1
Chester C.	Holywell T.	07.55	55-56	49	-	13

ALLON Joseph Ball
Gateshead, 12 November, 1966 E Yth (F)

League Club	Source	Date Signed	Seasons Played	Apps	Subs	Gls
Newcastle U.	YT	11.84	84-86	9	0	2
Swansea C.	Tr	07.87	87-88	27	7	12
Hartlepool U.	Tr	10.88	88-90	112	0	48
Chelsea	Tr	08.91	91-92	3	11	2
Port Vale	L	02.92	91	2	4	0
Brentford	Tr	11.92	92-93	38	7	19
Southend U.	L	09.93	93	2	1	0
Port Vale	Tr	03.94	93-94	13	10	9
Lincoln C.	Tr	07.95	95	3	1	0
Hartlepool U.	Tr	10.95	95-97	52	4	19

ALLOTT Mark Stephen
Manchester, 3 October, 1977 (CF)

League Club	Source	Date Signed	Seasons Played	Apps	Subs	Gls
Oldham Ath.	YT	10.95	96-97	10	17	3

ALLPRESS Timothy John
Hitchin, 27 January, 1971 (CD)

League Club	Source	Date Signed	Seasons Played	Apps	Subs	Gls
Luton T.	YT	07.89	89	1	0	0
Preston N.E.	L	10.91	91	7	2	0
Colchester U.	Tr	08.93	93-94	24	10	0

ALLSOP Norman
West Bromwich, 1 November, 1930 (IF)

League Club	Source	Date Signed	Seasons Played	Apps	Subs	Gls
West Bromwich A.	Hednesford T.	05.48				
Walsall	Worcester C.	10.53	53	9	-	0

ALLSOP William Henry
Ripley, 29 January, 1912 Died 1997 (FB)

League Club	Source	Date Signed	Seasons Played	Apps	Subs	Gls
Port Vale	Bolton W. (Am)	08.31	31-32	6	-	0
Halifax T.	Tr	05.34	34-46	203	-	0

ALLUM Albert Edward
Notting Hill, 15 October, 1930 (F)

League Club	Source	Date Signed	Seasons Played	Apps	Subs	Gls
Queens Park R.	Hereford U.	06.57	57	1	-	0

ALOISI John
Australia, 5 February, 1976 Australian Int (F)

League Club	Source	Date Signed	Seasons Played	Apps	Subs	Gls
Portsmouth	Cremonese (It)	08.97	97	33	5	12

ALSFORD Julian
Poole, 24 December, 1972 (CD)

League Club	Source	Date Signed	Seasons Played	Apps	Subs	Gls
Watford	YT	04.91	92-93	9	4	1
Chester C.	Tr	08.94	94-97	136	5	6

ALSOP Gilbert Arthur
Bristol, 10 September, 1908 Died 1992 (CF)

League Club	Source	Date Signed	Seasons Played	Apps	Subs	Gls
Coventry C.	Bath C.	12.29	29-30	16	-	4
Walsall	Tr	10.31	31-35	160	-	126
West Bromwich A.	Tr	11.35	35	1	-	0
Ipswich T.	Tr	06.37	38	9	-	2
Walsall	Tr	11.38	38-46	35	-	25

ALSOP Julian Mark
Nuneaton, 28 May, 1973 (F)

League Club	Source	Date Signed	Seasons Played	Apps	Subs	Gls
Bristol Rov.	Halesowen T.	02.97	96-97	20	13	4
Swansea C.	L	01.98	97	5	0	2
Swansea C.	Tr	03.98	97	7	0	1

ALSTON Adrian
Preston, 6 February, 1949 Australian Int (F)

League Club	Source	Date Signed	Seasons Played	Apps	Subs	Gls
Luton T.	Safeways (Aus)	08.74	74-75	26	3	8
Cardiff C.	Tr	10.75	75-76	44	4	16

ALSTON Alexander George
Preston, 26 February, 1937 (F)

League Club	Source	Date Signed	Seasons Played	Apps	Subs	Gls
Preston N.E.	Netherfield	05.55	57-62	102	-	26
Bury	Tr	03.63	62-65	86	0	22
Barrow	Tr	09.65	65-66	46	1	14

ALTY Colin
Southport, 23 October, 1944 (D)

League Club	Source	Date Signed	Seasons Played	Apps	Subs	Gls
Preston N.E.	Jnrs	10.61	62			
Southport	Tr	06.64	64-69	184	6	22

ALVES Paulo Lourenco
Portugal, 10 December, 1969 Portuguese Int (CF)

League Club	Source	Date Signed	Seasons Played	Apps	Subs	Gls
West Ham U. (L)	Sporting Lisbon (Por)	11.97	97	0	4	0

AMBLER Roy
Wakefield, 2 December, 1937 (IF)

League Club	Source	Date Signed	Seasons Played	Apps	Subs	Gls
Leeds U.	Jnrs	12.54				
Shrewsbury T.	Tr	01.59	58-60	29	-	8
Wrexham	Tr	05.61	61-62	21	-	13
York C.	Tr	11.62	62	12	-	3
Southport	Tr	07.63	63	11	-	0

AMBROSE Anthony **Leroy**
St Vincent (WI), 22 June, 1960 (M)

League Club	Source	Date Signed	Seasons Played	Apps	Subs	Gls
Charlton Ath.	Croydon	08.79	79-81	28	5	1

AMES Kenneth George
Canford, 17 September, 1933 E Sch (CF)

League Club	Source	Date Signed	Seasons Played	Apps	Subs	Gls
Portsmouth	Jnrs	09.50	53	2	-	0

AMES Percy Talbot
Bedford, 13 December, 1931 (G)

League Club	Source	Date Signed	Seasons Played	Apps	Subs	Gls
Tottenham H.	Bedford Ave.	05.51				
Colchester U.	Tr	05.55	55-64	397	-	0

AMES Trevor
Poole, 14 December, 1962 (F)

League Club	Source	Date Signed	Seasons Played	Apps	Subs	Gls
Hereford U.	Aston Villa (App)	10.80	80-81	5	3	0
Crystal Palace	Tr	10.81				

AMMANN Michael Anton
USA, 8 February, 1971 (G)

League Club	Source	Date Signed	Seasons Played	Apps	Subs	Gls
Charlton Ath.	L.A. Cobras (USA)	07.94	94-95	28	2	0

AMOKACHI Daniel Owofen
Nigeria, 30 December, 1972 Nigerian Int (F)

League Club	Source	Date Signed	Seasons Played	Apps	Subs	Gls
Everton	F.C. Bruges (Bel)	08.94	94-95	34	9	10

AMOR William George
Pewsey, 6 November, 1919 Died 1988 E Amat (OR)

League Club	Source	Date Signed	Seasons Played	Apps	Subs	Gls
Reading (Am)	Huntley & Palmers	12.47	47-51	66	-	12

AMOS Keith James
Walton-on-Thames, 13 January, 1932 (G)

League Club	Source	Date Signed	Seasons Played	Apps	Subs	Gls
Arsenal	Jnrs	05.52				
Aldershot	Tr	08.54	55-57	77	-	0

AMPADU Patrick **Kwame**
Bradford, 20 December, 1970 IR Yth/IRu21-4 (M)

League Club	Source	Date Signed	Seasons Played	Apps	Subs	Gls
Arsenal	YT	11.88	89	0	2	0
Plymouth Arg.	L	10.90	90	6	0	1
West Bromwich A.	L	03.91	90	3	4	0
West Bromwich A.	Tr	06.91	91-93	27	22	4
Swansea C.	Tr	02.94	93-97	128	19	12

AMPHLET Raymond Henry
Manchester, 25 September, 1922 (LB)

League Club	Source	Date Signed	Seasons Played	Apps	Subs	Gls
Cardiff C.	Guildford C.	04.48				
Newport Co.	Tr	04.49	49	13	-	0

AMPOFO Christopher John Kwasi
Paddington, 6 October, 1963 (CD)

League Club	Source	Date Signed	Seasons Played	Apps	Subs	Gls
West Ham U.	App	10.81				
Aldershot	Tr	08.83	83	4	0	0

ANDERS Henry (Harry)
St Helens, 28 November, 1926 Died 1994 (OR)

League Club	Source	Date Signed	Seasons Played	Apps	Subs	Gls
Preston N.E.	St Helens	08.45	47-52	69	-	4
Manchester C.	Tr	03.53	52-54	32	-	4
Port Vale	Tr	07.56	56	3	-	0
Accrington St.	Tr	06.57	57-59	114	-	18
Workington	Tr	07.60	60	7	-	1

ANDERS James
St Helens, 8 March, 1928 (OL)

League Club	Source	Date Signed	Seasons Played	Apps	Subs	Gls
Preston N.E.	St Helens	08.45				
Brentford	Tr	09.48	49-50	12	-	0
Bradford C.	Tr	06.51	51-52	51	-	11
Rochdale	Tr	07.53	53-56	123	-	28
Bradford P.A.	Tr	09.56	56	20	-	4
Accrington St.	Tr	01.57	56-59	129	-	29
Bradford P.A.	Buxton	09.60	60-61	39	-	8
Tranmere Rov.	Tr	11.61	61	8	-	1

ANDERS Jason Stuart
Littleborough, 13 March, 1974 (F)

League Club	Source	Date Signed	Seasons Played	Apps	Subs	Gls
Rochdale	YT	07.92	90-92	2	15	1

ANDERSEN Leif Erik
Norway, 19 April, 1971 (CD)

League Club	Source	Date Signed	Seasons Played	Apps	Subs	Gls
Crystal Palace	Moss F.K. (Nor)	01.96	96	19	11	1

ANDERSEN Nicholas John
Lincoln, 29 March, 1969 (M/RB)

League Club	Source	Date Signed	Seasons Played	Apps	Subs	Gls
Mansfield T.	YT	01.87	86-88	9	11	0
Lincoln C. (N/C)	Tr	08.89	89	1	0	0

ANDERSEN Vetle
Norway, 20 April, 1964 (D)

League Club	Source	Date Signed	Seasons Played	Apps	Subs	Gls
West Bromwich A. (N/C)	Lyngby (Den)	12.89	89	0	1	0

ANDERSON Arthur **Alan** Duncan
Edinburgh, 21 December, 1939 (WH)

League Club	Source	Date Signed	Seasons Played	Apps	Subs	Gls
Millwall	Falkirk	09.59	60-61	74	-	0
Scunthorpe U.	Tr	07.62	62	6	-	0

ANDERSON Alexander
Glasgow, 8 January, 1922 Died 1984 Lo1 (G)

League Club	Source	Date Signed	Seasons Played	Apps	Subs	Gls
Rochdale	Hearts	02.48	47	4	-	0
Southport	Dundalk	11.49	49-50	21	-	0

ANDERSON Alexander Ferguson
Monifieth, 15 November, 1921 (FB)

League Club	Source	Date Signed	Seasons Played	Apps	Subs	Gls
Southampton	Forfar Ath.	11.49	49-51	20	-	0
Exeter C.	Tr	06.52	52	6	-	0

ANDERSON Alexander (Sandy) Ogilvie Walker
Auchtermuchty, 20 February, 1930 (FB)

League Club	Source	Date Signed	Seasons Played	Apps	Subs	Gls
Southend U.	Newburgh Jnrs	04.50	50-62	452	-	8

ANDERSON Benjamin Cummings
Aberdeen, 18 February, 1946 (CD)

League Club	Source	Date Signed	Seasons Played	Apps	Subs	Gls
Blackburn Rov.	Peterlee	03.64	64-67	21	7	7
Bury	Tr	07.68	68-69	51	2	4
Crystal Palace	Cape Town C. (SA)	11.73	73	11	0	1

ANDERSON Christopher
Aberdeen, 30 August, 1925 Died 1986 (RH)

League Club	Source	Date Signed	Seasons Played	Apps	Subs	Gls
Hartlepool U.	Aberdeen	09.46	46	2	-	0

ANDERSON Christopher Shelley
East Wemyss, 28 November, 1928 Died 1996 (OR)

League Club	Source	Date Signed	Seasons Played	Apps	Subs	Gls
Blackburn Rov.	Lochore Welfare	08.50	50-51	13	-	1
Stockport Co.	Kidderminster Hrs	06.53	53	34	-	0
Southport	Tr	07.54	54	28	-	0

ANDERSON Colin Russell
Newcastle, 26 April, 1962 (LB/M))

League Club	Source	Date Signed	Seasons Played	Apps	Subs	Gls
Burnley	App	04.80	80-81	3	3	0
Torquay	North Shields	09.82	82-84	107	2	11
West Bromwich A.	Tr	03.85	85-90	131	9	10
Walsall	Tr	08.91	91	25	1	2
Hereford U.	Tr	08.92	92-93	67	3	1
Exeter C.	Tr	07.94	94-95	26	8	1

ANDERSON Dale
Newton Aycliffe, 23 August, 1970 (F)

League Club	Source	Date Signed	Seasons Played	Apps	Subs	Gls
Darlington	YT	09.88	86-88	4	11	0
Middlesbrough	Tr	07.90				

ANDERSON Darren Irwin
Merton, 6 September, 1966 E Yth (CD)

League Club	Source	Date Signed	Seasons Played	Apps	Subs	Gls
Charlton Ath.	Coventry C. (App)	03.84	83-84	10	0	1
Crewe Alex.	L	10.85	85	5	0	0
Aldershot	Tr	07.86	86-89	69	29	4

ANDERSON Desmond
Edinburgh, 9 January, 1938 S Sch (WH)

League Club	Source	Date Signed	Seasons Played	Apps	Subs	Gls
Millwall	Hibernian	06.61	61-63	46	-	1

ANDERSON John **Desmond**
Templepatrick (NI), 11 September, 1940 NI Amat/NI-5 (HB)

League Club	Source	Date Signed	Seasons Played	Apps	Subs	Gls
Exeter C.	Glenavon	08.62	62-65	142	2	1
Chesterfield	Tr	07.66	66-67	8	0	0

ANDERSON Douglas Eric
Hong Kong, 29 August, 1963 (LW)

League Club	Source	Date Signed	Seasons Played	Apps	Subs	Gls
Oldham Ath.	Port Glasgow	09.80	81-83	4	5	0
Tranmere Rov.	Tr	08.84	84-86	125	1	15
Plymouth Arg.	Tr	08.87	87	17	2	1
Cambridge U.	L	09.88	88	8	0	2
Northampton T.	L	12.88	88	4	1	0

ANDERSON Edward
Glasgow, 23 September, 1917 (FB)

League Club	Source	Date Signed	Seasons Played	Apps	Subs	Gls
Rochdale	Stirling A.	03.48	47	1	-	0

ANDERSON Edward Walton
Tynemouth, 17 July, 1911 Died 1979 (FB)

League Club	Source	Date Signed	Seasons Played	Apps	Subs	Gls
Wolverhampton W.	Worksop T.	12.29	30	3	-	0
Torquay U.	Tr	12.31	31-32	61	-	2
West Ham U.	Tr	06.33	33-34	26	-	2
Chester C.	Tr	06.35	35-36	23	-	0
Tranmere Rov.	Tr	07.37	37-47	74	-	0

ANDERSON Eric
Manchester, 12 July, 1931 Died 1990 (IF)

League Club	Source	Date Signed	Seasons Played	Apps	Subs	Gls
Liverpool		12.51	52-56	73	-	21
Barnsley	Tr	07.57	57	9	-	1

ANDERSON Gary Leslie
Bow, 20 October, 1955 (FB)

League Club	Source	Date Signed	Seasons Played	Apps	Subs	Gls
Tottenham H.	App	12.72				
Northampton T.	Tr	03.75	74-75	14	0	0

ANDERSON Geoffrey Thomas
Newcastle, 26 November, 1944 (W)

League Club	Source	Date Signed	Seasons Played	Apps	Subs	Gls
Birmingham C.	App	12.62	63	1	-	0
Mansfield T.	Tr	05.64	64-65	43	0	13
Lincoln C.	Tr	07.66	66	44	0	6

ANDERSON Ijah Massai
Hackney, 30 December, 1975 (LB)

League Club	Source	Date Signed	Seasons Played	Apps	Subs	Gls
Southend U.	Tottenham H. (YT)	08.94				
Brentford	Tr	07.95	95-97	88	0	3

ANDERSON James
Pelaw, 23 July, 1913 (LB)

League Club	Source	Date Signed	Seasons Played	Apps	Subs	Gls
Brentford	Blyth Spartans	07.39				
Carlisle U.	Tr	09.46	46	11	-	0

ANDERSON James McFarland
Glasgow, 25 December, 1932 (WH)

League Club	Source	Date Signed	Seasons Played	Apps	Subs	Gls
Bristol Rov.	R.A.O.C. Hilsea	04.53	54-56	24	-	0
Chester C.	Tr	06.57	57-59	62	-	0

ANDERSON John
Neilston, 8 December, 1929 S'B'/S-1 (G)

League Club	Source	Date Signed	Seasons Played	Apps	Subs	Gls
Leicester C.	Arthurlie	12.48	48-58	261	-	0
Peterborough U.	Tr	07.60				

ANDERSON John
Salford, 11 October, 1921 (WH)

League Club	Source	Date Signed	Seasons Played	Apps	Subs	Gls
Manchester U.	Jnrs	11.38	47-48	33	-	1
Nottingham F.	Tr	10.49	49-50	40	-	1

ANDERSON John Christopher Patrick
Dublin, 7 November, 1959 IR Yth/IRu21-1/IR-16 (D)

League Club	Source	Date Signed	Seasons Played	Apps	Subs	Gls
West Bromwich A.	App.	11.77				
Preston N.E.	Tr	08.79	79-81	47	4	0
Newcastle U.	Tr	09.82	82-90	283	16	14

ANDERSON John Curr
Dundee, 8 May, 1915 Died 1987 (CF)

League Club	Source	Date Signed	Seasons Played	Apps	Subs	Gls
Portsmouth	Stobswell	01.33	33-38	80	-	36
Aldershot	Tr	06.46	46	4	-	1

ANDERSON John Ephraim
Ridsdale, 7 June, 1931 (FB)

League Club	Source	Date Signed	Seasons Played	Apps	Subs	Gls
Grimsby T.	Langold Colly	05.54	55	3	-	0

ANDERSON John Hugh Todd
Johnstone, 11 January, 1937 (W)

League Club	Source	Date Signed	Seasons Played	Apps	Subs	Gls
Stoke C.	Johnstone Burgh	01.57	57-60	24	-	2

ANDERSON John Lochart
Glasgow, 5 April, 1928 (IF)

League Club	Source	Date Signed	Seasons Played	Apps	Subs	Gls
Northampton T.	Partick Thistle	06.53	53	14	-	5
Exeter C.	Tr	07.54	54	7	-	0
Wrexham	Dundee	06.56	56-58	98	-	27
Rochdale	Tr	07.59	59	28	-	5
Chester C.	Tr	07.60	60	17	-	2
Wrexham	Tr	08.61	61	1	-	0

ANDERSON Lee Charles
Tottington, 4 October, 1973 (RB)

League Club	Source	Date Signed	Seasons Played	Apps	Subs	Gls
Bury	YT	10.91	91-96	27	2	0
Doncaster Rov. (N/C)	Southport	03.97	96	6	0	0

ANDERSON Norman Hindmarsh
Hebburn, 30 November, 1930 (F)

League Club	Source	Date Signed	Seasons Played	Apps	Subs	Gls
Gateshead	Reyrolles	03.51	53-55	19	-	2

ANDERSON Percy Archibald
Cambridge, 22 September, 1930 (IF)

League Club	Source	Date Signed	Seasons Played	Apps	Subs	Gls
West Bromwich A.	Cambridge U.	09.51				
Stockport Co.	Tr	07.53	53	1	-	0

ANDERSON Peter Dennis
Devonport, 11 September, 1932 (W)

League Club	Source	Date Signed	Seasons Played	Apps	Subs	Gls
Plymouth Arg.	Oak Villa	07.50	52-62	241	-	41
Torquay U.	Tr	12.62	62-64	77	-	18

ANDERSON Peter Thomas
Hendon, 31 May, 1949 (M)

League Club	Source	Date Signed	Seasons Played	Apps	Subs	Gls
Luton T.	Hendon	02.71	70-75	178	3	34
Sheffield U.	Tampa Bay (USA)	09.78	78	28	2	12
Millwall	Tampa Bay (USA)	12.80	80-82	30	2	4

ANDERSON Philip Oswald
Portadown (NI), 5 January, 1948 (IF)

League Club	Source	Date Signed	Seasons Played	Apps	Subs	Gls
Bury	Portadown	05.66	66-69	5	4	1

ANDERSON Robert
Newton Mearns, 11 August, 1928 (W)

League Club	Source	Date Signed	Seasons Played	Apps	Subs	Gls
Leicester C.	Jnrs	01.46	46-47	19	-	2

ANDERSON Robert
Aberdeen, 21 January, 1937 (OR)

League Club	Source	Date Signed	Seasons Played	Apps	Subs	Gls
Chesterfield	Partick Thistle	08.59	59	4	-	0

ANDERSON Robert John
Portsmouth, 23 February, 1936 Died 1996 (W)

League Club	Source	Date Signed	Seasons Played	Apps	Subs	Gls
Mansfield T.	Chesterfield Tube	09.56	56-59	40	-	4

ANDERSON John **Robert**
Prestwick, 9 November, 1924 Died 1994 (G)

League Club	Source	Date Signed	Seasons Played	Apps	Subs	Gls
Middlesbrough	Blackhall Colly	11.45	47	1	-	0
Crystal Palace	Blackhall Colly	10.51	51-52	38	-	0
Bristol Rov.	Tr	03.53	52-53	10	-	0
Bristol C.	Tr	04.54	54-58	106	-	0

ANDERSON Robert Lymbun
Derry (NI), 23 April, 1926 Died 1986 (FB)

League Club	Source	Date Signed	Seasons Played	Apps	Subs	Gls
Doncaster Rov.	Derry C.	11.49	50-51	3	-	0

ANDERSON Ronald James
Gateshead, 3 July, 1922 Died 1984 (IF)

League Club	Source	Date Signed	Seasons Played	Apps	Subs	Gls
Bury		08.39	46	2	-	0
Crystal Palace	Tr	05.47				

ANDERSON Samuel
Manchester, 11 January, 1936 (FB)

League Club	Source	Date Signed	Seasons Played	Apps	Subs	Gls
Oldham Ath.	Oldham Amats	08.54	55-56	6	-	0

ANDERSON Stanley
Horden, 27 February, 1934 E Sch/Eu23-4/E-2 (WH)

League Club	Source	Date Signed	Seasons Played	Apps	Subs	Gls
Sunderland	Jnrs	03.51	52-63	402	-	31
Newcastle U.	Tr	11.63	63-65	81	0	13
Middlesbrough	Tr	11.65	65	21	0	2

ANDERSON Terence Keith
Woking, 11 March, 1944 Died 1980 E Yth (W)

League Club	Source	Date Signed	Seasons Played	Apps	Subs	Gls
Arsenal	App	08.61	62-64	25	-	6
Norwich C.	Tr	02.65	64-73	218	18	16
Colchester U.	L	02.74	73	4	0	0
Scunthorpe U.	Baltimore (USA)	09.74	74	10	0	0
Crewe Alex.	Tr	11.74	74	4	0	0
Colchester U.	Baltimore (USA)	08.75	75	13	3	0

ANDERSON Thomas Cowan
Haddington, 24 September, 1934 S Sch (IF)

League Club	Source	Date Signed	Seasons Played	Apps	Subs	Gls
Watford	Queen of South	12.56	56-57	52	-	12
Bournemouth	Tr	06.58	58	5	-	1
Queens Park R.	Tr	11.58	58	10	-	3
Torquay U.	Tr	07.59	59	9	-	4
Stockport Co.	Tr	06.60	60-61	60	-	17
Doncaster Rov.	Tr	11.61	61	16	-	3
Wrexham	Tr	03.62	61-62	12	-	3
Barrow	Hellas (Aus)	12.63	63	11	-	3
Watford	Hellas (Aus)	12.64	64-65	21	0	2
Leyton Orient	George Cross (Aus)	07.67	67	8	1	0

ANDERSON Trevor
Belfast, 3 March, 1951 NIu21-1/NI-22 (W)

League Club	Source	Date Signed	Seasons Played	Apps	Subs	Gls
Manchester U.	Portadown	10.72	72-73	13	6	2
Swindon T.	Tr	11.74	74-77	128	3	35
Peterborough U.	Tr	12.77	77-78	49	0	6

ANDERSON Vivian Alexander
Nottingham, 29 July, 1956 Eu21-1/E-'B'/EF Lge/E-30 (RB)

League Club	Source	Date Signed	Seasons Played	Apps	Subs	Gls
Nottingham F.	App	08.74	74-83	323	5	15
Arsenal	Tr	07.84	84-86	120	0	9
Manchester U.	Tr	05.87	87-90	50	4	2
Sheffield Wed.	Tr	01.91	90-92	60	10	8
Barnsley	Tr	07.93	93	20	0	3
Middlesbrough	Tr	07.94	94	2	0	0

ANDERSON William
Lochore (Fife), 6 November, 1926 (IF)

League Club	Source	Date Signed	Seasons Played	Apps	Subs	Gls
Southend U.	Hibernian	05.54	54-55	16	-	1

ANDERSON William Boston
Sunderland, 28 March, 1935 (WH)

League Club	Source	Date Signed	Seasons Played	Apps	Subs	Gls
Barnsley	Silksworth Jnrs	09.52	55	6	-	0
Hartlepool U.	Tr	02.56	55-60	179	-	11

ANDERSON William John
Liverpool, 24 January, 1947 (W)

League Club	Source	Date Signed	Seasons Played	Apps	Subs	Gls
Manchester U.	App	02.64	63-66	7	2	0
Aston Villa	Tr	01.67	66-72	229	2	36
Cardiff C.	Tr	02.73	72-76	122	4	12

ANDERSON William Ronald
Ponteland, 20 September, 1927 Died 1995 (G)

League Club	Source	Date Signed	Seasons Played	Apps	Subs	Gls
Newcastle U.	Throckley Welfare	02.47	46	1	-	0

ANDERSON William Ross
Kilmarnock, 13 November, 1919 Died 1981 (F)

League Club	Source	Date Signed	Seasons Played	Apps	Subs	Gls
Millwall	Dundee	07.44	46-47	32	-	6

ANDERSSON Anders Per
Tomelia, Sweden, 15 March, 1974 Swedish Int (M)

League Club	Source	Date Signed	Seasons Played	Apps	Subs	Gls
Blackburn Rov.	Malmo (Swe)	07.97	97	1	3	0

ANDERSSON Andreas Claes
Stockholm, Sweden, 10 April, 1974 Swedish Int (F)

League Club	Source	Date Signed	Seasons Played	Apps	Subs	Gls
Newcastle U.	A.C. Milan (It)	01.98	97	10	2	2

ANDERSSON Patrik Jonas
Sweden, 18 August, 1971 Swedish Int (D)

League Club	Source	Date Signed	Seasons Played	Apps	Subs	Gls
Blackburn Rov.	Malmo F.F. (Swe)	12.92	92-93	7	5	0

ANDERTON Darren Robert
Southampton, 3 March, 1972 E Yth/Eu21-12/E 'B'/E-22 (W)

League Club	Source	Date Signed	Seasons Played	Apps	Subs	Gls
Portsmouth	YT	02.90	90-91	53	9	7
Tottenham H.	Tr	06.92	92-97	131	16	22

ANDERTON John
Skelmersdale, 7 February, 1933 (FB)

League Club	Source	Date Signed	Seasons Played	Apps	Subs	Gls
Everton	Jnrs	03.51				
Torquay U.	Tr	07.54	54-57	40	-	2

ANDERTON Steven David
Lancaster, 2 October, 1969 (M)

League Club	Source	Date Signed	Seasons Played	Apps	Subs	Gls
Preston N.E.	YT	07.88	89	0	1	0

ANDERTON Sylvan James
Reading, 23 November, 1934 (WH)

League Club	Source	Date Signed	Seasons Played	Apps	Subs	Gls
Reading	Jnrs	06.52	52-58	155	-	18
Chelsea	Tr	03.59	58-61	76	-	2
Queens Park R.	Tr	01.62	61	4	-	0

ANDRADE Jose Manuel Gomes
Portugal, 1 June, 1970 (F)

League Club	Source	Date Signed	Seasons Played	Apps	Subs	Gls
Stoke C. (N/C)	Academica Coimbra (Por)	03.95	94	2	2	1
Stoke C.	Tr	08.97	97	4	8	1

ANDREW George
Glasgow, 24 November, 1945 Died 1993 (CH)

League Club	Source	Date Signed	Seasons Played	Apps	Subs	Gls
West Ham U.	Possilpark Jnrs	09.63	66	2	0	0
Crystal Palace	Tr	07.67				

ANDREW Matthew
Johnstone, 5 January, 1922 (HB)

League Club	Source	Date Signed	Seasons Played	Apps	Subs	Gls
Bristol C.		10.47				
Swansea C.	Tr	08.48	48-50	4	-	0
Workington	Tr	06.51	51	22	-	0

ANDREW Ronald Edward Harold
Bebington, 5 January, 1936 (CH)

League Club	Source	Date Signed	Seasons Played	Apps	Subs	Gls
Stoke C.	Ellesmere Port	05.54	57-63	115	-	1
Port Vale	Tr	06.64	64	8	-	1

ANDREWS Benjamin Phillip
Burton, 18 November, 1980 (LB)

League Club	Source	Date Signed	Seasons Played	Apps	Subs	Gls
Brighton & H.A.	YT	•	97	2	1	0

ANDREWS Cecil James
Alton, 1 November, 1930 Died 1986 (WH)

League Club	Source	Date Signed	Seasons Played	Apps	Subs	Gls
Portsmouth		01.49				
Crystal Palace	Tr	06.52	52-55	104	-	12
Queens Park R.	Tr	06.56	56-57	58	-	1

ANDREWS Derek
Bury, 14 December, 1934 (IF)

League Club	Source	Date Signed	Seasons Played	Apps	Subs	Gls
Rochdale		03.55	55	22	-	4

ANDREWS Gary Michael
Nottingham, 12 May, 1968 (FB)

League Club	Source	Date Signed	Seasons Played	Apps	Subs	Gls
Nottingham F.	App	09.85				
Peterborough U.	Tr	08.88	88-89	42	1	0

ANDREWS George
Dudley, 23 April, 1942 (CF)

League Club	Source	Date Signed	Seasons Played	Apps	Subs	Gls
Luton T.	Vono Sports	01.60				
Cardiff C.	Lower Gornal Ath.	10.65	65-66	43	0	21
Southport	Tr	02.67	66-69	115	2	41
Shrewsbury T.	Tr	11.69	69-72	123	1	49
Walsall	Tr	01.73	72-76	156	3	38

ANDREWS Glendon
Dudley, 11 February, 1945 (FB)

League Club	Source	Date Signed	Seasons Played	Apps	Subs	Gls
Manchester U.	Jnrs	09.63				
Wolverhampton W.	Tr	07.66				
Bradford P.A.	Tr	09.67	67-68	47	1	6

ANDREWS Ian Edmund
Nottingham, 1 December, 1964 E Yth/Eu21-1 (G)

League Club	Source	Date Signed	Seasons Played	Apps	Subs	Gls
Leicester C.	App	12.82	83-87	126	0	0
Swindon T.	L	01.84	83	1	0	0
Leeds U. (L)	Glasgow Celtic	12.88	88	1	0	0
Southampton	Glasgow Celtic	12.89	89-94	10	0	0
Bournemouth	Tr	09.94	94-95	64	0	0

ANDREWS James Patrick
Invergordon, 1 February, 1927 (OL)

League Club	Source	Date Signed	Seasons Played	Apps	Subs	Gls
West Ham U.	Dundee	11.51	51-55	114	-	21
Leyton Orient	Tr	06.56	56-58	36	-	8
Queens Park R.	Tr	06.59	59-61	82	-	16

ANDREWS John Edward
York, 3 February, 1950 (G)

League Club	Source	Date Signed	Seasons Played	Apps	Subs	Gls
York C. (Am)	Moor Lane Y.C.	08.68	68	11	0	0

ANDREWS Keri Anthony
Swansea, 28 April, 1968 W Yth (W)

League Club	Source	Date Signed	Seasons Played	Apps	Subs	Gls
Swansea C.	App	04.86	84-87	32	9	3

ANDREWS Leslie Lindon
Dudley, 29 October, 1953 (CF)

League Club	Source	Date Signed	Seasons Played	Apps	Subs	Gls
Wolverhampton W.	Jnrs	09.72				
Scunthorpe U.	L	03.74	73	7	2	1

ANDREWS Arthur **Percy**
Alton, 12 June, 1922 Died 1985 (LB)

League Club	Source	Date Signed	Seasons Played	Apps	Subs	Gls
York C.	Portsmouth (Am)	09.47	47-54	176	-	0

ANDREWS Phillip Donald
Andover, 14 September, 1976 (F)

League Club	Source	Date Signed	Seasons Played	Apps	Subs	Gls
Brighton & H.A.	YT	05.95	93-96	2	23	1

ANDREWS Wayne Michael Hill
Paddington, 25 November, 1977 (F)

League Club	Source	Date Signed	Seasons Played	Apps	Subs	Gls
Watford	YT	07.96	95-97	16	12	4

ANDRUSZEWSKI Emanuel (Manny) Franciszek
Eastleigh, 4 October, 1955 (FB)

League Club	Source	Date Signed	Seasons Played	Apps	Subs	Gls
Southampton	App	10.73	74-79	82	1	3
Aldershot	Tampa Bay (USA)	08.82	82	25	2	0

ANELKA Nicolas
France, 24 March, 1979 (F)

League Club	Source	Date Signed	Seasons Played	Apps	Subs	Gls
Arsenal	Paris St Germain (Fr)	03.97	96-97	16	14	6

ANGEL Mark
Newcastle, 23 August, 1975 (LW)

League Club	Source	Date Signed	Seasons Played	Apps	Subs	Gls
Sunderland	Walker Central	12.93				
Oxford U.	Tr	08.95	95-97	40	33	4

ANGELL Brett Ashley Mark
Marlborough, 20 August, 1968 (F)

League Club	Source	Date Signed	Seasons Played	Apps	Subs	Gls
Portsmouth (N/C)	YT	08.86				
Derby Co.	Cheltenham T.	02.88				
Stockport Co.	Tr	10.88	88-89	60	10	28
Southend U.	Tr	07.90	90-93	109	6	47
Everton	Tr	01.94	93	16	4	1
Sunderland	Tr	03.95	94-96	10	0	0
Sheffield U.	L	01.96	95	6	0	2
West Bromwich A.	L	03.96	95	0	3	0
Stockport Co.	Tr	08.96	96-97	75	4	33

ANGELL Darren James
Marlborough, 19 January, 1967 (D)

League Club	Source	Date Signed	Seasons Played	Apps	Subs	Gls
Portsmouth	Newbury T.	06.85				
Colchester U.	L	12.87	87	1	0	0
Lincoln C.	Cheltenham T.	07.88				

ANGELL Peter Frank
Eton, 11 January, 1932 Died 1979 (WH)

League Club	Source	Date Signed	Seasons Played	Apps	Subs	Gls
Queens Park R.	Slough T.	07.53	53-64	417	-	37

ANGUS John
Newcastle, 12 March, 1909 Died 1965 (FB)

League Club	Source	Date Signed	Seasons Played	Apps	Subs	Gls
Wolverhampton W.	Amble W.	09.28				
Exeter C.	Scunthorpe U.	05.30	30-47	246	-	1

ANGUS John
Warkworth, 2 September, 1938 E Yth/Eu23-7/EF Lge/E-1 (RB)

League Club	Source	Date Signed	Seasons Played	Apps	Subs	Gls
Burnley	Jnrs	09.55	56-71	438	1	4

ANGUS Michael Anthony
Middlesbrough, 28 October, 1960 (M)

League Club	Source	Date Signed	Seasons Played	Apps	Subs	Gls
Middlesbrough	Jnrs	08.78	79-81	35	2	1
Scunthorpe U.	L	09.82	82	20	0	2
Southend U.	Tr	08.83				
Darlington	Tr	03.84	83-84	18	0	7

ANGUS Terence Norman
Coventry, 14 January, 1966 (CD)

League Club	Source	Date Signed	Seasons Played	Apps	Subs	Gls
Northampton T.	V. S. Rugby	08.90	90-92	115	1	6
Fulham	Tr	07.93	93-96	107	15	5

ANNAN Richard Amondo
Leeds, 4 December, 1968 (LB)

League Club	Source	Date Signed	Seasons Played	Apps	Subs	Gls
Leeds U.	App	12.86				
Doncaster Rov.	Tr	10.87				
Crewe Alex.	Guiseley	05.92	92-93	17	2	1

ANNON Darren Carlton
Chelsea, 17 February, 1972 (W)

League Club	Source	Date Signed	Seasons Played	Apps	Subs	Gls
Brentford	Carshalton	03.94	93-95	14	6	2

ANSAH Andrew
Lewisham, 19 March, 1969 (W)

League Club	Source	Date Signed	Seasons Played	Apps	Subs	Gls
Brentford	Dorking	03.89	88-89	3	5	2
Southend U.	Tr	03.90	89-94	141	16	33
Brentford	L	11.94	94	2	1	1
Brentford	L	11.95	95	6	0	1
Peterborough U. (N/C)	Tr	03.96	95	0	2	1
Gillingham (N/C)	Tr	03.96	95	0	2	0
Leyton Orient (N/C)	Tr	12.96	96	0	2	0
Brighton & H.A. (N/C)	Heybridge Swifts	11.97	97	7	7	3

ANSELL Barry
Birmingham, 29 September, 1947 (FB)

League Club	Source	Date Signed	Seasons Played	Apps	Subs	Gls
Aston Villa	Jnrs	10.67	67	1	0	0

ANSELL William **John (Jack)**
Newport Pagnell, 4 August, 1921 (G)

League Club	Source	Date Signed	Seasons Played	Apps	Subs	Gls
Northampton T.	Bletchley Brickworks	03.48	47-51	131	-	0

ANSLOW Stanley Thomas
Hackney, 5 May, 1931 (LB)

League Club	Source	Date Signed	Seasons Played	Apps	Subs	Gls
Millwall	Eton Manor	03.51	51-58	131	-	13

ANTHONY Graham John
South Shields, 9 August, 1975 (M)

League Club	Source	Date Signed	Seasons Played	Apps	Subs	Gls
Sheffield U.	YT	07.93	94-96	0	3	0
Scarborough	L	03.96	95	2	0	0
Swindon T. (N/C)	Tr	03.97	96	3	0	0
Plymouth Arg. (N/C)	Tr	08.97	97	5	0	0
Carlisle U.	Tr	11.97	97	25	0	2

ANTHONY Thomas Henry
Hounslow, 16 August, 1943 (FB)

League Club	Source	Date Signed	Seasons Played	Apps	Subs	Gls
Brentford	Jnrs	12.61	62	33	-	1
Millwall	Coventry C. (trial)	11.65				

ANTHROBUS Stephen Anthony
Lewisham, 10 November, 1968 (W)

League Club	Source	Date Signed	Seasons Played	Apps	Subs	Gls
Millwall	Jnrs	08.86	87-89	19	2	4
Wimbledon	Tr	02.90	89-92	27	1	0
Peterborough U.	L	01.94	93	2	0	0
Chester C.	L	08.94	93	7	0	0
Shrewsbury T.	Tr	08.95	95-96	60	12	16
Crewe Alex.	Tr	03.97	96-97	37	3	6

ANTIC Radomir (Raddy)
Yugoslavia, 22 November, 1949 Yugoslav Int (M)

League Club	Source	Date Signed	Seasons Played	Apps	Subs	Gls
Luton T.	Real Zaragoza (Sp)	07.80	80-83	54	46	9

ANTONIO George Rowlands
Whitchurch, 20 October, 1914 Died 1997 (WH)

League Club	Source	Date Signed	Seasons Played	Apps	Subs	Gls
Stoke C.	Oswestry T.	02.36	35-46	84	-	13
Derby Co.	Tr	03.47	46-47	18	-	2
Doncaster Rov.	Tr	10.48	48-49	34	-	7
Mansfield T.	Tr	10.49	49-50	67	-	2

League Club	Source	Date Signed	Seasons Played	Career Record Apps	Subs	Gls

APPLEBY James Park
Shotton (Dm), 15 June, 1934 (CH)

League Club	Source	Date Signed	Seasons Played	Apps	Subs	Gls
Burnley	Wingate W.	02.53	56	1	-	0
Blackburn Rov.	Tr	02.58	58-61	2	-	0
Southport	Tr	10.61	61	13	-	0
Chester C.	Tr	06.62	62	1	-	0

APPLEBY Matthew Wilfred
Middlesbrough, 16 April, 1972 (CD)

League Club	Source	Date Signed	Seasons Played	Apps	Subs	Gls
Newcastle U.	YT	05.90	90-93	18	2	0
Darlington	L	11.93	93	10	0	1
Darlington	Tr	06.94	94-95	77	2	7
Barnsley	Tr	07.96	96-97	48	2	0

APPLEBY Richard Dean
Middlesbrough, 18 September, 1975 E Yth (RB/M)

League Club	Source	Date Signed	Seasons Played	Apps	Subs	Gls
Newcastle U.	YT	08.93				
Ipswich T.	Tr	12.95	95	0	3	0
Swansea C.	Tr	08.96	96-97	41	5	4

APPLEBY Robert
Warkworth, 15 January, 1940 (G)

League Club	Source	Date Signed	Seasons Played	Apps	Subs	Gls
Middlesbrough	Amble W.	05.57	59-66	99	0	0

APPLETON Colin Harry
Scarborough, 7 March, 1936 EF Lge (WH)

League Club	Source	Date Signed	Seasons Played	Apps	Subs	Gls
Leicester C.	Scarborough	03.54	54-65	277	0	19
Charlton Ath.	Tr	06.66	66	28	0	1
Barrow	Tr	08.67	67-68	40	4	1

APPLETON Michael Anthony
Salford, 4 December, 1975 (M)

League Club	Source	Date Signed	Seasons Played	Apps	Subs	Gls
Manchester U.	YT	07.94				
Lincoln C.	L	09.95	95	4	0	0
Grimsby T.	L	01.97	96	10	0	3
Preston N.E.	Tr	08.97	97	31	7	2

APPLETON Ronald
Cleator Moor, 24 September, 1932 (W)

League Club	Source	Date Signed	Seasons Played	Apps	Subs	Gls
Workington		02.53	52	3	-	0

APPLETON Stephen
Liverpool, 27 July, 1973 (CD)

League Club	Source	Date Signed	Seasons Played	Apps	Subs	Gls
Wigan Ath.	YT	09.90	90-92	31	17	1

APPLETON Thomas Henry
Stanley, 9 June, 1936 (HB)

League Club	Source	Date Signed	Seasons Played	Apps	Subs	Gls
Burnley	Annfield Plain	08.54				
Gateshead	Tr	08.58	58	26	-	0

ARBER Robert Leonard
Poplar, 13 January, 1951 (FB)

League Club	Source	Date Signed	Seasons Played	Apps	Subs	Gls
Arsenal	App	03.68				
Leyton Orient	Tr	07.70	71-72	31	0	0

ARBLASTER Michael Brian
Kensington, 6 June, 1943 (G)

League Club	Source	Date Signed	Seasons Played	Apps	Subs	Gls
Sheffield U.	Jnrs	07.62				
Chesterfield	Tr	12.64	64-66	55	0	0
Scunthorpe U.	Tr	06.67	67	10	0	0
Barnsley	Tr	05.68	67-73	111	0	0

ARCHDEACON Owen Duncan
Greenock, 4 March, 1966 S Yth/Su21-1 (W)

League Club	Source	Date Signed	Seasons Played	Apps	Subs	Gls
Barnsley	Glasgow Celtic	07.89	89-95	222	11	23
Carlisle U.	Tr	07.96	96-97	64	0	11

ARCHELL Graham Leonard
Islington, 8 February, 1950 (M)

League Club	Source	Date Signed	Seasons Played	Apps	Subs	Gls
Leyton Orient	Jnrs	11.67	67-68	5	2	0

ARCHER John (Dan)
Biddulph, 18 June, 1941 (IF)

League Club	Source	Date Signed	Seasons Played	Apps	Subs	Gls
Port Vale	Jnrs	07.58	59-60	10	-	3
Bournemouth	Tr	07.61	61-65	139	0	37
Crewe Alex.	Tr	09.66	66-67	59	0	14
Huddersfield T.	Tr	01.68	67	7	2	0
Chesterfield	Tr	05.69	69-71	116	0	22

ARCHER John George
Whitstable, 9 April, 1936 (G)

League Club	Source	Date Signed	Seasons Played	Apps	Subs	Gls
Grimsby T.	Whitstable T.	04.54	54	10	-	0

ARCHER Lee
Bristol, 6 November, 1972 (LW)

League Club	Source	Date Signed	Seasons Played	Apps	Subs	Gls
Bristol Rov.	YT	07.91	91-96	104	22	15

ARCHER Philip
Rotherham, 25 August, 1952 (FB)

League Club	Source	Date Signed	Seasons Played	Apps	Subs	Gls
Reading	Sheffield U. (App)	09.70	71	12	5	0

ARCHER Ronald
Barnsley, 3 September, 1933 E Sch (WH)

League Club	Source	Date Signed	Seasons Played	Apps	Subs	Gls
Barnsley	Jnrs	09.50	51-55	29	-	0

ARCHER William Henry
Scunthorpe, 5 February, 1914 Died 1992 (CH)

League Club	Source	Date Signed	Seasons Played	Apps	Subs	Gls
Lincoln C.		06.39				
Doncaster Rov.	Tr	10.45	46-47	14	-	0

ARCHIBALD John Murray
Carron, 19 March, 1917 (CF)

League Club	Source	Date Signed	Seasons Played	Apps	Subs	Gls
Wrexham		03.46	46	1	-	0

ARCHIBALD Steven
Glasgow, 27 September, 1956 Su21-5/S-27 (F)

League Club	Source	Date Signed	Seasons Played	Apps	Subs	Gls
Tottenham H.	Aberdeen	05.80	80-83	128	3	58
Blackburn Rov.	Barcelona (Sp)	12.87	87	20	0	6
Reading (N/C)	St Mirren	01.92	91	1	0	0
Fulham (N/C)		09.92	92	2	0	0

ARDILES Osvaldo (Ossie) Cesar
Argentina, 3 August, 1952 Argentinian Int (M)

League Club	Source	Date Signed	Seasons Played	Apps	Subs	Gls
Tottenham H.	Huracan (Arg)	07.78	78-87	221	16	16
Blackburn Rov.	L	03.88	87	5	0	0
Queens Park R.	Tr	08.88	88	4	4	0
Swindon T. (N/C)	Tr	07.89	89	0	2	0

ARDLEY Neal Christopher
Epsom, 1 September, 1972 Eu21-10 (RM)

League Club	Source	Date Signed	Seasons Played	Apps	Subs	Gls
Wimbledon	YT	07.91	90-97	123	16	10

ARDRON Walter
Swinton-on-Dearne, 19 September, 1918 Died 1978 (CF)

League Club	Source	Date Signed	Seasons Played	Apps	Subs	Gls
Rotherham U.	Denaby U.	12.38	38-48	123	-	98
Nottingham F.	Tr	07.49	49-55	182	-	123

ARENDSE Andre
Capetown, South Africa, 27 June, 1967 South African Int (G)

League Club	Source	Date Signed	Seasons Played	Apps	Subs	Gls
Fulham	Capetown Spurs (SA)	08.97	97	6	0	0

ARENTOFT Preben
Denmark, 1 November, 1942 (M)

League Club	Source	Date Signed	Seasons Played	Apps	Subs	Gls
Newcastle U.	Morton	03.69	68-70	46	4	2
Blackburn Rov.	Tr	09.71	71-73	94	0	3

ARGUE James
Glasgow, 26 November, 1911 Died 1978 (IF)

League Club	Source	Date Signed	Seasons Played	Apps	Subs	Gls
Birmingham C.	St Rochs	12.31				
Chelsea	Tr	05.33	33-46	118	-	30

ARINS Anthony Francis
Chesterfield, 26 October, 1958 (D)

League Club	Source	Date Signed	Seasons Played	Apps	Subs	Gls
Burnley	App	07.76	78-79	29	0	2
Leeds U.	Tr	05.80	81	0	1	0
Scunthorpe U.	Tr	11.81	81	20	0	1

ARKINS Vincent
Dublin, 18 September, 1970 IR Yth/IR U21-8/IR 'B' (F)

League Club	Source	Date Signed	Seasons Played	Apps	Subs	Gls
Notts Co.	Shelbourne	09.05	95-96	30	8	8

ARKWRIGHT Ian
Barnsley, 18 September, 1959 (W)

League Club	Source	Date Signed	Seasons Played	Apps	Subs	Gls
Wolverhampton W.	App	09.77	78	3	1	0
Wrexham	Tr	03.80	79-83	102	2	10
Torquay U.	L	03.84	83	2	0	0

ARMES Ivan William
Lowestoft, 6 April, 1924 (WH)

League Club	Source	Date Signed	Seasons Played	Apps	Subs	Gls
Norwich C.	Brooke Marine	11.46	46-49	61	-	1
Exeter C.	Tr	12.51	51-52	14	-	2

ARMFIELD James Christopher
Denton, 21 September, 1935 Eu23-9/EF Lge/E-43 (RB)

League Club	Source	Date Signed	Seasons Played	Apps	Subs	Gls
Blackpool	Jnrs	09.54	54-70	568	0	6

ARMITAGE Andrew Mark
Leeds, 17 October, 1968 (LB)

League Club	Source	Date Signed	Seasons Played	Apps	Subs	Gls
Leeds U. (N/C)	YT	08.87				
Rochdale	Tr	07.88	88	33	3	0

ARMITAGE Kenneth James
Sheffield, 23 October, 1920 Died 1952 (CH)

League Club	Source	Date Signed	Seasons Played	Apps	Subs	Gls
Leyton Orient	Gainsborough Trin.	04.46	46	7	-	0
Oldham Ath.	Tr	07.47	47	5	-	0

League Club	Source	Date Signed	Seasons Played	Career Record Apps	Subs	Gls
ARMITAGE Lewis						
Hull, 15 December, 1921						(F)
Rotherham U.		12.40	46-47	15	-	9
Grimsby T.	Tr	01.48	47	8	-	2
ARMITAGE Stanley Albert						
Woolwich, 5 June, 1919						(IL)
Queens Park R.		06.46	46	2	-	0
ARMSTRONG Adam John						
Blackpool, 6 June, 1925						(OL)
Chesterfield	Petershill	09.49	49	1	-	0
ARMSTRONG Alun						
Gateshead, 22 February, 1975						(F)
Newcastle U.	YT	08.93				
Stockport Co.	Tr	06.94	94-97	151	8	48
Middlesbrough	Tr	02.98	97	7	4	7
ARMSTRONG Christopher Peter						
Newcastle, 19 June, 1971 E 'B'						(F)
Wrexham	Llay Welfare	10.88	89-90	40	20	13
Millwall	Tr	08.91	91-92	11	17	5
Crystal Palace	Tr	09.92	92-94	118	0	45
Tottenham H.	Tr	06.95	95-97	61	6	25
ARMSTRONG Steven **Craig**						
South Shields, 23 May, 1975						(LB)
Nottingham F.	YT	06.92	97	4	14	0
Burnley	L	12.94	94	4	0	0
Bristol Rov.	L	01.96	95	13	1	0
Gillingham	L	10.96	96	10	0	0
Watford	L	01.97	96	15	0	0
ARMSTRONG David						
Durham, 26 December, 1954 Eu23-4/E' B'/E-3						(M)
Middlesbrough	App	01.72	71-80	357	2	59
Southampton	Tr	08.81	81-86	222	0	59
Bournemouth	Tr	07.87	87	6	3	2
ARMSTRONG David Thomas						
Mile End, 9 November, 1942						(W)
Millwall	Hornchurch	12.65	65-67	14	6	1
Brighton & H.A.	Tr	09.68	68-69	38	6	6
ARMSTRONG Derek James						
Carlisle, 16 March, 1939						(OL)
Blackpool		08.58	58	1	-	0
Carlisle U.	Morecambe	08.61	61	1	-	0
ARMSTRONG Eric						
Hebburn, 25 May, 1921 Died 1975						(WH)
West Ham U.	Cramlington W.	01.47	47	1	-	0
ARMSTRONG Gary Stephen						
West Ham, 2 January, 1958						(FB)
Gillingham	Jnrs	01.76	75-79	82	4	2
Wimbledon	Tr	03.80	79-81	71	0	0
Gillingham	Barnet	11.83	83	7	1	0
Crewe Alex.	Tr	08.84	84	31	0	0
ARMSTRONG George						
Felling, 9 August, 1944 E Yth/Eu23-5						(W)
Arsenal	Jnrs	08.61	61-76	490	10	53
Leicester C.	Tr	09.77	77-78	14	1	0
Stockport Co.	Tr	09.78	78	34	0	0
ARMSTRONG Gerard Joseph						
Belfast, 23 May, 1954 NI-63						(F)
Tottenham H.	Bangor (NI)	11.75	76-80	65	19	10
Watford	Tr	11.80	80-82	50	26	12
West Bromwich A.	Real Mallorca (Sp)	08.85	85	7	1	0
Chesterfield	L	01.86	85	12	0	1
Brighton & H.A.	Tr	07.86	86-88	30	17	6
Millwall	L	01.87	86	7	0	0
ARMSTRONG Gordon Ian						
Newcastle, 15 July, 1967						(LM)
Sunderland	App	07.85	84-95	331	18	50
Bristol C.	L	08.95	95	6	0	0
Northampton T.	L	01.96	95	4	0	1
Bury	Tr	07.96	96-97	49	20	4
ARMSTRONG James						
Ulverston, 14 September, 1943						(F)
Barrow	App	01.61	60-62	17	-	2
Chesterfield	Tr	07.63	63	7	-	0

League Club	Source	Date Signed	Seasons Played	Career Record Apps	Subs	Gls
ARMSTRONG John						
Airdrie, 5 September, 1936						(G)
Barrow	Bellshill	03.58	57-58	21	-	0
Nottingham F.	Tr	11.58	58-62	20	-	0
Portsmouth	Tr	02.63	62-66	79	0	0
Southport	Tr	08.67	67-70	86	0	0
ARMSTRONG Joseph						
Brighton, 16 November, 1931 Died 1986						(IF)
Southend U.		11.52				
Barrow	Tr	07.53	53-57	104	-	33
Workington	Tr	03.58	57-58	25	-	10
ARMSTRONG Joseph Michael						
Newcastle, 29 January, 1939						(IF)
Leeds U.	Leslie B.C.	05.57				
Gateshead	Tr	07.59	59	22	-	9
ARMSTRONG Keith Thomas						
Corbridge, 11 October, 1957						(W)
Sunderland	Jnrs	01.75	77	7	4	0
Newport Co.	L	08.78	78	3	1	0
Scunthorpe U.	L	10.78	78	0	1	0
Newcastle U.	Oulu (Fin)	06.79				
ARMSTRONG Kenneth						
Bradford, 3 June, 1924 Died 1984 EF Lge/E 'B'/E-1						(WH)
Chelsea	Bradford Rov.	12.46	47-56	362	-	25
ARMSTRONG Kenneth Charles						
Bridgnorth, 31 January, 1959						(CD)
Southampton	Kilmarnock	06.83	83	26	0	0
Notts Co.	L	03.84	83	10	0	0
Birmingham C.	Tr	08.84	84-85	58	0	1
Walsall	Tr	02.86				
ARMSTRONG Lee William						
Cockermouth, 19 October, 1972						(RB)
Carlisle U.	YT	07.91	90-91	12	8	0
ARMSTRONG Paul George						
Dublin, 5 October, 1978 IR u21-1						(M)
Brighton & H.A.	YT	07.97	97	12	8	0
ARMSTRONG John **Robert**						
Newcastle, 1 July, 1938						(F)
Darlington		07.59	59	1	-	0
ARMSTRONG Terence						
Barnsley, 10 July, 1958						(M)
Huddersfield T.	App	07.76	76-78	36	4	2
Port Vale	Tr	02.81	80-84	113	3	12
ARMSTRONG Thomas						
Carlisle, 27 February, 1920 Died 1985						(FB)
Carlisle U.	Holme Head	08.46	46	3	-	0
ARNELL Alan Jack						
Chichester, 25 November, 1933						(CF)
Liverpool	Worthing	03.54	53-60	69	-	33
Tranmere Rov.	Tr	02.61	60-62	68	-	34
Halifax T.	Tr	07.63	63	14	-	6
ARNISON Joseph **William**						
South Africa, 27 June, 1924 Died 1996						(CF)
Luton T.	Glasgow Rangers	08.48	48-50	44	-	19
ARNOLD Eric Arthur						
Kessingland, 13 September, 1922						(FB)
Norwich C.	Lowestoft T.	09.47	47-51	13	-	0
ARNOLD Ian						
Durham, 4 July, 1972						(F)
Middlesbrough	YT	01.90	90-91	0	3	0
Carlisle U.	Tr	08.92	92-94	34	13	11
ARNOLD James Alexander						
Stafford, 6 August, 1950 E Semi Pro						(G)
Blackburn Rov.	Stafford R.	06.79	79-80	58	0	0
Everton	Tr	08.81	81-83	48	0	0
Preston N.E.	L	10.82	82	6	0	0
Port Vale	Tr	08.85	85-86	53	0	0
ARNOLD John Walter Leonard						
Southwark, 6 December, 1954						(F)
Charlton Ath.	App	12.72	72-73	1	4	0

ARNOLD Roderick James
Wolverhampton, 3 June, 1952 (G)

League Club	Source	Date Signed	Seasons Played	Apps	Subs	Gls
Wolverhampton W.	App	06.70				
Mansfield T.	L	02.71	70	17	0	0
Mansfield T.	Tr	03.73	72-83	423	0	0

ARNOLD Stephen Frank
Willesden, 5 January, 1951 (M)

League Club	Source	Date Signed	Seasons Played	Apps	Subs	Gls
Crewe Alex.	App	01.69	68-70	13	2	0
Liverpool	Tr	09.70	70	1	1	0
Southport	L	01.72	71	16	0	3
Torquay U.	L	09.72	72	2	1	1
Rochdale	Tr	06.73	73	37	3	1

ARNOTT Andrew John
Chatham, 18 October, 1973 (CD/F)

League Club	Source	Date Signed	Seasons Played	Apps	Subs	Gls
Gillingham	YT	05.91	91-95	50	23	12
Leyton Orient	Tr	01.96	95-96	47	3	6
Fulham	Tr	06.97	97	0	1	0

ARNOTT John Henry
Sydenham, 6 September, 1932 (WH)

League Club	Source	Date Signed	Seasons Played	Apps	Subs	Gls
West Ham U.	Beckenham	07.54	53-54	6	-	2
Shrewsbury T.	Tr	08.55	55	30	-	6
Bournemouth	Tr	07.56	56-61	173	-	21
Gillingham	Tr	08.62	62-67	184	2	2

ARNOTT Kevin William
Gateshead, 28 September, 1958 (M)

League Club	Source	Date Signed	Seasons Played	Apps	Subs	Gls
Sunderland	App	09.76	76-81	132	1	16
Blackburn Rov.	L	11.81	81	17	0	2
Sheffield U.	Tr	06.82	82-86	120	1	11
Blackburn Rov.	L	11.82	82	11	1	1
Rotherham U.	L	03.83	82	9	0	2
Chesterfield	Vasalund (Swe)	11.87	87-89	67	4	4

ARNOTT William
Edinburgh, 29 May, 1935 (RH)

League Club	Source	Date Signed	Seasons Played	Apps	Subs	Gls
Crewe Alex.	Berwick R.	12.57	57	7	-	0

ARPHEXAD Pegguy Michel
Guadeloupe, 18 May, 1973 (G)

League Club	Source	Date Signed	Seasons Played	Apps	Subs	Gls
Leicester C.	Racing Club (Fr)	08.97	97	6	0	0

ARROWSMITH Alfred William
Manchester, 11 December, 1942 (CF)

League Club	Source	Date Signed	Seasons Played	Apps	Subs	Gls
Liverpool	Ashton U.	09.60	61-67	43	4	20
Bury	Tr	12.68	68-69	45	3	11
Rochdale	Tr	06.70	70-71	40	6	14

ARROWSMITH Brian William
Barrow, 2 July, 1940 (D)

League Club	Source	Date Signed	Seasons Played	Apps	Subs	Gls
Barrow	Vickers Sports	10.61	61-70	376	2	2

ARTHUR David Robert
Wolverhampton, 9 March, 1960 (FB)

League Club	Source	Date Signed	Seasons Played	Apps	Subs	Gls
West Bromwich A.	App	03.78	81	2	1	0
Walsall	Tr	08.82	82	8	1	0

ARTHUR John (Jackie)
Haslingdon, 14 December, 1917 Died 1986 (OR)

League Club	Source	Date Signed	Seasons Played	Apps	Subs	Gls
Everton	Blackburn Rov. (Am)	09.36				
Stockport Co.	Tr	05.38	38	2	-	0
Everton	Tr	11.40				
Chester C.	Tr	05.46	46	24	-	3
Rochdale	Tr	04.47	46-53	170	-	25

ARUNDEL Frank William
Plymouth, 20 February, 1939 Died 1994 (W)

League Club	Source	Date Signed	Seasons Played	Apps	Subs	Gls
Plymouth Arg.	Oak Villa	08.56	56	4	-	0
Torquay U.	Tr	07.59	59-60	6	-	0

ASABA Carl
Westminster, 28 January, 1973 (CF)

League Club	Source	Date Signed	Seasons Played	Apps	Subs	Gls
Brentford	Dulwich Hamlet	08.94	95-96	49	5	25
Colchester U.	L	02.95	94	9	3	2
Reading	Tr	08.97	97	31	1	8

ASANOVIC Aljosa
Croatia, 14 December, 1965 Croatian Int (LM)

League Club	Source	Date Signed	Seasons Played	Apps	Subs	Gls
Derby Co.	Hadjuk Split (Yug)	07.96	96-97	37	1	7

ASH Mark Christian
Sheffield, 22 January, 1968 (RB)

League Club	Source	Date Signed	Seasons Played	Apps	Subs	Gls
Rotherham U.	App	01.86	86-88	14	6	0
Scarborough	Tr	08.89	89-91	32	7	0

ASH Michael
Sheffield, 4 September, 1943 E Sch/E Yth (IF)

League Club	Source	Date Signed	Seasons Played	Apps	Subs	Gls
Sheffield U.	App	11.60	63	3	-	1
Scunthorpe U.	Tr	09.65	65-66	48	1	7

ASHALL George Henry
Killamarsh, 29 September, 1911 EF Lge (OL)

League Club	Source	Date Signed	Seasons Played	Apps	Subs	Gls
Wolverhampton W.	Frickley Colly	02.36	35-37	94	-	19
Coventry C.	Tr	07.38	38-47	62	-	10

ASHALL James
Normanton, 13 December, 1933 (FB)

League Club	Source	Date Signed	Seasons Played	Apps	Subs	Gls
Leeds U.	Hasland O.B.	10.51	55-60	89	-	0

ASHBEE Ian
Birmingham, 6 September, 1976 E Yth (M)

League Club	Source	Date Signed	Seasons Played	Apps	Subs	Gls
Derby Co.	YT	11.94	94	1	0	0
Cambridge U.	Tr	12.96	96-97	43	2	1

ASHBY Barry John
Harlesden, 21 November, 1970 (CD)

League Club	Source	Date Signed	Seasons Played	Apps	Subs	Gls
Watford	YT	12.88	89-93	101	13	3
Brentford	Tr	03.94	93-96	119	2	4
Gillingham	Tr	08.97	97	43	0	0

ASHCROFT Charles Thomas
Croston, 3 July, 1926 E 'B' (G)

League Club	Source	Date Signed	Seasons Played	Apps	Subs	Gls
Liverpool	Eccleston Jnrs	05.46	46-54	87	-	0
Ipswich T.	Tr	06.55	55	7	-	0
Coventry C.	Tr	06.57	57	19	-	0

ASHCROFT Lee
Preston, 7 September, 1972 Eu21-1 (W)

League Club	Source	Date Signed	Seasons Played	Apps	Subs	Gls
Preston N.E.	YT	07.91	90-92	78	13	13
West Bromwich A.	Tr	08.93	93-96	66	24	17
Notts Co.	L	03.96	95	4	2	0
Preston N.E.	Tr	09.96	96-97	63	1	22

ASHCROFT Llewellyn Lloyd
Flint, 10 July, 1921 (OR)

League Club	Source	Date Signed	Seasons Played	Apps	Subs	Gls
Tranmere Rov.	Flint T.	08.45	46	20	-	4

ASHCROFT William
Liverpool, 1 October, 1952 (F/CD)

League Club	Source	Date Signed	Seasons Played	Apps	Subs	Gls
Wrexham	Jnrs	10.70	70-77	196	23	72
Middlesbrough	Tr	09.77	77-81	139	20	21
Tranmere Rov.	T. Enschede (Neth)	08.85	85	16	7	2

ASHDJIAN John Anthony
Hackney, 13 September, 1972 (W)

League Club	Source	Date Signed	Seasons Played	Apps	Subs	Gls
Scarborough	Northampton T. (YT)	07.91	91-93	40	27	14

ASHE Armour Donald
Paisley, 14 October, 1925 Died 1968 (FB)

League Club	Source	Date Signed	Seasons Played	Apps	Subs	Gls
Stockport Co.	St Mirren	06.53	53	2	-	0
Accrington St.	Tr	09.53	53-57	162	-	0
Gateshead	Tr	11.57	57-58	54	-	1
Southport	Tr	07.59	59	14	-	2

ASHE Norman James
Walsall, 16 November, 1943 E Sch/E Yth (OR)

League Club	Source	Date Signed	Seasons Played	Apps	Subs	Gls
Aston Villa	App	05.61	59-60	5	-	0
Rotherham U.	Tr	03.63	62	6	-	1

ASHENDEN Russell Edward
South Ockenden, 4 February, 1961 (M)

League Club	Source	Date Signed	Seasons Played	Apps	Subs	Gls
Northampton T.	App	02.79	78-79	6	12	0

ASHENDEN Scott
Southend, 3 February, 1974 (W)

League Club	Source	Date Signed	Seasons Played	Apps	Subs	Gls
Southend U.	YT	06.92	92	4	1	0

ASHER Sydney James
Portsmouth, 24 December, 1930 Died 1994 (CF)

League Club	Source	Date Signed	Seasons Played	Apps	Subs	Gls
Portsmouth	Jnrs	08.48				
Northampton T.	Hastings U.	11.56	56	21	-	11

ASHER Thomas
Hatfield (Yk), 21 December, 1936 E Sch (IF)

League Club	Source	Date Signed	Seasons Played	Apps	Subs	Gls
Notts Co.	Wolverhampton W. (Am)	07.54	57-58	31	-	4

ASHFIELD George Owen
Manchester, 7 April, 1934 (CH)

League Club	Source	Date Signed	Seasons Played	Apps	Subs	Gls
Stockport Co.	Jnrs	09.51				
Aston Villa	Tr	03.54	55-57	9	-	0
Chester C.	Tr	02.59	58	5	-	0

League Club	Source	Date Signed	Seasons Played	Career Record Apps	Subs	Gls
ASHLEY John						
Clowne, 10 June, 1931						(G)
York C.	Frickley Colly	10.50	50	9	-	0
ASHLEY Kevin Mark						
Birmingham, 31 December, 1968						(RB)
Birmingham C.	App	12.86	86-90	56	1	1
Wolverhampton W.	Tr	09.90	90-92	87	1	1
Peterborough U.	Tr	08.94	94-95	36	0	0
Doncaster Rov.	L	03.96	95	3	0	0
ASHMAN George **Allan**						
Rotherham, 30 May, 1928						(CF)
Nottingham F.	Sheffield U. (Am)	04.46	48-49	13	-	3
Carlisle U.	Tr	06.51	51-57	206	-	101
ASHMAN Ronald George						
Whittlesey, 19 May, 1926						(D)
Norwich C.	Whittlesey	05.44	47-63	592	-	55
ASHMORE Alfred Maxwell						
Sheffield, 11 September, 1937						(G)
Sheffield U.		08.57	57	1	-	0
Bradford C.	Tr	07.61	61	9	-	0
Chesterfield	Tr	10.62	62	2	-	0
ASHMORE George **Arthur**						
Swadlincote, 11 August, 1946						(HB)
Doncaster Rov.	Frickley Colly	11.66	66-67	3	0	0
ASHTON Derek						
Worksop, 4 July, 1922						(FB)
Wolverhampton W.		09.41				
Aston Villa	Tr	05.46	46-48	8	-	0
ASHTON John						
Reading, 4 July, 1954						(F)
Reading	Jnrs	04.72	71-74	10	3	1
ASHTON Kenneth James						
Irlam, 12 December, 1936						(FB)
Stockport Co.	Bolton W. (Am)	09.56	57-61	39	-	0
ASHTON Roger William						
Llanidloes, 16 August, 1921 Died 1985						(G)
Wrexham		12.45				
Cardiff C.		04.48	47	1	-	0
Newport Co.	Bath C.	12.49	49-50	11	-	0
ASHURST John (Jack)						
Renton, 12 October, 1954						(CD)
Sunderland	App	10.71	72-79	129	11	4
Blackpool	Tr	10.79	79-80	53	0	3
Carlisle U.	Tr	08.81	81-85	194	0	2
Leeds U.	Tr	07.86	86-88	88	1	1
Doncaster Rov.	Tr	11.88	88-89	73	0	1
Doncaster Rov.	Bridlington T.	11.90	90-91	66	0	1
Rochdale (N/C)	Tr	08.92	92	1	0	1
ASHURST Leonard						
Liverpool, 10 March, 1939 E Yth/Eu23-1						(LB)
Sunderland	Prescot Cables	12.57	58-69	403	6	4
Hartlepool U.	Tr	03.71	70-72	42	4	2
ASHWORTH Alec						
Southport, 1 October, 1939 Died 1995						(IF)
Everton	Jnrs	05.57	57-59	12	-	3
Luton T.	Tr	10.60	60-61	63	-	20
Northampton T.	Tr	07.62	62	30	-	25
Preston N.E.	Tr	06.63	63-65	42	1	14
ASHWORTH Barry						
Stockport, 18 August, 1942						(WH)
Southend U.	Bangor C.	07.63	63-64	31	-	5
Hartlepool U.	Tr	03.65	64-65	45	0	4
Tranmere Rov.	Tr	07.66	66	21	0	3
Chester C.	Tr	08.67	67-69	117	2	11
ASHWORTH Frederick						
Oldham, 26 January, 1928						(CH)
Blackburn Rov.		10.48				
Shrewsbury T.	Tr	11.51	51-52	56	-	1
ASHWORTH Ian						
Blackburn, 17 December, 1958						(LW)
Manchester U.	App	12.75				
Crewe Alex.	Tr	07.79	79	7	6	0
ASHWORTH John						
Nottingham, 4 July, 1937 E Amat						(CH)
Portsmouth (Am)	Wealdstone	08.62	62	1	-	0
ASHWORTH Joseph Matthew						
Leeds, 6 January, 1943						(WH)
Bradford P.A.	Jnrs	01.60	61	3	-	0
York C.	Tr	05.62	62-64	57	-	0
Bournemouth	Tr	06.65	65-66	60	0	2
Southend U.	Tr	07.67	67	36	0	2
Rochdale	Tr	07.68	68-71	133	0	3
Chester C.	Tr	12.71	71	5	0	0
Stockport Co.	Tr	06.72	72	14	0	0
ASHWORTH Neil						
Southend, 16 January, 1968						(M)
Rochdale	YT	07.85	84	1	0	0
ASHWORTH Philip Anthony						
Burnley, 14 April, 1953						(F)
Blackburn Rov.	Nelson	01.75				
Bournemouth	Tr	09.75	75	30	1	2
Workington	Tr	07.76	76	38	1	7
Southport	Tr	08.77	77	22	2	9
Rochdale	Tr	07.78	78	9	2	0
Portsmouth	Tr	09.79	79	3	1	4
Scunthorpe U.	Tr	07.80	80	14	9	3
ASKEW William						
Lumley, 2 October, 1959						(LM)
Middlesbrough	App	10.77	79-81	10	2	0
Hull C.	Gateshead	09.82	82-89	247	6	19
Newcastle U.	Tr	03.90	89-90	5	1	0
Shrewsbury T.	L	01.91	90	5	0	0
ASKEY Colin						
Stoke, 3 October, 1932						(OR)
Port Vale	Jnrs	10.49	49-57	200	-	21
Walsall	Tr	07.58	58-61	83	-	12
Mansfield T.	Tr	06.62	62-63	30	-	2
ASKEY John Colin						
Stoke, 4 November, 1964 E Semi Pro						(M/F)
Macclesfield T.	Milton U.	N/L	97	37	2	6
ASPDEN John **Raymond**						
Darwen, 6 February, 1938						(CH)
Rochdale	Bolton W. (Am)	05.55	55-65	297	0	2
ASPIN Neil						
Gateshead, 12 April, 1965						(CD)
Leeds U.	App	10.82	81-88	203	4	5
Port Vale	Tr	07.89	89-97	315	3	3
ASPINALL Brendan James						
South Africa, 22 July, 1975						(CD)
Mansfield T.	Huddersfield T. (Jnrs)	07.94	94	13	7	0
ASPINALL John						
Ashton-u-Lyne, 27 April, 1916 Died 1996						(HB)
Oldham Ath.	Stalybridge Celtic	05.36	36-38	11	-	0
Bolton W.	Ashton Nat.	09.45	46-49	14	-	0
ASPINALL John Joseph						
Birkenhead, 15 March, 1959						(W)
Tranmere Rov.	Cammell Laird	10.82	82-84	100	7	25
Tranmere Rov.	Bangor C.	07.87	87	11	1	1
ASPINALL Warren						
Wigan, 13 September, 1967 E Yth						(M/F)
Wigan Ath.	App	08.85	84-85	39	12	22
Everton	Tr	05.86	85-86	0	7	0
Aston Villa	Tr	02.87	86-87	40	4	14
Portsmouth	Tr	08.88	88-93	97	35	21
Bournemouth	L	08.93	93	4	2	1
Swansea C.	L	10.93	93	5	0	0
Bournemouth	Tr	12.93	93-94	26	1	8
Carlisle U.	Tr	03.95	94-97	99	8	12
Brentford	Tr	11.97	97	24	0	3
ASPINALL Wayne						
Wigan, 10 December, 1964						(FB)
Wigan Ath.	Atherton Colly	06.83	83-84	8	0	0
ASPREY William						
Wolverhampton, 11 September, 1936						(D)
Stoke C.	Jnrs	09.53	53-65	304	0	23
Oldham Ath.	Tr	01.66	65-67	80	0	3
Port Vale	Tr	12.67	67-68	30	1	0

ASPRILLA Hinestroza **Faustino (Tino)** Hernan
Colombia, 10 November, 1969 Colombian Int (F)

League Club	Source	Date Signed	Seasons Played	Apps	Subs	Gls
Newcastle U.	Parma (It)	02.96	95-97	36	12	8

ASQUITH Beaumont
Wakefield, 16 September, 1910 Died 1977 (WH)

League Club	Source	Date Signed	Seasons Played	Apps	Subs	Gls
Barnsley	Painthorpe A.	07.33	34-38	105	-	40
Manchester U.	Tr	05.39				
Barnsley	Tr	07.42	46-47	40	-	5
Bradford C.	Tr	09.48	48-49	31	-	4

ASTALL Gordon
Horwich, 22 September, 1927 E 'B'/EF Lge/E-2 (OR)

League Club	Source	Date Signed	Seasons Played	Apps	Subs	Gls
Plymouth Arg.	Southampton (Am)	11.47	47-53	188	-	42
Birmingham C.	Tr	10.53	53-60	235	-	57
Torquay U.	Tr	07.61	61-62	33	-	10

ASTBURY Michael John
Leeds, 22 January, 1964 (G)

League Club	Source	Date Signed	Seasons Played	Apps	Subs	Gls
York C.	App	01.82	80-85	48	0	0
Peterborough U.	L	01.86	85	4	0	0
Darlington	Tr	03.86	85-86	38	0	0
Chester C.	Tr	07.87	87	5	0	0
Chesterfield	Tr	07.88	88	8	0	0

ASTBURY Thomas Arthur
Hawarden, 9 February, 1920 Died 1993 (RH)

League Club	Source	Date Signed	Seasons Played	Apps	Subs	Gls
Chester C.	Mold Alex.	05.38	46-54	303	-	38

ASTLE Jeffrey
Eastwood, 13 May, 1942 EF Lge/E-5 (CF)

League Club	Source	Date Signed	Seasons Played	Apps	Subs	Gls
Notts Co.	Jnrs	10.59	61-64	103	-	31
West Bromwich A.	Tr	09.64	64-73	290	2	137

ASTON John
Prestwich 3 September, 1921 EF Lge/E-17 (FB)

League Club	Source	Date Signed	Seasons Played	Apps	Subs	Gls
Manchester U.	Jnrs	04.46	46-53	253	-	29

ASTON John
Manchester, 28 June, 1947 Eu23-1 (OL)

League Club	Source	Date Signed	Seasons Played	Apps	Subs	Gls
Manchester U.	App	06.63	64-71	139	16	25
Luton T.	Tr	07.72	72-77	171	3	31
Mansfield T.	Tr	09.77	77	24	7	4
Blackburn Rov.	Tr	07.78	78-79	12	3	2

ASTON Alfred **John**
Newport, 29 July, 1930 Died 1992 (OL)

League Club	Source	Date Signed	Seasons Played	Apps	Subs	Gls
Newport Co.	Jnrs	04.48	47-50	6	-	1

ASTON Philip Thomas
Measham, 13 May, 1924 E Amat (WH)

League Club	Source	Date Signed	Seasons Played	Apps	Subs	Gls
Walsall	Measham Imperial	12.51	51	10	-	0

ASTON Stanley
Nuneaton, 10 May, 1940 (CH)

League Club	Source	Date Signed	Seasons Played	Apps	Subs	Gls
Hartlepool U.	Burton A.	12.66	66-67	20	1	0

ASTON Walter **Vivien**
Coseley, 16 October, 1918 (D)

League Club	Source	Date Signed	Seasons Played	Apps	Subs	Gls
Bury		12.36	38-47	23	-	0
Oldham Ath.	Tr	07.48	48-51	30	-	1
Chester C.	Tr	01.52				

ATHERSYCH Russell
Sheffield, 21 September, 1962 (M)

League Club	Source	Date Signed	Seasons Played	Apps	Subs	Gls
Chesterfield	App	09.80	81-82	11	9	0

ATHERTON Dewi Lewis
Bangor, 6 July, 1951 (M)

League Club	Source	Date Signed	Seasons Played	Apps	Subs	Gls
Blackburn Rov.	Jnrs	07.68	68-70	9	1	0

ATHERTON Francis **Gordon**
Horwich, 18 June, 1934 (WH)

League Club	Source	Date Signed	Seasons Played	Apps	Subs	Gls
Bury	Bury Amats	09.55	55-64	327	-	13
Swindon T.	Tr	12.64	64-65	31	0	0
Bury	Tr	01.66	65	7	0	0

ATHERTON James George
Queensferry, 2 April, 1923 W Amat (G)

League Club	Source	Date Signed	Seasons Played	Apps	Subs	Gls
Wrexham (Am)		07.47	47-48	18	-	0

ATHERTON Peter
Orrell, 6 April, 1970 E Sch/Eu21-1 (CD)

League Club	Source	Date Signed	Seasons Played	Apps	Subs	Gls
Wigan Ath.	YT	02.88	87-91	145	4	1
Coventry C.	Tr	08.91	91-93	113	1	0
Sheffield Wed.	Tr	06.94	94-97	141	0	6

ATKIN John **Michael**
Scunthorpe, 14 February, 1948 (CD)

League Club	Source	Date Signed	Seasons Played	Apps	Subs	Gls
Scunthorpe U.		09.69	69-74	116	6	0

ATKIN Paul Anthony
Nottingham, 3 September, 1969 E Sch/E Yth (CD)

League Club	Source	Date Signed	Seasons Played	Apps	Subs	Gls
Notts Co.	YT	07.87				
Bury	Tr	03.89	88-90	14	7	1
York C.	Tr	07.91	91-96	131	22	3
Leyton Orient	L	03.97	96	5	0	0
Scarborough	Tr	08.97	97	26	8	1

ATKINS Arthur Walter
Japan, 21 February, 1925 Died 1988 (CH)

League Club	Source	Date Signed	Seasons Played	Apps	Subs	Gls
Birmingham C.	Paget R.	11.48	49-53	97	-	0
Shrewsbury T.	Tr	06.54	54	16	-	0

ATKINS Dennis
Bradford, 8 November, 1938 (FB)

League Club	Source	Date Signed	Seasons Played	Apps	Subs	Gls
Huddersfield T.	Jnrs	12.55	59-66	194	0	0
Bradford C.	Tr	03.68	67-70	108	0	0

ATKINS Ian Leslie
Birmingham, 16 January, 1957 (D/M)

League Club	Source	Date Signed	Seasons Played	Apps	Subs	Gls
Shrewsbury T.	App	01.75	75-81	273	6	58
Sunderland	Tr	08.82	82-83	76	1	6
Everton	Tr	11.84	84-85	6	1	1
Ipswich T.	Tr	09.85	85-87	73	4	4
Birmingham C.	Tr	03.88	87-89	93	0	6
Birmingham C.	Colchester U.	09.91	91	5	3	0
Cambridge U. (N/C)	Tr	12.92	92	1	1	0
Doncaster Rov. (N/C)	Sunderland (N/C)	01.94	93	7	0	0

ATKINS Mark Nigel
Doncaster, 14 August, 1968 E Sch (M)

League Club	Source	Date Signed	Seasons Played	Apps	Subs	Gls
Scunthorpe U.	Jnrs	07.86	84-87	45	5	2
Blackburn Rov.	Tr	06.88	88-95	224	33	35
Wolverhampton W.	Tr	09.95	95-97	100	11	8

ATKINS Robert Gary
Leicester, 16 October, 1962 (CD)

League Club	Source	Date Signed	Seasons Played	Apps	Subs	Gls
Sheffield U.	Enderby T.	07.82	82-84	36	4	3
Preston N.E.	Tr	02.85	84-89	198	2	5

ATKINS Alfred James **Trevor**
Exeter, 17 August, 1941 (OR)

League Club	Source	Date Signed	Seasons Played	Apps	Subs	Gls
Exeter C.	Jnrs	08.58	57-59	3	-	3

ATKINS William Mark
Solihull, 9 May, 1939 (F)

League Club	Source	Date Signed	Seasons Played	Apps	Subs	Gls
Aston Villa	Birmingham G.P.O.	05.58				
Swindon T.	Tr	06.59	59-64	75	-	28
Halifax T.	Tr	08.65	65-66	74	0	34
Stockport Co.	Tr	03.67	66-68	92	0	37
Portsmouth	Tr	04.69	68-69	11	0	2
Halifax T.	Tr	11.69	69-72	123	2	37
Rochdale	Tr	12.72	72-73	25	0	7
Darlington	Tr	09.73	73-74	41	3	12

ATKINSON Brian
Rotherham, 16 November, 1934 (HB)

League Club	Source	Date Signed	Seasons Played	Apps	Subs	Gls
Sheffield U.		06.53				
Halifax T.	Tr	06.56	56-58	67	-	0

ATKINSON Brian
Darlington, 19 January, 1971 Eu21-6 (M)

League Club	Source	Date Signed	Seasons Played	Apps	Subs	Gls
Sunderland	YT	07.89	88-95	119	22	4
Carlisle U.	L	01.96	95	2	0	0
Darlington	Tr	08.96	96-97	54	8	5

ATKINSON Bryan Herbert
Saffron Walden, 15 April, 1934 Died 1989 (HB)

League Club	Source	Date Signed	Seasons Played	Apps	Subs	Gls
Watford	Bishops Stortford	06.54	55-56	20	-	0

ATKINSON Charles
Hull, 17 December, 1932 (WH)

League Club	Source	Date Signed	Seasons Played	Apps	Subs	Gls
Hull C.	Marist O.B.	05.50	53-55	37	-	2
Bradford P.A.	Tr	07.56	56-63	339	-	50
Bradford C.	Tr	06.64	64	16	-	1

ATKINSON Charles Brown Clayton
Haswell (Dm), 5 May, 1938 (CH)

League Club	Source	Date Signed	Seasons Played	Apps	Subs	Gls
Hartlepool U.	Eppleton C.W.	12.58	59-63	47	-	0

ATKINSON Dalian Robert
Shrewsbury, 21 March, 1968 E 'B' (F)

League Club	Source	Date Signed	Seasons Played	Apps	Subs	Gls
Ipswich T.	App	06.85	85-88	49	11	18
Sheffield Wed.	Tr	07.89	89	38	0	10
Aston Villa	Real Sociedad (Sp)	07.91	91-94	79	8	23
Manchester C. (L)	Fenerbahce (Tu)	03.97	96	7	1	2

League Club	Source	Date Signed	Seasons Played	Apps	Subs	Gls
ATKINSON David John						
Hull, 3 April, 1951						(OR)
Hartlepool U.	App	●	68	8	0	1
Charlton Ath.	Tr	05.69				
ATKINSON Frederick James						
Newcastle, 24 August, 1919 Died 1991						(RH)
Gateshead		12.45	46-48	32	-	6
ATKINSON Graeme						
Hull, 11 November, 1971						(W)
Hull C.	YT	05.90	89-94	129	20	23
Preston N.E.	Tr	10.94	94-97	63	16	6
Rochdale	L	12.97	97	5	1	0
Brighton & H.A.	Tr	03.98	97	9	0	0
ATKINSON Graham James						
Birmingham, 17 May, 1943						(IF)
Oxford U.	Aston Villa (Am)	02.60	62	18	-	4
Oxford U.	Cambridge U.	12.64	64-73	303	4	73
ATKINSON Harold						
Liverpool, 28 July, 1925						(CF)
Tranmere Rov.	Carlton	03.45	46-54	185	-	95
Chesterfield	Tr	07.55				
ATKINSON Hugh Anthony						
Dublin, 8 November, 1960 IRu21-1						(M/D)
Wolverhampton W.	App	11.78	79-81	38	8	3
Exeter C.	Tr	10.83	83	28	0	1
York C.	Tr	07.84	84	3	4	0
Darlington	L	03.85	84	7	0	0
ATKINSON Arthur **Ian**						
Carlisle, 19 December, 1932 Died 1995						(CF)
Carlisle U.		06.51	52-56	123	-	53
Exeter C.	Tr	07.57	57	8	-	2
ATKINSON John Edward						
Washington, 20 December, 1913 Died 1977 E Sch						(CH)
Bolton W.	Washington Colly	09.31	32-47	240	-	4
New Brighton	Tr	05.48	48-49	52	-	0
ATKINSON Jonathan David						
Ashington, 18 September, 1972						(F)
Darlington (N/C)	Morpeth T.	03.97	96	2	3	0
ATKINSON Patrick (Paddy) Darren						
Singapore, 22 May, 1970						(LB)
Hartlepool U.	Sheffield U. (YT)	08.88	88-89	9	12	3
York C.	Workington	11.95	95-97	36	5	0
ATKINSON Paul						
Chester-le-Street, 19 January, 1966 E Yth						(W)
Sunderland	App	11.83	83-87	46	14	5
Port Vale	Tr	06.88	88	4	0	3
Hartlepool U.	L	03.90	89	5	6	1
ATKINSON Paul Graham						
Otley, 14 August, 1961						(W)
Oldham Ath.	App	08.79	79-82	139	4	11
Watford	Tr	07.83	83	8	3	0
Oldham Ath.	Tr	08.85	85-87	29	4	1
Swansea C.	L	12.86	86	6	0	1
Bolton W.	L	02.87	86	2	1	0
Swansea C.	L	03.87	86	12	0	2
Burnley	Tr	07.88	88-89	18	4	1
ATKINSON Peter						
Middlesbrough, 13 September, 1924 Died 1972						(G)
Hull C.	Billingham Synth.	04.47	46-47	6	-	0
ATKINSON Peter						
Gainsborough, 14 December, 1949						(FB)
Rotherham U.		05.69	69	3	0	0
ATKINSON Peter Maurice Carl						
Spilsby, 20 September, 1929						(G)
Walsall	Walsall Y.M.C.A.	11.49	49-51	2	-	0
ATKINSON Ronald Frederick						
Liverpool, 18 March, 1939						(WH)
Aston Villa	B.S.A. Tools	05.56				
Oxford U.	Tr	07.59	62-71	383	1	14
ATKINSON Trevor						
Barnsley, 19 November, 1928						(OL)
Hull C.	Hull Amats	05.46	46	2	-	0
Barnsley	Tr	08.48				
ATKINSON Trevor						
Bishop Auckland, 23 November, 1942						(WH)
Darlington	Spennymoor U.	11.63	63-68	137	4	3
Bradford P.A.	Tr	01.69	68-69	59	1	6
ATKINSON Walter						
Gateshead, 31 August, 1920						(WH)
Norwich C.	Hexham Hearts	01.49	51	1	-	0
ATKINSON William						
Sunderland, 21 December, 1944						(W)
Birmingham C.	App	03.62				
Torquay U.	Tr	06.64	64	19	-	7
ATTEVELD Raymond						
Holland, 8 September, 1966						(FB/M)
Everton	Haarlem (Neth)	08.89	89-91	41	10	1
West Ham U.	L	02.92	91	1	0	0
Bristol C.	Tr	03.92	91-92	9	5	1
ATTHEY Nicholas						
Tantobie, 8 May, 1946						(M/D)
Walsall	App	07.63	63-76	429	10	17
ATTLEY Brian Robert						
Cardiff, 23 August, 1955						(D/M)
Cardiff C.	App	08.73	74-78	73	6	1
Swansea C.	Tr	02.79	78-81	83	6	6
Derby Co.	Tr	02.82	81-83	54	1	1
Oxford U.	L	03.83	82	5	0	0
ATTWELL Frederick **Reginald**						
Shifnal, 23 March, 1920 Died 1986 EF Lge						(WH)
West Ham U.	Denaby U.	04.38	37-46	5	-	0
Burnley	Tr	10.46	46-54	244	-	9
Bradford C.	Tr	10.54	54	24	-	0
ATYEO Peter **John** Walter						
Westbury, 7 February, 1932 Died 1993 E Yth/Eu23-2/EF Lge/E 'B'/E-6						(CF)
Portsmouth (Am)	Westbury U.	09.50	50	1	-	0
Bristol C.	Tr	06.51	51-65	596	0	314
AUGUSTE Joseph						
Trinidad (WI), 24 November, 1965						(F)
Exeter C. (N/C)	Hounslow	09.83	83	7	3	0
AULD Robert (Bertie)						
Glasgow, 23 March, 1938 S Lge/S-3						(OL)
Birmingham C.	Glasgow Celtic	05.61	61-64	126	-	26
AULD Walter Bottomley						
Bellshill, 9 July, 1929 Died 1988						(OL)
Middlesbrough	Bellshill Ath.	12.50	50	2	-	1
AUNGER Geoffrey Edward Ramer						
Canada, 4 February, 1968 Canadian Int						(F)
Luton T.	Vancouver 86ers (Can)	09.93	93	5	0	1
Chester C.	Sudbury T.	12.94	94	1	4	0
Stockport Co. (N/C)	Seattle Sounders (Can)	12.97	97	0	1	0
AUSTIN Dean Barry						
Hemel Hempstead, 26 April, 1970						(RB)
Southend U.	St Albans C.	03.90	89-91	96	0	2
Tottenham H.	Tr	06.92	92-96	117	7	0
AUSTIN John Frank						
Stoke, 6 July, 1933 E Sch						(FB)
Coventry C.	Jnrs	07.50	52-62	302	-	2
Torquay U.	Tr	01.63	62-63	24	-	0
AUSTIN Karl						
Stoke, 7 August, 1961						(G)
Port Vale (N/C)	Stafford R.	02.85	84	1	0	0
AUSTIN Kevin Levi						
Hackney, 12 February, 1973						(CD)
Leyton Orient	Saffron Walden T.	08.93	93-95	101	8	3
Lincoln C.	Tr	07.96	96-97	90	0	0
AUSTIN Roy Leonard						
Islington, 26 March, 1960						(F)
Doncaster Rov.	Millwall (App)	08.78	78	3	0	0
AUSTIN Terence Willis						
Isleworth, 1 February, 1954						(F)
Crystal Palace	Jnrs	06.72				
Ipswich T.	Tr	05.73	74-75	10	9	1
Plymouth Arg.	Tr	10.76	76-77	58	0	18

League Club	Source	Date Signed	Seasons Played	Apps	Subs	Gls
Walsall	Tr	03.78	77-78	44	3	19
Mansfield T.	Tr	03.79	78-80	84	0	31
Huddersfield T.	Tr	12.80	80-82	39	3	10
Doncaster Rov.	Tr	09.82	82	30	4	5
Northampton T.	Tr	08.83	83	42	1	10

AVERY Roger Joseph
Cambridge, 17 February, 1961 (F)

League Club	Source	Date Signed	Seasons Played	Apps	Subs	Gls
Cambridge U.	App	02.79	77	0	1	0

AVEYARD Walter
Hemsworth, 11 June, 1918 Died 1985 (IF)

League Club	Source	Date Signed	Seasons Played	Apps	Subs	Gls
Sheffield Wed.	Denaby U.	10.38	46	4	-	3
Birmingham C.	Tr	04.47	47	7	-	3
Port Vale	Tr	06.48	48-51	103	-	26
Accrington St.	Tr	03.52	51-52	24	-	4

AVIS Vernon Charles Sidney
Marylebone, 24 October, 1935 Died 1996 (FB)

League Club	Source	Date Signed	Seasons Played	Apps	Subs	Gls
Brentford	Jnrs	11.52	53-60	19	-	0

AVRAMOVIC Radojko (Raddy)
Yugoslavia, 29 November, 1949 Yugoslav Int (G)

League Club	Source	Date Signed	Seasons Played	Apps	Subs	Gls
Notts Co.	N.K.Rijeka (Yug)	08.79	79-82	149	0	0
Coventry C.	Montreal (USA)	09.83	83	18	0	0

AWFORD Andrew Terence
Worcester, 14 July, 1972 E Sch/E Yth/Eu21-9 (D)

League Club	Source	Date Signed	Seasons Played	Apps	Subs	Gls
Portsmouth	YT	07.89	88-97	228	14	1

AYLOTT Stephen John
Ilford, 3 September, 1951 (M)

League Club	Source	Date Signed	Seasons Played	Apps	Subs	Gls
West Ham U.	App	08.69				
Oxford U.	Tr	04.71	71-75	143	11	8
Brentford	Tr	07.76	76-77	6	1	0

AYLOTT Trevor Keith Charles
Bermondsey, 26 November, 1957 (F)

League Club	Source	Date Signed	Seasons Played	Apps	Subs	Gls
Chelsea	App	07.76	77-79	26	3	2
Barnsley	Tr	11.79	79-81	93	3	26
Millwall	Tr	08.82	82	32	0	5
Luton T.	Tr	03.83	82-83	32	0	10
Crystal Palace	Tr	07.84	84-85	50	3	12
Barnsley	L	02.86	85	9	0	0
Bournemouth	Tr	08.86	86-90	137	10	27
Birmingham C.	Tr	10.90	90-91	25	2	0
Oxford U.	Tr	09.91	91	35	2	6
Gillingham	Tr	07.92	92	8	2	2

AYORINDE Samuel Tayo
Nigeria, 20 October, 1974 (CF)

League Club	Source	Date Signed	Seasons Played	Apps	Subs	Gls
Leyton Orient	Nigeria	04.96	95-96	7	6	2

AYRE Colin
Ashington, 14 March, 1956 (W)

League Club	Source	Date Signed	Seasons Played	Apps	Subs	Gls
Newcastle U.	App	09.73				
Torquay U.	Telstar	09.76	76	2	0	0

AYRE Robert William
Berwick, 26 March, 1932 Eu23-2 (OR)

League Club	Source	Date Signed	Seasons Played	Apps	Subs	Gls
Charlton Ath.	Chippenham T.	07.52	52-57	109	-	48
Reading	Tr	05.58	58-59	57	-	24

AYRE William
Crookhill, 7 May, 1952 (CD)

League Club	Source	Date Signed	Seasons Played	Apps	Subs	Gls
Hartlepool U.	Scarborough	08.77	77-80	141	0	27
Halifax T.	Tr	01.81	80-81	63	0	5
Mansfield T.	Tr	08.82	82-83	67	0	7
Halifax T.	Tr	07.84	84-85	32	0	2

AYRES Frederick Edward
Stoke, 17 July, 1926 (CF)

League Club	Source	Date Signed	Seasons Played	Apps	Subs	Gls
Crewe Alex.		11.48	48	2	-	0

AYRES Harold
Redcar, 10 March, 1920 (WH)

League Club	Source	Date Signed	Seasons Played	Apps	Subs	Gls
Fulham	Clapton	07.46	46-48	38	-	8
Gillingham	Tr	06.50	50-54	136	-	2

AYRES Kenneth Edward
Oxford, 15 May, 1956 E Sch (F)

League Club	Source	Date Signed	Seasons Played	Apps	Subs	Gls
Manchester U.	App	06.73				
Crystal Palace	Tr	11.73	74	3	3	0

AYRIS John Patrick
Wapping, 8 January, 1953 E Yth (W)

League Club	Source	Date Signed	Seasons Played	Apps	Subs	Gls
West Ham U.	App	10.70	70-76	41	16	1

AYRTON Neil John
Lewisham, 11 February, 1962 (F)

League Club	Source	Date Signed	Seasons Played	Apps	Subs	Gls
Portsmouth	Maidstone U.	12.79	80	1	1	0

AYTON James
Barrhead, 15 October, 1923 Died 1988 (IF)

League Club	Source	Date Signed	Seasons Played	Apps	Subs	Gls
Leicester C.	Third Lanark	10.48	48-50	8	-	1
Shrewsbury T.	Tr	06.51	51	25	-	1

B

BAAH Peter Hayford
Littleborough, 1 May, 1973 (LW)

League Club	Source	Date Signed	Seasons Played	Apps	Subs	Gls
Blackburn Rov.	YT	06.91	91	1	0	0
Fulham	Tr	07.92	92-93	38	11	4

BAARDSEN Espen
USA, 7 December, 1977 (G)

League Club	Source	Date Signed	Seasons Played	Apps	Subs	Gls
Tottenham H.	San Francisco A.Bs (USA)	07.96	96-97	10	1	0

BABAYARO Celestine
Nigeria, 29 August, 1978 Nigerian Int (LWB)

League Club	Source	Date Signed	Seasons Played	Apps	Subs	Gls
Chelsea	Anderlecht (Bel)	06.97	97	8	0	0

BABB Philip Andrew
Lambeth, 30 November, 1970 IR 'B'/IR-25 (CD)

League Club	Source	Date Signed	Seasons Played	Apps	Subs	Gls
Millwall	YT	04.89				
Bradford C.	Tr	07.90	90-91	73	7	14
Coventry C.	Tr	07.92	92-94	70	7	3
Liverpool	Tr	09.94	94-97	100	3	1

BABER John Michael
Lambeth, 10 October, 1947 (W)

League Club	Source	Date Signed	Seasons Played	Apps	Subs	Gls
Southend U.	Charlton Ath. (App)	09.66	66-70	72	10	18

BABES John
Lurgan (NI), 20 November, 1929 (RB)

League Club	Source	Date Signed	Seasons Played	Apps	Subs	Gls
Arsenal	Glentoran	01.48				
Scunthorpe U.	Tr	09.50	50-51	9	-	0

BACCI Alfredo Giovanni
Bedlington, 15 July, 1922 Died 1993 (IF)

League Club	Source	Date Signed	Seasons Played	Apps	Subs	Gls
Chesterfield	West Sleekburn	08.50	50-51	6	-	2

BACKOS Desmond Patrick
South Africa, 13 November, 1950 (F)

League Club	Source	Date Signed	Seasons Played	Apps	Subs	Gls
Stoke C.	Los Angeles (USA)	10.77	77	1	1	0

BACON Cyril William
Hammersmith, 9 November, 1919 (WH)

League Club	Source	Date Signed	Seasons Played	Apps	Subs	Gls
Leyton Orient	Hayes	06.46	46-49	118	-	3

BACON Paul Darren
Newham, 20 December, 1970 (M)

League Club	Source	Date Signed	Seasons Played	Apps	Subs	Gls
Charlton Ath	YT	01.89	90-92	25	8	0

BACON Ronald Alfred Sydney
Fakenham, 4 March, 1935 (W)

League Club	Source	Date Signed	Seasons Played	Apps	Subs	Gls
Norwich C.	Holt	12.55	55-57	42	-	6
Gillingham	Tr	05.58	58-60	128	-	15

BACUZZI Reno **David**
Islington, 12 October, 1940 E Yth (FB)

League Club	Source	Date Signed	Seasons Played	Apps	Subs	Gls
Arsenal	Eastbourne	05.59	60-63	46	-	0
Manchester C.	Tr	04.64	64-65	56	1	0
Reading	Tr	09.66	66-69	107	0	1

BACUZZI Giuseppe (Joe) Luigi Davide
Holborn, 25 September, 1916 Died 1995 (FB)

League Club	Source	Date Signed	Seasons Played	Apps	Subs	Gls
Fulham	Tufnell Park	04.36	36-55	283	-	2

BADDELEY Kevin Stuart
Swindon, 12 March, 1962 (FB)

League Club	Source	Date Signed	Seasons Played	Apps	Subs	Gls
Bristol C.	App	03.80	80	1	0	0
Swindon T.	Tr	06.81	81-84	94	1	2

BADDELEY Lee Matthew
Cardiff, 12 July, 1974 W Yth/Wu21-2 (CD)

League Club	Source	Date Signed	Seasons Played	Apps	Subs	Gls
Cardiff C.	YT	08.91	90-96	112	21	1
Exeter C.	Tr	02.97	96-97	37	6	1

BADDOCK Stephen William
Kensington, 10 September, 1958 (W)

League Club	Source	Date Signed	Seasons Played	Apps	Subs	Gls
Bristol Rov.	Bristol Portway	07.85	85	14	3	3

BADES Brian Lawrence
Farnworth, 3 July, 1939 (W)

League Club	Source	Date Signed	Seasons Played	Apps	Subs	Gls
Accrington St.		02.60				
Chester C.		08.63	63	15	-	1

BADGER Colin Albert
Rotherham, 16 June, 1930 (F)

League Club	Source	Date Signed	Seasons Played	Apps	Subs	Gls
Rotherham U.		11.50	50	2	-	0

BADGER Leonard
Sheffield, 8 June, 1945 E Sch/E Yth/Eu23-13/EF Lge (RB)

League Club	Source	Date Signed	Seasons Played	Apps	Subs	Gls
Sheffield U.	App	08.62	62-75	457	1	7
Chesterfield	Tr	01.76	75-77	46	0	0

BADHAM John (Jack)
Birmingham, 31 January, 1919 Died 1992 (D)

League Club	Source	Date Signed	Seasons Played	Apps	Subs	Gls
Birmingham C.	Muntz Street Y.C.	05.46	47-56	175	-	4

BADMINTON Roger Geoffrey
Portsmouth, 15 September, 1947 (WH)

League Club	Source	Date Signed	Seasons Played	Apps	Subs	Gls
Brighton & H.A.	Jnrs	07.66	66	1	0	0

BAGNALL Reginald
Brinsworth, 22 November, 1926 (CH)

League Club	Source	Date Signed	Seasons Played	Apps	Subs	Gls
Notts Co.	Rotherham U. (Am)	06.45	46-47	9	-	0

BAIANO Francesco
Napoli, Italy, 24 February, 1968 Italian Int (M/F)

League Club	Source	Date Signed	Seasons Played	Apps	Subs	Gls
Derby Co.	Fiorentina (It)	08.97	97	30	3	12

BAILEY Alfred Benjamin
West Bromwich, 16 December, 1927 Died 1978 (CF)

League Club	Source	Date Signed	Seasons Played	Apps	Subs	Gls
Walsall (Am)	Darwen	09.53	53	1	-	0

BAILEY Anthony
Winsford, 3 December, 1939 (OR)

League Club	Source	Date Signed	Seasons Played	Apps	Subs	Gls
Crewe Alex. (Am)		05.59	59	3	-	0

BAILEY Anthony David
Burton, 23 September, 1946 (CD)

League Club	Source	Date Signed	Seasons Played	Apps	Subs	Gls
Derby Co.	Burton A.	09.70	71	1	0	0
Oldham Ath.	Tr	01.74	73-74	26	0	1
Bury	Tr	12.74	74-78	124	7	1

BAILEY William **Craig**
Airdrie, 6 July, 1944 (CF)

League Club	Source	Date Signed	Seasons Played	Apps	Subs	Gls
Brighton & H.A.	Kirkintilloch Rob Roy	12.61	62	4	-	1

BAILEY Danny Stephen
Leyton, 21 May, 1964 (M)

League Club	Source	Date Signed	Seasons Played	Apps	Subs	Gls
Bournemouth	App	●	80	1	1	0
Torquay U. (N/C)	Walthamstow Ave.	03.84	83	1	0	0
Exeter C.	Wealdstone	08.89	89-90	63	1	2
Reading	Tr	12.90	90-91	49	1	2
Fulham	L	07.92	92	2	1	0
Exeter C.	Tr	12.92	92-96	143	9	4

BAILEY David
Worksop, 11 January, 1957 (F)

League Club	Source	Date Signed	Seasons Played	Apps	Subs	Gls
Chesterfield	Jnrs	01.76	75	1	0	1

BAILEY Dennis
Church Hulme, 24 September, 1935 (OL)

League Club	Source	Date Signed	Seasons Played	Apps	Subs	Gls
Bolton W.	Jnrs	09.53	56	1	-	0
Port Vale	Tr	08.58	58	1	-	0

BAILEY Dennis Lincoln
Lambeth, 13 November, 1965 (F)

League Club	Source	Date Signed	Seasons Played	Apps	Subs	Gls
Fulham (N/C)	Barking	11.86				
Crystal Palace	Farnborough T.	12.87	87	0	5	1
Bristol Rov.	L	02.89	88	17	0	9
Birmingham C.	Tr	08.89	89-90	65	10	23
Bristol Rov.	L	03.91	90	6	0	1
Queens Park R.	Tr	06.91	91-93	32	7	10
Charlton Ath.	L	10.93	93	0	4	0
Watford	L	03.94	93	2	6	4
Brentford	L	01.95	94	6	0	3
Gillingham	Tr	08.95	95-97	63	25	11
Lincoln C. (N/C)	Tr	03.98	97	1	4	1

BAILEY Gary Richard
Ipswich, 9 August, 1958 Eu21-14/E 'B'/E-2 (G)

League Club	Source	Date Signed	Seasons Played	Apps	Subs	Gls
Manchester U.	Witts Univ. (SA)	01.78	78-86	294	0	0

BAILEY George Ernest
Doncaster, 31 October, 1958 E Sch (W)

League Club	Source	Date Signed	Seasons Played	Apps	Subs	Gls
Manchester U.	App	11.75				
Doncaster Rov.	L	02.78	77	3	0	0

BAILEY Thomas **Graham**
Dawley, 22 March, 1920 (FB)

League Club	Source	Date Signed	Seasons Played	Apps	Subs	Gls
Huddersfield T.	Jnrs	03.37	46	33	-	0
Sheffield U.	Tr	03.48	47-48	20	-	0

BAILEY Ian Craig
Middlesbrough, 20 October, 1956 (LB)

League Club	Source	Date Signed	Seasons Played	Apps	Subs	Gls
Middlesbrough	App	10.74	75-81	140	4	1
Doncaster Rov.	L	11.76	76	9	0	0

League Club	Source	Date Signed	Seasons Played	Apps	Subs	Gls
Carlisle U.	L	02.77	76	7	0	1
Bolton W.	L	11.81	81	5	0	0
Sheffield Wed.	Tr	08.82	82	35	0	0
Blackpool	L	10.84	84	3	0	0
Bolton W.	L	03.85	84	10	0	0
BAILEY John Andrew						
Lambeth, 6 May, 1969						(M)
Bournemouth	Enfield	07.95	95-97	106	10	6
BAILEY John Anthony						
Liverpool, 1 April, 1957						(LB)
Blackburn Rov.	App	04.75	75-78	115	5	1
Everton	Tr	07.79	79-85	171	0	3
Newcastle U.	Tr	10.85	85-87	39	1	0
Bristol C.	Tr	09.88	88-90	79	1	1
BAILEY John Stephen						
Oxford, 30 July, 1950						(WH)
Swindon T.	App	08.68	67	0	2	0
BAILEY Ernest **John (Jack)**						
Bristol, 17 June, 1921 Died 1986						(LB)
Bristol C.	B.A.C.	05.45	46-57	347	-	0
BAILEY Malcolm						
Halifax, 7 May, 1937						(M)
Bradford P.A.	Luddenfoot	04.58	57-58	10	-	1
Accrington St.	Tr	10.60	60	2	-	0
BAILEY Malcolm Roy						
Biddulph, 14 April, 1950						(WH)
Port Vale	Jnrs	05.67	68	2	0	0
BAILEY Mark						
Stoke, 12 August, 1976						(W)
Stoke C.	YT	07.94				
Rochdale	Tr	10.96	96-97	37	11	0
BAILEY Michael Alfred						
Wisbech, 27 February, 1942 Eu23-5/EF Lge/E-2						(M)
Charlton Ath	Jnrs	03.59	60-65	151	0	20
Wolverhampton W.	Tr	03.66	65-76	360	1	19
Hereford U.	Minnesota (USA)	08.78	78	13	3	1
BAILEY Neil						
Billinge, 26 September, 1958						(LM)
Burnley	App	07.76				
Newport Co.	Tr	09.78	78-83	129	5	7
Wigan Ath.	Tr	10.83	83-85	31	10	2
Stockport Co.	Tr	07.86	86-87	50	1	0
Newport Co.	L	03.87	86	8	1	1
Blackpool (N/C)	(Retired)	09.92	92-93	8	1	0
BAILEY Raymond Reginald						
Bedford, 16 May, 1944						(WH)
Gillingham	Bedford T.	05.66	66-70	154	6	7
Northampton T.	L	10.71	71	1	0	0
BAILEY Roy Norman						
Epsom, 26 May, 1932 Died 1993						(G)
Crystal Palace	Jnrs	06.49	49-55	118	-	0
Ipswich T.	Tr	03.56	55-64	315	-	0
BAILEY Steven John						
Bristol, 12 March, 1964						(M)
Bristol Rov.	App	03.82	81	15	1	1
BAILEY Terence						
Stoke, 18 December, 1947						(M)
Port Vale	Stafford R.	08.74	74-77	161	4	26
BAILIE Colin James						
Belfast, 31 March, 1964						(FB/M)
Swindon T.	App	03.82	81-84	105	2	4
Reading	Tr	07.85	85-87	83	1	1
Cambridge U.	Tr	08.88	88-91	104	15	3
BAILLIE Douglas						
Drycross, 27 January, 1937 S Sch/Su23-2						(CH)
Swindon T.	Airdrieonians	03.56	55	1	-	0
BAILLIE Joseph						
Glasgow, 26 February 1929 Died 1966 SF Lge/S' B'						(FB)
Wolverhampton W.	Gasgow Celtic	12.54	54	1	-	0
Bristol C.	Tr	06.56	56	10	-	0
Leicester C.	Tr	06.57	57-59	75	-	0
Bradford P.A.	Tr	06.60	60	7	-	1
BAILY Edward Francis						
Clapton, 6 August, 1925 EF Lge/E 'B'/E-9						(IL)
Tottenham H.	Jnrs	02.46	46-55	296	-	64
Port Vale	Tr	01.56	55-56	26	-	8
Nottingham F.	Tr	10.56	56-58	68	-	14
Leyton Orient	Tr	12.58	58-59	29	-	3
BAIN Alexander Edward						
Edinburgh, 22 January, 1936						(CF)
Huddersfield T.	Motherwell	08.57	57-58	29	-	11
Chesterfield	Tr	02.60	59	18	-	9
Bournemouth	Falkirk	08.61	61	8	-	4
BAIN James Alistair						
Blairgowrie, 14 December, 1919						(OL)
Chelsea	Gillingham	05.45	46	9	-	1
Swindon T.	Tr	05.47	47-53	235	-	40
BAIN John						
Falkirk, 23 June, 1957						(M)
Bristol C.	App	07.74	76-78	5	1	0
Brentford	L	02.77	76	17	1	1
BAIN John Shanks						
Calderbank, 20 July, 1946						(FB)
Bury	Clarkston	07.63	64-66	9	2	0
BAIN Kevin						
Kirkcaldy, 19 September, 1972 S Sch/S Yth/Su21-4						(M)
Rotherham U. (L)	Dundee	03.97	96	10	2	0
BAIN William Clark						
Alloa, 16 November, 1924						(F)
Hartlepool U.	Dunfermline Ath.	08.50	50	2	-	0
BAINBRIDGE Kenneth Victor						
Barking, 15 January, 1921						(OL)
West Ham U.	Leyton	11.44	46-49	80	-	16
Reading	Tr	06.50	50-52	89	-	32
Southend U.	Tr	02.53	52-54	78	-	25
BAINBRIDGE Peter Edgar						
Newton-on-Ouse, 30 January, 1958						(CD)
York C.	Middlesbrough (App)	11.77	77-78	9	0	0
Darlington	Tr	08.79	79	16	0	0
BAINBRIDGE Robert Esmond						
York, 22 February, 1931						(CF)
York C.	Terrys	04.54	53-54	4	-	0
BAINBRIDGE Terence						
Hartlepool, 23 December, 1962						(CD)
Hartlepool U.	Henry Smith Y.C.	12.81	81-83	34	3	1
BAINBRIDGE William						
Gateshead, 9 March, 1922						(IR)
Manchester U.	Ashington	12.45				
Bury	Tr	05.46	46	2	-	1
Tranmere Rov.	Tr	11.48	48-53	168	-	63
BAINES John Robert						
Colchester, 25 September, 1937						(CF)
Colchester U.	Colchester Casuals	01.60	60-62	4	-	0
BAINES Paul						
Burton, 15 January, 1972						(W)
Stoke C.	YT	07.90	90	1	1	0
BAINES Cecil **Peter**						
Manchester, 11 September, 1919 Died 1997						(IF)
Wrexham	Oldham Ath. (Am)	04.43	46	6	-	2
Crewe Alex.	Tr	11.46	46	7	-	0
Hartlepool U.	Tr	06.47	47	9	-	1
New Brighton	Tr	10.47	47	2	-	0
BAINES Stanley Norman						
Leicester, 28 July, 1920 Died 1990						(OL)
Leicester C.	Coalville T.	11.37	38	7	-	1
Northampton T.	Tr	07.46	46	1	-	0
BAINES Stephen John						
Newark, 23 June, 1954						(CD)
Nottingham F.	App	06.72	72	2	0	0
Huddersfield T.	Tr	07.75	75-77	113	1	10
Bradford C.	Tr	03.78	77-79	98	1	17
Walsall	Tr	07.80	80-81	47	1	5
Bury	L	12.81	81	7	0	0
Scunthorpe U.	Tr	08.82	82	37	1	1
Chesterfield	Tr	07.83	83-86	132	1	9

BAIRD Andrew Crawford
East Kilbride, 18 January, 1979 (F)

League Club	Source	Date Signed	Seasons Played	Apps	Subs	Gls
Wycombe W.	YT	03.98	97	0	2	0

BAIRD Douglas Francis Hogg
Falkirk, 26 November, 1935 Su23-1/SF Lge (RB)

League Club	Source	Date Signed	Seasons Played	Apps	Subs	Gls
Nottingham F.	Partick Thistle	09.60	60-62	32	-	0
Plymouth Arg.	Tr	10.63	63-67	147	1	1

BAIRD John **Gordon**
Nottingham, 14 January, 1924 (WH)

League Club	Source	Date Signed	Seasons Played	Apps	Subs	Gls
Mansfield T.	New Houghton	11.46	46-47	9	-	0

BAIRD Henry
Belfast, 17 August, 1913 Died 1973 NI Lge/NI-1 (WH)

League Club	Source	Date Signed	Seasons Played	Apps	Subs	Gls
Manchester U.	Linfield	01.37	36-37	49	-	15
Huddersfield T.	Tr	09.38	38	19	-	4
Ipswich T.	Tr	06.46	46-51	216	-	6

BAIRD Hugh
Bellshill, 14 March, 1930 S-1 (CF)

League Club	Source	Date Signed	Seasons Played	Apps	Subs	Gls
Leeds U.	Airdrieonians	06.57	57-58	45	-	22

BAIRD Ian James
Rotherham, 1 April, 1964 E Sch (F)

League Club	Source	Date Signed	Seasons Played	Apps	Subs	Gls
Southampton	App	04.82	82-84	20	2	5
Cardiff C.	L	11.83	83	12	0	6
Newcastle U.	L	12.84	84	4	1	1
Leeds U.	Tr	03.85	84-86	84	1	33
Portsmouth	Tr	06.87	87	20	0	1
Leeds U.	Tr	03.88	87-89	76	1	17
Middlesbrough	Tr	01.90	89-90	60	3	19
Bristol C.	Hearts	07.93	93-95	45	12	11
Plymouth Arg.	Tr	09.95	95	24	3	6
Brighton & H.A.	Tr	07.96	96-97	43	1	14

BAIRD Samuel
Denny, 13 May, 1930 SF Lge/S-7 (IF)

League Club	Source	Date Signed	Seasons Played	Apps	Subs	Gls
Preston N.E.	Clyde	06.54	54	15	-	2

BAIRSTOW David Leslie
Bradford, 1 September, 1951 Died 1998 (F)

League Club	Source	Date Signed	Seasons Played	Apps	Subs	Gls
Bradford C.	Jnrs	12.71	71-72	10	7	1

BAKER Alan Reeves
Tipton, 22 June, 1944 E Sch/E Yth (IF)

League Club	Source	Date Signed	Seasons Played	Apps	Subs	Gls
Aston Villa	App	07.61	60-65	92	1	13
Walsall	Tr	07.66	66-70	128	9	31

BAKER Charles Joseph
Turners Hill, 6 January, 1936 (G)

League Club	Source	Date Signed	Seasons Played	Apps	Subs	Gls
Brighton & H.A.	Horsham	05.60	60-62	81	-	0
Aldershot	Tr	07.64	64-65	28	0	0

BAKER Christopher
Maltby, 2 February, 1952 (F)

League Club	Source	Date Signed	Seasons Played	Apps	Subs	Gls
Barnsley (Am)		11.70	71	0	1	0

BAKER Clifford Henry
Bristol, 11 January, 1924 (IF)

League Club	Source	Date Signed	Seasons Played	Apps	Subs	Gls
Bristol Rov.	Coalpit Heath	01.47	46	5	-	2

BAKER Clive
Adwick-le-Street, 5 July, 1934 (F)

League Club	Source	Date Signed	Seasons Played	Apps	Subs	Gls
Doncaster Rov.		08.52				
Halifax T.	Tr	08.55	55-58	58	-	22

BAKER Clive Edward
North Walsham, 14 March, 1959 (G)

League Club	Source	Date Signed	Seasons Played	Apps	Subs	Gls
Norwich C.	Jnrs	07.77	77-80	14	0	0
Barnsley	Tr	08.84	84-90	291	0	0
Coventry C.	Tr	08.91				
Ipswich T.	Tr	08.92	92-94	47	1	0

BAKER Colin Walter
Cardiff, 18 December, 1934 Wu23-1/W-7 (WH)

League Club	Source	Date Signed	Seasons Played	Apps	Subs	Gls
Cardiff C.	Cardiff Nomads	03.53	53-65	293	1	18

BAKER Darren Spencer
Wednesbury, 28 June, 1965 W Sch (M)

League Club	Source	Date Signed	Seasons Played	Apps	Subs	Gls
Wrexham	Jnrs	08.83	82-83	18	6	1

BAKER David Henry
Penzance, 21 October, 1928 (CH)

League Club	Source	Date Signed	Seasons Played	Apps	Subs	Gls
Nottingham F.	Brush Sports	10.49	49	3	-	0

BAKER Douglas Graham
Lewisham, 8 April, 1947 (F)

League Club	Source	Date Signed	Seasons Played	Apps	Subs	Gls
Arsenal	App	05.64				
Millwall	Tr	06.66	66	4	1	1

BAKER Frank
Stoke, 22 October, 1918 Died 1989 (IF)

League Club	Source	Date Signed	Seasons Played	Apps	Subs	Gls
Stoke C.	Jnrs	05.36	36-49	161	-	32

BAKER Thomas **George**
Maerdy, 6 April, 1936 Wu23-2 (W)

League Club	Source	Date Signed	Seasons Played	Apps	Subs	Gls
Plymouth Arg.	Jnrs	10.53	54-59	78	-	16
Shrewsbury T.	Tr	06.60	60-61	52	-	5

BAKER Gerald
South Hiendley, 22 April, 1939 (FB)

League Club	Source	Date Signed	Seasons Played	Apps	Subs	Gls
Bradford P.A.	Jnrs	01.57	57-60	16	-	0

BAKER Gerard
Wigan, 16 September, 1938 (FB)

League Club	Source	Date Signed	Seasons Played	Apps	Subs	Gls
Nottingham F.	Wigan Ath.	12.59				
York C.	Tr	07.63	63-68	214	0	7

BAKER Gerard Austin
USA, 11 April, 1938 (CF)

League Club	Source	Date Signed	Seasons Played	Apps	Subs	Gls
Chelsea	Larkhall Thistle	06.55				
Manchester C.	St Mirren	11.60	60-61	37	0	14
Ipswich T.	Hibernian	12.63	63-67	135	0	58
Coventry C.	Tr	11.67	67-69	27	4	5
Brentford	L	10.69	69	8	0	2

BAKER Graham Edgar
Southampton, 3 December, 1958 Eu21-2 (M)

League Club	Source	Date Signed	Seasons Played	Apps	Subs	Gls
Southampton	App	12.76	77-81	111	2	22
Manchester C.	Tr	08.82	82-86	114	3	19
Southampton	Tr	06.87	87-89	57	3	8
Aldershot	L	03.90	89	7	0	2
Fulham	Tr	07.90	90-91	8	2	1

BAKER Joseph Henry
Liverpool, 17 July, 1940 S Sch/Eu23-6/E-8 (CF)

League Club	Source	Date Signed	Seasons Played	Apps	Subs	Gls
Arsenal	Torino (It)	08.62	62-65	144	0	93
Nottingham F.	Tr	03.66	65-68	117	1	41
Sunderland	Tr	07.69	69-70	39	1	12

BAKER Joseph Philip
London, 19 April, 1977 (W)

League Club	Source	Date Signed	Seasons Played	Apps	Subs	Gls
Leyton Orient	Charlton Ath. (YT)	05.95	95-97	23	48	3

BAKER Keith
Oxford, 15 October, 1956 E Sch (G)

League Club	Source	Date Signed	Seasons Played	Apps	Subs	Gls
Oxford U.	App	11.74				
Grimsby T.	L	08.75	75	1	0	0

BAKER Kieron Richard
Isle of Wight, 29 October, 1949 (G)

League Club	Source	Date Signed	Seasons Played	Apps	Subs	Gls
Bournemouth	Fulham (Am)	07.67	69-77	217	0	0
Brentford	L	02.73	72	6	0	0
Ipswich T.	Tr	08.78				

BAKER Mark
Swansea, 26 April, 1961 (F)

League Club	Source	Date Signed	Seasons Played	Apps	Subs	Gls
Swansea C.	Jnrs	09.78	78-79	3	8	2

BAKER David **Paul**
Newcastle, 5 January, 1963 (F)

League Club	Source	Date Signed	Seasons Played	Apps	Subs	Gls
Southampton	Bishop Auckland	06.84				
Carlisle U.	Tr	06.85	85-86	66	5	11
Hartlepool U.	Tr	07.87	87-91	192	5	67
Gillingham	Motherwell	01.93	92-94	58	4	16
York C.	Tr	10.94	94-95	36	12	18
Torquay U.	Tr	01.96	95-96	30	0	8
Scunthorpe U.	Tr	10.96	96	21	0	9
Hartlepool U.	Tr	03.97	96-97	22	0	7

BAKER Peter Robert
West Ham, 24 August, 1934 (FB)

League Club	Source	Date Signed	Seasons Played	Apps	Subs	Gls
Sheffield Wed.	Tottenham H. (Am)	11.54	57	11	-	0
Queens Park R.	Tr	03.61	60-62	27	-	0

BAKER Peter Russell Barker
Hampstead, 10 December, 1931 (FB)

League Club	Source	Date Signed	Seasons Played	Apps	Subs	Gls
Tottenham H.	Enfield	10.52	52-64	299	-	3

BAKER Roy Vincent
Bradford, 8 June, 1954 (F)

League Club	Source	Date Signed	Seasons Played	Apps	Subs	Gls
Bradford C.		07.72	72-74	39	7	11

BAKER Stephen
Newcastle, 2 December, 1961 (FB/M)

League Club	Source	Date Signed	Seasons Played	Apps	Subs	Gls
Southampton	App	12.79	80-87	61	12	0
Burnley	L	02.84	83	10	0	0
Leyton Orient	Tr	03.88	87-90	105	7	6
Bournemouth (N/C)	Tr	08.91	91	5	1	0

BAKER Steven Richard
Pontefract, 8 September, 1978 IRu21-2 (D)

League Club	Source	Date Signed	Seasons Played	Apps	Subs	Gls
Middlesbrough	YT	07.97	97	5	1	0

BAKER Terence
Southend, 3 November, 1965 (CD)

League Club	Source	Date Signed	Seasons Played	Apps	Subs	Gls
West Ham U.	App	11.83				
Colchester U.	Billericay T.	11.85	85-87	55	0	2

BAKER Thomas Arthur
Stepney, 9 August, 1939 (WH)

League Club	Source	Date Signed	Seasons Played	Apps	Subs	Gls
Bristol Rov.		10.56	62	1	-	0

BAKER Wayne Robert
Leeds, 4 December, 1965 (G)

League Club	Source	Date Signed	Seasons Played	Apps	Subs	Gls
Sheffield Wed.	App	12.83				
Darlington (N/C)	Whitby T.	11.86	86	5	0	0

BAKER William George
Penrhiwceiber, 3 October, 1920 W Sch/W-1 (LH)

League Club	Source	Date Signed	Seasons Played	Apps	Subs	Gls
Cardiff C.	Troedrhiw	01.38	38-54	293	-	5
Ipswich T.	Tr	06.55	55	20	-	0

BAKES Martin Stansfield
Bradford, 8 February, 1937 (OL)

League Club	Source	Date Signed	Seasons Played	Apps	Subs	Gls
Bradford C.	Jnrs	02.54	53-58	72	-	7
Scunthorpe U.	Tr	06.59	59-62	77	-	5

BAKEWELL Herbert
Barnsley, 8 March, 1921 (G)

League Club	Source	Date Signed	Seasons Played	Apps	Subs	Gls
Barnsley	Jnrs	02.39				
Newport Co.	Tr	09.46	46	8	-	0

BAKHOLT Kurt
Denmark 12 August, 1963 (M)

League Club	Source	Date Signed	Seasons Played	Apps	Subs	Gls
Queens Park R.	Vejle (Den)	01.86	85	0	1	0

B'ALAC Peta John
Exeter, 9 December, 1953 (G)

League Club	Source	Date Signed	Seasons Played	Apps	Subs	Gls
Plymouth Arg.	App	12.71	71-72	40	0	0
Hereford U.	L	08.73	73	2	0	0
Swansea C.	L	09.73	73	4	0	0

BALCOMBE Stephen William
Bangor, 2 September, 1961 Wu21-1 (F)

League Club	Source	Date Signed	Seasons Played	Apps	Subs	Gls
Leeds U.	App	06.79	81	1	0	1

BALDERSTONE John Christopher
Huddersfield, 16 November, 1940 (IF)

League Club	Source	Date Signed	Seasons Played	Apps	Subs	Gls
Huddersfield T.	Jnrs	05.58	59-64	117	-	24
Carlisle U.	Tr	06.65	65-74	369	7	68
Doncaster Rov.	Tr	07.75	75	38	1	1

BALDIE Douglas Wilson
Scoon, 16 April, 1921 (IF)

League Club	Source	Date Signed	Seasons Played	Apps	Subs	Gls
Bristol Rov.		04.46	46-47	8	-	4

BALDRIDGE Robert William
Sunderland, 26 November, 1932 (F)

League Club	Source	Date Signed	Seasons Played	Apps	Subs	Gls
Gateshead	Hendon Social	02.57	56-59	59	-	22

BALDRY Simon
Huddersfield, 12 February, 1976 (LW)

League Club	Source	Date Signed	Seasons Played	Apps	Subs	Gls
Huddersfield T.	YT	07.94	93-97	31	22	3

BALDRY William Joseph
Luton, 9 July, 1956 (LB)

League Club	Source	Date Signed	Seasons Played	Apps	Subs	Gls
Cambridge U.	Luton T. (Am)	03.76	75-77	27	0	0

BALDWIN Joseph George
Islington, 26 July, 1921 Died 1976 (WH)

League Club	Source	Date Signed	Seasons Played	Apps	Subs	Gls
Gillingham	Dartford	08.51	51	1	-	0

BALDWIN Harold
Saltley, 17 July, 1920 (G)

League Club	Source	Date Signed	Seasons Played	Apps	Subs	Gls
West Bromwich A.	Sutton T.	04.38	37	5	-	0
Brighton & H.A.	Tr	05.39	46-51	164	-	0
Walsall	Kettering T.	12.53	53-54	37	-	0

BALDWIN James
Blackburn, 12 January, 1922 Died 1985 (WH)

League Club	Source	Date Signed	Seasons Played	Apps	Subs	Gls
Blackburn Rov.	Mill Hill St Peter	12.45	46-49	88	-	0
Leicester C.	Tr	02.50	49-55	180	-	4

BALDWIN Thomas
Gateshead, 10 June, 1945 Eu23-2 (F)

League Club	Source	Date Signed	Seasons Played	Apps	Subs	Gls
Arsenal	Wrekenton Jnrs	12.62	64-66	17	0	7
Chelsea	Tr	09.66	66-74	182	5	74
Millwall	L	11.74	74	6	0	1
Manchester U.	L	01.75	74	2	0	0
Brentford (N/C)	Gravesend & Nft	10.77	77	4	0	1

BALL Alan James
Farnworth, 12 May, 1945 Eu23-8/EF Lge/E-72 (M)

League Club	Source	Date Signed	Seasons Played	Apps	Subs	Gls
Blackpool	App	05.62	62-65	116	0	41
Everton	Tr	08.66	66-71	208	0	66
Arsenal	Tr	12.71	71-76	177	0	45
Southampton	Tr	12.76	76-79	132	0	9
Blackpool	Vancouver (Can)	07.80	80	30	0	5
Southampton	Tr	03.81	80-82	63	0	2
Bristol Rov.	Eastern (HK)	01.83	82	17	0	2

BALL James Alan
Farnworth, 23 September, 1924 Died 1982 (IF)

League Club	Source	Date Signed	Seasons Played	Apps	Subs	Gls
Southport	Bolton B.F.	03.46	46	2	-	0
Birmingham C.	Tr	05.47				
Southport	Tr	02.48	47-49	41	-	9
Oldham Ath.	Tr	07.50	50	7	-	1
Rochdale	Tr	02.52	51	5	-	1

BALL Donald
Barnard Castle, 14 June, 1962 (CD)

League Club	Source	Date Signed	Seasons Played	Apps	Subs	Gls
Darlington	App	06.80	79-81	57	3	2

BALL Stephen Gary
St Austell, 15 December, 1959 (M)

League Club	Source	Date Signed	Seasons Played	Apps	Subs	Gls
Plymouth Arg.	App	12.77	79	0	1	0
Lincoln C.	Tr	10.79	79	3	0	0

BALL Geoffrey Hudson
Nottingham, 2 November, 1944 (FB)

League Club	Source	Date Signed	Seasons Played	Apps	Subs	Gls
Nottingham F.	Jnrs	02.63	64-65	3	0	0
Notts Co.	Tr	11.67	67-71	111	1	0

BALL John
Ince, 13 March, 1925 EF Lge (RB)

League Club	Source	Date Signed	Seasons Played	Apps	Subs	Gls
Manchester U.	Wigan Ath.	03.48	47-49	22	-	0
Bolton W.	Tr	09.50	50-57	200	-	2

BALL John (Jack) Albert
Brighton, 16 July, 1923 (G)

League Club	Source	Date Signed	Seasons Played	Apps	Subs	Gls
Brighton & H.A.	Vernon Ath.	02.43	46-52	113	-	0

BALL Joseph Howard
Walsall, 4 April, 1931 Died 1974 (W)

League Club	Source	Date Signed	Seasons Played	Apps	Subs	Gls
Ipswich T.	Banbury Spencer	08.51	51-52	32	-	2
Aldershot	Tr	06.54	54-55	31	-	5

BALL Keith
Walsall, 26 October, 1940 (G)

League Club	Source	Date Signed	Seasons Played	Apps	Subs	Gls
Walsall	Jnrs	01.59	58-61	11	-	0
Walsall	Worcester C.	05.65	66-67	34	0	0
Port Vale	Tr	11.68	68-71	130	0	0
Walsall	Stourbridge	11.72	72	2	0	0

BALL Kevin Anthony
Hastings, 12 November, 1964 (M/CD)

League Club	Source	Date Signed	Seasons Played	Apps	Subs	Gls
Portsmouth	Coventry C. (App)	10.82	83-89	96	9	4
Sunderland	Tr	08.90	90-97	281	5	19

BALL Michael John
Liverpool, 2 October, 1979 E Yth (LB)

League Club	Source	Date Signed	Seasons Played	Apps	Subs	Gls
Everton	YT	10.96	96-97	23	7	1

BALL Stephen
Leeds, 22 November, 1973 (LB/M)

League Club	Source	Date Signed	Seasons Played	Apps	Subs	Gls
Darlington	Leeds U. (YT)	08.92	92-93	30	12	3

BALL Steven James
Colchester, 2 September, 1969 (M)

League Club	Source	Date Signed	Seasons Played	Apps	Subs	Gls
Arsenal	YT	09.87				
Colchester U. (N/C)	Tr	12.89	89	3	1	0
Norwich C.	Tr	09.90	91	0	2	0
Colchester U.	Cambridge U. (N/C)	09.92	92-95	52	12	7

BALLAGHER John
Ashton-u-Lyne, 21 March, 1936 (IF)

League Club	Source	Date Signed	Seasons Played	Apps	Subs	Gls
Sheffield Wed.	Stalybridge Celtic	02.57	58	3	-	0

League Club	Source	Date Signed	Seasons Played	Apps	Subs	Gls
Doncaster Rov.	Tr	02.61	60-61	41	-	13
Gillingham	Tr	08.62	62-63	41	-	10

BALLANTYNE John **Dixon (Dick)**
Newburn, 16 September, 1927 (LB)

League Club	Source	Date Signed	Seasons Played	Apps	Subs	Gls
West Ham U.		05.46				
Hartlepool U.	Tr	07.50	50-51	13	-	0

BALLARD Edgar (Ted) Albert
Brentford, 16 June, 1920 (FB)

League Club	Source	Date Signed	Seasons Played	Apps	Subs	Gls
Leyton Orient	Hayes	04.46	46	26	-	1
Southampton	Tr	06.47	47-50	45	-	0
Leyton Orient	Tr	08.52				

BALMER John (Jack)
Liverpool, 6 February, 1916 Died 1984 (IF)

League Club	Source	Date Signed	Seasons Played	Apps	Subs	Gls
Liverpool	Collegiate O.B.	08.35	35-51	289	-	98

BALMER John **Michael**
Hexham, 25 May, 1946 (CF)

League Club	Source	Date Signed	Seasons Played	Apps	Subs	Gls
Leicester C.	App	01.64				
Halifax T.	Tr	05.65	65-66	28	0	9

BALMER Stuart Murray
Falkirk, 20 September, 1969 S Sch/S Yth (CD)

League Club	Source	Date Signed	Seasons Played	Apps	Subs	Gls
Charlton Ath.	Glasgow Celtic	08.90	90-97	201	26	8

BALOGUN Jesilimi Ayinde
Nigeria, 27 March, 1931 (F)

League Club	Source	Date Signed	Seasons Played	Apps	Subs	Gls
Queens Park R.	Skegness T.	09.56	56	13	-	3

BALSOM Clifford Gene
Torquay, 25 March, 1946 (FB)

League Club	Source	Date Signed	Seasons Played	Apps	Subs	Gls
Torquay U.	App	03.64	63	4	-	0
Swindon T.	Tr	06.64				

BALSON Michael John Charles
Bridport, 9 September, 1947 (D)

League Club	Source	Date Signed	Seasons Played	Apps	Subs	Gls
Exeter C.	Jnrs	08.65	66-73	273	3	9

BALTACHA Sergei
Ukraine, 17 February, 1958 USSR Int (M)

League Club	Source	Date Signed	Seasons Played	Apps	Subs	Gls
Ipswich T. (N/C)	Dinamo Kiev (USSR)	01.89	88-89	22	6	1

BAMBER John **David**
Whiston, 1 February, 1959 (F)

League Club	Source	Date Signed	Seasons Played	Apps	Subs	Gls
Blackpool	St Helens T.	09.79	79-82	81	5	29
Coventry C.	Tr	06.83	83	18	1	3
Walsall	Tr	03.84	83-84	17	3	7
Portsmouth	Tr	12.84	84	4	0	1
Swindon T.	Tr	11.85	85-87	103	3	31
Watford	Tr	06.88	88	16	2	3
Stoke C.	Tr	12.88	88-89	43	0	9
Hull C.	Tr	02.90	89-90	25	3	5
Blackpool	Tr	11.90	90-94	111	2	60

BAMBER Lee
Burnley, 31 October, 1968 (G)

League Club	Source	Date Signed	Seasons Played	Apps	Subs	Gls
Preston N.E. (N/C)	Leyland Motors	08.93	93	0	1	0

BAMBRIDGE Keith Graham
Rotherham, 1 September, 1935 (OL)

League Club	Source	Date Signed	Seasons Played	Apps	Subs	Gls
Rotherham U.	Masborough St Pauls	02.55	55-62	162	-	15
Darlington	Tr	12.64	64	6	-	0
Halifax T.	Tr	03.65	64-65	8	1	1

BAMBRIDGE Stephen Martin
Marylebone, 27 May, 1960 (F)

League Club	Source	Date Signed	Seasons Played	Apps	Subs	Gls
Aldershot	App	05.78	76	0	2	0

BAMFORD Harry Frank Ernest
Kingston, 8 April, 1914 Died 1949 (RB)

League Club	Source	Date Signed	Seasons Played	Apps	Subs	Gls
Brentford	Ealing Y.C.	05.39				
Brighton & H.A.	Tr	06.46	46	8	-	0

BAMFORD Henry (Harry) Charles
Bristol, 8 February, 1920 Died 1958 (FB)

League Club	Source	Date Signed	Seasons Played	Apps	Subs	Gls
Bristol Rov.	Ipswich T. (Am)	01.46	46-58	486	-	5

BANCROFT Paul Andrew
Derby, 10 September, 1964 (M)

League Club	Source	Date Signed	Seasons Played	Apps	Subs	Gls
Derby Co.	App	09.82				
Crewe Alex.	L	01.83	82	21	0	3
Northampton T.	Tr	07.84	84	15	1	0

BANFIELD Neil Anthony
Poplar, 20 January, 1962 E Sch/E Yth (CD)

League Club	Source	Date Signed	Seasons Played	Apps	Subs	Gls
Crystal Palace	App	08.79	80	2	1	0
Leyton Orient	Adelaide C. (Aus)	12.83	83-84	30	1	0

BANGER Nicholas Lee
Southampton, 25 February, 1971 (F)

League Club	Source	Date Signed	Seasons Played	Apps	Subs	Gls
Southampton	YT	04.89	90-94	18	37	8
Oldham Ath.	Tr	10.94	94-96	44	20	10
Oxford U	Tr	07.97	97	18	10	3

BANHAM Roy
Nottingham, 30 October, 1936 (CH)

League Club	Source	Date Signed	Seasons Played	Apps	Subs	Gls
Nottingham F.	Jnrs	11.53	55-56	2	-	0
Peterborough U.	Tr	07.58	60-61	16	-	0

BANJO Tunji Babajide
Kensington, 19 February, 1960 Nigerian Int (M)

League Club	Source	Date Signed	Seasons Played	Apps	Subs	Gls
Leyton Orient	App	03.77	77-81	20	7	1

BANKOLE Ademola
Nigeria, 9 September, 1969 (G)

League Club	Source	Date Signed	Seasons Played	Apps	Subs	Gls
Leyton Orient (N/C)	Nigeria	12.95				
Crewe Alex.	Tr	09.96	96-97	6	0	0

BANKS Alan
Liverpool, 5 October, 1938 (CF)

League Club	Source	Date Signed	Seasons Played	Apps	Subs	Gls
Liverpool	Rankin Boys	05.58	58-60	8	-	6
Exeter C.	Cambridge C.	10.63	63-65	85	0	43
Plymouth Arg.	Tr	06.66	66-67	19	0	5
Exeter C.	Tr	11.67	67-72	160	13	58

BANKS Christopher Noel
Stone, 12 November, 1965 (FB)

League Club	Source	Date Signed	Seasons Played	Apps	Subs	Gls
Port Vale	Jnrs	12.82	84-87	50	15	1
Exeter C.	Tr	06.88	88	43	2	1

BANKS Eric
Workington, 7 April, 1950 (W)

League Club	Source	Date Signed	Seasons Played	Apps	Subs	Gls
Workington	Jnrs	09.68	67-72	26	3	1

BANKS Francis Stanley
Hull, 21 August, 1945 (FB)

League Club	Source	Date Signed	Seasons Played	Apps	Subs	Gls
Southend U.	Jnrs	10.62	63-65	4	0	0
Hull C.	Tr	09.66	67-75	284	4	6
Southend U.	Tr	03.76	75-77	75	0	0

BANKS George Ernest
Wednesbury, 28 March, 1919 Died 1991 (CF)

League Club	Source	Date Signed	Seasons Played	Apps	Subs	Gls
West Bromwich A.	Brownhills Ath.	06.38	38	1	-	2
Mansfield T.	Tr	11.47	47-48	63	-	21

BANKS Gordon
Sheffield, 30 December, 1937 Eu23-2/EF Lge/E-73 (G)

League Club	Source	Date Signed	Seasons Played	Apps	Subs	Gls
Chesterfield	Rawmarsh Welfare	09.55	58	23	-	0
Leicester C.	Tr	05.59	59-66	293	0	0
Stoke C.	Tr	04.67	66-72	194	0	0

BANKS Ian Frederick
Mexborough, 9 January, 1961 (M)

League Club	Source	Date Signed	Seasons Played	Apps	Subs	Gls
Barnsley	App	01.79	78-82	158	6	37
Leicester C.	Tr	06.83	83-86	78	15	14
Huddersfield T.	Tr	09.86	86-87	78	0	17
Bradford C.	Tr	07.88	88	26	4	3
West Bromwich A.	Tr	03.89	88	2	2	0
Barnsley	Tr	07.89	89-91	87	9	7
Rotherham U.	Tr	07.92	92-93	76	0	8
Darlington	Tr	08.94	94	39	0	1

BANKS Jason Mark
Farnworth, 16 November, 1968 (D)

League Club	Source	Date Signed	Seasons Played	Apps	Subs	Gls
Wigan Ath.	App	11.86				
Chester C.	Atherton Colly	10.87	87	1	1	0

BANKS Kenneth
Wigan, 19 October, 1923 Died 1994 (WH)

League Club	Source	Date Signed	Seasons Played	Apps	Subs	Gls
Southport	Wigan Ath.	08.45	46-51	118	-	5

BANKS Ralph
Farnworth, 28 June, 1920 Died 1993 (FB)

League Club	Source	Date Signed	Seasons Played	Apps	Subs	Gls
Bolton W.	South Liverpool	12.40	46-52	104	-	0
Aldershot	Tr	01.54	53-54	44	-	1

BANKS Steven
Hillingdon, 9 February, 1972 (G)

League Club	Source	Date Signed	Seasons Played	Apps	Subs	Gls
West Ham U.	YT	03.90				
Gillingham	Tr	06.93	93-94	67	0	0
Blackpool	Tr	08.95	95-97	115	0	0

BANKS Thomas
Farnworth, 10 November, 1929 EF Lge/E-6 (FB)

League Club	Source	Date Signed	Seasons Played	Apps	Subs	Gls
Bolton W.	Jnrs	10.47	47-60	233	-	2

League Club	Source	Date Signed	Seasons Played	Apps	Subs	Gls
BANNAN Thomas Neilson						
Airdrie, 13 April, 1930						(CF)
Wrexham	Airdrieonians	06.51	51-54	158	-	60
Lincoln C.	Tr	06.55	55-56	67	-	19
Wrexham	Tr	08.57	57-58	68	-	23
Barrow	Tr	08.59	59-60	45	-	15
BANNER Arthur						
Sheffield, 28 June, 1918 Died 1980						(FB)
Doncaster Rov.	Lopham Street	03.37				
West Ham U.	Tr	05.38	38-47	27	-	0
Leyton Orient	Tr	02.48	47-52	164	-	1
BANNERMAN Telford Gordon						
Coupar Angus, 17 September, 1924						(W)
New Brighton	Blairgowrie Jnrs	01.49	48-50	35	-	3
BANNISTER Bruce Ian						
Bradford, 14 April, 1947						(F)
Bradford C.	Jnrs	08.65	65-71	199	9	60
Bristol Rov.	Tr	11.71	71-76	202	4	80
Plymouth Arg.	Tr	12.76	76	24	0	7
Hull C.	Tr	06.77	77-79	79	6	20
BANNISTER Edward						
Leyland, 2 June, 1920 Died 1991						(FB)
Leeds U.	Oaks Fold	05.46	46-49	44	-	1
Barnsley	Tr	07.50	50	32	-	0
BANNISTER Gary						
Warrington, 22 July, 1960 Eu21-1						(F)
Coventry C.	App	05.78	78-80	17	5	3
Sheffield Wed.	Tr	08.81	81-83	117	1	55
Queens Park R.	Tr	08.84	84-87	136	0	56
Coventry C.	Tr	03.88	87-89	39	4	11
West Bromwich A.	Tr	03.90	89-91	62	10	18
Oxford U.	L	03.92	91	7	3	2
Nottingham F.	Tr	08.92	92	27	4	8
Stoke C.	Tr	05.93	93	10	5	2
Lincoln C.	Hong Kong R. (HK)	09.94	94	25	4	7
Darlington	Tr	08.95	95	39	2	10
BANNISTER Jack						
Chesterfield, 26 January, 1942						(WH)
West Bromwich A.	Jnrs	08.59	59-62	9	-	0
Scunthorpe U.	Tr	06.64	64	9	-	0
Crystal Palace	Tr	07.65	65-68	117	3	7
Luton T.	Tr	10.68	68-70	79	4	0
Cambridge U.	Tr	05.71	71-73	28	4	0
BANNISTER James Henry						
Chesterfield, 1 February, 1929						(FB)
Chesterfield		12.50				
Shrewsbury T.	Tr	06.52	52-57	238	-	6
Northampton T.	Tr	07.58	58	24	-	0
Aldershot	Tr	08.59	59-60	85	-	0
BANNISTER Keith						
Sheffield, 13 November, 1930 E Yth						(WH)
Sheffield U.	Jnrs	05.48				
Birmingham C.	Tr	08.50	52-53	22	-	0
Wrexham	Tr	07.55	55	14	-	0
Chesterfield	Tr	12.55	55	21	-	1
Norwich C.	Tr	07.56	56	7	-	0
BANNISTER Keith						
Sheffield, 27 January, 1923						(FB)
Sheffield Wed.	Sheffield Y.M.C.A.	02.45	46-52	75	-	0
Chesterfield	Tr	06.53	53	17	-	0
BANNISTER Neville						
Brierfield, 21 July, 1937						(OR)
Bolton W.	Jnrs	07.54	55-60	26	-	4
Lincoln C.	Tr	03.61	60-63	68	-	16
Hartlepool U.	Tr	08.64	64	41	-	8
Rochdale	Tr	07.65	65	18	1	2
BANNISTER Paul Francis						
Stoke, 11 October, 1947						(F)
Port Vale	Jnrs	04.65	64-67	12	0	2
BANNON Eamonn John Peter						
Edinburgh, 18 April, 1958 S Sch/Su21-7/S Lge/S-11						(M)
Chelsea	Hearts	01.79	78-79	25	0	1
BANNON Ian						
Bury, 3 September, 1959						(CD)
Rochdale	App	09.77	76-79	112	10	0

League Club	Source	Date Signed	Seasons Played	Apps	Subs	Gls
BANNON Paul Anthony						
Dublin, 15 November, 1956						(F)
Nottingham F.	Jnrs	06.75				
Carlisle U.	Bridgend T.	02.79	78-83	126	13	45
Darlington	L	10.83	83	2	0	0
Bristol Rov.	Tr	01.84	83-84	27	2	8
Cardiff C.	L	08.84	84	3	1	0
Plymouth Arg.	L	11.84	84	0	2	0
BANOVIC Vjekoslav (Yakka)						
Yugoslavia, 12 November, 1956 Yugoslav Int						(G)
Derby Co.	Heidelberg (Aus)	09.80	81-83	35	0	0
BANTON Dale Conrad						
Kensington, 15 May, 1961						(F)
West Ham U.	App	05.79	79-81	2	3	0
Aldershot	Tr	08.82	82-84	105	1	47
York C.	Tr	11.84	84-88	129	9	49
Walsall	Tr	10.88	88	9	1	0
Grimsby T.	Tr	03.89	88	3	5	1
Aldershot	Tr	08.89	89-90	29	15	3
BANTON Geoffrey						
Ashton-u-Lyne, 16 March, 1957						(CD)
Plymouth Arg.	Bolton W. (App)	05.75	76-77	6	1	0
Fulham	Tr	07.78	78-81	37	1	3
BARACLOUGH Ian Robert						
Leicester, 4 December, 1970 E Yth						(LB)
Leicester C.	YT	12.88				
Wigan Ath.	L	03.90	89	8	1	2
Grimsby T.	L	12.90	90	1	3	0
Grimsby T.	Tr	08.91	92	1	0	0
Lincoln C.	Tr	08.92	92-93	68	5	10
Mansfield T.	Tr	06.94	94-95	47	0	5
Notts Co.	Tr	10.95	95-97	107	4	10
Queens Park R.	Tr	03.98	97	8	0	0
BARADA Taylor						
USA, 14 August, 1972						(G)
Colchester U. (N/C)	Notts Co. (N/C)	03.94	93	1	0	0
BARBARA Daniel						
France, 12 October, 1974						(F)
Darlington	Lourosa (Por)	12.96	96	1	5	1
BARBER David Eric						
Wombwell, 6 December, 1939 E Yth						(WH)
Barnsley	Jnrs	06.58	57-60	83	-	4
Preston N.E.	Tr	06.61	61-63	38	-	2
BARBER Eric						
Stockport, 25 March, 1926						(W)
Sheffield U.		02.47				
Bolton W.	Macclesfield T.	03.50				
Rochdale	Tr	04.51	50-51	17	-	2
BARBER Eric						
Dublin, 18 January, 1942 NI-2						(F)
Birmingham C.	Shelbourne	03.66	65-66	3	1	1
BARBER Frederick						
Ferryhill, 26 August, 1963						(G)
Darlington	App	08.81	82-85	135	0	0
Everton	Tr	03.86				
Walsall	Tr	10.86	86-90	153	0	0
Peterborough U.	L	10.89	89	6	0	0
Chester C.	L	10.90	90	3	0	0
Blackpool	L	11.90	90	2	0	0
Chester C.	L	03.91	90	5	0	0
Peterborough U.	Tr	08.91	91-94	63	0	0
Colchester U.	L	03.93	92	10	0	0
Luton T.	Tr	08.94				
Peterborough U.	L	12.94	94	5	0	0
Ipswich T.	L	11.95	95	1	0	0
Blackpool	L	12.95	95	1	0	0
Birmingham C.	Tr	01.96	95	1	0	0
BARBER John Nathaniel						
Tamworth, 9 October, 1929						(OL)
Swansea C.	Arsenal	08.50	50	4	-	0
Walsall	Tr	07.51	51	6	-	0
BARBER Keith						
London, 21 September, 1947						(G)
Luton T.	Dunstable T.	04.71	70-76	142	0	0
Swansea C.	Tr	07.77	77	42	0	0
Cardiff C.	L	09.78	78	2	0	0

League Club	Source	Date Signed	Seasons Played	Apps	Subs	Gls

BARBER Leonard
Stoke, 13 July, 1929 Died 1988 (CF)

League Club	Source	Date Signed	Seasons Played	Apps	Subs	Gls
Port Vale	Bury (Am)	06.47	49-54	47	-	12

BARBER Michael James
Plympton, 24 August, 1941 (OL)

League Club	Source	Date Signed	Seasons Played	Apps	Subs	Gls
Queens Park R.	Arsenal (Am)	12.59	60-62	63	-	11
Notts Co.	Tr	07.63	63-64	33	-	3

BARBER Philip Andrew
Tring, 10 June, 1965 (M)

League Club	Source	Date Signed	Seasons Played	Apps	Subs	Gls
Crystal Palace	Aylesbury U.	02.84	83-90	207	27	35
Millwall	Tr	07.91	91-93	104	6	12
Plymouth Arg.	L	12.94	94	4	0	0
Bristol C.	Tr	07.95	95	3	0	0
Mansfield T.	L	11.95	95	4	0	1
Fulham	L	01.96	95	13	0	1

BARBER William George
Bushey, 19 September, 1939 (WH)

League Club	Source	Date Signed	Seasons Played	Apps	Subs	Gls
Watford	Jnrs	03.57	56-59	25	-	0
Aldershot	Tr	08.62	62	1	-	0

BARCLAY Dominic Alexander
Bristol, 5 September, 1976 (F)

League Club	Source	Date Signed	Seasons Played	Apps	Subs	Gls
Bristol C.	YT	07.95	93-97	2	10	0

BARCLAY John Mitchell
Mid Calder, 8 September, 1921 (CF)

League Club	Source	Date Signed	Seasons Played	Apps	Subs	Gls
Bournemouth	Haddington	12.47	47-48	5	-	2

BARCLAY Robert Lindsay Guthrie
Perth, 13 November, 1922 Died 1991 (CF)

League Club	Source	Date Signed	Seasons Played	Apps	Subs	Gls
Preston N.E.		10.45				
Stockport Co.		08.48	48	1	-	0

BARCLAY William
Larkhall, 11 July, 1924 (OL)

League Club	Source	Date Signed	Seasons Played	Apps	Subs	Gls
Bury	Motherwell	03.49	48-49	17	-	0

BARDSLEY David John
Manchester, 11 September, 1964 E Yth/E-2 (RB)

League Club	Source	Date Signed	Seasons Played	Apps	Subs	Gls
Blackpool	App	11.82	81-83	45	0	0
Watford	Tr	11.83	83-87	97	3	7
Oxford U.	Tr	09.87	87-89	74	0	7
Queens Park R.	Tr	09.89	89-97	252	1	4

BARDSLEY Leslie
Stockport, 18 August, 1925 (WH)

League Club	Source	Date Signed	Seasons Played	Apps	Subs	Gls
Manchester C.	Jnrs	01.45				
Bury	Linfield	04.48	47-54	200	-	2
Barrow	Tr	09.55	55	21	-	0

BARFOOT Stuart John
Southampton, 10 December, 1975 (FB)

League Club	Source	Date Signed	Seasons Played	Apps	Subs	Gls
Bournemouth	YT	07.94	94	0	2	0

BARGH George Wolfenden
Garstang, 27 May, 1910 Died 1995 (IF)

League Club	Source	Date Signed	Seasons Played	Apps	Subs	Gls
Preston N.E.	Garstang	02.28	28-34	141	-	43
Sheffield Wed.	Tr	09.35	35	5	-	0
Bury	Tr	05.36	36-38	89	-	13
Chesterfield	Tr	06.39				
Bury	Tr	09.46	46	1	-	0

BARHAM Mark Francis
Folkestone, 12 July, 1962 E Yth/E-2 (RW)

League Club	Source	Date Signed	Seasons Played	Apps	Subs	Gls
Norwich C.	App	04.80	79-86	169	8	23
Huddersfield T.	Tr	07.87	87-88	25	2	1
Middlesbrough	Tr	11.88	88	3	1	0
West Bromwich A.	Tr	09.89	89	4	0	0
Brighton & H.A.	Tr	12.89	89-91	70	3	8
Shrewsbury T. (N/C)	Tr	09.92	92	7	1	1

BARK Robert
Stranraer, 27 January, 1926 (OL)

League Club	Source	Date Signed	Seasons Played	Apps	Subs	Gls
Barrow	Queen of South	04.48	48	1	-	0

BARKAS Samuel
Wardley, 29 December, 1909 Died 1989 EF Lge/E-5 (FB)

League Club	Source	Date Signed	Seasons Played	Apps	Subs	Gls
Bradford C.	Middle Dock	08.27	27-33	202	-	8
Manchester C.	Tr	04.34	33-46	175	-	1

BARKAS Thomas
Gateshead, 27 March, 1912 Died 1991 (IF)

League Club	Source	Date Signed	Seasons Played	Apps	Subs	Gls
Bradford C.	Washington Colly	09.32	32-34	16	-	2
Halifax T.	Tr	12.34	34-38	168	-	36
Rochdale	Tr	09.46	46-47	44	-	17
Stockport Co.	Tr	11.47	47-48	44	-	18
Carlisle U.	Tr	02.49	48	14	-	5

BARKE John **Lloyd**
Nuncargate, 16 December, 1912 Died 1976 (CH)

League Club	Source	Date Signed	Seasons Played	Apps	Subs	Gls
Sheffield U.	Scunthorpe U.	05.33	34-36	6	-	0
Mansfield T.	Tr	06.37	37-46	114	-	0

BARKE (NAYLOR) William Henry
Sheffield, 23 November, 1919 Died 1989 (IF)

League Club	Source	Date Signed	Seasons Played	Apps	Subs	Gls
Crystal Palace	Hampton Sports	01.39	46	18	-	9
Brentford	Tr	02.47	46	11	-	2
Leyton Orient	Tr	06.47	47-49	64	-	14

BARKER Donald
Long Eaton, 17 June, 1911 Died 1979 (IF)

League Club	Source	Date Signed	Seasons Played	Apps	Subs	Gls
Bradford P.A.	Notts Co. (Am)	01.34	33-36	55	-	15
Millwall	Tr	01.37	36-38	62	-	18
Brighton & H.A.	Tr	07.46	46	14	-	4

BARKER Geoffrey Arthur
Hull, 7 February, 1949 (CD)

League Club	Source	Date Signed	Seasons Played	Apps	Subs	Gls
Hull C.	Jnrs	03.67	68-70	29	1	2
Southend U.	L	12.70	70	25	0	0
Darlington	Tr	07.71	71-74	151	0	6
Reading	Tr	02.75	74-76	51	1	2
Grimsby T.	Tr	07.77	77-78	66	0	1

BARKER Gordon
Bramley, 6 July, 1931 (W)

League Club	Source	Date Signed	Seasons Played	Apps	Subs	Gls
Southend U.	Bishop Auckland	12.54	54-58	57	-	9

BARKER Thomas **Haydn**
Tyldesley, 12 January, 1936 (IF)

League Club	Source	Date Signed	Seasons Played	Apps	Subs	Gls
Southport	Boothstown	12.57	57-58	35	-	4

BARKER Jeffrey
Scunthorpe, 16 October, 1915 Died 1985 (FB)

League Club	Source	Date Signed	Seasons Played	Apps	Subs	Gls
Aston Villa	Scunthorpe U.	11.36	37	3	-	0
Huddersfield T.	Tr	11.45	46-47	67	-	0
Scunthorpe U.	Tr	08.48	50-51	73	-	1

BARKER John
Huddersfield, 4 July, 1948 (FB)

League Club	Source	Date Signed	Seasons Played	Apps	Subs	Gls
Scunthorpe U.	App	07.66	65-74	261	2	6

BARKER Keith
Stoke, 22 February, 1949 (G)

League Club	Source	Date Signed	Seasons Played	Apps	Subs	Gls
Cambridge U.		(N/L)				
Barnsley	Tr	03.71	71	9	0	0

BARKER Leonard
Salford, 26 March, 1924 Died 1991 (OR)

League Club	Source	Date Signed	Seasons Played	Apps	Subs	Gls
Stockport Co.		01.48	48-50	40	-	12

BARKER Allan **Michael**
Bishop Auckland, 23 February, 1956 (LB)

League Club	Source	Date Signed	Seasons Played	Apps	Subs	Gls
Newcastle U.	App	03.73	74-78	21	2	0
Gillingham	Tr	01.79	78-79	64	0	2
Hartlepool U.	Bishop Auckland	09.82	82-83	59	1	1

BARKER Richard Ian
Sheffield, 30 May, 1975 E Sch/E Yth (F)

League Club	Source	Date Signed	Seasons Played	Apps	Subs	Gls
Sheffield Wed.	Jnrs	07.93				
Doncaster Rov.	L	09.95	95	5	1	0
Brighton & H.A. (L)	Linfield	12.97	97	15	2	2

BARKER Richard Joseph
Loughborough, 23 November, 1939 (F)

League Club	Source	Date Signed	Seasons Played	Apps	Subs	Gls
Derby Co.	Burton A.	10.67	67-68	30	8	12
Notts Co.	Tr	12.68	68-70	99	13	36
Peterborough U.	Tr	09.71	71	36	0	9

BARKER Robert Campbell
Kinglassie (Fife), 1 December, 1927 (OL)

League Club	Source	Date Signed	Seasons Played	Apps	Subs	Gls
West Bromwich A.	Kelty R.	09.45	48	14	-	2
Shrewsbury T.	Tr	08.50	50	25	-	1

BARKER Simon
Farnworth, 4 November, 1964 Eu21-4 (M)

League Club	Source	Date Signed	Seasons Played	Apps	Subs	Gls
Blackburn Rov.	App	11.82	83-87	180	2	35
Queens Park R.	Tr	07.88	88-97	291	24	33

BARKER William
Stoke, 31 May, 1924 (CF)

League Club	Source	Date Signed	Seasons Played	Apps	Subs	Gls
Stoke C.		10.48	49	1	-	0

BARKS Edwin
Ilkeston, 1 September, 1921 Died 1989 (WH)

League Club	Source	Date Signed	Seasons Played	Apps	Subs	Gls
Nottingham F.	Heanor T.	04.39	46-48	66	-	5
Mansfield T.	Tr	01.49	48-54	213	-	6

BARKUS Lea Paul
Reading, 7 December, 1974 (F)

League Club	Source	Date Signed	Seasons Played	Apps	Subs	Gls
Reading	YT	08.92	91-92	8	7	1
Fulham	Tr	07.95	95	3	6	1

BARLEY Charles **Derek**
Highbury, 20 March, 1932 Died 1994 E Yth (CF)

League Club	Source	Date Signed	Seasons Played	Apps	Subs	Gls
Arsenal	Maidenhead U.	12.51				
Queens Park R.	Tr	05.53	53	4	-	0
Aldershot	Tr	07.54	54	2	-	0

BARLEY Peter James
Scunthorpe, 25 April, 1936 (G)

League Club	Source	Date Signed	Seasons Played	Apps	Subs	Gls
Scunthorpe U.	Leeds U. (Am)	10.53	53	5	-	0

BARLOW Andrew John
Oldham, 24 November, 1965 (LB)

League Club	Source	Date Signed	Seasons Played	Apps	Subs	Gls
Oldham Ath.	Jnrs	07.84	84-94	245	16	5
Bradford C.	L	11.93	93	2	0	0
Blackpool	Tr	07.95	95-96	77	3	2
Rochdale	Tr	07.97	97	35	3	0

BARLOW Colin James
Manchester, 14 November, 1935 (OR)

League Club	Source	Date Signed	Seasons Played	Apps	Subs	Gls
Manchester C.	Tarporley	12.56	57-62	179	-	78
Oldham Ath.	Tr	08.63	63	6	-	1
Doncaster Rov.	Tr	08.64	64	3	-	0

BARLOW Frank Charles
Sheffield, 15 October, 1946 E Sch (CD)

League Club	Source	Date Signed	Seasons Played	Apps	Subs	Gls
Sheffield U	Jnrs	09.65	65-71	116	5	2
Chesterfield	Tr	08.72	72-75	140	1	3

BARLOW Harold
Manchester, 25 October, 1925 (CH)

League Club	Source	Date Signed	Seasons Played	Apps	Subs	Gls
Crewe Alex.	Manchester C. (Am)	02.46	46-50	29	-	1

BARLOW Herbert
Rotherham, 22 July, 1916 (IF)

League Club	Source	Date Signed	Seasons Played	Apps	Subs	Gls
Barnsley	Silverwood Colly	07.35	35-37	58	-	12
Wolverhampton W.	Tr	06.38	38	3	-	1
Portsmouth	Tr	02.39	38-49	104	-	34
Leicester C.	Tr	12.49	49-51	42	-	9
Colchester U.	Tr	07.52	52-53	60	-	16

BARLOW Martin David
Barnstaple, 25 June, 1971 (W)

League Club	Source	Date Signed	Seasons Played	Apps	Subs	Gls
Plymouth Arg	YT	07.89	88-97	231	31	19

BARLOW Neil Keith
Bury, 24 March, 1978 (D)

League Club	Source	Date Signed	Seasons Played	Apps	Subs	Gls
Rochdale	YT	07.96	95	1	1	0

BARLOW Peter
Portsmouth, 9 January, 1950 (F)

League Club	Source	Date Signed	Seasons Played	Apps	Subs	Gls
Colchester U.	App	01.68	66-68	18	3	4
Workington	Tr	02.69	68-69	41	1	11
Hartlepool U.	Tr	07.70	70	8	3	0

BARLOW Philip Douglas
Shipley, 19 December, 1946 (WH)

League Club	Source	Date Signed	Seasons Played	Apps	Subs	Gls
Bradford C.	Guiseley	07.66	66	15	1	0
Lincoln C.	Tr	08.67	67	5	0	0

BARLOW Raymond John
Swindon, 17 August, 1926 E-1 (WH)

League Club	Source	Date Signed	Seasons Played	Apps	Subs	Gls
West Bromwich A.	Garrards	06.44	46-59	403	-	31
Birmingham C.	Tr	08.60	60	5	-	0

BARLOW Stuart
Liverpool, 16 July, 1968 (F)

League Club	Source	Date Signed	Seasons Played	Apps	Subs	Gls
Everton	Sherwood Park	06.90	90-95	24	47	10
Oldham Ath.	Tr	11.95	95-97	78	15	31
Wigan Ath.	Tr	03.98	97	9	0	3

BARMBY Jeffrey
Hull, 15 January, 1943 (CF)

League Club	Source	Date Signed	Seasons Played	Apps	Subs	Gls
York C. (Am)	Selby T.	03.63	62-63	2	-	0

BARMBY Nicholas Jonathan
Hull, 11 February, 1974 E Sch/E Yth/Eu21-4/E 'B'/E-10 (F)

League Club	Source	Date Signed	Seasons Played	Apps	Subs	Gls
Tottenham H.	YT	04.91	92-94	81	6	20
Middlesbrough	Tr	08.95	95-96	42	0	8
Everton	Tr	11.96	96-97	48	7	6

BARNARD Arthur
Tyldesley, 20 June, 1932 (G)

League Club	Source	Date Signed	Seasons Played	Apps	Subs	Gls
Bolton W.	Astley Colly	11.51	54-55	2	-	0
Stockport Co.	Tr	07.56	56-58	53	-	0
Southport	Tr	09.59	59	42	-	0

BARNARD Christopher Leslie
Cardiff, 1 August, 1947 (M)

League Club	Source	Date Signed	Seasons Played	Apps	Subs	Gls
Southend U.	App	08.65	65	4	4	0
Ipswich T.	Tr	07.66	66-70	18	3	0
Torquay U.	Tr	10.70	70-71	29	4	2
Charlton Ath.	Tr	01.72	71	0	1	0

BARNARD Darren Sean
West Germany, 30 November, 1971 E Sch/W-1 (LM)

League Club	Source	Date Signed	Seasons Played	Apps	Subs	Gls
Chelsea	Wokingham T.	07.90	91-93	18	11	2
Reading	L	11.94	94	3	1	0
Bristol C.	Tr	10.95	95-96	77	1	15
Barnsley	Tr	08.97	97	33	2	2

BARNARD Geoffrey
Southend, 23 March, 1946 (G)

League Club	Source	Date Signed	Seasons Played	Apps	Subs	Gls
Norwich C.	Jnrs	09.63	64-66	6	0	0
Scunthorpe U.	Tr	07.68	68-74	256	0	0
Scunthorpe U	Scarborough	09.76	76	6	0	0

BARNARD Leigh Kenneth
Worsley, 29 October, 1958 (M)

League Club	Source	Date Signed	Seasons Played	Apps	Subs	Gls
Portsmouth	App	10.76	77-81	71	8	8
Peterborough U.	L	03.82	81	1	3	0
Swindon T.	Tr	07.82	82-89	212	5	21
Exeter C.	L	02.85	84	6	0	2
Cardiff C.	Tr	10.89	89-90	61	2	8

BARNARD Mark
Sheffield, 27 November, 1975 (LB)

League Club	Source	Date Signed	Seasons Played	Apps	Subs	Gls
Rotherham U.	YT	07.94				
Darlington	Worksop T.	09.95	95-97	102	8	3

BARNARD Henry **Michael**
Portsmouth, 18 July , 1933 (IF)

League Club	Source	Date Signed	Seasons Played	Apps	Subs	Gls
Portsmouth	Gosport Borough	08.51	53-58	116	-	24

BARNARD Raymond Scholey
Middlesbrough, 16 April, 1933 E Sch (FB)

League Club	Source	Date Signed	Seasons Played	Apps	Subs	Gls
Middlesbrough	Jnrs	04.50	51-59	113	-	0
Lincoln C.	Tr	06.60	60-62	43	-	0

BARNES Andrew John
Croydon, 31 March, 1967 (F)

League Club	Source	Date Signed	Seasons Played	Apps	Subs	Gls
Crystal Palace	Sutton U.	09.91	91	0	1	0
Carlisle U.	L	12.93	93	2	0	0

BARNES Bernard Noel Preston
Plymouth, 25 December, 1937 (CF)

League Club	Source	Date Signed	Seasons Played	Apps	Subs	Gls
Plymouth Arg.	Bideford	01.55	56-57	4	-	1

BARNES Colin
Luton, 28 May, 1957 (F)

League Club	Source	Date Signed	Seasons Played	Apps	Subs	Gls
Torquay U.	Barnet	08.83	83-84	42	1	11

BARNES David
Paddington, 16 November, 1961 E Yth (LB)

League Club	Source	Date Signed	Seasons Played	Apps	Subs	Gls
Coventry C.	App	05.79	79-81	9	0	0
Ipswich T.	Tr	05.82	82-83	16	1	0
Wolverhampton W.	Tr	10.84	84-87	86	2	4
Aldershot	Tr	08.87	87-88	68	1	1
Sheffield U.	Tr	07.89	89-93	82	0	1
Watford	Tr	01.94	93-95	16	0	0
Colchester U.	Tr	08.96	96	11	0	0

BARNES David (Bobby) Oswald
Kingston, 17 December, 1962 E Yth (F)

League Club	Source	Date Signed	Seasons Played	Apps	Subs	Gls
West Ham U.	App	09.80	80-85	31	12	5
Scunthorpe U.	L	11.85	85	6	0	0
Aldershot	Tr	03.86	85-87	49	0	26
Swindon T.	Tr	10.87	87-88	43	2	13
Bournemouth	Tr	03.89	88-89	11	3	0
Northampton T.	Tr	10.89	89-91	97	1	37
Peterborough U.	Tr	02.92	91-93	42	7	9
Torquay U. (N/C)	Hong Kong	09.95	95	0	1	0

BARNES Eric
Wythenshawe, 29 November, 1937 (CH)

League Club	Source	Date Signed	Seasons Played	Apps	Subs	Gls
Crewe Alex.		01.58	57-69	347	2	1

BARNES John Charles Bryan
Jamaica (WI), 7 November, 1963 Eu21-3/EF Lge/E-79 (F)

League Club	Source	Date Signed	Seasons Played	Apps	Subs	Gls
Watford	Sudbury Court	07.81	81-86	232	1	65
Liverpool	Tr	07.87	87-96	310	4	84
Newcastle U	Tr	08.97	97	22	4	6

BARNES Kenneth Herbert
Birmingham, 16 March, 1929 EF Lge (WH)

League Club	Source	Date Signed	Seasons Played	Apps	Subs	Gls
Manchester C.	Stafford R.	05.50	51-60	258	-	18
Wrexham	Tr	05.61	61-64	132	-	24

League Club	Source	Date Signed	Seasons Played	Apps	Subs	Gls
BARNES Michael Frederick						
Reading, 17 September, 1963						(CD)
Reading	App	09.81	80-83	29	5	2
Northampton T.	Tr	08.84	84	19	0	1
BARNES Paul Lance						
Leicester, 16 November, 1967						(F)
Notts Co.	App	11.85	85-89	36	17	14
Stoke C.	Tr	03.90	89-91	10	14	3
Chesterfield	L	11.90	90	1	0	0
York C.	Tr	07.92	92-95	147	1	76
Birmingham C.	Tr	03.96	95-96	15	0	7
Burnley	Tr	09.96	96-97	63	2	30
Huddersfield T.	Tr	01.98	97	11	4	1
BARNES Peter						
St Albans, 29 June, 1938						(WH)
Watford	Jnrs	03.57	60-61	10	-	0
BARNES Peter Simon						
Manchester, 10 June, 1957 E Yth/Eu21-9/EF Lge/E-22						(W)
Manchester C.	App	08.74	74-78	108	7	15
West Bromwich A.	Tr	07.79	79-80	76	1	23
Leeds U.	Tr	08.81	81	31	0	1
Leeds U.	Real Betis (Sp)	08.83	83	25	2	4
Coventry C.	Tr	10.84	84	18	0	2
Manchester U.	Tr	07.85	85-86	19	1	2
Manchester C.	Tr	01.87	86	8	0	0
Bolton W.	L	10.87	87	2	0	0
Port Vale	L	12.87	87	3	0	0
Hull C.	Tr	03.88	87	11	0	0
Bolton W.	Farense (Por)	11.88	88	2	1	0
Sunderland	Tr	02.89	88	1	0	0
BARNES Philip Kenneth						
Sheffield, 2 March, 1979						(G)
Rotherham U.	YT	06.97	96	2	0	0
Blackpool	Tr	07.97	97	1	0	0
BARNES Richard Ian						
Wrexham, 6 September, 1975						(FB)
Wrexham	YT	05.94	94	0	1	0
BARNES Robert Alan						
Stoke, 26 November, 1969						(FB)
Manchester C.	YT	07.88				
Wrexham	Tr	06.89	89-90	8	1	0
BARNES Charles **Ronald**						
Bolton, 21 February, 1936 Died 1991						(OR)
Blackpool	Jnrs	05.54	56-58	9	-	0
Rochdale	Tr	06.59	59-60	91	-	7
Wrexham	Tr	07.61	61-63	88	-	24
Norwich C.	Tr	08.63	63	21	-	1
Peterborough U.	Tr	07.64	64-65	39	0	6
Torquay U.	Tr	01.66	65-68	110	4	25
BARNES Steven Leslie						
Harrow, 5 January, 1976						(W)
Birmingham C.	Welling U.	10.95	95	0	3	0
Brighton & H.A.	L	01.98	97	12	0	0
BARNES Walley						
Brecknock, 16 January, 1920 Died 1975 W-22						(FB)
Arsenal	Southampton (Am)	09.43	46-55	267	-	11
BARNES William						
Dumbarton, 16 March, 1939						(FB)
Bradford C.	Glencairn	04.58	58-60	59	-	0
Bradford P.A.	Scarborough	09.66	66-67	53	0	0
BARNESS Anthony						
Lewisham, 25 March, 1973						(LB)
Charlton Ath.	YT	03.91	91-92	21	6	1
Chelsea	Tr	09.92	92-94	12	2	0
Southend U.	L	02.96	95	5	0	0
Charlton Ath.	Tr	08.96	96-97	66	8	3
BARNETT George **Alan** Samuel						
Croydon, 4 November, 1934						(G)
Portsmouth	Croydon Amats	09.55	55-57	25	-	0
Grimsby T.	Tr	12.58	58-62	116	-	0
Exeter C.	Tr	07.63	63-65	57	0	0
Torquay U.	Tr	06.66				
BARNETT Benjamin James						
Islington, 18 December, 1969						(F)
Barnet	Maidenhead U.	08.93	93	0	2	0

League Club	Source	Date Signed	Seasons Played	Apps	Subs	Gls
BARNETT David						
Lambeth, 24 September, 1951						(CD)
Southend U.	App	09.69	68-72	48	9	0
BARNETT David Kwame						
Birmingham, 16 April, 1967						(CD)
Colchester U.	Windsor & Eton	08.88	88	19	1	0
West Bromwich A. (N/C)	Edmonton (Can)	10.89				
Walsall	Tr	07.90	90	4	1	0
Barnet	Kidderminster H.	02.92	91-93	58	1	3
Birmingham C.	Tr	12.93	93-96	45	1	0
Port Vale (L)	Dunfermline	03.98	97	8	1	1
BARNETT Gary Lloyd						
Stratford-on-Avon, 11 March, 1963						(W)
Coventry C.	App	01.81				
Oxford U.	Tr	07.82	82-85	37	8	9
Wimbledon	L	02.83	82	5	0	1
Fulham	L	12.84	84	0	2	1
Fulham	Tr	09.85	85-89	167	13	30
Huddersfield T.	Tr	07.90	90-93	92	8	11
Leyton Orient	Tr	08.93	93-94	47	16	7
BARNETT Geoffrey Colin						
Northwich, 16 October, 1946 E Sch/E Yth						(G)
Everton	App	05.64	65-67	10	0	0
Arsenal	Tr	10.69	69-75	39	0	0
BARNETT Graham						
Stoke, 17 May, 1936						(F)
Port Vale	Jnrs	06.56	58-59	49	-	34
Tranmere Rov.	Tr	03.60	59-60	32	-	11
Halifax T.	Tr	08.61	61	32	-	9
BARNETT Jason Vincent						
Shrewsbury, 21 April, 1976						(D/M)
Wolverhampton W.	YT	07.94				
Lincoln C.	Tr	10.95	95-97	93	8	2
BARNETT Thomas Andrew						
Muswell Hill, 12 October, 1936						(F)
Crystal Palace	Chatham T.	12.58	58-60	14	-	2
BARNEY Victor Charles						
Stepney, 3 April, 1922						(IF)
Reading	Oxford C.	09.46	46-48	45	-	12
Bristol C.	Tr	10.48	48	28	-	4
Grimsby T.	Tr	06.49	49	7	-	0
BARNEY Victor Roy						
Shipton (Ox), 18 November, 1947						(WH)
Bristol Rov.	App	12.65	66-69	30	1	3
BARNHOUSE David John						
Swansea, 19 March, 1975 W Sch/W Yth/Wu21-3						(RB)
Swansea C.	YT	07.93	91-95	18	5	0
BARNSLEY Andrew						
Sheffield, 9 June, 1962						(D)
Rotherham U.	Denaby U.	06.85	85	28	0	0
Sheffield U.	Tr	07.86	86-88	73	4	0
Rotherham U.	Tr	12.88	88-90	77	6	3
Carlisle U.	Tr	08.91	91-92	53	2	5
BARNSLEY Geoffrey Robert						
Bilston, 9 December, 1935						(G)
West Bromwich A.	Jnrs	12.52	54	1	-	0
Plymouth Arg.	Tr	06.57	57-60	132	-	0
Norwich C.	Tr	05.61	61	8	-	0
Torquay U.	Tr	12.62	63	6	-	0
BARNWELL John						
Newcastle, 24 December, 1938 E Yth/Eu23-1						(WH)
Arsenal	Bishop Auckland	11.56	56-63	138	-	23
Nottingham F.	Tr	03.64	63-69	172	8	22
Sheffield U.	Tr	04.70	70	9	0	2
BARNWELL-EDINBORO Jamie						
Hull, 26 December, 1975						(F)
Coventry C.	YT	07.94	95	0	1	0
Swansea C.	L	12.95	95	2	2	0
Wigan Ath.	L	02.96	95	2	8	1
Cambridge U.	Tr	03.96	95-97	53	10	12
BARON Kevin Mark Patrick						
Preston, 19 July, 1926 Died 1971						(IF)
Liverpool	Preston N.E. (Am)	08.45	47-53	140	-	32
Southend U.	Tr	05.54	54-58	138	-	45
Northampton T.	Tr	09.58	58	25	-	4
Aldershot	Wisbech T.	07.60	60	6	-	0

League Club	Source	Date Signed	Seasons Played	Career Record Apps	Subs	Gls
BARR Hugh Henry						
Ballymena (NI), 17 May, 1935 NI Sch/NI-3						(IF)
Coventry C.	Linfield	07.62	62-63	47	-	15
BARR John Millar						
Bridge of Weir, 9 September, 1917						(CH)
Queens Park R.	Third Lanark	05.39	46	4	-	0
BARR Robert Andrew						
Halifax, 5 December, 1969						(CD)
Halifax T.	YT	06.88	86-88	4	1	0
BARR William Joseph						
Halifax, 21 January, 1969						(CD)
Halifax T.	YT	07.87	87-92	178	18	13
Crewe Alex.	Tr	06.94	94-96	73	12	6
Carlisle U.	Tr	07.97	97	39	0	3
BARRAS Anthony						
Billingham, 29 March, 1971						(CD)
Hartlepool U.	YT	07.89	88-89	9	3	0
Stockport Co.	Tr	07.90	90-93	94	5	5
Rotherham U.	L	02.94	93	5	0	1
York C.	Tr	07.94	94-97	143	4	11
BARRASS Malcolm Williamson						
Blackpool, 15 December, 1924 EF Lge/E-3						(CH)
Bolton W.	Ford Motors	11.44	46-56	329	-	25
Sheffield U.	Tr	09.56	56	18	-	0
BARRATT Alfred George						
Kettering, 13 April, 1920						(CH)
Northampton T.	Kettering T.	07.38	38	1	-	0
Leicester C.	Stewart & Lloyds	09.46	47-48	4	-	0
Grimsby T.	Tr	07.50	50	23	-	0
Southport	Tr	07.51	51-55	198	-	0
BARRATT Anthony						
Salford, 18 October, 1965						(RB/M)
Grimsby T.	Billingham T.	08.85	85	20	2	0
Hartlepool U.	Billingham T.	12.86	86-88	93	5	4
York C.	Tr	03.89	88-94	116	31	11
BARRATT Henry (Harry)						
Oxford, 25 December, 1918 Died 1989						(D)
Coventry C.	Herberts Ath.	12.35	37-51	170	-	12
BARRATT Leslie Edwin						
Nuneaton, 13 August, 1945						(WH)
Barrow	App	08.62	62-63	10	-	0
Grimsby T.	Tr	07.64	64	4	-	1
Southport	Tr	07.65	65	9	1	0
BARRELL Leslie Peter						
Colchester, 30 August, 1932						(W)
Colchester U.	Lexden W.	12.56	56	4	-	1
BARRETT Arthur Henry						
Liverpool, 21 December, 1927						(CH)
Tranmere Rov.	Jnrs	03.45	46	1	-	0
BARRETT Colin						
Stockport, 3 August, 1952						(FB)
Manchester C.	Cheadle T.	05.70	72-75	50	3	0
Nottingham F.	Tr	03.76	75-78	64	5	4
Swindon T.	Tr	06.80	80	3	0	0
BARRETT Earl Delisser						
Rochdale, 28 April, 1967 Eu21-4/E 'B'/EF Lge/E-3						(D)
Manchester C.	YT	04.85	85-86	2	1	0
Chester C.	L	03.86	85	12	0	0
Oldham Ath.	Tr	11.87	87-91	181	2	7
Aston Villa	Tr	02.92	91-94	118	1	1
Everton	Tr	01.95	94-97	73	1	0
Sheffield U.	L	01.98	97	5	0	0
Sheffield Wed.	Tr	02.98	97	10	0	0
BARRETT James Guy						
West Ham, 5 November, 1930						(F)
West Ham U.	Jnrs	02.49	49-54	85	-	24
Nottingham F.	Tr	12.54	54-58	105	-	64
Birmingham C.	Tr	10.59	59	10	-	4
BARRETT John						
Birmingham, 26 March, 1931 E Yth						(WH)
Aston Villa	Jnrs	07.49				
Scunthorpe U.	Tr	06.54	54-55	17	-	0
BARRETT Kenneth Brian						
Bromsgrove, 5 May, 1938						(OL)
Aston Villa	Stoke Wks	02.57	58	5	-	3
Lincoln C.	Tr	06.59	59-62	17	-	4
BARRETT Leslie						
Chelsea, 22 October, 1947 Eu23-1						(OL)
Fulham	Jnrs	10.65	65-76	420	3	74
Millwall	Tr	10.77	77	8	0	1
BARRETT Michael John						
Bristol, 12 September, 1959 Died 1984						(W)
Bristol Rov.	Shirehampton	10.79	79-83	119	10	18
BARRETT Michael John						
Exeter, 20 October, 1963						(G)
Exeter C. (N/C)	Liskeard Ath.	12.94	94	4	0	0
BARRETT Charles **Roger**						
Doncaster, 19 October, 1946						(IF)
Doncaster Rov.	Doncaster U.	10.68	68	1	0	0
BARRETT Ronald Harold						
Reading, 22 July, 1939						(CF)
Grimsby T.	Maidenhead U.	08.58	58	3	-	0
BARRETT Scott						
Ilkeston, 2 April, 1963						(G)
Wolverhampton W.	Ilkeston T.	09.84	84-86	30	0	0
Stoke C.	Tr	07.87	87-89	51	0	0
Colchester U.	L	01.90	89	13	0	0
Stockport Co.	L	03.90	89	10	0	0
Gillingham	Tr	08.92	92-94	51	0	0
Cambridge U.	Tr	08.95	95-97	119	0	0
BARRETT George **Thomas**						
Salford, 16 March, 1934						(WH)
Manchester U.	Jnrs	08.52				
Plymouth Arg.	Tr	07.57	57-58	26	-	1
Chester C.	Tr	07.60	60	39	-	2
BARRICK Dean						
Hemsworth, 30 September, 1969						(M/LB)
Sheffield Wed.	YT	05.88	88-89	11	0	2
Rotherham U.	Tr	02.91	90-92	96	3	7
Cambridge U.	Tr	08.93	93-94	90	1	3
Preston N.E.	Tr	09.95	95-97	98	11	1
BARRIE John						
Blantyre, 17 May, 1925						(FB)
Cardiff C.	Thorniewood Ath.	07.48				
Tranmere Rov.	Tr	11.48	48-50	14	-	3
BARRITT Ronald						
Huddersfield, 15 April, 1919						(CF)
Doncaster Rov.	Wombwell	01.49	48-49	13	-	6
Leeds U.	Frickley Colly	04.51	51	6	-	1
York C.	Tr	07.52	52	5	-	0
BARRON James						
Blyth, 19 July, 1913 Died 1969						(G)
Blackburn Rov.	Blyth Spartans	03.35	35-38	76	-	0
Darlington	Tr	06.46	46	23	-	0
BARRON James						
Tantobie, 19 October, 1943						(G)
Wolverhampton W.	Newcastle W.E.	11.61	63-64	8	-	0
Chelsea	Tr	04.65	65	1	0	0
Oxford U.	Tr	03.66	65-69	152	0	0
Nottingham F.	Tr	07.70	70-73	155	0	0
Swindon T.	Tr	08.74	74-76	79	0	0
Peterborough U.	Connecticut (USA)	08.77	77-80	21	0	0
BARRON Michael James						
Chester-le-Street, 22 December, 1974						(CD)
Middlesbrough	YT	02.93	93-95	2	1	0
Hartlepool U.	L	09.96	96	16	0	0
Hartlepool U.	Tr	07.97	97	32	1	0
BARRON Paul George						
Woolwich, 16 September, 1953						(G)
Plymouth Arg.	Slough T.	07.76	76-77	44	0	0
Arsenal	Tr	07.78	78-79	8	0	0
Crystal Palace	Tr	08.80	80-82	90	0	0
West Bromwich A.	Tr	12.82	82-84	63	0	0
Stoke C.	L	01.85	84	1	0	0
Queens Park R.	Tr	03.85	85-86	32	0	0
Reading	L	12.86	86	4	0	0

League Club	Source	Date Signed	Seasons Played	Career Record Apps	Subs	Gls
BARRON Roger William						
Northampton, 30 June, 1947						(G)
Northampton T.	App	07.65	67-68	17	0	0
BARRON William						
Houghton-le-Spring, 26 October, 1917						(FB)
Charlton Ath.	Annfield Plain	10.37	37	3	-	2
Northampton T.	Tr	05.38	38-50	166	-	4
BARROW Graham						
Chorley, 13 June, 1954						(M)
Wigan Ath.	Altrincham	07.81	81-85	173	6	36
Chester C.	Tr	07.86	86-93	244	4	17
BARROW Lee Alexander						
Belper, 1 May, 1973						(CD)
Notts Co.	YT	07.91				
Scarborough	Tr	08.92	92	11	0	0
Torquay U.	Tr	02.93	92-97	154	10	5
BARROWCLIFF Paul Joseph						
Hillingdon, 15 June, 1969						(M)
Brentford	Stevenage Borough	08.97	97	5	6	0
BARROWCLIFFE Geoffrey						
Ilkeston, 18 October, 1931						(FB)
Derby Co.	Ilkeston T.	10.50	51-65	475	0	37
BARROWCLOUGH Stewart James						
Barnsley, 29 October, 1951 Eu23-5						(W)
Barnsley	App	11.69	69	9	0	0
Newcastle U.	Tr	08.70	70-77	201	18	21
Birmingham C.	Tr	05.78	78	26	3	2
Bristol Rov.	Tr	07.79	79-80	60	1	14
Barnsley	Tr	02.81	80-82	46	6	1
Mansfield T.	Tr	08.83	83-84	50	4	10
BARRY Gareth						
Hastings, 23 February, 1981						(CD)
Aston Villa	YT	02.98	97	1	1	0
BARRY George						
Islington, 19 September, 1967						(RB)
Leyton Orient (N/C)	Fisher 93	03.95	94	5	1	0
BARRY Kevin Anthony						
Woolwich, 13 September, 1930						(OL)
Charlton Ath.	Jnrs	12.47	52	3	-	0
BARRY Kevin Thomas						
Newcastle, 9 January, 1961						(G)
Darlington	Nottingham F. (App)	09.79	79-80	18	0	0
BARRY Michael James						
Hull, 22 May, 1953 Wu23-1						(M)
Huddersfield T.	App	06.70	70-72	21	5	0
Carlisle U.	Tr	05.73	73-76	73	8	10
Bristol Rov.	Tr	09.77	77-78	46	1	3
BARRY Patrick Percival						
Southampton, 25 October, 1920 Died 1994						(FB)
Southampton		02.40				
Blackburn Rov.	Hyde U.	05.48				
Bournemouth	Tr	05.50	50	4	-	0
BARRY Roy Alexander						
Edinburgh, 19 September, 1942						(CH)
Coventry C.	Dunfermline Ath.	10.69	69-72	82	1	2
Crystal Palace	Tr	09.73	73-74	41	1	1
BART-WILLIAMS Christopher Gerald						
Sierra Leone, 16 June, 1974 E Yth/Eu21-16/E 'B'						(M)
Leyton Orient	YT	07.91	90-91	34	2	2
Sheffield Wed.	Tr	11.91	91-94	95	29	16
Nottingham F.	Tr	07.95	95-97	79	3	5
BARTHOLOMEW Henry						
Motherwell, 18 January, 1920						(WH)
Exeter C.	Motherwell	05.47	47-48	66	-	6
Bournemouth	Tr	08.49				
Newport Co.	Tr	06.50	50	3	-	0
BARTLETT Frank						
Chester-le-Street, 8 November, 1930						(IF)
Barnsley	Blackhall Colly	08.50	52-62	297	-	68
Halifax T.	Tr	07.63	63	21	-	4

League Club	Source	Date Signed	Seasons Played	Career Record Apps	Subs	Gls
BARTLETT Frederick Leslie						
Reading, 5 March, 1913 Died 1968						(CH)
Queens Park R.		10.32	34-36	48	-	0
Leyton Orient	Tr	05.37	37-47	96	-	0
BARTLETT Gordon						
Chiswick, 3 December, 1955						(F)
Portsmouth	App	12.73	74	0	2	1
BARTLETT Kevin Francis						
Portsmouth, 12 October, 1962						(F)
Portsmouth	App	10.80	80-81	0	3	0
Cardiff C.	Fareham T.	09.86	86-88	60	22	25
West Bromwich A.	Tr	02.89	88-89	25	12	10
Notts Co.	Tr	03.90	89-92	86	13	32
Port Vale	L	09.92	92	5	0	1
Cambridge U.	Tr	03.93	92	3	5	1
BARTLETT Neal						
Southampton, 7 April, 1975 E Sch						(M)
Southampton	YT	07.93	92-93	4	4	0
Hereford U.	B.K. Haken (Fin)	09.96	96	0	3	0
BARTLETT Paul John						
Grimsby, 17 January, 1960						(W)
Derby Co.	App	12.77	77-79	7	6	0
BARTLETT Terence Richard						
Cleethorpes, 28 August, 1948						(OR)
Grimsby T. (Am)	Jnrs	08.67	67	1	0	0
BARTLEY Anthony						
Stalybridge, 8 March, 1938						(OL)
Bolton W.	Stalybridge Celtic	09.56				
Bury	Stalybridge Celtic	11.58	58-64	116	-	24
Oldham Ath.	Tr	09.64	64-65	48	2	13
Chesterfield	Tr	07.66	66	12	0	2
BARTLEY Carl Alexander						
Lambeth, 6 October, 1976						(F)
Fulham	YT	07.95	94	1	0	0
BARTLEY Daniel Robert						
Paulton, 3 October, 1947 E Yth						(OL)
Bristol C.	App	10.64	65-72	92	8	7
Swansea C.	Tr	08.73	73-79	195	4	8
Hereford U.	Tr	03.80	79-82	112	2	6
BARTLEY John Reginald						
Camberwell, 15 September, 1958						(F)
Millwall	Welling U.	10.80	80-81	39	1	8
BARTON Anthony Edward						
Sutton, 8 April, 1937 Died 1993 E Sch						(OR)
Fulham	Jnrs	05.54	53-58	49	-	8
Nottingham F.	Tr	12.59	59-61	22	-	1
Portsmouth	Tr	12.61	61-66	129	1	34
BARTON David						
Bishop Auckland, 9 May, 1959						(CD)
Newcastle U.	App	05.77	77-81	101	1	5
Blackburn Rov.	L	08.82	82	8	0	1
Darlington	Tr	02.83	82-83	49	0	3
BARTON Douglas Joseph						
Islington, 31 July, 1927						(FB)
Reading	Ford Sports	02.49	50-52	10	-	1
Newport Co.	Tr	01.53	52-53	23	-	0
BARTON Frank						
Barton-on-Humber, 22 October, 1947 E Yth						(M)
Scunthorpe U.	App	08.65	64-67	93	0	26
Carlisle U.	Tr	01.68	67-71	161	4	22
Blackpool	Tr	07.72	72	18	0	1
Grimsby T.	Tr	06.73	73-75	123	0	15
Bournemouth	Tr	06.76	76-77	66	0	13
Hereford U.	Tr	01.78	77-78	22	0	3
Bournemouth	Tr	09.78	78	22	0	2
BARTON John Birchall						
Wigan, 27 April, 1942						(G)
Preston N.E.	Jnrs	05.59	58-65	48	0	0
Blackburn Rov.	Tr	06.66	66-71	68	0	0
BARTON John Stanley						
Birmingham, 24 October, 1953						(RB)
Everton	Worcester C.	12.78	78-80	18	2	0
Derby Co.	Tr	03.82	81-83	68	1	1

League Club	Source	Date Signed	Seasons Played	Career Record Apps	Subs	Gls
BARTON Kenneth Rees						
Caernarfon, 20 September, 1937 Died 1982 W Sch						(FB)
Tottenham H.	Jnrs	10.56	60-63	4	-	0
Millwall	Tr	09.64				
Luton T.	Tr	12.64	64	11	-	0
BARTON Leslie						
Rochdale, 20 March, 1920						(D)
Bolton W.		09.46				
New Brighton	Tr	08.49	49-50	64	-	1
BARTON Michael Geoffrey						
Gainsborough, 23 September, 1973						(G)
Shrewsbury T.	YT	●	91	1	0	0
BARTON Peter						
Barrow, 3 April, 1951						(G)
Barrow	App	04.69	68	2	0	0
BARTON Charles **Reginald**						
Chester, 4 March, 1942						(G)
Chester C.	Jnrs	06.61	61-64	14	-	0
BARTON David **Roger**						
Jump, 25 September, 1946						(W)
Wolverhampton W.	App	10.63				
Lincoln C.	Tr	07.64	64-65	28	0	1
Barnsley	Tr	07.66	66-68	52	3	3
BARTON Warren Dean						
Stoke Newington, 19 March, 1969 E 'B'/E-3						(D/M)
Maidstone U.	Leytonstone & Ilford	07.89	89	41	1	0
Wimbledon	Tr	06.90	90-93	178	2	10
Newcastle U.	Tr	06.95	95-97	61	11	4
BARTRAM Andreas **Per**						
Denmark, 8 January, 1944						(CF)
Crystal Palace	Morton	08.69	69	8	2	2
BARTRAM Samuel						
South Shields, 22 January, 1914 Died 1981						(G)
Charlton Ath.	Boldon Villa	09.34	34-55	579	-	0
BARTRAM Vincent Lee						
Birmingham, 7 August, 1968						(G)
Wolverhampton W.	Jnrs	08.85	86-90	5	0	0
Blackpool	L	10.89	89	9	0	0
Bournemouth	Tr	07.91	91-93	132	0	0
Arsenal	Tr	08.94	94	11	0	0
Huddersfield T.	L	10.97	97	12	0	0
Gillingham	Tr	03.98	97	9	0	0
BARWOOD Daniel David						
Caerphilly, 25 February, 1981 W Yth						(LW)
Swansea C.	YT	●	97	1	2	1
BASEY Philip John						
Cardiff, 27 August, 1948						(OL)
Brentford	Jnrs	06.66	66	2	0	0
BASFORD John						
Crewe, 24 July, 1925 Died 1998						(IF)
Crewe Alex.		04.48	48-53	146	-	52
Chester C.	Tr	01.54	53	10	-	1
BASFORD Luke William						
Croydon, 6 January, 1980						(LWB)
Bristol Rov.	YT	●	97	5	2	0
BASHAM Michael						
Barking, 27 September, 1973 E Sch/E Yth						(D)
West Ham U.	YT	07.92				
Colchester U.	L	11.93	93	1	0	0
Swansea C.	Tr	03.94	93-95	27	2	1
Peterborough U.	Tr	12.95	95-96	17	2	1
Barnet	Tr	08.97	97	19	1	1
BASHAM Steven						
Southampton, 2 December, 1977						(F)
Southampton	YT	05.96	96-97	1	14	0
Wrexham	L	02.98	97	4	1	0
BASHIR Naseem						
Amersham, 12 September, 1969						(M)
Reading	Jnrs	06.88	89	1	2	1
BASON Brian						
Epsom, 3 September, 1955 E Sch						(M)
Chelsea	App	09.72	72-76	18	1	1
Plymouth Arg.	Tr	09.77	77-80	126	3	10
Crystal Palace	Tr	03.81	80-81	25	2	0
Portsmouth	L	01.82	81	9	0	0
Reading	Tr	08.82	82	41	0	0
BASS David						
Camberley, 29 November, 1974						(M)
Reading	YT	07.93	91-96	7	4	0
Rotherham U.	Tr	07.97	97	13	5	0
BASS Jonathan David						
Weston-super-Mare, 1 January, 1976 E Sch						(RB)
Birmingham C.	Jnrs	06.94	95-97	46	2	0
Carlisle U.	L	10.96	96	3	0	0
BASSETT David						
Stanmore, 4 September, 1944 E Amat						(D)
Wimbledon	Walton & Hersham	08.74	77	35	0	0
BASSETT George Raymond						
Birmingham, 12 May, 1943						(OL)
Coventry C.	Jnrs	08.61	61	1	-	0
BASSETT Graham Raymond						
Sunderland, 6 October, 1964						(F)
Hartlepool U.	Sunderland (App)	08.83	83	4	3	0
Burnley	Tr	03.84				
BASSETT William Edward George						
Merthyr Tydfil, 8 June, 1912 Died 1977						(CH)
Cardiff C.	Aberaman	08.34	34-38	154	-	2
Crystal Palace	Tr	09.42	46-48	70	-	0
BASSHAM Alan John						
Kensington, 3 October, 1933 E Sch						(FB)
Brentford	Jnrs	10.51	53-57	43	-	0
BASTIN Clifford Sydney						
Exeter, 14 March, 1912 Died 1991 E Sch/EF Lge/E-21						(OL)
Exeter C.	Jnrs	03.29	27-28	17	-	6
Arsenal	Tr	05.29	29-46	350	-	150
BASTOCK Paul Anthony						
Leamington, 19 May, 1970						(G)
Cambridge U.	Coventry C. (YT)	03.88	87-88	12	0	0
BASTOW Ian John						
Torquay, 12 August, 1971						(W)
Torquay U.	YT	03.89	88-89	7	4	0
BATCH Nigel Anthony						
Huddersfield, 9 November, 1957						(G)
Grimsby T.	Derby Co. (App)	07.76	76-86	348	0	0
Lincoln C.	Tr	07.87				
Darlington	Tr	09.88	88	30	0	0
Stockport Co.	L	03.89	88	12	0	0
Scunthorpe U.	(Retired)	08.91	91	1	0	0
BATCHELOR Edward						
Rugby, 4 August, 1930						(HB)
Wolverhampton W.	Jnrs	10.47				
Swindon T.	Tr	08.50	50-54	91	-	0
BATEMAN Albert						
Wortley, 13 June, 1924						(OR)
Huddersfield T.	Yorkshire I. & S. Wks	09.43	46-48	73	-	14
BATEMAN Arthur						
Audley, 12 June, 1918 Died 1984						(LB)
Crewe Alex.	Rolls Royce	11.42	46	3	-	0
BATEMAN Colin						
Hemel Hempstead, 22 October, 1930						(FB)
Watford	Hemel Hempstead	03.53	54-57	50	-	0
BATEMAN Ernest						
Hemel Hempstead, 5 April, 1929						(CH)
Watford	Hemel Hempstead	03.52	55-56	23	-	0
BATER Philip Thomas						
Cardiff, 26 October, 1955 Wu21-2						(FB)
Bristol Rov.	App	10.73	74-80	211	1	2
Wrexham	Tr	09.81	81-82	73	0	1
Bristol Rov.	Tr	09.83	83-85	90	8	1
Brentford	Tr	05.86	86	19	0	2
Cardiff C.	Tr	07.87	87-88	67	9	0

League Club	Source	Date Signed	Seasons Played	Career Record Apps	Subs	Gls
BATES Anthony Norman						
Blidworth, 6 April, 1938						(CF)
Notts Co.	Blidworth Colly	07.59	58	1	-	0
BATES Brian Frederick						
Beeston, 4 December, 1944						(W)
Notts Co.	Loughborough College	07.63	63-68	125	3	25
Mansfield T.	Tr	07.69	69	20	0	3
BATES Donald Lawson						
Brighton, 10 May, 1933						(WH)
Brighton & H.A.	Lewes	11.50	57	21	-	1
BATES Edric (Ted) Thornton						
Thetford, 3 May, 1918						(IF)
Norwich C.	Thetford T.	09.36				
Southampton	Tr	05.37	37-52	202	-	64
BATES Ernest						
Huddersfield, 10 June, 1935 Died 1995						(FB)
Huddersfield T.	Deighton Y.M.C.A.	08.55				
Bradford P.A.	Tr	05.57	57-58	44	-	0
BATES George Reginald						
Sheffield, 21 November, 1923 Died 1995						(OR)
Sheffield Wed.	Shardlows	03.45				
Darlington	Tr	07.46	46	3	-	0
BATES Jamie Alan						
Croydon, 24 February, 1968						(D)
Brentford	YT	08.86	86-97	372	20	17
BATES John Wilfred						
Newcastle, 28 April, 1942						(OR)
Hartlepool U.	Consett	03.66	65	11	0	0
BATES Keith						
Huddersfield, 1 September, 1933						(IL)
Halifax T. (Am)	Bradley R.	11.56	56	1	-	0
BATES Mark						
Walsall, 25 April, 1965						(FB)
Walsall	App	04.83	82-83	6	0	0
Shrewsbury T.	Tr	07.84	84	7	1	0
BATES Michael John						
Armthorpe, 19 September, 1947						(M)
Leeds U.	App	09.64	66-75	106	18	4
Walsall	Tr	06.76	76-77	84	1	4
Bradford C.	Tr	06.78	78-79	54	2	1
Doncaster Rov.	Tr	06.80	80	3	1	0
BATES Philip (Chic) Desmond						
West Bromwich, 28 November, 1949						(F)
Shrewsbury T.	Stourbridge	05.74	74-77	160	0	45
Swindon T.	Tr	01.78	77-79	50	13	15
Bristol Rov.	Tr	03.80	79-80	26	3	4
Shrewsbury T.	Tr	12.80	80-85	114	20	19
BATES William Henry						
Eaton Bray, 13 January, 1922						(OR)
Luton T.	Waterlows	09.41	46	1	-	0
Watford		07.48	48	13	-	1
BATEY Robert						
Greenhead, 18 October, 1912 Died 1988						(WH)
Carlisle U.	Tyne R.	09.32	32-33	23	-	0
Preston N.E.	Tr	03.34	34-38	78	-	0
Leeds U.	Tr	04.46	46	8	-	0
Southport	Tr	06.47	47	29	-	0
BATHGATE Sidney						
Aberdeen, 20 December, 1919 Died 1962						(FB)
Chelsea	Parkvale	09.46	46-52	135	-	0
BATSON Brendon Martin						
Grenada (WI), 6 February, 1953 E 'B'						(RB)
Arsenal	App	06.71	71-73	6	4	0
Cambridge U.	Tr	01.74	73-77	162	1	6
West Bromwich A.	Tr	02.78	77-82	172	0	1
BATT Victor Thomas						
Dorking, 13 March, 1943						(W)
Reading	Jnrs	08.61	61-62	15	-	0
BATTERSBY Anthony						
Doncaster, 30 August, 1975						(F)
Sheffield U.	YT	07.93	95	3	7	1

League Club	Source	Date Signed	Seasons Played	Career Record Apps	Subs	Gls
Southend U.	L	03.95	94	6	2	1
Notts Co.	Tr	01.96	95-96	20	19	8
Bury	Tr	03.97	96-97	37	11	8
BATTY David						
Leeds, 2 December, 1968 Eu21-7/E 'B'/E-35						(M)
Leeds U.	YT	07.87	87-93	201	10	4
Blackburn Rov.	Tr	10.93	93-95	53	1	1
Newcastle U.	Tr	03.96	95-97	75	0	3
BATTY Frederick Robson						
Stanley, 20 December, 1934						(CH)
Bradford P.A.	Stanley U.	01.56	55-58	56	-	0
BATTY Lawrence						
Westminster, 15 February, 1964						(G)
Fulham	Maidenhead U.	08.84	85-90	9	0	0
Brentford	Tr	02.91				
BATTY Michael						
Manchester, 10 July, 1944						(CH)
Manchester C.	App	07.61	62-64	13	-	0
BATTY Paul William						
Doncaster, 9 January, 1964						(M)
Swindon T.	App	01.82	82-84	102	6	7
Chesterfield	Tr	07.85	85	24	2	0
Exeter C.	Tr	07.86	86-90	98	13	11
BATTY Ronald Robson						
Lanchester, 5 October, 1925 Died 1971						(FB)
Newcastle U.	East Tanfield Colly	10.45	48-57	161	-	1
Gateshead	Tr	03.58	57-58	40	-	0
BATTY Stanley George						
Tottenham, 14 February, 1917						(WH)
Aston Villa	Finchley	11.37				
Newport Co.	Tr	12.45	46-47	60	-	3
BATTYE John Edward						
Scissett, 19 May, 1926						(WH)
Huddersfield T.	Jnrs	12.43	49-57	71	-	1
York C.	Tr	07.59	59	17	-	0
BAUGH John Robert						
Uganda, 23 February, 1956						(G)
Exeter C.	St Lukes College	02.77	76-77	20	0	0
BAULD Philip Spinelli						
Glasgow, 20 September, 1929 Died 1994						(WH)
Plymouth Arg.	Clyde	06.53				
Aldershot	Tr	07.54	54	3	-	0
BAURESS Gary Joseph						
Liverpool, 19 January, 1971						(M)
Tranmere Rov.	YT	08.89	89	1	0	0
BAVERSTOCK Raymond						
Southall, 3 December 1963						(FB)
Swindon T.	App	12.81	82	17	0	0
BAVIN John						
Ferriby, 25 May, 1921						(FB)
Tranmere Rov.	Arbroath	04.49	48	2	-	0
BAXTER James Cunningham						
Dunfermline, 8 November, 1925 Died 1994						(IF)
Barnsley	Dunfermline Ath.	08.45	46-51	222	-	54
Preston N.E.	Tr	07.52	52-58	245	-	65
Barnsley	Tr	07.59	59	26	-	3
BAXTER James Curran						
Hill O'Beath, 29 September, 1939 Su23-1/SF Lge/S-34						(M)
Sunderland	Glasgow Rangers	05.65	65-67	87	0	10
Nottingham F.	Tr	12.67	67-68	47	1	3
BAXTER Lawrence Raymond						
Leicester, 24 November, 1931						(OR)
Northampton T.		03.52	52-53	17	-	2
Norwich C.	Tr	11.54	54	5	-	0
Gillingham	Tr	10.55	55-56	61	-	7
Torquay U.	Tr	09.57	57-61	164	-	22
BAXTER Michael John						
Birmingham, 30 December, 1956 Died 1989						(CH)
Preston N.E.	App	12.74	74-80	209	1	17
Middlesbrough	Tr	08.81	81-83	122	0	7
Portsmouth	Tr	06.84				

League Club	Source	Date Signed	Seasons Played	Career Record Apps	Subs	Gls

BAXTER Paul Albert
Hackney, 22 April, 1964 (D)

League Club	Source	Date Signed	Seasons Played	Apps	Subs	Gls
Crystal Palace	Tottenham H. (App)	09.81	81	1	0	0

BAXTER Robert Denholm
Redcar, 4 February, 1937 (LB)

League Club	Source	Date Signed	Seasons Played	Apps	Subs	Gls
Darlington	Bo'ness	11.59	59-60	64	-	30
Brighton & H.A.	Tr	06.61	61-66	195	0	6
Torquay U.	Tr	07.67	67-68	58	4	6
Darlington	Tr	07.69	69	41	1	1

BAXTER Stuart William
Wolverhampton, 16 August, 1953 (CD)

League Club	Source	Date Signed	Seasons Played	Apps	Subs	Gls
Preston N.E.	App	10.71	72-74	34	7	1
Stockport Co.	Dundee	12.76	76	4	0	0

BAXTER William
Leven, 21 September, 1924 (WH)

League Club	Source	Date Signed	Seasons Played	Apps	Subs	Gls
Wolverhampton W.	Jnrs	03.45	48-53	43	-	1
Aston Villa	Tr	11.53	53-56	98	-	6

BAXTER William Alexander
Edinburgh, 23 April, 1939 (CH)

League Club	Source	Date Signed	Seasons Played	Apps	Subs	Gls
Ipswich T.	Broxburn Ath.	06.60	60-70	409	0	21
Hull C.	Tr	03.71	70-71	20	1	0
Watford	L	10.71	71	11	0	0
Northampton T.	Tr	06.72	72	41	0	4

BAXTER William Amelius
Nottingham, 6 September, 1917 Died 1992 (CH)

League Club	Source	Date Signed	Seasons Played	Apps	Subs	Gls
Nottingham F.	Berridge Road Inst.	12.36	37-46	15	-	0
Notts Co.	Tr	10.46	46-53	140	-	0

BAYES Ashley John
Lincoln, 19 April, 1972 E Yth (G)

League Club	Source	Date Signed	Seasons Played	Apps	Subs	Gls
Brentford	YT	07.90	89-92	4	0	0
Torquay U.	Tr	08.93	93-95	97	0	0
Exeter C.	Tr	07.96	96-97	86	0	0

BAYLEY Thomas Kenneth
Wednesbury, 25 June, 1921 Died 1996 (G)

League Club	Source	Date Signed	Seasons Played	Apps	Subs	Gls
Wrexham	Walsall (Am)	08.47	47	6	-	0

BAYLISS David Anthony
Liverpool, 8 June, 1976 (CD)

League Club	Source	Date Signed	Seasons Played	Apps	Subs	Gls
Rochdale	YT	06.95	94-97	71	11	2

BAYLISS Ronald
Belfast, 20 September, 1944 (D)

League Club	Source	Date Signed	Seasons Played	Apps	Subs	Gls
Reading		02.65	64-67	35	3	1
Bradford C.	Tr	07.68	68-69	35	4	0

BAYLY Martin Joseph
Dublin, 14 September, 1966 IR Yth/IRu21-1 (M)

League Club	Source	Date Signed	Seasons Played	Apps	Subs	Gls
Wolverhampton W.	App	07.84	83-84	9	1	0

BAYNHAM John
Rhondda, 21 April, 1918 Died 1995 (W)

League Club	Source	Date Signed	Seasons Played	Apps	Subs	Gls
Leyton Orient	Brentford (Am)	03.46	46-47	60	-	7
Swindon T.	Tr	08.48	48	4	-	1

BAYNHAM Ronald Leslie
Birmingham, 10 June, 1929 E 'B'/EF Lge/E-3 (G)

League Club	Source	Date Signed	Seasons Played	Apps	Subs	Gls
Luton T.	Worcester C.	11.51	52-64	388	-	0

BAZELEY Darren Shaun
Northampton, 5 October, 1972 Eu21-1 (W)

League Club	Source	Date Signed	Seasons Played	Apps	Subs	Gls
Watford	YT	05.91	89-97	151	49	19

BAZLEY John Alfred
Runcorn, 4 October, 1936 (OR)

League Club	Source	Date Signed	Seasons Played	Apps	Subs	Gls
Oldham Ath.	Bangor Univ.	10.56	56-61	130	-	19

BEACH Douglas Frederick
Watford, 2 February, 1920 (FB)

League Club	Source	Date Signed	Seasons Played	Apps	Subs	Gls
Luton T.	Sheffield Wed. (Am)	08.45	46	23	-	0
Southend U.	Tr	07.47	47-48	41	-	0

BEACOCK Gary Cedric
Scunthorpe, 22 January, 1960 (M)

League Club	Source	Date Signed	Seasons Played	Apps	Subs	Gls
Grimsby T.	Netherlands	05.80	80-82	10	7	0
Hereford U.	Tr	08.83	83-85	22	5	4

BEADLE Peter Clifford William James
Lambeth, 13 May, 1972 (F)

League Club	Source	Date Signed	Seasons Played	Apps	Subs	Gls
Gillingham	YT	05.90	88-91	42	25	14
Tottenham H.	Tr	06.92				
Bournemouth	L	03.93	92	9	0	2
Southend U.	L	03.94	93	8	0	1
Watford	Tr	09.94	94-95	12	11	1
Bristol Rov.	Tr	11.95	95-97	98	11	39

BEADNELL William
Sunderland, 25 January, 1933 (CF)

League Club	Source	Date Signed	Seasons Played	Apps	Subs	Gls
Chesterfield	Hylton Colly	06.50				
Middlesbrough		05.53				
Southport	Tr	05.54	54-55	63	-	19

BEAGRIE Peter Sidney
Middlesbrough, 28 November, 1965 Eu21-2/E'B' (LW)

League Club	Source	Date Signed	Seasons Played	Apps	Subs	Gls
Middlesbrough	Jnrs	09.83	84-85	24	8	2
Sheffield U.	Tr	08.86	86-87	81	3	11
Stoke C.	Tr	06.88	88-89	54	0	8
Everton	Tr	11.89	89-93	88	26	11
Sunderland	L	09.91	91	5	0	1
Manchester C.	Tr	03.94	93-96	46	6	3
Bradford C.	Tr	07.97	97	31	3	0
Everton	L	03.98	97	4	2	0

BEAL Philip
Godstone, 8 January, 1945 EYth (D)

League Club	Source	Date Signed	Seasons Played	Apps	Subs	Gls
Tottenham H.	App	01.62	63-74	330	3	1
Brighton & H.A.	Tr	07.75	75-76	9	1	0
Crewe Alex.	Memphis (USA)	08.79	79	4	0	0

BEALE John Michael
Portsmouth, 16 October, 1930 Died 1995 (WH)

League Club	Source	Date Signed	Seasons Played	Apps	Subs	Gls
Portsmouth	Jnrs	08.48	51-52	14	-	1

BEALL Matthew John
Enfield, 4 December, 1977 (M)

League Club	Source	Date Signed	Seasons Played	Apps	Subs	Gls
Cambridge U.	YT	03.96	95-97	73	8	7

BEAMAN Ralph Westley
Willenhall, 14 January, 1943 (F)

League Club	Source	Date Signed	Seasons Played	Apps	Subs	Gls
Walsall	Jnrs	12.60	61	1	-	0

BEAMENT Roger John
Croxley, 28 September, 1937 (G)

League Club	Source	Date Signed	Seasons Played	Apps	Subs	Gls
Watford (Am)	Croxley B.C.	07.56	56	1	-	0

BEAMISH Kenneth George
Bebington, 25 August, 1947 (F)

League Club	Source	Date Signed	Seasons Played	Apps	Subs	Gls
Tranmere Rov.	Jnrs	07.66	65-71	176	1	49
Brighton & H.A.	Tr	03.72	71-73	86	10	27
Blackburn Rov.	Tr	05.74	74-76	86	0	19
Port Vale	Tr	09.76	76-78	84	1	29
Bury	Tr	09.78	78-79	49	0	20
Tranmere Rov.	Tr	11.79	79-80	57	2	15
Swindon T.	Tr	08.81	81	1	1	0

BEAN Alan
Doncaster, 17 January, 1935 (CH)

League Club	Source	Date Signed	Seasons Played	Apps	Subs	Gls
Blackburn Rov.	Jnrs	04.52	52-54	2	-	0

BEAN Alfred Samuel
Lincoln, 25 August, 1915 Died 1993 (LB)

League Club	Source	Date Signed	Seasons Played	Apps	Subs	Gls
Lincoln C.	Lincoln Corries	05.35	34-48	174	-	10

BEAN Ronald Eric
Crayford, 10 April, 1926 Died 1992 (G)

League Club	Source	Date Signed	Seasons Played	Apps	Subs	Gls
Gillingham	Gravesend & Nft	06.51	51	3	-	0

BEANEY William Ronald
Southampton, 29 May, 1954 (FB)

League Club	Source	Date Signed	Seasons Played	Apps	Subs	Gls
Southampton	App	06.72	72-74	2	1	0

BEANLAND Anthony
Bradford, 11 January, 1944 (WH)

League Club	Source	Date Signed	Seasons Played	Apps	Subs	Gls
Blackpool	App	01.62				
Southport	Tr	07.62	62-65	143	0	3
Southend U.	Tr	03.66	65-66	57	0	3
Wrexham	Tr	07.67	67-68	84	0	5
Bradford P.A.	Tr	06.69	69	29	2	1

BEARD Malcolm
Cannock, 3 May, 1942 E Yth (WH)

League Club	Source	Date Signed	Seasons Played	Apps	Subs	Gls
Birmingham C.	Jnrs	05.59	60-70	349	1	26
Aston Villa	Tr	07.71	71-72	5	1	0

BEARD Mark
Roehampton, 8 October, 1974 (FB)

League Club	Source	Date Signed	Seasons Played	Apps	Subs	Gls
Millwall	YT	03.93	93-94	32	13	2
Sheffield U.	Tr	08.95	95-97	22	16	0
Southend U.	L	10.97	97	6	2	0

BEARDALL James Thomas
Whitefield, 18 October, 1946 (CF)

League Club	Source	Date Signed	Seasons Played	Apps	Subs	Gls
Blackburn Rov.	Bury (Am)	03.68	67-68	4	2	1
Oldham Ath.	Tr	05.69	69	21	1	10

BEARDS Allan
Normanton, 19 October, 1932 (OL)

League Club	Source	Date Signed	Seasons Played	Apps	Subs	Gls
Bolton W.	Whitewood Jnrs	10.50	50-53	14	-	2
Swindon T.	Tr	03.54	53-54	21	-	4
Stockport Co.	Tr	07.55	55	5	-	0

BEARDSHAW Ernest **Colin**
South Hetton, 26 November, 1912 Died 1977 (FB)

League Club	Source	Date Signed	Seasons Played	Apps	Subs	Gls
Gateshead (Am)	South Hetton Colly	02.36	35	12	-	0
Stockport Co.	Tr	05.36	37	18	-	0
Bradford C.	Tr	07.38	38	42	-	0
Southport	Cork U.	10.48	48-50	61	-	0

BEARDSLEY Donald Thomas
Alyth, 23 October, 1946 (FB)

League Club	Source	Date Signed	Seasons Played	Apps	Subs	Gls
Hull C.	App	11.64	66-72	128	2	0
Doncaster Rov.	L	03.72	71	10	0	0
Grimsby T.	Tr	08.73	73-74	66	0	0

BEARDSLEY Peter Andrew
Newcastle, 18 January, 1961 EF Lge/E'B'/E-59 (F)

League Club	Source	Date Signed	Seasons Played	Apps	Subs	Gls
Carlisle U.	Wallsend B.C.	08.79	79-81	93	11	22
Manchester U.	Vancouver (Can)	09.82				
Newcastle U.	Vancouver (Can)	09.83	83-86	146	1	61
Liverpool	Tr	07.87	87-90	120	11	46
Everton	Tr	08.91	91-92	81	0	25
Newcastle U.	Tr	07.93	93-96	126	3	47
Bolton W.	Tr	08.97	97	14	3	2
Manchester C.	L	02.98	97	5	1	0
Fulham	L	03.98	97	8	0	1

BEARDSMORE Russell Peter
Wigan, 28 September, 1968 Eu21-5 (M)

League Club	Source	Date Signed	Seasons Played	Apps	Subs	Gls
Manchester U.	App	09.86	88-90	30	26	4
Blackburn Rov.	L	12.91	91	1	1	0
Bournemouth	Tr	06.93	93-97	167	11	4

BEARPARK Ian Harper
Dursley, 13 January, 1939 (G)

League Club	Source	Date Signed	Seasons Played	Apps	Subs	Gls
Bristol Rov.	Stonehouse Violet	08.60	60	2	-	0

BEARRYMAN Henry William
Wandsworth, 26 September, 1924 (WH)

League Club	Source	Date Signed	Seasons Played	Apps	Subs	Gls
Chelsea	Jnrs	09.41				
Colchester U.	Tr	07.47	50-53	174	-	3

BEASANT David John
Willesden, 20 March, 1959 E 'B'/E-2 (G)

League Club	Source	Date Signed	Seasons Played	Apps	Subs	Gls
Wimbledon	Edgware T.	08.79	79-87	340	0	0
Newcastle U.	Tr	06.88	88	20	0	0
Chelsea	Tr	01.89	88-92	133	0	0
Grimsby T.	L	10.92	92	6	0	0
Wolverhampton W.	L	01.93	92	4	0	0
Southampton	Tr	11.93	93-96	86	2	0
Nottingham F.	Tr	08.97	97	41	0	0

BEASLEY Albert (Pat)
Stourbridge, 27 July, 1913 Died 1986 E-1 (WH)

League Club	Source	Date Signed	Seasons Played	Apps	Subs	Gls
Arsenal	Stourbridge	05.31	31-36	79	-	19
Huddersfield T.	Tr	10.36	36-38	108	-	24
Fulham	Tr	12.45	46-49	153	-	13
Bristol C.	Tr	08.50	50-51	66	-	5

BEASLEY Andrew
Sedgley, 15 February, 1964 (G)

League Club	Source	Date Signed	Seasons Played	Apps	Subs	Gls
Luton T.	App	02.82				
Mansfield T.	Tr	07.84	84-91	94	0	0
Peterborough U.	L	07.86	86	7	0	0
Scarborough	L	03.88	87	4	0	0
Bristol Rov.	L	03.93	92	1	0	0
Doncaster Rov.	Tr	07.93	93	37	0	0
Chesterfield	Tr	08.94	94-95	31	1	0

BEASON Malcolm Lloyd
Dulwich, 1 December, 1955 (M)

League Club	Source	Date Signed	Seasons Played	Apps	Subs	Gls
Crystal Palace	App	08.73				
Leyton Orient	Tr	09.75	75	0	1	0

BEATON William
Kincardine, 30 September, 1935 (G)

League Club	Source	Date Signed	Seasons Played	Apps	Subs	Gls
Aston Villa	Dunfermline Ath.	10.58	58	1	-	0

BEATTIE Andrew
Aberdeen, 11 August, 1913 Died 1983 S-7 (FB)

League Club	Source	Date Signed	Seasons Played	Apps	Subs	Gls
Preston N.E.	Inverurie Loco	05.35	34-46	125	-	5

BEATTIE Andrew Hugh
Liverpool, 9 February, 1964 (CD)

League Club	Source	Date Signed	Seasons Played	Apps	Subs	Gls
Cambridge U.	App	02.82	83-87	94	3	2

BEATTIE Bradley
Torquay, 20 August, 1957 (IF)

League Club	Source	Date Signed	Seasons Played	Apps	Subs	Gls
Torquay U.	App	●	73-74	2	2	0

BEATTIE George
Aberdeen, 16 June, 1925 (IF)

League Club	Source	Date Signed	Seasons Played	Apps	Subs	Gls
Southampton	Rosslyn Rosemount	08.47	47	1	-	0
Newport Co.	Gloucester C.	09.50	50-52	113	-	26
Bradford P.A.	Tr	07.53	53-54	53	-	16

BEATTIE James Scott
Lancaster, 27 February, 1978 (F)

League Club	Source	Date Signed	Seasons Played	Apps	Subs	Gls
Blackburn Rov.	YT	03.95	96-97	1	3	0

BEATTIE Thomas **Kevin**
Carlisle, 18 December, 1953 E Yth/E-9 (CD)

League Club	Source	Date Signed	Seasons Played	Apps	Subs	Gls
Ipswich T.	App	07.71	72-80	225	3	24
Colchester U. (N/C)	Tr	07.82	82	3	1	0
Middlesbrough	Tr	11.82	82	3	1	0

BEATTIE Richard Scott
Glasgow, 24 October, 1936 Died 1990 Su23-3/SF Lge (G)

League Club	Source	Date Signed	Seasons Played	Apps	Subs	Gls
Portsmouth	Glasgow Celtic	08.59	59-61	122	-	0
Peterborough U.	Tr	06.62	62	10	-	0

BEATTIE Robert
Stevenston, 24 January, 1916 Died 1984 S-1 (IF)

League Club	Source	Date Signed	Seasons Played	Apps	Subs	Gls
Preston N.E.	Kilmarnock	09.37	37-53	264	-	49

BEATTIE Stuart Richard
Stevenston, 10 July, 1967 (CD)

League Club	Source	Date Signed	Seasons Played	Apps	Subs	Gls
Doncaster Rov.	Glasgow Rangers	01.87	86-88	26	0	1

BEATTIE Thomas
Sheepwash, 12 March, 1921 Died 1988 (CF)

League Club	Source	Date Signed	Seasons Played	Apps	Subs	Gls
Gateshead	Morpeth T.	01.47	46-47	20	-	4

BEAUCHAMP Joseph Daniel
Oxford, 13 March, 1971 (W)

League Club	Source	Date Signed	Seasons Played	Apps	Subs	Gls
Oxford U.	YT	05.89	88-93	117	7	20
Swansea C.	L	10.91	91	5	0	2
West Ham U.	Tr	06.94				
Swindon T.	Tr	08.94	94-95	39	6	3
Oxford U.	Tr	10.95	95-97	105	16	27

BEAUMONT Alan
Liverpool, 9 January, 1927 (WH)

League Club	Source	Date Signed	Seasons Played	Apps	Subs	Gls
Chester C.	South Liverpool	09.48	48	5	-	0

BEAUMONT Christopher Paul
Sheffield, 5 December, 1965 (W)

League Club	Source	Date Signed	Seasons Played	Apps	Subs	Gls
Rochdale	Denaby U.	07.88	88	31	3	7
Stockport Co.	Tr	07.89	89-95	238	20	39
Chesterfield	Tr	07.96	96-97	61	11	2

BEAUMONT David Alan
Edinburgh, 10 December, 1963 S Yth/Su21-1 (CD)

League Club	Source	Date Signed	Seasons Played	Apps	Subs	Gls
Luton T.	Dundee U.	01.89	88-91	66	10	0

BEAUMONT Frank
Hoyland, 22 December, 1939 E Yth (IF)

League Club	Source	Date Signed	Seasons Played	Apps	Subs	Gls
Barnsley	Jnrs	12.57	57-61	107	-	37
Bury	Tr	09.61	61-63	68	-	12
Stockport Co.	Tr	09.64	64-65	52	3	4

BEAUMONT Nigel
Hemsworth, 11 February, 1967 (CD)

League Club	Source	Date Signed	Seasons Played	Apps	Subs	Gls
Bradford C.	YT	07.85	85	2	0	0
Wrexham	Tr	07.88	88-91	112	3	4

BEAVEN Kenneth
Bovingdon, 26 December, 1949 (F)

League Club	Source	Date Signed	Seasons Played	Apps	Subs	Gls
Luton T.	App	●	67	1	0	0

BEAVER David
Kirkby-in-Ashfield, 4 April, 1966 (M)

League Club	Source	Date Signed	Seasons Played	Apps	Subs	Gls
Notts Co.	App	04.84	84	1	0	0

BEAVON Cyril
Barnsley, 27 September, 1937 E Yth (RB)

League Club	Source	Date Signed	Seasons Played	Apps	Subs	Gls
Wolverhampton W.	Jnrs	12.54				
Oxford U.	Tr	01.59	62-68	271	2	7

BEAVON David George
Nottingham, 8 December, 1961 (D)

League Club	Source	Date Signed	Seasons Played	Apps	Subs	Gls
Notts Co.	App	12.79	80	5	0	0
Lincoln C.	Tr	11.81	81-82	7	1	0
Northampton T.	Tr	03.83	82	2	0	0

BEAVON Michael **Stuart**
Wolverhampton, 30 November, 1958 (M)

League Club	Source	Date Signed	Seasons Played	Apps	Subs	Gls
Tottenham H.	App	07.76	78-79	3	1	0
Notts Co.	L	12.79	79	6	0	0
Reading	Tr	07.80	80-89	380	16	44
Northampton T.	Tr	08.90	90-92	95	3	14

BEBBINGTON Richard **Keith**
Cuddington, 4 August, 1943 (W)

League Club	Source	Date Signed	Seasons Played	Apps	Subs	Gls
Stoke C.	Jnrs	08.60	62-65	99	2	17
Oldham Ath.	Tr	08.66	66-71	237	0	38
Rochdale	Tr	07.72	72-73	57	3	6

BEBBINGTON Peter Andrew
Oswestry, 13 October, 1946 (FB)

League Club	Source	Date Signed	Seasons Played	Apps	Subs	Gls
Leicester C.	Oswestry T.	10.65				
Barrow	Tr	11.67	67-68	51	1	3
Stockport Co.	Tr	07.69	69	16	1	1

BECK John Alexander
Edmonton, 25 May, 1954 (M)

League Club	Source	Date Signed	Seasons Played	Apps	Subs	Gls
Queens Park R.	App	05.72	72-75	32	8	1
Coventry C.	Tr	06.76	76-78	60	9	6
Fulham	Tr	10.78	78-81	113	1	12
Bournemouth	Tr	09.82	82-85	132	5	13
Cambridge U.	Tr	07.86	86-89	105	7	11

BECK Mikkel
Denmark, 12 May, 1973 Danish Int (F)

League Club	Source	Date Signed	Seasons Played	Apps	Subs	Gls
Middlesbrough	Fortuna Cologne (Ger)	09.96	96-97	53	11	19

BECKERS Peter
Dundee, 3 October, 1947 Died 1996 (OL)

League Club	Source	Date Signed	Seasons Played	Apps	Subs	Gls
Grimsby T.	Craigmore Thistle	11.64	64	1	-	0

BECKETT Roy Wilson
Stoke, 20 March, 1928 (D)

League Club	Source	Date Signed	Seasons Played	Apps	Subs	Gls
Stoke C.	Jnrs	04.45	50-53	14	-	1

BECKETT William
Liverpool, 4 July, 1915 (IF)

League Club	Source	Date Signed	Seasons Played	Apps	Subs	Gls
New Brighton	Litherland	11.34	34-35	25	-	4
Tranmere Rov.	Tr	07.36				
Blackpool	South Liverpool	04.37				
Bradford C.	Tr	07.38	38	5	-	1
Watford	Tr	05.39	46	7	-	1
Northampton T.	Tr	06.47				

BECKFORD Darren Richard Lorenzo
Manchester, 12 May, 1967 E Sch/E Yth (F)

League Club	Source	Date Signed	Seasons Played	Apps	Subs	Gls
Manchester C.	App	08.84	84-86	7	4	0
Bury	L	10.85	85	12	0	5
Port Vale	Tr	03.87	86-90	169	9	71
Norwich C.	Tr	07.91	91-92	32	6	8
Oldham Ath.	Tr	03.93	92-95	31	21	11
Preston N.E. (N/C)	Hearts	01.97	96	0	2	0
Walsall	Fulham (N/C)	03.97	96	3	5	0

BECKFORD Jason Neil
Manchester, 14 February, 1970 E Sch/E Yth (W)

League Club	Source	Date Signed	Seasons Played	Apps	Subs	Gls
Manchester C.	YT	08.87	87-90	8	12	1
Blackburn Rov.	L	03.91	90	3	1	0
Port Vale	L	09.91	91	4	1	1
Birmingham C.	Tr	01.92	91-92	5	2	2
Bury	L	03.94	93	3	0	0
Stoke C.	Tr	08.94	94	2	2	0
Millwall	Tr	12.94	94	6	3	0
Northampton T.	Tr	05.95	95	0	1	0

BECKHAM David Robert
Leytonstone, 2 May, 1975 E Yth/Eu21-9/E-18 (M)

League Club	Source	Date Signed	Seasons Played	Apps	Subs	Gls
Manchester U.	YT	01.93	94-97	95	15	24
Preston N.E.	L	02.95	94	4	1	2

BEDDOW Ronald Malcolm
Walsall, 11 May, 1936 (RB)

League Club	Source	Date Signed	Seasons Played	Apps	Subs	Gls
Walsall	Jnrs	10.54	54	1	-	0

BEDEAU Anthony Charles Osmond
Hammersmith, 24 March, 1974 (W)

League Club	Source	Date Signed	Seasons Played	Apps	Subs	Gls
Torquay U.	YT	07.97	95-97	18	28	6

BEDFORD Noel **Brian**
Ferndale, 24 December, 1933 (CF)

League Club	Source	Date Signed	Seasons Played	Apps	Subs	Gls
Reading	Beddau Y.C.	04.54	54	3	-	1
Southampton	Tr	07.55	55	5	-	2
Bournemouth	Tr	08.56	56-58	75	-	32
Queens Park R.	Tr	07.59	59-64	258	-	161
Scunthorpe U.	Tr	09.65	65-66	37	0	23
Brentford	Tr	09.66	66	21	0	10

BEDFORD Kevin Edward
Carshalton, 26 December, 1968 (LB)

League Club	Source	Date Signed	Seasons Played	Apps	Subs	Gls
Wimbledon	App	11.86	87	4	0	0
Aldershot	L	02.88	87	16	0	0
Colchester U.	Tr	07.88	88	24	2	0

BEDROSSIAN Ara
Cyprus, 2 June, 1967 Cypriot Int (M)

League Club	Source	Date Signed	Seasons Played	Apps	Subs	Gls
Fulham (N/C)	Apoel Limassol (Cyp)	03.93	92-94	34	8	1

BEDSON Raymond Arthur
Newcastle-u-Lyme, 4 February, 1929 (HB)

League Club	Source	Date Signed	Seasons Played	Apps	Subs	Gls
Crewe Alex.		08.52	53	2	-	0

BEE Francis Eric
Nottingham, 23 January, 1927 (IF)

League Club	Source	Date Signed	Seasons Played	Apps	Subs	Gls
Sunderland	Nottingham F. (Am)	06.47	47	5	-	1
Blackburn Rov.	Tr	03.49	48	4	-	0

BEEBY Oliver
Whetstone (Lei), 2 October, 1934 E Yth (FB)

League Club	Source	Date Signed	Seasons Played	Apps	Subs	Gls
Leicester C.		05.53	55	1	-	0
Notts Co.	Tr	06.59	59	13	-	0

BEECH Christopher
Congleton, 5 November, 1975 E Sch/E Yth (LWB)

League Club	Source	Date Signed	Seasons Played	Apps	Subs	Gls
Manchester C.	YT	11.92				
Cardiff C.	Tr	08.97	97	46	0	1

BEECH Christopher Stephen
Blackpool, 16 September, 1974 (M)

League Club	Source	Date Signed	Seasons Played	Apps	Subs	Gls
Blackpool	YT	07.93	92-95	53	29	4
Hartlepool U.	Tr	07.96	96-97	76	2	14

BEECH Cyril
Tamworth, 12 March, 1925 (OL)

League Club	Source	Date Signed	Seasons Played	Apps	Subs	Gls
Swansea C.	Merthyr Tydfil	08.49	49-53	133	-	29
Newport Co.	Worcester C.	07.55	55-56	39	-	8

BEECH Gilbert
Tamworth, 9 January, 1922 (FB)

League Club	Source	Date Signed	Seasons Played	Apps	Subs	Gls
Swansea C.	Merthyr Tydfil	11.49	49-57	157	-	2

BEECH Harry William
Kearsley, 7 January, 1946 (WH)

League Club	Source	Date Signed	Seasons Played	Apps	Subs	Gls
Bolton W.	Jnrs	06.64	65-66	14	1	0
Southport	Tr	07.67	67	2	2	0

BEECH Kenneth
Stoke, 18 March, 1958 (M)

League Club	Source	Date Signed	Seasons Played	Apps	Subs	Gls
Port Vale	App	01.76	74-80	169	6	18
Walsall	Tr	08.81	81-82	78	1	5
Peterborough U.	Tr	08.83	83-84	58	2	5

BEEKS Stephen John
Staines, 10 April, 1971 (M)

League Club	Source	Date Signed	Seasons Played	Apps	Subs	Gls
Aldershot	YT	07.89	89-90	0	3	0

BEEL William John Leonard
Leominster, 23 August, 1945 (G)

League Club	Source	Date Signed	Seasons Played	Apps	Subs	Gls
Shrewsbury T.	App	07.63	62-63	3	-	0
Birmingham C.	Tr	01.65	64	1	-	0

BEENEY Mark Raymond
Tunbridge Wells, 30 December, 1967 E Semi Pro (G)

League Club	Source	Date Signed	Seasons Played	Apps	Subs	Gls
Gillingham	Jnrs	08.86	86	2	0	0
Maidstone U.	Tr	02.87	89-90	50	0	0
Aldershot	L	03.90	89	7	0	0
Brighton & H.A.	Tr	03.91	90-92	68	1	0
Leeds U.	Tr	04.93	92-97	35	0	0

BEER Alan Desmond
Swansea, 11 March, 1950 W Amat (F)

League Club	Source	Date Signed	Seasons Played	Apps	Subs	Gls
Swansea C.	West End	02.71	70-71	9	5	3
Exeter C.	Weymouth	11.74	74-77	114	0	52

BEER Colin Edwin
Exeter, 15 August, 1936 (OR)

League Club	Source	Date Signed	Seasons Played	Apps	Subs	Gls
Exeter C.	Exbourne	05.56	56-57	5	-	2

League Club	Source	Date Signed	Seasons Played	Apps	Subs	Gls
BEESLEY Colin						
Stockton, 6 October, 1951						(W)
Sunderland	App	01.69	68	0	3	0
BEESLEY Michael Albert						
Epping Forest, 10 June, 1942						(IF)
West Ham U.	Jnrs	10.59	60	2	-	1
Southend U.	Tr	08.62	62-64	79	-	34
Peterborough U.	Tr	07.65	65-66	23	2	3
Southend U.	Tr	08.67	67-70	119	14	11
BEESLEY Paul						
Liverpool, 21 July, 1965						(CD)
Wigan Ath.	Marine	09.84	84-89	153	2	3
Leyton Orient	Tr	10.89	89	32	0	1
Sheffield U.	Tr	07.90	90-94	162	6	7
Leeds U.	Tr	08.95	95-96	19	3	0
Manchester C.	Tr	02.97	96-97	10	3	0
Port Vale	L	12.97	97	5	0	0
West Bromwich A.	L	03.98	97	8	0	0
BEESTON Carl Frederick						
Stoke, 30 June, 1967 Eu21-1						(M)
Stoke C.	App	06.85	84-96	224	12	13
Hereford U.	L	01.97	96-97	9	0	2
Southend U. (N/C)	Tr	08.97	97	5	1	0
BEESTON Thomas						
Gateshead, 26 April, 1933						(G)
Gateshead (Am)		09.56	56	1	-	0
BEETON Alan Matthew						
Watford, 4 October, 1978						(LWB)
Wycombe W.	YT	07.97	97	15	5	0
BEEVER Anthony						
Huddersfield, 18 September, 1974						(F)
Rochdale	YT	07.93	92	0	1	0
BEGG James Alexander						
Dumfries, 14 February, 1930 Died 1987						(G)
Liverpool	Auchinleck T.	04.52				
Bradford P.A.	Tr	08.53	53-54	10	-	0
BEGLIN James Martin						
Waterford, 29 July, 1963 IRu21-4/IR 'B'/IR-15						(LB)
Liverpool	Shamrock Rov.	05.83	84-86	64	0	2
Leeds U.	Tr	07.89	89	18	1	0
Plymouth Arg.	L	11.89	89	5	0	0
Blackburn Rov.	L	10.90	90	6	0	0
BEIGHTON Graham						
Sheffield, 1 July, 1939						(G)
Sheffield Wed.	Firthbrown Tools	03.59				
Stockport Co.	Tr	06.61	61-65	137	0	0
Wrexham	Tr	01.66	65	23	0	0
BEINLICH Stefan						
Germany, 13 January, 1972						(F)
Aston Villa	Bergman Bosnig (Ger)	10.91	91-93	7	9	1
BEIRNE Michael Andrew						
Manchester, 21 September, 1973						(F)
Doncaster Rov. (N/C)	Droylsden	02.97	96	1	0	0
BEKKER Jan Franciscus						
Cardiff, 24 December, 1951						(F)
Swansea C.	Bridgend T.	02.75	74-75	16	6	4
BELCHER James Alfred						
Stepney, 31 October, 1932						(WH)
Leyton Orient	Jnrs	03.50				
West Ham U.	Snowdown Colly	08.52				
Crystal Palace	Tr	06.54	54-57	128	-	22
Ipswich T.	Tr	05.58	58-59	27	-	0
Brentford	Tr	07.61	61	30	-	1
BELFIELD Michael Robert						
Wandsworth, 10 June, 1961						(F)
Wimbledon		03.80	79-82	16	8	4
BELFITT Roderick Michael						
Bournemouth, 30 October, 1945						(CF)
Leeds U.	Retford T.	07.63	64-71	57	18	17
Ipswich T.	Tr	11.71	71-72	40	0	13
Everton	Tr	11.72	72	14	2	2
Sunderland	Tr	10.73	73-74	36	3	4
Fulham	L	11.74	74	6	0	1
Huddersfield T.	Tr	02.75	74-75	34	0	8

League Club	Source	Date Signed	Seasons Played	Apps	Subs	Gls
BELFON Frank						
Wellingborough, 18 February, 1965						(W)
Northampton T.	Jnrs	04.82	81-84	64	15	15
BELFORD Dale						
Burton-on-Trent, 11 July, 1967						(G)
Aston Villa	App	07.85				
Notts Co.	Sutton Coldfield T.	03.87	87	1	0	0
BELL Alexander Stewart						
Auchinleck, 13 March, 1931						(G)
Exeter C.	Partick Thistle	08.54	54-57	40	-	0
Grimsby T.	Tr	07.58	58	8	-	0
BELL Andrew Donald						
Taunton, 6 May, 1956						(CF)
Exeter C.	Taunton T.	07.79	79	2	1	0
BELL Anthony						
North Shields, 27 February, 1955						(G)
Newcastle U.	App	03.73	74	1	0	0
BELL Arthur						
Sedgefield, 5 March, 1931						(RH)
Barrow	Hylton Colly	08.50	50	1	-	0
BELL Barry Russell						
Woolwich, 9 April, 1941						(CF)
Millwall	Jnrs	10.58	58	1	-	0
BELL Charles Thomas						
Sheffield, 21 March, 1945						(CH)
Sheffield U.	Jnrs	01.64	66	3	0	1
Chesterfield	Tr	06.68	68-72	149	3	12
BELL Colin						
Derby, 24 March, 1926						(WH)
Derby Co.	Holbrook	09.46	50-54	77	-	2
BELL Colin						
Hesleden (Dm), 26 February, 1946 Eu23-2/EF Lge/E-48						(M)
Bury	Horden Colly	07.63	63-65	82	0	25
Manchester C.	Tr	03.66	65-78	393	1	117
BELL David						
Edinburgh, 24 December, 1909 Died 1986						(FB)
Newcastle U.	Wallyford Bluebell	05.30	31-33	21	-	1
Derby Co.	Tr	06.34	34-38	52	-	0
Ipswich T.	Tr	10.38	38-49	171	-	3
BELL David John						
Carlisle, 13 September, 1939						(OR)
Carlisle U.	Jnrs	03.57	58	1	-	1
BELL Derek Martin						
Boston, 30 October, 1956						(F)
Derby Co.	App	10.74				
Halifax T.	Tr	05.75	75-78	104	8	21
Sheffield Wed.	L	03.76	75	5	0	1
Barnsley	Tr	10.78	78-79	45	1	20
Lincoln C.	Tr	11.79	79-82	69	14	33
Chesterfield	Tr	08.83	83	15	2	3
Scunthorpe U.	Tr	01.84	83-84	22	0	7
BELL Derek Stewart						
Newcastle, 19 December, 1963						(M)
Newcastle U.	App	12.81	81-82	3	1	0
BELL Douglas						
Paisley, 5 September, 1959 Su21-2						(M)
Shrewsbury T.	Hibernian	12.87	87-89	47	3	6
Hull C.	L	03.89	88	4	0	0
Birmingham C.	Tr	10.89	89-90	15	1	0
BELL Eric						
Manchester, 27 November, 1929 E 'B'/EF Lge						(WH)
Bolton W.	Manchester U. (Am)	11.49	50-57	102	-	1
BELL John Eric						
Bedlington, 13 February, 1922 EF Lge						(WH)
Blackburn Rov.	Blyth Spartans	05.45	46-56	323	-	9
BELL Ernest						
Hull, 22 July, 1918 Died 1968						(IF)
Hull C.	Blundell S.O.B.	03.36	36-37	22	-	4
Mansfield T.	Tr	05.38	38	28	-	1
Aldershot	Tr	07.39				
Hull C.	Tr	08.46	46	5	-	1

BELL Gary
Stourbridge, 4 April, 1947 (LB)

League Club	Source	Date Signed	Seasons Played	Apps	Subs	Gls
Cardiff C.	Lower Gornal Ath.	02.66	66-73	222	2	10
Hereford U.	L	03.74	73	8	0	0
Newport Co.	Tr	08.74	74-77	126	0	5

BELL George William
Newcastle, 26 March, 1937 (F)

League Club	Source	Date Signed	Seasons Played	Apps	Subs	Gls
Doncaster Rov.	St Marys B.C.	05.55	55	1	-	0
Cardiff C.	Frickley Colly	03.59				

BELL Graham Thomas
Middleton, 30 March, 1955 E Yth (M)

League Club	Source	Date Signed	Seasons Played	Apps	Subs	Gls
Oldham Ath.	Chadderton	12.73	74-78	166	4	9
Preston N.E.	Tr	03.79	78-82	140	3	9
Huddersfield T.	L	11.81	81	2	0	0
Carlisle U.	Tr	08.83	83	11	3	0
Bolton W.	Tr	02.84	83-85	86	6	3
Tranmere Rov.	Tr	08.86	86	41	1	4

BELL Harold
Liverpool, 22 November, 1924 Died 1994 (CH)

League Club	Source	Date Signed	Seasons Played	Apps	Subs	Gls
Tranmere Rov.	Jnrs	11.41	46-59	595	-	11

BELL Henry (Harry) Davey
Sunderland, 14 October, 1924 (WH)

League Club	Source	Date Signed	Seasons Played	Apps	Subs	Gls
Middlesbrough	Hylton Colly	09.45	46-54	290	-	9
Darlington	Tr	09.55	55-58	125	-	19

BELL Ian Charles
Middlesbrough, 14 November, 1958 (M)

League Club	Source	Date Signed	Seasons Played	Apps	Subs	Gls
Middlesbrough	App	12.76	77-80	10	0	1
Mansfield T.	Tr	07.81	81-82	82	2	12

BELL John Albert
Edinburgh, 25 April, 1936 (WH)

League Club	Source	Date Signed	Seasons Played	Apps	Subs	Gls
Swindon T.	Stirling A.	07.60	60-61	29	-	2

BELL John Henry
Morpeth, 29 August, 1919 Died 1994 (LB)

League Club	Source	Date Signed	Seasons Played	Apps	Subs	Gls
Gateshead		01.45	46-49	50	-	0

BELL John (Jackie) Russell
Evenwood, 17 October, 1939 Died 1991 (WH)

League Club	Source	Date Signed	Seasons Played	Apps	Subs	Gls
Newcastle U.	Jnrs	10.56	57-61	111	-	8
Norwich C.	Tr	07.62	62-63	48	-	3
Colchester U.	Tr	06.65	65	7	0	0

BELL Joseph
Sunderland, 28 July, 1924 (FB)

League Club	Source	Date Signed	Seasons Played	Apps	Subs	Gls
Sunderland		01.44				
Chesterfield	Stockton	05.46	47-48	37	-	0
Coventry C.	Tr	06.49	49-51	10	-	0

BELL Michael
Newcastle, 15 November, 1971 (LB/W)

League Club	Source	Date Signed	Seasons Played	Apps	Subs	Gls
Northampton T.	YT	07.90	89-94	133	20	10
Wycombe W.	Tr	10.94	94-96	117	1	5
Bristol C.	Tr	07.97	97	44	0	10

BELL Norman
Hylton Castle, 16 November, 1955 (CF)

League Club	Source	Date Signed	Seasons Played	Apps	Subs	Gls
Wolverhampton W.	App	11.73	75-81	58	22	17
Blackburn Rov.	Tr	11.81	81-83	57	4	10

BELL Peter
Grangemouth, 10 April, 1935 (HB)

League Club	Source	Date Signed	Seasons Played	Apps	Subs	Gls
Plymouth Arg.	Gairdoch Jnrs	07.54	55	1	-	0

BELL Raymond Lloyd
Seaham, 6 December, 1930 (G)

League Club	Source	Date Signed	Seasons Played	Apps	Subs	Gls
Lincoln C.	Seaham Colly	01.50	50	1	-	0

BELL Robert
Glasgow, 20 March, 1935 S Sch (IF)

League Club	Source	Date Signed	Seasons Played	Apps	Subs	Gls
Plymouth Arg.	Partick Thistle	11.55	55	2	-	1
Carlisle U.	Partick Thistle	06.59	59	1	-	0

BELL Robert Charles
Cambridge, 26 October, 1950 (CD)

League Club	Source	Date Signed	Seasons Played	Apps	Subs	Gls
Ipswich T.	Tottenham H. (App)	10.68	68-71	32	0	1
Blackburn Rov.	Tr	09.71	71	2	0	0
Crystal Palace	Tr	09.71	71-73	31	0	0
Norwich C.	L	02.72	71	3	0	0
York C.	Hellenic (SA)	02.77	76	5	0	0

BELL Robert McDicker
Ayr, 16 September, 1934 (FB)

League Club	Source	Date Signed	Seasons Played	Apps	Subs	Gls
Watford	Ayr U.	05.57	57-64	268	-	2

BELL Stanley
West Ham, 28 October, 1923 (OL)

League Club	Source	Date Signed	Seasons Played	Apps	Subs	Gls
Southend U.		07.48	48	3	-	0

BELL Stephen
Middlesbrough, 13 March, 1965 E Yth (LW)

League Club	Source	Date Signed	Seasons Played	Apps	Subs	Gls
Middlesbrough	App	05.82	81-84	79	6	12
Darlington	Whitby T.	03.87	86-87	28	12	3

BELL Sydney
Stepney, 8 January, 1920 (LB)

League Club	Source	Date Signed	Seasons Played	Apps	Subs	Gls
Southend U.	Monarchs	11.45	46-47	16	-	0

BELL Terence John
Nottingham, 1 August, 1944 (F)

League Club	Source	Date Signed	Seasons Played	Apps	Subs	Gls
Nottingham F.	Burton A.	08.64				
Manchester C.	Tr	10.64				
Portsmouth	Tr	11.64				
Hartlepool U.	Nuneaton Borough	07.66	66-69	111	6	34
Reading	Tr	03.73	69-72	82	5	20
Aldershot	Tr	07.73	73-77	112	12	49

BELL Thomas
Stanley, 14 June, 1924 (CH)

League Club	Source	Date Signed	Seasons Played	Apps	Subs	Gls
Millwall (Am)	Hammersmith U.	03.49	48	1	-	0

BELL Thomas Anthony
Crompton, 30 December, 1923 Died 1988 (FB)

League Club	Source	Date Signed	Seasons Played	Apps	Subs	Gls
Oldham Ath.	Mossley	12.46	46-51	170	-	0
Stockport Co.	Tr	08.52	52	31	-	0
Halifax T.	Tr	07.53	53-55	117	-	1

BELL William
Manchester, 16 June, 1953 (M)

League Club	Source	Date Signed	Seasons Played	Apps	Subs	Gls
Rochdale (N/C)	Hyde U.	05.74	74	5	1	0

BELL William John
Johnstone, 3 September, 1937 S Amat/S-2 (LB)

League Club	Source	Date Signed	Seasons Played	Apps	Subs	Gls
Leeds U.	Queens Park	07.60	60-67	204	0	15
Leicester C.	Tr	09.67	67-68	49	0	0
Brighton & H.A.	Tr	07.69	69	44	0	1

BELLAMY Arthur
Consett, 5 April, 1942 (M)

League Club	Source	Date Signed	Seasons Played	Apps	Subs	Gls
Burnley	Jnrs	06.59	62-71	204	13	29
Chesterfield	Tr	07.72	72-75	133	0	12

BELLAMY Craig Douglas
Cardiff, 13 July, 1979 W Sch/W Yth/Wu21-7/W-3 (M)

League Club	Source	Date Signed	Seasons Played	Apps	Subs	Gls
Norwich C.	YT	01.97	96-97	30	9	13

BELLAMY Gary
Worksop, 4 July, 1962 (CD)

League Club	Source	Date Signed	Seasons Played	Apps	Subs	Gls
Chesterfield	App	06.80	80-86	181	3	6
Wolverhampton W.	Tr	07.87	87-91	133	3	9
Cardiff C.	L	03.92	91	9	0	0
Leyton Orient	Tr	09.92	92-95	129	3	6

BELLAS William Joseph
Liverpool, 21 May, 1925 Died 1994 (CH)

League Club	Source	Date Signed	Seasons Played	Apps	Subs	Gls
Notts Co.	Marine	04.45				
Nottingham F.	Tr	05.46				
Southport	Tr	10.48	48-50	88	-	0
Grimsby T.	Tr	07.51	51	5	-	0

BELLETT Walter Ronald
Stratford, 14 November, 1933 E Yth (FB)

League Club	Source	Date Signed	Seasons Played	Apps	Subs	Gls
Chelsea	Barking	09.54	55-58	35	-	1
Plymouth Arg.	Tr	12.58	58-59	41	-	1
Leyton Orient	Chelmsford C.	01.61				
Chester C.	Tr	07.61	61	12	-	1
Wrexham	Tr	07.62	62	2	-	0
Tranmere Rov.	Tr	07.63				

BELLIS Alfred
Liverpool, 8 October, 1920 (OL)

League Club	Source	Date Signed	Seasons Played	Apps	Subs	Gls
Port Vale	Burnells Iron Wks	03.38	37-47	82	-	18
Bury	Tr	01.48	47-50	95	-	18
Swansea C.	Tr	08.51	51-52	43	-	12
Chesterfield	Tr	08.53	53	13	-	3

BELLIS Thomas **Gilbert**
Mold, 21 April, 1919 (D)

League Club	Source	Date Signed	Seasons Played	Apps	Subs	Gls
Wrexham	Buckley	05.38	38-48	95	-	1

BELLOTTI Derek Christopher
East Ham, 25 December, 1946 (G)

League Club	Source	Date Signed	Seasons Played	Apps	Subs	Gls
Gillingham	Bedford T.	07.66	66-69	35	0	0
Southend U.	L	10.70	70	3	0	0

League Club	Source	Date Signed	Seasons Played	Apps	Subs	Gls
Charlton Ath.	Tr	10.70	70-71	14	0	0
Southend U.	Tr	12.71	71-73	74	0	0
Swansea C.	Tr	05.74	74	19	0	0

BELLOTTI Ross Christopher
Tunbridge Wells, 15 May, 1978 (G)

League Club	Source	Date Signed	Seasons Played	Apps	Subs	Gls
Exeter C.	YT	07.96	94	1	1	0

BELSVIK Petter
Norway, 2 October, 1967 (F)

League Club	Source	Date Signed	Seasons Played	Apps	Subs	Gls
Southend U. (L)	I.K. Start (Nor)	11.95	95	3	0	1

BEMROSE Frank
Caistor, 20 October, 1935 (OL)

League Club	Source	Date Signed	Seasons Played	Apps	Subs	Gls
Grimsby T. (Am)	Caistor	08.58	58-60	2	-	0

BENALI Francis Vincent
Southampton, 30 December, 1968 E Sch (LB)

League Club	Source	Date Signed	Seasons Played	Apps	Subs	Gls
Southampton	App	12.86	88-96	225	28	1

BENBOW Ian Robert
Hereford, 9 January, 1969 (W)

League Club	Source	Date Signed	Seasons Played	Apps	Subs	Gls
Hereford U.	YT	07.87	87-90	60	23	4

BENCE Paul Ian
Littlehampton, 21 December, 1948 (D/M)

League Club	Source	Date Signed	Seasons Played	Apps	Subs	Gls
Brighton & H.A.	App	05.67	67	0	1	0
Reading	Tr	06.68	68-69	12	2	2
Brentford	Tr	07.70	70-76	238	6	6
Torquay U.	L	11.76	76	5	0	0

BENJAFIELD Brian James
Barton-on-Sea, 2 August, 1960 (M)

League Club	Source	Date Signed	Seasons Played	Apps	Subs	Gls
Bournemouth	Jnrs	01.79	78	2	0	0

BENJAMIN Christopher
Sheffield, 5 December, 1972 (F)

League Club	Source	Date Signed	Seasons Played	Apps	Subs	Gls
Chesterfield	YT	07.91	90-91	5	10	1

BENJAMIN Ian Tracey
Nottingham, 11 December, 1961 E Yth (F)

League Club	Source	Date Signed	Seasons Played	Apps	Subs	Gls
Sheffield U.	App	05.79	78-79	4	1	3
West Bromwich A.	Tr	08.79	80	1	1	0
Notts Co.	Tr	02.82				
Peterborough U.	Tr	08.82	82-83	77	3	14
Northampton T.	Tr	08.84	84-87	147	3	58
Cambridge U.	Tr	10.87	87	20	5	2
Chester C.	Tr	07.88	88	18	4	2
Exeter C.	Tr	02.89	88-89	30	2	4
Southend U.	Tr	03.90	89-92	122	0	33
Luton T.	Tr	11.92	92-93	7	6	2
Brentford	Tr	09.93	93-94	13	2	2
Wigan Ath.	Tr	09.94	94-95	13	7	6

BENJAMIN Trevor Junior
Kettering, 8 February, 1979 (F)

League Club	Source	Date Signed	Seasons Played	Apps	Subs	Gls
Cambridge U.	YT	02.97	95-97	17	20	5

BENJAMIN Tristan
St Kitts (WI), 1 April, 1957 (D)

League Club	Source	Date Signed	Seasons Played	Apps	Subs	Gls
Notts Co.	App	03.75	74-86	296	15	4
Chesterfield	Tr	07.87	87	32	2	0

BENN Alfred
Leeds, 26 January, 1926 (LH)

League Club	Source	Date Signed	Seasons Played	Apps	Subs	Gls
Leeds U.	East Leeds	01.47				
Southport	Tr	07.48	48	3	-	0

BENN Wayne
Pontefract, 7 August, 1976 (D/M)

League Club	Source	Date Signed	Seasons Played	Apps	Subs	Gls
Bradford C.	YT	06.94	94	8	2	0

BENNELLICK James Arthur
Torquay, 9 September, 1974 (M)

League Club	Source	Date Signed	Seasons Played	Apps	Subs	Gls
Torquay U.	YT	•	91	0	1	0

BENNETT Alan
Stoke, 5 November, 1931 E Yth (OL)

League Club	Source	Date Signed	Seasons Played	Apps	Subs	Gls
Port Vale	Jnrs	05.49	48-56	123	-	8
Crewe Alex.	Tr	09.57	57	10	-	0

BENNETT Albert
Chester-le-Street, 16 July, 1944 E Yth/Eu23-1 (CF)

League Club	Source	Date Signed	Seasons Played	Apps	Subs	Gls
Rotherham U.	Chester Moor Jnrs	10.61	61-64	108	-	64
Newcastle U.	Tr	07.65	65-68	85	0	22
Norwich C.	Tr	02.69	68-70	54	1	15

BENNETT Craig
Doncaster, 29 August, 1973 (F)

League Club	Source	Date Signed	Seasons Played	Apps	Subs	Gls
Doncaster Rov.	YT	07.91	90-92	5	3	0

BENNETT David Anthony
Manchester, 11 July, 1959 EF Lge (W)

League Club	Source	Date Signed	Seasons Played	Apps	Subs	Gls
Manchester C.	Jnrs	08.78	78-80	43	9	9
Cardiff C.	Tr	09.81	81-82	75	2	18
Coventry C.	Tr	07.83	83-88	157	15	25
Sheffield Wed.	Tr	03.89	88-89	20	8	0
Swindon T.	Tr	09.90	90	1	0	0
Shrewsbury T.	L	11.91	91	2	0	2

BENNETT David Michael
Southampton, 5 March, 1939 E Sch (W)

League Club	Source	Date Signed	Seasons Played	Apps	Subs	Gls
Arsenal	Jnrs	05.56				
Portsmouth	Tr	06.58				
Bournemouth	Tr	12.60	60-61	12	-	2

BENNETT David Paul
Oldham, 26 April, 1960 (W)

League Club	Source	Date Signed	Seasons Played	Apps	Subs	Gls
Norwich C.	Manchester C. (App)	08.78	78-83	64	7	9

BENNETT Dean
Wolverhampton, 13 December, 1977 (M)

League Club	Source	Date Signed	Seasons Played	Apps	Subs	Gls
West Bromwich A.	Aston Villa (Jnrs)	12.96	96	0	1	0

BENNETT Desmond
Doncaster, 30 October, 1963 (M)

League Club	Source	Date Signed	Seasons Played	Apps	Subs	Gls
Doncaster Rov.	App	06.80	80-81	0	2	0

BENNETT Donald
Wakefield, 18 December, 1933 E Yth (FB)

League Club	Source	Date Signed	Seasons Played	Apps	Subs	Gls
Arsenal	Jnrs	08.51				
Coventry C.	Tr	09.59	59-61	73	-	0

BENNETT Edgar William
Stoke, 29 March, 1929 (OR)

League Club	Source	Date Signed	Seasons Played	Apps	Subs	Gls
Luton T.	Vauxhall Motors	09.52	53	1	-	0

BENNETT Edward Ernest
Kilburn, 22 August, 1925 E Amat (G)

League Club	Source	Date Signed	Seasons Played	Apps	Subs	Gls
Queens Park R. (Am)	Southall	02.49	48	2	-	0
Watford	Southall	12.53	53-55	81	-	0

BENNETT Frank
Birmingham, 3 January, 1969 (W)

League Club	Source	Date Signed	Seasons Played	Apps	Subs	Gls
Southampton	Halesowen T.	02.93	93-95	5	14	1
Shrewsbury T.	L	10.96	96	2	2	3
Bristol Rov.	Tr	11.96	96-97	14	16	3

BENNETT Gary
Enfield, 13 November, 1970 (W)

League Club	Source	Date Signed	Seasons Played	Apps	Subs	Gls
Colchester U.	YT	11.88	88-93	65	22	13

BENNETT Gary Ernest
Manchester, 4 December, 1961 (CD)

League Club	Source	Date Signed	Seasons Played	Apps	Subs	Gls
Manchester C.	Ashton U.	09.79				
Cardiff C.	Tr	09.81	81-83	85	2	11
Sunderland	Tr	07.84	84-94	362	7	23
Carlisle U.	Tr	11.95	95	26	0	5
Scarborough	Tr	08.96	96-97	86	2	18

BENNETT Gary Michael
Liverpool, 20 September, 1963 (F)

League Club	Source	Date Signed	Seasons Played	Apps	Subs	Gls
Wigan Ath. (N/C)	Kirkby T.	10.84	84	10	10	3
Chester C.	Tr	08.85	85-88	109	17	36
Southend U.	Tr	11.88	88-89	36	6	6
Chester C.	Tr	03.90	89-91	71	9	15
Wrexham	Tr	08.92	92-94	120	1	77
Tranmere Rov.	Tr	07.95	95	26	3	9
Preston N.E.	Tr	03.96	95-96	15	9	4
Wrexham	Tr	02.97	96	15	0	5
Chester C.	Tr	07.97	97	37	4	11

BENNETT George Forest
South Shields, 16 March, 1938 (FB)

League Club	Source	Date Signed	Seasons Played	Apps	Subs	Gls
Burnley	Jnrs	04.55				
Barnsley	Tr	01.60	59-60	24	-	0

BENNETT Henry (Harry) Sylvester
Liverpool, 16 May, 1949 (WH)

League Club	Source	Date Signed	Seasons Played	Apps	Subs	Gls
Everton	Jnrs	03.67	67	2	1	0
Aldershot	Tr	01.71	70-72	77	12	7
Crewe Alex.	Tr	07.73	73	28	2	1

BENNETT Ian Michael
Worksop, 10 October, 1971 (G)

League Club	Source	Date Signed	Seasons Played	Apps	Subs	Gls
Newcastle U. (N/C)	Queens Park R. (YT)	03.89				
Peterborough U.	Tr	03.91	91-93	72	0	0
Birmingham C.	Tr	12.93	93-97	177	0	0

League Club	Source	Date Signed	Seasons Played	Career Record Apps	Subs	Gls

BENNETT John
Rotherham, 15 May, 1949 (OL)

League Club	Source	Date Signed	Seasons Played	Apps	Subs	Gls
Rotherham U.	App	●	65	1	0	0

BENNETT John Graham
Liverpool, 21 March, 1946 (LB)

League Club	Source	Date Signed	Seasons Played	Apps	Subs	Gls
Liverpool	App	04.63				
Chester C.	Tr	06.66	66-68	72	4	0

BENNETT Kenneth Edgar
Wood Green, 2 October, 1921 Died 1994 (IF)

League Club	Source	Date Signed	Seasons Played	Apps	Subs	Gls
Tottenham H.	Jnrs	10.40				
Southend U.	Tr	06.46	46-47	50	-	10
Bournemouth	Tr	06.48	48	19	-	1
Brighton & H.A.	Guildford C.	06.50	50-52	101	-	37
Crystal Palace	Tr	07.53	53	17	-	2

BENNETT Lawson Henry
Blackburn, 28 August, 1938 (OR)

League Club	Source	Date Signed	Seasons Played	Apps	Subs	Gls
Accrington St.	Darwen	05.58	58-60	29	-	2

BENNETT Leslie Donald
Wood Green, 10 January, 1918 (IF)

League Club	Source	Date Signed	Seasons Played	Apps	Subs	Gls
Tottenham H.	Jnrs	05.39	46-54	272	-	104
West Ham U.	Tr	12.54	54-55	26	-	3

BENNETT Martyn
Birmingham, 4 August, 1961 E Sch (CD)

League Club	Source	Date Signed	Seasons Played	Apps	Subs	Gls
West Bromwich A.	App	08.78	78-89	181	1	9

BENNETT Michael
Bolton, 24 December, 1962 E Yth (LB)

League Club	Source	Date Signed	Seasons Played	Apps	Subs	Gls
Bolton W.	App	01.80	79-82	62	3	1
Wolverhampton W.	Tr	06.83	83	6	0	0
Cambridge U.	Tr	03.84	83-85	76	0	0
Preston N.E.	Bradford C. (N/C)	09.86	86-89	85	1	1
Carlisle U.	Tr	07.90	90-91	21	3	0

BENNETT Michael Richard
Camberwell, 27 July, 1969 E Yth (W)

League Club	Source	Date Signed	Seasons Played	Apps	Subs	Gls
Charlton Ath.	App	04.87	86-89	24	11	2
Wimbledon	Tr	01.90	89-91	12	6	2
Brentford	Tr	07.92	92-93	40	6	4
Charlton Ath.	Tr	03.94	93-94	19	5	1
Millwall	Tr	05.95	95	1	1	0
Cardiff C. (N/C)	Tr	08.96	96	5	9	1
Leyton Orient (N/C)	Cambridge C.	12.97	97	1	1	0

BENNETT Paul
Liverpool, 30 January, 1961 (M)

League Club	Source	Date Signed	Seasons Played	Apps	Subs	Gls
Port Vale	Everton (App)	09.78	80-81	28	2	1

BENNETT Paul Reginald
Southampton, 4 February, 1952 (CD)

League Club	Source	Date Signed	Seasons Played	Apps	Subs	Gls
Southampton	App	11.69	71-75	116	0	1
Reading	Tr	07.76	76-78	105	0	3
Aldershot	Tr	08.79	79-81	112	1	2

BENNETT Peter Christopher
Plymouth, 29 November, 1939 (CF)

League Club	Source	Date Signed	Seasons Played	Apps	Subs	Gls
Exeter C.	Plymstock	08.59	59-60	6	-	5

BENNETT Peter Leigh
Hillingdon, 24 June, 1946 E Sch (M)

League Club	Source	Date Signed	Seasons Played	Apps	Subs	Gls
West Ham U.	App	07.63	63-70	38	4	3
Leyton Orient	Tr	10.70	70-78	195	4	13

BENNETT Richard John
Northampton, 16 February, 1945 E Yth (WH)

League Club	Source	Date Signed	Seasons Played	Apps	Subs	Gls
Peterborough U.	Wellingborough	08.63	63-64	4	-	0

BENNETT Robert
Harrow, 29 December, 1951 (CF)

League Club	Source	Date Signed	Seasons Played	Apps	Subs	Gls
Southend U.	Staines T.	06.72	72	1	0	0
Scunthorpe U.	L	10.73	73	2	1	0

BENNETT Ronald
Hinckley, 8 May, 1927 (OL)

League Club	Source	Date Signed	Seasons Played	Apps	Subs	Gls
Wolverhampton W.		01.45				
Portsmouth	Tr	07.48	49-51	8	-	1
Crystal Palace	Tr	01.52	51-52	27	-	5
Brighton & H.A.	Tr	07.53	53	3	-	0

BENNETT Sean
Newport, 3 September, 1970 (LB)

League Club	Source	Date Signed	Seasons Played	Apps	Subs	Gls
Newport Co.	Leeds U. (YT)	●	87	4	1	0

BENNETT Stanley Thomas
Birmingham, 18 September, 1944 (CH)

League Club	Source	Date Signed	Seasons Played	Apps	Subs	Gls
Walsall	App	09.62	63-74	378	8	12

BENNETT Thomas McNeill
Falkirk, 12 December, 1969 (M)

League Club	Source	Date Signed	Seasons Played	Apps	Subs	Gls
Aston Villa	App	12.87				
Wolverhampton W.	Tr	07.88	88-94	103	12	2
Stockport Co.	Tr	06.95	95-97	94	0	5

BENNETT Troy
Barnsley, 25 December, 1975 E Yth (M)

League Club	Source	Date Signed	Seasons Played	Apps	Subs	Gls
Barnsley	YT	12.93	92	2	0	0
Scarborough	Tr	03.97	96-97	28	11	3

BENNETT Walter
Doncaster, 15 December, 1918 (CF)

League Club	Source	Date Signed	Seasons Played	Apps	Subs	Gls
Barnsley	Mexborough	04.38	46-47	38	-	23
Doncaster Rov.	Tr	01.48	47-49	39	-	14
Halifax T.	Tr	01.50	49	7	-	1

BENNING Michael David
Croxley Green, 3 February, 1938 (OR)

League Club	Source	Date Signed	Seasons Played	Apps	Subs	Gls
Watford	Jnrs	09.56	58-61	103	-	14

BENNING Paul Martin
Watford, 7 June, 1963 (D)

League Club	Source	Date Signed	Seasons Played	Apps	Subs	Gls
Peterborough U. (N/C)	Hayes	12.87	87	2	0	0

BENNION John Raymond
Manchester, 2 April, 1934 (WH)

League Club	Source	Date Signed	Seasons Played	Apps	Subs	Gls
Burnley		01.52				
Hull C.	Tr	06.57	57-59	35	-	1
Stockport Co.	Tr	07.60	60	26	-	1
Barrow	Tr	07.61	61-62	16	-	0

BENNION Stanley
Chester, 9 February, 1938 (IF)

League Club	Source	Date Signed	Seasons Played	Apps	Subs	Gls
Wrexham	Jnrs	10.59	59-62	54	-	18
Chester C.	Tr	06.63	63	19	-	3

BENNYWORTH Ian Robert
Hull, 15 January, 1962 (CD)

League Club	Source	Date Signed	Seasons Played	Apps	Subs	Gls
Hull C.	App	01.80	79	1	0	0
Scarborough	Nuneaton Borough	08.86	87-89	88	1	3
Hartlepool U.	Tr	12.89	89-91	81	1	3

BENSKIN Dennis Walter
Nottingham, 28 May, 1947 (OL)

League Club	Source	Date Signed	Seasons Played	Apps	Subs	Gls
Notts Co. (Am)	Jnrs	05.65	65	4	0	1

BENSON John Harvey
Arbroath, 23 December, 1942 (FB)

League Club	Source	Date Signed	Seasons Played	Apps	Subs	Gls
Manchester C.	Jnrs	07.61	61-63	44	-	0
Torquay U.	Tr	06.64	64-70	233	7	7
Bournemouth	Tr	10.70	70-73	85	8	0
Exeter C.	L	03.73	72	4	0	0
Norwich C.	Tr	12.73	73-74	29	1	1
Bournemouth	Tr	01.75	74-78	56	1	0

BENSON Joseph Robert
Misterton, 7 January, 1933 (WH)

League Club	Source	Date Signed	Seasons Played	Apps	Subs	Gls
Scunthorpe U.		09.55	55	2	-	0

BENSON Ronald
Acomb, 26 March, 1925 (OR)

League Club	Source	Date Signed	Seasons Played	Apps	Subs	Gls
York C.	Holgates O.B.	10.47	49	20	-	3

BENSTEAD Graham Mark
Aldershot, 20 August, 1963 E Yth (G)

League Club	Source	Date Signed	Seasons Played	Apps	Subs	Gls
Queens Park R.	App	07.81				
Norwich C.	Tr	03.85	84-87	16	0	0
Colchester U.	L	08.87	87	18	0	0
Sheffield U.	Tr	03.88	87-88	47	0	0
Brentford	Tr	07.90	90-93	112	0	0
Brentford (N/C)	Rushden & Diamonds	07.97	97	1	0	0

BENSTOCK Danny
Hackney, 10 July, 1970 (M)

League Club	Source	Date Signed	Seasons Played	Apps	Subs	Gls
Leyton Orient	Barking	12.92	92-93	17	4	0

BENT Geoffrey
Salford, 27 September, 1932 Died 1958 (FB)

League Club	Source	Date Signed	Seasons Played	Apps	Subs	Gls
Manchester U.	Jnrs	04.51	54-56	12	-	0

BENT Graham William
Ruabon, 6 October, 1945 W Sch (W)

League Club	Source	Date Signed	Seasons Played	Apps	Subs	Gls
Wrexham	Aston Villa (App)	12.63	63-64	10	-	2

BENT Junior Antony
Huddersfield, 1 March, 1970 (W)

League Club	Source	Date Signed	Seasons Played	Apps	Subs	Gls
Huddersfield T.	YT	12.87	87-89	25	11	6
Burnley	L	11.89	89	7	2	3

League Club	Source	Date Signed	Seasons Played	Apps	Subs	Gls
Bristol C.	Tr	03.90	89-97	142	41	20
Stoke C.	L	03.92	91	1	0	0
Shrewsbury T.	L	10.96	96	6	0	0
Blackpool	Tr	08.97	97	25	11	3

BENT Marcus Nathan
Hammersmith, 19 May, 1978 Eu21-2 (W)

League Club	Source	Date Signed	Seasons Played	Apps	Subs	Gls
Brentford	YT	07.95	95-97	56	14	8
Crystal Palace	Tr	01.98	97	10	6	5

BENTALL Charles **Edward**
Helmsley, 28 January, 1922 Died 1947 (CH)

League Club	Source	Date Signed	Seasons Played	Apps	Subs	Gls
York C.	English Martyrs	10.45	46	1	-	0

BENTHAM Alan
Liverpool, 12 September, 1940 E Sch (FB)

League Club	Source	Date Signed	Seasons Played	Apps	Subs	Gls
Everton	Jnrs	11.57				
Southport	Tr	06.60	60-61	25	-	1

BENTHAM John James
South Elmsall, 3 March, 1963 (W)

League Club	Source	Date Signed	Seasons Played	Apps	Subs	Gls
York C.	App	03.81	81	22	1	0

BENTHAM Stanley Joseph
Leigh, 17 March, 1915 (WH)

League Club	Source	Date Signed	Seasons Played	Apps	Subs	Gls
Everton	Wigan Ath.	01.34	35-48	110	-	17

BENTLEY Alfred
Eythorne, 28 October, 1931 Died 1996 (G)

League Club	Source	Date Signed	Seasons Played	Apps	Subs	Gls
Coventry C.	Snowdown Colly	10.55	55-56	29	-	0
Gillingham	Margate	08.58	58-61	13	-	0

BENTLEY Anthony
Stoke, 20 December, 1939 (FB)

League Club	Source	Date Signed	Seasons Played	Apps	Subs	Gls
Stoke C.	Jnrs	12.56	58-60	44	-	15
Southend U.	Tr	05.61	61-70	379	3	14

BENTLEY David Alwyn
Worksop, 30 May, 1950 (M)

League Club	Source	Date Signed	Seasons Played	Apps	Subs	Gls
Rotherham U.	App	07.67	66-73	242	7	14
Mansfield T.	L	09.72	72	1	3	1
Chesterfield	Tr	06.74	74-76	53	2	1
Doncaster Rov.	Tr	08.77	77-79	87	2	4

BENTLEY John (Jack)
Liverpool, 17 February, 1942 (OR)

League Club	Source	Date Signed	Seasons Played	Apps	Subs	Gls
Everton	Jnrs	11.59	60	1	-	0
Stockport Co.	Tr	05.61	61-62	49	-	5

BENTLEY Keith James
Hull, 27 July, 1936 (IF)

League Club	Source	Date Signed	Seasons Played	Apps	Subs	Gls
Hull C.		11.57	57	4	-	0

BENTLEY Thomas Frank **Roy**
Bristol, 17 May, 1924 EF Lge/E 'B'/E-12 (CF)

League Club	Source	Date Signed	Seasons Played	Apps	Subs	Gls
Bristol C.	Jnrs	09.41				
Newcastle U.	Tr	06.46	46-47	48	-	22
Chelsea	Tr	01.48	47-56	324	-	128
Fulham	Tr	09.56	56-60	143	-	23
Queens Park R.	Tr	06.61	61-62	45	-	0

BENTLEY William John
Stoke, 21 October, 1947 E Sch/E Yth (LB)

League Club	Source	Date Signed	Seasons Played	Apps	Subs	Gls
Stoke C.	App	10.64	65-68	44	4	1
Blackpool	Tr	01.69	68-76	289	7	10
Port Vale	Tr	07.77	77-79	92	3	0

BENTON James
Wexford (IR), 9 April, 1975 (M)

League Club	Source	Date Signed	Seasons Played	Apps	Subs	Gls
Northampton T.	YT	●	91-92	6	4	1

BERESFORD David
Middleton, 11 November, 1978 E Sch/E Yth (RW)

League Club	Source	Date Signed	Seasons Played	Apps	Subs	Gls
Oldham Ath.	YT	07.94	93-96	32	32	2
Swansea C.	L	08.95	95	4	2	0
Huddersfield T.	Tr	03.97	96-97	11	3	1

BERESFORD John
Sheffield, 4 September, 1966 E Sch/E Yth/E 'B' (LB)

League Club	Source	Date Signed	Seasons Played	Apps	Subs	Gls
Manchester C.	App	09.83				
Barnsley	Tr	07.86	86-88	79	9	5
Portsmouth	Tr	03.89	88-91	102	5	8
Newcastle U.	Tr	07.92	92-97	176	3	3
Southampton	Tr	02.98	97	10	0	0

BERESFORD John Turner
Sunderland, 2 January, 1943 (WH)

League Club	Source	Date Signed	Seasons Played	Apps	Subs	Gls
Hartlepool U. (Am)		08.66	66	3	0	0

BERESFORD John William
Sheffield, 25 January, 1946 (IF)

League Club	Source	Date Signed	Seasons Played	Apps	Subs	Gls
Chesterfield	App	01.63	62-64	52	-	10
Notts Co.	Tr	05.65	65-66	49	1	13

BERESFORD Marlon
Lincoln, 2 September, 1969 (G)

League Club	Source	Date Signed	Seasons Played	Apps	Subs	Gls
Sheffield Wed.	YT	09.87				
Bury	L	08.89	89	1	0	0
Northampton T.	L	09.90	90	13	0	0
Crewe Alex.	L	02.91	90	3	0	0
Northampton T.	L	08.91	91	15	0	0
Burnley	Tr	08.92	92-97	240	0	0
Middlesbrough	Tr	03.98	97	3	0	0

BERESFORD Philip
Hollingwood, 30 November, 1944 (CF)

League Club	Source	Date Signed	Seasons Played	Apps	Subs	Gls
Chesterfield		01.64	63	7	-	3

BERESFORD Reginald
Chesterfield, 29 June, 1925 (F)

League Club	Source	Date Signed	Seasons Played	Apps	Subs	Gls
Notts Co.	Hardwick Colly	09.45	46	9	-	1

BERESFORD Reginald Harold
Walsall, 3 June, 1921 (IF)

League Club	Source	Date Signed	Seasons Played	Apps	Subs	Gls
Aston Villa	Jnrs	10.38				
Birmingham C.	Tr	09.46				
Crystal Palace	Tr	08.48	48	7	-	1

BERG Henning
Norway, 1 September, 1969 Norwegian Int (D)

League Club	Source	Date Signed	Seasons Played	Apps	Subs	Gls
Blackburn Rov.	Lillestrom (Nor)	01.93	92-96	154	5	4
Manchester U.	Tr	08.97	97	23	4	1

BERGER Patrik
Czechoslovakia, 10 November, 1973 Czechoslovakian Int (F)

League Club	Source	Date Signed	Seasons Played	Apps	Subs	Gls
Liverpool	Borussia Dortmund (Ger)	08.96	96-97	19	26	9

BERGKAMP Dennis
Holland, 18 May, 1969 Dutch Int (M)

League Club	Source	Date Signed	Seasons Played	Apps	Subs	Gls
Arsenal	Inter Milan (It)	07.95	95-97	89	1	39

BERGSSON Gudni
Iceland, 21 July, 1965 Icelandic Int (D)

League Club	Source	Date Signed	Seasons Played	Apps	Subs	Gls
Tottenham H.	Valur (Ice)	12.88	88-92	51	20	2
Bolton W.	Tr	03.95	94-97	106	4	9

BERKLEY Austin James
Dartford, 28 January, 1973 (W)

League Club	Source	Date Signed	Seasons Played	Apps	Subs	Gls
Gillingham	YT	05.91	91	0	3	0
Swindon T.	Tr	05.92	94	0	1	0
Shrewsbury T.	Tr	07.95	95-97	84	14	4

BERKOVIC Eyal
Israel, 2 April, 1972 Israeli Int (M)

League Club	Source	Date Signed	Seasons Played	Apps	Subs	Gls
Southampton (L)	Maccabi Tel Aviv (Isr)	10.96	96	26	2	4
West Ham U.	Tr	07.97	97	34	1	7

BERMINGHAM Alan
Liverpool, 11 September, 1944 (FB)

League Club	Source	Date Signed	Seasons Played	Apps	Subs	Gls
Wrexham	Skelmersdale U.	06.67	67-70	114	2	2

BERNAL Andrew
Australia, 16 May, 1966 Australian Int (D)

League Club	Source	Date Signed	Seasons Played	Apps	Subs	Gls
Ipswich T.	Sporting Gijon (Sp)	09.87	87	4	5	0
Reading	Sydney Olympic (Aus)	07.94	94-97	142	0	2

BERNARD Michael Peter
Shrewsbury, 10 January, 1948 E Yth/Eu23-3 (M)

League Club	Source	Date Signed	Seasons Played	Apps	Subs	Gls
Stoke C.	App	01.65	65-71	124	12	6
Everton	Tr	04.72	72-76	139	8	8
Oldham Ath.	Tr	07.77	77-78	6	0	0

BERNARD Paul Robert James
Edinburgh, 30 December, 1972 Su21-15/S 'B'/S-2 (M)

League Club	Source	Date Signed	Seasons Played	Apps	Subs	Gls
Oldham Ath.	YT	07.91	90-95	105	7	18

BERNARDEAU Olivier
France, 19 August, 1962 (W)

League Club	Source	Date Signed	Seasons Played	Apps	Subs	Gls
Chesterfield	Leeds U. (N/C)	08.86	86	5	4	0

BERRY David Gilbert
Newton-le-Willows, 1 June, 1945 (CH)

League Club	Source	Date Signed	Seasons Played	Apps	Subs	Gls
Blackpool	Jnrs	09.63				
Chester C.	Tr	07.64	66	0	1	0

BERRY George Frederick
West Germany, 19 November, 1957 W-5 (CD)

League Club	Source	Date Signed	Seasons Played	Apps	Subs	Gls
Wolverhampton W.	App	11.75	76-81	124	0	4

League Club	Source	Date Signed	Seasons Played	Apps	Subs	Gls
Stoke C.	Tr	08.82	82-89	229	8	27
Doncaster Rov.	L	08.84	84	1	0	0
Peterborough U.	Tr	07.90	90	28	4	6
Preston N.E.	Tr	08.91	91	4	0	0

BERRY Greg John
Grays, 5 March, 1971 (LW)

League Club	Source	Date Signed	Seasons Played	Apps	Subs	Gls
Leyton Orient	East Thurrock U.	07.89	89-91	68	12	14
Wimbledon	Tr	08.92	92-93	6	1	1
Millwall	Tr	03.94	93-96	23	11	1
Brighton & H.A.	L	08.95	95	6	0	2
Leyton Orient	L	03.96	95	4	3	0

BERRY John Andrew
Manchester, 27 August, 1965 (D)

League Club	Source	Date Signed	Seasons Played	Apps	Subs	Gls
Torquay U. (N/C)		01.84	83	1	0	0

BERRY Reginald **John**
Aldershot, 1 June, 1926 Died 1994 EF Lge/E 'B'/ E-4 (OR)

League Club	Source	Date Signed	Seasons Played	Apps	Subs	Gls
Birmingham C.	Aldershot Y.M.C.A.	12.44	47-51	104	-	6
Manchester U.	Tr	08.51	51-57	247	-	37

BERRY Leslie Dennis
Plumstead, 4 May, 1956 (CD)

League Club	Source	Date Signed	Seasons Played	Apps	Subs	Gls
Charlton Ath.	App	03.74	75-85	352	6	11
Brighton & H.A.	Tr	08.86	86	22	1	0
Gillingham	Tr	03.87	86-87	26	5	0
Maidstone U.	Tr	07.88	89-90	62	1	2

BERRY Michael James
Newbury, 14 February, 1955 (FB)

League Club	Source	Date Signed	Seasons Played	Apps	Subs	Gls
Southampton	App	02.73	74	2	0	0

BERRY Neil
Edinburgh, 6 April, 1963 S Yth (D)

League Club	Source	Date Signed	Seasons Played	Apps	Subs	Gls
Bolton W.	App	03.81	81-84	25	7	0

BERRY Norman
Bury, 15 August, 1922 (CF)

League Club	Source	Date Signed	Seasons Played	Apps	Subs	Gls
Bury (Am)	Bury Amats	05.46	46-47	23	-	6

BERRY Paul
Grays, 15 November, 1935 (CH)

League Club	Source	Date Signed	Seasons Played	Apps	Subs	Gls
Chelsea	Jnrs	04.53	56-57	3	-	0

BERRY Paul Alan
Oxford, 8 April, 1958 (F)

League Club	Source	Date Signed	Seasons Played	Apps	Subs	Gls
Oxford U.	App	04.76	76-81	98	12	20

BERRY Peter
Aldershot, 20 September, 1933 (OR)

League Club	Source	Date Signed	Seasons Played	Apps	Subs	Gls
Crystal Palace	Jnrs	08.51	53-57	151	-	27
Ipswich T.	Tr	05.58	58-59	38	-	6

BERRY Stephen Andrew
Liverpool, 4 April, 1963 (M)

League Club	Source	Date Signed	Seasons Played	Apps	Subs	Gls
Portsmouth	App	01.81	81-82	26	2	2
Aldershot	L	03.84	83	5	2	0
Sunderland	Tr	07.84	84-85	32	3	2
Newport Co.	Tr	12.85	85-86	60	0	6
Swindon T.	Tr	03.87	86-87	4	0	0
Aldershot	Tr	10.87	87-88	48	0	6
Northampton T.	Tr	10.88	88-90	95	7	7

BERRY Thomas
Clayton-le-Moors, 31 March, 1922 (CH)

League Club	Source	Date Signed	Seasons Played	Apps	Subs	Gls
Hull C.	Great Harwood	05.47	47-57	275	-	1

BERRY Trevor John
Haslemere, 1 August, 1974 E Yth (M)

League Club	Source	Date Signed	Seasons Played	Apps	Subs	Gls
Aston Villa	Bournemouth (YT)	04.92				
Rotherham U.	Tr	09.95	95-97	92	16	14

BERRY William
Mansfield, 4 April, 1934 (IF)

League Club	Source	Date Signed	Seasons Played	Apps	Subs	Gls
Mansfield T.	Langwith Colly	03.56	56	10	-	1

BERRYMAN Stephen Christopher
Blackburn, 26 December, 1966 (G)

League Club	Source	Date Signed	Seasons Played	Apps	Subs	Gls
Hartlepool U. (N/C)	Leyland Motors	03.90	89	1	0	0
Exeter C.	Tr	08.90				
Cambridge U.	Tr	03.91	90	1	0	0
Barnet (N/C)	Tr	08.91				

BERTI Nicola
Parma, 14 April, 1967 Italian Int (CM)

League Club	Source	Date Signed	Seasons Played	Apps	Subs	Gls
Tottenham H.	Inter Milan (It)	01.98	97	17	0	3

BERTOLINI John (Jack)
Alloa, 21 March, 1934 (WH)

League Club	Source	Date Signed	Seasons Played	Apps	Subs	Gls
Workington	Stirling A.	01.53	52-57	181	-	35
Brighton & H.A.	Tr	07.58	58-65	258	0	12

BERTRAM James **Terence**
Whitehaven, 3 February, 1953 (D/M)

League Club	Source	Date Signed	Seasons Played	Apps	Subs	Gls
Workington (Am)	Carlisle U. (App)	02.72	71	0	1	0

BERTSCHIN Christian Frederick
Kensington, 7 September, 1924 Died 1995 (F)

League Club	Source	Date Signed	Seasons Played	Apps	Subs	Gls
Reading	Ilford	08.47	47-48	12	-	1

BERTSCHIN Keith Edwin
Enfield, 25 August, 1956 E Yth/Eu21-3 (F)

League Club	Source	Date Signed	Seasons Played	Apps	Subs	Gls
Ipswich T.	Barnet	10.73	75-76	19	13	8
Birmingham C.	Tr	07.77	77-80	113	5	29
Norwich C.	Tr	08.81	81-84	112	2	29
Stoke C.	Tr	11.84	84-86	82	6	29
Sunderland	Tr	03.87	86-87	25	11	7
Walsall	Tr	08.88	88-89	40	15	9
Chester C.	Tr	11.90	90	14	5	0

BESAGNI Remo Giovanni
Clerkenwell, 22 April, 1935 (CF)

League Club	Source	Date Signed	Seasons Played	Apps	Subs	Gls
Crystal Palace	Jnrs	10.52	52	2	-	0

BEST Andrew Keith
Dorchester, 5 January, 1959 (RW)

League Club	Source	Date Signed	Seasons Played	Apps	Subs	Gls
Torquay U.	Teignmouth	11.84	84	14	4	2

BEST Cyril **Clyde**
Bermuda, 24 February, 1951 (CF)

League Club	Source	Date Signed	Seasons Played	Apps	Subs	Gls
West Ham U.	Bermuda	03.69	69-75	178	8	47

BEST David
Wareham, 6 September, 1943 (G)

League Club	Source	Date Signed	Seasons Played	Apps	Subs	Gls
Bournemouth	Jnrs	10.60	60-66	230	0	0
Oldham Ath.	Tr	09.66	66-68	98	0	0
Ipswich T.	Tr	10.68	68-73	168	0	0
Portsmouth	Tr	02.74	73-74	53	0	0
Bournemouth	Tr	07.75	75	2	0	0

BEST George
Belfast, 22 May, 1946 NI-37 (F)

League Club	Source	Date Signed	Seasons Played	Apps	Subs	Gls
Manchester U.	Jnrs	05.63	63-73	361	0	137
Stockport Co.	L	11.75	75	3	0	2
Fulham	Los Angeles (USA)	09.76	76-77	42	0	8
Bournemouth	Golden Bay (USA)	03.83	82	5	0	0

BEST John Bowers
Liverpool, 11 July, 1940 (WH)

League Club	Source	Date Signed	Seasons Played	Apps	Subs	Gls
Liverpool	Jnrs	05.58				
Tranmere Rov.	Tr	08.60	60	7	-	0

BEST Thomas Hubert
Milford Haven, 23 December, 1920 (CF)

League Club	Source	Date Signed	Seasons Played	Apps	Subs	Gls
Chester C.	Merthyr Tydfil	07.47	47-48	40	-	14
Cardiff C.	Tr	10.48	48-49	28	-	10
Queens Park R.	Tr	12.49	49	13	-	3

BEST William John Blaikley
Gartcosh, 7 September, 1943 (F)

League Club	Source	Date Signed	Seasons Played	Apps	Subs	Gls
Northampton T.	Pollok	07.62	63-67	38	2	11
Southend U.	Tr	01.68	67-72	225	1	106
Northampton T.	Tr	09.73	73-77	201	2	38

BESWETHERICK Jonathan Barry
Liverpool, 15 January, 1978 (LB)

League Club	Source	Date Signed	Seasons Played	Apps	Subs	Gls
Plymouth Arg.	YT	07.96	97	0	2	0

BESWICK Ivan
Manchester, 2 January, 1936 (FB)

League Club	Source	Date Signed	Seasons Played	Apps	Subs	Gls
Manchester U.		10.54				
Oldham Ath.	Tr	08.58	58-60	46	-	0

BESWICK Keith
Cardiff, 3 February, 1943 (G)

League Club	Source	Date Signed	Seasons Played	Apps	Subs	Gls
Millwall	Cardiff Corries	01.62	62	12	-	0
Newport Co.	Tr	08.64	64-66	58	0	0

BETMEAD Harry
Grimsby, 11 April, 1912 Died 1984 E-1 (CH)

League Club	Source	Date Signed	Seasons Played	Apps	Subs	Gls
Grimsby T.	Hay Cross	10.30	31-46	296	-	10

BETT Frederick
Scunthorpe, 5 December, 1920 (IF)

League Club	Source	Date Signed	Seasons Played	Apps	Subs	Gls
Sunderland	Scunthorpe U.	12.37	37-38	3	-	0
Coventry C.	Tr	05.46	46-48	27	-	11
Lincoln C.	Tr	09.48	48	14	-	2

BETTANY Colin David
Leicester, 15 June, 1932 (FB)

League Club	Source	Date Signed	Seasons Played	Apps	Subs	Gls
Crewe Alex.	Leicester C. (Am)	08.53	53-54	29	-	6
Birmingham C.	Tr	06.55				
Torquay U.	Tr	04.57	57-65	335	0	4

BETTANY John William
Maltby, 16 December, 1937 (WH)

League Club	Source	Date Signed	Seasons Played	Apps	Subs	Gls
Huddersfield T.	Thurcroft	09.60	60-64	59	-	6
Barnsley	Tr	03.65	64-69	194	4	25
Rotherham U.	Tr	06.70	70	16	0	1

BETTERIDGE Raymond **Michael**
Redditch, 11 August, 1924 (IF)

League Club	Source	Date Signed	Seasons Played	Apps	Subs	Gls
West Bromwich A.	Warslow Celtic	11.48	49-50	5	-	0
Swindon T.	Tr	07.51	51-53	108	-	23
Chester C.	Tr	03.54	53	8	-	1

BETTNEY Christopher John
Chesterfield, 27 October, 1977 (F)

League Club	Source	Date Signed	Seasons Played	Apps	Subs	Gls
Sheffield U.	YT	05.96	96	0	1	0
Hull C.	L	09.97	97	28	2	1

BETTS Antony Thomas
Derby, 31 October, 1953 E Yth (F)

League Club	Source	Date Signed	Seasons Played	Apps	Subs	Gls
Aston Villa	Jnrs	03.72	74	1	3	0
Southport	L	12.74	74	8	0	1
Port Vale	Tr	10.75	75	1	0	0

BETTS James **Barrie**
Barnsley, 18 September, 1932 (FB)

League Club	Source	Date Signed	Seasons Played	Apps	Subs	Gls
Barnsley	Jnrs	11.50	52-56	55	-	0
Stockport Co.	Tr	11.57	57-59	112	-	3
Manchester C.	Tr	06.60	60-63	101	-	5
Scunthorpe U.	Tr	08.64	64	7	-	0

BETTS Eric
Mansfield, 27 July, 1925 Died 1990 (OL)

League Club	Source	Date Signed	Seasons Played	Apps	Subs	Gls
Mansfield T.	Mansfield Villa	02.46	46	19	-	5
Coventry C.	Tr	08.47	47	1	-	0
Walsall	Nuneaton Borough	05.49	49	30	-	3
West Ham U.	Tr	04.50	50	3	-	1
Rochdale	Nuneaton Borough	10.51	51-52	52	-	8
Crewe Alex.	Tr	02.53	52-53	25	-	5
Wrexham	Tr	10.53	53-55	53	-	21
Oldham Ath.	Tr	02.56	55-56	26	-	5

BETTS Michael James
Barnsley, 21 September, 1956 (D)

League Club	Source	Date Signed	Seasons Played	Apps	Subs	Gls
Blackpool	App	10.73	75	4	3	0
Bury (N/C)	Northwich Vic.	11.80	80	1	0	0

BETTS Robert
Doncaster, 21 December, 1981 (F)

League Club	Source	Date Signed	Seasons Played	Apps	Subs	Gls
Doncaster Rov	YT	●	97	2	1	0

BETTS Simon Richard
Middlesbrough, 3 March, 1973 (FB)

League Club	Source	Date Signed	Seasons Played	Apps	Subs	Gls
Ipswich T.	YT	07.91				
Wrexham (N/C)	Tr	08.92				
Colchester U.	Scarborough (N/C)	12.92	92-97	160	3	9

BETTS Stuart
Barnsley, 21 September, 1956 (F)

League Club	Source	Date Signed	Seasons Played	Apps	Subs	Gls
Blackpool	App	10.73				
Halifax T.		09.76				
Crewe Alex. (N/C)	Tr	08.77	77	2	0	0

BEVAN Brian Edward
Bristol, 20 March, 1937 (OL)

League Club	Source	Date Signed	Seasons Played	Apps	Subs	Gls
Bristol C.	Bridgwater T.	02.56	57-59	2	-	0
Carlisle U.	Tr	03.60	59-60	27	-	2
Millwall	Tr	02.61	60	3	-	0

BEVAN Paul Philip
Shrewsbury, 20 October, 1952 (D)

League Club	Source	Date Signed	Seasons Played	Apps	Subs	Gls
Shrewsbury T.	App	10.70	70-72	66	5	1
Swansea C.	Tr	08.73	73-74	77	2	5
Crewe Alex.	Tr	07.75	75-79	170	2	7

BEVANS Stanley
Kingsley, 16 April, 1934 (OR)

League Club	Source	Date Signed	Seasons Played	Apps	Subs	Gls
Stoke C.	Jnrs	04.51	50-54	15	-	1

BEVIS David Roger
Southampton, 27 June, 1942 (G)

League Club	Source	Date Signed	Seasons Played	Apps	Subs	Gls
Ipswich T.	Jnrs	08.59	63-65	6	0	0

BEVIS William Ernest
Warsash, 29 September, 1918 Died 1994 (OR)

League Club	Source	Date Signed	Seasons Played	Apps	Subs	Gls
Portsmouth	Gosport Borough	07.36				
Southampton	Tr	06.37	37-46	82	-	16

BEWLEY David George
Bournemouth, 22 September, 1920 E Sch (WH)

League Club	Source	Date Signed	Seasons Played	Apps	Subs	Gls
Fulham	Gravesend & Nft	05.45	46-48	17	-	1
Reading	Tr	03.50	49-50	11	-	1
Fulham	Tr	11.50				
Watford	Tr	05.53	53-55	113	-	1

BEYNON Edgar Norman
Swansea, 3 May, 1940 (F)

League Club	Source	Date Signed	Seasons Played	Apps	Subs	Gls
Wrexham	R.A.F. Egypt	07.59	59	1	-	0

BEYNON Edwin Rees
Aberdare, 17 November, 1924 W Sch (WH)

League Club	Source	Date Signed	Seasons Played	Apps	Subs	Gls
Wrexham		01.47	46-51	72	-	21
Shrewsbury T.	Tr	10.51	51-54	91	-	6

BIBBO Salvatore
Basingstoke, 24 August, 1974 (G)

League Club	Source	Date Signed	Seasons Played	Apps	Subs	Gls
Sheffield U.	Crawley T.	08.93				
Chesterfield	L	02.95	94	0	1	0
Reading	Tr	08.96	96-97	7	0	0

BICKERSTAFFE John
St Helens, 8 November, 1918 Died 1982 (CH)

League Club	Source	Date Signed	Seasons Played	Apps	Subs	Gls
Bury	Peasley Cross	05.39	46-48	27	-	0
Lincoln C.	Tr	12.48	48-50	12	-	0
Halifax T.	Tr	09.51	51-52	37	-	0

BICKLE Michael John
Plymouth, 25 January, 1944 (CF)

League Club	Source	Date Signed	Seasons Played	Apps	Subs	Gls
Plymouth Arg.	St Austell	12.65	65-71	171	10	71
Gillingham	Tr	11.71	71-72	32	0	7

BICKLES David
West Ham, 6 April, 1944 E Yth (CH)

League Club	Source	Date Signed	Seasons Played	Apps	Subs	Gls
West Ham U.	App	07.61	63-66	24	1	0
Crystal Palace	Tr	10.67				
Colchester U.	Tr	09.68	68-69	68	0	3

BICKNELL Charles
Alfreton, 6 November, 1905 Died 1994 (FB)

League Club	Source	Date Signed	Seasons Played	Apps	Subs	Gls
Chesterfield	New Tupton Ivanhoe	10.27	28-30	79	-	0
Bradford C.	Tr	03.30	30-35	240	-	2
West Ham U.	Tr	03.36	35-46	137	-	1

BICKNELL John (Jack)
Edlington, 16 December, 1931 (IL)

League Club	Source	Date Signed	Seasons Played	Apps	Subs	Gls
Walsall	Retford T.	02.54	53	3	-	0

BICKNELL Roy
Doncaster, 19 February, 1926 (CH)

League Club	Source	Date Signed	Seasons Played	Apps	Subs	Gls
Wolverhampton W.	Jnrs	09.43				
Charlton Ath.	Tr	05.47	47-48	7	-	0
Bristol C.	Tr	06.49	49-50	21	-	0
Colchester U.	Gravesend & Nft	06.52	52-53	25	-	0

BICKNELL Stephen John
Rugby, 28 November, 1959 (W)

League Club	Source	Date Signed	Seasons Played	Apps	Subs	Gls
Leicester C.	App	12.76	76	6	1	0
Torquay U.	Tr	08.78	78	0	3	0

BIELBY Paul Anthony
Darlington, 24 November, 1956 E Yth (W)

League Club	Source	Date Signed	Seasons Played	Apps	Subs	Gls
Manchester U.	App	11.73	73	2	2	0
Hartlepool U.	Tr	11.75	75-77	74	21	8
Huddersfield T.	Tr	08.78	78	29	2	5

BIELBY Terence
Doncaster, 24 November, 1943 (FB)

League Club	Source	Date Signed	Seasons Played	Apps	Subs	Gls
Doncaster Rov.	Jnrs	01.61	60	1	-	0

BIGGINS Brian
Ellesmere Port, 19 May, 1940 (G)

League Club	Source	Date Signed	Seasons Played	Apps	Subs	Gls
Chester C.	Jnrs	06.57	57-58	5	-	0

BIGGINS Graham William
Chapeltown, 10 March, 1958 (G)

League Club	Source	Date Signed	Seasons Played	Apps	Subs	Gls
Doncaster Rov.	Rotherham U. (Am)	07.77	77	2	0	0

BIGGINS Stephen James
Lichfield, 20 June, 1954 (F)

League Club	Source	Date Signed	Seasons Played	Apps	Subs	Gls
Shrewsbury T.	Hednesford T.	12.77	77-81	140	6	41
Oxford U.	Tr	07.82	82-84	44	15	22
Derby Co.	Tr	10.84	84	8	2	1

League Club	Source	Date Signed	Seasons Played	Apps	Subs	Gls
Wolverhampton W.	L	03.85	84	4	0	0
Port Vale	L	03.86	85	1	3	0
Exeter C. (N/C)	Trelleborg (Swe)	10.86	86	14	0	2

BIGGINS Wayne
Sheffield, 20 November, 1961 (F)

League Club	Source	Date Signed	Seasons Played	Apps	Subs	Gls
Lincoln C.	App	11.79	80	8	0	1
Burnley	Matlock T.	02.84	83-85	78	0	30
Norwich C.	Tr	10.85	85-87	66	13	16
Manchester C.	Tr	07.88	88	29	3	9
Stoke C.	Tr	08.89	89-92	120	2	46
Barnsley	Tr	10.92	92-93	44	3	16
Stoke C.	Glasgow Celtic	03.94	93-94	18	9	6
Luton T.	L	01.95	94	6	1	1
Oxford U.	Tr	07.95	95	8	2	1
Wigan Ath.	Tr	11.95	95-96	35	16	5

BIGGS Alfred George
Bristol, 8 February, 1936 (CF)

League Club	Source	Date Signed	Seasons Played	Apps	Subs	Gls
Bristol Rov.	Jnrs	02.53	53-60	214	-	77
Preston N.E.	Tr	07.61	61-62	49	-	22
Bristol Rov.	Tr	10.62	62-67	210	0	101
Walsall	Tr	03.68	67-68	23	1	9
Swansea C.	Tr	11.68	68	16	0	4

BIGGS Anthony
Greenford, 17 April, 1936 E Amat (CF)

League Club	Source	Date Signed	Seasons Played	Apps	Subs	Gls
Arsenal	Hounslow T.	08.56	57-58	4	-	1
Leyton Orient	Tr	12.58	58-59	4	-	1

BIGNOT Marcus
Birmingham, 22 August, 1974 E Semi Pro (RB)

League Club	Source	Date Signed	Seasons Played	Apps	Subs	Gls
Crewe Alex.	Kidderminster Hrs	09.97	97	42	0	0

BILCLIFF Raymond
Blaydon, 24 May, 1931 (FB)

League Club	Source	Date Signed	Seasons Played	Apps	Subs	Gls
Middlesbrough	Spen Jnrs	05.49	51-60	182	-	0
Hartlepool U.	Tr	01.61	60-63	117	-	0

BILEY Alan Paul
Leighton Buzzard, 26 February, 1957 (F)

League Club	Source	Date Signed	Seasons Played	Apps	Subs	Gls
Cambridge U.	Luton T. (App)	07.75	75-79	160	5	75
Derby Co.	Tr	01.80	79-80	47	0	19
Everton	Tr	07.81	81	16	3	3
Stoke C.	L	03.82	81	8	0	1
Portsmouth	Tr	08.82	82-84	101	4	51
Brighton & H.A.	Tr	03.85	84-85	34	1	8
Cambridge U. (N/C)	New York (USA)	11.86	86	0	3	0

BILIC Slaven
Croatia, 11 September, 1968 Croatian Int (CD)

League Club	Source	Date Signed	Seasons Played	Apps	Subs	Gls
West Ham U.	Karlsruhe (Ger)	02.96	95-96	48	0	2
Everton	Tr	07.97	97	22	2	0

BILL Roger James
Creswell, 17 May, 1944 (OR)

League Club	Source	Date Signed	Seasons Played	Apps	Subs	Gls
Reading	Chelsea (Am)	09.62	62	4	-	0

BILLING Peter Graham
Liverpool, 24 October, 1964 (CD)

League Club	Source	Date Signed	Seasons Played	Apps	Subs	Gls
Everton	South Liverpool	01.86	85	1	0	0
Crewe Alex.	Tr	12.86	86-88	83	5	1
Coventry C.	Tr	06.89	89-92	51	7	1
Port Vale	Tr	02.93	92-94	23	3	0
Hartlepool U.	Tr	08.95	95	35	1	0
Crewe Alex.	Tr	08.96	96	9	6	0

BILLINGHAM John
Daventry, 3 December, 1914 Died 1981 (CF)

League Club	Source	Date Signed	Seasons Played	Apps	Subs	Gls
Northampton T.	Stead & Simpson	09.35	35	3	-	0
Bristol C.	Tr	07.37	37	7	-	0
Burnley	Tr	05.38	38-48	93	-	36
Carlisle U.	Tr	09.49	49-50	64	-	17
Southport	Tr	03.51	50-54	150	-	37

BILLINGHAM Peter Arnold
Brierley Hill, 8 October, 1938 (WH)

League Club	Source	Date Signed	Seasons Played	Apps	Subs	Gls
Walsall	Jnrs	10.55	55-59	99	-	9
West Bromwich A.	Tr	05.60	60	7	-	0

BILLINGS John
Doncaster, 30 March, 1944 (F)

League Club	Source	Date Signed	Seasons Played	Apps	Subs	Gls
Doncaster Rov.	Jnrs	05.61	62-64	18	-	4

BILLINGTON Brian Keith
Leicester, 28 April, 1951 (F)

League Club	Source	Date Signed	Seasons Played	Apps	Subs	Gls
Notts Co.	Leicester C. (Am)	10.69	69	4	3	0

BILLINGTON Charles Roy
Chesterfield, 8 November, 1927 Died 1985 (CH)

League Club	Source	Date Signed	Seasons Played	Apps	Subs	Gls
Aldershot	Chesterfield (Am)	12.46	46-55	212	-	11
Norwich C.	Tr	01.56	55-56	22	-	0
Watford	Tr	07.57	57	14	-	0
Mansfield T.	Tr	06.58	58	1	-	0

BILLINGTON David James
Oxford, 15 January, 1980 (M)

League Club	Source	Date Signed	Seasons Played	Apps	Subs	Gls
Peterborough U.	YT	●	96	2	3	0
Sheffield Wed.	Tr	04.97				

BILLINGTON Hugh John Richard
Ampthill, 24 February, 1916 Died 1988 (CF)

League Club	Source	Date Signed	Seasons Played	Apps	Subs	Gls
Luton T.	Waterlows	05.38	38-47	87	-	63
Chelsea	Tr	03.48	47-50	83	-	28

BILLINGTON Stanley
Wallasey, 23 February, 1937 E Yth (RB)

League Club	Source	Date Signed	Seasons Played	Apps	Subs	Gls
Everton	Jnrs	06.55				
Tranmere Rov.	Tr	07.60	60-63	93	-	0

BILLINGTON Wilfred Francis
Blackburn, 28 January, 1930 (G)

League Club	Source	Date Signed	Seasons Played	Apps	Subs	Gls
Blackburn Rov.		04.48				
Workington	Tr	07.54	54-57	52	-	0

BILLIO Patrizio
Treviso, Italy, 19 April, 1974 (CM)

League Club	Source	Date Signed	Seasons Played	Apps	Subs	Gls
Crystal Palace (N/C)	Monza (It)	03.98	97	1	2	0

BILLY Christopher Anthony
Huddersfield, 2 January, 1973 (RB/W)

League Club	Source	Date Signed	Seasons Played	Apps	Subs	Gls
Huddersfield T.	YT	07.91	91-94	76	18	4
Plymouth Arg.	Tr	08.95	95-97	107	11	8

BIMPSON James Louis
Rainford, 14 May, 1929 (CF)

League Club	Source	Date Signed	Seasons Played	Apps	Subs	Gls
Liverpool	Burscough	01.53	52-59	94	-	39
Blackburn Rov.	Tr	11.59	59-60	22	-	5
Bournemouth	Tr	02.61	60	11	-	1
Rochdale	Tr	08.61	61-62	54	-	16

BIMSON Stuart James
Liverpool, 29 September, 1969 (LB)

League Club	Source	Date Signed	Seasons Played	Apps	Subs	Gls
Bury	Macclesfield T.	02.95	94-96	36	0	0
Lincoln C.	Tr	11.96	96-97	20	7	1

BINCH David
Nottingham, 10 February, 1956 (F)

League Club	Source	Date Signed	Seasons Played	Apps	Subs	Gls
Doncaster Rov.		02.76	75-76	3	2	0

BINES Henry Melvin
Cardiff, 17 May, 1930 (WH)

League Club	Source	Date Signed	Seasons Played	Apps	Subs	Gls
Swindon T.		08.50	51-52	6	-	0

BING Douglas
Broadstairs, 27 October, 1928 (OR)

League Club	Source	Date Signed	Seasons Played	Apps	Subs	Gls
West Ham U.	Margate	01.51	51-54	29	-	3

BING Thomas Edward
Broadstairs, 24 November, 1931 (F)

League Club	Source	Date Signed	Seasons Played	Apps	Subs	Gls
Tottenham H.	Margate	09.54	57	1	-	0

BINGHAM John George
Ilkeston 23 September, 1949 (OL)

League Club	Source	Date Signed	Seasons Played	Apps	Subs	Gls
Manchester C.	Charlton Ath. (App)	10.67				
Oldham Ath.	Tr	07.69	69	16	1	3
Mansfield T.	Tr	08.70	70-71	18	3	0
Chester C.	L	03.72	71	7	0	1
Stockport Co.	Tr	07.72	72	16	4	3

BINGHAM William Laurence
Belfast, 5 August, 1931 IR Lge/NI-56 (OR)

League Club	Source	Date Signed	Seasons Played	Apps	Subs	Gls
Sunderland	Glentoran	11.50	50-57	206	-	45
Luton T.	Tr	07.58	58-60	87	-	27
Everton	Tr	10.60	60-62	86	-	23
Port Vale	Tr	08.63	63-64	40	-	6

BINGHAM William Peter
Swindon, 12 July, 1922 Died 1997 (HB)

League Club	Source	Date Signed	Seasons Played	Apps	Subs	Gls
Swindon T.		08.46	46-47	20	-	0

BINGLEY Walter
Sheffield, 17 April, 1930 (FB)

League Club	Source	Date Signed	Seasons Played	Apps	Subs	Gls
Bolton W.	Eccleshall M.W.	04.48	49-54	6	-	0
Sheffield Wed.	Tr	05.55	55-57	38	-	0
Swindon T.	Tr	01.58	57-59	101	-	0
York C.	Tr	08.60	60-62	130	-	5
Halifax T.	Tr	07.63	63-64	63	-	1

League Club	Source	Date Signed	Seasons Played	Apps	Subs	Gls
BINKS Martin John						
Romford, 15 September, 1953						(CD)
Colchester U.	Leyton Orient (App)	05.72	72	10	0	0
Cambridge U.	Tr	01.73	72	1	0	0
BINNEY Frederick Edward						
Plymouth, 12 August, 1946						(F)
Torquay U.	Launceston	10.66	67-69	24	10	10
Exeter C.	Tr	02.69	68-73	177	0	90
Brighton & H.A.	Tr	05.74	74-76	68	2	35
Plymouth Arg.	St Louis (USA)	10.77	77-79	67	4	39
Hereford U.	Tr	01.80	79-81	21	6	6
BINNIE Laurence						
Falkirk, 17 December, 1917						(HB)
Chesterfield	Camelon Jnrs	05.39				
Mansfield T.	Tr	11.46	46	20	-	0
BINNS Eric						
Halifax, 13 August, 1924						(CH)
Halifax T.	Huddersfield T. (Am)	05.46	46	6	-	1
Burnley	Goole T.	03.49	52-54	15	-	0
Blackburn Rov.	Tr	05.55	55-56	23	-	0
BIRBECK Joseph						
Stanley, 15 April, 1932						(LH)
Middlesbrough	Evenwood T.	04.53	53-58	38	-	0
Grimsby T.	Tr	07.59	59	18	-	0
BIRCH Alan						
West Bromwich, 12 August, 1956						(W)
Walsall	App	08.73	72-78	158	13	23
Chesterfield	Tr	07.79	79-80	90	0	35
Wolverhampton W.	Tr	08.81	81	13	2	0
Barnsley	Tr	02.82	81-82	43	1	10
Chesterfield	Tr	08.83	83	30	2	5
Rotherham U.	Tr	03.84	83-85	99	2	28
Scunthorpe U.	Tr	06.86	86-87	19	4	2
Stockport Co.	Tr	10.87	87	18	2	3
BIRCH Brian						
Southport, 9 April, 1938 E Sch/E Yth						(OR)
Bolton W.	Jnrs	04.55	54-63	165	-	23
Rochdale	Tr	07.64	64-65	60	1	6
BIRCH Brian						
Salford, 18 November, 1931 E Yth						(IF)
Manchester U.	Jnrs	05.49	49-51	11	-	4
Wolverhampton W.	Tr	03.52	51	3	-	1
Lincoln C.	Tr	12.52	52-54	56	-	15
Barrow	Tr	06.56	56-58	60	-	27
Exeter C.	Tr	09.58	58-59	19	-	1
Oldham Ath.	Tr	01.60	59-60	35	-	10
Rochdale	Tr	03.61	60-61	11	-	0
BIRCH Clifford						
Newport, 1 September, 1928 Died 1990						(OR)
Norwich C.	Ebbw Vale	12.46	49	5	-	3
Newport Co.	Tr	10.50	50-53	142	-	28
Colchester U.	Tr	06.54	54	12	-	3
BIRCH Harold Kelvin						
Crieff, 11 January, 1914 Died 1985						(WH)
Barrow	Bangor (NI)	09.45	46	26	-	2
BIRCH James Victor Tomlinson						
Ashover, 25 October, 1927						(IR)
Huddersfield T.	Grenoside	05.45				
Halifax T.		08.48	48	3	-	1
BIRCH Jeffrey						
Sheffield, 21 October, 1927						(OL)
Sheffield U.	Scarborough	09.47				
York C.	Tr	10.49	49	7	-	1
BIRCH Kenneth Joseph						
Birkenhead, 31 December, 1933						(WH)
Everton	Jnrs	08.51	55-57	43	-	1
Southampton	Tr	03.58	57-58	34	-	3
BIRCH Paul						
West Bromwich, 20 November, 1962						(M)
Aston Villa	App	07.80	83-90	153	20	16
Wolverhampton W.	Tr	02.91	90-95	128	14	15
Preston N.E.	L	03.96	95	11	0	2
Doncaster Rov.	Tr	07.96	96	26	1	2
Exeter C.	Tr	03.97	96-97	33	2	5

League Club	Source	Date Signed	Seasons Played	Apps	Subs	Gls
BIRCH Paul Anthony						
Reading, 3 December, 1968						(F)
Portsmouth	Arsenal (App)	01.87				
Brentford	Tr	12.87	87-88	13	5	2
BIRCH Trevor						
West Bromwich, 20 November, 1933						(WH)
Aston Villa	Accles & Pollock	01.52	54-59	22	-	0
Stockport Co.	Tr	11.60	60-61	43	-	0
BIRCH Trevor Nigel						
Ormskirk, 16 February, 1958						(M)
Liverpool	App	12.75				
Shrewsbury T.	Tr	03.79	78-79	23	2	4
Chester C.	Tr	07.80	80	30	1	0
BIRCH James **Walter**						
Ecclesfield, 5 October, 1917 Died 1991						(CH)
Huddersfield T.		05.39				
Rochdale	Tr	03.46	46-52	243	-	10
BIRCH William						
Southport, 20 October, 1944						(F)
West Bromwich A.	App	10.62				
Crystal Palace	Tr	06.63	63-64	6	-	0
BIRCHALL Paul William						
Liverpool, 3 September, 1957						(M)
Southport	Everton (Am)	03.77	76-77	16	3	1
BIRCHAM Bernard						
Philadelphia (Dm), 31 August, 1924						(G)
Sunderland	Jnrs	07.43				
Chesterfield	Tr	11.46				
Grimsby T.	Tr	06.48	49	8	-	0
Colchester U.	Tr	07.50	50	7	-	0
BIRCHAM Walter **Clive**						
Herrington (Dm), 7 September, 1939						(W)
Sunderland	Jnrs	09.56	58-59	28	-	2
Hartlepool U.	Tr	02.60	59-62	105	-	15
BIRCHAM Marc Stephen John						
Wembley, 11 May, 1978						(FB)
Millwall	YT	05.96	96-97	9	1	0
BIRCHENALL Alan John						
East Ham, 22 August, 1945 Eu23-4						(M)
Sheffield U.	Thorniewood Ath.	06.63	64-67	106	1	31
Chelsea	Tr	11.67	67-69	74	1	20
Crystal Palace	Tr	06.70	70-71	41	0	11
Leicester C.	Tr	09.71	71-76	156	7	12
Notts Co.	L	03.76	75	5	0	0
Notts Co.	San Jose (USA)	09.77	77	28	0	0
Blackburn Rov.	Memphis (USA)	07.78	78	17	1	0
Luton T.	Tr	03.79	78-79	9	1	0
Hereford U.	Tr	10.79	79	11	0	0
BIRCUMSHAW Anthony						
Mansfield, 8 February, 1945						(FB)
Notts Co.	App	02.62	60-65	148	0	1
Hartlepool U.	Tr	07.66	66-70	182	3	11
BIRCUMSHAW Peter Brian						
Mansfield, 29 August, 1938						(OL)
Notts Co.	Jnrs	07.56	56-61	72	-	40
Bradford C.	Tr	06.62	62	27	-	7
Stockport Co.	Tr	06.63	63	17	-	4
BIRD Adrian Lee						
Bristol, 8 July, 1969						(CD)
Birmingham C.	App	07.87	86-88	23	4	0
BIRD Anthony						
Cardiff, 1 September, 1974 W Yth/Wu21-8						(F)
Cardiff C.	YT	07.93	92-95	44	31	13
Swansea C.	Barry T.	08.97	97	35	6	14
BIRD John Charles						
Doncaster, 9 June, 1948						(CD)
Doncaster Rov.	Doncaster U.	03.67	67-70	48	2	3
Preston N.E.	Tr	03.71	70-75	166	0	9
Newcastle U.	Tr	08.75	75-79	84	3	5
Hartlepool U.	Tr	07.80	80-84	139	2	16
BIRD Francis **John**						
Cardiff, 21 November, 1940 W Sch						(FB)
Newport Co.	Jnrs	11.57	57-66	276	0	3
Swansea Co.	Tr	07.67	67	7	0	0

League Club	Source	Date Signed	Seasons Played	Career Record Apps	Subs	Gls
BIRD Kenneth Benjamin						
Norwich, 25 September, 1918 Died 1987 E Sch						(G)
Wolverhampton W.	Willenhall Rov.	05.37				
Bournemouth	Tr	10.38	38-52	249	-	0
BIRD Kevin						
Doncaster, 7 August, 1952						(CD)
Mansfield T.	Doncaster Rov. (Am)	07.72	72-82	372	5	55
Huddersfield T.	Tr	08.83	83	1	0	0
BIRD Ronald Philip						
Birmingham, 27 December, 1941 E Yth						(OL)
Birmingham C.	Jnrs	01.59				
Bradford P.A.	Tr	06.61	61-65	129	0	39
Bury	Tr	10.65	65	13	0	3
Cardiff C.	Tr	02.66	65-70	97	10	24
Crewe Alex.	Tr	07.71	71	19	1	0
BIRKBECK John David						
Lincoln, 1 October, 1932						(F)
Lincoln C.	Spilsby	01.52	54	2	-	0
BIRKETT Clifford						
Haydock, 17 September, 1933 Died 1997 E Sch						(OR)
Manchester U.	Jnrs	10.50	50	9	-	2
Southport	Tr	06.56	56	14	-	4
BIRKETT Ronald						
Warrington, 21 July, 1927 Died 1992						(OL)
Manchester C.	Crompton Rec.	01.46				
New Brighton	Tr	01.47	46-47	8	-	0
Oldham Ath.	Tr	08.48	48	4	-	0
Accrington St.	Tr	07.49	49	14	-	2
BIRKETT Wilfred						
Warrington, 26 June, 1922 Died 1993						(G)
Everton	Haydock C. & B.C.	02.44				
Southport	Tr	11.46	46-51	162	-	0
Shrewsbury T.	Tr	07.52	52	20	-	0
Southport	Tr	07.53	53	15	-	0
BIRKS Graham						
Sheffield, 25 January, 1942						(FB)
Sheffield Wed.	Jnrs	01.60	62	4	-	0
Peterborough U.	Tr	05.64	64-65	34	0	0
Southend U.	Tr	01.66	65-69	139	1	1
Chester C.	Tr	10.69	69-71	71	2	0
BIRMINGHAM Charles Henry						
Liverpool, 24 August, 1922 Died 1993						(IF)
Tranmere Rov.	Everton (Am)	08.46	46	2	-	1
BIRSE Charles Duncan Valentine						
Dundee, 26 October, 1916 Died 1995						(WH)
Watford	Hibernian	05.46	46	7	-	0
Northampton T.	Tr	07.47				
BIRTLES Garry						
Nottingham, 27 July, 1956 Eu21-2/E'B'/E-3						(F)
Nottingham F.	Long Eaton U.	12.76	76-80	87	0	32
Manchester U.	Tr	10.80	80-81	57	1	11
Nottingham F.	Tr	09.82	82-86	122	3	38
Notts Co.	Tr	06.87	87-88	62	1	9
Grimsby T.	Tr	07.89	89-91	54	15	9
BISHOP Charles Darren						
Nottingham, 16 February, 1968						(D)
Watford	Stoke C. (App)	04.86				
Bury	Tr	08.87	87-90	104	10	6
Barnsley	Tr	07.91	91-95	124	6	1
Preston N.E.	L	01.96	95	4	0	0
Burnley	L	03.96	95	9	0	0
Wigan Ath.	Tr	06.96	96-97	27	1	0
Northampton T.	Tr	12.97	97	7	0	0
BISHOP Edward Michael						
Liverpool, 28 November, 1962						(M)
Tranmere Rov.	Runcorn	03.88	87-90	46	30	19
Chester C.	Tr	12.90	90-95	97	18	26
Crewe Alex.	L	03.92	91	3	0	0
BISHOP Ian William						
Liverpool, 29 May, 1965 E 'B'						(M)
Everton	App	05.83	83	0	1	0
Crewe Alex.	L	03.84	83	4	0	0
Carlisle U.	Tr	10.84	84-87	131	1	14
Bournemouth	Tr	07.88	88	44	0	2
Manchester C.	Tr	07.89	89	18	1	2
West Ham U.	Tr	12.89	89-97	240	14	12
Manchester C.	Tr	03.98	97	4	2	0

League Club	Source	Date Signed	Seasons Played	Career Record Apps	Subs	Gls
BISHOP Peter Jason						
Sheffield, 4 January, 1944 E Yth						(OL)
Sheffield U.	Jnrs	04.63				
Chesterfield	Tr	05.65	65-70	78	3	7
BISHOP Raymond John						
Hengoed, 24 November, 1955						(F)
Cardiff C.	Cheltenham T.	01.77	77-80	92	10	25
Newport Co.	Tr	02.81	80-81	8	10	2
Torquay U.	Tr	08.82	82-83	33	7	8
BISHOP Sidney Harold Richard						
Tooting, 8 April, 1934						(CH)
Leyton Orient	Chertsey	06.52	53-64	296	-	4
BISHTON Dennis Roy						
Windsor, 22 September, 1950						(RB)
Reading	App	09.68	68	2	0	0
BISSELL Steven John						
Meriden, 8 October, 1958						(W)
Nottingham F.	App	10.76				
Blackpool	Tr	09.78	78	1	0	0
BISSET Thomas Alexander						
Croydon, 21 March, 1932						(FB)
Brighton & H.A.	Redhill	01.53	52-60	115	-	5
BISSETT Nicholas						
Fulham, 5 April, 1964						(CD)
Brighton & H.A.	Barnet	09.88	88-94	94	3	9
BITHELL Brian						
Manchester, 5 October, 1956						(D)
Stoke C.	App	10.73	76	16	1	0
Port Vale	L	09.77	77	2	0	0
Wimbledon	Tr	12.77	77	6	0	0
BJORNEBYE Stig-Inge						
Norway, 11 December, 1969 Norwegian Int						(LB)
Liverpool	Rosenborg (Nor)	12.92	92-97	112	4	2
BLACK Alan Douglas						
Glasgow, 4 June, 1943						(FB)
Sunderland	Dumbarton	08.64	64-65	4	2	0
Norwich C.	Tr	09.66	66-73	172	4	1
BLACK Andrew						
Stirling, 23 September, 1917 SF Lge/S-3						(CF)
Manchester C.	Hearts	06.46	46-49	139	-	47
Stockport Co.	Tr	08.50	50-52	94	-	38
BLACK Anthony						
Barrow, 15 July, 1969						(OR)
Wigan Ath.	Bamber Bridge	03.95	94-97	17	14	2
BLACK Ian Henderson						
Aberdeen, 27 March, 1924 S-1						(G)
Southampton	Aberdeen	12.47	47-49	97	-	0
Fulham	Tr	08.50	50-57	263	-	1
BLACK John						
Blackburn, 4 November, 1945 W Sch						(G)
Arsenal	App	02.63				
Swansea C.	App	12.64	64-65	15	0	0
BLACK John						
Helensburgh, 10 November, 1957						(W)
Wolverhampton W.	App	12.75	77-78	5	1	0
Bradford C.	Tr	01.80	79-82	50	5	13
Hereford U.	Tr	08.83	83	8	1	0
BLACK Kenneth George						
Stenhousemuir, 29 November, 1963 S Sch/S Yth						(M)
Portsmouth	Hearts	07.89	89-90	50	12	3
BLACK Kingsley Terence						
Luton, 22 June, 1968 E Sch/NIu21-1/NI 'B'/NI-30						(LW)
Luton T.	Jnrs	07.86	87-91	123	4	26
Nottingham F.	Tr	09.91	91-95	80	18	14
Sheffield U.	L	03.95	94	8	3	2
Millwall	L	09.95	95	1	2	1
Grimsby T.	Tr	07.96	96-97	43	20	2
BLACK Michael James						
Chigwell, 6 October, 1976 E Sch						(M)
Arsenal	YT	07.95				
Millwall	L	10.97	97	13	0	2

League Club	Source	Date Signed	Seasons Played	Apps	Subs	Gls
BLACK Neville						
Ashington, 19 June, 1931						(IF)
Newcastle U.	Pegswood	09.49				
Exeter C.	Tr	01.53	52	4	-	0
Rochdale	Tr	07.53	53-55	62	-	13
BLACK Russell Palmer						
Dumfries, 29 July, 1960						(F)
Sheffield U.	Gretna	08.84	84-85	10	4	0
Halifax T.	Tr	08.86	86-87	63	9	14
BLACK Simon Anthony						
Birmingham, 9 November, 1975						(F)
Birmingham C.	YT	06.94	93	2	0	0
Doncaster Rov.	Tr	07.96				
BLACKADDER Frederick						
Carlisle, 13 January, 1916 Died 1992						(CH)
Carlisle U. (Am)	Queens Park	05.37	37-46	3	-	0
BLACKBURN Alan						
Pleasley, 4 August, 1935						(OL)
West Ham U.	Jnrs	08.53	54-57	15	-	3
Halifax T.	Tr	11.57	57-60	124	-	35
BLACKBURN Colin						
Thirsk, 16 January, 1961						(W)
Middlesbrough	Jnrs	12.79	80	1	0	0
BLACKBURN Derrick John						
Ryhill, 5 July, 1931						(HB)
Burnley		06.53				
Chesterfield	Tr	06.54				
Swansea C.	Ossett T.	01.57	57	2	-	0
BLACKBURN Edwin Huitson						
Houghton-le-Spring, 18 April, 1957						(G)
Hull C.	App	09.74	74-79	68	0	0
York C.	Tr	04.80	80-81	76	0	0
Hartlepool U.	Tr	01.83	82-86	161	0	0
BLACKBURN Keith						
Manchester, 17 July, 1940						(IF)
Portsmouth	Bolton W. (Am)	07.59	60-63	34	-	8
BLACKBURN Kenneth Alan						
Wembley, 13 May, 1951						(F)
Brighton & H.A.	App	05.69	68	1	0	1
BLACKER James Arthur						
Leeds, 10 August, 1945						(CH)
Bradford C.	Jnrs	01.63	63-64	21	-	0
BLACKFORD Gary John						
Redhill, 25 September, 1968						(RB)
Barnet (N/C)	Fisher Ath.	07.91	91	2	4	0
BLACKHALL Mark Christopher						
Barking, 17 November, 1960						(F)
Leyton Orient	App	11.78	81-82	12	6	1
BLACKHALL Raymond						
Ashington, 19 February, 1957						(FB)
Newcastle U.	App	08.74	74-77	25	12	0
Sheffield Wed.	Tr	08.78	78-81	115	0	1
Mansfield T.	I.K. Tord (Swe)	11.82	82	15	0	0
BLACKHALL Sidney						
Ashington, 25 September, 1945						(F)
Bradford P.A.	App	10.62	63	1	-	0
BLACKLAW Adam Smith						
Aberdeen, 2 September, 1937 S Sch/Su23-2/S-3						(G)
Burnley	Jnrs	10.54	56-66	318	0	0
Blackburn Rov.	Tr	07.67	67-69	96	0	0
Blackpool	Tr	06.70	70	1	0	0
BLACKLER Martin John						
Swindon, 14 March, 1963						(M)
Swindon T.	App	03.81	82	8	1	0
BLACKLEY Arthur						
Carlisle, 31 January, 1939						(OR)
Chelsea	Jnrs	10.56				
Carlisle U.	Tr	11.60	60-61	38	-	7
BLACKLEY John Henderson						
Polmont, 12 May, 1948 Su23-4/S-7						(CD)
Newcastle U.	Hibernian	10.77	77-78	46	0	0
Preston N.E.	Tr	07.79	79-81	51	2	0
BLACKMAN Ronald Henry						
Portsmouth, 2 April, 1925						(CF)
Reading	Gosport Borough	03.47	46-53	218	-	158
Nottingham F.	Tr	06.54	54	11	-	3
Ipswich T.	Tr	07.55	55-57	27	-	12
BLACKMORE Clayton Graham						
Neath, 23 September, 1964 W Sch/W Yth/Wu21-3/W-39						(M/FB)
Manchester U.	App	09.82	83-92	150	36	19
Middlesbrough	Tr	07.94	94-97	45	8	4
Bristol C.	L	11.96	96	5	0	1
BLACKSHAW William						
Ashton-u-Lyne, 6 September, 1920 Died 1994						(OR)
Manchester C.	Audenshaw U.	05.38	38	3	-	0
Oldham Ath.	Tr	07.46	46-48	67	-	22
Crystal Palace	Tr	07.49	49-50	32	-	5
Rochdale	Tr	02.51				
BLACKSTONE Ian Kenneth						
Harrogate, 7 August, 1964						(F)
York C.	Harrogate R.I.	09.90	90-93	107	22	37
Scarborough	Tr	08.94	94	11	2	0
BLACKWELL Dean Robert						
Camden, 5 December, 1969 Eu21-6						(CD)
Wimbledon	YT	07.88	89-97	132	22	1
Plymouth Arg.	L	03.90	89	5	2	0
BLACKWELL Kevin Patrick						
Luton, 21 December, 1958						(G)
Scarborough	Barnet	11.86	87-89	44	0	0
Notts Co.	Tr	11.89				
Torquay U.	Tr	01.93	92	18	0	0
Huddersfield T. (N/C)	Tr	08.93	93-94	3	2	0
Plymouth Arg. (N/C)	Tr	08.95	95-96	24	0	0
BLACKWELL Paul						
Deeside, 13 January, 1963						(M)
Chester C.	Jnrs	09.81	81-84	89	5	3
BLACKWELL Stephen Geoffrey						
Wolverhampton, 8 June, 1967						(F)
Wolverhampton W.	YT	11.84	84	0	1	0
BLACKWELL Wilfred						
Maltby, 19 November, 1926 Died 1959						(OR)
Portsmouth		10.47				
Mansfield T.	Tr	08.48				
Aldershot	Tr	06.50	50	1	-	0
BLACKWOOD John Syme Duncan						
Cronberry, 25 July, 1935						(IF)
Accrington St. (Am)	Girvan Jnrs	10.58	58-59	4	-	1
BLACKWOOD Robert Rankin						
Edinburgh, 20 August, 1934 Died 1997 SF Lge						(WH)
Ipswich T.	Hearts	06.62	62-64	62	-	12
Colchester U.	Tr	05.65	65-67	104	1	6
BLADES Paul Andrew						
Peterborough, 5 January, 1965 E Yth						(D)
Derby Co.	App	12.82	82-89	157	9	1
Norwich C.	Tr	07.90	90-91	47	0	0
Wolverhampton W.	Tr	08.92	92-94	103	4	2
Rotherham U.	Tr	07.95	95-96	43	0	2
BLAGG Edward Arthur						
Worksop, 9 February, 1918 Died 1976						(CH)
Nottingham F.	Woodend	02.38	46-47	54	-	0
Southport	Tr	11.48	48	11	-	0
BLAIN Colin Anthony						
Urmston, 7 March, 1970						(M)
Halifax T.	YT	06.88	87-88	18	5	0
BLAIN James Donald						
Liverpool, 9 April, 1940						(M)
Everton	Jnrs	05.59				
Southport	Tr	02.60	59-62	127	-	40
Rotherham U.	Tr	12.62	62-63	23	-	1
Carlisle U.	Tr	04.64	64-65	41	0	7
Exeter C.	Tr	10.65	65-73	310	10	14

BLAIR Andrew
Kirkcaldy, 18 December, 1959 Su21-5 (M)

League Club	Source	Date Signed	Seasons Played	Apps	Subs	Gls
Coventry C.	App	10.77	78-80	90	3	6
Aston Villa	Tr	08.81	81-83	24	9	0
Wolverhampton W.	L	10.83	83	10	0	0
Sheffield Wed.	Tr	08.84	84-85	58	0	3
Aston Villa	Tr	03.86	85-87	19	2	1
Barnsley	L	03.88	87	6	0	0
Northampton T.	Tr	10.88	88	1	2	0

BLAIR Douglas
Ecclesfield, 26 June, 1921 (IF)

League Club	Source	Date Signed	Seasons Played	Apps	Subs	Gls
Blackpool		05.39				
Cardiff C.	Tr	08.47	48-53	201	-	28

BLAIR James
Calderbank, 13 January, 1947 (F)

League Club	Source	Date Signed	Seasons Played	Apps	Subs	Gls
Norwich C.	St Mirren	09.72	72-73	3	3	0

BLAIR James Alfred
Glasgow, 6 January, 1918 Died 1983 S-1 (IF)

League Club	Source	Date Signed	Seasons Played	Apps	Subs	Gls
Blackpool	Cardiff C. (Am)	06.35	37-46	50	-	7
Bournemouth	Tr	10.47	47-49	80	-	8
Leyton Orient	Tr	12.49	49-52	104	-	26

BLAIR Kenneth George
Portadown, 28 September, 1952 (M)

League Club	Source	Date Signed	Seasons Played	Apps	Subs	Gls
Derby Co.	Jnrs	06.70				
Halifax T.	Tr	10.74	74-75	42	1	4
Stockport Co.	L	02.76	75	7	0	0
Southport	Tr	08.76	76	17	0	0

BLAIR Ronald Victor
Coleraine (NI), 26 September, 1949 NI Sch/NI-5 (D)

League Club	Source	Date Signed	Seasons Played	Apps	Subs	Gls
Oldham Ath.	Coleraine	10.66	66-69	74	2	1
Rochdale	Tr	03.70	69-71	66	5	3
Oldham Ath.	Tr	08.72	72-80	285	10	22
Blackpool	Tr	08.81	81	35	1	3
Rochdale	Tr	08.82	82	3	0	0

BLAKE Antony John
Cofton Hackett, 26 February, 1927 (FB)

League Club	Source	Date Signed	Seasons Played	Apps	Subs	Gls
Birmingham C.	Rubery Owen	01.49	49	2	-	0
Gillingham	Tr	07.52	52	10	-	1

BLAKE James Bernard
Manchester, 5 May, 1966 (D)

League Club	Source	Date Signed	Seasons Played	Apps	Subs	Gls
Rochdale (N/C)	Jnrs	09.83	83	2	0	0

BLAKE Mark Antony
Nottingham, 16 December, 1970 E Sch/E Yth/Eu21-9 (M)

League Club	Source	Date Signed	Seasons Played	Apps	Subs	Gls
Aston Villa	YT	07.89	89-92	26	5	2
Wolverhampton W.	L	01.91	90	2	0	0
Portsmouth	Tr	08.93	93	15	0	0
Leicester C.	Tr	03.94	93-95	42	7	4
Walsall	Tr	08.96	96-97	51	10	5

BLAKE Mark Christopher
Portsmouth, 19 December, 1967 E Yth (CD)

League Club	Source	Date Signed	Seasons Played	Apps	Subs	Gls
Southampton	App	12.85	85-88	18	0	2
Colchester U.	L	09.89	89	4	0	1
Shrewsbury T.	L	03.90	89	10	0	0
Shrewsbury T.	Tr	07.90	90-93	132	0	3
Fulham	Tr	09.94	94-97	133	7	17

BLAKE Nathan Alexander
Cardiff, 27 January, 1972 W Yth/Wu21-5/W 'B'/W-7 (M)

League Club	Source	Date Signed	Seasons Played	Apps	Subs	Gls
Cardiff C.	Chelsea (YT)	03.90	89-93	113	18	35
Sheffield U.	Tr	02.94	93-95	55	14	34
Bolton W.	Tr	12.95	95-97	91	4	32

BLAKE Noel Lloyd George
Jamaica (WI), 12 January, 1962 (CD)

League Club	Source	Date Signed	Seasons Played	Apps	Subs	Gls
Aston Villa	Sutton Coldfield	08.79	79-81	4	0	0
Shrewsbury T.	L	03.82	81	6	0	0
Birmingham C.	Tr	09.82	82-83	76	0	5
Portsmouth	Tr	08.84	84-87	144	0	10
Leeds U.	Tr	07.88	88-89	51	0	4
Stoke C.	Tr	02.90	89-91	74	1	3
Bradford C.	L	02.92	91	6	0	0
Bradford C.	Tr	07.92	92-93	38	1	3
Exeter C.	Dundee	08.95	95-97	126	2	9

BLAKE Robert James
Middlesbrough, 4 March, 1976 (F)

League Club	Source	Date Signed	Seasons Played	Apps	Subs	Gls
Darlington	YT	07.94	94-96	54	14	21
Bradford C.	Tr	03.97	96-97	26	13	7

BLAKE Russell Timothy
Colchester, 24 July, 1935 (W)

League Club	Source	Date Signed	Seasons Played	Apps	Subs	Gls
Colchester U.		04.56	55-60	58	-	8

BLAKEMAN Alan
Oldham, 2 November, 1937 (F)

League Club	Source	Date Signed	Seasons Played	Apps	Subs	Gls
Rotherham U.	Ashton U.	05.58	58	2	-	0
Workington	Tr	01.59	58	14	-	8

BLAKEMAN Alec George
Headington, 11 June, 1918 Died 1994 (IF)

League Club	Source	Date Signed	Seasons Played	Apps	Subs	Gls
Brentford	Oxford C.	05.46	46-48	42	-	7
Sheffield U.	Tr	11.48	48	5	-	0
Bournemouth	Tr	02.49	48-49	25	-	8

BLAKEY David
Newburn, 22 August, 1929 (CH)

League Club	Source	Date Signed	Seasons Played	Apps	Subs	Gls
Chesterfield	Chevington Drift	05.47	48-66	617	0	20

BLAKIE James Shearlaw
Reston, 9 December, 1926 (F)

League Club	Source	Date Signed	Seasons Played	Apps	Subs	Gls
Barrow		08.50	50	9	-	1

BLAMEY Nathan
Plymouth, 10 June, 1977 (FB)

League Club	Source	Date Signed	Seasons Played	Apps	Subs	Gls
Southampton	YT	07.95				
Shrewsbury T.	Tr	02.97	96-97	15	0	1

BLAMPEY Stuart Leslie
North Ferriby, 13 June, 1951 (M)

League Club	Source	Date Signed	Seasons Played	Apps	Subs	Gls
Hull C.	Jnrs	08.68	69-74	61	11	1

BLANCHFLOWER Robert **Dennis (Danny)**
Belfast, 10 February, 1926 Died 1993 EF Lge/NI-56 (WH)

League Club	Source	Date Signed	Seasons Played	Apps	Subs	Gls
Barnsley	Glentoran	04.49	48-50	68	-	2
Aston Villa	Tr	03.51	50-54	148	-	10
Tottenham H.	Tr	12.54	54-63	337	-	15

BLANCHFLOWER John (Jackie)
Belfast, 7 March, 1933 Died 1998 NI Sch/NI-12 (CH)

League Club	Source	Date Signed	Seasons Played	Apps	Subs	Gls
Manchester U.	Jnrs	03.50	51-57	105	-	26

BLANEY Steven David
Orsett, 24 March, 1977 Wu21-3/E Sch (FB)

League Club	Source	Date Signed	Seasons Played	Apps	Subs	Gls
West Ham U.	YT	07.95				
Brentford	Tr	03.98	97	4	1	0

BLANKLEY Barry Steven
Aldershot, 27 October, 1964 (RB)

League Club	Source	Date Signed	Seasons Played	Apps	Subs	Gls
Southampton	App	10.82				
Aldershot	Tr	12.84	84-86	90	0	0

BLANT Colin
Rawtenstall, 7 October, 1946 (CD)

League Club	Source	Date Signed	Seasons Played	Apps	Subs	Gls
Burnley	Rossendale U.	08.64	66-69	46	7	7
Portsmouth	Tr	04.70	70-71	64	0	1
Rochdale	Tr	07.72	72-73	51	0	0
Darlington	Tr	01.74	73-75	89	0	0
Grimsby T.	Tr	08.76	76	9	0	0
Workington	Tr	11.76	76	21	0	0

BLATCHFORD Patrick John
Plymouth, 28 December, 1925 Died 1981 (OL)

League Club	Source	Date Signed	Seasons Played	Apps	Subs	Gls
Plymouth Arg.	Saltash U.	11.48	48-50	19	-	2
Leyton Orient	Tr	08.51	51-52	60	-	8

BLATHERWICK Steven Scott
Nottingham, 20 September, 1973 (CD)

League Club	Source	Date Signed	Seasons Played	Apps	Subs	Gls
Nottingham F.	Notts Co. (YT)	08.92	93-96	10	0	0
Wycombe W.	L	02.94	93	2	0	0
Hereford U.	L	09.95	95	10	0	1
Reading	L	03.97	96	6	1	0
Burnley	Tr	07.97	97	13	8	0

BLEANCH Norman Wesley Swan
Houghton-le-Spring, 19 August, 1940 (CF)

League Club	Source	Date Signed	Seasons Played	Apps	Subs	Gls
West Ham U.	Willington	02.60				
Southend U.	Tr	07.61	61	3	-	0
Bradford P.A.	Tr	11.61	61	9	-	3

BLEARS Brian Thomas
Prestatyn, 18 November, 1933 (IF)

League Club	Source	Date Signed	Seasons Played	Apps	Subs	Gls
Chester C.	Everton (Am)	07.54	54-55	2	-	0

BLEASDALE David George
St Helens, 23 March, 1965 (M)

League Club	Source	Date Signed	Seasons Played	Apps	Subs	Gls
Preston N.E.	Liverpool (App)	08.83	83	4	1	0

League Club	Source	Date Signed	Seasons Played	Career Record Apps	Subs	Gls

BLEASE Rory
Bebington, 16 August, 1960 (M)

League Club	Source	Date Signed	Seasons Played	Apps	Subs	Gls
Chester C. (N/C)	Caernarfon T.	12.84	84	4	0	0

BLENKINSOPP Thomas William
Bishop Auckland, 13 May, 1920 EF Lge (D)

League Club	Source	Date Signed	Seasons Played	Apps	Subs	Gls
Grimsby T.	West Auckland	03.39	46-47	74	-	10
Middlesbrough	Tr	05.48	48-52	98	-	0
Barnsley	Tr	11.52	52	8	-	0

BLICK Michael Robert
Berkeley, 20 September, 1948 (CH)

League Club	Source	Date Signed	Seasons Played	Apps	Subs	Gls
Swindon T.	App	09.66	67-70	6	0	0

BLINCOW Ernest
Walsall, 9 September, 1921 (OL)

League Club	Source	Date Signed	Seasons Played	Apps	Subs	Gls
Walsall (Am)	West Bromwich A. (Am)	01.47	46	1	-	0

BLINKER Reginald Waldie
Surinam, 4 June, 1969 Dutch Int (LW)

League Club	Source	Date Signed	Seasons Played	Apps	Subs	Gls
Sheffield Wed.	Feyenoord (Neth)	03.96	95-96	24	18	3

BLISSETT Gary Paul
Manchester, 29 June, 1964 (F)

League Club	Source	Date Signed	Seasons Played	Apps	Subs	Gls
Crewe Alex.	Altrincham	08.83	83-86	112	10	38
Brentford	Tr	03.87	86-92	220	13	79
Wimbledon	Tr	07.93	93-95	10	21	3
Wycombe W.	L	12.95	95	4	0	2
Crewe Alex.	L	03.96	95	10	0	1

BLISSETT Luther Loide
Jamaica (WI), 1 February, 1958 Eu21-4/E'B'/E-14 (F)

League Club	Source	Date Signed	Seasons Played	Apps	Subs	Gls
Watford	Jnrs	07.75	75-82	222	24	95
Watford	A.C. Milan (It)	08.84	84-88	113	14	44
Bournemouth	Tr	11.88	88-90	121	0	56
Watford	Tr	08.91	91	34	8	9
West Bromwich A.	L	10.92	92	3	0	1
Bury	Tr	08.93	93	8	2	1
Mansfield T.	L	12.93	93	4	1	1

BLIZZARD Leslie William Benjamin
Acton, 13 March, 1923 Died 1996 (WH)

League Club	Source	Date Signed	Seasons Played	Apps	Subs	Gls
Queens Park R.		07.41	46	5	-	0
Bournemouth	Tr	05.47	47	1	-	0
Leyton Orient	Yeovil T.	07.50	50-56	222	-	12

BLOCHEL Jozef Edward
Chalfont St Giles, 3 March, 1962 (F)

League Club	Source	Date Signed	Seasons Played	Apps	Subs	Gls
Southampton	App	03.80				
Wimbledon	L	01.82	81	6	0	1

BLOCK Michael John
Ipswich, 28 January, 1940 E Yth (OR)

League Club	Source	Date Signed	Seasons Played	Apps	Subs	Gls
Chelsea	Jnrs	02.57	57-61	37	-	6
Brentford	Tr	01.62	61-65	146	0	30
Watford	Tr	10.66	66	11	2	2

BLOCKLEY Jeffrey Paul
Leicester, 12 September, 1949 Eu23-10/EF Lge/E-1 (CD)

League Club	Source	Date Signed	Seasons Played	Apps	Subs	Gls
Coventry C.	App	06.67	68-72	144	2	6
Arsenal	Tr	10.72	72-74	52	0	1
Leicester C.	Tr	01.75	74-77	75	1	2
Notts Co.	Tr	06.78	78-79	57	2	5

BLONDEAU Patrick
Marseille, France, 27 January, 1968 French Int (RB)

League Club	Source	Date Signed	Seasons Played	Apps	Subs	Gls
Sheffield Wed.	Monaco (Fr)	07.97	97	5	1	0

BLONDEL Frederick
Lancaster, 31 October, 1923 Died 1989 (IF)

League Club	Source	Date Signed	Seasons Played	Apps	Subs	Gls
Bury	Morecambe	07.46	46	1	-	0

BLOOD John Foster
Nottingham, 2 October, 1914 Died 1992 (FB)

League Club	Source	Date Signed	Seasons Played	Apps	Subs	Gls
Notts Co	Johnson & Barnes	06.38	38	8	-	0
Exeter C.	Tr	05.39	46-47	39	-	1

BLOOMER Brian McGregor
Cleethorpes, 3 May, 1952 (F)

League Club	Source	Date Signed	Seasons Played	Apps	Subs	Gls
Scunthorpe U.	Brigg T.	08.78	78	3	4	1

BLOOMER James
Rutherglen, 10 April, 1926 (IF)

League Club	Source	Date Signed	Seasons Played	Apps	Subs	Gls
Hull C.	Strathclyde	02.48	47	4	-	2
Grimsby T.	Tr	07.49	49-54	109	-	42

BLOOMER James Moore
Glasgow, 22 August, 1947 (FB)

League Club	Source	Date Signed	Seasons Played	Apps	Subs	Gls
Grimsby T.	Jnrs	11.64	65-68	48	4	0

BLOOMER Robert Stephen
Sheffield, 21 June, 1966 (FB/M)

League Club	Source	Date Signed	Seasons Played	Apps	Subs	Gls
Chesterfield	Jnrs	08.85	85-89	120	21	15
Bristol Rov.	Tr	03.90	90-91	11	11	0

BLOOMFIELD Edward William Ashworth
Wisbech, 28 June, 1932 (OR)

League Club	Source	Date Signed	Seasons Played	Apps	Subs	Gls
Carlisle U.	Wisbech Cons. F.C.	08.53	53-55	5	-	1
Southport	Tr	07.56	56	2	-	0

BLOOMFIELD James Henry
Kensington, 15 February, 1934 Died 1983 Eu23-2/EF Lge (IF)

League Club	Source	Date Signed	Seasons Played	Apps	Subs	Gls
Brentford	Walthamstow Ave.	10.52	52-53	42	-	5
Arsenal	Tr	07.54	54-60	210	-	54
Birmingham C.	Tr	11.60	60-63	123	-	28
Brentford	Tr	06.64	64-65	44	0	4
West Ham U.	Tr	10.65	65	9	1	0
Plymouth Arg.	Tr	09.66	66-67	25	0	1
Leyton Orient	Tr	03.68	67-68	43	2	3

BLOOMFIELD Raymond George
Kensington, 15 October, 1944 E Sch/E Yth (W)

League Club	Source	Date Signed	Seasons Played	Apps	Subs	Gls
Arsenal	Jnrs	11.61				
Aston Villa	Tr	08.64	64-65	3	0	0

BLOOMFIELD William George
Kensington, 25 August, 1939 (IF)

League Club	Source	Date Signed	Seasons Played	Apps	Subs	Gls
Brentford	Jnrs	08.56	56-57	2	-	0

BLOOR Alan
Stoke, 16 March, 1943 E Yth (D)

League Club	Source	Date Signed	Seasons Played	Apps	Subs	Gls
Stoke C.	Jnrs	03.60	61-76	384	4	17
Port Vale	Tr	06.78	78	5	1	1

BLOOR Michael Bennett
Wrexham, 25 March, 1949 (FB)

League Club	Source	Date Signed	Seasons Played	Apps	Subs	Gls
Stoke C.	Newport (Salop)	04.67				
Lincoln C.	Tr	05.71	71-72	71	2	0
Darlington	Tr	08.73	73	7	0	0

BLOOR Robert
Stoke, 8 July, 1932 (LH)

League Club	Source	Date Signed	Seasons Played	Apps	Subs	Gls
Crewe Alex.		01.54	53-54	25	-	1

BLORE Reginald
Wrexham, 18 March, 1942 Wu23-4 (W)

League Club	Source	Date Signed	Seasons Played	Apps	Subs	Gls
Liverpool	Jnrs	05.59	59	1	-	0
Southport	Tr	07.60	60-63	139	-	55
Blackburn Rov.	Tr	11.63	63-65	11	0	0
Oldham Ath.	Tr	12.65	65-69	182	5	20

BLOSS Philip Kenneth
Colchester, 16 January, 1953 (M)

League Club	Source	Date Signed	Seasons Played	Apps	Subs	Gls
Colchester U.	App	01.71	70-72	32	2	2

BLOTT John Paul
Redcar, 26 February, 1965 (G)

League Club	Source	Date Signed	Seasons Played	Apps	Subs	Gls
Manchester C.	Jnrs	09.82				
Carlisle U.	Scunthorpe U. (N/C)	11.84	84	2	0	0
Newport Co. (N/C)	Mansfield T. (N/C)	03.87	86	1	0	0

BLOUNT Mark
Derby, 5 January, 1974 (D)

League Club	Source	Date Signed	Seasons Played	Apps	Subs	Gls
Sheffield U.	Gresley Rov.	02.94	94-95	11	2	0
Peterborough U. (N/C)	Tr	03.96	95	4	1	0

BLOWMAN Peter
Billingham, 12 December, 1949 (F)

League Club	Source	Date Signed	Seasons Played	Apps	Subs	Gls
Hartlepool U.		11.67	67-69	57	9	15

BLOXHAM James **Alexander**
Shirebrook, 2 July, 1920 Died 1982 (W)

League Club	Source	Date Signed	Seasons Played	Apps	Subs	Gls
Hull C.	Ollerton Colly.	10.47	47-49	33	-	2

BLUCK David
India, 31 January, 1930 (LH)

League Club	Source	Date Signed	Seasons Played	Apps	Subs	Gls
Aldershot (Am)		08.51	51	1	-	0

BLUE Archibald
Glasgow, 8 April, 1940 (CF)

League Club	Source	Date Signed	Seasons Played	Apps	Subs	Gls
Exeter C.	Hearts	07.61	61	34	-	6
Carlisle U.	Tr	07.62	62	2	-	1

BLUNDELL Alan
Birkenhead, 18 August, 1947 (WH)

League Club	Source	Date Signed	Seasons Played	Apps	Subs	Gls
Tranmere Rov	App	08.65	65-66	3	0	0

League Club	Source	Date Signed	Seasons Played	Career Record Apps	Subs	Gls
BLUNDELL Christopher Keith						
Billinge, 7 December, 1969						(CD)
Oldham Ath.	YT	07.88	87-88	2	1	0
Rochdale	Tr	09.90	90	10	4	0
BLUNSTONE Frank						
Crewe, 17 October, 1934 E Yth/Eu23-5/EF Lge/E-5						(OL)
Crewe Alex.	Jnrs	01.52	51-52	48	-	12
Chelsea	Tr	03.53	52-63	317	-	47
BLUNT David						
Goldthorpe, 29 April, 1949						(IF)
Bradford P.A. (Am)		03.68	67	2	0	0
Chester C.	Tr	06.68				
BLUNT Edwin						
Tunstall, 21 May, 1918 Died 1993						(WH)
Northampton T.	Lichfield T.	05.37	37-48	87	-	2
Accrington St.	Tr	07.49	49	9	-	1
BLUNT Jason						
Penzance, 16 August, 1977 E Yth						(M)
Leeds U.	YT	01.95	95-96	2	2	0
BLY Terence Geoffrey						
Fincham (Nk), 22 October, 1935						(CF)
Norwich C.	Bury T.	08.56	56-59	57	-	31
Peterborough U.	Tr	06.60	60-61	88	-	81
Coventry C.	Tr	07.62	62-63	32	-	26
Notts Co.	Tr	08.63	63-64	29	-	4
BLY William						
Newcastle, 15 May, 1920 Died 1982						(G)
Hull C.	Walkers Temp.	08.37	38-59	403	-	0
BLYTH James Anton						
Perth, 2 February, 1955 S-2						(G)
Preston N.E.	App	10.72	71	1	0	0
Coventry C.	Tr	10.72	75-81	151	0	0
Hereford U.	L	03.75	74	7	0	0
Birmingham C.	Tr	08.82	82	14	0	0
BLYTH John William						
Edinburgh, 26 May, 1947						(WH)
Halifax T.		05.67	66-67	5	0	0
BLYTH Melvyn Bernard						
Norwich, 28 July, 1944						(CD)
Scunthorpe U.	Great Yarmouth	11.67	67	27	0	3
Crystal Palace	Tr	07.68	68-74	213	3	9
Southampton	Tr	09.74	74-76	104	1	6
Crystal Palace	L	11.77	77	6	0	0
Millwall	Margate	11.78	78-80	75	0	0
BLYTHE John **David**						
Huddersfield, 21 July, 1947						(CF)
Hartlepool U. (Am)	Crook T.	01.70	69	1	1	0
BLYTHE John Alfred						
Darlington, 31 January, 1924						(CH)
Darlington		06.46	46-48	17	-	0
BOAG James						
Blairhall, 12 November, 1937						(G)
Exeter C.	Bath C.	10.62	62	2	-	0
BOAM Stuart William						
Kirkby-in-Ashfield, 28 January, 1948						(CD)
Mansfield T.	Kirkby B.C.	07.66	66-70	175	0	3
Middlesbrough	Tr	06.71	71-78	322	0	14
Newcastle U.	Tr	08.79	79-80	69	0	1
Mansfield T.	Tr	07.81	81-82	11	4	1
Hartlepool U. (N/C)	Tr	03.83	82	1	0	0
BOARDMAN Craig George						
Barnsley, 30 November, 1970						(CD)
Nottingham F.	YT	05.89				
Peterborough U.	Tr	08.93				
Scarborough	Halifax T.	08.95	95	6	3	0
BOARDMAN George						
Glasgow, 14 August, 1943 S Amat						(IF)
Shrewsbury T.	Queens Park	06.63	63-68	172	4	50
Barnsley	Tr	06.69	69-72	123	3	14
BOARDMAN Paul						
Tottenham, 6 November, 1967						(F)
Plymouth Arg.	Knowsley U.	08.92	92-93	2	1	1

League Club	Source	Date Signed	Seasons Played	Career Record Apps	Subs	Gls
BOATENG George						
Ghana, 5 September, 1975						(M)
Coventry C.	Feyenoord (Neth)	12.97	97	14	0	1
BOCHENSKI Simon						
Worksop, 6 December, 1975						(F)
Barnsley	YT	07.94	95	0	1	0
Scarborough	Tr	08.96	96	5	14	1
BODAK Peter John						
Birmingham, 12 August, 1961						(M)
Coventry C.	App	05.79	80-81	30	2	5
Manchester U.	Tr	08.82				
Manchester C.	Tr	12.82	82	12	2	1
Crewe Alex.	Antwerp (Bel)	12.86	86-87	49	4	7
Swansea C.	Tr	03.88	87-88	25	6	4
Walsall (N/C)	Happy Valley (HK)	08.90	90	3	1	1
BODEL Andrew Cunningham						
Clydebank, 12 February, 1957						(CD)
Oxford U.	App	02.75	75-79	128	0	11
BODELL Norman						
Oldham, 29 January, 1938						(D)
Rochdale		09.56	58-62	79	-	1
Crewe Alex.	Tr	05.63	63-66	108	1	2
Halifax T.	Tr	10.66	66-67	36	0	0
BODEN Christopher Desmond						
Wolverhampton, 13 October, 1973						(LB)
Aston Villa	YT	12.91	94	0	1	0
Barnsley	L	10.93	93	4	0	0
Derby Co.	Tr	03.95	94-95	8	2	0
Shrewsbury T.	L	01.96	95	5	0	0
BODEN John Gilbert						
Grimsby, 4 October, 1926						(OR)
Lincoln C.	Skegness T.	04.50	49-50	3	-	2
BODEN Kenneth						
Thrybergh, 5 July, 1950						(M)
Doncaster Rov.	Bridlington T.	03.77	76	1	0	0
BODIN Paul John						
Cardiff, 13 September, 1964 W Yth/Wu21-1/W-23						(LB)
Newport Co.	Chelsea (Jnrs)	01.82				
Cardiff C.	Tr	08.82	82-84	68	7	4
Newport Co.	Bath C.	01.88	87	6	0	1
Swindon T.	Tr	03.88	87-90	87	6	9
Crystal Palace	Tr	03.91	90-91	8	1	0
Newcastle U.	L	12.91	91	6	0	0
Swindon T.	Tr	01.92	91-95	140	6	28
Reading	Tr	07.96	96-97	40	1	1
Wycombe W.	L	09.97	97	5	0	0
BODLE Harold						
Adwick-le-Street, 4 October, 1920						(IF)
Rotherham U.	Ridgehill Ath.	05.38	38	9	-	0
Birmingham C.	Tr	12.38	38-48	95	-	32
Bury	Tr	03.49	48-51	119	-	40
Stockport Co.	Tr	10.52	52	29	-	6
Accrington St.	Tr	08.53	53-56	94	-	13
BODLEY Michael John						
Hayes, 14 September, 1967						(CD)
Chelsea	App	09.85	87	6	0	1
Northampton T.	Tr	01.89	88	20	0	0
Barnet	Tr	09.89	91-92	69	0	3
Southend U.	Tr	07.93	93-95	66	1	2
Gillingham	L	11.94	94	6	1	0
Birmingham C.	L	01.95	94	3	0	0
Peterborough U.	Tr	07.96	96-97	62	0	1
BOERE Jeroen Willem						
Holland, 18 November, 1967						(F)
West Ham U.	Go Ahead Eagles (Neth)	09.93	93-95	15	10	6
Portsmouth	L	03.94	93	4	1	0
West Bromwich A.	L	09.94	94	5	0	0
Crystal Palace	Tr	09.95	95	0	8	1
Southend U.	Tr	03.96	95-97	61	12	25
BOERSMA Philip						
Liverpool, 24 September, 1949						(M)
Liverpool	Jnrs	09.68	69-75	73	9	17
Wrexham	L	03.70	69	4	3	0
Middlesbrough	Tr	12.75	75-76	41	6	3
Luton T.	Tr	08.77	77-78	35	1	8
Swansea C.	Tr	09.78	78	15	3	1

BOERTIEN Paul
Haltwhistle, 20 January, 1979 (FB)

League Club	Source	Date Signed	Seasons Played	Apps	Subs	Gls
Carlisle U.	YT	05.97	97	8	1	0

BOGAN Thomas
Glasgow, 18 May, 1920 Died 1993 SF Lge (IF)

League Club	Source	Date Signed	Seasons Played	Apps	Subs	Gls
Preston N.E.	Glasgow Celtic	10.48	48	11	-	0
Manchester U.	Tr	08.49	49-50	29	-	7
Southampton	Aberdeen	12.51	51-52	8	-	2
Blackburn Rov.	Tr	08.53	53	1	-	0

BOGIE Ian
Newcastle, 6 December, 1967 E Sch (M)

League Club	Source	Date Signed	Seasons Played	Apps	Subs	Gls
Newcastle U.	App	12.85	86-88	7	7	0
Preston N.E.	Tr	02.89	88-90	67	12	12
Millwall	Tr	08.91	91-93	44	7	1
Leyton Orient	Tr	10.93	93-94	62	3	5
Port Vale	Tr	03.95	94-97	94	16	7

BOGIE Malcolm Fisher McKenzie
Edinburgh, 26 December, 1939 S Sch (IF)

League Club	Source	Date Signed	Seasons Played	Apps	Subs	Gls
Grimsby T.	Hibernian	07.63	63	1	-	0
Aldershot	Tr	07.64	64	2	-	1

BOHINEN Lars
Norway, 8 September, 1969 Norwegian Int (M)

League Club	Source	Date Signed	Seasons Played	Apps	Subs	Gls
Nottingham F.	Young Boys of Berne (Swi)	11.93	93-95	59	5	7
Blackburn Rov.	Tr	10.95	95-97	40	18	7
Derby Co.	Tr	03.98	97	9	0	1

BOLAM Thomas Edward
Newcastle, 8 July, 1924 (CH)

League Club	Source	Date Signed	Seasons Played	Apps	Subs	Gls
Barrow		08.50	50-51	35	-	0

BOLAND William John
Ennis (Ire), 6 August, 1975 IR Sch/IR Yth/IRu21-11/R 'B' (M)

League Club	Source	Date Signed	Seasons Played	Apps	Subs	Gls
Coventry C.	Jnrs	11.92	92-97	43	20	0

BOLDER Robert John
Dover, 2 October, 1958 (G)

League Club	Source	Date Signed	Seasons Played	Apps	Subs	Gls
Sheffield Wed.	Dover T.	03.77	77-82	196	0	0
Liverpool	Tr	08.83				
Sunderland	Tr	09.85	85	22	0	0
Charlton Ath.	Tr	08.86	86-92	249	0	0

BOLESAN Mirko
Italy, 6 May, 1975 (CD)

League Club	Source	Date Signed	Seasons Played	Apps	Subs	Gls
Cardiff C. (N/C)	Sestrese (It)	10.95	95	0	1	0

BOLI Roger Zokou
Ivory Coast, 29 June, 1965 (F)

League Club	Source	Date Signed	Seasons Played	Apps	Subs	Gls
Walsall	Lens (Fr)	08.97	97	41	0	12

BOLLAND Gordon Edward
Boston, 12 August, 1943 (IF)

League Club	Source	Date Signed	Seasons Played	Apps	Subs	Gls
Chelsea	Jnrs	08.60	61	2	-	0
Leyton Orient	Tr	03.62	61-63	63	-	19
Norwich C.	Tr	03.64	63-67	104	1	29
Charlton Ath.	Tr	11.67	67-68	9	2	2
Millwall	Tr	10.68	68-74	239	5	62

BOLLAND Paul Graham
Bradford, 23 December, 1979 (M)

League Club	Source	Date Signed	Seasons Played	Apps	Subs	Gls
Bradford C.	YT	03.98	97	2	8	0

BOLLANDS John Frederick
Middlesbrough, 11 July, 1935 (G)

League Club	Source	Date Signed	Seasons Played	Apps	Subs	Gls
Oldham Ath.	South Bank	05.53	54-55	23	-	0
Sunderland	Tr	03.56	55-59	61	-	0
Bolton W,	Tr	02.60	59	13	-	0
Oldham Ath.	Tr	09.61	61-65	131	0	0

BOLT Daniel Anthony
Wandsworth, 5 February, 1976 (LM)

League Club	Source	Date Signed	Seasons Played	Apps	Subs	Gls
Fulham	YT	07.94	94-95	9	4	2

BOLTON Anthony Gordon
Newport, 15 January, 1968 (W)

League Club	Source	Date Signed	Seasons Played	Apps	Subs	Gls
Charlton Ath.	Jnrs	01.85				
Newport Co.	Tr	08.86	86	6	2	0

BOLTON Ian Robert
Leicester, 13 July, 1953 (CD)

League Club	Source	Date Signed	Seasons Played	Apps	Subs	Gls
Notts Co.	Birmingham C. (App)	03.72	71-76	61	9	4
Lincoln C.	L	08.76	76	1	0	0
Watford	Tr	08.77	77-83	233	1	28
Brentford	Tr	12.83	83	14	0	1

BOLTON John (Jack) McCaig
Lesmahagow, 26 October, 1941 (D)

League Club	Source	Date Signed	Seasons Played	Apps	Subs	Gls
Ipswich T.	Raith Rov.	07.63	63-65	69	0	2

BOLTON Joseph
Birtley, 2 February, 1955 (LB)

League Club	Source	Date Signed	Seasons Played	Apps	Subs	Gls
Sunderland	App	02.72	71-80	264	9	11
Middlesbrough	Tr	07.81	81-82	59	0	1
Sheffield U.	Tr	08.83	83-85	109	0	2

BOLTON Lyall
Gateshead, 11 July, 1932 (WH)

League Club	Source	Date Signed	Seasons Played	Apps	Subs	Gls
Sunderland	Windy Nook Jnrs	08.50	55-56	3	-	0

BOLTON Nigel Alan
Bishop Auckland, 14 January, 1975 (F)

League Club	Source	Date Signed	Seasons Played	Apps	Subs	Gls
Darlington	Shildon	08.94	94	1	1	0

BOLTON Ronald (Danny)
Rotherham, 1 September, 1921 (G)

League Club	Source	Date Signed	Seasons Played	Apps	Subs	Gls
Bolton W.		05.39				
Rotherham U.	Owen & Dyson	06.48	48-54	151	-	0

BOLTON Ronald
Golborne, 21 January, 1938 (M)

League Club	Source	Date Signed	Seasons Played	Apps	Subs	Gls
Bournemouth	Crompton Rov.	04.58	58-65	199	0	31
Ipswich T.	Tr	10.65	65-67	21	1	0
Bournemouth	Tr	09.67	67-68	61	4	17

BONALAIR Thierry
Paris, France, 14 June, 1966 (M)

League Club	Source	Date Signed	Seasons Played	Apps	Subs	Gls
Nottingham F.	Neuchatel Xamax (Swi)	07.97	97	24	7	2

BOND Anthony
Preston, 23 December, 1913 Died 1991 (OR)

League Club	Source	Date Signed	Seasons Played	Apps	Subs	Gls
Blackburn Rov.	Dick Kerr's	04.32				
Wolverhampton W.	Chorley	11.36				
Torquay U.	Tr	06.37	37	15	-	0
Southport	Leyland Motors	08.45				
Accrington St.	Tr	05.46	46	29	-	4

BOND Dennis Joseph Thomas
Walthamstow, 17 March, 1947 E Sch/E Yth (M)

League Club	Source	Date Signed	Seasons Played	Apps	Subs	Gls
Watford	App	03.64	64-66	93	0	17
Tottenham H.	Tr	03.67	66-70	20	3	1
Charlton Ath.	Tr	10.70	70-72	70	5	3
Watford	Tr	02.73	72-77	178	1	20

BOND James **Ernest**
Preston, 4 May, 1929 (OL)

League Club	Source	Date Signed	Seasons Played	Apps	Subs	Gls
Manchester U.	Leyland Motors	12.50	51-52	20	-	4
Carlisle U.	Tr	09.52	52-58	194	-	23

BOND Graham Charles
Torquay, 30 December, 1932 (IF)

League Club	Source	Date Signed	Seasons Played	Apps	Subs	Gls
Torquay U.	Hele Spurs	09.51	53-60	128	-	46
Exeter C.	Tr	10.60	60	10	-	4
Torquay U.	Weymouth	10.61	61	5	-	1

BOND John
Dedham 17 December, 1932 EF Lge (FB)

League Club	Source	Date Signed	Seasons Played	Apps	Subs	Gls
West Ham U.	Colchester Casuals	03.50	51-64	381	-	32
Torquay U.	Tr	01.66	65-68	129	1	12

BOND Kevin John
West Ham, 22 June, 1957 (CD)

League Club	Source	Date Signed	Seasons Played	Apps	Subs	Gls
Norwich C.	Bournemouth (App)	07.74	75-80	137	5	12
Manchester C.	Seattle (USA)	09.81	81-84	108	2	11
Southampton	Tr	09.84	84-87	139	1	6
Bournemouth	Tr	08.88	88-91	121	5	4
Exeter C.	Tr	08.92	92-93	18	1	0

BOND Leonard Allan
Ilminster (Som), 12 February, 1954 (G)

League Club	Source	Date Signed	Seasons Played	Apps	Subs	Gls
Bristol C.	App	09.71	70-76	30	0	0
Exeter C.	L	11.74	74	30	0	0
Torquay U.	L	10.75	75	3	0	0
Scunthorpe U.	L	12.75	75	8	0	0
Colchester U.	L	01.76	75	3	0	0
Brentford	Tr	08.77	77-79	122	0	0
Exeter C.	Tr	10.80	80-83	138	0	0

BOND Richard
Blyth, 27 October, 1965 (F)

League Club	Source	Date Signed	Seasons Played	Apps	Subs	Gls
Blackpool	Blyth Spartans	12.91	92	0	1	0

BONDS William Arthur
Woolwich, 17 September, 1946 Eu23-2 (CD)

League Club	Source	Date Signed	Seasons Played	Apps	Subs	Gls
Charlton Ath.	App	09.64	64-66	95	0	1
West Ham U.	Tr	05.67	67-87	655	8	48

BONE James
Bridge of Allan, 22 September, 1949 Su23-3/S-2 (F)

League Club	Source	Date Signed	Seasons Played	Apps	Subs	Gls
Norwich C.	Partick Thistle	02.72	71-72	39	0	9
Sheffield U.	Tr	02.73	72-73	30	1	9

BONE John
Hartlepool, 19 December, 1930 (CH)

League Club	Source	Date Signed	Seasons Played	Apps	Subs	Gls
Sunderland	Wingate	05.51	54-56	11	-	0

BONER David
Queensferry, 12 October, 1941 S Sch (OR)

League Club	Source	Date Signed	Seasons Played	Apps	Subs	Gls
Everton	Jnrs	10.58				
Mansfield T.	Raith Rov.	07.63	63	12	-	1

BONETTI Ivano
Italy, 1 August, 1964 Italian Int (LM)

League Club	Source	Date Signed	Seasons Played	Apps	Subs	Gls
Grimsby T.	Torino (It)	09.95	95	19	0	3
Tranmere Rov.	Tr	08.96	96	9	4	1
Crystal Palace (N/C)	Bologna (It)	10.97	97	0	2	0

BONETTI Peter Phillip
Putney, 27 September, 1941 Eu23-12/EF Lge/E-7 (G)

League Club	Source	Date Signed	Seasons Played	Apps	Subs	Gls
Chelsea	Jnrs	05.59	59-78	600	0	0

BONNAR Patrick (Paddy)
Ballymena (NI), 27 November, 1920 LoI (OR)

League Club	Source	Date Signed	Seasons Played	Apps	Subs	Gls
Barnsley	Belfast Celtic	08.49	49	5	-	1
Aldershot	Tr	06.50	50-52	63	-	19

BONNELL Arnold
Barnsley, 23 March, 1921 (FB)

League Club	Source	Date Signed	Seasons Played	Apps	Subs	Gls
Barnsley	Jnrs	04.38	46-47	7	-	0
Rochdale	Tr	07.48	48	5	-	0

BONNER Bernard
Motherwell 22 July, 1927 (CF)

League Club	Source	Date Signed	Seasons Played	Apps	Subs	Gls
Wrexham	Airdrieonians	02.52	51	1	-	0

BONNER Mark
Ormskirk, 7 June, 1974 (M)

League Club	Source	Date Signed	Seasons Played	Apps	Subs	Gls
Blackpool	YT	06.92	91-97	156	22	14

BONNYMAN Philip
Glasgow, 6 February, 1954 (M)

League Club	Source	Date Signed	Seasons Played	Apps	Subs	Gls
Carlisle U.	Hamilton Academical	03.76	75-79	149	3	26
Chesterfield	Tr	03.80	79-81	98	1	25
Grimsby T.	Tr	08.82	82-86	146	5	15
Stoke C.	L	03.86	85	7	0	0
Darlington	Tr	07.87	87-88	49	1	5

BONSON Joseph
Barnsley, 19 June, 1936 Died 1991 (CF)

League Club	Source	Date Signed	Seasons Played	Apps	Subs	Gls
Wolverhampton W.	Jnrs	07.53	56	10	-	3
Cardiff C.	Tr	11.57	57-59	72	-	37
Scunthorpe U.	Tr	06.60	60-61	52	-	11
Doncaster Rov.	Tr	02.62	61	14	-	4
Newport Co.	Tr	06.62	62-63	83	-	47
Brentford	Tr	06.64	64-65	35	0	13
Lincoln C.	Tr	01.66	65-66	46	1	16

BOOGERS Marco
Netherlands, 12 January, 1967 (F)

League Club	Source	Date Signed	Seasons Played	Apps	Subs	Gls
West Ham U.	Sparta Rotterdam (Neth)	07.95	95	0	4	0

BOOK Anthony Keith
Bath, 4 September, 1934 (FB)

League Club	Source	Date Signed	Seasons Played	Apps	Subs	Gls
Plymouth Arg.	Bath C.	08.64	64-65	81	0	3
Manchester C.	Tr	07.66	66-73	242	2	4

BOOK Kim Alistair
Bath, 12 February, 1946 (G)

League Club	Source	Date Signed	Seasons Played	Apps	Subs	Gls
Bournemouth	Frome T.	07.67	67-68	2	0	0
Northampton T.	Tr	10.69	69-71	78	0	0
Mansfield T.	L	09.71	71	4	0	0
Doncaster Rov.	Tr	12.71	71-73	84	0	0

BOOKER Kenneth
Sheffield, 3 March, 1918 (CH)

League Club	Source	Date Signed	Seasons Played	Apps	Subs	Gls
Chesterfield	Dronfield	04.36	38-51	183	-	4
Shrewsbury T.	Tr	07.52	52	9	-	0

BOOKER Michael
Barnsley, 22 October, 1947 E Sch (FB)

League Club	Source	Date Signed	Seasons Played	Apps	Subs	Gls
Barnsley	App	10.65	66	0	2	0
Bradford P.A.	Tr	06.68	68	11	2	0

BOOKER Robert
Watford, 25 January, 1958 (M)

League Club	Source	Date Signed	Seasons Played	Apps	Subs	Gls
Brentford	Bedmond Social	10.78	78-88	207	44	42
Sheffield U.	Tr	11.88	88-91	91	18	13
Brentford	Tr	11.91	91-92	15	4	2

BOOKER Trevor Christopher
Lambeth, 26 February, 1969 (F)

League Club	Source	Date Signed	Seasons Played	Apps	Subs	Gls
Millwall (N/C)	Jnrs	07.86	86	1	2	0

BOORN Alan
Folkestone, 11 April, 1953 E Yth (M)

League Club	Source	Date Signed	Seasons Played	Apps	Subs	Gls
Brighton & H.A.	Coventry C. (Am)	08.71	72	2	0	0

BOOT Edmund
Rotherham, 13 October, 1915 (WH)

League Club	Source	Date Signed	Seasons Played	Apps	Subs	Gls
Sheffield U.	Denaby U.	10.35	35-36	41	-	0
Huddersfield T.	Tr	03.37	36-51	305	-	5

BOOT Michael Colin
Leicester, 17 December, 1947 E Sch (F)

League Club	Source	Date Signed	Seasons Played	Apps	Subs	Gls
Arsenal	App	12.64	66	3	1	2

BOOTH Andrew David
Huddersfield, 6 December, 1973 Eu21-3 (F)

League Club	Source	Date Signed	Seasons Played	Apps	Subs	Gls
Huddersfield T.	YT	06.92	91-95	109	14	54
Sheffield Wed.	Tr	07.96	96-97	53	5	17

BOOTH Anthony John
Biggin Hill, 20 June, 1961 (M)

League Club	Source	Date Signed	Seasons Played	Apps	Subs	Gls
Charlton Ath.	Jnrs	06.78	78-79	2	6	0

BOOTH Colin
Manchester, 30 December, 1934 Eu23-1 (IF)

League Club	Source	Date Signed	Seasons Played	Apps	Subs	Gls
Wolverhampton W.	Jnrs	01.52	54-59	78	-	26
Nottingham F.	Tr	10.59	59-61	87	-	39
Doncaster Rov.	Tr	08.62	62-63	88	-	57
Oxford U.	Tr	07.64	64-65	48	0	23

BOOTH David
Darton, 2 October, 1948 (FB)

League Club	Source	Date Signed	Seasons Played	Apps	Subs	Gls
Barnsley	Jnrs	05.67	68-71	161	3	8
Grimsby T.	Tr	06.72	72-77	199	1	7

BOOTH David Christopher
Wilmslow, 25 October, 1962 (M)

League Club	Source	Date Signed	Seasons Played	Apps	Subs	Gls
Stockport Co.	Jnrs	04.80	79-80	20	8	4

BOOTH Dennis
Ilkeston, 9 April, 1949 (M)

League Club	Source	Date Signed	Seasons Played	Apps	Subs	Gls
Charlton Ath.	App	04.66	66-70	67	10	5
Blackpool	Tr	07.71	71	12	0	0
Southend U.	Tr	03.72	71-73	77	1	1
Lincoln C.	Tr	02.74	73-77	162	0	9
Watford	Tr	10.77	77-79	97	3	2
Hull C.	Tr	05.80	80-84	121	2	2

BOOTH Grenville Vincent
Chester, 2 April, 1925 Died 1990 (LH)

League Club	Source	Date Signed	Seasons Played	Apps	Subs	Gls
Chester C.	Jnrs	08.48	48	8	-	0

BOOTH Kenneth Kershaw
Blackpool, 22 November, 1934 (IF)

League Club	Source	Date Signed	Seasons Played	Apps	Subs	Gls
Blackpool	Jnrs	01.52	54-56	2	-	1
Bradford P.A.	Tr	05.57	57-58	45	-	14
Workington	Tr	06.59	59	30	-	13
Southport	Tr	07.60	60	26	-	7

BOOTH Paul
Bolton, 7 December, 1965 (FB)

League Club	Source	Date Signed	Seasons Played	Apps	Subs	Gls
Bolton W.	App	12.83	84	1	0	0
Crewe Alex.	Tr	07.85	85	23	4	0

BOOTH Raymond
Wrexham, 5 September, 1949 (W)

League Club	Source	Date Signed	Seasons Played	Apps	Subs	Gls
Wrexham	Jnrs	10.67	66-68	5	0	0

BOOTH Samuel Stewart
Shotts, 20 April, 1926 (WH)

League Club	Source	Date Signed	Seasons Played	Apps	Subs	Gls
Exeter C.	Derry C.	08.51	51-53	62	-	0
Bradford C.	Tr	07.54	54	15	-	0

BOOTH William Samuel
Hove, 7 July, 1920 Died 1990 (CH/F)

League Club	Source	Date Signed	Seasons Played	Apps	Subs	Gls
Port Vale	Brighton & H.A. (Am)	02.39	38	9	-	0
Cardiff C.	Tr	05.39				
Brighton & H.A.	Tr	08.47	47-48	28	-	6

BOOTH Thomas Anthony
Manchester, 9 November, 1949 Eu23-4 (CD)

League Club	Source	Date Signed	Seasons Played	Apps	Subs	Gls
Manchester C.	Jnrs	08.67	68-81	380	2	25
Preston N.E.	Tr	10.81	81-84	84	0	2

BOOTH Wilfred
Mapplewell, 26 December, 1918 (F)

League Club	Source	Date Signed	Seasons Played	Apps	Subs	Gls
Halifax T.	Wombwell Ath.	12.47	47	5	-	2

BOOTHMAN James
Great Harwood, 2 December, 1920 Died 1980 (FB)

League Club	Source	Date Signed	Seasons Played	Apps	Subs	Gls
Oldham Ath.		01.46	46-47	44	-	0

BOOTHROYD Adrian Neil
Bradford, 8 February, 1971 (FB)

League Club	Source	Date Signed	Seasons Played	Apps	Subs	Gls
Huddersfield T.	YT	07.89	89	9	1	0
Bristol Rov.	Tr	06.90	90-91	10	6	0
Mansfield T.	Hearts	12.93	93-95	99	3	3
Peterborough U.	Tr	07.96	96	24	2	1

BOOTHWAY John
Manchester, 4 February, 1919 Died 1979 (CF)

League Club	Source	Date Signed	Seasons Played	Apps	Subs	Gls
Manchester C.		07.41				
Crewe Alex.	Tr	07.44	46	11	-	5
Wrexham	Tr	10.46	46-49	95	-	55

BOOTLE William
Ashton-u-Lyne, 9 January, 1926 (W)

League Club	Source	Date Signed	Seasons Played	Apps	Subs	Gls
Manchester C.	Jnrs	06.43	48-49	5	-	0
Crewe Alex.	Wigan Ath.	03.54	53-54	14	-	4

BOOTY Justin
Colchester, 2 June, 1976 (F)

League Club	Source	Date Signed	Seasons Played	Apps	Subs	Gls
Colchester U.	YT	08.94	93	0	1	0

BOOTY Martyn James
Kirby Muxloe, 30 May, 1971 (RB)

League Club	Source	Date Signed	Seasons Played	Apps	Subs	Gls
Coventry C.	YT	06.89	91-93	4	1	0
Crewe Alex.	Tr	10.93	93-95	95	1	5
Reading	Tr	01.96	95-97	55	1	1

BORBOKIS Vassilios
Greece, 10 February, 1969 Greek Int (WB)

League Club	Source	Date Signed	Seasons Played	Apps	Subs	Gls
Sheffield U.	AEK Athens (Gre)	07.97	97	36	0	2

BORG John Carmel Adam
Salford, 22 February, 1980 (M)

League Club	Source	Date Signed	Seasons Played	Apps	Subs	Gls
Doncaster Rov.	YT	●	97	1	0	0

BORLAND John Robert
Lancaster, 28 January, 1977 (M)

League Club	Source	Date Signed	Seasons Played	Apps	Subs	Gls
Burnley	YT	07.95	95	1	0	0
Scunthorpe U.	Tr	08.96	96	0	2	0

BOROTA Petar
Yugoslavia, 5 March, 1952 Yugoslav Int (G)

League Club	Source	Date Signed	Seasons Played	Apps	Subs	Gls
Chelsea	Partizan Belgrade (Yug)	03.79	78-81	107	0	0

BORROWS Brian
Liverpool, 20 December, 1960 E'B' (RB)

League Club	Source	Date Signed	Seasons Played	Apps	Subs	Gls
Everton	Jnrs	04.80	81-82	27	0	0
Bolton W.	Tr	03.83	82-84	95	0	0
Coventry C.	Tr	06.85	85-96	396	13	11
Bristol C.	L	09.93	93	6	0	0
Swindon T.	Tr	09.97	97	40	0	0

BORTHWICK Gary Michael
Slough, 30 November, 1955 (M)

League Club	Source	Date Signed	Seasons Played	Apps	Subs	Gls
Bournemouth	Barnet	03.78	77-79	66	8	4

BORTHWICK John Robert
Hartlepool, 24 March, 1964 (F)

League Club	Source	Date Signed	Seasons Played	Apps	Subs	Gls
Hartlepool U.	Owton Social	12.82	82-88	96	21	14
Darlington	Tr	08.89	90-91	57	18	15
York C.	Tr	07.92	92	28	5	8

BORTHWICK Walter Ross
Edinburgh, 4 April, 1948 (IF)

League Club	Source	Date Signed	Seasons Played	Apps	Subs	Gls
Brighton & H.A.	Morton	05.67	66	1	0	0

BOS Gijsbert
Netherlands, 22 February, 1973 (F)

League Club	Source	Date Signed	Seasons Played	Apps	Subs	Gls
Lincoln C.	Ijsselmeervogels (Neth)	03.96	95-96	28	6	6
Rotherham U.	Tr	08.97	97	6	10	4

BOSANCIC Jovo
Yugoslavia, 7 August, 1970 (M)

League Club	Source	Date Signed	Seasons Played	Apps	Subs	Gls
Barnsley	Uniao Madeira (Por)	08.96	96-97	30	12	3

BOSLEM William
Manchester, 11 January, 1958 (CD)

League Club	Source	Date Signed	Seasons Played	Apps	Subs	Gls
Rochdale	Jnrs	11.75	75-77	41	3	1

BOSNICH Mark John
Australia, 13 January, 1972 Australian Int (G)

League Club	Source	Date Signed	Seasons Played	Apps	Subs	Gls
Manchester U.	Jnrs	06.89	89-90	3	0	0
Aston Villa	Sydney Croatia (Aus)	02.92	91-97	164	0	0

BOSSONS Percy Lawrence Powell
Crewe, 10 January, 1924 Died 1950 (LB)

League Club	Source	Date Signed	Seasons Played	Apps	Subs	Gls
Crewe Alex.	West Ham U. (Am)	06.46	46-48	34	-	2

BOSTOCK Benjamin Roy
Mansfield, 19 April, 1929 Died 1993 (OR)

League Club	Source	Date Signed	Seasons Played	Apps	Subs	Gls
Crystal Palace	Jnrs	05.46	48	4	-	0

BOSWELL Alan Henry
West Bromwich, 8 August, 1943 (G)

League Club	Source	Date Signed	Seasons Played	Apps	Subs	Gls
Walsall	Jnrs	08.60	61-62	66	-	0
Shrewsbury T.	Tr	08.63	63-68	222	0	0
Wolverhampton W.	Tr	09.68	68	10	0	0
Bolton W.	Tr	10.69	69-70	51	0	0
Port Vale	Tr	08.72	72-73	86	0	0

BOSWELL James
Chester, 13 March, 1922 (WH)

League Club	Source	Date Signed	Seasons Played	Apps	Subs	Gls
Gillingham	Chester C. (Am)	07.46	50-57	342	-	6

BOTHAM Ian Terence
Heswall, 24 November, 1955 (D)

League Club	Source	Date Signed	Seasons Played	Apps	Subs	Gls
Scunthorpe U. (N/C)		03.80	79-84	7	4	0

BOTTIGLIERI Antonio (Tony)
Chatham, 29 May, 1962 (M)

League Club	Source	Date Signed	Seasons Played	Apps	Subs	Gls
Gillingham	App	04.80	79-81	5	3	0

BOTTOM Arthur Edwin
Sheffield, 28 February, 1930 (CF)

League Club	Source	Date Signed	Seasons Played	Apps	Subs	Gls
Sheffield U.	Jnrs	04.47	48-53	24	-	7
York C.	Tr	06.54	54-57	137	-	92
Newcastle U.	Tr	01.58	57-58	11	-	10
Chesterfield	Tr	11.58	58-59	33	-	6

BOTTOMLEY Paul
Harrogate, 11 September, 1965 (CD)

League Club	Source	Date Signed	Seasons Played	Apps	Subs	Gls
Doncaster Rov.	Bridlington T.	08.93	93	10	0	1

BOTTOMS Michael Charles
Fulham, 11 January, 1939 (F)

League Club	Source	Date Signed	Seasons Played	Apps	Subs	Gls
Queens Park R.	Harrow T.	07.60	60	2	-	0
Oxford U.	Tr	02.62				

BOUGHEN Dean
Hemsworth, 25 July, 1971 (D)

League Club	Source	Date Signed	Seasons Played	Apps	Subs	Gls
Newport Co.	YT	●	87	1	0	0

BOUGHEN Paul
South Kirkby, 17 September, 1949 (CH)

League Club	Source	Date Signed	Seasons Played	Apps	Subs	Gls
Barnsley	App	10.67	70	3	5	0

BOUGHEY Darren John
Stoke, 30 November, 1970 (RW)

League Club	Source	Date Signed	Seasons Played	Apps	Subs	Gls
Stoke C.	YT	07.89	89	4	3	0
Wigan Ath.	L	01.91	90	2	0	2
Exeter C.	L	03.91	90	8	0	1

BOULD Stephen Andrew
Stoke, 16 November, 1962 E 'B'/E-2 (CD)

League Club	Source	Date Signed	Seasons Played	Apps	Subs	Gls
Stoke C.	App	11.80	81-87	179	4	6
Torquay U.	L	10.82	82	9	0	0
Arsenal	Tr	06.88	88-97	257	11	5

BOULTER David Arthur
Stepney, 5 October, 1962 (FB)

League Club	Source	Date Signed	Seasons Played	Apps	Subs	Gls
Crystal Palace	App	07.80	81	16	0	0

BOULTON Clinton William
Stoke, 6 January, 1948 (D)

League Club	Source	Date Signed	Seasons Played	Apps	Subs	Gls
Port Vale	App	08.65	64-71	244	0	11
Torquay U.	Tr	11.71	71-78	260	2	34

BOULTON Colin Donald
Cheltenham, 12 September, 1945 (G)

League Club	Source	Date Signed	Seasons Played	Apps	Subs	Gls
Derby Co.	Cheltenham P.C.	08.64	64-77	272	0	0
Southampton	L	09.76	76	5	0	0
Lincoln C.	New York (USA)	07.80	80	4	0	0

BOULTON Frank Preece
Chipping Sodbury, 12 August, 1917 Died 1987 (G)

League Club	Source	Date Signed	Seasons Played	Apps	Subs	Gls
Arsenal	Bath C.	10.36	36-37	36	-	0
Derby Co.	Tr	08.38	38	39	-	0
Swindon T.	Tr	08.46	46-49	97	-	0

BOULTON Ralph
Grimsby, 22 July, 1923 Died 1992 (IF)

League Club	Source	Date Signed	Seasons Played	Apps	Subs	Gls
Grimsby T.		04.48	47-48	3	-	0

BOUND Matthew Terence
Melksham, 9 November, 1972 (CD)

League Club	Source	Date Signed	Seasons Played	Apps	Subs	Gls
Southampton	YT	05.91	91-93	2	3	0
Hull C.	L	08.93	93	7	0	1
Stockport Co.	Tr	10.94	94-96	44	0	5
Lincoln C.	L	09.95	95	3	1	0
Swansea C.	Tr	11.97	97	28	0	0

BOURNE Albert
Golborne, 30 September, 1934 (F)

League Club	Source	Date Signed	Seasons Played	Apps	Subs	Gls
Manchester C.		08.52				
Oldham Ath.	Tr	06.58	58-59	35	-	9

BOURNE George Frederick
Stoke, 5 March, 1932 (FB)

League Club	Source	Date Signed	Seasons Played	Apps	Subs	Gls
Stoke C.	Burslem Albion	06.50	52-55	100	-	1

BOURNE Jeffrey Albert
Repton, 19 June, 1948 (W)

League Club	Source	Date Signed	Seasons Played	Apps	Subs	Gls
Derby Co.	Burton A.	06.69	70-76	35	14	9
Crystal Palace	Tr	03.77	76-77	32	0	10
Sheffield U.	Atlanta (USA)	09.79	79	25	1	11

BOURNE Richard Adrian
Colchester, 9 December, 1954 (CD)

League Club	Source	Date Signed	Seasons Played	Apps	Subs	Gls
Colchester U.	Jnrs	04.73	71-72	3	1	0
Torquay U.	Bath C.	06.79	79-81	64	4	7

BOUSTON Bryan John
Hereford, 3 October, 1960 (FB)

League Club	Source	Date Signed	Seasons Played	Apps	Subs	Gls
Hereford U.	App	10.78	77	4	2	0

BOVINGTON Edward Ernest Perrian
Edmonton, 23 April, 1941 (WH)

League Club	Source	Date Signed	Seasons Played	Apps	Subs	Gls
West Ham U.	Jnrs	05.59	59-67	138	0	1

BOWATER Jason
Chesterfield, 5 April, 1978 (M)

League Club	Source	Date Signed	Seasons Played	Apps	Subs	Gls
Chesterfield	YT	●	96	0	1	0

BOWDEN John (Jack)
Manchester, 25 August, 1921 Died 1981 (WH)

League Club	Source	Date Signed	Seasons Played	Apps	Subs	Gls
Oldham Ath.	Jnrs	09.45	46-48	72	-	1

BOWDEN Jonathan Lee
Stockport, 21 January, 1963 (M)

League Club	Source	Date Signed	Seasons Played	Apps	Subs	Gls
Oldham Ath.	Jnrs	01.80	81-84	73	9	5
Port Vale	Tr	09.85	85-86	64	6	7
Wrexham	Tr	07.87	87-91	137	10	20
Rochdale	Tr	09.91	91-94	73	33	17

BOWDEN Peter William
Liverpool, 23 July, 1959 (M)

League Club	Source	Date Signed	Seasons Played	Apps	Subs	Gls
Doncaster Rov.	Jnrs	08.77	76-78	22	6	1

BOWEN Daniel
Llanwonno, 16 November, 1921 (OR)

League Club	Source	Date Signed	Seasons Played	Apps	Subs	Gls
Scunthorpe U.	Treharris	07.50	50	5	-	0

BOWEN David Lloyd
Maesteg, 7 June, 1928 Died 1995 W-19 (WH)

League Club	Source	Date Signed	Seasons Played	Apps	Subs	Gls
Northampton T.		07.47	47-48	12	-	0
Arsenal	Tr	07.50	50-58	146	-	2
Northampton T.	Tr	07.59	59	22	-	1

BOWEN Jason Peter
Merthyr Tydfil, 24 August, 1972 W Sch/W Yth/Wu21-5/W 'B'/W-2 (W)

League Club	Source	Date Signed	Seasons Played	Apps	Subs	Gls
Swansea C.	YT	07.90	90-94	93	31	26
Birmingham C.	Tr	07.95	95-96	35	13	7
Southampton	L	09.97	97	1	2	0
Reading	Tr	12.97	97	11	3	1

BOWEN Keith Bryn
Northampton, 26 February, 1958 W Sch (F)

League Club	Source	Date Signed	Seasons Played	Apps	Subs	Gls
Northampton T. (N/C)	Jnrs	08.76	76-81	61	4	24
Brentford	Tr	09.81	81-82	42	9	9
Colchester U.	Tr	03.83	82-85	115	1	38

BOWEN Mark Rosslyn
Neath, 7 December, 1963 W Sch/W Yth/Wu21-3/W-41 (LB)

League Club	Source	Date Signed	Seasons Played	Apps	Subs	Gls
Tottenham H.	App	12.81	83-86	14	3	2
Norwich C.	Tr	07.87	87-95	315	5	24
West Ham U.	Tr	07.96	96	15	2	1
Charlton Ath.	Shimizu S.P. (Jap)	09.97	97	34	2	0

BOWEN Stewart Anthony
West Bromwich, 12 December, 1972 (LB)

League Club	Source	Date Signed	Seasons Played	Apps	Subs	Gls
West Bromwich A.	YT	07.91	91	8	0	1

BOWEN Thomas Henry
West Bromwich, 21 August, 1924 (OR)

League Club	Source	Date Signed	Seasons Played	Apps	Subs	Gls
West Bromwich A.	Jnrs	04.44				
Newport Co.	Tr	07.46	46-49	37	-	6
Walsall	Tr	07.50	50-52	94	-	7

BOWER Daniel Neil
Woolwich, 20 November, 1976 (CD)

League Club	Source	Date Signed	Seasons Played	Apps	Subs	Gls
Fulham	YT	11.95	95	4	0	0

BOWER Kenneth
Huddersfield, 18 March, 1926 (CF)

League Club	Source	Date Signed	Seasons Played	Apps	Subs	Gls
Darlington		01.47	46-48	75	-	35
Rotherham U.	Tr	07.49	49	27	-	10

BOWER Mark James
Bradford, 23 January, 1980 (CD)

League Club	Source	Date Signed	Seasons Played	Apps	Subs	Gls
Bradford C.	YT	03.98	97	1	2	0

BOWERING Michael
Hull, 15 November, 1936 (W)

League Club	Source	Date Signed	Seasons Played	Apps	Subs	Gls
Hull C.		09.58	58-59	45	-	7
Chesterfield	Tr	06.60	60	16	-	1

BOWERS Ian (Danny)
Newcastle-u-Lyme, 16 January, 1955 (LB)

League Club	Source	Date Signed	Seasons Played	Apps	Subs	Gls
Stoke C.	Jnrs	06.73	74-77	35	4	2
Shrewsbury T.	L	03.78	77	6	0	0
Crewe Alex.	Tr	07.79	79-83	170	5	2

BOWERS John Anslow
Leicester, 14 November, 1939 (W)

League Club	Source	Date Signed	Seasons Played	Apps	Subs	Gls
Derby Co.	Derby Corries	02.57	59-65	65	0	19
Notts Co.	Tr	06.66	66	5	0	0

BOWERY Bertram Nathanial
St Kitts (WI), 29 October, 1954 (F)

League Club	Source	Date Signed	Seasons Played	Apps	Subs	Gls
Nottingham F.	Worksop T.	01.75	75-76	2	0	2
Lincoln C.	L	02.76	75	2	2	1

BOWEY Keith Alan
Newcastle, 9 May, 1960 (M)

League Club	Source	Date Signed	Seasons Played	Apps	Subs	Gls
Blackpool	App	03.78	78-79	3	0	1

BOWGETT Paul
Hitchin, 17 June, 1955 (CD)

League Club	Source	Date Signed	Seasons Played	Apps	Subs	Gls
Tottenham H.	Letchworth G.C.	02.78				
Wimbledon	Tr	03.79	78-79	41	0	0

BOWIE James Duncan
Aberdeen, 9 August, 1924 (IF)

League Club	Source	Date Signed	Seasons Played	Apps	Subs	Gls
Chelsea	Park Vale	01.44	47-50	76	-	18
Fulham	Tr	01.51	50-51	33	-	7
Brentford	Tr	03.52	51	9	-	0
Watford	Tr	07.52	52-55	125	-	39

BOWIE James McAvoy
Johnstone, 11 October, 1941 (M)

League Club	Source	Date Signed	Seasons Played	Apps	Subs	Gls
Oldham Ath.	Arthurlie Jnrs	07.62	62-71	331	2	37
Rochdale	Tr	10.72	72	1	2	0

BOWKER Keith
West Bromwich, 18 April, 1951 (F)

League Club	Source	Date Signed	Seasons Played	Apps	Subs	Gls
Birmingham C.	App	08.68	70-72	19	2	5
Exeter C.	Tr	12.73	73-75	110	0	38
Cambridge U.	Tr	05.76	76	12	5	1
Northampton T.	L	12.76	76	4	0	0
Exeter C.	Tr	08.77	77-79	93	9	28
Torquay U.	Tr	08.80	80-81	50	3	9

BOWLER Gerard Columba
Derry (NI), 8 June, 1919 NI-3 (CH)

League Club	Source	Date Signed	Seasons Played	Apps	Subs	Gls
Portsmouth	Distillery	08.46	46-48	8	-	0
Hull C.	Tr	08.49	49	38	-	0
Millwall	Tr	06.50	50-54	165	-	0

BOWLES John Charles
Cheltenham, 4 August, 1914 Died 1987 (G)

League Club	Source	Date Signed	Seasons Played	Apps	Subs	Gls
Newport Co.	Cheltenham T.	05.36	36	4	-	0
Accrington St.	Tr	06.37	37	12	-	0
Stockport Co.	Tr	07.38	38-52	275	-	0

BOWLES Paul Michael Anthony
Manchester, 31 May, 1957 (CD)

League Club	Source	Date Signed	Seasons Played	Apps	Subs	Gls
Crewe Alex.	App	05.75	74-79	174	4	20

League Club	Source	Date Signed	Seasons Played	Apps	Subs	Gls
Port Vale	Tr	10.79	79-81	98	0	6
Stockport Co.	Tr	06.82	82-84	67	3	0

BOWLES Stanley
Manchester, 24 December, 1948 EF Lge/E-5 (M)

League Club	Source	Date Signed	Seasons Played	Apps	Subs	Gls
Manchester C.	App	01.67	67-69	15	2	2
Bury	L	07.70	70	5	0	0
Crewe Alex.	Tr	09.70	70-71	51	0	18
Carlisle U.	Tr	10.71	71-72	33	0	12
Queens Park R.	Tr	09.72	72-79	255	0	70
Nottingham F.	Tr	12.79	79	19	0	2
Leyton Orient	Tr	07.80	80-81	46	0	7
Brentford	Tr	10.81	81-83	80	1	16

BOWLING Ian
Sheffield, 27 July, 1965 (G)

League Club	Source	Date Signed	Seasons Played	Apps	Subs	Gls
Lincoln C.	Gainsborough Trin.	10.88	88-92	59	0	0
Hartlepool U.	L	08.89	89	1	0	0
Bradford C.	Tr	03.93	92-94	36	0	0
Mansfield T.	Tr	08.95	95-97	123	0	0

BOWMAN Andrew
Pittenweem (Fife), 7 March, 1934 S Sch (WH)

League Club	Source	Date Signed	Seasons Played	Apps	Subs	Gls
Chelsea	Jnrs	06.51	53	1	-	0
Newport Co.	Hearts	08.61	61-62	69	-	7

BOWMAN David
Tonbridge, 10 March, 1964 Su21-1/S-6 (M)

League Club	Source	Date Signed	Seasons Played	Apps	Subs	Gls
Coventry C.	Hearts	12.84	84-85	38	2	2

BOWMAN David Michael
Scarborough, 16 December, 1960 (F)

League Club	Source	Date Signed	Seasons Played	Apps	Subs	Gls
Scarborough (N/C)	Bridlington T.	08.87	87	4	0	2

BOWMAN Richard David
Lewisham, 25 September, 1954 (M)

League Club	Source	Date Signed	Seasons Played	Apps	Subs	Gls
Charlton Ath.	App	03.73	72-76	93	3	7
Reading	Tr	12.76	76-80	194	0	30
Gillingham	Tr	08.81	81-82	26	0	6

BOWMAN Robert Alexander
Durham City, 21 November, 1975 E Yth (D)

League Club	Source	Date Signed	Seasons Played	Apps	Subs	Gls
Leeds U.	YT	11.92	92-95	4	3	0
Rotherham U.	Tr	02.97	96	13	0	0
Carlisle U.	Tr	08.97	97	6	1	1

BOWMAN Robert Craig Caldwell
Motherwell, 21 October, 1920 Died 1991 (RB)

League Club	Source	Date Signed	Seasons Played	Apps	Subs	Gls
New Brighton	Kilmarnock	01.49	48	18	-	0

BOWRON Kenneth
Newcastle, 10 April, 1939 (F)

League Club	Source	Date Signed	Seasons Played	Apps	Subs	Gls
Workington	Berwick R.	12.65	65-66	8	1	2

BOWRY Robert
Croydon, 19 May, 1971 (M)

League Club	Source	Date Signed	Seasons Played	Apps	Subs	Gls
Queens Park R.		08.90				
Crystal Palace	Carshalton Ath.	04.92	92-94	36	14	1
Millwall	Tr	07.95	95-97	100	9	5

BOWSTEAD Peter Edward
Cambridge, 10 May, 1944 (IF)

League Club	Source	Date Signed	Seasons Played	Apps	Subs	Gls
Oxford U.	Cambridge U.	10.62	62-63	8	-	2

BOWTELL Stephen John
Bethnal Green, 2 December, 1950 E Sch/E Yth (G)

League Club	Source	Date Signed	Seasons Played	Apps	Subs	Gls
Leyton Orient	App	01.68	67-71	8	0	0

BOWYER Francis
Stoke, 10 April, 1922 (IF)

League Club	Source	Date Signed	Seasons Played	Apps	Subs	Gls
Stoke C.	Jnrs	04.39	47-59	398	-	137

BOWYER Gary David
Manchester, 22 June, 1971 (LB/W)

League Club	Source	Date Signed	Seasons Played	Apps	Subs	Gls
Hereford U. (N/C)	Westfields	12.89	89	12	2	2
Nottingham F.	Tr	09.90				
Rotherham U.	Tr	08.95	95-96	33	5	2

BOWYER Ian
Little Sutton, 6 June, 1951 (M)

League Club	Source	Date Signed	Seasons Played	Apps	Subs	Gls
Manchester C.	App	08.68	68-70	42	8	13
Leyton Orient	Tr	06.71	71-72	75	3	19
Nottingham F.	Tr	10.73	73-80	222	17	49
Sunderland	Tr	01.81	80-81	15	0	1
Nottingham F.	Tr	01.82	81-86	203	3	19
Hereford U.	Tr	07.87	87-89	33	7	1

BOWYER Lee David
Newham, 3 January, 1977 E Yth/Eu21-8 (M)

League Club	Source	Date Signed	Seasons Played	Apps	Subs	Gls
Charlton Ath.	YT	04.94	94-95	46	0	8
Leeds U.	Tr	07.96	96-97	53	4	7

BOXALL Alan Ronald
Woolwich, 11 May, 1953 (CD)

League Club	Source	Date Signed	Seasons Played	Apps	Subs	Gls
Scunthorpe U.	Barton T.	08.80	80-83	50	4	1
Chesterfield	Tr	11.83	83	4	1	0

BOXALL Daniel James
Croydon, 24 August, 1977 IRu21-2 (D)

League Club	Source	Date Signed	Seasons Played	Apps	Subs	Gls
Crystal Palace	YT	04.95	95-97	5	3	0
Oldham Ath.	L	11.97	97	5	0	0
Oldham Ath.	L	02.98	97	12	0	0

BOXLEY John (Jack)
Birmingham, 31 May, 1931 (OL)

League Club	Source	Date Signed	Seasons Played	Apps	Subs	Gls
Bristol C.	Stourbridge	10.50	50-56	193	-	34
Coventry C.	Tr	12.56	56-59	92	-	17
Bristol C.	Tr	08.60	60	12	-	0

BOXSHALL Daniel
Bradford, 2 April, 1920 (W)

League Club	Source	Date Signed	Seasons Played	Apps	Subs	Gls
Queens Park R.	Salem Ath.	01.46	46-47	29	-	14
Bristol C.	Tr	05.48	48-49	52	-	10
Bournemouth	Tr	07.50	50-51	51	-	8
Rochdale	Tr	07.52	52-53	11	-	3

BOYAK Steven
Edinburgh, 4 September, 1976 Su21-1 (M)

League Club	Source	Date Signed	Seasons Played	Apps	Subs	Gls
Hull C. (L)	Glasgow Rangers	02.98	97	12	0	3

BOYCE Robert Alexander
Islington, 7 January, 1974 (M)

League Club	Source	Date Signed	Seasons Played	Apps	Subs	Gls
Colchester U.	Enfield	10.95	95	0	2	0

BOYCE Ronald William
West Ham, 6 January, 1943 E Sch/E Yth (M)

League Club	Source	Date Signed	Seasons Played	Apps	Subs	Gls
West Ham U.	Jnrs	05.60	60-72	275	7	21

BOYD Brian George
Carlisle, 4 January, 1938 (IL)

League Club	Source	Date Signed	Seasons Played	Apps	Subs	Gls
Carlisle U.	Raffles Rov.	08.55	58	4	-	0

BOYD Charles Michael
Liverpool, 20 September, 1969 (M)

League Club	Source	Date Signed	Seasons Played	Apps	Subs	Gls
Liverpool	YT	05.87				
Chesterfield (N/C)	Bristol Rov. (N/C)	11.90	90	0	1	0

BOYD Gordon
Glasgow, 27 March, 1958 S Sch (M)

League Club	Source	Date Signed	Seasons Played	Apps	Subs	Gls
Fulham	Glasgow Rangers	05.78	78	1	2	0
Barnsley	Glasgow Rangers	06.80	80	1	1	0
Scunthorpe U.	Tr	03.82	81	10	1	0

BOYD John (Jack)
Consett, 10 April, 1925 (FB)

League Club	Source	Date Signed	Seasons Played	Apps	Subs	Gls
Sunderland	Medomsley B.C.	05.45				
West Bromwich A.	Tr	06.48	48	1	-	0

BOYD John
U.S.A., 10 September, 1926 (OR)

League Club	Source	Date Signed	Seasons Played	Apps	Subs	Gls
Bristol C.	Gloucester C.	12.50	50-51	31	-	6

BOYD John Robertson
Carriden, 7 March, 1926 (CH)

League Club	Source	Date Signed	Seasons Played	Apps	Subs	Gls
Newport Co.	Bo'ness Jnrs	03.47	47	1	-	0

BOYD Leonard Arthur Miller
Plaistow, 11 November, 1923 E 'B' (WH)

League Club	Source	Date Signed	Seasons Played	Apps	Subs	Gls
Plymouth Arg.	Ilford	12.45	46-48	78	-	5
Birmingham C.	Tr	01.49	48-55	255	-	14

BOYD Stuart
Workington, 22 December, 1954 (RB)

League Club	Source	Date Signed	Seasons Played	Apps	Subs	Gls
Workington (Am)	Jnrs	08.73	73	1	2	0

BOYD Thomas
Glasgow, 24 November, 1965 S Yth/Su21-5/S'B'/S-58 (LB)

League Club	Source	Date Signed	Seasons Played	Apps	Subs	Gls
Chelsea	Motherwell	06.91	91	22	1	0

BOYD William
Hamilton, 18 October, 1958 S Yth (G)

League Club	Source	Date Signed	Seasons Played	Apps	Subs	Gls
Hull C.	App	10.77				
Doncaster Rov.	Tr	02.80	79-83	104	0	0

BOYDEN Joseph
Willenhall, 12 February, 1929 (LB)

League Club	Source	Date Signed	Seasons Played	Apps	Subs	Gls
Walsall	Jnrs	12.48	52	4	-	0

BOYER Philip John
Nottingham, 25 January, 1949 Eu23-2/E-1 (F)

League Club	Source	Date Signed	Seasons Played	Apps	Subs	Gls
Derby Co.	App	11.66				
York C.	Tr	07.68	68-70	108	1	27
Bournemouth	Tr	12.70	70-73	140	1	46
Norwich C.	Tr	12.74	73-76	115	1	34
Southampton	Tr	08.77	77-80	138	0	49
Manchester C.	Tr	11.80	80-82	17	3	3

BOYES Kenneth
Scarborough, 4 February, 1935 (CH)

League Club	Source	Date Signed	Seasons Played	Apps	Subs	Gls
York C.	Scarborough	10.55	57-65	53	0	2

BOYES Walter Edward
Sheffield, 5 January, 1913 Died 1960 EF Lge/E-3 (OL)

League Club	Source	Date Signed	Seasons Played	Apps	Subs	Gls
West Bromwich A.	Woodhouse M.U.	02.31	31-37	151	-	35
Everton	Tr	02.38	37-48	66	-	11
Notts Co.	Tr	08.49	49	3	-	1
Scunthorpe U.	Tr	08.50	50	13	-	2

BOYLAN Anthony
Hartlepool, 19 February, 1950 (M)

League Club	Source	Date Signed	Seasons Played	Apps	Subs	Gls
Hartlepool U. (Am)	Bishop Auckland	09.68	69-71	10	1	0

BOYLAN Lee Martin
Chelmsford, 2 September, 1978 IR Yth (F)

League Club	Source	Date Signed	Seasons Played	Apps	Subs	Gls
West Ham U.	YT	●	96	0	1	0

BOYLE David Walker
Tynemouth, 24 April, 1929 (IF)

League Club	Source	Date Signed	Seasons Played	Apps	Subs	Gls
Newcastle U.		10.47				
Barnsley	Berwick R.	03.51				
Crewe Alex.	Tr	06.52	52-53	25	-	3
Chesterfield	Tr	07.54	54-55	42	-	10
Bradford C.	Tr	07.56	56-60	92	-	13

BOYLE Henry
Glasgow, 22 April, 1924 Died 1988 (FB)

League Club	Source	Date Signed	Seasons Played	Apps	Subs	Gls
Southport	Murton Colly	07.47	47-49	88	-	0
Rochdale	Tr	06.50	50-55	175	-	0

BOYLE Ian Richard
Barnsley, 7 December, 1953 (CD)

League Club	Source	Date Signed	Seasons Played	Apps	Subs	Gls
Barnsley	App	12.71	72-73	19	2	0

BOYLE John
Motherwell, 25 December, 1946 (M)

League Club	Source	Date Signed	Seasons Played	Apps	Subs	Gls
Chelsea	Jnrs	08.64	64-73	188	10	10
Brighton & H.A.	L	09.73	73	10	0	0
Leyton Orient	Tr	12.73	73-74	18	0	0

BOYLE Lee David
North Shields, 22 January, 1972 (D)

League Club	Source	Date Signed	Seasons Played	Apps	Subs	Gls
Doncaster Rov.	Ipswich T. (YT)	07.90	91	2	1	0

BOYLE Terence David John
Ammanford, 29 October, 1958 W Sch/Wu21-1/W-2 (CD)

League Club	Source	Date Signed	Seasons Played	Apps	Subs	Gls
Tottenham H.	App	11.75				
Crystal Palace	Tr	01.78	77-80	24	2	1
Wimbledon	L	09.81	81	5	0	1
Bristol C.	Tr	10.81	81-82	36	1	0
Newport Co.	Tr	11.82	82-85	165	1	11
Cardiff C.	Tr	08.86	86-88	126	2	7
Swansea C.	Tr	08.89	89	27	0	1

BOYLE Wesley Samuel
Portadown, 30 March, 1979 NI Sch/NI Yth (W)

League Club	Source	Date Signed	Seasons Played	Apps	Subs	Gls
Leeds U.	YT	04.96	96	0	1	0

BOYLEN David
Prestbury, 26 October, 1947 (M)

League Club	Source	Date Signed	Seasons Played	Apps	Subs	Gls
Grimsby T.	Ryder Brow B.C.	07.65	66-77	370	14	34

BOZINOSKI Vlado
Macedonia, 30 March, 1964 Australian Int (M)

League Club	Source	Date Signed	Seasons Played	Apps	Subs	Gls
Ipswich T.	Sporting Lisbon (Por)	12.92	92	3	6	0

BRABIN Gary
Liverpool, 9 December, 1970 E Semi Pro (M)

League Club	Source	Date Signed	Seasons Played	Apps	Subs	Gls
Stockport Co.	YT	12.89	89-90	1	1	0
Doncaster Rov.	Runcorn	07.94	94-95	58	1	11
Bury	Tr	03.96	95	5	0	0
Blackpool	Tr	07.96	96-97	45	11	5

BRABROOK Peter
Greenwich, 8 November, 1937 E Yth/Eu23-9/EF Lge/E-3 (OR)

League Club	Source	Date Signed	Seasons Played	Apps	Subs	Gls
Chelsea	Jnrs	03.55	54-61	251	-	47
West Ham U.	Tr	10.62	62-67	167	0	33
Leyton Orient	Tr	07.68	68-70	70	2	6

BRACE Deryn Paul John
Haverfordwest, 15 March, 1975 W Yth/Wu21-8 (LB)

League Club	Source	Date Signed	Seasons Played	Apps	Subs	Gls
Norwich C.	YT	07.93				
Wrexham	Tr	04.94	93-97	61	4	2

BRACE Robert Leon
Edmonton, 19 December, 1964 (F)

League Club	Source	Date Signed	Seasons Played	Apps	Subs	Gls
Tottenham H.	App	12.82	83	0	1	0

BRACE Stuart Clive
Taunton, 21 September, 1942 (W)

League Club	Source	Date Signed	Seasons Played	Apps	Subs	Gls
Plymouth Arg.	Taunton T.	11.60	62-65	9	0	0
Watford	Tr	09.65	65	16	0	4
Mansfield T.	Tr	07.66	66-67	55	2	25
Peterborough U.	Tr	11.67	67-68	22	1	6
Grimsby T.	Tr	10.68	68-73	205	1	81
Southend U.	Tr	10.73	73-75	106	6	39

BRACEWELL Kenneth
Colne, 5 October, 1936 (FB)

League Club	Source	Date Signed	Seasons Played	Apps	Subs	Gls
Burnley	Trawden	04.57				
Tranmere Rov.	Tr	05.59	59-60	28	-	1
Lincoln C.	Canada	11.63	63-64	23	-	1
Bury	Margate	12.66	66	1	0	0
Rochdale	Toronto (Can)	03.68	67	5	0	0

BRACEWELL Paul William
Heswall, 19 July, 1962 Eu21-13/E-3 (M)

League Club	Source	Date Signed	Seasons Played	Apps	Subs	Gls
Stoke C.	App	02.80	79-82	123	6	5
Sunderland	Tr	07.83	83	38	0	4
Everton	Tr	05.84	84-88	95	0	7
Sunderland	Tr	08.89	89-91	112	1	2
Newcastle U.	Tr	06.92	92-94	64	9	3
Sunderland	Tr	05.95	95-97	76	1	0
Fulham	Tr	10.97	97	36	0	0

BRACEY Lee Michael Ian
Barking, 11 September, 1968 (G)

League Club	Source	Date Signed	Seasons Played	Apps	Subs	Gls
West Ham U.	YT	07.87				
Swansea C.	Tr	08.88	88-91	99	0	0
Halifax T.	Tr	10.91	91-92	73	0	0
Bury	Tr	08.93	93-95	65	2	0

BRACK Alistair Holland Brack
Aberdeen, 27 January, 1940 (FB)

League Club	Source	Date Signed	Seasons Played	Apps	Subs	Gls
Cardiff C.		09.61	62	1	-	0

BRADBURY Allen
Barnsley, 23 January, 1947 (WH)

League Club	Source	Date Signed	Seasons Played	Apps	Subs	Gls
Barnsley	App	01.65	64-69	68	1	9
Hartlepool U.	Kettering T.	01.71	70	7	0	0

BRADBURY Barry
Rochdale, 5 August, 1952 (FB)

League Club	Source	Date Signed	Seasons Played	Apps	Subs	Gls
Rochdale	Matthew Moss	08.72	72-73	12	2	0

BRADBURY Lee Michael
Isle of Wight, 3 July, 1975 Eu21-1 (CF)

League Club	Source	Date Signed	Seasons Played	Apps	Subs	Gls
Portsmouth	Cowes	08.95	95-96	41	13	15
Exeter C.	L	12.95	95	14	0	5
Manchester C.	Tr	08.97	97	23	4	7

BRADBURY Shaun
Birmingham, 11 February, 1974 (F)

League Club	Source	Date Signed	Seasons Played	Apps	Subs	Gls
Wolverhampton W.	YT	11.92	92	2	0	2

BRADBURY Terence Eugene
Paddington, 15 November, 1939 E Sch (WH)

League Club	Source	Date Signed	Seasons Played	Apps	Subs	Gls
Chelsea	Jnrs	07.57	60-61	29	-	1
Southend U.	Tr	09.62	62-65	160	1	19
Leyton Orient	Tr	06.66	66	25	2	0
Wrexham	Tr	06.67	67-68	77	1	3
Chester C.	Tr	06.69	69-70	90	0	2

BRADBURY William
Matlock, 3 April, 1933 (IF)

League Club	Source	Date Signed	Seasons Played	Apps	Subs	Gls
Coventry C.	Jnrs	05.50	51-54	24	-	7
Birmingham C.	Tr	11.54	54-55	3	-	2
Hull C.	Tr	10.55	55-59	178	-	82
Bury	Tr	02.60	59-60	18	-	4
Workington	Tr	11.60	60	23	-	5
Southport	Tr	08.61	61	11	-	2

BRADD Leslie John
Buxton, 5 November, 1947 (CF)

League Club	Source	Date Signed	Seasons Played	Apps	Subs	Gls
Rotherham U.	Earl Sterndale	03.66	67	3	0	0
Notts Co.	Tr	10.67	67-77	379	16	125
Stockport Co.	Tr	08.78	78-80	116	1	31
Wigan Ath.	Tr	07.81	81-82	57	6	25
Bristol Rov.	L	12.82	82	1	0	1

BRADER Alec
Horncastle, 6 October, 1942 (IF)

League Club	Source	Date Signed	Seasons Played	Apps	Subs	Gls
Grimsby T.	Horncastle U.	05.60	60	2	-	0

BRADFORD David William
Manchester, 22 February, 1953 (M)

League Club	Source	Date Signed	Seasons Played	Apps	Subs	Gls
Blackburn Rov.	App	08.71	71-73	58	6	3
Sheffield U.	Tr	07.74	74-76	54	6	3
Peterborough U.	L	10.76	76	4	0	0
West Bromwich A.	Tr	02.77				
Coventry C.	Washington (USA)	10.81	81	6	0	1

BRADFORD Geoffrey Reginald William
Bristol, 18 July, 1927 Died 1994 E-1 (CF)

League Club	Source	Date Signed	Seasons Played	Apps	Subs	Gls
Bristol Rov.	Soundwell	05.49	49-63	461	-	242

BRADFORD Lewis
Swadlincote, 24 November, 1916 Died 1984 (FB)

League Club	Source	Date Signed	Seasons Played	Apps	Subs	Gls
Preston N.E.		12.34				
Bradford C.	Kilmarnock	10.46	46-48	68	-	1
Newport Co.	Tr	11.48	48	24	-	0

BRADLEY Brendan Colin
Derry (NI), 7 June, 1950 (IF)

League Club	Source	Date Signed	Seasons Played	Apps	Subs	Gls
Lincoln C.	Finn Harps	07.72	72	31	0	12

BRADLEY Charles
York, 15 May, 1922 Died 1984 (IF)

League Club	Source	Date Signed	Seasons Played	Apps	Subs	Gls
York C.	York R.I.	10.41	46	10	-	2

BRADLEY Darren Michael
Birmingham, 24 November, 1965 E Yth (M/D)

League Club	Source	Date Signed	Seasons Played	Apps	Subs	Gls
Aston Villa	App	11.83	84-85	16	4	0
West Bromwich A.	Tr	03.86	85-94	236	18	9
Walsall	Tr	08.95	95-96	66	5	1

BRADLEY David
Salford, 16 January, 1958 E Sch (CD)

League Club	Source	Date Signed	Seasons Played	Apps	Subs	Gls
Manchester U.	App	01.75				
Wimbledon	L	03.78	77	7	0	0
Doncaster Rov.	Tr	08.78	78-79	67	0	5
Bury	Tr	08.80	80	8	0	0

BRADLEY David Hughes
Bolton, 6 December, 1953 (F)

League Club	Source	Date Signed	Seasons Played	Apps	Subs	Gls
Workington	Silcoms	09.75	75	8	0	1

BRADLEY Donald John
Annesley, 11 September, 1924 Died 1997 (FB)

League Club	Source	Date Signed	Seasons Played	Apps	Subs	Gls
West Bromwich A.	Clipstone Colly	09.43				
Mansfield T.	Tr	08.49	49-61	384	-	6

BRADLEY George Joseph
Maltby, 7 November, 1917 (D)

League Club	Source	Date Signed	Seasons Played	Apps	Subs	Gls
Rotherham U.	Maltby Hall O.B.	03.37	37-38	28	-	0
Newcastle U.	Tr	11.38	38	1	-	0
Millwall	Tr	09.46	46-49	74	-	2

BRADLEY Gordon
Sunderland, 23 November, 1933 (WH)

League Club	Source	Date Signed	Seasons Played	Apps	Subs	Gls
Bradford P.A.	Stanley U.	01.56	55-56	18	-	1
Carlisle U.	Tr	09.57	57-60	133	-	3

BRADLEY Gordon
Scunthorpe, 20 May, 1925 (G)

League Club	Source	Date Signed	Seasons Played	Apps	Subs	Gls
Leicester C.	Scunthorpe U.	11.42	46-49	69	-	0
Notts Co.	Tr	02.50	50-57	192	-	1

BRADLEY James
Greenock, 21 March, 1927 (W)

League Club	Source	Date Signed	Seasons Played	Apps	Subs	Gls
Shrewsbury T.	Third Lanark	07.52	52	1	-	0

BRADLEY John (Jack)
Hemsworth, 27 November, 1916 (IF)

League Club	Source	Date Signed	Seasons Played	Apps	Subs	Gls
Huddersfield T.	South Kirkby Colly	11.35				
Swindon T.	Tr	08.36	36-37	24	-	5
Chelsea	Tr	06.38				
Southampton	Tr	05.39	46-47	49	-	22
Bolton W.	Tr	10.47	47-50	92	-	19
Norwich C.	Tr	11.50	50-51	6	-	0

BRADLEY Keith
Ellesmere Port, 31 January, 1946 (D)

League Club	Source	Date Signed	Seasons Played	Apps	Subs	Gls
Aston Villa	App	06.63	64-71	115	7	2
Peterborough U.	Tr	11.72	72-75	106	3	0

BRADLEY Lee Herbert
Manchester, 27 May, 1957 (D)

League Club	Source	Date Signed	Seasons Played	Apps	Subs	Gls
Stockport Co.	App	08.75	75	39	1	4
Halifax T.	Tr	10.76	76-78	62	10	4

BRADLEY Noel Bernard
Ballycofey, 17 December, 1957 (D)

League Club	Source	Date Signed	Seasons Played	Apps	Subs	Gls
Manchester C.	St Roberts B.C.	11.78				
Bury	L	03.80	79	9	0	0
Bury	Tr	08.81	81	15	3	1
Chester C.	Tr	08.82	82	27	4	0

BRADLEY Patrick
Australia, 27 April, 1972 E Yth (FB)

League Club	Source	Date Signed	Seasons Played	Apps	Subs	Gls
Bury	YT	07.90	90	0	1	0

BRADLEY Peter Kenneth
Donnington, 18 March, 1955 (CD)

League Club	Source	Date Signed	Seasons Played	Apps	Subs	Gls
Shrewsbury T.	App	07.73	73	3	1	0

BRADLEY Ronald John
Bilston, 24 April, 1939 E Yth (WH)

League Club	Source	Date Signed	Seasons Played	Apps	Subs	Gls
West Bromwich A.	Jnrs	06.56	62	13	-	0
Norwich C.	Tr	07.64	64-65	4	0	0

BRADLEY Russell
Birmingham, 28 March, 1966 (CD)

League Club	Source	Date Signed	Seasons Played	Apps	Subs	Gls
Nottingham F.	Dudley T.	05.88				
Hereford U.	L	11.88	88	5	0	0
Hereford U.	L	03.89	88	7	0	1
Hereford U.	Tr	07.89	89-91	75	2	3
Halifax T.	Tr	09.91	91-92	54	2	3
Scunthorpe U.	Tr	06.93	93-96	116	3	5
Hartlepool U.	L	02.97	96	12	0	1
Hartlepool U.	Tr	07.97	97	43	0	1

BRADLEY Warren
Hyde, 20 June, 1933 E Amat/E-3 (OR)

League Club	Source	Date Signed	Seasons Played	Apps	Subs	Gls
Manchester U.	Bishop Auckland	11.58	58-61	63	-	20
Bury	Tr	03.62	61-62	13	-	1

BRADLEY William
Glasgow, 26 June, 1937 (IF)

League Club	Source	Date Signed	Seasons Played	Apps	Subs	Gls
Hartlepool U.	Ayr U.	07.63	63-65	98	0	15

BRADSHAW Alan
Blackburn, 14 September, 1941 (M)

League Club	Source	Date Signed	Seasons Played	Apps	Subs	Gls
Blackburn Rov.	Jnrs	07.63	62-64	11	-	2
Crewe Alex.	Tr	05.65	65-72	287	7	50

BRADSHAW Carl
Sheffield, 2 October, 1968 E Yth (RB)

League Club	Source	Date Signed	Seasons Played	Apps	Subs	Gls
Sheffield Wed.	App	08.86	86-88	16	16	4
Barnsley	L	08.86	86	6	0	1
Manchester C.	Tr	09.88	88	1	4	0
Sheffield U.	Tr	09.89	89-93	122	25	8
Norwich C.	Tr	07.94	94-97	55	10	2
Wigan Ath.	Tr	10.97	97	27	1	1

BRADSHAW Darren Shaun
Sheffield, 19 March, 1967 E Yth (RB/M)

League Club	Source	Date Signed	Seasons Played	Apps	Subs	Gls
Chesterfield	Matlock T.	08.87	87	18	0	0
York C.	Matlock T.	11.87	87-88	58	1	3
Newcastle U.	Tr	08.89	89-91	32	6	0
Peterborough U.	Tr	08.92	92-93	70	3	1
Plymouth Arg.	L	08.94	94	5	1	1
Blackpool	Tr	10.94	94-97	61	6	1

BRADSHAW George Frederick
Southport, 10 March, 1913 Died 1989 (G)

League Club	Source	Date Signed	Seasons Played	Apps	Subs	Gls
New Brighton	High Park Villa	09.33	33-34	83	-	0
Everton	Tr	11.34	34	2	-	0
Arsenal	Tr	03.35				
Doncaster Rov.	Tr	05.36	36-37	53	-	0
Bury	Tr	06.38	38-49	118	-	0
Oldham Ath.	Tr	07.50	50	1	-	0

BRADSHAW George Henry
Clay Cross, 24 March, 1920 (CF)

League Club	Source	Date Signed	Seasons Played	Apps	Subs	Gls
Chesterfield	Newstead Colly	04.46	47	7	-	1

BRADSHAW Mark
Ashton-u-Lyne, 7 September, 1969 (FB)

League Club	Source	Date Signed	Seasons Played	Apps	Subs	Gls
Blackpool	YT	12.87	86-90	34	8	1
York C.	L	04.91	90	0	1	0

League Club	Source	Date Signed	Seasons Played	Career Record Apps	Subs	Gls
BRADSHAW Paul						
Sheffield, 2 October, 1953 E Sch/E Yth						(W)
Burnley	App	10.70	74-76	11	2	2
Sheffield Wed.	Tr	09.76	76-77	62	2	9
BRADSHAW Paul William						
Altrincham, 28 April, 1956 E Yth/Eu21-4						(G)
Blackburn Rov.	App	07.73	73-77	78	0	0
Wolverhampton W.	Tr	09.77	77-83	200	0	0
West Bromwich A.	Vancouver (Can)	04.85	85	8	0	0
Bristol Rov. (N/C)	Walsall (Coach)	03.87	86	5	0	0
Newport Co. (N/C)	Tr	07.87	87	23	0	0
West Bromwich A.	Tr	08.88	88-89	6	0	0
Peterborough U.	Tr	06.90	90	39	0	0
BRADY Garry						
Glasgow, 7 September, 1976 S Yth						(M)
Tottenham H.	YT	09.93	97	0	9	0
BRADY Kieron						
Glasgow, 17 September, 1971 IRu21-3						(W)
Sunderland	YT	07.89	89-91	17	16	7
Doncaster Rov.	L	10.92	92	4	0	3
BRADY Matthew John						
Marylebone, 27 October, 1977						(M)
Barnet	YT	07.96	94-96	2	8	0
BRADY Patrick Joseph						
Dublin, 11 March, 1936						(LB)
Millwall	Home Farm	01.59	58-62	148	-	1
Queens Park R.	Tr	07.63	63-64	62	-	0
BRADY Paul James						
Marston Green, 26 March, 1961						(FB)
Birmingham C.	App	08.78				
Northampton T.	Tr	08.81	81-82	49	2	3
Crewe Alex.	Tr	02.83	82-83	42	1	1
BRADY Thomas **Raymond**						
Dublin, 3 June, 1937 IR-6						(CH)
Millwall	Home Farm	07.57	57-62	165	-	4
Queens Park R.	Tr	07.63	63-65	88	0	0
BRADY William (Liam)						
Dublin, 13 February, 1956 IR-72						(M)
Arsenal	App	08.73	73-79	227	8	43
West Ham U.	Ascoli (It)	03.87	86-89	79	10	8
BRAGG Walter Leonard						
London, 8 July, 1929						(D)
Brentford	Jnrs	01.47	46-56	161	-	6
BRAHAN Marcel Eric **Louis (Lou)**						
Stepney, 3 December, 1926 Died 1995						(CH)
Leyton Orient (Am)	Walthamstow Ave.	07.55	55	1	-	0
BRAIN Simon Anthony John						
Evesham, 31 March, 1966						(F)
Hereford U.	Cheltenham T.	12.90	90-93	81	6	20
BRAITHWAITE Leon Jerome						
Hackney, 17 December, 1972						(F)
Exeter C.	Bishops Stortford	11.95	95-97	40	26	9
BRAITHWAITE Robert Munn						
Belfast, 24 February, 1937 NI Sch/NI-10						(W)
Middlesbrough	Linfield	06.63	63-66	67	1	12
BRAMHALL John						
Warrington, 20 November, 1956						(CD)
Tranmere Rov.	Stockton Heath	07.76	76-81	164	6	7
Bury	Tr	03.82	81-85	165	2	17
Chester C.	L	11.85	85	4	0	0
Rochdale	Tr	08.86	86-87	86	0	13
Halifax T.	Tr	08.88	88-89	62	0	5
Scunthorpe U.	Tr	01.90	89-90	32	0	0
BRAMHALL Neil						
Blackpool, 16 October, 1965						(F)
Blackpool	App	10.83	82	0	3	0
BRAMLEY Arthur						
Mansfield, 25 March, 1929						(G)
Mansfield T.	Bentinck Colly	10.49	49-52	19	-	0
BRAMLEY Ernest						
Mansfield, 29 August, 1920 Died 1993						(RB)
Mansfield T.	Bolsover Colly	12.38	38-47	45	-	1
BRAMLEY John **Stewart**						
Scunthorpe, 19 April, 1946						(F)
Scunthorpe U.	App	04.64	64-66	35	0	3
BRAMMER David						
Bromborough, 28 February, 1975						(M)
Wrexham	YT	07.93	92-97	87	16	10
BRAMWELL John						
Ashton-in-Makerfield, 1 March, 1937						(FB)
Everton	Wigan Ath.	04.58	58-59	52	-	0
Luton T.	Tr	10.60	60-64	187	-	1
BRAMWELL Steven						
Stockport, 9 October, 1970						(M)
Oldham Ath.	YT	07.89	88	0	1	0
Crewe Alex.	Tr	05.90				
BRANAGAN James Patrick Stephen						
Urmston, 3 July, 1955						(FB)
Oldham Ath.	Jnrs	07.73	74-76	24	3	0
Huddersfield T.	Cape Town C. (SA)	11.77	77-78	37	1	0
Blackburn Rov.	Tr	10.79	79-86	290	4	5
Preston N.E.	Tr	05.87	87	3	0	0
York C.	Tr	10.87	87-88	40	2	1
BRANAGAN Keith Graham						
Fulham, 10 July, 1966 IR 'B'/IR-1						(G)
Cambridge U.	Jnrs	08.83	83-87	110	0	0
Millwall	Tr	03.88	89-91	46	0	0
Brentford	L	11.89	89	2	0	0
Gillingham	L	10.91	91	1	0	0
Bolton W.	Tr	07.92	92-97	200	0	0
BRANAGAN Kenneth						
Salford, 27 July, 1930 IR 'B'/IR-1						(FB)
Manchester C.	N.Salford B.C.	11.48	50-59	196	-	3
Oldham Ath.	Tr	10.60	60-65	177	0	5
BRANCA Marco						
Italy, 6 January, 1965						(CF)
Middlesbrough	Inter Milan (It)	02.98	97	11	0	9
BRANCH Graham						
Liverpool, 12 February, 1972						(W)
Tranmere Rov.	Heswall	05.91	91-97	55	47	10
Bury	L	11.92	92	3	1	1
Wigan Ath.	L	12.97	97	2	1	0
BRANCH Paul **Michael**						
Liverpool, 18 October, 1978 E Sch/E Yth/Eu21-2						(F)
Everton	YT	10.95	95-97	15	19	3
[BRANCO] LEAL Claudio Ibraim Vaz						
Brazil, 4 April, 1964 Brazilian Int						(LB)
Middlesbrough	Genoa (It)	03.96	95-96	6	3	0
BRAND Andrew (Drew) Scougal						
Edinburgh, 8 November, 1957						(G)
Everton	App	11.75	75-76	2	0	0
Crewe Alex.	L	02.77	76	14	0	0
Crewe Alex.	L	08.78	78	1	0	0
Hereford U.	Tr	05.80	80-81	54	0	0
Wrexham	L	11.82	82	1	0	0
Blackpool (N/C)	Witton A.	03.84	83	3	0	0
BRAND Kenneth Reginald						
Whitechapel, 28 April, 1938						(LB)
Millwall	Eton Manor	09.56	56-57	13	-	0
BRAND Ralph Laidlaw						
Edinburgh, 18 December, 1936 S Sch/Su23-1/SF Lge/S-8						(CF)
Manchester C.	Glasgow Rangers	08.65	65-66	20	0	2
Sunderland	Tr	08.67	67-68	31	0	7
BRAND Raymond Ernest						
Islington, 2 October, 1934						(CH)
Millwall	Hatfield	10.51	55-60	150	-	8
Southend U.	Tr	08.61	61-62	22	-	9
BRANDER George Milne						
Aberdeen, 1 November, 1929 Died 1995						(W)
Newcastle U.	Raith Rov.	03.52	52	5	-	2
BRANDON Kenneth Alfred						
Birmingham, 8 February, 1934 Died 1994						(OL)
Swindon T. (Am)	Kingstanding B.C.	01.53	52	5	-	0
Chester C.	Tr	06.53	53-55	36	-	6
Leicester C.	Tr	07.56				
Darlington	Tr	06.58	58	16	-	1

BRANFOOT Ian Grant
Gateshead, 26 January, 1947 (RB)

League Club	Source	Date Signed	Seasons Played	Apps	Subs	Gls
Sheffield Wed.	Gateshead	07.65	66-69	33	3	0
Doncaster Rov.	Tr	12.69	69-72	156	0	5
Lincoln C.	Tr	07.73	73-77	166	0	11

BRANNAN Gerard (Ged) Daniel
Prescot, 15 January, 1972 (M/FB)

League Club	Source	Date Signed	Seasons Played	Apps	Subs	Gls
Tranmere Rov.	YT	07.90	90-96	227	11	20
Manchester C.	Tr	03.97	96-97	38	5	4

BRANNAN Peter
Bradford, 7 April, 1947 (W)

League Club	Source	Date Signed	Seasons Played	Apps	Subs	Gls
Bradford P.A.		02.69	68-69	38	4	2

BRANNAN Robert
Bradford, 27 August, 1924 Died 1986 (OR)

League Club	Source	Date Signed	Seasons Played	Apps	Subs	Gls
Bradford C.		09.47	47-48	11	-	2

BRANNIGAN Kenneth
Glasgow, 8 June, 1965 (CD)

League Club	Source	Date Signed	Seasons Played	Apps	Subs	Gls
Sheffield Wed.	Queens Park	08.86	86	1	0	0
Stockport Co.	L	08.86	86	8	0	0
Doncaster Rov.	L	12.87	87	15	0	1

BRANSTON Guy Peter Bromley
Leicester, 9 January, 1979 (CH)

League Club	Source	Date Signed	Seasons Played	Apps	Subs	Gls
Leicester C.	YT	07.97				
Colchester U.	L	02.98	97	12	0	1

BRANSTON Terence George
Rugby, 25 July, 1938 (CH)

League Club	Source	Date Signed	Seasons Played	Apps	Subs	Gls
Northampton T.		10.58	60-66	244	2	2
Luton T.	Tr	06.67	67-70	100	1	9
Lincoln C.	Tr	09.70	70-72	99	1	1

BRASS Christopher Paul
Easington, 24 July, 1975 (CD)

League Club	Source	Date Signed	Seasons Played	Apps	Subs	Gls
Burnley	YT	07.93	94-97	83	10	1
Torquay U.	L	10.94	94	7	0	0

BRASS Robert Albert
Middlesbrough, 9 November, 1943 (HB)

League Club	Source	Date Signed	Seasons Played	Apps	Subs	Gls
Middlesbrough	Jnrs	06.62				
Hartlepool U.	Tr	10.64	64-65	27	1	0

BRASTED Gordon Albert
Burnham (Ex), 30 June, 1933 (CF)

League Club	Source	Date Signed	Seasons Played	Apps	Subs	Gls
Arsenal	Burnham Ramblers	12.53				
Gillingham	Tr	07.56	56	5	-	4

BRATLEY Charles **Tony**
Grimsby, 30 April, 1939 (FB)

League Club	Source	Date Signed	Seasons Played	Apps	Subs	Gls
Grimsby T.		08.57	58	2	-	0

BRATT Harold
Salford, 8 October, 1939 E Sch (WH)

League Club	Source	Date Signed	Seasons Played	Apps	Subs	Gls
Manchester U.	Jnrs	11.57				
Doncaster Rov.	Tr	05.61	61-62	54	-	0

BRATTAN Gary
Hull, 1 January, 1960 (M)

League Club	Source	Date Signed	Seasons Played	Apps	Subs	Gls
Hull C.	App	01.78				
Cambridge U. (N/C)	North Ferriby U.	08.87	87	7	1	0

BRAXTHWAITE John Roderick
Isleworth, 19 December, 1965 (F)

League Club	Source	Date Signed	Seasons Played	Apps	Subs	Gls
Fulham	Jnrs	07.84	85-86	7	5	2

BRAY Geoffrey Charles
Rochester, 30 May, 1951 (F)

League Club	Source	Date Signed	Seasons Played	Apps	Subs	Gls
Oxford U.	Erith & Belvedere	07.71	72-74	22	11	6
Swansea C.	Tr	07.75	75-76	43	3	20
Torquay U.	Tr	11.76	76	7	0	2

BRAY George
Oswaldtwistle, 11 November, 1918 (WH)

League Club	Source	Date Signed	Seasons Played	Apps	Subs	Gls
Burnley	Great Harwood T.	10.37	38-51	241	-	8

BRAY Ian Michael
Neath, 6 December, 1962 (LB)

League Club	Source	Date Signed	Seasons Played	Apps	Subs	Gls
Hereford U.	App	12.80	81-84	105	3	4
Huddersfield T.	Tr	07.85	85-89	87	2	1
Burnley	Tr	07.90	90-91	15	2	0

BRAY John
Rishton, 16 March, 1937 Died 1992 (FB)

League Club	Source	Date Signed	Seasons Played	Apps	Subs	Gls
Blackburn Rov.	Jnrs	03.54	59-64	153	-	2
Bury	Tr	04.65	65	32	0	0

BRAY Wayne
Bristol, 17 November, 1964 (M)

League Club	Source	Date Signed	Seasons Played	Apps	Subs	Gls
Bristol C.	App	11.81	81-82	28	1	2

BRAYSON Paul
Newcastle, 16 September, 1977 E Yth (F)

League Club	Source	Date Signed	Seasons Played	Apps	Subs	Gls
Newcastle U.	YT	08.95				
Swansea C.	L	01.97	96	11	0	5
Reading	Tr	03.98	97	2	4	1

BRAYTON Barry James
Carlisle, 29 September, 1938 (F)

League Club	Source	Date Signed	Seasons Played	Apps	Subs	Gls
Carlisle U.		01.60	59-66	160	1	35
Workington	Tr	02.67	66-67	43	0	8

BRAZIER Colin James
Birmingham, 6 June, 1957 E Semi Pro (CD)

League Club	Source	Date Signed	Seasons Played	Apps	Subs	Gls
Wolverhampton W.	Alvechurch	08.75	76-81	69	9	2
Birmingham C.	Jacksonville (USA)	09.82	82	10	1	1
Lincoln C.	A.P. Leamington	04.83	82	9	0	0
Walsall	Tr	08.83	83-86	114	1	4

BRAZIER Matthew Ronald
Leytonstone, 2 July, 1976 (M)

League Club	Source	Date Signed	Seasons Played	Apps	Subs	Gls
Queens Park R.	YT	07.94	95-97	36	13	2
Fulham	Tr	03.98	97	3	4	1

BRAZIL Alan Bernard
Glasgow, 15 June, 1959 Su21-8/S-13 (F)

League Club	Source	Date Signed	Seasons Played	Apps	Subs	Gls
Ipswich T.	App	05.77	77-82	143	11	70
Tottenham H.	Tr	03.83	82-83	29	2	9
Manchester U.	Tr	06.84	84-85	18	13	8
Coventry C.	Tr	01.86	85	15	0	2
Queens Park R.	Tr	06.86	86	1	3	0

BRAZIL Derek Michael
Dublin, 14 December, 1968 IR Sch/IR Yth/IRu21-7/IRu23-2/IR 'B' (CD)

League Club	Source	Date Signed	Seasons Played	Apps	Subs	Gls
Manchester U.	Rivermount B.C.	03.86	88-89	0	2	0
Oldham Ath.	L	11.90	90	1	0	0
Swansea C.	L	09.91	91	12	0	1
Cardiff C.	Tr	08.92	92-95	109	6	1

BRAZIL Gary Nicholas
Tunbridge Wells, 19 September, 1962 (F)

League Club	Source	Date Signed	Seasons Played	Apps	Subs	Gls
Sheffield U.	Crystal Palace (App)	08.80	80-84	39	23	9
Port Vale	L	08.84	84	6	0	3
Preston N.E.	Tr	02.85	84-88	163	3	58
Newcastle U.	Tr	02.89	88-89	7	16	2
Fulham	Tr	09.90	90-95	207	7	48
Cambridge U. (N/C)	Tr	08.96	96	1	0	1
Barnet	Tr	09.96	96	15	4	2

BREACKER Timothy Sean
Bicester, 2 July, 1965 Eu21-2 (RB)

League Club	Source	Date Signed	Seasons Played	Apps	Subs	Gls
Luton T.	App	05.83	83-90	204	6	3
West Ham U.	Tr	10.90	90-97	227	10	8

BREAKS Edward
Halifax, 29 December, 1919 (FB)

League Club	Source	Date Signed	Seasons Played	Apps	Subs	Gls
Halifax T.		07.48	48-54	179	-	1

BREARS Paul Arthur
Oldham, 25 September, 1954 (M)

League Club	Source	Date Signed	Seasons Played	Apps	Subs	Gls
Rochdale	Oldham Ath. (Am)	08.73	73-75	26	1	0

BREBNER Grant Iain
Edinburgh, 6 December, 1977 Su21-8 (M)

League Club	Source	Date Signed	Seasons Played	Apps	Subs	Gls
Manchester U.	Hutchinson Vale B.C.	03.95				
Cambridge U.	L	01.98	97	6	0	1

BRECKIN Ian
Rotherham, 24 February, 1975 (CD)

League Club	Source	Date Signed	Seasons Played	Apps	Subs	Gls
Rotherham U.	YT	11.93	93-96	130	2	6
Chesterfield	Tr	07.97	97	40	3	1

BRECKIN John
Sheffield, 27 July, 1953 (FB)

League Club	Source	Date Signed	Seasons Played	Apps	Subs	Gls
Rotherham U.	App	11.71	71-82	405	4	8
Darlington	L	10.72	72	4	0	0
Bury	Tr	02.83	82	17	0	0
Doncaster Rov.	Tr	08.83	83	17	1	0

BREEN Gary Patrick
Hendon, 12 December, 1973 IRu21-9/IR-15 (CD)

League Club	Source	Date Signed	Seasons Played	Apps	Subs	Gls
Maidstone U.	Jnrs	03.91	91	19	0	0
Gillingham	Tr	07.92	92-93	45	6	0
Peterborough U.	Tr	08.94	94-95	68	1	1
Birmingham C.	Tr	02.96	95-96	37	3	2
Coventry C.	Tr	02.97	96-97	38	1	1

BREITKREUTZ Matthias
Germany, 12 May, 1971 (M)

League Club	Source	Date Signed	Seasons Played	Apps	Subs	Gls
Aston Villa	Bergman Bosnig (Ger)	10.91	91-93	10	3	0

BREMNER Desmond George
Aberchirder 7 September, 1952 Su23-9/S-1 (M)

League Club	Source	Date Signed	Seasons Played	Apps	Subs	Gls
Aston Villa	Hibernian	09.79	79-84	170	4	9
Birmingham C.	Tr	09.84	84-88	167	1	5
Fulham	Tr	08.89	89	7	9	0
Walsall (N/C)	Tr	03.90	89	2	4	0

BREMNER Kevin Johnston
Banff, 7 October, 1957 (F)

League Club	Source	Date Signed	Seasons Played	Apps	Subs	Gls
Colchester U.	Keith	10.80	80-82	89	6	31
Birmingham C.	L	10.82	82	3	1	1
Wrexham	L	12.82	82	4	0	1
Plymouth Arg.	L	01.83	82	5	0	1
Millwall	Tr	02.83	82-84	87	9	32
Reading	Tr	08.85	85-86	60	4	21
Brighton & H.A.	Tr	07.87	87-89	125	3	35
Peterborough U.	Tr	07.90	90	13	4	3
Shrewsbury T. (L)	Dundee	03.92	91	7	0	2

BREMNER William John
Glasgow, 9 December, 1942 Died 1997 S Sch/Su23-4/S-54 (M)

League Club	Source	Date Signed	Seasons Played	Apps	Subs	Gls
Leeds U.	Jnrs	12.59	59-76	585	1	90
Hull C.	Tr	09.76	76-77	61	0	6
Doncaster Rov.	Tr	09.79	79-81	2	3	0

BRENEN Albert
South Shields, 5 October, 1915 Died 1995 (HB)

League Club	Source	Date Signed	Seasons Played	Apps	Subs	Gls
York C.	St John's College	08.38	38-50	204	-	13

BRENNAN Bryan
Halifax, 25 May, 1933 E Sch (CF)

League Club	Source	Date Signed	Seasons Played	Apps	Subs	Gls
Stockport Co.	Jnrs	06.50	50	4	-	0

BRENNAN Francis
Airdrie, 23 April, 1924 Died 1997 S-7 (CH)

League Club	Source	Date Signed	Seasons Played	Apps	Subs	Gls
Newcastle U.	Airdrieonians	05.46	46-55	318	-	3

BRENNAN Harry
Derby, 17 November, 1930 (IF)

League Club	Source	Date Signed	Seasons Played	Apps	Subs	Gls
Shrewsbury T.	Gresley Rov.	12.53	53-54	19	-	3

BRENNAN Ian
Easington, 25 March, 1953 (LB)

League Club	Source	Date Signed	Seasons Played	Apps	Subs	Gls
Burnley	App	10.70	74-79	173	2	11
Bolton W.	Tr	12.80	80-81	16	1	0

BRENNAN James
Downpatrick (NI), 29 February, 1932 (OL)

League Club	Source	Date Signed	Seasons Played	Apps	Subs	Gls
Birmingham C.	Glentoran	06.52				
Swindon T.	Tr	06.54	54-55	16	-	1

BRENNAN James Gerald
Canada, 8 May, 1977 (M)

League Club	Source	Date Signed	Seasons Played	Apps	Subs	Gls
Bristol C.	Sora Lazio (Can)	10.94	96-97	11	3	0

BRENNAN Malcolm
Manchester, 11 November, 1934 (IF)

League Club	Source	Date Signed	Seasons Played	Apps	Subs	Gls
Crewe Alex.		12.52	56	1	-	0

BRENNAN Mark Robert
Rossendale, 4 October, 1965 E Yth/Eu21-5 (LM)

League Club	Source	Date Signed	Seasons Played	Apps	Subs	Gls
Ipswich T.	App	04.83	83-87	165	3	19
Middlesbrough	Tr	07.88	88-89	61	4	6
Manchester C.	Tr	07.90	90-91	25	4	6
Oldham Ath.	Tr	11.92	92-95	82	8	7

BRENNAN Matthew Hyland
Glasgow, 3 January, 1943 (IF)

League Club	Source	Date Signed	Seasons Played	Apps	Subs	Gls
Luton T.	St Rochs	06.62	62	4	-	1

BRENNAN Michael
Salford, 17 May, 1952 (F)

League Club	Source	Date Signed	Seasons Played	Apps	Subs	Gls
Manchester C.	App	12.69	70-72	1	3	0
Stockport Co.	L	02.72	71	18	0	3
Rochdale	Tr	10.73	73-74	35	2	4

BRENNAN Patrick Joseph
Dublin, 1 March, 1924 Died 1991 (WH)

League Club	Source	Date Signed	Seasons Played	Apps	Subs	Gls
Brighton & H.A.	Shelbourne	08.48	48-50	45	-	0

BRENNAN Raymond John
Blackpool, 13 November, 1944 (F)

League Club	Source	Date Signed	Seasons Played	Apps	Subs	Gls
Blackburn Rov.	Wolverhampton W. (Am)	07.62				
Barrow	Tr	03.64	63-64	46	-	10

BRENNAN Robert Anderson
Belfast, 14 March, 1925 IR Lge/NI-5 (IF)

League Club	Source	Date Signed	Seasons Played	Apps	Subs	Gls
Luton T.	Distillery	10.47	47-48	69	-	22
Birmingham C.	Tr	07.49	49	39	-	7
Fulham	Tr	06.50	50-52	73	-	13
Norwich C.	Tr	07.53	53-59	225	-	44

BRENNAN James **Seamus** Anthony
Manchester, 6 May, 1937 IR-19 (FB)

League Club	Source	Date Signed	Seasons Played	Apps	Subs	Gls
Manchester U.	Jnrs	04.55	57-69	291	1	3

BRENNAN Stephen Anthony
Mile End, 3 September, 1958 (M)

League Club	Source	Date Signed	Seasons Played	Apps	Subs	Gls
Crystal Palace	App	02.76	76-77	2	1	1
Plymouth Arg.	Tr	08.78	78	6	0	0

BRENT Peter
Staveley, 18 November, 1937 Died 1988 (HB)

League Club	Source	Date Signed	Seasons Played	Apps	Subs	Gls
Chesterfield	Jnrs	01.55	59	2	-	0

BRENTANO Stephen Ronald
Hull, 9 November, 1961 (FB)

League Club	Source	Date Signed	Seasons Played	Apps	Subs	Gls
Hull C.	North Ferriby U.	03.82	84-86	11	1	0
Doncaster Rov. (N/C)	Bridlington T.	08.93	93	1	0	0

BRESLAN Geoffrey Francis
Torbay, 4 June, 1980 (M)

League Club	Source	Date Signed	Seasons Played	Apps	Subs	Gls
Exeter C.	YT	●	97	0	1	0

BRESSINGTON Graham
Eton, 8 July, 1966 (M/CD)

League Club	Source	Date Signed	Seasons Played	Apps	Subs	Gls
Lincoln C.	Wycombe W.	10.87	88-92	136	5	7
Southend U.	Tr	07.93	93-94	46	2	5

BRETHERTON Thomas
Chorley, 9 April, 1920 (IR)

League Club	Source	Date Signed	Seasons Played	Apps	Subs	Gls
Accrington St.	Leyland Motors	02.47	46	4	-	0

BRETT David Stephen
Chester, 8 April, 1961 (M)

League Club	Source	Date Signed	Seasons Played	Apps	Subs	Gls
Chester C.	Colwyn Bay	08.83	83-85	52	15	6

BRETT Ronald Alexander
Tilbury, 4 September, 1937 Died 1962 (CF)

League Club	Source	Date Signed	Seasons Played	Apps	Subs	Gls
Crystal Palace	Jnrs	09.54	55-58	36	-	12
West Ham U.	Tr	06.59	59-60	12	-	4
Crystal Palace	Tr	03.62	61	8	-	1

BRETTELL Raymond
Strood, 22 August, 1935 (IF)

League Club	Source	Date Signed	Seasons Played	Apps	Subs	Gls
Doncaster Rov. (Am)		01.61	60	8	-	1

BREVETT Rupis (Rufus) Emanuel
Derby, 24 September, 1969 (LB)

League Club	Source	Date Signed	Seasons Played	Apps	Subs	Gls
Doncaster Rov.	YT	06.88	87-90	106	3	3
Queens Park R.	Tr	02.91	90-97	141	11	1
Fulham	Tr	01.98	97	11	0	0

BREWER Anthony Peter
Edmonton, 20 May, 1932 Died 1989 (G)

League Club	Source	Date Signed	Seasons Played	Apps	Subs	Gls
Millwall	Jnrs	10.49	50-57	47	-	0
Northampton T.	Tr	12.57	58-60	87	-	0

BREWSTER George
Barmborough, 19 October, 1925 (F)

League Club	Source	Date Signed	Seasons Played	Apps	Subs	Gls
Bristol C.	Retford T.	09.49	49-50	13	-	3

BREWSTER John Robert
Creswell, 19 August, 1942 (WH)

League Club	Source	Date Signed	Seasons Played	Apps	Subs	Gls
Sheffield U.	Jnrs	04.60				
Torquay U.	Tr	08.64	64-65	21	0	2

BREWSTER William Clark
Kinglassie (Fife), 4 August, 1933 (G)

League Club	Source	Date Signed	Seasons Played	Apps	Subs	Gls
Chelsea	Dundonald Bluebell	08.51				
Southend U.	Tr	08.55	55	2	-	0

BRICE Gordon Henry John
Bedford, 4 May, 1924 (CH)

League Club	Source	Date Signed	Seasons Played	Apps	Subs	Gls
Luton T.	Jnrs	10.44	46	13	-	0
Wolverhampton W.	Tr	05.47	47	12	-	0
Reading	Tr	03.48	47-52	198	-	9
Fulham	Tr	12.52	52-55	87	-	1

BRICKLEY Dennis
Bradford, 9 September, 1929 E Yth (OR)

League Club	Source	Date Signed	Seasons Played	Apps	Subs	Gls
Bradford P.A.	Huddersfield T. (Am)	08.49	50-56	169	-	24

BRIDDON Samuel
Alfreton, 26 July, 1915 Died 1975 (LH)

League Club	Source	Date Signed	Seasons Played	Apps	Subs	Gls
Brentford	Port Vale (Am)	08.35	38	6	-	0
Swindon T.	Tr	07.39				
Swansea C.	Tr	01.46	46	18	-	0

BRIDGE Michael **John (Jack)**
Great Wakering, 6 June, 1932 (WH)

League Club	Source	Date Signed	Seasons Played	Apps	Subs	Gls
Southend U.	Jnrs	08.50	52-55	53	-	3

BRIDGER David James
Hartley Wintney, 8 November, 1941 (CH)

League Club	Source	Date Signed	Seasons Played	Apps	Subs	Gls
Reading		03.62	62-64	10	-	0

BRIDGES Barry John
Norwich, 29 April, 1941 E Sch/E Yth/EF Lge/E-4 (CF)

League Club	Source	Date Signed	Seasons Played	Apps	Subs	Gls
Chelsea	Jnrs	05.58	58-65	174	2	80
Birmingham C.	Tr	05.66	66-68	83	0	37
Queens Park R.	Tr	08.68	68-70	72	0	31
Millwall	Tr	09.70	70-71	77	0	27
Brighton & H.A.	Tr	09.72	72-73	56	10	14

BRIDGES Benjamin
Hull, 3 February, 1937 (IF)

League Club	Source	Date Signed	Seasons Played	Apps	Subs	Gls
Hull C.	Jnrs	08.55	57	1	-	0

BRIDGES Bernard
Doncaster, 28 February, 1959 (CD)

League Club	Source	Date Signed	Seasons Played	Apps	Subs	Gls
Scunthorpe U.	Jnrs	07.76	76-77	22	1	0

BRIDGES Harold
Burton, 30 June, 1915 Died 1989 (IL)

League Club	Source	Date Signed	Seasons Played	Apps	Subs	Gls
Manchester C.		04.37				
Tranmere Rov.	Tr	07.39	46-47	33	-	9

BRIDGES Michael
North Shields, 5 August, 1978 E Yth/Eu21-1 (F)

League Club	Source	Date Signed	Seasons Played	Apps	Subs	Gls
Sunderland	YT	11.95	95-97	18	31	8

BRIDGETT John
Walsall, 10 April, 1929 (CH/F)

League Club	Source	Date Signed	Seasons Played	Apps	Subs	Gls
West Bromwich A.	Jnrs	05.46				
Walsall	Tr	08.50	50-54	106	-	18

BRIDGETT Raymond Alwyn
Walsall, 5 April, 1947 (FB)

League Club	Source	Date Signed	Seasons Played	Apps	Subs	Gls
Nottingham F.	Jnrs	05.64	67-69	2	2	0

BRIDGWOOD Gerald
Stoke, 17 October, 1944 (M)

League Club	Source	Date Signed	Seasons Played	Apps	Subs	Gls
Stoke C.	App	10.61	60-68	90	5	6
Shrewsbury T.	Tr	02.69	68-72	113	4	7

BRIEN Anthony James
Dublin, 10 February, 1969 IR Yth (CD)

League Club	Source	Date Signed	Seasons Played	Apps	Subs	Gls
Leicester C.	App	02.87	87-88	12	4	1
Chesterfield	Tr	12.88	88-93	201	3	8
Rotherham U.	Tr	10.93	93-94	41	2	2
West Bromwich A.	Tr	07.95	95	2	0	0
Mansfield T.	L	02.96	95	4	0	0
Chester C.	L	03.96	95	8	0	0
Hull C.	Tr	07.96	96-97	43	4	1

BRIEN William Roy
Stoke, 11 November, 1930 Died 1987 (HB)

League Club	Source	Date Signed	Seasons Played	Apps	Subs	Gls
Port Vale		05.51	53	1	-	0

BRIER John David
Halifax, 3 April, 1941 (WH)

League Club	Source	Date Signed	Seasons Played	Apps	Subs	Gls
Burnley	Jnrs	06.58				
Halifax T.	Tr	08.61	61-65	78	2	0

BRIERLEY Keith
Dewsbury, 14 December, 1951 (CF)

League Club	Source	Date Signed	Seasons Played	Apps	Subs	Gls
Halifax T.	Jnrs	12.69	69-72	54	4	11

BRIERLEY Kenneth
Ashton-u-Lyne, 3 April, 1926 (OL)

League Club	Source	Date Signed	Seasons Played	Apps	Subs	Gls
Oldham Ath.	Range Boilers	04.45	46-47	58	-	5
Liverpool	Tr	02.48	47-52	58	-	8
Oldham Ath.	Tr	03.53	52-54	67	-	5

BRIGGS Alec Michael
Sheffiield, 21 June, 1939 (FB)

League Club	Source	Date Signed	Seasons Played	Apps	Subs	Gls
Bristol C.	Jnrs	04.57	57-69	349	2	1

BRIGGS Charles Edward
Newtown, 4 April, 1911 (G)

League Club	Source	Date Signed	Seasons Played	Apps	Subs	Gls
Fulham	Guildford C.	12.35				
Crystal Palace	Guildford C.	05.36				
Bradford P.A.	Guildford C.	05.37				
Halifax T.	Tr	03.38	37-38	52	-	0
Rochdale	Clyde	05.47	46-47	12	-	0
Chesterfield	Tr	12.47				

BRIGGS John **Cyril**
Salford, 24 November, 1918 E Sch (CH)

League Club	Source	Date Signed	Seasons Played	Apps	Subs	Gls
Manchester U.	Darwen	10.44				
Accrington St.	Tr	08.45	46-49	135	-	1
Southport	Tr	03.50	49	3	-	0

BRIGGS Gary
Leeds, 21 June, 1959 (CD)

League Club	Source	Date Signed	Seasons Played	Apps	Subs	Gls
Middlesbrough	App	05.77				
Oxford U.	Tr	01.78	77-88	418	2	18
Blackpool	Tr	06.89	89-94	137	0	4

BRIGGS George
Easington, 27 February, 1923 (CH)

League Club	Source	Date Signed	Seasons Played	Apps	Subs	Gls
Crystal Palace	Shotton Colly	11.47	48-54	150	-	4

BRIGGS John (Jackie)
Barnsley, 27 October, 1924 Died 1992 (IF)

League Club	Source	Date Signed	Seasons Played	Apps	Subs	Gls
Gillingham	Huddersfield T. (Am)	10.46	50-52	52	-	14

BRIGGS Malcolm Douglas
Sunderland, 14 September, 1961 (M)

League Club	Source	Date Signed	Seasons Played	Apps	Subs	Gls
Birmingham C.	App	08.79	78	0	1	0

BRIGGS Maxwell Francis
Norwich, 9 September, 1948 (M)

League Club	Source	Date Signed	Seasons Played	Apps	Subs	Gls
Norwich C.	Jnrs	12.67	68-73	127	8	1
Oxford U.	Tr	02.74	73-77	94	3	1

BRIGGS William **Ronald**
Belfast, 29 March, 1943 (G)

League Club	Source	Date Signed	Seasons Played	Apps	Subs	Gls
Manchester U.	Jnrs	03.60	60-61	9	-	0
Swansea C.	Tr	05.64	64	27	-	0
Bristol Rov.	Tr	06.65	65-67	35	0	0

BRIGGS Stephen
Leeds, 2 December, 1946 (CF)

League Club	Source	Date Signed	Seasons Played	Apps	Subs	Gls
Leeds U.	Jnrs	10.65				
Doncaster Rov.	Tr	02.69	68-72	114	7	34

BRIGGS Thomas Henry
Chesterfield, 27 November, 1923 Died 1984 E 'B' (CF)

League Club	Source	Date Signed	Seasons Played	Apps	Subs	Gls
Plymouth Arg.		03.46				
Grimsby T.	Tr	05.47	47-50	116	-	78
Coventry C.	Tr	01.51	50-51	11	-	7
Birmingham C.	Tr	09.51	51-52	50	-	22
Blackburn Rov.	Tr	12.52	52-57	194	-	140
Grimsby T.	Tr	03.58	57-58	19	-	9

BRIGGS Thomas Raymond
Rotherham, 11 May, 1919 (CH)

League Club	Source	Date Signed	Seasons Played	Apps	Subs	Gls
Huddersfield T.		02.46	46-49	45	-	0
Crewe Alex.	Tr	12.49	49-55	202	-	2

BRIGGS Walter
Middlesbrough, 29 November, 1922 Died 1990 (G)

League Club	Source	Date Signed	Seasons Played	Apps	Subs	Gls
Middlesbrough	Cochranes	05.47	46-47	2	-	0
Southport	Tr	06.48	48	4	-	0
Hartlepool U.	Tr	09.49	49-51	44	-	0

BRIGGS Wilson Waite
Gorebridge, 15 May, 1942 (FB)

League Club	Source	Date Signed	Seasons Played	Apps	Subs	Gls
Aston Villa	Arniston Rov.	08.59	61-62	2	-	0

BRIGHAM Harry
Selby, 19 November, 1914 Died 1978 (RB)

League Club	Source	Date Signed	Seasons Played	Apps	Subs	Gls
Stoke C.	Frickley Colly	05.36	36-46	104	-	0
Nottingham F.	Tr	11.46	46-47	35	-	2
York C.	Tr	07.48	48-49	56	-	5

BRIGHT David
Hexham, 24 December, 1946 (FB)

League Club	Source	Date Signed	Seasons Played	Apps	Subs	Gls
Sunderland	West Wylan Jnrs	08.65				
Preston N.E.	Tr	08.67	68	1	0	0
Oldham Ath.	Tr	03.69	68-69	19	0	0

BRIGHT David John
Bath, 5 September, 1972 (F)

League Club	Source	Date Signed	Seasons Played	Apps	Subs	Gls
Stoke C.	YT	07.91	90	0	1	0

BRIGHT Gerald
Northampton, 2 December, 1934 (CF)

League Club	Source	Date Signed	Seasons Played	Apps	Subs	Gls
Northampton T.		02.57	56-57	4	-	0

BRIGHT Mark Abraham
Stoke, 6 June, 1962 (F)

League Club	Source	Date Signed	Seasons Played	Apps	Subs	Gls
Port Vale	Leek T.	10.81	81-83	18	11	10
Leicester C.	Tr	07.84	84-86	26	16	6
Crystal Palace	Tr	11.86	86-92	224	3	92
Sheffield Wed.	Tr	09.92	92-96	112	21	48
Millwall	L	12.96	96	3	0	1
Charlton Ath.	Sion (Swi)	04.97	96-97	17	5	9

BRIGHT Stewart Linden
Colchester, 13 October, 1957 (RB)

League Club	Source	Date Signed	Seasons Played	Apps	Subs	Gls
Colchester U.	App	10.75	75-76	23	2	0

BRIGHTWELL David John
Lutterworth, 7 January, 1971 (CD)

League Club	Source	Date Signed	Seasons Played	Apps	Subs	Gls
Manchester C.	Jnrs	04.88	91-94	35	8	1
Chester C.	L	03.91	90	6	0	0
Lincoln C.	L	08.95	95	5	0	0
Stoke C.	L	09.95	95	0	1	0
Bradford C.	Tr	12.95	95-96	23	1	0
Blackpool	L	12.96	96	1	1	0
Northampton T	Tr	07.97	97	34	1	1

BRIGHTWELL Ian Robert
Lutterworth, 9 April, 1968 E Yth/Eu21-4 (M/RB)

League Club	Source	Date Signed	Seasons Played	Apps	Subs	Gls
Manchester C.	Jnrs	05.86	86-97	285	36	18

BRIGNALL Stephen James Charles
Tenterden, 12 June, 1960 (D)

League Club	Source	Date Signed	Seasons Played	Apps	Subs	Gls
Arsenal	App	05.78	78	0	1	0

BRIGNULL Philip Arthur
Stratford, 2 October, 1960 ESch (CD)

League Club	Source	Date Signed	Seasons Played	Apps	Subs	Gls
West Ham U.	App	09.78	78	0	1	0
Bournemouth	Tr	08.81	81-84	128	1	11
Wrexham	L	12.85	85	5	0	1
Cardiff C.	Tr	02.86	85-86	49	0	0
Newport Co.	Tr	08.87	87	3	0	0

BRILEY Leslie
Lambeth, 2 October, 1956 (M)

League Club	Source	Date Signed	Seasons Played	Apps	Subs	Gls
Chelsea	App	06.74				
Hereford U.	Tr	05.76	76-77	60	1	2
Wimbledon	Tr	02.78	77-79	59	2	2
Aldershot	Tr	03.80	79-83	157	0	3
Millwall	Tr	05.84	84-90	225	2	13
Brighton & H.A.	Tr	08.91	91	11	4	0

BRIMACOMBE Anthony
Plymouth, 6 August, 1939 (IF)

League Club	Source	Date Signed	Seasons Played	Apps	Subs	Gls
Plymouth Arg. (Am)	Barnet	12.65	65-67	15	2	0

BRIMACOMBE John
Plymouth, 25 November, 1958 (RB/M)

League Club	Source	Date Signed	Seasons Played	Apps	Subs	Gls
Plymouth Arg.	Saltash U.	08.85	85-89	93	5	3

BRIMS Donald
Auchendinny, 8 January, 1934 (WH)

League Club	Source	Date Signed	Seasons Played	Apps	Subs	Gls
Bradford P.A.	Motherwell	05.58	58-59	76	-	3

BRINDLE John James
Blackburn, 12 July, 1917 Died 1975 (IF)

League Club	Source	Date Signed	Seasons Played	Apps	Subs	Gls
Burnley		03.43				
Rochdale	Howard & Bullough	09.45				
Chelsea	Tr	03.46				
Rochdale	Tr	08.47	47	1	-	0
New Brighton	Tr	03.48	47	9	-	3

BRINDLE William
Liverpool, 29 January, 1950 (M)

League Club	Source	Date Signed	Seasons Played	Apps	Subs	Gls
Everton	App	08.67	67	1	0	0
Barnsley	Tr	05.70	70	0	1	0

BRINDLEY Christopher Peter
Stafford, 5 July, 1969 (CD)

League Club	Source	Date Signed	Seasons Played	Apps	Subs	Gls
Wolverhampton W.	Hednesford T.	11.86	86	7	0	0

BRINDLEY John
Ashbourne, 2 June, 1931 (IF)

League Club	Source	Date Signed	Seasons Played	Apps	Subs	Gls
Chesterfield	Buxton	12.53	53	1	-	0

BRINDLEY John Charles
Nottingham, 29 January, 1947 E Sch/E Yth (RB)

League Club	Source	Date Signed	Seasons Played	Apps	Subs	Gls
Nottingham F.	Jnrs	02.64	65-69	7	8	1
Notts Co.	Tr	05.70	70-75	221	2	0
Gillingham	Tr	07.76	76	19	1	1

BRINE Peter Kenneth
Greenwich, 18 July, 1953 (M)

League Club	Source	Date Signed	Seasons Played	Apps	Subs	Gls
Middlesbrough	App	09.70	72-77	59	20	6

BRINTON Ernest James
Bristol, 26 May, 1908 Died 1981 (LH)

League Club	Source	Date Signed	Seasons Played	Apps	Subs	Gls
Bristol C.	Avonmouth T.	02.30	29-36	249	-	7
Newport Co.	Tr	06.37	37-38	75	-	3
Aldershot	Tr	08.46	46	12	-	0

BRINTON John Victor
Avonmouth, 11 July, 1916 (W)

League Club	Source	Date Signed	Seasons Played	Apps	Subs	Gls
Bristol C.	Avonmouth T.	08.35	35-36	12	-	1
Newport Co.	Tr	07.37	37	6	-	0
Derby Co.	Tr	01.38	37	8	-	2
Stockport Co.	Tr	07.46	46-47	58	-	9
Leyton Orient	Tr	08.48	48	4	-	1

BRISCOE Anthony Maurice
Birmingham, 16 August, 1978 (F)

League Club	Source	Date Signed	Seasons Played	Apps	Subs	Gls
Shrewsbury T.	YT	●	96	0	1	0

BRISCOE James Edward
Clockface, 23 April, 1917 Died 1981 (OR)

League Club	Source	Date Signed	Seasons Played	Apps	Subs	Gls
Preston N.E.	St Helens T.	05.34	36	5	-	0
Northampton T.	Hearts	09.46	46-48	53	-	17

BRISCOE James Patrick
Swinton-on-Dearne, 14 October, 1923 (CF)

League Club	Source	Date Signed	Seasons Played	Apps	Subs	Gls
Sheffield Wed.	Jnrs	08.46	46	5	-	3

BRISCOE John
Huddersfield, 31 May, 1947 (CF)

League Club	Source	Date Signed	Seasons Played	Apps	Subs	Gls
Barnsley	Jnrs	10.66	66-67	11	0	5

BRISCOE Lee Stephen
Pontefract, 30 September, 1975 Eu21-5 (LB)

League Club	Source	Date Signed	Seasons Played	Apps	Subs	Gls
Sheffield Wed.	YT	05.94	93-97	36	10	0
Manchester C.	L	02.98	97	5	0	1

BRISCOE Robert Dean
Derby, 4 September, 1969 (LB)

League Club	Source	Date Signed	Seasons Played	Apps	Subs	Gls
Derby Co.	YT	09.87	89-90	10	3	1

BRISLEY Terence William
Stepney, 4 July, 1950 (M)

League Club	Source	Date Signed	Seasons Played	Apps	Subs	Gls
Leyton Orient	App	07.68	67-74	133	9	9
Southend U.	L	03.75	74	8	0	0
Millwall	Tr	07.75	75-77	106	1	14
Charlton Ath.	Tr	01.78	77-78	44	4	5
Portsmouth	Tr	07.79	79-80	55	0	13

BRISSETT Jason Curtis
Wanstead, 7 September, 1974 (LM)

League Club	Source	Date Signed	Seasons Played	Apps	Subs	Gls
Peterborough U.	Arsenal (YT)	06.93	93-94	27	8	0
Bournemouth	Tr	12.94	94-97	96	28	8

BRISSETT Trevor Anthony
Stoke, 2 January, 1961 (FB)

League Club	Source	Date Signed	Seasons Played	Apps	Subs	Gls
Stoke C.	Jnrs	04.78				
Port Vale	Tr	05.80	80-81	47	8	0
Darlington	Tr	08.82	82	10	2	0

BRISTOW George Andrew
Chiswick, 25 June, 1933 (WH)

League Club	Source	Date Signed	Seasons Played	Apps	Subs	Gls
Brentford	Jnrs	07.50	50-60	245	-	8
Queens Park R.	Tr	05.61				

BRISTOW Guy Austin
Kingsbury, 23 October, 1955 (CD)

League Club	Source	Date Signed	Seasons Played	Apps	Subs	Gls
Watford	App	07.73	74-76	18	5	0

BRITT Martin Charles
Leigh-on-Sea, 17 January, 1946 E Yth (CF)

League Club	Source	Date Signed	Seasons Played	Apps	Subs	Gls
West Ham U.	App	01.63	62-65	20	0	6
Blackburn Rov.	Tr	03.66	65	8	0	0

BRITTAN Colin
Bristol, 2 June, 1927 (WH)

League Club	Source	Date Signed	Seasons Played	Apps	Subs	Gls
Tottenham H.	North Bristol O.B.	10.48	50-57	41	-	1

BRITTEN Martyn Edward Walter
Bristol, 1 May, 1955 (W)

League Club	Source	Date Signed	Seasons Played	Apps	Subs	Gls
Bristol Rov.	App	05.73	74-76	17	3	2
Reading	Tr	08.77	77-78	6	2	0

BRITTON Gerard Joseph
Glasgow, 20 October, 1970 (F)

League Club	Source	Date Signed	Seasons Played	Apps	Subs	Gls
Reading (L)	Glasgow Celtic	11.91	91	0	2	0

BRITTON Ian
Dundee, 19 May, 1954 (W)

League Club	Source	Date Signed	Seasons Played	Apps	Subs	Gls
Chelsea	App	07.71	72-81	253	10	33

League Club	Source	Date Signed	Seasons Played	Apps	Subs	Gls
Blackpool	Dundee U.	12.83	83-85	100	6	15
Burnley	Tr	08.86	86-88	102	6	10

BRITTON James
Salford, 27 May, 1920 (WH)

League Club	Source	Date Signed	Seasons Played	Apps	Subs	Gls
Bradford P.A.	Lowestoft	01.46	46	1	-	0
Rochdale	Tr	12.47	47-48	20	-	0

BROAD Ronald
Sandbach, 18 August, 1933 (OL)

League Club	Source	Date Signed	Seasons Played	Apps	Subs	Gls
Crewe Alex. (Am)	Congleton T.	12.55	55	6	-	0

BROADBENT Albert Henry
West Bromwich, 20 August, 1934 (OL)

League Club	Source	Date Signed	Seasons Played	Apps	Subs	Gls
Notts Co.	Dudley T.	03.52	53-54	31	-	11
Sheffield Wed.	Tr	07.55	55-57	81	-	17
Rotherham U.	Tr	12.57	57-58	48	-	14
Doncaster Rov.	Tr	06.59	59-61	100	-	20
Lincoln C.	Tr	11.61	61-62	38	-	4
Doncaster Rov.	Tr	01.63	62-65	106	0	19
Bradford P.A.	Tr	10.65	65-66	56	0	11
Hartlepool U.	Tr	02.67	66-67	25	0	3

BROADBENT Graham
Halifax, 20 December, 1958 (F)

League Club	Source	Date Signed	Seasons Played	Apps	Subs	Gls
Halifax T.	Emley	09.88	88-90	13	19	3

BROADBENT Peter Frank
Dover, 15 May, 1933 Eu23-1/E 'B'/EF Lge/E-7 (IF)

League Club	Source	Date Signed	Seasons Played	Apps	Subs	Gls
Brentford	Jnrs	05.50	50	16	-	2
Wolverhampton W.	Tr	02.51	50-64	452	-	127
Shrewsbury T.	Tr	01.65	64-66	69	0	7
Aston Villa	Tr	10.66	66-68	60	4	2
Stockport Co.	Tr	10.69	69	31	0	1

BROADFOOT Joseph James
Lewisham, 4 March, 1940 (OR)

League Club	Source	Date Signed	Seasons Played	Apps	Subs	Gls
Millwall	Jnrs	01.58	58-63	225	-	60
Ipswich T.	Tr	10.63	63-65	81	0	17
Northampton T.	Tr	11.65	65	17	0	1
Millwall	Tr	07.66	66	26	0	5
Ipswich T.	Tr	02.67	66-67	19	1	2

BROADHURST Brian Walter
Sheffield, 24 November, 1938 (F)

League Club	Source	Date Signed	Seasons Played	Apps	Subs	Gls
Chesterfield	Hallam	10.61	61	7	-	0

BROADHURST Kevan
Dewsbury, 3 June, 1959 (D)

League Club	Source	Date Signed	Seasons Played	Apps	Subs	Gls
Birmingham C.	App	03.77	76-83	147	6	10
Walsall	L	11.79	79	3	0	0

BROADIS Ivan (Ivor) Arthur
Poplar, 18 December, 1922 EF Lge/E-14 (IF)

League Club	Source	Date Signed	Seasons Played	Apps	Subs	Gls
Carlisle U.	Tottenham H. (Am)	08.46	46-48	90	-	53
Sunderland	Tr	02.49	48-51	79	-	25
Manchester C.	Tr	10.51	51-53	74	-	10
Newcastle U.	Tr	10.53	53-54	42	-	15
Carlisle U.	Tr	07.55	55-58	157	-	33

BROADLEY Leslie
Goole, 10 August, 1930 (CF)

League Club	Source	Date Signed	Seasons Played	Apps	Subs	Gls
Scunthorpe U.	Goole T.	08.52	52	5	-	2

BROADLEY Patrick Joseph
Croy, 13 May, 1926 (LH)

League Club	Source	Date Signed	Seasons Played	Apps	Subs	Gls
Oldham Ath.	Sligo Rov.	06.51	51	4	-	0

BROCK Kevin Stanley
Bicester, 9 September, 1962 E Sch/Eu21-4/E 'B' (M)

League Club	Source	Date Signed	Seasons Played	Apps	Subs	Gls
Oxford U.	App	09.79	79-86	229	17	26
Queens Park R.	Tr	08.87	87-88	38	2	2
Newcastle U.	Tr	12.88	88-92	135	10	14
Cardiff C.	L	02.94	93	14	0	2

BROCKBANK Andrew
Millom, 23 September, 1961 (LB)

League Club	Source	Date Signed	Seasons Played	Apps	Subs	Gls
Blackpool	App	12.79	79-82	32	4	1

BROCKEN Budde Jan Peter Maria
Netherlands, 12 September, 1957 (M)

League Club	Source	Date Signed	Seasons Played	Apps	Subs	Gls
Birmingham C.	Willem Tilburg (Neth)	08.81	81	17	0	0

BROCKIE Vincent
Greenock, 2 February, 1969 (M/RB)

League Club	Source	Date Signed	Seasons Played	Apps	Subs	Gls
Leeds U.	YT	07.87	87	2	0	0
Doncaster Rov.	Tr	12.88	88-90	43	11	7

BROCKLEHURST John Fletcher
Horwich, 15 December, 1927 (WH)

League Club	Source	Date Signed	Seasons Played	Apps	Subs	Gls
Accrington St.	Stalybridge Celtic	05.52	52	34	-	0
Bradford P.A.	Stalybridge Celtic	08.54	54-55	47	-	1

BRODDLE Julian Raymond
Laughton, 1 November, 1964 (W/FB)

League Club	Source	Date Signed	Seasons Played	Apps	Subs	Gls
Sheffield U.	App	11.82	81	1	0	0
Scunthorpe U.	Tr	08.83	83-87	126	18	32
Barnsley	Tr	09.87	87-89	63	14	4
Plymouth Arg.	Tr	01.90	89	9	0	0
Scunthorpe U. (L)	St Mirren	09.92	92	5	0	0

BRODERICK Mortimer
Cork (Ire) 1 September, 1923 IRF Lge (IR)

League Club	Source	Date Signed	Seasons Played	Apps	Subs	Gls
Sheffield U.	Cork	08.50	50	2	-	0

BRODIE Charles (Chic) Thomas George
Duntocher, 22 February, 1937 S Sch (G)

League Club	Source	Date Signed	Seasons Played	Apps	Subs	Gls
Manchester C.	Partick Avondale	03.54				
Gillingham	Tr	07.57	57	18	-	0
Aldershot	Tr	07.58	58-60	95	-	0
Wolverhampton W.	Tr	02.61	60	1	-	0
Northampton T.	Tr	09.61	61-63	87	-	0
Brentford	Tr	11.63	63-70	199	0	0

BRODIE Eric
Rattray, 8 November, 1940 (WH)

League Club	Source	Date Signed	Seasons Played	Apps	Subs	Gls
Shrewsbury T.	Dundee U.	06.63	63-67	181	4	24
Chester C.	Tr	05.68	68-69	43	0	4
Tranmere Rov.	Tr	10.69	69-71	80	3	4

BRODIE John
Bedlington, 8 September, 1947 (FB)

League Club	Source	Date Signed	Seasons Played	Apps	Subs	Gls
Carlisle U.	Whitley Bay	12.67	67-68	8	1	0
Bradford P.A.	Tr	06.69	69	43	0	0
Port Vale	Tr	01.71	70-76	175	4	2

BRODIE Murray
Glasgow, 26 September, 1950 (M)

League Club	Source	Date Signed	Seasons Played	Apps	Subs	Gls
Leicester C.	Cumbernauld U.	10.69	69	3	0	2
Aldershot	Tr	09.70	70-82	449	11	84

BRODIE Stephen Eric
Sunderland, 14 January, 1973 (F)

League Club	Source	Date Signed	Seasons Played	Apps	Subs	Gls
Sunderland	YT	07.91	93-95	1	11	0
Doncaster Rov.	L	08.95	95	5	0	1
Scarborough	Tr	12.96	96-97	66	2	15

BROGAN David
Glasgow, 11 January, 1939 (F)

League Club	Source	Date Signed	Seasons Played	Apps	Subs	Gls
Luton T.	St Anthonys	09.60	60	4	-	0

BROGAN Frank Anthony
Glasgow, 3 August, 1942 (W)

League Club	Source	Date Signed	Seasons Played	Apps	Subs	Gls
Ipswich T.	Glasgow Celtic	06.64	64-69	201	2	58
Halifax T.	Tr	11.71	71-72	25	2	6

BROGAN James Andrew
Glasgow, 5 June, 1944 SF Lge/S-4 (FB)

League Club	Source	Date Signed	Seasons Played	Apps	Subs	Gls
Coventry C.	Glasgow Celtic	08.75	75	28	0	0

BROGDEN Lee Anthony
Leeds, 18 October, 1949 (W)

League Club	Source	Date Signed	Seasons Played	Apps	Subs	Gls
Rotherham U.	Ashley Road	12.67	67-71	79	7	17
Rochdale	Tr	03.72	71-73	48	9	7

BROLIN Tomas
Sweden, 29 November, 1969 Swedish Int (M)

League Club	Source	Date Signed	Seasons Played	Apps	Subs	Gls
Leeds U.	Parma (It)	11.95	95	17	2	4
Crystal Palace	Tr	01.98	97	13	0	0

BROLLS Norman
Wigtown, 26 September, 1933 (OR)

League Club	Source	Date Signed	Seasons Played	Apps	Subs	Gls
Bradford P.A.	Third Lanark	06.56	56	11	-	0

BROLLY Michael Joseph
Kilmarnock, 6 October, 1954 S Sch (W)

League Club	Source	Date Signed	Seasons Played	Apps	Subs	Gls
Chelsea	Jnrs	10.71	72-73	7	1	1
Bristol C.	Tr	06.74	74-75	27	3	2
Grimsby T.	Tr	09.76	76-81	246	8	27
Derby Co.	Tr	08.82	82	41	1	4
Scunthorpe U.	Tr	08.83	83-85	92	3	15

BROLLY Richard
York, 5 October, 1969 (W)

League Club	Source	Date Signed	Seasons Played	Apps	Subs	Gls
Wigan Ath.	Illinois Univ. (USA)	12.92	92	2	0	1

League Club	Source	Date Signed	Seasons Played	Career Record Apps	Subs	Gls
BROLLY Thomas Henry						
Belfast, 1 June, 1912 Died 1986 NI-4						(D)
Sheffield Wed.	Glenavon	05.33	33	2	-	0
Millwall	Tr	07.35	35-49	229	-	8
BROMAGE Russell						
Stoke, 9 November, 1959						(LB)
Port Vale	App	11.77	77-86	339	8	13
Oldham Ath.	L	10.83	83	2	0	0
Bristol C.	Tr	08.87	87-89	44	2	1
Brighton & H.A.	Tr	08.90	90	1	0	0
Maidstone U.	L	01.91	90	3	0	0
BROMILOW Geoffrey						
Farnworth, 14 September, 1945						(IF)
Bolton W. (Am)		10.68	68	3	2	0
BROMILOW George Joseph						
Southport, 4 December, 1930 E Yth/E Amat						(IF)
Southport (Am)	Northern Nomads	06.55	55-58	84	-	37
BROMLEY Brian						
Burnley, 20 March, 1946 E Yth						(M)
Bolton W.	App	03.63	62-68	165	1	25
Portsmouth	Tr	11.68	68-71	88	1	3
Brighton & H.A.	Tr	11.71	71-73	47	3	3
Reading	Tr	09.73	73-74	13	1	2
Darlington	L	02.75	74	3	0	0
BROMLEY Thomas Charles						
West Bromwich, 30 April, 1933						(IF)
Walsall (Am)	Swan Village	07.53	53	13	-	1
BROOK Daryl						
Holmfirth, 19 November, 1960						(M)
Huddersfield T.	App	11.78	78	1	0	0
BROOK Gary						
Dewsbury, 9 May, 1964						(F)
Newport Co.	Frickley Ath.	12.87	87	14	0	2
Scarborough	Tr	03.88	87-89	59	5	16
Blackpool	Tr	11.89	89-91	27	3	6
Notts Co.	L	09.90	90	0	1	0
Scarborough	L	10.90	90	8	0	0
BROOK Harold						
Sheffield, 15 October, 1921						(CF)
Sheffield U.	Hallam	04.43	46-53	229	-	89
Leeds U.	Tr	07.54	54-57	102	-	46
Lincoln C.	Tr	03.58	57	4	-	1
BROOK Lewis						
Halifax, 27 July, 1918 Died 1996						(FB)
Huddersfield T.	Halifax T. (Am)	05.36	37-46	18	-	6
Oldham Ath.	Tr	03.48	47-56	189	-	14
BROOKE David						
Barnsley, 23 November, 1975						(M)
Barnsley	YT	07.93				
Scarborough	Tr	08.96	96	28	6	2
BROOKE Garry James						
Bethnal Green, 24 November, 1960						(W)
Tottenham H.	App	10.78	80-84	49	24	15
Norwich C.	Tr	07.85	85-86	8	6	2
Wimbledon	Groningen (Neth)	08.88	88-89	5	7	0
Stoke C.	L	03.90	89	6	2	0
Brentford	Tr	08.90	90	8	3	1
Reading (N/C)	Tr	03.91	90	1	3	0
BROOKE Maurice						
Thurcroft, 4 June, 1925						(F)
Stockport Co.	Buxton	01.51	50	1	-	0
BROOKER Paul						
Hammersmith, 25 November, 1976						(RM)
Fulham	YT	07.95	95-97	13	42	4
BROOKES Colin						
Barnsley, 2 January, 1942 E Sch						(OL)
Barnsley	Jnrs	05.59	59-60	47	-	5
West Bromwich A.	Tr	06.61				
Peterborough U.	Tr	06.62				
Southport	Tr	07.63	63	20	-	2
BROOKES Darren Paul						
Sheffield, 7 July, 1973						(CD)
Doncaster Rov.	Worksop	07.97	97	9	2	0

League Club	Source	Date Signed	Seasons Played	Career Record Apps	Subs	Gls
BROOKES Eric						
Mapplewell, 3 February, 1944 E Sch/E Yth						(LB)
Barnsley	Jnrs	04.61	60-68	325	1	1
Northampton T.	Tr	07.69	69-70	81	0	1
Peterborough U.	Tr	06.71	71-72	41	1	1
BROOKES John Vincent						
Sheffield, 18 October, 1943						(IF)
Sheffield Wed.	Sheffield U. (Am)	09.64				
Southport	Tr	07.65	65	14	0	5
York C.	Tr	08.66	66	1	0	0
Stockport Co.	Cleveland (USA)	08.70	70	18	3	3
BROOKES Stanley Kevin						
Doncaster, 2 February, 1953						(CD)
Doncaster Rov.	App	02.71	71-76	230	5	7
BROOKES William Amos						
Dudley, 19 April, 1931						(WH)
West Bromwich A.	Churchfield	05.49	53-56	19	-	0
BROOKFIELD Anthony John						
Southport, 11 April, 1959						(F)
Southport (N/C)	Jnrs	07.76	76-77	14	5	1
BROOKIN William James						
Tilehurst, 14 June, 1919 Died 1976						(G)
Newport Co.	R.A.F. Hereford	08.46	46	2	-	0
BROOKING Trevor David						
Barking, 2 October, 1948 E Sch/E Yth/Eu23-1/EF Lge/E-47						(M)
West Ham U.	App	05.66	67-83	521	7	88
BROOKMAN Nicholas Anthony						
Manchester, 28 October, 1968						(M)
Bolton W.	Wrexham (N/C)	11.86	86-89	47	10	10
Stockport Co.	Tr	03.90	89	4	2	0
BROOKS Anthony						
Ince, 12 March, 1944						(F)
Blackpool	App	03.62				
Bury		08.63	63	1	-	0
Stockport Co.	Tr	06.64	64	2	-	0
BROOKS Christopher						
Mansfield, 6 June, 1972						(F)
Luton T.	Ilkeston T.	07.92				
Shrewsbury T.	L	02.93	92	1	0	0
BROOKS Harry						
Tibshelf, 2 June, 1915 Died 1994						(CF)
Doncaster Rov.	Heanor T.	01.37	36-38	5	-	0
Aldershot	Tr	06.39	46-47	23	-	14
BROOKS John						
Stoke, 8 March, 1927						(WH)
Stoke C.		12.46	50	2	-	0
BROOKS John						
Reading, 23 December, 1931 E-3						(IF)
Reading	Jnrs	04.49	49-52	46	-	5
Tottenham H.	Tr	02.53	52-59	166	-	46
Chelsea	Tr	12.59	59-60	46	-	6
Brentford	Tr	09.61	61-63	83	-	36
Crystal Palace	Tr	01.64	63	7	-	0
BROOKS John Terence						
Paddington, 23 August, 1947						(G)
Queens Park R.	App	08.65				
Ipswich T.	Tr	12.66				
Northampton T.	Tr	10.67	67	1	0	0
BROOKS Norman Harry						
Reading, 28 May, 1920 Died 1973						(OL)
Reading (Am)	Huntley & Palmer	11.46	46	1	-	0
BROOKS Shaun						
Reading, 9 October, 1962 E Sch/E Yth						(M)
Crystal Palace	App	10.79	79-83	47	7	4
Leyton Orient	Tr	10.83	83-86	140	8	26
Bournemouth	Tr	06.87	87-91	114	14	13
Bournemouth	Dorchester T.	10.94	94	1	0	0
Leyton Orient	Tr	11.94	94-95	42	8	2
BROOKS Stephen Michael						
Liverpool, 18 June, 1955						(CD)
Southport	Marine	02.77	76-77	65	0	3
Hartlepool U.	Tr	07.78	78-79	62	1	2
Halifax T. (N/C)	Barrow	03.85	84	16	0	0

BROOKS Thomas William

Tynemouth, 2 February, 1948 (D)

League Club	Source	Date Signed	Seasons Played	Apps	Subs	Gls
Lincoln C.	App	02.65	64-70	103	10	1

BROOME Frank Henry

Berkhamsted, 11 June, 1915 Died 1994 E-7 (CF)

League Club	Source	Date Signed	Seasons Played	Apps	Subs	Gls
Aston Villa	Berkhamsted	11.34	34-46	133	-	77
Derby Co.	Tr	09.46	46-49	112	-	45
Notts Co.	Tr	10.49	49-52	105	-	35
Brentford	Tr	07.53	53	6	-	1
Crewe Alex.	Tr	10.53	53-54	36	-	16

BROOMES Marlon Charles

Birmingham, 28 November, 1977 E Sch/E Yth/Eu21-2 (CD)

League Club	Source	Date Signed	Seasons Played	Apps	Subs	Gls
Blackburn Rov.	YT	11.94	97	2	2	0
Swindon T.	L	01.97	96	12	0	1

BROOMFIELD Desmond Stretton

Hove, 6 October, 1921 (WH)

League Club	Source	Date Signed	Seasons Played	Apps	Subs	Gls
Brighton & H.A.	Jnrs	01.47	46-47	20	-	0

BROOMFIELD Ian Lewis

Bristol, 17 December, 1950 (F)

League Club	Source	Date Signed	Seasons Played	Apps	Subs	Gls
Bristol C.	App	08.68	68-72	18	3	2
Stockport Co.	Tr	12.72	72-74	22	5	1
Workington	South Africa	10.75	75	3	0	0

BROOMFIELD John

Crewe, 6 June, 1934 (CH)

League Club	Source	Date Signed	Seasons Played	Apps	Subs	Gls
Crewe Alex. (Am)		10.56	56	1	-	0

BROOMHALL Keith Leslie

Stoke, 21 May, 1951 (FB)

League Club	Source	Date Signed	Seasons Played	Apps	Subs	Gls
Port Vale	App	●	68	1	1	0

BROPHY Hubert

Dublin, 2 September, 1948 NI Amat (F)

League Club	Source	Date Signed	Seasons Played	Apps	Subs	Gls
Crystal Palace	Shamrock Rov.	07.66	66	0	1	0

BROTHERSTON Noel

Dundonald, 18 November, 1956 Died 1995 NIu21-1/NI-27 (W)

League Club	Source	Date Signed	Seasons Played	Apps	Subs	Gls
Tottenham H.	App	04.74	75	1	0	0
Blackburn Rov.	Tr	07.77	77-86	307	10	40
Bury	Tr	06.87	87-88	32	6	4
Scarborough	L	10.88	88	5	0	0

BROUGH John Robert

Ilkeston, 8 January, 1973 (CD)

League Club	Source	Date Signed	Seasons Played	Apps	Subs	Gls
Notts Co.	YT	07.91				
Shrewsbury T.	Tr	07.92	92-93	7	9	1
Hereford U.	Telford	11.94	94-96	70	9	3

BROUGH Neil Keith

Daventry, 22 December, 1965 (W)

League Club	Source	Date Signed	Seasons Played	Apps	Subs	Gls
Northampton T.	App	12.83	83-84	6	6	0

BROUGH Paul

York, 24 January, 1965 (F)

League Club	Source	Date Signed	Seasons Played	Apps	Subs	Gls
York C. (N/C)	York R.I.	08.87	87	0	1	0

BROUGHTON Drewe Oliver

Hitchin, 25 October, 1978 (F)

League Club	Source	Date Signed	Seasons Played	Apps	Subs	Gls
Norwich C.	YT	05.97	96-97	3	6	1
Wigan Ath.	L	08.97	97	1	3	0

BROUGHTON Edward

Bradford, 9 February, 1925 (OR)

League Club	Source	Date Signed	Seasons Played	Apps	Subs	Gls
Bradford C.		09.45				
New Brighton	Tr	07.47	47	4	-	0
Crystal Palace	Tr	08.48	48-52	96	-	6

BROWN Alan

Lewes, 11 December, 1937 (CF)

League Club	Source	Date Signed	Seasons Played	Apps	Subs	Gls
Brighton & H.A.	Portslade	09.58	61	7	-	2
Exeter C.	Tr	01.62	61	11	-	3

BROWN Alan

Easington, 22 May, 1959 (F)

League Club	Source	Date Signed	Seasons Played	Apps	Subs	Gls
Sunderland	App	07.76	76-81	87	26	21
Newcastle U.	L	11.81	81	5	0	3
Shrewsbury T.	Tr	08.82	82-83	65	0	15
Doncaster Rov.	Tr	03.84	83-85	15	0	6

BROWN Albert Edward

Bristol, 4 March, 1934 (WH)

League Club	Source	Date Signed	Seasons Played	Apps	Subs	Gls
Crystal Palace	Exeter Univ.	08.56	57	3	-	0
Queens Park R.	Tr	07.59				

BROWN Albert Roy

Nottingham, 14 August, 1917 (W)

League Club	Source	Date Signed	Seasons Played	Apps	Subs	Gls
Nottingham F.	Sneinton	02.36	35-38	51	-	7
Wrexham	Tr	06.39	46	24	-	3
Mansfield T.	Tr	07.47	47	17	-	2

BROWN Alexander

Glasgow, 15 August, 1930 (FB)

League Club	Source	Date Signed	Seasons Played	Apps	Subs	Gls
Preston N.E.	Partick Thistle	06.57				
Carlisle U.	Tr	06.58	58-60	104	-	0

BROWN Alexander (Sandy) Dewar

Grangemouth, 24 March, 1939 SF Lge (FB)

League Club	Source	Date Signed	Seasons Played	Apps	Subs	Gls
Everton	Partick Thistle	09.63	63-70	176	33	9
Shrewsbury T.	Tr	05.71	71	21	0	0
Southport	Tr	07.72	72	17	2	0

BROWN Alexander Roy

Seaton Delaval, 21 November, 1914 (IF)

League Club	Source	Date Signed	Seasons Played	Apps	Subs	Gls
Chesterfield	Ashington	12.33	34	10	-	0
Darlington	Tr	06.35	35	5	-	0
Mansfield T.	Shrewsbury T.	11.46	46	5	-	0

BROWN Alistair

Midlothian, 12 April, 1951 (F)

League Club	Source	Date Signed	Seasons Played	Apps	Subs	Gls
Leicester C.	Jnrs	04.68	68-71	93	8	32
West Bromwich A.	Tr	03.72	71-82	254	25	72
Crystal Palace	Tr	03.83	82	11	0	2
Walsall	Tr	08.83	83	37	1	13
Port Vale	Tr	07.84	84-85	62	5	22

BROWN Allan Duncan

Leven, 12 October, 1926 SF Lge/S-14 (IF)

League Club	Source	Date Signed	Seasons Played	Apps	Subs	Gls
Blackpool	East Fife	12.50	50-56	157	-	68
Luton T.	Tr	02.57	56-60	151	-	51
Portsmouth	Tr	03.61	60-62	69	-	8

BROWN Allan Winston

Consett, 26 August, 1914 Died 1996 EF Lge (CH)

League Club	Source	Date Signed	Seasons Played	Apps	Subs	Gls
Huddersfield T.	Spen Black	03.33	34-38	57	-	0
Burnley	Tr	02.46	46-48	88	-	0
Notts Co.	Tr	10.48	48	13	-	0

BROWN Andrew

Liverpool, 17 August, 1963 (D)

League Club	Source	Date Signed	Seasons Played	Apps	Subs	Gls
Tranmere Rov. (N/C)	Jnrs	08.82	82	1	0	0

BROWN Andrew

Coatbridge, 20 February, 1915 Died 1973 (LB)

League Club	Source	Date Signed	Seasons Played	Apps	Subs	Gls
Cardiff C.	Cumbernauld Thistle	12.36	36-37	2	-	0
Torquay U.	Tr	06.38	38-46	34	-	5

BROWN Andrew Stewart

Edinburgh, 11 October, 1976 (F)

League Club	Source	Date Signed	Seasons Played	Apps	Subs	Gls
Leeds U.	St Johnstone (Jnrs)	04.95				
Hull C.	Tr	05.96	96-97	7	22	1

BROWN Anthony John

Oldham, 3 October, 1945 EF Lge/E-1 (M)

League Club	Source	Date Signed	Seasons Played	Apps	Subs	Gls
West Bromwich A.	App	10.63	63-79	561	13	218
Torquay U.	Jacksonville (USA)	10.81	81-82	38	7	11

BROWN Anthony John

Bradford, 17 September, 1958 (CD)

League Club	Source	Date Signed	Seasons Played	Apps	Subs	Gls
Leeds U.	Thackley	03.83	82-84	24	0	1
Doncaster Rov.	L	11.84	84	5	0	0
Doncaster Rov.	Tr	03.85	84-86	80	2	2
Scunthorpe U.	Tr	07.87	87-88	46	8	2
Rochdale	Tr	08.89	89-92	111	3	0

BROWN Robert **Beresford (Berry)**

Hartlepool, 6 September, 1927 (G)

League Club	Source	Date Signed	Seasons Played	Apps	Subs	Gls
Manchester U.	Blackhall Colly	08.46	47-48	4	-	0
Doncaster Rov.	Tr	01.49	48	4	-	0
Hartlepool U.	Stockton	08.51	51-55	126	-	0

BROWN Brian David

Shoreditch, 10 September, 1949 (FB)

League Club	Source	Date Signed	Seasons Played	Apps	Subs	Gls
Chelsea	App	11.66				
Millwall	Tr	03.68	68-74	186	4	5

BROWN Cyril

Ashington, 25 May, 1918 Died 1990 (IF)

League Club	Source	Date Signed	Seasons Played	Apps	Subs	Gls
Brentford	Felixstowe	01.39				
Sunderland	Tr	04.45				
Notts Co.	Tr	08.46	46	13	-	5
Rochdale	Tr	08.48	48-50	61	-	11

League Club	Source	Date Signed	Seasons Played	Career Record Apps	Subs	Gls
BROWN David						
Wallasey, 21 October, 1963						(D)
Tranmere Rov. (N/C)		08.82	82	1	0	0
BROWN David Alistair						
Bolton, 2 October, 1978						(F)
Manchester U.	YT	10.95				
Hull C.	L	03.98	97	7	0	2
BROWN David James						
Hartlepool, 28 January, 1957						(G)
Middlesbrough	Horden Colly	02.77	77	10	0	0
Plymouth Arg.	L	08.79	79	5	0	0
Oxford U.	Tr	10.79	79-80	21	0	0
Bury	Tr	09.81	81-84	146	0	0
Preston N.E.	Tr	06.86	86-88	74	0	0
Scunthorpe U.	L	01.89	88	5	0	0
Halifax T.	Tr	07.89	89-90	38	0	0
BROWN Dennis John						
Reading, 8 February, 1944						(IF)
Chelsea	Jnrs	06.62	63	10	-	1
Swindon T.	Tr	11.64	64-66	92	0	38
Northampton T.	Tr	02.67	66-68	41	5	10
Aldershot	Tr	07.69	69-74	237	8	55
BROWN William **Dewis**						
Doncaster, 4 June, 1919						(IF)
Stockport Co.		08.45	46-49	65	-	15
Rotherham U.	Tr	08.50	51	1	-	0
BROWN Douglas Alexander						
Poole, 21 March, 1958						(F)
Sheffield U.	Clydebank	03.79	78-79	17	8	2
BROWN Edward Alfred Cecil Henry						
St Pancras, 4 October, 1927 Died 1996						(CF)
Brentford		02.50				
Aldershot		08.53	53	3	-	0
BROWN Edwin						
Preston, 28 February, 1926						(CF)
Preston N.E.		08.48	48-50	36	-	6
Southampton	Tr	09.50	50-51	57	-	32
Coventry C.	Tr	03.52	51-54	85	-	50
Birmingham C.	Tr	10.54	54-58	158	-	74
Leyton Orient	Tr	01.59	58-60	63	-	28
BROWN Ernest						
Stockport, 30 May, 1923 Died 1980						(LH)
Manchester C.		04.44				
Aldershot	Tr	06.46	46	12	-	0
Accrington St.	Tr	08.49	49	2	-	0
BROWN Ernest Charles						
South Shields, 3 February, 1921 Died 1976						(IL)
Newcastle U.	South Shields	12.45				
Southend U.	Tr	02.47	46-47	6	-	0
BROWN Frederick						
Stratford, 6 December, 1931						(G)
Aldershot	Leytonstone	06.52	52-54	106	-	0
West Bromwich A.	Tr	05.55	55-57	11	-	0
Portsmouth	Tr	06.58	58-59	18	-	0
BROWN George						
Dennyloanhead, 12 January, 1932						(G)
Crewe Alex.	Stenhousemuir	06.57	57	38	-	0
BROWN George						
Sheffield, 18 October, 1934 Died 1995 E Sch						(RH)
Liverpool	Jnrs	10.51				
Chesterfield	Tr	05.53	53-54	66	-	5
BROWN George Donaldson						
Airdrie, 8 May, 1928						(IF)
Southport	Airdrieonians	04.51	50	1	-	0
Bradford P.A.	Clyde	07.56	56	17	-	2
BROWN Gordon						
Eastham, 30 June, 1933						(IF)
Wolverhampton W.	Jnrs	09.51				
Scunthorpe U.	Tr	12.52	52-56	164	-	72
Derby Co.	Tr	01.57	56-59	53	-	20
Southampton	Tr	03.60	59-60	8	-	2
Barrow	Tr	07.61	61-63	39	-	16
Southport	Tr	01.64	63	4	-	1

League Club	Source	Date Signed	Seasons Played	Career Record Apps	Subs	Gls
BROWN Gordon						
Dunfermline, 4 February, 1932						(OL)
Blackburn Rov.	Blairhall Colly	04.51				
Newport Co.	Tr	08.55	55-58	137	-	14
Gillingham	Tr	06.59	59-60	67	-	13
BROWN Gordon						
East Kilbride, 7 December, 1965						(D)
Rotherham U.	App	12.83	83	1	0	0
BROWN Gordon Steele						
Warsop, 21 March, 1929						(WH)
Nottingham F.	Jnrs	12.46				
York C.	Tr	06.50	50-57	322	-	25
BROWN Graham Cummings						
Matlock, 21 March, 1944						(G)
Millwall		12.64				
Mansfield T.	Crawley T.	08.69	69-73	142	0	0
Doncaster Rov.	Tr	07.74	74-75	53	0	0
Swansea C.	Portland (USA)	09.76	76	4	0	0
York C.	Portland (USA)	08.77	77-79	69	0	0
Rotherham U.	Tr	02.80	79-80	31	0	0
Mansfield T. (N/C)	Tr	01.82	81	1	0	0
BROWN Graham Frederick						
Leicester, 5 November, 1950						(F)
Leicester C.	App	11.68	69	0	1	0
BROWN Grant Ashley						
Sunderland, 19 November, 1969						(CD)
Leicester C.	YT	06.88	87-88	14	0	0
Lincoln C.	L	08.89	89	14	0	1
Lincoln C.	Tr	01.90	89-97	303	0	12
BROWN Gregory Jonathan						
Manchester, 31 July, 1978						(M)
Chester C.	YT	06.96	95-96	1	3	0
Macclesfield T. (N/C)	Tr	12.97	97	2	0	0
BROWN Harold Thomas						
Kingsbury, 9 April, 1924 Died 1982						(G)
Queens Park R.	Jnrs	04.41				
Notts Co.	Tr	04.46	46-48	93	-	0
Derby Co.	Tr	10.49	49-50	37	-	0
Queens Park R.	Tr	08.51	51-55	189	-	0
Plymouth Arg.	Tr	08.56	56-57	66	-	0
BROWN Henry Stanford						
Workington, 23 May, 1918 Died 1963						(CH)
Wolverhampton W.	Workington T.	02.37	38	2	-	0
Hull C.	Tr	05.46	46	22	-	0
BROWN Hugh						
Glasgow, 7 December, 1921 Died 1994 SF Lge/S-3						(WH)
Torquay U.	Partick Thistle	11.50	50-51	55	-	0
BROWN Ian O'Neill						
Ipswich, 11 September, 1965						(W)
Birmingham C.	YT	09.84				
Bristol C.	Chelmsford C.	05.93	93-94	5	7	1
Colchester U.	L	03.94	93	4	0	1
Northampton T.	Tr	12.94	94	23	0	4
BROWN Irvin						
Lewes, 20 September, 1935						(CH)
Brighton & H.A.	Jnrs	10.52	57	3	-	0
Bournemouth	Tr	09.58	58-62	65	-	2
BROWN James						
Cumnock, 16 February, 1924						(CF)
Chesterfield	Motherwell	05.48	48	5	-	2
Bradford C.	Tr	11.48	48	20	-	11
Carlisle U.	Queen of South	09.50	50-51	15	-	9
BROWN James						
Manchester, 5 October, 1935						(W)
Rochdale		04.57	56-60	52	-	4
BROWN James Birrell						
Stirling, 7 June, 1939						(WH)
Darlington	Dumbarton	09.60	60-62	14	-	0
BROWN James Grady						
Coatbridge, 11 May, 1952 Su23-4/S-1						(G)
Chesterfield	Albion Rov.	12.72	72-73	47	0	0
Sheffield U.	Tr	03.74	73-77	170	0	0
Cardiff C.	Chicago Sting (USA)	12.82	82	3	0	0
Chesterfield	Kettering T.	07.83	83-88	135	0	1

League Club	Source	Date Signed	Seasons Played	Career Record Apps	Subs	Gls
BROWN James Keith						
Bothwell, 3 October, 1953						(M)
Aston Villa	App	10.70	69-74	73	2	1
Preston N.E.	Tr	10.75	75-77	64	0	3
Portsmouth	Ethnikos (Gre)	02.80	79	5	0	0
BROWN Jeremy						
Newport, 13 June, 1961						(F)
Newport Co.	App	06.78	78	2	1	0
BROWN John						
Edinburgh, 6 March, 1940						(HB)
Colchester U.	Dunbar	09.61	62	1	-	0
BROWN John						
St Kew, 29 July, 1940						(IF)
Plymouth Arg.	Wadebridge	10.60	60-62	9	-	2
Bristol Rov.	Tr	07.63	63-67	156	0	32
BROWN John (Jackie)						
Belfast, 8 November, 1914 NI-10						(OR)
Wolverhampton W.	Belfast Celtic	12.34	34-36	27	-	6
Coventry C.	Tr	10.36	36-37	69	-	26
Birmingham C.	Tr	09.38	38	34	-	6
Ipswich T.	Barry T.	05.48	48-50	98	-	25
BROWN John Christopher						
Bradford, 30 December, 1947						(G)
Preston N.E.	App	03.65	66-74	67	0	0
Stockport Co.	L	11.70	70	26	0	0
Stockport Co.	Tr	07.75	75	15	0	0
Wigan Ath.	Tr	07.76	78-81	93	0	0
BROWN John Lewis						
Crook, 23 March, 1921 Died 1989						(RB)
York C.	Stanley U.	02.48	47-49	22	-	0
BROWN John Michael						
Streatham, 2 February, 1934						(CF)
Shrewsbury T. (Am)	Queens Park	05.53	53	5	-	3
BROWN John Thomas						
Edinburgh, 2 April, 1935 S Sch						(FB)
Tranmere Rov.	Third Lanark	01.61	60-61	33	-	0
Hartlepool U.	Tr	07.62	62-63	68	-	10
BROWN Jonathan						
Barnsley, 8 September, 1966						(FB)
Exeter C.	Denaby U.	06.90	90-94	149	15	3
BROWN Joseph						
Cramlington, 26 April, 1929						(WH)
Middlesbrough	Jnrs	04.46	49-50	11	-	0
Burnley	Tr	08.52	52	6	-	0
Bournemouth	Tr	06.54	54-59	215	-	5
Aldershot	Tr	07.60	60	5	-	0
BROWN Joseph Samuel						
Bebington, 7 May, 1920						(OL)
Chester C.	Port Sunlight	05.47	46-47	15	-	2
BROWN Keith						
Grimsby, 23 September, 1954						(OL)
Nottingham F.	App	09.72				
Grimsby T.	Tr	10.73	73-75	32	7	5
BROWN Keith						
Hucknall, 1 January, 1942 E Sch						(CF)
Notts Co.	Jnrs	01.59	58	8	-	4
Rotherham U.	Tr	07.59				
BROWN Keith						
Liverpool, 19 October, 1957						(FB)
Southport (N/C)	East Villa	11.76	76	4	0	0
BROWN Keith Gordon						
Coseley, 16 July, 1954						(FB)
Walsall	Jnrs	07.73	73-74	8	2	0
BROWN Keith Jack						
Bournemouth, 29 January, 1942						(FB)
Bournemouth	Pokesdown	09.60	63-64	15	-	0
BROWN Keith Timothy						
Bristol, 28 September, 1959						(F)
Bristol Rov.	Bristol St George	10.77	78-80	4	3	0

League Club	Source	Date Signed	Seasons Played	Career Record Apps	Subs	Gls
BROWN Kenneth						
Forest Gate, 16 February, 1934 E-1						(CH)
West Ham U.	Neville U.	10.51	52-66	386	0	4
Torquay U.	Tr	05.67	67-68	40	2	1
BROWN Kenneth Geoffrey						
Barnsley, 21 March, 1952						(M)
Barnsley	App	04.70	69-77	267	11	24
Bournemouth	Tr	06.78	78-79	29	3	4
BROWN Kenneth James						
Upminster, 11 July, 1967						(RB)
Norwich C.	Jnrs	07.85	86-87	24	1	0
Plymouth Arg.	Tr	08.88	88-90	126	0	4
West Ham U.	Tr	08.91	91-95	55	8	5
Huddersfield T.	L	09.95	95	5	0	0
Reading	L	10.95	95	12	0	1
Southend U.	L	03.96	95	6	0	0
Crystal Palace	L	03.96	95	5	1	2
Reading	L	09.96	96	5	0	0
Birmingham C.	Tr	12.96	96	11	0	0
Millwall	Tr	07.97	97	45	0	0
BROWN Kenneth James						
Coventry, 18 October, 1933						(IF)
Coventry C.		01.56				
Nottingham F.	Corby T.	11.56				
Bournemouth	Tr	07.57	57	6	-	1
Torquay U.	Tr	07.58	58	8	-	1
BROWN Kevan Barry						
Andover, 2 January, 1966						(RB)
Southampton	Jnrs	07.84				
Brighton & H.A.	Tr	02.87	86-88	52	1	0
Aldershot	Tr	11.88	88-90	108	2	2
BROWN Laurence						
Shildon, 22 August, 1937 E Amat						(CH)
Darlington (Am)	Bishop Auckland	03.59	58	3	-	0
Northampton T.	Bishop Auckland	10.60	60	33	-	22
Arsenal	Tr	08.61	61-63	101	-	2
Tottenham H.	Tr	04.63	63-65	62	0	3
Norwich C.	Tr	09.66	66-68	80	1	2
Bradford P.A.	Tr	12.68	68-69	36	0	1
BROWN Linton James						
Hull, 12 April, 1968						(F)
Halifax T. (N/C)	Guiseley	12.92	92	3	0	0
Hull C.	Tr	01.93	92-95	111	10	23
Swansea C.	Tr	03.96	95-97	16	11	3
Scarborough	L	08.97	97	4	0	1
BROWN Malcolm						
Salford, 13 December, 1956						(RB)
Bury	App	12.74	73-76	10	1	0
Huddersfield T.	Tr	05.77	77-82	256	0	16
Newcastle U.	Tr	08.83	84	39	0	0
Huddersfield T.	Tr	06.85	85-88	93	3	1
Rochdale (N/C)	Tr	02.89	88	11	0	0
Stockport Co.	Tr	07.89	89-90	71	0	3
Rochdale	Tr	08.91	91	18	0	1
BROWN Michael Anthony						
Birmingham, 8 February, 1968						(W)
Shrewsbury T.	App	02.86	86-90	174	16	9
Bolton W.	Tr	08.91	91-92	27	6	3
Shrewsbury T.	Tr	12.92	92-94	66	1	11
Preston N.E.	Tr	11.94	95-96	11	5	1
Rochdale	L	09.96	96	5	0	0
Shrewsbury T.	Tr	12.96	96-97	41	8	3
BROWN Michael John						
Walsall, 11 July, 1939						(FB)
Hull C.	Jnrs	10.58	59-65	8	0	0
Lincoln C.	Tr	07.67	67	39	0	0
BROWN Michael John						
Farnham Common, 11 April, 1944						(F)
Fulham	App	09.61	61-62	4	-	0
Millwall	Tr	02.65	64-66	47	5	11
Luton T.	Tr	07.67	67-68	9	5	2
Colchester U.	Tr	10.68	68-69	47	5	12
BROWN Michael John Leslie						
Swansea, 27 September, 1951 W Sch						(CD)
Crystal Palace	App	09.69				
Brighton & H.A.	Tr	06.73	73	5	3	1
Brentford	L	09.73	73	3	0	0

League Club	Source	Date Signed	Seasons Played	Apps	Subs	Gls
BROWN Michael Robert						
Hartlepool, 25 January, 1977 Eu21-4						(M)
Manchester C.	YT	09.94	95-97	41	17	0
Hartlepool U.	L	03.97	96	6	0	1
BROWN Monty Raymond						
Grimsby, 7 September, 1943						(CF)
Scunthorpe U.	Jnrs	07.63	64-65	19	0	6
BROWN Neil Richard						
Sheffiield, 16 January, 1966						(LB)
Chesterfield	App	11.83	83	4	0	0
BROWN Nicholas James						
Northampton, 25 January, 1973						(G)
Halifax T.	Norwich C. (YT)	07.91	91-92	2	0	0
BROWN Nicholas Lee						
Hull, 16 October, 1966						(FB)
Hull C.	YT	08.85	85-91	80	6	3
BROWN Owen John						
Liverpool, 4 September, 1960						(F)
Liverpool	Jnrs	11.78				
Carlisle U.	Tr	06.80	80	4	0	2
Tranmere Rov.	Tr	08.81	81	29	8	8
Crewe Alex.	Tr	08.82	82	1	0	0
Tranmere Rov.	Tr	10.82	82-83	47	9	12
Chester C.	Tr	08.84	84	9	1	3
BROWN Peter Barry						
Andover, 13 July, 1934						(F)
Southampton	Jnrs	01.52	53-57	16	-	3
Wrexham	Tr	07.58	58-59	33	-	9
BROWN Peter Ronald						
Hemel Hempstead, 1 September, 1961						(FB)
Wimbledon	Chelsea (App)	08.80	80-81	53	2	3
BROWN Philip						
South Shields, 30 May, 1959						(RB)
Hartlepool U.	St Hilda's Jnrs	07.78	79-84	210	7	8
Halifax T.	Tr	07.85	85-87	135	0	19
Bolton W.	Tr	06.88	88-93	254	2	14
Blackpool	Tr	07.94	94-95	33	11	5
BROWN Philip James						
Sheffield, 16 January, 1966						(W)
Chesterfield	App	10.83	82-86	82	5	19
Stockport Co.	Tr	12.86	86	23	0	1
Lincoln C.	Tr	08.87	88-89	32	11	3
BROWN Ralph						
Nottingham, 26 February, 1944						(F)
Aston Villa	App	03.61				
Notts Co.	Tr	05.62	62	18	-	3
BROWN Raymond Moscrop						
Carlisle, 11 February, 1928						(W)
Notts Co.	Queens Park	08.51	51	7	-	0
BROWN Richard Anthony						
Nottingham, 13 January, 1967						(FB)
Sheffield Wed.	Ilkeston T.	12.84				
Blackburn Rov.	Kettering T.	09.90	91-92	26	2	0
Maidstone U.	L	02.91	90	3	0	0
Stockport Co.	Tr	03.95	94	1	0	0
Blackpool	Tr	08.95	95	2	1	0
BROWN Richard Colin						
Sutton Coldfield, 25 December, 1973						(D)
Walsall	YT	03.92	91	6	3	0
BROWN Robert						
Glasgow, 9 August, 1924						(IF)
Derby Co.	Camerons	10.47				
Southend U.	Tr	07.48	48-49	12	-	0
Shrewsbury T.	Tr	07.50	50-52	104	-	41
Barnsley	Tr	07.53	53-56	120	-	55
Rotherham U.	Tr	09.56	56-57	42	-	12
BROWN Robert						
Carluke, 23 November, 1955						(D)
Workington	Jnrs	08.74	74-76	44	0	0
BROWN Robert						
Motherwell, 2 December, 1931						(FB)
Workington	Motherwell	05.56	56-67	418	1	2
BROWN Robert						
Bristol, 14 May, 1949						(IF)
Bristol Rov.	App	06.67	68-71	28	7	4
Newport Co.	L	03.70	69	8	1	0
BROWN Robert (Sailor) Albert John						
Great Yarmouth, 7 November, 1915						(IF)
Charlton Ath.	Gorleston	08.34	37-38	47	-	21
Nottingham F.	Tr	05.46	46-47	46	-	17
Aston Villa	Tr	10.47	47-48	30	-	9
BROWN Robert Christopher						
Plymouth, 24 November, 1953						(M)
Chelsea	Jnrs	08.72				
Sheffield Wed.	Tr	08.74	74-75	17	4	3
Aldershot	L	02.76	75	3	2	0
BROWN Robert Henry						
Streatham, 2 May, 1940 E Amat						(CF)
Fulham (Am)	Barnet	09.60	60-61	8	-	4
Watford	Tr	11.61	61-62	28	-	10
Northampton T.	Tr	12.63	63-66	50	0	22
Cardiff C.	Tr	10.66	66-67	50	0	24
BROWN Roger William						
Tamworth, 12 December, 1952						(CD)
Bournemouth	A.P. Leamington	02.78	77-78	63	0	3
Norwich C.	Tr	07.79	79	16	0	0
Fulham	Tr	03.80	79-83	141	0	18
Bournemouth	Tr	12.83	83-86	83	1	5
BROWN Ronald						
Ballymoney (NI), 20 March, 1923						(CF)
Plymouth Arg.	Linfield	04.45				
Hull C.	Tr	03.47	46	7	-	3
BROWN Ronald						
Sunderland, 26 December, 1944						(OR)
Blackpool	Whitley Bay	11.65	65-70	54	7	13
Plymouth Arg.	Tr	02.71	70-72	31	5	3
Bradford C.	Tr	09.72	72-74	90	7	11
BROWN Roy						
Middlesbrough, 10 June, 1925						(FB)
Darlington	Stockton W.E.	01.47	46-55	159	-	20
Hartlepool U.	Tr	08.56				
BROWN Roy						
Retford, 17 June, 1932						(F)
Doncaster Rov.	Gainsborough Trin.	05.53	53-56	26	-	6
BROWN Roy Eric						
Shoreham, 5 October, 1945						(G)
Tottenham H.	App	10.62	66	1	0	0
Reading	Tr	07.68	68-69	63	0	0
Notts Co.	Tr	07.70	70-74	113	0	0
Mansfield T. (N/C)	Tr	11.75	75	1	0	0
BROWN Henry **Roy**						
Stoke, 20 December, 1923 Died 1989						(CH/CF)
Stoke C.	Jnrs	08.42	46-52	70	-	14
Watford	Tr	07.53	53-57	142	-	40
BROWN Simon James						
Chelmsford, 3 December, 1976						(G)
Tottenham H.	YT	07.95				
Lincoln C.	L	12.97	97	1	0	0
BROWN Stanley						
Lewes, 15 September, 1941						(WH)
Fulham	Jnrs	05.59	60-72	348	5	16
Brighton & H.A.	L	10.72	72	9	0	0
Colchester U.	Tr	12.72	72	23	0	0
BROWN Steven Andrew John						
Peckham, 13 July, 1952						(W)
Millwall	App	06.70	69-74	47	23	5
BROWN Steven Byron						
Brighton, 13 May, 1972						(FB)
Charlton Ath.	YT	07.90	91-97	126	16	5
BROWN Steven Ferold						
Northampton, 6 July, 1966						(M)
Northampton T.	Jnrs	08.83	83-84	14	1	3
Northampton T.	Irthlingborough Diam.	07.89	89-93	145	13	19
Wycombe W.	Tr	02.94	93-97	152	9	11

League Club	Source	Date Signed	Seasons Played	Career Record Apps	Subs	Gls
BROWN Steven Robert						
Southend, 6 December, 1973						(F)
Southend U.	YT	07.92	92	10	0	2
Scunthorpe U.	Tr	07.93				
Colchester U.	Tr	08.93	93-94	56	6	17
Gillingham	Tr	03.95	94-95	8	1	2
Lincoln C.	Tr	10.95	95-97	47	25	8
BROWN Thomas						
Galashiels, 7 June, 1929						(IF)
Ipswich T.	Annbanks Jnrs	07.52	52-55	84	-	17
Walsall	Tr	06.56	56-57	38	-	9
BROWN Thomas						
Leven, 17 November, 1933						(CF)
Lincoln C.	Newburgh Jnrs	04.56	57	3	-	0
BROWN Thomas						
Troon, 26 October, 1919						(G)
Ipswich T.	Glenathon Jnrs	10.38	46-50	111	-	0
BROWN Thomas Emmerson						
Throckley, 8 September, 1935						(FB)
Middlesbrough	Jnrs	04.53	54-57	44	-	0
BROWN Thomas Graham						
Cowdenbeath, 11 August, 1924						(IF)
Portsmouth	Worcester C.	10.46	47	17	-	1
Watford	Tr	08.49	49-53	108	-	11
BROWN Thomas Hugh						
Liverpool, 8 May, 1930 E Yth						(WH)
Doncaster Rov.	South Liverpool	02.51	51-53	86	-	1
Swansea C.	Tr	12.55	55-58	69	-	0
BROWN Thomas Law						
Glenbuck, 17 April, 1921 Died 1966						(WH)
Millwall	Hearts	01.45	46-48	68	-	7
Charlton Ath.	Tr	10.48	48-49	34	-	1
Leyton Orient	Tr	08.50	50-52	99	-	5
BROWN Walter Sidney						
Oakengates, 8 February, 1921 Died 1989						(OR)
Walsall	Oakengates T.	10.40	46-47	20	-	4
BROWN Wayne Larry						
Southampton, 14 January, 1977						(G)
Bristol C.	YT	07.95	93	1	0	0
Chester C.	Weston-super-Mare	09.96	96-97	15	0	0
BROWN Wayne Lawrence						
Barking, 20 August, 1977						(CD)
Ipswich T.	YT	05.96	97	1	0	0
Colchester U.	L	10.97	97	0	2	0
BROWN Wesley Michael						
Manchester, 16 March, 1979 E Yth						(CD)
Manchester U.	YT	11.96	97	1	1	0
BROWN William						
Forfar, 17 September, 1928						(CF)
Accrington St.	Forfar Ath.	08.53	53	6	-	2
BROWN William						
Falkirk, 5 February, 1950						(F)
Burnley	Jnrs	02.67	68	0	1	0
Carlisle U.	Tr	07.69	69	16	3	8
Barrow	L	09.69	69	6	0	1
Newport Co.	Tr	08.70	70-74	166	2	50
Hereford U.	L	03.74	73	9	0	6
Brentford	Tr	11.74	74	16	0	9
Torquay U.	Tr	03.75	74-77	137	2	46
BROWN William						
Dawdon, 27 March, 1928						(HB)
Gateshead	Murton Colly	09.50	50-57	214	-	7
BROWN William						
Kilsyth, 21 February, 1929 Died 1987						(F)
Reading	Bridgeton Waverley	02.50				
Exeter C.	Tr	08.51	51	7	-	0
BROWN William						
Silvertown, 6 September, 1910 Died 1993						(RB)
Luton T.	Silvertown	03.30	30-34	49	-	4
Huddersfield T.	Tr	03.35	34-35	20	-	2
Brentford	Tr	03.37	36-46	92	-	2
Leyton Orient	Tr	05.47	46-47	26	-	0
BROWN William Charles						
Barking, 24 April, 1920 Died 1982						(CF)
Leyton Orient	Romford	08.46	46	2	-	1
BROWN William Dallas Fyfe						
Arbroath, 8 October, 1931 SF Lge/S 'B'/S-28						(G)
Tottenham H.	Dundee	06.59	59-65	222	0	0
Northampton T.	Tr	10.66	66	17	0	0
BROWN William Falconer						
Larkhall, 20 October, 1922 Died 1978						(FB)
Preston N.E.	Larkhall Thistle	01.42	46-49	40	-	0
Grimsby T.	Queen of South	06.51	51-57	265	-	1
BROWN William Frederick Thomas						
Croydon, 7 February, 1943						(CF)
Southampton		09.60				
Charlton Ath.	Tr	07.61				
Gillingham	Bedford T.	02.66	65-67	104	1	33
Portsmouth	Tr	06.68	68	8	0	2
Brentford	Tr	07.69	69	4	0	0
BROWN William Hutchinson						
Bedlington, 11 March, 1909 Died 1996						(FB)
Middlesbrough	West Stanley	12.28	31-38	256	-	2
Hartlepool U.	Tr	06.46	46-47	80	-	0
BROWN William Inglis						
Clydebank, 25 November, 1938						(G)
Accrington St.	St Mirren	08.59	59	29	-	0
Chester C.	Tr	06.60	60	41	-	0
BROWNBILL Derek Anthony						
Liverpool, 4 February, 1954						(F)
Liverpool	Jnrs	02.72	73	1	0	0
Port Vale	Tr	02.75	74-77	84	8	13
Wigan Ath.	Tr	09.78	78-79	32	16	8
BROWNE Corey Anthony						
Enfield, 2 July, 1970						(W)
Fulham	Kingsbury T.	08.91	91	1	0	0
BROWNE Paul						
Glasgow, 17 February, 1975						(CD)
Aston Villa	YT	07.93	95	2	0	0
BROWNE Robert James						
Derry (NI), 9 February, 1912 Died 1994 Lol/NI-6						(WH)
Leeds U.	Derry C.	10.35	35-46	107	-	0
York C.	Tr	08.47	47	5	-	0
BROWNE Stephen Logan						
Hackney, 21 June, 1964						(M)
Charlton Ath.	App	06.82	81	0	1	0
BROWNING Leonard James						
Doncaster, 30 March, 1928						(CF)
Leeds U.	Headingley R.	08.46	46-51	97	-	42
Sheffield U.	Tr	11.51	51-53	65	-	25
BROWNING Marcus Trevor						
Bristol, 22 April, 1971 W-5						(M)
Bristol Rov.	YT	07.89	89-96	152	22	13
Hereford U.	L	09.92	92	7	0	5
Huddersfield T.	Tr	02.97	96-97	23	4	0
BROWNLEE Thomas Courtney						
Carnwath, 21 May, 1935						(CF)
Walsall	Broxburn	09.56	57-58	30	-	14
York C.	Tr	12.58	58	9	-	2
Workington	Tr	06.59	59-60	25	-	2
Bradford C.	Netherfield	01.65	64-65	25	0	15
BROWNLIE John Jack						
Caldercruix, 11 March, 1952 Su23-5/S-7						(RB)
Newcastle U.	Hibernian	08.78	78-81	124	0	2
Middlesbrough	Tr	08.82	82	12	0	0
Hartlepool U.	Tr	08.84	84	19	0	1
BROWNLOW John (Jackie) Martin						
Belfast, 18 June, 1916 Died 1989						(W)
Ipswich T.	Gravesend & Nft	05.46	46	1	-	0
Hartlepool U.	Tr	10.48	48	3	-	0
BROWNRIGG Andrew David						
Sheffield, 2 August, 1976 S Sch						(CD)
Hereford U.	YT	01.95	94	8	0	0
Norwich C.	Tr	03.95				

League Club	Source	Date Signed	Seasons Played	Apps	Subs	Gls
BROWNSWORD Nathan **John (Jack)**						
Campsall, 15 May, 1923						(FB)
Hull C.	Frickley Colly	09.46	46	10	-	0
Scunthorpe U.	Tr	07.47	50-64	597	-	50
BRUCE Alexander Robert						
Dundee, 23 December, 1952 Su23-1						(F)
Preston N.E.	App	05.70	71-73	55	7	22
Newcastle U.	Tr	01.74	73-75	16	4	3
Preston N.E.	Tr	08.75	75-82	288	13	135
Wigan Ath.	Tr	08.83	83-84	35	8	7
BRUCE Marcelle Eugene						
U.S.A., 15 March, 1971						(RB)
Colchester U.	YT	07.89	89	28	1	1
BRUCE Paul Mark						
London, 18 February, 1978						(M)
Queens Park R.	YT	07.96	97	1	4	1
BRUCE Robert						
Belfast, 14 October, 1928						(OL)
Leicester C.	Larne T.	03.50				
Leyton Orient		11.51	51	1	-	0
BRUCE Stephen Roger						
Corbridge, 31 December, 1960 E Yth/E'B'/EF Lge						(CD)
Gillingham	App	10.78	79-83	203	2	29
Norwich C.	Tr	08.84	84-87	141	0	14
Manchester U.	Tr	12.87	87-95	309	0	36
Birmingham C.	Tr	06.96	96-97	70	2	2
BRUCK Dietmar Jurgen						
Germany, 19 April, 1944						(FB)
Coventry C.	App	05.62	60-70	181	8	7
Charlton Ath.	Tr	10.70	70-71	54	2	0
Northampton T.	Tr	06.72	72-73	41	0	0
BRUMWELL Phillip						
Darlington, 8 August, 1975						(D/M)
Sunderland	YT	06.94				
Darlington	Tr	08.95	95-97	73	28	1
BRUNFIELD Peter Stanley						
Maltby, 5 September, 1944						(HB)
Chesterfield		07.64	64	1	-	0
BRUNO Pasquale						
Lecce, Italy, 19 June, 1962						(CD)
Wigan Ath.	Hearts	02.98	97	1	0	0
BRUNSKILL Joseph						
Carlton, 22 April, 1932 Died 1989						(F)
Sunderland	Newcastle U. (Am)	04.50				
Oldham Ath.	Tr	05.54	54	12	-	2
BRUNT Geoffrey Reginald						
Nottingham, 24 November, 1926						(WH)
Notts Co.	Jnrs	09.49	49-53	29	-	1
BRUNT Malcolm Eric						
Sheffield, 5 December, 1946						(G)
Chesterfield	Sheffield Wed. (Am)	07.66	66	7	0	0
BRUSH Paul						
Plaistow, 22 February, 1958						(FB)
West Ham U.	App	02.76	77-84	144	7	1
Crystal Palace	Tr	09.85	85-87	50	0	3
Southend U.	Tr	01.88	87-89	69	4	1
BRUTON David Edward						
Dursley, 31 October, 1952						(CD)
Bristol C.	App	07.71	71-72	16	1	0
Swansea C.	Tr	08.73	73-78	185	8	19
Newport Co.	L	02.77	76	6	0	1
Newport Co.	Tr	10.78	78-80	79	3	9
BRUTON Michael						
Dursley, 6 May, 1958						(F)
Newport Co.	Gloucester C.	08.79	79	3	6	1
BRYAN Derek Kirk						
London, 11 November, 1974						(F)
Brentford	Hampton	08.97	97	2	9	2
BRYAN Ernest Newton						
Hawarden, 6 June, 1926						(RB)
Chester C.	Jnrs	11.45	48	1	-	0

League Club	Source	Date Signed	Seasons Played	Apps	Subs	Gls
BRYAN Marvin Lee						
Paddington, 2 August, 1975						(FB)
Queens Park R.	YT	08.92				
Doncaster Rov.	L	12.94	94	5	0	1
Blackpool	Tr	08.95	95-97	121	2	3
BRYAN Peter						
Ashbourne, 30 April, 1944						(FB)
Oxford U.	Botley Minors	07.61	62-65	18	0	0
BRYAN Peter Anthony						
Birmingham, 22 June, 1943						(FB)
Middlesbrough		08.61	64	4	-	0
Oldham Ath.	Tr	07.65	65	5	1	0
BRYANT Eric						
Birmingham, 18 November, 1921 Died 1995						(CF)
Mansfield T.		05.46	46-47	35	-	17
Plymouth Arg.	Yeovil T.	10.49	49-50	11	-	4
Leyton Orient	Tr	07.51	51	12	-	1
BRYANT Jeffrey Stephen						
Redhill, 27 November, 1953 E Yth						(D)
Wimbledon	Walton & Hersham	(N/L)	77-78	70	3	9
Bournemouth	Tr	06.79	79	16	0	2
BRYANT Matthew						
Bristol, 21 September, 1970						(CD)
Bristol C.	YT	07.89	90-95	201	2	7
Walsall	L	08.90	90	13	0	0
Gillingham	Tr	08.96	96-97	63	11	0
BRYANT Richard John						
Bristol, 20 June, 1963						(CD)
Bristol C.	D.R.G.	12.85	85	2	0	1
BRYANT Steven Paul						
Islington, 5 September, 1953						(LB)
Birmingham C.	App	07.71	74-75	34	2	1
Sheffield Wed.	L	08.76	76	2	1	0
Northampton T.	Tr	12.76	76-78	95	2	5
Portsmouth	Tr	03.79	78-81	111	0	5
Northampton T.	Tr	03.82	81	10	0	0
BRYCELAND Thomas						
Greenock, 1 March, 1939 S Sch						(IF)
Norwich C.	St Mirren	09.62	62-69	253	1	49
Oldham Ath.	Tr	03.70	69-71	66	1	10
BRYDON Ian Forrest						
Edinburgh, 22 March, 1927 Died 1973						(CF)
Darlington	St Johnstone	09.53	53	1	-	0
Accrington St.	Tr	11.53	53-54	27	-	19
Bradford P.A.	Tr	06.55	55	12	-	3
BRYDON Lee						
Stockton, 15 November, 1974						(CD)
Liverpool	YT	06.92				
Darlington	Tr	08.96	96-97	28	12	0
BRYSON James **Ian** Cook						
Kilmarnock, 26 November, 1962						(W)
Sheffield U.	Kilmarnock	08.88	88-92	138	17	36
Barnsley	Tr	08.93	93	16	0	3
Preston N.E.	Tr	11.93	93-96	141	10	19
Rochdale	Tr	07.97	97	12	3	1
BUCHAN Alistair Reid						
Aberdeen, 27 May, 1926						(WH)
Rochdale	Huntly	02.51	50-53	107	-	2
BUCHAN George						
Aberdeen, 2 May, 1950						(W)
Manchester U.	Aberdeen	05.73	73	0	3	0
Bury	Tr	08.74	74-75	57	8	6
BUCHAN Martin McLean						
Aberdeen, 6 March, 1949 Su23-3/S-34						(CD)
Manchester U.	Aberdeen	03.72	71-82	376	0	4
Oldham Ath.	Tr	08.83	83-84	28	0	0
BUCHAN Thomas						
Edinburgh, 6 December, 1915 Died 1980						(WH)
Blackpool	Woodhall Thistle	05.38	46-47	12	-	0
Carlisle U.	Tr	08.49	49	30	-	0
BUCHAN William Ralston Murray						
Grangemouth, 17 October, 1914 SF Lge						(IF)
Blackpool	Glasgow Celtic	11.37	37-47	90	-	34

League Club	Source	Date Signed	Seasons Played	Apps	Subs	Gls
Hull C.	Tr	01.48	47-48	40	-	12
Gateshead	Tr	11.49	49-51	88	-	16

BUCHANAN Cameron Campbell
Holytown, 31 July, 1928 (IF)

League Club	Source	Date Signed	Seasons Played	Apps	Subs	Gls
Wolverhampton W.	Jnrs	09.45				
Bournemouth	Tr	08.49	49-54	83	-	19
Norwich C.	Tr	10.56	56	3	-	0

BUCHANAN David
Newcastle, 23 June, 1962 E Yth/E Semi Pro (F)

League Club	Source	Date Signed	Seasons Played	Apps	Subs	Gls
Leicester C.	App	06.79	78-82	24	9	7
Northampton T.	L	10.82	82	3	2	0
Peterborough U.	Tr	08.83	83	13	3	4
Sunderland	Blyth Spartans	08.86	86-87	25	9	8
York C.	L	09.87	87	7	0	2

BUCHANAN John
Dingwall, 19 September, 1951 (M)

League Club	Source	Date Signed	Seasons Played	Apps	Subs	Gls
Northampton T.	Ross Co.	11.70	70-74	104	10	24
Cardiff C.	Tr	10.74	74-81	217	14	54
Northampton T.	Tr	09.81	81-82	66	3	6

BUCHANAN John
Bonnybridge, 9 June, 1928 (CF)

League Club	Source	Date Signed	Seasons Played	Apps	Subs	Gls
Derby Co.	Clyde	02.55	54-56	32	-	12
Bradford P.A.	Tr	12.57	57-62	164	-	67

BUCHANAN John (Jock)
Edinburgh, 3 January, 1935 (CF)

League Club	Source	Date Signed	Seasons Played	Apps	Subs	Gls
Newport Co.	Raith Rov.	08.61	61	31	-	7

BUCHANAN Peter Symington
Glasgow, 13 October, 1915 Died 1977 S-1 (IF)

League Club	Source	Date Signed	Seasons Played	Apps	Subs	Gls
Chelsea	Wishaw Jnrs	11.35	36-38	39	-	6
Fulham	Tr	03.46	46	20	-	1
Brentford	Tr	08.47	47-48	74	-	13

BUCHANAN William Mack
Tannockside, 29 July, 1924 (FB)

League Club	Source	Date Signed	Seasons Played	Apps	Subs	Gls
Carlisle U.	Motherwell	07.49	49	9	-	0
Barrow	Tr	10.49	49-55	242	-	0

BUCK Alan Michael
Colchester, 25 August, 1946 (G)

League Club	Source	Date Signed	Seasons Played	Apps	Subs	Gls
Colchester U.	Jnrs	07.64	64-68	38	0	0

BUCK Anthony Rowland
Clowne, 18 August, 1944 (CF)

League Club	Source	Date Signed	Seasons Played	Apps	Subs	Gls
Oxford U.	Eastbourne	08.62	62-67	30	5	6
Newport Co.	Tr	12.67	67-68	49	0	17
Rochdale	Tr	02.69	68-72	73	11	29
Bradford C.	L	01.72	71	3	0	0
Northampton T.	Tr	01.73	72-73	16	1	3

BUCK David Colin
Colchester, 25 August, 1946 (WH)

League Club	Source	Date Signed	Seasons Played	Apps	Subs	Gls
Colchester U.	Jnrs	05.65	65	0	1	0

BUCK George William
Abingdon, 25 January, 1941 (W)

League Club	Source	Date Signed	Seasons Played	Apps	Subs	Gls
Reading	Jnrs	01.58	58-60	31	-	4
Stockport Co.	Tr	07.62	62	3	-	0

BUCKINGHAM Colin Maurice Ernest
Plymouth, 12 August, 1943 (WH)

League Club	Source	Date Signed	Seasons Played	Apps	Subs	Gls
Plymouth Arg.	App	08.61	62-65	16	0	0
Exeter C.	Tr	09.65	65-66	29	0	0

BUCKINGHAM Victor Frederick
Greenwich, 23 October, 1915 Died 1995 (LB)

League Club	Source	Date Signed	Seasons Played	Apps	Subs	Gls
Tottenham H.	Jnrs	05.35	35-48	204	-	1

BUCKLAND Mark Christopher
Cheltenham, 18 August, 1961 (M)

League Club	Source	Date Signed	Seasons Played	Apps	Subs	Gls
Wolverhampton W.	A.P. Leamington	02.84	83-84	44	6	5

BUCKLE Herbert **Edward**
Southwark, 28 October, 1924 Died 1990 (W)

League Club	Source	Date Signed	Seasons Played	Apps	Subs	Gls
Manchester U.		11.45	46- 49	20	-	6
Everton	Tr	11.49	49-54	97	-	31
Exeter C.	Tr	07.55	55-56	65	-	12

BUCKLE Paul John
Hatfield, 16 December, 1970 (W)

League Club	Source	Date Signed	Seasons Played	Apps	Subs	Gls
Brentford	YT	07.89	87-92	42	15	1
Torquay U.	Tr	02.94	93-95	57	2	9
Exeter C.	Tr	10.95	95	22	0	2
Colchester U.	Wycombe W. (N/C)	11.96	96-97	57	5	5

BUCKLEY Alan Peter
Eastwood, 20 April, 1951 (F)

League Club	Source	Date Signed	Seasons Played	Apps	Subs	Gls
Nottingham F.	App	04.68	71-72	16	2	1
Walsall	Tr	08.73	73-78	241	0	125
Birmingham C.	Tr	10.78	78	24	4	8
Walsall	Tr	07.79	79-84	161	17	49

BUCKLEY Ambrose
Brinsley, 31 January, 1909 Died 1968 (LB)

League Club	Source	Date Signed	Seasons Played	Apps	Subs	Gls
Fulham	Sherwood Foresters	03.33	34-38	6	-	0
Doncaster Rov.	Tr	05.39				
Stockport Co.	Dartford	11.45	46	11	-	0

BUCKLEY Frank
Lichfield, 11 May, 1922 (WH)

League Club	Source	Date Signed	Seasons Played	Apps	Subs	Gls
Notts Co.	Jnrs	08.39				
Crystal Palace	Tr	11.46	47-50	69	-	0

BUCKLEY Gary
Manchester, 3 March, 1961 (M)

League Club	Source	Date Signed	Seasons Played	Apps	Subs	Gls
Manchester C.	App	04.78	80	4	2	0
Preston N.E.	Tr	10.81	81-82	27	7	2
Bury	Chorley	03.84	83-85	23	8	1

BUCKLEY Glen
Wigan, 31 August, 1960 (F)

League Club	Source	Date Signed	Seasons Played	Apps	Subs	Gls
Wigan Ath. (N/C)	Preston N.E. (N/C)	10.79	79	1	0	0

BUCKLEY Ian
Oldham, 8 October, 1953 E Yth (LB)

League Club	Source	Date Signed	Seasons Played	Apps	Subs	Gls
Oldham Ath.	App	12.71	71	5	0	0
Rochdale	L	02.74	73	6	0	0
Stockport Co.	Tr	08.75	75-76	55	10	2
Cambridge U.	Durban C. (SA)	11.77	77-80	51	6	2

BUCKLEY John William
East Kilbride, 18 May, 1962 (W)

League Club	Source	Date Signed	Seasons Played	Apps	Subs	Gls
Doncaster Rov.	Partick Thistle	07.84	84-85	79	5	11
Leeds U.	Tr	06.86	86-87	6	4	1
Leicester C.	L	03.87	86	1	4	0
Doncaster Rov.	L	10.87	87	6	0	0
Rotherham U.	Tr	11.87	87-90	85	20	13
Scunthorpe U.	Partick Thistle	08.91	91-92	39	4	8
Rotherham U.	Tr	02.93	92	2	2	0

BUCKLEY Michael John
Manchester, 4 November, 1953 E Yth/Eu23-1 (M)

League Club	Source	Date Signed	Seasons Played	Apps	Subs	Gls
Everton	App	06.71	71-77	128	7	10
Sunderland	Tr	08.78	78-82	117	4	7
Hartlepool U. (N/C)	Tr	08.83	83	6	0	0
Carlisle U.	Tr	09.83	83	24	1	2
Middlesbrough	Tr	06.84	84	27	0	0

BUCKLEY Neil Anthony
Hull, 25 September, 1968 (CD)

League Club	Source	Date Signed	Seasons Played	Apps	Subs	Gls
Hull C.	YT	12.86	86-91	55	5	3
Burnley	L	03.90	89	5	0	0

BUCKLEY Patrick McCabe
Leith, 12 August, 1946 (OL)

League Club	Source	Date Signed	Seasons Played	Apps	Subs	Gls
Wolverhampton W.	Third Lanark	02.64	64-67	28	1	8
Sheffield U.	Tr	01.68	67-70	9	6	2
Rotherham U.	Tr	06.72	72	1	2	0

BUCKLEY Steven
Eastwood, 16 October, 1953 (LB)

League Club	Source	Date Signed	Seasons Played	Apps	Subs	Gls
Luton T.	Burton A.	04.74	74-77	123	0	9
Derby Co.	Tr	01.78	77-85	323	0	21
Lincoln C.	Tr	08.86	86	36	0	2

BUDD Kevin John
Hillingdon, 20 March, 1962 (D)

League Club	Source	Date Signed	Seasons Played	Apps	Subs	Gls
Norwich C.	Bournemouth (App)	10.79				
Manchester C.	Tr	02.81				
Swansea C. (N/C)	Hillingdon Borough	11.85	85	1	0	0

BUGG Alec Alfred
Needham Market, 27 November, 1948 (G)

League Club	Source	Date Signed	Seasons Played	Apps	Subs	Gls
Ipswich T.	Jnrs	06.67	68-69	4	0	0
Bournemouth	L	02.70	69	4	0	0

BUICK Joseph Arnot Lorimer
Dundee, 1 July, 1933 (WH)

League Club	Source	Date Signed	Seasons Played	Apps	Subs	Gls
Lincoln C.	Broughty Ath.	10.55	55-61	31	-	3

BUIST James Gibb
Falkirk, 19 June, 1918 (W)

League Club	Source	Date Signed	Seasons Played	Apps	Subs	Gls
New Brighton	Dundee	08.46	46	21	-	6
Plymouth Arg.	Tr	06.47	48	1	-	0

League Club	Source	Date Signed	Seasons Played	Career Record Apps	Subs	Gls
BUKOVINA John Frank						
Barnsley, 2 February, 1964						(F)
Barnsley	App	02.82				
Doncaster Rov.	Tr	08.83	83	1	0	0
BUKOWSKI David						
Willington, 2 November, 1952						(CD)
Northampton T.	App	11.70	71-72	10	2	0
BULCH Robert Stephen						
Washington, 1 January, 1933						(WH)
Notts Co.	Washington	03.53	55-57	27	-	1
Darlington	Tr	06.58	58-59	44	-	1
BULL Gary William						
West Bromwich, 12 June, 1966						(F)
Southampton	Paget R.	10.86				
Cambridge U.	Tr	03.88	87-88	13	6	4
Barnet	Tr	03.89	91-92	83	0	37
Nottingham F.	Tr	07.93	93-94	4	8	1
Birmingham C.	L	09.94	94	10	0	6
Brighton & H.A.	L	08.95	95	10	0	2
Birmingham C.	Tr	12.95	95	3	3	0
York C.	Tr	03.96	95-97	66	17	11
BULL Michael						
Twickenham, 3 April, 1930						(W)
Brentford		09.48	52	3	-	0
Swindon T.	Tr	06.53	53-54	69	-	15
BULL Stephen George						
Tipton, 28 March, 1965 Eu21-5/E 'B'/E-13						(F)
West Bromwich A.	Tipton T.	08.85	85-86	2	2	2
Wolverhampton W.	Tr	11.86	86-97	450	9	246
BULL William						
Birmingham, 1 April, 1926						(CF)
Coventry C.		03.48	48	1	-	0
BULLESS Brian						
Hull, 4 September, 1933						(D)
Hull C.	Jnrs	10.50	52-63	326	-	30
BULLIMORE Alwyn Arthur						
Norwich, 22 October, 1933						(WH)
Norwich C.	Jnrs	10.53	56	1	-	0
BULLIMORE Wayne Alan						
Sutton-in-Ashfield, 12 September, 1970 E Yth						(M)
Manchester U.	YT	09.88				
Barnsley	Tr	03.91	91-92	27	8	1
Scunthorpe U.	Stockport Co. (N/C)	11.93	93-95	62	5	11
Bradford C.	Tr	12.95	95	1	1	0
Doncaster Rov.	L	09.96	96	4	0	0
Peterborough U.	Tr	03.97	96-97	10	11	1
BULLIONS James Law						
Bonnybridge, 12 March, 1924						(WH)
Derby Co.	Clowne	10.44	46-47	17	-	0
Leeds U.	Tr	11.47	47-49	35	-	0
Shrewsbury T.	Tr	09.50	50-53	131	-	2
BULLIVANT Terence Paul						
Lambeth, 23 September, 1956						(M)
Fulham	App	05.74	74-79	94	7	2
Aston Villa	Tr	11.79	79-81	10	3	0
Charlton Ath.	Tr	07.82	82	30	0	3
Brentford	Tr	07.83	83-85	36	1	2
BULLOCK Darren John						
Worcester, 12 February, 1969						(M)
Huddersfield T.	Nuneaton Borough	11.93	93-96	127	1	16
Swindon T.	Tr	02.97	96-97	38	6	1
BULLOCK Martin John						
Derby, 5 March, 1975 Eu21-1						(W)
Barnsley	Eastwood T.	09.93	94-97	72	59	1
BULLOCK Michael Edwin						
Stoke, 2 October, 1946 E Sch						(CF)
Birmingham C.	App	10.63	63-66	27	0	10
Oxford U.	Tr	06.67	67-68	58	1	15
Leyton Orient	Tr	10.68	68-75	267	10	65
Halifax T.	Tr	02.76	75-78	98	8	19
BULLOCK Norman						
Nuneaton, 26 March, 1932						(F)
Aston Villa	Coton Villa	09.49				
Chester C.	Tr	07.52	52-59	187	-	41

League Club	Source	Date Signed	Seasons Played	Career Record Apps	Subs	Gls
BULLOCK Peter Leonard						
Stoke, 17 November, 1941 E Sch/E Yth						(IF)
Stoke C.	Jnrs	11.58	57-61	44	-	14
Birmingham C.	Tr	03.62	61-64	27	-	3
Southend U.	Tr	02.65	64-65	12	0	2
Colchester U.	Tr	10.65	65-67	94	1	33
Exeter C.	Tr	07.68	68	14	0	2
Walsall	Tr	12.68	68	7	0	0
BULLOCK Simon John						
Stoke, 28 September, 1962						(F)
Halifax T.	Stoke C. (App)	09.80	80-81	15	2	1
BULLOCK Steven						
Stockport, 5 October, 1966						(D)
Oldham Ath.	Jnrs	07.84	83-85	10	8	0
Tranmere Rov.	Tr	08.86	86	25	5	1
Stockport Co.	Tr	08.87	87-90	106	14	0
BULMER Peter						
Liverpool, 31 August, 1965						(FB)
Chester C.	App	08.83	82-84	56	15	2
Preston N.E.	Rhyl	07.86	86	4	0	0
BULZIS Riccardo						
Bedford, 22 November, 1974						(F)
Northampton T.	YT	●	91	1	3	0
BUMPSTEAD David John						
Rainham, 6 November, 1935 E Amat						(WH)
Millwall	Tooting & Mitcham	06.58	57-61	84	-	8
Bristol Rov.	Tr	12.61	61-63	40	-	0
BUMSTEAD Charles Henry						
Croydon, 8 January, 1922						(G)
Millwall		03.43	46-47	12	-	0
Crystal Palace	Tr	08.48	48-51	53	-	0
BUMSTEAD John						
Rotherhithe, 27 November, 1958						(M)
Chelsea	App	11.76	78-90	314	25	38
Charlton Ath.	Tr	07.91	91-92	54	2	3
BUMSTEAD Raymond George						
Ringwood, 27 January, 1936						(OR)
Bournemouth	Ringwood	05.58	58-69	412	2	55
BUNBURY Alexander						
Guyana, 18 June, 1967 Canadian Int						(F)
West Ham U.	Montreal Supra (Can)	12.92	92	2	2	0
BUNCE Frederick						
Bushey, 16 February, 1938 Died 1991 E Yth						(OL)
Watford	Jnrs	10.55	55-62	150	-	34
BUNCE Paul Eric						
Coalville, 7 January, 1967						(W)
Leicester C.	App	01.85	86	5	1	0
Northampton T.	Tr	03.87	86-87	6	6	2
BUNCLARK Cyril						
Rotherham, 27 March, 1931						(F)
Rotherham U.		11.53	54	2	-	1
BUNKELL Raymond Keith						
Edmonton, 18 September, 1949 E Yth						(M)
Tottenham H.	App	06.67				
Swindon T.	Tr	06.71	71-73	52	4	3
Colchester U.	Tr	12.73	73-79	117	12	9
BUNN Frank Stephen						
Birmingham, 6 November, 1962						(F)
Luton T.	App	05.80	80-84	52	7	9
Hull C.	Tr	07.85	85-87	89	6	23
Oldham Ath.	Tr	12.87	87-89	75	3	26
BUNNER Henry Francis						
Manchester, 18 September, 1936						(CH)
Bury	Bury Amats	04.57	57-64	106	-	0
Stockport Co.	Tr	04.65	65	3	0	0
BUNTING Benjamin						
Rochdale, 14 February, 1923						(FB)
Oldham Ath.	Rochdale (Am)	08.46	46-47	32	-	0
BURBANKS William **Edwin**						
Campsall, 1 April, 1913 Died 1983						(OL)
Sunderland	Denaby U.	02.35	34-47	131	-	26

League Club	Source	Date Signed	Seasons Played	Apps	Subs	Gls
Hull C.	Tr	06.48	48-52	143	-	21
Leeds U.	Tr	07.53	53	13	-	1

BURBECK Ronald Thomas
Leicester, 27 February, 1934 E Yth (W)

League Club	Source	Date Signed	Seasons Played	Apps	Subs	Gls
Leicester C.	Jnrs	05.52	52-55	3	-	0
Middlesbrough	Tr	10.56	56-62	139	-	24
Darlington	Tr	08.63	63	18	-	1

BURCKITT John David
Coventry, 16 December, 1946 E Yth (FB)

League Club	Source	Date Signed	Seasons Played	Apps	Subs	Gls
Coventry C.	Jnrs	07.64	64	5	-	0
Bradford C.	L	03.67	66	9	-	0
Walsall	Tr	06.68				

BURDEN Brian
West Stockwith, 26 November, 1939 (G)

League Club	Source	Date Signed	Seasons Played	Apps	Subs	Gls
Lincoln C.	West Stockwith	03.61	60	1	-	0

BURDEN Ian
Bradford, 27 May, 1944 (CF)

League Club	Source	Date Signed	Seasons Played	Apps	Subs	Gls
York C. (Am)	Poppleton Road	10.65	65	3	0	2

BURDEN Thomas David
Andover, 21 February, 1924 (WH)

League Club	Source	Date Signed	Seasons Played	Apps	Subs	Gls
Wolverhampton W.	Jnrs	08.41				
Chester C.	Tr	11.45	46-47	82	-	39
Leeds U.	Tr	07.48	48-54	243	-	13
Bristol C.	Tr	10.54	54-60	231	-	20

BURDESS John
Newcastle, 10 April, 1946 (IF)

League Club	Source	Date Signed	Seasons Played	Apps	Subs	Gls
Oldham Ath.	App	04.64	63-64	3	-	0

BURGESS Albert **Campbell (Cam)**
Bebington, 21 September, 1919 Died 1978 (IF)

League Club	Source	Date Signed	Seasons Played	Apps	Subs	Gls
Bolton W.	Bromborough	02.38	46-47	5	-	3
Chester C.	Tr	10.48	48-51	111	-	64
Crystal Palace	Tr	09.51	51-52	47	-	40
York C.	Tr	07.53	53	32	-	14

BURGESS Daryl
Marston Green, 24 January, 1971 (CD)

League Club	Source	Date Signed	Seasons Played	Apps	Subs	Gls
West Bromwich A.	YT	07.89	89-97	278	5	9

BURGESS David John
Liverpool, 20 January, 1960 (FB)

League Club	Source	Date Signed	Seasons Played	Apps	Subs	Gls
Tranmere Rov.		08.81	81-85	217	1	1
Grimsby T.	Tr	08.86	86-87	66	3	0
Blackpool	Tr	07.88	88-92	101	0	1
Carlisle U.	L	02.93	92	6	0	0
Carlisle U.	Tr	06.93	93	36	4	1
Hartlepool U.	L	09.94	94	11	0	0

BURGESS Eric Robert Charles
Edgware, 27 October, 1944 (FB)

League Club	Source	Date Signed	Seasons Played	Apps	Subs	Gls
Watford	App	07.62	63-64	3	-	0
Torquay U.	Tr	07.65	65-67	73	2	0
Plymouth Arg.	Tr	07.68	68-69	14	1	0
Colchester U.	Plymouth C.	12.70	70-71	46	1	9

BURGESS Michael
Canada, 17 April, 1932 (CH/IF)

League Club	Source	Date Signed	Seasons Played	Apps	Subs	Gls
Bradford P.A.	Bradford C. (Am)	08.52				
Leyton Orient	Tr	07.53	53-55	31	-	12
Newport Co.	Tr	02.56	55-56	23	-	7
Bournemouth	Tr	06.57	57-60	109	-	34
Halifax T.	Tr	07.61	61-62	34	-	3
Gillingham	Tr	03.63	62-65	109	1	2
Aldershot	Tr	11.65	65	6	0	0

BURGESS Robert Buchanan Benwood
Glasgow, 1 April, 1927 (CF)

League Club	Source	Date Signed	Seasons Played	Apps	Subs	Gls
Walsall (Am)	Third Lanark	09.53	53	2	-	1

BURGESS William Arthur **Ronald**
Ebbw Vale, 9 April, 1917 W-32/EF Lge (WH)

League Club	Source	Date Signed	Seasons Played	Apps	Subs	Gls
Tottenham H.	Cwm Villa	05.36	38-53	297	-	14
Swansea C.	Tr	08.54	54-55	47	-	1

BURGESS Walter
Golborne, 19 June, 1921 Died 1988 (IF)

League Club	Source	Date Signed	Seasons Played	Apps	Subs	Gls
Halifax T.	Coleraine	11.46	46	13	-	2

BURGHER Symon George
Birmingham, 29 October, 1966 (M)

League Club	Source	Date Signed	Seasons Played	Apps	Subs	Gls
Exeter C.	YT	02.85	84	11	3	0

BURGIN Andrew
Sheffield, 6 March, 1947 (FB)

League Club	Source	Date Signed	Seasons Played	Apps	Subs	Gls
Sheffield Wed.	App	03.64	64	1	-	0
Rotherham U.	Tr	08.67	67	9	1	0
Halifax T.	Detroit (USA)	12.68	68-74	243	0	9
Blackburn Rov.	Tr	09.74	74-75	45	0	1

BURGIN Edward (Ted)
Bradfield (Yk), 29 April, 1927 E 'B' (G)

League Club	Source	Date Signed	Seasons Played	Apps	Subs	Gls
Sheffield U.	Alford T.	03.49	49-56	281	-	0
Doncaster Rov.	Tr	12.57	57	5	-	0
Leeds U.	Tr	03.58	58-60	58	-	0
Rochdale	Tr	01.61	60-65	207	0	0

BURGIN Eric
Sheffield, 4 January, 1924 (CH)

League Club	Source	Date Signed	Seasons Played	Apps	Subs	Gls
Sheffield U.		12.46				
York C.	Tr	05.49	49-50	23	-	0

BURGIN Terence
Nottingham, 9 October, 1938 (CF)

League Club	Source	Date Signed	Seasons Played	Apps	Subs	Gls
Reading		11.59	60	2	-	0

BURGIN Trevor
Darfield, 28 August, 1943 (HB)

League Club	Source	Date Signed	Seasons Played	Apps	Subs	Gls
Bradford P.A.	Wombwell	07.67	67	12	5	0

BURKE Charles
Arran, 13 September, 1921 Died 1995 (CF)

League Club	Source	Date Signed	Seasons Played	Apps	Subs	Gls
Bournemouth	Ardeer Rec.	06.39	46	25	-	6

BURKE David Ian
Liverpool, 6 August, 1960 E Yth (LB)

League Club	Source	Date Signed	Seasons Played	Apps	Subs	Gls
Bolton W.	App	08.77	78-80	65	4	1
Huddersfield T.	Tr	06.81	81-87	189	0	3
Crystal Palace	Tr	10.87	87-89	80	1	0
Bolton W.	Tr	07.90	90-93	104	2	0
Blackpool	Tr	07.94	94	23	0	0

BURKE John
Motherwell, 10 August, 1962 S Sch (W)

League Club	Source	Date Signed	Seasons Played	Apps	Subs	Gls
Sheffield U.	Motherwell	07.80				
Exeter C. (N/C)	Tr	03.83	82	3	0	0
Chester C. (N/C)	Tr	08.83	83	3	0	0

BURKE John Joseph
Dublin, 28 May, 1911 Died 1987 (G)

League Club	Source	Date Signed	Seasons Played	Apps	Subs	Gls
Chester C.	Shelbourne	07.31	31-35	80	-	0
Millwall	Tr	06.36	36-46	24	-	0
Gillingham	Tr	09.47	50	5	-	0

BURKE Mark Stephen
Solihull, 12 February, 1969 E Yth (W)

League Club	Source	Date Signed	Seasons Played	Apps	Subs	Gls
Aston Villa	Tr	02.87	86-87	5	2	0
Middlesbrough	Tr	12.87	87-89	32	25	6
Darlington	L	10.90	90	5	0	1
Wolverhampton W.	Tr	03.91	90-91	16	8	2
Luton T.	L	03.94	93	2	1	0
Port Vale	Tr	08.94	94	4	11	2

BURKE Marshall
Glasgow, 26 March, 1959 S Sch (M)

League Club	Source	Date Signed	Seasons Played	Apps	Subs	Gls
Burnley	App	03.77	77-79	22	2	5
Leeds U.	Tr	05.80				
Blackburn Rov.	Tr	12.80	80-81	34	5	7
Lincoln C.	Tr	10.82	82-83	49	1	7
Cardiff C.	L	12.83	83	3	0	0
Tranmere Rov.	Scarborough	09.84	84	3	0	0

BURKE Peter
Rotherham, 26 April, 1957 (CD)

League Club	Source	Date Signed	Seasons Played	Apps	Subs	Gls
Barnsley	App	04.75	74-76	36	0	1
Halifax T.	Tr	03.78	77-79	79	6	9
Rochdale	Tr	07.80	80-81	68	0	2

BURKE Peter Joseph
Fazackerley, 1 February, 1912 Died 1979 (CH)

League Club	Source	Date Signed	Seasons Played	Apps	Subs	Gls
Oldham Ath.	Prescot Cables	05.33	33-35	93	-	6
Norwich C.	Tr	12.35	35-38	114	-	0
Luton T.	Tr	06.39				
Southport	Tr	07.46	46	1	-	0

BURKE Richard
Ashton-u-Lyne, 28 October, 1920 (FB)

League Club	Source	Date Signed	Seasons Played	Apps	Subs	Gls
Blackpool	Jnrs	07.38	38	1	-	0
Newcastle U.	Tr	12.46	46	15	-	0
Carlisle U.	Tr	08.47	47-48	77	-	8

BURKE Robert Gallee
Ballymena (NI), 5 November, 1934 (IF)

League Club	Source	Date Signed	Seasons Played	Apps	Subs	Gls
Burnley	Albertville U.	09.55	55	19	-	5
Chester C.	Tr	06.58				

BURKE Ronald Stewart
Marske, 13 August, 1921 (CF)

League Club	Source	Date Signed	Seasons Played	Apps	Subs	Gls
Manchester U.	St Albans C.	08.46	46-48	28	-	16
Huddersfield T.	Tr	06.49	49-51	27	-	6
Rotherham U.	Tr	03.53	52-54	73	-	56
Exeter C.	Tr	06.55	55-56	42	-	14

BURKE Steven James
Nottingham, 29 September, 1960 E Yth (W)

League Club	Source	Date Signed	Seasons Played	Apps	Subs	Gls
Nottingham F.	App	03.78				
Queens Park R.	Tr	09.79	79-83	43	24	5
Millwall	L	10.83	83	7	0	1
Notts Co.	L	10.84	84	4	1	0
Lincoln C.	L	08.85	85	4	1	0
Brentford	L	03.86	85	10	0	1
Doncaster Rov.	Tr	08.86	86-87	50	7	8
Stockport Co.	L	10.87	87	5	0	0

BURKE Thomas
Greenock, 18 October, 1939 (F)

League Club	Source	Date Signed	Seasons Played	Apps	Subs	Gls
Barnsley	Clyde	02.63	62	1	-	0

BURKETT Jack William
Edmonton, 21 August, 1942 (FB)

League Club	Source	Date Signed	Seasons Played	Apps	Subs	Gls
West Ham U.	Jnrs	10.59	61-67	141	1	4
Charlton Ath.	Tr	06.68	68-69	8	0	0

BURKINSHAW George Allen
Barnsley, 1 October, 1922 Died 1982 (CH)

League Club	Source	Date Signed	Seasons Played	Apps	Subs	Gls
Barnsley	Woolley Colly	03.42				
Carlisle U.	Tr	09.46	46	25	-	0
Barnsley	Tr	06.47				
Bradford C.	Tr	11.48	48	12	-	0

BURKINSHAW Harry Keith
Darton, 23 June, 1935 (WH)

League Club	Source	Date Signed	Seasons Played	Apps	Subs	Gls
Liverpool	Denaby U.	11.53	54	1	-	0
Workington	Tr	12.57	57-64	293	-	9
Scunthorpe U.	Tr	05.65	65-67	107	1	3

BURKITT John (Jack) Orgill
Wednesbury, 19 January, 1926 (WH)

League Club	Source	Date Signed	Seasons Played	Apps	Subs	Gls
Nottingham F.	Darlaston	05.47	48-61	464	-	14

BURLEIGH Martin Stewart
Willington, 2 February, 1951 (G)

League Club	Source	Date Signed	Seasons Played	Apps	Subs	Gls
Newcastle U.	Willington	12.68	70-73	11	0	0
Darlington	Tr	10.74	74	30	0	0
Carlisle U.	Tr	06.75	75-76	26	0	0
Darlington	Tr	08.77	77-78	71	0	0
Hartlepool U.	Tr	10.79	79-81	84	0	0

BURLEY Craig William
Irvine, 24 September, 1971 S Sch/S Yth/Su21-7/S-28 (M)

League Club	Source	Date Signed	Seasons Played	Apps	Subs	Gls
Chelsea	YT	09.89	90-96	85	28	7

BURLEY George Elder
Cumnock, 3 June, 1956 S Sch/S Yth/Su21-5/Su23-2/S-11 (RB)

League Club	Source	Date Signed	Seasons Played	Apps	Subs	Gls
Ipswich T.	App	06.73	73-85	394	0	6
Sunderland	Tr	09.85	85-86	54	0	0
Gillingham	Tr	07.88	88	46	0	2
Colchester U. (N/C)	Ayr U.	08.94	94	5	2	0

BURLISON Robert Lyle
Newcastle, 29 March, 1920 Died 1987 (F)

League Club	Source	Date Signed	Seasons Played	Apps	Subs	Gls
Charlton Ath.	Horden Colly	09.39	46	1	-	0

BURLISON Thomas Henry
Edmondsley (Dm), 23 May, 1936 (WH)

League Club	Source	Date Signed	Seasons Played	Apps	Subs	Gls
Lincoln C.	Jnrs	12.53				
Hartlepool U.	Tr	07.57	57-63	148		5
Darlington	Tr	08.64	64	26	-	2

BURLURAUX Donald
Skelton, 8 June, 1951 (W)

League Club	Source	Date Signed	Seasons Played	Apps	Subs	Gls
Middlesbrough	Jnrs	07.68	70-71	4	1	0
York C.	L	12.71	71	3	0	1
Darlington	Tr	07.72	72-74	105	7	13

BURMAN Anthony Paul
Stockwell, 3 June, 1958 (F)

League Club	Source	Date Signed	Seasons Played	Apps	Subs	Gls
Charlton Ath.	Queens Park R. (App)	08.76	76-77	16	3	3

BURMAN Simon John
Ipswich, 26 November, 1965 (W)

League Club	Source	Date Signed	Seasons Played	Apps	Subs	Gls
Colchester U.	App	11.83	84-86	28	4	3

BURN John Haytor
South Shields, 21 January, 1930 (G)

League Club	Source	Date Signed	Seasons Played	Apps	Subs	Gls
Chelsea		10.48				
Chesterfield	Tr	08.50				
Carlisle U.		06.55	55	26	-	0

BURN Ralph Gordon
Alnwick, 9 November, 1931 (IF)

League Club	Source	Date Signed	Seasons Played	Apps	Subs	Gls
Northampton T.		08.50	50	1	-	0
Crewe Alex.	Tr	07.54	54	1	-	0

BURNDRED John Nigel
Stoke, 23 March, 1968 (F)

League Club	Source	Date Signed	Seasons Played	Apps	Subs	Gls
Port Vale (N/C)	Knypersley Vic.	02.95	94	0	1	0

BURNETT Alfred Price
Aberdeen, 23 July, 1922 Died 1977 (CF)

League Club	Source	Date Signed	Seasons Played	Apps	Subs	Gls
Barrow	Dundee	12.46	46-49	87	-	32
Lincoln C.	Tr	11.49	49	4	-	1

BURNETT Dennis Henry
Bermondsey, 27 September, 1944 (D)

League Club	Source	Date Signed	Seasons Played	Apps	Subs	Gls
West Ham U.	Jnrs	10.62	65-66	48	2	0
Millwall	Tr	08.67	67-73	257	0	3
Hull C.	Tr	10.73	73-74	46	0	2
Millwall	L	03.75	74	6	0	2
Brighton & H.A.	St Louis (USA)	09.75	75-76	41	3	1

BURNETT George Gordon
Liverpool, 11 February, 1920 Died 1985 (G)

League Club	Source	Date Signed	Seasons Played	Apps	Subs	Gls
Everton	Jnrs	09.38	46-50	47	-	0
Oldham Ath.	Tr	10.51	51-54	100	-	0

BURNETT John
Market Rasen, 24 June, 1939 (LB)

League Club	Source	Date Signed	Seasons Played	Apps	Subs	Gls
Grimsby T.	Gainsborough Trin.	07.58	58	1	-	0

BURNETT Wayne
Lambeth, 4 September 1971 E Yth (M)

League Club	Source	Date Signed	Seasons Played	Apps	Subs	Gls
Leyton Orient	YT	11.89	89-91	34	6	0
Blackburn Rov.	Tr	08.92				
Plymouth Arg.	Tr	08.93	93-95	61	9	3
Bolton W.	Tr	10.95	95-96	0	2	0
Huddersfield T.	Tr	09.96	96-97	44	6	0
Grimsby T.	Tr	01.98	97	20	1	1

BURNETT William John
Gateshead, 1 March, 1926 Died 1988 (OR)

League Club	Source	Date Signed	Seasons Played	Apps	Subs	Gls
Grimsby T.	Wardley Welfare	07.46	47	10	-	0
Hartlepool U.	Tr	11.48	48-53	194	-	17

BURNHAM Jason John
Mansfield, 8 May, 1973 (LB)

League Club	Source	Date Signed	Seasons Played	Apps	Subs	Gls
Northampton T.	YT	07.91	91-93	79	9	2
Chester C.	Tr	07.94	94-95	62	2	1

BURNS Anthony John
Edenbridge, 27 March, 1944 (G)

League Club	Source	Date Signed	Seasons Played	Apps	Subs	Gls
Arsenal	Tonbridge	03.63	64-65	31	0	0
Brighton & H.A.	Tr	07.66	66-68	54	0	0
Charlton Ath.	Tr	03.69	68-69	10	0	0
Crystal Palace	Durban U. (SA)	10.73	74-77	90	0	0
Brentford	L	01.77	76	6	0	0
Plymouth Arg.	Memphis (USA)	08.78	78	8	0	0

BURNS Barry Ross
Doncaster, 19 June, 1937 (F)

League Club	Source	Date Signed	Seasons Played	Apps	Subs	Gls
Rotherham U.	Dunscroft	10.54	57	5	-	4

BURNS Christopher
Manchester, 9 November, 1967 (M)

League Club	Source	Date Signed	Seasons Played	Apps	Subs	Gls
Portsmouth	Cheltenham T.	03.91	91-93	78	12	9
Swansea C.	L	12.93	93	4	0	0
Bournemouth	L	03.94	93	13	1	1
Swansea C. (N/C)	Tr	11.94	94	3	2	0
Northampton T.	Tr	01.95	94-96	62	4	9

BURNS David
Liverpool, 12 November, 1958 (LB)

League Club	Source	Date Signed	Seasons Played	Apps	Subs	Gls
Chester C.	App	10.76	76-81	66	12	2

BURNS Derek George
Bournemouth, 23 January, 1950 (M)

League Club	Source	Date Signed	Seasons Played	Apps	Subs	Gls
Bournemouth	App	01.68	68	3	1	0

BURNS Eric Owen
Newton Stewart, 8 March, 1945 (W)

League Club	Source	Date Signed	Seasons Played	Apps	Subs	Gls
Bradford P.A.	App	03.62	63-65	26	2	3
Barnsley	Tr	08.66	66	3	0	0

BURNS Francis
Glenboig, 17 October, 1948 S Sch/Su23-1/S-1 (LB)

League Club	Source	Date Signed	Seasons Played	Apps	Subs	Gls
Manchester U.	Jnrs	10.65	67-71	111	10	6
Southampton	Tr	06.72	72	20	1	0
Preston N.E.	Tr	08.73	73-80	271	2	9

BURNS Francis Joseph
Workington, 11 November, 1924 Died 1987 (WH)

League Club	Source	Date Signed	Seasons Played	Apps	Subs	Gls
Swansea C.	Wolverhampton W. (Am)	08.44	46-51	172	-	9
Southend U.	Tr	07.52	52-54	89	-	14
Crewe Alex.	Tr	11.56	56-57	30	-	7

BURNS Hugh
Lanark, 13 December, 1965 (LB)

League Club	Source	Date Signed	Seasons Played	Apps	Subs	Gls
Fulham (L)	Dunfermline Ath.	12.89	89	6	0	0

BURNS Kenneth
Glasgow, 23 September, 1953 Su23-2/S-20 (CD)

League Club	Source	Date Signed	Seasons Played	Apps	Subs	Gls
Birmingham C.	App	07.71	71-76	163	7	45
Nottingham F.	Tr	07.77	77-81	137	0	13
Leeds U.	Tr	10.81	81-83	54	2	2
Derby Co.	L	03.83	82	6	1	1
Derby Co.	Tr	02.84	83-84	30	1	1
Notts Co.	L	02.85	84	2	0	0
Barnsley (N/C)	Tr	08.85	85	19	2	0

BURNS Kinear (Ken)
Isle of Man, 24 September, 1923 (OR)

League Club	Source	Date Signed	Seasons Played	Apps	Subs	Gls
Tranmere Rov.	Ramsey	09.46	46	14	-	4
Southport	Tr	11.47	47	5	-	0

BURNS Leo Francis
Manchester, 3 August, 1932 (WH)

League Club	Source	Date Signed	Seasons Played	Apps	Subs	Gls
Oldham Ath.	Manchester C. (Am)	09.53	55	4	-	0

BURNS Leslie George Henry
Shepherds Bush, 22 June, 1944 (CH)

League Club	Source	Date Signed	Seasons Played	Apps	Subs	Gls
Charlton Ath.	Carshalton Ath.	03.67	66-67	8	0	0

BURNS Liam
Belfast, 30 October, 1978 NI Yth/NIu21-3 (CD)

League Club	Source	Date Signed	Seasons Played	Apps	Subs	Gls
Port Vale	YT	07.97	97	0	1	0

BURNS Michael Edward
Preston, 21 December, 1946 E Amat (F)

League Club	Source	Date Signed	Seasons Played	Apps	Subs	Gls
Blackpool	Skelmersdale U.	05.69	69-73	174	5	53
Newcastle U.	Tr	07.74	74-77	143	2	39
Cardiff C.	Tr	08.78	78	6	0	0
Middlesbrough	Tr	10.78	78-80	58	3	24

BURNS Michael Thomas
Coundon (Dm), 7 June, 1908 Died 1982 (G)

League Club	Source	Date Signed	Seasons Played	Apps	Subs	Gls
Newcastle U.	Chilton Colly	09.27	27-35	104	-	0
Preston N.E.	Tr	07.36	36-37	12	-	0
Ipswich T.	Tr	05.38	38-51	157	-	0

BURNS Neil James
Bellshill, 11 June, 1945 (F)

League Club	Source	Date Signed	Seasons Played	Apps	Subs	Gls
Mansfield T.	Bethesda	11.65	65-66	7	3	0

BURNS Oliver
Larkhall, 16 May, 1914 (IF)

League Club	Source	Date Signed	Seasons Played	Apps	Subs	Gls
Burnley	Glenavon	03.39				
Oldham Ath.	Tr	10.46	46	25	-	5
Halifax T.	Tr	09.47	47	27	-	5

BURNS Peter
Ulverston, 17 April, 1931 (CF)

League Club	Source	Date Signed	Seasons Played	Apps	Subs	Gls
Barrow	Askam U.	02.52	51	8	-	2

BURNS Philip Martin
Stockport, 18 December, 1966 (G)

League Club	Source	Date Signed	Seasons Played	Apps	Subs	Gls
Reading		03.89	90	12	0	0

BURNS William
Motherwell, 10 December, 1969 (D)

League Club	Source	Date Signed	Seasons Played	Apps	Subs	Gls
Manchester C.	YT	01.88				
Rochdale	Tr	07.89	89-90	68	3	2

BURNSIDE David Gort
Kingswood, 10 December, 1939 E Yth/Eu23-1 (IF)

League Club	Source	Date Signed	Seasons Played	Apps	Subs	Gls
West Bromwich A.	Jnrs	02.57	57-62	127	-	39
Southampton	Tr	10.62	62-64	61	-	22
Crystal Palace	Tr	12.64	64-66	54	4	8
Wolverhampton W.	Tr	09.66	66-67	38	2	5
Plymouth Arg.	Tr	03.68	67-70	105	0	15
Bristol C.	Tr	12.71	71	1	0	0
Colchester U.	Tr	03.72	71	13	0	0

BURRELL Gerald
Belfast, 6 September, 1926 (OR)

League Club	Source	Date Signed	Seasons Played	Apps	Subs	Gls
Huddersfield T.	St Mirren	12.53	53-55	59	-	9
Chesterfield	Tr	07.56	56-57	51	-	4

BURRELL Leslie Frank
Brighton, 8 August, 1917 (IF)

League Club	Source	Date Signed	Seasons Played	Apps	Subs	Gls
Crystal Palace	Margate	02.46	46-47	19	-	5
Ipswich T.	Tr	05.48				

BURRIDGE John
Workington, 3 December, 1951 (G)

League Club	Source	Date Signed	Seasons Played	Apps	Subs	Gls
Workington	App	12.69	68-70	27	0	0
Blackpool	Tr	04.71	70-75	134	0	0
Aston Villa	Tr	09.75	75-76	65	0	0
Southend U.	L	01.78	77	6	0	0
Crystal Palace	Tr	03.78	77-79	88	0	0
Queens Park R.	Tr	12.80	80-81	39	0	0
Wolverhampton W.	Tr	08.82	82-83	74	0	0
Derby Co.	L	09.84	84	6	0	0
Sheffield U.	Tr	10.84	84-86	109	0	0
Southampton	Tr	08.87	87-88	62	0	0
Newcastle U.	Tr	10.89	89-90	67	0	0
Newcastle U.	Hibernian	08.93				
Scarborough (N/C)	Tr	10.93	93	3	0	0
Lincoln C. (N/C)	Tr	12.93	93	4	0	0
Manchester C.	Falkirk	12.94	94	3	1	0
Darlington (N/C)	Witton A.	11.95	95	3	0	0

BURRIDGE Peter John
Harlow, 30 December, 1933 (IF)

League Club	Source	Date Signed	Seasons Played	Apps	Subs	Gls
Leyton Orient	Barnet	04.58	58-59	6	-	2
Millwall	Tr	08.60	60-61	87	-	58
Crystal Palace	Tr	06.62	62-65	114	0	42
Charlton Ath.	Tr	11.65	65-66	42	2	4

BURROWS Adrian Mark
Sutton-in-Ashfield, 16 January, 1959 (CD)

League Club	Source	Date Signed	Seasons Played	Apps	Subs	Gls
Mansfield T.		05.79	79-81	77	1	6
Northampton T.	Tr	08.82	82-83	88	0	4
Plymouth Arg.	Tr	07.84	84-93	272	5	14
Southend U.	L	09.87	87	6	0	0

BURROWS Alan
Thorne, 20 October, 1941 (HB)

League Club	Source	Date Signed	Seasons Played	Apps	Subs	Gls
Blackpool	Stockport Co. (Am)	05.59	59	1	-	0

BURROWS Arthur
Stockport, 4 December, 1919 (WH)

League Club	Source	Date Signed	Seasons Played	Apps	Subs	Gls
Stockport Co.	Jnrs	11.37	38-46	5	-	1
Accrington St.	Ashton U.	03.48	48	9	-	0

BURROWS David
Dudley, 25 October, 1968 Eu21-7/E'B'/EF Lge (LB)

League Club	Source	Date Signed	Seasons Played	Apps	Subs	Gls
West Bromwich A.	App	10.86	85-88	37	9	1
Liverpool	Tr	10.88	88-93	135	11	3
West Ham U.	Tr	09.93	93-94	29	0	1
Everton	Tr	09.94	94	19	0	0
Coventry C.	Tr	03.95	94-97	72	1	0

BURROWS David Williams
Ollerton, 7 April, 1961 (FB)

League Club	Source	Date Signed	Seasons Played	Apps	Subs	Gls
Lincoln C.	App	04.79	78	1	0	0

BURROWS Frank
Larkhall, 30 January, 1944 (CD)

League Club	Source	Date Signed	Seasons Played	Apps	Subs	Gls
Scunthorpe U.	Raith Rov.	06.65	65-67	106	0	4
Swindon T.	Tr	07.68	68-76	293	4	9
Mansfield T.	L	03.74	73	6	0	0

BURROWS Henry (Harry)
Haydock, 17 March, 1941 Eu23-1 (OL)

League Club	Source	Date Signed	Seasons Played	Apps	Subs	Gls
Aston Villa	Jnrs	03.58	59-64	147	-	53
Stoke C.	Tr	03.65	64-72	239	6	68
Plymouth Arg.	Tr	08.73	73-74	18	1	3

BURROWS Paul Samuel
Swansea, 2 October, 1967 W Yth (F)

League Club	Source	Date Signed	Seasons Played	Apps	Subs	Gls
Swansea C.	App	10.85	85	1	2	0

BURROWS Philip Arthur
Stockport, 8 April, 1946 (LB)

League Club	Source	Date Signed	Seasons Played	Apps	Subs	Gls
Manchester C.	Jnrs	07.64				
York C.	Tr	06.66	66-73	333	4	14

League Club	Source	Date Signed	Seasons Played	Career Record Apps	Subs	Gls
Plymouth Arg.	Tr	07.74	74-75	81	0	2
Hereford U.	Tr	08.76	76-79	110	0	2
Gillingham	L	10.77	77	5	0	0
BURSELL John **Clifford**						
Hull, 16 January, 1935 Died 1973						(IF)
Hull C.	Jnrs	11.52	52	2	-	2
BURT James Hamilton Laird						
Whitburn, 5 April, 1950						(FB)
Leicester C.	Whitburn Jnrs	06.67				
Aldershot	Tr	09.70	70-71	22	3	0
Northampton T.	Tr	07.72	72	16	5	0
Rochdale	Tr	09.73	73	4	0	0
BURTENSHAW Charles Edward						
Portslade, 16 October, 1922						(OR)
Luton T.	Southwick	01.48	48-49	11	-	1
Gillingham	Tr	10.49	50-51	28	-	5
BURTENSHAW Stephen						
Portslade, 23 November, 1935						(WH)
Brighton & H.A.	Jnrs	11.52	52-66	237	0	3
BURTENSHAW William Frederick						
Portslade, 13 December, 1925						(IR)
Luton T.	Southwick	08.48	48-49	1	-	0
Gillingham	Tr	10.49	50-51	39	-	7
BURTON Alan Richard						
Aldershot, 11 January, 1939						(W)
Aldershot	Alton T.	01.61	60-69	225	5	47
BURTON Alwyn (Ollie) Derek						
Chepstow, 11 November, 1941 W Sch/Wu23-5/W-9						(WH)
Newport Co.	Jnrs	12.58	58-60	53	-	8
Norwich C.	Tr	03.61	60-62	57	-	8
Newcastle U.	Tr	06.63	63-71	181	7	6
BURTON Bruce **Brian**						
Nottingham, 28 December, 1932						(OL)
Nottingham F.		07.51	54	1	-	0
BURTON Deon John						
Ashford, 25 October, 1976 Jamaican Int						(F)
Portsmouth	YT	02.94	93-96	42	20	10
Cardiff C.	L	12.96	96	5	0	2
Derby Co.	Tr	08.97	97	12	17	3
BURTON Ernest						
Sheffield, 2 September, 1921						(OR)
Sheffield Wed.		11.47				
York C.	Tr	08.48	48	3	-	0
BURTON Kenneth Owen						
Sheffield, 11 February, 1950						(FB)
Sheffield Wed.	App	05.67	68-71	55	2	2
Peterborough U.	L	03.73	72	3	1	0
Chesterfield	Tr	07.73	73-78	234	3	7
Halifax T.	Tr	08.80	80	26	1	1
BURTON Mark Anthony						
Penistone, 7 May, 1973						(M)
Barnsley	YT	06.91	92	5	0	0
BURTON Michael James						
Birmingham, 5 November, 1969						(W)
Birmingham C.	YT	07.88	88	0	4	0
Shrewsbury T.	Sheffield Wed. (N/C)	03.91	90	3	3	0
BURTON Nicholas John						
Bury St Edmunds, 10 February, 1975						(D)
Torquay U.	Portsmouth (YT)	08.93	93-94	14	2	2
BURTON Paul Stuart						
Hereford, 6 August, 1973						(F)
Hereford U.	YT	07.91	89-91	1	4	1
BURTON Royston						
Wokingham, 13 March, 1951						(G)
Oxford U.	Jnrs	09.70	71-82	397	0	0
BURTON Samuel						
Swindon, 10 November, 1926						(G)
Swindon T.	Jnrs	06.45	46-61	463	-	0
BURTON Simon Paul						
Farnworth, 29 December, 1973						(W)
Preston N.E.	YT	05.92	92-93	19	5	3

League Club	Source	Date Signed	Seasons Played	Career Record Apps	Subs	Gls
BURTON-GODWIN Osagyefo Lenin Ernesto						
Birmingham, 25 November, 1977						(RB)
Crystal Palace	YT	01.96	97	1	1	0
BURVILL Glenn						
Canning Town, 26 October, 1962						(M)
West Ham U.	App	09.80				
Aldershot	Tr	08.83	83-84	57	8	15
Reading	Tr	03.85	84-85	24	6	0
Fulham	L	03.86	85	9	0	2
Aldershot	Tr	07.86	86-90	177	18	23
BUSBY David Everett						
Paddington, 27 July, 1956						(F)
Brighton & H.A.	App	08.74	73-74	1	2	0
BUSBY Martin George						
High Wycombe, 24 March, 1953 E Yth						(M)
Queens Park R.	App	07.70	70-76	72	7	6
Portsmouth	L	02.76	75	6	0	1
Notts Co.	Tr	10.76	76-77	37	0	4
Queens Park R.	Tr	09.77	77-79	56	10	11
Burnley	L	02.80	79	4	0	1
BUSBY Vivian Dennis						
High Wycombe, 19 June, 1949						(F)
Luton T.	Wycombe W.	01.70	69-72	64	13	16
Newcastle U.	L	12.71	71	4	0	2
Fulham	Tr	08.73	73-76	114	4	29
Norwich C.	Tr	09.76	76-77	22	0	11
Stoke C.	Tr	11.77	77-79	33	17	9
Sheffield U.	L	01.80	79	3	0	1
Blackburn Rov.	Tulsa (USA)	02.81	80	8	0	1
York C. (N/C)	Tulsa (USA)	08.82	82-83	9	10	4
BUSH Brian						
Bristol, 25 April, 1925						(W)
Bristol Rov.	Soundwell	10.47	47-54	114	-	19
BUSH Terence Douglas						
Ingoldisthorpe, 29 January, 1943						(F)
Bristol C.	Jnrs	02.60	60-69	147	15	43
BUSH William **Thomas**						
Market Drayton, 22 February, 1914 Died 1969						(CH)
Liverpool	Shrewsbury T.	03.33	33-46	61	-	1
BUSHBY Alan						
Stainforth, 15 January, 1932 Died 1967						(WH)
Scunthorpe U.		08.52	52-58	218	-	10
Rochdale	Tr	07.59	59-60	66	-	0
BUSHBY Dennis Christopher						
Poole, 25 December, 1933						(WH)
Bournemouth		11.57	57	6	-	0
BUSHBY Thomas William						
Shildon, 21 August, 1914 Died 1998						(CH)
Southend U.	Shildon	10.34	34-38	40	-	13
Portsmouth	Tr	06.39				
Southampton	Tr	09.46	46	2	-	0
BUSHELL Alan						
Burnley, 4 September, 1932						(W)
Accrington St. (Am)	Wood Top	05.52	52	8	-	1
BUSHELL Mark John						
Northampton, 5 June, 1968						(FB)
Northampton T.	YT	09.85	84	1	0	0
BUSHELL Stephen Paul						
Manchester, 28 December, 1972						(M)
York C.	YT	02.91	90-97	156	18	10
BUSST David John						
Birmingham, 30 June, 1967						(CD)
Coventry C.	Moor Green	01.92	92-95	48	2	4
BUTCHER John Melvin						
Newcastle, 27 May, 1956						(G)
Blackburn Rov.		03.76	76-81	104	0	0
Oxford U.	Tr	07.82	82	16	0	0
Halifax T.	L	09.82	82	5	0	0
Bury	L	12.83	83	11	0	0
Chester C.	Tr	08.84	84-86	84	0	0
Bury	L	10.85	85	5	0	0
BUTCHER Reginald						
Prescot, 13 February, 1916						(FB)
Chester C.	Liverpool (Am)	11.38	38-49	155	-	1

BUTCHER Terence Ian
Singapore, 28 December, 1958 Eu21-7/E 'B'/E-77 (CD)

League Club	Source	Date Signed	Seasons Played	Apps	Subs	Gls
Ipswich T.	Jnrs	08.76	77-85	271	0	16
Coventry C. (N/C)	Glasgow Rangers	11.90	90	6	0	0
Sunderland	(Retired)	07.92	92	37	1	0

BUTLER Philip **Anthony**
Stockport, 28 September, 1972 (CD)

League Club	Source	Date Signed	Seasons Played	Apps	Subs	Gls
Gillingham	YT	05.91	90-95	142	6	5
Blackpool	Tr	07.96	96-97	78	1	0

BUTLER Barry
Stockton, 30 July, 1934 Died 1966 (CH)

League Club	Source	Date Signed	Seasons Played	Apps	Subs	Gls
Sheffield Wed.	South Bank	09.52	53-54	26	-	1
Norwich C.	Tr	07.57	57-65	303	0	3

BUTLER Barry Geoffrey
Farnworth, 4 June, 1962 (M/D)

League Club	Source	Date Signed	Seasons Played	Apps	Subs	Gls
Chester C.	Atherton L.R.	12.85	85-92	255	13	16

BUTLER Brian Francis
Salford, 4 July, 1966 (M/LB)

League Club	Source	Date Signed	Seasons Played	Apps	Subs	Gls
Blackpool	App	07.84	85-87	58	16	5
Stockport Co.	Tr	07.88	88	32	0	2
Halifax T.	Tr	07.89	89-90	44	12	4

BUTLER David
Thornaby, 23 March, 1945 (FB)

League Club	Source	Date Signed	Seasons Played	Apps	Subs	Gls
Workington	Stockton	11.64	64-70	195	4	7
Watford	Tr	11.70	70-75	168	0	2

BUTLER David John
Wolverhampton, 1 September, 1962 (W)

League Club	Source	Date Signed	Seasons Played	Apps	Subs	Gls
Wolverhampton W.	App	04.80				
Torquay U.	Tr	12.81	81	5	1	0

BUTLER David Joseph
Wednesbury, 30 March, 1953 (W)

League Club	Source	Date Signed	Seasons Played	Apps	Subs	Gls
West Bromwich A.	App	04.71				
Shrewsbury T.	Tr	06.73	73	5	5	0
Workington	L	03.74	73	10	0	0

BUTLER Dennis Anthony
Macclesfield, 24 June, 1944 (W)

League Club	Source	Date Signed	Seasons Played	Apps	Subs	Gls
Bolton W.	Jnrs	06.61	62-67	62	3	11
Rochdale	Tr	02.68	67-72	152	4	36

BUTLER Dennis George
Newbury, 4 August, 1952 (WH)

League Club	Source	Date Signed	Seasons Played	Apps	Subs	Gls
Reading	App	05.70	69-70	7	3	1

BUTLER Dennis Michael
Fulham, 7 March, 1943 (FB)

League Club	Source	Date Signed	Seasons Played	Apps	Subs	Gls
Chelsea	Jnrs	06.60	61-62	18	-	0
Hull C.	Tr	06.63	63-69	215	2	0
Reading	Tr	12.69	69-73	170	0	0

BUTLER Ernest
Middlesbrough, 28 August, 1924 (OR)

League Club	Source	Date Signed	Seasons Played	Apps	Subs	Gls
Southend U.	Stockton	08.48	48-51	36	-	3
Darlington	Tr	06.53	53	6	-	0

BUTLER Ernest Albert Edward
Chippenham, 13 May, 1919 (G)

League Club	Source	Date Signed	Seasons Played	Apps	Subs	Gls
Portsmouth	Bath C.	05.38	46-52	222	-	0

BUTLER Geoffrey
Middlesbrough, 26 September, 1946 (FB)

League Club	Source	Date Signed	Seasons Played	Apps	Subs	Gls
Middlesbrough	App	05.64	65-67	54	1	1
Chelsea	Tr	09.67	67	8	1	0
Sunderland	Tr	01.68	67-68	1	2	0
Norwich C.	Tr	10.68	68-75	151	2	1
Bournemouth	Tr	03.76	75-80	118	1	1
Peterborough U. (N/C)	Tr	08.81	81	39	0	0

BUTLER Ian
Darton, 1 February, 1944 E Yth (OL)

League Club	Source	Date Signed	Seasons Played	Apps	Subs	Gls
Rotherham U.	App	08.61	60-64	102	-	27
Hull C.	Tr	01.65	64-72	300	5	66
York C.	Tr	08.73	73-74	43	3	2
Barnsley	L	10.75	75	5	0	1

BUTLER John (Jackie)
Dawley, 16 October, 1920 Died 1984 (OL)

League Club	Source	Date Signed	Seasons Played	Apps	Subs	Gls
Shrewsbury T.	Dawley	08.50	50-53	58	-	8

BUTLER John Edward
Liverpool, 7 February, 1962 (RB/M)

League Club	Source	Date Signed	Seasons Played	Apps	Subs	Gls
Wigan Ath.	Prescot Cables	01.82	81-88	238	7	15
Stoke C.	Tr	12.88	88-94	258	4	7
Wigan Ath.	Tr	06.95	95-96	53	4	1

BUTLER John Herbert
Birmingham, 10 March, 1937 (CH)

League Club	Source	Date Signed	Seasons Played	Apps	Subs	Gls
Notts Co.	Eastwood Colly	10.57	58-61	109	-	0
Chester C.	Tr	05.62	62-67	220	2	0

BUTLER John Paul
Salford, 7 September, 1964 (M)

League Club	Source	Date Signed	Seasons Played	Apps	Subs	Gls
Blackpool	App	09.82	81-82	4	1	0

BUTLER Joseph William
Newcastle, 7 February, 1943 (LB/M)

League Club	Source	Date Signed	Seasons Played	Apps	Subs	Gls
Newcastle U.	Jnrs	09.60	63	3	-	0
Swindon T.	Tr	08.65	65-75	355	7	18
Aldershot	Tr	08.76	76-77	31	8	0

BUTLER Kenneth
Sunderland, 23 August, 1936 (OL)

League Club	Source	Date Signed	Seasons Played	Apps	Subs	Gls
Hartlepool U.	Whitburn	01.60	59-60	20	-	2

BUTLER Lee Simon
Sheffield, 30 May, 1966 (G)

League Club	Source	Date Signed	Seasons Played	Apps	Subs	Gls
Lincoln C.	Harworth C.I.	06.86	86	30	0	0
Aston Villa	Tr	08.87	88-90	8	0	0
Hull C.	L	03.91	90	4	0	0
Barnsley	Tr	07.91	91-95	118	2	0
Scunthorpe U.	L	02.96	95	2	0	0
Wigan Ath.	Tr	07.96	96-97	63	0	0

BUTLER Malcolm Partridge
Belfast, 6 August, 1913 Died 1987 NI-1 (FB)

League Club	Source	Date Signed	Seasons Played	Apps	Subs	Gls
Blackpool	Belfast Celtic	01.35	35-38	25	-	0
Accrington St.	Tr	07.47	47	32	-	0

BUTLER Martin
Hessle, 3 March, 1966 (W)

League Club	Source	Date Signed	Seasons Played	Apps	Subs	Gls
York C.	YT	10.84	84-88	40	25	9
Aldershot	L	12.85	85	2	0	1
Exeter C.	L	02.87	86	4	0	1
Carlisle U.	L	12.88	88	1	0	0
Scunthorpe U.	Tr	08.89	89	2	0	0
Scarborough (N/C)	Macclesfield T.	11.89	89	1	5	0

BUTLER Martin Neil
Wordsley, 15 September, 1974 (F)

League Club	Source	Date Signed	Seasons Played	Apps	Subs	Gls
Walsall	YT	05.93	93-96	43	31	8
Cambridge U.	Tr	08.97	97	28	3	10

BUTLER Michael Anthony
Barnsley, 27 January, 1951 (F)

League Club	Source	Date Signed	Seasons Played	Apps	Subs	Gls
Barnsley	Worsboro' Bridge	07.73	72-75	118	2	57
Huddersfield T.	Tr	03.76	75-77	73	6	22
Bournemouth	Tr	07.78	78-79	68	1	19
Bury	Tr	08.80	80-81	80	2	15

BUTLER Paul John
Manchester, 2 November, 1972 (CD)

League Club	Source	Date Signed	Seasons Played	Apps	Subs	Gls
Rochdale	YT	07.91	90-95	151	7	10
Bury	Tr	07.96	96-97	83	1	4

BUTLER Paul John
Stockton, 9 June, 1964 (W)

League Club	Source	Date Signed	Seasons Played	Apps	Subs	Gls
Wolverhampton W.	App	06.82	82-84	18	11	2
Hereford U.	L	01.84	83	16	0	2
Hereford U.	Tr	02.85	84-86	49	15	2
Hartlepool U.	Tr	07.87	87	6	3	0

BUTLER Peter James
Halifax, 27 August, 1966 (M)

League Club	Source	Date Signed	Seasons Played	Apps	Subs	Gls
Huddersfield T.	App	08.84	84-85	0	5	0
Cambridge U.	L	01.86	85	14	0	1
Bury	Tr	07.86	86	9	2	0
Cambridge U.	Tr	12.86	86-87	55	0	9
Southend U.	Tr	02.88	87-91	135	7	9
Huddersfield T.	L	03.92	91	7	0	0
West Ham U.	Tr	08.92	92-94	70	0	3
Notts Co.	Tr	10.94	94	20	0	0
Grimsby T.	L	01.96	95	3	0	0
West Bromwich A.	Tr	03.96	95-97	52	8	0

BUTLER Peter Leslie
Nottingham, 3 October, 1942 (G)

League Club	Source	Date Signed	Seasons Played	Apps	Subs	Gls
Notts Co.	Jnrs	11.60	61-65	44	0	0
Bradford C.	Tr	08.66	66	17	0	0

BUTLER Stanley
Stellington, 7 January, 1919 Died 1969 (OL)

League Club	Source	Date Signed	Seasons Played	Apps	Subs	Gls
West Bromwich A.	Scunthorpe U.	05.38	38-46	4	-	0
Southport	Tr	07.47	47	4	-	1

BUTLER Stephen
Birmingham, 27 January, 1962 E Semi Pro (F)

League Club	Source	Date Signed	Seasons Played	Apps	Subs	Gls
Brentford	Wokingham T.	12.84	84-85	18	3	3
Maidstone U.	Tr	08.86	89-90	76	0	41
Watford	Tr	03.91	90-92	40	22	9
Bournemouth	L	12.92	92	1	0	0
Cambridge U.	Tr	12.92	92-95	107	2	51
Gillingham	Tr	12.95	95-97	73	28	20

BUTLER Thomas
Atherton, 28 April, 1918 (OR)

League Club	Source	Date Signed	Seasons Played	Apps	Subs	Gls
Bolton W.	Astley	09.36				
Oldham Ath.	Macclesfield T.	02.38	37-38	45	-	9
Middlesbrough	Tr	03.39	38	2	-	0
Oldham Ath.	Tr	08.46	46	30	-	3
Accrington St.	Tr	07.47	47-52	218	-	26

BUTLER Walter Garth
Birmingham, 7 February, 1923 Died 1995 (FB)

League Club	Source	Date Signed	Seasons Played	Apps	Subs	Gls
Derby Co.		11.42				
Port Vale		06.46	46-50	128	-	0

BUTLIN Barry Desmond
Rosliston (Dy), 9 November, 1949 (F)

League Club	Source	Date Signed	Seasons Played	Apps	Subs	Gls
Derby Co.	Jnrs	01.67	67-72	4	0	0
Notts Co.	L	01.69	68-69	29	1	13
Luton T.	Tr	11.72	72-74	56	1	24
Nottingham F.	Tr	10.74	74-76	71	3	17
Brighton & H.A.	L	09.75	75	5	0	2
Reading	L	01.77	76	5	0	1
Peterborough U.	Tr	08.77	77-78	64	0	12
Sheffield U.	Tr	08.79	79-80	50	3	12

BUTT Leonard
Wilmslow, 26 August, 1910 Died 1994 (IF)

League Club	Source	Date Signed	Seasons Played	Apps	Subs	Gls
Stockport Co.	Ashton Nat.	08.28	29-30	8	-	1
Huddersfield T.	Macclesfield T.	05.35	35-36	67	-	11
Blackburn Rov.	Tr	01.37	36-46	110	-	44
York C.	Tr	01.47	46-47	25	-	2
Mansfield T.	Tr	10.47	47	15	-	4

BUTT Nicholas
Manchester, 21 January, 1975 E Sch/E Yth/Eu21-7/E-6 (M)

League Club	Source	Date Signed	Seasons Played	Apps	Subs	Gls
Manchester U.	YT	01.93	92-97	97	18	11

BUTT Robert
Chester, 27 March, 1946 (W)

League Club	Source	Date Signed	Seasons Played	Apps	Subs	Gls
Wrexham (Am)	Jnrs	01.65	64	3	-	0

BUTTERFIELD Daniel Paul
Boston, 21 November, 1979 E Yth (RWB)

League Club	Source	Date Signed	Seasons Played	Apps	Subs	Gls
Grimsby T.	YT	08.97	97	4	3	0

BUTTERFIELD John (Jack)
Barnsley, 30 August, 1922 (RB)

League Club	Source	Date Signed	Seasons Played	Apps	Subs	Gls
Burnley	Tamworth	02.46	47	3	-	0

BUTTERS Guy
Hillingdon, 30 October, 1969 Eu21-3 (CD)

League Club	Source	Date Signed	Seasons Played	Apps	Subs	Gls
Tottenham H.	YT	07.88	88-89	34	1	1
Southend U.	L	01.90	89	16	0	3
Portsmouth	Tr	09.90	90-96	148	6	6
Oxford U.	L	11.94	94	3	0	1
Gillingham	Tr	10.96	96-97	61	0	7

BUTTERWORTH Aidan James
Leeds, 7 November, 1961 E Sch (F)

League Club	Source	Date Signed	Seasons Played	Apps	Subs	Gls
Leeds U.	Jnrs	05.80	80-83	54	10	15
Doncaster Rov.	Tr	08.84	84-85	35	15	5

BUTTERWORTH David Albert
Bristol, 4 May, 1937 (WH)

League Club	Source	Date Signed	Seasons Played	Apps	Subs	Gls
Exeter C.	Guildford C.	12.57	57-59	26	-	0

BUTTERWORTH Garry Jeffrey
Whittlesey, 8 September, 1969 (LB)

League Club	Source	Date Signed	Seasons Played	Apps	Subs	Gls
Peterborough U.	YT	06.88	86-91	101	22	3

BUTTERWORTH Ian Stewart
Crewe, 25 January, 1964 Eu21-8 (CD)

League Club	Source	Date Signed	Seasons Played	Apps	Subs	Gls
Coventry C.	App	08.81	81-84	80	10	0
Nottingham F.	Tr	06.85	85-86	26	1	0
Norwich C.	L	09.86	86	4	0	0
Norwich C.	Tr	12.86	86-93	226	5	4

BUTTIGIEG John
Malta, 5 October, 1963 Maltese Int (D)

League Club	Source	Date Signed	Seasons Played	Apps	Subs	Gls
Brentford	Sliema W. (Malta)	11.88	88-89	24	16	0
Swindon T.	L	09.90	90	2	1	0

BUTTLE Stephen Arthur
Norwich, 1 January, 1953 (M)

League Club	Source	Date Signed	Seasons Played	Apps	Subs	Gls
Ipswich T.	App	01.71				
Bournemouth	Tr	08.73	73-76	136	3	12

BUTTRESS Michael David
Peterborough, 23 March, 1958 (FB)

League Club	Source	Date Signed	Seasons Played	Apps	Subs	Gls
Aston Villa	App	02.76	76-77	1	2	0
Gillingham	Tr	03.78	77-78	5	2	0

BUXTON Ian Raymond
Cromford, 17 April, 1938 (IF)

League Club	Source	Date Signed	Seasons Played	Apps	Subs	Gls
Derby Co.	Jnrs	03.59	59-67	144	1	41
Luton T.	Tr	09.67	67-68	46	1	14
Notts Co.	Tr	07.69	69	4	1	1
Port Vale	Tr	12.69	69	16	2	6

BUXTON Michael James
Corbridge, 29 May, 1943 (FB)

League Club	Source	Date Signed	Seasons Played	Apps	Subs	Gls
Burnley	Jnrs	06.60	62-67	16	2	0
Halifax T.	Tr	06.68	68-70	35	0	0

BUXTON Nicholas Gareth
Doncaster, 6 September, 1976 (G)

League Club	Source	Date Signed	Seasons Played	Apps	Subs	Gls
Scarborough	Goole T	10.97	97	3	0	0

BUXTON Stephen Christopher
Birmingham, 13 March, 1960 (F)

League Club	Source	Date Signed	Seasons Played	Apps	Subs	Gls
Wrexham	Jnrs	07.78	77-83	93	16	21
Stockport Co.	Tr	07.84	84	12	6	1
Wrexham	Altrincham	10.85	85-89	86	35	25

BYATT Dennis John
Hillingdon, 8 August, 1958 (CD)

League Club	Source	Date Signed	Seasons Played	Apps	Subs	Gls
Fulham	App	05.76				
Peterborough U.	Tr	07.78	78	2	1	0
Northampton T.	Tr	06.79	79-80	46	1	3

BYCROFT Sydney
Lincoln, 19 February, 1912 (CH)

League Club	Source	Date Signed	Seasons Played	Apps	Subs	Gls
Bradford C.	Notts Co. (Am)	07.32				
Hull C.	Tr	10.32				
Doncaster Rov.	Newark T.	01.36	35-51	333	-	2

BYERS Richard
Haltwhistle, 19 November, 1951 (CF)

League Club	Source	Date Signed	Seasons Played	Apps	Subs	Gls
Workington (Am)	Hadrian Paints	10.71	71	1	0	0

BYFIELD Darren
Birmingham, 29 September, 1976 (F)

League Club	Source	Date Signed	Seasons Played	Apps	Subs	Gls
Aston Villa	YT	02.94	97	1	6	0

BYNG David Graeme
Coventry, 9 July, 1977 (F)

League Club	Source	Date Signed	Seasons Played	Apps	Subs	Gls
Torquay U.	YT	07.95	93-95	12	12	3
Doncaster Rov.	Tr	02.96				

BYRNE Anthony Brendan
Rathdowney (IR), 2 February, 1946 IR-14 (D)

League Club	Source	Date Signed	Seasons Played	Apps	Subs	Gls
Millwall	Jnrs	08.63	63	1	-	0
Southampton	Tr	08.64	66-73	81	12	3
Hereford U.	Tr	08.74	74-76	54	1	0
Newport Co.	Tr	03.77	76-78	80	0	10

BYRNE Christopher Thomas
Liverpool, 9 February, 1975 (M)

League Club	Source	Date Signed	Seasons Played	Apps	Subs	Gls
Sunderland	Macclesfield T	06.97	97	4	4	0
Stockport Co.	Tr	11.97	97	21	5	7

BYRNE David Stuart
Hammersmith, 5 March, 1961 (RW)

League Club	Source	Date Signed	Seasons Played	Apps	Subs	Gls
Gillingham	Kingstonian	07.85	85	18	5	3
Millwall	Tr	07.86	86-87	52	11	6
Cambridge U.	L	09.88	88	4	0	0
Blackburn Rov.	L	02.89	88	4	0	0
Plymouth Arg.	Tr	03.89	88-90	52	7	2
Bristol Rov.	L	02.90	89	0	2	0
Watford	Tr	11.90	90	16	1	2
Reading	L	08.91	91	7	0	2
Fulham	L	01.92	91	5	0	0
Walsall (L)	Partick Thistle	02.94	93	5	0	0

BYRNE Gerald
Glasgow, 10 April, 1957 (M)

League Club	Source	Date Signed	Seasons Played	Apps	Subs	Gls
Cardiff C.	App	04.75	77-78	11	4	0

BYRNE Gerald
Liverpool, 29 August, 1938 Eu23-1/E-2 (LB)

League Club	Source	Date Signed	Seasons Played	Apps	Subs	Gls
Liverpool	Jnrs	08.55	57-68	273	1	2

BYRNE John
Cambuslang, 20 May, 1939 (IF)

League Club	Source	Date Signed	Seasons Played	Apps	Subs	Gls
Preston N.E.	Pollok Jnrs	03.58				
Tranmere Rov.	Queen of South	05.61	61	27	-	4
Barnsley	Hibernian	11.63	63-64	68	-	13
Peterborough U.	Tr	07.65	65-67	106	1	28
Northampton T.	Tr	12.67	67-68	40	0	4

BYRNE John Frederick
Manchester, 1 February, 1961 IR-23 (F)

League Club	Source	Date Signed	Seasons Played	Apps	Subs	Gls
York C.	App	01.79	79-84	167	8	55
Queens Park R.	Tr	10.84	84-87	108	18	30
Brighton & H.A.	Le Havre (Fr)	09.90	90-91	47	4	14
Sunderland	Tr	10.91	91-92	33	0	8
Millwall	Tr	10.92	92-93	12	5	1
Brighton & H.A.	L	03.93	92	5	2	2
Oxford U.	Tr	11.93	93-94	52	3	18
Brighton & H.A.	Tr	02.95	94-95	29	10	6

BYRNE John Joseph
West Horsley, 13 May, 1939 E Yth/Eu23-7/E-11 (CF)

League Club	Source	Date Signed	Seasons Played	Apps	Subs	Gls
Crystal Palace	Jnrs	05.56	56-61	203	-	85
West Ham U.	Tr	03.62	61-66	156	0	79
Crystal Palace	Tr	02.67	66-67	36	0	5
Fulham	Tr	03.68	67-68	16	3	2

BYRNE John Joseph Anthony
Wallasey, 24 March, 1949 (OR)

League Club	Source	Date Signed	Seasons Played	Apps	Subs	Gls
Tranmere Rov. (Am)	Cammell Laird	11.68	68	1	0	0

BYRNE Joseph
Workington, 24 April, 1929 Died 1993 (G)

League Club	Source	Date Signed	Seasons Played	Apps	Subs	Gls
Workington (Am)	Frizington	09.52	52	2	-	0

BYRNE Michael
Dublin, 14 January, 1960 (F)

League Club	Source	Date Signed	Seasons Played	Apps	Subs	Gls
Huddersfield T.	Shamrock Rov.	09.88	88-89	46	10	11

BYRNE Patrick Joseph
Dublin, 15 May, 1956 (M)

League Club	Source	Date Signed	Seasons Played	Apps	Subs	Gls
Leicester C.	Shelbourne	07.79	79-80	31	5	3

BYRNE Paul Peter
Dublin, 30 June, 1972 IR Sch/IR Yth/IRu21-1 (W)

League Club	Source	Date Signed	Seasons Played	Apps	Subs	Gls
Oxford U.	YT	07.89	89-91	4	2	0
Brighton & H.A. (L)	Glasgow Celtic	03.95	94	8	0	1
Southend U.	Glasgow Celtic	08.95	95-97	70	13	6

BYRNE Raymond
Newry (NI), 4 July, 1972 (D)

League Club	Source	Date Signed	Seasons Played	Apps	Subs	Gls
Nottingham F.	Newry T.	02.91				
Northampton T.	Tr	08.94	94	2	0	0

BYRNE Roger William
Manchester, 8 September, 1929 Died 1958 E 'B'/EF Lge/E-33 (FB)

League Club	Source	Date Signed	Seasons Played	Apps	Subs	Gls
Manchester U.	Ryder Brow B.C.	03.49	51-57	245	-	17

BYRNE Wesley John
Dublin, 9 February, 1977 IR Sch/IR Yth (LB)

League Club	Source	Date Signed	Seasons Played	Apps	Subs	Gls
Middlesbrough	YT	02.94				
Stoke C. (N/C)	Tr	07.96				
Darlington (N/C)	Tr	12.96	96	1	1	0

BYRNE William
Newcastle-u-Lyme, 22 October, 1918 (OR)

League Club	Source	Date Signed	Seasons Played	Apps	Subs	Gls
Port Vale		05.46	46	15	-	2
Crewe Alex.	Tr	07.47	47-48	18	-	1

BYROM David John
Padham, 6 January, 1965 (LB)

League Club	Source	Date Signed	Seasons Played	Apps	Subs	Gls
Blackburn Rov.	App	01.83				
Stockport Co.	Tr	10.84	84	3	0	0

BYROM John
Blackburn, 28 July, 1944 E Yth (F)

League Club	Source	Date Signed	Seasons Played	Apps	Subs	Gls
Blackburn Rov.	Jnrs	08.61	61-65	106	2	45
Bolton W.	Tr	06.66	66-75	296	8	113
Blackburn Rov.	Tr	09.76	76	15	1	5

BYROM Raymond
Blackburn, 2 January, 1935 (OL)

League Club	Source	Date Signed	Seasons Played	Apps	Subs	Gls
Accrington St.	Blackburn Rov. (Am)	01.56	57-58	9	-	1
Bradford P.A.	Tr	12.58	58-60	70	-	14

BYROM Thomas
Upton, 17 March, 1920 (WH)

League Club	Source	Date Signed	Seasons Played	Apps	Subs	Gls
Tranmere Rov.	Heswall	05.39	46	3	-	0

BYROM William
Blackburn, 30 March, 1915 Died 1989 (FB)

League Club	Source	Date Signed	Seasons Played	Apps	Subs	Gls
Burnley		08.37				
Queens Park R.	Tr	05.39				
Rochdale	Tr	06.46	46-47	30	-	0

BYRON Gordon Frank
Prescot, 4 September, 1953 (M)

League Club	Source	Date Signed	Seasons Played	Apps	Subs	Gls
Sheffield Wed.	App	07.71				
Lincoln C.	Tr	08.74	74	3	3	0

BYRON Paul
Preston, 9 May, 1965 (D)

League Club	Source	Date Signed	Seasons Played	Apps	Subs	Gls
Hartlepool U.	Blackburn Rov. (N/C)	08.86	86	1	0	0

BYWATER Noel Leslie
Lichfield, 8 December, 1920 (G)

League Club	Source	Date Signed	Seasons Played	Apps	Subs	Gls
Huddersfield T.		03.45				
Luton T.	Tr	09.46	46	19	-	0
Rochdale	Tr	12.47	47-48	34	-	0

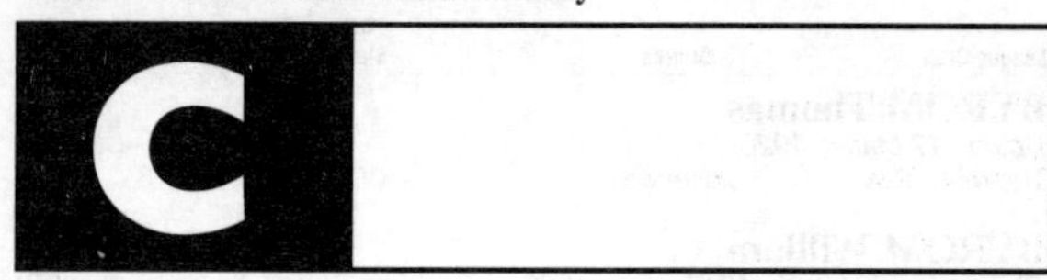

CABRIE David McArthur
Port Glasgow, 3 June, 1918 Died 1985 (WH)

League Club	Source	Date Signed	Seasons Played	Apps	Subs	Gls
Newport Co.	St Mirren	05.46	46	9	-	0

CADAMARTERI Daniel Leon
Bradford, 12 October, 1979 E Yth (F)

League Club	Source	Date Signed	Seasons Played	Apps	Subs	Gls
Everton	YT	10.96	96-97	15	12	4

CADDEN Joseph Young
Glasgow, 13 April, 1920 Died 1981 (CH)

League Club	Source	Date Signed	Seasons Played	Apps	Subs	Gls
Liverpool	Brooklyn W. (USA)	07.48	50	4	-	0
Grimsby T.	Tr	02.52	52	1	-	0
Accrington St.	Tr	06.53	53	17	-	0

CADE David
Hemsworth, 29 September, 1938 E Sch (F)

League Club	Source	Date Signed	Seasons Played	Apps	Subs	Gls
Barnsley	Doncaster Rov. (Am)	05.57				
Bradford P.A.	Tr	07.59	59	1	-	0

CADETTE Nathan Daniel
Cardiff, 6 January, 1980 W Yth (M)

League Club	Source	Date Signed	Seasons Played	Apps	Subs	Gls
Cardiff C.	YT	●	97	0	4	0

CADETTE Richard Raymond
Hammersmith, 21 March, 1965 (F)

League Club	Source	Date Signed	Seasons Played	Apps	Subs	Gls
Leyton Orient	Wembley	08.84	84	19	2	4
Southend U.	Tr	08.85	85-86	90	0	49
Sheffield U.	Tr	07.87	87	26	2	7
Brentford	Tr	07.88	88-91	67	20	20
Bournemouth	L	03.90	89	4	4	1
Millwall	Falkirk	10.94	94-96	19	5	5

CAESAR Gus Cassius
Tottenham, 5 March, 1966 Eu21-3 (CD)

League Club	Source	Date Signed	Seasons Played	Apps	Subs	Gls
Arsenal	App	02.84	85-89	27	17	0
Queens Park R	L	11.90	90	5	0	0
Cambridge U.	Tr	07.91				
Bristol C.	Tr	09.91	91	9	1	0
Colchester U.	Airdrieonians	08.94	94-95	62	0	3

CAFFREY Henry
Paisley, 15 February, 1966 (W)

League Club	Source	Date Signed	Seasons Played	Apps	Subs	Gls
Hereford U.	Clydebank	07.91	91	12	5	2

CAGIGAO Francis
Paddington, 10 November, 1969 (F)

League Club	Source	Date Signed	Seasons Played	Apps	Subs	Gls
Southend U.	Barcelona (Sp)	09.91	92	0	1	0

CAHILL Oliver Francis
Clonmell, 29 September, 1975 (LW)

League Club	Source	Date Signed	Seasons Played	Apps	Subs	Gls
Northampton T.	Clonmell	09.94	94-95	7	4	1

CAHILL Paul Gerard
Liverpool, 29 September, 1955 E Yth (D)

League Club	Source	Date Signed	Seasons Played	Apps	Subs	Gls
Coventry C.	App	01.73				
Portsmouth	Tr	02.75	74-77	95	2	2
Aldershot	L	01.78	77	2	0	0
Tranmere Rov.	California (USA)	10.78	78	5	0	0
Stockport Co.	Tr	02.79	78	3	0	0

CAHILL Thomas
Glasgow, 14 June, 1931 (LB)

League Club	Source	Date Signed	Seasons Played	Apps	Subs	Gls
Newcastle U.	Vale of Leven	12.51	52-53	4	-	0
Barrow	Tr	08.55	55-64	283	-	3

CAHILL Timothy
Sydney, Australia, 6 December, 1979 (M)

League Club	Source	Date Signed	Seasons Played	Apps	Subs	Gls
Millwall	Sydney U (Aus)	07.97	97	1	0	0

CAIG Antony
Whitehaven, 11 April, 1974 (G)

League Club	Source	Date Signed	Seasons Played	Apps	Subs	Gls
Carlisle U.	YT	07.92	92-97	186	0	0

CAIN James Patrick
Fishburn (Dm), 29 December, 1933 (WH)

League Club	Source	Date Signed	Seasons Played	Apps	Subs	Gls
Bristol C.	Stockton	05.57				
Hartlepool U.	South Shields	08.60	60-61	30	-	0

CAINE Brian
Nelson, 20 June, 1936 (G)

League Club	Source	Date Signed	Seasons Played	Apps	Subs	Gls
Blackpool	Accrington St. (Am)	02.57	57	1	-	0
Coventry C.	Tr	09.59	60	1	-	0
Northampton T.	Tr	07.61				
Barrow	Tr	10.61	61-63	109	-	0

CAINE William George
Barrow, 1 July, 1927 (CH)

League Club	Source	Date Signed	Seasons Played	Apps	Subs	Gls
Barrow	Barrow R.C.	07.52	51-54	12	-	0

CAIRNEY Charles (Chic)
Blantyre, 21 September, 1926 Died 1995 (RH)

League Club	Source	Date Signed	Seasons Played	Apps	Subs	Gls
Leyton Orient	Glasgow Celtic	10.50	50	4	-	0
Bristol Rov.	Barry T.	07.53	53-54	14	-	1

CAIRNEY James
Glasgow, 13 July, 1931 (HB)

League Club	Source	Date Signed	Seasons Played	Apps	Subs	Gls
Portsmouth	Shawfield Jnrs	09.49				
York C.	Tr	07.56	56-57	53	-	0

CAIRNS Colin
Alloa, 17 September, 1936 (IF)

League Club	Source	Date Signed	Seasons Played	Apps	Subs	Gls
Southend U.	Camelon Jnrs	02.58	58	2	-	0

CAIRNS John (Jackie) Greenfield
Newcastle, 13 April, 1922 Died 1988 (IL)

League Club	Source	Date Signed	Seasons Played	Apps	Subs	Gls
Hartlepool U.		03.48	47-49	16	-	2

CAIRNS Kevin William
Preston, 29 June, 1937 (LB)

League Club	Source	Date Signed	Seasons Played	Apps	Subs	Gls
Southport	Dundee U.	08.62	62-67	204	2	1

CAIRNS Robert Lynn
Choppington, 25 December, 1927 Died 1958 (FB)

League Club	Source	Date Signed	Seasons Played	Apps	Subs	Gls
Gateshead	Sunderland (Am)	09.48	48-56	141	-	0

CAIRNS Robert Seggie
Glenboig, 27 May, 1929 (WH)

League Club	Source	Date Signed	Seasons Played	Apps	Subs	Gls
Stoke C.	Ayr U.	12.53	53-60	175	-	9

CAIRNS Ronald
Chopwell, 4 April, 1934 (IF)

League Club	Source	Date Signed	Seasons Played	Apps	Subs	Gls
Blackburn Rov.	Consett	09.53	55-58	26	-	7
Rochdale	Tr	06.59	59-63	195	-	66
Southport	Tr	07.64	64	34	-	13

CAIRNS William Henry
Newcastle, 7 October, 1912 Died 1988 (IF)

League Club	Source	Date Signed	Seasons Played	Apps	Subs	Gls
Newcastle U.	Stargate Rov.	05.33	34-38	79	-	51
Gateshead	Tr	11.44			-	-
Grimsby T.	Tr	05.46	46-53	221	-	120

CAIZLEY Kevin
Jarrow, 2 December, 1968 (M)

League Club	Source	Date Signed	Seasons Played	Apps	Subs	Gls
Newcastle U.	YT	08.87				
Darlington	Tr	07.88	88	8	4	1

CAKEBREAD Gerald
Acton, 1 April, 1936 E Yth (G)

League Club	Source	Date Signed	Seasons Played	Apps	Subs	Gls
Brentford	Jnrs	06.55	54-63	348	-	0

CALDER William Carson
Greenock, 28 September, 1934 (CF)

League Club	Source	Date Signed	Seasons Played	Apps	Subs	Gls
Leicester C.	Port Glasgow	08.55	58	3	-	0
Bury	Tr	05.59	59-63	174	-	67
Oxford U.	Tr	11.63	63-66	66	1	28
Rochdale	Tr	11.66	66	7	1	1

CALDERBANK George **Raymond**
Manchester, 8 February, 1936 (IL)

League Club	Source	Date Signed	Seasons Played	Apps	Subs	Gls
Rochdale (Am)	Hyde U.	08.53	53	1	-	0

CALDERWOOD Colin
Glasgow, 20 January, 1965 S Sch/S-29 (CD)

League Club	Source	Date Signed	Seasons Played	Apps	Subs	Gls
Mansfield T.	Jnrs	03.82	81-84	97	3	1
Swindon T.	Tr	06.85	85-92	328	2	20
Tottenham H.	Tr	07.93	93-97	141	10	7

CALDERWOOD James
Glasgow, 28 February, 1955 Su23-1 (FB/M)

League Club	Source	Date Signed	Seasons Played	Apps	Subs	Gls
Birmingham C.	App	07.72	72-79	135	10	4
Cambridge U.	L	11.79	79	8	0	0

CALDWELL Anthony
Salford, 21 March, 1958 (F)

League Club	Source	Date Signed	Seasons Played	Apps	Subs	Gls
Bolton W.	Horwich R.M.I.	06.83	83-86	131	8	58
Bristol C.	Tr	07.87	87-88	9	8	3
Chester C.	L	01.88	87	4	0	0
Grimsby T.	Tr	09.88	88	2	1	0
Stockport Co.	Tr	10.88	88-89	23	3	6

CALDWELL David Lees
Clydebank, 7 May, 1932 (FB)

League Club	Source	Date Signed	Seasons Played	Apps	Subs	Gls
Rotherham U.	Aberdeen	05.60	60	1	-	0

CALDWELL David Wilson
Aberdeen, 31 July, 1960 (F)

League Club	Source	Date Signed	Seasons Played	Apps	Subs	Gls
Mansfield T.	Inverness Caledonian	06.79	79-84	145	12	57
Carlisle U.	L	12.84	84	4	0	0
Swindon T.	L	02.85	84	5	0	0
Chesterfield	Tr	07.85	85-87	66	4	17
Torquay U.	Tr	11.87	87	24	0	4
Torquay U. (L)	KW Overpelt (Bel)	12.89	89	17	0	6
Chesterfield	KW Overpelt (Bel)	10.90	90-91	27	5	4

CALDWELL Garrett Evan James
U.S.A., 6 November, 1973 (G)

League Club	Source	Date Signed	Seasons Played	Apps	Subs	Gls
Colchester U.	Princeton Univ.	09.95	96	6	0	0

CALDWELL Peter James
Dorchester, 5 June, 1972 E Sch (G)

League Club	Source	Date Signed	Seasons Played	Apps	Subs	Gls
Queens Park R.	YT	03.90				
Leyton Orient	Tr	07.95	95-96	31	0	0

CALDWELL Terence
Wakefield, 5 December, 1938 E Yth (LB)

League Club	Source	Date Signed	Seasons Played	Apps	Subs	Gls
Huddersfield T.	Jnrs	06.57	59	4	-	0
Leeds U.	Tr	12.59	59-60	20	-	0
Carlisle U.	Tr	07.61	61-69	340	4	1
Barrow	Tr	07.70	70-71	29	1	0

CALEB Graham Stuart
Oxford, 25 May, 1945 (CH)

League Club	Source	Date Signed	Seasons Played	Apps	Subs	Gls
Luton T.	App	05.63	63-64	20	-	0

CALLACHAN Ralph
Edinburgh, 29 April, 1955 (M)

League Club	Source	Date Signed	Seasons Played	Apps	Subs	Gls
Newcastle U.	Hearts	02.77	77	9	0	0

CALLAGHAN Aaron Joseph
Dublin, 8 October, 1966 IR Yth/IRu21-2 (CD)

League Club	Source	Date Signed	Seasons Played	Apps	Subs	Gls
Stoke C.	App	10.84	84-86	10	5	0
Crewe Alex.	L	11.85	85	8	0	0
Oldham Ath.	Tr	10.86	86-87	11	5	2
Crewe Alex.	Tr	05.88	88-91	148	10	6
Preston N.E.	Tr	08.92	92-93	34	2	2

CALLAGHAN Christopher
Sandbach, 25 August, 1930 (FB)

League Club	Source	Date Signed	Seasons Played	Apps	Subs	Gls
Crewe Alex.	Bideford	12.52	53-56	45	-	0

CALLAGHAN Ernest
Birmingham, 21 January, 1910 Died 1972 (RB)

League Club	Source	Date Signed	Seasons Played	Apps	Subs	Gls
Aston Villa	Atherstone T.	09.30	32-46	125	-	0

CALLAGHAN Frederick John
Fulham, 19 December, 1944 (LB)

League Club	Source	Date Signed	Seasons Played	Apps	Subs	Gls
Fulham	App	08.62	63-73	291	4	9

CALLAGHAN Henry William
Glasgow, 20 March, 1929 (OL)

League Club	Source	Date Signed	Seasons Played	Apps	Subs	Gls
Ipswich T.	Kirkintilloch Rob Roy	09.54	54	1	-	0

CALLAGHAN Ian Michael
Prescot, 5 August, 1969 (M)

League Club	Source	Date Signed	Seasons Played	Apps	Subs	Gls
Bolton W.	YT	07.87	87	1	0	0

CALLAGHAN Ian Robert
Liverpool, 10 April, 1942 Eu23-4/EF Lge/E-4 (OR)

League Club	Source	Date Signed	Seasons Played	Apps	Subs	Gls
Liverpool	Jnrs	03.60	59-77	637	3	50
Swansea C.	Fort Lauderdale (USA)	09.78	78-79	76	0	1
Crewe Alex.	Cork Hibs	10.81	81	15	0	0

CALLAGHAN Nigel Ian
Singapore, 12 September, 1962 Eu21-9/E 'B' (W)

League Club	Source	Date Signed	Seasons Played	Apps	Subs	Gls
Watford	App	07.80	80-86	209	13	41
Derby Co.	Tr	02.87	86-88	76	0	10
Aston Villa	Tr	02.89	88-90	24	2	1
Derby Co.	L	09.90	90	12	0	1
Watford	L	03.91	90	6	6	1
Huddersfield T.	L	01.92	91	8	0	0

CALLAGHAN Robert
Glasgow, 5 October, 1931 Died 1991 (OR)

League Club	Source	Date Signed	Seasons Played	Apps	Subs	Gls
Scunthorpe U.	Duntocher H.	08.55	55	19	-	6
Barrow	Tr	10.56	56-57	40	-	10

CALLAGHAN William
Glasgow, 7 February, 1930 (IR)

League Club	Source	Date Signed	Seasons Played	Apps	Subs	Gls
Ipswich T.	Great Perth Jnrs	07.52	52-54	21	-	7

CALLAGHAN William Andrew
Glasgow, 9 December, 1941 (OR)

League Club	Source	Date Signed	Seasons Played	Apps	Subs	Gls
Barnsley	Dumbarton	08.64	64	15	-	0

CALLAGHAN William Francis
Ebbw Vale, 26 February, 1924 Died 1981 (LB)

League Club	Source	Date Signed	Seasons Played	Apps	Subs	Gls
Aldershot	Frickley Colly	06.49	49	1	-	0

CALLAGHAN William Thomas
Dunfermline, 23 March, 1967 (F)

League Club	Source	Date Signed	Seasons Played	Apps	Subs	Gls
Walsall (L)	Dunfermline Ath.	09.88	88	2	0	1

CALLAN Dennis
Merthyr Tydfil, 27 July, 1932 (WH)

League Club	Source	Date Signed	Seasons Played	Apps	Subs	Gls
Cardiff C.	Troedyrhiw	07.52	55	1	-	0
Exeter C.	L	05.54	54	10	-	1

CALLAN Francis Thomas Moore
Dundalk, 24 May, 1935 (F)

League Club	Source	Date Signed	Seasons Played	Apps	Subs	Gls
Doncaster Rov.	Dundalk	11.57	57-58	28	-	6

CALLAND Albert
Bishop Auckland, 10 September, 1929 (CF)

League Club	Source	Date Signed	Seasons Played	Apps	Subs	Gls
Torquay U.	Langley Park	03.50	51-53	24	-	11

CALLAND Edward (Ted)
Hedley Hope, 15 June, 1932 Died 1995 (CF)

League Club	Source	Date Signed	Seasons Played	Apps	Subs	Gls
Fulham	Durham C.	04.52				
Torquay U.	Tr	09.52	52-56	47	-	21
Exeter C.	Tr	07.57	57-59	105	-	49
Port Vale	Tr	08.60	60	12	-	3
Lincoln C.	Tr	07.61	61	7	-	3

CALLAND Ralph
Lanchester, 5 July, 1916 (FB)

League Club	Source	Date Signed	Seasons Played	Apps	Subs	Gls
Charlton Ath.		05.37				
Torquay U.	Tr	05.39	46-53	207	-	14

CALLENDER John (Jack)
West Wylam, 2 April, 1923 (WH)

League Club	Source	Date Signed	Seasons Played	Apps	Subs	Gls
Gateshead	Jnrs	05.39	46-57	470	-	41

CALLENDER Norman
Newburn, 9 June, 1924 Died 1990 (RH)

League Club	Source	Date Signed	Seasons Played	Apps	Subs	Gls
Darlington		06.46	46-48	27	-	1

CALLENDER Thomas Sanderson
Bywell, 20 September, 1920 E Sch (WH)

League Club	Source	Date Signed	Seasons Played	Apps	Subs	Gls
Lincoln C.	Jnrs	09.37	38	23	-	0
Gateshead	Tr	11.45	46-56	439	-	61

CALLOWAY Laurence John
Birmingham, 17 June, 1945 (LB/M)

League Club	Source	Date Signed	Seasons Played	Apps	Subs	Gls
Wolverhampton W.	App	10.62				
Rochdale	Tr	07.64	64-67	161	1	4
Blackburn Rov.	Tr	03.68	67-69	17	8	1
Southport	Tr	08.70	70	45	0	7
York C.	Tr	06.71	71-72	54	1	3
Shrewsbury T.	Tr	12.72	72-74	77	5	3

CALOW Charles John Herbert
Belfast, 30 September, 1931 NI Amat (G)

League Club	Source	Date Signed	Seasons Played	Apps	Subs	Gls
Bradford P.A.	Cliftonville	06.52	52	1	-	0

CALVER Reginald **John**
Glasgow, 22 September, 1938 (WH)

League Club	Source	Date Signed	Seasons Played	Apps	Subs	Gls
Burnley	Jnrs	09.55				
Southport	Tr	07.61	61	2	-	0

CALVERLEY Alfred
Huddersfield, 24 November, 1917 Died 1991 (W)

League Club	Source	Date Signed	Seasons Played	Apps	Subs	Gls
Huddersfield T.		11.43				
Mansfield T.	Tr	06.46	46	30	-	1
Arsenal	Tr	03.47	46	11	-	0
Preston N. E.	Tr	07.47	47	13	-	0
Doncaster Rov.	Tr	12.47	47-52	142	-	11

CALVERT Clifford Alistair
York, 21 April, 1954 E Yth (FB/M)

League Club	Source	Date Signed	Seasons Played	Apps	Subs	Gls
York C.	Jnrs	07.72	72-75	62	5	0
Sheffield U.	Tr	09.75	75-78	78	3	5

CALVERT Joseph William Herbert
Bullcroft, 3 February, 1907 (G)

League Club	Source	Date Signed	Seasons Played	Apps	Subs	Gls
Bristol Rov.	Frickley Colly	05.31	31	42	-	0
Leicester C.	Tr	05.32	32-47	72	-	0
Watford	Tr	02.48	47	5	-	0

CALVERT Mark Robert
Consett, 11 September, 1970 (W)

League Club	Source	Date Signed	Seasons Played	Apps	Subs	Gls
Hull C.	YT	07.89	88-92	24	6	1
Scarborough	Tr	08.93	93-94	68	4	5

CALVERT John **Steven**
Barrow, 2 April, 1952 (M)

League Club	Source	Date Signed	Seasons Played	Apps	Subs	Gls
Barrow (Am)	Jnrs	08.70	71	22	0	4

CALVO-GARCIA Alexander
Ordizia, Spain, 1 January, 1972 (M)

League Club	Source	Date Signed	Seasons Played	Apps	Subs	Gls
Scunthorpe U.	Eibar (Sp)	10.96	96-97	46	11	7

CAMDEN Christopher Eric
Birkenhead, 28 May, 1963 (F)

League Club	Source	Date Signed	Seasons Played	Apps	Subs	Gls
Chester C.	Poulton Vic.	12.83	83	9	0	2
Tranmere R. (N/C)	Oswestry T.	03.87	86	2	1	1

CAME Mark Raymond
Exeter, 14 September, 1961 (CD)

League Club	Source	Date Signed	Seasons Played	Apps	Subs	Gls
Bolton W.	Winsford U.	04.84	84-92	188	7	7
Chester C.	Tr	12.92	92-93	47	0	1
Exeter C.	Tr	07.94	94-95	70	0	5

CAMERON Alexander Ramsey
Leith, 5 October, 1943 (RB)

League Club	Source	Date Signed	Seasons Played	Apps	Subs	Gls
Oldham Ath.	Hibernian	05.64	64	15	-	0

CAMERON Daniel
Dundee, 9 November, 1953 (FB)

League Club	Source	Date Signed	Seasons Played	Apps	Subs	Gls
Sheffield Wed.	App	07.71	73-75	31	0	1
Colchester U.	L	02.75	74	5	0	0
Preston N. E.	Tr	04.76	75-80	120	2	0

CAMERON Daniel
Dublin, 16 June, 1922 (CH)

League Club	Source	Date Signed	Seasons Played	Apps	Subs	Gls
Everton	Shelbourne	07.48	48	1	-	0

CAMERON David
Glasgow, 10 March, 1936 (IF)

League Club	Source	Date Signed	Seasons Played	Apps	Subs	Gls
Bradford C.	Glencalrn	04.58	58	7	-	2

CAMERON Duncan George Brown
Uddingston 1 February, 1936 (OR)

League Club	Source	Date Signed	Seasons Played	Apps	Subs	Gls
Swindon T.		09.56	56-57	2	-	0

CAMERON Hugh Gibson
Blantyre, 1 February, 1927 (W)

League Club	Source	Date Signed	Seasons Played	Apps	Subs	Gls
Torquay U.	Clyde	05.48	48-50	120	-	17
Newcastle U.	Tr	04.51	51	2	-	0
Bury	Tr	03.52	51-53	29	-	1
Workington	Tr	11.53	53-55	54	-	4

CAMERON John (Jack)
Dalmuir, 7 March, 1931 (FB)

League Club	Source	Date Signed	Seasons Played	Apps	Subs	Gls
Hartlepool U.	Dumbarton	11.53	53-59	175	-	0

CAMERON John Alexander
Greenock, 29 November, 1929 (WH)

League Club	Source	Date Signed	Seasons Played	Apps	Subs	Gls
Bradford P.A.	Motherwell	07.56	56	3	-	0

CAMERON Robert
Greenock, 23 November, 1932 S Sch (IF)

League Club	Source	Date Signed	Seasons Played	Apps	Subs	Gls
Queens Park R	Port Glasgow	06.50	50-58	256	-	59
Leeds U.	Tr	07.59	59-61	58	-	9
Southend U.	Gravesend & Nft	10.63	63	3	-	0

CAMERON Rodney Peter
Newcastle, 11 April, 1939 (FB)

League Club	Source	Date Signed	Seasons Played	Apps	Subs	Gls
Bradford C.	Newcastle W.E.	08.57	58	1	-	0

CAMERON Stuart John
Liverpool, 28 November, 1966 (G)

League Club	Source	Date Signed	Seasons Played	Apps	Subs	Gls
Preston N.E.	YT	08.83	83	1	0	0

CAMMACK Stephen Richard
Sheffield, 20 March, 1954 E Yth (F)

League Club	Source	Date Signed	Seasons Played	Apps	Subs	Gls
Sheffield U.	App	05.71	71-75	21	15	5
Chesterfield	Tr	01.76	75-78	95	18	21
Scunthorpe U.	Tr	09.79	79-80	84	0	27
Lincoln C.	Tr	07.81	81	18	0	6
Scunthorpe U.	Tr	03.82	81-86	159	2	83
Port Vale	L	12.85	85	1	2	0
Stockport Co.	L	01.86	85	3	1	1

CAMP Stephen
Manchester, 8 February, 1954 (F)

League Club	Source	Date Signed	Seasons Played	Apps	Subs	Gls
Fulham	Leatherhead	09.75	75-76	4	1	0
Peterborough U.	Tr	08.77	77	6	1	1

CAMPBELL Alan James
Arbroath, 21 January, 1948 S Yth/Su23-1 (M)

League Club	Source	Date Signed	Seasons Played	Apps	Subs	Gls
Charlton Ath.	Jnrs	02.65	65-70	196	2	28
Birmingham C.	Tr	10.70	70-75	169	6	11
Cardiff C.	Tr	03.76	75-80	165	2	2
Carlisle U.	Tr	11.80	80-81	29	2	2

CAMPBELL Thomas **Alan**
Belfast, 11 September, 1944 (FB)

League Club	Source	Date Signed	Seasons Played	Apps	Subs	Gls
Grimsby T.	Coleraine	10.70	70-72	84	1	0

CAMPBELL Andrew Paul
Stockton, 18 April, 1979 E Yth (F)

League Club	Source	Date Signed	Seasons Played	Apps	Subs	Gls
Middlesbrough	YT	07.96	95-97	6	6	0

CAMPBELL Charles
Oban, 27 February, 1928 (WH)

League Club	Source	Date Signed	Seasons Played	Apps	Subs	Gls
Oldham Ath.	Rutherglen Glencairn	11.49	49	2	-	0

CAMPBELL Daniel
Oldham, 3 February, 1944 (CH)

League Club	Source	Date Signed	Seasons Played	Apps	Subs	Gls
West Bromwich A.	Droylsden	11.62	65-67	8	0	0
Stockport Co.	Los Angeles (USA)	01.69	68-69	31	0	3
Bradford P.A.	Tr	03.70	69	10	0	1

CAMPBELL David
Wrexham, 18 February, 1947 (W)

League Club	Source	Date Signed	Seasons Played	Apps	Subs	Gls
Wrexham	Jnrs	07.65	64-66	41	2	7

CAMPBELL David Alistair
Edinburgh, 2 November, 1958 (CD)

League Club	Source	Date Signed	Seasons Played	Apps	Subs	Gls
Charlton Ath.	Jnrs	06.77	75-79	71	5	3

CAMPBELL David Anthony
Derry (NI), 2 June, 1965 NI-10 (M)

League Club	Source	Date Signed	Seasons Played	Apps	Subs	Gls
Nottingham F.	App	06.83	84-87	35	6	3
Notts Co.	L	02.87	86	18	0	2
Charlton Ath.	Tr	10.87	87-88	26	4	1
Plymouth Arg.	L	03.89	88	1	0	0
Bradford C.	Tr	03.89	88-89	27	8	4
Rotherham U. (N/C)	Shamrock Rov.	11.92	92	0	1	0
Burnley	West Bromwich A. (N/C)	03.93	92	7	1	0
Lincoln C.	L	02.94	93	2	2	1
Wigan Ath (N/C)	Tr	08.94	94	7	0	0
Cambridge U. (N/C)	Tr	01.95	94	1	0	0

CAMPBELL David Martin
Dublin, 13 September, 1969 (CD)

League Club	Source	Date Signed	Seasons Played	Apps	Subs	Gls
Huddersfield T.	Bohemians	08.90	90-91	4	0	0

CAMPBELL Donald
Bootle, 19 October, 1932 E Yth (FB)

League Club	Source	Date Signed	Seasons Played	Apps	Subs	Gls
Liverpool	Jnrs	11.50	53-57	47	-	2
Crewe Alex.	Tr	07.58	58-61	149	-	1
Gillingham	Tr	09.62	62-63	29	-	0

CAMPBELL Dougald
Kirkintilloch, 14 December, 1922 (OR)

League Club	Source	Date Signed	Seasons Played	Apps	Subs	Gls
Queens Park R		03.48				
Crewe Alex.	Tr	07.49	49	34	-	0
Barrow	Tr	08.50	50-51	30	-	3
Grimsby T.	Tr	10.51	51	6	-	0

CAMPBELL Frank
Dunkeld, 23 December, 1950 (WH)

League Club	Source	Date Signed	Seasons Played	Apps	Subs	Gls
Grimsby T.	Jnrs	03.68	68	4	0	0

CAMPBELL Gary
Belfast, 4 April, 1966 (M)

League Club	Source	Date Signed	Seasons Played	Apps	Subs	Gls
Arsenal	App	01.84				
Leyton Orient (N/C)	Leyton-Wingate	01.90	89	4	4	0

CAMPBELL Anthony **Glen**
Leyland, 26 February, 1965 (G)

League Club	Source	Date Signed	Seasons Played	Apps	Subs	Gls
Preston N. E.	App	02.83	82-84	18	0	0

CAMPBELL Gregory Robert
Portsmouth, 13 July, 1965 (F)

League Club	Source	Date Signed	Seasons Played	Apps	Subs	Gls
West Ham U.	App	10.82	84-85	3	2	0
Brighton & H. A.	L	02.87	86	0	2	0
Plymouth Arg.	Sparta Rotterdam (Neth)	11.88	88-89	21	14	6
Northampton T.	Tr	07.90	90-91	32	15	7

CAMPBELL James
Glasgow, 25 November, 1918 (OR)

League Club	Source	Date Signed	Seasons Played	Apps	Subs	Gls
Leicester C.	Glasgow Celtic	10.43				
Walsall	Tr	10.46	46-47	14	-	1

CAMPBELL James (Jock)
East Kilbride, 11 November, 1922 Died 1983 (FB)

League Club	Source	Date Signed	Seasons Played	Apps	Subs	Gls
Charlton Ath.	R.A.F. Brize Norton	01.45	46-57	255	-	1

CAMPBELL James Charles
St Pancras, 11 April, 1937 Died 1994 (OR)

League Club	Source	Date Signed	Seasons Played	Apps	Subs	Gls
West Bromwich A.	Maidenhead U.	10.55	57-58	31	-	9
Portsmouth	Tr	07.59	59-61	50	-	12
Lincoln C.	Tr	05.62	62-63	63	-	16

CAMPBELL Jamie
Birmingham, 21 October, 1972 (D/M)

League Club	Source	Date Signed	Seasons Played	Apps	Subs	Gls
Luton T.	YT	07.91	91-93	10	26	1
Mansfield T.	L	11.94	94	3	0	1
Cambridge U.	L	03.95	94	12	0	0
Barnet	Tr	07.95	95-96	50	17	5
Cambridge U.	Tr	08.97	97	46	0	2

CAMPBELL John
West Wylam, 23 July, 1928 (OL)

League Club	Source	Date Signed	Seasons Played	Apps	Subs	Gls
Gateshead		11.49	49-55	183	-	48

CAMPBELL John
Alexandria, 22 September, 1934 (FB)

League Club	Source	Date Signed	Seasons Played	Apps	Subs	Gls
Chesterfield	Motherwell	08.59	59	1	-	0

CAMPBELL John
Liverpool, 17 March, 1922 (WH)

League Club	Source	Date Signed	Seasons Played	Apps	Subs	Gls
Liverpool		04.43				
Blackburn Rov.	Tr	12.45	46-55	224	-	19
Oldham Ath.	Tr	07.56	56	26	-	5

CAMPBELL John Peter
Derry, 28 June, 1923 Died 1968 LoI/NI-2 (OL)

League Club	Source	Date Signed	Seasons Played	Apps	Subs	Gls
Fulham	Belfast Celtic	03.49	49-52	62	-	4

CAMPBELL Joseph
Glasgow, 28 March, 1925 (IF)

League Club	Source	Date Signed	Seasons Played	Apps	Subs	Gls
Leyton Orient	Glasgow Celtic	07.49	49	5	-	1
Gillingham	Tr	09.50	50	12	-	2

CAMPBELL Kevin Joseph
Lambeth, 4 February, 1970 Eu21-4/E 'B' (F)

League Club	Source	Date Signed	Seasons Played	Apps	Subs	Gls
Arsenal	YT	02.88	87-94	124	42	46
Leyton Orient	L	01.89	88	16	0	9
Leicester C.	L	11.89	89	11	0	5
Nottingham F.	Tr	07.95	95-97	79	1	32

CAMPBELL Leslie
Wigan, 26 July, 1935 (OL)

League Club	Source	Date Signed	Seasons Played	Apps	Subs	Gls
Preston N. E.	Wigan Ath.	06.53	53-59	64	-	6
Blackpool	Tr	07.60	60	11	-	0
Tranmere Rov.	Tr	06.61	61-63	99	-	9

CAMPBELL Michael
Oban, 19 November, 1966 (M)

League Club	Source	Date Signed	Seasons Played	Apps	Subs	Gls
Hereford U. (N/C)		08.88	88	1	0	0

CAMPBELL Neil Andrew
Middlesbrough, 26 January, 1977 (F)

League Club	Source	Date Signed	Seasons Played	Apps	Subs	Gls
York C.	YT	06.95	96-97	6	6	1
Scarborough	Tr	09.97	97	20	14	7

CAMPBELL Paul Andrew
Middlesbrough, 29 January, 1980 (F)

League Club	Source	Date Signed	Seasons Played	Apps	Subs	Gls
Darlington	YT	●	97	4	2	1

CAMPBELL Paul John
Newcastle, 7 October, 1964 (M)

League Club	Source	Date Signed	Seasons Played	Apps	Subs	Gls
Hartlepool U.	Gateshead	10.83	83	1	2	0
Burnley	Tr	03.84				

CAMPBELL Philip Anthony
Barnsley, 16 October, 1961 (W)

League Club	Source	Date Signed	Seasons Played	Apps	Subs	Gls
Sheffield Wed.	App	10.79	80	0	1	0

CAMPBELL Raymond Martin John
Downpatrick (NI), 3 October, 1968 (W)

League Club	Source	Date Signed	Seasons Played	Apps	Subs	Gls
Nottingham F.	App	10.86				
Hereford U.	L	01.88	87	4	0	0

CAMPBELL Robert
Liverpool, 23 April, 1937 EYth (WH)

League Club	Source	Date Signed	Seasons Played	Apps	Subs	Gls
Liverpool	Jnrs	05.54	58-60	24	-	2
Portsmouth	Wigan Ath.	11.61	61-65	60	1	2
Aldershot	Tr	07.66	66	2	3	0

CAMPBELL Robert Inglis
Glasgow, 28 June, 1922 S-5 (OR)

League Club	Source	Date Signed	Seasons Played	Apps	Subs	Gls
Chelsea	Falkirk	05.47	47-53	188	-	36
Reading	Tr	08.54	54-57	94	-	12

CAMPBELL Robert McFaul
Belfast, 13 September, 1956 NI Yth/NI-2 (F)

League Club	Source	Date Signed	Seasons Played	Apps	Subs	Gls
Aston Villa	App	01.74	73-74	7	3	1
Halifax T.	L	02.75	74	14	1	0
Huddersfield T.	Tr	04.75	75-76	30	1	9
Sheffield U.	Tr	07.77	77	35	2	11
Huddersfield T.	Vancouver (Can)	09.78	78	7	0	3
Halifax T.	Tr	10.78	78	19	3	3
Bradford C.	Brisbane C. (Aus)	12.79	79-82	147	1	76
Derby Co.	Tr	08.83	83	11	0	4
Bradford C.	Tr	11.83	83-86	126	0	45
Wigan Ath.	Tr	10.86	86-87	61	8	27

CAMPBELL Roy
Congleton, 19 October, 1934 (WH)

League Club	Source	Date Signed	Seasons Played	Apps	Subs	Gls
Crewe Alex.		12.55	55-56	14	-	0

CAMPBELL Sean
Bristol, 31 December, 1974 (W)

League Club	Source	Date Signed	Seasons Played	Apps	Subs	Gls
Colchester U.	YT	07.93	93	1	3	0

CAMPBELL Stuart Pearson
Corby, 9 December, 1977 Su21-4 (M)

League Club	Source	Date Signed	Seasons Played	Apps	Subs	Gls
Leicester C.	YT	07.96	96-97	10	11	0

CAMPBELL Sulzeer (Sol) Jeremiah
Newham, 18 September, 1974 E Yth/Eu21-11/E 'B'/E-20 (CD)

League Club	Source	Date Signed	Seasons Played	Apps	Subs	Gls
Tottenham H.	YT	09.92	92-97	159	9	2

CAMPBELL Thomas McMillan
Glasgow, 20 February, 1935 (CF)

League Club	Source	Date Signed	Seasons Played	Apps	Subs	Gls
Tranmere Rov.	Dundee U.	06.61	61	4	-	0

CAMPBELL William Gibson
Belfast, 2 July, 1944 NIu23-3/NI-6 (W)

League Club	Source	Date Signed	Seasons Played	Apps	Subs	Gls
Sunderland	Distillery	09.64	64-65	5	0	0

CAMPBELL Winston Richard
Sheffield, 9 October, 1962 (W)

League Club	Source	Date Signed	Seasons Played	Apps	Subs	Gls
Barnsley	App	10.80	79-86	121	7	9
Doncaster Rov.	L	01.83	82	3	0	0
Rotherham U.	Tr	09.86	86-87	67	2	9

CANDLIN Maurice Hall
Jarrow, 11 November, 1921 Died 1992 (CH)

League Club	Source	Date Signed	Seasons Played	Apps	Subs	Gls
Northampton T.	Partick Thistle	02.49	49-52	139	-	1
Shrewsbury T.	Tr	07.53	53-54	69	-	2

CANHAM Anthony
Leeds, 8 June, 1960 (LW)

League Club	Source	Date Signed	Seasons Played	Apps	Subs	Gls
York C.	Harrogate R.I.	01.85	84-94	309	38	57
Hartlepool U.	Tr	08.95	95	25	4	1

CANHAM Scott Walter
Newham, 5 November, 1974 (M)

League Club	Source	Date Signed	Seasons Played	Apps	Subs	Gls
West Ham U.	YT	07.93				
Torquay U.	L	11.95	95	3	0	0
Brentford	L	01.96	95	14	0	0
Brentford	Tr	08.96	96-97	24	11	1

CANN Darren John
Torquay, 17 June, 1968 (CD)

League Club	Source	Date Signed	Seasons Played	Apps	Subs	Gls
Torquay U.	YT	06.87	86-87	12	1	0

CANN Ralph Graham
Sheffield, 17 November, 1934 (CH)

League Club	Source	Date Signed	Seasons Played	Apps	Subs	Gls
Mansfield T.		05.57	57	1	-	0

CANNELL Paul Anthony
Newcastle, 2 September, 1953 (F)

League Club	Source	Date Signed	Seasons Played	Apps	Subs	Gls
Newcastle U.	Jnrs	07.72	73-77	48	1	13
Mansfield T.	Washington (USA)	01.82	81-82	29	1	4

CANNELL Stuart
Doncaster, 31 December, 1958 (CD)

League Club	Source	Date Signed	Seasons Played	Apps	Subs	Gls
Doncaster Rov.	Bentley Vic.	03.78	77-78	22	4	0

CANNING Leslie **Daniel**
Pontypridd, 21 February, 1926 (G)

League Club	Source	Date Signed	Seasons Played	Apps	Subs	Gls
Cardiff C.	Abercynon	07.45	46-47	80	-	0
Swansea C.	Tr	01.49	48-50	47	-	0
Nottingham F.	Tr	07.51	51	5	-	0

League Club	Source	Date Signed	Seasons Played	Career Record Apps	Subs	Gls
CANNING Lawrence (Larry)						
Cowdenbeath, 1 November, 1925						(RH)
Aston Villa	Paget R.	10.47	48-53	39	-	3
Northampton T.	Kettering T.	06.56	56	2	-	0
CANNON James						
Coatbridge, 19 March, 1927						(IF)
Darlington	Third Lanark	06.56	56	12	-	1
CANNON James Anthony						
Glasgow, 2 October, 1953						(CD)
Crystal Palace	App	05.71	72-87	568	3	30
CANOVILLE Dean						
Perivale, 30 November, 1978						(M)
Millwall	Jnrs	12.95	96	0	2	0
CANOVILLE Paul Kenneth						
Hillingdon, 4 March, 1962						(W)
Chelsea	Hillingdon Borough	12.81	81-85	53	26	11
Reading	Tr	08.86	86-87	16	0	4
CANTELLO Leonard						
Manchester, 11 September, 1951 E Yth/Eu23-8						(M)
West Bromwich A.	App	10.68	68-78	297	4	13
Bolton W.	Tr	06.79	79-81	89	1	3
Hereford U. (N/C)	Altrincham	01.83	82	1	0	0
Bury (N/C)	Tr	02.83	82	8	1	1
CANTONA Eric						
France, 24 May, 1966 French Int						(F)
Leeds U.	Nimes (Fr)	02.92	91-92	18	10	9
Manchester U.	Tr	11.92	92-96	142	1	64
CANTONA Joel						
France, 26 October, 1967						(M)
Stockport Co. (N/C)	Ujpest Dozsa (Hun)	03.94	93	0	3	0
CANTWELL Noel Eucharia						
Cork (Ire), 28 December, 1932 IR-36						(LB)
West Ham U.	Cork Celtic	09.52	52-60	248	-	11
Manchester U.	Tr	11.60	60-66	123	-	6
CANVIN Cyril Edward						
Hemel Hempstead, 23 January, 1924 Died 1950						(IL)
Leyton Orient	Apsley	03.47	46	3	-	0
CAPE John Phillips						
Carlisle, 16 November, 1911 Died 1994						(OR)
Carlisle U.	Penrith	05.29	29	15	-	2
Newcastle U.	Tr	01.30	29-33	51	-	18
Manchester U.	Tr	01.34	33-36	59	-	18
Queens Park R	Tr	06.37	37-38	61	-	13
Carlisle U.	Scarborough	10.46	46	3	-	0
CAPEL Frederick John						
Manchester, 14 January, 1927 Died 1990						(FB)
Chesterfield	Goslings	06.48	49-56	285	-	16
CAPEL John Elwyn						
Newport, 31 March, 1937 W Sch						(OR)
Newport Co.	Jnrs	12.55	55	3	-	0
CAPEL Maurice John						
Crewe, 15 February, 1935						(CF)
Crewe Alex.	Whitchurch Alport	04.56	55-56	6	-	0
CAPEL Thomas						
Chorlton, 27 June, 1922						(IF)
Manchester C.	Droylsden	11.41	46-47	9	-	2
Chesterfield	Tr	10.47	47-48	62	-	27
Birmingham C.	Tr	06.49	49	8	-	2
Nottingham F.	Tr	11.49	49-53	154	-	69
Coventry C.	Tr	06.54	54-55	36	-	19
Halifax T.	Tr	10.55	55	7	-	1
CAPEWELL Ronald						
Sheffield, 26 July, 1929						(G)
Sheffield Wed.		03.50	52-53	29	-	0
Hull C.	Tr	07.54	54	1	-	0
CAPLETON Melvin David						
Hackney, 24 October, 1973						(G)
Southend U.	YT	06.92				
Blackpool	Tr	07.93	94-95	9	2	0

League Club	Source	Date Signed	Seasons Played	Career Record Apps	Subs	Gls
CAPPER John (Jack)						
Wrexham, 23 July, 1931						(CH)
Wrexham	Jnrs	11.49	52-54	48	-	0
Lincoln C.	Headington U.	01.56	55-58	21	-	0
Chester C.	Tr	09.59	59-60	36	-	0
CAPSTICK Albert Lewin						
South Kirkby, 2 January, 1928						(IF)
Accrington St.	Fleetwood	08.48	48	1	-	0
CARBERRY Robert (Bert)						
Glasgow, 16 January, 1931						(WH)
Norwich C.	Avondale	01.49	53-54	5	-	0
Gillingham	Bedford T.	07.56	56	1	-	0
Port Vale	Tr	07.57	57	29	-	0
Exeter C.	Tr	08.58				
CARBERRY James						
Liverpool, 13 October, 1969						(W)
Everton	YT	06.88				
Wigan Ath.	Tr	06.89	89-91	30	35	6
CARBERRY Lawrence James						
Liverpool, 18 January, 1936						(RB)
Ipswich T.	Bootle	05.56	56-64	257	-	0
Barrow	Tr	07.65	65-66	17	0	0
CARBON Matthew Phillip						
Nottingham, 8 June, 1975 Eu21-4						(CD)
Lincoln C.	YT	04.93	92-95	66	3	10
Derby Co.	Tr	03.96	95-97	11	9	0
West Bromwich A.	Tr	01.98	97	16	0	1
CARBONE Benito						
Italy, 14 August, 1971						(M)
Sheffield Wed.	Inter Milan (It)	10.96	96-97	52	6	15
CARDEN Paul Andrew						
Liverpool, 29 March, 1979						(F)
Blackpool	YT	07.97	96	0	1	0
Rochdale	Tr	03.98	97	3	4	0
CARDEW Norman						
South Shields, 7 November, 1938						(IF)
Darlington (Am)	South Shields	07.65	65	6	0	0
CARDWELL Louis						
Blackpool, 20 August, 1912 Died 1986						(CH)
Blackpool	Whitegate Jnrs	04.30	30-37	133	-	6
Manchester C.	Tr	09.38	38-46	39	-	0
Crewe Alex.	Netherfield	10.47	47-48	25	-	0
CAREY Alan William						
Greenwich, 21 August, 1975						(F)
Reading	YT	07.94	93-94	0	3	0
CAREY Brian Patrick						
Cork, 31 May, 1968 IRu21-1/IR-3						(CD)
Manchester U.	Cork C.	09.89				
Wrexham	L	01.91	90	3	0	0
Wrexham	L	12.91	91	13	0	1
Leicester C.	Tr	07.93	93-95	51	7	1
Wrexham	Tr	07.96	96-97	81	0	1
CAREY John James						
Dublin, 23 February, 1919 Died 1995 IR-29/NI-7						(FB)
Manchester U.	St James Gate	11.36	37-52	304	-	16
CAREY Louis Anthony						
Bristol, 22 January, 1977 Su21-1						(D/M)
Bristol C.	YT	07.95	95-97	99	4	0
CAREY Peter Richard						
Barking, 14 April, 1933						(LB/WH)
Leyton Orient	Barking	10.57	56-59	34	-	2
Queens Park R	Tr	07.60	60	15	-	1
Colchester U.	Tr	11.60	60	10	-	0
Aldershot	Tr	08.61	61-62	47	-	0
CAREY Richard						
Paisley, 19 November, 1927						(WH)
Southport	Cowdenbeath	07.49	49	1	-	0
CAREY Shaun Peter						
Kettering, 13 May, 1976 IRu21-2						(M)
Norwich C.	YT	07.94	95-97	25	12	0

CARGILL David Anderson
Arbroath, 21 July, 1936 (OL)

League Club	Source	Date Signed	Seasons Played	Apps	Subs	Gls
Burnley	Jnrs	07.53	53-55	5	-	0
Sheffield Wed.	Tr	09.56	56-57	10	-	0
Derby Co.	Tr	04.58	58-60	56	-	8
Lincoln C.	Tr	12.60	60	9	-	0

CARGILL James Gordon
Alyth, 22 September, 1945 S Sch (G)

League Club	Source	Date Signed	Seasons Played	Apps	Subs	Gls
Nottingham F.	Jnrs	09.62	64-65	2	0	0
Notts Co.	Tr	07.66	66	10	0	0

CARLESS Ernest Francis
Barry, 9 September, 1912 Died 1987 (IF)

League Club	Source	Date Signed	Seasons Played	Apps	Subs	Gls
Cardiff C. (Am)	Wolverhampton W.(Am)	10.32	32	2	-	0
Plymouth Arg.	Barry T.	12.46	46	4	-	0

CARLIN Patrick
Dunscroft, 17 December, 1929 (RB)

League Club	Source	Date Signed	Seasons Played	Apps	Subs	Gls
Bradford P. A.	Dunscroft	07.53	53	6	-	0

CARLIN William
Liverpool, 6 October, 1940 E Sch/E Yth (M)

League Club	Source	Date Signed	Seasons Played	Apps	Subs	Gls
Liverpool	Jnrs	05.58	59	1	-	0
Halifax T.	Tr	08.62	62-64	95	-	32
Carlisle U.	Tr	10.64	64-67	92	1	21
Sheffield U.	Tr	09.67	67-68	36	0	3
Derby Co.	Tr	08.68	68-70	89	0	14
Leicester C.	Tr	10.70	70-71	31	0	1
Notts Co.	Tr	09.71	71-73	57	3	2
Cardiff C.	Tr	11.73	73	22	0	1

CARLINE Peter
Chesterfield, 2 March, 1951 (WH)

League Club	Source	Date Signed	Seasons Played	Apps	Subs	Gls
Chesterfield	Jnrs	09.70	70	2	0	0

CARLING Terence Patrick
Otley, 26 February, 1939 (G)

League Club	Source	Date Signed	Seasons Played	Apps	Subs	Gls
Leeds U.	Dawsons	11.56	60-61	5	-	0
Lincoln C.	Tr	07.62	62-63	84	-	0
Walsall	Tr	06.64	64-66	101	0	0
Chester C.	Tr	12.66	66-70	199	0	0

CARLISLE Clarke James
Preston, 14 October, 1979 (CD)

League Club	Source	Date Signed	Seasons Played	Apps	Subs	Gls
Blackpool	YT	08.97	97	8	3	2

CARLSON George Edward
Liverpool, 27 July, 1925 (CF)

League Club	Source	Date Signed	Seasons Played	Apps	Subs	Gls
Tranmere Rov.		09.47	47-48	2	-	0

CARLTON David George
Stepney, 24 November, 1952 (M)

League Club	Source	Date Signed	Seasons Played	Apps	Subs	Gls
Fulham	App	12.69	71-72	5	4	0
Northampton T.	Tr	10.73	73-76	99	5	6
Brentford	Tr	10.76	76-79	138	2	7
Northampton T.	Tr	09.80	80-81	76	0	1

CARMICHAEL John (Jack)
Newcastle, 11 November, 1948 (CD)

League Club	Source	Date Signed	Seasons Played	Apps	Subs	Gls
Arsenal	Possilpark Jnrs	11.66				
Peterborough U.	Tr	01.71	70-79	331	21	5
Swindon T.	New England (USA)	09.80				
Peterborough U. (N/C)	Jacksonville (USA)	01.83	82	5	1	0

CARMICHAEL Matthew
Singapore, 13 May, 1964 (CD/F)

League Club	Source	Date Signed	Seasons Played	Apps	Subs	Gls
Lincoln C.	Basingstoke T.	08.89	89-92	113	20	18
Scunthorpe U.	Tr	07.93	93-94	51	11	20
Barnet	L	09.94	94	2	1	0
Preston N.E.	Tr	03.95	94	7	3	3
Mansfield T. (N/C)	Tr	08.95	95	1	0	1
Doncaster Rov.	Tr	08.95	95	19	8	4
Darlington	Tr	02.96	95	11	2	2

CARMODY Michael Joseph
Huddersfield, 9 February, 1966 (LB)

League Club	Source	Date Signed	Seasons Played	Apps	Subs	Gls
Huddersfield T.	Emley	12.84	84	8	0	0
Tranmere R. (N/C)	Emley	09.86	86	2	0	0

CARNABY Brian James
Plymouth, 14 December, 1947 (M)

League Club	Source	Date Signed	Seasons Played	Apps	Subs	Gls
Reading	Arcadia Shepherds (SA)	07.72	72-76	136	9	10

CARNEY Leonard Francis
Liverpool, 30 May, 1915 Died 1996 (IF)

League Club	Source	Date Signed	Seasons Played	Apps	Subs	Gls
Liverpool (Am)	Collegiate O.B.	07.46	46-47	6	-	1

CARNEY Stephen
Wallsend, 22 September, 1957 (D)

League Club	Source	Date Signed	Seasons Played	Apps	Subs	Gls
Newcastle U.	Blyth Spartans	10.79	79-84	125	9	1
Carlisle U.	L	03.85	84	6	0	0
Darlington	Tr	08.85	85	10	2	0
Rochdale	L	01.86	85	4	0	0
Hartlepool U.	Tr	03.86	85	7	0	0

CAROLAN Joseph Francis
Dublin, 8 September, 1937 IR-2 (FB)

League Club	Source	Date Signed	Seasons Played	Apps	Subs	Gls
Manchester U.	Home Farm	02.56	58-60	66	-	0
Brighton & H. A.	Tr	12.60	60-61	33	-	0

CAROLIN Brian
Ashington, 6 December, 1939 (HB)

League Club	Source	Date Signed	Seasons Played	Apps	Subs	Gls
Gateshead		08.57	57-59	17	-	0

CARPENTER Richard
Sheppey, 30 September, 1972 (M)

League Club	Source	Date Signed	Seasons Played	Apps	Subs	Gls
Gillingham	YT	05.91	90-96	107	15	4
Fulham	Tr	09.96	96-97	49	9	7

CARPENTER Stephen
Torquay, 23 September, 1960 (M)

League Club	Source	Date Signed	Seasons Played	Apps	Subs	Gls
Torquay U. (N/C)		04.86	85	2	0	0

CARPENTER Thomas Albert Edward
Carshalton, 11 March, 1925 (G)

League Club	Source	Date Signed	Seasons Played	Apps	Subs	Gls
Watford	Harrow T.	11.50	50	4	-	0

CARR Ashley
Crowland, 15 August, 1968 (M)

League Club	Source	Date Signed	Seasons Played	Apps	Subs	Gls
Peterborough U.	Jnrs	08.86	86-88	9	6	0

CARR Clifford Paul
Hackney, 19 June, 1964 Eu21-1 (LB)

League Club	Source	Date Signed	Seasons Played	Apps	Subs	Gls
Fulham	App	06.82	82-86	136	9	14
Stoke C.	Tr	07.87	87-90	116	8	1
Shrewsbury T. (N/C)	Tr	08.91	91	1	0	1
Mansfield T.	Telford U.	10.91	91	20	0	0
Chesterfield	Tr	08.92	92-93	62	3	2

CARR Darren John
Bristol, 4 September, 1968 (CD)

League Club	Source	Date Signed	Seasons Played	Apps	Subs	Gls
Bristol Rov.	YT	08.86	85-87	26	4	0
Newport Co.	L	10.87	87	4	0	0
Newport Co.	Tr	01.88	87	5	0	0
Sheffield U.	Tr	03.88	87-88	12	1	1
Crewe Alex.	Tr	09.90	90-92	96	8	5
Chesterfield	Tr	07.93	93-97	84	2	4

CARR David
Wheatley Hill (Dm), 19 January, 1937 (IF)

League Club	Source	Date Signed	Seasons Played	Apps	Subs	Gls
Darlington	Spennymoor U.	05.57	57-61	132	-	42
Workington	Tr	07.62	62-64	108	-	47
Watford	Tr	02.65	64-65	10	0	3

CARR David
Aylesham (Kt), 31 January, 1957 (D)

League Club	Source	Date Signed	Seasons Played	Apps	Subs	Gls
Luton T.	App	01.75	76-78	39	4	0
Lincoln C.	Tr	07.79	79-82	165	3	4
Torquay U.	Tr	08.83	83	34	0	0

CARR Derek Henry
Blidworth, 1 September, 1927 (RH)

League Club	Source	Date Signed	Seasons Played	Apps	Subs	Gls
Birmingham C.	Lockheed Leamington	02.48	49	3	-	0

CARR Edward Miller
Wheatley Hill (Dm), 3 October, 1917 (CF)

League Club	Source	Date Signed	Seasons Played	Apps	Subs	Gls
Arsenal	Margate	05.35	37-38	12	-	7
Huddersfield T.	Tr	10.45	46	2	-	0
Newport Co.	Tr	10.46	46-49	98	-	48
Bradford C.	Tr	10.49	49-52	94	-	49
Darlington	Tr	08.53	53	7	-	0

CARR Everton Dale
Antigua (WI), 11 January, 1961 (FB)

League Club	Source	Date Signed	Seasons Played	Apps	Subs	Gls
Leicester C.	App	01.79	78-80	11	1	0
Halifax T.	Tr	08.81	81-82	49	4	0
Rochdale	Tr	03.83	82	9	0	0

CARR Francis
Maltby, 21 April, 1919 (IF)

League Club	Source	Date Signed	Seasons Played	Apps	Subs	Gls
Rotherham U.		09.41				
York C.	Tr	08.46	46	7	-	3

CARR Franz Alexander
Preston, 24 September, 1966 E Yth/Eu21-9 (W)

League Club	Source	Date Signed	Seasons Played	Apps	Subs	Gls
Blackburn Rov.	App	07.84				

League Club	Source	Date Signed	Seasons Played	Apps	Subs	Gls
Nottingham F.	Tr	08.84	85-90	122	9	17
Sheffield Wed.	L	12.89	89	9	3	0
West Ham U.	L	03.91	90	1	2	0
Newcastle U.	Tr	06.91	91-92	20	5	3
Sheffield U.	Tr	01.93	92-93	18	0	4
Leicester C.	Tr	09.94	94	12	1	1
Aston Villa	Tr	02.95	94-95	1	2	0
Bolton W.	Reggiana (It)	10.97	97	0	5	0
West Bromwich A.	Tr	02.98	97	1	3	0

CARR Graham Gordon
Darlington, 8 December, 1970 (G)

League Club	Source	Date Signed	Seasons Played	Apps	Subs	Gls
Hartlepool U. (N/C)	YT	08.89	89	1	0	0

CARR William **Graham**
Corbridge, 25 October, 1944 E Yth (CH)

League Club	Source	Date Signed	Seasons Played	Apps	Subs	Gls
Northampton T.	Jnrs	08.62	62-67	84	1	0
York C.	Tr	06.68	68	32	1	1
Bradford P. A.	Tr	07.69	69	42	0	2

CARR John (Jackie)
Bishopbriggs, 12 January, 1924 (IF)

League Club	Source	Date Signed	Seasons Played	Apps	Subs	Gls
Gillingham	Alloa Ath.	06.48	50	11	-	2

CARR John William
South Africa, 10 June, 1926 (OL)

League Club	Source	Date Signed	Seasons Played	Apps	Subs	Gls
Huddersfield T.	Durban Railways (SA)	10.50	50	1	-	0

CARR Kevin
Morpeth, 6 November, 1958 (G)

League Club	Source	Date Signed	Seasons Played	Apps	Subs	Gls
Newcastle U.	Burnley (App)	07.76	77-84	173	0	0
Carlisle U.	Tr	08.85	85-86	17	0	0
Darlington	L	11.86	86	3	0	0
Hartlepool U.	Middlesbrough (N/C)	07.87	87	31	0	0

CARR Lance Lanyon
South Africa, 18 February, 1910 Died 1983 (OL)

League Club	Source	Date Signed	Seasons Played	Apps	Subs	Gls
Liverpool	Boksburg (SA)	08.33	33-35	31	-	8
Newport Co.	Tr	10.36	36-38	25	-	0
Bristol Rov.	Tr	08.46	46	42	-	8

CARR Peter
Bishop Middleham, 25 August, 1951 (FB)

League Club	Source	Date Signed	Seasons Played	Apps	Subs	Gls
Darlington	App	08.69	67-72	131	4	1
Carlisle U.	Tr	11.72	72-77	202	2	1
Hartlepool U.	New England (USA)	10.79	79	22	0	0

CARR Peter
Rawmarsh, 16 November, 1960 (M)

League Club	Source	Date Signed	Seasons Played	Apps	Subs	Gls
Rotherham U.	App	11.78	78-81	31	5	3

CARR Stanley Rushton
Southport, 1 June, 1926 (FB)

League Club	Source	Date Signed	Seasons Played	Apps	Subs	Gls
Southport	Brockhouse	10.45				
New Brighton	Tr	08.48	48	1	-	0

CARR Stephen
Dublin, 29 August, 1976 IR Sch/IR Yth/IRu21-12 (RB)

League Club	Source	Date Signed	Seasons Played	Apps	Subs	Gls
Tottenham H.	YT	09.93	93-97	62	3	0

CARR William McInanny
Cambridge, 6 January, 1950 Su23-4/S-6 (M)

League Club	Source	Date Signed	Seasons Played	Apps	Subs	Gls
Coventry C.	App	07.67	67-74	245	7	33
Wolverhampton W.	Tr	03.75	74-81	231	6	21
Millwall	Tr	08.82	82	8	0	1

CARR-LAWTON Colin
South Shields, 5 September, 1978 (F)

League Club	Source	Date Signed	Seasons Played	Apps	Subs	Gls
Burnley	YT	01.97	97	0	1	0

CARRAGHER James Lee
Bootle, 28 January, 1978 E Yth/Eu21-11/E 'B' (M)

League Club	Source	Date Signed	Seasons Played	Apps	Subs	Gls
Liverpool	YT	10.96	96-97	18	4	1

CARRAGHER Matthew
Liverpool, 14 January, 1976 (RB)

League Club	Source	Date Signed	Seasons Played	Apps	Subs	Gls
Wigan Ath.	YT	11.93	93-96	102	17	0
Port Vale	Tr	07.97	97	26	0	0

CARRICK Matthew **David**
Evenwood, 5 December, 1946 Died 1989 (W)

League Club	Source	Date Signed	Seasons Played	Apps	Subs	Gls
Wolverhampton W.	App	12.64				
Wrexham	Tr	07.66	66-67	20	4	3
Port Vale	Altrincham	01.69	68	14	2	1
Preston N. E.	Witton A.	11.73	73	0	2	0
Rochdale	Tr	03.74	73-74	25	1	4

CARRICK William Francis
Dublin, 26 September, 1952 (G)

League Club	Source	Date Signed	Seasons Played	Apps	Subs	Gls
Manchester U.	App	09.70				
Luton T.	Tr	07.72	72	4	0	0

CARRINGTON Andrew
Grimsby, 14 November, 1936 (CH)

League Club	Source	Date Signed	Seasons Played	Apps	Subs	Gls
Grimsby T.	Jnrs	09.55	59-60	4	-	0

CARRODUS Francis
Altrincham, 31 May, 1949 (W)

League Club	Source	Date Signed	Seasons Played	Apps	Subs	Gls
Manchester C.	Altrincham	11.69	69-73	33	9	1
Aston Villa	Tr	08.74	74-78	150	0	7
Wrexham	Tr	12.79	79-81	97	0	6
Birmingham C.	Tr	08.82	82	7	1	0
Bury	Tr	10.83	83	31	3	1

CARROLL Alfred
Bradford, 6 March, 1920 Died 1994 (CH)

League Club	Source	Date Signed	Seasons Played	Apps	Subs	Gls
Bradford C.	Metallic Packing	03.48	48-49	28	-	0

CARROLL David Francis
Paisley, 20 September, 1966 E Sch (RM)

League Club	Source	Date Signed	Seasons Played	Apps	Subs	Gls
Wycombe W.	Ruislip Manor	07.88	93-97	205	5	31

CARROLL John
Limerick (IR), 11 May, 1923 (CF)

League Club	Source	Date Signed	Seasons Played	Apps	Subs	Gls
West Ham U.	Limerick	05.48	48	5	-	0

CARROLL Joseph
Bury, 6 January, 1957 (F)

League Club	Source	Date Signed	Seasons Played	Apps	Subs	Gls
Oldham Ath.	Jnrs	07.75	75	3	1	0
Halifax T.	Tr	09.76	76-78	76	6	14

CARROLL Michael
Aberdeen, 10 September, 1952 S Sch (F)

League Club	Source	Date Signed	Seasons Played	Apps	Subs	Gls
Grimsby T.	Liverpool (App)	03.71	70	0	1	0

CARROLL Michael
Blaydon, 4 October, 1961 (W)

League Club	Source	Date Signed	Seasons Played	Apps	Subs	Gls
Chesterfield	Whickham	09.81	81-82	5	1	1

CARROLL Robert
Greenford, 15 February, 1968 (F)

League Club	Source	Date Signed	Seasons Played	Apps	Subs	Gls
Southampton	App	02.86				
Brentford	Gosport Borough	09.86	86-87	24	10	8

CARROLL Roy Eric
Enniskillen, 30 September, 1977 NI Yth/NIu21-2/NI-1 (G)

League Club	Source	Date Signed	Seasons Played	Apps	Subs	Gls
Hull C.	YT	09.95	95-96	46	0	0
Wigan Ath.	Tr	04.97	97	29	0	0

CARROLL Thomas Roger
Dublin, 18 August, 1942 IR Amat/IRu23-1/IR-17 (RB)

League Club	Source	Date Signed	Seasons Played	Apps	Subs	Gls
Ipswich T.	Cambridge C.	07.66	66-71	115	2	2
Birmingham C.	Tr	10.71	71-72	38	0	0

CARRUTHERS Alexander Neilson
Loganlea, 12 May, 1915 Died 1977 (OR)

League Club	Source	Date Signed	Seasons Played	Apps	Subs	Gls
Bolton W.	Falkirk	02.37	36-37	26	-	4
Rochdale	Falkirk	05.46	46	13	-	4

CARRUTHERS Eric
Edinburgh, 2 February, 1953 (F)

League Club	Source	Date Signed	Seasons Played	Apps	Subs	Gls
Derby Co.	Hearts	01.75	76	0	1	0

CARRUTHERS John
Dumfries, 2 August, 1926 Died 1997 (W)

League Club	Source	Date Signed	Seasons Played	Apps	Subs	Gls
Carlisle U.		07.49	49	2	-	0
Workington	Tr	07.51	51	3	-	0

CARRUTHERS Martin George
Nottingham, 7 August, 1972 (F)

League Club	Source	Date Signed	Seasons Played	Apps	Subs	Gls
Aston Villa	YT	07.90	91-92	2	2	0
Hull C.	L	10.92	92	13	0	6
Stoke C.	Tr	07.93	93-96	60	31	13
Peterborough U.	Tr	11.96	96-97	50	3	19

CARSLEY Lee Kevin
Birmingham, 28 February, 1974 IRu21-1/IR-6 (M)

League Club	Source	Date Signed	Seasons Played	Apps	Subs	Gls
Derby Co.	YT	07.92	94-97	102	14	4

CARSON Alexander McPhee
Clarkston, 12 November, 1942 (CH)

League Club	Source	Date Signed	Seasons Played	Apps	Subs	Gls
Northampton T.	Jnrs	11.59	60-61	8	-	0
Aldershot	Tr	05.63	63-64	5	-	0

League Club	Source	Date Signed	Seasons Played	Career Record Apps	Subs	Gls
CARSON Thomas						
Dumbarton, 26 March, 1959						(G)
Ipswich T. (L)	Dundee	01.88	87	1	0	0
CARSS Anthony John						
Alnwick, 31 March, 1976						(LM)
Blackburn Rov.	Bradford C. (YT)	08.94				
Darlington	Tr	08.95	95-96	33	24	2
Cardiff C.	Tr	07.97	97	36	6	1
CARSTAIRS James Wood						
St Andrews (Fife), 29 January, 1971						(LB)
Arsenal	YT	03.89				
Brentford	L	02.91	90	8	0	0
Cambridge U.	Tr	07.91				
Stockport Co.	Tr	11.91	91-92	33	1	1
CARTER Brian						
Dorchester, 17 November, 1938						(WH)
Portsmouth	Weymouth	01.56	57-60	44	-	0
Bristol Rov.	Tr	07.61	61	4	-	0
CARTER Darren (Danny) Stephen						
Hackney, 29 June, 1969						(LW)
Leyton Orient	Billericay T.	07.88	88-94	168	20	22
Peterborough U.	Tr	06.95	95-96	33	12	1
CARTER Donald Frederick						
Midsomer Norton, 11 September, 1921						(W)
Bury	Stourbridge	01.39	46-47	56	-	27
Blackburn Rov.	Tr	06.48	48	2	-	0
New Brighton	Tr	11.48	48-50	105	-	19
CARTER Geoffrey						
Northwich, 14 February, 1943						(OL)
West Bromwich A.	Jnrs	02.60	59-64	25	-	3
Bury	Tr	07.66	66	4	0	0
Bradford C.	Tr	08.67	67	1	0	0
CARTER Horatio (Raich) Stratton						
Sunderland, 21 December, 1913 Died 1994 E Sch/EF Lge/E-13						(IF)
Sunderland	Jnrs	11.31	32-38	246	-	118
Derby Co.	Tr	12.45	46-47	63	-	34
Hull C.	Tr	04.48	47-51	136	-	57
CARTER Ian Noel						
Birmingham, 20 September, 1967 Canadian Int						(FB)
Peterborough U.	Winnipeg (Can)	02.94	93	9	2	0
CARTER James William Charles						
Hammersmith, 9 November, 1965						(RW)
Crystal Palace	App	11.83				
Queens Park R	Tr	09.85				
Millwall	Tr	03.87	86-90	99	11	11
Liverpool	Tr	01.91	90	2	3	0
Arsenal	Tr	10.91	91-94	18	7	2
Oxford U.	L	03.94	93	5	0	0
Oxford U.	L	12.94	94	3	1	0
Portsmouth	Tr	07.95	95-97	60	12	5
CARTER Joseph						
Bingley, 23 April, 1920 Died 1978						(G)
Walsall	Jnrs	11.36				
Notts Co.		09.44				
Hull C.	Tr	06.46	46	5	-	0
Bournemouth	Tr	03.47				
CARTER Lee Richard						
Dartford, 22 March, 1970						(CD)
Northampton T. (N/C)	YT	07.88	87	0	1	0
CARTER Leslie Alan						
Farnborough, 24 October, 1960 E Sch						(F)
Crystal Palace	App	11.77	80	1	1	0
Bristol C.	Tr	02.82	81	16	0	0
CARTER Mark Colin						
Liverpool, 17 December, 1960 E Semi Pro						(F)
Barnet	Runcorn	02.91	91-93	62	20	30
Bury	Tr	09.93	93-96	113	21	62
Rochdale	Tr	07.97	97	7	4	2
CARTER Michael						
Warrington, 18 April, 1960						(W)
Bolton W.	App	07.77	79-81	37	12	8
Mansfield T.	L	03.79	78	18	0	4
Swindon T.	L	03.82	81	4	1	0
Plymouth Arg.	Tr	08.82	82	6	6	1
Hereford U.	Tr	03.83	82-86	91	6	11
Wrexham	Tr	07.87	87-88	25	9	6
CARTER Raymond						
Chester, 1 May, 1951						(M)
Chester C.	Jnrs	09.71	71-73	56	6	0
Crewe Alex.	Tr	07.74	74	26	0	3
CARTER Raymond						
East Grinstead, 1 June, 1933						(IF)
Torquay U.	Brixham	08.58	58-59	3	-	1
Exeter C.	Tr	10.60	60-62	105	-	50
CARTER Roger Frank						
Great Yarmouth, 11 October, 1937						(WH)
Aston Villa	Gorleston	12.55				
Torquay U.	Tr	07.60	60	5	-	0
CARTER Roy William						
Torpoint, 19 February, 1954						(M)
Hereford U.	Falmouth	04.75	74-77	64	7	9
Swindon T.	Tr	12.77	77-82	193	7	34
Torquay U.	Tr	10.82	82-83	27	0	8
Bristol Rov.	L	12.82	82	4	0	1
Newport Co.	Tr	09.83	83-86	150	2	21
Exeter C.	Tr	06.87	87	37	4	2
CARTER Stanley Albert						
Exeter, 6 September, 1928						(CH)
Exeter C.	Heavitree U.	11.49	50-51	2	-	0
CARTER Stephen Charles						
Great Yarmouth, 23 April, 1953						(W)
Manchester C.	App	08.70	70-71	4	2	2
Notts Co.	Tr	02.72	71-78	172	16	21
Derby Co.	Tr	08.78	78-79	32	1	1
Bournemouth	Notts Co. (N/C)	03.82	81-83	42	4	1
Torquay U.	Tr	07.84	84	16	0	1
CARTER Stephen George						
Sunderland, 13 April, 1972						(LW)
Scarborough	Manchester U. (YT)	07.90	90-91	33	4	3
CARTER Sydney Youles						
Chesterfield, 28 July, 1916 Died 1978						(CF)
Mansfield T.	Macclesfield T.	05.38	38-46	39	-	10
CARTER Timothy Douglas						
Bristol, 5 October, 1967 E Yth						(G)
Bristol Rov.	App	10.85	85-87	47	0	0
Newport Co.	L	12.87	87	1	0	0
Sunderland	Tr	12.87	87-92	37	0	0
Carlisle U.	L	03.88	87	4	0	0
Bristol C.	L	09.88	88	3	0	0
Birmingham C.	L	11.91	91	2	0	0
Hartlepool U.	Tr	08.92	93	18	0	0
Millwall	Tr	01.94	93-94	4	0	0
Oxford U.	Tr	08.95	95	12	0	0
Millwall	Tr	12.95	95-97	62	0	0
CARTER Wilfred						
West Bromwich, 4 October, 1933						(IF)
West Bromwich A.	Jnrs	01.51	51-56	57	-	12
Plymouth Arg.	Tr	03.57	57-63	253	-	134
Exeter C.	Tr	05.64	64-65	48	0	6
CARTER William Henry John						
Woking, 14 September, 1945						(WH)
Leyton Orient	Jnrs	10.64	65-66	26	3	3
CARTLIDGE David Thomas						
Leicester, 9 April, 1940						(WH)
Leicester C.	Jnrs	10.57				
Bradford C.	Tr	06.61	61	6	-	3
Chester C.	Tr	11.61	61-62	19	-	0
CARTWRIGHT Ian James						
Birmingham, 13 November, 1964						(M)
Wolverhampton W.	App	09.82	82-85	59	2	3
CARTWRIGHT John William						
Brixworth, 5 November, 1940 E Yth						(IF)
West Ham U.	Jnrs	11.57	59-60	4	-	0
Crystal Palace	Tr	05.61	61-62	11	-	1
CARTWRIGHT Lee						
Rawtenstall, 19 September, 1972						(M)
Preston N.E.	YT	07.91	90-97	198	34	16
CARTWRIGHT Leslie						
Aberdare, 4 March, 1952 Wu23-4/W-7						(M)
Coventry C.	Jnrs	05.70	73-76	50	18	4
Wrexham	Tr	06.77	77-81	111	4	6

League Club	Source	Date Signed	Seasons Played	Apps	Subs	Gls
Cambridge U.	Tr	03.82	81-84	52	8	1
Southend U.	L	09.83	83	2	2	0

CARTWRIGHT Mark Neville
Chester, 13 January, 1973 (G)

League Club	Source	Date Signed	Seasons Played	Apps	Subs	Gls
Stockport Co. (N/C)	York C. (YT)	08.91				
Wrexham	U.S.A.	03.94	96-97	7	0	0

CARTWRIGHT Michael
Birmingham, 9 October, 1946 (FB)

League Club	Source	Date Signed	Seasons Played	Apps	Subs	Gls
Coventry C.		08.65				
Notts Co.	Tr	06.67	67-68	15	1	0
Bradford C.	L	11.67	67	1	-	0

CARTWRIGHT Neil Andrew
Stourbridge, 20 February, 1971 (M)

League Club	Source	Date Signed	Seasons Played	Apps	Subs	Gls
West Bromwich A.	YT	07.89	88-91	5	6	0

CARTWRIGHT Peter
Newcastle, 23 August, 1957 (M)

League Club	Source	Date Signed	Seasons Played	Apps	Subs	Gls
Newcastle U.	North Shields	06.79	79-82	57	8	3
Scunthorpe U.	L	12.82	82	2	2	1
Darlington	Tr	03.83	82-83	48	2	5

CARTWRIGHT Stephen Raymond
Tamworth, 8 January, 1965 (FB)

League Club	Source	Date Signed	Seasons Played	Apps	Subs	Gls
Colchester U.	Tamworth	08.88	88	10	0	0

CARTWRIGHT William John
Malpas, 11 June, 1922 (CH)

League Club	Source	Date Signed	Seasons Played	Apps	Subs	Gls
Tranmere Rov.		02.41	46-47	9	-	1

CARTY Stephen Francis
Dunfermline, 12 January, 1934 (FB)

League Club	Source	Date Signed	Seasons Played	Apps	Subs	Gls
Crewe Alex.	Blairhall	05.57	56-59	37	-	0

CARVER David Francis
Wickersley, 16 April, 1944 (FB)

League Club	Source	Date Signed	Seasons Played	Apps	Subs	Gls
Rotherham U.	App	01.62	61-64	82	-	0
Cardiff C.	Tr	01.66	65-72	210	1	1
Swansea C.	L	12.72	72	3	0	0
Hereford U.	Tr	08.73	73	14	0	0
Doncaster Rov.	Tr	03.74	73-74	29	1	0

CARVER Gerald Francis
Worcester, 27 June, 1935 (WH)

League Club	Source	Date Signed	Seasons Played	Apps	Subs	Gls
Notts Co.	Jnrs	08.52	53-65	279	1	10

CARVER John William
Newcastle, 16 January, 1965 (FB)

League Club	Source	Date Signed	Seasons Played	Apps	Subs	Gls
Newcastle U.	App	01.83				
Cardiff C.	Tr	07.85	85	13	0	0

CASCARINO Anthony Guy
Orpington, 1 September, 1962 IR-76 (F)

League Club	Source	Date Signed	Seasons Played	Apps	Subs	Gls
Gillingham	Crockenhill	01.82	81-86	209	10	78
Millwall	Tr	06.87	87-89	105	0	42
Aston Villa	Tr	03.90	89-90	43	3	11
Chelsea	Glasgow Celtic	02.92	91-93	35	5	8

CASE James Robert
Liverpool, 18 May, 1954 Eu23-1 (M)

League Club	Source	Date Signed	Seasons Played	Apps	Subs	Gls
Liverpool	South Liverpool	05.73	74-80	170	16	23
Brighton & H. A.	Tr	08.81	81-84	124	3	10
Southampton	Tr	03.85	84-90	213	2	10
Bournemouth	Tr	07.91	91	38	2	1
Halifax T.	Tr	07.92	92	17	4	2
Wrexham (N/C)	Tr	02.93	92	1	3	0
Darlington (N/C)	British Wanneroo (Aus)	10.93	93	1	0	0
Brighton & H.A.	Sittingbourne	12.93	93-95	30	2	0

CASE Norman
Prescot, 1 September, 1925 Died 1973 LoI (CF)

League Club	Source	Date Signed	Seasons Played	Apps	Subs	Gls
Sunderland	Ards	09.49	49-50	4	-	2
Watford	Tr	12.50	50	10	-	4
Rochdale	Tr	02.52	51	2	-	0

CASEY Gerald Hugh
Birkenhead, 25 August, 1941 (M)

League Club	Source	Date Signed	Seasons Played	Apps	Subs	Gls
Tranmere Rov.	Holyhead T.	08.67	67-69	49	3	5

CASEY Leonard John
Hackney, 24 May, 1931 (WH)

League Club	Source	Date Signed	Seasons Played	Apps	Subs	Gls
Chelsea	Leyton	02.54	55-58	34	-	0
Plymouth Arg.	Tr	12.58	58-59	44	-	0

CASEY Paul
West Germany, 6 October, 1961 (M/RB)

League Club	Source	Date Signed	Seasons Played	Apps	Subs	Gls
Sheffield U.	App	06.79	79-81	23	2	1
Lincoln C.	Boston U.	03.88	88-90	44	5	4

CASEY Paul
Great Yarmouth, 29 July, 1969 (G)

League Club	Source	Date Signed	Seasons Played	Apps	Subs	Gls
Cambridge U. (N/C)	YT	07.87	87	1	0	0

CASEY Ryan Peter
Coventry, 3 January, 1979 IR Yth (W)

League Club	Source	Date Signed	Seasons Played	Apps	Subs	Gls
Swansea C.	YT	05.97	96-97	5	11	0

CASEY Terence David
Abergwynfi, 5 September, 1943 (WH)

League Club	Source	Date Signed	Seasons Played	Apps	Subs	Gls
Leeds U.	Jnrs	10.60	61	3	-	0

CASEY Thomas
Combe (NI), 11 March, 1930 NI-12 (WH)

League Club	Source	Date Signed	Seasons Played	Apps	Subs	Gls
Leeds U.	Bangor (NI)	05.49	49	4	-	0
Bournemouth	Tr	08.50	50-51	66	-	1
Newcastle U.	Tr	08.52	52-57	116	-	8
Portsmouth	Tr	07.58	58	24	-	1
Bristol C.	Tr	03.59	58-62	122	-	9

CASH Stuart Paul
Tipton, 5 September, 1965 (LB)

League Club	Source	Date Signed	Seasons Played	Apps	Subs	Gls
Nottingham F.	Halesowen T.	09.89				
Rotherham U.	L	03.90	89	8	0	1
Brentford	L	09.90	90	11	0	0
Shrewsbury T.	L	09.91	91	8	0	1
Chesterfield	Tr	08.92	92-93	27	2	0

CASHLEY Alec **Raymond**
Bristol, 23 October, 1951 (G)

League Club	Source	Date Signed	Seasons Played	Apps	Subs	Gls
Bristol C.	Jnrs	09.70	70-80	227	0	1
Hereford U.	L	01.81	80	20	0	0
Bristol Rov.	(Retired)	08.82	83-84	53	0	0
Chester C. (N/C)	Trowbridge T.	10.85	85	9	0	0

CASHMORE Norman
Aldershot, 24 March, 1939 (WH)

League Club	Source	Date Signed	Seasons Played	Apps	Subs	Gls
Aldershot	Woking	07.63	64	7	-	0

CASKEY Darren Mark
Basildon, 21 August, 1974 E Sch/E Yth (M)

League Club	Source	Date Signed	Seasons Played	Apps	Subs	Gls
Tottenham H.	YT	03.92	93-95	20	12	4
Watford	L	10.95	95	6	0	1
Reading	Tr	02.96	95-97	60	13	2

CASKEY William Thomas
Belfast, 12 October, 1953 NI-7 (F)

League Club	Source	Date Signed	Seasons Played	Apps	Subs	Gls
Derby Co.	Glentoran	09.78	78-79	26	2	3

CASLEY John
Torquay, 27 April, 1926 (G)

League Club	Source	Date Signed	Seasons Played	Apps	Subs	Gls
Torquay U.		06.47	47	1	-	0

CASPER Christopher Martin
Burnley, 28 April, 1975 E Yth/Eu21-1 (CD)

League Club	Source	Date Signed	Seasons Played	Apps	Subs	Gls
Manchester U.	YT	02.93	96	0	2	0
Bournemouth	L	01.96	95	16	0	1
Swindon T.	L	09.97	97	8	1	1

CASPER Frank
Barnsley, 9 December, 1944 EF Lge (F)

League Club	Source	Date Signed	Seasons Played	Apps	Subs	Gls
Rotherham U.	App	07.62	62-66	101	1	25
Burnley	Tr	06.67	67-75	230	7	74

CASS David William Royce
Forest Gate, 27 March, 1962 (G)

League Club	Source	Date Signed	Seasons Played	Apps	Subs	Gls
Leyton Orient (N/C)	Billericay T.	03.87	86	7	0	0
Leyton Orient	Billericay T.	02.88				

CASSELL James
Prestwick, 23 April, 1947 (IF)

League Club	Source	Date Signed	Seasons Played	Apps	Subs	Gls
Bury		07.70	70	2	1	0

CASSELLS Keith Barrington
Islington, 10 July, 1957 (F)

League Club	Source	Date Signed	Seasons Played	Apps	Subs	Gls
Watford	Wembley	11.77	78-80	6	6	0
Peterborough U.	L	01.80	79	8	0	0
Oxford U.	Tr	11.80	80-81	43	2	13
Southampton	Tr	03.82	81-82	13	6	4
Brentford	Tr	02.83	82-84	80	6	28
Mansfield T.	Tr	08.85	85-88	162	1	52

CASSIDY Andrew Duncan
Leeds, 1 March, 1959 (G)

League Club	Source	Date Signed	Seasons Played	Apps	Subs	Gls
Stockport Co.		02.77	77-78	5	0	0

CASSIDY Francis James Augustine
Watford, 20 August, 1964 (M)

League Club	Source	Date Signed	Seasons Played	Apps	Subs	Gls
Watford	App	08.82				

League Club	Source	Date Signed	Seasons Played	Apps	Subs	Gls
Plymouth Arg.	L	02.84	83	1	0	0
Peterborough U.	Tr	08.84	84-85	44	2	9

CASSIDY James Toner
Falkirk, 1 December, 1943 (FB/W)

League Club	Source	Date Signed	Seasons Played	Apps	Subs	Gls
Oxford U.	East Stirling	07.63	63	5	-	0
Barrow	Tr	03.65	64	5	-	0

CASSIDY Laurence
Manchester, 10 March, 1923 (F)

League Club	Source	Date Signed	Seasons Played	Apps	Subs	Gls
Manchester U.		02.47	47-51	4	-	0
Oldham Ath.	Tr	07.56	56	4	-	1

CASSIDY Nigel
Sudbury, 7 December, 1945 (CF)

League Club	Source	Date Signed	Seasons Played	Apps	Subs	Gls
Norwich C.	Lowestoft	07.67	67-68	2	1	0
Scunthorpe U.	Tr	12.68	68-70	88	0	35
Oxford U.	Tr	11.70	70-73	113	3	33
Cambridge U.	Tr	03.74	73-75	52	2	13

CASSIDY Thomas
Belfast, 18 November, 1950 NI-24 (M)

League Club	Source	Date Signed	Seasons Played	Apps	Subs	Gls
Newcastle U.	Coleraine	10.70	70-79	170	10	22
Burnley	Tr	07.80	80-82	70	2	4

CASSIDY William
Gateshead, 30 June, 1917 (WH)

League Club	Source	Date Signed	Seasons Played	Apps	Subs	Gls
Gateshead	Close Wks	01.36	35-52	132	-	6

CASSIDY William Pitt
Hamilton, 4 October, 1940 Died 1995 (IF)

League Club	Source	Date Signed	Seasons Played	Apps	Subs	Gls
Rotherham U.	Glasgow Rangers	08.61	61-62	25	-	1
Brighton & H. A.	Tr	11.62	62-66	113	5	25
Cambridge U.	Detroit (USA)	10.68	70	27	4	6

CASTLE Stephen Charles
Ilford, 17 May, 1966 (M)

League Club	Source	Date Signed	Seasons Played	Apps	Subs	Gls
Leyton Orient	App	05.84	84-91	232	11	55
Plymouth Arg.	Tr	06.92	92-94	98	3	35
Birmingham C.	Tr	07.95	95-96	16	7	1
Gillingham	L	02.96	95	5	1	1
Leyton Orient	L	02.97	96	4	0	1
Peterborough U.	Tr	05.97	97	34	3	3

CASTLEDINE Gary John
Dumfries, 27 March, 1970 (M)

League Club	Source	Date Signed	Seasons Played	Apps	Subs	Gls
Mansfield T.	Shirebrook Colly	01.91	91-94	43	23	3

CASTLEDINE Stewart Mark
Wandsworth, 22 January, 1973 (M)

League Club	Source	Date Signed	Seasons Played	Apps	Subs	Gls
Wimbledon	YT	07.91	91-97	17	10	4
Wycombe W.	L	08.95	95	7	0	3

CASWELL Brian Leonard
Wednesbury, 14 February, 1956 (M/FB)

League Club	Source	Date Signed	Seasons Played	Apps	Subs	Gls
Walsall	App	09.73	72-84	388	12	17
Doncaster Rov.	Tr	08.85	85	15	0	2
Leeds U.	Tr	11.85	85-86	9	0	0
Wolverhampton W.	L	01.87	86	1	0	0

CASWELL Peter Donald
Leatherhead, 16 January, 1957 (G)

League Club	Source	Date Signed	Seasons Played	Apps	Subs	Gls
Crystal Palace	App	08.75	76-77	3	0	0
Crewe Alex.	Tr	08.78	78	22	0	0

CATER Ronald
Fulham, 2 February, 1922 (WH)

League Club	Source	Date Signed	Seasons Played	Apps	Subs	Gls
West Ham U.	Leytonstone	01.44	46-49	63	-	0
Leyton Orient	Tr	06.51	51	13	-	0

CATERER Brian
Hayes, 23 January, 1943 (CH)

League Club	Source	Date Signed	Seasons Played	Apps	Subs	Gls
Brentford (Am)	Chesham U.	05.68	68	1	0	0

CATLEUGH George Charles
Horden, 11 June, 1932 Died 1996 (WH)

League Club	Source	Date Signed	Seasons Played	Apps	Subs	Gls
Watford	Nuneaton Borough	05.54	54-64	293	-	15

CATLEY John William
Grimsby, 16 March, 1945 (OR)

League Club	Source	Date Signed	Seasons Played	Apps	Subs	Gls
Grimsby T.	Jnrs	07.62	62	2	-	0

CATLIN Robert
Wembley, 22 June, 1965 (G)

League Club	Source	Date Signed	Seasons Played	Apps	Subs	Gls
Notts Co.	Marconi (Aus)	08.92	92-93	3	0	0
Birmingham C.	L	03.93	92	8	0	0

CATON Thomas Stephen
Liverpool, 6 October, 1962 Died 1993 E Sch/E Yth/Eu21-14 (CD)

League Club	Source	Date Signed	Seasons Played	Apps	Subs	Gls
Manchester C.	App	10.79	79-83	164	1	8
Arsenal	Tr	12.83	83-85	81	0	2
Oxford U.	Tr	02.87	86-87	50	3	3
Charlton Ath.	Tr	11.88	88-90	56	1	5

CATON William Clifford
Stoke, 11 September, 1924 (IF)

League Club	Source	Date Signed	Seasons Played	Apps	Subs	Gls
Stoke C.	Jnrs	09.41	47-49	22	-	2
Carlisle U.	Tr	04.50	49-51	64	-	16
Chesterfield	Tr	10.52	52	7	-	0
Crewe Alex.	Worcester C.	07.54	54	38	-	8

CATTERICK Harry
Darlington, 26 November, 1919 Died 1985 (CF)

League Club	Source	Date Signed	Seasons Played	Apps	Subs	Gls
Everton	Cheadle Heath	03.37	46-51	59	-	19
Crewe Alex.	Tr	12.51	51-52	24	-	11

CATTLIN Christopher John
Milnrow, 25 June, 1946 Eu23-1 (LB)

League Club	Source	Date Signed	Seasons Played	Apps	Subs	Gls
Huddersfield T.	Burnley (Am)	08.64	64-67	59	2	1
Coventry C.	Tr	03.68	67-75	213	4	0
Brighton & H. A.	Tr	06.76	76-78	95	0	1

CATTRELL Gordon William
Sunderland, 18 December, 1954 E Sch (M)

League Club	Source	Date Signed	Seasons Played	Apps	Subs	Gls
Leeds U.	App	01.72				
Darlington	Tr	08.73	73-75	96	6	5

CAUGHEY Mark
Belfast, 27 August, 1960 (F)

League Club	Source	Date Signed	Seasons Played	Apps	Subs	Gls
Burnley (L)	Hibernian	02.87	86	8	0	0

CAUGHTER Alan David
Bangor, 19 February, 1946 (FB)

League Club	Source	Date Signed	Seasons Played	Apps	Subs	Gls
Chester C.	Jnrs	08.69	69	1	1	0

CAULFIELD Graham William
Leeds, 18 July, 1943 (CF)

League Club	Source	Date Signed	Seasons Played	Apps	Subs	Gls
York C. (Am)	Frickley Colly	02.67	66	9	0	2
Bradford C. (Am)	Tr	07.67	67	1	0	0

CAVACO Luis Miguel Pasaro
Portugal, 1 March, 1972 (W)

League Club	Source	Date Signed	Seasons Played	Apps	Subs	Gls
Stockport Co.	Estoril (Por)	08.96	96-97	19	10	5

CAVANAGH Irvin
Rochdale, 31 July, 1924 (IL)

League Club	Source	Date Signed	Seasons Played	Apps	Subs	Gls
Bury		05.48	49	1	-	0

CAVANAGH Thomas Henry
Liverpool, 29 June, 1928 (WH)

League Club	Source	Date Signed	Seasons Played	Apps	Subs	Gls
Preston N. E.		08.49				
Stockport Co.	Tr	01.50	49-51	32	-	2
Huddersfield T.	Tr	05.52	52-55	93	-	29
Doncaster Rov.	Tr	05.56	56-58	119	-	16
Bristol C.	Tr	07.59	59	24	-	6
Carlisle U.	Tr	06.60	60	34	-	4

CAVANAH John
Salford, 4 August, 1961 (RB)

League Club	Source	Date Signed	Seasons Played	Apps	Subs	Gls
Rochdale (N/C)	Barrow	09.84	84	14	3	0

CAVE Michael John
Weymouth, 28 January, 1949 Died 1985 (M)

League Club	Source	Date Signed	Seasons Played	Apps	Subs	Gls
Torquay U.	Weymouth	07.68	68-70	106	8	17
Bournemouth	Tr	07.71	71-73	91	8	17
Plymouth Arg.	L	03.72	71	8	0	4
York C.	Tr	08.74	74-76	94	2	13
Bournemouth	Tr	02.77	76-77	42	0	3

CAVEN John
Edinburgh, 6 July, 1934 (OL)

League Club	Source	Date Signed	Seasons Played	Apps	Subs	Gls
Brentford	Kilmarnock	10.57	57-58	7	-	1

CAVEN John (Joe) Brown
Kirkintilloch, 11 October, 1936 (CF)

League Club	Source	Date Signed	Seasons Played	Apps	Subs	Gls
Brighton & H. A.	Airdrieonians	03.62	61-62	10	-	0

CAVENER Philip
Tynemouth, 2 June, 1961 (W)

League Club	Source	Date Signed	Seasons Played	Apps	Subs	Gls
Burnley	App	05.79	79-82	55	14	4
Bradford C.	L	03.83	82	9	0	2
Gillingham	Tr	10.83	83	4	6	1
Northampton T.	Tr	08.84	84-85	41	4	11
Peterborough U.	Tr	03.86	85	9	1	0

CAWLEY Peter
Walton-on-Thames, 15 September, 1965 (CD)

League Club	Source	Date Signed	Seasons Played	Apps	Subs	Gls
Wimbledon	Chertsey T.	01.87	88	1	0	0

League Club	Source	Date Signed	Seasons Played	Career Record Apps	Subs	Gls
Bristol Rov.	L	02.87	86	9	1	0
Fulham	L	12.88	88	3	2	0
Bristol Rov.	Tr	07.89	89	1	2	0
Southend U.	Tr	07.90	90	6	1	1
Exeter C.	Tr	11.90	90	7	0	0
Barnet (N/C)	Tr	11.91	91	3	0	0
Colchester U.	Tr	10.92	92-97	178	2	8
CAWSTON Mervyn William						
Diss, 4 February, 1952	*E Sch*					(G)
Norwich C.	App	07.69	70	4	0	0
Southend U.	L	08.74	74	10	0	0
Newport Co.	L	01.76	75	4	0	0
Gillingham	Tr	05.76	76	19	0	0
Southend U.	Chicago (USA)	08.78	78-83	189	0	0
Stoke C.	Tr	03.84				
Southend U. (N/C)	Chelmsford C.	11.84	84	9	0	0
CAWTHORN Paul James						
Pontefract, 26 May, 1975						(W)
Scarborough	YT	12.93	92-93	8	3	1
CAWTHORNE Graham John						
Doncaster, 30 September, 1958						(CD)
Grimsby T.	Harworth Colly	11.79	79	1	0	0
Doncaster Rov.	Tr	03.82	81-82	33	0	1
CECERE Michele (Mike) Joseph						
Chester, 4 January, 1968						(F)
Oldham Ath.	App	01.86	86-88	35	17	8
Huddersfield T.	Tr	11.88	88-89	50	4	8
Stockport Co.	L	03.90	89	0	1	0
Walsall	Tr	08.90	90-93	92	20	32
Exeter C.	Tr	01.94	93-95	34	9	11
Rochdale	Tr	07.96	96	2	2	1
CEGIELSKI Wayne						
Blackwood, 11 January, 1956	*Wu21-2*					(CD)
Tottenham H.	App	05.73				
Northampton T.	L	03.75	74	11	0	0
Wrexham	Schalke 04 (Ger)	09.76	76-81	112	11	0
Port Vale	Tr	08.82	82-84	91	1	5
Hereford U.	Tr	07.85	85-86	46	4	2
CHADBOURNE William						
Mansfield, 29 October, 1922						(IF)
Mansfield T.	South Normanton	04.47	46-47	9	-	3
CHADWICK Clifton						
Bolton, 26 January, 1914						(OR)
Oldham Ath.	Fleetwood	10.33	33	18	-	6
Middlesbrough	Tr	02.34	33-38	93	-	27
Hull C.	Tr	09.46	46	23	-	7
Darlington	Tr	07.47	47	37	-	5
CHADWICK David Edwin						
India, 19 August, 1943						(W)
Southampton	Jnrs	10.60	61-65	25	0	1
Middlesbrough	Tr	07.66	66-69	100	2	3
Halifax T.	Tr	01.70	69-71	95	0	15
Bournemouth	Tr	02.72	71-73	29	7	4
Torquay U.	L	12.72	72	10	0	0
Gillingham	Tr	09.74	74	35	0	3
CHADWICK Frank Robert						
Blackburn, 9 November, 1927						(WH)
Blackburn Rov.	Jnrs	06.46	48-52	11	-	1
York C.	Tr	07.55				
CHADWICK Frederick William						
Manchester, 8 November, 1913	*Died 1987*					(CF)
Wolverhampton W.	British Dyes	05.35				
Newport Co.	Tr	09.36	36-37	40	-	18
Ipswich T.	Tr	06.38	38-46	40	-	18
Bristol Rov.	Tr	07.47	47	6	-	1
CHADWICK Graham						
Oldham, 8 April, 1942						(WH)
Manchester C.	Jnrs	03.62	62-63	12	-	0
Walsall	Tr	08.64	64	9	-	0
Chester C.	Tr	07.65	65-66	11	1	0
CHADWICK Harold						
Oldham, 25 January, 1919	*Died 1987*					(OR)
Grimsby T.		05.45				
Tranmere Rov.		03.48	47-48	9	-	0
CHADWICK Keith Michael						
Stoke, 10 March, 1953						(F)
Port Vale	Nantwich T.	09.73	73-75	29	12	7
CHADWICK Simon Leslie						
Liverpool, 15 March, 1968						(F)
Wrexham	Jnrs	08.85	85	1	1	0
CHALK Martyn Peter Glyn						
Southampton, 30 August, 1969						(W)
Derby Co.	Louth U.	01.90	91	4	3	1
Stockport Co.	Tr	06.94	94-95	29	14	6
Wrexham	Tr	02.96	95-97	68	20	6
CHALK Stephen Roger						
Southampton, 15 October, 1957						(G)
Bournemouth	App	10.75	75-77	11	0	0
Charlton Ath.	Tr	06.78				
CHALKLIN Geoffrey						
Swindon, 1 October, 1956	*E Sch*					(D)
Swindon T.	App	10.74	75	3	0	0
CHALLENDER Gregory Louis						
Rochdale, 5 February, 1973						(M)
Preston N.E.	Mossley	05.93	93	5	5	2
CHALLINOR David Paul						
Chester, 2 October, 1975	*E Sch/E Yth*					(CD)
Tranmere Rov.	Bromborough Pool	07.94	96-97	32	5	1
CHALLIS Roger Leonard Alfred						
Rochester, 3 August, 1943	*E Yth*					(FB)
Gillingham	Jnrs	07.61	60-62	10	-	0
Crewe Alex.	Tr	08.64	64	3	-	0
CHALLIS Stanley Marcel						
Lympstone, 22 April, 1918						(OL)
Exeter C.	Lympstone	09.45	46	4	-	1
CHALLIS Trevor Michael						
Paddington, 23 October, 1975	*E Yth/Eu21-1*					(LB)
Queens Park R.	YT	07.94	95-96	12	1	0
CHALMERS Grant						
Guernsey, 12 September, 1969						(M)
Brentford	Northerners	08.92	92	9	2	1
CHALMERS Leonard Austin						
Geddington, 4 September, 1936						(RB)
Leicester C.	Corby T.	01.56	57-65	171	0	4
Notts Co.	Tr	07.66	66-67	51	0	1
CHALMERS Paul						
Glasgow, 31 October, 1963	*S Yth*					(F)
Bradford C. (L)	Glasgow Celtic	01.86	85	2	0	0
Swansea C.	St Mirren	11.89	89-91	39	19	13
CHAMBERLAIN Alec Francis Roy						
March, 20 June, 1964						(G)
Ipswich T.	Ramsey T.	07.81				
Colchester U.	Tr	08.82	82-86	188	0	0
Everton	Tr	07.87				
Tranmere Rov.	L	11.87	87	15	0	0
Luton T.	Tr	07.88	88-92	138	0	0
Sunderland	Tr	07.93	93-95	89	1	0
Watford	Tr	07.96	96-97	50	0	0
CHAMBERLAIN Derek Colin						
Nottingham, 6 January, 1933						(FB)
Aston Villa	Parliament St M.	11.53				
Mansfield T.	Tr	11.56	56-57	43	-	0
York C.	Tr	07.58				
CHAMBERLAIN Glyn						
Chesterfield, 29 July, 1957						(D)
Burnley	App	11.74				
Chesterfield	Tr	12.76	76-78	17	1	0
Halifax T.	Tr	08.81	81	35	0	0
CHAMBERLAIN Kenneth Russell						
South Africa, 30 June, 1926						(CH)
Charlton Ath.	Parkhill (SA)	10.51	52-56	42	-	0
CHAMBERLAIN Mark Valentine						
Stoke, 19 November, 1961	*E Sch/Eu21-4/E-8*					(W)
Port Vale	App	04.79	78-81	90	6	18
Stoke C.	Tr	08.82	82-85	110	2	17
Sheffield Wed.	Tr	09.85	85-87	32	34	8
Portsmouth	Tr	08.88	88-93	143	24	20
Brighton & H.A.	Tr	08.94	94	12	7	2
Exeter C.	Tr	08.95	95-96	51	8	4

CHAMBERLAIN Neville Patrick
Stoke, 22 January, 1960 (F)

League Club	Source	Date Signed	Seasons Played	Apps	Subs	Gls
Port Vale	App	01.78	77-82	133	8	32
Stoke C.	Tr	09.82	82-83	7	0	0
Newport Co.	L	11.83	83	6	0	2
Plymouth Arg.	L	03.84	83	7	4	3
Newport Co.	Tr	07.84	84	39	2	13
Mansfield T.	Tr	07.85	85-86	56	5	19
Doncaster Rov.	Tr	08.87	87	22	7	4

CHAMBERLAIN Peter Michael
Liverpool, 30 June, 1935 (CH)

League Club	Source	Date Signed	Seasons Played	Apps	Subs	Gls
Leicester C.		09.56				
Swindon T.	Tr	06.57	57-62	80	-	6
Aldershot	Tr	10.62	62-64	46	-	1

CHAMBERLAIN Trevor (Tosh) Charles
Camden Town, 11 July, 1934 E Sch/E Yth (OL)

League Club	Source	Date Signed	Seasons Played	Apps	Subs	Gls
Fulham	Jnrs	07.51	54-64	187	-	59

CHAMBERS Brian Mark
Newcastle, 31 October, 1949 E Sch (M)

League Club	Source	Date Signed	Seasons Played	Apps	Subs	Gls
Sunderland	Jnrs	08.67	70-72	53	10	5
Arsenal	Tr	06.73	73	1	0	0
Luton T.	Tr	02.74	74-76	73	3	9
Millwall	Tr	07.77	77-78	54	5	9
Bournemouth	Tr	07.79	79-80	39	3	7
Halifax T.	Tr	03.81	80	10	0	1

CHAMBERS David Martin
Barnsley, 6 June, 1947 (W)

League Club	Source	Date Signed	Seasons Played	Apps	Subs	Gls
Rotherham U.	App	06.65	65-67	23	5	2
Southend U.	Cambridge U.	10.68	68-70	52	10	5
York C.	Tr	03.71	70-71	8	8	1

CHAMBERS John Frederick
Birmingham, 7 October, 1949 (M)

League Club	Source	Date Signed	Seasons Played	Apps	Subs	Gls
Aston Villa	App	10.66	68	1	1	0
Southend U.	Tr	07.69	69	6	1	0

CHAMBERS Leroy Dean
Sheffield, 25 October, 1972 (F)

League Club	Source	Date Signed	Seasons Played	Apps	Subs	Gls
Sheffield Wed.	YT	06.91				
Chester C.	Tr	08.94	94-96	29	4	1
Macclesfield T.	Boston U.	12.97	97	17	4	4

CHAMBERS Paul Anthony
Wolverhampton, 14 January, 1965 (D)

League Club	Source	Date Signed	Seasons Played	Apps	Subs	Gls
Plymouth Arg.	App	01.83				
Torquay U. (N/C)	Saltash U.	10.84	84	1	1	0

CHAMBERS Philip Martin
Barnsley, 10 November, 1953 E Sch (LB)

League Club	Source	Date Signed	Seasons Played	Apps	Subs	Gls
Barnsley	App	11.71	70-84	441	1	7
Rochdale (N/C)	Tr	08.85	85	9	1	0
Hartlepool U.	Tr	11.85	85	29	0	0

CHAMBERS Stephen
Worksop, 20 July, 1968 (M/RB)

League Club	Source	Date Signed	Seasons Played	Apps	Subs	Gls
Mansfield T.	Sheffield Wed. (App)	11.86	86-90	42	15	0

CHAMPELOVIER Leslie William
Kensington, 23 April, 1933 E Amat (IF)

League Club	Source	Date Signed	Seasons Played	Apps	Subs	Gls
Brighton & H. A. (Am)	Hayes	05.57	57	1	-	0

CHANDLER Dean Andrew Robert
Ilford, 6 May, 1976 (CD)

League Club	Source	Date Signed	Seasons Played	Apps	Subs	Gls
Charlton Ath.	YT	04.94	94-95	1	1	1
Torquay U.	L	03.97	96	4	0	0
Lincoln C.	Tr	08.97				

CHANDLER Frederick Ernest John
Hythe, 2 August, 1912 (IL)

League Club	Source	Date Signed	Seasons Played	Apps	Subs	Gls
Reading	Portsmouth (Am)	05.32	32-35	41	-	13
Blackpool	Tr	10.35	35	15	-	3
Swindon T.	Tr	05.36	36	22	-	7
Crewe Alex.	Tr	05.37	37-46	80	-	22

CHANDLER Ian
Sunderland, 20 March, 1968 E Sch (F)

League Club	Source	Date Signed	Seasons Played	Apps	Subs	Gls
Barnsley	Jnrs	08.86	86	8	4	4
Stockport Co.	L	08.87	87	4	1	0
Aldershot	Tr	08.88	88	5	4	2

CHANDLER Jeffrey George
Hammersmith, 19 June, 1959 IRu21-1/IR-2 (W)

League Club	Source	Date Signed	Seasons Played	Apps	Subs	Gls
Blackpool	App	08.76	77-78	31	6	7
Leeds U.	Tr	09.79	79-80	21	5	2
Bolton W.	Tr	10.81	81-84	152	5	36
Derby Co.	Tr	07.85	85-86	45	1	9
Mansfield T.	L	11.86	86	6	0	0
Bolton W.	Tr	07.87	87-89	18	6	4
Cardiff C.	Tr	11.89	89-90	21	4	1

CHANDLER Raymond
Bath, 14 August, 1931 (G)

League Club	Source	Date Signed	Seasons Played	Apps	Subs	Gls
Bristol Rov.	Bristol C. (Am)	06.53	53-54	12	-	0
Swindon T.	Tr	06.56	56-58	35	-	0

CHANDLER Richard (Ricky) David
Bristol, 26 September, 1961 E Sch (F)

League Club	Source	Date Signed	Seasons Played	Apps	Subs	Gls
Bristol C.	App	10.78	80-82	57	4	13

CHANDLER Robin Anthony Sydney
Luton, 19 December, 1942 E Sch (CF)

League Club	Source	Date Signed	Seasons Played	Apps	Subs	Gls
Luton T.	Jnrs	12.61	60-64	13	-	0

CHANNING Justin Andrew
Chichester, 19 November, 1968 E Yth (D/M)

League Club	Source	Date Signed	Seasons Played	Apps	Subs	Gls
Queens Park R	App	08.86	86-92	42	13	5
Bristol Rov.	Tr	10.92	92-95	121	9	10
Leyton Orient	Tr	07.96	96-97	69	5	5

CHANNON Michael Roger
Orcheston, 28 November, 1948 Eu23-9/EF Lge/E-46 (F)

League Club	Source	Date Signed	Seasons Played	Apps	Subs	Gls
Southampton	App	12.65	65-76	388	4	157
Manchester C.	Tr	07.77	77-79	71	1	24
Southampton	Tr	09.79	79-81	119	0	28
Newcastle U.	Tr	09.82	82	4	0	1
Bristol Rov.	Tr	10.82	82	4	5	0
Norwich C.	Tr	12.82	82-84	84	4	16
Portsmouth	Tr	08.85	85	34	0	6

CHAPMAN Campbell
Sutton-in-Ashfield, 28 June, 1963 (M)

League Club	Source	Date Signed	Seasons Played	Apps	Subs	Gls
Peterborough U.	App	06.81				
Wolverhampton W.	Bilston T.	12.84	84-85	47	6	4
Crewe Alex. (N/C)	Preston N.E. (N/C)	11.86	86	0	1	0

CHAPMAN Cavan
Emsworth, 11 September, 1967 (F)

League Club	Source	Date Signed	Seasons Played	Apps	Subs	Gls
Wolverhampton W.	YT	07.84	84	1	0	0

CHAPMAN Daniel Graham
Deptford, 21 November, 1974 (M)

League Club	Source	Date Signed	Seasons Played	Apps	Subs	Gls
Millwall	YT	03.93	94	4	8	0
Leyton Orient	Tr	07.95	95-96	69	9	4

CHAPMAN Darren Peter
Lincoln, 15 November, 1974 (M)

League Club	Source	Date Signed	Seasons Played	Apps	Subs	Gls
Lincoln C.	YT	●	91	0	1	0

CHAPMAN Daryl Mark
Kenilworth, 17 September, 1963 (F)

League Club	Source	Date Signed	Seasons Played	Apps	Subs	Gls
Derby Co.	Jnrs	07.82				
Crewe Alex. (N/C)	Tr	03.83	82	3	3	2

CHAPMAN Edwin
Blackburn, 2 May, 1919 Died 1977 (CF)

League Club	Source	Date Signed	Seasons Played	Apps	Subs	Gls
Blackburn Rov.	Darwen	05.36				
Accrington St.	Tr	07.38	38	4	-	1
Oldham Ath.	Tr	06.39				
Stockport Co.	Tr	08.46	46	9	-	3

CHAPMAN Edwin Maude
East Ham, 3 August, 1923 (IF)

League Club	Source	Date Signed	Seasons Played	Apps	Subs	Gls
West Ham U.	Romford	09.42	48	7	-	3

CHAPMAN Gary Anthony
Bradford, 1 May, 1964 (F)

League Club	Source	Date Signed	Seasons Played	Apps	Subs	Gls
Bradford C.	Frickley Ath.	08.88	88-89	2	3	0
Notts Co.	L	09.89	89	10	0	4
Notts Co.	Tr	02.90	89-90	3	12	0
Mansfield T.	L	10.90	90	6	0	0
Exeter C.	Tr	09.91	91-92	20	4	5
Torquay U.	Tr	02.93	92	6	2	0
Darlington	Tr	08.93	93-94	57	17	9

CHAPMAN George
Burton, 8 October, 1920 (IL)

League Club	Source	Date Signed	Seasons Played	Apps	Subs	Gls
West Bromwich A.	Donisthorpe	12.38				
Brighton & H. A.	Tr	07.46	46-47	43	-	12

CHAPMAN Harold
Liverpool, 4 March, 1921 (WH)

League Club	Source	Date Signed	Seasons Played	Apps	Subs	Gls
Aston Villa	Ellesmere Port	02.47	47	6	-	0
Notts Co.	Tr	03.49	48-50	53	-	1

CHAPMAN Ian Russell
Brighton, 31 May, 1970 (LB/M)

League Club	Source	Date Signed	Seasons Played	Apps	Subs	Gls
Brighton & H. A.	YT	06.87	86-95	265	16	14
Gillingham	Tr	08.96	96	20	3	1

CHAPMAN John
Sacriston (Dm), 24 May, 1945 (D)

League Club	Source	Date Signed	Seasons Played	Apps	Subs	Gls
Workington	Stockton	02.63	63-65	28	0	1
Reading	Tr	06.66	66-68	102	1	2
Stockport Co.	Tr	07.69	69-71	87	2	5

CHAPMAN Kenneth Arthur
Coventry, 25 April, 1932 (F)

League Club	Source	Date Signed	Seasons Played	Apps	Subs	Gls
Blackpool	Jnrs	08.49				
Crewe Alex.	Tr	07.53	53	24	-	8
Bradford C.	Tr	07.54	54	26	-	4

CHAPMAN Kenneth Freeman Raymond
Grimsby, 16 November, 1948 (OL)

League Club	Source	Date Signed	Seasons Played	Apps	Subs	Gls
Grimsby T. (Am)	Louth U.	06.68	69	6	1	0

CHAPMAN Lee Roy
Lincoln, 5 December, 1959 Eu21-1/E'B' (F)

League Club	Source	Date Signed	Seasons Played	Apps	Subs	Gls
Stoke C.	Jnrs	06.78	79-81	95	4	34
Plymouth Arg.	L	12.78	78	3	1	0
Arsenal	Tr	08.82	82-83	15	8	4
Sunderland	Tr	12.83	83	14	1	3
Sheffield Wed.	Tr	08.84	84-87	147	2	63
Nottingham F.	Niort (Fr)	10.88	88-89	48	0	15
Leeds U.	Tr	01.90	89-92	133	4	62
Portsmouth	Tr	08.93	93	5	0	2
West Ham U.	Tr	09.93	93-94	33	7	8
Southend U.	L	01.95	94	1	0	1
Ipswich T.	Tr	01.95	94-95	11	11	1
Leeds U.	L	01.96	95	2	0	0
Swansea C. (N/C)	Tr	03.96	95	7	0	4

CHAPMAN Leslie
Oldham, 27 September, 1948 (M)

League Club	Source	Date Signed	Seasons Played	Apps	Subs	Gls
Oldham Ath.	Huddersfield T. (Am)	01.67	66-69	75	1	9
Huddersfield T.	Tr	09.69	69-74	120	14	8
Oldham Ath.	Tr	12.74	74-78	186	1	11
Stockport Co.	Tr	05.79	79	32	0	1
Bradford C.	Tr	02.80	79-82	137	2	3
Rochdale	Tr	06.83	83-84	87	1	0
Stockport Co.	Tr	07.85	85	38	0	3
Preston N. E.	Tr	07.86	86-87	50	3	1

CHAPMAN Neville
Cockfield (Dm), 15 September, 1941 Died 1993 (RB)

League Club	Source	Date Signed	Seasons Played	Apps	Subs	Gls
Middlesbrough	Jnrs	11.58	61-66	51	2	0
Darlington	Tr	09.67	67-68	31	1	0

CHAPMAN Paul Christopher
Cardiff, 28 September, 1951 (D)

League Club	Source	Date Signed	Seasons Played	Apps	Subs	Gls
Plymouth Arg.	App	10.69	69	2	1	0

CHAPMAN Philip Edward
Lichfield, 27 January, 1925 (CF)

League Club	Source	Date Signed	Seasons Played	Apps	Subs	Gls
Walsall	Cannock T.	09.48	48-50	63	-	36

CHAPMAN Reginald
Eccles, 14 June, 1928 (W)

League Club	Source	Date Signed	Seasons Played	Apps	Subs	Gls
Crewe Alex.	Hereford U.	05.50	50-51	21	-	1

CHAPMAN Reginald Frederick James
Shepherds Bush, 7 September, 1921 Died 1992 (CH)

League Club	Source	Date Signed	Seasons Played	Apps	Subs	Gls
Queens Park R.		08.44	46-52	97	-	2

CHAPMAN Robert (Sammy) Dennis
Aldridge, 18 August, 1946 (CD)

League Club	Source	Date Signed	Seasons Played	Apps	Subs	Gls
Nottingham F.	Jnrs	08.63	63-76	347	12	17
Notts Co.	Tr	08.77	77	42	0	0
Shrewsbury T.	Tr	07.78	78-79	36	1	6

CHAPMAN Rodger Anthony
Doncaster, 20 November, 1944 (G)

League Club	Source	Date Signed	Seasons Played	Apps	Subs	Gls
Rotherham U.		01.65	64	2	-	0
Doncaster Rov.	Tr	12.65	65	5	0	0

CHAPMAN Roy Clifford
Birmingham, 18 March, 1934 Died 1983 (IF)

League Club	Source	Date Signed	Seasons Played	Apps	Subs	Gls
Aston Villa	Kynoch Wks	02.52	53-57	19	-	8
Lincoln C.	Tr	11.57	57-61	105	-	45
Mansfield T.	Tr	08.61	61-64	136	-	78
Lincoln C.	Tr	01.65	64-66	69	1	31
Port Vale	Tr	08.67	67-68	76	0	35
Chester C.	Tr	06.69	69	9	0	3

CHAPMAN Samuel Edward Campbell
Belfast, 16 February, 1938 NI 'B' (IF)

League Club	Source	Date Signed	Seasons Played	Apps	Subs	Gls
Mansfield T.	Shamrock Rov.	10.56	56-57	50	-	25
Portsmouth	Tr	02.58	57-61	48	-	10
Mansfield T.	Tr	12.61	61-63	105	-	15

CHAPMAN Stuart
Morpeth, 6 May, 1951 (IF)

League Club	Source	Date Signed	Seasons Played	Apps	Subs	Gls
Port Vale	App	07.69	66-69	6	3	0

CHAPMAN Vernon William
Leicester, 9 May, 1921 (OR)

League Club	Source	Date Signed	Seasons Played	Apps	Subs	Gls
Leicester C.	Bath C.	01.42	46	1	-	0
Leyton Orient	Tr	07.47	47-48	31	-	7

CHAPMAN Vincent John
Newcastle, 5 December, 1967 (LB)

League Club	Source	Date Signed	Seasons Played	Apps	Subs	Gls
Huddersfield T.	Tow Law T.	01.88	87	4	2	0
Rochdale	Tr	07.89	89-90	23	1	1

CHAPPELL Larratt (Lol)
Ecclesfield, 19 December, 1930 Died 1988 (CF)

League Club	Source	Date Signed	Seasons Played	Apps	Subs	Gls
Barnsley	Jnrs	05.49	52-58	218	-	94
Doncaster Rov.	Tr	08.59	59-60	34	-	5

CHAPPELL Leslie Alan
Nottingham, 6 February, 1947 (M)

League Club	Source	Date Signed	Seasons Played	Apps	Subs	Gls
Rotherham U.	App	02.65	65-67	106	2	37
Blackburn Rov.	Tr	05.68	68	7	0	0
Reading	Tr	07.69	69-74	193	8	78
Doncaster Rov.	Tr	12.74	74-75	57	1	10
Swansea C.	Tr	07.76	76-77	65	2	5

CHAPPLE Philip Richard
Norwich, 26 November, 1966 (CD)

League Club	Source	Date Signed	Seasons Played	Apps	Subs	Gls
Norwich C.	YT	07.85				
Cambridge U.	Tr	03.88	87-92	183	4	19
Charlton Ath.	Tr	08.93	93-97	128	14	15

CHAPPLE Shaun Ronald
Swansea, 14 February, 1973 W Sch/Wu21-10/W 'B' (M)

League Club	Source	Date Signed	Seasons Played	Apps	Subs	Gls
Swansea C.	YT	07.91	91-97	72	35	9

CHARD Philip John
Corby, 16 October, 1960 (M/FB)

League Club	Source	Date Signed	Seasons Played	Apps	Subs	Gls
Peterborough U.	Corby T.	01.79	78-84	153	19	18
Northampton T.	Tr	08.85	85-87	113	2	27
Wolverhampton W.	Tr	03.88	87-89	26	8	5
Northampton T.	Tr	10.89	89-93	155	8	19

CHARLERY Kenneth Leroy
Stepney, 28 November, 1964 (F)

League Club	Source	Date Signed	Seasons Played	Apps	Subs	Gls
Maidstone U.	Fisher Ath.	03.89	89-90	41	18	11
Peterborough U.	Tr	03.91	90-92	45	6	19
Watford	Tr	10.92	92-93	45	3	13
Peterborough U.	Tr	12.93	93-94	70	0	24
Birmingham C.	Tr	07.95	95	8	9	4
Southend U.	L	01.96	95	2	1	0
Peterborough U.	Tr	02.96	95-96	55	1	12
Stockport Co.	Tr	03.97	96	8	2	0
Barnet	Tr	08.97	97	18	14	6

CHARLES Clive Michael
Bow, 3 October, 1951 EYth (FB)

League Club	Source	Date Signed	Seasons Played	Apps	Subs	Gls
West Ham U.	App	08.69	71-73	12	2	0
Cardiff C.	Tr	03.74	73-76	75	2	5

CHARLES Gary Andrew
Newham, 13 April, 1970 Eu21-4/E-2 (FB)

League Club	Source	Date Signed	Seasons Played	Apps	Subs	Gls
Nottingham F.	YT	11.87	88-92	54	2	1
Leicester C.	L	03.89	88	5	3	0
Derby Co.	Tr	07.93	93-94	61	0	3
Aston Villa	Tr	01.95	94-97	62	6	2

CHARLES Jeremy Melvyn
Swansea, 26 September, 1959 Wu21-2/W-19 (F)

League Club	Source	Date Signed	Seasons Played	Apps	Subs	Gls
Swansea C.	App	01.77	76-83	224	23	53
Queens Park R	Tr	11.83	83	10	2	5
Oxford U.	Tr	02.85	84-86	41	5	13

CHARLES John William
Canning Town, 20 September, 1944 E Yth (FB)

League Club	Source	Date Signed	Seasons Played	Apps	Subs	Gls
West Ham U.	App	05.62	62-69	117	1	1

CHARLES William **John**
Swansea, 27 December, 1931 W-38 (CF)

League Club	Source	Date Signed	Seasons Played	Apps	Subs	Gls
Leeds U.	Jnrs	01.49	48-56	297	-	150
Leeds U.	Juventus (It)	08.62	62	11	-	3
Cardiff C.	Roma (It)	08.63	63-65	65	1	19

CHARLES Lee
Hillingdon, 20 August, 1971 (F)

League Club	Source	Date Signed	Seasons Played	Apps	Subs	Gls
Queens Park R.	Chertsey T.	08.95	95-96	6	10	1
Barnet	L	09.95	95	2	3	0
Cambridge U.	L	02.98	97	7	0	1

CHARLES Melvyn
Swansea, 14 May, 1935 Wu23-1/W-31 (CF)

League Club	Source	Date Signed	Seasons Played	Apps	Subs	Gls
Swansea C.	Leeds U. (Am)	05.52	52-58	233	-	69
Arsenal	Tr	04.59	59-61	60	-	26
Cardiff C.	Tr	02.62	61-64	81	-	24
Port Vale	Portmadoc	02.67	66	7	0	0

CHARLES Robert John
Burlesdon, 26 December, 1941 E Sch/E Yth (G)

League Club	Source	Date Signed	Seasons Played	Apps	Subs	Gls
Southampton	Jnrs	04.59	59-60	26	-	0

CHARLES Stephen
Sheffield, 10 May, 1960 E Sch (M)

League Club	Source	Date Signed	Seasons Played	Apps	Subs	Gls
Sheffield U.	Sheffield Univ.	01.80	79-84	112	11	10
Wrexham	Tr	10.84	84-86	111	2	37
Mansfield T.	Tr	07.87	87-92	231	6	39
Scunthorpe U.	L	11.92	92	4	0	0
Scarborough	Tr	02.93	92-95	134	0	20

CHARLESWORTH Arnold
Sheffield, 6 July, 1930 (IF)

League Club	Source	Date Signed	Seasons Played	Apps	Subs	Gls
West Bromwich A.	Boston U.	03.52				
Rotherham U.	Tr	08.53				
York C.	Tr	04.54	54	1	-	0

CHARLESWORTH Stanley
Conisborough, 10 March, 1920 (CH)

League Club	Source	Date Signed	Seasons Played	Apps	Subs	Gls
Grimsby T.	Wath W.	12.37	38-46	2	-	0
Barnsley	Tr	12.46	46	7	-	0

CHARLESWORTH Terence
Scunthorpe, 13 July, 1933 (G)

League Club	Source	Date Signed	Seasons Played	Apps	Subs	Gls
Scunthorpe U.		06.52	52-56	19	-	0

CHARLTON Harold
Newcastle, 22 June, 1951 (M)

League Club	Source	Date Signed	Seasons Played	Apps	Subs	Gls
Middlesbrough	App	07.68	70-74	8	2	0
Hartlepool U.	L	01.76	75	2	1	0
Chesterfield	Tr	03.76	75-76	17	4	0
Darlington	Buxton	08.79	79-81	69	3	4

CHARLTON John (Jack)
Ashington, 8 May, 1935 EF Lge/E-35 (CH)

League Club	Source	Date Signed	Seasons Played	Apps	Subs	Gls
Leeds U.	Jnrs	05.52	52-72	628	0	70

CHARLTON John
(G)

League Club	Source	Date Signed	Seasons Played	Apps	Subs	Gls
Gateshead (Am)		08.49	49	1	-	0

CHARLTON Kevin
Atherstone, 12 September, 1954 E Semi Pro (G)

League Club	Source	Date Signed	Seasons Played	Apps	Subs	Gls
Wolverhampton W.	App	09.72				
Bournemouth	Tr	12.73	73-74	21	0	0
Hereford U.	Tr	06.75	75-77	52	0	0
Scarborough (N/C)	Telford U.	09.88	88	3	0	0

CHARLTON Robert
Ashington, 11 October, 1937 E Sch/E Yth/Eu23-6/EF Lge/E-106 (IF)

League Club	Source	Date Signed	Seasons Played	Apps	Subs	Gls
Manchester U.	Jnrs	10.54	56-72	604	2	199
Preston N. E.	Tr	05.74	74	38	0	8

CHARLTON Simon Thomas
Huddersfield, 25 October, 1971 E Yth (LB)

League Club	Source	Date Signed	Seasons Played	Apps	Subs	Gls
Huddersfield T.	YT	07.89	89-92	121	3	1
Southampton	Tr	06.93	93-97	104	10	2
Birmingham C.	Tr	12.97	97	23	1	0

CHARLTON Stanley
Exeter, 28 June, 1929 E Amat (FB)

League Club	Source	Date Signed	Seasons Played	Apps	Subs	Gls
Leyton Orient	Bromley	11.52	52-55	151	-	1
Arsenal	Tr	11.55	55-58	99	-	0
Leyton Orient	Tr	12.58	58-64	216	-	1

CHARLTON Wilfred Sydney
Blyth, 12 September, 1933 (WH)

League Club	Source	Date Signed	Seasons Played	Apps	Subs	Gls
Huddersfield T.	Jnrs	11.50				
Southport	Tr	07.54	54-56	109	-	8
Tranmere Rov.	Tr	06.57	57-60	92	0	4

CHARNLEY James **Charles (Chic)**
Glasgow, 11 June, 1963 (M)

League Club	Source	Date Signed	Seasons Played	Apps	Subs	Gls
Bolton W. (L)	St Mirren	03.92	91	3	0	0

CHARNLEY Derek Lawrence
Doncaster, 7 May, 1954 (F)

League Club	Source	Date Signed	Seasons Played	Apps	Subs	Gls
Scunthorpe U.		02.73	72-75	28	10	3

CHARNLEY Raymond Ogden
Lancaster, 29 May, 1935 E-1 (CF)

League Club	Source	Date Signed	Seasons Played	Apps	Subs	Gls
Blackpool	Morecambe	05.57	57-67	363	0	193
Preston N. E.	Tr	12.67	67	23	0	4
Wrexham	Tr	07.68	68	19	1	5
Bradford P. A.	Tr	01.69	68-69	59	0	15

CHARNOCK Philip Anthony
Southport, 14 February, 1975 (M)

League Club	Source	Date Signed	Seasons Played	Apps	Subs	Gls
Liverpool	YT	03.93				
Blackpool	L	02.96	95	0	4	0
Crewe Alex.	Tr	09.96	96-97	57	8	4

CHARTER Raymond
Ashton-u-Lyne, 10 January, 1950 (FB/M)

League Club	Source	Date Signed	Seasons Played	Apps	Subs	Gls
Blackburn Rov.	App	01.68	69-70	13	5	0
Stockport Co.	Tr	07.71	71-73	87	4	2

CHARVET Laurent Jean
Beziers, France, 8 May, 1973 (RWB)

League Club	Source	Date Signed	Seasons Played	Apps	Subs	Gls
Chelsea (L)	Cannes (Fr)	01.98	97	7	4	2

CHASE Charles Thomas
Steyning, 31 January, 1924 (WH)

League Club	Source	Date Signed	Seasons Played	Apps	Subs	Gls
Watford	Brighton & H.A. (Am)	09.46	46-47	16	-	1
Crystal Palace	Tr	07.48	48-49	55	-	2

CHATHAM Alexander Whyte
Glasgow, 7 July, 1936 (G)

League Club	Source	Date Signed	Seasons Played	Apps	Subs	Gls
Barrow		12.58	58	1	-	0

CHATHAM Raymond Harold
Wolverhampton, 20 July, 1924 (CH)

League Club	Source	Date Signed	Seasons Played	Apps	Subs	Gls
Wolverhampton W.	Jnrs	06.45	46-53	76	-	0
Notts Co.	Tr	01.54	53-58	127	-	4

CHATTERLEY Lawson (Lew) Colin
Birmingham, 15 February, 1945 E Yth (M)

League Club	Source	Date Signed	Seasons Played	Apps	Subs	Gls
Aston Villa	App	02.62	62-70	149	4	26
Doncaster Rov.	L	03.71	70	9	0	0
Northampton T.	Tr	09.71	71	23	0	2
Grimsby T.	Tr	02.72	71-73	72	1	16
Southampton	Tr	03.74	73-74	7	2	0
Torquay U.	Tr	02.75	74-76	55	2	10

CHATTERTON Nicholas John
Norwood, 18 May, 1954 (M)

League Club	Source	Date Signed	Seasons Played	Apps	Subs	Gls
Crystal Palace	Jnrs	03.72	73-78	142	9	31
Millwall	Tr	11.78	78-85	258	6	56
Colchester U.	Tr	09.86	86-88	47	2	8

CHAYTOR Kenneth
Trimdon (Dm), 18 November, 1937 (IF)

League Club	Source	Date Signed	Seasons Played	Apps	Subs	Gls
Oldham Ath.	Jnrs	11.54	54-59	77	-	20

CHEADLE Thomas
Stoke, 8 April, 1919 Died 1993 (CH)

League Club	Source	Date Signed	Seasons Played	Apps	Subs	Gls
Port Vale		05.46	46-56	333	-	14
Crewe Alex.	Tr	07.57	57-58	37	-	0

CHEESEBROUGH Albert
Burnley, 17 January, 1935 Eu23-1 (IF)

League Club	Source	Date Signed	Seasons Played	Apps	Subs	Gls
Burnley	Jnrs	01.52	51-58	142	-	35
Leicester C.	Tr	06.59	59-62	122	-	40
Port Vale	Tr	07.63	63-64	57	-	13
Mansfield T.	Tr	07.65	65-66	24	0	0

CHEESEWRIGHT John Anthony
Romford, 12 January, 1973 (G)

League Club	Source	Date Signed	Seasons Played	Apps	Subs	Gls
Southend U. (N/C)	Tottenham H. (YT)	03.91				
Birmingham C. (N/C)	Tr	11.91	91	1	0	0
Colchester U.	Braintree T.	01.94	93-94	40	0	0
Wycombe W.	Hong Kong	03.96	96	18	0	0

CHEESLEY Paul Martyn
Bristol, 20 October, 1953 (F)

League Club	Source	Date Signed	Seasons Played	Apps	Subs	Gls
Norwich C.	App	10.71	72-73	10	3	1
Bristol C.	Tr	12.73	73-76	61	3	20

CHEETHAM Hugh David
Manchester, 3 February, 1958 (M)

League Club	Source	Date Signed	Seasons Played	Apps	Subs	Gls
Crewe Alex.	App	01.76	75-78	90	6	0
Reading	Tr	07.79	79-80	10	2	0

CHEETHAM Michael Martin
Netherlands, 30 June, 1967 (M)

League Club	Source	Date Signed	Seasons Played	Apps	Subs	Gls
Ipswich T.	Basingstoke T.	10.88	88-89	1	3	0
Cambridge U.	Tr	10.89	89-93	123	9	22
Chesterfield	Tr	07.94	94	5	0	0
Colchester U.	Tr	03.95	94-95	33	4	3

CHEETHAM Roy Alexander John
Eccles, 21 December, 1939 (D/M)

League Club	Source	Date Signed	Seasons Played	Apps	Subs	Gls
Manchester C.	Jnrs	12.56	57-67	127	5	4
Charlton Ath.	Detroit (USA)	10.68				
Chester C.	Tr	12.68	68-71	122	2	8

CHEETHAM Thomas
Liverpool, 8 December, 1950 (F)

League Club	Source	Date Signed	Seasons Played	Apps	Subs	Gls
Southport	Cambridge Park	12.69	69-70	24	2	4

CHEETHAM Thomas Miles
Newcastle, 11 October, 1910 Died 1993 (CF)

League Club	Source	Date Signed	Seasons Played	Apps	Subs	Gls
Queens Park R		08.35	36-38	116	-	80
Brentford	Tr	02.39	38	17	-	8
Lincoln C.	Tr	10.45	46-47	47	-	29

CHENERY Benjamin Roger
Ipswich, 28 January, 1977 (D)

League Club	Source	Date Signed	Seasons Played	Apps	Subs	Gls
Luton T.	YT	03.95	95-96	2	0	0
Cambridge U.	Tr	07.97	97	36	0	2

CHENEY Dennis
Coalville, 30 June, 1924 (IF)

League Club	Source	Date Signed	Seasons Played	Apps	Subs	Gls
Leicester C.	Jnrs	11.41	47-48	2	-	0
Watford	L	02.48	47	18	-	5
Bournemouth	Tr	10.48	48-53	157	-	47
Aldershot	Tr	06.54	54-55	53	-	19

CHENHALL John Colin
Bristol, 23 July, 1927 (FB)

League Club	Source	Date Signed	Seasons Played	Apps	Subs	Gls
Arsenal	Maidenhead U.	11.45	51-52	16	-	0
Fulham	Tr	07.53	53-57	91	-	0

CHEREDNIK Alexei
USSR, 12 December, 1960 USSR Int (RB)

League Club	Source	Date Signed	Seasons Played	Apps	Subs	Gls
Southampton	Dnepr (USSR)	02.90	89-90	19	4	0

CHERRY Rex Aubrey
Penistone, 11 November, 1933 (CF)

League Club	Source	Date Signed	Seasons Played	Apps	Subs	Gls
Gillingham		03.53	52-53	10	-	4

CHERRY Steven Reginald
Nottingham, 5 August, 1960 EYth (G)

League Club	Source	Date Signed	Seasons Played	Apps	Subs	Gls
Derby Co.	App	03.78	79-83	77	0	0
Port Vale	L	11.80	80	4	0	0
Walsall	Tr	08.84	84-85	71	0	0
Plymouth Arg.	Tr	10.86	86-88	73	0	0
Chesterfield	L	12.88	88	10	0	0
Notts Co.	Tr	02.89	88-94	266	0	0
Watford	Tr	07.95	95	4	0	0
Plymouth Arg.	Tr	02.96	95	16	0	0
Rotherham U.	Tr	07.96	96	20	0	0

CHERRY Trevor John
Huddersfield, 23 February, 1948 EF Lge/E-27 (D)

League Club	Source	Date Signed	Seasons Played	Apps	Subs	Gls
Huddersfield T.	Jnrs	07.65	66-71	185	3	12
Leeds U.	Tr	06.72	72-82	394	6	24
Bradford C.	Tr	12.82	82-84	92	0	0

CHESSELL Samuel
Shirebrook, 9 July, 1921 Died 1996 (FB)

League Club	Source	Date Signed	Seasons Played	Apps	Subs	Gls
Mansfield T.	Welbeck Colly	09.45	46-53	256	-	7

CHESTERS Colin Wayne
Crewe, 21 November, 1959 (F)

League Club	Source	Date Signed	Seasons Played	Apps	Subs	Gls
Derby Co.	App	11.77	77-78	6	3	1
Crewe Alex.	Tr	09.79	79-81	52	9	6

CHETTLE Stephen
Nottingham, 27 September, 1968 Eu21-12 (CD)

League Club	Source	Date Signed	Seasons Played	Apps	Subs	Gls
Nottingham F.	App	08.86	87-97	356	14	8

CHEUNG Chi-Doy
Hong Kong, 30 July, 1941 (F)

League Club	Source	Date Signed	Seasons Played	Apps	Subs	Gls
Blackpool	Tung Wah (HK)	10.60	60-61	2	-	1

CHEW John (Jackie)
Blackburn, 13 May, 1920 (OR)

League Club	Source	Date Signed	Seasons Played	Apps	Subs	Gls
Burnley	Blackburn Rov. (Am)	05.45	46-53	225	-	39
Bradford C.	Tr	06.54	54	36	-	4

CHEW John
Longton, 25 November, 1915 Died 1984 (FB)

League Club	Source	Date Signed	Seasons Played	Apps	Subs	Gls
Luton T.		11.42				
Port Vale	Tr	03.46	46	9	-	0

CHIEDOZIE John Okay
Nigeria, 18 April, 1960 Nigerian Int (W)

League Club	Source	Date Signed	Seasons Played	Apps	Subs	Gls
Leyton Orient	App	04.77	76-80	131	14	20
Notts Co.	Tr	08.81	81-83	110	1	16
Tottenham H.	Tr	08.84	84-86	45	8	12
Derby Co.	Tr	08.88	88	2	0	0
Notts Co. (N/C)	Tr	01.90	89	0	1	0
Chesterfield (N/C)	Tr	03.90	89	5	2	0

CHILCOTT Kenneth
Rhondda, 17 March, 1920 (OR)

League Club	Source	Date Signed	Seasons Played	Apps	Subs	Gls
Bristol C.	Eastville U.	10.37	37-48	46	-	6

CHILDS Albert (Bert) Robert
Liverpool, 25 September, 1930 E Amat (FB)

League Club	Source	Date Signed	Seasons Played	Apps	Subs	Gls
Liverpool (Am)	Northern Nomads	09.53	53	2	-	0

CHILDS Gary Paul Colin
Birmingham, 19 April, 1964 E Yth (W)

League Club	Source	Date Signed	Seasons Played	Apps	Subs	Gls
West Bromwich A.	App	02.82	81-83	2	1	0
Walsall	Tr	10.83	83-86	120	11	17
Birmingham C.	Tr	07.87	87-88	39	16	2
Grimsby T.	Tr	07.89	89-96	204	29	26

CHILTON Allenby
Sunderland, 16 September, 1918 Died 1996 E-2 (CH)

League Club	Source	Date Signed	Seasons Played	Apps	Subs	Gls
Manchester U.	Seaham Colly	11.38	46-54	352	-	3
Grimsby T.	Tr	03.55	54-56	63	-	0

CHILTON Anthony Julian Thomas
Cockermouth, 7 September, 1965 (FB)

League Club	Source	Date Signed	Seasons Played	Apps	Subs	Gls
Sunderland	App	09.83				
Burnley (N/C)	Tr	02.85	84	1	0	0
Hartlepool U. (N/C)	Tr	10.85	85	3	0	0

CHILTON Christopher Roy
Sproatley, 25 June, 1943 (CF)

League Club	Source	Date Signed	Seasons Played	Apps	Subs	Gls
Hull C.	Jnrs	07.60	60-71	415	0	193
Coventry C.	Tr	09.71	71	26	1	3

CHILTON Frederick
Washington, 10 July, 1935 (FB)

League Club	Source	Date Signed	Seasons Played	Apps	Subs	Gls
Sunderland	Usworth Colly	05.53	56-57	3	-	0

CHILVERS Geoffrey Thomas
Epsom, 31 January, 1925 E Sch (WH)

League Club	Source	Date Signed	Seasons Played	Apps	Subs	Gls
Crystal Palace	Sutton U.	03.45	48-53	118	-	1

CHILVERS Gordon Malcolm
Norwich, 15 November, 1933 (G)

League Club	Source	Date Signed	Seasons Played	Apps	Subs	Gls
Walsall	Fordhouses B.C.	04.52	51-57	123	-	0

CHINAGLIA Giorgio
Italy, 24 January, 1947 Italian Int (CF)

League Club	Source	Date Signed	Seasons Played	Apps	Subs	Gls
Swansea C.	App	04.65	64-65	4	1	1

CHINE Athumani Khamiss
Tanzania, 12 March, 1967 (M)

League Club	Source	Date Signed	Seasons Played	Apps	Subs	Gls
Walsall (N/C)		03.92	91	4	1	0

CHIPPENDALE Brian Albert
Bradford, 29 October, 1964 (M)

League Club	Source	Date Signed	Seasons Played	Apps	Subs	Gls
York C.	Bradford C. (App)	10.83	83-84	2	6	0
Halifax T.	L	11.84	84	1	1	0
Burnley (N/C)	Tr	08.85	85	6	2	0
Preston N. E. (N/C)	Tr	10.85	85	5	1	0

CHISHOLM Gordon William
Glasgow, 8 April, 1960 (CD)

League Club	Source	Date Signed	Seasons Played	Apps	Subs	Gls
Sunderland	App	04.78	78-85	192	5	10

CHISHOLM Jack Richardson
Edmonton, 9 October, 1924 Died 1977 (CH)

League Club	Source	Date Signed	Seasons Played	Apps	Subs	Gls
Tottenham H.	Jnrs	10.42	47	2	-	0
Brentford	Tr	10.47	47-48	49	-	1
Sheffield U.	Tr	03.49	48-49	21	-	1
Plymouth Arg.	Tr	12.49	49-53	175	-	2

CHISHOLM Kenneth McTaggart
Glasgow, 12 April, 1925 Died 1990 (IF)

League Club	Source	Date Signed	Seasons Played	Apps	Subs	Gls
Leeds U.	Partick Thistle	01.48	47-48	40	-	17
Leicester C.	Tr	01.49	48-49	42	-	17
Coventry C.	Tr	03.50	49-51	68	-	34

League Club	Source	Date Signed	Seasons Played	Career Record Apps	Subs	Gls
Cardiff C.	Tr	03.52	51-53	63	-	13
Sunderland	Tr	01.54	53-55	78	-	33
Workington	Tr	08.56	56-57	39	-	15
CHISHOLM Wilfred						
Hebburn, 23 May, 1921						(G)
Grimsby T.	Newcastle U. (Am)	09.46	46-50	92	-	0
CHISNALL Joseph **Philip**						
Manchester, 27 October, 1942 E Sch/Eu23-1						(M)
Manchester U.	Jnrs	11.59	61-63	35	-	8
Liverpool	Tr	04.64	64	6	-	1
Southend U.	Tr	08.67	67-70	137	5	28
Stockport Co.	Tr	09.71	71	30	0	2
CHISWICK Peter John Henry						
Romford, 19 September, 1929 Died 1962						(G)
West Ham U.	Jnrs	07.47	53-54	19	-	0
Gillingham	Tr	07.56	56	14	-	0
CHITTY Wilfred Sidney						
Walton-on-Thames, 10 July, 1912 Died 1997						(OL)
Chelsea	Woking	03.30	31-37	45	-	16
Plymouth Arg.	Tr	12.38	38	3	-	1
Reading	Tr	08.39	46-47	23	-	7
CHIVERS Gary Paul Stephen						
Stockwell, 15 May, 1960						(D)
Chelsea	App	07.78	78-82	128	5	4
Swansea C.	Tr	08.83	83	10	0	0
Queens Park R	Tr	02.84	84-86	58	2	0
Watford	Tr	09.87	87	14	0	0
Brighton & H.A.	Tr	03.88	87-92	215	2	14
Bournemouth (N/C)	Lyn (Nor)	11.93	93-94	29	2	2
CHIVERS Martin Harcourt						
Southampton, 27 April, 1945 Eu23-17/EF Lge/E-24						(F)
Southampton	Jnrs	09.62	62-67	174	1	97
Tottenham H.	Tr	01.68	67-75	268	10	118
Norwich C.	Servette (Swi)	07.78	78	11	0	4
Brighton & H. A.	Tr	03.79	78-79	4	1	1
CHMILOWSKY Roman						
Bradford, 19 April, 1959						(G)
Halifax T. (Am)	Jnrs	04.77	76	1	0	0
CHOLERTON William						
Derby, 1 January, 1949						(FB)
Derby Co.	App	12.66	66	1	0	0
CHOULES Leonard George						
Orpington, 29 January, 1932						(CH)
Crystal Palace	Sutton U.	05.51	52-61	258	-	2
CHRISTENSEN Thomas Anton						
Denmark, 20 July, 1961						(W)
Leicester C. (N/C)	Elche (Sp)	11.85	85	1	1	0
Portsmouth (N/C)	Tr	11.85	85	3	0	2
CHRISTIE David						
Salford, 26 February, 1973						(W)
Preston N.E.	YT	07.91	91-92	1	3	0
Halifax T.	Tr	01.93	92	6	3	0
CHRISTIE Derrick Hugh Michael						
Hackney, 15 March, 1957						(W)
Northampton T.	App	03.75	73-78	116	22	18
Cambridge U.	Tr	11.78	78-83	132	6	19
Reading	Tr	07.84	84	8	6	1
Cardiff C.	Tr	10.85	85	18	1	2
Peterborough U.	Tr	08.86	86	6	2	0
CHRISTIE Frank						
Perth, 17 December, 1927 Died 1996						(WH)
Liverpool	Scone Jnrs	03.49	49	4	-	0
CHRISTIE Iyseden						
Coventry, 14 November, 1976						(F)
Coventry C.	YT	05.95	95	0	1	0
Bournemouth	L	11.96	96	3	1	0
Mansfield T.	L	02.97	96	8	0	0
Mansfield T.	Tr	06.97	97	26	13	10
CHRISTIE John Alexander						
Fraserburgh, 26 September, 1929						(G)
Southampton	Ayr U.	01.51	50-58	197	-	0
Walsall	Tr	06.59	59-62	102	-	0

League Club	Source	Date Signed	Seasons Played	Career Record Apps	Subs	Gls
CHRISTIE Trevor John						
Newcastle, 28 February, 1959						(F)
Leicester C.	App	12.76	77-78	28	3	8
Notts Co.	Tr	06.79	79-83	158	29	63
Nottingham F.	Tr	07.84	84	14	0	5
Derby Co.	Tr	02.85	84-85	65	0	22
Manchester C.	Tr	08.86	86	9	0	3
Walsall	Tr	10.86	86-88	91	8	22
Mansfield T.	Tr	03.89	88-90	88	4	24
CHRISTOPHER Paul Anthony						
Poole, 19 June, 1954						(F)
Bournemouth	App	11.71				
Mansfield T.	Tr	07.73	73	7	1	1
CHUNG Cyril (Sammy)						
Abingdon, 16 July, 1932						(WH)
Reading	Headington U.	11.51	53-54	22	-	12
Norwich C.	Tr	01.55	54-56	47	-	9
Watford	Tr	06.57	57-64	220	-	22
CHURCH Garry						
Pontefract, 20 September, 1944						(HB)
Bradford P. A.	Great Preston Jnrs	07.62	63	4		0
CHURCH John						
Lowestoft, 17 September, 1919						(OL)
Norwich C.	Lowestoft	09.36	37-49	110	-	16
Colchester U.	Tr	07.50	50-53	118	-	20
CHURCHILL Trevor						
Barnsley, 20 November, 1923						(G)
Reading	Sheffield U. (Am)	09.46	46	10	-	0
Leicester C.	Tr	08.47				
Rochdale	Tr	01.49	48-52	110	-	0
Swindon T.	Tr	05.53	53	11	-	0
CHURCHOUSE Gary						
Wembley, 1 February, 1957						(M)
Charlton Ath.	Windsor & Eton	03.79	78-79	13	5	0
CHURMS Dennis John						
Rotherham, 8 May, 1931						(IF)
Rotherham U.	Spurley Hey	04.50	53-55	15	-	0
Coventry C.	Tr	06.56	56	10	-	2
Exeter C.	Tr	03.57	56-57	44	-	8
CINI Joseph						
Malta Maltese Int						(OR)
Queens Park R. (Am)	Floriana (Malta)	08.59	59	7	-	1
CIRCUIT Steven						
Sheffield, 11 April, 1972						(M)
Sheffield U.	YT	07.90				
Halifax T. (N/C)	Stafford R.	03.93	92	0	1	0
CITRON Gerald Conrad						
Manchester, 8 April, 1935						(OL)
Chester C. (Am)	Corinthian Casuals	10.59	59	2	-	0
CLACK Frank Edward						
Witney, 30 March, 1912 Died 1995						(G)
Birmingham C.	Witney T.	05.33	33-38	60	-	0
Brentford	Tr	07.39				
Bristol C.	Tr	05.47	46-48	67	-	0
CLAESEN Nicolas Pieter Josef						
Belgium, 1 October, 1962 Belgian Int						(F)
Tottenham H.	Standard Liége (Bel)	10.86	86-87	37	13	18
CLAMP Edward						
Burton, 13 November, 1922 Died 1990						(G)
Derby Co.	Gresley Rov.	11.47	48	1	-	0
Oldham Ath.	Tr	07.49	49	3	-	0
CLAMP Harold **Edwin**						
Coalville, 14 September, 1934 Died 1995 E Sch/EF Lge/E-4						(WH)
Wolverhampton W.	Jnrs	04.52	53-61	214	-	23
Arsenal	Tr	11.61	61-62	22	-	1
Stoke C.	Tr	09.62	62-63	50	-	2
Peterborough U.	Tr	10.64	64	8	-	0
CLAMP Martin						
Coventry, 31 January, 1948						(G)
Coventry C.	Jnrs	01.66				
Plymouth Arg.	Tr	07.68	69	8	0	0

League Club	Source	Date Signed	Seasons Played	Apps	Subs	Gls
CLANCY John Patrick						
Ealing, 5 July, 1949						(W)
Bristol C.	Tottenham H. (App)	03.67				
Bradford P. A.	Tr	07.67	67-68	52	4	2
CLAPHAM Graham Leslie						
Lincoln, 23 September, 1947						(M)
Newcastle U.	App	09.65				
Shrewsbury T.	Tr	08.67	67-71	74	16	5
Chester C.	Tr	01.72	71-72	37	4	7
CLAPHAM James Richard						
Lincoln, 7 December, 1975						(LB)
Tottenham H.	YT	07.94	96	0	1	0
Leyton Orient	L	01.97	96	6	0	0
Bristol Rov.	L	03.97	96	4	1	0
Ipswich T.	Tr	01.98	97	22	0	0
CLAPHAM Keith						
Fareham, 9 September, 1952						(CD)
Bournemouth	App	09.70				
Exeter C.	Tr	07.72	72-76	79	12	0
CLAPTON Daniel Robert						
Stepney, 22 July, 1934 Died 1986 EF Lge/E-1						(OR)
Arsenal	Leytonstone	08.53	54-61	207	-	25
Luton T.	Tr	09.62	62	10	-	0
CLAPTON Dennis Patrick						
Hackney, 12 October, 1939 E Yth						(CF)
Arsenal	Jnrs	08.58	59-60	4	-	0
Northampton T.	Tr	08.61	61	1	-	0
CLARE Daryl Adam						
Jersey, 1 August, 1978 IRu21-1						(M)
Grimsby T.	YT	12.95	95-97	8	15	3
CLARE James Edward						
Islington, 6 November, 1959						(F)
Chelsea	App	08.78	80	0	1	0
Charlton Ath	Tr	08.81				
CLARIDGE Stephen Edward						
Portsmouth, 10 April, 1966						(F)
Bournemouth	Fareham T.	09.84	84-85	3	4	1
Crystal Palace	Weymouth	08.88				
Aldershot	Tr	10.88	88-89	58	4	19
Cambridge U.	Tr	02.90	89-91	56	23	28
Luton T.	Tr	07.92	92	15	1	2
Cambridge U.	Tr	11.92	92-93	53	0	18
Birmingham C.	Tr	01.94	93-95	86	2	35
Leicester C.	Tr	03.96	95-97	53	10	17
Portsmouth	L	01.98	97	10	0	2
Wolverhampton W.	Tr	03.98	97	4	1	0
CLARK Albert Henry						
Ashington, 24 July, 1921 Died 1977						(WH)
Newcastle U.	North Shields	01.48	48	1	-	0
CLARK Alexander (Sandy)						
Lanark, 28 October, 1956						(F)
West Ham U.	Airdrieonians	06.82	82	26	0	7
CLARK Anthony John						
Lambeth, 7 April, 1977						(F)
Wycombe W.	Jnrs	07.95	94-95	2	2	0
CLARK Benjamin						
North Shields, 14 April, 1933						(WH)
Sunderland	North Shields	08.50				
Derby Co.	Yeovil T.	05.54	54-57	16	-	0
Barrow	Tr	02.59	58-63	202	-	7
CLARK Brian Donald						
Bristol, 13 January, 1943						(F)
Bristol C.	Jnrs	03.60	60-66	195	0	83
Huddersfield T.	Tr	10.66	66-67	28	4	11
Cardiff C.	Tr	02.68	67-72	178	4	75
Bournemouth	Tr	10.72	72-73	28	2	12
Millwall	Tr	09.73	73-74	66	5	17
Cardiff C.	Tr	05.75	75	19	2	1
Newport Co.	Tr	08.76	76-78	72	8	18
CLARK Clive						
Leeds, 19 December, 1940 Eu23-1						(OL)
Leeds U.	Jnrs	01.58				
Queens Park R.	Tr	08.58	58-60	58	-	7
West Bromwich A.	Tr	01.61	60-68	300	1	80
Queens Park R.	Tr	06.69	69	7	1	1
Preston N. E.	Tr	01.70	69-72	71	1	9
Southport	Tr	07.73	73	7	1	1
CLARK David George						
Leyton, 19 January, 1938						(CH)
Leyton Orient	Leyton	12.61	61-62	4	-	0
CLARK Dean Wayne						
Hillingdon, 31 March, 1980						(M)
Brentford	YT	10.97	97	0	4	0
CLARK Derek						
Newcastle, 10 August, 1931						(IR)
Lincoln C.	Durham C.	12.51	51	4	-	1
CLARK Derrick Bryan						
Leyburn, 27 December, 1935						(F)
Darlington		03.55	54-55	5	-	1
CLARK Frederick **Donald**						
Bristol, 25 October, 1917						(CF)
Bristol C.	North Bristol O.B.	05.37	38-50	117	-	67
CLARK Frank Albert						
Rowlands Gill, 9 September, 1943 E Yth/E Amat/EF Lge						(LB)
Newcastle U.	Crook T.	11.62	63-74	388	1	0
Nottingham F.	Tr	07.75	75-78	116	1	1
CLARK Graham John						
Aberdeen, 20 January, 1961 S Sch						(M)
Sheffield U.	App	10.78				
Darlington	Tr	08.79	79	6	0	0
CLARK Harold						
Cloughdene, 30 March, 1913						(OL)
Accrington St.	Manchester C. (Am)	12.44				
Gateshead	Tr	06.46	46	23	-	1
CLARK Harold Maurice						
Newcastle, 29 December, 1932						(IF)
Darlington		07.51	50-56	142	-	20
Sheffield Wed.	Tr	10.57	57	1	-	0
Hartlepool U.	Tr	08.58	58-60	118	-	43
CLARK Henry (Harry)						
Sunderland, 11 September, 1934						(IF)
Sunderland	St Benets	05.56	56	6	-	0
CLARK Howard William						
Coventry, 19 September, 1968						(M/CD)
Coventry C.	App	09.86	88-90	9	11	1
Darlington	L	09.91	91	5	0	0
Shrewsbury T.	Tr	12.91	91-92	51	5	0
Hereford U.	Tr	07.93	93-94	52	3	7
CLARK Ian David						
Stockton, 23 October, 1974						(W)
Doncaster Rov.	Stockton	08.95	95-97	23	22	3
Hartlepool U.	Tr	10.97	97	19	5	7
CLARK James Donald						
Dornoch, 1 May, 1923 Died 1994						(FB)
Exeter C.	Aberdeen	08.48	48-52	95	-	5
Bradford C.	L	09.52	52	6	-	0
CLARK John Brown						
Edinburgh, 22 September, 1964 S Yth						(CD)
Stoke C.	Dundee U.	02.94	93-94	17	0	0
CLARK Jonathan						
Swansea, 12 November, 1958 W Sch/Wu21-2						(M)
Manchester U.	App	11.75	76	0	1	0
Derby Co.	Tr	09.78	78-80	48	5	3
Preston N. E.	Tr	08.81	81-86	107	3	10
Bury	Tr	12.86	86	13	1	1
Carlisle U.	Tr	08.87	87-88	48	1	2
CLARK Joseph Thomas Henry						
Bermondsey, 2 March, 1920						(FB)
Leyton Orient	Gravesend & Nft	02.46	46	18	-	0
CLARK Lee Robert						
Wallsend, 27 October, 1972 E Sch/E Yth/Eu21-11						(M)
Newcastle U.	YT	12.89	90-96	153	42	23
Sunderland	Tr	06.97	97	46	0	13
CLARK Martin Alan						
Accrington, 12 September, 1970						(CD)
Rotherham U.	Southport	06.97	97	28	0	0

CLARK Martin John
Motherwell, 13 October, 1968 (M)

League Club	Source	Date Signed	Seasons Played	Apps	Subs	Gls
Nottingham F.	Clyde	02.89				
Mansfield T.	L	03.90	89	14	0	1
Mansfield T.	Tr	08.90	90-91	31	2	0

CLARK Neville
Gateshead, 9 October, 1930 (RH)

League Club	Source	Date Signed	Seasons Played	Apps	Subs	Gls
Grimsby T.	Chilton Colly	12.48				
Sunderland		12.49				
Hartlepool U.	Tr	08.53	53	2	-	0

CLARK Paul Peterson
Benfleet, 14 September, 1958 E Sch/E Yth (CD)

League Club	Source	Date Signed	Seasons Played	Apps	Subs	Gls
Southend U.	App	07.76	76-77	29	4	1
Brighton & H. A.	Tr	11.77	77-80	69	10	9
Reading	L	10.81	81	2	0	0
Southend U.	Tr	08.82	82-90	269	7	3
Gillingham	Tr	07.91	91-93	87	3	1
Cambridge U. (N/C)	Chelmsford C.	10.95	95	2	0	0

CLARK Joseph Peter
Doncaster, 22 January, 1938 (WH)

League Club	Source	Date Signed	Seasons Played	Apps	Subs	Gls
Wolverhampton W.	Jnrs	03.55				
Doncaster Rov.	Tr	07.59	59	14	-	8
Mansfield T.	Tr	06.60	60	2	-	0
Stockport Co.	Hereford U.	08.65	65	21	0	2
Crewe Alex.	Tr	07.66	66	2	0	0

CLARK Ronald
Airdrie, 21 May, 1932 (OL)

League Club	Source	Date Signed	Seasons Played	Apps	Subs	Gls
Gillingham	Kilmarnock	07.56	56-57	33	-	6
Oldham Ath.	Tr	06.58	58	4	-	0

CLARK Simon
Boston, 12 March, 1967 (D)

League Club	Source	Date Signed	Seasons Played	Apps	Subs	Gls
Peterborough U.	Stevenage Borough	03.94	93-96	102	5	3
Leyton Orient	Tr	06.97	97	39	0	5

CLARK Steven
Baldock, 20 September, 1964 (FB)

League Club	Source	Date Signed	Seasons Played	Apps	Subs	Gls
Cambridge U.	App	09.82	83-85	63	3	0

CLARK Thomas Henry
Luton, 5 October, 1924 Died 1981 (IF)

League Club	Source	Date Signed	Seasons Played	Apps	Subs	Gls
Aston Villa	Vauxhall Motors	04.47				
Walsall	Tr	05.48	48	9	-	2

CLARK William
Larkhall, 25 February, 1932 (CF)

League Club	Source	Date Signed	Seasons Played	Apps	Subs	Gls
Queens Park R.	Petershill	02.54	53-55	95	-	32

CLARK William Raymond
Christchurch, 19 May, 1967 (CD)

League Club	Source	Date Signed	Seasons Played	Apps	Subs	Gls
Bournemouth	YT	09.84	84-87	4	0	0
Bristol Rov.	Tr	10.87	87-96	235	13	14
Exeter C.	Tr	11.97	97	31	0	3

CLARKE Adrian James
Cambridge, 28 September, 1974 E Sch/E Yth (M)

League Club	Source	Date Signed	Seasons Played	Apps	Subs	Gls
Arsenal	YT	07.93	94-95	4	3	0
Rotherham U.	L	12.96	96	1	1	0
Southend U.	Tr	03.97	96-97	49	3	5

CLARKE Alan
Houghton Regis, 10 April, 1942 (OR)

League Club	Source	Date Signed	Seasons Played	Apps	Subs	Gls
Luton T.	Jnrs	10.61	61-62	9	-	0

CLARKE Alfred
Ashton-u-Lyne, 23 August, 1926 (CF)

League Club	Source	Date Signed	Seasons Played	Apps	Subs	Gls
Crewe Alex.	Stalybridge Celtic	02.48	47-48	22	-	12
Burnley	Tr	12.48	48-51	24	-	6
Oldham Ath.	Tr	08.52	52-53	43	-	12
Halifax T.	Tr	03.54	53-55	71	-	22

CLARKE Allan John
Willenhall, 31 July, 1946 Eu23-6/E-19 (F)

League Club	Source	Date Signed	Seasons Played	Apps	Subs	Gls
Walsall	App	08.63	63-65	72	0	41
Fulham	Tr	03.66	65-67	85	1	45
Leicester C.	Tr	06.68	68	36	0	12
Leeds U.	Tr	07.69	69-77	270	3	110
Barnsley	Tr	06.78	78-79	47	0	15

CLARKE Allen Frederick
Crayford, 2 December, 1952 (G)

League Club	Source	Date Signed	Seasons Played	Apps	Subs	Gls
Charlton Ath.	App	07.71	71	2	0	0
Bristol Rov.	L	09.71	71	1	0	0
Exeter C.	Tr	02.73	72-73	16	0	0

CLARKE Ambrose
Liverpool, 10 September, 1945 (WH)

League Club	Source	Date Signed	Seasons Played	Apps	Subs	Gls
Everton	Red Triangle	06.64				
Southport	Tr	01.66	65-70	193	4	4
Barrow	Tr	07.71	71	45	1	0

CLARKE Andrew Weston
Islington, 22 July, 1967 E Semi Pro (F)

League Club	Source	Date Signed	Seasons Played	Apps	Subs	Gls
Wimbledon	Barnet	02.91	90-97	74	96	17

CLARKE Brian Roy
Eastbourne, 10 October, 1968 (CD)

League Club	Source	Date Signed	Seasons Played	Apps	Subs	Gls
Gillingham	YT	06.87	88-91	42	2	0

CLARKE Christopher Elliott
Battersea, 11 December, 1946 (OL)

League Club	Source	Date Signed	Seasons Played	Apps	Subs	Gls
Millwall	Chelsea (App)	12.63	64-65	19	0	4
Watford	Tr	08.66	66	1	1	0

CLARKE Christopher John
Barnsley, 1 May, 1974 (G)

League Club	Source	Date Signed	Seasons Played	Apps	Subs	Gls
Bolton W.	YT	07.92				
Rochdale	Tr	07.94	94-95	30	0	0

CLARKE Colin
Glasgow, 4 April, 1946 (CD)

League Club	Source	Date Signed	Seasons Played	Apps	Subs	Gls
Arsenal	Arthurlie Jnrs	10.63				
Oxford U.	Tr	07.65	65-77	443	1	23
Plymouth Arg.	Los Angeles (USA)	09.78	78	35	0	3

CLARKE Colin John
Newry (NI), 30 October, 1962 NI-35 (F)

League Club	Source	Date Signed	Seasons Played	Apps	Subs	Gls
Ipswich T.	App	10.80				
Peterborough U.	Tr	07.81	81-83	76	6	18
Gillingham	L	03.84	83	8	0	1
Tranmere Rov.	Tr	07.84	84	45	0	22
Bournemouth	Tr	06.85	85	46	0	26
Southampton	Tr	06.86	86-88	82	0	36
Bournemouth	L	12.88	88	3	1	2
Queens Park R	Tr	03.89	88-89	39	7	11
Portsmouth	Tr	06.90	90-92	68	17	18

CLARKE Darrell James
Mansfield, 16 December, 1977 (M)

League Club	Source	Date Signed	Seasons Played	Apps	Subs	Gls
Mansfield T.	YT	07.96	95-97	44	13	6

CLARKE David Alan
Nottingham, 3 December, 1964 E Yth (LB)

League Club	Source	Date Signed	Seasons Played	Apps	Subs	Gls
Notts Co.	App	12.82	82-86	113	10	8
Lincoln C.	Tr	07.87	88-93	141	6	9
Doncaster Rov.	Tr	01.94	93	15	1	0

CLARKE David Arthur
Long Eaton, 25 September, 1946 (W)

League Club	Source	Date Signed	Seasons Played	Apps	Subs	Gls
Nottingham F.	Derby Co. (Am)	05.64				
Notts Co.	Tr	07.66	66	23	1	0

CLARKE David Leslie
Newcastle, 24 July, 1949 E Semi Pro (G)

League Club	Source	Date Signed	Seasons Played	Apps	Subs	Gls
Newcastle U.	Felham B.C.	06.67				
Doncaster Rov.	Tr	08.69	69	3	0	0
Darlington	L	03.70	69	11	0	0

CLARKE Dean Brian
Hereford, 28 July, 1977 (RB)

League Club	Source	Date Signed	Seasons Played	Apps	Subs	Gls
Hereford U.	YT	07.95	93-95	8	3	0

CLARKE Dennis
Stockton, 18 January, 1948 (FB)

League Club	Source	Date Signed	Seasons Played	Apps	Subs	Gls
West Bromwich A.	App	02.65	66-68	19	2	0
Huddersfield T.	Tr	01.69	68-73	172	0	3
Birmingham C.	Tr	09.73	73-74	14	0	0

CLARKE Derek
Willenhall, 19 February, 1950 (F)

League Club	Source	Date Signed	Seasons Played	Apps	Subs	Gls
Walsall	App	12.67	67	6	0	2
Wolverhampton W.	Tr	05.68	68-69	2	3	0
Oxford U.	Tr	10.70	70-75	172	6	35
Leyton Orient	Tr	08.76	76-78	30	6	6
Carlisle U.	L	10.78	78	0	1	0

CLARKE Donald Leslie
Poole, 29 June, 1931 Died 1993 (IF)

League Club	Source	Date Signed	Seasons Played	Apps	Subs	Gls
Cardiff C.		08.54				
Brighton & H. A.	Tr	06.55	55	2	-	0

CLARKE Douglas
Bolton, 19 January, 1934 (OR)

League Club	Source	Date Signed	Seasons Played	Apps	Subs	Gls
Bury	Darwen	02.52	53-55	37	-	16

League Club	Source	Date Signed	Seasons Played	Apps	Subs	Gls
Hull C.	Tr	11.55	55-64	368	-	79
Torquay U.	Tr	07.65	65-67	116	4	21
CLARKE Frank James						
Willenhall, 15 July, 1942						(F)
Shrewsbury T.	Willenhall	11.61	61-67	188	0	77
Queens Park R.	Tr	02.68	67-69	67	0	17
Ipswich T.	Tr	03.70	69-72	62	4	15
Carlisle U.	Tr	08.73	73-77	121	5	30
CLARKE Frederick Jeffrey						
Crewe, 3 January, 1931						(CH)
Crewe Alex.		11.51	53-54	3	-	0
CLARKE Frederick Robert George						
Banbridge (NI), 4 November, 1941						(FB)
Arsenal	Glenavon	11.60	61-64	26	-	0
CLARKE Gary						
Boston, 6 November, 1960						(W)
Bristol Rov.	App	11.78	78-79	6	5	0
CLARKE George Edmund						
Ipswich, 27 April, 1921 Died 1981						(CH)
Ipswich T.		11.46	46-52	34	-	1
CLARKE Gerald						
Barrow Hill, 4 January, 1936						(RB)
Chesterfield	Oaks Fold	03.55	54-67	382	0	21
CLARKE Graham Peter						
Nottingham, 11 August, 1935 E Yth						(FB)
Southampton		06.53	57-58	3	-	0
CLARKE Henry (Harry)						
Sunderland, 26 November, 1960						(M)
Hartlepool U.	Middlesbrough (N/C)	08.79	81	5	2	1
CLARKE Henry (Harry) Alfred						
Woodford, 23 February, 1923 E 'B'/E-1						(CH)
Tottenham H.	Lovells Ath.	03.49	48-56	295	-	4
CLARKE James **Henry**						
Sheffield, 27 March, 1921						(CF)
Rotherham U.	Goole T.	05.37	37-38	54	-	12
Darlington	Tr	04.46	46	19	-	17
Leeds U.	Tr	02.47	46	14	-	1
Darlington	Tr	11.47	47-48	37	-	25
Hartlepool U.	Tr	11.49	49	7	-	1
Darlington	Stockton	09.52	52	14	-	12
CLARKE Isaac (Ike)						
Tipton, 9 January, 1915						(IF)
West Bromwich A.	T. E. Wesley	01.37	37-47	108	-	39
Portsmouth	Tr	11.47	47-52	116	-	49
CLARKE James						
West Bromwich, 7 December, 1923						(LB)
Nottingham F.		05.47	47-53	18	-	0
CLARKE Jeffrey Derek						
Hemsworth, 18 January, 1954						(CD)
Manchester C.	Jnrs	01.72	74	13	0	0
Sunderland	Tr	06.75	75-81	178	3	6
Newcastle U.	Tr	08.82	82-86	124	0	4
Brighton & H. A.	L	08.84	84	4	0	0
CLARKE John Leslie						
Northampton, 23 October, 1946 E Yth						(CD)
Northampton T.	Jnrs	07.65	66-74	228	5	1
CLARKE William **John**						
Bargoed, 26 December, 1940						(G)
Newport Co.	Bargoed Y.M.C.A.	05.59	59-61	12	-	0
CLARKE Kelvin Leslie						
Wolverhampton, 16 July, 1957						(D)
Walsall	App	07.75	74-78	4	5	0
CLARKE Kevin						
Drogheda (IR), 29 April, 1923						(F)
Barrow	Drogheda	12.45	46	13	-	1
CLARKE Patrick **Kevin** Noel						
Santry, 3 December, 1921 LoI/IR-2						(HB)
Swansea C.	Drumcondra	11.48	48-51	10	-	0

League Club	Source	Date Signed	Seasons Played	Apps	Subs	Gls
CLARKE Malcolm McQueen						
Clydebank, 29 June, 1944						(M)
Leicester C.	Johnstone Burgh	07.65	65	0	1	0
Cardiff C.	Tr	08.67	67-68	43	2	5
Bristol C.	Tr	07.69	69	2	1	0
Hartlepool U.	Tr	07.70	70-71	29	4	0
CLARKE Matthew John						
Sheffield, 3 November, 1973						(G)
Rotherham U.	YT	07.92	92-95	123	1	0
Sheffield Wed.	Tr	07.96	96-97	2	2	0
CLARKE Michael						
Sheffield, 28 November, 1944						(LB)
Sheffield U.	App	01.62				
Aldershot	Tr	06.64	64	5	-	0
Halifax T.	Tr	07.65	65-66	50	1	1
CLARKE Michael Darren						
Marston Green, 22 December, 1967						(LB/W)
Barnsley	Birmingham C. (App)	11.86	86-88	37	3	3
Scarborough	Tr	08.89	89-90	31	6	1
CLARKE Nicholas John						
Walsall, 20 August, 1967						(CD)
Wolverhampton W.	Jnrs	02.85	85-91	73	8	1
Mansfield T.	Tr	12.91	91-93	39	4	5
Chesterfield	L	02.93	92	7	0	0
Doncaster Rov.	L	12.93	93	5	0	0
CLARKE Norman (Nobby) Frederick						
Birmingham, 31 October, 1934 E Yth						(WH)
Aston Villa	Jnrs	07.53	54	1	-	0
Torquay U.	Tr	07.56	56-58	55	-	0
CLARKE Norman Samson						
Ballylougham (NI), 1 April, 1942 NIu23-2						(W)
Sunderland	Ballymena	02.62	62	4	-	0
CLARKE Paul Stewart						
Chesterfield, 25 September, 1950 E Sch						(CD)
Liverpool	App	10.67				
Rochdale	Tr	08.69	69-71	10	1	0
CLARKE Peter Anthony						
Bolton, 6 July, 1949						(G)
Bolton W.	Jnrs	06.69	70	13	0	0
Stockport Co.	Tr	07.71	71-74	49	0	0
CLARKE Raymond Charles						
Hackney, 25 September, 1952 E Yth						(F)
Tottenham H.	App	10.69	72	0	1	0
Swindon T.	Tr	06.73	73	11	3	2
Mansfield T.	Tr	08.74	74-75	91	0	52
Brighton & H. A.	Bruges (Bel)	10.79	79	30	0	8
Newcastle U.	Tr	07.80	80	14	0	2
CLARKE Allan **Robert**						
Liverpool, 13 October, 1941						(IF)
Chester C.	Liverpool (Jnrs)	10.61	61-62	30	-	5
CLARKE Royston James						
Newport, 1 June, 1925 W-22						(OL)
Cardiff C.	Jnrs	12.42	46	39	-	11
Manchester C.	Tr	04.47	46-57	349	-	73
Stockport Co.	Tr	09.58	58	25	-	5
CLARKE Simon Nathan						
Chelmsford, 23 September, 1971						(LM)
West Ham U.	YT	03.90	90-92	0	3	0
CLARKE Stephen						
Saltcoats, 29 August, 1963 S Yth/Su21-8/S 'B'/S-6						(D)
Chelsea	St Mirren	01.87	86-97	321	9	7
CLARKE Stuart Anthony						
Hull, 25 January, 1961						(M)
Torquay U.	Jnrs	02.78	78	4	1	0
CLARKE Thomas						
Ardrossan, 12 April, 1946						(G)
Carlisle U.	Airdrieonians	07.70	71-74	23	0	0
Preston N. E.	Tr	07.75	75	3	0	0
CLARKE Timothy Joseph						
Stourbridge, 16 May, 1965						(G)
Coventry C.	Halesowen T.	10.90				
Huddersfield T.	Tr	07.91	91-92	70	0	0
Rochdale	L	02.93	92	2	0	0

League Club	Source	Date Signed	Seasons Played	Apps	Subs	Gls
Shrewsbury T.	Altrincham	10.93	94-95	30	1	0
York C.	Witton A.	09.96	96	17	0	0
Scunthorpe U.	Tr	02.97	96-97	56	0	0

CLARKE Wayne
Wolverhampton, 28 February, 1961 E Sch/E Yth (F)

League Club	Source	Date Signed	Seasons Played	Apps	Subs	Gls
Wolverhampton W.	App	03.78	77-83	129	19	30
Birmingham C.	Tr	08.84	84-86	92	0	38
Everton	Tr	03.87	86-88	46	11	18
Leicester C.	Tr	07.89	89	10	1	1
Manchester C.	Tr	01.90	89-91	7	14	2
Shrewsbury T.	L	10.90	90	7	0	6
Stoke C.	L	03.91	90	9	0	3
Wolverhampton W.	L	09.91	91	1	0	0
Walsall	Tr	07.92	92	39	0	21
Shrewsbury T.	Tr	08.93	93-94	53	6	22

CLARKE William Arthur
Newport, 17 April, 1923 Died 1994 W Amat (WH)

League Club	Source	Date Signed	Seasons Played	Apps	Subs	Gls
Ipswich T. (Am)		02.47	46	3	-	0

CLARKSON David James
Preston, 1 February, 1968 (M)

League Club	Source	Date Signed	Seasons Played	Apps	Subs	Gls
Brighton & H.A.	Sunshine G.C. (Aus)	09.91	91	4	9	0

CLARKSON Ian Stewart
Solihull, 4 December, 1970 (RB)

League Club	Source	Date Signed	Seasons Played	Apps	Subs	Gls
Birmingham C.	YT	12.88	88-92	125	11	0
Stoke C.	Tr	09.93	93-95	72	3	0
Northampton T.	Tr	08.96	96-97	87	0	1

CLARKSON Philip Ian
Garstang, 13 November, 1968 (M/F)

League Club	Source	Date Signed	Seasons Played	Apps	Subs	Gls
Crewe Alex.	Fleetwood T.	10.91	91-95	76	22	27
Scunthorpe U.	L	10.95	95	4	0	1
Scunthorpe U.	Tr	02.96	95-96	45	3	18
Blackpool	Tr	02.97	96-97	59	3	18

CLAXTON Thomas
Rochdale, 17 October, 1944 (W)

League Club	Source	Date Signed	Seasons Played	Apps	Subs	Gls
Bury	Burnley (Am)	03.63	63-68	97	4	3

CLAY John Harfield
Stockport, 22 November, 1946 (IF)

League Club	Source	Date Signed	Seasons Played	Apps	Subs	Gls
Manchester C.	App	05.64	67	1	1	0

CLAYPOLE Anthony William
Kettering, 13 February, 1937 (FB)

League Club	Source	Date Signed	Seasons Played	Apps	Subs	Gls
Northampton T.	Jnrs	03.54	56-61	116	-	1

CLAYTON Edward
Bethnal Green, 7 May, 1937 (IF)

League Club	Source	Date Signed	Seasons Played	Apps	Subs	Gls
Tottenham H.	Eton Manor	12.57	57-67	88	4	20
Southend U.	Tr	03.68	67-69	70	3	16

CLAYTON Gary
Sheffield, 2 February, 1963 E Semi Pro (M/RB)

League Club	Source	Date Signed	Seasons Played	Apps	Subs	Gls
Doncaster Rov.	Burton A.	08.86	86	34	1	5
Cambridge U.	Tr	06.87	87-93	166	13	17
Peterborough U.	L	01.91	90	4	0	0
Huddersfield T.	Tr	02.94	93-94	15	4	1
Plymouth Arg.	Tr	08.95	95-97	32	6	2
Torquay U.	Tr	08.97	97	41	0	2

CLAYTON Gordon
Wednesbury, 3 November, 1936 Died 1991 E Sch/E Yth (G)

League Club	Source	Date Signed	Seasons Played	Apps	Subs	Gls
Manchester U.	Jnrs	11.53	56	2	-	0
Tranmere Rov.	Tr	11.59	59-60	4	-	0

CLAYTON John
Elgin, 20 August, 1961 (F)

League Club	Source	Date Signed	Seasons Played	Apps	Subs	Gls
Derby Co.	App	12.78	78-81	21	3	4
Chesterfield	Bulova (HK)	06.83	83	25	8	5
Tranmere Rov.	Tr	07.84	84-85	47	0	35
Plymouth Arg.	Tr	08.85	85-87	68	9	21
Burnley	Volendam (Neth)	08.92	92	3	0	1

CLAYTON John Michael
St Asaph, 28 March, 1937 (WH)

League Club	Source	Date Signed	Seasons Played	Apps	Subs	Gls
Everton	Jnrs	06.55				
Southport	Tr	07.59	59-60	32	-	3

CLAYTON Kenneth
Preston, 6 April, 1933 (WH)

League Club	Source	Date Signed	Seasons Played	Apps	Subs	Gls
Blackburn Rov.	Jnrs	05.50	52-58	72	-	0

CLAYTON Lewis
Barnsley, 7 June, 1924 (WH)

League Club	Source	Date Signed	Seasons Played	Apps	Subs	Gls
Barnsley	Monkton Ath.	03.42				
Carlisle U.	Tr	09.46	46	24	-	0
Barnsley	Tr	06.47	48-49	15	-	0
Queens Park R	Tr	08.50	50-53	91	-	5
Bournemouth	Tr	05.55	55-56	40	-	1
Swindon T.	Tr	06.57	57-58	35	-	2

CLAYTON Paul Spencer
Dunstable, 4 January, 1965 (F)

League Club	Source	Date Signed	Seasons Played	Apps	Subs	Gls
Norwich C.	App	01.83	83-85	8	5	0
Darlington	Tr	03.88	87-88	20	2	3
Crewe Alex.	Tr	01.89	88-90	51	9	12

CLAYTON Ronald
Hull, 18 January, 1937 (IF)

League Club	Source	Date Signed	Seasons Played	Apps	Subs	Gls
Arsenal	Hereford U.	01.58				
Brighton & H. A.	Tr	09.58	58-59	14	-	3

CLAYTON Ronald
Preston, 5 August, 1934 Eu23-6/EF Lge/E 'B'/E-35 (WH)

League Club	Source	Date Signed	Seasons Played	Apps	Subs	Gls
Blackburn Rov.	Jnrs	08.51	50-68	579	2	15

CLAYTON Roy Charles
Dudley, 18 February, 1950 (F)

League Club	Source	Date Signed	Seasons Played	Apps	Subs	Gls
Oxford U.	Warley Borough	08.69	69-72	49	4	8

CLEARY George
Bedford, 25 May, 1947 (F)

League Club	Source	Date Signed	Seasons Played	Apps	Subs	Gls
Cambridge U.	Dunstable	12.75	75	5	3	0

CLEARY William
Middlesbrough, 20 April, 1931 Died 1991 (WH)

League Club	Source	Date Signed	Seasons Played	Apps	Subs	Gls
Sunderland	South Bank East End	05.49				
Norwich C.	Tr	05.52	53-55	18	-	0
Port Vale	Wisbech T.	11.57	57	8	-	0

CLEAVER Christopher William
Hitchin, 24 March, 1979 (F)

League Club	Source	Date Signed	Seasons Played	Apps	Subs	Gls
Peterborough U.	YT	03.97	96-97	10	17	3

CLEEVELY Nigel Robert
Cheltenham, 23 December, 1945 (OL)

League Club	Source	Date Signed	Seasons Played	Apps	Subs	Gls
Derby Co.	Jnrs	07.64	64-66	15	1	3

CLEGG David Lee
Liverpool, 23 October, 1976 (M)

League Club	Source	Date Signed	Seasons Played	Apps	Subs	Gls
Liverpool	YT	05.95				
Hartlepool U.	Tr	07.96	96	24	11	2

CLEGG Donald
Huddersfield, 2 June, 1921 (G)

League Club	Source	Date Signed	Seasons Played	Apps	Subs	Gls
Huddersfield T.	I.C.I.	05.40	46-47	3	-	0
Bury	Tr	07.48	48-49	15	-	0
Stoke C.	Tr	06.50	50	2	-	0

CLEGG Malcolm Brook
Leeds, 9 April, 1936 (CF)

League Club	Source	Date Signed	Seasons Played	Apps	Subs	Gls
Bradford P.A. (Am)	Bradford Rov.	01.58	57	6	-	0

CLEGG Michael Jamie
Ashton-u-Lyne, 3 July, 1977 Eu21-2 (FB)

League Club	Source	Date Signed	Seasons Played	Apps	Subs	Gls
Manchester U.	YT	07.95	96-97	4	3	0

CLEGG Tony
Bradford, 8 November, 1965 (D)

League Club	Source	Date Signed	Seasons Played	Apps	Subs	Gls
Bradford C.	App	11.83	83-86	40	7	2
York C.	Tr	08.87	87-88	38	3	3

CLELAND Peter Melville
Glasgow, 8 May, 1932 Died 1990 (F)

League Club	Source	Date Signed	Seasons Played	Apps	Subs	Gls
Norwich C.	Cheltenham T.	08.58	58	3	-	0

CLELLAND Crawford
USA, 3 December, 1930 (IF)

League Club	Source	Date Signed	Seasons Played	Apps	Subs	Gls
Plymouth Arg.	Aberdeen	06.55	55	2	-	0

CLELLAND David
Larkhall, 18 March, 1924 (OR)

League Club	Source	Date Signed	Seasons Played	Apps	Subs	Gls
Arsenal		08.46				
Brighton & H. A.	Tr	01.48	47	8	-	1
Crystal Palace	Tr	09.49	49	2	-	0
Scunthorpe U.	Weymouth	07.50	50	16	-	8

CLEMENCE Raymond Neal
Skegness, 5 August, 1948 Eu23-4/EF Lge/E-61 (G)

League Club	Source	Date Signed	Seasons Played	Apps	Subs	Gls
Scunthorpe U.	Notts Co. (Jnr)	08.65	65-66	48	0	0
Liverpool	Tr	06.67	69-80	470	0	0
Tottenham H.	Tr	08.81	81-87	240	0	0

League Club	Source	Date Signed	Seasons Played	Career Record Apps	Subs	Gls
CLEMENCE Stephen Neal						
Liverpool, 31 March, 1978 E Sch/E Yth						(M)
Tottenham H.	YT	04.95	97	12	5	0
CLEMENT Andrew David						
Cardiff, 12 November, 1967 W Yth						(FB/M)
Wimbledon	App	10.85	86-88	14	12	0
Bristol Rov.	L	03.87	86	5	1	0
Newport Co.	L	12.87	87	5	0	1
Plymouth Arg.	Woking	12.90	90-91	28	14	0
CLEMENT David Thomas						
Battersea, 2 February, 1948 Died 1982 E Yth/E-5						(RB)
Queens Park R.	Jnrs	07.65	66-78	403	4	21
Bolton W.	Tr	06.79	79-80	33	0	0
Fulham	Tr	10.80	80	17	1	0
Wimbledon	Tr	10.81	81	9	0	2
CLEMENT Neil						
Reading, 3 October, 1978 E Sch/E Yth						(D)
Chelsea	YT	10.95	96	1	0	0
CLEMENTS Andrew Paul						
Swinton, 11 October, 1955						(CD)
Bolton W.	App	10.73	77	1	0	0
Port Vale	L	02.77	76	2	1	0
York C.	Tr	11.77	77-80	146	2	6
CLEMENTS David						
Lame (NI), 15 September, 1945 NI Amat/NIu23-3/NI-48						(LB)
Wolverhampton W.	Portadown	01.63				
Coventry C.	Tr	07.64	64-71	228	2	26
Sheffield Wed.	Tr	08.71	71-73	78	0	0
Everton	Tr	09.73	73-75	81	2	6
CLEMENTS Kenneth Henry						
Middleton, 9 April, 1955						(CD)
Manchester C.	Jnrs	07.75	75-78	116	3	0
Oldham Ath.	Tr	09.79	79-84	204	2	2
Manchester C.	Tr	03.85	84-87	104	2	1
Bury	Tr	03.88	87-89	66	15	1
Shrewsbury T.	Limerick	10.90	90	19	1	0
CLEMENTS Paul Robert						
Greenwich, 7 November, 1946 E Amat						(M)
Oldham Ath.	Skelmersdale U.	06.71	71-72	32	3	0
CLEMENTS Stanley						
Portsmouth, 25 June, 1923						(CH)
Southampton	Gosport Borough	07.44	46-54	116	-	1
CLEMENTS Steven						
Slough, 26 September, 1972						(M)
Arsenal	YT	11.90				
Hereford U.	Tr	07.93	93	2	5	0
CLEMPSON Frank						
Salford, 27 May, 1930 Died 1970						(WH/IF)
Manchester U.	Adelphi B.C.	09.48	49-52	15	-	2
Stockport Co.	Tr	02.53	52-58	246	-	35
Chester C.	Tr	07.59	59-60	67	-	8
CLEWLOW Sidney John						
Wallasey, 8 November, 1919 Died 1989						(WH)
New Brighton	Poulton Vic.	02.39				
Wolverhampton W.	Tr	05.39				
New Brighton	Tr	08.46	46	1	-	0
CLEWS Malcolm Derek						
Tipton, 12 March, 1931						(OL)
Wolverhampton W.	Jnrs	03.48	51	1	-	0
Lincoln C.	Tr	02.54	53-54	7	-	0
CLIFF Edward						
Liverpool, 30 September, 1951						(FB)
Burnley	App	10.68	70-72	21	0	0
Notts Co.	Tr	09.73	73	5	0	0
Lincoln C.	L	10.74	74	3	0	0
Tranmere Rov.	Chicago (USA)	09.76	76-78	44	6	4
Rochdale	Tr	09.79	79-80	25	1	0
CLIFF John George						
Middlesbrough, 7 November, 1946						(F)
Middlesbrough	App	11.63				
Halifax T.	Tr	07.66	66	1	0	0
CLIFF Philip Robert						
Rotherham, 20 November, 1947						(W)
Sheffield U.	Jnrs	11.65	66-69	16	6	5
Chesterfield	Tr	02.71	70-72	30	1	2
CLIFFORD Darren Robert						
Bristol, 2 November, 1966						(M)
Exeter C.	App	11.84	84	0	1	0
CLIFFORD Mark Robert						
Nottingham, 11 September, 1977						(RB)
Mansfield T.	YT	07.96	94-96	4	0	0
CLIFTON Brian						
Whitchurch (Hants), 15 March, 1934						(WH)
Southampton	Whitchurch	02.53	57-62	111	-	35
Grimsby T.	Tr	10.62	62-65	104	0	5
CLIFTON Bryan						
Bentley, 13 February, 1939						(WH)
Doncaster Rov.		10.58	58	2	-	0
CLIFTON Henry						
Newburn, 28 May, 1914						(IF)
Chesterfield	Scotswood	08.33	33-37	122	-	66
Newcastle U.	Tr	06.38	38	29	-	15
Grimsby T.	Tr	02.46	46-48	69	-	23
CLINCH Peter John						
Coventry, 15 October, 1950						(CH)
Oxford U.	App	08.69	69	2	0	0
CLINTON Thomas Joseph						
Dublin, 13 April, 1926 IR-3						(FB)
Everton	Dundalk	03.48	48-53	73	-	4
Blackburn Rov.	Tr	04.55	55	6	-	0
Tranmere Rov.	Tr	06.56	56	9	-	0
CLISH Colin						
Hetton, 14 January, 1944						(LB)
Newcastle U.	Jnrs	01.61	61-63	20	-	0
Rotherham U.	Tr	12.63	63-67	128	0	4
Doncaster Rov.	Tr	02.68	67-71	99	1	4
CLISH Thomas Partridge						
Wheatley Hill (Dm), 19 October, 1932						(G)
West Ham U.	Wheatley Hill	09.53				
Darlington	Tr	07.55	55-57	52	-	0
CLISS David Laurence						
Enfield, 15 November, 1939 E Yth						(IF)
Chelsea	Jnrs	11.56	57-61	24	-	1
CLISS Tony						
March, 22 September, 1959						(W)
Peterborough U.	Jnrs	08.77	77-82	65	20	11
Crewe Alex.	Tr	12.82	82-86	109	4	11
CLITHEROE Lee John						
Chorley, 18 November, 1978						(RW)
Oldham Ath.	YT	07.97	97	1	2	0
CLODE Mark James						
Plymouth, 24 February, 1973						(FB)
Plymouth Arg.	YT	03.91				
Swansea C.	Tr	07.93	93-97	107	10	3
CLOSE Dennis **Brian**						
Rawdon, 24 February, 1931 E Yth						(CF)
Leeds U.	Jnrs	02.49				
Arsenal	Tr	08.50				
Bradford C.	Tr	10.52	52	6	-	2
CLOSE Shaun Charles						
Islington, 8 September, 1966						(F)
Tottenham H.	YT	08.84	86-87	3	6	0
Bournemouth	Tr	01.88	87-88	28	11	8
Swindon T.	Tr	09.89	89-92	13	31	1
Barnet	Tr	08.93	93	21	6	2
CLOUGH Brian Howard						
Middlesbrough, 21 March, 1935 Eu23-3/E 'B'/EF Lge/E-2						(CF)
Middlesbrough	Great Broughton Jnrs	05.53	55-60	213	-	197
Sunderland	Tr	07.61	61-64	61	-	54
CLOUGH James						
Newcastle, 30 August, 1918						(OL)
Southport	Seaton Bum	02.39	38-46	45	-	10
Crystal Palace	Tr	09.47	47-48	67	-	12
Southend U.	Tr	05.49	49	34	-	7
Barrow	Tr	07.50	50	17	-	3

CLOUGH Nigel Howard
Sunderland, 19 March, 1966 Eu21-15/E 'B'/EF Lge/E-14 (F)

League Club	Source	Date Signed	Seasons Played	Apps	Subs	Gls
Nottingham F.	A.C. Hunters	09.84	84-92	307	4	101
Liverpool	Tr	06.93	93-95	29	10	7
Manchester C.	Tr	01.96	95-96	33	5	4
Nottingham F.	L	12.96	96	10	3	1
Sheffield Wed.	L	09.97	97	1	0	0

CLOVER William Arthur
Bracknell, 19 February, 1920 (FB)

League Club	Source	Date Signed	Seasons Played	Apps	Subs	Gls
Reading		02.46	46-49	44	-	4

CLOWES John Alan
Alton (Staffs), 5 November, 1929 (F)

League Club	Source	Date Signed	Seasons Played	Apps	Subs	Gls
Stoke C.	Crewe Alex. (Am)	06.50	50	2	-	2
Shrewsbury T.	Tr	06.52	52-53	11	-	2
Stoke C.	Wellington T.	08.55	55	2	-	0

CLUGSTON James
Belfast, 30 October, 1934 NI Sch (F)

League Club	Source	Date Signed	Seasons Played	Apps	Subs	Gls
Liverpool	Distillery	01.52				
Portsmouth	Glentoran	01.57	56	1	-	0

CLUNIE James Robertson
Kirkcaldy, 4 September, 1933 (CH)

League Club	Source	Date Signed	Seasons Played	Apps	Subs	Gls
Bury	St Mirren	07.65	65	10	0	0

CLUROE Malcolm
Nottingham, 6 February, 1935 (IF)

League Club	Source	Date Signed	Seasons Played	Apps	Subs	Gls
Nottingham F.		11.54	54	1	-	0

CLUTTON Nigel
Chester, 12 February, 1954 (F)

League Club	Source	Date Signed	Seasons Played	Apps	Subs	Gls
Chester C. (N/C)	Blacon	12.77	77	1	0	0

CLYDESDALE William
Fallin, 14 September, 1935 (FB)

League Club	Source	Date Signed	Seasons Played	Apps	Subs	Gls
Hartlepool U.	Aberdeen	08.60	60	14	-	0

COADY John
Dublin, 25 August, 1960 (M)

League Club	Source	Date Signed	Seasons Played	Apps	Subs	Gls
Chelsea	Shamrock Rov.	12.86	86-87	9	7	2

COADY Lewis
Liverpool, 20 September, 1976 (M)

League Club	Source	Date Signed	Seasons Played	Apps	Subs	Gls
Wrexham	YT	07.95	94	2	0	0
Doncaster Rov. (N/C)	Tr	03.97	96	1	0	0

COADY Michael Liam
Dipton (Dm), 1 October, 1958 (D)

League Club	Source	Date Signed	Seasons Played	Apps	Subs	Gls
Sunderland	App	07.76	76-79	4	2	0
Carlisle U.	Tr	07.80	80-81	48	3	1
Wolverhampton W.	Sydney Olympic (Aus)	01.85	84-85	14	1	1

COAK Timothy David
Southampton, 16 January, 1958 (LB)

League Club	Source	Date Signed	Seasons Played	Apps	Subs	Gls
Southampton	App	01.76	76-77	4	0	0

COAKLEY Thomas
Bellshill, 21 May, 1947 (OR)

League Club	Source	Date Signed	Seasons Played	Apps	Subs	Gls
Arsenal	Motherwell	05.66	66	9	0	1

COATES David Plews
Newcastle, 11 April, 1935 (WH)

League Club	Source	Date Signed	Seasons Played	Apps	Subs	Gls
Hull C.	Shiney Row	10.52	56-59	62	-	13
Mansfield T.	Tr	03.60	59-63	159	-	17
Notts Co.	Tr	07.64	64-66	66	0	1

COATES Frank
Farrington, 16 April, 1922 (OR)

League Club	Source	Date Signed	Seasons Played	Apps	Subs	Gls
Blackburn Rov.	Leyland Motors	01.43				
Accrington St.	Leyland Motors	01.48	47	4	-	0

COATES John Albert
Southport, 3 June, 1944 (G)

League Club	Source	Date Signed	Seasons Played	Apps	Subs	Gls
Southport	Burscough	02.65	64	5	-	0
Chester C.	Tr	08.66	66	1	0	0
Southport (N/C)	Morecambe	07.76	76	16	0	0

COATES John Alfred
Limehouse, 13 May, 1920 (OR)

League Club	Source	Date Signed	Seasons Played	Apps	Subs	Gls
Crystal Palace (Am)		08.46	46	4	-	0

COATES Jonathan Simon
Swansea, 27 June, 1975 W Yth/Wu21-5 (W)

League Club	Source	Date Signed	Seasons Played	Apps	Subs	Gls
Swansea C.	YT	07.93	93-97	87	24	11

COATES Ralph
Hetton-le-Hole, 26 April, 1946 Eu23-8/EF Lge/E-4 (M/W)

League Club	Source	Date Signed	Seasons Played	Apps	Subs	Gls
Burnley	App	06.63	64-70	214	2	26
Tottenham H.	Tr	05.71	71-77	173	15	14
Leyton Orient	St Georges (Aus)	10.78	78-80	76	0	12

COATSWORTH Frederick William
Lincoln, 5 July, 1948 (F)

League Club	Source	Date Signed	Seasons Played	Apps	Subs	Gls
Scunthorpe U.	Jnrs	07.65	65-66	15	0	2

COATSWORTH Gary
Sunderland, 7 October, 1968 (M/FB)

League Club	Source	Date Signed	Seasons Played	Apps	Subs	Gls
Barnsley		02.87	87	3	3	0
Darlington	Tr	08.89	90-91	15	7	2
Leicester C.	Tr	10.91	91-93	27	5	4

COATSWORTH John Robert
Newcastle, 21 May, 1935 (CF)

League Club	Source	Date Signed	Seasons Played	Apps	Subs	Gls
Gateshead	Crook T.	03.57	56	16	-	4

COBB Gary Edward
Luton, 6 August, 1968 (W)

League Club	Source	Date Signed	Seasons Played	Apps	Subs	Gls
Luton T.	App	08.86	86-87	6	3	0
Northampton T.	L	10.88	88	1	0	0
Swansea C.	L	08.89	89	5	0	0
Fulham	Tr	08.90	90-91	8	14	0

COBB Paul Mark
Aveley, 13 December, 1972 (F)

League Club	Source	Date Signed	Seasons Played	Apps	Subs	Gls
Leyton Orient	Purfleet	11.90	90-91	3	2	0

COBB Walter **William**
Newark, 29 September, 1940 (IF)

League Club	Source	Date Signed	Seasons Played	Apps	Subs	Gls
Nottingham F.	Ransome & Marles	09.59	60-62	30	-	5
Plymouth Arg.	Tr	10.63	63-64	31	-	0
Brentford	Tr	10.64	64-66	69	2	23
Lincoln C.	Tr	11.66	66-67	67	0	10

COCHRAN Albert George
Ebbw Vale, 26 November, 1939 (G)

League Club	Source	Date Signed	Seasons Played	Apps	Subs	Gls
Plymouth Arg.	Ilford	09.59				
Leyton Orient	Tr	07.60	60	1	-	0

COCHRANE Alan
Belfast, 16 March, 1956 (W)

League Club	Source	Date Signed	Seasons Played	Apps	Subs	Gls
Shrewsbury T.	App	03.74	73-74	3	0	0

COCHRANE Colin
Sutton-in-Ashfield, 26 August, 1921 Died 1985 (IF)

League Club	Source	Date Signed	Seasons Played	Apps	Subs	Gls
Mansfield T.		09.47	47	1	-	0

COCHRANE David
Portadown (NI), 14 August, 1920 NI-12 (OR)

League Club	Source	Date Signed	Seasons Played	Apps	Subs	Gls
Leeds U.	Portadown	08.37	37-50	172	-	28

COCHRANE George Napier
Glasgow, 27 February, 1931 (IF)

League Club	Source	Date Signed	Seasons Played	Apps	Subs	Gls
New Brighton	Arthurlie	07.50	50	2	-	0

COCHRANE Hugh
Glasgow, 9 February, 1943 (IF)

League Club	Source	Date Signed	Seasons Played	Apps	Subs	Gls
Barnsley	Dundee U.	08.63	63	5	-	0

COCHRANE James
Kingswinford 26 October, 1935 (IF)

League Club	Source	Date Signed	Seasons Played	Apps	Subs	Gls
Birmingham C.	Jnrs	10.52	52-53	3	-	1
Walsall	Tr	06.58	58	6	-	1

COCHRANE James Kyle
Glasgow, 14 January, 1954 (LB)

League Club	Source	Date Signed	Seasons Played	Apps	Subs	Gls
Middlesbrough	Drumchapel	05.71	73	3	0	0
Darlington	Tr	02.75	74-79	222	1	5
Torquay U.	Tr	08.80	80	16	0	0

COCHRANE John
Bellshill, 27 April, 1959 (F)

League Club	Source	Date Signed	Seasons Played	Apps	Subs	Gls
Preston N. E.	App	02.77	76-78	3	2	2

COCHRANE John James
Belfast, 11 May, 1944 (IF)

League Club	Source	Date Signed	Seasons Played	Apps	Subs	Gls
Brighton & H. A.	Jnrs	10.61	61-62	14	-	3
Exeter C.	Tr	08.63	63	2	-	0

COCHRANE George **Terence**
Killyleagh (NI), 23 January, 1953 NI-26 (W)

League Club	Source	Date Signed	Seasons Played	Apps	Subs	Gls
Burnley	Coleraine	10.76	76-78	62	5	13
Middlesbrough	Tr	10.78	78-82	96	15	7
Gillingham	Tr	10.83	83-85	105	2	17

League Club	Source	Date Signed	Seasons Played	Apps	Subs	Gls
Millwall (N/C)	Dallas (USA)	11.86	86	1	0	0
Hartlepool U. (N/C)	Tr	01.87	86	2	0	0

COCKBURN Henry
Ashton-u-Lyne, 14 September, 1921 E 'B'/EF Lge/E-13 (WH)

League Club	Source	Date Signed	Seasons Played	Apps	Subs	Gls
Manchester U.	Goslings	08.44	46-54	243	-	4
Bury	Tr	10.54	54-55	35	-	0

COCKBURN Keith
Barnsley, 2 September, 1948 (OL)

League Club	Source	Date Signed	Seasons Played	Apps	Subs	Gls
Barnsley	Jnrs	11.66	66	1	0	0
Bradford P. A.	Tr	07.68	68	16	0	1
Grimsby T.	Tr	01.69	68-69	15	4	2

COCKBURN William Robb
Shotton, 3 May, 1937 Died 1995 (WH)

League Club	Source	Date Signed	Seasons Played	Apps	Subs	Gls
Burnley	Murton Jnrs	08.55				
Gillingham	Tr	06.60	60-61	62	-	1

COCKCROFT Victor Herbert
Birmingham, 25 February, 1941 E Yth (FB)

League Club	Source	Date Signed	Seasons Played	Apps	Subs	Gls
Wolverhampton W.	Jnrs	12.59				
Northampton T.	Tr	07.62	62-66	46	1	1
Rochdale	Tr	06.67	67	42	0	0

COCKELL David John
Ashford (Mx), 1 August, 1939 (WH)

League Club	Source	Date Signed	Seasons Played	Apps	Subs	Gls
Queens Park R.	Hounslow	08.60	60-61	9	-	0

COCKER Leslie
Stockport, 13 March, 1924 Died 1979 (F)

League Club	Source	Date Signed	Seasons Played	Apps	Subs	Gls
Stockport Co.		08.47	46-52	173	-	43
Accrington St.	Tr	08.53	53-57	122	-	48

COCKER Leslie James Robert
Wolverhampton, 18 September, 1939 E Yth (WH)

League Club	Source	Date Signed	Seasons Played	Apps	Subs	Gls
Wolverhampton W.	Jnrs	06.58	60	1	-	0

COCKERILL Glenn
Grimsby, 25 August, 1959 (M)

League Club	Source	Date Signed	Seasons Played	Apps	Subs	Gls
Lincoln C.	Louth U.	11.76	76-79	65	6	10
Swindon T.	Tr	12.79	79-80	23	3	1
Lincoln C.	Tr	08.81	81-83	114	1	25
Sheffield U.	Tr	03.84	83-85	62	0	10
Southampton	Tr	10.85	85-93	272	15	32
Leyton Orient	Tr	12.93	93-95	89	1	7
Fulham	Tr	07.96	96-97	32	8	1
Brentford (N/C)	Tr	11.97	97	23	0	0

COCKERILL John
Grimsby, 12 July, 1961 (M)

League Club	Source	Date Signed	Seasons Played	Apps	Subs	Gls
Grimsby T.	Stafford R.	08.88	88-91	99	8	19

COCKERILL Ronald
Chapeltown, 28 February, 1935 (WH)

League Club	Source	Date Signed	Seasons Played	Apps	Subs	Gls
Huddersfield T.	Jnrs	05.52	55-57	40	-	1
Grimsby T.	Tr	08.58	58-67	293	1	28

COCKHILL Andrew James
Bowden, 11 October, 1967 (F)

League Club	Source	Date Signed	Seasons Played	Apps	Subs	Gls
Stockport Co.	Derby Co. (YT)	08.86	86	3	0	0

COCKRAM Allan Charles
Kensington, 8 October, 1963 (W)

League Club	Source	Date Signed	Seasons Played	Apps	Subs	Gls
Tottenham H.	App	01.81	83	2	0	0
Bristol Rov. (N/C)	Tr	08.85	85	1	0	0
Brentford	Farnborough T.	03.88	87-90	66	24	14
Reading (N/C)	Woking	10.91	91	2	4	1

COCKROFT Hubert
Barnsley, 21 November, 1918 Died 1979 (LH)

League Club	Source	Date Signed	Seasons Played	Apps	Subs	Gls
Barnsley		06.38				
Bradford C.		05.46	46	27	-	0
Halifax T.	Tr	07.47	47	10	-	1
Bradford C.	Peterborough U.	05.50				

COCKROFT Joseph
Barnsley, 20 June, 1911 Died 1994 (WH)

League Club	Source	Date Signed	Seasons Played	Apps	Subs	Gls
Rotherham U.	Wombwell	02.31	30-31	3	-	1
West Ham U.	Gainsborough Trin.	03.33	32-38	251	-	3
Sheffield Wed.	Dartford	11.45	46-48	87	-	2
Sheffield U.	Tr	11.48	48	12	-	0

COCKS Alan William
Burscough, 7 May, 1951 (CF)

League Club	Source	Date Signed	Seasons Played	Apps	Subs	Gls
Chelsea	App	04.69				
Brentford	L	01.70	69	11	0	2
Southport	Tr	07.70	70	24	1	7

CODD Ronald William
Sheffield, 3 December, 1928 (OR)

League Club	Source	Date Signed	Seasons Played	Apps	Subs	Gls
Bolton W.	Meynell Y.C.	03.50	50-53	31	-	5
Sheffield Wed.	L	03.53	52	2	-	0
Barrow	Tr	10.54	54-55	45	-	11

CODDINGTON John William
Worksop, 16 December, 1937 (CH)

League Club	Source	Date Signed	Seasons Played	Apps	Subs	Gls
Huddersfield T.	Jnrs	01.55	55-66	332	0	17
Blackburn Rov.	Tr	06.67	67-69	72	1	3
Stockport Co.	Tr	01.70	69-70	52	0	0

CODNER Robert Andrew George
Walthamstow, 23 January, 1965 E Semi Pro (M)

League Club	Source	Date Signed	Seasons Played	Apps	Subs	Gls
Leicester C.	Tottenham H. (Jnrs)	09.83				
Brighton & H. A.	Barnet	09.88	88-94	257	9	39
Reading (N/C)	Tr	09.95	95	3	1	0
Peterborough U. (N/C)	Tr	03.96	95	1	1	0
Barnet	Tr	03.96	95-96	28	4	1
Southend U. (N/C)	Tr	03.97	96	3	1	0

COE Norman Clive
Swansea, 6 December, 1940 (G)

League Club	Source	Date Signed	Seasons Played	Apps	Subs	Gls
Arsenal	Jnrs	08.58				
Northampton T.	Tr	07.60	60-65	58	0	0

COEN Lawrence
Lowestoft, 4 December, 1914 Died 1972 E Sch (LB)

League Club	Source	Date Signed	Seasons Played	Apps	Subs	Gls
West Bromwich A.	Milford Haven	10.32	36	7	-	4
Coventry C.	Tr	06.38	38-47	20	-	3

COFFEY Michael James Joseph
Liverpool, 29 September, 1958 (M)

League Club	Source	Date Signed	Seasons Played	Apps	Subs	Gls
Everton	App	07.76				
Mansfield T.	Tr	07.78	78	2	1	0

COFFILL Peter Terence
Romford, 14 February, 1957 (W)

League Club	Source	Date Signed	Seasons Played	Apps	Subs	Gls
Watford	App	02.75	75-77	56	7	6
Torquay U.	Tr	11.77	77-80	101	21	11
Northampton T.	Tr	07.81	81-82	64	5	3

COFFIN Geoffrey William
Chester, 17 August, 1924 (CH/CF)

League Club	Source	Date Signed	Seasons Played	Apps	Subs	Gls
Chester C.		05.47	47-54	151	-	35

COGGINS Philip Reginald
Bristol, 10 July, 1940 (OR)

League Club	Source	Date Signed	Seasons Played	Apps	Subs	Gls
Bristol C.	Dorset House B.C.	10.58	59	4	-	0
Bristol Rov.	Tr	07.60	60	4	-	0

COGLAN Alan
Barrow, 14 December, 1936 Died 1987 (G)

League Club	Source	Date Signed	Seasons Played	Apps	Subs	Gls
Barrow	Jnrs	04.54	53-61	51	-	0

COHEN Abraham (Avi)
Egypt, 14 November, 1956 Israeli Int (LB)

League Club	Source	Date Signed	Seasons Played	Apps	Subs	Gls
Liverpool	Macabbi Tel Aviv (Isr)	07.79	79-80	16	2	1

COHEN George Reginald
Kensington, 22 October, 1939 Eu23-8/EF Lge/E-37 (RB)

League Club	Source	Date Signed	Seasons Played	Apps	Subs	Gls
Fulham	Jnrs	10.56	56-68	408	0	6

COHEN Jacob
Israel, 25 September, 1956 Israeli Int (LB)

League Club	Source	Date Signed	Seasons Played	Apps	Subs	Gls
Brighton & H. A.	Macabbi Tel Aviv (Isr)	10.80	80	3	3	0

COKER Adewunmi (Ade) Olarewaju
Nigeria, 19 May, 1954 (F)

League Club	Source	Date Signed	Seasons Played	Apps	Subs	Gls
West Ham U.	App	12.71	71-73	9	1	3
Lincoln C.	L	12.74	74	6	0	1

COLBOURNE Neil
Swinton, 25 August, 1956 (G)

League Club	Source	Date Signed	Seasons Played	Apps	Subs	Gls
Rochdale (N/C)	Hyde U.	03.80	79	1	0	0

COLBRIDGE Clive
Hull, 27 April, 1934 (OL)

League Club	Source	Date Signed	Seasons Played	Apps	Subs	Gls
Leeds U.	Hull C. (Am)	05.52				
York C.	Tr	05.55	55-57	37	-	14
Workington	Tr	09.57	57-58	46	-	8
Crewe Alex.	Tr	10.58	58	29	-	8
Manchester C.	Tr	05.59	59-61	62	-	12
Wrexham	Tr	02.62	61-64	108	-	33

COLCOMBE Scott
West Bromwich, 15 December, 1971 (LB/W)

League Club	Source	Date Signed	Seasons Played	Apps	Subs	Gls
West Bromwich A.	YT	07.90				

League Club	Source	Date Signed	Seasons Played	Apps	Subs	Gls
Torquay U.	Tr	08.91	91-94	78	11	1
Doncaster Rov.	Tr	07.95	95-96	30	12	4

COLDICOTT Stacy
Redditch, 29 April, 1974 (M)

League Club	Source	Date Signed	Seasons Played	Apps	Subs	Gls
West Bromwich A.	YT	03.92	92-97	64	40	3
Cardiff C.	L	08.96	96	6	0	0

COLDRICK Graham George
Newport, 6 November, 1945 W Sch/Wu23-2 (D)

League Club	Source	Date Signed	Seasons Played	Apps	Subs	Gls
Cardiff C.	App	11.62	63-69	91	5	2
Newport Co.	Tr	03.70	69-74	156	1	10

COLDWELL George **Cecil**
Dungworth, 12 January, 1929 (RB)

League Club	Source	Date Signed	Seasons Played	Apps	Subs	Gls
Sheffield U.	Norton Woodseats	09.51	51-66	409	1	2

COLE Andrew Alexander
Nottingham, 15 October, 1971 E Sch/E Yth/Eu21-8/E 'B'/E-2 (F)

League Club	Source	Date Signed	Seasons Played	Apps	Subs	Gls
Arsenal	YT	10.89	90	0	1	0
Fulham	L	09.91	91	13	0	3
Bristol C.	Tr	03.92	91-92	41	0	20
Newcastle U.	Tr	03.93	92-94	69	1	55
Manchester U.	Tr	01.95	94-97	90	15	45

COLE David Andrew
Barnsley, 28 September, 1962 (CD)

League Club	Source	Date Signed	Seasons Played	Apps	Subs	Gls
Sunderland		10.83				
Swansea C.	Tr	09.84	84	7	1	0
Swindon T.	Tr	02.85	84-86	69	0	3
Torquay U.	Tr	11.86	86-88	107	3	6
Rochdale	Tr	07.89	89-90	73	11	7
Exeter C.	Tr	08.91	91	0	2	0

COLE George **Douglas**
Heswall, 2 July, 1916 Died 1959 (D)

League Club	Source	Date Signed	Seasons Played	Apps	Subs	Gls
Sheffield U.		05.37	37	1	-	0
Chester C.	Tr	05.39	46-47	20	-	0

COLE James Edward
Wrexham, 14 August, 1925 (RB)

League Club	Source	Date Signed	Seasons Played	Apps	Subs	Gls
Bolton W.	Wrexham (Am)	05.47				
Chester C.	Tr	08.49	49	1	-	0

COLE Michael Edward
Ilford, 9 June, 1937 (FB)

League Club	Source	Date Signed	Seasons Played	Apps	Subs	Gls
Norwich C.	Harwich & Parkeston	08.56	55-57	3	-	0

COLE Michael Washington
Hillingdon, 3 September, 1966 (F)

League Club	Source	Date Signed	Seasons Played	Apps	Subs	Gls
Ipswich T.	App	11.83	84-87	24	14	3
Port Vale	L	01.88	87	4	0	1
Fulham	Tr	03.88	87-90	45	3	4

COLE, Roy
Barnsley, 8 December, 1953 (CD)

League Club	Source	Date Signed	Seasons Played	Apps	Subs	Gls
Barnsley	App	12.71	71-73	6	0	0

COLEMAN Anthony George
Ellesmere Port, 2 May, 1945 (OL)

League Club	Source	Date Signed	Seasons Played	Apps	Subs	Gls
Tranmere Rov.	Stoke C. (App)	10.62	62-63	8	-	0
Preston N. E.	Tr	05.64	64	5	-	1
Doncaster Rov.	Bangor C.	11.65	65-66	58	0	11
Manchester C.	Tr	03.67	66-69	82	1	12
Sheffield Wed.	Tr	10.69	69	25	1	2
Blackpool	Tr	08.70	70	17	0	0
Southport	Durban C. (SA)	11.73	73	22	1	1
Stockport Co.	Tr	06.74	74-75	28	2	3

COLEMAN Christopher
Swansea, 10 June, 1970 W Sch/W Yth/Wu21-3/W-19 (LB)

League Club	Source	Date Signed	Seasons Played	Apps	Subs	Gls
Swansea C.	Manchester C. (Jnrs)	08.87	87-90	159	1	2
Crystal Palace	Tr	07.91	91-95	143	11	13
Blackburn Rov.	Tr	12.95	95-96	27	1	0
Fulham	Tr	12.97	97	26	0	1

COLEMAN David Houston
Hackney, 8 April, 1967 (LB)

League Club	Source	Date Signed	Seasons Played	Apps	Subs	Gls
Bournemouth	Jnrs	09.84	85-90	40	10	2
Colchester U.	L	02.88	87	6	0	1

COLEMAN David John
Colchester, 27 March, 1942 (F)

League Club	Source	Date Signed	Seasons Played	Apps	Subs	Gls
Colchester U.	Harwich & Parkeston	11.61	61-62	2	-	1

COLEMAN Edward
Middlesbrough, 23 September, 1957 (F)

League Club	Source	Date Signed	Seasons Played	Apps	Subs	Gls
Middlesbrough	App	09.75	75	1	0	0
Workington	L	03.77	76	10	2	1

COLEMAN Geoffrey James
Bedworth, 13 May, 1936 (FB)

League Club	Source	Date Signed	Seasons Played	Apps	Subs	Gls
Northampton T.	Bedworth T.	05.55	55-58	18	-	0

COLEMAN Gordon Michael
Nottingham, 11 February, 1954 (M)

League Club	Source	Date Signed	Seasons Played	Apps	Subs	Gls
Preston N. E.	Padstow Y.C.	09.73	73-82	248	21	25
Bury	Tr	08.83	83	24	5	0

COLEMAN John Henry
Hucknall, 3 March, 1946 (WH)

League Club	Source	Date Signed	Seasons Played	Apps	Subs	Gls
Nottingham F.	Jnrs	03.63				
Mansfield T.	Tr	08.66	66-67	43	0	1
York C.	Tr	07.68	68	8	3	3

COLEMAN Keith
Washington, 24 May, 1951 (FB)

League Club	Source	Date Signed	Seasons Played	Apps	Subs	Gls
Sunderland	App	06.68	71-72	49	0	2
West Ham U.	Tr	09.73	73-76	96	5	0
Darlington	K.V. Mechelen (Bel)	07.79	79	25	0	0

COLEMAN Neville (Tim) James
Prescot, 29 January, 1930 (OR)

League Club	Source	Date Signed	Seasons Played	Apps	Subs	Gls
Stoke C.	Gorleston	01.55	53-58	114	-	46
Crewe Alex.	Tr	02.59	58-60	73	-	16

COLEMAN Nicholas
Crayford, 6 May, 1966 (LB)

League Club	Source	Date Signed	Seasons Played	Apps	Subs	Gls
Millwall	App	01.84	84-89	87	1	0
Swindon T.	L	09.85	85	13	0	4

COLEMAN Philip
Woolwich, 8 September, 1960 (D)

League Club	Source	Date Signed	Seasons Played	Apps	Subs	Gls
Millwall	App	08.78	78-80	23	13	1
Colchester U.	Tr	02.81	80-83	82	4	6
Wrexham	L	09.83	83	17	0	2
Exeter C. (N/C)	Chelmsford C.	12.84	84	6	0	0
Aldershot	Tr	02.85	84-85	45	0	5
Millwall	Dulwich Hamlet	09.86	86	8	2	0
Colchester U. (N/C)	Finland	12.88	88	6	4	0

COLEMAN Simon
Worksop, 13 March, 1968 (CD)

League Club	Source	Date Signed	Seasons Played	Apps	Subs	Gls
Mansfield T.	Jnrs	07.85	86-89	96	0	7
Middlesbrough	Tr	09.89	89-90	51	4	2
Derby Co.	Tr	08.91	91-93	62	8	2
Sheffield Wed.	Tr	01.94	93-94	11	5	1
Bolton W.	Tr	10.94	94-95	34	0	5
Wolverhampton W.	L	09.97	97	3	1	0
Southend U.	Tr	02.98	97	14	0	0

COLES Arthur
Crediton, 28 January, 1914 (D)

League Club	Source	Date Signed	Seasons Played	Apps	Subs	Gls
Exeter C.	Copplestone	06.37	37-48	16	-	0

COLES David Andrew
Wandsworth, 15 June, 1964 (G)

League Club	Source	Date Signed	Seasons Played	Apps	Subs	Gls
Birmingham C.	App	04.82				
Mansfield T.	Tr	03.83	82	3	0	0
Aldershot	Tr	08.83	83-87	120	0	0
Newport Co.	L	01.88	87	14	0	0
Brighton & H.A. (N/C)	H.J.K. Helsinki (Fin)	02.89	88	1	0	0
Aldershot	Tr	07.89	89-90	30	0	0
Fulham	Tr	08.91				

COLEY William Ernest
Wolverhampton, 17 September, 1916 Died 1974 (WH)

League Club	Source	Date Signed	Seasons Played	Apps	Subs	Gls
Wolverhampton W.	Jnrs	09.33	36	2	-	0
Bournemouth	Tr	09.37	37	13	-	0
Torquay U.	Tr	07.38	38-46	61	-	2
Northampton T.	Tr	08.47	47-50	104	-	7
Exeter C.	Tr	07.51	51	8	-	0

COLFAR Raymond Joseph
Liverpool, 4 December, 1935 (OL)

League Club	Source	Date Signed	Seasons Played	Apps	Subs	Gls
Crystal Palace	Sutton U.	11.58	58-60	41	-	6
Oxford U.	Cambridge U.	08.62	62-63	18	-	4

COLGAN Nicholas Vincent
Drogheda (Ire), 19 September, 1973 IR Sch/IR Yth/IRu21-9/IR 'B' (G)

League Club	Source	Date Signed	Seasons Played	Apps	Subs	Gls
Chelsea	YT	10.92	96	1	0	0
Brentford	L	10.97	97	5	0	0
Reading	L	02.98	97	5	0	0

COLGAN Walter
Castleford, 3 April, 1937 (FB)

League Club	Source	Date Signed	Seasons Played	Apps	Subs	Gls
Queens Park R.	Ashley Road	07.54	57-58	3	-	0

League Club	Source	Date Signed	Seasons Played	Apps	Subs	Gls

COLKIN Lee
Nuneaton, 15 July, 1974 (LB/M)

League Club	Source	Date Signed	Seasons Played	Apps	Subs	Gls
Northampton T.	YT	07.90	91-96	74	25	3
Leyton Orient	L	08.97	97	5	6	0

COLL Owen Oliver
Donegal, 9 April, 1976 IRu21-5 (CD)

League Club	Source	Date Signed	Seasons Played	Apps	Subs	Gls
Tottenham H.	Enfield R.	07.94				
Bournemouth	Tr	03.96	95-96	24	0	0

COLL William (Liam) Sean
Carrick, 16 December, 1929 (OR)

League Club	Source	Date Signed	Seasons Played	Apps	Subs	Gls
Accrington St.		08.49	49-50	13	-	0

COLLARD James Bruce
Hetton-le-Hole, 21 August, 1953 (D/M)

League Club	Source	Date Signed	Seasons Played	Apps	Subs	Gls
West Bromwich A.	App	05.71				
Scunthorpe U.	Tr	07.73	73	21	1	0

COLLARD Ian
Hetton-le-Hole, 31 August, 1947 (M)

League Club	Source	Date Signed	Seasons Played	Apps	Subs	Gls
West Bromwich A.	App	11.64	64-68	63	6	7
Ipswich T.	Tr	05.69	69-74	83	9	5
Portsmouth	L	09.75	75	1	0	0

COLLETON Anthony
Manchester, 17 January, 1974 (F)

League Club	Source	Date Signed	Seasons Played	Apps	Subs	Gls
Rochdale	YT	•	90	0	1	0

COLLETT Andrew Alfred
Stockton, 28 October, 1973 (G)

League Club	Source	Date Signed	Seasons Played	Apps	Subs	Gls
Middlesbrough	YT	03.92	92	2	0	0
Bristol Rov.	L	10.94	94	4	0	0
Bristol Rov.	Tr	03.95	94-97	104	0	0

COLLETT Ernest
Sheffield, 17 November, 1914 Died 1980 (WH)

League Club	Source	Date Signed	Seasons Played	Apps	Subs	Gls
Arsenal	Oughtibridge W.M.C.	04.33	37-46	20	-	0

COLLIER Alan Stanley
Markyate, 24 March, 1938 E Sch/E Yth (G)

League Club	Source	Date Signed	Seasons Played	Apps	Subs	Gls
Luton T.	Jnrs	05.55	58-60	10	-	0

COLLIER Austin
Dewsbury, 24 July, 1914 Died 1991 (WH)

League Club	Source	Date Signed	Seasons Played	Apps	Subs	Gls
Mansfield T.	Frickley Colly	05.38	38	21	-	0
York C.	Tr	05.39	46	10	-	0
Rochdale	Queen of South	04.47	46-47	6	-	0
Halifax T.	Tr	11.47	47	1	-	0

COLLIER Daniel Joseph
Eccles, 15 January, 1974 (CD)

League Club	Source	Date Signed	Seasons Played	Apps	Subs	Gls
Wolverhampton W.	YT	07.92				
Crewe Alex.	Tr	06.94	94-95	5	6	0

COLLIER Darren James
Stockton, 1 December, 1967 (G)

League Club	Source	Date Signed	Seasons Played	Apps	Subs	Gls
Blackburn Rov.	Middlesbrough (N/C)	12.87	88-90	27	0	0
Darlington	Tr	07.93	93-94	44	0	0

COLLIER David
Bangor, 2 October, 1957 (FB)

League Club	Source	Date Signed	Seasons Played	Apps	Subs	Gls
Shrewsbury T.	App	10.75	74-76	20	0	4
Crewe Alex.	Tr	08.77	77	24	2	1

COLLIER Gary Bernard
Bristol, 4 February, 1955 (CD)

League Club	Source	Date Signed	Seasons Played	Apps	Subs	Gls
Bristol C.	App	11.72	72-78	193	0	3
Coventry C.	Tr	07.79	79	2	0	0

COLLIER Geoffrey Heywood
Blackpool, 25 July, 1950 (F)

League Club	Source	Date Signed	Seasons Played	Apps	Subs	Gls
Notts Co.	Macclesfield T.	07.73	73	0	3	0

COLLIER Graham Ronald
Nottingham, 12 September, 1951 (M)

League Club	Source	Date Signed	Seasons Played	Apps	Subs	Gls
Nottingham F.	App	03.69	69-70	13	2	2
Scunthorpe U.	Tr	07.72	72-76	155	6	19
Barnsley	Tr	08.77	77	22	2	2
York C.	Buxton	09.78	78	5	0	0

COLLIER James Robert
Stockport, 24 August, 1952 (M)

League Club	Source	Date Signed	Seasons Played	Apps	Subs	Gls
Stockport Co.	App	03.70	68-73	101	6	12

COLLINDRIDGE Colin
Barnsley, 15 November, 1920 (OL)

League Club	Source	Date Signed	Seasons Played	Apps	Subs	Gls
Sheffield U.	Barugh Green	01.39	46-49	142	-	52
Nottingham F.	Tr	08.50	50-53	151	-	45
Coventry C.	Tr	06.54	54-55	34	-	6

COLLINGS Paul Wallace
Liverpool, 30 September, 1968 (G)

League Club	Source	Date Signed	Seasons Played	Apps	Subs	Gls
Tranmere Rov.	Ellesmere Port	08.88	88-90	4	0	0
Bury (N/C)	Altrincham	08.93	93	1	0	0

COLLINGWOOD Graham
South Kirkby, 8 December, 1954 (M)

League Club	Source	Date Signed	Seasons Played	Apps	Subs	Gls
Barnsley	App	12.72	73-74	12	2	0

COLLINS Albert Desmond
Chesterfield, 15 April, 1923 (W)

League Club	Source	Date Signed	Seasons Played	Apps	Subs	Gls
Chesterfield	Jnrs	01.41	46	8	-	0
Halifax T.	Tr	11.46	46-47	44	-	10
Carlisle U.	Tr	02.48	47-48	20	-	3
Barrow	Tr	12.48	48-49	55	-	7
Bournemouth	Tr	08.50	50	5	-	1
Shrewsbury T.	Tr	08.51	51	9	-	2
Accrington St.	Tr	07.52	52	17	-	2

COLLINS Andrew Balsillie
Carlisle, 20 October, 1958 (FB)

League Club	Source	Date Signed	Seasons Played	Apps	Subs	Gls
Carlisle U.	Carlisle Spartans	09.77	77-81	47	7	1

COLLINS Anthony Norman
Kensington, 19 March, 1926 (IF)

League Club	Source	Date Signed	Seasons Played	Apps	Subs	Gls
Sheffield Wed.	Brentford (Am)	11.47				
York C.	Tr	07.49	49	10	-	1
Watford	Tr	08.50	50-52	90	-	8
Norwich C.	Tr	07.53	53-54	29	-	2
Torquay U.	Tr	07.55	55-56	89	-	17
Watford	Tr	07.57	57	17	-	1
Crystal Palace	Tr	11.57	57-58	55	-	14
Rochdale	Tr	06.59	59-60	47	-	5

COLLINS Benjamin Victor
Kislingbury, 9 March, 1928 (CH)

League Club	Source	Date Signed	Seasons Played	Apps	Subs	Gls
Northampton T.	Jnrs	04.48	48-58	213	-	0

COLLINS Darren
Winchester, 24 May, 1967 (F)

League Club	Source	Date Signed	Seasons Played	Apps	Subs	Gls
Northampton T.	Petersfield U.	01.89	88-90	40	11	9

COLLINS David Dennis
Dublin, 30 October, 1971 IR Yth/IRu21-6 (M/D)

League Club	Source	Date Signed	Seasons Played	Apps	Subs	Gls
Liverpool	YT	11.88				
Wigan Ath.	L	01.92	91	9	0	0
Oxford U.	Tr	07.92	92-94	33	9	0

COLLINS John Douglas
Blackwell, 28 August, 1945 (M)

League Club	Source	Date Signed	Seasons Played	Apps	Subs	Gls
Grimsby T.	Rotherham U. (App)	06.63	63-68	96	7	9
Burnley	Tr	09.68	68-75	172	15	18
Plymouth Arg.	Tr	05.76	76	22	1	2
Sunderland	Tr	03.77	76-77	4	2	0
Rochdale	Tulsa (USA)	01.79	78	6	2	0

COLLINS Eamonn Anthony Stephen
Dublin, 22 October, 1965 IR Yth/IRu21-4 (M)

League Club	Source	Date Signed	Seasons Played	Apps	Subs	Gls
Southampton	App	10.83	84	1	2	0
Portsmouth	Tr	05.86	86	4	1	0
Exeter C.	L	11.87	87	8	1	0
Colchester U.	Tr	05.89	89	39	0	2
Exeter C.	Tr	07.92	92	8	3	0

COLLINS George Cornelius
Hengoed, 6 August, 1935 (CF)

League Club	Source	Date Signed	Seasons Played	Apps	Subs	Gls
Bristol Rov.	Ton Pentre	06.60	60	2	-	1

COLLINS Glyn
Hereford, 18 January, 1946 (G)

League Club	Source	Date Signed	Seasons Played	Apps	Subs	Gls
Brighton & H.A. (Am)		03.66	65	2	0	0

COLLINS Graham Frank
Bury, 5 February, 1947 (WH)

League Club	Source	Date Signed	Seasons Played	Apps	Subs	Gls
Rochdale	Jnrs	09.65	66	7	0	0

COLLINS James
Sorn, 21 December, 1937 (IF)

League Club	Source	Date Signed	Seasons Played	Apps	Subs	Gls
Tottenham H.	Lugar Boswell Thistle	06.56	61	2	-	0
Brighton & H. A.	Tr	10.62	62-66	199	2	44

COLLINS James Ian
Liverpool, 28 May, 1978 (M)

League Club	Source	Date Signed	Seasons Played	Apps	Subs	Gls
Crewe Alex.	YT	07.96	97	0	1	0

COLLINS James Kenneth
Colne, 7 November, 1923 Died 1996 (IF)

League Club	Source	Date Signed	Seasons Played	Apps	Subs	Gls
Barrow	Derby Co. (Am)	09.47	47-54	295	-	52
Chester C.	Tr	07.55	55-56	48	-	11

COLLINS James Patrick
Urmston, 27 December, 1966 (RB)

League Club	Source	Date Signed	Seasons Played	Apps	Subs	Gls
Oldham Ath.	YT	08.84	83	0	1	0
Bury	Tr	10.86	86-87	10	1	0

COLLINS Jeremy David
Plymouth, 21 December, 1961 (M)

League Club	Source	Date Signed	Seasons Played	Apps	Subs	Gls
Plymouth Arg.	App	01.80	80-81	4	0	0
Torquay U.	Falmouth	08.83	83	6	0	0

COLLINS John Joseph
Manchester, 30 January, 1945 (FB)

League Club	Source	Date Signed	Seasons Played	Apps	Subs	Gls
Blackburn Rov.	Jnrs	02.63				
Stockport Co.	Tr	01.64	63-65	84	0	1

COLLINS John Lindsay
Rhymney, 21 January, 1949 W Sch/Wu23-7 (FB)

League Club	Source	Date Signed	Seasons Played	Apps	Subs	Gls
Tottenham H.	App	03.66	65-67	2	0	0
Portsmouth	Tr	05.71	71-73	71	3	0
Halifax T.	Tr	08.74	74-75	82	0	1
Sheffield Wed.	Tr	07.76	76	7	0	0
Barnsley	Tr	12.76	76-79	129	1	1

COLLINS John William
Chiswick, 10 August, 1942 (IF)

League Club	Source	Date Signed	Seasons Played	Apps	Subs	Gls
Queens Park R	Jnrs	08.59	59-66	172	0	46
Oldham Ath.	Tr	10.66	66	20	1	8
Reading	Tr	08.67	67-68	82	3	28
Luton T.	Tr	08.69	69-70	40	2	10
Cambridge U.	Tr	02.71	70-72	93	4	16

COLLINS Kenneth John
Pontypridd, 11 October, 1933 (FB)

League Club	Source	Date Signed	Seasons Played	Apps	Subs	Gls
Fulham	Ynysybwl	05.52	55-58	32	-	0

COLLINS Kevin
Birmingham, 21 July, 1964 (D)

League Club	Source	Date Signed	Seasons Played	Apps	Subs	Gls
Shrewsbury T.	Boldmere St Michael	01.84	83	1	0	0

COLLINS Lee
Bellshill, 3 February, 1974 (M)

League Club	Source	Date Signed	Seasons Played	Apps	Subs	Gls
Swindon T.	Albion Rov.	11.95	95-97	27	8	1

COLLINS Lynn
Neath, 30 April, 1948 (FB)

League Club	Source	Date Signed	Seasons Played	Apps	Subs	Gls
Newport Co.	Jnrs	06.66	66-67	17	0	0

COLLINS Michael Anthony
South Africa, 27 July, 1953 (F)

League Club	Source	Date Signed	Seasons Played	Apps	Subs	Gls
Wolverhampton W.	Jnrs	08.71				
Swindon T.	Stafford R.	07.73	73	2	4	0

COLLINS Michael Joseph Anthony
Bermondsey, 1 February, 1938 (CH)

League Club	Source	Date Signed	Seasons Played	Apps	Subs	Gls
Luton T.	Jnrs	03.55	59-61	8	-	0

COLLINS Michael Thomas
Belfast, 6 September, 1977 NI Yth (M)

League Club	Source	Date Signed	Seasons Played	Apps	Subs	Gls
Darlington (N/C)	Sheffield U. (YT)	08.96	96	0	1	0

COLLINS Ronald Michael
Middlesbrough, 8 June, 1933 (G)

League Club	Source	Date Signed	Seasons Played	Apps	Subs	Gls
Chelsea	Redcar	11.51	53	1	-	0
Watford	Tr	07.57	57-58	43	-	0

COLLINS Paul
West Ham, 11 August, 1966 E Yth (M)

League Club	Source	Date Signed	Seasons Played	Apps	Subs	Gls
Gillingham	App	08.84	84-86	30	7	3

COLLINS Peter John
Chelmsford, 29 November, 1948 (CH)

League Club	Source	Date Signed	Seasons Played	Apps	Subs	Gls
Tottenham H.	Chelmsford C.	01.68	68-72	77	6	4

COLLINS Robert Lionel
Winchester, 12 August, 1939 (G)

League Club	Source	Date Signed	Seasons Played	Apps	Subs	Gls
Newport Co. (Am)	Winchester C.	03.63	62	1	-	0

COLLINS Robert Young
Glasgow, 16 February, 1931 SF Lge/S-31 (IF)

League Club	Source	Date Signed	Seasons Played	Apps	Subs	Gls
Everton	Glasgow Celtic	09.58	58-61	133	-	42
Leeds U.	Tr	03.62	61-66	149	0	24
Bury	Tr	02.67	66-68	74	1	5
Oldham Ath.	Morton	10.72	72	6	1	0

COLLINS Roderick
Dublin, 7 August, 1962 (F)

League Club	Source	Date Signed	Seasons Played	Apps	Subs	Gls
Mansfield T.	Dundalk	12.85	85-86	11	5	1
Newport Co.	Tr	08.87	87	5	2	1

COLLINS Ronald (Sam) Dudley
Bristol, 13 January, 1923 (IF)

League Club	Source	Date Signed	Seasons Played	Apps	Subs	Gls
Bristol C.		11.44	46-47	14	-	2
Torquay U.	Tr	06.48	48-57	355	-	204

COLLINS Samuel Jason
Pontefract, 5 June, 1977 (CD)

League Club	Source	Date Signed	Seasons Played	Apps	Subs	Gls
Huddersfield T.	YT	07.94	96-97	12	2	0

COLLINS Simon
Pontefract, 16 December, 1973 (M)

League Club	Source	Date Signed	Seasons Played	Apps	Subs	Gls
Huddersfield T.	YT	07.92	92-96	31	21	3
Plymouth Arg.	Tr	03.97	96-97	41	3	3

COLLINS Stephen Mark
Stamford, 21 March, 1962 (LB)

League Club	Source	Date Signed	Seasons Played	Apps	Subs	Gls
Peterborough U.	App	08.79	78-82	92	2	1
Southend U.	Tr	08.83	83-84	51	0	0
Lincoln C.	Tr	03.85	84-85	24	0	0
Peterborough U.	Tr	12.85	85-88	114	8	2

COLLINS Terence James
Penrhiwceiber, 8 January, 1943 (IF)

League Club	Source	Date Signed	Seasons Played	Apps	Subs	Gls
Swansea C.	Ton Pentre	03.67	67	1	0	0

COLLINS Wayne Anthony
Manchester, 4 March, 1969 (M)

League Club	Source	Date Signed	Seasons Played	Apps	Subs	Gls
Crewe Alex.	Winsford U.	07.93	93-95	102	15	14
Sheffield Wed.	Tr	08.96	96-97	16	15	6
Fulham	Tr	01.98	97	10	3	1

COLLINS William Hanna
Belfast, 15 February, 1920 (WH)

League Club	Source	Date Signed	Seasons Played	Apps	Subs	Gls
Luton T.	Distillery	02.48	47-48	7	-	0
Gillingham	Tr	10.49	50	13	-	0

COLLINSON Clifford
Middlesbrough, 3 March, 1920 Died 1990 (G)

League Club	Source	Date Signed	Seasons Played	Apps	Subs	Gls
Manchester U.	Urmston B.C.	09.46	46	7	-	0

COLLINSON Leslie
Hull, 2 December, 1935 (WH)

League Club	Source	Date Signed	Seasons Played	Apps	Subs	Gls
Hull C.	Jnrs	09.56	56-66	296	1	14
York C.	Tr	02.67	66-67	35	0	2

COLLINSON Roger
Rawmarsh, 5 December, 1940 Died 1989 E Sch/E Yth (FB)

League Club	Source	Date Signed	Seasons Played	Apps	Subs	Gls
Bristol C.	Doncaster Rov. (Am)	10.58	59-60	50	-	1
Stockport Co.	Tr	0761	61	2	-	0

COLLYMORE Stanley Victor
Cannock, 22 January, 1971 E-3 (F)

League Club	Source	Date Signed	Seasons Played	Apps	Subs	Gls
Wolverhampton W. (N/C)	YT	07.89				
Crystal Palace	Stafford R.	12.90	90-92	4	16	1
Southend U.	Tr	11.92	92	30	0	15
Nottingham F.	Tr	07.93	93-94	64	1	41
Liverpool	Tr	07.95	95-96	55	6	26
Aston Villa	Tr	05.97	97	23	2	6

COLMAN Edward
Salford, 1 November, 1936 Died 1958 (WH)

League Club	Source	Date Signed	Seasons Played	Apps	Subs	Gls
Manchester U.	Jnrs	11.53	55-57	85	-	1

COLOMBO Donald Simon
Poplar, 26 October, 1928 (OL)

League Club	Source	Date Signed	Seasons Played	Apps	Subs	Gls
Portsmouth	Barking	03.53				
Walsall	Tr	12.53	53	20	-	1

COLQUHOUN Edmund Peter Skiruing
Prestonpans, 29 March, 1945 S-9 (CD)

League Club	Source	Date Signed	Seasons Played	Apps	Subs	Gls
Bury	Jnrs	03.62	63-66	81	0	2
West Bromwich A.	Tr	02.67	66-68	46	0	1
Sheffield U.	Tr	10.68	68-77	360	3	21

COLQUHOUN John
Stirling, 3 June, 1940 (M)

League Club	Source	Date Signed	Seasons Played	Apps	Subs	Gls
Oldham Ath.	Stirling A.	08.61	61-64	163	-	33
Scunthorpe U.	Tr	06.65	65-68	149	0	23
Oldham Ath.	Tr	11.68	68-69	68	2	6

COLQUHOUN John Mark
Stirling, 14 July, 1963 S-1 (W)

League Club	Source	Date Signed	Seasons Played	Apps	Subs	Gls
Millwall	Hearts	08.91	91	27	0	3
Sunderland	Tr	07.92	92	12	8	0

COLRAIN John James
Glasgow, 4 February, 1937 Died 1984 Su23-1 (F)

League Club	Source	Date Signed	Seasons Played	Apps	Subs	Gls
Ipswich T.	Clyde	06.63	63-65	55	1	17

COLVAN Hugh
Port Glasgow, 24 September, 1925 (IL)

League Club	Source	Date Signed	Seasons Played	Apps	Subs	Gls
Rochdale	Hibernian	02.48	47	1	-	0

COLVILLE Henry
Kirkcaldy, 12 February, 1924 (OL)

League Club	Source	Date Signed	Seasons Played	Apps	Subs	Gls
Chester C.	East Fife	08.47	47	4	-	1

COLVILLE Robert John
Nuneaton, 27 April, 1963 W Semi Pro (F)

League Club	Source	Date Signed	Seasons Played	Apps	Subs	Gls
Oldham Ath.	Rhos U.	02.84	83-86	22	10	4
Bury	Tr	10.86	86-87	5	6	1
Stockport Co.	Tr	09.87	87-88	67	4	19
York C.	Tr	06.89	89	17	7	0

COMERFORD Patrick
Chester-le-Street, 30 November, 1925 (WH)

League Club	Source	Date Signed	Seasons Played	Apps	Subs	Gls
Shrewsbury T.	Bedford T.	07.52	52	7	-	0

COMFORT Alan
Aldershot, 8 December, 1964 E Yth (LW)

League Club	Source	Date Signed	Seasons Played	Apps	Subs	Gls
Queens Park R	App	10.82				
Cambridge U.	Tr	09.84	84-85	61	2	5
Leyton Orient	Tr	03.86	85-88	145	5	46
Middlesbrough	Tr	07.89	89	15	0	2

COMLEY Leonard George
Swansea, 25 January, 1922 (IF)

League Club	Source	Date Signed	Seasons Played	Apps	Subs	Gls
Swansea C.	Jnrs	10.45	46-47	28	-	7
Newport Co.	Tr	10.48	48-50	76	-	29
Scunthorpe U.	Tr	03.51	50	12	-	5

COMMON Alan Robert
Stannington, 16 December, 1954 (FB)

League Club	Source	Date Signed	Seasons Played	Apps	Subs	Gls
West Bromwich A.	App	12.72				
Stockport Co.	Tr	07.73	73	2	1	0

COMMONS Michael
Adwick-le-Street, 18 April, 1940 (CF)

League Club	Source	Date Signed	Seasons Played	Apps	Subs	Gls
Lincoln C.	Wath W.	05.58	59-60	2	-	1
Workington	Tr	07.61	61-63	74	-	36
Chesterfield	Tr	07.64	64	10	-	1

COMPTON Denis Charles Scott
Hendon, 23 May, 1918 Died 1997 (OL)

League Club	Source	Date Signed	Seasons Played	Apps	Subs	Gls
Arsenal	Nunhead	05.35	36-49	54	-	15

COMPTON John Frederick
Poplar, 27 August, 1937 (LB)

League Club	Source	Date Signed	Seasons Played	Apps	Subs	Gls
Chelsea	Jnrs	02.55	55-59	12	-	0
Ipswich T.	Tr	07.60	60-63	111	-	0
Bournemouth	Tr	07.64	64	27	-	1

COMPTON Leslie Harry
Woodford, 12 September, 1912 Died 1984 EF Lge/E-2 (CH)

League Club	Source	Date Signed	Seasons Played	Apps	Subs	Gls
Arsenal	Hampstead T.	02.32	31-51	253	-	5

COMPTON Paul David
Stroud, 6 June, 1961 (CD)

League Club	Source	Date Signed	Seasons Played	Apps	Subs	Gls
Bournemouth	Trowbridge T.	10.80	80-82	64	0	0
Aldershot (N/C)	Tr	12.83	83	13	0	0
Torquay U.	Tr	02.84	83-86	95	0	4
Newport Co.	Tr	12.86	86	27	0	2
Torquay U. (N/C)	Bashley	08.91	91-92	19	2	0

COMPTON Roy
Lambeth, 8 November, 1954 (F)

League Club	Source	Date Signed	Seasons Played	Apps	Subs	Gls
Swindon T.	Millwall (App)	11.72	73	4	0	2

COMPTON Terence David
Bristol, 28 November, 1931 Died 1991 (CH)

League Club	Source	Date Signed	Seasons Played	Apps	Subs	Gls
Bristol C.	Jnrs	12.48	51-57	44	-	0

COMSTIVE Paul Thomas
Southport, 25 November, 1961 (M)

League Club	Source	Date Signed	Seasons Played	Apps	Subs	Gls
Blackburn Rov.	Jnrs	10.79	80-82	3	3	0
Rochdale	L	09.82	82	9	0	2
Wigan Ath.	Tr	08.83	83-84	35	0	2
Wrexham	Tr	11.84	84-86	95	4	8
Burnley	Tr	07.87	87-88	81	1	17
Bolton W.	Tr	09.89	89-90	42	7	3
Chester C.	Tr	11.91	91-92	55	2	6

COMYN Andrew John
Wakefield, 2 August, 1968 (CD)

League Club	Source	Date Signed	Seasons Played	Apps	Subs	Gls
Aston Villa	Alvechurch	08.89	89-90	12	3	0
Derby Co.	Tr	08.91	91-92	59	4	1
Plymouth Arg.	Tr	08.93	93-94	76	0	5
West Bromwich A. (N/C)	Tr	03.96	95	3	0	0

CONBOY Francis Joseph Anthony
Marylebone, 5 September, 1947 (WH)

League Club	Source	Date Signed	Seasons Played	Apps	Subs	Gls
Chelsea	App	07.65				
Luton T.	Tr	10.66	66	19	0	1

CONDE James Patrick
Cresswell, 19 July, 1944 (CF)

League Club	Source	Date Signed	Seasons Played	Apps	Subs	Gls
Wolverhampton W.	Jnrs	05.62				
Scunthorpe U.	Tr	06.63	63	4	-	1

CONDIE James
Hamilton, 24 July, 1926 (W)

League Club	Source	Date Signed	Seasons Played	Apps	Subs	Gls
Walsall	Kilsyth R.	12.47	47-49	49	-	2

CONEY Dean Henry
Dagenham, 18 September, 1963 Eu21-4 (F)

League Club	Source	Date Signed	Seasons Played	Apps	Subs	Gls
Fulham	App	05.81	80-86	209	2	56
Queens Park R.	Tr	06.87	87-88	36	12	7
Norwich C.	Tr	03.89	88-89	12	5	1

CONLEY Brian John
Thurnscoe, 21 November, 1948 (WH)

League Club	Source	Date Signed	Seasons Played	Apps	Subs	Gls
Sheffield U.	App	01.66				
Bradford P. A.	Tr	12.68	68-69	11	2	0

CONLEY John **Joseph**
Whitstable, 27 September, 1920 Died 1991 (CF)

League Club	Source	Date Signed	Seasons Played	Apps	Subs	Gls
Torquay U.	Charlton Ath. (Jnrs)	05.39	46-50	156	-	72

CONLON Barry John
Drogheda, 1 October, 1978 IRu21-1 (F)

League Club	Source	Date Signed	Seasons Played	Apps	Subs	Gls
Manchester C.	Queens Park R. (YT)	08.97	97	1	6	0
Plymouth Arg.	L	02.98	97	13	0	2

CONLON Bryan
Shildon, 14 January, 1943 (F)

League Club	Source	Date Signed	Seasons Played	Apps	Subs	Gls
Newcastle U.	Jnrs	05.61				
Darlington	South Shields	08.64	64-67	71	3	27
Millwall	Tr	11.67	67-68	40	1	13
Norwich C.	Tr	12.68	68-69	29	0	8
Blackburn Rov.	Tr	05.70	70-71	43	2	7
Crewe Alex.	L	01.72	71	4	0	1
Cambridge U.	Tr	03.72	71-72	17	1	3
Hartlepool U.	Tr	09.72	72-73	38	3	3

CONLON Paul Robert
Sunderland, 5 January, 1978 (F)

League Club	Source	Date Signed	Seasons Played	Apps	Subs	Gls
Hartlepool U.	YT	•	95	11	4	4
Sunderland	Tr	07.96				
Doncaster Rov.	Tr	08.97	97	4	10	1

CONMY Oliver Martin
Mulrany (Ire), 13 November, 1939 IR-5 (W)

League Club	Source	Date Signed	Seasons Played	Apps	Subs	Gls
Huddersfield T.	St Paulinus Y.C.	05.59	60-62	3	-	0
Peterborough U.	Tr	05.64	64-71	251	12	34

CONN Alfred James
Edinburgh, 5 April, 1952 Su23-3/S-2 (M)

League Club	Source	Date Signed	Seasons Played	Apps	Subs	Gls
Tottenham H.	Glasgow Rangers	07.74	74-76	35	3	6
Blackpool	Hearts	03.81	80	3	0	0

CONNACHAN Edward Devlin
Prestonpans, 27 August, 1935 SF Lge/S-2 (G)

League Club	Source	Date Signed	Seasons Played	Apps	Subs	Gls
Middlesbrough	Dunfermline Ath.	08.63	63-65	95	0	0

CONNAUGHTON Patrick **John**
Wigan, 23 September, 1949 E Yth (G)

League Club	Source	Date Signed	Seasons Played	Apps	Subs	Gls
Manchester U.	App	10.66	71	3	0	0
Halifax T.	L	09.69	69	3	0	0
Torquay U.	L	10.71	71	22	0	0
Sheffield U.	Tr	10.72	73	12	0	0
Port Vale	Tr	06.74	74-79	191	0	0

CONNEALLY Martin
Lichfield, 2 February, 1962 (G)

League Club	Source	Date Signed	Seasons Played	Apps	Subs	Gls
Walsall	App	02.80	80	3	0	0

CONNELL James David
Blackburn, 24 May, 1951 (OL)

League Club	Source	Date Signed	Seasons Played	Apps	Subs	Gls
Bury	Blackburn Rov. (App)	02.68	69	9	0	2

CONNELL Peter McArthur
East Kilbride, 26 November, 1927 Died 1995 (FB)

League Club	Source	Date Signed	Seasons Played	Apps	Subs	Gls
Northampton T.	Morton	05.51	51	13	-	0

CONNELL Roger
Seaford, 8 September, 1946 E Amat (F)

League Club	Source	Date Signed	Seasons Played	Apps	Subs	Gls
Wimbledon	Walton & Hersham	08.74	77-78	30	2	14

CONNELL Thomas Eugene
Newry (NI), 25 November, 1957 (CD)

League Club	Source	Date Signed	Seasons Played	Apps	Subs	Gls
Manchester U.	Coleraine	08.78	78	2	0	0

CONNELLY Dean
Jersey, 6 January, 1970 S Sch/S Yth (M)

League Club	Source	Date Signed	Seasons Played	Apps	Subs	Gls
Arsenal	YT	02.88				
Barnsley	Tr	06.90	90-92	7	6	0
Wigan Ath.	L	10.91	91	12	0	2
Carlisle U.	L	08.92	92	0	3	0
Wigan Ath.	Tr	02.93	92-93	15	5	1
Stockport Co.	Tr	07.94				

CONNELLY Edward John
Dumbarton, 9 December, 1916 Died 1990 (IF)

League Club	Source	Date Signed	Seasons Played	Apps	Subs	Gls
Newcastle U.	Rosslyn Pk	03.35	35-37	25	-	8
Luton T.	Tr	03.38	37-38	50	-	16
West Bromwich A.	Tr	08.39				
Luton T.	Tr	04.46	46-47	38	-	8
Leyton Orient	Tr	06.48	48-49	32	-	5
Brighton & H.A.	Tr	10.49	49	6	-	1

CONNELLY John Michael
St Helens, 18 July, 1938 Eu23-1/EF Lge/E-20 (OR)

League Club	Source	Date Signed	Seasons Played	Apps	Subs	Gls
Burnley	St Helens T.	11.56	56-63	215	-	86
Manchester U.	Tr	04.64	64-66	79	1	22
Blackburn Rov.	Tr	09.66	66-69	148	1	36
Bury	Tr	06.70	70-72	128	0	37

CONNELLY Sean Patrick
Sheffield, 26 June, 1970 (RB)

League Club	Source	Date Signed	Seasons Played	Apps	Subs	Gls
Stockport Co.	Hallam	08.91	92-97	206	5	2

CONNER Richard (Dick) John
Jarrow, 13 August, 1931 (WH)

League Club	Source	Date Signed	Seasons Played	Apps	Subs	Gls
Newcastle U.	Jnrs	01.50				
Grimsby T.	South Shields	08.52	53-58	186	-	8
Southampton	Tr	07.59	59-60	78	-	2
Tranmere Rov.	Tr	07.61	61	4	-	0
Aldershot	Tr	07.62	62	6	-	0

CONNING Terence **Peter**
Liverpool, 18 October, 1964 (W)

League Club	Source	Date Signed	Seasons Played	Apps	Subs	Gls
Rochdale	Altrincham	08.86	86	39	0	1

CONNOLLY David James
Willesden, 6 June, 1977 IR-13 (F)

League Club	Source	Date Signed	Seasons Played	Apps	Subs	Gls
Watford	YT	11.94	94-96	19	7	10

CONNOLLY John
Barrhead, 13 June, 1950 Su23-2/S-1 (W)

League Club	Source	Date Signed	Seasons Played	Apps	Subs	Gls
Everton	St Johnstone	03.72	71-75	105	3	16
Birmingham C.	Tr	09.76	76-77	49	8	9
Newcastle U.	Tr	05.78	78-79	42	7	10

CONNOLLY Karl Andrew
Prescot, 9 February, 1970 (F)

League Club	Source	Date Signed	Seasons Played	Apps	Subs	Gls
Wrexham	Napoli (Liverpool)	07.91	91-97	259	14	68

CONNOLLY Michael
Stainforth, 8 September, 1938 (W)

League Club	Source	Date Signed	Seasons Played	Apps	Subs	Gls
Doncaster Rov. (Am)	Jnrs	03.57	56	3	-	0
Wolverhampton W	Tr	09.59				
Stockport Co.	Halifax T. (Am)	11.60	59-60	6	-	0

CONNOLLY Patrick Joseph
Newcastle-u-Lyme, 27 July, 1941 (CF)

League Club	Source	Date Signed	Seasons Played	Apps	Subs	Gls
Crewe Alex.		01.61	60-62	9	-	3
Colchester U.	Macclesfield T.	07.64	64	21	-	7

CONNOR David Richard
Wythenshawe, 27 October, 1945 (FB)

League Club	Source	Date Signed	Seasons Played	Apps	Subs	Gls
Manchester C.	Jnrs	11.62	64-71	130	11	10
Preston N. E.	Tr	01.72	71-72	29	0	0

CONNOR Harold
Liverpool, 26 December, 1929 (W)

League Club	Source	Date Signed	Seasons Played	Apps	Subs	Gls
Stoke C. (Am)	Marine	03.53	52-53	4	-	2

CONNOR James
Sunderland, 28 November, 1938 (OL)

League Club	Source	Date Signed	Seasons Played	Apps	Subs	Gls
Darlington (Am)	Stanley U.	09.65	65	3	0	0

CONNOR James Richard
Twickenham, 22 August, 1974 (M)

League Club	Source	Date Signed	Seasons Played	Apps	Subs	Gls
Millwall	YT	11.92	94-95	8	1	0

CONNOR James Terence
Stockport, 31 January, 1959 (D)

League Club	Source	Date Signed	Seasons Played	Apps	Subs	Gls
Stockport Co.	Jnrs	02.79	78	1	1	0

CONNOR John
Stockport, 15 May, 1965 (G)

League Club	Source	Date Signed	Seasons Played	Apps	Subs	Gls
Stockport Co. (N/C)	Jnrs	08.80	81	1	0	0

CONNOR John
Ashton-u-Lyne, 1 February, 1914 Died 1978 (FB)

League Club	Source	Date Signed	Seasons Played	Apps	Subs	Gls
Bolton W.	Mossley	10.34	34-38	29	-	0
Tranmere Rov.	Tr	06.47	47-48	46	-	3

CONNOR John (Jack) Ferguson
Maryport, 25 July, 1934 (CH)

League Club	Source	Date Signed	Seasons Played	Apps	Subs	Gls
Huddersfield T.	Jnrs	10.52	54-60	85	-	10
Bristol C.	Tr	10.60	60-70	354	1	10

CONNOR John (Jack) Thomas
Todmorden, 21 December, 1919 (CF)

League Club	Source	Date Signed	Seasons Played	Apps	Subs	Gls
Ipswich T.	Albion Rov.	11.44	46	12	-	4
Carlisle U.	Tr	12.46	46-47	39	-	12
Rochdale	Ards	12.48	48-50	82	-	42
Bradford C.	Tr	04.51	50-51	14	-	7
Stockport Co.	Tr	10.51	51-56	206	-	132
Crewe Alex.	Tr	09.56	56	27	-	4

CONNOR Kevin Holland
Radcliffe, 12 January, 1945 (RB)

League Club	Source	Date Signed	Seasons Played	Apps	Subs	Gls
Rochdale		01.66	65-66	21	4	1

CONNOR Paul
Bishop Auckland, 12 January, 1979 (F)

League Club	Source	Date Signed	Seasons Played	Apps	Subs	Gls
Middlesbrough	YT	07.96				
Hartlepool U.	L	02.98	97	4	1	0

CONNOR Robert
Bradford, 13 October, 1925 (G)

League Club	Source	Date Signed	Seasons Played	Apps	Subs	Gls
Bradford C.	Salts	11.49	49-50	28	-	0
Wrexham	Tr	07.51	51-53	77	-	0

CONNOR Terence Fitzroy
Leeds, 9 November, 1962 E Yth/Eu21-1 (F)

League Club	Source	Date Signed	Seasons Played	Apps	Subs	Gls
Leeds U.	App	11.79	79-82	83	13	19
Brighton & H. A.	Tr	03.83	82-86	153	3	51
Portsmouth	Tr	06.87	87-89	42	6	14
Swansea C.	Tr	08.90	90-91	39	0	6
Bristol C.	Tr	09.91	91-92	11	5	1
Swansea C.	L	11.92	92	3	0	0

CONNORS John Joseph Aloysius
Stockton, 21 August, 1927 (HB)

League Club	Source	Date Signed	Seasons Played	Apps	Subs	Gls
Darlington		03.48	47-51	65	-	0

CONROY Gerard (Terry) Anthony Francis
Dublin, 2 October, 1946 IR-26 (F)

League Club	Source	Date Signed	Seasons Played	Apps	Subs	Gls
Stoke C.	Glentoran	03.67	67-78	244	27	49
Crewe Alex.	Bulova (HK)	01.80	79-80	37	0	5

CONROY Michael George
Johnstone, 31 July, 1957 (M)

League Club	Source	Date Signed	Seasons Played	Apps	Subs	Gls
Blackpool	Hibernian	08.84	84-85	66	0	2
Wrexham	Tr	07.86	86	23	2	2
Leyton Orient	Tr	07.87	87	2	1	0

CONROY Michael Kevin
Glasgow, 31 December, 1965 (F)

League Club	Source	Date Signed	Seasons Played	Apps	Subs	Gls
Reading	St Mirren	09.88	88-90	65	15	7
Burnley	Tr	07.91	91-92	76	1	30
Preston N.E.	Tr	08.93	93-94	50	7	22
Fulham	Tr	08.95	95-97	88	6	32
Blackpool	Tr	03.98	97	5	1	0

CONROY Richard
Bradford, 29 July, 1927 Died 1991 (CH)

League Club	Source	Date Signed	Seasons Played	Apps	Subs	Gls
Bradford C.	Swain House	02.48	48-52	158	-	0
Bradford P.A.	Tr	10.53	53-55	57	-	0

CONROY Maurice **Richard**
Bradford, 26 April, 1919 (D)

League Club	Source	Date Signed	Seasons Played	Apps	Subs	Gls
Fulham		05.37				
Accrington St.	Tr	09.44	46-48	87	-	1
Scunthorpe U.	Tr	09.50	50	1	-	0

CONROY Robert Bell
Kirkintilloch, 20 June, 1929 Died 1978 (LB)

League Club	Source	Date Signed	Seasons Played	Apps	Subs	Gls
Bury	Ashfield Jnrs	10.51	55-61	217	-	2
Tranmere Rov.	Tr	07.62	62-64	103	-	1

CONROY Steven Harold
Chesterfield, 19 December, 1956 (G)

League Club	Source	Date Signed	Seasons Played	Apps	Subs	Gls
Sheffield U.	App	06.74	77-82	104	0	0
Rotherham U. (N/C)	Tr	02.83	82	5	0	0
Rochdale	Tr	06.83	83-84	49	0	0
Rotherham U.	Tr	01.85				

CONSTABLE Shaun
Maidstone, 21 March, 1968 (LW)

League Club	Source	Date Signed	Seasons Played	Apps	Subs	Gls
Scunthorpe U. (N/C)	Leeds Univ.	02.93	92	2	5	0

CONSTANTINE David
Ashton-u-Lyne, 2 February, 1957 E Semi Pro (FB)

League Club	Source	Date Signed	Seasons Played	Apps	Subs	Gls
Bury	Hyde U.	02.79	78-81	67	3	2

CONSTANTINE James
Ashton-u-Lyne, 16 February, 1920 (CF)

League Club	Source	Date Signed	Seasons Played	Apps	Subs	Gls
Rochdale	Ashton Nat.	01.45				
Manchester C.	Tr	04.45	46	18	-	12
Bury	Tr	08.47	47	32	-	14
Millwall	Tr	05.48	48-51	141	-	74

CONSTANTINOU Costakis
Cyprus, 24 September, 1968 Cypriot Int (CD)

League Club	Source	Date Signed	Seasons Played	Apps	Subs	Gls
Barnet (L)	Omoninia Nicosia (Cyp)	10.96	96	1	0	0

CONWAY Andrew
South Shields, 17 February, 1923 Died 1996 (CF)

League Club	Source	Date Signed	Seasons Played	Apps	Subs	Gls
Hull C.	North Shields	06.47	47-48	6	-	5
Stockport Co.	Dartford	07.50				

CONWAY Christopher
Dundee, 23 July, 1928 (G)

League Club	Source	Date Signed	Seasons Played	Apps	Subs	Gls
Bury	Ayr U.	09.54	54-55	44	-	0

CONWAY James
Motherwell, 27 August, 1940 S Sch (CF)

League Club	Source	Date Signed	Seasons Played	Apps	Subs	Gls
Norwich C.	Glasgow Celtic	05.61	61-63	42	-	13
Southend U.	Tr	10.63	63-64	31	-	9

CONWAY James Patrick
Dublin, 10 August, 1946 IR Amat/IR-20 (OR)

League Club	Source	Date Signed	Seasons Played	Apps	Subs	Gls
Fulham	Bohemians	05.66	66-75	312	4	67
Manchester C.	Tr	08.76	76	11	2	1

CONWAY John
Dublin, 11 July, 1951 (W)

League Club	Source	Date Signed	Seasons Played	Apps	Subs	Gls
Fulham	Bohemians	08.71	71-74	30	8	6

CONWAY John George
Gateshead, 24 January, 1931 (F)

League Club	Source	Date Signed	Seasons Played	Apps	Subs	Gls
Gateshead		05.53	53-54	4	-	0

CONWAY Michael Denis
Sheffield, 11 March, 1956 (W)

League Club	Source	Date Signed	Seasons Played	Apps	Subs	Gls
Brighton & H. A.	App	03.74	72-73	1	1	1
Swansea C.	Tr	12.75	75-77	56	5	11

CONWAY Patrick
Newcastle, 19 September, 1968 (M)

League Club	Source	Date Signed	Seasons Played	Apps	Subs	Gls
Cambridge U. (N/C)	YT	10.85	85-86	2	0	0

CONWAY Paul James
Wandsworth, 17 April, 1970 USA u21 Int (F)

League Club	Source	Date Signed	Seasons Played	Apps	Subs	Gls
Carlisle U.		10.93	93-96	75	14	22
Northampton T.	Tr	06.97	97	2	1	0
Scarborough	L	12.97	97	13	0	2

CONWAY Thomas
Stoke, 7 November, 1933 (IF)

League Club	Source	Date Signed	Seasons Played	Apps	Subs	Gls
Port Vale	Jnrs	05.51	55	15	-	4

CONWELL Anthony
Bradford, 17 January, 1932 (FB)

League Club	Source	Date Signed	Seasons Played	Apps	Subs	Gls
Sheffield Wed.	Jnrs	02.49	53-54	44	-	0
Huddersfield T.	Tr	07.55	55-58	106	-	2
Derby Co.	Tr	06.59	59-61	98	-	1
Doncaster Rov.	Tr	07.62	62-63	35	-	0

COOK Aaron
Caerphilly, 6 December, 1979 (LB)

League Club	Source	Date Signed	Seasons Played	Apps	Subs	Gls
Portsmouth	YT	●	97	1	0	0

COOK Andrew Charles
Romsey, 10 August, 1969 (LB)

League Club	Source	Date Signed	Seasons Played	Apps	Subs	Gls
Southampton	App	06.87	87-90	11	5	1
Exeter C.	Tr	09.91	91-92	70	0	1
Swansea C.	Tr	07.93	93-95	54	8	0
Portsmouth	Tr	12.96	96-97	7	2	0
Millwall	Tr	01.98	97	3	0	0

COOK Anthony
Bristol, 8 October, 1929 Died 1996 (G)

League Club	Source	Date Signed	Seasons Played	Apps	Subs	Gls
Bristol C.	Clifton St Vincent	01.50	52-63	320	-	0

COOK Anthony
Hemel Hempstead, 17 September, 1976 (M)

League Club	Source	Date Signed	Seasons Played	Apps	Subs	Gls
Colchester U.	YT	●	93	1	1	0

COOK Anthony
Crewe, 26 December, 1961 (M)

League Club	Source	Date Signed	Seasons Played	Apps	Subs	Gls
Crewe Alex. (N/C)	Winsford U.	05.81	81	2	1	0

COOK Charles Ivor
Cheltenham, 28 January, 1937 (FB)

League Club	Source	Date Signed	Seasons Played	Apps	Subs	Gls
Bristol C.	Gloucester C.	02.57	56-57	2	-	0

COOK Garry John
Northampton, 31 March, 1978 (M)

League Club	Source	Date Signed	Seasons Played	Apps	Subs	Gls
Hereford U.	YT	07.96	96	17	3	0

COOK James Steven
Oxford, 2 August, 1979 (W)

League Club	Source	Date Signed	Seasons Played	Apps	Subs	Gls
Oxford U.	YT	07.97	97	9	11	2

COOK Jason Peter
Edmonton, 29 December, 1969 (M)

League Club	Source	Date Signed	Seasons Played	Apps	Subs	Gls
Tottenham H.	YT	07.88				
Southend U.	Tr	07.89	89-90	29	1	1
Colchester U.	Tr	09.91	92-93	30	5	1

COOK Jeffrey William
Hartlepool, 14 March, 1953 (F)

League Club	Source	Date Signed	Seasons Played	Apps	Subs	Gls
Stoke C.	Hellenic (SA)	10.77	77-81	22	8	5
Bradford C.	L	02.79	78	8	0	1
Plymouth Arg.	L	12.79	79	4	3	5
Plymouth Arg.	Tr	10.81	81-82	54	1	21
Halifax T.	Tr	08.83	83-84	49	7	9

COOK John Albert
Iron Acton, 27 June, 1929 (IF)

League Club	Source	Date Signed	Seasons Played	Apps	Subs	Gls
Bristol Rov.	Jnrs	09.46	46	2	-	0

COOK Leslie
Blackburn, 11 November, 1924 Died 1996 E Sch (WH)

League Club	Source	Date Signed	Seasons Played	Apps	Subs	Gls
Blackburn Rov.	Jnrs	11.41	46-48	76	-	0
Coventry C.	Tr	07.49	49-53	88	-	0

COOK Malcolm Ian
Glasgow, 24 May, 1943 (WH)

League Club	Source	Date Signed	Seasons Played	Apps	Subs	Gls
Bradford P. A.	Motherwell	07.63	63-64	45	-	2
Newport Co.	Tr	07.65	65	30	2	0

COOK Mark Richard
Boston, 7 August, 1970 (M)

League Club	Source	Date Signed	Seasons Played	Apps	Subs	Gls
Lincoln C.	YT	08.88	88-89	7	0	0

COOK Maurice
Hemel Hempstead, 10 December, 1931 (CF)

League Club	Source	Date Signed	Seasons Played	Apps	Subs	Gls
Watford	Berkhamsted	05.53	53-57	208	-	68
Fulham	Tr	02.58	57-64	221	-	89
Reading	Tr	05.65	65	12	0	2

COOK Michael
Enfield, 9 April, 1951 (FB)

League Club	Source	Date Signed	Seasons Played	Apps	Subs	Gls
Colchester U.	Leyton Orient (Am)	07.69	69-83	609	4	21

COOK Michael John
Stroud, 18 October, 1968 (M)

League Club	Source	Date Signed	Seasons Played	Apps	Subs	Gls
Coventry C.	YT	03.87				
York C.	L	08.87	87	6	0	1
Cambridge U.	Tr	06.89	89-90	12	5	1
York C.	L	11.90	90	3	3	0

COOK Michael John
Sutton, 25 January, 1950 (CF)

League Club	Source	Date Signed	Seasons Played	Apps	Subs	Gls
Crystal Palace	App	02.68	67	1	0	0
Brentford	Tr	08.69	69	16	4	4

COOK Mitchell Christopher
Scarborough, 15 October, 1961 (M/LB)

League Club	Source	Date Signed	Seasons Played	Apps	Subs	Gls
Darlington	Scarborough	08.84	84-85	34	0	4

League Club	Source	Date Signed	Seasons Played	Career Record Apps	Subs	Gls
Middlesbrough	Tr	09.85	85	3	3	0
Scarborough	Tr	08.86	87-88	61	20	10
Halifax T.	Tr	07.89	89-90	52	2	2
Scarborough	L	10.90	90	9	0	1
Darlington	Tr	03.91	90-91	35	1	4
Blackpool	Tr	03.92	91-94	66	2	0
Hartlepool U.	Tr	11.94	94	22	2	0
Scarborough (N/C)	Guiseley	03.96	95	2	0	0

COOK Paul Anthony
Liverpool, 22 February, 1967 (M)

League Club	Source	Date Signed	Seasons Played	Apps	Subs	Gls
Wigan Ath.	Marine	07.84	84-87	77	6	14
Norwich C.	Tr	05.88	88-89	3	3	0
Wolverhampton W.	Tr	11.89	89-93	191	2	19
Coventry C.	Tr	08.94	94-95	35	2	3
Tranmere Rov.	Tr	02.96	95-97	54	6	4
Stockport Co.	Tr	10.97	97	25	0	3

COOK Peter Henry
Hull, 1 February, 1927 Died 1960 (W)

League Club	Source	Date Signed	Seasons Played	Apps	Subs	Gls
Hull C.	Kingston Wolves	06.46	46-47	5	-	0
Bradford C.	Scarborough	05.49	49	1	-	0
Crewe Alex.	Tr	08.50	50-52	45	-	7

COOK Reuben
Gateshead, 9 March, 1933 (WH)

League Club	Source	Date Signed	Seasons Played	Apps	Subs	Gls
Arsenal	Tow Law T.	11.51				
Leyton Orient	Tr	01.56	56	2	-	0

COOK Robert Kenneth
Letchworth, 13 June, 1924 Died 1997 (W)

League Club	Source	Date Signed	Seasons Played	Apps	Subs	Gls
Reading	Letchworth T.	03.48				
Tottenham H.	Tr	07.49	49	3	-	0
Watford	Tr	08.51	51-52	53	-	8

COOK Trevor
Blidworth, 2 July, 1956 (F)

League Club	Source	Date Signed	Seasons Played	Apps	Subs	Gls
Mansfield T.	App	07.74	73	1	0	0

COOKE Alan
Nantwich, 28 December, 1930 Died 1990 (LB)

League Club	Source	Date Signed	Seasons Played	Apps	Subs	Gls
Crewe Alex.		08.55	55	8	-	0

COOKE Andrew Roy
Shrewsbury, 2 January, 1974 (F)

League Club	Source	Date Signed	Seasons Played	Apps	Subs	Gls
Burnley	Newtown	05.95	95-97	55	33	33

COOKE Barry Anthony
Wolverhampton, 22 January, 1938 EYth (WH)

League Club	Source	Date Signed	Seasons Played	Apps	Subs	Gls
West Bromwich A.	Erdington	05.55				
Northampton T.	Tr	07.59	59-61	58	-	1

COOKE Charles
St Monance (Fife), 14 October, 1942 Su23-4/SF Lge/S-16 (M)

League Club	Source	Date Signed	Seasons Played	Apps	Subs	Gls
Chelsea	Dundee	04.66	66-72	204	8	15
Crystal Palace	Tr	10.72	72-73	42	2	0
Chelsea	Tr	01.74	73-77	85	2	7

COOKE David Frederick
Birmingham, 29 November, 1946 (FB)

League Club	Source	Date Signed	Seasons Played	Apps	Subs	Gls
Wolverhampton W.	Jnrs	07.65				
Stockport Co.	Tr	07.68	68	3	0	0

COOKE Edward John
Barnsley, 18 March, 1942 (G)

League Club	Source	Date Signed	Seasons Played	Apps	Subs	Gls
Port Vale	Jnrs	06.60	60-63	7	-	0

COOKE Gordon
Crewe, 31 May, 1928 (IR)

League Club	Source	Date Signed	Seasons Played	Apps	Subs	Gls
Crewe Alex.	Jnrs	05.48	48	2	-	0

COOKE Jason
Birmingham, 13 July, 1971 (F)

League Club	Source	Date Signed	Seasons Played	Apps	Subs	Gls
Torquay U. (N/C)	Brierley Hill T.	10.95	95	1	0	0

COOKE John
Salford, 25 April, 1962 E Yth (W)

League Club	Source	Date Signed	Seasons Played	Apps	Subs	Gls
Sunderland	App	11.79	79-84	42	13	4
Carlisle U.	L	11.84	84	5	1	2
Sheffield Wed.	Tr	06.85				
Carlisle U.	Tr	10.85	85-87	105	1	11
Stockport Co.	Tr	07.88	88-89	54	4	7
Chesterfield	Tr	07.90	90-91	48	5	8

COOKE Joseph
Dominica (WI), 15 February, 1955 (CD/F)

League Club	Source	Date Signed	Seasons Played	Apps	Subs	Gls
Bradford C.	App	05.72	71-78	184	20	62
Peterborough U.	Tr	01.79	78	18	0	5
Oxford U.	Tr	08.79	79-80	71	1	13
Exeter C.	T	06.81	81	17	0	3

League Club	Source	Date Signed	Seasons Played	Apps	Subs	Gls
Bradford C.	Tr	01.82	81-83	61	1	6
Rochdale	Tr	07.84	84-85	75	0	4
Wrexham	Tr	07.86	86-87	49	2	4

COOKE Peter Charles
Northampton, 15 January, 1962 (M)

League Club	Source	Date Signed	Seasons Played	Apps	Subs	Gls
Northampton T.	Jnrs	07.80	80	4	1	1

COOKE Richard Edward
Islington, 4 September, 1965 E Yth/Eu21-1 (W)

League Club	Source	Date Signed	Seasons Played	Apps	Subs	Gls
Tottenham H.	App	05.83	83-85	9	2	2
Birmingham C.	L	09.86	86	5	0	0
Bournemouth	Tr	01.87	86-88	63	9	15
Luton T.	Tr	03.89	88-89	3	14	1
Bournemouth	Tr	03.91	90-92	38	15	2

COOKE Robert (Robbie) Leslie
Rotherham, 16 February, 1957 (F)

League Club	Source	Date Signed	Seasons Played	Apps	Subs	Gls
Mansfield T.	App	02.75	76-77	7	8	1
Peterborough U.	Grantham	05.80	80-82	115	0	51
Cambridge U.	Tr	02.83	82-84	62	3	14
Brentford	Tr	12.84	84-87	122	1	53
Millwall	Tr	12.87	87	4	0	1

COOKE Terence Arthur
Wrexham, 21 February, 1962 (F)

League Club	Source	Date Signed	Seasons Played	Apps	Subs	Gls
Chester C.	App	02.80	80-82	37	12	11

COOKE Terence John
Birmingham, 5 August, 1976 E Yth/Eu21-4 (W)

League Club	Source	Date Signed	Seasons Played	Apps	Subs	Gls
Manchester U.	YT	07.94	95	1	3	0
Sunderland	L	01.96	95	6	0	0
Birmingham C.	L	11.96	96	1	3	0

COOKE Wilfred Hodson
Crewe, 10 October, 1915 Died 1985 (WH)

League Club	Source	Date Signed	Seasons Played	Apps	Subs	Gls
Bradford C.	Leeds U. (Am)	08.35	36-37	21	-	2
Leeds U.	Tr	07.38				
Fulham	Tr	07.39				
Crewe Alex.	Tr	02.46	46	12	-	2

COOKE William Henry
Whittington, 7 March, 1919 Died 1992 (FB)

League Club	Source	Date Signed	Seasons Played	Apps	Subs	Gls
Bournemouth		04.38				
Luton T.	Tr	01.46	46-52	211	-	4
Shrewsbury T.	Tr	07.53	53	4	-	0
Watford	Tr	07.54	54	10	-	0

COOKSEY Scott Andrew
Birmingham, 24 June, 1972 (G)

League Club	Source	Date Signed	Seasons Played	Apps	Subs	Gls
Derby Co.	YT	07.90				
Shrewsbury T.	Tr	02.91				
Peterborough U.	Bromsgrove Rov.	12.93	93-94	15	0	0

COOKSON James
Liverpool, 22 August, 1927 Died 1993 (FB)

League Club	Source	Date Signed	Seasons Played	Apps	Subs	Gls
Everton		10.45				
Southport	Tr	08.49	49-51	55	-	1

COOKSON Steven John
Wolverhampton, 19 February, 1972 (F)

League Club	Source	Date Signed	Seasons Played	Apps	Subs	Gls
Torquay U.	YT	07.90	89-90	7	5	1

COOLE William
Manchester, 27 January, 1925 (OR)

League Club	Source	Date Signed	Seasons Played	Apps	Subs	Gls
Mansfield T.		01.48	47-53	182	-	35
Notts Co.	Tr	10.53	53-55	42	-	5
Barrow	Tr	07.56	56-58	56	-	3

COOLING Roy
Barnsley, 9 December, 1921 (IF)

League Club	Source	Date Signed	Seasons Played	Apps	Subs	Gls
Barnsley	Mitchell M.W.	03.42	46	6	-	3
Mansfield T.	Tr	09.47	47-49	65	-	14

COOMBE Mark Andrew
Torquay, 17 September, 1968 (G)

League Club	Source	Date Signed	Seasons Played	Apps	Subs	Gls
Bristol C.	Bournemouth (YT)	08.87				
Colchester U. (N/C)	Carlisle U. (N/C)	10.88	88	3	0	0
Torquay U.	Tr	12.88	88	8	0	0

COOMBES Jeffrey
Porth, 1 April, 1954 W Sch (M)

League Club	Source	Date Signed	Seasons Played	Apps	Subs	Gls
Bristol Rov.	App	04.72	72-74	10	1	1

COOMBES Lee Edward
York, 5 July, 1966 (D)

League Club	Source	Date Signed	Seasons Played	Apps	Subs	Gls
Sheffield Wed.	App	07.84				
Scunthorpe U.	Tr	08.85				
Chesterfield	Tr	07.86	86	1	2	0

COOMBS Francis Henry
East Ham, 24 April, 1925 (G)

League Club	Source	Date Signed	Seasons Played	Apps	Subs	Gls
Bristol C.	Dartford	06.49	49	24	-	0
Southend U.	Tr	06.50	50	20	-	0
Colchester U.	Tr	07.51	51-53	38	-	0

COOMBS Paul Andrew
Bristol, 4 September, 1970 (F)

League Club	Source	Date Signed	Seasons Played	Apps	Subs	Gls
Aldershot	YT	07.89	88-90	9	7	1

COOP James Yates
Horwich, 17 September, 1927 Died 1996 (OL)

League Club	Source	Date Signed	Seasons Played	Apps	Subs	Gls
Sheffield U.	Shrewsbury T.	05.46	47-48	9	-	1
York C.	Tr	07.49	49-50	12	-	4

COOP Michael Anthony
Grimsby, 10 July, 1948 (RB)

League Club	Source	Date Signed	Seasons Played	Apps	Subs	Gls
Coventry C.	App	01.66	66-80	413	12	18
York C.	L	11.74	74	4	0	0
Derby Co.	Tr	07.81	81	17	1	0

COOPER Adrian Stanley John
Reading, 16 January, 1957 E Sch (M)

League Club	Source	Date Signed	Seasons Played	Apps	Subs	Gls
Reading	App	01.75	73-75	14	0	2

COOPER Arthur
Etruria, 16 March, 1921 (LH)

League Club	Source	Date Signed	Seasons Played	Apps	Subs	Gls
Port Vale	Shelton St Marks	08.41	46	4	-	0

COOPER Charles
Farnworth, 14 June, 1941 (FB)

League Club	Source	Date Signed	Seasons Played	Apps	Subs	Gls
Bolton W.	Jnrs	05.59	60-68	79	4	0
Barrow	Tr	07.69	69-70	54	0	0

COOPER Colin Terence
Sedgefield, 28 February, 1967 Eu21-8/E-2 (D)

League Club	Source	Date Signed	Seasons Played	Apps	Subs	Gls
Middlesbrough	Jnrs	06.84	85-90	183	5	6
Millwall	Tr	07.91	91-92	77	0	6
Nottingham F.	Tr	06.93	93-97	179	1	20

COOPER David Andrew
Lambeth, 25 June, 1971 (F)

League Club	Source	Date Signed	Seasons Played	Apps	Subs	Gls
Wimbledon	YT	07.89				
Plymouth Arg.	Tr	03.91	90	0	3	0

COOPER David Barry Ernest
Hatfield, 7 March, 1973 (FB)

League Club	Source	Date Signed	Seasons Played	Apps	Subs	Gls
Exeter C.	Luton T. (YT)	08.91	91-94	39	9	0

COOPER Douglas
Eston, 18 October, 1936 (F)

League Club	Source	Date Signed	Seasons Played	Apps	Subs	Gls
Middlesbrough	Jnrs	10.53	54-56	5	-	0
Rotherham U.	Tr	01.59	58	14	-	5
Hartlepool U.	Tr	08.60	60	16	-	6

COOPER Frederick John
West Ham, 18 November, 1934 Died 1972 E Sch (FB)

League Club	Source	Date Signed	Seasons Played	Apps	Subs	Gls
West Ham U.	Jnrs	12.51	56-57	4	-	0

COOPER Gary
Hammersmith, 20 November, 1965 E Sch/E Yth (M)

League Club	Source	Date Signed	Seasons Played	Apps	Subs	Gls
Queens Park R.	App	06.83	84	1	0	0
Brentford	L	09.85	85	9	1	0
Maidstone U.	Fisher Ath.	03.89	89-90	53	7	7
Peterborough U.	Tr	03.91	90-93	83	5	10
Birmingham C.	Tr	12.93	93-95	58	4	2

COOPER Gary Smethurst
Horwich, 15 February, 1955 (F)

League Club	Source	Date Signed	Seasons Played	Apps	Subs	Gls
Rochdale	Horwich R.M.I.	12.73	73-76	81	10	14
Southport	Tr	08.77	77	13	7	5

COOPER Geoffrey Victor
Kingston, 27 December, 1960 (LB)

League Club	Source	Date Signed	Seasons Played	Apps	Subs	Gls
Brighton & H.A.	Bognor Regis T.	12.87	87-88	2	5	0
Barnet	Tr	07.89	91-94	55	13	4

COOPER George
Kingswinford, 1 October, 1932 Died 1994 (IF)

League Club	Source	Date Signed	Seasons Played	Apps	Subs	Gls
Crystal Palace	Brierley Hill Alliance	01.55	54-58	69	-	27
Rochdale	Tr	01.59	58-59	32	-	9

COOPER Graham
Huddersfield, 22 May, 1962 (W)

League Club	Source	Date Signed	Seasons Played	Apps	Subs	Gls
Huddersfield T.	Emley	03.84	83-87	61	13	13
Wrexham	Tr	08.88	88-90	50	13	17
York C.	L	11.90	90	2	0	0
Halifax T.	Tr	01.91	90-91	32	7	4

COOPER Ian Laurence
Bradford, 21 September, 1946 (LB)

League Club	Source	Date Signed	Seasons Played	Apps	Subs	Gls
Bradford C.	Jnrs	08.66	65-76	442	1	4

COOPER James Else
Blackpool, 13 January, 1928 (F)

League Club	Source	Date Signed	Seasons Played	Apps	Subs	Gls
Accrington St.	Fleetwood	06.52	52	7	-	1

COOPER James Ernest
Chester, 19 January, 1942 (W)

League Club	Source	Date Signed	Seasons Played	Apps	Subs	Gls
Chester C.	Jnrs	09.59	59-61	91	-	17
Southport	Tr	06.62	62	28	-	7
Blackpool	Tr	07.63	63	4	-	0
Mansfield T.	Tr	05.64	64	7	-	4
Crewe Alex.	Tr	07.65	65	6	0	0

COOPER James Thomson
Glasgow, 28 December, 1939 (OR)

League Club	Source	Date Signed	Seasons Played	Apps	Subs	Gls
Brighton & H. A.	Airdrieonians	08.62	62-63	41	-	6
Hartlepool U.	Tr	07.65	65	19	0	1

COOPER Joseph
Reddish, 16 February, 1918 Died 1992 (LB)

League Club	Source	Date Signed	Seasons Played	Apps	Subs	Gls
Blackpool		01.38				
Crewe Alex.	Tr	07.39	46	3	-	0

COOPER Joseph
Gateshead, 15 October, 1934 (HB)

League Club	Source	Date Signed	Seasons Played	Apps	Subs	Gls
Newcastle U.	Winlaton Mill	09.52	53-57	6	-	0

COOPER Kevin Lee
Derby, 8 February, 1973 (LW)

League Club	Source	Date Signed	Seasons Played	Apps	Subs	Gls
Derby Co.	YT	07.93	94-95	0	2	0
Stockport Co.	L	03.97	96-97	41	9	11

COOPER Leigh Vernon
Reading, 7 May, 1961 (LB)

League Club	Source	Date Signed	Seasons Played	Apps	Subs	Gls
Plymouth Arg.	App	05.79	79-89	316	7	15
Aldershot	Tr	08.90	90	33	0	2

COOPER Leonard Arnold
Lower Gornal, 11 May, 1936 Died 1992 E Yth (OL)

League Club	Source	Date Signed	Seasons Played	Apps	Subs	Gls
Wolverhampton W.	Jnrs	05.53				
Walsall		02.56	55	5	-	2

COOPER Mark David
Watford, 5 April, 1967 (F)

League Club	Source	Date Signed	Seasons Played	Apps	Subs	Gls
Cambridge U.	App	10.84	83-86	62	9	17
Tottenham H.	Tr	03.87				
Shrewsbury T.	L	09.87	87	6	0	2
Gillingham	Tr	10.87	87	38	11	11
Leyton Orient	Tr	02.89	88-93	117	33	45
Barnet	Tr	07.94	94-95	58	9	19
Northampton T.	Tr	08.96	96	37	4	10

COOPER Mark Nicholas
Wakefield, 18 December, 1968 (M)

League Club	Source	Date Signed	Seasons Played	Apps	Subs	Gls
Bristol C.	YT	09.87				
Exeter C.	Tr	10.89	89-91	46	4	12
Southend U.	L	03.90	89	4	1	0
Birmingham C.	Tr	09.91	91-92	30	9	4
Fulham	Tr	11.92	92-93	10	4	0
Huddersfield T.	L	03.93	92	10	0	4
Wycombe W. (N/C)	Tr	01.94	93	0	2	1
Exeter C.	Tr	02.94	93-95	78	10	20
Hartlepool U.	Tr	07.96	96	33	0	9
Macclesfield T.	L	09.97	97	8	0	2
Leyton Orient (N/C)	Tr	12.97	97	0	1	0

COOPER Neale James
India, 24 November, 1963 S Yth/Su21-13 (CD)

League Club	Source	Date Signed	Seasons Played	Apps	Subs	Gls
Aston Villa	Aberdeen	07.86	86-87	19	1	0
Reading	Glasgow Rangers	07.91	91	6	1	0

COOPER Neil
Aberdeen, 12 August, 1959 S Sch (CD)

League Club	Source	Date Signed	Seasons Played	Apps	Subs	Gls
Barnsley	Aberdeen	01.80	79-81	57	3	6
Grimsby T.	Tr	03.82	81-83	47	0	2

COOPER Paul
Darlington, 24 December, 1975 (M)

League Club	Source	Date Signed	Seasons Played	Apps	Subs	Gls
Darlington	YT	07.93	93	1	0	0

COOPER Paul David
Brierley Hill, 21 December, 1953 (G)

League Club	Source	Date Signed	Seasons Played	Apps	Subs	Gls
Birmingham C.	App	07.71	71-73	17	0	0
Ipswich T.	Tr	03.74	73-86	447	0	0
Leicester C.	Tr	06.87	87-88	56	0	0
Manchester C.	Tr	03.89	88-89	15	0	0
Stockport Co.	Tr	08.90	90	22	0	0

League Club	Source	Date Signed	Seasons Played	Apps	Subs	Gls
COOPER Paul Terence						
Birmingham, 12 July, 1957						(FB)
Huddersfield T.	App	08.75	76	2	0	0
Grimsby T.	Tr	07.77	77	3	0	0
COOPER Richard David						
Wembley, 7 May, 1965						(M)
Sheffield U.	App	05.83	82-84	2	4	0
Lincoln C.	Tr	08.85	85-86	57	4	2
Exeter C.	Tr	07.87	87-88	55	7	2
COOPER Robert Charles						
Sutton Coldfield, 3 September, 1966						(M)
Leicester C.	YT	05.85				
Tranmere Rov.	L	12.85	85	3	2	0
COOPER Ronald						
Peterborough, 28 August, 1938						(FB)
Peterborough U.	Jnrs	(N/L)	63-67	132	0	1
COOPER Stephen Brian						
Birmingham, 22 June, 1964						(F)
Birmingham C.	Moor Green	11.83				
Halifax T.	L	12.83	83	7	0	1
Newport Co.	Tr	09.84	84	38	0	11
Plymouth Arg.	Tr	08.85	85-87	58	15	15
Barnsley	Tr	08.88	88-90	62	15	13
Tranmere Rov.	Tr	12.90	90-92	16	16	3
Peterborough U.	L	03.92	91	2	7	0
Wigan Ath.	L	12.92	92	4	0	0
York C.	Tr	08.93	93-94	37	1	6
COOPER Steven Milne						
Worcester, 14 December, 1955 E Yth						(F)
Torquay U.	Stourbridge	03.78	77-83	219	15	77
COOPER Terence						
Castleford, 12 July, 1944 E-20						(LB)
Leeds U.	App	07.62	63-74	240	10	7
Middlesbrough	Tr	03.75	74-77	105	0	1
Bristol C.	Tr	07.78	78	11	0	0
Bristol Rov.	Tr	08.79	79-81	53	6	0
Doncaster Rov.	Tr	11.81	81	20	0	0
Bristol C.	Tr	08.82	82-84	38	22	1
COOPER Terence						
Cwmbran, 11 March, 1950						(CD)
Newport Co.	Jnrs	07.68	67-69	64	4	1
Notts Co.	Tr	07.70	71-72	3	6	0
Lincoln C.	L	12.71	71	3	0	0
Lincoln C.	Tr	08.72	72-78	265	2	12
Scunthorpe U.	L	11.77	77	4	0	0
Bradford C.	Tr	06.79	79-80	47	1	2
Rochdale	Tr	08.81	81	35	0	2
COOPER William George Edward						
York, 2 November, 1917 Died 1978						(F)
Bradford C.	Halifax T. (Am)	09.46	46-47	7	-	4
COOTE Adrian						
Great Yarmouth, 13 September, 1978 NIu21-2						(F)
Norwich C.	YT	07.97	97	11	12	2
COOTE Kenneth Alexander						
Paddington, 19 May, 1928						(D)
Brentford	Wembley T.	05.49	49-63	514	-	14
COPE Charles **Anthony**						
Doncaster, 17 January, 1941						(WH)
Doncaster Rov.	Jnrs	09.58	58-59	8	-	0
COPE James Andrew						
Solihull, 4 October, 1977						(M)
Shrewsbury T.	YT	07.96	95-96	3	1	0
COPE Ronald						
Crewe, 5 October, 1934 E Sch						(CH)
Manchester U.	Jnrs	10.51	56-60	93	-	2
Luton T.	Tr	08.61	61-62	28	-	0
COPELAND Edward						
Hetton-le-Hole, 19 May, 1921						(OR)
Hartlepool U.	Easington Colly	06.44	46-47	38	-	9
COPELAND Michael Wilfred						
Newport, 31 December, 1954						(FB)
Newport Co.	Jnrs	07.73	73	3	1	0

League Club	Source	Date Signed	Seasons Played	Apps	Subs	Gls
COPELAND William **Philip**						
Workington, 16 September, 1936						(CH)
Workington		02.57	60-62	11	-	0
COPELAND Simon Dean						
Sheffield, 10 October, 1968						(RB)
Sheffield U.	YT	06.87				
Rochdale	Tr	07.88	88	27	1	0
COPESTAKE Oliver Francis Reginald						
Mansfield, 1 September, 1921 Died 1953						(IF)
Mansfield T.	Church Warsop	01.46	46	33	-	7
COPLEY Dennis Irwin						
Misterton (Nts), 21 December, 1921						(IF)
Lincoln C.	Norwich C. (Am)	09.46	46	1	-	0
COPLEY Gary						
Rotherham, 30 December, 1960						(G)
Barnsley (N/C)	App	01.79	78	1	0	0
COPP Leonard James Henry						
Aberystwyth, 7 October, 1940						(IF)
Leeds U.	Jnrs	10.57				
Shrewsbury T.	Tr	07.58	60	2	-	1
COPPELL Stephen James						
Liverpool, 9 July, 1955 Eu23-1/EF Lge/E-42						(W)
Tranmere Rov.	Liverpool Univ.	01.74	73-74	35	3	10
Manchester U.	Tr	02.75	74-82	320	2	54
CORAZZIN Giancarlo (Carlo) Michele						
Canada, 25 December, 1971 Canadian Int						(F)
Cambridge U.	Vancouver 86ers (Can)	12.93	93-95	104	1	39
Plymouth Arg.	Tr	03.96	95-97	61	13	23
CORBETT Alexander McLennan						
Saltcoats, 20 April, 1921						(G)
New Brighton	Ayr U.	07.46	46-47	58	-	0
Hull C.	Tr	01.48	47	8	-	0
Hartlepool U.	Weymouth	07.53	53	7	-	0
CORBETT Anthony						
Bilston, 28 April, 1940 E Yth						(FB)
Woverhampton W.	Jnrs	05.59				
Shrewsbury T.	Tr	07.60	60-61	8	-	0
CORBETT Arthur Beech						
Birmingham, 17 August, 1928						(IF)
Walsall	Sutton T.	12.49	49-50	25	-	5
CORBETT David Frank						
Marshfield, 15 April, 1940						(OR)
Swindon T.	Jnrs	08.58	58-61	68	-	3
Plymouth Arg.	Tr	02.62	61-66	84	0	8
CORBETT George						
Newcastle, 11 May, 1925						(FB)
Sheffield Wed.	Shildon Jnrs	05.45				
West Bromwich A.	Spennymoor U.	03.51	51	1	-	0
Workington	Tr	07.53	53	9	-	0
CORBETT James John						
Hackney, 6 July, 1980						(M/F)
Gillingham	YT	01.98	97	8	8	2
CORBETT John						
Bow, 9 January, 1920						(F)
Hartlepool U.		09.43				
Swansea C.		08.45				
Crystal Palace		09.46	46	1	-	1
CORBETT Norman George						
Falkirk, 23 June, 1919 Died 1990						(WH)
West Ham U.	Hearts	04.37	36-49	166	-	3
CORBETT Patrick Avalon						
Hackney, 12 February, 1963 EYth						(CD)
Tottenham H.	App	10.80	81-82	3	2	1
Leyton Orient	Tr	08.83	83-85	77	0	2
CORBETT Peter						
Preston, 5 March, 1934						(G)
Preston N. E.		06.56				
Workington	Tr	08.57	57-58	11	-	0
Oldham Ath.	Tr	07.59	59	10	-	0

CORBETT Robert
Newburn, 16 March, 1922 Died 1988 (FB)

League Club	Source	Date Signed	Seasons Played	Apps	Subs	Gls
Newcastle U.	Throckley Welfare	08.43	46-51	46	-	1
Middlesbrough	Tr	12.51	51-56	92	-	0
Northampton T.	Tr	08.57	57	8	-	1

CORBETT William
Wolverhampton, 29 July, 1920 (LB)

League Club	Source	Date Signed	Seasons Played	Apps	Subs	Gls
Doncaster Rov.		01.42	46-47	37	-	0
Bristol C.	Tr	06.48	48	1	-	0

CORBETT William
Falkirk, 31 August, 1922 (CH)

League Club	Source	Date Signed	Seasons Played	Apps	Subs	Gls
Preston N. E.	Glasgow Celtic	06.48	48	19	-	0
Leicester C.	Tr	08.49	49	16	-	0

CORBIN Kirk De Vere
Barbados (WI), 12 March, 1955 (FB)

League Club	Source	Date Signed	Seasons Played	Apps	Subs	Gls
Cambridge U.	Wokingham T.	01.78	78	3	0	0

CORBISHLEY Colin
Stoke, 13 June, 1939 (WH)

League Club	Source	Date Signed	Seasons Played	Apps	Subs	Gls
Port Vale		10.59	60-61	11	-	0
Chester C.	Tr	08.62	62-64	83	-	11

CORDELL John **Graham**
Walsall, 6 December, 1928 Died 1984 (G)

League Club	Source	Date Signed	Seasons Played	Apps	Subs	Gls
Aston Villa	Walsall Star	09.49	51-52	5	-	0
Rochdale	Tr	05.53	53-54	15	-	0

CORDEN Stephen
Eston, 9 January, 1967 (M)

League Club	Source	Date Signed	Seasons Played	Apps	Subs	Gls
Middlesbrough	YT	06.84	85	1	0	0

CORDEN Simon **Wayne**
Leek, 1 November, 1975 (LW)

League Club	Source	Date Signed	Seasons Played	Apps	Subs	Gls
Port Vale	YT	09.94	94-97	26	22	1

CORDER Peter Robert
Loughton, 12 December, 1966 (G)

League Club	Source	Date Signed	Seasons Played	Apps	Subs	Gls
Tottenham H.	App	10.84				
Peterborough U.	L	10.85	85	2	0	0

CORDICE Neil Anthony
Amersham, 7 April, 1960 (F)

League Club	Source	Date Signed	Seasons Played	Apps	Subs	Gls
Northampton T.	Wycombe W.	07.78	78	4	4	1

CORDJOHN Barry Ronald
Oxford, 5 September, 1942 (FB)

League Club	Source	Date Signed	Seasons Played	Apps	Subs	Gls
Charlton Ath.	Jnrs	06.60				
Aldershot	Tr	07.63				
Portsmouth	Tr	07.64	64	14	-	0

CORDNER Scott
Glasgow, 3 August, 1972 (M)

League Club	Source	Date Signed	Seasons Played	Apps	Subs	Gls
Chesterfield	YT	●	90	1	3	1

CORE John
Ripponden, 29 March, 1929 (CF)

League Club	Source	Date Signed	Seasons Played	Apps	Subs	Gls
Halifax T. (Am)		09.49	49-53	29	-	14

CORFIELD Ernest
Wigan, 18 January, 1931 (IF)

League Club	Source	Date Signed	Seasons Played	Apps	Subs	Gls
Bolton W.	Jnrs	04.48	49-51	6	-	0
Stockport Co.	Tr	07.53	53	2	-	0

CORICA Stephen Christopher
Australia, 24 March, 1973 Australian Int (RW)

League Club	Source	Date Signed	Seasons Played	Apps	Subs	Gls
Leicester C.	Marconi (Aus)	08.95	95	16	0	2
Wolverhampton W.	Tr	02.96	95-97	50	4	2

CORISH Robert
Liverpool, 13 September, 1958 (FB)

League Club	Source	Date Signed	Seasons Played	Apps	Subs	Gls
Derby Co.	Jnrs	08.76	77	0	1	0

CORK Alan Graham
Derby, 4 March, 1959 (F)

League Club	Source	Date Signed	Seasons Played	Apps	Subs	Gls
Derby Co.	Jnrs	07.77				
Lincoln C.	L	09.77	77	5	0	0
Wimbledon	Tr	02.78	78-91	352	78	145
Sheffield U.	Tr	03.92	91-93	25	29	7
Fulham	Tr	08.94	94	11	4	3

CORK David
Doncaster, 28 October, 1962 (F)

League Club	Source	Date Signed	Seasons Played	Apps	Subs	Gls
Arsenal	App	06.80	83	5	2	1
Huddersfield T.	Tr	07.85	85-87	104	6	25
West Bromwich A.	L	09.88	88	1	3	0
Scunthorpe U. (N/C)	Tr	02.89	88	8	7	0
Darlington	Tr	07.89	90-91	53	11	11

CORK David
Doncaster, 8 October, 1959 (M)

League Club	Source	Date Signed	Seasons Played	Apps	Subs	Gls
Manchester U.	App	10.76				
Doncaster Rov.	Tr	08.78	78-79	9	0	1

CORKAIN Stephen
Middlesbrough, 25 February, 1967 (M)

League Club	Source	Date Signed	Seasons Played	Apps	Subs	Gls
Hull C.	Jnrs	06.85	86	5	0	1

CORKHILL Robert Douglas
Barrow, 20 November, 1943 (OL)

League Club	Source	Date Signed	Seasons Played	Apps	Subs	Gls
Barrow	Holker C.O.B.	08.63	63-64	8	-	1

CORKHILL William Grant
Belfast, 23 April, 1910 Died 1978 (WH)

League Club	Source	Date Signed	Seasons Played	Apps	Subs	Gls
Notts Co.	Marine	05.31	31-37	166	-	9
Cardiff C.	Tr	05.38	38	23	-	0
Notts Co.	Tr	11.45	46-51	98	-	0

CORMACK Peter Barr
Edinburgh, 17 July, 1946 S Amat/Su23-5/SF Lge/S-9 (M)

League Club	Source	Date Signed	Seasons Played	Apps	Subs	Gls
Nottingham F.	Hibernian	03.70	69-71	74	0	15
Liverpool	Tr	07.72	72-75	119	6	21
Bristol C.	Tr	11.76	76-79	59	8	15

CORNER Brian
Glasgow, 6 January, 1961 (M)

League Club	Source	Date Signed	Seasons Played	Apps	Subs	Gls
Fulham	App	01.79	80	1	2	0

CORNER David Edward
Sunderland, 15 May, 1966 EYth (CD)

League Club	Source	Date Signed	Seasons Played	Apps	Subs	Gls
Sunderland	App	04.84	84-87	33	0	1
Cardiff C.	L	09.85	85	6	0	0
Peterborough U.	L	03.88	87	9	0	0
Leyton Orient	Tr	07.88	88	4	0	0
Darlington	Tr	07.89	90	13	2	0

CORNER James **Norman**
Horden, 16 February, 1943 (CH/CF)

League Club	Source	Date Signed	Seasons Played	Apps	Subs	Gls
Hull C.	Horden Colly	08.62	63-66	5	0	4
Lincoln C.	Tr	10.67	67-68	44	1	12
Bradford C.	Tr	01.69	68-71	105	5	16

CORNES James **Stuart**
Usk, 4 March, 1960 (CD)

League Club	Source	Date Signed	Seasons Played	Apps	Subs	Gls
Hereford U.	App	01.78	77-81	91	2	3

CORNFIELD Alan Henry
Dudley, 19 December, 1940 (OL)

League Club	Source	Date Signed	Seasons Played	Apps	Subs	Gls
Shrewsbury T.	Lower Gornal Ath.	11.59	59-61	9	-	0

CORNFORTH John Michael
Whitley Bay, 7 October, 1967 W-2 (M)

League Club	Source	Date Signed	Seasons Played	Apps	Subs	Gls
Sunderland	App	10.85	84-90	21	11	2
Doncaster Rov.	L	11.86	86	6	1	3
Shrewsbury T.	L	11.89	89	3	0	0
Lincoln C.	L	01.90	89	9	0	1
Swansea C.	Tr	07.91	91-95	147	2	16
Birmingham C.	Tr	03.96	95	8	0	0
Wycombe W.	Tr	12.96	96-97	26	8	5
Peterborough U.	L	02.98	97	3	1	0

CORNISH Ricky George
Newham, 1 December, 1970 (LB)

League Club	Source	Date Signed	Seasons Played	Apps	Subs	Gls
Aldershot	Cornard U.	11.90	90	7	2	0

CORNOCK Walter Berkeley
Australia, 1 January, 1921 (G)

League Club	Source	Date Signed	Seasons Played	Apps	Subs	Gls
Oldham Ath.		01.41				
Rochdale	Hereford U.	11.47	47	1	-	0

CORNWELL Ellis
Coppull, 14 November, 1913 Died 1986 (FB)

League Club	Source	Date Signed	Seasons Played	Apps	Subs	Gls
Accrington St.	Chorley	11.45	46	5	-	0

CORNWELL John Anthony
Bethnal Green, 13 October, 1964 (M/CD)

League Club	Source	Date Signed	Seasons Played	Apps	Subs	Gls
Leyton Orient	App	10.82	81-86	194	9	35
Newcastle U.	Tr	07.87	87-88	28	5	1
Swindon T.	Tr	12.88	88-89	7	18	0
Southend U.	Tr	08.90	90-92	92	9	5
Cardiff C.	L	08.93	93	5	0	2
Brentford	L	09.93	93	4	0	0
Northampton T.	L	02.94	93	13	0	1

League Club	Source	Date Signed	Seasons Played	Apps	Subs	Gls
CORNWELL Kevin John						
Birmingham, 10 December,1941						(IF)
Oxford U.	Banbury Spencer	07.62	62-63	26	-	10
CORR John Joseph						
Glasgow, 18 December, 1946						(W)
Arsenal	Possilpark Jnrs	07.65				
Exeter C.	Tr	07.67	67-70	73	6	19
CORR Patrick						
Creagh (NI), 31 March, 1927 NI Amat/Lol						(WH)
Burnley	Coleraine	10.51	51	1	-	0
CORR Peter Joseph						
Dundalk (Ire), 22 June, 1923 IR-4						(OR)
Preston N. E.	Dundalk	04.47	46	3	-	0
Everton	Tr	08.48	48-49	24	-	2
CORRIGAN Francis Joseph						
Liverpool, 13 November, 1952						(M)
Blackpool	Ormskirk	08.72				
Walsall	Tr	07.73	73	1	0	0
Wigan Ath.	Northwich Vic.	(N/L)	78-80	113	3	12
CORRIGAN Thomas **Joseph**						
Manchester, 18 November, 1948 Eu21-3/EF Lge/E'B'/E-9						(G)
Manchester C.	Sale	01.67	68-82	476	0	0
Brighton & H. A.	Seattle (USA)	09.83	83	36	0	0
Norwich C.	L	09.84	84	3	0	0
Stoke C.	L	10.84	84	9	0	0
CORT Carl Edward Richard						
Bermondsey, 1 November, 1977						(F)
Wimbledon	YT	06.96	96-97	16	7	4
Lincoln C.	L	02.97	96	5	1	1
CORTHINE Peter Alan						
Highbury, 19 July, 1937						(IF)
Chelsea	Leytonstone	12.57	59	2	-	0
Southend U.	Tr	03.60	59-61	73	-	24
COSSLETT Michael Paul						
Barry, 17 April, 1957						(CD)
Newport Co.	Barry T.	02.78	77-78	2	0	0
COSTELLO John						
Prestonpans, 23 March, 1920						(FB)
Southend U.		08.52				
Barrow	Tr	07.53	53	6	-	0
COSTELLO Matthew						
Airdrie, 4 August, 1924 Died 1987						(OR)
Chesterfield	New Stevenston	05.49	49-51	18	-	2
Chester C.	Tr	07.52	52	9	-	2
COSTELLO Mortimer (Lou) Daniel						
Barking, 8 July, 1936						(WH/CF)
Aldershot (Am)	Leyton	05.56	56	28	-	7
Southend U.	Tr	05.57	57-64	251	-	15
COSTELLO Nigel Graham						
Catterick, 22 November, 1968						(W)
York C. (N/C)	YT	07.87	86-87	2	2	0
COSTELLO Peter						
Halifax, 31 October, 1969						(F)
Bradford C.	YT	07.88	88-89	11	9	2
Rochdale	Tr	07.90	90	31	3	10
Peterborough U.	Tr	03.91	90-92	3	5	0
Lincoln C.	L	09.91	91	3	0	0
Lincoln C.	Tr	09.92	92-93	28	10	7
COTHLIFF Harold Thomas						
Liverpool, 24 March, 1916 Died 1976						(RH)
Manchester C.	Prestcot Cables	04.36				
Nottingham F.	Tr	05.37				
Torquay U.	Tr	06.38	38-47	65	-	1
COTON Anthony Philip						
Tamworth, 19 May, 1961 E'B'						(G)
Birmingham C.	Mile Oak Rov.	10.78	80-84	94	0	0
Watford	Tr	09.84	84-89	233	0	0
Manchester C.	Tr	07.90	90-94	162	1	0
Manchester U.	Tr	01.96				
Sunderland	Tr	07.96	96	10	0	0
COTON Paul Stanley						
Birmingham, 9 February, 1949						(FB)
Walsall	App	02.67	66	1	0	0
COTTAM John Edward						
Worksop, 5 June, 1950						(CD)
Nottingham F.	App	04.68	70-75	92	3	4
Mansfield T.	L	11.72	72	2	0	1
Lincoln C.	L	03.73	72	1	0	0
Chesterfield	Tr	08.76	76-78	120	0	7
Chester C.	Tr	07.79	79-81	117	3	1
COTTEE Antony Richard						
West Ham, 11 July, 1965 EYth/Eu21-8/E-7						(F)
West Ham U.	App	09.82	82-87	203	9	92
Everton	Tr	08.88	88-94	161	23	72
West Ham U.	Tr	09.94	94-96	63	4	23
Leicester C.	Selangor (Mal)	08.97	97	7	12	4
Birmingham C.	L	11.97	97	4	1	1
COTTERELL Leo Spencer						
Cambridge, 2 September, 1974 E Sch/E Yth						(RB)
Ipswich T.	YT	07.93	94	0	2	0
Bournemouth	Tr	06.96	96	2	7	0
COTTERILL Stephen John						
Cheltenham, 20 July, 1964						(F)
Wimbledon	Burton A.	02.89	88-92	10	7	6
Brighton & H.A.	L	08.92	92	11	0	4
Bournemouth	Tr	08.93	93-94	44	1	15
COTTEY Philip Anthony						
Swansea, 2 June, 1966						(M)
Swansea C.	App	06.84	84	2	1	0
COTTINGTON Brian Anthony						
Hammersmith, 14 February, 1965						(D)
Fulham	App	02.83	83-86	67	6	1
COTTON Frederick Joseph						
Halesowen, 12 March, 1932						(IF)
Crystal Palace		08.56	56	4	-	0
COTTON John						
Stoke, 2 March, 1930						(FB)
Stoke C.		05.52	53	2	-	0
Crewe Alex.	Tr	10.55	55	14	-	0
COTTON Perry						
Bromley, 11 November, 1965						(M/F)
Scunthorpe U.	Nelson U. (NZ)	12.88	88-90	24	9	2
COTTON Roy William						
Hammersmith, 14 November, 1955 E Yth						(W)
Brentford (Am)	Jnrs	09.73	73	1	1	0
Leyton Orient	Tr	07.74	75	0	3	0
Aldershot	Tr	07.76	77	5	0	0
COTTON Russell Andrew						
Wellington, 4 April, 1960						(M)
Colchester U.	App	04.78	77-81	33	4	1
COTTON Terence						
Liverpool, 25 January, 1946 W Amat						(CF)
Swansea C.	Ammanford	06.68	68-70	12	1	1
COUCH Alan						
Neath, 15 March, 1953						(M)
Cardiff C.	Jnrs	08.70	71-72	7	4	0
COUCH Geoffrey Raymond						
Scunthorpe, 3 April, 1953						(F)
Scunthorpe U.	Crowle	03.78	77-79	22	4	5
COUGHLAN Derek James						
Cork, 2 January, 1977						(CD)
Brighton & H.A.	YT	05.95	95	1	0	0
COUGHLAN Graham						
Dublin, 18 November, 1974						(CD)
Blackburn Rov.	Bray W.	10.95				
Swindon T.	L	03.97	96	3	0	0
COUGHLIN Dennis Michael						
Houghton-le-Spring, 26 November, 1937						(CF)
Barnsley	Durham C.	10.57				
Bournemouth	Yeovil T.	03.63	62-65	86	2	41
Swansea C.	Tr	08.66	66-67	38	1	11
Exeter C.	L	03.68	67	13	0	2
COUGHLIN James						
Cheltenham, 26 July, 1953						(F)
Hereford U.	Albion Rov.	03.77	76	1	1	1

COUGHLIN Russell James
Swansea, 15 February, 1960 W Sch/W Yth (M)

League Club	Source	Date Signed	Seasons Played	Apps	Subs	Gls
Manchester C.	App	02.78				
Blackburn Rov.	Tr	03.79	78-80	22	2	0
Carlisle U.	Tr	10.80	80-83	114	16	13
Plymouth Arg.	Tr	07.84	84-87	128	3	18
Blackpool	Tr	12.87	87-89	100	2	8
Shrewsbury T.	L	09.90	90	4	1	0
Swansea C.	Tr	10.90	90-92	99	2	2
Exeter C.	Tr	07.93	93-95	64	4	0
Torquay U.	Tr	10.95	95	22	3	0

COULBAULT Regis Arnaud Vincent
Brignoles, France, 12 August, 1972 (M)

League Club	Source	Date Signed	Seasons Played	Apps	Subs	Gls
Southend U.	Toulon (Fr)	10.97	97	30	4	4

COULL George Thomson
Dundee, 10 August, 1935 (IF)

League Club	Source	Date Signed	Seasons Played	Apps	Subs	Gls
Millwall	Dundee Downfield	08.56	56	6	-	1

COULSON William John
Newcastle, 14 January, 1950 (W)

League Club	Source	Date Signed	Seasons Played	Apps	Subs	Gls
Newcastle U.	Consett	09.71				
Southend U.	Tr	10.73	73-75	51	1	4
Aldershot	L	02.75	74	3	0	0
Huddersfield T.	L	11.75	75	2	0	0
Darlington	L	01.76	75	11	2	1

COUPE Joseph
Carlisle, 15 July, 1924 (FB)

League Club	Source	Date Signed	Seasons Played	Apps	Subs	Gls
Carlisle U.	Swift Rov.	09.47	48-50	31	-	0
Rochdale	Tr	10.51	51	8	-	0
Workington	Tr	10.52	52	6	-	0

COUPLAND Joseph
Glasgow, 10 April, 1920 (FB)

League Club	Source	Date Signed	Seasons Played	Apps	Subs	Gls
Bradford C.	Ayr U.	08.50	50-51	18	-	0
Carlisle U.	Tr	07.52	52-53	3	-	0

COURT Colin
Winchester, 25 March, 1964 (G)

League Club	Source	Date Signed	Seasons Played	Apps	Subs	Gls
Reading (N/C)	Andover T.	07.81	81	1	0	0

COURT Colin Raymond
Ebbw Vale, 3 September,1937 W Sch (W)

League Club	Source	Date Signed	Seasons Played	Apps	Subs	Gls
Chelsea	Jnrs	09.54				
Torquay U.	Tr	05.59	59-60	27	-	5

COURT David John
Mitcham, 1 March, 1944 (M)

League Club	Source	Date Signed	Seasons Played	Apps	Subs	Gls
Arsenal	App	01.62	62-69	168	7	17
Luton T.	Tr	07.70	70-71	50	2	0
Brentford	Tr	08.72	72	8	4	1

COURT Harold John
Rhymney, 13 June, 1919 Died 1975 (IF)

League Club	Source	Date Signed	Seasons Played	Apps	Subs	Gls
Cardiff C.	Llanbradach	03.39	38	1	-	0
Swindon T.	Dundee	06.50	50	16	-	2

COUSANS William Eric
Doncaster, 10 September, 1929 (W)

League Club	Source	Date Signed	Seasons Played	Apps	Subs	Gls
Walsall	Goole T.	08.54	54	4	-	1
Gillingham	Tr	09.55	55	2	-	0

COUSINS Anthony James
Dublin, 25 August, 1969 IRu21-6 (F)

League Club	Source	Date Signed	Seasons Played	Apps	Subs	Gls
Liverpool	Dundalk	10.90				
Hereford U.	L	11.92	92	3	0	0

COUSINS Harold
Chesterfield, 25 Sepember, 1907 Died 1981 (WH)

League Club	Source	Date Signed	Seasons Played	Apps	Subs	Gls
Chesterfield	North Wingfield	10.26	26-31	85	-	0
Swindon T.	Tr	08.32	32-46	240	-	1

COUSINS Jason Michael
Hayes, 14 October, 1970 (RB)

League Club	Source	Date Signed	Seasons Played	Apps	Subs	Gls
Brentford	YT	07.89	89-90	20	1	0
Wycombe W.	Tr	07.91	93-97	167	7	3

COUSINS Kenneth Frank
Bristol, 6 August, 1922 (G)

League Club	Source	Date Signed	Seasons Played	Apps	Subs	Gls
Bristol C.	Brislington	03.46	46	3	-	0

COUTTS Roger Alexander
Barrow, 18 December, 1944 (OR)

League Club	Source	Date Signed	Seasons Played	Apps	Subs	Gls
Barrow	Walney Rov.	08.64	64	2	-	0

COUZENS Andrew
Shipley, 4 June, 1975 Eu21-3 (D/M)

League Club	Source	Date Signed	Seasons Played	Apps	Subs	Gls
Leeds U.	YT	03.93	94-96	17	11	1
Carlisle U.	Tr	07.97	97	18	9	2

COVERDALE Andrew (Drew)
Middlesbrough, 20 September, 1969 (FB)

League Club	Source	Date Signed	Seasons Played	Apps	Subs	Gls
Middlesbrough	YT	07.88				
Darlington	Tr	07.89	90-91	24	6	3

COWAN Donald
Durham, 17 August, 1931 (G)

League Club	Source	Date Signed	Seasons Played	Apps	Subs	Gls
Darlington		11.52	52-53	17	-	0

COWAN Ian
Falkirk, 27 November, 1944 (OR)

League Club	Source	Date Signed	Seasons Played	Apps	Subs	Gls
Southend U.	Dunfermline Ath.	07.70	70	3	0	0

COWAN James Clews
Paisley, 16 June, 1926 Died 1968 SF Lge/S-25 (G)

League Club	Source	Date Signed	Seasons Played	Apps	Subs	Gls
Sunderland	Morton	06.53	53	28	-	0

COWAN John
Belfast, 8 January, 1949 NI-1 (M)

League Club	Source	Date Signed	Seasons Played	Apps	Subs	Gls
Newcastle U.	Crusaders	02.67	69-72	6	3	0
Darlington	Drogheda	08.75	75	10	0	0

COWAN Thomas
Bellshill, 28 August, 1969 (LB)

League Club	Source	Date Signed	Seasons Played	Apps	Subs	Gls
Sheffield U.	Glasgow Rangers	07.91	91-93	45	0	0
Stoke C.	L	10.93	93	14	0	0
Huddersfield T.	Tr	03.94	93-96	132	0	7

COWANS Gordon Sidney
Cornforth (Dm), 27 October, 1958 EYth/Eu21-5/E'B'/E-10 (M)

League Club	Source	Date Signed	Seasons Played	Apps	Subs	Gls
Aston Villa	App	09.76	75-84	276	10	42
Aston Villa	Bari (It)	07.88	88-91	114	3	7
Blackburn Rov.	Tr	11.91	91-92	49	1	2
Aston Villa	Tr	07.93	93	9	2	0
Derby Co.	Tr	02.94	93-94	36	0	0
Wolverhampton W.	Tr	12.94	94-95	31	6	0
Sheffield U.	Tr	12.95	95	18	2	0
Bradford C.	Tr	07.96	96	23	1	0
Stockport Co.	Tr	03.97	96	6	1	0
Burnley (N/C)	Tr	08.97	97	5	1	0

COWDRILL Barry James
Birmingham, 3 January, 1957 (FB)

League Club	Source	Date Signed	Seasons Played	Apps	Subs	Gls
West Bromwich A.	Sutton Coldfield T.	04.79	79-87	127	4	0
Rotherham U.	L	10.85	85	2	0	0
Bolton W.	Tr	07.88	88-91	117	2	4
Rochdale	Tr	02.92	91	15	0	1

COWE Steven Mark
Gloucester, 29 September, 1974 (F)

League Club	Source	Date Signed	Seasons Played	Apps	Subs	Gls
Aston Villa	YT	07.93				
Swindon T.	Tr	03.96	95-97	40	26	9

COWELL George **Robert**
Trimdon, 5 December, 1922 Died 1996 (FB)

League Club	Source	Date Signed	Seasons Played	Apps	Subs	Gls
Newcastle U.	Blackhall Colly	10.43	46-54	289	-	0

COWEN John Michael
Lewisham, 1 December, 1944 EYth (G)

League Club	Source	Date Signed	Seasons Played	Apps	Subs	Gls
Chelsea	App	10.62				
Watford	Tr	10.64	64-66	17	0	0

COWIE Andrew David
Motherwell, 11 March, 1913 Died 1972 (WH)

League Club	Source	Date Signed	Seasons Played	Apps	Subs	Gls
Swindon T.	Aberdeen	07.48	48-50	89	-	4

COWIE George Alexander
Buckie, 9 May, 1961 (M)

League Club	Source	Date Signed	Seasons Played	Apps	Subs	Gls
West Ham U.	App	08.78	81-82	6	2	0

COWLEY Carl
Stepney, 10 July, 1965 (CD)

League Club	Source	Date Signed	Seasons Played	Apps	Subs	Gls
Millwall	App	10.82	83	2	1	0

COWLEY Francis
Stepney, 28 November, 1957 (W)

League Club	Source	Date Signed	Seasons Played	Apps	Subs	Gls
Derby Co.	Sutton U.	08.77				
Wimbledon	Tr	02.78	77-78	5	3	0

COWLING Christopher
Scunthorpe, 19 September, 1962 (M/F)

League Club	Source	Date Signed	Seasons Played	Apps	Subs	Gls
Scunthorpe U.	App	12.79	79-84	117	17	26

COWLING David Roy
Doncaster, 27 November, 1958 (LW)

League Club	Source	Date Signed	Seasons Played	Apps	Subs	Gls
Mansfield T.	App	11.76				
Huddersfield T.	Tr	08.77	78-87	331	9	43
Scunthorpe U.	L	11.87	87	1	0	0
Reading	L	12.87	87	2	0	0

League Club	Source	Date Signed	Seasons Played	Apps	Subs	Gls
Reading	Tr	03.88	87	7	1	1
Scunthorpe U.	Tr	08.88	88-90	85	4	5
COWLING Jason Paul						
Cambridge, 12 August, 1969						(M)
Cambridge U. (N/C)	Jnrs	07.87	86	0	2	0
COWSILL Charles Mills						
Farnworth, 5 May, 1929						(OR)
Bury		05.50				
Workington		11.51	51	1	-	0
COX Alan William						
Liverpool, 4 September, 1920 Died 1993						(OR)
Tranmere Rov.		03.41	46-47	8	-	1
COX Albert Edward Harrison						
Rotherham, 24 June, 1917						(FB)
Sheffield U.	Woodhouse Mill	04.35	35-51	267	-	5
Halifax T.	Tr	07.52	52-53	53	-	1
COX Brian Roy						
Sheffield, 7 May, 1961						(G)
Sheffield Wed.	App	02.79	78-80	22	0	0
Huddersfield T.	Tr	03.82	81-87	213	0	0
Mansfield T.	Tr	08.88	88-89	54	0	0
Hartlepool U.	Tr	08.90	90	34	0	0
COX David						
Dukinfield, 16 September, 1936						(CF)
Stockport Co.	Oldham Ath. (Am)	10.55	56-57	7	-	4
COX Frederick James Arthur						
Reading, 1 November,1920 Died 1973						(OR)
Tottenham H.	Jnrs	08.38	38-48	99	-	15
Arsenal	Tr	09.49	49-52	79	-	9
West Bromwich A.	Tr	07.53	53	4	-	1
COX Geoffrey						
Arley, 30 November, 1934						(IF)
Birmingham C.	Jnrs	12.51	52-56	35	-	3
Torquay U.	Tr	12.57	57-66	260	1	62
COX Graham Paul						
Willesden, 30 April, 1959						(G)
Brentford	App	04.77	76-77	4	0	0
Aldershot (N/C)	Hillingdon Borough	01.85	84-85	13	0	0
COX Ian Gary						
Croydon, 25 March, 1971						(CD/W)
Crystal Palace	Carshalton	03.94	94-95	2	13	0
Bournemouth	Tr	03.96	95-97	98	0	11
COX Keith						
Ilkeston, 26 January, 1936						(FB)
Charlton Ath.	Heanor T.	04.54	56-58	14	-	0
COX Mark Louis						
Birmingham, 4 October, 1959						(F)
Lincoln C.	App	09.77	76-77	3	2	0
Doncaster Rov.	Tr	09.78	78	10	5	3
COX Maurice						
Torquay, 1 October, 1959						(F)
Torquay U.	Jnrs	01.80	78-81	49	13	13
Huddersfield T. (N/C)	Tr	08.82	82	3	1	1
COX Neil James						
Scunthorpe, 8 October, 1971 Eu21-6						(RB)
Scunthorpe U.	YT	03.90	90	17	0	1
Aston Villa	Tr	02.91	91-93	26	16	3
Middlesbrough	Tr	07.94	94-96	103	3	3
Bolton W.	Tr	05.97	97	20	1	1
COX Paul Richard						
Nottingham, 6 January, 1972						(CD)
Notts Co.	YT	08.89	91-94	39	5	1
Hull C.	L	12.94	94	5	0	1
COX Ronald Bert						
Foleshill, 2 May, 1919						(CH)
Coventry C.	Wyken Pippin	10.45	46-51	29	-	0
COX Samuel						
Mexborough, 30 October, 1920 Died 1985						(FB)
West Bromwich A.	Denaby U.	05.48	48	2	-	0
Accrington St.	Tr	07.51	51	43	-	0
Scunthorpe U.	Tr	07.52	52	3	-	0

League Club	Source	Date Signed	Seasons Played	Apps	Subs	Gls
COXHILL David						
Motherwell, 10 April, 1952						(M)
Millwall	Jnrs	06.70	70-71	6	2	0
Gillingham	Tr	07.73	73-74	32	2	1
COXON Eric **Gary**						
Liverpool, 31 May, 1946						(FB)
Blackburn Rov.	Everton (App)	12.63	66-67	10	0	0
COXON John						
Whitley Bay, 7 April, 1922						(FB)
Darlington (Am)	Hartley	05.46	46	1	-	0
COXON William George						
Derby, 28 April, 1933						(OL)
Derby Co.	Jnrs	05.50				
Norwich C.	Ilkeston T.	05.52	52-57	98	-	24
Lincoln C.	Tr	03.58	57-58	11	-	6
Bournemouth	Tr	11.58	58-65	199	1	37
COY Robert Anthony						
Birmingham, 30 November, 1961						(CD)
Wolverhampton W.	App	11.79	81-83	40	3	0
Chester C.	Tr	03.84	83-85	93	0	2
Northampton T.	Tr	08.86	86	15	2	0
COYLE Anthony						
Glasgow, 17 January, 1960						(W)
Stockport Co.	Albion Rov.	12.79	79-85	215	4	28
Chesterfield	Tr	06.86	86-87	71	5	4
Stockport Co.	Tr	08.88	88	23	0	3
Exeter C. (N/C)	Northwich Vic.	11.89	89	1	0	0
COYLE Francis (Fay)						
Derry (NI), 1 April, 1924 NI Amat/NI-4						(CF)
Nottingham F.	Coleraine	03.58	57	3	-	0
COYLE Owen Columba						
Glasgow, 14 July, 1966 IRu21-2/IR 'B'/IR-1						(F)
Bolton W.	Airdrieonians	06.93	93-95	35	19	12
COYLE Robert Irvine						
Belfast, 31 January, 1948 NI-5						(M)
Sheffield Wed.	Glentoran	03.72	72-73	38	2	2
Grimsby T.	Tr	10.74	74	24	0	1
COYLE Ronald Paul						
Glasgow, 19 August, 1961						(M)
Middlesbrough	Glasgow Celtic	12.86	86	1	2	0
Rochdale	Tr	08.87	87	23	1	1
COYLE William						
Newcastle, 24 October, 1926						(CH)
Darlington (Am)	West Auckland	05.49	49	16	-	0
COYNE Brian						
Glasgow, 13 December, 1959						(M)
Shrewsbury T.	Glasgow Celtic	06.79	79	1	0	0
COYNE Cyril						
Barnsley, 21 May, 1924 Died 1981						(WH)
Leeds U.	Barnsley Main Colly	10.44				
Halifax T.	Stalybridge Celtic	06.51	51	4	-	0
COYNE Daniel						
Prestatyn, 27 August, 1973 W Sch/W Yth/Wu21-9/W-1						(G)
Tranmere Rov.	YT	05.92	92-97	93	1	0
COYNE Gerard Aloyoius						
Hebburn, 9 August, 1948						(CF)
York C.	Reyrolles	08.66	66	2	0	0
COYNE John David						
Liverpool, 18 July, 1951						(F)
Tranmere Rov.		08.71	71	12	3	3
Hartlepool U.	Tr	07.72	72-73	47	8	10
Stockport Co.	Wigan Ath.	11.75	75	3	1	0
COYNE Peter David						
Manchester, 13 November, 1958						(F)
Manchester U.	App	11.75	75	1	1	1
Crewe Alex.	Ashton U.	08.77	77-80	113	21	47
Swindon T.	Hyde U.	08.84	84-88	99	11	30
Aldershot	L	08.89	89	3	0	0
COYNE Thomas						
Glasgow, 14 November, 1962 IR 'B'/IR-21						(F)
Tranmere Rov.	Glasgow Celtic	03.93	92	9	3	1

COZENS John William
Hammersmith, 14 May, 1946 (F)

League Club	Source	Date Signed	Seasons Played	Apps	Subs	Gls
Notts Co.	Hillingdon Borough	08.70	70-72	41	4	13
Peterborough U.	Tr	11.72	72-77	127	5	41
Cambridge U.	Tr	12.77	77-79	52	9	3

CRABBE Stephen Allan **John (Buster)**
Weymouth, 20 October, 1954 (M)

League Club	Source	Date Signed	Seasons Played	Apps	Subs	Gls
Southampton	App	10.72	74-76	8	4	0
Gillingham	Tr	01.76	76-80	181	0	13
Carlisle U.	Tr	08.81	81	26	0	4
Hereford U.	Tr	08.82	82	15	1	2
Crewe Alex.	Tr	08.83	83-85	75	0	7
Torquay U.	Tr	09.85	85	27	2	2

CRABTREE Richard Edward
Exeter, 6 February, 1955 (G)

League Club	Source	Date Signed	Seasons Played	Apps	Subs	Gls
Bristol Rov.	App	02.73	71	7	0	0
Doncaster Rov.	L	10.74	74	1	0	0
Torquay U. (N/C)	Tr	08.75	75	1	0	0
Exeter C. (N/C)	Dawlish	07.83	83	1	0	0

CRADDOCK Jody Darryl
Bromsgrove, 25 July, 1975 (CD)

League Club	Source	Date Signed	Seasons Played	Apps	Subs	Gls
Cambridge U.	Christchurch	08.93	93-96	142	3	4
Sunderland	Tr	08.97	97	31	1	0

CRADDOCK Leonard **Miller**
Newent, 21 September, 1926 Died 1960 (F)

League Club	Source	Date Signed	Seasons Played	Apps	Subs	Gls
Newport Co.	Chelsea (Am)	05.46	46	7	-	0
Aston Villa	Hereford U.	09.48	48-50	34	-	10

CRAGGS John Edward
Flint Hill (Dm), 31 October, 1948 E Yth (RB)

League Club	Source	Date Signed	Seasons Played	Apps	Subs	Gls
Newcastle U.	App	12.65	66-70	50	2	1
Middlesbrough	Tr	08.71	71-81	408	1	12
Newcastle U.	Tr	08.82	82	10	2	0
Darlington	Tr	08.83	83-84	53	1	0

CRAIG Albert Hughes
Glasgow, 3 January, 1962 (W)

League Club	Source	Date Signed	Seasons Played	Apps	Subs	Gls
Newcastle U.	Hamilton Academical	02.87	86-88	6	4	0
Northampton T.	L	01.89	88	2	0	1

CRAIG Benjamin
Leadgate, 6 December, 1915 Died 1982 (FB)

League Club	Source	Date Signed	Seasons Played	Apps	Subs	Gls
Huddersfield T.	Eden Colly	01.34	33-38	99	-	0
Newcastle U.	Tr	11.38	38-49	66	-	0

CRAIG David James
Belfast, 8 June, 1944 NI Yth/NIu23-1/NI-25 (RB)

League Club	Source	Date Signed	Seasons Played	Apps	Subs	Gls
Newcastle U.	App	04.62	63-77	346	5	8

CRAIG William **David**
Liverpool, 27 December, 1921 Died 1994 (OR)

League Club	Source	Date Signed	Seasons Played	Apps	Subs	Gls
Blackpool	Marine	05.46				
Southport	Tr	08.48	48	5	-	2

CRAIG Derek Malcolm
Hexham, 28 July, 1952 (CD)

League Club	Source	Date Signed	Seasons Played	Apps	Subs	Gls
Newcastle U.	Jnrs	08.69				
Darlington	San Jose (USA)	09.75	75-79	186	1	10
York C.	Tr	05.80	80-81	53	0	1

CRAIG James Philip
Glasgow, 30 April, 1943 S-1 (FB)

League Club	Source	Date Signed	Seasons Played	Apps	Subs	Gls
Sheffield Wed.	Hellenic (SA)	12.72	72-73	5	1	0

CRAIG Joseph
Logie, 14 May, 1954 Su23-4/S-1 (F)

League Club	Source	Date Signed	Seasons Played	Apps	Subs	Gls
Blackburn Rov.	Glasgow Celtic	09.78	78-80	44	4	8

CRAIG Robert
Consett, 16 June, 1928 (FB)

League Club	Source	Date Signed	Seasons Played	Apps	Subs	Gls
Sunderland	Jnrs	11.45	49	1	-	0

CRAIG Robert McAllister
Airdrie, 8 April, 1935 (IF)

League Club	Source	Date Signed	Seasons Played	Apps	Subs	Gls
Sheffield Wed.	Third Lanark	11.59	59-61	84	-	25
Blackburn Rov.	Tr	04.62	61-62	8	-	3
Oldham Ath.	St Johnstone	03.64	63-64	18	-	4

CRAIG Thomas Brooks
Glasgow, 21 November,1950 S Sch/Su21-1/Su23-9/S-1 (M)

League Club	Source	Date Signed	Seasons Played	Apps	Subs	Gls
Sheffield Wed.	Aberdeen	05.69	68-74	210	4	38
Newcastle U.	Tr	12.74	74-77	122	2	22
Aston Villa	Tr	01.78	77-78	27	0	2
Swansea C.	Tr	07.78	79-80	47	5	9
Carlisle U.	Tr	03.82	81-84	92	6	10

CRAIG William James
Aberdeen, 11 September, 1929 (D)

League Club	Source	Date Signed	Seasons Played	Apps	Subs	Gls
Millwall	Dundee	08.56	56-58	21	-	1

CRAINIE Daniel
Kilsyth, 24 May, 1962 Su21-1 (W)

League Club	Source	Date Signed	Seasons Played	Apps	Subs	Gls
Wolverhampton W.	Glasgow Celtic	12.83	83-85	63	1	4
Blackpool	L	03.85	84	6	0	0

CRAKER Laurence David
Aylesbury, 1 March, 1953 (M)

League Club	Source	Date Signed	Seasons Played	Apps	Subs	Gls
Chelsea	App	08.70				
Watford	Jewish Guild	11.72	72-76	60	6	4

CRAM Robert
Hetton-le-Hole, 19 November, 1939 (RB)

League Club	Source	Date Signed	Seasons Played	Apps	Subs	Gls
West Bromwich A.	Jnrs	01.57	59-66	141	0	25
Colchester U.	Vancouver (Can)	01.70	69-71	99	1	4

CRAMB Colin
Lanark, 23 June, 1974 (F)

League Club	Source	Date Signed	Seasons Played	Apps	Subs	Gls
Southampton	Hamilton Academical	06.93	93	0	1	0
Doncaster Rov.	Hearts	12.95	95-96	60	2	25
Bristol C.	Tr	07.97	97	34	6	9

CRAMPTON David William
Bearpark (Dm), 9 June, 1949 (G)

League Club	Source	Date Signed	Seasons Played	Apps	Subs	Gls
Blackburn Rov.	Spennymoor U.	03.68				
Darlington	Tr	07.69	69	14	0	0

CRAMPTON Paul
Cleethorpes, 28 January, 1953 (FB)

League Club	Source	Date Signed	Seasons Played	Apps	Subs	Gls
Grimsby T.	App	●	70	0	1	0

CRANE Andrew David
Ipswich, 3 January, 1967 (LB)

League Club	Source	Date Signed	Seasons Played	Apps	Subs	Gls
Ipswich T.	App	04.84				
Shrewsbury T.	Tr	06.87				
Hereford U.	Tr	07.88	88	30	2	0

CRANE Steven John
Grays, 3 June, 1972 (F)

League Club	Source	Date Signed	Seasons Played	Apps	Subs	Gls
Charlton Ath.	YT	07.90				
Gillingham	USA	03.93	92-93	3	10	1
Torquay U. (N/C)	New Zealand	12.96	96	0	2	0

CRANFIELD Harold Richard
Chesterton, 25 December, 1917 Died 1990 (OL)

League Club	Source	Date Signed	Seasons Played	Apps	Subs	Gls
Fulham	Cambridge T.	12.37	46	1	-	0
Bristol Rov.	Tr	06.47	47	24	-	2

CRANGLE James Patrick
Glasgow, 4 April, 1953 (W)

League Club	Source	Date Signed	Seasons Played	Apps	Subs	Gls
York C.	Campsie B.W.	08.72	72	4	0	0

CRANSON Ian
Easington, 2 July, 1964 Eu21-5 (CD)

League Club	Source	Date Signed	Seasons Played	Apps	Subs	Gls
Ipswich T.	App	07.82	83-87	130	1	4
Sheffield Wed.	Tr	03.88	87-88	29	1	0
Stoke C.	Tr	07.89	89-96	220	3	9

CRANSTON Nicholas Geoffrey
Carlisle, 20 October, 1972 (M)

League Club	Source	Date Signed	Seasons Played	Apps	Subs	Gls
Carlisle U.	YT	01.92	91	0	2	0

CRANSTON William
Kilmarnock, 18 January, 1942 (WH)

League Club	Source	Date Signed	Seasons Played	Apps	Subs	Gls
Blackpool	Saxone Y.C.	08.60	61-64	33	-	0
Preston N. E.	Tr	12.64	64-69	80	7	1
Oldham Ath.	Tr	07.70	69-72	98	2	2

CRAVEN Dean
Shrewsbury, 17 February, 1979 (RM)

League Club	Source	Date Signed	Seasons Played	Apps	Subs	Gls
West Bromwich A.	YT	07.97				
Shrewsbury T.	Tr	03.98	97	1	0	0

CRAVEN John Roland
St Annes, 15 May, 1947 Died 1996 (M)

League Club	Source	Date Signed	Seasons Played	Apps	Subs	Gls
Blackpool	App	01.65	65-70	154	9	24
Crystal Palace	Tr	09.71	71-72	56	7	14
Coventry C.	Tr	05.73	73-76	86	3	8
Plymouth Arg.	Tr	01.77	76-77	45	0	3

CRAVEN Michael Anthony
Birkenhead, 20 November, 1957 (G)

League Club	Source	Date Signed	Seasons Played	Apps	Subs	Gls
Chester C.	Jnrs	09.75	76	4	0	0

CRAVEN Peter
West Germany, 30 June, 1968 (W)

League Club	Source	Date Signed	Seasons Played	Apps	Subs	Gls
Halifax T. (N/C)	Guiseley	03.93	92	7	0	0

CRAVEN Stephen Joseph
Birkenhead, 17 September, 1957 (M)

League Club	Source	Date Signed	Seasons Played	Apps	Subs	Gls
Tranmere Rov.		03.78	77-81	106	8	17
Crewe Alex.	Tr	08.82	82	26	3	3
Tranmere Rov.	Caernarfon T.	07.87	87	6	7	0

CRAVEN Terence
Barnsley, 27 November, 1944 E Yth (WH)

League Club	Source	Date Signed	Seasons Played	Apps	Subs	Gls
Barnsley	Jnrs	06.63	64	3	-	0

CRAWFORD Alan Paterson
Rotherham, 30 October, 1953 (W)

League Club	Source	Date Signed	Seasons Played	Apps	Subs	Gls
Rotherham U.	App	10.71	73-78	233	4	49
Mansfield T.	L	01.73	72	1	1	0
Chesterfield	Tr	08.79	79-81	88	6	20
Bristol C.	Tr	08.82	82-84	85	7	26
Exeter C.	Tr	07.85	85	33	0	3

CRAWFORD Andrew
Filey, 30 January, 1959 (F)

League Club	Source	Date Signed	Seasons Played	Apps	Subs	Gls
Derby Co.	App	01.77	77-79	16	5	4
Blackburn Rov.	Tr	10.79	79-81	56	0	21
Bournemouth	Tr	11.81	81-82	31	2	10
Cardiff C.	Tr	08.83	83	6	0	1
Middlesbrough	Tr	10.83	83	8	1	1
Stockport Co. (N/C)		12.84	84	6	0	2
Torquay U. (N/C)	Tr	02.85	84	3	0	0

CRAWFORD John Robert **Bruce**
Preston, 10 October, 1938 Eu23-1 (WH)

League Club	Source	Date Signed	Seasons Played	Apps	Subs	Gls
Blackpool	Jnrs	05.56	59-64	98	-	7
Tranmere Rov.	Tr	09.65	65-66	24	2	5

CRAWFORD Campbell Hackett Rankin
Alexandria, 1 December, 1943 S Sch (FB)

League Club	Source	Date Signed	Seasons Played	Apps	Subs	Gls
West Bromwich A.	Jnrs	12.60	63-66	10	0	0
Exeter C.	Tr	07.67	67-73	224	10	3

CRAWFORD Peter **Graeme**
Falkirk, 7 August, 1947 (G)

League Club	Source	Date Signed	Seasons Played	Apps	Subs	Gls
Sheffield U.	East Stirling	09.68	69-70	2	0	0
Mansfield T.	L	07.71	71	2	0	0
York C.	Tr	10.71	71-76	235	0	0
Scunthorpe U.	Tr	08.77	77-79	104	0	0
York C.	Tr	01.80	79	17	0	0
Rochdale	Tr	09.80	80-82	70	0	0

CRAWFORD James
U.S.A., 1 May, 1973 IRu21-2 (M)

League Club	Source	Date Signed	Seasons Played	Apps	Subs	Gls
Newcastle U.	Bohemians	03.95	96	0	2	0
Rotherham U.	L	09.96	96	11	0	0
Reading	Tr	03.98	97	5	1	0

CRAWFORD James Cherrie
Bellshill, 27 September, 1930 (IF)

League Club	Source	Date Signed	Seasons Played	Apps	Subs	Gls
Leicester C.	Jnrs	10.47	50-53	10	-	2
Plymouth Arg.	Tr	03.54	53-55	25	-	4

CRAWFORD John (Ian)
Edinburgh, 14 July, 1934 Su23-1 (OL)

League Club	Source	Date Signed	Seasons Played	Apps	Subs	Gls
West Ham U.	Hearts	07.61	61-62	24	-	5
Scunthorpe U.	Tr	02.63	62-63	35	-	2
Peterborough U.	Tr	07.64	64-68	172	0	6

CRAWFORD John (Ian) Campbell
Falkirk, 27 June, 1922 Died 1996 (F)

League Club	Source	Date Signed	Seasons Played	Apps	Subs	Gls
Oldham Ath.	Ayr U.	07.52	52-53	24	-	8
Halifax T.	Tr	07.54	54	11	-	2

CRAWFORD Raymond
Portsmouth, 13 July, 1936 EF Lge/E-2 (CF)

League Club	Source	Date Signed	Seasons Played	Apps	Subs	Gls
Portsmouth	Jnrs	12.54	57-58	19	-	9
Ipswich T.	Tr	09.58	58-63	197	-	143
Wolverhampton W.	Tr	09.63	63-64	57	-	39
West Bromwich A.	Tr	02.65	64-65	14	0	6
Ipswich T.	Tr	03.66	65-68	123	0	61
Charlton Ath.	Tr	03.69	68-69	21	0	7
Colchester U.	Kettering T.	06.70	70	45	0	24

CRAWFORD Stephen
Dunfermline, 9 January, 1974 Su21-19/S-1 (F)

League Club	Source	Date Signed	Seasons Played	Apps	Subs	Gls
Millwall	Raith Rov.	07.96	96	40	2	11

CRAWLEY Thomas
Hamilton, 10 November, 1911 Died 1977 (CF/CH)

League Club	Source	Date Signed	Seasons Played	Apps	Subs	Gls
Preston N. E.	Motherwell	05.35	35	2	-	0
Coventry C.	Tr	02.36	35-46	42	-	16

CRAWSHAW Cyril
Eccles, 2 March, 1916 (IF)

League Club	Source	Date Signed	Seasons Played	Apps	Subs	Gls
Rochdale	Rossendale U.	11.36	36	2	-	0
Exeter C.	Queen of South	07.39				
Hull C.	Stalybridge Celtic	06.46	46	2	-	2

CREAMER Peter Anthony
Hartlepool, 20 September, 1953 E Sch (D)

League Club	Source	Date Signed	Seasons Played	Apps	Subs	Gls
Middlesbrough	App	10.70	72-73	9	0	0
York C.	L	11.75	75	4	0	0
Doncaster Rov.	Tr	12.75	75-76	31	1	0
Hartlepool U.	Tr	10.76	76-77	63	0	3
Rochdale (N/C)	Gateshead	12.78	78	18	2	0

CREANE Gerard Martin
Lincoln, 2 February, 1962 (CD)

League Club	Source	Date Signed	Seasons Played	Apps	Subs	Gls
Lincoln C.	App	02.80	78-82	6	1	0

CREANEY Gerard Thomas
Coatbridge, 13 April, 1970 Su21-11/S 'B' (CF)

League Club	Source	Date Signed	Seasons Played	Apps	Subs	Gls
Portsmouth	Glasgow Celtic	01.94	93-95	60	0	32
Manchester C.	Tr	09.95	95-97	8	13	4
Oldham Ath.	L	03.96	95	8	1	2
Ipswich T.	L	10.96	96	6	0	1
Burnley	L	09.97	97	9	1	8
Chesterfield	L	01.98	97	3	1	0

CREASER Glyn Robert
Camden, 1 September, 1959 (CD)

League Club	Source	Date Signed	Seasons Played	Apps	Subs	Gls
Wycombe W.	Barnet	09.88	93-94	17	2	2

CRELLIN Andrew
Gainsborough, 11 October, 1954 (FB)

League Club	Source	Date Signed	Seasons Played	Apps	Subs	Gls
Doncaster Rov.	Ashby Inst.	03.74	74	4	0	0

CRERAND Daniel Bruno
Barton, 5 May, 1969 (M)

League Club	Source	Date Signed	Seasons Played	Apps	Subs	Gls
Rochdale (N/C)	Chapel Villa	02.88	87	3	0	0

CRERAND Patrick Timothy
Glasgow, 19 February, 1939 Su23-1/SF Lge/S-16 (RH)

League Club	Source	Date Signed	Seasons Played	Apps	Subs	Gls
Manchester U.	Glasgow Celtic	02.63	62-70	304	0	10

CRESSWELL Corbett Eric
Birkenhead, 3 August, 1932 E Amat (CH)

League Club	Source	Date Signed	Seasons Played	Apps	Subs	Gls
Carlisle U.	Bishop Auckland	03.58	57-58	14	-	2

CRESSWELL Peter Frank
Chesterfield, 9 November, 1935 (OR)

League Club	Source	Date Signed	Seasons Played	Apps	Subs	Gls
Derby Co.	Heanor T.	04.54	54-56	12	-	2

CRESSWELL Philip
Hucknall, 11 May, 1933 Died 1993 (OR)

League Club	Source	Date Signed	Seasons Played	Apps	Subs	Gls
Coventry C.	Jnrs	05.50	54	2	-	0

CRESSWELL Richard Paul Wesley
Bridlington, 20 September, 1977 (F)

League Club	Source	Date Signed	Seasons Played	Apps	Subs	Gls
York C.	YT	11.95	95-96	18	15	1
Mansfield T.	L	03.97	96-97	5	0	1

CRIBLEY Alexander
Liverpool, 1 April, 1957 (CD)

League Club	Source	Date Signed	Seasons Played	Apps	Subs	Gls
Liverpool		06.78				
Wigan Ath.	Tr	10.80	80-87	268	3	16

CRICHTON George
Leslie (Fife), 11 December, 1925 (FB)

League Club	Source	Date Signed	Seasons Played	Apps	Subs	Gls
Workington	Loughborough College	(N/L)	51	4	-	0

CRICHTON Paul Andrew
Pontefract, 3 October, 1968 (G)

League Club	Source	Date Signed	Seasons Played	Apps	Subs	Gls
Nottingham F.	Jnrs	05.86				
Notts Co.	L	09.86	86	5	0	0
Darlington	L	01.87	86	5	0	0
Peterborough U.	L	03.87	86	4	0	0
Darlington	L	09.87	87	3	0	0
Swindon T.	L	12.87	87	4	0	0
Rotherham U.	L	03.88	87	6	0	0
Torquay U.	L	08.88	88	13	0	0
Peterborough U.	Tr	11.88	88-89	47	0	0
Doncaster Rov.	Tr	08.90	90-92	77	0	0
Grimsby T.	Tr	07.93	93-95	133	0	0
West Bromwich A.	Tr	09.96	96-97	32	0	0

League Club	Source	Date Signed	Seasons Played	Apps	Subs	Gls
CRICKETT Norman						
Carlisle, 13 October, 1932						(OR)
Carlisle U.		11.52	55	1	-	0
CRICKMORE Charles Alfred						
Hull, 11 February, 1942						(OL)
Hull C.	Jnrs	02.59	59-61	53	-	13
Bournemouth	Tr	07.62	62-65	128	0	17
Gillingham	Tr	06.66	66-67	53	0	13
Rotherham U.	Tr	11.67	67	7	1	1
Norwich C.	Tr	01.68	67-69	54	2	9
Notts Co.	Tr	03.70	69-71	59	0	11
CRICKSON George (Gerry) Edward						
Dover, 21 September, 1934 Died 1991 E Sch/ E Yth						(WH)
Queens Park R.	Jnrs	09.51	52-55	5	-	0
CRIPPS Henry (Harry) Richard						
East Dereham, 29 April, 1941 Died 1995						(LB)
West Ham U.	Jnrs	09.58				
Millwall	Tr	06.61	61-74	390	10	37
Charlton Ath.	Tr	10.74	74-75	17	3	4
CRIPSEY Brian Samuel						
Hull, 26 June, 1931						(OL)
Hull C.	Brunswick Inst.	11.51	52-58	145	-	19
Wrexham	Tr	09.58	58-59	27	-	3
CRISP Richard Ian						
Stourbridge, 23 May, 1972						(M)
Aston Villa	YT	07.90				
Scunthorpe U.	L	03.93	92	6	2	0
CRISP Ronald James						
Datchet, 24 September, 1938						(WH)
Watford	Dulwich Hamlet	01.61	60-64	89	-	14
Brentford	Tr	08.65	65-66	17	1	0
CRISPIN Timothy						
Leicester, 7 June, 1948						(FB)
Notts Co.	Jnrs	07.66	66-67	8	0	0
CRITTENDEN Nicholas John						
Ascot, 11 November, 1978						(M)
Chelsea	YT	07.97	97	0	2	0
CROCI Laurent						
Montbeliard, France, 8 December, 1964						(M)
Carlisle U. (N/C)	Bordeaux (Fr)	10.97	97	1	0	0
CROCKER Marcus Alan						
Plymouth, 8 October, 1974						(F)
Plymouth Arg.	YT	06.93	92-94	4	6	0
CROFT Alec Robert						
Chester, 17 June, 1937						(W)
Chester C.		08.58	58-60	53	-	3
CROFT Brian Graham Alexander						
Chester, 27 September, 1967						(W)
Chester C.	YT	07.86	85-87	36	23	3
Cambridge U.	Tr	10.88	88	12	5	2
Chester C.	Tr	08.89	89-91	90	24	3
Queens Park R.	Tr	08.92				
Shrewsbury T.	L	12.93	93	4	0	0
Torquay U. (N/C)	Tr	08.95	95	0	1	0
Stockport Co. (N/C)	Witton A.	10.95	95	0	3	0
CROFT Charles						
Dewsbury, 26 November, 1918						(LH)
Huddersfield T.		05.39				
Mansfield T.	Tr	05.47	47-49	85	-	5
CROFT Gary						
Burton, 17 February, 1974 Eu21-4						(LB)
Grimsby T.	YT	07.92	90-95	139	10	3
Blackburn Rov.	Tr	03.96	95-97	23	5	1
CROFT Stuart Dunbar						
Ashington, 12 April, 1954						(CD)
Hull C.	App	04.72	72-80	187	3	4
Portsmouth	Tr	03.81	80	6	0	1
York C.	Tr	08.81	81	14	0	0
CROKER Edgar (Ted) Alfred						
Kingston, 13 February, 1924 Died 1992						(LB)
Charlton Ath.	Dartford	07.48	50	8	-	0

League Club	Source	Date Signed	Seasons Played	Apps	Subs	Gls
CROKER Peter Harry Lucas						
Kingston, 21 December, 1921						(RB)
Charlton Ath.	Bromley	11.45	46-50	59	-	0
Watford	Tr	06.52	52	23	-	0
CROMACK David Charles						
Leeds, 22 December, 1948						(G)
Doncaster Rov.	Hull C. (Am)	11.66	66	8	0	0
CROMACK Victor						
Mansfield, 17 March, 1920 Died 1984						(G)
Mansfield T.		01.46	46	10	-	0
CROMBIE Dean Malcolm						
Lincoln, 9 August, 1957						(D)
Lincoln C.	Ruston Sports	02.77	76-77	33	0	0
Grimsby T.	Tr	08.78	78-86	316	4	3
Reading	L	11.86	86	4	0	0
Bolton W.	Tr	08.87	87-90	90	5	1
Lincoln C.	Tr	01.91	90	0	1	0
CROMBIE Thomas Ronald						
Kirkcaldy, 3 June, 1930						(LB)
Blackpool	Jeanfield Swifts	08.51				
Gillingham	Tr	07.55	55-56	17	-	0
CROMPTON Alan						
Bolton, 6 March, 1958						(M)
Sunderland	App	03.75				
Blackburn Rov.	Tr	07.76	76	2	2	0
Wigan Ath.	Tr	07.78	78-79	7	7	0
CROMPTON David Gerald						
Wigan, 6 March, 1945						(WH)
Rochdale (Am)		11.66	66-67	15	2	0
CROMPTON Dennis						
Bolton, 12 March, 1942						(WH)
Burnley	Wigan Ath.	12.59				
Doncaster Rov.	Tr	06.63	63	23	-	0
CROMPTON John (Jack)						
Chorlton, 18 December, 1921						(G)
Manchester U.	Goslings	01.45	46-55	191	-	0
CROMPTON Paul **Jonathan**						
Orrell, 25 January, 1970						(F)
Wigan Ath.	YT	07.88	89	1	0	0
CROMPTON Stephen Wynn						
Wrexham, 3 December, 1958						(F)
Hereford U.	Wolverhampton W.(App)	02.77	76-78	30	4	6
CROMPTON Steven Geoffrey						
Lymm 20 April, 1968						(G)
Manchester C.	Jnrs	05.86				
Carlisle U.	Tr	07.87	87	10	0	0
Stockport Co. (N/C)	Tr	02.88	87	2	0	0
CRONIN Dennis						
Altrincham, 30 October, 1967						(F)
Manchester U.	App	10.85				
Stockport Co.	Tr	08.87	87	11	4	1
Crewe Alex.	Tr	08.88	88	12	3	2
CRONIN Thomas Patrick						
Richmond, 17 December, 1932						(WH)
Fulham	East Sheen Ath.	09.50	53-54	2	-	0
Reading	Tr	06.56	56-57	30	-	4
CROOK Alfred Rowland						
Brewood, 13 August, 1923						(FB)
Wolverhampton W.	Boulton Paul	05.45	48	1	-	0
CROOK George						
Easington, 30 January, 1935						(IF)
Oldham Ath.		02.53	53-57	57	-	13
Middlesbrough	Tr	11.58				
CROOK Ian Stewart						
Romford, 18 January, 1963 E'B'						(M)
Tottenham H.	App	08.80	81-85	10	10	1
Norwich C.	Tr	06.86	86-96	314	27	18
CROOK Leslie Ronald						
Manchester, 26 June, 1949						(M)
Oxford U.	Manchester Amats	10.68	68	1	0	0
Hartlepool U.	Tr	07.70	70	23	2	3

League Club	Source	Date Signed	Seasons Played	Career Record Apps	Subs	Gls
CROOK Walter						
Chorley, 28 April, 1913 Died 1988						(FB)
Blackburn Rov.	Jnrs	01.31	31-46	218	-	2
Bolton W.	Tr	05.47	47	28	-	0
CROOK William Charles						
Cannock, 7 June, 1926						(WH)
Wolverhampton W.	Jnrs	08.45	46-52	196	-	1
Walsall	Tr	10.54	54-55	45	-	2
CROOKES Robert Eastland						
Retford, 29 February, 1924						(IF)
Notts Co.	Retford T.	06.49	49-55	177	-	45
CROOKS Garth Anthony						
Stoke, 10 March, 1958 Eu21-4						(F)
Stoke C.	App	03.76	75-79	141	6	48
Tottenham H.	Tr	07.80	80-84	121	4	48
Manchester U.	L	11.83	83	6	1	2
West Bromwich A.	Tr	08.85	85-86	39	1	16
Charlton Ath.	Tr	03.87	86-90	41	15	15
CROOKS Lee Robert						
Wakefield, 14 January, 1978 E Yth						(D)
Manchester C.	YT	01.95	96-97	11	9	0
CROOKS Paul						
Durham, 12 October, 1966						(F)
Stoke C.	Caernarfon T.	08.86	86	0	1	0
CROOKS Samuel Dickinson						
Bearpark, 16 January, 1908 Died 1981 EF Lge/E-26						(OR)
Durham C.	Tow Law	06.26	26	15	-	4
Derby Co.	Tr	04.27	27-46	408	-	101
CROPLEY Alexander James						
Aldershot, 16 January, 1951 Su23-3/S-2						(M)
Arsenal	Hibernian	12.74	74-76	29	1	5
Aston Villa	Tr	09.78	76-79	65	2	7
Newcastle U.	L	02.80	79	3	0	0
Portsmouth	Toronto (Can)	09.81	81	8	2	2
CROPLEY John Thomas						
Edinburgh, 27 September, 1924						(WH)
Aldershot	Tranent Jnrs	10.46	47-53	162	-	3
CROSBIE Robert Crichton						
Glasgow, 2 September, 1925 Died 1994						(CF)
Bury		05.47	47-48	9	-	5
Bradford P. A.	Tr	05.49	49-53	139	-	72
Hull C.	Tr	10.53	53-54	61	-	22
Grimsby T.	Tr	07.55	55-56	65	-	45
CROSBY Andrew Keith						
Rotherham, 3 March, 1973						(CD)
Doncaster Rov.	Leeds U. (YT)	07.91	91-92	41	10	0
Darlington	Tr	12.93	93-97	179	2	3
CROSBY Gary						
Sleaford, 8 May, 1964						(W)
Lincoln C. (N/C)	Lincoln U.	08.86	86	6	1	0
Nottingham F.	Grantham	12.87	87-93	139	13	12
Grimsby T.	L	08.93	93	2	1	0
Huddersfield T.	Tr	09.94	94-96	35	9	6
CROSBY Geoffrey John						
Stoke, 24 August, 1931						(IF)
Stockport Co.	Leek T.	09.52	52-53	5	-	1
CROSBY Malcolm						
South Shields, 4 July, 1954						(M)
Aldershot	App	07.72	71-81	272	22	23
York C.	Tr	11.81	81-84	99	4	4
Wrexham	L	09.84	84	5	1	0
CROSBY Philip Alan						
Leeds, 9 November, 1962 E Yth						(LB)
Grimsby T.	App	09.80	79-82	34	5	1
Rotherham U.	Tr	08.83	83-88	181	2	2
Peterborough U.	Tr	08.89	89-90	85	2	0
York C.	Tr	07.91	91	25	0	0
CROSLAND John Ronald						
St Annes, 10 November, 1922 E 'B'						(FB)
Blackpool	Ansdell Rov.	05.46	46-53	68	-	0
Bournemouth	Tr	06.54	54-56	106	-	0

League Club	Source	Date Signed	Seasons Played	Career Record Apps	Subs	Gls
CROSS David						
Bury, 8 December, 1950						(F)
Rochdale	Jnrs	08.69	69-71	50	9	20
Norwich C.	Tr	10.71	71-73	83	1	21
Coventry C.	Tr	11.73	73-76	90	1	30
West Bromwich A.	Tr	11.76	76-77	38	0	18
West Ham U.	Tr	12.77	77-81	178	1	77
Manchester C.	Tr	08.82	82	31	0	12
Oldham Ath.	Vancouver (Can)	10.83	83	18	4	6
West Bromwich A.	Vancouver (Can)	10.84	84	16	0	2
Bolton W.	Tr	06.85	85	19	1	8
Bury	L	01.86	85	12	1	0
CROSS Graham Frederick						
Leicester, 15 November, 1943						(CD)
Leicester C.	App	11.60	60-75	495	3	29
Chesterfield	L	03.76	75	12	0	0
Brighton & H. A.	Tr	06.76	76	46	0	3
Preston N. E.	Tr	07.77	77-78	45	0	1
Lincoln C.	Enderby T.	03.79	78	19	0	0
CROSS James Keith						
Liverpool, 3 December, 1926						(RH)
Everton		10.50				
Swindon T.	Tr	07.53	53-57	154	-	5
CROSS John (Jack)						
Bury, 5 February, 1927						(CF)
Bournemouth	Guildford C.	06.47	47-53	137	-	64
Northampton T.	Tr	10.53	53	10	-	8
Sheffield U.	Tr	02.54	53-55	44	-	16
Reading	Tr	10.55	55	15	-	6
CROSS Jonathan Neil						
Wallasey, 2 March, 1975						(W)
Wrexham	YT	11.92	91-97	92	27	12
Hereford U.	L	12.96	96	5	0	1
CROSS Mark						
Abergavenny, 6 May, 1976						(LW)
Hereford U.	YT	●	92	0	1	0
CROSS Michael John						
Walkden, 25 April, 1956						(LB)
Bolton W.	App	04.74				
Stockport Co.	Tr	07.75	75	27	0	2
CROSS Nicholas Jeremy Rowland						
Birmingham, 7 February, 1961						(F)
West Bromwich A.	App	02.79	80-84	68	37	15
Walsall	Tr	08.85	85-87	107	2	45
Leicester C.	Tr	01.88	87-88	54	4	15
Port Vale	Tr	06.89	89-93	120	24	39
Hereford U.	Tr	07.94	94-95	56	9	14
CROSS Paul						
Barnsley, 31 October, 1965						(LB)
Barnsley	App	10.83	82-91	115	4	0
Preston N.E.	L	09.91	91	5	0	0
Hartlepool U.	Tr	01.92	91-93	73	1	1
Darlington	Tr	11.93	93-94	39	0	2
CROSS Roger George						
East Ham, 20 October, 1948						(F)
West Ham U.	App	07.64	68-69	5	2	1
Leyton Orient	L	10.68	68	4	2	2
Brentford	Tr	03.70	69-71	62	0	20
Fulham	Tr	09.71	71-72	39	1	8
Brentford	Tr	12.72	72-76	141	4	52
Millwall	Tr	01.77	76-78	14	4	0
CROSS Roy						
Wednesbury, 4 December, 1947						(CH)
Walsall	Jnrs	07.66	66-69	11	1	0
Port Vale	Tr	07.70	70-74	136	0	1
CROSS Ryan						
Plymouth, 11 October, 1972						(RB)
Plymouth Arg.	YT	03.91	90-91	18	1	0
Hartlepool U.	Tr	06.92	92-93	49	1	2
Bury	Tr	12.93	93-95	40	2	0
CROSS Stephen Charles						
Wolverhampton, 22 December, 1959						(M/FB)
Shrewsbury T.	App	12.77	76-85	240	22	33
Derby Co.	Tr	06.86	86-91	42	31	3
Bristol Rov.	Tr	09.91	91-92	37	6	2

CROSSAN Edward
Derry (NI), 17 November, 1925 NI-3 (IF)

League Club	Source	Date Signed	Seasons Played	Apps	Subs	Gls
Blackburn Rov.	Derry C.	11.47	47-56	287	-	73
Tranmere Rov.	Tr	08.57	57	39	-	6

CROSSAN Errol Gilmour
Canada, 6 October, 1930 (OR)

League Club	Source	Date Signed	Seasons Played	Apps	Subs	Gls
Manchester C.	Isle of Man	01.54				
Gillingham	Tr	07.55	55-56	76	-	16
Southend U.	Tr	08.57	57-58	40	-	11
Norwich C.	Tr	09.58	58-60	102	-	28
Leyton Orient	Tr	01.61	60	8	-	2

CROSSAN John Andrew
Derry (NI), 29 November, 1938 NI-24 (IF)

League Club	Source	Date Signed	Seasons Played	Apps	Subs	Gls
Sunderland	Standard Liége (Bel)	10.62	62-64	82	-	39
Manchester C.	Tr	01.65	64-66	94	0	24
Middlesbrough	Tr	08.67	67-69	54	2	7

CROSSLEY James
Belfast, 19 July, 1922 (LB)

League Club	Source	Date Signed	Seasons Played	Apps	Subs	Gls
Portsmouth	Cliftonville	04.45				
Reading	Tr	07.46	46	1	-	0

CROSSLEY Mark Geoffrey
Sheffield, 16 June, 1969 Eu21-3/W 'B'/W-1 (G)

League Club	Source	Date Signed	Seasons Played	Apps	Subs	Gls
Nottingham F.	YT	07.87	88-96	270	1	0
Millwall	L	02.98	97	13	0	0

CROSSLEY Matthew John William
Basingstoke, 18 March, 1968 (CD)

League Club	Source	Date Signed	Seasons Played	Apps	Subs	Gls
Wycombe W.	Overton U.	02.88	93-96	93	3	3

CROSSLEY Paul
Rochdale, 14 August, 1948 Died 1996 (W)

League Club	Source	Date Signed	Seasons Played	Apps	Subs	Gls
Rochdale	Jnrs	09.65	65-66	17	0	2
Preston N. E.	Tr	11.66	66-67	3	0	0
Southport	L	09.68	68	10	0	2
Tranmere Rov.	Tr	06.69	69-75	186	17	37
Chester C.	Tr	09.75	75-77	93	6	26

CROSSLEY Richard Mark
Huddersfield, 5 September, 1970 (CD)

League Club	Source	Date Signed	Seasons Played	Apps	Subs	Gls
York C.	Northwich Vic.	10.89	89-90	6	0	0

CROSSLEY Roy
Hebden Bridge, 16 October, 1923 (CF)

League Club	Source	Date Signed	Seasons Played	Apps	Subs	Gls
Huddersfield T.		05.46				
Halifax T.		09.48	48-50	41	-	15

CROSSLEY Russell
Hebden Bridge, 25 June, 1927 (G)

League Club	Source	Date Signed	Seasons Played	Apps	Subs	Gls
Liverpool	Jnrs	06.47	50-53	68	-	0
Shrewsbury T.	Tr	07.54	54-59	173	-	0

CROSSLEY Terence Gordon
Rockferry, 24 February, 1936 (OL)

League Club	Source	Date Signed	Seasons Played	Apps	Subs	Gls
Oldham Ath.	Bangor Univ.	08.57	57	2	-	1

CROSSON David
Bishop Auckland, 24 November, 1952 (RB)

League Club	Source	Date Signed	Seasons Played	Apps	Subs	Gls
Newcastle U.	Jnrs	11.70	73-74	6	0	0
Darlington	Tr	08.75	75-79	115	13	2

CROTTY Colin
Aberfan, 12 February, 1951 (F)

League Club	Source	Date Signed	Seasons Played	Apps	Subs	Gls
Swansea C. (Am)	Jnrs	08.68	68	1	1	1

CROUCH Nigel John
Colchester, 24 November, 1958 (FB)

League Club	Source	Date Signed	Seasons Played	Apps	Subs	Gls
Ipswich T.	App	11.76				
Lincoln C.	L	08.79	79	7	0	0
Colchester U.	Tr	07.80	80	9	1	0

CROWE Alexander Allan
Motherwell, 24 November, 1924 Died 1997 (IF)

League Club	Source	Date Signed	Seasons Played	Apps	Subs	Gls
Ipswich T.	St Mirren	05.53	53-54	50	-	9

CROWE Charles Alfred
Newcastle, 30 October, 1924 (WH)

League Club	Source	Date Signed	Seasons Played	Apps	Subs	Gls
Newcastle U.	Wallsend St Luke	10.44	46-56	178	-	5
Mansfield T.	Tr	02.57	56-57	37	-	0

CROWE Christopher
Newcastle, 11 June, 1939 S Sch/E Yth/Eu23-4/E-1 (IF)

League Club	Source	Date Signed	Seasons Played	Apps	Subs	Gls
Leeds U.	Jnrs	06.56	56-59	95	-	27
Blackburn Rov.	Tr	03.60	59-61	51	-	6
Wolverhampton W.	Tr	02.62	61-63	83	-	24
Nottingham F.	Tr	08.64	64-66	73	0	12
Bristol C.	Tr	01.67	66-68	66	1	13
Walsall	Tr	09.69	69	10	3	1

CROWE Dean Anthony
Stockport, 6 June, 1979 (F)

League Club	Source	Date Signed	Seasons Played	Apps	Subs	Gls
Stoke C.	YT	09.96	97	10	6	4

CROWE Glen Michael
Dublin, 25 December, 1977 IR Yth/IRu21-2 (F)

League Club	Source	Date Signed	Seasons Played	Apps	Subs	Gls
Wolverhampton W.	YT	07.96	95-97	6	4	1
Exeter C.	L	02.97	96	10	0	5
Cardiff C.	L	10.97	97	7	1	1

CROWE Mark Anthony
Southwold, 21 January, 1965 (CD)

League Club	Source	Date Signed	Seasons Played	Apps	Subs	Gls
Norwich C.	App	01.83	82	0	1	0
Torquay U.	Tr	07.85	85-86	57	0	2
Cambridge U.	Tr	12.86	86-87	51	0	0

CROWE Matthew Jackson
Bathgate, 4 July, 1932 (WH)

League Club	Source	Date Signed	Seasons Played	Apps	Subs	Gls
Bradford P. A.	Bathgate Thistle	07.49	52	1	-	0
Norwich C.	Partick Thistle	05.57	57-61	186	-	14
Brentford	Tr	07.62	62-63	73	-	0

CROWE Michael
Ulverston, 13 August, 1942 (IF)

League Club	Source	Date Signed	Seasons Played	Apps	Subs	Gls
Barrow	Ulverston Ath.	08.60	60-62	15	-	1

CROWE Victor Herbert
Abercynon, 31 January, 1932 W-16 (WH)

League Club	Source	Date Signed	Seasons Played	Apps	Subs	Gls
Aston Villa	West Bromwich A.(Am)	06.52	54-63	294	-	10
Peterborough U.	Tr	07.64	64-66	56	0	0

CROWN David Ian
Enfield, 16 February, 1958 (F)

League Club	Source	Date Signed	Seasons Played	Apps	Subs	Gls
Brentford	Walthamstow Ave.	07.80	80-81	44	2	8
Portsmouth	Tr	10.81	81-82	25	3	2
Exeter C.	L	03.83	82	6	1	3
Reading	Tr	08.83	83-84	87	1	15
Cambridge U.	Tr	07.85	85-87	106	0	44
Southend U.	Tr	11.87	87-89	113	0	61
Gillingham	Tr	06.90	90-92	83	3	38

CROWSHAW Allan Alfred
Bloxwich 12 December, 1932 (OL)

League Club	Source	Date Signed	Seasons Played	Apps	Subs	Gls
West Bromwich A.	Bloxwich Strollers	05.50	54-55	11	-	2
Derby Co.	Tr	06.56	56-57	18	-	6
Millwall	Tr	05.58	58-59	49	-	10

CROWTHER Kenneth
Halifax, 17 December, 1924 Died 1994 (IF)

League Club	Source	Date Signed	Seasons Played	Apps	Subs	Gls
Burnley	Halifax T. (Am)	09.45				
Bradford P. A.	Tr	07.48	48	6	-	1
Rochdale	Tr	08.50	50	2	-	0

CROWTHER Stanley
Bilston, 3 September, 1935 Eu23-3 (WH)

League Club	Source	Date Signed	Seasons Played	Apps	Subs	Gls
Aston Villa	Bilston	08.55	56-57	50	-	4
Manchester U.	Tr	02.58	57-58	13	-	0
Chelsea	Tr	12.58	58-59	51	-	0
Brighton & H. A.	Tr	03.61	60	4	-	0

CROWTHER Stephen John
Romiley, 16 January, 1955 (FB)

League Club	Source	Date Signed	Seasons Played	Apps	Subs	Gls
Stockport Co.		01.74	73-74	42	2	4
Hartlepool U.	Tr	07.75	75	3	0	0

CROY John
Falkirk, 23 February, 1925 Died 1979 (FB)

League Club	Source	Date Signed	Seasons Played	Apps	Subs	Gls
Northampton T.	Third Lanark	07.50	51-54	25	-	0

CROZIER Joseph
Coatbridge, 2 December, 1914 Died 1985 (G)

League Club	Source	Date Signed	Seasons Played	Apps	Subs	Gls
Brentford	East Fife	05.37	37-48	200	-	0

CRUDGINGTON Geoffrey
Wolverhampton, 14 February, 1952 E Sch (G)

League Club	Source	Date Signed	Seasons Played	Apps	Subs	Gls
Aston Villa	Wolverhampton W. (Jnr)	09.69	70-71	4	0	0
Bradford C.	L	03.71	70	1	0	0
Crewe Alex.	Tr	03.72	71-77	250	0	0
Swansea C.	Tr	07.78	78-79	52	0	0
Plymouth Arg.	Tr	10.79	79-87	326	0	0

CRUICKSHANK Frank James
Polmont, 20 November,1931 (FB)

League Club	Source	Date Signed	Seasons Played	Apps	Subs	Gls
Notts Co.	Nuneaton Borough	01.50	53-59	151	-	5

CRUICKSHANK George Philip
Malaya, 22 July, 1931 (OL)

League Club	Source	Date Signed	Seasons Played	Apps	Subs	Gls
Carlisle U.	Queen of South	08.57	57	14	-	0

CRUICKSHANK John Paul
Oldham, 18 January, 1960 (M)

League Club	Source	Date Signed	Seasons Played	Apps	Subs	Gls
Blackpool	App	08.77				
Bury	Tr	07.79	79-82	65	17	4

CRUMBLEHULME Kevin
Manchester, 17 June, 1952 (M)

League Club	Source	Date Signed	Seasons Played	Apps	Subs	Gls
Oldham Ath.	App	07.70	71	2	0	0

CRUMPLIN Ian
Leamington, 12 September, 1954 (F)

League Club	Source	Date Signed	Seasons Played	Apps	Subs	Gls
Hartlepool U.	Blue Star	06.78	78	25	4	5

CRUMPLIN John Leslie
Bath, 26 May, 1967 (W/FB)

League Club	Source	Date Signed	Seasons Played	Apps	Subs	Gls
Brighton & H. A.	Bognor Regis T.	02.87	86-93	173	34	7

CRUSE Peter Leonard
Camden, 10 January, 1951 E Amat (M)

League Club	Source	Date Signed	Seasons Played	Apps	Subs	Gls
Arsenal	Slough T.	04.72				
Luton T.	Tr	07.73	73	3	1	0
Shrewsbury T.	L	02.74	73	2	0	0

CRUTCHLEY Wilfred Ronald
Walsall, 20 June, 1922 Died 1987 (WH)

League Club	Source	Date Signed	Seasons Played	Apps	Subs	Gls
Walsall		03.45	46-49	62	-	4
Shrewsbury T.	Tr	09.50	50-53	146	-	1

CRUYFF Jordi
Netherlands, 9 February, 1974 Dutch Int (F)

League Club	Source	Date Signed	Seasons Played	Apps	Subs	Gls
Manchester U.	Barcelona (Sp)	08.96	96-97	14	7	3

CRYLE George
Aberdeen, 10 April, 1928 (WH)

League Club	Source	Date Signed	Seasons Played	Apps	Subs	Gls
Wolverhampton W.	Jnrs	02.46				
Reading	Tr	06.48	48-50	8	-	2
Swindon T.	Ayr U.	08.52	52	12	-	0

CUBIE Neil George
South Africa, 3 November, 1932 (WH)

League Club	Source	Date Signed	Seasons Played	Apps	Subs	Gls
Bury	Clyde (SA)	10.56				
Hull C.	Tr	07.57	57	4	-	0

CUDDIHEY Russell Francis
Rawtenstall, 8 September, 1939 (WH)

League Club	Source	Date Signed	Seasons Played	Apps	Subs	Gls
Accrington St.		09.60	60	10	-	0

CUDDY Paul
Kendal, 21 February, 1959 E Semi Pro (D)

League Club	Source	Date Signed	Seasons Played	Apps	Subs	Gls
Rochdale (N/C)	Jnrs	08.77	77	0	1	0

CUERVO Philippe
Calais, France, 13 August, 1969 (D/M)

League Club	Source	Date Signed	Seasons Played	Apps	Subs	Gls
Swindon T.	St Etienne (Fr)	08.97	97	14	9	0

CUFF Patrick Joseph
Middlesbrough, 19 March, 1952 E Sch (G)

League Club	Source	Date Signed	Seasons Played	Apps	Subs	Gls
Middlesbrough	App	05.69	73-77	31	0	0
Grimsby T.	L	09.71	71	2	0	0
Millwall	Tr	08.78	78	42	0	0
Darlington	Tr	06.80	80-82	110	0	0

CUGGY Michael Steven
Wallsend, 18 March, 1971 (F)

League Club	Source	Date Signed	Seasons Played	Apps	Subs	Gls
Maidstone U.	Blyth Spartans	06.91	91	1	12	1

CULLEN Anthony Scott
Gateshead, 30 September, 1969 (W)

League Club	Source	Date Signed	Seasons Played	Apps	Subs	Gls
Sunderland	Newcastle U. (YT)	09.88	88-91	11	18	0
Carlisle U.	L	12.89	89	2	0	1
Rotherham U.	L	01.91	90	3	0	1
Bury	L	10.91	91	4	0	0
Swansea C.	Tr	08.92	92	20	7	3

CULLEN David Jonathan
Bishop Auckland, 10 January, 1973 (M)

League Club	Source	Date Signed	Seasons Played	Apps	Subs	Gls
Doncaster Rov.	YT	09.91	90-91	8	1	0
Hartlepool U. (N/C)	Morpeth T.	03.97	96-97	33	1	12
Sheffield U.	Tr	01.98	97	0	2	0

CULLEN Shane Jonathan Raymond
Oxford, 9 October, 1962 (FB)

League Club	Source	Date Signed	Seasons Played	Apps	Subs	Gls
Reading	App	10.80	79-81	14	5	0

CULLEN Michael Joseph
Glasgow, 3 July, 1931 S 'B'/S-1 (IF)

League Club	Source	Date Signed	Seasons Played	Apps	Subs	Gls
Luton T.	Douglasdale Jnrs	08.49	51-57	112	-	16
Grimsby T.	Tr	04.58	58-62	178	-	35
Derby Co.	Tr	12.62	62-64	24	-	5

CULLEN Patrick Joseph
Mexborough, 9 August, 1949 IR Amat (F)

League Club	Source	Date Signed	Seasons Played	Apps	Subs	Gls
Halifax T.	Mexborough	05.68	67-73	1	5	0

CULLERTON Michael Joseph
Edinburgh, 25 November, 1948 (M)

League Club	Source	Date Signed	Seasons Played	Apps	Subs	Gls
Port Vale		01.66	65-68	95	2	22
Chester C.	L	03.69	68	5	2	0
Derby Co.	Tr	07.69				
Port Vale	Stafford R.	07.75	75-77	67	16	28

CULLING Gary
Braintree, 6 April, 1972 (RB)

League Club	Source	Date Signed	Seasons Played	Apps	Subs	Gls
Colchester U.	Braintree T.	08.94	94	2	0	0

CULLINGFORD Robert
Bradford, 3 December, 1953 (D)

League Club	Source	Date Signed	Seasons Played	Apps	Subs	Gls
Bradford C. (Am)	Jnrs	10.69	69-71	1	1	0

CULLIP Daniel
Bracknell, 17 September, 1976 (CD)

League Club	Source	Date Signed	Seasons Played	Apps	Subs	Gls
Oxford U.	YT	07.95				
Fulham	Tr	07.96	96-97	41	9	2
Brentford	Tr	02.98	97	13	0	0

CULLIS Stanley
Ellesmere Port, 25 October, 1916 EF Lge/E-12 (CH)

League Club	Source	Date Signed	Seasons Played	Apps	Subs	Gls
Wolverhampton W.	Ellesmere Port	02.34	34-46	152	-	0

CULLUM Arthur Richard
Colchester, 28 January, 1931 (F)

League Club	Source	Date Signed	Seasons Played	Apps	Subs	Gls
Colchester U.		01.51	50-53	2	-	1

CULLUM Riley Granville
West Ham, 2 April, 1923 Died 1996 (IF)

League Club	Source	Date Signed	Seasons Played	Apps	Subs	Gls
Charlton Ath.	Dartford	10.47	49-52	32	-	6

CULPIN Paul
Kirby Muxloe, 8 February, 1962 E Semi Pro (F)

League Club	Source	Date Signed	Seasons Played	Apps	Subs	Gls
Leicester C.	Jnrs	05.81				
Coventry C.	Nuneaton Borough	06.85	85-86	5	4	2
Northampton T.	Tr	10.87	87-89	52	11	23
Peterborough U.	Tr	10.89	89-91	30	17	14
Hereford U. (N/C)	Tr	02.92	91	1	1	0

CULVERHOUSE Ian Brett
Bishops Stortford, 22 September, 1964 E Yth (RB)

League Club	Source	Date Signed	Seasons Played	Apps	Subs	Gls
Tottenham H.	App	09.82	83	1	1	0
Norwich C.	Tr	10.85	85-93	295	1	1
Swindon T.	Tr	12.94	94-97	95	2	0

CUMBES James
Manchester, 4 May, 1944 (G)

League Club	Source	Date Signed	Seasons Played	Apps	Subs	Gls
Tranmere Rov.	Runcorn	09.65	66-69	137	0	0
West Bromwich A.	Tr	08.69	69-71	64	0	0
Aston Villa	Tr	10.71	71-75	157	0	0
Southport (N/C)	Portland (USA)	01.78	77	19	0	0

CUMMING David Scott
Aberdeen, 6 May, 1910 Died 1993 S-1 (G)

League Club	Source	Date Signed	Seasons Played	Apps	Subs	Gls
Middlesbrough	Aberdeen	10.36	36-46	135	-	0

CUMMING Gordon Robert Riddell
Johnstone, 23 January, 1948 (M)

League Club	Source	Date Signed	Seasons Played	Apps	Subs	Gls
Arsenal	Glasgow U.	01.65				
Reading	Tr	12.69	69-77	277	18	51

CUMMING Robert
Airdrie, 7 December, 1955 (W/FB)

League Club	Source	Date Signed	Seasons Played	Apps	Subs	Gls
Grimsby T.	Baillieston Jnrs	03.74	74-86	338	27	58
Lincoln C.	Tr	07.87	88-89	40	1	5

CUMMINGS George Wilfred
Falkirk, 5 June, 1913 Died 1987 SF Lge/S-9 (FB)

League Club	Source	Date Signed	Seasons Played	Apps	Subs	Gls
Aston Villa	Partick Thistle	11.35	35-48	210	-	0

CUMMINGS John
Greenock, 5 May, 1944 (CF)

League Club	Source	Date Signed	Seasons Played	Apps	Subs	Gls
Port Vale	Aberdeen	08.65	65	2	1	0

CUMMINGS Robert Douglas
Ashington, 17 November, 1935 (CF)

League Club	Source	Date Signed	Seasons Played	Apps	Subs	Gls
Newcastle U.	New Hartley Jnrs	05.54				
Newcastle U.	Aberdeen	10.63	63-65	43	1	14

League Club	Source	Date Signed	Seasons Played	Apps	Subs	Gls
Darlington	Tr	10.65	65-67	73	1	43
Hartlepool U.	Tr	02.68	67-68	48	4	12

CUMMINGS Thomas Smith
Sunderland, 12 September, 1928 E 'B/EF Lge (CH)

League Club	Source	Date Signed	Seasons Played	Apps	Subs	Gls
Burnley	Stanley U.	10.47	48-62	434	-	3
Mansfield T.	Tr	03.63	62-63	10	-	0

CUMMINS George Patrick
Dublin, 12 March, 1931 IR-19 (IF)

League Club	Source	Date Signed	Seasons Played	Apps	Subs	Gls
Everton	St Patricks Ath.	11.50	51-52	24	-	0
Luton T.	Tr	08.53	53-60	184	-	21
Hull C.	Cambridge C.	11.62	62-63	21	-	2

CUMMINS James William Heywood
Hebburn, 15 February, 1925 Died 1981 (CF)

League Club	Source	Date Signed	Seasons Played	Apps	Subs	Gls
Southport	Horden Colly	09.49	49	9	-	1

CUMMINS Stanley
Ferryhill, 6 December, 1958 (M)

League Club	Source	Date Signed	Seasons Played	Apps	Subs	Gls
Middlesbrough	App	12.76	76-79	39	5	9
Sunderland	Tr	11.79	79-82	132	1	29
Crystal Palace	Tr	08.83	83-84	27	1	7
Sunderland	Tr	10.84	84	13	4	0

CUMNER Reginald **Horace**
Aberdare, 31 March, 1918 (OL)

League Club	Source	Date Signed	Seasons Played	Apps	Subs	Gls
Hull C.	Margate	01.38	37	12	-	4
Arsenal	Tr	05.38	38	12	-	2
Notts Co.	Tr	08.46	46-47	66	-	11
Watford	Tr	07.48	48-50`	62	-	7
Scunthorpe U.	Tr	09.50	50-52	102	-	21
Bradford C.	Tr	08.53				

CUNDY Jason Victor
Wimbledon, 12 November, 1969 Eu21-3 (CD)

League Club	Source	Date Signed	Seasons Played	Apps	Subs	Gls
Chelsea	YT	08.88	90-91	40	1	2
Tottenham H.	Tr	03.92	91-95	23	3	1
Crystal Palace	L	12.95	95	4	0	0
Bristol C.	L	08.96	96	6	0	1
Ipswich T.	Tr	10.96	96-97	53	1	5

CUNLIFFE Arthur
Blackrod, 5 February, 1909 Died 1986 (OL)

League Club	Source	Date Signed	Seasons Played	Apps	Subs	Gls
Blackburn Rov.	Chorley	01.28	29-32	129	-	47
Aston Villa	Tr	05.33	32-35	69	-	11
Middlesbrough	Tr	12.35	35-36	27	-	5
Burnley	Tr	04.37	37	9	-	0
Hull C.	Tr	06.38	38	42	-	20
Rochdale	Tr	08.45	46	23	-	5

CUNLIFFE James **Graham**
Hindley, 16 June, 1936 (WH)

League Club	Source	Date Signed	Seasons Played	Apps	Subs	Gls
Bolton W.		01.55	57-62	25	-	0
Rochdale	Tr	07.64	64	36	-	0

CUNLIFFE James
Adlington, 4 October, 1941 (CF)

League Club	Source	Date Signed	Seasons Played	Apps	Subs	Gls
Stockport Co. (Am)	Horwich R.M.I.	11.60	60	1	-	0

CUNLIFFE James Nathaniel
Blackrod, 5 July, 1912 Died 1986 E-1 (IF)

League Club	Source	Date Signed	Seasons Played	Apps	Subs	Gls
Everton	Adlington	05.30	32-38	174	-	73
Rochdale	Tr	09.46	46	2	-	0

CUNLIFFE John (Dickie)
Wigan, 4 February, 1930 Died 1975 (OL)

League Club	Source	Date Signed	Seasons Played	Apps	Subs	Gls
Port Vale		12.50	50-59	283	-	52
Stoke C.	Tr	09.59	59	26	-	3

CUNLIFFE Reginald
Wigan, 4 December, 1920 (LB)

League Club	Source	Date Signed	Seasons Played	Apps	Subs	Gls
Swansea C.	Wigan Ath.	06.46	46-47	2	-	0

CUNLIFFE Robert
Manchester, 17 May, 1945 (IF)

League Club	Source	Date Signed	Seasons Played	Apps	Subs	Gls
Manchester C.	App	08.62	63	3	-	1
York C.	Tr	06.65	65	11	1	2

CUNLIFFE Robert Arthur
Ashton-in-Makefield, 27 December, 1928 (OL)

League Club	Source	Date Signed	Seasons Played	Apps	Subs	Gls
Manchester C.	Jnrs.	01.46	49-55	44	-	9
Chesterfield	Tr	06.56	56-57	62	-	19
Southport	Tr	07.58	58	17	-	2

CUNNING Robert Robertson
Dunfermline, 12 February, 1930 (OL)

League Club	Source	Date Signed	Seasons Played	Apps	Subs	Gls
Sunderland	Port Glasgow	06.50	50	5	-	0

CUNNINGHAM Anthony Eugene
Jamaica (WI), 12 November, 1957 (F)

League Club	Source	Date Signed	Seasons Played	Apps	Subs	Gls
Lincoln C.	Stourbridge	05.79	79-82	111	12	32
Barnsley	Tr	09.82	82-83	40	2	11
Sheffield Wed.	Tr	11.83	83	26	2	5
Manchester C.	Tr	07.84	84	16	2	1
Newcastle U.	Tr	02.85	84-86	37	10	4
Blackpool	Tr	07.87	87-88	71	0	17
Bury	Tr	07.89	89-90	55	3	17
Bolton W.	Tr	03.91	90	9	0	4
Rotherham U.	Tr	08.91	91-92	65	4	24
Doncaster Rov.	Tr	07.93	93	19	6	1
Wycombe W.	Tr	03.94	93	4	1	0

CUNNINGHAM David
Kirkcaldy, 10 August, 1953 (W)

League Club	Source	Date Signed	Seasons Played	Apps	Subs	Gls
Southend U.	Brechin C.	04.73	73-76	55	4	4
Hartlepool U.	L	03.77	76	10	2	1
Swindon T.	Tr	06.77	77-78	18	5	3
Peterborough U.	L	11.78	78	4	0	1
Aston Villa	Tr	12.78				
Hereford U.	Tr	08.79	79	28	2	2
Newport Co.	Tr	08.80				

CUNNINGHAM Edward Milburn
South Shields, 20 March, 1928 (WH)

League Club	Source	Date Signed	Seasons Played	Apps	Subs	Gls
Blackburn Rov.		09.49				
Chesterfield	North Shields	08.52	52-54	56	-	0

CUNNINGHAM Edwin
Jarrow, 20 September, 1919 (W)

League Club	Source	Date Signed	Seasons Played	Apps	Subs	Gls
Bristol C.		05.39	46	1	-	0

CUNNINGHAM Daniel **Harvey**
Manchester, 11 September, 1968 (W)

League Club	Source	Date Signed	Seasons Played	Apps	Subs	Gls
Doncaster Rov.	Droylsden	02.97	96-97	43	1	1

CUNNINGHAM Hugh
Kirkintilloch, 5 April, 1947 (HB)

League Club	Source	Date Signed	Seasons Played	Apps	Subs	Gls
Fulham	Glasgow Celtic	05.66	67	0	1	0

CUNNINGHAM Ian
Glasgow, 6 September, 1956 (RB)

League Club	Source	Date Signed	Seasons Played	Apps	Subs	Gls
Bournemouth	App	08.74	74-80	180	8	4

CUNNINGHAM John
Derry (NI), 30 November, 1966 NI Yth (W)

League Club	Source	Date Signed	Seasons Played	Apps	Subs	Gls
Mansfield T.	Jnrs	08.84	84	3	1	0

CUNNINGHAM Kenneth Edward
Dublin, 28 June, 1971 IR Yth/IRu21-4/IR 'B'/IR-16 (RB)

League Club	Source	Date Signed	Seasons Played	Apps	Subs	Gls
Millwall	Tolka Rov.	09.89	89-94	132	4	1
Wimbledon	Tr	11.94	94-97	128	1	0

CUNNINGHAM Kenneth Rankin
Glasgow, 26 October, 1941 (CF)

League Club	Source	Date Signed	Seasons Played	Apps	Subs	Gls
Hartlepool U.	Falkirk	07.63	63	2	-	0

CUNNINGHAM Laurence
Consett, 20 October, 1921 (FB)

League Club	Source	Date Signed	Seasons Played	Apps	Subs	Gls
Barnsley	Consett U.	11.45	46-47	51	-	1
Bournemouth	Tr	06.48	48-56	273	-	0

CUNNINGHAM Lawrence Paul
Holloway, 8 March, 1956 Died 1989 Eu21-6/E-6 (W)

League Club	Source	Date Signed	Seasons Played	Apps	Subs	Gls
Leyton Orient	App	07.74	74-76	72	3	15
West Bromwich A.	Tr	03.77	76-78	81	5	21
Manchester U.	Real Madrid (Sp)	03.83	82	3	2	1
Leicester C. (N/C)	Marseille (Fr)	10.85	85	13	2	0
Wimbledon (N/C)	Charleroi (Bel)	02.88	87	6	0	2

CUNNINGHAM Thomas Edward
Bethnal Green, 7 October, 1955 (CD)

League Club	Source	Date Signed	Seasons Played	Apps	Subs	Gls
Chelsea	App	10.73				
Queens Park R	Tr	05.75	76-78	27	3	2
Wimbledon	Tr	03.79	78-81	99	0	12
Leyton Orient	Tr	09.81	81-86	162	0	17

CUNNINGHAM William Carruthers
Cowdenbeath, 22 February, 1925 S-8 (FB)

League Club	Source	Date Signed	Seasons Played	Apps	Subs	Gls
Preston N. E.	Airdrieonians	07.49	49-62	440	-	3
Southport	Tr	03.64	64	12	-	0

CUNNINGHAM William Edward
Belfast, 20 February, 1930 NI-30 (FB)

League Club	Source	Date Signed	Seasons Played	Apps	Subs	Gls
Leicester C.	St Mirren	12.54	54-59	127	-	4

CUNNINGHAM William Livingstone
Paisley, 11 July, 1938 (WH)

League Club	Source	Date Signed	Seasons Played	Apps	Subs	Gls
Barnsley	Third Lanark	07.64	64	24	-	0

CUNNINGTON Shaun Gary
Bourne, 4 January, 1966 (M/LB)

League Club	Source	Date Signed	Seasons Played	Apps	Subs	Gls
Wrexham	Jnrs	01.84	82-87	196	3	12
Grimsby T.	Tr	02.88	87-91	182	0	13
Sunderland	Tr	07.92	92-94	52	6	8
West Bromwich A.	Tr	08.95	95-96	8	5	0
Notts Co.	Tr	03.97	96-97	9	8	0

CURBISHLEY Llewellyn (Alan) Charles
Forest Gate, 8 November, 1957 E Sch/E Yth/Eu21-1 (M)

League Club	Source	Date Signed	Seasons Played	Apps	Subs	Gls
West Ham U.	App	08.75	74-78	78	7	5
Birmingham C.	Tr	07.79	79-82	128	2	11
Aston Villa	Tr	03.83	82-84	34	2	1
Charlton Ath.	Tr	12.84	84-86	62	1	6
Brighton & H. A.	Tr	08.87	87-89	111	5	13
Charlton Ath.	Tr	07.90	90-93	22	6	0

CURCIC Sasa
Yugoslavia, 14 February, 1972 Yugoslav Int (M)

League Club	Source	Date Signed	Seasons Played	Apps	Subs	Gls
Bolton W.	Partizan Belgrade (Yug)	10.95	95	28	0	4
Aston Villa	Tr	08.96	96-97	20	9	0
Crystal Palace	Tr	03.98	97	6	2	1

CURETON Jamie
Chippenham, 28 August, 1975 E Yth (F)

League Club	Source	Date Signed	Seasons Played	Apps	Subs	Gls
Norwich C.	YT	02.93	94-95	13	16	6
Bournemouth	L	09.95	95	0	5	0
Bristol Rov.	Tr	09.96	96-97	72	9	24

CURLE Keith
Bristol, 14 November, 1963 E'B'/EF Lge/E-3 (CD)

League Club	Source	Date Signed	Seasons Played	Apps	Subs	Gls
Bristol Rov.	App	11.81	81-82	21	11	4
Torquay U.	Tr	11.83	83	16	0	5
Bristol C.	Tr	03.84	83-87	113	8	1
Reading	Tr	10.87	87-88	40	0	0
Wimbledon	Tr	10.88	88-90	91	2	3
Manchester C.	Tr	08.91	91-95	171	0	11
Wolverhampton W.	Tr	08.96	96-97	60	1	3

CURLEY Thomas
Glasgow, 11 June, 1945 (OR)

League Club	Source	Date Signed	Seasons Played	Apps	Subs	Gls
Brentford	Glasgow Celtic	08.65	65-66	40	0	6
Crewe Alex.	Tr	08.67	67-68	48	4	7

CURLEY William
Trimdon, 20 November, 1945 (FB)

League Club	Source	Date Signed	Seasons Played	Apps	Subs	Gls
Darlington	App	11.63	62-64	29	0	1

CURRAN Christopher
Birmingham, 17 September, 1971 (D)

League Club	Source	Date Signed	Seasons Played	Apps	Subs	Gls
Torquay U.	YT	07.90	89-95	144	8	4
Plymouth Arg.	Tr	12.95	95-96	26	4	0
Exeter C.	Tr	07.97	97	9	0	0

CURRAN Christopher Patrick
Heywood, 6 January, 1971 (D)

League Club	Source	Date Signed	Seasons Played	Apps	Subs	Gls
Crewe Alex.	YT	09.89	89-90	2	3	0
Scarborough	Tr	03.92	91-92	40	0	4
Carlisle U.	Tr	07.93	93	4	2	1

CURRAN Edward (Terry)
Hemsworth, 20 March, 1955 (W)

League Club	Source	Date Signed	Seasons Played	Apps	Subs	Gls
Doncaster Rov.	Jnrs	07.73	73-75	67	1	11
Nottingham F.	Tr	08.75	75-76	46	2	12
Bury	L	10.77	77	2	0	0
Derby Co.	Tr	11.77	77	26	0	2
Southampton	Tr	08.78	78	25	1	0
Sheffield Wed.	Tr	03.79	78-81	122	3	35
Sheffield U.	Tr	08.82	82	31	2	3
Everton	L	12.82	82	7	0	1
Everton	Tr	09.83	83-84	12	5	0
Huddersfield T.	Tr	07.85	85	33	1	7
Hull C.	Panionis (Gre)	10.86	86	4	0	0
Sunderland	Tr	11.86	86	9	0	1
Grimsby T.	Grantham	11.87	87	10	2	0
Chesterfield (N/C)	Tr	03.88	87	0	1	0

CURRAN Frank
Royton, 31 May, 1917 (IF)

League Club	Source	Date Signed	Seasons Played	Apps	Subs	Gls
Southport	Washington Colly	08.35	35-36	16	-	3
Accrington St.	Tr	02.37	36-37	34	-	14
Bristol Rov.	Tr	06.38	38	27	-	21
Bristol C.	Tr	05.39				
Bristol Rov.	Tr	05.46	46	11	-	3
Tranmere Rov.	Shrewsbury T.	06.47	47	17	-	7

CURRAN Hugh Patrick
Glasgow, 25 September, 1943 S-5 (F)

League Club	Source	Date Signed	Seasons Played	Apps	Subs	Gls
Millwall	Corby T.	03.64	63-65	57	0	26
Norwich C.	Tr	01.66	65-68	112	0	46
Wolverhampton W.	Tr	01.69	68-71	77	5	40
Oxford U.	Tr	09.72	72-74	69	1	28
Bolton W.	Tr	09.74	74-76	40	7	13
Oxford U.	Tr	07.77	77-78	30	5	11

CURRAN James
Macclesfield, 24 September, 1947 (G)

League Club	Source	Date Signed	Seasons Played	Apps	Subs	Gls
Newcastle U.	Jnrs	10.64				
Oldham Ath.		12.66	66	3	0	0
Crewe Alex.	Tr	04.67	68	3	0	0

CURRAN John
Glasgow, 22 June, 1924 Died 1985 (G)

League Club	Source	Date Signed	Seasons Played	Apps	Subs	Gls
Shrewsbury T.	East Fife	08.56	56	24	-	0
Watford	Tr	06.57	57	30	-	0

CURRAN Patrick James
Sunderland, 13 November, 1917 (IF)

League Club	Source	Date Signed	Seasons Played	Apps	Subs	Gls
Sunderland	Sunderland St Patrick	10.36	37	1	-	0
Ipswich T.	Tr	10.38	38	7	-	1
Watford	Tr	06.39				
Bradford C.	Tr	06.47	47	5	-	1

CURRAN Terence William
Staines, 29 June, 1940 (IF)

League Club	Source	Date Signed	Seasons Played	Apps	Subs	Gls
Brentford	Tottenham H. (Am)	09.57	60	5	-	0

CURRIE Anthony William
Edgware, 1 January, 1950 E Yth/Eu23-13/EF Lge/E-17 (M)

League Club	Source	Date Signed	Seasons Played	Apps	Subs	Gls
Watford	App	05.67	67	17	1	9
Sheffield U.	Tr	02.68	67-75	313	0	55
Leeds U.	Tr	06.76	76-78	102	0	11
Queens Park R	Tr	08.79	79-82	79	2	5
Torquay U. (N/C)	Chesham U.	02.84	83-84	14	0	1

CURRIE Charles
Belfast, 17 April, 1920 LoI (WH)

League Club	Source	Date Signed	Seasons Played	Apps	Subs	Gls
Bradford P. A.	Belfast Celtic	06.49	49-53	118	-	2

CURRIE Darren Paul
Hampstead, 29 November, 1974 (LW)

League Club	Source	Date Signed	Seasons Played	Apps	Subs	Gls
West Ham U.	YT	07.93				
Shrewsbury T.	L	09.94	94	10	2	2
Shrewsbury T.	L	02.95	94	5	0	0
Leyton Orient	L	11.95	95	9	1	0
Shrewsbury T.	Tr	02.96	95-97	46	20	8
Plymouth Arg.	Tr	03.98	97	5	2	0

CURRIE David Norman
Stockton, 27 November, 1962 EF Lge (F)

League Club	Source	Date Signed	Seasons Played	Apps	Subs	Gls
Middlesbrough		02.82	81-85	94	19	31
Darlington	Tr	06.86	86-87	76	0	33
Barnsley	Tr	02.88	87-89	80	0	30
Nottingham F.	Tr	01.90	89	4	4	1
Oldham Ath.	Tr	08.90	90-91	17	14	3
Barnsley	Tr	09.91	91-93	53	22	12
Rotherham U.	L	10.92	92	5	0	2
Huddersfield T.	L	01.94	93	7	0	1
Carlisle U.	Tr	07.94	94-96	84	5	13
Scarborough	Tr	01.97	96	16	0	6

CURRIE James Adam Campbell
Glasgow, 25 April, 1932 (F)

League Club	Source	Date Signed	Seasons Played	Apps	Subs	Gls
Exeter C.	Falkirk	06.56	56-57	54	-	19
Workington	Tr	10.57	57-59	23	-	8

CURRIE James Thomson
Bridge of Allan, 6 August, 1948 (WH)

League Club	Source	Date Signed	Seasons Played	Apps	Subs	Gls
Scunthorpe U.		09.68	68-69	4	2	0

CURRIE John
Motherwell, 14 March, 1935 (IR)

League Club	Source	Date Signed	Seasons Played	Apps	Subs	Gls
Accrington St.	Cleland Jnrs	11.53	53-54	16	-	3

CURRIE John Edward
Liverpool, 18 March, 1921 Died 1984 (OR)

League Club	Source	Date Signed	Seasons Played	Apps	Subs	Gls
Bournemouth (Am)	Stafford R.	10.46	46	8	-	2
Port Vale	Tr	06.47	47	9	-	0

CURRIE John Gemmell
Dumfries, 7 April, 1939 S Sch (WH)

League Club	Source	Date Signed	Seasons Played	Apps	Subs	Gls
Leicester C.	Jnrs	04.57				
Workington	Tr	07.61	61-62	55	-	2
Chester C.	Tr	07.63	63	2	-	0

CURRIE Malcolm
Glasgow, 5 February, 1932 Died 1996 (D)

League Club	Source	Date Signed	Seasons Played	Apps	Subs	Gls
Bradford C.	Rutherglen Glencairn	07.56	56-60	136	-	1

League Club	Source	Date Signed	Seasons Played	Apps	Subs	Gls

CURRY Robert
Gateshead, 2 November, 1918 (IR)

League Club	Source	Date Signed	Seasons Played	Apps	Subs	Gls
Sheffield W.		10.37	37	1	-	0
Colchester U.	Gainsborough Trin.	(N/L)	50	32	-	14

CURRY Sean Patrick
Liverpool, 13 November, 1966 (F)

League Club	Source	Date Signed	Seasons Played	Apps	Subs	Gls
Liverpool	App	07.84				
Blackburn Rov.	Tr	01.87	86-88	25	13	6
Hartlepool U.	Tr	08.89	89	0	1	0
Preston N. E.	Tr	09.89				

CURRY William Morton
Longbenton, 12 October, 1935 Died 1990 E-u23-1 (CF)

League Club	Source	Date Signed	Seasons Played	Apps	Subs	Gls
Newcastle U.	Jnrs	10.53	54-58	80	-	36
Brighton & H. A.	Tr	07.59	59-60	49	-	26
Derby Co.	Tr	10.60	60-64	148	-	67
Mansfield T.	Tr	02.65	64-67	102	0	53
Chesterfield	Tr	01.68	67-68	14	0	2

CURTIN Douglas James
Penarth, 15 September, 1947 W Sch (OL)

League Club	Source	Date Signed	Seasons Played	Apps	Subs	Gls
Mansfield T.	Cardiff C. (App)	11.65	65	3	0	0

CURTIS Alan Thomas
Pentre, 16 April, 1954 Wu21-1/Wu23-1/W-35 (F/M)

League Club	Source	Date Signed	Seasons Played	Apps	Subs	Gls
Swansea C.	Jnrs	07.72	72-78	244	4	72
Leeds U.	Tr	06.79	79-80	28	0	5
Swansea C.	Tr	12.80	80-83	82	8	21
Southampton	Tr	11.83	83-85	43	7	5
Stoke C.	L	03.86	85	3	0	0
Cardiff C.	Tr	07.86	86-89	122	3	10
Swansea C.	Tr	10.89	89	21	5	3

CURTIS Andrew
Rotherham, 2 December, 1972 (W)

League Club	Source	Date Signed	Seasons Played	Apps	Subs	Gls
York C.	YT	07.91	90-91	6	6	0
Peterborough U. (N/C)	Kettering T.	09.92	92	8	3	1
York C.	(Retired)	07.95	95	0	1	0
Scarborough (N/C)	Tr	01.96	95	3	2	0

CURTIS Dermot Patrick
Dublin, 26 August, 1932 IR-17 (CF)

League Club	Source	Date Signed	Seasons Played	Apps	Subs	Gls
Bristol C.	Shelbourne	12.56	56-57	26	-	16
Ipswich T.	Tr	09.58	58-62	41	-	17
Exeter C.	Tr	08.63	63-65	91	0	23
Torquay U.	Tr	08.66	66	12	0	1
Exeter C.	Tr	06.67	67-68	64	2	10

CURTIS George Edward
Grays, 3 December, 1919 (WH)

League Club	Source	Date Signed	Seasons Played	Apps	Subs	Gls
Arsenal	Anglo Purfleet	04.37	38-46	13	-	0
Southampton	Tr	08.47	47-51	174	-	11

CURTIS George William
Dover, 5 May, 1939 E Yth (CH)

League Club	Source	Date Signed	Seasons Played	Apps	Subs	Gls
Coventry C.	Snowdown Colly	05.56	55-69	483	4	11
Aston Villa	Tr	12.69	69-71	51	0	3

CURTIS John
Poulton-le-Fylde, 2 September, 1954 (FB)

League Club	Source	Date Signed	Seasons Played	Apps	Subs	Gls
Blackpool	App	09.72	73-76	96	6	0
Blackburn Rov.	Tr	07.77	77-78	9	1	0
Wigan Ath.	Tr	03.79	78-80	32	0	0

CURTIS John Charles
Nuneaton, 3 September, 1978 E Sch/E Yth/Eu21-6/E'B' (FB)

League Club	Source	Date Signed	Seasons Played	Apps	Subs	Gls
Manchester U.	YT	10.95	97	3	5	0

CURTIS William Norman
Dinnington, 10 September, 1924 (FB)

League Club	Source	Date Signed	Seasons Played	Apps	Subs	Gls
Sheffield Wed.	Gainsborough Trin.	01.50	50-59	310	-	21
Doncaster Rov.	Tr	08.60	60	39	-	3

CURTIS Paul Anthony Ernest
Woolwich, 1 July, 1963 (FB)

League Club	Source	Date Signed	Seasons Played	Apps	Subs	Gls
Charlton Ath.	App	07.81	82-84	69	3	5
Northampton T.	Tr	07.85	85	27	0	1
Northampton T. (N/C)	Corby T.	08.92	92	22	0	1

CURTIS Robert Anthony
Mansfield, 21 May, 1972 (CD)

League Club	Source	Date Signed	Seasons Played	Apps	Subs	Gls
Northampton T.	Boston U.	06.94	94	13	0	0

CURTIS Robert Dennis
Langwith, 25 January, 1950 (RB)

League Club	Source	Date Signed	Seasons Played	Apps	Subs	Gls
Charlton Ath.	App	02.67	66-67	324	13	34
Mansfield T.	Tr	02.78	77-79	69	4	7

CURTIS Thomas David
Exeter, 1 March, 1973 (M)

League Club	Source	Date Signed	Seasons Played	Apps	Subs	Gls
Derby Co.	Jnrs	07.91				
Chesterfield	Tr	08.93	93-97	194	4	9

CURTIS Mark Wayne
Neath, 22 February, 1967 (RB)

League Club	Source	Date Signed	Seasons Played	Apps	Subs	Gls
Cardiff C.	Swansea C. (Jnr)	10.84	85	24	3	2

CURWEN Eric
Blackpool, 16 September, 1947 E Sch (FB)

League Club	Source	Date Signed	Seasons Played	Apps	Subs	Gls
Everton	App	05.65				
Southport	Tr	12.66	66-68	89	0	0

CURZON Terence
Winsford, 26 May, 1936 (OL)

League Club	Source	Date Signed	Seasons Played	Apps	Subs	Gls
Crewe Alex.	Bolton W. (Am)	10.53	53-56	11	-	1

CUSACK David Stephen
Thurcroft, 6 June, 1956 (CD/F)

League Club	Source	Date Signed	Seasons Played	Apps	Subs	Gls
Sheffield Wed.	App	06.74	75-77	92	3	1
Southend U.	Tr	09.78	78-82	186	0	17
Millwall	Tr	03.83	82-84	98	0	9
Doncaster Rov.	Tr	07.85	85-87	100	0	4
Rotherham U.	Tr	12.87	87	18	0	0
Doncaster Rov. (N/C)	Boston U.	08.89	89	1	0	0

CUSACK Nicholas John
Maltby, 24 December, 1965 (F)

League Club	Source	Date Signed	Seasons Played	Apps	Subs	Gls
Leicester C.	Alvechurch	06.87	87	5	11	1
Peterborough U.	Tr	07.88	88	44	0	10
Darlington	Motherwell	01.92	91	21	0	6
Oxford U.	Tr	07.92	92-93	48	13	10
Wycombe W.	L	03.94	93	2	2	1
Fulham	Tr	11.94	94-97	109	7	14
Swansea C.	Tr	10.97	97	32	0	0

CUSH Wilbur
Lurgan (NI), 10 June, 1928 Died 1981 LoI/NI-26 (WH)

League Club	Source	Date Signed	Seasons Played	Apps	Subs	Gls
Leeds U.	Glenavon	11.57	57-59	87	-	9

CUSHIN Edward
Whitehaven, 27 January, 1927 (FB)

League Club	Source	Date Signed	Seasons Played	Apps	Subs	Gls
Workington	Lowca	(N/L)	51-55	119	-	4

CUSHLEY John
Blantyre, 21 January, 1943 (CH)

League Club	Source	Date Signed	Seasons Played	Apps	Subs	Gls
West Ham U.	Glasgow Celtic	07.67	67-69	38	0	0

CUSHLOW Richard
Shotton (Dm), 15 June, 1920 (CH)

League Club	Source	Date Signed	Seasons Played	Apps	Subs	Gls
Chesterfield	Murton Colly	05.46	46-47	34	-	0
Sheffield U.	Tr	12.47				
Derby Co.	Tr	03.48	48-49	2	-	0
Crystal Palace	Tr	02.51	50-51	28	-	0

CUTBUSH William John
Malta, 28 June, 1949 (RB)

League Club	Source	Date Signed	Seasons Played	Apps	Subs	Gls
Tottenham H.	App	09.66				
Fulham	Tr	07.72	72-76	131	3	3
Sheffield U.	Tr	03.77	76-80	126	3	1

CUTHBERT Ean Richardson
Hurlford, 5 February, 1942 (FB)

League Club	Source	Date Signed	Seasons Played	Apps	Subs	Gls
Blackpool	Alyth U.	07.59				
Stockport Co.	Tr	07.63	63-65	93	0	0
Crewe Alex.	Bangor C.	11.66	66	1	0	0

CUTHBERTSON James
Sunderland, 7 December, 1947 (W)

League Club	Source	Date Signed	Seasons Played	Apps	Subs	Gls
Bradford C.	App	07.66	66-67	25	3	7

CUTHBERTSON John
Glasgow, 10 March, 1932 (IF)

League Club	Source	Date Signed	Seasons Played	Apps	Subs	Gls
Mansfield T.		10.53	53	3	-	0

CUTLER Christopher Paul
Manchester, 7 April, 1964 (M/F)

League Club	Source	Date Signed	Seasons Played	Apps	Subs	Gls
Bury	Jnrs	08.81	81-84	8	15	3
Crewe Alex.	Tr	08.85	85-89	116	24	24

CUTLER Neil Anthony
Birmingham, 3 September, 1976 E Sch/E Yth (G)

League Club	Source	Date Signed	Seasons Played	Apps	Subs	Gls
West Bromwich A.	YT	09.93				
Chester C.	L	03.96	95	1	0	0
Crewe Alex.	Tr	07.96				
Chester C.	L	08.96	96	5	0	0

League Club	Source	Date Signed	Seasons Played	Apps	Subs	Gls
CUTLER Paul						
Welwyn Garden City, 18 June, 1946						(OL)
Crystal Palace	App	04.64	64-65	10	0	1
CUTLER Reginald Victor						
Blackheath, 17 February, 1935						(W)
West Bromwich A.	Jnrs	02.52	51-54	5	-	0
Bournemouth	Tr	06.56	56-58	96	-	21
Portsmouth	Tr	09.58	58-61	100	-	13
Stockport Co.	Tr	07.62	62	34	-	0
CUTTING Frederick Charles						
North Walsham, 4 December, 1921 Died 1997						(IF)
Leicester C.		01.46				
Norwich C.	Tr	09.46				
Colchester U.	Tr	12.47	50-51	29	-	12
CUTTING Jack Andrew						
Fleetwood, 15 April, 1924 Died 1985						(IF)
Oldham Ath.		11.46	46	4	-	1
Accrington St.	Fleetwood	06.48	48	23	-	5
CUTTING Stanley William						
St Faiths (Nk), 21 September, 1914						(RH)
Southampton	Norwich C. (Am)	05.37	38	3	-	0
Exeter C.	Tr	07.39	46-47	38	-	2
CYGAN Paul						
Doncaster, 4 March, 1972						(M)
Doncaster Rov.	YT	●	89	0	1	0
CYRUS Andrew						
Lambeth, 30 September, 1976						(LB)
Crystal Palace	YT	08.95	96	1	0	0
Exeter C.	Tr	07.97	97	17	4	0
CZUCZMAN Mychaljo (Mike)						
Carlisle, 27 May, 1953						(D)
Grimsby T.	Preston N.E. (App)	08.71	71-75	107	6	6
Scunthorpe U.	Tr	08.76	76-78	115	1	1
Stockport Co.	Tr	05.79	79	36	0	7
Grimsby T.	San Jose (USA)	09.80	80-81	9	0	0
York C.	Tr	11.81	81	17	0	0

League Club	Source	Date Signed	Seasons Played	Apps	Subs	Gls

League Club	Source	Date Signed	Seasons Played	Apps	Subs	Gls
DABIZAS Nikolaos						
Amyndaeo, Greece, 3 August, 1973 Greek Int						(CD)
Newcastle U.	Olympiakos (Gre)	03.98	97	10	1	1
DA COSTA Hugo Alexandre						
Portugal, 4 November, 1973						(CD)
Stoke C. (N/C)	Benfica (Por)	08.96	96	1	1	0
DADLEY Peter Robin						
Farnham, 10 December, 1948						(OR)
Aldershot	App	12.66	66	1	0	1
DAGG Henry Cable						
Sunderland, 4 March, 1924						(CF)
Lincoln C. (Am)	Boston U.	12.46	46	1	-	1
DAGGER John **Leslie**						
Longtown, 25 April, 1933						(OR)
Preston N.E.	West Auckland	05.56	56-60	61	-	8
Carlisle U.	Tr	06.61	61-62	74	-	9
Southport	Tr	07.63	63-64	81	-	9
DAHLIN Martin						
Udevalla, Sweden, 16 April, 1968 Swedish Int						(CF)
Blackburn Rov.	Roma (It)	07.97	97	11	10	4
DAILEY James						
Airdrie, 8 September, 1927						(CF)
Sheffield Wed.	Third Lanark	10.46	46-48	37	-	24
Birmingham C.	Tr	02.49	48-51	41	-	14
Exeter C.	Tr	08.52	52-53	45	-	13
Workington	Tr	12.53	53-57	176	-	74
Rochdale	Tr	10.57	57-58	53	-	25
DAILLY Christian Eduard						
Dundee, 23 October, 1973 S Sch/S Yth/Su21-34/S 'B'/S-13						(D/M)
Derby Co.	Dundee U.	08.96	95-97	61	5	4
DAILLY Marcus Graham						
Dundee, 1 October, 1975						(M)
Exeter C.	Dundee	08.96	96	8	9	0
DAINES Barry Raymond						
Braintree, 30 September, 1951 E Yth						(G)
Tottenham H.	App	09.69	71-80	146	0	0
Mansfield T. (N/C)	Hong Kong	10.83	83	21	0	0
DAINTY Albert						
Lancaster, 4 December, 1923 Died 1979						(CF)
Preston N.E.	Standfast Dyers	10.42	46	1	-	1
Stockport Co.	Tr	04.47	46-48	36	-	16
Southport	Tr	02.49	48-50	48	-	11
DAINTY James Anthony						
Coleshill, 21 January, 1954						(W)
Walsall	Jnrs	10.71	71-72	4	1	0
DAIR Jason						
Dunfermline, 15 June, 1974 S Sch						(LM)
Millwall	Raith Rov.	07.96	96	21	3	1
DAISH Liam Sean						
Portsmouth, 23 September, 1968 IRu21-5/IR 'B'/IR-5						(CD)
Portsmouth	App	09.86	86	1	0	0
Cambridge U.	Tr	07.88	88-93	138	1	4
Birmingham C.	Tr	01.94	93-95	72	1	3
Coventry C.	Tr	02.96	95-96	31	0	2
DAKIN Simon Mark						
Nottingham, 30 November, 1974						(RB)
Derby Co. (N/C)	YT	07.93				
Hull C.	Tr	03.94	93-95	29	7	1
DALE Alan George						
Moorends, 20 September, 1958						(F)
Scunthorpe U.	App	09.76	75-76	1	2	0
DALE Carl						
Colwyn Bay, 29 April, 1966						(F)
Chester C.	Bangor C.	05.88	88-90	106	10	41
Cardiff C.	Tr	08.91	91-97	188	25	71
DALE Christopher						
York, 16 April, 1950						(OL)
York C. (Am)	Hull C. (Am)	05.68	68	5	0	0
DALE Eric						
Manchester, 6 July, 1924						(OR)
Shrewsbury T.		(N/L)	50	1	-	0
DALE Gordon						
Worksop, 20 May, 1928 Died 1996						(OL)
Chesterfield	Worksop T.	02.48	48-50	92	-	3
Portsmouth	Tr	07.51	51-56	114	-	18
Exeter C.	Tr	10.57	57-60	124	-	8
DALE Joseph						
Northwich, 3 July, 1921						(OR)
Manchester U.	Witton A.	06.47	47	2	-	0
Port Vale	Tr	04.48	47-48	9	-	1
DALE Leo						
Esh Winning, 11 October, 1933						(W)
Doncaster Rov.	Durham C.	02.54	54	1	-	0
DALE Robert Jenkins						
Manchester, 31 October, 1931						(IF)
Bury	Altrincham	09.51	52-53	15	-	2
Colchester U.	Tr	12.53	53-56	127	-	12
DALE Frederick **William**						
Doncaster, 26 October, 1925						(W)
Halifax T.	Scunthorpe U.	08.49	49-51	69	-	16
Southport	Tr	07.52	52-53	47	-	5
Accrington St.	Tr	07.54	54	1	-	0
Crewe Alex.	Tr	10.54	54	4	-	3
DALEY Alan James						
Mansfield, 11 October, 1927						(OL)
Mansfield T.	Pleasley B.C.	09.46				
Hull C.	Tr	07.47	47	7	-	0
Doncaster Rov.	Worksop T.	03.50	49	1	-	1
Scunthorpe U.	Boston U.	07.52	52	35	-	8
Mansfield T.	Corby T.	11.53	53-55	97	-	25
Stockport Co.	Tr	02.56	55-57	73	-	17
Crewe Alex.	Tr	06.58	58	14	-	1
Coventry C.	Tr	11.58	58-60	56	-	10
DALEY Anthony Mark						
Birmingham, 18 October, 1967 E Yth/E 'B'/E-7						(RW)
Aston Villa	App	05.85	84-93	189	44	31
Wolverhampton W.	Tr	06.94	94-97	16	5	3
DALEY Peter John						
Liverpool, 14 February, 1970						(M)
Southend U.	Knowsley U.	09.89	89	0	5	1
DALEY Phillip						
Liverpool, 12 April, 1967						(F)
Wigan Ath.	Newton	10.89	89-93	152	9	39
Lincoln C.	Tr	08.94	94-95	25	7	5
DALEY Stephen						
Barnsley, 15 April, 1953 E Yth/E'B'						(M)
Wolverhampton W.	App	06.71	71-78	191	21	38
Manchester C.	Tr	09.79	79-80	47	1	4
Burnley	Seattle (USA)	11.83	83	20	3	4
Walsall	San Diego (USA)	08.85	85	28	0	1
DALEY Thomas Edward						
Grimsby, 15 November, 1933						(G)
Grimsby T.	Jnrs	08.51	51-56	14	-	0
Huddersfield T.	Tr	03.57	56	1	-	0
West Bromwich A.	Tr	08.58				
DALGLISH Kenneth Mathieson						
Glasgow, 4 March, 1951 Su23-4/S-102						(F)
Liverpool	Glasgow Celtic	08.77	77-89	342	13	118
DALGLISH Paul						
Glasgow, 18 February, 1977						(F)
Liverpool	Glasgow Celtic	08.96				
Newcastle U.	Tr	11.97				
Bury	L	11.97	97	1	11	0
DALL David Graham						
St Andrews, 10 October, 1957						(CD)
Scunthorpe U.	Grantham	10.79	79-81	77	0	2
DALLAS William Robert Dempster						
Glasgow, 6 March, 1931						(CH)
Luton T.		09.52				
Wrexham	St Mirren	07.57	57	8	-	0

League Club	Source	Date Signed	Seasons Played	Apps	Subs	Gls
DALLI Jean						
Enfield, 13 August, 1976						(FB)
Colchester U. (N/C)	Jnrs	08.94	94	1	0	0
DALLING Nigel Aubrey						
Swansea, 20 February, 1959						(M)
Swansea C.	App	02.77	74-77	3	5	0
DALLMAN William						
Mansfield, 8 August, 1918 Died 1988						(CH)
Mansfield T.	Rufford Colly	03.47	46-47	5	-	0
DALRYMPLE Malcolm Owen						
Bedford, 8 October, 1951 E Yth						(G)
Luton T.	Jnrs	07.70				
Bristol Rov.	Margate	10.71	71-72	7	0	0
Watford	Tr	07.73	73	5	0	0
DALTON George						
Dilston, 4 September, 1941						(FB)
Newcastle U.	Jnrs	11.58	60-66	85	0	2
Brighton & H.A.	Tr	06.67	67	24	0	0
DALTON Paul						
Middlesbrough, 25 April, 1967						(LW)
Manchester U.	Brandon U.	05.88				
Hartlepool U.	Tr	03.89	88-91	140	11	37
Plymouth Arg.	Tr	06.92	92-94	93	5	25
Huddersfield T.	Tr	08.95	95-97	72	17	22
DALTON Richard **Timothy**						
London, 14 October, 1965						(G)
Coventry C.	App	09.83				
Notts Co.	Tr	07.84	85	1	0	0
Bradford C.	Boston U.	09.86				
Tranmere Rov.	L	12.86	86	1	0	0
DALY Gerard Anthony						
Dublin, 30 April, 1954 IRu21-1/IR-47						(M)
Manchester U.	Bohemians	04.73	73-76	107	4	23
Derby Co.	Tr	03.77	76-79	111	1	31
Coventry C.	Tr	08.80	80-83	82	2	19
Leicester C.	L	01.83	82	17	0	1
Birmingham C.	Tr	08.84	84-85	31	1	1
Shrewsbury T.	Tr	10.85	85-86	55	0	8
Stoke C.	Tr	03.87	86-87	17	5	1
Doncaster Rov.	Tr	07.88	88	37	2	4
DALY Maurice Celsus						
Dublin, 28 November, 1955 IRu21-4/IR-2						(FB)
Wolverhampton W.	Home Farm	07.73	75-77	28	4	0
DALY Patrick						
Dublin, 4 December, 1927 LoI/IR-1						(FB)
Aston Villa	Shamrock Rov.	11.49	49	3	-	0
DALY Patrick John						
Manchester, 3 January, 1941						(OL)
Blackburn Rov.	Jnrs	01.58	59-60	3	-	0
Southport	Tr	02.62	61	10	-	0
DALY Ronald George						
Clerkenwell, 22 July, 1930 Died 1996						(IF)
Watford		10.50	50	3	-	0
DALZIEL Gordon						
Motherwell, 16 March, 1962						(M)
Manchester C.	Glasgow Rangers	12.83	83	4	1	0
DALZIEL Ian						
South Shields, 24 October, 1962						(D)
Derby Co.	App	10.79	81-82	22	0	4
Hereford U.	Tr	05.83	83-87	137	13	8
Carlisle U.	Tr	07.88	88-92	90	1	2
DAMERELL Mark Anthony						
Plymouth, 31 July, 1965						(W)
Plymouth Arg.	St Blazey	11.89	89-91	0	6	0
Exeter C. (N/C)	Tr	12.91	91	1	0	0
DANCE Trevor						
Hetton-le-Hole, 31 July, 1958						(G)
Port Vale	App	07.76	76-80	84	0	0
DANDO Philip						
Liverpool, 8 June, 1952						(G)
Liverpool	Jnrs	09.69				
Barrow	L	10.70	70	9	0	0

League Club	Source	Date Signed	Seasons Played	Apps	Subs	Gls
DANGERFIELD Christopher George						
Coleshill, 9 August, 1955						(F)
Wolverhampton W.	App	08.73				
Port Vale	Portland (USA)	09.76	76	0	2	0
DANGERFIELD David Anthony						
Tetbury, 27 September, 1951 E Sch						(M)
Swindon T.	App	08.69	68-72	16	4	0
[DANI] CARVALHO Daniel da Cruz						
Portugal, 2 November, 1976 Portuguese u21 Int						(F)
West Ham U. (L)	Sporting Lisbon (Por)	02.96	95	3	6	2
DANIEL Alan Winstone						
Ashford, 5 April, 1940						(FB)
Luton T.	Bexleyheath & Welling	01.58	58-63	50	-	3
DANIEL Melville						
Llanelli, 26 January, 1916 Died 1997						(IF)
Luton T.	Ashford T.	09.44	46-48	53	-	20
Aldershot	Tr	06.49	49	28	-	1
DANIEL Peter Aylmer						
Ripley, 22 December, 1946						(D)
Derby Co.	App	12.64	65-78	188	7	7
DANIEL Peter William						
Hull, 12 December, 1955 Eu21-7/Eu23-3						(M/RB)
Hull C.	Jnrs	09.73	74-77	113	0	9
Wolverhampton W.	Tr	05.78	78-83	157	0	13
Sunderland	Tr	08.84	84-85	33	1	0
Lincoln C.	Tr	11.85	85-86	55	0	2
Burnley	Tr	07.87	87-88	40	1	0
DANIEL Raymond Christopher						
Luton, 10 December, 1964						(LB)
Luton T.	App	09.82	82-85	14	8	4
Gillingham	L	09.83	83	5	0	0
Hull C.	Tr	06.86	86-88	55	3	3
Cardiff C.	Tr	08.89	89-90	56	0	1
Portsmouth	Tr	11.90	90-94	91	9	4
Notts Co.	L	10.94	94	5	0	0
Walsall	Tr	08.95	95-96	31	4	0
DANIEL William **Raymond**						
Swansea, 2 November, 1928 Died 1997 W-21						(CH)
Arsenal	Swansea C. (Am)	10.46	48-52	87	-	5
Sunderland	Tr	06.53	53-56	136	-	6
Cardiff C.	Tr	10.57	57	6	-	0
Swansea C.	Tr	03.58	57-59	45	-	7
DANIEL Thomas						
Oldham, 14 April, 1923						(IF)
Bury	Castleton Gabriels	12.46	47-57	276	-	58
DANIELS Bernard (Barney) Joseph						
Salford, 24 November, 1950						(F)
Manchester U.	Jnrs	04.69				
Manchester C.	Ashton U.	04.73	73-74	9	4	2
Chester C.	Tr	07.75	75	8	1	1
Stockport Co.	Tr	07.76	76-77	45	2	17
DANIELS Douglas						
Salford, 21 August, 1924						(G)
New Brighton	Manchester C. (Am)	08.47	47	25	-	0
Chesterfield	Tr	07.48				
Accrington St.	Tr	10.49	49-52	112	-	0
DANIELS Graham David						
Farnborough, 9 April, 1962						(W)
Cambridge U.	Cardiff Corries	11.83	83-84	37	2	4
DANIELS Henry (Harry) Augustus George						
Kensington, 25 June, 1920						(LH)
Queens Park R.	Kensington Sports	10.44	46-47	14	-	0
Brighton & H.A.	Tr	08.48	48-49	32	-	0
York C.	Tr	08.50	50	4	-	2
DANIELS John						
St Helens, 8 January, 1925						(G)
Lincoln C.	British Cider	05.46	46	17	-	0
New Brighton		03.48	48	3	-	0
DANIELS Scott Charles						
Benfleet, 22 November, 1969						(CD)
Colchester U.	YT	06.88	87-89	64	9	0
Exeter C.	Tr	08.91	91-94	114	3	7
Northampton T.	Tr	01.95	94	5	3	0

League Club	Source	Date Signed	Seasons Played	Apps	Subs	Gls
DANIELS Stephen Richard						
Leeds, 17 December, 1961						(LB)
Doncaster Rov.	App	10.79	79	0	1	0
DANKS Derek Peter						
Cheadle, 15 February, 1931						(IF)
Northampton T.		11.53	54	1	-	0
DANN Terence Edward						
Shoreditch, 6 July, 1936						(IF)
Plymouth Arg.	Penzance	07.59	59	8	-	0
Torquay U.	Sittingbourne	07.62	62	1	-	0
DANSKIN Jason						
Winsford, 28 December, 1967						(M)
Everton	YT	07.85	84	1	0	0
Mansfield T.	Tr	03.87	86	10	0	0
Hartlepool U.	L	01.88	87	3	0	0
DANSKIN Robert						
Newcastle, 28 May, 1908 Died 1985						(CH)
Leeds U.	Wallsend U.	05.29	30-31	5	-	1
Bradford P.A.	Tr	12.32	32-47	261	-	6
DANZEY Michael James						
Widnes, 8 February, 1971						(F)
Nottingham F.	YT	05.89				
Chester C.	L	02.90	89	0	2	0
Peterborough U. (N/C)		01.91	90	0	1	0
Cambridge U.	St Albans C.	10.92	92-94	18	9	3
Scunthorpe U.	L	02.94	93	3	0	1
DARBY Alan						
Sheffield, 3 June, 1942						(G)
Doncaster Rov.	Goole T.	06.59	60	1	-	0
DARBY Douglas						
Bolton-on-Dearne, 26 December, 1919 Died 1963						(CF)
Wolverhampton W.	Wath W.	09.41				
Walsall	Tr	05.46	46	15	-	4
DARBY Duane Anthony						
Warley, 17 October, 1973						(F)
Torquay U.	YT	07.92	91-94	60	48	26
Doncaster Rov.	Tr	07.95	95	8	9	4
Hull C.	Tr	03.96	95-97	75	3	27
DARBY Julian Timothy						
Farnworth, 3 October, 1967 E Sch						(M)
Bolton W.	YT	08.85	85-93	258	12	36
Coventry C.	Tr	10.93	93-94	52	3	5
West Bromwich A.	Tr	11.95	95-96	32	7	1
Preston N.E.	Tr	06.97	97	6	6	0
Rotherham U.	L	03.98	97	3	0	0
DARBY Lee Alan						
Salford, 20 September, 1969						(M)
Portsmouth	YT	10.86	87	1	0	0
DARBYSHIRE Harold						
Leeds, 22 October, 1931						(IF)
Leeds U.		02.50				
Halifax T.	Tr	07.52	52-56	161	-	32
Bury	Tr	08.57	57-58	29	-	12
Darlington	Tr	06.59	59	15	-	2
D'ARCY Arnold Joseph						
Blackburn, 13 January, 1933						(OL)
Accrington St.	St Matthews Y.C.	03.52	51-52	38	-	9
Swindon T.	Wigan Ath.	11.56	56-63	223	-	29
D'ARCY Colin Robert						
Wirral, 5 August, 1954						(G)
Everton		04.73				
Bury	Tr	01.75	74	4	0	0
Wigan Ath.	Tr	01.79				
D'ARCY Francis Anthony						
Liverpool, 8 December, 1946						(FB)
Everton	App	08.64	65-70	8	8	0
Tranmere Rov.	Tr	07.72	72	7	1	1
D'ARCY Michael Edmund						
Dublin, 8 March, 1933						(G)
Oldham Ath.	Dundalk	09.54	54-55	45	-	0
D'ARCY Seamus (Jimmy) Donal						
Newry (NI), 14 December, 1921 Died 1985 NI-5						(IF)
Charlton Ath.	Ballymena	03.48	47-50	13	-	1
Chelsea	Tr	10.51	51-52	23	-	12
Brentford	Tr	10.52	52	13	-	3
D'ARCY Thomas McDonald						
Edinburgh, 22 June, 1932 Died 1985						(F)
Bournemouth	Hibernian	09.54				
Southend U.	Hibernian	05.56	56-57	4	-	0
DARE Kevin John						
Finchley, 15 November, 1959						(FB)
Crystal Palace	App	02.77	80-81	6	0	0
DARE Reginald Arthur						
Blandford, 26 November, 1921 Died 1993						(CF)
Southampton	Windsor & Eton	06.49				
Exeter C.	Tr	08.50	50	6	-	0
DARE William Thomas Charles						
Willesden, 14 February, 1927 Died 1994						(CF)
Brentford	Hendon	11.48	48-54	208	-	63
West Ham U.	Tr	01.55	54-58	111	-	44
DAREY Jeffrey Arthur						
Hammersmith, 26 February, 1934 E Amat						(CF)
Brighton & H.A.	Hendon	03.57	56-60	10	-	2
DARFIELD Stuart Charles						
Leeds, 12 April, 1950						(WH)
Bradford P.A.	Wolverhampton W. (App)	07.68	68	15	2	0
DARGIE Ian Charles						
Camberwell, 3 October, 1931						(CH)
Brentford	Tonbridge	02.52	51-62	263	-	2
DARK Trevor Charles						
St Helier, 29 January, 1961						(W)
Birmingham C.	App	01.79	78	2	3	1
DARKE Peter George						
Exeter, 21 December, 1953						(D)
Plymouth Arg.	App	12.71	71-76	94	7	2
Exeter C.	L	10.76	76	5	0	0
Torquay U.	Tr	07.77	77-78	58	1	0
DARLING Henry **Leonard**						
Gillingham, 9 August, 1911 Died 1958						(WH)
Gillingham	Chatham T.	05.32	32	14	-	0
Brighton & H.A.	Tr	08.33	33-47	199	-	5
DARLING Malcolm						
Arbroath, 4 July, 1947						(F)
Blackburn Rov.	Luncarty Jnrs	10.64	65-69	114	14	30
Norwich C.	Tr	05.70	70-71	16	0	5
Rochdale	Tr	10.71	71-73	82	4	16
Bolton W.	Tr	09.73	73	6	2	0
Chesterfield	Tr	08.74	74-76	100	4	33
Stockport Co.	L	03.77	76	11	0	2
Sheffield Wed.	Tr	08.77	77	1	1	0
Hartlepool U.	Tr	09.77	77	2	2	0
Bury (N/C)	Morecambe	03.78	77	1	1	0
DARLINGTON Jermaine Christopher						
Hackney, 11 April, 1974						(W)
Charlton Ath.	YT	06.92	91	1	1	0
DARMODY Aubrey						
Swansea, 17 May, 1921						(FB)
Norwich C.	Cardiff Nomads	10.46	46	2	-	0
DARRACOTT Terence Michael						
Liverpool, 6 December, 1950						(FB)
Everton	App	07.68	67-78	138	10	0
Wrexham	Tulsa (USA)	09.79	79	22	0	0
DARRAS Frederick Guy Albert						
France, 19 August, 1974						(D)
Swindon T.	Bastia (Fr)	08.96	96-97	42	7	0
DARRELL Michael Alan						
Bilston, 14 January, 1947						(M)
Birmingham C.	App	01.65	65-68	10	4	2
Newport Co.	L	10.70	70	8	0	0
Gillingham	L	12.70	70	19	2	1
Peterborough U.	Tr	05.71	71-72	32	10	6
DARTON Scott Richard						
Ipswich, 27 March, 1975						(CD)
West Bromwich A.	YT	10.92	92-94	15	0	0
Blackpool	Tr	01.95	94-96	31	11	1

League Club	Source	Date Signed	Seasons Played	Apps	Subs	Gls
DARVELL Roger Derek						
High Wycombe, 10 February, 1931						(CH)
Charlton Ath.	Rickmansworth	12.53				
Gillingham	Tr	07.57	57	3	-	0
Southport	Tr	07.58	58-64	256	-	1
DARWIN George Hedworth						
Chester-le-Street, 16 May, 1932						(IF)
Huddersfield T.	Kimblesworth Jnrs	05.50				
Mansfield T.	Tr	11.53	53-56	126	-	63
Derby Co.	Tr	05.57	57-60	94	-	32
Rotherham U.	Tr	10.60	60	2	-	2
Barrow	Tr	07.61	61-63	92	-	28
DAUBNEY Raymond						
Oldham, 7 December, 1946						(OR)
Rochdale		12.66	66-67	12	0	2
DAUGHTRY Paul William						
Oldham, 14 February, 1973						(W)
Stockport Co.	Winsford U.	01.94				
Hartlepool U.	Droylsden	11.94	94	14	1	0
D'AURIA David Alan						
Swansea, 26 March, 1970 W Yth						(M)
Swansea C.	YT	07.88	87-90	27	18	6
Scarborough	Barry T.	08.94	94-95	49	3	8
Scunthorpe U.	Tr	12.95	95-97	103	4	18
DAVENPORT Carl						
Farnworth, 30 May, 1944						(CF)
Preston N.E.	App	05.62				
Stockport Co.	Tr	03.63	62-63	16	-	3
DAVENPORT Peter						
Birkenhead, 24 March, 1961 E'B'/E-1						(F)
Nottingham F.	Cammell Laird	01.82	81-85	114	4	54
Manchester U.	Tr	03.86	85-88	73	19	22
Middlesbrough	Tr	11.88	88-89	53	6	7
Sunderland	Tr	07.90	90-92	72	27	15
Stockport Co.	St Johnstone	03.95	94	3	3	1
Macclesfield T.	Southport	01.97	97	2	2	1
DAVEY Frederick						
Crediton, 13 April, 1924						(HB)
Exeter C.	Crediton T.	08.47	47-55	276	-	3
DAVEY Nigel Geoffrey						
Garforth, 20 June, 1946						(FB)
Leeds U.	Jnrs	02.64	67-70	13	1	0
Rotherham U.	Tr	07.74				
DAVEY Simon						
Swansea, 1 October, 1970						(M)
Swansea C.	YT	07.89	86-91	37	12	4
Carlisle U.	Tr	08.92	92-94	105	0	18
Preston N.E.	Tr	02.95	94-97	97	9	21
Darlington	L	09.97	97	10	1	0
DAVEY Stephen Gilbert Richard						
Plymouth, 5 September, 1948 E Yth						(W)
Plymouth Arg.	App	07.66	66-74	213	11	47
Hereford U.	Tr	08.75	75-77	104	3	32
Portsmouth	Tr	06.78	78-80	83	10	8
Exeter C.	Tr	08.81	81	15	0	0
DAVEY Stuart						
Haslington, 4 January, 1938						(FB)
Crewe Alex.	Jnrs	08.56	56	1	-	0
DAVIDS Neil Graham						
Bingley, 22 September, 1955 E Yth						(CD)
Leeds U.	App	08.73				
Norwich C.	Tr	04.75	75	2	0	0
Northampton T.	L	09.75	75	9	0	0
Stockport Co.	L	01.76	75	5	0	1
Swansea C.	Tr	07.77	77	9	0	0
Wigan Ath.	Tr	07.78	78-80	66	2	1
DAVIDSON Adam Richmond						
Invergowrie, 28 November, 1929						(OR)
Sheffield Wed.		03.48				
Colchester U.	Tr	08.51	51	19	-	0
DAVIDSON Alan Edward						
Australia, 1 June, 1960 Australian Int						(FB)
Nottingham F.	South Melbourne (Aus)	11.84	84	3	0	0

League Club	Source	Date Signed	Seasons Played	Apps	Subs	Gls
DAVIDSON Alexander Morrison						
Langholm, 6 June, 1920						(IF)
Chelsea	Hibernian	08.46	46	2	-	0
Crystal Palace	Tr	08.48	48	10	-	2
DAVIDSON Andrew						
Douglas Water, 13 July, 1932						(RB)
Hull C.	Jnrs	09.49	52-67	520	0	18
DAVIDSON Angus Gordon						
Forfar, 2 October, 1948						(M)
Grimsby T.	Dundee	11.65	65-68	46	5	1
Scunthorpe U.	Tr	07.69	69-76	304	17	45
DAVIDSON Brian						
Workington, 23 August, 1951						(OL)
Workington (Am)	Jnrs	08.72	72	1	0	0
DAVIDSON Callum Iain						
Stirling, 25 June, 1976 Su21-2						(LB)
Blackburn Rov.	St Johnstone	02.98	97	1	0	0
DAVIDSON David						
Govan Hill, 20 August, 1934						(HB)
Manchester C.	Jnrs	08.51	53	1	-	0
Workington	Tr	07.58	58	3	-	0
DAVIDSON David Blyth Logie						
Lanark, 25 March, 1920 Died 1954						(WH)
Bradford P.A.	Douglas Water Thistle	05.38	46	13	-	0
Leyton Orient	Tr	01.47	46-49	84	-	1
DAVIDSON David Craighogie						
Douglas Water, 19 March, 1926 Died 1996						(W)
Hull C.	Douglas Water Thistle	10.46	46-47	22	-	4
DAVIDSON Dennis James						
Aberdeen, 18 May, 1937						(WH)
Portsmouth	Jnrs	05.54	59	1	-	0
DAVIDSON Douglas Bell						
Dundee, 2 December, 1918 Died 1968						(IF)
Blackpool	East Fife	10.48	48-49	14	-	0
Reading	Tr	04.50	49-50	11	-	1
DAVIDSON Duncan						
Elgin, 5 July, 1954						(F)
Manchester C.	See Bee (HK)	09.83	83	2	4	1
DAVIDSON Ian						
Goole, 31 January, 1947						(M)
Hull C.	Jnrs	02.65	66-67	5	1	1
Scunthorpe U.	L	09.68	68	32	3	0
York C.	Tr	06.69	69-70	82	4	4
Bournemouth	Tr	07.71	71	7	2	0
Stockport Co.	Tr	05.72	72-73	74	4	6
DAVIDSON Ian						
East Lothian, 8 September, 1937						(WH)
Preston N.E.	Kilmarnock	12.62	62-64	67	-	1
Middlesbrough	Tr	02.65	64-66	46	0	0
Darlington	Tr	09.67	67	27	0	0
DAVIDSON John Summers						
Stonehouse (LK), 6 November, 1931						(IF)
Walsall	Alloa Ath.	08.55	55	5	-	0
DAVIDSON Jonathan Stewart						
Cheadle, 1 March, 1970						(D)
Derby Co.	YT	07.88	89-91	7	5	0
Preston N.E.	Tr	07.92	92	18	3	1
Chesterfield	L	03.93	92	0	1	0
DAVIDSON Peter Edward						
Newcastle, 31 October, 1956						(W)
Queens Park R.	Berwick R.	07.79	79	0	1	0
DAVIDSON Robert Trimming						
Lochgelly (Fife), 27 April, 1913 Died 1988						(IF)
Arsenal	St Johnstone	02.35	34-37	57	-	13
Coventry C.	Tr	11.37	37-47	47	-	9
DAVIDSON Roger						
Islington, 27 October, 1948 E Sch						(M)
Arsenal	App	11.65	67	0	1	0
Portsmouth	Tr	06.69	69	3	0	0
Fulham	Tr	08.70	70	1	0	0
Lincoln C.	Tr	10.71	71	6	0	0
Aldershot	L	02.72	71	12	0	2

League Club | Source | Date Signed | Seasons Played | Career Record: Apps | Subs | Gls

DAVIDSON Ross James
Chertsey, 13 November, 1973 (RB)

League Club	Source	Date Signed	Seasons Played	Apps	Subs	Gls
Sheffield U.	Walton & Hersham	06.93	94-95	2	0	0
Chester C.	Tr	01.96	95-97	83	0	5

DAVIDSON Victor Salvatore Ferla
Glasgow, 8 November, 1950 (M)

League Club	Source	Date Signed	Seasons Played	Apps	Subs	Gls
Blackpool	Motherwell	07.78	78	23	2	3

DAVIE Alexander (Sandy) Grimmond
Dundee, 10 June, 1945 (G)

League Club	Source	Date Signed	Seasons Played	Apps	Subs	Gls
Luton T.	Dundee	09.68	68-69	58	0	0
Southampton	Tr	05.70	70	1	0	0

DAVIE James Graham
Cambuslang, 7 September, 1922 Died 1984 (WH)

League Club	Source	Date Signed	Seasons Played	Apps	Subs	Gls
Preston N.E.	Kilmarnock	06.48	48-49	28	-	0
Northampton T.	Tr	07.50	50-52	75	-	1
Shrewsbury T.	Tr	07.53				

DAVIE John (Jock)
Dunfermline, 19 February, 1913 Died 1994 (CF)

League Club	Source	Date Signed	Seasons Played	Apps	Subs	Gls
Brighton & H.A.	Margate	05.36	36-38	89	-	39
Barnsley	Stockton	12.46	46	6	-	0

DAVIE William Clark
Paisley, 7 January, 1925 Died 1996 (IF)

League Club	Source	Date Signed	Seasons Played	Apps	Subs	Gls
Luton T.	St Mirren	12.50	50-51	42	-	9
Huddersfield T.	Tr	12.51	51-56	113	-	16
Walsall	Tr	07.57	57	7	-	0

DAVIES Alan
Manchester, 5 December, 1961 Died 1992 Wu21-6/W-13 (W)

League Club	Source	Date Signed	Seasons Played	Apps	Subs	Gls
Manchester U.	App	12.78	81-83	6	1	0
Newcastle U.	Tr	08.85	85-86	20	1	1
Charlton Ath.	L	03.86	85	1	0	0
Carlisle U.	L	11.86	86	4	0	1
Swansea C.	Tr	07.87	87-88	84	0	8
Bradford C.	Tr	06.89	89	24	2	1
Swansea C.	Tr	08.90	90-91	41	2	4

DAVIES Albert John Victor
Greenwich, 19 April, 1935 (G)

League Club	Source	Date Signed	Seasons Played	Apps	Subs	Gls
Millwall		10.56	57	1	-	0

DAVIES Albert Llewellyn
Pontypridd, 11 March, 1933 (OR)

League Club	Source	Date Signed	Seasons Played	Apps	Subs	Gls
Newport Co.	Merthyr Tydfil	04.51	50	1	-	0

DAVIES Alexander McLean
Dundonald, 21 May, 1920 Died 1964 (OR)

League Club	Source	Date Signed	Seasons Played	Apps	Subs	Gls
Sheffield Wed.		04.45				
Lincoln C.	Tr	07.45	46-48	37	-	9

DAVIES Andrew Jonathan
Wolverhampton, 6 June, 1972 (CD)

League Club	Source	Date Signed	Seasons Played	Apps	Subs	Gls
Torquay U. (YT)	YT	07.88	88-89	9	4	0
Hartlepool U.	Tr	06.90	90-91	4	3	0
Torquay U.	Tr	08.92	92	1	2	0

DAVIES Brian
Doncaster, 21 August, 1947 (F)

League Club	Source	Date Signed	Seasons Played	Apps	Subs	Gls
Sheffield Wed.	App	08.64	65	3	0	1

DAVIES Byron
Llanelli, 5 February, 1932 (HB)

League Club	Source	Date Signed	Seasons Played	Apps	Subs	Gls
Leeds U.	Llanelli	05.52	53	1	-	0
Newport Co.	Tr	06.56				

DAVIES Cecil Joseph
Aberbargoed, 26 March, 1918 Died 1994 W Sch (WH)

League Club	Source	Date Signed	Seasons Played	Apps	Subs	Gls
Charlton Ath.	Lovells Ath.	03.35				
Barrow	Tr	06.38	38-46	76	-	3
Millwall	Tr	07.47	47-48	31	-	0

DAVIES Colin Frank
Shrewsbury, 12 April, 1936 (CH)

League Club	Source	Date Signed	Seasons Played	Apps	Subs	Gls
Port Vale		06.59	59-60	13	-	0

DAVIES Cyril
Swansea, 7 September, 1948 W Sch/Wu23-4/W-1 (M)

League Club	Source	Date Signed	Seasons Played	Apps	Subs	Gls
Swansea C.	App	09.66				
Carlisle U.	Tr	06.68	68	1	1	0
Charlton Ath.	Yeovil T.	05.70	70-72	70	6	6

DAVIES David (Dai) Daniel
Aberdare, 5 December, 1914 Died 1984 (IF)

League Club	Source	Date Signed	Seasons Played	Apps	Subs	Gls
Hull C.	Aberaman Ath.	08.35	35-46	141	-	30

DAVIES David Ivor
Bridgend, 21 July, 1932 (CF)

League Club	Source	Date Signed	Seasons Played	Apps	Subs	Gls
Leyton Orient	Harwich & Parkeston	04.53	53	4	-	0

DAVIES David John
Neath, 21 May, 1952 (CD)

League Club	Source	Date Signed	Seasons Played	Apps	Subs	Gls
Swansea C.	Afan Lido	07.73	73-74	27	1	0

DAVIES David Lamb
Pontypridd, 11 July, 1956 (W)

League Club	Source	Date Signed	Seasons Played	Apps	Subs	Gls
Swansea C.	App	07.74	72	0	1	0
Crewe Alex.	Tr	03.75	74-80	196	13	26

DAVIES William **David (Dai)**
Ammanford, 1 April, 1948 Wu23-3/W-52 (G)

League Club	Source	Date Signed	Seasons Played	Apps	Subs	Gls
Swansea C.	Ammanford	08.69	69-70	9	0	0
Everton	Tr	12.70	70-76	82	0	0
Swansea C.	L	02.74	73	6	0	0
Wrexham	Tr	09.77	77-80	144	0	0
Swansea C.	Tr	07.81	81-82	71	0	0
Tranmere Rov.	Tr	06.83	83	42	0	0

DAVIES Dudley
Shoreham, 27 December, 1924 (OR)

League Club	Source	Date Signed	Seasons Played	Apps	Subs	Gls
Charlton Ath.	Lancing T.	01.58				
Leyton Orient	Tr	05.50	50-51	17	-	2

DAVIES Edmund
Oswestry, 5 June, 1927 (CF)

League Club	Source	Date Signed	Seasons Played	Apps	Subs	Gls
Arsenal	Liverpool (Am)	08.48				
Queens Park R.	Tr	04.50	50	1	-	1
Crewe Alex.	Tr	07.51	51	7	-	0

DAVIES Edward
Burslem, 3 May, 1923 Died 1995 (CF)

League Club	Source	Date Signed	Seasons Played	Apps	Subs	Gls
Port Vale		01.43	46	3	-	0

DAVIES Eric
Manchester, 20 February, 1943 Died 1988 (CF)

League Club	Source	Date Signed	Seasons Played	Apps	Subs	Gls
Southport	Southport Trin.	03.62	61-64	3	-	0

DAVIES Frederick
Liverpool, 22 August, 1939 (G)

League Club	Source	Date Signed	Seasons Played	Apps	Subs	Gls
Wolverhampton W.	Llandudno	04.57	61-67	156	0	0
Cardiff C.	Tr	01.68	67-69	99	0	0
Bournemouth	Tr	07.70	70-73	134	0	0

DAVIES Gareth
Cardiff, 6 October, 1959 (M)

League Club	Source	Date Signed	Seasons Played	Apps	Subs	Gls
Cardiff C. (N/C)	Sully	11.86	86	1	1	0

DAVIES Gareth Melville
Hereford, 11 December, 1973 Wu21-8 (CD)

League Club	Source	Date Signed	Seasons Played	Apps	Subs	Gls
Hereford U.	YT	04.92	91-94	91	4	1
Crystal Palace	Tr	07.95	95-97	22	5	2
Cardiff C.	L	02.97	96	6	0	2
Reading	Tr	12.97	97	17	1	0

DAVIES Geoffrey Peter
Ellesmere Port, 1 July, 1947 (M)

League Club	Source	Date Signed	Seasons Played	Apps	Subs	Gls
Chester C.	Wigan Ath.	08.72	72-73	18	14	5
Wrexham	Tr	10.73	73-75	64	3	15
Port Vale	Tr	08.76	76	7	0	0
Hartlepool U.	L	11.76	76	5	0	1
Wimbledon	San Jose (USA)	08.77	77	23	0	1

DAVIES George
Oswestry, 1 March, 1927 (WH)

League Club	Source	Date Signed	Seasons Played	Apps	Subs	Gls
Sheffield Wed.	Oswestry T.	06.50	50-54	98	-	1
Chester C.	Tr	07.56	56-57	35	-	4

DAVIES Edward George **Gladstone (Glen)**
Swansea, 30 June, 1950 (CD)

League Club	Source	Date Signed	Seasons Played	Apps	Subs	Gls
Swansea C.	Jnrs	07.70	70-75	138	12	14

DAVIES Glen
Brighton, 20 July, 1976 (CD)

League Club	Source	Date Signed	Seasons Played	Apps	Subs	Gls
Burnley	YT	07.94				
Hartlepool U.	Tr	06.96	96-97	48	4	1

DAVIES Glyn
Swansea, 31 May, 1932 (WH)

League Club	Source	Date Signed	Seasons Played	Apps	Subs	Gls
Derby Co.	Jnrs	07.49	53-61	200	-	5
Swansea C.	Tr	07.62	62	17	-	1

DAVIES Gordon
Manchester, 4 September, 1932 (IF)

League Club	Source	Date Signed	Seasons Played	Apps	Subs	Gls
Manchester C.	Ashton U.	12.51	51-54	13	-	5
Chester C.	Tr	06.57	57	22	-	5
Southport	Tr	08.58	58	11	-	1

DAVIES Gordon John
Merthyr Tydfil, 3 August, 1955 W Sch/W-18 (F)

League Club	Source	Date Signed	Seasons Played	Apps	Subs	Gls
Fulham	Merthyr Tydfil	03.78	77-84	244	3	114
Chelsea	Tr	11.84	84-85	11	2	6
Manchester C.	Tr	10.85	85-86	31	0	9
Fulham	Tr	10.86	86-90	120	27	45
Wrexham	Tr	08.91	91	21	1	4

DAVIES Graham Golding
Swansea, 3 October, 1921 W Sch (G)

League Club	Source	Date Signed	Seasons Played	Apps	Subs	Gls
Swansea C.		02.42				
Watford	Tr	06.47	47-48	9	-	0

DAVIES Grant
Barrow, 13 October, 1959 (CD)

League Club	Source	Date Signed	Seasons Played	Apps	Subs	Gls
Preston N.E.	App	10.77				
Newport Co.	Tr	07.78	78-82	147	3	1
Exeter C.	L	02.83	82	7	0	0

DAVIES Ian Claude
Bristol, 29 March, 1957 Wu21-1 (LB)

League Club	Source	Date Signed	Seasons Played	Apps	Subs	Gls
Norwich C.	App	03.75	73-78	29	3	2
Newcastle U.	Tr	06.79	79-81	74	1	3
Manchester C.	Tr	08.82	82-83	7	0	0
Bury	L	11.82	82	14	0	0
Brentford	L	11.83	83	2	0	0
Cambridge U.	L	02.84	83	5	0	0
Carlisle U.	Tr	08.84	84	4	0	0
Exeter C.	Tr	12.84	84	5	0	0
Bristol Rov.(N/C)	Yeovil T.	08.85	85	13	1	1
Swansea C.(N/C)	Tr	11.85	85	11	0	0

DAVIES John Gerwyn
Llandysul, 18 November, 1959 (G)

League Club	Source	Date Signed	Seasons Played	Apps	Subs	Gls
Cardiff C.	App	11.77	78-79	7	0	0
Hull C.	Tr	07.80	80-82	24	0	0
Notts Co.	L	03.86	85	10	0	0

DAVIES John Robert
Portsmouth, 26 September, 1933 (OR)

League Club	Source	Date Signed	Seasons Played	Apps	Subs	Gls
Portsmouth	Jnrs	05.52	53-54	2	-	0
Scunthorpe U.	Tr	07.55	55-57	67	-	10
Walsall	Tr	01.59	58-60	65	-	16

DAVIES John William
Holt, 14 November, 1916 W Sch (WH)

League Club	Source	Date Signed	Seasons Played	Apps	Subs	Gls
Chester C.	Troedyrhiw	12.34	35-36	18	-	1
Everton	Tr	07.37	46	1	-	0
Plymouth Arg.	Tr	02.47	46-47	33	-	0
Bristol C.	Tr	05.48	48	30	-	1

DAVIES Joseph
Birkenhead, 30 January, 1926 (W)

League Club	Source	Date Signed	Seasons Played	Apps	Subs	Gls
Chester C.	Bromborough	04.48	47-51	55	-	10

DAVIES Edward **Keith**
Birkenhead, 19 February, 1934 (IF)

League Club	Source	Date Signed	Seasons Played	Apps	Subs	Gls
Tranmere Rov.		07.53	53	1	-	0

DAVIES Kenneth
Doncaster, 20 September, 1923 (OL)

League Club	Source	Date Signed	Seasons Played	Apps	Subs	Gls
Wolverhampton W.		01.44				
Walsall	Tr	06.46	46-47	28	-	5
Brighton & H.A.	Tr	05.48	48-49	36	-	5

DAVIES Kenneth Frank
Stockton, 22 December, 1970 (M)

League Club	Source	Date Signed	Seasons Played	Apps	Subs	Gls
Hartlepool U.	YT	07.89	89-90	4	2	0

DAVIES Kevin
Hereford, 1 April, 1963 (M)

League Club	Source	Date Signed	Seasons Played	Apps	Subs	Gls
Hereford U. (N/C)	Westfields	07.85	85	0	1	0

DAVIES Kevin Cyril
Sheffield, 26 March, 1977 E Yth/Eu21-1 (F)

League Club	Source	Date Signed	Seasons Played	Apps	Subs	Gls
Chesterfield	YT	04.94	93-96	113	16	22
Southampton	Tr	05.97	97	20	5	9

DAVIES Lawrence
Abergavenny, 3 September, 1977 W Yth (CF)

League Club	Source	Date Signed	Seasons Played	Apps	Subs	Gls
Leeds U.	YT	08.96				
Bradford C.	Tr	07.97	97	1	3	0
Darlington	L	12.97	97	2	0	0

DAVIES Leonard
(G)

League Club	Source	Date Signed	Seasons Played	Apps	Subs	Gls
Southend U.		11.45	46	3	-	0

DAVIES David **Lyn**
Neath, 29 September, 1947 W Sch/Wu23-1 (G)

League Club	Source	Date Signed	Seasons Played	Apps	Subs	Gls
Cardiff C.	App	10.65	65-66	16	0	0
Swansea C.	Llanelli	07.72	72	3	0	0

DAVIES Malcolm
Aberdare, 26 June, 1931 (OR)

League Club	Source	Date Signed	Seasons Played	Apps	Subs	Gls
Plymouth Arg.	Aberaman	04.49	52-56	84	-	15

DAVIES Mark
Swansea, 9 August, 1972 (D)

League Club	Source	Date Signed	Seasons Played	Apps	Subs	Gls
Swansea C.	YT	07.91	91	1	0	0

DAVIES Martin Lemuel
Swansea, 28 June, 1974 W Yth (G)

League Club	Source	Date Signed	Seasons Played	Apps	Subs	Gls
Coventry C.	YT	07.92				
Cambridge U.	Tr	08.95	95	16	0	0

DAVIES Michael John
Stretford, 19 January, 1966 (RB/M)

League Club	Source	Date Signed	Seasons Played	Apps	Subs	Gls
Blackpool	App	01.84	83-94	276	34	16

DAVIES Paul
St Asaph, 10 October, 1952 W Sch (CF)

League Club	Source	Date Signed	Seasons Played	Apps	Subs	Gls
Arsenal	App	11.69	71	0	1	0
Charlton Ath.	Tr	08.72	72-74	51	6	9

DAVIES Paul Andrew
Kidderminster, 9 October, 1960 E Semi Pro (F)

League Club	Source	Date Signed	Seasons Played	Apps	Subs	Gls
Cardiff C.	Oldswinford	10.78	79-80	1	1	0

DAVIES Peter
Llanelli, 8 March, 1936 (WH)

League Club	Source	Date Signed	Seasons Played	Apps	Subs	Gls
Arsenal	Llanelli	11.57				
Swansea C.	Tr	03.59	58-64	134	-	4
Brighton & H.A.	Tr	07.65	65	6	0	0

DAVIES Peter
Merthyr Tydfil, 1 July, 1942 W Amat (IF)

League Club	Source	Date Signed	Seasons Played	Apps	Subs	Gls
Newport Co. (Am)	Merthyr Tydfil	05.64	64	1	-	0

DAVIES Leonard **Raymond**
Wallasey, 3 October, 1931 (IF)

League Club	Source	Date Signed	Seasons Played	Apps	Subs	Gls
Tranmere Rov.		10.49	51-57	120	-	28

DAVIES Reginald Walter
Tipton, 10 October, 1933 (G)

League Club	Source	Date Signed	Seasons Played	Apps	Subs	Gls
West Bromwich A.	Jnrs	01.51	53-54	4	-	0
Walsall	Tr	07.55	55-56	53	-	0
Millwall	Tr	05.58	58-62	199	-	0
Leyton Orient	Tr	07.63	63	11	-	0
Port Vale	Tr	07.64	64	13	-	0
Leyton Orient	Tr	03.65	64-65	16	0	0

DAVIES Ellis **Reginald**
Glyncorrwg, 27 May, 1929 W-6 (IF)

League Club	Source	Date Signed	Seasons Played	Apps	Subs	Gls
Southend U.	Southampton (Am)	07.49	49-50	41	-	18
Newcastle U.	Tr	04.51	51-58	157	-	49
Swansea C.	Tr	10.58	58-61	108	-	29
Carlisle U.	Tr	06.62	62-63	65	-	13

DAVIES Robert Griffith
Blaenau Ffestiniog, 19 October, 1913 Died 1978 (CH)

League Club	Source	Date Signed	Seasons Played	Apps	Subs	Gls
Nottingham F.	Blaenau Ffestiniog	11.36	36-46	55	-	0

DAVIES Roger
Wolverhampton, 25 October, 1950 Eu23-1 (F)

League Club	Source	Date Signed	Seasons Played	Apps	Subs	Gls
Derby Co.	Worcester C.	09.71	72-75	98	16	31
Preston N.E.	L	08.72	72	2	0	0
Leicester C.	Bruges (Bel)	12.77	77-78	22	4	6
Derby Co.	Tulsa (USA)	09.79	79	22	0	3
Darlington	Fort Lauderdale (USA)	11.83	83	10	0	1

DAVIES Ronald (Roy) Alfred
South Africa, 23 August, 1924 Died 1973 (W)

League Club	Source	Date Signed	Seasons Played	Apps	Subs	Gls
Luton T.	Clyde	05.51	51-56	150	-	26

DAVIES Ronald George
Swansea, 13 November, 1935 (WH)

League Club	Source	Date Signed	Seasons Played	Apps	Subs	Gls
Swansea C.	Tower U.	05.58	58	2	-	0
Plymouth Arg.	Tr	06.59				

DAVIES Ronald Thomas
Merthyr Tydfil, 21 September, 1932 (FB)

League Club	Source	Date Signed	Seasons Played	Apps	Subs	Gls
Cardiff C.	Merthyr Tydfil	10.52	55-57	32	-	3
Southampton	Tr	03.58	57-63	161	-	0
Aldershot	Tr	08.64	64-66	84	1	1

League Club	Source	Date Signed	Seasons Played	Career Record Apps	Subs	Gls
DAVIES Ronald Tudor						
Holywell, 25 May, 1942 Wu23-3/W-29						(CF)
Chester C.	Jnrs	07.59	59-62	94	-	44
Luton T.	Tr	10.62	62-63	32	-	21
Norwich C.	Tr	09.63	63-65	113	0	58
Southampton	Tr	08.66	66-72	239	1	134
Portsmouth	Tr	04.73	73-74	59	0	18
Manchester U.	Tr	11.74	74	0	8	0
Millwall	L	11.75	75	3	0	0
DAVIES Roy						
Ealing, 25 October, 1953						(M)
Reading	Slough T.	09.77	77	37	0	2
Torquay U.	Tr	08.78	78-79	65	5	6
Wimbledon	Tr	08.80	80	6	3	0
DAVIES Roy Martin						
Cardiff, 19 August, 1971 W Yth						(RB)
Newport Co.	YT	●	87	0	2	0
Chelsea	YT	07.89				
DAVIES Simon						
Haverfordwest, 23 October, 1979 W Yth						(M)
Peterborough U.	YT	07.97	97	4	2	0
DAVIES Simon Ithel						
Winsford, 23 April, 1974 W-1						(M)
Manchester U.	YT	07.92	94-95	4	7	0
Exeter C.	L	12.93	93	5	1	1
Huddersfield T.	L	10.96	96	3	0	0
Luton T.	Tr	08.97	97	8	12	1
DAVIES Steven Easman						
Liverpool, 16 July, 1960						(W)
Port Vale	Congleton T.	12.87	87	1	5	0
DAVIES Wilfred Gordon						
Swansea, 31 July, 1915 Died 1992						(RB)
Swansea C.		03.34	37-46	25	-	0
DAVIES William						
Middlesbrough, 16 May, 1930						(CH)
Hull C.	St. Mary's C.O.B.	04.49				
Leeds U.	Tr	08.50				
Reading	Scarborough	12.52	54-60	202	-	0
DAVIES William						
Troedyrhiw, 22 June, 1910 Died 1995						(OL)
Watford	New Tredegar	07.30	30-49	284	-	69
DAVIES William						
Wirksworth, 27 September, 1975						(CD)
Derby Co.	YT	07.94	94	1	1	0
DAVIES William						
						(OR)
Crewe Alex.	Droylsden	02.47	46	11	-	3
DAVIES William McIntosh						
Glasgow, 31 May, 1964						(M)
Leicester C.	St Mirren	08.90	90	5	1	0
DAVIES Ronald **Wyn**						
Caernarfon, 20 March, 1942 Wu23-4/W-34						(F)
Wrexham	Caernarfon	04.60	60-61	55	-	21
Bolton W.	Tr	03.62	61-66	155	0	66
Newcastle U.	Tr	10.66	66-70	181	0	40
Manchester C.	Tr	08.71	71-72	45	0	8
Manchester U.	Tr	09.72	72	15	1	4
Blackpool	Tr	06.73	73-74	34	2	5
Crystal Palace	L	08.74	74	3	0	0
Stockport Co.	Tr	08.75	75	28	2	7
Crewe Alex.	Tr	08.76	76-77	50	5	13
DAVIN Joseph James						
Dumbarton, 13 February, 1942 S Sch						(FB)
Ipswich T.	Hibernian	07.63	63-65	77	0	0
DAVIS Arron Spencer						
Wanstead, 11 February, 1972						(FB)
Torquay U.	YT	08.91	91-92	20	4	0
Colchester U. (N/C)	Dorchester T.	08.94	94	4	0	0
DAVIS Craig						
Rotherham, 12 October, 1977						(G)
Rotherham U.	YT	06.96				
Doncaster Rov. (N/C)	Tr	11.97	97	15	0	0

League Club	Source	Date Signed	Seasons Played	Career Record Apps	Subs	Gls
DAVIS Cyril						
Birmingham, 21 July, 1925 Died 1992						(CF)
Walsall (Am)	Hednesford T.	05.48	48	1	-	0
DAVIS Darren John						
Sutton-in-Ashfield, 5 February, 1967 E Yth						(D)
Notts Co.	App	02.85	83-87	90	2	1
Lincoln C.	Tr	08.88	88-90	97	5	4
Maidstone U.	Tr	03.91	90-91	31	0	2
Scarborough	Frickley Ath.	08.93	93-94	46	2	3
Lincoln C. (N/C)	Grantham T.	09.95	95	3	0	0
DAVIS Derek Edgar Counsell						
Colwyn Bay, 19 June, 1922 Died 1985						(G)
Norwich C.	Plymouth Arg. (Am)	10.45	46-47	26	-	0
Torquay U.	Tr	08.48	48-50	89	-	0
DAVIS Edward						
Brackley, 8 March, 1922						(F)
Newport Co.	R.A.F. Hereford	10.46	46	3	-	1
DAVIS Eric William Charles						
Plymouth, 26 February, 1932						(CF)
Plymouth Arg.	Tavistock	08.52	52-56	63	-	29
Scunthorpe U.	Tr	07.57	57-58	40	-	20
Chester C.	Tr	02.59	58-59	31	-	11
Oldham Ath.	Tr	09.60	60	2	-	1
DAVIS Joseph **Frederick**						
Bloxwich, 23 May, 1929 Died 1996						(WH)
Reading	Bloxwich Strollers	12.52	53-54	63	-	1
Wrexham	Tr	07.55	55-60	230	-	12
DAVIS Gareth						
Bangor, 11 July, 1949 Wu23-4/W-3						(CD)
Wrexham	Colwyn Bay	10.67	67-82	482	8	9
DAVIS Gordon						
Newcastle, 14 December, 1930						(HB)
Gateshead	Everton (Am)	11.49	51-56	87	-	0
DAVIS Ian						
Hull, 1 February, 1965						(M)
Hull C.	App	02.83	81-82	25	3	1
DAVIS John Leslie						
Hackney, 31 March, 1957						(FB)
Gillingham	Arsenal (App)	07.75	75	2	1	1
Sheffield Wed.	Tr	10.76	76	1	0	0
DAVIS Joseph						
Glasgow, 22 May, 1941						(LB)
Carlisle U.	Hibernian	12.69	69-71	75	4	0
DAVIS Joseph						
Bristol, 24 August, 1938						(CH)
Bristol Rov.	Jnrs	03.56	60-66	210	1	4
Swansea C.	Tr	03.67	66-67	38	0	0
DAVIS Kelvin Geoffrey						
Bedford, 29 September, 1976 E Yth/Eu21-3						(G)
Luton T.	YT	07.94	93-97	48	0	0
Torquay U.	L	09.94	94	2	0	0
Hartlepool U.	L	08.97	97	2	0	0
DAVIS Kenneth Edward						
Romsey, 6 February, 1933						(F)
Bristol C.	Jnrs	05.52	52	1	-	0
DAVIS Leonard Philip						
Cork, 31 July, 1931						(CF)
Arsenal		11.49				
Walsall	Tr	02.54	53-54	25	-	5
DAVIS Mark Ronald						
Wallsend, 12 October, 1969						(M)
Darlington	YT	●	86	0	2	0
DAVIS Michael Vernon						
Bristol, 19 October, 1974						(F)
Bristol Rov.	Yate T.	05.93	92-95	3	14	1
Hereford U.	L	08.94	94	1	0	1
DAVIS Neil						
Bloxwich, 15 August, 1973						(CF)
Aston Villa	Redditch U.	05.91	95	0	2	0
Wycombe W.	L	10.96	96	13	0	0

DAVIS Paul Edward
Newham, 31 January, 1968 (D)

League Club	Source	Date Signed	Seasons Played	Apps	Subs	Gls
Queens Park R.	App	12.85				
Aldershot	Tr	08.87	87	1	0	0

DAVIS Paul Vincent
Dulwich, 9 December, 1961 Eu21-11/E'B'/EF Lge (M)

League Club	Source	Date Signed	Seasons Played	Apps	Subs	Gls
Arsenal	App	07.79	79-94	331	20	30
Brentford	Tr	09.95	95	5	0	0

DAVIS Richard Daniel
Birmingham, 22 January, 1922 E Sch (CF)

League Club	Source	Date Signed	Seasons Played	Apps	Subs	Gls
Sunderland	Morris & J.	02.39	46-53	144	-	72
Darlington	Tr	05.54	54-56	93	-	32

DAVIS Richard Frederick
Plymouth, 14 November, 1943 (FB)

League Club	Source	Date Signed	Seasons Played	Apps	Subs	Gls
Plymouth Arg.	App	11.61	62-63	23	-	0
Southampton	Tr	07.64	64	1	-	0
Bristol C.	Tr	07.65	67-68	8	0	0
Barrow	Tr	03.69	68-69	50	0	0

DAVIS Sean
Clapham, 20 September, 1979 (M)

League Club	Source	Date Signed	Seasons Played	Apps	Subs	Gls
Fulham	YT	●	96	0	1	0

DAVIS Solomon Sebastian
Cheltenham, 4 September, 1979 (D)

League Club	Source	Date Signed	Seasons Played	Apps	Subs	Gls
Swindon T.	YT	●	97	5	1	0

DAVIS Stephen Mark
Hexham, 30 October, 1968 (CD)

League Club	Source	Date Signed	Seasons Played	Apps	Subs	Gls
Southampton	YT	07.87	89-90	5	1	0
Burnley	L	11.89	89	7	2	0
Notts Co.	L	03.91	90	0	2	0
Burnley	Tr	08.91	91-94	162	0	22
Luton T.	Tr	07.95	95-97	117	1	15

DAVIS Steven Peter
Birmingham, 26 July, 1965 E Yth (CD)

League Club	Source	Date Signed	Seasons Played	Apps	Subs	Gls
Crewe Alex.	Stoke C. (App)	08.83	83-87	140	5	1
Burnley	Tr	10.87	87-90	147	0	11
Barnsley	Tr	07.91	91-96	103	4	10
York C.	L	09.97	97	2	0	1
Oxford U.	Tr	02.98	97	15	0	2

DAVISON Aidan John
Sedgefield, 11 May, 1968 NI 'B'/NI-3 (G)

League Club	Source	Date Signed	Seasons Played	Apps	Subs	Gls
Notts Co.	Billingham Synth.	03.88	88	1	0	0
Bury	Tr	10.89				
Millwall	Tr	08.91	91-92	34	0	0
Bolton W.	Tr	07.93	93-95	35	2	0
Hull C.	L	11.96	96	9	0	0
Bradford C.	Tr	03.97	96	10	0	0
Grimsby T.	Tr	07.97	97	42	0	0

DAVISON Alan
Sunderland, 8 September, 1931 (FB)

League Club	Source	Date Signed	Seasons Played	Apps	Subs	Gls
Norwich C.		09.49				
Darlington		08.51	51	1	-	0

DAVISON Arthur
Hackney, 21 December, 1915 (RB)

League Club	Source	Date Signed	Seasons Played	Apps	Subs	Gls
Stockport Co.		09.45				
Torquay U.		11.46	46	1	-	0

DAVISON Daniel
Newcastle, 11 November, 1947 (FB)

League Club	Source	Date Signed	Seasons Played	Apps	Subs	Gls
Barrow	Newcastle U. (Am)	09.65	66-69	7	0	0

DAVISON Edward
Seaham, 15 April, 1933 (CH)

League Club	Source	Date Signed	Seasons Played	Apps	Subs	Gls
Hartlepool U.	Seaham Jnrs	08.53	53	1	-	0

DAVISON James Hawkins
Sunderland, 1 November, 1942 (OR)

League Club	Source	Date Signed	Seasons Played	Apps	Subs	Gls
Sunderland	Jnrs	11.59	59-62	62	-	10
Bolton W.	Tr	11.63	63	21	-	1

DAVISON Joseph Henry
Newcastle, 29 July, 1919 Died 1983 (RB)

League Club	Source	Date Signed	Seasons Played	Apps	Subs	Gls
Darlington	Throckley Welfare	01.47	46-53	239	-	7

DAVISON Robert
South Shields, 17 July, 1959 (F)

League Club	Source	Date Signed	Seasons Played	Apps	Subs	Gls
Huddersfield T.	Seaham Colly	07.80	80	1	1	0
Halifax T.	Tr	08.81	81-82	63	0	29
Derby Co.	Tr	12.82	82-87	203	3	83
Leeds U.	Tr	11.87	87-91	79	12	31
Derby Co.	L	09.91	91	10	0	8
Sheffield U.	L	03.92	91	6	5	4
Leicester C.	Tr	08.92	92	21	4	6
Sheffield U.	Tr	09.93	93-94	9	3	1
Rotherham U.	Tr	10.94	94-95	20	2	4
Hull C.	L	11.95	95	11	0	4

DAVOCK Michael
St Helens, 27 April, 1935 (OL)

League Club	Source	Date Signed	Seasons Played	Apps	Subs	Gls
Stockport Co.	St Helens T.	01.57	56-63	235	-	41

D'AVRAY Jean **Michael (Mich)**
South Africa, 19 February, 1962 Eu21-2 (F)

League Club	Source	Date Signed	Seasons Played	Apps	Subs	Gls
Ipswich T.	App	05.79	79-89	170	41	37
Leicester C.	L	02.87	86	3	0	0

DAVY Stephen
Norwich, 9 April, 1955 (FB)

League Club	Source	Date Signed	Seasons Played	Apps	Subs	Gls
Scunthorpe U.	West Ham U. (N/C)	08.77	77-81	126	8	1

DAWE Simon
Plymouth, 16 March, 1977 (M)

League Club	Source	Date Signed	Seasons Played	Apps	Subs	Gls
Plymouth Arg.	YT	07.95	94	3	1	0

DAWES Derek Malcolm
Dawley, 23 June, 1944 (IF)

League Club	Source	Date Signed	Seasons Played	Apps	Subs	Gls
Shrewsbury T.	App	06.62	61-62	9	-	0

DAWES Frederick William
Frimley Green, 2 May, 1911 Died 1989 (LB)

League Club	Source	Date Signed	Seasons Played	Apps	Subs	Gls
Northampton T.	Frimley Green	03.30	29-35	161	-	1
Crystal Palace	Tr	02.36	35-49	222	-	2

DAWES Ian Michael
Aldershot, 5 January, 1965 E Sch (D)

League Club	Source	Date Signed	Seasons Played	Apps	Subs	Gls
Newcastle U.	Jnrs	06.83				
Northampton T.	Tr	06.85	85	3	2	0

DAWES Ian Robert
Croydon, 22 February, 1963 E Sch (LB)

League Club	Source	Date Signed	Seasons Played	Apps	Subs	Gls
Queens Park R.	App	12.80	81-87	229	0	3
Millwall	Tr	08.88	88-94	219	6	5

DAWES Malcolm
Trimdon, 3 March, 1944 (D)

League Club	Source	Date Signed	Seasons Played	Apps	Subs	Gls
Darlington		03.62				
Aldershot	Horden Colly	08.65	65-69	160	4	2
Hartlepool U.	Tr	07.70	70-75	193	2	12
Workington	Tr	11.75	75-76	49	2	1

DAWKINS Derek Anthony
Edmonton, 29 November, 1959 (FB/M)

League Club	Source	Date Signed	Seasons Played	Apps	Subs	Gls
Leicester C.	App	11.77	77	3	0	0
Mansfield T.	Tr	12.78	78-80	73	0	0
Bournemouth	Tr	08.81	81-82	4	4	0
Torquay U.	Weymouth	02.84	83-88	153	22	7

DAWKINS Trevor Andrew
Southend, 7 October, 1945 E Sch/E Yth (M)

League Club	Source	Date Signed	Seasons Played	Apps	Subs	Gls
West Ham U.	App	10.62	64-66	5	1	0
Crystal Palace	Tr	10.67	67-70	24	1	3
Brentford	L	09.71	71	3	1	0

DAWS Anthony
Sheffield, 10 September, 1966 E Sch/E Yth (F)

League Club	Source	Date Signed	Seasons Played	Apps	Subs	Gls
Notts Co.	App	09.84	84-85	6	2	1
Sheffield U.	Tr	08.86	86	7	4	3
Scunthorpe U.	Tr	06.87	87-92	166	17	63
Grimsby T.	Tr	03.93	92-93	14	2	1
Lincoln C.	Tr	02.94	93-95	42	9	13
Scarborough	Tr	08.96	96	4	2	0

DAWS Nicholas John
Manchester, 15 March, 1970 (M)

League Club	Source	Date Signed	Seasons Played	Apps	Subs	Gls
Bury	Altrincham	08.92	93-97	223	13	9

DAWSON Alexander
Glasgow, 23 October, 1933 (W)

League Club	Source	Date Signed	Seasons Played	Apps	Subs	Gls
Queens Park R.	Gourock Jnrs	02.57	56-58	59	-	5

DAWSON Alexander Downie
Aberdeen, 21 February, 1940 S Sch (CF)

League Club	Source	Date Signed	Seasons Played	Apps	Subs	Gls
Manchester U.	Jnrs	04.57	56-61	80	-	45
Preston N.E.	Tr	10.61	61-66	197	0	114
Bury	Tr	03.67	66-68	49	1	21
Brighton & H.A.	Tr	12.68	68-70	53	4	26
Brentford	L	09.70	70	10	0	6

DAWSON Alistair John
Govan, 25 February, 1958 S Yth/Su21-8/S-5 (CD)

League Club	Source	Date Signed	Seasons Played	Apps	Subs	Gls
Blackburn Rov.	Glasgow Rangers	08.87	87-89	32	8	0

DAWSON Carl Michael
Harwich, 24 June, 1934 Died 1991 (G)

League Club	Source	Date Signed	Seasons Played	Apps	Subs	Gls
Lincoln C. (Am)	Jnrs	05.50	50	1	-	0

DAWSON Edward
Chester-le-Street, 16 January, 1913 Died 1970 (G)

League Club	Source	Date Signed	Seasons Played	Apps	Subs	Gls
Manchester C.	Blyth Spartans	12.34				
Bristol C.	Tr	05.36	36-38	66	-	0
Gateshead	Tr	08.46	46-48	83	-	0

DAWSON George
Glasgow, 13 September, 1930 (WH)

League Club	Source	Date Signed	Seasons Played	Apps	Subs	Gls
Queens Park R.	Motherwell	05.55	55	1	-	0

DAWSON James
Stoneyburn, 21 December, 1927 (OL)

League Club	Source	Date Signed	Seasons Played	Apps	Subs	Gls
Leicester C.	Polkemmet	05.46	46-48	5	-	0
Portsmouth	Tr	06.49	49	1	-	0

DAWSON Jason
Burslem, 9 February, 1971 (F)

League Club	Source	Date Signed	Seasons Played	Apps	Subs	Gls
Rochdale	Port Vale (YT)	07.89	89-90	37	18	7

DAWSON Owen John
Hatfield, 7 March, 1943 E Yth (FB)

League Club	Source	Date Signed	Seasons Played	Apps	Subs	Gls
Portsmouth	Jnrs	06.60				
Swindon T.	Tr	06.62	62-70	196	7	4

DAWSON Peter
Crewe, 19 January, 1933 (RB)

League Club	Source	Date Signed	Seasons Played	Apps	Subs	Gls
Crewe Alex.		01.54	55	2	-	0

DAWSON Joseph **Reginald**
Sheffield, 4 October, 1914 Died 1973 (OL)

League Club	Source	Date Signed	Seasons Played	Apps	Subs	Gls
Rotherham U.		01.39	38-46	32	-	2

DAWSON Richard
Sheffield, 12 April, 1967 (G)

League Club	Source	Date Signed	Seasons Played	Apps	Subs	Gls
Grimsby T.	Stoke C. (Jnrs)	08.84	84	1	0	0

DAWSON Richard
Chesterfield, 19 January, 1960 (F)

League Club	Source	Date Signed	Seasons Played	Apps	Subs	Gls
Rotherham U.	App	01.78	77-79	21	3	3
Doncaster Rov.	Tr	02.81	80-81	39	4	14
Chesterfield	Tr	08.82	82	6	6	0

DAWSON Richard
York, 6 July, 1962 (D)

League Club	Source	Date Signed	Seasons Played	Apps	Subs	Gls
York C.	New Earswick	07.80	81-82	45	0	0

DAWSON Robert
South Shields, 31 January, 1935 (FB)

League Club	Source	Date Signed	Seasons Played	Apps	Subs	Gls
Leeds U.	South Shields	11.53	53	1	-	0
Gateshead	Tr	11.55	55-59	118	-	1

DAWSON Robert Anthony
Bentley, 21 June, 1944 (G)

League Club	Source	Date Signed	Seasons Played	Apps	Subs	Gls
Doncaster Rov.		12.64	65-66	28	0	0

DAWSON Thomas
Middlesbrough, 6 February, 1915 Died 1972 (IF)

League Club	Source	Date Signed	Seasons Played	Apps	Subs	Gls
Darlington	Whitby T.	12.36	36-37	20	-	4
Charlton Ath.	Spennymoor U.	02.39	38-46	23	-	2
Brentford	Tr	08.47	47	36	-	10
Swindon T.	Tr	05.48	48-49	65	-	15

DAWSON William
Glasgow, 5 February, 1931 Died 1991 (CF)

League Club	Source	Date Signed	Seasons Played	Apps	Subs	Gls
Northampton T.	Ashfield Jnrs	03.55	54-55	14	-	7

DAWTRY Kevin Austin
Southampton, 15 June, 1958 (M)

League Club	Source	Date Signed	Seasons Played	Apps	Subs	Gls
Southampton	App	06.76	78	0	1	0
Crystal Palace	Tr	05.80				
Bournemouth	Tr	03.81	80-83	58	7	11
Reading	L	09.82	82	4	0	0

DAY Albert
Camberwell, 7 March, 1918 Died 1983 (F)

League Club	Source	Date Signed	Seasons Played	Apps	Subs	Gls
Brighton & H.A.	Hastings & St Lennards	08.38				
Ipswich T.	Tr	05.46	46-48	63	-	25
Watford	Tr	08.49	49	4	-	1

DAY Christopher Nicholas
Waltham Cross, 28 July, 1975 E Yth/Eu21-6 (G)

League Club	Source	Date Signed	Seasons Played	Apps	Subs	Gls
Tottenham H.	YT	04.93				
Crystal Palace	Tr	08.96	96	24	0	0
Watford	Tr	07.97				

DAY Clive Anthony
Grays, 27 January, 1961 (FB)

League Club	Source	Date Signed	Seasons Played	Apps	Subs	Gls
Fulham	App	08.78	80-81	2	8	0
Mansfield T.	L	08.82	82	10	2	1
Aldershot	Tr	08.83	83-84	53	7	0

DAY Eric Charles
Dartford, 6 November, 1921 (OR)

League Club	Source	Date Signed	Seasons Played	Apps	Subs	Gls
Southampton	R.A.F. Ford	04.45	46-56	398	-	145

DAY Graham George
Bristol, 22 November, 1953 (CD)

League Club	Source	Date Signed	Seasons Played	Apps	Subs	Gls
Bristol Rov.	Bristol St George	05.73	74-78	129	1	1

DAY Burcombe **James**
Watford, 9 May, 1931 (CF)

League Club	Source	Date Signed	Seasons Played	Apps	Subs	Gls
Watford	Berkhamsted T.	12.51	51	3	-	0

DAY John (Jack) Norman
Northfleet, 21 January, 1924 (G)

League Club	Source	Date Signed	Seasons Played	Apps	Subs	Gls
Gillingham	Brighton & H.A. (Am)	07.50	50	1	-	0

DAY Keith David
Grays, 29 November, 1962 (CD)

League Club	Source	Date Signed	Seasons Played	Apps	Subs	Gls
Colchester U.	Aveley	08.84	84-86	113	0	12
Leyton Orient	Tr	07.87	87-92	184	8	9

DAY Mervyn Richard
Chelmsford, 26 June, 1955 E Yth/Eu23-5 (G)

League Club	Source	Date Signed	Seasons Played	Apps	Subs	Gls
West Ham U.	App	03.73	73-78	194	0	0
Leyton Orient	Tr	07.79	79-82	170	0	0
Aston Villa	Tr	08.83	83-84	30	0	0
Leeds U.	Tr	01.85	84-92	227	0	0
Luton T.	L	03.92	91	4	0	0
Sheffield U.	L	04.92	91	1	0	0
Carlisle U.	Tr	07.93	93	16	0	0

DAY Roger Arthur
Romford, 3 December, 1939 E Amat (F)

League Club	Source	Date Signed	Seasons Played	Apps	Subs	Gls
Watford (Am)	Enfield	12.61	61	1	-	0

DAY William
Middlesbrough, 27 December, 1936 (OR)

League Club	Source	Date Signed	Seasons Played	Apps	Subs	Gls
Middlesbrough	South Bank	05.55	55-61	120	-	18
Newcastle U.	Tr	03.62	61-62	13	-	1
Peterborough U.	Tr	04.63	62-63	18	-	2

DAYKIN Reginald **Brian**
Long Eaton, 4 August, 1937 (WH)

League Club	Source	Date Signed	Seasons Played	Apps	Subs	Gls
Derby Co.	Long Eaton U.	11.55	59-61	4	-	1
Notts Co.	Tr	07.62	62	3	-	0

DEACON David Benjamin
Broome, 10 March, 1929 Died 1990 (FB)

League Club	Source	Date Signed	Seasons Played	Apps	Subs	Gls
Ipswich T.	Bungay	11.50	50-59	66	-	0

DEACY Eamonn Stephen
Galway (Ire), 1 October, 1958 IR-4 (FB)

League Club	Source	Date Signed	Seasons Played	Apps	Subs	Gls
Aston Villa	Galway Rov.	03.79	79-83	27	6	1
Derby Co.	L	10.83	83	5	0	0

DEACY Michael
Cardiff, 29 November, 1943 (CH)

League Club	Source	Date Signed	Seasons Played	Apps	Subs	Gls
Newport Co.		08.66	66-69	46	1	2

DEACY Nicholas Simon
Cardiff, 19 July, 1953 Wu21-1/Wu23-1/W-12 (CD)

League Club	Source	Date Signed	Seasons Played	Apps	Subs	Gls
Hereford U.	Merthyr Tydfill	09.74	74	13	4	2
Workington	L	12.74	74	5	0	2
Hull C.	Vitesse Arnhem (Neth)	02.80	79-81	80	7	7
Bury	Happy Valley (HK)	10.83	83	30	1	0

DEAKIN Alan Roy
Birmingham, 27 November, 1941 Eu23-6 (WH)

League Club	Source	Date Signed	Seasons Played	Apps	Subs	Gls
Aston Villa	Jnrs	12.58	59-69	230	1	9
Walsall	Tr	10.69	69-71	46	4	0

DEAKIN Frederick Arthur
Birmingham, 5 February, 1920 (FB)

League Club	Source	Date Signed	Seasons Played	Apps	Subs	Gls
Birmingham C.		01.38				
Crystal Palace	Tr	09.46	46-47	6	-	0

League Club	Source	Date Signed	Seasons Played	Career Record Apps	Subs	Gls
DEAKIN John						
Stocksbridge, 29 September, 1966						(M)
Doncaster Rov.	Barnsley (YT)	08.85	85-86	21	2	0
Birmingham C.	Shepshed Charterhouse	09.89	89	3	4	0
Carlisle U.	Tr	08.91	91	3	0	0
DEAKIN Michael Raymond Frederick						
Birmingham, 25 October, 1933						(CF)
Crystal Palace	Bromsgrove Rov.	11.54	54-59	143	-	56
Northampton T.	Tr	10.59	59-60	44	-	31
Aldershot	Tr	01.61	60-61	17	-	5
DEAKIN Peter						
Normanton, 25 March, 1938						(IF)
Bolton W.	Jnrs	05.55	57-63	63	-	13
Peterborough U.	Tr	06.64	64-66	74	1	34
Bradford P.A.	Tr	09.66	66-67	36	0	9
Peterborough U.	Tr	09.67	67	16	0	1
Brentford	Tr	07.68	68	7	1	2
DEAKIN Raymond John						
Liverpool, 19 June, 1959						(LB)
Everton	App	06.77				
Port Vale	Tr	08.81	81	21	2	6
Bolton W.	Tr	08.82	82-84	104	1	2
Burnley	Tr	07.85	85-90	212	1	6
DEAKIN William Edward						
Maltby, 19 January, 1925						(OL)
Barnsley	Sunnyside W.M.C.	05.49	49-51	25	-	3
Chester C.	Tr	07.52	52	27	-	5
DEAN Alan John						
Aldershot, 20 January, 1950						(FB)
Aldershot	App	01.68	66-67	3	0	0
DEAN Andrew Geoffrey						
Salford, 27 November, 1966						(D)
Rochdale (N/C)	Burnley (Jnrs)	10.83	83	1	0	0
DEAN Brian Robert						
Stockport, 10 September, 1947						(FB)
Blackpool	Jnrs	09.64	67	0	1	0
Barrow	Tr	07.69	69-70	44	2	0
DEAN George Charles						
Walsall, 22 February, 1930						(WH)
Walsall	Hillery Street O.B.	05.50	50-53	72	-	13
DEAN Joby						
Edwinstowe, 25 November, 1934						(WH)
Queens Park R.	Thoresby Colly	11.52	55-56	16	-	0
Bradford P.A.	Sutton T.	12.57	57-58	53	-	1
DEAN Joseph						
Manchester, 4 April, 1939 E Sch/E Yth						(G)
Bolton W.	Jnrs	04.56	55-59	17	-	0
Carlisle U.	Tr	07.62	62-69	137	0	0
Barrow	Tr	07.70	70-71	41	0	0
DEAN Mark Christopher						
Northwich, 18 November, 1964						(D)
Chester C.	App	10.82	81-82	23	2	0
DEAN Michael James						
Weymouth, 9 March, 1978						(M)
Bournemouth	YT	07.96	95-97	17	8	0
DEAN Norman						
Corby, 13 September, 1944						(F)
Southampton	Corby T.	04.63	65	18	0	11
Cardiff C.	Tr	03.67	66-68	20	1	3
Barnsley	Tr	09.68	68-72	58	2	19
DEAN Raymond George						
Abingdon, 15 December, 1945						(CH)
Reading		05.66	66-68	50	4	0
Aldershot	Tr	07.69	69-74	256	0	7
DEANE Brian Christopher						
Leeds, 7 February, 1968 E'B'/E-3						(F)
Doncaster Rov.	Jnrs	12.85	85-87	59	7	12
Sheffield U.	Tr	07.88	88-92	197	0	82
Leeds U.	Tr	07.93	93-96	131	7	32
Sheffield U.	Tr	07.97	97	24	0	11
DEANS John (Dixie) Kelty						
Johnstone, 30 July, 1946 S-2						(F)
Luton T.	Glasgow Celtic	06.76	76	13	1	6
Carlisle U.	L	02.77	76	4	0	2
DEANS Raymond Alexander						
Lanark, 24 January, 1966 S Yth						(F)
Doncaster Rov.	Clyde	02.85	84-85	18	1	5
DEANS Thomas Sneddon						
Shieldhill, 7 January, 1922 SF Lge						(FB)
Notts Co.	Clyde	10.49	49-55	239	-	0
DEAR Brian Charles						
Plaistow, 18 September, 1943 E Sch						(CF)
West Ham U.	App	11.60	62-68	63	2	33
Brighton & H.A.	L	03.67	66	7	0	5
Fulham	Tr	02.69	68	13	0	7
Millwall	Tr	07.69	69	5	1	0
West Ham U.	Woodford T.	10.70	70	4	0	0
DEAR Gerald Albert						
Kensington, 5 January, 1937						(D)
Swindon T.		07.56	56	4	-	0
DEARDEN Kevin Charles						
Luton, 8 March, 1970						(G)
Tottenham H.	YT	07.88	92	0	1	0
Cambridge U.	L	03.89	88	15	0	0
Hartlepool U.	L	08.89	89	10	0	0
Swindon T.	L	03.90	89	1	0	0
Peterborough U.	L	08.90	90	7	0	0
Hull C.	L	01.91	90	3	0	0
Rochdale	L	08.91	91	2	0	0
Birmingham C.	L	03.92	91	12	0	0
Brentford	Tr	09.93	93-97	198	0	0
DEARDEN William						
Oldham, 11 February, 1944						(F)
Oldham Ath.	Jnrs	09.63	64-66	32	3	2
Crewe Alex.	Tr	12.66	66-67	44	3	7
Chester C.	Tr	06.68	68-69	85	0	22
Sheffield U.	Tr	04.70	70-75	170	5	61
Chester C.	Tr	02.76	75-76	35	1	7
Chesterfield	Tr	08.77	77-78	18	9	2
DEARSON Donald John						
Ynysybwl, 13 May, 1914 Died 1990 W Amat/W-3						(IF)
Birmingham C.	Barry T.	04.34	34-46	131	-	17
Coventry C.	Tr	02.47	46-49	84	-	10
Walsall	Tr	03.50	49-50	51	-	13
DEARY John Steele						
Ormskirk, 18 October, 1962						(M)
Blackpool	App	03.80	80-88	285	18	43
Burnley	Tr	07.89	89-94	209	6	23
Rochdale	Tr	01.95	94-96	90	1	10
D'EATH Stephen Victor						
Elmswell (Sk), 19 September, 1949 S Sch						(G)
West Ham U.	App	06.67	68	1	0	0
Reading	Tr	11.69	69-81	471	0	0
DEBENHAM Robert Karl						
Doncaster, 28 November, 1979						(FB)
Doncaster Rov.	YT	•	97	4	2	0
DEBONT Andrew Cornelius						
Wolverhampton, 7 February, 1974						(G)
Wolverhampton W.	YT	07.92				
Hartlepool U.	L	10.95	95	1	0	0
Hereford U.	L	03.96	95	8	0	0
Hereford U.	Tr	08.96	96	27	0	0
DEEGAN Mark						
Liverpool, 12 November, 1971 W Semi Pro						(G)
Oxford U.	Holywell T.	08.94	94	2	0	0
DEEHAN John Matthew						
Solihull, 6 August, 1957 E Yth/Eu21-7						(F)
Aston Villa	App	04.75	75-79	107	3	41
West Bromwich A.	Tr	09.79	79-81	44	3	5
Norwich C.	Tr	12.81	81-85	158	4	62
Ipswich T.	Tr	06.86	86-87	45	4	11
Manchester C.	Tr	07.88				
Barnsley	Tr	01.90	90	3	8	2
DEELEY Norman Victor						
Wednesbury, 30 November, 1933 E Sch/E-2						(OR)
Wolverhampton W.	Jnrs	12.50	51-61	206	-	66
Leyton Orient	Tr	02.62	61-63	73	-	9
DEERE Stephen Herbert						
Burnham Market, 31 March, 1948						(CD)
Scunthorpe U.	Norwich C. (Am)	11.67	67-72	232	6	20

League Club	Source	Date Signed	Seasons Played	Apps	Subs	Gls
Hull C.	Tr	06.73	73-74	65	1	2
Barnsley	L	10.75	75	4	0	0
Stockport Co.	L	12.75	75	6	0	0
Scunthorpe U.	Scarborough	02.78	77-79	105	0	2

DE FREITAS Fabian
Surinam, 28 July, 1972 (F)

League Club	Source	Date Signed	Seasons Played	Apps	Subs	Gls
Bolton W.	Volendam (Neth)	08.94	94-95	24	16	7

DE GARIS James Frederick
Worcester, 9 October, 1952 (M)

League Club	Source	Date Signed	Seasons Played	Apps	Subs	Gls
Arsenal	App	06.70				
Bournemouth	Tr	09.71	71-73	8	4	0
Torquay U.	Tr	03.74	73	7	2	0

DE GOEY Eduard Franciscus
Gouda, Holland, 20 December, 1966 Dutch Int (G)

League Club	Source	Date Signed	Seasons Played	Apps	Subs	Gls
Chelsea	Feyenoord (Neth)	07.97	97	28	0	0

DE GOEY Leendert
Netherlands, 29 February, 1952 (M)

League Club	Source	Date Signed	Seasons Played	Apps	Subs	Gls
Sheffield U.	Sparta Rotterdam (Neth)	08.79	79	33	0	5

DE GRUCHY Raymond Philip
Guernsey, 18 May, 1932 (FB)

League Club	Source	Date Signed	Seasons Played	Apps	Subs	Gls
Nottingham F.		08.53				
Grimsby T.	Tr	05.54	54-57	74	-	2
Chesterfield	Tr	06.58	58	1	-	0

DEGRYSE Marc
Belgium, 4 September, 1965 Belgian Int (M)

League Club	Source	Date Signed	Seasons Played	Apps	Subs	Gls
Sheffield Wed.	Anderlecht (Bel)	07.95	95	30	4	8

DELANEY James
Stoneyburn, 3 September, 1914 Died 1989 SF Lge/S-13 (W)

League Club	Source	Date Signed	Seasons Played	Apps	Subs	Gls
Manchester U.	Glasgow Celtic	02.46	46-50	164	-	25

DELANEY James Christopher
London, 22 July, 1945 (CF)

League Club	Source	Date Signed	Seasons Played	Apps	Subs	Gls
Newport Co. (Am)	Port Talbot	07.69	69	1	0	0

DELANEY John Joseph
Slough, 3 February, 1942 E Amat (CD)

League Club	Source	Date Signed	Seasons Played	Apps	Subs	Gls
Bournemouth	Wycombe W.	08.73	73-74	25	0	0

DELANEY Louis
Bothwell, 28 February, 1921 (FB)

League Club	Source	Date Signed	Seasons Played	Apps	Subs	Gls
Arsenal	Nunhead	05.43				
Crystal Palace	Tr	11.49	49	3	-	0

DELAP Rory John
Sutton Coldfield, 6 July, 1976 IRu21-4/IR 'B' (M/F)

League Club	Source	Date Signed	Seasons Played	Apps	Subs	Gls
Carlisle U.	YT	07.94	92-97	40	25	7
Derby Co.	Tr	02.98	97	10	3	0

DELAPENHA Lloyd **Lindbergh (Lindy)**
Jamaica (WI), 20 May, 1927 (F)

League Club	Source	Date Signed	Seasons Played	Apps	Subs	Gls
Portsmouth	Arsenal (Am)	04.48	48-49	7	-	0
Middlesbrough	Tr	04.50	49-57	260	-	90
Mansfield T.	Tr	06.58	58-60	115	-	27

DELF Barrie
Southend, 5 June, 1961 (G)

League Club	Source	Date Signed	Seasons Played	Apps	Subs	Gls
Southend U. (N/C)		03.83	82	1	0	0

DELGADO Robert Allan
Cardiff, 29 January, 1949 (CD)

League Club	Source	Date Signed	Seasons Played	Apps	Subs	Gls
Luton T.	Barry T.	02.70				
Carlisle U.	Tr	07.71	72-73	25	10	3
Workington	L	10.73	73	7	0	0
Rotherham U.	Tr	12.73	73-75	69	1	5
Chester C.	Tr	10.75	75-78	125	3	8
Port Vale	Tr	12.78	78-79	41	0	0

DELLAS Traianos
Thessaloniki, Greece, 31 January, 1976 (CB)

League Club	Source	Date Signed	Seasons Played	Apps	Subs	Gls
Sheffield U.	Aris Salonika (Gre)	08.97	97	5	4	0

DELLOW Ronald William
Crosby, 13 July, 1914 (OR)

League Club	Source	Date Signed	Seasons Played	Apps	Subs	Gls
Blackburn Rov.	Liverpool (Am)	08.33				
Mansfield T.	Tr	06.34	34	24	-	10
Manchester C.	Tr	01.35	34	10	-	4
Tranmere Rov.	Tr	03.36	35-38	105	-	29
Carlisle U.	Tr	08.39	46	16	-	5

DELVE John Frederick
Ealing, 27 September, 1953 (M)

League Club	Source	Date Signed	Seasons Played	Apps	Subs	Gls
Queens Park R.	App	07.71	72-73	9	6	0
Plymouth Arg.	Tr	07.74	74-77	127	5	6
Exeter C.	Tr	03.78	77-82	215	0	20
Hereford U.	Tr	06.83	83-86	116	2	11
Exeter C. (N/C)	Gloucester C.	10.87	87	12	1	1

DEMAINE David Jack
Cleveleys, 7 May, 1942 (W)

League Club	Source	Date Signed	Seasons Played	Apps	Subs	Gls
Blackpool	Jnrs	07.60				
Tranmere Rov.	Tr	08.61	61	2	-	0
Southport	Tr	07.62	62	5	-	0

DEMANGE Kenneth John Philip Petit
Dublin, 3 September, 1964 IR Yth/IRu21-5/IR-2 (M)

League Club	Source	Date Signed	Seasons Played	Apps	Subs	Gls
Liverpool	Home Farm	08.83				
Scunthorpe U.	L	12.86	86	3	0	2
Leeds U.	Tr	09.87	87	14	1	1
Hull C.	Tr	03.88	87-90	48	20	1
Cardiff C.	L	11.90	90	5	0	0
Cardiff C.	L	03.91	90	10	0	0

DEMETRIOS Cristakis
Dudley, 26 October, 1973 (M)

League Club	Source	Date Signed	Seasons Played	Apps	Subs	Gls
Walsall	YT	08.92	92	3	4	1

DEMPSEY John
Cumbernauld, 22 June, 1913 (IF)

League Club	Source	Date Signed	Seasons Played	Apps	Subs	Gls
Ipswich T.	Queen of South	06.48	48	22	-	5

DEMPSEY John Thomas
Hampstead, 15 March, 1946 IR-19 (CD)

League Club	Source	Date Signed	Seasons Played	Apps	Subs	Gls
Fulham	App	03.64	64-68	149	0	4
Chelsea	Tr	01.69	68-75	161	4	4

DEMPSEY John William
Birkenhead, 2 April, 1951 (FB)

League Club	Source	Date Signed	Seasons Played	Apps	Subs	Gls
Tranmere Rov.	App	04.69	67-71	52	1	1

DEMPSEY Mark Anthony
Dublin, 10 December, 1972 IR Yth/IRu21-5 (LW)

League Club	Source	Date Signed	Seasons Played	Apps	Subs	Gls
Gillingham	YT	08.90	90-92	27	21	2
Leyton Orient	Tr	07.94	94	43	0	1
Shrewsbury T.	Tr	07.95	95-97	62	18	3

DEMPSEY Mark James
Manchester, 14 January, 1964 (M)

League Club	Source	Date Signed	Seasons Played	Apps	Subs	Gls
Manchester U.	App	01.82	85	1	0	0
Swindon T.	L	01.85	84	5	0	0
Sheffield U.	Tr	08.86	86-87	60	3	8
Chesterfield	L	09.88	88	3	0	0
Rotherham U.	Tr	10.88	88-90	71	4	7

DENHAM Charles
Hartlepool, 28 April, 1937 (CF)

League Club	Source	Date Signed	Seasons Played	Apps	Subs	Gls
Hartlepool U. (Am)	West Amats	11.58	58	5	-	3

DENHAM John William
Middleton, 6 November, 1925 (LH)

League Club	Source	Date Signed	Seasons Played	Apps	Subs	Gls
Hull C.	Yorkshire Amats	06.48				
Hartlepool U.	Tr	08.49	49	1	-	0

DENIAL Geoffrey
Stocksbridge, 31 January, 1932 (WH)

League Club	Source	Date Signed	Seasons Played	Apps	Subs	Gls
Sheffield U.		01.52	52-54	10	-	0
Oxford U.	Tr	09.56	62	6	-	0

DENNEHY Jeremiah (Miah)
Cork, 29 March, 1950 IRu23-1IR-11 (W)

League Club	Source	Date Signed	Seasons Played	Apps	Subs	Gls
Nottingham F.	Cork Hibs	01.73	72-74	37	4	4
Walsall	Tr	07.75	75-77	123	5	22
Bristol Rov.	Tr	07.78	78-79	47	5	6

DENNIS Alan George
Colchester, 22 December, 1951 (CH)

League Club	Source	Date Signed	Seasons Played	Apps	Subs	Gls
Colchester U.	Jnrs	08.70	69-70	2	3	0

DENNIS John **Anthony**
Eton, 1 December, 1963 (W)

League Club	Source	Date Signed	Seasons Played	Apps	Subs	Gls
Plymouth Arg.	App	12.81	81-82	7	2	0
Exeter C.	Tr	08.83	83	3	1	0
Cambridge U.	Slough T.	02.89	88-92	89	22	10
Chesterfield	Tr	06.93	93	4	6	0
Colchester U.	Tr	08.94	94-95	56	9	5
Lincoln C.	Tr	07.96	96	23	5	2

DENNIS Kevin Jason
Islington, 14 December, 1976 (LW)

League Club	Source	Date Signed	Seasons Played	Apps	Subs	Gls
Brentford	Arsenal (YT)	07.96	96-97	9	8	0

DENNIS Mark Earl
Lambeth, 2 May, 1961 E Yth/Eu21-3 (LB)

League Club	Source	Date Signed	Seasons Played	Apps	Subs	Gls
Birmingham C.	App	08.78	78-82	130	0	1
Southampton	Tr	11.83	83-86	95	0	2
Queens Park R.	Tr	05.87	87-88	26	2	0
Crystal Palace	Tr	08.89	89-90	8	1	0

DENNISON Charles Robert
Hull, 12 September, 1932 (FB)

League Club	Source	Date Signed	Seasons Played	Apps	Subs	Gls
Hull C.	Jnrs	07.54	54-57	24	-	1

DENNISON Robert (Robbie)
Banbridge (NI), 30 April, 1963 NI Yth/NI 'B'/NI-17 (W)

League Club	Source	Date Signed	Seasons Played	Apps	Subs	Gls
West Bromwich A.	Glenavon	09.85	85-86	9	7	1
Wolverhampton W.	Tr	03.87	86-96	264	29	40
Swansea C.	L	10.95	95	9	0	0

DENNISON Robert Smith
Ambleside, 6 March, 1912 Died 1996 (CH)

League Club	Source	Date Signed	Seasons Played	Apps	Subs	Gls
Newcastle U.	Radcliffe U.	05.29	32-33	11	-	2
Nottingham F.	Tr	05.34	34	15	-	5
Fulham	Tr	06.35	35-38	31	-	0
Northampton T.	Tr	09.45	46-47	55	-	0

DENNY Paul Nicholas
Croydon, 5 September, 1957 (M)

League Club	Source	Date Signed	Seasons Played	Apps	Subs	Gls
Southend U.	App	09.75	76	8	1	2
Wimbledon	Tr	08.77	77-80	87	16	11

DENTON Edward John
Oxford, 18 May, 1970 (M)

League Club	Source	Date Signed	Seasons Played	Apps	Subs	Gls
Oxford U.	YT	07.88	87	0	2	0
Watford	Witney T.	02.91	90	0	2	0

DENTON Peter Robert
Gorleston, 1 March, 1946 (OR)

League Club	Source	Date Signed	Seasons Played	Apps	Subs	Gls
Coventry C.	App	03.64	65-67	10	0	1
Luton T.	Tr	01.68	67-68	4	1	0

DENTON Roger William
Stretford, 6 January, 1953 (FB)

League Club	Source	Date Signed	Seasons Played	Apps	Subs	Gls
Bolton W.	Jnrs	05.71	71	3	1	0
Bradford C.	Tr	07.72	72-73	25	5	0
Rochdale	L	02.74	73	2	0	0

DENYER Albert
Swindon, 6 December, 1924 (OR)

League Club	Source	Date Signed	Seasons Played	Apps	Subs	Gls
Swindon T.		10.45	46	7	-	1
Cardiff C.	Tr	05.48				

DENYER Peter Russell
Haslemere, 26 November, 1957 (M)

League Club	Source	Date Signed	Seasons Played	Apps	Subs	Gls
Portsmouth	App	12.75	75-78	123	7	15
Northampton T.	Tr	07.79	79-82	138	9	28

DENYS Ryan Hayden
Brentford, 16 August, 1978 (RW)

League Club	Source	Date Signed	Seasons Played	Apps	Subs	Gls
Brentford	YT	07.97	97	12	7	1

DEPEAR Ernest **Roland (Roly)**
Spalding, 10 December, 1923 (CH)

League Club	Source	Date Signed	Seasons Played	Apps	Subs	Gls
Leeds U.	Boston U.	05.48	48	4	-	0
Newport Co.	Tr	06.49	49	16	-	0
Shrewsbury T.	Tr	07.50	50-51	74	-	5

DEPLACIDO Michael Stephen
Scarborough, 9 March, 1954 E Yth (W)

League Club	Source	Date Signed	Seasons Played	Apps	Subs	Gls
York C.	Jnrs	03.72	71-72	4	7	0

DEPLIDGE William
Bradford, 12 November, 1924 (IF)

League Club	Source	Date Signed	Seasons Played	Apps	Subs	Gls
Bradford P.A.	Jnrs	08.42	46-55	274	-	62

DERBYSHIRE Thomas
Manchester, 10 December, 1930 (G)

League Club	Source	Date Signed	Seasons Played	Apps	Subs	Gls
Hartlepool U. (Am)	E. Yorks Regt	08.50	50	1	-	0

DERKO Tadeusz **Franciszek (Franco)**
Italy, 22 December, 1946 (FB)

League Club	Source	Date Signed	Seasons Played	Apps	Subs	Gls
Mansfield T.	App	01.65	66	1	0	0

DERRETT Stephen Clifford
Cardiff, 16 October, 1947 W Sch/Wu23-3/W-4 (FB)

League Club	Source	Date Signed	Seasons Played	Apps	Subs	Gls
Cardiff C.	App	10.65	66-71	61	5	0
Carlisle U.	Tr	04.72	72	13	0	0
Aldershot	L	10.73	73	4	0	0
Rotherham U.	Tr	12.73	73-75	79	2	2
Newport Co.	Tr	06.76	76-77	61	0	0

DERRICK Albert Edward
Newport, 8 September, 1908 Died 1975 (OR)

League Club	Source	Date Signed	Seasons Played	Apps	Subs	Gls
Newport Co.		10.35	35-38	125	-	48
Swindon T.	Tr	01.46	46	1	-	0

DERRICK Edward **Albert**
Newport, 6 August, 1939 (IF)

League Club	Source	Date Signed	Seasons Played	Apps	Subs	Gls
Newport Co.		12.60	60	3	-	1
Newport Co.	Hereford U.	07.69	69	25	2	8

DERRICK Jantzen Stuart
Bristol, 10 January, 1943 E Sch (W)

League Club	Source	Date Signed	Seasons Played	Apps	Subs	Gls
Bristol C.	Jnrs	01.60	59-70	253	6	31
Mansfield T.	L	03.71	70	2	1	0

DERRY Shaun Peter
Nottingham, 6 December, 1977 (M)

League Club	Source	Date Signed	Seasons Played	Apps	Subs	Gls
Notts Co.	YT	04.96	95-97	76	3	4
Sheffield U.	Tr	01.98	97	8	4	0

DESBOROUGH Michael
Newham, 28 November, 1969 (G)

League Club	Source	Date Signed	Seasons Played	Apps	Subs	Gls
Colchester U. (N/C)	Chelmsford C.	10.93	93	1	0	0

DESMEULES Rodney Leo
Newbury, 23 September, 1948 (WH)

League Club	Source	Date Signed	Seasons Played	Apps	Subs	Gls
Swindon T.	App	10.66	66-67	4	0	0

DESMOND Peter
Cork (Ire), 26 October, 1926 Died 1990 LoI/IR-4 (IF)

League Club	Source	Date Signed	Seasons Played	Apps	Subs	Gls
Middlesbrough	Shelbourne	05.49	49	2	-	0
Southport	Tr	08.50	50	12	-	2
York C.	Tr	12.51	51	1	-	0
Hartlepool U.	Fleetwood	08.53	53	1	-	0

DE SOUZA Miquel Juan
Newham, 11 February, 1970 (F)

League Club	Source	Date Signed	Seasons Played	Apps	Subs	Gls
Charlton Ath.	Clapton	07.89				
Bristol C.	Tr	08.90				
Birmingham C.	Dagenham & Redbridge	02.94	93-94	5	10	0
Bury	L	11.94	94	2	1	0
Wycombe W.	Tr	01.95	94-96	73	10	29
Peterborough U.	Tr	03.97	96-97	16	16	5

DEVANEY Philip Charles
Huyton, 12 February, 1969 (F)

League Club	Source	Date Signed	Seasons Played	Apps	Subs	Gls
Burnley	App	02.87	86-87	8	5	1

DEVANNEY Allan
Otley, 5 September, 1941 (CF)

League Club	Source	Date Signed	Seasons Played	Apps	Subs	Gls
Bradford C.	Jnrs	02.59	59-61	12	-	4

DEVERALL Harold (Jackie) Reginald
Petersfield, 5 May, 1916 E Sch (WH)

League Club	Source	Date Signed	Seasons Played	Apps	Subs	Gls
Reading	Maidenhead U.	11.37	38-47	74	-	9
Leyton Orient	Tr	08.48	48-52	115	-	2

DEVEREUX Anthony William John
Gibraltar, 6 January, 1940 (FB)

League Club	Source	Date Signed	Seasons Played	Apps	Subs	Gls
Aldershot	Chelsea (Am)	11.58	59-65	132	0	0

DEVEREUX James Anthony
Aldershot, 20 February, 1970 (D)

League Club	Source	Date Signed	Seasons Played	Apps	Subs	Gls
Aldershot	YT	07.88	88-89	0	2	0

DEVEREUX Robert
Bury St Edmunds, 31 January, 1971 (M)

League Club	Source	Date Signed	Seasons Played	Apps	Subs	Gls
Colchester U.	Ipswich T. (YT)	05.89	89	1	1	0
Colchester U. (N/C)	Cornard U.	08.92	92	3	3	0

DEVEY Raymond
Birmingham, 19 December, 1917 (WH)

League Club	Source	Date Signed	Seasons Played	Apps	Subs	Gls
Birmingham C.	Shirley Jnrs	08.37	46	1	-	0
Mansfield T.	Tr	08.47	47-49	76	-	4

DEVINE John **Henry**
Liverpool, 9 July, 1933 (OR)

League Club	Source	Date Signed	Seasons Played	Apps	Subs	Gls
Chester C.	Rhyl	07.55	55	1	-	0

DEVINE John Anthony
Dublin, 11 November, 1958 IRu21-2/IR-12 (M)

League Club	Source	Date Signed	Seasons Played	Apps	Subs	Gls
Arsenal	App	10.76	77-82	86	3	0
Norwich C.	Tr	08.83	83-84	51	2	3
Stoke C.	Tr	11.85	85	15	0	1

DEVINE Peter
Blackburn, 25 May, 1960 (W)

League Club	Source	Date Signed	Seasons Played	Apps	Subs	Gls
Bristol C.	Vancouver (Can)	07.81	81	19	2	1

League Club	Source	Date Signed	Seasons Played	Apps	Subs	Gls
Blackburn Rov. (N/C)	Tr	09.82	82-83	8	0	2
Burnley	Tr	06.84	84-85	46	10	4

DEVINE Sean Thomas
Lewisham, 6 September, 1972 IR 'B' (F)

League Club	Source	Date Signed	Seasons Played	Apps	Subs	Gls
Millwall	YT	05.91				
Barnet	Famagusta (Cyp)	10.95	95-97	102	4	46

DEVINE Stephen Bernard
Strabane (NI), 11 December, 1964 NI Yth (D)

League Club	Source	Date Signed	Seasons Played	Apps	Subs	Gls
Wolverhampton W.	App	12.82				
Derby Co.	Tr	03.83	83-84	10	1	0
Stockport Co.	Tr	08.85	85	2	0	0
Hereford U.	Tr	10.85	85-92	261	11	4

DEVINE William
Whitletts, 22 August, 1933 (OL)

League Club	Source	Date Signed	Seasons Played	Apps	Subs	Gls
Watford	St Mirren	03.58	57-58	30	-	6
Accrington St.	Partick Thistle	05.60	60	46	-	6

DE VITO Claudio Gaeatano
Peterborough, 21 July, 1978 (CF)

League Club	Source	Date Signed	Seasons Played	Apps	Subs	Gls
Northampton T. (N/C)	YT	07.96				
Barnet (N/C)	Tr	03.98	97	0	1	0

DEVITT Bernard **Malcolm**
Bradford, 26 January, 1937 (IF)

League Club	Source	Date Signed	Seasons Played	Apps	Subs	Gls
Bradford C.	Bradford Rov.	03.59	58-62	100	-	13

DEVLIN Alan Thomas
Edinburgh, 10 October, 1953 (F)

League Club	Source	Date Signed	Seasons Played	Apps	Subs	Gls
Exeter C.	Dundee U.	11.73	73	1	0	0

DEVLIN Douglas Paul Keith
Glasgow, 17 March, 1953 (M)

League Club	Source	Date Signed	Seasons Played	Apps	Subs	Gls
Wolverhampton W.	App	06.71				
Walsall	Tr	07.72	72	15	3	0

DEVLIN Ernest
Gateshead, 6 March, 1920 Died 1976 (FB)

League Club	Source	Date Signed	Seasons Played	Apps	Subs	Gls
Gateshead		08.42				
West Ham U.	Tr	06.46	46-52	70	-	0
Darlington	Tr	02.54	53-56	115	-	1

DEVLIN John
Airdrie, 11 December, 1917 (IF)

League Club	Source	Date Signed	Seasons Played	Apps	Subs	Gls
Walsall	Kilmarnock	12.47	47-51	159	-	50

DEVLIN Joseph
Cleland, 12 March, 1931 (OR)

League Club	Source	Date Signed	Seasons Played	Apps	Subs	Gls
Accrington St.	Falkirk	07.53	53-56	114	-	18
Rochdale	Tr	09.56	56-57	38	-	7
Bradford P.A.	Tr	11.57	57-58	34	-	3
Carlisle U.	Tr	07.59	59	5	-	0

DEVLIN Mark Andrew
Irvine, 18 January, 1973 S Yth (M)

League Club	Source	Date Signed	Seasons Played	Apps	Subs	Gls
Stoke C.	YT	04.91	90-96	39	16	2
Exeter C.	Tr	10.97	97	31	2	2

DEVLIN Paul John
Birmingham, 14 April, 1972 (W)

League Club	Source	Date Signed	Seasons Played	Apps	Subs	Gls
Notts Co.	Stafford R.	02.92	91-95	132	9	25
Birmingham C.	Tr	02.96	95-97	61	15	28
Sheffield U.	Tr	03.98	97	4	6	1

DEVLIN William
Glasgow, 30 May, 1931 (W)

League Club	Source	Date Signed	Seasons Played	Apps	Subs	Gls
Carlisle U.	Peterborough U.	08.56	56	28	-	6

DEVONSHIRE Alan Ernest
Park Royal, 13 April, 1956 E-8 (M)

League Club	Source	Date Signed	Seasons Played	Apps	Subs	Gls
West Ham U.	Southall	10.76	76-89	345	13	29
Watford	Tr	07.90	90-91	23	2	1

DEVONSHIRE Leslie Ernest
West Ham, 13 June, 1926 (W)

League Club	Source	Date Signed	Seasons Played	Apps	Subs	Gls
Brentford	Wealdstone	05.48				
Chester C.	Tr	06.50	50	44	-	4
Crystal Palace	Tr	08.51	51-54	83	-	12

DE VOS Jason Richard
Canada, 2 January, 1974 Canadian Int (CD)

League Club	Source	Date Signed	Seasons Played	Apps	Subs	Gls
Darlington	Montreal Impact (Can)	11.96	96-97	31	1	3

DEVRIES Roger Stuart
Hull, 25 October, 1950 (LB)

League Club	Source	Date Signed	Seasons Played	Apps	Subs	Gls
Hull C.	Jnrs	09.67	70-79	314	4	0
Blackburn Rov.	Tr	07.80	80	13	0	0
Scunthorpe U.	Tr	10.81	81	6	0	1

DEWHURST Robert Matthew
Keighley, 10 September, 1971 (CD)

League Club	Source	Date Signed	Seasons Played	Apps	Subs	Gls
Blackburn Rov.	YT	10.90	90	13	0	0
Darlington	L	12.91	91	11	0	1
Huddersfield T.	L	10.92	92	7	0	0
Hull C.	Tr	11.93	93-97	128	2	13

DEWICK John Albert
Rotherham, 28 November, 1919 (G)

League Club	Source	Date Signed	Seasons Played	Apps	Subs	Gls
Notts Co.		10.46	46	1	-	0

DEWIS George Ranger
Burbage, 22 January, 1913 Died 1994 (CF)

League Club	Source	Date Signed	Seasons Played	Apps	Subs	Gls
Leicester C.	Nuneaton T.	10.33	33-49	116	-	45

DE WOLF John
Netherlands, 10 December, 1962 Dutch Int (CD)

League Club	Source	Date Signed	Seasons Played	Apps	Subs	Gls
Wolverhampton W.	Feyenoord (Neth)	12.94	94-95	27	1	5

DEWS George
Ossett, 5 June, 1921 (IF)

League Club	Source	Date Signed	Seasons Played	Apps	Subs	Gls
Middlesbrough		08.46	46-47	33	-	8
Plymouth Arg.	Tr	10.47	47-54	257	-	76
Walsall	Tr	06.55	55	9	-	1

DEWSBURY John
Swansea, 16 February, 1932 (FB)

League Club	Source	Date Signed	Seasons Played	Apps	Subs	Gls
Swansea C.	Jnrs	07.50	52	9	-	0
Newport Co.	Tr	08.55	55	2	-	0

DEWSNIP George Edward
Little Hulton, 6 May, 1956 (W)

League Club	Source	Date Signed	Seasons Played	Apps	Subs	Gls
Southport	Preston N.E. (App)	06.74	74-76	83	4	11

DEY Geoffrey
Chesterfield, 11 January, 1964 E Yth (M)

League Club	Source	Date Signed	Seasons Played	Apps	Subs	Gls
Sheffield U.	App	01.82				
Scunthorpe U.	Tr	08.83	83-84	17	0	1

DEYNA Kazimierz
Poland, 23 October, 1947 Died 1989 Polish Int (F)

League Club	Source	Date Signed	Seasons Played	Apps	Subs	Gls
Manchester C.	Legia Warsaw (Pol)	11.78	78-80	34	4	12

DE ZEEUW Adrianus (Arjan) Johannes
Holland, 16 April, 1970 (CD)

League Club	Source	Date Signed	Seasons Played	Apps	Subs	Gls
Barnsley	Telstar (Neth)	11.95	95-97	100	0	3

DIA Aly
Senegal, 20 August, 1965 Senegelese Int (F)

League Club	Source	Date Signed	Seasons Played	Apps	Subs	Gls
Southampton (N/C)	Lubeck (Ger)	11.96	96	0	1	0

DIAMOND Anthony John
Rochdale, 23 August, 1968 NIu23-1 (F)

League Club	Source	Date Signed	Seasons Played	Apps	Subs	Gls
Blackburn Rov.	YT	06.86	86-88	9	17	3
Wigan Ath.	L	10.88	88	6	0	2
Blackpool	Tr	08.89	89	2	1	1

DIAMOND Barry
Dumbarton, 20 February, 1960 (F)

League Club	Source	Date Signed	Seasons Played	Apps	Subs	Gls
Rochdale	Barrow	07.84	84-85	50	2	16
Stockport Co.	L	12.85	85	6	0	0
Halifax T.	Tr	02.86	85-86	17	5	3
Wrexham	L	01.87	86	2	2	0

DIAZ Isidro (Izzy)
Spain, 15 May, 1972 (RW)

League Club	Source	Date Signed	Seasons Played	Apps	Subs	Gls
Wigan Ath.	Balaguer (Sp)	07.95	95-96	57	19	16
Wolverhampton W.	Tr	08.97	97	1	0	0
Wigan Ath.	Tr	12.97	97	1	1	0

DIBBLE Andrew Gerald
Cwmbran, 8 May, 1965 W Sch/W Yth/Wu21-3/W-3 (G)

League Club	Source	Date Signed	Seasons Played	Apps	Subs	Gls
Cardiff C.	App	08.82	81-83	62	0	0
Luton T.	Tr	07.84	84-87	30	0	0
Sunderland	L	02.86	85	12	0	0
Huddersfield T.	L	03.87	86	5	0	0
Manchester C.	Tr	06.88	88-96	113	3	0
Middlesbrough	L	02.91	90	19	0	0
Bolton W.	L	09.91	91	13	0	0
West Bromwich A.	L	02.92	91	9	0	0
Sheffield U.	Tr	08.87				
Luton T.	Tr	09.97	97	1	0	0
Middlesbrough	Tr	01.98	97	2	0	0

DIBBLE Christopher
Morden, 10 October, 1960 E Sch (M)

League Club	Source	Date Signed	Seasons Played	Apps	Subs	Gls
Millwall	App	11.77	77-81	49	14	5
Wimbledon	Tr	07.82	82-83	7	2	0

DIBDEN William **Keith**
Totton, 17 December, 1933 (F)

League Club	Source	Date Signed	Seasons Played	Apps	Subs	Gls
Southampton	Jnrs	01.52				
Gillingham	Tr	07.57	57	1	-	0

DI CANIO Paolo
Rome, Italy, 9 July, 1968 (F)

League Club	Source	Date Signed	Seasons Played	Apps	Subs	Gls
Sheffield Wed.	Glasgow Celtic	08.97	97	34	1	12

DICHIO Daniele (Danny) Salvatore Ernest
Hammersmith, 19 October, 1974 E Sch/Eu21-1 (F)

League Club	Source	Date Signed	Seasons Played	Apps	Subs	Gls
Queens Park R.	YT	05.93	94-96	56	19	20
Barnet	L	03.94	93	9	0	2
Sunderland	Lecce (It)	01.98	97	2	11	0

DICK Alistair John
Stirling, 25 April, 1965 S Sch/S Yth (W)

League Club	Source	Date Signed	Seasons Played	Apps	Subs	Gls
Tottenham H.	App	05.82	81-85	16	1	2

DICK George White
Torphichen, 12 June, 1921 Died 1960 (IF)

League Club	Source	Date Signed	Seasons Played	Apps	Subs	Gls
Blackpool		08.46	46-47	46	-	13
West Ham U.	Tr	10.48	48	14	-	1
Carlisle U.	Tr	07.49	49-50	52	-	23
Stockport Co.	Tr	10.50	50	25	-	12
Workington	Tr	10.51	51-52	56	-	16

DICK John Hart
Glasgow, 19 March, 1930 S 'B'/S-1 (IF)

League Club	Source	Date Signed	Seasons Played	Apps	Subs	Gls
West Ham U.	Crittalls Ath.	06.53	53-62	326	-	153
Brentford	Tr	09.62	62-64	72	-	45

DICK Thomas Woods
Glasgow, 19 July, 1936 (CF)

League Club	Source	Date Signed	Seasons Played	Apps	Subs	Gls
Bradford P.A.	Third Lanark	06.60	60	4	-	0

DICK Peter **Watt (Wattie)**
Newmains, 20 August, 1927 (WH)

League Club	Source	Date Signed	Seasons Played	Apps	Subs	Gls
Accrington St.	Third Lanark	06.55	55-58	125	-	37
Bradford P.A.	Tr	12.58	58-62	155	-	2

DICKENS Alan William
Plaistow, 3 September, 1964 E Yth/Eu21-1 (M)

League Club	Source	Date Signed	Seasons Played	Apps	Subs	Gls
West Ham U.	App	08.82	82-88	173	19	23
Chelsea	Tr	08.89	89-91	39	9	1
West Bromwich A.	L	12.92	92	3	0	1
Brentford	Tr	02.93	92	13	2	1
Colchester U.	Tr	09.93	93	28	4	3

DICKENS Leo
Hemsworth, 16 March, 1927 (RB)

League Club	Source	Date Signed	Seasons Played	Apps	Subs	Gls
Rotherham U.	Frickley Colly	07.50				
Chester C.	Tr	07.52	52	7	-	0

DICKENSON Kevin James
Hackney, 24 November, 1962 (LB)

League Club	Source	Date Signed	Seasons Played	Apps	Subs	Gls
Charlton Ath.	Tottenham H. (App)	04.80	79-84	72	3	1
Leyton Orient	Tr	07.85	85-91	190	2	3

DICKER Leslie Raymond
Stockwell, 20 December, 1926 (OL)

League Club	Source	Date Signed	Seasons Played	Apps	Subs	Gls
Tottenham H.	Chelmsford C.	06.51	52	10	-	2
Southend U.	Tr	07.53	53-54	17	-	7

DICKIE Alan Leonard
Charlton, 30 January, 1944 (G)

League Club	Source	Date Signed	Seasons Played	Apps	Subs	Gls
West Ham U.	App	02.62	61-65	12	0	0
Coventry C.	Tr	03.67	67	2	0	0
Aldershot	Tr	07.68	68	7	0	0

DICKIE Murdoch McFarlane
Dumbarton, 28 December, 1919 (OR)

League Club	Source	Date Signed	Seasons Played	Apps	Subs	Gls
Port Vale		10.44				
Chelsea	Guildford C.	04.45	46	1	-	0
Bournemouth	Tr	02.47	46-47	16	-	2

DICKINS Matthew James
Sheffield, 3 September, 1970 (G)

League Club	Source	Date Signed	Seasons Played	Apps	Subs	Gls
Sheffield U.	YT	07.89				
Lincoln C.	Tr	02.91	90-91	27	0	0
Blackburn Rov.	Tr	03.92	91	1	0	0
Blackpool	L	01.93	92	19	0	0
Rochdale	L	10.94	94	4	0	0
Stockport Co.	Tr	02.95	94-95	12	1	0

DICKINSON James
South Elmsall, 26 September, 1931 (FB)

League Club	Source	Date Signed	Seasons Played	Apps	Subs	Gls
Barrow	Pontefract	08.51	51-57	67	-	0

DICKINSON James William
Alton, 24 April, 1925 Died 1982 EF Lge/E 'B'/E-48 (WH)

League Club	Source	Date Signed	Seasons Played	Apps	Subs	Gls
Portsmouth	Jnrs	01.44	46-64	764	-	9

DICKINSON Leonard
South Elmsall, 6 March, 1942 (IF)

League Club	Source	Date Signed	Seasons Played	Apps	Subs	Gls
Sheffield Wed.	Jnrs	02.60				
Oldham Ath.	Tr	06.61	61	5	-	2

DICKINSON Martin John
Leeds, 14 March, 1963 (CD)

League Club	Source	Date Signed	Seasons Played	Apps	Subs	Gls
Leeds U.	App	05.80	79-85	100	3	2
West Bromwich A.	Tr	02.86	85-87	46	4	2
Sheffield U.	Tr	07.88	88	0	1	0

DICKINSON Patrick James
Canada, 6 May, 1978 (M)

League Club	Source	Date Signed	Seasons Played	Apps	Subs	Gls
Hull C.	YT	07.97	96-97	2	2	0

DICKINSON Ronald Arthur
Coventry, 29 June, 1930 (CH)

League Club	Source	Date Signed	Seasons Played	Apps	Subs	Gls
Shrewsbury T. (Am)	Nuneaton Borough	05.53	53	11	-	0
Coventry C.	Tr	06.54				

DICKOV Paul
Livingston, 1 November, 1972 S Sch/S Yth/Su21-4 (F)

League Club	Source	Date Signed	Seasons Played	Apps	Subs	Gls
Arsenal	YT	12.90	92-96	6	15	3
Luton T.	L	10.93	93	8	7	1
Brighton & H.A.	L	03.94	93	8	0	5
Manchester C.	Tr	08.96	96-97	46	13	14

DICKS Alan Victor
Kennington, 29 August, 1934 (WH)

League Club	Source	Date Signed	Seasons Played	Apps	Subs	Gls
Chelsea	Jnrs	09.51	52-57	33	-	1
Southend U.	Tr	11.58	58-61	85	-	2
Coventry C.	Tr	02.62				

DICKS Julian Andrew
Bristol, 8 August, 1968 Eu21-4/E 'B' (LB)

League Club	Source	Date Signed	Seasons Played	Apps	Subs	Gls
Birmingham C.	App	03.86	85-87	83	6	1
West Ham U.	Tr	03.88	87-93	159	0	29
Liverpool	Tr	09.93	93	24	0	3
West Ham U.	Tr	10.94	94-96	94	0	21

DICKS Ronald William
Kennington, 13 April, 1924 (WH)

League Club	Source	Date Signed	Seasons Played	Apps	Subs	Gls
Middlesbrough	Dulwich Hamlet	05.43	47-58	316	-	10

DICKSON Adam
Hamilton, 4 January, 1929 (G)

League Club	Source	Date Signed	Seasons Played	Apps	Subs	Gls
Leicester C.	Thorniewood Ath.	06.51	51-54	16	-	0

DICKSON Joseph James March
Liverpool, 31 January, 1934 Died 1992 E Yth (F)

League Club	Source	Date Signed	Seasons Played	Apps	Subs	Gls
Liverpool	Jnrs	06.52	55	6	-	3

DICKSON William
Lurgan (NI), 15 April, 1923 NI-12 (WH)

League Club	Source	Date Signed	Seasons Played	Apps	Subs	Gls
Notts Co.	Glenavon	11.45	46-47	21	-	2
Chelsea	Tr	11.47	47-52	101	-	4
Arsenal	Tr	10.53	53-55	29	-	1
Mansfield T.	Tr	07.56	56	19	-	0

DIGBY Derek Francis
Teignmouth, 14 May, 1931 (W)

League Club	Source	Date Signed	Seasons Played	Apps	Subs	Gls
Exeter C.	Dawlish	08.49	51-52	31	-	2
Southampton	Tr	09.53	53-54	15	-	2

DIGBY Fraser Charles
Sheffield, 23 April, 1967 E Sch/E Yth/Eu21-5 (G)

League Club	Source	Date Signed	Seasons Played	Apps	Subs	Gls
Manchester U.	App	04.85				
Swindon T.	Tr	09.86	86-97	417	0	0

DIGHTON Richard Anthony
Peterborough, 26 July, 1951 (G)

League Club	Source	Date Signed	Seasons Played	Apps	Subs	Gls
Peterborough U.	Coventry C. (App)	11.69	70-71	8	0	0
Stockport Co.	L	10.70	70	1	0	0

DIGNAM Joseph Colquhoun
Glasgow, 10 January, 1931 (IF)

League Club	Source	Date Signed	Seasons Played	Apps	Subs	Gls
Wrexham	Alloa Ath.	07.57	57	8	-	0

DIGWEED Perry Michael
Westminster, 26 October, 1959 (G)

League Club	Source	Date Signed	Seasons Played	Apps	Subs	Gls
Fulham	App	08.77	76-80	15	0	0
Brighton & H.A.	Tr	01.81	80-92	179	0	0
Chelsea	L	02.88	87	3	0	0
Wimbledon	Tr	08.93				
Watford	Tr	12.93	93-94	28	1	0

League Club	Source	Date Signed	Seasons Played	Career Record Apps	Subs	Gls
DIJKSTRA Meindert						
Netherlands, 28 February, 1967						(D)
Notts Co.	Willem II Tilburg (Neth)	08.92	92-93	27	2	1
DIJKSTRA Sieb						
Netherlands, 20 October, 1966						(G)
Queens Park R.	Motherwell	07.94	94	11	0	0
Bristol C.	L	09.95	95	8	0	0
Wycombe W.	L	03.96	95	13	0	0
DI LELLA Gustavo Martin						
Buenos Aires, Argentine, 6 October, 1973						(M/F)
Darlington	Blyth Spartans	12.97	97	0	5	0
Hartlepool U. (N/C)	Blyth Spartans	03.98	97	1	4	2
DILLON Andrew						
Salford, 20 January, 1969						(G)
Newport Co.	YT	07.87	86-87	15	0	0
DILLON John						
Coatbridge, 9 November, 1942						(OL)
Sunderland	Jnrs	11.59	60-61	18	-	1
Brighton & H.A.	Tr	07.62	62	21	-	3
Crewe Alex.	Tr	07.63	63	5	-	1
DILLON Kevin Paul						
Sunderland, 18 December, 1959 E Yth/Eu21-1						(M)
Birmingham C.	App	07.77	77-82	181	5	15
Portsmouth	Tr	03.83	82-88	206	9	45
Newcastle U.	Tr	07.89	89-90	62	0	0
Reading	Tr	07.91	91-93	100	1	4
DILLON Michael Leslie						
Highgate, 29 September, 1952 E Sch/E Yth						(CD)
Tottenham H.	App	12.69	72-73	21	3	1
Millwall	L	12.74	74	4	0	0
Swindon T.	L	03.75	74	7	2	0
DILLON Paul William						
Limerick, 22 October, 1978 IR Yth/IRu21-1						(CD)
Rotherham U.	YT	03.97	96-97	25	4	1
DILLON Vincent						
Manchester, 2 October, 1923						(CF)
Bolton W.		04.48	47-50	17	-	2
Tranmere Rov.	Tr	02.51	50-52	33	-	17
DILLSWORTH Edward						
Sierra Leone, 16 April, 1946						(WH)
Lincoln C. (Am)	Wealdstone	03.67	66	2	0	0
DI MATTEO Roberto						
Switzerland, 29 May, 1970 Italian Int						(M)
Chelsea	Lazio (It)	07.96	96-97	61	3	11
DIMMER Hyam						
Scotstown, 14 March, 1914 Died 1990						(IF)
Aldershot	Ayr U.	08.46	46	7	-	1
Bristol C.	Tr	05.47	47	1	-	0
DIMOND Stuart						
Manchester, 3 January, 1920						(CF)
Manchester U.		12.42				
Bradford C.	Tr	11.45	46	9	-	1
DINE John McQuade						
Newton Stewart, 3 May, 1940						(G)
Bradford P.A.	Bulford U.	08.62	62-64	32	-	0
DINEEN Jack Anthony						
Brighton, 23 September, 1970						(M)
Brighton & H.A.	Jnrs	09.87				
Scarborough (N/C)	Crawley T.	01.94	93	1	1	0
DINGWALL William **Norman**						
Gateshead, 29 July, 1923						(F)
Sheffield U.		03.46				
Halifax T.	Tr	07.47	47	9	-	0
DINNING Anthony						
Wallsend, 12 April, 1975						(CD)
Newcastle U.	YT	10.93				
Stockport Co.	Tr	06.94	94-97	75	25	8
DINSDALE Peter						
Bradford, 19 October, 1938						(WH)
Huddersfield T.	Yorkshire Amats	01.56	59-66	213	1	8
Bradford P.A.	Tr	08.67	67	9	0	0

League Club	Source	Date Signed	Seasons Played	Career Record Apps	Subs	Gls
DISLEY Martin						
Ormskirk, 24 June, 1971						(F)
Crewe Alex.	YT	09.89	89-91	0	2	0
DITCHBURN Edwin (Ted) George						
Gillingham, 24 October, 1921 E 'B'/EF Lge/E-6						(G)
Tottenham H.	Jnrs	05.39	46-58	418	-	0
DIUK Wayne John						
Nottingham, 26 May, 1980						(M)
Notts Co.	YT	●	96-97	0	2	0
DIVERS John						
Clydebank, 6 August, 1911 Died 1984 S-1						(IF)
Oldham Ath.	Morton	08.47	47	1	-	0
DIVERS John Rice						
Glasgow, 24 November, 1931						(F)
Exeter C.	Clyde	05.56	56	12	-	1
DIX Richard						
South Shields, 17 January, 1924 Died 1990						(OL)
Bradford P.A.	Jnrs	08.44	46-47	18	-	5
Bradford C.	North Shields	08.52	52	8	-	1
DIX Ronald William						
Bristol, 5 September, 1912 E Sch/EF Lge/E-1						(IF)
Bristol Rov.	Jnrs	02.28	27-31	101	-	33
Blackburn Rov.	Tr	05.32	32	38	-	14
Aston Villa	Tr	05.33	32-36	97	-	30
Derby Co.	Tr	02.37	36-38	94	-	35
Tottenham H.	Tr	06.39	46-47	36	-	5
Reading	Tr	11.47	47-48	44	-	13
DIXEY Richard						
Wigston, 2 September, 1956						(CD)
Burnley	Enderby T.	12.74	74	3	0	0
Stockport Co.	L	02.76	75	14	0	1
DIXON Andrew						
Louth, 19 April, 1968						(FB)
Grimsby T.	YT	05.86	86-88	35	3	0
Southend U.	Tr	08.89	89	24	0	0
DIXON Andrew Paul						
Hartlepool, 5 August, 1968						(M)
Hartlepool U.	Jnrs	07.87	86-87	7	7	1
Hartlepool U. (N/C)	R.A.E.C. Mons (Bel)	11.95	95	3	0	0
DIXON Arthur						
Middleton, 17 November, 1921						(IF)
Northampton T.	Hearts	11.49	49-51	68	-	21
Leicester C.	Tr	10.51	51-52	11	-	0
DIXON Benjamin Marcus Alexander						
Lincoln, 16 September, 1974						(LB/W)
Lincoln C.	YT	11.92	91-95	33	10	0
Blackpool	Tr	07.96	96-97	9	9	0
DIXON Cecil Hubert						
Trowbridge, 28 March, 1935						(OR)
Cardiff C.	Trowbridge T.	07.54	54-56	21	-	1
Newport Co.	Tr	07.57	57-60	107	-	15
Northampton T.	Tr	08.61	61	15	-	4
DIXON Colin						
Newcastle, 24 September, 1963						(D)
Southampton	App	09.81				
Hartlepool U.		11.83	83	1	0	0
DIXON David						
Seaham, 3 November, 1951						(FB)
Middlesbrough	App	11.68	69	1	0	0
DIXON John Thomas						
Hebburn, 10 December, 1923						(IF)
Aston Villa	Spennymoor U.	01.46	46-60	392	-	132
DIXON John William						
Hartlepool, 12 March, 1934						(FB)
Hartlepool U.	Throston W.	10.57	58-60	35	-	2
DIXON Joseph						
Newcastle-u-Lyme, 24 September, 1916						(CF)
Northampton T.	Audley U.	04.45				
Port Vale	Tr	10.46	46	1	-	0

DIXON Kerry Michael
Luton, 24 July, 1961 Eu21-1/E-8 (F)

League Club	Source	Date Signed	Seasons Played	Apps	Subs	Gls
Tottenham H.	Chesham U.	07.78				
Reading	Dunstable	07.80	80-82	110	6	51
Chelsea	Tr	08.83	83-91	331	4	147
Southampton	Tr	07.92	92	8	1	2
Luton T.	Tr	02.93	92-94	66	9	19
Millwall	Tr	03.95	94-95	24	7	9
Watford	Tr	01.96	95	8	3	0
Doncaster Rov.	Tr	08.96	96	13	3	3

DIXON Kevin Lynton
Consett, 27 July, 1960 (W)

League Club	Source	Date Signed	Seasons Played	Apps	Subs	Gls
Carlisle U.	Tow Law T.	08.83	83	5	4	0
Hartlepool U.	L	10.83	83	6	0	3
Hartlepool U.	Tr	08.84	84-86	103	4	26
Scunthorpe U.	L	01.86	85	14	0	2
Scunthorpe U.	Tr	08.87	87	37	4	4
Hartlepool U.	Tr	06.88	88	14	0	4
York C.	Tr	11.88	88-89	33	5	8
Scarborough	L	02.90	89	3	0	0

DIXON Lee Michael
Manchester, 17 March, 1964 EF Lge/E'B'/E-21 (RB)

League Club	Source	Date Signed	Seasons Played	Apps	Subs	Gls
Burnley	Jnrs	07.82	82-83	4	0	0
Chester C.	Tr	02.84	83-84	56	1	1
Bury	Tr	07.85	85	45	0	6
Stoke C.	Tr	07.86	86-87	71	0	5
Arsenal	Tr	01.88	87-97	346	6	20

DIXON Michael
Willesden, 14 March, 1937 (CF)

League Club	Source	Date Signed	Seasons Played	Apps	Subs	Gls
Luton T.	Hitchin T.	04.57	58-60	3	-	0
Coventry C.	Tr	05.61	61	18	-	12

DIXON Michael George
Reading, 12 October, 1943 Died 1993 E Sch (G)

League Club	Source	Date Signed	Seasons Played	Apps	Subs	Gls
Reading	Jnrs	08.61	62-67	113	0	0
Aldershot	Tr	07.69	69-70	38	0	0

DIXON Milton
Manchester, 30 March, 1925 (OR)

League Club	Source	Date Signed	Seasons Played	Apps	Subs	Gls
Huddersfield T.		02.48				
Stockport Co.	Tr	10.50	50	21	-	2

DIXON Paul Kenneth
Derry (NI), 22 February, 1960 (CD)

League Club	Source	Date Signed	Seasons Played	Apps	Subs	Gls
Burnley	App	02.78	78-81	23	1	1

DIXON Raymond
Denaby, 31 December, 1930 (F)

League Club	Source	Date Signed	Seasons Played	Apps	Subs	Gls
Rotherham U.	Denaby U.	06.55	55-56	14	-	4

DIXON Robert
Felling, 11 January, 1936 (OL)

League Club	Source	Date Signed	Seasons Played	Apps	Subs	Gls
Arsenal	Crook T.	08.57				
Workington	Tr	11.58	58	28	-	5
West Bromwich A.	Tr	05.59	59	7	-	1

DIXON Stanley
Burnley, 28 August, 1920 Died 1996 (CH)

League Club	Source	Date Signed	Seasons Played	Apps	Subs	Gls
Plymouth Arg.	Hapton U.	12.38	46-50	60	-	1

DIXON Thomas Charles
Newcastle, 8 June, 1929 (CF)

League Club	Source	Date Signed	Seasons Played	Apps	Subs	Gls
West Ham U.	Newcastle U. (Am)	02.51	52-54	39	-	21
Reading	Tr	03.55	54-58	123	-	64
Brighton & H.A.	Tr	10.58	58-59	35	-	12
Workington	Tr	07.60	60-61	53	-	17
Barrow	Tr	10.61	61-62	62	-	23

DIXON Wilfred Edward
Wood Green, 20 February, 1950 (RB)

League Club	Source	Date Signed	Seasons Played	Apps	Subs	Gls
Arsenal	App	02.68				
Reading	Tr	07.69	69-72	150	3	0
Colchester U.	Tr	08.73				
Swindon T.	Tr	09.73	73-76	134	6	10
Aldershot	Tr	07.77	77-79	114	6	6

DOBBIE Harold
Bishop Auckland, 20 February, 1923 Died 1988 (IF)

League Club	Source	Date Signed	Seasons Played	Apps	Subs	Gls
Middlesbrough	South Bank	12.46	46-49	23	-	6
Plymouth Arg.	Tr	03.50	49-53	30	-	6
Torquay U.	Tr	10.53	53-56	110	-	47

DOBBIN James
Dunfermline, 17 September, 1963 S Yth (M)

League Club	Source	Date Signed	Seasons Played	Apps	Subs	Gls
Doncaster Rov.	Glasgow Celtic	03.84	83-86	56	8	13
Barnsley	Tr	09.86	86-90	116	13	12
Grimsby T.	Tr	07.91	91-95	154	10	21
Rotherham U.	Tr	08.96	96	17	2	0
Doncaster Rov.	Tr	08.97	97	28	3	0
Scarborough	Tr	03.98	97	1	0	0
Grimsby T.	Tr	03.98	97	1	1	0

DOBBING Robert
Sunderland, 27 June, 1949 (LB)

League Club	Source	Date Signed	Seasons Played	Apps	Subs	Gls
Coventry C.	App	06.67				
Hartlepool U.	Tr	07.69	69	34	0	1

DOBBINS Lionel Wayne
Bromsgrove, 30 August, 1968 (FB/M)

League Club	Source	Date Signed	Seasons Played	Apps	Subs	Gls
West Bromwich A.	App	08.86	86-90	30	15	0
Torquay U.	Tr	07.91	91	18	3	1

DOBBS Eric
Forehoe, 15 October, 1920 (FB)

League Club	Source	Date Signed	Seasons Played	Apps	Subs	Gls
Coventry C.		08.46	46-47	5	-	0
Bristol Rov.	Tr	07.48				

DOBBS Gerald Francis
Lambeth, 24 January, 1971 (M)

League Club	Source	Date Signed	Seasons Played	Apps	Subs	Gls
Wimbledon	YT	07.89	91-93	21	12	1
Cardiff C.	L	09.95	95	3	0	0

DOBIE Mark Walter Graham
Carlisle, 8 November, 1963 (F)

League Club	Source	Date Signed	Seasons Played	Apps	Subs	Gls
Carlisle U.(N/C)	Workington	12.86	86	2	4	0
Cambridge U.	Gretna	12.90				
Torquay U.	Tr	08.91	91	18	2	2
Darlington	Tr	08.92	92	35	1	8

DOBIE Robert Scott
Workington, 10 October, 1978 (F)

League Club	Source	Date Signed	Seasons Played	Apps	Subs	Gls
Carlisle U.	YT	05.97	96-97	9	16	2

DOBING Brian George
Sheffield, 29 December, 1937 Died 1995 (G)

League Club	Source	Date Signed	Seasons Played	Apps	Subs	Gls
Crewe Alex.	Knutsford	04.59	58	1	-	0

DOBING Peter Alan
Manchester, 1 December, 1938 Eu23-7/EF Lge (IF)

League Club	Source	Date Signed	Seasons Played	Apps	Subs	Gls
Blackburn Rov.	Jnrs	12.55	55-60	179	-	88
Manchester C.	Tr	07.61	61-62	82	-	31
Stoke C.	Tr	08.63	63-72	303	4	82

DOBSON Anthony John
Coventry, 5 February, 1969 Eu21-4 (D)

League Club	Source	Date Signed	Seasons Played	Apps	Subs	Gls
Coventry C.	App	07.86	86-90	51	3	1
Blackburn Rov.	Tr	01.91	90-92	36	5	0
Portsmouth	Tr	09.93	93-96	48	5	2
Oxford U.	L	12.94	94	5	0	0
Peterborough U.	L	01.96	95	4	0	0
West Bromwich A.	Tr	08.97	97	6	5	0

DOBSON Brian Ashley
Colchester, 1 March, 1934 (CH)

League Club	Source	Date Signed	Seasons Played	Apps	Subs	Gls
Colchester U.		01.56	55-59	24	-	0

DOBSON Colin
Middlesbrough, 9 May, 1940 Eu23-2 (W)

League Club	Source	Date Signed	Seasons Played	Apps	Subs	Gls
Sheffield Wed.	Jnrs	11.57	61-65	177	0	49
Huddersfield T.	Tr	08.66	66-70	149	6	50
Brighton & H.A.	L	01.72	71	2	2	0
Bristol Rov.	Tr	07.72	72-75	62	0	4

DOBSON George Richard
Chiswick, 24 August, 1949 (W)

League Club	Source	Date Signed	Seasons Played	Apps	Subs	Gls
Brentford	App	08.67	66-69	75	11	10

DOBSON Ian
Hull, 3 October, 1957 (CD)

League Club	Source	Date Signed	Seasons Played	Apps	Subs	Gls
Hull C.	App	10.75	75-79	86	6	7
Hereford U.	Tr	06.80	80-81	41	0	5

DOBSON John Martin
Blackburn, 14 February, 1948 EF Lge/E-5 (M)

League Club	Source	Date Signed	Seasons Played	Apps	Subs	Gls
Bolton W.	Jnrs	07.66				
Burnley	Tr	08.67	67-74	220	4	43
Everton	Tr	08.74	74-78	190	0	29
Burnley	Tr	08.79	79-83	186	0	20
Bury	Tr	03.84	83-85	60	1	4

DOBSON Paul
Hartlepool, 17 December, 1962 (F)

League Club	Source	Date Signed	Seasons Played	Apps	Subs	Gls
Hartlepool U.	Newcastle U. (Jnrs)	11.81	81-82	23	8	8
Hartlepool U.	Horden Colly	12.83	83-85	60	20	24
Torquay U.	Tr	07.86	86-87	63	14	38

League Club	Source	Date Signed	Seasons Played	Apps	Subs	Gls
Doncaster Rov.	Tr	08.88	88	22	2	10
Scarborough	Tr	02.89	88-90	54	7	22
Halifax T.	L	10.90	90	1	0	1
Hereford U.	L	11.90	90	6	0	1
Lincoln C.	Tr	01.91	90-91	13	8	5
Darlington	Tr	08.92	92	4	10	2

DOBSON Robert **Peter**
Frimley, 13 June, 1925 (F)

League Club	Source	Date Signed	Seasons Played	Apps	Subs	Gls
Ipswich T.	Wisbech T.	10.49	49-53	30	-	5

DOBSON Ryan Adam
Wellington, 24 September, 1978 (RB)

League Club	Source	Date Signed	Seasons Played	Apps	Subs	Gls
Chester C.	YT	07.97	97	6	0	0

DOBSON Warren Edward
North Shields, 5 November, 1978 (G)

League Club	Source	Date Signed	Seasons Played	Apps	Subs	Gls
Hartlepool U.	Queens Park R. (YT)	08.97	97	1	0	0

DOCHERTY Bernard
Bellshill, 11 August, 1941 (IF)

League Club	Source	Date Signed	Seasons Played	Apps	Subs	Gls
Notts Co.	Cambuslang	08.64	64	25	-	2

DOCHERTY James
Greenock, 21 April, 1926 (IF)

League Club	Source	Date Signed	Seasons Played	Apps	Subs	Gls
Northampton T.	Glasgow Celtic	07.50	50	1	-	0

DOCHERTY James
Clydebank, 22 April, 1929 (WH)

League Club	Source	Date Signed	Seasons Played	Apps	Subs	Gls
Doncaster Rov.	Airdrieonians	05.51	51	11	-	4
Crewe Alex.	Limerick C.	02.57	56	2	-	0

DOCHERTY James
Broxburn, 8 November, 1956 (IF)

League Club	Source	Date Signed	Seasons Played	Apps	Subs	Gls
Chelsea	East Stirling	03.79	78	2	1	0

DOCHERTY John
Glasgow, 28 February, 1935 (WH)

League Club	Source	Date Signed	Seasons Played	Apps	Subs	Gls
Colchester U.	Hearts	06.63	63-64	77	-	2

DOCHERTY John
Glasgow, 29 April, 1940 (OR)

League Club	Source	Date Signed	Seasons Played	Apps	Subs	Gls
Brentford	St Rochs	07.59	60	17	-	2
Sheffield U.	Tr	03.61	60-65	41	0	9
Brentford	Tr	12.65	65-67	97	0	31
Reading	Tr	02.68	67-69	45	1	7
Brentford	Tr	03.70	70-73	137	4	34

DOCHERTY Michael
Preston, 29 October, 1950 E Yth (FB)

League Club	Source	Date Signed	Seasons Played	Apps	Subs	Gls
Burnley	App	11.67	68-75	149	4	0
Manchester C.	Tr	04.76	75-76	8	0	0
Sunderland	Tr	12.76	76-78	72	1	6

DOCHERTY Peter
Hebburn, 14 February, 1929 (OL)

League Club	Source	Date Signed	Seasons Played	Apps	Subs	Gls
Fulham		09.49				
Darlington	Tr	09.50	50	3	-	1

DOCHERTY Thomas
Penshaw (Dm), 15 April, 1924 (OL)

League Club	Source	Date Signed	Seasons Played	Apps	Subs	Gls
Lincoln C.	Murton Colly	07.47	47-49	45	-	3
Norwich C.	Tr	06.50	50-52	85	-	4
Reading	Tr	07.53	53-54	53	-	2
Newport Co.	Tr	06.55	55-57	108	-	1

DOCHERTY Thomas Henderson
Glasgow, 24 August, 1928 S 'B'/S-25 (WH)

League Club	Source	Date Signed	Seasons Played	Apps	Subs	Gls
Preston N.E.	Glasgow Celtic	11.49	49-57	324	-	5
Arsenal	Tr	08.58	58-60	83	-	1
Chelsea	Tr	09.61	61	4	-	0

DOCKER Ian
Gravesend, 12 September, 1969 (M)

League Club	Source	Date Signed	Seasons Played	Apps	Subs	Gls
Gillingham	YT	09.87	87-90	73	14	3

DOCKER John Barry
Coventry, 25 September, 1947 (F)

League Club	Source	Date Signed	Seasons Played	Apps	Subs	Gls
Coventry C.	Jnrs	08.65				
Torquay U.	L	07.67	67	4	1	0

DODD Alan
Stoke, 20 September, 1953 Eu23-6 (D)

League Club	Source	Date Signed	Seasons Played	Apps	Subs	Gls
Stoke C.	App	10.70	72-82	349	7	3
Wolverhampton W.	Tr	11.82	82-84	88	0	5
Stoke C.	Tr	01.85	84	16	0	0
Port Vale (N/C)	Elfsborg (Swe)	11.86	86	2	0	0

DODD James Edward
Wallasey, 12 December, 1933 (F)

League Club	Source	Date Signed	Seasons Played	Apps	Subs	Gls
Tranmere Rov.	Upton	05.56	56-59	63	-	22

DODD Jason Robert
Bath, 2 November, 1970 Eu21-8 (RB)

League Club	Source	Date Signed	Seasons Played	Apps	Subs	Gls
Southampton	Bath C.	03.89	89-97	215	16	7

DODD William
Bedlington, 30 September, 1936 (F)

League Club	Source	Date Signed	Seasons Played	Apps	Subs	Gls
Burnley	Whitley Bay	02.56				
Workington	Tr	09.58	58	1	-	1

DODD William Dickinson
Chester-le-Street, 25 August, 1933 Died 1982 (WH)

League Club	Source	Date Signed	Seasons Played	Apps	Subs	Gls
Shrewsbury T.	Derby Co. (Am)	08.50	50-54	28	-	1
Southport	Tr	06.57	57-58	70	-	2

DODDS Ephraim (Jock)
Grangemouth, 7 September, 1915 (CF)

League Club	Source	Date Signed	Seasons Played	Apps	Subs	Gls
Huddersfield T.	Medomsley	02.33				
Lincoln C.	Tr	03.33				
Sheffield U.	Tr	05.34	34-38	178	-	114
Blackpool	Tr	03.39	38	12	-	10
Everton	Shamrock Rov.	11.46	46-48	55	-	36
Lincoln C.	Tr	10.48	48-49	60	-	38

DODDS Gerald
Sheffield, 4 January, 1935 (OR)

League Club	Source	Date Signed	Seasons Played	Apps	Subs	Gls
Sheffield U.	Jnrs	02.52				
Chesterfield	Tr	06.55	55	4	-	0
Scunthorpe U.	South Shields	05.59				

DODDS Leslie
Newcastle, 12 October, 1936 E Sch (G)

League Club	Source	Date Signed	Seasons Played	Apps	Subs	Gls
Sunderland	Jnrs	10.53	54-55	6	-	0

DODDS Robert
Gateshead, 1 July, 1923 (WH)

League Club	Source	Date Signed	Seasons Played	Apps	Subs	Gls
Darlington		02.47	46-48	34	-	1

DODDS Thomas Black
South Shields, 20 December, 1918 (IF)

League Club	Source	Date Signed	Seasons Played	Apps	Subs	Gls
Aston Villa	North Shields	01.39	46	1	-	0
Swansea C.	Tr	01.47	46-47	11	-	2

DODDS William
New Cumnock, 5 February, 1969 (F)

League Club	Source	Date Signed	Seasons Played	Apps	Subs	Gls
Chelsea	App	05.86	86-88	0	3	0

DODGE William Charles
Hackney, 10 March, 1937 (WH)

League Club	Source	Date Signed	Seasons Played	Apps	Subs	Gls
Tottenham H.	Eton Manor	10.57	58-59	6	-	0
Crystal Palace	Tr	07.62	62	3	-	0

DODGIN Norman
Gateshead, 1 November, 1921 (WH)

League Club	Source	Date Signed	Seasons Played	Apps	Subs	Gls
Newcastle U.	Whitehall B.C.	08.40	47-49	84	-	1
Reading	Tr	06.50	50	13	-	1
Northampton T.	Tr	09.51	51-52	19	-	1
Exeter C.	Tr	08.53	53-54	33	-	1

DODGIN William
Gateshead, 4 November, 1931 Eu23-1 (CH)

League Club	Source	Date Signed	Seasons Played	Apps	Subs	Gls
Fulham	Southampton (Am)	09.49	51-52	35	-	0
Arsenal	Tr	12.52	52-59	191	-	0
Fulham	Tr	03.61	60-63	69	-	0

DODSON David Alfred
Gravesend, 20 January, 1940 E Yth (OL)

League Club	Source	Date Signed	Seasons Played	Apps	Subs	Gls
Arsenal	Jnrs	11.57				
Swansea C.	Tr	07.59	59-61	30	-	12
Portsmouth	Tr	12.61	61-64	53	-	15
Aldershot	Tr	01.65	64-66	59	0	12

DOHERTY Gary Michael Thomas
Carndonagh, 31 January, 1980 E Yth (F)

League Club	Source	Date Signed	Seasons Played	Apps	Subs	Gls
Luton T.	YT	07.97	97	1	9	0

DOHERTY James Clarkson
Douglas, 31 January, 1957 (F)

League Club	Source	Date Signed	Seasons Played	Apps	Subs	Gls
Notts Co.	Cumnock Jnrs	07.79	79-80	6	2	0

DOHERTY John Herbert
Manchester, 12 March, 1935 (IF)

League Club	Source	Date Signed	Seasons Played	Apps	Subs	Gls
Manchester U.	Jnrs	03.52	52-57	25	-	7
Leicester C.	Tr	10.57	57	12	-	5

DOHERTY John Michael
Ewell, 26 April, 1936 (CF)

League Club	Source	Date Signed	Seasons Played	Apps	Subs	Gls
Fulham	Chelsea (Am)	09.54	56-61	49	-	7
Aldershot	South Coast U. (Aus)	01.65	64-65	18	0	1

DOHERTY Michael
Liverpool, 8 March, 1961 E Semi Pro (F)

League Club	Source	Date Signed	Seasons Played	Apps	Subs	Gls
Reading	Basingstoke T.	10.82	82	23	2	5

DOHERTY Neil
Barrow, 21 February, 1969 (W)

League Club	Source	Date Signed	Seasons Played	Apps	Subs	Gls
Watford	YT	07.87				
Birmingham C.	Barrow	02.94	93-95	15	8	2
Northampton T.	L	02.96	95	3	6	1

DOHERTY Peter Dermont
Magherafelt (NI), 5 June, 1913 Died 1990 NI-16 (IF)

League Club	Source	Date Signed	Seasons Played	Apps	Subs	Gls
Blackpool	Glentoran	11.33	33-35	83	-	28
Manchester C.	Tr	02.36	35-38	119	-	74
Derby Co.	Tr	12.45	46	15	-	7
Huddersfield T.	Tr	12.46	46-48	83	-	33
Doncaster Rov.	Tr	06.49	49-52	103	-	55

DOHERTY Thomas Edward
Bristol, 17 March, 1979 (M)

League Club	Source	Date Signed	Seasons Played	Apps	Subs	Gls
Bristol C.	YT	07.97	97	22	8	2

DOIG Russell
Millport, 17 January, 1964 (W)

League Club	Source	Date Signed	Seasons Played	Apps	Subs	Gls
Leeds U.	East Stirling	07.86	86-87	3	3	0
Peterborough U.	L	10.86	86	7	0	0
Hartlepool U.	Tr	03.88	87-89	22	11	2

DOLAN Andrew
Glasgow, 2 August, 1920 (IF)

League Club	Source	Date Signed	Seasons Played	Apps	Subs	Gls
Bury	Raith Rov.	08.48	48	10	-	2
Accrington St.	Tr	09.49	49	19	-	4

DOLAN Eamonn John
Dagenham, 20 September, 1967 IR Yth/IRu21-5 (F)

League Club	Source	Date Signed	Seasons Played	Apps	Subs	Gls
West Ham U.	App	03.85	86-89	9	6	3
Bristol C.	L	02.89	88	3	0	0
Birmingham C.	Tr	12.90	90-91	6	6	1
Exeter C.	Tr	09.91	91-92	15	11	4

DOLAN Patrick Daniel
Dagenham, 20 September, 1967 IR Yth/IRu21-3 (D)

League Club	Source	Date Signed	Seasons Played	Apps	Subs	Gls
Arsenal	App	07.85				
Walsall	Tr	08.86	86	1	0	0

DOLAN Terence Peter
Bradford, 11 June, 1950 (M)

League Club	Source	Date Signed	Seasons Played	Apps	Subs	Gls
Bradford P.A.	Bradford C. (Am)	04.69	68-69	46	2	0
Huddersfield T.	Tr	10.70	71-75	157	5	14
Bradford C.	Tr	08.76	76-80	191	4	43
Rochdale	Tr	08.81	81	42	1	1

DOLBY Christopher John
Dewsbury, 4 September, 1974 (W)

League Club	Source	Date Signed	Seasons Played	Apps	Subs	Gls
Rotherham U.	YT	08.93	93-94	0	3	0
Bradford C.	Tr	07.95				

DOLBY Peter
Derby, 18 May, 1940 (CH)

League Club	Source	Date Signed	Seasons Played	Apps	Subs	Gls
Shrewsbury T.	Heanor T.	02.60	60-75	303	21	21

DOLBY Tony Christopher
Greenwich, 16 June, 1974 (LM)

League Club	Source	Date Signed	Seasons Played	Apps	Subs	Gls
Millwall	YT	10.91	92-96	38	28	3
Barnet	L	02.94	93	13	3	2

DOLDING Desmond **Leonard**
India, 13 December, 1922 Died 1954 (W)

League Club	Source	Date Signed	Seasons Played	Apps	Subs	Gls
Chelsea	Wealdstone	07.45	46-47	26	-	2
Norwich C.	Tr	07.48	48-49	12	-	1

DOLING Stuart James
Newport (IOW), 28 October, 1972 E Yth (M)

League Club	Source	Date Signed	Seasons Played	Apps	Subs	Gls
Portsmouth	YT	06.90	91-94	20	17	4
Doncaster Rov.	A.F.C. Lymington	10.95	95-96	3	3	0

DOMINEY Barry William
Edmonton, 21 October, 1955 (CD)

League Club	Source	Date Signed	Seasons Played	Apps	Subs	Gls
Colchester U.	Enfield W.M.C.	01.74	73-76	56	15	3

DOMINGUEZ Jose Manuel Martins
Portugal, 16 February, 1974 Portuguese Int (W)

League Club	Source	Date Signed	Seasons Played	Apps	Subs	Gls
Birmingham C.	Benfica (Por)	03.94	93-94	15	20	3
Tottenham H.	Sporting Lisbon (Por)	08.97	97	8	10	2

DONACHIE Daniel James
Manchester, 17 May, 1973 (FB)

League Club	Source	Date Signed	Seasons Played	Apps	Subs	Gls
Carlisle U.	Radcliffe Borough	01.96	95	0	1	0

DONACHIE William
Glasgow, 5 October, 1951 Su23-2/S-35 (LB)

League Club	Source	Date Signed	Seasons Played	Apps	Subs	Gls
Manchester C.	Jnrs	12.68	69-79	347	4	2
Norwich C.	Portland (USA)	09.81	81	11	0	0
Burnley	Portland (USA)	11.82	82-84	60	0	3
Oldham Ath.	Tr	07.84	84-90	158	11	3

DONAGHY Barry
Consett, 21 March, 1956 E Yth (M)

League Club	Source	Date Signed	Seasons Played	Apps	Subs	Gls
West Bromwich A.	App	05.73	73-74	4	2	1
Workington	Tr	12.75	75-76	40	4	3

DONAGHY Malachy (Mal) Martin
Belfast, 13 September, 1957 NIu21-1/NI-91 (CD)

League Club	Source	Date Signed	Seasons Played	Apps	Subs	Gls
Luton T.	Larne T.	06.78	78-88	410	0	16
Manchester U.	Tr	10.88	88-91	76	13	0
Luton T.	L	12.89	89	5	0	0
Chelsea	Tr	08.92	92-93	63	5	3

DONALD Alexander
Kirkliston, 5 June, 1948 (W)

League Club	Source	Date Signed	Seasons Played	Apps	Subs	Gls
Port Vale	Jnrs	10.65	65-67	41	2	0

DONALD Ian Richard
Aberdeen, 28 November, 1951 S Sch (FB)

League Club	Source	Date Signed	Seasons Played	Apps	Subs	Gls
Manchester U.	Jnrs	07.69	72	4	0	0

DONALD Warren Ramsay
Uxbridge, 7 October, 1964 E Sch (M)

League Club	Source	Date Signed	Seasons Played	Apps	Subs	Gls
West Ham U.	App	10.82	83	1	1	0
Northampton T.	L	03.85	84	11	0	2
Northampton T.	Tr	10.85	85-89	169	8	11
Colchester U.	Tr	07.90	92	8	2	0

DONALDSON Andrew
Newcastle, 22 March, 1925 Died 1987 (CF)

League Club	Source	Date Signed	Seasons Played	Apps	Subs	Gls
Newcastle U.	Vickers Armstrong	09.43	46-48	19	-	6
Middlesbrough	Tr	01.49	48-50	21	-	7
Exeter C.	Peterborough U.	09.53	53-54	39	-	16

DONALDSON Brian Leslie
Hove, 3 April, 1936 (OR)

League Club	Source	Date Signed	Seasons Played	Apps	Subs	Gls
Chelsea	Jnrs	07.53				
Swindon T.	Tr	10.57	57	1	-	0

DONALDSON David
Hounslow, 28 December, 1941 (D)

League Club	Source	Date Signed	Seasons Played	Apps	Subs	Gls
Wimbledon	Walton & Hersham	08.74	77-78	61	0	0

DONALDSON David John
Islington, 12 November, 1954 E Sch (RB)

League Club	Source	Date Signed	Seasons Played	Apps	Subs	Gls
Arsenal	App	07.72				
Millwall	Tr	06.73	73-79	215	1	1
Cambridge U.	Tr	02.80	79-83	130	2	0

DONALDSON Frederick Lewis
Stoke, 7 April, 1937 (FB)

League Club	Source	Date Signed	Seasons Played	Apps	Subs	Gls
Port Vale	Jnrs	07.54	54-59	47	-	4
Exeter C.	Tr	08.60	60	36	-	6
Chester C.	Tr	07.61	61	20	-	0

DONALDSON James Dent
South Shields, 11 June, 1927 (WH)

League Club	Source	Date Signed	Seasons Played	Apps	Subs	Gls
Chesterfield	South Shields	11.48	49-50	17	-	4
Newport Co.	Tr	08.51	51-52	36	-	1

DONALDSON Leslie Darcy Robert
Glasgow, 30 July, 1922 Died 1990 (IF)

League Club	Source	Date Signed	Seasons Played	Apps	Subs	Gls
Wrexham	Rhyl	06.50	50-51	30	-	6

DONALDSON O'Neill McKay
Birmingham, 24 November, 1969 (F)

League Club	Source	Date Signed	Seasons Played	Apps	Subs	Gls
Shrewsbury T.	Hinckley T.	11.91	91-93	15	13	4
Doncaster Rov.	Tr	08.94	94	7	2	2
Mansfield T.	L	12.94	94	4	0	6
Sheffield Wed.	Tr	01.95	94-97	4	10	3
Oxford U.	L	01.98	97	6	0	2
Stoke C.	Tr	03.98	97	2	0	0

DONALDSON Robert Stone
South Shields, 26 February, 1921 Died 1990 (D)

League Club	Source	Date Signed	Seasons Played	Apps	Subs	Gls
Newcastle U.		01.43				
Hartlepool U.	Tr	07.47	47-51	131	-	4

DONALDSON William
Wallaceton, 20 January, 1920 Died 1977 (OL)

League Club	Source	Date Signed	Seasons Played	Apps	Subs	Gls
Bradford P.A.	Leith Ath.	05.46	46-50	45	-	6
Mansfield T.	Tr	10.50	50-51	52	-	10

DONCEL-VARCARCEL Antonio
Spain, 31 January, 1967 (CD)

League Club	Source	Date Signed	Seasons Played	Apps	Subs	Gls
Hull C.	Ferrol (Sp)	08.96	96-97	30	8	2

DONE Cyril Charles
Liverpool, 21 October, 1920 Died 1993 (CF)

League Club	Source	Date Signed	Seasons Played	Apps	Subs	Gls
Liverpool	Bootle B.B.	01.38	46-51	93	-	32
Tranmere Rov.	Tr	05.52	52-54	87	-	61
Port Vale	Tr	12.54	54-56	52	-	34

DONEGAL Glenville Paul
Northampton, 20 June, 1969 (F)

League Club	Source	Date Signed	Seasons Played	Apps	Subs	Gls
Northampton T.	YT	08.87	87-89	7	14	3
Maidstone U.	Aylesbury U.	08.91	91	9	5	1

DONIS Georgios
Greece, 22 October, 1969 Greek Int (LW)

League Club	Source	Date Signed	Seasons Played	Apps	Subs	Gls
Blackburn Rov.	Panathanaikos (Gre)	07.96	96	11	11	2

DONN Nigel
Maidstone, 2 March, 1962 (M)

League Club	Source	Date Signed	Seasons Played	Apps	Subs	Gls
Gillingham	App	02.80	80-81	2	1	0
Leyton Orient	Karpalo (Fin)	08.82	82	22	1	2

DONNELLAN Gary
Kensington, 3 July, 1962 (W)

League Club	Source	Date Signed	Seasons Played	Apps	Subs	Gls
Chelsea	App	07.80				
Watford	Tr	11.80				
Reading	Tr	11.81	81-82	33	8	5

DONNELLAN Leo John
Willesden, 19 January, 1965 IRu21-1 (M)

League Club	Source	Date Signed	Seasons Played	Apps	Subs	Gls
Chelsea	App	08.82				
Leyton Orient	L	12.84	84	6	0	0
Fulham	Tr	08.85	85-89	54	25	4

DONNELLY Andrew
Lanark, 1 May, 1943 (G)

League Club	Source	Date Signed	Seasons Played	Apps	Subs	Gls
Millwall	Clyde	05.63				
Torquay U.	Weymouth	08.67	67-71	160	0	0

DONNELLY Darren Charles
Liverpool, 28 December, 1971 (F)

League Club	Source	Date Signed	Seasons Played	Apps	Subs	Gls
Blackburn Rov.	YT	06.90	90	1	1	0
Chester C.	Tr	08.93	93	0	9	0

DONNELLY James
Cork (Ire), 6 May, 1919 (IF)

League Club	Source	Date Signed	Seasons Played	Apps	Subs	Gls
Accrington St.	Sligo Rov.	08.51	51	4	-	1

DONNELLY John
Glasgow, 8 March, 1961 (W)

League Club	Source	Date Signed	Seasons Played	Apps	Subs	Gls
Leeds U.	Dumbarton	03.83	82-84	36	4	4

DONNELLY John
Broxburn, 17 December, 1936 (FB)

League Club	Source	Date Signed	Seasons Played	Apps	Subs	Gls
Preston N.E.	Glasgow Celtic	04.62	62-66	56	1	1

DONNELLY Mark Paul
Leeds, 22 December, 1979 (M)

League Club	Source	Date Signed	Seasons Played	Apps	Subs	Gls
Doncaster Rov.	YT	•	96-97	8	3	1

DONNELLY Paul Anthony
Liverpool, 23 December, 1971 (W)

League Club	Source	Date Signed	Seasons Played	Apps	Subs	Gls
Halifax T.	YT	03.90	88-90	9	4	0

DONNELLY Peter
Hull, 22 September, 1936 (CF)

League Club	Source	Date Signed	Seasons Played	Apps	Subs	Gls
Doncaster Rov.	Jnrs	03.54	53-56	6	-	1
Scunthorpe U.	Tr	07.58	58-59	39	-	19
Cardiff C.	Tr	06.60	60-61	30	-	8
Swansea C.	Tr	10.61	61	16	-	3
Brighton & H.A.	Tr	07.62	62-64	56	-	13
Bradford C.	Tr	03.65	64-65	13	0	5

DONNELLY Peter James
Chester, 11 May, 1965 (M)

League Club	Source	Date Signed	Seasons Played	Apps	Subs	Gls
Chester C. (N/C)	YT	08.83	83	1	0	0

DONOVAN Daniel (Don) Christopher
Cork (Ire), 23 December, 1929 IR-5 (FB)

League Club	Source	Date Signed	Seasons Played	Apps	Subs	Gls
Everton	Dalymount Rov.	05.49	51-57	179	-	2
Grimsby T.	Tr	08.58	58-63	238	-	1

DONOVAN Francis James
Pembroke, 21 February, 1919 W Amat (OR)

League Club	Source	Date Signed	Seasons Played	Apps	Subs	Gls
Swansea C.	Pembroke Borough	05.50	50	15	-	2

DONOVAN Kevin
Halifax, 17 December, 1971 (RM)

League Club	Source	Date Signed	Seasons Played	Apps	Subs	Gls
Huddersfield T.	YT	10.89	89-92	11	9	1
Halifax T.	L	02.92	91	6	0	0
West Bromwich A.	Tr	10.92	92-96	139	29	19
Grimsby T.	Tr	07.97	97	46	0	16

DONOVAN Terence Christopher
Liverpool, 27 February, 1958 IRu21-1/IR-1 (F)

League Club	Source	Date Signed	Seasons Played	Apps	Subs	Gls
Grimsby T.	Louth U.	08.76	76-78	52	12	23
Aston Villa	Tr	09.79	79-81	17	0	6
Oxford U.	L	02.83	82	3	0	0
Burnley	Tr	02.83	82-83	13	2	6
Rotherham U.	Tr	09.83	83-84	9	4	0
Blackpool	L	10.84	84	2	0	0

DONOWA Brian **Louie**
Ipswich, 24 September, 1964 Eu21-3 (W)

League Club	Source	Date Signed	Seasons Played	Apps	Subs	Gls
Norwich C.	App	09.82	82-85	56	6	11
Stoke C.	L	12.85	85	4	0	1
Ipswich T.	Willem II Tilburg (Neth)	08.89	89	17	6	1
Bristol C.	Tr	08.90	90	11	13	3
Birmingham C.	Tr	08.91	91-92	78	38	18
Burnley	L	01.93	92	4	0	0
Shrewsbury T.	L	01.94	93	4	0	0
Walsall	L	10.96	96	6	0	1
Peterborough U.	Tr	12.96	96	16	6	1
Walsall	Tr	08.97	97	5	1	0

DOOLAN John
Liverpool, 7 May, 1974 (M)

League Club	Source	Date Signed	Seasons Played	Apps	Subs	Gls
Everton	YT	06.92				
Mansfield T.	Tr	09.94	94-97	128	3	10
Barnet	Tr	01.98	97	17	0	0

DOOLAN John
Liverpool, 10 November, 1968 (RB/M)

League Club	Source	Date Signed	Seasons Played	Apps	Subs	Gls
Wigan Ath.	Knowsley U.	03.92	91-95	29	9	1

DOOLEY Derek
Sheffield, 13 December, 1929 (CF)

League Club	Source	Date Signed	Seasons Played	Apps	Subs	Gls
Lincoln C. (Am)	Jnrs	09.46	46	2	-	2
Sheffield Wed.	Tr	06.47	49-52	61	-	62

DOOLEY George
Chesterfield, 29 December, 1922 (IF)

League Club	Source	Date Signed	Seasons Played	Apps	Subs	Gls
Chesterfield	Parkhouse Colly	06.45				
Halifax T.	Tr	12.46	46	11	-	2

DOONAN Thomas
West Calder, 5 October, 1922 (CF)

League Club	Source	Date Signed	Seasons Played	Apps	Subs	Gls
Bradford C.	Albion Rov.	06.49	49	13	-	7
Tranmere Rov.	Tr	07.50	50	4	-	2

DOONER Gary James
St Helens, 14 September, 1970 (W)

League Club	Source	Date Signed	Seasons Played	Apps	Subs	Gls
Stockport Co.	YT	•	88	1	0	0

DORAN Robert Rennie
Carlisle, 26 December, 1933 (CH)

League Club	Source	Date Signed	Seasons Played	Apps	Subs	Gls
Carlisle U.		10.52	53-61	107	-	0

DORAN Terence
Jarrow, 2 April, 1940

League Club	Source	Date Signed	Seasons Played	Apps	Subs	Gls
Gateshead (Am)	St. Mary's B.C.	09.59	59	1	-	0

DORE Leslie **Charles** Albert
Portsmouth, 22 January, 1931 (G)

League Club	Source	Date Signed	Seasons Played	Apps	Subs	Gls
Portsmouth	Fleetlands B.C.	05.50	51-53	18	-	0

DORIGO Anthony Robert
Australia, 31 December, 1965 Eu21-11/E'B'/E-15 (LB)

League Club	Source	Date Signed	Seasons Played	Apps	Subs	Gls
Aston Villa	App	07.83	83-86	106	5	1
Chelsea	Tr	05.87	87-90	146	0	11
Leeds U.	Tr	05.91	91-96	168	3	5

DORLING George John
Edmonton, 27 July, 1918 Died 1987 (FB)

League Club	Source	Date Signed	Seasons Played	Apps	Subs	Gls
Tottenham H.	Jnrs	03.46				
Gillingham	Tr	05.47	50	10	-	0

DORMAN Donald
Birmingham, 18 September, 1922 Died 1997 (IF/WH)

League Club	Source	Date Signed	Seasons Played	Apps	Subs	Gls
Birmingham C.	Jnrs	05.46	46-51	59	-	4
Coventry C.	Tr	09.51	51-54	90	-	29
Walsall	Tr	10.54	54-56	116	-	34

DORNAN Andrew
Aberdeen, 19 August, 1961 S Sch/S Yth (RB)

League Club	Source	Date Signed	Seasons Played	Apps	Subs	Gls
Walsall	Motherwell	08.86	86-89	117	1	1

DORNAN Peter
Belfast, 30 June, 1953 (M)

League Club	Source	Date Signed	Seasons Played	Apps	Subs	Gls
Sheffield U.	Linfield	12.76	76	1	2	0
Swindon T.	Linfield	02.79	78	0	1	0

DORNER Mario
Baden, Austria, 21 March, 1970 (F)

League Club	Source	Date Signed	Seasons Played	Apps	Subs	Gls
Darlington	Motherwell	10.97	97	25	2	10

DORNEY Alan John
Bermondsey, 18 May, 1947 (CD)

League Club	Source	Date Signed	Seasons Played	Apps	Subs	Gls
Millwall	Jnrs	05.65	68-76	249	3	1

DORSETT Richard (Dickie)
Brownhills, 3 December, 1919 (IF/WH)

League Club	Source	Date Signed	Seasons Played	Apps	Subs	Gls
Wolverhampton W.	Jnrs	12.36	37-46	46	-	32
Aston Villa	Tr	09.46	46-52	257	-	32

DOUGALL Cornelius (Neil)
Falkirk, 7 November, 1921 S-1 (IF)

League Club	Source	Date Signed	Seasons Played	Apps	Subs	Gls
Burnley	Jnrs	03.40				
Birmingham C.	Tr	10.45	46-48	93	-	15
Plymouth Arg.	Tr	03.49	48-58	274	-	26

DOUGAL James
Denny, 3 October, 1913 S-1 (IF)

League Club	Source	Date Signed	Seasons Played	Apps	Subs	Gls
Preston N.E.	Falkirk	01.34	33-46	171	-	51
Carlisle U.	Tr	10.46	46-48	70	-	15
Halifax T.	Tr	10.48	48	22	-	2

DOUGAL John (Jack)
Falkirk, 7 August, 1934 E Amat (CH)

League Club	Source	Date Signed	Seasons Played	Apps	Subs	Gls
Halifax T. (Am)	Pegasus	05.56	56	2	-	0

DOUGALL Thomas
Wishaw, 17 May, 1921 Died 1997 (OR)

League Club	Source	Date Signed	Seasons Played	Apps	Subs	Gls
Coventry C.		09.45				
Brentford	Tr	08.47	47	2	-	0
Sunderland	Tr	11.48	48	3	-	0

DOUGALL William
Falkirk, 30 October, 1923 (WH)

League Club	Source	Date Signed	Seasons Played	Apps	Subs	Gls
Preston N.E.	Glasgow Rangers	12.47	47-48	22	-	2
Barnsley	Tr	08.52	52	21	-	0

DOUGAN Alexander Derek
Belfast, 20 January, 1938 NI Sch/NI 'B'/NI-43 (CF)

League Club	Source	Date Signed	Seasons Played	Apps	Subs	Gls
Portsmouth	Distillery	08.57	57-58	33	-	9
Blackburn Rov.	Tr	03.59	58-60	59	-	26
Aston Villa	Tr	08.61	61-62	51	-	19
Peterborough U.	Tr	06.63	63-64	77	-	38
Leicester C.	Tr	05.65	65-66	68	0	35
Wolverhampton W.	Tr	03.67	66-74	244	14	95

DOUGAN George
Glasgow, 22 March, 1939 (WH)

League Club	Source	Date Signed	Seasons Played	Apps	Subs	Gls
Ipswich T.	Yiewsley	03.63	62-63	17	-	0

DOUGAN John McKechnie
Glasgow, 12 January, 1931 Died 1995 (IF)

League Club	Source	Date Signed	Seasons Played	Apps	Subs	Gls
Brighton & H.A.	Bellshill Ath.	12.51				
Torquay U.	Tr	02.54	53-54	20	-	3

DOUGAN Maxwell Spalding
Stoneyburn, 23 May, 1938 S Amat (D)

League Club	Source	Date Signed	Seasons Played	Apps	Subs	Gls
Leicester C.	Queens Park	09.63	63-66	9	0	0
Luton T.	Tr	12.66	66-69	117	1	0

DOUGHERTY Paul
Leamington, 12 May, 1966 (M)

League Club	Source	Date Signed	Seasons Played	Apps	Subs	Gls
Wolverhampton W.	App	05.84	83-86	24	17	3
Torquay U.	L	02.85	84	5	0	0

DOUGHERTY Victor
Glasgow, 17 January, 1955 (FB)

League Club	Source	Date Signed	Seasons Played	Apps	Subs	Gls
Bury	App	01.73	72	9	0	0

DOUGHTY Eric
Radstock, 9 April, 1932 (LB)

League Club	Source	Date Signed	Seasons Played	Apps	Subs	Gls
Arsenal	Peasedown	05.51				
Plymouth Arg.	Tr	07.58	58	1	-	0

DOUGLAS Bryan
Blackburn, 27 May, 1934 Eu23-5/E 'B'/EF Lge/E-36 (OR)

League Club	Source	Date Signed	Seasons Played	Apps	Subs	Gls
Blackburn Rov.	Jnrs	04.52	54-68	438	0	100

DOUGLAS Colin Francis
Kilmarnock, 9 September, 1962 (D)

League Club	Source	Date Signed	Seasons Played	Apps	Subs	Gls
Doncaster Rov.	Glasgow Celtic	11.81	81-85	202	10	48
Rotherham U.	Tr	07.86	86-87	82	1	4
Doncaster Rov.	Tr	08.88	88-92	182	10	5

DOUGLAS James Stewart
Sunderland, 16 September, 1941 (CF)

League Club	Source	Date Signed	Seasons Played	Apps	Subs	Gls
Hartlepool U (Am)	Evenwood T.	10.62	62	13	-	4

DOUGLAS John
Stockton, 13 March, 1961 (F)

League Club	Source	Date Signed	Seasons Played	Apps	Subs	Gls
Darlington (N/C)	Stockton	01.86	85	3	0	0

DOUGLAS John Stuart
Hartlepool, 1 December, 1917 (WH)

League Club	Source	Date Signed	Seasons Played	Apps	Subs	Gls
Hartlepool U. (Am)	Trimdon Grange	09.38	38	5	-	0
Middlesbrough	Tr	09.45	46	2	-	0
Hartlepool U.	Tr	11.48	48-49	27	-	1

DOUGLAS Patrick George
Baschurch, 17 September, 1951 (M)

League Club	Source	Date Signed	Seasons Played	Apps	Subs	Gls
Shrewsbury T.	App	07.69	68	12	1	1

DOUGLAS Stuart Anthony
Enfield, 9 April, 1978 (M)

League Club	Source	Date Signed	Seasons Played	Apps	Subs	Gls
Luton T.	YT	05.96	95-97	10	24	2

DOUGLASS Norman
Sunderland, 14 May, 1930 (FB)

League Club	Source	Date Signed	Seasons Played	Apps	Subs	Gls
Chelsea	Crook T.	03.52				
Exeter C.	Tr	06.53	53-54	63	-	0

DOVE Henry William
Stepney, 11 March, 1932 (CH)

League Club	Source	Date Signed	Seasons Played	Apps	Subs	Gls
Arsenal	Essex Co. Cadets	08.50				
Millwall	Tr	04.58	58	7	-	0

DOVEY Alan Raymond
Stepney, 18 July, 1952 (G)

League Club	Source	Date Signed	Seasons Played	Apps	Subs	Gls
Chelsea	App	07.69				
Brighton & H.A.	Tr	03.71	70-72	6	0	0

DOW Andrew James
Dundee, 7 February, 1973 Su21-3 (LB)

League Club	Source	Date Signed	Seasons Played	Apps	Subs	Gls
Chelsea	Dundee	07.93	93-95	14	1	0
Bradford C.	L	10.94	94	5	0	0

DOW David
Manchester, 10 June, 1947 (CH)

League Club	Source	Date Signed	Seasons Played	Apps	Subs	Gls
Rochdale (Am)	Avorton	02.66	66-67	8	0	0

DOWD Henry (Harry) William
Salford, 4 July, 1938 (G)

League Club	Source	Date Signed	Seasons Played	Apps	Subs	Gls
Manchester C.	Blackley I.C.I.	07.60	61-69	181	0	1
Stoke C.	L	10.69	69	3	0	0
Oldham Ath.	Tr	12.70	70-73	121	0	0

DOWD Hugh Oliver
Lurgan (NI), 19 May, 1951 NI-3 (CD)

League Club	Source	Date Signed	Seasons Played	Apps	Subs	Gls
Sheffield Wed.	Glenavon	07.74	74-78	110	2	0
Doncaster Rov.	Tr	08.79	79-82	94	0	3

DOWE Jens
Germany, 1 June, 1968 (M)

League Club	Source	Date Signed	Seasons Played	Apps	Subs	Gls
Wolverhampton W. (L)	S.V. Hamburg (Ger)	10.96	96	5	3	0

DOWELL Wayne Anthony
Easington, 28 December, 1973 (LB)

League Club	Source	Date Signed	Seasons Played	Apps	Subs	Gls
Burnley	YT	03.93	94-95	6	0	0
Carlisle U.	L	03.96	95	2	5	0
Rochdale	Tr	07.96	96	6	1	0
Doncaster Rov.	Tr	08.97	97	1	0	0

DOWEY Walter Leslie
Lockton, 12 June, 1923 (LB)

League Club	Source	Date Signed	Seasons Played	Apps	Subs	Gls
Crewe Alex.		04.45	47-48	15	-	0

DOWIE Iain
Hatfield, 9 January, 1965 NIu21-1/NIu23-1/NI-49 (F)

League Club	Source	Date Signed	Seasons Played	Apps	Subs	Gls
Luton T.	Hendon	12.88	88-90	53	13	15
Fulham	L	09.89	89	5	0	1
West Ham U.	Tr	03.91	90	12	0	4
Southampton	Tr	08.91	91-94	115	7	30
Crystal Palace	Tr	01.95	94-95	19	0	6
West Ham U.	Tr	09.95	95-97	58	10	8
Queens Park R.	Tr	01.98	97	9	2	1

DOWIE John
Hamilton, 12 December, 1955 (M)

League Club	Source	Date Signed	Seasons Played	Apps	Subs	Gls
Fulham	App	05.73	73-76	32	5	2
Doncaster Rov.	Glasgow Celtic	07.79	79-80	21	0	0

DOWKER Thomas
Liverpool, 7 November, 1922 (OL)

League Club	Source	Date Signed	Seasons Played	Apps	Subs	Gls
Oldham Ath.	South Liverpool	07.47	47	1	-	0

DOWLER Michael
Caldicot, 12 October, 1957 W Sch (G)

League Club	Source	Date Signed	Seasons Played	Apps	Subs	Gls
Newport Co.	Hereford U. (App)	10.75	75-80	19	0	0

DOWLING Michael Leslie
Bodmin, 3 October, 1952 (FB)

League Club	Source	Date Signed	Seasons Played	Apps	Subs	Gls
Plymouth Arg.	App	10.70	69-73	27	4	0

DOWMAN Stephen John
Ilford, 15 April, 1958 (CD)

League Club	Source	Date Signed	Seasons Played	Apps	Subs	Gls
Colchester U.	App	04.76	76-79	150	4	21
Wrexham	Tr	07.80	80-82	87	0	2
Charlton Ath.	Tr	08.83	83-84	60	1	5
Newport Co.	Tr	08.85	85	9	0	1
Cambridge U.	Tr	10.85	85-86	45	0	3

DOWN David Frederick
Bristol, 7 July, 1948 (CF)

League Club	Source	Date Signed	Seasons Played	Apps	Subs	Gls
Bristol C.	App	09.65	66-67	6	1	3
Bradford P.A.	Tr	10.67	67-68	39	0	7
Oldham Ath.	Tr	09.68	68	9	0	1
Swindon T.	Tr	08.69	69-70	1	1	0

DOWN William Frederick
Bristol, 8 November, 1963 (D)

League Club	Source	Date Signed	Seasons Played	Apps	Subs	Gls
Bristol C.	App	10.81	81	1	0	0

DOWNES Christopher Bryan
Sheffield, 17 January, 1969 (FB/M)

League Club	Source	Date Signed	Seasons Played	Apps	Subs	Gls
Sheffield U.	YT	06.87	88	2	0	0
Scarborough	L	03.88	87	2	0	0
Stockport Co.	Tr	08.89	89	10	1	1
Crewe Alex. (N/C)	Tr	08.91	91	1	1	0

DOWNES Eric
Wigan, 25 August, 1926 (CH)

League Club	Source	Date Signed	Seasons Played	Apps	Subs	Gls
Rochdale	Chester C. (Am)	05.49	50-53	54	-	0

DOWNES Robert David
Bloxwich, 18 August, 1949 (W)

League Club	Source	Date Signed	Seasons Played	Apps	Subs	Gls
West Bromwich A.	Jnrs	08.66				
Peterborough U.	Tr	09.67	67-68	23	3	3
Rochdale	Tr	08.69	69-73	164	10	10
Watford	Tr	05.74	74-79	192	7	19
Barnsley	Tr	03.80	79-80	43	0	1
Blackpool	Tr	07.82	82-83	27	1	3

DOWNES Steven Fleming
Leeds, 2 December, 1949 (F)

League Club	Source	Date Signed	Seasons Played	Apps	Subs	Gls
Rotherham U.	Leeds M.D.B.C.	04.67	67-69	54	5	18
Sheffield Wed.	Tr	12.69	69-71	26	4	4
Chesterfield	Tr	08.72	72-73	37	4	11
Halifax T.	Tr	07.74	74-75	38	12	12
Blackburn Rov.	L	03.76	75	6	0	0

DOWNES Walter John
Hammersmith, 9 June, 1961 (M)

League Club	Source	Date Signed	Seasons Played	Apps	Subs	Gls
Wimbledon	App	01.79	78-86	194	14	14
Newport Co.	L	12.87	87	4	0	2
Sheffield U.	Tr	02.88	87	6	3	1

DOWNIE John Dennis
Lanark, 19 July, 1925 (IF)

League Club	Source	Date Signed	Seasons Played	Apps	Subs	Gls
Bradford P.A.	Lanark A.T.C.	12.44	46-48	86	-	33
Manchester U.	Tr	03.49	48-52	110	-	35
Luton T.	Tr	08.53	53	26	-	12
Hull C.	Tr	07.54	54	27	-	5
Mansfield T.	Wisbech T.	10.58	58	18	-	4
Darlington	Tr	05.59	59	15	-	2

DOWNIE Mitchell
Irvine, 9 February, 1923 (G)

League Club	Source	Date Signed	Seasons Played	Apps	Subs	Gls
Bradford P.A.	Airdrieonians	08.50	50-53	156	-	0
Lincoln C.	Tr	05.54	54-58	157	-	0
Bradford C.	Goole T.	09.59	59-62	134	-	0
Doncaster Rov.	Tr	09.63	63	7	-	0

DOWNING David William
Bideford, 6 October, 1969 (W)

League Club	Source	Date Signed	Seasons Played	Apps	Subs	Gls
York C.	YT	●	87	1	0	0

DOWNING Derrick Graham
Doncaster, 3 November, 1945 (W)

League Club	Source	Date Signed	Seasons Played	Apps	Subs	Gls
Middlesbrough	Frickley Colly	02.65	65-71	172	10	39
Leyton Orient	Tr	05.72	72-74	100	4	12
York C.	Tr	07.75	75-76	44	3	2
Hartlepool U.	Tr	07.77	77	40	0	4

DOWNING Keith Gordon
Oldbury, 23 July, 1965 (M)

League Club	Source	Date Signed	Seasons Played	Apps	Subs	Gls
Notts Co.	Mile Oak Rov.	05.84	84-86	23	0	1
Wolverhampton W.	Tr	07.87	87-92	169	22	8
Birmingham C.	Tr	07.93	93	1	0	0
Stoke C.	Tr	08.94	94	16	0	0
Cardiff C.	Tr	08.95	95	3	1	0
Hereford U.	Tr	09.95	95-96	45	0	0

DOWNS David
Glasgow, 7 March, 1934 Died 1978 (LB)

League Club	Source	Date Signed	Seasons Played	Apps	Subs	Gls
Plymouth Arg.		11.57				
Torquay U.	Tr	07.59	59	3	-	0

DOWNS Gregory
Nottingham, 13 December, 1958 (LB)

League Club	Source	Date Signed	Seasons Played	Apps	Subs	Gls
Norwich C.	App	12.76	77-84	162	7	7
Torquay U.	L	11.77	77	1	0	1
Coventry C.	Tr	07.85	85-89	142	4	4
Birmingham C.	Tr	07.90	90	16	1	0
Hereford U.	Tr	06.91	91-94	105	3	2

DOWNS Ronald Henry
Southwark, 27 August, 1932 (W)

League Club	Source	Date Signed	Seasons Played	Apps	Subs	Gls
Crystal Palace	Grove U.	12.52	52-53	23	-	2

DOWNSBOROUGH Peter
Halifax, 13 September, 1943 (G)

League Club	Source	Date Signed	Seasons Played	Apps	Subs	Gls
Halifax T.	Jnrs	09.60	59-64	148	-	0
Swindon T.	Tr	08.65	65-72	274	0	0
Brighton & H.A.	L	08.73	73	3	0	0
Bradford C.	Tr	11.73	73-78	225	0	0

DOWSETT Gilbert (Dickie) James
Chelmsford, 3 July, 1931 (CF)

League Club	Source	Date Signed	Seasons Played	Apps	Subs	Gls
Tottenham H.	Sudbury T.	05.52	54	1	-	1
Southend U.	Tr	05.55	55	20	-	4
Southampton	Tr	07.56	56	2	-	0
Bournemouth	Tr	06.57	57-62	169	-	79
Crystal Palace	Tr	11.62	62-64	54	-	22

DOWSON Alan Paul
Gateshead, 17 June, 1970 (LB)

League Club	Source	Date Signed	Seasons Played	Apps	Subs	Gls
Millwall	YT	05.88	90	1	0	0
Fulham	L	01.90	89	4	0	0
Bradford C.	Tr	07.91	91	16	2	0
Darlington	Tr	08.92	92	30	2	0

DOWSON John Simpson
Ashington, 18 September, 1926 Died 1989 (OR)

League Club	Source	Date Signed	Seasons Played	Apps	Subs	Gls
Manchester C.		03.50				
Darlington	Peterborough U.	06.52	52-53	65	-	11

DOYLE John **Alexander (Ally)**
Limavady (NI), 25 October, 1949 (FB)

League Club	Source	Date Signed	Seasons Played	Apps	Subs	Gls
Oldham Ath.	Coleraine	10.66	67-68	31	2	0

DOYLE Joseph **Brian**
Salford, 15 July, 1930 Died 1992 (FB)

League Club	Source	Date Signed	Seasons Played	Apps	Subs	Gls
Stoke C.	Lostock Gralam	03.51	52	17	-	0
Exeter C.	Tr	04.54	54-56	100	-	0
Bristol Rov.	Tr	08.57	57-59	43	-	1

DOYLE Ian Patrick
Torquay, 27 February, 1959 (W)

League Club	Source	Date Signed	Seasons Played	Apps	Subs	Gls
Bristol C.	Barnstaple	12.78	79-80	2	1	0

DOYLE Jeffrey Noel
Dublin, 25 February, 1967 (M)

League Club	Source	Date Signed	Seasons Played	Apps	Subs	Gls
Coventry C.	App	02.85				
Peterborough U.	Tr	08.86	86	13	1	0

DOYLE John Joseph
Oxford, 8 February, 1960 (FB)

League Club	Source	Date Signed	Seasons Played	Apps	Subs	Gls
Oxford U.	App	02.78	77-81	66	0	0
Torquay U.	Tr	08.82	82	40	1	3

DOYLE Robert **Leslie**
Liverpool, 28 June, 1927 (D)

League Club	Source	Date Signed	Seasons Played	Apps	Subs	Gls
Everton	Jnrs	05.45				
Exeter C.	Tr	08.49	49-54	82	-	0

DOYLE Maurice
Ellesmere Port, 17 October, 1969 (M)

League Club	Source	Date Signed	Seasons Played	Apps	Subs	Gls
Crewe Alex.	YT	07.88	87-88	6	2	2
Queens Park R.	Tr	04.89	92-93	6	0	0
Crewe Alex.	L	01.91	90	6	1	2
Millwall	Tr	05.95	95-97	42	24	1

DOYLE Michael
Manchester, 25 November, 1946 Eu23-8/EF Lge/E-5 (CD)

League Club	Source	Date Signed	Seasons Played	Apps	Subs	Gls
Manchester C.	App	05.64	64-77	441	7	32
Stoke C.	Tr	06.78	78-81	115	0	5
Bolton W.	Tr	01.82	81-82	40	0	2
Rochdale	Tr	08.83	83	24	0	1

DOYLE Robert
Dumbarton, 27 December, 1953 (M)

League Club	Source	Date Signed	Seasons Played	Apps	Subs	Gls
Barnsley	Jnrs	12.72	72-75	148	1	16
Peterborough U.	Tr	07.76	76-78	130	0	10
Blackpool	Tr	07.79	79-80	47	2	2
Portsmouth	Tr	12.80	80-85	169	8	16
Hull C.	Tr	08.85	85-86	43	0	2

DOYLE Stephen Charles
Neath, 2 June, 1958 W Yth/Wu21-2 (M)

League Club	Source	Date Signed	Seasons Played	Apps	Subs	Gls
Preston N.E.	App	06.75	74-81	178	19	8
Huddersfield T.	Tr	09.82	82-86	158	3	6
Sunderland	Tr	09.86	86-88	99	1	2
Hull C.	Tr	08.89	89-90	47	0	2
Rochdale	Tr	11.90	90-93	115	6	1

DOZZELL Jason Irvin Winans
Ipswich, 9 December, 1967 E Yth/Eu21-9 (M)

League Club	Source	Date Signed	Seasons Played	Apps	Subs	Gls
Ipswich T.	App	12.84	83-92	312	20	52
Tottenham H.	Tr	08.93	93-96	68	16	13
Ipswich T. (N/C)	Tr	10.97	97	8	0	1
Northampton T. (N/C)	Tr	12.97	97	18	3	4

DRAKE Kenneth Lawrence
Skipton, 17 February, 1922 (CH)

League Club	Source	Date Signed	Seasons Played	Apps	Subs	Gls
Halifax T.		01.47	46-51	132	-	0

DRAKE Leonard George
Dorchester, 26 July, 1937 (CF)

League Club	Source	Date Signed	Seasons Played	Apps	Subs	Gls
Bristol Rov.	Dorchester T.	08.57	58-59	8	-	0

DRAKE Raymond Bradwell
Stockport, 24 October, 1934 (CF)

League Club	Source	Date Signed	Seasons Played	Apps	Subs	Gls
Stockport Co.	Bramhall	03.55	56-57	23	-	19

DRAKE Robert James
Southgate, 7 September, 1943 (FB)

League Club	Source	Date Signed	Seasons Played	Apps	Subs	Gls
Fulham	Chelsea (Am)	12.61	63-67	15	0	0

DRAKE Stephen
Goole, 27 August, 1948 (G)

League Club	Source	Date Signed	Seasons Played	Apps	Subs	Gls
Huddersfield T.	Leeds U. (Am)	06.66				
Scunthorpe U.	Tr	07.67	67-69	23	0	0

DRAPER Derek
Swansea, 11 May, 1943 Wu23-1 (M)

League Club	Source	Date Signed	Seasons Played	Apps	Subs	Gls
Swansea C.	Jnrs	05.62	62-65	61	0	10
Derby Co.	Tr	04.66	66	8	0	1
Bradford P.A.	Tr	09.67	67-68	60	3	9
Chester C.	Tr	01.69	68-76	316	6	54

DRAPER Mark Andrew
Long Eaton, 11 November, 1970 Eu21-3 (M)

League Club	Source	Date Signed	Seasons Played	Apps	Subs	Gls
Notts Co.	YT	12.88	88-93	206	16	40
Leicester C.	Tr	07.94	94	39	0	5
Aston Villa	Tr	07.95	95-97	95	1	5

DRAPER Richard Walter William
Leamington, 26 September, 1932 (CF)

League Club	Source	Date Signed	Seasons Played	Apps	Subs	Gls
Northampton T.	Lockheed Leamington	06.55	55-56	49	-	20

DREWERY Michael Stephen
Snettisham, 16 January, 1949 (G)

League Club	Source	Date Signed	Seasons Played	Apps	Subs	Gls
Peterborough U.	Snettisham	07.67	68-73	209	0	0

DREYER John Brian
Alnwick, 11 June, 1963 (CD)

League Club	Source	Date Signed	Seasons Played	Apps	Subs	Gls
Oxford U.	Wallingford T.	01.85	86-87	57	3	2
Torquay U.	L	12.85	85	5	0	0
Fulham	L	03.86	85	12	0	2
Luton T.	Tr	06.88	88-93	212	2	13
Stoke C.	Tr	07.94	94-96	32	17	3
Bolton W.	L	03.95	94	1	1	0
Bradford C.	Tr	11.96	96-97	42	3	1

DRING Raymond
Lincoln, 13 February, 1924 E Sch (G)

League Club	Source	Date Signed	Seasons Played	Apps	Subs	Gls
Huddersfield T. (Am)		06.47	47	4	-	0

DRINKELL Kevin Smith
Grimsby, 18 June, 1960 (F)

League Club	Source	Date Signed	Seasons Played	Apps	Subs	Gls
Grimsby T.	App	06.78	76-84	242	30	89
Norwich C.	Tr	08.85	85-87	121	0	50
Coventry C.	Glasgow Rangers	10.89	89-91	34	7	5
Birmingham C.	L	10.91	91	5	0	2

DRINKWATER Charles John
Willesden, 25 June, 1914 Died 1998 (OL)

League Club	Source	Date Signed	Seasons Played	Apps	Subs	Gls
Aston Villa	Walthamstow Ave.	11.35	35	2	-	1
Charlton Ath.	Tr	07.38	38	3	-	0
Watford	Tr	01.45	46	1	-	0

DRINKWATER James Arthur
Northwich, 10 February, 1918 Died 1996 (FB)

League Club	Source	Date Signed	Seasons Played	Apps	Subs	Gls
Torquay U.	St Mirren	06.52	52-53	67	-	1

DRINKWATER Raymond
Jarrow, 18 May, 1931 (G)

League Club	Source	Date Signed	Seasons Played	Apps	Subs	Gls
Portsmouth	Guildford C.	11.55	56	8	-	0
Queens Park R.	Tr	02.58	57-62	199	-	0

DRISCOLL Andrew
Staines, 21 October, 1971 (RW)

League Club	Source	Date Signed	Seasons Played	Apps	Subs	Gls
Brentford	YT	03.90	88-91	10	4	2

DRIVER Allenby
Blackwell (Dy), 29 September, 1918 (IF)

League Club	Source	Date Signed	Seasons Played	Apps	Subs	Gls
Sheffield Wed.	Mansfield Shoes	04.36	37-38	6	-	3
Luton T.	Tr	10.46	46-47	41	-	13
Norwich C.	Tr	01.48	47-49	49	-	19
Ipswich T.	Tr	01.50	49-51	86	-	25
Walsall	Tr	07.52	52	26	-	2

DRIVER Philip Anthony
Huddersfield, 10 August, 1959 (W)

League Club	Source	Date Signed	Seasons Played	Apps	Subs	Gls
Wimbledon	Bedford T.	12.78	78-80	7	9	3
Chelsea	Tr	09.80	80-82	25	19	4
Wimbledon	Tr	07.83	83-84	2	2	0

DROY Michael Robert
Highbury, 7 May, 1951 (CD)

League Club	Source	Date Signed	Seasons Played	Apps	Subs	Gls
Chelsea	Slough T.	09.70	70-84	263	9	13
Luton T.	L	11.84	84	2	0	0
Crystal Palace	Tr	03.85	84-86	49	0	7
Brentford	Tr	11.86	86	19	0	3

DRUCE Mark Andrew
Oxford, 3 March, 1974 (F)

League Club	Source	Date Signed	Seasons Played	Apps	Subs	Gls
Oxford U.	YT	12.91	91-95	18	34	4
Rotherham U.	Tr	09.96	96-97	21	13	4

DRUMMOND Ian Phillip
Brechin, 27 August, 1923 (FB)

League Club	Source	Date Signed	Seasons Played	Apps	Subs	Gls
Portsmouth		05.45				
Bournemouth	Tr	06.49	49-55	265	-	1

DRUMMY Dermot
Hackney, 16 January, 1961 (M)

League Club	Source	Date Signed	Seasons Played	Apps	Subs	Gls
Arsenal	App	01.79				
Blackpool	L	03.80	79	4	1	0

DRURY Adam James
Cambridge, 29 August, 1978 (LB)

League Club	Source	Date Signed	Seasons Played	Apps	Subs	Gls
Peterborough U.	YT	07.96	95-97	29	8	1

DRURY Charles (Chuck) Edward
Darlaston, 4 July, 1937 E Yth (WH)

League Club	Source	Date Signed	Seasons Played	Apps	Subs	Gls
West Bromwich A.	F.H. Lloyds	02.55	57-63	146	-	1
Bristol C.	Tr	08.64	64-66	51	0	2
Bradford P.A.	Tr	03.68	67-68	31	0	1

DRURY George Benjamin
Hucknall, 22 January, 1914 Died 1972 (IF)

League Club	Source	Date Signed	Seasons Played	Apps	Subs	Gls
Sheffield Wed.	Heanor T.	09.34	36-37	44	-	9
Arsenal	Tr	03.38	37-46	38	-	3
West Bromwich A.	Tr	10.46	46-47	29	-	8
Watford	Tr	07.48	48-49	35	-	3

DRURY James Welsh
Cumnock, 29 May, 1924 (OL)

League Club	Source	Date Signed	Seasons Played	Apps	Subs	Gls
Rochdale	Stirling A.	05.51	51	4	-	1
Carlisle U.	Tr	08.52	52-53	35	-	5
Southport	Tr	07.54	54	24	-	2

DRYBURGH Thomas James Douglas
Kirkcaldy, 23 April, 1923 (OL)

League Club	Source	Date Signed	Seasons Played	Apps	Subs	Gls
Aldershot	Lochgelly Albert	06.47	47	19	-	2
Rochdale	Tr	07.48	48-49	77	-	17
Leicester C.	Tr	09.50	50-53	95	-	29
Hull C.	Tr	05.54	54	23	-	3
Oldham Ath.	Kings Lynn	08.57	57	1	-	0
Rochdale	Tr	11.57	57	5	-	0

DRYDEN John (Jackie) George
Sunderland, 16 September, 1919 (OR)

League Club	Source	Date Signed	Seasons Played	Apps	Subs	Gls
Charlton Ath.	Washington Chem.	03.46				
Swindon T.	Hylton Colly	05.47	47	21	-	3
Leyton Orient	Tr	06.48	48-49	40	-	10

DRYDEN Richard Andrew
Stroud, 14 June, 1969 (CD)

League Club	Source	Date Signed	Seasons Played	Apps	Subs	Gls
Bristol Rov.	YT	07.87	86-88	12	1	0
Exeter C.	L	09.88	88	6	0	0
Exeter C.	Tr	03.89	88-90	86	0	13
Notts Co.	Tr	07.91	91-92	30	1	1
Plymouth Arg.	L	11.92	92	5	0	0
Birmingham C.	Tr	03.93	92-94	48	0	0
Bristol C.	Tr	12.94	94-95	32	5	2
Southampton	Tr	08.96	96-97	39	3	1

DRYHURST Carl David
Sutton Coldfield, 8 November, 1960 (F)

League Club	Source	Date Signed	Seasons Played	Apps	Subs	Gls
Halifax T.	Sutton Coldfield T.	11.79	79	4	4	0

DRYSDALE Brian
Wingate (Dm), 24 February, 1943 (LB)

League Club	Source	Date Signed	Seasons Played	Apps	Subs	Gls
Lincoln C.	Jnrs	09.60	59-64	21	-	0
Hartlepool U.	Tr	07.65	65-68	169	1	2
Bristol C.	Tr	05.69	69-76	280	2	3
Reading	L	02.77	76	16	0	0
Oxford U.	Tr	07.77	77	15	0	0

DRYSDALE Jason
Bristol, 17 November, 1970 E Yth (LB)

League Club	Source	Date Signed	Seasons Played	Apps	Subs	Gls
Watford	YT	09.88	89-93	135	10	11
Newcastle U.	Tr	08.94				
Swindon T.	Tr	03.95	94-97	35	7	0
Northampton T.	Tr	03.98	97	1	0	0

DUBERRY Michael Wayne
Enfield, 14 October, 1975 Eu21-5 (CD)

League Club	Source	Date Signed	Seasons Played	Apps	Subs	Gls
Chelsea	YT	06.93	93-97	59	2	1
Bournemouth	L	09.95	95	7	0	0

DUBLIN Dion
Leicester, 22 April, 1969 E-3 (F)

League Club	Source	Date Signed	Seasons Played	Apps	Subs	Gls
Norwich C.	Oakham U.	03.88				
Cambridge U.	Tr	08.88	88-91	133	23	53
Manchester U.	Tr	08.92	92-93	4	8	2
Coventry C.	Tr	09.94	94-97	134	1	58

DUBLIN Keith Barry Lennox
High Wycombe, 29 January, 1966 E Yth (D)

League Club	Source	Date Signed	Seasons Played	Apps	Subs	Gls
Chelsea	App	01.84	83-86	50	1	0
Brighton & H.A.	Tr	08.87	87-89	132	0	5
Watford	Tr	07.90	90-93	165	3	2
Southend U.	Tr	07.94	94-97	169	1	9

DUBOIS Joseph Martin
Monkstown (NI), 27 December, 1927 Died 1987 NI Amat (OR)

League Club	Source	Date Signed	Seasons Played	Apps	Subs	Gls
Doncaster Rov.	Brantwood	05.49	49-51	31	-	5
Grimsby T.	Bedford T.	07.53	53	6	-	1
Halifax T.	Tr	07.54	54-56	78	-	10

DUCHART Alexander
Falkirk, 3 May, 1933 (OL)

League Club	Source	Date Signed	Seasons Played	Apps	Subs	Gls
Southend U.	Hibernian	05.56	56	8	-	2

DUCK George Thomas
Tottenham, 22 February, 1952 (F)

League Club	Source	Date Signed	Seasons Played	Apps	Subs	Gls
Millwall	App	02.70				
Southend U.	Tr	06.71	71	3	0	0

DUCKHOUSE Edward
Walsall, 9 April, 1918 Died 1978 (CH)

League Club	Source	Date Signed	Seasons Played	Apps	Subs	Gls
Birmingham C.	Streetly Wks	08.38	38-49	119	-	4
Northampton T.	Tr	08.50	50-51	68	-	0

DUCROS Andrew John
Evesham, 16 September, 1977 E Sch/E Yth (W)

League Club	Source	Date Signed	Seasons Played	Apps	Subs	Gls
Coventry C.	YT	09.94	96-97	2	6	0

DUDDY John Michael
Manchester, 8 February, 1956 (M)

League Club	Source	Date Signed	Seasons Played	Apps	Subs	Gls
Oldham Ath.	App	02.74				
Stockport Co.	Tr	03.76	75	6	0	0

DUDLEY Craig Bryan
Ollerton, 12 September, 1979 (F)

League Club	Source	Date Signed	Seasons Played	Apps	Subs	Gls
Notts Co.	YT	04.97	96-97	11	16	3
Shrewsbury T.	L	01.98	97	3	1	0

DUDLEY Frank Ernest
Southend, 9 May, 1925 (IF)

League Club	Source	Date Signed	Seasons Played	Apps	Subs	Gls
Southend U.	Jnrs	10.45	46-48	88	-	32
Leeds U.	Tr	08.49	49-50	64	-	23
Southampton	Tr	02.51	50-53	67	-	32
Cardiff C.	Tr	09.53	53	4	-	1
Brentford	Tr	12.53	53-56	72	-	32

DUDLEY James George
Gartcosh, 24 August, 1928 S 'B' (WH)

League Club	Source	Date Signed	Seasons Played	Apps	Subs	Gls
West Bromwich A.	Jnrs	05.46	49-59	285	-	9
Walsall	Tr	12.59	59-63	167	-	3

DUDLEY Philip William
Basildon, 17 February, 1959 (FB)

League Club	Source	Date Signed	Seasons Played	Apps	Subs	Gls
Southend U.	App	02.77	77-82	109	3	3

DUDLEY Reginald Arthur
Hemel Hempstead, 3 February, 1915 Died 1994 E Amat (FB)

League Club	Source	Date Signed	Seasons Played	Apps	Subs	Gls
Millwall	Apsley	03.35	35-46	42	-	0
Queens Park R.	Tr	12.46	46-49	58	-	0
Watford	Tr	07.50	50	1	-	0

DUERDEN Harold
Barnsley, 5 March, 1948 (WH)

League Club	Source	Date Signed	Seasons Played	Apps	Subs	Gls
Barnsley	App	09.65	65-66	24	1	1

DUERDEN Ian Christopher
Burnley, 27 March, 1978 (F)

League Club	Source	Date Signed	Seasons Played	Apps	Subs	Gls
Burnley	YT	07.96	97	1	0	0

DUFF Damien Anthony
Ballyboden, 2 March, 1979 IR Sch/IR Yth/IR 'B'/IR-2 (F)

League Club	Source	Date Signed	Seasons Played	Apps	Subs	Gls
Blackburn Rov.	Lourdes Celtic	03.96	96-97	18	9	4

DUFF William
Winchburgh, 6 February, 1935 Su23-1/SF Lge (G)

League Club	Source	Date Signed	Seasons Played	Apps	Subs	Gls
Charlton Ath.	Hearts	12.56	56-61	213	-	0
Peterborough U.	Tr	05.63	63-66	118	0	0

DUFF William Francis Andrew
Littleborough, 16 December, 1938 (OL)

League Club	Source	Date Signed	Seasons Played	Apps	Subs	Gls
Rochdale	Jnrs	05.56				
Scunthorpe U.	Tr	10.58				
Grimsby T.	Tr	10.59	59	3	-	1
Accrington St.	Toronto (Can)	10.60	60	14	-	3

DUFFETT Edgar
Worcester, 29 August, 1926 (IF)

League Club	Source	Date Signed	Seasons Played	Apps	Subs	Gls
Norwich C.	West Bromwich A. (Am)	11.47				
Carlisle U.	Tr	08.50	50-52	47	-	8

DUFFEY Christopher Paul
Kirkby, 8 January, 1952 (W)

League Club	Source	Date Signed	Seasons Played	Apps	Subs	Gls
Bolton W.	App	09.69	69-71	8	0	0
Crewe Alex.	L	09.72	72	6	0	3
Crewe Alex.	Tr	07.73	73-74	54	3	12
Bury	Tr	10.74	74	17	4	8
Shrewsbury T.	Tr	05.75	75	4	4	1
Rochdale	L	11.75	75	2	0	0

DUFFIELD Martin John
Park Royal, 28 February, 1964 E Yth (M)

League Club	Source	Date Signed	Seasons Played	Apps	Subs	Gls
Queens Park R.	App	01.82	82	0	1	0
Bournemouth	L	09.83	83	6	0	1
Charlton Ath.	L	11.84	84	1	0	0

DUFFIELD Peter
Middlesbrough, 4 February, 1969 (W)

League Club	Source	Date Signed	Seasons Played	Apps	Subs	Gls
Middlesbrough	App	11.86				
Sheffield U.	Tr	08.87	87-91	34	24	16
Halifax T.	L	03.88	87	12	0	6
Rotherham U.	L	03.91	90	17	0	5
Blackpool	L	08.92	92	3	2	1
Crewe Alex.	L	01.93	92	0	2	0
Stockport Co.	L	03.93	92	6	1	4

DUFFIN Lionel Joseph
Ulverston, 8 August, 1945 (G)

League Club	Source	Date Signed	Seasons Played	Apps	Subs	Gls
Barrow	Jnrs	07.64	64-67	46	0	0

League Club	Source	Date Signed	Seasons Played	Career Record Apps	Subs	Gls
DUFFY Alan						
Stanley, 20 December, 1949 E Yth						(M)
Newcastle U.	App	03.67	68-69	2	2	0
Brighton & H.A.	Tr	01.70	69-71	34	16	8
Tranmere Rov.	Tr	03.72	71-72	29	4	2
Darlington	Tr	08.73	73	19	5	0
DUFFY Christopher						
Wemyss, 21 October, 1918 Died 1978						(OL)
Charlton Ath.	Leith Ath.	09.45	46-52	162	-	33
DUFFY Christopher John						
Eccles, 31 October, 1973						(LB/W)
Crewe Alex.	YT	06.92				
Wigan Ath.	Tr	07.93	93-94	15	16	1
DUFFY Darrell Gerard						
Birmingham, 18 January, 1971 E Yth						(D)
Aston Villa	YT	07.89	88	1	0	0
Scunthorpe U.	Moor Green	02.93	92	4	0	0
DUFFY Gerald						
Middlewich, 12 September, 1934						(CF)
Oldham Ath.	Middlewich	05.56	56-58	58	-	21
DUFFY John						
Dunfermline, 6 September, 1943						(LH)
Darlington	Dunfermline Ath.	08.63	63	10	-	1
DUFFY John						
Glasgow, 24 April, 1922						(FB)
Norwich C.	Clyde	03.49	49-53	78	-	0
DUFFY John Gerard						
Dundee, 24 August, 1929						(WH)
Southend U.	Glasgow Celtic	05.54	54-59	114	-	4
DUFFY Michael Kevin						
Leicester, 12 June, 1961						(M)
Leicester C.	Jnrs	07.78	78-79	7	5	1
DUFFY Vincent Gerard						
Nottingham, 21 September, 1962						(M)
Scunthorpe U.	Nottingham F. (App)	12.80	80-81	3	5	0
DUGDALE Alan						
Liverpool, 11 September, 1952 E Yth						(CD)
Coventry C.	App	11.69	72-77	139	3	0
Charlton Ath.	Tr	10.77	77-78	34	0	0
Barnsley	L	08.79	79	7	0	0
DUGDALE Gordon						
Liverpool, 21 February, 1924 Died 1986						(LB)
Everton	Jnrs	06.47	47-49	58	-	0
DUGDALE James Robert						
Liverpool, 15 January, 1932 E 'B'/EF Lge						(CH)
West Bromwich A.	Harrowby	06.52	52-55	63	-	0
Aston Villa	Tr	01.56	55-61	215	-	3
Queens Park R.	Tr	10.62	62	10	-	0
DUGGAN Andrew James						
Bradford, 19 September, 1967						(CD)
Barnsley	YT	07.85	86	1	1	1
Rochdale	L	11.87	87	3	0	0
Huddersfield T.	Tr	09.88	88-89	29	0	3
Hartlepool U.	L	08.90	90	2	0	0
Rochdale	Tr	03.91	90	1	0	0
DUGGAN Edward John						
West Ham, 27 July, 1922 Died 1982						(IF)
Luton T.	Jnrs	08.39	46-48	48	-	20
Queens Park R.	Tr	02.49	48-50	47	-	5
Luton T.	Bedford T.	02.56				
DUGGAN James						
Droitwich, 17 November, 1920 Died 1982						(IF)
West Bromwich A.	Droitwich O.B.	12.39	46	25	-	8
DUGGINS Eric Edward						
Tamworth, 24 November, 1928 Died 1992						(FB)
Portsmouth	Atherstone T.	08.48				
Southend U.	Tr	07.52	52-53	28	-	0
DUGGINS Gordon						
Tamworth, 8 December, 1932						(CF)
Barnsley	Gresley Rov.	11.55	55-57	17	-	6

League Club	Source	Date Signed	Seasons Played	Career Record Apps	Subs	Gls
DUGGINS John Austin						
Tamworth, 4 August, 1931						(F)
Portsmouth	Atherstone T.	06.50				
Walsall	Tr	08.52	52	16	-	3
DUGNOLLE John Henry						
India, 24 March, 1914 Died 1977						(HB)
Brighton & H.A.	Southwick	10.34	35-37	7	-	0
Plymouth Arg.	Tunbridge Wells	02.39	38	4	-	0
Brighton & H.A.	Tr	08.46	46-47	59	-	0
DUGUID Karl Anthony						
Hitchin, 21 March, 1978						(F)
Colchester U.	YT	07.96	95-97	23	34	7
DUKE George Edward						
Chichester, 6 September, 1920 Died 1988						(G)
Luton T.	Southwick	01.39	46-48	16	-	0
Bournemouth	Tr	05.49	49	10	-	0
DUKES Harold Parkinson						
Portsmouth, 31 March, 1912 Died 1988						(G)
Norwich C.	Ipswich T.	08.34	34-38	105	-	0
Norwich C.	Bedford T.	09.46	46	13	-	0
DULIN Michael Charles						
Stepney, 25 October, 1935						(OR)
Tottenham H.	Jnrs	11.52	55-57	10	-	2
DULSON Garry						
Nottingham, 21 December, 1953						(D)
Nottingham F.	App	10.71				
Port Vale	Tr	10.74	74-77	108	2	3
Crewe Alex.	Tr	11.78	78-79	33	5	0
DUMIGHAN Joseph						
Langley Park (Dm), 25 September, 1938						(F)
Sunderland	Jnrs	11.55				
Darlington	Tr	07.58	58	4	-	1
DUMITRESCU Ilie						
Romania, 6 January, 1969 Romanian Int						(F)
Tottenham H.	Steaua Bucharest (Rom)	08.94	94-95	16	2	4
West Ham U.	Tr	03.96	95-96	5	5	0
DUNBAR Ian						
Newcastle, 6 June, 1971 E Sch						(F)
Hartlepool U. (N/C)	Jnrs	08.89	89-90	1	2	0
DUNCAN Andrew						
Hexham, 20 October, 1977 E Sch						(CB)
Manchester U.	YT	07.96				
Cambridge U.	Tr	01.98	97	18	1	0
DUNCAN Cameron						
Shotts, 4 August, 1965 S Yth						(G)
Sunderland	Jnrs	07.84	85	1	0	0
DUNCAN Colin John						
Plymstock, 5 August, 1957						(M)
Oxford U.	App	12.74	74-79	188	1	6
Gillingham	Tr	01.80	79-83	83	2	5
Reading	Tr	09.83	83-84	56	0	3
Aldershot	Tr	08.85	85	15	0	0
DUNCAN David Millar						
East Fife, 21 November, 1921 Died 1991 SF Lge/S-3						(OL)
Crewe Alex.	Raith Rov.	08.55	55	22	-	0
DUNCAN Douglas (Dally)						
Aberdeen, 14 October, 1909 Died 1990 S-14						(W)
Hull C.	Aberdeen	08.28	28-31	111	-	47
Derby Co.	Tr	03.32	31-46	261	-	63
Luton T.	Tr	10.46	46-47	32	-	4
DUNCAN George						
Glasgow, 16 January, 1937						(W)
Southend U.	Glasgow Rangers	06.60	60	6	-	2
Chesterfield	Tr	08.61	61-64	140	-	13
DUNCAN James Robert						
Hull, 2 April, 1938						(F)
Hull C.	Jnrs	04.55	55-59	26	-	3
Bradford C.	Tr	06.60	60	18	-	5
DUNCAN John Gillespie						
Glasgow, 10 December, 1926						(F)
Newcastle U.	Ayr U.	11.50	51-52	5	-	3

League Club	Source	Date Signed	Seasons Played	Career Record Apps	Subs	Gls

DUNCAN John Pearson
Dundee, 22 February, 1949 SF Lge (F)

League Club	Source	Date Signed	Seasons Played	Apps	Subs	Gls
Tottenham H.	Dundee	10.74	74-78	101	2	53
Derby Co.	Tr	09.78	78-80	35	1	12
Scunthorpe U.	Tr	06.81	81-82	3	6	0

DUNCAN Joseph James
Liverpool, 24 February, 1950 (OR)

League Club	Source	Date Signed	Seasons Played	Apps	Subs	Gls
Wrexham (Am)	Jnrs	12.68	68	1	0	0

DUNCAN Robert
Kirkcaldy, 2 November, 1943 (FB)

League Club	Source	Date Signed	Seasons Played	Apps	Subs	Gls
Southend U.	Jnrs	08.61	61	1	-	0

DUNCAN Thomas Montgomerie
Portsay, 15 July, 1936 (IF)

League Club	Source	Date Signed	Seasons Played	Apps	Subs	Gls
Newport Co. (L)	Airdrieonians	03.58	57	1	-	0

DUNCLIFFE Michael John
Brighton, 17 September, 1947 (FB)

League Club	Source	Date Signed	Seasons Played	Apps	Subs	Gls
Brighton & H.A.	App	09.65	66-67	22	0	0
Grimsby T.	Tr	06.68	68-69	71	1	0
Peterborough U.	Tr	07.70	70-72	120	0	0

DUNDERDALE William **Leonard**
Gainsborough, 6 February, 1915 Died 1989 (CF)

League Club	Source	Date Signed	Seasons Played	Apps	Subs	Gls
Walsall	Goole T.	03.36	35-37	32	-	19
Watford	Tr	05.38	38	30	-	18
Leeds U.	Tr	03.39	38	3	-	0
Watford	Tr	04.46	46-47	44	-	15

DUNFORD Neil
Rochdale, 18 July, 1967 (G)

League Club	Source	Date Signed	Seasons Played	Apps	Subs	Gls
Rochdale (N/C)	Castleton Gabriels	09.93	94	2	0	0

DUNGEY James Andrew
Plymouth, 7 February, 1978 E Sch/E Yth (G)

League Club	Source	Date Signed	Seasons Played	Apps	Subs	Gls
Plymouth Arg.	YT	10.95	94-96	9	1	0
Exeter C.	Tr	12.97	97	1	0	0

DUNGWORTH John Henry
Rotherham, 30 March, 1955 (F)

League Club	Source	Date Signed	Seasons Played	Apps	Subs	Gls
Huddersfield T.	App	04.72	72-74	18	5	1
Barnsley	L	10.74	74	2	1	1
Oldham Ath.	Tr	03.75	75	2	2	0
Rochdale	L	03.77	76	14	0	3
Aldershot	Tr	09.77	77-79	105	0	58
Shrewsbury T.	Tr	11.79	79-81	81	5	17
Hereford U.	L	10.81	81	7	0	3
Mansfield T.	Tr	08.82	82-83	50	6	16
Rotherham U.	Tr	02.84	83-87	176	10	16

DUNKLEY Malcolm
Wolverhampton, 12 July, 1961 (F)

League Club	Source	Date Signed	Seasons Played	Apps	Subs	Gls
Lincoln C.	Bromsgrove Rov.	02.89	88	9	2	4

DUNKLEY Maurice Edward Frank
Kettering, 19 February, 1914 Died 1989 (OR)

League Club	Source	Date Signed	Seasons Played	Apps	Subs	Gls
Northampton T.	Kettering T.	12.36	36-37	26	-	5
Manchester C.	Tr	03.38	37-46	51	-	5
Northampton T.	Kettering T.	07.49	49	4	-	0

DUNKLEY Robert
Stoke, 6 April, 1922 (OL)

League Club	Source	Date Signed	Seasons Played	Apps	Subs	Gls
Stoke C.		01.41				
Barrow	Tr	08.46	46	11	-	0

DUNLEAVY Christopher
Liverpool, 30 December, 1949 (CD)

League Club	Source	Date Signed	Seasons Played	Apps	Subs	Gls
Everton	Jnrs	03.68				
Southport	Tr	07.69	69-73	145	2	9
Chester C.	Tr	09.73	73-76	74	2	0
Halifax T.	Tr	10.76	76-80	181	0	13

DUNLOP Albert
Liverpool, 21 April, 1932 Died 1990 (G)

League Club	Source	Date Signed	Seasons Played	Apps	Subs	Gls
Everton	Jnrs	08.49	56-62	211	-	0
Wrexham	Tr	11.63	63-64	15	-	0

DUNLOP William **Rex**
Dumfries, 21 September, 1927 (WH)

League Club	Source	Date Signed	Seasons Played	Apps	Subs	Gls
Workington	Glasgow Rangers	11.53	53-55	110	-	20

DUNLOP William Lumsden
Airdrie, 20 December, 1926 (IF)

League Club	Source	Date Signed	Seasons Played	Apps	Subs	Gls
Exeter C.	Dunfermline Ath.	07.50	50	4	-	0
Bristol Rov.	Ilfracombe	05.52				
Bradford P.A.	Tr	05.53	53	36	-	12
Darlington	Tr	10.54	54	18	-	2

DUNMORE David Gerald Ivor
Whitehaven, 8 February, 1934 (CF)

League Club	Source	Date Signed	Seasons Played	Apps	Subs	Gls
York C.	Cliftonville	05.52	51-53	48	-	25
Tottenham H.	Tr	02.54	53-59	75	-	23
West Ham U.	Tr	03.60	59-60	36	-	16
Leyton Orient	Tr	03.61	60-64	147	-	54
York C.	Tr	06.65	65-66	61	2	13

DUNN Barry
Middlesbrough, 17 December, 1939 (F)

League Club	Source	Date Signed	Seasons Played	Apps	Subs	Gls
Doncaster Rov.		02.58				
Halifax T.	Tr	09.59	59-60	7	-	1

DUNN Barry
Sunderland, 15 February, 1952 (W)

League Club	Source	Date Signed	Seasons Played	Apps	Subs	Gls
Sunderland	Blue Star	09.79	79-80	16	7	2
Preston N.E.	Tr	10.81	81	8	0	1
Darlington	Tr	08.82	82	16	0	4

DUNN Brian James
Boston, 4 October, 1940 (OL)

League Club	Source	Date Signed	Seasons Played	Apps	Subs	Gls
Grimsby T.	Jnrs	10.57				
Hartlepool U.	Tr	06.58	58-60	27	-	1

DUNN Iain George William
Goole, 1 April, 1970 E Sch/E Yth (W)

League Club	Source	Date Signed	Seasons Played	Apps	Subs	Gls
York C.	Jnrs	07.88	88-90	46	31	11
Chesterfield	Tr	08.91	91	8	5	1
Huddersfield T.	Goole T.	12.92	92-96	62	58	14
Scunthorpe U.	L	09.96	96	3	0	0
Chesterfield	Tr	02.97	96-97	10	8	0

DUNN James
Edinburgh, 25 November, 1923 (IF)

League Club	Source	Date Signed	Seasons Played	Apps	Subs	Gls
Wolverhampton W.	Maghull Ath.	11.42	46-52	123	-	33
Derby Co.	Tr	11.52	52-54	57	-	21

DUNN James
Rutherglen, 23 October, 1922 (FB)

League Club	Source	Date Signed	Seasons Played	Apps	Subs	Gls
Leeds U.	Rutherglen Glencairn	06.47	47-58	422	-	1
Darlington	Tr	07.59	59	27	-	0

DUNN John Alfred
Barking, 21 June, 1944 (G)

League Club	Source	Date Signed	Seasons Played	Apps	Subs	Gls
Chelsea	App	02.62	62-65	13	0	0
Torquay U.	Tr	10.66	66-67	44	0	0
Aston Villa	Tr	01.68	67-70	101	0	0
Charlton Ath.	Tr	07.71	71-74	104	0	0

DUNN Joseph
Glasgow, 20 September, 1925 (CH)

League Club	Source	Date Signed	Seasons Played	Apps	Subs	Gls
Preston N.E.	Clyde	08.51	51-60	223	-	2

DUNN Norman
South Shields, 20 October, 1928 (CH)

League Club	Source	Date Signed	Seasons Played	Apps	Subs	Gls
Aldershot	Murton Colly	08.51	52	1	-	0
Darlington	Tr	07.54				

DUNN Richard
Easington, 23 December, 1919 Died 1986 (IF)

League Club	Source	Date Signed	Seasons Played	Apps	Subs	Gls
West Ham U.	Ferryhill Ath.	02.38	46-47	11	-	2
Hartlepool U.	Tr	08.49	49	13	-	2

DUNN William Charles
Hebburn, 25 March, 1920 Died 1982 (G)

League Club	Source	Date Signed	Seasons Played	Apps	Subs	Gls
Darlington		05.46	46-55	340	-	0

DUNNE Anthony Peter
Dublin, 24 July, 1941 IR-33 (LB)

League Club	Source	Date Signed	Seasons Played	Apps	Subs	Gls
Manchester U.	Shelbourne	04.60	60-72	414	0	2
Bolton W.	Tr	08.73	73-78	166	4	0

DUNNE Austin
Limerick (Ire), 31 July, 1934 (WH)

League Club	Source	Date Signed	Seasons Played	Apps	Subs	Gls
Colchester U.	Limerick	10.53	54	1	-	0

DUNNE James Christopher
Dublin, 1 December, 1947 IR-1 (CD)

League Club	Source	Date Signed	Seasons Played	Apps	Subs	Gls
Millwall	Shelbourne	02.66				
Torquay U.	Tr	07.67	67-69	125	1	13
Fulham	Tr	07.70	70-73	142	1	2
Torquay U.	Tr	04.76	75-78	119	3	6

DUNNE James Patrick
Dublin, 16 March, 1935 LoI/IR-3 (IF)

League Club	Source	Date Signed	Seasons Played	Apps	Subs	Gls
Leicester C.		09.53	54-55	4	-	0
Peterborough U.	St Patricks Ath.	07.60	60-61	4	-	1

DUNNE Joseph John
Dublin, 25 May, 1973 IR Sch/IR Yth/IRu21-1 (RB)

League Club	Source	Date Signed	Seasons Played	Apps	Subs	Gls
Gillingham	YT	08.90	90-95	108	7	1
Colchester U.	Tr	03.96	95-97	47	18	3

DUNNE Patrick Anthony Joseph
Dublin, 9 February, 1943 IR-5/IRu23-1 (G)

League Club	Source	Date Signed	Seasons Played	Apps	Subs	Gls
Everton	Jnrs	05.60				
Manchester U.	Shamrock Rov.	05.64	64-65	45	0	0
Plymouth Arg.	Tr	02.67	66-70	152	0	0

DUNNE Richard Patrick
Dublin, 21 September, 1979 IR Sch/IR Yth/IR 'B' (CD)

League Club	Source	Date Signed	Seasons Played	Apps	Subs	Gls
Everton	YT	10.96	96-97	8	2	0

DUNNE Seamus
Wicklow (Ire), 13 April, 1930 IR-15 (FB)

League Club	Source	Date Signed	Seasons Played	Apps	Subs	Gls
Luton T.	Shelbourne	07.50	51-60	301	-	0

DUNNE Thomas
Dublin, 19 March, 1927 Died 1988 LoI (WH)

League Club	Source	Date Signed	Seasons Played	Apps	Subs	Gls
Leicester C.	Shamrock Rov.	11.49	50-53	33	-	0
Exeter C.	Tr	07.54	54-55	37	-	1
Shrewsbury T.	Tr	08.56	56	3	-	0
Southport	Tr	07.57	57	21	-	0

DUNNE Thomas Joseph
Glasgow, 22 June, 1946 (IF)

League Club	Source	Date Signed	Seasons Played	Apps	Subs	Gls
Leyton Orient	St Anthonys	05.64	64	1	-	0

DUNNIGAN John Young
Dalmuir, 30 November, 1920 (OR)

League Club	Source	Date Signed	Seasons Played	Apps	Subs	Gls
Barrow	Bridgeton Waverley	09.45	46	1	-	0

DUNNING William Samuel
Bury, 15 November, 1952 (W)

League Club	Source	Date Signed	Seasons Played	Apps	Subs	Gls
Blackburn Rov.	App	11.70	70-71	10	3	2

DUNPHY Eamonn Martin
Dublin, 3 August, 1945 IRu23-1/IR-23 (M)

League Club	Source	Date Signed	Seasons Played	Apps	Subs	Gls
Manchester U.	App	08.62				
York C.	Tr	08.65	65	22	0	3
Millwall	Tr	01.66	65-73	267	7	24
Charlton Ath.	Tr	11.73	73-74	39	3	3
Reading	Tr	07.75	75-76	74	3	3

DUNPHY Nicholas Owen
Sutton Coldfield, 3 August, 1974 (CD)

League Club	Source	Date Signed	Seasons Played	Apps	Subs	Gls
Peterborough U.	Hednesford T.	08.94	94	0	2	0

DUNPHY Sean
Maltby, 5 November, 1970 (CD)

League Club	Source	Date Signed	Seasons Played	Apps	Subs	Gls
Barnsley	YT	06.89	89	5	1	0
Lincoln C.	Tr	07.90	91-93	48	5	2
Doncaster Rov.	L	10.93	93	1	0	0
Scarborough	L	08.94	94	10	0	0

DUNS Leonard
Newcastle, 28 September, 1916 Died 1989 (OR)

League Club	Source	Date Signed	Seasons Played	Apps	Subs	Gls
Sunderland	Newcastle W.E.	10.33	35-51	215	-	45

DUNWELL Peter Matthew
Ecclesfield, 22 November, 1938 (OL)

League Club	Source	Date Signed	Seasons Played	Apps	Subs	Gls
Lincoln C.	Ecclesfield	09.58	59-60	14	-	1

DUNWELL Richard Kirk
Islington, 17 June, 1971 (F)

League Club	Source	Date Signed	Seasons Played	Apps	Subs	Gls
Aldershot	Millwall (N/C)	11.90	90	0	1	0
Barnet	Collier Row	10.95	95-96	4	10	1

DUQUEMIN Leonard Stanley
Guernsey, 17 July, 1924 (CF)

League Club	Source	Date Signed	Seasons Played	Apps	Subs	Gls
Tottenham H.	Vauxbelets	09.46	47-56	274	-	114

DURANDT Clifford Michael
South Africa, 16 April, 1940 (OL)

League Club	Source	Date Signed	Seasons Played	Apps	Subs	Gls
Wolverhampton W.	Marist Bros (SA)	06.57	58-61	43	-	9
Charlton Ath.	Tr	03.63	62-64	36	-	4

DURBAN William **Alan**
Bridgend, 7 July, 1941 Wu23-14/W-27 (M)

League Club	Source	Date Signed	Seasons Played	Apps	Subs	Gls
Cardiff C.	Jnrs	09.58	59-62	52	-	9
Derby Co.	Tr	07.63	63-72	336	10	93
Shrewsbury T.	Tr	09.73	73-77	150	6	32

DURHAM Raymond **Denis**
East Halton, 26 September, 1923 (LH)

League Club	Source	Date Signed	Seasons Played	Apps	Subs	Gls
Hull C.	East Halton	04.47	46-58	267	-	7

DURHAM Jonathan Simon
Rotherham, 12 June, 1965 (F)

League Club	Source	Date Signed	Seasons Played	Apps	Subs	Gls
Rotherham U.	App	06.83	83	4	3	1
Torquay U.	Tr	03.85	84-85	20	4	2

DURIE David George
Blackpool, 13 August, 1931 (IF)

League Club	Source	Date Signed	Seasons Played	Apps	Subs	Gls
Blackpool	Oxford Amats	05.52	52-63	301	-	84
Chester C.	Tr	09.64	64-66	87	2	4

DURIE Gordon Scott
Paisley, 6 December, 1965 Su21-4/S 'B'/S-43 (F)

League Club	Source	Date Signed	Seasons Played	Apps	Subs	Gls
Chelsea	Hibernian	04.86	85-90	115	8	51
Tottenham H.	Tr	08.91	91-93	58	0	11

DURKAN Kieron John
Chester, 1 December, 1973 IRu21-3 (W)

League Club	Source	Date Signed	Seasons Played	Apps	Subs	Gls
Wrexham	YT	07.92	91-95	43	7	3
Stockport Co.	Tr	02.96	95-97	52	12	4
Macclesfield T.	Tr	03.98	97	2	2	0

DURKIN John
Hill O' Beath, 18 April, 1930 (IF)

League Club	Source	Date Signed	Seasons Played	Apps	Subs	Gls
Gillingham	Hearts	08.53	53-54	30	-	5

DURKIN William
Bradford, 29 September, 1921 (IF)

League Club	Source	Date Signed	Seasons Played	Apps	Subs	Gls
Bradford C.		01.47	46-47	28	-	1
Rotherham U.	Tr	08.48	48	2	-	0
Aldershot	Tr	08.49	49-53	129	-	17

DURNIN John Paul
Bootle, 18 August, 1965 (F)

League Club	Source	Date Signed	Seasons Played	Apps	Subs	Gls
Liverpool	Waterloo Dock	03.86				
West Bromwich A.	L	10.88	88	5	0	2
Oxford U.	Tr	02.89	88-92	140	21	44
Portsmouth	Tr	07.93	93-97	100	53	24

DURRANT Frederick
Dover, 19 June, 1921 (CF)

League Club	Source	Date Signed	Seasons Played	Apps	Subs	Gls
Brentford	Folkestone T.	05.39	46	4	-	3
Queens Park R.	Tr	09.46	46-48	51	-	26
Exeter C.	Tr	02.49	48-49	17	-	5

DURRANT Iain
Glasgow, 29 October, 1966 S Yth/Su21-4/S-11 (M)

League Club	Source	Date Signed	Seasons Played	Apps	Subs	Gls
Everton (L)	Glasgow Rangers	10.94	94	4	1	0

DURRANT Lee Roger
Great Yarmouth, 18 December, 1973 E Sch (LM)

League Club	Source	Date Signed	Seasons Played	Apps	Subs	Gls
Ipswich T.	YT	07.92	93	3	4	0

DURRANT Paul
East Howdon, 21 February, 1943 (OL)

League Club	Source	Date Signed	Seasons Played	Apps	Subs	Gls
Wolverhampton W.	Sunderland (Am)	07.61				
Bury	Tr	07.62	63-64	21	-	6
Doncaster Rov.	Tr	07.65	65-66	13	2	1

DURRELL Joseph Timothy
Stepney, 15 March, 1953 (OL)

League Club	Source	Date Signed	Seasons Played	Apps	Subs	Gls
West Ham U.	App	10.70	71	5	1	0
Bristol C.	Tr	07.73	73-74	5	3	0
Cardiff C.	L	08.75	75	2	0	0
Gillingham	Tr	11.75	75-76	43	6	9

DURSUN Peter Muhamet Ali
Denmark, 8 January, 1975 (F)

League Club	Source	Date Signed	Seasons Played	Apps	Subs	Gls
Southend U.	Aarhus Fremad (Den)	11.96	96	0	1	0

DUTHIE Ian Martin
Forfar, 18 January, 1930 (F)

League Club	Source	Date Signed	Seasons Played	Apps	Subs	Gls
Huddersfield T.	Forfar Celtic	06.49	49-52	7	-	0
Bradford C.	Tr	06.54	54-55	28	-	4

DUTHIE James
Rescobie, 23 September, 1923 (WH)

League Club	Source	Date Signed	Seasons Played	Apps	Subs	Gls
Grimsby T.		09.49	48-50	40	-	0
Hull C.	Tr	06.51	51-52	17	-	3
Southend U.	Tr	05.53	53-57	160	-	8

DUTHOIT John (Jack)
Leeds, 4 November, 1918 (LB)

League Club	Source	Date Signed	Seasons Played	Apps	Subs	Gls
Leeds U.	Carlton U.	04.45				
York C.	Tr	05.46	46-49	36	-	0

DUTTON Charles Alfred
Rugeley, 10 April, 1934 (CF)

League Club	Source	Date Signed	Seasons Played	Apps	Subs	Gls
Coventry C.	Derby Co. (Am)	10.52	53-55	27	-	8
Northampton T.	Tr	03.56	55-56	10	-	2

DUTTON Leonard Lewis
Cardiff, 17 January, 1922 W Sch (WH)

League Club	Source	Date Signed	Seasons Played	Apps	Subs	Gls
Arsenal	Jnrs	05.39				
Norwich C.	Tr	08.46	46-52	139	-	11

DUXBURY Lee Edward
Skipton, 7 October, 1969 (M)

League Club	Source	Date Signed	Seasons Played	Apps	Subs	Gls
Bradford C.	YT	07.88	88-94	204	5	25
Rochdale	L	01.90	89	9	1	0
Huddersfield T.	Tr	12.94	94-95	29	0	2
Bradford C.	Tr	11.95	95-96	63	0	7
Oldham Ath.	Tr	03.97	96-97	48	2	5

DUXBURY Michael
Blackburn, 1 September, 1959 Eu21-7/E-10 (FB/M)

League Club	Source	Date Signed	Seasons Played	Apps	Subs	Gls
Manchester U.	App	10.76	80-89	274	25	6
Blackburn Rov.	Tr	08.90	90-91	25	2	0
Bradford C.	Tr	01.92	91-93	64	1	0

DWIGHT Royston Edward
Dartford, 9 January, 1933 (OR)

League Club	Source	Date Signed	Seasons Played	Apps	Subs	Gls
Fulham	Jnrs	06.50	54-57	72	-	54
Nottingham F.	Tr	07.58	58-59	44	-	21
Coventry C.	Gravesend & Nft	01.62	61-62	31	-	8
Millwall	Tr	01.64	63-64	7	-	2

DWYER Robert **Alan**
Liverpool, 5 October, 1952 (FB)

League Club	Source	Date Signed	Seasons Played	Apps	Subs	Gls
Wrexham	Halewood Y.C.	10.73	74-80	169	11	2
Stockport Co.	Tr	10.81	81	4	0	0

DWYER Noel Michael
Dublin, 30 October, 1934 Died 1992 IR 'B'/IR-14 (G)

League Club	Source	Date Signed	Seasons Played	Apps	Subs	Gls
Wolverhampton W.	Ormeau	08.53	57	5	-	0
West Ham U.	Tr	12.58	58-59	36	-	0
Swansea C.	Tr	08.60	60-64	140	-	0
Plymouth Arg.	Tr	01.65	64-65	26	0	0
Charlton Ath.	Tr	12.65	65	6	0	0

DWYER Philip John
Cardiff, 28 October, 1953 W Sch/W Yth/Wu21-1/Wu23-5/W-10 (D)

League Club	Source	Date Signed	Seasons Played	Apps	Subs	Gls
Cardiff C.	Jnrs	10.71	72-84	466	5	41
Rochdale	L	03.85	84	15	0	1

DYAS Gordon
Hednesford, 17 May, 1936 (W)

League Club	Source	Date Signed	Seasons Played	Apps	Subs	Gls
Walsall	Hednesford T.	06.55	55	12	-	0

DYCHE Sean Mark
Kettering, 28 June, 1971 (D)

League Club	Source	Date Signed	Seasons Played	Apps	Subs	Gls
Nottingham F.	YT	05.89				
Chesterfield	Tr	02.90	89-96	219	12	8
Bristol C.	Tr	07.97	97	10	1	0

DYE Dean Charles
Lincoln, 4 March, 1969 (F)

League Club	Source	Date Signed	Seasons Played	Apps	Subs	Gls
Charlton Ath.	Lincoln U.	06.91				
Lincoln C. (N/C)	Tr	10.91	91	0	2	0

DYER Alexander Constantine
West Ham, 14 November, 1965 (W)

League Club	Source	Date Signed	Seasons Played	Apps	Subs	Gls
Blackpool	Watford (App)	10.83	83-86	101	7	19
Hull C.	Tr	02.87	86-88	59	1	14
Crystal Palace	Tr	11.88	88-89	16	1	2
Charlton Ath.	Tr	10.90	90-92	60	18	13
Oxford U.	Tr	07.93	93-94	62	14	6
Lincoln C. (N/C)	Tr	08.95	95	1	0	0
Barnet	Tr	09.95	95	30	5	2
Huddersfield T.	F.A. Maia (Por)	08.97	97	8	4	1
Notts Co.	Tr	03.98	97	10	0	0

DYER Joseph **Alexander**
Crewe, 13 April, 1913 Died 1984 (OL/LB)

League Club	Source	Date Signed	Seasons Played	Apps	Subs	Gls
Crewe Alex.		10.33	33-36	51	-	9
Plymouth Arg.	Tr	02.37	36-46	53	-	3

DYER Bruce Antonio
Ilford, 13 April, 1975 Eu21-11 (F)

League Club	Source	Date Signed	Seasons Played	Apps	Subs	Gls
Watford	YT	04.93	92-93	29	2	6
Crystal Palace	Tr	03.94	93-97	90	39	35

DYER Keiron Courtney
Ipswich, 29 December, 1978 E Yth/Eu21-6/E 'B' (LM)

League Club	Source	Date Signed	Seasons Played	Apps	Subs	Gls
Ipswich T.	YT	01.97	96-97	43	11	4

DYER Paul David
Leicester, 24 January, 1953 (D/M)

League Club	Source	Date Signed	Seasons Played	Apps	Subs	Gls
Notts Co.		09.72	72-73	1	6	0
Colchester U.	Tr	07.75	75-79	124	20	4

DYER Peter Robert Francis
Devonport, 12 October, 1937 (G)

League Club	Source	Date Signed	Seasons Played	Apps	Subs	Gls
Plymouth Arg.	Oak Villa	06.55	55-56	8	-	0

DYER Raymond
Stockport, 12 May, 1938 (F)

League Club	Source	Date Signed	Seasons Played	Apps	Subs	Gls
Stockport Co.	Bolton W. (Am)	09.56	56	1	-	0

DYER Stephen Paul
Chelmsford, 21 March, 1954 (D)

League Club	Source	Date Signed	Seasons Played	Apps	Subs	Gls
Southend U.	App	03.72	72-76	60	8	0

DYKE Charles
Caerphilly, 23 September, 1926 (OR)

League Club	Source	Date Signed	Seasons Played	Apps	Subs	Gls
Chelsea	Troedyrhiw	11.47	47-50	24	-	2

DYKES Donald William
Spilsby, 8 June, 1930 (WH)

League Club	Source	Date Signed	Seasons Played	Apps	Subs	Gls
Lincoln C.	M. & B.D.C.	06.49	49-58	95	-	4

DYMOND William Henry
Dawlish, 13 February, 1920 (OR)

League Club	Source	Date Signed	Seasons Played	Apps	Subs	Gls
Bristol C.		09.45	46	8	-	1
Exeter C.	Tr	06.47	47-48	41	-	7

DYSON John **Barry**
Oldham, 6 September, 1942 Died 1995 (IF)

League Club	Source	Date Signed	Seasons Played	Apps	Subs	Gls
Bury	Jnrs	09.60				
Tranmere Rov.	Tr	07.62	62-66	174	0	100
Crystal Palace	Tr	09.66	66-67	33	1	9
Watford	Tr	01.68	67-68	38	0	19
Leyton Orient	Tr	12.68	68-72	154	6	28
Colchester U.	Tr	07.73	73-74	41	1	6

DYSON Geoffrey
Huddersfield, 16 March, 1923 Died 1989 (IF)

League Club	Source	Date Signed	Seasons Played	Apps	Subs	Gls
Huddersfield T.	Jnrs	03.46				
Bradford C.	Tr	06.47	47	1	-	0
Accrington St.	Tr	01.48	47-48	20	-	1

DYSON Jack
Oldham, 8 July, 1934 Eu23-1 (IF)

League Club	Source	Date Signed	Seasons Played	Apps	Subs	Gls
Manchester C.	Nelson	05.52	55-59	63	-	26

DYSON James
Seaham, 16 December, 1935 (G)

League Club	Source	Date Signed	Seasons Played	Apps	Subs	Gls
Hartlepool U.	Seaham Colly	04.55	54-58	63	-	0

DYSON Jonathan Paul
Mirfield, 18 December, 1971 (D)

League Club	Source	Date Signed	Seasons Played	Apps	Subs	Gls
Huddersfield T.	Jnrs	12.90	92-97	125	16	3

DYSON Keith
Consett, 10 February, 1950 Eu23-1 (F)

League Club	Source	Date Signed	Seasons Played	Apps	Subs	Gls
Newcastle U.	Jnrs	08.68	68-71	74	2	22
Blackpool	Tr	10.71	71-75	91	3	30

DYSON Paul Ian
Birmingham, 27 December, 1959 Eu21-4 (CD)

League Club	Source	Date Signed	Seasons Played	Apps	Subs	Gls
Coventry C.	App	06.77	78-82	140	0	5
Stoke C.	Tr	07.83	83-85	106	0	5
West Bromwich A.	Tr	03.86	85-88	64	0	5
Darlington	Tr	03.89	88	12	0	3
Crewe Alex.	Tr	08.89	89	30	1	2

DYSON Terence Kent
Malton, 29 November, 1934 (OL)

League Club	Source	Date Signed	Seasons Played	Apps	Subs	Gls
Tottenham H.	Scarborough	04.55	54-64	184	-	41
Fulham	Tr	06.65	65	21	1	3
Colchester U.	Tr	08.68	68-69	53	3	4

DZIADULEWICZ Mark
Wimbledon, 29 January, 1960 (M)

League Club	Source	Date Signed	Seasons Played	Apps	Subs	Gls
Southend U.	App	02.78				
Wimbledon	Chelmsford C.	02.79	78-79	22	6	1

DZIEKANOWSKI Dariusz (Jackie) Pavel
Poland, 30 September, 1962 Polish Int (F)

League Club	Source	Date Signed	Seasons Played	Apps	Subs	Gls
Bristol C.	Glasgow Celtic	01.92	91-92	40	3	7

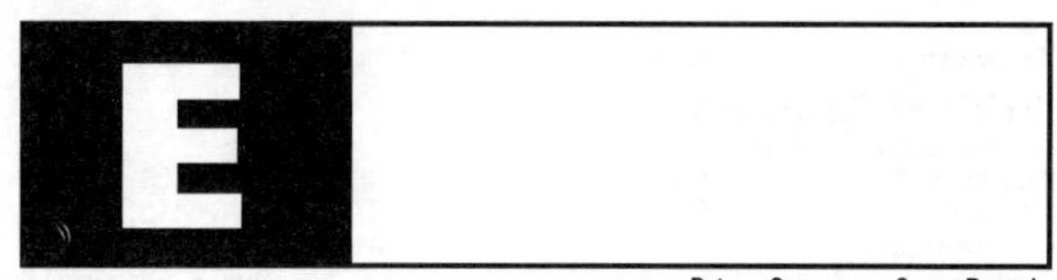

League Club	Source	Date Signed	Seasons Played	Career Record Apps	Subs	Gls
EADEN Nicholas Jeremy						
Sheffield, 12 December, 1972						(RB)
Barnsley	Jnrs	06.91	92-97	205	6	8
EADES Kevin Michael						
Rotherham, 11 March, 1959						(OR)
Rotherham U.	App	03.77	75	1	0	0
EADES Terence Gerald						
Banbridge (NI), 5 March, 1944						(CD)
Cambridge U.	Chelmsford C.	03.69	70-76	248	0	5
Watford	L	09.76	76	4	0	0
EADIE Darren Malcolm						
Chippenham, 10 June, 1975 E Yth/Eu21-7						(LW)
Norwich C.	YT	02.93	93-97	120	13	31
EADIE Douglas						
Edinburgh, 22 September, 1946						(OL)
West Ham U.		09.66	66	2	0	0
Leyton Orient	L	09.67	67	2	0	0
EADIE Gordon						
Glasgow , 17 November, 1950						(OL)
Bury (Am)	Glasgow U.	06.67	67	2	0	0
EADIE James						
Alexandria, 4 February, 1947						(G)
Cardiff C.	Kirkintilloch Rob Roy	09.66	69-71	43	0	0
Chester C.	L	08.72	72	6	0	0
Bristol Rov.	Tr	02.73	72-76	183	0	0
EAGLES Alan James						
Willesden, 6 September, 1933 Died 1995						(FB)
Leyton Orient	Carshalton Ath.	09.57	57-60	75	-	0
Colchester U.	Tr	01.61	60	16	-	1
Queens Park R.	Tr	08.61				
Aldershot	Tr	11.61	61-62	15	-	1
EALING William						
Tamworth, 12 March, 1930						(CF)
Blackburn Rov.		02.50				
Walsall	Tr	07.52	52	1	-	0
EAMES Terence						
Croydon, 13 October, 1957						(FB)
Wimbledon	Crystal Palace (Am)	(N/L)	77-79	46	1	1
EAMES William Alan						
Malta, 20 September, 1957						(M)
Portsmouth	App	09.75	75	9	2	1
Brentford	Tr	08.78	78	2	0	1
EARL Albert (Sam) Thomas						
Gateshead, 10 February, 1915						(IF)
Bury	Dunston C.W.S.	03.32	33-36	35	-	7
York C.	Rhyl Ath.	07.37	37-38	58	-	9
Stockport Co.	Tr	08.46	46-47	42	-	12
Rochdale	Tr	11.47	47	4	-	1
New Brighton	Tr	03.48	47	9	-	1
EARL Stanley James William						
Alton, 9 July, 1929						(FB)
Portsmouth	Alton T.	11.49	50-51	8	-	0
Leyton Orient	Tr	07.53	53-55	33	-	0
Swindon T.	Tr	11.56	56-57	23	-	0
EARL Steven						
Scunthorpe, 31 August, 1956						(F)
Scunthorpe U. (Am)	Appleby Frodingham	09.74	74	7	0	1
Scunthorpe U.	Appleby Frodingham	11.78	78-79	30	2	9
EARLAM Donald Stuart						
Altrincham, 25 June, 1931 Died 1988						(LH)
Southport (Am)	Broad Heath C.	08.54	54	2	-	0
EARLE Robert (Robbie) Fitzgerald						
Newcastle-u-Lyme, 27 January, 1965 Jamaican Int						(M)
Port Vale	Jnrs	07.82	82-90	284	10	77
Wimbledon	Tr	07.91	91-97	222	2	51

League Club	Source	Date Signed	Seasons Played	Career Record Apps	Subs	Gls
EARLE Stephen John						
Feltham, 1 November, 1945						(F)
Fulham	App	11.63	63-73	285	6	98
Leicester C.	Tr	11.73	73-77	91	8	20
Peterborough U.	L	11.77	77	1	0	0
EARLES Patrick John						
Titchfield (Hants), 22 March, 1955 E Sch						(F)
Southampton	App	11.72	74-76	4	8	1
Reading	Tr	01.77	76-82	240	7	68
EARLS Michael Patrick Marien						
Limerick (Ire), 25 March, 1954						(CD)
Southampton	App	03.72	73-74	8	0	0
Aldershot	Tr	06.75	75-78	68	5	0
EARLY Michael						
Dumbarton, 4 April, 1928 Died 1995						(OR)
Watford	Strathleven	06.46	46	5	-	1
EARNSHAW Robert						
Zambia, 6 April, 1981						(F)
Cardiff C.	YT	●	97	0	5	0
EARNSHAW Robert Ian						
Rotherham, 15 March, 1943						(OR)
Barnsley	Jnrs	06.62	62-72	219	6	35
EASDALE John						
Dumbarton, 16 January, 1919						(CH)
Liverpool		02.37	46	2	-	0
Stockport Co.	Tr	09.48	48	6	-	0
EAST Keith Michael George						
Southampton, 31 October, 1944						(CF)
Portsmouth	App	06.63				
Swindon T.	Tr	05.64	64-66	43	2	21
Stockport Co.	Tr	12.66	66-67	23	2	7
Bournemouth	Tr	11.67	67-69	93	1	34
Northampton T.	Tr	07.70	70	26	3	7
Crewe Alex.	Tr	07.71	71	32	2	8
EASTER Graham Paul						
Epsom, 26 September, 1969						(W)
West Bromwich A.	YT	07.88				
Huddersfield T.	Tr	03.89				
Crewe Alex.	Tr	07.89	89	0	3	0
Preston N.E. (N/C)	Finland	10.90	90	1	0	0
EASTHAM Brian						
Bolton, 26 April, 1937						(FB)
Bury		09.58	58-66	188	1	3
Rochdale	Toronto (Can)	07.67	67	13	0	0
EASTHAM George Edward						
Blackpool, 23 September, 1936 Eu23-6/EF Lge/E-19						(IF)
Newcastle U.	Ards	05.56	56-59	124	-	29
Arsenal	Tr	10.60	60-65	207	0	41
Stoke C.	Tr	08.66	66-73	184	10	4
EASTHAM George Richard						
Blackpool, 13 September, 1913 E-1						(IF)
Bolton W.	Southshore Wed.	08.32	32-36	114	-	16
Brentford	Tr	05.37	37-38	49	-	1
Blackpool	Tr	11.38	38-46	45	-	9
Swansea C.	Tr	08.47	47	15	-	0
Rochdale	Tr	06.48	48	2	-	0
Lincoln C.	Tr	01.49	48-49	27	-	1
EASTHAM Henry (Harry)						
Blackpool, 30 June, 1917						(IF)
Blackpool	Jnrs	06.34				
Liverpool	Tr	02.36	36-46	63	-	3
Tranmere Rov.	Tr	05.48	48-52	154	-	13
Accrington St.	Tr	07.53	53	42	-	3
EASTHAM Stanley						
Bolton, 26 November, 1913 E Amat						(RH)
Liverpool		05.38				
Exeter C.	Tr	04.46				
Stockport Co.	Tr	06.46	46	14	-	1
EASTHOPE Joseph Donald						
Liverpool, 26 September, 1929 Died 1993						(OL)
Everton		04.50	52	2	-	0
Stockport Co.	Tr	06.54	54	9	-	2
EASTMAN Donald John						
Eastry, 9 August, 1923						(FB)
Crystal Palace (Am)	Jnrs	08.46	46	1	-	0

League Club	Source	Date Signed	Seasons Played	Career Record Apps	Subs	Gls
EASTOE Peter Robert						
Tamworth, 2 August, 1953 E Yth						(F)
Wolverhampton W.	App	06.71	71-73	4	2	0
Swindon T.	Tr	11.73	73-75	91	0	43
Queens Park R.	Tr	03.76	76-78	69	3	15
Everton	Tr	03.79	78-81	88	7	26
West Bromwich A.	Tr	08.82	82	30	1	8
Leicester C.	L	10.83	83	5	0	1
Huddersfield T.	L	03.84	83	8	2	0
Walsall	L	08.84	84	6	0	1
Leicester C.	L	10.84	84	6	0	1
Wolverhampton W.	L	02.85	84	8	0	0
EASTON Clint Jude						
Barking, 1 October, 1977 E Yth						(M)
Watford	YT	07.96	96-97	25	4	1
EASTON Henry (Harry) Blair						
Shoreham, 12 September, 1938						(F)
Crystal Palace	Jnrs	11.56	59-61	8	-	1
EASTWAY Raymond John						
Croydon, 12 April, 1929 Died 1989						(RB)
Watford		08.49	51	12	-	0
EASTWOOD Eric						
Heywood, 24 March, 1916 Died 1991						(CH)
Manchester C.	Heywood St James	04.35	38-46	16	-	0
Port Vale	Tr	03.47	46-48	28	-	1
EASTWOOD Phillip John						
Blackburn, 6 April, 1978						(F)
Burnley	YT	07.96	97	1	2	0
EASTWOOD Raymond						
Manchester, 1 January, 1913						(FB)
Aldershot	Altrincham	06.38	38	9	-	0
Accrington St.	Tr	07.46	46	3	-	0
EATON Jason Cord						
Bristol, 29 January, 1969						(F)
Bristol Rov.	Jnrs	06.87	87	0	3	0
Bristol C.	Clevedon T.	03.89	88-89	6	7	1
EATON Joseph David						
Cuckney, 16 May, 1931						(IF)
Mansfield T.	Langwith B.C.	08.51	52-53	4	-	1
EATON Stephen Paul						
Liverpool, 25 December, 1959						(FB)
Tranmere Rov.	Jnrs	06.77	78	1	0	0
EAVES David Michael Curtis						
Blackpool, 13 February, 1973						(M)
Preston N.E.	YT	07.91	90-92	2	5	0
EAVES Ernest						
Ashton-in-Makerfield, 4 January, 1927						(CF)
New Brighton	Newton-le-Willows	10.48	48-50	14	-	3
EBANKS Michael **Wayne** Anthony						
Birmingham, 2 October, 1964						(RB/M)
West Bromwich A.	App	04.82	83	6	1	0
Stoke C.	L	08.84	84	10	0	0
Port Vale	Tr	03.85	84-86	36	3	0
Cambridge U. (N/C)	Tr	08.87	87	3	1	0
EBBRELL John Keith						
Bromborough, 1 October, 1969 E Sch/E Yth/Eu21-14/E'B'						(M)
Everton	YT	11.86	88-96	207	10	13
Sheffield U.	Tr	03.97	96	1	0	0
EBDON Marcus						
Pontypool, 17 October, 1970 W Yth/Wu21-2						(M)
Everton	YT	07.89				
Peterborough U.	Tr	07.91	91-96	136	11	15
Chesterfield	Tr	03.97	96-97	40	5	3
EBDON Richard George						
Ottery St Mary, 3 May, 1913 Died 1987						(CF)
Exeter C.	Ottery St Mary	12.35	35-47	138	-	50
Torquay U.	Tr	07.48	48	5	-	1
ECCLES Peter Edward						
Dublin, 24 August, 1962 IR-1						(CD)
Leicester C.	Dundalk	10.88	88	1	0	0

League Club	Source	Date Signed	Seasons Played	Career Record Apps	Subs	Gls
ECCLES Terence Stuart						
Leeds, 2 March, 1952						(CF)
Blackburn Rov.	App	08.69	69-72	33	13	6
Mansfield T.	Tr	07.73	73-76	115	3	47
Huddersfield T.	Tr	01.77	76-77	41	5	6
York C.	Ethnikos (Gre)	09.79	79-80	64	0	18
ECCLESHARE Keith						
Bolton, 14 December, 1950 E Yth						(FB)
Bury	App	12.68	68-71	79	3	0
ECCLESTON Stuart Ian						
Stoke, 4 October, 1961						(CD)
Stoke C.	App	10.79				
Hull C.	Tr	01.81	80-81	22	1	0
Port Vale	Tr	10.82				
ECKERSALL Michael William						
Bury, 3 February, 1939						(WH)
Torquay U.	Mossley	10.59	60-62	28	-	2
Stockport Co.	Tr	07.63	63-65	39	1	2
ECKERSLEY William						
Southport, 16 July, 1925 Died 1982 EF Lge/E 'B'/E-17						(FB)
Blackburn Rov.	High Park	03.48	47-60	406	-	20
ECKHARDT Jeffrey Edward						
Sheffield, 7 October, 1965						(CD/M)
Sheffield U.	Jnrs	08.84	84-87	73	1	2
Fulham	Tr	11.87	87-93	245	4	25
Stockport Co.	Tr	07.94	94-95	56	6	7
Cardiff C.	Tr	08.96	96-97	53	3	8
ECONOMOU Jon						
Holloway, 25 October, 1961						(M)
Bristol C.	App	10.79	81-83	62	3	3
EDDOLLS John Douglas						
Bristol, 19 August, 1919 Died 1994						(G)
Bristol C.	Peasedown	09.45	46	6	-	0
Bristol Rov.	Tr	08.48				
EDDS Ernest Frederick						
Portsmouth, 19 March, 1926						(OL)
Plymouth Arg.	Portsmouth (Am)	10.46	46-49	59	-	18
Blackburn Rov.	Tr	12.49	49-50	18	-	3
Torquay U.	Tr	06.51	51-53	84	-	34
Plymouth Arg.	Tr	10.53	53-54	26	-	4
Swindon T.	Tr	07.55	55	3	-	0
EDDY Keith						
Barrow, 23 October, 1944						(M)
Barrow	Holker C.O.B.	06.62	62-65	127	1	5
Watford	Tr	07.66	66-71	239	1	26
Sheffield U.	Tr	08.72	72-75	113	1	16
EDELSTON Maurice						
Hull, 27 April, 1918 Died 1976 E Amat						(CF)
Fulham (Am)	Jnrs	07.35	35-37	4	-	0
Brentford (Am)	Tr	12.37	37-38	21	-	6
Reading	Tr	05.39	46-51	202	-	70
Northampton T.	Tr	07.52	52-53	40	-	17
EDEN Alan						
Sunderland, 8 October, 1958						(M)
Lincoln C.	Lambton Street B.C.	08.77	77-78	5	2	0
EDEN Anthony Frederick						
Birmingham, 15 March, 1941						(CH)
Aston Villa	Jnrs	04.58				
Walsall	Tr	07.60	60-62	14	-	0
EDESON Matthew Kirk						
Beverley, 11 August, 1976						(F)
Hull C.	YT	07.94	92-94	0	5	0
EDEY Cecil						
Manchester, 12 March, 1965						(D)
Macclesfield T. (N/C)	Witton A.	10.95	97	9	4	0
EDGAR Edward (Ted)						
Jarrow, 31 October, 1956						(G)
Newcastle U.	App	08.74				
Hartlepool U.	Tr	07.76	76-78	75	0	0
EDGAR John (Tich)						
Barnsley, 9 April, 1936						(IF)
Barnsley	Jnrs	05.54	55-57	22	-	6
Gillingham	Tr	06.58	58	45	-	23

League Club	Source	Date Signed	Seasons Played	Apps	Subs	Gls
York C.	Tr	06.59	59-60	47	-	16
Hartlepool U.	Tr	06.61	61-62	72	-	31
Exeter C.	Tr	07.63	63	6	-	0
EDGAR John David						
Aldershot, 1 December, 1930						(IF)
Darlington	Ferryhill Ath.	12.54	54-55	12	-	0
EDGE Harold **Anthony**						
Hoylake, 14 March, 1937						(CF)
Bristol Rov.	Devizes	08.59	59-60	13	-	4
EDGE Declan John						
Malaysia, 18 September, 1965 New Zealand Int						(F)
Notts Co.	Gisborne C. (NZ)	12.85	85	7	3	2
EDGE Derek						
Hanley, 14 February, 1942						(OR)
Port Vale	Stoke C. (Am)	09.60	61	2	-	0
EDGHILL Richard Arlon						
Oldham, 23 September, 1974 Eu21-3/E 'B'						(FB)
Manchester C.	YT	07.92	93-97	85	0	0
EDGLEY Brian Kenneth						
Shrewsbury, 26 August, 1937						(IF)
Shrewsbury T.	Jnrs	02.56	55-59	113	-	12
Cardiff C.	Tr	07.60	60	10	-	1
Brentford	Tr	06.61	61-62	31	-	9
Barnsley	Tr	11.62	62	4	-	0
EDINBURGH Justin Charles						
Brentwood, 18 December, 1969						(LB)
Southend U.	YT	07.88	88-89	36	1	0
Tottenham H.	Tr	07.90	90-97	169	20	1
[EDINHO] Amaral Neto Edon Do						
Brazil, 21 February, 1967						(F)
Bradford C.	V.S.C. Guimaraes (Por)	02.97	96-97	49	7	15
EDISBURY William						
Leigh, 12 November, 1937						(FB)
Bolton W.	Jnrs	10.56	56-57	2	-	0
EDMONDS Darren						
Watford, 12 April, 1971						(LW)
Leeds U.	YT	05.89				
Ipswich T.	Tr	09.91	91	0	2	0
Scarborough (N/C)	Tr	08.92	92	0	1	0
Halifax T. (N/C)	Mossley	11.92	92	0	2	0
EDMONDS Derek James						
Newcastle, 9 November, 1950 E Yth						(G)
Leeds U.	App	11.67				
Watford	Tr	05.70	70-71	15	0	0
Southport	Cape Town (SA)	07.74	74	2	0	0
EDMONDS Neil Anthony						
Accrington, 18 October, 1968						(M)
Oldham Ath.	YT	06.86	86-87	3	2	0
Rochdale	Tr	09.88	88-89	36	7	8
EDMONDSON Douglas **Barry**						
Southport, 10 February, 1943						(WH)
Southport	Blackpool (Am)	12.61	61	1	-	0
EDMONDSON Darren Stephen						
Coniston, 4 November, 1971						(CD)
Carlisle U.	YT	07.90	90-96	205	9	8
Huddersfield T.	Tr	03.97	96-97	25	4	0
EDMONDSON Stanley Glasgow						
Bacup, 10 August, 1922 Died 1977						(OR)
Bradford C. (Am)	Bacup Borough	05.46	46	3	-	0
EDMUNDS Paul						
Doncaster, 2 December, 1957						(W)
Leicester C.	Troston Welfare	04.79	79-80	8	0	2
Bournemouth	Tr	07.81	81	13	1	2
EDMUNDS Redvern Esmond						
Risca, 10 January, 1943 W Sch						(OL)
Portsmouth	Jnrs	06.60	60	5	-	0
Newport Co.	Tr	07.61	61	4	-	0
EDWARDS Alistair Martin						
Australia, 21 June, 1968 Australian Int						(F)
Brighton & H.A. (N/C)	Sydney Olympic (Aus)	11.89	89	1	0	0
Millwall	Selangor (Mal)	12.94	94	3	1	0

League Club	Source	Date Signed	Seasons Played	Apps	Subs	Gls
EDWARDS Andrew David						
Epping, 17 September, 1971						(CD)
Southend U.	YT	12.89	88-94	141	6	5
Birmingham C.	Tr	07.95	95-96	37	3	1
Peterborough U.	Tr	11.96	96-97	71	0	2
EDWARDS Andrew John						
Wrexham, 28 March, 1965 W Yth						(W)
Wrexham	Jnrs	08.83	82-85	89	25	27
EDWARDS Brian Allan						
Portsmouth, 6 October, 1930						(FB)
Portsmouth	Jnrs	10.48	51	1	-	0
EDWARDS George **Bryan**						
Leeds, 27 October, 1930						(WH)
Bolton W.	Jnrs	10.47	50-64	482	-	8
EDWARDS Christian Nicholas Howells						
Caerphilly, 23 November, 1975 Wu21-7/W 'B'/W-1						(CD)
Swansea C.	YT	07.94	94-97	113	2	4
Nottingham F.	Tr	03.98				
EDWARDS Clifford						
Carmarthen, 4 December, 1928						(G)
Swansea C.		10.51	52	1	-	0
EDWARDS Clifford Ivor						
Cannock, 8 March, 1921 Died 1989						(WH)
West Bromwich A.	Cannock T.	10.38	46-47	40	-	1
Bristol C.	Tr	06.48	48-49	33	-	3
EDWARDS Emmanuel **Conroy (Roy)**						
Sheffield, 26 November, 1920						(IL)
Lincoln C.		06.47	47-48	6	-	0
EDWARDS David						
						(F)
Wrexham (Am)		11.49	49	1	-	1
EDWARDS David James						
Treharris, 10 December, 1934						(WH)
Fulham	Treharris	05.52	56-63	38	-	0
EDWARDS David John						
Bridgnorth, 13 January, 1974						(M)
Walsall	YT	01.92	91-92	16	11	1
EDWARDS David Samuel						
Bargoed, 11 September, 1916 Died 1990						(OL)
Newport Co.	Deri	09.37	37	1	-	0
Ipswich T.	Gloucester C.	06.39				
Swindon T.	Tr	06.46	46	3	-	1
EDWARDS Dean Stephen						
Wolverhampton, 25 February, 1962						(F)
Shrewsbury T.	App	02.80	79-81	7	6	1
Wolverhampton W.	Telford U.	10.85	85-86	28	3	9
Exeter C.	Tr	03.87	86-87	51	3	17
Torquay U.	Tr	08.88	88-91	98	18	26
Exeter C.	Tr	12.91	91	4	0	0
Northampton T. (N/C)	Tr	02.92	91	7	0	0
EDWARDS Dennis						
Slough, 19 January, 1937 E Amat						(IF)
Charlton Ath.	Wycombe W.	02.59	58-64	171	-	61
Portsmouth	Tr	01.65	64-67	69	2	14
Brentford	L	09.67	67	11	0	2
Aldershot	Tr	12.67	67	11	3	1
EDWARDS Donald						
Wrexham, 2 August, 1930 Died 1995						(G)
Norwich C.	Wrexham Vic.	09.47	47	2	-	0
EDWARDS Duncan						
Dudley, 1 October, 1936 Died 1958 E Sch/E Yth/Eu23-6/E 'B'/EF Lge/E-18						(WH)
Manchester U.	Jnrs	10.53	52-57	151	-	20
EDWARDS Edward						
Seaham, 13 February, 1936						(FB)
Hartlepool U.	Dawdon Jnrs	02.57	57	1	-	0
EDWARDS James **Elfyn**						
Aberystwyth, 4 May, 1960						(CD)
Wrexham	Jnrs	07.78				
Tranmere Rov.	Tr	07.79	79-80	62	0	1

League Club	Source	Date Signed	Seasons Played	Career Record Apps	Subs	Gls
EDWARDS George						
Treherbert, 2 December, 1920 W Amat/W-12						(OL)
Swansea C. (Am)	Jnrs	05.38	38	2	-	0
Birmingham C.	Tr	07.44	46-48	84	-	9
Cardiff C.	Tr	12.48	48-54	194	-	34
EDWARDS George Robert						
Norwich, 1 April, 1918 Died 1993						(F)
Norwich C.	Yarmouth Caledonians	04.36	35-37	9	-	1
Aston Villa	Tr	06.38	38-50	138	-	34
EDWARDS Jeffrey **Gordon**						
Wrexham, 14 October, 1935 W Sch						(CH)
Bolton W.	Jnrs	10.52	58	3	-	0
EDWARDS Henry Patrick						
Wigan, 13 February, 1932						(IF)
Blackpool		06.51				
Southport	Tr	08.53	54	1	-	0
EDWARDS Howard						
Tipton, 2 June, 1919 Died 1992						(WH)
Derby Co.	Stourbridge	01.47				
Crewe Alex.	Tr	06.52	52	5	-	0
EDWARDS Robert **Ian**						
Wrexham, 30 January, 1955 Wu21-2/W-4						(F)
West Bromwich A.	Rhyl	02.73	74-76	13	3	3
Chester C.	Tr	11.76	76-79	104	0	36
Wrexham	Tr	11.79	79-81	71	4	20
Crystal Palace	Tr	07.82	82	16	2	4
EDWARDS John (Jack)						
Salford, 23 February, 1924 Died 1979						(IF)
Nottingham F.	Long Eaton U.	05.44	46-48	77	-	20
Southampton	Tr	06.49	49-51	82	-	16
Notts Co.	Kidderminster Hrs	11.52	52-53	25	-	3
EDWARDS John						
Wrexham, 23 May, 1940						(G)
Wrexham (Am)	Bradley Sports	10.65	65	1	0	0
EDWARDS John (Jack) Francis						
Wath-on-Dearne, 27 December, 1921						(WH)
Rotherham U.	Manvers Main Colly	09.44	46-53	296	-	9
EDWARDS William **John (Jack)**						
Risca, 6 July, 1929						(FB)
Crystal Palace	Lovells Ath.	09.49	49-58	223	-	0
Rochdale	Tr	06.59	59-60	68	-	1
EDWARDS Keith						
Middlesbrough, 16 July, 1957						(F)
Sheffield U.	Jnrs	08.75	75-77	64	6	29
Hull C.	Tr	08.78	78-81	130	2	57
Sheffield U.	Tr	09.81	81-85	183	8	114
Leeds U.	Tr	08.86	86-87	28	10	6
Hull C.	Aberdeen	03.88	87-89	55	0	29
Stockport Co.	Tr	09.89	89	26	1	10
Huddersfield T.	L	03.90	89	6	4	4
Huddersfield T.	Tr	08.90	90	10	8	4
Plymouth Arg.	L	12.90	90	3	0	1
EDWARDS Keith Barry						
Chester, 10 June, 1944						(CF)
Chester C. (Am)	Buckley W.	03.66	65-66	3	0	0
EDWARDS Malcolm **Keith**						
Briton Ferry, 26 September, 1952 W Sch						(CD)
Leeds U.	App	10.69	71	0	1	0
EDWARDS Leonard Owen						
Wrexham, 30 May, 1930						(WH)
Sheffield Wed.	Wrexham (Am)	01.51	51	2	-	0
Brighton & H. A.	Tr	03.54	54	6	-	0
Crewe Alex.	Tr	12.55	55-56	40	-	0
EDWARDS Leslie Raymond						
Guildford, 12 April, 1924						(LB)
Bristol Rov.	Nailsea U.	05.48	50-56	47	-	0
EDWARDS Levi Wilfred						
Manchester, 10 September, 1961						(M)
Crewe Alex.	Ashton U.	08.85	85	10	3	0
Stockport Co.	Altrincham	09.86	86-87	40	9	5
EDWARDS Malcolm						
Wrexham, 25 October, 1939 W Sch/Wu23-2						(LB)
Bolton W.	Jnrs	11.56	56-60	14	-	1

League Club	Source	Date Signed	Seasons Played	Career Record Apps	Subs	Gls
Chester C.	Tr	02.61	60-61	43	-	5
Tranmere Rov.	Tr	07.62	62-63	34	-	2
Barrow	Tr	07.64	64-68	177	0	9
EDWARDS Matthew David						
Hammersmith, 15 June, 1971						(W)
Tottenham H.	YT	07.89				
Reading	L	03.91	90	6	2	0
Peterborough U.	Tr	03.92				
Brighton & H.A.	Tr	08.92	92-93	49	11	6
EDWARDS Michael						
Birkenhead, 10 September, 1974						(M)
Tranmere Rov.	YT	07.93	94	2	1	0
EDWARDS Michael						
Hessle, 25 April, 1980						(CD)
Hull C.	YT	●	97	20	1	0
EDWARDS Neil Anthony						
Rowley Regis, 14 March, 1966						(F)
Wolverhampton W.	Oldswinford	08.85	85-87	26	3	7
EDWARDS Neil Robert						
Liverpool, 2 July, 1967						(F)
Burnley	Liverpool (App)	08.85	85	0	1	0
EDWARDS Neil Ryan						
Aberdare, 5 December, 1970 W Sch/W Yth/Wu21-1						(G)
Leeds U.	YT	03.89				
Stockport Co.	Tr	09.91	91-96	163	1	0
Rochdale	Tr	11.97	97	27	0	0
EDWARDS Nigel Steven						
Wrexham, 31 December, 1950 Wu23-3						(FB)
Chester C.	Blackburn Rov. (Am)	09.68	68-77	281	10	15
Aldershot	Tr	07.78	78-81	137	0	6
Chester C.	Tr	06.82	82	8	0	1
EDWARDS Patrick Kenneth						
Wolverhampton, 9 December, 1939						(F)
Walsall	Jnrs	10.57	58	1	-	0
Chesterfield	Tr	07.59				
EDWARDS Paul						
Liverpool, 22 February, 1965						(G)
Crewe Alex.	Leek T.	02.89	88-91	29	0	0
Shrewsbury T.	Tr	08.92	92-97	203	0	0
EDWARDS Paul						
Manchester, 1 January, 1980						(FB)
Doncaster Rov. (N/C)	Ashton U.	02.98	97	5	4	0
EDWARDS Paul Francis						
Crompton, 7 October, 1947 Eu23-3/EF Lge						(CD)
Manchester U.	Jnrs	02.65	69-72	52	2	0
Oldham Ath.	Tr	09.72	72-77	108	4	7
Stockport Co.	L	01.77	76	2	0	0
Stockport Co.	Tr	08.78	78-79	64	3	2
EDWARDS Paul Ronald						
Birkenhead, 25 December, 1963						(LB)
Crewe Alex.	Altrincham	01.88	87-89	82	4	6
Coventry C.	Tr	03.90	89-91	32	4	0
Wolverhampton W.	Tr	08.92	92-93	43	3	0
West Bromwich A.	Tr	01.94	93-95	48	3	0
Bury	L	02.96	95	4	0	0
EDWARDS Reginald Ernest						
Rugeley, 28 January, 1953						(G)
Port Vale	Nuneaton Borough	08.72	72-74	8	0	0
EDWARDS Reginald Charles						
Newton-le-Willows, 24 July, 1919						(OL)
Luton T.	Alloa Ath.	11.45				
Accrington St.	Tr	08.46	46-48	66	-	10
EDWARDS Richard						
Hartlepool, 9 November, 1964						(G)
Hartlepool U. (N/C)		08.86	86	1	0	0
EDWARDS Richard Leonard						
Kingsbury, 5 November, 1943						(FB)
Luton T.	Admult	06.64	64-65	15	2	1
EDWARDS Richard Thomas						
Kirkby-in-Ashfield, 20 November, 1942						(D)
Notts Co.	Jnrs	10.59	59-66	221	0	20
Mansfield T.	Tr	03.67	66-67	45	0	1

League Club	Source	Date Signed	Seasons Played	Apps	Subs	Gls
Aston Villa	Tr	03.68	67-69	68	0	2
Torquay U.	Tr	06.70	70-72	99	3	5
Mansfield T.	Tr	07.73	73	31	2	1
EDWARDS Robert						
Manchester, 23 February, 1970						(F)
Crewe Alex.	YT	07.88	87-95	110	45	44
Huddersfield T.	Tr	03.96	95-97	63	21	11
EDWARDS Robert Henry						
Guildford, 22 May, 1931						(IF)
Chelsea	Woking	11.51	52-54	13	-	2
Swindon T.	Tr	07.55	55-59	173	-	65
Norwich C.	Tr	12.59	59	1	-	0
Northampton T.	Tr	03.61	60-61	23	-	10
EDWARDS Robert William						
Cockermouth, 1 July, 1973 W Yth/Wu21-17/W 'B'/W-4						(M)
Carlisle U.	YT	04.90	89-90	48	0	5
Bristol C.	Tr	03.91	91-97	169	24	5
EDWARDS Ronald						
Liverpool, 11 July, 1927						(IF)
Chesterfield	South Liverpool	07.53	53	13	-	2
EDWARDS Russell James						
Beckenham, 21 December, 1973						(CD)
Crystal Palace	Jnrs	06.92				
Barnet	L	03.94	93	5	0	1
EDWARDS Stanley						
West Bromwich, 11 December, 1942						(OL)
Everton	Jnrs	12.59				
Port Vale	Tr	05.61	61-62	49	-	9
EDWARDS Stanley Llewellyn						
Dawdon, 17 October, 1926 Died 1989						(CF)
Chelsea	Horden Colly	10.49				
Colchester U.	Tr	06.52	52	16	-	5
Leyton Orient	Tr	06.53	53	2	-	1
EDWARDS Stephen Gerald						
Birkenhead, 11 January, 1958						(D)
Oldham Ath.	App	01.76	77-82	77	3	0
Crewe Alex.	Tr	02.83	82-83	57	1	1
Rochdale	Tr	07.84	84	4	0	0
Tranmere Rov.	Tr	10.84	84-86	72	0	6
EDWARDS Walter **Thomas**						
Llanelli, 13 March, 1923						(OL)
Fulham	Workington	08.46	47	2	-	0
Southend U.	Tr	03.48	47-48	12	-	1
Leicester C.	Tr	12.48	48	3	-	1
Walsall	Bath C.	05.52	52	12	-	0
EDWARDS Leonard **Trevor**						
Rhondda, 24 January, 1937 Wu23-2/W-2						(FB)
Charlton Ath.	Jnrs	05.55	56-59	64	-	0
Cardiff C.	Tr	06.60	60-63	73	-	3
EDWARDS Walter						
Mansfield, 26 June, 1924						(W)
Mansfield T.	Woodhouse	11.47	47-48	25	-	5
Leeds U.	Tr	03.49	48	2	-	0
Leicester C.	Tr	08.49				
EDWARDS William						
Paddington, 8 January, 1952						(D)
Wimbledon	Walton & Hersham	08.74	77	21	0	2
EDWARDS William Inman						
Bowburn (Dm), 10 December, 1933						(CF)
Middlesbrough	Bowburn	03.52	52-54	16	-	4
EDWARDSON Barry John						
Hindley, 4 November, 1972						(M)
Wigan Ath.	YT	07.91	91	0	1	0
EDWARDSON John Philemon						
Manchester, 9 March, 1944						(HB)
Crystal Palace	Bethesda	11.66				
Crewe Alex.	L	01.68	67	1	0	0
EDWORTHY Marc						
Barnstaple, 24 December, 1972						(RB)
Plymouth Arg.	YT	03.91	91-94	52	17	1
Crystal Palace	Tr	06.95	95-97	119	4	0

League Club	Source	Date Signed	Seasons Played	Apps	Subs	Gls
EELES Anthony George						
Chatham, 15 November, 1970						(M)
Gillingham	YT	07.89	88-92	54	19	5
EGAN Christopher Anthony						
Limerick, 6 August, 1953						(OL)
Derby Co.	Cork Celtic	10.73				
Newport Co.	Tr	08.76	76	5	2	0
EGAN John						
Kilsyth, 19 August, 1937						(W)
Halifax T.	Stenhousemuir	10.59	59	5	-	0
Accrington St.	Tr	08.60	60	1	-	0
EGDELL Ernest						
Newcastle, 29 May, 1922						(CH)
Darlington (Am)	Consett	08.46	46	1	-	0
EGERTON Frank						
Atherton, 5 April, 1926						(FB)
Blackburn Rov.	Atherton Colly	04.44				
Accrington St.	Tr	06.47	47-48	8	-	0
EGGLESTONE Patrick						
Penrith, 17 March, 1927						(G)
Bradford C. (Am)	Portsmouth (Am)	05.48	48	2	-	0
Halifax T.	Tr	09.49	49	20	-	0
Shrewsbury T.	Tr	08.50	50-52	109	-	0
Wrexham	Tr	02.53	52-55	84	-	0
EGGLESTON Thomas						
Consett, 21 February, 1920						(LH)
Derby Co.	Jnrs	02.37				
Leicester C.	Tr	08.46	46-47	34	-	2
Watford	Tr	02.48	47-52	177	-	6
EGLINGTON Thomas Joseph						
Dublin, 15 January, 1923 IR-24/NI-6						(OL)
Everton	Shamrock Rov.	07.46	46-56	394	-	76
Tranmere Rov.	Tr	06.57	57-60	172	-	36
EHIOGU Ugochuku						
Hackney, 3 November, 1972 Eu21-15/E 'B'/E-1						(CD)
West Bromwich A.	YT	•	90	0	2	0
Aston Villa	Tr	07.91	91-97	168	11	9
EISENTRAGER Alois (Alec) Bernhard						
Germany, 20 July, 1927						(IF)
Bristol C.	Trowbridge T.	01.50	49-57	228	-	47
EKELUND Ronald Michael						
Denmark, 21 August, 1972 Danish Int						(F)
Southampton (L)	Barcelona (Sp)	09.94	94	15	2	5
Manchester C. (L)	Barcelona (Sp)	12.95	95	2	2	0
EKNER Daniel						
Sweden, 5 February, 1927 Died 1975						(CF)
Portsmouth (Am)	Sweden	11.49	49	5	-	0
EKOKU Efangwu (Efan) Goziem						
Manchester, 8 June, 1967 Nigerian Int						(F)
Bournemouth	Sutton U.	05.90	90-92	43	19	21
Norwich C.	Tr	03.93	92-94	26	11	15
Wimbledon	Tr	10.94	94-97	91	10	31
ELAD Diodene **Efon**						
Hillingdon, 5 September, 1970						(M)
Northampton T. (N/C)	Fortuna Köln (Ger)	01.94	93	8	2	0
Cambridge U. (N/C)	Tr	08.94	94	2	1	0
Mansfield T. (N/C)	Tr	02.95	94	0	2	0
ELDER Alexander Russell						
Lisburn (NI), 25 April, 1941 NI Sch/NIu23-1/NI-40						(LB)
Burnley	Glentoran	01.59	59-66	271	0	15
Stoke C.	Tr	08.67	67-72	80	3	1
ELDER Alexander Yeoman Pirrie						
Perth, 11 September, 1923						(IF)
Hartlepool U.	Dundee U.	08.51	51-52	65	-	20
ELDER James						
Scone, 5 March, 1928						(WH)
Portsmouth	Jeanfield Swifts	09.45	49	1	-	0
Colchester U.	Tr	07.50	50-54	199	-	15
ELEY Kevin						
Mexborough, 4 March, 1968						(W)
Rotherham U.	App	03.86	83-86	3	10	0
Chesterfield	Tr	08.87	87-89	72	9	2

ELGIN Robert Brown
Edinburgh, 23 June, 1949 (M)

League Club	Source	Date Signed	Seasons Played	Apps	Subs	Gls
Stockport Co.	Hearts	07.69	69-70	30	5	3

ELI Roger
Bradford, 11 September, 1965 (W)

League Club	Source	Date Signed	Seasons Played	Apps	Subs	Gls
Leeds U.	App	09.83	84-85	1	1	0
Wolverhampton W.	Tr	01.86	85-86	16	2	0
Crewe Alex (N/C)	Cambridge U. (N/C)	09.87	87	20	7	1
York C. (N/C)	Pontefract Colly	11.88	88	3	1	1
Bury	Tr	12.88	88	0	2	0
Burnley	Tr	07.89	89-92	70	29	20
Scunthorpe U. (N/C)	Hong Kong	02.95	94	0	2	0

ELKINS Gary
Wallingford, 4 May, 1966 E Yth (LB)

League Club	Source	Date Signed	Seasons Played	Apps	Subs	Gls
Fulham	App	12.83	84-89	100	4	2
Exeter C.	L	12.89	89	5	0	0
Wimbledon	Tr	08.90	90-95	100	10	3
Swindon T.	Tr	09.96	96	19	4	1

ELLAM Roy
Hemsworth, 13 January, 1943 (CH)

League Club	Source	Date Signed	Seasons Played	Apps	Subs	Gls
Bradford C.	Jnrs	05.61	61-65	149	0	12
Huddersfield T.	Tr	01.66	66-71	206	0	8
Leeds U.	Tr	08.72	72-73	9	2	0
Huddersfield T.	Tr	07.74	74	18	0	2

ELLAWAY William John
Crediton, 12 October, 1932 (IF)

League Club	Source	Date Signed	Seasons Played	Apps	Subs	Gls
Exeter C.	Barnstaple	11.54	53-55	31	-	9
Bournemouth	Tr	06.56	56-57	4	-	0

ELLERINGTON William
Southampton, 30 June, 1923 E Sch/EF Lge/E 'B'/E-2 (FB)

League Club	Source	Date Signed	Seasons Played	Apps	Subs	Gls
Southampton	Fatfield Colly	09.40	46-55	227	-	10

ELLINGTON Lee Simon
Bradford, 3 July, 1980 (M)

League Club	Source	Date Signed	Seasons Played	Apps	Subs	Gls
Hull C.	YT	●	96-97	4	5	2

ELLIOTT Andrew
Ashton-u-Lyne, 21 November, 1963 (M)

League Club	Source	Date Signed	Seasons Played	Apps	Subs	Gls
Manchester C.	App	11.81	81	1	0	0
Chester C.	Sligo Rov.	09.83	83	24	8	3

ELLIOTT Andrew
Newcastle, 2 May, 1974 (M)

League Club	Source	Date Signed	Seasons Played	Apps	Subs	Gls
Hartlepool U. (N/C)	Spennymoor U.	02.97	96-97	2	6	0

ELLIOTT Anthony Robert
Nuneaton, 30 November, 1969 E Sch/E Yth (G)

League Club	Source	Date Signed	Seasons Played	Apps	Subs	Gls
Birmingham C.	YT	12.86				
Hereford U.	Tr	12.88	88-91	75	0	0
Huddersfield T.	Tr	07.92	92	15	0	0
Carlisle U.	Tr	06.93	93-95	21	1	0
Cardiff C.	Tr	07.96	96-97	38	1	0
Scarborough	Tr	02.98	97	15	0	0

ELLIOTT Bernard (Bryn) Harry
Beeston, 3 May, 1925 (WH)

League Club	Source	Date Signed	Seasons Played	Apps	Subs	Gls
Nottingham F.	Beeston B.C.	10.42	47-48	10	-	0
Southampton	Tr	10.49	49-57	235	-	2

ELLIOTT Charles Standish
Bolsover, 24 April, 1912 (FB)

League Club	Source	Date Signed	Seasons Played	Apps	Subs	Gls
Chesterfield	Sheffield Wed. (Am)	11.30				
Coventry C.	Tr	08.31	31-47	95	-	2

ELLIOTT David
Tantobie, 10 February, 1945 (M)

League Club	Source	Date Signed	Seasons Played	Apps	Subs	Gls
Sunderland	App	02.62	63-66	30	1	1
Newcastle U.	Tr	12.66	66-70	78	2	4
Southend U.	Tr	02.71	70-74	173	4	9
Newport Co.	Tr	07.75	75	21	0	0
Newport Co.	Bangor C.	10.78	78	0	2	0

ELLIOTT Eamonn Gerard
Belfast, 27 August, 1971 (M)

League Club	Source	Date Signed	Seasons Played	Apps	Subs	Gls
Carlisle U.	YT	07.90	90	3	1	0

ELLIOTT Edward (Ted)
Carlisle, 24 May, 1919 Died 1984 (G)

League Club	Source	Date Signed	Seasons Played	Apps	Subs	Gls
Carlisle U.		12.37	37-38	11	-	0
Wolverhampton W.	Tr	02.39	46-47	7	-	0
Chester C.	Tr	10.48	48-50	59	-	0
Halifax T.	Tr	11.50	50-51	33	-	0

ELLIOTT Frederick **Francis** George
Lambeth, 23 July, 1929 (G)

League Club	Source	Date Signed	Seasons Played	Apps	Subs	Gls
Swansea C.	Merthyr Tydfil	09.49				
Stoke C.	Tr	12.52	52-53	22	-	0
Fulham	Tr	03.54	53-55	25	-	0
Mansfield T.	Tr	07.56	56-57	63	-	0

ELLIOTT Harvey
Middleton, 21 January, 1922 Died 1996 (IF)

League Club	Source	Date Signed	Seasons Played	Apps	Subs	Gls
Hull C.		12.46	46	4	-	0

ELLIOTT Ian
Barrow, 16 December, 1953 (G)

League Club	Source	Date Signed	Seasons Played	Apps	Subs	Gls
Barrow	Jnrs	●	69	1	0	0

ELLIOTT John
Eden Valley, 6 May, 1938 (IR)

League Club	Source	Date Signed	Seasons Played	Apps	Subs	Gls
Carlisle U.	Jnrs	08.55	55-57	2	-	1

ELLIOTT John Walter
Warkworth (Nd), 23 December, 1946 (OL)

League Club	Source	Date Signed	Seasons Played	Apps	Subs	Gls
Notts Co.	Ashington	08.67	67-68	61	3	7

ELLIOTT Kevan
Chilton (Dm), 5 September, 1958 (F)

League Club	Source	Date Signed	Seasons Played	Apps	Subs	Gls
Hartlepool U.	App	09.76	75-76	24	3	1

ELLIOTT Lee
Ormskirk, 5 May, 1970 (F)

League Club	Source	Date Signed	Seasons Played	Apps	Subs	Gls
Crewe Alex.	Everton (YT)	06.88	88	1	0	0

ELLIOTT Richard **Mark**
Rhondda, 20 March, 1959 (M)

League Club	Source	Date Signed	Seasons Played	Apps	Subs	Gls
Brighton & H. A.	Merthyr Tydfil	02.77	76	3	0	0
Cardiff C.	Tr	09.79	79	6	1	0
Bournemouth	L	01.80	79	4	0	0
Wimbledon (N/C)	Ton Pentre	02.82	81	7	4	1

ELLIOTT Matthew Stephen
Wandsworth, 1 November, 1968 S-3 (CD)

League Club	Source	Date Signed	Seasons Played	Apps	Subs	Gls
Charlton Ath.	Epsom & Ewell	05.88				
Torquay U.	Tr	03.89	88-91	123	1	15
Scunthorpe U.	Tr	03.92	91-93	61	0	8
Oxford U.	Tr	11.93	93-96	148	0	21
Leicester C.	Tr	01.97	96-97	53	0	11

ELLIOTT Paul Marcellus
Lewisham, 18 March, 1964 E Yth/Eu21-3/E-'B' (CD)

League Club	Source	Date Signed	Seasons Played	Apps	Subs	Gls
Charlton Ath.	App	03.81	81-82	61	2	1
Luton T.	Tr	03.83	82-85	63	3	4
Aston Villa	Tr	12.85	85-86	56	1	7
Chelsea	Glasgow Celtic	07.91	91-92	42	0	3

ELLIOTT Raymond Charles
Eastleigh, 11 June, 1947 (F)

League Club	Source	Date Signed	Seasons Played	Apps	Subs	Gls
Charlton Ath.	App	06.65				
Exeter C.	Tr	03.66	65-66	28	0	3

ELLIOTT Raymond John
Rhondda, 23 March, 1929 (OR)

League Club	Source	Date Signed	Seasons Played	Apps	Subs	Gls
Millwall	Woking	11.46	47-48	2	-	0

ELLIOTT Robert James
Newcastle, 25 December, 1973 E Yth/Eu21-2 (LB)

League Club	Source	Date Signed	Seasons Played	Apps	Subs	Gls
Newcastle U.	YT	04.91	90-96	71	8	9
Bolton W.	Tr	07.97	97	4	0	0

ELLIOTT Shaun
Haltwhistle, 26 January, 1957 E 'B' (CD)

League Club	Source	Date Signed	Seasons Played	Apps	Subs	Gls
Sunderland	App	01.75	76-85	316	5	11
Norwich C.	Tr	08.86	86-87	29	2	2
Blackpool	Tr	08.88	88-89	66	1	0

ELLIOTT Stephen Blair
Haltwhistle, 15 September, 1958 (F)

League Club	Source	Date Signed	Seasons Played	Apps	Subs	Gls
Nottingham F.	App	09.76	78	4	0	0
Preston N.E.	Tr	03.79	78-83	202	6	70
Luton T.	Tr	07.84	84	12	0	3
Walsall	Tr	12.84	84-85	68	1	21
Bolton W.	Tr	07.86	86-88	57	3	11
Bury	Tr	09.88	88	31	0	11
Rochdale	Tr	10.89	89-90	46	6	9

ELLIOTT Steven William
Derby, 29 October, 1978 Eu21-3 (CD)

League Club	Source	Date Signed	Seasons Played	Apps	Subs	Gls
Derby Co.	YT	03.97	97	3	0	0

ELLIOTT Stuart Thomas
Hendon, 27 August, 1977 (CD)

League Club	Source	Date Signed	Seasons Played	Apps	Subs	Gls
Newcastle U.	YT	08.95				

League Club	Source	Date Signed	Seasons Played	Apps	Subs	Gls
Hull C.	L	02.97	96	3	0	0
Swindon T.	L	02.98	97	1	1	0

ELLIOTT William
Poole, 23 October, 1961 (M)

League Club	Source	Date Signed	Seasons Played	Apps	Subs	Gls
Plymouth Arg.	App	03.79				
Bournemouth	Tr	05.80	80	6	5	1

ELLIOTT William Bethwaite
Workington, 6 August, 1919 Died 1966 (OR)

League Club	Source	Date Signed	Seasons Played	Apps	Subs	Gls
Carlisle U.	Jnrs	11.36				
Wolverhampton W.	Dudley T.	07.37				
Bournemouth	Tr	05.38	38	10	-	1
West Bromwich A.	Tr	12.38	38-50	170	-	39

ELLIOTT William Henry
Bradford, 20 March, 1925 EF Lge/E-5 (OL)

League Club	Source	Date Signed	Seasons Played	Apps	Subs	Gls
Bradford P.A.	Jnrs	04.42	46-50	176	-	21
Burnley	Tr	09.51	51-52	74	-	14
Sunderland	Tr	06.53	53-58	193	-	23

ELLIS Alan
Alfreton, 17 November, 1951 (M)

League Club	Source	Date Signed	Seasons Played	Apps	Subs	Gls
Charlton Ath.	App	11.69	70-72	9	5	0

ELLIS Anthony Joseph
Salford, 20 October, 1964 (F)

League Club	Source	Date Signed	Seasons Played	Apps	Subs	Gls
Oldham Ath.	Horwich R.M.I.	08.86	86-87	5	3	0
Preston N.E.	Tr	10.87	87-89	80	6	27
Stoke C.	Tr	12.89	89-91	66	11	19
Preston N.E.	Tr	08.92	92-93	70	2	48
Blackpool	Tr	07.94	94-97	140	6	55
Bury	Tr	12.97	97	21	1	6

ELLIS David
(W)

League Club	Source	Date Signed	Seasons Played	Apps	Subs	Gls
Bury	Pollok Jnrs	04.47				
Halifax T.	Tr	01.48	47	3	-	0
Barrow	Tr	10.48	48	1	-	0

ELLIS Glenn Douglas
Dagenham, 31 October, 1957 E Sch (G)

League Club	Source	Date Signed	Seasons Played	Apps	Subs	Gls
Ipswich T.	App	10.75				
Colchester U.	L	12.76	76	2	0	0

ELLIS Keith Duncan
Sheffield, 6 November, 1935 (CF)

League Club	Source	Date Signed	Seasons Played	Apps	Subs	Gls
Sheffield Wed.	Jnrs	04.55	54-63	102	-	52
Scunthorpe U.	Tr	03.64	63	10	-	5
Cardiff C.	Tr	09.64	64	22	-	10
Lincoln C.	Tr	06.65	65	7	0	0

ELLIS Kenneth
Buckley, 22 January, 1928 (W)

League Club	Source	Date Signed	Seasons Played	Apps	Subs	Gls
Chester C. (Am)	Jnrs	05.46	46	1	-	0
Wrexham (Am)		05.49	49	5	-	0

ELLIS Kenneth
Sunderland, 29 May, 1948 Died 1992 (D/F)

League Club	Source	Date Signed	Seasons Played	Apps	Subs	Gls
Hartlepool U.	Scarborough	07.71	71	32	2	4
Darlington	Verna (Bel)	07.79	79	21	0	0

ELLIS Kevin Edward
Tiptree, 11 May, 1977 (LB)

League Club	Source	Date Signed	Seasons Played	Apps	Subs	Gls
Ipswich T.	YT	08.95	94	1	0	0

ELLIS Mark Edward
Bradford, 6 January, 1962 (W)

League Club	Source	Date Signed	Seasons Played	Apps	Subs	Gls
Bradford C.	Trinity Ath.	08.80	80-89	190	28	30
Halifax T.	Tr	10.90	90-91	33	4	4

ELLIS Neil James
Wirral, 30 April, 1969 (LW)

League Club	Source	Date Signed	Seasons Played	Apps	Subs	Gls
Chester C.	Bangor C.	06.90	90	13	8	1
Maidstone U.	Tr	07.91	91	22	6	0

ELLIS Peter James
Portsmouth, 20 March, 1956 (CD)

League Club	Source	Date Signed	Seasons Played	Apps	Subs	Gls
Portsmouth	App	03.74	73-83	225	21	1
Southend U.	Tr	09.84	84	12	0	1

ELLIS Samuel
Ashton-u-Lyne, 12 September, 1946 Eu23-3 (CD)

League Club	Source	Date Signed	Seasons Played	Apps	Subs	Gls
Sheffield Wed.	Smiths (Manchester)	09.64	65-70	155	2	1
Mansfield T.	Tr	01.72	71-72	64	0	7
Lincoln C.	Tr	05.73	73-76	173	0	33
Watford	Tr	08.77	77-78	30	4	4

ELLIS Sydney Carey
Charlton, 16 August, 1931 Eu23-1 (FB)

League Club	Source	Date Signed	Seasons Played	Apps	Subs	Gls
Charlton Ath.	Crystal Palace (Am)	05.49	53-57	48	-	0
Brighton & H. A.	Tr	11.57	57-58	42	-	0

ELLISON Anthony **Lee**
Bishop Auckland, 13 January, 1973 (F)

League Club	Source	Date Signed	Seasons Played	Apps	Subs	Gls
Darlington	YT	11.90	90-93	54	18	17
Hartlepool U.	L	03.93	92	3	1	1
Leicester C.	Tr	08.94				
Crewe Alex.	Tr	08.95	95-96	3	1	2
Hereford U. (N/C)	Halifax T.	10.96	96	0	1	0
Darlington	Bishop Auckland	03.98	97	4	4	3

ELLISON Norman
Bebington, 2 November, 1929 (F)

League Club	Source	Date Signed	Seasons Played	Apps	Subs	Gls
Tranmere Rov.		10.49	49-50	2	-	0

ELLISON Raymond
Newcastle, 31 December, 1950 (FB)

League Club	Source	Date Signed	Seasons Played	Apps	Subs	Gls
Newcastle U.	App	10.68	71	5	0	0
Sunderland	Tr	03.73	72	2	0	0
Torquay U.	Tr	07.74	74	11	5	0
Workington	Tr	07.75	75-76	57	0	3

ELLISON William **Roy**
Newbiggin, 5 July, 1948 (M)

League Club	Source	Date Signed	Seasons Played	Apps	Subs	Gls
Newcastle U.	App	06.66				
Barrow	Tr	02.68	67-70	76	9	7
Hartlepool U.	L	10.70	70	5	0	0

ELLISON Samuel Walter
Leadgate, 27 August, 1923 Died 1994 (OR)

League Club	Source	Date Signed	Seasons Played	Apps	Subs	Gls
Sunderland	Mid. Crusaders	10.45	46	3	-	0
Reading	Consett	06.49	49	4	-	0

ELLSON Peter Edward
Audlem, 21 August, 1925 (G)

League Club	Source	Date Signed	Seasons Played	Apps	Subs	Gls
Crewe Alex.	Crewe R.P.	05.49	48-55	219	-	0

ELMES Timothy
Croydon, 28 September, 1962 (M)

League Club	Source	Date Signed	Seasons Played	Apps	Subs	Gls
Chelsea	App	07.80	80	2	2	0

ELMS James Brian
Manchester, 16 September, 1940 E Yth (OL)

League Club	Source	Date Signed	Seasons Played	Apps	Subs	Gls
Manchester U.	Jnrs	04.58				
Crewe Alex.	Tr	10.60	60	1	-	0

ELSBY Ian Christopher
Newcastle-u-Lyme, 13 September, 1960 (M/D)

League Club	Source	Date Signed	Seasons Played	Apps	Subs	Gls
Port Vale	Jnrs	06.78	78-80	32	11	1

ELSBY James
Newcastle-u-Lyme, 1 August, 1928 Died 1987 (FB)

League Club	Source	Date Signed	Seasons Played	Apps	Subs	Gls
Port Vale		05.47	48-53	12	-	0

ELSE Frederick
Golborne, 31 March, 1933 E 'B' (G)

League Club	Source	Date Signed	Seasons Played	Apps	Subs	Gls
Preston N.E.	Wigan Ath.	08.53	53-60	215	-	0
Blackburn Rov.	Tr	08.61	61-65	187	0	0
Barrow	Tr	07.66	66-69	148	0	0

ELSEY William **John**
Swansea, 23 December, 1938 W Sch (F)

League Club	Source	Date Signed	Seasons Played	Apps	Subs	Gls
Swansea C.	Jnrs	04.56	56	1	-	0
Wrexham	Tr	05.59				

ELSEY Karl William
Swansea, 20 November, 1958 (M)

League Club	Source	Date Signed	Seasons Played	Apps	Subs	Gls
Queens Park R.	Pembroke Borough	01.79	78-79	6	1	0
Newport Co.	Tr	07.80	80-83	114	9	15
Cardiff C.	Tr	09.83	83-84	59	0	5
Gillingham	Tr	08.85	85-87	126	2	13
Reading	Tr	08.88	88	41	3	3
Maidstone U.	Tr	07.89	89-90	70	2	5
Gillingham	Tr	08.91	91	25	2	3

ELSTRUP Lars
Denmark, 24 March, 1963 Danish Int (F)

League Club	Source	Date Signed	Seasons Played	Apps	Subs	Gls
Luton T.	B.K. Odense (Den)	08.89	89-90	50	10	19

ELSWORTHY John
Newport, 26 July, 1931 (WH)

League Club	Source	Date Signed	Seasons Played	Apps	Subs	Gls
Ipswich T.	Newport Co. (Am)	05.49	49-64	396	-	44

ELVY Reginald
Leeds, 25 November, 1920 Died 1991 (G)

League Club	Source	Date Signed	Seasons Played	Apps	Subs	Gls
Halifax T.		03.44	46	22	-	0

League Club	Source	Date Signed	Seasons Played	Apps	Subs	Gls
Bolton W.	Tr	03.47	47-49	31	-	0
Blackburn Rov.	Tr	11.51	51-55	192	-	0
Northampton T.	Tr	07.56	56-58	67	-	0

ELWELL Terence Thomas
Newport, 13 April, 1926 (FB)

League Club	Source	Date Signed	Seasons Played	Apps	Subs	Gls
Swansea C.	Barry T.	08.48	48-50	48	-	0
Swindon T.	Tr	07.52	52-53	61	-	0

ELWISS Michael Walter
Doncaster, 2 May, 1954 (F)

League Club	Source	Date Signed	Seasons Played	Apps	Subs	Gls
Doncaster Rov.	Jnrs	07.71	71-73	96	1	30
Preston N.E.	Tr	02.74	73-77	191	1	60
Crystal Palace	Tr	07.78	78	19	1	7
Preston N.E.	L	03.80	79	8	2	3

ELWOOD Joseph Patrick
Belfast, 26 October, 1939 NI Sch/NIu23-1/NI 'B' (OL)

League Club	Source	Date Signed	Seasons Played	Apps	Subs	Gls
Leyton Orient	Glenavon	04.58	58-65	101	2	25

EMANUEL William **John (Ivor)**
Treherbert, 5 April, 1948 W Amat/W-2 (M)

League Club	Source	Date Signed	Seasons Played	Apps	Subs	Gls
Bristol C.	Ferndale	05.71	71-75	124	4	10
Swindon T.	L	01.76	75	6	0	0
Gillingham	L	02.76	75	4	0	0
Newport Co.	Tr	06.76	76-77	79	0	4

EMBERSON Carl Wayne
Epsom, 13 July, 1973 (G)

League Club	Source	Date Signed	Seasons Played	Apps	Subs	Gls
Millwall	YT	05.91				
Colchester U.	L	12.92	92	13	0	0
Colchester U.	Tr	07.94	94-97	141	1	0

EMBERY Benjamin James
Barking, 10 October, 1944 (RB)

League Club	Source	Date Signed	Seasons Played	Apps	Subs	Gls
Tottenham H.	App	06.62				
Exeter C.	Tr	06.66	66-67	36	3	0

EMBLEN Neil Robert
Bromley, 19 June, 1971 (CD/M)

League Club	Source	Date Signed	Seasons Played	Apps	Subs	Gls
Millwall	Sittingbourne	11.93	93	12	0	0
Wolverhampton W.	Tr	07.94	94-96	80	8	9
Crystal Palace	Tr	08.97	97	8	5	0
Wolverhampton W.	Tr	03.98	97	6	1	0

EMBLEN Paul David
Bromley, 3 April, 1976 (F)

League Club	Source	Date Signed	Seasons Played	Apps	Subs	Gls
Charlton Ath.	Tonbridge	05.97	97	0	4	0
Brighton & H.A.	L	11.97	97	15	0	4

EMBLETON Daniel Charles
Liverpool, 27 March, 1975 (G)

League Club	Source	Date Signed	Seasons Played	Apps	Subs	Gls
Liverpool	YT	04.93				
Walsall (N/C)	Tr	08.94	94	0	1	0

EMBLETON David
Newcastle, 14 September, 1952 (D)

League Club	Source	Date Signed	Seasons Played	Apps	Subs	Gls
Newcastle U.	App	08.71				
Bury	Tr	07.72	72	6	1	0
Hartlepool U.	Tr	07.73	73-75	24	2	0

EMENALO Michael
Nigeria, 14 July, 1965 Nigerian Int (LB)

League Club	Source	Date Signed	Seasons Played	Apps	Subs	Gls
Notts Co.	Eintracht Trier (Ger)	08.94	94	7	0	0

EMERSON Dean
Salford, 27 December, 1962 (M)

League Club	Source	Date Signed	Seasons Played	Apps	Subs	Gls
Stockport Co.	East Manchester F.C.	02.82	81-84	156	0	7
Rotherham U.	Tr	07.85	85-86	55	0	8
Coventry C.	Tr	10.86	86-91	98	16	0
Hartlepool U.	Tr	07.92	92-93	44	1	1
Stockport Co.	Tr	11.93	93-94	8	3	0
Preston N.E.	Tr	11.94	94	1	0	0

EMERSON Moises Costa
Brazil, 12 April, 1972 (M)

League Club	Source	Date Signed	Seasons Played	Apps	Subs	Gls
Middlesbrough	F.C. Porto (Por)	07.96	96-97	53	0	8

EMERY Anthony John
Lincoln, 4 November, 1927 (CH)

League Club	Source	Date Signed	Seasons Played	Apps	Subs	Gls
Lincoln C.	Jnrs	08.47	46-58	402	-	1
Mansfield T.	Tr	06.59	59-60	26	-	0

EMERY Dennis
Sandy, 4 October, 1933 (IF)

League Club	Source	Date Signed	Seasons Played	Apps	Subs	Gls
Tottenham H.	Eynesbury Rov.	12.51				
Peterborough U.	Eynesbury Rov.	07.54	60-62	68	-	29

EMERY Donald Kenneth James
Cardiff, 11 June, 1920 Died 1993 W Sch (LB)

League Club	Source	Date Signed	Seasons Played	Apps	Subs	Gls
Swindon T.	Cardiff C. (Am)	06.37	37-47	69	-	3

EMERY James
Lisburn (NI), 2 March, 1940 (IR)

League Club	Source	Date Signed	Seasons Played	Apps	Subs	Gls
Exeter C.	Distillery	08.59				
Barrow	Tr	07.60	60	2	-	0

EMERY Stephen Roger
Ledbury, 7 February, 1956 (M)

League Club	Source	Date Signed	Seasons Played	Apps	Subs	Gls
Hereford U.	App	02.74	73-79	203	1	10
Derby Co.	Tr	09.79	79-81	73	2	4
Newport Co.	Tr	03.83				
Hereford U.	Tr	06.83	83-84	72	3	2
Wrexham	Tr	08.85	85	8	1	0

EMERY Terence George
Bristol, 8 September, 1936 (WH)

League Club	Source	Date Signed	Seasons Played	Apps	Subs	Gls
Bristol C.		02.57	56-57	11	-	0

EMMANUEL John **Gary**
Swansea, 1 February, 1954 Wu23-1 (M)

League Club	Source	Date Signed	Seasons Played	Apps	Subs	Gls
Birmingham C.	App	07.71	74-78	61	10	6
Bristol Rov.	Tr	12.78	78-80	59	6	2
Swindon T.	Tr	07.81	81-83	109	2	8
Newport Co.	Tr	07.84	84	12	0	0
Bristol C. (N/C)	Tr	08.85	85	2	0	0
Swansea C.	Tr	08.85	85-87	104	7	5

EMMANUEL David **Leonard**
Treboreth, 3 September, 1917 W Sch (FB)

League Club	Source	Date Signed	Seasons Played	Apps	Subs	Gls
Swansea C.		04.36	37-46	52	-	1
Newport Co.	Tr	05.47	46-47	33	-	7

EMMERSON Mark
Cuddington, 7 August, 1965 (M)

League Club	Source	Date Signed	Seasons Played	Apps	Subs	Gls
Wrexham (N/C)	Jnrs	08.82	82	1	1	0

EMMERSON Morris
Sunniside (Dm), 23 October, 1942 E Sch (G)

League Club	Source	Date Signed	Seasons Played	Apps	Subs	Gls
Middlesbrough	Jnrs	10.59	62	10	-	0
Peterborough U.	Tr	07.63	63	7	-	0

EMMERSON Wayne Edward
Canada, 2 November, 1947 (CF)

League Club	Source	Date Signed	Seasons Played	Apps	Subs	Gls
Manchester U.	Jnrs	09.65				
Crewe Alex.	Tr	07.68	68	6	1	1

EMPTAGE Albert Taylor
Grimsby, 26 December, 1917 EF Lge (WH)

League Club	Source	Date Signed	Seasons Played	Apps	Subs	Gls
Manchester C.	Scunthorpe U.	02.37	37-50	136	-	1
Stockport Co.	Tr	01.51	50-52	36	-	1

EMSON Paul David
Lincoln, 22 October, 1958 (W)

League Club	Source	Date Signed	Seasons Played	Apps	Subs	Gls
Derby Co.	Brigg T.	09.78	78-82	112	15	13
Grimsby T.	Tr	08.83	83-85	90	7	15
Wrexham	Tr	07.86	86-87	42	7	5
Darlington	Tr	08.88	88-90	39	9	5

ENDEAN Barry
Chester-le-Street, 22 March, 1946 (F)

League Club	Source	Date Signed	Seasons Played	Apps	Subs	Gls
Watford	Pelton Fell	09.68	68-70	72	5	28
Charlton Ath.	Tr	02.71	70-71	27	0	1
Blackburn Rov.	Tr	10.71	71-74	65	14	18
Huddersfield T.	Tr	03.75	74-75	8	4	1
Workington	L	10.75	75	8	0	2
Hartlepool U.	Tr	03.76	75-76	24	1	5

ENDERSBY Scott Ian Glenn
Lewisham, 20 February, 1962 E Yth (G)

League Club	Source	Date Signed	Seasons Played	Apps	Subs	Gls
Ipswich T.	App	03.79				
Tranmere Rov.	Tr	07.81	81-82	79	0	0
Swindon T.	Tr	08.83	83-85	85	0	0
Carlisle U.	Tr	11.85	85-86	52	0	0
York C.	Tr	07.87	87-88	35	0	0
Cardiff C.	L	12.87	87	4	0	0

ENES Roberto Manuel
Australia, 22 August, 1975 Australian Int (M)

League Club	Source	Date Signed	Seasons Played	Apps	Subs	Gls
Portsmouth	Sydney U. (Aus)	10.97	97	1	4	0

ENGLAND Frederick Watson
Holmfirth, 11 July, 1923 (IF)

League Club	Source	Date Signed	Seasons Played	Apps	Subs	Gls
Halifax T. (Am)	Huddersfield T. (Am)	05.46	46-47	18	-	1

League Club	Source	Date Signed	Seasons Played	Career Record Apps	Subs	Gls
ENGLAND Michael						
Kingswood, 4 January, 1961 (CD)						
Bristol Rov.	App	01.79	78	1	0	0
Bristol Rov.	Forest Green Rov.	09.85	85	17	0	0
ENGLAND Harold **Michael**						
Holywell, 2 December, 1941 Wu23-11/W-44 (CH)						
Blackburn Rov.	Jnrs	04.59	59-65	165	0	21
Tottenham H.	Tr	08.66	66-74	300	0	14
Cardiff C.	Tr	08.75	75	40	0	1
ENGLEFIELD Grahame William Elwyn						
Eltham, 21 September, 1931 (WH)						
Charlton Ath.	Jnrs	01.49				
Norwich C.	Tr	05.54	55-56	22	-	0
ENGLISH Anthony Karl						
Luton, 19 October, 1966 E Yth (CD)						
Colchester U.	Coventry C. (App)	12.84	84-95	345	6	42
ENGLISH John (Jack)						
Darlington, 19 March, 1923 Died 1985 (OR)						
Northampton T.	Bristol C. (Am)	10.46	47-59	301	-	135
ENGLISH Robert Harold						
Stockport, 19 April, 1939 (WH)						
Manchester U.	Jnrs	03.57				
Southport	Tr	11.61	61-62	20	-	0
ENGLISH Thomas Steven						
Cirencester, 18 October, 1961 E Yth (F)						
Coventry C.	App	06.79	79-81	62	4	17
Leicester C.	Tr	09.82	82-83	29	15	3
Rochdale (N/C)	Tr	09.84	84	3	0	1
Plymouth Arg. (N/C)	Tr	09.84	84	0	4	1
Colchester U.	Canberra C. (Aus)	11.85	85-86	34	13	17
Colchester U.	Bishops Stortford	10.89	89	12	1	3
ENGWELL Michael Leonard						
Grays, 27 September, 1966 (F)						
Southend U.	Jnrs	08.84	84-85	7	2	3
Crewe Alex. (N/C)	Tr	10.86	86	0	2	0
ENNIS Mark						
Bradford, 6 January, 1962 (D)						
Rochdale (N/C)	Joiners Libs	11.83	83	1	0	0
ENTWISTLE Robert Peter						
Bury, 6 October, 1938 (F)						
Rochdale (Am)	Macclesfield T.	03.59	58	1	-	0
Accrington St.	Tr	09.60	60	2	-	0
Hartlepool U.	Llandudno	10.64	64	14	-	3
ENTWISTLE Wayne Peter						
Bury, 6 August, 1958 E Yth (F)						
Bury	App	08.76	76-77	25	6	7
Sunderland	Tr	11.77	77-79	43	2	13
Leeds U.	Tr	10.79	79	7	4	2
Blackpool	Tr	11.80	80-81	27	5	6
Crewe Alex.	Tr	03.82	81	11	0	0
Wimbledon	Tr	07.82	82	4	5	3
Bury	Grays Ath.	08.83	83-84	80	3	32
Carlisle U.	Tr	06.85	85	8	1	2
Bolton W.	Tr	10.85	85	5	3	0
Burnley	L	08.86	86	6	2	2
Stockport Co.	Tr	10.86	86-87	38	11	8
Bury (N/C)	Tr	08.88	88	0	2	0
Wigan Ath.	Tr	10.88	88	24	5	6
Hartlepool U. (N/C)	Altrincham	09.89	89	2	0	0
EPHGRAVE George Arthur						
Reading, 29 April, 1918 (G)						
Aston Villa	Northfleet	10.36				
Swindon T.	Tr	03.39	38	1	-	0
Southampton	Tr	09.46	46-47	36	-	0
Norwich C.	Tr	07.48	48-50	5	-	0
Watford	Tr	08.51	51	4	-	0
ERANIO Stefano						
Genoa, Italy, 29 December, 1966 Italian Int (M)						
Derby Co.	AC Milan (It)	07.97	97	23	0	5
ERIKSSON Jan						
Sweden, 24 August, 1967 Swedish Int (CD)						
Sunderland	Helsingborg (Swe)	01.97	96	1	0	0
ESDAILLE Darren						
Manchester, 4 November, 1974 (D/M)						
Doncaster Rov.	Hyde U.	01.97	96-97	37	3	1
ESDAILLE David						
Manchester, 22 July, 1963 (M)						
Wrexham (N/C)	Winsford U.	08.92	92	4	0	0
Bury	Tr	01.93	92	1	5	0
Doncaster Rov. (N/C)	Hyde U.	08.97	97	10	3	0
ESHELBY Paul						
Sheffield, 29 May, 1970 (W)						
Exeter C.	Endcliffe U.	12.89	89-90	10	9	1
Scarborough	Tr	03.91	90	2	1	0
ESSER Edward **David**						
Altrincham, 20 June, 1957 (M)						
Everton	App	05.75				
Rochdale	Tr	07.77	77-81	169	11	24
ESSERS Pierre						
Netherlands, 20 February, 1959 (F)						
Walsall (N/C)	Charleroi (Bel)	09.91	91	1	0	0
ETHERIDGE Brian George						
Northampton, 4 March, 1944 E Yth (IF)						
Northampton T.	Jnrs	07.62	61-64	17	-	1
Brentford	Tr	02.66	65-66	22	0	2
ETHERIDGE Richard **Keith**						
Ivybridge, 14 May, 1944 (F)						
Plymouth Arg.	St Blazey	07.66	66-67	30	1	5
ETHERIDGE Robert James						
Gloucester, 21 March, 1934 Died 1988 (WH)						
Bristol C.	Gloucester C.	09.56	56-63	259	-	42
ETHERINGTON Matthew						
Truro, 14 August, 1981 (F)						
Peterborough U.	Jnrs	●	96-97	3	0	0
EUELL Jason Joseph						
Lambeth, 6 February, 1977 Eu21-2 (F)						
Wimbledon	YT	06.95	95-97	22	13	8
EUSTACE Peter						
Stocksbridge, 31 July, 1944 (M)						
Sheffield Wed.	App	06.62	62-69	189	3	21
West Ham U.	Tr	01.70	69-71	41	2	6
Rotherham U.	L	03.72	71	6	0	1
Sheffield Wed.	Tr	08.72	72-74	48	8	4
Peterborough U.	Tr	07.75	75	42	1	5
EUSTACE Scott Douglas						
Leicester, 13 June, 1975 (CD)						
Leicester C.	YT	07.93	93	0	1	0
Mansfield T.	Tr	06.95	95-97	90	8	6
EVANS Allan James						
Dunfermline, 12 October, 1956 S-4 (CD)						
Aston Villa	Dunfermline Ath.	05.77	77-88	374	6	51
Leicester C.	Tr	08.89	89	14	0	0
Darlington	Brisbane U. (Aus)	03.91	90	0	1	0
EVANS Alun James						
Penrycadery, 1 December, 1922 (WH/IF)						
West Bromwich A.	Wilden	01.43	47	18	-	0
EVANS Alun William						
Stourport, 30 September, 1949 E Sch/E Yth/Eu23-4 (F)						
Wolverhampton W.	App	10.66	67-68	20	2	4
Liverpool	Tr	09.68	68-71	77	2	21
Aston Villa	Tr	06.72	72-73	53	7	11
Walsall	Tr	12.75	75-77	78	9	7
EVANS Andrew David Stanley						
Swansea, 3 October, 1957 W Sch/W Yth/Wu21-1 (W)						
Bristol Rov.	App	09.75	75-77	34	8	2
EVANS David **Andrew**						
Aberystwyth, 25 November, 1975 W Yth (F)						
Cardiff C.	YT	12.94	93-95	5	10	0
EVANS Anthony						
Liverpool, 11 January, 1954 (F)						
Blackpool	Formby	06.73	74	4	2	0
Cardiff C.	Tr	06.75	75-78	120	4	47
Birmingham C.	Tr	07.79	79-82	62	4	28
Crystal Palace	Tr	08.83	83	19	2	7
Wolverhampton W.	Tr	06.84	84	20	3	5
Bolton W.	L	02.85	84	4	0	0
Swindon T.	Tr	08.85	85	8	2	0

League Club	Source	Date Signed	Seasons Played	Apps	Subs	Gls
EVANS Anthony William						
Colchester, 14 March, 1960						(M)
Colchester U.	App	03.78	77-80	20	9	2
EVANS Arthur						
Urmston, 13 May, 1933 E Yth						(G)
Bury	Jnrs	06.50	50	2	-	0
Stockport Co.	Tr	08.52				
Gillingham	Tr	09.53	53-54	14	-	0
EVANS Bernard						
Chester, 4 January, 1937						(CF)
Wrexham	Jnrs	08.54	54-60	114	-	47
Queens Park R.	Tr	10.60	60-62	78	-	35
Oxford U.	Tr	12.62	62-63	13	-	3
Tranmere Rov.	Tr	10.63	63	12	-	5
Crewe Alex.	Tr	07.64				
EVANS Bernard Royden						
Rotherhithe, 7 October, 1929						(IL)
Millwall		03.50				
Watford	Tr	08.51	51	2	-	1
EVANS Brian Clifford						
Brynmawr, 2 December, 1942 Wu23-2/W-7						(W)
Swansea C.	Abergavenny Thistle	07.63	63-72	351	4	58
Hereford U.	Tr	08.73	73-74	44	4	9
EVANS Ceri Lee						
Christchurch, 2 October, 1963						(CD)
Oxford U.	Oxford Univ.	02.89	88-92	113	3	3
EVANS Charles John						
West Bromwich, 4 February, 1923						(IF)
West Bromwich A.	Cordley Vic.	08.41	1946	1	-	0
EVANS Christopher Brian						
Rhondda, 13 October, 1962						(RB)
Arsenal	App	06.80				
Stoke C.	Tr	08.81				
York C.	Tr	08.82	82-85	93	3	1
Darlington	Tr	10.85	85-86	58	0	1
EVANS Andrew **Clive**						
Heswall, 1 May, 1957						(W/FB)
Tranmere Rov.	App	05.75	76-80	175	3	27
Wigan Ath.	Tr	07.81	81	29	3	2
Crewe Alex.	Tr	08.82	82	26	2	7
Stockport Co.	Tr	08.83	83-87	158	2	23
Lincoln C.	Tr	09.87	88	42	0	2
EVANS Darren						
Wolverhampton, 30 September, 1974						(RB)
Aston Villa	YT	07.93				
Hereford U.	Tr	09.95	95	24	0	0
EVANS David						
Chester, 4 April, 1967						(RB)
Chester C.	App	05.84	83-84	15	1	1
EVANS David (Dai)						
Colwyn Bay, 19 June, 1934						(G)
Crewe Alex.	Llandudno	03.57	56-59	50	-	0
EVANS David Gordon						
West Bromwich, 20 May, 1958						(CD)
Aston Villa	App	02.76	78	2	0	0
Halifax T.	Tr	06.79	79-83	218	0	9
Bradford C.	Tr	06.84	84-89	222	1	3
Halifax T.	Tr	08.90	90-91	68	5	1
EVANS David Thom						
Peterlee, 6 April, 1959						(F)
Hartlepool U.		07.78	78-79	2	2	0
EVANS Dennis						
Chester, 23 July, 1935						(FB)
Wrexham		03.55	55-57	11	-	0
Tranmere Rov.	Tr	06.58	58-59	3	-	0
EVANS Dennis Joseph						
Ellesmere Port, 18 May, 1930						(FB)
Arsenal	Ellesmere Port	01.51	53-59	189	-	10
EVANS David **Douglas**						
Ystradygynlais, 27 September, 1956						(W)
Norwich C.	App	08.74	76-79	14	4	1
Cambridge U.	Tr	03.80	79-80	11	1	2

League Club	Source	Date Signed	Seasons Played	Apps	Subs	Gls
EVANS Elfed						
Ferndale, 28 August, 1926 Died 1988						(IF)
Cardiff C.	Treharris	05.49	49-51	46	-	18
Torquay U.	L	03.51	50	12	-	6
West Bromwich A.	Tr	06.52	52	17	-	3
Wrexham	Tr	06.55	55-56	34	-	16
Southport	Tr	12.56	56	13	-	0
EVANS Emrys Brian						
Tonypandy, 16 September, 1930						(IF)
Newport Co.	Tottenham H. (Am)	08.52	52	18	-	4
EVANS Frederick John						
Petersfield, 20 May, 1923						(IF)
Portsmouth		01.45	46	9	-	2
Notts Co.	Tr	07.47	47-50	39	-	14
Crystal Palace	Tr	03.51	50-52	52	-	11
Rochdale	Tr	06.53	53	12	-	0
EVANS Gareth John						
Coventry, 14 January, 1967						(F)
Coventry C.	App	01.85	85-86	5	2	0
Rotherham U.	Tr	10.86	86-87	62	1	13
Stoke C. (L)	Hibernian	10.90	90	5	0	1
Northampton T. (L)	Hibernian	12.90	90	2	0	0
EVANS Gary Neil						
Doncaster, 20 December, 1968						(F)
Chesterfield	Thorne Colly	08.91	91	1	4	0
EVANS George Albert						
Wrexham, 6 July, 1935						(WH)
Wrexham	Oswestry T.	07.57	57-62	175	-	9
Chester C.	Tr	06.63	63-68	109	4	0
EVANS Gwyn						
Ton Pentre, 24 December, 1935						(CH)
Crystal Palace	Treorchy	03.55	58-62	80	-	0
EVANS Henry (Harry) Alfred						
Lambeth, 17 April, 1919 Died 1962						(IF)
Southampton	Woking	10.43	46	1	-	0
Exeter C.	Tr	04.47	47-48	41	-	6
Aldershot	Tr	03.49	48-49	16	-	5
EVANS Hubert William Richard						
Swansea, 10 August, 1922						(WH)
Swansea C.	Jnrs	08.39				
Newport Co.	Lovells Ath.	04.51	50-51	14	-	1
EVANS Gwilym **Hugh**						
Ynysybwl, 12 December, 1919						(IF)
Birmingham C.	Redditch U.	12.47	48-49	11	-	0
Bournemouth	Tr	06.50	50	22	-	8
Walsall	Tr	08.51	51	36	-	12
Watford	Tr	08.52	52	7	-	2
EVANS Ian Peter						
Egham, 30 January, 1952 Wu23-2/W-13						(CD)
Queens Park R.	App	01.70	70-73	39	0	2
Crystal Palace	Tr	09.74	74-77	137	0	14
Barnsley	Tr	12.79	79-82	102	0	3
Exeter C.	L	08.83	83	4	0	0
Cambridge U.	L	10.83	83	1	0	0
EVANS Ivor James						
Cardiff, 25 October, 1933						(IF)
Portsmouth	Guest Keen	09.56	56	1	-	0
EVANS Jason Stuart						
Telford, 22 January, 1974						(D)
Shrewsbury T.	YT	07.92	92	0	1	0
EVANS John						
Hetton-le-Hole, 21 October, 1932						(IF)
Norwich C.	Jnrs	10.49				
Sunderland	Tr	08.54	54	1	-	0
EVANS John (Taffy) Alwyn						
Aberystwyth, 22 October, 1922 Died 1956						(FB)
Millwall	Aberystwyth	09.43	46-49	73	-	2
Leyton Orient	Tr	06.50	50-53	149	-	0
EVANS John Charles						
Torquay, 24 March, 1947						(OR)
Torquay U.	App	04.65	64-65	6	0	1

League Club	Source	Date Signed	Seasons Played	Apps	Subs	Gls
EVANS John David						
Liverpool, 13 March, 1938						(IF)
Liverpool		05.58				
Bournemouth	Tr	05.59				
Stockport Co.		10.62	62-63	52	-	20
Carlisle U.	Tr	02.64	63-65	78	0	37
Exeter C.	Tr	03.66	65-66	11	1	2
Barnsley	Tr	11.66	66-70	165	5	54
EVANS John David						
Chester, 24 March, 1941						(FB)
Chester C.		08.61	61-64	40	-	0
EVANS John Joseph						
Coventry, 11 March, 1926						(CF)
Coventry C.	Mod Machines	06.47	48-50	8	-	1
EVANS John Llewelyn						
Wattstown, 4 October, 1937						(HB)
Gillingham	Lovells Ath.	04.56	57	7	-	0
EVANS John Randall						
Rhondda, 28 July, 1932						(FB)
Swansea C.	Jnrs	08.50	51	14	-	0
Bristol Rov.	Tr	06.53				
EVANS John William						
Tilbury, 28 August, 1929 EF Lge						(IF)
Charlton Ath.	Tilbury Bata	05.50	50-53	90	-	38
Liverpool	Tr	12.53	53-57	96	-	49
Colchester U.	Tr	11.57	57-59	56	-	22
EVANS Keith						
Trealaw, 15 September, 1953						(CD)
Swansea C.	App	08.71	70-72	14	0	0
EVANS Kenneth Philip						
Swansea, 17 July, 1931						(G)
Swansea C.	Carmarthen	06.50	54-56	13	-	0
Walsall	Tr	08.57	57	2	-	0
EVANS Leslie						
Rhondda, 26 December, 1924						(CH)
Cardiff C.		09.45				
Torquay U.	Tr	07.47	47	24	-	0
EVANS Leslie Norman						
Kingswinford, 13 October, 1929						(OL)
Cardiff C.	Brierley Hill Alliance	10.50	50-51	3	-	0
Plymouth Arg.	Tr	06.52				
EVANS Mark						
Leeds, 24 August, 1970						(G)
Bradford C.	YT	07.88	88-91	12	0	0
Scarborough	Tr	08.92	92-93	46	0	0
EVANS Maurice George						
Didcot, 22 September, 1936						(WH)
Reading	Jnrs	09.53	55-66	407	0	13
EVANS Medwyn John						
Brynteg, 8 November, 1964 W Sch						(M)
Wrexham	Jnrs	08.83	82-83	13	4	0
EVANS Michael						
West Bromwich, 3 August, 1946						(LB)
Walsall	Vono	05.64	65-72	229	2	7
Swansea C.	Tr	12.72	72-74	92	0	7
Crewe Alex.	Tr	07.75	75-76	62	0	4
EVANS Michael Graham						
Llanidloes, 4 June, 1947 W Sch/Wu23-2						(D)
Wolverhampton W.	App	07.64				
Wrexham	Tr	07.66	66-78	368	15	19
EVANS Michael James						
Plymouth, 1 January, 1973 IR-1						(F)
Plymouth Arg.	YT	03.91	90-96	130	33	38
Southampton	Tr	03.97	96-97	14	8	4
West Bromwich A.	Tr	10.97	97	2	8	1
EVANS Nicholas						
Trimdon, 23 November, 1925 Died 1992						(OR)
New Brighton (Am)	Heselden	03.47	46	1	-	0
EVANS Nicholas John						
Bedford, 6 July, 1958						(F)
Queens Park R.	App	07.76				
Peterborough U.	Tr	08.77				
Barnet	Wycombe W.	01.91	91-93	16	23	8
EVANS Oswald Vernon						
Llanelli, 2 September, 1916 Died 1986						(G)
Fulham	Milford Haven	02.46	46	1	-	0
EVANS Paul						
Kiveton Park, 24 February, 1949						(G)
Sheffield Wed.	Jnrs	02.66				
Mansfield T.	Boston U.	10.75	75	6	0	0
EVANS Paul Alan						
Brentwood, 14 September, 1964						(F)
Cardiff C.	Jnrs	09.82	83	0	2	0
Newport Co. (N/C)	Brecon Corries	07.87	87	9	1	2
EVANS Paul Simon						
Oswestry, 1 September 1974 W Yth/Wu21-4						(M)
Shrewsbury T.	YT	07.93	91-97	146	20	20
EVANS, Philip						
Swansea, 14 May, 1957						(CD)
Swansea C.	Jnrs	08.75	75	9	0	0
EVANS Denzil **Ralph**						
Hungerford, 9 October, 1915 Died 1996						(IF)
Bury		07.35				
Halifax T.	Yeovil T.	07.36	36	21	-	1
Watford	Tr	07.37	37-47	88	-	30
EVANS Raymond						
Mansfield, 27 November, 1927						(CF)
Coventry C.		05.48				
Mansfield T.	Stafford R.	11.49	49-52	39	-	12
EVANS Raymond						
Carlisle, 8 October, 1929						(G)
Crewe Alex.	Hightown Y.C.	10.48	48-50	21	-	0
EVANS Raymond						
Preston, 21 June, 1933						(W)
Preston N.E.	Jnrs	05.51	53-56	33	-	2
Bournemouth	Tr	06.59	59-60	36	-	9
EVANS Raymond Leslie						
Edmonton, 20 September, 1949 E Yth						(RB)
Tottenham H.	App	06.67	68-74	130	4	2
Millwall	Tr	01.75	74-76	74	0	3
Fulham	Tr	03.77	76-78	86	0	6
Stoke C.	Tr	08.79	79-81	94	0	1
EVANS Reginald						
Consett, 18 March, 1939						(F)
Newcastle U.	Jnrs	03.56	58	4	-	0
Charlton Ath.	Tr	03.59	58-59	14	-	2
EVANS Reuben						
Dublin, 19 March, 1941						(IF)
Bradford P. A.	Glasgow Rangers	06.63	63	13	-	5
EVANS Richard William						
Ebbw Vale, 12 April, 1968						(W)
Bristol Rov.	Weymouth	08.91	91-93	9	6	1
Exeter C.	L	10.92	92	5	0	2
EVANS Robert						
Glasgow, 16 July, 1927 SF Lge/S-48						(CH)
Chelsea	Glasgow Celtic	05.60	60	32	-	0
Newport Co.	Tr	06.61	61	31	-	0
EVANS Ronald						
St Helens, 21 February, 1929						(WH)
Stockport Co.	Bolton W. (Am)	07.50	50-53	6	-	0
EVANS Roy Quintin Echlin						
Crosby, 4 October, 1948 E Sch						(LB)
Liverpool	App	10.65	69-73	9	0	0
EVANS Royston Sidney						
Parkmill, 5 June, 1943 Died 1969 Wu23-3/W-1						(FB)
Swansea C.	Jnrs	07.60	62-67	215	2	7
EVANS John **Royston**						
Lampeter, 9 February, 1939						(W)
Wolverhampton W.	Bangor C.	08.56				
Wrexham	Tr	07.57				
Chester C.	Tr	10.57	57-59	23	-	3
Halifax T.	Tr	10.60	60	7	-	0

EVANS Stewart John
Maltby, 15 November, 1960 (CD/F)

League Club	Source	Date Signed	Seasons Played	Apps	Subs	Gls
Rotherham U.	App	11.78				
Sheffield U.	Gainsborough Trin.	11.80				
Wimbledon	Tr	03.82	81-85	165	10	50
West Bromwich A.	Tr	08.86	86	13	1	1
Plymouth Arg.	Tr	03.87	86-88	36	9	10
Rotherham U.	Tr	11.88	88-90	45	20	14
Torquay U.	L	03.91	90	15	0	5
Crewe Alex.	Tr	09.91	91-93	74	9	12

EVANS Terence William
Hammersmith, 12 April, 1965 (CD)

League Club	Source	Date Signed	Seasons Played	Apps	Subs	Gls
Brentford	Hillingdon Borough	07.85	85-92	228	1	23
Wycombe W.	Tr	08.93	93-96	128	8	16

EVANS Terry
Pontypridd, 8 January, 1976 Wu21-4 (RB)

League Club	Source	Date Signed	Seasons Played	Apps	Subs	Gls
Cardiff C.	YT	07.94	93-95	12	2	0

EVANS Thomas Raymond
Doncaster, 31 December, 1976 (G)

League Club	Source	Date Signed	Seasons Played	Apps	Subs	Gls
Sheffield U.	YT	07.95				
Crystal Palace	Tr	06.96				
Scunthorpe U.	Tr	08.97	97	5	0	0

EVANS Duncan **Wayne**
Abermule, 25 August, 1971 (FB)

League Club	Source	Date Signed	Seasons Played	Apps	Subs	Gls
Walsall	Welshpool	08.93	93-97	167	5	1

EVANS William Emmanuel
Birmingham, 5 September, 1921 Died 1960 (IF)

League Club	Source	Date Signed	Seasons Played	Apps	Subs	Gls
Aston Villa	Linread Wks	09.46	46-48	7	-	3
Notts Co.	Tr	06.49	49-52	96	-	14
Gillingham	Tr	07.53	53-54	89	-	12
Grimsby T.	Tr	06.55	55-57	102	-	28

EVANS Wyndham Edgar
Llanelli, 19 March, 1951 (FB)

League Club	Source	Date Signed	Seasons Played	Apps	Subs	Gls
Swansea C.	Stoke C. (Am)	02.71	70-82	349	5	19
Swansea C. (N/C)	Llanelli	12.83	83-84	35	2	0

EVANSON John Michael
Newcastle-u-Lyme, 10 May, 1947 (M)

League Club	Source	Date Signed	Seasons Played	Apps	Subs	Gls
Oxford U.	Towcester	02.65	66-73	144	10	10
Blackpool	Tr	02.74	73-75	63	4	0
Fulham	Tr	08.76	76-78	84	11	5
Bournemouth	Tr	07.79	79-80	52	1	2

EVELEIGH Gordon
Lymington, 26 July, 1922 (OL)

League Club	Source	Date Signed	Seasons Played	Apps	Subs	Gls
Bristol C.	Guildford C.	05.48	48	2	-	0

EVERALL William Frederick
Nantwich, 18 July, 1928 (LB)

League Club	Source	Date Signed	Seasons Played	Apps	Subs	Gls
Crewe Alex.		08.53	53	1	-	0

EVERETT Harold
Worksop, 9 June, 1922 (LB)

League Club	Source	Date Signed	Seasons Played	Apps	Subs	Gls
Notts Co.	Rufford Colly	04.43				
Mansfield T.	Tr	09.46	46	15	-	0

EVERETT Harry
Worksop, 11 November, 1920 (LH)

League Club	Source	Date Signed	Seasons Played	Apps	Subs	Gls
Mansfield T.	Warsop Main	08.45	46	3	-	0

EVERETT Michael
Mile End, 21 March, 1958 (F)

League Club	Source	Date Signed	Seasons Played	Apps	Subs	Gls
Leyton Orient	Crystal Palace (App)	03.76	75	0	1	0

EVERINGHAM Nicholas
Hull, 1 February, 1973 (M)

League Club	Source	Date Signed	Seasons Played	Apps	Subs	Gls
Oldham Ath.	YT	07.92				
Halifax T. (N/C)	Tr	02.93	92	0	2	0

EVERITT Michael Dennis
Clacton, 16 January, 1941 (LB)

League Club	Source	Date Signed	Seasons Played	Apps	Subs	Gls
Arsenal	Jnrs	02.58	59-60	9	-	1
Northampton T.	Tr	02.61	60-66	206	1	15
Plymouth Arg.	Tr	03.67	66-67	29	0	0
Brighton & H. A.	Tr	07.68	68-69	24	3	1

EVERITT Richard Ewart
Carlisle, 3 May, 1922 (W)

League Club	Source	Date Signed	Seasons Played	Apps	Subs	Gls
Darlington	Sheffield W. (Am)	07.45	46	1	-	0

EVERS Sean Anthony
Hitchin, 10 October, 1977 (M)

League Club	Source	Date Signed	Seasons Played	Apps	Subs	Gls
Luton T.	YT	05.96	95-97	16	9	3

EVERSHAM Paul Jonathan
Hereford, 28 January, 1975 (M)

League Club	Source	Date Signed	Seasons Played	Apps	Subs	Gls
Hereford U.	YT	07.93	93-94	6	7	1

EVES John Robert
Sunderland, 28 February, 1922 (FB)

League Club	Source	Date Signed	Seasons Played	Apps	Subs	Gls
Sunderland		11.41				
Darlington	Tr	09.46	46-51	177	-	1

EVES Melvyn James
Wednesbury, 10 September, 1956 E'B' (F)

League Club	Source	Date Signed	Seasons Played	Apps	Subs	Gls
Wolverhampton W.	Jnrs	07.75	77-83	169	11	44
Huddersfield T.	L	03.84	83	7	0	4
Sheffield U.	Tr	12.84	84-85	25	1	10
Gillingham	Tr	08.86	86-87	19	8	9
Mansfield T.	L	10.87	87	3	0	0

EVTUSHOK Aleksandr
Ukraine, 11 January, 1970 Ukranian Int (CD)

League Club	Source	Date Signed	Seasons Played	Apps	Subs	Gls
Coventry C.	Dnepr (Ukr)	02.97	96	3	0	0

EWING David
Logierait, 10 May, 1929 (CH)

League Club	Source	Date Signed	Seasons Played	Apps	Subs	Gls
Manchester C.	Luncarty Jnrs	06.49	52-61	279	-	1
Crewe Alex.	Tr	07.62	62-63	48	-	0

EWING Thomas
Larkhall, 2 May, 1937 SF Lge/S-2 (OR)

League Club	Source	Date Signed	Seasons Played	Apps	Subs	Gls
Aston Villa	Partick Thistle	02.62	61-63	39	-	4

EWING Thomas McCall Halliday
Musselburgh, 8 August, 1934 (WH)

League Club	Source	Date Signed	Seasons Played	Apps	Subs	Gls
Doncaster Rov.	Jnrs	08.51	51-57	39	-	6

EXLEY William
Bradford, 2 May, 1924 (G)

League Club	Source	Date Signed	Seasons Played	Apps	Subs	Gls
Bradford C. (Am)		08.52	52	2	-	0

EYDELIE Jean-Jacques
France, 3 February, 1966 (M)

League Club	Source	Date Signed	Seasons Played	Apps	Subs	Gls
Walsall (L)	Sion (Fr)	03.98	97	10	1	0

EYRE St **Frederick**
Manchester, 3 February, 1944 (WH)

League Club	Source	Date Signed	Seasons Played	Apps	Subs	Gls
Manchester C.	App	07.61				
Lincoln C.	Tr	07.63				
Bradford P.A.	Rossendale U.	12.69	69	1	0	0

EYRE John Robert
Hull, 9 October, 1974 (F)

League Club	Source	Date Signed	Seasons Played	Apps	Subs	Gls
Oldham Ath.	YT	07.93	93-94	4	6	1
Scunthorpe U.	L	12.94	94	9	0	8
Scunthorpe U.	Tr	07.95	95-97	110	13	28

EYRE Ernest **Leslie**
Ilkeston, 7 January, 1922 Died 1991 (IF)

League Club	Source	Date Signed	Seasons Played	Apps	Subs	Gls
Norwich C.	Cardiff C. (Am)	07.46	46-51	185	-	58
Bournemouth	Tr	11.51	51-52	38	-	10

EYRE Richard Paul
Poynton, 15 September, 1976 (RW)

League Club	Source	Date Signed	Seasons Played	Apps	Subs	Gls
Port Vale	YT	06.95	97	0	1	0

EYRES David
Liverpool, 26 February, 1964 (LW)

League Club	Source	Date Signed	Seasons Played	Apps	Subs	Gls
Blackpool	Rhyl	08.89	89-92	147	11	38
Burnley	Tr	07.93	93-97	171	4	37
Preston N.E.	Tr	10.97	97	26	2	4

FACEY Delroy Michael
Huddersfield, 22 April, 1980 (F)

League Club	Source	Date Signed	Seasons Played	Apps	Subs	Gls
Huddersfield T.	YT	05.97	96-97	2	4	0

FACEY Kenneth William
Hackney, 12 October, 1927 (F/WH)

League Club	Source	Date Signed	Seasons Played	Apps	Subs	Gls
Leyton Orient	Leyton	06.52	52-60	301	-	74

FADIDA Aharon
Israel, 20 September, 1961 (F)

League Club	Source	Date Signed	Seasons Played	Apps	Subs	Gls
Aldershot	Hapoel Haifa (Isr)	12.85	85-86	9	5	6

FAGAN Bernard
Houghton-le-Spring, 29 January, 1949 (W)

League Club	Source	Date Signed	Seasons Played	Apps	Subs	Gls
Sunderland	App	02.66				
Northampton T.	Tr	07.69	69	6	0	0

FAGAN Christopher James
Manchester, 5 June, 1950 (FB)

League Club	Source	Date Signed	Seasons Played	Apps	Subs	Gls
Liverpool		07.70	70	1	0	0
Tranmere Rov.	Tr	07.71	71-74	77	7	2

FAGAN Fionan (Paddy)
Dublin, 7 June, 1930 IR'B'/IR-8 (W)

League Club	Source	Date Signed	Seasons Played	Apps	Subs	Gls
Hull C.	Transport (Dublin)	03.51	51-53	26	-	2
Manchester C.	Tr	12.53	53-59	153	-	34
Derby Co.	Tr	03.60	59-60	24	-	6

FAGAN George
Dundee, 27 September, 1934 (FB)

League Club	Source	Date Signed	Seasons Played	Apps	Subs	Gls
Leeds U.	Dundee St Joseph	11.53				
Halifax T.	Tr	06.58	58-61	67	-	3

FAGAN Joseph
Liverpool, 12 March, 1921 (CH)

League Club	Source	Date Signed	Seasons Played	Apps	Subs	Gls
Manchester C.	Earlestown	10.38	46-50	148	-	2
Bradford P. A.	Nelson	08.53	53	3	-	0

FAGAN Michael Jeffrey
Newcastle, 22 June, 1960 (D)

League Club	Source	Date Signed	Seasons Played	Apps	Subs	Gls
Hartlepool U.	Carlisle U. (N/C)	08.79	79-82	36	1	1

FAGAN William
Inveresk, 20 February, 1917 Died 1992 (IF)

League Club	Source	Date Signed	Seasons Played	Apps	Subs	Gls
Preston N.E.	Glasgow Celtic	10.36	36-37	35	-	6
Liverpool	Tr	10.37	37-51	158	-	47

FAHY Alan
Liverpool, 27 January, 1973 (M)

League Club	Source	Date Signed	Seasons Played	Apps	Subs	Gls
Doncaster Rov. (N/C)	Barrow	03.97	96	0	5	0

FAHY John Joseph
Paisley, 13 May, 1943 (CF)

League Club	Source	Date Signed	Seasons Played	Apps	Subs	Gls
Oxford U.	Bedford T.	01.64	63-65	23	0	14

FAIRBROTHER Barrie Edward
Hackney, 30 December, 1950 (F)

League Club	Source	Date Signed	Seasons Played	Apps	Subs	Gls
Leyton Orient	App	01.69	69-74	171	17	41
Millwall	Tr	06.74	75-76	12	3	1

FAIRBROTHER Ian Andrew
Bootle, 2 October, 1966 (M)

League Club	Source	Date Signed	Seasons Played	Apps	Subs	Gls
Liverpool	App	07.84				
Bury	Tr	02.87	86-87	16	10	3
Wrexham	L	10.87	87	7	0	0

FAIRBROTHER John (Jack)
Burton, 16 August, 1917 (G)

League Club	Source	Date Signed	Seasons Played	Apps	Subs	Gls
Preston N. E.	Burton T.	03.37	46	41	-	0
Newcastle U.	Tr	07.47	47-51	132	-	0

FAIRBROTHER John
Cricklewood, 12 February, 1941 (CF)

League Club	Source	Date Signed	Seasons Played	Apps	Subs	Gls
Watford	Bennetts End	08.59	60-62	40	-	19
Peterborough U.	Worcester C.	05.65	65-67	69	3	37
Northampton T.	Tr	02.68	67-71	135	5	56
Mansfield T.	Tr	09.71	71-72	83	2	38
Torquay U.	Tr	06.73	73	15	0	3

FAIRCHILD Michael Peter
Brixworth, 24 November, 1942 (OR)

League Club	Source	Date Signed	Seasons Played	Apps	Subs	Gls
Luton T.	Lowestoft T.	11.60	60-63	21	-	1
Reading	Tr	07.64	64-65	24	0	6

FAIRCLOUGH Courtney (Chris) Huw
Nottingham, 12 April, 1964 Eu21-7/E'B' (CD)

League Club	Source	Date Signed	Seasons Played	Apps	Subs	Gls
Nottingham F.	App	10.81	82-86	102	5	1
Tottenham H.	Tr	06.87	87-88	60	0	5
Leeds U.	Tr	03.89	88-94	187	6	21
Bolton W.	Tr	07.95	95-97	89	1	8

FAIRCLOUGH Cyril
Radcliffe, 21 April, 1923 (FB)

League Club	Source	Date Signed	Seasons Played	Apps	Subs	Gls
Bury	Urmston	09.45	46-57	191	-	2

FAIRCLOUGH David
Liverpool, 5 January, 1957 Eu21-1 (F)

League Club	Source	Date Signed	Seasons Played	Apps	Subs	Gls
Liverpool	App	01.74	75-82	64	34	34
Norwich C.	Luzern (Switz)	03.85	84	1	1	0
Oldham Ath.	Tr	08.85	85	6	11	1
Tranmere Rov.	Beveren (Bel)	08.89	89	3	11	1
Wigan Ath.	Tr	08.90	90	4	3	1

FAIRCLOUGH Michael Joseph
Drogheda (Ire), 22 October, 1952 IR-2 (M)

League Club	Source	Date Signed	Seasons Played	Apps	Subs	Gls
Huddersfield T.	Drogheda	08.71	71-74	25	10	2

FAIRCLOUGH Wayne Ricks
Nottingham, 27 April, 1968 (D/M)

League Club	Source	Date Signed	Seasons Played	Apps	Subs	Gls
Notts Co.	App	04.86	85-89	39	32	0
Mansfield T.	Tr	03.90	89-93	131	10	12
Chesterfield	Tr	06.94	94-95	12	3	0
Scarborough	L	03.96	95	7	0	0

FAIRFAX Raymond John
Smethwick, 13 November, 1941 (FB)

League Club	Source	Date Signed	Seasons Played	Apps	Subs	Gls
West Bromwich A.	Jnrs	08.59	62-67	79	2	0
Northampton T.	Tr	06.68	68-70	116	0	2

FAIRHURST John
Bentley, 15 March, 1944 (WH)

League Club	Source	Date Signed	Seasons Played	Apps	Subs	Gls
Doncaster Rov.	App	07.61	61-65	21	0	0

FAIRLEY Thomas
Houghton-le-Spring, 12 October, 1932 (G)

League Club	Source	Date Signed	Seasons Played	Apps	Subs	Gls
Sunderland	Bankhead Jnrs	10.51	52	2	-	0
Carlisle U.	Tr	05.56	56-58	55	-	0

FAIRWEATHER Carlton
Camberwell, 22 September, 1961 (W)

League Club	Source	Date Signed	Seasons Played	Apps	Subs	Gls
Wimbledon	Tooting & Mitcham	12.84	84-91	118	20	26
Carlisle U.	Tr	08.93	93	11	1	1

FAIRWEATHER John Wilson
Dornoch, 12 August, 1924 Died 1989 (RH)

League Club	Source	Date Signed	Seasons Played	Apps	Subs	Gls
Blackburn Rov.		04.44				
Carlisle U.		11.48	49	1	-	0

FALANA Wade
Westminster, 7 January, 1970 (F)

League Club	Source	Date Signed	Seasons Played	Apps	Subs	Gls
Doncaster Rov. (N/C)	Tooting & Mitcham	10.92	92	2	2	0
Chesterfield (N/C)	Scarborough (N/C)	03.93	92	4	1	0

FALCO Mark Peter
Hackney, 22 October, 1960 E Yth (F)

League Club	Source	Date Signed	Seasons Played	Apps	Subs	Gls
Tottenham H.	App	07.78	78-86	162	12	68
Chelsea	L	11.82	82	3	0	0
Watford	Tr	10.86	86	33	0	14
Queens Park R.	Glasgow Rangers	12.87	87-90	65	22	27
Millwall	Tr	08.91	91	19	2	4

FALCONER Andrew Gordon
South Africa, 27 June, 1925 (IF)

League Club	Source	Date Signed	Seasons Played	Apps	Subs	Gls
Blackpool	South Africa	09.49	49	4	-	0

FALCONER Henry
Newcastle, 22 December, 1954 (FB)

League Club	Source	Date Signed	Seasons Played	Apps	Subs	Gls
Bournemouth	Burnley (App)	07.72	74	4	3	0

FALCONER William Henry
Aberdeen, 5 April, 1966 S Sch/S Yth (LB/M)

League Club	Source	Date Signed	Seasons Played	Apps	Subs	Gls
Watford	Aberdeen	06.88	88-90	85	13	12
Middlesbrough	Tr	08.91	91-92	47	6	10
Sheffield U.	Tr	08.93	93	21	2	3

FALDER David Edward James
Liverpool, 21 October, 1922 (CH)

League Club	Source	Date Signed	Seasons Played	Apps	Subs	Gls
Everton	Wigan Ath.	12.45	49-50	25	-	0

FALLON Henry (Harry)
Paisley, 28 April, 1942 (G)

League Club	Source	Date Signed	Seasons Played	Apps	Subs	Gls
York C.	St Johnstone	09.65	65-67	67	0	0

FALLON Kevin Barry
Maltby, 3 December, 1948 (CH)

League Club	Source	Date Signed	Seasons Played	Apps	Subs	Gls
Rotherham U.	App	12.65				
Southend U.	Sligo Rov.	07.70	70	4	0	0

FALLON Peadar (Peter) Domnal
Dublin, 19 October, 1922 (WH)

League Club	Source	Date Signed	Seasons Played	Apps	Subs	Gls
Exeter C.		06.47	47-52	110	-	8
Queens Park R.	Tr	08.53	53	1	-	0

FALLON Shaun
Widnes, 10 September, 1970 (LB)

League Club	Source	Date Signed	Seasons Played	Apps	Subs	Gls
Wigan Ath.	YT	07.89	88-89	2	1	0

FALLON Stephen Paul
Whittlesey, 3 August, 1956 (CD)

League Club	Source	Date Signed	Seasons Played	Apps	Subs	Gls
Cambridge U.	Kettering T.	12.74	74-86	405	5	27

FALLON William Joseph
Larne, 14 January, 1912 Died 1989 (OL)

League Club	Source	Date Signed	Seasons Played	Apps	Subs	Gls
Notts Co.	Dublin Dolphins	02.34	33-37	120	-	20
Sheffield Wed.	Tr	03.38	37-38	44	-	12
Notts Co.	Tr	06.46	46	15	-	3
Exeter C.	Tr	06.47	47	8	-	2

FANTHAM John
Sheffield, 6 February, 1939 Eu23-1/EF Lge/E-1 (IF)

League Club	Source	Date Signed	Seasons Played	Apps	Subs	Gls
Sheffield Wed.	Jnrs	10.56	57-69	381	7	147
Rotherham U.	Tr	10.69	69-70	46	5	8

FAREY John Albert
Darlington, 22 July, 1922 Died 1962 (G)

League Club	Source	Date Signed	Seasons Played	Apps	Subs	Gls
Sunderland		02.44				
Carlisle U.		11.47	47	2	-	0

FARINA Frank
Australia, 5 September, 1964 Australian Int (F)

League Club	Source	Date Signed	Seasons Played	Apps	Subs	Gls
Notts Co. (L)	Bari (It)	03.92	91	1	2	0

FARLEY Alexander
Finchley, 11 May, 1925 (LB)

League Club	Source	Date Signed	Seasons Played	Apps	Subs	Gls
Leyton Orient	Cromwell Ath.	11.45	46-47	15	-	0
Bournemouth	Tr	06.48				

FARLEY Henry Brian
Craven Arms, 1 January, 1927 Died 1962 (CH)

League Club	Source	Date Signed	Seasons Played	Apps	Subs	Gls
Tottenham H.	Chelmsford C.	07.49	51	1	-	0

FARLEY John Denis
Middlesbrough, 21 September, 1951 (W)

League Club	Source	Date Signed	Seasons Played	Apps	Subs	Gls
Watford	Stockton	07.69	70-73	97	8	8
Halifax T.	L	09.71	71	6	0	3
Wolverhampton W.	Tr	05.74	74-77	35	5	0
Blackpool	L	10.76	76	1	0	0
Hull C.	Tr	05.78	78-79	59	1	5
Bury	Tr	08.80	80	17	1	2

FARM George Neil
Edinburgh, 13 July, 1924 S-10 (G)

League Club	Source	Date Signed	Seasons Played	Apps	Subs	Gls
Blackpool	Hibernian	09.48	48-59	461	-	1

FARMER Frederick Brian Webb
Wordsley, 29 July, 1933 (FB)

League Club	Source	Date Signed	Seasons Played	Apps	Subs	Gls
Birmingham C.	Stourbridge	07.54	56-61	118	-	0
Bournemouth	Tr	01.62	61-64	132	-	0

FARMER James Edward (Ted)
Rowley Regis, 21 January, 1940 Eu23-2 (CF)

League Club	Source	Date Signed	Seasons Played	Apps	Subs	Gls
Wolverhampton W.	Jnrs	08.57	60-63	57	-	44

FARMER John
Biddulph, 31 August, 1947 Eu23-1 (G)

League Club	Source	Date Signed	Seasons Played	Apps	Subs	Gls
Stoke C.	Jnrs	01.65	65-74	163	0	0
Leicester C.	L	12.74	74	2	0	0

FARMER Kevin John
Ramsgate, 24 January, 1960 (CD/F)

League Club	Source	Date Signed	Seasons Played	Apps	Subs	Gls
Leicester C.	App	11.77	77	1	0	0
Northampton T.	Tr	08.79	79-81	70	7	12

FARMER Michael Chester
Leicester, 22 November, 1944 (WH)

League Club	Source	Date Signed	Seasons Played	Apps	Subs	Gls
Birmingham C.	App	04.62	63	1	-	1
Lincoln C.	Tr	05.65	65	21	1	0

FARMER Ronald James
Guernsey, 6 March, 1936 (WH)

League Club	Source	Date Signed	Seasons Played	Apps	Subs	Gls
Nottingham F.	Jnrs	05.53	57	9	-	0
Coventry C.	Tr	11.58	58-67	281	4	48
Notts Co.	Tr	10.67	67-68	69	0	5

FARMER Terence
Maltby, 11 May, 1931 (CF)

League Club	Source	Date Signed	Seasons Played	Apps	Subs	Gls
Rotherham U.	Gainsborough Trin.	07.52	52-57	61	-	23
York C.	Tr	01.58	57-59	66	-	28

FARMER William Henry
Guernsey, 24 November, 1927 (G)

League Club	Source	Date Signed	Seasons Played	Apps	Subs	Gls
Nottingham F.	St Martins	05.51	53-56	52	-	0
Oldham Ath.	Tr	07.57	57	5	-	0

FARNABY Craig
Stockton, 8 August, 1967 (M)

League Club	Source	Date Signed	Seasons Played	Apps	Subs	Gls
Hartlepool U. (N/C)	Jnrs	10.84	84	5	0	0
Middlesbrough	Tr	11.85				
Halifax T.	Tr	09.86	86	7	3	1
Stockport Co.	Shotton Comrades	09.87	87	17	5	1

FARNEN Austin Leslie
St Helens, 17 September, 1919 Died 1985 (CH)

League Club	Source	Date Signed	Seasons Played	Apps	Subs	Gls
Watford		05.46	46-48	77	-	0
Bradford C.	Tr	05.49	49	8	-	0

FARNSWORTH Peter Albert
Barnsley, 17 May, 1946 (WH)

League Club	Source	Date Signed	Seasons Played	Apps	Subs	Gls
Barnsley	App	09.63	64	1	-	0

FARNWORTH Simon
Chorley, 28 October, 1963 E Sch (G)

League Club	Source	Date Signed	Seasons Played	Apps	Subs	Gls
Bolton W.	App	09.81	83-85	113	0	0
Stockport Co.	L	09.86	86	10	0	0
Tranmere Rov.	L	01.87	86	7	0	0
Bury	Tr	03.87	86-89	105	0	0
Preston N. E.	Tr	06.90	90-92	81	0	0
Wigan Ath.	Tr	07.93	93-95	126	0	0

FARQUHAR Douglas Methven
Buckhaven, 11 June, 1921 (WH)

League Club	Source	Date Signed	Seasons Played	Apps	Subs	Gls
Arsenal	St Andrews U.	05.44				
Reading	Tr	09.50	50-51	9	-	1

FARR Brian Sydney
Swindon, 19 October, 1930 (WH)

League Club	Source	Date Signed	Seasons Played	Apps	Subs	Gls
Swindon T.		04.51	50-51	11	-	0

FARR Ian
Swindon, 13 February, 1958 (F)

League Club	Source	Date Signed	Seasons Played	Apps	Subs	Gls
Swindon T.	App	●	75	0	1	0

FARR Thomas (Chick) Francis
Bathgate, 19 February, 1914 Died 1980 (G)

League Club	Source	Date Signed	Seasons Played	Apps	Subs	Gls
Bradford P. A.	Broxburn Ath.	09.34	34-49	294	-	0

FARRALL Alec
Hoylake, 3 March, 1936 E Sch (WH)

League Club	Source	Date Signed	Seasons Played	Apps	Subs	Gls
Everton	Jnrs	03.53	52-56	5	-	0
Preston N. E.	Tr	05.57	57-59	27	-	9
Gillingham	Tr	07.60	60-64	202	-	19
Lincoln C.	Tr	06.65	65	20	0	2
Watford	Tr	07.66	66-67	47	1	8

FARRAR John Norman
St Helens, 6 May, 1928 Died 1988 (RH)

League Club	Source	Date Signed	Seasons Played	Apps	Subs	Gls
Manchester C.		03.48				
Crewe Alex.	Tr	01.51	50	2	-	0

FARRELL Andrew James
Colchester, 7 October, 1965 (W/D)

League Club	Source	Date Signed	Seasons Played	Apps	Subs	Gls
Colchester U.	App	09.83	83-86	98	7	6
Burnley	Tr	08.87	87-93	237	20	19
Wigan Ath.	Tr	09.94	94-95	51	3	1
Rochdale	Tr	07.96	96-97	77	3	6

FARRELL Arthur
Huddersfield, 1 November, 1920 (FB)

League Club	Source	Date Signed	Seasons Played	Apps	Subs	Gls
Bradford P. A.		05.40	46-50	156	-	4
Barnsley	Tr	05.51	51	18	-	0

FARRELL David William
Birmingham, 11 November, 1971 (LW)

League Club	Source	Date Signed	Seasons Played	Apps	Subs	Gls
Aston Villa	Redditch U.	01.92	92-93	5	1	0
Scunthorpe U.	L	01.93	92	4	1	1
Wycombe W.	Tr	09.95	95-96	44	16	6
Peterborough U.	Tr	07.97	97	40	2	6

League Club	Source	Date Signed	Seasons Played	Career Record Apps	Subs	Gls
FARRELL Gerard William						
Liverpool, 19 March, 1952						(FB)
Wolverhampton W.	App	03.70				
Blackburn Rov.	Tr	10.71	71-72	21	1	1
FARRELL Gregory James Philip						
Motherwell, 19 March, 1944						(OR)
Birmingham C.	App	03.61	62-63	4	-	0
Cardiff C.	Tr	03.64	63-66	93	1	8
Bury	Tr	03.67	66-69	83	0	15
FARRELL John						
Clunie, 22 June, 1933						(OL)
Accrington St.	Perth Celtic	08.54	54	2	-	0
FARRELL Kevin **Michael**						
Ilkley, 13 March, 1959						(M)
Scunthorpe U.	App	03.77	75-77	5	4	1
FARRELL Paul Anthony						
Liverpool, 1 November, 1958						(F)
Southport	App	●	75	0	2	0
FARRELL Peter Desmond						
Dublin, 16 August, 1922 IR-28/NI-7						(WH)
Everton	Shamrock Rov.	08.46	46-56	422	-	13
Tranmere Rov.	Tr	10.57	57-59	114	-	1
FARRELL Peter John						
Liverpool, 10 January, 1957						(M)
Bury	Ormskirk	09.75	75-78	49	5	9
Port Vale	Tr	11.78	78-81	85	4	10
Rochdale	Tr	08.82	82-84	71	2	17
Crewe Alex.	Tr	09.84	84	7	1	1
Crewe Alex.	Iceland	11.85	85	19	1	1
FARRELL Raymond Leo						
Cardiff, 31 May, 1933						(CF)
Crystal Palace	Treharris	05.57	57-58	5	-	0
FARRELL Sean Paul						
Watford, 28 February, 1969						(F)
Luton T.	App	02.87	89-91	14	11	1
Colchester U.	L	03.88	87	4	5	1
Northampton T.	L	09.91	91	4	0	1
Fulham	Tr	12.91	91-93	93	1	31
Peterborough U.	Tr	08.94	94-96	49	17	20
Notts Co.	Tr	10.96	96-97	42	7	16
FARRELL Stephen Edward						
Kilmarnock, 8 March, 1973						(M)
Stoke C.	YT	07.91	89	0	2	0
FARRELLY Gareth						
Dublin, 28 August, 1975 IR Sch/IR Yth/IRu21-11/IR 'B'/IR-5						(M)
Aston Villa	YT	01.92	95-96	2	6	0
Rotherham U.	L	03.95	94	9	1	2
Everton	Tr	07.97	97	18	8	1
FARRELLY Michael						
Manchester, 1 November, 1962 E Sch/E Semi Pro						(M)
Preston N. E.		06.81	81-84	77	5	4
FARRELLY Stephen						
Liverpool, 27 March, 1965 E Semi Pro						(G)
Rotherham U.	Macclesfield T.	07.95	96	7	0	0
FARRIMOND Sydney						
Hindley, 17 July, 1940 E Yth						(LB)
Bolton W.	Jnrs	01.58	58-70	364	1	1
Tranmere Rov.	Tr	02.71	70-73	132	2	0
FARRINGTON John Robert						
Lynemouth, 19 June, 1947						(W)
Wolverhampton W.	App	06.65	66-69	31	3	2
Leicester C.	Tr	10.69	69-73	115	3	18
Cardiff C.	Tr	11.73	73-74	23	0	6
Northampton T.	Tr	10.74	74-79	224	8	29
FARRINGTON Mark Anthony						
Liverpool, 15 June, 1965						(F)
Norwich C.	Everton (App)	05.83	83-84	11	3	2
Cambridge U.	L	03.85	84	10	0	1
Cardiff C.	Tr	07.85	85	24	7	3
Brighton & H.A.	Feyenoord (Neth)	08.91	91-93	15	13	4
Hereford U. (N/C)	A.I.F. (Nor)	10.94	94	0	1	0
FARRINGTON Roy Arthur						
Tonbridge, 6 June, 1925						(IF)
Crystal Palace		11.47	47-48	3	-	0

League Club	Source	Date Signed	Seasons Played	Career Record Apps	Subs	Gls
FARROW Desmond Albert						
Peterborough, 11 February, 1926						(LH)
Queens Park R.	Leicester C. (Am)	11.44	48-52	118	-	7
Stoke C.	Tr	10.52	52-53	8	-	0
FARROW George Henry						
Whitburn, 4 October, 1913 Died 1980						(WH)
Stockport Co.	Jnrs	10.30	31	6	-	0
Wolverhampton W.	Tr	01.32	32	10	-	0
Bournemouth	Tr	07.33	33-35	106	-	12
Blackpool	Tr	06.36	36-47	144	-	16
Sheffield U.	Tr	01.48	47	1	-	0
FASCIONE Joseph Victor						
Coatbridge, 5 February, 1945						(W)
Chelsea	Kirkintilloch Rob Roy	10.62	65-68	22	7	1
FASHANU John						
Kensington, 18 September, 1962 E-2						(F)
Norwich C.	Cambridge U. (Jnrs)	10.79	81-82	6	1	1
Crystal Palace	L	08.83	83	1	0	0
Lincoln C.	Tr	09.83	83-84	31	5	11
Millwall	Tr	11.84	84-85	50	0	12
Wimbledon	Tr	03.86	85-93	271	5	107
Aston Villa	Tr	08.94	94	11	2	3
FASHANU Justinus (Justin) Soni						
Hackney, 19 February, 1961 Died 1998 E Yth/Eu21-11/E 'B'						(F)
Norwich C.	App	12.78	78-80	84	6	35
Nottingham F.	Tr	08.81	81	31	1	3
Southampton	L	08.82	82	9	0	3
Notts Co.	Tr	12.82	82-84	63	1	20
Brighton & H.A.	Tr	06.85	85	16	0	2
Manchester C. (N/C)	(Retired)	10.89	89	0	2	0
West Ham U. (N/C)	Tr	11.89	89	2	0	0
Leyton Orient (N/C)	Tr	03.90	89	3	2	0
Torquay U.	Leatherhead	12.91	91-92	41	0	15
FAULKES Brian Keith						
Abingdon, 10 April, 1945						(FB)
Reading	Jnrs	09.63	63-66	23	2	0
Northampton T.	Tr	07.67	67-68	51	1	2
Torquay U.	Tr	07.69	69	6	0	0
FAULKNER David Peter						
Sheffield, 8 October, 1975 E Sch/E Yth						(CD)
Sheffield Wed.	YT	12.92				
Darlington	Tr	08.96	96	2	2	0
FAULKNER John Gilbert						
Orpington, 10 March, 1948						(CD)
Leeds U.	Sutton U.	03.70	69	2	0	0
Luton T.	Tr	03.72	72-77	209	0	6
FAULKNER Kenneth Gordon						
Smethwick, 10 September, 1923 E Sch						(OL)
Birmingham C.	Smethwick Highfield	09.44	46	2	-	0
FAULKNER Michael						
Conisborough, 3 January, 1950						(WH)
Sheffield U.	App	12.67				
Oldham Ath.	Tr	07.69	69	1	0	0
FAULKNER Raymond Arthur						
Horncastle, 26 May, 1934						(OR)
Grimsby T.	Jnrs	10.54	54	5	-	1
FAULKNER Roy Vincent						
Manchester, 28 June, 1935						(IF)
Manchester C.	Jnrs	12.52	55	7	-	4
Walsall	Tr	03.58	57-60	100	-	45
FAULKNER Stephen Andrew						
Sheffield, 18 December, 1954						(CD)
Sheffield U.	App	02.72	72-76	14	1	0
Stockport Co.	L	03.78	77	3	1	0
York C.	Tr	05.78	78-80	90	0	7
FAWCETT Brian						
Barmborough, 14 February, 1932 Died 1991						(OR)
Scunthorpe U.	Bentley Colly	02.55	54	1	-	0
Bradford P.A.	Tr	07.56				
FAWCETT Roy						
Hunslet, 20 January, 1938						(F)
Blackpool	Jnrs	03.55	55-59	3	-	0
FAWELL Derek Stuart						
Hartlepool, 22 March 1944						(CF)
Notts Co.	Spennymoor U.	10.64	64	1	-	0
Lincoln C.	Tr	09.65	65	4	0	0

FAWLEY Ronald
Ashton-u-Lyne, 22 April, 1927 Died 1982 (OL/LB)

League Club	Source	Date Signed	Seasons Played	Apps	Subs	Gls
Oldham Ath.	Ashton U.	08.50	50-57	94	-	9

FAZACKERLEY Derek William
Preston, 5 November, 1951 (CD)

League Club	Source	Date Signed	Seasons Played	Apps	Subs	Gls
Blackburn Rov.	App	10.69	70-86	593	3	23
Chester C.	Tr	01.87	86-87	66	0	0
York C.	Tr	07.88	88	16	0	0
Bury	Tr	12.88	88	7	7	0

FAZACKERLEY Michael Alexander
Manchester, 8 April, 1932 (FB)

League Club	Source	Date Signed	Seasons Played	Apps	Subs	Gls
Bradford P. A.	Bradford C. (Am)	08.55	55	2	-	0

FEALEY Nathan James
Aldershot, 12 March, 1973 (CD)

League Club	Source	Date Signed	Seasons Played	Apps	Subs	Gls
Reading	YT	07.91	91	1	0	0

FEAR, Keith William
Bristol, 8 May, 1952 (F)

League Club	Source	Date Signed	Seasons Played	Apps	Subs	Gls
Bristol C.	Jnrs	06.69	70-76	126	25	32
Hereford U.	L	09.77	77	6	0	0
Blackburn Rov.	L	12.77	77	5	0	2
Plymouth Arg.	Tr	02.78	77-79	40	5	9
Brentford	L	11.79	79	7	1	2
Chester C.	Tr	01.80	79-80	41	3	3

FEAR Peter Stanley
Sutton, 10 September, 1973 Eu21-3 (M)

League Club	Source	Date Signed	Seasons Played	Apps	Subs	Gls
Wimbledon	YT	07.92	92-97	51	20	4

FEAR Vivien James
Bristol, 24 October, 1955 (F)

League Club	Source	Date Signed	Seasons Played	Apps	Subs	Gls
Hereford U.	Bristol C. (App)	07.74	74	2	1	0

FEARNLEY Gordon
Bradford, 25 January, 1950 (F)

League Club	Source	Date Signed	Seasons Played	Apps	Subs	Gls
Sheffield Wed.	Jnrs	07.68				
Bristol Rov.	Tr	07.70	70-76	95	26	21

FEARNLEY Harrison (Harry) Lockhead
Dewsbury, 27 May, 1923 (G)

League Club	Source	Date Signed	Seasons Played	Apps	Subs	Gls
Leeds U.	Bradford P.A. (Am)	11.45	46-48	28	-	0
Halifax T.	Tr	01.49	48	3	-	0
Newport Co.	Tr	07.49	49-52	103	-	0
Rochdale	Selby T.	07.55	55	1	-	0

FEARNLEY Henry (Harry)
Penistone, 16 June, 1935 (G)

League Club	Source	Date Signed	Seasons Played	Apps	Subs	Gls
Huddersfield T.	Jnrs	12.52	55-62	90	-	0
Oxford U.	Tr	10.63	63-65	90	0	0
Doncaster Rov.	Tr	02.66	65-66	32	0	0

FEARON Ronald Thomas
Romford, 19 November, 1960 (G)

League Club	Source	Date Signed	Seasons Played	Apps	Subs	Gls
Reading	Dover T.	02.80	80-82	61	0	0
Ipswich T.	Sutton U.	08.87	87-88	28	0	0
Brighton & H. A.	L	09.88	88	7	0	0
Walsall (N/C)	Sutton U.	02.93	92	1	0	0
Leyton Orient	Ashford T.	08.95	95	18	0	0

FEASEY Paul Cedric
Hull, 4 May, 1933 (CH)

League Club	Source	Date Signed	Seasons Played	Apps	Subs	Gls
Hull C.	Jnrs	05.50	52-64	271	-	0

FEATHERSTONE James Lee
Wharfdale, 12 November, 1979 (F)

League Club	Source	Date Signed	Seasons Played	Apps	Subs	Gls
Scunthorpe U.	Blackburn Rov. (YT)	03.98	97	0	1	0

FEATHERSTONE Keith
Bradford, 30 August, 1935 (G)

League Club	Source	Date Signed	Seasons Played	Apps	Subs	Gls
Bradford P.A. (Am)	Wyke Celtic	12.55	55	1	-	0

FEE Gregory Paul
Halifax, 24 June, 1964 (CD)

League Club	Source	Date Signed	Seasons Played	Apps	Subs	Gls
Bradford C.	YT	05.83	82-83	6	1	0
Sheffield Wed.	Boston U.	08.87	87-89	16	10	0
Preston N.E.	L	09.90	90	10	0	0
Northampton T.	L	11.90	90	1	0	0
Preston N.E.	L	01.91	90	5	0	0
Leyton Orient	L	03.91	90	4	1	0
Mansfield T.	Tr	03.91	90-92	50	4	7
Chesterfield	L	12.92	92	10	0	0

FEEHAN John **Ignatius (Sonny)**
Dublin, 17 September, 1926 Died 1995 (G)

League Club	Source	Date Signed	Seasons Played	Apps	Subs	Gls
Manchester U.	Waterford	11.48	49	12	-	0
Northampton T.	Tr	08.50	50-51	39	-	0
Brentford	Tr	08.54	54-58	30	-	0

FEELEY Andrew James
Hereford, 30 September, 1961 (FB/M)

League Club	Source	Date Signed	Seasons Played	Apps	Subs	Gls
Hereford U.	App	08.79	78-79	50	1	3
Leicester C.	Trowbridge T.	02.84	83-86	74	2	0
Brentford	Tr	08.87	87-88	57	10	0
Bury	Tr	07.89	89-90	46	11	3

FEELY Peter John
City of London, 3 January, 1950 E Yth/E Amat (F)

League Club	Source	Date Signed	Seasons Played	Apps	Subs	Gls
Chelsea	Enfield	05.70	70-72	4	1	2
Bournemouth	Tr	02.73	72-73	8	1	2
Fulham	Tr	07.74				
Gillingham	Tr	10.74	74-75	41	0	22
Sheffield Wed.	Tr	02.76	75-76	17	2	2
Stockport Co.	L	01.77	76	2	0	0

FEENEY James McBurney
Belfast, 23 June, 1921 Died 1985 NI-2 (FB)

League Club	Source	Date Signed	Seasons Played	Apps	Subs	Gls
Swansea C.	Linfield	12.46	46-49	88	-	0
Ipswich T.	Tr	03.50	49-55	214	-	0

FEENEY Joseph
Glasgow, 21 July, 1926 Died 1992 (F)

League Club	Source	Date Signed	Seasons Played	Apps	Subs	Gls
Sunderland	St Theresa's	07.47				
Chester C.	Rhyl	09.51	51	5	-	0

FEENEY Mark Anthony
Derry (NI), 26 July, 1974 (M)

League Club	Source	Date Signed	Seasons Played	Apps	Subs	Gls
Barnsley	YT	07.93	92	0	2	0

FELGATE David Wynne
Blaenau Ffestiniog, 4 March, 1960 W Sch/W-1 (G)

League Club	Source	Date Signed	Seasons Played	Apps	Subs	Gls
Bolton W.	Jnrs	08.78				
Rochdale	L	10.78	78	35	0	0
Crewe Alex.	L	09.79	79	14	0	0
Rochdale	L	03.80	79	12	0	0
Lincoln C.	Tr	09.80	80-84	198	0	0
Cardiff C.	L	11.84	84	4	0	0
Grimsby T.	Tr	02.85	84-86	36	0	0
Bolton W.	L	02.86	85	15	0	0
Bolton W.	Tr	02.87	86-91	223	0	0
Chester C.	Wolverhampton W. (N/C)	10.93	93-94	71	1	0
Wigan Ath.	Tr	07.95	95	3	0	0

FELIX Gary
Manchester, 31 October, 1957 (M)

League Club	Source	Date Signed	Seasons Played	Apps	Subs	Gls
Leeds U.	App	11.75				
Chester C.	Manchester C. (N/C)	01.79	78	8	0	0

FELL Geoffrey Mark
Carlisle, 8 May, 1960 (F)

League Club	Source	Date Signed	Seasons Played	Apps	Subs	Gls
Carlisle U.	Jnrs	06.77	77-79	0	3	0

FELL Gerald Charles
Newark, 1 March, 1951 (F)

League Club	Source	Date Signed	Seasons Played	Apps	Subs	Gls
Brighton & H. A.	Long Eaton U.	11.74	74-77	65	14	19
Southend U.	Tr	11.77	77-79	43	2	10
Torquay U.	Tr	07.80	80-81	50	0	12
York C.	L	03.82	81	2	3	0

FELL James Irving
Grimsby, 4 January, 1936 (OL)

League Club	Source	Date Signed	Seasons Played	Apps	Subs	Gls
Grimsby T.	Waltham	04.54	56-60	166	-	35
Everton	Tr	03.61	60-61	27	-	4
Newcastle U.	Tr	03.62	61-62	49	-	16
Walsall	Tr	07.63	63	21	-	4
Lincoln C.	Tr	01.64	63-65	63	0	10

FELL Leslie James
Leyton, 16 December, 1920 (OR)

League Club	Source	Date Signed	Seasons Played	Apps	Subs	Gls
Charlton Ath.	Gravesend U.	12.45	46-51	13	-	2
Crystal Palace	Tr	10.52	52-53	65	-	6

FELLOWES William James
Bradford, 15 March, 1910 Died 1987 (WH)

League Club	Source	Date Signed	Seasons Played	Apps	Subs	Gls
Plymouth Arg.	Tavistock T.	07.27	29-32	5	-	0
Leyton Orient	Tr	07.33	33-34	78	-	1
Luton T.	Tr	05.35	35-37	110	-	3
Exeter C.	Tr	06.38	38-46	56	-	1

FELLOWS Geoffrey Allan
West Bromwich, 26 July, 1944 (LB)

League Club	Source	Date Signed	Seasons Played	Apps	Subs	Gls
Aston Villa	App	10.61				
Shrewsbury T.	Tr	06.65	65-72	277	4	3

FELLOWS Gregory Frederick Arthur
Dudley, 10 October, 1953 (CF)

League Club	Source	Date Signed	Seasons Played	Apps	Subs	Gls
Aston Villa	App	09.71				
Crewe Alex.	L	02.73	72	3	0	1
Manchester U.	Tr	08.73				

FELLOWS Stewart
Stockton, 9 October, 1948 (WH)

League Club	Source	Date Signed	Seasons Played	Apps	Subs	Gls
Newcastle U.	App	03.66				
York C.	Tr	06.67	67	0	2	0

FELTON Graham MacLean
Cambridge, 1 March, 1949 E Yth (W)

League Club	Source	Date Signed	Seasons Played	Apps	Subs	Gls
Northampton T.	Cambridge U.	09.66	66-75	243	13	25
Barnsley	L	02.76	75	12	0	2
Barnsley	Tr	07.76	76	24	0	3

FELTON Kenneth Carl
Blackhall (Dm), 18 February, 1949 (LB)

League Club	Source	Date Signed	Seasons Played	Apps	Subs	Gls
Darlington	Jnrs	04.67	67-69	50	2	8

FELTON Robert Francis Foster
Gateshead, 12 August, 1918 Died 1982 (FB)

League Club	Source	Date Signed	Seasons Played	Apps	Subs	Gls
Everton	Tr	08.37				
Port Vale	Tr	06.38	38	10	-	0
Crystal Palace	Tr	09.46	46	1	-	0

FELTON Vivien Edward
Southgate, 13 August, 1929 (CH)

League Club	Source	Date Signed	Seasons Played	Apps	Subs	Gls
Crystal Palace	Barnet	08.54	54-55	2	-	0

FENCOTT Kenneth Sydney
Walsall, 27 December, 1943 (F)

League Club	Source	Date Signed	Seasons Played	Apps	Subs	Gls
Aston Villa	App	01.61	61-63	3	-	0
Lincoln C.	Tr	06.64	64-66	67	6	13

FENN Neale Michael Charles
Edmonton, 18 January, 1977 IR Yth/IRu21-4/IR 'B' (F)

League Club	Source	Date Signed	Seasons Played	Apps	Subs	Gls
Tottenham H.	YT	07.95	96-97	0	8	0
Leyton Orient	L	01.98	97	3	0	0
Norwich C.	L	03.98	97	6	1	1

FENNEY Stanley
Barry, 21 June, 1923 (LB)

League Club	Source	Date Signed	Seasons Played	Apps	Subs	Gls
Barrow	Stranraer	12.45	46	26	-	0

FENOUGHTY Thomas
Rotherham, 7 June, 1941 (M)

League Club	Source	Date Signed	Seasons Played	Apps	Subs	Gls
Sheffield U.	Sheffield F.C.	11.63	63-68	47	2	4
Chesterfield	Tr	07.69	69-71	98	3	15

FENSOME Andrew Brian
Northampton, 18 February, 1969 (FB)

League Club	Source	Date Signed	Seasons Played	Apps	Subs	Gls
Norwich C.	App	02.87				
Cambridge U.	Bury T.	11.89	89-93	122	4	1
Preston N.E.	Tr	10.93	93-95	93	0	1
Rochdale	Tr	07.96	96-97	80	2	0

FENTON Benjamin Robert Vincent
West Ham, 28 October, 1918 (WH)

League Club	Source	Date Signed	Seasons Played	Apps	Subs	Gls
West Ham U.	Jnrs	10.35	37-38	21	-	9
Millwall	Tr	03.39	38-46	20	-	7
Charlton Ath.	Tr	01.47	46-54	264	-	22
Colchester U.	Tr	02.55	54-57	103	-	15

FENTON Alexander Ewan
Dundee, 17 November, 1929 (WH)

League Club	Source	Date Signed	Seasons Played	Apps	Subs	Gls
Blackpool	Dundee N.E.	11.46	48-58	203	-	20
Wrexham	Tr	05.59	59	24	-	0

FENTON Graham Anthony
Wallsend, 22 May, 1974 Eu21-1 (W)

League Club	Source	Date Signed	Seasons Played	Apps	Subs	Gls
Aston Villa	YT	02.92	93-95	16	16	3
West Bromwich A.	L	01.94	93	7	0	3
Blackburn Rov.	Tr	11.95	95-96	9	18	7
Leicester C.	Tr	08.97	97	9	14	3

FENTON Michael
Stockton, 30 October, 1913 E-1 (CF)

League Club	Source	Date Signed	Seasons Played	Apps	Subs	Gls
Middlesbrough	South Bank E.E.	03.33	32-49	240	-	147

FENTON Ronald
South Shields, 21 September, 1940 (IF)

League Club	Source	Date Signed	Seasons Played	Apps	Subs	Gls
Burnley	Jnrs	09.57	60-61	11	-	1
West Bromwich A.	Tr	11.62	62-64	59	-	16
Birmingham C.	Tr	01.65	64-67	28	5	7
Brentford	Tr	01.68	67-69	87	4	19

FENTON Stephen James
Hartlepool, 25 February, 1951 E Yth (M)

League Club	Source	Date Signed	Seasons Played	Apps	Subs	Gls
Middlesbrough	Jnrs	08.69				
Bradford C.	Tr	06.72	72	9	1	1

FENTON William Hartes
Hartlepool, 23 June, 1926 Died 1973 (OL)

League Club	Source	Date Signed	Seasons Played	Apps	Subs	Gls
Barnsley		11.44				
Blackburn Rov.	Horden Colly	12.48	48-50	33	-	7
York C.	Tr	05.51	51-57	258	-	118

FENWICK Paul
Camden, 25 August, 1969 (CD)

League Club	Source	Date Signed	Seasons Played	Apps	Subs	Gls
Birmingham C.	Winnipeg Fury (Can)	11.92	92-93	9	10	0

FENWICK Terence William
Seaham, 17 November, 1959 E Yth/Eu21-11/E-20 (D)

League Club	Source	Date Signed	Seasons Played	Apps	Subs	Gls
Crystal Palace	App	12.76	77-80	62	8	0
Queens Park R.	Tr	12.80	80-87	256	0	33
Tottenham H.	Tr	12.87	87-92	90	3	8
Leicester C.	L	10.90	90	8	0	1
Swindon T.	Tr	09.93	93-94	25	3	0

FERDINAND Leslie
Acton, 18 December, 1966 E 'B'/E-17 (F)

League Club	Source	Date Signed	Seasons Played	Apps	Subs	Gls
Queens Park R.	Hayes	04.87	86-94	152	11	80
Brentford	L	03.88	87	3	0	0
Newcastle U.	Tr	06.95	95-96	67	1	41
Tottenham H.	Tr	08.97	97	19	2	5

FERDINAND Rio Gavin
Peckham, 7 November, 1978 E Yth/Eu21-4/E-3 (CD)

League Club	Source	Date Signed	Seasons Played	Apps	Subs	Gls
West Ham U.	YT	11.95	95-97	46	5	2
Bournemouth	L	11.96	96	10	0	0

FEREBEE Stewart Raymond
Carshalton, 6 September, 1960 (F)

League Club	Source	Date Signed	Seasons Played	Apps	Subs	Gls
York C.	Harrogate R.A.	07.79	79-80	7	6	0
Darlington (N/C)	Harrogate T.	03.87	86	9	0	0
Halifax T.	Tr	07.87	87	6	6	0

FEREDAY Wayne
Warley, 16 June, 1963 Eu21-5/EF Lge (W)

League Club	Source	Date Signed	Seasons Played	Apps	Subs	Gls
Queens Park R.	App	09.80	80-88	167	29	21
Newcastle U.	Tr	06.89	89-90	27	6	0
Bournemouth	Tr	11.90	90-91	20	3	0
West Bromwich A.	Tr	12.91	91-93	39	9	3
Cardiff C.	Tr	03.94	93-94	43	1	2

FERGUSON Alexander Stirling Brown
Lochore, 5 August, 1903 Died 1974 (G)

League Club	Source	Date Signed	Seasons Played	Apps	Subs	Gls
Wigan Bor.	Vale of Clyde	11.24	24	1	-	0
Gillingham	Tr	06.25	25-26	67	-	0
Swansea C.	Tr	02.27	26-35	270	-	0
Bury	Tr	06.36	36-37	63	-	0
Newport Co.	Tr	06.38	38	41	-	0
Bristol C.	Tr	05.46	46	32	-	0
Swindon T.	Tr	09.47	47	7	-	0

FERGUSON Archibald
Lochore, 9 December, 1918 (G)

League Club	Source	Date Signed	Seasons Played	Apps	Subs	Gls
Doncaster Rov.	Raith Rov.	12.41	46-47	61	-	0
Wrexham	Tr	07.48	48-52	126	-	0

FERGUSON James Brian
Irvine, 14 December, 1960 (M)

League Club	Source	Date Signed	Seasons Played	Apps	Subs	Gls
Newcastle U.	Mansfield T. (App)	01.79	79	4	1	1
Hull C.	Tr	12.80	80-81	24	4	2
Southend U.	Goole T.	08.83	83-84	31	3	6
Chesterfield	Tr	10.84	84	30	1	0

FERGUSON Charles
Glasgow, 22 April, 1930 (FB)

League Club	Source	Date Signed	Seasons Played	Apps	Subs	Gls
Accrington St.	Hamilton Academical	05.54	54	1	-	0
Rochdale	Tr	09.55	55-58	150	-	3
Oldham Ath.	Tr	07.59	59-60	57	-	0

FERGUSON Darren
Glasgow, 9 February, 1972 S Yth/Su21-5 (M)

League Club	Source	Date Signed	Seasons Played	Apps	Subs	Gls
Manchester U.	YT	07.90	90-93	20	7	0
Wolverhampton W.	Tr	01.94	93-97	92	21	4

FERGUSON David Dyer
Bonnybridge, 11 March, 1929 (OL)

League Club	Source	Date Signed	Seasons Played	Apps	Subs	Gls
Coventry C.	Alloa Ath.	10.56	56	4	-	0

FERGUSON Derek
Glasgow, 31 July, 1967 S Sch/S Yth/Su21-5/S-2 (M)

League Club	Source	Date Signed	Seasons Played	Apps	Subs	Gls
Sunderland	Hearts	07.93	93-94	64	0	0

FERGUSON Donald
Canada, 2 January, 1963 Canadian 'B' Int (G)

League Club	Source	Date Signed	Seasons Played	Apps	Subs	Gls
Wrexham (N/C)		01.86	85	20	0	0

League Club	Source	Date Signed	Seasons Played	Apps	Subs	Gls
FERGUSON Duncan						
Stirling, 27 December, 1971 S Sch/S Yth/Su21-7/S 'B'/S-7						(CF)
Everton	Glasgow Rangers	10.94	94-97	97	6	34
FERGUSON Edward Brodie						
Whitburn, 10 September, 1949						(M)
Rotherham U.	Dumbarton	02.71	70-73	63	4	5
Grimsby T.	L	11.71	71	1	1	0
FERGUSON Hubert						
Belfast, 23 May, 1926 Died 1994						(FB)
Bradford C.	Ballymena	07.48	48-52	132	-	0
Halifax T.	Tr	09.54	54-57	95	-	0
FERGUSON Iain John						
Newarthill, 4 August, 1962						(F)
Charlton Ath. (L)	Hearts	11.89	89	1	0	0
Bristol C. (L)	Hearts	03.90	89	8	3	2
FERGUSON James Cameron Mars						
Glasgow, 20 February, 1935						(G)
Oldham Ath.	Falkirk	05.59	59	36	-	0
Crewe Alex.	Tr	08.60	60-61	26	-	0
Darlington	Tr	07.62	62	32	-	0
FERGUSON John (Jackie)						
Maybole, 29 August, 1939						(OR)
Southend U.	Airdrieonians	06.67	67	13	1	2
FERGUSON John Theodore Hever						
Edinburgh, 14 June, 1939						(OL)
Oldham Ath.	St Andrews U.	11.56	56	1	-	0
FERGUSON Mark						
Liverpool, 6 November, 1960						(W)
Tranmere Rov.		08.81	81-84	71	16	13
FERGUSON Martin Murphy						
Glasgow, 21 December, 1942						(IF)
Barnsley	Partick Thistle	08.65	65	40	0	17
Doncaster Rov.	Tr	07.66	66	3	0	0
FERGUSON Michael John						
Newcastle, 3 October, 1954						(F)
Coventry C.	App	12.71	74-80	121	6	51
Everton	Tr	08.81	81	7	1	4
Birmingham C.	Tr	11.82	82-84	22	0	9
Coventry C.	L	03.84	83	7	0	3
Brighton & H. A.	Tr	09.84	84-85	17	0	6
Colchester U.	Tr	03.86	85-86	25	1	11
FERGUSON Michael Kevin						
Burnley, 9 March, 1943						(M)
Accrington St.	Plymouth Arg. (Am)	07.60	60	23	-	1
Blackburn Rov.	Tr	03.62	62-67	220	0	29
Aston Villa	Tr	05.68	68-69	38	0	2
Queens Park R.	Tr	11.69	69-72	67	1	2
Cambridge U.	Tr	07.73	73	39	0	4
Rochdale	Tr	07.74	74-75	68	1	5
Halifax T.	I.A. Akranes (Ice)	12.76	76	2	0	0
FERGUSON Robert						
Kilwinning, 1 March, 1945 Su23-1/SF Lge/S-7						(G)
West Ham U.	Kilmarnock	06.67	67-79	240	0	0
Sheffield Wed.	L	02.74	73	5	0	0
FERGUSON Robert						
Grangetown, 27 July, 1917						(G)
Middlesbrough	Hurworth Jnrs	08.35	36-37	10	-	0
York C.	Tr	05.39	46	26	-	0
FERGUSON Robert Burnett						
Dudley (Nd), 8 January, 1938						(FB)
Newcastle U.	Jnrs	05.55	55-62	11	-	0
Derby Co.	Tr	10.62	62-65	121	0	0
Cardiff C.	Tr	12.65	65-68	87	1	0
Newport Co.	Barry T.	07.69	69-70	71	0	2
FERGUSON Ronald Charles						
Accrington, 9 February, 1957						(F)
Sheffield Wed.	App	02.75	74	10	1	1
Scunthorpe U.	L	12.75	75	3	0	0
Darlington	Tr	02.76	75-79	101	13	18
FERN Rodney Alan						
Burton, 13 December, 1948						(F)
Leicester C.	Measham Imps	12.66	67-71	133	19	32
Luton T.	Tr	06.72	72-74	34	5	5
Chesterfield	Tr	06.75	75-78	150	2	54
Rotherham U.	Tr	06.79	79-82	98	7	34

League Club	Source	Date Signed	Seasons Played	Apps	Subs	Gls
FERNANDES Tamer Hasan						
Paddington, 7 December, 1974 E Yth						(G)
Brentford	YT	07.93	93-96	10	2	0
FERNEY Martin John						
Lambeth, 8 November, 1971						(M)
Fulham	YT	07.90	90-94	49	11	1
FERNIE James						
Kirkcaldy, 31 October, 1936						(IF)
Doncaster Rov.	Arbroath	10.58	58-60	89	-	31
FERNIE William						
Kinglassie, 22 November, 1928 SF Lge/S 'B'/S-12						(IF)
Middlesbrough	Glasgow Celtic	12.58	58-60	65	-	3
FERNS Philip						
Liverpool, 14 November, 1937						(FB)
Liverpool		09.57	62-64	27	-	1
Bournemouth	Tr	08.65	65	46	0	0
Mansfield T.	Tr	08.66	66-67	55	1	1
FERNS Philip David						
Liverpool, 12 September, 1961						(LB)
Bournemouth	App	02.79	78-80	94	1	6
Charlton Ath.	Tr	08.81	81-82	35	3	1
Wimbledon	L	12.82	82	7	0	0
Blackpool	Tr	08.83	83-84	44	3	0
Aldershot	Tr	07.85	85	24	0	2
FERRETT Christopher Andrew						
Poole, 10 February, 1971						(M)
Bournemouth	YT	•	94	0	1	0
FERRIDAY Leslie						
Manchester, 3 June, 1929						(WH)
Walsall	Buxton	05.54	54	32	-	1
FERRIER Henry (Harry)						
Ratho, 20 May, 1920						(FB)
Barnsley		09.37				
Portsmouth	Tr	03.46	46-53	241	-	8
FERRIER John						
Edinburgh, 6 October, 1927						(LB)
Brighton & H. A.		10.46	46	1	-	1
Exeter C.	Clyde	05.56	56	31	-	0
FERRIER Ronald Johnson						
Cleethorpes, 26 April, 1914 Died 1991						(IF)
Grimsby T.	Grimsby W.	05.33				
Manchester U.	Tr	05.35	35-37	18	-	4
Oldham Ath.	Tr	03.38	37-46	45	-	25
Lincoln C.	Tr	08.47				
FERRIS John Owner						
Bristol, 4 September, 1939						(G)
Torquay U.	Minehead	09.58	58	3	-	0
FERRIS Paul James						
Lisburn (NI), 10 July, 1965						(W)
Newcastle U.	App	03.83	81-84	1	10	0
FERRIS Raymond Osborn						
Newry (NI), 22 September, 1920 Died 1994 NI-3						(WH)
Crewe Alex.	Cambridge T.	03.45	46-48	101	-	23
Birmingham C.	Tr	03.49	48-52	93	-	3
FERRIS Samuel						
Motherwell, 14 March, 1951						(F)
Chesterfield	Albion Rov.	03.72	71-73	25	6	3
Workington	L	02.74	73	2	1	0
FERRY Gordon						
Sunderland, 22 December, 1943						(CH)
Arsenal	App	01.61	64	11	-	0
Leyton Orient	Tr	05.65	65	42	0	0
FERRY William						
Sunderland, 21 November, 1966						(F)
Scunthorpe U.	YT	09.84	84-86	2	3	0
Barnsley	Tr	11.86	86	3	1	1
FESTA Gianluca						
Sardinia, 15 March, 1969						(CD)
Middlesbrough	Inter Milan (It)	01.97	96-97	51	0	3

League Club	Source	Date Signed	Seasons Played	Career Record Apps	Subs	Gls
FETTIS Alan William						
Belfast, 1 February, 1971 NI Sch/NI Yth/NI 'B'/NI-22						(G)
Hull C.	Ards	07.91	91-95	131	4	2
West Bromwich A.	L	11.95	95	3	0	0
Nottingham F.	Tr	01.96	96	4	0	0
Blackburn Rov.	Tr	09.97	97	7	1	0
FEUER Anthony **Ian**						
USA, 20 May, 1971						(G)
West Ham U.	Los Angeles Salsa (USA)	03.94				
Peterborough U.	L	02.95	94	16	0	0
Luton T.	Tr	09.95	95-97	97	0	0
FEWINGS Patrick John Henry						
Barnstaple, 21 January, 1931						(OR)
Torquay U.	Barnstaple	11.53	53-54	8	-	0
FEWINGS Paul John						
Hull, 18 February, 1978						(F)
Hull C.	YT	08.95	94-97	32	25	2
FICKLING Ashley						
Sheffield, 15 November, 1972 E Sch						(CD)
Sheffield U.	Jnrs	07.91				
Darlington	L	11.92	92	14	0	0
Darlington	L	08.93	93	1	0	0
Grimsby T.	Tr	03.95	94-96	26	13	2
Darlington	L	03.98	97	8	0	0
FIDLER Dennis John						
Stockport, 22 June, 1938						(OL)
Manchester C.	Manchester U. (Am)	01.57	57-58	5	-	1
Port Vale	Tr	06.60	60-61	38	-	12
Grimsby T.	Tr	10.61	61	9	-	3
Halifax T.	Tr	04.63	62-66	142	1	40
Darlington	Tr	10.66	66-67	32	2	3
FIDLER Frank						
Middleton, 16 August, 1924						(CF)
Manchester U.	Jnrs	08.41				
Wrexham	Witton A.	05.50	50-51	36	-	15
Leeds U.	Tr	10.51	51-52	22	-	8
Bournemouth	Tr	12.52	52-54	61	-	32
FIDLER Richard Michael						
Sheffield, 26 October, 1976 E Sch						(LM)
Leeds U.	Jnrs	07.95				
Hull C. (N/C)	Tr	12.95	95	0	1	0
FIDLER Thomas George						
Hounslow, 4 September, 1933 Died 1992						(CF)
Queens Park R.	Hounslow	05.54	54	12	-	2
FIELD Anthony						
Halifax, 6 July, 1946						(F)
Halifax T.	Jnrs	07.63	63-65	21	0	3
Barrow	Tr	08.66	66-67	36	2	16
Southport	Tr	03.68	67-71	127	6	41
Blackburn Rov.	Tr	10.71	71-73	104	2	45
Sheffield U.	Tr	03.74	73-75	63	3	13
FIELD Anthony Frederick						
Chester, 23 May, 1942						(CF)
Chester C.		08.61	60	2	-	0
Southport	Tr	07.62				
FIELD Norman						
Durham, 27 August, 1927 Died 1993						(WH)
Portsmouth		08.45				
Mansfield T.	Tr	06.50	51-52	20	-	0
FIELDER Colin Michael Raynor						
Winchester, 5 January, 1964						(M)
Aldershot	App	01.82	81-86	56	12	8
FIELDING John Arnold						
Liverpool, 2 September, 1939						(IF)
Southport	Wigan Ath.	03.61	60-62	76	-	21
Brentford	Tr	03.63	62-65	82	0	18
Grimsby T.	Tr	12.65	65-66	29	1	8
FIELDING Mark John						
Bury, 10 November, 1956						(FB)
Preston N.E.	App	11.74	74	9	0	0
FIELDING Michael Anthony						
Liverpool, 3 December, 1965						(FB)
Barnsley	Everton (YT)	08.84				
Rochdale	L	10.84	84	6	0	0

League Club	Source	Date Signed	Seasons Played	Career Record Apps	Subs	Gls
FIELDING Paul Anthony						
Oldham, 4 December, 1955						(M)
Rochdale	App	12.73	72-75	65	7	5
FIELDING Alfred **Walter**						
Edmonton, 26 November, 1919						(IF)
Everton	Walthamstow Ave.	09.45	46-58	380	-	49
Southport	Tr	01.59	58-59	20	-	1
FIELDING William						
Broadhurst, 17 June, 1915						(G)
Cardiff C.	Hurst	05.36	36-38	50	-	0
Bolton W.	Tr	06.44				
Manchester U.	Tr	01.47	46	6	-	0
FIELDS Alfred George						
Canning Town, 15 November, 1918						(CH)
Arsenal	Margate	05.37	38-50	19	-	0
FIELDS Maurice John Bernard						
Chester, 12 August, 1935						(F)
Chester C.		08.55	55-57	20	-	1
FIFE Adrian						
Peterborough, 13 September, 1969						(F)
Peterborough U. (N/C)	YT	07.88	86-87	1	1	0
FIFIELD David						
Plymouth, 10 December, 1966						(M)
Torquay U.	YT	●	83	0	1	0
FIGGINS Philip Eric						
Portsmouth, 20 August, 1955						(G)
Portsmouth	Waterlooville	07.73	74-77	36	0	0
FILAN John Richard						
Australia, 8 February, 1970 Australian Int						(G)
Cambridge U.	Budapest St George (Aus)	03.93	92-94	68	0	0
Coventry C.	Tr	03.95	94-96	15	1	0
Blackburn Rov.	Tr	07.97	97	7	0	0
FILBY Ian Frederick						
Woodford, 9 October, 1954						(W)
Leyton Orient	App	10.72				
Brentford	L	09.74	74	1	2	0
FILLERY Michael Christopher						
Mitcham, 17 September, 1960 E Sch/E Yth						(M)
Chelsea	App	08.78	78-82	156	5	32
Queens Park R.	Tr	08.83	83-86	95	2	9
Portsmouth	Tr	07.87	87-90	62	5	6
Oldham Ath.	Tr	10.90	90	1	1	0
Millwall	L	03.91	90	1	0	0
Torquay U.	L	09.91	91	4	0	0
FILSON Robert **Martin**						
St Helens, 25 June, 1968						(CD)
Wrexham (N/C)	Preston N.E. (N/C)	02.89	88-89	0	2	0
FINAN Robert Joseph						
Dalmuir, 1 March, 1912 Died 1983						(CF)
Blackpool	Yoker Ath.	08.33	33-38	173	-	82
Crewe Alex.	Tr	09.47	47-48	59	-	14
FINC Robert						
Rochdale, 13 February, 1959						(M)
Rochdale (N/C)	Milton	10.77	77	0	1	0
FINCH Derek						
Arley, 29 July, 1940						(FB)
West Bromwich A.	Jnrs	08.57				
Aldershot	Tr	06.60	60	3	-	0
FINCH Desmond Richard						
Worksop, 26 February, 1950						(G)
Mansfield T.		03.69	68-70	4	0	0
FINCH John						
Lambeth, 5 July, 1966						(CD)
Fulham	Dorking	12.90	90-91	6	1	0
FINCH Michael						
Stockton, 30 June, 1965						(G)
Hartlepool U. (N/C)		12.83	83-84	3	0	0
FINCH Robert John						
Camberwell, 24 August, 1948 Died 1978						(FB)
Queens Park R.	App	08.66	67-68	5	1	0

FINCH Roy
Barry, 7 April, 1922 (OL)

League Club	Source	Date Signed	Seasons Played	Apps	Subs	Gls
Swansea C.	Barians	08.39				
West Bromwich A.	Tr	06.44	46-48	15	-	1
Lincoln C.	Tr	02.49	48-58	275	-	57

FINCHAM, Gordon Richard
Hornchurch, 8 January, 1935 (CH)

League Club	Source	Date Signed	Seasons Played	Apps	Subs	Gls
Leicester C.	Fletton	11.52	52-57	50	-	0
Plymouth Arg.	Tr	07.58	58-62	136	-	4
Luton T.	Tr	07.63	63-64	64	-	0

FINDLAY John (Jake) Williamson
Blairgowrie, 13 July, 1954 (G)

League Club	Source	Date Signed	Seasons Played	Apps	Subs	Gls
Aston Villa	App	06.72	73-76	14	0	0
Luton T.	Tr	11.78	78-84	167	0	0
Barnsley	L	09.83	83	6	0	0
Derby Co.	L	01.84	83	1	0	0
Swindon T.	Tr	07.85	85	4	0	0
Portsmouth	Tr	01.86				
Coventry C.	Tr	08.86				

FINLAY Allan Jackson
Edinburgh, 9 January, 1939 S Sch (IF)

League Club	Source	Date Signed	Seasons Played	Apps	Subs	Gls
Newport Co.	Hearts	07.61	61	20	-	1

FINLAY Darren Jonathan
Belfast, 19 December, 1973 NI Yth/NI 'B' (LM)

League Club	Source	Date Signed	Seasons Played	Apps	Subs	Gls
Queens Park R.	YT	05.92				
Doncaster Rov.	Tr	08.94	94	6	2	1

FINLAY John
Birtley, 16 February, 1919 Died 1985 (IF)

League Club	Source	Date Signed	Seasons Played	Apps	Subs	Gls
Sunderland	Ouston Jnrs	05.38	46	1	-	0

FINLAY John
Glasgow, 1 July, 1925 (OR)

League Club	Source	Date Signed	Seasons Played	Apps	Subs	Gls
New Brighton	Clyde	03.51	50	15	-	2
Leeds U.	Tr	06.51	51	1	-	0
Walsall	Yeovil T.	08.53	53	11	-	0

FINLAY Kenneth
Pegswood, 24 March, 1926 (LB/WH)

League Club	Source	Date Signed	Seasons Played	Apps	Subs	Gls
Aldershot	Aberdeen	08.50	50	7	-	0

FINLAY Patrick
Birkenhead, 18 March, 1938 (OL)

League Club	Source	Date Signed	Seasons Played	Apps	Subs	Gls
Tranmere Rov.		08.59	61	3	-	0

FINLAYSON Malcolm John
Bowhill, 14 June, 1930 (G)

League Club	Source	Date Signed	Seasons Played	Apps	Subs	Gls
Millwall	Renfrew Jnrs	02.48	47-55	230	-	0
Wolverhampton W.	Tr	08.56	56-63	179	-	0

FINLEY Alan James
Liverpool, 10 December, 1967 (CD)

League Club	Source	Date Signed	Seasons Played	Apps	Subs	Gls
Shrewsbury T.	Marine	06.88	88-89	60	3	2
Stockport Co.	Tr	08.90	90-93	63	3	5
Carlisle U.	L	12.92	92	1	0	0
Rochdale	L	12.93	93	1	0	0

FINLEY Gary
Liverpool, 14 November, 1970 (CD)

League Club	Source	Date Signed	Seasons Played	Apps	Subs	Gls
Doncaster Rov. (N/C)	Netherfield	08.97	97	6	1	0

FINLEY Thomas
Frizington, 6 October, 1933 (FB)

League Club	Source	Date Signed	Seasons Played	Apps	Subs	Gls
Workington	Northside Jnrs	01.56	55-59	94	-	2
Southport	Tr	02.60	59	6	-	0

FINN Michael Gerard
Liverpool, 1 May, 1954 (G)

League Club	Source	Date Signed	Seasons Played	Apps	Subs	Gls
Burnley	App	12.71	73-74	4	0	0

FINN Neil Edward
Barking, 29 December, 1978 (G)

League Club	Source	Date Signed	Seasons Played	Apps	Subs	Gls
West Ham U.	YT	●	95	1	0	0

FINNAN Stephen John
Limerick, 20 April, 1976 IR u21-8/IR 'B' (W)

League Club	Source	Date Signed	Seasons Played	Apps	Subs	Gls
Birmingham C.	Welling U.	06.95	95-96	9	6	1
Notts Co.	L	03.96	95	14	3	2
Notts Co.	Tr	10.96	96-97	59	8	5

FINNEGAN John
Glasgow, 3 July, 1943 (FB)

League Club	Source	Date Signed	Seasons Played	Apps	Subs	Gls
Millwall	Clyde	06.63	63	6	-	0

FINNEY Alan
Langwith, 31 October, 1933 Eu23-3/E 'B' (OR)

League Club	Source	Date Signed	Seasons Played	Apps	Subs	Gls
Sheffield Wed.	Jnrs	11.50	50-65	455	0	83
Doncaster Rov.	Tr	01.66	65-66	30	0	3

FINNEY Richard **Kenneth**
St Helens, 10 March, 1929 (W)

League Club	Source	Date Signed	Seasons Played	Apps	Subs	Gls
Stockport Co.		12.47	47-57	191	-	33
Tranmere Rov.	Tr	03.58	57-62	180	-	26

FINNEY Kevin
Newcastle-u-Lyme, 19 October, 1969 (M)

League Club	Source	Date Signed	Seasons Played	Apps	Subs	Gls
Port Vale	YT	06.87	87-89	20	17	1
Lincoln C.	Tr	07.91	91-92	31	6	2

FINNEY John **Richard**
Rotherham, 14 March, 1956 E Yth (W)

League Club	Source	Date Signed	Seasons Played	Apps	Subs	Gls
Rotherham U.	Jnrs	07.74	73-80	236	0	68

FINNEY Shaun Barry
York, 5 October, 1966 (F)

League Club	Source	Date Signed	Seasons Played	Apps	Subs	Gls
Scunthorpe U.	Nottingham F. (App)	10.84	84	1	1	0

FINNEY Stephen Kenneth
Hexham, 31 October, 1973 (W)

League Club	Source	Date Signed	Seasons Played	Apps	Subs	Gls
Preston N.E.	YT	05.92	91-92	1	5	1
Manchester C.	Tr	02.93				
Swindon T.	Tr	06.95	95-97	47	26	18
Cambridge U.	L	10.97	97	4	3	2

FINNEY Thomas
Belfast, 6 November, 1952 NI-14 (M)

League Club	Source	Date Signed	Seasons Played	Apps	Subs	Gls
Luton T.	Crusaders	08.73	73	13	1	5
Sunderland	Tr	07.74	74-75	8	7	1
Cambridge U.	Tr	08.76	76-83	259	9	56
Brentford	Tr	02.84	83-84	19	1	2
Cambridge U.	Tr	12.84	84-85	64	0	5

FINNEY Thomas
Preston, 5 April, 1922 EF Lge/E-76 (F)

League Club	Source	Date Signed	Seasons Played	Apps	Subs	Gls
Preston N. E.	Jnrs	01.40	46-59	433	-	187

FINNEY Charles **William** Thomas
Stoke, 5 September, 1931 (IF)

League Club	Source	Date Signed	Seasons Played	Apps	Subs	Gls
Stoke C.	Crewe Alex. (Am)	05.49	52-54	57	-	14
Birmingham C.	Tr	11.55	55-56	14	-	0
Queens Park R.	Tr	05.57	57	10	-	1
Crewe Alex.	Tr	07.58	58	1	-	0
Rochdale	Tr	09.58	58	31	-	1

FINNIESTON Stephen James
Edinburgh, 30 November, 1954 S Yth (F)

League Club	Source	Date Signed	Seasons Played	Apps	Subs	Gls
Chelsea	App	12.71	74-77	78	2	34
Cardiff C.	L	10.74	74	9	0	2
Sheffield U.	Tr	06.78	78	23	0	4

FINNIGAN Anthony
Wimbledon, 17 October, 1962 E Yth (M)

League Club	Source	Date Signed	Seasons Played	Apps	Subs	Gls
Fulham	App	10.80				
Crystal Palace	Corinthian Casuals	02.85	84-87	94	11	10
Blackburn Rov.	Tr	07.88	88-89	21	15	0
Hull C.	Tr	07.90	90	15	3	1
Swindon T.	Tr	03.91	90	2	1	0
Brentford (N/C)	Hong Kong	01.92	91	3	0	0
Barnet (N/C)	Hong Kong	09.93	93	5	1	1
Fulham (N/C)	Dulwich Hamlet	09.94	94-95	8	5	0

FINNIGAN Denis Vincent
Sheffield, 23 March, 1940 Died 1994 (CH)

League Club	Source	Date Signed	Seasons Played	Apps	Subs	Gls
Sheffield U.		04.59	59-66	14	0	0
Chesterfield	Tr	09.68	68-69	27	0	0

FINNIGAN John Francis
Wakefield, 29 March, 1976 (M)

League Club	Source	Date Signed	Seasons Played	Apps	Subs	Gls
Nottingham F.	YT	05.93				
Lincoln C.	L	03.98	97	6	0	0

FINNIGAN Raymond William
Wallsend, 22 January, 1947 (FB)

League Club	Source	Date Signed	Seasons Played	Apps	Subs	Gls
Newcastle U.	App	01.65				
Darlington	Tr	07.66	66-67	8	4	0

FINNIGAN Thomas **Trevor**
Bedlington, 14 October, 1952 E Semi Pro (F)

League Club	Source	Date Signed	Seasons Played	Apps	Subs	Gls
Everton		05.71				
Blackpool	Runcorn	03.77	76-77	13	4	3
Bournemouth	Tr	01.78	77-78	23	2	5

League Club	Source	Date Signed	Seasons Played	Career Record Apps	Subs	Gls
FINNIS Harold Alexander						
Liverpool, 21 November, 1920 Died 1991						(LB)
Everton		06.46	46	1	-	0
FIOCCA Paul						
Italy, 13 January, 1955						(M)
Swindon T.	App	01.73	73	1	0	0
FIORE Mark Joseph						
Southwark, 18 November, 1969						(LW)
Wimbledon	YT	07.88	88	1	0	0
Plymouth Arg.	Tr	03.90	89-92	74	9	8
FIRM Neil John						
Bradford, 23 January, 1958						(CD)
Leeds U.	App	01.76	79-81	11	1	0
Oldham Ath.	L	03.82	81	9	0	0
Peterborough U.	Tr	08.82	82-84	71	1	3
FIRMAN Kenneth						
Felling, 5 February, 1941						(IL)
Gateshead (Am)	Jarrow Mercantile	02.59	58	1	-	0
FIRMANI Edward Ronald						
South Africa, 7 August, 1933						(IF)
Charlton Ath.	Clyde (SA)	02.50	51-54	100	-	50
Charlton Ath.	Sampdorla (It)	10.63	63-64	55	-	32
Southend U.	Tr	06.65	65-66	55	0	24
Charlton Ath.	Tr	03.67	66-67	10	0	6
FIRMANI Peter Walter						
South Africa, 14 February, 1936						(FB)
Charlton Ath.	Marist Bros (SA)	09.53	55-58	31	-	2
FIRTH Francis (Franny) Martin						
Dewsbury, 27 May, 1956						(W)
Huddersfield T.	App	11.73	73-76	26	1	4
Halifax T.	Tr	02.78	77-81	157	11	19
Bury	Tr	08.82	82	33	0	4
FISH Mark Anthony						
Capetown, South Africa, 14 March, 1974 South African Int						(CD)
Bolton W.	Lazio (It)	09.97	97	22	0	2
FISHENDEN Paul						
Hillingdon, 2 August, 1963						(F)
Wimbledon	App	10.81	81-85	57	18	25
Fulham	L	12.85	85	3	0	0
Millwall	L	09.86	86	3	0	0
Leyton Orient	L	10.86	86	4	0	0
Crewe Alex.	Tr	02.88	87-89	79	2	25
FISHER Alexander James						
Southampton, 30 January, 1973						(RB)
Aldershot	YT	07.91	90	2	0	0
FISHER James **Bernard**						
York, 23 February, 1934						(G)
Hull C.	Jnrs	11.55	55-62	126	-	0
Bradford C.	Tr	07.63	63-64	60	-	0
FISHER Charles Kitchener						
Pontypridd, 4 January, 1915 Died 1986						(LB)
Swansea	Lovells Ath.	08.39	46-47	65	-	0
FISHER Frederick						
Hetton-le-Hole, 28 November, 1924						(OR)
Reading	Slough T.	08.44	46-51	139	-	24
Shrewsbury T.	Tr	07.52	52-53	64	-	9
Leyton Orient	Tr	07.54	54	2	-	1
FISHER Frederick Thomas						
Wednesbury, 12 January, 1920 Died 1993						(FB)
Grimsby T.	Fallings Heath	05.37	38-50	166	-	0
Rochdale	Tr	06.51	51	1	-	0
FISHER George Sidney						
Bermondsey, 19 June, 1925						(FB)
Millwall		12.44	46-54	286	-	4
Fulham	Tr	11.54	54	8	-	0
Colchester U.	Tr	09.55	55-59	163	-	6
FISHER Hugh Donnelly						
Glasgow, 9 January, 1944						(M)
Blackpool	Gowan Bank Y.C.	08.62	63-66	51	3	1
Southampton	Tr	03.67	66-76	297	5	7
Southport	Tr	03.77	76-77	60	0	1

League Club	Source	Date Signed	Seasons Played	Career Record Apps	Subs	Gls
FISHER James						
Barrow, 12 June, 1934						(IF)
Barrow	Holker C.O.B.	10.55	52-57	10	-	1
FISHER John Alfred						
Bermondsey, 19 June, 1925						(FB)
Millwall		05.46	47-48	3	-	0
Bournemouth	Tr	06.49	49-52	52	-	0
FISHER Kenneth Douglas Walter						
Bitterne, 30 September, 1921 Died 1989						(FB)
Southampton	Bitterne Nomads	09.46				
Watford	Tr	08.47	47-50	106	-	2
FISHER Leslie Barry						
Southampton, 8 January, 1948						(FB)
Blackpool		12.67	68	1	0	0
FISHER Neil John						
St Helens, 7 November, 1970						(M)
Bolton W.	YT	07.89	91-94	17	7	1
Chester C.	Tr	06.95	95-97	91	17	4
FISHER Paul						
Mansfield, 19 January, 1951						(FB)
Huddersfield T.		02.69				
Darlington	Tr	06.70	70	2	1	0
FISHER Peter McArthur						
Edinburgh, 17 February, 1920						(FB)
Northampton T.		09.47	47	8	-	0
Shrewsbury T.	Tr	08.50	50-51	39	-	0
Wrexham	Tr	10.51	51-53	85	-	0
FISHER Philip John						
Carmarthen, 10 January, 1958						(W)
Exeter C.	Bridgend T.	02.81	80-81	9	2	1
Swansea C. (N/C)	Merthyr Tydfil	03.85	84	2	0	0
FISHER Robert Paul						
Wembley, 3 August, 1956						(FB)
Leyton Orient	App	08.73	73-82	308	6	4
Cambridge U.	Tr	11.82	82-83	42	0	0
Brentford	Tr	02.84	83-84	44	1	0
FISHER Ronald						
Sheffield, 9 March, 1923 Died 1987						(RB)
Halifax T.		08.50	50	6	-	0
FISHER Stanley						
Barnsley, 29 September, 1924						(CF)
Barnsley	Rockingham Colly	09.44	46	1	-	0
Halifax T.	Tr	01.47	46-47	26	-	7
FISHLOCK Murray Edward						
Marlborough, 23 September, 1973						(LB)
Hereford U.	Trowbridge T.	09.94	95-96	67	4	4
FITCH Barry Edward						
Brighton, 19 November, 1943						(FB)
Brighton & H.A.	Jnrs	11.61	63	1	-	0
FITTON John						
Oldham, 12 January, 1951						(G)
Oldham Ath.	Jnrs	10.68	69	3	0	0
FITZGERALD Michael **Alfred**						
Conisbrough, 25 January, 1911 Died 1981						(WH)
Reading	Denaby U.	08.34	34-35	6	-	1
Queens Park R.	Tr	05.36	36-38	94	-	1
Aldershot	Tr	11.45	46-47	59	-	1
FITZGERALD Gary Michael						
Hampstead, 27 October, 1976						(CD)
Watford	YT	11.94	94	1	0	0
FITZGERALD Peter Joseph						
Waterford, 17 June, 1937 LoI/IR-5						(F)
Leeds U.	Sparta Rotterdam (Neth)	08.60	60	8	-	0
Chester C.	Tr	07.61	61-63	80	-	12
FITZGERALD Scott Brian						
Westminster, 13 August, 1969 IRu21-4/IR 'B'						(CD)
Wimbledon	YT	07.87	89-95	95	11	1
Sheffield U.	L	11.95	95	6	0	0
Millwall	L	10.96	96	7	0	0
Millwall	Tr	07.97	97	16	2	0

League Club	Source	Date Signed	Seasons Played	Career Record Apps	Subs	Gls
FITZHENRY Neil						
Wigan, 24 September, 1978						(CD)
Wigan Ath.	YT	07.97	97	1	2	0
FITZPATRICK Anthony Charles						
Glasgow, 3 March, 1956 Su21-5						(M)
Bristol C.	St Mirren	08.79	79-80	75	0	1
FITZPATRICK Gary Gerard						
Birmingham, 5 August, 1971 IR Yth						(M)
Leicester C.	YT	01.90	89	0	1	0
FITZPATRICK John Herbert Norton						
Aberdeen, 18 August, 1946						(WH)
Manchester U.	Jnrs	09.63	64-72	111	6	8
FITZPATRICK Paul James						
Oxford, 5 October, 1965						(D/M)
Bolton W.	Tranmere Rov. (Jnrs)	03.85	84-85	13	1	0
Bristol C.	Tr	08.86	86-88	40	4	7
Carlisle U.	Tr	10.88	88-90	106	3	4
Preston N. E.	L	12.88	88	2	0	0
Leicester C.	Tr	07.91	91-92	21	6	4
Birmingham C.	Tr	01.93	92	7	0	0
Bury	L	03.93	92	8	1	0
Northampton T. (N/C)	Hamilton Academical	02.94	93	1	1	1
FITZPATRICK Peter						
Bebington, 27 April, 1929						(IF)
New Brighton (Am)		01.50	49	1	-	0
FITZPATRICK Trevor Joseph James						
Frimley, 19 February, 1980						(F)
Southend U.	YT	●	97	1	2	0
FITZSIMONS Arthur Gerard						
Dublin, 16 December, 1929 LoI/IR-26						(IF)
Middlesbrough	Shelbourne	05.49	49-58	223	-	49
Lincoln C.	Tr	03.59	58	7	-	0
Mansfield T.	Tr	08.59	59-60	62	-	23
FITZSIMONS Eric James						
Oldham, 23 October, 1948						(IR)
Bradford P.A. (Am)		02.70	69	1	0	0
FJORTOFT Jan-Aage						
Norway, 10 January, 1967 Norwegian Int						(F)
Swindon T.	Rapid Vienna (Aut)	07.93	93-94	62	10	28
Middlesbrough	Tr	03.95	94-96	37	4	10
Sheffield U.	Tr	01.97	96-97	30	4	19
Barnsley	Tr	01.98	97	12	3	6
FLACK Douglas						
Staines, 24 October, 1920						(G)
Fulham	Jnrs	12.38	48-52	54	-	0
Walsall	Tr	08.53	53	11	-	0
FLACK William **Leonard** Wallace						
Cambridge, 1 June, 1916 Died 1995 E Sch						(FB)
Norwich C.	Cambridge T.	07.33	34-46	49	-	0
FLACK Steven Richard						
Cambridge, 29 May, 1971						(F)
Cardiff C.	Cambridge C.	11.95	95-96	6	5	1
Exeter C.	Tr	09.96	96-97	57	11	18
FLAHAVAN Aaron Adam						
Southampton, 15 December, 1975						(G)
Portsmouth	YT	02.94	96-97	50	0	0
FLANAGAN Daniel Christopher						
Dublin, 24 November, 1924						(CF)
Notts Co. (Am)	Dundalk	12.46	46	2	-	2
Manchester C.	Shelbourne	02.47				
Bradford C.	Tr	12.47	47	13	-	6
FLANAGAN Michael Anthony						
Ilford, 9 November, 1952 E Yth						(F)
Charlton Ath.	Tottenham H. (Jnrs)	08.71	71-78	241	13	85
Crystal Palace	Tr	08.79	79-80	56	0	8
Queens Park R.	Tr	12.80	80-83	71	7	20
Charlton Ath.	Tr	01.84	83-85	89	4	24
Cambridge U. (N/C)	Tr	09.86	86	7	2	3
FLANAGAN Shaun						
Doncaster, 25 December, 1960						(M)
Doncaster Rov.	App	01.79	78-80	41	9	3

League Club	Source	Date Signed	Seasons Played	Career Record Apps	Subs	Gls
FLANNIGAN Raymond John						
Margate, 15 March, 1949						(FB)
Reading	Margate	02.70	70-71	36	4	0
FLASH Richard Garfield						
Birmingham, 8 April, 1976						(LW)
Manchester U.	YT	07.94				
Wolverhampton W.	Tr	09.95				
Watford	Tr	07.96	96	0	1	0
Lincoln C.	L	10.97	97	2	3	0
FLATLEY Albert Austin						
Bradford, 5 September, 1919 Died 1987						(IF)
York C.	Wolverhampton W (Am)	02.39	38	4	-	0
Port Vale	Tr	06.39				
Bradford P.A.	Tr	07.44				
Bury	Tr	12.46				
Workington	Alessandria (It)	11.51	51	8	-	0
FLATT Colin Harold						
Blythburgh, 30 January, 1940						(CF)
Leyton Orient	Wisbech T.	05.65	65	32	1	8
Southend U.	Tr	06.66	66	20	2	8
FLATTS Mark Michael						
Islington, 14 October, 1972 E Yth						(W)
Arsenal	YT	12.90	92-94	9	7	0
Cambridge U.	L	10.93	93	5	0	1
Brighton & H.A.	L	12.93	93	9	1	1
Bristol C.	L	03.95	94	4	2	0
Grimsby T.	L	03.96	95	4	1	0
FLAVELL John Alfred						
Brierley Hill, 15 May, 1929						(FB)
West Bromwich A.	Lye T.	05.47				
Walsall	Tr	09.53	53	22	-	0
FLAVELL Robert William						
Berwick, 7 March, 1956						(FB)
Burnley	App	03.73				
Halifax T.	Tr	02.76	75-77	91	0	7
Chesterfield	Tr	08.78	78	27	2	2
Barnsley	Tr	07.79	79	25	0	0
Halifax T. (N/C)	Tr	12.80	80	1	0	0
FLAY Stephen						
Poole, 2 October, 1954						(FB)
Oxford U.	App	10.72	73-74	3	0	0
FLECK Robert William						
Glasgow, 11 August, 1965 S Yth/Su21-6/S-4						(F)
Norwich C.	Glasgow Rangers	12.87	87-91	130	13	39
Chelsea	Tr	08.92	92-93	35	5	3
Bolton W.	L	12.93	93	6	1	1
Bristol C.	L	01.95	94	10	0	1
Norwich C.	Tr	08.95	95-97	93	11	16
Reading	Tr	03.98	97	3	2	0
FLEET Stephen						
Urmston, 2 July, 1937						(G)
Manchester C.	Jnrs	02.55	57-60	5	-	0
Wrexham	Tr	06.63	63-65	79	0	0
Stockport Co.	Tr	01.66	65-67	36	0	0
FLEETING James Taylor						
Glasgow, 8 April, 1955						(CD)
Norwich C.	Kilbirnie Ladeside	04.75	76	0	1	0
FLEETWOOD Steven Robert						
Sheffield, 27 February, 1962						(M)
Rotherham U. (N/C)		02.87	86	0	1	0
FLEMING Bernard James						
Middlesbrough, 8 January, 1937						(FB)
Grimsby T.	R.A.F. Binbrook	04.57	57-60	22	-	0
Workington	Tr	07.61	61	19	-	0
Chester C.	Tr	05.62	62-63	64	-	0
FLEMING Charles						
Culross, 12 July, 1927 Died 1997 S-1						(CF)
Sunderland	East Fife	01.55	54-57	107	-	62
FLEMING Craig						
Calder, 6 October, 1971						(D)
Halifax T.	YT	03.90	88-90	56	1	0
Oldham Ath.	Tr	08.91	91-96	158	6	1
Norwich C.	Tr	06.97	97	20	2	1

FLEMING Curtis
Manchester, 8 October, 1968 IR Yth/IRu21-5/IRu23-2/IR-10 (RB)

League Club	Source	Date Signed	Seasons Played	Apps	Subs	Gls
Middlesbrough	St Patricks Ath.	08.91	91-97	172	15	2

FLEMING Francis Joseph
South Shields, 21 December, 1945 (G)

League Club	Source	Date Signed	Seasons Played	Apps	Subs	Gls
Darlington		07.64	64	2	-	0

FLEMING Gary James
Derry (NI), 17 February, 1967 NIu23-1/NI-31 (FB)

League Club	Source	Date Signed	Seasons Played	Apps	Subs	Gls
Nottingham F.	App	11.84	84-87	71	3	0
Manchester C.	Tr	08.89	89	13	1	0
Notts Co.	L	03.90	89	3	0	0
Barnsley	Tr	03.90	89-95	236	3	0

FLEMING George Keith
Gourock, 25 February, 1935 (IF)

League Club	Source	Date Signed	Seasons Played	Apps	Subs	Gls
Watford	Morton	06.58	58-59	27	-	10
Carlisle U.	Tr	06.60	60	7	-	0
Barrow	Tr	09.60	60	17	-	3

FLEMING Haydn Valentine
Islington, 14 March, 1978 (RB)

League Club	Source	Date Signed	Seasons Played	Apps	Subs	Gls
Cardiff C.	YT	07.96	95-96	29	3	0

FLEMING James
Tannochside, 4 November, 1952 (M)

League Club	Source	Date Signed	Seasons Played	Apps	Subs	Gls
Carlisle U.	Manchester U. (App)	07.71				
Barrow	L	01.72	71	1	1	0

FLEMING James Freeburn
Glasgow, 7 January, 1929 (FB)

League Club	Source	Date Signed	Seasons Played	Apps	Subs	Gls
Workington	Stirling A.	05.54	54-57	89	-	1

FLEMING James Paterson
Alloa, 7 January, 1942 (OL)

League Club	Source	Date Signed	Seasons Played	Apps	Subs	Gls
Luton T.	Partick Thistle	11.60	60-62	66	-	9

FLEMING John (Ian) Hares
Maybole, 15 January, 1953 (W)

League Club	Source	Date Signed	Seasons Played	Apps	Subs	Gls
Sheffield Wed.	Aberdeen	02.79	78-79	13	0	1

FLEMING John Joseph
Nottingham, 1 July, 1953 (M)

League Club	Source	Date Signed	Seasons Played	Apps	Subs	Gls
Oxford U.	Jnrs	09.70	71-74	67	8	2
Lincoln C.	Tr	07.75	75-78	109	12	17
Port Vale	Tr	03.80	79	3	0	0

FLEMING Mark John
Hammersmith, 11 August, 1969 (LB)

League Club	Source	Date Signed	Seasons Played	Apps	Subs	Gls
Queens Park R.	YT	01.88	87-88	1	2	0
Brentford	Tr	07.89	89-90	33	2	1

FLEMING Michael Anthony
India, 23 February, 1928 (IF)

League Club	Source	Date Signed	Seasons Played	Apps	Subs	Gls
Tranmere Rov.		09.53	53-57	115	-	8

FLEMING Neil
Felixstowe, 9 January, 1950 (CH)

League Club	Source	Date Signed	Seasons Played	Apps	Subs	Gls
Lincoln C. (Am)	Lincoln Claytons	07.73	73	1	0	0

FLEMING Paul
Halifax, 6 September, 1967 (RB)

League Club	Source	Date Signed	Seasons Played	Apps	Subs	Gls
Halifax T.	YT	09.85	85-90	135	4	1
Mansfield T.	Tr	07.91	91-94	65	3	0

FLEMING Terence Maurice
Marston Green, 5 January, 1973 (FB/M)

League Club	Source	Date Signed	Seasons Played	Apps	Subs	Gls
Coventry C.	YT	07.91	90-92	8	5	0
Northampton T.	Tr	08.93	93	26	5	1
Preston N.E.	Tr	07.94	94-95	25	7	2
Lincoln C.	Tr	12.95	95-97	94	5	3

FLETCHER Alan Frederick
Pendleton, 28 October, 1917 Died 1984 (IF)

League Club	Source	Date Signed	Seasons Played	Apps	Subs	Gls
Blackpool		01.37				
Bournemouth		06.38	38	12	-	0
Bristol Rov.	Tr	06.39				
Crewe Alex.		09.47	47	1	-	0

FLETCHER Andrew Michael
Saltburn, 12 August, 1971 (F)

League Club	Source	Date Signed	Seasons Played	Apps	Subs	Gls
Middlesbrough	YT	05.89				
Scarborough	Tr	02.91	90-91	15	12	6

FLETCHER Carl Neil
Surrey Heath, 7 April, 1980 (M)

League Club	Source	Date Signed	Seasons Played	Apps	Subs	Gls
Bournemouth	YT	●	97	0	1	0

FLETCHER Christopher Columba
Buncrana (Ire), 14 June, 1933 (F)

League Club	Source	Date Signed	Seasons Played	Apps	Subs	Gls
Brentford	Cheltenham T.	12.57	57	3	-	0

FLETCHER Douglas
Sheffield, 17 September, 1930 (IF)

League Club	Source	Date Signed	Seasons Played	Apps	Subs	Gls
Sheffield Wed.	Hillsborough B.C.	01.48	48-49	4	-	0
Bury	Tr	05.51	51-55	67	-	17
Scunthorpe U.	Tr	07.56	56-57	54	-	26
Darlington	Tr	07.58	58	43	-	13
Halifax T.	Tr	06.59	59	20	-	4

FLETCHER Gavin
Bellshill, 30 October, 1941 (IF)

League Club	Source	Date Signed	Seasons Played	Apps	Subs	Gls
Bradford C.	Third Lanark	07.63	63	8	-	1

FLETCHER Hugh Malcolm
Lochgilphead, 8 April, 1933 (FB/F)

League Club	Source	Date Signed	Seasons Played	Apps	Subs	Gls
Carlisle U.	Glasgow Celtic	05.56	56-60	124	-	18

FLETCHER James
Houghton-le-Spring, 6 November, 1934 (CF)

League Club	Source	Date Signed	Seasons Played	Apps	Subs	Gls
Doncaster Rov.	Appleton Colly	01.58	57-59	45	-	15
Stockport Co.	Tr	01.60	59-60	61	-	19

FLETCHER James Alfred
Wouldham, 10 November, 1931 E Amat (IF)

League Club	Source	Date Signed	Seasons Played	Apps	Subs	Gls
Gillingham	Maidstone U.	07.57	57	23	-	8
Southend U.	Tr	07.58				

FLETCHER James Robert
Brewood, 23 December, 1926 (F)

League Club	Source	Date Signed	Seasons Played	Apps	Subs	Gls
Birmingham C.	Bilston U.	06.50				
Chester C.	Tr	07.51	51	23	-	9

FLETCHER John
Sheffield, 22 February, 1943 (FB)

League Club	Source	Date Signed	Seasons Played	Apps	Subs	Gls
Doncaster Rov.		06.61	61	1	-	0

FLETCHER Joseph Michael
Manchester, 25 September, 1946 (CF)

League Club	Source	Date Signed	Seasons Played	Apps	Subs	Gls
Rochdale	Manchester C. (Am)	01.67	66-68	55	2	21
Grimsby T.	Tr	07.69	69	11	0	1
Barrow	Tr	10.69	69	7	1	1

FLETCHER Kenneth
Liverpool, 31 December, 1931 (FB)

League Club	Source	Date Signed	Seasons Played	Apps	Subs	Gls
Everton	Jnrs	08.49				
Chester C.	Tr	07.53	53-55	34	-	0

FLETCHER Leonard Gerald George
Hammersmith, 28 April, 1929 (WH)

League Club	Source	Date Signed	Seasons Played	Apps	Subs	Gls
Ipswich T.	R.A.F. Didcot	11.49	49-54	20	-	0

FLETCHER Mark Robert John
Barnsley, 1 April, 1965 (FB)

League Club	Source	Date Signed	Seasons Played	Apps	Subs	Gls
Barnsley	App	04.83	83	1	0	0
Bradford C.	Tr	06.84	84	4	2	0

FLETCHER Paul John
Bolton, 13 January, 1951 Eu23-4 (F)

League Club	Source	Date Signed	Seasons Played	Apps	Subs	Gls
Bolton W.	App	11.68	68-70	33	3	5
Burnley	Tr	03.71	70-79	291	2	71
Blackpool	Tr	02.80	79-81	19	1	8

FLETCHER Peter
Manchester, 2 December, 1953 (F)

League Club	Source	Date Signed	Seasons Played	Apps	Subs	Gls
Manchester U.	App	12.70	72-73	2	5	0
Hull C.	Tr	05.74	74-75	26	10	5
Stockport Co.	Tr	05.76	76-77	43	8	13
Huddersfield T.	Tr	07.78	78-81	83	16	36

FLETCHER James **Rodney**
Preston, 23 September, 1945 (F)

League Club	Source	Date Signed	Seasons Played	Apps	Subs	Gls
Leeds U.	Colne	12.62				
Crewe Alex.	Madeley College	03.67	66	1	0	0
Lincoln C.	Tr	08.67	67-70	86	4	29
Scunthorpe U.	Tr	06.71	71-73	97	1	30
Grimsby T.	Tr	11.73	73-74	9	3	1

FLETCHER Steven Mark
Hartlepool, 26 July, 1972 (F)

League Club	Source	Date Signed	Seasons Played	Apps	Subs	Gls
Hartlepool U.	YT	08.90	90-91	19	13	4
Bournemouth	Tr	07.92	92-97	175	16	36

FLEWIN Reginald
Portsmouth, 28 November, 1920 (CH)

League Club	Source	Date Signed	Seasons Played	Apps	Subs	Gls
Portsmouth	Ryde Sports	11.37	38-52	150	-	0

FLEXNEY Paul
Glasgow, 18 January, 1965 (CD)

League Club	Source	Date Signed	Seasons Played	Apps	Subs	Gls
Northampton T.	Clyde	08.88	88	12	0	0

FLINT Kenneth
Nottingham, 12 November, 1923 (OL)

League Club	Source	Date Signed	Seasons Played	Apps	Subs	Gls
Tottenham H.	Bedford T.	07.47	47	5	-	1
Aldershot	Tr	07.50	50-57	324	-	70
Leyton Orient	Tr	06.58	58	4	-	0

FLITCROFT David John
Bolton, 14 January, 1974 (M)

League Club	Source	Date Signed	Seasons Played	Apps	Subs	Gls
Preston N.E.	YT	05.92	92	4	4	2
Lincoln C.	L	09.93	93	2	0	0
Chester C.	Tr	12.93	93-97	104	21	12

FLITCROFT Garry William
Bolton, 6 November, 1972 E Sch/E Yth/Eu21-10 (M)

League Club	Source	Date Signed	Seasons Played	Apps	Subs	Gls
Manchester C.	YT	07.91	92-95	109	6	13
Bury	L	03.92	91	12	0	0
Blackburn Rov.	Tr	03.96	95-97	58	6	3

FLO Jostein
Norway, 3 October, 1964 Norwegian Int (F)

League Club	Source	Date Signed	Seasons Played	Apps	Subs	Gls
Sheffield U.	Sogndal (Nor)	08.93	93-95	74	10	19

FLO Tore Andre
Norway, 15 June, 1973 Norwegian Int (CF)

League Club	Source	Date Signed	Seasons Played	Apps	Subs	Gls
Chelsea	Brann Bergen (Nor)	08.97	97	16	18	11

FLOCKETT Thomas William
Ferryhill, 17 July, 1927 Died 1997 (FB)

League Club	Source	Date Signed	Seasons Played	Apps	Subs	Gls
Chesterfield	Spennymoor U.	04.49	49-56	200	-	1
Bradford C.	Tr	06.57	57-62	227	-	1

FLOOD Edward David
Liverpool, 19 November, 1952 (FB)

League Club	Source	Date Signed	Seasons Played	Apps	Subs	Gls
Liverpool	App	11.69				
Tranmere Rov.	Tr	07.72	72-80	313	2	6
York C.	Tr	08.81	81	13	2	0

FLOOD John Ernest
Southampton, 21 October, 1932 E Sch (OR)

League Club	Source	Date Signed	Seasons Played	Apps	Subs	Gls
Southampton	Jnrs	11.49	52-57	122	-	28
Bournemouth	Tr	06.58	58	17	-	3

FLOOD John Gerard
Glasgow, 25 December, 1960 (W)

League Club	Source	Date Signed	Seasons Played	Apps	Subs	Gls
Sheffield U.	App	10.78	78-80	16	3	1

FLOOD Paul Anthony
Dublin, 29 June, 1948 (W)

League Club	Source	Date Signed	Seasons Played	Apps	Subs	Gls
Brighton & H.A.	Bohemians	06.67	67-70	32	3	7

FLOUNDERS Andrew John
Hull, 13 December, 1963 (F)

League Club	Source	Date Signed	Seasons Played	Apps	Subs	Gls
Hull C.	App	12.81	80-86	126	33	54
Scunthorpe U.	Tr	03.87	86-90	186	10	87
Rochdale	Tr	07.91	91-93	82	3	31
Rotherham U.	L	02.93	92	6	0	2
Carlisle U.	L	10.93	93	5	0	1
Carlisle U.	L	02.94	93	1	2	0
Northampton T.	Halifax T.	12.94	94	2	0	0

FLOWER Anthony John
Nottingham, 2 January, 1945 (W)

League Club	Source	Date Signed	Seasons Played	Apps	Subs	Gls
Notts Co.	Jnrs	01.62	61-66	127	2	17
Halifax T.	Tr	07.67	67-69	78	1	6

FLOWER Johannes (John) Graham
Northampton, 9 December, 1964 (CD)

League Club	Source	Date Signed	Seasons Played	Apps	Subs	Gls
Sheffield U.	Corby T.	08.89				
Aldershot	Tr	10.90	90	30	2	2

FLOWERS John Edward
Edlington, 26 August, 1944 (WH)

League Club	Source	Date Signed	Seasons Played	Apps	Subs	Gls
Stoke C.	App	09.61	63-65	8	0	0
Doncaster Rov.	Tr	08.66	66-70	162	2	4
Port Vale	Tr	08.71	71	34	0	0

FLOWERS Malcolm Thomas
Mansfield, 9 August, 1938 (CH)

League Club	Source	Date Signed	Seasons Played	Apps	Subs	Gls
Mansfield T.	Jnrs	08.56	56	3	-	0

FLOWERS Paul Anthony
Stepney, 7 September, 1974 (CD)

League Club	Source	Date Signed	Seasons Played	Apps	Subs	Gls
Colchester U.	YT	08.93	92	2	1	0

FLOWERS Ronald
Doncaster, 28 July, 1934 Eu23-2/EF Lge/E-49 (WH)

League Club	Source	Date Signed	Seasons Played	Apps	Subs	Gls
Wolverhampton W.	Jnrs	08.51	52-66	467	0	33
Northampton T.	Tr	09.67	67-68	61	1	4

FLOWERS Timothy David
Kenilworth, 3 February, 1967 E Yth/Eu21-3/E-10 (G)

League Club	Source	Date Signed	Seasons Played	Apps	Subs	Gls
Wolverhampton W.	App	08.84	84-85	63	0	0
Southampton	Tr	06.86	86-93	192	0	0
Swindon T.	L	03.87	86	2	0	0
Swindon T.	L	11.87	87	5	0	0
Blackburn Rov.	Tr	11.93	93-97	165	1	0

FLOYD Ronald Charles
Coventry, 17 August, 1932 (G)

League Club	Source	Date Signed	Seasons Played	Apps	Subs	Gls
West Bromwich A.	Jnrs	11.49				
Crewe Alex.	Tr	07.53	53-54	39	-	0

FLYNN Brian
Port Talbot, 12 October, 1955 W Sch/Wu23-2/W-66 (M)

League Club	Source	Date Signed	Seasons Played	Apps	Subs	Gls
Burnley	App	10.72	73-77	115	5	8
Leeds U.	Tr	11.77	77-82	152	2	11
Burnley	L	03.82	81	2	0	0
Burnley	Tr	11.82	82-84	76	4	11
Cardiff C.	Tr	11.84	84-85	32	0	0
Doncaster Rov.	Tr	11.85	85	27	0	0
Bury	Tr	07.86	86	19	0	0
Doncaster Rov. (N/C)	Limerick	08.87	87	18	6	1
Wrexham	Tr	02.88	87-92	91	9	5

FLYNN John Edward
Workington, 20 March, 1948 (CD)

League Club	Source	Date Signed	Seasons Played	Apps	Subs	Gls
Workington	Jnrs	09.67	66-68	35	3	0
Sheffield U.	Tr	07.69	69-77	185	5	8
Rotherham U.	Tr	07.78	78-79	30	1	1

FLYNN Michael Anthony
Oldham, 23 February, 1969 (CD)

League Club	Source	Date Signed	Seasons Played	Apps	Subs	Gls
Oldham Ath.	App	02.87	87-88	37	3	1
Norwich C.	Tr	12.88				
Preston N. E.	Tr	12.89	89-92	134	2	7
Stockport Co.	Tr	03.93	92-97	224	1	12

FLYNN Peter
Glasgow, 11 October, 1936 (WH)

League Club	Source	Date Signed	Seasons Played	Apps	Subs	Gls
Leeds U.	Jnrs	10.53	53	1	-	0
Bradford P. A.	Tr	06.57	58-65	130	1	9

FLYNN Sean Michael
Birmingham, 13 March, 1968 (RM)

League Club	Source	Date Signed	Seasons Played	Apps	Subs	Gls
Coventry C.	Halesowen T.	12.91	91-94	90	7	9
Derby Co.	Tr	08.95	95-96	39	20	3
Stoke C.	L	03.97	96	5	0	0
West Bromwich A.	Tr	08.97	97	30	5	2

FLYNN William
Kirkmalden, 2 January, 1927 (OL)

League Club	Source	Date Signed	Seasons Played	Apps	Subs	Gls
Rotherham U.	Maybold Jnrs	07.49	49	6	-	0

FOAN Albert Thomas
Rotherhithe, 30 October, 1923 (IF)

League Club	Source	Date Signed	Seasons Played	Apps	Subs	Gls
Norwich C.	B.A.O.R. Germany	04.47	47-49	18	-	4
West Ham U.	Tr	07.50	50-56	53	-	6

FOGARTY Ambrose Gerald
Dublin, 11 September, 1933 IR-11 (IF)

League Club	Source	Date Signed	Seasons Played	Apps	Subs	Gls
Sunderland	Glentoran	10.57	57-63	152	-	37
Hartlepool U.	Tr	11.63	63-66	127	0	22

FOGARTY Kenneth Anthony
Manchester, 25 January, 1955 (CD)

League Club	Source	Date Signed	Seasons Played	Apps	Subs	Gls
Stockport Co.	App	11.72	71-79	265	4	6

FOGARTY William Francis
Dulwich, 27 June, 1957 (M)

League Club	Source	Date Signed	Seasons Played	Apps	Subs	Gls
Gillingham	App	07.75	75-76	25	4	0
Charlton Ath.	Tr	12.76				

FOGG David
Liverpool, 28 May, 1951 (FB)

League Club	Source	Date Signed	Seasons Played	Apps	Subs	Gls
Wrexham		05.70	70-75	159	2	0
Oxford U.	Tr	07.76	76-84	289	4	16

FOGG Ronald William James
Tilbury, 3 June, 1938 (CF)

League Club	Source	Date Signed	Seasons Played	Apps	Subs	Gls
Southend U. (Am)	Grays Ath.	08.59	59	2	-	0
Aldershot	Weymouth	07.63	63-64	64	-	28

FOGGO Kenneth Taylor
Perth, 7 November, 1943 S Sch (OR)

League Club	Source	Date Signed	Seasons Played	Apps	Subs	Gls
West Bromwich A.	Peebles Y.M.C.A.	11.60	62-67	128	1	29
Norwich C.	Tr	10.67	67-72	181	4	54
Portsmouth	Tr	01.73	72-74	47	13	3
Southend U.	Tr	09.75	75	30	0	6

FOGGON Alan
Chester-le-Street, 23 February, 1950 E Yth (W)

League Club	Source	Date Signed	Seasons Played	Apps	Subs	Gls
Newcastle U.	App	11.67	67-70	54	7	14
Cardiff C.	Tr	08.71	71-72	14	3	1
Middlesbrough	Tr	10.72	72-75	105	10	45
Manchester U.	Tr	07.76	76	0	3	0
Sunderland	Tr	09.76	76	7	1	0
Southend U.	Tr	06.77	77	22	0	0
Hartlepool U.	L	02.78	77	18	0	2

FOLAN Anthony Stephen
Lewisham, 18 September, 1978 IRu21-2 (LM)

League Club	Source	Date Signed	Seasons Played	Apps	Subs	Gls
Crystal Palace	YT	09.95	97	0	1	0

FOLDS Robert James
Bedford, 18 April, 1949 (LB)

League Club	Source	Date Signed	Seasons Played	Apps	Subs	Gls
Gillingham	App	04.67	68-70	38	5	1
Northampton T.	Tr	08.71	71	29	1	0

FOLEY Charles
Salford, 7 January, 1952 (M)

League Club	Source	Date Signed	Seasons Played	Apps	Subs	Gls
Stockport Co.	App	01.70	69-70	6	1	0

FOLEY Dominic Joseph
Cork, 7 July, 1976 IRu21-8 (F)

League Club	Source	Date Signed	Seasons Played	Apps	Subs	Gls
Wolverhampton W.	St James Gate	08.95	95-97	2	13	1
Watford	L	02.98	97	2	6	1

FOLEY Peter
Bicester, 10 September, 1956 IR Yth (F)

League Club	Source	Date Signed	Seasons Played	Apps	Subs	Gls
Oxford U.	App	09.74	74-82	262	15	71
Gillingham	L	02.83	82	5	0	0
Aldershot	Bulova (HK)	08.84	84	6	3	2
Exeter C. (N/C)		03.87	86	1	0	0

FOLEY Peter Allan
Edinburgh, 28 June, 1944 (W)

League Club	Source	Date Signed	Seasons Played	Apps	Subs	Gls
Workington	Preston Ath.	02.65	64-66	74	0	14
Scunthorpe U.	Tr	07.67	67-68	15	2	3
Chesterfield	Tr	08.69	69	2	0	0

FOLEY Stephen Paul
Clacton, 21 June, 1953 (M)

League Club	Source	Date Signed	Seasons Played	Apps	Subs	Gls
Colchester U.	App	09.71	71-81	273	10	54

FOLEY Steven
Liverpool, 4 October, 1962 (M)

League Club	Source	Date Signed	Seasons Played	Apps	Subs	Gls
Liverpool	App	09.80				
Fulham	L	12.83	83	2	1	0
Grimsby T.	Tr	08.84	84	31	0	2
Sheffield U.	Tr	08.85	85-86	56	10	14
Swindon T.	Tr	06.87	87-91	142	9	23
Stoke C.	Tr	01.92	91-93	106	1	10
Lincoln C.	Tr	07.94	94	15	1	0
Bradford C. (N/C)	Tr	08.95	95	0	1	0

FOLEY Terence
Portsmouth, 8 February, 1938 (CF)

League Club	Source	Date Signed	Seasons Played	Apps	Subs	Gls
Portsmouth	Ryde	05.59	59	7	-	0
Chesterfield	Tr	07.60	60	28	-	11

FOLEY Theodore Cornelius
Dublin, 2 April, 1937 IR-9 (FB)

League Club	Source	Date Signed	Seasons Played	Apps	Subs	Gls
Exeter C.	Home Farm	03.55	55-60	155	-	1
Northampton T.	Tr	05.61	61-66	204	0	8
Charlton Ath.	Tr	08.67	67	6	0	0

FOLEY William
Bellshill, 25 June, 1960 (F)

League Club	Source	Date Signed	Seasons Played	Apps	Subs	Gls
Swansea C. (N/C)	Frickley Ath.	01.86	85	4	1	2
Cardiff C. (N/C)	Tr	03.86	85	5	2	1

FOLLAN Edward Harvey
Greenock, 3 October, 1929 (IF)

League Club	Source	Date Signed	Seasons Played	Apps	Subs	Gls
Aston Villa	Prescot Cables	06.52	54-55	34	-	7

FOLLAND Robert
Hartlepool, 3 December, 1940 (CF)

League Club	Source	Date Signed	Seasons Played	Apps	Subs	Gls
Hartlepool U.	Newcastle U. (Am)	05.59	59-62	58	-	24

FOLLAND Robert William
Swansea, 16 September, 1979 W Yth (M)

League Club	Source	Date Signed	Seasons Played	Apps	Subs	Gls
Oxford U.	YT	•	97	0	2	0

FOOT Daniel Francis
Edmonton, 6 September, 1975 (FB)

League Club	Source	Date Signed	Seasons Played	Apps	Subs	Gls
Southend U.	Tottenham H. (YT)	08.94	94	2	1	0

FOOTE Christopher Robert Thomas
Bournemouth, 19 November, 1950 (M)

League Club	Source	Date Signed	Seasons Played	Apps	Subs	Gls
Bournemouth	App	08.68	68-69	44	1	2
Cambridge U.	Tr	03.71	70-73	76	10	6

FOOTITT Donald
Grantham, 24 May, 1929 Died 1995 (G)

League Club	Source	Date Signed	Seasons Played	Apps	Subs	Gls
Lincoln C.	St Johns	01.47	46	24	-	0
Crewe Alex.	Tr	07.49	49	1	-	0

FORAN Mark James
Aldershot, 30 October, 1973 (CD)

League Club	Source	Date Signed	Seasons Played	Apps	Subs	Gls
Millwall	YT	11.90				
Sheffield U.	Tr	08.93	94-95	10	1	1
Rotherham U.	L	08.94	94	3	0	0
Wycombe W.	L	08.95	95	5	0	0
Peterborough U.	Tr	02.96	95-97	22	3	1
Lincoln C.	L	01.97	96	1	1	0
Oldham Ath.	L	03.97	96	0	1	0
Crewe Alex.	Tr	12.97	97	10	2	1

FORBES Adrian Emmanuel
Ealing, 23 January, 1979 E Yth (W)

League Club	Source	Date Signed	Seasons Played	Apps	Subs	Gls
Norwich C.	YT	01.97	96-97	31	12	4

FORBES Alexander Rooney
Dundee, 21 January, 1925 S-14 (WH)

League Club	Source	Date Signed	Seasons Played	Apps	Subs	Gls
Sheffield U.	Dundee N.E.	12.44	46-47	61	-	6
Arsenal	Tr	02.48	47-55	217	-	20
Leyton Orient	Tr	08.56	56	8	-	0
Fulham	Tr	11.57	57	4	-	0

FORBES Dudley Douglas
South Africa, 19 April, 1926 (WH)

League Club	Source	Date Signed	Seasons Played	Apps	Subs	Gls
Charlton Ath.	Marist Bros (SA)	12.47	48-50	57	-	1

FORBES Duncan Scott
Edinburgh, 19 June, 1941 (CD)

League Club	Source	Date Signed	Seasons Played	Apps	Subs	Gls
Colchester U.	Musselburgh	09.61	61-68	270	0	2
Norwich C.	Tr	09.68	68-80	289	6	10
Torquay U.	L	10.76	76	7	0	0

FORBES George
Dukinfield, 21 July, 1914 (CH)

League Club	Source	Date Signed	Seasons Played	Apps	Subs	Gls
Blackburn Rov.	Hyde U.	01.37	36	2	-	1
Barrow	Tr	06.46	46-50	177	-	3

FORBES Graeme Scott Alexander
Forfar, 29 July, 1958 (CD)

League Club	Source	Date Signed	Seasons Played	Apps	Subs	Gls
Walsall	Motherwell	09.86	86-89	173	0	9

FORBES Richard John
Ashford (Kt), 12 March, 1955 (M)

League Club	Source	Date Signed	Seasons Played	Apps	Subs	Gls
Exeter C.	Woking	07.79	77-80	55	4	5
Plymouth Arg.	Bideford	08.83	83	3	0	0

FORBES Steven Dudley
Stoke Newington, 24 December, 1975 (M)

League Club	Source	Date Signed	Seasons Played	Apps	Subs	Gls
Millwall	Sittingbourne	07.94	94-95	0	5	0
Colchester U.	Tr	03.97	96-97	26	10	2

FORBES William
Glasgow, 25 May, 1922 (WH)

League Club	Source	Date Signed	Seasons Played	Apps	Subs	Gls
Wolverhampton W.	Dunfermline Ath.	09.46	46-49	71	-	23
Preston N.E.	Tr	12.49	49-55	192	-	7
Carlisle U.	Tr	07.56	56-57	26	-	0

FORD Alan Lenane
Ferndale, 28 October, 1925 Died 1963 (G)

League Club	Source	Date Signed	Seasons Played	Apps	Subs	Gls
Workington (Am)		07.51	51-53	39	-	0

FORD Andrew Carl
Minehead, 4 May, 1954 (FB)

League Club	Source	Date Signed	Seasons Played	Apps	Subs	Gls
Bournemouth	Minehead	07.72				
Southend U.	Tr	05.73	73-76	135	3	3
Swindon T.	Tr	08.77	77-79	92	6	0
Gillingham	Tr	07.80	80-81	62	0	3

FORD Anthony Michael
Bristol, 26 November, 1944 E Yth (FB)

League Club	Source	Date Signed	Seasons Played	Apps	Subs	Gls
Bristol C.	App	11.61	61-69	170	1	10
Bristol Rov.	Tr	12.69	69-70	28	0	1

FORD Clive
Oldbury, 10 April, 1945 (F)

League Club	Source	Date Signed	Seasons Played	Apps	Subs	Gls
Wolverhampton W.	App	10.62	64	2	-	0

League Club	Source	Date Signed	Seasons Played	Apps	Subs	Gls
Walsall	Tr	12.64	64-66	11	3	0
Lincoln C.	Tr	02.67	66-67	48	1	16

FORD Colin
Lewisham, 18 September, 1960 (FB)

League Club	Source	Date Signed	Seasons Played	Apps	Subs	Gls
Gillingham	App	09.78	79	1	0	0

FORD David
Sheffield, 2 March, 1945 Eu23-2 (IF)

League Club	Source	Date Signed	Seasons Played	Apps	Subs	Gls
Sheffield Wed.	App	01.63	65-69	117	5	31
Newcastle U.	Tr	12.69	69-70	24	2	3
Sheffield U.	Tr	01.71	70-72	21	6	2
Halifax T.	Tr	08.73	73-75	83	2	6

FORD Francis Martin
Bridgend, 3 February, 1967 (D)

League Club	Source	Date Signed	Seasons Played	Apps	Subs	Gls
Cardiff C.	YT	03.85	84	1	1	0

FORD Frederick George Luther
Dartford, 10 December, 1916 Died 1981 (RH)

League Club	Source	Date Signed	Seasons Played	Apps	Subs	Gls
Charlton Ath.	Erith & Belvedere	03.36	36-37	22	-	0
Millwall	Tr	11.45	46	9	-	0
Carlisle U.	Tr	07.47	47	28	-	0

FORD Gary
York, 8 February, 1961 (RW)

League Club	Source	Date Signed	Seasons Played	Apps	Subs	Gls
York C.	App	02.79	78-86	359	7	53
Leicester C.	Tr	06.87	87	15	1	2
Port Vale	Tr	12.87	87-90	66	9	12
Walsall	L	03.90	89	13	0	2
Mansfield T.	Tr	03.91	90-92	88	0	7
Hartlepool U. (N/C)	Harstad (Nor)	09.95	95	2	1	0

FORD Jonathan Steven
Birmingham, 12 April, 1968 (FB)

League Club	Source	Date Signed	Seasons Played	Apps	Subs	Gls
Swansea C.	Cradley T.	08.91	91-94	145	15	7
Bradford C.	Tr	07.95	95	18	1	0
Gillingham	Tr	08.96	96	2	2	0
Barnet	Tr	02.97	96-97	32	0	1

FORD Kenneth
Sheffield, 1 December, 1940 (OR)

League Club	Source	Date Signed	Seasons Played	Apps	Subs	Gls
Sheffield Wed.	Jnrs	03.60				
Oldham Ath.	Tr	06.61	61	5	-	1

FORD Mark
Pontefract, 10 October, 1975 E Yth/Eu21-2 (M)

League Club	Source	Date Signed	Seasons Played	Apps	Subs	Gls
Leeds U.	YT	03.93	93-96	27	2	1
Burnley	Tr	07.97	97	32	4	1

FORD Michael Paul
Bristol, 9 February, 1966 (D)

League Club	Source	Date Signed	Seasons Played	Apps	Subs	Gls
Leicester C.	App	02.84				
Cardiff C.	Devizes T.	09.84	84-87	144	1	13
Oxford U.	Tr	06.88	88-97	273	16	18

FORD Peter Leslie
Stoke, 10 August, 1933 (HB)

League Club	Source	Date Signed	Seasons Played	Apps	Subs	Gls
Stoke C.	West Bromwich A. (Am)	05.53	56-58	14	-	0
Port Vale	Tr	09.59	59-62	104	-	5

FORD Robert John
Bristol, 22 September, 1974 (M)

League Club	Source	Date Signed	Seasons Played	Apps	Subs	Gls
Oxford U.	YT	10.92	93-97	104	12	7
Sheffield U.	Tr	11.97	97	20	3	1

FORD Robert Milloy
Rutherglen, 13 August, 1934 (IF)

League Club	Source	Date Signed	Seasons Played	Apps	Subs	Gls
Aldershot	Vale of Clyde	07.57	57	2	-	0

FORD Stephen Derek
Shoreham, 17 February, 1959 (F)

League Club	Source	Date Signed	Seasons Played	Apps	Subs	Gls
Stoke C.	Lewes	07.81	81	1	1	0

FORD Stuart Trevor
Sheffield, 20 July, 1971 (G)

League Club	Source	Date Signed	Seasons Played	Apps	Subs	Gls
Rotherham U.	YT	07.89	89-91	5	0	0
Scarborough	L	03.92	91	6	0	0
Scarborough	Tr	08.92	92	22	0	0
Doncaster Rov.	Tr	08.93	93	4	2	0
Scarborough	Tr	07.94	94	6	0	0

FORD Tony
Grimsby, 14 May, 1959 E'B' (W)

League Club	Source	Date Signed	Seasons Played	Apps	Subs	Gls
Grimsby T.	App	05.77	75-85	321	34	55
Sunderland	L	03.86	85	8	1	1
Stoke C.	Tr	07.86	86-88	112	0	13
West Bromwich A.	Tr	03.89	88-91	114	0	15
Grimsby T.	Tr	11.91	91-93	59	9	3

League Club	Source	Date Signed	Seasons Played	Apps	Subs	Gls
Bradford C.	L	09.93	93	5	0	0
Scunthorpe U.	Tr	08.94	94-95	73	3	9
Mansfield T.	Barrow	10.96	96-97	58	3	5

FORD Trevor
Swansea, 1 October, 1923 W-38 (CF)

League Club	Source	Date Signed	Seasons Played	Apps	Subs	Gls
Swansea C.	Jnrs	05.42	46	16	-	9
Aston Villa	Tr	01.47	46-50	120	-	60
Sunderland	Tr	10.50	50-53	108	-	67
Cardiff C.	Tr	12.53	53-56	96	-	39
Newport Co.	P.S.V. Eindhoven (Neth)	07.60	60	8	-	3

FORDE Clevere
London, 14 November, 1958 (W)

League Club	Source	Date Signed	Seasons Played	Apps	Subs	Gls
Plymouth Arg.	Hounslow	12.78	78	4	1	0

FORDE Stephen
South Kirkby, 29 August, 1914 Died 1992 (FB)

League Club	Source	Date Signed	Seasons Played	Apps	Subs	Gls
Sheffield Wed.	South Elmsall	01.33				
Rotherham U.	Tr	04.33	32-36	116	-	1
West Ham U.	Tr	01.37	37-51	170	-	1

FOREMAN Darren
Southampton, 12 February, 1968 E Sch (F)

League Club	Source	Date Signed	Seasons Played	Apps	Subs	Gls
Barnsley	Fareham T.	08.86	86-89	33	14	8
Crewe Alex.	Tr	03.90	89-90	19	4	4
Scarborough	Tr	03.91	90-94	77	20	35

FOREMAN Dennis Joseph
South Africa, 1 February, 1933 (OL)

League Club	Source	Date Signed	Seasons Played	Apps	Subs	Gls
Brighton & H.A.	Hibernians (SA)	03.52	52-60	211	-	63

FOREMAN Alexander George
Walthamstow, 1 March, 1914 Died 1969 E Amat (CF)

League Club	Source	Date Signed	Seasons Played	Apps	Subs	Gls
West Ham U.	Walthamstow Ave.	03.38	38	6	-	1
Tottenham H.	Tr	02.46	46	36	-	14

FOREMAN Matthew
Gateshead, 15 February, 1975 (M)

League Club	Source	Date Signed	Seasons Played	Apps	Subs	Gls
Sheffield U.	YT	07.93				
Scarborough (N/C)	Tr	03.96	95	1	3	0

FOREMAN William Ernest
Havant, 3 February, 1958 (M)

League Club	Source	Date Signed	Seasons Played	Apps	Subs	Gls
Bristol Rov.	Bournemouth (App)	05.76	76-77	0	2	0

FORGAN Thomas Carr
Middlesbrough, 12 October, 1929 (G)

League Club	Source	Date Signed	Seasons Played	Apps	Subs	Gls
Hull C.	Sutton Est.	05.49	53	10	-	0
York C.	Tr	06.54	54-65	388	0	0

FORINTON Howard Lee
Boston, 18 September, 1975 (CF)

League Club	Source	Date Signed	Seasons Played	Apps	Subs	Gls
Birmingham C.	Yeovil	07.97	97	0	1	0

FORMAN Matthew Charles
Evesham, 8 September, 1967 (M)

League Club	Source	Date Signed	Seasons Played	Apps	Subs	Gls
Aston Villa	App	09.85				
Wolverhampton W.	Tr	08.86	86	24	1	4

FORMBY Kevin
Ormskirk, 22 July, 1971 (LB)

League Club	Source	Date Signed	Seasons Played	Apps	Subs	Gls
Rochdale	Burscough	03.94	93-96	59	8	1

FORREST Craig Lorne
Canada, 20 September, 1967 Canadian Int (G)

League Club	Source	Date Signed	Seasons Played	Apps	Subs	Gls
Ipswich T.	App	08.85	88-96	263	0	0
Colchester U.	L	03.88	87	11	0	0
Chelsea	L	03.97	96	2	1	0
West Ham U.	Tr	07.97	97	13	0	0

FORREST Ernest
Sunderland, 19 February, 1919 Died 1987 (WH)

League Club	Source	Date Signed	Seasons Played	Apps	Subs	Gls
Bolton W.	Usworth Colly	01.38	38-47	69	-	1
Grimsby T.	Tr	05.48	48	33	-	1
Millwall	Tr	06.49	49	37	-	4

FORREST Gerald
Stockton, 21 January, 1957 (RB)

League Club	Source	Date Signed	Seasons Played	Apps	Subs	Gls
Rotherham U.	South Bank	02.77	77-85	357	0	8
Southampton	Tr	12.85	85-89	112	3	0
Rotherham U.	Tr	08.90	90	32	2	0

FORREST James
Glasgow, 22 September, 1944 S Sch/Su23-2/S-5 (CF)

League Club	Source	Date Signed	Seasons Played	Apps	Subs	Gls
Preston N.E.	Glasgow Rangers	03.67	66-67	24	2	3

FORREST James
Dalkeith, 14 November, 1929 Died 1994 (F)

League Club	Source	Date Signed	Seasons Played	Apps	Subs	Gls
Leeds U.	Musselburgh	12.50				
Accrington St.	Tr	11.51	51	5	-	2

FORREST John Anthony
Tottington, 9 October, 1947 (G)

League Club	Source	Date Signed	Seasons Played	Apps	Subs	Gls
Bury	Jnrs	03.66	67-80	430	0	0

FORREST Keith
Hartlepool, 18 February, 1951 (IF)

League Club	Source	Date Signed	Seasons Played	Apps	Subs	Gls
Hartlepool U. (Am)	St James	07.69	69-70	4	2	0

FORREST John **Robert**
Rossington, 13 May, 1931 (IF)

League Club	Source	Date Signed	Seasons Played	Apps	Subs	Gls
Leeds U.	Retford T.	12.52	52-58	119	-	36
Notts Co.	Tr	02.59	58-61	117	-	37

FORREST William
Carriden, 19 January, 1945 (WH)

League Club	Source	Date Signed	Seasons Played	Apps	Subs	Gls
Carlisle U.	Hearts	07.62	62-63	10	-	0
Brighton & H. A.	Tr	07.64				

FORRESTER Anthony Charles
Parkstone, 14 January, 1940 (OR)

League Club	Source	Date Signed	Seasons Played	Apps	Subs	Gls
West Bromwich A.	Jnrs	03.57	58	6	-	3
Southend U.	Tr	04.59	59	10	-	1

FORRESTER George Hogg
Edinburgh, 28 August, 1934 (FB)

League Club	Source	Date Signed	Seasons Played	Apps	Subs	Gls
Sunderland	Raith Rov.	03.53				
Accrington St.	Eyemouth U.	02.60	59-60	54	-	0

FORRESTER George Larmouth
Cannock, 8 June, 1927 Died 1981 (WH)

League Club	Source	Date Signed	Seasons Played	Apps	Subs	Gls
Gillingham		08.47	50-54	100	-	3
Reading	Tr	07.55	55	6	-	2

FORRESTER Jamie Mark
Bradford, 1 November, 1974 E Sch/E Yth (M)

League Club	Source	Date Signed	Seasons Played	Apps	Subs	Gls
Leeds U.	Auxerre (Fr)	10.92	92-93	7	2	0
Southend U.	L	09.94	94	3	2	0
Grimsby T.	L	03.95	94	7	2	1
Grimsby T.	Tr	10.95	95-96	27	14	6
Scunthorpe U.	Tr	03.97	96-97	53	2	17

FORRESTER Paul
Edinburgh, 3 November, 1972 (F)

League Club	Source	Date Signed	Seasons Played	Apps	Subs	Gls
Middlesbrough	Musselburgh Windsor	03.93	93	0	1	0

FORSTER Derek
Newcastle, 19 February, 1949 E Sch (G)

League Club	Source	Date Signed	Seasons Played	Apps	Subs	Gls
Sunderland	App	02.66	64-71	18	0	0
Charlton Ath.	Tr	07.73	73	9	0	0
Brighton & H. A.	Tr	07.74	74	3	0	0

FORSTER Geoffrey Patrick
Middlesbrough, 3 August, 1954 (F)

League Club	Source	Date Signed	Seasons Played	Apps	Subs	Gls
Rochdale (N/C)	Winnybanks	11.78	78	0	1	0
Hartlepool U.	Whitby T.	05.80	80	10	4	4

FORSTER Leslie James
Newcastle, 22 July, 1915 Died 1986 (OR)

League Club	Source	Date Signed	Seasons Played	Apps	Subs	Gls
Blackpool	Walker Celtic	04.37	38	2	-	0
York C.	Tr	09.46	46	10	-	2
Gateshead	Tr	02.47	46-47	15	-	3

FORSTER Mark Erwin
Middlesbrough, 1 November, 1964 (F)

League Club	Source	Date Signed	Seasons Played	Apps	Subs	Gls
Leicester C.	Guisborough T.	06.83				
Darlington	Tr	03.84	83-85	31	7	13

FORSTER Martyn Gerald
Kettering, 1 February, 1963 E Sch (FB)

League Club	Source	Date Signed	Seasons Played	Apps	Subs	Gls
Northampton T.	Kettering T.	10.83	83	41	1	0

FORSTER Nicholas Michael
Caterham, 8 September, 1973 Eu21-4 (F)

League Club	Source	Date Signed	Seasons Played	Apps	Subs	Gls
Gillingham	Horley T.	05.92	92-93	54	13	24
Brentford	Tr	06.94	94-96	108	1	39
Birmingham C.	Tr	01.97	96-97	16	19	6

FORSTER Ronald
Stockton, 19 August, 1935 (OR)

League Club	Source	Date Signed	Seasons Played	Apps	Subs	Gls
Darlington	Shotton Colly	05.56	56-59	57	-	4

FORSTER Stanley Gerard
Sandwich, 1 November, 1943 (OL)

League Club	Source	Date Signed	Seasons Played	Apps	Subs	Gls
Crystal Palace	Margate	11.61	62	2	-	1

FORSYTH Alexander
Swinton (Merse), 5 February, 1952 Su23-1/SF Lge/S-10 (LB)

League Club	Source	Date Signed	Seasons Played	Apps	Subs	Gls
Manchester U.	Partick Thistle	12.72	72-77	99	2	4

FORSYTH Alexander Simpson Hutchinson
Falkirk, 29 September, 1928 (OL)

League Club	Source	Date Signed	Seasons Played	Apps	Subs	Gls
Darlington	Falkirk	08.52	52	26	-	7

FORSYTH Robert **Campbell**
Plean, 5 May, 1934 SF Lge/S-4 (G)

League Club	Source	Date Signed	Seasons Played	Apps	Subs	Gls
Southampton	Kilmarnock	12.65	65-67	48	0	0

FORSYTH David
Falkirk, 5 May, 1945 (FB)

League Club	Source	Date Signed	Seasons Played	Apps	Subs	Gls
Leyton Orient	Kirkintilloch Rob Roy	05.64	65-66	32	-	0

FORSYTH John Thomson
Dalmuir, 20 December, 1918 (OL)

League Club	Source	Date Signed	Seasons Played	Apps	Subs	Gls
Luton T.	Dumbarton	08.42				
New Brighton	Tr	07.46	46-47	64	-	4
Chester C.	Tr	07.48	48	32	-	1

FORSYTH Michael Eric
Liverpool, 20 March, 1966 E Yth/Eu21-1/E'B' (LB)

League Club	Source	Date Signed	Seasons Played	Apps	Subs	Gls
West Bromwich A.	App	11.83	83-85	28	1	0
Derby Co.	Tr	03.86	86-94	323	2	8
Notts Co.	Tr	02.95	94	7	0	0
Hereford U.	L	09.96	96	12	0	0
Wycombe W.	Tr	12.96	96-97	47	1	2

FORSYTH Richard Michael
Dudley, 3 October, 1970 E Semi Pro (M)

League Club	Source	Date Signed	Seasons Played	Apps	Subs	Gls
Birmingham C.	Kidderminster Hrs.	07.95	95	12	14	2
Stoke C.	Tr	07.96	96-97	77	0	15

FORSYTH William Alan
Auchterderran, 29 March, 1932 (FB)

League Club	Source	Date Signed	Seasons Played	Apps	Subs	Gls
Blackburn Rov.	Bowhill Rov.	08.49				
Southport	Tr	07.52	52-56	55	-	5

FORSYTHE Robert Haddon
Belfast, 27 February, 1925 (OR)

League Club	Source	Date Signed	Seasons Played	Apps	Subs	Gls
Bradford C.	Ballymoney	07.48	48	1	-	0

FORT Samuel Marsh
Doncaster, 27 April, 1929 (FB)

League Club	Source	Date Signed	Seasons Played	Apps	Subs	Gls
Walsall	Retford T.	02.54	53-54	28	-	0

FORTUNE-WEST Leo Paul Osborne
Stratford, 9 April, 1971 (F)

League Club	Source	Date Signed	Seasons Played	Apps	Subs	Gls
Gillingham	Stevenage Borough	07.95	95-97	48	19	18
Leyton Orient	L	03.97	96	1	4	0

FOSS Sidney Lacy Richard
Barking, 28 November, 1912 Died 1995 (LH)

League Club	Source	Date Signed	Seasons Played	Apps	Subs	Gls
Chelsea	Southall	05.36	36-47	41	-	3

FOSTER Adrian Michael
Kidderminster, 19 March, 1971 (F)

League Club	Source	Date Signed	Seasons Played	Apps	Subs	Gls
West Bromwich A.	YT	07.89	89-91	13	14	2
Torquay U.	Tr	07.92	92-93	55	20	24
Gillingham	Tr	08.94	94-95	28	12	9
Exeter C.	L	03.96	95	4	3	0
Hereford U.	Tr	08.96	96	42	1	16

FOSTER Alan
South Shields, 20 November, 1934 (CF)

League Club	Source	Date Signed	Seasons Played	Apps	Subs	Gls
Crewe Alex.	Northwich Vic.	08.59	59-60	19	-	7

FOSTER Anthony Joseph
Dublin, 13 February, 1949 (IF)

League Club	Source	Date Signed	Seasons Played	Apps	Subs	Gls
Arsenal	Jnrs	02.66				
Oldham Ath.	Tr	09.66	66-67	8	1	0

FOSTER Barry
Worksop, 21 September, 1951 E Yth (FB)

League Club	Source	Date Signed	Seasons Played	Apps	Subs	Gls
Mansfield T.	Jnrs	07.70	71-81	282	5	0

FOSTER George **Clifford**
Wigan, 14 January, 1931 (IF)

League Club	Source	Date Signed	Seasons Played	Apps	Subs	Gls
Southport (Am)	Burscough	08.51	51-52	10	-	2

FOSTER Colin
Bulwell (Nts), 26 December, 1952 (CD)

League Club	Source	Date Signed	Seasons Played	Apps	Subs	Gls
Mansfield T.	App	12.70	71-78	195	10	17
Peterborough U.	Tr	06.79	79-80	71	0	5

FOSTER Colin John
Chislehurst, 16 July, 1964 (CD)

League Club	Source	Date Signed	Seasons Played	Apps	Subs	Gls
Leyton Orient	App	02.82	81-86	173	1	10
Nottingham F.	Tr	02.87	86-89	68	4	5
West Ham U.	Tr	09.89	89-93	88	5	5

League Club	Source	Date Signed	Seasons Played	Apps	Subs	Gls
Notts Co.	L	01.94	93	9	0	0
Watford	Tr	03.94	93-95	66	0	7
Cambridge U.	Tr	03.97	96-97	33	0	1

FOSTER Craig Andrew
Australia, 15 April, 1969 Australian Int (M)

League Club	Source	Date Signed	Seasons Played	Apps	Subs	Gls
Portsmouth	Marconi (Aus)	09.97	97	13	3	2

FOSTER Deane
Reading, 22 August, 1966 (D)

League Club	Source	Date Signed	Seasons Played	Apps	Subs	Gls
Reading	YT	03.85	84	0	2	0

FOSTER Emanuel (Manny)
Newcastle-u-Lyme, 4 December, 1921 (G)

League Club	Source	Date Signed	Seasons Played	Apps	Subs	Gls
Stoke C.	Mow Cop	12.43	46	1	-	0

FOSTER George Walter
Plymouth, 26 September, 1956 (CD)

League Club	Source	Date Signed	Seasons Played	Apps	Subs	Gls
Plymouth Arg.	App	09.74	73-81	201	11	6
Torquay U.	L	10.76	76	6	0	3
Exeter C.	L	12.81	81	28	0	0
Derby Co.	Tr	06.82	82	30	0	0
Mansfield T.	Tr	08.83	83-92	373	0	0

FOSTER Ian James
Liverpool, 11 November, 1976 E Sch (M)

League Club	Source	Date Signed	Seasons Played	Apps	Subs	Gls
Hereford U.	Liverpool (NC)	07.96	96	4	15	0

FOSTER John Colin
Manchester, 19 September, 1973 E Sch (RB)

League Club	Source	Date Signed	Seasons Played	Apps	Subs	Gls
Manchester C.	YT	07.92	93-96	17	2	0
Carlisle U.	Tr	03.98	97	7	0	0

FOSTER Karl Adolphus
Birmingham, 15 September, 1965 (F)

League Club	Source	Date Signed	Seasons Played	Apps	Subs	Gls
Shrewsbury T.	App	09.83	82	1	1	0

FOSTER Lee
Bishop Auckland, 21 October, 1977 (RM)

League Club	Source	Date Signed	Seasons Played	Apps	Subs	Gls
Hartlepool U.	YT	●	95	0	1	0

FOSTER Martin
Sheffield, 29 October, 1977 (M)

League Club	Source	Date Signed	Seasons Played	Apps	Subs	Gls
Leeds U.	YT	06.96				
Blackpool	L	12.97	97	1	0	0

FOSTER Michael Sidney
Leicester, 3 February, 1939 (W)

League Club	Source	Date Signed	Seasons Played	Apps	Subs	Gls
Leicester C.		08.59				
Colchester U.	Tr	05.61	61	36	-	8
Norwich C.	Tr	09.62				
Millwall	Tr	07.63	63	13	-	2

FOSTER Nigel
Sutton-in-Ashfield, 23 March, 1968 (D)

League Club	Source	Date Signed	Seasons Played	Apps	Subs	Gls
Mansfield T.	YT	08.85	84	1	0	0

FOSTER Robert John
Sheffield, 19 July, 1929 E 'B' (IF)

League Club	Source	Date Signed	Seasons Played	Apps	Subs	Gls
Chesterfield	Jnrs	09.47	48-50	4	-	0
Preston N. E.	Tr	07.51	51-56	99	-	40
Rotherham U.	Tr	05.58	58	1	-	0

FOSTER Ronald Edmund
Islington, 22 November, 1938 (IF)

League Club	Source	Date Signed	Seasons Played	Apps	Subs	Gls
Leyton Orient	Clapton	03.57	59-62	72	-	17
Grimsby T.	Tr	12.62	62-65	129	0	24
Reading	Tr	07.66	66-67	44	1	5
Brentford	Dallas (USA)	03.69	68	3	1	0

FOSTER Stephen
Mansfield, 3 December, 1974 (CD)

League Club	Source	Date Signed	Seasons Played	Apps	Subs	Gls
Mansfield T. (N/C)	YT	07.93	93	2	3	0
Bristol Rov.	Woking	05.97	97	32	2	0

FOSTER Stephen Brian
Portsmouth, 24 September, 1957 Eu21-1/E-3 (CD)

League Club	Source	Date Signed	Seasons Played	Apps	Subs	Gls
Portsmouth	App	09.75	75-78	101	8	6
Brighton & H. A.	Tr	07.79	79-83	171	1	6
Aston Villa	Tr	03.84	83-84	15	0	3
Luton T.	Tr	11.84	84-88	163	0	11
Oxford U.	Tr	07.89	89-91	95	0	9
Brighton & H.A.	Tr	08.92	92-95	115	0	7

FOSTER Trevor
Walsall, 11 January, 1941 (F)

League Club	Source	Date Signed	Seasons Played	Apps	Subs	Gls
Walsall	Jnrs	07.59	59-64	63	-	13

FOSTER Wayne Paul
Leigh, 11 September, 1963 E Yth (M)

League Club	Source	Date Signed	Seasons Played	Apps	Subs	Gls
Bolton W.	App	08.81	81-84	92	13	13
Preston N. E.	Tr	06.85	85	25	6	3
Hartlepool U. (L)	Hearts	10.94	94	4	0	1

FOSTER Winston Arthur
Birmingham, 1 November, 1941 (CH)

League Club	Source	Date Signed	Seasons Played	Apps	Subs	Gls
Birmingham C.	Jnrs	11.58	60-68	151	1	2
Crewe Alex.	L	03.69	68	13	0	0
Plymouth Arg.	Tr	06.69	69-70	33	0	0

FOTHERGILL Ashley Grove
Harrogate, 3 October, 1969 (M)

League Club	Source	Date Signed	Seasons Played	Apps	Subs	Gls
Rochdale	Middlesbrough (YT)	10.88	88	8	1	0

FOTHERINGHAM James Gibb
Hamilton, 19 December, 1933 Died 1977 (CH)

League Club	Source	Date Signed	Seasons Played	Apps	Subs	Gls
Arsenal	Jnrs	03.51	54-58	72	-	0
Northampton T.	Hearts	08.59	59	11	-	0

FOTIADIS Andrew
Hitchin, 6 September, 1977 E Sch (F)

League Club	Source	Date Signed	Seasons Played	Apps	Subs	Gls
Luton T.	Jnrs	07.96	96-97	14	18	4

FOULDS Albert
Salford, 8 August, 1919 (IF)

League Club	Source	Date Signed	Seasons Played	Apps	Subs	Gls
Chester C.	Altrincham	08.48	48	31	-	14
Rochdale	Yeovil T.	09.50	50-52	61	-	24
Crystal Palace	Tr	07.53	53	17	-	4
Crewe Alex.	Tr	01.54	53	14	-	2

FOULKES Reginald Ernest
Shrewsbury, 23 February, 1923 E Sch (CH)

League Club	Source	Date Signed	Seasons Played	Apps	Subs	Gls
Walsall	Birmingham C. (Am)	08.45	46-49	160	-	6
Norwich C.	Tr	05.50	50-55	216	-	8

FOULKES William Anthony
St Helens, 5 January, 1932 Eu23-2/EF Lge/E-1 (D)

League Club	Source	Date Signed	Seasons Played	Apps	Subs	Gls
Manchester U.	Whiston B.C.	08.51	52-69	563	3	7

FOULKES William Isaiah
Merthyr Tydfil, 29 May, 1926 Died 1979 W-11 (OR)

League Club	Source	Date Signed	Seasons Played	Apps	Subs	Gls
Cardiff C.		02.45				
Chester C.	Winsford U.	05.48	48-51	118	-	14
Newcastle U.	Tr	10.51	51-53	58	-	8
Southampton	Tr	08.54	54	23	-	1
Chester C.	Tr	07.56	56-60	178	-	23

FOUNTAIN John (Jack)
Leeds, 27 May, 1932 (WH)

League Club	Source	Date Signed	Seasons Played	Apps	Subs	Gls
Sheffield U.	Ashley Road	11.49	50-55	31	-	0
Swindon T.	Tr	01.57	56-59	81	-	2
York C.	Tr	08.60	60-63	130	-	3

FOWLER Derek William
Torquay, 28 November, 1961 (D/M)

League Club	Source	Date Signed	Seasons Played	Apps	Subs	Gls
Torquay U.	S.T.C. Paignton	03.84	83-85	65	8	4

FOWLER Jason Kenneth
Bristol, 20 August, 1974 (M)

League Club	Source	Date Signed	Seasons Played	Apps	Subs	Gls
Bristol C.	YT	07.93	92-95	16	9	0
Cardiff C.	Tr	06.96	96-97	75	0	10

FOWLER John
Edinburgh, 17 October, 1933 (LB)

League Club	Source	Date Signed	Seasons Played	Apps	Subs	Gls
Colchester U.	Bonnyrigg Rose	06.55	55-67	415	0	5

FOWLER John Anthony
Preston, 27 October, 1974 (M)

League Club	Source	Date Signed	Seasons Played	Apps	Subs	Gls
Cambridge U.	YT	04.92	92-95	30	11	0
Preston N.E.	L	02.93	92	5	1	0

FOWLER John (Jack) Barry
Sheffield, 13 April, 1935 (F)

League Club	Source	Date Signed	Seasons Played	Apps	Subs	Gls
Sheffield U.		07.54				
Halifax T.	Tr	06.56	56-58	19	-	3

FOWLER Lee Edward
Eastwood, 26 January, 1970 (LB/M)

League Club	Source	Date Signed	Seasons Played	Apps	Subs	Gls
Stoke C.	YT	07.88	87-91	42	7	0
Preston N.E.	Tr	07.92	92	29	3	2
Doncaster Rov.	Tr	12.93	93	7	4	0

FOWLER Martin
York, 17 January, 1957 (M)

League Club	Source	Date Signed	Seasons Played	Apps	Subs	Gls
Huddersfield T.	App	01.74	73-77	62	11	2
Blackburn Rov.	Tr	07.78	78-79	36	2	0
Hartlepool U.	L	03.80	79	6	0	0

League Club	Source	Date Signed	Seasons Played	Apps	Subs	Gls
Stockport Co.	Tr	08.80	80-81	74	1	6
Scunthorpe U.	Tr	09.82	82	15	3	0

FOWLER Henry **Norman**
Stockton, 3 September, 1919 Died 1990 E Sch (FB)

League Club	Source	Date Signed	Seasons Played	Apps	Subs	Gls
Middlesbrough	South Bank	09.36	37-38	7	-	0
Hull C.	Tr	09.46	46-49	52	-	0
Gateshead	Tr	11.49	49-51	64	-	0

FOWLER Robert (Robbie) Bernard
Liverpool, 9 April, 1975 E Yth/Eu21-8/E 'B'/E-7 (F)

League Club	Source	Date Signed	Seasons Played	Apps	Subs	Gls
Liverpool	YT	04.92	93-97	156	4	92

FOWLER Thomas
Prescot, 16 December, 1924 (OL)

League Club	Source	Date Signed	Seasons Played	Apps	Subs	Gls
Northampton T.	Everton (Am)	03.45	46-61	521	-	84
Aldershot	Tr	12.61	61-62	14	-	0

FOWLER Tony
Birmingham, 3 October, 1962 (G)

League Club	Source	Date Signed	Seasons Played	Apps	Subs	Gls
Torquay U.	Foxhole U.	03.85	84-85	9	0	0

FOX Alan
Holywell, 10 July, 1936 Wu23-1 (CH)

League Club	Source	Date Signed	Seasons Played	Apps	Subs	Gls
Wrexham	Jnrs	04.54	53-63	350	-	3
Hartlepool U.	Tr	06.64	64-65	58	0	0
Bradford C.	Tr	10.65	65	33	0	0

FOX Geoffrey Roy
Bristol, 19 January, 1925 Died 1994 (FB)

League Club	Source	Date Signed	Seasons Played	Apps	Subs	Gls
Ipswich T.	M.C.W.	08.45	46	11	-	1
Bristol Rov.	Tr	06.47	47-54	276	-	2
Swindon T.	Tr	10.55	55-56	48	-	0

FOX Kevin
Sheffield, 22 September, 1960 (G)

League Club	Source	Date Signed	Seasons Played	Apps	Subs	Gls
Lincoln C.	Jnrs	03.78	79	4	0	0

FOX Mark Stephen
Basingstoke, 17 November, 1975 (W)

League Club	Source	Date Signed	Seasons Played	Apps	Subs	Gls
Brighton & H.A.	YT	07.94	93-96	8	17	1

FOX Matthew Christopher
Birmingham, 13 July, 1971 (CD)

League Club	Source	Date Signed	Seasons Played	Apps	Subs	Gls
Birmingham C.	YT	07.89	88-90	12	2	0
Northampton T. (N/C)		03.93	92	0	1	0

FOX Oscar
Clowne, 1 January, 1921 Died 1990 (IF/WH)

League Club	Source	Date Signed	Seasons Played	Apps	Subs	Gls
Sheffield Wed.		10.43	46-49	44	-	3
Mansfield T.	Tr	06.50	50-56	248	-	30

FOX Peter David
Scunthorpe, 5 July, 1957 (G)

League Club	Source	Date Signed	Seasons Played	Apps	Subs	Gls
Sheffield Wed.	App	06.75	72-76	49	0	0
Barnsley	L	12.77	77	1	0	0
Stoke C.	Tr	03.78	78-92	409	0	0
Exeter C.	Tr	07.93	93-96	107	1	0

FOX Raymond
Manchester, 13 December, 1934 (OL)

League Club	Source	Date Signed	Seasons Played	Apps	Subs	Gls
Oldham Ath. (Am)		08.57	57	1	-	0

FOX Raymond Victor
Bristol, 28 January, 1921 (FB)

League Club	Source	Date Signed	Seasons Played	Apps	Subs	Gls
Bristol C.	St Aldheims	10.46	46-48	23	-	0

FOX Reginald Allan
Edmonton, 16 October, 1929 (FB)

League Club	Source	Date Signed	Seasons Played	Apps	Subs	Gls
Fulham	Tufnell Park	12.49				
Brighton & H. A.	Tr	10.52	52-55	20	-	0

FOX Ruel Adrian
Ipswich, 14 January, 1968 E 'B' (W)

League Club	Source	Date Signed	Seasons Played	Apps	Subs	Gls
Norwich C.	App	01.86	86-93	148	24	22
Newcastle U.	Tr	02.94	93-95	56	2	12
Tottenham H.	Tr	10.95	95-97	77	6	10

FOX Simon Michael
Basingstoke, 28 August, 1977 (F)

League Club	Source	Date Signed	Seasons Played	Apps	Subs	Gls
Brighton & H.A.	YT	05.95	93-96	6	15	0

FOX Stephen Douglas
Tamworth, 17 February, 1958 (W)

League Club	Source	Date Signed	Seasons Played	Apps	Subs	Gls
Birmingham C.	App	02.76	76-78	26	3	1
Wrexham	Tr	12.78	78-82	136	6	10
Port Vale	Tr	10.82	82-83	71	3	6
Chester C.	Tr	07.84	84-85	29	4	4

FOX Walter
Bolsover, 10 April, 1921 (FB)

League Club	Source	Date Signed	Seasons Played	Apps	Subs	Gls
Mansfield T.	Creswell Colly	05.46	46-49	62	-	0

FOXON David **Neil**
Nottingham, 10 July, 1948 (W)

League Club	Source	Date Signed	Seasons Played	Apps	Subs	Gls
Scunthorpe U.	Notts Co. (Am)	08.65	66-67	20	2	1

FOXTON David **Graham**
Harrogate, 2 October, 1949 (FB)

League Club	Source	Date Signed	Seasons Played	Apps	Subs	Gls
Scunthorpe U.	App	10.67	67-72	148	6	1

FOXTON John (Jack) Dixon
Salford, 17 June, 1921 (LH)

League Club	Source	Date Signed	Seasons Played	Apps	Subs	Gls
Portsmouth	Bolton W. (Am)	05.45	46	1	-	0
Swindon T.	Tr	09.48	48-50	49	-	0

FOY David Lee
Coventry, 20 October, 1972 (M)

League Club	Source	Date Signed	Seasons Played	Apps	Subs	Gls
Birmingham C.	YT	07.91	92	3	0	0
Scunthorpe U.	L	03.93	92	1	2	0

FOY John Joseph
Liverpool, 28 April, 1950 (OL)

League Club	Source	Date Signed	Seasons Played	Apps	Subs	Gls
Southport (Am)	Ormskirk	08.74	74	1	0	0

FOYLE Martin John
Salisbury, 2 May, 1963 (F)

League Club	Source	Date Signed	Seasons Played	Apps	Subs	Gls
Southampton	App	08.80	82-83	6	6	1
Aldershot	Tr	07.84	84-86	98	0	35
Oxford U.	Tr	03.87	86-90	120	6	36
Port Vale	Tr	06.91	91-97	181	58	67

FRAIL Stephen
Glasgow, 10 August, 1969 (D)

League Club	Source	Date Signed	Seasons Played	Apps	Subs	Gls
Tranmere Rov.	Hearts	01.98	97	4	2	0

FRAIN David
Sheffield, 11 October, 1962 (M)

League Club	Source	Date Signed	Seasons Played	Apps	Subs	Gls
Sheffield U.	Dronfield U.	09.85	85-87	35	9	6
Rochdale	Tr	07.88	88	42	0	12
Stockport Co.	Tr	07.89	89-94	176	11	12
Mansfield T.	L	09.94	94	4	2	0

FRAIN John William
Birmingham, 8 October, 1968 (M/LB)

League Club	Source	Date Signed	Seasons Played	Apps	Subs	Gls
Birmingham C.	App	10.86	85-96	265	9	23
Northampton T.	Tr	01.97	96-97	58	0	1

FRAIN Peter John Andrew
Birmingham, 18 March, 1965 (F)

League Club	Source	Date Signed	Seasons Played	Apps	Subs	Gls
West Bromwich A.	App	03.82				
Mansfield T.	L	01.84	83	1	1	0

FRAME William James
Castle Douglas, 1 August, 1939 (G)

League Club	Source	Date Signed	Seasons Played	Apps	Subs	Gls
Workington		11.58	58	9	-	0

FRAME William Lammie
Carluke, 7 May, 1912 Died 1993 (FB)

League Club	Source	Date Signed	Seasons Played	Apps	Subs	Gls
Leicester C.	Shawfield Jnrs	10.33	34-49	220	-	0

FRANCE Anthony
Sheffield, 11 April, 1939 (IF)

League Club	Source	Date Signed	Seasons Played	Apps	Subs	Gls
Huddersfield T.	Jnrs	04.56	57-59	9	-	2
Darlington	Tr	12.61	61-62	47	-	9
Stockport Co.	Tr	07.63	63	30	-	8

FRANCE Darren Brian
Hull, 8 August, 1967 (F)

League Club	Source	Date Signed	Seasons Played	Apps	Subs	Gls
Hull C.	North Ferriby U.	11.91	91-92	19	24	7
Doncaster Rov.	Tr	08.93	93	0	1	0

FRANCE Gary
Worksop, 18 June, 1955 (CF)

League Club	Source	Date Signed	Seasons Played	Apps	Subs	Gls
Sheffield U.	App	06.73	73-74	1	1	0

FRANCE Gary Lawton
Stalybridge, 5 May, 1946 (IF)

League Club	Source	Date Signed	Seasons Played	Apps	Subs	Gls
Burnley	Stalybridge Celtic	04.66	66-67	1	2	0
Bury	Tr	07.68	68	0	1	0

FRANCE John (Jack)
Stalybridge, 30 November, 1913 Died 1995 (WH)

League Club	Source	Date Signed	Seasons Played	Apps	Subs	Gls
Swindon T.	Bath C.	08.37	37	1	-	0
Halifax T.	Bath C.	06.39	46-47	50	-	1

FRANCE Michael **Paul**
Holmfirth, 10 September, 1968 (CD)

League Club	Source	Date Signed	Seasons Played	Apps	Subs	Gls
Huddersfield T.	YT	06.87	87-88	7	4	0
Bristol C.	Tr	07.89				
Burnley	Tr	07.90	90-91	7	1	0

FRANCE Peter
Huddersfield, 27 March, 1936 (G)

League Club	Source	Date Signed	Seasons Played	Apps	Subs	Gls
Huddersfield T.		09.56				
Bradford P.A.	Tr	05.57	57	16	-	0

FRANCIS Carlos (Carl) Everton
West Ham, 21 August, 1962 (W)

League Club	Source	Date Signed	Seasons Played	Apps	Subs	Gls
Birmingham C.	App	08.80	82	2	3	0
Hereford U.	L	12.83	83	5	0	0

FRANCIS Damien Jerome
London, 27 February, 1979 (CF)

League Club	Source	Date Signed	Seasons Played	Apps	Subs	Gls
Wimbledon	YT	03.97	97	0	2	0

FRANCIS George Edward
Acton, 4 February, 1934 (CF)

League Club	Source	Date Signed	Seasons Played	Apps	Subs	Gls
Brentford	Jnrs	01.53	54-60	228	-	110
Queens Park R.	Tr	05.61	61	2	-	1
Brentford	Tr	10.61	61	32	-	14
Gillingham	Tr	08.62	62-63	51	-	19

FRANCIS Gerald
South Africa, 6 December, 1933 (OR)

League Club	Source	Date Signed	Seasons Played	Apps	Subs	Gls
Leeds U.	Johannesburg (SA)	07.57	57-61	46	-	9
York C.	Tr	10.61	61	16	-	4

FRANCIS Gerald Charles James
Chiswick, 6 December, 1951 Eu23-6/E-12 (M)

League Club	Source	Date Signed	Seasons Played	Apps	Subs	Gls
Queens Park R.	App	06.69	69-78	290	5	53
Crystal Palace	Tr	07.79	79-80	59	0	7
Queens Park R.	Tr	02.81	80-81	17	0	4
Coventry C.	Tr	02.82	81-82	50	0	2
Exeter C.	Tr	08.83	83	28	0	3
Cardiff C. (N/C)	Tr	09.84	84	7	0	0
Swansea C. (N/C)	Tr	10.84	84	3	0	0
Portsmouth (N/C)	Tr	11.84	84	3	0	0
Bristol Rov. (N/C)	Tr	09.85	85-87	33	0	0

FRANCIS John Andrew
Dewsbury, 21 November, 1963 (F)

League Club	Source	Date Signed	Seasons Played	Apps	Subs	Gls
Halifax T. (N/C)	Emley	02.85	84	1	3	0
Sheffield U.	Emley	09.88	88-89	14	28	6
Burnley	Tr	01.90	89-91	99	2	27
Cambridge U.	Tr	08.92	92	15	14	3
Burnley	Tr	03.93	92-95	44	32	10
Scunthorpe U. (N/C)	Tr	08.96	96	1	4	0

FRANCIS Keith Roy
Yeovil, 22 July, 1929 (WH)

League Club	Source	Date Signed	Seasons Played	Apps	Subs	Gls
Leyton Orient	Yeovil T.	06.50	50	3	-	0

FRANCIS Kevin Michael Derek
Birmingham, 6 December, 1967 St Kitts & Nevis Int (F)

League Club	Source	Date Signed	Seasons Played	Apps	Subs	Gls
Derby Co.	Mile Oak Rov.	02.89	89-90	0	10	0
Stockport Co.	Tr	02.91	90-94	147	5	88
Birmingham C.	Tr	01.95	94-97	32	41	13
Oxford U.	Tr	02.98	97	15	0	7

FRANCIS Lee Charles
Walthamstow, 24 October, 1969 (M/RB)

League Club	Source	Date Signed	Seasons Played	Apps	Subs	Gls
Arsenal	YT	11.87				
Chesterfield	L	03.90	89	2	0	0
Chesterfield	Tr	06.90	90-91	63	5	2

FRANCIS Sean Robert
Birmingham, 1 August, 1972 (F)

League Club	Source	Date Signed	Seasons Played	Apps	Subs	Gls
Birmingham C.	YT	07.90	90-91	0	6	0
Northampton T.	Telford U.	08.93	93	0	1	0

FRANCIS Stephen Stuart
Billericay, 29 May, 1964 E Yth (G)

League Club	Source	Date Signed	Seasons Played	Apps	Subs	Gls
Chelsea	App	04.82	81-85	71	0	0
Reading	Tr	02.87	86-92	216	0	0
Huddersfield T.	Tr	08.93	93-97	183	0	0

FRANCIS Terence
Hartlepool, 18 June, 1943 (IF)

League Club	Source	Date Signed	Seasons Played	Apps	Subs	Gls
Hartlepool U.	Billingham Synthonia	12.63	63-64	18	-	4

FRANCIS Thomas George
Bermondsey, 30 October, 1920 Died 1996 (G)

League Club	Source	Date Signed	Seasons Played	Apps	Subs	Gls
Millwall	Cheltenham T.	05.46	46	1	-	0

FRANCIS Trevor John
Plymouth, 19 April, 1954 E Yth/Eu23-5/E-52 (F)

League Club	Source	Date Signed	Seasons Played	Apps	Subs	Gls
Birmingham C.	App	05.71	70-78	278	2	119
Nottingham F.	Tr	02.79	78-81	69	1	28
Manchester C.	Tr	09.81	81	26	0	12
Queens Park R.	Glasgow Rangers	03.88	87-89	30	2	12
Sheffield Wed.	Tr	02.91	89-93	29	47	5

FRANCOMBE Peter
Cardiff, 4 August, 1963 (D)

League Club	Source	Date Signed	Seasons Played	Apps	Subs	Gls
Cardiff C.	Crystal Palace (App)	09.81	81	2	1	0

FRANDSEN Per
Denmark, 6 February, 1970 Danish Int (M)

League Club	Source	Date Signed	Seasons Played	Apps	Subs	Gls
Bolton W.	F.C. Copenhagen (Den)	08.96	96-97	78	1	7

FRANKLAND Anthony
Greenwich, 11 October, 1972 (W/FB)

League Club	Source	Date Signed	Seasons Played	Apps	Subs	Gls
Exeter C.	YT	07.90	89-90	3	4	0

FRANKLIN Graham Nigel
Bicester, 25 January, 1957 (F)

League Club	Source	Date Signed	Seasons Played	Apps	Subs	Gls
Southend U.	Lowestoft T.	12.77	77-79	1	5	1

FRANKLIN Jeffrey Terence
Darlington, 8 December, 1973 (W)

League Club	Source	Date Signed	Seasons Played	Apps	Subs	Gls
Torquay U.	Millwall (YT)	●	91	1	1	0

FRANKLIN John
Stockton, 27 November, 1924 (OL)

League Club	Source	Date Signed	Seasons Played	Apps	Subs	Gls
Middlesbrough		12.43				
Darlington	Bath C.	08.47	47	8	-	3

FRANKLIN Neil
Stoke, 24 January, 1922 Died 1996 EF Lge/E-27 (CH)

League Club	Source	Date Signed	Seasons Played	Apps	Subs	Gls
Stoke C.	Jnrs	01.39	46-49	142	-	0
Hull C.	Santa Fe (Col)	02.51	50-55	95	-	0
Crewe Alex.	Tr	02.56	55-57	66	-	4
Stockport Co.	Tr	10.57	57	20	-	0

FRANKLIN Neil John
Lincoln, 10 March, 1969 (FB)

League Club	Source	Date Signed	Seasons Played	Apps	Subs	Gls
Lincoln C.	YT	06.87	86	15	0	0
Lincoln C. (N/C)	Nykopings (Swe)	10.88	88	0	1	0

FRANKLIN Paul Leslie
Hainault, 5 October, 1963 (CD)

League Club	Source	Date Signed	Seasons Played	Apps	Subs	Gls
Watford	App	08.81	82-86	32	0	0
Shrewsbury T.	L	10.86	86	6	0	0
Swindon T.	L	11.86	86	5	0	1
Reading	Tr	06.87	87-88	17	3	0

FRANKLIN Stanley Thomas
Shrewsbury, 16 September, 1919 (CH)

League Club	Source	Date Signed	Seasons Played	Apps	Subs	Gls
Blackpool	Kenwood Jnrs	05.38				
Crewe Alex.	Tr	04.46	46-47	28	-	0

FRANKLIN William Michael
Tiverton, 3 March, 1955 (G)

League Club	Source	Date Signed	Seasons Played	Apps	Subs	Gls
Charlton Ath.	App	03.73	72-74	13	0	0

FRANKS Albert John
Boldon, 13 April, 1936 (WH)

League Club	Source	Date Signed	Seasons Played	Apps	Subs	Gls
Newcastle U.	Boldon Colly	12.53	56-59	72	-	4
Lincoln C.	Glasgow Rangers	11.61	61-62	58	-	5

FRANKS Colin James
Willesden, 16 April, 1951 (CD)

League Club	Source	Date Signed	Seasons Played	Apps	Subs	Gls
Watford	Wealdstone	07.69	69-72	99	13	8
Sheffield U.	Tr	07.73	73-78	139	11	7

FRANKS Kenneth
Motherwell, 24 April, 1944 (OL)

League Club	Source	Date Signed	Seasons Played	Apps	Subs	Gls
Brighton & H. A.		06.62	62	1	-	0

FRASER Andrew McKnight
Newtongrange, 29 August, 1940 (CH)

League Club	Source	Date Signed	Seasons Played	Apps	Subs	Gls
Hartlepool U.	Hearts	10.61	61-63	82	-	2

FRASER John **Cameron (Cammie)**
Blackford, 24 May, 1941 Su23-2 (FB)

League Club	Source	Date Signed	Seasons Played	Apps	Subs	Gls
Aston Villa	Dunfermline Ath.	10.62	62-63	33	-	1
Birmingham C.	Tr	02.65	64-65	38	1	0

FRASER David McLean
Newtongrange, 6 June, 1937 (OL)

League Club	Source	Date Signed	Seasons Played	Apps	Subs	Gls
Hull C.	Jnrs	07.54	55-57	11	-	7
Mansfield T.	Tr	07.58	58	6	-	1

League Club	Source	Date Signed	Seasons Played	Career Record Apps	Subs	Gls
FRASER Douglas Michael						
Busby, 8 December, 1941 S-2						(D)
West Bromwich A.	Aberdeen	09.63	63-70	255	2	8
Nottingham F.	Tr	01.71	70-72	85	0	3
Walsall	Tr	07.73	73	26	1	0
FRASER Gordon						
Elgin, 27 November, 1943						(CF)
Cardiff C.	Forres Mechs	01.61	62	4	-	0
Millwall	Tr	09.63	63	5	-	0
Newport Co.	Barry T.	08.66	66	11	2	2
FRASER James						
Coatbridge, 17 November, 1932						(FB)
Barrow	Bellshill Ath.	03.58	57-58	32	-	0
FRASER John						
Hammersmith, 12 July, 1953						(RB)
Fulham	App	06.71	71-75	55	1	1
Brentford	Tr	07.76	76-79	121	2	6
FRASER John Watson						
Belfast, 15 September, 1938						(OR)
Sunderland	Glentoran	03.59	58-59	22	-	1
Portsmouth	Tr	06.60	60	1	-	0
Watford	Margate	07.62	62-63	24	-	3
FRASER Robert						
Glasgow, 23 January, 1917						(CH)
Newcastle U.	Hibernian	01.47	46-48	26	-	0
FRASER Stuart Thomas						
Edinburgh, 9 January, 1980						(LB)
Luton T.	YT	04.98	97	1	0	0
FRASER William Alexander						
Australia, 24 February, 1929 Died 1996 S-2						(G)
Sunderland	Airdrieonians	03.54	53-58	127	-	0
Nottingham F.	Tr	12.58	58	2	-	0
FRASER William Thomas						
Edinburgh, 12 August, 1945						(OL)
Huddersfield T.	Jnrs	04.63	63-64	8	-	2
FREAR Bryan						
Cleckheaton, 8 July, 1933						(IF)
Huddersfield T.	Jnrs	09.50	51-56	37	-	10
Chesterfield	Tr	02.57	56-63	281	-	84
Halifax T.	Tr	07.64	64	35	-	5
FREEBURN William Openshaw						
Hamilton, 7 April, 1930						(FB)
Grimsby T.	East Stirling	08.51	51-54	34	-	0
FREEDMAN Douglas Alan						
Glasgow, 21 January, 1974 S Sch/Su21-8/S 'B'						(F)
Queens Park R.	YT	05.92				
Barnet	Tr	07.94	94-95	47	0	27
Crystal Palace	Tr	09.95	95-97	72	18	31
Wolverhampton W.	Tr	10.97	97	25	4	10
FREEMAN Alfred						
Bethnal Green, 2 January, 1920						(IF)
Southampton		11.43	46	7	-	2
Crystal Palace	Tr	04.48	48	2	-	0
FREEMAN Andrew James						
Reading, 8 September, 1977						(M)
Reading	YT	07.96	95	0	1	0
FREEMAN Anthony						
Melton Mowbray, 29 August, 1928						(OR)
Notts Co.	Melton T.	01.46	46-49	44	-	2
FREEMAN Clive Richard						
Leeds, 12 September, 1962						(LB/M)
Swansea C.	Bridlington T.	08.90	90-91	10	4	0
Carlisle U.	L	01.92	91	4	0	0
Doncaster Rov.	Altrincham	08.93	93	23	2	2
FREEMAN Darren Barry Andduet						
Brighton, 22 August, 1973						(W)
Gillingham	Horsham	01.95	94-95	4	8	0
Fulham	Tr	07.96	96-97	32	14	9
FREEMAN Donald Richard						
Dartford, 29 August, 1921						(WH)
Charlton Ath.	Dartford	03.46				
Bristol C.	Tr	05.49	49	8	-	0
Watford	Tr	11.50				
Gillingham	Tr	06.51				
FREEMAN Henry (Harry) George						
Worcester, 4 November, 1918 Died 1997						(FB)
Fulham	Woodstock T.	10.37	38-51	179	-	6
Walsall	Tr	10.52	52	20	-	1
FREEMAN Neil						
Northampton, 16 February, 1955						(G)
Arsenal	Jnrs	06.72				
Grimsby T.	Tr	03.74	73-75	33	0	0
Southend U.	Tr	07.76	76-77	69	0	0
Birmingham C.	Tr	07.78	78-79	31	0	0
Walsall	L	08.80	80	8	0	0
Huddersfield T.	L	01.81	80	18	0	0
Peterborough U.	Tr	09.81	81	41	0	0
Northampton T. (N/C)	Tr	08.82	82	22	0	0
FREEMAN Neville Frank						
Brixworth, 25 January, 1925 Died 1984						(G)
Northampton T.		10.49	50	1	-	0
FREEMAN Ronald Peter **Percy**						
Newark, 4 July, 1945						(F)
West Bromwich A.	Stourbridge	04.68	69	2	1	0
Lincoln C.	Tr	06.70	70-72	76	4	30
Reading	Tr	01.73	72-74	53	7	13
Lincoln C.	Tr	01.75	74-76	62	10	34
FREESTONE Christopher Mark						
Nottingham, 4 September, 1971						(F)
Middlesbrough	Arnold T.	12.94	94-97	2	7	1
Carlisle U.	L	03.97	96	3	2	2
Northampton T.	Tr	12.97	97	23	2	11
FREESTONE Roger						
Caerleon, 19 August, 1968 W Sch/W Yth/Wu21-1						(G)
Newport Co.	YT	04.86	86	13	0	0
Chelsea	Tr	04.87	86-88	42	0	0
Swansea C.	L	09.89	89	14	0	0
Hereford U.	L	03.90	89	8	0	0
Swansea C.	Tr	09.91	91-97	311	1	3
FREESTONE Trevor						
Market Bosworth, 16 February, 1954						(F)
Peterborough U.	Jnrs	01.73	72	2	1	1
FREIMANIS Edward						
Latvia, 22 February, 1920 Died 1993 Latvian Int						(CF)
Northampton T.	Peterborough U.	05.48	48-49	19	-	4
FRENCH George Noah						
Colchester, 10 November, 1926						(FB)
Colchester U. (Am)		05.52	52-53	3	-	0
FRENCH (LAFITE) Graham Edward						
Wolverhampton, 6 April, 1945 E Yth						(W)
Shrewsbury T.	App	11.62	61-62	27	-	1
Swindon T.	Tr	08.63	63	5	-	0
Watford	Tr	08.64	64	4	-	0
Luton T.	Wellington T.	10.65	65-72	180	2	22
Reading	L	11.73	73	3	0	0
Southport	Boston Minutemen (USA)	03.76	75	2	0	0
FRENCH James Robert						
Stockton, 27 November, 1926						(IF)
Middlesbrough		08.45				
Northampton T.		08.51	51	1	-	0
Darlington	Tr	08.53	53-54	52	-	8
FRENCH John (Jack) William						
Stockton, 19 January, 1925						(WH)
Middlesbrough		10.43				
Southend U.	Tr	02.47	46-52	182	-	19
Nottingham F.	Tr	11.52	52-55	80	-	8
Southend U.	Tr	07.56	56	5	-	0
FRENCH Jonathan Charles						
Bristol, 25 September, 1976						(M/F)
Bristol Rov.	YT	07.95	95-97	8	9	1
FRENCH Michael John						
Eastbourne, 7 May, 1955 E Yth						(F)
Queens Park R.	App	05.73				
Brentford	Tr	02.75	74-76	56	9	16
Swindon T.	Tr	02.77	76-77	5	5	1
Doncaster Rov.	Tr	07.78	78	36	0	5

League Club	Source	Date Signed	Seasons Played	Apps	Subs	Gls
Aldershot	Tr	05.79	79-81	70	4	16
Rochdale	Tr	08.82	82	35	1	11

FRENCH Nigel Peter
Swansea, 24 March, 1968 (W)

League Club	Source	Date Signed	Seasons Played	Apps	Subs	Gls
Swansea	App	03.86	85-86	13	13	3

FRENCH Raymond
Wigton, 16 December, 1946 (CH)

League Club	Source	Date Signed	Seasons Played	Apps	Subs	Gls
Workington (Am)	Wigton	11.73	73	2	0	0

FRETWELL David
Wakefield, 18 February, 1952 (CD)

League Club	Source	Date Signed	Seasons Played	Apps	Subs	Gls
Bradford C.	Jnrs	07.70	70-77	247	6	5
Wigan Ath.	Chicago (USA)	10.78	78-80	111	1	0

FRIAR John **Paul**
Glasgow, 6 June, 1963 S Yth (LB)

League Club	Source	Date Signed	Seasons Played	Apps	Subs	Gls
Leicester C.	App	08.80	80-82	56	2	0
Rotherham U.	Tr	02.83	82-83	20	0	0
Charlton Ath	Tr	07.84	84-85	36	0	0
Northampton T.	L	03.86	85	14	0	0
Aldershot	Tr	08.86	86	29	0	1

FRIDAY Robin
Hammersmith, 27 July, 1952 Died 1991 (F)

League Club	Source	Date Signed	Seasons Played	Apps	Subs	Gls
Reading	Hayes	02.74	73-76	121	0	46
Cardiff C.	Tr	12.76	76-77	20	1	6

FRIDAY Terence John
Sittingbourne, 1 May, 1936 (G)

League Club	Source	Date Signed	Seasons Played	Apps	Subs	Gls
Gillingham (Am)	Sheppey U.	03.61	60	2	-	0

FRIDGE Leslie Francis
Inverness, 27 August, 1968 S Yth/Su21-1 (G)

League Club	Source	Date Signed	Seasons Played	Apps	Subs	Gls
Chelsea	App	09.85	85	1	0	0

FRIEDEL Bradley Howard
USA, 18 May, 1971 USA Int (G)

League Club	Source	Date Signed	Seasons Played	Apps	Subs	Gls
Liverpool	Columbus Crew (USA)	12.97	97	11	0	0

FRIEL Bernard (Benny) James
Glasgow, 16 September, 1941 (IF)

League Club	Source	Date Signed	Seasons Played	Apps	Subs	Gls
Southend U.	Dumbarton	06.63	63-64	17	-	8

FRIEL George Patrick
Reading, 11 October, 1970 (W)

League Club	Source	Date Signed	Seasons Played	Apps	Subs	Gls
Reading	YT	06.89	89-90	10	6	1

FRIEL John Patrick
Glasgow, 1 September, 1923 (IF)

League Club	Source	Date Signed	Seasons Played	Apps	Subs	Gls
New Brighton	Third Lanark	06.50	50	3	-	0
Torquay U.	Queen of South	10.52				

FRIEL Peter
Wishaw, 27 March, 1939 (W)

League Club	Source	Date Signed	Seasons Played	Apps	Subs	Gls
Workington	Cambuslang R.	08.61	61	4	-	0

FRIEND Barry Neil
Wandsworth, 13 October, 1951 E Amat (W)

League Club	Source	Date Signed	Seasons Played	Apps	Subs	Gls
Fulham	Leatherhead	10.73	73	2	1	0

FRITH David William Malcolm
Liverpool, 17 March, 1929 (FB)

League Club	Source	Date Signed	Seasons Played	Apps	Subs	Gls
Blackpool	Jnrs	05.49	52-56	32	-	0
Tranmere Rov.	Tr	08.58	58-62	177	-	0

FRITH William
Sheffield, 9 June, 1912 Died 1996 (WH)

League Club	Source	Date Signed	Seasons Played	Apps	Subs	Gls
Mansfield T.	Worksop	04.30				
Chesterfield	Tr	05.31	31	9	-	3
Coventry C.	Tr	05.32	32-46	169	-	4

FRIZZELL James Letson
Greenock, 16 February, 1937 (IF/WH)

League Club	Source	Date Signed	Seasons Played	Apps	Subs	Gls
Oldham Ath.	Morton	05.60	60-69	308	9	56

FROGGATT John (Jack)
Sheffield, 17 November, 1922 Died 1993 EF Lge/E-13 (OL/HB)

League Club	Source	Date Signed	Seasons Played	Apps	Subs	Gls
Portsmouth		09.45	46-53	280	-	67
Leicester C.	Tr	03.54	53-57	143	-	18

FROGGATT John Lawrence
Sutton-in-Ashfield, 13 December, 1945 (F)

League Club	Source	Date Signed	Seasons Played	Apps	Subs	Gls
Notts Co.	East Kirkby Colly	06.64	63-64	4	-	0
Colchester U.	Boston U.	07.74	74-77	155	0	29
Port Vale	Tr	02.78	77-78	12	2	3
Northampton T.	Tr	09.78	78	42	0	12

FROGGATT Redfern
Sheffield, 23 August, 1924 EF Lge/E'B'/E-4 (IF)

League Club	Source	Date Signed	Seasons Played	Apps	Subs	Gls
Sheffield Wed.	Sheffield Y.M.C.A.	08.42	46-59	434	-	140

FROGGATT Stephen Junior
Lincoln, 9 March, 1973 Eu21-2 (LW)

League Club	Source	Date Signed	Seasons Played	Apps	Subs	Gls
Aston Villa	YT	01.91	91-93	30	5	2
Wolverhampton W.	Tr	07.94	94-97	91	7	7

FRONTZECK Michael
Germany, 26 March, 1964 German Int (D)

League Club	Source	Date Signed	Seasons Played	Apps	Subs	Gls
Manchester C.	Borussia M-Gladbach (Ger)	01.96	95-96	19	4	0

FROST Brian Philip
Sheffield, 5 June, 1938 (F)

League Club	Source	Date Signed	Seasons Played	Apps	Subs	Gls
Chesterfield	Oswestry T.	05.59	59-64	103	-	20

FROST Desmond
Congleton, 3 August, 1926 Died 1993 (CF)

League Club	Source	Date Signed	Seasons Played	Apps	Subs	Gls
Leeds U.	Congleton T.	04.49	49-50	10	-	2
Halifax T.	Tr	01.51	50-53	117	-	55
Rochdale	Tr	11.53	53-54	16	-	6
Crewe Alex.	Tr	09.54	54-55	42	-	12

FROST John (Jack)
Wallsend, 13 February, 1920 Died 1988 (G)

League Club	Source	Date Signed	Seasons Played	Apps	Subs	Gls
Grimsby T.	North Shields	07.39				
York C.	Tr	07.48	48-51	45	-	0

FROST Lee Adrian
Woking, 4 December, 1957 (W)

League Club	Source	Date Signed	Seasons Played	Apps	Subs	Gls
Chelsea	App	07.76	77-79	11	3	5
Brentford	L	10.78	78	5	1	0
Brentford	Tr	12.80	80	15	0	3

FROST Ronald Albert
Stockport, 16 January, 1947 (W)

League Club	Source	Date Signed	Seasons Played	Apps	Subs	Gls
Manchester C.	App	05.64	63	2	-	1

FROST Stanley
Northampton, 19 October, 1922 (OR)

League Club	Source	Date Signed	Seasons Played	Apps	Subs	Gls
Leicester C.	Northampton T. (Am)	03.41				
Northampton T.	Tr	01.47	46	6	-	1

FROWEN John
Trelewis, 11 October, 1931 (D)

League Club	Source	Date Signed	Seasons Played	Apps	Subs	Gls
Cardiff C.	Nelson	05.51	52-57	35	-	0
Bristol Rov.	Tr	08.58	58-62	84	-	0
Newport Co.	Tr	03.63	62-65	67	1	0

FRUDE Roger Gordon
Plymouth, 19 November, 1946 Died 1996 (IF)

League Club	Source	Date Signed	Seasons Played	Apps	Subs	Gls
Bristol Rov.	App	12.64	63-67	38	3	8
Mansfield T.	Tr	09.67	67-68	14	1	0
Brentford	Tr	07.69	69	1	1	0

FRY Barry Francis
Bedford, 7 April, 1945 E Sch (IF)

League Club	Source	Date Signed	Seasons Played	Apps	Subs	Gls
Manchester U.	App	04.62				
Bolton W.	Tr	05.64	64	3	-	1
Luton T.	Tr	07.65	65	6	0	0
Leyton Orient	Gravesend & Nft	12.66	66	2	1	0
Leyton Orient	Bedford T.	06.67	67	5	5	0

FRY Christopher David
Cardiff, 23 October, 1969 W Yth (W)

League Club	Source	Date Signed	Seasons Played	Apps	Subs	Gls
Cardiff C.	YT	07.88	88-90	22	33	1
Hereford U.	Tr	07.91	91-93	76	14	10
Colchester U.	Tr	10.93	93-96	102	28	16
Exeter C.	Tr	07.97	97	16	12	1

FRY David Paul
Bournemouth, 5 January, 1960 (G)

League Club	Source	Date Signed	Seasons Played	Apps	Subs	Gls
Crystal Palace	App	01.77	77-82	40	0	0
Gillingham	Tr	07.83	83-84	49	0	0
Torquay U.	Millwall (N/C)	10.85	85	30	0	0

FRY Keith Frederick
Cardiff, 11 April, 1941 W Sch (OR)

League Club	Source	Date Signed	Seasons Played	Apps	Subs	Gls
Newport Co.	Jnrs	10.58	58-61	58	-	2
Notts Co.	Tr	02.62	61-63	73	-	9
Chesterfield	Merthyr Tydfil	01.66	65	2	0	1

FRY Robert Philip
Pontypridd, 29 June, 1935 (G)

League Club	Source	Date Signed	Seasons Played	Apps	Subs	Gls
Crystal Palace		04.56	55	6	-	0
Queens Park R.	Bath C.	08.57	57	1	-	0

League Club	Source	Date Signed	Seasons Played	Apps	Subs	Gls
FRY Roger Norman						
Southampton, 18 August, 1948						(LB)
Southampton	Jnrs	10.67	70-71	23	0	0
Walsall	Tr	07.73	73-76	120	0	1
FRYATT James Edward						
Southampton, 2 September, 1940						(CF)
Charlton Ath.	Jnrs	10.57	59	5	-	3
Southend U.	Tr	06.60	60-62	61	-	24
Bradford P.A.	Tr	06.63	63-65	101	0	38
Southport	Tr	03.66	65-66	39	0	15
Torquay U.	Tr	03.67	66-67	27	0	11
Stockport Co.	Tr	10.67	67-68	45	0	28
Blackburn Rov.	Tr	10.68	68-69	29	8	5
Oldham Ath.	Tr	02.70	69-71	76	0	40
Southport	Tr	11.71	71-73	102	2	24
Stockport Co.	Tr	09.74	74	1	0	1
Torquay U.	Tr	12.74	74	3	0	0
FRYE John Marr						
Ardrossan, 27 July, 1933						(IF)
Sheffield Wed.	St Mirren	01.61				
Tranmere Rov.	Tr	10.61	61	21	-	6
FRYER John Hilary						
Manchester, 24 June, 1924						(CF)
Oldham Ath.	Goslings	04.47	47	9	-	3
FUCCILLO Pasquale (Lil)						
Bedford, 2 May, 1956						(M)
Luton T.	App	07.74	74-82	153	7	24
Southend U.	Tulsa (USA)	12.83	83-84	40	5	4
Peterborough U. (N/C)	Tr	08.85	85-86	82	0	3
Cambridge U. (N/C)	Malta	01.88	87	18	1	2
FUCHS Uwe						
Germany, 23 July, 1966						(F)
Middlesbrough (L)	Kaiserslautern (Ger)	01.95	94	13	2	9
Millwall	Kaiserslautern (Ger)	07.95	95	21	11	5
FUDGE Michael Henry						
Bristol, 5 December, 1945						(IF)
West Bromwich A.	App	12.63	63-64	13	-	5
Exeter C.	Tr	06.67	67	32	2	6
FUGLESTAD Erik						
Stavanger, Norway, 13 August, 1974						(WB)
Norwich C.	Viking Stavanger (Nor)	11.97	97	23	1	2
FULBROOK Gary						
Bath, 4 May, 1966						(D)
Swindon T.	YT	09.84	84	0	1	0
Carlisle U.	Bath C.	09.87	87	6	0	0
FULLAM John Rowan						
Dublin, 22 March, 1940 IR 'B'/IR-11						(WH)
Preston N. E.	Home Farm	10.58	59-60	49	-	6
FULLARTON James						
Glasgow, 20 July, 1974 Su21-17						(M)
Crystal Palace	Bastia	08.97	97	19	6	1
FULLBROOK John Frederick Albert						
Grays, 15 July, 1918 Died 1992						(FB)
Leyton Orient	Plymouth Arg. (Am)	04.46	46-47	36	-	1
FULLER William James						
Brixton, 6 April, 1944						(FB)
Crystal Palace	Jnrs	01.63	62-64	3	-	0
FULLERTON George						
Ballymena (NI), 14 June, 1939						(G)
Leeds U.	Glentoran	05.58				
Barrow	Distillery	07.60	60	12	-	0
FULTON Bryce						
Kilwinning, 7 August, 1935						(FB)
Manchester U.	Jnrs	03.53				
Plymouth Arg.	Tr	08.57	57-63	176	-	0
Exeter C.	Tr	07.64	64-65	37	0	0
FULTON Raymond Hamilton						
Hendon, 24 September, 1953						(FB)
Leyton Orient	West Ham U. (App)	08.72	72	1	0	0
FULTON Stephen						
Greenock, 10 August, 1970 Su21-7						(M)
Bolton W.	Glasgow Celtic	07.93	93	4	0	0
Peterborough U.	L	12.93	93	3	0	0

League Club	Source	Date Signed	Seasons Played	Apps	Subs	Gls
FUNNELL Anthony						
Eastbourne, 20 August, 1957						(F)
Southampton	Eastbourne	01.77	77-78	13	4	8
Gillingham	Tr	03.79	78-79	27	6	10
Brentford	Tr	03.80	79-80	29	3	8
Bournemouth	Tr	09.81	81-82	59	5	22
FUNNELL Simon Paul						
Brighton, 8 August, 1974						(F)
Brighton & H.A.	YT	07.92	91-94	14	14	2
FURIE John Patrick Christopher						
Hammersmith, 13 May, 1948						(FB)
Watford	App	05.66	66	0	1	0
Gillingham	Tr	07.67	67	17	0	0
FURLONG Carl David						
Liverpool, 18 October, 1976						(F)
Wigan Ath.	YT	07.95	93-94	1	2	0
FURLONG Paul Anthony						
Wood Green, 1 October, 1968 E Semi Pro						(F)
Coventry C.	Enfield	07.91	91	27	10	4
Watford	Tr	07.92	92-93	79	0	37
Chelsea	Tr	05.94	94-95	44	20	13
Birmingham C.	Tr	07.96	96-97	61	7	25
FURNELL Andrew Paul						
Peterborough, 13 February, 1977 E Yth						(F)
Peterborough U.	YT	01.95	93-95	9	10	1
FURNELL James						
Manchester, 23 November, 1937						(G)
Burnley	Jnrs	11.54	59-60	2	-	0
Liverpool	Tr	02.62	61-63	28	-	0
Arsenal	Tr	11.63	63-67	141	0	0
Rotherham U.	Tr	09.68	68-69	76	0	0
Plymouth Arg.	Tr	12.70	70-75	183	0	0
FURNESS William Isaac						
Washington, 8 June, 1909 Died 1980 E-1						(IF)
Leeds U.	Usworth Colly	08.28	29-36	243	-	62
Norwich C.	Tr	06.37	37-46	93	-	21
FURNISS Frederick						
Sheffield, 10 July, 1922						(FB)
Sheffield U.	Hallam	01.43	46-54	279	-	14
Chesterfield	Tr	08.55				
FURPHY Keith						
Stockton, 30 July, 1958						(LW)
Queens Park R.	Sheffield U. (App)	10.76				
Plymouth Arg.	Baltimore (USA)	08.87	87	6	0	1
FURPHY Kenneth						
Stockton, 28 May, 1931						(WH)
Everton		11.50				
Darlington	Runcorn	08.53	53-61	316	-	5
Workington	Tr	07.62	62-64	105	-	3
Watford	Tr	11.64	64-67	95	6	1
FURSDON Alan Harry						
Grantham, 16 October, 1947						(FB)
Swindon T.		09.65				
Oxford U.		05.67	68	0	1	0
FURY Paul						
Swansea, 16 March, 1955 W Sch						(FB)
Swansea C.	App	•	71-72	11	0	0
FUSCHILLO Paul Michael						
Islington, 20 October, 1948 E Amat						(FB)
Blackpool	Wycombe W.	07.71	71-73	8	3	0
Brighton & H. A.	Tr	02.74	73-74	17	0	1
FUTCHER Graham						
Chester, 15 June, 1953						(F)
Chester C.	Jnrs	08.71	71-72	5	5	0
FUTCHER Paul						
Chester, 25 September, 1956 Eu21-11						(CD)
Chester C.	App	01.74	72-73	20	0	0
Luton T.	Tr	06.74	74-77	131	0	1
Manchester C.	Tr	06.78	78-79	36	1	0
Oldham Ath.	Tr	08.80	80-82	98	0	1
Derby Co.	Tr	01.83	82-83	35	0	0
Barnsley	Tr	03.84	83-89	229	1	0
Halifax T.	Tr	07.90	90	15	0	0
Grimsby T.	Tr	01.91	90-94	131	1	0

League Club	Source	Date Signed	Seasons Played	Career Record Apps	Subs	Gls
FUTCHER Ronald						
Chester, 25 September, 1956						(F)
Chester C.	App	01.74	73	4	0	0
Luton T.	Tr	06.74	74-77	116	4	40
Manchester C.	Tr	08.78	78	10	7	7
Barnsley	N.A.C. Breda (Neth)	12.84	84	18	1	5
Oldham Ath.	Tr	07.85	85-86	65	0	30
Bradford C.	Tr	03.87	86-87	35	7	18
Port Vale	Tr	08.88	88-89	46	6	20
Burnley	Tr	11.89	89-90	52	5	25
Crewe Alex.	Tr	07.91	91	18	3	4
FUTRE Paulo Jorge						
Portugal, 28 February, 1966 Portuguese Int						(F)
West Ham U.	A.C. Milan (It)	07.96	96	4	5	0
FYFE Tony						
Carlisle, 23 February, 1962						(F)
Carlisle U.	Penrith	09.87	87-89	28	20	12
Scarborough	L	12.89	89	6	0	1
Halifax T.	Tr	01.90	89-90	13	3	0
Carlisle U.	Tr	10.90	90-91	33	9	8

G

GABBIADINI Marco
Nottingham, 20 January, 1968 Eu21-2/E 'B'/EF Lge (F)

League Club	Source	Date Signed	Seasons Played	Apps	Subs	Gls
York C.	App	09.85	84-87	42	18	14
Sunderland	Tr	09.87	87-91	155	2	75
Crystal Palace	Tr	09.91	91	15	0	5
Derby Co.	Tr	01.92	91-96	163	25	50
Birmingham C.	L	10.96	96	0	2	0
Oxford U.	L	01.97	96	5	0	1
Stoke C.	Panionis (Gre)	12.97	97	2	6	0
York C.	Tr	02.98	97	5	2	1

GABBIADINI Riccardo
Newport, 11 March, 1970 (F)

League Club	Source	Date Signed	Seasons Played	Apps	Subs	Gls
York C.	YT	•	87	0	1	0
Sunderland	Tr	06.88	89	0	1	0
Blackpool	L	09.89	89	5	0	3
Grimsby T.	L	10.89	89	3	0	1
Brighton & H.A.	L	03.90	89	0	1	0
Crewe Alex.	L	10.90	90	1	1	0
Hartlepool U.	Tr	03.91	90-91	2	12	2
Scarborough	Tr	03.92	91	3	4	1
Carlisle U.	Tr	08.92	92	18	6	3

GABRIEL James
Dundee, 16 October, 1940 S Sch/Su23-6/S-2 (WH)

League Club	Source	Date Signed	Seasons Played	Apps	Subs	Gls
Everton	Dundee	03.60	59-66	255	1	33
Southampton	Tr	07.67	67-71	190	1	25
Bournemouth	Tr	07.72	72-73	53	0	4
Swindon T.	L	10.73	73	6	0	0
Brentford	Tr	03.74	73	9	0	0

GADDES Graham **Robert**
Byfleet, 27 September, 1941 E Yth (G)

League Club	Source	Date Signed	Seasons Played	Apps	Subs	Gls
Portsmouth	Jnrs	06.60	59	1	-	0

GADSBY Kenneth
Chesterfield, 3 July, 1916 (LB)

League Club	Source	Date Signed	Seasons Played	Apps	Subs	Gls
Leeds U.	Middlecliffe Rov.	10.34	36-47	78	-	0

GADSBY Matthew John
Sutton Coldfield, 6 September, 1979 (M)

League Club	Source	Date Signed	Seasons Played	Apps	Subs	Gls
Walsall	YT	02.98	97	0	1	0

GADSBY Michael David
Oswestry, 1 August, 1947 (G)

League Club	Source	Date Signed	Seasons Played	Apps	Subs	Gls
Notts Co.	Ashbourne	01.68	67	11	0	0
York C.	Tr	07.69	69	13	0	0
Grimsby T.	L	09.70	70	2	0	0
Bradford C.	L	12.70	70	6	0	0
Hartlepool U.	Tr	07.71	71	21	0	0

GADSTON Joseph Edward
Hanwell, 13 September, 1945 (CF)

League Club	Source	Date Signed	Seasons Played	Apps	Subs	Gls
Brentford	West Ham U. (Am)	08.64				
Bristol Rov.	Cheltenham T.	06.68	68	10	1	5
Exeter C.	Tr	11.69	69-71	85	0	31
Aldershot	Tr	07.72	72	2	2	0
Hartlepool U.	L	02.73	72	1	0	0

GAFFNEY Terence
Hartlepool, 15 February, 1952 (M)

League Club	Source	Date Signed	Seasons Played	Apps	Subs	Gls
Hartlepool U.	Billingham Synth.	07.77	77	10	3	1

GAGE Kevin William
Chiswick, 21 April, 1964 E Yth (M/FB)

League Club	Source	Date Signed	Seasons Played	Apps	Subs	Gls
Wimbledon	App	01.82	80-86	135	33	15
Aston Villa	Tr	07.87	87-90	113	2	8
Sheffield U.	Tr	11.91	91-95	107	5	7
Preston N.E.	Tr	03.96	95-96	20	3	0
Hull C.	Tr	09.97	97	8	2	0

GAGE Larry Albert
Walthamstow, 10 September, 1922 Died 1996 (G)

League Club	Source	Date Signed	Seasons Played	Apps	Subs	Gls
Leyton Orient	Walthamstow Ave.	08.43				
Fulham	Tr	08.44				
Aldershot	Tr	07.46	46-47	39	-	0
Fulham	Canada	08.48	48	3	-	0
Gillingham	Tr	06.50	50	40	-	0

GAGE Wakely Alexander John
Northampton, 5 May, 1958 (CD)

League Club	Source	Date Signed	Seasons Played	Apps	Subs	Gls
Northampton T.	Desborough T.	10.79	79-84	215	3	17
Chester C.	Tr	08.85	85	17	0	1
Peterborough U.	Tr	11.85	85-86	73	0	1
Crewe Alex.	Tr	06.87	87-88	45	9	1

GAGER Horace Edwin
West Ham, 25 January, 1917 Died 1984 (CH)

League Club	Source	Date Signed	Seasons Played	Apps	Subs	Gls
Luton T.	Vauxhall Motors	11.37	46-47	59	-	2
Nottingham F.	Tr	02.48	47-54	258	-	11

GAILLARD Marcel Jean Elie
Belgium, 15 January, 1927 Died 1976 (W)

League Club	Source	Date Signed	Seasons Played	Apps	Subs	Gls
Crystal Palace	Tonbridge	02.48	47-49	21	-	3
Portsmouth	Tr	02.51	50-52	58	-	7

GALBRAITH Walter McMurray
Glasgow, 26 May, 1918 Died 1995 (LB)

League Club	Source	Date Signed	Seasons Played	Apps	Subs	Gls
New Brighton	Clyde	09.48	48-50	109	-	1
Grimsby T.	Tr	08.51	51-52	77	-	0
Accrington St.	Tr	06.53	53	21	-	0

GALE Anthony Peter
Westminster, 19 November, 1959 E Yth/Eu21-1 (CD)

League Club	Source	Date Signed	Seasons Played	Apps	Subs	Gls
Fulham	App	08.77	77-83	277	0	19
West Ham U.	Tr	07.84	84-93	293	7	5
Blackburn Rov.	Tr	08.94	94	15	0	0
Crystal Palace	Tr	09.95	95	2	0	0

GALE Colin Maurice
Pontypridd, 31 August, 1932 (CH)

League Club	Source	Date Signed	Seasons Played	Apps	Subs	Gls
Cardiff C.	Jnrs	07.50	53-55	12	-	0
Northampton T.	Tr	03.56	55-60	211	-	0

GALE Darren
Port Talbot, 25 October, 1963 Wu21-2 (F)

League Club	Source	Date Signed	Seasons Played	Apps	Subs	Gls
Swansea C.	App	10.80	81-84	26	11	6
Exeter C.	Tr	09.85	85-86	19	1	5

GALE Ian James
Slough, 3 March, 1961 (M)

League Club	Source	Date Signed	Seasons Played	Apps	Subs	Gls
Millwall	App	03.78	78	4	1	0

GALE Shaun Michael
Reading, 8 October, 1969 (FB)

League Club	Source	Date Signed	Seasons Played	Apps	Subs	Gls
Portsmouth	YT	07.88	90	2	1	0
Barnet	Tr	07.94	94-96	109	5	5
Exeter C.	Tr	06.97	97	42	1	4

GALE Thomas
Washington, 4 November, 1920 Died 1975 (CH)

League Club	Source	Date Signed	Seasons Played	Apps	Subs	Gls
Sheffield Wed.	Gateshead (Am)	04.45	46	6	-	0
York C.	Tr	08.47	47-48	76	-	0

GALL Benny
Denmark, 14 March, 1971 (G)

League Club	Source	Date Signed	Seasons Played	Apps	Subs	Gls
Shrewsbury T.	Dordrecht D.G. (Neth)	08.96	96-97	34	0	0

GALL Mark Ian
Brixton, 14 May, 1963 (F)

League Club	Source	Date Signed	Seasons Played	Apps	Subs	Gls
Maidstone U.	Greenwich Borough	02.88	89-91	69	16	31
Brighton & H. A.	Tr	10.91	91	30	1	13

GALL Norman Albert
Wallsend, 30 September, 1942 (CH)

League Club	Source	Date Signed	Seasons Played	Apps	Subs	Gls
Brighton & H. A.	Gateshead	03.62	62-73	427	13	4

GALLACHER Bernard
Johnstone, 22 March, 1967 (LB)

League Club	Source	Date Signed	Seasons Played	Apps	Subs	Gls
Aston Villa	App	03.85	86-90	55	2	0
Blackburn Rov.	L	11.90	90	4	0	0
Doncaster Rov. (N/C)	Tr	09.91	91	2	0	0
Brighton & H.A.	Tr	10.91	91-92	45	0	1
Northampton T. (N/C)		01.94	93	5	0	0

GALLACHER Connor
Derry (NI), 24 April, 1922 (IF)

League Club	Source	Date Signed	Seasons Played	Apps	Subs	Gls
Middlesbrough	Lochee Harp	01.47	46	1	-	0
Hull C.	Tr	05.47	47	18	-	3
Rochdale	Tr	03.48	47	6	-	1

GALLACHER John Anthony
Glasgow, 26 January, 1969 (W)

League Club	Source	Date Signed	Seasons Played	Apps	Subs	Gls
Newcastle U.	Falkirk	06.89	89-90	22	7	6
Hartlepool U.	Tr	08.92	92-93	18	5	2

GALLACHER Kevin William
Clydebank, 23 November, 1966 S Yth/Su21-7/S 'B'/S-39 (F)

League Club	Source	Date Signed	Seasons Played	Apps	Subs	Gls
Coventry C.	Dundee U.	01.90	89-92	99	1	28
Blackburn Rov.	Tr	03.93	92-97	116	7	41

GALLACHER Patrick
Glasgow, 9 January, 1913 Died 1983 (IF)

League Club	Source	Date Signed	Seasons Played	Apps	Subs	Gls
Blackburn Rov.	Third Lanark	10.36	36-37	11	-	0
Bournemouth	Tr	06.38	38-47	35	-	3

GALLAGHER Barry Patrick
Bradford, 7 April, 1961 (M)

League Club	Source	Date Signed	Seasons Played	Apps	Subs	Gls
Bradford C.	App	04.79	77-82	66	5	22
Mansfield T.	L	01.83	82	2	1	0
Halifax T.	Tr	03.83	82-85	110	5	27

GALLAGHER Brian
Oldham, 22 July, 1938 (FB)

League Club	Source	Date Signed	Seasons Played	Apps	Subs	Gls
Bury	Ashton U.	10.56	57-64	130	-	1
Carlisle U.	Tr	05.65	65-66	42	2	1
Stockport Co.	Tr	07.67	67	13	0	0

GALLAGHER Ian
Hartlepool, 30 May, 1978 (M)

League Club	Source	Date Signed	Seasons Played	Apps	Subs	Gls
Hartlepool U.	YT	07.96	95	1	0	0

GALLAGHER James
Manchester, 2 September, 1911 Died 1972 (CH)

League Club	Source	Date Signed	Seasons Played	Apps	Subs	Gls
Bury	Tr	01.36				
Notts Co.	Tr	08.37	37-38	23	-	2
Exeter C.	Tr	06.39				
Exeter C.	Notts Co. (coach)	09.48	48	1	-	0

GALLAGHER John (Jackie) Christopher
Wisbech, 6 April, 1958 (F)

League Club	Source	Date Signed	Seasons Played	Apps	Subs	Gls
Lincoln C.	March T.	02.76	76	1	0	0
Peterborough U.	Kings Lynn	04.80	79-80	11	2	1
Torquay U. (N/C)	Hong Kong	08.82	82	38	4	7
Peterborough U.	Wisbech T.	08.85	85-86	78	4	20
Wolverhampton W.	Tr	06.87	87-88	10	17	4

GALLAGHER Joseph Anthony
Liverpool, 11 January, 1955 E 'B' (CD)

League Club	Source	Date Signed	Seasons Played	Apps	Subs	Gls
Birmingham C.	App	01.72	73-80	281	5	17
Wolverhampton W.	Tr	08.81	81-82	31	0	0
West Ham U.	Tr	12.82	82	8	1	0
Burnley	Tr	08.83	83-86	46	1	3
Halifax T.	L	10.83	83	4	0	0

GALLAGHER Michael
Cambuslang, 16 January, 1932 Died 1975 (OL)

League Club	Source	Date Signed	Seasons Played	Apps	Subs	Gls
Bolton W.	Benburb	01.52				
West Bromwich A.	Tr	12.52	52	1	-	0

GALLAGHER Nicholas
Boston, 28 January, 1971 E Sch (W)

League Club	Source	Date Signed	Seasons Played	Apps	Subs	Gls
Doncaster Rov.	Jnrs	05.89	89	0	1	0

GALLAGHER Thomas Duncan
Nottingham, 25 August, 1974 (RB/M)

League Club	Source	Date Signed	Seasons Played	Apps	Subs	Gls
Notts Co.	YT	06.92	93-96	42	1	2

GALLANT David
Middlesbrough, 12 October, 1949 (F)

League Club	Source	Date Signed	Seasons Played	Apps	Subs	Gls
Leeds U.	Jnrs	12.66				
Darlington	L	01.68	67	1	0	0

GALLEGO Antonio
Spain, 2 June, 1924 (G)

League Club	Source	Date Signed	Seasons Played	Apps	Subs	Gls
Norwich C.	Cambridge T.	03.47	46	1	-	0

GALLEGO Jose Augustin
Spain, 8 April, 1923 (OL)

League Club	Source	Date Signed	Seasons Played	Apps	Subs	Gls
Brentford	Abbey U.	01.47	46-47	6	-	0
Southampton	Tr	05.48	48	1	-	0
Colchester U.	Tr	(N/L)	50	4	-	0

GALLEN Joseph Martin
Hammersmith, 2 September, 1972 IRu21-6 (F)

League Club	Source	Date Signed	Seasons Played	Apps	Subs	Gls
Watford	YT	05.91				
Exeter C.	L	12.92	92	6	0	0
Shrewsbury T.	Tr	07.93	93	4	2	1

GALLEN Kevin Andrew
Chiswick, 21 September, 1975 E Sch/E Yth/Eu21-4 (F)

League Club	Source	Date Signed	Seasons Played	Apps	Subs	Gls
Queens Park R.	YT	09.92	94-97	78	18	24

GALLEY Gordon Walter
Worksop, 4 February, 1930 (OL)

League Club	Source	Date Signed	Seasons Played	Apps	Subs	Gls
Sheffield Wed.	Jnrs	06.47				
Darlington	Tr	10.48	48-51	60	-	12

GALLEY John Edward
Clowne, 7 May, 1944 (CF)

League Club	Source	Date Signed	Seasons Played	Apps	Subs	Gls
Wolverhampton W.	Jnrs	05.61	62-64	5	-	2
Rotherham U.	Tr	12.64	64-67	108	0	46
Bristol C.	Tr	12.67	67-72	172	0	84
Nottingham F.	Tr	12.72	72-74	31	6	6
Peterborough U.	L	10.74	74	7	0	1
Hereford U.	Tr	12.74	74-76	77	3	10

GALLEY Keith John
Worksop, 17 October, 1955 (F)

League Club	Source	Date Signed	Seasons Played	Apps	Subs	Gls
Southport	Morecambe	12.75	75-76	50	10	11

GALLEY Maurice
Clowne, 10 August, 1934 (WH)

League Club	Source	Date Signed	Seasons Played	Apps	Subs	Gls
Chesterfield	Jnrs	07.52	54-58	55	-	5

GALLEY Thomas
Cannock, 4 August, 1915 EF Lge/E-2 (IF/WH)

League Club	Source	Date Signed	Seasons Played	Apps	Subs	Gls
Wolverhampton W.	Notts Co. (Am)	04.34	34-47	183	-	41
Grimsby T.	Tr	11.47	47-48	32	-	2

GALLIER William Henry
Cannock, 24 April, 1932 (LB)

League Club	Source	Date Signed	Seasons Played	Apps	Subs	Gls
West Bromwich A.	Beaudesert Sports	07.53				
Walsall	Tr	06.55	55	10	-	0

GALLIERS Steven
Preston, 21 August, 1957 (M)

League Club	Source	Date Signed	Seasons Played	Apps	Subs	Gls
Wimbledon	Chorley	06.77	77-81	148	7	10
Crystal Palace	Tr	10.81	81	8	5	0
Wimbledon	Tr	08.82	82-87	145	1	5
Bristol C.	L	02.87	86	9	0	0
Bristol C.	Tr	09.87	87-88	65	3	6
Maidstone U.	Tr	07.89	89	7	1	0

GALLIMORE Anthony Mark
Crewe, 21 February, 1972 (LB)

League Club	Source	Date Signed	Seasons Played	Apps	Subs	Gls
Stoke C.	YT	07.90	89-91	6	5	0
Carlisle U.	L	10.91	91	8	0	0
Carlisle U.	L	02.92	91	8	0	0
Carlisle U.	Tr	03.93	93-95	124	0	9
Grimsby T.	Tr	03.96	95-97	80	7	4

GALLIMORE Leonard
Northwich, 14 September, 1912 Died 1978 (FB)

League Club	Source	Date Signed	Seasons Played	Apps	Subs	Gls
Preston N. E.	Bainton Vic.	01.32	33-36	9	-	0
Watford	Tr	05.37	37-46	64	-	0

GALLOGLY Charles
Banbridge (NI), 16 June, 1925 NI-2 (FB)

League Club	Source	Date Signed	Seasons Played	Apps	Subs	Gls
Huddersfield T.	Glenavon	12.49	49-51	76	-	0
Watford	Tr	08.52	52-53	47	-	0
Bournemouth	Tr	07.54				

GALLON John William
Burradon (Nd), 12 February, 1914 Died 1993 (IF)

League Club	Source	Date Signed	Seasons Played	Apps	Subs	Gls
Bradford C.	Bedlington U.	06.36	36-37	20	-	5
Bradford P. A.	Tr	02.38	37-38	31	-	1
Swansea C.	Tr	06.39				
Gateshead	Tr	03.46	46	20	-	2

GALLOWAY John
Bo'ness, 29 October, 1918 (IF)

League Club	Source	Date Signed	Seasons Played	Apps	Subs	Gls
Chelsea	Glasgow Rangers	08.46	46-47	4	-	0

GALLOWAY Michael
Oswestry, 30 May, 1965 S Yth/Su21-2/S-1 (CD)

League Club	Source	Date Signed	Seasons Played	Apps	Subs	Gls
Mansfield T.	Berwick R.	09.83	83-85	39	15	3
Halifax T.	Tr	02.86	85-87	79	0	5
Leicester C. (L)	Glasgow Celtic	02.95	94	4	1	0

GALLOWAY Michael Anthony
Nottingham, 13 October, 1974 (M)

League Club	Source	Date Signed	Seasons Played	Apps	Subs	Gls
Notts Co.	YT	06.93	94-96	17	4	0
Gillingham	L	03.97	96-97	38	10	2

GALLOWAY Steven George
West Germany, 13 February, 1963 (F)

League Club	Source	Date Signed	Seasons Played	Apps	Subs	Gls
Crystal Palace	Sutton U.	10.84	84-85	3	2	1
Cambridge U.	L	03.86	85	0	1	0

GALVIN Anthony
Huddersfield, 12 July, 1956 IR-29 (LW)

League Club	Source	Date Signed	Seasons Played	Apps	Subs	Gls
Tottenham H.	Goole T.	01.78	78-86	194	7	20
Sheffield Wed.	Tr	08.87	87-88	21	15	1
Swindon T.	Tr	08.89	89	6	5	0

GALVIN Christopher
Huddersfield, 24 November, 1951 E Yth (M)

League Club	Source	Date Signed	Seasons Played	Apps	Subs	Gls
Leeds U.	App	11.68	69-72	7	1	0
Hull C.	Tr	08.73	73-78	132	11	11

League Club	Source	Date Signed	Seasons Played	Career Record Apps	Subs	Gls
York C.	L	12.76	76	22	0	6
Stockport Co.	Tr	04.79	78-80	67	1	3
GALVIN David						
Denaby, 5 October, 1946						(CD)
Wolverhampton W.	Jnrs	05.65	68	5	0	0
Gillingham	Tr	10.69	69-76	239	6	17
Wimbledon	Tr	08.77	77-78	73	0	7
GAMBARO Enzo						
Italy, 23 February, 1966						(M)
Grimsby T. (N/C)	A.C. Milan (It)	03.96	95	0	1	0
GAMBLE Bradley David						
Southwark, 4 February, 1975						(F)
Leyton Orient	YT	07.93	93	0	1	0
GAMBLE Francis						
Liverpool, 21 August, 1961						(W)
Derby Co.	Burscough	05.81	81-82	5	1	2
Rochdale (N/C)	Barrow	12.84	84-85	41	5	9
GAMBLE Simon **William**						
Cottam (Nts), 5 March, 1968						(F)
Lincoln C.	App	01.86	85-88	44	20	14
GAMBLIN Derek						
Havant, 7 April, 1943 E Amat						(FB)
Portsmouth (Am)	Sutton U.	07.65	65	1	0	0
GAMBRILL Brian Daniel						
Whitstable, 23 December, 1943						(G)
Millwall	Whitstable	12.65	65	1	0	0
GAME Kirk Michael						
Southend, 22 October, 1966						(D)
Colchester U.	Southend U. (App)	08.85	85-86	28	1	0
GAMMON Stephen George						
Swansea, 24 September, 1939 Wu23-2						(WH)
Cardiff C.	Jnrs	04.58	58-64	67	-	1
GANE Alan						
Chiswick, 11 June, 1950						(M)
Hereford U.	Slough T.	09.73	73	6	3	1
GANNON Edward						
Dublin, 3 January, 1921 Died 1989 IR-14						(WH)
Notts Co.	Shelbourne	08.46	46-48	107	-	2
Sheffield Wed.	Tr	03.49	48-54	204	-	4
GANNON James Paul						
Southwark, 7 September, 1968						(M/CD)
Sheffield U.	Dundalk	04.89				
Halifax T.	L	02.90	89	2	0	0
Stockport Co.	Tr	03.90	89-97	302	14	52
Notts Co.	L	01.94	93	2	0	0
GANNON John Spencer						
Wimbledon, 18 December, 1966						(M)
Wimbledon	App	12.84	85-87	13	3	2
Crewe Alex.	L	12.86	86	14	1	0
Sheffield U.	Tr	02.89	89-95	162	12	6
Middlesbrough	L	11.93	93	6	1	0
Oldham Ath.	Tr	03.96	95-96	6	0	0
GANNON Michael John						
Liverpool, 2 February, 1943						(D)
Everton	Jnrs	02.60	61	3	-	0
Scunthorpe U.	Tr	05.62	62-63	15	-	0
Crewe Alex.	Tr	10.64	64-69	206	4	2
GARBETT William **Edward**						
Dawley, 14 September, 1949						(W)
Shrewsbury T.	App	09.67	67-68	7	4	2
Barrow	Tr	07.69	69-71	119	0	27
Stockport Co.	Tr	07.72	72-73	63	7	11
GARBETT Terence Graham						
Lanchester, 9 September, 1945						(M)
Middlesbrough	Stockton	08.63	65	7	0	1
Watford	Tr	08.66	66-71	196	4	46
Blackburn Rov.	Tr	09.71	71-73	90	0	6
Sheffield U.	Tr	02.74	73-75	26	5	0
GARBUTT Eric **John** Edward						
Scarborough, 27 March, 1920 Died 1997						(G)
Newcastle U.	Billingham Synth.	01.39	46-49	52	-	0
GARBUTT Peter						
Corbridge, 28 December, 1939 E Amat						(CD)
Carlisle U.	Crook T.	08.64	64-70	133	2	12
GARBUTT Raymond Hardiman						
Middlesbrough, 9 May, 1925 Died 1994						(CF)
Manchester C.	South Bank	09.47				
Watford	Spennymoor U.	05.50	50	22	-	8
Brighton & H.A.	Tr	03.51	50-51	32	-	17
Workington	Tr	10.52	52	8	-	2
GARDE Rémi						
France, 3 April, 1966 French Int						(D/M)
Arsenal	Strasbourg (Fr)	08.96	96-97	13	8	0
GARDINER Douglas						
Douglas, 29 March, 1917						(WH)
Luton T.	Auchinleck Talbot	05.38	46-50	121	-	1
GARDINER John						
Chester-le-Street, 5 November, 1914						(IF)
Southend U. (Am)	Holfords	05.46	46	1	-	0
GARDINER Mark Christopher						
Cirencester, 25 December, 1966						(LB/W)
Swindon T.	App	09.84	83-86	7	3	1
Torquay U.	Tr	02.87	86-87	37	12	4
Crewe Alex.	Tr	08.88	88-94	179	14	35
Chester C.	L	03.95	94	2	1	0
Macclesfield T.	Frederikstad (Nor)	10.95	97	7	0	2
GARDINER Matthew						
Birmingham, 28 March, 1974						(FB)
Torquay U.	YT	07.92	92	5	2	0
GARDINER William Silcock						
Larbert, 15 August, 1929 S 'B'						(CF)
Leicester C.	Glasgow Rangers	08.55	55-57	69	-	48
Reading	Tr	11.58	58-59	8	-	2
GARDNER Charles Claridge						
Dundee, 17 March, 1925						(WH/IF)
Aldershot	St Mirren	08.50	50	6	-	0
GARDNER Charles **Donald**						
Jamaica (WI), 30 August, 1955						(M)
Wolverhampton W.	App	08.73	74	1	2	0
GARDNER Frederick Charles						
Foleshill, 4 June, 1922 Died 1979						(IF)
Birmingham C.		09.40				
Coventry C.	Tr	05.46	46-48	13	-	3
Newport Co.	Tr	05.49	49	4	-	2
GARDNER James						
Dunfermline, 27 September, 1967						(W)
Scarborough (N/C)	St Mirren	08.95	95	5	1	1
Cardiff C.	Tr	09.95	95-96	51	12	5
Exeter C.	Tr	07.97	97	19	4	1
GARDNER Lee						
Ayr, 11 July, 1970						(M)
Oxford U. (L)	Aberdeen	03.91	90	2	5	0
GARDNER Paul Anthony						
Southport, 22 September, 1957						(RB)
Blackpool	App	09.75	76-81	149	3	1
Bury	Tr	08.82	82-83	90	0	0
Swansea C. (N/C)	Tr	10.84	84	4	0	0
Wigan Ath. (N/C)	Preston N.E. (N/C)	01.85	84	5	0	0
GARDNER Stephen David						
Barnsley, 7 October, 1958 E Sch						(M)
Ipswich T.	App	10.75				
Oldham Ath.	Tr	12.77	77-80	41	12	2
GARDNER Stephen George						
Middlesbrough, 3 July, 1968						(CD)
Manchester U.	App	07.86				
Burnley	Tr	07.87	87-89	93	2	0
Bradford C.	Glossop N.E.	08.91	91	14	0	0
Bury		10.92	92	1	0	0
GARDNER Thomas						
Liverpool, 17 March, 1923						(OR)
Liverpool	South Liverpool	10.46				
Everton	Tr	06.47	47	1	-	0

GARDNER Thomas
Huyton, 28 May, 1910 Died 1970 E-2 (WH)

League Club	Source	Date Signed	Seasons Played	Apps	Subs	Gls
Liverpool	Orrell	04.29	29	5	-	0
Grimsby T.	Tr	06.31	31	13	-	0
Hull C.	Tr	05.32	32-33	66	-	2
Aston Villa	Tr	02.34	33-37	77	-	1
Burnley	Tr	04.38	38	39	-	3
Wrexham	Tr	12.45	46	33	-	4

GARGAN John
York, 6 June, 1928 (WH)

League Club	Source	Date Signed	Seasons Played	Apps	Subs	Gls
York C.	Cliftonville	08.45	46	1	-	0

GARIANI Moshe
Israel, 18 June, 1957 Israeli Int (M)

League Club	Source	Date Signed	Seasons Played	Apps	Subs	Gls
Brighton & H.A.	Macabbi Netanya (Isr)	06.80	80	0	1	0

GARLAND Christopher Stephen
Bristol, 24 April, 1949 Eu23-1 (F)

League Club	Source	Date Signed	Seasons Played	Apps	Subs	Gls
Bristol C.	App	05.66	66-71	142	1	31
Chelsea	Tr	09.71	71-74	89	3	22
Leicester C.	Tr	02.75	74-76	52	3	15
Bristol C.	Tr	12.76	76-82	53	11	11

GARLAND David
Grimsby, 18 June, 1948 (F)

League Club	Source	Date Signed	Seasons Played	Apps	Subs	Gls
Grimsby T.	Jnrs	07.65	65	2	0	0
Scunthorpe U.	Tr	07.67				

GARLAND Peter John
Croydon, 20 January, 1971 E Yth (M)

League Club	Source	Date Signed	Seasons Played	Apps	Subs	Gls
Tottenham H.	YT	07.89	90	0	1	0
Newcastle U.	Tr	03.92	91	0	2	0
Charlton Ath.	Tr	12.92	92-95	40	13	2
Wycombe W.	L	03.95	94	5	0	0
Leyton Orient	Tr	07.96	96	13	8	0

GARLAND Ronald
Middlesbrough, 28 July, 1931 Died 1989 (CF)

League Club	Source	Date Signed	Seasons Played	Apps	Subs	Gls
Oldham Ath.	South Bank St Peter	12.51	54-55	9	-	3

GARNER Alan Henry
Lambeth, 2 February, 1951 (CD)

League Club	Source	Date Signed	Seasons Played	Apps	Subs	Gls
Millwall	App	02.69	70	2	0	0
Luton T.	Tr	07.71	71-74	88	0	3
Watford	Tr	02.75	74-79	200	0	15
Portsmouth	Tr	02.80	79-81	36	0	2

GARNER Andrew
Stonebroom Dby), 8 March, 1966 (F/M)

League Club	Source	Date Signed	Seasons Played	Apps	Subs	Gls
Derby Co.	App	12.83	83-87	48	23	17
Blackpool	Tr	08.88	88-92	151	8	37

GARNER Darren John
Plymouth, 10 December, 1971 (M)

League Club	Source	Date Signed	Seasons Played	Apps	Subs	Gls
Plymouth Arg.	YT	03.89	88-92	22	5	1
Rotherham U.	Dorchester T.	06.95	95-97	98	3	6

GARNER Paul
Doncaster, 1 December, 1955 E Yth (LB)

League Club	Source	Date Signed	Seasons Played	Apps	Subs	Gls
Huddersfield T.	App	12.72	72-75	96	0	2
Sheffield U.	Tr	11.75	75-83	248	3	7
Gillingham	L	09.83	83	5	0	0
Mansfield T.	Tr	09.84	84-88	102	9	8

GARNER Simon
Boston, 23 November, 1959 (F)

League Club	Source	Date Signed	Seasons Played	Apps	Subs	Gls
Blackburn Rov.	App	07.78	78-91	455	29	168
West Bromwich A.	Tr	08.92	92-93	25	8	8
Wycombe W.	Tr	02.94	93-95	53	13	15
Torquay U.	L	01.96	95	10	1	1

GARNER Timothy
Hitchin, 30 March, 1961 (G)

League Club	Source	Date Signed	Seasons Played	Apps	Subs	Gls
Northampton T. (N/C)	Kidderminster Hrs	03.86	85	2	0	0

GARNER William
Stirling, 24 July, 1955 (CD)

League Club	Source	Date Signed	Seasons Played	Apps	Subs	Gls
Rochdale (L)	Alloa Ath.	10.82	82	4	0	0

GARNER William David
Leicester, 14 December, 1947 (F)

League Club	Source	Date Signed	Seasons Played	Apps	Subs	Gls
Notts Co.	Jnrs	07.66	66	2	0	0
Southend U.	Bedford T.	11.69	69-72	101	1	41
Chelsea	Tr	09.72	72-78	94	11	31
Cambridge U.	Tr	11.78	78-79	17	7	3
Brentford (N/C)	Chelmsford C.	08.83	83	2	1	1

GARNETT Malcolm John
Wickersley, 8 September, 1943 (CH)

League Club	Source	Date Signed	Seasons Played	Apps	Subs	Gls
Doncaster Rov.	Jnrs	07.61	61	1	-	0

GARNETT Shaun Maurice
Wallasey, 22 November, 1969 (CD)

League Club	Source	Date Signed	Seasons Played	Apps	Subs	Gls
Tranmere Rov.	YT	06.88	87-95	110	2	5
Chester C.	L	10.92	92	9	0	0
Preston N.E.	L	12.92	92	10	0	2
Wigan Ath.	L	02.93	92	13	0	1
Swansea C.	Tr	03.96	95-96	15	0	0
Oldham Ath.	Tr	09.96	96-97	54	3	4

GARNEYS Thomas Thurston
West Ham, 25 August, 1923 (CF)

League Club	Source	Date Signed	Seasons Played	Apps	Subs	Gls
Notts Co.	Leytonstone	08.48				
Brentford	Chingford T.	12.49	49-50	12	-	2
Ipswich T.	Tr	05.51	51-58	248	-	123

GARNHAM Stuart Edward
Selby, 30 November, 1955 (G)

League Club	Source	Date Signed	Seasons Played	Apps	Subs	Gls
Wolverhampton W.	App	12.73				
Northampton T.	L	09.74	74	1	0	0
Peterborough U.	Tr	03.77	76	2	0	0
Northampton T.	L	\`08.77	77	11	0	0

GARRATT Geoffrey
Whitehaven, 2 February, 1930 (OL)

League Club	Source	Date Signed	Seasons Played	Apps	Subs	Gls
Barrow	Barrow Social	09.51	52	2	-	0
Workington	Tr	08.53	53	2	-	0

GARRETT Archibald Campbell
Lesmahagow, 17 June, 1919 Died 1994 (CF)

League Club	Source	Date Signed	Seasons Played	Apps	Subs	Gls
Preston N. E.	Hearts	12.38	38	2	-	2
Northampton T.	Hearts	09.46	46-47	51	-	35
Birmingham C.	Tr	12.47	47-48	18	-	5
Northampton T.	Tr	12.48	48-50	43	-	15

GARRETT James Edward
Dumfries, 15 March, 1939 (W)

League Club	Source	Date Signed	Seasons Played	Apps	Subs	Gls
Carlisle U.	Queen of South	08.63	63	1	-	0

GARRETT Leonard George
Hackney, 14 May, 1936 E Yth (FB)

League Club	Source	Date Signed	Seasons Played	Apps	Subs	Gls
Arsenal	Eton Manor	05.54				
Ipswich T.	Tr	05.58	58	1	-	0

GARRETT Scott
Gateshead, 9 January, 1974 (RB)

League Club	Source	Date Signed	Seasons Played	Apps	Subs	Gls
Hartlepool U.	YT	05.92	93-94	14	1	0

GARRETT Thomas
South Shields, 28 February, 1926 EF Lge/E-3 (FB)

League Club	Source	Date Signed	Seasons Played	Apps	Subs	Gls
Blackpool	Horden Colly	10.44	46-60	308	-	3
Millwall	Tr	05.61	61	12	-	0

GARRITY Kenneth
Blackburn, 6 August, 1935 (F)

League Club	Source	Date Signed	Seasons Played	Apps	Subs	Gls
Accrington St.		02.56	58-59	37	-	5

GARROW Herbert Alexander
Elgin, 24 January, 1942 (G)

League Club	Source	Date Signed	Seasons Played	Apps	Subs	Gls
Newcastle U.	Fochabers	02.60	60-62	4	-	0

GARTH James Russell
Glasgow, 1 May, 1922 Died 1968 (F)

League Club	Source	Date Signed	Seasons Played	Apps	Subs	Gls
Preston N.E.	Morton	11.46	46-47	23	-	7

GARTLAND Paul
Shipley, 8 February, 1959 (FB)

League Club	Source	Date Signed	Seasons Played	Apps	Subs	Gls
Huddersfield T.	App	02.77	76-78	8	0	0

GARTON William Francis
Salford, 15 March, 1965 (CD)

League Club	Source	Date Signed	Seasons Played	Apps	Subs	Gls
Manchester U.	App	03.83	84-88	39	2	0
Birmingham C.	L	03.86	85	5	0	0

GARVEY Brian
Hull, 3 July, 1937 (D)

League Club	Source	Date Signed	Seasons Played	Apps	Subs	Gls
Hull C.	Jnrs	01.58	57-64	232	-	3
Watford	Tr	07.65	65-69	179	1	2
Colchester U.	Tr	06.70	70-71	75	2	1

GARVEY James
Motherwell, 4 June, 1919 (WH)

League Club	Source	Date Signed	Seasons Played	Apps	Subs	Gls
Northampton T.	Corby T.	05.39				
Leicester C.	Tr	06.46	46-48	15	-	0

GARVEY Stephen Hugh
Stalybridge, 22 November, 1973 (W)

League Club	Source	Date Signed	Seasons Played	Apps	Subs	Gls
Crewe Alex.	YT	10.91	90-97	68	40	8
Chesterfield	L	10.97	97	2	1	0

GARVIE John
Bellshill, 16 October, 1927 Died 1996 (CF)

League Club	Source	Date Signed	Seasons Played	Apps	Subs	Gls
Preston N. E.	Hibernian	08.49	49	5	-	0
Lincoln C.	Tr	08.50	50-55	183	-	73
Carlisle U.	Tr	05.56	56	25	-	6

GARWOOD Colin Arthur
Heacham (Nfk), 29 June, 1949 E Yth (F)

League Club	Source	Date Signed	Seasons Played	Apps	Subs	Gls
Peterborough U.	Jnrs	07.67	67-70	58	8	30
Oldham Ath.	Tr	07.71	71-74	84	9	35
Huddersfield T.	Tr	12.74	74-75	22	6	8
Colchester U.	Tr	02.76	75-77	83	4	25
Portsmouth	Tr	03.78	77-79	62	9	34
Aldershot	Tr	02.80	79-81	79	2	25

GARWOOD Jason
Birmingham, 23 March, 1969 (W)

League Club	Source	Date Signed	Seasons Played	Apps	Subs	Gls
Leicester C.	App	03.87				
Northampton T.	L	09.88	88	5	1	0

GARWOOD Leonard Frank
India, 28 July, 1923 Died 1979 (WH)

League Club	Source	Date Signed	Seasons Played	Apps	Subs	Gls
Tottenham H.	Hitchin T.	05.46	48	2	-	0

GASCOIGNE Paul John
Gateshead, 27 May, 1967 E Yth/Eu21-13/E 'B'/E-57 (M)

League Club	Source	Date Signed	Seasons Played	Apps	Subs	Gls
Newcastle U.	App	05.85	84-87	83	9	21
Tottenham H.	Tr	07.88	88-90	91	1	19
Middlesbrough	Glasgow Rangers	03.98	97	7	0	0

GASKELL Alec
Leigh, 30 July, 1932 (CF)

League Club	Source	Date Signed	Seasons Played	Apps	Subs	Gls
Southport	Manchester U. (Am)	11.52	51-53	44	-	18
Newcastle U.	Tr	10.53	53	1	-	0
Mansfield T.	Tr	06.54	54-55	42	-	17
Tranmere Rov.	Tr	06.57	57	6	-	6

GASKELL John **David**
Wigan, 5 October, 1940 E Sch/E Yth (G)

League Club	Source	Date Signed	Seasons Played	Apps	Subs	Gls
Manchester U.	Jnrs	10.57	57-66	96	0	0
Wrexham	Wigan Ath.	06.69	69-71	95	0	0

GASKELL Edward
Bridbury, 19 December, 1916 (G)

League Club	Source	Date Signed	Seasons Played	Apps	Subs	Gls
Brentford		05.38	47-51	34	-	0

GASKELL Ronald
Worsley, 1 March, 1926 (WH)

League Club	Source	Date Signed	Seasons Played	Apps	Subs	Gls
Southport	Walkden Yard	05.50	49-50	2	-	0

GASTON Raymond
Belfast, 22 December, 1946 NIu23-1/NI-1 (CF)

League Club	Source	Date Signed	Seasons Played	Apps	Subs	Gls
Wolverhampton W.	Coleraine	05.65				
Oxford U.	Coleraine	09.68	68	12	0	2
Lincoln C.	L	02.70	69	4	0	1

GATE Kenneth Bruce
Hartlepool, 26 October, 1948 (FB)

League Club	Source	Date Signed	Seasons Played	Apps	Subs	Gls
Hartlepool U. (Am)	St Josephs	08.68	68	1	0	0

GATER Roy
Stoke, 22 June, 1940 (CH)

League Club	Source	Date Signed	Seasons Played	Apps	Subs	Gls
Port Vale	Jnrs	04.60	60-61	5	-	0
Bournemouth	Tr	07.62	62-68	216	0	3
Crewe Alex.	Tr	01.69	68-72	156	0	5

GATES Eric Lazenby
Ferryhill, 28 June, 1955 E-2 (F)

League Club	Source	Date Signed	Seasons Played	Apps	Subs	Gls
Ipswich T.	App	10.72	73-84	267	29	73
Sunderland	Tr	08.85	85-89	163	18	43
Carlisle U.	Tr	06.90	90	33	5	8

GATES William Lazenby
Ferryhill, 8 May, 1944 E Yth (CH)

League Club	Source	Date Signed	Seasons Played	Apps	Subs	Gls
Middlesbrough	Jnrs	10.61	61-73	277	6	12

GATTING Stephen Paul
Willesden, 29 May, 1959 (CD)

League Club	Source	Date Signed	Seasons Played	Apps	Subs	Gls
Arsenal	App	03.77	78-80	50	8	5
Brighton & H. A.	Tr	09.81	81-90	313	3	19
Charlton Ath.	Tr	08.91	91-92	61	3	3

GAUDEN Allan
Ashington, 20 November, 1944 (W)

League Club	Source	Date Signed	Seasons Played	Apps	Subs	Gls
Sunderland	Jnrs	03.62	65-67	40	4	6
Darlington	Tr	10.68	68-71	125	3	39
Grimsby T.	Tr	02.72	71-72	54	1	12
Hartlepool U.	Tr	08.73	73-74	63	0	15
Gillingham	Tr	12.74	74-75	41	0	3

GAUDINO Maurizio
Germany, 12 December, 1966 German Int (M)

League Club	Source	Date Signed	Seasons Played	Apps	Subs	Gls
Manchester C. (L)	Eintracht Frankfurt (Ger)	12.94	94	17	3	3

GAUGHAN Steven Edward
Doncaster, 14 April, 1970 (M/FB)

League Club	Source	Date Signed	Seasons Played	Apps	Subs	Gls
Doncaster Rov.	Hatfield Main	01.88	87-89	42	25	3
Sunderland	Tr	06.90				
Darlington	Tr	01.92	91-95	159	12	15
Chesterfield	Tr	08.96	96-97	16	4	0
Darlington	Tr	11.97	97	23	1	1

GAULD James
Aberdeen, 9 May, 1929 (IF)

League Club	Source	Date Signed	Seasons Played	Apps	Subs	Gls
Charlton Ath.	Waterford	05.55	55-56	47	-	21
Everton	Tr	10.56	56	23	-	7
Plymouth Arg.	Tr	10.57	57-58	64	-	25
Swindon T.	Tr	08.59	59	40	-	14
Mansfield T.	St Johnstone	11.60	60	4	-	3

GAVAN John Thomas
Walsall, 8 December, 1939 (G)

League Club	Source	Date Signed	Seasons Played	Apps	Subs	Gls
Aston Villa	Walsall Wood	11.62	62-65	9	0	0
Doncaster Rov.	Tr	07.67	67-68	21	0	0

GAVIN John Thomas
Limerick (Ire), 20 April, 1928 IR-7 (OR)

League Club	Source	Date Signed	Seasons Played	Apps	Subs	Gls
Norwich C.	Limerick	08.48	48-54	203	-	76
Tottenham H.	Tr	10.54	54-55	32	-	15
Norwich C.	Tr	11.55	55-57	109	-	46
Watford	Tr	07.58	58	43	-	12
Crystal Palace	Tr	05.59	59-60	66	-	15

GAVIN Mark Wilson
Baillieston, 10 December, 1963 (W)

League Club	Source	Date Signed	Seasons Played	Apps	Subs	Gls
Leeds U.	App	12.81	82-84	20	10	3
Hartlepool U.	L	03.85	84	7	0	0
Carlisle U.	Tr	07.85	85	12	1	1
Bolton W.	Tr	03.86	85-86	48	1	3
Rochdale	Tr	08.87	87	23	0	6
Bristol C.	Hearts	10.88	88-89	62	7	6
Watford	Tr	08.90	90	8	5	0
Bristol C.	Tr	12.91	91-93	34	7	2
Exeter C.	Tr	02.94	93-95	73	4	4
Scunthorpe U.	Tr	08.96	96	10	1	0
Hartlepool U.	Tr	09.97	97	0	3	0

GAVIN Patrick John
Hammersmith, 5 June, 1967 (F)

League Club	Source	Date Signed	Seasons Played	Apps	Subs	Gls
Gillingham	Hanwell T.	03.89	88	13	0	7
Leicester C.	Tr	06.89	90	1	2	0
Gillingham	L	09.89	89	18	16	1
Peterborough U.	Tr	03.91	90-92	18	5	5
Northampton T. (N/C)	Barnet (N/C)	02.93	92	13	1	4
Wigan Ath.	Tr	07.93	93-94	37	5	8

GAVIN Patrick Joseph
Drogheda (Ire), 6 June, 1929 IR 'B'/LoI (FB)

League Club	Source	Date Signed	Seasons Played	Apps	Subs	Gls
Doncaster Rov.	Dundalk	06.53	53-59	145	-	6

GAWLER Ronald Victor
Canterbury, 10 July, 1924 (WH)

League Club	Source	Date Signed	Seasons Played	Apps	Subs	Gls
Southend U.	Canterbury C.	06.49	49-50	8	-	1

GAY Geoffrey
Romford, 4 February, 1957 (M)

League Club	Source	Date Signed	Seasons Played	Apps	Subs	Gls
Bolton W.	App	01.75				
Exeter C.	L	03.77	76	5	1	0
Southport	Tr	08.77	77	40	0	5
Wigan Ath.	Tr	07.78	78	1	0	0

GAYLE Andrew Keith
Manchester, 17 September, 1970 (W)

League Club	Source	Date Signed	Seasons Played	Apps	Subs	Gls
Oldham Ath.	YT	07.89	88	0	1	0
Crewe Alex.	Tr	02.90	89	0	1	0
Bury	Tr	08.90				

GAYLE Brian Wilbert
Kingston, 6 March, 1965 (CD)

League Club	Source	Date Signed	Seasons Played	Apps	Subs	Gls
Wimbledon	App	11.82	84-87	76	7	3
Manchester C.	Tr	07.88	88-89	55	0	3
Ipswich T.	Tr	01.90	89-91	58	0	4
Sheffield U.	Tr	09.91	91-95	115	2	9
Exeter C.	Tr	08.96	96	10	0	0

League Club	Source	Date Signed	Seasons Played	Career Record Apps	Subs	Gls
Rotherham U.	Tr	10.96	96	19	1	0
Bristol Rov.	Tr	03.97	96-97	23	0	0
Shrewsbury T.	Tr	12.97	97	23	0	0
GAYLE Howard Anthony						
Liverpool, 18 May, 1958 Eu21-3						(W)
Liverpool	Jnrs	11.77	80	3	1	1
Fulham	L	01.80	79	14	0	0
Newcastle U.	L	11.82	82	8	0	2
Birmingham C.	Tr	01.83	82-83	45	1	9
Sunderland	Tr	08.84	84-85	39	9	4
Stoke C.	Dallas (USA)	03.87	86	4	2	2
Blackburn Rov.	Tr	07.87	87-91	97	19	29
Halifax T. (N/C)	Tr	08.92	92	2	3	0
GAYLE John						
Bromsgrove, 30 July, 1964						(F)
Wimbledon	Burton A.	03.89	88-90	17	3	2
Birmingham C.	Tr	11.90	90-92	39	5	10
Walsall	L	08.93	93	4	0	1
Coventry C.	Tr	09.93	93	3	0	0
Burnley	Tr	08.94	94	7	7	3
Stoke C.	Tr	01.95	94-96	14	12	4
Gillingham	L	03.96	95	9	0	3
Northampton T.	Tr	02.97	96-97	35	13	7
GAYLE Marcus Anthony						
Hammersmith, 27 September, 1970 E Yth/Jamaican Int						(W/F)
Brentford	YT	07.89	88-93	118	38	22
Wimbledon	Tr	03.94	93-97	108	25	17
GAYLE Mark Samuel Roye						
Bromsgrove, 21 October, 1969						(G)
Leicester C.	YT	07.88				
Blackpool	Tr	07.89				
Walsall	Worcester C.	06.91	91-93	74	1	0
Crewe Alex.	Tr	12.93	93-96	82	1	0
Chesterfield	L	10.97	97	5	0	0
GAYNOR James Michael						
Dublin, 22 August, 1928 LoI						(OR)
Ipswich T.	Shamrock Rov.	03.52	51-52	47	-	3
Aldershot	Tr	09.53	53-57	165	-	39
GAYNOR Leonard Alfred						
Greasley, 22 September, 1925						(IF)
Hull C.	Eastwood Colly	04.48	50	2	-	0
Bournemouth	Tr	06.51	51-53	51	-	12
Southampton	Tr	03.54	53	12	-	1
Aldershot	Tr	02.55	54-56	62	-	9
Oldham Ath.	Tr	07.57	57	5	-	0
GAYNOR Thomas						
Limerick, 29 January, 1963						(F)
Doncaster Rov.	Limerick	12.86	86-87	28	5	7
Nottingham F.	Tr	10.87	87-91	43	14	10
Newcastle U.	L	11.90	90	4	0	1
Millwall	Tr	03.93	92	0	3	0
GAZZARD Gerald						
Westbury, 15 March, 1925						(IF)
West Ham U.	Penzance	05.49	49-53	119	-	29
Brentford	Tr	01.54	53	13	-	6
GEARD Leonard						
Hammersmith, 12 February, 1934						(WH)
Fulham	Jnrs	05.51				
Brentford	Tr	03.53	54-55	4	-	0
GEBBIE Robert (Bert) Brown Robertson						
Cambuslang, 18 November, 1934						(G)
Bradford P. A.	Queen of South	07.60	60-63	112	-	0
GEDDES Andrew						
Motherwell, 6 September, 1922 Died 1958						(WH)
Bradford C.	Kilmarnock	06.49	49-50	30	-	4
Mansfield T.	Tr	08.51	51	11	-	2
Halifax T.	Tr	07.52	52-54	50	-	4
GEDDES Gavin John						
Brighton, 7 October, 1972						(W)
Brighton & H.A.	Wick	07.93	93	7	5	1
GEDDES James George						
Burntisland, 25 May, 1942						(WH)
Bradford P. A.	Third Lanark	08.65	65	1	0	0
GEDDES Paul						
Paisley, 19 April, 1961						(M)
Leicester C.	Kilbirnie Ladeside	04.79				
Wimbledon (N/C)	Hibernian	11.81	81	2	0	0

League Club	Source	Date Signed	Seasons Played	Career Record Apps	Subs	Gls
GEDDIS David						
Carlisle, 12 March, 1958 E Yth						(F)
Ipswich T.	App	08.75	76-78	26	17	5
Luton T.	L	02.77	76	9	4	4
Aston Villa	Tr	09.79	79-82	43	4	12
Luton T.	L	12.82	82	4	0	0
Barnsley	Tr	09.83	83-84	45	0	24
Birmingham C.	Tr	12.84	84-86	45	1	18
Brentford	L	11.86	86	4	0	0
Shrewsbury T.	Tr	02.87	86-88	36	3	11
Swindon T.	Tr	10.88	88	8	2	3
Darlington	Tr	03.90	90	2	11	0
GEDNEY Christopher						
Boston, 1 September, 1945						(IF)
Lincoln C. (Am)	Jnrs	05.62	62-65	9	0	1
GEE Alan						
Chesterfield, 16 March, 1932						(OL)
Rotherham U. (Am)		08.52	52	2	-	0
GEE James Percival						
Plymouth, 6 June, 1932						(G)
Plymouth Arg. (Am)	Launceston T.	08.56	56	1	-	0
GEE Philip John						
Pelsall, 19 December, 1964						(F)
Derby Co.	Gresley Rov.	09.85	85-91	107	17	26
Leicester C.	Tr	03.92	91-95	35	18	9
Plymouth Arg.	L	01.95	94	6	0	0
GEIDMINTIS Anthony Joseph						
Stepney, 30 July, 1949 Died 1993						(D)
Workington	App	08.66	64-75	323	5	37
Watford	Tr	07.76	76-77	48	1	0
Northampton T.	Tr	02.78	77-78	63	0	1
Halifax T.	Tr	07.79	79	10	2	0
GELDARD Albert						
Bradford, 11 April, 1914 Died 1989 E Sch/EF Lge/E-4						(OR)
Bradford P. A.	Jnrs	09.29	29-32	34	-	1
Everton	Tr	11.32	32-37	167	-	31
Bolton W.	Tr	06.38	38-46	29	-	1
GELSON Peter William John						
Hammersmith, 18 October, 1941						(CH)
Brentford	Jnrs	03.60	61-74	468	3	17
GEMMELL Andrew						
Greenock, 27 July, 1945						(W)
Bradford C.	Morton	01.67	66	3	0	0
GEMMELL Eric						
Manchester, 7 April, 1921						(CF)
Manchester C.	Manchester U. (Am)	03.46				
Oldham Ath.	Tr	06.47	47-53	195	-	109
Crewe Alex.	Tr	02.54	53-54	15	-	5
Rochdale	Tr	09.54	54-55	65	-	32
GEMMELL James						
Sunderland, 17 November, 1911 Died 1992						(FB)
Bury	West Stanley	03.30	30-38	257	-	0
Southport	Tr	08.45	46	25	-	0
GEMMELL Matthew						
Glasgow, 10 March, 1931						(IF)
Portsmouth	Shawfield Jnrs	09.51	53-54	3	-	0
Swindon T.	Tr	10.54	54	8	-	2
GEMMELL Thomas						
Glasgow, 16 October, 1943 SF Lge/S-18						(FB)
Nottingham F.	Glasgow Celtic	12.71	71-72	39	0	6
GEMMILL Archibald						
Paisley, 24 March, 1947 Su23-1/S-43						(M)
Preston N. E.	St Mirren	06.67	67-70	93	6	13
Derby Co.	Tr	09.70	70-77	261	0	17
Nottingham F.	Tr	09.77	77-78	56	2	4
Birmingham C.	Tr	08.79	79-81	97	0	12
Wigan Ath. (N/C)	Jacksonville (USA)	09.82	82	11	0	0
Derby Co.	Tr	11.82	82-83	63	0	8
GEMMILL Scot						
Paisley, 2 January, 1971 Su21-4/S 'B'/S-13						(M)
Nottingham F.	YT	01.90	90-97	210	15	21
GENAUX Regis Herve						
Belgium, 31 August, 1973 Belgian Int						(FB)
Coventry C.	Standard Liege (Bel)	08.96	96	3	1	0

League Club	Source	Date Signed	Seasons Played	Career Record Apps	Subs	Gls

GENDALL Richard Martin
Wrexham, 25 September, 1960 (M)

Chester C.	App	09.78	80	4	1	0

GENNOE Terence William
Shrewsbury, 16 March, 1953 (G)

Bury	Bricklayer Sports	06.73	72-73	3	0	0
Halifax T.	Tr	05.75	75-77	78	0	0
Southampton	Tr	02.78	78-79	36	0	0
Crystal Palace	L	01.81	80	3	0	0
Blackburn Rov.	Tr	08.81	81-90	289	0	0

GENOVESE Domenico
Peterborough, 2 February, 1961 (F)

Peterborough U.	Cambridge C.	03.88	87-88	8	8	1

GENTLE Justin
Enfield, 6 June, 1974 (F)

Luton T.	Boreham Wood	07.93				
Colchester U.	Tr	03.94	93	0	2	0

GEORGE Charles Frederick
Islington, 10 October, 1950 Eu23-5/E-1 (F)

Arsenal	App	03.68	69-74	113	20	31
Derby Co.	Tr	07.75	75-78	106	0	34
Southampton	Tr	12.78	78-80	44	0	11
Nottingham F.	L	01.80	79	2	0	0
Bournemouth	Bulova (HK)	03.82	81	2	0	0
Derby Co.	Tr	03.82	81	11	0	2

GEORGE Daniel Stephen
Lincoln, 22 October, 1978 (D)

Nottingham F.	YT	10.95				
Doncaster Rov.	Tr	01.98	97	16	2	1

GEORGE Frank Richard
Stepney, 20 November, 1933 (G)

Leyton Orient	Carshalton Ath.	07.54	56-62	119	-	0
Watford	Tr	07.63	64	10	-	0

GEORGE Liam Brendan
Luton, 2 February, 1979 IR Yth (F)

Luton T.	YT	01.97	97	1	0	0

GEORGE Richard (Ricki) Stuart
Barnet, 28 June, 1946 (W)

Tottenham H.	App	10.63				
Watford	Tr	08.64	64	4	-	0
Bournemouth	Tr	05.65	65	2	1	0
Oxford U.	Tr	07.66	66	6	0	0

GEORGE Ronald Anthony
Bristol, 14 August, 1922 Died 1989 (FB)

Crystal Palace	Bristol Aero.	02.47	48-53	122	-	2
Colchester U.	Tr	07.54	54	5	-	0

GEORGESON Roderick Bruce
Egypt, 31 July, 1948 (CF)

Port Vale	Bo'ness U.	01.66	65-66	26	1	6

GEORGIOU George Jordaris
Camden, 19 August, 1972 (F)

Fulham	Wembley	08.91	91	1	3	0

GERHARDI Hugh
South Africa, 5 May, 1933 (IF)

Liverpool	Thistle (SA)	08.52	52	6	-	0

GERMAINE Gary
Birmingham, 2 August, 1976 Su21-1 (G)

West Bromwich A.	YT	07.94				
Scunthorpe U.	L	03.96	95	11	0	0
Shrewsbury T.	L	01.98	97	1	0	0

GERMAN David
Sheffield, 16 October, 1973 (RB)

Halifax T.	YT	07.92	90-92	30	9	2

GERNON Frederick (Irvin) Anthony John
Birmingham, 30 December, 1962 E Yth /Eu21-1 (D)

Ipswich T.	App	01.80	81-86	76	0	0
Northampton T.	L	11.86	86	9	0	0
Gillingham	Tr	03.87	86-87	33	2	1
Reading	Tr	09.88	88-89	21	4	0
Northampton T.	Tr	10.89	89-91	47	1	1

GERRARD Paul William
Heywood, 22 January, 1973 Eu21-18 (G)

Oldham Ath.	YT	11.91	92-95	118	1	0
Everton	Tr	07.96	96-97	8	1	0

GERRIE Sydney
Aberdeen, 14 June, 1927 (IF)

Hull C.	Dundee	11.50	50-56	146	-	59

GERULA Stanislaw (Stan) Eugeniusz
Poland, 21 February, 1914 Died 1979 Polish Amat Int (G)

Leyton Orient (Am)	Carpathians (Pol)	05.48	48-49	30	-	0

GHAZGHAZI Sufyan
Honiton, 24 August, 1977 E Sch/E Yth (F)

Exeter C.	YT	07.96	96-97	2	13	0

GIALLANZA Gaetano
Dornach, Switzerland, 6 June, 1974 (F)

Bolton W. (L)	Nantes (Fr)	03.98	97	0	3	0

GIAMATTEI Aaron Pietro
Reading, 11 October, 1973 (M)

Reading	YT	07.92	91	0	2	0

GIBB Alistair Stuart
Salisbury, 17 February, 1976 (M)

Norwich C.	YT	07.94				
Northampton T.	L	09.95	95	9	0	1
Northampton T.	Tr	02.96	95-97	15	52	3

GIBB James **Barry**
Workington, 21 May, 1940 (WH)

Workington	Jnrs	07.60	59-60	6	-	0

GIBB Dean Alan
Newcastle, 26 October, 1966 (M)

Hartlepool U.	Brandon U.	07.86	86-87	32	16	3

GIBB Thomas
Bathgate, 13 December, 1944 Su23-1 (M)

Newcastle U.	Partick Thistle	08.68	68-74	190	9	12
Sunderland	Tr	06.75	75-76	7	3	1
Hartlepool U.	Tr	07.77	77	40	0	4

GIBBENS Kevin
Southampton, 4 November, 1979 (M)

Southampton	YT	01.98	97	2	0	0

GIBBINS Edward
Shoreditch, 24 March, 1926 (CH)

Tottenham H.	Jnrs	09.46	52	1	-	0

GIBBINS Roger Graeme
Enfield, 6 September, 1955 E Sch (M/CD)

Tottenham H.	App	12.72				
Oxford U.	Tr	08.75	75	16	3	2
Norwich C.	Tr	06.76	76-77	47	1	12
Cambridge U.	New England (USA)	09.79	79-81	97	3	12
Cardiff C.	Tr	08.82	82-85	135	4	17
Swansea C.	Tr	10.85	85	35	0	6
Newport Co.	Tr	08.86	86-87	79	0	8
Torquay U.	Tr	03.88	87-88	32	1	5
Cardiff C.	Newport Co.	03.89	88-92	132	10	7

GIBBON Malcolm
North Shields, 24 October, 1950 (WH)

Port Vale	App	•	66-67	4	1	0

GIBBONS Albert (Jack) Henry
Fulham, 10 April, 1914 E Amat (CF)

Tottenham H. (Am)	Kingstonian	07.37	37	27	-	13
Brentford (Am)	Tr	08.38	38	12	-	1
Bradford P. A.	Tottenham H. (Am)	05.46	46	42	-	21
Brentford	Tr	08.47	47-48	56	-	16

GIBBONS Arthur Thomas
Greatham, 24 May, 1937 (HB)

Hartlepool U.		09.58	58	13	-	0

GIBBONS David
Belfast, 4 November, 1952 (FB)

Manchester C.	App	08.70				
Stockport Co.	L	02.72	71	1	0	0

GIBBONS Ian Kenneth
Stoke, 8 February, 1970 (RW)

Stoke C.	YT	•	87	0	1	0

GIBBONS John Ronald
Charlton, 8 April, 1925 (CF)

Queens Park R.	Dartford	12.47	48	8	-	2
Ipswich T.	Tr	05.49	49	11	-	3
Tottenham H.	Tr	03.50				

GIBBONS Leonard
Wirral, 27 November, 1930 (FB)

League Club	Source	Date Signed	Seasons Played	Apps	Subs	Gls
Wolverhampton W.	Jnrs	02.48	51-53	25	-	0

GIBBS Alan Martin
Orpington, 7 February, 1934 (F)

League Club	Source	Date Signed	Seasons Played	Apps	Subs	Gls
Cardiff C.		10.54				
Swindon T.	Tr	05.56	56	16	-	5

GIBBS Brian Richard
Shaftesbury, 6 October, 1936 (IF)

League Club	Source	Date Signed	Seasons Played	Apps	Subs	Gls
Bournemouth	Gosport Borough	10.57	57-62	58	-	15
Gillingham	Tr	10.62	62-68	259	0	101
Colchester U.	Tr	09.68	68-71	153	4	40

GIBBS Derek William
Fulham, 22 December, 1934 (IF)

League Club	Source	Date Signed	Seasons Played	Apps	Subs	Gls
Chelsea	Jnrs	04.55	56-60	23	-	5
Leyton Orient	Tr	11.60	60-62	33	-	4
Queens Park R.	Tr	08.63	63-64	27	-	0

GIBBS Nigel James
St Albans, 20 November, 1965 E Yth/Eu21-5 (RB)

League Club	Source	Date Signed	Seasons Played	Apps	Subs	Gls
Watford	App	11.83	83-97	362	12	5

GIBBS Paul Derek
Gorleston, 26 October, 1972 (LB)

League Club	Source	Date Signed	Seasons Played	Apps	Subs	Gls
Colchester U.	Diss T.	03.95	94-96	39	14	3
Torquay U.	Tr	07.97	97	40	1	7

GIBBS Peter Leslie
Rhodesia, 24 August, 1956 (G)

League Club	Source	Date Signed	Seasons Played	Apps	Subs	Gls
Watford	Tring T.	07.75	75-76	4	0	0

GIBLIN Edward **John**
Stoke, 29 June, 1923 (HB)

League Club	Source	Date Signed	Seasons Played	Apps	Subs	Gls
Stoke C.	Tunstall B.C.	04.43	47	1	-	0

GIBSON Aidan Michael
Newcastle-u-Lyme, 17 May, 1963 (M)

League Club	Source	Date Signed	Seasons Played	Apps	Subs	Gls
Derby Co.	App	05.81	80-81	0	2	0
Exeter C.	Tr	07.82	82	17	1	1

GIBSON Alexander Pollock Stitt
Kirkconnel (Ayrs), 28 November, 1939 (CH)

League Club	Source	Date Signed	Seasons Played	Apps	Subs	Gls
Notts Co.	Auchinleck Talbot	04.59	59-68	344	3	10

GIBSON Alexander Rose
Glasgow, 25 January, 1925 (FB)

League Club	Source	Date Signed	Seasons Played	Apps	Subs	Gls
Hull C.	Clyde	03.50	49-50	21	-	0

GIBSON Alfred
Castleford, 9 September, 1919 Died 1988 (CH)

League Club	Source	Date Signed	Seasons Played	Apps	Subs	Gls
Rotherham U.		10.45	46-53	152	-	0

GIBSON Archibald Boyle
Dailly, 30 December, 1933 (WH)

League Club	Source	Date Signed	Seasons Played	Apps	Subs	Gls
Leeds U.	Colyston Jnrs	05.51	54-59	169	-	5
Scunthorpe U.	Tr	07.60	60-63	138	-	5

GIBSON Brian
Huddersfield, 22 February, 1928 (FB)

League Club	Source	Date Signed	Seasons Played	Apps	Subs	Gls
Huddersfield T.	Paddock Ath.	05.51	51-60	157	-	1

GIBSON Charles
Dumbarton, 12 June, 1961 (M)

League Club	Source	Date Signed	Seasons Played	Apps	Subs	Gls
Shrewsbury T.	St Anthony's	03.81	81	2	4	0

GIBSON Colin Hayward
Middlesbrough, 16 September, 1923 Died 1992 Eu21-1/E 'B'/EF Lge (OR)

League Club	Source	Date Signed	Seasons Played	Apps	Subs	Gls
Cardiff C.	Penarth Pont.	04.44	46-47	71	-	16
Newcastle U.	Tr	07.48	48	23	-	5
Aston Villa	Tr	02.49	48-55	158	-	24
Lincoln C.	Tr	01.56	55-56	36	-	12

GIBSON Colin John
Bridport, 6 April, 1960 E Sch/Eu21-1/E 'B' (LB/M)

League Club	Source	Date Signed	Seasons Played	Apps	Subs	Gls
Aston Villa	App	04.78	78-85	181	4	10
Manchester U.	Tr	11.85	85-89	74	5	9
Port Vale	L	09.90	90	5	1	2
Leicester C.	Tr	12.90	90-93	50	9	4
Blackpool (N/C)	Tr	08.94	94	1	1	0
Walsall	Tr	09.94	94	31	2	0

GIBSON David
Seaham, 14 February, 1958 (M)

League Club	Source	Date Signed	Seasons Played	Apps	Subs	Gls
Hull C.	App	12.75	75-77	19	5	0
Scunthorpe U.	Tr	07.78	78-79	15	6	1

GIBSON David James
Runcorn, 18 March, 1931 (OR)

League Club	Source	Date Signed	Seasons Played	Apps	Subs	Gls
Everton	Jnrs	08.50	50-51	3	-	0
Swindon T.	Tr	11.54	54-56	70	-	6

GIBSON David Wedderburn
Winchburgh, 23 September, 1938 S-7 (IF)

League Club	Source	Date Signed	Seasons Played	Apps	Subs	Gls
Leicester C.	Hibernian	01.62	61-69	274	6	41
Aston Villa	Tr	09.70	70-71	16	3	1
Exeter C.	Tr	01.72	71-72	69	2	3

GIBSON Thomas Richard **Donald**
Manchester, 12 May, 1929 (WH)

League Club	Source	Date Signed	Seasons Played	Apps	Subs	Gls
Manchester U.	Jnrs	08.47	50-54	108	-	0
Sheffield Wed.	Tr	06.55	55-59	80	-	2
Leyton Orient	Tr	06.60	60	8	-	0

GIBSON Frank Alec
Croxley Green, 7 June, 1914 (OR)

League Club	Source	Date Signed	Seasons Played	Apps	Subs	Gls
Watford (Am)	Rickmansworth	05.46	46	1	-	0

GIBSON Henry (Harry)
Newcastle, 17 April, 1930 Died 1993 (CH)

League Club	Source	Date Signed	Seasons Played	Apps	Subs	Gls
Fulham	Spennymoor U.	11.52	54	1	-	0
Aldershot	Kings Lynn	08.56	56	3	-	0

GIBSON Ian Stewart
Newton Stewart, 30 March, 1943 S Sch/Su23-2 (M)

League Club	Source	Date Signed	Seasons Played	Apps	Subs	Gls
Accrington St. (Am)	Jnrs	07.58	58	9	-	3
Bradford P. A.	Jnrs	04.60	59-61	88	-	18
Middlesbrough	Tr	03.62	61-65	168	-	44
Coventry C.	Tr	07.66	66-69	90	3	13
Cardiff C.	Tr	07.70	70-72	89	1	11
Bournemouth	Tr	10.72	72-73	17	3	0

GIBSON James
Belfast, 4 September,1940 (WH)

League Club	Source	Date Signed	Seasons Played	Apps	Subs	Gls
Newcastle U.	Linfield	01.59	58-60	2	-	1
Luton T.	Cambridge U.	02.65	64-65	31	1	0

GIBSON Joseph
Banknock, 20 March, 1926 (F)

League Club	Source	Date Signed	Seasons Played	Apps	Subs	Gls
Ipswich T.	Polkemmet Jnrs	09.47	48	1	-	0
West Ham U.	Tr	07.49				

GIBSON Michael James
Derby, 15 July, 1939 E Yth (G)

League Club	Source	Date Signed	Seasons Played	Apps	Subs	Gls
Shrewsbury T.	Nuneaton Borough	03.60	60-62	76	-	0
Bristol C.	Tr	04.63	62-71	331	0	0
Gillingham	Tr	07.72	72-73	80	0	0

GIBSON Paul Richard
Sheffield, 1 November, 1976 (G)

League Club	Source	Date Signed	Seasons Played	Apps	Subs	Gls
Manchester U.	YT	07.95				
Mansfield T.	L	10.97	97	13	0	0

GIBSON Reginald
Tideswell, 15 May, 1919 Died 1991 (CH)

League Club	Source	Date Signed	Seasons Played	Apps	Subs	Gls
Manchester U.		09.38				
Plymouth Arg.	Tr	02.46	46	6	-	0
Exeter C.	Tr	06.47	47-48	40	-	0

GIBSON Robert
Washington, 29 December, 1916 Died 1995 (IF)

League Club	Source	Date Signed	Seasons Played	Apps	Subs	Gls
Southend U.		06.45	46	2	-	0

GIBSON Robert Henry
Ashington, 5 August, 1927 Died 1989 (CF)

League Club	Source	Date Signed	Seasons Played	Apps	Subs	Gls
Hull C.	Aberdeen	10.49	49	12	-	5
Lincoln C.	Ashington	05.51	51-54	41	-	20
Gateshead	Peterborough U.	03.57	56-58	49	-	27

GIBSON Simon John
Nottingham, 10 December, 1964 (CD)

League Club	Source	Date Signed	Seasons Played	Apps	Subs	Gls
Chelsea	App	12.82				
Swindon T.	Tr	11.83	83-84	29	2	3
Preston N. E.	Tr	12.84	84-85	42	0	5
Rochdale	Tr	08.86	86	3	2	0

GIBSON John **Stephen**
Huddersfield, 2 May, 1949 (D)

League Club	Source	Date Signed	Seasons Played	Apps	Subs	Gls
Bradford P.A.	Huddersfield T. (Am)	12.67	67-68	28	4	0

GIBSON Terence Bradley
Walthamstow, 23 December, 1962 E Sch/E Yth (F)

League Club	Source	Date Signed	Seasons Played	Apps	Subs	Gls
Tottenham H.	App	01.80	79-82	16	2	4
Coventry C.	Tr	08.83	83-85	97	1	43
Manchester U.	Tr	01.86	85-86	14	9	1
Wimbledon	Tr	08.87	87-92	80	6	21

League Club	Source	Date Signed	Seasons Played	Apps	Subs	Gls
Swindon T.	L	03.92	91	8	1	1
Peterborough U. (N/C)	Tr	12.93	93	1	0	0
Barnet	Tr	02.94	93-94	24	8	5

GIBSON William
Lanark, 24 June, 1959 (FB)

League Club	Source	Date Signed	Seasons Played	Apps	Subs	Gls
Leicester C.	Easthouses B.C.	07.79	80-81	28	0	0

GIBSON William
Glasgow, 17 September, 1926 (FB)

League Club	Source	Date Signed	Seasons Played	Apps	Subs	Gls
Brentford	Arsenal (Am)	01.47				
Tranmere Rov.	Tr	06.51	51-53	72	-	1

GIDMAN John
Liverpool, 10 January, 1954 E Yth/Eu23-4/E-1 (RB)

League Club	Source	Date Signed	Seasons Played	Apps	Subs	Gls
Aston Villa	Liverpool (App)	08.71	72-79	196	1	9
Everton	Tr	10.79	79-80	64	0	2
Manchester U.	Tr	08.81	81-85	94	1	4
Manchester C.	Tr	10.86	86-87	52	1	1
Stoke C.	Tr	08.88	88	7	3	0
Darlington	Tr	02.89	88	13	0	1

GIGGS Ryan Joseph
Cardiff, 29 November, 1973 E Sch/W Yth/Wu21-1/W-21 (F)

League Club	Source	Date Signed	Seasons Played	Apps	Subs	Gls
Manchester U.	YT	12.90	90-97	217	19	50

GILBERG Harold
Edmonton, 27 June, 1923 Died 1994 (IF/WH)

League Club	Source	Date Signed	Seasons Played	Apps	Subs	Gls
Tottenham H.	Jnrs	09.44	46-47	2	-	0
Queens Park R.	Tr	08.51	51-52	66	-	12
Brighton & H. A.	Tr	12.52	52-55	67	-	3

GILBERT Carl Graham
Folkestone, 20 March, 1948 (CF)

League Club	Source	Date Signed	Seasons Played	Apps	Subs	Gls
Gillingham	Jnrs	10.65	67-69	28	2	11
Bristol Rov.	Tr	12.69	69-70	38	7	15
Rotherham U.	Tr	03.71	70-73	78	16	36

GILBERT David George
Smethwick, 5 August, 1940 (OR)

League Club	Source	Date Signed	Seasons Played	Apps	Subs	Gls
Chesterfield	Redditch	05.60	60	22	-	2

GILBERT David James
Lincoln, 22 June, 1963 (LM)

League Club	Source	Date Signed	Seasons Played	Apps	Subs	Gls
Lincoln C.	App	06.81	80-81	15	15	1
Scunthorpe U. (N/C)	Tr	08.82	82	1	0	0
Northampton T.	Boston U.	06.86	86-88	120	0	21
Grimsby T.	Tr	03.89	88-94	259	0	41
West Bromwich A.	Tr	08.95	95-97	46	16	6
York C.	L	03.97	96	9	0	1
Grimsby T.	L	08.97	97	5	0	0

GILBERT Kenneth Robert
Aberdeen, 8 March, 1975 S Sch/S Yth (RB/M)

League Club	Source	Date Signed	Seasons Played	Apps	Subs	Gls
Hull C.	Aberdeen	01.96	95-96	21	11	1

GILBERT Noel Albert
North Walsham, 25 December, 1931 (OR)

League Club	Source	Date Signed	Seasons Played	Apps	Subs	Gls
Norwich C.	North Walsham	08.55	55	1	-	0

GILBERT Phillip Leonard
Sandwich, 11 September, 1944 (IF)

League Club	Source	Date Signed	Seasons Played	Apps	Subs	Gls
Brighton & H. A.	Ramsgate	01.62	61-63	6	-	3

GILBERT Timothy Hew
South Shields, 28 August, 1958 Died 1995 (FB)

League Club	Source	Date Signed	Seasons Played	Apps	Subs	Gls
Sunderland	App	08.76	76-79	34	2	3
Cardiff C.	Tr	02.81	80-81	33	0	1
Darlington	Tr	08.82	82-83	62	3	3

GILBERT William Albert
Lewisham, 10 November, 1959 E Sch/E Yth/Eu21-11 (CD)

League Club	Source	Date Signed	Seasons Played	Apps	Subs	Gls
Crystal Palace	App	12.76	77-83	235	2	3
Portsmouth	Tr	06.84	84-88	133	7	0
Colchester U.		10.89	89	26	1	0
Maidstone U. (N/C)	Tr	10.90	90	2	2	0

GILBERT William Arthur
Newcastle, 7 November, 1925 (G)

League Club	Source	Date Signed	Seasons Played	Apps	Subs	Gls
Coventry C.	Murton Colly	09.48	51-52	14	-	0
Stockport Co.	Snowdown Colly	07.54	54	33	-	0

GILCHRIST Alexander
Motherwell, 28 September, 1923 Died 1989 (OR)

League Club	Source	Date Signed	Seasons Played	Apps	Subs	Gls
Cardiff C.		05.48	48	1	-	0

GILCHRIST John Skidmore
Wishaw, 5 September, 1939 Died 1991 S Sch (FB)

League Club	Source	Date Signed	Seasons Played	Apps	Subs	Gls
Millwall	Airdrieonians	03.61	60-68	279	0	10
Fulham	Tr	07.69	69	20	3	1
Colchester U.	Tr	07.70	70-71	41	0	1

GILCHRIST Paul Anthony
Dartford, 5 January, 1951 (F)

League Club	Source	Date Signed	Seasons Played	Apps	Subs	Gls
Charlton Ath.	App	03.68	69	5	2	0
Doncaster Rov.	Tr	07.71	71	22	0	8
Southampton	Tr	03.72	71-76	96	11	17
Portsmouth	Tr	03.77	76-77	38	1	3
Swindon T.	Tr	08.78	78-79	10	7	6
Hereford U.	Tr	03.80	79	11	0	1

GILCHRIST Philip Alexander
Stockton-on-Tees, 25 August, 1973 (CD)

League Club	Source	Date Signed	Seasons Played	Apps	Subs	Gls
Nottingham F.	YT	12.90				
Middlesbrough	Tr	01.92				
Hartlepool U.	Tr	11.92	92-94	77	5	0
Oxford U.	Tr	02.95	94-97	133	4	8

GILCHRIST Robert Cook
Bellshill, 17 August, 1932 (FB)

League Club	Source	Date Signed	Seasons Played	Apps	Subs	Gls
Aldershot	Dumfermline Ath.	06.52	52-56	47	-	0

GILDER Carlton Eric
Chelmsford, 25 July, 1957 (F)

League Club	Source	Date Signed	Seasons Played	Apps	Subs	Gls
Cambridge U.	Jnrs	01.75	74-75	0	2	0

GILES Albert Edgar
Swansea, 4 May, 1924 (WH)

League Club	Source	Date Signed	Seasons Played	Apps	Subs	Gls
Bristol Rov.	Jnrs	05.41	46	1	-	0

GILES Christopher Joseph
Dublin, 17 July, 1928 IR-1 (OR)

League Club	Source	Date Signed	Seasons Played	Apps	Subs	Gls
Doncaster Rov.	Drumcondra	06.50	50-51	27	-	4
Aldershot	Tr	08.53				

GILES David Charles
Cardiff, 21 September, 1956 W Sch/Wu21-4/W-12 (W)

League Club	Source	Date Signed	Seasons Played	Apps	Subs	Gls
Cardiff C.	App	09.74	74-78	51	8	3
Wrexham	Tr	12.78	78-79	38	0	3
Swansea C.	Tr	11.79	79-81	49	5	13
Leyton Orient	L	11.81	81	3	0	2
Crystal Palace	Tr	03.82	81-83	83	5	6
Birmingham C.	Tr	08.84				
Newport Co.	Tr	10.84	84	28	4	1
Cardiff C.	Tr	09.85	85-86	50	0	0

GILES James Archer
Kidlington, 21 April, 1946 (CD)

League Club	Source	Date Signed	Seasons Played	Apps	Subs	Gls
Swindon T.	Kidlington	03.65	65-67	12	1	0
Aldershot	Tr	10.68	68-70	80	1	3
Exeter C.	Tr	03.71	70-74	183	0	8
Charlton Ath.	Tr	06.75	75-77	`92	1	6
Exeter C.	Tr	12.77	77-80	130	0	5

GILES John
Walsall, 4 June, 1933 (IF)

League Club	Source	Date Signed	Seasons Played	Apps	Subs	Gls
Walsall	Hednesford T.	12.50	52	1	-	0

GILES John Edgar
Bristol, 7 November, 1947 (M)

League Club	Source	Date Signed	Seasons Played	Apps	Subs	Gls
Bristol C.	App	06.65	66	3	0	1
Bradford P. A.	L	03.68	67	9	0	0
Exeter C.	Tr	05.69	69-71	55	5	2

GILES Michael John
Dublin, 6 November, 1940 IR-60 (M)

League Club	Source	Date Signed	Seasons Played	Apps	Subs	Gls
Manchester U.	Home Farm	11.57	59-62	99	-	10
Leeds U.	Tr	08.63	63-74	380	3	88
West Bromwich A.	Tr	06.75	75-76	74	1	3

GILES Martin William
Shrewsbury, 1 January, 1979 (LB)

League Club	Source	Date Signed	Seasons Played	Apps	Subs	Gls
Chester C.	YT	07.97	97	8	2	0

GILES Paul Anthony
Cardiff, 21 February, 1961 Wu21-3 (W)

League Club	Source	Date Signed	Seasons Played	Apps	Subs	Gls
Cardiff C.	Jnrs	06.79	80-82	17	7	1
Exeter C.	L	03.82	81	9	0	1
Newport Co. (N/C)	Excelsior (Neth)	12.84	84	0	1	0
Newport Co.	Merthyr Tydfil	03.87	86-87	28	1	2

GILES Philip Richard
Walsall, 8 October, 1929 E Yth (OL)

League Club	Source	Date Signed	Seasons Played	Apps	Subs	Gls
Walsall	Jnrs	05.48	48-52	68	-	14

GILES Terence
Halifax, 25 March, 1943 (F)

League Club	Source	Date Signed	Seasons Played	Apps	Subs	Gls
Halifax T. (Am)		09.61	61-62	2	-	1

GILFILLAN Robert
Dunfermline, 14 March, 1926 (IF)

League Club	Source	Date Signed	Seasons Played	Apps	Subs	Gls
Blackpool	Jeanfield Swifts	07.47				
Rochdale	Cowdenbeath	06.51	51-53	62	-	11

GILFILLAN Robert Inglis
Cowdenbeath, 29 June, 1938 (F)

League Club	Source	Date Signed	Seasons Played	Apps	Subs	Gls
Newcastle U.	Cowdenbeath	10.59	59-60	7	-	2
Southend U.	Raith Rov.	06.63	63-65	65	1	33
Doncaster Rov.	Tr	11.65	65-70	178	8	33

GILKES Michael Earl Glenis McDonald
Hackney, 20 July, 1965 (LW)

League Club	Source	Date Signed	Seasons Played	Apps	Subs	Gls
Reading	Leicester C. (Jnrs)	07.84	84-96	348	45	43
Chelsea	L	01.92	91	0	1	0
Southampton	L	03.92	91	4	2	0
Wolverhampton W.	Tr	03.97	96-97	8	0	1

GILL Anthony Dean
Bradford, 6 March, 1968 (FB)

League Club	Source	Date Signed	Seasons Played	Apps	Subs	Gls
Manchester U.	App	03.86	86-88	5	5	1

GILL Colin John Peter
Swindon, 20 January, 1933 (G)

League Club	Source	Date Signed	Seasons Played	Apps	Subs	Gls
Swindon T.		10.55	55	1	-	0

GILL Eric Norman
St Pancras, 3 November, 1930 (G)

League Club	Source	Date Signed	Seasons Played	Apps	Subs	Gls
Charlton Ath.	Broomfields	04.48	51	1	-	0
Brighton & H. A.	Tr	06.52	52-59	280	-	0

GILL Frank
Manchester, 5 December, 1948 (OL)

League Club	Source	Date Signed	Seasons Played	Apps	Subs	Gls
Manchester U.	App	12.65				
Tranmere Rov.	Tr	07.68	68-70	70	4	8

GILL Gary
Middlesbrough, 28 November, 1964 (M)

League Club	Source	Date Signed	Seasons Played	Apps	Subs	Gls
Middlesbrough	App	11.82	83-89	69	8	2
Hull C.	L	12.83	83	0	1	0
Darlington	Tr	12.89	90-91	55	1	9
Cardiff C.	Tr	03.92	91	3	3	1

GILL Jeremy Morley
Clevedon, 8 September, 1970 E Semi Pro (M)

League Club	Source	Date Signed	Seasons Played	Apps	Subs	Gls
Birmingham C.	Yeovil	07.97	97	3	0	0

GILL John Barry Anthony
Wednesbury, 3 February, 1941 (CH)

League Club	Source	Date Signed	Seasons Played	Apps	Subs	Gls
Nottingham F.	Jnrs	03.58				
Mansfield T.	Tr	07.61	61-65	138	1	0
Hartlepool U.	Tr	02.66	65-70	201	3	1

GILL Joseph
Sunderland, 10 November, 1945 (G)

League Club	Source	Date Signed	Seasons Played	Apps	Subs	Gls
Hartlepool U. (Am)	Ashington	01.69	68	4	0	0

GILL Kenneth
Swindon, 5 November, 1955 (W)

League Club	Source	Date Signed	Seasons Played	Apps	Subs	Gls
Newport Co. (N/C)	Forest Green Rov.	09.85	85	13	6	1

GILL Matthew James
Norwich, 8 November, 1980 (M)

League Club	Source	Date Signed	Seasons Played	Apps	Subs	Gls
Peterborough U.	YT	03.98	97	2	0	0

GILL Mervyn John
Exeter, 13 April, 1931 (G)

League Club	Source	Date Signed	Seasons Played	Apps	Subs	Gls
Portsmouth (Am)	Bideford	08.53	53	6	-	0
Southampton	Woking	04.56	55	1	-	0
Torquay U.	Tr	09.56	56-61	159	-	0

GILL Raymond
Manchester, 8 December, 1924 (D)

League Club	Source	Date Signed	Seasons Played	Apps	Subs	Gls
Manchester C.		09.47	48-49	8	-	0
Chester C.	Tr	06.51	51-61	406	-	3

GILLARD Ian Terry
Hammersmith, 9 October, 1950 Eu23-5/E-3 (LB)

League Club	Source	Date Signed	Seasons Played	Apps	Subs	Gls
Queens Park R.	App	10.68	68-81	403	5	9
Aldershot	Tr	07.82	82-85	83	0	2

GILLARD Kenneth Joseph
Dublin, 30 April, 1972 IRu21-1 (FB)

League Club	Source	Date Signed	Seasons Played	Apps	Subs	Gls
Luton T.	YT	05.89				
Northampton T.	Tr	03.93	92-93	22	1	0

GILLESPIE Gary Thompson
Bonnybridge, 5 July, 1960 Su21-8/S-13 (CD)

League Club	Source	Date Signed	Seasons Played	Apps	Subs	Gls
Coventry C.	Falkirk	03.78	78-82	171	1	6
Liverpool	Tr	07.83	83-90	152	4	14
Coventry C.	Glasgow Celtic	08.94	94	2	1	0

GILLESPIE Ian Colin
Plymouth, 6 May, 1913 Died 1988 (F)

League Club	Source	Date Signed	Seasons Played	Apps	Subs	Gls
Crystal Palace	Harwich & Parkeston	02.37	36-38	21	-	4
Ipswich T.	Tr	04.66	46	6	-	1

GILLESPIE Keith Robert
Bangor (NI), 18 February, 1975 NI Sch/NI Yth/NIu21-1/NI-21 (W)

League Club	Source	Date Signed	Seasons Played	Apps	Subs	Gls
Manchester U.	YT	02.93	94	3	6	1
Wigan Ath.	L	09.93	93	8	0	4
Newcastle U.	Tr	01.95	94-97	89	17	11

GILLESPIE Norman
Edinburgh, 20 April, 1940 (IF)

League Club	Source	Date Signed	Seasons Played	Apps	Subs	Gls
Wrexham	Falkirk	12.63	63	3	-	0

GILLESPIE Patrick
Bellshill, 22 September, 1922 (WH/G)

League Club	Source	Date Signed	Seasons Played	Apps	Subs	Gls
Watford	Partick Thistle	07.45	46	6	-	0
Northampton T.	Tr	08.47	47	1	-	0
Doncaster Rov.	Tr	11.47	47-48	8	-	1

GILLETT David John
Edinburgh, 2 April, 1951 (D)

League Club	Source	Date Signed	Seasons Played	Apps	Subs	Gls
Crewe Alex.	Hibernian	08.72	72-74	64	5	2

GILLIAM Reginald Charles
Farnham, 19 February, 1931 (G)

League Club	Source	Date Signed	Seasons Played	Apps	Subs	Gls
Aldershot	Farnham T.	02.56	56	1	-	0

GILLIBRAND Ian Victor
Blackburn, 24 November, 1948 (D)

League Club	Source	Date Signed	Seasons Played	Apps	Subs	Gls
Arsenal	App	12.65				
Wigan Ath.	Tr	(N/L)	78	7	0	0

GILLIES Donald George
Glencoe, 20 June, 1951 Su23-1 (F/FB)

League Club	Source	Date Signed	Seasons Played	Apps	Subs	Gls
Bristol C.	Morton	03.73	72-79	183	17	26
Bristol Rov.	Tr	06.80	80-81	56	3	0

GILLIES John
Glasgow, 22 October, 1918 (OL)

League Club	Source	Date Signed	Seasons Played	Apps	Subs	Gls
Brentford	St Mirren	05.46	46	5	-	0

GILLIES Matthew Muirhead
Loganlea, 12 August, 1921 (CH)

League Club	Source	Date Signed	Seasons Played	Apps	Subs	Gls
Bolton W.	R.A.F. Weeton	10.42	46-51	145	-	1
Leicester C.	Tr	01.52	51-54	103	-	0

GILLIGAN Augustus (Gus) Anthony
Abingdon, 19 August, 1959 (F)

League Club	Source	Date Signed	Seasons Played	Apps	Subs	Gls
Swindon T.	App	08.77	77	3	1	0
Doncaster Rov.	L	09.78	78	1	0	0

GILLIGAN James Martin
Hammersmith, 24 January, 1964 EYth (F)

League Club	Source	Date Signed	Seasons Played	Apps	Subs	Gls
Watford	App	08.81	81-84	18	9	6
Lincoln C.	L	10.82	82	0	3	0
Grimsby T.	Tr	08.85	85	19	5	4
Swindon T.	Tr	06.86	86	13	4	5
Newport Co.	L	02.87	86	4	1	1
Lincoln C.	Tr	03.87	86	11	0	1
Cardiff C.	Tr	07.87	87-89	99	0	35
Portsmouth	Tr	10.89	89	24	8	5
Swansea C.	Tr	08.90	90-91	60	2	23

GILLIGAN John
Abingdon, 2 May, 1957 (M)

League Club	Source	Date Signed	Seasons Played	Apps	Subs	Gls
Swindon T.	App	10.75	75-76	2	4	0
Huddersfield T.	L	09.76	76	0	1	0
Northampton T.	L	01.77	76	5	0	1

GILLIGAN Malcolm
Cardiff, 11 October, 1942 (OR)

League Club	Source	Date Signed	Seasons Played	Apps	Subs	Gls
Swansea C.		05.62	62	2	-	0

GILLIVER Allan Henry
Swallownest, 3 August, 1944 (CF)

League Club	Source	Date Signed	Seasons Played	Apps	Subs	Gls
Huddersfield T.	Jnrs	08.61	62-65	45	0	22
Blackburn Rov.	Tr	06.66	66-67	32	2	9
Rotherham U.	Tr	05.68	68	24	3	2
Brighton & H. A.	Tr	07.69	69-70	54	3	19
Lincoln C.	Tr	02.71	70-71	33	4	8
Bradford C.	Tr	06.72	72-73	68	2	30
Stockport Co.	Tr	06.74	74	22	3	5
Bradford C. (N/C)	Boston U.	08.78	78	1	1	0

League Club	Source	Date Signed	Seasons Played	Career Record Apps	Subs	Gls
GILLOTT Peter						
Barnsley, 20 July, 1935 EYth						(FB)
Barnsley	Jnrs	05.53	55-58	5	-	0
GILMOUR George Reynolds						
Barrhead, 7 May, 1919 Died 1987						(RH)
Halifax T.		09.48	48-49	37	-	2
GILMOUR Ronald						
Workington, 28 February, 1935						(HB)
Workington	Jnrs	12.52	53	2	-	0
GILPIN James						
Edinburgh, 12 June, 1945						(OL)
Bradford P. A.	Raith Rov.	08.65	65	10	1	1
GILROY Joseph						
Glasgow, 19 October, 1941						(CF)
Fulham	Clyde	10.67	67-68	23	1	8
GILZEAN Alan John						
Coupar Angus, 22 October, 1938 Su23-3/SF Lge/S-22						(CF)
Tottenham H.	Dundee	12.64	64-73	335	8	93
GILZEAN Ian Roger						
Enfield, 10 December, 1969						(F)
Tottenham H.	YT	07.88				
Doncaster Rov. (L)	Dundee	02.93	92	3	0	0
Northampton T.	Dundee	08.93	93	29	4	10
GINOLA David						
France, 25 January, 1967 French Int						(W)
Newcastle U.	Paris St Germain (Fr)	07.95	95-96	54	4	6
Tottenham H.,	Tr	07.97	97	34	0	6
GINTER Anthony						
Plymouth, 6 November, 1974						(M)
Torquay U.	YT	●	92	1	0	0
GINTY Rory Vincent						
Galway, 23 January, 1977						(W)
Crystal Palace	YT	11.94	97	2	3	0
GIPP David Thomas						
Stratford, 13 July, 1969						(F)
Brighton & H. A.	App	07.86	86-87	1	4	0
GIRLING Howard (Dickie) Milton						
Birmingham, 24 May, 1922 Died 1992						(OL)
Crystal Palace		10.43	46	26	-	6
Brentford	Tr	02.47	46-49	86	-	7
Bournemouth	Tr	07.51	51	4	-	0
GISBOURNE Charles Joseph						
Bury, 7 October, 1952						(D)
Bury	App	10.70	72-74	13	3	1
Crewe Alex.	Tr	10.74	74	5	1	0
GISLASON Valur Fannar						
Reykjavic, Iceland, 8 September, 1977						(M)
Arsenal	Fram (Ice)	07.96				
Brighton & H.A.	L	10.97	97	7	0	0
GISSING John William						
Stapleford, 24 November, 1938						(OR)
Notts Co.	Stapleford B.C.	07.56	57-60	22	-	1
Chesterfield	Tr	07.61	61	2	-	0
GITSHAM James William						
Hammersmith, 12 May, 1942						(FB)
Brentford	Jnrs	07.59	60-62	54	-	0
GITTENS Jonathan Antoni						
Birmingham, 22 January, 1964						(CD)
Southampton	Paget R.	10.85	85-86	18	0	0
Swindon T.	Tr	07.87	87-90	124	2	6
Southampton	Tr	03.91	90-91	16	3	0
Middlesbrough	L	02.92	91	9	3	1
Middlesbrough	Tr	07.92	92	13	0	0
Portsmouth	Tr	08.93	93-95	81	2	2
Torquay U.	Tr	08.96	96-97	78	0	9
GIUMMARRA William Giorgio						
Ontario, Canada, 26 August, 1971						(LM)
Darlington	Montreal Impact (Can)	08.97	97	0	4	0
GIVEN Seamus John						
Lifford (IR), 20 April, 1976 IR Yth/IRu21-5/IR-17						(G)
Blackburn Rov.	Glasgow Celtic (Jnrs)	08.94	96	2	0	0
Swindon T.	L	08.95	95	5	0	0
Sunderland	L	01.96	95	17	0	0
Newcastle U.	Tr	07.97	97	24	0	0
GIVENS Daniel (Don) Joseph						
Limerick (Ire), 9 August, 1949 IR-56						(F)
Manchester U.	App	12.66	69	4	4	1
Luton T.	Tr	04.70	70-71	80	3	19
Queens Park R.	Tr	07.72	72-77	242	0	77
Birmingham C.	Tr	08.78	78-80	49	10	10
Bournemouth	L	03.80	79	5	0	4
Sheffield U.	Tr	03.81	80	11	0	3
GLADWIN Robin						
Harlow, 12 August, 1940						(FB)
Norwich C.	Chelmsford C.	01.66	65-67	16	0	0
Oxford U.	Tr	07.68	68-69	44	0	0
GLAISTER George						
Bywell, 18 May, 1918						(OL)
Blackburn Rov.	North Shields	05.37	46	8	-	1
Stockport Co.	Tr	04.47	46-49	92	-	21
Halifax T.	Tr	08.50	50	34	-	7
Accington St.	Tr	09.51	51	24	-	1
GLASBY Herbert						
Bradford, 21 September, 1919						(OR)
Bradford P. A.	Aldershot (Am)	05.46	46-48	11	-	1
GLASGOW Byron Fitzgerald						
Clapham, 18 February, 1979						(M)
Reading	YT	08.96	96-97	3	4	0
GLASS James Robert						
Epsom, 1 August, 1973						(G)
Crystal Palace	YT	07.91				
Portsmouth	L	02.95	94	3	0	0
Bournemouth	Tr	03.96	95-97	94	0	0
GLAVIN Ronald Michael						
Glasgow, 27 March, 1951 S-1						(M)
Barnsley	Glasgow Celtic	06.79	79-83	171	5	73
Barnsley (N/C)	Belenenses (Por)	08.85	85	5	1	0
Stockport Co. (N/C)	Tr	08.86	86	5	5	1
GLAZIER William James						
Nottingham, 2 August, 1943 Eu23-3/EF Lge						(G)
Crystal Palace	Jnrs	10.61	61-64	106	-	0
Coventry C.	Tr	10.64	64-74	346	0	0
Brentford	Tr	06.75	75	9	0	0
GLAZZARD James						
Normanton, 23 April, 1923 Died 1996						(CF)
Huddersfield T.	Altofts	10.43	46-55	299	-	141
Everton	Tr	09.56	56	3	-	0
Mansfield T.	Tr	12.56	56-57	21	-	10
GLAZZARD Malcolm						
Bebington, 1 July, 1931						(OL)
Liverpool	Jnrs	05.49				
Accrington St.	Tr	08.51	51	1	-	0
GLEADALL Dennis						
Sheffield, 15 February, 1934						(CH)
Bury		08.54				
Bradford P. A.	Tr	07.56	56-57	34	-	0
GLEADALL Edward						
Sheffield, 21 August, 1931 Died 1993						(OR)
Bury		01.52	51-56	74	-	17
Scunthorpe U.	Tr	03.57	56-57	6	-	2
GLEASURE Peter Francis						
Luton, 8 October, 1960						(G)
Millwall	App	08.78	80-82	55	0	0
Northampton T.	Tr	03.83	82-90	344	0	0
Gillingham	L	03.91	90	3	0	0
GLEAVE Colin						
Stockport, 6 April, 1919						(D)
Stockport Co.		02.38	46-47	57	-	1
GLEDHILL Samuel						
Castleford, 7 July, 1913 Died 1994						(D)
York C.	Altofts	09.36	36-48	123	-	6
GLEDSTONE Peter Hayward						
Ferndown, 4 May, 1934						(LB)
Bournemouth	Bournemouth G.W.	11.55	57-63	131	-	2

League Club	Source	Date Signed	Seasons Played	Career Record Apps	Subs	Gls
GLEESON Percy						
Acton, 18 July, 1921						(IF)
Brentford	Hounslow T.	03.47	47	9	-	1
GLEGHORN Nigel William						
Seaham, 12 August, 1962						(W/M)
Ipswich T.	Seaham Red Star	08.85	85-87	54	12	11
Manchester C.	Tr	08.88	88-89	27	7	7
Birmingham C.	Tr	09.89	89-92	142	0	33
Stoke C.	Tr	10.92	92-95	162	4	26
Burnley	Tr	07.96	96-97	33	1	4
Brentford	L	11.97	97	11	0	1
Northampton T.	L	02.98	97	3	5	1
GLENDINNING Brian						
Newcastle, 26 December, 1934						(CF)
Darlington	Felham B.C.	05.55	55	12	-	2
GLENDINNING Kevin						
Corbridge, 23 January, 1962						(LB)
Darlington	Jnrs	08.80	80	4	0	0
GLENDON Kevin William						
Manchester, 21 June, 1961						(M)
Manchester C.	App	06.79				
Crewe Alex.	Tr	08.80	80	3	1	0
Burnley	Hyde U.	12.83	83	4	0	0
GLENN David Anthony						
Wigan, 30 November, 1962						(RB)
Wigan Ath.	App	11.80	80-82	68	4	4
Blackburn Rov.	Tr	08.83	83-84	23	1	0
Chester C.	Tr	07.85	85-88	70	3	1
GLENNON Christopher David						
Manchester, 29 October, 1949						(F)
Manchester C.	App	11.67	68-69	3	1	0
Tranmere Rov.	L	01.71	70	2	0	0
GLIDDEN Gilbert Swinburne						
Sunderland, 15 December, 1915 Died 1988 E Sch						(WH)
Sunderland	Jnrs	02.32				
Port Vale	Tr	05.35	35	5	-	1
Reading	Tr	05.36	36-49	111	-	25
Leyton Orient	Tr	11.50	50	1	-	0
GLOSSOP Terence						
Sheffield, 10 May, 1940						(OR)
Chesterfield		05.59	59	7	-	1
GLOVER Alexander						
Glasgow, 28 February, 1922						(OR)
Bradford P. A.	Partick Thistle	03.48	47-49	48	-	5
Luton T.	Tr	09.49	49-50	56	-	6
Blackburn Rov.	Tr	09.51	51-53	65	-	4
Barrow	Tr	08.54	54-57	86	-	7
GLOVER Allan Richard						
Staines, 21 October, 1950						(M)
Queens Park R.	App	03.68	68	5	1	0
West Bromwich A.	Tr	06.69	69-76	84	8	9
Southend U.	L	01.76	75	0	1	0
Brentford	L	10.76	76	6	0	0
Leyton Orient	Tr	03.77	76-77	37	0	5
Brentford	Tr	11.78	78-79	21	2	2
GLOVER Arthur						
Barnsley, 27 March, 1918						(CH)
Barnsley	Jnrs	03.35	37-52	186	-	5
GLOVER Benjamin David						
Birmingham, 30 November, 1946						(HB)
Coventry C.		10.66	66	0	1	0
GLOVER Bevil Arthur						
Salford, 25 March, 1926						(CH)
Stockport Co.	Cheadle	01.48	47-53	137	-	1
Rochdale	Tr	03.54	53-58	169	-	1
GLOVER Dean Victor						
West Bromwich, 29 December, 1963						(CD)
Aston Villa	App	12.81	84-86	25	3	0
Sheffield U.	L	10.86	86	5	0	0
Middlesbrough	Tr	06.87	87-88	44	6	5
Port Vale	Tr	02.89	88-97	354	9	15
GLOVER Gerard John						
Liverpool, 27 September, 1946 E Sch/E Yth						(WH)
Everton	App	08.64	64-65	2	1	0
Mansfield T.	Tr	09.67	67	18	1	0

League Club	Source	Date Signed	Seasons Played	Career Record Apps	Subs	Gls
GLOVER John James						
Workington, 6 February, 1935						(F)
Workington	Marsh B.C.	10.54	54	2	-	0
GLOVER Edward **Lee**						
Kettering, 24 April, 1970 S Yth/Su21-3						(F)
Nottingham F.	YT	04.87	87-93	61	15	9
Leicester C.	L	09.89	89	3	2	1
Barnsley	L	01.90	89	8	0	0
Luton T.	L	09.91	91	1	0	0
Port Vale	Tr	08.94	94-95	38	14	7
Rotherham U.	Tr	08.96	96-97	52	7	18
Huddersfield T.	L	03.97	96	11	0	0
GLOVER Leonard						
Kennington, 31 January, 1944						(LW)
Charlton Ath.	Jnrs	05.62	62-67	177	0	20
Leicester C.	Tr	11.67	67-75	245	7	38
GLOVER Peter						
Bradford, 16 October, 1936						(WH)
Bradford C.		11.57	57	1	-	0
GLOZIER Robert						
West Ham, 20 November, 1948 E Sch						(FB)
West Ham U.	App	05.66				
Torquay U.	Tr	08.69	69-71	57	0	1
GLYNN Terence Robert						
Hackney, 17 December, 1958						(F)
Leyton Orient	App	12.76	76	1	1	0
GOAD Alan Michael						
Hailsham, 8 August, 1948						(D)
Exeter C.	Jnrs	12.65				
Hartlepool U.	Tr	07.67	67-77	366	9	11
GOALEN Harold **Keith**						
Hindley, 24 May, 1933						(OL)
Stockport Co.	Jnrs	04.53	50-55	18	-	2
GOATER Leonard **Shaun**						
Bermuda, 25 February, 1970 Bermudan Int						(F)
Manchester U.	Jnrs	05.89				
Rotherham U.	Tr	10.89	89-95	169	40	70
Notts Co.	L	11.93	93	1	0	0
Bristol C.	Tr	07.96	96-97	67	8	40
Manchester C.	Tr	03.98	97	7	0	3
GOBLE Stephen Richard						
Erpingham (Nfk), 5 September, 1960						(LW)
Norwich C.	App	09.78	79-80	30	0	2
Norwich C.	Groningen (Neth)	08.84	84			
Cambridge C. (N/C)	Utrecht (Neth)	02.88	87	1	1	0
GODBOLD Daryl Martin						
Ipswich, 5 September, 1964						(FB)
Norwich C.	App	09.82	83	0	2	0
Colchester U.	Tr	08.84	84	4	2	1
GODBOLD Harold						
Springwell, 31 January, 1939						(W)
Sunderland	Usworth Colly	05.56	57-59	12	-	1
Hartlepool U.	Tr	01.61	60-62	65	-	8
Lincoln C.	Boston U.	03.66	65-66	22	0	3
GODDARD Howard John						
Over Wallop (Hants), 10 May, 1957						(F)
Bournemouth	App	07.74	72-75	62	2	18
Swindon T.	Tr	06.76	76	10	3	0
Newport Co.	Tr	08.77	77-81	101	4	42
Blackpool	L	09.81	81	4	0	2
Bournemouth	Tr	12.81	81	6	3	2
Aldershot	Tr	08.82	82	26	2	9
GODDARD Karl Eric						
Leeds, 29 December, 1967 E Sch						(M/LB)
Manchester U.	App	12.85				
Bradford C.	Tr	06.86	86-89	67	6	0
Exeter C.	L	12.89	89	0	1	0
Colchester U.	L	01.90	89	16	0	1
Hereford U.	Tr	09.90	90-91	8	1	1
GODDARD Paul						
Harlington, 12 October, 1959 Eu21-8/E-1						(F)
Queens Park R.	App	07.77	77-79	63	7	23
West Ham U.	Tr	08.80	80-86	159	11	54
Newcastle U.	Tr	11.86	86-87	61	0	19
Derby Co.	Tr	08.88	88-89	49	0	15

League Club	Source	Date Signed	Seasons Played	Apps	Subs	Gls
Millwall	Tr	12.89	89-90	17	3	1
Ipswich T.	Tr	01.91	90-93	59	13	13

GODDARD Raymond
Fulham, 13 February, 1949 (G)

League Club	Source	Date Signed	Seasons Played	Apps	Subs	Gls
Leyton Orient	Fulham (App)	02.67	66-73	278	0	0
Millwall	Tr	11.74	75-77	80	0	0
Wimbledon	Tr	02.78	77-80	119	0	1

GODDARD Raymond
Sheffield, 17 October, 1920 Died 1974 (CH)

League Club	Source	Date Signed	Seasons Played	Apps	Subs	Gls
Wolverhampton W.	Red Rov.	09.38	38	4	-	0
Chelsea	Tr	09.46	46-47	14	-	1
Plymouth Arg.	Tr	07.48	48-49	43	-	1
Exeter C.	Tr	12.49	49-53	130	-	2

GODDARD-CRAWLEY Richard Lewis
Burnt Oak, 31 March, 1978 (CD)

League Club	Source	Date Signed	Seasons Played	Apps	Subs	Gls
Brentford	Arsenal (YT)	07.96	96	0	1	0

GODDEN Anthony Leonard
Gillingham, 2 August, 1955 (G)

League Club	Source	Date Signed	Seasons Played	Apps	Subs	Gls
West Bromwich A.	Ashford T.	08.75	76-85	267	0	0
Luton T.	L	03.83	82	12	0	0
Walsall	L	10.83	83	19	0	0
Chelsea	Tr	03.86	85-86	34	0	0
Birmingham C.	Tr	07.87	87-88	29	0	0
Bury	L	12.88	88	1	0	0
Peterborough U.	Tr	07.89	89	24	0	0

GODDERIDGE Alan Edward
Tamworth, 23 May, 1928 (HB)

League Club	Source	Date Signed	Seasons Played	Apps	Subs	Gls
Swansea C.	Tamworth	10.50	51	1	-	0
Walsall	Tr	07.52	52	3	-	0

GODDING Earl George
Hawarden, 6 January, 1934 (G)

League Club	Source	Date Signed	Seasons Played	Apps	Subs	Gls
Wrexham	Jnrs	04.54	52-58	21	-	0
Workington	Tr	08.59	59	10	-	0

GODFREY Anthony William
Wokingham, 30 April, 1939 (G)

League Club	Source	Date Signed	Seasons Played	Apps	Subs	Gls
Southampton	Basingstoke	04.58	58-65	141	0	0
Aldershot	Tr	12.65	65-69	171	0	0
Rochdale	Tr	07.70	70-71	71	0	0
Aldershot	Tr	07.72	72-75	68	0	0

GODFREY Brian Cameron
Flint, 1 May, 1940 Wu23-1/W-3 (IF)

League Club	Source	Date Signed	Seasons Played	Apps	Subs	Gls
Everton	Flint Alex.	05.58	59	1	-	0
Scunthorpe U.	Tr	06.60	60-63	87	-	24
Preston N. E.	Tr	10.63	63-67	121	1	52
Aston Villa	Tr	09.67	67-70	139	4	22
Bristol Rov.	Tr	05.71	71-72	79	2	16
Newport Co.	Tr	06.73	73-75	117	1	14

GODFREY Kevin
Kennington, 24 February, 1960 (W)

League Club	Source	Date Signed	Seasons Played	Apps	Subs	Gls
Leyton Orient	App	03.77	77-87	255	30	63
Plymouth Arg.	L	02.86	85	7	0	1
Brentford	Maidenhead U.	10.88	88-92	101	39	17

GODFREY Paul
Derby, 27 September, 1972 (LM)

League Club	Source	Date Signed	Seasons Played	Apps	Subs	Gls
Chesterfield	YT	•	90	2	0	0

GODFREY Peter Ronald
Woolwich, 15 March, 1938 (OR)

League Club	Source	Date Signed	Seasons Played	Apps	Subs	Gls
Charlton Ath.	Jnrs	11.55	60	1	-	0
Gillingham	Tr	07.61	61-64	66	-	9
Chesterfield	Tr	07.65	65	27	0	2
Exeter C.	Tr	06.66	66	42	0	4

GODFREY Warren
Liverpool, 31 March, 1973 (M)

League Club	Source	Date Signed	Seasons Played	Apps	Subs	Gls
Liverpool	YT	05.91				
Barnsley	Tr	07.92	92	1	7	0

GODSELL John Dryburgh
Lassodie, 13 September, 1924 (LB)

League Club	Source	Date Signed	Seasons Played	Apps	Subs	Gls
Huddersfield T.	Forfar Ath.	06.46				
Bradford C.	Tr	09.48	49	9	-	0
Southport	Tr	08.51	51	3	-	0

GODWIN Donald John
Aberbargoed, 5 July, 1932 (OL)

League Club	Source	Date Signed	Seasons Played	Apps	Subs	Gls
Cardiff C.	Bargoed	12.53	56	2	-	0

GODWIN Robert Geoffrey
Wootton Bassett, 3 February, 1928 (IF)

League Club	Source	Date Signed	Seasons Played	Apps	Subs	Gls
Swindon T.		09.51	51	2	-	0

GODWIN Thomas Fergus
Dublin, 20 August, 1927 Died 1996 LoI/IR-13 (G)

League Club	Source	Date Signed	Seasons Played	Apps	Subs	Gls
Leicester C.	Shamrock Rov.	10.49	49-51	45	-	0
Bournemouth	Tr	06.52	52-61	357	-	0

GODWIN Verdi
Blackburn, 11 February, 1926 (F)

League Club	Source	Date Signed	Seasons Played	Apps	Subs	Gls
Blackburn Rov.	Jnrs	03.46	46-47	27	-	6
Manchester C.	Tr	06.48	48	8	-	3
Stoke C.	Tr	06.49	49	22	-	2
Mansfield T.	Tr	01.50	49-50	31	-	9
Middlesbrough	Tr	11.51				
Grimsby T.	Tr	01.52	51	1	-	0
Brentford	Tr	03.52	51-52	7	-	1
Southport	Tr	07.54	54	17	-	2
Barrow	Tr	08.55	55	16	-	3
Tranmere Rov.	Tr	08.56	56	14	-	2

GOFFIN William Charles
Tamworth, 12 December, 1920 Died 1987 (W)

League Club	Source	Date Signed	Seasons Played	Apps	Subs	Gls
Aston Villa	Jnrs	12.37	46-53	156	-	36
Walsall	Tr	08.54	54	8	-	1

GOLAC Ivan
Yugoslavia, 15 June, 1950 Yugoslav Int (FB)

League Club	Source	Date Signed	Seasons Played	Apps	Subs	Gls
Southampton	Partizan Belgrade (Yug)	11.78	78-81	143	1	4
Bournemouth	L	11.82	82	9	0	0
Manchester C.	L	03.83	82	2	0	0
Southampton	Bjelasica (Yug)	03.84	83-85	24	0	0
Portsmouth	L	01.85	84	8	0	0

GOLDBERG (GAUNT) Leslie
Leeds, 3 January, 1918 E Sch (FB)

League Club	Source	Date Signed	Seasons Played	Apps	Subs	Gls
Leeds U.	Jnrs	05.35	37-46	31	-	0
Reading	Tr	03.47	46-49	71	-	1

GOLDER James
Manchester, 28 March, 1955 (M)

League Club	Source	Date Signed	Seasons Played	Apps	Subs	Gls
Stockport Co.	App	•	71	0	1	0

GOLDIE James
Denny, 29 June, 1940 (F)

League Club	Source	Date Signed	Seasons Played	Apps	Subs	Gls
Luton T.	Kilsyth R.	04.62	62	7	-	2
York C.	Tr	06.63	63	22	-	7

GOLDIE Peter
Dumbarton, 7 June, 1934 (FB)

League Club	Source	Date Signed	Seasons Played	Apps	Subs	Gls
Aldershot	Glasgow Celtic	06.58	58	5	-	0

GOLDING Norman **John** William
Southwark, 23 January, 1937 (W)

League Club	Source	Date Signed	Seasons Played	Apps	Subs	Gls
Queens Park R.	Tonbridge	08.59	59-60	30	-	6

GOLDRING Mark
Brighton, 17 September, 1972 (G)

League Club	Source	Date Signed	Seasons Played	Apps	Subs	Gls
Chesterfield	YT	07.91	91	7	0	0

GOLDSMITH Craig Stephen William
Peterborough, 27 August, 1963 (LW)

League Club	Source	Date Signed	Seasons Played	Apps	Subs	Gls
Peterborough U.	Mirrlees Blackstone	08.88	88-89	39	7	6
Carlisle U.	Tr	12.89	89-90	21	9	1

GOLDSMITH Martin
Walsall, 4 November, 1969 (F)

League Club	Source	Date Signed	Seasons Played	Apps	Subs	Gls
Walsall	YT	08.88	88-90	2	5	2

GOLDSMITH Martin Sidney
Carmarthen, 25 May, 1962 (F)

League Club	Source	Date Signed	Seasons Played	Apps	Subs	Gls
Cambridge U.	Carmarthen T.	04.80	80-83	28	7	5
Cardiff C.	Tr	01.84	83	3	6	2

GOLDTHORPE Robert James
Osterley, 6 December, 1950 (CD)

League Club	Source	Date Signed	Seasons Played	Apps	Subs	Gls
Crystal Palace	Jnrs	07.68	71	1	0	0
Charlton Ath.	Tr	12.72	72-75	70	8	6
Aldershot	L	02.76	75	16	0	0
Brentford	Tr	07.76	76	19	0	2

GOLDTHORPE Wayne
Staincross, 19 September, 1957 (F)

League Club	Source	Date Signed	Seasons Played	Apps	Subs	Gls
Huddersfield T.	App	09.75	75-77	19	7	7
Hartlepool U.	L	12.76	76	6	1	1
Hartlepool U.	Tr	08.78	78-79	43	4	8
Crewe Alex.	Tr	10.79	79	0	1	0

GOLLEY Mark Anthony
Beckenham, 28 October, 1962 (CD)

League Club	Source	Date Signed	Seasons Played	Apps	Subs	Gls
Maidstone U.	Sutton U.	(N/L)	89-90	77	4	3

GOLLOGLY John
Bridlington, 4 July, 1962 (M)

League Club	Source	Date Signed	Seasons Played	Apps	Subs	Gls
Hartlepool U. (N/C)	Whitby T.	03.85	84-86	29	2	5

GOMERSALL Victor
Manchester, 17 June, 1942 (FB)

League Club	Source	Date Signed	Seasons Played	Apps	Subs	Gls
Manchester C.	Jnrs	07.60	61-65	39	0	0
Swansea C.	Tr	08.66	66-70	179	1	6

GONZAGUE Michael Alexander Granville
Canning Town, 27 March, 1975 (D)

League Club	Source	Date Signed	Seasons Played	Apps	Subs	Gls
Southend U.	YT	07.93				
Hereford U.	Tr	08.94	94	2	1	0

GOOCH James Arthur George
West Ham, 11 July, 1921 (G)

League Club	Source	Date Signed	Seasons Played	Apps	Subs	Gls
Preston N. E.	Becontree	05.42	46-51	135	-	0
Bradford C.	Tr	07.53	53	22	-	0
Watford	Tr	07.54	55-56	43	-	0

GOOD John Russell
Portsmouth, 29 January, 1933 (OR)

League Club	Source	Date Signed	Seasons Played	Apps	Subs	Gls
Nottingham F.		06.53				
Bury	Tr	06.54				
Tranmere Rov.	Buxton	07.55	55	5	-	0

GOODACRE Samuel David
Chesterfield, 1 December, 1970 E Sch (F)

League Club	Source	Date Signed	Seasons Played	Apps	Subs	Gls
Sheffield Wed.	Jnrs	07.89				
Scunthorpe U.	Tr	07.91	92-94	24	20	12

GOODALL Bernard
Islington, 4 October, 1937 (FB)

League Club	Source	Date Signed	Seasons Played	Apps	Subs	Gls
Reading		07.59	59-61	98	-	0
Carlisle U.	Tr	07.63	63	1	-	0
Halifax T.	Tr	11.64	64	23	-	0

GOODALL David George
Madeley (Staffs), 18 May, 1943 (CH)

League Club	Source	Date Signed	Seasons Played	Apps	Subs	Gls
Shrewsbury T.	Jnrs	05.61	61	1	-	0

GOODCHILD Gary Dean
Chelmsford, 27 January, 1958 E Sch (F)

League Club	Source	Date Signed	Seasons Played	Apps	Subs	Gls
Arsenal	App	01.75				
Hereford U.	Tr	06.76	76	1	3	0
Reading	Tr	09.77	77	0	1	0
Crystal Palace	Kramfors (Swe)	12.79	79-80	0	2	0

GOODCHILD John
Gateshead, 2 January, 1939 (F)

League Club	Source	Date Signed	Seasons Played	Apps	Subs	Gls
Sunderland	Ludworth Jnrs	09.56	57-60	44	-	21
Brighton & H. A.	Tr	05.61	61-65	162	1	44
York C.	Tr	06.66	66	29	0	6
Darlington	Tr	07.67	67	2	0	0

GOODE Terence Joseph
Islington, 29 October, 1961 (F)

League Club	Source	Date Signed	Seasons Played	Apps	Subs	Gls
Birmingham C.	App	09.79	80	0	2	0

GOODEN Ty Michael
Canvey Island, 23 October, 1972 (LW)

League Club	Source	Date Signed	Seasons Played	Apps	Subs	Gls
Swindon T.	Wycombe W.	09.93	93-97	74	24	8

GOODEVE Kenneth George Alfred
Manchester, 3 September, 1950 (CD)

League Club	Source	Date Signed	Seasons Played	Apps	Subs	Gls
Manchester U.	App	09.67				
Luton T.	Tr	04.70	70-72	9	6	0
Brighton & H. A.	Tr	12.73	73	5	1	0
Watford	Tr	06.74	74-75	67	0	4

GOODFELLOW Derwick Ormond
Shilbottle (Nd), 26 June, 1914 (G)

League Club	Source	Date Signed	Seasons Played	Apps	Subs	Gls
Gateshead		03.35	34-35	30	-	0
Sheffield Wed.	Tr	05.36	36-46	69	-	0
Middlesbrough	Tr	06.47	47	36	-	0

GOODFELLOW James
Sunderland, 16 September, 1943 (M)

League Club	Source	Date Signed	Seasons Played	Apps	Subs	Gls
Port Vale	Bishop Auckland	06.66	66-68	76	9	10
Workington	Tr	07.69	69-73	199	0	15
Rotherham U.	Tr	01.74	73-77	192	0	8
Stockport Co.	Tr	08.78	78	2	1	0

GOODFELLOW James Boyd
Edinburgh, 30 July, 1938 (F)

League Club	Source	Date Signed	Seasons Played	Apps	Subs	Gls
Leicester C.	Third Lanark	05.63	63-67	96	2	26
Mansfield T.	Tr	03.68	67-70	96	4	14

GOODFELLOW Sydney
Newcastle-under-Lyme, 6 July, 1915 (WH)

League Club	Source	Date Signed	Seasons Played	Apps	Subs	Gls
Port Vale	Hanley	11.36	36	16	-	1
Rochdale	Glentoran	05.38	38	41	-	2
Chesterfield	Tr	04.39	46-47	80	-	0
Doncaster Rov.	Tr	05.48	48-49	65	-	2
Oldham Ath.	Tr	09.50	50-51	72	-	2
Accrington St.	Tr	06.52	52	28	-	3

GOODGAME Anthony Alan
Hammersmith, 19 February, 1946 (FB)

League Club	Source	Date Signed	Seasons Played	Apps	Subs	Gls
Fulham	App	02.64				
Leyton Orient	Tr	08.66	66	7	1	0

GOODHIND Warren Ernest
South Africa, 16 August, 1977 (D/M)

League Club	Source	Date Signed	Seasons Played	Apps	Subs	Gls
Barnet	YT	07.96	96-97	23	15	1

GOODING Michael Charles
Newcastle, 12 April, 1959 (M)

League Club	Source	Date Signed	Seasons Played	Apps	Subs	Gls
Rotherham U.	Bishop Auckland	07.79	79-82	90	12	9
Chesterfield	Tr	12.82	82	12	0	0
Rotherham U.	Tr	09.83	83-86	149	7	33
Peterborough U.	Tr	08.87	87-88	47	0	21
Wolverhampton W.	Tr	09.88	88-89	43	1	4
Reading	Tr	12.89	89-96	303	11	26

GOODING Raymond
Hartlepool, 16 February, 1959 (M)

League Club	Source	Date Signed	Seasons Played	Apps	Subs	Gls
Coventry C.	App	06.76	76-81	46	3	5
Bristol C.	L	03.82	81	3	0	0
Plymouth Arg.	Tr	08.82	82	7	0	1

GOODISON Christopher **Wayne**
Wakefield, 23 September, 1964 (FB)

League Club	Source	Date Signed	Seasons Played	Apps	Subs	Gls
Barnsley	App	09.82	82-85	31	5	0
Crewe Alex.	Tr	09.86	86-88	90	4	1
Rochdale	Tr	07.89	89-90	78	1	4

GOODLASS Ronald
Liverpool, 6 September, 1953 E Sch (W)

League Club	Source	Date Signed	Seasons Played	Apps	Subs	Gls
Everton	App	07.71	75-77	31	4	2
Fulham	Den Haag (Neth)	09.80	80	21	1	2
Scunthorpe U.	Tr	03.82	81	9	0	0
Tranmere Rov.	Hong Kong	12.83	83-84	19	2	0

GOODMAN Donald Ralph
Leeds, 9 May, 1966 (F)

League Club	Source	Date Signed	Seasons Played	Apps	Subs	Gls
Bradford C.	Collingham	07.84	83-86	65	5	14
West Bromwich A.	Tr	03.87	86-91	140	18	60
Sunderland	Tr	12.91	91-94	112	4	40
Wolverhampton W.	Tr	12.94	94-97	115	10	33

GOODMAN John
Kings Lynn, 8 September, 1935 (G)

League Club	Source	Date Signed	Seasons Played	Apps	Subs	Gls
Crewe Alex.		10.58	58	1	-	0

GOODMAN Jonathan
Walthamstow, 2 June, 1971 IR-4 (F)

League Club	Source	Date Signed	Seasons Played	Apps	Subs	Gls
Millwall	Bromley	08.90	90-94	97	12	35
Wimbledon	Tr	11.94	94-96	28	31	11

GOODMAN Malcolm John
Solihull, 6 May, 1961 (D)

League Club	Source	Date Signed	Seasons Played	Apps	Subs	Gls
Halifax T.	Bromsgrove Rov.	09.79	79-82	70	16	1

GOODRIDGE Gregory Ronald St Clair
Barbados (WI), 10 July, 1971 Barbados Int (W)

League Club	Source	Date Signed	Seasons Played	Apps	Subs	Gls
Torquay U.	Lambada (St V)	03.94	93-94	32	6	4
Queens Park R.	Tr	08.95	95	0	7	1
Bristol C.	Tr	08.96	96-97	47	12	12

GOODWIN Craig
Wrexham, 12 February, 1974 (LB)

League Club	Source	Date Signed	Seasons Played	Apps	Subs	Gls
Chester C.	Aston Villa (YT)	08.92	92	3	2	0

GOODWIN David
Nantwich, 15 October, 1954 (F)

League Club	Source	Date Signed	Seasons Played	Apps	Subs	Gls
Stoke C.	App	06.72	73-77	22	4	3
Workington	L	10.76	76	7	0	0
Mansfield T.	Tr	11.77	77-79	42	4	5
Bury	Tr	09.80	80	2	2	0
Rochdale	Tr	08.81	81	34	5	6
Crewe Alex.	Tr	08.82	82	4	3	0

League Club	Source	Date Signed	Seasons Played	Apps	Subs	Gls
GOODWIN Eric						
Chesterfield, 6 March, 1929						(CH)
Mansfield T.	St Aidan Stags	09.53	53-54	9	-	0
GOODWIN Frederick						
Heywood, 28 June, 1933						(WH)
Manchester U.		10.53	54-59	95	-	7
Leeds U.	Tr	03.60	59-63	107	-	2
Scunthorpe U.	Tr	12.64	65	5	1	1
GOODWIN Frederick James						
Stockport, 4 January, 1944						(M)
Wolverhampton W.	Jnrs	01.61	61-65	44	1	0
Stockport Co.	Tr	01.66	65-69	171	5	20
Blackburn Rov.	Tr	03.70	69-71	63	1	4
Southport	Tr	10.71	71	10	2	0
Port Vale	Tr	08.72	72	27	0	2
Stockport Co.	Macclesfield T.	08.74	74	29	0	1
GOODWIN Ian David						
Irlam, 14 November, 1950						(CD)
Coventry C.	Oldham Ath. (App)	12.68	70	4	0	0
Brighton & H.A.	Tr	10.70	70-73	52	4	0
GOODWIN John William						
Worcester, 29 September, 1920 Died 1995						(OR)
Birmingham C.	Worcester C.	05.46	46-48	32	-	8
Brentford	Tr	04.49	49-53	131	-	22
GOODWIN Leslie						
Manchester, 30 April, 1924						(W)
Oldham Ath.	Haughton Green	08.44	46	7	-	0
Southport	Tr	07.47	47-48	16	-	2
GOODWIN Mark Adrian						
Sheffield, 23 February, 1960						(M)
Leicester C.	App	11.77	77-80	69	22	8
Notts Co.	Tr	03.81	80-86	226	11	23
Walsall	Tr	07.87	87-89	81	11	2
GOODWIN Samuel Gourlay						
Tarbolton (Ayrs), 14 March, 1943						(M)
Crystal Palace	Airdrieonians	09.71	71	18	7	0
GOODWIN Shaun Lee						
Rotherham, 14 June, 1969						(M)
Rotherham U.	YT	07.87	87-97	258	22	39
GOODWIN Stephen Alan						
Oldham, 23 February, 1954						(M)
Norwich C.	App	02.72	70-74	2	1	0
Scunthorpe U.	L	09.73	73	2	0	0
Southend U.	Tr	06.75	75-78	68	7	10
GOODYEAR Clive						
Lincoln, 15 January, 1961						(D)
Luton T.	Lincoln U.	10.78	79-83	85	5	4
Plymouth Arg.	Tr	08.84	84-86	99	7	5
Wimbledon	Tr	07.87	87-89	25	1	0
Brentford	Tr	03.91	90	10	0	0
GOODYEAR George William						
Luton, 5 July, 1916						(WH)
Luton T.	Hitchin T.	10.38	46	10	-	0
Southend U.	Tr	07.47	47-48	59	-	1
Crystal Palace	Tr	06.49				
GORAM Andrew Lewis						
Bury, 13 April, 1964 Su21-1/S-43						(G)
Oldham Ath.	West Bromwich A.(App)	08.81	81-87	195	0	0
GORAM Lewis Albert						
Edinburgh, 2 July, 1926 Died 1989						(G)
Bury	Third Lanark	06.50	50-56	111	-	0
GORDINE Barry						
Stepney, 1 September, 1948						(G)
Sheffield U.	Gravesend & Nft.	06.68				
Oldham Ath.	Tr	12.68	68-70	83	0	0
GORDON Andrew						
Bathgate, 6 July, 1944						(CF)
Darlington (Am)	West Auckland	08.69	69	1	2	0
GORDON Colin Kenneth						
Stourbridge, 17 January, 1963						(F)
Swindon T.	Oldbury U.	10.84	84-85	70	2	34
Wimbledon	Tr	06.86	86	2	1	0
Gillingham	L	02.87	86	4	0	2
Reading	Tr	07.87	87-88	23	1	9
Bristol C.	L	03.88	87	8	0	4
Fulham	Tr	10.88	88	12	5	2
Birmingham C.	Tr	06.89	89-90	17	9	3
Hereford U.	L	09.90	90	6	0	0
Walsall	L	12.90	90	6	0	1
Bristol Rov.	L	01.91	90	1	3	0
Leicester C.	Tr	07.91	91-92	18	6	5
GORDON Dale Andrew						
Great Yarmouth, 9 January, 1967 E Sch/E Yth/Eu21-4/E 'B'						(W)
Norwich C.	App	01.84	84-91	194	12	31
West Ham U.	Glasgow Rangers	07.93	93-95	8	1	1
Peterborough U.	L	03.95	94	6	0	1
Millwall	L	03.96	95	6	0	0
Bournemouth	Tr	08.96	96	14	2	1
GORDON Dean Dwight						
Croydon, 10 February, 1973 Eu21-13						(LB)
Crystal Palace	YT	07.91	91-97	181	20	20
GORDON Dennis William						
Bilston, 7 June, 1924						(OR)
West Bromwich A.	Oxford C.	09.47	47-51	27	-	2
Brighton & H.A.	Tr	07.52	52-60	277	-	62
GORDON Kenyatta **Gavin**						
Manchester, 24 June, 1979						(F)
Hull C.	YT	07.96	95-97	22	16	9
Lincoln C.	Tr	11.97	97	9	4	3
GORDON Henry						
Glasgow, 10 December, 1931						(HB)
Bury	Petershill	06.51	51-56	24	-	0
GORDON Henry Alexander						
Livingston, 25 July, 1940						(WH)
Bradford P.A.	Dundee U.	08.65	65-66	61	0	2
GORDON James						
Fauldhouse, 23 October, 1915 Died 1996						(WH)
Newcastle U.	Wishaw Jnrs	04.35	34-38	132	-	2
Middlesbrough	Tr	11.45	46-53	231	-	3
GORDON James Stephen						
Birmingham, 3 September, 1955 E Sch						(G)
Luton T.	Blackpool (App)	09.73				
Lincoln C.	Tr	07.74	76-77	4	0	0
Scunthorpe U.	Reading (N/C)	09.78	79-80	34	0	0
GORDON John Duncan Sinclair						
Portsmouth, 11 September, 1931						(IF)
Portsmouth	Jnrs	01.49	51-58	209	-	69
Birmingham C.	Tr	09.58	58-60	96	-	32
Portsmouth	Tr	03.61	60-66	234	0	37
GORDON Neville Spencer Damian						
Greenwich, 15 November, 1975						(F)
Millwall	YT	05.94				
Reading	Tr	08.95	95	0	1	0
GORDON Peter John						
Northampton, 21 May, 1932 Died 1990						(OR)
Norwich C.	L	12.49	53-57	160	-	34
Watford	Tr	07.58	58-59	43	-	13
Exeter C.	Tr	07.60	60-61	67	-	11
Newport Co.	Tr	07.62	62	8	-	1
GORDON Robert Baxter						
Ormiston, 5 September, 1923						(IF)
Millwall	Armadale Jnrs	01.45	46-47	5	-	0
GORDON William James						
Carlisle, 22 November, 1926 Died 1983						(CF)
Carlisle U.		08.48	48	15	-	4
Barrow	Tr	07.50	49-57	301	-	145
Workington	Tr	03.58	57-58	33	-	7
GORE Ian George						
Prescot, 10 January, 1968						(CD)
Birmingham C.	YT	05.86				
Blackpool	Southport	01.88	88-94	196	4	0
Torquay U.	Tr	08.95	95	25	0	2
Doncaster Rov.	Tr	03.96	95-97	65	1	1
GORE Shaun Michael						
West Ham, 21 September, 1968						(D)
Fulham	YT	06.86	85-88	25	1	0
Halifax T.	L	02.91	90	15	0	0

League Club	Source	Date Signed	Seasons Played	Career Record		
				Apps	Subs	Gls
GORE Thomas John						
Liverpool, 26 November, 1953						(M)
Wigan Ath.	Tranmere Rov. (N/C)	(N/L)	78-80	102	0	14
Bury	Tr	10.80	80-82	118	1	15
Port Vale	Tr	07.83	83	33	3	2
GORIN Edward (Ted) Rosser						
Cardiff, 2 March, 1924						(CF)
Cardiff C.	Grange A.	10.48	48-49	6	-	2
Scunthorpe U.	Tr	07.50	50	26	-	12
Shrewsbury T.	Tr	01.51	50-51	18	-	3
GORING Harry (Peter)						
Bishops Cleeve, 2 January 1927 Died 1994						(CF/WH)
Arsenal	Cheltenham T.	01.48	49-58	220	-	51
GORMAN Andrew David						
Cardiff, 13 September, 1974						(D)
Cardiff C.	YT	●	91-92	8	4	1
GORMAN John						
Winchburgh, 16 August, 1949						(LB)
Carlisle U.	Glasgow Celtic	09.70	70-76	228	1	5
Tottenham H.	Tr	11.76	76-78	30	0	0
GORMAN Keith						
Bishop Auckland, 13 October, 1966						(W)
Ipswich T.	App	01.84				
Colchester U.	L	09.86	86	0	1	0
Darlington	Tr	01.87	86	4	3	2
GORMAN Paul Anthony						
Dublin, 6 August, 1963 IR Yth/IRu21-1						(M/FB)
Arsenal	App	10.80	81-83	5	1	0
Birmingham C.	Tr	06.84	84	6	0	0
Carlisle U.	Tr	03.85	84-89	137	11	7
Shrewsbury T.	Tr	11.89	89-91	58	6	1
Carlisle U.	Tr	12.91	91	5	0	0
GORMAN Paul Michael						
Macclesfield, 18 September, 1968						(F)
Doncaster Rov.	YT	07.87	87-88	1	15	2
Charlton Ath.	Fisher Ath.	03.91	90-93	19	21	8
GORMAN William Charles						
Sligo (Ire), 13 July, 1911 Died 1978 IR-13/NI-4						(FB)
Bury	Sheltleston Jnrs	09.34	36-38	52	-	0
Brentford	Tr	12.38	38-49	125	-	0
GORMLEY Edward Joseph						
Dublin, 23 October, 1968 IRu21-3						(M)
Tottenham H.	Bray W.	11.87				
Chesterfield	L	11.88	88	4	0	0
Doncaster Rov.	Tr	07.90	90-92	110	8	16
GORMLEY Philip						
Greenock, 13 October, 1924 Died 1998						(CF/WH)
Aldershot	Glasgow Celtic	08.50	50-52	65	-	9
GORNALL John						
Preston, 28 March, 1941						(CH)
Preston N. E.	Jnrs	07.60	61-62	4	-	0
GORRIE David Alexander						
Liverpool, 21 January, 1943						(WH)
Everton	Jnrs	05.60				
Stockport Co.	Tr	07.62	62	18	-	0
GORRY Martin Christopher						
Derby, 29 December, 1954						(FB)
Barnsley	Jnrs	05.73	75-76	34	0	3
Newcastle U.	Tr	10.76	77	0	1	0
Hartlepool U.	Tr	07.78	78-79	59	0	0
GORTON Andrew William						
Salford, 23 September, 1966						(G)
Oldham Ath.	YT	07.84	85-87	26	0	0
Stockport Co.	L	12.86	86	14	0	0
Tranmere Rov.	L	05.88	87	1	0	0
Stockport Co.	Tr	08.88	88	34	0	0
Lincoln C.	Tr	08.89	89	20	0	0
Oldham Ath.	Glossop N.E.	02.91				
Crewe Alex. (N/C)	Tr	03.91	90	3	0	0
GOSLIN Richard William						
Bovey Tracey, 31 October, 1956						(F)
Torquay U.	Nottingham F. (App)	04.74	73-75	14	5	2

League Club	Source	Date Signed	Seasons Played	Career Record		
				Apps	Subs	Gls
GOSNEY Andrew Robert						
Southampton, 8 November, 1963 E Yth						(G)
Portsmouth	App	11.81	81-91	48	0	0
York C.	L	10.91	91	5	0	0
Birmingham C.	Tr	07.92	92	21	0	0
Exeter C. (N/C)		10.93	93	1	0	0
GOSS Jeremy						
Cyprus, 11 May, 1965 W-9						(M)
Norwich C.	Jnrs	03.83	83-95	155	33	14
GOTSMANOV Sergei Anaiolyenich						
USSR, 17 March, 1959						(F)
Brighton & H.A. (N/C)	Dinamo Minsk (USSR)	02.90	89	14	2	4
Southampton	Dinamo Minsk (USSR)	08.90	90	2	6	0
GOTTS James						
Seaton Delaval, 17 January, 1917						(OR)
Brentford	Ashington	01.46				
Brighton & H. A.	Tr	07.46	46	2	-	0
GOUCK Andrew Scott						
Blackpool, 8 June, 1972						(M)
Blackpool	YT	07.90	89-95	121	27	12
Rochdale	Tr	07.96	96-97	58	8	8
GOUGH Alan						
Watford, 10 March, 1971 IR Yth/IRu21-5						(G)
Portsmouth	Jnrs	07.89				
Fulham	Tr	06.92	92	3	0	0
GOUGH Anthony Michael						
Bath, 18 March, 1940						(M)
Bristol Rov.	Bath C.	05.58	58	1	-	0
Swindon T.	Bath C.	07.70	70	24	1	2
Torquay U.	Hereford U.	07.72	72	2	0	0
GOUGH Charles Storrar						
Glasgow, 21 May, 1939						(WH)
Charlton Ath.	Alton T.	06.63	64	4	-	0
GOUGH Keith						
Willenhall, 4 February, 1953 E Sch						(W)
Walsall	App	02.71	69-71	11	4	0
Oxford U.	Tr	07.72	72-74	32	7	5
GOUGH Matthew **Michael**						
Beeston, 29 December, 1935						(LH)
Aldershot		05.56	56-58	20	-	1
GOUGH Raymond John						
Belfast, 8 February, 1938						(WH)
Exeter C.	Linfield	10.63				
Millwall	Tr	10.64	64	13	-	0
GOUGH Richard Charles						
Sweden, 5 April, 1962 Su21-5/S-61						(CD)
Tottenham H.	Dundee U.	08.86	86-87	49	0	2
GOUGH Robert George						
Birmingham, 20 July, 1949						(F)
Walsall	App	07.67	66	1	0	0
Port Vale	Tr	07.68	68-73	189	21	33
Stockport Co.	L	02.73	73	6	0	0
Southport	Tr	07.74	74-75	61	0	16
Colchester U.	Tr	01.76	75-80	195	1	65
GOULD John **Barrie**						
Ammanford, 18 January, 1944						(WH)
Arsenal	App	11.61				
Chelsea	Tr	02.64				
Peterborough U.	Tr	07.65	65	18	0	3
GOULD Geoffrey						
Blackburn, 7 January, 1945						(OL)
Bradford P. A.	App	01.62	62-68	129	2	18
Lincoln C.	L	02.68	67	1	0	0
Notts Co.	Tr	07.69	69	1	0	0
GOULD Henry (Harry)						
Birkenhead, 5 January, 1925						(IF)
Tranmere Rov.	Park Villa	09.46	46-48	5	-	2
Southport	Northwich Vic.	09.50	50	16	-	2
Tranmere Rov.	Tr	07.51				
GOULD Jonathan Alan						
Paddington, 18 July, 1968 S 'B'						(G)
Halifax T.	Clevedon T.	07.90	90-91	32	0	0
West Bromwich A.	Tr	01.92				

League Club	Source	Date Signed	Seasons Played	Apps	Subs	Gls
Coventry C.	Tr	07.92	92-94	25	0	0
Bradford C.	Tr	03.96	95-96	18	0	0
Gillingham	L	10.96	96	3	0	0

GOULD Robert Alfred
Coventry, 12 June, 1946 (F)

League Club	Source	Date Signed	Seasons Played	Apps	Subs	Gls
Coventry C.	App	06.64	63-67	78	4	40
Arsenal	Tr	02.68	67-69	57	8	16
Wolverhampton W.	Tr	06.70	70-71	39	1	18
West Bromwich A.	Tr	09.71	71-72	52	0	18
Bristol C.	Tr	12.72	72-73	35	0	15
West Ham U.	Tr	11.73	73-75	46	5	15
Wolverhampton W.	Tr	12.75	75-76	24	10	13
Bristol Rov.	Tr	10.77	77-78	35	1	12
Hereford U.	Tr	09.78	78-79	42	3	13

GOULD Trevor Roy
Coventry, 5 March, 1950 E Sch (M)

League Club	Source	Date Signed	Seasons Played	Apps	Subs	Gls
Coventry C.	Jnrs	07.67	69	9	0	0
Northampton T.	Tr	10.70	70-72	102	3	6

GOULD Walter
Thrybergh, 25 September, 1938 (OR)

League Club	Source	Date Signed	Seasons Played	Apps	Subs	Gls
Sheffield U.	Rawmarsh Welfare	02.58	58	5	-	1
York C.	Tr	02.61	60-63	120	-	25
Brighton & H. A.	Tr	01.64	63-67	166	2	45

GOULDEN Albert Edward
Salford, 5 February, 1945 (FB)

League Club	Source	Date Signed	Seasons Played	Apps	Subs	Gls
Bolton W.	Jnrs	02.62	62	1	-	0

GOULDEN Leonard Arthur
West Ham, 9 July, 1912 Died 1995 E Sch/EF Lge/E-14 (IF)

League Club	Source	Date Signed	Seasons Played	Apps	Subs	Gls
West Ham U.	Jnrs	04.33	32-38	239	-	54
Chelsea	Tr	08.45	46-49	99	-	17

GOULDEN Roy Leonard
Ilford, 22 September, 1937 E Sch (IF)

League Club	Source	Date Signed	Seasons Played	Apps	Subs	Gls
Arsenal	Jnrs	09.54	58	1	-	0
Southend U.	Tr	05.61	61	9	-	2
Ipswich T.	Tr	07.62				

GOULDING Eric
Winsford, 22 November, 1924 (RB)

League Club	Source	Date Signed	Seasons Played	Apps	Subs	Gls
Everton	Over A.	10.45				
Crewe Alex.	Tr	10.46	46	1	-	0

GOULDING Stephen
Mexborough, 21 January, 1954 (FB)

League Club	Source	Date Signed	Seasons Played	Apps	Subs	Gls
Sheffield U.	App	05.71	71-75	28	0	0

GOULET Brent
USA, 19 June, 1964 (F)

League Club	Source	Date Signed	Seasons Played	Apps	Subs	Gls
Bournemouth	Seattle (USA)	11.87	87	2	4	0
Crewe Alex.	L	01.88	87	2	1	3

GOULOOZE Richard
Netherlands, 16 November, 1967 (M)

League Club	Source	Date Signed	Seasons Played	Apps	Subs	Gls
Derby Co.	Heerenveen (Neth)	09.92	92	7	5	0

GOUNDRY William
Middlesbrough, 28 March, 1934 (WH)

League Club	Source	Date Signed	Seasons Played	Apps	Subs	Gls
Brentford	Huddersfield T. (Am)	05.55	55-60	141	-	12

GOURLAY Archibald Murdoch
Greenock, 29 June, 1969 (M)

League Club	Source	Date Signed	Seasons Played	Apps	Subs	Gls
Newcastle U.	Morton	03.88	88-90	2	1	0
Hartlepool U. (N/C)	Motherwell	09.94	94	0	1	0

GOVAN Alexander
Glasgow, 16 June, 1929 (OL)

League Club	Source	Date Signed	Seasons Played	Apps	Subs	Gls
Plymouth Arg.	Jnrs	09.46	46-52	110	-	27
Birmingham C.	Tr	06.53	53-57	165	-	53
Portsmouth	Tr	03.58	57-58	11	-	2
Plymouth Arg.	Tr	09.58	58-59	32	-	8

GOVAN Charles Pearson
Belfast, 12 January, 1943 NI Sch (IF)

League Club	Source	Date Signed	Seasons Played	Apps	Subs	Gls
Burnley	Jnrs	01.60				
Mansfield T.	Tr	06.63	63-64	11	-	0

GOVIER Stephen
Watford, 6 April, 1952 (CD)

League Club	Source	Date Signed	Seasons Played	Apps	Subs	Gls
Norwich C.	App	07.69	70-73	22	0	1
Brighton & H. A.	Tr	04.74	74	12	0	1
Grimsby T.	Tr	12.74	74-76	23	1	0

GOW Gerald
Glasgow, 29 May, 1952 Su23-1 (M)

League Club	Source	Date Signed	Seasons Played	Apps	Subs	Gls
Bristol C.	Jnrs	06.69	69-80	368	7	48
Manchester C.	Tr	10.80	80-81	26	0	5
Rotherham U.	Tr	01.82	81-82	58	0	4
Burnley	Tr	08.83	83	8	1	0

GOWANS Peter Taylor
Dundee, 25 May, 1944 (W)

League Club	Source	Date Signed	Seasons Played	Apps	Subs	Gls
Crewe Alex.	Glasgow Celtic	07.63	63-66	141	0	43
Aldershot	Tr	07.67	67-69	111	2	27
Rochdale	Tr	07.70	70-73	136	8	21
Southport	Tr	07.74	74	3	1	0

GOWLING Alan Edwin
Stockport, 16 March, 1949 E Amat/Eu23-1 (F)

League Club	Source	Date Signed	Seasons Played	Apps	Subs	Gls
Manchester U.	Manchester Univ.	04.67	67-71	64	7	18
Huddersfield T.	Tr	06.72	72-74	128	0	58
Newcastle U.	Tr	08.75	75-77	91	1	30
Bolton W.	Tr	03.78	77-81	147	2	28
Preston N. E.	Tr	09.82	82	37	3	5

GOY Peter John
Beverley, 8 June, 1938 (G)

League Club	Source	Date Signed	Seasons Played	Apps	Subs	Gls
Arsenal	Jnrs	06.55	58	2	-	0
Southend U.	Tr	10.60	60-63	118	-	0
Watford	Tr	07.64	64	27	-	0
Huddersfield T.	Tr	07.65	66	4	0	0

GRACE Derek George
Chiswick, 29 December, 1944 (IF)

League Club	Source	Date Signed	Seasons Played	Apps	Subs	Gls
Exeter C.	Queens Park R. (App)	05.62	62-64	40	-	4
Gillingham	Tr	07.65	65	4	0	0

GRACE John Michael
Dublin, 16 February, 1964 (G)

League Club	Source	Date Signed	Seasons Played	Apps	Subs	Gls
Colchester U.	Tolka Rov.	07.89	89	19	0	0

GRAFTON Stanley Thomas
Wolverhampton, 2 April, 1923 Died 1953 (WH)

League Club	Source	Date Signed	Seasons Played	Apps	Subs	Gls
Aldershot	Bilston T.	08.47	47-48	2	-	0

GRAHAM Allan
Ryhope, 23 October, 1937 (FB)

League Club	Source	Date Signed	Seasons Played	Apps	Subs	Gls
Sunderland	Silksworth Jnrs	05.55	57	3	-	0

GRAHAM Arthur
Glasgow, 26 October, 1952 Su23-3/S-10 (W)

League Club	Source	Date Signed	Seasons Played	Apps	Subs	Gls
Leeds U.	Aberdeen	07.77	77-82	222	1	37
Manchester U.	Tr	08.83	83	33	4	5
Bradford C.	Tr	06.85	85-86	28	3	2

GRAHAM Benjamin
Pontypool, 23 September, 1975 (D)

League Club	Source	Date Signed	Seasons Played	Apps	Subs	Gls
Cardiff C.	YT	07.94	93	0	1	0

GRAHAM Deiniol William Thomas
Cannock, 4 October, 1969 W Yth/Wu21-1 (F)

League Club	Source	Date Signed	Seasons Played	Apps	Subs	Gls
Manchester U.	YT	10.87	87-89	1	1	0
Barnsley	Tr	08.91	91-93	18	20	2
Preston N.E.	L	10.92	92	8	0	0
Carlisle U.	L	11.93	93	2	0	1
Stockport Co.	Tr	06.94	94	5	6	2
Scunthorpe U. (N/C)	Tr	08.95	95	1	2	1

GRAHAM Donald
Oldham, 2 April, 1953 (FB)

League Club	Source	Date Signed	Seasons Played	Apps	Subs	Gls
Bury	Hyde U.	10.79	79-80	3	4	0

GRAHAM Douglas
Morpeth, 15 July, 1921 Died 1993 (FB)

League Club	Source	Date Signed	Seasons Played	Apps	Subs	Gls
Newcastle U.	Barrington U.	08.40	46-50	71	-	0
Preston N. E.	Tr	11.50				
Lincoln C.	Tr	12.51	51-56	182	-	0

GRAHAM George
Coatbridge, 30 November, 1944 S Sch/Su23-2/S-13 (F/M)

League Club	Source	Date Signed	Seasons Played	Apps	Subs	Gls
Aston Villa	App	12.61	62-63	8	-	2
Chelsea	Tr	07.64	64-66	72	0	35
Arsenal	Tr	09.66	66-72	219	8	59
Manchester U.	Tr	12.72	72-74	41	2	2
Portsmouth	Tr	11.74	74-76	61	0	5
Crystal Palace	Tr	11.76	76-77	43	1	2

GRAHAM Gerald Wilson
Aspatria (Cumb), 31 January, 1941 (WH)

League Club	Source	Date Signed	Seasons Played	Apps	Subs	Gls
Blackpool	Jnrs	08.59				
Peterborough U.	Tr	07.60	60-63	17	-	1
Mansfield T.	Tr	06.64	64	18	-	3
Workington	Worcester C.	07.68	68	6	0	0

GRAHAM James
Glasgow, 5 November, 1969 (LB)

League Club	Source	Date Signed	Seasons Played	Apps	Subs	Gls
Bradford C.	YT	09.88	88-89	6	1	0
Rochdale	L	11.89	89	11	0	0
Rochdale	Tr	07.90	90-93	120	6	1
Hull C.	Tr	08.94	94-95	63	0	1

GRAHAM John
Leyland, 26 April, 1926 (IF)

League Club	Source	Date Signed	Seasons Played	Apps	Subs	Gls
Aston Villa	Leyland Wks	11.46	46-48	10	-	3
Wrexham	Tr	06.49	49-51	45	-	7
Rochdale	Tr	02.53	52	10	-	1
Bradford C.	Tr	07.53	53	18	-	1

GRAHAM John (Jackie) Joseph
Glasgow, 16 July, 1946 (M)

League Club	Source	Date Signed	Seasons Played	Apps	Subs	Gls
Brentford	Guildford C.	07.70	70-79	371	3	38

GRAHAM William George Leonard
Belfast, 17 October, 1925 NI-14 (FB)

League Club	Source	Date Signed	Seasons Played	Apps	Subs	Gls
Doncaster Rov.	Brantwood	10.49	50-58	303	-	3
Torquay U.	Tr	11.58	58	20	-	0

GRAHAM Leslie
Manchester, 14 May, 1924 Died 1998 (IF)

League Club	Source	Date Signed	Seasons Played	Apps	Subs	Gls
Blackburn Rov.	Flixton	04.47	47-52	150	-	42
Newport Co.	Tr	02.53	52-54	97	-	40
Watford	Tr	07.55	56-57	90	-	26
Newport Co.	Tr	09.57	57-58	65	-	15

GRAHAM Malcolm
Crigglestone, 26 January, 1934 (IF)

League Club	Source	Date Signed	Seasons Played	Apps	Subs	Gls
Barnsley	Hall Green	04.53	54-58	109	-	35
Bristol C.	Tr	05.59	59	14	-	8
Leyton Orient	Tr	06.60	60-62	75	-	29
Queens Park R.	Tr	07.63	63	21	-	7
Barnsley	Tr	07.64	64	20	-	5

GRAHAM Mark Roland
Newry, 24 October, 1974 NI Sch/NI Yth/NI 'B' (RB)

League Club	Source	Date Signed	Seasons Played	Apps	Subs	Gls
Queens Park R.	YT	05.93	96	16	2	0

GRAHAM Michael Anthony
Lancaster, 24 February, 1959 (D)

League Club	Source	Date Signed	Seasons Played	Apps	Subs	Gls
Bolton W.	App	02.77	77-80	43	3	0
Swindon T.	Tr	07.81	81-84	141	0	1
Mansfield T.	Tr	07.85	85-88	132	1	1
Carlisle U.	Tr	09.88	88-91	137	1	3

GRAHAM Milton Mackay
Hackney, 2 November, 1962 (M)

League Club	Source	Date Signed	Seasons Played	Apps	Subs	Gls
Bournemouth	Jnrs	05.81	81-84	54	19	12
Chester C.	Tr	08.85	85-88	123	6	10
Peterborough U.	Tr	07.89	89	10	5	2

GRAHAM Peter
Barnsley, 19 April, 1947 (M)

League Club	Source	Date Signed	Seasons Played	Apps	Subs	Gls
Barnsley	Worsboro' Bridge	01.67	66-69	16	3	1
Halifax T.	L	03.70	69	6	0	0
Darlington	Tr	06.70	70-73	118	1	43
Lincoln C.	Tr	09.73	73-77	142	16	47
Cambridge U.	Tr	06.78	78-79	35	3	0

GRAHAM Ralph Cowell
Durham, 29 December, 1929 (W)

League Club	Source	Date Signed	Seasons Played	Apps	Subs	Gls
Doncaster Rov.	Broadway Ath.	05.47	48-49	15	-	0
Southport	Tr	07.50	50-51	29	-	9

GRAHAM Richard Ean
Dewsbury, 28 November, 1974 (CD)

League Club	Source	Date Signed	Seasons Played	Apps	Subs	Gls
Oldham Ath.	YT	07.93	93-97	114	8	9

GRAHAM Douglas Richard (Dick)
Corby, 6 May, 1922 (G)

League Club	Source	Date Signed	Seasons Played	Apps	Subs	Gls
Leicester C.	Northampton T. (Am)	11.44				
Crystal Palace	Tr	12.45	46-50	155	-	0

GRAHAM Robert
Motherwell, 22 November, 1944 (F)

League Club	Source	Date Signed	Seasons Played	Apps	Subs	Gls
Liverpool	App	11.61	64-71	96	5	31
Coventry C.	Tr	03.72	71-72	19	-	3
Tranmere Rov.	L	01.73	72	10	0	3

GRAHAM Thomas
Glasgow, 31 March, 1955 (M)

League Club	Source	Date Signed	Seasons Played	Apps	Subs	Gls
Aston Villa	Arthurlie	04.78				
Barnsley	Tr	12.78	78-79	36	2	13
Halifax T.	Tr	10.80	80-81	68	3	17
Doncaster Rov. (N/C)	Tr	08.82	82	9	2	2
Scunthorpe U.	Tr	03.83	82-85	102	7	21
Scarborough	Tr	08.86	87-89	104	7	11
Halifax T.	Tr	01.90	89-91	56	2	4

GRAHAM William Reynolds
Carlisle, 8 May, 1929 (WH)

League Club	Source	Date Signed	Seasons Played	Apps	Subs	Gls
Workington		07.51				
Carlisle U.	Consett	01.54	53-60	35	-	2

GRAHAM William Valentine
Armagh (NI), 14 February, 1959 (M)

League Club	Source	Date Signed	Seasons Played	Apps	Subs	Gls
Brentford	Northampton T. (App)	08.77	77-80	42	6	3

GRAINGER Colin
Hemsworth, 10 June, 1933 EF Lge/E-7 (OL)

League Club	Source	Date Signed	Seasons Played	Apps	Subs	Gls
Wrexham	South Elmsall	10.50	50-52	5	-	0
Sheffield U.	Tr	07.53	53-56	88	-	26
Sunderland	Tr	02.57	56-59	120	-	14
Leeds U.	Tr	07.60	60	33	-	5
Port Vale	Tr	10.61	61-63	39	-	6
Doncaster Rov.	Tr	08.64	64-65	40	0	4

GRAINGER Dennis
Barnsley, 5 March, 1920 Died 1986 (W)

League Club	Source	Date Signed	Seasons Played	Apps	Subs	Gls
Southport	South Kirkby	10.38				
Leeds U.	Tr	10.45	46-47	37	-	5
Wrexham	Tr	12.47	47-50	98	-	12
Oldham Ath.	Tr	06.51	51	3	-	0

GRAINGER John (Jack)
South Elmsall, 17 July, 1912 Died 1976 (FB)

League Club	Source	Date Signed	Seasons Played	Apps	Subs	Gls
Barnsley	Royston Colly	08.32	32	1	-	0
Southport	Tr	08.33	33-46	222	-	0

GRAINGER John (Jack)
Darton, 3 April, 1924 Died 1983 E 'B' (OR)

League Club	Source	Date Signed	Seasons Played	Apps	Subs	Gls
Rotherham U.	Frickley Colly	11.45	47-56	352	-	112
Lincoln C.	Tr	06.57	57-58	42	-	14

GRAINGER Martin Robert
Enfield, 23 August, 1972 (LB)

League Club	Source	Date Signed	Seasons Played	Apps	Subs	Gls
Colchester U.	YT	07.92	89-93	37	9	7
Brentford	Tr	10.93	93-95	100	1	12
Birmingham C.	Tr	03.96	95-97	56	8	5

GRANGER Keith William
Southampton, 5 October, 1968 (G)

League Club	Source	Date Signed	Seasons Played	Apps	Subs	Gls
Southampton	App	10.86	85	2	0	0
Darlington	Tr	12.87	87	23	0	0

GRANGER Michael
Leeds, 7 October, 1931 (G)

League Club	Source	Date Signed	Seasons Played	Apps	Subs	Gls
York C.	Cliftonville	12.51	54-61	71	-	0
Hull C.	Tr	07.62	62	2	-	0
Halifax T.	Tr	07.53	63-64	2	-	0

GRANT Alan James
Havant, 6 January, 1935 (HB)

League Club	Source	Date Signed	Seasons Played	Apps	Subs	Gls
Brighton & H. A.	Gosport Borough	04.56	56	1	-	0
Exeter C.	Tr	06.60	60	4	-	0

GRANT Alick Frank
Radstock, 11 August, 1916 (G)

League Club	Source	Date Signed	Seasons Played	Apps	Subs	Gls
Bury	Sheffield U. (Am)	08.37				
Aldershot	Tr	05.38	38	5	-	0
Leicester C.	Tr	12.41	46	2	-	0
Derby Co.	Tr	11.46	46-47	12	-	0
Newport Co.	Tr	11.48	48	20	-	0
Leeds U.	Tr	08.49				
York C.	Tr	03.50	49	3	-	0

GRANT Anthony
Drogheda, 20 August, 1976 IR Sch/IR Yth (F)

League Club	Source	Date Signed	Seasons Played	Apps	Subs	Gls
Leeds U.	YT	08.94				
Preston N.E.	Tr	11.95	95	0	1	0

GRANT Anthony James
Liverpool, 14 November, 1974 Eu21-1 (M)

League Club	Source	Date Signed	Seasons Played	Apps	Subs	Gls
Everton	YT	07.93	94-97	30	13	2
Swindon T.	L	01.96	95	3	0	1

GRANT Bernard
Airdrie, 23 May, 1920 Died 1984 (IF)

League Club	Source	Date Signed	Seasons Played	Apps	Subs	Gls
Exeter C.	Third Lanark	07.47	48	2	-	0

GRANT Brian Patrick
Coatbridge, 10 May, 1943 (FB)

League Club	Source	Date Signed	Seasons Played	Apps	Subs	Gls
Nottingham F.	Jnrs	05.60	60-64	18	-	0
Hartlepool U.	Tr	01.66	65-66	35	0	0
Cambridge U.	Bradford C. (trial)	(N/L)	70	14	0	0

GRANT Cyril
Wath, 10 July, 1920 (CF)

League Club	Source	Date Signed	Seasons Played	Apps	Subs	Gls
Lincoln C.	Mexborough	06.39				
Arsenal	Tr	07.46	46	2	-	0
Fulham	Tr	12.46	46-47	14	-	4
Southend U.	Tr	03.48	47-54	175	-	63

GRANT David
Sheffield, 2 June, 1960 (LB)

League Club	Source	Date Signed	Seasons Played	Apps	Subs	Gls
Sheffield Wed.	App	02.78	77-81	132	1	4
Oxford U.	Tr	07.82	82-83	24	0	1
Chesterfield	L	09.83	83	7	0	0
Cardiff C.	Tr	03.84	83-84	25	0	0
Rochdale	Tr	03.85	84-86	97	0	2

GRANT David Bell
Edinburgh, 31 July, 1943 (F)

League Club	Source	Date Signed	Seasons Played	Apps	Subs	Gls
Reading	Third Lanark	05.63	63-64	17	-	3

GRANT David John
Liverpool, 18 December, 1947 E Sch (WH)

League Club	Source	Date Signed	Seasons Played	Apps	Subs	Gls
Everton	App	12.65				
Wrexham	Tr	09.66	66	6	5	0

GRANT Edward Anthony
Greenock, 1 October, 1928 (IF)

League Club	Source	Date Signed	Seasons Played	Apps	Subs	Gls
Sheffield U.	Weymouth	05.50	50	4	-	0
Grimsby T.	Tr	07.52	52-53	15	-	5

GRANT Gareth Michael
Leeds, 6 September, 1980 (F)

League Club	Source	Date Signed	Seasons Played	Apps	Subs	Gls
Bradford C.	YT	04.98	97	1	2	0

GRANT James
Airdrie, 10 June, 1940 (OR)

League Club	Source	Date Signed	Seasons Played	Apps	Subs	Gls
Scunthorpe U.	Larkhall Thistle	11.58	58	1	-	0

GRANT James
(OL)

League Club	Source	Date Signed	Seasons Played	Apps	Subs	Gls
Brighton & H.A. (Am)		12.46	46	1	-	0

GRANT John (Jackie) Albert
Gateshead, 8 September, 1924 (WH)

League Club	Source	Date Signed	Seasons Played	Apps	Subs	Gls
Everton	High Spen Ath.	12.42	46-54	121	-	10
Rochdale	Tr	05.56	56-58	102	-	3
Southport	Tr	01.59	58-59	40	-	0

GRANT Kenneth
High Spen, 13 November, 1938 (CF)

League Club	Source	Date Signed	Seasons Played	Apps	Subs	Gls
Gateshead (Am)	Crook T.	12.58	58	5	-	0

GRANT Kimberley Tyrone
Ghana, 25 September, 1972 Ghanaian Int (F)

League Club	Source	Date Signed	Seasons Played	Apps	Subs	Gls
Charlton Ath.	YT	03.91	90-95	74	49	18
Luton T.	Tr	03.96	95-96	18	17	5
Millwall	Tr	08.97	97	31	8	8

GRANT Peter
Glasgow, 30 August, 1965 S Sch/S Yth/Su21-10/S 'B'/S-2 (M)

League Club	Source	Date Signed	Seasons Played	Apps	Subs	Gls
Norwich C.	Glasgow Celtic	08.97	97	33	2	3

GRANT Peter John
Glasgow, 11 April, 1968 (D)

League Club	Source	Date Signed	Seasons Played	Apps	Subs	Gls
Stockport Co.	Ipswich T. (App)	07.86	86	1	0	0

GRANT Robert
Edinburgh, 25 September, 1940 (CF)

League Club	Source	Date Signed	Seasons Played	Apps	Subs	Gls
Carlisle U.	St Johnstone	07.62	62	2	-	1

GRANT Stephen Hubert
Birr, 14 April, 1977 IRu21-2 (F)

League Club	Source	Date Signed	Seasons Played	Apps	Subs	Gls
Sunderland	Athlone T.	08.95				
Stockport Co.	Shamrock Rov.	09.97	97	9	7	3

GRANT Wilfred
Ashington, 31 August, 1920 Died 1990 E 'B' (CF)

League Club	Source	Date Signed	Seasons Played	Apps	Subs	Gls
Manchester C.	Morpeth T.	02.43				
Southampton	Tr	10.46	46-49	61	-	12
Cardiff C.	Tr	03.50	49-54	155	-	65
Ipswich T.	Tr	10.54	54-56	75	-	22

GRANT William Fraser
Perth, 7 October, 1933 (HB)

League Club	Source	Date Signed	Seasons Played	Apps	Subs	Gls
Gillingham	Brechin C.	08.56	56	1	-	0

GRANVILLE Daniel Patrick
Islington, 19 January, 1975 Eu21-4 (LB)

League Club	Source	Date Signed	Seasons Played	Apps	Subs	Gls
Cambridge U.	YT	05.93	93-96	89	10	7
Chelsea	Tr	03.97	96-97	12	6	0

GRANVILLE John Hubert
Tobago (WI), 6 May, 1956 Trinidadian Int (G)

League Club	Source	Date Signed	Seasons Played	Apps	Subs	Gls
Millwall (N/C)	Slough T.	10.85	85	6	0	0

GRANVILLE Anthony **Ralph**
Glasgow, 23 April, 1931

League Club	Source	Date Signed	Seasons Played	Apps	Subs	Gls
Gateshead	Clyde	10.57	57	2	-	0

GRANVILLE Norman **Trevor**
Newport, 25 November, 1919 Died 1992 (OR)

League Club	Source	Date Signed	Seasons Played	Apps	Subs	Gls
Newport Co.	Cliftonville	01.46	46	1	-	0
Exeter C.	Tr	10.46	46-47	20	-	1

GRANYCOMBE Neil
Middlesbrough, 23 October, 1958 (F)

League Club	Source	Date Signed	Seasons Played	Apps	Subs	Gls
Hartlepool U. (N/C)	South Bank	02.81	80	1	0	0

GRAPES Stephen Philip
Norwich, 25 February, 1953 (M)

League Club	Source	Date Signed	Seasons Played	Apps	Subs	Gls
Norwich C.	App	07.70	70-76	34	7	3
Bournemouth	L	03.76	75	7	0	1
Cardiff C.	Tr	10.76	76-81	138	9	6
Torquay U.	Tr	08.82	82	31	0	0

GRATRIX Roy
Salford, 9 February, 1932 E 'B'/EF Lge (CH)

League Club	Source	Date Signed	Seasons Played	Apps	Subs	Gls
Blackpool	Taylor Bros	03.53	53-64	400	-	0
Manchester C.	Tr	09.64	64	15	-	0

GRATTAN James
Belfast, 30 November, 1958 (F)

League Club	Source	Date Signed	Seasons Played	Apps	Subs	Gls
Sunderland	App	10.76				
Mansfield T.	L	11.78	78	1	0	0

GRATTON Dennis
Rotherham, 21 April, 1934 (CH)

League Club	Source	Date Signed	Seasons Played	Apps	Subs	Gls
Sheffield U.	Worksop T.	10.52	55-58	6	-	0
Lincoln C.	Tr	09.59	59-60	45	-	0

GRAVER Andrew Martin
Lanchester, 12 September, 1927 (CF)

League Club	Source	Date Signed	Seasons Played	Apps	Subs	Gls
Newcastle U.	Annfield Plain	09.47	49	1	-	0
Lincoln C.	Tr	09.50	50-54	172	-	107
Leicester C.	Tr	12.54	54	11	-	3
Lincoln C.	Tr	07.55	55	15	-	4
Stoke C.	Tr	11.55	55-56	37	-	12
Lincoln C.	Boston U.	10.58	58-60	89	-	33

GRAVES Mark Terence
Isleworth, 14 December, 1960 (F)

League Club	Source	Date Signed	Seasons Played	Apps	Subs	Gls
Plymouth Arg.	App	09.78	77-80	24	9	3

GRAVES Robert Edward
Marylebone, 7 November, 1942 (G)

League Club	Source	Date Signed	Seasons Played	Apps	Subs	Gls
Lincoln C.	Kirton	04.60	59-64	77	-	0

GRAVES Wayne Alan
Scunthorpe, 18 September, 1980 (D/M)

League Club	Source	Date Signed	Seasons Played	Apps	Subs	Gls
Scunthorpe U.	YT	●	97	0	3	0

GRAVETTE Warren
Thetford, 13 September, 1968 (M)

League Club	Source	Date Signed	Seasons Played	Apps	Subs	Gls
Tottenham H.	App	08.86				
Brentford	Tr	07.87	87	1	4	0

GRAY Alan Muir
Carlisle, 2 May, 1974 (RB)

League Club	Source	Date Signed	Seasons Played	Apps	Subs	Gls
Doncaster Rov.	Richmond Univ. (USA)	08.96	96	1	0	0
Darlington	Bishop Auckland	08.97	97	6	0	0
Carlisle U.	Tr	02.98	97	0	1	0

GRAY Alexander David
Arbroath, 7 November, 1936 (FB)

League Club	Source	Date Signed	Seasons Played	Apps	Subs	Gls
Burnley	Dundee Violet	06.54				
Cardiff C.	Arbroath	03.57	58	1	-	0

GRAY Andrew
Southampton, 25 October, 1973 (F)

League Club	Source	Date Signed	Seasons Played	Apps	Subs	Gls
Reading	YT	07.92	91-93	8	9	3
Leyton Orient	Tr	07.94	94-95	16	16	3

GRAY Andrew Arthur
Lambeth, 22 February, 1964 Eu21-2/E-1 (M)

League Club	Source	Date Signed	Seasons Played	Apps	Subs	Gls
Crystal Palace	Dulwich Hamlet	11.84	84-87	91	7	27
Aston Villa	Tr	11.87	87-88	34	3	4
Queens Park R.	Tr	02.89	88	11	0	2
Crystal Palace	Tr	08.89	89-91	87	3	12
Tottenham H.	Tr	02.92	91-93	23	10	3
Swindon T.	L	12.92	92	3	0	0

League Club	Source	Date Signed	Seasons Played	Career Record Apps	Subs	Gls
Bury	Falkirk	07.97	97	21	0	1
Millwall	Tr	01.98	97	12	0	1
GRAY Andrew David						
Harrogate, 15 November, 1977 S Yth						(LW)
Leeds U.	YT	07.95	95-96	13	9	0
Bury	L	12.97	97	4	2	1
GRAY Andrew Mullen						
Glasgow, 30 November, 1955 Su23-4/S-20						(F)
Aston Villa	Dundee U.	10.75	75-78	112	1	54
Wolverhampton W.	Tr	09.79	79-83	130	3	38
Everton	Tr	11.83	83-84	44	5	14
Aston Villa	Tr	07.85	85-86	53	1	5
Notts Co.	L	08.87	87	3	1	0
West Bromwich A.	Tr	09.87	87-88	32	3	10
GRAY David						
Coupar Angus, 8 February, 1922						(FB)
Preston N.E.	Glasgow Rangers	05.47	47	36	-	0
Blackburn Rov.	Tr	08.48	48-52	107	-	5
GRAY David Downie						
Clydebank, 13 April, 1923						(WH)
Bradford C.	Queensbury	09.48	48-55	242	-	13
GRAY Edward						
Bellshill, 19 October, 1934 S Sch						(IF)
Barrow	Yeovil T.	12.57	57-58	17	-	4
Accrington St.	Tr	07.59	59	6	-	0
GRAY Edwin (Eddie)						
Glasgow, 17 January, 1948 S Sch/Su23-2/S-12						(W)
Leeds U.	Jnrs	01.65	65-83	442	13	52
GRAY Francis Tierney						
Glasgow, 27 October, 1954 S Sch/Su23-5/S-32						(LB)
Leeds U.	App	11.71	72-78	188	5	17
Nottingham F.	Tr	08.79	79-80	81	0	5
Leeds U.	Tr	05.81	81-84	139	0	10
Sunderland	Tr	07.85	85-88	118	28	8
Darlington	Tr	07.89	90-91	49	0	7
GRAY Gareth						
Longridge, 24 February, 1970						(G)
Bolton W.	Darwen	02.88				
Rochdale	Tr	07.90	91	6	0	0
GRAY George						
Glasgow, 6 October, 1929						(OR)
Carlisle U.	Vale of Clyde	11.47	47	1	-	1
Scunthorpe U.	Sligo Rov.	08.51	51	9	-	3
GRAY George James Pope						
Sunderland, 7 July, 1925 Died 1995						(WH)
Grimsby T.	Derby Co. (Am)	01.47	50	3	-	0
Swindon T.	Tr	07.51	51-52	45	-	0
Darlington	Tr	07.53	53	6	-	0
GRAY George Walter						
Canning Town, 30 November, 1922						(CF)
Aldershot	West Ham U. (Am)	02.47	46-47	9	-	0
GRAY Harry						
Hemsworth, 26 October, 1918 Died 1989						(IF)
Barnsley	Ardsley Rec.	02.38	46	7	-	1
Bournemouth	Tr	12.46	46-47	30	-	7
Southend U.	Tr	06.48	48-49	19	-	0
GRAY Ian James						
Manchester, 25 February, 1975						(G)
Oldham Ath.	YT	07.93				
Rochdale	L	11.94	94	12	0	0
Rochdale	Tr	07.95	95-96	66	0	0
Stockport Co.	Tr	07.97	97	3	0	0
GRAY Irvine William						
Hoyland, 27 February, 1933						(W)
Barnsley		09.52				
Gillingham	Tr	08.56	56	9	-	0
GRAY Kevin John						
Sheffield, 7 January, 1972						(CD)
Mansfield T.	YT	07.90	88-93	129	12	3
Huddersfield T.	Tr	07.94	94-97	113	4	2
GRAY Mark Stuart						
Pembroke, 24 November, 1959						(F)
Swansea C.	App	09.77	77	1	1	0

League Club	Source	Date Signed	Seasons Played	Career Record Apps	Subs	Gls
Fulham	Tr	01.78				
Leyton Orient	Tr	02.79	78	1	1	0
GRAY Martin David						
Stockton, 17 August, 1971						(M)
Sunderland	YT	02.90	91-95	46	18	1
Aldershot	L	01.91	90	3	2	0
Fulham	L	10.95	95	6	0	0
Oxford U.	Tr	03.96	95-97	75	6	4
GRAY Matthew						
Renfrew, 11 July, 1936						(IF)
Manchester C.	Third Lanark	03.63	62-66	87	4	21
GRAY Michael						
						(IF)
Aldershot	Glenavon	09.46	46	7	-	1
Watford	Tr	06.47	47	10	-	3
GRAY Michael						
Sunderland, 3 August, 1974						(LW)
Sunderland	YT	07.92	92-97	170	19	12
GRAY Nigel Robert						
Fulham, 2 November, 1956						(CD)
Leyton Orient	App	07.74	74-82	233	0	4
Charlton Ath.	L	12.82	82	3	0	0
Swindon T.	Tr	07.83	83-84	33	0	1
Brentford	L	03.84	83	16	0	1
Aldershot	L	09.84	84	4	0	0
GRAY Robert **Paul**						
Portsmouth, 28 January, 1970						(F)
Luton T.	YT	06.88	89	2	5	1
Wigan Ath.	Tr	05.91	91	2	3	0
GRAY Philip						
Belfast, 2 October, 1968 NI Sch/NI Yth/NIu23-1/NI-20						(F)
Tottenham H.	App	08.86	86-90	4	5	0
Barnsley	L	01.90	89	3	0	0
Fulham	L	11.90	90	3	0	0
Luton T.	Tr	08.91	91-92	54	5	22
Sunderland	Tr	07.93	93-95	108	7	34
Luton T.	Fortuna Sittard (Neth)	09.97	97	14	3	2
GRAY Robert						
Cambuslang, 18 June, 1927						(IR)
Lincoln C.	Wishaw Jnrs	10.49	49	2	-	0
GRAY Robert						
Glasgow, 8 June, 1953 S Sch						(M)
Workington	Nottingham F. (App)	08.72	72	0	1	0
GRAY Robert						
Newcastle, 14 December, 1923						(G)
Gateshead	Newcastle U. (Am)	03.44	47-58	432	-	0
GRAY Robert Henry William						
Aberdeen, 21 January, 1951						(G)
Torquay U. (Am)	Inverurie Loco.	11.69	69	2	0	0
GRAY Roland (Ron)						
North Shields, 25 June, 1920						(WH)
Sheffield U.	Boldon Colly	05.38				
Lincoln C.	Tr	05.39				
Watford	Tr	08.45	46	16	-	0
GRAY Stewart Alexander						
Doncaster, 16 October, 1950						(D)
Doncaster Rov.	App	09.68	67-70	53	5	0
Grimsby T.	Tr	09.70	70-76	263	1	2
Doncaster Rov. (N/C)	Frickley Ath.	03.78	77	6	0	0
GRAY Stuart						
Hallogate, 18 December, 1973 Su21-7						(FB)
Reading	Glasgow Celtic	03.98	97	7	0	0
GRAY Stuart						
Withernsea, 19 April, 1960						(M/LB)
Nottingham F.	Withernsea Y.C.	12.80	80-82	48	1	3
Bolton W.	L	03.83	82	10	0	0
Barnsley	Tr	08.83	83-87	117	3	23
Aston Villa	Tr	11.87	87-90	102	4	9
Southampton	Tr	09.91	91	10	2	0
GRAY Terence Ian						
Bradford, 3 June, 1954 E Yth						(W)
Huddersfield T.	Ashley Road	08.72	73-78	146	17	36
Southend U.	Tr	07.79	79-81	106	4	28

League Club	Source	Date Signed	Seasons Played	Apps	Subs	Gls
Bradford C.	Tr	08.82	82-84	72	4	15
Preston N. E.	Tr	10.84	84-85	40	0	1
GRAY William Mair						
Coventry, 3 December, 1931						(WH)
Coventry C.	Jnrs	12.48	51	2	-	0
GRAY William Patrick						
Ashington, 24 May, 1927 E 'B'						(W)
Leyton Orient	Dinnington Colly	05.47	47-48	19	-	1
Chelsea	Tr	03.49	48-52	146	-	12
Burnley	Tr	08.53	53-56	120	-	30
Nottingham F.	Tr	06.57	57-62	201	-	29
Millwall	Tr	12.63	63-64	20	-	1
GRAYDON Raymond Jack						
Bristol, 21 July, 1947 EYth						(W)
Bristol Rov.	App	09.65	65-70	131	2	33
Aston Villa	Tr	06.71	71-76	188	4	68
Coventry C.	Tr	07.77	77	17	3	5
Oxford U.	Washington (USA)	11.78	78-80	36	6	10
GRAYSON Barry John						
Manchester, 12 October, 1944						(F)
Manchester U.	App	11.61				
Bury	Tr	01.65	64	1	-	0
GRAYSON Neil						
York, 1 November, 1964						(W/F)
Doncaster Rov. (N/C)	Rowntree Mackintosh	03.90	89-90	21	8	6
York C.	Tr	03.91	90	0	1	0
Chesterfield	Tr	08.91	91	10	6	0
Northampton T.	Boston U.	06.94	94-96	103	17	31
GRAYSON Simon Darrell						
Sheffield, 21 October, 1968						(F)
Sheffield U.	App	10.86				
Chesterfield	L	11.87	87	7	1	0
Hartlepool U.	Tr	04.88	87-89	39	5	13
GRAYSON Simon Nicholas						
Ripon, 16 December, 1969						(RB/M)
Leeds U.	YT	06.88	87	2	0	0
Leicester C.	Tr	03.92	91-96	175	13	4
Aston Villa	Tr	07.97	97	28	5	0
GRAYSTON Neil James						
Keighley, 25 November, 1975						(LB)
Bradford C.	YT	05.94	93-95	7	0	0
GRAZIOLI Guiliano Stefano Luigi						
Marylebone, 23 March, 1975						(F)
Peterborough U.	Wembley	10.95	95-96	2	5	1
GREALISH Anthony Patrick						
Paddington, 21 September, 1956 IR Yth/IR-44						(M)
Leyton Orient	App	07.74	74-78	169	2	10
Luton T.	Tr	08.79	79-80	78	0	2
Brighton & H. A.	Tr	07.81	81-83	95	5	6
West Bromwich A.	Tr	03.84	83-85	55	10	5
Manchester C.	Tr	10.86	86	11	0	0
Rotherham U.	Tr	08.87	87-89	105	5	7
Walsall	Tr	08.90	90-91	32	4	1
GREATREX Edward John						
Nuneaton, 18 November, 1936						(G)
Norwich C.	Jnrs	06.54	57	1	-	0
GREAVES Daniel Thomas						
Upminster, 31 January, 1963						(F)
Southend U.	Tottenham H. (Jnrs)	01.81	81-83	30	19	14
Cambridge U. (N/C)	Dagenham	09.84	84	2	2	1
GREAVES Ian Denzil						
Crompton, 26 May, 1932						(FB)
Manchester U.	Buxton	05.53	54-59	67	-	0
Lincoln C.	Tr	12.60	60	11	-	0
Oldham Ath.	Tr	05.61	61-62	22	-	0
GREAVES James Peter						
East Ham, 20 February, 1940 E Yth/Eu23-12/EF Lge/E-57						(IF)
Chelsea	Jnrs	05.57	57-60	157	-	124
Tottenham H.	AC Milan (It)	12.61	61-69	321	0	220
West Ham U.	Tr	03.70	69-70	36	2	13
GREAVES Mark Andrew						
Hull, 22 January, 1975						(CD)
Hull C.	Brigg T.	06.96	96-97	40	15	4

League Club	Source	Date Signed	Seasons Played	Apps	Subs	Gls
GREAVES Philip						
Chesterfield, 5 September, 1961						(W)
Chesterfield (N/C)	Alfreton T.	10.86	86	5	0	0
GREAVES Roy						
Farnworth, 4 April, 1947						(M)
Bolton W.	Jnrs	01.65	65-79	487	8	66
Rochdale	Seattle (USA)	11.82	82	19	2	0
GREAVES Steven Ronald						
Chelsea, 17 January, 1970						(D)
Fulham	YT	07.88	87	0	1	0
Preston N. E.	Tr	08.90	90	2	0	0
Ipswich T.	Tr	01.91				
Scunthorpe U.	Tr	08.92	92	9	6	0
GREEN Adrian						
Leicester, 22 October, 1957						(M)
Leicester C.	App	06.76				
Rochdale	L	12.77	77	7	0	0
Aldershot	Tr	07.78	78-79	7	14	0
GREEN Alan Paul						
Worcester, 1 January, 1954 E Yth						(F)
Coventry C.	App	01.71	71-78	98	19	30
GREEN Alan Peter Charles						
Fordingbridge, 19 April, 1951						(F)
Bournemouth	Jnrs	07.69				
Mansfield T.	Tr	07.72	72	1	0	0
GREEN Allan						
Darfield, 14 December, 1939						(FB)
Barnsley	Dodworth Colly	01.59	60-61	19	-	0
York C.	Tr	07.62				
GREEN Anthony						
Glasgow, 13 October, 1946 S-6						(M)
Blackpool	Albion Rov.	05.67	66-71	123	0	13
Newcastle U.	Tr	10.71	71-72	33	0	3
GREEN Arthur						
Liverpool, 28 April, 1928 Died 1992						(FB)
Huddersfield T.	Burscough	02.51	51	3	-	0
GREEN Brian Geoffrey						
Droylsden, 5 June, 1935						(CF)
Rochdale	Haggate Lads	08.55	54-58	46	-	8
Southport	Tr	03.59	58-59	20	-	7
Barrow	Colwyn Bay	09.60	60	3	-	0
Exeter C.	Altrincham	08.62	62	9	-	1
Chesterfield	Tr	02.63	62	2	-	0
GREEN Clive Peter						
Portsmouth, 6 December, 1959						(F)
Portsmouth	Jnrs	07.76	76-77	34	6	4
GREEN Colin Robert						
Wrexham, 10 February, 1942 Wu23-7/W-15						(FB)
Everton	Jnrs	02.59	60-61	15	-	1
Birmingham C.	Tr	12.62	62-70	183	0	1
Wrexham	L	01.71	70	3	0	0
GREEN Donald						
Needham Market, 30 November, 1924 Died 1996						(CH)
Ipswich T.	Bramford	03.47	46-51	52	-	0
GREEN Donald						
Blackburn, 13 May, 1932 Died 1992						(LB)
Accrington St. (Am)	Blackburn Rov. (Am)	05.52	52	12	-	0
GREEN Francis James						
Nottingham, 25 August, 1980						(F)
Peterborough U.	Ilkeston T.	03.98	97	2	2	1
GREEN Frederick Zeanes						
Sheffield, 9 September, 1916						(FB)
Torquay U.	Mosborough Trin.	06.35	35-37	86	-	0
Brighton & H.A.	Tr	06.38	38-47	26	-	0
GREEN George Frederick						
Halifax, 21 December, 1914 Died 1995						(WH)
Bradford P. A.		05.36	36	2	-	0
Huddersfield T.	Tr	10.44	46-47	9	-	1
Reading	Tr	10.47	47-48	44	-	6
GREEN Horace						
Barnsley, 23 April, 1918						(FB)
Halifax T.	Worsboro' Bridge	11.36	37-48	156	-	6
Lincoln C.	Tr	02.49	48-54	212	-	14

League Club	Source	Date Signed	Seasons Played	Career Record Apps	Subs	Gls
GREEN Ivan David						
Bexhill, 29 July, 1933						(IF)
Millwall		09.53	54	1	-	0
GREEN John						
Warrington, 22 May, 1939						(WH)
Tranmere Rov.	Stockton Heath	02.58	58	17	-	5
Blackpool	Tr	03.59	59-66	135	0	9
Port Vale	Tr	09.67	67-70	92	2	7
GREEN John Richard						
Rotherham, 7 March, 1958						(CD)
Rotherham U.	App	03.76	75-83	247	1	8
Scunthorpe U.	Tr	09.83	83-85	100	0	4
Darlington	Tr	10.85	85-86	45	0	2
Rotherham U.	Tr	12.86	86-88	84	1	3
GREEN Kenneth						
Plaistow, 27 April, 1924 E 'B'/EF Lge						(FB)
Birmingham C.	Millwall (Am)	11.43	47-58	401	-	3
GREEN Kenneth						
Hull, 20 November, 1929						(CF)
Grimsby T.	Selby T.	04.51	51	1	-	0
GREEN Leonard Hope						
Bishop Auckland, 2 October, 1936						(FB)
Darlington		10.55	55-60	48	-	0
GREEN Leslie						
Atherstone, 17 October, 1941						(G)
Hull C.	Atherstone T.	08.60	61	4	-	0
Hartlepool U.	Burton A.	11.65	65-66	34	0	0
Rochdale	Tr	04.67	67	44	0	0
Derby Co.	Tr	05.68	68-70	107	0	0
GREEN Melvyn						
Hull, 20 October, 1951						(CD)
Hull C.	App	10.69	71-72	10	0	0
Cambridge U.	Tr	07.74	74	3	0	0
GREEN Michael Clive						
Carlisle, 8 September, 1946						(CD)
Carlisle U.	App	09.64	65	2	0	0
Gillingham	Tr	07.68	68-70	131	1	24
Bristol Rov.	Tr	07.71	71-73	74	3	2
Plymouth Arg.	Tr	07.74	74-76	108	0	8
Torquay U.	Tr	03.77	76-78	88	0	7
GREEN Michael John						
Southend, 20 November, 1957						(D)
Exeter C.	App	11.75	76	0	1	0
GREEN Philip						
Cardiff, 30 October, 1957						(F)
Newport Co. (N/C)	Barry T.	03.84	83-84	11	5	2
GREEN Richard (Rick)						
Scunthorpe, 23 November, 1952						(F)
Scunthorpe U.	Appleby Frodingham	09.75	75-76	66	0	19
Chesterfield	Tr	02.77	76-77	45	3	13
Notts Co.	Tr	06.78	78	6	3	0
Scunthorpe U.	Tr	08.79	79-81	66	5	19
GREEN Richard Edward						
Wolverhampton, 22 November, 1967						(D)
Shrewsbury T.	YT	07.86	86-89	120	5	5
Swindon T.	Tr	10.90				
Gillingham	Tr	03.92	91-97	206	10	16
GREEN Harry **Rodney**						
Halifax, 24 June, 1939						(CF)
Halifax T.		08.60	60-61	9	-	2
Bradford P. A.	Tr	06.62	62	19	-	6
Bradford C.	Tr	01.63	62-63	66	-	39
Gillingham	Tr	07.64	64	33	-	17
Grimsby T.	Tr	08.65	65-66	65	0	20
Charlton Ath.	Tr	02.67	66	3	1	1
Luton T.	Tr	08.67	67	9	2	3
Watford	Tr	08.68	68-69	19	11	8
GREEN Roger						
Cardiff, 20 September, 1944						(D)
Newport Co.	Barry T.	01.72	71	1	0	0
GREEN Ronald Rex						
Birmingham, 3 October, 1956						(G)
Walsall	Alvechurch	06.77	77-83	163	0	0
Shrewsbury T.	Tr	06.84	84	19	0	0
Bristol Rov.	Tr	02.85	84-85	56	0	0
Scunthorpe U.	Tr	08.86	86-87	78	0	0
Wimbledon	Tr	08.88	88	4	0	0
Shrewsbury T.	L	09.88	88	17	0	0
Walsall	Tr	03.89	88-90	67	0	0
Colchester U. (N/C)	Kidderminster Hrs	11.92	92	4	0	0
GREEN Roy						
Loughborough, 8 June, 1931						(IF)
Reading	Bloxwich Strollers	12.52	55-56	14	-	3
GREEN Norman **Russell**						
Donington (Lincs), 13 August, 1933						(WH)
Lincoln C.	Quadring	08.51				
Lincoln C.	Corby T.	05.57	57-63	125	-	8
GREEN Scott Paul						
Walsall, 15 January, 1970						(RB/W)
Derby Co.	YT	07.88				
Bolton W.	Tr	03.90	89-96	166	54	25
Wigan Ath.	Tr	06.97	97	37	1	1
GREEN Stanley						
West Bromwich, 6 September, 1928						(CH)
Bristol Rov.	Accles & Pollock	03.52	51	1	-	0
GREEN Thomas						
Birkenhead, 18 September, 1926 Died 1952						(RH)
Southport	West Lancs A.T.C.	05.46	46	4	-	0
GREEN William						
Newcastle, 22 December, 1950						(CD)
Hartlepool U.	Jnrs	06.69	69-72	128	3	9
Carlisle U.	Tr	07.73	73-75	119	0	4
West Ham U.	Tr	06.76	76-77	35	0	1
Peterborough U.	Tr	07.78	78	30	0	0
Chesterfield	Tr	06.79	79-82	160	0	5
Doncaster Rov.	Tr	06.83	83	10	1	1
GREEN William Charles						
Hull, 9 October, 1927 Died 1996						(D)
Wolverhampton W.	Jnrs	09.45				
Walsall	Tr	09.49	49-53	180	-	8
Wrexham	Tr	06.54	54-56	60	-	2
GREENACRE Christopher Mark						
Wakefield, 23 December, 1977						(F)
Manchester C.	YT	07.95	96-97	2	5	1
Cardiff C.	L	08.97	97	11	0	2
Blackpool	L	03.98	97	2	2	0
GREENALL Colin Anthony						
Billinge, 30 December, 1963 E Yth						(CD)
Blackpool	App	01.81	80-86	179	4	9
Gillingham	Tr	09.86	86-87	62	0	5
Oxford U.	Tr	02.88	87-89	67	0	2
Bury	L	01.90	89	3	0	0
Bury	Tr	07.90	90-91	66	2	5
Preston N.E.	Tr	03.92	91-92	29	0	1
Chester C.	Tr	08.93	93	42	0	1
Lincoln C.	Tr	07.94	94-95	43	0	3
Wigan Ath.	Tr	09.95	95-97	122	0	8
GREENALL George Edward						
Liverpool, 5 November, 1937						(CH)
Manchester C.	Jnrs	11.58				
Oldham Ath.	Tr	09.60	60	25	-	0
GREENAWAY Arthur Robert						
Swindon, 5 April, 1928						(IF)
Plymouth Arg.		08.47				
Exeter C.	Tr	05.50	50	1	-	0
Swansea C.	Tr	10.51				
GREENAWAY Brian Joseph						
Hammersmith, 26 September, 1957						(W)
Fulham	App	06.75	76-80	68	17	8
GREENE David Michael						
Luton, 26 October, 1973 IRu21-14						(CD)
Luton T.	Jnrs	09.91	92-94	18	1	0
Colchester U.	L	11.95	95	14	0	1
Brentford	L	03.96	95	11	0	0
Colchester U.	Tr	06.96	96-97	82	0	6
GREENER Ronald						
Easington, 31 January, 1934						(CH)
Newcastle U.	Easington Colly	05.51	53	3	-	0
Darlington	Tr	08.55	55-66	442	-	5

GREENHALGH Brian Arthur
Chesterfield, 20 February, 1947 (F)

League Club	Source	Date Signed	Seasons Played	Apps	Subs	Gls
Preston N. E.	App	02.65	65-67	19	0	9
Aston Villa	Tr	09.67	67-68	37	3	12
Leicester C.	Tr	02.69	68	2	2	0
Huddersfield T.	Tr	06.69	69-70	15	0	0
Cambridge U.	Tr	07.71	71-73	116	0	47
Bournemouth	Tr	02.74	73-74	23	1	7
Torquay U.	L	06.74	74	9	0	1
Watford	Tr	03.75	74-75	17	1	1

GREENHALGH James Radcliffe
Manchester, 25 August, 1923 (WH)

League Club	Source	Date Signed	Seasons Played	Apps	Subs	Gls
Hull C.	Newton Heath	08.46	46-50	148	-	5
Bury	Tr	12.50	50-54	122	-	1
Gillingham	Wigan Ath.	07.56	56	16	-	0

GREENHALGH Laurence (Loz) Lee
Salford, 2 April, 1974 (LB)

League Club	Source	Date Signed	Seasons Played	Apps	Subs	Gls
Bury	YT	07.92	92	2	0	0

GREENHALGH Norman
Bolton, 10 August, 1914 Died 1995 EF Lge (LB)

League Club	Source	Date Signed	Seasons Played	Apps	Subs	Gls
Bolton W.		09.33				
New Brighton	Tr	10.35	35-37	77	-	8
Everton	Tr	01.38	37-48	106	-	1

GREENHOFF Brian
Barnsley, 28 April, 1953 Eu23-4/E'B'/E-18 (CD)

League Club	Source	Date Signed	Seasons Played	Apps	Subs	Gls
Manchester U.	App	06.70	73-78	218	3	13
Leeds U.	Tr	08.79	79-81	68	4	1
Rochdale	Hong Kong	03.83	82-83	15	1	0

GREENHOFF Frank
Barnsley, 3 March, 1924 (OL)

League Club	Source	Date Signed	Seasons Played	Apps	Subs	Gls
Barnsley	Manchester C. (Am)	09.47				
Bradford C.	Tr	10.48	48-51	81	-	11

GREENHOFF James
Barnsley, 19 June, 1946 Eu23-5/EF Lge (F)

League Club	Source	Date Signed	Seasons Played	Apps	Subs	Gls
Leeds U.	App	08.63	62-68	88	6	21
Birmingham C.	Tr	08.68	68	31	0	14
Stoke C.	Tr	08.69	69-76	274	0	76
Manchester U.	Tr	11.76	76-80	94	3	26
Crewe Alex.	Tr	12.80	80	11	0	4
Port Vale	Toronto (Can)	08.81	81-82	44	4	5
Rochdale	Tr	03.83	82-83	16	0	0

GREENING Jonathan
Scarborough, 2 January, 1979 E Yth (M/F)

League Club	Source	Date Signed	Seasons Played	Apps	Subs	Gls
York C.	YT	12.96	96-97	5	20	2
Manchester U.	Tr	03.98				

GREENMAN Christopher
Bristol, 22 December, 1968 E Sch (CD)

League Club	Source	Date Signed	Seasons Played	Apps	Subs	Gls
Coventry C.	Jnrs	07.88	91-92	5	1	0
Peterborough U.	Tr	03.93	92-93	32	2	0

GREENOUGH Richard (Ricky) Anthony
Mexborough, 30 May, 1961 (CD)

League Club	Source	Date Signed	Seasons Played	Apps	Subs	Gls
Chester C.	Alfreton T.	01.85	84-87	123	9	15
Scarborough	Tr	07.88				
York C.	Tr	11.88	88-89	28	1	1

GREENSMITH Ronald
Sheffield, 22 January, 1933 (OL)

League Club	Source	Date Signed	Seasons Played	Apps	Subs	Gls
Sheffield Wed.	Shiregreen W.M.C.	01.54	54-57	5	-	0
York C.	Tr	01.58	57-59	42	-	1

GREENWAY Mark
Halifax, 19 April, 1966 (LB)

League Club	Source	Date Signed	Seasons Played	Apps	Subs	Gls
Halifax T.	App	04.84	83-84	15	1	1

GREENWELL Donald
Chester-le-Street, 4 January, 1924 (HB)

League Club	Source	Date Signed	Seasons Played	Apps	Subs	Gls
York C.		12.46	46	1	-	0

GREENWOOD Alexander John
Fulham, 17 June, 1933 (FB)

League Club	Source	Date Signed	Seasons Played	Apps	Subs	Gls
Chelsea	Ferryhill Ath.	09.53				
Crystal Palace	Tr	05.54	54	2	-	0
Darlington	Scarborough	06.55	55	8	-	0

GREENWOOD John Jones
Manchester, 22 January, 1921 Died 1994 (WH)

League Club	Source	Date Signed	Seasons Played	Apps	Subs	Gls
Manchester C.		09.46	48	1	-	0
Exeter C.	Tr	06.49	49	31	-	2
Aldershot	Tr	03.51	50	12	-	0
Halifax T.	Tr	11.51				

GREENWOOD Nigel Patrick
Preston, 27 November, 1966 (F)

League Club	Source	Date Signed	Seasons Played	Apps	Subs	Gls
Preston N.E.	App	09.84	84-85	36	9	14
Bury	Tr	08.86	86-89	78	32	24
Preston N.E.	Tr	02.90	89-91	24	6	4
Halifax T.	Tr	07.92	92	21	4	5

GREENWOOD Patrick (Paddy) George
Hull, 17 October, 1946 (D)

League Club	Source	Date Signed	Seasons Played	Apps	Subs	Gls
Hull C.	Jnrs	11.64	65-71	137	12	3
Barnsley	Tr	11.71	71-73	110	1	6
Nottingham F.	Tr	10.74	74	15	0	0

GREENWOOD Peter
Todmorden, 11 September, 1924 (WH)

League Club	Source	Date Signed	Seasons Played	Apps	Subs	Gls
Burnley		10.46				
Chester C.	Tr	07.48	48-51	62	-	3

GREENWOOD Peter
Rawtenstall, 30 April, 1938 (F)

League Club	Source	Date Signed	Seasons Played	Apps	Subs	Gls
Bury	Bolton W. (Am)	10.56	56	1	-	0

GREENWOOD Ronald
Burnley, 11 November, 1921 E 'B' (CH)

League Club	Source	Date Signed	Seasons Played	Apps	Subs	Gls
Chelsea	Belfast Celtic	10.43				
Bradford P. A.	Tr	12.45	46-47	59	-	0
Brentford	Tr	03.49	48-52	142	-	1
Chelsea	Tr	10.52	52-54	65	-	0
Fulham	Tr	02.55	54-55	42	-	0

GREENWOOD Roy Thornton
Leeds, 26 September, 1952 (W)

League Club	Source	Date Signed	Seasons Played	Apps	Subs	Gls
Hull C.	App	10.70	71-75	118	8	24
Sunderland	Tr	01.76	75-78	45	11	9
Derby Co.	Tr	01.79	78-79	26	5	1
Swindon T.	Tr	02.80	79-81	49	4	7
Huddersfield T.	Tr	08.82	82-83	5	3	0
Tranmere Rov.	L	11.83	83	3	0	0

GREENWOOD Roy Tony
Croydon, 22 May, 1931 (FB)

League Club	Source	Date Signed	Seasons Played	Apps	Subs	Gls
Crystal Palace	Beckenham	11.54	54-58	111	-	0

GREER Ross
Australia, 23 September, 1967 (F)

League Club	Source	Date Signed	Seasons Played	Apps	Subs	Gls
Chester C. (N/C)	Floreat Athena (Aus)	11.89	89	2	0	0

GREETHAM Harold
Grimsby, 7 March, 1930 (FB)

League Club	Source	Date Signed	Seasons Played	Apps	Subs	Gls
Grimsby T.	Jnrs	06.50	50	4	-	0

GREGAN Sean Matthew
Guisborough, 29 March, 1974 (CD)

League Club	Source	Date Signed	Seasons Played	Apps	Subs	Gls
Darlington	YT	12.91	91-96	129	7	4
Preston N.E.	Tr	11.96	96-97	54	2	3

GREGG Frank
Stourbridge, 9 October, 1942 (FB)

League Club	Source	Date Signed	Seasons Played	Apps	Subs	Gls
Walsall	Jnrs	10.59	60-72	389	4	3

GREGG Henry (Harry)
Derry (NI), 27 October, 1932 NI Sch/NI Amat/ILol/NI-25 (G)

League Club	Source	Date Signed	Seasons Played	Apps	Subs	Gls
Doncaster Rov.	Coleraine	10.52	52-57	93	-	0
Manchester U.	Tr	12.57	57-66	210	0	0
Stoke C.	Tr	12.66	66	2	0	0

GREGG Matthew Stephen
Cheltenham, 30 November, 1978 (G)

League Club	Source	Date Signed	Seasons Played	Apps	Subs	Gls
Torquay U.	YT	07.97	95-97	21	0	0

GREGOIRE Roland Barry
Liverpool, 23 November, 1958 (F)

League Club	Source	Date Signed	Seasons Played	Apps	Subs	Gls
Halifax T.	Jnrs	08.76	77	5	0	0
Sunderland	Tr	11.77	77-78	6	3	1

GREGORY Anthony Charles
Luton, 16 May, 1937 E Yth (OL/LH)

League Club	Source	Date Signed	Seasons Played	Apps	Subs	Gls
Luton T.	Vauxhall Motors	05.55	55-59	59	-	17
Watford	Tr	03.60	59-63	107	-	14

GREGORY Anthony Gerard
Doncaster, 21 March, 1968 E Sch/E Yth (M)

League Club	Source	Date Signed	Seasons Played	Apps	Subs	Gls
Sheffield Wed.	App	01.86	85-88	14	4	1
Halifax T.	Tr	08.90	90-91	16	1	1

GREGORY Anthony Thomas
Dawley, 10 March, 1947 (FB)

League Club	Source	Date Signed	Seasons Played	Apps	Subs	Gls
Shrewsbury T.	App	03.65	64-75	286	8	0

GREGORY Brian
Belfast, 11 January, 1955 (F)

League Club	Source	Date Signed	Seasons Played	Apps	Subs	Gls
Gillingham	Jnrs	08.74	74	1	1	0
Luton T.	Margate	06.76				

GREGORY Charles Frederick
Doncaster, 24 October, 1911 Died 1985 (FB)

League Club	Source	Date Signed	Seasons Played	Apps	Subs	Gls
Doncaster Rov.	Brodsworth Colly	10.28	29	13	-	3
Manchester C.	Tr	03.30	31-33	21	-	2
Reading	Tr	03.34	33-37	128	-	6
Crystal Palace	Tr	12.37	37-38	43	-	9
Hartlepool U.	Tr	06.46	46	21	-	0
Rotherham U.	Tr	02.47	46	1	-	0

GREGORY David Harry
Peterborough, 6 October, 1951 (F)

League Club	Source	Date Signed	Seasons Played	Apps	Subs	Gls
Peterborough U.	Chatteris T.	08.73	73-76	125	17	32
Stoke C.	Tr	06.77	77	22	1	3
Blackburn Rov.	Tr	07.78	78	5	0	3
Bury	Tr	09.78	78-79	50	2	13
Portsmouth	Tr	12.79	79-81	63	10	18
Wrexham	Tr	08.82	82-85	145	8	31
Peterborough U.	Tr	08.86	86	16	15	8

GREGORY David Peter
London, 19 February, 1960 (FB)

League Club	Source	Date Signed	Seasons Played	Apps	Subs	Gls
Millwall	Crystal Palace (N/C)	08.78	78-80	52	0	2

GREGORY David Spencer
Sudbury, 23 January, 1970 (M/RB)

League Club	Source	Date Signed	Seasons Played	Apps	Subs	Gls
Ipswich T.	YT	03.87	88-94	16	16	2
Hereford U.	L	01.95	94	2	0	0
Peterborough U.	Tr	07.95	95	0	3	0
Colchester U.	Tr	12.95	95-97	81	11	6

GREGORY Ernest
Stratford, 10 November, 1921 E 'B' (G)

League Club	Source	Date Signed	Seasons Played	Apps	Subs	Gls
West Ham U.	Leytonstone	05.39	46-59	382	-	0

GREGORY Gordon (Harry)
Hackney, 24 October, 1943 E Yth (M)

League Club	Source	Date Signed	Seasons Played	Apps	Subs	Gls
Leyton Orient	Jnrs	10.61	62-65	79	0	12
Charlton Ath.	Tr	08.66	66-70	146	3	24
Aston Villa	Tr	10.70	70-71	18	6	2
Hereford U.	Tr	08.72	72-74	71	2	6

GREGORY John Charles
Scunthorpe, 11 May, 1954 E-6 (M)

League Club	Source	Date Signed	Seasons Played	Apps	Subs	Gls
Northampton T.	App	05.72	72-76	187	0	8
Aston Villa	Tr	06.77	77-78	59	6	10
Brighton & H.A.	Tr	07.79	79-80	72	0	7
Queens Park R.	Tr	06.81	81-85	159	2	36
Derby Co.	Tr	11.85	85-87	103	0	22
Portsmouth	(Team Coach)	07.89				
Plymouth Arg. (N/C)	Tr	01.90	89	3	0	0
Bolton W. (N/C)	Tr	03.90	89	2	5	0

GREGORY John Ernest
Shoreditch, 24 September, 1926 Died 1995 (IF)

League Club	Source	Date Signed	Seasons Played	Apps	Subs	Gls
West Ham U.	Bromley	06.51	51-52	24	-	6
Scunthorpe U.	Tr	06.53	53-56	147	-	63
Aldershot	Tr	06.57	57	6	-	2

GREGORY John Graham
Hounslow, 16 May, 1977 (G)

League Club	Source	Date Signed	Seasons Played	Apps	Subs	Gls
Fulham	YT	•	94	0	1	0

GREGORY John (Jack) Leslie
Southampton, 25 January, 1925 (FB)

League Club	Source	Date Signed	Seasons Played	Apps	Subs	Gls
Southampton	Jnrs	12.44	46-54	66	-	0
Leyton Orient	Tr	07.55	55-58	91	-	0
Bournemouth	Tr	07.59	59	17	-	0

GREGORY Neil Richard
Zambia, 7 October, 1972 (F)

League Club	Source	Date Signed	Seasons Played	Apps	Subs	Gls
Ipswich T.	YT	02.92	94-97	18	27	9
Chesterfield	L	02.94	93	2	1	1
Scunthorpe U.	L	03.95	94	10	0	7
Torquay U.	L	11.96	96	5	0	0
Peterborough U.	L	11.97	97	2	1	1
Colchester U.	Tr	01.98	97	12	3	7

GREGORY Paul Gordon
Sheffield, 26 July, 1961 (G)

League Club	Source	Date Signed	Seasons Played	Apps	Subs	Gls
Chesterfield	App	07.79	80-83	23	0	0
Doncaster Rov.	Tr	03.84	84	1	0	0
Scunthorpe U.	Tr	10.84	84-86	69	0	0
Halifax T.	L	09.86	86	6	0	0

GREGSON Colin
Newcastle, 19 January, 1958 (M)

League Club	Source	Date Signed	Seasons Played	Apps	Subs	Gls
West Bromwich A.	App	01.76				
Sheffield Wed.	Tr	07.77	77	1	1	0

GREGSON John
Skelmersdale, 17 May, 1939 (W)

League Club	Source	Date Signed	Seasons Played	Apps	Subs	Gls
Blackpool	Skelmersdale U.	05.57	57-58	3	-	1
Chester C.	Tr	05.62	62	32	-	5
Shrewsbury T.	Tr	03.63	62-64	56	-	6
Mansfield T.	Tr	11.64	64-66	75	1	5
Lincoln C.	Tr	06.67	67	31	5	3
Cambridge U.	Tr	07.68	70	32	0	0

GREGSON Peter George
Blackpool, 12 May, 1953 (G)

League Club	Source	Date Signed	Seasons Played	Apps	Subs	Gls
Southport	Blackpool (App)	07.71	71-72	35	0	0

GREIG John **Robert**
Sunderland, 13 September, 1949 (W)

League Club	Source	Date Signed	Seasons Played	Apps	Subs	Gls
Leicester C.	App	01.67				
Workington	Tr	02.68	67	4	1	0

GRENFELL Stephen John
Enfield, 27 October, 1966 (M/LB)

League Club	Source	Date Signed	Seasons Played	Apps	Subs	Gls
Tottenham H.	App	08.84				
Colchester U.	Tr	10.86	86-88	67	3	1

GRESTY Philip
Tarporley, 2 June, 1953 (OL)

League Club	Source	Date Signed	Seasons Played	Apps	Subs	Gls
Crewe Alex. (Am)	Jnrs	07.71	74	3	1	0

GREW Mark Stuart
Bilston, 15 February, 1958 (G)

League Club	Source	Date Signed	Seasons Played	Apps	Subs	Gls
West Bromwich A.	Jnrs	06.76	81-82	33	0	0
Wigan Ath.	L	12.78	78	4	0	0
Leicester C.	Tr	07.83	83	5	0	0
Oldham Ath.	L	10.83	83	5	0	0
Ipswich T.	Tr	03.84	84	6	0	0
Fulham	L	09.85	85	4	0	0
West Bromwich A.	L	01.86	85	1	0	0
Port Vale	Tr	06.86	86-91	184	0	0
Blackburn Rov.	L	10.90	90	13	0	0
Cardiff C.	Tr	08.92	92-93	21	0	0

GREWCOCK Neil
Leicester, 26 April, 1962 (W)

League Club	Source	Date Signed	Seasons Played	Apps	Subs	Gls
Leicester C.	App	07.79	79-80	7	1	1
Gillingham	Tr	03.82	81-82	30	4	4
Burnley	Shepshed Charthouse	06.84	84-90	180	22	27

GREY William **Brian**
Swansea, 7 September, 1948 (IF)

League Club	Source	Date Signed	Seasons Played	Apps	Subs	Gls
Swansea C.	App	09.66	67-69	28	3	9

GREYGOOSE Dean
Torquay, 18 December, 1964 E Yth (G)

League Club	Source	Date Signed	Seasons Played	Apps	Subs	Gls
Cambridge U.	App	11.82	83-84	26	0	0
Lincoln C.	L	09.85	85	6	0	0
Leyton Orient	Tr	12.85	85	1	0	0
Crystal Palace	Tr	08.86				
Crewe Alex.	Tr	08.87	87-92	205	0	0

GRIBBIN Brian Thomas
Newcastle, 2 June, 1954 (FB)

League Club	Source	Date Signed	Seasons Played	Apps	Subs	Gls
Hartlepool U.	Jnrs	07.73	72	1	0	0

GRICE Michael John
Woking, 3 November, 1931 (W)

League Club	Source	Date Signed	Seasons Played	Apps	Subs	Gls
Colchester U.	Lowestoft T.	06.52	52-55	106	-	14
West Ham U.	Tr	03.56	55-60	142	-	18
Coventry C.	Tr	08.61	61	37	-	6
Colchester U.	Tr	06.62	62-65	138	1	13

GRIDELET Philip Raymond
Hendon, 30 April, 1967 E Semi Pro (M)

League Club	Source	Date Signed	Seasons Played	Apps	Subs	Gls
Barnsley	Barnet	09.90	90-92	3	3	0
Rotherham U.	L	03.93	92	9	0	0
Southend U.	Tr	09.93	93-97	149	27	10

GRIEMINK Bart
Netherlands, 29 March, 1972 (G)

League Club	Source	Date Signed	Seasons Played	Apps	Subs	Gls
Birmingham C.	W.K. Emmen (Neth)	11.95	95	20	0	0
Peterborough U.	Tr	10.96	96	27	0	0

GRIERSON Darrell Philip
Blackpool, 13 October, 1968 (G)

League Club	Source	Date Signed	Seasons Played	Apps	Subs	Gls
Tranmere Rov.	App	10.86	86	4	0	0

GRIEVE David
Selkirk, 15 February, 1929 (W)

League Club	Source	Date Signed	Seasons Played	Apps	Subs	Gls
Reading	Dalry Thistle	02.52	51-53	19	-	1
Crystal Palace	Tr	04.54	54	22	-	4

GRIEVE Richard Maxwell
Aberdeen, 29 June, 1924 (IL)

League Club	Source	Date Signed	Seasons Played	Apps	Subs	Gls
Rochdale	Montrose	05.50				
Wrexham	Tr	09.50	50	1	-	0

GRIEVES Kenneth James
Australia, 27 August, 1925 Died 1992 (G)

League Club	Source	Date Signed	Seasons Played	Apps	Subs	Gls
Bury	Wigan Ath.	04.47	47-49	59	-	0
Bolton W.	Tr	12.51	51-55	49	-	0
Stockport Co.	Tr	07.57	57	39	-	0

GRIEVSON Henry (Harry)
Easington, 10 April, 1941 (WH)

League Club	Source	Date Signed	Seasons Played	Apps	Subs	Gls
Sunderland	Jnrs	04.58				
Southend U.	Tr	07.61	61	24	-	1

GRIFFIN Andrew
Billinge, 7 March, 1979 E Yth (LB)

League Club	Source	Date Signed	Seasons Played	Apps	Subs	Gls
Stoke C.	YT	09.96	96-97	52	5	2
Newcastle U.	Tr	01.98	97	4	0	0

GRIFFIN Colin Raymond
Dudley, 8 January, 1956 (CD)

League Club	Source	Date Signed	Seasons Played	Apps	Subs	Gls
Derby Co.	App	01.74				
Shrewsbury T.	Tr	01.76	75-88	402	4	7

GRIFFIN Frank Albert
Swinton, 28 March, 1928 (OR)

League Club	Source	Date Signed	Seasons Played	Apps	Subs	Gls
Shrewsbury T.	St Augustines	03.51	50	37	-	5
West Bromwich A.	Tr	04.51	50-58	240	-	47
Northampton T.	Tr	07.59	59	16	-	0

GRIFFIN Kevin Russell
Plymouth, 5 October, 1953 (F)

League Club	Source	Date Signed	Seasons Played	Apps	Subs	Gls
Bristol C.	App	09.71	71-74	5	3	0
Mansfield T.	L	03.75	74	4	0	2
Cambridge U.	L	09.75	75	7	1	1

GRIFFIN William
Bircotes, 24 September, 1940 (IF)

League Club	Source	Date Signed	Seasons Played	Apps	Subs	Gls
Sheffield Wed.	Jnrs	09.57	58-62	35	-	20
Bury	Tr	12.62	62-65	84	4	22
Workington	Tr	02.66	65-68	82	0	16
Rotherham U.	Tr	01.69	68-69	14	3	1

GRIFFITH Cohen
Guyana, 26 December, 1962 Wu21-1 (W)

League Club	Source	Date Signed	Seasons Played	Apps	Subs	Gls
Cardiff C.	Kettering T.	10.89	89-94	205	29	39

GRIFFITHS Arfon Trevor
Wrexham, 23 August, 1941 Wu23-3/W-17 (M)

League Club	Source	Date Signed	Seasons Played	Apps	Subs	Gls
Wrexham	Jnrs	05.59	59-60	41	-	8
Arsenal	Tr	01.61	60-61	15	-	2
Wrexham	Tr	09.62	62-78	544	6	112

GRIFFITHS Ashley Russell
Barry, 5 January, 1961 W Sch/W Yth (M)

League Club	Source	Date Signed	Seasons Played	Apps	Subs	Gls
Bristol Rov.	App	01.79	79-80	6	1	0
Torquay U.	Tr	08.81				

GRIFFITHS Barry
Manchester, 21 November, 1940 (G)

League Club	Source	Date Signed	Seasons Played	Apps	Subs	Gls
Blackburn Rovers	Jnrs	07.62	59-62	2	-	0

GRIFFITHS Brian
Ruabon, 21 November, 1933 (IF)

League Club	Source	Date Signed	Seasons Played	Apps	Subs	Gls
Wrexham		05.52	52-57	22	-	11
Chester C.	Tr	07.58	58	2	-	1

GRIFFITHS Bryan
Liverpool, 21 November, 1938 (FB)

League Club	Source	Date Signed	Seasons Played	Apps	Subs	Gls
Everton	Jnrs	03.56	58	2	-	0
Southport	Tr	06.60	60-62	117	-	1

GRIFFITHS Bryan Kenneth
St Helens, 26 January, 1965 (LW)

League Club	Source	Date Signed	Seasons Played	Apps	Subs	Gls
Wigan Ath.	St Helens T.	11.88	88-92	176	13	44
Blackpool	Tr	07.93	93-94	54	3	17
Scarborough	L	12.94	94	5	0	1

GRIFFITHS Carl Brian
Welshpool, 16 July, 1971 W Yth/Wu21-2/W 'B' (F)

League Club	Source	Date Signed	Seasons Played	Apps	Subs	Gls
Shrewsbury T.	YT	09.88	88-93	110	33	54
Manchester C.	Tr	10.93	93-94	11	7	4
Portsmouth	Tr	08.95	95	2	12	2
Peterborough U.	Tr	03.96	95-96	6	10	2
Leyton Orient	L	10.96	96	5	0	3
Leyton Orient	Tr	03.97	96-97	39	2	21

GRIFFITHS Clive Leslie
Pontypridd, 22 January, 1955 W Sch/Wu23-2 (CD)

League Club	Source	Date Signed	Seasons Played	Apps	Subs	Gls
Manchester U.	App	01.72	73	7	0	0
Plymouth Arg.	L	07.74	74	10	1	0
Tranmere Rov.	Tr	11.75	75-76	59	0	0

GRIFFITHS David
Woking, 13 December, 1937 (WH)

League Club	Source	Date Signed	Seasons Played	Apps	Subs	Gls
Portsmouth		03.56				
Aldershot	Tr	08.57	58-59	5	-	0

GRIFFITHS David
Newport, 20 May, 1962 (D)

League Club	Source	Date Signed	Seasons Played	Apps	Subs	Gls
Newport Co. (N/C)	Cwmbran T.	03.88	87	0	1	0

GRIFFITHS David Bernard
Liverpool, 25 May, 1951 (FB)

League Club	Source	Date Signed	Seasons Played	Apps	Subs	Gls
Tranmere Rov.	Jnrs	02.70	69	6	0	0

GRIFFITHS Dennis
Ruabon, 12 August, 1935 (WH)

League Club	Source	Date Signed	Seasons Played	Apps	Subs	Gls
Wrexham	Jnrs	08.52	53-57	67	-	3

GRIFFITHS Douglas James
Birmingham, 23 October, 1948 (CH)

League Club	Source	Date Signed	Seasons Played	Apps	Subs	Gls
Wolverhampton W.	App	10.66				
Stockport Co.	Tr	07.68	68-69	20	1	0

GRIFFITHS Estyn
Mold, 22 July, 1927 W Amat (CH)

League Club	Source	Date Signed	Seasons Played	Apps	Subs	Gls
Wrexham		04.50	50-51	10	-	0

GRIFFITHS Evan Gareth
Aylesham (Kt), 19 April, 1943 (WH)

League Club	Source	Date Signed	Seasons Played	Apps	Subs	Gls
Gillingham	Jnrs	07.61	60	1	-	0

GRIFFITHS Gareth John
Winsford, 10 April, 1970 (CD)

League Club	Source	Date Signed	Seasons Played	Apps	Subs	Gls
Port Vale	Rhyl	02.93	93-97	90	4	4
Shrewsbury T.	L	10.97	97	6	0	0

GRIFFITHS George
Warrington, 23 June, 1924 (FB)

League Club	Source	Date Signed	Seasons Played	Apps	Subs	Gls
Bury	Newton Park	03.42	46-53	241	-	7
Halifax T.	Tr	06.54	54-57	166	-	14

GRIFFITHS Gerald Leslie
Swansea, 15 December, 1934 W Sch (WH)

League Club	Source	Date Signed	Seasons Played	Apps	Subs	Gls
Swansea C.	Jnrs	06.52				
Crewe Alex.	Tr	06.56	56	21	0	3

GRIFFITHS Harry Stanley
Liverpool, 17 November, 1912 Died 1981 (CH)

League Club	Source	Date Signed	Seasons Played	Apps	Subs	Gls
Everton		08.32				
Port Vale	Tr	05.35	35-46	103	-	3

GRIFFITHS James Henry (Harry)
Swansea, 4 January, 1931 Died 1978 W-1 (OR)

League Club	Source	Date Signed	Seasons Played	Apps	Subs	Gls
Swansea C.	Jnrs	06.49	49-63	424	-	68

GRIFFITHS Ian James
Birkenhead, 17 April, 1960 (OL)

League Club	Source	Date Signed	Seasons Played	Apps	Subs	Gls
Tranmere Rov.	Jnrs	02.79	78-82	110	6	5
Rochdale	Tr	08.83	83-84	40	2	5
Port Vale (N/C)	Tr	09.84	84	9	3	0
Wigan Ath.	Tr	07.85	85-87	73	9	7
Wigan Ath.	Mazda Hiroshima (Jap)	08.90	90	6	5	0
Wrexham	Tr	03.91	90-91	14	0	0

GRIFFITHS Ivor
Port Talbot, 19 June, 1918 Died 1993 (IF)

League Club	Source	Date Signed	Seasons Played	Apps	Subs	Gls
Chester C.	Tottenham H. (Am)	09.46	46	1	-	0

GRIFFITHS James Thomas
Gowerton, 5 October, 1941 (CF)

League Club	Source	Date Signed	Seasons Played	Apps	Subs	Gls
Stockport Co.		03.63	62	3	-	0

GRIFFITHS Jeffrey Kenneth
Swansea, 19 March, 1957 (F)

League Club	Source	Date Signed	Seasons Played	Apps	Subs	Gls
Swansea C. (N/C)		04.76	75-77	6	7	1

GRIFFITHS John
Oldbury, 16 June, 1951 (M)

League Club	Source	Date Signed	Seasons Played	Apps	Subs	Gls
Aston Villa	App	11.68	68-69	1	2	0
Stockport Co.	Tr	05.70	70-74	167	15	31

GRIFFITHS George **Keith**
Chester, 30 December, 1927 (G)

League Club	Source	Date Signed	Seasons Played	Apps	Subs	Gls
Chester C.	Rhyl	07.55	55-58	54	-	0

GRIFFITHS Kenneth George
Cardiff, 11 November, 1925 Died 1985 (IF)

League Club	Source	Date Signed	Seasons Played	Apps	Subs	Gls
Cardiff C.	Jnrs	06.43				
Torquay U.	L	01.48	47-48	11	-	1
Newport Co.	Tr	09.49	49	14	-	6

GRIFFITHS Kenneth James
Stoke, 2 April, 1930 (IF)

League Club	Source	Date Signed	Seasons Played	Apps	Subs	Gls
Port Vale	Northwood Mission	03.50	49-57	179	-	52
Mansfield T.	Tr	01.58	57-58	42	-	7

GRIFFITHS William **Malwyn**
Merthyr Tydfil, 8 March, 1919 Died 1969 W-11 (OR)

League Club	Source	Date Signed	Seasons Played	Apps	Subs	Gls
Arsenal	Merthyr Tydfil	02.37	37	9	-	5
Leicester C.	Tr	09.38	38-55	373	-	66

GRIFFITHS Neil
Newcastle-u-Lyme, 12 October, 1951 (FB)

League Club	Source	Date Signed	Seasons Played	Apps	Subs	Gls
Chester C.		11.70	70-73	89	1	5
Port Vale	Tr	12.73	73-80	214	4	13
Crewe Alex.	Tr	08.81	81	32	2	1

GRIFFITHS Neil
Halifax, 4 September, 1972 (D)

League Club	Source	Date Signed	Seasons Played	Apps	Subs	Gls
Halifax T.	YT	07.91	90-92	2	2	0

GRIFFITHS Peter James
Barnstaple, 14 August, 1957 (W)

League Club	Source	Date Signed	Seasons Played	Apps	Subs	Gls
Stoke C.	Bideford	11.80	80-83	46	14	5
Bradford C.	L	03.84	83	2	0	0
Port Vale	Tr	07.84	84-85	32	4	4

GRIFFITHS Raymond
Llanelli, 26 September, 1931 (WH)

League Club	Source	Date Signed	Seasons Played	Apps	Subs	Gls
Chester C.	Stockton Heath	09.55	55-59	18	-	0

GRIFFITHS Richard David
Colchester, 21 March, 1942 (FB)

League Club	Source	Date Signed	Seasons Played	Apps	Subs	Gls
Colchester U.	Jnrs	06.61	61-64	48	-	0

GRIFFITHS Robert William
Aldridge, 15 September, 1942 (WH)

League Club	Source	Date Signed	Seasons Played	Apps	Subs	Gls
Stoke C.	Rhyl	09.60				
Chester C.	Tr	07.62	62	2	-	0

GRIFFITHS Roger David Norman
Hereford, 20 February, 1945 (FB)

League Club	Source	Date Signed	Seasons Played	Apps	Subs	Gls
Hereford U.	Worcester C.	07.70	72	7	2	0

GRIFFITHS Stephen
Billingham, 28 November, 1957 (F)

League Club	Source	Date Signed	Seasons Played	Apps	Subs	Gls
Hartlepool U.	App	•	74	0	1	0

GRIFFITHS James **Stephen**
Barnsley, 23 February, 1914 (IF)

League Club	Source	Date Signed	Seasons Played	Apps	Subs	Gls
Chesterfield	Thurnscoe Vic.	10.34				
Halifax T.	Tr	07.37	37-38	76	-	14
Portsmouth	Tr	06.39				
Aldershot	Tr	06.46	46	42	-	9
Barnsley	Tr	07.47	47-50	65	-	29
York C.	Tr	06.51	51-52	74	-	12

GRIFFITHS Vernon
Birmingham, 14 June, 1936 (WH)

League Club	Source	Date Signed	Seasons Played	Apps	Subs	Gls
Coventry C.	Sheldon T.	02.57	57-58	15	-	1

GRIFFITHS William
Earlestown, 13 January, 1921 Died 1964 (CH)

League Club	Source	Date Signed	Seasons Played	Apps	Subs	Gls
Bury	Earlestown	05.39	46-51	191	-	11

GRIFFITHS William Edward
Warrington, 23 May, 1944 (W)

League Club	Source	Date Signed	Seasons Played	Apps	Subs	Gls
Torquay U.	App	05.62	62	1	-	0

GRIFFITHS Wyn Rhys
Blaengwynfi, 17 October, 1919 (G)

League Club	Source	Date Signed	Seasons Played	Apps	Subs	Gls
Cardiff C. (Am)		08.47	47	1	-	0
Newport Co. (Am)		01.52	51	3	-	0

GRIGGS Robert John
Petersfield, 12 December, 1952 (CD)

League Club	Source	Date Signed	Seasons Played	Apps	Subs	Gls
Aldershot	App	07.70	68-69	3	1	0

GRIMANDI Gilles
Gap, France, 11 November, 1970 (D)

League Club	Source	Date Signed	Seasons Played	Apps	Subs	Gls
Arsenal	Monaco (Fr)	06.97	97	16	6	1

GRIMES Augustine **Ashley**
Dublin, 2 August, 1957 IRu21-6/IR-17 (LB)

League Club	Source	Date Signed	Seasons Played	Apps	Subs	Gls
Manchester U.	Bohemians	03.77	77-82	62	28	10
Coventry C.	Tr	08.83	83	29	3	1
Luton T.	Tr	08.84	84-88	85	2	3
Stoke C. (N/C)	Osasuna (Sp)	01.92	91	4	6	1

GRIMES Vincent
Scunthorpe, 13 May, 1954 (M)

League Club	Source	Date Signed	Seasons Played	Apps	Subs	Gls
Hull C.	App	05.72	73-77	84	5	9
Bradford C.	L	12.77	77	7	0	1
Scunthorpe U.	Tr	01.78	77-81	143	0	12

GRIMLEY Thomas William
Worksop, 1 November, 1920 Died 1976 (G)

League Club	Source	Date Signed	Seasons Played	Apps	Subs	Gls
West Bromwich A.	Swallownest	04.39	46-47	30	-	0
New Brighton	Tr	08.48	48-50	94	-	0

GRIMSDITCH Samuel **Walker**
Farnworth, 10 August, 1920 Died 1996 (G)

League Club	Source	Date Signed	Seasons Played	Apps	Subs	Gls
Southport	Rossendale U.	11.45	46	10	-	0

GRIMSHAW Anthony
Manchester, 8 December, 1957 (M)

League Club	Source	Date Signed	Seasons Played	Apps	Subs	Gls
Manchester U.	App	12.74	75	0	1	0

GRIMSHAW Christopher Anthony
Accrington, 1 October, 1965 (M)

League Club	Source	Date Signed	Seasons Played	Apps	Subs	Gls
Burnley	App	10.83				
Crewe Alex.	Tr	03.84	83	1	2	0
Bury	Tr	08.84	84-85	1	2	0

GRIMSHAW Colin George
Betchworth (Sy), 16 September, 1925 Died 1995 (WH)

League Club	Source	Date Signed	Seasons Played	Apps	Subs	Gls
Arsenal	Redhill	06.48				
Crystal Palace	Tr	10.52	52	32	-	3

GRINNEY Ian George
Crediton, 8 March, 1936 (OR)

League Club	Source	Date Signed	Seasons Played	Apps	Subs	Gls
Exeter C.	Crediton	09.54	55	2	-	0

GRIPTON Ernest **William**
Tipton, 2 July, 1920 Died 1981 (CH)

League Club	Source	Date Signed	Seasons Played	Apps	Subs	Gls
West Bromwich A.	Jnrs	11.37	38-47	13	-	0
Luton T.	Tr	06.48	48	3	-	0
Bournemouth	Tr	07.50	50-51	79	-	0

GRITT Stephen John
Bournemouth, 31 October, 1957 (M)

League Club	Source	Date Signed	Seasons Played	Apps	Subs	Gls
Bournemouth	App	07.76	76	4	2	3
Charlton Ath.	Tr	07.77	77-88	320	27	24
Walsall	Tr	07.89	89	20	0	1
Charlton Ath.	Tr	02.90	89-92	15	18	1

GROBBELAAR Bruce David
South Africa, 6 October, 1957 Zimbabwe Int/EF Lge (G)

League Club	Source	Date Signed	Seasons Played	Apps	Subs	Gls
Crewe Alex. (N/C)	Vancouver W. (Can)	12.79	79	24	0	1
Liverpool	Vancouver W. (Can)	03.81	81-93	440	0	0
Stoke C.	L	03.93	92	4	0	0
Southampton	Tr	08.94	94-95	32	0	0
Plymouth Arg.	Tr	08.96	96	36	0	0
Oxford U.	Tr	09.97				
Sheffield Wed.	Tr	09.97				
Oldham Ath. (N/C)	Tr	12.97	97	4	0	0

GROCOCK Christopher Richard
Grimsby, 30 October, 1968 (W)

League Club	Source	Date Signed	Seasons Played	Apps	Subs	Gls
Grimsby T.	Jnrs	06.87	85-88	18	25	1

GRODAS Frode
Norway, 24 October, 1964 Norwegian Int (G)

League Club	Source	Date Signed	Seasons Played	Apps	Subs	Gls
Chelsea	Lillestrom (Nor)	09.96	96	20	1	0

GROENENDIJK Alfons
Netherlands, 17 May, 1964 (M)

League Club	Source	Date Signed	Seasons Played	Apps	Subs	Gls
Manchester C.	Ajax (Neth)	07.93	93	9	0	0

GROGAN John
Paisley, 30 October, 1915 Died 1976 (CH)

League Club	Source	Date Signed	Seasons Played	Apps	Subs	Gls
Leicester C.	Shawfield Jnrs	10.33	35-46	46	-	0
Mansfield T.	Tr	09.47	47-51	201	-	0

GROOMBRIDGE David Henry
Croydon, 13 April, 1930 (G)

League Club	Source	Date Signed	Seasons Played	Apps	Subs	Gls
Leyton Orient	Hayes	06.51	51-59	133	-	0

League Club	Source	Date Signed	Seasons Played	Career Record Apps	Subs	Gls
GROOME Patrick Bernard						
Nottingham, 16 March, 1934						(FB)
Notts Co.	Jnrs	11.51	52-57	40	-	0
GROTIER Peter David						
Stratford, 18 October, 1950						(G)
West Ham U.	App	03.68	68-72	50	0	0
Cardiff C.	L	11.73	73	2	0	0
Lincoln C.	Tr	08.74	74-79	233	0	0
Cardiff C.	Tr	12.79	79-81	38	0	0
Grimsby T.	Tr	03.82	82-84	10	0	0
GROVES Alan James						
Southport, 24 October, 1948 Died 1978						(W)
Southport	Blowick	12.68	68-69	10	4	2
Chester C.	Tr	07.70	70	21	1	3
Shrewsbury T.	Tr	02.71	70-72	76	0	11
Bournemouth	Tr	10.72	72-73	31	5	4
Oldham Ath.	Tr	02.74	73-77	136	4	12
Blackpool	Tr	11.77	77	11	4	1
GROVES Edward **Gwynfryn**						
Merthyr Tydfil, 24 July, 1930 W Amat						(G)
Swansea C.	Troedyrhiw	06.52	52-53	27	-	0
GROVES John						
Worksop, 16 September, 1933						(WH)
Luton T.	Jnrs	10.50	53-62	218	-	16
Bournemouth	Tr	09.63	63-64	54	-	0
GROVES Kenneth Ernest Leonard						
Eton, 9 October, 1921						(G)
Preston N. E.	Windsor & Eton	03.39				
Reading	Tr	08.46	46	4	-	0
GROVES Paul						
Derby, 28 February, 1966						(M)
Leicester C.	Burton A.	04.88	87-88	7	9	1
Lincoln C.	L	08.89	89	8	0	1
Blackpool	Tr	01.90	89-91	106	1	21
Grimsby T.	Tr	08.92	92-95	183	1	38
West Bromwich A.	Tr	07.96	96	27	2	4
Grimsby T.	Tr	07.97	97	46	0	7
GROVES Perry						
Bow, 19 April, 1965						(F)
Colchester U.	App	06.82	81-86	142	14	26
Arsenal	Tr	09.86	86-92	91	65	21
Southampton	Tr	08.92	92	13	2	2
GROVES Victor George						
Stepney, 5 November, 1932 E Yth/E Amat/Eu23-1/E 'B'						(IF/WH)
Tottenham H. (Am)	Leytonstone	06.52	52-53	4	-	3
Leyton Orient	Walthamstow Ave.	10.54	54-55	42	-	24
Arsenal	Tr	11.55	55-63	185	-	31
GROZIER William						
Cumnock, 24 August, 1956						(FB)
Mansfield T.	App	08.74	73	1	0	0
GRUBB Alan Johnstone						
Leven, 5 February, 1928						(W)
Tottenham H.	East Fife	03.52	52	2	-	0
Walsall	Tr	08.53	53	15	-	0
GRUMMETT James						
Hoyland, 31 July, 1918 Died 1996						(WH)
Lincoln C.	Ruston Sports	09.43	45-51	165	-	12
Accrington St.	Tr	09.52	52	40	-	1
GRUMMETT James						
Maltby, 11 July, 1945 EYth						(CD)
Lincoln C.	Jnrs	06.63	63-70	246	5	19
Aldershot	Tr	07.71	71-72	81	0	6
Chester C.	Tr	06.73	73	15	1	0
Rochdale	Tr	12.73	73-74	32	1	2
GRUMMITT Peter Malcolm						
Bourne, 19 August, 1942 Eu23-3/EF Lge						(G)
Nottingham F.	Bourne T.	05.60	60-69	313	0	0
Sheffield Wed.	Tr	01.70	69-72	121	0	0
Brighton & H. A.	Tr	12.73	73-76	136	0	0
GRUNDY Brian						
Atherton, 9 May, 1945						(W)
Bury	Wigan Ath.	11.67	67-70	94	6	10

League Club	Source	Date Signed	Seasons Played	Career Record Apps	Subs	Gls
GRYBA John **Raymond**						
Liverpool, 19 August, 1935						(IF)
Liverpool	Jnrs	08.52				
Southport	R.A.O.C. Feltham	10.55	55-57	72	-	14
GUARD Anthony Francis						
Swansea, 19 April, 1964						(M)
Swansea C.	App	04.82	83	1	0	0
GUBBINS Ralph Grayham						
Ellesmere Port, 31 January, 1932						(IF)
Bolton W.	Shell Mex	10.52	52-59	97	-	15
Hull C.	Tr	10.59	59-60	45	-	10
Tranmere Rov.	Tr	03.61	60-63	107	-	37
GUDMUNDSSON Albert						
Iceland, 5 October, 1923 Died 1994 Icelandic Int						(IF)
Arsenal (Am)	Glasgow Rangers	09.46	46	2	-	0
GUDMUNDSSON Niklas						
Sweden, 29 February, 1972 Swedish Int						(F)
Blackburn Rov.	Halmstads (Swe)	12.95	95-96	1	5	0
Ipswich T.	L	03.97	96	2	6	2
GUENTCHEV Bontcho Lubomisov						
Bulgaria, 7 July, 1964 Bulgarian Int						(M)
Ipswich T.	Sporting Lisbon (Por)	12.92	92-94	39	22	6
Luton T.	Tr	08.95	95-96	40	22	10
GUEST Brendan John						
Barnsley, 19 December, 1958 E Yth						(RB)
Lincoln C.	App	12.76	76-79	99	5	2
Swindon T.	Tr	07.80				
GUEST Gladstone						
Rotherham, 26 June, 1917						(IF)
Rotherham U.	Rawmarsh Welfare	12.39	46-55	358	-	135
GUEST William Francis						
Birmingham, 8 February, 1914 Died 1994						(OL)
Birmingham C.	Kingswinford Bromley	02.32	33-36	76	-	15
West Ham U.	Tr	03.36	36	3	-	1
Blackburn Rov.	Tr	01.37	36-46	88	-	30
Walsall	Tr	08.47	47	5	-	0
GUILD Alan Nicoll						
Forfar, 27 March, 1947 S Amat						(CD)
Luton T.	East Fife	07.69	70	1	0	0
Cambridge U.	Tr	05.71	71-73	117	10	1
GUILD James						
Glasgow, 10 December, 1928						(WH)
New Brighton	Dunoon Ath.	09.50	50	2	-	0
GUINAN Stephen						
Birmingham, 24 December, 1975						(F)
Nottingham F.	YT	01.93	95-97	2	4	0
Darlington	L	12.95	95	3	0	1
Burnley	L	03.97	96	0	6	0
Crewe Alex.	L	03.98	97	3	0	0
GULLAN Stanley Knox						
Edinburgh, 26 January, 1926						(G)
Queens Park R.	Clyde	07.49	50-54	48	-	0
GULLIT Ruud						
Sampdoria, 1 September, 1962 Dutch Int						(D/M)
Chelsea	Sampdoria (It)	07.95	95-97	37	12	4
GULLIVER Joffre						
Merthyr Tydfil, 2 August, 1915						(FB)
Southend U.		08.34				
Leeds U.		03.38				
Reading	Tr	06.39	46-50	161	-	0
Swindon T.	Tr	08.51	51	11	-	0
GULLIVER Terence Reginald						
Salisbury, 30 September, 1944						(FB)
Bournemouth	Weymouth	08.66	66-71	162	1	2
GUMMER Jason Craig						
Tredegar, 27 October, 1967 W Yth						(M)
Cardiff C.	YT	07.85	85-89	28	6	5
Torquay U.	L	03.89	88	7	0	1
GUNBY Peter						
Leeds, 20 November, 1934						(WH)
Leeds U.		09.55				
Bradford C.	Tr	07.56	56	3	-	0

League Club	Source	Date Signed	Seasons Played	Career Record Apps	Subs	Gls
GUNN Alfred						
West Germany, 11 July, 1924						(CF)
Nottingham F.		02.47	46	2	-	0
GUNN Alistair Robert						
Broughty Ferry, 2 November, 1924						(OR)
Huddersfield T.	Dundee	01.51	50-53	83	-	11
Bournemouth	Tr	06.54	54	27	-	2
GUNN Andrew Charles						
Barking, 2 February, 1971						(LW)
Watford	YT	03.89				
Crewe Alex.	Tr	02.90	89-90	2	2	0
GUNN Bryan James						
Thurso, 22 December, 1963 S Sch/S Yth/Su21-9/S 'B'/S-6						(G)
Norwich C.	Aberdeen	10.86	86-97	390	0	0
GUNN Brynley Charles						
Kettering, 21 August, 1958						(D)
Nottingham F.	App	08.75	75-84	129	2	1
Shrewsbury T.	L	11.85	85	9	0	0
Walsall	L	01.86	85	6	0	0
Mansfield T.	L	03.86	85	5	0	0
Peterborough U.	Tr	08.86	86-88	130	1	14
Chesterfield	Tr	07.89	89-91	89	2	10
GUNNING Henry (Harry)						
Leigh-on-Sea, 8 February, 1932						(OL)
West Ham U.	Gravesend & Nft.	06.52	52	1	-	0
Crystal Palace	Tr	05.54	54-56	63	-	4
Reading	Tr	05.57	57	13	-	1
GUNNING James Michael						
Helensburgh, 25 June, 1929 Died 1993						(OR)
Manchester C.	Hibernian	11.50	50-52	13	-	0
Barrow	Weymouth	07.54	54	10	-	1
GUNNLAUGSSON Arnar Bergmann						
Iceland, 6 March, 1973 Icelandic Int						(CF)
Bolton W.	I.A. Akranes (Ice)	08.97	97	2	13	0
GUNTER David Reginald						
Portsmouth, 4 March, 1933						(FB)
Southampton	Portsmouth (Am)	05.55	55	7	-	0
GUNTER Philip Edward						
Portsmouth, 6 January, 1932 Eu23-1/E 'B'						(D)
Portsmouth	Jnrs	08.49	51-63	321	-	2
Aldershot	Tr	07.64	64-65	78	0	8
GUNTHORPE Kenneth						
Sheffield, 14 November, 1938						(HB)
Rotherham U.		05.58	58	2	-	0
GUPPY Stephen						
Winchester, 29 March, 1969 E Semi Pro/Eu21-1/E 'B'						(M)
Wycombe W.		09.89	93	41	0	8
Newcastle U.	Tr	08.94				
Port Vale	Tr	11.94	94-96	102	3	12
Leicester C.	Tr	02.97	96-97	49	1	2
GURINOVICH Igor Nikolaivich						
U.S.S.R., 5 March, 1960 Russian Int						(F)
Brighton & H.A. (N/C)	Dinamo Minsk (USSR)	11.90	90	3	1	1
GURNEY Andrew Robert						
Bristol, 25 January, 1974						(RM)
Bristol Rov.	YT	07.92	93-96	100	8	9
Torquay U.	Tr	07.97	97	44	0	9
GURR Gerald Robert						
Brighton, 20 October, 1946						(G)
Southampton	Guildford C.	03.64	66-69	42	0	0
Aldershot	Tr	03.71	70-71	55	0	0
GUSCOTT Lindon						
Lambeth, 29 March, 1972						(F)
Gillingham	YT	07.89	88	0	2	0
GUSCOTT Raymond Melvin						
Newport, 18 November, 1957 W Sch						(M)
Bristol Rov.	App	11.75	76	1	0	0
Newport Co.	Minehead	10.77	77	12	5	1
GUTHRIE Christopher William						
Hexham, 7 September, 1953 E Sch						(F)
Newcastle U.	App	01.71	71	3	0	0
Southend U.	Tr	11.72	72-74	107	1	35
Sheffield U.	Tr	05.75	75-76	58	2	15
Swindon T.	Tr	07.77	77-78	44	1	12
Fulham	Tr	09.78	78-79	49	1	15
Millwall	Tr	03.80	79	7	0	1
GUTHRIE James Wallace Taylor						
Leith, 6 August, 1912 Died 1981						(WH)
Portsmouth	Dundee	08.37	37-38	76	-	1
Crystal Palace	Guildford C.	10.46	46	5	-	0
GUTHRIE Peter John						
Newcastle, 10 October, 1961						(G)
Tottenham H.	Weymouth	01.88				
Swansea C.	L	02.88	87	14	0	0
Bournemouth	Barnet	08.90	90	10	0	0
GUTHRIE Ralph						
Hartlepool, 13 September, 1932 Died 1996						(G)
Arsenal	Tow Law T.	05.53	54	2	-	0
Hartlepool U.	Tr	07.56	56-57	78	-	0
GUTHRIE Ronald George						
Gosforth, 19 April, 1944						(LB)
Newcastle U.	Jnrs	07.63	66-72	52	3	2
Sunderland	Tr	01.73	72-74	66	0	1
GUTTRIDGE Ronald						
Widnes, 28 April, 1916						(LB)
Aston Villa	Prescot Cables	03.37	46-47	15	-	0
Brighton & H. A.	Tr	06.48	48-49	17	-	0
GUTTRIDGE William Henry						
Darlaston, 4 March, 1931						(FB)
Wolverhampton W.	Metroshaft Wks	03.48	51-53	6	-	0
Walsall	Tr	11.54	54-61	198	-	0
GUTZMORE Leon Johnson Fitzgerald						
Camden, 30 October, 1976						(F)
Cambridge U. (N/C)	YT	09.95	95	0	2	0
GUY Alan						
Jarrow, 8 September, 1957						(M)
Newcastle U.	App	09.75	76-78	3	1	0
Peterborough U.	Tr	03.79	78-80	42	11	4
GUY Edward Frederick						
Seaham, 6 February, 1956						(G)
Hartlepool U.	App	02.74	74	1	0	0
GUY Harold George						
Wolverhampton, 1 January, 1932						(CH)
West Bromwich A.	Jnrs	03.50	50	1	-	0
GUY Ivor						
Chipping Sodbury, 27 February, 1926 Died 1986						(FB)
Bristol C.	Hambrook Villa	10.44	45-56	404	-	2
GUY Richard **James**						
Swansea, 29 January, 1921 Died 1990						(WH)
Norwich C.	R.A.F. St Athan	08.46	46-47	12	-	1
GUY Keith						
Seaham, 19 May, 1959						(M)
Newcastle U.	App	06.77				
Hartlepool U.	Tr	06.78	78	7	3	0
GUY Michael James						
Limavady (NI), 4 February, 1953						(M)
Sheffield U.	Coleraine	03.78	77-78	12	6	2
Crewe Alex.	Tr	09.79	79-80	54	1	7
GUY Richard						
Greenwich, 6 January, 1949						(G)
Wimbledon	Tooting & Mitcham	01.68	77	13	0	0
GUY Ronald						
Salford, 25 April, 1936						(CF)
Stockport Co.		09.58	58-59	9	-	2
GWATKIN Philip **Arthur**						
Harrow, 5 August, 1929						(OR)
Wrexham		10.52	53-55	56	-	8
Tranmere Rov.	Tr	06.56	56	21	-	6
GWINNETT Melvyn Lawrence						
Worcester, 14 May, 1963						(G)
Peterborough U.	Stourbridge	05.81				

League Club	Source	Date Signed	Seasons Played	Career Record Apps	Subs	Gls
Hereford U. (N/C)	Tr	09.82	82	1	0	0
Bradford C.	Gloucester C.	06.84				
Exeter C.	Tr	08.85	85-88	46	0	0

GWYTHER David Jeffrey Andrew
Birmingham, 6 December, 1948 *Wu23-2* (F)

League Club	Source	Date Signed	Seasons Played	Apps	Subs	Gls
Swansea C.	South Gower	03.66	65-72	213	5	58
Halifax T.	Tr	08.73	73-75	104	0	26
Rotherham U.	Tr	02.76	75-79	162	0	45
Newport Co.	Tr	12.79	79-82	84	21	29
Crewe Alex.	L	01.82	81	7	0	1
Newport Co. (N/C)	Port Talbot Ath.	03.85	84	1	1	0

GYMER John Paul
Romford, 11 November, 1966 (W)

League Club	Source	Date Signed	Seasons Played	Apps	Subs	Gls
Southend U.	App	08.84	83-86	30	25	12
Crewe Alex.	Tr	07.87	87	10	5	5

GYNN Michael
Peterborough, 19 August, 1961 (M)

League Club	Source	Date Signed	Seasons Played	Apps	Subs	Gls
Peterborough U.	App	04.79	78-82	152	4	33
Coventry C.	Tr	08.83	83-92	206	35	32
Stoke C.	Tr	08.93	93	14	7	0

League Club | Source | Date Signed | Seasons Played | Career Record Apps Subs Gls

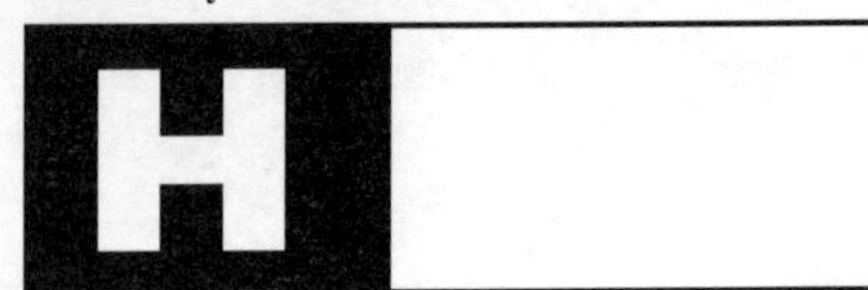

League Club	Source	Date Signed	Seasons Played	Career Record Apps	Subs	Gls
HAAG Kelly Jason						
Enfield, 6 October, 1970						(F)
Brentford	YT	07.89	89	1	4	0
Fulham	Tr	08.90	90-92	35	32	9
Barnet	Tr	08.93	93	31	7	8
HAALAND Alf-Inge Rasdal						
Norway, 23 November, 1972 Norwegian Int						(M)
Nottingham F.	Bryne (Nor)	01.94	93-96	66	9	7
Leeds U.	Tr	07.97	97	26	6	7
HAASZ John						
Hungary, 7 July, 1937						(WH)
Swansea C.		09.60	60	1	-	0
Workington	Tr	07.61	61-62	50	-	17
HABBIN Richard (Dick) Leonard						
Cambridge, 6 January, 1949						(M)
Reading	Cambridge U.	03.69	69-74	204	14	42
Rotherham U.	Tr	01.75	74-77	79	5	19
Doncaster Rov.	Tr	09.77	77-78	57	3	12
HACKETT Bernard Edward Kenneth						
Ramsbottom, 7 September, 1933						(CF)
Aston Villa		11.53				
Chester C.	Tr	07.55	55-56	21	-	4
HACKETT Gary Stuart						
Stourbridge, 11 October, 1962						(W)
Shrewsbury T.	Bromsgrove Rov.	07.83	83-86	142	8	17
Stoke C.	Aberdeen	03.88	87-89	64	9	7
West Bromwich A.	Tr	03.90	89-92	26	18	3
Peterborough U.	Tr	09.93	93	18	4	1
Chester C.	Tr	09.94	94	30	5	5
HACKETT Warren James						
Newham, 16 December, 1971 St Lucian Int						(LB)
Leyton Orient	Tottenham H. (YT)	07.90	90-93	74	2	3
Doncaster Rov.	Tr	07.94	94-95	46	0	2
Mansfield T.	Tr	10.95	95-97	90	1	5
HACKING John						
Blackpool, 24 August, 1925						(G)
Accrington St.	Blackburn Rov. (Am)	09.45	46	8	-	0
Stockport Co.	Tr	11.46	46-49	4	-	0
HACKING Robert Edward						
Blackburn, 30 March, 1918						(WH)
Luton T.	Blackburn Rov. (Am)	04.45	46	1	-	0
Brighton & H.A.	Tr	08.47	47	17	-	2
Southport	Tr	08.48	48-53	181	-	6
HADDAOUI Riffi						
Denmark, 24 March, 1971						(M)
Torquay U. (N/C)	Avarta (Den)	03.96	95	0	2	0
HADDINGTON Harold						
Scarborough, 7 August, 1931						(FB)
Bradford P.A.	Jnrs	02.49	52	2	-	0
West Bromwich A.	Tr	05.53				
Walsall	Tr	07.55	55-60	226	-	0
HADDINGTON William **Raymond**						
Bradford, 18 November, 1923 Died 1994						(IF)
Bradford C.	Bradford P.A. (Am)	09.46				
Oldham Ath.	Tr	08.47	47-50	117	-	63
Manchester C.	Tr	11.50	50	6	-	4
Stockport Co.	Tr	12.51	51	11	-	4
Bournemouth	Tr	07.52	52	2	-	0
Rochdale	Tr	10.52	52-53	38	-	12
Halifax T.	Tr	11.53	53	8	-	0
HADDOCK Andrew Edwin Robinson						
Edinburgh, 5 May, 1946						(W)
Chester C.	Jnrs	08.63	63	12	-	0
Crewe Alex.	Tr	08.64	64	4	-	0
Rotherham U.	Falkirk	12.66	66	4	0	0
Bradford P.A.	Chelmsford C.	12.67	67	5	0	0
Chester C.	Tr	03.68	67	10	0	1
HADDOCK Henry (Harry)						
Glasgow, 26 July, 1925						(FB)
Exeter C. (Am)	Renfrew Jnrs	05.46	46	1	-	0
HADDOCK Peter Murray						
Newcastle, 9 December, 1961						(D)
Newcastle U.	App	12.79	81-85	53	4	0
Burnley	L	03.86	85	7	0	0
Leeds U.	Tr	07.86	86-90	106	12	1
HADDON Henry (Harry) Llewellyn						
Cardiff, 8 April, 1923						(IF)
Cardiff C.		04.46				
Newport Co.	Bangor C.	02.47	46-48	10	-	1
Bristol Rov.	Tr	11.48	48	2	-	0
HADDOW Paul Andrew						
Blackpool, 11 October, 1978						(M)
Blackpool	YT	07.97	97	0	1	0
HADDRICK Robert						
West Ham, 1 May, 1950						(CH)
Southend U.	App	●	66	2	0	0
HADLEY Anthony Paul Frederick						
Upminster, 5 July, 1955						(CD)
Southend U.	Basildon U.	07.74	74-82	241	21	16
Colchester U.	Tr	08.83	83	44	1	0
Southend U.	Tr	08.84	84	31	1	3
HADLEY Stewart						
Dudley, 30 December, 1973						(F)
Derby Co.	Halesowen T.	07.92				
Mansfield T.	Tr	02.94	93-97	100	24	31
HADLINGTON John (Jack)						
Brierley Hill, 16 August, 1933						(OL)
Walsall	Cradley Heath	02.54	53	1	-	0
HADZIABDIC Dzemal						
Yugoslavia, 25 July, 1953 Yugoslav Int						(LB)
Swansea C.	Velez Mostar (Yug)	08.80	80-82	87	2	2
HAFFEY Francis						
Glasgow, 28 November, 1938 S-2						(G)
Swindon T.	Glasgow Celtic	10.64	64	4	-	0
HAGAN James						
Monkstown (NI), 10 August, 1956						(CD)
Coventry C.	Larne T.	11.77	78	12	1	0
Torquay U.	L	09.79	79	7	0	0
Coventry C.	Seiko (HK)	07.81	81	3	0	0
Birmingham C.	Tr	05.82	82-86	124	13	0
Colchester U. (N/C)	Celta Vigo (Sp)	11.89	89	2	0	0
HAGAN James						
Washington, 21 January, 1918 Died 1998 E Sch/EF Lge/E-1						(IF)
Derby Co.	Washington Colly	01.35	35-38	30	-	7
Sheffield U.	Tr	11.38	38-57	361	-	116
HAGUE Keith						
Hull, 25 May, 1946						(CH)
York C.	Goole T.	10.65	65	0	1	0
HAGUE Neil						
Thurcroft, 1 December, 1949 E Yth						(M/D)
Rotherham U.	App	12.66	67-71	134	11	23
Plymouth Arg.	Tr	11.71	71-73	98	0	15
Bournemouth	Tr	07.74	74-75	89	0	7
Huddersfield T.	Tr	06.76	76	25	0	2
Darlington	Tr	05.77	77-78	80	0	4
HAGUE Paul						
Consett, 16 September, 1972						(CD)
Gillingham	YTS	05.91	90-93	8	1	0
Leyton Orient	Tr	09.94	94	17	1	1
HAIG Richard Neil						
Pontypridd, 29 December, 1970						(F)
Cardiff C.	YTS	07.89	88-89	1	4	0
HAIGH Gordon						
Barnsley, 18 August, 1921						(IF)
Burnley	Ransome & Marles	11.45	46-49	18	-	3
Bournemouth	Tr	04.50	49-50	17	-	3
Watford	Tr	08.51	51	29	-	5

League Club	Source	Date Signed	Seasons Played	Career Record Apps	Subs	Gls
HAIGH Graham						
Huddersfield, 16 September, 1946						(WH)
Halifax T.	App	●	64	1	-	0
HAIGH John (Jack)						
Rotherham, 10 September, 1928						(IF)
Liverpool	Gainsborough Trin.	10.49	50-51	11	-	3
Scunthorpe U.	Tr	08.52	52-59	329	-	66
Doncaster Rov.	Tr	07.60	60-61	72	-	6
HAIGH Paul						
Scarborough, 4 May, 1958 Eu21-1						(D)
Hull C.	App	06.75	74-80	179	1	8
Carlisle U.	Tr	11.80	80-86	228	5	4
Hartlepool U.	Tr	07.87	87-88	49	1	0
HAILS Julian						
Lincoln, 20 November, 1967						(W)
Fulham	Hemel Hempstead	08.90	91-94	99	10	12
Southend U.	Tr	12.94	94-97	132	17	6
HAILS William						
Nettlesworth (Dm), 19 February, 1935						(OR)
Lincoln C.	Jnrs	03.53	53-54	9	-	0
Peterborough U.	Tr	(N/L)	60-62	94	-	27
Northampton T.	Tr	11.62	62-63	59	-	13
Luton T.	Tr	06.64	64	3	-	0
HAILWOOD David John						
Blackpool, 17 October, 1954						(W)
Mansfield T.		07.73	74	1	0	0
HAINES Donald Noah						
Ynysybwl, 23 September, 1925						(FB)
Bournemouth		10.48				
Newport Co.	Yeovil T.	12.50	50-53	78	-	1
HAINES Ivan Gerald						
Chatham, 14 September, 1968						(CD)
Gillingham	YT	06.87	87-90	45	6	0
HAINES John (Jack) Thomas William						
Evesham, 24 April, 1920 Died 1987 E-1						(IF)
Liverpool	Cheltenham T.	11.37				
Swansea C.	Tr	06.39	46	28	-	7
Leicester C.	Tr	06.47	47	12	-	3
West Bromwich A.	Tr	03.48	47-49	59	-	23
Bradford P.A.	Tr	12.49	49-53	136	-	34
Rochdale	Tr	10.53	53-54	60	-	16
Chester C.	Tr	07.55	55-56	47	-	8
HAINES Keith Harry						
Wigston, 19 December, 1937 E Yth						(CH)
Leeds U.	Matlock T.	05.59				
Lincoln C.	Tr	07.60	60-62	13	-	0
HAINES Mervyn John						
Ynysybwl, 2 May, 1923						(W)
Bournemouth		10.48				
Newport Co.	Yeovil T.	05.50	50	14	-	2
HAINSWORTH Leonard						
Rotherham, 25 January, 1918 Died 1990						(FB)
Rotherham U.		03.39	38-47	32	-	8
Doncaster Rov.	Tr	07.48	48-50	65	-	0
Workington	Tr	07.51	51-52	75	-	0
HAIR George						
Ryton, 28 April, 1925 Died 1994						(OL)
Newcastle U.	Spen Jnrs	05.43	46-48	23	-	7
Grimsby T.	Tr	02.49	48-50	68	-	8
HAIR Kenneth **Grenville** Arthur						
Burton, 16 November, 1931 Died 1968						(FB)
Leeds U.	Jnrs	11.48	50-63	443	-	1
HAIRE Garry						
Sedgefield, 24 July, 1963						(W)
Oxford U.	App	07.81				
Bradford C.	Whitley Bay	06.83	83-84	43	6	13
Darlington	Tr	02.85	84-85	16	9	2
Rochdale	L	10.85	85	3	0	0
HALBERT Paul John						
St Albans, 28 October, 1973						(F)
Aldershot	YT	●	90	0	3	0
HALE Alfred						
Waterford (Ire), 28 August, 1939 IR Amat/IR-13						(IF)
Aston Villa	Waterford	06.60	60-61	5	-	1
Doncaster Rov.	Tr	07.62	62-64	119	-	42
Newport Co.	Tr	08.65	65	34	0	21
HALE Denzil (Paddy) William						
Clevedon, 7 April, 1928						(CH)
Bristol Rov.	Clevedon T.	02.52	53-58	120	-	12
HALE Kenneth Oliver						
Blyth, 18 September, 1939						(IF)
Newcastle U.	Jnrs	10.56	57-62	30	-	15
Coventry C.	Tr	12.62	62-65	98	1	27
Oxford U.	Tr	03.66	65-67	64	2	13
Darlington	Tr	05.68	68-71	173	0	25
Halifax T.	Tr	07.72	72-73	52	0	4
HALE Joseph **Richard (Dixie)**						
Waterford (Ire), 29 May, 1935 LoI						(WH)
Swansea C.	Waterford	10.59	59-60	34	-	3
Barrow	Tr	07.61	61-63	118	-	16
Workington	Tr	08.64	64-66	131	0	10
Watford	Tr	07.67	67-69	95	3	7
HALES Derek David						
Rainham (Kt), 15 December, 1951						(F)
Luton T.	Dartford	03.72	72	5	2	1
Charlton Ath.	Tr	10.73	73-76	126	3	72
Derby Co.	Tr	12.76	76-77	22	1	4
West Ham U.	Tr	09.77	77	23	1	10
Charlton Ath.	Tr	07.78	78-84	186	5	76
Gillingham	Tr	03.85	84-85	31	9	9
HALES John McKendrick						
Glasgow, 15 May, 1940						(W)
Brentford	St Rochs	09.58	58-63	62	-	7
HALES Kevin Peter						
Dartford, 13 January, 1961						(M)
Chelsea	App	01.79	79-82	18	2	2
Leyton Orient	Tr	08.83	83-92	285	15	23
HALES Richard Joseph						
Gillingham, 24 August, 1925						(RB)
Gillingham (Am)	Sittingbourne	08.51	51	5	-	0
HALES William Henry						
Gillingham, 6 January, 1920 Died 1984						(CF)
Gillingham (Am)	Sittingbourne	07.50	50-51	15	-	9
HALEY John						
Sunderland, 24 April, 1932 Died 1956						(WH)
Gateshead		09.53	53-56	38	-	2
HALFORD Carl						
Ashton u Lyne, 27 November, 1958						(M)
Manchester C.	App	08.76				
Stockport Co.	Tr	07.77	77-78	65	9	5
Bury	Tr	08.79	79-80	31	0	2
HALL Albert Edward Benjamin						
Barry, 3 September, 1918 Died 1998 W Sch						(OR)
Tottenham H.	Jnrs	10.35	35-46	40	-	10
Plymouth Arg.	Tr	07.47	47	9	-	0
HALL Alexander Frank						
Grimsby, 17 September, 1909 Died 1992						(WH)
Grimsby T.	Cleethorpes T.	05.29	29-47	358	-	4
HALL Allan Samuel						
Urmston, 26 May, 1938 E Yth						(WH)
Oldham Ath.	Manchester U. (Am)	11.57	57-60	74	-	5
HALL Almerick George						
Hove, 12 November, 1912 Died 1994						(IF)
Brighton & H.A.	Southwick	02.31				
Tottenham H.	Tr	09.33	34-35	16	-	3
Southend U.	Tr	05.37	37-38	37	-	10
Bradford C.	Tr	06.39				
West Ham U.	Tr	12.45	46-48	50	-	11
HALL Anthony David						
Billingham, 17 January, 1969						(D)
Tranmere Rov.	Billingham T.	08.87	87	0	1	0
Hartlepool U.	Tr	10.87	87	0	1	0

League Club	Source	Date Signed	Seasons Played	Apps	Subs	Gls

HALL Arthur
Sheffield, 23 November, 1925 (W)

League Club	Source	Date Signed	Seasons Played	Apps	Subs	Gls
Chesterfield	Gainsborough Trin.	07.47	47-48	23	-	4
Scunthorpe U.	Goole T.	08.51	51	15	-	5

HALL Arthur Brian
Witney, 24 March, 1937 (W)

League Club	Source	Date Signed	Seasons Played	Apps	Subs	Gls
Bristol Rov.	Witney T.	07.59	60-61	2	-	0

HALL Bernard Roy
Clevedon, 8 July, 1942 (G)

League Club	Source	Date Signed	Seasons Played	Apps	Subs	Gls
Bristol Rov.	Jnrs	09.59	61-66	163	0	0

HALL Brian Samuel
Derby, 9 March, 1939 (OL/LB)

League Club	Source	Date Signed	Seasons Played	Apps	Subs	Gls
Mansfield T.	Belper T.	04.59	58-64	72	-	19
Colchester U.	Tr	03.65	64-72	324	5	28

HALL Brian William
Glasgow, 22 January, 1946 (M)

League Club	Source	Date Signed	Seasons Played	Apps	Subs	Gls
Liverpool	Manchester Univ.	07.68	68-75	140	13	15
Plymouth Arg.	Tr	07.76	76-77	49	2	16
Burnley	Tr	11.77	77-79	39	4	3

HALL Colin Thomas
Wolverhampton, 2 February, 1948 E Yth (W)

League Club	Source	Date Signed	Seasons Played	Apps	Subs	Gls
Nottingham F.	Jnrs	03.66	67-69	27	9	2
Bradford C.	Tr	06.70	70-71	65	1	7
Bristol C.	Tr	07.72	72	0	1	0
Hereford U.	L	09.72	72	5	0	0

HALL David
Doncaster, 26 September, 1960 (CD)

League Club	Source	Date Signed	Seasons Played	Apps	Subs	Gls
Scunthorpe U.	App	09.78	78-79	16	1	0

HALL David Henry
Sheffield, 16 March, 1954 (M)

League Club	Source	Date Signed	Seasons Played	Apps	Subs	Gls
Sheffield Wed.	App	03.72				
Bradford C.	Tr	07.75	75-76	51	3	3

HALL Kenneth Dennis
Southwell, 24 December, 1930 (FB)

League Club	Source	Date Signed	Seasons Played	Apps	Subs	Gls
Portsmouth	Jnrs	09.48	52-53	10	-	0
Reading	Tr	08.54	54	13	-	0
Bournemouth	Tr	07.55				

HALL Derek Robert
Ashton-under-Lyne, 5 January, 1965 (M)

League Club	Source	Date Signed	Seasons Played	Apps	Subs	Gls
Coventry C.	App	10.82	82	1	0	0
Torquay U.	Tr	03.84	83-84	55	0	6
Swindon T.	Tr	07.85	85	9	1	0
Southend U.	Tr	08.86	86-88	120	3	15
Halifax T.	Tr	07.89	89-90	48	1	4
Hereford U.	Tr	07.91	91-93	98	5	18
Rochdale	Tr	08.94	94-95	14	9	2

HALL Frederick
Norwich, 20 October, 1914 (G)

League Club	Source	Date Signed	Seasons Played	Apps	Subs	Gls
Norwich C.	Hellesden Hospital	09.34	35-46	90	-	0

HALL Frederick
Worksop, 24 November, 1924 (CF)

League Club	Source	Date Signed	Seasons Played	Apps	Subs	Gls
Birmingham C.	Whitwell O.B.	03.47	46-48	5	-	2

HALL Frederick Wilkinson
Chester-le-Street, 18 November, 1917 Died 1989 (CH)

League Club	Source	Date Signed	Seasons Played	Apps	Subs	Gls
Blackburn Rov.	Ouston Jnrs	11.35	36-38	29	-	0
Sunderland	Tr	08.46	46-54	215	-	1
Barrow	Tr	09.55	55	16	-	1

HALL Gareth David
Croydon, 12 March, 1969 E Sch/Wu21-1/W-9 (RB)

League Club	Source	Date Signed	Seasons Played	Apps	Subs	Gls
Chelsea	App	05.86	86-95	120	18	4
Sunderland	Tr	12.95	95-97	41	7	0
Brentford	L	10.97	97	6	0	0

HALL Ian
Whitehaven, 28 November, 1950 (D)

League Club	Source	Date Signed	Seasons Played	Apps	Subs	Gls
Workington	Jnrs	07.72	71-73	25	11	1
Southport	Tr	07.74	74	0	1	0

HALL Ian William
Bolsover, 27 December, 1939 E Sch/E Yth (IF/WH)

League Club	Source	Date Signed	Seasons Played	Apps	Subs	Gls
Derby Co.	Wolverhampton W. (Am)	09.59	59-61	44	-	13
Mansfield T.	Tr	09.62	62-67	145	0	10

HALL James
Bootle, 5 October, 1959 (M)

League Club	Source	Date Signed	Seasons Played	Apps	Subs	Gls
Blackpool	App	10.77	78	1	0	0
Blackburn Rov.	Tr	07.80				

HALL James Franklin
Manchester, 7 May, 1945 (FB)

League Club	Source	Date Signed	Seasons Played	Apps	Subs	Gls
Oldham Ath.	Mather & Platt	07.66	65	2	0	0

HALL James Leonard
Northampton, 21 March, 1945 E Yth (F)

League Club	Source	Date Signed	Seasons Played	Apps	Subs	Gls
Northampton T.	Jnrs	07.63	63-67	54	2	7
Peterborough U.	Tr	12.67	67-74	298	4	122
Northampton T.	Tr	01.75	74-77	69	0	28
Cambridge U.	L	12.76	76	24	0	15

HALL Jeffrey James
Scunthorpe, 7 September, 1929 Died 1959 EF Lge/E 'B'/E-17 (FB)

League Club	Source	Date Signed	Seasons Played	Apps	Subs	Gls
Birmingham C.	Bradford P.A. (Am)	05.50	50-58	227	-	1

HALL John (Jack)
Doncaster, 19 November, 1931 (CF)

League Club	Source	Date Signed	Seasons Played	Apps	Subs	Gls
Doncaster Rov.		08.51	51	2	-	0

HALL John Franklin
Bramley, 18 April, 1944 (OR)

League Club	Source	Date Signed	Seasons Played	Apps	Subs	Gls
Bradford C.	Jnrs	05.62	62-73	417	13	63

HALL Joseph Edgar
Sherburn (Dm), 10 April, 1934 (IF)

League Club	Source	Date Signed	Seasons Played	Apps	Subs	Gls
Fulham	Jnrs	10.51	55	1	-	0

HALL Lancelot
Darlington, 23 January, 1915 Died 1985 (CH)

League Club	Source	Date Signed	Seasons Played	Apps	Subs	Gls
Luton T.		01.37				
Barrow	Tr	07.38	38-48	108	-	1

HALL Leigh
Hereford, 10 June, 1975 (M)

League Club	Source	Date Signed	Seasons Played	Apps	Subs	Gls
Hereford U. (N/C)	Ledbury T.	03.95	94-95	0	2	0

HALL Leslie Frederick
St Albans, 1 October, 1921 (CH)

League Club	Source	Date Signed	Seasons Played	Apps	Subs	Gls
Luton T.	St Albans C.	08.43	47-54	79	-	0

HALL Marcus Thomas
Coventry, 24 March, 1976 Eu21-8/E 'B' (LB)

League Club	Source	Date Signed	Seasons Played	Apps	Subs	Gls
Coventry C.	YT	07.94	94-97	56	12	1

HALL Mark
Doncaster, 11 May, 1970 (RB)

League Club	Source	Date Signed	Seasons Played	Apps	Subs	Gls
Doncaster Rov.	YT	06.88	87-88	1	1	0

HALL Mark Anthony
Islington, 13 January, 1973 (W)

League Club	Source	Date Signed	Seasons Played	Apps	Subs	Gls
Southend U.	Tottenham H. (YT)	08.91	91-92	4	8	0
Barnet	L	09.93	93	3	0	0
Torquay U.	Tr	07.95	95	22	7	0

HALL Paul Anthony
Manchester, 3 July, 1972 Jamaican Int (W)

League Club	Source	Date Signed	Seasons Played	Apps	Subs	Gls
Torquay U.	YT	07.90	89-92	77	16	1
Portsmouth	Tr	03.93	92-97	148	40	37

HALL Peter
Stoke, 29 September, 1939 (W)

League Club	Source	Date Signed	Seasons Played	Apps	Subs	Gls
Port Vale	Stoke C. (Am)	05.58	58-60	16	-	4
Bournemouth	Tr	07.61				
Gillingham	Bedford T.	11.67	67	9	0	1

HALL Richard Anthony
Ipswich, 14 March 1972 E Yth/Eu21-11 (CD)

League Club	Source	Date Signed	Seasons Played	Apps	Subs	Gls
Scunthorpe U.	YT	03.90	89-90	22	0	3
Southampton	Tr	02.91	90-95	119	7	12
West Ham U.	Tr	07.96	96	7	0	0

HALL Richard Frank
Weymouth, 3 July, 1945 (WH)

League Club	Source	Date Signed	Seasons Played	Apps	Subs	Gls
Bournemouth	Weymouth	06.67	67	8	3	0

HALL Ronald
Dudley, 8 February, 1933 (WH)

League Club	Source	Date Signed	Seasons Played	Apps	Subs	Gls
Walsall	Cradley Heath	06.54	54-55	2	-	0

HALL Stanley Arthur
Southgate, 18 February, 1917 (G)

League Club	Source	Date Signed	Seasons Played	Apps	Subs	Gls
Leyton Orient	Finchley	03.38	38-46	26	-	0

HALL Wayne
Rotherham, 25 October, 1968 (LB)

League Club	Source	Date Signed	Seasons Played	Apps	Subs	Gls
Darlington	Hatfield Main	12.88				
York C.	Tr	03.89	88-97	288	16	8

League Club	Source	Date Signed	Seasons Played	Apps	Subs	Gls
HALL Wilfred						
St Helens, 14 October, 1934						(G)
Stoke C.	Earlestown	10.53	54-59	45	-	0
Ipswich T.	Tr	06.60	60-62	16	-	0
HALL William						
Gosport, 24 August, 1930						(CF)
Gillingham	Gosport Borough	09.52	52	9	-	0
HALL William Furness						
Walton-le-Dale, 6 February, 1926 Died 1986						(G)
Preston N.E.	Jnrs	02.48	47	7	-	0
Blackpool	Tr	07.49	52	3	-	0
Reading	Tr	07.53	53	16	-	0
HALL William Wilson						
Liverpool, 3 June, 1917						(W)
Liverpool	Thorndale	11.43				
Southport	Tr	06.46	46	16	-	1
HALLAM Anthony Kenneth						
Chesterfield, 9 October, 1946						(FB)
Chesterfield	App	10.64	65-66	5	1	0
HALLAM Norman Henry						
Stoke, 23 October, 1920						(WH)
Port Vale	Chelsea (Am)	05.46	46-52	63	-	4
Halifax T.	Tr	10.53	53	3	-	0
HALLARD William						
St Helens, 28 August, 1913 Died 1980						(WH)
Bury	Runcorn	08.35	35	1	-	0
Bradford P.A.	Tr	06.37	37-38	69	-	5
Rochdale	Tr	06.46	46	17	-	2
Accrington St.	Tr	03.47	46	3	-	0
HALLAS Geoffrey						
Oldham, 8 December, 1930						(FB)
West Ham U.	Warminster	03.54	54	3	-	0
HALLE Gunnar						
Norway, 11 August, 1965 Norwegian Int						(RB)
Oldham Ath.	Lillestrom (Nor)	02.91	90-96	185	3	17
Leeds U.	Tr	12.96	96-97	51	2	2
HALLETT Thomas Reginald						
Glyn-Neath, 10 April, 1939 W Sch						(CH)
Leeds U.	Jnrs	04.56				
Swindon T.	Tr	07.63	63-65	26	0	0
Bradford C.	Tr	06.66	66-70	177	2	2
HALLIDAY Brian						
Farnworth, 19 January, 1938						(OR)
Stockport Co.	Bolton W. (Am)	10.58	58	1	-	0
HALLIDAY Brian Joseph						
Liverpool, 30 December, 1944						(W)
Liverpool	Jnrs	05.63				
Tranmere Rov.	Tr	07.65				
Crewe Alex.	Tr	10.65	65	1	0	0
HALLIDAY Bruce						
Sunderland, 3 January, 1961						(CD)
Newcastle U.	App	01.79	80-81	32	0	1
Darlington	L	09.82	82	7	0	0
Bury	Tr	11.82	82	29	0	0
Bristol C.	Tr	08.83	83-84	52	1	0
Hereford U.	Tr	06.85	85-86	61	1	6
HALLIDAY Gary						
Bradford, 9 May, 1951						(F)
Bradford P.A.	Jnrs	08.68	68	0	1	0
HALLIDAY Stephen William						
Sunderland, 3 May, 1976						(F)
Hartlepool U.	YT	07.94	93-97	111	29	25
HALLIDAY Thomas						
Ardrossan, 28 April, 1940						(CF)
Cardiff C.	Dumbarton	10.63	63-64	16	-	2
HALLOWS Paul Charles Richard						
Chester, 22 June, 1950						(FB)
Bolton W.	App	10.67	68-73	45	2	0
Rochdale	Tr	05.74	74-79	197	0	2
HALLWORTH Jonathan Geoffrey						
Stockport, 26 October, 1965						(G)
Ipswich T.	App	05.83	85-87	45	0	0
Bristol Rov.	L	01.85	84	2	0	0
Oldham Ath.	Tr	02.89	88-96	171	3	0
Cardiff C.	Tr	08.97	97	43	0	0
HALLYBONE James Michael						
Leytonstone, 15 May, 1962						(M)
Leyton Orient	App	05.80	81	5	3	0
Halifax T.	Tr	07.82	82	11	5	0
HALOM Victor Lewis						
Burton, 3 October, 1948						(F)
Charlton Ath.	App	01.66	65-67	9	3	0
Leyton Orient	Tr	08.67	67-68	53	0	12
Fulham	Tr	11.68	68-71	66	6	22
Luton T.	Tr	09.71	71-72	57	2	17
Sunderland	Tr	02.73	72-75	110	3	35
Oldham Ath.	Tr	07.76	76-79	121	2	43
Rotherham U.	Tr	02.80	79-80	19	1	2
HALPIN John Thomas						
Manchester, 5 June, 1927						(RB)
Bury		11.48	48	2	-	0
Shrewsbury T.	Tr	08.51	51-52	42	-	0
HALPIN John William						
Broxburn, 15 November, 1961 S Yth						(LW)
Carlisle U.	Glasgow Celtic	10.84	84-90	148	5	17
Rochdale	Tr	07.91	91	22	9	1
HALSALL Alan						
Menai Bridge, 17 November, 1940						(G)
Blackpool	Skelmersdale U.	04.62	61	2	-	0
Oldham Ath.	Tr	07.63	63	2	-	0
HALSALL Michael						
Bootle, 21 July, 1961						(M)
Liverpool	App	05.79				
Birmingham C.	Tr	03.83	82-84	35	1	3
Carlisle U.	Tr	10.84	84-86	92	0	11
Grimsby T.	Tr	02.87	86	12	0	0
Peterborough U.	Tr	07.87	87-93	248	1	29
HALSEY Mark Alan						
Romford, 1 December, 1959						(M)
Norwich C.	App	12.77	77-79	3	0	0
HALSTEAD Roy						
Whitworth, 26 July, 1931						(IR)
Burnley	Jnrs	06.53				
Chester C.	Tr	06.54	54	21	-	4
HALTON Reginald Lloyd						
Leek, 11 July, 1916 Died 1988						(WH)
Manchester U.	Cheddington M.H.	10.36	36	4	-	1
Notts Co.	Tr	06.37	37	6	-	0
Bury	Tr	11.37	37-48	114	-	19
Chesterfield	Tr	12.48	48-50	61	-	10
Leicester C.	Tr	09.50	50-51	64	-	3
HAM Michael Thomas						
Plymouth, 6 December, 1963						(CD)
Plymouth Arg.	App	12.81	81-84	16	1	0
HAM Robert Stanley						
Bradford, 29 March, 1942						(F)
Bradford P.A.	Jnrs	10.61	61-62	25	-	6
Grimsby T.	Gainsborough Trin.	02.64	63	2	-	1
Bradford P.A.	Tr	08.64	64-67	134	0	47
Bradford C.	Tr	02.68	67-70	115	0	40
Preston N.E.	Tr	10.70	70-71	43	0	14
Rotherham U.	Tr	10.71	71-72	67	1	24
Bradford C.	Tr	07.73	73-74	72	1	24
HAMER John						
Bradford, 5 April, 1944						(LH)
Bradford C. (Am)		04.64	64	1	-	0
HAMER Kevin John						
Merthyr Tydfil, 2 February, 1969						(CD)
Newport Co.	YT	07.87	85-87	15	2	1
HAMILL Rory						
Coleraine (NI), 4 May, 1976 NI Sch/NI Yth						(LW)
Fulham	Portstewart	11.94	94-95	24	24	7

HAMILL Stewart Peter
Glasgow, 22 January, 1960 (W)

League Club	Source	Date Signed	Seasons Played	Apps	Subs	Gls
Leicester C.	Pollok Jnrs	09.80	80-81	10	0	2
Scunthorpe U.	L	03.82	81	4	0	0
Northampton T.	Nuneaton Borough	03.86	85	3	0	1
Scarborough	Altrincham	07.87	87	19	9	3

HAMILTON Alexander McGregor
Kirkcolm, 21 November, 1937 (WH)

League Club	Source	Date Signed	Seasons Played	Apps	Subs	Gls
Accrington St.	Drumore Jnrs	08.57	58-60	82	-	0
York C.	Tr	03.62	61	11	-	0

HAMILTON Bryan
Belfast, 21 December, 1946 NIu23-2/NI-50 (M)

League Club	Source	Date Signed	Seasons Played	Apps	Subs	Gls
Ipswich T.	Linfield	08.71	71-75	142	11	43
Everton	Tr	11.75	75-76	38	3	5
Millwall	Tr	07.77	77-78	48	1	6
Swindon T.	Tr	11.78	78-80	19	5	1
Tranmere Rov.	Tr	10.80	80-84	95	14	6

HAMILTON Charles McDermott
Glasgow, 16 June, 1933 (OR)

League Club	Source	Date Signed	Seasons Played	Apps	Subs	Gls
Plymouth Arg.	Jnrs	07.50				
Stockport Co.	Tr	11.55	55	7	-	1

HAMILTON David
South Shields, 7 November, 1960 E Yth (M)

League Club	Source	Date Signed	Seasons Played	Apps	Subs	Gls
Sunderland	App	09.78				
Blackburn Rov.	Tr	01.81	80-85	104	10	7
Cardiff C.	L	03.85	84	10	0	0
Wigan Ath.	Tr	07.86	86-88	97	6	7
Chester C.	Tr	08.89	89	26	2	0
Burnley	Tr	08.90	90-91	11	4	0

HAMILTON David Stewart
Carlisle, 8 February, 1919 (IF)

League Club	Source	Date Signed	Seasons Played	Apps	Subs	Gls
Newcastle U.	Shawfield Jnrs	05.39				
Southend U.	Tr	05.46	46	4	-	0

HAMILTON Derrick (Des) Vivian
Bradford, 15 August, 1976 Eu21-1 (M)

League Club	Source	Date Signed	Seasons Played	Apps	Subs	Gls
Bradford C.	YT	06.94	93-96	67	21	5
Newcastle U.	Tr	03.97	97	7	5	0

HAMILTON Edward
Glasgow, 17 January, 1927 (IL)

League Club	Source	Date Signed	Seasons Played	Apps	Subs	Gls
Barnsley	Dundalk	04.49	49	1	-	0

HAMILTON Gary James
Glasgow, 27 December, 1965 S Yth (M)

League Club	Source	Date Signed	Seasons Played	Apps	Subs	Gls
Middlesbrough	App	06.83	82-88	217	12	25
Darlington	L	09.91	91	11	0	2

HAMILTON Hugh Hare
Newton Mearns, 16 June, 1942 (W)

League Club	Source	Date Signed	Seasons Played	Apps	Subs	Gls
Hartlepool U.	Falkirk	07.63	63-65	38	1	7

HAMILTON Ian
Thornbury, 12 September, 1940 (IF)

League Club	Source	Date Signed	Seasons Played	Apps	Subs	Gls
Bristol Rov.	Jnrs	01.58	58-67	149	0	60
Exeter C.	L	10.67	67	4	0	1
Newport Co.	Tr	07.68	68	11	2	2

HAMILTON Ian (Chico) Michael
Streatham, 31 October, 1950 E Yth (M)

League Club	Source	Date Signed	Seasons Played	Apps	Subs	Gls
Chelsea	App	01.68	66	3	2	2
Southend U.	Tr	09.68	68	34	2	11
Aston Villa	Tr	06.69	69-75	189	19	40
Sheffield U.	Tr	07.76	76-77	55	5	13

HAMILTON Ian Richard
Stevenage, 14 December, 1967 (M)

League Club	Source	Date Signed	Seasons Played	Apps	Subs	Gls
Southampton	App	12.85				
Cambridge U.	Tr	03.88	87-88	23	1	1
Scunthorpe U.	Tr	12.88	88-91	139	6	18
West Bromwich A.	Tr	06.92	92-97	229	11	23
Sheffield U.	Tr	03.98	97	8	0	1

HAMILTON Ian Walter
South Shields, 21 July, 1956 (M)

League Club	Source	Date Signed	Seasons Played	Apps	Subs	Gls
Darlington	Boldon Colly	11.79	79-81	99	4	19

HAMILTON James
Baillieston, 14 June, 1955 (M)

League Club	Source	Date Signed	Seasons Played	Apps	Subs	Gls
Sunderland	App	06.72	71-73	8	8	2
Plymouth Arg.	Tr	11.75	76	6	2	0
Bristol Rov.	Tr	12.76	76-77	16	4	1
Carlisle U.	Tr	09.77	77-81	150	4	12
Hartlepool U.	Gretna	11.82	82	2	1	0

HAMILTON John
Larkhall, 22 January, 1935 Su23-2/SF Lge (W)

League Club	Source	Date Signed	Seasons Played	Apps	Subs	Gls
Watford	Hearts	05.67	67	7	1	2

HAMILTON John Turner
Glasgow, 10 July, 1949 (F)

League Club	Source	Date Signed	Seasons Played	Apps	Subs	Gls
Millwall	Glasgow Rangers	06.78	78	1	1	0

HAMILTON Neville Roy
Leicester, 19 April, 1960 (M)

League Club	Source	Date Signed	Seasons Played	Apps	Subs	Gls
Leicester C.	App	11.77	77	4	0	0
Mansfield T.	Tr	01.79	78-80	84	5	4
Rochdale	Tr	08.81	81-83	72	2	5
Wolverhampton W.	Tr	07.84				

HAMILTON Robert Menzies
Edinburgh, 25 April, 1924 (W)

League Club	Source	Date Signed	Seasons Played	Apps	Subs	Gls
Chester C.	Hearts	11.45	46-47	68	-	10

HAMILTON William
Hamilton, 1 September, 1918 (WH)

League Club	Source	Date Signed	Seasons Played	Apps	Subs	Gls
Preston N.E.	Blantyre Celtic	09.37	46	37	-	0

HAMILTON William Murdoch
Airdrie, 16 February, 1938 Died 1976 SF Lge/S-1 (IF)

League Club	Source	Date Signed	Seasons Played	Apps	Subs	Gls
Sheffield U.	Drumpelier	02.56	56-60	79	-	21
Middlesbrough	Tr	02.61	60-61	10	-	1
Aston Villa	Hibernian	08.65	65-66	49	0	9

HAMILTON William Robert
Belfast, 9 May, 1957 NIu21-1/NI-41 (F)

League Club	Source	Date Signed	Seasons Played	Apps	Subs	Gls
Queens Park R.	Linfield	04.78	78-79	9	3	2
Burnley	Tr	11.79	79-83	200	0	58
Oxford U.	Tr	08.84	84-86	32	0	12

HAMLET Alan Graham
Watford, 30 September, 1977 (RB)

League Club	Source	Date Signed	Seasons Played	Apps	Subs	Gls
Barnet	YT	07.96	94	3	0	0

HAMLETT Thomas **Lawrence (Lol)**
Stoke, 24 January, 1917 Died 1986 (FB)

League Club	Source	Date Signed	Seasons Played	Apps	Subs	Gls
Bolton W.	Congleton T.	05.38	46-48	72	-	9
Port Vale	Tr	05.49	49-51	109	-	0

HAMMILL John
Irvine, 8 January, 1924 (RH)

League Club	Source	Date Signed	Seasons Played	Apps	Subs	Gls
Newport Co.	Arbroath	04.47	46-47	12	-	0

HAMMOND Albert William Arthur
Hanwell, 5 February, 1924 Died 1989 (IF)

League Club	Source	Date Signed	Seasons Played	Apps	Subs	Gls
Brentford	Queens Park R. (Am)	01.46				
Exeter C.	Tr	06.46	46	2	-	0

HAMMOND Andrew Bendall
Rotherham, 21 November, 1978 (F)

League Club	Source	Date Signed	Seasons Played	Apps	Subs	Gls
Doncaster Rov.	YT	•	97	1	0	0

HAMMOND Cyril Samuel
Woolwich, 10 October, 1927 (WH)

League Club	Source	Date Signed	Seasons Played	Apps	Subs	Gls
Charlton Ath.	Erith & Belvedere	04.46	50-57	201	-	2
Colchester U.	Tr	07.58	58-60	95	-	5

HAMMOND Geoffrey
Sudbury, 24 March, 1950 (FB)

League Club	Source	Date Signed	Seasons Played	Apps	Subs	Gls
Ipswich T.	Jnrs	07.68	70-73	52	3	2
Manchester C.	Tr	09.74	74-75	33	1	2
Charlton Ath.	Tr	07.76	76	15	1	0

HAMMOND Nicholas David
Hornchurch, 7 September, 1967 (G)

League Club	Source	Date Signed	Seasons Played	Apps	Subs	Gls
Arsenal	App	07.85				
Bristol Rov.	L	08.86	86	3	0	0
Swindon T.	Tr	06.87	87-94	65	2	0
Plymouth Arg.	Tr	08.95	95	4	0	0
Reading	Tr	02.96	95-97	24	0	0

HAMMOND Paul Anthony
Nottingham, 26 July, 1953 (G)

League Club	Source	Date Signed	Seasons Played	Apps	Subs	Gls
Crystal Palace	App	07.71	72-76	117	0	0

HAMON Christopher Anthony
Jersey, 27 April, 1970 (F)

League Club	Source	Date Signed	Seasons Played	Apps	Subs	Gls
Swindon T.	St Peter (Jersey)	07.92	92-94	3	5	1

HAMPSHIRE Paul
Guildford, 10 October, 1961 (F)

League Club	Source	Date Signed	Seasons Played	Apps	Subs	Gls
Aldershot	Jnrs	06.79	80-81	4	1	2

HAMPSON Alan
Prescot, 31 December, 1927 (IF)

League Club	Source	Date Signed	Seasons Played	Apps	Subs	Gls
Everton		08.49	50	1	-	0
Halifax T.	Tr	11.52	52-55	121	-	32
Bradford C.	Tr	07.56	56	6	-	4

HAMPSON Eric
Stafford, 11 November, 1921 (WH)

League Club	Source	Date Signed	Seasons Played	Apps	Subs	Gls
Stoke C.	Stafford R.	05.39	48-51	8	-	0

HAMPSON Raymond Geoffrey
Manchester, 27 July, 1932 (OR)

League Club	Source	Date Signed	Seasons Played	Apps	Subs	Gls
Manchester U.	Jnrs	04.51				
Reading	Tr	04.53				
Aldershot	Tr	07.55	55-56	21	-	2
Bournemouth	Tr	07.57	57-58	15	-	2

HAMPTON Derek
Saltburn, 25 April, 1952 (W)

League Club	Source	Date Signed	Seasons Played	Apps	Subs	Gls
Hartlepool U.	Whitby T.	11.79	79-81	66	8	18

HAMPTON Ivan Keith
Heanor, 15 October, 1942 (FB)

League Club	Source	Date Signed	Seasons Played	Apps	Subs	Gls
Notts Co.	Rotherham U. (Am)	03.61	60-66	139	2	1
Halifax T.	Tr	07.67	67-68	57	2	1
Peterborough U.	Tr	07.69	69	3	1	0

HAMPTON Peter John
Oldham, 12 September, 1954 E Yth (LB)

League Club	Source	Date Signed	Seasons Played	Apps	Subs	Gls
Leeds U.	App	09.71	72-79	63	5	2
Stoke C.	Tr	08.80	80-83	134	4	4
Burnley	Tr	08.84	84-86	116	2	2
Rochdale	Tr	08.87	87	19	0	1
Carlisle U.	Tr	12.87	87	12	0	0

HAMSHER John James
Lambeth, 14 January, 1978 (RB)

League Club	Source	Date Signed	Seasons Played	Apps	Subs	Gls
Fulham	YT	07.96	95	0	3	0

HAMSON Gary
Sandiacre, 24 August, 1959 (LM)

League Club	Source	Date Signed	Seasons Played	Apps	Subs	Gls
Sheffield U.	App	11.76	76-78	107	1	8
Leeds U.	Tr	07.79	79-85	126	8	3
Bristol C.	Tr	07.86	86	12	0	2
Port Vale	Tr	12.86	86-87	36	2	3

HAMSTEAD George William
Rotherham, 24 January, 1946 (W)

League Club	Source	Date Signed	Seasons Played	Apps	Subs	Gls
York C.	Rotherham U. (Am)	09.64	64-65	32	3	1
Barnsley	Tr	07.66	66-70	147	2	22
Bury	Tr	07.71	71-78	189	7	29
Rochdale	L	01.77	76	3	1	0

HANBY Robert James
Pontefract, 24 December, 1974 (D)

League Club	Source	Date Signed	Seasons Played	Apps	Subs	Gls
Barnsley	YT	07.93				
Scarborough	Tr	08.96	96	1	3	0

HANCOCK Anthony Eric
Manchester, 31 January, 1967 (F)

League Club	Source	Date Signed	Seasons Played	Apps	Subs	Gls
Stockport Co.	Stockport Georgians	12.88	88	12	10	5
Burnley	Tr	06.89	89	9	8	0
Preston N.E.	Tr	01.90				

HANCOCK Barry John
Stoke, 30 December, 1938 (IF)

League Club	Source	Date Signed	Seasons Played	Apps	Subs	Gls
Port Vale		07.57	60-63	21	-	1
Crewe Alex.	Tr	08.64	64	3	-	0

HANCOCK Charles Raymond
Stoke, 16 February, 1925 (G)

League Club	Source	Date Signed	Seasons Played	Apps	Subs	Gls
Port Vale	Birches Head	05.48	48-55	50	-	0

HANCOCK David Jeffrey
Exeter, 24 July, 1938 (WH)

League Club	Source	Date Signed	Seasons Played	Apps	Subs	Gls
Plymouth Arg.	Jnrs	09.55	56	2	-	0
Torquay U.	Tr	01.59	58-63	177	-	12
Exeter C.	Tr	03.64	63-64	40	-	3

HANCOCK Kenneth Paul
Hanley, 25 November, 1937 (G)

League Club	Source	Date Signed	Seasons Played	Apps	Subs	Gls
Port Vale	Stoke C. (Am)	12.58	58-64	241	-	0
Ipswich T.	Tr	12.64	64-68	163	0	0
Tottenham H.	Tr	03.69	69-70	3	0	0
Bury	Tr	07.71	71-72	35	0	0

HANCOCK Michael
Newport, 17 February, 1954 W Sch (CD)

League Club	Source	Date Signed	Seasons Played	Apps	Subs	Gls
Newport Co.	Jnrs	08.73	71-75	51	9	2

HANCOCKS John
Oakengates, 30 April, 1919 Died 1994 EF Lge/E-3 (OR)

League Club	Source	Date Signed	Seasons Played	Apps	Subs	Gls
Walsall	Oakengates T.	08.38	38	30	-	9
Wolverhampton W.	Tr	05.46	46-55	343	-	158

HANCOX David Thomas
Conisbrough, 2 October, 1947 (CF)

League Club	Source	Date Signed	Seasons Played	Apps	Subs	Gls
Sheffield U.	App	09.65				
Chester C.	Tr	07.67	67	17	2	4

HANCOX Paul Anthony
Manchester, 22 July, 1970 (M)

League Club	Source	Date Signed	Seasons Played	Apps	Subs	Gls
Rochdale	YT	●	87	0	2	0

HANCOX Raymond
Mansfield, 1 May, 1929 (F)

League Club	Source	Date Signed	Seasons Played	Apps	Subs	Gls
Crystal Palace	Sutton U.	08.50	50-52	20	-	3
Southend U.	Tr	06.53				

HANCOX Richard
Wolverhampton, 4 October, 1968 (F/FB)

League Club	Source	Date Signed	Seasons Played	Apps	Subs	Gls
Torquay U.	Stourport Swifts	03.93	92-96	56	26	10

HAND Eoin Kevin Joseph Colin
Dublin, 30 March, 1946 IR-20 (CD)

League Club	Source	Date Signed	Seasons Played	Apps	Subs	Gls
Swindon T.	Drumcondra	06.64				
Portsmouth	Drumcondra	10.68	68-75	259	1	13
Portsmouth	Shamrock Rov.	12.77	77-78	15	2	2

HANDFORD Philip Michael
Chatham, 18 July, 1964 (M)

League Club	Source	Date Signed	Seasons Played	Apps	Subs	Gls
Gillingham	App	07.82	82-83	29	3	1
Wimbledon	Tr	08.84	84	7	0	0
Crewe Alex.	L	01.86	85	9	0	0

HANDLEY Brian
Wakefield, 21 June, 1936 Died 1982 (CF)

League Club	Source	Date Signed	Seasons Played	Apps	Subs	Gls
Aston Villa	Goole T.	09.57	59	3	-	0
Torquay U.	Tr	09.60	60-63	80	-	33
Rochdale	Bridgwater T.	02.66	65	3	0	0

HANDSCOMBE Malcolm
Normanton, 29 June, 1934 (CH)

League Club	Source	Date Signed	Seasons Played	Apps	Subs	Gls
Chester C. (Am)		05.57	57	4	-	0

HANDYSIDE Peter David
Dumfries, 31 July, 1974 Su21-7 (CD)

League Club	Source	Date Signed	Seasons Played	Apps	Subs	Gls
Grimsby T.	YT	11.92	92-97	134	6	1

HANDYSIDES Ian Robert
Jarrow, 14 December, 1962 Died 1990 E Yth (W)

League Club	Source	Date Signed	Seasons Played	Apps	Subs	Gls
Birmingham C.	App	01.80	80-83	44	18	2
Walsall	Tr	01.84	83-85	58	8	11
Birmingham C.	Tr	03.86	85-87	53	3	4
Wolverhampton W.	L	09.86	86	11	0	2

HANFORD Harry
Blaengwynfi, 9 October, 1907 Died 1996 W Sch/W-7 (CH)

League Club	Source	Date Signed	Seasons Played	Apps	Subs	Gls
Swansea C.	Ton Pentre	05.26	27-35	200	-	0
Sheffield Wed.	Tr	02.36	35-38	85	-	1
Exeter C.	Tr	05.46	46	36	-	0

HANKEY Albert Edward
Stoke, 24 May, 1914 (G)

League Club	Source	Date Signed	Seasons Played	Apps	Subs	Gls
Southend U.	Charlton Ath. (Am)	10.37	37-49	125	-	0

HANKIN Raymond
Wallsend, 21 February, 1956 E Yth/Eu23-3 (F)

League Club	Source	Date Signed	Seasons Played	Apps	Subs	Gls
Burnley	App	02.73	72-76	110	2	37
Leeds U.	Tr	09.76	76-79	82	1	32
Arsenal	Vancouver (Can)	11.81				
Middlesbrough	Vancouver (Can)	09.82	82	19	2	1
Peterborough U.	Tr	09.83	83-84	31	2	8
Wolverhampton W.	Tr	03.85	84	9	1	1

HANKINSON James
Preston, 1 July, 1928 (IF)

League Club	Source	Date Signed	Seasons Played	Apps	Subs	Gls
Preston N.E.		09.47				
Chester C.	Tr	06.50	50	15	-	1

HANLON John James
Manchester, 12 October, 1917 (CF)

League Club	Source	Date Signed	Seasons Played	Apps	Subs	Gls
Manchester U.	St Wilfreds	11.35	38-48	63	-	20
Bury	Tr	10.48	48-49	31	-	1

HANLON Richard Kenneth
Wembley, 26 May, 1978 (M/F)

League Club	Source	Date Signed	Seasons Played	Apps	Subs	Gls
Southend U.	Chelsea (YT)	07.96	96	1	1	0

League Club	Source	Date Signed	Seasons Played	Apps	Subs	Gls
HANLON Stephen Henry						
Chester, 18 July, 1963 (M)						
Crewe Alex.	App	07.81	80-82	23	4	0
HANLON Walter						
Glasgow, 23 September, 1919 (OL)						
Brighton & H.A.	Clyde	08.46	46-47	72	-	4
Bournemouth	Tr	05.48	48	19	-	3
Crystal Palace	Tr	07.49	49-54	126	-	8
HANMER Gareth Craig						
Shrewsbury, 12 October, 1973 (RB)						
West Bromwich A.	Newtown	06.96				
Shrewsbury T.	Tr	07.97	97	39	0	1
HANN Ralph						
Whitburn (Dm), 4 July, 1911 Died 1990 (CH)						
Derby Co.	Newcastle Swifts	03.32	32-38	115	-	0
Crystal Palace	Tr	04.47	46	1	-	0
HANNABY Cyril						
Doncaster, 11 October, 1923 (G)						
Wolverhampton W.	Wath W.	03.44				
Hull C.	Tr	08.46	46-47	17	-	0
Halifax T.	Tr	02.48	47	2	-	0
HANNAH George						
Liverpool, 11 December, 1928 Died 1990 NIF Lge (IF)						
Newcastle U.	Linfield	09.49	49-56	167	-	41
Lincoln C.	Tr	09.57	57-58	38	-	4
Manchester C.	Tr	09.58	58-63	114	-	15
Notts Co.	Tr	07.64	64-65	25	0	1
Bradford C.	Tr	10.65	65	29	1	2
HANNAH John						
Wakefield, 25 October, 1962 (F)						
Darlington (N/C)	Fryston Colly	10.83	83-84	15	7	7
HANNAH William King						
Shotts, 6 August, 1921 Died 1978 (IF)						
Preston N.E.	Albion Rov.	12.47	47-49	15	-	4
Barrow	Tr	02.51	50-53	106	-	16
HANNAM David Vincent						
Islington, 10 May, 1944 (W)						
Brighton & H.A.	Jnrs	06.61	62	5	-	2
HANNAWAY John (Jack)						
Bootle, 22 October, 1927 (WH)						
Manchester C.	Seaforth Fellows	04.50	51-56	64	-	0
Gillingham	Tr	06.57	57-59	126	-	4
Southport	Tr	06.60	60-61	73	-	2
HANNIGAN Al-James						
Islington, 26 January, 1971 (CD)						
Arsenal	YT	03.89				
Torquay U.	L	03.90	89	5	2	0
HANNIGAN Brendan						
Dublin, 3 September, 1943 (F)						
Wrexham	Shelbourne	12.65	65	7	0	2
HANNIGAN Ernest						
Glasgow, 23 January, 1943 (W)						
Preston N.E.	Queen of South	08.64	64-67	97	0	29
Coventry C.	Tr	11.67	67-69	43	4	6
Torquay U.	L	12.69	69	2	0	0
HANNIGAN John Leckie						
Barrhead, 17 February, 1933 (W)						
Sunderland	Morton	07.55	55-57	33	-	8
Derby Co.	Tr	05.58	58-60	72	-	19
Bradford P.A.	Tr	06.61	61-63	96	-	26
HANSBURY Roger						
Barnsley, 26 January, 1955 (G)						
Norwich C.	App	01.73	74-80	78	0	0
Cambridge U.	L	11.77	77	11	0	0
Burnley	Eastern (HK)	08.83	83-84	83	0	0
Cambridge U.	Tr	07.85	85	37	0	0
Birmingham C.	Tr	03.86	86-89	57	0	0
Sheffield U.	L	10.87	87	5	0	0
Wolverhampton W.	L	03.89	88	3	0	0
Colchester U.	L	08.89	89	4	0	0
Cardiff C.	Tr	10.89	89-91	99	0	0
HANSELL Ronald Arthur Robert						
Norwich, 3 October, 1930 (IF)						
Norwich C.	Norwich St B.	06.50	53-55	29	-	7
Chester C.	Tr	06.56	56	36	-	9
HANSEN Allan David						
Alloa, 13 June, 1955 Su23-3/S-26 (CD)						
Liverpool	Partick Thistle	04.77	77-89	434	0	8
HANSEN Edwin						
Denmark, 21 January, 1920 (IF)						
Grimsby T. (Am)	Koge K.B. (Den)	12.46	46	1	-	0
HANSEN Karl						
Denmark, 4 July, 1921 Died 1990 (IF)						
Huddersfield T. (Am)	Denmark	01.49	48	15	-	2
HANSEN Vergard						
Norway, 8 August, 1969 (RB)						
Bristol C.	Stromsgodset (Nor)	11.94	94-95	36	1	0
HANSON David Paul						
Huddersfield, 19 November, 1968 (CF)						
Bury (N/C)	Farsley Celtic	07.93	93	1	0	0
Leyton Orient	Hednesford T.	10.95	95-97	26	22	5
Chesterfield	L	03.97	96	3	0	1
HANSON Frederick						
Sheffield, 23 May, 1915 Died 1967 (OL)						
Crystal Palace	Indus Sports	05.35	34	1	-	0
Rotherham U.	Tr	03.36	36-46	108	-	29
HANSON John						
Bradford, 3 December, 1962 (F)						
Bradford C.	App	12.80	80	1	0	0
HANSON Neil						
Blackburn, 16 June, 1964 (F)						
Preston N.E.	App	09.81				
Halifax T.	Tr	08.83	83	1	1	0
HANSON Stanley						
Bootle, 27 December, 1915 Died 1987 (G)						
Bolton W.	Southport (Am)	10.35	36-55	384	-	0
HANVEY Keith						
Manchester, 18 January, 1952 (CD)						
Manchester C.	Jnrs	08.71				
Swansea C.	Tr	07.72	72	11	0	0
Rochdale	Tr	07.73	73-76	121	0	10
Grimsby T.	Tr	02.77	76-77	54	0	2
Huddersfield T.	Tr	07.78	78-83	205	0	14
Rochdale	Tr	07.84	84	15	0	0
HAPGOOD Edris **Anthony**						
Kettering, 13 June, 1930 (OR)						
Burnley		03.48	51	7	-	2
Watford	Tr	07.53	53	1	-	0
HAPGOOD Leon Duane						
Torbay, 7 August, 1979 (M)						
Torquay U.	YT	●	96-97	15	8	3
HARBACH Peter Colin						
Carlisle, 30 April, 1967 (F)						
Newcastle U.	App	04.85				
Carlisle U.	Tr	08.87	87	0	7	0
HARBER William Hudson						
Hitchin, 3 December, 1944 (W)						
Swindon T.	App	12.61	62	2	-	0
Luton T.	Tr	09.64	64-65	28	0	3
HARBERTSON Ronald						
Redcar, 23 December, 1929 (IF)						
Newcastle U.	North Shields	01.49				
Bradford C.	Tr	08.50	50	16	-	1
Brighton & H.A.	Tr	10.51				
Bradford C.	Tr	05.52	53	13	-	3
Grimsby T.	Tr	07.54	54	26	-	6
Darlington	Ashington	01.57	56-57	49	-	21
Lincoln C.	Tr	03.58	57-59	57	-	22
Wrexham	Tr	03.60	59-60	28	-	13
Darlington	Tr	01.61	60	14	-	2
Lincoln C.	Tr	07.61	61	29	-	3
HARBEY Graham Keith						
Chesterfield, 29 August, 1964 (LB)						
Derby Co.	App	08.82	83-86	35	5	1
Ipswich T.	Tr	07.87	87-89	53	6	1
West Bromwich A.	Tr	11.89	89-91	97	0	2
Stoke C.	Tr	07.92	92-93	18	1	0

League Club	Source	Date Signed	Seasons Played	Apps	Subs	Gls

HARBOTTLE Mark Stuart
Nottingham, 26 September, 1968 E Yth (F)

League Club	Source	Date Signed	Seasons Played	Apps	Subs	Gls
Notts Co.	App	09.86	85	1	3	1
Doncaster Rov.	L	01.88	87	4	0	0

HARBURN Peter Arthur Patrick
Shoreditch, 18 June, 1931 (CF)

League Club	Source	Date Signed	Seasons Played	Apps	Subs	Gls
Brighton & H.A.	Portsmouth (Am)	02.56	54-57	126	-	61
Everton	Tr	08.58	58	4	-	1
Scunthorpe U.	Tr	01.59	58-59	20	-	8
Workington	Tr	10.59	59-60	67	-	23

HARBURN William Nicholson
Stockton, 19 November, 1923 (CF)

League Club	Source	Date Signed	Seasons Played	Apps	Subs	Gls
Darlington (Am)		06.47	47	1	-	0

HARBY Michael John
Nottingham, 7 November, 1948 (G)

League Club	Source	Date Signed	Seasons Played	Apps	Subs	Gls
Nottingham F.	Jnrs	07.66	67	3	0	0

HARDCASTLE Cyril
Halifax, 22 November, 1919 Died 1982 (CF)

League Club	Source	Date Signed	Seasons Played	Apps	Subs	Gls
Bradford C. (Am)		09.48	48	4	-	1

HARDCASTLE Peter David
Leeds, 27 January, 1949 E Amat (FB)

League Club	Source	Date Signed	Seasons Played	Apps	Subs	Gls
Blackpool	Skelmersdale U.	07.71	71-73	29	7	0
Plymouth Arg.	Tr	07.74	74-75	12	2	1
Bradford C.	Tr	07.76	76-77	62	0	1

HARDEN Leo
Hartlepool, 7 May, 1923 (OL)

League Club	Source	Date Signed	Seasons Played	Apps	Subs	Gls
Hartlepool U.	Railways Ath.	05.46	46-55	169	-	47

HARDIE John Clarke
Edinburgh, 7 February, 1938 (G)

League Club	Source	Date Signed	Seasons Played	Apps	Subs	Gls
Oldham Ath.	Falkirk	07.60	60	17	-	0
Chester C.	Tr	07.61	61-62	84	-	0
Bradford P.A.	Tr	12.63	63-69	265	0	0
Crystal Palace	Tr	08.70				

HARDING Alan
Sunderland, 14 May, 1948 (W)

League Club	Source	Date Signed	Seasons Played	Apps	Subs	Gls
Darlington	Spennymoor U.	01.70	69-72	125	4	38
Lincoln C.	Tr	03.73	72-78	203	6	38
Hartlepool U.	Tr	03.79	78-82	79	5	8

HARDING David
Liverpool, 14 August, 1946 (F)

League Club	Source	Date Signed	Seasons Played	Apps	Subs	Gls
Wrexham		09.65	65	9	1	0

HARDING Edward (Ted) James
Croydon, 5 April, 1925 (FB)

League Club	Source	Date Signed	Seasons Played	Apps	Subs	Gls
Crystal Palace	Coalville	11.44	46-52	151	-	0

HARDING Kevin
Isleworth, 19 March, 1957 (M/FB)

League Club	Source	Date Signed	Seasons Played	Apps	Subs	Gls
Brentford	App	●	73-74	8	0	0

HARDING Paul John
Mitcham, 6 March, 1964 (M)

League Club	Source	Date Signed	Seasons Played	Apps	Subs	Gls
Notts Co.	Barnet	09.90	90-92	45	9	1
Southend U.	L	08.93	93	2	3	0
Watford	L	11.93	93	1	1	0
Birmingham C.	Tr	12.93	93-94	19	3	0
Cardiff C.	Tr	08.95	95	36	0	0

HARDING Stephen John
Bristol, 23 July, 1956 (CD)

League Club	Source	Date Signed	Seasons Played	Apps	Subs	Gls
Bristol C.	App	07.74	75	2	0	0
Southend U.	L	01.76	75	2	0	0
Grimsby T.	L	09.76	76	8	0	0
Bristol Rov.	Tr	06.77	77-79	37	1	1
Brentford	L	01.80	79	3	1	0

HARDISTY John (Bob) Roderick Elliott
Chester-le-Street, 1 February, 1921 Died 1986 E Amat (WH)

League Club	Source	Date Signed	Seasons Played	Apps	Subs	Gls
Darlington (Am)	Bishop Auckland	12.46	46-48	6	-	0

HARDMAN Colin Arthur
Altrincham, 13 November, 1955 (W)

League Club	Source	Date Signed	Seasons Played	Apps	Subs	Gls
Stockport Co.		03.76	75-76	6	3	1

HARDMAN John Alan
Bury, 17 December, 1940 (HB)

League Club	Source	Date Signed	Seasons Played	Apps	Subs	Gls
Rochdale	Bess' Boys	08.60	60-66	40	0	2

HARDS Neil Andrew
Portsmouth, 28 January, 1962 (G)

League Club	Source	Date Signed	Seasons Played	Apps	Subs	Gls
Plymouth Arg.	App	01.80	79-82	6	0	0

HARDSTAFF Cecil
Crewe, 14 November, 1931 (RB)

League Club	Source	Date Signed	Seasons Played	Apps	Subs	Gls
Crewe Alex.	Wolverhampton W. (Am)	06.49	49	1	-	0

HARDWICK George Francis Moutry
Saltburn, 2 February, 1920 EF Lge/E-13 (FB)

League Club	Source	Date Signed	Seasons Played	Apps	Subs	Gls
Middlesbrough	South Bank	04.37	37-50	143	-	5
Oldham Ath.	Tr	11.50	50-55	190	-	14

HARDWICK Kenneth
West Auckland, 27 January, 1924 Died 1983 (G)

League Club	Source	Date Signed	Seasons Played	Apps	Subs	Gls
Doncaster Rov.	Rossington Colly	04.45	47-56	308	-	0
Scunthorpe U.	Tr	04.57	56-59	96	-	0
Barrow	Tr	12.59	59	12	-	0

HARDWICK Steven
Mansfield, 6 September, 1956 E Yth (G)

League Club	Source	Date Signed	Seasons Played	Apps	Subs	Gls
Chesterfield	Jnrs	07.74	74-76	38	0	0
Newcastle U.	Tr	12.76	77-82	92	0	0
Oxford U.	Tr	02.83	82-87	156	0	0
Crystal Palace	L	03.86	85	3	0	0
Sunderland	L	08.87	87	6	0	0
Huddersfield T.	Tr	07.88	88-90	109	0	0

HARDY Edwin Malcolm
Chesterfield, 16 October, 1953 (G)

League Club	Source	Date Signed	Seasons Played	Apps	Subs	Gls
Chesterfield	Jnrs	08.71	72	6	0	0

HARDY Gordon (Bob) Douglas
Kingston, 23 May, 1923 (CH)

League Club	Source	Date Signed	Seasons Played	Apps	Subs	Gls
Millwall	Charlton Rov.	08.45	46	3	-	0
Southport	Tr	07.48	48-49	16	-	0
Bournemouth	Tr	06.50	51-53	76	-	0

HARDY Herbert Thomas
Barrow, 6 December, 1929 (IF)

League Club	Source	Date Signed	Seasons Played	Apps	Subs	Gls
Barrow		05.52	51	2	-	1

HARDY Jason Paul
Manchester, 14 December, 1969 (LB)

League Club	Source	Date Signed	Seasons Played	Apps	Subs	Gls
Burnley	YT	07.88	86-91	38	5	1
Halifax T.	L	01.92	91	0	4	0
Halifax T.	Tr	07.92	92	20	2	2
Rochdale	Prestwich Heys	08.95	95	5	2	0

HARDY John Henry
Chesterfield, 15 June, 1910 Died 1978 (CH)

League Club	Source	Date Signed	Seasons Played	Apps	Subs	Gls
Chesterfield	Unstone	12.34	34-36	48	-	1
Hull C.	Tr	07.37	37-38	65	-	0
Lincoln C.	Tr	05.39	46	18	-	0

HARDY Paul Alan
Plymouth, 29 August, 1975 (M)

League Club	Source	Date Signed	Seasons Played	Apps	Subs	Gls
Torquay U.	YT	08.93	93	0	1	0

HARDY Philip
Chester, 9 April, 1973 IRu21-9 (LB)

League Club	Source	Date Signed	Seasons Played	Apps	Subs	Gls
Wrexham	YT	11.90	89-97	264	1	0

HARDY Robin
Worksop, 18 January, 1941 (WH)

League Club	Source	Date Signed	Seasons Played	Apps	Subs	Gls
Sheffield Wed.	Jnrs	02.58	61-63	30	-	1
Rotherham U.	Tr	02.65	64-65	42	0	2
Cambridge U.		(N/L)	70	15	1	0

HARDY William
Whitehaven, 23 August, 1929 (HB)

League Club	Source	Date Signed	Seasons Played	Apps	Subs	Gls
Workington	Queen of South	10.51	51-53	55	-	2

HARDYMAN Paul George
Portsmouth, 11 March, 1964 Eu21-2 (LB)

League Club	Source	Date Signed	Seasons Played	Apps	Subs	Gls
Portsmouth	Waterlooville	07.83	83-88	113	4	3
Sunderland	Tr	07.89	89-91	101	5	9
Bristol Rov.	Tr	08.92	92-94	54	13	5
Wycombe W.	Tr	08.95	95	12	3	0
Barnet	Tr	08.96	96	13	3	2

HARE Matthew
Barnstaple, 26 December, 1976 (M/RB)

League Club	Source	Date Signed	Seasons Played	Apps	Subs	Gls
Exeter C.	YT	08.95	95-97	31	14	1

HARE Thomas
Motherwell, 1 April, 1944 (FB)

League Club	Source	Date Signed	Seasons Played	Apps	Subs	Gls
Southampton	Fauldhouse U.	04.63	65	13	0	0
Luton T.	Tr	07.67	67	12	0	0

HAREIDE Aage Fridhjof
Norway, 23 September, 1953 Norwegian Int (D)

League Club	Source	Date Signed	Seasons Played	Apps	Subs	Gls
Manchester C.	Molde F.K. (Nor)	10.81	81-82	17	7	0
Norwich C.	Tr	11.82	82-83	38	2	2

HAREWOOD Marlon Anderson
Hampstead, 25 August, 1979 (CF)

League Club	Source	Date Signed	Seasons Played	Apps	Subs	Gls
Nottingham F.	YT	09.96	97	1	0	0

HARFIELD Leslie Philip
Southampton, 22 November, 1952 E Sch/E Yth (W)

League Club	Source	Date Signed	Seasons Played	Apps	Subs	Gls
Southampton	App	11.69	70	2	0	1
Luton T.	Tr	09.72	72	0	1	0

HARFORD Michael Gordon
Sunderland, 12 February, 1959 E'B'/E-2 (F)

League Club	Source	Date Signed	Seasons Played	Apps	Subs	Gls
Lincoln C.	Lambton Street B.C.	07.77	77-80	109	6	41
Newcastle U.	Tr	12.80	80	18	1	4
Bristol C.	Tr	08.81	81	30	0	11
Birmingham C.	Tr	03.82	81-84	92	0	25
Luton T.	Tr	12.84	84-89	135	4	57
Derby Co.	Tr	01.90	89-91	58	0	15
Luton T.	Tr	09.91	91	29	0	12
Chelsea	Tr	08.92	92	27	1	9
Sunderland	Tr	03.93	92	10	1	2
Coventry C.	Tr	07.93	93	0	1	1
Wimbledon	Tr	08.94	94-96	37	24	8

HARFORD Paul Raymond Thomas
Chelmsford, 21 October, 1974 (M)

League Club	Source	Date Signed	Seasons Played	Apps	Subs	Gls
Blackburn Rov.	Arsenal (YT)	08.93				
Wigan Ath.	L	09.94	94	3	0	0
Shrewsbury T.	L	12.94	94	3	3	0

HARFORD Raymond Thomas
Halifax, 1 June, 1945 (CD)

League Club	Source	Date Signed	Seasons Played	Apps	Subs	Gls
Charlton Ath.	Jnrs	05.64	65	3	0	0
Exeter C.	Tr	01.66	65-66	55	0	1
Lincoln C.	Tr	07.67	67-70	161	0	10
Mansfield T.	Tr	06.71	71	7	0	0
Port Vale	Tr	12.71	71-72	20	0	1
Colchester U.	Tr	01.73	72-74	107	1	4

HARGREAVES Allan
Dewsbury, 29 March, 1931 (CF)

League Club	Source	Date Signed	Seasons Played	Apps	Subs	Gls
Bradford C.		07.54	54-55	4	-	1

HARGREAVES Christian
Cleethorpes, 12 May, 1972 (F)

League Club	Source	Date Signed	Seasons Played	Apps	Subs	Gls
Grimsby T.	YT	12.89	89-92	15	36	5
Scarborough	L	03.93	92	2	1	0
Hull C.	Tr	07.93	93-94	34	15	0
West Bromwich A.	Tr	07.95	95	0	1	0
Hereford U.	Tr	02.96	95-96	57	4	5

HARGREAVES David
Accrington, 27 August, 1954 (F)

League Club	Source	Date Signed	Seasons Played	Apps	Subs	Gls
Blackburn Rov.	Accrington St.	12.77	77	2	0	0

HARGREAVES John (Jack)
Rotherham, 1 May, 1915 Died 1978 (OL)

League Club	Source	Date Signed	Seasons Played	Apps	Subs	Gls
Leeds U.		08.34	35-38	45	-	10
Bristol C.	Tr	08.45	46	26	-	9
Reading	Tr	04.47	46-47	15	-	1

HARGREAVES Joseph Albert
Accrington, 30 October, 1915 Died 1992 (CH)

League Club	Source	Date Signed	Seasons Played	Apps	Subs	Gls
Rochdale	Rossendale U.	10.45	46-47	35	-	24

HARGREAVES Thomas
Blackburn, 29 October, 1917 (CF)

League Club	Source	Date Signed	Seasons Played	Apps	Subs	Gls
Blackburn Rov.	Crosshill	10.36	37	4	-	2
Rochdale	Tr	05.46	46	7	-	0

HARGREAVES Wilfred Oscar
Rawmarsh, 15 December, 1921 Died 1993 (RH)

League Club	Source	Date Signed	Seasons Played	Apps	Subs	Gls
Rotherham U.	Rawmarsh Welfare	03.45	46-47	3	-	0

HARKER Christopher Joseph
Shiremoor, 29 June, 1937 (G)

League Club	Source	Date Signed	Seasons Played	Apps	Subs	Gls
Newcastle U.	Jnrs	03.55	57	1	-	0
Bury	Aberdeen	12.61	61-66	178	0	0
Grimsby T.	Tr	06.67	67	10	0	0
Rochdale	Tr	07.68	68-69	92	0	0

HARKES John Andrew
U.S.A., 8 March, 1967 USA Int (RB/M)

League Club	Source	Date Signed	Seasons Played	Apps	Subs	Gls
Sheffield Wed.	North Carolina (USA)	10.90	90-92	59	22	7
Derby Co.	Tr	08.93	93-95	67	7	2
West Ham U.	L	10.95	95	6	5	0

HARKIN James
Brinsworth, 8 August, 1913 Died 1988 (IF)

League Club	Source	Date Signed	Seasons Played	Apps	Subs	Gls
Doncaster Rov.	Rossington Main Colly	08.34	34	1	-	0
Mansfield T.	Shrewsbury T.	02.39	38-46	23	-	5

HARKIN Maurice Presley
Derry, 16 August, 1979 NI Yth (RW)

League Club	Source	Date Signed	Seasons Played	Apps	Subs	Gls
Wycombe W.	YT	02.97	96-97	13	26	2

HARKIN John **Terence**
Derry (NI), 14 September, 1941 NIu23-1/NI-5 (CF)

League Club	Source	Date Signed	Seasons Played	Apps	Subs	Gls
Port Vale	Coleraine	09.62	62-63	27	-	11
Crewe Alex.	Tr	06.64	64	42	-	34
Cardiff C.	Tr	08.65	65	19	2	10
Notts Co.	Tr	09.66	66	27	1	10
Southport	Tr	07.67	67-68	63	1	31
Shrewsbury T.	Tr	03.69	68-70	79	0	30

HARKNESS James
Edinburgh, 19 May, 1940 (G)

League Club	Source	Date Signed	Seasons Played	Apps	Subs	Gls
Carlisle U.	Hamilton Academical	08.61	61-62	16	-	0

HARKNESS Steven
Carlisle, 27 August, 1971 E Yth (LB)

League Club	Source	Date Signed	Seasons Played	Apps	Subs	Gls
Carlisle U.	YT	03.89	88	12	1	0
Liverpool	Tr	07.89	91-97	86	10	2
Huddersfield T.	L	09.93	93	5	0	0
Southend U.	L	02.95	94	6	0	0

HARKNESS William (James) Jardine
Dumfries, 21 July, 1918 Died 1995 (IF)

League Club	Source	Date Signed	Seasons Played	Apps	Subs	Gls
Carlisle U.		10.47				
Workington		(N/L)	51	7	-	1

HARKOUK Rachid Peter
Chelsea, 19 May, 1956 Algerian Int (F)

League Club	Source	Date Signed	Seasons Played	Apps	Subs	Gls
Crystal Palace	Feltham	06.76	76-77	51	3	21
Queens Park R.	Tr	06.78	78-79	15	5	3
Notts Co.	Tr	06.80	80-85	124	20	39

HARLAND Stanley Clarence
Liverpool, 19 June, 1940 (WH)

League Club	Source	Date Signed	Seasons Played	Apps	Subs	Gls
Everton	New Brighton	12.59				
Bradford C.	Tr	07.61	61-63	120	-	20
Carlisle U.	Tr	06.64	64-65	77	0	7
Swindon T.	Tr	08.66	66-71	237	0	6
Birmingham C.	Tr	12.71	71-72	37	1	0

HARLE David
Denaby, 15 August, 1963 E Yth (M)

League Club	Source	Date Signed	Seasons Played	Apps	Subs	Gls
Doncaster Rov.	App	11.80	79-81	48	13	3
Exeter C.	Tr	07.82	82-83	42	1	6
Doncaster Rov.	Tr	09.83	83-85	80	3	17
Leeds U.	Tr	12.85	85	3	0	0
Bristol C.	Tr	03.86	85-86	23	0	2
Scunthorpe U.	Tr	11.86	86-88	88	1	10
Peterborough U.	Tr	03.89	88-89	21	1	2
Doncaster Rov.	Tr	03.90	89-91	39	6	3

HARLE Michael James Lee
Lewisham, 31 October, 1972 (LB/M)

League Club	Source	Date Signed	Seasons Played	Apps	Subs	Gls
Gillingham	YT	●	90	1	1	0
Millwall	Sittingbourne	11.93	96	12	9	1
Bury	L	12.95	95	0	1	0
Barnet	Tr	07.97	97	42	1	2

HARLEY Albert George
Chester, 17 April, 1940 Died 1993 (WH)

League Club	Source	Date Signed	Seasons Played	Apps	Subs	Gls
Shrewsbury T.	Jnrs	04.57	56-64	220	-	14
Swansea C.	Tr	09.64	64-65	25	1	0
Crewe Alex.	Guildford C.	07.66	66	22	0	4
Stockport Co.	Tr	02.67	66-68	77	3	11
Chester C.	Tr	06.69	69	3	0	1

HARLEY Alexander
Glasgow, 20 April, 1936 Died 1969 (CF)

League Club	Source	Date Signed	Seasons Played	Apps	Subs	Gls
Manchester C.	Third Lanark	08.62	62	40	-	23
Birmingham C.	Tr	08.63	63-64	28	-	9

HARLEY James
Methil, 2 February, 1917 Died 1989 (FB)

League Club	Source	Date Signed	Seasons Played	Apps	Subs	Gls
Liverpool	Hill of Beath	04.34	35-47	114	-	0

HARLEY Richard **John**
March, 22 April, 1949 (M)

League Club	Source	Date Signed	Seasons Played	Apps	Subs	Gls
Reading	Stevenage T.	09.69	69-72	64	10	6
Aldershot	Tr	07.73	73-74	16	12	0
Hartlepool U. (N/C)	Wokingham T.	09.76	76	4	0	1

League Club	Source	Date Signed	Seasons Played	Apps	Subs	Gls
HARLEY Jonathan						
Maidstone, 26 September, 1979 E Yth						(LM)
Chelsea	YT	03.97	97	0	3	0
HARLEY Lee						
Crewe, 7 July, 1967						(F)
Chester C.	YT	●	85	0	1	0
HARLEY Leslie						
Chester, 26 September, 1946						(OR)
Chester C.	Jnrs	09.64	64-66	22	3	3
Blackpool	Tr	07.67				
Rochdale	L	02.68	67	5	0	0
HARLOCK Desmond Southern						
Blaenau Ffestiniog, 20 December, 1922 Died 1981						(OR)
Tranmere Rov.		03.42	46-53	151	-	17
HARMAN Peter Robert						
Guildford, 11 October, 1950						(CF)
Bournemouth	App	08.68	69	1	0	0
Reading	Tr	08.71	71-72	34	2	9
HARMER Thomas Charles						
Hackney, 2 February, 1928 E 'B'						(IF)
Tottenham H.	Finchley	08.48	51-59	205	-	47
Watford	Tr	10.60	60-61	63	-	6
Chelsea	Tr	09.62	62-63	8	-	1
HARMON Darren John						
Northampton, 30 January, 1973						(M)
Notts Co.	YT	07.91				
Shrewsbury T.	Tr	02.92	91-92	1	5	2
Northampton T.	Tr	10.92	92-94	76	13	12
HARMSTON Michael James						
Sheffield, 7 April, 1950						(FB)
Sheffield U.	App	05.67	68	5	0	0
Southend U.	L	12.70	70	1	0	0
HARMSWORTH Lee Anthony						
Southwark, 27 October, 1967						(G)
Charlton Ath.	App	10.85	84	3	0	0
HARNBY Donald Reed						
Darlington, 20 July, 1923						(FB)
Newcastle U.	Spennymoor U.	05.45				
York C.	Tr	08.47	47	1	-	0
Grimsby T.	Spennymoor U.	09.49	49-51	34	-	0
HARNEY David						
Jarrow, 2 March, 1947						(CF)
Grimsby T.	Jnrs	11.64				
Scunthorpe U.	Tr	07.67	67-68	20	5	1
Brentford	Tr	10.69	69	0	1	0
HARNEY Stephen Graham						
Bradford, 18 February, 1951						(RB)
Bradford C. (Am)	Drum Rov.	07.68	68-70	13	1	0
HAROLD Michael Lloyd						
Stockport, 22 September, 1943						(FB)
Stockport Co.	Manchester C. (Am)	08.64	64	4	-	0
HARPER Alan						
Liverpool, 1 November, 1960 E Yth						(D/M)
Liverpool	App	04.78				
Everton	Tr	06.83	83-87	103	24	4
Sheffield Wed.	Tr	07.88	88-89	32	3	0
Manchester C.	Tr	12.89	89-90	46	4	1
Everton	Tr	08.91	91-92	45	6	0
Luton T.	Tr	09.93	93	40	1	1
Burnley	Tr	08.94	94-95	30	1	0
Cardiff C.	L	11.95	95	5	0	0
HARPER Antony Frederick						
Oxford, 26 May, 1925 Died 1982						(WH)
Brentford	Headington U.	04.48	48-54	173	-	6
HARPER Colin George						
Ipswich, 25 July, 1946						(LB)
Ipswich T.	Jnrs	08.64	65-74	144	4	5
Grimsby T.	L	12.76	76	3	0	0
Cambridge U.	L	02.77	76	15	0	0
Port Vale	Tr	08.77	77	4	0	0
HARPER David						
Peckham, 29 September, 1938 E Yth						(WH)
Millwall	Jnrs	05.57	57-64	165	-	4
Ipswich T.	Tr	03.65	64-66	70	2	2
Swindon T.	Tr	07.67	67	4	0	0
Leyton Orient	Tr	10.67	67-70	82	3	4
HARPER Dennis						
Tipton, 12 October, 1936						(IF)
Birmingham C.	Darlaston	08.56	56	1	-	0
HARPER Donald						
Blackwell (Dby), 26 October, 1921 Died 1990						(OR)
Chesterfield		12.43				
Mansfield T.	Tr	07.46	46	21	-	1
HARPER Ian Thomas						
Scunthorpe, 23 November, 1944						(FB)
Scunthorpe U.	Jnrs	07.62	63-64	21	-	0
HARPER Ivor Roy						
Watford, 23 June, 1933						(IF)
Watford (Am)	Hemel Hempstead	10.51	51	3	-	0
HARPER Joseph John						
Muirhead (Lk), 12 January, 1920 Died 1987						(FB)
Watford	Twechar U.	05.37	46-51	159	-	1
HARPER Joseph Montgomery						
Greenock, 11 January, 1948 Su23-2/SF Lge/S-4						(CF)
Huddersfield T.	Morton	03.67	66-67	26	2	4
Everton	Aberdeen	12.72	72-73	40	3	12
HARPER Kenneth						
Barnsley, 15 April, 1917 Died 1994						(FB)
Walsall		03.35	37-38	22	-	1
Bradford C.	Tr	01.46	46-48	50	-	0
HARPER Kenneth						
Farnworth, 27 April, 1924						(CH)
Blackpool		12.45				
Rochdale		12.47				
Shrewsbury T.	Hindsford	08.50	50	1	-	0
HARPER Lee Charles Phillip						
Chelsea, 30 October, 1971						(G)
Arsenal	Sittingbourne	06.94	96	1	0	0
Queens Park R.	Tr	07.97	97	36	0	0
HARPER Lee James						
Bridlington, 24 March, 1975						(D)
Scarborough	YT	03.94	93	0	2	0
HARPER Robert						
Glasgow, 6 June, 1920 Died 1980						(OL)
Huddersfield T.	Ayr U.	06.46				
Newport Co.	Tr	11.46	46-49	114	-	12
Southend U.	Tr	07.50	50	6	-	0
HARPER Stephen Alan						
Easington, 14 March, 1975						(G)
Newcastle U.	Seaham Red Star	07.93				
Bradford C.	L	09.95	95	1	0	0
Hartlepool U.	L	08.97	97	15	0	0
Huddersfield T.	L	12.97	97	24	0	0
HARPER Steven James						
Newcastle-u-Lyme, 3 February, 1969						(W)
Port Vale	YT	06.87	87-88	16	12	2
Preston N.E.	Tr	03.89	88-90	57	20	10
Burnley	Tr	07.91	91-92	64	5	8
Doncaster Rov.	Tr	08.93	93-95	56	9	11
Mansfield T.	Tr	09.95	95-97	112	3	12
HARRIES Paul Graham						
Sydney, Australia, 19 November, 1977						(F)
Portsmouth	NSW Soccer Acad. (Aus)	09.97	97	0	1	0
HARRIGAN Duncan						
Paisley, 26 June, 1921						(CF)
Crewe Alex.	St Mirren (Am)	08.46	46-47	55	-	24
Aston Villa	Tr	04.48				
Chester C.	Tr	10.48	48	20	-	4
HARRINGTON Alan Charles						
Penarth, 17 November, 1933 W-11						(FB)
Cardiff C.	Cardiff Nomads	10.51	52-65	349	0	6
HARRINGTON Colin Andrew						
Bicester, 3 April, 1943						(OL)
Oxford U.	Wolverhampton W. (Am)	10.62	62-70	230	4	29
Mansfield T.	Tr	06.71	71	7	6	0

HARRINGTON Justin David
Truro, 18 September, 1975 (M)

League Club	Source	Date Signed	Seasons Played	Apps	Subs	Gls
Norwich C.	YT	07.94				
Leicester C.	Tr	08.96				
Bournemouth	Tr	07.97	97	4	4	0

HARRINGTON Paul
Hartlepool, 26 September, 1964 (M)

League Club	Source	Date Signed	Seasons Played	Apps	Subs	Gls
Hartlepool U.		04.83	83	0	2	0

HARRINGTON Philip
Bangor, 20 November, 1963 W Yth (G)

League Club	Source	Date Signed	Seasons Played	Apps	Subs	Gls
Chester C.	App	11.81	81-84	76	0	0
Blackpool	Tr	03.85				
Burnley	L	11.85	85	2	0	0
Preston N.E.	L	02.86	85	2	0	0

HARRIOTT Marvin Lee
Dulwich, 20 April, 1974 E Sch/E Yth (RB)

League Club	Source	Date Signed	Seasons Played	Apps	Subs	Gls
Oldham Ath.	West Ham U. (YT)	04.92				
Barnsley	Tr	04.93				
Leyton Orient	L	10.93	93	8	0	0
Bristol C.	Tr	12.93	93-94	36	0	0

HARRIS Alan John
Northampton, 28 December, 1942 E Sch/E Yth (LB)

League Club	Source	Date Signed	Seasons Played	Apps	Subs	Gls
Chelsea	Jnrs	06.60	60-64	70	-	0
Coventry C.	Tr	11.64	64-65	60	0	0
Chelsea	Tr	05.66	66	12	2	0
Queens Park R.	Tr	07.67	67-70	90	4	0
Plymouth Arg.	Tr	03.71	70-72	64	0	0
Cambridge U.	Tr	07.73	73	6	0	0

HARRIS Albert Edward
Bootle, 21 November, 1931 (G)

League Club	Source	Date Signed	Seasons Played	Apps	Subs	Gls
Everton	Maghull	01.55	55	5	-	0
Tranmere Rov.	Tr	05.57	57-59	33	-	0
Southport	Tr	07.60	60-64	159	-	0

HARRIS Alexander
Hong Kong, 22 October, 1934 (OR)

League Club	Source	Date Signed	Seasons Played	Apps	Subs	Gls
Blackpool	Jnrs	11.51	52-57	21	-	4

HARRIS Andrew
Birmingham, 17 November, 1970 (M)

League Club	Source	Date Signed	Seasons Played	Apps	Subs	Gls
Birmingham C.	YT	07.89	89	0	1	0
Oxford U.	L	10.91	91	1	0	0
Exeter C.	Tr	11.91	91-93	32	6	1

HARRIS Andrew David Douglas
South Africa, 26 February, 1977 (D)

League Club	Source	Date Signed	Seasons Played	Apps	Subs	Gls
Liverpool	YT	03.94				
Southend U.	Tr	07.96	96-97	69	2	0

HARRIS Anthony Thomas
Berrington (Salop), 20 December, 1945 (HB)

League Club	Source	Date Signed	Seasons Played	Apps	Subs	Gls
Shrewsbury T.	App	07.63	63-66	54	1	4
Bradford P.A.	Tr	07.68	68	10	0	0

HARRIS Arthur
Coventry, 28 July, 1914 Died 1973 (RH)

League Club	Source	Date Signed	Seasons Played	Apps	Subs	Gls
Southend U.	Nuneaton T.	07.36	36-46	114	-	1

HARRIS Brian
Bebington, 16 May, 1935 E Yth (WH)

League Club	Source	Date Signed	Seasons Played	Apps	Subs	Gls
Everton	Port Sunlight	01.54	55-66	310	0	23
Cardiff C.	Tr	10.66	66-70	147	2	0
Newport Co.	Tr	07.71	71-73	85	0	0

HARRIS Carl Stephen
Neath, 3 November, 1956 W Sch/Wu23-1/W-24 (W)

League Club	Source	Date Signed	Seasons Played	Apps	Subs	Gls
Leeds U.	App	11.73	74-81	123	30	26
Charlton Ath.	Tr	07.82	82-84	73	3	7
Bury	Leeds U. (N/C)	12.85	85-86	33	5	4
Rochdale (N/C)	Cardiff C. (N/C)	01.88	87-88	24	1	3
Exeter C.	Tr	12.88	88	11	5	1

HARRIS Christopher Robert
Hastings, 23 January, 1957 (F)

League Club	Source	Date Signed	Seasons Played	Apps	Subs	Gls
Millwall	Bexhill U.	10.76	76	3	0	0

HARRIS David
Stoke, 19 November, 1953 (CD)

League Club	Source	Date Signed	Seasons Played	Apps	Subs	Gls
Port Vale		08.73	73-78	175	1	8
Halifax T.	Tr	07.79	79-80	69	2	3

HARRIS Frederick
Birmingham, 2 July, 1912 EF Lge (IF/WH)

League Club	Source	Date Signed	Seasons Played	Apps	Subs	Gls
Birmingham C.	Osborne Ath.	04.33	34-49	280	-	61

HARRIS Gary Wayne
Birmingham, 31 May, 1959 (W)

League Club	Source	Date Signed	Seasons Played	Apps	Subs	Gls
Cardiff C.	App	05.77	78-79	4	0	0

HARRIS Geoffrey Robert
Heywood, 1 February, 1956 (F)

League Club	Source	Date Signed	Seasons Played	Apps	Subs	Gls
Oldham Ath.	App	02.74				
Halifax T.	Tr	07.75	75-76	10	5	1

HARRIS George
Stanley, 24 August, 1936 (F)

League Club	Source	Date Signed	Seasons Played	Apps	Subs	Gls
Preston N.E.	Craghead	08.57				
Southport	Tr	07.59	59	1	-	0

HARRIS George Alfred
Lambeth, 10 June, 1940 (OL)

League Club	Source	Date Signed	Seasons Played	Apps	Subs	Gls
Newport Co.	Woking	07.61	61	31	-	8
Watford	Tr	04.62	61-65	162	1	55
Reading	Tr	07.66	66-69	134	2	56
Cambridge U.	Tr	07.70	70-71	33	2	11

HARRIS Gerald William
Bridgnorth, 8 October, 1935 Eu23-4 (FB)

League Club	Source	Date Signed	Seasons Played	Apps	Subs	Gls
Wolverhampton W.	Bebington	01.54	56-65	235	0	2
Walsall	Tr	04.66	65-67	13	2	1

HARRIS Gordon
Worksop, 2 June, 1940 Eu23-2/EF Lge/E-1 (OL)

League Club	Source	Date Signed	Seasons Played	Apps	Subs	Gls
Burnley	Firbeck Colly	01.58	58-67	258	0	69
Sunderland	Tr	01.68	67-71	124	1	16

HARRIS Gordon William
Campmuir, 19 February, 1945 (FB)

League Club	Source	Date Signed	Seasons Played	Apps	Subs	Gls
Cardiff C.	Forfar Ath.	03.65	64	5	-	0

HARRIS Derek **Harold**
Undy, 2 November, 1933 (IF/WH)

League Club	Source	Date Signed	Seasons Played	Apps	Subs	Gls
Newport Co.	Undy U.	09.54	54-57	157	-	56
Portsmouth	Tr	07.58	58-70	378	2	48
Newport Co.	L	10.70	70	17	0	2

HARRIS James
Birkenhead, 18 August, 1933 Eu23-1/EF Lge (CF)

League Club	Source	Date Signed	Seasons Played	Apps	Subs	Gls
Everton	Jnrs	09.51	55-60	191	-	65
Birmingham C.	Tr	12.60	60-63	93	-	37
Oldham Ath.	Tr	07.64	64-65	28	1	9

HARRIS James Christopher
Swansea, 28 June, 1979 (F)

League Club	Source	Date Signed	Seasons Played	Apps	Subs	Gls
Swansea C.	Mumbles R.	07.97	97	0	6	0

HARRIS Jamie
Exeter, 4 February, 1969 (F)

League Club	Source	Date Signed	Seasons Played	Apps	Subs	Gls
Exeter C.	YT	08.86	87-88	6	8	1

HARRIS Jason Andre Sebastian
Sutton, 24 November, 1976 (F)

League Club	Source	Date Signed	Seasons Played	Apps	Subs	Gls
Crystal Palace	YT	07.95	96	0	2	0
Bristol Rov.	L	11.96	96	5	1	2
Lincoln C.	L	08.97	97	0	1	0
Leyton Orient	Tr	09.97	97	21	14	6

HARRIS Jason Mark
Rochdale, 26 December, 1969 (M)

League Club	Source	Date Signed	Seasons Played	Apps	Subs	Gls
Burnley	YT	07.88	86	4	0	0

HARRIS Jeffrey Bruce
Stepney, 11 June, 1942 E Amat (WH)

League Club	Source	Date Signed	Seasons Played	Apps	Subs	Gls
Leyton Orient	Enfield	05.64	64	14	-	0

HARRIS John
Glasgow, 30 June, 1917 Died 1988 (D)

League Club	Source	Date Signed	Seasons Played	Apps	Subs	Gls
Swansea C.	Swindon T. (Am)	08.34	36-38	28	-	4
Tottenham H.	Tr	02.39				
Wolverhampton W.	Tr	05.39				
Chelsea	Tr	08.45	46-55	326	-	14
Chester C.	Tr	07.56	56	27	-	1

HARRIS John Patrick
Bermondsey, 20 December, 1931 (IF)

League Club	Source	Date Signed	Seasons Played	Apps	Subs	Gls
Millwall (Am)		06.56	56	1	-	0

HARRIS David **John**
Gornal, 3 April, 1939 (FB)

League Club	Source	Date Signed	Seasons Played	Apps	Subs	Gls
Wolverhampton W.	Jnrs	05.58	61-62	3	-	0
Walsall	Tr	01.65	64-68	74	0	2

HARRIS Thomas **John**
Swansea, 18 May, 1934 (CH)

League Club	Source	Date Signed	Seasons Played	Apps	Subs	Gls
Leeds U.		11.51				
Halifax T.	Tr	10.55	55-56	9	-	0

HARRIS Joseph
Belfast, 8 April, 1929 (CF)

League Club	Source	Date Signed	Seasons Played	Apps	Subs	Gls
Blackburn Rov.	Distillery	01.51	50-51	35	-	15
Oldham Ath.	Tr	03.53	52-53	27	-	4

HARRIS Joseph Anthony
Liverpool, 20 September, 1926 (OR)

League Club	Source	Date Signed	Seasons Played	Apps	Subs	Gls
Everton		07.50	50-52	14	-	4

HARRIS Thomas **Kevin**
Dublin, 20 February, 1918 (WH)

League Club	Source	Date Signed	Seasons Played	Apps	Subs	Gls
Notts Co.		09.45				
Brentford		08.48	48	4	-	0

HARRIS Leonard James
Nuneaton, 29 May, 1949 (FB)

League Club	Source	Date Signed	Seasons Played	Apps	Subs	Gls
Nottingham F.	Jnrs	06.66	68-69	2	0	0
Doncaster Rov.	L	09.70	70	4	0	0

HARRIS Leslie
Llanfair, 1 November, 1941 (FB)

League Club	Source	Date Signed	Seasons Played	Apps	Subs	Gls
Swansea C.	Aberystwyth Univ.	08.63	63-64	4	-	0

HARRIS Leslie Henry
Stocksbridge, 29 May, 1955 (F)

League Club	Source	Date Signed	Seasons Played	Apps	Subs	Gls
Barnsley	Jnrs	05.74	75-76	11	15	2

HARRIS Mark Andrew
Reading, 15 July, 1963 (CD)

League Club	Source	Date Signed	Seasons Played	Apps	Subs	Gls
Crystal Palace	Wokingham T.	02.88	88	0	2	0
Burnley	L	08.89	89	4	0	0
Swansea C.	Tr	09.89	89-94	228	0	14
Gillingham	Tr	08.95	95-96	63	2	3
Cardiff C.	Tr	08.97	97	38	0	1

HARRIS Martin
Doncaster, 22 December, 1955 (W)

League Club	Source	Date Signed	Seasons Played	Apps	Subs	Gls
Workington	Grimsby T. (App)	07.74	74-76	97	9	13
Hartlepool U.	Tr	12.77	77	0	1	0

HARRIS Neil
Glasgow, 9 February, 1920 (CF)

League Club	Source	Date Signed	Seasons Played	Apps	Subs	Gls
Queens Park R.		09.46	46	1	-	1

HARRIS Neil
Orsett, 12 July, 1977 (F)

League Club	Source	Date Signed	Seasons Played	Apps	Subs	Gls
Millwall	Chelmsford	03.98	97	2	1	0

HARRIS Neil John
Manchester, 7 November, 1969 (W)

League Club	Source	Date Signed	Seasons Played	Apps	Subs	Gls
Crewe Alex.	YT	07.88	87	3	0	0

HARRIS Paul Edwin
Hackney, 19 May, 1953 (CD)

League Club	Source	Date Signed	Seasons Played	Apps	Subs	Gls
Leyton Orient	App	07.70	70-74	96	0	4
Swansea C.	Tr	07.75	75-76	47	2	2

HARRIS Peter
Neath, 9 August, 1953 (W)

League Club	Source	Date Signed	Seasons Played	Apps	Subs	Gls
Newport Co.	App	08.71	70-72	20	11	1

HARRIS Peter Philip
Portsmouth, 19 December, 1925 EF Lge/E-2 (OR)

League Club	Source	Date Signed	Seasons Played	Apps	Subs	Gls
Portsmouth	Gosport Borough	11.44	46-59	479	-	193

HARRIS Philip
Swindon, 18 December, 1958 (M)

League Club	Source	Date Signed	Seasons Played	Apps	Subs	Gls
Swindon T.	App	●	76	0	1	0

HARRIS Ronald Edward
Hackney, 13 November, 1944 E Sch/E Yth/Eu23-4 (D)

League Club	Source	Date Signed	Seasons Played	Apps	Subs	Gls
Chelsea	App	11.61	61-79	646	9	13
Brentford	Tr	05.80	80-83	60	1	0

HARRIS Thomas
Chelsea, 8 November, 1924 (IF)

League Club	Source	Date Signed	Seasons Played	Apps	Subs	Gls
Fulham		09.47				
Leyton Orient	Tr	09.51	51-52	31	-	11
Colchester U.	Tr	06.53	53	3	-	0

HARRIS Thomas
Ogmore, 15 February, 1916 (G)

League Club	Source	Date Signed	Seasons Played	Apps	Subs	Gls
Charlton Ath.		08.39				
Plymouth Arg.	Aberaman	05.48	48	3	-	0

HARRIS William **Thomas**
Aberbargoed, 30 June, 1913 (FB)

League Club	Source	Date Signed	Seasons Played	Apps	Subs	Gls
Watford	New Tredegar	04.33	35-48	94	-	6

HARRIS Trevor John
Colchester, 6 February, 1936 (WH)

League Club	Source	Date Signed	Seasons Played	Apps	Subs	Gls
Colchester U.	Jnrs	07.54	54-62	103	-	6

HARRIS William
Dudley, 1 December, 1918 Died 1996 (G)

League Club	Source	Date Signed	Seasons Played	Apps	Subs	Gls
West Bromwich A.	Whiteheath	02.37	37	2	-	0
Oldham Ath.	Tr	06.46	46	32	-	0
Accrington St.	Tr	08.47	47-49	99	-	0

HARRIS William Charles
Swansea, 31 October, 1928 Died 1989 W-6 (IF/WH)

League Club	Source	Date Signed	Seasons Played	Apps	Subs	Gls
Hull C.	Llanelli	03.50	49-53	131	-	6
Middlesbrough	Tr	03.54	53-64	360	-	69
Bradford C.	Tr	03.65	64-65	9	0	1

HARRISON Andrew Frank
Long Eaton, 13 September, 1957 (FB)

League Club	Source	Date Signed	Seasons Played	Apps	Subs	Gls
Scarborough	Kettering T.	(N/L)	87	3	1	0

HARRISON Anthony Leslie
Gateshead, 9 January, 1954 (G)

League Club	Source	Date Signed	Seasons Played	Apps	Subs	Gls
Southport	Whitley Bay	02.77	76-77	48	0	0
Carlisle U.	Tr	06.78	80	8	0	0

HARRISON Bernard Reginald Stanhope
Worcester, 28 September, 1934 (W)

League Club	Source	Date Signed	Seasons Played	Apps	Subs	Gls
Crystal Palace	Portsmouth (Am)	10.55	55-58	92	-	12
Southampton	Tr	08.59	59	3	-	0
Exeter C.	Tr	07.60	60	18	-	4

HARRISON Christopher Colin
Launceston, 17 October, 1956 (D)

League Club	Source	Date Signed	Seasons Played	Apps	Subs	Gls
Plymouth Arg.	App	10.74	75-84	315	9	7
Swansea C.	Tr	09.85	85-87	114	3	14

HARRISON Colin George
Pelsall, 18 March, 1946 (M/D)

League Club	Source	Date Signed	Seasons Played	Apps	Subs	Gls
Walsall	Jnrs	11.63	64-81	453	20	33

HARRISON Craig
Gateshead, 10 November, 1977 (D)

League Club	Source	Date Signed	Seasons Played	Apps	Subs	Gls
Middlesbrough	YT	07.96	97	16	4	0

HARRISON Derek
Littlethorpe, 9 February, 1950 (CD)

League Club	Source	Date Signed	Seasons Played	Apps	Subs	Gls
Leicester C.	App	02.67				
Torquay U.	Tr	01.71	70-74	124	3	4
Colchester U.	Tr	06.75	75	5	2	0

HARRISON Eric George
Hebden Bridge, 5 February, 1938 (WH)

League Club	Source	Date Signed	Seasons Played	Apps	Subs	Gls
Halifax T.	Mytholmroyd	07.57	57-63	199	-	10
Hartlepool U.	Tr	08.64	64-65	81	0	4
Barrow	Tr	07.66	66-68	127	3	1
Southport	Tr	06.69	69-70	75	0	0
Barrow	Tr	07.71	71	31	1	1

HARRISON Francis John
Gateshead, 12 November, 1931 Died 1981 E Yth (FB)

League Club	Source	Date Signed	Seasons Played	Apps	Subs	Gls
Hull C.	Jnrs	05.49	52-59	199	-	0

HARRISON Francis Nicholas
Middlesbrough, 19 September, 1963 (LB)

League Club	Source	Date Signed	Seasons Played	Apps	Subs	Gls
Middlesbrough	Guisborough T.	09.82				
Lincoln C. (N/C)	Carnegie College	11.85	85	0	1	0
Halifax T.	Guiseley	03.87	86-89	48	6	1

HARRISON Garry Mark
Northampton, 12 March, 1975 (M)

League Club	Source	Date Signed	Seasons Played	Apps	Subs	Gls
Northampton T.	Aston Villa (YT)	12.93	93-94	7	0	0

HARRISON Gerald Randall
Lambeth, 15 April, 1972 E Sch (D/M)

League Club	Source	Date Signed	Seasons Played	Apps	Subs	Gls
Watford	YT	12.89	89-90	6	3	0
Bristol C.	Tr	06.91	91-93	25	13	1
Cardiff C.	L	01.92	91	10	0	1
Hereford U.	L	11.93	93	6	0	0
Huddersfield T.	Tr	03.94				
Burnley	Tr	08.94	94-97	116	8	3

HARRISON Harry
Sunderland, 26 June, 1917 (FB)

League Club	Source	Date Signed	Seasons Played	Apps	Subs	Gls
Chesterfield	Houghton Colly	06.37				
Southport	Tr	07.39	46-50	135	-	1

HARRISON Herbert
Burnley, 23 January, 1916 (OR)

League Club	Source	Date Signed	Seasons Played	Apps	Subs	Gls
Accrington St. (Am)	Morecambe	10.47	47	3	-	0

HARRISON James Charles
Leicester, 12 February, 1921 (FB)

League Club	Source	Date Signed	Seasons Played	Apps	Subs	Gls
Leicester C.	Jnrs	12.41	46-48	81	-	1
Aston Villa	Tr	07.49	49	8	-	1
Coventry C.	Tr	07.51	51-52	20	-	2

HARRISON James Herbert
Hammersmith, 31 July, 1928 (CF)

League Club	Source	Date Signed	Seasons Played	Apps	Subs	Gls
Queens Park R.		02.52	52	6	-	1

HARRISON John
Swansea, 30 September, 1932 (G)

League Club	Source	Date Signed	Seasons Played	Apps	Subs	Gls
Crewe Alex.		08.56	56	2	-	0

HARRISON John Gilbert
Worksop, 18 May, 1946 (W)

League Club	Source	Date Signed	Seasons Played	Apps	Subs	Gls
Sheffield U.	Worksop T.	01.67				
Lincoln C.	Tr	07.68	68	4	0	0

HARRISON John James
York, 7 June, 1961 (FB)

League Club	Source	Date Signed	Seasons Played	Apps	Subs	Gls
York C.	App	06.79	79	8	0	0

HARRISON John Michael
Stepney, 16 January, 1958 (W)

League Club	Source	Date Signed	Seasons Played	Apps	Subs	Gls
Charlton Ath.	App	01.76	75	5	0	2

HARRISON John Walter
Leicester, 27 September, 1927 (FB)

League Club	Source	Date Signed	Seasons Played	Apps	Subs	Gls
Aston Villa		08.48				
Colchester U.	Tr	07.50	50-56	237	-	1

HARRISON Kenneth
Stockton, 20 January, 1926 (OR)

League Club	Source	Date Signed	Seasons Played	Apps	Subs	Gls
Hull C.	Billingham Synth.	04.47	46-54	238	-	47
Derby Co.	Tr	07.54	54-55	15	-	3

HARRISON Lee David
Billericay, 12 September, 1971 G)

League Club	Source	Date Signed	Seasons Played	Apps	Subs	Gls
Charlton Ath.	YT	07.90				
Gillingham	L	03.92	91	2	0	0
Fulham	Tr	12.92	94-95	11	1	0
Barnet	Tr	07.96	96-97	67	0	0

HARRISON Mark Simon
Derby, 11 December, 1960 (G)

League Club	Source	Date Signed	Seasons Played	Apps	Subs	Gls
Southampton	App	12.78				
Port Vale	Tr	02.80	80-81	70	0	0
Stoke C.	Tr	08.82	82	7	0	0

HARRISON Michael
Leicester, 21 December, 1952 (CD)

League Club	Source	Date Signed	Seasons Played	Apps	Subs	Gls
Birmingham C.	App	02.70	70-71	3	0	0
Southend U.	Tr	07.72	72	16	0	0

HARRISON Michael John
Ilford, 18 April, 1940 E Sch/Eu23-3 (OL)

League Club	Source	Date Signed	Seasons Played	Apps	Subs	Gls
Chelsea	Jnrs	04.57	56-62	61	-	8
Blackburn Rov.	Tr	09.62	62-67	160	0	40
Plymouth Arg.	Tr	09.67	67	15	0	3
Luton T.	Tr	06.68	68-69	28	3	6

HARRISON Peter
Sleaford, 25 October, 1927 (W)

League Club	Source	Date Signed	Seasons Played	Apps	Subs	Gls
Leeds U.	Peterborough U.	01.49	49-51	65	-	9
Bournemouth	Tr	08.52	52-56	172	-	34
Reading	Tr	06.57	57-58	39	-	5
Southport	Tr	07.59	59-61	126	-	22

HARRISON Ralph
Clayton-le-Moors, 18 December, 1926 (OL)

League Club	Source	Date Signed	Seasons Played	Apps	Subs	Gls
Leeds U.	Great Harwood	01.49	49	2	-	0

HARRISON Raymond William
Boston, 21 June, 1921 (CF)

League Club	Source	Date Signed	Seasons Played	Apps	Subs	Gls
Burnley	Boston U.	04.46	46-49	60	-	19
Doncaster Rov.	Tr	01.50	49-53	126	-	47
Grimsby T.	Tr	07.54	54	38	-	7

HARRISON Reginald Frederick
Derby, 22 May, 1923 (OR)

League Club	Source	Date Signed	Seasons Played	Apps	Subs	Gls
Derby Co.	Jnrs	03.44	46-54	254	-	52

HARRISON Robert Alan
Chatham, 25 December, 1947 (IF)

League Club	Source	Date Signed	Seasons Played	Apps	Subs	Gls
Gillingham	Jnrs	06.67	66	1	0	0

HARRISON John **Robert**
Manchester, 23 December, 1930 (OR)

League Club	Source	Date Signed	Seasons Played	Apps	Subs	Gls
Carlisle U.		02.53	52-54	67	-	16
Stockport Co.	Tr	07.56				

HARRISON Ronald
Hebburn, 15 May, 1923 (F)

League Club	Source	Date Signed	Seasons Played	Apps	Subs	Gls
Darlington	Gateshead (Am)	08.45	46	8	-	3
Gateshead	Tr	07.47	47	6	-	1

HARRISON Steven John
Blackpool, 26 December, 1952 (LB)

League Club	Source	Date Signed	Seasons Played	Apps	Subs	Gls
Blackpool	App	12.70	71-77	141	7	0
Watford	Vancouver (Can)	09.78	78-80	82	1	0
Charlton Ath.	Tr	07.81	81	3	0	0

HARRISON Terence John
Thornaby, 12 September, 1950 (CF)

League Club	Source	Date Signed	Seasons Played	Apps	Subs	Gls
Newcastle U.	Stockton	11.67				
Barrow	Tr	07.70	70	4	0	0

HARRISON Thomas Edward
Edinburgh, 22 January, 1974 S Sch/S Yth (M)

League Club	Source	Date Signed	Seasons Played	Apps	Subs	Gls
York C.	Clyde	01.97	96	0	1	0
Carlisle U.	Tr	08.97	97	6	4	0

HARRISON Walter Edward
Coalville, 16 January, 1923 Died 1979 E 'B' (WH)

League Club	Source	Date Signed	Seasons Played	Apps	Subs	Gls
Leicester C.	Jnrs	08.45	46-50	125	-	3
Chesterfield	Tr	12.50	50-52	74	-	12

HARRISON Wayne
Stockport, 15 November, 1967 (F)

League Club	Source	Date Signed	Seasons Played	Apps	Subs	Gls
Oldham Ath.	App	12.84	84	5	1	1
Liverpool	Tr	03.85				
Crewe Alex.	L	12.88	88	3	0	0

HARRISON Wayne Moffat
Whitehaven, 16 October, 1957 (M)

League Club	Source	Date Signed	Seasons Played	Apps	Subs	Gls
Workington (N/C)	Everton (Jnrs)	08.75	75	1	3	0
Blackpool	Sheffield Wed. (N/C)	09.79	79-81	81	5	6
Carlisle U. (N/C)	Workington	08.87	87	1	1	0

HARRITY Michael David
Sheffield, 5 October, 1946 (FB)

League Club	Source	Date Signed	Seasons Played	Apps	Subs	Gls
Rotherham U.		10.65	65-68	36	5	0
Doncaster Rov.	Tr	09.68	68	2	1	0

HARROLD Mark Anthony
Huddersfield, 29 January, 1957 (M)

League Club	Source	Date Signed	Seasons Played	Apps	Subs	Gls
Halifax T.	Jnrs	08.74	74-75	8	5	1

HARROP Jack
Manchester, 25 June, 1929 Died 1977 (FB)

League Club	Source	Date Signed	Seasons Played	Apps	Subs	Gls
Swansea C.		08.52	52-53	10	-	0
Watford	Tr	07.56	56-59	111	-	0

HARROP Robert
Manchester, 25 August, 1936 (CH)

League Club	Source	Date Signed	Seasons Played	Apps	Subs	Gls
Manchester U.	Benchill Y.C.	05.54	57-58	10	-	0
Tranmere Rov.	Tr	11.59	59-60	41	-	2

HARROW Andrew
Kirkcaldy, 6 November, 1956 (F)

League Club	Source	Date Signed	Seasons Played	Apps	Subs	Gls
Luton T.	Raith Rov.	09.80	80	3	1	0

HARROWER James
Alva, 18 August, 1935 Su23-1 (IF)

League Club	Source	Date Signed	Seasons Played	Apps	Subs	Gls
Liverpool	Hibernian	01.58	57-60	96	-	21
Newcastle U.	Tr	03.61	60-61	5	-	0

HARROWER James Swanson
Dunfermline, 19 June, 1924 Died 1992 (FB)

League Club	Source	Date Signed	Seasons Played	Apps	Subs	Gls
Accrington St.	Third Lanark	12.54	54-60	246	-	2

HARROWER Steven Gordon
Exeter, 9 October, 1961 (RB)

League Club	Source	Date Signed	Seasons Played	Apps	Subs	Gls
Exeter C.	Dawlish	01.84	83-89	165	22	10

HARROWER William
Dunfermline, 13 April, 1922 (IF)

League Club	Source	Date Signed	Seasons Played	Apps	Subs	Gls
Torquay U.	Third Lanark	05.46	46-47	16	-	3
Exeter C.	Tr	07.48	48-51	85	-	11

HARSLEY Paul
Scunthorpe, 29 May, 1978 (M)

League Club	Source	Date Signed	Seasons Played	Apps	Subs	Gls
Grimsby T.	YT	07.96				
Scunthorpe U.	Tr	07.97	97	11	4	1

HARSTON John (Jack)
Barnsley, 7 October, 1920 (FB)

League Club	Source	Date Signed	Seasons Played	Apps	Subs	Gls
Wolverhampton W.		10.37				
Barnsley	Tr	09.38	46-48	20	-	1
Bradford C.	Tr	06.49	49	24	-	1

HART Alan Michael
Woolwich, 21 February, 1956 (M)

League Club	Source	Date Signed	Seasons Played	Apps	Subs	Gls
Charlton Ath.	App	02.74	74	3	0	2
Millwall	Tr	06.75	75	13	3	0

HART Andrew
Yarmouth, 14 January, 1963 (D)

League Club	Source	Date Signed	Seasons Played	Apps	Subs	Gls
Norwich C.	App	01.81	81	0	1	0

HART Brian Patrick
Farnworth, 14 July, 1959 (CD)

League Club	Source	Date Signed	Seasons Played	Apps	Subs	Gls
Rochdale	Bolton W. (App)	07.77	77-79	73	5	0

HART Harold
Sheffield, 29 September, 1926 (IF)

League Club	Source	Date Signed	Seasons Played	Apps	Subs	Gls
Rotherham U.		12.45	49	10	-	4
Coventry C.	Tr	06.50	50-51	10	-	1
Grimsby T.	Tr	12.52	52	13	-	3

HART John Paul
Golborne, 8 June, 1928 (IF)

League Club	Source	Date Signed	Seasons Played	Apps	Subs	Gls
Manchester C.	Jnrs	06.45	47-60	169	-	67

HART John Leslie
Ashton-u-Lyne, 28 February, 1917 Died 1996 (CH)

League Club	Source	Date Signed	Seasons Played	Apps	Subs	Gls
Bury	Ashton National	12.36	38-53	280	-	1

HART Nigel
Golborne, 1 October, 1958 (CD)

League Club	Source	Date Signed	Seasons Played	Apps	Subs	Gls
Wigan Ath.		08.78	79	1	0	0
Leicester C.	Tr	10.79				
Blackpool	Tr	08.81	81-82	36	1	0
Crewe Alex.	Tr	11.82	82-86	139	3	10
Bury	Tr	02.87	86-87	33	12	2
Stockport Co.	Tr	07.88	88-89	38	1	2
Chesterfield	Tr	08.89	89-90	45	1	2
York C. (N/C)	Tr	02.91	90	1	0	0

HART Paul Anthony
Golborne, 4 May, 1953 (CD)

League Club	Source	Date Signed	Seasons Played	Apps	Subs	Gls
Stockport Co.	Jnrs	09.70	70-72	87	0	5
Blackpool	Tr	06.73	73-77	143	0	17
Leeds U.	Tr	03.78	77-82	191	0	16
Nottingham F.	Tr	05.83	83-84	70	0	1
Sheffield Wed.	Tr	08.85	85-86	52	0	2
Birmingham C.	Tr	12.86	86	1	0	0
Notts Co.	Tr	06.87	87	23	0	0

HART Peter
Wickersley, 6 September, 1949 (FB)

League Club	Source	Date Signed	Seasons Played	Apps	Subs	Gls
Bradford P.A. (Am)	Rotherham U. (App)	03.68	67	3	0	0

HART Peter Osborne
Mexborough, 14 August, 1957 (CD)

League Club	Source	Date Signed	Seasons Played	Apps	Subs	Gls
Huddersfield T.	App	08.74	73-79	208	2	7
Walsall	Tr	08.80	80-89	389	1	12

HART Roy Ernest
Acton, 30 May, 1933 E Sch (CH)

League Club	Source	Date Signed	Seasons Played	Apps	Subs	Gls
Brentford	Jnrs	06.50	54	2	-	0

HART Marvin Stuart
Derby, 15 January, 1941 (OR)

League Club	Source	Date Signed	Seasons Played	Apps	Subs	Gls
Exeter C.	Long Eaton U.	08.67	67	20	2	1

HART William Robert
North Shields, 1 April, 1923 Died 1990 (RH)

League Club	Source	Date Signed	Seasons Played	Apps	Subs	Gls
Newcastle U.		09.40				
Chesterfield	Tr	03.45	46	1	-	0
Bradford C.	Tr	05.47	46-48	25	-	0

HARTBURN John
Houghton-le-Spring, 20 December, 1920 (OL)

League Club	Source	Date Signed	Seasons Played	Apps	Subs	Gls
Queens Park R.	Yeovil T.	03.47	47-48	58	-	11
Watford	Tr	09.49	49-50	66	-	19
Millwall	Tr	03.51	50-53	104	-	29
Leyton Orient	Tr	06.54	54-57	112	-	36

HARTE Ian Patrick
Drogheda, 31 August, 1977 IRu21-3/IR-18 (LM)

League Club	Source	Date Signed	Seasons Played	Apps	Subs	Gls
Leeds U.	YT	12.95	95-97	24	6	2

HARTENBERGER Uwe
Germany, 1 February, 1968 (F)

League Club	Source	Date Signed	Seasons Played	Apps	Subs	Gls
Reading	Bayer Uerdingen (Ger)	09.93	93-94	8	16	4

HARTERY John
Waterford (Ire), 25 November, 1920 LoI (RB)

League Club	Source	Date Signed	Seasons Played	Apps	Subs	Gls
Plymouth Arg.	Limerick	06.48	49	1	-	0

HARTFIELD Charles Joseph
Lambeth, 4 September, 1971 E Yth (M/FB)

League Club	Source	Date Signed	Seasons Played	Apps	Subs	Gls
Arsenal	YT	09.89				
Sheffield U.	Tr	08.91	91-96	45	11	1
Fulham	L	02.97	96	1	1	0
Swansea C.	Tr	11.97	97	22	0	2

HARTFORD Richard Asa
Clydebank, 24 October, 1950 Su21-1/Su23-5/S-50 (M)

League Club	Source	Date Signed	Seasons Played	Apps	Subs	Gls
West Bromwich A.	Jnrs	11.67	67-73	206	8	18
Manchester C.	Tr	08.74	74-78	184	1	22
Nottingham F.	Tr	07.79	79	3	0	0
Everton	Tr	08.79	79-81	81	0	6
Manchester C.	Tr	10.81	81-83	75	0	7
Norwich C.	Fort Lauderdale (USA)	10.84	84	28	0	2
Bolton W.	Tr	07.85	85-86	81	0	8
Stockport Co.	Tr	06.87	87-88	42	3	0
Oldham Ath.	Tr	03.89	88	3	4	0
Shrewsbury T.	Tr	08.89	89-90	22	3	0

HARTLAND Michael Leo
Dunfermline, 7 January, 1944 (M)

League Club	Source	Date Signed	Seasons Played	Apps	Subs	Gls
Oxford U.	Nuneaton Borough	06.63	63-64	19	-	6
Barrow	Tr	07.65	65-70	169	7	20
Crewe Alex.	Tr	12.70	70	3	0	2
Southport	Tr	07.71	71-72	32	5	4

HARTLE Barry
Salford, 8 August, 1939 (OL/LB)

League Club	Source	Date Signed	Seasons Played	Apps	Subs	Gls
Watford	Jnrs	08.56	58-59	39	-	7
Sheffield U.	Tr	06.60	60-65	101	0	16
Carlisle U.	Tr	07.66	66-67	28	1	1
Stockport Co.	Tr	09.67	67-69	88	0	1
Oldham Ath.	Tr	06.70	70	8	1	2
Southport	Tr	07.71	71	37	4	6

HARTLE Leslie Roy
Bromsgrove, 4 October, 1931 EF Lge (FB)

League Club	Source	Date Signed	Seasons Played	Apps	Subs	Gls
Bolton W.	Bromsgrove Rov.	02.51	52-65	446	1	11

HARTLEY Edmund
Burnley, 5 May, 1932 (OR)

League Club	Source	Date Signed	Seasons Played	Apps	Subs	Gls
Burnley	Jnrs	11.50				
Oldham Ath.	Rossendale U.	07.56	56	1	-	0

HARTLEY Paul
Glasgow, 19 October, 1976 Su21-1 (W)

League Club	Source	Date Signed	Seasons Played	Apps	Subs	Gls
Millwall	Hamilton Academical	07.96	96	35	9	4

HARTLEY Thomas William
Gateshead, 7 May, 1917 Died 1984 (IF)

League Club	Source	Date Signed	Seasons Played	Apps	Subs	Gls
Gateshead	Birtley B.C.	02.36	35-36	5	-	1
Bury	Tr	05.38				
Chesterfield	Tr	05.39				
Leicester C.	North Shields	01.48				
Watford	Tr	02.48	47	6	-	1

HARTLEY Trevor John
Doncaster, 16 March, 1947 (W)

League Club	Source	Date Signed	Seasons Played	Apps	Subs	Gls
West Ham U.	Jnrs	07.64	66-68	4	1	0
Bournemouth	Tr	07.69	69-70	35	7	2

HARTNETT James Benedict
Dublin, 21 March, 1927 Died 1988 LoI/IR-2 (OL)

League Club	Source	Date Signed	Seasons Played	Apps	Subs	Gls
Middlesbrough	Dundalk	06.48	48-54	48	-	8
Hartlepool U.	Barry T.	09.57	57	7	-	1
York C.	Tr	08.58	58	2	-	1

HARTSON John
Swansea, 5 April, 1975 W Yth/Wu21-9/W-15 (F)

League Club	Source	Date Signed	Seasons Played	Apps	Subs	Gls
Luton T.	YT	12.92	93-94	32	22	11
Arsenal	Tr	01.95	94-96	43	10	14
West Ham U.	Tr	02.97	96-97	43	0	20

HARVEY Alexander
Ayr, 28 September, 1928 (IF)

League Club	Source	Date Signed	Seasons Played	Apps	Subs	Gls
Chesterfield	Saltcoats Vic.	11.50	50-52	26	-	9

HARVEY Alexander
Kirkconnel (Ayrs), 28 August, 1925 (LH)

League Club	Source	Date Signed	Seasons Played	Apps	Subs	Gls
Carlisle U.	Queen of South	08.46	46	1	-	0

HARVEY Brian
Liverpool, 12 January, 1947 (WH)

League Club	Source	Date Signed	Seasons Played	Apps	Subs	Gls
Chester C.	Sheffield Wed. (App)	09.64	64	1	-	0

HARVEY Bryan Robert
Stepney, 26 August, 1938 (G)

League Club	Source	Date Signed	Seasons Played	Apps	Subs	Gls
Newcastle U.	Wisbech T.	09.58	58-60	86	-	0
Blackpool	Cambridge C.	02.62	61-63	11	-	0
Northampton T.	Tr	10.63	63-67	165	0	0

HARVEY James Colin
Liverpool, 16 November, 1944 Eu23-5/EF Lge/E-1 (M)

League Club	Source	Date Signed	Seasons Played	Apps	Subs	Gls
Everton	App	10.62	63-74	317	3	18
Sheffield Wed.	Tr	09.74	74-75	45	0	2

HARVEY David
Hetton-le-Hole, 15 February, 1954 (OR)

League Club	Source	Date Signed	Seasons Played	Apps	Subs	Gls
Hartlepool U.	App	●	70	3	2	0

HARVEY David
Leeds, 7 February, 1948 S-16 (G)

League Club	Source	Date Signed	Seasons Played	Apps	Subs	Gls
Leeds U.	Jnrs	02.65	65-79	276	0	0
Leeds U.	Vancouver (Can)	09.82	82-84	73	0	0
Bradford C. (N/C)	Tr	02.85	84	6	0	0

HARVEY Gary
Colchester, 19 November, 1961 (F)

League Club	Source	Date Signed	Seasons Played	Apps	Subs	Gls
Colchester U.	App	11.79	79-80	6	0	2

HARVEY James
Lurgan (NI), 2 May, 1958 NIu23-1 (M)

League Club	Source	Date Signed	Seasons Played	Apps	Subs	Gls
Arsenal	Glenavon	08.77	77-78	2	1	0
Hereford U.	Tr	03.80	79-86	276	2	39
Bristol C.	Tr	03.87	86-87	2	1	0
Wrexham	L	09.87	87	6	0	0
Tranmere Rov.	Tr	10.87	87-91	174	10	18
Crewe Alex.	Tr	07.92	92	16	1	0

HARVEY Joseph
Doncaster, 11 June, 1918 Died 1989 (WH)

League Club	Source	Date Signed	Seasons Played	Apps	Subs	Gls
Bradford P.A.	Edlington R.	05.36	36	3	-	0
Wolverhampton W.	Tr	11.36				
Bournemouth	Tr	05.37	37-38	3	-	0
Newcastle U.	Tr	10.45	46-52	224	-	12

HARVEY William Keith
Crediton, 25 December, 1934 (CH)

League Club	Source	Date Signed	Seasons Played	Apps	Subs	Gls
Exeter C.	Crediton	08.52	52-68	483	0	28

HARVEY Lawrence (Lol)
Heanor, 25 July, 1934 (FB)

League Club	Source	Date Signed	Seasons Played	Apps	Subs	Gls
Coventry C.	Jnrs	07.51	51-60	140	-	1

HARVEY Lee Derek
Harlow, 21 December, 1966 E Yth (W/FB)

League Club	Source	Date Signed	Seasons Played	Apps	Subs	Gls
Leyton Orient	App	12.84	83-92	135	49	23
Nottingham F.	Tr	08.93	93	0	2	0
Brentford	Tr	11.93	93-96	87	18	6

HARVEY Leighton
Neath, 27 August, 1959 (W)

League Club	Source	Date Signed	Seasons Played	Apps	Subs	Gls
Swansea C.	App	●	75-76	1	1	0

HARVEY Martin
Belfast, 19 September, 1941 NI Sch/NIu23-3/NI 'B'/NI-33 (WH)

League Club	Source	Date Signed	Seasons Played	Apps	Subs	Gls
Sunderland	Jnrs	09.58	59-71	310	4	5

HARVEY Richard George
Letchworth, 17 April, 1969 E Sch/E Yth (LB)

League Club	Source	Date Signed	Seasons Played	Apps	Subs	Gls
Luton T.	App	01.87	86-97	134	27	4
Blackpool	L	10.92	92	4	1	0

HARVEY William Derek
Doncaster, 30 September, 1934 (FB)

League Club	Source	Date Signed	Seasons Played	Apps	Subs	Gls
Doncaster Rov.	Jnrs	11.51	52	2	-	0

HARVEY William James
Clydebank, 23 November, 1929 (IF)

League Club	Source	Date Signed	Seasons Played	Apps	Subs	Gls
Bradford P.A.	Dunfermline Ath.	01.59	58-59	26	-	1

HARWOOD Lee
Southall, 4 October, 1960 (CD)

League Club	Source	Date Signed	Seasons Played	Apps	Subs	Gls
Southampton	App	10.78				
Wimbledon	Tr	01.79	78	1	0	0
Port Vale	Leatherhead	02.80	79-80	19	0	1

HARWOOD Richard Andrew
Sheffield, 13 September, 1960 (M)

League Club	Source	Date Signed	Seasons Played	Apps	Subs	Gls
Sheffield U.	App	07.78	78	2	1	0

HASELDEN John James
Doncaster, 3 August, 1943 (CD)

League Club	Source	Date Signed	Seasons Played	Apps	Subs	Gls
Rotherham U.	Denaby U.	02.62	61-68	98	2	0
Doncaster Rov.	Tr	09.68	68-73	168	4	20
Mansfield T.	L	02.72	71	4	0	0

HASFORD Jason Miles
Manchester, 1 April, 1971 (F)

League Club	Source	Date Signed	Seasons Played	Apps	Subs	Gls
Rochdale	Manchester C. (YT)	07.89	89	0	1	0

HASKINS Anthony John
Northampton, 26 July, 1935 (FB)

League Club	Source	Date Signed	Seasons Played	Apps	Subs	Gls
Northampton T.		01.59	59-61	8	-	0

HASLAM Graham
Doncaster, 29 April, 1956 (G)

League Club	Source	Date Signed	Seasons Played	Apps	Subs	Gls
Rotherham U.	App	04.74	75	2	0	0

HASLAM Harry
Manchester, 30 July, 1921 Died 1986 (FB)

League Club	Source	Date Signed	Seasons Played	Apps	Subs	Gls
Oldham Ath.	Rochdale (Am)	05.46	46	2	-	0
Brighton & H.A.	Tr	09.47				
Leyton Orient	Tr	07.48	48	7	-	0

HASLEGRAVE Sean Matthew
Stoke, 7 June, 1951 (M)

League Club	Source	Date Signed	Seasons Played	Apps	Subs	Gls
Stoke C.	Jnrs	11.68	70-75	106	7	5
Nottingham F.	Tr	07.76	76	5	2	1
Preston N.E.	Tr	09.77	77-80	111	2	2
Crewe Alex.	Tr	08.81	81-82	78	4	1
York C.	Tr	07.83	83-86	137	5	0
Torquay U.	Tr	08.87	87-88	32	4	1

HASPELL Alan
Northwich, 23 January, 1943 (IF)

League Club	Source	Date Signed	Seasons Played	Apps	Subs	Gls
Burnley	Jnrs	01.60				
Doncaster Rov.	Tr	07.63	63	1	-	0

HASSALL Harold William
Tyldesley, 4 March, 1929 EF Lge/E-5 (IF)

League Club	Source	Date Signed	Seasons Played	Apps	Subs	Gls
Huddersfield T.	Astley	09.46	48-51	74	-	26
Bolton W.	Tr	01.52	51-54	102	-	34

HASSALL Wilfred
Prestwich, 23 September, 1923 (FB)

League Club	Source	Date Signed	Seasons Played	Apps	Subs	Gls
Hull C.	R.M. Alsager	09.46	46-52	141	-	3

HASSELBAINK Jerrel
Surinam, 27 March, 1972 Dutch Int (F)

League Club	Source	Date Signed	Seasons Played	Apps	Subs	Gls
Leeds U.	Boavista (Por)	07.97	97	30	3	16

HASSELL Richard (Rick)
Coatbridge, 12 January, 1951 (WH)

League Club	Source	Date Signed	Seasons Played	Apps	Subs	Gls
Carlisle U.	Jnrs	01.69	68-69	3	3	0

HASSELL Robert John Francis
Derby, 4 June, 1980 (CD)

League Club	Source	Date Signed	Seasons Played	Apps	Subs	Gls
Mansfield T.	YT	●	97	8	1	0

HASSELL Thomas William
Southampton, 5 April, 1919 Died 1984 (W)

League Club	Source	Date Signed	Seasons Played	Apps	Subs	Gls
Southampton	Romsey T.	02.40				
Aldershot	Tr	05.46	46-49	114	-	15
Brighton & H.A.	Tr	08.50	50	11	-	4

HASTIE John Kenneth George
South Africa, 6 September, 1928 (IF)

League Club	Source	Date Signed	Seasons Played	Apps	Subs	Gls
Leeds U.	Clyde Ath. (SA)	08.52	52	4	-	2

HASTY Patrick (Paddy) Joseph
Belfast, 17 March, 1934 NI Amat (CF)

League Club	Source	Date Signed	Seasons Played	Apps	Subs	Gls
Leyton Orient (Am)	Tooting & Mitcham	07.58	58	2	-	2
Queens Park R. (Am)	Tr	10.59	59	1	-	0
Aldershot	Tooting & Mitcham	03.61	60-62	35	-	14

HATCH Peter Derek
Wargrave, 22 October, 1949 (LB/M)

League Club	Source	Date Signed	Seasons Played	Apps	Subs	Gls
Oxford U.	App	10.66	67-72	15	4	2
Exeter C.	Tr	12.73	73-81	343	3	18

HATCHER Clifford
Keynsham, 27 June, 1925 (G)

League Club	Source	Date Signed	Seasons Played	Apps	Subs	Gls
Reading		06.46	47-48	2	-	0

HATCHER Douglas Terence
Carshalton, 6 March, 1962 (G)

League Club	Source	Date Signed	Seasons Played	Apps	Subs	Gls
Fulham	App	03.80				
Aldershot (N/C)	Wokingham T.	08.83	83	1	0	0

HATELEY Anthony
Derby, 13 June, 1941 (CF)

League Club	Source	Date Signed	Seasons Played	Apps	Subs	Gls
Notts Co.	Jnrs	06.58	58-62	131	-	77
Aston Villa	Tr	08.63	63-66	127	0	68
Chelsea	Tr	10.66	66	26	1	6
Liverpool	Tr	07.67	67-68	42	0	17
Coventry C.	Tr	09.68	68	17	0	4
Birmingham C.	Tr	08.69	69-70	28	0	6
Notts Co.	Tr	11.70	70-71	57	0	32
Oldham Ath.	Tr	07.72	73	1	4	1

HATELEY Mark Wayne
Derby, 7 November, 1961 E Yth/Eu21-10/E-32 (F)

League Club	Source	Date Signed	Seasons Played	Apps	Subs	Gls
Coventry C.	App	12.78	78-82	86	6	25
Portsmouth	Tr	06.83	83	38	0	22
Queens Park R.	Glasgow Rangers	11.95	95-96	18	9	3
Leeds U.	L	08.96	96	5	1	0
Hull C.	Glasgow Rangers	08.97	97	4	5	0

HATHAWAY Ian Ashley
Wordsley, 22 August, 1968 (W)

League Club	Source	Date Signed	Seasons Played	Apps	Subs	Gls
Mansfield T.	Bedworth U.	03.89	88-90	21	23	2
Rotherham U.	Tr	03.91	90-91	5	8	1
Torquay U.	Tr	07.93	93-96	114	26	14
Colchester U.	Tr	07.97	97	5	7	0

HATSELL Dennis
Sheffield, 9 June, 1930 Died 1998 (CF)

League Club	Source	Date Signed	Seasons Played	Apps	Subs	Gls
Preston N.E.	Jnrs	06.48	53-59	115	-	54

HATTER Stephen John
East Ham, 21 October, 1958 (CD)

League Club	Source	Date Signed	Seasons Played	Apps	Subs	Gls
Fulham	App	05.76	77-80	25	1	1
Exeter C.	L	09.82	82	11	0	1
Wimbledon	Tr	11.82	82-84	83	1	4
Southend U.	Tr	03.85	84-85	62	0	2

HATTON Cyril
Nottingham, 14 September, 1918 Died 1987 (IF)

League Club	Source	Date Signed	Seasons Played	Apps	Subs	Gls
Notts Co.	Grantham Co-op.	07.36	36-38	62	-	15
Queens Park R.	Tr	04.46	46-52	162	-	64
Chesterfield	Tr	06.53	53	36	-	10

HATTON David Howcroft
Farnworth, 30 October, 1943 (CD)

League Club	Source	Date Signed	Seasons Played	Apps	Subs	Gls
Bolton W.	Jnrs	11.60	61-69	231	0	8
Blackpool	Tr	09.69	69-75	249	1	6
Bury	Tr	08.76	76-78	96	1	2

HATTON Robert James
Hull, 10 April, 1947 (F)

League Club	Source	Date Signed	Seasons Played	Apps	Subs	Gls
Wolverhampton W.	Jnrs	11.64	66	10	0	7
Bolton W.	Tr	03.67	66-67	23	1	2
Northampton T.	Tr	10.68	68	29	4	7
Carlisle U.	Tr	07.69	69-71	93	0	37
Birmingham C.	Tr	10.71	71-75	170	5	58
Blackpool	Tr	07.76	76-77	75	0	32
Luton T.	Tr	07.78	78-79	81	1	29
Sheffield U.	Tr	07.80	80-82	92	3	34
Cardiff C.	Tr	12.82	82	29	1	9

HAUGHEY Frederick
Conisborough, 12 May, 1921 (LB)

League Club	Source	Date Signed	Seasons Played	Apps	Subs	Gls
Bradford C. (Am)	Halifax T. (Am)	08.46	46	3	-	0

HAUGHEY William
Glasgow, 20 December, 1932 (IF)

League Club	Source	Date Signed	Seasons Played	Apps	Subs	Gls
Everton	Larkhall Thistle	06.56	56-57	4	-	1

HAUSER Peter Benjamin
South Africa, 20 April, 1934 (IF/WH)

League Club	Source	Date Signed	Seasons Played	Apps	Subs	Gls
Blackpool	South Africa	11.55	57-61	83	-	10
Chester C.	Cheltenham T.	08.63	63-66	117	4	3

HAUSER Thomas
West Germany, 10 April, 1965 (F)

League Club	Source	Date Signed	Seasons Played	Apps	Subs	Gls
Sunderland	F.C. Basel (Swi)	02.89	88-91	22	31	9

HAVENGA William Stephanus
South Africa, 6 November, 1924 (IF)

League Club	Source	Date Signed	Seasons Played	Apps	Subs	Gls
Birmingham C.	Bremner O.B. (SA)	07.48	49	1	-	0
Luton T.	Tr	05.50	50-51	18	-	6
Ipswich T.	Tr	01.52	51-52	19	-	3

HAVENHAND Keith
Dronfield, 11 September, 1937 E Yth (IF)

League Club	Source	Date Signed	Seasons Played	Apps	Subs	Gls
Chesterfield	Jnrs	09.54	53-61	176	-	58
Derby Co.	Tr	10.61	61	26	-	14
Oxford U.	Tr	12.63	63-64	12	-	3

HAVERSON Paul Timothy
Chigwell, 19 February, 1959 E Sch (D)

League Club	Source	Date Signed	Seasons Played	Apps	Subs	Gls
Queens Park R.	App	08.76				
Wimbledon	Tr	10.78	78-79	27	1	2

HAVERTY Joseph
Dublin, 17 February, 1936 IR-32 (OL)

League Club	Source	Date Signed	Seasons Played	Apps	Subs	Gls
Arsenal	St Patricks Ath.	07.54	54-60	114	-	25
Blackburn Rov.	Tr	08.61	61-62	27	-	1
Millwall	Tr	09.62	62-63	68	-	8
Bristol Rov.	Glasgow Celtic	12.64	64	13	-	1

HAWDEN Kenneth
Huddersfield, 16 September, 1931 (F)

League Club	Source	Date Signed	Seasons Played	Apps	Subs	Gls
Derby Co.	Ashenhurst S.C.	04.53	53	2	-	0

HAWES Steven Robert
High Wycombe, 17 July, 1978 (M)

League Club	Source	Date Signed	Seasons Played	Apps	Subs	Gls
Sheffield U.	YT	03.96	95-96	1	3	0
Doncaster Rov.	L	09.97	97	7	1	0
Doncaster Rov. (N/C)	Tr	02.98	97	1	2	0

HAWKE Warren Robert
Durham, 20 September, 1970 (F)

League Club	Source	Date Signed	Seasons Played	Apps	Subs	Gls
Sunderland	YT	11.88	88-92	7	18	1
Chesterfield	L	09.91	91	7	0	1
Carlisle U.	L	10.92	92	8	0	2
Northampton T.	L	03.93	92	7	0	1
Scarborough (N/C)	Raith Rov.	12.93	93	0	1	0

HAWKER David
Hull, 29 November, 1958 (M)

League Club	Source	Date Signed	Seasons Played	Apps	Subs	Gls
Hull C.	App	08.76	77-79	33	2	2
Darlington	Tr	03.80	79-82	84	4	2

HAWKER Philip Nigel
Solihull, 7 December, 1962 E Yth (D/M)

League Club	Source	Date Signed	Seasons Played	Apps	Subs	Gls
Birmingham C.	App	06.80	80-82	34	1	1
Walsall	Tr	12.82	82-89	159	18	10
West Bromwich A.	Tr	09.90	90	1	0	0

HAWKES Barry
Easington (Dm), 21 March, 1938 (IF)

League Club	Source	Date Signed	Seasons Played	Apps	Subs	Gls
Luton T.	Shotton Colly	11.55	58-59	8	-	0
Darlington	Tr	06.60	60	13	-	3
Hartlepool U.	Tr	07.61	61	9	-	0

HAWKES Kenneth Kilby
Easington (Dm), 6 May, 1933 (FB)

League Club	Source	Date Signed	Seasons Played	Apps	Subs	Gls
Luton T.	Shotton Colly	10.51	57-60	90	-	1
Peterborough U.	Tr	06.61	61	1	-	0

HAWKINGS Barry
Birmingham, 7 November, 1931 (IF)

League Club	Source	Date Signed	Seasons Played	Apps	Subs	Gls
Coventry C.	Jnrs	01.49	53-55	34	-	12
Lincoln C.	Tr	03.56	55-56	15	-	6
Northampton T.	Tr	06.57	57-58	65	-	25

HAWKINS Bertram
Bristol, 29 September, 1923 (CF)

League Club	Source	Date Signed	Seasons Played	Apps	Subs	Gls
Bristol Rov.	De Veys	08.47				
Bristol C.	Tr	05.49	49	8	-	4
West Ham U.	Bath C.	09.51	51-52	34	-	16
Queens Park R.	Tr	06.53	53	8	-	3

HAWKINS David John
Kingston, 11 August, 1931 (CF)

League Club	Source	Date Signed	Seasons Played	Apps	Subs	Gls
Gillingham (Am)	Sheppey U.	01.56	55	14	-	8

HAWKINS Dennis Ronald
Swansea, 22 October, 1947 W Sch/Wu23-6 (F)

League Club	Source	Date Signed	Seasons Played	Apps	Subs	Gls
Leeds U.	App	10.64	66-67	2	0	0
Shrewsbury T.	Tr	10.68	68-69	50	8	9
Chester C.	L	09.70	70	6	1	1
Workington	L	03.72	71	6	0	1
Newport Co.	Tr	05.72	72	9	0	1

HAWKINS Graham Norman
Darlaston, 5 March, 1946 (CD)

League Club	Source	Date Signed	Seasons Played	Apps	Subs	Gls
Wolverhampton W.	App	06.63	64-67	28	6	0
Preston N.E.	Tr	01.68	67-73	241	4	3
Blackburn Rov.	Tr	06.74	74-77	108	1	4
Port Vale	Tr	01.78	77-79	61	1	3

League Club	Source	Date Signed	Seasons Played	Career Record Apps	Subs	Gls

HAWKINS Harry
Middlesbrough, 24 November, 1915 Died 1992 (CF)

League Club	Source	Date Signed	Seasons Played	Apps	Subs	Gls
Middlesbrough	South Bank E.E.	02.35	35	1	-	0
Watford	Tr	06.37	37	5	-	0
Southport	Tr	07.38	38-46	79	-	30
Gateshead	Tr	06.47	47	27	-	12
Hartlepool U.	Tr	03.48	47-48	30	-	4

HAWKINS Herbert Henry
Lambeth, 15 July, 1923 Died 1982 (CF)

League Club	Source	Date Signed	Seasons Played	Apps	Subs	Gls
Leyton Orient	Gravesend & Nft	06.51	51-52	5	-	0

HAWKINS Nigel Sean
Bristol, 7 September, 1968 (F)

League Club	Source	Date Signed	Seasons Played	Apps	Subs	Gls
Bristol C.	YT	02.87	87-88	8	10	2
Blackpool	Tr	10.89	89	4	3	0

HAWKINS Peter Michael
Swansea, 18 December, 1951 W Sch (F)

League Club	Source	Date Signed	Seasons Played	Apps	Subs	Gls
Northampton T.	App	12.68	68-73	49	10	10

HAWKSBY John Frederick
York, 12 June, 1942 E Yth (IF)

League Club	Source	Date Signed	Seasons Played	Apps	Subs	Gls
Leeds U.	Jnrs	06.59	60-62	37	-	2
Lincoln C.	Tr	08.64	64-65	64	1	4
York C.	Tr	03.66	65-67	72	2	7

HAWKSFORD Edward
Liverpool, 7 November, 1931 (OR)

League Club	Source	Date Signed	Seasons Played	Apps	Subs	Gls
Mansfield T.	R.A.O.C. Chilwell	03.52	52	1	-	0

HAWKSWORTH Anthony
Sheffield, 15 January, 1938 E Sch/E Yth (G)

League Club	Source	Date Signed	Seasons Played	Apps	Subs	Gls
Manchester U.	Jnrs	04.55	56	1	-	0

HAWKSWORTH Derek Marshall
Bradford, 16 July, 1927 E 'B' (OL)

League Club	Source	Date Signed	Seasons Played	Apps	Subs	Gls
Bradford C.	Huddersfield T. (Am)	10.48	48-50	75	-	20
Sheffield U.	Tr	12.50	50-57	255	-	88
Huddersfield T.	Tr	05.58	58-59	55	-	14
Lincoln C.	Tr	02.60	59-60	36	-	14
Bradford C.	Tr	01.61	60-61	44	-	8

HAWLEY Alan James
Woking, 7 June, 1946 (FB)

League Club	Source	Date Signed	Seasons Played	Apps	Subs	Gls
Brentford	App	06.63	62-73	315	3	4

HAWLEY John East
Withernsea, 8 May, 1954 (F)

League Club	Source	Date Signed	Seasons Played	Apps	Subs	Gls
Hull C.	Jnrs	04.72	72-77	101	13	22
Leeds U.	Tr	04.78	78-79	30	3	16
Sunderland	Tr	10.79	79-80	25	0	11
Arsenal	Tr	09.81	81-82	14	6	3
Leyton Orient	L	10.82	82	4	0	1
Hull C.	L	12.82	82	3	0	1
Bradford C.	Happy Valley(HK)	09.83	83-84	61	6	28
Scunthorpe U.	Tr	07.85	85	18	3	7

HAWORTH Gary
Bury, 25 April, 1959 (F)

League Club	Source	Date Signed	Seasons Played	Apps	Subs	Gls
Rochdale (N/C)	Radcliffe Borough	08.84	84	1	0	0

HAWORTH Herbert
Accrington, 6 May, 1920 Died 1993 (IF)

League Club	Source	Date Signed	Seasons Played	Apps	Subs	Gls
Accrington St. (Am)	Woodcock Amats	10.46	46	2	-	0

HAWORTH Robert John
Edgware, 21 November, 1975 (F)

League Club	Source	Date Signed	Seasons Played	Apps	Subs	Gls
Fulham	YT	07.93	93-94	7	14	1

HAWORTH Simon Owen
Cardiff, 30 March, 1977 W Yth/Wu21-6/W 'B'/W-5 (F)

League Club	Source	Date Signed	Seasons Played	Apps	Subs	Gls
Cardiff C.	YT	08.95	95-96	27	10	9
Coventry C.	Tr	06.97	97	4	6	0

HAWSON Alexander
Dalbeattie, 23 October, 1923 (RH)

League Club	Source	Date Signed	Seasons Played	Apps	Subs	Gls
Rochdale	Aberdeen	12.48	48	1	-	0

HAWTHORNE Mark
Glasgow, 31 October, 1973 (M)

League Club	Source	Date Signed	Seasons Played	Apps	Subs	Gls
Crystal Palace	Jnrs	06.92				
Sheffield U. (N/C)	Tr	08.94				
Torquay U.	Walsall (N/C)	03.95	94-96	43	15	2

HAWTHORNE Mark
Sunderland, 21 August, 1979 (CD)

League Club	Source	Date Signed	Seasons Played	Apps	Subs	Gls
Doncaster Rov.	YT	12.96	97	7	1	0

HAWTIN Craig Scott
Buxton, 29 March, 1970 (FB)

League Club	Source	Date Signed	Seasons Played	Apps	Subs	Gls
Chester C.	Port Vale (YT)	09.88	87-88	6	1	1
Burnley (N/C)	Tr	08.89				

HAY Alan Browning
Dunfermline, 28 November, 1958 (LB)

League Club	Source	Date Signed	Seasons Played	Apps	Subs	Gls
Bolton W.	Dundee	03.77				
Bristol C.	Tr	07.78	79-81	72	2	1
York C.	Tr	08.82	82-85	147	3	2
Tranmere Rov.	Tr	08.86	86	27	1	0
York C. (N/C)	Hill of Beath	12.88	88	1	0	0
Sunderland	Tr	02.89	88	1	0	0
Torquay U.	Tr	09.89	89-90	10	0	0

HAY Christopher Drummond
Glasgow, 28 August, 1974 (F)

League Club	Source	Date Signed	Seasons Played	Apps	Subs	Gls
Swindon T.	Glasgow Celtic	08.97	97	30	6	14

HAY Darran Andrew
Hitchin, 17 December, 1969 (F)

League Club	Source	Date Signed	Seasons Played	Apps	Subs	Gls
Cambridge U.	Biggleswade T.	03.94	93-94	7	22	3
Cambridge U. (L)	Woking	10.96	96	0	4	0

HAY David
Paisley, 29 January, 1948 Su23-3/SF Lge/S-27 (D)

League Club	Source	Date Signed	Seasons Played	Apps	Subs	Gls
Chelsea	Glasgow Celtic	08.74	74-78	107	1	2

HAYCOCK Frederick Joseph
Liverpool, 19 April, 1912 Died 1989 (F)

League Club	Source	Date Signed	Seasons Played	Apps	Subs	Gls
Aston Villa	Prescot Cables	02.34	36-38	99	-	28
Wrexham	Tr	12.45	46	6	-	1

HAYCOCK Thomas Paul
Sheffield, 8 July, 1962 (F)

League Club	Source	Date Signed	Seasons Played	Apps	Subs	Gls
Rotherham U.	Burton A.	08.86	86-89	77	20	22

HAYDE Michael Patrick
St Helens, 20 June, 1971 (FB)

League Club	Source	Date Signed	Seasons Played	Apps	Subs	Gls
Chester C.	Liverpool (YT)	08.89	89	0	1	0

HAYDOCK Frank
Eccles, 29 November, 1940 (CH)

League Club	Source	Date Signed	Seasons Played	Apps	Subs	Gls
Manchester U.	Jnrs	12.58	60-62	6	-	0
Charlton Ath.	Tr	08.63	63-65	84	0	4
Portsmouth	Tr	12.65	65-68	71	0	1
Southend U.	Tr	01.69	68-69	29	3	4

HAYDOCK William Edward
Salford, 19 January, 1936 (FB/W)

League Club	Source	Date Signed	Seasons Played	Apps	Subs	Gls
Manchester C.	Buxton	03.59	59-60	3	-	1
Crewe Alex.	Tr	03.61	60-64	142	-	30
Grimsby T.	Tr	11.64	64	21	-	4
Stockport Co.	Tr	08.65	65-70	257	4	3
Southport	Port Elizabeth (SA)	11.71	71	7	0	0

HAYDON Nicholas
Barking, 18 August, 1978 (M)

League Club	Source	Date Signed	Seasons Played	Apps	Subs	Gls
Colchester U.	YT	08.95	96-97	9	9	1

HAYES Adrian Michael
Norwich, 22 May, 1978 (M)

League Club	Source	Date Signed	Seasons Played	Apps	Subs	Gls
Cambridge U.	YT	07.96	95-97	25	9	0

HAYES Austin William Patrick
Hammersmith, 15 July, 1958 Died 1986 IRu21-1/IR-1 (W)

League Club	Source	Date Signed	Seasons Played	Apps	Subs	Gls
Southampton	App	07.76	76-79	22	9	5
Millwall	Tr	02.81	80-82	40	7	5
Northampton T.	Tr	08.83	83-84	60	3	14

HAYES Hugh
Bangor, 23 June, 1925 (WH)

League Club	Source	Date Signed	Seasons Played	Apps	Subs	Gls
Ipswich T.	Bangor	06.46	48-49	9	-	0

HAYES Joseph
Kearsley, 20 January, 1936 Eu23-2 (IF)

League Club	Source	Date Signed	Seasons Played	Apps	Subs	Gls
Manchester C.	Jnrs	08.53	53-64	331	-	142
Barnsley	Tr	07.65	65	26	0	3

HAYES Martin
Walthamstow, 21 March, 1966 Eu21-3 (W)

League Club	Source	Date Signed	Seasons Played	Apps	Subs	Gls
Arsenal	App	11.83	85-89	70	32	26
Wimbledon (L)	Glasgow Celtic	09.92	91	1	1	0
Swansea C.	Glasgow Celtic	01.93	92-94	44	17	8

HAYES Michael
Newport, 11 September, 1954 (D)

League Club	Source	Date Signed	Seasons Played	Apps	Subs	Gls
Newport Co. (N/C)	Dairy U.	01.76	75	4	0	0

League Club	Source	Date Signed	Seasons Played	Apps	Subs	Gls
HAYES Michael Charles						
Aberdare, 24 April, 1944 W Sch						(WH)
Swansea C.	Jnrs	06.61	62	3	-	0
HAYES Philip Henry						
Chiswick, 23 December, 1935						(F)
Millwall	Slough T.	12.56	56-58	16	-	1
HAYES Samuel						
Accrington, 21 June, 1920 Died 1959						(G)
Accrington St. (Am)	Blackburn Rov. (Am)	10.46	46	13	-	0
HAYES Stephen Charles						
Smethwick, 28 January, 1952						(CD)
Shrewsbury T.	Warley Borough	02.74	74-79	69	3	0
Torquay U.	L	09.75	75	1	0	0
Torquay U.	Tr	07.80	80	25	0	0
HAYES William						
Runcorn, 8 June, 1919						(HB)
Oldham Ath.	Halton Jnrs	01.37	38-50	126	-	3
HAYES William						
Newcastle-u-Lyme, 2 March, 1918 Died 1996						(CH)
Crewe Alex.	R.O.F. Radway Green	09.46	46	29	-	0
HAYES William Edward						
Cork (Ire), 7 November, 1915 IR-2/NI-4						(FB)
Huddersfield T.	Jnrs	04.33	34-49	181	-	5
Burnley	Tr	02.50	49-50	12	-	0
HAYES William John						
Limerick (Ire), 30 March, 1928 LoI/IR Amat/IR-1						(G)
Wrexham	Limerick	07.50	50	14	-	0
Torquay U.	Ellesmere Port	08.52	52-55	54	-	0
HAYFIELD Matthew Anthony						
Bristol, 8 August, 1975						(M)
Bristol Rov.	YT	07.94	95-97	24	17	0
HAYHURST Stanley Henry						
Leyland, 13 May, 1925						(G)
Blackburn Rov.	Leyland Motors	01.43	46-48	27	-	0
Tottenham H.	Tr	10.48				
Barrow	Tr	06.50	50	26	-	0
Grimsby T.	Tr	01.51	50-52	62	-	0
HAYLES Barrington Edward						
Lambeth, London, 17 May, 1972						(F)
Bristol Rov.	Stevenage Borough	06.97	97	45	0	23
HAYLOCK Garry Andrew						
Bradford, 31 December, 1970						(F)
Huddersfield T.	YT	07.89	90-91	10	3	4
HAYLOCK Paul						
Lowestoft, 24 March, 1963						(RB)
Norwich C.	App	01.81	81-85	154	1	3
Gillingham	Tr	08.86	86-89	149	3	0
Maidstone U.	Tr	03.91	90-91	47	1	1
Shrewsbury T.	Tr	09.92	92	16	2	1
Barnet	Woking	10.93	93	18	2	0
HAYMAN James						
Ramsbottom, 19 February, 1928						(FB)
Bury	Radcliffe Borough	11.50	50	5	-	0
HAYNES Arthur Edwin						
Birmingham, 23 May, 1924 Died 1990						(OR)
Aston Villa		01.46	46	4	-	0
Walsall	Tr	05.48	48	2	-	0
HAYNES Eric						
Sheffield, 18 June, 1936						(F)
Rotherham U.	Thorncliffe	04.56	55	1	-	0
HAYNES John Norman						
Edmonton, 17 October, 1934 E Sch/E Yth/Eu23-8/E 'B'/EF Lge/E-56						(IF)
Fulham	Jnrs	05.52	52-69	594	0	146
HAYNES Junior Lloyd						
Croydon, 6 April, 1976						(F)
Barnet	Tottenham H. (YT)	08.94	94	2	4	0
HAYRETTIN Hakan						
Enfield, 4 February, 1970						(M)
Leyton Orient	YT	07.88				
Barnet	Tr	08.89	91-92	0	6	0

League Club	Source	Date Signed	Seasons Played	Apps	Subs	Gls
Torquay U.	L	01.93	92	3	1	0
Wycombe W.	Tr	07.93	93	15	4	1
Cambridge U.	Tr	08.94	94	15	2	0
Doncaster Rov.	Tr	07.95				
HAYS Christopher **John (Jack)**						
Ashington, 12 December, 1918 Died 1983						(OR)
Bradford P.A.	Ipswich T.	08.38	38	17	-	0
Burnley	Tr	05.39	46-50	146	-	12
Bury	Tr	09.51	51-52	27	-	2
HAYTER James Edward						
Sandown (IoW), 9 April, 1979						(F)
Bournemouth	YT	07.97	96-97	0	7	0
HAYTON Eric						
Carlisle, 14 January, 1922						(WH/OR)
Carlisle U.		08.45	46-50	49	-	5
Rochdale	Tr	05.51	51	12	-	0
Workington	Tr	10.52	52	19	-	0
HAYWARD Andrew William						
Barnsley, 21 June, 1970						(M/F)
Rotherham U.	Frickley Ath.	08.94	94-97	93	27	15
HAYWARD Carl **Basil**						
Leek, 7 April, 1928 Died 1989						(CH/CF)
Port Vale	Northwood Heath	05.46	46-57	349	-	55
Portsmouth	Tr	07.58	58-59	44	-	4
HAYWARD Douglas Stanworth						
Wellington, 23 August, 1920						(FB)
Huddersfield T.	Jnrs	05.39				
Bristol Rov.	Barry T.	09.46	46	1	-	0
Newport Co.	Tr	11.46	46-55	259	-	11
HAYWARD Lionel **Eric**						
Newcastle-u-Lyme, 2 August, 1917 Died 1976						(CH)
Port Vale	Wardles	08.34	34-36	35	-	0
Blackpool	Tr	07.37	37-51	269	-	0
HAYWARD Keith William						
Hove, 21 November, 1951						(G)
Charlton Ath.	App	●	68	1	0	0
HAYWARD Steven Lee						
Pelsall, 8 September, 1971 E Yth						(M)
Derby Co.	Jnrs	09.88	89-94	15	11	1
Carlisle U.	Tr	03.95	94-95	88	2	14
Fulham	Tr	06.97	97	32	3	4
HAYWOOD Clive						
Ramsgate, 1 November, 1960						(F)
Coventry C.	App	08.78	80	1	0	0
HAYWOOD Raymond						
Dudley, 12 January, 1949						(F)
Shrewsbury T.	Stourbridge	05.74	74-76	75	12	27
Northampton T.	Tr	03.77	76-77	14	2	2
HAZAN Alon						
Ashdod, Israel, 14 September, 1967 Israeli Int						(M)
Watford	Ironi Ashdod (Isr)	01.98	97	7	3	0
HAZARD Michael						
Sunderland, 5 February, 1960						(M)
Tottenham H.	App	02.78	79-85	73	18	13
Chelsea	Tr	09.85	85-89	78	3	9
Portsmouth	Tr	01.90	89	8	0	1
Swindon T.	Tr	09.90	90-93	112	7	17
Tottenham H.	Tr	11.93	93-94	15	13	2
HAZEL Clifford						
Woolwich, 14 September, 1937						(IF)
Gillingham	Hastings U.	07.55	57	2	-	0
Millwall	Tr	07.58				
HAZEL Desmond St Lloyd						
Bradford, 15 July, 1967						(W)
Sheffield Wed.	App	07.85	87	5	1	0
Grimsby T.	L	10.86	86	9	0	2
Rotherham U.	Tr	07.88	88-94	204	34	30
Chesterfield	Tr	03.95	95	16	5	0
HAZEL Ian						
Merton, 1 December, 1967						(M)
Wimbledon	App	12.85	87-88	4	3	0
Bristol Rov.	L	02.89	88	3	0	0
Bristol Rov.	Tr	07.89	89-90	4	10	0
Maidstone U. (N/C)	Tr	03.92	91	6	2	0

HAZEL Julian
Luton, 25 September, 1973 (F)

League Club	Source	Date Signed	Seasons Played	Apps	Subs	Gls
Colchester U. (N/C)	YT	08.92	92	2	0	0

HAZELDEN Walter
Ashton-in-Makerfield, 13 February, 1941 E Yth (IF)

League Club	Source	Date Signed	Seasons Played	Apps	Subs	Gls
Aston Villa	Jnrs	02.58	57-58	17	-	5

HAZELL Anthony Philip
High Wycombe, 19 September, 1947 E Yth (D)

League Club	Source	Date Signed	Seasons Played	Apps	Subs	Gls
Queens Park R.	Jnrs	10.64	64-74	362	7	4
Millwall	Tr	12.74	74-78	153	0	6
Crystal Palace	Tr	11.78	78	5	0	0
Charlton Ath.	Tr	09.79	79-80	37	0	0

HAZELL Robert Joseph
Jamaica (WI), 14 June, 1959 E Yth/Eu21-1/E 'B' (CD)

League Club	Source	Date Signed	Seasons Played	Apps	Subs	Gls
Wolverhampton W.	App	05.77	77-78	32	1	1
Queens Park R.	Tr	09.79	79-83	100	6	8
Leicester C.	Tr	09.83	83-84	41	0	2
Wolverhampton W.	L	09.85	85	1	0	0
Reading	Luton T. (trial)	11.86	86	4	0	0
Port Vale	Tr	12.86	86-88	81	0	1

HAZLEDINE Albert Victor
Royton, 28 July, 1918 (LH)

League Club	Source	Date Signed	Seasons Played	Apps	Subs	Gls
Halifax T.	West Ham U. (Am)	11.45	46	10	-	2

HAZLEDINE Donald
Arnold, 10 July, 1929 (IF)

League Club	Source	Date Signed	Seasons Played	Apps	Subs	Gls
Derby Co.	Notts Regent	08.51	52-53	26	-	6
Northampton T.	Tr	06.54	54	22	-	4

HAZLEDINE Geoffrey
Arnold, 27 February, 1932 (F)

League Club	Source	Date Signed	Seasons Played	Apps	Subs	Gls
Derby Co.	Notts Regent	07.52	53	1	-	0
Southport	Boston U.	07.57	57	29	-	5

HAZLETT George
Glasgow, 10 March, 1923 (OR)

League Club	Source	Date Signed	Seasons Played	Apps	Subs	Gls
Bury	Belfast Celtic	08.49	49-51	101	-	9
Cardiff C.	Tr	08.52	52	7	-	1
Millwall	Tr	05.53	53-57	131	-	10

HAZZLETON James
Bolton, 29 September, 1930 Died 1991 (IF)

League Club	Source	Date Signed	Seasons Played	Apps	Subs	Gls
Bury	Atherton Colly	05.50				
Rochdale	Tr	08.51	51	11	-	1
Accrington St.	Tr	07.52	52	4	-	0

HEAD Bertram James
Midsomer Norton, 8 June, 1916 (D)

League Club	Source	Date Signed	Seasons Played	Apps	Subs	Gls
Torquay U.	Midsomer Norton	10.36	36-50	222	-	6
Bury	Tr	02.52	51-52	22	-	0

HEAD David George
Midsomer Norton, 11 August, 1940 (IF)

League Club	Source	Date Signed	Seasons Played	Apps	Subs	Gls
Swindon T.	Jnrs	08.58				
Arsenal	Tr	03.59				
Reading	Tr	07.60	60	12	-	0
Bristol Rov.	Tr	07.61				

HEAD Michael
Hull, 13 April, 1933 (OR)

League Club	Source	Date Signed	Seasons Played	Apps	Subs	Gls
Hull C.	Bridlington C.U.	12.53	54	3	-	0

HEALD Gregory James
Enfield, 26 September, 1971 E Sch (CD)

League Club	Source	Date Signed	Seasons Played	Apps	Subs	Gls
Peterborough U.	Enfield	07.94	94-96	101	4	6
Barnet	Tr	08.97	97	43	0	3

HEALD Oliver Richard
Canada, 13 March, 1975 (F)

League Club	Source	Date Signed	Seasons Played	Apps	Subs	Gls
Port Vale	North Vancouver (Can)	09.93				
Scarborough	Tr	08.95	95	1	8	1

HEALD Paul Andrew
Wath, 20 September, 1968 (G)

League Club	Source	Date Signed	Seasons Played	Apps	Subs	Gls
Sheffield U.	YT	06.87				
Leyton Orient	Tr	11.88	88-94	176	0	0
Coventry C.	L	03.92	91	2	0	0
Swindon T.	L	03.94	93	1	1	0
Wimbledon	Tr	07.95	95-96	20	0	0

HEALE Gary John
Canvey Island, 15 July, 1958 (F)

League Club	Source	Date Signed	Seasons Played	Apps	Subs	Gls
Luton T.	Canvey	12.76	77	7	0	1
Exeter C.	L	12.77	77	3	1	0
Reading	Tr	08.79	79-81	68	8	20

HEALER Ernest
Birtley, 13 November, 1941 (IF)

League Club	Source	Date Signed	Seasons Played	Apps	Subs	Gls
Darlington		08.61				
Brighton & H.A.	Berwick R.	10.63	63	3	-	1

HEALEY Daniel Kevin
Manchester, 22 October, 1953 (W)

League Club	Source	Date Signed	Seasons Played	Apps	Subs	Gls
Manchester U.	App	01.71				
Bolton W.	Tr	05.73				
Workington	Tr	07.74	74	13	4	2

HEALEY Jonathan Peter
Morecambe, 30 December, 1966 (M)

League Club	Source	Date Signed	Seasons Played	Apps	Subs	Gls
Oldham Ath.	YT	06.85				
Crewe Alex.	Alsager College	12.87	87	7	3	2

HEALEY Ronald
Manchester, 30 August, 1952 IR-2 (G)

League Club	Source	Date Signed	Seasons Played	Apps	Subs	Gls
Manchester C.	App	10.69	70-73	30	0	0
Coventry C.	L	12.71	71	3	0	0
Preston N.E.	L	12.73	73	6	0	0
Cardiff C.	Tr	03.74	73-81	216	0	0

HEALEY William Richard Ernest
Liverpool, 22 May, 1926 (FB)

League Club	Source	Date Signed	Seasons Played	Apps	Subs	Gls
Arsenal	Chorley	05.49				
Fulham	Tr	12.52	52	1	-	0
Hartlepool U.	Tr	08.55	55	6	-	0

HEALY Patrick (Felix) Joseph
Derry (NI), 27 September, 1955 NI-4 (M)

League Club	Source	Date Signed	Seasons Played	Apps	Subs	Gls
Port Vale	Finn Harps	10.78	78-79	40	1	2

HEANEY Anthony James
Plymouth, 9 May, 1940 E Yth (FB)

League Club	Source	Date Signed	Seasons Played	Apps	Subs	Gls
Southampton	Jnrs	06.58	60	1	-	0

HEANEY Neil Andrew
Middlesbrough, 3 November, 1971 E Yth/Eu21-6 (W)

League Club	Source	Date Signed	Seasons Played	Apps	Subs	Gls
Arsenal	YT	11.89	91-93	4	3	0
Hartlepool U.	L	01.91	90	2	1	0
Cambridge U.	L	01.92	91	9	4	2
Southampton	Tr	03.94	93-96	42	19	5
Manchester C.	Tr	11.96	96-97	13	5	1
Charlton Ath.	L	03.98	97	4	2	0

HEAP Stuart
Nelson, 7 February, 1965 (M)

League Club	Source	Date Signed	Seasons Played	Apps	Subs	Gls
Tranmere Rov. (N/C)	Clitheroe	03.85	84	0	3	0

HEARD Timothy **Patrick**
Hull, 17 March, 1960 E Yth (LB/M)

League Club	Source	Date Signed	Seasons Played	Apps	Subs	Gls
Everton	App	03.78	78-79	10	1	0
Aston Villa	Tr	10.79	79-82	20	4	2
Sheffield Wed.	Tr	01.83	82-84	22	3	3
Newcastle U.	Tr	09.84	84	34	0	2
Middlesbrough	Tr	08.85	85	25	0	2
Hull C.	Tr	03.86	85-87	79	1	5
Rotherham U.	Tr	07.88	88-89	41	3	7
Cardiff C.	Tr	08.90	90-91	45	1	4
Hull C. (N/C)	Tr	08.92	92	3	1	0

HEARN Frank Guy
Camden, 5 November, 1929 (IF)

League Club	Source	Date Signed	Seasons Played	Apps	Subs	Gls
Torquay U.		08.50				
Northampton T.	Tr	10.51				
Crystal Palace	Tr	06.54	54	8	-	1

HEARY Thomas Mark
Dublin, 14 February, 1979 IR Sch/IR Yth (M)

League Club	Source	Date Signed	Seasons Played	Apps	Subs	Gls
Huddersfield T.	YT	02.96	96-97	4	4	0

HEASLEGRAVE Samuel Edward
Smethwick, 1 October, 1916 Died 1975 (IR)

League Club	Source	Date Signed	Seasons Played	Apps	Subs	Gls
West Bromwich A.	Brierley Hill Alliance	10.34	36-38	49	-	16
Northampton T.	Tr	10.45	46-47	42	-	4

HEATH Adrian Paul
Stoke, 11 January, 1961 Eu21-8/E 'B' (F)

League Club	Source	Date Signed	Seasons Played	Apps	Subs	Gls
Stoke C.	App	01.79	78-81	94	1	16
Everton	Tr	01.82	81-88	206	20	71
Aston Villa	Espanol (Sp)	08.89	89	8	1	0
Manchester C.	Tr	02.90	89-91	58	17	4
Stoke C.	Tr	03.92	91	5	1	0
Burnley	Tr	08.92	92-95	109	6	29
Sheffield U.	Tr	12.95	95	0	4	0
Burnley (N/C)	Tr	03.96	96	1	4	0

League Club	Source	Date Signed	Seasons Played	Career Record Apps	Subs	Gls
HEATH Dennis John						
Chiswick, 28 September, 1934						(OR)
Brentford	Jnrs	09.52	54-60	123	-	20
HEATH Donald						
Stockton, 26 December, 1944						(W)
Middlesbrough	App	12.62				
Norwich C.	Tr	07.64	64-67	79	3	15
Swindon T.	Tr	09.67	67-69	82	6	2
Oldham Ath.	Tr	07.70	70-71	43	2	1
Peterborough U.	Tr	07.72	72	43	1	4
Hartlepool U.	Tr	07.73	73-74	36	1	2
HEATH Duncan Nigel						
Stoke, 23 October, 1961						(D)
Aston Villa	App	07.79				
Crewe Alex.	Tr	11.80	81	17	6	0
HEATH Herbert George						
Wolverhampton, 29 March, 1970						(CD)
Exeter C.	Walsall Wood	02.89	88	3	2	0
HEATH John						
Heywood, 5 June, 1936						(G)
Bury	Blackburn Rov. (Am)	09.56	56-61	8	-	0
Tranmere Rov.	Tr	01.62	61-63	58	-	0
Rochdale	Wigan Ath.	02.66	65	6	0	0
HEATH Michael						
Hull, 7 February, 1974						(G)
Tottenham H.	YT	05.92				
Scunthorpe U. (N/C)	Tr	12.93	93	1	1	0
HEATH Michael						
Hillingdon, 9 January, 1953						(IF)
Brentford (Am)	Walton & Hersham	04.71	70	1	0	0
HEATH Norman Harry						
Wolverhampton, 31 January, 1924 Died 1983						(G)
West Bromwich A.	Meadows B.C.	10.43	47-53	121	-	0
HEATH Philip Adrian						
Stoke, 24 November, 1964						(LW)
Stoke C.	App	10.82	82-87	144	12	17
Oxford U.	Tr	06.88	88-89	24	13	1
Cardiff C.	Tr	03.91	90	11	0	1
Aldershot	Tr	08.91				
HEATH Robert						
Stoke, 31 August, 1978						(M)
Stoke C.	YT	07.96	97	4	2	0
HEATH Seamus Martin James Paul						
Belfast, 6 December, 1961						(D/M)
Luton T.	Jnrs	04.79				
Lincoln C.	L	08.82	82	6	1	0
Wrexham	Tr	08.83	83	32	0	1
Tranmere Rov.	Tr	08.84	84	6	11	0
HEATH Stephen Dennis						
Hull, 15 November, 1977 E Yth						(CD)
Leeds U.	YT	11.94				
Carlisle U.	Tr	07.96	96	0	1	0
HEATH Richard **Terence**						
Leicester, 17 November, 1943						(M)
Leicester C.	App	11.61	62-63	8	-	2
Hull C.	Tr	05.64	64-67	27	6	1
Scunthorpe U.	Tr	03.68	67-72	174	2	49
Lincoln C.	Tr	02.73	72-73	17	0	1
HEATH William Henry Mansell						
Bournemouth, 15 April, 1934						(G)
Bournemouth	Jnrs	12.51	56-57	34	-	0
Lincoln C.	Tr	11.58	58-61	84	-	0
HEATH William John						
Stepney, 26 June, 1920 Died 1994						(FB)
Queens Park R.		09.45	46-52	96	-	3
HEATHCOCK Adrian						
Dudley, 26 January, 1975						(W)
Hereford U.	YT	●	92	1	1	0
HEATHCOTE Michael						
Kelloe (Dm), 10 September, 1965						(CD)
Sunderland	Spennymoor U.	08.87	87-89	6	3	0
Halifax T.	L	12.87	87	7	0	1
York C.	L	01.90	89	3	0	0
Shrewsbury T.	Tr	07.90	90-91	43	1	6
Cambridge U.	Tr	09.91	91-94	123	5	13
Plymouth Arg.	Tr	07.95	95-97	121	1	9
HEATHCOTE Peter George Samuel						
Leicester, 13 November, 1932						(G)
Southend U.	Jnrs	11.51	51	2	-	0
HEATHCOTE Wilfred						
Hemsworth, 29 June, 1911 Died 1991						(CF)
Queens Park R.		10.43	46	5	-	1
Millwall	Tr	12.46	46	8	-	2
HEATHER Leslie **John**						
Winchcombe (Glos), 25 April, 1933						(IF)
Mansfield T.	Belper T.	08.52	53	1	-	0
HEATON James **Michael**						
Sheffield, 15 January, 1947 Died 1995						(FB)
Sheffield U.	App	11.64	66-70	31	2	0
Blackburn Rov.	Tr	10.71	71-75	168	2	1
HEATON Paul John						
Hyde, 24 January, 1961						(M)
Oldham Ath.	App	01.79	77-83	124	12	28
Rochdale	Tr	03.84	83-85	85	4	9
HEATON William Henry						
Leeds, 26 August, 1918 Died 1990						(OL)
Leeds U.	Whitkirk	12.37	46-48	59	-	6
Southampton	Tr	02.49	48	15	-	0
Rochdale	Tr	11.50	50	5	-	0
HEAVISIDE John						
Ferryhill, 7 October, 1943						(LB)
Darlington (Am)	Bishops Middleham	08.63	63	2	-	0
HEBBERD Trevor Neal						
Winchester, 19 June, 1958						(M)
Southampton	App	06.76	76-81	69	28	8
Bolton W.	L	09.81	81	6	0	0
Leicester C.	L	11.81	81	4	0	1
Oxford U.	Tr	03.82	81-87	260	0	37
Derby Co.	Tr	08.88	88-90	70	11	10
Portsmouth (N/C)	Tr	10.91	91	1	3	0
Chesterfield	Tr	11.91	91-93	67	7	1
Lincoln C.	Tr	07.94	94	20	5	0
HEBDITCH Alan						
Wigan, 11 October, 1961						(D)
Bradford C.	Leeds U. (Jnrs)	08.80	80	2	0	0
HECKINBOTTOM Paul						
Barnsley, 17 July, 1977						(LB)
Sunderland	Manchester U. (YT)	07.95				
Scarborough	L	10.97	97	28	1	0
HECKMAN Ronald Ernest						
Peckham, 23 November, 1929 Died 1990 E Amat						(OL)
Leyton Orient	Bromley	07.55	55-57	87	-	38
Millwall	Tr	11.57	57-59	92	-	21
Crystal Palace	Tr	07.60	60-62	84	-	25
HECTOR Kevin James						
Leeds, 2 November, 1944 EF Lge/E-2						(F)
Bradford P.A.	Jnrs	07.62	62-66	176	0	113
Derby Co.	Tr	09.66	66-77	426	4	147
Derby Co.	Vancouver (Can)	10.80	80-81	52	4	8
HEDLEY Graeme						
Easington (Dm), 1 March, 1957						(M)
Middlesbrough	App	03.75	76-81	36	14	6
Sheffield Wed.	L	02.78	77	6	0	1
Darlington	L	03.79	78	14	0	1
York C.	L	10.81	81	5	0	1
Hartlepool U.	Horden Colly	08.84	84	32	-	9
HEDLEY John (Jack) Robert						
Willington Quay, 11 December, 1923 Died 1985						(FB)
Everton	North Shields	04.45	47-49	54	-	0
Sunderland	Tr	08.50	50-58	269	-	0
Gateshead	Tr	07.59	59	11	-	0
HEDMAN Magnus Carl						
Stockholm, Sweden, 19 March, 1973 Swedish Int						(G)
Coventry C.	A.I.K. Solna (Swe)	07.97	97	14	0	0
HEDMAN Rudolph (Rudi) Gideon						
Lambeth, 16 November, 1964						(D)
Colchester U.		02.84	83-88	166	10	10

League Club	Source	Date Signed	Seasons Played	Career Record Apps	Subs	Gls
Crystal Palace	Tr	12.88	88-91	10	11	0
Leyton Orient	L	12.89	89	5	0	0
HEDWORTH Christopher						
Wallsend, 5 January, 1964						(D)
Newcastle U.	App	01.82	82-85	8	1	0
Barnsley	Tr	08.86	86-87	19	6	0
Halifax T.	Tr	08.88	88-89	38	0	0
Blackpool	Tr	09.90	90-91	24	0	0
HEELEY David **Mark**						
Peterborough, 8 September, 1959						(W)
Peterborough U.	App	11.76	75-76	12	5	3
Arsenal	Tr	09.77	77-78	9	6	1
Northampton T.	Tr	03.80	79-82	84	8	5
HEENAN Thomas						
Glasgow, 16 June, 1932						(IF)
Bradford P.A.	Stirling A.	05.58	58	5	-	1
HEEPS James Andrew						
Luton, 16 May, 1971						(G)
Swansea C.	YT	07.89	89	1	0	0
HEESOM Darren Lea						
Warrington, 8 May, 1968						(LB)
Burnley	App	12.85	85-86	36	2	1
HEFFER Paul Victor						
West Ham, 21 December, 1947						(CH)
West Ham U.	Jnrs	08.65	66-71	11	4	0
HEFFER Robert William						
Mildenhall, 9 November, 1935						(W)
Norwich C.	R.A.F. St Faiths	04.56	56	2	-	1
HEFFERNAN Thomas Patrick						
Dublin, 30 April, 1955						(RB)
Tottenham H.	Dunleary Celtic	10.77				
Bournemouth	Tr	05.79	79-82	152	2	21
Sheffield U.	Tr	08.83	83-84	82	0	5
Bournemouth	Tr	06.85	85-87	58	5	6
HEFFRON Charles Alphonsus						
Belfast, 13 August, 1927						(G)
Bradford P.A.	Belfast Celtic	06.49	51-52	25	-	0
HEGAN Daniel						
Coatbridge, 14 June, 1943 NI-7						(M)
Sunderland	Albion Rov.	09.61				
Ipswich T.	Tr	07.63	63-68	207	0	34
West Bromwich A.	Tr	05.69	69	13	1	2
Wolverhampton W.	Tr	05.70	70-73	49	4	6
Sunderland	Tr	11.73	73	3	3	0
HEGARTY Kevin Michael						
Edinburgh, 30 July, 1950						(F)
Carlisle U.	Hearts	09.71	71	1	6	0
HEGGARTY James Patrick						
Larne (NI), 4 August, 1965						(CD)
Brighton & H.A.	Larne T.	09.84				
Burnley	Tr	08.85	85	33	3	1
HEGGIE William Campbell						
Perth, 7 June, 1927						(CF)
New Brighton	Jeanfield Swifts	02.51	50	10	-	5
Leeds U.	Tr	06.51				
Wrexham	Tr	08.52	52-54	33	-	13
Accrington St.	Winsford U.	02.55	54	1	-	0
HEGGS Carl Sydney						
Leicester, 11 October, 1970						(LW)
West Bromwich A.	Leicester U.	08.91	91-94	13	27	3
Bristol Rov.	L	01.95	94	2	3	1
Swansea C.	Tr	07.95	95-96	33	13	7
Northampton T.	Tr	07.97	97	21	12	4
HEGINBOTHAM Brian						
Hyde, 3 October, 1937						(FB)
Stockport Co.	Jnrs	10.54	58-59	11	-	0
HEIDENSTROM Bjorn						
Norway, 15 January, 1968						(M)
Leyton Orient (L)	Odd Grenland (Nor)	12.96	96	3	1	0
HEIGHWAY Stephen Derek						
Dublin, 25 November, 1947 IR-34						(W)
Liverpool	Skelmersdale U.	05.70	70-80	312	17	50

League Club	Source	Date Signed	Seasons Played	Career Record Apps	Subs	Gls
HEINOLA Antti Juhani						
Helsinki, Finland, 20 March, 1973 Finnish Int						(LWB)
Queens Park R.	Heracles (Neth)	01.98	97	0	10	0
HELDER Glenn						
Netherlands, 28 October, 1968 Dutch Int						(F)
Arsenal	Vitesse Arnhem (Neth)	02.95	94-96	27	12	1
HELLAWELL John Rodney						
Keighley, 20 December, 1943						(IF)
Bradford C.	Salts	06.63	62-64	48	-	13
Rotherham U.	Tr	01.65	64-65	9	1	3
Darlington	Tr	07.66	66	6	3	1
Bradford P.A.		10.68	68	1	0	0
HELLAWELL Michael Stephen						
Keighley, 30 June, 1938 E-2						(OR)
Queens Park R.	Salts	08.55	55-56	45	-	7
Birmingham C.	Tr	05.57	57-64	178	-	30
Sunderland	Tr	01.65	64-66	43	1	2
Huddersfield T.	Tr	09.66	66-67	45	1	1
Peterborough U.	Tr	12.68	68	9	0	0
HELLEWELL Keith						
Barnsley, 1 April, 1944						(G)
Doncaster Rov.	Jnrs	05.61	62-63	12	-	0
HELLIN Anthony						
Merthyr Tydfil, 26 September, 1944 W Sch						(LB)
Swindon T.	App	06.62				
Torquay U.	Tr	07.64	64-65	29	0	1
HELLIN Matthew Karl						
Merthyr Tydfil, 12 September, 1966						(D)
Aston Villa	App	09.84				
Wolverhampton W.	Tr	08.86	86	1	0	0
HELLINGS Dennis Raymond						
Lincoln, 9 December, 1923 Died 1996						(IF)
Lincoln C.	Ransome & Marles	12.45	46	3	-	0
HELLIWELL David						
Blackburn, 28 March, 1948						(W)
Blackburn Rov.	App	05.66	66-68	15	0	1
Lincoln C.	Tr	05.69	69	11	2	1
Workington	Tr	07.70	70-75	184	13	20
Rochdale	Tr	07.76	76	20	11	3
HELLIWELL Ian						
Rotherham, 7 November, 1962						(F)
York C.	Matlock T.	10.87	87-90	158	2	40
Scunthorpe U.	Tr	08.91	91-92	78	2	22
Rotherham U.	Tr	08.93	93-94	47	5	4
Stockport Co.	Tr	01.95	94-95	35	4	13
Burnley	Tr	02.96	95	3	1	0
Mansfield T.	L	09.96	96	4	1	1
Chester C.	L	10.96	96	8	1	1
Doncaster Rov.	L	11.97	97	8	0	1
HEMMERMAN Jeffrey Lawrence						
Hull, 25 February, 1955						(F)
Hull C.	App	03.73	73-76	45	14	10
Scunthorpe U.	L	09.75	75	4	1	1
Port Vale	Tr	06.77	77	13	2	5
Portsmouth	Tr	07.78	78-81	114	9	40
Cardiff C.	Tr	07.82	82-83	54	1	22
HEMMING Christopher Andrew John						
Stoke, 13 April, 1966						(CD)
Stoke C.	Jnrs	04.84	83-88	85	8	2
Wigan Ath.	L	01.89	88	4	0	0
Hereford U.	Tr	08.89	89-90	39	2	3
HEMMINGS Anthony George						
Burton, 21 September, 1967 E Semi Pro						(LW)
Wycombe W.	Northwich Vic.	09.93	93-95	28	21	12
HEMSLEY Edward (Ted) John Orton						
Stoke, 1 September, 1943						(D)
Shrewsbury T.	Jnrs	07.61	60-68	234	1	21
Sheffield U.	Tr	08.68	68-76	247	0	8
Doncaster Rov.	Tr	07.77	77-78	32	0	1
HEMSTEAD Derek William						
Scunthorpe, 22 May, 1943						(FB)
Scunthorpe U.	Jnrs	05.60	60-68	248	0	2
Carlisle U.	Tr	07.69	69-72	96	1	1

HEMSTOCK Brian
Goldthorpe, 9 February, 1949 (F)

League Club	Source	Date Signed	Seasons Played	Apps	Subs	Gls
Barnsley	Jnrs	12.66	66	1	0	0
Bradford P.A.	Tr	07.68	68	4	0	0

HENCHER Kenneth Ernest Edward
Romford, 2 February, 1928 (CH)

League Club	Source	Date Signed	Seasons Played	Apps	Subs	Gls
Millwall		12.49	49-55	48	-	0

HENCHER Nicholas
Wrexham, 24 August, 1961 (W)

League Club	Source	Date Signed	Seasons Played	Apps	Subs	Gls
Wrexham (N/C)	Lex XI	08.85	85-87	26	6	5

HENCHOZ Stephane
Billens, Switzerland, 7 September, 1974 Swiss Int (D)

League Club	Source	Date Signed	Seasons Played	Apps	Subs	Gls
Blackburn Rov.	Hamburg (Ger)	07.97	97	36	0	0

HENDERSON Anthony Joseph
Newcastle, 14 January, 1954 (CH)

League Club	Source	Date Signed	Seasons Played	Apps	Subs	Gls
Rotherham U.	App	01.72	73	5	1	0

HENDERSON Brian Charles
Allendale (Nd), 12 June, 1930 (FB)

League Club	Source	Date Signed	Seasons Played	Apps	Subs	Gls
Carlisle U.		05.50				
Darlington	Tr	07.52	52-63	422	-	3

HENDERSON Damian Michael
Leeds, 12 May, 1973 (F)

League Club	Source	Date Signed	Seasons Played	Apps	Subs	Gls
Leeds U.	YT	07.91				
Scarborough	Tr	08.93	93	17	0	5
Scunthorpe U.	Tr	12.93	93-94	31	6	4
Hereford U.	L	01.95	94	5	0	0
Hartlepool U.	Tr	03.95	94-95	45	3	6

HENDERSON George
Hartlepool, 7 March, 1946 (CF)

League Club	Source	Date Signed	Seasons Played	Apps	Subs	Gls
Hartlepool U. (Am)	Bishop Auckland	11.70	70	1	0	0

HENDERSON John
Johnshaven, 22 September, 1941 (IF)

League Club	Source	Date Signed	Seasons Played	Apps	Subs	Gls
Charlton Ath.	Montrose Vic.	06.59	62	4	-	1
Exeter C.	Tr	11.62	62-63	46	-	14
Doncaster Rov.	Tr	07.64	64	10	-	0
Chesterfield	Tr	07.65	65	28	0	3

HENDERSON John (Jackie) Gillespie
Glasgow, 17 January, 1932 S 'B'/S-7 (CF)

League Club	Source	Date Signed	Seasons Played	Apps	Subs	Gls
Portsmouth	Jnrs	01.49	51-57	217	-	70
Wolverhampton W.	Tr	03.58	57-58	9	-	3
Arsenal	Tr	10.58	58-61	103	-	29
Fulham	Tr	01.62	61-63	45	-	7

HENDERSON John Swinton Pryde
Glasgow, 13 October, 1923 (IF)

League Club	Source	Date Signed	Seasons Played	Apps	Subs	Gls
Rotherham U.	Third Lanark	11.53	53-54	47	-	7
Leeds U.	Tr	03.55	54-55	15	-	4

HENDERSON Joseph
Cleland, 21 December, 1924 (G)

League Club	Source	Date Signed	Seasons Played	Apps	Subs	Gls
Northampton T.	Albion Rov.	05.49				
Accrington St.	Stenhousemuir	07.53	53	14	-	0

HENDERSON Kevin Malcolm
Ashington, 8 June, 1974 (F)

League Club	Source	Date Signed	Seasons Played	Apps	Subs	Gls
Burnley	Morpeth T.	12.97	97	0	7	0

HENDERSON William Martin Melville
Kirkcaldy, 3 May, 1956 (F)

League Club	Source	Date Signed	Seasons Played	Apps	Subs	Gls
Leicester C.	Philadelphia (USA)	10.78	78-80	79	12	12
Chesterfield	Tr	09.81	81-83	87	0	23
Port Vale	Tr	10.83	83	27	0	7

HENDERSON Michael Robert
Newcastle, 31 March, 1956 (RB/M)

League Club	Source	Date Signed	Seasons Played	Apps	Subs	Gls
Sunderland	App	03.74	75-78	81	3	2
Watford	Tr	11.79	79-81	50	1	0
Cardiff C.	Tr	03.82	81	11	0	0
Sheffield U.	Tr	08.82	82-84	65	2	0
Chesterfield	Tr	01.85	84-88	135	1	10

HENDERSON Peter
Berwick, 29 September, 1952 (W)

League Club	Source	Date Signed	Seasons Played	Apps	Subs	Gls
Chester C.	Witton A.	12.78	78-79	59	5	10
Gillingham	Tr	07.80	80	6	1	3
Crewe Alex.	L	09.81	81	6	1	0
Chester C.	Tr	12.81	81	28	0	5

HENDERSON Raymond
Wallsend, 31 March, 1937 (OR)

League Club	Source	Date Signed	Seasons Played	Apps	Subs	Gls
Middlesbrough	Ashington	05.57	57-60	9	-	5
Hull C.	Tr	06.61	61-67	226	3	54
Reading	Tr	10.68	68	5	0	0

HENDERSON Stanley
Barrow, 15 October, 1925 Died 1980 (OR)

League Club	Source	Date Signed	Seasons Played	Apps	Subs	Gls
Barrow	Holker C.O.B.	06.46	46-47	25	-	3

HENDERSON James Stewart
Bridge of Allan, 5 June, 1947 S Sch (FB)

League Club	Source	Date Signed	Seasons Played	Apps	Subs	Gls
Chelsea	Jnrs	07.64				
Brighton & H.A.	Tr	07.65	65-72	198	0	1
Reading	Tr	06.73	73-82	159	7	6

HENDERSON Thomas
Consett, 6 April, 1949 (W)

League Club	Source	Date Signed	Seasons Played	Apps	Subs	Gls
Bradford P.A.	Tow Law T.	02.69	68-69	22	0	3
York C.	Tr	10.70	70-71	63	1	7

HENDERSON Thomas
Burnley, 1 October, 1927 (OR)

League Club	Source	Date Signed	Seasons Played	Apps	Subs	Gls
Burnley	Jnrs	08.45	48	2	-	0

HENDERSON Thomas Wedlock
Larkhall, 25 July, 1943 (W)

League Club	Source	Date Signed	Seasons Played	Apps	Subs	Gls
Leeds U.	St Mirren	11.62	62-64	24	-	2
Bury	Tr	06.65	65	7	0	1
Swindon T.	Tr	01.66	65	11	0	3
Stockport Co.	Tr	07.66	66	17	2	4

HENDERSON William
Baillieston, 24 January, 1944 S Sch/Su23-2/SF Lge/S-29 (W)

League Club	Source	Date Signed	Seasons Played	Apps	Subs	Gls
Sheffield Wed.	Glasgow Rangers	07.72	72-73	42	6	5

HENDERSON William John
Closeburn, 21 February, 1920 Died 1965 (G)

League Club	Source	Date Signed	Seasons Played	Apps	Subs	Gls
Rochdale	Queen of South	07.46	46	17	-	0
Southport	Tr	06.47	47	20	-	0

HENDON Ian Michael
Ilford, 5 December, 1971 E Yth/Eu21-7 (D)

League Club	Source	Date Signed	Seasons Played	Apps	Subs	Gls
Tottenham H.	YT	12.89	90-91	0	4	0
Portsmouth	L	01.92	91	1	3	0
Leyton Orient	L	03.92	91	5	1	0
Barnsley	L	03.93	92	6	0	0
Leyton Orient	Tr	08.93	93-96	130	1	5
Birmingham C.	L	03.95	94	4	0	0
Notts Co.	Tr	02.97	96-97	50	0	0

HENDRIE John Grattan
Lennoxtown, 24 October, 1963 S Yth (RW)

League Club	Source	Date Signed	Seasons Played	Apps	Subs	Gls
Coventry C.	App	05.81	81-83	15	6	2
Hereford U.	L	01.84	83	6	0	0
Bradford C.	Tr	06.84	84-87	173	0	46
Newcastle U.	Tr	06.88	88	34	0	4
Leeds U.	Tr	06.89	89	22	5	5
Middlesbrough	Tr	06.90	90-95	181	11	44
Barnsley	Tr	10.96	96-97	43	13	6

HENDRIE Lee Andrew
Birmingham, 18 May, 1977 E Yth/Eu21-2/E 'B' (M)

League Club	Source	Date Signed	Seasons Played	Apps	Subs	Gls
Aston Villa	YT	05.94	95-97	15	9	3

HENDRIE Paul
Glasgow, 27 March, 1954 (M)

League Club	Source	Date Signed	Seasons Played	Apps	Subs	Gls
Birmingham C.	Kirkintilloch Rob Roy	03.72	72-75	19	3	1
Bristol Rov.	Portland (USA)	09.77	77-78	17	13	1
Halifax T.	Tr	07.79	79-83	187	0	11
Stockport Co.	Tr	08.84	84-88	114	7	5

HENDRY Edward Colin James
Keith, 7 December, 1965 S 'B'/S-35 (CD)

League Club	Source	Date Signed	Seasons Played	Apps	Subs	Gls
Blackburn Rov.	Dundee	03.87	86-89	99	3	22
Manchester C.	Tr	11.89	89-91	57	6	5
Blackburn Rov.	Tr	11.91	91-97	229	5	12

HENDRY Ian
Glasgow, 19 October, 1959 (M)

League Club	Source	Date Signed	Seasons Played	Apps	Subs	Gls
Aston Villa	App	09.77				
Hereford U.	Tr	02.79	78-79	21	0	0

HENDRY John
Glasgow, 6 January, 1970 Su21-1 (F)

League Club	Source	Date Signed	Seasons Played	Apps	Subs	Gls
Tottenham H.	Dundee	07.90	90-93	5	12	5
Charlton Ath.	L	02.92	91	1	4	1
Swansea C.	L	10.94	94	8	0	2

HENLEY Leslie Donald
Lambeth, 26 September, 1922 Died 1996 E Sch (IF)

League Club	Source	Date Signed	Seasons Played	Apps	Subs	Gls
Arsenal	Jnrs	09.40				
Reading	Tr	12.46	46-52	181	-	28

HENNESSEY William **Terence**
Llay, 1 September, 1942 W Sch/Wu23-6/W-39 (CD)

League Club	Source	Date Signed	Seasons Played	Apps	Subs	Gls
Birmingham C.	Jnrs	09.59	60-65	178	0	3
Nottingham F.	Tr	11.65	65-69	159	0	5
Derby Co.	Tr	02.70	69-72	62	1	4

HENNIGAN Michael
Rotherham, 20 December, 1942 (CH)

League Club	Source	Date Signed	Seasons Played	Apps	Subs	Gls
Sheffield Wed.	Rotherham U. (Am)	03.61				
Southampton	Tr	06.62	63	3	-	0
Brighton & H.A.	Tr	07.64	64	4	-	0

HENNIN Derek
Prescot, 28 December, 1931 Died 1989 E Yth (WH)

League Club	Source	Date Signed	Seasons Played	Apps	Subs	Gls
Bolton W.	Prescot Cables	06.49	53-60	164	-	8
Chester C.	Tr	02.61	60-61	54	-	4

HENNINGS Roberts Iva
Glyncorrwg, 30 December, 1931 (F)

League Club	Source	Date Signed	Seasons Played	Apps	Subs	Gls
Swansea C.		10.49	55-56	10	-	1

HENRY Anthony
Houghton-le-Spring, 26 November, 1957 (M)

League Club	Source	Date Signed	Seasons Played	Apps	Subs	Gls
Manchester C.	App	12.74	76-81	68	11	6
Bolton W.	Tr	09.81	81-82	70	0	22
Oldham Ath.	Tr	03.83	82-87	185	5	25
Stoke C.	Tr	11.87	87-88	59	3	11
Shrewsbury T.	Mazda (Jap)	08.91	91	39	1	7

HENRY Charles Anthony
Acton, 13 February, 1962 (M)

League Club	Source	Date Signed	Seasons Played	Apps	Subs	Gls
Swindon T.	App	02.80	80-88	200	23	26
Torquay U.	L	02.87	86	6	0	1
Northampton T.	L	03.87	86	4	0	1
Aldershot	Tr	08.89	89-90	81	0	18

HENRY Gerald Robert
Hemsworth, 5 October, 1920 Died 1979 (IF)

League Club	Source	Date Signed	Seasons Played	Apps	Subs	Gls
Leeds U.	Outwood Stormcocks	10.37	38-47	44	-	4
Bradford P.A.	Tr	11.47	47-49	79	-	31
Sheffield Wed.	Tr	02.50	49-51	40	-	7
Halifax T.	Tr	12.51	51-52	24	-	3

HENRY Gordon
Troon, 9 October, 1930 (CH/CF)

League Club	Source	Date Signed	Seasons Played	Apps	Subs	Gls
Aldershot	St Mirren	06.56	56-63	175	-	15

HENRY Liburd Algernon
Dominica (WI), 29 August, 1967 (F)

League Club	Source	Date Signed	Seasons Played	Apps	Subs	Gls
Watford	Leytonstone & Ilford	11.87	88-89	8	2	1
Halifax T.	L	09.88	88	1	4	0
Maidstone U.	Tr	06.90	90-91	61	6	9
Gillingham	Tr	06.92	92-93	37	5	2
Peterborough U.	Tr	08.94	94	22	10	7

HENRY Nicholas Ian
Liverpool, 21 February, 1969 (M)

League Club	Source	Date Signed	Seasons Played	Apps	Subs	Gls
Oldham Ath.	YT	06.87	87-96	264	9	19
Sheffield U.	Tr	02.97	96-97	10	0	0

HENRY Ronald Patrick
Shoreditch, 17 August, 1934 E-1 (LB)

League Club	Source	Date Signed	Seasons Played	Apps	Subs	Gls
Tottenham H.	Redbourne	03.52	54-65	247	0	1

HENSHAW Gary
Leeds, 18 February, 1965 (W)

League Club	Source	Date Signed	Seasons Played	Apps	Subs	Gls
Grimsby T.	App	02.83	83-86	46	4	9
Bolton W.	Tr	06.87	87-90	49	21	4
Rochdale	L	03.90	89	8	1	1

HENSON Anthony Harold
Dronfield, 15 October, 1960 (M)

League Club	Source	Date Signed	Seasons Played	Apps	Subs	Gls
Chesterfield	Alfreton T.	11.81	81-82	26	2	0

HENSON Leonard
Hull, 6 August, 1921 (WH)

League Club	Source	Date Signed	Seasons Played	Apps	Subs	Gls
Gillingham		05.50	50	8	-	0

HENSON Philip Michael
Manchester, 30 March, 1953 (M)

League Club	Source	Date Signed	Seasons Played	Apps	Subs	Gls
Manchester C.	App	07.70	71-74	12	4	0
Swansea C.	L	07.72	72	1	0	0
Sheffield Wed.	Tr	02.75	74-76	65	8	9
Stockport Co.	Sparta Rotterdam (Neth)	09.78	78-79	65	2	13
Rotherham U.	Tr	02.80	79-83	87	5	7

HENWOOD Rodney Charles
Portsmouth, 27 November, 1931 (OL)

League Club	Source	Date Signed	Seasons Played	Apps	Subs	Gls
Portsmouth	Kingston B.C.	05.50	53	2	-	0

HEPBURN John
Paisley, 10 March, 1921 (OR)

League Club	Source	Date Signed	Seasons Played	Apps	Subs	Gls
Workington	Morton	08.51	51	1	-	0

HEPPELL George
Hartlepool, 2 September, 1916 Died 1993 (G)

League Club	Source	Date Signed	Seasons Played	Apps	Subs	Gls
Wolverhampton W.		09.36				
Port Vale	Tr	05.37	37-51	193	-	0

HEPPLE Gordon
Sunderland, 16 September, 1925 Died 1980 (FB)

League Club	Source	Date Signed	Seasons Played	Apps	Subs	Gls
Middlesbrough	North Sands	07.45	46-53	41	-	0
Norwich C.	Tr	06.54	54	5	-	0

HEPPLE John Andrew
Middlesbrough, 12 March, 1970 (F)

League Club	Source	Date Signed	Seasons Played	Apps	Subs	Gls
Sunderland	YT	07.87				
Hartlepool U.	L	03.89	88	1	1	0

HEPPLEWHITE George
Edmondsley (Dm), 5 September, 1919 Died 1989 (CH)

League Club	Source	Date Signed	Seasons Played	Apps	Subs	Gls
Huddersfield T.	Horden Colly	05.39	46-50	156	-	3
Preston N.E.	Tr	03.51				
Bradford C.	Tr	07.53	53-54	57	-	2

HEPPLEWHITE Wilson
Washington, 11 June, 1946 (OL)

League Club	Source	Date Signed	Seasons Played	Apps	Subs	Gls
Carlisle U.	Crook T.	03.65	65	3	0	0
Hartlepool U.	Tr	07.67	67-68	50	2	2

HEPPOLETTE Richard (Ricky) Alfred William
India, 8 April, 1949 (M)

League Club	Source	Date Signed	Seasons Played	Apps	Subs	Gls
Preston N.E.	App	09.64	67-72	149	5	13
Leyton Orient	Tr	12.72	72-76	113	0	10
Crystal Palace	Tr	10.76	76	13	2	0
Chesterfield	Tr	02.77	76-78	46	1	3
Peterborough U.	Tr	08.79	79	5	0	0

HEPTON Stanley
Leeds, 3 December, 1932 (WH/IF)

League Club	Source	Date Signed	Seasons Played	Apps	Subs	Gls
Blackpool	Ashley Road	03.50	52-56	7	-	3
Huddersfield T.	Tr	08.57	57-58	6	-	1
Bury	Tr	06.59	59	14	-	3
Rochdale	Tr	07.60	60-63	149	-	21
Southport	Tr	07.64	64	22	-	2

HEPWORTH Maurice
Hexham, 6 September, 1953 (FB)

League Club	Source	Date Signed	Seasons Played	Apps	Subs	Gls
Sunderland	App	09.70	70	2	0	0
Darlington	L	01.75	74	4	0	0

HEPWORTH Ronald
Barnsley, 25 January, 1919 (FB)

League Club	Source	Date Signed	Seasons Played	Apps	Subs	Gls
Chesterfield		05.36				
Bradford P.A.	Tr	05.39	46-50	101	-	0

HERBERT Craig Justin
Coventry, 9 November, 1975 (CD)

League Club	Source	Date Signed	Seasons Played	Apps	Subs	Gls
West Bromwich A.	Torquay U. (YT)	03.94	94	8	0	0
Shrewsbury T.	Tr	07.97	97	23	1	0

HERBERT David Ronald
Sheffield, 23 January, 1956 (F)

League Club	Source	Date Signed	Seasons Played	Apps	Subs	Gls
Sheffield Wed.	App	01.74	74-75	12	5	5

HERBERT Frank
Stocksbridge, 29 June, 1916 Died 1972 (RH)

League Club	Source	Date Signed	Seasons Played	Apps	Subs	Gls
Sheffield Wed.		05.38				
Bury	Tr	10.45				
Oldham Ath.	Tr	06.46	46	4	-	0

HERBERT Rikki Lloyd
New Zealand, 10 April, 1961 New Zealand Int (CD)

League Club	Source	Date Signed	Seasons Played	Apps	Subs	Gls
Wolverhampton W.	Sydney Olympic (Aus)	10.84	84-85	44	1	0

HERBERT Robert
Glasgow, 21 November, 1925 (WH)

League Club	Source	Date Signed	Seasons Played	Apps	Subs	Gls
Doncaster Rov.	Blantyre Vic.	06.50	50-55	108	-	15

HERBERT William **Stanley**
Whitehaven, 29 August, 1946 (IF)

League Club	Source	Date Signed	Seasons Played	Apps	Subs	Gls
Workington (Am)	Jnrs	09.66	66	1	0	0

League Club	Source	Date Signed	Seasons Played	Apps	Subs	Gls
HERBERT Trevor Ernest						
Reading, 3 June, 1929						(CF)
Leyton Orient		08.49				
Crystal Palace	Tr	07.50	50	8	-	2
HERD Alexander						
Bowhill, 8 November, 1911 Died 1982 SF Lge						(IF)
Manchester C.	Hamilton Academical	02.33	32-47	257	-	107
Stockport Co.	Tr	03.48	47-51	111	-	35
HERD David George						
Hamilton, 15 April, 1934 S-5						(CF)
Stockport Co.	Jnrs	04.51	50-53	15	-	6
Arsenal	Tr	08.54	54-60	166	-	97
Manchester U.	Tr	07.61	61-67	201	1	114
Stoke C.	Tr	07.68	68-69	39	5	11
HERD George						
Gartcosh, 6 May, 1936 Su23-2/SF Lge/S-5						(IF)
Sunderland	Clyde	04.61	60-68	275	3	47
Hartlepool U.	Tr	06.70	70	10	5	0
HERD Stuart						
Stone, 25 February, 1974						(M)
Torquay U. (N/C)	Rossington Main	10.92	92	5	2	0
HERITAGE Peter Mark						
Bexhill, 8 November, 1960						(F)
Gillingham	Hythe T.	08.89	89-90	42	15	11
Hereford U.	Tr	02.91	90-91	55	2	9
Doncaster Rov.	Tr	07.92	92	25	6	2
HERNON James						
Cleland, 6 December, 1924						(IF)
Leicester C.	Mossvale Y.M.C.A.	04.42	46-47	31	-	7
Bolton W.	Tr	09.48	48-50	43	-	2
Grimsby T.	Tr	08.51	51-53	91	-	23
Watford	Tr	07.54	54-55	43	-	10
HEROD Dennis John						
Stoke, 27 October, 1923						(G)
Stoke C.	Jnrs	01.41	46-52	191	-	1
Stockport Co.	Tr	07.53	53	33	-	0
HERON Brian						
Glasgow, 19 June, 1948						(W)
Oxford U.	Dumbarton	07.74	74-76	40	3	8
Scunthorpe U.	Tr	07.77	77	20	5	1
HERON Thomas Russell Ferrie						
Irvine, 31 March, 1936						(LB)
Manchester U.	Portadown	03.58	57-60	3	-	0
York C.	Tr	05.61	61-65	192	0	6
HERON William Bolton						
Washington, 29 March, 1932						(IF)
Gateshead		02.55	54-56	21	-	1
HERRERA Roberto						
Torquay, 12 June, 1970						(FB)
Queens Park R.	YT	02.88	88-90	4	2	0
Torquay U.	L	03.92	91	11	0	0
Torquay U.	L	10.92	92	5	0	0
Fulham	Tr	10.93	93-97	143	2	1
HERRING David **Harry**						
Hartlepool, 4 January, 1939						(F)
Hartlepool U.	Caledonians	08.58	58	2	-	0
HERRING Paul John						
Hyde, 1 July, 1973						(M)
Rochdale	YT	07.91	90	0	1	0
HERRINGTON Eric						
Rotherham, 30 October, 1943						(CH)
Doncaster Rov.	Jnrs	01.61	61	1	-	0
HERRIOT James						
Airdrie, 20 December, 1939 SF Lge/S-8						(G)
Birmingham C.	Dunfermline Ath.	05.65	65-69	181	0	0
Mansfield T.	L	11.70	70	5	0	0
HERRITTY Alan Michael						
Newport, 24 October, 1941 W Sch						(FB)
Newport Co.	Jnrs	12.58	59-61	28	-	0
HERRITTY William Raymond						
Newport, 2 September, 1938						(IR)
Newport Co.	Jnrs	05.57	56-62	62	-	12

League Club	Source	Date Signed	Seasons Played	Apps	Subs	Gls
HERRON Alan						
Ashington, 6 October, 1932						(CH)
Blackburn Rov.	Newcastle U. (Am)	08.50	55-56	4	-	0
HERRON John						
Widdrington (Nd), 2 March, 1938						(F)
Leeds U.		10.56				
Gateshead	Tr	06.57	57-58	8	-	0
HESELTINE George Victor						
Wolverhampton, 25 March, 1926						(IF)
Walsall	Hednesford T.	02.49	48-49	8	-	0
HESELTINE Wayne Alan						
Bradford, 3 December, 1969						(FB)
Manchester U.	YT	12.87				
Oldham Ath.	Tr	12.89	89	1	0	0
Bradford C.	Tr	08.92	92-93	51	3	1
HESFORD Iain						
Zambia, 4 March, 1960 E Yth/Eu21-7						(G)
Blackpool	App	08.77	77-82	202	0	0
Sheffield Wed.	Tr	08.83				
Fulham	L	01.85	84	3	0	0
Notts Co.	L	11.85	85	10	0	0
Sunderland	Tr	08.86	86-88	97	0	0
Hull C.	Tr	12.88	88-90	91	0	0
Maidstone U.	Tr	08.91	91	42	0	1
HESFORD Robert Taylor						
Bolton, 13 April, 1916 Died 1982						(G)
Huddersfield T.	South Shore	09.33	34-49	203	-	0
HESKEY Emile William Ivanhoe						
Leicester, 11 January, 1978 E Yth/Eu21-11/E 'B'						(CF)
Leicester C.	YT	10.95	94-97	91	10	27
HESLOP Brian						
Carlisle, 4 August, 1947						(D)
Carlisle U.	App	08.65	65-66	5	0	0
Sunderland	Tr	05.67	67-70	57	1	0
Northampton T.	Tr	03.71	70-71	49	1	0
Workington	Tr	09.72	72-75	139	1	5
HESLOP George Wilson						
Wallsend, 1 July, 1940						(CH)
Newcastle U.	Dudley Welfare	02.59	59-61	27	-	0
Everton	Tr	03.62	62-65	10	0	0
Manchester C.	Tr	09.65	65-71	159	3	1
Bury	Tr	08.72	72	37	0	0
HESLOP Norman						
Bolton, 1 August, 1920						(IF)
Southport	Bolton W. (Am)	10.46	46-47	30	-	4
HESSENTHALER Andrew						
Dartford, 17 August, 1965 E Semi Pro						(M)
Watford	Redbridge Forest	09.91	91-95	195	0	11
Gillingham	Tr	08.96	96-97	80	0	2
HESSEY Sean Peter						
Whiston, 19 September, 1978						(CD/M)
Leeds U.	Liverpool (YT)	09.97				
Wigan Ath.	Tr	12.97				
Huddersfield T.	Tr	03.98	97	0	1	0
HETHERINGTON Robert **Brent**						
Carlisle, 6 December, 1961						(F)
Carlisle U.	Workington	08.87	87-89	61	27	23
HETHERINGTON Henry (Harry)						
Chester-le-Street, 7 November, 1928 Died 1987						(OR)
Sunderland	Shiney Row	05.46	47	2	-	0
Gateshead	Tr	01.49	48	2	-	1
HETHERINGTON Thomas Burns						
Newcastle, 22 January, 1911 Died 1968						(G)
Burnley	Walker Celtic	12.33	33-38	67	-	0
Barnsley	Jarrow	02.39				
Gateshead	Tr	10.46	46	1	-	0
HETHERSTON Peter						
Bellshill, 6 November, 1964						(W)
Watford	Falkirk	07.87	87	2	3	0
Sheffield U.	Tr	02.88	87	11	0	0
HETZKE Stephen Edward Richard						
Marlborough, 3 June, 1955						(CD)
Reading	App	06.73	71-81	254	7	23

League Club	Source	Date Signed	Seasons Played	Career Record Apps	Subs	Gls
Blackpool	Tr	07.82	82-85	140	0	18
Sunderland	Tr	03.86	85-86	31	0	0
Chester C.	Tr	06.87	87	14	0	0
Colchester U.	Tr	03.88	87-88	27	2	2

HEWARD Brian John
Lincoln, 17 July, 1935 (CH)

League Club	Source	Date Signed	Seasons Played	Apps	Subs	Gls
Scunthorpe U.	Jnrs	03.54	53-60	137	-	0
Lincoln C.	Tr	07.61	61-65	97	0	1

HEWARD Graham Keith
Newcastle, 13 October, 1965 (F)

League Club	Source	Date Signed	Seasons Played	Apps	Subs	Gls
Cambridge U.	App	10.83	83	1	0	0

HEWIE John Davidson
South Africa, 13 December, 1927 Su23-1/S'B'/S-19 (FB)

League Club	Source	Date Signed	Seasons Played	Apps	Subs	Gls
Charlton Ath.	Arcadia Shepherds (SA)	10.49	51-65	495	0	37

HEWITT Daren Peter
Chichester, 1 September, 1969 (M)

League Club	Source	Date Signed	Seasons Played	Apps	Subs	Gls
Aldershot	YT	08.88	88	0	2	0

HEWITT Gerald
Sheffield, 28 January, 1935 (WH)

League Club	Source	Date Signed	Seasons Played	Apps	Subs	Gls
Sheffield U.	Jnrs	07.54	55-56	3	-	0
Workington	Tr	06.58				

HEWITT Harold
Chesterfield, 24 June, 1919 (OR)

League Club	Source	Date Signed	Seasons Played	Apps	Subs	Gls
Mansfield T.	Chesterfield (Am)	11.45	46	1	-	0

HEWITT James (Jamie) Robert
Chesterfield, 17 May, 1968 (D/M)

League Club	Source	Date Signed	Seasons Played	Apps	Subs	Gls
Chesterfield	YT	04.86	85-91	240	9	14
Doncaster Rov.	Tr	08.92	92-93	32	1	0
Chesterfield	Tr	10.93	93-97	169	7	10

HEWITT John
Aberdeen, 9 February, 1963 S Sch/S Yth/Su21-6 (M)

League Club	Source	Date Signed	Seasons Played	Apps	Subs	Gls
Middlesbrough (L)	Glasgow Celtic	09.91	91	0	2	0

HEWITT Leonard
Wrexham, 20 March, 1920 Died 1979 (CF)

League Club	Source	Date Signed	Seasons Played	Apps	Subs	Gls
Wrexham		05.46	46	5	-	2

HEWITT Martin
Hartlepool, 24 July, 1965 (F)

League Club	Source	Date Signed	Seasons Played	Apps	Subs	Gls
Hartlepool U. (N/C)		08.84	85-86	11	3	2

HEWITT Richard (Dick)
South Elmsall, 25 May, 1943 (M)

League Club	Source	Date Signed	Seasons Played	Apps	Subs	Gls
Huddersfield T.	Moorthorpe B.C.	05.61				
Bradford C.	Tr	07.64	64	20	-	7
Barnsley	Tr	07.65	65-68	97	2	20
York C.	Tr	03.69	68-71	87	4	7

HEWITT Ronald
Chesterfield, 25 January, 1924 (G)

League Club	Source	Date Signed	Seasons Played	Apps	Subs	Gls
Sheffield U.	Youlgreave	11.44				
Lincoln C.	Tr	08.46	48	3	-	0

HEWITT Ronald
Flint, 21 June, 1928 W-5 (IF)

League Club	Source	Date Signed	Seasons Played	Apps	Subs	Gls
Wolverhampton W.		07.48				
Walsall	Tr	10.49	49	8	-	2
Darlington	Tr	06.50	50	36	-	3
Wrexham	Tr	07.51	51-56	204	-	83
Cardiff C.	Tr	06.57	57-58	64	-	27
Wrexham	Tr	07.59	59	27	-	11
Coventry C.	Tr	03.60	59-61	59	-	23
Chester C.	Tr	03.62	61-62	29	-	6

HEWITT Stephen
Hull, 17 April, 1973 (G)

League Club	Source	Date Signed	Seasons Played	Apps	Subs	Gls
Scarborough	YT	01.92	91	2	0	0

HEWKINS Kenneth John Robert
South Africa, 30 October, 1929 (G)

League Club	Source	Date Signed	Seasons Played	Apps	Subs	Gls
Fulham	Clyde Ath. (SA)	11.55	55-61	38	-	0

HEWLETT Matthew Paul
Bristol, 25 February, 1976 E Yth (M)

League Club	Source	Date Signed	Seasons Played	Apps	Subs	Gls
Bristol C.	YT	08.93	93-97	98	12	8

HEWSON Patrick Carroll
Gateshead, 2 June, 1926 (FB)

League Club	Source	Date Signed	Seasons Played	Apps	Subs	Gls
West Bromwich A.	Crook T.	11.50				
Gateshead	Tr	07.53	53-57	130	-	0

HEY Antoine
Berlin, Germany, 19 September, 1970 (RM)

League Club	Source	Date Signed	Seasons Played	Apps	Subs	Gls
Birmingham C.	Fortuna Cologne (Ger)	07.97	97	8	1	0

HEYDON Cecil
Birkenhead, 24 May, 1919 (WH)

League Club	Source	Date Signed	Seasons Played	Apps	Subs	Gls
New Brighton	Victory Social	02.39	38	1	-	0
Derby Co.	Tr	06.39				
Doncaster Rov.	Tr	10.45	46-47	6	-	0
Rochdale	Tr	07.48	48	1	-	0

HEYDON John (Jack)
Birkenhead, 19 October, 1928 (WH)

League Club	Source	Date Signed	Seasons Played	Apps	Subs	Gls
Liverpool	Everton (Am)	01.49	50-52	63	-	0
Millwall	Tr	05.53	53-55	75	-	1
Tranmere Rov.	Tr	07.56	56-60	76	-	1

HEYES Darren Lee
Swansea, 11 January, 1967 E Sch/E Yth (G)

League Club	Source	Date Signed	Seasons Played	Apps	Subs	Gls
Nottingham F.	App	01.84				
Wrexham	L	01.87	86	2	0	0
Scunthorpe U. (N/C)	Tr	07.87	87	3	0	0

HEYES George
Bolton, 16 November, 1937 (G)

League Club	Source	Date Signed	Seasons Played	Apps	Subs	Gls
Rochdale	Jnrs	04.56	58-59	24	-	0
Leicester C.	Tr	07.60	60-65	25	0	0
Swansea C.	Tr	09.65	65-68	99	0	0
Barrow	Tr	07.69	69	26	0	0

HEYES Kenneth
Haydock, 4 January, 1936 E Sch/E Yth (FB)

League Club	Source	Date Signed	Seasons Played	Apps	Subs	Gls
Everton	Jnrs	02.53				
Preston N.E.	Tr	05.57	59	3	-	0

HEYS Michael
Preston, 23 June, 1938 (G)

League Club	Source	Date Signed	Seasons Played	Apps	Subs	Gls
Preston N.E.	Jnrs	05.57				
Barrow	Tr	03.59	58-61	70	-	0
Workington	Tr	08.62				
Halifax T.		11.63	63	1	-	0

HEYWOOD Albert Edward
Hartlepool, 12 May, 1913 Died 1989 (G)

League Club	Source	Date Signed	Seasons Played	Apps	Subs	Gls
Sunderland	Spennymoor U.	03.37	38	4	-	0
Hartlepool U.	Tr	05.46	46	39	-	0

HEYWOOD David Ian
Wolverhampton, 25 July, 1967 (LB)

League Club	Source	Date Signed	Seasons Played	Apps	Subs	Gls
Wolverhampton W.	YT	11.84	84	7	0	0

HIBBARD Mark Andrew
Hereford, 12 August, 1977 (LB)

League Club	Source	Date Signed	Seasons Played	Apps	Subs	Gls
Hereford U.	YT	07.96	96	5	2	1

HIBBERD Stuart
Sheffield, 11 October, 1961 (W)

League Club	Source	Date Signed	Seasons Played	Apps	Subs	Gls
Lincoln C.	App	10.79	80-82	36	6	3

HIBBITT Kenneth
Bradford, 3 January, 1951 Eu23-1 (M)

League Club	Source	Date Signed	Seasons Played	Apps	Subs	Gls
Bradford P.A.	App	11.68	67-68	13	2	0
Wolverhampton W.	Tr	11.68	68-83	447	19	89
Coventry C.	Tr	08.84	84-85	42	5	4
Bristol Rov.	Tr	08.86	86-88	51	2	5

HIBBITT Terence Arthur
Bradford, 1 December, 1947 Died 1994 (M)

League Club	Source	Date Signed	Seasons Played	Apps	Subs	Gls
Leeds U.	Jnrs	12.64	65-70	32	15	9
Newcastle U.	Tr	08.71	71-75	138	0	7
Birmingham C.	Tr	08.75	75-77	110	0	11
Newcastle U.	Tr	05.78	78-80	89	1	5

HIBBS Garry Thomas
Hammersmith, 26 January, 1957 (M)

League Club	Source	Date Signed	Seasons Played	Apps	Subs	Gls
Leyton Orient	App	07.74	75	1	0	0
Aldershot	Tr	02.77	76	4	2	0

HICK Leslie David
York, 23 April, 1927 (OR)

League Club	Source	Date Signed	Seasons Played	Apps	Subs	Gls
Bradford C.		07.48	48	1	-	0

HICKIE George Noel Ellerton
Hawarden, 25 December, 1922 Died 1994 (FB)

League Club	Source	Date Signed	Seasons Played	Apps	Subs	Gls
Barnsley		05.46				
Carlisle U.	Tr	09.46	46	1	-	0

HICKLIN Albert **William**
Dudley, 20 September, 1924 (WH)

League Club	Source	Date Signed	Seasons Played	Apps	Subs	Gls
Birmingham C.	West Bromwich A. (Am)	03.45				

League Club	Source	Date Signed	Seasons Played	Apps	Subs	Gls
Watford	Tr	06.47	47	21	-	5
West Bromwich A.	Tr	05.48				

HICKMAN Geoffrey Brian
West Bromwich, 7 January, 1950 (G)

League Club	Source	Date Signed	Seasons Played	Apps	Subs	Gls
West Bromwich A.	App	01.68				
Bradford P.A.	Tr	06.69	69	9	0	0

HICKMAN Michael Frederick Thomas
Elstead (Sy), 2 October, 1946 (M)

League Club	Source	Date Signed	Seasons Played	Apps	Subs	Gls
Brighton & H.A.	Jnrs	06.65	65-67	12	3	0
Grimsby T.	Tr	06.68	68-74	247	7	48
Blackburn Rov.	Tr	02.75	74-75	23	3	8
Torquay U.	Tr	10.75	75-76	17	0	1

HICKS Anthony John
Swindon, 20 August, 1945 (G)

League Club	Source	Date Signed	Seasons Played	Apps	Subs	Gls
Swindon T.	App	10.62	64-66	51	0	0

HICKS James Michael
Ipswich, 16 September, 1960 (CD)

League Club	Source	Date Signed	Seasons Played	Apps	Subs	Gls
Exeter C. (N/C)	St Lukes College	09.83	83	3	0	0
Oxford U.	Tr	08.84				
Fulham	Tr	08.85	85-87	39	1	1

HICKS Keith
Oldham, 9 August, 1954 E Yth (CD)

League Club	Source	Date Signed	Seasons Played	Apps	Subs	Gls
Oldham Ath.	App	08.72	71-79	240	2	11
Hereford U.	Tr	09.80	80-84	201	0	2
Rochdale	Tr	07.85	85-86	32	0	1

HICKS Martin
Stratford-on-Avon, 27 February, 1957 (CD)

League Club	Source	Date Signed	Seasons Played	Apps	Subs	Gls
Charlton Ath.	Stratford T.	02.77				
Reading	Tr	02.78	77-90	499	1	23
Birmingham C.	Tr	08.91	91-92	57	3	1

HICKS Stuart Jason
Peterborough, 30 May, 1967 (CD)

League Club	Source	Date Signed	Seasons Played	Apps	Subs	Gls
Peterborough U.	YT	07.84				
Colchester U.	Wisbech T.	03.88	87-89	57	7	0
Scunthorpe U.	Tr	08.90	90-91	67	0	0
Doncaster Rov.	Tr	08.92	92	36	0	0
Huddersfield T.	Tr	08.93	93	20	2	1
Preston N.E.	Tr	03.94	93-94	11	1	0
Scarborough	Tr	02.95	94-96	81	4	2
Leyton Orient	Tr	08.97	97	35	0	0

HICKSON David
Salford, 30 October, 1929 (CF)

League Club	Source	Date Signed	Seasons Played	Apps	Subs	Gls
Everton	Ellesmere Port	05.48	51-55	139	-	63
Aston Villa	Tr	09.55	55	12	-	1
Huddersfield T.	Tr	11.55	55-56	54	-	28
Everton	Tr	08.57	57-59	86	-	32
Liverpool	Tr	11.59	59-60	60	-	37
Bury	Cambridge C.	01.62	61	8	-	0
Tranmere Rov.	Tr	08.62	62-63	45	-	21

HICKSON George **Geoffrey**
Crewe, 26 September, 1939 (G)

League Club	Source	Date Signed	Seasons Played	Apps	Subs	Gls
Stoke C.	Blackburn Rov. (Am)	08.57	59-60	11	-	0
Crewe Alex.	Tr	07.62	62-66	105	0	0
Port Vale	L	08.68	68	17	0	0
Southport	Tr	12.68	68	3	0	0

HICKTON John
Chesterfield, 24 September, 1944 (F)

League Club	Source	Date Signed	Seasons Played	Apps	Subs	Gls
Sheffield Wed.	Jnrs	01.62	63-65	52	1	21
Middlesbrough	Tr	09.66	66-77	395	20	159
Hull C.	L	01.77	76	6	0	1

HICKTON Roy
Chesterfield, 19 September, 1948 (FB)

League Club	Source	Date Signed	Seasons Played	Apps	Subs	Gls
Chesterfield	App	11.65	68-70	48	2	1

HIDEN Martin
Stainz, Austria, 11 March, 1973 Austrian Int (D)

League Club	Source	Date Signed	Seasons Played	Apps	Subs	Gls
Leeds U.	Rapid Vienna (Aut)	02.98	97	11	0	0

HIGGINBOTTOM Andrew John
Chesterfield, 22 October, 1964 (M)

League Club	Source	Date Signed	Seasons Played	Apps	Subs	Gls
Chesterfield	App	10.82	82	1	2	0
Everton	Tr	07.83				
Cambridge U.	Tr	08.84	84	1	0	0
Crystal Palace		09.85	85-86	16	7	2

HIGGINBOTTOM Daniel John
Manchester, 29 December, 1978 (D)

League Club	Source	Date Signed	Seasons Played	Apps	Subs	Gls
Manchester U.	YT	07.97	97	0	1	0

HIGGINBOTTOM Michael
Sheffield, 13 October, 1962 (M)

League Club	Source	Date Signed	Seasons Played	Apps	Subs	Gls
Chesterfield (N/C)		08.83	83	3	1	0

HIGGINS Andrew Martin
Bolsover, 12 February, 1960 (CD)

League Club	Source	Date Signed	Seasons Played	Apps	Subs	Gls
Chesterfield	App	02.78	78	1	0	0
Port Vale	Tr	02.81	80-81	11	3	0
Hartlepool U.	Tr	09.82	82	3	1	1
Rochdale	Kings Lynn	03.83	82-83	31	2	6
Chester C.	Tr	07.84	84	16	3	1

HIGGINS Augustine (Ossie) Robert
Dublin, 19 January, 1931 (CF)

League Club	Source	Date Signed	Seasons Played	Apps	Subs	Gls
Aston Villa	Shamrock Rov.	11.49				
Ipswich T.	Tr	07.52	52	2	-	0

HIGGINS Charles
Bellshill, 12 May, 1921 (LB)

League Club	Source	Date Signed	Seasons Played	Apps	Subs	Gls
Chester C.	Arbroath	08.46	46	11	-	0

HIGGINS David Anthony
Liverpool, 19 August, 1961 (RB)

League Club	Source	Date Signed	Seasons Played	Apps	Subs	Gls
Tranmere Rov.	Eagle	08.83	83-84	27	1	0
Tranmere Rov.	Caernarfon T.	07.87	87-96	315	4	12

HIGGINS Frederick Thomas
Hackney, 21 January, 1930 (CH)

League Club	Source	Date Signed	Seasons Played	Apps	Subs	Gls
Crystal Palace	Wood Green	03.52	52-53	11	-	0

HIGGINS George
Batley, 12 September, 1932 (HB)

League Club	Source	Date Signed	Seasons Played	Apps	Subs	Gls
Huddersfield T.	Jnrs	12.49				
Halifax T.	Tr	07.57	57	5	-	0

HIGGINS George
Dundee, 16 June, 1925 Died 1993 (FB)

League Club	Source	Date Signed	Seasons Played	Apps	Subs	Gls
Blackburn Rov.	Lochee Harp	10.46	46-50	53	-	0
Bolton W.	Tr	07.51	51-53	69	-	0
Grimsby T.	Tr	05.54	54-56	47	-	0

HIGGINS James
Dublin, 3 February, 1926 IR-1 (CF)

League Club	Source	Date Signed	Seasons Played	Apps	Subs	Gls
Birmingham C.	Dundalk	11.49	49-52	50	-	12

HIGGINS John Oldfield
Bakewell, 15 November, 1932 (CH)

League Club	Source	Date Signed	Seasons Played	Apps	Subs	Gls
Bolton W.	Buxton	10.50	52-60	183	-	0

HIGGINS John Wilson
Kilmarnock, 27 January, 1933 (FB)

League Club	Source	Date Signed	Seasons Played	Apps	Subs	Gls
Swindon T.	St Mirren	05.59	59-60	28	-	0

HIGGINS Mark Nicholas
Buxton, 29 September, 1958 E Sch/E Yth (CD)

League Club	Source	Date Signed	Seasons Played	Apps	Subs	Gls
Everton	App	08.76	76-83	150	2	6
Manchester U.	(Retired)	12.85	85	6	0	0
Bury	Tr	01.87	86-88	67	1	0
Stoke C.	Tr	09.88	88-89	37	2	1

HIGGINS Michael
Haslingden, 5 September, 1956 (W)

League Club	Source	Date Signed	Seasons Played	Apps	Subs	Gls
Blackburn Rov.	App	12.73				
Workington	Tr	07.76	76	11	4	1

HIGGINS Peter
Blidworth, 1 August, 1944 (CH)

League Club	Source	Date Signed	Seasons Played	Apps	Subs	Gls
Oxford U.	Blidworth Y.C.	07.62	62-68	35	5	0
Crewe Alex.	Tr	06.69	69-71	56	3	0

HIGGINS Peter Clive
Cardiff, 12 November, 1950 (W)

League Club	Source	Date Signed	Seasons Played	Apps	Subs	Gls
Bristol Rov.	App	02.69	68-72	36	1	5
Doncaster Rov.	Tr	07.73	73-75	63	5	10
Torquay U.	L	03.76	75	3	1	1

HIGGINS Robert James
Bolsover, 23 December, 1958 (CD)

League Club	Source	Date Signed	Seasons Played	Apps	Subs	Gls
Burnley	App	07.76	77	3	0	0
Hartlepool U.	L	11.79	79	2	0	0
Rochdale	Tr	10.80	80	4	1	0

HIGGINS Ronald Valentine
Silvertown, 14 February, 1923 (CF)

League Club	Source	Date Signed	Seasons Played	Apps	Subs	Gls
Leyton Orient (Am)	Green & Siley Wks	12.49	49	2	-	0
Brighton & H.A.	Tonbridge	01.52	51	8	-	0
Queens Park R.	Tr	01.53	52	3	-	1

HIGGINS William Charles
Birkenhead, 26 February, 1924 Died 1981 (F)

League Club	Source	Date Signed	Seasons Played	Apps	Subs	Gls
Everton	Tranmere Rov. (Am)	03.46	46-49	48	-	8

HIGGINSON Thomas
Newtongrange, 6 January, 1937 (WH)

League Club	Source	Date Signed	Seasons Played	Apps	Subs	Gls
Brentford	Kilmarnock	06.59	59-69	383	5	15

HIGGS Shane Peter
Oxford, 13 May, 1977 (G)

League Club	Source	Date Signed	Seasons Played	Apps	Subs	Gls
Bristol Rov.	YT	07.95	96-97	10	0	0

HIGH David Henry
Reading, 22 February, 1941 E Yth (FB)

League Club	Source	Date Signed	Seasons Played	Apps	Subs	Gls
Reading	Jnrs	02.58	59-63	72	-	2

HIGH Sidney William
Waterbeach, 30 September, 1922 (OR)

League Club	Source	Date Signed	Seasons Played	Apps	Subs	Gls
Luton T.	Cambridge U.	10.46				
Watford	Tr	08.48	48	7	-	3

HIGHAM John Peter
Liverpool, 22 November, 1954 (CD)

League Club	Source	Date Signed	Seasons Played	Apps	Subs	Gls
Liverpool	App	05.74				
Southport	Tr	01.76	75-77	96	0	1

HIGHAM Peter
Wigan, 8 November, 1930 (CF)

League Club	Source	Date Signed	Seasons Played	Apps	Subs	Gls
Portsmouth (Am)	Wigan Ath.	11.49	49	1	-	0
Bolton W.	Tr	11.50				
Preston N.E.	Tr	05.52	53-54	15	-	10
Nottingham F.	Tr	08.55	55-57	61	-	20
Doncaster Rov.	Tr	03.58	57-58	22	-	6

HIGNETT Alan James
Liverpool, 1 November, 1946 E Sch (FB)

League Club	Source	Date Signed	Seasons Played	Apps	Subs	Gls
Liverpool	App	11.63	64	1	-	0
Chester C.	Tr	08.66	66	6	0	0

HIGNETT Craig John
Prescot, 12 January, 1970 (W)

League Club	Source	Date Signed	Seasons Played	Apps	Subs	Gls
Crewe Alex.	Liverpool (YT)	05.88	88-92	108	13	42
Middlesbrough	Tr	11.92	92-97	126	30	33

HILAIRE Vince Mark
Forest Hill, 10 October, 1959 E Yth/Eu21-9/E'B' (LW)

League Club	Source	Date Signed	Seasons Played	Apps	Subs	Gls
Crystal Palace	App	10.76	76-83	239	16	29
Luton T.	Tr	07.84	84	5	1	0
Portsmouth	Tr	11.84	84-87	144	2	25
Leeds U.	Tr	07.88	88-89	42	2	6
Stoke C.	L	11.89	89	5	0	1
Stoke C.	Tr	11.90	90	10	0	2
Exeter C.	Tr	09.91	91	24	9	4

HILDERSLEY Ronald
Kirkcaldy, 6 April, 1965 (M)

League Club	Source	Date Signed	Seasons Played	Apps	Subs	Gls
Manchester C.	App	04.83	82	1	0	0
Chester C.	L	01.84	83	9	0	0
Chester C.	Tr	07.84	84	5	4	0
Rochdale (N/C)	Tr	08.85	85	12	4	0
Preston N.E.	Tr	06.86	86-87	54	4	3
Cambridge U.	L	02.88	87	9	0	3
Blackburn Rov.	Tr	07.88	88-89	25	5	4
Wigan Ath.	Tr	08.90	90	4	0	0
Halifax T.		11.91	91-92	21	10	2

HILDITCH Mark
Royton, 20 August, 1960 (F)

League Club	Source	Date Signed	Seasons Played	Apps	Subs	Gls
Rochdale	Jnrs	11.78	77-82	184	13	40
Tranmere Rov.	Tr	08.83	83-85	47	2	12
Wigan Ath.	Altrincham	09.86	86-89	89	14	26
Rochdale	Tr	08.90	90-91	12	4	2

HILEY Scott Patrick
Plymouth, 27 September, 1968 (RB)

League Club	Source	Date Signed	Seasons Played	Apps	Subs	Gls
Exeter C.	YT	08.86	87-92	205	5	12
Birmingham C.	Tr	03.93	92-95	49	0	0
Manchester C.	Tr	02.96	95-96	4	5	0

HILL Alan
Barnsley, 3 November, 1943 (G)

League Club	Source	Date Signed	Seasons Played	Apps	Subs	Gls
Barnsley	Jnrs	04.61	60-65	133	0	0
Rotherham U.	Tr	06.66	66-68	81	0	0
Nottingham F.	Tr	03.69	68-69	41	0	0

HILL Alan George
Chester, 22 June, 1955 (FB)

League Club	Source	Date Signed	Seasons Played	Apps	Subs	Gls
Wrexham	Jnrs	07.73	74-82	173	26	7

HILL Ernest Alan
Bromborough, 1 July, 1933 (OL)

League Club	Source	Date Signed	Seasons Played	Apps	Subs	Gls
Tranmere Rov. (Am)	Bebington	11.56	56	6	-	1

HILL Alistair Greenwood
Glasgow, 25 April, 1934 (OR)

League Club	Source	Date Signed	Seasons Played	Apps	Subs	Gls
Bristol C.	Dundee	11.59	59	3	-	0

HILL Andrew Robert
Ilkeston, 10 November, 1960 (F)

League Club	Source	Date Signed	Seasons Played	Apps	Subs	Gls
Derby Co.	Kimberley T.	06.81	81-83	19	3	2
Carlisle U.	Tr	09.83	83-85	73	12	15

HILL Andrew Rowland
Maltby, 20 January, 1965 E Yth (RB)

League Club	Source	Date Signed	Seasons Played	Apps	Subs	Gls
Manchester U.	App	01.83				
Bury	Tr	07.84	84-90	264	0	10
Manchester C.	Tr	12.90	90-94	91	7	6
Port Vale	Tr	08.95	95-97	96	4	1

HILL Arthur
Chesterfield, 12 November, 1921 (OR)

League Club	Source	Date Signed	Seasons Played	Apps	Subs	Gls
Chesterfield		09.46	47	1	-	0

HILL Bert
Paddington, 8 March, 1930 (WH)

League Club	Source	Date Signed	Seasons Played	Apps	Subs	Gls
Chelsea	Jnrs	05.50				
Colchester U.	Tr	10.52	52-57	105	-	3

HILL Brian
Sheffield, 6 October, 1937 Died 1968 (FB)

League Club	Source	Date Signed	Seasons Played	Apps	Subs	Gls
Sheffield Wed.	Jnrs	04.55	56-65	116	1	1

HILL Brian
Mansfield, 15 December, 1942 (OL)

League Club	Source	Date Signed	Seasons Played	Apps	Subs	Gls
Grimsby T.	Ollerton Colly	08.60	60-66	180	0	26
Huddersfield T.	Tr	11.66	66-68	85	3	6
Blackburn Rov.	Tr	09.69	69-70	34	3	4
Torquay U.	Tr	07.71	71	6	1	1

HILL Brian William
Bedworth, 31 July, 1941 (D)

League Club	Source	Date Signed	Seasons Played	Apps	Subs	Gls
Coventry C.	Jnrs	08.58	57-70	240	4	7
Bristol C.	L	03.71	70	7	0	0
Torquay U.	Tr	10.71	71-72	49	0	1

HILL Charles (Midge) John
Cardiff, 6 September, 1918 (IF)

League Club	Source	Date Signed	Seasons Played	Apps	Subs	Gls
Cardiff C.		06.38	38-46	19	-	4
Torquay U.	Tr	07.47	47-48	63	-	15
Queens Park R.	Tr	03.49	48-49	21	-	1
Swindon T.	Tr	09.50	50	4	-	0

HILL Clinton Scott
Knowsley, 19 October, 1978 (D)

League Club	Source	Date Signed	Seasons Played	Apps	Subs	Gls
Tranmere Rov.	YT	07.97	97	13	1	0

HILL Colin Frederick
Uxbridge, 12 November, 1963 NI-26 (CD)

League Club	Source	Date Signed	Seasons Played	Apps	Subs	Gls
Arsenal	App	08.81	82-84	46	0	1
Colchester U.	Maritimo (Port)	10.87	87-88	64	5	0
Sheffield U.	Tr	07.89	89-91	77	5	1
Leicester C.	Tr	03.92	91-96	140	5	0
Northampton T.	Trelleborg (Swe)	11.97	97	27	0	0

HILL Daniel Ronald
Enfield, 1 October, 1974 E Yth/Eu21-4 (M)

League Club	Source	Date Signed	Seasons Played	Apps	Subs	Gls
Tottenham H.	YT	09.92	92-94	4	6	0
Birmingham C.	L	11.95	95	5	0	0
Watford	L	02.96	95	1	0	0
Cardiff C.	L	02.98	97	7	0	0

HILL David
Bradford, 25 May, 1965 (F)

League Club	Source	Date Signed	Seasons Played	Apps	Subs	Gls
Bradford C. (N/C)	YT	08.82	82-83	2	3	1

HILL David
Kettering, 28 September, 1953 (G)

League Club	Source	Date Signed	Seasons Played	Apps	Subs	Gls
Northampton T.	App	07.70	70	1	0	0

HILL David Michael
Nottingham, 6 June, 1966 (M)

League Club	Source	Date Signed	Seasons Played	Apps	Subs	Gls
Scunthorpe U.	YT	02.85	83-87	139	1	10
Ipswich T.	Tr	07.88	88-90	54	7	0
Scunthorpe U.	L	03.91	90	8	1	1
Scunthorpe U.	Tr	09.91	91-92	55	1	5
Lincoln C.	Tr	07.93	93-94	52	6	6
Chesterfield	L	08.94	94	3	0	0

League Club	Source	Date Signed	Seasons Played	Career Record Apps	Subs	Gls
HILL Dennis						
Willenhall, 16 August, 1929						(OL)
Birmingham C.	Darlaston	06.51	53-55	4	-	0
HILL Dilwyn						
Rhondda, 1 April, 1937 Died 1963						(IF)
Exeter C.	Pontypridd	06.55	57-59	14	-	3
HILL Frank Robert						
Forfar, 21 May, 1906 Died 1993 S-3						(WH)
Arsenal	Aberdeen	05.32	32-35	76	-	4
Blackpool	Tr	06.36	36-37	45	-	8
Southampton	Tr	09.37	37-38	51	-	4
Crewe Alex.	Preston N.E. (coach)	07.44	46-47	20	-	0
HILL Frederick						
Sheffield, 17 January, 1940 Eu23-10/EF Lge/E-2						(IF)
Bolton W.	Jnrs	03.57	57-68	373	2	74
Halifax T.	Tr	07.69	69	25	0	3
Manchester C.	Tr	05.70	70-72	28	7	3
Peterborough U.	Tr	08.73	73-74	73	2	7
HILL Geoffrey Raymond						
Carlisle, 31 August, 1929						(D)
Carlisle U.		10.49	49-57	190	-	0
HILL Gordon Alec						
Sunbury, 1 April, 1954 Eu23-1/E-6						(W)
Millwall	Southall	01.73	72-75	79	7	20
Manchester U.	Tr	11.75	75-77	100	1	39
Derby Co.	Tr	04.78	77-79	22	2	5
Queens Park R.	Tr	11.79	79-80	10	4	1
HILL Henry Alec						
Lambeth, 19 September, 1947						(M)
Ipswich T.	Canada	03.69				
Gillingham	South Africa	07.71	71	0	1	0
Hereford U. (N/C)	South Africa	11.78	78	0	1	0
HILL James						
Wilshaw, 19 August, 1931						(OL)
Coventry C.	Jnrs	08.48	49-55	66	-	8
Millwall	Tr	07.56	56	1	-	0
Shrewsbury T.	Tr	07.57	57	8	-	0
HILL James William Thomas						
Balham, 22 July, 1928						(IF)
Brentford	Reading (Am)	05.49	49-51	83	-	10
Fulham	Tr	03.52	51-60	276	-	41
HILL Matthew **James**						
Carrickfergus (NI), 31 October, 1935 NI Amat/NI 'B'/NI-7						(IF)
Newcastle U.	Linfield	07.57	57	11	-	2
Norwich C.	Tr	07.58	58-62	161	-	55
Everton	Tr	08.63	63	7	-	1
Port Vale	Tr	10.65	65-67	63	0	8
HILL John Ernest						
Yeovil, 29 November, 1948						(FB)
Bournemouth	App	08.66	67	3	1	0
HILL Jonathan William						
Wigan, 20 August, 1970						(LM)
Rochdale	Crewe Alex. (YT)	07.89	89-90	25	11	1
HILL Keith John						
Bolton, 17 May, 1969						(CD)
Blackburn Rov.	Jnrs	05.87	87-92	89	7	4
Plymouth Arg.	Tr	09.92	92-95	117	6	2
Rochdale	Tr	07.96	96-97	79	1	5
HILL Kenneth						
Walsall, 28 April, 1938						(WH)
Walsall	Bescot U.	11.56	58-62	115	-	1
Norwich C.	Tr	07.63	63-65	44	0	0
Walsall	Tr	10.66	66	15	0	0
HILL Kenneth George						
Canterbury, 7 March, 1953 E Semi Pro						(CD)
Gillingham	App	03.71	71-76	120	5	7
Lincoln C.	L	12.74	74	1	0	0
HILL Kevin						
Exeter, 6 March, 1976						(LM)
Torquay U.	Torrington	08.97	97	31	6	7
HILL Leonard Winston						
Caerleon, 14 April, 1941 W Yth						(M)
Newport Co.	Lovells Ath.	11.62	62-69	267	2	52

League Club	Source	Date Signed	Seasons Played	Career Record Apps	Subs	Gls
Swansea C.	Tr	07.70	70	12	0	1
Newport Co.	Tr	01.72	71-73	93	4	13
HILL Mark Stephen						
Perivale, 21 January, 1961						(FB)
Queens Park R.	App	07.79				
Brentford	Tr	07.80	80-81	54	2	3
HILL Maurice						
Halifax, 2 May, 1920 Died 1966						(CH)
Everton	Park Side	05.39				
New Brighton	Tr	07.46	46-47	73	-	0
HILL Michael Richard						
Hereford, 3 December, 1947 W-2						(CF)
Sheffield U.	Bethesda Ath.	09.65	66-69	35	2	9
Ipswich T.	Tr	10.69	69-72	63	3	18
Crystal Palace	Tr	12.73	73-75	43	2	6
HILL Paul James						
Nottingham, 28 January, 1973						(D)
Peterborough U.	YT	07.89	90	1	0	0
HILL Peter						
Heanor, 8 August, 1931						(IF)
Coventry C.	Jnrs	08.48	48-61	285	-	73
HILL Raymond William						
Stourbridge, 15 February, 1936						(F)
Coventry C.	Redditch U.	11.57	57-58	14	-	5
HILL Richard Wilfred						
Hinckley, 20 September, 1963						(LW)
Leicester C.	Jnrs	11.81				
Northampton T.	Nuneaton Borough	06.85	85-86	86	0	46
Watford	Tr	05.87	87	2	2	0
Oxford U.	Tr	09.87	87-88	48	15	13
HILL Ricky Anthony						
Hammersmith, 5 March, 1959 E Yth/E-3						(M)
Luton T.	App	05.76	75-88	429	7	54
Leicester C.	Le Havre (Fr)	08.90	90	19	7	0
HILL Robert						
Edinburgh, 9 June, 1938						(IF)
Colchester U.	Jnrs	06.55	55-64	240	-	20
HILL Stephen (Mandy) Thomas						
Blackpool, 15 February, 1940 Eu23-4						(W)
Blackpool	Jnrs	05.59	59-63	71	-	1
Tranmere Rov.	Tr	09.64	64-67	130	0	10
HILL William						
Sheffield, 6 January, 1936						(F)
York C.	Rawmarsh Welfare	02.54	56-59	29	-	3
HILL William Henry						
Sutton-in-Ashfield, 15 March, 1920						(IF)
Mansfield T.	Skegby M.W.	11.47	47	2	-	0
HILL William Leslie						
Uxbridge, 9 June, 1930						(F)
Queens Park R.	Uxbridge T.	04.51	51	10	-	1
HILLARD Douglas Alfred						
Bristol, 10 August, 1935 Died 1997						(FB)
Bristol Rov.	Bristol M.H.	05.57	58-67	313	5	12
HILLARD John Gordon						
Aberdeen, 3 September, 1916						(OR)
Torquay U.		09.46	46	6	-	0
HILLEY David						
Glasgow, 20 December, 1938 Su23-1/SF Lge						(IF)
Newcastle U.	Third Lanark	08.62	62-67	194	0	31
Nottingham F.	Tr	12.67	67-70	72	16	14
HILLIER Barry Guy						
Redcar, 8 April, 1936						(FB)
Southampton	Jnrs	04.53	57-58	9	-	0
HILLIER David						
Blackheath, 19 December, 1969 Eu21-1						(M)
Arsenal	YT	02.88	90-96	82	22	2
Portsmouth	Tr	11.96	96-97	51	0	4
HILLIER John (Jack)						
Halsall, 10 September, 1933						(G)
Chester C. (Am)	Bootle	11.54	54	6	-	0

HILLMAN Dennis Victor
Southend, 27 November, 1918 Died 1994 (OR)

League Club	Source	Date Signed	Seasons Played	Apps	Subs	Gls
Brighton & H.A.		11.44				
Colchester U.	Tr	(N/L)	50	4	-	0
Gillingham	Tr	08.51	51	21	-	0

HILLS John David
Blackpool, 21 April, 1978 (LB)

League Club	Source	Date Signed	Seasons Played	Apps	Subs	Gls
Blackpool	YT	10.95				
Everton	Tr	11.95	96	1	2	0
Swansea C.	L	01.97	96	11	0	0
Swansea C.	L	08.97	97	7	0	0
Blackpool	Tr	01.98	97	19	0	1

HILLS John Raymond
Northfleet, 24 February, 1934 (FB)

League Club	Source	Date Signed	Seasons Played	Apps	Subs	Gls
Tottenham H.	Gravesend & Nft	08.53	57-59	29	-	0
Bristol Rov.	Tr	07.61	61	7	-	0

HILLYARD Ronald William
Rotherham, 31 March, 1952 (G)

League Club	Source	Date Signed	Seasons Played	Apps	Subs	Gls
York C.	Jnrs	12.69	69-73	61	0	0
Hartlepool U.	L	01.72	71	23	0	0
Gillingham	Tr	07.74	74-90	563	0	0

HILTON Damian Alan
Norwich, 6 September, 1977 (F)

League Club	Source	Date Signed	Seasons Played	Apps	Subs	Gls
Norwich C.	YT	07.96				
Brighton & H.A.	Tr	03.98	97	4	1	0

HILTON David
Barnsley, 10 November, 1977 E Sch/E Yth (D)

League Club	Source	Date Signed	Seasons Played	Apps	Subs	Gls
Manchester U.	YT	12.94				
Darlington	Tr	08.97	97	0	1	0

HILTON Gary
Manchester, 4 March, 1961 (G)

League Club	Source	Date Signed	Seasons Played	Apps	Subs	Gls
Bury (N/C)		08.83	83	1	0	0

HILTON John (Jack)
Rochdale, 20 February, 1925 (CF)

League Club	Source	Date Signed	Seasons Played	Apps	Subs	Gls
Wrexham	Hyde U.	07.50	50	3	-	0

HILTON Joseph
Barnburgh (Yks), 20 July, 1931 Died 1995 (IF/WH)

League Club	Source	Date Signed	Seasons Played	Apps	Subs	Gls
Leeds U.	Jnrs	09.48	49	1	-	0
Chester C.	Tr	08.50	50-53	61	-	9

HILTON Mark Gerard
Middleton, 15 January, 1960 (M)

League Club	Source	Date Signed	Seasons Played	Apps	Subs	Gls
Oldham Ath.	App	01.78	77-80	48	2	2
Bury	Tr	08.81	81-82	29	3	3

HILTON Maurice
Stockton, 14 March, 1979 (FB)

League Club	Source	Date Signed	Seasons Played	Apps	Subs	Gls
Doncaster Rov.	YT	●	97	9	1	0

HILTON Patrick John
Aylesham (Kt), 1 May, 1954 (W)

League Club	Source	Date Signed	Seasons Played	Apps	Subs	Gls
Brighton & H.A.	Canterbury C.	02.73	72-73	18	2	2
Blackburn Rov.	Tr	05.74	74	16	0	2
Gillingham	Tr	09.75	75-76	16	10	1
Aldershot	L	03.77	76	12	1	0
Southport	Tr	07.77	77	22	5	5

HILTON Paul
Oldham, 8 October, 1959 (CD/F)

League Club	Source	Date Signed	Seasons Played	Apps	Subs	Gls
Bury	Chadderton	07.78	78-83	136	12	39
West Ham U.	Tr	02.84	83-88	47	13	7

HILTON Peter Bowes
Tamworth, 20 March, 1929 Died 1968 (FB)

League Club	Source	Date Signed	Seasons Played	Apps	Subs	Gls
West Bromwich A.	Tamworth	07.49				
Swindon T.	Tr	07.53	53-55	50	-	0

HIMSWORTH Gary Paul
Pickering, 19 December, 1969 (M)

League Club	Source	Date Signed	Seasons Played	Apps	Subs	Gls
York C.	YT	01.88	87-90	74	14	8
Scarborough	Tr	12.90	90-92	83	9	6
Darlington	Tr	07.93	93-95	86	8	8
York C.	Tr	02.96	95-97	48	8	3

HINCE Paul Frank
Manchester, 2 March, 1945 (W)

League Club	Source	Date Signed	Seasons Played	Apps	Subs	Gls
Manchester C.	Pinnington Celtic	10.66	66-67	7	0	4
Charlton Ath.	Tr	02.68	67-68	23	0	2
Bury	Tr	12.68	68-69	38	0	3
Crewe Alex.	Tr	07.70	70	23	3	2

HINCH James Andrew
Sheffield, 8 November, 1947 (F)

League Club	Source	Date Signed	Seasons Played	Apps	Subs	Gls
Tranmere Rov.	Portmadoc	03.70	69-70	36	3	10
Plymouth Arg.	Tr	02.71	70-73	102	5	28
Hereford U.	Tr	10.73	73	22	5	7
York C.	Tr	07.74	74-76	56	12	12
Southport	L	03.75	74	7	0	2
Sheffield Wed.	Tr	10.77	77	0	1	0
Barnsley	Tr	12.77	77	9	3	4

HINCHCLIFFE Alan Arthur
Chesterfield, 8 December, 1936 (G)

League Club	Source	Date Signed	Seasons Played	Apps	Subs	Gls
Sheffield Wed.	Jnrs	12.53	56	2	-	0
Chesterfield	Tr	07.59				

HINCHCLIFFE Andrew George
Manchester, 5 February, 1969 E Yth/Eu21-1/E-6 (LB)

League Club	Source	Date Signed	Seasons Played	Apps	Subs	Gls
Manchester C.	App	06.86	87-89	107	5	8
Everton	Tr	07.90	90-97	170	12	6
Sheffield Wed.	Tr	01.98	97	15	0	1

HINCHCLIFFE Thomas
Denaby, 6 December, 1913 Died 1978 (IF)

League Club	Source	Date Signed	Seasons Played	Apps	Subs	Gls
Grimsby T.	Denaby U.	10.33	36-37	27	-	5
Huddersfield T.	Tr	02.38	37-38	13	-	4
Derby Co.	Tr	11.38	38	6	-	1
Nottingham F.	Tr	05.46	46	1	-	0

HINCHLEY Gary
Guisborough, 14 November, 1968 (RB)

League Club	Source	Date Signed	Seasons Played	Apps	Subs	Gls
Darlington	Jnrs	08.86	86-87	13	1	0
Darlington	Guisborough T.	02.92	91-92	13	0	1

HINCHLIFFE John (Jack)
Tillicoultry, 4 June, 1938 S Sch (WH)

League Club	Source	Date Signed	Seasons Played	Apps	Subs	Gls
Aston Villa	Jnrs	09.56	57	2	-	0
Workington	Tr	06.58	58-61	116	-	4
Hartlepool U.	Tr	10.61	61-63	88	-	8

HINDLE Frank Johnston
Blackburn, 22 June, 1925 (FB)

League Club	Source	Date Signed	Seasons Played	Apps	Subs	Gls
Blackburn Rov.		01.43				
Chester C.	Tr	06.49	49-50	81	-	0
Bradford P.A.	Tr	04.51	50-56	204	-	0

HINDLE John (Jack)
Preston, 10 November, 1921 Died 1987 (G)

League Club	Source	Date Signed	Seasons Played	Apps	Subs	Gls
Preston N.E.	Clifton B.C.	11.46	47	1	-	0
Barrow	Tr	05.48	48-49	84	-	0
Aston Villa	Tr	06.50	50	15	-	0
Barrow	Tr	08.51	51-55	182	-	0

HINDLE Thomas
Keighley, 22 February, 1921 (IF)

League Club	Source	Date Signed	Seasons Played	Apps	Subs	Gls
Leeds U.	Keighley T.	09.43	46-48	43	-	2
York C.	Tr	02.49	48-49	19	-	3
Halifax T.	Tr	09.49	49-51	85	-	17
Rochdale	Tr	03.52	51	6	-	1

HINDLEY Frank
Worksop, 2 November, 1914 (CF)

League Club	Source	Date Signed	Seasons Played	Apps	Subs	Gls
Nottingham F.	Netherton U.	12.37	38	6	-	3
Brighton & H.A.	Tr	05.39	46	10	-	4

HINDLEY Peter
Worksop, 19 May, 1944 Eu23-1 (RB)

League Club	Source	Date Signed	Seasons Played	Apps	Subs	Gls
Nottingham F.	Jnrs	06.61	62-73	366	0	10
Coventry C.	Tr	01.74	73-75	33	0	0
Peterborough U.	Tr	07.76	76-78	112	0	1

HINDMARCH Robert
Morpeth, 27 April, 1961 E Yth (CD)

League Club	Source	Date Signed	Seasons Played	Apps	Subs	Gls
Sunderland	App	04.78	77-83	114	1	2
Portsmouth	L	12.83	83	2	0	0
Derby Co.	Tr	07.84	84-89	164	0	9
Wolverhampton W.	Tr	06.90	90	40	0	2

HINDMARSH Edward
Sunderland, 7 September, 1921 (WH)

League Club	Source	Date Signed	Seasons Played	Apps	Subs	Gls
Sunderland		10.43				
Carlisle U.	Tr	07.45	46	15	-	0

HINDMARSH John William
Crook, 26 December, 1919 Died 1994 (FB)

League Club	Source	Date Signed	Seasons Played	Apps	Subs	Gls
Portsmouth	Willington	04.39	46-50	55	-	0
Swindon T.	Tr	07.51	51	11	-	0

HINDSON Gordon
Stanley, 8 January, 1950 (W)

League Club	Source	Date Signed	Seasons Played	Apps	Subs	Gls
Newcastle U.	Jnrs	08.68	68-71	7	0	1

League Club	Source	Date Signed	Seasons Played	Apps	Subs	Gls
Luton T.	Tr	10.71	71-74	62	6	3
Carlisle U.	L	09.75	75	1	2	0
Blackburn Rov.	Tr	10.75	75	10	0	0

HINE Mark
Middlesbrough, 18 May, 1964 (M)

League Club	Source	Date Signed	Seasons Played	Apps	Subs	Gls
Grimsby T.	Whitby T.	10.83	84-85	20	2	1
Darlington	Tr	06.86	86-88	126	2	8
Peterborough U.	Tr	01.90	89-90	55	0	7
Scunthorpe U.	Tr	03.91	90-91	19	3	2
Doncaster Rov.	Tr	06.92	92	18	7	1

HINES Derek Jabez
Swadlincote, 8 February, 1931 E Yth (CF)

League Club	Source	Date Signed	Seasons Played	Apps	Subs	Gls
Leicester C.	Jnrs	03.48	47-60	299	-	116
Shrewsbury T.	Tr	11.61	61-62	16	-	5

HINNIGAN Joseph Peter
Liverpool, 3 December, 1955 (FB)

League Club	Source	Date Signed	Seasons Played	Apps	Subs	Gls
Wigan Ath.	South Liverpool	(N/L)	78-79	66	0	10
Sunderland	Tr	02.80	79-82	63	0	4
Preston N.E.	Tr	12.82	82-83	51	1	8
Gillingham	Tr	08.84	84-86	99	4	7
Wrexham	Tr	07.87	87	28	1	1
Chester C.	Tr	08.88	88-89	52	2	2

HINSHELWOOD Daniel Martin
Bromley, 12 December, 1975 E Yth (RB)

League Club	Source	Date Signed	Seasons Played	Apps	Subs	Gls
Nottingham F.	YT	12.92				
Portsmouth	Tr	02.96	95	5	0	0
Torquay U.	L	03.97	96	7	2	0

HINSHELWOOD Martin Alan
Reading, 16 June, 1953 (M)

League Club	Source	Date Signed	Seasons Played	Apps	Subs	Gls
Crystal Palace	App	08.70	72-77	66	3	4

HINSHELWOOD Paul Alexander
Bristol, 14 August, 1956 Eu21-2 (RB)

League Club	Source	Date Signed	Seasons Played	Apps	Subs	Gls
Crystal Palace	App	08.73	73-82	271	5	22
Oxford U.	Tr	08.83	83-84	45	0	7
Millwall	Tr	01.85	84-86	59	2	2
Colchester U.	Tr	09.86	86-87	81	0	6

HINSHELWOOD Walter Alexander Alan
Lambeth, 27 October, 1929 (OR)

League Club	Source	Date Signed	Seasons Played	Apps	Subs	Gls
Fulham	Jnrs	10.46	46-50	17	-	1
Chelsea	Tr	01.51	50	12	-	1
Fulham	Tr	05.51	51	2	-	0
Reading	Tr	12.52	52-55	135	-	31
Bristol C.	Tr	02.56	55-59	148	-	16
Millwall	Tr	06.60	60	19	-	1
Newport Co.	Canada	11.61	61	3	-	0

HINSHELWOOD William Douglas
Airdrie, 11 May, 1935 (WH)

League Club	Source	Date Signed	Seasons Played	Apps	Subs	Gls
Hartlepool U.	Airdrieonians	07.63	63	17	-	3

HINSLEY George
Sheffield, 19 July, 1914 Died 1989 (HB)

League Club	Source	Date Signed	Seasons Played	Apps	Subs	Gls
Barnsley	Denaby U.	09.35	35-38	9	-	0
Bradford C.	Tr	10.38	38-48	114	-	17
Halifax T.	Tr	07.49	49	32	-	0

HINTON Alan Thomas
West Bromwich, 6 October, 1942 E Yth/Eu23-7/E-3 (OL)

League Club	Source	Date Signed	Seasons Played	Apps	Subs	Gls
Wolverhampton W.	Jnrs	10.59	61-63	75	-	29
Nottingham F.	Tr	01.64	63-67	108	4	24
Derby Co.	Tr	09.67	67-75	240	13	64

HINTON Edward (Ted)
Belfast, 20 May, 1922 Died 1988 NI-7 (G)

League Club	Source	Date Signed	Seasons Played	Apps	Subs	Gls
Fulham	Distillery	08.46	46-48	82	-	0
Millwall	Tr	07.49	49-51	91	-	0

HINTON Marvin
Norwood, 2 February, 1940 Eu23-3 (CH)

League Club	Source	Date Signed	Seasons Played	Apps	Subs	Gls
Charlton Ath.	Jnrs	04.57	57-63	131	-	2
Chelsea	Tr	08.63	63-74	257	8	3

HINTON Ronald
Keighley, 27 November, 1943 (CH)

League Club	Source	Date Signed	Seasons Played	Apps	Subs	Gls
Doncaster Rov.	App	07.61				
Chesterfield	Tr	07.63	63	1	-	0

HIPKIN Reginald Willmont
Syderstone (Nk), 31 December, 1921 (RH)

League Club	Source	Date Signed	Seasons Played	Apps	Subs	Gls
Wolverhampton W.	Norwich C. (Am)	07.39				
Charlton Ath.	Tr	09.46	47	2	-	0
Brighton & H.A.	Tr	02.48	47-48	15	-	1

HIRD Robert Keith Bryan
Annfield Plain, 25 November, 1939 Died 1967 (G)

League Club	Source	Date Signed	Seasons Played	Apps	Subs	Gls
Sunderland	Annfield Plain	09.57	60	1	-	0
Darlington	Tr	07.63	63	17	-	0

HIRD Kevin
Colne, 11 February, 1955 (M)

League Club	Source	Date Signed	Seasons Played	Apps	Subs	Gls
Blackburn Rov.	App	02.73	73-78	129	3	20
Leeds U.	Tr	03.79	78-83	165	16	19
Burnley	Tr	08.84	84-85	83	0	23

HIRON Raymond Michael Charles
Gosport, 22 July, 1943 (F)

League Club	Source	Date Signed	Seasons Played	Apps	Subs	Gls
Portsmouth	Fareham T.	05.64	64-74	323	7	110
Reading	Tr	07.75	75-77	88	4	14

HIRONS Paul Terence
Bath, 6 March, 1971 (F)

League Club	Source	Date Signed	Seasons Played	Apps	Subs	Gls
Torquay U.	Bristol C. (YT)	01.89	88-89	10	11	0

HIRST David Eric
Cudworth, 7 December, 1967 E Yth/Eu21-7/E'B'/E-3 (F)

League Club	Source	Date Signed	Seasons Played	Apps	Subs	Gls
Barnsley	App	11.85	85	26	2	9
Sheffield Wed.	Tr	08.86	86-97	261	33	106
Southampton	Tr	10.97	97	28	0	9

HIRST Keith Richard Halliwell
Bradford, 15 October, 1932 (OR)

League Club	Source	Date Signed	Seasons Played	Apps	Subs	Gls
Bradford P.A.	Lowmoor Celtic	01.54	53	1	-	0

HIRST Lee William
Sheffield, 26 January, 1969 (CD)

League Club	Source	Date Signed	Seasons Played	Apps	Subs	Gls
Scarborough	Sheffield Parks	02.90	89-92	107	1	6
Coventry C.	Tr	07.93				
Lincoln C.	L	12.93	93	7	0	0

HIRST Malcolm William
Cudworth, 28 December, 1937 (CF)

League Club	Source	Date Signed	Seasons Played	Apps	Subs	Gls
Barnsley	Darfield Colly	05.56	56	1	-	0

HIRST Martyn Paul
Batley, 26 October, 1961 E Sch (M)

League Club	Source	Date Signed	Seasons Played	Apps	Subs	Gls
Bristol C.	Bath Univ.	10.83	83-85	36	5	1
Torquay U.	L	09.85	85	4	0	0

HISLOP Terence **Kona**
Hackney, 21 December, 1970 (LW)

League Club	Source	Date Signed	Seasons Played	Apps	Subs	Gls
Hartlepool U.	Livingston	09.96	96	23	4	0

HISLOP Neil (Shaka)
Hackney, 22 February, 1969 Eu21-1 (G)

League Club	Source	Date Signed	Seasons Played	Apps	Subs	Gls
Reading	Howard Univ. (USA)	09.92	92-94	104	0	0
Newcastle U.	Tr	08.95	95-97	53	0	0

HITCHCOCK Alan Peter
Bracknell, 5 October, 1949 (FB)

League Club	Source	Date Signed	Seasons Played	Apps	Subs	Gls
Reading	App	10.67	68-69	4	0	0

HITCHCOCK Kevin Joseph
Canning Town, 5 October, 1962 (G)

League Club	Source	Date Signed	Seasons Played	Apps	Subs	Gls
Nottingham F.	Barking	08.83				
Mansfield T.	L	02.84	83	14	0	0
Mansfield T.	Tr	06.84	84-87	168	0	0
Chelsea	Tr	03.88	87-96	90	3	0
Northampton T.	L	12.90	90	17	0	0

HITCHEN Henry (Harry)
Liverpool, 22 October, 1922 Died 1993 (WH)

League Club	Source	Date Signed	Seasons Played	Apps	Subs	Gls
New Brighton	Formby	09.46	46-47	70	-	2
Sheffield U.	Tr	05.48	48-52	154	-	15
Bury	Tr	05.53	53	2	-	0

HITCHEN Steven James
Salford, 28 November, 1976 (FB)

League Club	Source	Date Signed	Seasons Played	Apps	Subs	Gls
Blackburn Rov.	YT	07.95				
Macclesfield T.	Tr	07.97	97	1	1	0

HITCHEN Trevor
Sowerby Bridge, 25 September, 1926 (WH)

League Club	Source	Date Signed	Seasons Played	Apps	Subs	Gls
Notts Co.	Halifax T. (Am)	05.45				
Southport	Wellington T.	01.49	48-55	242	-	34
Oldham Ath.	Tr	08.56	56	3	-	0
Southport	Wigan Ath.	08.58	58	5	-	0

HITCHENS Gerald Archibald
Cannock, 8 October, 1934 Died 1983 Eu23-1/EF Lge/E-7 (CF)

League Club	Source	Date Signed	Seasons Played	Apps	Subs	Gls
Cardiff C.	Kidderminster Hrs	01.55	54-57	95	-	40
Aston Villa	Tr	12.57	57-60	132	-	78

HITCHON John
Carlisle, 30 August, 1919 Died 1985 (G)

League Club	Source	Date Signed	Seasons Played	Apps	Subs	Gls
Carlisle U.		04.47	46-49	5	-	0

HJELDE Jon Olav
Levanger, Norway, 30 April, 1972 (CD)

League Club	Source	Date Signed	Seasons Played	Apps	Subs	Gls
Nottingham F.	Rosenborg (Nor)	08.97	97	23	5	1

HOADLEY Philip Frederick William
Battersea, 6 January, 1952 E Yth (CD)

League Club	Source	Date Signed	Seasons Played	Apps	Subs	Gls
Crystal Palace	App	01.69	67-71	63	11	1
Leyton Orient	Tr	10.71	71-77	255	0	9
Norwich C.	Tr	08.78	78-81	74	3	0

HOBBINS Sidney George
Plumstead, 6 May, 1916 Died 1984 (G)

League Club	Source	Date Signed	Seasons Played	Apps	Subs	Gls
Charlton Ath.	Bromley	05.34	37-46	2	-	0
Millwall	Tr	05.48	48	15	-	0
Leyton Orient	Tr	12.49	49	11	-	0

HOBBIS Harold Henry Frederick
Dartford, 9 March, 1913 Died 1991 E-2 (OL)

League Club	Source	Date Signed	Seasons Played	Apps	Subs	Gls
Charlton Ath.	Bromley	03.31	31-47	248	-	76

HOBBS John Eric
Swanage, 17 April, 1930 (CF)

League Club	Source	Date Signed	Seasons Played	Apps	Subs	Gls
Bournemouth	Swanage	10.52	53-54	6	-	1

HOBBS Ronald George
Aldershot, 23 August, 1921 (W)

League Club	Source	Date Signed	Seasons Played	Apps	Subs	Gls
Aldershot	Woking	11.44	46-53	169	-	14

HOBSON Albert
Glossop, 7 April, 1925 (OR)

League Club	Source	Date Signed	Seasons Played	Apps	Subs	Gls
Blackpool	Glossop	08.45	47-53	62	-	3
Huddersfield T.	Tr	07.54	54-55	9	-	0
York C.	Tr	03.56	55-56	22	-	1

HOBSON Gary
North Ferriby, 12 November, 1972 (CD)

League Club	Source	Date Signed	Seasons Played	Apps	Subs	Gls
Hull C.	YT	07.91	90-95	135	7	0
Brighton & H.A.	Tr	03.96	95-97	74	5	1

HOBSON Gordon
Sheffield, 27 November, 1957 (F)

League Club	Source	Date Signed	Seasons Played	Apps	Subs	Gls
Lincoln C.	Sheffield R.	12.77	77-84	260	12	73
Grimsby T.	Tr	06.85	85-86	50	2	18
Southampton	Tr	11.86	86-87	32	1	8
Lincoln C.	Tr	09.88	88-89	61	0	23
Exeter C.	Tr	08.90	90-91	37	1	7
Walsall (N/C)	Tr	09.91	91	3	0	0

HOBSON John
Barnsley, 1 June, 1946 (W)

League Club	Source	Date Signed	Seasons Played	Apps	Subs	Gls
Blackpool	Jnrs	09.63				
Barnsley	Tr	07.65	65-68	30	6	7
Notts Co.	Tr	05.69	69-70	46	3	6

HOBSON Norman
Shrewsbury, 22 August, 1933 (FB)

League Club	Source	Date Signed	Seasons Played	Apps	Subs	Gls
Shrewsbury T.	Oswestry T.	10.54	55-60	212	-	5

HOBSON Wilfred
Consett, 26 January, 1932 (WH)

League Club	Source	Date Signed	Seasons Played	Apps	Subs	Gls
Oldham Ath.	West Stanley	01.53	54-58	170	-	1
Gateshead	Tr	06.59	59	31	-	1

HOCKADAY David
Sedgefield, 9 November, 1957 (W/FB)

League Club	Source	Date Signed	Seasons Played	Apps	Subs	Gls
Blackpool	Billingham Synth.	06.75	76-82	131	16	24
Swindon T.	Tr	08.83	83-90	227	18	7
Hull C.	Tr	09.90	90-91	72	0	2
Stoke C.	L	03.93	92	7	0	0
Shrewsbury T.	Tr	08.93	93-94	46	2	0

HOCKEY Trevor
Keighley, 1 May, 1943 Died 1987 W-9 (M)

League Club	Source	Date Signed	Seasons Played	Apps	Subs	Gls
Bradford C.	Jnrs	05.60	59-61	53	-	5
Nottingham F.	Tr	11.61	61-63	73	-	6
Newcastle U.	Tr	11.63	63-65	52	0	3
Birmingham C.	Tr	11.65	65-70	195	1	8
Sheffield U.	Tr	01.71	70-72	68	0	4
Norwich C.	Tr	02.73	72	13	0	0
Aston Villa	Tr	06.73	73	24	0	1
Bradford C.	Tr	06.74	74-75	43	1	1

HOCKING Matthew James
Boston, 30 January, 1978 (D)

League Club	Source	Date Signed	Seasons Played	Apps	Subs	Gls
Sheffield U.	YT	05.96				
Hull C.	Tr	09.97	97	31	0	1

HOCKLEY Wayne
Paignton, 6 September, 1978 (F)

League Club	Source	Date Signed	Seasons Played	Apps	Subs	Gls
Torquay U.	YT	●	96	0	2	0

HOCKTON Daniel John
Barking, 7 February, 1979 (F)

League Club	Source	Date Signed	Seasons Played	Apps	Subs	Gls
Millwall	YT	03.97	96-97	10	18	3

HODDER Kenneth
Stockport, 20 August, 1930 (CH)

League Club	Source	Date Signed	Seasons Played	Apps	Subs	Gls
Stockport Co.	Jnrs	03.49	51-63	258	-	1

HODDER Stephen John
Sheffield, 18 October, 1971 (LB)

League Club	Source	Date Signed	Seasons Played	Apps	Subs	Gls
Nottingham F.	YT	07.90				
Notts Co.	Tr	03.91				
Doncaster Rov.	Tr	07.92	92	1	1	0

HODDLE Carl
Harlow, 8 March, 1967 (M)

League Club	Source	Date Signed	Seasons Played	Apps	Subs	Gls
Tottenham H.	App	07.84				
Leyton Orient	Bishops Stortford	07.89	89-90	19	9	2
Barnet	Tr	07.91	91-94	80	12	3

HODDLE Glenn
Hayes, 27 October, 1957 E Yth/Eu21-12/E 'B'/E-53 (M)

League Club	Source	Date Signed	Seasons Played	Apps	Subs	Gls
Tottenham H.	App	04.75	75-86	371	7	88
Swindon T.	A.S. Monaco (Fr)	08.91	91-92	63	1	1
Chelsea	Tr	06.93	93-94	19	12	1

HODDY Kevin Raymond
Romford, 6 January, 1968 (M)

League Club	Source	Date Signed	Seasons Played	Apps	Subs	Gls
Fulham	App	01.86	86-88	13	9	1

HODGE Eric
Edmonton, 1 June, 1928 Died 1963 (G)

League Club	Source	Date Signed	Seasons Played	Apps	Subs	Gls
Tottenham H.		08.48				
Newport Co.	Tr	08.49	49	7	-	0

HODGE Eric Richard Carew
South Africa, 3 April, 1933 (CH)

League Club	Source	Date Signed	Seasons Played	Apps	Subs	Gls
Brighton & H.A.	South Africa	10.56	57	4	-	0
Aldershot	Tr	07.59	59	17	-	0

HODGE James Oswald
Perth, 23 October, 1926 (LB)

League Club	Source	Date Signed	Seasons Played	Apps	Subs	Gls
Newport Co.	York C. (Am)	08.46	46	1	-	0

HODGE John
Skelmersdale, 1 April, 1969 (W)

League Club	Source	Date Signed	Seasons Played	Apps	Subs	Gls
Exeter C.	Falmouth	09.91	91-92	57	8	10
Swansea C.	Tr	07.93	93-95	87	25	10
Walsall	Tr	09.96	96-97	67	9	12

HODGE Martin John
Southport, 4 February, 1959 (G)

League Club	Source	Date Signed	Seasons Played	Apps	Subs	Gls
Plymouth Arg.	App	02.77	77-78	43	0	0
Everton	Tr	07.79	79-80	25	0	0
Preston N.E.	L	12.81	81	28	0	0
Oldham Ath.	L	07.82	82	4	0	0
Gillingham	L	01.83	82	4	0	0
Preston N.E.	L	02.83	82	16	0	0
Sheffield Wed.	Tr	08.83	83-87	197	0	0
Leicester C.	Tr	08.88	88-90	75	0	0
Hartlepool U.	Tr	08.91	91-92	69	0	0
Rochdale	Tr	07.93	93	42	0	0
Plymouth Arg.	Tr	08.94	94	17	0	0

HODGE Robert William
Exeter, 30 April, 1954 (W)

League Club	Source	Date Signed	Seasons Played	Apps	Subs	Gls
Exeter C.		07.74	74-78	120	8	18
Colchester U.	Tr	09.78	78-80	87	5	14
Torquay U.	Tr	08.81	81	3	1	1

HODGE Stephen Brian
Nottingham, 25 October, 1962 Eu21-8/E 'B'/E-24 (LM)

League Club	Source	Date Signed	Seasons Played	Apps	Subs	Gls
Nottingham F.	App	10.80	81-85	122	1	30
Aston Villa	Tr	08.85	85-86	53	0	12
Tottenham H.	Tr	12.86	86-87	44	1	7
Nottingham F.	Tr	08.88	88-90	79	3	20
Leeds U.	Tr	07.91	91-93	28	26	10
Derby Co.	L	08.94	94	10	0	2
Queens Park R.	Tr	10.94	94	15	0	0
Watford (N/C)	Tr	12.95	95	2	0	0
Leyton Orient (N/C)	Hong Kong	08.97	97	1	0	0

HODGES Cyril Leslie
Hackney, 18 September, 1919 Died 1979 (F)

League Club	Source	Date Signed	Seasons Played	Apps	Subs	Gls
Arsenal	Eton Manor	04.45	46	2	-	0
Brighton & H.A.	Tr	10.46	46	9	-	3

HODGES David
Ross-on-Wye, 17 January, 1970 (M)

League Club	Source	Date Signed	Seasons Played	Apps	Subs	Gls
Mansfield T.	Jnrs	08.87	86-90	67	18	7
Torquay U.	Tr	01.91	90-91	8	8	0
Shrewsbury T. (N/C)	Bolton W. (N/C)	08.92	92	1	0	0

HODGES Glyn Peter
Streatham, 30 April, 1963 W Yth/Wu21-5/W 'B'/W-18 (LM)

League Club	Source	Date Signed	Seasons Played	Apps	Subs	Gls
Wimbledon	App	02.81	80-86	200	32	49
Newcastle U.	Tr	07.87	87	7	0	0
Watford	Tr	10.87	87-89	82	4	15
Crystal Palace	Tr	07.90	90	5	2	0
Sheffield U.	Tr	01.91	90-95	116	31	19
Derby Co.	Tr	02.96	95	1	8	0
Hull C.	Sin Tao (HK)	08.97	97	13	5	4
Nottingham F.	Tr	02.98				

HODGES Kevin
Bridport, 12 June, 1960 (M)

League Club	Source	Date Signed	Seasons Played	Apps	Subs	Gls
Plymouth Arg.	App	03.78	78-92	502	28	81
Torquay U.	L	01.92	91	3	0	0
Torquay U.	Tr	12.92	92-96	49	19	4

HODGES Lee Leslie
Plaistow, 2 March, 1978 (LW)

League Club	Source	Date Signed	Seasons Played	Apps	Subs	Gls
West Ham U.	YT	03.95	97	0	2	0
Exeter C.	L	09.96	96	16	1	0
Leyton Orient	L	02.97	96	3	0	0
Plymouth Arg.	L	11.97	97	9	0	0

HODGES Lee Leslie
Epping, 4 September, 1973 E Yth (F)

League Club	Source	Date Signed	Seasons Played	Apps	Subs	Gls
Tottenham H.	YT	02.92	92	0	4	0
Plymouth Arg.	L	02.93	92	6	1	2
Wycombe W.	L	12.93	93	2	2	0
Barnet	Tr	05.94	94-96	94	11	26
Reading	Tr	07.97	97	20	4	6

HODGES Leonard Herbert
Bristol, 17 February, 1920 Died 1959 (IR)

League Club	Source	Date Signed	Seasons Played	Apps	Subs	Gls
Bristol Rov.	Soundwell	08.46	46-49	118	-	20
Swansea C.	Tr	08.50	50	2	-	0
Reading	Tr	08.51	51-52	6	-	2

HODGES Mark
Sheffield, 24 October, 1971 (CD)

League Club	Source	Date Signed	Seasons Played	Apps	Subs	Gls
Rotherham U.	YT	07.90	90	3	1	0

HODGETTS Frank
Dudley, 30 September, 1924 (OL)

League Club	Source	Date Signed	Seasons Played	Apps	Subs	Gls
West Bromwich A.	Jnrs	10.42	46-48	67	-	11
Millwall	Tr	08.49	49-52	34	-	6

HODGKINS Jeffrey
Portsmouth, 8 October, 1942 (CF)

League Club	Source	Date Signed	Seasons Played	Apps	Subs	Gls
Portsmouth	Jnrs	06.60	60	3	-	0

HODGKINSON Alan
Maltby, 16 August, 1936 Eu23-7/EF Lge/E-5 (G)

League Club	Source	Date Signed	Seasons Played	Apps	Subs	Gls
Sheffield U.	Worksop T.	08.53	54-70	576	0	0

HODGKINSON Derek John
Weston-super-Mare, 30 April, 1944 (IF)

League Club	Source	Date Signed	Seasons Played	Apps	Subs	Gls
Manchester C.	Margate	08.61	63	1	-	1
Stockport Co.	Tr	06.64	64-65	46	0	9

HODGKINSON Edwin
Ilkeston, 27 November, 1920 (WH)

League Club	Source	Date Signed	Seasons Played	Apps	Subs	Gls
Leeds U.		12.46	46-47	2	-	0
Halifax T.	Tr	07.48	48-49	12	-	2

HODGKISS Robert
Farnworth, 22 March, 1918 (FB)

League Club	Source	Date Signed	Seasons Played	Apps	Subs	Gls
Southport	Walkden Meths	11.38	38	10	-	0
Everton	Tr	08.46				
Southport	Tr	07.47	47-48	20	-	0

HODGKISSON William **Kenneth**
West Bromwich, 12 March, 1933 (IF)

League Club	Source	Date Signed	Seasons Played	Apps	Subs	Gls
West Bromwich A.	Jnrs	04.50	52-55	21	-	4
Walsall	Tr	01.56	55-65	335	1	57

HODGSON Brian George
Cleethorpes, 29 January, 1936 (F)

League Club	Source	Date Signed	Seasons Played	Apps	Subs	Gls
Grimsby T.	Askern W.M.C.	09.56	56	7	-	1
Workington	Tr	10.59	59	1	-	0

HODGSON David James
Gateshead, 6 August, 1960 Eu21-6 (F)

League Club	Source	Date Signed	Seasons Played	Apps	Subs	Gls
Middlesbrough	Jnrs	08.78	78-81	116	9	16
Liverpool	Tr	08.82	82-83	21	7	4
Sunderland	Tr	08.84	84-85	32	8	5
Norwich C.	Tr	07.86	86	3	3	1
Middlesbrough	L	02.87	86	2	0	0
Sheffield Wed.	Jerez (Sp)	08.88	88	6	5	1
Swansea C. (N/C)	Metz (Fr)	03.92	91	1	2	0

HODGSON Donald
Liversedge, 22 December, 1922 Died 1995 (IF)

League Club	Source	Date Signed	Seasons Played	Apps	Subs	Gls
Bradford P.A.	Bradford U.	04.48	48-51	41	-	7
York C.	Tr	08.52				

HODGSON Douglas John
Australia, 27 February, 1969 (CD)

League Club	Source	Date Signed	Seasons Played	Apps	Subs	Gls
Sheffield U.	Heidelberg (Aus)	07.94	94-96	24	6	1
Plymouth Arg.	L	08.95	95	3	2	0
Burnley	L	10.96	96	1	0	0
Oldham Ath.	Tr	02.97	96-97	33	7	4

HODGSON Gordon Henry
Newcastle, 13 October, 1952 E Yth (M)

League Club	Source	Date Signed	Seasons Played	Apps	Subs	Gls
Newcastle U.	Jnrs	06.71	71-73	8	1	0
Mansfield T.	Tr	05.74	74-78	184	0	23
Oxford U.	Tr	09.78	78-79	66	1	3
Peterborough U.	Tr	08.80	80-81	82	1	5

HODGSON John Percival
Seaham, 10 May, 1922 (G)

League Club	Source	Date Signed	Seasons Played	Apps	Subs	Gls
Leeds U.	Murton Colly	11.43	46-47	20	-	0
Middlesbrough	Tr	03.48	47-54	13	-	0

HODGSON John (Jack) Venner
Seaham, 30 September, 1913 Died 1970 (FB)

League Club	Source	Date Signed	Seasons Played	Apps	Subs	Gls
Grimsby T.	Seaham Colly	01.32	32-47	212	-	2
Doncaster Rov.	Tr	01.48	47-51	96	-	2

HODGSON Kenneth
Newcastle, 19 January, 1942 (F)

League Club	Source	Date Signed	Seasons Played	Apps	Subs	Gls
Newcastle U.	Jnrs	05.59	60	6	-	0
Scunthorpe U.	Tr	12.61	61-63	88	-	30
Bournemouth	Tr	06.64	64-65	77	1	24
Colchester U.	Tr	07.66	66-68	56	1	19

HODGSON Lawrence
Birkenhead, 19 January, 1917 Died 1980 (FB)

League Club	Source	Date Signed	Seasons Played	Apps	Subs	Gls
Tranmere Rov.	Silver Green	01.39	46-50	78	-	0

HODGSON Michael
Newcastle, 6 July, 1945 (OR)

League Club	Source	Date Signed	Seasons Played	Apps	Subs	Gls
Hartlepool U. (Am)	Billingham Synth.	08.64	64	1	-	0

HODGSON Noel
Workington, 25 December, 1938 (W)

League Club	Source	Date Signed	Seasons Played	Apps	Subs	Gls
Workington	Jnrs	08.57	57-62	51	-	12

HODGSON Ronald
Birkenhead, 2 November, 1922 (CH)

League Club	Source	Date Signed	Seasons Played	Apps	Subs	Gls
Tranmere Rov.	Jnrs	02.41				
Manchester C.	Tr	10.44	46	1	-	0
Southport	Tr	06.47	47-48	42	-	1
Crewe Alex.	Tr	02.49	48-49	31	-	0

HODGSON Samuel
Seaham, 21 January, 1919 (WH)

League Club	Source	Date Signed	Seasons Played	Apps	Subs	Gls
Grimsby T.	Seaham Colly	01.36	46-47	21	-	0
Mansfield T.	Tr	07.48	48	2	-	0

HODGSON William
Glasgow, 9 July, 1935 (IF)

League Club	Source	Date Signed	Seasons Played	Apps	Subs	Gls
Sheffield U.	St Johnstone	05.57	57-63	152	-	32
Leicester C.	Tr	09.63	63-64	46	-	10
Derby Co.	Tr	06.65	65-67	78	0	17
Rotherham U.	Tr	09.67	67	9	0	0
York C.	Tr	12.67	67-69	98	0	3

HODKINSON Andrew James
Ashton-u-Lyne, 4 November, 1965 E Sch (W)

League Club	Source	Date Signed	Seasons Played	Apps	Subs	Gls
Oldham Ath.	Bolton W. (App)	08.83	83-84	4	1	1
Stockport Co.	Tr	08.85	85-87	114	4	18
Scunthorpe U.	Tr	08.88	88-89	59	3	8

HODKINSON David
Lancaster, 18 January, 1945 (OL)

League Club	Source	Date Signed	Seasons Played	Apps	Subs	Gls
Oldham Ath.	App	02.63	61	2	-	0

HODSON Simeon Paul
Lincoln, 5 March, 1966 (RB)

League Club	Source	Date Signed	Seasons Played	Apps	Subs	Gls
Notts Co.	App	03.84	83-84	27	0	0
Charlton Ath.	Tr	03.85	84	5	0	0

League Club	Source	Date Signed	Seasons Played	Career Record Apps	Subs	Gls
Lincoln C.	Tr	01.86	85-86	54	2	0
Newport Co.	Tr	08.87	87	34	0	1
West Bromwich A.	Tr	03.88	87-92	78	5	0
Doncaster Rov. (N/C)	Tr	09.92	92	15	0	0
Mansfield T.	Kidderminster Hrs	02.93	92	17	0	0
HODSON Stuart William						
Peterborough, 5 November, 1950						(D)
Peterborough U.	Chatteris T.	11.74	74-76	24	10	0
HOEKMAN Daniel						
Netherlands, 21 September, 1964						(M)
Manchester C. (N/C)	Den Haag (Neth)	10.91	91	0	1	0
HOGAN Charles						
Bury, 23 April, 1926 Died 1992						(OR)
Bury	Spartan Ath.	06.48	47	1	-	0
Accrington St.	Tr	08.49	49-50	56	-	4
Southport	Tr	08.51	51	9	-	1
Rochdale	Tr	08.52	52	3	-	0
HOGAN Thomas **Eric**						
Cork, 17 December, 1971						(M)
Birmingham C.	Cobh Ramblers	08.91	91	0	1	0
HOGAN Roy David						
Hartlepool, 24 September, 1960						(M)
Hartlepool U.	App	09.78	77-82	133	10	15
Hartlepool U.	Crook T.	12.83	83-86	138	3	17
HOGAN John **Terence**						
Hartlepool, 3 June, 1933						(IR)
Hartlepool U.		08.57	57	9	-	1
HOGAN William James						
Salford, 9 January, 1924						(OR)
Manchester C.		05.42	48	3	-	0
Carlisle U.	Tr	09.49	49-55	190	-	26
HOGARTH Gordon						
Sunderland, 18 November, 1936						(WH)
Gateshead	Throckley Welfare	06.57	57-58	12	-	0
HOGG Adam						
Airdrie, 26 April, 1934						(FB)
Swindon T.	Airdrieonians	06.56	56	1	-	0
HOGG Derek						
Stockton, 4 November, 1930 EF Lge						(OL)
Leicester C.	Chorley	10.52	52-57	161	-	26
West Bromwich A.	Tr	04.58	58-60	81	-	11
Cardiff C.	Tr	10.60	60-61	41	-	7
HOGG Frederick William						
Bishop Auckland, 24 April, 1918						(IF/WH)
Luton T.		12.36	37	4	-	0
Mansfield T.	Tr	11.45	46-47	45	-	8
Halifax T.	Tr	10.47	47-49	49	-	3
HOGG Graeme James						
Aberdeen, 17 June, 1964 S Yth/Su21-4						(CD)
Manchester U.	App	06.82	83-87	82	1	1
West Bromwich A.	L	11.87	87	7	0	0
Portsmouth	Tr	08.88	88-90	97	3	2
Notts Co.	Hearts	01.95	94-97	66	0	0
Brentford	Tr	01.98	97	17	0	2
HOGG Graham Stuart						
Neath, 15 January, 1922 W Amat						(F)
Cardiff C.	Cardiff Corries	06.48	48	1	-	0
HOGG John						
Blyth, 7 October, 1931						(F)
Sunderland		12.49				
Portsmouth	Blyth Spartans	12.54				
Gateshead	Peterborough U.	07.57	57-59	80	-	21
HOGG Matthew						
Dinnington (Nd), 14 April, 1941						(RB)
Newcastle U.	Jnrs	05.59				
Darlington	Tr	07.61	61	1	-	0
HOGG Anthony **Raymond**						
Lowick (Nd), 11 December, 1929						(FB)
Aston Villa	Berwick R.	03.55	54-56	21	-	0
Mansfield T.	Tr	07.58	58-59	11	-	0
Peterborough U.	Tr	08.60	60	2	-	0

League Club	Source	Date Signed	Seasons Played	Career Record Apps	Subs	Gls
HOGGAN David Matthew						
Falkirk, 10 August, 1961						(M)
Bolton W.	App	08.79	79-82	83	10	11
HOGGART Dennis Joseph						
Glasgow, 2 January, 1939						(IF)
Leeds U.	Ferndale Ath.	02.57				
York C.	Tr	08.60	60-63	45	-	11
Stockport Co.	Tr	08.64	64-65	30	0	6
HOGGETH Gary Denis						
South Shields, 7 October, 1979						(G)
Doncaster Rov.	YT	●	97	8	0	0
HOLAH Eric Tansley						
Hull, 3 August, 1937						(CF)
Hull C. (Am)	Malet Lambert O.B.	06.60	60	1	-	1
Bradford C.	Tr	08.61	61	4	-	2
HOLBROOK Ian Clifford						
Knutsford, 24 November, 1955						(G)
Bolton W.	Jnrs	07.74				
Stockport Co.	Tr	07.76	76	37	0	0
HOLBROOK Leigh William						
Belper, 6 August, 1979						(CD)
Mansfield T.	YT	●	96	0	1	0
HOLBROOK Stephen						
Richmond (NYorks), 16 September, 1952 E Sch						(W)
Hull C.	App	09.70	70-71	2	1	0
Darlington	Tr	06.72	72-76	104	12	12
HOLBUTT Barry Lewis						
Birmingham, 11 February, 1943						(CF)
Aston Villa	Jnrs	10.60				
Walsall	Nuneaton Borough	03.65	65	0	1	0
HOLCROFT Peter Ian						
Liverpool, 3 January, 1976						(M)
Everton	YT	07.94				
Swindon T.	Tr	11.96	96	2	1	0
Exeter C.	L	08.97	97	3	3	0
HOLD John David						
Southampton, 28 March, 1948						(F)
Bournemouth	App	11.64	65-70	80	5	25
Crewe Alex.	L	01.69	68	0	2	0
Northampton T.	Tr	08.71	71-72	42	2	11
HOLD Oscar						
Carlton (Yk), 19 October, 1918						(IF)
Barnsley	Denaby U.	08.37				
Aldershot	Tr	04.39	46	14	-	3
Norwich C.	Tr	03.47	46-48	44	-	18
Notts Co.	Tr	10.48	48	19	-	9
Everton	Chelmsford C.	02.50	49-50	22	-	5
Queens Park R.	Tr	02.52	51-52	5	-	1
HOLDEN Alan						
Haslingden, 12 October, 1941						(WH)
Blackburn Rov.	Jnrs	01.62	63	1	-	0
Stockport Co.	Tr	07.66	66	1	0	0
HOLDEN Andrew Ian						
Flint, 14 September, 1962 Wu21-1/W-1						(CD)
Chester C.	Rhyl	08.83	83-86	100	0	17
Wigan Ath.	Tr	10.86	86-88	48	1	4
Oldham Ath.	Tr	01.89	88-94	22	0	4
HOLDEN Albert **Douglas**						
Manchester, 28 September, 1930 E Yth/EF Lge/E-5						(OR)
Bolton W.	Jnrs	01.50	51-62	419	-	40
Preston N.E.	Tr	11.62	62-64	89	-	13
HOLDEN Melville George						
Dundee, 25 August, 1954 Died 1981						(F)
Preston N.E.	App	09.72	72-74	69	3	22
Sunderland	Tr	05.75	75-77	66	7	23
Blackpool	Tr	07.78	78	2	1	0
HOLDEN Richard (Rick) William						
Skipton, 9 September, 1964						(LW)
Burnley (N/C)	Carnegie College	03.86	85	0	1	0
Halifax T.	Tr	09.86	86-87	66	1	12
Watford	Tr	03.88	87-88	42	0	8
Oldham Ath.	Tr	08.89	89-91	125	4	19
Manchester C.	Tr	08.92	92-93	49	1	3
Oldham Ath.	Tr	10.93	93-94	46	14	9
Blackpool	Tr	09.95	95	19	3	2

HOLDEN Robert
Sunderland, 28 October, 1965 (F)

League Club	Source	Date Signed	Seasons Played	Apps	Subs	Gls
Scunthorpe U.	Sunderland (App)	09.83	83	6	1	1

HOLDEN Simon John
Littleborough, 9 March, 1968 (M)

League Club	Source	Date Signed	Seasons Played	Apps	Subs	Gls
Rochdale	Jnrs	07.85				
Rochdale	Wheatsheaf	01.87	86-87	35	14	4

HOLDEN Stephen Anthony
Luton, 4 September, 1972 E Semi Pro (CD)

League Club	Source	Date Signed	Seasons Played	Apps	Subs	Gls
Leicester C.	YT	03.91	91	1	0	0
Carlisle U.	L	10.92	92	8	0	0
Carlisle U.	Tr	02.93	92-93	14	0	1

HOLDEN James Stewart
Grange Moor (Yks), 21 April, 1942 (D)

League Club	Source	Date Signed	Seasons Played	Apps	Subs	Gls
Huddersfield T.	Jnrs	04.59	60-64	28	-	2
Oldham Ath.	Tr	07.65	65-66	39	3	5
Rochdale	Tr	01.67	66	21	0	0

HOLDEN William
Bolton, 1 April, 1928 E 'B' (CF)

League Club	Source	Date Signed	Seasons Played	Apps	Subs	Gls
Burnley	Everton (Am)	11.49	50-55	187	-	75
Sunderland	Tr	12.55	55	19	-	5
Stockport Co.	Tr	10.56	56-58	87	-	37
Bury	Tr	03.59	58-61	101	-	33
Halifax T.	Tr	06.62	62	37	-	11

HOLDER Alan Maurice
Oxford, 10 December, 1931 (WH)

League Club	Source	Date Signed	Seasons Played	Apps	Subs	Gls
Nottingham F.		04.52	54	3	-	0
Lincoln C.	Tr	07.55	55	1	-	0
Tranmere Rov.	Tr	12.56	56	13	-	1

HOLDER Colin Walter
Cheltenham, 6 January, 1944 (CF)

League Club	Source	Date Signed	Seasons Played	Apps	Subs	Gls
Coventry C.	App	05.61	60-61	9	-	4

HOLDER David James
Cheltenham, 15 December, 1943 (CH)

League Club	Source	Date Signed	Seasons Played	Apps	Subs	Gls
Notts Co.	Cardiff C. (Am)	10.62	63	8	-	0
Barrow	Tr	07.64	64	29	-	0

HOLDER Philip
Kilburn, 19 January, 1952 E Yth (M)

League Club	Source	Date Signed	Seasons Played	Apps	Subs	Gls
Tottenham H.	App	02.69	71-73	9	4	1
Crystal Palace	Tr	02.75	74-77	93	2	5
Bournemouth	Memphis (USA)	03.79	78-79	58	0	4

HOLDER Stephen William
Nottingham, 21 April, 1952 (OR)

League Club	Source	Date Signed	Seasons Played	Apps	Subs	Gls
Notts Co.	App	04.70	69	0	1	0

HOLDING Edwin John
Wolverhampton, 15 October, 1930 (RB/F)

League Club	Source	Date Signed	Seasons Played	Apps	Subs	Gls
Walsall		01.49	50-53	39	-	6
Barrow		07.54	54	5	-	5

HOLDSWORTH David Gary
Walthamstow, 8 November, 1968 E Yth/Eu21-1 (CD)

League Club	Source	Date Signed	Seasons Played	Apps	Subs	Gls
Watford	App	11.86	88-95	249	9	10
Sheffield U.	Tr	10.96	96-97	77	0	3

HOLDSWORTH Dean Christopher
Walthamstow, 8 November, 1968 E 'B' (F)

League Club	Source	Date Signed	Seasons Played	Apps	Subs	Gls
Watford	App	11.86	87-89	2	14	3
Carlisle U.	L	02.88	87	4	0	1
Port Vale	L	03.88	87	6	0	2
Swansea C.	L	08.88	88	4	1	1
Brentford	L	10.88	88	2	5	1
Brentford	Tr	09.89	89-91	106	4	53
Wimbledon	Tr	07.92	92-97	148	21	58
Bolton W.	Tr	10.97	97	17	3	3

HOLE Alan Vincent
Swansea, 26 December, 1930 (CH)

League Club	Source	Date Signed	Seasons Played	Apps	Subs	Gls
Swansea C.		07.53	53	20	-	0

HOLE Barrington (Barry) Gerard
Swansea, 16 September, 1942 W Sch/Wu23-5/W-30 (WH)

League Club	Source	Date Signed	Seasons Played	Apps	Subs	Gls
Cardiff C.	Jnrs	09.59	59-65	211	0	16
Blackburn Rov.	Tr	07.66	66-68	79	0	13
Aston Villa	Tr	09.68	68-69	47	0	6
Swansea C.	Tr	07.70	70-71	78	0	3

HOLE David Colin
Swansea, 1 September, 1932 W Sch (WH)

League Club	Source	Date Signed	Seasons Played	Apps	Subs	Gls
Swansea C.	Jnrs	03.50	53	1	-	0

HOLLAND Christopher James
Whalley, 11 September, 1975 E Yth/Eu21-10 (M)

League Club	Source	Date Signed	Seasons Played	Apps	Subs	Gls
Preston N.E.	YT	●	93	0	1	0
Newcastle U.	Tr	01.94	93	2	1	0
Birmingham C.	Tr	09.96	96-97	30	12	0

HOLLAND David William
Chorley, 6 March, 1935 (IF/WH)

League Club	Source	Date Signed	Seasons Played	Apps	Subs	Gls
Stockport Co.	Horwich R.M.I.	06.59	59-60	25	-	4

HOLLAND Kenneth
Doncaster, 18 April, 1922 (IF)

League Club	Source	Date Signed	Seasons Played	Apps	Subs	Gls
Bury	Wolverhampton W. (Am)	09.44				
Bournemouth	Tr	09.48	48	3	-	0

HOLLAND Matthew Rhys
Bury, 11 April, 1974 (M)

League Club	Source	Date Signed	Seasons Played	Apps	Subs	Gls
West Ham U.	YT	07.92				
Bournemouth	Tr	01.95	94-96	97	7	18
Ipswich T.	Tr	07.97	97	46	0	10

HOLLAND Patrick George
Poplar, 13 September, 1950 (W)

League Club	Source	Date Signed	Seasons Played	Apps	Subs	Gls
West Ham U.	App	04.69	68-80	227	18	23
Bournemouth	L	03.71	70	10	0	0

HOLLAND Paul
Lincoln, 18 July, 1973 E Sch/E Yth/Eu21-4 (M)

League Club	Source	Date Signed	Seasons Played	Apps	Subs	Gls
Mansfield T.	Jnrs	07.91	90-94	149	0	25
Sheffield U.	Tr	06.95	95	11	7	1
Chesterfield	Tr	01.96	95-97	72	5	8

HOLLAND Eric Reginald
Sutton-in-Ashfield, 23 January, 1940 E Sch/E Yth (FB)

League Club	Source	Date Signed	Seasons Played	Apps	Subs	Gls
Manchester U.	Jnrs	05.57				
Wrexham	Tr	03.60	59-65	118	0	0
Chester C.	Tr	03.66	65-66	5	1	0

HOLLAND Robert James
Willesden, 18 August, 1965 (LB)

League Club	Source	Date Signed	Seasons Played	Apps	Subs	Gls
Crewe Alex. (N/C)	Harrow Borough	09.85	85	7	0	0

HOLLAND Simon Luke David
Sunderland, 26 March, 1973 (F)

League Club	Source	Date Signed	Seasons Played	Apps	Subs	Gls
Doncaster Rov.	YT	01.91	90	1	0	0

HOLLETT Ivan Ronald
Pinxton, 22 April, 1940 (CF)

League Club	Source	Date Signed	Seasons Played	Apps	Subs	Gls
Mansfield T.	Sutton T.	08.58	58-64	98	-	40
Chesterfield	Tr	12.64	64-68	157	0	62
Crewe Alex.	Tr	11.68	68-70	55	4	19
Cambridge U.	Tr	11.70	70-71	37	1	13
Hereford U.	Tr	01.72	72	11	0	2

HOLLEY Thomas
Sunderland, 15 November, 1913 Died 1992 (CH)

League Club	Source	Date Signed	Seasons Played	Apps	Subs	Gls
Barnsley	Sunderland (Am)	09.32	33-35	75	-	4
Leeds U.	Tr	07.36	36-48	162	-	1

HOLLIDAY Edwin
Leeds, 7 June, 1939 Eu23-5/EF Lge/E-3 (OL)

League Club	Source	Date Signed	Seasons Played	Apps	Subs	Gls
Middlesbrough	Jnrs	08.56	57-61	134	-	17
Sheffield Wed.	Tr	03.62	61-63	55	-	12
Middlesbrough	Tr	06.65	65	23	0	4
Workington	Hereford U.	02.68	67-68	56	0	4
Peterborough U.	Tr	07.69	69	12	4	1

HOLLIDAY John Richard
Penrith, 13 March, 1970 (CD)

League Club	Source	Date Signed	Seasons Played	Apps	Subs	Gls
Carlisle U.		09.89	90-92	19	0	0

HOLLIDAY Kenneth Joseph
Darwen, 19 August, 1925 (D)

League Club	Source	Date Signed	Seasons Played	Apps	Subs	Gls
Blackburn Rov.	Darwen	10.46	47-51	29	-	0
Accrington St.	Tr	07.52	52-54	96	-	5
Barrow	Tr	09.55	55	5	-	0

HOLLIFIELD Michael
Middlesbrough, 2 May, 1961 (LB)

League Club	Source	Date Signed	Seasons Played	Apps	Subs	Gls
Wolverhampton W.	App	04.79	80-81	21	0	0
Hull C.	Tr	08.83	83-84	45	0	1
Tranmere Rov.	Tr	07.85	85	0	1	0

HOLLINS David Michael
Bangor, 4 February, 1938 Wu23-2/W-11 (G)

League Club	Source	Date Signed	Seasons Played	Apps	Subs	Gls
Brighton & H.A.	Merrow	11.55	57-60	66	-	0
Newcastle U.	Tr	03.61	60-66	112	0	0
Mansfield T.	Tr	02.67	66-69	111	0	0
Nottingham F.	L	03.70	69	9	0	0
Aldershot	Tr	07.70	70	16	0	0

HOLLINS John William
Guildford, 16 July, 1946 E Yth/Eu23-12/E'B'/EF Lge/E-1 (M)

League Club	Source	Date Signed	Seasons Played	Apps	Subs	Gls
Chelsea	App	07.63	63-74	436	0	47
Queens Park R.	Tr	06.75	75-78	148	3	6
Arsenal	Tr	07.79	79-82	123	4	9
Chelsea	Tr	06.83	83	29	0	1

HOLLINSHEAD Shaun
Sandbach, 21 February, 1961 (M)

League Club	Source	Date Signed	Seasons Played	Apps	Subs	Gls
Crewe Alex.	App	●	77	2	3	0

HOLLIS Andrew
Huntingdon, 16 September, 1963 (F)

League Club	Source	Date Signed	Seasons Played	Apps	Subs	Gls
Cambridge U.	Ramsey T.	04.87	86-87	3	1	0

HOLLIS Harry
Shotton, 12 December, 1913 Died 1982 (FB)

League Club	Source	Date Signed	Seasons Played	Apps	Subs	Gls
Chester C.		09.40				
Wrexham	Connahs Quay	08.46	46	1	-	0

HOLLIS Kenneth **Michael**
Loughborough, 14 November, 1949 (F)

League Club	Source	Date Signed	Seasons Played	Apps	Subs	Gls
Leicester C.	App	11.66				
Barrow	Tr	07.69	69-71	88	3	13
Chester C.	Tr	07.72	72	34	3	8
Stockport Co.	Tr	07.73	73-75	106	6	33
Reading	Tr	03.76	75-76	18	7	6

HOLLIS Roy Walter
Yarmouth, 24 December, 1925 (CF)

League Club	Source	Date Signed	Seasons Played	Apps	Subs	Gls
Norwich C.	Great Yarmouth	05.47	47-51	96	-	52
Tottenham H.	Tr	12.52	52	3	-	1
Southend U.	Tr	02.54	53-59	240	-	120

HOLLIS Stephen John
Liverpool, 22 August, 1972 (FB)

League Club	Source	Date Signed	Seasons Played	Apps	Subs	Gls
Liverpool	YT	05.90				
Wigan Ath.	Knowsley U.	08.93	93	0	1	0

HOLLOW Michael John
Nazeing (Ex), 5 September, 1943 (FB)

League Club	Source	Date Signed	Seasons Played	Apps	Subs	Gls
Leyton Orient	Bishops Stortford	08.62	63-64	34	-	0
Peterborough U.	Tr	07.65	65	14	0	1

HOLLOWAY Christopher David
Swansea, 5 February, 1980 (M)

League Club	Source	Date Signed	Seasons Played	Apps	Subs	Gls
Exeter C.	YT	●	97	4	2	0

HOLLOWAY Darren
Bishop Auckland, 3 October, 1977 Eu21-1 (RB)

League Club	Source	Date Signed	Seasons Played	Apps	Subs	Gls
Sunderland	YT	10.95	97	32	0	0
Carlisle U.	L	08.97	97	5	0	0

HOLLOWAY Ian Scott
Kingswood, 12 March, 1963 (RW)

League Club	Source	Date Signed	Seasons Played	Apps	Subs	Gls
Bristol Rov.	App	03.81	80-84	104	7	14
Wimbledon	Tr	07.85	85	19	0	2
Brentford	Tr	03.86	85-87	27	3	2
Torquay U.	L	01.87	86	5	0	0
Bristol Rov.	Tr	08.87	87-90	179	0	26
Queens Park R.	Tr	08.91	91-95	130	17	4
Bristol Rov.	Tr	07.96	96-97	63	7	1

HOLLOWBREAD John Frederick
Enfield, 2 January, 1934 (G)

League Club	Source	Date Signed	Seasons Played	Apps	Subs	Gls
Tottenham H.	Enfield	01.52	58-63	67	-	0
Southampton	Tr	05.64	64-65	36	0	0

HOLLUND Martin
Stord, Norway, 11 August, 1975 (G)

League Club	Source	Date Signed	Seasons Played	Apps	Subs	Gls
Hartlepool U.	SK Brann Bergen (Nor)	11.97	97	28	0	0

HOLLYMAN Kenneth Charles
Cardiff, 18 November, 1922 (WH)

League Club	Source	Date Signed	Seasons Played	Apps	Subs	Gls
Cardiff C.	Cardiff Nomads	04.42	46-53	188	-	8
Newport Co.	Tr	11.53	53-59	231	-	4

HOLLYWOOD Dennis Fallan
Govan, 3 November, 1944 Su23-1 (LB)

League Club	Source	Date Signed	Seasons Played	Apps	Subs	Gls
Southampton	App	12.61	62-71	234	0	4

HOLMAN Harold Western
Exeter, 25 September, 1920 Died 1977 (CF)

League Club	Source	Date Signed	Seasons Played	Apps	Subs	Gls
Exeter C.	Budleigh Salterton	12.46	46	4	-	2

HOLMAN Harold William
Exeter, 16 November, 1957 E Sch (F)

League Club	Source	Date Signed	Seasons Played	Apps	Subs	Gls
Exeter C.	Chelsea (App)	07.76	76-78	47	5	9
Peterborough U.	Tr	12.78	78	9	0	1

HOLME Philip Charles
Briton Ferry, 21 June, 1947 (F)

League Club	Source	Date Signed	Seasons Played	Apps	Subs	Gls
Swansea C.	Bridgend T.	03.71	70-71	19	4	5
Hull C.	Tr	07.72	72-73	29	9	11

HOLMES Albert Valentine
Ecclesfield, 14 February, 1942 (FB)

League Club	Source	Date Signed	Seasons Played	Apps	Subs	Gls
Chesterfield	E.M.Gas Board	06.61	61-75	467	3	10

HOLMES Andrew John
Stoke, 7 January, 1969 (CD)

League Club	Source	Date Signed	Seasons Played	Apps	Subs	Gls
Stoke C.	App	01.87	87-89	6	2	0
Doncaster Rov.	Tr	07.90	90	10	1	0

HOLMES Barry
Bradford, 4 October, 1942 (W)

League Club	Source	Date Signed	Seasons Played	Apps	Subs	Gls
Halifax T.	Ossett A.	09.66	66-72	82	8	8

HOLMES Albert **Colin**
Winchester, 28 March, 1939 E Yth (HB)

League Club	Source	Date Signed	Seasons Played	Apps	Subs	Gls
Southampton	Jnrs	02.57	59	1	-	0

HOLMES Bert Harold Frank
Norwich, 27 September, 1924 (CH)

League Club	Source	Date Signed	Seasons Played	Apps	Subs	Gls
Norwich C.	Gothic	08.47	48-54	58	-	1

HOLMES Daniel
Clophill (Beds), 13 June, 1972 (M)

League Club	Source	Date Signed	Seasons Played	Apps	Subs	Gls
Middlesbrough	YT	01.90				
Bournemouth (N/C)	Tr	07.91	92	0	1	0

HOLMES David James
Derby, 22 November, 1971 (F)

League Club	Source	Date Signed	Seasons Played	Apps	Subs	Gls
Scarborough	YT	07.91	89-91	4	7	1

HOLMES Ian Michael
Wombwell, 8 December, 1950 (M)

League Club	Source	Date Signed	Seasons Played	Apps	Subs	Gls
Sheffield U.	Jnrs	01.68	71-72	4	2	0
York C.	Tr	07.73	73-77	152	7	30
Huddersfield T.	Tr	10.77	77-79	65	8	21

HOLMES James Paul
Dublin, 11 November, 1953 IR-30 (LB)

League Club	Source	Date Signed	Seasons Played	Apps	Subs	Gls
Coventry C.	App	11.70	71-76	122	6	6
Tottenham H.	Tr	03.77	76-78	81	0	2
Leicester C. (N/C)	Vancouver (Can)	10.82	82	2	0	0
Brentford (N/C)	Tr	02.83	82	4	0	0
Torquay U. (N/C)	Tr	03.83	82-83	25	0	3
Peterborough U.	Tr	11.83	83-85	48	1	7

HOLMES Joseph
Clay Cross, 10 February, 1926 (WH)

League Club	Source	Date Signed	Seasons Played	Apps	Subs	Gls
Chesterfield	Parkhouse Colly	09.46	47-51	29	-	3

HOLMES Kyle Jonathon
Abergavenny, 25 September, 1959 (M)

League Club	Source	Date Signed	Seasons Played	Apps	Subs	Gls
Hereford U.	App	10.77	77-79	25	3	3

HOLMES Lee John
Aveley, 28 September, 1955 (F)

League Club	Source	Date Signed	Seasons Played	Apps	Subs	Gls
Brentford	Haringey Borough	06.79	79	26	2	6

HOLMES Matthew Jason
Luton, 1 August, 1969 (M)

League Club	Source	Date Signed	Seasons Played	Apps	Subs	Gls
Bournemouth	YT	08.88	88-91	105	9	8
Cardiff C.	L	03.89	88	0	1	0
West Ham U.	Tr	08.92	92-94	63	13	4
Blackburn Rov.	Tr	08.95	95	8	1	1
Charlton Ath.	Tr	07.97	97	10	6	1

HOLMES Michael Arthur
Blackpool, 9 September, 1965 (M)

League Club	Source	Date Signed	Seasons Played	Apps	Subs	Gls
Bradford C. (N/C)	Yeadon Celtic	07.84	84	0	5	0
Wolverhampton W.	Burnley (N/C)	11.85	85-87	74	9	13
Huddersfield T.	Tr	07.88	88	3	4	0
Cambridge U.	Tr	02.89	88	7	4	0
Rochdale	Tr	07.89	89-90	47	8	7
Torquay U.	Tr	12.90	90-91	34	6	3
Carlisle U.	Tr	02.92	91-92	33	1	4
Northampton T. (N/C)	Tr	03.93	92	6	0	0

HOLMES Nicholas Charles
Southampton, 11 November, 1954 (M)

League Club	Source	Date Signed	Seasons Played	Apps	Subs	Gls
Southampton	App	11.72	73-86	437	7	56

HOLMES Paul
Stocksbridge, 18 February, 1968 (RB)

League Club	Source	Date Signed	Seasons Played	Apps	Subs	Gls
Doncaster Rov.	App	02.86	85-87	42	5	1
Torquay U.	Tr	08.88	88-91	127	11	4

League Club	Source	Date Signed	Seasons Played	Apps	Subs	Gls
Birmingham C.	Tr	06.92	92	12	0	0
Everton	Tr	03.93	92-95	21	0	0
West Bromwich A.	Tr	01.96	95-97	85	1	1

HOLMES Roger William
Scunthorpe, 9 September, 1942 (M)

League Club	Source	Date Signed	Seasons Played	Apps	Subs	Gls
Lincoln C.	Jnrs	09.59	59-71	276	2	36

HOLMES Stanley
Easington, 27 November, 1920 Died 1994 (RB)

League Club	Source	Date Signed	Seasons Played	Apps	Subs	Gls
Hartlepool U.		07.47	49	1	-	0

HOLMES Steven Peter
Middlesbrough, 13 January, 1971 (CD)

League Club	Source	Date Signed	Seasons Played	Apps	Subs	Gls
Lincoln C. (N/C)	YT	07.89				
Preston N.E.	Guisborough T.	03.94	94-95	13	0	1
Hartlepool U.	L	03.95	94	5	0	2
Lincoln C.	L	10.95	95	12	0	1
Lincoln C.	Tr	03.96	95-97	84	1	9

HOLMES Thomas
Hemsworth, 14 December, 1934 (IF)

League Club	Source	Date Signed	Seasons Played	Apps	Subs	Gls
Barnsley	Hemsworth Y.C.	03.53	54-58	35	-	7
Halifax T.	Tr	07.59	59-60	50	-	15
Chesterfield	Tr	07.61	61	20	-	3

HOLMES William
Hunslet, 29 October, 1926 E Amat (CF)

League Club	Source	Date Signed	Seasons Played	Apps	Subs	Gls
Doncaster Rov. (Am)	Wolverhampton W. (Am)	10.50	50	2	-	0
Blackburn Rov. (Am)	Morecambe	01.52	51-52	21	-	16
Bradford C.	Morecambe	09.53	53	22	-	5
Southport	Tr	07.54	54-55	56	-	21

HOLMES William Gerald
Balham, 4 February, 1951 Died 1988 (F)

League Club	Source	Date Signed	Seasons Played	Apps	Subs	Gls
Millwall	Woking	07.70	70	0	1	0
Luton T.	Tr	07.73	73	0	1	0
Wimbledon	Barnet	07.75	77	15	0	5
Hereford U.	Tr	11.77	77-78	21	10	5
Brentford	Tr	08.79	79	8	7	2

HOLSGROVE John William
Southwark, 27 September, 1945 E Yth (CD)

League Club	Source	Date Signed	Seasons Played	Apps	Subs	Gls
Crystal Palace	Tottenham H. (Am)	02.64	64	18	-	2
Wolverhampton W.	Tr	05.65	65-70	178	2	7
Sheffield Wed.	Tr	06.71	71-74	103	1	5
Stockport Co.	Tr	08.75	75	9	0	0

HOLSGROVE Paul
Telford, 26 August, 1969 (M)

League Club	Source	Date Signed	Seasons Played	Apps	Subs	Gls
Aldershot	YT	02.87	87-88	0	3	0
Luton T.	Wokingham T.	01.91	90-91	1	1	0
Millwall	Heracles (Neth)	08.92	92	3	8	0
Reading	Tr	08.94	94-97	63	7	6
Grimsby T.	L	09.97	97	3	7	0
Crewe Alex. (N/C)	Tr	11.97	97	7	1	1
Stoke C.	Tr	01.98	97	11	1	1

HOLT Andrew
Stockport, 21 April, 1978 (CD)

League Club	Source	Date Signed	Seasons Played	Apps	Subs	Gls
Oldham Ath.	YT	07.96	96-97	7	8	1

HOLT David
Padiham, 26 February, 1952 (D)

League Club	Source	Date Signed	Seasons Played	Apps	Subs	Gls
Bury	App	10.69	69-74	174	4	9
Oldham Ath.	Tr	12.74	74-79	141	1	1
Burnley	Tr	07.80	80-82	84	0	1

HOLT David Ephraim
Sunniside (Dm), 7 January, 1945 (CH)

League Club	Source	Date Signed	Seasons Played	Apps	Subs	Gls
Blackburn Rov.	Jnrs	04.63	65-66	10	0	0

HOLT George
Halifax, 28 February, 1927 (IF)

League Club	Source	Date Signed	Seasons Played	Apps	Subs	Gls
Halifax T.		07.47	47-53	57	-	11

HOLT Michael Andrew
Burnley, 28 July, 1977 (F)

League Club	Source	Date Signed	Seasons Played	Apps	Subs	Gls
Blackburn Rov.	YT	07.95				
Preston N.E.	Tr	08.96	96-97	12	21	5

HOLT Raymond
Thorne, 29 October, 1939 (CH)

League Club	Source	Date Signed	Seasons Played	Apps	Subs	Gls
Huddersfield T.	Moor End	08.58	61-63	16	-	0
Oldham Ath.	Tr	07.65	65	14	1	0
Halifax T.	Tr	07.66	66-67	86	0	0
Scunthorpe U.	Tr	07.68	68-69	50	0	0

HOLT William Kenneth
Boldon, 31 March, 1926 (CH)

League Club	Source	Date Signed	Seasons Played	Apps	Subs	Gls
Blackburn Rov.	Boldon Colly	01.49	48-52	78	-	0
Barrow	Weymouth	06.54	54-56	72	-	0

HOLTHAM Dean Mark
Pontypridd, 30 September, 1963 (D)

League Club	Source	Date Signed	Seasons Played	Apps	Subs	Gls
Cardiff C.	App	09.81				
Swansea C.	Tr	08.82	82	6	0	0
Newport Co. (N/C)	Ebbw Vale	09.87	87	4	2	0

HOLTON Clifford Charles
Oxford, 29 April, 1929 Died 1996 (CF)

League Club	Source	Date Signed	Seasons Played	Apps	Subs	Gls
Arsenal	Oxford C.	11.47	50-58	198	-	83
Watford	Tr	10.58	58-61	120	-	84
Northampton T.	Tr	09.61	61-62	62	-	50
Crystal Palace	Tr	12.62	62-64	101	-	40
Watford	Tr	05.65	65	24	0	12
Charlton Ath.	Tr	02.66	65	18	0	7
Leyton Orient	Tr	07.66	66-67	47	0	17

HOLTON James Allan
Lesmahagow, 11 April, 1951 Died 1993 Su23-1/S-15 (CD)

League Club	Source	Date Signed	Seasons Played	Apps	Subs	Gls
West Bromwich A.	Jnrs	04.68				
Shrewsbury T.	Tr	06.71	71-72	67	0	4
Manchester U.	Tr	01.73	72-74	63	0	5
Sunderland	Tr	09.76	76	15	0	0
Coventry C.	Tr	03.77	76-79	91	0	0
Sheffield Wed.	Tr	08.81				

HOLTON Patrick Carr
Hamilton, 23 December, 1935 (FB)

League Club	Source	Date Signed	Seasons Played	Apps	Subs	Gls
Chelsea	Motherwell	03.59	58	1	-	0
Southend U.	Tr	08.60	60	11	-	0

HOLWYN Jermaine Titano Benito
Netherlands, 16 April, 1973 (D)

League Club	Source	Date Signed	Seasons Played	Apps	Subs	Gls
Port Vale	Ajax (Neth)	07.95	96	5	2	0

HOLYOAK Philip
Sunderland, 22 May, 1959 (CD)

League Club	Source	Date Signed	Seasons Played	Apps	Subs	Gls
Tottenham H.	App	05.77				
Scunthorpe U.	L	02.78	77	1	0	0

HOLZMAN Mark Robin
Bracknell, 21 February, 1973 (FB)

League Club	Source	Date Signed	Seasons Played	Apps	Subs	Gls
Reading	YT	07.91	91-92	23	9	1

HOMER Christopher
Stockton, 16 April, 1977 (M)

League Club	Source	Date Signed	Seasons Played	Apps	Subs	Gls
Hartlepool U.	YT	07.95	94-96	2	5	0

HONE Mark Joseph
Croydon, 31 March, 1968 E Semi Pro (RB)

League Club	Source	Date Signed	Seasons Played	Apps	Subs	Gls
Crystal Palace	Jnrs	07.85	87-88	4	0	0
Southend U.	Welling U.	08.94	94-95	50	6	0
Lincoln C.	Tr	07.96	96-97	48	5	2

HONEYWOOD Brian Roy
Chelmsford, 8 May, 1949 (WH)

League Club	Source	Date Signed	Seasons Played	Apps	Subs	Gls
Ipswich T.	App	05.67				
Colchester U.	Tr	06.68	68	12	6	0

HONOR Christian Robert
Bristol, 5 June, 1968 (D)

League Club	Source	Date Signed	Seasons Played	Apps	Subs	Gls
Bristol C.	App	06.86	85-89	44	16	1
Torquay U.	L	11.86	86	3	0	0
Hereford U.	L	12.89	89	2	1	0
Swansea C.	L	01.91	90	2	0	0
Cardiff C. (L)	Airdrieonians	02.95	94	10	0	0

HONOUR Brian
Horden, 16 February, 1964 (RM)

League Club	Source	Date Signed	Seasons Played	Apps	Subs	Gls
Darlington	App	02.82	81-83	59	15	4
Hartlepool U.	Peterlee Newtown	02.85	84-94	301	18	25

HONOUR John
Horden, 1 November, 1953 (M)

League Club	Source	Date Signed	Seasons Played	Apps	Subs	Gls
West Bromwich A.	App	05.71				
Hartlepool U.	Tr	07.72	72-75	107	5	6
Workington	Tr	03.76	75-76	38	1	1

HOOD Derek
Washington, 17 December, 1958 (M/FB)

League Club	Source	Date Signed	Seasons Played	Apps	Subs	Gls
West Bromwich A.	App	12.76				
Hull C.	Tr	08.77	77-79	20	4	0
York C.	Tr	02.80	79-87	287	13	32

League Club	Source	Date Signed	Seasons Played	Apps	Subs	Gls
HOOD George William						
Houghton-le-Spring, 27 November, 1920						(RB)
Gateshead		10.47	47-48	30	-	0
HOOD Owen Glyn						
Pontypool, 12 March, 1925						(WH)
West Bromwich A.	Nuffield Wks	09.45	46-49	69	-	0
HOOD Henry (Harry) Anthony						
Glasgow, 3 October, 1944 Su23-1						(CF)
Sunderland	Clyde	11.64	64-66	31	0	9
HOOD John (Jack) O'Dorman						
Glasgow, 8 January, 1938						(CF)
Everton	Shettleston	10.56				
Tranmere Rov.	Tr	12.59	59	3	-	2
HOOD Melvyn Arthur						
Reading, 5 October, 1939						(F)
Reading	Jnrs	10.56	56-57	10	-	0
HOOD Ronald						
Cowdenbeath, 18 November, 1922						(IF)
Aldershot	Hamilton Academical	08.47	47	14	-	8
Rochdale	Tr	11.48	48	9	-	1
HOOKER Alan Thomas						
Exeter, 23 June, 1956						(FB)
Exeter C.	Jnrs	07.74	74-76	46	4	0
HOOKER Jonathan William						
City of London, 31 March, 1972						(LW)
Brentford	Hertford T.	11.94	94-95	4	1	0
HOOKER Keith William						
Fleet, 31 January, 1950						(WH)
Brentford	App	02.68	66-68	24	8	2
HOOKS Paul						
Wallsend, 30 May, 1959						(M)
Notts Co.	App	06.77	76-82	144	29	30
Derby Co.	Tr	03.83	82-84	46	2	4
HOOKS Victor Ronald						
Belfast, 4 July, 1955						(F)
Grimsby T.	Manchester U. (App)	10.72	72	0	1	0
HOOLE David John						
Chesterfield, 16 October, 1970						(M/RB)
Chesterfield	YT	07.89	88-89	6	8	0
HOOLEY Joseph Winston						
Hoyland, 26 December, 1938						(W)
Barnsley	Jnrs	04.56	56	1	-	0
Sheffield U.	Tr	12.57				
Workington	Tr	06.58	58	6	-	2
Bradford P.A.	Holbeach U.	11.59	59-60	13	-	4
Accrington St.	Bedford T.	10.61				
HOOLICKIN Garry John						
Middleton, 29 October, 1957						(D)
Oldham Ath.	App	07.75	76-86	209	2	2
HOOLICKIN Stephen						
Manchester, 13 December, 1951						(RB)
Oldham Ath.	App	12.69	69-72	8	0	0
Bury	Tr	08.73	73-76	140	0	5
Carlisle U.	Tr	10.76	76-80	143	0	2
Hull C.	Tr	12.80	80-81	31	0	0
HOOPER Dean Raymond						
Harefield, 13 April, 1971						(W)
Swindon T.	Hayes	03.95	94	0	4	0
Peterborough U.	L	12.95	95	4	0	0
HOOPER Harry						
Pittington (Dm), 14 June, 1933 Eu23-2/EF Lge/E 'B'						(OR)
West Ham U.	Hylton Colly	11.50	50-55	119	-	39
Wolverhampton W.	Tr	03.56	56	39	-	19
Birmingham C.	Tr	12.57	57-60	105	-	34
Sunderland	Tr	09.60	60-62	65	-	16
HOOPER Harry Reed						
Burnley, 16 December, 1910 Died 1970						(FB)
Nelson	Nelson Trades	11.28	29	8	-	0
Sheffield U.	Tr	02.30	30-38	269	-	12
Hartlepool U.	Tr	07.47	47-49	66	-	4

League Club	Source	Date Signed	Seasons Played	Apps	Subs	Gls
HOOPER Lyndon						
Guyana, 30 May, 1966 Canadian Int						(M)
Birmingham C.	Toronto Blizzard (Can)	09.93	93	1	4	0
HOOPER Michael Dudley						
Bristol, 10 February, 1964						(G)
Bristol C.	Mangotsfield U.	11.83	84	1	0	0
Wrexham	Tr	02.85	84-85	34	0	0
Liverpool	Tr	10.85	86-92	50	1	0
Leicester C.	L	09.90	90	14	0	0
Newcastle U.	Tr	09.93	93-94	23	2	0
HOOPER Percy George William						
Lambeth, 17 December, 1914 Died 1997						(G)
Tottenham H.	Islington Corries	01.35	34-38	97	-	0
Swansea C.	Tr	03.47	46-47	12	-	0
HOOPER Peter John						
Teignmouth, 2 February, 1933 EF Lge						(OL)
Bristol Rov.	Dawlish	05.53	53-61	297	-	101
Cardiff C.	Tr	07.62	62	40	-	22
Bristol C.	Tr	07.63	63-65	54	0	14
HOOPER Stuart Robert John						
Lytham St Annes, 16 June, 1970						(F)
Burnley	Jnrs	07.88	88	0	1	0
HOOPER Wynne						
Neath, 5 June, 1952 W Yth						(W)
Newport Co.	App	06.70	68-76	165	14	22
Swindon T.	Tr	12.76	76	4	2	0
Aldershot	Tr	07.77	77-78	21	19	1
HOPE Alexander John Henry						
Musselburgh, 22 June, 1924						(OL)
Swindon T.	Morton	06.54	54	11	-	1
HOPE Christopher Jonathan						
Sheffield, 14 November, 1972						(CD)
Nottingham F.	Darlington (YT)	08.90				
Scunthorpe U.	Tr	07.93	93-97	189	8	11
HOPE Darren						
Stoke, 3 April, 1971						(W)
Stoke C.	YT	07.89				
Stockport Co.	Tr	03.90	89	4	0	0
HOPE Eric						
Oakengates, 2 December, 1927						(IF)
Manchester C.		01.46				
Shrewsbury T.	Tr	08.50	50-51	27	-	3
Wrexham	Tr	10.51	51-53	37	-	9
HOPE George						
Haltwhistle, 4 April, 1954						(F)
Newcastle U.	App	04.72	73	6	0	1
Charlton Ath.	Tr	06.75	75-76	13	0	2
York C.	Tr	11.76	76-77	34	8	8
HOPE James Gibson						
Glasgow, 11 September, 1919						(OL)
Manchester C.	Ardeer Rec.	02.39	46	7	-	0
HOPE James Greatrix						
East Wemyss, 4 October, 1919 Died 1993						(HB)
New Brighton	East Fife	08.47	47-49	43	-	0
HOPE John William March						
Shildon, 30 March, 1949						(G)
Darlington	App	05.67	64-68	14	0	0
Newcastle U.	Tr	03.69	68	1	0	0
Sheffield U.	Tr	01.71	70-73	63	0	0
Hartlepool U.	Tr	07.75	75	23	0	0
HOPE Mark Bryan						
Isleworth, 13 June, 1970						(CD)
Darlington (N/C)	Porthleven	01.97	96	1	0	0
HOPE Richard Paul						
Middlesbrough, 22 June, 1978						(CD)
Blackburn Rov.	YT	08.95				
Darlington	Tr	01.97	96-97	54	1	1
HOPE Robert						
Bridge of Allan, 28 September, 1943 S Sch/Su23-1/S-2						(M)
West Bromwich A.	Jnrs	09.60	59-71	331	5	33
Birmingham C.	Tr	06.72	72-75	33	1	5
Sheffield Wed.	Tr	09.76	76-77	39	3	7

HOPGOOD Ronald Frederick
Balham, 24 November, 1934 Died 1990 (G)

League Club	Source	Date Signed	Seasons Played	Apps	Subs	Gls
Crystal Palace	Spicers Ath.	05.57	57-59	14	-	0

HOPKIN David
Greenock, 21 August, 1970 S 'B'/S-4 (M)

League Club	Source	Date Signed	Seasons Played	Apps	Subs	Gls
Chelsea	Morton	09.92	92-94	21	19	1
Crystal Palace	Tr	07.95	95-96	79	4	21
Leeds U.	Tr	07.97	97	22	3	1

HOPKIN Gareth Gersom
Swansea, 12 April, 1923 (W)

League Club	Source	Date Signed	Seasons Played	Apps	Subs	Gls
Swansea C.		11.46	47	2	-	0

HOPKINS Anthony
Pontypool, 17 February, 1971 (LB/W)

League Club	Source	Date Signed	Seasons Played	Apps	Subs	Gls
Newport Co.	YT	•	87	2	4	0
Bristol C.	Chelsea (YT)	10.89				
Aldershot	Ebbw Vale	02.91	90	9	1	0

HOPKINS Brian
Derby, 15 March, 1933 (OR)

League Club	Source	Date Signed	Seasons Played	Apps	Subs	Gls
Port Vale (Am)	Keele Univ.	08.57	57	2	-	0

HOPKINS Idris Morgan
Merthyr Tydfil, 11 October, 1910 Died 1994 W-12 (OR)

League Club	Source	Date Signed	Seasons Played	Apps	Subs	Gls
Crystal Palace	Ramsgate Ath.	05.32	32	4	-	0
Brentford	Tr	11.32	32-46	290	-	77
Bristol C.	Tr	05.47	47	24	-	0

HOPKINS Jeffrey
Swansea, 14 April, 1964 W Yth/Wu21-5/W-16 (CD)

League Club	Source	Date Signed	Seasons Played	Apps	Subs	Gls
Fulham	App	09.81	80-87	213	6	4
Crystal Palace	Tr	08.88	88-89	70	0	2
Plymouth Arg.	L	10.91	91	8	0	0
Bristol Rov.	Tr	03.92	91	4	2	0
Reading	Tr	07.92	92-96	127	4	3

HOPKINS Kelvin Robert
Perivale, 26 July, 1953 (G)

League Club	Source	Date Signed	Seasons Played	Apps	Subs	Gls
Aldershot	App	07.71	70-71	2	0	0

HOPKINS Melvyn
Ystrad, 7 November, 1934 Wu23-1/W-34 (FB)

League Club	Source	Date Signed	Seasons Played	Apps	Subs	Gls
Tottenham H.	Jnrs	05.52	52-63	219	-	0
Brighton & H.A.	Tr	10.64	64-66	57	1	2
Bradford P.A.	Ballymena U.	01.69	68-69	29	1	0

HOPKINS Oliver Thomas
South Kirkby, 15 November, 1935 (CH)

League Club	Source	Date Signed	Seasons Played	Apps	Subs	Gls
Barnsley	Burntwood	03.54	57-60	50	-	10
Peterborough U.	Tr	07.61	61-64	104	-	0

HOPKINS Robert Arthur
Birmingham, 25 October, 1961 (M)

League Club	Source	Date Signed	Seasons Played	Apps	Subs	Gls
Aston Villa	App	07.79	79-82	1	2	1
Birmingham C.	Tr	03.83	82-86	123	0	20
Manchester C.	Tr	08.86	86	7	0	1
West Bromwich A.	Tr	10.86	86-88	81	2	11
Birmingham C.	Tr	03.89	88-90	43	7	9
Shrewsbury T.	Tr	06.91	91	18	9	3
Colchester U. (N/C)	South China (HK)	02.93	92	13	1	1

HOPKINSON Alan
Chapeltown, 15 April, 1953 (F)

League Club	Source	Date Signed	Seasons Played	Apps	Subs	Gls
Barnsley	App	04.71	70-73	24	3	5

HOPKINSON Edward
Royton, 29 October, 1935 Eu23-6/EF Lge/E-14 (G)

League Club	Source	Date Signed	Seasons Played	Apps	Subs	Gls
Oldham Ath. (Am)	Jnrs	06.51	51	3	-	0
Bolton W.	Tr	11.52	56-69	519	0	0

HOPKINSON Gordon
Sheffield, 19 June, 1933 (FB)

League Club	Source	Date Signed	Seasons Played	Apps	Subs	Gls
Doncaster Rov.	Beighton M.W.	06.57	57	10	-	0
Bristol C.	Tr	07.58	58-60	67	-	1

HOPKINSON Ian John
Newcastle, 19 October, 1950 (F)

League Club	Source	Date Signed	Seasons Played	Apps	Subs	Gls
Barrow	Newcastle U. (App)	01.69	68-70	17	5	1
Workington	Tr	07.71	71	13	6	7
Darlington	Berwick R.	12.72	72	7	2	1

HOPKINSON Michael Edward
Ambergate (Dy), 24 February, 1942 (D)

League Club	Source	Date Signed	Seasons Played	Apps	Subs	Gls
Derby Co.	Jnrs	07.59	60-67	112	3	4
Mansfield T.	Tr	07.68	68-69	46	0	1
Port Vale	Tr	07.70	70	12	1	0

HOPKINSON Paul Edward
Royton, 17 January, 1958 (G)

League Club	Source	Date Signed	Seasons Played	Apps	Subs	Gls
Stockport Co.	Manchester C. (App)	10.75	75-76	39	0	0

HOPKINSON Stanley
Kiveton Park, 15 March, 1922 (G)

League Club	Source	Date Signed	Seasons Played	Apps	Subs	Gls
Watford (Am)	Hemel Hempstead	05.47	46	1	-	0

HOPPER Allan
Newcastle, 17 July, 1937 (RB)

League Club	Source	Date Signed	Seasons Played	Apps	Subs	Gls
Newcastle U.		10.59				
Barnsley	South Shields	03.61	61-64	135	-	4
Bradford C.	Tr	07.65	65	8	0	0

HOPPER Anthony
Carlisle, 31 May, 1976 (RB/M)

League Club	Source	Date Signed	Seasons Played	Apps	Subs	Gls
Carlisle U.	YT	07.94	92-97	33	17	1

HOPPER William
Bishop Auckland, 20 February, 1938 (CF)

League Club	Source	Date Signed	Seasons Played	Apps	Subs	Gls
Halifax T.	West Auckland	12.61	61-62	35	-	9
Workington	Tr	07.63	63-64	46	-	14
Darlington	Tr	07.65	65	6	0	0

HORACE Alain
Madagascar, 4 December, 1971 (M)

League Club	Source	Date Signed	Seasons Played	Apps	Subs	Gls
Hartlepool U. (N/C)	Mulhouse (Fr)	10.96	96	0	1	0

HORE Kenneth **John**
St Austell, 10 February, 1947 (D)

League Club	Source	Date Signed	Seasons Played	Apps	Subs	Gls
Plymouth Arg.	App	12.64	64-75	393	7	17
Exeter C.	Tr	03.76	75-79	193	0	0

HORLOCK Kevin
Bexley, 1 November, 1972 NI 'B'/NI-12 (M)

League Club	Source	Date Signed	Seasons Played	Apps	Subs	Gls
West Ham U.	YT	07.91				
Swindon T.	Tr	08.92	92-96	151	12	22
Manchester C.	Tr	01.97	96-97	43	0	9

HORMANTSCHUK Peter Anthony
Coventry, 11 September, 1962 (FB)

League Club	Source	Date Signed	Seasons Played	Apps	Subs	Gls
Coventry C.	App	09.80	81-83	18	6	1

HORN Graham Roy
Westminster, 23 August, 1954 (G)

League Club	Source	Date Signed	Seasons Played	Apps	Subs	Gls
Arsenal	App	04.72				
Portsmouth	L	06.72	72	22	0	0
Luton T.	Tr	02.73	72-74	58	0	0
Brentford	L	11.75	75	3	0	0
Charlton Ath.	Los Angeles (USA)	12.76				
Southend U.	Kettering T.	12.77	77-78	9	0	0
Aldershot	Tr	01.80	79-81	9	0	0
Torquay U.	Tr	08.82	82-83	47	0	0

HORN Robert Ian
Westminster, 15 December, 1961 E Yth (G)

League Club	Source	Date Signed	Seasons Played	Apps	Subs	Gls
Crystal Palace	App	04.79				
Barnsley	Tr	11.80	81-83	67	0	0
Cambridge U.	L	11.83	83	8	0	0
Crystal Palace	Tr	07.84				

HORN William
Glasgow, 13 May, 1938 (OL)

League Club	Source	Date Signed	Seasons Played	Apps	Subs	Gls
Brentford	Kilmarnock	10.58	58	1	-	0

HORNBY Eric
Birkenhead, 31 March, 1923 (FB)

League Club	Source	Date Signed	Seasons Played	Apps	Subs	Gls
Tranmere Rov.	Jnrs	11.44	47-48	32	-	0
Crewe Alex.	Tr	08.49	49-50	4	-	0

HORNBY Ronald
Rochdale, 13 April, 1914 Died 1962 (OL)

League Club	Source	Date Signed	Seasons Played	Apps	Subs	Gls
Rochdale (Am)	Rochdale St Clements	02.32	31	2	-	0
Oldham Ath.	Tr	07.33				
Burnley	Stalybridge Celtic	05.34	34-47	123	-	16

HORNE Alfred
Brixworth, 6 September, 1926 (WH)

League Club	Source	Date Signed	Seasons Played	Apps	Subs	Gls
Northampton T.		09.44	48	1	-	0

HORNE Barry
St Asaph, 18 May, 1962 W-59 (M)

League Club	Source	Date Signed	Seasons Played	Apps	Subs	Gls
Wrexham	Rhyl	06.84	84-86	136	0	16
Portsmouth	Tr	07.87	87-88	66	4	7
Southampton	Tr	03.89	88-91	111	1	6
Everton	Tr	07.92	92-95	118	5	3
Birmingham C.	Tr	06.96	96	33	0	0
Huddersfield T.	Tr	10.97	97	29	1	0

HORNE Brian Simon
Billericay, 5 October, 1967 E Yth/Eu21-5 (G)

League Club	Source	Date Signed	Seasons Played	Apps	Subs	Gls
Millwall	App	10.85	86-90	163	0	0
Middlesbrough	L	09.92	92	3	1	0
Stoke C.	L	10.92	92	1	0	0
Portsmouth	Tr	12.92	93	3	0	0
Hartlepool U.	Tr	08.94	94-95	73	0	0

HORNE Desmond Tolton
South Africa, 12 December, 1939 (OL)

League Club	Source	Date Signed	Seasons Played	Apps	Subs	Gls
Wolverhampton W.	Jnrs	12.56	58-60	40	-	16
Blackpool	Tr	03.61	60-65	117	1	17

HORNE George
Glasgow, 23 November, 1933 (OL)

League Club	Source	Date Signed	Seasons Played	Apps	Subs	Gls
Carlisle U.	Maryhill Jnrs	08.57	57	4	-	2

HORNE John Robert
Dudley, 4 November, 1961 (FB)

League Club	Source	Date Signed	Seasons Played	Apps	Subs	Gls
Walsall	App	11.79	79-81	10	6	1

HORNE Kenneth William
Burton, 25 June, 1926 (FB)

League Club	Source	Date Signed	Seasons Played	Apps	Subs	Gls
Blackpool	Wolverhampton W. (Am)	06.49				
Brentford	Tr	05.50	50-59	223	-	1

HORNE Henry **Leslie**
Dudley, 2 May, 1923 Died 1986 (CH)

League Club	Source	Date Signed	Seasons Played	Apps	Subs	Gls
West Bromwich A.	Netherton W.	04.48	49-51	13	-	0
Plymouth Arg.	Tr	07.52				
Walsall	Tr	11.52	52-53	52	-	1

HORNE Stanley Frederick
Clanfield, 17 December, 1944 (M)

League Club	Source	Date Signed	Seasons Played	Apps	Subs	Gls
Aston Villa	App	12.61	63	6	-	0
Manchester C.	Tr	09.65	65-67	48	2	0
Fulham	Tr	02.69	68-72	73	6	0
Chester C.	Tr	08.73	73	17	1	0
Rochdale	Tr	12.73	73-74	48	0	5

HORNER Philip Matthew
Leeds, 10 November, 1966 E Yth (CD/M)

League Club	Source	Date Signed	Seasons Played	Apps	Subs	Gls
Leicester C.	App	11.84	86-87	7	3	0
Rotherham U.	L	03.86	85	3	1	0
Halifax T.	Tr	08.88	88-89	70	2	4
Blackpool	Tr	09.90	90-94	184	3	22

HORNER William
Cassop (Dm), 7 September, 1942 (D)

League Club	Source	Date Signed	Seasons Played	Apps	Subs	Gls
Middlesbrough	Jnrs	09.59	60-68	184	3	11
Darlington	Tr	06.69	69-74	211	7	5

HORNSBY Brian Geoffrey
Great Shelford (Camb), 10 September, 1954 E Sch/E Yth (M)

League Club	Source	Date Signed	Seasons Played	Apps	Subs	Gls
Arsenal	App	07.72	72-75	23	3	6
Shrewsbury T.	Tr	06.76	76-77	75	0	16
Sheffield Wed.	Tr	03.78	77-81	102	4	25
Chester C.	L	11.81	81	4	0	0
Carlisle U.	Edmonton (Can)	08.82	82-83	9	1	1
Chesterfield	L	12.83	83	1	0	0

HORNSBY John
Ferryhill, 3 August, 1945 (OL)

League Club	Source	Date Signed	Seasons Played	Apps	Subs	Gls
Colchester U.	Evenwood T.	10.64	65	11	0	1

HOROBIN Roy
Brownhills, 10 March, 1935 (IF)

League Club	Source	Date Signed	Seasons Played	Apps	Subs	Gls
West Bromwich A.	Jnrs	10.52	55-57	54	-	6
Notts Co.	Tr	11.58	58-61	123	-	37
Peterborough U.	Tr	06.62	62-63	80	-	20
Crystal Palace	Tr	07.64	64	4	-	0

HORREY Rowland George
Bishop Auckland, 7 March, 1943 (W)

League Club	Source	Date Signed	Seasons Played	Apps	Subs	Gls
Blackburn Rov.	Ferryhill Ath.	12.63	64-65	3	0	0
York C.	Tr	07.66	66-67	74	0	9
Cambridge U.	Tr	07.68	70-71	37	1	4

HORRIDGE Peter
Manchester, 31 May, 1934 (FB)

League Club	Source	Date Signed	Seasons Played	Apps	Subs	Gls
Manchester C.	Newton Heath P.	11.52	58	3	-	0
Crewe Alex.	Tr	06.59				

HORRIGAN Kenneth Peter
Gravesend, 7 December, 1919 (WH)

League Club	Source	Date Signed	Seasons Played	Apps	Subs	Gls
Carlisle U.	Imp.Paper Mill	08.46	46	16	-	1

HORRIX Dean Victor
Maidenhead, 21 November, 1961 Died 1990 (F)

League Club	Source	Date Signed	Seasons Played	Apps	Subs	Gls
Millwall	App	04.79	80-82	65	7	19
Gillingham	Tr	03.83	82	7	7	0
Reading	Tr	08.83	83-87	135	23	35
Cardiff C.	L	02.87	86	9	0	3
Millwall	Tr	03.88	87-89	5	6	1
Bristol C.	Tr	03.90	89	3	0	0

HORROBIN Thomas
Askern, 8 August, 1943 (FB)

League Club	Source	Date Signed	Seasons Played	Apps	Subs	Gls
Sheffield Wed.	Jnrs	08.60	62	3	-	0

HORSBURGH John James
Edinburgh, 17 November, 1936 (G)

League Club	Source	Date Signed	Seasons Played	Apps	Subs	Gls
Oldham Ath.	Dundee	08.61	61	1	-	0

HORSCROFT Grant
Fletching (E Sx), 30 July, 1961 (CD)

League Club	Source	Date Signed	Seasons Played	Apps	Subs	Gls
Brighton & H.A.	Lewes	03.87	87	2	0	0

HORSFALL Frank **George**
Australia, 19 September, 1924 Died 1992 (WH)

League Club	Source	Date Signed	Seasons Played	Apps	Subs	Gls
Southampton		05.47	46	2	-	0
Southend U.	Tr	07.49	49	1	-	0

HORSFALL Thomas William
Hamilton, 7 January, 1951 (W)

League Club	Source	Date Signed	Seasons Played	Apps	Subs	Gls
Southend U.	Dover T.	11.72	72-73	11	5	1
Bury	L	11.73	73	0	1	0
Scunthorpe U.	L	11.73	73	5	0	2
Cambridge U.	Tr	12.74	74-76	79	4	28
Halifax T.	Tr	07.77	77	15	1	3

HORSFIELD Alec
Selby, 4 August, 1921 Died 1991 (IF)

League Club	Source	Date Signed	Seasons Played	Apps	Subs	Gls
Arsenal	Selby T.	11.46				
Bradford P.A.	Tr	12.50	50	4	-	2

HORSFIELD Arthur
Newcastle, 5 July, 1946 E Yth (F)

League Club	Source	Date Signed	Seasons Played	Apps	Subs	Gls
Middlesbrough	App	07.63	63-68	107	4	51
Newcastle U.	Tr	01.69	68	7	2	3
Swindon T.	Tr	06.69	69-71	107	1	42
Charlton Ath.	Tr	06.72	72-75	139	0	54
Watford	Tr	09.75	75-76	78	0	16

HORSFIELD Geoffrey
Barnsley, 1 November, 1973 (F)

League Club	Source	Date Signed	Seasons Played	Apps	Subs	Gls
Scarborough	Jnrs	07.92	92-93	12	0	1

HORSMAN Leslie
Burley-in-Wharfedale, 26 May, 1920 Died 1996 (CH)

League Club	Source	Date Signed	Seasons Played	Apps	Subs	Gls
Bradford P.A.	Guiseley	06.45	46-52	239	-	18
Halifax T.	Tr	08.53	53-56	120	-	8

HORSTEAD John **Barry**
Brigg, 8 May, 1935 (D)

League Club	Source	Date Signed	Seasons Played	Apps	Subs	Gls
Scunthorpe U.	Jnrs	05.56	56-67	316	4	3

HORSWILL Michael Frederick
Annfield Plain, 6 March, 1953 (M)

League Club	Source	Date Signed	Seasons Played	Apps	Subs	Gls
Sunderland	App	03.70	71-73	68	1	3
Manchester C.	Tr	03.74	73-74	11	3	0
Plymouth Arg.	Tr	06.75	75-77	98	4	3
Hull C.	Tr	07.78	78-81	82	2	6
Carlisle U. (N/C)	Happy Valley (HK)	08.83	83	1	0	0

HORTON Brian
Hednesford, 4 February, 1949 (M)

League Club	Source	Date Signed	Seasons Played	Apps	Subs	Gls
Port Vale	Hednesford T.	07.70	70-75	232	4	33
Brighton & H.A.	Tr	02.76	75-80	217	1	33
Luton T.	Tr	08.81	81-83	118	0	8
Hull C.	Tr	07.84	84-86	38	0	0

HORTON Duncan
Maidstone, 18 February, 1967 (M/LB)

League Club	Source	Date Signed	Seasons Played	Apps	Subs	Gls
Charlton Ath. (N/C)	App	02.85	84	1	0	0
Barnet	Welling U.	03.91	91-92	52	5	3
Wycombe W.	Tr	08.93	93	15	0	0

HORTON Henry
Ledbury, 18 April, 1923 (WH)

League Club	Source	Date Signed	Seasons Played	Apps	Subs	Gls
Blackburn Rov.	Worcester C.	01.47	46-50	92	-	5
Southampton	Tr	06.51	51-53	75	-	12
Bradford P.A.	Tr	05.54	54	26	-	0

HORTON Joseph **Kenneth**
Preston, 26 August, 1922 (IF)

League Club	Source	Date Signed	Seasons Played	Apps	Subs	Gls
Preston N.E.	Jnrs	10.45	46-52	166	-	36
Hull C.	Tr	10.52	52-54	76	-	16
Barrow	Tr	08.55	55	22	-	4

League Club	Source	Date Signed	Seasons Played	Career Record Apps	Subs	Gls
HORTON Leonard						
Darlaston, 17 September, 1923 Died 1987						(CH)
Walsall		06.47	46	1	-	0
HORTON Leslie						
Salford, 12 July, 1921						(D)
Rochdale	Tyldesley U.	04.41				
Oldham Ath.	Tr	01.43	46-47	79	-	2
Carlisle U.	Tr	08.48	48-49	66	-	0
Rochdale	Tr	04.50				
York C.	Tr	07.50	50	21	-	0
Halifax T.	Tr	03.51	50-51	34	-	1
HORTON William George						
Aldershot, 27 August, 1942						(IF)
Aldershot	Chelsea (Jnrs)	11.61	62-64	9	-	1
HORWOOD Neil Kenneth						
Peterhead, 4 August, 1964						(F)
Grimsby T.	Kings Lynn	08.86	86	0	1	0
Halifax T.	L	12.86	86	3	0	0
Tranmere Rov.	L	03.87	86	4	0	1
Cambridge U. (N/C)	Tr	08.87	87	4	10	2
HOSIE James England						
Aberdeen, 3 April, 1940						(OR)
Barnsley	Aberdeen	07.62	62	37	-	0
HOSKER Robert Charles						
Cannock, 27 February, 1955						(W)
Middlesbrough	App	03.72				
York C.	Tr	08.73	75-76	16	9	1
HOSKIN James **Ashley**						
Accrington, 27 March, 1968						(LW)
Burnley	App	12.85	85-88	72	16	11
HOSKIN Michael Andrew						
Chesterfield, 3 November, 1966						(D)
Chesterfield (N/C)	YT	08.84	83-84	1	1	0
HOSKINS John Frederick						
Southampton, 10 May, 1931						(OL)
Southampton	Winchester C.	07.52	52-58	220	-	64
Swindon T.	Tr	07.59	59	10	-	3
HOTTE Mark Stephen						
Bradford, 27 September, 1978						(CD)
Oldham Ath.	YT	07.97	97	0	1	0
HOTTE Timothy Alwin						
Bradford, 4 October, 1963						(F)
Huddersfield T.	Arsenal (App)	09.81	81-82	14	2	4
Halifax T.	Harrogate T.	08.85	85	2	2	0
Hull C.	North Ferriby U.	10.87	87-88	1	4	0
York C.	L	09.88	88	1	1	0
HOTTIGER Marc						
Switzerland, 7 November, 1967 Swiss Int						(FB)
Newcastle U.	Sion (Swi)	08.94	94-95	38	1	1
Everton	Tr	03.96	95-96	13	4	1
HOUCHEN Keith Morton						
Middlesbrough, 25 July, 1960						(F)
Hartlepool U.	Chesterfield (Jnrs)	02.78	77-81	160	10	65
Leyton Orient	Tr	03.82	81-83	74	2	20
York C.	Tr	03.84	83-85	56	11	19
Scunthorpe U.	Tr	03.86	85	9	0	3
Coventry C.	Tr	06.86	86-88	43	11	7
Port Vale	Hibernian	08.91	91-92	44	5	10
Hartlepool U.	Tr	08.93	93-96	104	5	27
HOUGH David John						
Crewe, 20 February, 1966 W Yth						(RB)
Swansea C.	App	02.84	83-91	202	25	9
HOUGH Frederick Alan						
Stoke, 23 December, 1935						(OR)
Port Vale		06.55	57	4	-	0
HOUGH Harry						
Ecclesfield, 26 September, 1924						(G)
Barnsley	Thorncliffe Welfare	09.47	47-58	346	-	0
Bradford P.A.	Tr	06.59	59-60	57	-	0
HOUGH John						
Halifax, 9 June, 1954						(G)
Halifax T.	Irish Dems	09.79	79	1	0	0
HOUGH Thomas						
Preston, 17 January, 1922						(IF)
Preston N.E.	Jnrs	05.39				
Barrow	Tr	10.46	46	3	-	0
HOUGHTON Harry **Brian (Bud)**						
India, 1 September, 1936 Died 1994						(CF)
Bradford P.A.	St Wrefords Y.C.	10.55	55-57	28	-	7
Birmingham C.	Tr	10.57	57-58	4	-	1
Southend U.	Tr	10.58	58-60	68	-	32
Oxford U.	Tr	03.61	62-63	53	-	17
Lincoln C.	Tr	10.63	63-64	54	-	22
HOUGHTON William **Eric**						
Billingborough, 29 June, 1910 Died 1996 EF Lge/E-7						(OL)
Aston Villa	Billingborough	08.27	29-46	361	-	160
Notts Co.	Tr	12.46	46-48	55	-	10
HOUGHTON Frank Calvert						
Preston, 15 February, 1926 Died 1994						(IF/WH)
Newcastle U.	Ballymena	12.47	47-50	55	-	10
Exeter C.	Tr	08.54	54-56	27	-	10
HOUGHTON Keith						
Backworth, 10 March, 1954 E Semi Pro						(CD)
Carlisle U.	Blyth Spartans	01.80	79-82	82	5	2
Lincoln C.	Tr	08.83	83	26	0	0
HOUGHTON Kenneth						
Rotherham, 18 October, 1939						(IF)
Rotherham U.	Silverwood Colly	05.60	60-64	149	-	56
Hull C.	Tr	01.65	64-72	253	11	79
Scunthorpe U.	Tr	06.73	73	33	0	5
HOUGHTON Peter						
Liverpool, 30 November, 1954						(F)
Wigan Ath.	South Liverpool	(N/L)	78-83	169	16	62
Preston N.E.	Tr	10.83	83-84	52	4	16
Wrexham	L	11.84	84	5	0	2
Chester C.	Tr	08.85	85-87	78	7	13
HOUGHTON Raymond James						
Glasgow, 9 January, 1962 IR-73						(M)
West Ham U.	Jnrs	07.79	81	0	1	0
Fulham	Tr	07.82	82-85	129	0	16
Oxford U.	Tr	09.85	85-87	83	0	10
Liverpool	Tr	10.87	87-91	147	6	28
Aston Villa	Tr	07.92	92-94	83	12	6
Crystal Palace	Tr	03.95	94-96	69	3	7
Reading	Tr	07.97	97	20	5	1
HOUGHTON Scott Aaron						
Hitchin, 22 October, 1971 E Sch/E Yth						(F)
Tottenham H.	YT	07.90	91	0	10	2
Ipswich T.	L	03.91	90	7	1	1
Gillingham	L	12.92	92	3	0	0
Charlton Ath.	L	02.93	92	6	0	0
Luton T.	Tr	08.93	93-94	7	9	1
Walsall	Tr	09.94	94-95	76	2	14
Peterborough U.	Tr	07.96	96-97	50	12	12
HOUGHTON William Gascoigne						
Hemsworth, 20 February, 1939 E Yth						(D)
Barnsley	Jnrs	08.57	57-63	206	-	10
Watford	Tr	07.64	64-65	48	0	2
Ipswich T.	Tr	06.66	66-68	107	0	3
Leicester C.	Tr	07.69	69	6	1	0
Rotherham U.	Tr	01.70	69-73	139	0	1
HOULAHAN Harold						
Coundon (Dm), 14 February, 1930						(IL)
Newcastle U.	Durham C.	02.51				
Oldham Ath.	Tr	05.52	52-53	6	-	3
Darlington	Tr	01.54	53-54	23	-	8
HOULT Alan John						
Hinckley, 7 October, 1957 E Sch						(F)
Leicester C.	Jnrs	09.75				
Hull C.	L	01.78	77	3	0	1
Lincoln C.	L	03.78	77	2	2	1
Bristol Rov.	Tr	07.78				
HOULT Russell						
Leicester, 22 November, 1972						(G)
Leicester C.	YT	03.91	92	10	0	0
Lincoln C.	L	08.91	91	2	0	0
Bolton W.	L	11.93	93	3	1	0
Lincoln C.	L	08.94	94	15	0	0
Derby Co.	Tr	02.95	94-97	88	2	0

League Club	Source	Date Signed	Seasons Played	Career Record Apps	Subs	Gls
HOUNSLEA William Hudson						
Liverpool, 15 August, 1926						(RB)
New Brighton	Unity B.C.	12.47	47	16	-	0
Chester C.	Tr	08.48	48	1	-	0
HOUSAM Arthur						
Sunderland, 1 October, 1917 Died 1975						(WH)
Sunderland	Hylton Colly	05.37	37-47	55	-	2
HOUSDEN Dennis						
Islington, 15 March, 1953						(F)
Gillingham	App	08.71	71-72	12	4	1
HOUSEMAN Peter						
Battersea, 24 December, 1945 Died 1977						(W)
Chelsea	App	12.62	63-74	252	17	20
Oxford U.	Tr	05.75	75-76	65	0	2
HOUSHAM Steven James						
Gainsborough, 24 February, 1976						(RB/M)
Scunthorpe U.	YT	12.93	94-97	73	17	4
HOUSLEY Stuart						
Doncaster, 15 September, 1948						(W)
Grimsby T.	App	07.66	66-68	34	0	3
HOUSTON David						
Glasgow, 7 July, 1948						(WH)
Cardiff C.	Jnrs	07.65	65-66	17	1	0
Crystal Palace	Tr	01.67				
HOUSTON Graham Robert						
Gibraltar, 24 February, 1960						(W)
Preston N.E.	Jnrs	03.78	79-84	90	38	11
Burnley (N/C)	Tr	09.85				
Wigan Ath.	Tr	06.86	86	16	1	4
Carlisle U. (N/C)	Northwich Vic.	10.87	87	8	8	1
HOUSTON Joseph						
Wishaw, 27 February, 1926						(G)
Aldershot	Dunfermline Ath.	07.51	51-52	47	-	0
HOUSTON Stewart Mackie						
Dunoon, 20 August, 1949 Su23-2/S-1						(D)
Chelsea	Port Glasgow	08.67	67-69	6	3	0
Brentford	Tr	03.72	71-73	77	0	9
Manchester U.	Tr	12.73	73-79	204	1	13
Sheffield U.	Tr	07.80	80-82	93	1	1
Colchester U.	Tr	08.83	83-85	106	1	5
HOVI Thomas Henning						
Norway, 5 January, 1972						(D)
Charlton Ath. (L)	Hamar K. (Nor)	01.95	94	0	2	0
HOW Trevor Anthony						
Amersham, 8 August, 1957						(FB)
Watford	App	03.75	74-79	90	1	2
HOWARD Andrew Paul						
Southport, 15 March, 1973						(F)
Blackpool	Liverpool (YT)	09.91	91	0	1	0
Rochdale	Fleetwood T.	07.92	92-93	4	16	3
HOWARD Barry Peter						
Ashton-u-Lyne, 19 February, 1950 E Semi Pro						(F)
Stockport Co.	Runcorn	02.78	77	12	1	1
HOWARD David Frederick						
Hartlepool, 3 June, 1962						(F)
Newcastle U.	Jnrs	07.79				
Hartlepool U.	Tr	03.81	80-81	6	3	4
HOWARD Francis Henry						
Acton, 30 January, 1931						(OL)
Brighton & H.A.	Guildford C.	05.50	50-58	200	-	26
HOWARD Jonathan						
Sheffield, 7 October, 1971						(F)
Rotherham U.	YT	07.90	90-93	25	11	5
Chesterfield	Tr	12.94	94-97	73	39	18
HOWARD Lee						
Worksop, 6 February, 1967						(W)
Mansfield T.	YT	●	84	0	1	0
HOWARD Mark Edward						
Kings Lynn, 21 October, 1964						(W)
Stockport Co.	Kings Lynn	04.88	87-89	13	6	2
Cambridge U.	L	03.89	88	0	2	0
HOWARD Matthew Jones						
Watford, 5 December, 1970						(D)
Brentford	YT	●	87	0	1	0
HOWARD Michael Anthony						
Birkenhead, 2 December, 1978						(D)
Tranmere Rov.	YT	07.97				
Swansea C.	Tr	02.98	97	2	1	0
HOWARD Patrick						
Dodworth, 7 October, 1947						(CD)
Barnsley	Jnrs	10.65	65-71	176	1	6
Newcastle U.	Tr	09.71	71-76	182	2	7
Arsenal	Tr	09.76	76	15	1	0
Birmingham C.	Tr	08.77	77-78	40	0	0
Bury	Tr	07.79	79-81	117	1	5
HOWARD Richard James						
Birkenhead, 10 June, 1943						(G)
Chester C.	Chester Tech. College	09.65	65	1	0	0
HOWARD Stanley						
Chorley, 1 July, 1934						(W)
Huddersfield T.	Chorley	07.52	57-59	62	-	13
Bradford C.	Tr	06.60	60	18	-	6
Barrow	Tr	01.61	60-63	86	-	22
Halifax T.	Tr	07.64	64	21	-	1
HOWARD Steven John						
Durham, 10 May, 1976						(M/F)
Hartlepool U.	Tow Law T.	08.95	95-97	92	22	21
HOWARD Terence						
Stepney, 26 February, 1966 E Yth						(D)
Chelsea	App	02.84	84-86	6	0	0
Crystal Palace	L	01.86	85	4	0	0
Chester C.	L	01.87	86	2	0	0
Leyton Orient	Tr	03.87	86-94	323	5	31
Wycombe W.	Tr	02.95	94-95	56	3	2
HOWARD Trevor Edward						
Kings Lynn, 2 June, 1949						(M)
Norwich C.	App	07.67	67-73	81	42	13
Bournemouth	Tr	08.74	74-75	86	0	11
Cambridge U.	Tr	07.76	76-78	105	0	5
HOWARTH Frank						
Budleigh Salterton, 17 November, 1964						(D)
Exeter C.	App	11.82	81-84	21	16	1
HOWARTH Jack						
Crook, 27 February, 1945						(CF)
Chelsea	Stanley U.	10.63				
Swindon T.	Tr	10.64	64	2	-	0
Aldershot	Tr	07.65	65-71	258	1	113
Rochdale	Tr	01.72	71-72	40	0	12
Aldershot	Tr	11.72	72-76	163	0	58
Bournemouth	Tr	01.77	76-77	39	3	6
Southport (N/C)	Dorchester T.	03.78	77	9	0	1
HOWARTH Lee						
Bolton, 3 January, 1968						(CD)
Peterborough U.	Chorley	08.91	91-93	56	6	0
Mansfield T.	Tr	08.94	94-95	56	1	2
Barnet	Tr	01.96	95-97	101	1	5
HOWARTH Neil						
Farnworth, 15 November, 1971 E Semi Pro						(CD)
Burnley	YT	07.90	89	0	1	0
Macclesfield T.	Tr	09.93	97	38	3	3
HOWARTH Sydney						
Bristol, 28 June, 1923						(CF)
Aston Villa	Merthyr Tydfil	06.48	48-49	8	-	2
Swansea C.	Tr	09.50	50-51	39	-	7
Walsall	Tr	09.52	52	6	-	0
HOWAT Ian Stuart						
Wrexham, 29 July, 1958						(F)
Chester C.	App	07.76	76-81	48	9	10
Crewe Alex.	Tr	02.82	81	16	1	1
HOWCROFT Brian						
Farnworth, 20 June, 1938						(FB)
Bury	Jnrs	09.56	57-58	20	-	0
HOWDON Stephen						
Prudhoe, 1 February, 1922						(F)
Newcastle U.	Hexham Hearts	08.41				
Gateshead	Tr	11.44	46	2	-	1

League Club	Source	Date Signed	Seasons Played	Apps	Subs	Gls
HOWE Albert (Bert) Richard Henry						
Greenwich, 16 November, 1938						(FB)
Crystal Palace	Faversham	12.58	58-66	192	1	0
Leyton Orient	Tr	01.67	66-68	91	0	0
Colchester U.	Tr	07.69	69	29	0	1
HOWE Anthony Valentine						
Colchester, 14 February, 1939						(OL)
Colchester U.	Colchester Casuals	03.60	60	10	-	2
Southend U.	Haverhill Rov.	07.64	64	2	-	0
HOWE Denis Cecil						
West Ham, 14 September, 1928						(CH)
West Ham U.		05.49				
Darlington	Tr	08.51	51-53	89	-	1
Southend U.	Tr	08.54	54-57	101	-	0
Aldershot	Tr	07.58	58	33	-	0
HOWE Donald						
Wakefield, 26 November, 1917 Died 1978						(WH)
Bolton W.	Jnrs	11.34	36-51	266	-	35
HOWE Donald						
Wolverhampton, 12 October, 1935 Eu23-6/E 'B'/EF Lge/E-23						(FB)
West Bromwich A.	Jnrs	11.52	55-63	342	-	17
Arsenal	Tr	04.64	64-66	70	0	1
HOWE Edward John Frank						
Amersham, 29 November, 1977 Eu21-2						(D)
Bournemouth	YT	07.96	95-97	42	16	1
HOWE Ernest James						
Chiswick, 15 February, 1953						(CD)
Fulham	Hounslow	10.73	73-77	68	2	10
Queens Park R.	Tr	12.77	77-81	89	0	3
Portsmouth	Tr	08.82	82-83	35	0	4
HOWE Frederick						
Bredbury, 24 September, 1912 Died 1984						(CF)
Stockport Co.	Wilmslow	09.31	31-32	2	-	0
Liverpool	Hyde U.	03.35	34-37	89	-	36
Manchester C.	Tr	06.38	38	6	-	5
Grimsby T.	Tr	10.38	38	29	-	15
Oldham Ath.	Tr	07.46	46	30	-	20
HOWE George						
Wakefield, 10 January, 1924 Died 1971						(FB)
Huddersfield T.	Carlton U.	05.42	46-53	40	-	0
York C.	Tr	06.54	54-60	307	-	0
HOWE Herbert Alexander						
Rugby, 1 April, 1916 Died 1972						(LB)
Leicester C.	Leicester Nomads	02.37	38-46	28	-	0
Notts Co.	Tr	07.47	47-48	52	-	0
HOWE Jeremy Raymond						
Dewsbury, 5 September, 1973 E Yth						(M)
Bradford C.	YT	07.92	91	3	0	0
HOWE John (Jack) Robert						
Hartlepool, 7 October, 1915 Died 1987 E-3						(FB)
Hartlepool U.		06.34	34-35	24	-	0
Derby Co.	Tr	03.36	35-49	223	-	2
Huddersfield T.	Tr	10.49	49-50	29	-	1
HOWE Robert John						
Chadwell St Mary, 22 December, 1945						(CD)
West Ham U.	App	01.63	66-71	68	7	4
Bournemouth	Tr	01.72	71-73	100	0	6
HOWE Stephen **Robert**						
Cramlington, 6 November, 1973 E Yth						(F)
Nottingham F.	YT	12.90	93-96	6	8	2
Ipswich T.	L	01.97	96	2	1	0
Swindon T.	Tr	01.98	97	9	1	0
HOWELL David Christopher						
Hammersmith, 10 October, 1958 E Semi Pro						(CD)
Barnet	Enfield	07.90	91-92	57	0	3
Southend U.	Tr	07.93	93	6	0	0
Birmingham C. (N/C)	(Retired)	10.94	94	2	0	0
HOWELL Graham Frank						
Urmston, 18 February, 1951						(FB)
Manchester C.	App	10.68				
Bradford C.	Tr	06.71	71-72	45	0	0
Brighton & H.A.	Tr	08.72	72-73	40	4	0
Cambridge U.	Tr	07.74	74-75	68	3	3

League Club	Source	Date Signed	Seasons Played	Apps	Subs	Gls
HOWELL James Alexander						
Rustington, 19 February, 1977 E Yth						(M)
Arsenal	YT	07.95				
Portsmouth	Tr	08.96				
Torquay U. (N/C)	Tr	03.97	96	2	2	0
HOWELL Reginald William						
Wolverhampton, 12 August, 1938						(G)
Plymouth Arg.		11.56	56	1	-	0
Aston Villa	Tr	02.58				
HOWELL Ronald Roger						
Tottenham, 22 May, 1949						(M)
Millwall	App	03.67	66-69	7	7	0
Cambridge U.	Tr	09.70	70	10	2	1
Swindon T.	Kettering T.	07.72	72	22	3	1
Brighton & H.A.	Tr	07.73	73	26	1	9
HOWELLS David						
Guildford, 15 December, 1967 E Yth						(M)
Tottenham H.	YT	01.85	85-97	238	39	22
HOWELLS Gareth Jonathan						
Guildford, 13 June, 1970						(G)
Tottenham H.	YT	07.88				
Torquay U.	Tr	08.90	90-91	83	0	0
HOWELLS Jeffrey Denis						
Shoreham, 26 September, 1940						(WH)
Millwall	Fulham (Am)	10.57	58-60	55	-	3
HOWELLS Peter						
Middlesbrough, 23 September, 1932 Died 1993						(W)
Sheffield Wed.		10.53	54-55	3	-	1
Hartlepool U.	Tr	11.56	56	1	-	0
HOWELLS Raymond						
Rhondda, 27 June, 1926						(OL)
Crystal Palace		06.47	46-49	25	-	5
Exeter C.	Tr	07.51	51-52	15	-	3
HOWELLS Roger William						
Swansea, 18 September, 1931						(FB)
Swansea C.	Llanelli	03.50				
Darlington	Tr	02.53	52-53	2	-	0
Swansea C.	Tr	07.54				
HOWELLS Ronald						
Ferndale, 3 August, 1935						(WH)
Wolverhampton W.	Nuneaton Borough	11.52	55-57	9	-	0
Portsmouth	Tr	03.59	58-60	65	-	2
Scunthorpe U.	Tr	06.61	61-62	69	-	4
Walsall	Tr	07.63	63	13	-	0
HOWELLS Ronald Gilbert						
Llanelli, 12 January, 1927 W-2						(G)
Swansea C.		04.48	47	9	-	0
Cardiff C.	Barry T.	07.50	51-56	154	-	0
Chester C.	Worcester C.	09.58	58-59	80	-	0
HOWELLS William Mansel						
Grimsby, 20 March, 1943						(CH)
Grimsby T.	Jnrs	10.61	63	6	-	0
HOWES Shaun Colin						
Norwich, 7 November, 1977						(LB)
Cambridge U.	YT	07.96	95	0	1	0
Leyton Orient	Tr	11.96	96	3	2	0
HOWEY Lee Matthew						
Sunderland, 1 April, 1969						(CD/F)
Ipswich T.	YT	10.86				
Sunderland	Bishop Auckland	03.93	92-96	39	30	8
Burnley	Tr	08.97	97	21	2	0
HOWEY Peter						
Kinsley, 23 January, 1958						(W)
Huddersfield T.	App	01.76	76-78	20	2	3
Leeds U.	Tr	07.79				
Newport Co.	Tr	11.79				
HOWEY Stephen Norman						
Sunderland, 26 October, 1971 E-4						(CD)
Newcastle U.	YT	12.89	88-97	146	22	6
HOWFIELD Robert Michael						
Watford, 3 December, 1936						(F)
Watford	Bushey U.	09.57	57-58	47	-	9
Crewe Alex.	Tr	07.59	59	5	-	0

League Club	Source	Date Signed	Seasons Played	Apps	Subs	Gls
Aldershot	Tr	10.59	59-61	76	-	44
Watford	Tr	07.62	62-63	45	-	13
Fulham	Tr	11.63	63-64	26	-	9
Aldershot	Tr	08.65	65-66	33	1	10

HOWIE Scott
Glasgow, 4 January, 1972 Su21-5 (G)

League Club	Source	Date Signed	Seasons Played	Apps	Subs	Gls
Norwich C.	Clyde	08.93	93	1	1	0
Reading	Motherwell	03.98	97	7	0	0

HOWITT David John
Birmingham, 4 August, 1952 (FB)

League Club	Source	Date Signed	Seasons Played	Apps	Subs	Gls
Birmingham C.	App	08.69	72	2	0	0
Bury	Tr	08.73	73	11	9	4
Workington	Tr	07.74	74	30	5	1
Aldershot	Tr	06.75	75-79	126	11	2

HOWITT Robert Gibb
Glasgow, 15 July, 1929 SF Lge (IF/WH)

League Club	Source	Date Signed	Seasons Played	Apps	Subs	Gls
Sheffield U.	Partick Thistle	07.55	55-57	88	-	30
Stoke C.	Tr	04.58	58-62	133	-	14

HOWLETT Gary Patrick
Dublin, 2 April, 1963 IR Yth/IRu21-4/IR-1 (M)

League Club	Source	Date Signed	Seasons Played	Apps	Subs	Gls
Coventry C.	Home Farm	11.80				
Brighton & H.A.	Tr	08.82	82-84	30	2	2
Bournemouth	Tr	12.84	84-86	56	4	7
Aldershot	L	08.87	87	1	0	0
Chester C.	L	12.87	87	6	0	1
York C.	Tr	01.88	87-90	94	7	13

HOWLETT Robert Victor
West Ham, 12 December, 1948 (CD)

League Club	Source	Date Signed	Seasons Played	Apps	Subs	Gls
Chelsea	App	12.65				
Southend U.	Tr	09.67	67-68	4	2	0
Colchester U.	Tr	07.69	69	10	6	0

HOWSAM Alfred **Dennis**
Sheffield, 21 October, 1922 Died 1981 (CF)

League Club	Source	Date Signed	Seasons Played	Apps	Subs	Gls
Sheffield Wed.		11.45				
Chesterfield	Tr	03.47	46-47	12	-	4
Halifax T.	Tr	06.48	48	19	-	4

HOWSHALL Gerald Thomas
Stoke, 27 October, 1944 (WH)

League Club	Source	Date Signed	Seasons Played	Apps	Subs	Gls
West Bromwich A.	App	05.62	63-67	43	2	3
Norwich C.	Tr	11.67	67-70	36	4	0

HOY Kristian
Doncaster, 27 April, 1976 (F)

League Club	Source	Date Signed	Seasons Played	Apps	Subs	Gls
Doncaster Rov. (N/C)	Jnrs	07.94	94	0	1	0

HOY Robert
Halifax, 10 January, 1950 E Yth (W)

League Club	Source	Date Signed	Seasons Played	Apps	Subs	Gls
Huddersfield T.	App	11.67	66-74	140	4	18
Blackburn Rov.	Tr	03.75	74-75	13	6	0
Halifax T.	Tr	06.76	76	30	0	7
York C.	Tr	08.77	77	10	4	1
Rochdale	Tr	12.77	77-80	61	5	12

HOY Roger Ernest
Bow, 6 December, 1946 (D/M)

League Club	Source	Date Signed	Seasons Played	Apps	Subs	Gls
Tottenham H.	Jnrs	05.64	65-67	10	0	0
Crystal Palace	Tr	09.68	68-69	54	0	6
Luton T.	Tr	06.70	70	32	0	0
Cardiff C.	Tr	08.71	71-72	14	2	0

HOYLAND Jamie William
Sheffield, 23 January, 1966 E Yth (M/CD)

League Club	Source	Date Signed	Seasons Played	Apps	Subs	Gls
Manchester C.	App	11.83	83-84	2	0	0
Bury	Tr	07.86	86-89	169	3	35
Sheffield U.	Tr	07.90	90-94	72	17	6
Bristol C.	L	03.94	93	6	0	0
Burnley	Tr	10.94	94-97	77	10	4
Carlisle U.	L	11.97	97	5	0	0

HOYLAND Thomas
Sheffield, 14 June, 1932 (WH)

League Club	Source	Date Signed	Seasons Played	Apps	Subs	Gls
Sheffield U.	Jnrs	10.49	49-60	181	-	18
Bradford C.	Tr	10.61	61-62	27	-	6

HOYLE Colin Roy
Wirksworth, 15 January, 1972 (CD)

League Club	Source	Date Signed	Seasons Played	Apps	Subs	Gls
Arsenal	YT	01.90				
Chesterfield	L	02.90	89	3	0	0
Barnsley	Tr	06.90				
Bradford C.	Tr	08.92	92-93	55	7	1
Notts Co.	Tr	08.94	94-95	5	0	0
Mansfield T.	L	10.94	94	4	1	0

HOYLE Herbert
Baildon, 22 April, 1920 (G)

League Club	Source	Date Signed	Seasons Played	Apps	Subs	Gls
Wolverhampton W.		05.46				
Exeter C.	Tr	08.46	46-49	82	-	0
Bristol Rov.	Tr	05.50	50-52	105	-	0

HREIDARSSON Hermann
Iceland, 11 July, 1974 Icelandic Int (CD)

League Club	Source	Date Signed	Seasons Played	Apps	Subs	Gls
Crystal Palace	IBV (Ice)	08.97	97	26	4	2

HRISTOV Georgi
Macedonia, 30 January, 1976 Macedonian Int (F)

League Club	Source	Date Signed	Seasons Played	Apps	Subs	Gls
Barnsley	Partizan Belgrade (Yug)	07.97	97	11	12	4

HUBBARD John (Jack)
Barnsley, 24 March, 1925 (WH)

League Club	Source	Date Signed	Seasons Played	Apps	Subs	Gls
Notts Co.		02.45	46	13	-	2
Scunthorpe U.	Scarborough	08.50	50-59	359	-	12

HUBBARD John Gaulton
South Africa, 16 December, 1930 SF Lge (OL)

League Club	Source	Date Signed	Seasons Played	Apps	Subs	Gls
Bury	Glasgow Rangers	04.59	59-61	109	-	29

HUBBARD Philip John
Lincoln, 25 January, 1949 (M)

League Club	Source	Date Signed	Seasons Played	Apps	Subs	Gls
Lincoln C.	App	07.66	65-71	150	2	41
Norwich C.	Tr	12.71	71-72	6	4	1
Grimsby T.	Tr	10.72	72-75	144	2	37
Lincoln C.	Tr	08.76	76-79	99	9	11

HUBBARD Terence John
Pontypool, 6 November, 1950 W Sch/Wu23-2 (M)

League Club	Source	Date Signed	Seasons Played	Apps	Subs	Gls
Swindon T.	App	11.68	70-75	83	1	2

HUBBICK David
South Shields, 16 March, 1960 (F)

League Club	Source	Date Signed	Seasons Played	Apps	Subs	Gls
Ipswich T.	App	01.78				
Wimbledon	Tr	09.80	80-81	22	4	6
Colchester U. (N/C)	Dagenham	10.83	83-84	4	11	1

HUBBICK Henry (Harry) Edward
Jarrow, 12 November, 1910 Died 1992 (FB)

League Club	Source	Date Signed	Seasons Played	Apps	Subs	Gls
Burnley	Blyth Spartans	03.35	35-36	58	-	1
Bolton W.	Tr	02.37	36-46	128	-	0
Port Vale	Tr	10.47	47-48	50	-	1
Rochdale	Tr	01.49	48-50	90	-	0

HUCKER Ian **Peter**
Hampstead, 28 October, 1959 Eu21-2 (G)

League Club	Source	Date Signed	Seasons Played	Apps	Subs	Gls
Queens Park R.	App	07.77	80-85	160	0	0
Oxford U.	Tr	02.87	86-89	66	0	0
West Bromwich A.	L	01.88	87	7	0	0
Millwall	Tr	11.89				
Aldershot	Tr	11.90	90	27	0	0

HUCKERBY Darren Carl
Nottingham, 23 April, 1976 Eu21-4/E 'B' (F)

League Club	Source	Date Signed	Seasons Played	Apps	Subs	Gls
Lincoln C.	YT	07.93	93-95	20	8	5
Newcastle U.	Tr	11.95	95	0	1	0
Millwall	L	09.96	96	6	0	3
Coventry C.	Tr	11.96	96-97	53	6	19

HUDD David Clive
Bristol, 9 July, 1944 (IF)

League Club	Source	Date Signed	Seasons Played	Apps	Subs	Gls
Bristol Rov.	Jnrs	07.63	64	5	-	1

HUDDART David Joseph
Maryport, 18 November, 1937 (G)

League Club	Source	Date Signed	Seasons Played	Apps	Subs	Gls
Aldershot		06.61				
Gillingham	Tr	07.62	62-64	10	-	0

HUDDLESTONE Edward Thomas
Nottingham, 29 September, 1935 (CF)

League Club	Source	Date Signed	Seasons Played	Apps	Subs	Gls
Nottingham F.	Blackpool (Am)	12.56	56	1	-	0

HUDGELL Arthur John
Hackney, 28 December, 1920 (FB)

League Club	Source	Date Signed	Seasons Played	Apps	Subs	Gls
Crystal Palace	Eton Manor	12.37	46	25	-	1
Sunderland	Tr	01.47	46-56	260	-	0

HUDSON Alan Anthony
Chelsea, 21 June, 1951 Eu23-10/E-2 (M)

League Club	Source	Date Signed	Seasons Played	Apps	Subs	Gls
Chelsea	App	06.68	68-73	144	1	10
Stoke C.	Tr	01.74	73-76	105	0	9
Arsenal	Tr	12.76	76-77	36	0	0
Chelsea	Seattle (USA)	08.83				
Stoke C.	Tr	01.84	83-85	38	1	0

League Club	Source	Date Signed	Seasons Played	Apps	Subs	Gls
HUDSON Albert George						
Swansea, 17 June, 1920 W Sch						(IL)
Fulham	Caerau	08.37	46	1	-	0
HUDSON Carl Bernard						
Bradford, 10 October, 1966						(CD)
Rochdale	Bradford C. (YT)	08.86	86	13	2	1
HUDSON Charles Arthur						
Stamford, 3 April, 1920						(CF)
Accrington St. (Am)	Guiseley	06.46	46	11	-	3
HUDSON Christopher Ben						
Rotherham, 13 March, 1951						(FB)
Rotherham U.	App	03.86	68-71	53	9	1
HUDSON Colin Arthur Richard						
Chepstow, 5 October, 1935						(OR)
Newport Co.	Undy U.	04.54	53-56	82	-	21
Cardiff C.	Tr	07.57	57-60	61	-	9
Brighton & H.A.	Tr	06.61	61	1	-	0
Newport Co.	Tr	02.62	62	30	-	2
HUDSON Daniel Robert						
Doncaster, 25 June, 1979						(M)
Rotherham U.	YT	06.97	97	6	4	0
HUDSON Gary						
West Auckland, 1 November, 1955						(G)
Preston N.E. (Am)		08.73	73	1	-	0
HUDSON Gary Paul						
Bradford, 25 February, 1951						(FB)
Bradford P.A.	Jnrs	07.68	67-69	38	1	0
HUDSON Geoffrey Alan						
Leeds, 14 October, 1931						(FB)
Bradford P.A.	Jnrs	12.49	50-56	95	-	0
Bradford C.	Tr	02.57	56-58	34	-	0
Halifax T.	Tr	08.59	59-60	52	-	0
Exeter C.	Tr	07.61	61	41	-	0
Crewe Alex.	Tr	07.62	62	1	-	0
Gillingham	Tr	07.63	63-64	81	-	1
Lincoln C.	Tr	05.65	65	33	0	0
Rotherham U.	Tr	06.66				
HUDSON George (Garth)						
Southampton, 26 October, 1923						(CH)
Portsmouth		08.45	47	1	-	0
Swindon T.	Tr	09.48	48-59	401	-	11
HUDSON George Anthony						
Manchester, 14 March, 1937						(CF)
Blackburn Rov.		01.58	58	4	-	1
Accrington St.	Tr	07.60	60	44	-	35
Peterborough U.	Tr	10.61	61-62	65	-	39
Coventry C.	Tr	04.63	62-65	113	0	62
Northampton T.	Tr	03.66	65-66	18	0	6
Tranmere Rov.	Tr	01.67	66-68	53	1	20
HUDSON John (Jackie)						
Blaydon, 5 October, 1921						(OR)
Chesterfield	West Stanley	10.46	46-51	169	-	33
Shrewsbury T.	Bangor C.	09.53	53-54	48	-	20
HUDSON Christopher **John**						
Middleton, 25 November, 1964						(LW)
Oldham Ath.	Manchester C. (Jnrs)	09.82	82-83	16	4	0
Rochdale (N/C)	Sweden	02.87	86	18	1	1
HUDSON Morris						
Barnsley, 12 September, 1930						(FB)
Barnsley	Jnrs	01.49	50-53	36	-	0
Bradford C.	Tr	07.55	55	4	-	0
HUDSON Raymond James						
Slough, 21 November, 1937						(FB)
Reading	Jnrs	11.54	55-58	11	-	0
HUDSON Raymond Wilfred						
Gateshead, 24 March, 1955						(M)
Newcastle U.	App	03.73	73-77	16	4	1
HUDSON Stanley Robert						
Fulham, 10 February, 1923 Died 1951						(OL)
Queens Park R.		09.48	48-49	22	-	7

League Club	Source	Date Signed	Seasons Played	Apps	Subs	Gls
HUDSON William Albert						
Swansea, 10 March, 1928 W Amat						(OR)
Leeds U.	Pembroke Borough	05.51	51	4	-	0
Sheffield U.	Tr	05.52	53	1	-	0
Mansfield T.	Tr	05.54	54	8	-	1
HUFFER Philip						
Bedworth, 23 January, 1932 Died 1995						(CH)
Derby Co.	Bedworth T.	10.53				
Northampton T.	Tr	05.54	54	1	-	0
HUGGINS John Edward Minden						
India, 24 February, 1930						(IF)
Aldershot	Alton T.	12.55	55	6	-	5
HUGHES Aaron William						
Magherafelt, 8 November, 1979 NI Yth/NI 'B'/NI-3						(D)
Newcastle U.	YT	03.97	97	4	0	0
HUGHES Adrian Francis						
Billinge, 19 December, 1970						(CD)
Preston N.E.	YT	03.89	87-91	91	9	3
HUGHES Alan						
Wallasey, 5 October, 1948						(CF)
Liverpool	Jnrs	09.66				
Chester C.	L	11.67	67	9	0	2
HUGHES Allan Leslie						
Swansea, 11 March, 1951						(FB)
Swansea C.	App	03.69	68	2	0	0
HUGHES Andrew John						
Manchester, 2 January, 1978						(M)
Oldham Ath.	YT	01.96	95-97	18	15	1
Notts Co.	Tr	01.98	97	12	3	2
HUGHES Anthony						
Liverpool, 3 October, 1973 E Yth						(CD)
Crewe Alex.	YT	06.92	92-93	18	5	1
HUGHES Arthur						
Linlithgow, 23 November, 1927						(IF)
Notts Co.	Jeanfield Swifts	07.49				
Nottingham F.	Tr	05.51				
Grimsby T.	Canterbury C.	06.54	54	25	-	11
Gillingham	Tr	05.55	55	5	-	1
HUGHES Brian						
Skewen, 22 November, 1937 W Sch/Wu23-2						(WH)
Swansea C.	Jnrs	07.56	58-68	231	0	6
HUGHES Brian David						
Ludgershall, 20 August, 1962						(M)
Swindon T.	App	07.80	80-82	67	3	5
Torquay U.	Tr	08.83	83	33	5	6
HUGHES Bryan						
Liverpool, 19 June, 1976						(M)
Wrexham	YT	07.94	93-96	71	23	12
Birmingham C.	Tr	03.97	96-97	44	7	5
HUGHES Ceri Morgan						
Pontypridd, 26 February, 1971 W Yth/W 'B'/W-6						(M)
Luton T.	YT	07.89	89-96	157	18	17
Wimbledon	Tr	07.97	97	13	4	1
HUGHES Charles						
Manchester, 17 September, 1927						(W)
Manchester U.	Jnrs	09.46				
Leeds U.	Tr	09.50	50-51	21	-	2
HUGHES Charles James						
Blackpool, 7 September, 1939						(G)
Wrexham		10.58	59-60	35	-	0
HUGHES Darren John						
Prescot, 6 October, 1965						(LB/M)
Everton	App	10.83	83-84	3	0	0
Shrewsbury T.	Tr	06.85	85-86	34	3	1
Brighton & H.A.	Tr	09.86	86	26	0	2
Port Vale	Tr	09.87	87-91	183	1	4
Northampton T.	(Retired)	01.95	94-95	19	2	0
Exeter C.	Tr	11.95	95-96	58	4	1
HUGHES David James						
Liverpool, 23 September, 1951						(OR)
Wrexham (Am)		05.70	70	1	0	0

HUGHES David James
Connah's Quay, 27 April, 1943 (OR)

League Club	Source	Date Signed	Seasons Played	Apps	Subs	Gls
Wrexham	Jnrs	05.61				
Tranmere Rov.	Tr	07.62	62	2	-	0

HUGHES David Robert
Blackburn, 7 September, 1948 (W)

League Club	Source	Date Signed	Seasons Played	Apps	Subs	Gls
Preston N.E.	Jnrs	09.65	66-71	22	9	0
Southport	Tr	07.72	72	40	0	1
Bury	Tr	08.73	73	12	0	3
Southport	Tr	11.73	73-76	109	4	4
Crewe Alex. (N/C)		08.78	78	12	1	0

HUGHES David Robert
St Albans, 30 December, 1972 E Sch/Wu21-1 (M)

League Club	Source	Date Signed	Seasons Played	Apps	Subs	Gls
Southampton	Jnrs	07.91	93-97	15	30	3

HUGHES David Thomas
Birmingham, 19 March, 1958 (M)

League Club	Source	Date Signed	Seasons Played	Apps	Subs	Gls
Aston Villa	App	02.76	76	3	1	1
Lincoln C.	Tr	04.77	77-80	61	1	1
Scunthorpe U.	Tr	06.81	81	17	4	0
Lincoln C.	Tr	03.82				

HUGHES Robert **David**
Wrexham, 1 February, 1978 W Yth/Wu21-9/W 'B' (CD)

League Club	Source	Date Signed	Seasons Played	Apps	Subs	Gls
Aston Villa	YT	07.96	96	4	3	0
Carlisle U.	L	03.98	97	1	0	0

HUGHES Denis
Stoke, 9 April, 1931 Died 1990 (OR)

League Club	Source	Date Signed	Seasons Played	Apps	Subs	Gls
Stoke C.	Jnrs	09.48	50	1	-	0

HUGHES Derek
Wrexham, 22 November, 1940 (OR)

League Club	Source	Date Signed	Seasons Played	Apps	Subs	Gls
Wrexham (Am)	Druids U.	07.61	61	1	-	0

HUGHES Emlyn Walter
Barrow, 28 August, 1947 Eu23-8/EF Lge/E-62 (D/M)

League Club	Source	Date Signed	Seasons Played	Apps	Subs	Gls
Blackpool	Jnrs	09.64	65-66	27	1	0
Liverpool	Tr	03.67	66-78	474	0	35
Wolverhampton W.	Tr	08.79	79-80	56	2	2
Rotherham U.	Tr	09.81	81-82	55	1	6
Hull C.	Tr	03.83	82	9	0	0
Swansea C.	Mansfield T. (N/C)	09.83	83	7	0	0

HUGHES Thomas **Glynfor**
Wrexham, 29 November, 1931 Died 1995 (OR)

League Club	Source	Date Signed	Seasons Played	Apps	Subs	Gls
Sheffield Wed.		01.51				
Wrexham	Tr	08.52	52-54	92	-	20
Newport Co.	Tr	07.55	55	4	-	0

HUGHES Gordon
Washington, 19 June, 1936 (OR)

League Club	Source	Date Signed	Seasons Played	Apps	Subs	Gls
Newcastle U.	Tow Law T.	08.56	56-62	133	-	18
Derby Co.	Tr	08.63	63-67	184	0	22
Lincoln C.	Tr	03.68	67-70	117	0	9

HUGHES Thomas **Gwynfor**
Blaenau Ffestiniog, 7 May, 1922 (IF/WH)

League Club	Source	Date Signed	Seasons Played	Apps	Subs	Gls
Northampton T.	Blaenau Ffestiniog	12.45	46-55	225	-	15

HUGHES Harold James
Nuneaton, 8 October, 1929 (CH)

League Club	Source	Date Signed	Seasons Played	Apps	Subs	Gls
Southport	Symingtons	08.50				
Chelsea	Tr	02.51	51	1	-	0
Bournemouth	Tr	06.52	52-57	77	-	2
Gillingham	Tr	07.58	58-62	204	-	15

HUGHES Harry Anthony
Maltby, 12 August, 1937 (FB)

League Club	Source	Date Signed	Seasons Played	Apps	Subs	Gls
Rotherham U.		06.59	59	1	-	0

HUGHES Ian
Bangor, 2 August, 1974 W Yth/Wu21-12 (D/M)

League Club	Source	Date Signed	Seasons Played	Apps	Subs	Gls
Bury	YT	11.91	91-97	137	23	1
Blackpool	Tr	12.97	97	20	1	0

HUGHES Ian James
Sunderland, 24 August, 1961 Wu21-1 (D)

League Club	Source	Date Signed	Seasons Played	Apps	Subs	Gls
Sunderland	App	08.79	79	1	0	0
Barnsley	Tr	07.81				

HUGHES Robert **Ian**
Cefn Mawr, 17 March, 1946 (OR)

League Club	Source	Date Signed	Seasons Played	Apps	Subs	Gls
Wrexham	Oswestry T.	02.66	65	9	0	3
Bradford P.A.	Tr	07.67	67	13	0	0

HUGHES Iorwerth
Abergele, 26 May, 1925 Died 1993 W Amat/W-4 (G)

League Club	Source	Date Signed	Seasons Played	Apps	Subs	Gls
Luton T.	Llandudno	04.49	49-50	36	-	0
Cardiff C.	Tr	08.51	51	26	-	0
Newport Co.	Worcester C.	08.53	53-57	106	-	0

HUGHES James Horace
Leeds, 28 August, 1918 Died 1979 (D)

League Club	Source	Date Signed	Seasons Played	Apps	Subs	Gls
Fulham		09.46	46	1	-	0

HUGHES John
Edinburgh, 19 September, 1964 (F)

League Club	Source	Date Signed	Seasons Played	Apps	Subs	Gls
Swansea C.	Berwick R.	11.89	89	16	8	4

HUGHES John
Coatbridge, 3 April, 1943 Su23-4/SF Lge/S-8 (CF)

League Club	Source	Date Signed	Seasons Played	Apps	Subs	Gls
Crystal Palace	Glasgow Celtic	10.71	71-72	20	0	4
Sunderland	Tr	01.73	72	1	0	0

HUGHES John
West Bromwich, 13 September, 1929 (IF)

League Club	Source	Date Signed	Seasons Played	Apps	Subs	Gls
Walsall	Golden Lion	05.50	50-52	44	-	10

HUGHES John Gareth
Prestatyn, 18 February, 1942 (CF)

League Club	Source	Date Signed	Seasons Played	Apps	Subs	Gls
Chester C.	Rhyl	07.62	62	2	-	0

HUGHES John Ifor
Bangor, 4 May, 1951 (W)

League Club	Source	Date Signed	Seasons Played	Apps	Subs	Gls
Blackpool	Jnrs	07.69	69-70	5	3	0
Southport	L	03.71	70	7	1	1
Stockport Co.	Altrincham	01.76	75	11	1	3

HUGHES John Michael
Manchester, 29 November, 1962 (M)

League Club	Source	Date Signed	Seasons Played	Apps	Subs	Gls
Bury	Winsford U.	11.80	81-82	1	1	0

HUGHES John Norman
Tamworth, 10 July, 1921 (W)

League Club	Source	Date Signed	Seasons Played	Apps	Subs	Gls
Birmingham C.	Tamworth Castle	06.47	47-48	6	-	0

HUGHES Kenneth David
Barmouth, 9 January, 1966 (G)

League Club	Source	Date Signed	Seasons Played	Apps	Subs	Gls
Crystal Palace	Jnrs	08.85				
Shrewsbury T.	Tr	07.86	86-91	74	0	0
Wrexham	Tr	08.92	92	8	0	0

HUGHES Lawrie
Liverpool, 2 March, 1924 E 'B'/E-3 (CH)

League Club	Source	Date Signed	Seasons Played	Apps	Subs	Gls
Liverpool	Tranmere Rov. (Am)	02.43	46-57	303	-	1

HUGHES Lee
Birmingham, 22 May, 1976 E Semi Pro (CF)

League Club	Source	Date Signed	Seasons Played	Apps	Subs	Gls
West Bromwich A.	Kidderminster Hrs	05.97	97	18	19	14

HUGHES Lyndon James
Smethwick, 16 September, 1950 E Sch/E Yth (FB/M)

League Club	Source	Date Signed	Seasons Played	Apps	Subs	Gls
West Bromwich A.	App	01.68	68-74	89	9	3
Peterborough U.	Tr	07.75	75-77	75	2	5

HUGHES Mark
Port Talbot, 3 February, 1962 W Sch (CD)

League Club	Source	Date Signed	Seasons Played	Apps	Subs	Gls
Bristol Rov.	App	02.80	79-83	73	1	3
Torquay U.	L	12.82	82	9	0	1
Swansea C.	Tr	07.84	84	12	0	0
Bristol C.	Tr	02.85	84-85	21	1	0
Tranmere Rov.	Tr	09.85	85-93	258	8	9
Shrewsbury T.	Tr	07.94	94-95	20	2	0

HUGHES Mark Christopher
Swindon, 17 July, 1967 W Yth (M)

League Club	Source	Date Signed	Seasons Played	Apps	Subs	Gls
Swindon T.	App	●	83	0	1	0

HUGHES Leslie **Mark**
Wrexham, 1 November, 1963 W Sch/W Yth/Wu21-5/W-66 (F)

League Club	Source	Date Signed	Seasons Played	Apps	Subs	Gls
Manchester U.	App	11.80	83-85	85	4	37
Manchester U.	Barcelona (Sp)	07.88	88-94	251	5	82
Chelsea	Tr	07.95	95-97	88	7	25

HUGHES Michael Eamonn
Larne (NI), 2 August, 1971 NI Sch/NI Yth/NIu21-1/NIu23-2/NI-42 (W)

League Club	Source	Date Signed	Seasons Played	Apps	Subs	Gls
Manchester C.	Carrick R.	08.88	88-91	25	1	1
West Ham U. (L)	Strasbourg (Fr)	11.94	94	15	2	2
West Ham U. (L)	Strasbourg (Fr)	10.95	95	28	0	0
West Ham U.	Strasbourg (Fr)	08.96	96-97	33	5	3
Wimbledon	Tr	09.97	97	29	0	4

League Club	Source	Date Signed	Seasons Played	Career Record Apps	Subs	Gls
HUGHES Michael Richard						
Bridgend, 19 August, 1964 W Yth						(G)
Swansea C.	App	08.82	83-87	139	0	0
HUGHES Edward **Michael (Blodwyn)**						
Llaniloes, 3 September, 1940						(WH)
Cardiff C.	Jnrs	12.58	58	1	-	0
Exeter C.	Tr	07.61	61-62	36	-	0
Chesterfield	Tr	07.63	63-68	208	2	9
HUGHES Patrick Joseph						
Coatbridge, 28 February, 1945						(OL)
Darlington	St Mirren	08.65	65	3	0	0
HUGHES Paul						
Denton, 19 December, 1968						(FB)
Bolton W.	YT	07.87	87-89	12	1	0
HUGHES John **Paul**						
Hammersmith, 19 April, 1976 E Sch						(M)
Chelsea	YT	07.94	96-97	13	8	2
HUGHES Philip Anthony						
Belfast, 19 November, 1964 NI Yth/NI-3						(G)
Leeds U.	Manchester U. (App)	01.83	83-84	6	0	0
Bury	Tr	07.85	85-87	80	0	0
Wigan Ath.	Tr	11.87	87-90	99	0	0
Scarborough	Rochdale (N/C)	10.91	91	17	0	0
HUGHES Richard						
Barrow, 27 December, 1950						(F)
Barrow (Am)	Jnrs	08.70	71	0	2	0
HUGHES Ronald						
Mold, 1 July, 1930						(RB/WH)
Chester C.	Mold Alex.	09.50	51-61	399	-	21
HUGHES Ronald Hardwick						
Workington, 17 August, 1955						(G)
Workington	R.N.A.D.	12.75	75	15	0	0
HUGHES Roy						
Manchester, 13 August, 1949						(M)
Bury	App	09.66	67-71	45	3	1
HUGHES Stephen John						
Reading, 18 September, 1976 E Sch/E Yth/Eu21-8						(M)
Arsenal	YT	07.95	94-97	17	16	3
HUGHES Stephen John						
Warrington, 4 January, 1958						(F)
Crewe Alex. (N/C)	Manchester C. (App)	03.76	75	0	2	0
HUGHES Stephen (Billy) John						
Folkestone, 29 July, 1960						(M)
Gillingham	Jnrs	07.77	75-80	110	16	8
Crystal Palace	Tr	07.81	81	3	4	0
Wimbledon (N/C)	Tr	03.82	81	2	0	0
HUGHES Terence Philip						
Llaniloes, 10 March, 1953						(F)
Shrewsbury T.	App	03.71	69-73	67	5	22
HUGHES Thomas Alexander						
Dalmuir, 11 July, 1947 Su23-2						(G)
Chelsea	Clydebank	07.65	66-69	11	0	0
Aston Villa	Tr	06.71	71	16	0	0
Brighton & H.A.	L	02.73	72	3	0	0
Hereford U.	Tr	08.73	73-81	240	0	0
HUGHES Walter Cyril Joseph						
Liverpool, 15 March, 1934						(OR)
Liverpool	Winsford U.	10.54				
Sheffield U.	Winsford U.	01.56	55	2	-	0
Bradford P.A.	Wisbech T.	04.57	56-57	20	-	0
Southport	Tr	02.58	57	11	-	0
HUGHES Byron **Wayne**						
Port Talbot, 8 March, 1958 W Sch/Wu21-3						(M)
West Bromwich A.	App	03.76	76-77	3	3	2
Cardiff C.	Tulsa (USA)	10.79	79-81	42	4	1
HUGHES William						
Glasgow, 3 March, 1929						(OR)
York C.	Newcastle U. (Am)	05.51	51-61	349	-	55
HUGHES William						
Ballymena (NI), 9 May, 1929 NI-1						(OR)
Bolton W.	Larne T.	08.48	48-52	47	-	2
Bournemouth	Tr	06.53	53	16	-	1

League Club	Source	Date Signed	Seasons Played	Career Record Apps	Subs	Gls
HUGHES William						
Coatbridge, 30 December, 1948 S-1						(F)
Sunderland	Jnrs	02.66	66-76	264	23	74
Derby Co.	Tr	08.77	77	17	2	8
Leicester C.	Tr	12.77	77-78	36	1	5
Carlisle U.	L	09.79	79	5	0	0
HUGHES William (Archie) Arthur						
Holyhead, 2 February, 1919 Died 1992 W-5						(G)
Huddersfield T.	Newry T.	05.39				
Tottenham H.	Tr	12.45	46-47	2	-	0
Blackburn Rov.	Tr	10.48	48-49	27	-	0
Rochdale	Tr	09.50	50	9	-	0
Crystal Palace	Tr	02.51	50-51	18	-	0
HUGHES William Henry						
Cardiff, 2 October, 1920 Died 1995 W Sch						(CH)
Hartlepool U.	Newcastle U. (Am)	05.46	46-49	124	-	2
HUGHES William Marshall						
Llanelli, 6 March, 1918 Died 1981 W-10						(FB)
Birmingham C.	Watchers Celtic	05.35	35-46	104	-	0
Luton T.	Tr	07.47	47	31	-	0
Chelsea	Tr	03.48	47-50	93	-	0
HUGHES Zacari David						
Australia, 6 June, 1971						(CD)
Rochdale	YT	08.89	87	2	0	0
HUGHTON Christopher William Gerard						
Stratford, 11 December, 1958 IR-53						(FB)
Tottenham H.	Jnrs	06.77	79-89	293	4	12
West Ham U.	Tr	11.90	90-91	32	1	0
Brentford	Tr	03.92	91-92	32	0	0
HUGHTON Henry Timothy						
Stratford, 18 November, 1959 IRu21-1						(D)
Leyton Orient	App	12.76	78-81	104	7	2
Crystal Palace	Tr	07.82	82-85	113	5	1
Brentford	Tr	09.86	86	5	3	0
Leyton Orient	Tr	12.86	86-87	16	2	0
HUGO Roger Victor						
Woking, 6 September, 1942						(IF)
West Ham U.	Jnrs	10.60	63	3	-	2
Watford	Tr	05.65	65	24	1	6
HUKIN Arthur						
Sheffield, 22 October, 1937 Died 1983						(F)
Sheffield Wed.	Jnrs	10.54	54	6	-	3
HULBERT Robin James						
Plymouth, 14 March, 1980 E Sch/E Yth						(M)
Swindon T.	YT	09.97	97	0	1	0
HULL Alan Edward						
Southend, 4 September, 1962						(F)
Leyton Orient	Barking	05.87	87-90	54	25	17
HULL Gary						
Sheffield, 21 June, 1956						(FB)
Sheffield Wed.	App	06.74	75	6	2	0
HULL Jeffrey						
Southend, 25 August, 1960						(W)
Southend U.	App	08.78	78-80	10	5	1
Colchester U.	Basildon U.	12.82	82-85	82	1	10
HULLETT William Alexander						
Liverpool, 19 November, 1915 Died 1982						(CF)
Everton		12.35				
New Brighton	Tr	01.37	36	13	-	8
Plymouth Arg.	Tr	10.37	37-38	29	-	20
Manchester U.	Tr	03.39				
Cardiff C.	Merthyr Tydfil	02.48	47-48	27	-	15
Nottingham F.	Tr	11.48	48	13	-	2
HULLIGAN Michael John						
Liverpool, 28 February, 1923 Died 1978						(W)
Liverpool		12.42				
Port Vale	Tr	07.48	48-54	197	-	22
HULME Eric Martin						
Houghton-le-Spring, 14 January, 1949						(G)
Nottingham F.	Spennymoor U.	03.70	71	5	0	0
Lincoln C.	Tr	09.72	72-73	23	0	0
HULME John						
Mobberley, 6 February, 1945						(CD)
Bolton W.	Jnrs	02.62	62-71	186	2	7

League Club	Source	Date Signed	Seasons Played	Apps	Subs	Gls
Notts Co.	L	03.72	71	8	0	0
Reading	Tr	07.72	72-73	86	1	0
Bury	Tr	07.74	74-75	86	0	5

HULME Kevin
Farnworth, 2 December, 1967 (M/F)

League Club	Source	Date Signed	Seasons Played	Apps	Subs	Gls
Bury	Radcliffe Borough	03.89	88-92	82	28	21
Chester C.	L	10.89	89	4	0	0
Doncaster Rov.	Tr	07.93	93	33	1	8
Bury	Tr	08.94	94-95	24	5	0
Lincoln C.	Tr	09.95	95	4	1	0

HULMES Gary Anthony
Manchester, 28 February, 1957 (F)

League Club	Source	Date Signed	Seasons Played	Apps	Subs	Gls
Rochdale	Manchester C. (Jnr)	12.74	74-75	4	6	1

HULSE Robert Arthur
Crewe, 5 November, 1948 E Yth (CF)

League Club	Source	Date Signed	Seasons Played	Apps	Subs	Gls
Stoke C.	Nantwich T.	04.67	67	2	0	0

HULSE Robert James
Gateshead, 5 January, 1957 (M)

League Club	Source	Date Signed	Seasons Played	Apps	Subs	Gls
Darlington (N/C)	Stade Quimper (Fr)	09.83	83	3	1	0

HUMBLE Douglas
Weardale, 16 February, 1920 Died 1989 (CF)

League Club	Source	Date Signed	Seasons Played	Apps	Subs	Gls
Sunderland	Bishop Auckland	05.45				
Southport	Tr	06.47	47	11	-	4

HUMBLE James **Wilfred**
Ashington, 10 May, 1936 Died 1985 (FB)

League Club	Source	Date Signed	Seasons Played	Apps	Subs	Gls
Mansfield T.	Ashington	05.59	59-65	198	0	1

HUME Robert
Kirkintilloch, 18 March, 1941 (OL)

League Club	Source	Date Signed	Seasons Played	Apps	Subs	Gls
Middlesbrough	Glasgow Rangers	09.62	62	19	-	5

HUME William Sanderson
Armadale, 18 December, 1935 (IF)

League Club	Source	Date Signed	Seasons Played	Apps	Subs	Gls
Birmingham C.	Dunfermline Ath.	02.58	58-59	10	-	2

HUMES Anthony
Blyth, 19 March, 1966 (CD)

League Club	Source	Date Signed	Seasons Played	Apps	Subs	Gls
Ipswich T.	App	05.83	86-91	107	13	10
Wrexham	Tr	03.92	91-97	181	6	8

HUMES James
Carlisle, 6 August, 1942 (W)

League Club	Source	Date Signed	Seasons Played	Apps	Subs	Gls
Preston N.E.	Jnrs	09.59	59-61	18	-	1
Bristol Rov.	Tr	06.62	62	2	-	0
Chester C.	Tr	07.63	63-66	124	0	31
Barnsley	Tr	07.67	67	7	0	1

HUMPHREY John
Paddington, 31 January, 1961 (RB)

League Club	Source	Date Signed	Seasons Played	Apps	Subs	Gls
Wolverhampton W.	App	01.79	79-84	149	0	3
Charlton Ath.	Tr	07.85	85-89	194	0	3
Crystal Palace	Tr	06.90	90-94	153	7	2
Reading	L	12.93	93	8	0	0
Charlton Ath.	Tr	07.95	95	28	0	0
Gillingham	Tr	08.96	96	9	0	0
Brighton & H.A.	Tr	01.97	96-97	22	0	0

HUMPHREY John Mark
Guildford, 2 July, 1969 (F)

League Club	Source	Date Signed	Seasons Played	Apps	Subs	Gls
Millwall	Leatherhead	02.91				
Exeter C.	L	12.91	91	2	0	0

HUMPHREY Thomas Robson
Houghton-le-Spring, 27 October, 1937 (OR)

League Club	Source	Date Signed	Seasons Played	Apps	Subs	Gls
Aldershot		03.59	58-60	22	-	3

HUMPHREYS Alan
Chester, 18 October, 1939 (G)

League Club	Source	Date Signed	Seasons Played	Apps	Subs	Gls
Shrewsbury T.	Jnrs	10.56	56-59	32	-	0
Leeds U.	Tr	02.60	59-61	40	-	0
Mansfield T.	Gravesend & Nft.	01.64	64-67	58	0	0
Chesterfield	Tr	07.68	68-69	51	0	0

HUMPHREYS Derek John Beattie
Belfast, 5 October, 1949 (G)

League Club	Source	Date Signed	Seasons Played	Apps	Subs	Gls
Arsenal	Jnrs	10.66				
Sunderland	Crusaders	11.67				
Hartlepool U.	L	10.69	69	4	0	0

HUMPHREYS Gerald
Llandudno, 14 January, 1946 W Sch/Wu23-5 (W)

League Club	Source	Date Signed	Seasons Played	Apps	Subs	Gls
Everton	App	09.63	65-69	12	0	2
Crystal Palace	Tr	06.70	70	4	7	0
Crewe Alex.	Tr	01.72	71-76	184	9	30

HUMPHREYS John Stephen
Farnworth, 18 July, 1964 (F)

League Club	Source	Date Signed	Seasons Played	Apps	Subs	Gls
Oldham Ath.	App	07.82	82-83	7	6	0
Rochdale	L	03.84	83	6	0	0

HUMPHREYS John Vaughan
Llandudno, 13 January, 1920 Died 1954 W-1 (CH)

League Club	Source	Date Signed	Seasons Played	Apps	Subs	Gls
Everton	Llandudno	04.43	46-50	53	-	0

HUMPHREYS Percy Ronald
Bradford, 28 October, 1924 (OR)

League Club	Source	Date Signed	Seasons Played	Apps	Subs	Gls
Halifax T.	Boothtown	11.43	46	3	-	1

HUMPHREYS Richard John
Sheffield, 30 November, 1977 Eu21-3 (M/F)

League Club	Source	Date Signed	Seasons Played	Apps	Subs	Gls
Sheffield Wed.	YT	02.96	95-97	17	24	3

HUMPHREYS Ronald
Tonypandy, 4 April, 1925 (FB)

League Club	Source	Date Signed	Seasons Played	Apps	Subs	Gls
Southend U.	Snowdown Colly	05.45	46	3	-	0

HUMPHRIES Charles William
Birmingham, 19 March, 1922 Died 1995 (FB)

League Club	Source	Date Signed	Seasons Played	Apps	Subs	Gls
Walsall	Paget R.	09.46	47	6	-	0

HUMPHRIES David William
Wolverhampton, 10 August, 1939 (CH)

League Club	Source	Date Signed	Seasons Played	Apps	Subs	Gls
Shrewsbury T.		03.60	60	3	-	0

HUMPHRIES Glenn
Hull, 11 August, 1964 E Yth (CD)

League Club	Source	Date Signed	Seasons Played	Apps	Subs	Gls
Doncaster Rov.	App	08.82	80-87	174	6	8
Lincoln C.	L	03.87	86	9	0	0
Bristol C.	Tr	10.87	87-90	81	4	0
Scunthorpe U.	Tr	03.91	90-92	71	1	5
Hull C.	Golden (HK)	08.95	95	9	3	0

HUMPHRIES Mark
Glasgow, 23 December, 1971 (LB)

League Club	Source	Date Signed	Seasons Played	Apps	Subs	Gls
Leeds U.	Aberdeen	06.93				
Bristol C.	Tr	10.94	94	4	0	0

HUMPHRIES Robert
Hindhead, 4 July, 1933 (WH)

League Club	Source	Date Signed	Seasons Played	Apps	Subs	Gls
Sheffield U.		12.55				
Brighton & H.A.	Tr	11.56	56	10	-	2
Millwall	Tr	08.57	57-59	47	-	4

HUMPHRIES Stephen Rodney
Hull, 29 May, 1961 E Semi Pro (G)

League Club	Source	Date Signed	Seasons Played	Apps	Subs	Gls
Leicester C.	App	09.78				
Doncaster Rov.	Tr	06.81	81	13	0	0
Cardiff C.	Tr	08.82	82	1	0	0
Wrexham	Tr	09.82	82	2	0	0
Oldham Ath.	Tr	10.82				
Leicester C.	Tr	01.83				

HUMPHRIES William McCauley
Belfast, 8 June, 1936 NI-14 (OR)

League Club	Source	Date Signed	Seasons Played	Apps	Subs	Gls
Leeds U.	Ards	09.58	58-59	25	-	2
Coventry C.	Ards	04.62	61-64	109	-	23
Swansea C.	Tr	03.65	64-67	143	0	22

HUMPSTON Ronald
Derby, 14 December, 1923 (G)

League Club	Source	Date Signed	Seasons Played	Apps	Subs	Gls
Portsmouth		01.46	47-50	9	-	0
Huddersfield T.	Tr	11.51	51	5	-	0

HUNT Andrew
Grays, 9 June, 1970 (F)

League Club	Source	Date Signed	Seasons Played	Apps	Subs	Gls
Newcastle U.	Kettering T.	01.91	90-91	34	9	11
West Bromwich A.	Tr	03.93	92-97	201	11	76

HUNT David
Durham, 5 March, 1980 (LB)

League Club	Source	Date Signed	Seasons Played	Apps	Subs	Gls
Darlington	YT	•	96	0	1	0

HUNT David
Leicester, 17 April, 1959 (M)

League Club	Source	Date Signed	Seasons Played	Apps	Subs	Gls
Derby Co.	App	04.77	77	5	0	0
Notts Co.	Tr	03.78	77-86	331	5	28
Aston Villa	Tr	06.87	87-88	12	1	0
Mansfield T.	Tr	06.89	89	21	1	0

HUNT Dennis Perrior
Portsmouth, 8 September, 1937 (FB)

League Club	Source	Date Signed	Seasons Played	Apps	Subs	Gls
Gillingham		09.58	58-67	319	2	6
Brentford	Tr	06.68	68	12	0	0

HUNT Douglas Arthur
Shipton, 19 May, 1914 Died 1989 (CF)

League Club	Source	Date Signed	Seasons Played	Apps	Subs	Gls
Tottenham H.	Gravesend & Nft	03.34	34-36	17	-	6
Barnsley	Tr	03.37	36-37	36	-	17
Sheffield Wed.	Tr	03.38	37-38	42	-	30
Leyton Orient	Tr	04.46	46-47	61	-	16

HUNT George Harold
Bethnal Green, 5 March, 1917 Died 1990 (CH)

League Club	Source	Date Signed	Seasons Played	Apps	Subs	Gls
Charlton Ath.	Bexleyheath	05.37				
Barnsley	Tr	05.38				
Watford	Tr	06.46	47-49	35	-	0

HUNT George Samuel
Barnsley, 22 February, 1910 Died 1996 E-3 (CF)

League Club	Source	Date Signed	Seasons Played	Apps	Subs	Gls
Chesterfield	Regent Street Congs	09.29	29	14	-	9
Tottenham H.	Tr	06.30	30-36	185	-	125
Arsenal	Tr	10.37	37	18	-	3
Bolton W.	Tr	02.38	37-46	45	-	24
Sheffield Wed.	Tr	11.46	46-47	32	-	8

HUNT Reginald **George** Albert
Swindon, 27 February, 1922 Died 1987 (RB)

League Club	Source	Date Signed	Seasons Played	Apps	Subs	Gls
Swindon T.		01.47	48-57	306	-	0

HUNT James Malcolm
Derby, 17 December, 1976 (M)

League Club	Source	Date Signed	Seasons Played	Apps	Subs	Gls
Notts Co.	YT	07.94	95-96	15	4	1
Northampton T.	Tr	08.97	97	14	7	0

HUNT Jonathan Richard
Camden, 2 November, 1971 (M)

League Club	Source	Date Signed	Seasons Played	Apps	Subs	Gls
Barnet	Jnrs	07.90	91-92	12	21	0
Southend U.	Tr	07.93	93-94	41	8	6
Birmingham C.	Tr	09.94	94-96	67	10	18
Derby Co.	Tr	05.97	97	7	12	1

HUNT Mark Geoffrey
Farnworth, 5 October, 1969 (F)

League Club	Source	Date Signed	Seasons Played	Apps	Subs	Gls
Rochdale	YT	●	86-87	1	1	1

HUNT Morgan Marshall
Bridgend, 5 March, 1931 (RH)

League Club	Source	Date Signed	Seasons Played	Apps	Subs	Gls
Doncaster Rov.	Askern Welfare	02.52	53-57	50	-	2
Norwich C.	Tr	07.58	58	7	-	0
Port Vale	Tr	08.59	59	2	-	0

HUNT Paul Craig
Swindon, 8 October, 1970 (F)

League Club	Source	Date Signed	Seasons Played	Apps	Subs	Gls
Swindon T.	YT	07.89	89-92	5	6	0

HUNT Paul Leslie
Hereford, 7 March, 1959 (D)

League Club	Source	Date Signed	Seasons Played	Apps	Subs	Gls
Hereford U.	Coventry C. (App)	06.77	78-80	41	10	4

HUNT Peter John
Stepney, 2 July, 1952 E Yth (M)

League Club	Source	Date Signed	Seasons Played	Apps	Subs	Gls
Southend U.	App	09.69	68-71	49	7	1
Charlton Ath.	Tr	12.72	72-76	138	20	6
Gillingham	Tr	08.77	77	23	0	0

HUNT Ralph Robert Arthur
Portsmouth, 14 August, 1933 Died 1964 (CF)

League Club	Source	Date Signed	Seasons Played	Apps	Subs	Gls
Portsmouth	Jnrs	08.50	52-53	5	-	0
Bournemouth	Tr	02.54	53-54	33	-	7
Norwich C.	Tr	07.55	55-57	124	-	67
Derby Co.	Tr	08.58	58	24	-	10
Grimsby T.	Tr	08.59	59-60	53	-	39
Swindon T.	Tr	07.61	61	21	-	13
Port Vale	Tr	12.61	61	14	-	6
Newport Co.	Tr	07.62	62-63	83	-	37
Chesterfield	Tr	07.64	64	17	-	5

HUNT Richard Anthony
Reading, 5 January, 1971 (CD)

League Club	Source	Date Signed	Seasons Played	Apps	Subs	Gls
Aldershot	Queens Park R. (YT)	07.89	89	1	1	0

HUNT Robert
Liverpool, 4 September, 1934 (WH)

League Club	Source	Date Signed	Seasons Played	Apps	Subs	Gls
Wrexham		07.56				
Chester C.	Tr	05.58	58-60	84	-	2

HUNT Robert
Newcastle, 20 September, 1966 (G)

League Club	Source	Date Signed	Seasons Played	Apps	Subs	Gls
Halifax T. (N/C)	Barnsley (YT)	01.85	84	3	0	0

HUNT Robert Rex
Colchester, 1 October, 1942 (F)

League Club	Source	Date Signed	Seasons Played	Apps	Subs	Gls
Colchester U.	Jnrs	11.59	59-63	149	-	81
Northampton T.	Tr	03.64	63-65	40	0	10
Millwall	Tr	09.66	66-67	43	0	13
Ipswich T.	Tr	11.67	67-70	16	10	4
Charlton Ath.	Tr	09.70	70-72	34	2	11
Northampton T.	L	11.72	72	5	0	3
Reading	Tr	01.73	72-73	15	1	3

HUNT Roger
Golborne, 20 July, 1938 EF Lge/E-34 (F)

League Club	Source	Date Signed	Seasons Played	Apps	Subs	Gls
Liverpool	Stockton Heath	05.59	59-69	401	3	245
Bolton W.	Tr	12.69	69-71	72	4	24

HUNT Roger (Ernie) Patrick
Swindon, 17 March, 1943 Eu23-3 (F)

League Club	Source	Date Signed	Seasons Played	Apps	Subs	Gls
Swindon T.	Jnrs	03.60	59-65	214	0	82
Wolverhampton W.	Tr	09.65	65-67	74	0	32
Everton	Tr	09.67	67	12	2	3
Coventry C.	Tr	03.68	67-73	140	6	45
Doncaster Rov.	L	01.73	72	9	0	1
Bristol C.	Tr	12.73	73-74	9	3	2

HUNT Ronald Geoffrey
Paddington, 19 December, 1945 (CH)

League Club	Source	Date Signed	Seasons Played	Apps	Subs	Gls
Queens Park R.	App	03.63	64-72	214	5	1

HUNT Ronald Malcolm
Colchester, 26 September, 1933 (WH)

League Club	Source	Date Signed	Seasons Played	Apps	Subs	Gls
Colchester U.	Jnrs	10.51	51-63	176	-	4

HUNT Simon
Chester, 17 November, 1962 (M)

League Club	Source	Date Signed	Seasons Played	Apps	Subs	Gls
Wrexham	Jnrs	08.81	81-83	102	6	18

HUNT Stephen Kenneth
Birmingham, 4 August, 1956 E-2 (W)

League Club	Source	Date Signed	Seasons Played	Apps	Subs	Gls
Aston Villa	App	01.74	74-76	4	3	1
Coventry C.	New York (USA)	08.78	78-83	178	7	27
West Bromwich A.	Tr	03.84	83-85	68	0	15
Aston Villa	Tr	03.86	85-87	61	1	6

HUNT William Edmund
Colchester, 25 November, 1934 (CH)

League Club	Source	Date Signed	Seasons Played	Apps	Subs	Gls
Colchester U.	Jnrs	08.53	55	1	-	0

HUNT William Sylvester
Halesowen, 19 November, 1934 (FB)

League Club	Source	Date Signed	Seasons Played	Apps	Subs	Gls
Aston Villa	Jnrs	01.52	52	1	-	0

HUNT-BROWN Peter Barry
Halifax, 19 February, 1937 (CF)

League Club	Source	Date Signed	Seasons Played	Apps	Subs	Gls
Halifax T. (Am)	Elland U.	12.58	58	1	-	0

HUNTER Allan
Sion Mills (NI), 30 June, 1946 NI Amat/NIu23-1/NI-53 (CD)

League Club	Source	Date Signed	Seasons Played	Apps	Subs	Gls
Oldham Ath.	Coleraine	01.67	66-68	83	0	1
Blackburn Rov.	Tr	06.69	69-71	84	0	1
Ipswich T.	Tr	09.71	71-80	280	0	8
Colchester U.	Tr	05.82	81-82	18	1	0

HUNTER Barry Victor
Coleraine, 18 November, 1968 NI Yth/NI 'B'/NI-11 (CD)

League Club	Source	Date Signed	Seasons Played	Apps	Subs	Gls
Newcastle U.	Coleraine	11.87				
Wrexham	Crusaders	08.93	93-95	88	3	4
Reading	Tr	07.96	96	26	1	2

HUNTER Christopher Paul
Hong Kong, 18 January, 1964 (F)

League Club	Source	Date Signed	Seasons Played	Apps	Subs	Gls
Preston N.E.	App	09.81	82	0	1	0
Preston N.E.	Chorley	09.84	84	3	3	0

HUNTER Donald
Thorne, 10 March, 1927 (WH)

League Club	Source	Date Signed	Seasons Played	Apps	Subs	Gls
Huddersfield T.	Jnrs	03.44	48-50	26	-	1
Halifax T.	Tr	08.51	51	11	-	0
Southport	Tr	08.52	52-56	174	-	1

HUNTER Edward
Tillicoultry, 7 March, 1928 (WH)

League Club	Source	Date Signed	Seasons Played	Apps	Subs	Gls
Accrington St.	Falkirk	08.54	54-58	169	-	4

HUNTER Geoffrey
Hull, 27 October, 1959 (M)

League Club	Source	Date Signed	Seasons Played	Apps	Subs	Gls
Manchester U.	App	11.76				
Crewe Alex.	Tr	08.79	79-80	86	1	8
Port Vale	Tr	08.81	81-86	218	3	15
Wrexham	Tr	08.87	87-90	116	6	15

HUNTER George Irvine
Troon, 29 August, 1930 Died 1990 (G)

League Club	Source	Date Signed	Seasons Played	Apps	Subs	Gls
Derby Co.	Glasgow Celtic	06.54	54	19	-	0

League Club	Source	Date Signed	Seasons Played	Apps	Subs	Gls
Exeter C.	Tr	08.55	55-58	147	-	0
Darlington	Yiewsley	06.61	61	20	-	0
Lincoln C.	Burton A.	09.65	65	1	0	0

HUNTER Gordon Greig
Lyneham, 8 November, 1954 (D)

League Club	Source	Date Signed	Seasons Played	Apps	Subs	Gls
York C.	Shrewsbury T. (Am)	07.73	73-77	70	7	1

HUNTER John Dixon
Backworth, 20 September, 1934 (G)

League Club	Source	Date Signed	Seasons Played	Apps	Subs	Gls
Gateshead		08.54	55	4	-	0

HUNTER John Smith
Coalburn, 26 May, 1934 (OL)

League Club	Source	Date Signed	Seasons Played	Apps	Subs	Gls
Rotherham U.	Coltness U.	06.56	56	5	-	1
Carlisle U.	Tr	07.57	57	1	-	0
Barrow	Kings Lynn	07.59	59-60	24	-	0

HUNTER Alvin **Junior**
Lambeth, 1 February, 1975 (M)

League Club	Source	Date Signed	Seasons Played	Apps	Subs	Gls
Cambridge U.	YT	05.93	93-94	26	14	0

HUNTER Lee
Oldham, 5 October, 1969 (M)

League Club	Source	Date Signed	Seasons Played	Apps	Subs	Gls
Colchester U.	YT	06.88	87-88	5	4	0

HUNTER Leslie
Middlesbrough, 15 January, 1958 (CD)

League Club	Source	Date Signed	Seasons Played	Apps	Subs	Gls
Chesterfield	App	08.75	75-81	156	9	8
Scunthorpe U.	Tr	07.82	82-83	61	0	8
Chesterfield	Tr	01.84	83-85	99	0	9
Scunthorpe U.	Tr	03.86	85-86	49	0	5
Chesterfield	Lincoln C.	12.87	87-88	31	0	3

HUNTER Michael
Hexham, 27 May, 1948 (F)

League Club	Source	Date Signed	Seasons Played	Apps	Subs	Gls
Blackpool		01.66				
Darlington	Tr	07.67	67	2	1	0

HUNTER Norman
Gateshead, 29 October, 1943 Eu23-3/E-28 (CD)

League Club	Source	Date Signed	Seasons Played	Apps	Subs	Gls
Leeds U.	Jnrs	04.61	62-76	540	0	18
Bristol C.	Tr	10.76	76-78	108	0	4
Barnsley	Tr	06.79	79-82	28	3	0

HUNTER Paul
Kirkcaldy, 30 August, 1968 Su21-3 (F)

League Club	Source	Date Signed	Seasons Played	Apps	Subs	Gls
Hull C.	East Fife	03.90	89-92	37	31	11

HUNTER Philip
Hartlepool, 28 September, 1950 (OR)

League Club	Source	Date Signed	Seasons Played	Apps	Subs	Gls
Hartlepool U. (Am)	Jnrs	08.69	69	1	0	0

HUNTER Reginald John
Colwyn Bay, 25 October, 1938 (W)

League Club	Source	Date Signed	Seasons Played	Apps	Subs	Gls
Manchester U.	Colwyn Bay	11.56	58	1	-	0
Wrexham	Tr	02.60	59-61	34	-	3

HUNTER Robert
Gateshead, 25 March, 1951 (W)

League Club	Source	Date Signed	Seasons Played	Apps	Subs	Gls
Hartlepool U.		02.71	70	1	0	0

HUNTER Robert Russell
Shotts, 12 March, 1931 (OR)

League Club	Source	Date Signed	Seasons Played	Apps	Subs	Gls
Swindon T.	Motherwell	08.54	54	16	-	3

HUNTER Roy Ian
Middlesbrough, 29 October, 1973 (M)

League Club	Source	Date Signed	Seasons Played	Apps	Subs	Gls
West Bromwich A.	YT	03.92	91-93	3	6	1
Northampton T.	Tr	08.95	95-97	80	18	9

HUNTER William Nibb
Cambuslang, 7 April, 1942 (IF)

League Club	Source	Date Signed	Seasons Played	Apps	Subs	Gls
Bradford P.A.	Glasgow Rangers	07.64	64	14	-	0

HUNTLEY John
Great Lumley, 5 November, 1967 (D)

League Club	Source	Date Signed	Seasons Played	Apps	Subs	Gls
Darlington (N/C)	Chester-le-Street	10.85	85	5	1	0

HUNTLEY Keith Stanley Murray
Swansea, 12 February, 1931 Died 1995 W Amat (OL)

League Club	Source	Date Signed	Seasons Played	Apps	Subs	Gls
Swansea C.		08.50	50	2	-	0

HUNTLEY Richard Bernard
Sunderland, 5 January, 1949 (CH)

League Club	Source	Date Signed	Seasons Played	Apps	Subs	Gls
Sunderland	Jnrs	08.67	68	1	0	0

HUNTON Keith
Workington, 18 July, 1961 (G)

League Club	Source	Date Signed	Seasons Played	Apps	Subs	Gls
Carlisle U. (N/C)	Workington	02.87	86	3	0	0

HURDLE Augustus (Gus) Athel
Kensington, 14 October, 1973 Barbadan Int (RB)

League Club	Source	Date Signed	Seasons Played	Apps	Subs	Gls
Fulham	YT	07.92				
Brentford	Tr	10.93	94-97	63	8	0

HURFORD David George
Sodbury, 17 January, 1945 (OR)

League Club	Source	Date Signed	Seasons Played	Apps	Subs	Gls
Bristol Rov.	App	01.63	62-64	6	-	0

HURLEY Charles John
Cork, 4 October, 1936 IR-40 (CH)

League Club	Source	Date Signed	Seasons Played	Apps	Subs	Gls
Millwall	Jnrs	10.53	53-57	105	-	2
Sunderland	Tr	09.57	57-68	357	1	23
Bolton W.	Tr	06.69	69-70	41	1	3

HURLEY Christopher Joseph
Hornchurch, 20 November, 1943 (CF)

League Club	Source	Date Signed	Seasons Played	Apps	Subs	Gls
Millwall	Rainham T.	03.64	63-64	4	-	2

HURLEY William Henry
Leytonstone, 11 December, 1959 E Sch (F)

League Club	Source	Date Signed	Seasons Played	Apps	Subs	Gls
Leyton Orient	App	01.77	76	1	1	0

HURLOCK Terence Alan
Hackney, 22 September, 1958 E 'B' (M)

League Club	Source	Date Signed	Seasons Played	Apps	Subs	Gls
Brentford	Leytonstone & Ilford	08.80	80-85	220	0	18
Reading	Tr	02.86	85-86	29	0	0
Millwall	Tr	02.87	86-89	103	1	8
Southampton	Glasgow Rangers	09.91	91-93	59	2	0
Millwall	Tr	03.94	93	13	0	0
Fulham	Tr	07.94	94	27	0	1

HURLSTONE Gary
Mexborough, 25 April, 1963 (F)

League Club	Source	Date Signed	Seasons Played	Apps	Subs	Gls
York C. (N/C)	Hatfield Main	03.89	88	1	1	0

HURRELL William
Newcastle, 15 September, 1955 (CH)

League Club	Source	Date Signed	Seasons Played	Apps	Subs	Gls
Northampton T.	App	08.72	72	5	0	0

HURRELL William Provan
Dundee, 28 January, 1920 (IF)

League Club	Source	Date Signed	Seasons Played	Apps	Subs	Gls
Millwall	Raith Rov.	01.46	46-52	121	-	32
Queens Park R.	Tr	07.53	53	6	-	1

HURST Charles
Denton, 25 January, 1919 (RH)

League Club	Source	Date Signed	Seasons Played	Apps	Subs	Gls
Bristol Rov.		09.38				
Oldham Ath.		01.43				
Rochdale	Tr	06.46	46	4	-	1

HURST Christopher Mark
Barnsley, 3 October, 1973 (M)

League Club	Source	Date Signed	Seasons Played	Apps	Subs	Gls
Huddersfield T.	Emley	08.97	97	1	2	0

HURST Geoffrey Charles
Ashton-u-Lyne, 8 December, 1941 E Yth/Eu23-4/EF Lge/E-49 (F)

League Club	Source	Date Signed	Seasons Played	Apps	Subs	Gls
West Ham U.	Jnrs	04.59	59-71	410	1	180
Stoke C.	Tr	08.72	72-74	103	5	30
West Bromwich A.	Tr	08.75	75	10	0	2

HURST Glynn
Barnsley, 17 January, 1976 (F)

League Club	Source	Date Signed	Seasons Played	Apps	Subs	Gls
Barnsley	Tottenham H. (YT)	07.94	94-96	0	8	0
Swansea C.	L	12.95	95	2	0	1
Mansfield T.	L	11.96	96	5	1	0

HURST Gordon
Oldham, 9 October, 1924 Died 1980 EF Lge (W)

League Club	Source	Date Signed	Seasons Played	Apps	Subs	Gls
Charlton Ath.	Ramsgate	05.46	46-57	369	-	75

HURST Graham John
Oldham, 23 November, 1967 (M)

League Club	Source	Date Signed	Seasons Played	Apps	Subs	Gls
Rochdale	YT	07.85	84	0	1	0

HURST John
Blackpool, 6 February, 1947 E Sch/Eu23-9 (CD)

League Club	Source	Date Signed	Seasons Played	Apps	Subs	Gls
Everton	App	10.64	65-75	336	11	29
Oldham Ath.	Tr	06.76	76-80	169	1	2

HURST George **John (Jack)**
Bolton, 27 October, 1914 (CH)

League Club	Source	Date Signed	Seasons Played	Apps	Subs	Gls
Bolton W.	Lever Bridge	05.33	34-46	60	-	2
Oldham Ath.	Tr	02.47	46-50	98	-	2

HURST Lee Jason
Nuneaton, 21 September, 1970 (M)

League Club	Source	Date Signed	Seasons Played	Apps	Subs	Gls
Coventry C.	YT	05.89	90-92	46	3	2

HURST Paul Michael
Sheffield, 25 September, 1974 (M/LB)

League Club	Source	Date Signed	Seasons Played	Apps	Subs	Gls
Rotherham U.	YT	08.93	93-97	87	30	4

HURST William Robert
Brierfield, 4 March, 1921 (W)

League Club	Source	Date Signed	Seasons Played	Apps	Subs	Gls
Burnley	Jnrs	03.38				
Plymouth Arg.	Tr	06.39	46	4	-	0
Bury	Nelson	09.47	47	1	-	0
Accrington St.	Northwich Vic.	10.48	48	1	-	0

HUSBAND James
Newcastle, 15 October, 1947 E Sch/E Yth/Eu23-5 (F)

League Club	Source	Date Signed	Seasons Played	Apps	Subs	Gls
Everton	App	10.64	64-73	158	7	44
Luton T.	Tr	11.73	73-77	138	5	44

HUSSEY Malcolm Frederick
Darfield, 11 September, 1933 (CH)

League Club	Source	Date Signed	Seasons Played	Apps	Subs	Gls
Rotherham U.	Jnrs	04.52	52-55	24	-	1
Scunthorpe U.	Tr	08.56	56-57	23	-	0
Rochdale	Tr	03.59	58	1	-	0

HUTCHINGS Carl Emil
Hammersmith, 24 September, 1974 (M/RB)

League Club	Source	Date Signed	Seasons Played	Apps	Subs	Gls
Brentford	YT	07.93	93-97	144	18	7

HUTCHINGS Christopher
Winchester, 5 July, 1957 (FB)

League Club	Source	Date Signed	Seasons Played	Apps	Subs	Gls
Chelsea	Harrow Borough	07.80	80-83	83	4	3
Brighton & H.A.	Tr	11.83	83-87	153	0	4
Huddersfield T.	Tr	12.87	87-89	110	0	10
Walsall	Tr	08.90	90	40	0	0
Rotherham U.	Tr	07.91	91-93	76	2	4

HUTCHINGS Denis George
Axminster, 1 December, 1924 Died 1990 (OR)

League Club	Source	Date Signed	Seasons Played	Apps	Subs	Gls
Exeter C.	Axminster	04.47	46-51	82	-	13

HUTCHINS Donald
Middlesbrough, 8 May, 1948 (W)

League Club	Source	Date Signed	Seasons Played	Apps	Subs	Gls
Leicester C.	Stockton	02.66	67-68	4	0	0
Plymouth Arg.	Tr	07.69	69-71	94	1	23
Blackburn Rov.	Tr	07.72	72-73	37	3	6
Bradford C.	Tr	06.74	74-80	252	4	44

HUTCHINSON James Barry
Sheffield, 27 January, 1936 (IF)

League Club	Source	Date Signed	Seasons Played	Apps	Subs	Gls
Chesterfield	Bolton W. (Am)	04.53	54-59	154	-	16
Derby Co.	Tr	07.60	60-63	107	-	51
Lincoln C.	Weymouth	07.65	65	24	0	18
Darlington	Tr	02.66	65-66	28	2	14
Halifax T.	Tr	11.66	66	25	0	14
Rochdale	Tr	07.67	67	27	0	3

HUTCHINSON Colin
Lanchester, 20 October, 1936 (IF)

League Club	Source	Date Signed	Seasons Played	Apps	Subs	Gls
Stoke C.	Jnrs	11.53	54-57	9	-	0

HUTCHINSON David Norman
Grimsby, 25 September, 1941 (CF)

League Club	Source	Date Signed	Seasons Played	Apps	Subs	Gls
Scunthorpe U.	Brigg T.	07.71	71	5	4	0

HUTCHINSON Douglas
Gateshead, 3 May, 1922 (CF)

League Club	Source	Date Signed	Seasons Played	Apps	Subs	Gls
Gateshead	Stirling A.	08.46	46	3	-	0

HUTCHINSON George Henry
Castleford, 31 October, 1929 Died 1996 (W)

League Club	Source	Date Signed	Seasons Played	Apps	Subs	Gls
Huddersfield T.	Jnrs	01.47	47	1	-	0
Sheffield U.	Tr	03.48	48-52	73	-	10
Tottenham H.	Tr	06.53	53	5	-	1
Leeds U.	Tr	08.55	55	11	-	5
Halifax T.	Tr	07.56	56-57	44	-	12

HUTCHINSON Ian
Derby, 4 August, 1948 Eu23-2 (CF)

League Club	Source	Date Signed	Seasons Played	Apps	Subs	Gls
Chelsea	Cambridge U.	07.68	68-75	112	7	44

HUTCHINSON Ian Nicholas
Stockton, 7 November, 1972 (M/LB)

League Club	Source	Date Signed	Seasons Played	Apps	Subs	Gls
Halifax T.	YT	07.91	90-91	7	1	1
Gillingham	Cork C.	09.94	94	1	4	0

HUTCHINSON James Arthur
Sheffield, 28 December, 1915 (IF)

League Club	Source	Date Signed	Seasons Played	Apps	Subs	Gls
Sheffield U.	Aqueduct	11.37				
Bournemouth	Tr	06.46	46	8	-	3
Lincoln C.	Tr	11.46	46-48	85	-	55
Oldham Ath.	Tr	02.49	48-49	14	-	3

HUTCHINSON John (Jack)
Basford, 1 June, 1921 (FB)

League Club	Source	Date Signed	Seasons Played	Apps	Subs	Gls
Nottingham F.		08.43	46-58	241	-	0

HUTCHINSON Keith Graham
South Shields, 7 September, 1920 Died 1986 (FB)

League Club	Source	Date Signed	Seasons Played	Apps	Subs	Gls
Darlington		05.46	46-48	31	-	0

HUTCHINSON Colin Mark
Stoke, 2 November, 1963 (M)

League Club	Source	Date Signed	Seasons Played	Apps	Subs	Gls
Aston Villa	App	11.81				
Leicester C.	Tr	08.83				
Carlisle U.	L	08.84	84	6	0	0
Northampton T.	Tr	02.85	84	1	1	0

HUTCHINSON Paul
Eaglescliffe, 20 February, 1953 (FB)

League Club	Source	Date Signed	Seasons Played	Apps	Subs	Gls
Darlington	Jnrs	09.71	71-72	8	2	0

HUTCHINSON Robert
Glasgow, 19 June, 1953 (M)

League Club	Source	Date Signed	Seasons Played	Apps	Subs	Gls
Wigan Ath.	Hibernian	07.80	80	34	1	3
Tranmere Rov.	Tr	08.81	81-82	32	3	6
Mansfield T.	Tr	10.82	82-83	35	0	3
Tranmere Rov.	Tr	01.84	83	21	0	4
Bristol C.	Tr	07.84	84-86	89	3	10
Walsall	Tr	02.87	86-87	8	8	0
Blackpool	L	09.87	87	3	3	0
Carlisle U.	L	01.88	87	12	1	2

HUTCHINSON Robert Wayne
Bolton, 9 May, 1955 (F)

League Club	Source	Date Signed	Seasons Played	Apps	Subs	Gls
Rochdale	Radcliffe Borough	12.74	74	2	0	1

HUTCHINSON Simon
Sheffield, 24 September, 1969 E Sch (M)

League Club	Source	Date Signed	Seasons Played	Apps	Subs	Gls
Manchester U.	YT	09.87				
Wycombe W.	Eastwood T.	09.90	93-94	2	10	0

HUTCHISON Donald
Gateshead, 9 May, 1971 S 'B' (M)

League Club	Source	Date Signed	Seasons Played	Apps	Subs	Gls
Hartlepool U.	YT	03.90	89-90	19	5	3
Liverpool	Tr	11.90	91-92	33	12	7
West Ham U.	Tr	08.94	94-95	30	5	11
Sheffield U.	Tr	01.96	95-97	70	8	5
Everton	Tr	02.98	97	11	0	1

HUTCHISON Thomas
Cardenden, 22 September, 1947 Su23-1/S-17 (LW)

League Club	Source	Date Signed	Seasons Played	Apps	Subs	Gls
Blackpool	Alloa Ath.	02.68	67-72	163	2	10
Coventry C.	Tr	10.72	72-80	312	2	24
Manchester C.	Tr	10.80	80-81	44	2	4
Burnley	Bulova (HK)	08.83	83-84	92	0	4
Swansea C.	Tr	07.85	85-90	163	15	9

HUTT Geoffrey
Duffield, 28 September, 1949 (FB)

League Club	Source	Date Signed	Seasons Played	Apps	Subs	Gls
Huddersfield T.	App	09.67	68-75	245	0	4
Blackburn Rov.	L	09.75	75	10	0	1
York C.	Haarlem (Neth)	02.77	76-77	63	0	1
Halifax T.	Tr	04.78	78-79	75	1	0

HUTT Stephen Graham
Middlesbrough, 19 February, 1979 (CD)

League Club	Source	Date Signed	Seasons Played	Apps	Subs	Gls
Hartlepool U.	YT	07.97	95-97	4	1	0

HUTTON Alexander Shaw
Edinburgh, 10 October, 1941 (FB)

League Club	Source	Date Signed	Seasons Played	Apps	Subs	Gls
Southend U.		08.63	64	1	-	0

HUTTON John (Jack)
Bellshill, 23 April, 1944 (W)

League Club	Source	Date Signed	Seasons Played	Apps	Subs	Gls
Scunthorpe U.	Hamilton Academical	06.63	63-65	53	1	7

HUTTON Joseph
Dundee, 18 November, 1927 (IF)

League Club	Source	Date Signed	Seasons Played	Apps	Subs	Gls
Reading	Albion Rov.	10.50	49-50	8	-	0
Stoke C.	Ayr U.	12.53	53-56	34	-	7
Gillingham	Tr	08.57	57	36	-	6
Millwall	Tr	08.58	58-59	24	-	9

League Club	Source	Date Signed	Seasons Played	Apps	Subs	Gls
HUTTON Thomas Osborne						
Gateshead, 10 September, 1922						(FB)
Accrington St.	Red Rose	05.45	46	18	-	0
Carlisle U.	Tr	08.47	47-48	44	-	0
Rochdale	Tr	08.49				
Tranmere Rov.	Nelson	08.50				
HUXFORD Clifford George						
Stroud, 8 June, 1937						(WH)
Chelsea	Jnrs	02.55	58	6	-	0
Southampton	Tr	05.59	59-66	276	2	4
Exeter C.	Tr	06.67	67	40	1	1
HUXFORD Colin John						
Stroud, 26 May, 1944 E Yth						(FB)
Chelsea	App	10.61				
Swindon T.	Tr	11.62	62	1	-	0
HUXFORD Richard John						
Scunthorpe, 25 July, 1969						(FB)
Barnet	Kettering T.	08.92	92	33	0	1
Millwall	Tr	07.93	93-94	25	7	0
Birmingham C.	L	02.94	93	5	0	0
Bradford C.	Tr	10.94	94-96	55	6	2
Peterborough U.	L	10.96	96	7	0	0
Burnley	Tr	01.97	96-97	6	7	0
HYATT John William						
Feltham, 20 December, 1932						(CF)
Crystal Palace		08.54	54	1	-	0
HYDE Frank Lomas						
Wath, 11 January, 1927						(G)
Bradford C.	Wath W.	12.48	48-51	34	-	0
HYDE Gary Stuart						
Wolverhampton, 28 December, 1969						(W)
Darlington	YT	07.88	87-88	31	7	3
Leicester C.	Tr	04.90				
Scunthorpe U.	Tr	08.91	91	1	7	0
HYDE Graham						
Doncaster, 10 November, 1970						(M)
Sheffield Wed.	YT	05.88	91-97	126	45	11
HYDE Micah Anthony						
Newham, 10 November, 1974						(M)
Cambridge U.	YT	05.93	93-96	89	18	13
Watford	Tr	07.97	97	40	0	4
HYDE Paul David						
Hayes, 7 April, 1963						(G)
Wycombe W.	Hayes	07.91	93-95	105	0	0
Leicester C.	Tr	02.96				
Leyton Orient	Tr	02.97	96-97	37	0	0
HYDE Stephen Leslie						
High Wycombe, 18 December, 1943						(W)
Oxford U.	Wycombe W.	01.65	64-65	9	0	0
HYDES Arthur						
Barnsley, 24 November, 1910 Died 1990						(IF)
Leeds U.	Ardsley Rec.	05.30	30-36	127	-	74
Newport Co.	Tr	05.38	38	27	-	13
Exeter C.	Tr	02.46	46	4	-	0
HYMERS Thomas						
Thorne, 29 April, 1935						(FB)
Doncaster Rov.	Frickley Colly	11.58	59-60	23	-	0
HYND John **Roger** Shankly						
Falkirk, 2 February, 1942						(CD)
Crystal Palace	Glasgow Rangers	07.69	69	29	1	0
Birmingham C.	Tr	07.70	70-75	162	8	4
Oxford U.	L	10.75	75	5	0	0
Walsall	Tr	12.75	75-77	89	0	1
HYSEN Glenn Ingvar						
Sweden, 30 October, 1959 Swedish Int						(CD)
Liverpool	Fiorentina (It)	07.89	89-91	70	2	2
HYSLOP Christian Terence						
Watford, 14 June, 1972						(LB)
Southend U.	YT	04.90	90-92	16	3	0
Northampton T.	L	12.93	93	8	0	0
Colchester U.	Tr	02.94	93	8	0	0
HYSON Matthew Alexander						
Stockton, 2 May, 1976						(M)
Hartlepool U.	YT	07.94	94	1	4	0

I

I'ANSON Paul
Shipley, 31 May, 1946 (WH)

League Club	Source	Date Signed	Seasons Played	Apps	Subs	Gls
Bradford P.A.	App	06.64	63-67	49	1	2

IBBOTSON Daniel
Morecambe, 5 October, 1968 (W)

League Club	Source	Date Signed	Seasons Played	Apps	Subs	Gls
Preston N.E.	YT	●	85	1	0	0

IBBOTSON Dennis
Rotherham, 4 December, 1920 E Sch (FB)

League Club	Source	Date Signed	Seasons Played	Apps	Subs	Gls
Rotherham U. (Am)	Rotherham Y.M.C.A.	11.46	46	4	-	0

IBBOTSON Wilfred
Sheffield, 1 October, 1926 (IF)

League Club	Source	Date Signed	Seasons Played	Apps	Subs	Gls
Sheffield Wed.	Jnrs	04.44	47	1	-	0
Mansfield T.	Tr	08.48	48	2	-	0

ICETON Osborne Lloyd
Workington, 30 March, 1920 Died 1994 (OL)

League Club	Source	Date Signed	Seasons Played	Apps	Subs	Gls
Preston N.E.		05.38				
Carlisle U.	Tr	10.46	46-49	77	-	17
Tranmere Rov.	Tr	06.50	50-54	140	-	18

ICKE David Vaughan
Leicester, 29 May, 1952 (G)

League Club	Source	Date Signed	Seasons Played	Apps	Subs	Gls
Coventry C.	App	09.69				
Hereford U.	Tr	08.71	72	37	0	0

IDDON Harold
Preston, 20 February, 1921 (OR)

League Club	Source	Date Signed	Seasons Played	Apps	Subs	Gls
Preston N.E.	Jnrs	02.43				
Barrow	Tr	10.46	46	25	-	6
Southport	Tr	06.47	47-48	42	-	3

IGA Andrew
Uganda, 9 December, 1977 (G)

League Club	Source	Date Signed	Seasons Played	Apps	Subs	Gls
Millwall	Jnrs	06.95	96	0	1	0

IGGLEDEN Horatio (Ray)
Hull, 17 March, 1925 (IF)

League Club	Source	Date Signed	Seasons Played	Apps	Subs	Gls
Leicester C.	Jnrs	03.42	46-47	11	-	2
Leeds U.	Tr	01.49	48-54	169	-	47
Exeter C.	Tr	07.55	55	27	-	8

IGOE Samuel Gary
Feltham, 30 September, 1975 (M)

League Club	Source	Date Signed	Seasons Played	Apps	Subs	Gls
Portsmouth	YT	02.94	95-97	47	47	5

IKIN David
Stoke, 18 February, 1946 (G)

League Club	Source	Date Signed	Seasons Played	Apps	Subs	Gls
Port Vale		08.65	65	2	0	0

ILES Richard
Bristol, 21 May, 1967 (D)

League Club	Source	Date Signed	Seasons Played	Apps	Subs	Gls
Bristol Rov. (N/C)	Longwell Green	03.86	85	1	0	0

ILES Robert John
Leicester, 2 September, 1955 (G)

League Club	Source	Date Signed	Seasons Played	Apps	Subs	Gls
Bournemouth	App	02.73				
Chelsea	Weymouth	06.78	78-82	14	0	0

ILEY James
South Kirkby, 15 December, 1935 Eu23-1/EF Lge (WH)

League Club	Source	Date Signed	Seasons Played	Apps	Subs	Gls
Sheffield U.	Jnrs	06.53	54-57	99	-	7
Tottenham H.	Tr	08.57	57-58	53	-	1
Nottingham F.	Tr	07.59	59-62	93	-	4
Newcastle U.	Tr	09.62	62-68	227	5	15
Peterborough U.	Tr	01.69	68-72	64	4	4

ILIC Sasa
Melborne, Australia, 18 July, 1972 Macedonian Int (G)

League Club	Source	Date Signed	Seasons Played	Apps	Subs	Gls
Charlton Ath.	St Leonards Stamcroft	10.97	97	14	0	0

ILLINGWORTH Jeremy Marcus
Huddersfield, 20 May, 1977 (M)

League Club	Source	Date Signed	Seasons Played	Apps	Subs	Gls
Huddersfield T.	YT	06.95	96	2	1	0

ILLMAN Neil David
Doncaster, 29 April, 1975 (CF)

League Club	Source	Date Signed	Seasons Played	Apps	Subs	Gls
Middlesbrough	YT	03.93	93	0	1	0
Plymouth Arg.	Tr	03.96	96-97	13	18	4
Cambridge U.	L	03.96	95	1	4	0
Exeter C. (N/C)	Tr	12.97	97	6	2	2

IMLACH Michael Thomas
Croydon, 19 September, 1962 (FB)

League Club	Source	Date Signed	Seasons Played	Apps	Subs	Gls
Preston N.E.	Everton (App)	08.80				
Leeds U.	Tr	11.81				
Peterborough U.	Tr	08.82	82-83	37	5	1
Tranmere Rov.	Tr	08.84	84	4	0	0

IMLACH James John Stuart
Lossiemouth, 6 January, 1932 S-4 (OL)

League Club	Source	Date Signed	Seasons Played	Apps	Subs	Gls
Bury	Lossiemouth	10.52	52-53	71	-	14
Derby Co.	Tr	05.54	54	36	-	2
Nottingham F.	Tr	07.55	55-59	184	-	43
Luton T.	Tr	06.60	60	8	-	0
Coventry C.	Tr	10.60	60-61	73	-	11
Crystal Palace	Tr	07.62	62-64	35	-	2
Crystal Palace	Chelmsford C.	02.66	65-66	16	0	1

IMMEL Eike
Germany, 27 November, 1960 German Int (G)

League Club	Source	Date Signed	Seasons Played	Apps	Subs	Gls
Manchester C.	V.F.B. Stuttgart (Ger)	08.95	95-96	42	0	0

IMPEY Andrew Rodney
Hammersmith, 13 September, 1971 Eu21-1 (W)

League Club	Source	Date Signed	Seasons Played	Apps	Subs	Gls
Queens Park R.	Yeading	06.90	91-96	177	10	13
West Ham U.	Tr	09.97	97	19	0	0

IMPEY John Edward
Exeter, 11 August, 1954 E Sch/E Yth (CD)

League Club	Source	Date Signed	Seasons Played	Apps	Subs	Gls
Cardiff C.	App	08.72	72-74	13	8	0
Bournemouth	Tr	07.75	75-82	280	4	7
Torquay U.	Tr	08.83	83-84	72	0	0
Exeter C.	Tr	08.85	85	26	0	0
Torquay U.	Tr	07.86	86-87	58	0	2

IMRIE Adam Lyle
Annan, 1 October, 1933 (OR)

League Club	Source	Date Signed	Seasons Played	Apps	Subs	Gls
Carlisle U.	Kilmarnock	05.57	57	10	-	5

INCE Paul Emerson Carlyle
Ilford, 21 October, 1967 E Yth/Eu21-2/E 'B'/E-43 (M)

League Club	Source	Date Signed	Seasons Played	Apps	Subs	Gls
West Ham U.	YT	07.85	86-89	66	6	7
Manchester U.	Tr	09.89	89-94	203	3	24
Liverpool	Inter Milan (It)	07.97	97	31	0	8

INGEBRIGTSEN Kaare
Norway, 11 November, 1965 Norwegian Int (M)

League Club	Source	Date Signed	Seasons Played	Apps	Subs	Gls
Manchester C.	Rosenborg (Nor)	01.93	92-93	4	11	0

INGER James
Nottingham, 10 August, 1953 (G)

League Club	Source	Date Signed	Seasons Played	Apps	Subs	Gls
Walsall (Am)	Long Eaton U.	03.73	72	2	0	0

INGESSON Klas
Sweden, 20 August, 1968 Swedish Int (M)

League Club	Source	Date Signed	Seasons Played	Apps	Subs	Gls
Sheffield Wed.	P.S.V. Eindhoven (Neth)	09.94	94-95	12	6	2

INGHAM Anthony
Harrogate, 18 February, 1925 (FB)

League Club	Source	Date Signed	Seasons Played	Apps	Subs	Gls
Leeds U.	Harrogate T.	04.47	47-49	3	-	0
Queens Park R.	Tr	06.50	50-62	514	-	3

INGHAM Frederick Roy
Manchester, 3 April, 1954 (F)

League Club	Source	Date Signed	Seasons Played	Apps	Subs	Gls
Stockport Co.	App	04.72	71-72	12	7	1
Blackburn Rov.	Tr	08.73				
Exeter C.	Falmouth	03.78	77-78	4	4	1

INGHAM Gary
Rotherham, 9 October, 1964 (G)

League Club	Source	Date Signed	Seasons Played	Apps	Subs	Gls
Rotherham U. (N/C)	Bridlington T.	03.93				
Doncaster Rov. (N/C)	Tr	03.94	93	1	0	0
Doncaster Rov.	Gainsborough Tr.	08.97	97	10	0	0

INGHAM John Robert
Hebburn, 18 October, 1924 (OR)

League Club	Source	Date Signed	Seasons Played	Apps	Subs	Gls
Gateshead	Newburn	08.47	47-57	431	-	109

INGHAM William Charles
Stakeford (Nd), 22 October, 1952 (M)

League Club	Source	Date Signed	Seasons Played	Apps	Subs	Gls
Burnley	App	11.69	71-79	181	30	22
Bradford C.	Tr	08.80	80-81	78	0	4

INGLE Stephen Paul
Bradford, 22 October, 1946 (FB)

League Club	Source	Date Signed	Seasons Played	Apps	Subs	Gls
Bradford C.	App	08.64	64-66	89	1	15
Southend U.	Tr	01.67	66	14	1	3

League Club	Source	Date Signed	Seasons Played	Apps	Subs	Gls
Wrexham	Tr	07.67	67-71	145	4	5
Stockport Co.	Tr	07.72	72	29	0	0
Southport	Tr	07.73	73	2	0	0
Darlington	Tr	10.73	73	8	0	0
INGLETHORPE Alexander Matthew						
Epsom, 14 November, 1971						(F)
Watford	Jnrs	07.90	90-93	2	10	2
Barnet	L	03.95	94	5	1	3
Leyton Orient	Tr	05.95	94-97	78	6	26
INGLIS James McDougal						
Glasgow, 14 February, 1924						(CF)
Bury	Falkirk	05.50	50	2	-	0
INGLIS John						
Gateshead, 5 August, 1933						(G)
Gateshead (Am)	Blyth Spartans	06.57	57	2	-	0
INGLIS John Francis						
Leven, 19 May, 1947						(CF)
Aston Villa	Glenrothes	09.65	67	1	1	0
Crewe Alex.	Tr	07.68	68-69	46	1	10
INGRAM Alexander David						
Edinburgh, 2 January, 1945 S Amat/SF Lge						(CF)
Nottingham F.	Ayr U.	12.69	69-70	28	0	3
INGRAM Christopher David						
Cardiff, 5 December, 1976						(RW)
Cardiff C.	YT	08.95	95	4	4	1
INGRAM Stuart **Denevan (Denny)**						
Sunderland, 27 June, 1976						(RB)
Hartlepool U.	YT	07.94	93-97	149	5	6
INGRAM Gerald						
Merthyr Tydfil, 28 January, 1951 W Sch						(M)
Swansea C.		08.70	70-72	35	2	1
INGRAM Gerald						
Beverley, 19 August, 1947						(F)
Blackpool	Hull Brunswick	03.67	66-67	33	1	18
Preston N.E.	Tr	09.68	68-71	107	3	40
Bradford C.	Tr	03.72	71-76	171	3	60
INGRAM Godfrey Patrick						
Luton, 26 October, 1959 E Sch/E Yth						(F)
Luton T.	App	10.77	77-81	22	5	6
Northampton T.	L	03.80	79	10	0	4
Cardiff C.	San Jose (USA)	09.82	82	7	4	2
Peterborough U. (N/C)	St Louis (USA)	08.92	92	0	1	0
INGRAM Rae						
Manchester, 6 December, 1974						(LB)
Manchester C.	YT	07.93	95-96	18	5	0
Macclesfield T.	L	03.98	97	5	0	0
INMAN Niall Edward						
Wakefield, 6 February, 1978 IRu21-5						(M)
Peterborough U.	YT	07.96	95-97	5	3	1
INNES Gary John						
Consett, 7 October, 1977 E Yth						(F)
Darlington	Sheffield U. (YT)	07.96	96	1	14	0
INNES Mark						
Glasgow, 27 September, 1978						(FB/M)
Oldham Ath.	YT	10.95	97	2	2	0
INSKIP Frederick Clive						
Cheadle, 20 October, 1924						(OR)
Nottingham F.		12.44				
Crewe Alex.	Tr	04.48	47-48	26	-	4
INWOOD Gordon Frederick						
Kislingbury, 18 June, 1928						(OL)
West Bromwich A.	Rushden T.	01.49	49	10	-	0
Hull C.	Tr	05.50	50	3	-	0
IORFA Dominic						
Nigeria, 1 October, 1968 Nigerian Int						(F)
Queens Park R.	Royal Antwerp (Bel)	03.90	89-91	1	7	0
Peterborough U.	Galatasaray (Tur)	10.92	92-93	27	33	9
Southend U.	Tr	08.94	94-95	5	5	1
IOVAN Stefan						
Romania, 23 August, 1960						(D)
Brighton & H.A.	Steava Bucarest (Rom)	03.91	90-91	4	2	0

League Club	Source	Date Signed	Seasons Played	Apps	Subs	Gls
IPPOLITO Mario						
Peterborough, 16 April, 1964						(F)
Peterborough U.	Jnrs	04.83	82	8	0	3
IRELAND Jeffrey John Charles						
Paddington, 1 December, 1935						(OR)
Tottenham H.	Finchley	11.57	57-58	3	-	0
Shrewsbury T.	Tr	06.59	59	38	-	3
IRELAND Jeremy						
Chester, 14 September, 1938						(IF/WH)
Chester C.		09.57	57-61	40	-	8
IRELAND Roy Peter						
Exeter, 3 February, 1961						(M)
Exeter C.	App	02.79	78-80	17	4	0
IRELAND Simon Piers						
Barnstaple, 23 November, 1971 E Sch						(W)
Huddersfield T.	Jnrs	07.90	90-92	10	9	0
Wrexham	L	03.92	91	2	3	0
Blackburn Rov.	Tr	11.92	92	0	1	0
Mansfield T.	Tr	03.94	93-96	89	5	11
Doncaster Rov.	L	10.96	96	9	0	1
Doncaster Rov.	Tr	01.97	96-97	52	0	1
IRONS Kenneth						
Liverpool, 4 November, 1970						(M)
Tranmere Rov.	YT	11.89	89-97	270	38	39
IRONSIDE Ian						
Sheffield, 8 March, 1964						(G)
Barnsley	Jnrs	09.82				
Scarborough	North Ferriby U.	03.88	87-90	88	0	0
Middlesbrough	Tr	08.91	91-92	12	1	0
Scarborough	L	03.92	91	7	0	0
Stockport Co.	Tr	09.93	93-94	17	2	0
Scarborough	Tr	03.95	94-96	88	0	0
Oldham Ath.	Tr	07.97				
IRONSIDE Roy						
Sheffield, 28 May, 1935						(G)
Rotherham U.	Jnrs	07.54	56-64	220	-	0
Barnsley	Tr	07.65	65-68	113	0	0
IRVIN Derek Vincent						
Stockton, 23 August, 1943						(W)
Middlesbrough		09.61				
Watford	Brechin C.	06.67	67	0	2	1
IRVINE Alan James						
Broxburn, 20 November, 1962						(F)
Liverpool	Falkirk	11.86	86	0	2	0
Shrewsbury T.	Dundee U.	02.88	87-88	32	5	6
IRVINE James **Alan**						
Glasgow, 12 July, 1958						(RW)
Everton	Queens Park	05.81	81-83	51	9	4
Crystal Palace	Tr	08.84	84-86	108	1	12
Blackburn Rov.	Dundee U.	10.89	89-91	40	18	3
IRVINE Archibald						
Coatbridge, 25 June, 1946						(M)
Sheffield Wed.	Airdrieonians	09.68	68-69	25	4	1
Doncaster Rov.	Tr	12.69	69-74	220	8	16
Scunthorpe U.	Tr	07.75	75	22	1	1
IRVINE James						
Whitburn, 17 August, 1940 S Sch						(CF)
Middlesbrough	Dundee U.	05.64	64-66	90	1	37
Barrow	Hearts	07.70	70-71	67	0	17
IRVINE Robert James						
Carrickfergus (NI), 17 January, 1942 NI Sch/NIu23-1/NI-8						(G)
Stoke C.	Linfield	06.63	63-65	25	0	0
IRVINE Samuel						
Glasgow, 7 January, 1956						(M)
Shrewsbury T.	App	01.74	72-77	198	9	18
Stoke C.	Tr	06.78	78-79	67	0	10
IRVINE Stuart Christopher						
Hartlepool, 1 March, 1979						(F)
Hartlepool U.	YT	07.97	96-97	3	10	1
IRVINE William John						
Carrickfergus (NI), 18 June, 1943 NI Sch/NIu23-3/NI-23						(CF)
Burnley	Jnrs	06.60	62-67	124	2	78
Preston N.E.	Tr	03.68	67-70	77	4	27

League Club	Source	Date Signed	Seasons Played	Apps	Subs	Gls
Brighton & H.A.	Tr	03.71	70-72	66	3	27
Halifax T.	Tr	12.72	72	9	1	1

IRVING David
Cockermouth, 10 September, 1951 E Yth (F)

League Club	Source	Date Signed	Seasons Played	Apps	Subs	Gls
Workington	Jnrs	05.70	70-72	57	8	16
Everton	Tr	01.73	73-75	4	2	0
Sheffield U.	Tr	09.75	75	0	2	0
Oldham Ath.	Tr	06.76	76-77	18	3	7

IRVING Gerald
Maryport, 19 September, 1937 (W)

League Club	Source	Date Signed	Seasons Played	Apps	Subs	Gls
Workington		08.56	56	1	-	0

IRVING Richard James
Halifax, 10 September, 1975 E Sch/E Yth (F)

League Club	Source	Date Signed	Seasons Played	Apps	Subs	Gls
Manchester U.	YT	10.92				
Nottingham F.	Tr	07.95	95	0	1	0
Macclesfield T.	Tr	10.97	97	6	3	0

IRVING Russell
Wallsend, 4 January, 1964 (F)

League Club	Source	Date Signed	Seasons Played	Apps	Subs	Gls
Ipswich T.	App	05.81				
Colchester U.	Tr	08.84	84-85	36	14	9

IRWIN Cecil
Ellington (Nd), 8 April, 1942 E Yth (RB)

League Club	Source	Date Signed	Seasons Played	Apps	Subs	Gls
Sunderland	Jnrs	04.59	58-71	312	3	1

IRWIN Colin Thomas
Liverpool, 9 February, 1957 (CD)

League Club	Source	Date Signed	Seasons Played	Apps	Subs	Gls
Liverpool	Jnrs	12.74	79-80	26	3	3
Swansea C.	Tr	08.81	81-83	48	0	0

IRWIN Joseph **Denis**
Cork, 31 October, 1965 IR Sch/IR Yth/IRu21-3/IRu23-1/IR 'B'/IR-48 (RB)

League Club	Source	Date Signed	Seasons Played	Apps	Subs	Gls
Leeds U.	App	10.83	83-85	72	0	1
Oldham Ath.	Tr	05.86	86-89	166	1	4
Manchester U.	Tr	06.90	90-97	275	6	17

IRWIN William
Newtonards (NI), 23 July, 1951 NI Amat (G)

League Club	Source	Date Signed	Seasons Played	Apps	Subs	Gls
Cardiff C.	Bangor C.	10.71	71-77	180	0	0

ISAAC James
Cramlington, 23 October, 1916 Died 1993 (IF)

League Club	Source	Date Signed	Seasons Played	Apps	Subs	Gls
Huddersfield T.	Cramlington	11.34	36-38	33	-	8
Bradford C.	Tr	04.45	46	24	-	3
Hartlepool U.	Tr	07.47	47-48	56	-	9

ISAAC Robert Charles
Hackney, 30 November, 1965 E Yth (CD)

League Club	Source	Date Signed	Seasons Played	Apps	Subs	Gls
Chelsea	App	11.83	84-86	9	0	0
Brighton & H.A.	Tr	02.87	86-88	30	0	0

ISAAC William (Peter) Henry
Pontypridd, 16 May, 1935 (G)

League Club	Source	Date Signed	Seasons Played	Apps	Subs	Gls
Stoke C.		03.53				
Northampton T.	Barry T.	07.58	59	8	-	0

ISAACS Anthony Brian
Middlesbrough, 8 April, 1973 (M)

League Club	Source	Date Signed	Seasons Played	Apps	Subs	Gls
Darlington	YT	07.91	91-93	37	14	2

ISAIAS Marques Soares
Brazil, 17 November, 1963 (M)

League Club	Source	Date Signed	Seasons Played	Apps	Subs	Gls
Coventry C.	Benfica (Por)	08.95	95-96	9	3	2

ISHERWOOD Dennis
Brierley Hill, 20 January, 1947 (FB)

League Club	Source	Date Signed	Seasons Played	Apps	Subs	Gls
Birmingham C.	App	01.64	66	5	0	1

ISHERWOOD Dennis
Northwich, 9 January, 1924 Died 1974 (F)

League Club	Source	Date Signed	Seasons Played	Apps	Subs	Gls
Wrexham		08.44				
Chester C.	Tr	04.46	46	3	-	0

ISHERWOOD Roy Edward
Blackburn, 24 January, 1934 (OR)

League Club	Source	Date Signed	Seasons Played	Apps	Subs	Gls
Blackburn Rov.	Nelson	10.57	57-61	49	-	9

ISMAEL Valerien
Strasbourg, France, 28 September, 1975 (CD)

League Club	Source	Date Signed	Seasons Played	Apps	Subs	Gls
Crystal Palace	Strasbourg (Fr)	01.98	97	13	0	0

ITHELL William **James**
Hawarden, 7 February, 1916 Died 1986 (CH)

League Club	Source	Date Signed	Seasons Played	Apps	Subs	Gls
Bolton W.		11.36				
Swindon T.	Tr	05.46	46-49	107	-	1

IVERSON Robert Thomas James
Folkestone, 17 October, 1910 Died 1953 (IF/WH)

League Club	Source	Date Signed	Seasons Played	Apps	Subs	Gls
Lincoln C.	Ramsgate P.W.	09.33	33	41	-	13
Wolverhampton W.	Tr	02.35	34-36	37	-	7
Aston Villa	Tr	12.36	36-47	135	-	9

IVERSON Steffen
Norway, 10 November, 1976 (F)

League Club	Source	Date Signed	Seasons Played	Apps	Subs	Gls
Tottenham H.	Rosenborg (Nor)	12.96	96-97	24	5	6

IVEY George Harrison
Stanley, 29 October, 1923 Died 1979 (W)

League Club	Source	Date Signed	Seasons Played	Apps	Subs	Gls
York C.	West Stanley	06.48	48-50	79	-	13

IVEY Paul Henry Winspear
Westminster, 1 April, 1961 (F)

League Club	Source	Date Signed	Seasons Played	Apps	Subs	Gls
Birmingham C.	App	01.79	78-80	4	3	0
Chesterfield (N/C)	Kettering T.	12.82	82	0	6	0

IZZET Mustafa (Muzzy) Kemmel
Mile End, 31 October, 1974 (M)

League Club	Source	Date Signed	Seasons Played	Apps	Subs	Gls
Chelsea	YT	05.93				
Leicester C.	Tr	03.96	95-97	78	2	8

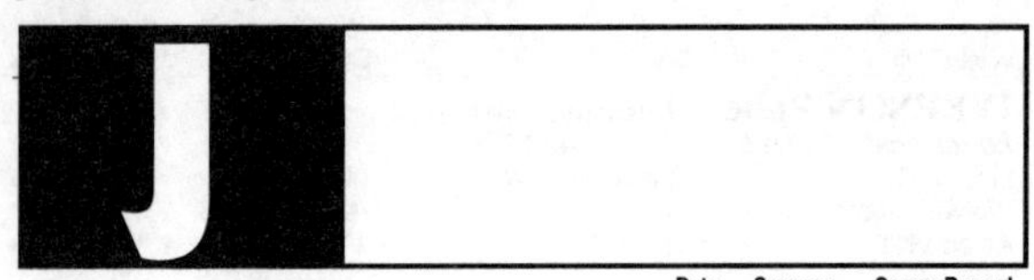

League Club	Source	Date Signed	Seasons Played	Career Record Apps	Subs	Gls
JACK Andrew						
Glasgow, 30 June, 1923						(F)
Tranmere Rov.	Wishaw Jnrs	06.48	48	3	-	3
JACK Rodney Alphonso						
St Vincent (WI), 28 September, 1972 St Vincent Int						(F)
Torquay U.	Lambada (StV)	10.95	95-97	82	5	24
JACK James **Ross**						
Inverness, 21 March, 1959						(F)
Everton	App	02.77	78	1	0	1
Norwich C.	Tr	12.79	80-82	31	25	10
Lincoln C.	Tr	08.83	83-84	52	8	16
JACK Vincent						
Fortrose, 6 August, 1933						(CH)
Bury	Inverness Jnrs	04.54	55-56	10	-	0
Swindon T.	Tr	10.56	56-58	26	-	0
Accrington St.	Tr	07.59	59	22	-	0
JACKETT Frank						
Pontardawe, 5 July, 1927						(WH)
Watford	Pontardawe Ath.	11.49	49-52	14	-	0
Leyton Orient	Tr	07.53	53	4	-	0
JACKETT Kenneth Francis						
Watford, 5 January, 1962 W Yth/Wu21-2/W-31						(M/LB)
Watford	App	01.80	79-89	330	7	25
JACKMAN Clive Edward James						
Farnborough, 21 February, 1936						(G)
Aldershot	Jnrs	05.53	52-56	38	-	0
West Bromwich A.	Tr	06.57	57-58	21	-	0
JACKMAN Derek Clive						
Colchester, 20 August, 1927						(WH)
Crystal Palace	Chelmsford C.	03.45				
West Ham U.	Tr	08.48	48-50	8	-	0
JACKS George Charles						
Stepney, 14 March, 1946						(M)
Queens Park R.	App	01.64	64	1	-	0
Millwall	Tr	07.65	65-70	144	7	5
Gillingham	Tr	07.72	72-75	159	0	20
JACKSON Alan						
Swadlincote, 22 August, 1938						(IF)
Wolverhampton W.	Jnrs	08.55	57-58	4	-	1
Bury	Tr	06.59	59-62	124	-	43
Brighton & H.A.	Tr	11.62	62-63	21	-	5
JACKSON Alan Edward						
Scunthorpe, 14 February, 1938 Died 1996						(W)
Lincoln C.	Brigg T.	11.58	58-60	4	-	0
JACKSON Albert						
Manchester, 12 September, 1943						(CH)
Oldham Ath.	Manchester U. (Jnrs)	12.62	63-65	22	0	4
JACKSON Alec						
Tipton, 29 May, 1937 EF Lge						(F)
West Bromwich A.	Jnrs	09.54	54-63	192	-	50
Birmingham C.	Tr	06.64	64-66	78	0	11
Walsall	Tr	02.67	66-67	36	2	7
JACKSON Alexander James						
Glasgow, 28 November, 1935						(CF)
Birmingham C.	Shettleston	04.58	58	6	-	6
Plymouth Arg.	Tr	03.60	59-63	67	-	23
JACKSON Alexander Wilson						
Lesmahagow, 2 October, 1921						(WH)
York C.	Huddersfield T. (Am)	09.46	46-49	50	-	5
JACKSON Thomas **Anthony**						
Tarleton (Lancs), 16 August, 1942						(FB)
Southport	St Gerards	08.62	62-64	12	-	0
JACKSON Arnold						
Manchester, 10 November, 1925						(IF)
Shrewsbury T.		(N/L)	50-53	144	-	39
Stockport Co.	Tr	06.54	54-58	153	-	48
JACKSON Charles **Barry**						
Askrigg, 2 February, 1938						(CH)
York C.	Cliftonville	12.56	58-69	481	1	9
JACKSON Brian						
Maltby, 2 February, 1936						(WH)
Rotherham U.	Maltby Main	09.54	55-64	131	-	6
Barnsley	Tr	07.65	65	29	0	0
JACKSON Brian Harvill						
Walton-on-Thames, 1 April, 1933 E Sch						(OR)
Leyton Orient	Arsenal (Am)	10.50	50-51	38	-	2
Liverpool	Tr	11.51	51-57	124	-	12
Port Vale	Tr	07.58	58-61	159	-	29
Peterborough U.	Tr	07.62	62-63	47	-	4
Lincoln C.	Tr	05.64	64	10	-	1
JACKSON Christopher Dean						
Barnsley, 16 January, 1976 E Sch/E Yth						(CF)
Barnsley	YT	01.93	92-95	16	7	2
JACKSON Clifford						
Swindon, 3 September, 1941 E Sch						(F)
Swindon T.	Jnrs	09.58	58-62	91	-	30
Plymouth Arg.	Tr	06.63	63-66	72	0	19
Crystal Palace	Tr	09.66	66-69	100	6	26
Torquay U.	Tr	08.70	70-73	114	13	13
JACKSON Craig						
Renishaw (Dby), 17 January, 1969						(CD)
Notts Co.	YT	08.86	85-86	3	2	0
JACKSON Darren						
Edinburgh, 25 July, 1966 S-26						(W)
Newcastle U.	Meadowbank Thistle	10.86	86-88	53	16	7
JACKSON Darren William						
Keynsham, 24 September, 1971						(CD)
Oxford U.	YT	05.90	89-93	11	3	0
Reading	L	02.93	92	5	0	0
JACKSON David						
Stoke, 23 January, 1937						(IF/WH)
Wrexham (Am)	Jnrs	07.54	54	7	-	1
Bradford C.	Marine	03.55	54-60	250	-	61
Tranmere Rov.	Tr	07.61	61-62	38	-	5
Halifax T.	Tr	07.63	63-64	66	-	2
JACKSON David Kenneth George						
Solihull, 28 August, 1978						(LB)
Shrewsbury T.	YT	●	95	0	1	0
JACKSON David Patrick						
Bradford, 16 September, 1958						(F)
Manchester U.	App	09.75				
Bradford C.	Tr	09.78	78	9	3	3
JACKSON Dennis Leonard						
Birmingham, 8 March, 1932						(FB)
Aston Villa	Hednesford T.	10.54	56-58	8	-	0
Millwall	Tr	05.59	59-60	80	-	0
JACKSON Elliot						
Swindon, 27 August, 1977						(G)
Oxford U.	YT	07.96	96-97	6	0	0
JACKSON Ernest						
Sheffield, 11 June, 1914 Died 1996						(WH)
Sheffield U.	Atlas & Norfolk	09.32	32-48	229	-	8
JACKSON Gary Andrew						
Swinton, 30 September, 1964						(M)
Manchester C.	Jnrs	10.81	81	6	2	0
Exeter C.	Tr	09.85	85-86	34	1	2
JACKSON George						
Liverpool, 14 January, 1911						(FB)
Everton	Walton Parish	05.32	34-47	75	-	0
JACKSON George						
Stretford, 10 February, 1952						(M)
Stoke C.	App	07.69	71	8	0	0
JACKSON Harold						
Halifax, 20 July, 1917 Died 1996						(FB)
Halifax T.	Sowerby W.E.	08.36	36-46	49	-	3
Stockport Co.	Tr	08.47	47	2	-	0

League Club	Source	Date Signed	Seasons Played	Apps	Subs	Gls
JACKSON Harry						
Blackburn, 30 December, 1918 Died 1984						(CF)
Burnley	Darwen	01.42				
Manchester C.	Tr	06.46	46-47	8	-	2
Preston N.E.	Tr	12.47	47-48	18	-	5
Blackburn Rov.	Tr	12.48	48	1	-	0
Chester C.	Tr	07.49	49	21	-	10
JACKSON Harry						
Shaw, 12 May, 1934						(F)
Oldham Ath.	Jnrs	06.51	51-55	10	-	1
Rochdale	Tr	10.55	55	1	-	1
JACKSON James						
Glasgow, 26 March, 1931						(CF)
Notts Co.	Mapperley Celtic	03.49	48-57	113	-	47
JACKSON James						
Glasgow,, 1 January, 1921						(IF)
Bolton W.		06.39	47-49	11	-	1
Carlisle U.	Tr	07.50	50-54	100	-	23
JACKSON James Potter						
Glasgow, 4 August, 1924						(WH)
Bury	Third Lanark	05.50	50	1	-	0
JACKSON James William						
Ashington, 30 December, 1933 E Sch						(FB)
Newcastle U.	Jnrs	01.51				
Aldershot	Tr	07.55	55-60	197	-	19
JACKSON John						
Newcastle-u-Lyme, 7 January, 1923 Died 1992						(F)
Stoke C.	Alsager	05.41	46-47	4	-	3
JACKSON John Keith						
Hammersmith, 5 September, 1942 E Yth/EF Lge						(G)
Crystal Palace	Jnrs	03.62	64-73	346	0	0
Leyton Orient	Tr	10.73	73-78	226	0	0
Millwall	Tr	08.79	79-80	79	0	0
Ipswich T.	Tr	08.81	81	1	0	0
Hereford U.	Tr	08.82	82	4	0	0
JACKSON Joseph George						
Wolverhampton, 22 April, 1966						(M)
Wolverhampton W.	Jnrs	08.83	83	1	0	0
JACKSON Justin Jonathan						
Nottingham, 10 December, 1974						(F)
Notts Co.	Woking	09.97	97	4	11	1
JACKSON Kirk Stewart						
Barnsley, 16 October, 1976						(F)
Sheffield U.	YT	05.95				
Scunthorpe U.	Tr	07.96	96	0	4	1
Chesterfield	Tr	08.97	97	0	3	0
JACKSON Leonard						
Stockport, 10 May, 1923						(RB)
Manchester C.		01.45				
Rochdale	Tr	09.45	46-47	61	-	0
JACKSON Leonard Wilfred						
Birmingham, 6 September, 1922 Died 1990						(RB)
Birmingham C.		09.46				
Northampton T.	Tr	07.48	48	2	-	0
JACKSON Mark Graham						
Leeds, 30 September, 1977 E Yth						(CD/M)
Leeds U.	YT	07.95	95-97	11	8	0
JACKSON Matthew Alan						
Leeds, 19 October, 1971 E Sch/Eu21-10						(RB)
Luton T.	Jnrs	07.90	91	7	2	0
Preston N.E.	L	03.91	90	3	1	0
Everton	Tr	10.91	91-95	132	6	4
Charlton Ath.	L	03.96	95	8	0	0
Queens Park R.	L	08.96	96	7	0	0
Birmingham C.	L	10.96	96	10	0	0
Norwich C.	Tr	12.96	96-97	58	2	5
JACKSON Maurice						
Barnsley, 6 November, 1928 Died 1971						(FB)
Barnsley	Carlton U.	09.49	49-55	34	-	0
Barrow	Tr	08.56	56-58	74	-	0
JACKSON Michael James						
Runcorn, 4 December, 1973 E Yth						(CD)
Crewe Alex.	YT	06.92	91-92	5	0	0

League Club	Source	Date Signed	Seasons Played	Apps	Subs	Gls
Bury	Tr	08.93	93-96	123	2	9
Preston N.E.	Tr	03.97	96-97	46	1	2
JACKSON Nigel Anthony						
Pudsey, 27 June, 1950						(FB)
Scunthorpe U.	App	07.68	68-72	112	6	5
JACKSON Norman Edward						
Bradford, 6 July, 1925						(FB)
Sheffield Wed.	Manningham Mills	10.48	49-52	31	-	0
Bristol C.	Tr	06.54	54-55	8	-	0
Oldham Ath.	Tr	07.56	56	2	-	0
JACKSON Peter						
Stoke, 23 January, 1937 Died 1991						(WH)
Wrexham (Am)	Jnrs	07.54	54	7	-	1
Bradford C.	Marine	03.55	54-60	199	-	15
Tranmere Rov.	Tr	07.61	61-64	81	-	3
JACKSON Peter Alan						
Bradford, 6 April, 1961						(CD)
Bradford C.	App	04.79	78-86	267	11	24
Newcastle U.	Tr	10.86	86-88	60	0	3
Bradford C.	Tr	09.88	88-89	55	3	5
Huddersfield T.	Tr	09.90	90-93	152	3	3
Chester C.	Tr	09.94	94-96	100	0	3
JACKSON Philip John						
Manchester, 8 September, 1958						(M)
Stockport Co.	Manchester C. (App)	08.76	76-77	15	3	1
JACKSON Richard						
Whitby, 18 April, 1980						(FB)
Scarborough	YT	03.98	97	2	0	0
JACKSON Richard George						
Rotherham, 13 December, 1932						(G)
Rotherham U.	Jnrs	07.51				
York C.	Tr	08.54				
Rotherham U.		07.56	56	1	-	0
JACKSON Robert						
Middleton, 5 June, 1934						(RB/WH)
Oldham Ath.	Jnrs	08.51	51-54	29	-	1
Lincoln C.	Tr	03.55	55-63	235	-	0
JACKSON Robert Gary						
Altrincham, 9 February, 1973						(F)
Walsall	Manchester C. (YT)	03.91	90-91	8	2	2
JACKSON Robert Gristwood						
Cornsay (Dm), 12 May, 1915 Died 1991						(WH)
Southend U.	Stanley U.	07.34	35-47	93	-	0
JACKSON Ronald						
Crook, 15 October, 1919 Died 1980						(FB)
Wrexham		09.45	46-49	108	-	0
Leicester C.	Tr	12.49	49-54	161	-	0
JACKSON Royston Leonard						
Swindon, 22 October, 1931						(WH)
Swindon T.		11.53	54	2	-	0
JACKSON Thomas						
Belfast, 3 November, 1946 NIu23-1/NI-35						(M)
Everton	Glentoran	02.68	67-70	30	2	0
Nottingham F.	Tr	10.70	70-74	73	8	6
Manchester U.	Tr	07.75	75-76	18	1	0
JACKSON William Patrick						
Liverpool, 8 December, 1924 Died 1974						(IF)
Swindon T.		10.47	48-49	4	-	1
Tranmere Rov.	Tr	04.51	51-53	14	-	1
JACOBS Francis Arthur						
Bristol, 22 April, 1940						(WH)
Bristol C.	Jnrs	05.58	59-60	5	-	0
JACOBS Stephen Douglas						
West Ham, 5 July, 1961						(D)
Coventry C.	App	11.78	79-83	94	7	0
Brighton & H.A.	Tr	06.84	84-85	47	1	3
Charlton Ath.	Tr	08.86				
Gillingham	Tr	12.86	86	6	1	0
JACOBS Trevor Frederick						
Bristol, 28 November, 1946						(FB)
Bristol C.	Jnrs	07.65	66-72	130	1	3
Plymouth Arg.	L	09.72	72	4	0	0
Bristol Rov.	Tr	05.73	73-75	82	0	3

JACOBS Wayne Graham
Sheffield, 3 February, 1969 (LB)

League Club	Source	Date Signed	Seasons Played	Apps	Subs	Gls
Sheffield Wed.	App	01.87	87	5	1	0
Hull C.	Tr	03.88	87-91	127	2	4
Rotherham U.	Tr	08.93	93	40	2	2
Bradford C.	Tr	08.94	94-97	139	2	6

JACOBSEN Viggo Lund
Denmark, 11 August, 1953 (M)

League Club	Source	Date Signed	Seasons Played	Apps	Subs	Gls
Charlton Ath.	Kastrup (Den)	11.79	79	9	0	0

JACQUES Anthony
Oddington (Oxon), 10 October, 1942 (WH)

League Club	Source	Date Signed	Seasons Played	Apps	Subs	Gls
Oxford U.	Jnrs	(N/L)	62	7	-	0

JACQUES Joseph
Consett, 12 September, 1944 Died 1981 (WH)

League Club	Source	Date Signed	Seasons Played	Apps	Subs	Gls
Preston N.E.	Jnrs	09.61				
Lincoln C.	Tr	05.64	64	22	-	0
Darlington	Tr	07.65	65-69	150	3	5
Southend U.	Tr	10.69	69-72	85	2	0
Gillingham	Tr	11.72	72-74	73	0	1
Hartlepool U.	Dartford	01.76	75	5	0	0

JAGGER George Newman
Great Houghton, 30 September, 1941 (W)

League Club	Source	Date Signed	Seasons Played	Apps	Subs	Gls
Barnsley	Houghton Main	06.60	60-62	45	-	2

JAGIELKA Stephen
Manchester, 10 March, 1978 (F)

League Club	Source	Date Signed	Seasons Played	Apps	Subs	Gls
Stoke C.	YT	07.96				
Shrewsbury T.	Tr	07.97	97	4	12	1

JAGO Gordon Harold
Poplar, 22 October, 1932 E Sch/E Yth (CH)

League Club	Source	Date Signed	Seasons Played	Apps	Subs	Gls
Charlton Ath.	Dulwich Hamlet	05.51	54-61	137	-	1

JAKEMAN Leslie
Nuneaton, 14 March, 1930 (WH)

League Club	Source	Date Signed	Seasons Played	Apps	Subs	Gls
Derby Co.	Atherstone T.	06.47				
Leicester C.	Hinckley Ath.	05.51	54	1	-	0

JAKUB Yanek (Joe)
Falkirk, 7 December, 1956 (M/FB)

League Club	Source	Date Signed	Seasons Played	Apps	Subs	Gls
Burnley	App	12.73	75-79	42	0	0
Bury	Tr	10.80	80-86	262	3	27
Chester C.	A.Z.67 Alkmaar (Neth)	08.88	88	42	0	1
Burnley	Tr	07.89	89-92	161	2	8
Chester C.	Tr	08.93	93	35	1	0
Wigan Ath.	Colwyn Bay	09.94	94	16	0	0

JALES Richard
Chiswick, 3 April, 1922 (FB)

League Club	Source	Date Signed	Seasons Played	Apps	Subs	Gls
Bradford C.		06.45				
Aldershot	Tr	05.46	46-50	78	-	1

JALINK Nicolaas
Netherlands, 22 June, 1964 (M)

League Club	Source	Date Signed	Seasons Played	Apps	Subs	Gls
Port Vale	Waalwijk (Neth)	07.91	91	20	8	1

JAMES Anthony Craig
Sheffield, 27 June, 1967 (CD)

League Club	Source	Date Signed	Seasons Played	Apps	Subs	Gls
Lincoln C.	Gainsborough Trin.	08.88	88-89	24	5	0
Leicester C.	Tr	08.89	89-93	79	28	11
Hereford U.	Tr	07.94	94-95	35	0	4
Plymouth Arg.	Tr	08.96	96	34	0	1

JAMES Anthony Ralph
Swansea, 24 February, 1960 (M)

League Club	Source	Date Signed	Seasons Played	Apps	Subs	Gls
Swansea C.	App	12.77	77-79	6	5	1

JAMES Thomas **Anthony** George
Ynysybwl, 16 September, 1919 (WH)

League Club	Source	Date Signed	Seasons Played	Apps	Subs	Gls
Brighton & H.A.	Folkestone T.	06.39	46-48	69	-	20
Bristol Rov.	Tr	06.49	49-50	21	-	5

JAMES Christopher
Sheffield, 16 January, 1969 (RB)

League Club	Source	Date Signed	Seasons Played	Apps	Subs	Gls
Scarborough	Worksop T.	08.91	91	12	1	0

JAMES David
Swansea, 29 September, 1917 Died 1981 (CF)

League Club	Source	Date Signed	Seasons Played	Apps	Subs	Gls
Chelsea	Mossley	04.38				
Swansea C.	Tr	06.47	47	12	-	7

JAMES David
Cambuslang, 12 December, 1942 (OR)

League Club	Source	Date Signed	Seasons Played	Apps	Subs	Gls
Brighton & H.A.	Blantyre Vic.	05.62	62	5	-	0

JAMES David Benjamin
Welwyn Garden City, 1 August, 1970 E Yth/Eu21-10/E 'B'/E-1 (G)

League Club	Source	Date Signed	Seasons Played	Apps	Subs	Gls
Watford	YT	07.88	90-91	89	0	0
Liverpool	Tr	07.92	92-97	187	1	0

JAMES David John
Southend, 11 March, 1948 (LB/M)

League Club	Source	Date Signed	Seasons Played	Apps	Subs	Gls
West Ham U.	App	03.65				
Torquay U.	Tr	05.67	67	8	0	0

JAMES Walter **George**
Swansea, 15 June, 1924 W Sch (FB/CF)

League Club	Source	Date Signed	Seasons Played	Apps	Subs	Gls
Swansea C.	Tawe U.	08.42	49	4	-	0
Newport Co.	Tr	07.50	50-51	13	-	5

JAMES Edward **Glyn**
Llangollen, 17 December, 1941 Wu23-2/W-9 (CH)

League Club	Source	Date Signed	Seasons Played	Apps	Subs	Gls
Blackpool	Jnrs	05.59	60-74	393	6	22

JAMES John Brian
Stone, 24 October, 1948 (F)

League Club	Source	Date Signed	Seasons Played	Apps	Subs	Gls
Port Vale	Jnrs	04.66	65-72	202	8	39
Chester C.	Tr	02.73	72-75	97	1	40
Tranmere Rov.	Tr	09.75	75-77	59	14	22

JAMES John Edward
Birmingham, 19 February, 1934 (WH)

League Club	Source	Date Signed	Seasons Played	Apps	Subs	Gls
Birmingham C.	Jnrs	03.51	52-53	5	-	2
Torquay U.	Tr	06.55	55-60	125	-	11

JAMES John Stanley
South Shields, 12 September, 1923 (FB)

League Club	Source	Date Signed	Seasons Played	Apps	Subs	Gls
Bradford P.A.	South Shields	08.44	49-50	13	-	1

JAMES Joseph
Bootle, 9 September, 1954 (CD)

League Club	Source	Date Signed	Seasons Played	Apps	Subs	Gls
Liverpool	Jnrs	01.74				
Southport	Tr	07.75	75	11	2	0

JAMES Julian Colin
Tring, 22 March, 1970 Eu21-2 (RB)

League Club	Source	Date Signed	Seasons Played	Apps	Subs	Gls
Luton T.	YT	06.88	87-97	262	20	13
Preston N.E.	L	09.91	91	6	0	0

JAMES Keith Andrew
Hillingdon, 18 August, 1961 E Yth (FB)

League Club	Source	Date Signed	Seasons Played	Apps	Subs	Gls
Portsmouth	App	07.79	78-79	5	1	0

JAMES Leighton
Loughor (Glam), 16 February, 1953 W Sch/Wu23-7/W-54 (LW)

League Club	Source	Date Signed	Seasons Played	Apps	Subs	Gls
Burnley	App	02.70	70-75	180	1	44
Derby Co.	Tr	10.75	75-77	67	1	15
Queens Park R.	Tr	10.77	77-78	27	1	4
Burnley	Tr	09.78	78-79	76	0	9
Swansea C.	Tr	04.80	79-82	88	10	27
Sunderland	Tr	01.83	82-83	50	2	4
Bury	Tr	08.84	84	46	0	5
Newport Co.	Tr	08.85	85	21	7	2
Burnley	Tr	08.86	86-88	75	4	13

JAMES Leslie
(OL)

League Club	Source	Date Signed	Seasons Played	Apps	Subs	Gls
Darlington (Am)		05.53	53	4	-	0

JAMES Lutel
Manchester, 2 June, 1972 (F)

League Club	Source	Date Signed	Seasons Played	Apps	Subs	Gls
Scarborough (N/C)	Yorkshire Amats	02.93	92	0	6	0

JAMES Martin Christopher
Slough, 18 February, 1953 (CD)

League Club	Source	Date Signed	Seasons Played	Apps	Subs	Gls
Reading	Jnrs	08.71	71	21	0	0

JAMES Martin Joseph
Crosby, 18 May, 1971 (LW/B)

League Club	Source	Date Signed	Seasons Played	Apps	Subs	Gls
Preston N.E.	YT	07.89	90-92	92	6	11
Stockport Co.	Tr	03.93	92-93	13	19	0
Rotherham U.	Tr	08.94	94-96	40	4	0

JAMES Paul John
Cardiff, 11 November, 1963 Canadian Int (M)

League Club	Source	Date Signed	Seasons Played	Apps	Subs	Gls
Doncaster Rov.	Hamilton (Can)	11.87	87	7	1	0

JAMES Percy George Burge
Rhondda, 9 March, 1917 Died 1993 W Amat (OL)

League Club	Source	Date Signed	Seasons Played	Apps	Subs	Gls
Luton T.	Oxford C.	08.49	49	2	-	1

JAMES Robert (Robbie) Mark
Swansea, 23 March, 1957 Died 1998 Wu21-3/W-47 (F/M)

League Club	Source	Date Signed	Seasons Played	Apps	Subs	Gls
Swansea C.	App	04.74	72-82	386	8	99
Stoke C.	Tr	07.83	83-84	48	0	6

League Club	Source	Date Signed	Seasons Played	Apps	Subs	Gls
Queens Park R.	Tr	10.84	84-86	78	9	5
Leicester C.	Tr	06.87	87	21	2	0
Swansea C.	Tr	01.88	87-89	82	8	16
Bradford C.	Tr	08.90	90-91	89	0	6
Cardiff C.	Tr	08.92	92-93	51	0	2
JAMES Ronald						
Birmingham, 16 March, 1922						(WH)
Birmingham C.		10.47				
Northampton T.	Tr	07.48	48	4	-	1
JAMES Royston William						
Bristol, 19 February, 1941 Died 1990						(CF)
Bristol Rov.	Old Georgians	07.60	60	1	-	0
JAMES Steven Robert						
Coseley, 29 November, 1949 E Yth						(CD)
Manchester U.	App	12.66	68-74	129	0	4
York C.	Tr	01.76	75-79	105	0	1
JAMES Tyrone Selwyn						
Paddington, 19 September, 1956						(D)
Fulham	Jnrs	09.74	75-77	18	2	0
Plymouth Arg.	Tr	03.78	77-81	77	4	0
Torquay U.	L	03.83	82	13	0	1
JAMES William John						
Cardiff, 18 October, 1921 Died 1980						(CF)
Cardiff C.	Cardiff Corries	08.39	46	6	-	2
JAMESON John Charles						
Belfast, 11 March, 1958						(W)
Huddersfield T.	Bangor (NI)	03.77	77	1	0	0
JAMIESON Ian						
Edinburgh, 22 October, 1934						(F)
Crewe Alex.	Third Lanark	08.56	56	4	-	2
Birmingham C.	Tr	07.57				
JAMIESON John (Ian) Wallace						
Dumbarton, 14 October, 1928						(WH)
Coventry C.	Aberdeen	01.49	48-57	181	-	6
JANKOVIC Bozo						
Yugoslavia, 22 May, 1951 Died 1993 Yugoslav Int						(F)
Middlesbrough	Zeljeznicar (Yug)	02.79	79-80	42	8	16
JANNEY Mark						
Romford, 2 December, 1977						(F)
Tottenham H.	YT	07.96				
Brentford	L	03.97	96	1	1	1
JANSEN Matthew Brooke						
Carlisle, 20 October, 1977 E Yth						(F)
Carlisle U.	YT	01.96	96-97	26	16	10
Crystal Palace	Tr	02.98	97	5	3	3
JANSSON Jan						
Sweden, 26 January, 1968 Swedish Int						(M)
Port Vale	Norrkoping (Swe)	11.96	96-97	32	12	6
JANTUNEN Pertti Kalevi						
Finland, 25 June, 1952 Finnish Int						(M)
Bristol C.	Eskilstuna (Swe)	03.79	78-79	7	1	1
JARDINE Alexander						
Cleland, 12 April, 1926 Died 1978						(RB)
Millwall	Dundee U.	08.50	50-57	299	-	25
JARDINE Frederick						
Edinburgh, 27 September, 1941						(LB)
Luton T.	Dundee U.	05.61	61-69	218	2	9
Torquay U.	Tr	02.71	70-71	11	0	0
JARMAN Harold James						
Bristol, 4 May, 1939						(OR)
Bristol Rov.	Clifton St Vincent	08.59	59-72	440	12	127
Newport Co.	Tr	05.73	73	34	6	8
JARMAN John Emlyn						
Rhymney, 4 February, 1931						(WH)
Wolverhampton W.	Lowhill Y.C.	07.49				
Barnsley	Tr	10.50	51-55	45	-	1
Walsall	Tr	06.56	56-57	37	-	2
JARMAN Lee						
Cardiff, 16 December, 1977 W Yth/Wu21-7						(CD)
Cardiff C.	YT	08.95	95-97	76	11	0

League Club	Source	Date Signed	Seasons Played	Apps	Subs	Gls
JARMAN William Brynmor						
Pontypridd, 18 July, 1920 Died 1984						(CF)
Bury	Llanbradach	10.46	46	10	-	1
JARRIE Frederick						
Hartlepool, 2 August, 1922						(G)
Hartlepool U. (Am)		08.47	47	1	-	0
JARVIS Alan Leslie						
Wrexham, 4 August, 1943 W-3						(M)
Everton	Jnrs	07.61				
Hull C.	Tr	06.64	65-70	148	11	12
Mansfield T.	Tr	03.71	70-72	76	6	0
JARVIS Antony						
Radcliffe, 19 March, 1964						(F)
Oldham Ath.	Irlam T.	03.86				
Crewe Alex.	Tr	10.86	86	6	3	1
JARVIS John **Brian**						
Bangor-on-Dee, 26 August, 1933						(WH)
Wrexham		07.52	53-58	64	-	3
Oldham Ath.	Tr	07.59	59-62	88	-	2
JARVIS Harry						
Maltby, 8 October, 1928						(WH)
Notts Co.	Worksop T.	05.51	52-54	29	-	0
JARVIS Joseph						
Farnworth, 27 June, 1929						(FB)
Stockport Co.		09.53	54-56	43	-	0
JARVIS Mervin John						
Bristol, 20 October, 1924 Died 1994						(OL)
Bristol C.		05.48	48	4	-	0
JARVIS Nicholas Charles						
Mansfield, 19 September, 1955						(LB)
Scunthorpe U.	Grantham	07.80	80	21	0	0
JARVIS Nigel Brian						
Totnes, 6 November, 1963						(FB)
Plymouth Arg.	App	11.81				
Torquay U. (N/C)	Yeovil T.	02.85	84	8	3	0
JASPER Brian						
Plymouth, 25 November, 1933						(FB)
Plymouth Arg.	Astor Inst.	07.54	56	2	-	0
JASPER Dale William						
Croydon, 14 January, 1964						(M/D)
Chelsea	App	01.82	83-84	10	0	0
Brighton & H.A.	Tr	05.86	86-87	44	5	6
Crewe Alex.	Tr	07.88	88-91	103	8	2
JAYES Brian						
Leicester, 13 December, 1932						(WH)
Leicester C.	Jnrs	07.54	55	3	-	0
Mansfield T.	Tr	07.56	56-59	115	-	1
JAYES Carl Geoffrey						
Leicester, 15 March, 1954 E Sch						(G)
Leicester C.	Jnrs	06.71	74	5	0	0
Northampton T.	Tr	11.77	77-79	68	0	0
JAYES Alfred **Gordon**						
Leicester, 26 September, 1923 E Sch						(IF)
Notts Co.	Leicester C. (Am)	11.46	46-47	27	-	7
JEAN Earl Jude						
St Lucia (WI), 9 October, 1971 St Lucian Int						(F)
Ipswich T. (N/C)	Felgueires (Por)	12.96	96	0	1	0
Rotherham U.	Tr	01.97	96	7	11	6
Plymouth Arg.	Tr	08.97	97	16	20	4
JEAVONS Patrick William Peter						
Deptford, 5 July, 1946						(G)
Lincoln C.	Gravesend & Nft	02.66	65	1	0	0
JEFFELS Simon						
Barnsley, 18 January, 1966 E Yth						(CD)
Barnsley	App	01.84	83-87	39	3	0
Preston N.E.	L	10.87	87	1	0	0
Carlisle U.	Tr	07.88	88-91	75	2	5
JEFFERIES Alfred James						
Oxford, 9 February, 1922						(G)
Brentford	Oxford C.	09.47	49-53	116	-	0
Torquay U.	Tr	06.54	54	45	-	0

JEFFERS Francis
Liverpool, 25 January, 1981 E Yth (F)

League Club	Source	Date Signed	Seasons Played	Apps	Subs	Gls
Everton	YT	●	97	0	1	0

JEFFERS John Joseph
Liverpool, 5 October, 1968 E Sch (LW)

League Club	Source	Date Signed	Seasons Played	Apps	Subs	Gls
Liverpool	App	10.86				
Port Vale	Tr	12.88	88-94	147	33	10
Shrewsbury T.	L	01.95	94	3	0	1
Stockport Co.	Tr	11.95	95-96	46	11	6

JEFFERSON Arthur
Goldthorpe (Yks), 14 December, 1916 Died 1997 (FB)

League Club	Source	Date Signed	Seasons Played	Apps	Subs	Gls
Queens Park R.	Peterborough U.	02.36	36-49	211	-	1
Aldershot	Tr	03.50	49-54	170	-	0

JEFFERSON Derek
Morpeth, 5 September, 1948 (CD)

League Club	Source	Date Signed	Seasons Played	Apps	Subs	Gls
Ipswich T.	App	02.66	67-72	163	3	1
Wolverhampton W.	Tr	10.72	72-75	41	1	0
Sheffield Wed.	L	10.76	76	5	0	0
Hereford U.	Tr	11.76	76-77	39	0	0

JEFFERSON Stanley
Goldthorpe (Yks), 26 June, 1931 Died 1973 (FB)

League Club	Source	Date Signed	Seasons Played	Apps	Subs	Gls
Aldershot	Dearne Ath.	08.52	52-57	80	-	0
Southend U.	Tr	07.58				

JEFFREY Alick James
Rawmarsh, 29 January, 1939 E Sch/E Yth/E Amat/Eu23-2 (IF)

League Club	Source	Date Signed	Seasons Played	Apps	Subs	Gls
Doncaster Rov.	Jnrs	02.56	54-56	71	-	34
Doncaster Rov.	Skegness	12.63	63-68	190	1	95
Lincoln C.	Tr	01.69	68-69	19	3	3

JEFFREY Andrew Samuel
Motherwell, 15 January, 1972 (RB)

League Club	Source	Date Signed	Seasons Played	Apps	Subs	Gls
Leicester C.	YT	02.90				
Cambridge U.	Cambridge C.	07.93	93-95	82	13	2

JEFFREY Michael Richard
Liverpool, 11 August, 1971 (F)

League Club	Source	Date Signed	Seasons Played	Apps	Subs	Gls
Bolton W.	YT	02.89	88-91	9	6	0
Doncaster Rov.	Tr	03.92	91-93	48	1	19
Newcastle U.	Tr	10.93	93	2	0	0
Rotherham U.	Tr	06.95	95	22	0	5

JEFFREY Robert
Aberdeen, 24 May, 1920 (WH)

League Club	Source	Date Signed	Seasons Played	Apps	Subs	Gls
Derby Co.		12.43				
Exeter C.	Aberdeen	10.47	47	7	-	0

JEFFREY William Greenwood
Helensburgh, 25 October, 1956 (M)

League Club	Source	Date Signed	Seasons Played	Apps	Subs	Gls
Oxford U.	App	10.73	73-81	311	3	24
Blackpool	Tr	06.82	82	12	2	1
Northampton T.	Tr	03.83	82-83	53	1	5

JEFFRIES Derek
Manchester, 22 March, 1951 (CD)

League Club	Source	Date Signed	Seasons Played	Apps	Subs	Gls
Manchester C.	App	08.68	69-72	64	9	0
Crystal Palace	Tr	09.73	73-75	107	0	1
Peterborough U.	L	10.76	76	7	0	0
Millwall	L	03.77	76	10	1	0
Chester C.	Tr	07.77	77-80	116	5	2

JEFFRIES Ronald James
Birmingham, 24 March, 1930 (CF)

League Club	Source	Date Signed	Seasons Played	Apps	Subs	Gls
Aston Villa	Moor Green	12.50	50	2	-	0
Walsall	Tr	11.53	53	3	-	0

JEFFRIES William Arthur
Acton, 11 March, 1921 Died 1981 (IF)

League Club	Source	Date Signed	Seasons Played	Apps	Subs	Gls
Mansfield T.		03.46	46	2	-	0
Hull C.	Tr	01.47				

JELLY Horace **Edward (Ted)**
Leicester, 28 August, 1921 (FB)

League Club	Source	Date Signed	Seasons Played	Apps	Subs	Gls
Leicester C.	Belgrave U.	05.46	46-50	56	-	1
Plymouth Arg.	Tr	08.51	52-53	11	-	0

JEMSON Nigel Bradley
Preston, 10 October, 1969 Eu21-1 (F)

League Club	Source	Date Signed	Seasons Played	Apps	Subs	Gls
Preston N.E.	YT	06.87	85-87	28	4	8
Nottingham F.	Tr	03.88	89-91	45	2	13
Bolton W.	L	12.88	88	4	1	0
Preston N.E.	L	03.89	88	6	3	2
Sheffield Wed.	Tr	09.91	91-93	26	25	9
Grimsby T.	L	09.93	93	6	0	2
Notts Co.	Tr	09.94	94-95	7	7	1
Watford	L	01.95	94	3	1	0
Rotherham U.	L	02.96	95	16	0	5
Oxford U.	Tr	07.96	96-97	68	0	27
Bury	Tr	02.98	97	11	4	1

JENKIN Kenneth
Grimsby, 27 November, 1931 (OR)

League Club	Source	Date Signed	Seasons Played	Apps	Subs	Gls
Grimsby T.	Jnrs	07.50	50-53	23	-	6

JENKINS Brian
Treherbert, 1 August, 1935 (W)

League Club	Source	Date Signed	Seasons Played	Apps	Subs	Gls
Cardiff C.	Cwmparc	04.57	56-60	30	-	7
Exeter C.	Tr	06.61	61-62	73	-	12
Bristol Rov.	Tr	07.63	63	7	-	0

JENKINS David John
Bristol, 2 September, 1946 (F)

League Club	Source	Date Signed	Seasons Played	Apps	Subs	Gls
Arsenal	App	10.63	67-68	16	1	3
Tottenham H.	Tr	10.68	68-69	11	3	2
Brentford	Tr	07.72	72	13	5	1
Hereford U.	Tr	03.73	72-73	18	4	3
Newport Co.	L	03.74	73	6	0	1
Shrewsbury T.	Tr	08.74	74	2	0	1
Workington	South Africa	10.75	75	6	0	0

JENKINS Iain
Prescot, 24 November, 1972 NI 'B'/NI-5 (D)

League Club	Source	Date Signed	Seasons Played	Apps	Subs	Gls
Everton	YT	06.91	90-92	3	2	0
Bradford C.	L	12.92	92	6	0	0
Chester C.	Tr	08.93	93-97	155	5	1

JENKINS Iorweth Clifford
Neath, 11 December, 1959 W Sch (D)

League Club	Source	Date Signed	Seasons Played	Apps	Subs	Gls
Chelsea	App	08.78				
Brentford	Tr	11.79	79-80	12	3	1

JENKINS Lee David
Pontypool, 28 June, 1979 W Sch/W Yth/Wu21-1 (RW)

League Club	Source	Date Signed	Seasons Played	Apps	Subs	Gls
Swansea C.	YT	12.96	96-97	35	9	2

JENKINS Lee Robert
Birmingham, 17 March, 1961 E Yth (M)

League Club	Source	Date Signed	Seasons Played	Apps	Subs	Gls
Aston Villa	App	01.79	78-79	0	3	0
Port Vale	Tr	11.80	80	1	0	0
Birmingham C.	Rovaniemi (Fin)	10.85	85	1	0	0

JENKINS James **Lindley**
West Bromwich, 6 April, 1954 (M)

League Club	Source	Date Signed	Seasons Played	Apps	Subs	Gls
Birmingham C.	App	07.71	73	2	0	0
Walsall	Tr	07.74	74	3	0	0

JENKINS Peter Leslie
Bow, 7 February, 1947 (FB)

League Club	Source	Date Signed	Seasons Played	Apps	Subs	Gls
Charlton Ath.	Chelsea (App)	03.65	65	2	0	0

JENKINS Randolph Joseph
Sligo (Ire), 5 September, 1925 (IF)

League Club	Source	Date Signed	Seasons Played	Apps	Subs	Gls
Walsall		01.45				
Northampton T.	Tr	06.46	46-47	18	-	6
Fulham	Tr	05.48				
Gillingham	Tr	06.50	50	2	-	0

JENKINS Reginald
Millbrook, 7 October, 1938 (IF)

League Club	Source	Date Signed	Seasons Played	Apps	Subs	Gls
Plymouth Arg.	Truro C.	10.57	58-59	16	-	3
Exeter C.	Tr	12.60	60	20	-	6
Torquay U.	Tr	07.61	61-63	88	-	23
Rochdale	Tr	06.64	64-72	294	11	119

JENKINS Ross Anthony
Kensington, 4 November, 1951 (F)

League Club	Source	Date Signed	Seasons Played	Apps	Subs	Gls
Crystal Palace	App	11.69	71-72	15	0	2
Watford	Tr	11.72	72-82	312	27	118

JENKINS Stephen Robert
Merthyr Tydfil, 16 July, 1972 W Yth/Wu21-2/W-10 (RB)

League Club	Source	Date Signed	Seasons Played	Apps	Subs	Gls
Swansea C.	YT	07.90	90-95	155	10	1
Huddersfield T.	Tr	11.95	95-97	92	1	2

JENKINS Thomas Ernest
Bethnal Green, 2 December, 1947 (OL)

League Club	Source	Date Signed	Seasons Played	Apps	Subs	Gls
Leyton Orient		01.66	65	1	0	0
Reading	Margate	07.69	69	21	0	5
Southampton	Tr	12.69	69-72	84	0	4
Swindon T.	Tr	11.72	72-75	89	11	4

JENKINS Thomas Frederick
Stockton, 5 December, 1925 (IF)

League Club	Source	Date Signed	Seasons Played	Apps	Subs	Gls
Chelsea	Queen of South	07.49	49	5	-	0
Leicester C.	Kettering T.	07.54				

League Club	Source	Date Signed	Seasons Played	Career Record Apps	Subs	Gls
JENKINSON Leigh						
Thorne, 9 July, 1969						(LW)
Hull C.	YT	06.87	87-92	95	35	13
Rotherham U.	L	09.90	90	5	2	0
Coventry C.	Tr	03.93	92-94	22	10	1
Birmingham C.	L	11.93	93	2	1	0
JENNINGS Dennis Bernard						
Kidderminster, 20 July, 1910 Died 1996						(OL/LB)
Huddersfield T.	Kidderminster Hrs	10.30	30-32	33	-	5
Grimsby T.	Tr	09.32	32-35	99	-	29
Birmingham C.	Tr	01.36	35-49	192	-	12
JENNINGS Kentoine (Jed)						
Bermuda, 15 October, 1971 Bermudan Int						(FB)
Hereford U.	Pembroke (Ber)	08.91	91-92	11	5	0
JENNINGS Nicholas						
Wellington (Som), 18 January, 1946						(OL)
Plymouth Arg.	Wellington	08.63	63-66	98	0	11
Portsmouth	Tr	01.67	66-73	198	8	45
Aldershot	L	11.73	73	4	0	1
Exeter C.	Tr	05.74	74-77	119	5	15
JENNINGS Patrick Anthony						
Newry (NI), 12 June, 1945 NI Yth/NIu23-1/NI-119						(G)
Watford	Newry T.	05.63	62-63	48	-	0
Tottenham H.	Tr	06.64	64-76	472	0	0
Arsenal	Tr	08.77	77-84	237	0	0
JENNINGS Roy Thomas Edward						
Swindon, 31 December, 1931 E Yth						(CH)
Brighton & H.A.	Southampton (Am)	05.52	52-63	276	-	22
JENNINGS William John						
Hackney, 20 February, 1952 E Yth						(F)
Watford	Jnrs	04.70	70-74	80	13	33
West Ham U.	Tr	09.74	74-78	89	10	34
Leyton Orient	Tr	08.79	79-81	64	3	21
Luton T.	Tr	03.82	81	0	2	1
JENNINGS Henry **William**						
Norwich, 7 January, 1920 Died 1969						(CF)
Northampton T.		10.38	38-46	11	-	2
Ipswich T.	Tr	05.47	47-50	102	-	41
Rochdale	Tr	06.51	51	3	-	1
Crystal Palace	Tr	09.51				
JENSEN John Faxe						
Denmark, 3 May, 1965 Danish Int						(M)
Arsenal	Brondby (Den)	07.92	92-95	93	5	1
JENSEN Hans **Viggo**						
Denmark, 29 March, 1921 Danish Int						(LB/IF)
Hull C.	Esbjerg (Den)	10.48	48-56	308	-	51
JEPPSON Hans						
Sweden, 10 May, 1925 Swedish Int						(CF)
Charlton Ath. (Am)	Djurgardens (Swe)	01.51	50	11	-	9
JEPSON Arthur						
Selston (Nts), 12 July, 1915 Died 1997						(G)
Mansfield T. (Am)	Newark T.	11.34	34	2	-	0
Port Vale	Grantham	06.38	38	39	-	0
Stoke C.	Tr	09.46	46-47	28	-	0
Lincoln C.	Tr	12.48	48-49	58	-	0
JEPSON Charles **Barry**						
Alfreton, 29 December, 1929						(CF)
Chesterfield	Jnrs	11.48				
Mansfield T.	Ilkeston T.	03.54	53-56	55	-	36
Chester C.	Tr	01.57	56-59	89	-	42
Southport	Tr	11.59	59	24	-	7
JEPSON Ronald Francis						
Stoke, 12 May, 1963						(F)
Port Vale	Nantwich T.	03.89	88-90	12	10	0
Peterborough U.	L	01.90	89	18	0	5
Preston N.E.	Tr	02.91	90-91	36	2	8
Exeter C.	Tr	07.92	92-93	51	3	21
Huddersfield T.	Tr	12.93	93-95	95	12	36
Bury	Tr	07.96	96-97	31	16	9
Oldham Ath.	Tr	01.98	97	9	0	4
JERKAN Nicola						
Croatia, 8 December, 1964 Croatian Int						(D/M)
Nottingham F.	Real Oviedo (Sp)	07.96	96	14	0	0
JERVIS William John						
Liverpool, 22 January, 1942						(OR)
Blackburn Rov.	Jnrs	01.59				
Gillingham	Tr	07.61	61	1	-	0
JESS Eoin						
Aberdeen, 13 December, 1970 Su21-14/S 'B'/S-14						(M)
Coventry C.	Aberdeen	02.96	95-96	28	11	1
JESSOP Thomas **Stanley**						
Liverpool, 5 August, 1932 Died 1996						(F)
Southport	Kidderminster Hrs	08.53	53	11	-	1
JESSOP William						
Preston, 2 April, 1922 Died 1994						(OL)
Preston N.E.	Jnrs	09.40	46	4	-	0
Stockport Co.	Tr	04.47	46-47	17	-	4
Oldham Ath.	Tr	02.48	47-50	94	-	16
Wrexham	Tr	06.51	51	14	-	2
JEST Sydney Thomas						
Ramsgate, 4 June, 1943						(FB)
Brighton & H.A.	Ramsgate	12.61	61-62	12	-	0
JEWELL Paul						
Liverpool, 28 September, 1964						(F/M)
Liverpool	App	09.82				
Wigan Ath	Tr	12.84	84-87	117	20	35
Bradford C.	Tr	07.88	88-96	217	52	56
Grimsby T.	L	08.95	95	2	3	1
JEWELL Ronald Percival						
Plymouth, 6 December, 1920						(OR)
Torquay U.	Plymouth Arg. (Am)	09.46	46	1	-	0
JEZZARD Bedford Alfred George						
Clerkenwell, 19 October, 1927 EF Lge/E 'B'/E-2						(CF)
Fulham	Croxley B.C.	10.48	48-55	292	-	154
JINKS James Thomas						
Camberwell, 19 August, 1916 Died 1981						(CF)
Millwall	Downham Com.	11.38	38-47	45	-	16
Fulham	Tr	08.48	48-49	11	-	3
Luton T.	Tr	03.50	49-50	9	-	2
Aldershot	Tr	09.51	51	5	-	0
JOACHIM Julian Kevin						
Peterborough, 20 September, 1974 E Yth/Eu21-9						(F)
Leicester C.	YT	09.92	92-95	77	22	25
Aston Villa	Tr	02.96	95-97	23	29	13
JOBLING Keith Allen						
Grimsby, 26 March, 1934						(CH)
Grimsby T.	Jnrs	07.53	53-68	450	0	5
JOBLING Kevin Andrew						
Sunderland, 1 January, 1968						(M/LB)
Leicester C.	App	01.86	86-87	4	5	0
Grimsby T.	Tr	02.88	87-97	251	34	10
JOBSON Richard Ian						
Holderness, 9 May, 1963 E'B'						(CD)
Watford	Burton A.	11.82	82-84	26	2	4
Hull C.	Tr	02.85	84-90	219	2	17
Oldham Ath.	Tr	09.90	90-95	188	1	10
Leeds U.	Tr	10.95	95-96	22	0	1
Southend U.	L	01.98	97	8	0	1
Manchester C.	Tr	03.98	97	6	0	1
JOEL Stephen Philip						
Liverpool, 13 October, 1954						(M)
Southport (N/C)	Portmadoc	11.77	77	0	1	0
JOHANNESON Albert Louis						
South Africa, 12 March, 1940 Died 1995						(OL)
Leeds U.	Germiston Callies (SA)	04.61	60-69	170	2	48
York C.	Tr	07.70	70-71	26	0	3
JOHANSEN Martin						
Glostrud, Denmark, 22 July, 1972 Danish Int						(M)
Coventry C.	F.C. Copenhagen (Den)	07.97	97	0	2	0
JOHANSEN Michael Bro						
Denmark, 22 July, 1972 Danish Int						(W)
Bolton W.	F.C. Copenhagen (Den)	08.96	96-97	28	21	6
JOHANSEN Stig						
Norway, 13 June, 1972 Norwegian Int						(F)
Southampton	F.K. Bodo Glimpt (Nor)	08.97	97	3	3	0
Bristol C.	L	02.98	97	2	1	0

JOHN Dennis Carl
Swansea, 27 January, 1935 (FB)

League Club	Source	Date Signed	Seasons Played	Apps	Subs	Gls
Plymouth Arg.	Jnrs	02.52	55-56	3	-	0
Swansea C.	Tr	08.58	58	4	-	0
Scunthorpe U.	Tr	08.59	59-61	88	-	0
Millwall	Tr	06.62	62-65	101	5	6

JOHN Dilwyn
Rhondda, 3 June, 1944 Wu23-1 (G)

League Club	Source	Date Signed	Seasons Played	Apps	Subs	Gls
Cardiff C.	Jnrs	06.61	61-66	88	0	0
Swansea C.	Tr	03.67	66-69	80	0	0

JOHN Malcolm
Bridgend, 9 December, 1950 (F)

League Club	Source	Date Signed	Seasons Played	Apps	Subs	Gls
Bristol Rov.	Swansea C. (Am)	09.71	71-73	4	1	2
Northampton T.	Tr	03.74	73-74	34	7	8

JOHN Raymond Charles
Swansea, 22 November, 1932 (IF/WH)

League Club	Source	Date Signed	Seasons Played	Apps	Subs	Gls
Barnsley	Tottenham H. (Am)	05.53				
Exeter C.	Tr	07.54	54-58	144	-	18
Oldham Ath.	Tr	12.58	58-59	32	-	5

JOHN Stephen Paul
Brentwood, 22 December, 1966 (D)

League Club	Source	Date Signed	Seasons Played	Apps	Subs	Gls
Leyton Orient	App	12.84	85-86	23	0	0

JOHNROSE Leonard
Preston, 29 November, 1969 (M/F)

League Club	Source	Date Signed	Seasons Played	Apps	Subs	Gls
Blackburn Rov.	YT	06.88	87-91	20	22	11
Preston N.E.	L	01.92	91	1	2	1
Hartlepool U.	Tr	02.92	91-93	59	7	11
Bury	Tr	12.93	93-97	155	6	18

JOHNS Mark
Bristol, 17 May, 1959 (F)

League Club	Source	Date Signed	Seasons Played	Apps	Subs	Gls
Bristol Rov. (N/C)	Bristol Manor Farm	09.86	86	2	0	1

JOHNS Nicholas Paul
Bristol, 8 June, 1957 (G)

League Club	Source	Date Signed	Seasons Played	Apps	Subs	Gls
Millwall	Minehead	02.76	76-77	50	0	0
Sheffield U. (L)	Tampa Bay (USA)	09.78	78	1	0	0
Charlton Ath.	Tr	12.78	78-87	288	0	0
Queens Park R.	Tr	12.87	87-88	10	0	0
Maidstone U.	L	10.89	89	2	0	0
Maidstone U.	Tr	03.90	89-90	40	0	0

JOHNS Francis **Stanley**
Liverpool, 28 June, 1924 Died 1985 (IF)

League Club	Source	Date Signed	Seasons Played	Apps	Subs	Gls
West Ham U.	South Liverpool	08.50	50	6	-	2

JOHNSEN Erland
Norway, 5 April, 1967 Norwegian Int (CD)

League Club	Source	Date Signed	Seasons Played	Apps	Subs	Gls
Chelsea	Bayern Munchen (Ger)	11.89	89-96	135	10	1

JOHNSEN Jean **Ronny**
Norway, 10 June, 1969 Norwegian Int (D/M)

League Club	Source	Date Signed	Seasons Played	Apps	Subs	Gls
Manchester U.	Besiktas (Tur)	07.96	96-97	44	9	2

JOHNSON Alan
Stoke, 13 March, 1947 (OR)

League Club	Source	Date Signed	Seasons Played	Apps	Subs	Gls
Port Vale	Jnrs	09.64	65	2	0	1

JOHNSON Alan Keith
Wigan, 19 February, 1971 (CD)

League Club	Source	Date Signed	Seasons Played	Apps	Subs	Gls
Wigan Ath.	YT	03.89	88-93	163	17	13
Lincoln C.	Tr	02.94	93-95	57	6	0
Preston N.E.	L	09.95	95	2	0	0
Rochdale	Tr	08.96	96	46	0	4

JOHNSON Albert
Morpeth, 7 September, 1923 Died 1989 (FB)

League Club	Source	Date Signed	Seasons Played	Apps	Subs	Gls
Bradford C.	Ashington	05.47	46-49	35	-	0

JOHNSON Albert
Weaverham, 15 July, 1920 (OR)

League Club	Source	Date Signed	Seasons Played	Apps	Subs	Gls
Everton	P.C.I.	05.39	46-47	9	-	0
Chesterfield	Tr	09.48	48	19	-	1

JOHNSON Andrew James
Bristol, 2 May, 1974 E Yth (M)

League Club	Source	Date Signed	Seasons Played	Apps	Subs	Gls
Norwich C.	YT	03.92	91-96	56	10	13
Nottingham F.	Tr	07.97	97	24	10	4

JOHNSON Arthur
Liverpool, 23 January, 1933 (G)

League Club	Source	Date Signed	Seasons Played	Apps	Subs	Gls
Blackburn Rov.	Jnrs	01.50	51	1	-	0
Halifax T.	Tr	03.55	54-59	216	-	0
Wrexham	Tr	06.60	60-61	52	-	0
Chester C.	L	08.62	62	3	-	0

JOHNSON Brian
Gateshead, 20 March, 1936 (CF)

League Club	Source	Date Signed	Seasons Played	Apps	Subs	Gls
Millwall		10.57	57	7	-	2

JOHNSON Brian
Newcastle, 12 November, 1948 (OR)

League Club	Source	Date Signed	Seasons Played	Apps	Subs	Gls
Sunderland	App	11.65				
Luton T.	Tr	07.66	66-67	9	1	0

JOHNSON Brian Arthur Bentley
Nantwich, 28 May, 1930 (F)

League Club	Source	Date Signed	Seasons Played	Apps	Subs	Gls
Wrexham		04.50	50-51	14	-	2

JOHNSON Brian Frederick
Isleworth, 21 October, 1955 (W)

League Club	Source	Date Signed	Seasons Played	Apps	Subs	Gls
Plymouth Arg.	App	08.73	73-80	186	11	40
Torquay U.	L	01.79	78	5	0	2
Torquay U.	L	09.81	81	2	0	0

JOHNSON Brian Joseph
Huyton, 29 October, 1948 (M)

League Club	Source	Date Signed	Seasons Played	Apps	Subs	Gls
Tranmere Rov.	Jnrs	05.67	68	0	1	0

JOHNSON Christopher
Brighton, 25 January, 1979 (M)

League Club	Source	Date Signed	Seasons Played	Apps	Subs	Gls
Watford	YT	02.97	96	1	0	0

JOHNSON Damien Michael
Lisburn, 18 November, 1978 NI Yth/NIu21-3 (RW)

League Club	Source	Date Signed	Seasons Played	Apps	Subs	Gls
Blackburn Rov.	YT	02.96				
Nottingham F.	L	01.98	97	5	1	0

JOHNSON David
Blackburn, 17 April, 1950 (G)

League Club	Source	Date Signed	Seasons Played	Apps	Subs	Gls
Tranmere Rov.	Atherstone T.	07.74	74	3	0	0
Southport	L	01.76	75	6	0	0

JOHNSON David
South Shields, 19 November, 1955 E Yth (F)

League Club	Source	Date Signed	Seasons Played	Apps	Subs	Gls
Bristol C.	Doncaster Rov. (Am)	05.74				
Hartlepool U.	Tr	02.75	74	1	0	0

JOHNSON David Alan
Dinnington, 29 October, 1970 (F)

League Club	Source	Date Signed	Seasons Played	Apps	Subs	Gls
Sheffield Wed.	YT	07.89	91	5	1	0
Hartlepool U.	L	10.91	91	7	0	2
Hartlepool U.	L	11.92	92	3	0	0
Lincoln C.	Tr	08.93	93-95	75	14	13

JOHNSON David Anthony
Jamaica (WI), 15 August, 1976 E 'B' (F)

League Club	Source	Date Signed	Seasons Played	Apps	Subs	Gls
Manchester U.	YT	07.94				
Bury	Tr	07.95	95-97	72	25	17
Ipswich T.	Tr	11.97	97	30	1	20

JOHNSON David Donald
Northampton, 10 March, 1967 (LB)

League Club	Source	Date Signed	Seasons Played	Apps	Subs	Gls
Northampton T.	Irthlingboro Diamonds	07.89	89-91	23	25	0

JOHNSON David Edward
Liverpool, 23 October, 1951 E-8 (F)

League Club	Source	Date Signed	Seasons Played	Apps	Subs	Gls
Everton	App	04.69	70-72	47	3	11
Ipswich T.	Tr	11.72	72-75	134	3	35
Liverpool	Tr	08.76	76-81	128	20	55
Everton	Tr	08.82	82-83	32	8	4
Barnsley	L	02.84	83	4	0	1
Manchester C.	Tr	03.84	83	4	2	1
Preston N.E.	Tulsa (USA)	10.84	84	20	4	3

JOHNSON David Nicholas Conrad
Gloucester, 26 December, 1962 (W)

League Club	Source	Date Signed	Seasons Played	Apps	Subs	Gls
Watford	Redhill	03.82	81-83	4	3	0
Peterborough U.	Tr	08.84	84-85	28	7	4

JOHNSON Dennis
Sunderland, 20 May, 1934 (F)

League Club	Source	Date Signed	Seasons Played	Apps	Subs	Gls
Hartlepool U.	Seaham Colly	02.54	57	2	-	0

JOHNSON Eric
Northwich, 25 May, 1927 Died 1992 (WH/W)

League Club	Source	Date Signed	Seasons Played	Apps	Subs	Gls
Coventry C.	Winsford U.	09.52	52-56	91	-	7
Torquay U.	Tr	07.57	57-58	49	-	1

JOHNSON Eric
Birkenhead, 16 December, 1944 (WH)

League Club	Source	Date Signed	Seasons Played	Apps	Subs	Gls
Wrexham	Everton (Am)	06.63	63-65	28	0	0

League Club	Source	Date Signed	Seasons Played	Career Record Apps	Subs	Gls
JOHNSON Gary Jack						
Peckham, 14 September, 1959						(F)
Chelsea	App	09.77	78-80	16	3	9
Brentford	Tr	12.80	80-82	55	5	13
Aldershot	P.G.R. (SA)	08.85	85-87	73	2	20
JOHNSON Gavin						
Stowmarket, 10 October, 1970						(LM)
Ipswich T.	YT	02.89	88-94	114	18	11
Luton T.	Tr	07.95	95	4	1	0
Wigan Ath.	Tr	12.95	95-97	82	2	8
JOHNSON George						
Manchester, 27 April, 1936						(IF)
Rochdale	Gerrards	12.54	54	1	-	0
Southport	Ashton U.	01.63	62	6	-	0
JOHNSON George						
Esh (Dm), 6 October, 1932						(OL)
Lincoln C.	Langley Park Jnrs	09.51	51	3	-	1
JOHNSON Glen William						
Barrow, 7 March, 1952 E Yth						(G)
Arsenal	App	07.69				
Doncaster Rov.	Tr	06.70	70-72	95	0	0
Walsall	L	12.72	72	3	0	0
Aldershot	Tr	07.73	73-82	424	0	0
JOHNSON Glenn Paul						
Australia, 16 July, 1972						(F)
Cardiff C.	Blacktown C. (Aus)	03.96	95	1	4	0
JOHNSON Lloyd **Glenn**						
Canada, 22 April, 1951						(F)
West Bromwich A.	Vancouver (Can)	10.69	71	2	1	0
JOHNSON Ian **Grant**						
Dundee, 24 March, 1972 Su21-6						(M)
Huddersfield T.	Dundee U.	11.97	97	28	1	1
JOHNSON William **Herbert**						
Stockton, 4 June, 1916						(WH)
Charlton Ath.	Spennymoor U.	03.39	46-52	142	-	1
JOHNSON Howard						
Sheffield, 17 July, 1925						(CH)
Sheffield U.	Norton Woodseats	03.51	50-56	92	-	0
York C.	Tr	08.57	57	28	-	0
JOHNSON Ian						
Oldham, 11 November, 1960						(FB)
Rochdale	Chadderton	09.84	84-86	74	7	1
JOHNSON Ian						
Newcastle, 14 February, 1969						(CD)
Northampton T.	Gateshead	11.87	88	2	1	0
Torquay U.	Whitley Bay	11.92	92	9	0	1
JOHNSON Ian						
Sunderland, 1 September, 1975						(W)
Middlesbrough	YT	01.94	93	1	1	0
Bradford C.	Tr	01.95	94	1	1	0
JOHNSON James						
Stockton, 26 February, 1923 Died 1987						(CF)
Grimsby T.	York C. (Am)	03.45	46-49	6	-	1
Carlisle U.	Tr	03.51	50	8	-	0
JOHNSON Jeffrey						
Manchester, 29 October, 1950 E Semi Pro						(M)
Stockport Co.	Hyde U.	09.76	76	6	2	0
JOHNSON Jeffrey David						
Cardiff, 26 November, 1953 W Sch						(M)
Manchester C.	App	12.70	70-71	4	2	0
Swansea C.	L	07.72	72	37	2	4
Crystal Palace	Tr	12.73	73-75	82	5	4
Sheffield Wed.	Tr	07.76	76-80	175	5	6
Newport Co.	Tr	08.81	81	34	0	2
Gillingham	Tr	09.82	82-84	85	3	4
Port Vale	Tr	07.85	85	10	0	1
JOHNSON John (Jack)						
Hazel Grove, 11 December, 1921						(OR)
Stockport Co.	Tr	01.41				
Millwall	Tr	12.45	46-56	309	-	46
JOHNSON John						
South Shields, 4 February, 1929						(F)
Manchester C.		05.49				
Gateshead	North Shields	01.51	50-54	73	-	13
JOHNSON John William						
Newcastle, 12 February, 1919 Died 1975						(OR)
Huddersfield T.	Leicester Nomads	06.36	36-38	18	-	2
Grimsby T.	Tr	04.39	46-47	44	-	2
JOHNSON Joseph						
South Kirkby, 16 May, 1916						(RH)
Doncaster Rov.	Scarborough	12.38				
Southport	Folkestone T.	12.46	46	5	-	0
JOHNSON Joseph Robert						
Greenock, 13 September, 1920						(IF)
Lincoln C.	Glasgow Rangers	11.52	52	11	-	2
Workington	Tr	07.53	53	38	-	5
JOHNSON Kenneth						
Hartlepool, 15 February, 1931						(IF)
Hartlepool U.	Seaton H.T.	05.49	49-63	384	-	98
JOHNSON Kevin Peter						
Doncaster, 29 August, 1952						(M)
Sheffield Wed.	App	07.70	70	0	1	0
Southend U.	Tr	09.72	72-73	13	4	1
Gillingham	L	02.74	73	1	0	0
Workington	Tr	07.74	74	15	0	1
Hartlepool U.	Tr	02.75	74-76	60	1	8
Huddersfield T.	Tr	09.76	76-77	80	1	23
Halifax T.	Tr	08.78	78-80	51	6	10
Hartlepool U.	Tr	01.81	80-83	74	13	3
JOHNSON Marvin Anthony						
Wembley, 29 October, 1968						(CD)
Luton T.	App	12.86	87-97	246	14	6
JOHNSON Michael						
York, 4 October, 1933						(W)
Newcastle U.	Jnrs	04.51				
Brighton & H.A.	Blyth Spartans	12.55	56	2	-	0
Fulham	Gloucester C.	08.58	58-61	23	-	6
Doncaster Rov.	Tr	07.62	62	15	-	2
Barrow	Tr	03.63	62	12	-	1
JOHNSON Michael George						
Swansea, 13 October, 1941 Wu23-2/W-1						(CH)
Swansea C.	Jnrs	10.58	59-65	167	0	1
JOHNSON Michael James						
Oxford, 24 February, 1928						(IF)
Preston N.E.	Lytham St Annes	09.50				
Accrington St.	Tr	06.51	51	3	-	0
JOHNSON Michael Owen						
Nottingham, 4 July, 1973						(CD)
Notts Co.	YT	07.91	91-94	102	5	0
Birmingham C.	Tr	09.95	95-97	81	25	3
JOHNSON Neil Joseph						
Grimsby, 3 December, 1946						(W)
Tottenham H.	App	06.64	65-70	27	7	5
Charlton Ath.	L	02.71	70	1	0	0
Torquay U.	Tr	07.71	71	5	1	1
JOHNSON Nigel Meridon						
Rotherham, 23 June, 1964						(CD)
Rotherham U.	App	08.82	82-84	89	0	1
Manchester C.	Tr	06.85	85	4	0	0
Rotherham U.	Tr	07.87	87-92	172	3	9
JOHNSON Owen Edmund						
Grimsby, 13 November, 1919						(OL)
Derby Co.		11.37				
Bradford C.	Tr	10.46	46	10	-	1
JOHNSON Paul						
Stoke, 25 May, 1959						(LB)
Stoke C.	App	05.77	78-80	33	1	0
Shrewsbury T.	Tr	05.81	81-86	178	2	3
York C.	Tr	07.87	87-88	83	0	1
JOHNSON Paul						
Scunthorpe, 10 May, 1963						(G)
Scunthorpe U.	App	05.81	81	2	0	0
Scunthorpe U. (N/C)		01.85	85	12	0	0

League Club	Source	Date Signed	Seasons Played	Apps	Subs	Gls
JOHNSON Paul Anthony						
Stoke, 19 September, 1955						(M)
Stoke C.	App	06.73	76-81	51	5	0
Chester C.	Tr	08.82	82	18	1	0
JOHNSON Peter						
Rotherham, 31 July, 1931						(RB)
Rotherham U.	Rawmarsh Welfare	03.53	53-57	153	-	23
Sheffield Wed.	Tr	12.57	57-64	181	-	6
Peterborough U.	Tr	07.65	65-66	42	0	1
JOHNSON Peter Edward						
Harrogate, 5 October, 1958						(LB)
Middlesbrough	App	10.76	77-79	42	1	0
Newcastle U.	Tr	10.80	80	16	0	0
Bristol C.	L	09.82	82	20	0	0
Doncaster Rov.	Tr	03.83	82	12	0	0
Darlington	Tr	08.83	83-84	89	0	2
Crewe Alex. (N/C)	Whitby T.	10.85	85	8	0	0
Exeter C. (N/C)	Whitby T.	03.86	85	5	0	0
Southend U.	Tr	08.86	86-88	126	0	3
Gillingham	Tr	08.89	89-90	67	2	2
Peterborough U. (N/C)		10.91	91	11	0	0
JOHNSON Peter James						
Hackney, 18 February, 1954						(W)
Leyton Orient	Tottenham H. (Am)	04.72	71-72	1	2	0
Crystal Palace	Greece	10.74	74-75	5	2	0
Bournemouth	Tr	06.76	76-78	99	8	11
JOHNSON Victor **Ralph**						
Hethersett (Nk), 15 April, 1922						(CF)
Norwich C.	Chesterfield (Am)	05.46	46	18	-	8
Leyton Orient	Tr	04.47	47-48	7	-	2
JOHNSON Richard Mark						
Australia, 27 April, 1974						(M)
Watford	YT	05.92	91-97	144	20	13
JOHNSON Richard (Dick) Raymond						
Liverpool, 20 February, 1953						(G)
Tranmere Rov.	Jnrs	08.72	71-81	355	0	0
JOHNSON Robert Emmerson Oliver						
Fencehouses (Dm), 25 October, 1911 Died 1982						(CH)
Burnley	Bishop Auckland	09.34	34-48	78	-	0
JOHNSON Robert Nicholas						
Kensington, 30 March, 1962						(D)
Arsenal	App	02.80				
Brentford	Tr	03.81	80-81	2	0	0
JOHNSON Robert (Rob) Simon						
Bedford, 22 February, 1962						(FB)
Luton T.	App	08.79	83-88	91	6	0
Lincoln C.	L	08.83	83	4	0	0
Leicester C.	Tr	08.89	89-90	19	6	0
Barnet (N/C)	Tr	08.91	91	2	0	0
JOHNSON Rodney						
Leeds, 8 January, 1945 E Yth						(M/F)
Leeds U.	Jnrs	03.62	62-67	18	4	4
Doncaster Rov.	Tr	03.68	67-70	106	1	23
Rotherham U.	Tr	12.70	70-73	108	2	8
Bradford C.	Tr	12.73	73-78	190	2	16
JOHNSON Ross Yorke						
Brighton, 2 January, 1976						(CD)
Brighton & H.A.	YT	07.94	93-97	79	10	0
JOHNSON Roy						
Swindon, 18 May, 1933						(CF)
Swindon T.		04.52	52-55	31	-	4
JOHNSON Samuel						
Barnton, 10 February, 1919						(RB)
Hull C.	Northwich Vic.	04.47	46-47	10	-	0
JOHNSON Seth Art Maurice						
Birmingham, 12 March, 1979 E Yth						(FB)
Crewe Alex.	YT	07.96	96-97	47	4	2
JOHNSON Stephen Anthony						
Liverpool, 23 June, 1957						(F)
Bury	Altrincham	11.77	77-82	139	15	52
Rochdale	Tr	08.83	83	17	2	7
Wigan Ath.	Tr	02.84	83-84	50	1	18
Bristol C.	Tr	03.85	84-85	14	7	3
Rochdale	L	12.85	85	3	3	1
Chester C.	L	03.86	85	10	0	6
Scunthorpe U.	Tr	07.86	86-87	59	13	20
Chester C.	Tr	08.88	88	35	3	10
Rochdale	Huskvarna (Swe)	10.89	89	20	4	4
JOHNSON Steven						
Nottingham, 23 March, 1961						(LB)
Mansfield T.	App	03.79	80	1	0	0
JOHNSON Terence						
Newcastle, 30 August, 1949						(W)
Newcastle U.	Longbenton Jnrs	05.67				
Darlington	L	11.69	69	4	0	1
Southend U.	Tr	01.71	70-74	155	2	35
Brentford	Tr	11.74	74-76	98	3	27
JOHNSON Thomas (Tucker)						
Gateshead, 21 September, 1921						(IF)
Gateshead		09.41	46-47	52	-	19
Nottingham F.	Tr	08.48	48-51	68	-	27
JOHNSON Thomas						
Stockton, 5 March, 1926						(LH)
Middlesbrough		01.45				
Darlington	Tr	08.47	47	6	-	1
Bradford P.A.		08.52	52	1	-	0
JOHNSON Thomas						
Ecclesfield, 4 May, 1911 Died 1983						(CH)
Sheffield U.	Ecclesfield	09.28	29-38	182	-	0
Lincoln C.	Tr	03.46	46-48	75	-	0
JOHNSON Thomas						
Newcastle, 15 January, 1971 Eu21-7						(F)
Notts Co.	YT	01.89	88-91	100	18	47
Derby Co.	Tr	03.92	91-94	91	7	30
Aston Villa	Tr	01.95	94-96	38	19	13
JOHNSTON Alan Keith						
Workington, 23 September, 1944						(FB)
Blackpool	Jnrs	10.61				
Workington	Tr	07.62	62-64	65	-	0
JOHNSTON Allan						
Glasgow, 14 December, 1973 Su21-3/S 'B'						(W)
Sunderland	Rennes (Fr)	03.97	96-97	42	4	12
JOHNSTON Clement						
Stoneyburn, 3 September, 1933						(IF)
Walsall	Haddington	08.56	56	7	-	1
JOHNSTON Craig Peter						
South Africa, 25 June, 1960 Eu21-2						(F/W)
Middlesbrough	App	02.78	77-80	61	3	16
Liverpool	Tr	04.81	81-87	165	25	30
JOHNSTON David Douglas						
Scothern (Lincs), 17 September, 1941						(FB)
Leicester C.	Bishop Auckland	02.60				
Exeter C.	Tr	05.62	62	10	-	0
Stockport Co.	Tr	07.63	63	26	-	0
JOHNSTON George						
Glasgow, 21 March, 1947						(F)
Cardiff C.	Jnrs	05.64	64-66	57	3	21
Arsenal	Tr	03.67	67-68	17	4	3
Birmingham C.	Tr	05.69	69	6	3	1
Walsall	L	09.70	70	5	0	1
Fulham	Tr	10.70	70-71	33	6	12
Hereford U.	Tr	08.72	72	15	3	5
Newport Co.	Tr	09.73	73	2	1	0
JOHNSTON Henry (Harry)						
Manchester, 26 September, 1919 Died 1973 EF Lge/E-10						(CH)
Blackpool	Droylsden Ath.	10.36	37-54	386	-	11
JOHNSTON Ian						
Workington, 19 September, 1957						(CD)
Workington	Jnrs	08.75	74-76	46	2	0
JOHNSTON James						
Aberdeen, 12 April, 1923						(WH)
Leicester C.	Aberdeen	04.47	48-49	35	-	0
Reading	Tr	05.50	50-52	120	-	0
Swindon T.	Tr	03.53	52-54	75	-	0
JOHNSTON John						
Belfast, 2 May, 1947 NIu23-1						(M)
Blackpool	Glentoran	11.68	68-71	19	5	2

League Club	Source	Date Signed	Seasons Played	Apps	Subs	Gls
Halifax T.	L	10.71	71	3	1	1
Bradford C.	Tr	07.72	72-73	55	4	4
Southport	Tr	07.74	74-75	82	0	6
Halifax T.	Tr	07.76	76-78	67	6	7
JOHNSTON Leslie Hamilton						
Glasgow, 16 August, 1920 S-2						(IF)
Stoke C.	Glasgow Celtic	10.49	49-52	88	-	22
Shrewsbury T.	Tr	07.53	53	16	-	6
JOHNSTON Maurice (Mo) John Giblin						
Glasgow, 30 April, 1963 Su21-3/S-38						(F)
Watford	Partick Thistle	11.83	83-84	37	1	23
Everton	Glasgow Rangers	11.91	91-92	28	6	10
JOHNSTON Christopher **Patrick (Paddy)**						
Dublin, 16 July, 1924 Died 1971 LoI						(WH)
Middlesbrough	Shelbourne	12.47	47-48	3	-	0
Grimsby T.	Tr	02.49	48-56	250	-	16
JOHNSTON Robert						
Carlisle, 28 January, 1933						(WH)
Carlisle U.	Jnrs	11.51	51-59	120	-	1
JOHNSTON Ronald						
Glasgow, 3 April, 1921 Died 1995						(CF)
Rochdale	Glasgow Perthshire	11.47	47	17	-	7
Exeter C.	Tr	06.48	48	10	-	2
Brighton & H.A.	Headington U.	11.50	50	1	-	0
JOHNSTON Stanley						
Wallsend, 23 February, 1934						(F)
Fulham	Jnrs	08.51				
Gateshead	Durham C.	09.54	54	10	-	1
JOHNSTON Thomas Bourhill						
Loanhead, 18 August, 1927						(CF)
Darlington	Kilmarnock	04.51	51	27	-	9
Oldham Ath.	Tr	03.52	51	5	-	3
Norwich C.	Tr	06.52	52-54	60	-	28
Newport Co.	Tr	10.54	54-55	63	-	46
Leyton Orient	Tr	02.56	55-57	87	-	70
Blackburn Rov.	Tr	03.58	57-58	36	-	21
Leyton Orient	Tr	02.59	58-60	93	-	51
Gillingham	Tr	09.61	61	35	-	10
JOHNSTON Thomas Deans						
Coldstream, 30 December, 1918 Died 1994						(LH/OL)
Nottingham F.	Peterborough U.	05.44	46-47	64	-	26
Notts Co.	Tr	08.48	48-56	267	-	88
JOHNSTON William						
						(G)
Barrow	Morton	04.47	46	1	-	0
JOHNSTON William Cecil						
Dungannon, 21 May, 1942 NI-2						(IF)
Oldham Ath.	Glenavon	06.66	66-68	28	1	6
JOHNSTON William James						
Sunderland, 3 September, 1948						(F)
Northampton T.	Durham C.	07.67	67	0	1	0
JOHNSTON William McClure						
Glasgow, 19 December, 1946 Su23-2/SF Lge/S-22						(W)
West Bromwich A.	Glasgow Rangers	12.72	72-78	203	4	18
Birmingham C.	Vancouver (Can)	10.79	79	15	0	0
JOHNSTONE Cyril						
Hamilton, 21 December, 1920						(FB)
Exeter C.	Hamilton Academical	07.47	47-50	134	-	0
JOHNSTONE Derek Joseph						
Dundee, 4 November, 1953 Su23-6/S-14						(F)
Chelsea	Glasgow Rangers	09.83	83-84	1	3	0
JOHNSTONE Eric						
Newcastle, 22 March, 1943						(OL)
Carlisle U.	Tow Law T.	06.63	63-64	15	-	3
Darlington	Tr	07.65	65-66	27	1	10
JOHNSTONE Glenn Paul						
Kenya, 5 June, 1967						(G)
Preston N.E.	Lancaster C.	01.93	92	10	0	0
JOHNSTONE Ian Donaldson						
Galashiels, 2 March, 1939						(IF)
Colchester U.	Ormiston Primrose	06.58	58-59	2	-	0

League Club	Source	Date Signed	Seasons Played	Apps	Subs	Gls
JOHNSTONE James Connolly						
Uddingston, 30 September, 1944 Su23-2/SF Lge/S-23						(W)
Sheffield U.	Glasgow Celtic	11.75	75-76	11	0	2
JOHNSTONE Robert						
Cleland, 13 September, 1918						(WH)
Tranmere Rov.	Raith Rov.	09.46	46-47	40	-	0
JOHNSTONE Robert						
Selkirk, 7 September, 1929 SF Lge/S-17						(IF)
Manchester C.	Hibernian	03.55	54-59	124	-	42
Oldham Ath.	Hibernian	10.60	60-64	143	-	36
JOHNSTONE Robert Gordon						
Edinburgh, 19 November, 1934						(WH)
West Ham U.	Ormiston Primrose	04.53	56	2	-	0
Ipswich T.	Tr	07.57	57-58	35	-	4
JOHNSTONE Stanley						
Shiremoor, 28 October, 1940						
Gateshead	Durham C.	12.58	58	5	-	1
JOICEY Brian						
Blaydon, 19 December, 1945						(F)
Coventry C.	North Shields	06.69	69-71	31	8	9
Sheffield Wed.	Tr	08.71	71-75	144	1	48
Barnsley	Tr	07.76	76-78	77	16	43
JOL Maarten Cornelius						
Netherlands, 16 January, 1956						(M)
West Bromwich A.	Twente Enschede (Neth)	10.81	81-83	63	1	4
Coventry C.	Tr	07.84	84	15	0	0
JOLLEY Charles						
Bebington, 3 March, 1936 E Yth						(CF)
Tranmere Rov.	Liverpool (Am)	07.53	53-54	6	-	2
Chester C.	Tr	05.55	55	7	-	3
JOLLEY Terence Arthur						
Greenhithe, 13 April, 1959						(F)
Gillingham	Jnrs	11.76	76-79	14	7	5
JONES Alan						
Abermodda, 13 January, 1944						(OR)
Wrexham		07.64	64	2	-	0
JONES Alan						
Grimethorpe, 21 January, 1951						(W)
Huddersfield T.	App	12.68	70-72	30	2	0
Halifax T.	Tr	08.73	73-76	109	0	6
Chesterfield	Tr	09.76	76-77	39	0	5
Lincoln C.	Tr	11.77	77-78	24	2	4
Bradford C.	Tr	09.79	79	16	3	1
Rochdale	Tr	08.80	80	40	4	5
JONES Alan Hugh						
Wrexham, 22 September, 1949 W Sch						(CH)
Shrewsbury T.	App	05.67	68	3	0	0
JONES Alan Michael						
Swansea, 6 October, 1945						(CD)
Swansea C.	App	10.63	64-67	59	0	5
Hereford U.	Tr	07.68	72-73	52	1	2
Southport	Tr	08.74	74-75	49	0	2
JONES Alan William Edward						
Edmonton, 19 September, 1940						(CF)
Fulham	Jnrs	04.58	59	7	-	3
JONES John **Alan**						
Wrexham, 12 September, 1939						(G)
Cardiff C.	Druids	06.57	57	1	-	0
Exeter C.	Tr	07.59	59-61	90	-	0
Norwich C.	Tr	07.62	62	9	-	0
Wrexham	Tr	08.63	63	18	-	0
JONES Alexander						
Blackburn, 27 November, 1964						(CD)
Oldham Ath.	App	12.82	82-84	7	1	0
Stockport Co.	L	10.84	84	3	0	0
Preston N.E.	Tr	06.86	86-89	100	1	3
Carlisle U.	Tr	09.89	89-90	62	0	4
Rochdale	Tr	06.91	91	12	1	0
Rochdale	Motherwell	10.92	92-93	31	2	2
JONES Alfred						
Liverpool, 2 March, 1937						(FB)
Leeds U.	Marine	04.60	60-61	25	-	0
Lincoln C.	Tr	06.62	62-66	179	1	3

League Club	Source	Date Signed	Seasons Played	Apps	Subs	Gls
JONES Allan Powell						
Flint, 6 January, 1940 W Sch						(FB)
Liverpool	Jnrs	05.57	59-62	5	-	0
Brentford	Tr	08.63	63-69	244	5	3
JONES Allan Raymond						
Burton, 3 November, 1941						(W)
Aston Villa	Jnrs	11.58	61	1	-	0
JONES Andrew Mark						
Wrexham, 9 January, 1963 W-6						(F)
Port Vale	Rhyl	06.85	85-87	87	3	49
Charlton Ath.	Tr	09.87	87-90	51	15	15
Port Vale	L	02.89	88	8	9	3
Bristol C.	L	11.89	89	2	2	1
Bournemouth	Tr	10.90	90-91	36	4	8
Leyton Orient	Tr	10.91	91-92	44	15	13
JONES Anthony Peter						
Birmingham, 12 November, 1937						(IF/WH)
Oxford U.	Birmingham C. (Am)	09.59	62-67	226	0	42
Newport Co.	Tr	11.67	67-68	53	1	9
JONES Arthur						
Harphurey,						(OR)
Rochdale	Goslings	06.45	46	1	-	0
JONES Barrie						
Barnsley, 31 October, 1938						(CF)
Notts Co.		09.61	61-63	42	-	15
JONES Barrie Spencer						
Swansea, 10 October, 1941 Wu23-8/W-15						(OR)
Swansea C.	Jnrs	04.59	59-64	166	-	23
Plymouth Arg.	Tr	09.64	64-66	98	1	9
Cardiff C.	Tr	03.67	66-69	107	0	18
JONES Barry						
Prescot, 30 June, 1970						(D)
Liverpool	Prescot Cables	01.89				
Wrexham	Tr	07.92	92-97	184	11	5
York C.	Tr	12.97	97	23	0	2
JONES Thomas **Benjamin**						
Frodsham, 23 March, 1920 Died 1972						(W)
Tranmere Rov.	Ellesmere Port	09.41	46-47	54	-	19
Chelsea	Tr	11.47	47-51	55	-	11
Accrington St.	Tr	07.53	53	14	-	0
JONES Bernard						
Coventry, 10 April, 1934						(IF)
Northampton T.		10.52	53-55	43	-	16
Cardiff C.	Tr	03.56	55-56	9	-	0
Shrewsbury T.	Tr	07.57	57-58	43	-	15
JONES Bernard						
Stoke, 27 September, 1924						(W)
Port Vale	Longport	10.48	48	6	-	0
JONES Brian (Bryn)						
Barnsley, 15 September, 1938						(FB)
Barnsley	Jnrs	05.57	57-58	14	-	0
York C.	Tr	05.59	59	1	-	0
JONES Brian						
Doncaster, 5 September, 1933						(D)
Walsall		11.53	53	2	-	0
JONES Bryn Edward						
Flint, 26 May, 1939						(FB)
Watford	Holywell	01.63	62	2	-	0
Chester C.	Tr	08.64	64-66	30	0	0
JONES Brynley						
Llandrindod Wells, 8 February, 1948 W Sch/Wu23-1						(M)
Cardiff C.	App	02.66	66-67	1	2	0
Newport Co.	L	02.69	68	13	0	0
Bristol Rov.	Tr	06.69	69-74	84	6	6
JONES Brynley						
St Asaph, 16 May, 1959						(M)
Chester C.	App	05.77	76-81	149	13	17
JONES Brynley Roy						
Swansea, 20 May, 1931 Died 1990						(FB)
Swansea C.	Jnrs	09.51	52-57	121	-	4
Newport Co.	Tr	06.58	58-59	71	-	11
Bournemouth	Tr	02.60	59-63	118	-	5
Northampton T.	Tr	10.63	63	7	-	0
Watford	Tr	11.63	63-66	90	1	1

League Club	Source	Date Signed	Seasons Played	Apps	Subs	Gls
JONES Brynmor						
Merthyr Tydfil, 14 February, 1912 Died 1985 W-17						(IF)
Wolverhampton W.	Aberaman	10.33	33-37	163	-	52
Arsenal	Tr	08.38	38-48	71	-	7
Norwich C.	Tr	06.49	49	23	-	1
JONES Christopher Harry						
Jersey, 18 April, 1956 Eu21-1						(F)
Tottenham H.	App	05.73	74-81	149	15	37
Manchester C.	Tr	09.82	82	3	0	0
Crystal Palace	Tr	11.82	82	18	0	3
Charlton Ath.	Tr	09.83	83	17	6	2
Leyton Orient	Tr	09.84	84-86	106	1	19
JONES Christopher Martin Nigel						
Altrincham, 19 November, 1945						(F)
Manchester C.	Jnrs	05.64	66-67	6	1	2
Swindon T.	Tr	07.68	68-71	49	19	18
Oldham Ath.	L	01.72	71	3	0	1
Walsall	Tr	02.72	71-72	54	5	14
York C.	Tr	06.73	73-75	94	1	33
Huddersfield T.	Tr	08.76	76	9	5	2
Doncaster Rov.	Tr	07.77	77-78	14	6	4
Darlington	L	01.78	77	14	2	3
Rochdale	Tr	12.78	78-79	51	5	19
JONES Clifford William						
Swansea, 7 February, 1935 Wu23-1/EF Lge/W-59						(W)
Swansea C.	Jnrs	05.52	52-57	168	-	47
Tottenham H.	Tr	02.58	57-68	314	4	135
Fulham	Tr	10.68	68-69	23	2	2
JONES Cobi N'Gai						
U.S.A., 16 June, 1970 USA Int						(W)
Coventry C.	U.S.S.F. (USA)	09.94	94	16	5	2
JONES Colin Malcolm						
Birmingham, 30 October, 1963						(W)
West Bromwich A.	App	10.81				
Mansfield T. (N/C)		01.85	84	5	0	0
JONES George **Colin**						
Chester, 8 September, 1940						(WH)
Chester C.	Jnrs	03.60	59	3	-	0
JONES Cyril						
Rhos, 17 July, 1920 Died 1995						(RB)
Wrexham	Johnstown	02.42	46	29	-	0
JONES David						
Blaenau Ffestiniog, 8 September, 1914						(G)
Stoke C.	Colwyn Bay U.	03.37	38	1	-	0
Carlisle U.	Tr	05.39	46-47	66	-	0
JONES David						
Wrexham, 6 May, 1971 W Sch						(W)
Aston Villa	YT	06.89				
Wrexham	Tr	01.92	91	0	1	0
JONES David						
Whitwell (Dby), 9 April, 1914						(WH)
Bury	Worksop T.	08.34	34-49	257	-	12
JONES David						
Orpington, 3 March, 1935						(G)
Swansea C.		12.55	56-57	3	-	0
JONES David						
Aberdare, 7 January, 1932						(G)
Brentford	Dover T.	12.51				
Reading	Tr	07.53	53-60	215	-	0
Aldershot	Tr	07.61	61-65	187	0	0
JONES David						
Harrow, 3 July, 1964						(F)
Chelsea	New Zealand	11.87				
Bury (N/C)	Barnet	09.88	88	0	1	0
Leyton Orient (N/C)	Barnet	12.88	88	0	2	0
Burnley (N/C)	Barnet	02.89	88	4	0	0
Ipswich T. (N/C)	U.S.A.	10.89				
Doncaster Rov.	Tr	11.89	89-90	34	6	14
Bury	Tr	09.91	91	0	9	0
Hull C.		02.93	92	11	1	1
JONES David (Dai) Albert Brynmawr						
Neath, 31 March, 1941 W Yth						(F)
Millwall	Ton Pentre	03.64	63-64	12	-	3
Newport Co.	Tr	07.65	65-67	81	0	25
Mansfield T.	Tr	11.67	67-71	116	14	32
Newport Co.	Tr	11.71	71-73	43	4	12

JONES David Edward
Chester, 5 March, 1936 (OL)

League Club	Source	Date Signed	Seasons Played	Apps	Subs	Gls
Wrexham	Saltney	04.55	56-58	71	-	11
Crewe Alex.	Tr	07.59	59	1	-	1

JONES David Edward
Gosport, 11 February,1952 Wu23-4/W-8 (CD)

League Club	Source	Date Signed	Seasons Played	Apps	Subs	Gls
Bournemouth	App	01.70	70-74	128	6	5
Nottingham F.	Tr	08.74	74	36	0	1
Norwich C.	Tr	09.75	75-79	120	3	4

JONES David Frederick
Brixham, 18 May, 1950 (M)

League Club	Source	Date Signed	Seasons Played	Apps	Subs	Gls
Arsenal	App	02.68				
Oxford U.	Middlesbrough (trial)	10.68	68-70	17	4	0
Torquay U.	Tr	07.72	72	0	1	0

JONES David Henry
Tetbury, 4 August, 1937 (WH/LB)

League Club	Source	Date Signed	Seasons Played	Apps	Subs	Gls
Leeds U.	Gloucester C.	12.54				
Crewe Alex.	Tr	05.60	60	14	-	0

JONES David Hillary
Bradford, 29 December, 1950 (W)

League Club	Source	Date Signed	Seasons Played	Apps	Subs	Gls
Wolverhampton W.		08.68				
York C.	Tr	08.70	70	3	0	0

JONES David John
Ruabon, 16 September, 1952 (F)

League Club	Source	Date Signed	Seasons Played	Apps	Subs	Gls
Hereford U.	Telford U.	05.78	78-79	44	3	11

JONES David (Dai) Owen
Cardiff, 28 October, 1910 Died 1971 W-7 (FB)

League Club	Source	Date Signed	Seasons Played	Apps	Subs	Gls
Leyton Orient	Ebbw Vale	08.31	31-32	55	-	0
Leicester C.	Tr	05.33	32-46	226	-	4
Mansfield T.	Tr	10.47	47-48	74	-	0

JONES David Richard
Onllwyn (Glam), 18 January, 1946 (G)

League Club	Source	Date Signed	Seasons Played	Apps	Subs	Gls
Derby Co.		07.65				
Newport Co.	Burton A.	05.68	67-68	3	0	0

JONES David Ronald
Liverpool, 17 August, 1956 E Yth/Eu21-1 (CD)

League Club	Source	Date Signed	Seasons Played	Apps	Subs	Gls
Everton	App	05.74	75-78	79	7	1
Coventry C.	Tr	06.79	79-80	8	3	0
Preston N.E.	Seiko (HK)	08.83	83-84	50	0	1

JONES David Wilmott Llewellyn
Runcorn, 9 April, 1940 E Yth (IF)

League Club	Source	Date Signed	Seasons Played	Apps	Subs	Gls
Crewe Alex. (Am)	Jnrs	05.56	56	10	-	1
Birmingham C.	Tr	04.57	57-58	9	-	0
Millwall	Tr	12.59	59-63	165	-	71

JONES Denys John
Aberdare, 19 October, 1930 (OR)

League Club	Source	Date Signed	Seasons Played	Apps	Subs	Gls
Norwich C.	Yarmouth T.	04.51	51-52	5	-	2

JONES Frederick William **Derek**
Ellesmere Port, 24 April, 1929 (FB)

League Club	Source	Date Signed	Seasons Played	Apps	Subs	Gls
Tranmere Rov.	Ellesmere Port	07.53	53-60	155	-	19

JONES Desmond
Rhondda, 15 March, 1930 Died 1987 (W)

League Club	Source	Date Signed	Seasons Played	Apps	Subs	Gls
Swansea C.	Jnrs	01.48				
Bristol Rov.	Tr	06.52	52	6	-	0
Workington	Tr	07.54	54-59	210	-	23

JONES Dilwyn Bowen
Swansea, 2 January, 1937 (WH)

League Club	Source	Date Signed	Seasons Played	Apps	Subs	Gls
Leeds U.	Jnrs	01.54				
Crewe Alex.	Tr	02.58	57-58	19	-	1

JONES Edward William George
Finchley, 17 September, 1952 W Sch (FB)

League Club	Source	Date Signed	Seasons Played	Apps	Subs	Gls
Tottenham H.	Jnrs	10.70				
Millwall	Tr	07.73	73-75	58	1	0

JONES Edwin Morris
Abercynon, 20 March, 1914 Died 1984 W Sch (OR)

League Club	Source	Date Signed	Seasons Played	Apps	Subs	Gls
Bolton W. (Am)	Abercynon	04.33	33	1	-	1
Swindon T.	Tr	05.36	36-46	124	-	18

JONES Eric
Ulverston, 23 June, 1931 (W)

League Club	Source	Date Signed	Seasons Played	Apps	Subs	Gls
Preston N.E.	Notts Co. (Am)	01.52	53-54	13	-	0
Nottingham F.	Tr	09.55	55-57	18	-	3
Doncaster Rov.	Tr	03.58	57-58	15	-	2
Accrington St.	Tr	07.59	59	18	-	0
Southport	Tr	07.60	60-61	76	-	18

JONES Eric John
Dover, 5 March, 1938 (HB)

League Club	Source	Date Signed	Seasons Played	Apps	Subs	Gls
Coventry C.	Snowdown Colly	05.55	55-60	14	-	0

JONES Eric Norman
Birmingham, 5 February, 1915 Died 1985 (W)

League Club	Source	Date Signed	Seasons Played	Apps	Subs	Gls
Wolverhampton W.	Kidderminster Hrs	10.36	36	3	-	0
Portsmouth	Tr	11.37	37	1	-	0
Stoke C.	Tr	09.38				
West Bromwich A.	Tr	05.39				
Brentford	Tr	12.45				
Crewe Alex.	Tr	07.46	46-47	53	-	14

JONES Ernest
Ruabon, 9 December, 1919 (F)

League Club	Source	Date Signed	Seasons Played	Apps	Subs	Gls
Chester C.	Bangor C.	08.49	49-50	6	-	1

JONES Ernest
Bristol, 12 May, 1919 (LH)

League Club	Source	Date Signed	Seasons Played	Apps	Subs	Gls
Bristol C.	Jnrs	08.39	46-47	27	-	1

JONES William **Ernest** Arthur
Swansea, 12 November, 1920 W-4 (W)

League Club	Source	Date Signed	Seasons Played	Apps	Subs	Gls
Swansea C.	Bolton W. (Am)	10.43	46	37	-	3
Tottenham H.	Tr	06.47	46-48	56	-	14
Southampton	Tr	05.49	49-51	44	-	4
Bristol C.	Tr	11.51	51-53	50	-	7

JONES Frank
Llandudno, 3 October, 1960 Wu21-1 (D)

League Club	Source	Date Signed	Seasons Played	Apps	Subs	Gls
Wrexham	Jnrs	07.79	78-80	8	0	0
Wrexham	Finland	09.84	84-86	30	1	0

JONES Frederick Arthur
Stoke, 21 October, 1922 Died 1989 (RB)

League Club	Source	Date Signed	Seasons Played	Apps	Subs	Gls
Port Vale	South Liverpool	06.46	46	12	-	1

JONES Frederick George
Gelligaer, 11 January, 1938 Wu23-2 (OL)

League Club	Source	Date Signed	Seasons Played	Apps	Subs	Gls
Arsenal	Hereford U.	01.58				
Brighton & H.A.	Tr	09.58	58-60	69	-	14
Swindon T.	Tr	12.60	60	18	-	1
Grimsby T.	Tr	07.61	61-62	58	-	9
Reading	Tr	07.63	63	30	-	5

JONES Gareth Anthony
Cardiff, 18 June, 1952 (W)

League Club	Source	Date Signed	Seasons Played	Apps	Subs	Gls
Torquay U.		10.72	72-73	11	5	0
Bournemouth	Tr	03.74	73-74	1	3	0

JONES Gary
Huddersfield, 6 April, 1969 (F)

League Club	Source	Date Signed	Seasons Played	Apps	Subs	Gls
Doncaster Rov.	Rossington Main	01.89	88-89	10	10	2
Southend U.	Boston U.	06.93	93-95	47	23	16
Lincoln C.	L	09.93	93	0	4	2
Notts Co.	Tr	03.96	95-97	80	9	36
Scunthorpe U.	L	02.97	96	9	2	5

JONES Gary Kenneth
Prescot, 5 January, 1951 (W)

League Club	Source	Date Signed	Seasons Played	Apps	Subs	Gls
Everton	Jnrs	10.68	70-75	76	6	12
Birmingham C.	Tr	07.76	76-77	33	2	1

JONES Gary Roy
Birkenhead, 3 June, 1977 (M)

League Club	Source	Date Signed	Seasons Played	Apps	Subs	Gls
Swansea C.	Caernarfon T.	07.97	97	3	5	0
Rochdale	Tr	01.98	97	17	0	2

JONES Gary Steven
Chester, 10 May, 1975 (M/F)

League Club	Source	Date Signed	Seasons Played	Apps	Subs	Gls
Tranmere Rov.	YT	07.93	93-97	75	46	20

JONES Garry Edwin
Wythenshawe, 11 December, 1950 (F)

League Club	Source	Date Signed	Seasons Played	Apps	Subs	Gls
Bolton W.	App	01.68	68-78	195	8	41
Sheffield U.	L	02.75	74	3	0	1
Blackpool	Tr	11.78	78-79	18	9	5
Hereford U.	Tr	08.80	80	21	4	4

JONES George
Wrexham, 19 July, 1930 (WH)

League Club	Source	Date Signed	Seasons Played	Apps	Subs	Gls
Wrexham		08.50	50-53	113	-	5

JONES George Alexander
Radcliffe, 21 April, 1945 E Yth (F)

League Club	Source	Date Signed	Seasons Played	Apps	Subs	Gls
Bury	App	06.62	61-63	63	-	14
Blackburn Rov.	Tr	03.64	63-66	36	3	14
Bury	Tr	11.66	66-72	249	7	100
Oldham Ath.	Tr	03.73	72-75	63	8	19

League Club	Source	Date Signed	Seasons Played	Career Record Apps	Subs	Gls
Halifax T.	Tr	02.76	75-76	18	1	4
Southport	Tr	01.77	76-77	54	1	11
JONES George Henry						
Sheffield, 27 November, 1918 Died 1995						(OL)
Sheffield U.	Woodburn Alliance	08.36	36-50	141	-	35
Barnsley	Tr	02.51	50-51	22	-	6
JONES Gerald						
Burslem, 30 December, 1945						(W)
Stoke C.	App	06.63	64-66	7	0	0
JONES Gerald Kenneth						
Newport, 21 April, 1950						(W)
Luton T.	Barry T.	07.72				
Crewe Alex.	L	02.73	72	6	1	1
JONES Glanville						
Merthyr Tydfil, 27 February, 1921						(OL)
Hull C.	Merthyr Tydfil	06.46	46	7	-	0
Bournemouth	Tr	05.47	48	9	-	3
Crewe Alex.	Tr	03.49	48	12	-	1
JONES Glyn						
Rotherham, 8 April, 1936 E Yth						(F)
Sheffield U.	Rotherham U. (Am)	06.54	55-57	29	-	4
Rotherham U.	Tr	12.57	57-58	23	-	6
Mansfield T.	Tr	07.59	59-60	45	-	18
JONES Glyn Alan						
Newport, 29 March, 1959						(G)
Bristol Rov.	App	03.77	77-79	9	0	0
Shrewsbury T.	Tr	07.80				
Newport Co. (N/C)	Newport Y.M.C.A.	09.83	83	3	0	0
JONES Gordon Edward						
Sedgefield, 6 March, 1943 E Yth/Eu23-9						(FB)
Middlesbrough	Jnrs	03.60	60-72	457	5	4
Darlington	Tr	02.73	72-74	80	5	5
JONES Graeme Anthony						
Gateshead, 13 March, 1970						(F)
Doncaster Rov.	Bridlington T.	08.93	93-95	80	12	26
Wigan Ath.	Tr	07.96	96-97	67	6	40
JONES Graham						
Worsley, 2 June, 1959						(CD)
Luton T.	App	06.76	75-79	31	8	0
Torquay U.	Tr	01.80	79-82	114	0	6
Stockport Co.	Tr	07.83	83	32	3	2
JONES Graham						
Bradford, 5 October, 1957						(D)
Bradford C. (N/C)	Jnrs	06.76	75-77	1	3	0
JONES Graham Osborne						
Wrexham, 16 September, 1949						(CH)
Wrexham	Jnrs	10.67	67	3	0	0
JONES Grenville Arthur						
Nuneaton, 23 November, 1932 Died 1991 E Sch/E Yth						(OR)
West Bromwich A.	Jnrs	12.49	53	2	-	0
Wrexham	Tr	06.55	55-60	241	-	36
JONES Daniel John **Gwilym**						
Cardigan, 3 April, 1925 Died 1992						(CF)
Torquay U.	Abergwynfi	09.47	47	6	-	1
JONES Gwyn						
Newport, 20 November, 1932						(IF)
Leeds U.	Llanelli	08.50				
York C.	Tr	09.53				
Walsall	Tr	11.53	53	10	-	0
JONES Gwynfor						
Llandwrog, 20 March, 1935						(FB)
Wolverhampton W.	Caernarfon T.	09.55	55-61	21	-	0
Bristol Rov.	Tr	08.62	62-65	153	0	0
JONES Harold						
Liverpool, 22 May, 1933						(HB)
Liverpool	Jnrs	02.52	53	1	-	0
JONES Harvey Cunningham						
Rhos, 16 August, 1936						(WH)
Wrexham (Am)	Liverpool (Am)	11.59	59	13	-	0
Chester C.	Tr	08.60	60	19	-	0

League Club	Source	Date Signed	Seasons Played	Career Record Apps	Subs	Gls
JONES Haydn						
Caernarfon, 8 May, 1946						(FB)
Wrexham	Caernarfon T.	06.64	64-65	13	1	1
JONES Henry (Jerry)						
Hartlepool, 28 September, 1918						(WH)
Hartlepool U.	Belle Vue Congs	09.46	46-48	75	-	1
JONES Herbert Neville						
Mold, 20 January, 1929						(IF)
Wrexham	Colwyn Bay	07.51	51	1	-	0
JONES Ian Michael						
Germany, 26 August, 1976 W Yth						(FB)
Cardiff C.	YT	07.95	93-95	3	0	0
JONES Idwal						
Ton Pentre, 3 August, 1924						(OR)
Swansea C.	Ton Pentre	10.46	46	4	-	0
JONES Islwyn						
Merthyr Tydfil, 8 April, 1935						(CH)
Cardiff C.	Jnrs	11.52	54-55	26	-	0
JONES Ivor						
Rhondda, 1 April, 1925						(OR)
Crystal Palace		06.46	46	1	-	1
JONES James						
Manchester						(IF)
Hull C. (Am)		05.47	46	1	-	0
JONES James Alfred						
Birkenhead, 31 August, 1927						(G)
Everton		12.45				
New Brighton	Tr	08.50	50	32	-	0
Lincoln C.	Tr	08.51	51-53	76	-	0
Accrington St.	Tr	02.54	53-54	46	-	0
Rochdale	Tr	09.55	55-60	177	-	0
JONES Benjamin **James**						
Rhondda, 16 November, 1919 Died 1976 W Amat						(FB)
Watford	Slough T.	09.47	47-53	158	-	0
JONES Jason Andrew						
Wrexham, 10 May, 1979 W Yth						(G)
Swansea C.	Liverpool	12.97	97	1	0	0
JONES John						
Gourock						(IL)
Bradford C.	Third Lanark	09.46	46	2	-	1
JONES John (Jack)						
Wrexham, 9 April, 1921						(IF)
Wrexham		09.46	46-47	20	-	1
Doncaster Rov.	Tr	07.48	48	6	-	0
New Brighton	Tr	08.49	49-50	77	-	11
JONES John Edward						
Bromborough, 3 July, 1913 Died 1995						(FB)
Everton	Ellesmere Port	03.32	33-37	98	-	10
Sunderland	Tr	12.45	46	24	-	0
JONES John Morris						
Llanelli, 31 October, 1924						(OL)
Fulham	Larne	01.47	47	1	-	0
Millwall	Tr	03.50	49-50	27	-	7
JONES John Thomas						
Holywell, 25 November, 1916 Died 1978 W Sch						(G)
Port Vale		12.36	36	3	-	0
Northampton T.	Tr	05.37	38-47	71	-	0
Oldham Ath.	Tr	08.48	48	22	-	0
JONES Jonathan Berwyn						
Wrexham, 27 October, 1978						(F)
Chester C.	YT	03.97	96-97	5	19	2
JONES Joseph Patrick						
Llandudno, 4 March, 1955 Wu23-4/W-72						(D)
Wrexham	Jnrs	01.73	72-74	98	0	2
Liverpool	Tr	07.75	75-77	72	0	3
Wrexham	Tr	10.78	78-82	145	1	6
Chelsea	Tr	10.82	82-84	76	2	2
Huddersfield T.	Tr	08.85	85-86	67	1	3
Wrexham	Tr	08.87	87-91	131	1	11

League Club	Source	Date Signed	Seasons Played	Career Record Apps	Subs	Gls

JONES Keith
Nantyglo, 23 October, 1928 W-1 (G)

League Club	Source	Date Signed	Seasons Played	Apps	Subs	Gls
Aston Villa	Kidderminster Hrs	05.46	47-56	185	-	0
Port Vale	Tr	07.57	57-58	64	-	0
Crewe Alex.	Tr	04.59	58-59	46	-	0
Southport	Tr	07.60				

JONES Keith Aubrey
Dulwich, 14 October, 1965 E Sch/E Yth (M)

League Club	Source	Date Signed	Seasons Played	Apps	Subs	Gls
Chelsea	App	08.83	82-86	43	9	7
Brentford	Tr	09.87	87-91	167	2	13
Southend U.	Tr	10.91	91-94	88	2	11
Charlton Ath.	Tr	09.94	94-97	113	6	4

JONES Kenneth
Easington, 1 October, 1936 E Sch (FB)

League Club	Source	Date Signed	Seasons Played	Apps	Subs	Gls
Sunderland	Jnrs	10.53	59	10	-	0
Hartlepool U.	Tr	01.61	60-61	33	-	0

JONES Kenneth
Aberdare, 2 January, 1936 Wu23-1 (G)

League Club	Source	Date Signed	Seasons Played	Apps	Subs	Gls
Cardiff C.	Jnrs	05.53	57-58	24	-	0
Scunthorpe U.	Tr	12.58	58-63	168	-	0
Charlton Ath.	Tr	09.64	64-65	25	0	0
Exeter C.	Tr	06.66	66	17	0	0

JONES Kenneth
Havercroft, 26 June, 1944 (FB)

League Club	Source	Date Signed	Seasons Played	Apps	Subs	Gls
Bradford P.A.	Monckton Colly	09.61	62-64	100	-	3
Southampton	Tr	06.65	65-69	79	0	0
Cardiff C.	Tr	07.71	71	6	0	0

JONES Kenneth Boothroyd
Ruabon, 11 May, 1937 (FB)

League Club	Source	Date Signed	Seasons Played	Apps	Subs	Gls
Wrexham	Jnrs	05.54	57-59	31	-	0
Crystal Palace	Tr	06.60	60	4	-	0
Swindon T.	Tr	03.61	60-61	35	-	0

JONES Kenneth Brian
Keighley, 9 February, 1941 (M)

League Club	Source	Date Signed	Seasons Played	Apps	Subs	Gls
Southend U.		10.60	60-63	87	-	34
Millwall	Tr	09.64	64-69	175	3	11
Colchester U.	Tr	11.69	69-71	73	4	23

JONES Kevin Richard
Wrexham, 16 February, 1974 (FB)

League Club	Source	Date Signed	Seasons Played	Apps	Subs	Gls
Wrexham	YT	08.92	91-93	8	1	0

JONES Lee
Pontypridd, 9 August, 1970 (G)

League Club	Source	Date Signed	Seasons Played	Apps	Subs	Gls
Swansea C.	A.F.C. Porth	03.94	94-97	6	0	0
Bristol Rov.	Tr	03.98	97	8	0	0

JONES Philip Lee
Wrexham, 29 May, 1973 W Yth/Wu21-14/W 'B'/W-2 (F)

League Club	Source	Date Signed	Seasons Played	Apps	Subs	Gls
Wrexham	YT	07.91	90-91	24	15	9
Liverpool	Tr	03.92	94-96	0	3	0
Crewe Alex.	L	09.93	93	4	4	1
Wrexham	L	01.96	95	20	0	8
Wrexham	L	01.97	96	2	4	0
Tranmere Rov.	Tr	03.97	96-97	37	5	14

JONES Leonard
Barnsley, 9 June, 1913 (OR)

League Club	Source	Date Signed	Seasons Played	Apps	Subs	Gls
Barnsley	Huddersfield T. (Am)	08.33	34-37	57	-	0
Plymouth Arg.	Chelmsford C.	05.39	46-48	39	-	2
Southend U.	Tr	08.49	49	29	-	0
Colchester U.	Tr	07.50	50-52	71	-	3

JONES Leslie
Ynysybwl, 8 December, 1922 Died 1983 (IF)

League Club	Source	Date Signed	Seasons Played	Apps	Subs	Gls
Millwall	Barry T.	12.47	48-51	7	-	1

JONES Leslie Albert
Wrexham, 9 November, 1940 W Sch (IF)

League Club	Source	Date Signed	Seasons Played	Apps	Subs	Gls
Bolton W.	Jnrs	11.57				
Tranmere Rov.	Tr	07.62	62-64	68	-	29
Chester C.	Tr	04.65	65-68	132	3	35

JONES Leslie Clifford
Mountain Ash, 1 January, 1930 (FB)

League Club	Source	Date Signed	Seasons Played	Apps	Subs	Gls
Luton T.	Craig Ath.	10.50	50-57	98	-	1
Aston Villa	Tr	01.58	57	5	-	0

JONES Leslie Jenkin
Aberdare, 1 July, 1911 Died 1981 W-11 (IF)

League Club	Source	Date Signed	Seasons Played	Apps	Subs	Gls
Cardiff C.	Aberdare Ath.	08.29	29-33	139	-	31
Coventry C.	Tr	01.34	33-37	138	-	70
Arsenal	Tr	11.37	37-38	46	-	3
Swansea C.	Tr	06.46	46	2	-	0
Brighton & H.A.	Barry T.	08.48	48	3	-	0

JONES Linden
New Tredegar, 5 March, 1961 Wu21-3 (RB/M)

League Club	Source	Date Signed	Seasons Played	Apps	Subs	Gls
Cardiff C.	App	03.79	78-83	142	3	2
Newport Co.	Tr	09.83	83-86	141	0	6
Reading	Tr	07.87	87-91	147	5	8

JONES Mark
Barnsley, 15 June, 1933 Died 1958 E Sch (CH)

League Club	Source	Date Signed	Seasons Played	Apps	Subs	Gls
Manchester U.	Jnrs	07.50	50-57	103	-	1

JONES Mark
Brownhills, 4 January, 1968 (RW/B)

League Club	Source	Date Signed	Seasons Played	Apps	Subs	Gls
Walsall	App	01.86	87	6	2	0
Exeter C.	L	11.88	88	5	0	0
Hereford U.	Tr	08.89	89	40	2	7

JONES Mark
Berinsfield (Oxon), 26 September, 1961 (M)

League Club	Source	Date Signed	Seasons Played	Apps	Subs	Gls
Oxford U.	App	09.79	79-85	101	28	7
Swindon T.	Tr	09.86	86	39	1	9
Cardiff C.	Tr	08.90	90-91	33	3	2

JONES Mark
Romford, 4 August, 1979 (LB)

League Club	Source	Date Signed	Seasons Played	Apps	Subs	Gls
Southend U.	YT	●	96	0	1	0

JONES Mark
Bristol, 2 December, 1965 (M)

League Club	Source	Date Signed	Seasons Played	Apps	Subs	Gls
Bristol C.	App	●	82	0	1	0

JONES Mark Anthony Waldron
Warley, 22 October, 1961 (RB)

League Club	Source	Date Signed	Seasons Played	Apps	Subs	Gls
Aston Villa	App	07.79	81-83	24	0	0
Brighton & H.A.	Tr	03.84	83-84	9	0	0
Birmingham C.	Tr	10.84	84-86	33	1	0
Shrewsbury T.	Tr	03.87				
Hereford U.	Tr	06.87	87-90	155	1	2

JONES Mark David
Doncaster, 2 October, 1958 (M)

League Club	Source	Date Signed	Seasons Played	Apps	Subs	Gls
Doncaster Rov.	App	11.75	75-77	10	3	0

JONES Mark Richard
Mansfield, 21 December, 1965 (CD)

League Club	Source	Date Signed	Seasons Played	Apps	Subs	Gls
Notts Co.	App	12.83	83-84	4	2	0

JONES Mark Thomas
Liverpool, 16 September, 1960 (FB)

League Club	Source	Date Signed	Seasons Played	Apps	Subs	Gls
Preston N.E.	Runcorn	02.84	83-85	76	0	3

JONES Matthew Leon
Chiswick, 9 October, 1970 (W)

League Club	Source	Date Signed	Seasons Played	Apps	Subs	Gls
Southend U.	YT	05.89	88-89	2	3	0

JONES John Mervyn
Bangor, 30 April, 1931 (W)

League Club	Source	Date Signed	Seasons Played	Apps	Subs	Gls
Liverpool	Bangor C.	12.51	51-52	4	-	0
Scunthorpe U.	Tr	08.53	53-58	240	-	27
Crewe Alex.	Tr	06.59	59-60	84	-	14
Chester C.	Tr	08.61	61-62	63	-	10
Lincoln C.		10.63	63	1	-	0

JONES Michael
Sunderland, 24 March, 1947 (CD)

League Club	Source	Date Signed	Seasons Played	Apps	Subs	Gls
Derby Co.	Jnrs	11.64				
Notts Co.	Tr	07.69	69-72	82	18	1
Peterborough U.	Tr	08.73	73-75	82	6	4

JONES Michael Alan
Sutton-in-Ashfield, 4 December, 1942 (FB)

League Club	Source	Date Signed	Seasons Played	Apps	Subs	Gls
Mansfield T.	Mansfield Co-op.	10.60	62-65	91	0	0

JONES Michael David
Worksop, 24 April, 1945 Eu23-9/E-3 (CF)

League Club	Source	Date Signed	Seasons Played	Apps	Subs	Gls
Sheffield U.	App	11.62	62-67	149	0	63
Leeds U.	Tr	09.67	67-73	215	4	77

JONES Michael Howard
Llangurig, 25 August, 1938 (W)

League Club	Source	Date Signed	Seasons Played	Apps	Subs	Gls
Shrewsbury T.		07.59	58-61	22	-	1

JONES Michael Keith
Berkhamsted, 8 January, 1945 (FB)

League Club	Source	Date Signed	Seasons Played	Apps	Subs	Gls
Fulham	App	01.63				
Chelsea	Tr	12.64				
Leyton Orient	Tr	02.66	65-71	223	5	16
Charlton Ath.	Tr	12.71	71-73	58	1	0

JONES William **Morris**
Liverpool, 30 November, 1919 Died 1993 (IF)

League Club	Source	Date Signed	Seasons Played	Apps	Subs	Gls
Port Vale	South Liverpool	06.46	46-47	53	-	26
Swindon T.	Tr	11.47	47-49	94	-	48
Crystal Palace	Tr	05.50	50	17	-	3
Watford	Tr	03.51	50-51	27	-	7

JONES Murray Lee
Bexley, 7 October, 1964 (F)

League Club	Source	Date Signed	Seasons Played	Apps	Subs	Gls
Southend U.	App	08.82				
Crystal Palace	Carshalton Ath.	10.89				
Bristol C.	Tr	08.90				
Doncaster Rov.	L	10.90	90	5	0	0
Exeter C.	Tr	01.91	90	16	4	3
Grimsby T.	Tr	07.91	91	14	14	3
Brentford	Tr	07.92	92	6	10	0

JONES Nathan Jason
Rhondda, 28 May, 1973 (M)

League Club	Source	Date Signed	Seasons Played	Apps	Subs	Gls
Luton T.	Merthyr	06.95				
Southend U.	Nomincia (Sp)	08.97	97	34	5	0

JONES Norman Glyn
Rhostyllen, 15 November, 1923 W Sch (G)

League Club	Source	Date Signed	Seasons Played	Apps	Subs	Gls
Wrexham	Jnrs	09.41	46	1	-	0

JONES Patrick James
Plymouth, 7 September, 1920 Died 1990 (FB)

League Club	Source	Date Signed	Seasons Played	Apps	Subs	Gls
Plymouth Arg.	Astor Inst.	03.47	46-57	425	-	2

JONES Paul Anthony
Walsall, 6 September, 1965 (M)

League Club	Source	Date Signed	Seasons Played	Apps	Subs	Gls
Walsall	App	09.83	82-89	125	18	15
Wrexham	L	03.89	88	5	0	0
Wolverhampton W.	Tr	11.89	89-90	7	7	0

JONES Paul Bernard
Ellesmere Port, 13 May, 1953 (CD)

League Club	Source	Date Signed	Seasons Played	Apps	Subs	Gls
Bolton W.	App	06.70	70-82	441	4	38
Huddersfield T.	Tr	07.83	83-85	73	0	8
Oldham Ath.	Tr	12.85	85-86	32	0	1
Blackpool	Tr	03.87	86-87	31	6	0
Rochdale	Galway U.	03.89	88	14	0	2
Stockport Co.	Tr	06.89	89	25	0	0

JONES Paul Philip
Birkenhead, 2 October, 1976 (LB)

League Club	Source	Date Signed	Seasons Played	Apps	Subs	Gls
Wrexham	YT	07.95	96	6	0	0

JONES Paul Stanley
Stockport, 10 September, 1953 (M)

League Club	Source	Date Signed	Seasons Played	Apps	Subs	Gls
Manchester U.	App	12.70				
Mansfield T.	Tr	06.73	73	15	5	1

JONES Paul Steven
Chirk, 18 April, 1967 W-5 (G)

League Club	Source	Date Signed	Seasons Played	Apps	Subs	Gls
Wolverhampton W.	Kidderminster Hrs	07.91	92-95	33	0	0
Stockport Co.	Tr	07.96	96	46	0	0
Southampton	Tr	07.97	97	38	0	0

JONES Paul Timothy
Solihull, 6 February, 1974 (W)

League Club	Source	Date Signed	Seasons Played	Apps	Subs	Gls
Birmingham C.	YT	02.92	91	0	1	0

JONES Peter
Caerphilly, 22 September, 1957 (LB)

League Club	Source	Date Signed	Seasons Played	Apps	Subs	Gls
Newport Co.	Merthyr Tydfil	08.85	85-86	54	1	1

JONES Peter Alfred
Ellesmere Port, 25 November, 1949 E Sch/E Yth (FB)

League Club	Source	Date Signed	Seasons Played	Apps	Subs	Gls
Burnley	App	05.67	68-69	2	0	0
Swansea C.	Tr	07.71	71-73	80	0	1

JONES Ernest **Peter**
Salford, 30 November, 1937 E Yth (D)

League Club	Source	Date Signed	Seasons Played	Apps	Subs	Gls
Manchester U.	Jnrs	04.55	57	1	-	0
Wrexham	Tr	03.60	59-65	225	1	7
Stockport Co.	Tr	07.66	66-67	51	3	1

JONES Philip Andrew
Liverpool, 1 December, 1969 (RB)

League Club	Source	Date Signed	Seasons Played	Apps	Subs	Gls
Everton	YT	06.88	87	0	1	0
Blackpool	L	03.90	89	6	0	0
Wigan Ath.	Tr	01.91	90-92	84	2	2
Bury (N/C)	Tr	08.93	93	4	0	0

JONES Philip Eric
Ellesmere Port, 30 March, 1948 (IF)

League Club	Source	Date Signed	Seasons Played	Apps	Subs	Gls
Blackpool	Jnrs	01.66				
Wrexham	Blackburn Rov. (trial)	05.67	66	1	0	0

JONES Philip Howard
Middlesbrough, 12 September, 1961 (M)

League Club	Source	Date Signed	Seasons Played	Apps	Subs	Gls
Sheffield U.	App	06.79	78-80	25	3	1

JONES Ralph
Maesteg, 19 May, 1921 Died 1997 (FB)

League Club	Source	Date Signed	Seasons Played	Apps	Subs	Gls
Leicester C.		10.44				
Newport Co.	Tr	05.46	46-47	19	-	0
Bristol Rov.	Tr	12.47	47-49	13	-	1

JONES Raymond Michael
Chester, 4 June, 1944 (FB)

League Club	Source	Date Signed	Seasons Played	Apps	Subs	Gls
Chester C.	Jnrs	10.62	62-68	169	1	0

JONES Richard John
Usk, 26 April, 1969 (M)

League Club	Source	Date Signed	Seasons Played	Apps	Subs	Gls
Newport Co.	YT	07.87	86-87	31	10	1
Hereford U.	Tr	08.88	88-92	142	6	9
Swansea C. (N/C)	Tr	07.93	93	6	1	0

JONES Richard Kenneth
Llanelli, 16 April, 1926 (FB)

League Club	Source	Date Signed	Seasons Played	Apps	Subs	Gls
Coventry C.	Llanelli	11.49	51-55	83	-	0

JONES Gordon **Richard**
Llanrwst, 25 June, 1932 (WH)

League Club	Source	Date Signed	Seasons Played	Apps	Subs	Gls
Crewe Alex.	Holyhead	01.57	56-61	76	-	2

JONES Robert
Coventry, 17 November, 1964 (F)

League Club	Source	Date Signed	Seasons Played	Apps	Subs	Gls
Leicester C.	Manchester C. (App)	09.82	82-85	12	3	3
Walsall	Tr	08.86	86	1	4	0

JONES Robert Marc
Wrexham, 5 November, 1971 W Sch/E Yth/Eu21-2/E-8 (RB)

League Club	Source	Date Signed	Seasons Played	Apps	Subs	Gls
Crewe Alex.	YT	12.88	87-91	59	16	2
Liverpool	Tr	10.91	91-97	182	1	0

JONES Robert Stanley
Bristol, 28 October, 1938 (F)

League Club	Source	Date Signed	Seasons Played	Apps	Subs	Gls
Bristol Rov.	Soundwell	05.56	57-66	250	0	64
Northampton T.	Tr	09.66	66	17	0	1
Swindon T.	Tr	02.67	66	11	0	0
Bristol Rov.	Tr	08.67	67-72	160	11	37

JONES Robert Stuart
Liverpool, 12 November, 1971 (M)

League Club	Source	Date Signed	Seasons Played	Apps	Subs	Gls
Wrexham	YT	07.90	89-90	5	2	1

JONES Robert William
Liverpool, 28 March, 1933 Died 1998 (G)

League Club	Source	Date Signed	Seasons Played	Apps	Subs	Gls
Southport	Jnrs	07.51	51-52	22	-	0
Chester C.	Tr	08.53	53-57	166	-	0
Blackburn Rov.	Tr	03.58	58-65	49	0	0

JONES Roderick
Rhiwderyn, 14 June, 1946 (F/D)

League Club	Source	Date Signed	Seasons Played	Apps	Subs	Gls
Newport Co.	Lovells Ath.	10.69	69-78	271	17	65

JONES Rodney Ernest
Ashton-u-Lyne, 23 September, 1945 (G)

League Club	Source	Date Signed	Seasons Played	Apps	Subs	Gls
Rotherham U.	Ashton U.	06.65	65-66	36	0	0
Burnley	Tr	03.67	67-68	9	0	0
Rochdale	Tr	06.71	71-73	19	0	0

JONES Roger
Upton-on-Severn, 8 November, 1946 Eu23-1 (G)

League Club	Source	Date Signed	Seasons Played	Apps	Subs	Gls
Portsmouth	App	11.64				
Bournemouth	Tr	05.65	65-69	160	0	0
Blackburn Rov.	Tr	01.70	69-75	242	0	0
Newcastle U.	Tr	03.76	75	5	0	0
Stoke C.	Tr	02.77	76-79	101	0	0
Derby Co	Tr	07.80	80-81	59	0	0
Birmingham C.	L	02.82	81	4	0	0
York C.	Tr	08.82	82-84	122	0	0

JONES Ronald
Crewe, 9 April, 1918 Died 1987 (OL)

League Club	Source	Date Signed	Seasons Played	Apps	Subs	Gls
Crewe Alex.	Heslington Vic.	05.37	37-46	3	-	2

JONES Ronald John
Rhondda, 27 February, 1926 Died 1991 (CF)

League Club	Source	Date Signed	Seasons Played	Apps	Subs	Gls
Swansea C.		07.49				
Scunthorpe U.	Tr	08.50	50	3	-	0

JONES Roy
Stoke, 20 December, 1924 (CH)

League Club	Source	Date Signed	Seasons Played	Apps	Subs	Gls
Stoke C.	Jnrs	10.43	47-49	7	-	0

League Club	Source	Date Signed	Seasons Played	Career Record Apps	Subs	Gls
JONES Roy John						
Clacton, 26 July, 1942						(G)
Swindon T.		10.67	67-71	34	0	0
JONES Ryan Anthony						
Sheffield, 23 July, 1973 Wu21-4/W 'B'/W-1						(M)
Sheffield Wed.	YT	06.91	92-94	36	5	6
Scunthorpe U.	L	01.96	95	11	0	3
JONES Samuel						
Lurgan (NI), 14 September, 1911 Died 1993 NI-2						(WH)
Blackpool	Distillery	10.33	33-46	168	-	7
JONES Scott						
Sheffield, 1 May, 1975						(LB)
Barnsley	YT	02.94	95-97	28	6	1
Mansfield T.	L	08.97	97	6	0	0
JONES Thomas **Selwyn**						
Rhos, 3 April, 1929 Died 1995						(OR)
Everton		07.49				
Sheffield Wed.		08.51				
Leyton Orient	Tr	07.52	52	6	-	0
JONES Shane Graham						
Tredegar, 8 November, 1972						(M)
Hereford U.	YT	08.91	89-91	12	26	1
JONES Sidney						
Rothwell, 15 February, 1921 Died 1977						(FB)
Arsenal	Kippax Jnrs	05.39				
Walsall	Tr	07.48	48-51	146	-	1
JONES Eric **Sidney**						
Wrexham, 10 October, 1921 Died 1981						(OL)
Bolton W.	Jnrs	05.39				
Norwich C.	Tr	12.45	46-47	40	-	9
JONES Simon Christopher						
Nettleham (Lincs), 16 May, 1945						(G)
Rochdale	Gainsborough Trin.	06.63	63-66	47	0	0
Chester C.	Bangor C.	10.67	67	3	0	0
JONES Stanley						
						(OL)
Crewe Alex.		08.47	47	2	-	0
JONES Stanley George						
Highley, 16 November, 1938						(CH)
Walsall	Kidderminster Hrs	05.56	57-59	30	-	0
West Bromwich A.	Tr	05.60	60-66	239	0	2
Walsall	Tr	03.68	67-72	204	2	7
JONES Stephen Alexander						
Plymouth, 11 March, 1974						(F)
Plymouth Arg.	YT	07.92	91	0	1	0
JONES Stephen Anthony						
Wrexham, 28 November, 1962						(F)
Wrexham	Jnrs	08.81	80-81	3	2	0
Crewe Alex.	Tr	08.82	82	6	4	1
JONES Stephen Gary						
Cambridge, 17 March, 1970						(F)
West Ham U.	Billericay T.	11.92	92-94	8	8	4
Bournemouth	Tr	10.94	94-95	71	3	26
West Ham U.	Tr	05.96	96	5	3	0
Charlton Ath.	Tr	02.97	96-97	20	5	7
Bournemouth	L	12.97	97	5	0	4
JONES Stephen Robert						
Bristol, 25 December, 1970						(D)
Swansea C.	Cheltenham T.	11.95	95-96	62	1	1
JONES Stephen Russell						
Eastbourne, 25 July, 1957						(FB)
Queens Park R.	App	10.74				
Walsall	Tr	01.79	78	15	0	0
Wimbledon	Tr	07.79	79-82	77	2	0
JONES Samuel **Stephen** Thomas						
Harrogate, 6 September, 1955						(G)
Bradford C.	App	09.73	72	2	0	0
JONES Steven						
Stockton, 31 January, 1974						(G)
Hartlepool U.	YT	05.92	91-95	45	3	0
JONES Steven Francis						
Liverpool, 18 October, 1960						(M)
Manchester U.	App.	10.77				
Port Vale	Tr	05.79	79-80	24	1	2
JONES Steven Wynn						
Wrexham, 23 October, 1964						(LB)
Wrexham	Jnrs	08.83	82-83	9	1	1
JONES Tecwyn						
Holywell, 3 January, 1930						(FB)
Brentford		03.50	51-52	5	-	0
Wrexham	Tr	07.53	53	4	-	0
JONES Tecwyn Lloyd						
Ruabon, 27 January, 1941 Wu23-1						(WH)
Wrexham	Jnrs	05.59	61-64	57	-	2
Colchester U.	Tr	10.64	64-65	28	0	0
Crewe Alex.	Tr	10.65	65	8	0	0
JONES Thomas						
Aldershot, 7 October, 1964 E Semi Pro						(M)
Swindon T.	Aberdeen	09.88	88-91	162	6	12
Reading	Tr	09.92	92-95	63	16	2
JONES Thomas Edwin						
Liverpool, 11 April, 1930 E Yth						(CH)
Everton	Jnrs	01.48	50-61	383	-	14
JONES Thomas George						
Connahs Quay, 12 October, 1917 W Sch/W-17						(CH)
Wrexham	Llanerch Celtic	11.34	35	6	-	0
Everton	Tr	03.36	36-49	165	-	4
JONES Thomas William						
Oakengates, 23 March, 1907 Died 1980						(IF)
West Bromwich A.	Oakengates T.	07.29				
Burnley	Tr	11.30	30-33	94	-	24
Blackpool	Tr	09.33	33-37	155	-	40
Grimsby T.	Tr	07.38	38-46	48	-	8
JONES Trevor						
Aberdare, 27 January, 1923 Died 1983						(W)
Plymouth Arg.	Aberaman	05.48				
Watford	Tr	08.49	49	15	-	2
JONES Vaughan						
Tonyrefail, 8 September, 1959 W Yth/Wu21-2						(LB)
Bristol Rov.	App	09.77	76-81	93	8	3
Newport Co.	Tr	08.82	82-83	67	1	4
Cardiff C.	Tr	07.84	84	11	0	0
Bristol Rov.	Tr	12.84	84-92	277	3	9
JONES Vincent (Vinny) Peter						
Watford, 5 January, 1965 W-9						(M)
Wimbledon	Wealdstone	11.86	86-88	77	0	9
Leeds U.	Tr	06.89	89-90	44	2	5
Sheffield U.	Tr	09.90	90-91	35	0	2
Chelsea	Tr	08.91	91-92	42	0	4
Wimbledon	Tr	09.92	92-97	171	6	12
Queens Park R.	Tr	03.98	97	7	0	1
JONES Walter						
Lurgan (NI), 4 April, 1925						(WH)
Blackpool	Linfield	12.47				
Doncaster Rov.	Tr	06.50	50-52	69	-	2
York C.	Grimsby T. (trial)	11.54	54	1	-	0
JONES Walter Schofield						
Rochdale, 9 January, 1925						(CF)
Rochdale	St Chads	11.46	46	2	-	2
JONES Philip **Wayne**						
Treorchy, 20 October, 1948 Wu23-6/W-1						(M)
Bristol Rov.	Jnrs	10.66	66-72	218	6	28
JONES William Henry						
Macclesfield, 13 May, 1921 EF Lge/E 'B'/E-2						(WH)
Liverpool	Hayfield St Mathews	09.38	46-53	257	-	17
JONES William John						
Aberbargoed, 5 May, 1925						(OR)
Ipswich T.	Bargoed	04.49	49-54	33	-	1
JONES William John Beattie						
Liverpool, 6 June, 1924 Died 1995						(F)
Manchester C.		05.48	48-49	3	-	0
Chester C.	Tr	06.51	51	29	-	4

JONES Charles **Wilson**
Wrexham, 29 April, 1914 Died 1986 W-2 (CF)

League Club	Source	Date Signed	Seasons Played	Apps	Subs	Gls
Wrexham	Brymbo Green	08.32	32-33	6	-	3
Birmingham C.	Tr	09.34	34-46	135	-	63
Nottingham F.	Tr	09.47	47	7	-	5

JONSSON Sigurdur (Siggi)
Iceland, 27 September, 1966 Icelandic Int (M)

League Club	Source	Date Signed	Seasons Played	Apps	Subs	Gls
Sheffield Wed.	Akranes (Ice)	02.85	84-88	59	8	4
Barnsley	L	01.86	85	5	0	0
Arsenal	Tr	07.89	89-90	2	6	1

JOPLING Joseph
South Shields, 21 April, 1951 (FB)

League Club	Source	Date Signed	Seasons Played	Apps	Subs	Gls
Aldershot	Horton Westhoe	08.69	69-70	35	0	2
Leicester C.	Tr	09.70	70-73	2	1	0
Torquay U.	L	01.74	73	6	0	0
Aldershot	Tr	03.74	73-83	321	11	11

JORDAN Brian Athol
Doncaster, 31 January, 1932 (CH)

League Club	Source	Date Signed	Seasons Played	Apps	Subs	Gls
Derby Co.		10.51				
Rotherham U.	Denaby U.	07.53	53-58	38	-	0
Middlesbrough	Tr	11.58	58	5	-	0
York C.	Tr	07.60	60	8	-	0

JORDAN Clarence (Clarrie)
South Kirkby, 20 June, 1922 Died 1992 (CF)

League Club	Source	Date Signed	Seasons Played	Apps	Subs	Gls
Doncaster Rov.	Upton Colly	04.40	46-47	60	-	47
Sheffield Wed.	Tr	02.48	47-54	92	-	36

JORDAN Colin
Hemsworth, 2 June, 1934 (FB)

League Club	Source	Date Signed	Seasons Played	Apps	Subs	Gls
Bradford P.A.	Fitzwilliam Y.C.	04.52	53-56	27	-	0

JORDAN David Charles
Gillingham, 26 October, 1971 (F)

League Club	Source	Date Signed	Seasons Played	Apps	Subs	Gls
Gillingham	YT	06.90	90	0	2	0

JORDAN Gerald
Seaham, 4 April, 1949 (FB)

League Club	Source	Date Signed	Seasons Played	Apps	Subs	Gls
Northampton T.	Jnrs	06.66	66	1	0	0

JORDAN John
Glasgow, 25 February, 1924 (OR)

League Club	Source	Date Signed	Seasons Played	Apps	Subs	Gls
Reading	Glasgow Celtic	10.48	48	3	-	0
Brentford	Tr	10.49				

JORDAN John William
Bromley, 8 November, 1921 (IF)

League Club	Source	Date Signed	Seasons Played	Apps	Subs	Gls
Tottenham H.	Grays Ath.	08.47	47	24	-	10
Birmingham C.	Juventus (It)	03.49	48-49	24	-	2
Sheffield Wed.	Tr	09.50	50	10	-	2

JORDAN Joseph
Carluke, 15 December, 1951 Su23-1/S-52 (F)

League Club	Source	Date Signed	Seasons Played	Apps	Subs	Gls
Leeds U.	Morton	10.70	71-77	139	31	35
Manchester U.	Tr	01.78	77-80	109	0	37
Southampton	Verona (It)	08.84	84-86	48	0	12
Bristol C.	Tr	02.87	86-89	38	19	8

JORDAN Michael John
Exeter, 8 January, 1956 (W)

League Club	Source	Date Signed	Seasons Played	Apps	Subs	Gls
Exeter C.		07.75	75-76	15	3	3

JORDAN Roy Antony
Plymouth, 17 April, 1978 (W)

League Club	Source	Date Signed	Seasons Played	Apps	Subs	Gls
Hereford U.	YT	•	96	1	0	0

JORDAN Scott Douglas
Newcastle, 19 July, 1975 (M)

League Club	Source	Date Signed	Seasons Played	Apps	Subs	Gls
York C.	YT	10.92	92-97	64	31	5

JORDAN Timothy Edwin
Littleborough, 12 April, 1960 (F)

League Club	Source	Date Signed	Seasons Played	Apps	Subs	Gls
Oldham Ath.	Jnrs	06.78	78-79	2	3	0

JOSEPH Francis
Kilburn, 6 March, 1960 (F)

League Club	Source	Date Signed	Seasons Played	Apps	Subs	Gls
Wimbledon	Hillingdon Borough	11.80	80-81	42	9	14
Brentford	Tr	07.82	82-86	103	7	44
Wimbledon	L	03.87	86	2	3	1
Reading	Tr	07.87	87	5	6	2
Bristol Rov.	L	01.88	87	3	0	0
Aldershot	L	03.88	87	9	1	2
Sheffield U.	Tr	07.88	88	5	8	3
Gillingham	Tr	03.89	88-89	12	6	1
Crewe Alex.	Tr	12.89	89	9	7	2
Fulham	Tr	08.90	90	2	2	0
Barnet (N/C)	Racing Ghent (Bel)	10.91	91	1	0	0

JOSEPH Leon
Stepney, 26 February, 1920 Died 1983 E Amat (OL)

League Club	Source	Date Signed	Seasons Played	Apps	Subs	Gls
Tottenham H. (Am)	Leytonstone	02.47	46	1	-	0

JOSEPH Marc Ellis
Leicester, 10 November, 1976 (RB)

League Club	Source	Date Signed	Seasons Played	Apps	Subs	Gls
Cambridge U.	YT	05.95	95-97	52	9	0

JOSEPH Matthew Nathan Adolphus
Bethnal Green, 30 September, 1972 E Yth (M/D)

League Club	Source	Date Signed	Seasons Played	Apps	Subs	Gls
Arsenal	YT	11.90				
Gillingham (N/C)	Tr	12.92				
Cambridge U.	Ilves (Fin)	11.93	93-97	157	2	6
Leyton Orient	Tr	01.98	97	14	0	1

JOSEPH Roger Anthony
Paddington, 24 December, 1965 E'B' (RB)

League Club	Source	Date Signed	Seasons Played	Apps	Subs	Gls
Brentford	Southall	10.84	84-87	103	1	2
Wimbledon	Tr	08.88	88-94	155	7	0
Millwall	L	03.95	94	5	0	0
Leyton Orient (N/C)		11.96	96	15	0	0
West Bromwich A. (N/C)	Tr	02.97	96	0	2	0
Leyton Orient	Tr	08.97	97	13	12	0

JOSLIN Philip James
Kingsteignton, 1 September, 1916 Died 1981 (G)

League Club	Source	Date Signed	Seasons Played	Apps	Subs	Gls
Torquay U.	Plymouth Arg. (Am)	01.36	35-47	135	-	0
Cardiff C.	Tr	05.48	48-50	108	-	0

JOSLYN Roger Douglas William
Colchester, 7 May, 1950 (M)

League Club	Source	Date Signed	Seasons Played	Apps	Subs	Gls
Colchester U.	Jnrs	05.68	67-70	92	7	4
Aldershot	Tr	10.70	70-74	186	0	17
Watford	Tr	11.74	74-79	178	4	17
Reading	Tr	11.79	79-81	67	1	1

JOVANOVIC Nikola
Yugoslavia, 18 September, 1952 Yugoslav Int (CD)

League Club	Source	Date Signed	Seasons Played	Apps	Subs	Gls
Manchester U.	Red Star Belgrade (Yug)	01.80	79-80	20	1	4

JOWETT Harold Uttley
Halifax , 15 November, 1923 (OR)

League Club	Source	Date Signed	Seasons Played	Apps	Subs	Gls
Halifax T.		09.50	50	9	-	1

JOWETT Sylvester **James**
Sheffield, 27 January, 1926 (OL)

League Club	Source	Date Signed	Seasons Played	Apps	Subs	Gls
York C. (Am)	Sheffield U. (Am)	09.46	46	1	-	0

JOWETT Kenneth Stuart
Bradford, 9 March, 1927 Died 1993 (W)

League Club	Source	Date Signed	Seasons Played	Apps	Subs	Gls
Halifax T.	Fryston Colly	02.47	46-48	29	-	2

JOY Bernard
Fulham, 29 October, 1911 Died 1984 E Amat (CH)

League Club	Source	Date Signed	Seasons Played	Apps	Subs	Gls
Fulham (Am)	Corinthian Casuals	02.31	33	1	-	0
Arsenal (Am)	Corinthian Casuals	05.35	35-46	86	-	0

JOY Brian William
Salford, 26 February, 1951 (FB)

League Club	Source	Date Signed	Seasons Played	Apps	Subs	Gls
Blackburn Rov.	Coventry C. (Am)	08.68				
Torquay U.	Tr	08.69	69	26	1	0
Tranmere Rov.	Tr	06.70	70	21	0	1
Doncaster Rov.	Tr	07.72	72	28	6	1
Exeter C.	Tr	07.73	73-75	89	1	2
York C.	San Diego (USA)	09.76	76	18	0	0

JOY David Frederick
Barnard Castle, 23 September, 1943 E Yth (FB)

League Club	Source	Date Signed	Seasons Played	Apps	Subs	Gls
Huddersfield T.	Evenwood T.	07.62	65	1	0	0
York C.	Tr	06.67	67	13	2	0

JOY Harold Cuthbert
Ebbw Vale, 8 January, 1921 (CF)

League Club	Source	Date Signed	Seasons Played	Apps	Subs	Gls
Norwich C.	Lovells Ath.	02.47	46	8	-	4
Newport Co.	Tr	01.48	47	2	-	0

JOYCE Anthony John
Wembley, 24 September, 1971 (LB)

League Club	Source	Date Signed	Seasons Played	Apps	Subs	Gls
Queens Park R.	YT	03.90				
Aldershot (N/C)	Tr	05.91	90	3	0	0

JOYCE Christopher
Dumbarton, 19 April, 1933 (IF)

League Club	Source	Date Signed	Seasons Played	Apps	Subs	Gls
Nottingham F.	Vale of Leven	09.56	57	10	-	0
Notts Co.	Tr	07.59	59-61	62	-	18

JOYCE Eric
Durham, 3 July, 1924 Died 1977 (RH)

League Club	Source	Date Signed	Seasons Played	Apps	Subs	Gls
Bradford C.	Eppleton Colly	11.45	46	5	-	0

JOYCE John
Easington, 6 January, 1949 (OR)

League Club	Source	Date Signed	Seasons Played	Apps	Subs	Gls
Hartlepool U. (Am)	Peterlee Jnrs	03.67	66-68	4	0	0

JOYCE Joseph Patrick
Consett, 18 March, 1961 (RB)

League Club	Source	Date Signed	Seasons Played	Apps	Subs	Gls
Barnsley	Jnrs	11.79	79-90	332	2	4
Scunthorpe U.	Tr	02.91	90-92	91	0	2
Carlisle U.	Tr	08.93	93-94	45	5	0
Darlington	L	09.93	93	4	0	0

JOYCE Nicholas John
Leeds, 27 July, 1947 (W)

League Club	Source	Date Signed	Seasons Played	Apps	Subs	Gls
Bradford C. (Am)	Ashley Road	11.71	71	5	0	1

JOYCE Sean William
Doncaster, 15 February, 1967 (M)

League Club	Source	Date Signed	Seasons Played	Apps	Subs	Gls
Doncaster Rov.	YT	09.86	85-87	39	2	2
Exeter C.	L	11.86	86	1	0	0
Torquay U.	Tr	08.88	88-92	143	15	15

JOYCE Walter
Oldham, 10 September, 1937 (WH)

League Club	Source	Date Signed	Seasons Played	Apps	Subs	Gls
Burnley	Jnrs	10.54	60-63	70	-	3
Blackburn Rov.	Tr	02.64	63-67	119	1	4
Oldham Ath.	Tr	09.67	67-69	68	3	2

JOYCE Warren Garton
Oldham, 20 January, 1965 (M)

League Club	Source	Date Signed	Seasons Played	Apps	Subs	Gls
Bolton W.	Jnrs	06.82	82-87	180	4	17
Preston N.E.	Tr	10.87	87-91	170	7	34
Plymouth Arg.	Tr	05.92	92	28	2	3
Burnley	Tr	07.93	93-95	65	5	9
Hull C.	L	01.95	94	9	0	3
Hull C.	Tr	07.96	96-97	90	0	9

JUDD Jeremy Laurence
Bristol, 18 June, 1965 (G)

League Club	Source	Date Signed	Seasons Played	Apps	Subs	Gls
Bournemouth	Jnrs	07.82				
Torquay U. (N/C)	Dorchester T.	08.84	84	2	0	0

JUDD Michael David
Southampton, 18 June, 1948 (F)

League Club	Source	Date Signed	Seasons Played	Apps	Subs	Gls
Southampton	App	08.65	67-69	14	1	3

JUDD Walter James
Salisbury, 25 October, 1926 Died 1964 (F)

League Club	Source	Date Signed	Seasons Played	Apps	Subs	Gls
Southampton	Nomansland	08.49	50-52	34	-	13

JUDGE Alan Graham
Kingsbury, 14 May, 1960 (G)

League Club	Source	Date Signed	Seasons Played	Apps	Subs	Gls
Luton T.	Jnrs	01.78	79-82	11	0	0
Reading	Tr	09.82	82-84	77	0	0
Oxford U.	Tr	12.84	85-90	80	0	0
Lincoln C.	L	11.85	85	2	0	0
Cardiff C.	L	10.87	87	8	0	0
Hereford U.	Tr	07.91	91-93	105	0	0

JUDGES Barry John
Gillingham, 23 September, 1940 (CH)

League Club	Source	Date Signed	Seasons Played	Apps	Subs	Gls
Gillingham	Jnrs	12.57	57-58	3	-	0

JUKES Norman Geoffrey
Leeds, 14 October, 1932 (RB)

League Club	Source	Date Signed	Seasons Played	Apps	Subs	Gls
Huddersfield T.		07.51				
York C.	Tr	10.53	53	1	-	0

JULES Mark Anthony
Bradford, 5 September, 1971 (LW)

League Club	Source	Date Signed	Seasons Played	Apps	Subs	Gls
Bradford C.	YT	07.90				
Scarborough	Tr	08.91	91-92	57	20	16
Chesterfield	Tr	05.93	93-97	136	27	4

JULIANS Leonard Bruce
Tottenham, 19 June, 1933 Died 1993 (CF)

League Club	Source	Date Signed	Seasons Played	Apps	Subs	Gls
Leyton Orient	Walthamstow Ave.	06.55	55-58	66	-	35
Arsenal	Tr	12.58	58-59	18	-	7
Nottingham F.	Tr	06.60	60-63	58	-	24
Millwall	Tr	01.64	63-66	125	0	58

JULIUSSEN Albert Laurence
Blyth, 20 February, 1920 (CF)

League Club	Source	Date Signed	Seasons Played	Apps	Subs	Gls
Portsmouth	Dundee	03.48	47	7	-	4
Everton	Tr	09.48	48	10	-	1

JUMP Stewart Paul
Crumpsall, 27 January, 1952 (D)

League Club	Source	Date Signed	Seasons Played	Apps	Subs	Gls
Stoke C.	App	07.69	70-73	36	8	1
Crystal Palace	Tr	12.73	73-77	79	2	2
Fulham	L	01.77	76	3	0	0

[JUNINHO] JUNIOR Oswaldo Giroldo
Brazil, 22 February, 1973 Brazilian Int (M)

League Club	Source	Date Signed	Seasons Played	Apps	Subs	Gls
Middlesbrough	Sao Paulo (Br)	11.95	95-96	54	2	14

JUPP Duncan Alan
Haslemere, 25 January, 1975 Su21-10 (FB)

League Club	Source	Date Signed	Seasons Played	Apps	Subs	Gls
Fulham	YT	07.93	92-95	101	4	2
Wimbledon	Tr	06.96	96-97	9	0	0

JURYEFF Ian Martin
Gosport, 24 November, 1962 (F)

League Club	Source	Date Signed	Seasons Played	Apps	Subs	Gls
Southampton	App	11.80	83	0	2	0
Mansfield T.	L	03.84	83	12	0	5
Reading	L	11.84	84	7	0	1
Leyton Orient	Tr	02.85	84-88	106	5	45
Ipswich T.	L	02.89	88	0	2	0
Halifax T.	Tr	08.89	89	15	2	7
Hereford U.	Tr	12.89	89-90	25	3	4
Halifax T.	Tr	09.90	90-92	72	0	13
Darlington	Tr	08.92	92	25	8	6
Scunthorpe U.	Tr	08.93	93-94	41	3	13

KABIA James Paul
Mansfield, 11 November, 1954 (F)

League Club	Source	Date Signed	Seasons Played	Apps	Subs	Gls
Chesterfield	App	11.72	72-73	10	1	1

KABIA Jason Thomas
Sutton-in-Ashfield, 28 May, 1969 (F)

League Club	Source	Date Signed	Seasons Played	Apps	Subs	Gls
Lincoln C.	Oakham U.	01.92	91-92	17	11	4
Doncaster Rov.	L	01.93	92	5	0	0

KAILE Gordon Walter
Blandford Camp, 7 December, 1924 Died 1988 (OL)

League Club	Source	Date Signed	Seasons Played	Apps	Subs	Gls
Nottingham F.		05.45	47-49	65	-	8
Preston N.E.	Tr	07.51	51-53	7	-	1
Exeter C.	Tr	08.54	54	6	-	1

KAISER Rudolph Hendrik
Netherlands, 26 December, 1960 (W)

League Club	Source	Date Signed	Seasons Played	Apps	Subs	Gls
Coventry C.	Antwerp (Bel)	08.81	81	11	5	3

KALAC Zeljko
Australia, 16 December, 1972 Australian Int (G)

League Club	Source	Date Signed	Seasons Played	Apps	Subs	Gls
Leicester C.	Sydney U. (Aus)	10.95	95	1	0	0

KALOGERACOS Vasilios
Perth, Australia, 21 March, 1975 (F)

League Club	Source	Date Signed	Seasons Played	Apps	Subs	Gls
Stockport Co.	Perth Glory (Aus)	08.97	97	0	2	0

KAMARA Abdul Salam
Southampton, 10 February, 1974 (M)

League Club	Source	Date Signed	Seasons Played	Apps	Subs	Gls
Southampton	Jnrs	08.92				
Bristol C.	Tr	03.93	93	0	1	0

KAMARA Allan
Sheffield, 15 July, 1958 (FB)

League Club	Source	Date Signed	Seasons Played	Apps	Subs	Gls
York C.	Kiveton Park	07.79	79	10	0	0
Darlington	Tr	06.80	80-82	134	0	1
Scarborough	Burton A.	11.87	87-90	158	1	2
Halifax T.	Tr	08.91	91-92	34	2	0

KAMARA Christopher
Middlesbrough, 25 December, 1957 (M)

League Club	Source	Date Signed	Seasons Played	Apps	Subs	Gls
Portsmouth	App	12.75	75-76	56	7	7
Swindon T.	Tr	08.77	77-80	133	14	21
Portsmouth	Tr	08.81	81	11	0	0
Brentford	Tr	10.81	81-84	150	2	28
Swindon T.	Tr	08.85	85-87	86	1	6
Stoke C.	Tr	07.88	88-89	60	0	5
Leeds U.	Tr	01.90	89-91	15	5	1
Luton T.	Tr	11.91	91-92	49	0	0
Sheffield U.	L	11.92	92	6	2	0
Middlesbrough	L	02.93	92	3	2	0
Sheffield U.	Tr	07.93	93	15	1	0
Bradford C.	Tr	07.94	94	22	1	3

KAMINSKY Jason Mario George
Leicester, 5 December, 1973 (F)

League Club	Source	Date Signed	Seasons Played	Apps	Subs	Gls
Nottingham F.	YT	07.91	91	0	1	0

KAMMARK Pontus Sven
Sweden, 5 April, 1969 Swedish Int (CD)

League Club	Source	Date Signed	Seasons Played	Apps	Subs	Gls
Leicester C.	I.F.K. Gothenburg (Swe)	11.95	95-97	45	1	0

KANCHELSKIS Andrei
Ukraine, 23 January, 1969 Russian Int (RW)

League Club	Source	Date Signed	Seasons Played	Apps	Subs	Gls
Manchester U.	Shakytor Donetsk (USSR)	03.91	90-94	96	27	28
Everton	Tr	08.95	95-96	52	0	21

KANE Alan
Falkirk, 20 January, 1957 (M)

League Club	Source	Date Signed	Seasons Played	Apps	Subs	Gls
Portsmouth	Hibernian	03.75	74-75	6	1	0

KANE John Peter
Hackney, 15 December, 1960 (D)

League Club	Source	Date Signed	Seasons Played	Apps	Subs	Gls
Leyton Orient	App	12.78	78	0	1	0

KANE Leonard Russell
Belfast, 27 January, 1926 (FB)

League Club	Source	Date Signed	Seasons Played	Apps	Subs	Gls
Preston N.E.	Glentoran	05.47	48-49	5	-	0
Plymouth Arg.	Tr	01.50				

KANE Paul James
Edinburgh, 8 September, 1965 S Yth (M/RB)

League Club	Source	Date Signed	Seasons Played	Apps	Subs	Gls
Oldham Ath.	Hibernian	01.91	90-91	13	8	0
Barnsley (L)	Aberdeen	08.95	95	4	0	0

KANE Peter
Petershill, 4 April, 1939 (IF)

League Club	Source	Date Signed	Seasons Played	Apps	Subs	Gls
Northampton T.	Queens Park	10.59	59	28	-	16
Arsenal	Tr	07.60	60	4	-	1
Northampton T.	Tr	09.63	63	18	-	8
Crewe Alex.	Tr	03.64	63-66	82	1	31

KANE Robert
Cambuslang, 11 May, 1911 Died 1985 (CH)

League Club	Source	Date Signed	Seasons Played	Apps	Subs	Gls
Leeds U.	St Rochs	08.35	35-46	57	-	0

KAPENGWE Emment
Zambia, 27 March, 1943 (OR)

League Club	Source	Date Signed	Seasons Played	Apps	Subs	Gls
Aston Villa	Atlanta (USA)	09.69	69	3	0	0

KAPLER Konrad
Poland, 25 February, 1925 Died 1991 (OL)

League Club	Source	Date Signed	Seasons Played	Apps	Subs	Gls
Rochdale	Glasgow Celtic	05.49	49	4	-	0

KARAA Roch Di
Tunisia, 3 April, 1964 (G)

League Club	Source	Date Signed	Seasons Played	Apps	Subs	Gls
Darlington		03.85	84	1	0	0

KARL Steffen
East Germany, 3 February, 1970 (W)

League Club	Source	Date Signed	Seasons Played	Apps	Subs	Gls
Manchester C. (L)	Borussia Dortmund (Ger)	03.94	93	4	2	1

KASULE Victor
Glasgow, 28 May, 1965 (W)

League Club	Source	Date Signed	Seasons Played	Apps	Subs	Gls
Shrewsbury T.	Meadowbank Thistle	01.88	87-89	28	12	4

KATALINIC Ivan
Yugoslavia, 17, May, 1951 Yugoslav Int (G)

League Club	Source	Date Signed	Seasons Played	Apps	Subs	Gls
Southampton	Red Star Belgrade (Yug)	02.80	79-81	48	0	0

KATCHOURO Petr
Belarus, 2 August, 1972 Belarus Int (F)

League Club	Source	Date Signed	Seasons Played	Apps	Subs	Gls
Sheffield U.	Dinamo Minsk (Belarus)	07.96	96-97	34	22	12

KAVANAGH Eamonn Anthony
Manchester, 5 January, 1954 (M)

League Club	Source	Date Signed	Seasons Played	Apps	Subs	Gls
Manchester C.	Jnrs	06.71				
Rochdale	Tr	10.73	73	2	2	0
Workington	Bury (N/C)	03.74	73-76	123	6	11
Scunthorpe U.	Tr	08.77	77-79	69	8	3

KAVANAGH Edward Mark
Glasgow, 20 July, 1941 (OR)

League Club	Source	Date Signed	Seasons Played	Apps	Subs	Gls
Notts Co.	Cambuslang	05.64	64	25	-	4

KAVANAGH Graham Anthony
Dublin, 2 December, 1973 IR Sch/IR Yth/IRu21-9/IR 'B'/IR-1 (M)

League Club	Source	Date Signed	Seasons Played	Apps	Subs	Gls
Middlesbrough	Home Farm	08.91	92-95	22	13	3
Darlington	L	02.94	93	5	0	0
Stoke C.	Tr	09.96	96-97	76	6	9

KAVANAGH Jason Colin
Meriden, 23 November, 1971 E Sch/E Yth (RB)

League Club	Source	Date Signed	Seasons Played	Apps	Subs	Gls
Derby Co.	YT	12.88	90-95	74	25	1
Wycombe W.	Tr	11.96	96-97	70	2	1

KAVANAGH Michael
Dublin, 31 December, 1927 (OL)

League Club	Source	Date Signed	Seasons Played	Apps	Subs	Gls
Brighton & H.A.	Bohemians	02.48	48-49	26	-	7

KAVANAGH Peter John
Ilford, 3 November, 1938 (OL)

League Club	Source	Date Signed	Seasons Played	Apps	Subs	Gls
Fulham	Dagenham	10.56				
Everton	Romford	02.61	60	6	-	0

KAVELASHVILI Mikhail
Georgia, 22 July, 1971 Georgian Int (F)

League Club	Source	Date Signed	Seasons Played	Apps	Subs	Gls
Manchester C.	Spartak Vladikavkaz (Rus)	03.96	95-96	9	19	3

KAY Anthony Herbert
Sheffield, 13 May, 1937 Eu23-7/EF Lge/E-1 (LH)

League Club	Source	Date Signed	Seasons Played	Apps	Subs	Gls
Sheffield Wed.	Jnrs	05.54	54-62	179	-	10
Everton	Tr	12.62	62-63	50	-	4

KAY James
Preston, 3 May, 1932 (IF)

League Club	Source	Date Signed	Seasons Played	Apps	Subs	Gls
Stockport Co.	Leyland Motors	05.53	54-55	9	-	3
Crewe Alex.	Tr	12.56	56	4	-	0

KAY John
Great Lumley, 29 January, 1964 (RB)

League Club	Source	Date Signed	Seasons Played	Apps	Subs	Gls
Arsenal	App	08.81	82-83	13	1	0
Wimbledon	Tr	07.84	84-86	63	0	2
Middlesbrough	L	01.85	84	8	0	0
Sunderland	Tr	07.87	87-93	196	3	0
Shrewsbury T.	L	03.96	95	7	0	0
Preston N.E. (N/C)	Tr	08.96	96	7	0	0
Scarborough	Tr	09.96	96-97	74	0	0

KAY Kenneth
Newark, 9 March, 1920 Died 1986 (OL)

League Club	Source	Date Signed	Seasons Played	Apps	Subs	Gls
Mansfield T.	Ransome & Marles	06.47	47	1	-	0

KAY Robert (Roy)
Edinburgh, 24 October, 1949 (FB)

League Club	Source	Date Signed	Seasons Played	Apps	Subs	Gls
York C.	Hearts	07.78	78-81	160	0	8

KAYE Arthur
Darton, 9 May, 1933 E Sch/Eu23-1/EF Lge (OR)

League Club	Source	Date Signed	Seasons Played	Apps	Subs	Gls
Barnsley	Jnrs	05.50	50-58	265	-	54
Blackpool	Tr	05.59	59-60	38	-	9
Middlesbrough	Tr	11.60	60-64	164	-	38
Colchester U.	Tr	06.65	65-66	48	1	2

KAYE David Nicholas
Huddersfield, 14 November, 1959 (G)

League Club	Source	Date Signed	Seasons Played	Apps	Subs	Gls
Rotherham U.	App	11.77				
Chester C. (N/C)	Mexborough T.	03.85	84-85	10	0	0

KAYE George Henry (Harry)
Liverpool, 19 April, 1919 Died 1992 (WH)

League Club	Source	Date Signed	Seasons Played	Apps	Subs	Gls
Liverpool		04.41	46	1	-	0
Swindon T.	Tr	05.47	47-52	170	-	5

KAYE John
Goole, 3 March, 1940 EF Lge (D/CF)

League Club	Source	Date Signed	Seasons Played	Apps	Subs	Gls
Scunthorpe U.	Goole T.	09.60	60-62	77	-	25
West Bromwich A.	Tr	06.63	63-71	281	3	45
Hull C.	Tr	11.71	71-73	71	1	9

KAYE Peter John
Huddersfield, 4 February, 1979 (F)

League Club	Source	Date Signed	Seasons Played	Apps	Subs	Gls
Huddersfield T.	YT	09.96	96	0	1	0

KEAN Robert Steven
Luton, 3 June, 1978 (M)

League Club	Source	Date Signed	Seasons Played	Apps	Subs	Gls
Luton T.	YT	05.96	97	0	1	0

KEAN Stephen
Glasgow, 30 September, 1967 (W)

League Club	Source	Date Signed	Seasons Played	Apps	Subs	Gls
Swansea C. (L)	Glasgow Celtic	02.87	86	3	1	0

KEANE Robert David
Dublin, 8 July, 1980 IR 'B'/IR-3 (F)

League Club	Source	Date Signed	Seasons Played	Apps	Subs	Gls
Wolverhampton W.	YT	07.97	97	34	4	11

KEANE Roy Maurice
Cork, 10 August, 1971 IR Sch/IR Yth/IRu21-4/IR-38 (M)

League Club	Source	Date Signed	Seasons Played	Apps	Subs	Gls
Nottingham F	Cobh Ramblers	05.90	90-92	114	0	22
Manchester U.	Tr	07.93	93-97	116	5	17

KEANE Thomas Joseph
Dublin, 16 September, 1968 IR Yth (M)

League Club	Source	Date Signed	Seasons Played	Apps	Subs	Gls
Bournemouth	App	09.86	85-87	1	2	0
Colchester U.	Tr	12.87	87	9	7	0

KEANE Thomas Roderick
Limerick (Ire), 31 August, 1922 IR-4/NI-1 (FB)

League Club	Source	Date Signed	Seasons Played	Apps	Subs	Gls
Swansea C.	Limerick	06.47	47-54	164	-	0

KEAR Michael Philip
Coleford, 27 May, 1943 (OR)

League Club	Source	Date Signed	Seasons Played	Apps	Subs	Gls
Newport Co.	Cinderford T.	08.63	63	6	-	0
Nottingham F.	Tr	12.63	63-66	26	1	5
Middlesbrough	Tr	09.67	67-69	56	2	7
Barnsley	L	08.70	70	6	0	1

KEARNEY Mark James
Ormskirk, 12 June, 1962 (M/LB)

League Club	Source	Date Signed	Seasons Played	Apps	Subs	Gls
Everton	Marine	10.81				
Mansfield T.	Tr	03.83	82-90	248	2	29
Bury	Tr	01.91	90-93	109	4	5

KEARNEY Michael Joseph
Glasgow, 18 February, 1953 (F)

League Club	Source	Date Signed	Seasons Played	Apps	Subs	Gls
Shrewsbury T.	Petershill	12.72	72-76	143	6	41
Chester C.	Tr	03.77	76-77	37	1	5
Reading	Tr	01.78	77-79	78	9	24
Chester C.	Tr	07.80	80	9	0	0
Reading	Tr	10.80	80-82	57	1	12

KEARNEY Noel Michael
Ipswich, 7 October, 1942 (F)

League Club	Source	Date Signed	Seasons Played	Apps	Subs	Gls
Ipswich T.	Jnrs	10.60				
Colchester U.	Tr	09.64	64	3	-	0

KEARNEY Sidney Francis
Liverpool, 28 March, 1917 Died 1982 (LH)

League Club	Source	Date Signed	Seasons Played	Apps	Subs	Gls
Leicester C.	Crowndale	08.36				
Tranmere Rov.	Tr	05.37	37-38	31	-	3
Accrington St.	Tr	11.38	38-46	30	-	7
Bristol C.	Tr	01.47	46-49	65	-	5

KEARNS Frederick Thomas
Dublin, 8 January, 1927 Died 1987 IR-1 (CF)

League Club	Source	Date Signed	Seasons Played	Apps	Subs	Gls
West Ham U.	Shamrock Rov.	05.48	49-53	43	-	14
Norwich C.	Tr	06.54	54-55	28	-	11

KEARNS Jamie Adam
Hammersmith, 28 October, 1971 (FB)

League Club	Source	Date Signed	Seasons Played	Apps	Subs	Gls
Cambridge U. (N/C)	YT	07.90	90	1	0	0

KEARNS Michael
Banbury, 26 November, 1950 IR-18 (G)

League Club	Source	Date Signed	Seasons Played	Apps	Subs	Gls
Oxford U.	App	07.68	69-71	67	0	0
Plymouth Arg.	L	10.72	72	1	0	0
Charlton Ath.	L	02.73	72	4	0	0
Walsall	Tr	07.73	73-78	249	0	0
Wolverhampton W.	Tr	07.79	79-80	9	0	0
Walsall	Tr	08.82	82-84	26	0	0

KEARNS Michael David
Nuneaton, 10 March, 1938 (D)

League Club	Source	Date Signed	Seasons Played	Apps	Subs	Gls
Coventry C.	Stockingford	09.55	57-67	344	0	14

KEARNS Oliver Anthony
Banbury, 12 June, 1956 (F)

League Club	Source	Date Signed	Seasons Played	Apps	Subs	Gls
Reading	Banbury U.	03.77	76-79	75	11	40
Oxford U.	Tr	08.81	81	9	9	4
Walsall	Tr	08.82	82	31	7	11
Hereford U.	Tr	06.83	83-87	166	4	58
Wrexham	Tr	12.87	87-89	36	10	14

KEARNS Peter Vincent
Aldershot, 26 March, 1937 (IF)

League Club	Source	Date Signed	Seasons Played	Apps	Subs	Gls
Plymouth Arg.	Wellingborough T.	04.56	56-59	65	-	8
Aldershot	Corby T.	12.62	62-67	184	1	64
Lincoln C.	Tr	03.68	67-68	45	1	11

KEARTON Jason Brett
Australia, 9 July, 1969 (G)

League Club	Source	Date Signed	Seasons Played	Apps	Subs	Gls
Everton	Brisbane Lions (Aus)	10.88	92-94	3	3	0
Stoke C.	L	08.91	91	16	0	0
Blackpool	L	01.92	91	14	0	0
Notts Co.	L	01.95	94	10	0	0
Crewe Alex.	Tr	10.96	96-97	73	0	0

KEATES Dean Scott
Walsall, 30 June, 1978 (D)

League Club	Source	Date Signed	Seasons Played	Apps	Subs	Gls
Walsall	YT	08.96	96-97	33	2	1

KEATING, Brian Alfred
Lewisham, 19 March, 1935 (CF)

League Club	Source	Date Signed	Seasons Played	Apps	Subs	Gls
Crewe Alex. (Am)	Barry T.	07.56	56-57	7	-	1

KEATING Dennis Joseph
Cork (Ire), 18 October, 1940 (OL)

League Club	Source	Date Signed	Seasons Played	Apps	Subs	Gls
Chester C.	Saltney Jnrs	06.62	62	1	-	0

KEATING Patrick Joseph
Cork (Ire), 17 September, 1930 (OL)

League Club	Source	Date Signed	Seasons Played	Apps	Subs	Gls
Sheffield U.	Cork	02.50	50	3	-	0
Bradford P.A.	Wisbech T.	09.53	53	2	-	0
Chesterfield	Tr	10.53	53-56	95	-	21

KEATING Robert
Oldham, 24 June, 1917 Died 1985 (W)

League Club	Source	Date Signed	Seasons Played	Apps	Subs	Gls
Oldham Ath.		08.41				
Accrington St.	Hereford U.	12.46	46	5	-	0

KEAY John (Jack) Paul
Glasgow, 14 June, 1960 (CD)

League Club	Source	Date Signed	Seasons Played	Apps	Subs	Gls
Shrewsbury T.	Glasgow Celtic (Jnrs)	07.77	77-81	152	3	20
Wrexham	Tr	09.82	82-85	156	0	9

KEE Paul James
Derry, 21 February, 1967 NI Yth (F)

League Club	Source	Date Signed	Seasons Played	Apps	Subs	Gls
Mansfield T.	App	01.84	83	0	1	0
Nottingham F.	Tr	01.85				

League Club	Source	Date Signed	Seasons Played	Apps	Subs	Gls
KEE Paul Victor						
Belfast, 8 November, 1969 NI Yth/NIu21-1/NI-9						(G)
Oxford U.	Ards	05.88	89-93	56	0	0
KEEBLE Brian Beverley						
Holbeach, 11 July, 1938						(LB)
Grimsby T.	Holbeach U.	05.59	59-64	172	-	1
Darlington	Tr	07.65	65-68	154	0	2
KEEBLE Christopher Mark						
Colchester, 17 September, 1978						(M)
Ipswich T.	YT	06.97	97	0	1	0
KEEBLE Walter **Frederick**						
Coventry, 30 August, 1919						(IF)
Grimsby T.	Albion Rov.	09.46	46	7	-	1
Notts Co.	Tr	07.47	47	4	-	1
KEEBLE Matthew						
Chipping Norton, 8 September, 1972						(F)
Oxford U.	YT	05.91	92-93	1	1	0
KEEBLE Victor Albert William						
Colchester, 25 June, 1930						(CF)
Colchester U.	King George Y.C.	(N/L)	50-51	46	-	23
Newcastle U.	Tr	02.52	51-57	104	-	56
West Ham U.	Tr	10.57	57-59	76	-	45
KEEFE David Edward						
Dagenham, 23 June, 1957						(W)
Southend U.	App	07.75	74-75	4	2	1
Torquay U.	Tr	08.77	77	2	0	0
KEEGAN Gerard (Ged) Anthony						
Bradford, 3 October, 1955 Eu21-1						(M)
Manchester C.	App	03.73	74-78	32	5	2
Oldham Ath.	Tr	02.79	78-82	139	5	5
Mansfield T.	Tr	10.83	83	18	0	1
Rochdale	Tr	07.84	84	2	0	0
KEEGAN Joseph **Kevin**						
Armthorpe, 14 February, 1951 Eu23-5/E-63						(F)
Scunthorpe U.	App	12.68	68-70	120	4	17
Liverpool	Tr	05.71	71-76	230	0	68
Southampton	S.V. Hamburg (Ger)	07.80	80-81	68	0	37
Newcastle U.	Tr	08.82	82-83	78	0	48
KEELAN Kevin Damien						
India, 5 January, 1941						(G)
Aston Villa	Jnrs	07.58	59-60	5	-	0
Stockport Co.	Tr	04.61	60	3	-	0
Wrexham	Kidderminster Hrs	11.61	61-62	68	-	0
Norwich C.	Tr	07.63	63-79	571	0	0
KEELEY Andrew James						
Basildon, 16 September, 1956 E Yth						(D)
Tottenham U.	App	01.74	76	5	1	0
Sheffield U.	Tr	12.77	77-80	28	0	0
Scunthorpe U.	Tr	07.81	81-82	75	2	1
KEELEY Damian						
Salford, 14 February, 1963						(F)
Torquay U. (N/C)		09.81	81	1	2	0
KEELEY Glenn Matthew						
Barking, 1 September, 1954 E Yth						(CD)
Ipswich T.	App	08.72	72-73	4	0	0
Newcastle U.	Tr	07.74	74-75	43	1	2
Blackburn Rov.	Tr	08.76	76-86	365	5	23
Everton	L	10.82	82	1	0	0
Oldham Ath.	Tr	08.87	87	10	1	0
Colchester U.	L	02.88	87	4	0	0
Bolton W.	Tr	09.88	88	20	0	0
KEELEY John Henry						
Plaistow, 27 July, 1961						(G)
Southend U.	App	07.79	79-84	63	0	0
Brighton & H.A.	Chelmsford C.	08.86	86-89	138	0	0
Oldham Ath.	Tr.	08.90	91-92	2	0	0
Oxford U.	L	11.91	91	6	0	0
Reading	L	02.92	91	6	0	0
Chester C.	L	08.92	92	4	0	0
Colchester U.	Tr	07.93	93	15	0	0
Stockport Co.	Chelmsford C.	03.94	93-94	20	0	0
Peterborough U.	Tr	01.95	94	3	0	0
KEELEY John (Jack) James						
Liverpool, 18 October, 1936 E Sch/E Yth						(IF)
Everton	Jnrs	05.54	57	4	-	1
Accrington St.	Tr	07.59	59	10	-	1
Southport	Tr	12.59	59	4	-	0
KEELEY Nolan Bruce						
Fakenham, 24 May, 1951						(M)
Scunthorpe U.	Yarmouth T.	07.73	72-79	255	4	37
Lincoln C.	Tr	01.80	79-80	52	0	3
KEELEY Raymond						
Battersea, 25 December, 1946						(IF)
Charlton Ath.	App	12.64	64	1	-	0
Exeter C.	Tr	03.66	65-66	45	1	10
Mansfield T.	Crawley T.	06.68	68-69	48	4	5
KEELEY Walter						
Manchester, 1 April, 1921 Died 1995						(IF)
Accrington St.		12.44	46-47	48	-	21
Bury	Tr	10.47	47	7	-	0
Port Vale	Tr	01.48	47-48	18	-	3
Accrington St.	Tr	09.48	48-51	101	-	35
Rochdale	Tr	10.51	51	4	-	0
KEEN Alan						
Barrow, 29 May, 1930						(IF)
Barrow	Barrow Social	05.49	49-53	95	-	14
Chesterfield	Tr	07.54	54-55	54	-	12
Bradford P.A.	Cheltenham T.	02.57	56	11	-	1
Carlisle U.	Cheltenham T.	09.58	58-59	7	-	0
KEEN Herbert						
Barrow, 9 September, 1926 Died 1993						(OL)
Barrow	Netherfield	07.53	53	8	-	0
KEEN John						
Barrow, 26 January, 1929						(WH)
Barrow	West Bromwich A. (Am)	01.48	47-58	273	-	19
Workington	Tr	07.59	59	19	-	0
KEEN Kevin Ian						
Amersham, 25 February, 1967 E Sch/E Yth						(RM)
West Ham U.	App	03.84	86-92	187	32	21
Wolverhampton W.	Tr	07.93	93-94	37	5	7
Stoke C.	Tr	10.94	94-97	84	26	7
KEEN Michael Andrew Charles						
Wrexham, 12 February, 1963 W Sch						(G)
Chester C.	Jnrs	09.81				
Wrexham (N/C)	Lex XI	06.85	85	5	0	0
KEEN Michael Thomas						
High Wycombe, 19 March, 1940						(WH)
Queens Park R.	Jnrs	06.58	59-68	393	0	39
Luton T.	Tr	01.69	68-71	143	1	11
Watford	Tr	07.72	72-74	124	2	5
KEEN Nigel John						
Barrow, 23 October, 1961						(M)
Manchester U.	App	02.79				
Preston N.E.	Barrow	05.85	85	24	0	0
KEENAN Gerald Patrick						
Liverpool, 25 July, 1954						(FB)
Bury	Skelmersdale	04.75	74-78	69	2	3
Port Vale	Tr	09.78	78-81	105	1	7
Rochdale	Tr	11.82	82-83	35	0	1
KEENAN William George						
Llanelli, 29 December, 1918 Died 1993						(OL)
Everton	Hereford U.	01.39				
Newport Co.	Tr	06.46	46	4	-	1
KEENE Douglas Charles						
Hendon, 30 August, 1928 Died 1986						(W)
Brentford	Jnrs	09.47	48-49	13	-	1
Brighton & H.A.	Tr	06.50	50-52	61	-	10
Colchester U.	Tr	07.53	53	22	-	1
KEEP Vernon						
Chester, 23 May, 1963						(M)
Wrexham (N/C)	Connahs Quay	10.84	84	0	1	0
KEERS James						
Stanley, 10 December, 1931						(OR)
Darlington	Evenwood T.	03.52	51-55	73	-	15
KEERY Stanley						
Derby, 9 September, 1931						(WH)
Shrewsbury T.	Blackburn Rov. (Am)	08.52	52	15	-	2
Newcastle U.	Tr	11.52	52-56	19	-	1

League Club	Source	Date Signed	Seasons Played	Apps	Subs	Gls
Mansfield T.	Tr	05.57	57-58	53	-	17
Crewe Alex.	Tr	10.58	58-64	254	-	23

KEETCH Robert David
Tottenham, 25 October, 1941 Died 1996 (CH)

League Club	Source	Date Signed	Seasons Played	Apps	Subs	Gls
Fulham	West Ham U. (Am)	04.59	62-65	106	0	2
Queens Park R.	Tr	11.66	66-68	49	3	0

KEETLEY Ernest **Albert**
Nottingham, 22 February, 1930 (FB)

League Club	Source	Date Signed	Seasons Played	Apps	Subs	Gls
Bury		03.50	50	4	-	0
Bournemouth	Tr	07.52	53-57	86	-	0

KEETON Albert
Chesterfield, 15 January, 1918 Died 1996 (RB)

League Club	Source	Date Signed	Seasons Played	Apps	Subs	Gls
Torquay U.	Mosborough Trin.	06.37	37-47	77	-	0

KEIGHLEY John **Paul**
Ribchester (Lancs), 15 February, 1961 (M)

League Club	Source	Date Signed	Seasons Played	Apps	Subs	Gls
Bolton W.	App	02.79				
Crewe Alex.	Tr	08.81	81	25	4	0

KEIR Colin William
Bournemouth, 14 January, 1938 (W)

League Club	Source	Date Signed	Seasons Played	Apps	Subs	Gls
Portsmouth	Jnrs	05.55				
Workington	Tr	06.59	59	4	-	0

KEIRS John
Irvine, 14 August, 1947 Died 1995 (CH)

League Club	Source	Date Signed	Seasons Played	Apps	Subs	Gls
Charlton Ath.	Annbank U.	06.65	65-70	73	5	1

KEISTER John Edward Samuel
Manchester, 11 November, 1970 Sierra Leone Int (M)

League Club	Source	Date Signed	Seasons Played	Apps	Subs	Gls
Walsall	Faweh F.C.	09.93	93-97	76	27	2

KEITH Adrian John
Colchester, 16 December, 1962 (D)

League Club	Source	Date Signed	Seasons Played	Apps	Subs	Gls
West Ham U.	App	12.80				
Colchester U. (N/C)		12.82	82	4	0	0

KEITH Richard (Dick) Matthewson
Belfast, 15 May, 1933 Died 1967 NI 'B'/NI-23 (RB)

League Club	Source	Date Signed	Seasons Played	Apps	Subs	Gls
Newcastle U.	Linfield	09.56	56-63	208	-	2
Bournemouth	Tr	02.64	63-65	47	0	0

KEIZEWEED Orpheo **Henk**
Netherlands, 21 November, 1968 (F)

League Club	Source	Date Signed	Seasons Played	Apps	Subs	Gls
Oldham Ath. (N/C)	Rodez (Fr)	03.93	92	0	1	0

KELL George **Allan**
Spennymoor, 9 April, 1949 (WH)

League Club	Source	Date Signed	Seasons Played	Apps	Subs	Gls
Darlington (Am)		08.66	67	0	2	0

KELL Leonard William
Billingham, 27 May, 1932 (IF)

League Club	Source	Date Signed	Seasons Played	Apps	Subs	Gls
Chelsea	Jnrs	02.52	53	3	-	0
Norwich C.	Tr	06.54	54	2	-	0

KELLARD Robert Sydney William
Edmonton, 1 March, 1943 E Yth (M)

League Club	Source	Date Signed	Seasons Played	Apps	Subs	Gls
Southend U.	Jnrs	05.60	59-62	106	-	15
Crystal Palace	Tr	09.63	63-65	77	0	6
Ipswich T.	Tr	11.65	65	13	0	3
Portsmouth	Tr	03.66	65-67	91	0	8
Bristol C.	Tr	07.68	68-69	77	0	6
Leicester C.	Tr	08.70	70-71	48	0	8
Crystal Palace	Tr	09.71	71-72	44	2	4
Portsmouth	Tr	12.72	72-74	62	1	6
Hereford U.	L	01.75	74	3	0	1
Torquay U.	South Africa	09.75	75	2	0	0

KELLER Kasey
U.S.A., 27 November, 1969 USA Int (G)

League Club	Source	Date Signed	Seasons Played	Apps	Subs	Gls
Millwall	Portland Univ. (USA)	02.92	91-95	176	0	0
Leicester C.	Tr	08.96	96-97	63	0	0

KELLEY Alan William
Liverpool, 24 December, 1952 (FB)

League Club	Source	Date Signed	Seasons Played	Apps	Subs	Gls
Southport	App	12.70	70-71	17	6	2
Crewe Alex.	Tr	08.72	72-75	105	2	0

KELLEY Stanley Robert
Foleshill, 14 June, 1920 Died 1993 (FB)

League Club	Source	Date Signed	Seasons Played	Apps	Subs	Gls
Coventry C.	Herberts Ath.	08.39	46	4	-	0

KELLOCK William
Glasgow, 7 February, 1954 S Sch (M)

League Club	Source	Date Signed	Seasons Played	Apps	Subs	Gls
Cardiff C.	Aston Villa (App)	02.72	71-72	33	2	2
Norwich C.	Tr	06.73	73	1	2	0

League Club	Source	Date Signed	Seasons Played	Apps	Subs	Gls
Millwall	Tr	07.74				
Peterborough U.	Kettering T.	08.79	79-81	134	0	43
Luton T.	Tr	07.82	82	2	5	0
Wolverhampton W.	Tr	03.83	82-83	12	0	3
Southend U.	Tr	09.83	83-84	53	0	8
Port Vale	Tr	12.84	84	10	1	4
Halifax T.	Tr	07.85	85	41	2	17

KELLOW Tony
Falmouth, 1 May, 1952 (F)

League Club	Source	Date Signed	Seasons Played	Apps	Subs	Gls
Exeter C.	Falmouth	07.76	76-78	107	0	40
Blackpool	Tr	11.78	78-79	57	0	23
Exeter C.	Tr	03.80	79-83	140	3	61
Plymouth Arg.	Tr	11.83	83	8	2	2
Swansea C. (N/C)	Tr	10.84	84	0	1	0
Newport Co. (N/C)	Tr	11.84	84	17	3	8
Exeter C.	Tr	07.85	85-87	51	31	28

KELLY Alan James Alexander
Dublin, 5 July 1936, IR-47 (G)

League Club	Source	Date Signed	Seasons Played	Apps	Subs	Gls
Preston N.E.	Drumcondra	04.58	60-73	447	0	0

KELLY Alan Thomas
Preston, 11 August, 1968 IR Yth/IRu21-3/IRu23-1/IR-20 (G)

League Club	Source	Date Signed	Seasons Played	Apps	Subs	Gls
Preston N.E.	YT	09.85	85-91	142	0	0
Sheffield U.	Tr	07.92	92-97	191	3	0

KELLY Anthony Gerald
Prescot, 1 October, 1964 (M)

League Club	Source	Date Signed	Seasons Played	Apps	Subs	Gls
Liverpool	App	09.82				
Wigan Ath.	Prescot Cables	01.84	83-85	98	3	15
Stoke C.	Tr	04.86	85-86	33	3	4
West Bromwich A.	Tr	07.87	87	26	0	1
Chester C.	L	09.88	88	5	0	0
Colchester U.	L	10.88	88	13	0	2
Shrewsbury T.	Tr	01.89	88-90	100	1	15
Bolton W.	Tr	08.91	91-94	103	3	5
Port Vale (N/C)	Tr	09.94	94	3	1	1
Millwall (N/C)	Tr	10.94	94	1	1	0
Peterborough U.	Tr	12.94	94	12	1	2
Wigan Ath.	Tr	07.95	95	2	0	0

KELLY Nyree **Anthony** Okpara
Meriden, 14 February, 1966 (W)

League Club	Source	Date Signed	Seasons Played	Apps	Subs	Gls
Bristol C. (N/C)	Jnrs	09.82	82	2	4	1
Stoke C.	St Albans C.	01.90	89-92	33	25	5
Hull C.	L	01.92	91	6	0	1
Cardiff C.	L	10.92	92	5	0	1
Bury	Tr	09.93	93-94	53	4	10
Leyton Orient	Tr	07.95	95-96	38	5	4
Colchester U.	L	10.96	96	2	1	0

KELLY Arthur
Belfast, 12 March, 1914 Died 1973 (CF)

League Club	Source	Date Signed	Seasons Played	Apps	Subs	Gls
Barrow	Belfast Celtic	09.46	46	8	-	2

KELLY Bernard
New Stevenson, 21 October, 1932 S 'B'/SF Lge (IF)

League Club	Source	Date Signed	Seasons Played	Apps	Subs	Gls
Leicester C.	Raith Rov.	07.58	58	24	-	13
Nottingham F.	Tr	04.59	58	2	-	0

KELLY Bernard Alexander
Kensington, 21 August, 1928 OR)

League Club	Source	Date Signed	Seasons Played	Apps	Subs	Gls
Brentford	Bath C.	08.50	50	1	-	1

KELLY Brian Leslie
Ilkley, 22 May, 1943 (FB)

League Club	Source	Date Signed	Seasons Played	Apps	Subs	Gls
Bradford C.	Jnrs	05.60	61-64	83	-	2
Doncaster Rov.	Tr	01.65	64-67	130	1	3
York C.	Tr	07.68	68-69	32	1	0

KELLY William **Brian**
Isleworth, 25 September, 1937 (CF)

League Club	Source	Date Signed	Seasons Played	Apps	Subs	Gls
Queens Park R.	Dover T.	11.58	58	6	-	0

KELLY Christopher Miles
Epsom, 14 October, 1948 E Amat (F)

League Club	Source	Date Signed	Seasons Played	Apps	Subs	Gls
Millwall	Leatherhead	01.75	74	9	2	0

KELLY David Thomas
Birmingham, 25 November, 1965 IRu21-3/IRu23-1/IR 'B'/IR-26 (F)

League Club	Source	Date Signed	Seasons Played	Apps	Subs	Gls
Walsall	Alvechurch	12.83	83-87	115	32	63
West Ham U.	Tr	08.88	88-89	29	12	7
Leicester C.	Tr	03.90	89-91	63	3	22
Newcastle U.	Tr	12.91	91-92	70	0	35
Wolverhampton W.	Tr	06.93	93-95	76	7	26
Sunderland	Tr	09.95	95-96	32	2	2
Tranmere Rov.	Tr	08.97	97	28	1	11

League Club	Source	Date Signed	Seasons Played	Career Record Apps	Subs	Gls
KELLY Desmond Charles James Jude						
Limerick (Ire), 1 November, 1950						(G)
Norwich C.	Limerick	07.70				
Colchester U.	Tr	06.72	72	1	0	0
KELLY Donald Joseph						
Market Harborough, 2 July, 1922						(CF)
Torquay U.	Coventry C. (Am)	07.47	46-47	5	-	3
KELLY Douglas Cain						
Barnsley, 30 May, 1934						(CF)
Barnsley	Jnrs	08.51	52-54	18	-	7
Bradford C.	Tr	06.55	55-56	43	-	14
Chesterfield	Tr	06.57	57	1	-	1
KELLY Edward Patrick						
Glasgow, 7 February, 1951						(M)
Arsenal	Jnrs	02.68	69-75	168	7	13
Queens Park R.	Tr	09.76	76	28	0	1
Leicester C.	Tr	07.77	77-79	85	0	3
Notts Co.	Tr	07.80	80	26	1	1
Bournemouth	Tr	08.81	81	13	0	0
Leicester C.	Tr	12.81	81-82	34	0	0
Torquay U. (N/C)	Melton T.	10.84	84-85	35	0	1
KELLY Errington Edison						
St Vincent (WI), 8 April, 1958						(W)
Bristol Rov.	Ledbury T.	09.81	81-82	12	6	3
Lincoln C. (N/C)	Tr	01.83	82	0	2	0
Bristol C.	Tr	02.83	82	4	1	1
Coventry C.	Tr	08.83				
Peterborough U.	Tr	03.84	83-85	59	13	22
Peterborough U.		12.86	86-87	36	10	6
KELLY Frederick Charles						
Wednesbury, 11 February, 1921						(CF)
Walsall		12.45	46-47	16	-	6
KELLY Garry						
Drogheda (IR), 9 July, 1974 IR Sch/IR Yth/IRu21-5/IR-28						(RB)
Leeds U.	Home Farm	09.91	91-97	186	4	2
KELLY Gary Alexander						
Preston, 3 August, 1966 IRu21-8/IRu23-1/IR 'B'						(G)
Newcastle U.	App	06.84	86-89	53	0	0
Blackpool	L	10.88	88	5	0	0
Bury	Tr	10.89	89-95	236	0	0
Oldham Ath.	Tr	08.96	96-97	68	0	0
KELLY Gavin John						
Beverley, 29 September, 1968						(G)
Hull C.	YT	05.87	88-89	11	0	0
Bristol Rov.	Tr	06.90	90-93	30	0	0
Scarborough	Tr	08.94	94-95	30	0	0
KELLY George Lawson						
Aberdeen, 29 June, 1933						(IF)
Stoke C	Aberdeen	02.56	55-57	67	-	35
Cardiff C.	Tr	05.58	58	8	-	4
Stockport Co.	Tr	07.59	59	34	-	4
KELLY Hugh Redmond						
Lurgan, 17 August, 1919 Died 1977 LoI/NI-4						(G)
Fulham	Belfast Celtic	03.49	49	25	-	0
Southampton	Tr	08.50	50	28	-	0
Exeter C.	Tr	06.52	52-55	99	-	0
KELLY Hugh Thomas						
Culross, 23 July 1923 S'B'-1/S-1						(WH)
Blackpool	Jeanfield Swifts	08.44	46-59	429	-	5
KELLY James						
Bellshill, 4 June, 1933						(CF)
Preston N.E.	Peterborough U.	05.55				
Swindon T.	Tr	02.58	57-58	30	-	14
Walsall	Tr	02.59	58	8	-	1
KELLY James						
Liverpool, 14 February, 1973						(M)
Wrexham	YT	07.91	90-91	11	10	0
Wolverhampton W.	Tr	02.92	91-93	4	3	0
Walsall	L	03.93	92	7	3	2
Wrexham	L	03.94	93	9	0	0
KELLY James						
Bradford, 1 July, 1938						(WH)
Halifax T.	Queensbury U.	10.62	63	3	-	0

League Club	Source	Date Signed	Seasons Played	Career Record Apps	Subs	Gls
KELLY James						
Morpeth, 11 August, 1931						(WH)
Watford	Blyth Spartans	03.49	50-54	119	-	4
Blackpool	Tr	10.54	54-60	198	-	9
KELLY James						
Aldergrove (NI), 6 February, 1954						(W)
Wolverhampton W.	Cliftonville	12.71	73-77	20	2	0
Wrexham	L	09.75	75	4	0	0
Walsall	Tr	08.76	78-79	19	7	3
KELLY James						
						(CF)
Barrow		02.46	46	1	-	0
KELLY James Edward						
Seaham, 29 December, 1907 Died 1984						(FB)
Southport	Murton Colly	11.28	28-30	7	-	0
Barrow	Tr	08.31	31-32	63	-	0
Grimsby T.	Tr	03.33	32-37	160	-	3
Bradford P.A.	Tr	05.38	38	2	-	0
York C.	Tr	12.38	38	24	-	0
Barrow	Trondheim (Nor)	06.46	46	1	-	0
KELLY James Lawrence						
Holborn, 14 July, 1926 Died 1996						(IF)
Gillingham	Dartford	05.51	51	3	-	0
KELLY James Patrick						
Sacriston (Dm), 22 November, 1951						(FB)
Hartlepool U.		08.70	71	5	0	0
KELLY James Patrick						
Drogheda (Ire), 16 February, 1925						(OL)
Tottenham H.	Glenavon	07.49				
Carlisle U.	Tr	02.50	49-51	42	-	6
KELLY James William						
Carlisle, 2 May, 1957						(M)
Manchester U.	App	05.74	75	0	1	0
KELLY John						
Bebington, 20 October, 1960 IRu21-2						(W/M)
Tranmere Rov.	Cammell Laird	09.79	79-81	55	9	9
Preston N.E.	Tr	10.81	81-84	120	10	27
Chester C.	Tr	08.85	85-86	85	0	17
Swindon T.	Tr	06.87	87	3	4	1
Oldham Ath.	Tr	11.87	87-88	51	1	6
Walsall	Tr	08.89	89-90	36	3	1
Huddersfield T.	L	03.90	89	9	1	1
Huddersfield T.	Tr	02.91	90-91	16	2	0
Chester C.	Tr	07.92	92	24	7	1
KELLY John Carmichael						
Paisley, 21 February, 1921 S-2						(W)
Barnsley	Morton	12.45	46-52	217	-	25
Halifax T.	Morton	07.56	56-57	38	-	2
KELLY John Gerald						
Glasgow, 14 December, 1935 S Sch						(WH)
Crewe Alex.	Third Lanark	08.59	59	20	-	1
KELLY Lawrence						
Wolverhampton, 28 April, 1925						(LB)
Wolverhampton W.	Jnrs	03.43	47-49	60	-	0
Huddersfield T.	Tr	10.50	50-56	225	-	2
KELLY Mark David						
Blackpool, 7 October, 1966						(M)
Shrewsbury T.		12.85				
Cardiff C.	Tr	06.87	87-89	93	12	2
Fulham	Tr	06.90	90-92	55	9	2
KELLY Mark John						
Sutton, 27 November, 1969 E Yth/IRu21-3/IRu23-2/IR-4						(W)
Portsmouth	YT	11.86	87-90	24	25	2
KELLY Michael						
						(OL)
Wolverhampton W.		06.39				
Crewe Alex.	Tr	11.45	46	15	-	2
KELLY Michael John						
Northampton, 18 October, 1942 E Amat						(G)
Queens Park R.	Wimbledon	03.66	67-69	54	0	0
Birmingham C.	Tr	08.70	70-74	62	0	0

KELLY Michael Lawrence
Belvedere, 22 October, 1954 (M)

League Club	Source	Date Signed	Seasons Played	Apps	Subs	Gls
Millwall	App	10.72	72-74	16	2	2
Charlton Ath.	Tr	12.74	74	10	0	3

KELLY Noel
Dublin, 28 December, 1921 Died 1991 LoI/IR-1 (IF)

League Club	Source	Date Signed	Seasons Played	Apps	Subs	Gls
Arsenal	Glentoran	10.47	49	1	-	0
Crystal Palace	Tr	03.50	49-50	42	-	5
Nottingham F.	Tr	08.51	51-54	48	-	11
Tranmere Rov.	Tr	07.55	55-56	52	-	6

KELLY Norman
Belfast, 10 October, 1970 NI Yth/NIu21-1 (M)

League Club	Source	Date Signed	Seasons Played	Apps	Subs	Gls
Oldham Ath.	YT	07.89	87-88	0	2	0
Wigan Ath.	L	10.89	89	0	4	0

KELLY Patrick
South Africa, 9 April, 1918 Died 1985 NI-1 (G)

League Club	Source	Date Signed	Seasons Played	Apps	Subs	Gls
Barnsley	Aberdeen	10.46	46-50	144	-	0
Crewe Alex.	Tr	02.52	51-52	38	-	0

KELLY Patrick
Kirkcaldy, 26 April, 1978 S Yth (D)

League Club	Source	Date Signed	Seasons Played	Apps	Subs	Gls
Newcastle U.	Glasgow Celtic	08.97				
Reading	L	03.98	97	3	0	0

KELLY Paul Anthony
Eccles, 6 March, 1971 (M)

League Club	Source	Date Signed	Seasons Played	Apps	Subs	Gls
Manchester C.	YT	02.90				
Crewe Alex.	Tr	02.92	91	0	1	0

KELLY Paul Leon Marvin
Hillingdon, 24 February, 1974 (M)

League Club	Source	Date Signed	Seasons Played	Apps	Subs	Gls
Fulham	YT	07.92	91-93	4	2	0

KELLY Paul Michael
Bexley, 12 October, 1969 E Yth (M)

League Club	Source	Date Signed	Seasons Played	Apps	Subs	Gls
West Ham U.	YT	06.88	89	0	1	0

KELLY Peter Anthony
Glasgow, 6 December, 1956 (FB)

League Club	Source	Date Signed	Seasons Played	Apps	Subs	Gls
Newcastle U.	App	07.74	75-80	31	2	0

KELLY James **Philip** Vincent
Dublin, 10 July, 1939 IR-5 (FB)

League Club	Source	Date Signed	Seasons Played	Apps	Subs	Gls
Wolverhampton W.	Sheldon T.	09.57	58-61	16	-	0
Norwich C.	Tr	08.62	62-66	114	1	2

KELLY Raymond
Athlone, 29 December, 1976 IRu21-4 (F)

League Club	Source	Date Signed	Seasons Played	Apps	Subs	Gls
Manchester C.	Athlone T.	08.94	97	1	0	0
Wrexham	L	10.97	97	5	1	1
Wrexham	L	03.98	97	0	4	0

KELLY Robert
Kirkcaldy, 16 November, 1919 (WH)

League Club	Source	Date Signed	Seasons Played	Apps	Subs	Gls
Millwall	Raith Rov.	06.46	46-47	52	-	1
Bury	Tr	05.48	48	9	-	0

KELLY Robert Anthony
Birmingham, 21 December, 1964 (M)

League Club	Source	Date Signed	Seasons Played	Apps	Subs	Gls
Leicester C.	App	12.82	83-86	17	7	1
Tranmere Rov.	L	12.84	84	5	0	2
Wolverhampton W.	Tr	03.87	86-88	13	3	2

KELLY Russell
Ballymoney, 10 August, 1976 IR Sch/IR Yth (M)

League Club	Source	Date Signed	Seasons Played	Apps	Subs	Gls
Chelsea	YT	07.95				
Leyton Orient	L	03.96	95	5	1	0
Darlington (N/C)	Tr	08.96	96	13	10	2

KELLY Terence James
Gateshead, 14 May, 1942 (CF)

League Club	Source	Date Signed	Seasons Played	Apps	Subs	Gls
Newcastle U.	Jnrs	05.60				
Lincoln C.	Tr	07.62	62	8	-	3

KELLY Terence William John
Luton, 16 January, 1932 (CH)

League Club	Source	Date Signed	Seasons Played	Apps	Subs	Gls
Luton T.	Vauxhall Motors	04.50	54-62	136	-	1

KELLY Thomas John
Bellshill, 28 March, 1964 (M/LB)

League Club	Source	Date Signed	Seasons Played	Apps	Subs	Gls
Hartlepool U.	Queen of South	08.85	85	14	1	0
Torquay U.	Tr	07.86	86-88	116	4	0
York C.	Tr	06.89	89	35	0	2
Exeter C.	Tr	03.90	89-92	76	12	9
Torquay U.	Tr	01.93	92-95	109	8	8

KELLY Thomas William
Darlington, 22 November, 1919 (FB)

League Club	Source	Date Signed	Seasons Played	Apps	Subs	Gls
Darlington		11.37	37-50	157	-	3
York C.	Tr	08.51				

KELLY Walter Muir
Cowdenbeath, 15 April, 1929 (CF)

League Club	Source	Date Signed	Seasons Played	Apps	Subs	Gls
Bury	Raith Rov.	08.52	52-56	160	-	76
Doncaster Rov.	Tr	06.57	57	29	-	6
Stockport Co.	Tr	03.58	57-59	47	-	12
Chester C.	Tr	08.59	59-60	56	-	24

KELLY William Muir
Cowdenbeath, 14 August, 1922 Died 1996 (CH)

League Club	Source	Date Signed	Seasons Played	Apps	Subs	Gls
Blackburn Rov.	Airdrieonians	09.51	51-56	186	-	1
Accrington St.	Mossley	09.57	57	24	-	0

KELSALL Charles
Hawarden, 15 April, 1921 (LB)

League Club	Source	Date Signed	Seasons Played	Apps	Subs	Gls
Wrexham		08.39	46-51	39	-	0

KELSEY Alfred **John (Jack)**
Llansamlet, 19 November, 1929 Died 1992 EF Lge/W-41 (G)

League Club	Source	Date Signed	Seasons Played	Apps	Subs	Gls
Arsenal	Winch Wen	08.49	50-61	327	-	0

KEMBER Stephen Dennis
Croydon, 8 December, 1948 Eu23-3 (M)

League Club	Source	Date Signed	Seasons Played	Apps	Subs	Gls
Crystal Palace	App	12.65	65-71	216	2	35
Chelsea	Tr	09.71	71-74	125	5	13
Leicester C.	Tr	07.75	75-78	115	2	6
Crystal Palace	Tr	10.78	78-79	39	3	1

KEMP David Michael
Harrow, 20 February, 1953 (F)

League Club	Source	Date Signed	Seasons Played	Apps	Subs	Gls
Crystal Palace	Slough T.	04.75	74-76	32	3	10
Portsmouth	Tr	11.76	76-77	63	1	32
Carlisle U.	Tr	03.78	77-79	60	1	22
Plymouth Arg.	Tr	09.79	79-81	82	2	39
Gillingham	L	12.81	81	9	0	2
Brentford	L	03.82	81	3	0	1

KEMP Frederick George
Italy, 27 February, 1946 (M)

League Club	Source	Date Signed	Seasons Played	Apps	Subs	Gls
Wolverhampton W.	App	06.63	64	3	-	0
Southampton	Tr	06.65	65-69	58	3	10
Blackpool	Tr	11.70	70-71	20	2	1
Halifax T.	Tr	12.71	71-73	106	5	10
Hereford U.	Tr	07.74	74	12	1	2

KEMP John
Clydebank, 11 April, 1934 (OL)

League Club	Source	Date Signed	Seasons Played	Apps	Subs	Gls
Leeds U.	Clyde	12.57	58	1	-	0
Barrow	Tr	03.59	58-63	170	-	46
Crewe Alex.	Tr	12.63	63-65	47	0	7

KEMP Raymond William
Bristol, 18 January, 1922 Died 1989 (G)

League Club	Source	Date Signed	Seasons Played	Apps	Subs	Gls
Reading (Am)	Grays Ath.	09.49	49	3	-	0

KEMP Robert McAlpine
Falkirk, 15 August, 1941 (OL)

League Club	Source	Date Signed	Seasons Played	Apps	Subs	Gls
Carlisle U.	Falkirk	11.60	60	1	-	0

KEMP Samuel Patrick
Stockton, 29 August, 1932 Died 1987 (OR)

League Club	Source	Date Signed	Seasons Played	Apps	Subs	Gls
Sunderland	Whitby T.	03.52	52-56	17	-	2
Sheffield U.	Tr	02.57	56-57	16	-	1
Mansfield T.	Tr	05.58	58	3	-	1
Gateshead	Tr	10.58	58	7	-	1

KEMP Stephen Duncan
Shrewsbury, 2 May, 1955 (CD)

League Club	Source	Date Signed	Seasons Played	Apps	Subs	Gls
Shrewsbury T.	App	07.73	72-73	7	1	0

KENDAL Stephen James
Birtley, 4 August, 1961 (M)

League Club	Source	Date Signed	Seasons Played	Apps	Subs	Gls
Nottingham F.	App	08.79	81	1	0	0
Chesterfield	Tr	12.82	82-86	122	3	14
Torquay U. (N/C)	Tr	10.86	86	4	0	0

KENDALL Harold **Arnold**
Halifax, 6 April, 1925 (W)

League Club	Source	Date Signed	Seasons Played	Apps	Subs	Gls
Bradford C.	Ossett T.	02.49	48-52	113	-	13
Rochdale	Tr	09.53	53-56	111	-	25
Bradford P.A.	Tr	09.56	56-58	90	-	12

KENDALL Howard
Ryton-on-Tyne, 22 May, 1946 E Sch/E Yth/Eu23-6/EF Lge (M)

League Club	Source	Date Signed	Seasons Played	Apps	Subs	Gls
Preston N.E.	App	05.63	62-66	104	0	13

League Club	Source	Date Signed	Seasons Played	Apps	Subs	Gls
Everton	Tr	03.67	66-73	227	2	21
Birmingham C.	Tr	02.74	73-76	115	0	16
Stoke C.	Tr	08.77	77-78	82	0	9
Blackburn Rov.	Tr	07.79	79-80	79	0	6
Everton (N/C)	Tr	08.81	81	4	0	0

KENDALL Ian
Blackburn, 11 December, 1947 (OL)

League Club	Source	Date Signed	Seasons Played	Apps	Subs	Gls
Blackburn Rov.	App	12.65				
Southport	Tr	08.67	67	1	1	0

KENDALL James Briden
Birtley, 4 October, 1922 (IF)

League Club	Source	Date Signed	Seasons Played	Apps	Subs	Gls
Barrow	Gateshead U.	05.47	46-48	44	-	16
Gateshead	Tr	11.48	48-51	57	-	21
Barrow	Tr	10.51	51-52	22	-	6
Accrington St.	Tr	09.52	52	26	-	8

KENDALL Mark
Blackwood (Mon), 20 September, 1958 W Sch/W Yth/Wu21-1 (G)

League Club	Source	Date Signed	Seasons Played	Apps	Subs	Gls
Tottenham H.	App	07.76	78-80	29	0	0
Chesterfield	L	11.79	79	9	0	0
Newport Co.	Tr	09.80	80-86	272	0	0
Wolverhampton W.	Tr	12.86	86-89	147	0	0
Swansea C.	Tr	07.90	90-91	12	0	0
Burnley	L	12.91	91	2	0	0

KENDALL Mark Ivor
Nuneaton, 10 December, 1961 E Yth (G)

League Club	Source	Date Signed	Seasons Played	Apps	Subs	Gls
Aston Villa	App	11.79				
Northampton T.	Tr	06.82	82	11	0	0
Birmingham C.	Tr	02.84	83	1	0	0

KENDALL Paul Scott
Halifax, 19 October, 1964 (CD)

League Club	Source	Date Signed	Seasons Played	Apps	Subs	Gls
Halifax T.	App	10.82	81-85	91	15	4
Scarborough	Tr	07.86	87	22	5	1
Halifax T.	Tr	03.88	87	9	1	0

KENNA Jeffrey Jude
Dublin, 27 August, 1970 IR Sch/IR Yth/IRu21-8/IR 'B'/IR-24 (FB)

League Club	Source	Date Signed	Seasons Played	Apps	Subs	Gls
Southampton	YT	04.89	90-94	110	4	4
Blackburn Rov.	YT	03.95	94-97	115	0	1

KENNEDY Alan Philip
Sunderland, 31 August, 1954 Eu23-6/E-2 (LB)

League Club	Source	Date Signed	Seasons Played	Apps	Subs	Gls
Newcastle U.	App	08.72	72-77	155	3	9
Liverpool	Tr	08.78	78-85	249	2	15
Sunderland	Tr	09.85	85-86	54	0	2
Hartlepool U. (N/C)	Beerschot (Bel)	10.87	87	4	1	0
Wigan Ath.	Grantham	12.87	87	22	0	0
Wrexham (N/C)	Colne Dynamoes	03.90	89-90	15	1	0

KENNEDY Andrew John
Stirling, 8 October, 1964 S Yth (F)

League Club	Source	Date Signed	Seasons Played	Apps	Subs	Gls
Birmingham C.	Seiko (HK)	03.85	84-87	51	25	19
Sheffield U.	L	03.87	86	8	1	1
Blackburn Rov.	Tr	06.88	88-89	49	10	23
Watford	Tr	08.90	90-91	17	8	4
Bolton W.	L	10.91	91	1	0	0
Brighton & H.A.	Tr	09.92	92-93	34	8	10
Gillingham (N/C)	Tr	09.94	94	0	2	0

KENNEDY David
Birkenhead, 14 February, 1949 (W)

League Club	Source	Date Signed	Seasons Played	Apps	Subs	Gls
Tranmere Rov.	Jnrs	05.67	67-69	16	1	0
Chester C.	Tr	05.70	70-73	79	8	9
Torquay U.	Tr	09.73	73-76	144	7	7

KENNEDY David
Sunderland, 30 November, 1950 (CD)

League Club	Source	Date Signed	Seasons Played	Apps	Subs	Gls
Leeds U.	App	05.68	69	2	0	1
Lincoln C.	Tr	07.71	71	6	2	1

KENNEDY Gordon McKay
Dundee, 15 April, 1924 (FB)

League Club	Source	Date Signed	Seasons Played	Apps	Subs	Gls
Blackpool		10.43	46-49	8	-	0
Bolton W.	Tr	09.50	50	17	-	0
Stockport Co.	Tr	08.53	53	20	-	1

KENNEDY John
Newtonards (NI), 4 September, 1939 (G)

League Club	Source	Date Signed	Seasons Played	Apps	Subs	Gls
Lincoln C.	Glasgow Celtic	07.67	67-73	251	0	0

KENNEDY John
Kilwinning, 26 February, 1941 (IF)

League Club	Source	Date Signed	Seasons Played	Apps	Subs	Gls
Charlton Ath.	Saltcoats Vic.	03.62	61-64	46	-	8
Exeter C.	Tr	11.65	65-66	40	1	6

KENNEDY John Neil
Newmarket, 19 August, 1978 (LB)

League Club	Source	Date Signed	Seasons Played	Apps	Subs	Gls
Ipswich T.	YT	06.97	97	0	1	0

KENNEDY Joseph Peter
Cleator Moor, 15 November, 1925 Died 1986 E 'B' (CH)

League Club	Source	Date Signed	Seasons Played	Apps	Subs	Gls
West Bromwich A.	Altrincham	12.48	48-60	364	-	3
Chester C.	Tr	06.61	61	35	-	0

KENNEDY, Keith Vernon
Sunderland, 5 March, 1952 (LB)

League Club	Source	Date Signed	Seasons Played	Apps	Subs	Gls
Newcastle U.	App	07.70	71	1	0	0
Bury	Tr	10.72	72-81	405	0	4
Mansfield T.	Tr	08.82	82	32	2	0

KENNEDY Malcolm Stephen John
Swansea, 13 October, 1939 (HB)

League Club	Source	Date Signed	Seasons Played	Apps	Subs	Gls
Swansea C.	Jnrs	05.57	57-60	19	-	0

KENNEDY Mark
Dublin, 15 May, 1976 IR Sch/IR Yth/IRu21-7/IR-18 (LW)

League Club	Source	Date Signed	Seasons Played	Apps	Subs	Gls
Millwall	YT	05.92	92-94	37	6	9
Liverpool	Tr	03.95	94-97	5	11	0
Queens Park R.	L	01.98	97	8	0	2
Wimbledon	Tr	03.98	97	4	0	0

KENNEDY Michael Francis Martin
Salford, 9 April, 1961 IRu21-4/IR-2 (M)

League Club	Source	Date Signed	Seasons Played	Apps	Subs	Gls
Halifax T.	App	01.79	78-79	74	2	4
Huddersfield T.	Tr	08.80	80-81	80	1	9
Middlesbrough	Tr	08.82	82-83	68	0	5
Portsmouth	Tr	06.84	84-87	129	0	4
Bradford C.	Tr	01.88	87-88	45	0	2
Leicester C.	Tr	03.89	88	9	0	0
Luton T.	Tr	08.89	89	30	2	0
Stoke C.	Tr	08.90	90-91	51	1	3
Chesterfield	Tr	08.92	92	19	8	1
Wigan Ath.	Tr	07.93	93	15	2	1

KENNEDY Patrick Antony
Dublin, 9 October, 1934 (FB)

League Club	Source	Date Signed	Seasons Played	Apps	Subs	Gls
Manchester U.	Jnrs	02.53	54	1	-	0
Blackburn Rov.	Tr	08.56	57	3	-	0
Southampton	Tr	07.59	59	2	-	0

KENNEDY Peter Henry James
Lurgan, 10 September, 1973 NI 'B' (LW)

League Club	Source	Date Signed	Seasons Played	Apps	Subs	Gls
Notts Co.	Portadown	08.96	96	20	2	0
Watford	Tr	07.97	97	34	0	11

KENNEDY Raymond
Seaton Delaval, 28 July, 1951 Eu23-6/E-17 (M/F)

League Club	Source	Date Signed	Seasons Played	Apps	Subs	Gls
Arsenal	App	11.68	69-73	156	2	53
Liverpool	Tr	07.74	74-81	272	3	51
Swansea C.	Tr	01.82	81-83	42	0	2
Hartlepool U.	Tr	11.83	83	18	5	3

KENNEDY Robert
Motherwell, 23 June, 1937 Su23-1 (FB)

League Club	Source	Date Signed	Seasons Played	Apps	Subs	Gls
Manchester C.	Kilmarnock	07.61	61-68	216	3	9
Grimsby T.	Tr	03.69	68-70	84	0	1

KENNEDY Stephen
Ashton-u-Lyne, 22 July, 1965 (FB)

League Club	Source	Date Signed	Seasons Played	Apps	Subs	Gls
Burnley	App	07.83	83-86	18	0	0

KENNERLEY Kevin Robert
Chester, 26 April, 1954 (M)

League Club	Source	Date Signed	Seasons Played	Apps	Subs	Gls
Burnley	Arsenal (App)	05.72	75	6	0	1
Port Vale	Tr	05.76	76-77	16	8	1
Swansea C.	L	02.78	77	2	0	0

KENNING Michael John
Birmingham, 18 August, 1940 (W)

League Club	Source	Date Signed	Seasons Played	Apps	Subs	Gls
Aston Villa	Jnrs	10.59	60	3	-	0
Shrewsbury T.	Tr	05.61	61-62	62	-	17
Charlton Ath.	Tr	11.62	62-66	152	2	43
Norwich C.	Tr	12.66	66-67	44	0	9
Wolverhampton W.	Tr	01.68	67-68	35	6	5
Charlton Ath.	Tr	03.69	68-71	60	7	12
Watford	Tr	12.71	71-72	35	6	2

KENNON Neil Sandilands
South Africa, 28 November, 1933 (G)

League Club	Source	Date Signed	Seasons Played	Apps	Subs	Gls
Huddersfield T.	Bulawayo (Rhod)	08.56	56-58	78	-	0
Norwich C.	Tr	02.59	58-64	213	-	0
Colchester U.	Tr	03.65	64-66	76	0	0

League Club	Source	Date Signed	Seasons Played	Career Record Apps	Subs	Gls
KENNY Frederick						
Manchester, 14 January, 1923 Died 1985						(FB)
Stockport Co.	Manchester C. (Am)	12.47	48-56	204	-	0
KENNY Vincent						
Sheffield, 29 December, 1924						(FB)
Sheffield Wed.	Atlas Wks	11.45	46-54	144	-	0
Carlisle U.	Tr	07.55	55-57	103	-	3
KENNY William Aidan						
Liverpool, 23 October, 1951						(M)
Everton	App	07.69	70-74	10	2	0
Tranmere Rov.	Tr	03.75	74-76	36	18	6
KENNY William Aidan						
Liverpool, 19 September, 1973 Eu21-1						(M)
Everton	YT	06.92	92	16	1	1
Oldham Ath.	Tr	08.94	94	4	0	0
KENT Kevin Joseph						
Stoke, 19 March, 1965						(W)
West Bromwich A.	App	12.82	83	1	1	0
Newport Co.	Tr	07.84	84	23	10	1
Mansfield T.	Tr	08.85	85-90	223	6	36
Port Vale	Tr	03.91	90-95	87	28	7
KENT Michael John						
Dinnington, 12 January, 1951						(M)
Wolverhampton W.	Wath W.	08.68	69-71	0	2	0
Gillingham	L	03.71	70	11	0	0
Sheffield Wed.	Tr	09.73	73	4	0	0
KENT Paul						
Rotherham, 23 February, 1954						(FB)
Norwich C.	App	02.72	73	1	2	0
Halifax T.	Tr	08.76	76	12	0	0
KENT Terence Ian						
Battersea, 21 October, 1939						(OL)
Southend U.		05.58	58	1	-	0
Millwall	Tr	08.60				
KENTON Darren Edward						
Wandsworth, 13 September, 1978						(CD/M)
Norwich C.	YT	07.97	97	7	4	0
KENWORTHY Anthony David						
Leeds, 30 October, 1958 E Yth						(CD)
Sheffield U.	App	07.76	75-85	281	5	34
Mansfield T.	Tr	03.86	85-89	98	2	0
KENWORTHY Jonathan Raymond						
St Asaph, 18 August, 1974 W Yth/Wu21-4						(W)
Tranmere Rov.	YT	07.93	93-95	14	12	2
Chester C.	L	12.95	95	5	2	1
KENWORTHY Stephen						
Wrexham, 6 November, 1959						(LB)
Wrexham	Jnrs	11.77	77-80	19	1	0
Bury	Tr	08.81	82	14	0	0
KENYON Frederick						
Carlisle, 14 September, 1922						(CH)
Carlisle U.		09.43	47-48	4	-	0
KENYON John Francis						
Blackburn, 2 December, 1953						(F)
Blackburn Rov.	Great Harwood	12.72	72-75	32	14	7
KENYON Roger Norton						
Blackpool, 4 January, 1949						(CD)
Everton	App	09.66	67-78	254	13	6
Bristol C.	Vancouver (Can)	10.79	79	4	0	0
KENYON Roy						
Manchester, 10 March, 1933						(F)
Leeds U.	Bolton W. (Am)	12.50				
Southport	Worcester C.	09.54	54	1	-	0
KEOUGH Daniel Peter						
Bacup, 31 January, 1963						(M)
Manchester U.	App	02.80				
Exeter C.	Bury (N/C)	10.85	85-86	71	1	0
KEOWN Martin Raymond						
Oxford, 24 July, 1966 E Yth/Eu21-8/E 'B'/E-18						(CD)
Arsenal	App	01.84	85	22	0	0
Brighton & H.A.	L	02.85	84	16	0	0

League Club	Source	Date Signed	Seasons Played	Career Record Apps	Subs	Gls
Brighton & H.A.	L	08.85	85	5	2	1
Aston Villa	Tr	06.86	86-88	109	3	3
Everton	Tr	08.89	89-92	92	4	0
Arsenal	Tr	02.93	92-97	147	18	2
KERFOOT Eric						
Ashton-u-Lyne, 31 July, 1924 Died 1980						(WH)
Leeds U.	Stalybridge Celtic	12.49	49-58	336	-	9
Chesterfield	Tr	07.59	59	9	-	0
KERFOOT Jason John Thomas						
Preston, 17 April, 1973						(M)
Preston N.E.	YT	07.91	90-91	0	4	0
KERNAGHAN Alan Nigel						
Otley, 25 April, 1967 NI Sch/IR-22						(CD)
Middlesbrough	App	03.85	84-93	172	40	16
Charlton Ath.	L	01.91	90	13	0	0
Manchester C.	Tr	09.93	93-97	55	8	1
Bolton W.	L	08.94	94	9	2	0
Bradford C.	L	02.96	95	5	0	0
KERNAN Anthony Paul						
Letterkenny (Ire), 31 August, 1963 IR Yth						(M)
Wolverhampton W.	App	01.81	81	1	0	0
KERNICK Dudley Henry John						
Camelford, 29 August, 1921						(IF)
Torquay U.	Tintagel	01.39	46-47	38	-	7
Northampton T.	Tr	08.48				
Birmingham C.	Tr	12.48				
KERR Albert Wigham						
Lanchester, 11 August, 1917 Died 1979						(OR)
Aston Villa	Medomsley Jnrs	07.36	36-46	29	-	4
KERR Andrew						
Lugar, 29 June, 1931 S 'B'/SF Lge/S-2						(CF)
Manchester C	Partick Thistle	06.59	59	10	-	0
Sunderland	Kilmarnock	04.63	62-63	18	-	5
KERR Andrew Alphonso						
West Bromwich, 7 April, 1966						(CD)
Shrewsbury T.	YT	04.84	84-85	9	1	0
Cardiff C.	Tr	08.86	86	31	0	1
Wycombe W.	Telford U.	09.88	93	12	2	3
KERR Archibald						
Motherwell, 30 August, 1935						(OR)
Shrewsbury T.	Motherwell	01.57	56	13	-	0
KERR Charles Currie						
Glasgow, 10 December, 1933						(OR)
Carlisle U.	Morton	08.56	56-57	9	-	3
Barrow		07.59	59	20	-	3
KERR David						
Glasgow, 4 December, 1936						(F)
Liverpool	Bridgeton Waverley	04.56				
Southport	Tr	07.58	58	32	-	4
KERR David William						
Dumfries, 6 September, 1974						(D/M)
Manchester C.	YT	09.91	92-95	4	2	0
Mansfield T.	L	09.95	95	4	1	0
Mansfield T.	Tr	07.96	96-97	16	11	2
KERR Dylan						
Malta, 14 January, 1967						(FB)
Sheffield Wed.	YT	09.84				
Leeds U.	Arcadia Shepherds (SA)	01.89	88-92	6	7	0
Doncaster Rov.	L	08.91	91	7	0	1
Blackpool	L	12.91	91	12	0	1
Reading	Tr	07.93	93-95	84	5	5
Carlisle U. (N/C)	Tr	09.96	96	0	1	0
KERR George Adams McDonald						
Alexandria, 9 January, 1943						(IF)
Barnsley	Vale of Leven	05.60	61-65	166	0	40
Bury	Tr	03.66	65-66	15	0	2
Oxford U.	Tr	09.66	66-67	40	1	5
Scunthorpe U.	Tr	02.68	67-72	151	6	32
KERR James						
Newcastle, 3 March, 1932 Died 1994						(OL)
Lincoln C.	Blyth Spartans	11.52	52-53	15	-	1
Oldham Ath.	Tr	06.54	54-55	34	-	4

League Club	Source	Date Signed	Seasons Played	Apps	Subs	Gls
KERR James Peter						
Glasgow, 2 September, 1949 S Sch						(M)
Bury	Jnrs	09.66	65-69	150	2	37
Blackburn Rov.	Tr	05.70	70	11	0	0
KERR John						
Birkenhead, 23 November, 1959						(F)
Tranmere Rov.	App	11.77	78-82	145	9	38
Bristol C.	Tr	08.83	83	13	1	4
Stockport Co.	Tr	01.84	83-84	47	0	16
Bury	Tr	03.85	84-85	21	10	4
KERR John Joseph						
Canada, 6 March, 1965 USA Int						(F)
Portsmouth	Harrow Borough	08.87	87	2	2	0
Peterborough U.	L	12.87	87	10	0	1
Millwall	San Diego (USA)	02.93	92-94	21	22	8
Walsall (N/C)	Chesham U.	11.95	95	0	1	0
KERR Paul Andrew						
Portsmouth, 9 June, 1964						(M)
Aston Villa	App	05.82	83-86	16	8	3
Middlesbrough	Tr	01.87	86-90	114	11	13
Millwall	Tr	03.91	90-91	42	2	14
Port Vale	Tr	07.92	92-93	58	5	15
Leicester C.	L	03.94	93	4	3	2
Wycombe W. (N/C)	Tr	10.94	94	0	1	1
KERR Peter						
Paisley, 25 September, 1943						(IF)
Reading	Third Lanark	05.63	63-64	41	-	7
KERR Peter						
Glasgow, 3 January, 1928						(IR)
Hartlepool U.	Maryhill Hearts	09.49	49	2	-	0
KERR Robert						
Alexandria, 16 November, 1947						(M)
Sunderland	Jnrs	11.64	66-78	355	13	56
Blackpool	Tr	03.79	78-79	18	4	2
Hartlepool U.	Tr	07.80	80-81	48	1	2
KERR Robert						
West Lothian, 10 July, 1942						(CF)
Millwall	Arbroath	08.62	62	1	-	0
KERR Robert James						
Coatbridge, 29 November, 1929						(IF)
Darlington	Third Lanark	10.52	52	10	-	2
KERR James **Stewart**						
Motherwell, 13 November, 1974 Su21-10						(G)
Brighton & H.A. (L)	Glasgow Celtic	11.94	94	2	0	0
KERRAY James Rillay						
Stirling, 2 December, 1935						(IF)
Huddersfield T.	Dunfermline Ath.	08.60	60-61	54	-	12
Newcastle U.	Tr	02.62	61-62	38	-	10
KERRIGAN Donald McDonald						
West Kilbride, 7 May, 1941 Died 1990						(OR)
Fulham	Dunfermline Ath.	02.68	67-68	4	2	1
Lincoln C.	L	03.69	68	12	0	0
KERRIGAN Steven John						
Baillieston, 9 October, 1972						(F)
Shrewsbury T.	Ayr U.	01.98	97	11	3	2
KERRINS Patrick Michael						
Fulham, 13 September, 1936						(OL)
Queens Park R.	Jnrs	12.53	53-59	146	-	30
Crystal Palace	Tr	06.60	60	5	-	0
Southend U.	Tr	07.61	61	11	-	0
KERRINS Wayne Michael						
Brentwood, 5 August, 1965						(M/LB)
Fulham	App	08.83	84-88	51	15	1
Port Vale	L	03.85	84	6	2	0
Leyton Orient	L	03.89	88	3	0	0
KERRY Brian Philip						
Maltby, 18 December, 1948						(F)
Grimsby T.	App	01.66	65	0	1	0
Huddersfield T.	Tr	04.67				
KERRY Christopher Brian						
Chesterfield, 15 April, 1976						(F)
Mansfield T. (N/C)	YT	07.94	93	1	1	0

League Club	Source	Date Signed	Seasons Played	Apps	Subs	Gls
KERRY David Thomas						
Derby, 6 February, 1937 E Yth						(CF)
Preston N.E.	Derby Co. (Am)	05.55				
Chesterfield	Tr	07.61	61-62	55	-	23
Rochdale	Tr	07.63	63	12	-	4
KERSHAW Alan Derek						
Southport, 23 April, 1954						(FB)
Preston N.E.	App	09.72				
Southport	Tr	07.74	74	19	5	0
KERSLAKE David						
Stepney, 19 June, 1966 E Sch/E Yth/Eu21-1						(FB)
Queens Park R.	App	06.83	84-89	38	20	6
Swindon T.	Tr	11.89	89-92	133	2	1
Leeds U.	Tr	03.93	92	8	0	0
Tottenham H.	Tr	09.93	93-95	34	3	0
Swindon T.	L	11.96	96-97	10	0	0
Ipswich T.	Tr	08.97	97	2	5	0
Wycombe W.	L	12.97	97	9	1	0
Swindon T.	Tr	03.98	97	10	0	0
KERSLAKE Michael						
Bethnal Green, 27 February, 1958 E Yth						(FB)
Fulham	App	10.75	75-77	1	2	0
Brighton & H.A.	Tr	06.78				
KETSBAIA Temuri						
Georgia, 18 March, 1968 Georgian Int						(M)
Newcastle U.	A.E.K. Athens (Gre)	07.97	97	16	15	3
KETTERIDGE Stephen Jack						
Stevenage, 7 November, 1959						(M)
Wimbledon	Derby Co. (App)	04.78	78-84	229	8	32
Crystal Palace	Tr	08.85	85-86	58	1	6
Leyton Orient	Tr	07.87	87-88	26	5	1
Cardiff C.	L	10.88	88	6	0	2
KETTLE Albert Henry						
Colchester, 3 June, 1922						(RB)
Colchester U.	Arkwright Sports	(N/L)	50-54	23	-	0
KETTLE Brian						
Prescot, 22 April, 1956 E Yth						(FB)
Liverpool	App	05.73	75-76	3	0	0
Wigan Ath.	Houston (USA)	08.80	80	14	0	1
KETTLEBOROUGH Keith Frank						
Rotherham, 29 June, 1935						(IF)
Rotherham U.	Rotherham Y.M.C.A.	12.55	55-60	118	-	19
Sheffield U.	Tr	12.60	60-65	154	0	17
Newcastle U.	Tr	12.65	65-66	30	0	0
Doncastle Rov.	Tr	12.66	66-67	35	1	0
Chesterfield	Tr	11.67	67-68	66	0	3
KETTLEY Spencer						
Rhondda, 22 May, 1921						(WH)
Luton T.	Newbury T.	08.44	46	1	-	0
KEVAN David John						
Wigtown, 31 August, 1968						(M)
Notts Co.	App	08.86	85-89	82	7	3
Cardiff C.	L	09.89	89	6	1	0
Stoke C.	Tr	01.90	89-93	78	3	2
Maidstone U.	L	02.91	90	3	0	0
Bournemouth	Tr	03.94	93	0	1	0
KEVAN Derek Tennyson						
Ripon, 6 March, 1935 Eu23-4/EF Lge/E-14						(IF)
Bradford P.A.	Ripon Y.M.C.A.	10.52	52	15	-	8
West Bromwich A.	Tr	07.53	55-62	262	-	157
Chelsea	Tr	03.63	62	7	-	1
Manchester C.	Tr	08.63	63-64	67	-	48
Crystal Palace	Tr	07.65	65	21	0	5
Peterborough U.	Tr	03.66	65-66	16	1	2
Luton T.	Tr	12.66	66	11	0	4
Stockport Co.	Tr	03.67	66-67	38	2	10
KEWELL Harold						
Australia, 22 September, 1978 Australian Int						(LB)
Leeds U.	A.I.S. (Aus)	12.95	95-97	28	4	5
KEWLEY John **Kevin**						
Liverpool, 2 March, 1955						(M)
Liverpool	App	03.72	77	0	1	0
KEY Daniel Charles						
Darlington, 2 November, 1977						(M)
Darlington (N/C)	YT	07.96	96	0	3	0

KEY John Peter
Kensington, 5 November, 1937 (OR)

League Club	Source	Date Signed	Seasons Played	Apps	Subs	Gls
Fulham	Jnrs	05.56	58-65	163	0	29
Coventry C.	Tr	05.66	66-67	27	1	7
Leyton Orient	Tr	03.68	67-68	9	1	0

KEY Lance William
Kettering, 13 May, 1968 (G)

League Club	Source	Date Signed	Seasons Played	Apps	Subs	Gls
Sheffield Wed.	Histon	04.90				
Oldham Ath.	L	10.93	93	2	0	0
Oxford U.	L	01.95	94	6	0	0
Lincoln C.	L	08.95	95	5	0	0
Hartlepool U.	L	12.95	95	1	0	0
Rochdale	L	03.96	95-97	19	0	0
Sheffield U.	Dundee U.	03.97				
Rochdale	Tr	08.97	97	19	0	0

KEY Richard Martin
Cambridge, 13 April, 1956 (G)

League Club	Source	Date Signed	Seasons Played	Apps	Subs	Gls
Exeter C.	Coventry C. (Jnrs)	07.75	75-77	109	0	0
Cambridge U.	Tr	08.78	78-82	52	0	0
Northampton T.	L	11.82	82	2	0	0
Leyton Orient	Tr	08.83	83	42	0	0
Brentford	Tr	08.84	84	1	0	0
Sunderland	Tr	10.84				
Cambridge U.	L	03.85	84	13	0	0
Brentford (N/C)	Tr	08.85	85	3	0	0

KEYES Anthony Joseph
Salford, 29 October, 1953 (M)

League Club	Source	Date Signed	Seasons Played	Apps	Subs	Gls
Stockport Co.	Witton A.	10.71	71-73	7	1	0

KEYS Paul Andrew
Ipswich, 4 September, 1962 (F)

League Club	Source	Date Signed	Seasons Played	Apps	Subs	Gls
Luton T.		07.81				
Halifax T.	L.	03.82	81	1	1	0

KEYWORTH Kenneth
Rotherham, 24 February, 1934 (CF/WH)

League Club	Source	Date Signed	Seasons Played	Apps	Subs	Gls
Rotherham U.	Wolverhampton W. (Am)	01.52	55-57	85	-	6
Leicester C.	Tr	05.58	58-64	177	-	63
Coventry C.	Tr	12.64	64	7	-	3
Swindon T.	Tr	08.65	65	6	0	0

KHARINE Dmitri Victorvitch
Russia, 16 August, 1968 Russian Int (G)

League Club	Source	Date Signed	Seasons Played	Apps	Subs	Gls
Chelsea	C.S.K.A. Moscow (Rus)	12.92	92-97	117	0	0

KICHENBRAND Donald Basil
South Africa, 13 August, 1933 (CF)

League Club	Source	Date Signed	Seasons Played	Apps	Subs	Gls
Sunderland	Glasgow Rangers	03.58	57-59	53	-	28

KIDD Brian
Manchester, 29 May, 1949 E Yth/Eu23-10/EF Lge/E-2 (F)

League Club	Source	Date Signed	Seasons Played	Apps	Subs	Gls
Manchester U.	App	06.66	67-73	195	8	52
Arsenal	Tr	08.74	74-75	77	0	30
Manchester C.	Tr	07.76	76-78	97	1	44
Everton	Tr	03.79	78-79	40	0	12
Bolton W.	Tr	05.80	80-81	40	3	14

KIDD John Oliver
Birkenhead, 15 January, 1936 (F)

League Club	Source	Date Signed	Seasons Played	Apps	Subs	Gls
Tranmere Rov.	Everton (Am)	08.55	55-58	34	-	4

KIDD Ryan Andrew
Radcliffe, 6 October, 1971 (CD)

League Club	Source	Date Signed	Seasons Played	Apps	Subs	Gls
Port Vale	YT	07.90	91	1	0	0
Preston N.E.	Tr	07.92	92-97	168	13	6

KIDD William Edward
Morpeth, 31 January, 1907 Died 1978 (FB)

League Club	Source	Date Signed	Seasons Played	Apps	Subs	Gls
Chesterfield	Pegswood U.	03.32	31-47	316	-	2

KIELY Dean Lawrence
Salford, 10 October, 1970 E Sch/E Yth (G)

League Club	Source	Date Signed	Seasons Played	Apps	Subs	Gls
Coventry C.	YT	10.87				
York C.	Tr	03.90	90-95	210	0	0
Bury	Tr	08.96	96-97	92	0	0

KIERAN Leonard Vincent
Birkenhead, 25 July, 1926 Died 1981 (WH)

League Club	Source	Date Signed	Seasons Played	Apps	Subs	Gls
Tranmere Rov.	Jnrs	09.43	47-56	346	-	6

KIERNAN Daniel James
Northampton, 16 December, 1973 (M)

League Club	Source	Date Signed	Seasons Played	Apps	Subs	Gls
Northampton T.	YT	•	91	6	3	0

KIERNAN Frederick William
Dublin, 7 July 1919 Died 1981 IR-5 (G)

League Club	Source	Date Signed	Seasons Played	Apps	Subs	Gls
Southampton	Shamrock Rov.	10.51	51-55	132	-	0

KIERNAN Joseph
Coatbridge, 22 October, 1942 (WH)

League Club	Source	Date Signed	Seasons Played	Apps	Subs	Gls
Sunderland	Jnrs	11.59	62	1	-	0
Northampton T.	Tr	07.63	63-71	305	3	13

KIERNAN Thomas
Coatbridge, 20 October, 1918 Died 1991 SF Lge (IF)

League Club	Source	Date Signed	Seasons Played	Apps	Subs	Gls
Stoke C.	Glasgow Celtic	09.47	47-48	28	-	6
Luton T.	Tr	11.48	48-50	55	-	10

KIERNAN William Edward
Penge, 22 May, 1925 E 'B' (OL)

League Club	Source	Date Signed	Seasons Played	Apps	Subs	Gls
Charlton Ath.	Hong Kong	07.49	49-60	378	-	89

[KIKO] CHARANA Manuel Henrique Baptista Gomes
Portugal, 24 October, 1976 (M)

League Club	Source	Date Signed	Seasons Played	Apps	Subs	Gls
Stockport Co.	Belenenses (Por)	12.96	96	0	3	0

KILBANE Farrell Noel
Preston, 21 October, 1974 (CD)

League Club	Source	Date Signed	Seasons Played	Apps	Subs	Gls
Preston N.E.	Cambridge U. (YT)	07.93	93	0	1	0

KILBANE Kevin Daniel
Preston, 1 February, 1977 IRu21-8/IR-3 (LW)

League Club	Source	Date Signed	Seasons Played	Apps	Subs	Gls
Preston N.E.	YT	07.95	95-96	39	8	3
West Bromwich A.	Tr	06.97	97	42	1	4

KILCLINE Brian
Nottingham, 7 May, 1962 Eu21-2 (CD)

League Club	Source	Date Signed	Seasons Played	Apps	Subs	Gls
Notts Co.	App	05.80	79-83	156	2	9
Coventry C.	Tr	06.84	84-90	173	0	28
Oldham Ath.	Tr	08.91	91	8	0	0
Newcastle U.	Tr	02.92	91-93	20	12	0
Swindon T.	Tr	01.94	93-94	16	1	0
Mansfield T.	Tr	12.95	95-96	48	2	3

KILEY Thomas James
Swansea, 15 June, 1924 (CH)

League Club	Source	Date Signed	Seasons Played	Apps	Subs	Gls
Swansea C.		06.47	49-56	130	-	2

KILFORD Ian Anthony
Bristol, 6 October, 1973 (M)

League Club	Source	Date Signed	Seasons Played	Apps	Subs	Gls
Nottingham F.	YT	04.91	93	0	1	0
Wigan Ath.	L	12.93	93	2	1	2
Wigan Ath.	Tr	07.94	94-97	111	19	27

KILFORD John Douglas
Derby, 8 November, 1938 (FB)

League Club	Source	Date Signed	Seasons Played	Apps	Subs	Gls
Notts Co.	Derby Corries	07.57	58	26	-	0
Leeds U.	Tr	02.59	58-61	21	-	0

KILGALLON Mark Christopher
Glasgow, 20 December, 1962 (D)

League Club	Source	Date Signed	Seasons Played	Apps	Subs	Gls
Hull C.	Ipswich T. (App)	08.80	80	0	1	0

KILGANNON John
Stenhousemuir, 26 June, 1936 Died 1967 (F)

League Club	Source	Date Signed	Seasons Played	Apps	Subs	Gls
Luton T.	Stenhousemuir	04.59	58-59	13	-	1

KILKELLY Thomas Francis
Galway (Ire), 22 August, 1955 IR Yth (D)

League Club	Source	Date Signed	Seasons Played	Apps	Subs	Gls
Leicester C.	App	07.73				
Northampton T.	L	09.74	74	2	2	0

KILKENNY James
Stanley, 21 November, 1934 (WH)

League Club	Source	Date Signed	Seasons Played	Apps	Subs	Gls
Doncaster Rov.	Annfield Plain	05.52	55-60	131	-	1

KILLARNEY Arthur
Huddersfield, 26 February, 1921 (IR)

League Club	Source	Date Signed	Seasons Played	Apps	Subs	Gls
Halifax T.		05.46	46	2	-	0

KILLIN Harold Roy
Canada, 18 July, 1929 (FB)

League Club	Source	Date Signed	Seasons Played	Apps	Subs	Gls
Manchester U		04.49				
Lincoln C.	Tr	08.52	53	7	-	0

KILMORE Kevin
Scunthorpe, 11 November, 1959 E Yth (M)

League Club	Source	Date Signed	Seasons Played	Apps	Subs	Gls
Scunthorpe U.	Jnrs	01.77	76-79	93	9	28
Grimsby T.	Tr	09.79	79-82	70	32	27
Rotherham U.	Tr	08.83	83-84	82	2	20
Lincoln C.	K.F.C. Geel (Bel)	01.86	85-86	40	6	6

KILNER Andrew William
Bolton, 11 October, 1966 E Yth (LW)

League Club	Source	Date Signed	Seasons Played	Apps	Subs	Gls
Burnley	App	07.84	85	2	3	0
Stockport Co.	Jonsereds (Swe)	12.90	90-91	34	8	14

League Club	Source	Date Signed	Seasons Played	Apps	Subs	Gls
Rochdale	L	01.92	91	3	0	0
Bury (N/C)	Tr	08.92	92	4	1	0

KILNER John Ian
Bolton, 3 October, 1959 (G)

League Club	Source	Date Signed	Seasons Played	Apps	Subs	Gls
Preston N.E.	App	10.77				
Halifax T.	Tr	02.79	78-81	114	0	0
Wigan Ath. (N/C)	South Africa	07.83	83	4	0	0

KILSHAW Edmund (Eddie) Ainsworth
Prescot, 25 December, 1919 (OR)

League Club	Source	Date Signed	Seasons Played	Apps	Subs	Gls
Bury	Prescot Cables	10.37	37-48	111	-	13
Sheffield Wed.	Tr	12.48	48	17	-	1

KILSHAW Frederick
Wrexham, 24 August, 1916 (IR)

League Club	Source	Date Signed	Seasons Played	Apps	Subs	Gls
Leicester C.		01.45				
New Brighton	Tr	07.46	46	8	-	1

KIMBERLEY Samuel **Kenneth**
Walsall, 7 August, 1920 (G)

League Club	Source	Date Signed	Seasons Played	Apps	Subs	Gls
Walsall	Cannock Colly	05.46	46	1	-	0

KIMBLE Alan Frank
Dagenham, 6 August, 1966 (LB)

League Club	Source	Date Signed	Seasons Played	Apps	Subs	Gls
Charlton Ath.	Jnrs	08.84	84	6	0	0
Exeter C.	L	08.85	85	1	0	0
Cambridge U.	Tr	08.86	86-92	295	4	24
Wimbledon	Tr	07.93	93-97	122	5	0

KIMBLE Gary Leslie
Dagenham, 6 August, 1966 (LW)

League Club	Source	Date Signed	Seasons Played	Apps	Subs	Gls
Charlton Ath.	Jnrs	08.84	84	7	2	1
Exeter C.	L	08.85	85	1	0	0
Cambridge U.	Tr	08.86	86-87	39	2	2
Doncaster Rov.	Tr	10.87	87-88	60	5	1
Fulham	Tr	08.89	89	1	2	0
Maidstone U. (N/C)	Tr	10.89				
Gillingham	St Albans C.	02.90	89-90	35	13	1
Peterborough U.	Tr	07.91	91	30	0	4

KINDER Vladimir
Czechoslovakia, 9 March, 1969 Slovakian Int (D)

League Club	Source	Date Signed	Seasons Played	Apps	Subs	Gls
Middlesbrough	Slovan Bratislava (Cz)	01.97	96-97	29	3	3

KINDON Stephen Michael
Warrington, 17 December, 1950 E Yth (W/F)

League Club	Source	Date Signed	Seasons Played	Apps	Subs	Gls
Burnley	App	12.67	68-71	102	7	28
Wolverhampton W.	Tr	07.72	72-77	111	27	28
Burnley	Tr	11.77	77-79	73	3	18
Huddersfield T.	Tr	12.79	79-81	69	4	35

KING Adam
Hillingdon, 4 October, 1969 E Yth (M)

League Club	Source	Date Signed	Seasons Played	Apps	Subs	Gls
West Ham U.	YT	06.88				
Plymouth Arg.	Tr	03.90	89-90	9	7	0

KING Alan
Gateshead, 25 November, 1947 (OL)

League Club	Source	Date Signed	Seasons Played	Apps	Subs	Gls
Hartlepool U. (Am)	Horden Colly	08.67	67	0	1	0

KING Alan John
Birkenhead, 18 January, 1945 (WH)

League Club	Source	Date Signed	Seasons Played	Apps	Subs	Gls
Tranmere Rov.	Jnrs	07.62	62-71	342	0	33

KING Andrew Edward
Luton, 14 August, 1956 Eu21-2 (M)

League Club	Source	Date Signed	Seasons Played	Apps	Subs	Gls
Luton T	App	07.74	74-75	30	3	9
Everton	Tr	04.76	75-79	150	1	38
Queens Park R.	Tr	09.80	80-81	28	2	9
West Bromwich A.	Tr	09.81	81	21	4	4
Everton	Tr	07.82	82-83	43	1	11
Wolverhampton W.	Cambuur (Neth)	01.85	84-85	28	0	10
Luton T.	Tr	12.85	85	3	0	0
Aldershot	Tr	08.86	86	36	0	11

KING Andrew John
Thatcham, 30 March, 1970 (F)

League Club	Source	Date Signed	Seasons Played	Apps	Subs	Gls
Reading	Tr	06.88	88	0	1	0

KING, Barry
Chesterfield, 30 March, 1935 (OR)

League Club	Source	Date Signed	Seasons Played	Apps	Subs	Gls
Chelsea	Norton Woodseats	02.58				
Reading	Tr	03.58	57	3	-	0

KING Michael **Bryan**
Bishops Stortford, 18 May, 1947 (G)

League Club	Source	Date Signed	Seasons Played	Apps	Subs	Gls
Millwall	Chelmsford C.	06.67	67-74	302	0	0
Coventry C.	Tr	08.75	75	23	0	0

KING David John
Hull, 24 October, 1940 (IF)

League Club	Source	Date Signed	Seasons Played	Apps	Subs	Gls
Hull C.	Jnrs	10.58	59-62	65	-	24

KING David Martin
Colchester, 18 September, 1962 (M)

League Club	Source	Date Signed	Seasons Played	Apps	Subs	Gls
Derby Co.	App	09.80				
York C. (N/C)	Gresley Rov.	03.83	82	0	1	0

KING Dennis
Bearpark (Dm), 16 September, 1932 Died 1988 (W)

League Club	Source	Date Signed	Seasons Played	Apps	Subs	Gls
Bradford P.A.		09.50				
Oldham Ath.	Spennymoor U.	05.54	54-55	22	-	7

KING Derek Albert
Hackney, 15 August, 1929 (CH)

League Club	Source	Date Signed	Seasons Played	Apps	Subs	Gls
Tottenham H.	Jnrs	08.50	51-54	19	-	0
Swansea C.	Tr	08.56	56	5	-	0

KING George
Warkworth (Nd), 5 January, 1923 (CF)

League Club	Source	Date Signed	Seasons Played	Apps	Subs	Gls
Newcastle U.		08.46	46	2	-	0
Hull C.	Tr	03.48	47-48	3	-	0
Port Vale	Tr	04.49	48-49	10	-	5
Barrow	Tr	02.50	49-51	86	-	35
Bradford C.	Tr	01.52	51-52	23	-	9
Gillingham	Tr	10.52	52	19	-	5

KING Gerald Henry
Radnor, 7 April, 1947 W Sch (W)

League Club	Source	Date Signed	Seasons Played	Apps	Subs	Gls
Cardiff C.	Jnrs	06.64	64	6	-	0
Torquay U.	Tr	06.65	65	17	0	2
Luton T.	Tr	06.66	66	21	1	4
Newport Co.	Tr	07.67	67-68	49	3	9

KING Jeffrey
Fauldhouse, 9 November, 1953 (M)

League Club	Source	Date Signed	Seasons Played	Apps	Subs	Gls
Derby Co.	Albion Rov.	04.74	75-77	12	2	0
Notts Co.	L	01.76	75	3	0	0
Portsmouth	L	03.76	75	4	0	0
Walsall	Tr	11.77	77-78	50	1	4
Sheffield Wed.	Tr	08.79	79-81	54	3	5
Sheffield U.	Tr	01.82	81-82	35	2	5
Chesterfield (N/C)	Tr	10.83	83	1	0	0

KING John
Ferndale, 29 November, 1933 Died 1982 W Sch/W-1 (G)

League Club	Source	Date Signed	Seasons Played	Apps	Subs	Gls
Swansea C.	Jnrs	02.51	50-63	368	-	0

KING John (Jake)
Glasgow, 29 January, 1955 (RB)

League Club	Source	Date Signed	Seasons Played	Apps	Subs	Gls
Shrewsbury T.	App	01.73	71-81	304	2	20
Wrexham	Tr	08.82	82-84	91	1	5
Cardiff C.	Tr	11.84	84-85	30	0	0

KING John (Ian) Aitken
Loanhead, 27 May, 1937 S Sch (CH)

League Club	Source	Date Signed	Seasons Played	Apps	Subs	Gls
Leicester C.	Arniston Rov.	06.57	57-65	244	0	6
Charlton Ath.	Tr	03.66	65-67	63	0	0

KING John Allen
Marylebone, 15 April, 1938 (WH)

League Club	Source	Date Signed	Seasons Played	Apps	Subs	Gls
Everton	Jnrs	03.56	57-59	48	-	1
Bournemouth	Tr	07.60	60	21	-	1
Tranmere R.	Tr	02.61	60-67	239	2	4
Port Vale	Tr	07.68	68-70	99	2	0

KING John Charles
Great Gidding (Hunts), 5 November, 1926 (WH)

League Club	Source	Date Signed	Seasons Played	Apps	Subs	Gls
Leicester C.	Peterborough U.	09.44	46-54	197	-	5

KING John William
Wrenbury (Ches), 9 August, 1932 (CF)

League Club	Source	Date Signed	Seasons Played	Apps	Subs	Gls
Crewe Alex.	Jnrs	10.49	50-53	48	-	17
Stoke C.	Tr	09.53	53-60	284	-	106
Cardiff C.	Tr	08.61	61	33	-	6
Crewe Alex.	Tr	06.62	62-66	178	0	43

KING Martyn Noel Geoffrey
Birmingham, 23 August, 1937 (CF)

League Club	Source	Date Signed	Seasons Played	Apps	Subs	Gls
Colchester U.	Pegasus	05.56	56-64	212	-	130
Wrexham	Tr	10.64	64-65	45	0	15

KING Peter
Liverpool, 5 July, 1964 (M)

League Club	Source	Date Signed	Seasons Played	Apps	Subs	Gls
Liverpool	App	07.82				
Crewe Alex.	Tr	08.83	83-84	55	9	5

KING Peter Charles
Worcester, 3 April, 1943 (F)

League Club	Source	Date Signed	Seasons Played	Apps	Subs	Gls
Cardiff C.	Worcester C.	09.60	61-73	352	2	66

KING Philip Geoffrey
Bristol, 28 December, 1967 E'B' (LB)

League Club	Source	Date Signed	Seasons Played	Apps	Subs	Gls
Exeter C.	App	01.85	84-85	24	3	0
Torquay U.	Tr	07.86	86	24	0	3
Swindon T.	Tr	02.87	86-89	112	4	4
Sheffield Wed.	Tr	11.89	89-93	124	5	2
Notts Co.	L	10.93	93	6	0	0
Aston Villa	Tr	08.94	94	13	3	0
West Bromwich A.	L	10.95	95	4	0	0
Swindon T.	Tr	03.97	96	5	0	0
Blackpool	L	10.97	97	6	0	0

KING Raymond
Warkworth, 15 August, 1924 E 'B' (G)

League Club	Source	Date Signed	Seasons Played	Apps	Subs	Gls
Newcastle U.		04.42				
Leyton Orient	Tr	10.46	46	1	-	0
Port Vale	Ashington	05.49	49-56	252	-	0

KING Robert David
Merthyr Tydfil, 2 September, 1977 W Yth (RB)

League Club	Source	Date Signed	Seasons Played	Apps	Subs	Gls
Swansea C.	Torquay U. (YT)	07.96	96	2	0	0

KING Robert Edward
Edinburgh, 7 September, 1941 (FB)

League Club	Source	Date Signed	Seasons Played	Apps	Subs	Gls
Southend U.	Glasgow Rangers	08.63	63-65	77	2	2

KING Frederick **Robert**
Northampton, 19 September, 1919 (OR)

League Club	Source	Date Signed	Seasons Played	Apps	Subs	Gls
Northampton T.		10.37	37-38	42	-	6
Wolverhampton W.	Tr	11.39	46	6	-	3
Northampton T.	Tr	12.47	47-49	56	-	17

KING Simon
Ebbw Vale, 19 July, 1964 (D)

League Club	Source	Date Signed	Seasons Played	Apps	Subs	Gls
Newport Co. (N/C)	Cwmbran T.	10.84	84	1	0	0

KING Thomas
Edinburgh, 18 July, 1933 (G)

League Club	Source	Date Signed	Seasons Played	Apps	Subs	Gls
Watford	Ormiston Primrose	03.54	55	20	-	0

KING Thomas Frederick
Barrow, 2 April, 1934 (WH)

League Club	Source	Date Signed	Seasons Played	Apps	Subs	Gls
Barrow	Holker C.O.B.	03.53	52-59	73	-	1

KINGSHOTT Frederick John
Camden, 20 June, 1929 (G)

League Club	Source	Date Signed	Seasons Played	Apps	Subs	Gls
Doncaster Rov.	Eastbourne U.	02.53	52	2	-	0
Gillingham	Tr	11.55	55-56	45	-	0

KINGSNORTH Thomas Henry
Sittingbourne, 16 April, 1917 Died 1992 (CH)

League Club	Source	Date Signed	Seasons Played	Apps	Subs	Gls
Gillingham	Lloyds Paper Mill	09.46	50	29	-	0

KINGSTON Andrew Keith
Oxford, 21 February, 1959 E Sch/E Yth (RB)

League Club	Source	Date Signed	Seasons Played	Apps	Subs	Gls
Oxford U.	App	10.76	76-81	44	6	0

KINKLADZE Georgiou
Georgia, 6 November, 1973 Georgian Int (M)

League Club	Source	Date Signed	Seasons Played	Apps	Subs	Gls
Manchester C.	Dinamo Tbilisi (Geo)	08.95	95-97	105	1	20

KINLOCH Thomas Sutherland
Glasgow, 22 February, 1927 Died 1994 (WH)

League Club	Source	Date Signed	Seasons Played	Apps	Subs	Gls
Carlisle U.	Falkirk	05.50	50-55	184	-	15
Workington	Tr	07.56	56-57	70	-	12
Southport	Tr	02.58	57-58	53	-	0

KINNAIRD Paul
Glasgow, 11 November, 1966 S Yth (W)

League Club	Source	Date Signed	Seasons Played	Apps	Subs	Gls
Norwich C.	App	11.84				
Shrewsbury T. (L)	Partick Thistle	02.93	92	4	0	1
Scarborough (N/C)	Dunfermline Ath.	10.95	95	3	0	0

KINNEAR Joseph Patrick
Dublin, 27 December, 1946 IR-25 (RB)

League Club	Source	Date Signed	Seasons Played	Apps	Subs	Gls
Tottenham H.	St Albans C.	02.65	65-75	189	7	2
Brighton & H.A.	Tr	08.75	75	15	1	1

KINNELL George
Dunfermline, 22 December, 1937 (CH)

League Club	Source	Date Signed	Seasons Played	Apps	Subs	Gls
Stoke C.	Aberdeen	11.63	63-65	89	2	6
Oldham Ath.	Tr	08.66	66	12	0	8
Sunderland	Tr	10.66	66-68	67	2	3
Middlesbrough	Tr	10.68	68	12	1	1

KINSELL Thomas **Henry (Harry)**
Cannock, 31 May, 1921 (FB)

League Club	Source	Date Signed	Seasons Played	Apps	Subs	Gls
West Bromwich A.	Jnrs	06.38	46-48	83	-	0
Bolton W.	Tr	06.49	49	17	-	0
Reading	Tr	05.50	50	12	-	0
West Ham U.	Tr	01.51	50-54	101	-	2

KINSELLA Antony Steven
Grays, 30 October, 1961 IRu21-2 (LW)

League Club	Source	Date Signed	Seasons Played	Apps	Subs	Gls
Millwall	App	11.78	78-80	55	6	1
Ipswich T.	Tampa Bay (USA)	04.82	82-83	7	2	0
Millwall	Tr	06.84	84-85	20	2	1
Doncaster Rov.	Enfield	02.87	86-87	29	1	4

KINSELLA Leonard
Alexandria, 14 May, 1946 (M)

League Club	Source	Date Signed	Seasons Played	Apps	Subs	Gls
Burnley	App	05.63	65-69	7	6	0
Carlisle U.	Tr	09.70	70-71	10	4	0
Rochdale	Tr	09.71	71-73	82	3	4

KINSELLA Mark Anthony
Dublin, 12 August, 1972 IR Yth/IRu21-8/IR 'B'/IR-2 (M)

League Club	Source	Date Signed	Seasons Played	Apps	Subs	Gls
Colchester U.	YT	08.89	89-96	174	6	27
Charlton Ath.	Tr	09.96	96-97	83	0	12

KINSELLA Patrick Gerard
Liverpool, 8 November, 1943 (M)

League Club	Source	Date Signed	Seasons Played	Apps	Subs	Gls
Liverpool	Jnrs	11.60				
Tranmere Rov.	Bangor C.	08.66	66	1	0	0
Stockport Co.	Rhyl	10.68	68	12	1	0

KINSEY Albert John
Liverpool, 19 September, 1945 E Sch (F)

League Club	Source	Date Signed	Seasons Played	Apps	Subs	Gls
Manchester U.	App	10.62				
Wrexham	Tr	03.66	65-72	245	8	84
Crewe Alex.	Tr	03.73	72-74	30	2	1

KINSEY Brian Robert
Charlton, 4 March, 1938 (LB)

League Club	Source	Date Signed	Seasons Played	Apps	Subs	Gls
Charlton Ath.	Bromley	09.56	56-70	371	6	19

KINSEY Noel
Treorchy, 24 December, 1925 W-7 (IF)

League Club	Source	Date Signed	Seasons Played	Apps	Subs	Gls
Cardiff C.	Jnrs	06.44				
Norwich C.	Tr	05.47	47-52	223	-	57
Birmingham C.	Tr	05.53	53-57	149	-	48
Port Vale	Tr	02.58	57-60	72	-	6

KINSEY Stephen
Manchester, 2 January, 1963 E Yth (W)

League Club	Source	Date Signed	Seasons Played	Apps	Subs	Gls
Manchester C.	App	01.80	80-85	87	14	15
Chester C.	L	09.82	82	3	0	1
Chesterfield	L	11.82	82	3	0	0
Rochdale (N/C)	Tacoma (USA)	10.91	91	3	3	1

KIPPAX Dennis Hobson
Sheffield, 7 August, 1926 Died 1970 (OR)

League Club	Source	Date Signed	Seasons Played	Apps	Subs	Gls
Sheffield Wed.	Stocksbridge Wks	03.46	46	1	-	0

KIPPAX Frederick **Peter**
Burnley, 17 July, 1922 Died 1987 E Amat/EF Lge (OL)

League Club	Source	Date Signed	Seasons Played	Apps	Subs	Gls
Burnley (Am)	Jnrs	07.46	46-47	32	-	6
Liverpool (Am)	Tr	01.49	48	1	-	0

KIRBY Alan
Barrow, 19 December, 1926 (G)

League Club	Source	Date Signed	Seasons Played	Apps	Subs	Gls
Notts Co.		05.45				
Barrow		09.47	50-51	21	-	0

KIRBY Denis
Leeds, 8 November, 1924 (WH)

League Club	Source	Date Signed	Seasons Played	Apps	Subs	Gls
Leeds U.	Jnrs	09.42	47	8	-	0

KIRBY Eric
Sheffield, 12 October, 1926 (WH)

League Club	Source	Date Signed	Seasons Played	Apps	Subs	Gls
Sheffield Wed.		12.49	50	1	-	0
York C.	Tr	08.52	52	1	-	0

KIRBY George
Liverpool, 20 December, 1933 (CF)

League Club	Source	Date Signed	Seasons Played	Apps	Subs	Gls
Everton	Jnrs	06.52	55-57	26	-	9
Sheffield Wed.	Tr	03.59	59	3	-	0
Plymouth Arg.	Tr	01.60	59-62	93	-	38
Southampton	Tr	09.62	62-63	63	-	28
Coventry C.	Tr	03.64	63-64	18	-	10
Swansea C.	Tr	10.64	64	26	-	8
Walsall	Tr	05.65	65-66	74	1	25
Brentford	New York (USA)	10.68	68	5	0	1

KIRBY Ryan Mark
Chingford, 6 September, 1974 (RB)

League Club	Source	Date Signed	Seasons Played	Apps	Subs	Gls
Arsenal	YT	07.93				
Doncaster Rov.	Tr	07.94	94-95	73	5	0
Wigan Ath. (N/C)	Tr	08.96	96	5	1	0
Northampton T. (N/C)	Tr	09.96	96	0	1	0

KIRK Henry (Harry) Joseph
Saltcoats, 25 August, 1944 (W)

League Club	Source	Date Signed	Seasons Played	Apps	Subs	Gls
Middlesbrough	Ardeer Rec.	05.63	63	1	-	0
Darlington	Dumbarton	06.67	67-69	59	3	7
Hartlepool U.	Tr	10.69	69-70	42	3	5
Scunthorpe U.	Tr	11.70	70-72	112	0	16
Stockport Co.	Tr	09.73	73-74	60	8	7

KIRK James
Tarbolton (Ayrs), 12 November, 1925 (G)

League Club	Source	Date Signed	Seasons Played	Apps	Subs	Gls
Bury	St Mirren	08.51	51-53	79	-	0
Colchester U.	Tr	06.54	54	32	-	0
Torquay U.	Tr	08.55	55	39	-	0
Aldershot	Tr	07.56	56	5	-	0

KIRK John Francis
Leicester, 7 February, 1922 (OL)

League Club	Source	Date Signed	Seasons Played	Apps	Subs	Gls
Nottingham F.		08.48				
Darlington	Tr	08.51	51	31	-	4

KIRK John McCrae
Canada, 13 March, 1930 (IF)

League Club	Source	Date Signed	Seasons Played	Apps	Subs	Gls
Portsmouth	Montrose	01.51				
Accrington St.	Tr	03.53	52-53	14	-	1

KIRK Roy
Bolsover, 11 June, 1929 Died 1984 (D)

League Club	Source	Date Signed	Seasons Played	Apps	Subs	Gls
Leeds U.	Bolsover Colly	10.48	50-51	34	-	1
Coventry C.	Tr	03.52	51-59	330	-	6

KIRK Stephen David
Kirkcaldy, 3 January, 1963 (FB)

League Club	Source	Date Signed	Seasons Played	Apps	Subs	Gls
Stoke C.	East Fife	05.80	81	12	0	0

KIRKALDIE John (Jack)
Coventry, 2 August, 1917 Died 1985 (OR)

League Club	Source	Date Signed	Seasons Played	Apps	Subs	Gls
Southend U.	Nuneaton T.	02.36				
West Ham U.	Tr	02.37	36-38	11	-	1
Doncaster Rov.	Tr	04.39	38-47	53	-	17

KIRKBY John
U.S.A., 29 November, 1929 Died 1953 (FB)

League Club	Source	Date Signed	Seasons Played	Apps	Subs	Gls
Stoke C.	Jnrs	12.46	48	1	-	0
Wrexham	Tr	08.51	51-52	5	-	0

KIRKHAM John
Ellesmere Port, 16 June, 1918 Died 1982 (F)

League Club	Source	Date Signed	Seasons Played	Apps	Subs	Gls
Wolverhampton W.	Ellesmere Port	03.36	37-38	13	-	5
Bournemouth	Tr	10.38	38-46	47	-	26

KIRKHAM John Kenneth
Wednesbury, 13 May, 1941 E Yth/Eu23-2 (WH)

League Club	Source	Date Signed	Seasons Played	Apps	Subs	Gls
Wolverhampton W.	Jnrs	05.58	59-64	100	-	12
Peterborough U.	Tr	11.65	65-67	46	0	2
Exeter C.	Tr	07.68	68	31	1	6

KIRKHAM Paul
Manchester, 5 July, 1969 (F)

League Club	Source	Date Signed	Seasons Played	Apps	Subs	Gls
Huddersfield T.	Manchester U. (YT)	09.87	87	0	1	0

KIRKHAM Peter Jonathan
Newcastle, 28 October, 1974 (M)

League Club	Source	Date Signed	Seasons Played	Apps	Subs	Gls
Darlington	Newcastle U. (YT)	08.93	93-94	5	8	0

KIRKHAM Raymond Neville
Thame, 16 December, 1934 (G)

League Club	Source	Date Signed	Seasons Played	Apps	Subs	Gls
Mansfield T.	Thorne T.	12.57	57-59	42	-	0

KIRKHAM Reginald
Ormskirk, 8 May, 1919 (FB)

League Club	Source	Date Signed	Seasons Played	Apps	Subs	Gls
Wolverhampton W.	Ormskirk	03.46				
Burnley	Tr	03.47	48-50	13	-	1

KIRKHAM Royce
Ollerton, 17 October, 1937 (FB)

League Club	Source	Date Signed	Seasons Played	Apps	Subs	Gls
Notts Co.	Ollerton Colly	05.55	56	1	-	0

KIRKLAND James William
Bedford, 30 October, 1946 (FB)

League Club	Source	Date Signed	Seasons Played	Apps	Subs	Gls
Grimsby T.	Aberdeen	07.70	70	12	0	0

KIRKMAN Alan John
Bolton, 21 June, 1936 (IF)

League Club	Source	Date Signed	Seasons Played	Apps	Subs	Gls
Manchester C.	Bacup Borough	02.56	56-58	7	-	6
Rotherham U.	Tr	03.59	58-63	144	-	58
Newcastle U.	Tr	09.63	63	5	-	1
Scunthorpe U.	Tr	12.63	63-64	32	-	5
Torquay U.	Tr	07.65	65-66	59	0	8
Workington	Tr	01.67	66-67	56	0	3

KIRKMAN Kenneth Roy
Bolton, 20 March, 1931 (OR)

League Club	Source	Date Signed	Seasons Played	Apps	Subs	Gls
Bournemouth	Lomax's	07.51				
Southport	Tr	08.53	53	1	-	0

KIRKMAN Norman
Bolton, 6 June, 1920 Died 1995 (FB)

League Club	Source	Date Signed	Seasons Played	Apps	Subs	Gls
Burnley		09.39				
Rochdale	Tr	09.46	46-47	53	-	0
Chesterfield	Tr	12.47	47-48	41	-	0
Leicester C.	Tr	08.49	49	12	-	0
Southampton	Tr	07.50	50-51	20	-	0
Exeter C.	Tr	03.52	51-52	11	-	1

KIRKPATRICK John
Annan, 3 March, 1919 (WH/IF)

League Club	Source	Date Signed	Seasons Played	Apps	Subs	Gls
Carlisle U.	Jnrs	11.37	46	34	-	2

KIRKPATRICK Roger Whitworth
Sculcotes, 29 May, 1923 (WH/OL)

League Club	Source	Date Signed	Seasons Played	Apps	Subs	Gls
Chester C.		08.47	47-52	111	-	26

KIRKUP Brian Alexander
Burnham, 16 April, 1932 (CF)

League Club	Source	Date Signed	Seasons Played	Apps	Subs	Gls
Reading	Bedford T.	08.55	55-57	55	-	19
Northampton T.	Tr	07.58	58-59	26	-	7
Aldershot	Tr	11.59	59-61	59	-	15

KIRKUP Frank William
Spennymoor, 12 January, 1939 (OL)

League Club	Source	Date Signed	Seasons Played	Apps	Subs	Gls
Blackburn Rov.	Spennymoor U.	02.57				
Workington	Tr	06.59	59-62	140	-	31
Carlisle U.	Tr	12.62	62-64	76	-	15
Notts Co.	Tr	06.65	65	29	0	3
Workington		11.66	66	8	0	0

KIRKUP Graeme Stuart
Cramlington, 31 May, 1965 (RB)

League Club	Source	Date Signed	Seasons Played	Apps	Subs	Gls
Exeter C.	App	05.83	81-85	102	5	1

KIRKUP Joseph Robert
Hexham, 17 December, 1939 E Yth/Eu23-3 (FB)

League Club	Source	Date Signed	Seasons Played	Apps	Subs	Gls
West Ham U.	Jnrs	05.57	58-65	165	0	6
Chelsea	Tr	03.66	65-67	48	5	2
Southampton	Tr	02.68	67-73	169	0	3

KIRKWOOD Ian
Edinburgh, 29 November, 1932 (IR)

League Club	Source	Date Signed	Seasons Played	Apps	Subs	Gls
Reading	Wokingham T.	02.53	52-54	5	-	1

KIRKWOOD John Fleming
Falkirk, 27 February, 1932 (G)

League Club	Source	Date Signed	Seasons Played	Apps	Subs	Gls
Reading	Blairhall Colly	12.49	52-53	31	-	0

KIRMAN Harold
Hull, 3 December, 1930 (FB)

League Club	Source	Date Signed	Seasons Played	Apps	Subs	Gls
Hull C.	Fred Askew Y.C.	12.50				
Gillingham	Tr	07.52	53	8	-	0
Hull C.		01.55	55	2	-	0

KIRSTEN Kenneth
South Africa, 28 October, 1922 (LB)

League Club	Source	Date Signed	Seasons Played	Apps	Subs	Gls
Charlton Ath.	Park Villa	03.48				
Aldershot	Tr	08.51	51	5	-	0

KIRTLEY John **Harold**
Washington, 23 May, 1930 (IF)

League Club	Source	Date Signed	Seasons Played	Apps	Subs	Gls
Sunderland	Fatfield Jnrs	05.48	48-54	95	-	18
Cardiff C.	Tr	05.55	55	38	-	4
Gateshead	Tr	03.57	56-59	96	-	14

KIRTON John
Aberdeen, 4 March, 1916 Died 1996 (WH)

League Club	Source	Date Signed	Seasons Played	Apps	Subs	Gls
Stoke C.	Banks o'Dee	11.35	36-52	219	-	2
Bradford C.	Tr	07.53	53	8	-	0

KISBY Christopher Nigel
Pudsey, 7 November, 1952 (D)

League Club	Source	Date Signed	Seasons Played	Apps	Subs	Gls
Scunthorpe U.	App	10.70	70-72	30	9	2
Workington	Tr	08.73	73-76	162	2	2
Southport	Tr	08.77	77	42	0	1

KITCHEN David (Sam) Edward
Germany, 11 June, 1967 (D)

League Club	Source	Date Signed	Seasons Played	Apps	Subs	Gls
Leyton Orient	Frickley Ath.	08.92	92-93	35	8	1
Doncaster Rov.	Tr	02.94	93-94	21	1	1

KITCHEN John (Jack)
Whitehaven, 28 February, 1925 Died 1992 (CH)

League Club	Source	Date Signed	Seasons Played	Apps	Subs	Gls
Barnsley	Ketts. Ath.	10.44	46-51	53	-	0

KITCHEN Michael **Peter**
Mexborough, 16 February, 1952 (F)

League Club	Source	Date Signed	Seasons Played	Apps	Subs	Gls
Doncaster Rov.	Jnrs	07.70	70-76	221	7	89
Leyton Orient	Tr	07.77	77-78	64	1	28
Fulham	Tr	02.79	78-79	21	3	6
Cardiff C.	Tr	08.80	80-81	64	3	21
Leyton Orient	Happy Valley (HK)	12.82	82-83	46	3	21
Chester C. (N/C)	Dagenham	03.85	84	3	2	1

KITCHENER Barry Raymond
Dagenham, 11 December, 1947 (CD)

League Club	Source	Date Signed	Seasons Played	Apps	Subs	Gls
Millwall	App	08.65	66-81	518	5	25

KITCHENER Raymond Alan
Baldock, 31 October, 1930 (OL)

League Club	Source	Date Signed	Seasons Played	Apps	Subs	Gls
Chelsea	Hitchin T.	07.54	55	1	-	0
Norwich C.	Tr	09.56	56	18	-	0

KITCHENER William Harry
Arlesey, 3 November, 1946 (FB)

League Club	Source	Date Signed	Seasons Played	Apps	Subs	Gls
West Ham U.	App	11.63	66-67	11	0	0
Torquay U.	L	09.66	66	25	0	3
Torquay U.	Tr	12.67	67-70	142	0	5
Bournemouth	Tr	07.71	71	36	0	2

KITCHING Phillip John
Lewisham, 30 September, 1967 (M)

League Club	Source	Date Signed	Seasons Played	Apps	Subs	Gls
York C. (N/C)	Bradford C. (N/C)	08.87	87	7	6	0

KITE Philip David
Bristol, 26 October, 1962 E Sch/E Yth (G)

League Club	Source	Date Signed	Seasons Played	Apps	Subs	Gls
Bristol Rov.	App	10.80	80-83	96	0	0
Southampton	Tr	08.84	84-85	4	0	0
Middlesbrough	L	03.86	85	2	0	0
Gillingham		02.87	86-88	70	0	0
Bournemouth	Tr	08.89	89	7	0	0
Sheffield U.	Tr	08.90	90-91	11	0	0
Mansfield T.	L	11.91	91	11	0	0
Plymouth Arg.	L	09.92	92	2	0	0
Rotherham U.	L	10.92	92	1	0	0
Crewe Alex.	L	11.92	92	5	0	0
Stockport Co.	L	03.93	92	5	0	0
Cardiff C.	Tr	07.93	93	17	1	0
Bristol C.	Tr	08.94	94-95	5	1	0
Bristol Rov.	Tr	08.96				

KITSON Paul
Murton, 9 January, 1971 Eu21-7 (F)

League Club	Source	Date Signed	Seasons Played	Apps	Subs	Gls
Leicester C.	YT	12.88	89-91	39	11	6
Derby Co.	Tr	03.92	91-94	105	0	36
Newcastle U.	Tr	09.94	94-96	26	10	10
West Ham U.	Tr	02.97	96-97	26	1	12

KIWOMYA Andrew Derek
Huddersfield, 1 October, 1967 E Yth (W)

League Club	Source	Date Signed	Seasons Played	Apps	Subs	Gls
Barnsley	YT	07.85	85	1	0	0
Sheffield Wed.	Tr	10.86				
Rotherham U.	Dundee	10.93	93	4	3	0
Scunthorpe U. (N/C)	Halifax T.	03.95	94	9	0	3
Bradford C.	Tr	07.95	95-96	27	16	3
Luton T.	L	03.97	96	5	0	1
Burnley	L	09.97	97	1	2	0
Notts Co.	Tr	12.97	97	0	2	0

KIWOMYA Christopher Mark
Huddersfield, 2 December, 1969 (F)

League Club	Source	Date Signed	Seasons Played	Apps	Subs	Gls
Ipswich T.	YT	03.87	88-94	197	28	51
Arsenal	Tr	01.95	94	5	9	3

KJELDBERG Jakob
Denmark, 21 October, 1969 Danish Int (CD)

League Club	Source	Date Signed	Seasons Played	Apps	Subs	Gls
Chelsea	Silkeborg (Den)	08.93	93-94	52	0	2

KLETZENBAUER Carl **Frank**
Coventry, 21 July, 1936 Died 1996 (FB)

League Club	Source	Date Signed	Seasons Played	Apps	Subs	Gls
Coventry C.	Coventry M.S.C.	03.56	56-63	122	-	3
Walsall	Tr	03.64	63-64	12	-	0

KLINSMANN Jurgen
Germany, 30 July, 1964 German Int (F)

League Club	Source	Date Signed	Seasons Played	Apps	Subs	Gls
Tottenham H.	A.S. Monaco (Fr)	08.94	94	41	0	20
Tottenham H.	Sampdoria (It)	12.97	97	15	0	9

KLONER Hymie
Poland, 23 May, 1929 (WH)

League Club	Source	Date Signed	Seasons Played	Apps	Subs	Gls
Birmingham C.	Marist Bros (SA)	11.50	50	1	-	0

KLUG Bryan Paul
Coventry, 8 October, 1960 E Yth (M)

League Club	Source	Date Signed	Seasons Played	Apps	Subs	Gls
Ipswich T.	App	11.77				
Wimbledon	L	03.80	79	10	1	0
Chesterfield	Tr	08.83	83	27	7	2
Peterborough U.	Tr	08.84	84	39	0	2

KNAPP Anthony
Newstead (Nts), 13 October, 1936 EF Lge (CH)

League Club	Source	Date Signed	Seasons Played	Apps	Subs	Gls
Leicester C.	Jnrs	12.53	55-60	86	-	0
Southampton	Tr	08.61	61-66	233	0	2
Coventry C.	Tr	08.67	67	11	0	0
Tranmere Rov.	Los Angeles (USA)	10.69	69-70	36	0	1

KNIGHT Alan Edward
Balham, 3 July, 1961 E Yth/Eu21-2 (G)

League Club	Source	Date Signed	Seasons Played	Apps	Subs	Gls
Portsmouth	App	03.79	77-97	662	0	0

KNIGHT Anthony
Romford, 6 March, 1959 (G)

League Club	Source	Date Signed	Seasons Played	Apps	Subs	Gls
Luton T.	App	05.76	76-77	6	0	0
Brighton & H.A.	Dover T.	08.79				

KNIGHT Arnold William
Guisborough, 30 May, 1919 (IF)

League Club	Source	Date Signed	Seasons Played	Apps	Subs	Gls
Leeds U.		10.37				
Plymouth Arg.	Tr	07.47	47	7	-	0
Bradford C.	Tr	02.48	47-48	7	-	0

KNIGHT Brian
Dundee, 28 March, 1949 (FB)

League Club	Source	Date Signed	Seasons Played	Apps	Subs	Gls
Huddersfield T.	Dundee	07.69				
Northampton T.	Tr	10.69	69	9	3	0

KNIGHT Brian Thomas Arthur
High Wycombe, 14 November, 1946 (OL)

League Club	Source	Date Signed	Seasons Played	Apps	Subs	Gls
Reading	App	11.64	64-65	4	0	1

KNIGHT Craig
Wrexham, 24 October, 1973 (D)

League Club	Source	Date Signed	Seasons Played	Apps	Subs	Gls
Wrexham	YT	07.92	91	1	0	0

KNIGHT Frank
Hucknall, 26 October, 1921 Died 1993 (LH)

League Club	Source	Date Signed	Seasons Played	Apps	Subs	Gls
Nottingham F.		05.43	46-49	48	-	1

KNIGHT George Rollinson
Bolton, 12 May, 1921 (IR)

League Club	Source	Date Signed	Seasons Played	Apps	Subs	Gls
Burnley	Jnrs	05.38	38-46	9	-	2

KNIGHT Graham John
Rochester, 5 January, 1952 (FB/M)

League Club	Source	Date Signed	Seasons Played	Apps	Subs	Gls
Gillingham	App	01.70	70-78	229	16	10

KNIGHT Ian John
Hartlepool, 26 October, 1966 Eu21-2 (CD)

League Club	Source	Date Signed	Seasons Played	Apps	Subs	Gls
Barnsley	App	10.84				
Sheffield Wed.	Tr	08.85	85-88	21	0	0
Scunthorpe U.	L	08.89	89	2	0	0
Grimsby T.	Tr	01.90	89-91	16	5	2
Carlisle U. (N/C)	Tr	08.92	92	1	0	0

KNIGHT Jason George
Australia, 16 September, 1974 (M)

League Club	Source	Date Signed	Seasons Played	Apps	Subs	Gls
Doncaster Rov.	Hinckley Ath.	08.95	95	1	3	0

KNIGHT Jeffrey William
Sudbury, 10 December, 1926 (IF)

League Club	Source	Date Signed	Seasons Played	Apps	Subs	Gls
Derby Co.		05.46				
Walsall	Tr	08.52	52	4	-	0

KNIGHT John (Jack)
Bolton, 12 September, 1922 Died 1996 (IL)

League Club	Source	Date Signed	Seasons Played	Apps	Subs	Gls
Burnley	Jnrs	08.45	46-48	26	-	5
Preston N.E.	Tr	12.48	48-49	39	-	7
Chesterfield	Tr	07.51	51	35	-	6
Exeter C.	Tr	08.52	52-53	56	-	6

KNIGHT Keith
Cheltenham, 16 February, 1969 E Sch (W)

League Club	Source	Date Signed	Seasons Played	Apps	Subs	Gls
Reading	Cheltenham T.	09.88	88-90	39	4	8

KNIGHT Lyndon Alan
Lydbrook (Glos), 3 February, 1961 (G)

League Club	Source	Date Signed	Seasons Played	Apps	Subs	Gls
Hereford U.	App	02.79	78	2	0	0

KNIGHT Peter Richard
Brighton, 12 November, 1939 (W)

League Club	Source	Date Signed	Seasons Played	Apps	Subs	Gls
Brighton & H.A.	Lewes	01.64	63-65	9	1	1

KNIGHT Peter Robert
Ilford, 26 December, 1937 (OR)

League Club	Source	Date Signed	Seasons Played	Apps	Subs	Gls
Southend U.		06.58				
Nottingham F.	Tr	08.59	59	4	-	0
Oxford U.	Tr	07.60	62-64	94	-	12
Reading	Tr	11.64	64-65	26	0	3

KNIGHT Richard
Burton, 31 August, 1974 (RB)

League Club	Source	Date Signed	Seasons Played	Apps	Subs	Gls
Walsall	YT	03.92	92-93	27	2	1

KNIGHT Terrie George
Camden, 1 February, 1932 (G)

League Club	Source	Date Signed	Seasons Played	Apps	Subs	Gls
Aldershot (Am)	Alton T.	10.58	58	4	-	0

KNIGHTON Kenneth
Darton, 20 February, 1944 (M)

League Club	Source	Date Signed	Seasons Played	Apps	Subs	Gls
Wolverhampton W.	App	02.61	64-66	13	3	0
Oldham Ath.	Tr	11.66	66-67	45	0	4
Preston N.E.	Tr	11.67	67-68	62	0	3
Blackburn Rov.	Tr	06.69	69-70	70	0	11
Hull C.	Tr	03.71	70-72	79	1	9
Sheffield Wed.	Tr	08.73	73-75	71	5	2

KNIGHTS Anthony Frank
Grimsby, 13 March, 1940 (LH)

League Club	Source	Date Signed	Seasons Played	Apps	Subs	Gls
Grimsby T.	Jnrs	06.58	59-63	75	-	1
Luton T.	Tr	08.64	64	2	-	0
Aldershot	Tr	07.65	65	20	0	0

KNILL Alan Richard
Eton, 8 October, 1964 W Yth/W-1 (CD)

League Club	Source	Date Signed	Seasons Played	Apps	Subs	Gls
Southampton	App	10.82				
Halifax T.	Tr	07.84	84-86	118	0	6
Swansea C.	Tr	08.87	87-88	89	0	3
Bury	Tr	08.89	89-93	141	3	8
Cardiff C.	L	09.93	93	4	0	0
Scunthorpe U.	Tr	11.93	93-96	131	0	8
Rotherham U.	Tr	07.97	97	38	0	3

KNOTT Gareth Raymond
Blackwood, 19 January, 1976 W Yth/Wu21-1 (M)

League Club	Source	Date Signed	Seasons Played	Apps	Subs	Gls
Tottenham H.	YT	07.94				
Gillingham	L	02.95	94	5	0	0

KNOTT Herbert
Goole, 5 December, 1914 Died 1986 (CF)

League Club	Source	Date Signed	Seasons Played	Apps	Subs	Gls
Walsall	Brierley Hill Alliance	08.37	39	9	-	2
Hull C.	Brierley Hill Alliance	10.40	46	6	-	1

KNOTT William Francis
Leeds, 16 March, 1934 E Yth (IL)

League Club	Source	Date Signed	Seasons Played	Apps	Subs	Gls
Leeds U.	Jnrs	05.51				
Walsall	Tr	02.55	54	1	-	0

KNOWLES James Barry
Wigan, 25 April, 1959 (LB)

League Club	Source	Date Signed	Seasons Played	Apps	Subs	Gls
Wigan Ath.	Barrow	10.84	84-87	124	3	3

KNOWLES Cameron
Ripon, 19 September, 1969 (M)

League Club	Source	Date Signed	Seasons Played	Apps	Subs	Gls
Chesterfield (N/C)		08.93	93	1	0	0

KNOWLES Christopher James
Stone, 4 February, 1978 (G)

League Club	Source	Date Signed	Seasons Played	Apps	Subs	Gls
Chester C. (N/C)	Peterborough U. (YT)	08.96	96	2	0	0

KNOWLES Cyril Barry
Fitzwilliam, 13 July, 1944 Died 1991 Eu23-6/EF Lge/E-4 (LB)

League Club	Source	Date Signed	Seasons Played	Apps	Subs	Gls
Middlesbrough	Monckton Colly	10.62	62-63	37	-	0
Tottenham H.	Tr	05.64	64-75	402	1	15

KNOWLES Darren Thomas
Sheffield, 8 October, 1970 (RB/M)

League Club	Source	Date Signed	Seasons Played	Apps	Subs	Gls
Sheffield U.	YT	07.89				
Stockport Co.	Tr	09.89	89-92	51	12	0
Scarborough	Tr	08.93	93-96	139	5	2
Hartlepool U.	Tr	03.97	96-97	53	0	1

KNOWLES John David
Halifax, 11 April, 1941 (G)

League Club	Source	Date Signed	Seasons Played	Apps	Subs	Gls
Halifax T.	Jnrs	12.58	58-62	72	-	0
Bury	Tr	07.63	64	1	-	0
Bradford C.	Tr	08.66	66	21	0	0

KNOWLES Harold Frederick
Hednesford, 6 September, 1932 (OL)

League Club	Source	Date Signed	Seasons Played	Apps	Subs	Gls
Walsall	Excelsior	09.50	50	9	-	1
Cardiff C.	Worcester C.	02.59	58-59	8	-	0

KNOWLES James
Preston, 31 July, 1934 (G)

League Club	Source	Date Signed	Seasons Played	Apps	Subs	Gls
Preston N.E.	Jnrs	10.57	57	2	-	0
Barrow	Tr	08.58	58-59	11	-	0

KNOWLES Peter
Fitzwilliam, 30 September, 1945 E Yth/Eu23-4 (IF)

League Club	Source	Date Signed	Seasons Played	Apps	Subs	Gls
Wolverhampton W.	App	10.62	63-69	171	3	61

KNOWLES Raymond
Willesden, 30 September, 1952 (F)

League Club	Source	Date Signed	Seasons Played	Apps	Subs	Gls
Wimbledon	Southall	07.78	78-79	31	8	6

KNOX James Hay
Brechin, 26 November, 1935 (F)

League Club	Source	Date Signed	Seasons Played	Apps	Subs	Gls
Coventry C.	Raith Rov.	05.57	57	2	-	0

KNOX Robert Preston
Ulverston, 26 February, 1946 (F)

League Club	Source	Date Signed	Seasons Played	Apps	Subs	Gls
Barrow	Jnrs	07.65	64-71	94	12	19

KNOX Thomas
Glasgow, 5 September, 1939 (OL)

League Club	Source	Date Signed	Seasons Played	Apps	Subs	Gls
Chelsea	East Stirling	06.62	62-64	20	-	0
Newcastle U.	Tr	02.65	64-66	24	1	1
Mansfield T.	Tr	03.67	66-67	34	0	5
Northampton T.	Tr	11.67	67-68	28	2	0

KNOX William Jess
Kilmarnock, 9 September, 1937 S Sch (WH)

League Club	Source	Date Signed	Seasons Played	Apps	Subs	Gls
Barrow	Third Lanark	07.59	59	1	-	0

KOENEN Franciscus Leonardus Albertus
Netherlands, 4 November, 1958 Dutch u21 Int (M)

League Club	Source	Date Signed	Seasons Played	Apps	Subs	Gls
Newcastle U.	Nijmegen (Neth)	08.80	80	11	1	1

KOFFMAN Sidney John (Jack)
Prestwich, 3 August, 1920 Died 1977 (OL)

League Club	Source	Date Signed	Seasons Played	Apps	Subs	Gls
Manchester U.	Northwich Vic.	08.45				
Hull C.	Tr	06.46	46	4	-	0
Oldham Ath.	Congleton T.	06.47	47	3	-	0

KONCHESKY Paul Martyn
Barking, 15 May, 1981 E Yth (D)

League Club	Source	Date Signed	Seasons Played	Apps	Subs	Gls
Charlton Ath.	YT	•	97	2	1	0

KOORDES Rogier
Netherlands, 13 June, 1972 (M)

League Club	Source	Date Signed	Seasons Played	Apps	Subs	Gls
Port Vale	Telstar (Neth)	02.97	96-97	16	7	0

KOPEL Frank
Falkirk, 28 March, 1949 S Sch (FB)

League Club	Source	Date Signed	Seasons Played	Apps	Subs	Gls
Manchester U.	Jnrs	04.66	67-68	8	2	0
Blackburn Rov.	Tr	03.69	68-71	23	2	0

KOPEL Scott
Blackburn, 25 February, 1970 (M)

League Club	Source	Date Signed	Seasons Played	Apps	Subs	Gls
Chesterfield (N/C)	Dundee U.	05.93	92	1	0	0

KOSMINA Alexander John
Australia, 17 August, 1956 (F)

League Club	Source	Date Signed	Seasons Played	Apps	Subs	Gls
Arsenal	Polonia (Aus)	03.78	78	0	1	0

KOTTILA Mika
Finland, 22 September, 1974 (F)

League Club	Source	Date Signed	Seasons Played	Apps	Subs	Gls
Hereford U. (L)	Rovàniemi (Fin)	11.96	96	11	2	1

KOVACEVIC Darko
Yugoslavia, 18 November, 1973 Yugoslav Int (F)

League Club	Source	Date Signed	Seasons Played	Apps	Subs	Gls
Sheffield Wed.	Red Star Belgrade (Yug)	12.95	95	8	8	4

KOWALSKI Andrew Michael
Mansfield, 26 February, 1953 (M)

League Club	Source	Date Signed	Seasons Played	Apps	Subs	Gls
Chesterfield	Alfreton T.	02.73	72-82	354	11	30
Doncaster Rov.	Tr	07.83	83-84	45	7	1
Peterborough U.	Tr	08.85	85	35	0	3
Chesterfield	Tr	08.86	86	19	9	1

League Club	Source	Date Signed	Seasons Played	Apps	Subs	Gls
KOWENICKI Ryszard Stefan						
Poland, 22 December, 1948						(M)
Oldham Ath.	Widzew Lodz (Pol)	12.79	79-80	40	2	5
KOZLUK Robert						
Mansfield, 5 August, 1977 Eu21-2						(RWB)
Derby Co.	YT	02.96	97	6	3	0
KOZMA Istvan						
Hungary, 3 December, 1964 Hungarian Int						(M)
Liverpool	Dunfermline Ath.	02.92	91-92	3	3	0
KRAAY Hans						
Netherlands, 22 December, 1959						(M)
Brighton & H.A.	N.A.C. Breda (Neth)	02.84	83-84	19	4	3
KRISTENSEN Bjorn						
Denmark, 10 October, 1963 Danish Int						(M/CD)
Newcastle U.	Aarhus G.F. (Den)	03.89	88-91	69	11	4
Bristol C.	L	11.92	92	4	0	0
Portsmouth	Tr	03.93	92-94	56	15	1
KRIZAN Ales						
Slovenia, 25 July, 1971 Slovenian Int						(D)
Barnsley	Marbor Branik (Slov)	07.97	97	12	0	0
KRUSE Patrick Karl						
Biggleswade, 30 November, 1953						(CD)
Leicester C.	App	02.72	73	2	0	0
Mansfield T.	L	09.74	74	6	0	1
Torquay U.	Tr	03.75	74-76	79	0	4
Brentford	Tr	03.77	76-81	186	0	12
Northampton T.	L	02.82	81	18	0	0
KRUSZYNSKI Zbigniew (Detzi)						
Germany, 14 October, 1961						(M)
Wimbledon	F.C. 08 Homburg (Ger)	12.88	88-91	65	6	4
Brentford	L	03.92	91	8	0	0
Brentford	Tr	08.92	92	5	1	0
Coventry C. (N/C)	Saarbrucken (Ger)	09.93	93	1	1	0
Peterborough U.	Tr	12.93	93	2	1	0
KRZYWICKI Ryzsard (Dick) Lech						
Penley, 2 February, 1947 Wu23-3/W-8						(W)
West Bromwich A.	App	02.65	64-69	51	6	9
Huddersfield T.	Tr	03.70	69-73	39	8	7
Scunthorpe U.	L	02.73	72	2	0	0
Northampton T.	L	11.73	73	8	0	3
Lincoln C.	Tr	07.74	74-75	55	13	11
KUBICKI Dariusz						
Poland, 6 June, 1963 Polish Int						(RB)
Aston Villa	Legia Warsaw (Pol)	08.91	91-93	24	1	0
Sunderland	Tr	03.94	93-96	135	1	0
Wolverhampton W.	Tr	08.97	97	12	0	0
Tranmere Rov.	L	03.98	97	12	0	0
KUBICKI Eryk						
Poland						(OL)
York C. (Am)	Polish Army	10.46	46	5	-	0
KUHL Martin						
Frimley, 10 January, 1965						(M)
Birmingham C.	App	01.83	82-86	103	8	5
Sheffield U.	Tr	03.87	86-87	38	0	4
Watford	Tr	02.88	87	4	0	0
Portsmouth	Tr	09.88	88-92	146	11	27
Derby Co.	Tr	09.92	92-94	68	0	1
Notts Co.	L	09.94	94	2	0	0
Bristol C.	Tr	12.94	94-96	85	9	7
KULCSAR George						
Hungary, 12 August, 1967 Australian Int						(M)
Bradford C.	Royal Antwerp (Bel)	03.97	96-97	23	3	1
Queens Park R.	Tr	12.97	97	11	1	0
KULKOV Vassili						
Russia, 11 June, 1966 Russian Int						(M)
Millwall (L)	Moscow Spartak (Rus)	01.96	95	6	0	0
KURILA John						
Glasgow, 10 April, 1941						(WH)
Northampton T.	Glasgow Celtic	08.62	62	40	-	1
Bristol C.	Tr	08.63	63	6	-	0
Northampton T.	Tr	11.63	63-67	105	3	3
Southend U.	Tr	07.68	68-69	87	1	1
Colchester U.	Tr	05.70	70-71	53	0	4
Lincoln C.	Tr	12.71	71	23	1	0

League Club	Source	Date Signed	Seasons Played	Apps	Subs	Gls
KURZ Frederick John						
Grimsby, 3 September, 1918 Died 1978						(CF)
Grimsby T.	Grimsby Y.M.C.A.	05.36	38	3	-	0
Crystal Palace	Tr	12.45	46-50	148	-	48
KVARME Bjorn Tore						
Norway, 17 June, 1972 Norwegian Int						(LB)
Liverpool	Rosenborg (Nor)	01.97	96-97	37	1	0
KWIATKOWSKI Richard						
Peterborough, 7 April, 1948						(FB/M)
Peterborough U.	Jnrs	07.67	67-71	49	11	0
KYDD David Richard						
Croydon, 22 December, 1945						(WH)
Brighton & H.A.	App	09.63	65	2	-	0
KYDD Michael Robert						
Hackney, 21 May, 1977						(F)
Cambridge U.	YT	05.95	94-97	71	23	20
KYLE Maurice						
Darlington, 8 November, 1937 Died 1981						(CH)
Wolverhampton W.	Jnrs	09.55				
Oxford U.	Tr	02.59	62-69	275	-	2
Southend U.	L	03.70	69	8	-	0
KYNMAN David John						
Hull, 20 May, 1962						(M)
Hull C.	App	05.80	80-81	11	-	0
KYRATZOGLOU Alexandros Bassilios						
Armidale, Australia, 27 August, 1974						(F)
Oldham Ath. (N/C)	I.E.K. Athens (Gre)	10.97	97	0	1	0

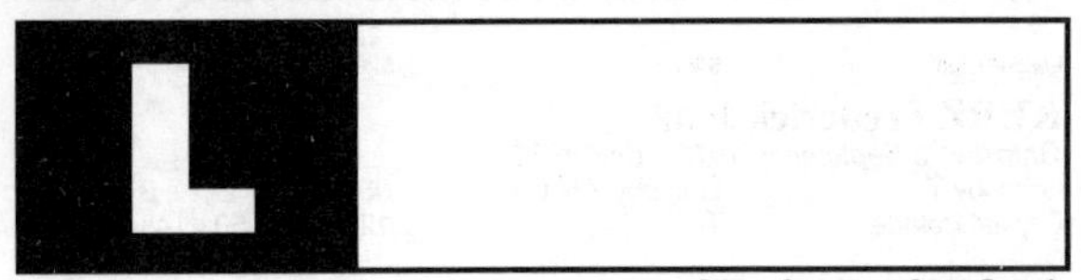

LABONE Brian Leslie
Liverpool, 23 January, 1940 E-26/Eu23-7/EF Lge (CH)

League Club	Source	Date Signed	Seasons Played	Apps	Subs	Gls
Everton	Jnrs	07.57	57-71	451	0	2

LACEY Anthony John
Leek, 18 March, 1944 (FB/M)

League Club	Source	Date Signed	Seasons Played	Apps	Subs	Gls
Stoke C.	Leek C.S.O.B.	10.65	67-68	2	2	0
Port Vale	Tr	02.70	69-74	194	7	9
Rochdale	Tr	07.75	75-76	83	0	0

LACEY Damien James
Bridgend, 3 August, 1977 (LB/M)

League Club	Source	Date Signed	Seasons Played	Apps	Subs	Gls
Swansea C.	YT	07.96	96-97	25	7	1

LACEY Desmond
Dublin, 3 August, 1925 Died 1974 (OR)

League Club	Source	Date Signed	Seasons Played	Apps	Subs	Gls
Chester C. (Am)		07.46	46	1	-	0

LACEY William
Tynemouth, 17 November, 1931 Died 1988 (CF)

League Club	Source	Date Signed	Seasons Played	Apps	Subs	Gls
Middlesbrough		05.52				
Aldershot	Tr	02.53	52-58	210	-	59
Reading	Tr	07.59	59-62	90	-	40

LACK Harry
Bolsover, 29 November, 1930 (OL)

League Club	Source	Date Signed	Seasons Played	Apps	Subs	Gls
Leeds U.		07.51				
Blackburn Rov.	Tr	08.52				
Chesterfield	Tr	08.53	53	1	-	0

LACKENBY George
Newcastle, 22 May, 1931 (D)

League Club	Source	Date Signed	Seasons Played	Apps	Subs	Gls
Newcastle U.	Jnrs	10.50	51-56	19	-	0
Exeter C.	Tr	12.56	56	24	-	4
Carlisle U.	Tr	07.57	57-58	46	-	0
Gateshead	Tr	07.59	59	43	-	2
Hartlepool U.	Tr	08.60	60-62	86	-	1

LACY John
Liverpool, 14 August, 1951 (CD)

League Club	Source	Date Signed	Seasons Played	Apps	Subs	Gls
Fulham	Kingstonian	06.71	72-77	164	4	7
Tottenham H.	Tr	07.78	78-82	99	5	2
Crystal Palace	Tr	08.83	83	24	3	0

LADD Ian Martin
Peterborough, 22 November, 1958 (CD)

League Club	Source	Date Signed	Seasons Played	Apps	Subs	Gls
Notts Co.		09.77	77	1	0	0

LAHTINEN Aki Arimo
Finland, 31 October, 1958 Finnish Int (CD)

League Club	Source	Date Signed	Seasons Played	Apps	Subs	Gls
Notts Co.	O.P.S. Oulu (Fin)	09.81	81-84	37	8	2

LAIDLAW John
Aldershot, 5 July, 1936 (RB)

League Club	Source	Date Signed	Seasons Played	Apps	Subs	Gls
Colchester U.	Easthouses	06.57	59-60	41	-	1

LAIDLAW Joseph Daniel
Whickham, 12 July, 1950 (M)

League Club	Source	Date Signed	Seasons Played	Apps	Subs	Gls
Middlesbrough	App	08.67	67-71	104	5	20
Carlisle U.	Tr	07.72	72-75	146	5	44
Doncaster Rov.	Tr	06.76	76-78	127	1	27
Portsmouth	Tr	06.79	79-80	60	0	19
Hereford U.	Tr	12.80	80-81	61	1	8
Mansfield T.	Tr	07.82	82	4	0	0

LAIDLER John (Jackie) Ralph
Windermere, 5 January, 1919 (OL)

League Club	Source	Date Signed	Seasons Played	Apps	Subs	Gls
Barrow		09.36	36-38	40	-	6
Carlisle U.	Netherfield	06.46	46	27	-	3

LAIDMAN Frederick
Durham, 20 June, 1913 Died 1987 (IF)

League Club	Source	Date Signed	Seasons Played	Apps	Subs	Gls
Everton		12.36				
Bristol C.	Tr	06.38	38	10	-	1
Darlington	Stockton	07.48	49	2	-	0

LAIGHT Ellis Stanley
Birmingham, 30 June, 1976 (F)

League Club	Source	Date Signed	Seasons Played	Apps	Subs	Gls
Torquay U.	YT	07.95	93-96	18	23	3

LAING David
Strathmiglo (Fife), 20 February, 1925 SF Lge (WH)

League Club	Source	Date Signed	Seasons Played	Apps	Subs	Gls
Gillingham	Hibernian	08.57	57-58	82	-	5

LAING James **Frederick**
Glasgow, 25 February, 1920 (IF)

League Club	Source	Date Signed	Seasons Played	Apps	Subs	Gls
Luton T.	Ashfield Jnrs	06.38				
Middlesbrough	Tr	07.47				
Bristol Rov.	Tr	07.48	48	2	-	0

LAING Robert Smith
Glasgow, 1 February, 1925 Died 1985 (OL)

League Club	Source	Date Signed	Seasons Played	Apps	Subs	Gls
Birmingham C.	Falkirk	03.46	47-49	19	-	2
Watford	Tr	06.50	50-51	60	-	8

LAIRD Alexander
Newmains, 2 June, 1926 (OR)

League Club	Source	Date Signed	Seasons Played	Apps	Subs	Gls
Chelsea	Stirling A.	11.51				
Notts Co.	Tr	07.53	53	1	-	0

LAIRD Alexander Watson
Edinburgh, 23 October, 1928 (FB)

League Club	Source	Date Signed	Seasons Played	Apps	Subs	Gls
Barrow	Dunfermline Ath.	11.57	57	22	-	0
Scunthorpe U.	Tr	08.58				

LAIRD David Sands
Rutherglen, 11 February, 1936 (IF)

League Club	Source	Date Signed	Seasons Played	Apps	Subs	Gls
Aldershot	St Mirren	07.57				
Northampton T.	St Mirren	06.60	60	12	-	1

LAIRD David Wilson
Clackmannan, 9 May, 1926 (WH)

League Club	Source	Date Signed	Seasons Played	Apps	Subs	Gls
Aldershot	Alloa Ath.	05.48	48-53	127	-	22

LAISBY Jonathan
Ulverston, 27 March, 1957 (G)

League Club	Source	Date Signed	Seasons Played	Apps	Subs	Gls
Liverpool	App	04.75				
Workington (N/C)	Barrow	03.77	76	2	0	0

LAITT David John
Colchester, 1 November, 1946 (FB)

League Club	Source	Date Signed	Seasons Played	Apps	Subs	Gls
Colchester U.	Colchester Casuals	08.65	65	0	1	0

LAKE Huw Gilwyn Taylor
Swansea, 20 August, 1963 W Sch (M)

League Club	Source	Date Signed	Seasons Played	Apps	Subs	Gls
Swansea C.	App	08.81	82-83	14	5	2

LAKE Leslie Eric
Luton, 29 January, 1923 Died 1976 (FB)

League Club	Source	Date Signed	Seasons Played	Apps	Subs	Gls
Luton T.	Holly R.	09.41	46-50	59	-	0

LAKE Michael Charles
Denton, 16 November, 1966 E Semi Pro (M)

League Club	Source	Date Signed	Seasons Played	Apps	Subs	Gls
Sheffield U.	Macclesfield T.	10.89	89-92	19	16	4
Wrexham	Tr	11.92	92-94	56	2	6

LAKE Paul Andrew
Denton, 28 October, 1968 Eu21-5/E'B' (M)

League Club	Source	Date Signed	Seasons Played	Apps	Subs	Gls
Manchester C.	YT	05.87	86-92	106	4	7

LAKIN Barry
Dartford, 19 September, 1973 (M)

League Club	Source	Date Signed	Seasons Played	Apps	Subs	Gls
Leyton Orient	YT	07.92	92-95	41	13	2

LAKING George Edward
Harthill (Yks), 17 March, 1913 (FB)

League Club	Source	Date Signed	Seasons Played	Apps	Subs	Gls
Wolverhampton W.	Dinnington	05.34	35-36	27	-	0
Middlesbrough	Tr	10.36	36-46	94	-	1

LALLY Patrick Anthony
Paddington, 11 January, 1952 (M/CD)

League Club	Source	Date Signed	Seasons Played	Apps	Subs	Gls
Millwall	App	01.70	69	1	0	0
York C.	Tr	07.71	71-72	64	7	5
Swansea C.	Tr	08.73	73-78	152	8	10
Aldershot	L	10.75	75	3	0	0
Doncaster Rov.	Tr	09.78	78-81	118	4	0

LAMA Bernard Pascal
St Symphorien, France, 7 April, 1963 French Int (G)

League Club	Source	Date Signed	Seasons Played	Apps	Subs	Gls
West Ham U.	St Paris Germain (Fr)	12.97	97	12	0	0

LAMB Alan
Gateshead, 30 January, 1970 (F)

League Club	Source	Date Signed	Seasons Played	Apps	Subs	Gls
Nottingham F.	YT	02.88				
Hereford U.	L	03.89	88	9	1	2
Hartlepool U.	Tr	09.89	89-90	4	10	0
Newcastle U.	Brandon U.	10.91				

League Club	Source	Date Signed	Seasons Played	Apps	Subs	Gls
LAMB Alan David						
Falkirk, 3 July, 1952 Su23-1						(M)
Preston N.E.	App	05.70	72-76	76	4	2
Port Vale	Tr	03.77	76-77	54	0	3
LAMB Thomas **Harold**						
Kingswinford, 20 April, 1928						(FB)
Aston Villa	Wordsley	10.49				
Scunthorpe U.	Tr	06.54	54-55	36	-	0
LAMB Harry Edward						
Bebington, 3 June, 1925 Died 1982						(IF)
Tranmere Rov.	Jnrs	08.42	47-52	88	-	12
LAMB Paul						
Plumstead, 12 September, 1974						(M)
Northampton T.	YT	●	92	2	1	0
LAMB Stephen Percy						
Leigh-on Sea, 2 October, 1955						(M)
Southend U.	App	10.73	74-75	6	1	0
LAMBDEN Victor David						
Bristol, 24 October, 1925 Died 1996						(CF)
Bristol Rov.	Oldland	10.45	46-54	269	-	117
LAMBERT Anton James						
Nottingham, 29 November, 1959						(M)
Scunthorpe U.	Long Eaton U.	07.80	80-81	35	4	4
LAMBERT Brian						
Sutton-in-Ashfield, 10 July, 1936						(FB)
Mansfield T.	Sutton T.	10.54	54-59	24	-	0
LAMBERT David						
Ruabon, 7 July, 1939						(FB)
Cardiff C.		03.59				
Wrexham	Tr	07.63	63	5	-	0
LAMBERT Eric Victor						
Derby, 4 August, 1920 Died 1979						(CH)
Derby Co.	Nottingham F. (Am)	10.44				
Hartlepool U.	Tr	06.46	46	16	-	0
LAMBERT John **Gilbert**						
Preston, 16 March, 1937 Died 1986						(OL)
Preston N.E.	Jnrs	03.55	58-60	22	-	6
LAMBERT Christopher **James**						
Henley, 14 September, 1973						(M)
Reading	YT	07.92	92-97	76	48	16
LAMBERT Kenneth						
Sheffield, 7 June, 1928						(IF)
Barnsley	Ecclesfield	01.50	50-51	11	-	2
Gillingham	Tr	07.52	52	37	-	10
Swindon T.	Tr	07.53	53-54	30	-	5
Bradford C.	Tr	11.54	54	19	-	4
LAMBERT Martin Clive						
Southampton, 24 September, 1965 E Sch/E Yth						(F)
Brighton & H.A.	App	08.83	83	2	1	0
Torquay U.	Tr	07.85	85	4	2	2
Brighton & H.A.	Sedan (Fr)	07.89	89	0	1	0
LAMBERT Matthew Roy						
Morecambe, 28 September, 1971						(D)
Preston N.E.	YT	07.90	90-91	11	5	2
Bury	Tr	06.92				
LAMBERT Michael Arnold						
Balsham (Cam), 20 May, 1950						(W)
Ipswich T.	Newmarket	11.67	68-78	180	30	39
Peterborough U.	Tr	07.79	79-80	15	6	2
LAMBERT Raymond						
Holywell, 18 July, 1922 W Sch/W-5						(FB)
Liverpool	Jnrs	07.39	46-55	308	-	2
LAMBERT Roy						
Hoyland, 16 July, 1933						(WH)
Rotherham U.	Thorncliffe Colly	07.54	56-64	307	-	6
Barnsley	Tr	11.65	65	3	0	0
LAMBLE John						
Reading, 10 November, 1948						(W)
Reading	App	11.66	67	3	2	0

League Club	Source	Date Signed	Seasons Played	Apps	Subs	Gls
LAMBOURDE Bernard						
Guadaloupe, 11 May, 1971						(CD)
Chelsea	Bordeaux (Fr)	07.97	97	5	2	0
LAMBOURNE Dennis James						
Swansea, 7 October, 1945						(CF)
Wrexham	Llanelli	07.64	64-65	15	0	4
LAMBTON George **Colin**						
Newcastle, 21 February, 1942						(WH)
Newcastle U.	Chester Moor	02.60				
Doncaster Rov.	Tr	07.63	63	6	-	0
LAMBTON William Ernest						
Nottingham, 2 December, 1914 Died 1976						(G)
Nottingham F.	Basford N.E.	05.35				
Exeter C.		04.46				
Doncaster Rov.	Tr	10.46	46	3	-	0
LAMIE Robert						
Newarthill, 28 December, 1928						(IF)
Cardiff C.	Stonehouse Violet	10.49	49-50	6	-	1
Swansea C.	Tr	03.51	51	2	-	0
LAMONT David						
Glasgow, 2 April, 1949						(HB)
Colchester U.	App	04.67	67	0	1	0
LAMONT William Turnbull						
Glasgow, 25 December, 1926 Died 1996						(FB)
New Brighton	Kilmarnock	07.50	50	27	-	0
Tranmere Rov.	Tr	09.51	51-55	143	-	3
LAMPARD Frank James						
Romford, 21 June, 1978 E Yth/Eu21-6/E 'B'						(M)
West Ham U.	YT	07.95	95-97	30	16	5
Swansea C.	L	10.95	95	8	1	1
LAMPARD Frank Richard George						
East Ham, 20 September, 1948 E Yth/Eu23-4/E-2						(FB)
West Ham U.	App	09.65	67-84	546	5	18
Southend U.	Tr	08.85	85	34	0	1
LAMPE Derek Stanley						
Edmonton, 20 May, 1937 E Yth						(CH)
Fulham	Jnrs	05.54	56-62	88	-	0
LAMPKIN Kevin						
Liverpool, 20 December, 1972						(M)
Liverpool	YT	05.91				
Huddersfield T.	Tr	07.92	92	13	0	0
Mansfield T.	Tr	02.94	93-95	35	7	3
LAMPKIN Stephen Charles Arthur						
Keighley, 15 October, 1964						(M)
Bradford C.		03.83	82-83	5	2	1
LAMPTEY Nii Odartey						
Ghana, 10 December, 1974 Ghanaian Int						(M)
Aston Villa	P.S.V. Eindhoven (Neth)	08.94	94	1	5	0
Coventry C.	Anderlecht (Bel)	08.95	95	3	3	0
LANCASHIRE Carl Peter						
Blackpool, 17 January, 1969						(M)
Blackpool	YT	06.87	87	2	5	0
LANCASHIRE Graham						
Blackpool, 19 October, 1972						(F)
Burnley	YT	06.91	90-94	11	20	8
Halifax	L	11.92	92	2	0	0
Chester C.	L	01.94	93	10	1	7
Preston N.E.	Tr	12.94	94-95	11	12	2
Wigan Ath.	Tr	01.96	95-97	20	10	12
Rochdale	Tr	10.97	97	20	7	9
LANCASTER Brian						
Bradford, 8 May, 1939						(CH)
Torquay U.		07.60	61	18	-	0
LANCASTER David						
Preston, 8 September, 1961						(F)
Blackpool	Colne Dynamoes	08.90	90	7	1	1
Chesterfield	L	02.91	90	12	0	4
Chesterfield	Tr	08.91	91-92	66	3	16
Rochdale	Tr	07.93	93	37	3	14
Bury	Halifax T.	03.95	94-95	4	6	1
Rochdale	Tr	02.96	95-96	14	6	2

LANCASTER Desmond Charles
Burnley, 16 July, 1937 (F)

League Club	Source	Date Signed	Seasons Played	Apps	Subs	Gls
Burnley	Jnrs	08.54	56	1	-	0
Darlington	Tr	03.58	57-58	31	-	18
Tranmere Rov.	Tr	06.59	59	1	-	0

LANCASTER Joseph Gerard
Stockport, 28 April, 1926 (G)

League Club	Source	Date Signed	Seasons Played	Apps	Subs	Gls
Manchester U.	Heaton Mersey O.B.	02.50	49	2	-	0
Accrington St.	Tr	11.50	50	1	-	0

LANCASTER Raymond
Maltby, 17 August, 1941 (WH)

League Club	Source	Date Signed	Seasons Played	Apps	Subs	Gls
Rotherham U.	Jnrs	11.58	60-64	63	-	2
Grimsby T.	Tr	12.64	64-66	16	2	0
Lincoln C.	Tr	01.67	66-67	24	0	0

LANCELOTTE Eric Charles
India, 26 February, 1917 (IF)

League Club	Source	Date Signed	Seasons Played	Apps	Subs	Gls
Charlton Ath.	Jnrs	05.35	37-47	40	-	6
Brighton & H.A.	Tr	02.48	47-49	60	-	14

LANDON Richard John
Worthing, 22 March, 1970 (F)

League Club	Source	Date Signed	Seasons Played	Apps	Subs	Gls
Plymouth Arg.	Bedworth U.	01.94	93-94	21	9	12
Stockport Co.	Tr	07.95	95-96	7	6	4
Rotherham U.	L	03.97	96	7	1	0
Macclesfield T.	Tr	07.97	97	6	12	7

LANDSBOROUGH Murray
Thornhill, 30 December, 1915 Died 1987 (FB)

League Club	Source	Date Signed	Seasons Played	Apps	Subs	Gls
Carlisle U.	Kilmarnock	08.47	47	1	-	0

LANE Frank
Wallasey, 20 July, 1948 (G)

League Club	Source	Date Signed	Seasons Played	Apps	Subs	Gls
Tranmere Rov.	Stanley Arms	08.68	69-71	76	0	0
Liverpool	Tr	09.71	72	1	0	0
Notts Co.	Tr	07.75	75	2	0	0

LANE Henry (Harry)
Cannock, 21 March, 1909 Died 1977 (F)

League Club	Source	Date Signed	Seasons Played	Apps	Subs	Gls
Birmingham C.	Bloxwich Strollers	12.29	30	2	-	0
Southend U.	Tr	05.33	33-37	155	-	50
Plymouth Arg.	Tr	03.38	37-38	47	-	8
Southend U.	Tr	05.46	46-48	65	-	14

LANE John George
Birmingham, 10 November, 1931 (CF)

League Club	Source	Date Signed	Seasons Played	Apps	Subs	Gls
Birmingham C.	Boldmere St Michael	09.49	52-55	46	-	14
Notts Co.	Tr	07.56	56-58	57	-	19

LANE Kevin John
Willenhall, 11 May, 1957 (F)

League Club	Source	Date Signed	Seasons Played	Apps	Subs	Gls
Torquay U.	Walsall (App)	08.75	75-76	17	13	5

LANE Martin John
Altrincham, 12 April, 1961 (D)

League Club	Source	Date Signed	Seasons Played	Apps	Subs	Gls
Manchester U.	Jnrs	05.79				
Chester C.	Tr	08.82	82-86	175	0	3
Coventry C.	Tr	01.87	86-87	0	3	0
Wrexham	L	10.88	88	6	0	0
Chester C.	Tr	01.89	88-90	97	2	0
Walsall	Tr	08.91	91	6	4	0

LANE Michael Edward
Wellington (Som), 6 December, 1966 (FB)

League Club	Source	Date Signed	Seasons Played	Apps	Subs	Gls
Exeter C.	App	12.84	83	1	0	0

LANE Sean Brendon
Bristol, 16 January, 1964 E Sch (M)

League Club	Source	Date Signed	Seasons Played	Apps	Subs	Gls
Hereford U.	App	03.81	80-82	39	11	3
Derby Co.	Tr	05.83	83	1	0	0

LANG Gavin
Larkhall, 21 March, 1926 Died 1989 (OL)

League Club	Source	Date Signed	Seasons Played	Apps	Subs	Gls
Chester C.	Spalding U.	08.56	56	3	-	0

LANG Gavin Thomas
Hereford, 10 November, 1951 (W)

League Club	Source	Date Signed	Seasons Played	Apps	Subs	Gls
Chester C.	Newcastle U. (App)	11.69				
Crewe Alex.	Tr	09.70	70	3	0	1

LANG Malcolm Christian
Barnsley, 14 January, 1941 (OL)

League Club	Source	Date Signed	Seasons Played	Apps	Subs	Gls
York C.	Bridlington T.	08.63	63	12	-	2

LANG Thomas
Larkhall, 3 April, 1905 Died 1988 (OL)

League Club	Source	Date Signed	Seasons Played	Apps	Subs	Gls
Newcastle U.	Larkhall Thistle	10.26	27-34	215	-	53
Huddersfield T.	Tr	12.34	34-35	24	-	5
Manchester U.	Tr	12.35	35-36	12	-	1
Swansea C.	Tr	04.37	37	33	-	1
Ipswich T.	Queen of South	10.46	46	5	-	1

LANGAN David Francis
Dublin, 15 February, 1957 IR-25 (RB)

League Club	Source	Date Signed	Seasons Played	Apps	Subs	Gls
Derby Co.	App	02.75	76-79	143	0	1
Birmingham C.	Tr	07.80	80-82	92	0	3
Oxford U.	Tr	08.84	84-87	112	2	2
Leicester C.	L	10.87	87	5	0	0
Bournemouth	Tr	12.87	87	19	1	0
Peterborough U.	Tr	08.88	88	18	1	0

LANGAN Kevin
Jersey, 7 April, 1978 (RB)

League Club	Source	Date Signed	Seasons Played	Apps	Subs	Gls
Bristol C.	YT	07.96	97	0	3	0

LANGE Anthony Stephen
West Ham, 10 December, 1964 (G)

League Club	Source	Date Signed	Seasons Played	Apps	Subs	Gls
Charlton Ath.	App	12.82	83-85	12	0	0
Aldershot	L	08.85	85	7	0	0
Aldershot	Tr	07.86	86-88	125	0	0
Wolverhampton W.	Tr	07.89	89-90	8	0	0
Aldershot	L	11.90	90	2	0	0
Torquay U.	L	09.91	91	1	0	0
West Bromwich A.	Tr	08.92	92-94	45	3	0
Fulham	Tr	07.95	95-96	59	0	0

LANGFORD Craig Brian
Solihull, 12 March, 1975 (CD)

League Club	Source	Date Signed	Seasons Played	Apps	Subs	Gls
Hereford U.	YT	07.93	92-93	4	1	0

LANGFORD John William
Kirkby-in-Ashfield, 4 August, 1937 (OL)

League Club	Source	Date Signed	Seasons Played	Apps	Subs	Gls
Nottingham F.	Leicester C. (Am)	08.55	55	4	-	0
Notts Co.	Tr	08.58	58	16	-	0

LANGFORD Timothy
Kingswinford, 12 September, 1965 (F)

League Club	Source	Date Signed	Seasons Played	Apps	Subs	Gls
Wycombe W.	Telford U.	03.93	93-94	19	16	8

LANGLAND John
Easington, 9 November, 1929 (F)

League Club	Source	Date Signed	Seasons Played	Apps	Subs	Gls
Sunderland		06.48				
Chesterfield	Consett	01.51	52-53	7	-	0
Hartlepool U.	Blyth Spartans	07.58	58-59	38	-	11

LANGLEY Geoffrey Ralph
Gateshead, 31 March, 1962 (F)

League Club	Source	Date Signed	Seasons Played	Apps	Subs	Gls
Bolton W.	App	03.80	81	3	3	0

LANGLEY Ernest **James**
Kilburn, 7 February, 1929 EF Lge/E 'B'/E-3 (LB)

League Club	Source	Date Signed	Seasons Played	Apps	Subs	Gls
Leeds U.	Guildford C.	06.52	52	9	-	3
Brighton & H.A.	Tr	07.53	53-56	166	-	14
Fulham	Tr	02.57	56-64	323	-	31
Queens Park R.	Tr	07.65	65-66	86	1	9

LANGLEY Kevin James
St Helens, 24 May, 1964 (M)

League Club	Source	Date Signed	Seasons Played	Apps	Subs	Gls
Wigan Ath.	App	05.82	81-85	156	4	6
Everton	Tr	07.86	86	16	0	2
Manchester C.	Tr	03.87	86	9	0	0
Chester C.	L	01.88	87	9	0	0
Birmingham C.	Tr	03.88	87-89	74	2	2
Wigan Ath.	Tr	09.90	90-93	151	6	6

LANGLEY Richard John
Lambeth, 20 March, 1965 (FB)

League Club	Source	Date Signed	Seasons Played	Apps	Subs	Gls
Fulham	Corinthian Casuals	11.86	86-90	43	7	0

LANGLEY Thomas William
Lambeth, 8 February, 1958 E Sch/E Yth/Eu21-1 (F)

League Club	Source	Date Signed	Seasons Played	Apps	Subs	Gls
Chelsea	App	04.75	74-79	129	13	40
Queens Park R.	Tr	08.80	80	24	1	8
Crystal Palace	Tr	03.81	80-82	54	5	8
Coventry C.	A.E.K. Athens (Gre)	03.84	83	2	0	0
Wolverhampton W.	Tr	07.84	84	22	1	4
Aldershot	L	03.85	84	16	0	4
Aldershot	South China (HK)	08.86	86-87	80	1	21
Exeter C.	Tr	07.88	88	14	7	2

LANGMAN Hedley **Neil**
Tavistock, 21 February, 1932 (F)

League Club	Source	Date Signed	Seasons Played	Apps	Subs	Gls
Plymouth Arg.	Tavistock	09.53	53-57	97	-	49
Colchester U.	Tr	11.57	57-60	128	-	49

LANGMAN Peter John Henry
Bere Alston, 1 April, 1928 (CH)

League Club	Source	Date Signed	Seasons Played	Apps	Subs	Gls
Plymouth Arg.	Tavistock	06.51	54-57	90	-	0

League Club	Source	Date Signed	Seasons Played	Apps	Subs	Gls
LANGRIDGE John						
Newcastle, 14 November, 1957						(F)
Hartlepool U. (N/C)	Easington Colly	10.82	82	5	1	0
LANGSTRETH Horace **Lawrence**						
Blackburn, 19 July, 1931 Died 1990						(FB)
Accrington St.	Blackburn Rov. (Am)	07.53	53	3	-	0
Torquay U.	Netherfield	08.56	56	1	-	0
LANGTON Robert						
Ormskirk, 8 September, 1918 Died 1996 E 'B'/EF Lge/E-11						(OL)
Blackburn Rov.	Burscough Vic.	09.38	38-47	107	-	24
Preston N.E.	Tr	08.48	48-49	55	-	14
Bolton W.	Tr	11.49	49-52	118	-	16
Blackburn Rov.	Tr	09.53	53-55	105	-	33
LANSDOWNE William						
Epping, 28 April, 1959						(F)
West Ham U.	Jnrs	06.78	78-79	5	4	1
Charlton Ath.	Tr	07.81	81-82	28	4	4
Gillingham	L	01.83	82	6	0	2
LANSDOWNE William Thomas Michael						
Shoreditch, 9 November, 1935						(WH)
West Ham U.	Woodford T.	02.56	55-62	57	-	5
LAPPER Michael Steven						
U.S.A., 28 August, 1970 USA Int						(CD)
Southend U.	U.S.S.F. (USA)	08.95	95-96	46	6	1
LAPOT Stanley						
Edinburgh, 20 January, 1944						(WH)
Preston N.E.	Smeaton B.C.	06.62	62-66	16	3	2
LARAMAN Peter Kenneth						
Rochester, 24 October, 1940 E Yth						(IF)
Charlton Ath.	Jnrs	02.58	58-59	2	-	1
Torquay U.	Tr	07.61	61	9	-	5
LARGE Frank						
Leeds, 26 January, 1940						(CF)
Halifax T.	Halifax B.R.	06.59	58-61	133	-	50
Queens Park R.	Tr	06.62	62	18	-	5
Northampton T.	Tr	03.63	62-63	47	-	30
Swindon T.	Tr	03.64	63-64	17	-	4
Carlisle U.	Tr	09.64	64-65	51	0	18
Oldham Ath.	Tr	12.65	65-66	34	0	18
Northampton T.	Tr	12.66	66-67	37	0	15
Leicester C.	Tr	11.67	67	26	0	8
Fulham	Tr	06.68	68-69	20	4	3
Northampton T.	Tr	08.69	69-72	134	2	43
Chesterfield	Tr	11.72	72-73	46	0	15
LARKIN Anthony Gerard						
Liverpool, 12 January, 1956						(D)
Wrexham	Jnrs	07.75				
Shrewsbury T.	Tr	07.78	78-80	54	1	0
Carlisle U.	Tr	07.81	81-82	47	2	2
Hereford U.	Tr	03.83	82-84	28	7	2
LARKIN Bernard (Bunny) Patrick						
Birmingham, 11 January, 1936						(WH/IF)
Birmingham C.	Jnrs	07.54	56-59	79	-	23
Norwich C.	Tr	03.60	59-61	41	-	12
Doncaster Rov.	Tr	09.61	61	25	-	12
Watford	Tr	06.62	62-64	49	-	3
Lincoln C.	Tr	11.64	64-65	25	2	3
LARKIN Gordon Thomas						
Hartlepool, 12 October, 1958						(W)
Hartlepool U.		07.77	77-79	5	9	1
LARKIN James Thomas						
Canada, 23 October, 1975						(G)
Cambridge U. (N/C)	Canada	01.98	97	1	0	0
LARMOUR Albert Andrew James						
Belfast, 27 May, 1951						(CD)
Cardiff C.	Linfield	07.72	72-78	152	2	0
Torquay U.	Tr	06.79	79-81	46	4	4
LARMOUR David James						
Belfast, 23 August, 1977 NI Sch/NI Yth						(F)
Doncaster Rov.	Liverpool (YT)	08.96	96	3	17	0
LARNACH Ian James						
Ferryhill, 10 July, 1951						(F)
Darlington	App	07.69	69	1	1	1
LARNACH Michael						
Lybster, 9 November, 1952						(F)
Newcastle U.	Clydebank	12.77	77	12	1	0
LA RONDE Everald						
East Ham, 24 January, 1963						(FB)
West Ham U.	App	01.81	81	6	1	0
Bournemouth	Tr	09.83	83-84	24	0	0
Peterborough U.	L	01.85	84	8	0	0
LARSEN Stig Olav						
Bergen, Norway, 26 September, 1973						(CF)
Hartlepool U. (N/C)	Fana I.L. (Nor)	12.97	97	0	4	0
LARYEA Benjamin Michael						
Ghana, 20 March, 1962						(F)
Torquay U. (N/C)	Maidenhead U.	03.84	83-84	10	2	3
LASKEY Russell George						
Norwich, 17 March, 1937						(F)
Norwich C.	Gothic	01.56	56	4	-	2
LATCHAM Leslie Arnold						
Crook, 22 December, 1942						(LM)
Burnley	Jnrs	01.60	64-70	149	4	10
Plymouth Arg.	Tr	07.71	71-72	83	0	13
Bradford C.	Tr	07.73	73	15	0	2
LATCHFORD David Barry						
Birmingham, 9 April, 1949						(G)
Birmingham C.	App	07.66	68-77	206	0	0
Bury	Motherwell	03.79	78	2	0	0
LATCHFORD Peter William						
Birmingham, 27 September, 1952 Eu23-2						(G)
West Bromwich A.	App	10.69	72-74	81	0	0
LATCHFORD Robert Dennis						
Birmingham, 18 January, 1951 E Yth/Eu23-6/EF Lge/E-12						(F)
Birmingham C.	App	08.68	68-73	158	2	68
Everton	Tr	02.74	73-80	235	1	106
Swansea C.	Tr	07.81	81-83	87	0	35
Coventry C.	N.A.C. Breda (Neth)	07.84	84	11	1	2
Lincoln C.	Tr	08.85	85	14	1	2
Newport Co.	Tr	01.86	85	20	0	5
LATHAM David Colin						
Manchester, 17 October, 1943						(W)
Manchester U.	App	10.61				
Southport	Tr	07.63	63	22	-	0
LATHAM Harry						
Sheffield, 9 January, 1921 Died 1983						(CH)
Sheffield U.	Jnrs	10.38	46-52	190	-	1
LATHAM Leslie						
Foleshill, 31 December, 1917 E Sch						(CH)
Aston Villa		10.36				
Coventry C.	Tr	10.46	46	1	-	0
LATHAN John George						
Sunderland, 12 April, 1952						(M)
Sunderland	App	04.69	69-73	41	12	14
Mansfield T.	Tr	02.74	73-75	72	2	14
Carlisle U.	Tr	02.76	75-77	55	6	8
Barnsley	L	02.77	76	6	1	0
Portsmouth	Tr	03.78	77-79	56	2	4
Mansfield T.	Tr	08.79	79	29	0	1
LATIMER Frank Jackson						
Sunderland, 3 October, 1923 Died 1994						(WH)
Brentford	Snowdown Colly	11.45	46-55	171	-	3
LAUGHTON Denis						
Dingwall, 22 January, 1948						(D)
Newcastle U.	Morton	10.73	73-74	7	0	0
LAUNDERS Brian Terence						
Dublin, 8 January, 1976 IR Yth/IRu21-9						(F)
Crystal Palace		09.93	94-95	1	3	0
Crewe Alex.	Tr	08.96	96	6	3	0
LAUREL John Albert						
Bexleyheath, 11 June, 1935 E Yth						(CH)
Tottenham H.	Jnrs	07.52				
Ipswich T.	Tr	06.59	60-62	4	-	0
LAURENT Pierre						
France, 13 December, 1970						(F)
Leeds U.	Bastia (Fr)	03.97	96	2	2	0

League Club	Source	Date Signed	Seasons Played	Apps	Subs	Gls
LAURSEN Jacob						
Denmark, 6 October, 1971 Danish Int						(D)
Derby Co.	Silkeborg (Den)	07.96	96-97	62	2	2
LAVERICK Michael George						
Castle Eden, 13 March, 1954						(M)
Mansfield T.	Jnrs	01.72	72-75	73	16	13
Southend U.	Tr	10.76	76-78	108	2	18
Huddersfield T.	Tr	07.79	79-81	74	0	9
York C.	Tr	01.82	81-82	38	3	6
Huddersfield T.	L	01.83	82	2	0	0
LAVERICK Peter Henry						
Cleethorpes, 29 January, 1939						(IF)
Grimsby T.	Jnrs	03.56	57-60	4	-	0
LAVERICK Robert						
Castle Eden, 11 June, 1938 E Yth						(OL)
Chelsea	Jnrs	06.55	56-57	7	-	0
Everton	Tr	02.59	58-59	22	-	6
Brighton & H.A.	Tr	06.60	60-61	63	-	20
Coventry C.	Tr	07.62	62	4	-	0
LAVERTY Patrick James						
Gorseinon, 24 May, 1934						(IF)
Sheffield U.	Wellington T.	05.56	56-59	7	-	0
Southend U.	Tr	07.60	60	21	-	6
LAVERY James						
Lennoxtown, 13 December, 1948						(G)
Scunthorpe U.		08.66	67	15	0	0
Scunthorpe U.	Brigg T.	08.74	74	11	0	0
LAVERY John						
Belfast, 24 November, 1919 NI Sch						(OL)
Bradford C.	Dundalk	08.48	48	5	-	0
Halifax T.	Tr	09.48	48	3	-	1
LAVIN Gerard						
Corby, 5 February, 1974 Su21-7						(FB/W)
Watford	YT	05.92	91-95	121	5	3
Millwall	Tr	11.95	95-97	29	7	0
LAW Brian John						
Merthyr Tydfil, 1 January, 1970 W Sch/W Yth/Wu21-2/W-1						(CD)
Queens Park R.	YT	08.87	87-90	19	1	0
Wolverhampton W.	(Retired)	12.94	94-96	26	5	1
Millwall	Tr	07.97	97	40	0	4
LAW Cecil Richard						
Rhodesia, 10 March, 1930						(OL)
Derby Co.	Alexandra (SA)	08.51	52-53	33	-	2
Bury	Tr	05.54	54-55	44	-	5
LAW Denis						
Aberdeen, 24 February, 1940 Su23-3/EF Lge/S-55						(IF)
Huddersfield T.	Jnrs	02.57	56-59	81	-	16
Manchester C.	Tr	03.60	59-60	44	-	21
Manchester U.	Torino (It)	08.62	62-72	305	4	171
Manchester C.	Tr	07.73	73	22	2	9
LAW Marcus William						
Coventry, 28 September, 1975						(G)
Bristol Rov.	YT	07.94	94	2	0	0
LAW Nicholas						
Greenwich, 8 September, 1961 E Sch						(CD)
Arsenal	App	07.79				
Barnsley	Tr	08.81	81-85	113	1	1
Blackpool	Tr	08.85	85-86	64	2	1
Plymouth Arg.	Tr	03.87	86-87	37	1	5
Notts Co.	Tr	06.88	88-89	44	3	4
Scarborough	L	11.89	89	12	0	0
Rotherham U.	Tr	07.90	90-93	126	2	4
Chesterfield	Tr	10.93	93-96	108	3	11
Hereford U.	Tr	10.96	96	14	0	0
LAWFORD Craig Brian						
Dewsbury, 25 November, 1972						(FB/M)
Bradford C.	YT	07.91	89-93	13	7	1
Hull C.	Tr	08.94	94-95	45	17	3
LAWLER Christopher						
Liverpool, 20 October, 1943 E Yth/Eu23-4/EF Lge/E-4						(RB)
Liverpool	Jnrs	10.60	62-74	406	0	41
Portsmouth	Tr	10.75	75-76	35	1	0
Stockport Co.	Tr	08.77	77	33	3	3
LAWLER James Henry						
Dublin, 20 November, 1923						(WH)
Portsmouth	Glentoran	10.47				
Southend U.	Tr	01.49	48-56	269	-	17
LAWLER Joseph (Robin) Frederick						
Dublin, 28 August, 1925 Died 1998 LoI/IR-8						(D)
Fulham	Belfast Celtic	03.49	49-61	281	-	0
LAWLESS Arthur **Trevor**						
Retford, 23 March, 1932						(CH)
Plymouth Arg.	Worcester C.	07.55	55	8	-	0
Oldham Ath.	Tr	07.56	56	9	-	0
Aldershot	Tr	07.57	57	2	-	0
Southport	Tr	07.58	58	15	-	0
LAWLOR James Joseph						
Dublin, 10 May, 1933						(CH)
Doncaster Rov.	Drumcondra	08.52	54	9	-	0
Bradford C.	Coleraine	03.57	56-61	153	-	5
LAWLOR John Boscoe						
Bellshill, 30 January, 1937 S Sch						(OL)
Aldershot	Kilmarnock	05.59	59-60	57	-	18
LAWLOR John Christopher						
Dublin, 3 December, 1922 IR-3						(IF)
Doncaster Rov.	Drumcondra	06.50	50-54	128	-	46
LAWRENCE Cyril						
Salford, 12 June, 1920						(OR)
Blackpool	Jnrs	02.46				
Rochdale	Tr	04.47	46-49	44	-	5
Wrexham	Tr	09.50	50-51	50	-	9
LAWRENCE David						
Poole, 12 May, 1933						(FB)
Bristol Rov.	Poole T.	06.55	56	5	-	0
Reading	Tr	06.57	57-58	23	-	0
LAWRENCE David William						
Swansea, 18 January, 1947 W Amat						(FB)
Swansea C.	Merthyr Tydfil	05.67	67-70	94	3	2
LAWRENCE George Randolph						
Kensington, 14 September, 1962						(W)
Southampton	App	09.80	81-82	7	3	1
Oxford U.	L	03.82	81	15	0	4
Oxford U.	Tr	11.82	82-84	63	0	21
Southampton	Tr	01.85	84-86	58	12	11
Millwall	Tr	07.87	87-88	26	2	4
Bournemouth	Tr	08.89	89-91	47	28	5
Portsmouth (N/C)	Weymouth	02.93	92	0	12	0
LAWRENCE James Hubert						
Balham, 8 March, 1970						(RW)
Sunderland	Cowes (IoW)	10.93	93	2	2	0
Doncaster Rov.	Tr	03.94	93-94	16	9	3
Leicester C.	Tr	01.95	94-96	21	26	1
Bradford C.	Tr	06.97	97	38	5	3
LAWRENCE Keith Derek						
Sidcup, 25 March, 1954						(CD)
Chelsea	App	03.72				
Brentford	Tr	05.74	74-75	78	0	1
LAWRENCE Leslie Oliver						
Rowley Regis, 18 May, 1957						(F)
Shrewsbury T.	Stourbridge	02.75	75-76	10	4	2
Torquay U.	Telford U.	07.77	77-81	170	19	45
Port Vale	Tr	08.82	82	5	3	0
Aldershot	Tr	07.83	83	39	0	22
Rochdale	Tr	08.84	84	15	0	4
Burnley	Tr	11.84	84-85	22	9	8
Peterborough U.	Tr	07.86	86-87	28	5	8
Cambridge U.	Tr	02.88	87	11	2	0
LAWRENCE Mark						
Stockton, 4 December, 1958						(M)
Hartlepool U.		08.77	77-83	155	13	24
Port Vale	L	03.83	82	10	1	0
LAWRENCE Matthew James						
Northampton, 19 June, 1974						(RB/M)
Wycombe W.	Grays Ath.	01.96	95-96	13	3	1
Fulham	Tr	02.97	96-97	56	2	0

LAWRENCE Thomas Johnstone
Dailly (Ayrs), 14 May, 1940 Su23-1/S-3 (G)

League Club	Source	Date Signed	Seasons Played	Apps	Subs	Gls
Liverpool	Jnrs	10.57	62-70	306	0	0
Tranmere Rov.	Tr	09.71	71-73	80	0	0

LAWRENSON Mark Thomas
Preston, 2 June, 1957 IR-38 (D)

League Club	Source	Date Signed	Seasons Played	Apps	Subs	Gls
Preston N.E.	Jnrs	08.74	74-76	73	0	2
Brighton & H.A.	Tr	07.77	77-80	152	0	5
Liverpool	Tr	08.81	81-87	233	8	11

LAWRENSON Thomas
Preston, 24 May, 1929 Died 1996 (W)

League Club	Source	Date Signed	Seasons Played	Apps	Subs	Gls
Preston N.E.	Leyland Motors	04.49	54	1	-	0
Southport	Tr	07.55	55-56	37	-	0

LAWRIE Samuel
Glasgow, 15 December, 1934 Died 1979 (OR)

League Club	Source	Date Signed	Seasons Played	Apps	Subs	Gls
Middlesbrough	Jnrs	02.52	51-56	36	-	5
Charlton Ath.	Tr	11.56	56-62	193	-	70
Bradford P.A.	Tr	10.62	62-65	72	1	16

LAWS Brian
Wallsend, 14 October, 1961 E 'B'/EF Lge (RB)

League Club	Source	Date Signed	Seasons Played	Apps	Subs	Gls
Burnley	App	10.79	79-82	125	0	12
Huddersfield T.	Tr	08.83	83-84	56	0	1
Middlesbrough	Tr	03.85	84-87	103	5	12
Nottingham F.	Tr	07.88	88-93	136	11	4
Grimsby T.	Tr	12.94	94-96	30	16	2
Darlington (N/C)	Tr	11.96	96	10	0	0
Scunthorpe U. (N/C)	Tr	01.97	96-97	11	7	0

LAWS Jonathan
Peterborough, 1 September, 1964 (M)

League Club	Source	Date Signed	Seasons Played	Apps	Subs	Gls
Wolverhampton W.	App	09.82				
Mansfield T.	Tr	03.83	82	0	1	0

LAWSON Allan
Kirkintilloch, 13 September, 1941 (CD)

League Club	Source	Date Signed	Seasons Played	Apps	Subs	Gls
Oldham Ath.	Glasgow Celtic	06.64	64-69	128	10	1

LAWSON David
Wallsend, 22 December, 1947 (G)

League Club	Source	Date Signed	Seasons Played	Apps	Subs	Gls
Newcastle U.	Jnrs	04.66				
Bradford P.A.	Shrewsbury T. (trial)	10.67	67-68	13	0	0
Huddersfield T.	Tr	05.69	70-71	51	0	0
Everton	Tr	06.72	72-76	124	0	0
Luton T.	Tr	10.78	78	5	0	0
Stockport Co.	Tr	03.79	78-80	106	0	0

LAWSON Ian James
Huddersfield, 4 November, 1977 (F)

League Club	Source	Date Signed	Seasons Played	Apps	Subs	Gls
Huddersfield T.	YT	01.95	96-97	11	25	3

LAWSON Frederick Ian Allison
Ouston (Dm), 24 March, 1939 E Yth (CF)

League Club	Source	Date Signed	Seasons Played	Apps	Subs	Gls
Burnley	Jnrs	03.56	56-60	23	-	7
Leeds U.	Tr	03.62	61-64	44	-	17
Crystal Palace	Tr	06.65	65	15	2	6
Port Vale	Tr	08.66	66	7	1	0

LAWSON James Joseph
Middlesbrough, 11 December, 1947 (W)

League Club	Source	Date Signed	Seasons Played	Apps	Subs	Gls
Middlesbrough	Jnrs	12.64	65-67	25	6	3
Huddersfield T.	Tr	08.68	68-75	234	11	42
Halifax T.	Tr	06.76	76-78	93	0	9

LAWSON John Richard
York, 3 February, 1925 Died 1990 (OR)

League Club	Source	Date Signed	Seasons Played	Apps	Subs	Gls
York C.	Dringhouses	08.44	46	1	-	0

LAWSON Norman
Hetton-le-Hole, 6 April, 1935 (OL)

League Club	Source	Date Signed	Seasons Played	Apps	Subs	Gls
Bury	Hednesford T.	09.55	55-57	56	-	8
Swansea C.	Tr	07.58	58-59	24	-	3
Watford	Tr	07.60				

LAWSON William
Dundee, 28 November, 1947 (W)

League Club	Source	Date Signed	Seasons Played	Apps	Subs	Gls
Sheffield Wed.	Brechin C.	10.69	69-70	9	1	0

LAWTHER William Ian
Belfast, 20 October, 1939 NI 'B'/NI-4 (CF)

League Club	Source	Date Signed	Seasons Played	Apps	Subs	Gls
Sunderland	Crusaders	03.58	59-60	75	-	41
Blackburn Rov.	Tr	07.61	61-62	59	-	21
Scunthorpe U.	Tr	07.63	63-64	60	-	22
Brentford	Tr	11.64	64-67	138	1	43
Halifax T.	Tr	08.68	68-70	87	14	23
Stockport Co.	Tr	07.71	71-75	158	6	29

LAWTON Craig Thomas
Deeside, 5 January, 1972 W Sch/W Yth/Wu21-1/W 'B' (M)

League Club	Source	Date Signed	Seasons Played	Apps	Subs	Gls
Manchester U.	YT	07.90				
Port Vale	Tr	08.94	94-95	2	1	0

LAWTON James Michael
Middlesbrough, 6 July, 1942 (CF)

League Club	Source	Date Signed	Seasons Played	Apps	Subs	Gls
Darlington	Middlesbrough (Am)	10.61	61-65	120	0	60
Swindon T.	Tr	09.65	65-66	11	0	3
Watford	Tr	03.67	66-67	10	3	1
Darlington	Tr	03.68	67-68	22	0	3

LAWTON John Kenneth
Woore (Salop), 6 July, 1936 (F)

League Club	Source	Date Signed	Seasons Played	Apps	Subs	Gls
Stoke C.	Jnrs	06.54	55	9	-	3

LAWTON Hubert Malcolm
Leeds, 7 November, 1935 (FB)

League Club	Source	Date Signed	Seasons Played	Apps	Subs	Gls
Leeds U.	Jnrs	11.52				
Bradford P.A.	Tr	06.57	57-62	113	-	0

LAWTON Norbert (Nobby)
Manchester, 25 March, 1940 (M)

League Club	Source	Date Signed	Seasons Played	Apps	Subs	Gls
Manchester U.	Jnrs	04.58	59-62	36	-	6
Preston N.E.	Tr	03.63	62-67	143	0	22
Brighton & H.A.	Tr	09.67	67-70	112	0	12
Lincoln C.	Tr	02.71	70-71	20	0	0

LAWTON Peter
Barnsley, 25 February, 1944 (FB)

League Club	Source	Date Signed	Seasons Played	Apps	Subs	Gls
Barnsley	Jnrs	05.62	62-63	2	-	0

LAWTON Thomas
Bolton, 6 October, 1919 Died 1996 EF Lge/E-23 (CF)

League Club	Source	Date Signed	Seasons Played	Apps	Subs	Gls
Burnley	Jnrs	03.36	35-36	25	-	16
Everton	Tr	01.37	36-38	87	-	65
Chelsea	Tr	11.45	46-47	42	-	30
Notts Co.	Tr	11.47	47-51	151	-	90
Brentford	Tr	03.52	51-53	50	-	17
Arsenal	Tr	09.53	53-55	35	-	13

LAWTON William
Ashton-u-Lyne, 4 June, 1920 (WH)

League Club	Source	Date Signed	Seasons Played	Apps	Subs	Gls
Oldham Ath.	Ferranti	02.45	46-48	10	-	0
Chester C.	Tr	10.49				

LAY Peter John
West Ham, 4 December, 1931 (FB)

League Club	Source	Date Signed	Seasons Played	Apps	Subs	Gls
Nottingham F.		04.53	54	1	-	0
Queens Park R.	Tr	07.56	56	1	-	0

LAYBOURNE Keith Ernest
Sunderland, 27 January, 1959 (LB)

League Club	Source	Date Signed	Seasons Played	Apps	Subs	Gls
Lincoln C.	Lambton Street B.C.	07.77	77-78	18	0	1

LAYNE David (Bronco) Richard
Sheffield, 29 July, 1939 (CF)

League Club	Source	Date Signed	Seasons Played	Apps	Subs	Gls
Rotherham U.	Jnrs	07.57	57-58	11	-	4
Swindon T.	Tr	06.59	59-60	41	-	28
Bradford C.	Tr	12.60	60-61	65	-	44
Sheffield Wed.	Tr	02.62	62-63	74	-	52
Sheffield Wed.	(Retired)	06.72				
Hereford U.	L	12.72	72	4	0	0

LAYTON Alan
Bury, 27 November, 1928 (OR)

League Club	Source	Date Signed	Seasons Played	Apps	Subs	Gls
Bolton W.		04.49				
Barrow	Tr	10.50	50-55	142	-	19

LAYTON John Henry
Hereford, 29 June, 1951 (CD)

League Club	Source	Date Signed	Seasons Played	Apps	Subs	Gls
Hereford U.	Gloucester C.	09.74	74-79	198	2	13
Newport Co. (N/C)	Trowbridge T.	01.84	83	1	0	0

LAYTON William Herbert
Birmingham, 13 January, 1915 Died 1984 (WH)

League Club	Source	Date Signed	Seasons Played	Apps	Subs	Gls
Reading	Shirley T.	03.37	37-46	51	-	17
Bradford P.A.	Tr	01.47	46-48	47	-	5
Colchester U.	Tr	08.50	50	7	-	0

LAZARIDIS Stanley
Australia, 16 August, 1972 Australian Int (LW)

League Club	Source	Date Signed	Seasons Played	Apps	Subs	Gls
West Ham U.	West Adelaide (Aus)	09.95	95-97	42	12	3

LAZARUS Mark
Stepney, 5 December, 1938 (W)

League Club	Source	Date Signed	Seasons Played	Apps	Subs	Gls
Leyton Orient	Barking	11.57	58-60	20	-	4
Queens Park R.	Tr	09.60	60-61	37	-	19
Wolverhampton W.	Tr	09.61	61	9	-	3

League Club	Source	Date Signed	Seasons Played	Apps	Subs	Gls
Queens Park R.	Tr	02.62	61-63	81	-	28
Brentford	Tr	01.64	63-65	62	0	20
Queens Park R.	Tr	11.65	65-67	86	2	29
Crystal Palace	Tr	11.67	67-69	63	0	17
Leyton Orient	Tr	10.69	69-71	81	1	14
LAZARUS Paul						
Stepney, 4 September, 1962						(F)
Charlton Ath.	Jnrs	08.80	80	2	0	1
Wimbledon	T.P.S. Turun (Fin)	10.81	81	17	1	6
LEA Cyril						
Wrexham, 5 August, 1934 W Amat/W-2						(WH)
Leyton Orient	Bradley R.	07.57	57-64	205	-	0
Ipswich T.	Tr	11.64	64-68	103	4	2
LEA Harold						
Wigan, 14 September, 1931						(G)
Stockport Co.	Horwich R.M.I.	05.58	58-63	117	-	0
LEA Leslie						
Manchester, 5 October, 1942						(W)
Blackpool	Jnrs	10.59	60-67	159	1	13
Cardiff C.	Tr	11.67	67-69	75	1	7
Barnsley	Tr	08.70	70-75	198	7	32
LEA William Thomas						
Wigan, 27 May, 1924						(OL)
Stockport Co. (Am)		11.59	59	1	-	0
LEABURN Carl Winston						
Lewisham, 30 March, 1969						(F)
Charlton Ath.	App	03.87	86-97	276	46	53
Northampton T.	L	03.90	89	9	0	0
Wimbledon	Tr	01.98	97	15	1	4
LEACH Albert						
Bolton, 10 July, 1931						(G)
Shrewsbury T.		11.51	51	2	-	0
LEACH Brian Ernest						
Reading, 20 July, 1932						(WH)
Reading		11.50	52-56	108	-	1
LEACH John Norman						
Whitehaven, 17 January, 1919						(OL)
Barrow	Barrow Celtic	09.47	47-49	74	-	10
LEACH Michael John Christopher						
Hackney, 16 January, 1947 Died 1992 E Yth						(M)
Queens Park R.	App	02.64	64-77	291	22	61
Cambridge U.	Detroit (USA)	09.78	78	18	1	1
LEADBEATER Richard Paul						
Dudley, 21 October, 1977						(F)
Wolverhampton W.	YT	07.96	96	0	1	0
LEADBETTER Albert						
Newton-le-Willows, 17 August, 1921 Died 1994						(OL)
Accrington St. (Am)	Earlestown	12.46	46	4	-	0
LEADBETTER James Hunter						
Edinburgh, 15 July, 1928						(OL)
Chelsea	Edinburgh Thistle	07.49	51	3	-	0
Brighton & H.A.	Tr	08.52	52-54	107	-	29
Ipswich T.	Tr	06.55	55-64	344	-	43
LEADBITTER Christopher Jonathan						
Middlesbrough, 17 October, 1967						(LM)
Grimsby T.	App	09.85				
Hereford U.	Tr	08.86	86-87	32	4	1
Cambridge U.	Tr	08.88	88-92	144	32	18
Bournemouth	Tr	08.93	93-94	45	9	3
Plymouth Arg.	Tr	07.95	95-96	46	6	1
Torquay U.	Dorchester T.	11.97	97	21	5	1
LEADBITTER John						
Sunderland, 7 May, 1953						(CD)
Sunderland	App	05.70				
Darlington	Tr	08.72	72	15	4	0
LEAF Andrew Keith						
York, 18 January, 1962						(FB)
York C.	App	01.80	79	1	0	0
LEAHY Stephen David						
Battersea, 23 September, 1959 E Sch						(F)
Crystal Palace	App	10.76	80-81	3	1	0

League Club	Source	Date Signed	Seasons Played	Apps	Subs	Gls
LEAKE Albert George						
Stoke, 7 April, 1930 E Yth						(WH)
Port Vale	Stoke C. (Am)	02.50	50-59	269	-	34
LEAMON Frederick William						
Jersey, 11 May, 1919 Died 1981						(CF)
Newport Co.	Bath C.	02.46	46	4	-	3
Bristol Rov.	Tr	10.46	46-47	43	-	21
Brighton & H.A.	Tr	07.49	49	11	-	4
LEAN David Reginald						
Plymouth, 28 August, 1945						(CD)
Plymouth Arg.	Embankment	08.69	69-70	44	1	0
LEANING Andrew John						
Goole, 18 May, 1963						(G)
York C.	Rowntree-Mackintosh	06.85	85-86	69	0	0
Sheffield U.	Tr	05.87	87	21	0	0
Bristol C.	Tr	09.88	88-92	75	0	0
Lincoln C.	Tr	03.94	93-95	36	0	0
Chesterfield	Tr	10.96	96-97	14	0	0
LEAR Graham John						
Exeter, 18 December, 1930						(G)
Exeter C. (Am)	Exeter T.	06.50	50-51	20	-	0
LEARY Stuart Edward						
South Africa, 30 April, 1933 Died 1988 Eu23-1						(CF)
Charlton Ath.	Clyde (SA)	02.50	51-61	376	-	153
Queens Park R.	Tr	12.62	62-65	94	0	29
LEATH Terence Charles						
Liverpool, 6 November, 1934						(FB)
Southport	Birchfield Rov.	03.59	58-59	17	-	0
LEATHER Maurice Peate						
Eastleigh, 9 November, 1929 E Yth						(G)
Portsmouth	Southampton (Am)	01.50	50-52	18	-	0
LEAVER Derek						
Blackburn, 13 November, 1930						(IF)
Blackburn Rov.		05.49	50-54	14	-	5
Bournemouth	Tr	07.55	55	29	-	5
Crewe Alex.	Tr	03.56	55-56	28	-	6
LEAVY Stephen Francis						
Longford (Ire), 18 June, 1925 Died 1996 LoI						(FB)
Swansea C.	Sligo Rov.	07.50	50-57	36	-	1
LE BIHAN Neil Ernest						
Croydon, 14 March, 1976						(M)
Peterborough U.	Tottenham H. (YT)	07.94	94-96	21	10	0
LEBOUEF Frank						
France, 22 January, 1968 French Int						(CD)
Chelsea	Strasbourg (Fr)	07.96	96-97	58	0	11
LECK Derek Alan						
Deal, 8 February, 1937						(WH)
Millwall	Leyton Y.C.	05.55	55-57	7	-	2
Northampton T.	Tr	06.58	58-65	246	0	45
Brighton & H.A.	Tr	11.65	65-66	29	1	0
LE CORNU Craig Douglas						
Birkenhead, 17 September, 1960						(M)
Liverpool	App	09.78				
Tranmere Rov.	Tr	12.80	80	3	3	0
LEDGARD Ian						
Stockport, 9 February, 1948						(IF)
Blackburn Rov.	Leeds U. (Am)	07.67				
Stockport Co.	Tr	10.67	67-68	4	4	0
LEDGER Robert Hardy						
Chester-le-Street, 5 October, 1937						(OR)
Huddersfield T.	Jnrs	10.54	55-61	58	-	7
Oldham Ath.	Tr	05.62	62-67	221	1	37
Mansfield T.	Tr	11.67	67-69	51	6	14
Barrow	Tr	10.69	69	21	1	2
LEDGER Roy						
Barnsley, 9 December, 1930 Died 1992						(IF)
Barnsley	Jnrs	04.48	50	1	-	0
LEDGERTON Terence						
Liverpool, 7 October, 1930						(OL)
Brentford		05.50	51-53	40	-	8
Millwall	Tr	05.54	54	6	-	2

LEE Alan Robert
West Germany, 19 June, 1960 (W)

League Club	Source	Date Signed	Seasons Played	Apps	Subs	Gls
Leicester C.	Philadelphia (USA)	02.79	78-79	6	0	0

LEE Alfred
Farnworth, 11 June, 1927 Died 1991 (WH)

League Club	Source	Date Signed	Seasons Played	Apps	Subs	Gls
Bolton W.		10.48				
Oldham Ath.	Tr	07.50	50	3	-	1

LEE Andrew Gerard
Liverpool, 14 September, 1962 (D)

League Club	Source	Date Signed	Seasons Played	Apps	Subs	Gls
Tranmere Rov.	Stafford R.	07.84	84	14	4	0
Cambridge U. (N/C)	Tr	09.85	85	8	1	0

LEE Anthony
Manchester, 4 June, 1937 (OL)

League Club	Source	Date Signed	Seasons Played	Apps	Subs	Gls
Southport (Am)	Cheadle Rov.	02.58	57-58	10	-	1

LEE John **Anthony** Lee
Edgware, 26 November, 1947 (F)

League Club	Source	Date Signed	Seasons Played	Apps	Subs	Gls
Leicester C.		10.65				
Bradford C.	Tr	07.67	67	6	2	3
Darlington	Stockton	05.68	68	10	4	0

LEE Christian
Aylesbury, 8 October, 1976 (F)

League Club	Source	Date Signed	Seasons Played	Apps	Subs	Gls
Northampton T.	Doncaster Rov. (YT)	07.95	95-97	16	24	7

LEE Christopher
Batley, 18 June, 1971 (M)

League Club	Source	Date Signed	Seasons Played	Apps	Subs	Gls
Bradford C.	YT	07.89				
Rochdale	Tr	06.90	90	24	2	2
Scarborough	Tr	03.91	90-92	75	3	3
Hull C.	Tr	07.93	93-95	104	12	5

LEE Colin
Torquay, 12 June, 1956 (F/CD)

League Club	Source	Date Signed	Seasons Played	Apps	Subs	Gls
Bristol C.	App	06.74				
Hereford U.	L	11.74	74	7	2	0
Torquay U.	Tr	01.77	76-77	35	0	14
Tottenham H.	Tr	10.77	77-79	57	5	18
Chelsea	Tr	01.80	79-86	167	18	36
Brentford	Tr	07.87	87-88	20	4	1

LEE David John
Bristol, 26 November, 1969 E Yth/Eu21-10 (M/CD)

League Club	Source	Date Signed	Seasons Played	Apps	Subs	Gls
Chelsea	YT	10.88	88-97	119	32	11
Reading	L	01.92	91	5	0	5
Plymouth Arg.	L	03.92	91	9	0	1
Portsmouth	L	08.94	94	4	1	0
Sheffield U.	L	12.97	97	5	0	0

LEE David Mark
Manchester, 5 November, 1967 (W)

League Club	Source	Date Signed	Seasons Played	Apps	Subs	Gls
Bury	YT	08.86	85-91	203	5	35
Southampton	Tr	08.91	91-92	11	9	0
Bolton W.	Tr	11.92	92-96	124	31	17
Wigan Ath.	Tr	07.97	97	41	2	5

LEE Eric George
Chester, 18 October, 1922 E Amat (CH)

League Club	Source	Date Signed	Seasons Played	Apps	Subs	Gls
Chester C.	Jnrs	05.46	46-56	363	-	10

LEE Francis
Chorley, 17 February, 1944 (W)

League Club	Source	Date Signed	Seasons Played	Apps	Subs	Gls
Preston N.E.	Jnrs	11.61	62-70	144	9	22
Southport	Tr	11.70	70-73	115	0	21
Stockport Co.	Tr	07.74	74	13	0	1

LEE Francis (Franny) Henry
Westhoughton, 29 April, 1944 E Yth/EF Lge/E-27 (F)

League Club	Source	Date Signed	Seasons Played	Apps	Subs	Gls
Bolton W.	Jnrs	05.61	60-67	189	0	92
Manchester C.	Tr	10.67	67-73	248	1	112
Derby Co.	Tr	08.74	74-75	62	0	24

LEE Garth
Sheffield, 39 September, 1943 E Yth (OL)

League Club	Source	Date Signed	Seasons Played	Apps	Subs	Gls
Sheffield U.	Jnrs	05.61				
Chester C.	Tr	09.63	63-64	28	-	7

LEE Gary
Doncaster, 30 April, 1966 (D)

League Club	Source	Date Signed	Seasons Played	Apps	Subs	Gls
Doncaster Rov. (N/C)	YT	07.84	84	1	0	0

LEE George Thomas
York, 4 June, 1919 Died 1991 (OL)

League Club	Source	Date Signed	Seasons Played	Apps	Subs	Gls
York C.	Jnrs	06.36	36-46	37	-	11
Nottingham F.	Tr	08.47	47-48	76	-	20
West Bromwich A.	Tr	07.49	49-57	271	-	59

LEE Gordon Francis
Cannock, 13 July, 1934 (FB)

League Club	Source	Date Signed	Seasons Played	Apps	Subs	Gls
Aston Villa	Hednesford T.	10.55	58-64	118	-	2
Shrewsbury T.	Tr	07.66	66	2	0	0

LEE Graeme Barry
Middlesbrough, 31 May, 1978 (CD)

League Club	Source	Date Signed	Seasons Played	Apps	Subs	Gls
Hartlepool U.	YT	07.96	95-97	61	6	3

LEE Harry
Mexborough, 13 January, 1933 (IF)

League Club	Source	Date Signed	Seasons Played	Apps	Subs	Gls
Derby Co.	Thomas Hill Y.C.	10.50				
Mansfield T.		08.55	55	3	-	2

LEE James
Rotherham, 26 January, 1926 (FB)

League Club	Source	Date Signed	Seasons Played	Apps	Subs	Gls
Wolverhampton W.	Wath W.	02.45				
Hull C.	Tr	10.48	49	3	-	1
Halifax T.	Tr	02.51	50-51	26	-	0
Chelsea	Tr	10.51				
Leyton Orient	Tr	07.54	54-55	67	-	1
Swindon T.	Tr	11.56	56-58	35	-	0

LEE Jason Benedict
Forest Gate, 9 May, 1971 (F)

League Club	Source	Date Signed	Seasons Played	Apps	Subs	Gls
Charlton Ath.	YT	05.89	89	0	1	0
Stockport Co.	L	02.91	90	2	0	0
Lincoln C.	Tr	03.91	90-92	86	7	21
Southend U.	Tr	08.93	93	18	6	3
Nottingham F.	Tr	03.94	93-96	41	35	14
Charlton Ath.	L	02.97	96	7	1	3
Grimsby T.	L	03.97	96	2	5	2
Watford	Tr	06.97	97	35	1	10

LEE Jeffrey Wreathall
Dewsbury, 3 October, 1945 (LB)

League Club	Source	Date Signed	Seasons Played	Apps	Subs	Gls
Halifax T.	Huddersfield T. (Am)	01.65	64-72	231	9	2
Peterborough U.	Tr	08.73	73-77	170	2	12

LEE John (Jack)
Sileby (Leics), 4 November, 1920 E-1 (CF)

League Club	Source	Date Signed	Seasons Played	Apps	Subs	Gls
Leicester C.	Quorn	02.41	46-49	123	-	74
Derby Co.	Tr	07.50	50-53	93	-	54
Coventry C.	Tr	11.54	54	15	-	8

LEE Michael James
Chester, 27 June, 1938 W Sch (OL)

League Club	Source	Date Signed	Seasons Played	Apps	Subs	Gls
West Bromwich A.	Saltney Jnrs	08.56	56	1	-	0
Crewe Alex.	Tr	06.58	58	1	-	0

LEE Norman Thomas
Trealaw, 29 May, 1939 (WH)

League Club	Source	Date Signed	Seasons Played	Apps	Subs	Gls
Tottenham H.	Jnrs	11.57				
Bournemouth	Tr	09.61				
Southend U.	Tr	02.62	61-62	22	-	1

LEE Paul Andrew
Oxford, 30 May, 1952 (F)

League Club	Source	Date Signed	Seasons Played	Apps	Subs	Gls
Hereford U.	Oxford C.	09.72	73-74	21	7	5

LEE Raymond Maurice
Bristol, 19 September, 1970 (W)

League Club	Source	Date Signed	Seasons Played	Apps	Subs	Gls
Arsenal	YT	10.88				
Scarborough (N/C)		02.91	90	2	8	0

LEE Richard (Dick)
Sheffield, 11 September, 1944 (WH)

League Club	Source	Date Signed	Seasons Played	Apps	Subs	Gls
Rotherham U.	Jnrs	05.63				
Notts Co.	Tr	06.64				
Mansfield T.	Tr	08.65	65	3	1	0
Halifax T.	Tr	07.66	66-67	16	0	0

LEE Robert
Newcastle, 23 December, 1957 (M)

League Club	Source	Date Signed	Seasons Played	Apps	Subs	Gls
Doncaster Rov.	App	05.74	74	1	0	0
Scunthorpe U.	Tr	07.76	76-77	17	2	0

LEE Robert Gordon
Melton Mowbray, 2 February, 1953 (F)

League Club	Source	Date Signed	Seasons Played	Apps	Subs	Gls
Leicester C.	Blaby B.C.	02.72	71-76	55	8	17
Doncaster Rov.	L	08.74	74	14	0	4
Sunderland	Tr	09.76	76-79	101	8	32
Bristol Rov.	Tr	08.80	80	19	4	2
Carlisle U.	Tr	08.81	81-82	47	8	12
Darlington	Hong Kong	08.83	83	5	0	0

LEE Robert Martin
West Ham, 1 February, 1966 Eu21-2/E 'B'/E-18 (RW)

League Club	Source	Date Signed	Seasons Played	Apps	Subs	Gls
Charlton Ath.	Hornchurch	07.83	83-92	274	24	59
Newcastle U.	Tr	09.92	92-97	206	3	43

League Club	Source	Date Signed	Seasons Played	Apps	Subs	Gls
LEE Samuel						
Liverpool, 7 February, 1959 E Yth/Eu21-6/E-14						(M)
Liverpool	App	04.76	77-85	190	7	13
Queens Park R.	Tr	08.86	86	29	1	0
Southampton	Osasuna (Sp)	01.90	89	0	2	0
Bolton W.	Tr	10.90	90	4	0	0
LEE Frederick **Stuart**						
Manchester, 11 February, 1953						(F)
Bolton W.	App	02.71	71-74	77	8	20
Wrexham	Tr	11.75	75-77	46	8	12
Stockport Co.	Tr	08.78	78-79	49	0	21
Manchester C.	Tr	09.79	79	6	1	2
LEE Terence William George						
Stepney, 20 September, 1952 Died 1996						(G)
Tottenham H.	Jnrs	05.70	73	1	0	0
Torquay U.	Tr	07.75	75-77	106	0	0
Newport Co.	Tr	11.78	78	1	0	0
LEE Thomas Joseph						
Horden, 19 December, 1949						(F)
Hartlepool U.		11.68	69	6	0	0
LEE Trevor Carl						
Lewisham, 3 July, 1954						(F)
Millwall	Epsom & Ewell	10.75	75-78	99	9	22
Colchester U.	Tr	11.78	78-80	95	1	35
Gillingham	Tr	01.81	80-82	43	4	14
Leyton Orient	L	10.82	82	5	0	0
Bournemouth	Tr	11.82	82-83	28	6	9
Cardiff C.	Tr	12.83	83	21	0	5
Northampton T.	Tr	07.84	84	24	0	0
Fulham (N/C)	Tr	03.85	84	1	0	0
LEE William Richard						
Darwen, 24 October, 1919 Died 1996						(WH)
Blackburn Rov.	Pleasington	08.38	38	1	-	0
Barrow	Tr	05.47	46-52	158	-	1
LEEBROOK Peter David						
Saltburn, 18 September, 1968						(RB)
Burnley	YT	05.87	86-87	52	0	0
LEECH Frederick						
Stalybridge, 5 December, 1923						(CF)
Bradford C.	Hurst	12.45	46	7	-	2
LEECH Vincent Graham						
Littleborough, 6 December, 1940						(D)
Blackburn Rov.	Burnley (Am)	04.59				
Bury	Tr	07.61	61-67	108	3	0
Rochdale	Tr	07.68	68-70	59	1	1
LEEDER Frederick						
Seaton Delaval, 15 September, 1936						(FB)
Everton	Seaton Delaval	03.55	57	1	-	0
Darlington	Tr	07.58	58-59	21	-	0
Southport	Tr	07.60	60-61	63	-	0
LEEDHAM John Richard						
Carshalton, 8 November, 1942						(WH)
Millwall	Epsom & Ewell	10.62	62-63	9	-	0
Walsall	Tr	05.64	64	13	-	0
Leyton Orient	Tr	08.65				
LEEK Kenneth						
Ynysybwl, 26 July, 1935 Wu23-1/W-13						(CF)
Northampton T.	Pontypridd	08.52	55-57	71	-	27
Leicester C.	Tr	05.58	58-60	93	-	34
Newcastle U.	Tr	06.61	61	13	-	6
Birmingham C.	Tr	11.61	61-64	104	-	49
Northampton T.	Tr	12.64	64-65	16	0	4
Bradford C.	Tr	11.65	65-67	99	0	25
LEEMING Clifford						
Turton, 2 February, 1920						(IF)
Bury	Bolton W. (Am)	10.46	46	1	-	0
Tranmere Rov.	Tr	07.47	47	13	-	2
LEES Alfred						
Worsley, 28 July, 1923						(CH)
Bolton W.		05.47	47	2	-	0
New Brighton	Tr	08.49	49-50	72	-	0
Crewe Alex.	Tr	09.51	51-55	185	-	5
LEES Geoffrey						
Rotherham, 1 October, 1933						(HB)
Barnsley	Jnrs	03.51				
Bradford C.	Tr	07.55	55	3	-	0
LEES Norman						
Newcastle, 18 November, 1948						(D)
Hull C.	App	11.66	66-70	4	1	0
Hartlepool U.	L	12.70	70	20	0	1
Darlington	Tr	07.71	71-76	108	12	5
LEES Terence						
Stoke, 30 June, 1952						(FB)
Stoke C.	App	07.69	70-73	17	7	0
Crewe Alex.	L	03.75	74	6	0	0
Port Vale	Tr	08.75	75	40	1	2
Birmingham C.	J.C. Roda (Neth)	07.79	79-80	11	1	0
Newport Co.	Tr	08.81	81	25	0	0
Scunthorpe U.	Stafford R.	09.84	84	30	1	0
LEES Walter Joseph						
Glasgow, 2 February, 1947						(CD)
Watford	Kilsyth R.	06.68	68-75	220	6	10
LEESE Lars						
Germany, 18 August, 1969						(G)
Barnsley	Bayern Leverkusen (Ger)	07.97	97	8	1	0
LEESE William						
Stoke, 10 March, 1961						(CD)
Port Vale	App	03.79	79	1	0	0
LEESON Donald						
Askern, 25 August, 1935						(G)
Barnsley	Askern B.C.	05.54	56-60	97	-	0
LEET Norman David						
Leicester, 13 March, 1962						(FB)
Leicester C.	Jnrs	06.80	80-82	19	0	0
LE FLEM Richard (Flip) Peter						
Bradford-on-Avon, 12 July, 1942 Eu23-1						(OL)
Nottingham F.	Guernsey	05.60	60-63	132	-	18
Wolverhampton W.	Tr	01.64	63-64	19	-	5
Middlesbrough	Tr	02.65	64-65	9	0	1
Leyton Orient	Tr	03.66	65-66	11	0	2
LEGATE Roland Arthur						
Arlesey, 4 May, 1939						(OL)
Luton T.	Jnrs	05.56	56-61	15	-	8
LEGG Andrew						
Neath, 28 July, 1966 W-4						(LW)
Swansea C.	Briton Ferry	08.88	88-92	155	8	29
Notts Co.	Tr	07.93	93-95	85	4	9
Birmingham C.	Tr	02.96	95-96	31	14	5
Ipswich T.	L	11.97	97	6	0	1
Reading	Tr	02.98	97	10	0	0
LEGG Richard Desmond						
Chippenham, 23 April, 1952						(F)
Swindon T.	Chippenham T.	08.71	71-73	13	7	3
LEGG William Campbell						
Bradford, 17 April, 1948						(LB)
Huddersfield T.	App	05.65	64-68	54	2	4
LEGGAT Graham						
Aberdeen, 20 June, 1934 Su23-1/SF Lge/S-18						(W)
Fulham	Aberdeen	08.58	58-66	251	3	127
Birmingham C.	Tr	01.67	66-67	13	3	3
Rotherham U.	Tr	07.68	68	13	3	7
LEGGETT Peter Robert						
Newton-le-Willows, 16 December, 1943						(W)
Swindon T.	Weymouth	05.62	63-64	15	-	1
Brighton & H.A.	Tr	07.65	65	2	1	0
Cambridge U.	Chelmsford C.	01.70	70	21	0	0
LEIGH Dennis						
Barnsley, 26 February, 1949						(LB)
Doncaster Rov.	App	03.67	66-67	34	2	1
Rotherham U.	Tr	02.68	67-72	153	7	10
Lincoln C.	Tr	02.73	72-78	201	5	3
LEIGH Ian Reginald						
Ilfracombe, 11 June, 1962						(G)
Bournemouth	Swaythling	10.79	81-85	123	0	0
Bristol C.	L	01.85	84	1	0	0
Torquay U.	L	09.85	85	4	0	0
LEIGH Mark Brian						
Manchester, 4 October, 1961						(M)
Stockport Co. (N/C)	Manchester C. (App)	11.79	80-83	6	5	1

League Club	Source	Date Signed	Seasons Played	Apps	Subs	Gls
LEIGH Peter						
Wythenshawe, 4 March, 1939						(LB)
Manchester C.	Stamford Lads	08.57	59	2	-	0
Crewe Alex.	Tr	06.61	61-71	430	0	3
LEIGHTON Anthony						
Leeds, 27 November, 1939 Died 1978						(CF)
Leeds U.	Ashley Road	12.56				
Doncaster Rov.	Tr	06.59	59-61	83	-	45
Barnsley	Tr	05.62	62-64	107	-	59
Huddersfield T.	Tr	01.65	64-67	89	1	40
Bradford C.	Tr	03.68	67-69	84	4	23
LEIGHTON James						
Johnstone, 24 July, 1958 Su21-1/S-89						(G)
Manchester U.	Aberdeen	05.88	88-89	73	0	0
Reading	L	11.91	91	8	0	0
LEIPER John						
Aberdeen, 26 June, 1938						(G)
Plymouth Arg.	Aberdeen E.E.	04.58	60-66	75	0	0
LEISHMAN Graham						
Salford, 6 April, 1968						(F)
Mansfield T.	Irlam T.	12.88	88-90	8	19	3
LEISHMAN Thomas						
Stenhousemuir, 3 September, 1937						(WH)
Liverpool	St Mirren	11.59	59-62	107	-	6
LEITCH Andrew Buchanan						
Exeter, 27 March, 1950						(F)
Swansea C.		07.75	75	15	2	6
LEITCH Grant						
South Africa, 31 October, 1972						(W)
Blackpool	Jnrs	08.90	91-93	13	12	1
LEITCH Donald **Scott**						
Motherwell, 6 October, 1969						(M)
Swindon T.	Hearts	03.96	95-97	68	1	1
LEIVERS William Ernest						
Bolsover, 29 January, 1932						(FB)
Chesterfield	Jnrs	02.50	51-52	27	-	0
Manchester C.	Tr	11.53	54-63	250	-	4
Doncaster Rov.	Tr	07.64	64-65	24	0	1
LELLO Cyril Frank						
Ludlow, 24 February, 1920						(WH)
Everton	Shrewsbury T.	09.47	47-56	237	-	9
Rochdale	Tr	11.56	56	11	-	0
LEMAN Dennis						
Newcastle, 1 December, 1954 E Sch						(M)
Manchester C.	App	12.71	73-75	10	7	1
Sheffield Wed.	Tr	12.76	76-81	89	15	9
Wrexham	L	02.82	81	17	0	1
Scunthorpe U.	Tr	08.82	82-83	38	0	3
LEMON Arthur						
Neath, 25 January, 1931						(F)
Nottingham F.		02.51	52-54	24	-	1
LEMON Paul Andrew						
Middlesbrough, 3 June, 1966						(M)
Sunderland	App	05.84	84-88	91	16	15
Carlisle U.	L	12.84	84	2	0	0
Walsall	L	11.89	89	2	0	0
Reading	L	12.89	89	3	0	0
Chesterfield	Tr	09.90	90-92	80	5	9
LENAGH Steven Michael						
Durham, 21 March, 1979						(CD)
Chesterfield	Sheffield Wed. (YT)	11.97	97	0	3	0
LENARDUZZI Robert Italo						
Canada, 1 May, 1955 Canadian Int						(D)
Reading	App	05.73	71-75	63	4	2
LENG Michael						
Rotherham, 14 June, 1952						(D)
Rotherham U.	App	07.71	71-75	94	7	2
Workington	Tr	07.76	76	43	0	2
LENIHAN Michael Martin						
Swansea, 15 October, 1946						(F)
Swansea C.	Swansea G.P.O.	08.72	72-73	9	4	0
LENNARD David						
Manchester, 31 December, 1944						(M)
Bolton W.	Jnrs	12.61	62-68	114	5	3
Halifax T.	Tr	07.69	69-71	97	0	16
Blackpool	Tr	10.71	71-72	42	3	9
Cambridge U.	Tr	08.73	73-74	39	1	6
Chester C.	Tr	09.74	74-75	73	2	11
Stockport Co.	Tr	07.76	76	39	0	4
Bournemouth	Tr	09.77	77-78	56	3	4
LENNON Alexander Vincent						
Glasgow, 25 October, 1925 Died 1992						(IL)
Rotherham U.		11.44				
Queens Park R.		01.47	48	1	-	0
Mansfield T.	Tr	02.49	48	3	-	0
LENNON Neil Francis						
Lurgan (NI), 25 June, 1971 NI Yth/NIu21-2/NIu23-1/NI 'B'/NI-21						(M)
Manchester C.	YT	08.89	87	1	0	0
Crewe Alex.	Tr	08.90	90-95	142	5	15
Leicester C.	Tr	02.96	95-97	86	1	4
LENNOX Stephen John Martin						
Aberdeen, 14 November, 1964						(M)
Stoke C.	App	12.81	82	1	1	0
Torquay U.	L	12.83	83	11	0	0
LEONARD Carleton Craig						
Oswestry, 3 February, 1958						(FB)
Shrewsbury T.	Jnrs	09.75	75-82	224	3	1
Hereford U.	Tr	06.83	83-84	29	1	0
Cardiff C. (N/C)	Tr	07.85	85	4	0	0
LEONARD Christopher						
Jarrow, 11 July, 1927						(CH)
Darlington	South Shields	03.52	51-53	26	-	0
LEONARD Gary Alan						
Newcastle, 28 November, 1965						(M)
West Bromwich A.	App	11.83				
Shrewsbury T.	Tr	07.85	85-87	48	18	1
Hereford U.	L	03.88	87	11	0	1
Bury	Tr	07.88	88	4	5	1
Stockport Co.	Tr	03.89	88-89	15	2	1
LEONARD Gary Edward						
Northampton, 23 March, 1962						(M)
Northampton T.	App	03.80	79-80	2	0	0
LEONARD Henry (Harry)						
Jarrow, 19 May, 1924						(FB)
Bradford P.A.	Darlington (Am)	05.45	47	1	-	0
Hartlepool U.	Tr	11.48	48	2	-	0
LEONARD Keith Andrew						
Birmingham, 10 November, 1950						(F)
Aston Villa	Highgate U.	04.72	72-75	36	2	11
Port Vale	L	11.73	73	12	1	1
LEONARD Mark Anthony						
St Helens, 27 September, 1962						(F)
Everton	Witton A.	02.82				
Tranmere Rov.	L	03.83	82	6	1	0
Crewe Alex.	Tr	06.83	83-84	51	3	15
Stockport Co.	Tr	02.85	84-86	73	0	23
Bradford C.	Tr	09.86	86-91	120	37	29
Rochdale	Tr	03.92	91	9	0	1
Preston N.E.	Tr	08.92	92	19	3	1
Chester C.	Tr	08.93	93-94	28	4	8
Wigan Ath.	Tr	09.94	94-95	60	4	12
Rochdale	Tr	07.96	96-97	72	0	6
LEONARD Michael Christopher						
Carshalton, 9 May, 1959						(G)
Halifax T.	Epsom & Ewell	07.76	76-79	69	0	0
Notts Co.	Tr	09.79	79-88	204	0	0
Chesterfield	Tr	03.89	88-93	175	1	0
Halifax T.	L	11.90	90	3	0	0
LEONARD Patrick Desmond						
Dublin, 25 July, 1929						(IF)
Bristol Rov.	Bath C.	07.52	52-53	14	-	2
Colchester U.	Tr	07.54	54	34	-	5
LEONARD Stanley						
Hawarden, 8 October, 1924 Died 1995						(OR)
Chester C. (Am)		01.47	46	1	-	0

League Club	Source	Date Signed	Seasons Played	Apps	Subs	Gls

LEONHARDSEN Oyvind
Norway, 17 August, 1970 Norwegian Int (M)

League Club	Source	Date Signed	Seasons Played	Apps	Subs	Gls
Wimbledon	Rosenborg (Nor)	11.94	94-96	73	3	13
Liverpool	Tr	06.97	97	27	1	6

LE ROUX Daniel Leow
South Africa, 25 November, 1933 South African Am Int (OR)

League Club	Source	Date Signed	Seasons Played	Apps	Subs	Gls
Arsenal	Queens Park (SA)	02.57	57	5	-	0

LE SAUX Graeme Pierre
Jersey, 17 October, 1968 Eu21-4/E 'B'/E-29 (LB)

League Club	Source	Date Signed	Seasons Played	Apps	Subs	Gls
Chelsea	St Pauls (Jersey)	12.87	88-92	77	13	8
Blackburn Rov.	Tr	03.93	92-96	127	2	7
Chelsea	Tr	08.97	97	26	0	1

LESLIE John Alexander
Plumstead, 25 October, 1955 (F)

League Club	Source	Date Signed	Seasons Played	Apps	Subs	Gls
Wimbledon	Dulwich Hamlet	12.75	77-82	242	11	85
Gillingham	Tr	08.83	83-84	60	5	12
Millwall	Tr	08.85	85-86	12	7	2

LESLIE Lawrence Grant
Edinburgh, 17 March, 1935 SF Lge/S-5 (G)

League Club	Source	Date Signed	Seasons Played	Apps	Subs	Gls
West Ham U.	Airdrieonians	06.61	61-62	57	-	0
Stoke C.	Tr	10.63	63-65	78	0	0
Millwall	Tr	07.66	66-67	67	0	0
Southend U.	Tr	07.68	68	13	0	0

LESLIE Maurice Harrington
India, 19 August, 1923 (FB)

League Club	Source	Date Signed	Seasons Played	Apps	Subs	Gls
Swindon T.		06.47	46	1	-	0

LESLIE Steven
Dumfries, 6 February, 1976 (M)

League Club	Source	Date Signed	Seasons Played	Apps	Subs	Gls
Stoke C.	Jnrs	03.93	94	0	1	0

LESLIE Steven Robert William
Hornsey, 2 August, 1952 E Yth (M)

League Club	Source	Date Signed	Seasons Played	Apps	Subs	Gls
Colchester U.	Jnrs	05.71	70-83	412	22	40

LESSLIE Kenneth Gordon
West Ham, 4 January, 1923 Died 1991 (OR)

League Club	Source	Date Signed	Seasons Played	Apps	Subs	Gls
Ipswich T.		08.47				
Watford	Tr	07.48	48	7	-	1

LESTER Abraham Bennett (Benny)
Sheffield, 10 February, 1920 (CF)

League Club	Source	Date Signed	Seasons Played	Apps	Subs	Gls
Hull C.	Selby T.	09.46	46-47	27	-	17
Lincoln C.	Tr	01.48	47-48	37	-	10
Stockport Co.	Tr	08.49	49	8	-	2

LESTER Jack William
Sheffield, 8 October, 1975 E Sch (F)

League Club	Source	Date Signed	Seasons Played	Apps	Subs	Gls
Grimsby T.	Jnrs	07.94	94-97	44	30	9
Doncaster Rov.	L	09.96	96	5	6	1

LESTER Leslie James
Cardiff, 17 November, 1923 Died 1991 (LH)

League Club	Source	Date Signed	Seasons Played	Apps	Subs	Gls
Cardiff C.	Cardiff Corries	04.44				
Torquay U.	Tr	08.48	48-49	31	-	1
Newport Co.	Tr	09.50	50	2	-	0

LESTER Michael John Anthony
Manchester, 4 August, 1954 (M)

League Club	Source	Date Signed	Seasons Played	Apps	Subs	Gls
Oldham Ath.	App	08.72	72-73	26	1	2
Manchester C.	Tr	11.73	73-76	1	1	0
Stockport Co.	L	08.75	75	8	1	1
Grimsby T.	Washington (USA)	11.77	77-79	45	3	10
Barnsley	Tr	10.79	79-80	64	0	11
Exeter C.	Tr	08.81	81	18	1	6
Bradford C.	Tr	02.82	81-82	46	3	2
Scunthorpe U.	Tr	03.83	82-85	106	0	9
Hartlepool U.	L	01.86	85	11	0	1
Stockport Co.	Tr	09.86	86	11	0	0
Blackpool	Sweden	12.87	87	11	0	1

LETHERAN Glanville
Neath, 1 May, 1956 Wu21-2/Wu23-1 (G)

League Club	Source	Date Signed	Seasons Played	Apps	Subs	Gls
Leeds U.	App	05.73	74	1	0	0
Scunthorpe U.	L	08.76	76	27	0	0
Chesterfield	Tr	12.77	77-79	63	0	0
Swansea C.	Tr	09.79	79	21	0	0

LE TISSIER Matthew Paul
Guernsey, 14 October, 1968 E Yth/E 'B'/E-8 (W/F)

League Club	Source	Date Signed	Seasons Played	Apps	Subs	Gls
Southampton	App	10.86	86-97	346	37	151

LEUTY Leon Harry
Shrewsbury, 23 October, 1920 Died 1955 EF Lge/E 'B' (CH)

League Club	Source	Date Signed	Seasons Played	Apps	Subs	Gls
Derby Co.	Notts Co. (Am)	05.44	46-49	131	-	1
Bradford P.A.	Tr	03.50	49-50	19	-	0
Notts Co.	Tr	09.50	50-55	188	-	3

LEVER Arthur Richard
Cardiff, 25 March, 1920 W-1 (FB)

League Club	Source	Date Signed	Seasons Played	Apps	Subs	Gls
Cardiff C.	Jnrs	08.43	46-50	156	-	9
Leicester C.	Tr	09.50	50-53	119	-	0
Newport Co.	Tr	07.54	54-56	72	-	0

LEVER Mark
Beverley, 29 March, 1970 (CD)

League Club	Source	Date Signed	Seasons Played	Apps	Subs	Gls
Grimsby T.	YT	07.88	87-97	293	9	8

LEVERTON Ronald (Tot)
Worksop, 8 May, 1926 (IF)

League Club	Source	Date Signed	Seasons Played	Apps	Subs	Gls
Nottingham F.	Jnrs	10.43	46-53	103	-	36
Notts Co.	Tr	10.53	53-55	45	-	5
Walsall	Tr	07.56	56	17	-	2

LEVY Anthony Samuel
Edmonton, 20 October, 1959 (M)

League Club	Source	Date Signed	Seasons Played	Apps	Subs	Gls
Plymouth Arg.	App	10.77	78	0	1	0
Torquay U.	Tr	07.79	79	8	5	1

LEVY Leonard
Stepney, 24 December, 1926 (G)

League Club	Source	Date Signed	Seasons Played	Apps	Subs	Gls
Aldershot	Guildford C.	10.50	50	2	-	0

LEWIN Derek James
Manchester, 18 May, 1930 E Amat (IF)

League Club	Source	Date Signed	Seasons Played	Apps	Subs	Gls
Oldham Ath. (Am)	St Annes Ath.	08.53	53-54	10	-	1
Accrington St. (Am)	Bishop Auckland	10.57	57	1	-	0

LEWIN Dennis Ronald
Edmonton, 21 June, 1920 Died 1985 (FB)

League Club	Source	Date Signed	Seasons Played	Apps	Subs	Gls
Bradford C.		09.43				
Fulham	Tr	06.46	46-48	41	-	0
Gillingham	Tr	06.50	50-54	191	-	1

LEWINGTON Raymond
Lambeth, 7 September, 1956 (M)

League Club	Source	Date Signed	Seasons Played	Apps	Subs	Gls
Chelsea	App	02.74	75-78	80	5	4
Wimbledon (L)	Vancouver (Can)	09.79	79	23	0	0
Fulham	Tr	03.80	79-84	172	2	20
Sheffield U.	Tr	07.85	85	36	0	0
Fulham	Tr	07.86	86-89	58	2	1

LEWIS Alan Trevor
Oxford, 19 August, 1954 E Yth (LB)

League Club	Source	Date Signed	Seasons Played	Apps	Subs	Gls
Derby Co.	App	05.72	72	2	0	0
Peterborough U.	Tr	03.74	73	10	0	1
Brighton & H.A.	Tr	01.75	74	3	0	0
Reading	Tr	07.77	77-81	147	4	5

LEWIS Allan
Pontypridd, 31 May, 1971 (D)

League Club	Source	Date Signed	Seasons Played	Apps	Subs	Gls
Cardiff C.	YT	07.89	89-91	27	23	0

LEWIS Benjamin
Chelmsford, 22 June, 1977 (CD)

League Club	Source	Date Signed	Seasons Played	Apps	Subs	Gls
Colchester U.	YT	03.96	95	1	1	0
Southend U.	Tr	08.97	97	14	0	1

LEWIS Bernard
Merthyr Tydfil, 12 March, 1945 Wu23-5 (OL)

League Club	Source	Date Signed	Seasons Played	Apps	Subs	Gls
Cardiff C.	Jnrs	04.64	63-67	87	1	7
Watford	Tr	12.67	67-69	41	10	9
Southend U.	Tr	09.70	70-71	55	3	6

LEWIS Brian
Woking, 26 January, 1943 (M)

League Club	Source	Date Signed	Seasons Played	Apps	Subs	Gls
Crystal Palace	Jnrs	04.60	60-62	32	-	4
Portsmouth	Tr	07.63	63-66	134	0	24
Coventry C.	Tr	01.67	66-67	33	2	2
Luton T.	Tr	07.68	68-69	45	5	22
Oxford U.	Tr	01.70	69-70	12	2	4
Colchester U.	Tr	12.70	70-71	48	0	17
Portsmouth	Tr	04.72	71-74	44	16	8

LEWIS Charles Reginald
Liverpool, 11 May, 1921 (OL)

League Club	Source	Date Signed	Seasons Played	Apps	Subs	Gls
Halifax T.	South Liverpool	10.47	47-48	24	-	4

LEWIS David Sandbrook
Cardigan, 12 February, 1936 (W)

League Club	Source	Date Signed	Seasons Played	Apps	Subs	Gls
Swansea C.		12.57	57-58	19	-	1
Torquay U.	Tr	07.60	60	16	-	2

LEWIS Dennis George
Rhondda, 21 April, 1925 Died 1996 (WH/IF)

League Club	Source	Date Signed	Seasons Played	Apps	Subs	Gls
Swansea C.		08.46				
Torquay U.	Tr	08.47	47-58	442	-	31

LEWIS Derek Ivor Edwin
Edmonton, 10 June, 1929 Died 1953 (IF)

League Club	Source	Date Signed	Seasons Played	Apps	Subs	Gls
Gillingham	Fulham (Am)	05.50	50-51	48	-	31
Preston N.E.	Tr	02.52	51-52	37	-	14

LEWIS Dudley Keith
Swansea, 17 November, 1962 W Sch/Wu21-9/W-1 (CD)

League Club	Source	Date Signed	Seasons Played	Apps	Subs	Gls
Swansea C.	App	11.79	80-88	228	2	2
Huddersfield T.	Tr	07.89	89-90	32	2	0
Halifax T.	L	10.91	91	11	0	0
Wrexham	Tr	03.92	91	8	1	0
Halifax T. (N/C)	Tr	08.92	92	10	3	0
Torquay U.	Tr	12.92	92	9	0	0

LEWIS Edward
Manchester, 3 January, 1935 (FB/F)

League Club	Source	Date Signed	Seasons Played	Apps	Subs	Gls
Manchester U.	Jnrs	01.52	52-55	20	-	9
Preston N.E.	Tr	12.55	55-56	12	-	2
West Ham U.	Tr	11.56	56-57	31	-	12
Leyton Orient	Tr	06.58	58-63	143	-	5

LEWIS Edward
West Bromwich, 21 June, 1926 (G)

League Club	Source	Date Signed	Seasons Played	Apps	Subs	Gls
West Bromwich A.	Jnrs	11.44				
Leyton Orient	Tr	03.46	46	5	-	0

LEWIS Frederick Arthur
Bradford-on-Avon, 27 July, 1923 (FB)

League Club	Source	Date Signed	Seasons Played	Apps	Subs	Gls
Chelsea	Aylesbury T.	03.46	46-52	23	-	0
Colchester U.	Tr	07.53	53-54	85	-	0

LEWIS Thomas **George**
Merthyr Tydfil, 20 October, 1913 Died 1981 (CF)

League Club	Source	Date Signed	Seasons Played	Apps	Subs	Gls
Watford	New Tredegar	05.34	36-38	25	-	11
Southampton	Tr	07.46	46-47	43	-	12
Brighton & H.A.	Tr	06.48	48	24	-	8

LEWIS Glyndwr
Abertillery, 3 July, 1921 Died 1992 (W)

League Club	Source	Date Signed	Seasons Played	Apps	Subs	Gls
Crystal Palace		05.42	46-47	60	-	4
Bristol C.	Tr	07.48	48	18	-	0

LEWIS Gwynfor
Bangor, 22 April, 1931 Died 1995 W Yth (CF)

League Club	Source	Date Signed	Seasons Played	Apps	Subs	Gls
Everton	Jnrs	05.48	51-55	10	-	6
Rochdale	Tr	06.56	56	27	-	11
Chesterfield	Tr	02.57	56-60	123	-	58

LEWIS Idris
Tonypandy, 26 August, 1915 Died 1996 (OR)

League Club	Source	Date Signed	Seasons Played	Apps	Subs	Gls
Swansea C.		05.35	35-37	66	-	2
Sheffield Wed.	Tr	08.38	38	18	-	7
Swansea C.	Tr	03.39	38	12	-	2
Bristol Rov.	Tr	07.46	46	13	-	2
Newport Co.	Tr	10.46	46-47	27	-	4

LEWIS James Leonard
Hackney, 26 June, 1927 E Amat (CF)

League Club	Source	Date Signed	Seasons Played	Apps	Subs	Gls
Leyton Orient (Am)	Walthamstow Ave.	11.50	50	4	-	0
Chelsea (Am)	Walthamstow Ave.	09.52	52-57	90	-	38

LEWIS John
Tredegar, 15 October, 1955 Wu21-1 (M)

League Club	Source	Date Signed	Seasons Played	Apps	Subs	Gls
Cardiff C.	Pontllanfraith	08.78	78-83	135	5	9
Newport Co.	Tr	09.83	83-87	153	0	8
Swansea C.	Tr	10.87	87	25	0	0

LEWIS John (Jack)
Tamworth, 1 May, 1920 Died 1988 (G)

League Club	Source	Date Signed	Seasons Played	Apps	Subs	Gls
Walsall	Boldmere St Michael	12.45	46-52	271	-	0

LEWIS John (Jack)
Walsall, 26 August, 1919 (WH)

League Club	Source	Date Signed	Seasons Played	Apps	Subs	Gls
Crystal Palace	West Bromwich A. (Am)	07.38	38-49	124	-	5
Bournemouth	Tr	11.49	49-50	25	-	1
Reading	Tr	07.51	51-52	74	-	17

LEWIS John
Walsall, 6 October, 1923 (WH)

League Club	Source	Date Signed	Seasons Played	Apps	Subs	Gls
West Bromwich A.	Jnrs	10.45				
Mansfield T.	Tr	08.48	48-52	163	-	11

LEWIS John George
Hackney, 9 May, 1954 E Yth (M)

League Club	Source	Date Signed	Seasons Played	Apps	Subs	Gls
Leyton Orient	Tottenham H. (Am)	07.72	72	0	2	0

LEWIS Frederick **John (Jack)**
Long Eaton, 22 March, 1948 Wu23-1 (F)

League Club	Source	Date Signed	Seasons Played	Apps	Subs	Gls
Lincoln C.	Long Eaton U.	03.67	66-69	47	15	9
Grimsby T.	Tr	01.70	69-76	231	27	74
Blackburn Rov.	Tr	08.77	77	24	4	6
Doncaster Rov.	Tr	08.78	78-79	48	16	10

LEWIS Karl **Junior**
Wembley, 9 October, 1973 (W)

League Club	Source	Date Signed	Seasons Played	Apps	Subs	Gls
Fulham	YT	07.92	92	4	2	0

LEWIS Kenneth
Cardiff, 7 November, 1924 (FB)

League Club	Source	Date Signed	Seasons Played	Apps	Subs	Gls
Torquay U.		01.50	50-52	27	-	0

LEWIS Kenneth
Bangor, 12 October, 1929 Died 1990 (IF)

League Club	Source	Date Signed	Seasons Played	Apps	Subs	Gls
Walsall	Bangor C.	03.54	53-54	19	-	1
Scunthorpe U.	Worcester C.	08.56	56	1	-	0

LEWIS Kevin
Ellesmere Port, 19 September, 1940 E Yth (W)

League Club	Source	Date Signed	Seasons Played	Apps	Subs	Gls
Sheffield U.	Jnrs	10.57	57-59	62	-	23
Liverpool	Tr	06.60	60-62	71	-	39
Huddersfield T.	Tr	08.63	63-64	45	-	13

LEWIS Kevin
Hull, 17 October, 1970 (D)

League Club	Source	Date Signed	Seasons Played	Apps	Subs	Gls
Stoke C. (YT)	YT	07.87	87	0	1	0

LEWIS Kevin William
Hull, 25 September, 1952 E Sch (FB)

League Club	Source	Date Signed	Seasons Played	Apps	Subs	Gls
Manchester U.	App	09.69				
Stoke C.	Tr	07.72	72-75	15	0	0
Crewe Alex.	Tr	06.79	79-81	117	5	2

LEWIS Michael
Birmingham, 15 February, 1965 E Yth (M)

League Club	Source	Date Signed	Seasons Played	Apps	Subs	Gls
West Bromwich A.	App	02.82	81-84	22	2	0
Derby Co.	Tr	11.84	84-87	37	6	1
Oxford U.	Tr	08.88	88-95	276	24	7

LEWIS Morgan Rees
Bournemouth, 8 September, 1965 (M)

League Club	Source	Date Signed	Seasons Played	Apps	Subs	Gls
Bournemouth	Jnrs	07.84	83-86	11	1	0

LEWIS Neil Anthony
Wolverhampton, 28 June, 1974 (LB/M)

League Club	Source	Date Signed	Seasons Played	Apps	Subs	Gls
Leicester C.	YT	07.92	92-96	53	14	1
Peterborough U.	Tr	06.97	97	31	3	0

LEWIS Norman
Shifnal, 28 May, 1927 (LB)

League Club	Source	Date Signed	Seasons Played	Apps	Subs	Gls
Shrewsbury T.	Oakengates T.	08.50	50-52	62	-	0
Newport Co.	Gravesend & Nft.	06.54	54	15	-	0

LEWIS Paul Samuel
Ystrad, 27 September, 1956 W Yth (G)

League Club	Source	Date Signed	Seasons Played	Apps	Subs	Gls
Bristol Rov.	App	10.74	75	1	0	0

LEWIS Reginald
Bilston, 7 March, 1920 E 'B' (CF)

League Club	Source	Date Signed	Seasons Played	Apps	Subs	Gls
Arsenal	Jnrs	03.37	37-51	154	-	103

LEWIS Roland
Sandbach, 21 September, 1925 (F)

League Club	Source	Date Signed	Seasons Played	Apps	Subs	Gls
Port Vale	Congleton T.	03.50	50-53	7	-	0

LEWIS Ronald
Belfast, 10 February, 1932 (IF)

League Club	Source	Date Signed	Seasons Played	Apps	Subs	Gls
Burnley	Glentoran	06.49				
Barrow	Tr	05.54	54	5	-	1

LEWIS Russell
Blaengwynfi, 15 September, 1956 (CD)

League Club	Source	Date Signed	Seasons Played	Apps	Subs	Gls
Swindon T.	Bridgend T.	10.76	76-82	175	6	7
Northampton T.	Tr	08.83	83-85	131	1	6

LEWIS Terence John
Newport, 22 October, 1950 W Sch (WH)

League Club	Source	Date Signed	Seasons Played	Apps	Subs	Gls
Cardiff C.	App	10.68	68-69	2	0	0

LEWIS Trevor
Blackwood (Mon), 6 January, 1921 (W)

League Club	Source	Date Signed	Seasons Played	Apps	Subs	Gls
Coventry C.	Redditch U.	02.48	47-52	11	-	0
Gillingham	Tr	02.53	52-54	26	-	4

League Club	Source	Date Signed	Seasons Played	Apps	Subs	Gls
LEWIS William						
Cardiff, 4 July, 1923 (OR)						
Cardiff C.	Jnrs	07.41	46-47	9	-	0
Newport Co.	Tr	10.47	47-49	49	-	11
LEWIS William Albert						
Silvertown, 23 November, 1921 E Sch (FB)						
Blackpool	West Ham U. (Am)	07.45	46-49	30	-	0
Norwich C.	Tr	11.49	49-55	232	-	1
LEWORTHY David John						
Portsmouth, 22 October, 1962 (F)						
Portsmouth	App	09.80	81	0	1	0
Tottenham H.	Fareham T.	08.84	84-85	8	3	3
Oxford U.	Tr	12.85	85-88	25	12	8
Shrewsbury T.	L	10.87	87	6	0	3
Reading	Tr	07.89	89-91	23	21	7
LEY Oliver Albert **George**						
Exminster, 7 April, 1946 (LB)						
Exeter C.	Hitchin T.	09.63	63-66	93	0	7
Portsmouth	Tr	05.67	66-72	183	1	10
Brighton & H.A.	Tr	09.72	72-73	47	0	0
Gillingham	Tr	08.74	74-75	87	0	2
LEYDEN Daron Spencer						
Warley, 20 February, 1970 (D)						
Torquay U.	YT	07.88	88	7	2	0
LEYFIELD John George						
Chester, 5 August, 1923 (WH)						
Wrexham	Chester C. (Am)	07.46	46-49	34	-	1
Southport	Tr	08.50	50	26	-	0
LEYLAND Harry Kenneth						
Liverpool, 12 May, 1930 (G)						
Everton	Jnrs	08.50	51-55	36	-	0
Blackburn Rov.	Tr	08.56	56-60	166	-	0
Tranmere Rov.	Tr	03.61	60-65	180	0	0
LIBURD Richard John						
Nottingham, 26 September, 1973 (FB)						
Middlesbrough	Eastwood T.	03.93	93	41	0	1
Bradford C.	Tr	07.94	94-96	75	3	3
Carlisle U.	Tr	02.98	97	9	0	0
LIDDELL Andrew Mark						
Leeds, 28 June, 1973 Su21-11 (F)						
Barnsley	YT	06.91	91-97	139	51	34
LIDDELL Gary						
Stirling, 27 August, 1954 (F)						
Leeds U.	App	09.71	72-74	2	1	0
Grimsby T.	Tr	03.77	76-80	90	15	22
Doncaster Rov.	Hearts	03.82	81-82	25	12	4
LIDDELL John Cairney						
Stirling, 13 December, 1933 (CF)						
Oldham Ath.	St Johnstone	09.60	60-61	23	-	10
LIDDELL John Gilbert Hay						
Edinburgh, 17 April, 1915 Died 1986 (IL)						
Leyton Orient		03.44				
Bolton W.	Tr	09.46				
Brighton & H.A.	Tr	03.47	46	4	-	1
LIDDELL William Beveridge						
Dunfermline, 10 January, 1922 S-28 (F)						
Liverpool	Lochgelly Viollet	04.39	46-60	495	-	216
LIDDLE Bryan						
Durham, 23 June, 1961 (LB)						
Hartlepool U.	Brandon U.	08.84	84	12	1	0
LIDDLE Craig George						
Chester-le-Street, 21 October, 1971 (M)						
Aston Villa	YT	07.90				
Middlesbrough	Blyth Spartans	07.94	94-97	20	5	0
Darlington	L	02.98	97	15	0	0
LIDDLE Daniel Hamilton Sneddon						
Bo'ness, 19 February, 1912 Died 1982 S-3 (IF)						
Leicester C.	East Fife	05.32	32-38	255	-	64
Mansfield T.	Tr	07.46	46	1	-	0
LIDDLE David						
Malta, 21 May, 1957 (M/CD)						
Northampton T.	App	05.75	77-78	28	3	3
LIDDLE Gavin						
Houghton-le-Spring, 9 May, 1963 (FB)						
Darlington	Hartlepool U. (App)	08.81	81-82	33	0	4
LIDDLE Kenneth						
Gateshead, 6 October, 1928 (F)						
Sunderland		12.49				
Darlington	Tr	06.50	50	1	-	0
LIDDLE Thomas Blenkarn						
Middleton, 22 April, 1921 Died 1994 (D)						
Bournemouth		02.47	47	1	-	0
LIEVESLEY Dennis						
Chesterfield, 19 September, 1919 Died 1997 (CH)						
Aldershot		08.46	46-48	8	-	0
LIGGITT Norman						
Thornaby, 21 July, 1941 (CH)						
Middlesbrough	Jnrs	08.59				
Southend U.	Tr	07.62	62	1	-	0
LIGHT Daniel						
Chiswick, 10 July, 1948 (W)						
Crystal Palace	App	12.65	66-67	18	1	5
Colchester U.	Tr	08.68	68-69	65	2	14
LIGHT James Power						
Oxford, 13 January, 1954 (FB)						
Oxford U.	App	01.72	72-75	64	0	1
LIGHTBOURNE Kyle Lavince						
Bermuda, 29 September, 1968 Bermudan Int (CF)						
Scarborough		12.92	92	11	8	3
Walsall	Tr	09.93	93-96	158	7	65
Coventry C.	Tr	07.97	97	1	6	0
Fulham	L	01.98	97	4	0	2
Stoke City	Tr	02.98	97	9	4	2
LIGHTBOWN Trevor						
Blackburn, 21 November, 1939 (CF)						
Accrington St. (Am)	Burnley (Am)	08.59	59	8	-	0
Bradford P.A. (Am)	Tr	08.60	60	2	-	0
LIGHTENING Arthur Douglas						
South Africa, 1 August, 1936 (G)						
Nottingham F.	Queens Park (SA)	12.56	57-58	6	-	0
Coventry C.	Tr	11.58	58-62	150	-	0
Middlesbrough	Tr	08.62	62	15	-	0
LIGHTFOOT Christopher Ian						
Warrington, 1 April, 1970 (M/CD)						
Chester C.	YT	07.88	87-94	263	14	31
Wigan Ath.	Tr	07.95	95	11	3	1
Crewe Alex.	Tr	03.96	95-97	28	16	2
LIGHTLY Brian Sydney						
Portsmouth, 12 May, 1936 (WH)						
Exeter C.	Portsmouth (Am)	06.57	57	4	-	0
LIGHTOWLER Gerard						
Bradford, 5 September, 1940 (FB)						
Bradford P.A.	St Bede's	12.58	58-67	206	2	1
Bradford C.	Los Angeles (USA)	10.68	68	11	0	0
LILEY Henry John Gerald						
Trowbridge, 19 August, 1918 (G)						
Bristol Rov.	Dockland Settlement	10.46	46-49	27	-	0
LILL David Arthur						
Aldbrough, 17 February, 1947 (M)						
Hull C.	Jnrs	03.65	66-69	16	2	2
Rotherham U.	Tr	10.69	69-70	33	6	5
Cambridge U.	Tr	07.71	71-75	166	6	22
LILL James Alfred						
Barnsley, 4 June, 1933 (OL)						
Mansfield T.	Wentworth	03.54	53-55	3	-	0
LILL Michael James						
Barking, 3 August, 1936 E Yth (OL)						
Wolverhampton W.	Storey Ath.	06.54	57-59	30	-	15
Everton	Tr	02.60	59-61	31	-	11
Plymouth Arg.	Tr	06.62	62	21	-	7
Portsmouth	Tr	03.63	62-64	39	-	5
LILLEY Derek Symon						
Paisley, 9 February, 1974 S Yth (F)						
Leeds U.	Morton	03.97	96-97	4	15	1

LILLIS Jason Warren
Chatham, 1 October, 1969 (F)

League Club	Source	Date Signed	Seasons Played	Apps	Subs	Gls
Gillingham	YT	10.87	87-88	15	14	3
Maidstone U.	Jaro (Fin)	07.89	89-91	57	18	18
Carlisle U.	L	02.91	90	4	0	1
Walsall	Sittingbourne	10.93	93	14	10	6
Cambridge U. (N/C)	Tr	09.94	94	14	5	4

LILLIS Mark Anthony
Manchester, 17 January, 1960 (F/M)

League Club	Source	Date Signed	Seasons Played	Apps	Subs	Gls
Huddersfield T.	Manchester C. (Jnr)	07.78	78-84	199	7	56
Manchester C.	Tr	06.85	85	39	0	11
Derby Co.	Tr	08.86	86-87	6	9	1
Aston Villa	Tr	09.87	87-88	30	1	4
Scunthorpe U.	Tr	09.89	89-90	62	6	24
Stockport Co.	Tr	09.91	91	9	2	2

LILWALL Stephen
Birmingham, 15 February, 1970 (LB)

League Club	Source	Date Signed	Seasons Played	Apps	Subs	Gls
West Bromwich A.	Kidderminster H.	06.92	92-94	71	2	0

LILYGREEN Christopher Laurence
Newport, 9 June, 1965 (F)

League Club	Source	Date Signed	Seasons Played	Apps	Subs	Gls
Newport Co.	Jnrs	08.83	83-84	18	13	4

LIM Harvey Choun
Halesworth, 30 August, 1967 (G)

League Club	Source	Date Signed	Seasons Played	Apps	Subs	Gls
Norwich C.	YT	07.85				
Gillingham	Ornskoldsvik (Swe)	11.89	89-92	90	0	0

LIMBER Nicholas
Doncaster, 23 January, 1974 (LB)

League Club	Source	Date Signed	Seasons Played	Apps	Subs	Gls
Doncaster Rov.	YT	01.92	90-91	13	0	1
Manchester C.	Tr	01.92				
Peterborough U.	L	10.92	92	2	0	0
Doncaster Rov.	Tr	03.94	93	3	1	0

LIMBERT Marc
Hawarden, 3 October, 1973 (FB)

League Club	Source	Date Signed	Seasons Played	Apps	Subs	Gls
Chester C.	YT	07.92	92	12	2	0

LIMPAR Anders Erik
Sweden, 24 August, 1965 Swedish Int (LW)

League Club	Source	Date Signed	Seasons Played	Apps	Subs	Gls
Arsenal	Cremonese (It)	07.90	90-93	76	20	17
Everton	Tr	03.94	93-96	51	15	5
Birmingham C.	Tr	01.97	96	3	1	0

LINACRE John Edward
Middlesbrough, 13 December, 1955 (M)

League Club	Source	Date Signed	Seasons Played	Apps	Subs	Gls
Hartlepool U.	Whitby T.	07.77	77-81	192	4	12
Hartlepool U.	Hamrun (Malta)	12.83	83	15	0	0

LINACRE Philip
Middlesbrough, 17 May, 1962 (F)

League Club	Source	Date Signed	Seasons Played	Apps	Subs	Gls
Hartlepool U.	Coventry C. (App)	08.80	80-82	59	4	10
Hartlepool U.	Whitby T.	01.84	83	19	0	7
Darlington	Newcastle Blue Star	03.90	90	6	2	3

LINACRE William
Chesterfield, 10 August, 1924 (F)

League Club	Source	Date Signed	Seasons Played	Apps	Subs	Gls
Chesterfield	Jnrs	02.44	46-47	22	-	3
Manchester C.	Tr	10.47	47-49	75	-	6
Middlesbrough	Tr	09.49	49-51	31	-	2
Hartlepool U.	Goole T.	08.53	53-55	89	-	10
Mansfield T.	Tr	10.55	55	13	-	0

LINAKER John Edward
Southport, 14 January, 1927 (OR)

League Club	Source	Date Signed	Seasons Played	Apps	Subs	Gls
Manchester C.	Everton (Am)	08.45				
Southport	Tr	11.46	46	15	-	1
Nottingham F.	Tr	09.47	48-49	15	-	2
York C.	Tr	06.50	50-51	59	-	16
Hull C.	Tr	10.51	51-52	26	-	3
York C.	Tr	05.53	53-55	39	-	4
Crewe Alex.	Scarborough	07.57	57	34	-	3

LINDLEY Edwin
Epworth (Lincs), 22 April, 1931 Died 1951 (IF)

League Club	Source	Date Signed	Seasons Played	Apps	Subs	Gls
Nottingham F.	Scunthorpe U.	10.49	49	1	-	0
Scunthorpe U.	Tr	08.51				

LINDLEY William **Maurice**
Keighley, 5 December, 1915 Died 1994 (CH)

League Club	Source	Date Signed	Seasons Played	Apps	Subs	Gls
Everton	Keighley T.	03.36	47-51	51	-	0

LINDORES William Robert Hope
Newcastleton, 3 May, 1933 S Sch (FB)

League Club	Source	Date Signed	Seasons Played	Apps	Subs	Gls
Barrow	Hearts Liddleston	07.59	59	5	-	0

LINDSAY Alec
Bury, 27 February, 1948 E Yth/E-4 (LB)

League Club	Source	Date Signed	Seasons Played	Apps	Subs	Gls
Bury	App	03.65	64-68	126	0	14
Liverpool	Tr	03.69	69-76	168	2	12
Stoke C.	Tr	08.77	77	20	0	3

LINDSAY David
Dumbarton, 23 September, 1919 Died 1993 (CH)

League Club	Source	Date Signed	Seasons Played	Apps	Subs	Gls
Luton T.	St Mirren	05.48	48	7	-	0
Barnsley	Tr	11.48	48-51	78	-	3

LINDSAY David
Cambuslang, 29 June, 1922 (FB)

League Club	Source	Date Signed	Seasons Played	Apps	Subs	Gls
Sunderland	Blantyre Vic.	08.46	46	1	-	0
Southend U.	Tr	05.48	48-50	52	-	1

LINDSAY David James
Romford, 17 May, 1966 (LB)

League Club	Source	Date Signed	Seasons Played	Apps	Subs	Gls
Crystal Palace	App	05.84	83-85	18	3	0

LINDSAY Hugh Murray
Ickenham, 23 August, 1938 E Amat (IF)

League Club	Source	Date Signed	Seasons Played	Apps	Subs	Gls
Southampton (Am)	Kingstonian	07.60	60	2	-	0

LINDSAY Ian
Canonble, 10 February, 1944 (G)

League Club	Source	Date Signed	Seasons Played	Apps	Subs	Gls
Workington	Hearts Liddleston	11.64	64-65	10	0	0

LINDSAY James Young
Hamilton, 12 July, 1949 (M)

League Club	Source	Date Signed	Seasons Played	Apps	Subs	Gls
West Ham U.	Jnrs	08.66	68-70	36	3	2
Watford	Tr	08.71	71-73	64	1	12
Colchester U.	Tr	07.74	74	45	0	6
Hereford U.	Tr	08.75	75-76	79	0	6
Shrewsbury T.	Tr	08.77	77-80	80	6	0

LINDSAY John McArthur
Cambuslang, 11 December, 1921 (CF)

League Club	Source	Date Signed	Seasons Played	Apps	Subs	Gls
Sheffield Wed.	Morton	03.45	46	1	-	1
Bury	Tr	10.46	46	11	-	7
Carlisle U.	Tr	08.47	47-50	103	-	46
Southport	Tr	03.51	50-51	50	-	20
Carlisle U.	Wigan Ath.	01.55	54	13	-	2

LINDSAY John Smith
Auchinleck, 8 August, 1924 (FB)

League Club	Source	Date Signed	Seasons Played	Apps	Subs	Gls
Everton	Glasgow Rangers	03.51	50-53	105	-	2
Bury	Worcester C.	05.56	56	7	-	0

LINDSAY Laurence
Dumbarton, 7 October, 1921 (CH)

League Club	Source	Date Signed	Seasons Played	Apps	Subs	Gls
Crewe Alex.	Hibernian	01.48	47-48	40	-	0

LINDSAY Malcolm
Ashington, 26 September, 1940 (CF)

League Club	Source	Date Signed	Seasons Played	Apps	Subs	Gls
Cambridge U.	Kings Lynn	02.70	70	6	0	0

LINDSAY Mark Edward
Lambeth, 6 March, 1955 (M)

League Club	Source	Date Signed	Seasons Played	Apps	Subs	Gls
Crystal Palace	App	03.73	73-74	27	3	0

LINDSEY Barry
Scunthorpe, 17 April, 1944 (WH)

League Club	Source	Date Signed	Seasons Played	Apps	Subs	Gls
Scunthorpe U.	App	05.61	61-70	210	7	13

LINDSEY Keith
Scunthorpe, 25 November, 1946 (RB)

League Club	Source	Date Signed	Seasons Played	Apps	Subs	Gls
Scunthorpe U.	App	12.64	65	15	0	0
Doncaster Rov.	Tr	07.66	66	16	2	0
Southend U.	Cambridge U.	01.69	68-71	89	2	4
Port Vale	Tr	12.71	71-72	24	0	0
Gillingham	Tr	12.72	72-74	73	0	5

LINDSEY Scott
Walsall, 4 May, 1972 (M)

League Club	Source	Date Signed	Seasons Played	Apps	Subs	Gls
Gillingham	Bridlington T.	07.94	94	11	1	0

LINEKER Gary Winston
Leicester, 30 November, 1960 E'B'/E-80 (F)

League Club	Source	Date Signed	Seasons Played	Apps	Subs	Gls
Leicester C.	App	11.89	78-84	187	7	95
Everton	Tr	07.85	85	41	0	30
Tottenham H.	Barcelona (Sp)	07.89	89-91	105	0	67

LINES Barry
Northampton, 16 May, 1942 (OL)

League Club	Source	Date Signed	Seasons Played	Apps	Subs	Gls
Northampton T.	Bletchley T.	09.60	60-69	259	7	48

LINEY Patrick
Paisley, 14 July, 1936 (G)

League Club	Source	Date Signed	Seasons Played	Apps	Subs	Gls
Bradford P.A.	St Mirren	06.66	66	11	0	0
Bradford C.	Tr	09.67	67-71	147	0	0

LINFORD John Russell
Norwich, 6 December, 1957 (F)

League Club	Source	Date Signed	Seasons Played	Apps	Subs	Gls
Ipswich T.	Gorleston	08.81				
Colchester U.	L	01.83	82	7	0	0
Southend U.	L	03.83	82	6	0	3
Birmingham C.	L	11.84	84	1	1	0

LING Martin
West Ham, 15 July, 1966 (M)

League Club	Source	Date Signed	Seasons Played	Apps	Subs	Gls
Exeter C.	App	01.84	82-85	110	8	14
Swindon T.	Tr	07.86	86	2	0	0
Southend U.	Tr	10.86	86-90	126	12	30
Mansfield T.	L	01.91	90	3	0	0
Swindon T.	Tr	03.91	90-95	132	18	10
Leyton Orient	Tr	07.96	96-97	85	5	3

LINGER Paul Hayden
Stepney, 20 December, 1974 (M)

League Club	Source	Date Signed	Seasons Played	Apps	Subs	Gls
Charlton Ath.	YT	07.93	92-95	5	18	1
Leyton Orient	Tr	09.97	97	1	2	0
Brighton & H.A.	Tr	12.97	97	17	2	0

LINIGHAN Andrew
Hartlepool, 18 June, 1962 E 'B' (CD)

League Club	Source	Date Signed	Seasons Played	Apps	Subs	Gls
Hartlepool U.	Henry Smiths B.C.	09.80	80-83	110	0	4
Leeds U.	Tr	05.84	84-85	66	0	3
Oldham Ath.	Tr	01.86	85-87	87	0	6
Norwich C.	Tr	03.88	87-89	86	0	8
Arsenal	Tr	06.90	90-96	101	17	5
Crystal Palace	Tr	01.97	96-97	45	0	2

LINIGHAN Brian
Hartlepool, 2 November, 1973 (RB)

League Club	Source	Date Signed	Seasons Played	Apps	Subs	Gls
Sheffield Wed.	YT	06.92	93	1	0	0
Bury	Tr	07.97				

LINIGHAN William Brian
Hartlepool, 17 May, 1936 (HB)

League Club	Source	Date Signed	Seasons Played	Apps	Subs	Gls
Lincoln C.		12.53				
Darlington	L	10.58	58	1	-	1

LINIGHAN David
Hartlepool, 9 January, 1965 EF Lge (CD)

League Club	Source	Date Signed	Seasons Played	Apps	Subs	Gls
Hartlepool U.	Jnrs	03.82	81-85	84	7	5
Derby Co.	Tr	08.86				
Shrewsbury T.	Tr	12.86	86-87	65	0	1
Ipswich T.	Tr	06.88	88-95	275	2	12
Blackpool	Tr	11.95	95-97	97	3	5

LINK Thomas Henry
Halifax, 15 December, 1918 Died 1990 (OR)

League Club	Source	Date Signed	Seasons Played	Apps	Subs	Gls
Bradford C.		05.48	47-48	6	-	0

LINNECOR Albert (Bert) Roy
Birmingham, 30 November, 1933 (IF/WH)

League Club	Source	Date Signed	Seasons Played	Apps	Subs	Gls
Birmingham C.	Jnrs	05.52	55-56	17	-	0
Lincoln C.	Tr	04.57	56-63	264	-	52

LINNELL John Lovell Leonard
Northampton, 2 January, 1944 (WH)

League Club	Source	Date Signed	Seasons Played	Apps	Subs	Gls
Northampton T.	Jnrs	09.63				
Peterborough U.	Tr	07.67	67	24	2	1

LINNEY David William
Birmingham, 5 September, 1961 (RB)

League Club	Source	Date Signed	Seasons Played	Apps	Subs	Gls
Birmingham C.	App	09.79	81	0	1	0
Oxford U.	Tr	08.82	82	26	0	0

LINSTREM Kenneth Richard
Salford, 12 October, 1928 Died 1996 (WH)

League Club	Source	Date Signed	Seasons Played	Apps	Subs	Gls
Crewe Alex.	Stockport Co. (Am)	06.50	50-51	13	-	1
Bournemouth	Tr	08.52				

LINTERN Melvin
Seaton Delaval, 17 May, 1950 (IF)

League Club	Source	Date Signed	Seasons Played	Apps	Subs	Gls
Port Vale	Jnrs	03.68	66	0	1	0

LINTON Desmond Martin
Birmingham, 5 September, 1971 (RB/M)

League Club	Source	Date Signed	Seasons Played	Apps	Subs	Gls
Leicester C.	YT	01.90	89-91	6	5	0
Luton T.	Tr	10.91	91-96	65	18	1
Peterborough U.	Tr	03.97	96-97	33	5	0

LINTON Ivor
West Bromwich, 20 November, 1959 (M)

League Club	Source	Date Signed	Seasons Played	Apps	Subs	Gls
Aston Villa	App	09.77	76-81	16	11	0
Peterborough U.	Tr	08.82	82-83	24	3	3
Birmingham C.	Tr	12.83	83	3	1	0

LINTON James
Glasgow, 2 December, 1930 (G)

League Club	Source	Date Signed	Seasons Played	Apps	Subs	Gls
Notts Co.	Kirkintilloch Rob Roy	11.52	52-58	114	-	0
Watford	Tr	07.59	59-62	71	-	0

LINTON Malcolm Wilton
Southend, 13 February, 1952 (CD)

League Club	Source	Date Signed	Seasons Played	Apps	Subs	Gls
Leyton Orient	Southend U. (Am)	08.72	72-74	14	5	0

LINTON Thomas
Falkirk, 15 October, 1920 (FB)

League Club	Source	Date Signed	Seasons Played	Apps	Subs	Gls
Southend U.		05.45	46-48	67	-	0

LINWOOD Alexander Bryce
Glasgow, 13 March, 1920 SF Lge/S-1 (IF)

League Club	Source	Date Signed	Seasons Played	Apps	Subs	Gls
Middlesbrough	St Mirren	06.46	46	14	-	3

LIPTROTT David
Stockport, 26 February, 1965 (F)

League Club	Source	Date Signed	Seasons Played	Apps	Subs	Gls
Stockport Co. (N/C)	Jnrs	09.82	82	0	1	0

LISBIE Kevin Anthony
Hackney, 17 October, 1978 E Yth (F)

League Club	Source	Date Signed	Seasons Played	Apps	Subs	Gls
Charlton Ath.	YT	05.96	96-97	5	37	2

LISHMAN Douglas John
Birmingham, 14 September, 1923 Died 1994 E 'B'/EF Lge (IF)

League Club	Source	Date Signed	Seasons Played	Apps	Subs	Gls
Walsall	Paget R.	08.46	46-47	59	-	26
Arsenal	Tr	07.48	48-55	226	-	125
Nottingham F.	Tr	03.56	55-56	38	-	22

LISTER Alexander (Sandy) Duncan
Glasgow, 20 January, 1924 (IF)

League Club	Source	Date Signed	Seasons Played	Apps	Subs	Gls
Rochdale	Alloa Ath.	05.52	52	2	-	0

LISTER Eric
Willenhall, 13 August, 1933 (OL)

League Club	Source	Date Signed	Seasons Played	Apps	Subs	Gls
Notts Co.	Wolverhampton W. (Am)	09.51	54-56	8	-	0

LISTER Herbert (Bert) Francis
Manchester, 4 October, 1939 (CF)

League Club	Source	Date Signed	Seasons Played	Apps	Subs	Gls
Manchester C.	Jnrs	11.57	58	2	-	0
Oldham Ath.	Tr	10.60	60-64	135	-	81
Rochdale	Tr	01.65	64-66	56	0	16
Stockport Co.	Tr	01.67	66	16	0	11

LISTER Stephen Haley
Doncaster, 17 November, 1961 (M/CD)

League Club	Source	Date Signed	Seasons Played	Apps	Subs	Gls
Doncaster Rov.	App	05.79	78-84	228	8	30
Scunthorpe U.	Tr	07.85	85-91	176	6	30
York C.	L	03.91	90	4	0	1

LITCHFIELD Peter
Manchester, 27 July, 1956 (G)

League Club	Source	Date Signed	Seasons Played	Apps	Subs	Gls
Preston N.E.	Droylsden	01.79	80-84	107	0	0
Bradford C.	Tr	07.85	85-88	88	0	0
Oldham Ath.	L	10.88	88	3	0	0
Scunthorpe U.	Tr	07.89	89-90	25	0	0

LITHGO Gordon
Hartlepool, 14 August, 1942 (OL)

League Club	Source	Date Signed	Seasons Played	Apps	Subs	Gls
Hartlepool U.	Jnrs	08.59	60-63	37	-	8

LITT Stephen Eric
Carlisle, 21 May, 1954 (CD)

League Club	Source	Date Signed	Seasons Played	Apps	Subs	Gls
Luton T.	Blackpool (App)	06.72	73-75	15	0	0
Northampton T.	Minnesota (USA)	09.77	77	19	1	0

LITTLE Alan
Horden, 5 February, 1955 (M)

League Club	Source	Date Signed	Seasons Played	Apps	Subs	Gls
Aston Villa	App	01.73	74	2	1	0
Southend U.	Tr	12.74	74-76	102	1	12
Barnsley	Tr	08.77	77-79	91	0	14
Doncaster Rov.	Tr	12.79	79-82	84	1	11
Torquay U.	Tr	10.82	82-83	51	0	4
Halifax T.	Tr	11.83	83-84	68	0	6
Hartlepool U.	Tr	07.85	85	12	0	1

LITTLE Barry Brian
Greenwich, 25 August, 1964 Died 1994 E Yth (M)

League Club	Source	Date Signed	Seasons Played	Apps	Subs	Gls
Charlton Ath.	App	07.82	82	2	0	1

LITTLE Brian
Horden, 25 November, 1953 E-1 (F)

League Club	Source	Date Signed	Seasons Played	Apps	Subs	Gls
Aston Villa	App	03.71	71-79	242	5	60

LITTLE Colin Campbell
Wythenshawe, 4 November, 1972 (F)

League Club	Source	Date Signed	Seasons Played	Apps	Subs	Gls
Crewe Alex.	Hyde U.	02.96	95-97	39	30	14

LITTLE George
Newcastle, 30 June, 1915 (W)

League Club	Source	Date Signed	Seasons Played	Apps	Subs	Gls
Doncaster Rov.	Throckley Welfare	08.36	36-47	50	-	11
York C.	Tr	12.47	47	15	-	2

LITTLE Glen Matthew
Wimbledon, 15 October, 1975 (M)

League Club	Source	Date Signed	Seasons Played	Apps	Subs	Gls
Crystal Palace	YT	07.94				
Burnley	Glentoran	11.96	96-97	24	9	4

LITTLE John (Jackie)
Gateshead, 17 May, 1912 (W)

League Club	Source	Date Signed	Seasons Played	Apps	Subs	Gls
Ipswich T.	Needham Market	11.37	38-49	146	-	20

LITTLE Ronald
Carlisle, 24 January, 1934 (OR)

League Club	Source	Date Signed	Seasons Played	Apps	Subs	Gls
Carlisle U. (Am)	Sowerby Hearts	05.55	55	5	-	0

LITTLE Roy
Manchester, 1 June, 1931 (FB)

League Club	Source	Date Signed	Seasons Played	Apps	Subs	Gls
Manchester C.	Greenwood Vic.	08.49	52-58	168	-	2
Brighton & H.A.	Tr	10.58	58-60	83	-	0
Crystal Palace	Tr	05.61	61-62	38	-	1

LITTLEJOHN Adrian Sylvester
Wolverhampton, 26 September, 1970 E Yth (F)

League Club	Source	Date Signed	Seasons Played	Apps	Subs	Gls
Walsall	West Bromwich A. (YT)	05.89	89-90	26	18	1
Sheffield U.	Tr	08.91	91-94	44	25	12
Plymouth Arg.	Tr	09.95	95-97	100	10	29
Oldham Ath.	Tr	03.98	97	5	0	3

LITTLEJOHN Roy Derek
Bournemouth, 2 June, 1933 E Amat (CF)

League Club	Source	Date Signed	Seasons Played	Apps	Subs	Gls
Bournemouth (Am)	Jnrs	05.52	52-55	22	-	2

LITTLEJOHNS Colin
Liverpool, 8 September, 1968 (M)

League Club	Source	Date Signed	Seasons Played	Apps	Subs	Gls
Cambridge U. (N/C)	YT	10.85	85-86	10	2	0

LITTLER Joseph Eric
St Helens, 14 April, 1929 (CF)

League Club	Source	Date Signed	Seasons Played	Apps	Subs	Gls
Leicester C.	Stubshaw Cross	05.51	51-54	5	-	2
Lincoln C.	Tr	12.54	54	6	-	2
Wrexham	Tr	06.55	55	12	-	1
Crewe Alex.	Tr	12.55	55	10	-	2

LITTLER Thomas
Stockport, 6 March, 1936 (OL)

League Club	Source	Date Signed	Seasons Played	Apps	Subs	Gls
Stockport Co.		04.55	55	1	-	0

LIVERMORE Douglas Ernest
Prescot, 27 December, 1947 (M)

League Club	Source	Date Signed	Seasons Played	Apps	Subs	Gls
Liverpool	Jnrs	11.65	67-70	13	3	0
Norwich C.	Tr	11.70	70-74	113	1	4
Bournemouth	L	03.75	74	10	0	0
Cardiff C.	Tr	08.75	75-77	84	4	5
Chester C.	Tr	10.77	77-78	71	0	6

LIVERSIDGE Ronald
Huddersfield, 12 September, 1934 (CF)

League Club	Source	Date Signed	Seasons Played	Apps	Subs	Gls
Bradford C.	Ossett T.	10.56	56-58	48	-	27

LIVESEY Charles Edward
West Ham, 6 February, 1938 (CF)

League Club	Source	Date Signed	Seasons Played	Apps	Subs	Gls
Southampton	Custom House	03.56	58	25	-	14
Chelsea	Tr	05.59	59-60	39	-	17
Gillingham	Tr	08.61	61-62	47	-	17
Watford	Tr	10.62	62-63	64	-	26
Northampton T.	Tr	08.64	64-65	28	0	4
Brighton & H.A.	Tr	09.65	65-68	124	2	28

LIVESEY John (Jack)
Preston, 8 March, 1924 Died 1988 (IF)

League Club	Source	Date Signed	Seasons Played	Apps	Subs	Gls
Preston N.E.	Jnrs	04.44				
Bury	Tr	05.46	46	7	-	1
Doncaster Rov.	Tr	01.47	47	3	-	0
Rochdale	Tr	04.48	47-50	113	-	36
Southport	Tr	07.51	51	31	-	9

LIVETT Simon Robert
East Ham, 8 January, 1969 (M)

League Club	Source	Date Signed	Seasons Played	Apps	Subs	Gls
West Ham U.	App	01.87	90	1	0	0
Leyton Orient	Tr	08.92	92-93	16	8	0
Cambridge U.	Tr	10.93	93-94	12	0	0

LIVIE Gordon
Billingham, 10 June, 1932 (D)

League Club	Source	Date Signed	Seasons Played	Apps	Subs	Gls
Leicester C.	Jnrs	12.49				
Mansfield T.	Tr	07.52	52-53	21	-	0

LIVINGSTONE Archibald
Pencaitland, 15 November, 1915 Died 1961 (IF)

League Club	Source	Date Signed	Seasons Played	Apps	Subs	Gls
Newcastle U.	Ormiston Primrose	05.35	35-37	33	-	5
Bury	Tr	06.38	38	23	-	8
Everton	Tr	05.46	46	4	-	2
Southport	Tr	06.47	47	23	-	2

LIVINGSTONE Glen
Birmingham, 13 October, 1972 E Yth (G)

League Club	Source	Date Signed	Seasons Played	Apps	Subs	Gls
Aston Villa	YT	01.91				
Walsall (N/C)	York C. (N/C)	03.94	93	2	1	0

LIVINGSTONE Joseph
Middlesbrough, 18 June, 1942 (CF)

League Club	Source	Date Signed	Seasons Played	Apps	Subs	Gls
Middlesbrough	Jnrs	01.60	60-62	20	-	7
Carlisle U.	Tr	11.62	62-65	79	1	41
Hartlepool U.	Tr	05.66	65-66	15	0	5

LIVINGSTONE Stephen
Middlesbrough, 8 September, 1969 (F)

League Club	Source	Date Signed	Seasons Played	Apps	Subs	Gls
Coventry C.	YT	07.86	86-90	17	14	5
Blackburn Rov.	Tr	01.91	90-92	25	5	10
Chelsea	Tr	03.93	92-93	0	1	0
Port Vale	L	09.93	93	4	1	0
Grimsby T.	Tr	10.93	93-97	140	32	33

LIVINGSTONE Wilfred Egerton
Barrow, 22 October, 1919 (CF)

League Club	Source	Date Signed	Seasons Played	Apps	Subs	Gls
Barrow	Holker Street O.B.	09.47	47-48	4	-	0

LIVINGSTONE William
Coventry, 13 August, 1964 S Yth (F)

League Club	Source	Date Signed	Seasons Played	Apps	Subs	Gls
Wolverhampton W.	App	08.82	82-83	21	3	4
Derby Co.	Tr	07.84				

LIVINGSTONE William Rennison
Greenock, 8 February, 1929 (CH)

League Club	Source	Date Signed	Seasons Played	Apps	Subs	Gls
Reading	Ardeer Rec.	04.49	49-54	49	-	2
Chelsea	Tr	06.55	56-57	20	-	0
Brentford	Tr	07.59	59	19	-	0

LIVSEY Gordon William
Keighley, 24 January, 1947 (G)

League Club	Source	Date Signed	Seasons Played	Apps	Subs	Gls
Wrexham	Kettering T.	01.67	67-70	79	0	0
Chester C.	Tr	08.71	71	44	0	0
Hartlepool U.	Kettering T.	12.77	77	6	0	0

LLEWELLYN Andrew David
Bristol, 26 February, 1966 E Yth (FB)

League Club	Source	Date Signed	Seasons Played	Apps	Subs	Gls
Bristol C.	App	02.84	82-93	296	12	3
Exeter C.	L	03.94	93	15	0	0
Hereford U. (N/C)	Tr	10.94	94	3	1	0

LLEWELLYN Christopher Mark
Merthyr, 29 August, 1979 W Yth/Wu21-3/W 'B'/W-2 (F)

League Club	Source	Date Signed	Seasons Played	Apps	Subs	Gls
Norwich C.	YT	01.97	97	10	5	4

LLEWELLYN David John
Cardiff, 9 August, 1949 Wu23-1 (W)

League Club	Source	Date Signed	Seasons Played	Apps	Subs	Gls
West Ham U.	Jnrs	08.66	69-71	2	4	0
Peterborough U.	Tr	08.73	73-74	11	2	3
Mansfield T.	L	08.74	74	6	2	0

LLEWELLYN Herbert (Bert) Arthur
Golborne, 5 February, 1939 E Yth (CF)

League Club	Source	Date Signed	Seasons Played	Apps	Subs	Gls
Everton	Jnrs	05.56	56-57	11	-	2
Crewe Alex.	Tr	07.58	58-60	96	-	51
Port Vale	Tr	11.60	60-62	88	-	42
Northampton T.	Tr	02.63	62	1	-	0
Walsall	Tr	02.64	63-64	17	-	6

LLOYD Barry David
Uxbridge, 19 February, 1949 E Yth (M)

League Club	Source	Date Signed	Seasons Played	Apps	Subs	Gls
Chelsea	App	02.66	66-68	8	2	0
Fulham	Tr	12.68	68-75	249	8	29
Hereford U.	Tr	10.76	76	12	2	0
Brentford	Tr	06.77	77	26	5	4

LLOYD Brian William
St Asaph, 18 March, 1948 Wu23-2/W-3 (G)

League Club	Source	Date Signed	Seasons Played	Apps	Subs	Gls
Stockport Co.	Rhyl	03.67	67-68	32	0	0
Southend U.	Tr	09.69	69-70	46	0	0
Wrexham	Tr	08.71	71-77	266	0	0
Chester C.	Tr	09.77	77-79	94	0	0
Port Vale	L	02.81	80	16	0	0
Stockport Co.	Tr	08.81	81-82	91	0	1

LLOYD Clifford
Frodsham, 14 November, 1916 (LB)

League Club	Source	Date Signed	Seasons Played	Apps	Subs	Gls
Liverpool		11.37				
Fulham		12.43	46	2	-	0
Bristol Rov.	Margate	05.50				

LLOYD Robert **Clive**
Merthyr Tydfil, 4 September, 1945 (IF)

League Club	Source	Date Signed	Seasons Played	Apps	Subs	Gls
Norwich C.	App	09.62				
Cardiff C.	Tr	08.64	64	2	-	0

LLOYD David
Gateshead, 1 June, 1928 (CF)

League Club	Source	Date Signed	Seasons Played	Apps	Subs	Gls
Sheffield U.		09.49				
York C.	Tr	03.51	50	1	-	0

LLOYD Frank
Barnsley, 16 January, 1928 (LH)

League Club	Source	Date Signed	Seasons Played	Apps	Subs	Gls
Bradford C.		07.51	51-53	24	-	0

LLOYD Robert **Geoffrey**
Wrexham, 18 August, 1942 (CF)

League Club	Source	Date Signed	Seasons Played	Apps	Subs	Gls
Wrexham	Llangollen	10.66	66	13	1	5
Bradford P.A.	Tr	07.67	67	32	0	10

LLOYD Graham
Liverpool, 10 January, 1951 (G)

League Club	Source	Date Signed	Seasons Played	Apps	Subs	Gls
Liverpool	App	01.68				
Portsmouth	Motherwell	07.75	75-76	73	0	0

LLOYD Harold Demane
Flint, 12 March, 1920 Died 1984 (G)

League Club	Source	Date Signed	Seasons Played	Apps	Subs	Gls
Tranmere Rov.	Flint T.	10.45	45-56	188	-	0

LLOYD John David
Hitchin, 10 December, 1944 (LB)

League Club	Source	Date Signed	Seasons Played	Apps	Subs	Gls
Swindon T.	App	01.62				
Oxford U.	Tr	10.64	65-68	68	4	0
Aldershot	Tr	02.69	68-69	11	2	0

LLOYD John Walter
Rossett (Fife), 15 February, 1948 (OR)

League Club	Source	Date Signed	Seasons Played	Apps	Subs	Gls
Wrexham (Am)	Jnrs	08.65	65-66	2	0	0

LLOYD Joseph Millington
Shotton, 30 September, 1910 Died 1996 (WH)

League Club	Source	Date Signed	Seasons Played	Apps	Subs	Gls
Everton	Connah's Quay	02.31				
Swansea C.		08.32	32-38	212	-	0
Wrexham	Tr	07.46	46	20	-	0

LLOYD Kevin Gareth
Llaniloes, 26 September, 1970 (LB)

League Club	Source	Date Signed	Seasons Played	Apps	Subs	Gls
Hereford U.	Caersws	11.94	94-95	49	2	3
Cardiff C.	Tr	08.96	96-97	27	6	1

LLOYD Kevin John James
Wolverhampton, 12 June, 1958 (F)

League Club	Source	Date Signed	Seasons Played	Apps	Subs	Gls
Cardiff C.	Darlaston	05.79	79	0	1	0
Gillingham	Tr	07.80	80	0	1	0

LLOYD Laurence (Larry) Valentine
Bristol, 6 October, 1948 E Yth/Eu23-8/E-4 (CD)

League Club	Source	Date Signed	Seasons Played	Apps	Subs	Gls
Bristol Rov.	Jnrs	07.67	68	43	0	1
Liverpool	Tr	04.69	69-73	150	0	4
Coventry C.	Tr	08.74	74-76	50	0	5
Nottingham F.	Tr	10.76	76-80	148	0	6
Wigan Ath.	Tr	03.81	80-82	52	0	2

LLOYD Norman Philip
Neath, 8 March, 1930 (WH)

League Club	Source	Date Signed	Seasons Played	Apps	Subs	Gls
Cardiff C.		03.48				
Torquay U.	Tr	08.49	52-56	29	-	1

LLOYD Norman William McLean
Torrance, 6 September, 1949 (M)

League Club	Source	Date Signed	Seasons Played	Apps	Subs	Gls
Preston N.E.	Jnrs	09.66	68-70	18	2	6
Stockport Co.	L	01.71	70	10	0	0
Southport	Tr	07.71	71-73	93	10	13
Stockport Co.	Tr	07.74	74	36	2	2

LLOYD Peter John
Pattingham (Staffs), 26 April, 1933 (OL)

League Club	Source	Date Signed	Seasons Played	Apps	Subs	Gls
Walsall	Pattingham	03.51	53	5	-	0

LLOYD Philip Rowan
Hemsworth 26 December, 1964 (CD)

League Club	Source	Date Signed	Seasons Played	Apps	Subs	Gls
Middlesbrough	App	12.82				
Barnsley (N/C)	Tr	09.83				
Darlington	Tr	03.84	83-86	127	0	3
Torquay U.	Tr	08.87	87-91	169	1	7

LLOYD William **Stanley**
West Auckland, 1 October, 1924 E Sch (W)

League Club	Source	Date Signed	Seasons Played	Apps	Subs	Gls
Sunderland	Jnrs	12.41	46-47	24	-	5
Grimsby T.	Tr	08.48	48-52	148	-	23
Scunthorpe U.	Worksop T.	07.54	54	1	-	0

LLOYD William Frederick
Poplar, 10 July, 1934 (G)

League Club	Source	Date Signed	Seasons Played	Apps	Subs	Gls
Millwall	Bromley	08.56	56-57	74	-	0

LLOYD William Lorraine
Rhondda, 22 May, 1915 Died 1978 (D)

League Club	Source	Date Signed	Seasons Played	Apps	Subs	Gls
Swindon T.	Milford Haven	08.39	46-50	107	-	2

LOADWICK Derek
Middlesbrough, 4 October, 1956 (D/M)

League Club	Source	Date Signed	Seasons Played	Apps	Subs	Gls
Leeds U.	App	10.73				
Stockport Co.	Tr	07.76	76-78	84	0	0
Hartlepool U.	Tr	10.78	78-79	49	2	1

LOASBY Alan Arthur
Wellingborough, 19 March, 1937 (IF)

League Club	Source	Date Signed	Seasons Played	Apps	Subs	Gls
Luton T.	Jnrs	04.54				
Northampton T.	Tr	07.58	58	2	-	0

LOBBETT Patrick Sidney **John**
Exeter, 8 January, 1938 (G)

League Club	Source	Date Signed	Seasons Played	Apps	Subs	Gls
Exeter C.	Barnstaple	03.56	58-60	44	-	0

LOCHERTY Joseph
Dundee, 5 September, 1925 (IF)

League Club	Source	Date Signed	Seasons Played	Apps	Subs	Gls
Sheffield Wed.	Dundee	09.47	48-49	10	-	0
Colchester U.	Tr	07.50	50	10	-	1

LOCHHEAD Andrew Lorimar
Lenzie, 9 March, 1941 Su23-1 (CF)

League Club	Source	Date Signed	Seasons Played	Apps	Subs	Gls
Burnley	Renfrew Jnrs	12.58	60-68	225	1	101
Leicester C.	Tr	10.68	68-69	40	4	12
Aston Villa	Tr	02.70	69-72	127	4	34
Oldham Ath.	Tr	08.73	73-74	44	1	10

LOCK Anthony Charles
Harlow, 3 September, 1976 (F)

League Club	Source	Date Signed	Seasons Played	Apps	Subs	Gls
Colchester U.	YT	04.95	94-97	15	26	8

LOCK Frank William
Whitechapel, 12 March, 1922 Died 1985 (LB)

League Club	Source	Date Signed	Seasons Played	Apps	Subs	Gls
Charlton Ath.	Finchley	12.45	46-53	222	-	8
Liverpool	Tr	12.53	53-54	41	-	0
Watford	Tr	06.55	55-56	42	-	1

LOCK Kevin Joseph
Plaistow, 27 December, 1953 E Yth/Eu23-4 (D)

League Club	Source	Date Signed	Seasons Played	Apps	Subs	Gls
West Ham U.	App	12.71	71-77	122	10	2
Fulham	Tr	05.78	78-84	210	1	27
Southend U.	Tr	08.85	85	10	0	0

LOCKE Adam Spencer
Croydon, 20 August, 1970 (RB/M)

League Club	Source	Date Signed	Seasons Played	Apps	Subs	Gls
Crystal Palace	YT	06.88				
Southend U.	Tr	08.90	90-93	56	17	4
Colchester U.	L	10.93	93	4	0	0
Colchester U.	Tr	09.94	93-96	64	15	8
Bristol C.	Tr	07.97	97	35	2	1

LOCKE Gary Robert
Willesden, 12 July, 1954 E Yth (RB)

League Club	Source	Date Signed	Seasons Played	Apps	Subs	Gls
Chelsea	App	07.71	72-82	270	2	3
Crystal Palace	Tr	01.83	82-85	84	0	1

LOCKE Leslie Cameron
Perth, 24 January, 1934 S Amat (IF)

League Club	Source	Date Signed	Seasons Played	Apps	Subs	Gls
Queens Park R.	Bromley	05.58	56-59	76	-	24

LOCKER Stephen
Ashington, 5 November, 1970 (D)

League Club	Source	Date Signed	Seasons Played	Apps	Subs	Gls
Hartlepool U.	Nottingham F. (YT)	09.88	88	0	1	0

LOCKETT Philip Barry
Stockport, 6 September, 1972 (M)

League Club	Source	Date Signed	Seasons Played	Apps	Subs	Gls
Rochdale	YT	07.91	89-90	1	2	0

LOCKHART Crichton (Jock)
Aberuthven, 6 March, 1930 (W)

League Club	Source	Date Signed	Seasons Played	Apps	Subs	Gls
Southend U.	Chertsey	08.50	50-56	45	-	11
Rochdale	Tr	06.57	57	40	-	11

LOCKHART Keith Samuel
Wallsend, 19 July 1964 (W)

League Club	Source	Date Signed	Seasons Played	Apps	Subs	Gls
Cambridge U.	App	07.82	81-85	55	3	8
Wolverhampton W.	Tr	03.86	85-86	24	1	4
Hartlepool U. (N/C)	Tr	12.86	86	2	0	0

LOCKHART Norman
Belfast, 4 March, 1924 NI-8 (OL)

League Club	Source	Date Signed	Seasons Played	Apps	Subs	Gls
Swansea C.	Linfield	10.46	46-47	47	-	13
Coventry C.	Tr	10.47	47-52	182	-	41
Aston Villa	Tr	09.52	52-55	74	-	10
Bury	Tr	11.56	56-57	41	-	6

LOCKIE Alexander James
South Shields, 11 April, 1915 (CH)

League Club	Source	Date Signed	Seasons Played	Apps	Subs	Gls
Sunderland	South Shields	09.35	36-38	40	-	1
Notts Co.	Tr	09.46	46	23	-	0

LOCKIER Maurice Reginald
Bristol, 27 November, 1924 (OL)

League Club	Source	Date Signed	Seasons Played	Apps	Subs	Gls
Bristol Rov.		07.47	49	2	-	0

LOCKWOOD Edward
Goldthorpe, 4 August, 1925 (FB)

League Club	Source	Date Signed	Seasons Played	Apps	Subs	Gls
Scunthorpe U.	Denaby U.	06.51	51-52	9	-	0

LOCKWOOD Matthew Dominic
Southend, 17 October, 1976 (M/LB)

League Club	Source	Date Signed	Seasons Played	Apps	Subs	Gls
Queens Park R.	Southend U. (YT)	05.95				
Bristol Rov.	Tr	07.96	96-97	58	5	1

LOCKWOOD Roy
Barnsley, 20 June, 1933 E Yth (FB)

League Club	Source	Date Signed	Seasons Played	Apps	Subs	Gls
Sheffield Wed.	Jnrs	04.51				
Norwich C.	Tr	09.55	55-57	36	-	0

LODGE Frank
Oldham, 28 November, 1919 Died 1973 (CF)

League Club	Source	Date Signed	Seasons Played	Apps	Subs	Gls
Stockport Co. (Am)	Ward Street O.B.	03.47	46	1	-	0

LODGE George Raymond
Wallsend, 27 January, 1943 (OL)

League Club	Source	Date Signed	Seasons Played	Apps	Subs	Gls
Workington		12.61				
Newcastle U.	Tr	07.62				
Barrow	Tr	07.63	63	6	-	0

LODGE Thomas **Joseph**
Huddersfield, 16 April, 1921 (LH)

League Club	Source	Date Signed	Seasons Played	Apps	Subs	Gls
Huddersfield T.	Jnrs	08.39	46-47	2	-	0

LODGE Paul
Liverpool, 13 February, 1961 E Sch (M)

League Club	Source	Date Signed	Seasons Played	Apps	Subs	Gls
Everton	App	02.79	80-81	20	4	0
Wigan Ath.	L	08.82	82	5	0	1
Rotherham U.	L	01.83	82	4	0	0
Preston N.E.	Tr	02.83	82-83	36	2	0
Bolton W.	Tr	07.84	84	4	0	0
Port Vale	L	11.84	84	3	0	0
Stockport Co.	Tr	03.85	84-85	10	3	2

LODGE Robert William
Retford, 1 July, 1941 (OR)

League Club	Source	Date Signed	Seasons Played	Apps	Subs	Gls
Sheffield Wed.		05.59	60	3	-	2
Doncaster Rov.	Tr	05.61	61	23	-	4

LOFTHOUSE Nathaniel (Nat)
Bolton, 27 August, 1925 E 'B'/EF Lge/E-33 (CF)

League Club	Source	Date Signed	Seasons Played	Apps	Subs	Gls
Bolton W.	Jnrs	08.42	46-60	452	-	255

LOFTUS Robert
Liverpool, 15 December, 1931 (IF)

League Club	Source	Date Signed	Seasons Played	Apps	Subs	Gls
Bradford P.A.	Llanelli	12.55	55	3	-	0

LOFTY James Kenneth
Farnham, 5 December, 1945 (W)

League Club	Source	Date Signed	Seasons Played	Apps	Subs	Gls
Reading	Jnrs	05.63	63	2	-	0
Birmingham C.	Tr	07.64				

LOGAN David
Middlesbrough, 5 December, 1963 (LB)

League Club	Source	Date Signed	Seasons Played	Apps	Subs	Gls
Mansfield T.	Whitby T.	06.84	84-86	67	0	1
Northampton T.	Tr	02.87	86-87	39	2	1
Halifax T.	Tr	08.88	88	3	0	0
Stockport Co.	Tr	10.88	88-89	60	0	4
Scarborough	Tr	08.90	90-91	54	1	1

LOGAN Douglas
Aberdeen, 30 August, 1933 Died 1984 (WH)

League Club	Source	Date Signed	Seasons Played	Apps	Subs	Gls
Southampton	R.A.F. Lamport	01.54	55-57	21	-	0

LOGAN Gordon Taylor
Kirkliston, 3 October, 1949 S Yth (FB)

League Club	Source	Date Signed	Seasons Played	Apps	Subs	Gls
Port Vale		03.67	66-69	33	2	1

LOGAN John William
Easington, 16 August, 1912 Died 1980 (WH)

League Club	Source	Date Signed	Seasons Played	Apps	Subs	Gls
Charlton Ath.		07.34				
Darlington	Tr	05.35	35-36	65	-	5
Barnsley	Tr	03.37	36-46	99	-	5
Sheffield Wed.	Tr	01.47	46	4	-	0

LOGAN Richard Anthony
Barnsley, 24 May, 1969 (M)

League Club	Source	Date Signed	Seasons Played	Apps	Subs	Gls
Huddersfield T.	Gainsborough Trin.	11.93	93-95	35	10	1
Plymouth Arg.	Tr	10.95	95-97	67	19	12

LOGGIE David McKie
Newbiggin, 31 May, 1957 (F)

League Club	Source	Date Signed	Seasons Played	Apps	Subs	Gls
Burnley	App	06.74	75-77	6	1	0
York C.	Tr	06.78	78-79	47	3	11

LOGIE James Tullis
Edinburgh, 23 November, 1919 Died 1984 S-1 (IF)

League Club	Source	Date Signed	Seasons Played	Apps	Subs	Gls
Arsenal	Lochore Welfare	06.39	46-54	296	-	68

LOGUE Samuel Walker
Glasgow, 9 April, 1934 (IF)

League Club	Source	Date Signed	Seasons Played	Apps	Subs	Gls
Accrington St.	Clyde	06.60	60	2	-	0

LOHMAN Johannas (Jan) Hermanus Petrus
Netherlands, 18 February, 1959 Dutch u21 Int (W)

League Club	Source	Date Signed	Seasons Played	Apps	Subs	Gls
Watford	Lokeren (Bel)	10.81	81-85	51	12	6

LOMAS Albert
Tyldesley, 14 October, 1924 (G)

League Club	Source	Date Signed	Seasons Played	Apps	Subs	Gls
Leeds U.	Bolton W. (Am)	09.48	48	1	-	0
Rochdale	Mossley	05.50	50	9	-	0
Chesterfield	Tr	07.51	51	29	-	0

LOMAS Andrew James
Hartlepool, 26 April, 1965 (G)

League Club	Source	Date Signed	Seasons Played	Apps	Subs	Gls
Cambridge U. (L)	Stevenage Borough	03.95	94	2	0	0

LOMAS Clive Ian
Ealing, 18 January, 1947 (WH)

League Club	Source	Date Signed	Seasons Played	Apps	Subs	Gls
Watford	App	01.65	65	6	1	0

LOMAS James Duncan
Chesterfield, 18 October, 1977 (M)

League Club	Source	Date Signed	Seasons Played	Apps	Subs	Gls
Chesterfield	YT	09.96	96-97	2	4	0

LOMAS Peter
Oldham, 9 May, 1933 (FB)

League Club	Source	Date Signed	Seasons Played	Apps	Subs	Gls
Southport	Royton Amats	04.52	51-56	18	-	0

LOMAS Stephen Martin
Germany, 18 January, 1974 NI Sch/NI Yth/NI 'B'/NI-26 (M)

League Club	Source	Date Signed	Seasons Played	Apps	Subs	Gls
Manchester C.	YT	01.91	93-96	102	9	8
West Ham U.	Tr	03.97	96-97	40	0	2

LOMAX Geoffrey William
Droylsden, 6 July, 1964 (D)

League Club	Source	Date Signed	Seasons Played	Apps	Subs	Gls
Manchester C.	Jnrs	07.81	82-84	23	2	1
Wolverhampton W.	L	10.85	85	5	0	0
Carlisle U.	Tr	12.85	85-86	37	0	0
Rochdale	Tr	07.87	87-88	70	1	0

LOMBARDO Attilio
Maria la Fossa, Italy, 6 January, 1966 Italian Int (M)

League Club	Source	Date Signed	Seasons Played	Apps	Subs	Gls
Crystal Palace	Juventus (It)	08.97	97	21	3	5

LONERGAN Darren
Cork, 28 January, 1974 (D)

League Club	Source	Date Signed	Seasons Played	Apps	Subs	Gls
Oldham Ath.	Waterford	09.94	95	1	1	0

LONG Christopher
Hatfield, 7 February, 1948 (OL)

League Club	Source	Date Signed	Seasons Played	Apps	Subs	Gls
Luton T.	Hatfield T.	02.66	65	1	0	0

LONG John William
Southampton, 8 May, 1921 (FB)

League Club	Source	Date Signed	Seasons Played	Apps	Subs	Gls
Exeter C.	Chester C. (Am)	04.46	46	1	-	0

LONG Nigel
Doncaster, 31 March, 1955 (M)

League Club	Source	Date Signed	Seasons Played	Apps	Subs	Gls
Doncaster Rov. (N/C)		05.74	74	1	0	0

LONG Herbert Raymond
Stickney (Lincs), 4 October, 1936 (CH)

League Club	Source	Date Signed	Seasons Played	Apps	Subs	Gls
Lincoln C.	Louth U.	12.58	59	1	-	0

LONG Terence Anthony
Beaconsfield, 17 November, 1934 (D)

League Club	Source	Date Signed	Seasons Played	Apps	Subs	Gls
Crystal Palace	Wycombe W.	05.55	55-68	432	10	16

LONG Trevor George
Smethwick, 1 July, 1931 (W)

League Club	Source	Date Signed	Seasons Played	Apps	Subs	Gls
Wolverhampton W.	Mitchell & Butlers	12.50				
Gillingham	Tr	07.52	52-54	67	-	15
Reading	Tr	07.55	55	12	-	5

LONG Wilfred Roy
Wallasey, 28 December, 1922 Died 1993 (OL)

League Club	Source	Date Signed	Seasons Played	Apps	Subs	Gls
New Brighton (Am)	Everton (Am)	07.46	46	2	-	0

LONGBOTTOM (LANGLEY) Arthur
Leeds, 30 January, 1933 (IF)

League Club	Source	Date Signed	Seasons Played	Apps	Subs	Gls
Queens Park R.	Methley U.	03.54	54-60	201	-	62
Port Vale	Tr	05.61	61-62	52	-	18
Millwall	Tr	01.63	62	10	-	1
Oxford U.	Tr	08.63	63-64	34	-	14
Colchester U.	Tr	10.64	64	33	-	12

LONGDEN Colin
Rotherham, 21 July, 1933 E Sch (OR)

League Club	Source	Date Signed	Seasons Played	Apps	Subs	Gls
Rotherham U.	Jnrs	08.50	52	3	-	0
York C.	Tr	08.55	57	2	-	0

LONGDEN David Paul
Morley, 28 September, 1962 (LB)

League Club	Source	Date Signed	Seasons Played	Apps	Subs	Gls
Barnsley	App	09.80	81-82	5	0	0
Scunthorpe U.	Tr	08.83	83-92	364	4	0

LONGDON Charles William
Mansfield, 6 May, 1917 Died 1986 (WH)

League Club	Source	Date Signed	Seasons Played	Apps	Subs	Gls
Brighton & H.A.	Folkestone T.	05.39				
Bournemouth	Tr	05.46	46	9	-	1
Rochdale	Tr	07.47	47	2	-	0

LONGHORN Dennis
Hythe (Hants), 12 September, 1950 (M)

League Club	Source	Date Signed	Seasons Played	Apps	Subs	Gls
Bournemouth	App	08.68	67-71	23	7	1
Mansfield T.	Tr	12.71	71-73	93	3	5
Sunderland	Tr	02.74	73-76	35	5	3
Sheffield U.	Tr	10.76	76-77	34	2	1
Aldershot	Tr	02.78	77-79	46	7	3
Colchester U.	Tr	05.80	80-82	62	9	0

LONGHURST David John
Northampton, 15 January, 1965 Died 1990 (F)

League Club	Source	Date Signed	Seasons Played	Apps	Subs	Gls
Nottingham F.	App	01.83				
Halifax T.	Tr	07.85	85-86	85	0	24
Northampton T.	Tr	06.87	87-88	34	3	7
Peterborough U.	Tr	10.88	88-89	51	7	7
York C.	Tr	01.90	89-90	6	0	2

LONGLAND John
Southampton, 24 September, 1932 (WH)

League Club	Source	Date Signed	Seasons Played	Apps	Subs	Gls
Brighton & H.A.		04.54	54	3	-	0

LONGLEY Nicholas
Mexborough, 21 May, 1961 (G)

League Club	Source	Date Signed	Seasons Played	Apps	Subs	Gls
Crewe Alex.		05.81	81-85	23	0	0

LONGLEY Scott Edward
Wakefield, 16 July, 1973 (M)

League Club	Source	Date Signed	Seasons Played	Apps	Subs	Gls
Halifax T.	YT	07.92	91	1	0	0

LONGRIDGE George Paterson
Glasgow, 23 August, 1931 (G)

League Club	Source	Date Signed	Seasons Played	Apps	Subs	Gls
Leyton Orient	Dennistoun Jnrs	07.50				
Darlington	Tr	09.51	51	2	-	0

LONGWORTH Steven Paul
Preston, 6 February, 1980 (M)

League Club	Source	Date Signed	Seasons Played	Apps	Subs	Gls
Blackpool	YT	●	97	0	2	0

LONSDALE Joseph Stanley
Washington, 13 April, 1931 (WH)

League Club	Source	Date Signed	Seasons Played	Apps	Subs	Gls
Huddersfield T.	Seaham Jnrs	12.48				
Halifax T.	Tr	03.55	54-59	202	-	21
Hartlepool U.	Tr	11.60	60	9	-	0

LORAM Mark Julian
Paignton, 13 August, 1967 (M/F)

League Club	Source	Date Signed	Seasons Played	Apps	Subs	Gls
Torquay U.	Brixham Villa	01.85	84-85	50	2	8
Queens Park R.	Tr	05.86				
Torquay U.	Tr	03.87	86-91	188	21	41
Stockport Co.	L	03.92	91	1	3	0
Exeter C.	L	09.92	92	2	1	0
Torquay U. (N/C)	Minehead	08.93	93	0	1	0

LORD Albert Ernest
Farnworth, 10 September, 1944 (G)

League Club	Source	Date Signed	Seasons Played	Apps	Subs	Gls
Bolton W.	Jnrs	01.63				
Southport	Tr	03.66	65	16	0	0

LORD Barry
Goole, 17 November, 1937 (G)

League Club	Source	Date Signed	Seasons Played	Apps	Subs	Gls
Hull C.	Goole Buchanan	04.56	58-60	5	-	0

LORD Frank
Oldham, 13 March, 1936 (CF)

League Club	Source	Date Signed	Seasons Played	Apps	Subs	Gls
Rochdale	Jnrs	10.53	53-60	122	-	54
Crewe Alex.	Tr	07.61	61-63	108	-	68
Plymouth Arg.	Tr	11.63	63-65	69	1	23
Stockport Co.	Tr	02.66	65-66	27	0	18
Blackburn Rov.	Tr	12.66	66	10	0	1
Chesterfield	Tr	06.67	67	12	0	6
Plymouth Arg.	Tr	10.67	68	6	0	2

LORD William Graham
Rawtenstall, 9 July, 1936 (FB)

League Club	Source	Date Signed	Seasons Played	Apps	Subs	Gls
Accrington St.	Rossendale U.	07.57	58-60	67	-	0

LORD Malcolm
Driffield, 25 October, 1946 (M)

League Club	Source	Date Signed	Seasons Played	Apps	Subs	Gls
Hull C.	Jnrs	08.65	66-78	271	27	24

LORD Walter
Grimsby, 1 November, 1933 (IF)

League Club	Source	Date Signed	Seasons Played	Apps	Subs	Gls
Grimsby T.	Jnrs	08.51	52-53	7	-	1
Lincoln C.	Tr	05.56	56	1	-	0

LORENSON Roy Vicent
Liverpool, 8 April, 1932 (CH)

League Club	Source	Date Signed	Seasons Played	Apps	Subs	Gls
Halifax T.	St Elizabeths	02.52	51-60	216	-	7
Tranmere Rov.	Tr	10.60	60-61	14	-	0

LORENZO Nestor Gabriel
Argentina, 28 February, 1966 Argentinian Int (CD)

League Club	Source	Date Signed	Seasons Played	Apps	Subs	Gls
Swindon T	F.C. Bari (It)	10.90	90-91	20	4	2

LORIMER Peter Patrick
Dundee, 14 December, 1946 S Sch/S Yth/Su23-2/S-21 (F)

League Club	Source	Date Signed	Seasons Played	Apps	Subs	Gls
Leeds U.	Jnrs	12.63	62-78	430	20	151
York C.	Toronto (Can)	09.79	79	29	0	8
Leeds U.	Vancouver (Can)	03.84	83-85	74	2	17

LORMOR Anthony
Ashington, 29 October, 1970 (F)

League Club	Source	Date Signed	Seasons Played	Apps	Subs	Gls
Newcastle U.	YT	02.88	87-88	6	2	3
Lincoln C.	Tr	01.90	89-93	90	10	30
Peterborough U.	Tr	07.94	94	2	3	0
Chesterfield	Tr	12.94	94-97	97	16	35
Preston N.E.	Tr	11.97	97	9	3	3
Notts Co.	L	02.98	97	2	5	0

LORNIE John
Aberdeen, 2 March, 1939 S Sch (IF)

League Club	Source	Date Signed	Seasons Played	Apps	Subs	Gls
Leicester C.	Banks o'Dee	03.58	58-60	8	-	3
Luton T.	Tr	06.61	61-62	19	-	6
Carlisle U.	Tr	06.63	63	4	-	0
Tranmere Rov.	Tr	06.64	64-65	33	2	7

LOSKA Anthony Stephen Patrick
Chesterton, 11 February, 1950 (LB)

League Club	Source	Date Signed	Seasons Played	Apps	Subs	Gls
Shrewsbury T.	App	03.68	68-70	12	0	0
Port Vale	Tr	07.71	71-73	74	6	5
Chester C.	Tr	12.73	73-76	103	7	5
Halifax T.	Tr	10.76	76-78	101	1	0

LOSS Colin Paul
Brentwood, 15 August, 1973 (M)

League Club	Source	Date Signed	Seasons Played	Apps	Subs	Gls
Derby Co. (N/C)	Norwich C. (YT)	11.91				
Bristol C.	Gresley Rov.	03.94	94	3	2	0

League Club	Source	Date Signed	Seasons Played	Apps	Subs	Gls
LOUGH John Douglas						
Gateshead, 31 October, 1922 Died 1987						(IF)
Gateshead (Am)		09.46	46	1	-	0
LOUGHLAN Antony John						
Croydon, 19 January, 1970						(W)
Nottingham F.	Leicester U.	08.89	90	2	0	1
Lincoln C. (N/C)	Kettering T.	10.93	93	4	8	2
LOUGHLAN John						
Coatbridge, 12 June, 1943						(FB)
Leicester C.		08.61				
Crystal Palace	Morton	09.68	68-71	58	2	0
Wrexham	L	03.72	71	5	0	0
LOUGHNANE John **Brian**						
Manchester, 16 August, 1930						(W)
Leeds U.		08.52				
Shrewsbury T.	Tr	07.53	53-55	42	-	7
Bournemouth	Tr	07.56	56-58	43	-	6
LOUGHNANE Peter Brian						
Bournemouth, 18 March, 1958						(W)
Manchester U.	App	03.75				
Shrewsbury T.	Tr	02.77	76-78	24	7	4
LOUGHRAN Joseph Lane						
Consett, 12 August, 1915 Died 1994						(FB)
Birmingham C.	Dudley Colly	08.33	35-36	31	-	2
Luton T.	Tr	05.37	37-38	25	-	0
Burnley	TR	07.39	46-49	65	-	0
Southend U.	Tr	09.49	49-52	147	-	1
LOUGHTON Michael George						
Colchester, 8 December, 1942						(CH)
Colchester U.	Jnrs	08.61	64-67	121	1	7
LOUKES Gordon						
Sheffield, 15 June, 1928						(OL)
Sheffield U.		04.49	50	1	-	0
Southend U.	Tr	07.51	51	2	-	0
LOVATT John (Jack)						
Burton, 23 August, 1941						(CF)
West Bromwich A.	Jnrs	12.58	60-62	18	-	5
LOVATT John						
Middlesbrough, 21 January, 1962						(FB)
Derby Co.	App	01.80	81	2	2	0
LOVE Alastair James						
Edinburgh, 9 May, 1955						(M)
West Bromwich A.	Melbourne Thistle	03.73				
Southend U.	Tr	05.74	74	6	5	0
Newport Co.	Tr	07.75	75	41	1	2
LOVE Andrew Mark						
Grimsby, 28 March, 1979						(G)
Grimsby T.	YT	07.96	96	3	0	0
LOVE Ian James						
Cardiff, 1 March, 1958						(F)
Swansea C.	Barry T.	08.86	86-88	33	8	9
Torquay U.	Tr	03.89	88	8	1	0
Cardiff C. (N/C)	Tr	09.89	89	1	1	0
LOVE John						
Eynsham, 11 March, 1937						(OL)
Oxford U.	Wolverhampton W. (Am)	03.55	62-63	25	-	5
LOVE John Ernest						
Uxbridge, 22 April, 1951						(CD)
Crystal Palace	Staines T.	01.75	74	1	0	0
LOVE John Thomson						
Edinburgh, 18 March, 1924						(IF)
Nottingham F.	Albion Rov.	02.49	48-51	59	-	21
Walsall	Llanelli	03.55	54-55	40	-	11
LOVE Michael John						
Stockport, 27 November, 1973						(M)
Wigan Ath.	Hinckley Ath.	01.96	96	0	3	0
LOVELL Alan John						
Swansea, 17 May, 1940						(OL)
Swansea C.	Jnrs	06.57				
Stockport Co.	Tr	07.60	60	1	-	0

League Club	Source	Date Signed	Seasons Played	Apps	Subs	Gls
LOVELL Frederick						
Crewe, 18 June, 1929						(IF)
Notts Co. (Am)	Loughborough College	04.53	52-53	7	-	2
LOVELL Mark Anthony						
Kensington, 20 January, 1961						(M)
Fulham	App	08.78	77-78	4	2	0
LOVELL Michael Graham						
Doncaster, 28 October, 1946						(FB)
Doncaster Rov.	App	10.64	65	2	0	0
LOVELL Stephen John						
Swansea, 16 July, 1960 W Sch/W-6						(F)
Crystal Palace	App	08.77	80-82	68	6	3
Stockport Co.	L	10.79	79	12	0	0
Millwall	Tr	03.83	82-85	143	3	43
Swansea C.	L	02.87	86	2	0	1
Gillingham	Tr	02.87	86-92	222	11	94
Bournemouth (N/C)	Tr	11.92	92	3	0	0
LOVELL Stuart Andrew						
Sydney (Aus), 9 January, 1972						(F)
Reading	YT	07.90	90-97	177	50	58
LOVELL Trevor						
Halifax, 19 January, 1940						(W)
Halifax T. (Am)	Jnrs	08.60	60-62	9	-	0
LOVEMAN Robert Leith						
Greenock, 30 September, 1921 Died 1986						(G)
Newport Co.	Ballieston Jnrs	03.48	47-48	20	-	0
LOVERIDGE James Charles						
Swansea, 19 October, 1962 W Sch/Wu21-3						(M)
Swansea C.	App	11.79	79-84	40	7	4
Charlton Ath.	Tr	06.85	85	5	1	0
LOVERIDGE John						
Wolverhampton, 28 February, 1959						(M)
West Bromwich A.	App	03.77				
Walsall	Tr	08.81	81	23	3	2
LOVERING John						
Nuneaton, 10 December, 1922						(LH)
Coventry C.	Holbrooks O.B.	06.46	46-47	6	-	0
LOVESEY William Samuel						
Marylebone, 8 December, 1922 Died 1994						(WH)
Swindon T.	Wolverhampton W. (Am)	05.45	46	4	-	0
LOVETT Eric						
Radcliffe, 20 August, 1925						(CH)
Accrington St.		11.49	49-50	41	-	1
LOVETT Graham John						
Birmingham, 5 August, 1947						(M)
West Bromwich A.	App	11.64	64-70	106	8	8
Southampton	L	11.71	71	3	0	0
LOVETT John Ernest						
Portsmouth, 31 October, 1940						(OR)
Portsmouth		09.58				
Millwall	Tr	03.60	59	6	-	2
LOVETT Percy Reginald						
Bayston, 1 August, 1920 Died 1982						(G)
Everton	Kenwood Jnrs	08.38				
Wrexham	Tr	02.47	46	13	-	0
LOVIE James Theirs Harrison						
Peterhead, 19 September, 1932						(WH/W)
Bury	Peterhead	01.57	57-59	51	-	10
Bournemouth	Tr	07.60	60	9	-	0
Chesterfield	Tr	07.61	61-63	95	-	7
LOW Gordon Alexander						
Aberdeen, 11 July, 1940						(WH)
Huddersfield T.	Jnrs	07.57	57-60	67	-	6
Bristol C.	Tr	03.61	60-67	203	2	12
Stockport Co.	Tr	07.68	68-69	63	1	7
Crewe Alex.	Tr	08.70	70	5	0	0
LOW Joshua David						
Bristol, 15 February, 1979 W Yth						(W)
Bristol Rov.	YT	08.96	95-97	6	8	0
LOW Norman Harvey						
Aberdeen, 23 March, 1914 Died 1994						(CH)
Liverpool	Rosehill	10.33	34-36	13	-	0
Newport Co.	Tr	11.36	36-46	112	-	0
Norwich C.	Tr	10.46	46-49	150	-	0

LOW Anthony Roy
Watford, 8 July, 1944 E Sch (IF)

League Club	Source	Date Signed	Seasons Played	Apps	Subs	Gls
Tottenham H.	Jnrs	07.61	64-66	6	2	1
Watford	Tr	02.67	66-68	25	1	4

LOWDEN George
Isleworth, 2 March, 1933 (FB)

League Club	Source	Date Signed	Seasons Played	Apps	Subs	Gls
Brentford	Jnrs	05.51	53-56	29	-	0

LOWDER Thomas
Worksop, 17 October, 1924 (OL)

League Club	Source	Date Signed	Seasons Played	Apps	Subs	Gls
Rotherham U.	Crystal Palace (Am)	08.47	48	8	-	5
Southampton	Boston U.	10.49	49-52	39	-	2
Southend U.	Tr	05.53	53	21	-	3

LOWE David Anthony
Liverpool, 30 August, 1965 E Yth/Eu21-2 (RW)

League Club	Source	Date Signed	Seasons Played	Apps	Subs	Gls
Wigan Ath.	App	06.83	82-86	179	9	40
Ipswich T.	Tr	06.87	87-91	121	13	37
Port Vale	L	03.92	91	8	1	2
Leicester C.	Tr	07.92	92-95	68	26	22
Port Vale	L	02.94	93	18	1	5
Wigan Ath.	Tr	03.96	95-97	80	12	25

LOWE Edward
Halesowen, 11 July, 1925 E-3 (WH)

League Club	Source	Date Signed	Seasons Played	Apps	Subs	Gls
Aston Villa	Kynoch Wks	05.45	46-49	104	-	3
Fulham	Tr	05.50	50-62	473	-	8
Notts Co.	Tr	09.63	63-64	9	-	0

LOWE Garry
Prescot, 21 February, 1967 (FB)

League Club	Source	Date Signed	Seasons Played	Apps	Subs	Gls
Bury	YT	06.86	85	3	1	0

LOWE Gary Walter
Manchester, 25 September, 1959 (M)

League Club	Source	Date Signed	Seasons Played	Apps	Subs	Gls
Crystal Palace	App	10.76				
Manchester C.	Tr	12.79				
Hereford U.	Tr	06.80	80	9	0	0

LOWE Kenneth
Sedgefield, 6 November, 1961 E Semi Pro (M)

League Club	Source	Date Signed	Seasons Played	Apps	Subs	Gls
Hartlepool U.	App	11.78	81-83	50	4	3
Scarborough (L)	Barrow	01.88	87	4	0	0
Barnet	Barrow	03.91	91-92	55	17	5
Stoke City	Tr	08.93	93	3	6	0
Birmingham C.	Tr	12.93	93-95	14	7	3
Carlisle U.	L	09.94	94	1	1	0
Hartlepool U.	L	08.95	95	13	0	3
Darlington (N/C)	Tr	03.97	96-97	10	4	0

LOWE Matthew Ian
Birmingham, 25 February, 1974 (G)

League Club	Source	Date Signed	Seasons Played	Apps	Subs	Gls
Torquay U.	YT	07.92	91-93	30	0	0

LOWE Nicholas Paul
Oxford, 28 October, 1952 (CD)

League Club	Source	Date Signed	Seasons Played	Apps	Subs	Gls
Oxford U.	App	07.70	72-76	71	0	3
Halifax T.	L	08.74	74	9	0	0

LOWE Reginald
Halesowen, 15 December, 1926 (LB)

League Club	Source	Date Signed	Seasons Played	Apps	Subs	Gls
Aston Villa	Finchley	08.44				
Fulham	Tr	05.50	50-52	66	-	0

LOWE Simon John
Westminster, 26 December, 1962 (F)

League Club	Source	Date Signed	Seasons Played	Apps	Subs	Gls
Barnsley	Ossett T.	12.83	83	2	0	0
Halifax T.	Tr	07.84	84-85	74	3	19
Hartlepool U.	Tr	08.86	86	12	2	1
Colchester U.	Tr	12.86	86-87	32	4	8
Scarborough	Tr	11.87	87	14	2	3

LOWE Terence John
Cheadle, 27 May, 1943 (FB)

League Club	Source	Date Signed	Seasons Played	Apps	Subs	Gls
Port Vale	Stoke C. (Am)	06.60	61-65	55	0	0

LOWELL Eric James
Cheadle, 8 March, 1935 (IF)

League Club	Source	Date Signed	Seasons Played	Apps	Subs	Gls
Derby Co.	Jnrs	03.52	53	1	-	1
Stoke C.	Tr	05.55	55	7	-	3

LOWERY Anthony William
Wallsend, 6 July, 1961 (M)

League Club	Source	Date Signed	Seasons Played	Apps	Subs	Gls
West Bromwich A.	Ashington	03.81	81	1	0	0
Walsall	L	02.82	81	4	2	1
Mansfield T.	Tr	04.83	82-90	249	3	19
Walsall	L	10.90	90	6	0	0
Carlisle U.		10.91	91	6	1	0

LOWERY Harry
Egremont (Cumb), 26 February, 1918 (WH)

League Club	Source	Date Signed	Seasons Played	Apps	Subs	Gls
West Bromwich A.	Cleator Moor Celtic	05.35	37	17	-	0
Northampton T.	Tr	11.45	46-48	76	-	2

LOWERY Jeremiah
Newcastle, 19 October, 1924 (G)

League Club	Source	Date Signed	Seasons Played	Apps	Subs	Gls
Newcastle U.	C.A. Parsons	06.47	49-51	6	-	0
Lincoln C.	Tr	03.52	52-53	51	-	0
Barrow	Peterborough U.	06.56	56-57	86	-	0
Crewe Alex.	Tr	07.58	58	4	-	0

LOWERY Stewart
Thornaby, 21 February, 1951 (IF)

League Club	Source	Date Signed	Seasons Played	Apps	Subs	Gls
Watford	Bishop Auckland	01.70				
Walsall	L	11.70	70	0	2	0

LOWES Arnold Richardson
Sunderland, 27 February, 1919 Died 1994 (WH)

League Club	Source	Date Signed	Seasons Played	Apps	Subs	Gls
Sheffield Wed.	Washington Chemicals	10.37	38-47	42	-	8
Doncaster Rov.	Tr	02.48	47-50	72	-	3

LOWES Barry Thomas
Barrow, 16 March, 1939 (OR)

League Club	Source	Date Signed	Seasons Played	Apps	Subs	Gls
Barrow	Holker Street O.B.	01.60	59-61	55	-	15
Blackpool	Tr	11.61				
Workington	Tr	08.62	62-65	121	0	34
Bury	Tr	02.66	65-66	33	0	6
Coventry C.	Tr	03.67	66	3	0	0
Swindon T.	Tr	08.67	67	2	0	0

LOWEY John Anthony
Manchester, 7 March, 1958 (M)

League Club	Source	Date Signed	Seasons Played	Apps	Subs	Gls
Manchester U.	App	03.75				
Blackburn Rov.	Chicago (USA)	07.77				
Port Vale	Tr	12.77				
Sheffield Wed.	California (USA)	10.78	78-79	35	7	4
Blackburn Rov.	Tr	11.80	80-85	136	5	14
Wigan Ath.	Tr	07.86	86	1	2	0
Chesterfield	L	11.86	86	2	0	0
York C.	L	03.87	86	3	3	0
Preston N.E.	Tr	08.87	87	4	0	1
Chester C.	Tr	03.88	87	9	0	0

LOWIS Paul Noble
Shap, 17 October, 1937 (WH)

League Club	Source	Date Signed	Seasons Played	Apps	Subs	Gls
Blackpool	B.A.B.C.	05.57				
Stockport Co.	Tr	06.59	59	9	-	0

LOWNDES Nathan Peter
Salford, 2 June, 1977 (F)

League Club	Source	Date Signed	Seasons Played	Apps	Subs	Gls
Leeds U.	YT	04.95				
Watford	Tr	10.95	96-97	1	6	0

LOWNDES Stephen Robert
Cwmbran, 17 June, 1960 Wu21-4/W-10 (W)

League Club	Source	Date Signed	Seasons Played	Apps	Subs	Gls
Newport Co.	Jnrs	10.77	77-82	200	8	39
Millwall	Tr	08.83	83-85	95	1	16
Barnsley	Tr	08.86	86-89	108	8	20
Hereford U.	Tr	10.90	90-91	45	4	4

LOWNDS Mark Usher
Sunderland, 28 November, 1940 (WH)

League Club	Source	Date Signed	Seasons Played	Apps	Subs	Gls
Luton T.	Ryhope Colly	01.60	61-64	59	-	3

LOWREY Patrick
Newcastle, 11 October, 1950 E Sch (W)

League Club	Source	Date Signed	Seasons Played	Apps	Subs	Gls
Sunderland	Newcastle U. (App)	11.67	68-71	13	2	3
Darlington	R.U. Bruges (Bel)	08.75	75	14	6	2
Workington	Tr	07.76	76	15	0	3

LOWRIE George
Rhondda, 19 December, 1919 Died 1989 W-4 (CF)

League Club	Source	Date Signed	Seasons Played	Apps	Subs	Gls
Swansea C.	Tonypandy	01.37				
Preston N.E.	Tr	12.37	37	5	-	0
Coventry C.	Tr	06.39	46-47	56	-	44
Newcastle U.	Tr	03.48	47-49	12	-	5
Bristol C.	Tr	09.49	49-51	48	-	21
Coventry C.	Tr	02.52	51-52	27	-	12

LOWRIE Thomas
Glasgow, 14 January, 1928 (WH)

League Club	Source	Date Signed	Seasons Played	Apps	Subs	Gls
Manchester U.	Troon Ath.	08.47	48-49	13	-	0
Oldham Ath.	Aberdeen	08.52	52-54	79	-	5

LOWRY Brian Thomas
Manchester, 12 December, 1936 (OR)

League Club	Source	Date Signed	Seasons Played	Apps	Subs	Gls
Grimsby T.	Manchester U. (Am)	08.54	54-55	12	-	1
Aldershot	Tr	07.56				

League Club	Source	Date Signed	Seasons Played	Career Record Apps	Subs	Gls
LOWRY Thomas						
Prescot, 26 August, 1945						(RB)
Liverpool	App	04.63	64	1	-	0
Crewe Alex.	Tr	07.66	66-77	435	1	2
LOWTHER Shaun						
North Shields, 24 January, 1962						(D)
Peterborough U.	Middlesbrough (N/C)	01.85	84	1	0	0
LOWTHORPE Adam						
Hull, 7 August, 1975						(FB)
Hull C.	YT	07.93	93-97	70	11	3
LOXLEY Anthony Dale						
Nottingham, 14 December, 1959						(CD)
Lincoln C.	App	12.77	78	1	0	0
LOXLEY Herbert (Bert)						
Matlock, 3 February, 1934						(WH)
Notts Co.	Jnrs	03.52	54-63	245	-	9
Mansfield T.	Tr	07.64				
Lincoln C.	Lockheed Leamington	10.66	66	7	0	0
LOYDEN Edward						
Liverpool, 22 December, 1945						(CF)
Blackpool	Jnrs	12.63	64	2	-	0
Carlisle U.	Tr	06.66				
Chester C.	Tr	07.67	67	37	0	22
Shrewsbury T.	Tr	05.68	68	11	1	2
Barnsley	Tr	12.68	68-70	64	1	23
Chester C.	Tr	11.70	70-71	62	0	26
Tranmere Rov.	Tr	06.72	72-73	61	0	22
LUCAS Alec Leroy						
Wrexham, 1 December, 1945 Wu23-1						(FB)
Wrexham	Queens Park R. (App)	08.65	65-66	51	4	0
LUCAS Brian Andrew						
Farnborough (Hants), 31 January, 1961						(M)
Aldershot	Jnrs	07.78	79-83	112	13	19
LUCAS David Anthony						
Preston, 23 November, 1977 E Yth						(G)
Preston N.E.	YT	12.94	95-97	9	0	0
Darlington	L	12.95	95	6	0	0
Darlington	L	10.96	96	7	0	0
Scunthorpe U.	L	12.96	96	6	0	0
LUCAS Frederick Charles						
Erith, 29 September, 1933						(IF/WH)
Charlton Ath.	Jnrs	01.52	55-63	185	-	29
Crystal Palace	Tr	10.63	63-64	16	-	0
LUCAS Peter **Malcolm**						
Wrexham, 7 October, 1938 Wu23-1/W-4						(WH)
Leyton Orient	Bradley R.	09.58	58-64	157	-	6
Norwich C.	Tr	09.64	64-69	180	3	8
Torquay U.	Tr	03.70	69-73	118	4	3
LUCAS Oliver Henry						
Paisley, 14 January, 1923						(FB)
Leyton Orient	St Mirren	07.48	48-49	2	-	0
LUCAS Paul						
Coseley, 27 April, 1936 Died 1992						(IF)
Aston Villa	Jnrs	04.54				
Gillingham	Tr	08.56	56-57	44	-	7
LUCAS Richard						
Chapeltown, 22 September, 1970						(FB)
Sheffield U.	YT	07.89	90-91	8	2	0
Preston N.E.	Tr	12.92	92-93	47	3	0
Lincoln C.	L	10.94	94	4	0	0
Scarborough	Tr	07.95	95-96	63	9	0
Hartlepool U.	Tr	03.97	96-97	49	0	2
LUCAS Richard John						
Witney, 22 January, 1948						(FB)
Oxford U.	Jnrs	07.65	67-74	190	1	2
LUCAS Robert Walter						
Bethnal Green, 6 January, 1925						(G)
Crystal Palace	Hendon	06.46	46	4	-	0
LUCAS William Henry						
Newport, 15 January, 1918 W-7						(WH/IF)
Wolverhampton W.	Treharris	05.36				
Swindon T.	Tr	05.37	37-47	141	-	32
Swansea C.	Tr	03.48	47-53	203	-	35
Newport Co.	Tr	12.53	53-57	94	-	6
LUCKETT Paul						
Coventry, 12 January, 1957						(FB)
Halifax T.	Coventry C. (App)	08.74	74-75	26	1	0
Hartlepool U.	Tr	03.76	75-76	19	0	0
LUCKETTI Christopher James						
Littleborough, 28 September, 1971						(CD)
Rochdale	YT	●	88	1	0	0
Stockport Co.	Tr	08.90				
Halifax T.	Tr	07.91	91-92	73	5	2
Bury	Tr	10.93	93-97	192	0	7
LUDDEN Dominic James						
Basildon, 30 March, 1974 E Sch						(LB)
Leyton Orient	Billericay T.	07.92	92-93	50	8	1
Watford	Tr	08.94	94-96	28	5	0
LUDFORD George Albert						
Barnet, 22 March, 1915						(WH)
Tottenham H.	Jnrs	05.36	36-49	75	-	7
LUDLAM Craig						
Sheffield, 8 November, 1976						(RB)
Sheffield Wed.	YT	05.95				
Notts Co.	L	10.96	96	1	0	0
LUDLAM Steven John						
Chesterfield, 18 October, 1955						(M)
Sheffield U.	App	01.73	75-76	26	1	1
Carlisle U.	Tr	05.77	77-79	90	6	11
Chester C.	Tr	07.80	80-82	100	2	12
LUFF Neil John						
Bletchley, 9 April, 1969						(M)
Gillingham	Jnrs	06.87	87	0	1	0
LUGG Raymond						
Jarrow, 18 July, 1948						(M)
Middlesbrough	Jnrs	07.65	66-68	34	3	3
Watford	Tr	11.69	69-71	51	8	3
Plymouth Arg.	Tr	07.72	72	22	2	1
Crewe Alex.	Tr	07.73	73-77	183	2	10
Bury	Tr	07.78	78-79	68	3	2
LUKE George						
Hetton-le-Hole, 9 November, 1948 E Sch						(WH)
Newcastle U.	App	03.66				
Chelsea	Tr	03.67	66	1	0	0
LUKE George Baron						
Lanchester, 20 October, 1932						(CF)
Sheffield U.		01.52	53-54	7	-	0
Scunthorpe U.	Tr	05.56	56	18	-	6
LUKE George Thomas						
Newcastle, 17 December, 1933						(OL)
Newcastle U.	Jnrs	12.50				
Hartlepool U.	Tr	10.53	53-59	186	-	60
Newcastle U.	Tr	10.59	59-60	27	-	4
Darlington	Tr	01.61	60-62	68	-	10
LUKE Noel Emmanuel						
Birmingham, 28 December, 1964						(W/RB)
West Bromwich A.	App	04.82	82-83	8	1	1
Mansfield T.	Tr	07.84	84-85	41	9	9
Peterborough U.	Tr	08.86	86-92	270	7	27
Rochdale	L	03.93	92	2	1	0
LUKE William						
Aberdeen, 19 April, 1932						(IL)
Crewe Alex.	East Fife	10.55	55	1	-	0
LUKIC Jovan (John)						
Chesterfield, 11 December, 1960 E Yth/Eu21-7/E'B'						(G)
Leeds U.	App	12.78	79-82	146	0	0
Arsenal	Tr	07.83	83-89	223	0	0
Leeds U.	Tr	06.90	90-95	209	0	0
Arsenal	Tr	07.96	96	15	0	0
LUMBY James Anthony						
Grimsby, 2 October, 1954						(F)
Grimsby T.	Jnrs	10.72	73-74	28	3	12
Scunthorpe U.	Brigg T.	03.77	76-77	55	0	29
Carlisle U.	Tr	04.78	77-78	24	3	7
Tranmere Rov.	Tr	07.79	79-80	43	3	21
Mansfield T.	Tr	01.81	80-81	49	2	18
LUMLEY Robert						
Consett, 6 January, 1933						(IF)
Charlton Ath.	Jnrs	01.50	53-54	6	-	0

League Club	Source	Date Signed	Seasons Played	Apps	Subs	Gls
Hartlepool U.	Tr	02.55	54-57	107	-	19
Chesterfield	Tr	12.57	57-58	25	-	2
Gateshead	Tr	06.59	59	40	-	5
Hartlepool U.	Tr	07.60	60	38	-	6
LUMLEY Ilderton **Thomas**						
Consett, 9 December, 1924						(IF)
Charlton Ath.	Consett	12.48	48-51	37	-	10
Barnsley	Tr	03.52	51-55	146	-	36
Darlington	Tr	08.56	56	15	-	3
LUMSDEN Alexander						
Falkirk, 24 May, 1946						(F)
Southend U.	Camelon Jnrs	02.66	65-66	2	0	0
LUMSDEN James Murdoch						
Glasgow, 7 November, 1947						(M)
Leeds U.	Jnrs	11.66	66-69	3	1	0
Southend U.	Tr	09.70	70	12	1	0
LUMSDEN John David						
Newcastle, 30 July, 1956						(RB)
Stoke C.	App	08.73	75-77	26	2	0
Port Vale	L	03.78	77	5	0	0
LUMSDEN John Ivor						
Heanor, 1 July, 1942						(LB)
Aston Villa	Jnrs	07.59				
Workington	Tr	02.52	61-67	249	2	7
Chesterfield	Tr	03.68	67-70	94	0	0
LUMSDEN John Watson						
Edinburgh, 15 December, 1960						(M)
Stoke C.	East Fife	02.80	79-81	2	4	0
LUMSDON Christopher						
Newcastle, 15 December, 1979						(LW)
Sunderland	YT	07.97	97	1	0	0
LUND Gary James						
Grimsby, 13 September, 1964 E Sch/Eu21-3						(F)
Grimsby T.	Jnrs	07.83	83-85	47	13	24
Lincoln C.	Tr	08.86	86	41	3	13
Notts Co.	Tr	06.87	87-94	223	25	62
Hull C.	L	08.92	92	5	0	2
Hull C.	L	01.93	92	6	0	1
Hull C.	L	03.95	94	11	0	3
Chesterfield	Tr	12.95	95-96	13	5	1
LUNDEKVAM Claus						
Norway, 22 February, 1973 Norwegian Int						(CD)
Southampton	S.K. Brann (Nor)	09.96	96-97	59	1	0
LUNDON Sean						
Liverpool, 7 March, 1969						(LB/M)
Chester C.	YT	12.86	86-90	48	8	4
LUNDSTRUM Colin Francis						
Colchester, 9 October, 1938						(W)
Ipswich T.	West Ham U. (Am)	11.56	57-59	13	-	1
Colchester U.	Tr	08.61	61	1	-	0
LUNN Dennis						
Barnsley, 20 November, 1938						(CH)
Doncaster Rov.	Wombwell	10.58	59-61	85	-	0
LUNN George						
Bolton-on-Dearne, 28 June, 1915						(CH)
Aston Villa	Frickley Colly	05.38				
Birmingham C.	Tr	09.46				
Watford	Tr	10.47	47	5	-	0
LUNN Grant						
Guildford, 26 August, 1967						(G)
Aldershot (N/C)	Chelsea (App)	08.85	85	9	0	0
LUNN Henry (Harry)						
Lurgan (NI), 2 March, 1925 Died 1980						(OR)
Notts Co.	Lurgan	07.46	46	24	-	5
Portsmouth	Tr	07.47	47	1	-	0
Swindon T.	Tr	05.48	48-53	195	-	30
LUNN Jack						
Barnsley, 14 October, 1937 Died 1988						(OL)
Barnsley	Jnrs	05.56	56-60	56	-	19
Chesterfield	Tr	07.61	61	40	-	13
LUNN William John						
Lurgan (NI), 8 May, 1923 NI Sch						(IF)
West Bromwich A.	Glenavon	02.46	46-47	10	-	5

League Club	Source	Date Signed	Seasons Played	Apps	Subs	Gls
Bournemouth	Tr	02.48	47-49	47	-	19
Newport Co.	Tr	07.50	50-51	6	-	1
LUNNISS Roy Evan						
Islington, 4 November, 1939						(FB)
Crystal Palace	Carshalton Ath.	04.60	59-62	25	-	1
Portsmouth	Tr	06.63	63-65	69	0	1
Luton T.	South Africa	12.66	66	1	0	0
LUNT Kenneth Vincent						
Runcorn, 20 November, 1979 E Sch/E Yth						(M)
Crewe Alex.	YT	06.97	97	29	12	2
LUNT Robert John						
Widnes, 11 December, 1973						(LW)
Wrexham	YT	●	90-91	1	8	0
LUSCOMBE Lee James						
Guernsey, 16 July, 1971						(W)
Southampton	YT	04.89				
Brentford	Tr	10.91	91-92	29	13	6
Millwall	Tr	06.93	93	0	2	0
Doncaster Rov.	Tr	02.94	93	5	3	0
LUSTED Leslie Reginald						
Reading, 20 September, 1931						(IF)
Leyton Orient	Harwich & Parkeston	12.52	52-53	23	-	6
Aldershot	Tr	07.54	54-55	10	-	1
LUTTON Robert (Bert) John						
Banbridge (NI), 13 July, 1950 NI-6						(W)
Wolverhampton W.	Jnrs	09.67	68-70	16	5	1
Brighton & H.A.	Tr	09.71	71-72	18	11	4
West Ham U.	Tr	01.73	72-73	8	4	1
LYALL George						
Wick, 4 May, 1947						(M)
Preston N.E.	Raith Rov.	03.66	65-71	90	15	16
Nottingham F.	Tr	05.72	72-75	108	8	24
Hull C.	Tr	12.75	75-76	42	0	5
LYALL John Angus						
Ilford, 24 February, 1940 E Yth						(LB)
West Ham U.	Jnrs	05.57	59-62	31	-	0
LYDERSEN Pal						
Norway, 10 September, 1965 Norwegian Int						(FB)
Arsenal	F.K. Start (Nor)	11.91	91-92	12	3	0
LYDIATE Jason Lee						
Manchester, 29 October, 1971						(CD)
Manchester U.	YT	07.90				
Bolton W.	Tr	03.92	91-94	29	1	0
Blackpool	Tr	03.95	94-97	81	5	2
LYDON George **Michael**						
Sunderland, 25 November, 1933 E Sch						(OL)
Sunderland	Jnrs	12.50				
Leeds U.	Tr	06.54	54	4	-	1
Gateshead	Tr	11.55	55-58	106	-	24
LYMAN Colin Charles						
Northampton, 9 March, 1914 Died 1986						(OL)
Southend U.	Rushden T.	03.34	33	1	-	0
Northampton T.	Tr	11.34	34-37	85	-	31
Tottenham H.	Tr	10.37	37-38	46	-	10
Port Vale	Tr	05.46	46	11	-	1
Nottingham F.	Tr	10.46	46	23	-	9
Notts Co.	Tr	08.47	47	21	-	5
LYNAM Christopher Anthony						
Manchester, 22 January, 1962						(W)
Manchester U.	App	01.80				
Carlisle U.	Ryoden (HK)	08.86	86	1	1	0
LYNCH Anthony Junior						
Paddington, 20 January, 1966						(W)
Brentford	Jnrs	01.84	83-85	35	10	6
Barnet	Wealdstone	10.90	91-93	18	18	4
LYNCH Barry John						
Birmingham, 8 June, 1951						(FB)
Aston Villa	App	01.69	68-69	2	0	0
Grimsby T.	Atlanta (USA)	09.72	72	10	4	0
Scunthorpe U.	Tr	07.73	73-74	62	2	0
Torquay U.	Portland T. (USA)	09.75	75-76	67	3	2
LYNCH Christopher John						
Middlesbrough, 18 November, 1974						(LB/M)
Hartlepool U.	Halifax T. (YT)	05.93	92-95	38	12	2

League Club	Source	Date Signed	Seasons Played	Apps	Subs	Gls
LYNCH John						
Uddingston, 22 September, 1917						(G)
Workington	St Mirren	10.52	52	2	-	0
LYNCH Patrick						
Belfast, 22 January, 1950						(D)
Middlesbrough	Cliftonville	06.70	71	0	1	0
LYNCH Terence John						
Newport, 17 May, 1952						(G)
Newport Co.	Jnrs	11.69	69-71	56	0	0
LYNCH Thomas Michael						
Limerick, 10 October, 1964						(M/LB)
Sunderland	Limerick	08.88	88	4	0	0
Shrewsbury T.	Tr	01.90	89-95	220	14	14
LYNE Michael George Anthony						
Kettering, 20 March, 1938						(G)
Preston N.E.	Jnrs	03.56	58	2	-	0
Bournemouth	Tr	06.59	59-60	17	-	0
LYNE Neil George Francis						
Leicester, 4 April, 1970						(W)
Nottingham F.	Leicester U.	08.89				
Walsall	L	03.90	89	6	1	0
Shrewsbury T.	L	03.91	90	16	0	6
Shrewsbury T.	Tr	07.91	91-92	61	3	11
Cambridge U.	Tr	01.93	92-93	5	12	0
Chesterfield	L	09.93	93	3	0	1
Chesterfield	L	03.94	93	2	1	0
Hereford U.	Tr	07.94	94-95	49	14	2
Northampton T. (N/C)	Tr	08.96	96	1	0	0
LYNEX Steven Charles						
West Bromwich, 23 January, 1958						(W)
West Bromwich A.	App	01.76				
Birmingham C.	Shamrock Rov.	04.79	78-80	28	18	10
Leicester C.	Tr	02.81	80-86	200	13	57
Birmingham C.	L	10.86	86	10	0	2
West Bromwich A.	Tr	03.87	86-87	26	3	3
Cardiff C.	Tr	07.88	88-89	56	6	2
LYNN Francis						
Consett, 29 May, 1929						(OL)
Grimsby T	Blackhall Colly	12.47	48	2	-	0
LYNN Joseph						
Cramlington, 31 January, 1925 Died 1992						(IF/WH)
Huddersfield T.	Cramlington	05.47	49	5	-	0
Exeter C.	Tr	06.50	50	29	-	2
Rochdale	Tr	07.51	51-55	193	-	23
LYNN Samuel						
St Helens, 25 December, 1920 Died 1995						(WH)
Manchester U.	Jnrs	01.38	47-49	13	-	0
Bradford P.A.	Tr	02.51	50-52	73	-	0
LYNN Stanley						
Bolton, 18 June, 1928						(FB)
Accrington St.	Whitworths	07.47	46-49	35	-	2
Aston Villa	Tr	03.50	50-61	281	-	36
Birmingham C.	Tr	10.61	61-65	131	0	26
LYNN William						
Newcastle, 20 January, 1947						(OL)
Huddersfield T.		07.65	65-66	4	0	0
Rotherham U.	Tr	04.67				
LYON David Edward						
Oldham, 21 November, 1948						(M)
Bolton W.	App	11.66				
Southport	Wigan Ath.	09.76	76	11	2	1
LYON David George						
Bowden, 18 January, 1951						(CD)
Bury	App	01.69	68-71	65	6	0
Huddersfield T.	Tr	09.71	71-73	24	1	0
Mansfield T.	L	11.73	73	2	0	0
Cambridge U.	Tr	07.74	74-76	84	1	11
Northampton T.	Tr	10.77	77	6	0	0
LYON Thomas King						
Clydebank, 17 March, 1915						(CF)
Blackpool	Albion Rov.	03.37	36-37	7	-	0
Chesterfield	Tr	09.38	38-47	41	-	22
New Brighton	Tr	07.48	48	36	-	7
LYONS Andrew						
Blackpool, 19 October, 1966						(W)
Crewe Alex.	Fleetwood T.	10.92	92-93	7	4	2
Wigan Ath.	Tr	10.93	93-95	79	8	27
LYONS Barry						
Shirebrook, 14 March, 1945						(W)
Rotherham U.	Jnrs	09.62	63-66	125	0	23
Nottingham F.	Tr	11.66	66-72	201	2	28
York C.	Tr	09.73	73-75	80	5	11
Darlington	Tr	07.76	76-78	97	0	10
LYONS Brian						
Darfield, 3 December, 1948						(CH)
Bradford P.A. (Am)	Houghton Colly	03.68	67	3	0	0
LYONS Darren Peter						
Manchester, 9 November, 1966						(W)
Bury	Ashton U.	03.92	91-92	23	13	7
LYONS Albert **Edward**						
Manchester, 20 May, 1920 Died 1996						(FB)
Bury		04.45	47-48	2	-	0
Millwall	Tr	03.50	49-51	6	-	0
Crewe Alex.	Tr	07.52	52-53	23	-	0
Rochdale	Tr	12.53	53-54	19	-	1
LYONS George William						
Manchester, 1 May, 1935						(OR)
Rochdale		12.53	53-56	29	-	4
LYONS John Patrick						
Hawarden, 8 November, 1956 Died 1982						(F)
Wrexham	Jnrs	06.75	74-78	63	23	23
Millwall	Tr	07.79	79-80	55	0	20
Cambridge U.	Tr	10.80	80-81	20	1	6
Colchester U.	Tr	02.82	81-82	31	2	9
LYONS Michael						
Liverpool, 8 December, 1951 Eu23-5/E'B'						(CD)
Everton	App	07.69	70-81	364	26	48
Sheffield Wed.	Tr	08.82	82-85	129	0	12
Grimsby T.	Tr	11.85	85-86	50	0	4
LYONS Michael Charles						
Iron Acton (Glos), 31 January, 1932						(FB)
Bristol C.	Jnrs	06.50	50-51	2	-	0
Bristol Rov.	Tr	07.53	53	2	-	0
Bournemouth	Tr	07.56	56-58	105	-	0
Swindon T.	Tr	11.59	59	2	-	0
LYONS Paul						
Leigh, 24 June, 1977						(LB/M)
Rochdale	Manchester U. (YT)	09.95	95	1	2	0
LYONS Terence						
Bradford, 14 April, 1929 Died 1986						(OL)
Burnley		10.49	50	12	-	3
Bradford P.A.	Tr	09.51	51-52	38	-	6
LYSKE James Herbert Alexander						
Portadown, 7 October, 1932						(FB)
Sunderland	Glenavon	11.57				
Darlington	Tr	02.58	57-58	16	-	0
LYTHGOE Arnold						
Bolton, 7 March, 1922						(LH)
Accrington St.	Ashton National	09.45	46	10	-	0
LYTHGOE Derrick						
Bolton, 5 May, 1933						(W)
Blackpool	Jnrs	05.50	55-57	4	-	1
Norwich C.	Tr	03.58	57-61	62	-	22
Bristol C.	Tr	08.62	62-63	13	-	2
LYTHGOE Philip						
Norwich, 18 December, 1959						(W)
Norwich C.	App	12.77	77-79	9	3	1
Bristol Rov.	L	09.78	78	6	0	0
Oxford U.	Tr	08.80	80-81	23	5	3
LYTTLE Desmond						
Wolverhampton, 24 September, 1971						(RB)
Leicester C.	YT	01.90				
Swansea C.	Worcester C.	07.92	92	46	0	1
Nottingham F.	Tr	07.93	93-97	172	3	3

League Club	Source	Date Signed	Seasons Played	Apps	Subs	Gls
MABBUTT Gary Vincent						
Bristol, 23 August, 1961 E Yth/Eu21-7/E'B'/E-16						(CD)
Bristol Rov.	App	01.79	78-81	122	9	10
Tottenham H.	Tr	08.82	82-97	458	19	27
MABBUTT Kevin Richard						
Bristol, 5 December, 1958						(F)
Bristol C.	App	01.76	77-81	112	17	29
Crystal Palace	Tr	10.81	81-84	67	8	22
MABBUTT Raymond William						
Aylesbury, 13 March, 1936						(WH)
Bristol Rov.	Oxford C.	08.56	57-68	392	3	27
Newport Co.	Tr	09.69	69-70	39	7	14
MABEE Gary Lee						
Oxford, 1 February, 1955						(F)
Tottenham H.	App	02.72				
Northampton T.	Tr	08.74	74-75	29	4	13
McADAM David Frederick						
Hereford, 3 April, 1923						(FB)
Leeds U.	Stapenhill W.	05.48	48-49	24	-	0
Wrexham	Tr	05.50	50	10	-	0
McADAM Neil Bernard						
East Kilbride, 30 July, 1957						(G)
Port Vale	Northwich Vic.	08.82	82	2	0	0
McADAM Steven						
Portadown (NI), 2 April, 1960						(FB)
Burnley	Portadown	05.78	79	5	0	0
Wigan Ath	Barnsley (N/C)	11.80	80-81	26	0	0
McADAM Thomas Ian						
Glasgow, 9 April, 1954						(CD)
Stockport Co.	Glasgow Celtic	08.86	86	5	0	1
McADAMS William John						
Belfast, 20 January, 1934 NI-15						(CF)
Manchester C.	Distillery	12.53	53-59	127	-	62
Bolton W.	Tr	09.60	60-61	44	-	26
Leeds U.	Tr	12.61	61	11	-	3
Brentford	Tr	07.62	62-64	75	-	36
Queens Park R.	Tr	09.64	64-65	33	0	11
Barrow	Tr	07.66	66-67	53	0	9
McALEA Robert Joseph						
Belfast, 13 September, 1920						(IF)
Bradford C.	Ballymoney	07.48	48	4	-	0
McALEER Frank						
Glasgow, 16 October, 1945						(M)
Barrow	Morton	08.70	70	9	1	0
McALINDEN James						
Belfast, 31 December, 1917 Died 1993 LoI/IR-2/NI-4						(IF)
Portsmouth	Belfast Celtic	12.38	38-47	53	-	9
Stoke C.	Tr	09.47	47-48	33	-	2
Southend U.	Tr	10.48	48-53	217	-	12
McALINDEN Robert						
Salford, 22 May, 1946						(W)
Manchester C.	Aston Villa (App)	05.64	63	1	-	0
Port Vale	Tr	09.65				
Bournemouth	Los Angeles (USA)	09.76	76	1	0	0
McALINDON Gareth Edward						
Hexham, 6 April, 1977						(F)
Carlisle U.	Newcastle U. (YT)	07.95	95-97	19	24	5
McALINDON John						
Carlisle, 25 December, 1930						(CF)
Shrewsbury T.	Glasgow Celtic	05.57	57	12	-	3
McALISTER Thomas Gerald						
Clydebank, 10 December, 1952						(G)
Sheffield U.	App	05.70	71-75	63	0	0
Rotherham U.	Tr	01.76	75-78	159	0	0
Blackpool	Tr	07.79	79	16	0	0
Swindon T.	Tr	05.80	80	1	0	0
Bristol Rov.	L	02.81	80	13	0	0
West Ham U.	Tr	05.81	81-88	85	0	0
Colchester U.	L	02.89	88	20	0	0
McALLE John Edward						
Liverpool, 31 January, 1950						(CD)
Wolverhampton W.	App	02.67	67-80	394	12	0
Sheffield U.	Tr	08.81	81	18	0	0
Derby Co.	Tr	04.82	81-83	51	7	1
McALLISTER Brian						
Glasgow, 30 November, 1970 S-3						(D)
Wimbledon	YT	02.89	89-97	74	11	0
Plymouth Arg.	L	12.90	90	7	1	0
Crewe Alex.	L	03.96	95	13	0	1
McALLISTER Donald						
Radcliffe, 26 May, 1953						(D)
Bolton W.	App	06.70	69-74	155	1	2
Tottenham H.	Tr	02.75	74-80	168	4	9
Charlton Ath.	Tr	08.81	81-82	55	0	6
Rochdale (N/C)	Vitoria Setubal (Por))	11.84	84	3	0	0
McALLISTER Gary						
Motherwell, 25 December, 1964 Su21-1/S'B'/S-56						(M)
Leicester C.	Motherwell	08.85	85-89	199	2	46
Leeds U.	Tr	06.90	90-95	230	1	31
Coventry C.	Tr	07.96	96-97	52	0	6
McALLISTER James						
Barrhead, 30 October, 1931						(IF)
Millwall	Neilston Jnrs	06.54	54-55	20	-	6
Bradford P.A.	Morton	05.59	59-60	43	-	14
McALLISTER Kevin						
Falkirk, 8 November, 1962						(W)
Chelsea	Falkirk	05.85	85-90	78	28	7
McALONE Robert						
Whitehaven, 16 February, 1928						(CH)
Workington		(N/L)	51-53	68	-	3
McALOON Gerald Padua						
Glasgow, 13 September, 1916 Died 1987						(IF)
Brentford	St Francis	06.34	37-38	21	-	9
Wolverhampton W.	Tr	03.39	38	2	-	1
Brentford	Tr	12.45	46	7	-	4
McANDREW Anthony						
Glasgow, 11 April, 1956						(CD)
Middlesbrough	App	08.73	73-81	245	2	13
Chelsea	Tr	09.82	82-83	20	0	4
Middlesbrough	Tr	09.84	84-85	66	0	2
Darlington	(Retired)	11.88	88	11	0	0
Hartlepool U.	Tr	03.89	88	4	0	0
MacANDREW Robert						
Derby, 6 April, 1943						(HB)
Derby Co.	Jnrs	06.61	63	1	-	0
McANEARNEY James						
Dundee, 20 March, 1935						(IF)
Sheffield Wed.	Jnrs	03.52	53-59	38	-	10
Plymouth Arg.	Tr	01.60	59-63	135	-	34
Watford	Tr	11.63	63-66	84	2	19
Bradford C.	Tr	09.66	66-67	41	4	5
McANEARNEY Thomas						
Dundee, 6 January, 1933						(WH)
Sheffield Wed.	Dundee St Stephens	10.51	52-64	352	-	19
Peterborough U.	Tr	11.65	65	12	0	0
Aldershot	Tr	03.66	65-68	106	0	3
McANESPIE Stephen						
Kilmarnock, 1 February, 1972 S Yth						(RB)
Bolton W.	Raith Rov.	09.95	95-97	19	5	0
Fulham	Tr	11.97	97	2	2	0
Bradford C.	L	03.98	97	7	0	0
McAREAVEY Paul						
Belfast, 3 December, 1980						(M)
Swindon T.	YT	●	97	0	1	0
McAREE Rodney Joseph						
Dungannon, 19 August, 1974 NI Sch/NI Yth						(M)
Liverpool	YT	08.91				
Bristol C.	Tr	07.94	94	4	2	0
Fulham	Dungannon Swifts	12.95	95-97	22	6	3

MACARI Luigi (Lou)
Edinburgh, 7 June, 1949 Su23-2/S-24 (F)

League Club	Source	Date Signed	Seasons Played	Apps	Subs	Gls
Manchester U.	Glasgow Celtic	01.73	72-83	311	18	78
Swindon T.	Tr	07.84	84-85	33	3	3

MACARI Michael
Kilwinning, 4 February, 1973 (F)

League Club	Source	Date Signed	Seasons Played	Apps	Subs	Gls
Stoke C.	West Ham U. (YT)	07.91	96	15	15	3

MACARI Paul
Manchester, 23 August, 1976 (F)

League Club	Source	Date Signed	Seasons Played	Apps	Subs	Gls
Stoke C.	Jnrs	08.93	97	0	3	0

McARTHUR Barry
Nottingham, 4 May, 1947 (CF)

League Club	Source	Date Signed	Seasons Played	Apps	Subs	Gls
Nottingham F.	Jnrs	05.65	65	7	1	4
Barrow	Tr	07.69	69	5	2	0
York C.	Tr	12.69	69	1	0	0

McARTHUR Thomas
Neilston, 23 April, 1925 Died 1994 (CH)

League Club	Source	Date Signed	Seasons Played	Apps	Subs	Gls
Leicester C.	Neilston Vic.	01.47	46-53	97	-	0
Plymouth Arg.	Tr	01.54	53	2	-	0

McARTHUR Walter
Doncaster, 21 March, 1912 Died 1980 (WH)

League Club	Source	Date Signed	Seasons Played	Apps	Subs	Gls
Bristol Rov.	Goldthorpe Colly	01.33	32-49	261	-	14

McATEER Andrew William
Preston, 24 April, 1961 (LB)

League Club	Source	Date Signed	Seasons Played	Apps	Subs	Gls
Preston N.E.	App	04.79	79-86	236	2	8
Blackpool	Tr	12.86	86-87	37	4	0
Preston N.E.	Tr	05.88	88	11	2	1

McATEER Jason Wynn
Birkenhead, 18 June, 1971 IR 'B'/IR-25 (RB/M)

League Club	Source	Date Signed	Seasons Played	Apps	Subs	Gls
Bolton W.	Marine	01.92	92-95	109	5	8
Liverpool	Tr	09.95	95-97	78	9	3

McAUGHTRIE David
Cumnock, 30 January, 1963 (CD)

League Club	Source	Date Signed	Seasons Played	Apps	Subs	Gls
Stoke C.	App	01.81	80-83	48	3	2
Carlisle U.	Tr	07.84	84	28	0	1
York C.	Tr	06.85	85-86	64	0	1
Darlington	Tr	07.87	87-88	36	3	0

MACAULAY Archibald Renwick
Falkirk, 30 July, 1915 Died 1993 S-7 (IF/WH)

League Club	Source	Date Signed	Seasons Played	Apps	Subs	Gls
West Ham U.	Glasgow Rangers	06.37	37-46	83	-	29
Brentford	Tr	10.46	46	26	-	2
Arsenal	Tr	07.47	47-49	103	-	1
Fulham	Tr	06.50	50-52	48	-	4

McAULEY Hugh Albert
Bootle, 8 January, 1953 (W)

League Club	Source	Date Signed	Seasons Played	Apps	Subs	Gls
Liverpool	App	01.70				
Tranmere Rov.	L	08.73	73	13	0	1
Plymouth Arg.	Tr	10.74	74-76	76	1	7
Charlton Ath.	Tr	12.76	76-77	55	0	9
Tranmere Rov.	Tr	08.78	78	41	2	0
Carlisle U.	Tr	07.79	79-80	14	3	1

MACAULEY James Austin Russell
Edinburgh, 19 October, 1922 (WH)

League Club	Source	Date Signed	Seasons Played	Apps	Subs	Gls
Chelsea	Edinburgh Thistle	10.46	46-49	86	-	5
Aldershot	Tr	08.51	51	31	-	3

McAULEY Patrick Comerford
Motherwell, 31 July, 1921 Died 1970 SF Lge (WH)

League Club	Source	Date Signed	Seasons Played	Apps	Subs	Gls
Luton T.	Glasgow Celtic	12.50	50	8	-	1

McAULEY Sean
Sheffield, 23 June, 1972 S Yth/Su21-1 (LB)

League Club	Source	Date Signed	Seasons Played	Apps	Subs	Gls
Manchester U.	YT	07.90				
Chesterfield (L)	St Johnstone	11.94	94	1	0	1
Hartlepool U.	St Johnstone	07.95	95-96	84	0	1
Scunthorpe U.	Tr	03.97	96-97	39	5	1

McAULEY Stephen Roy
Lytham, 4 March, 1969 (CD)

League Club	Source	Date Signed	Seasons Played	Apps	Subs	Gls
Manchester C.	YT	11.87				
Crewe Alex.	Fleetwood T.	03.92	91-96	161	4	20

McAVENNIE Frank
Glasgow, 22 November, 1959 S Yth/Su21-5/S-5 (F)

League Club	Source	Date Signed	Seasons Played	Apps	Subs	Gls
West Ham U.	St Mirren	06.85	85-87	85	0	33
West Ham U.	Glasgow Celtic	03.89	88-91	49	19	16
Aston Villa	Tr	08.92	92	0	3	0
Swindon T. (L)	Glasgow Celtic	02.94	93	3	4	0

McAVOY Alan Joseph
Wigton (Cumb), 4 October, 1963 (M)

League Club	Source	Date Signed	Seasons Played	Apps	Subs	Gls
Blackpool		02.81	81	6	0	0

McAVOY Douglas Haig
Kilmarnock, 29 November, 1918 (IF)

League Club	Source	Date Signed	Seasons Played	Apps	Subs	Gls
Liverpool	Kilmarnock	12.47	47-48	2	-	0

McBAIN Alan
Aberdeen, 10 February, 1940 (FB)

League Club	Source	Date Signed	Seasons Played	Apps	Subs	Gls
Swansea C.	Aberdeen E.E.	01.59				
Carlisle U.	Tr	06.60	60-62	70	-	0
Luton T.	Tr	06.63	63-64	60	-	0

McBAIN Gordon Archibald
Blantyre, 4 December, 1934 (W)

League Club	Source	Date Signed	Seasons Played	Apps	Subs	Gls
Rochdale	Kilmarnock	05.58	58	10	-	1

McBAIN Neil
Campbeltown, 15 November, 1895 Died 1974 S-3 (WH)

League Club	Source	Date Signed	Seasons Played	Apps	Subs	Gls
Manchester U.	Ayr U.	11.21	21-22	42	-	2
Everton	Tr	01.23	22-25	97	-	1
Liverpool	St Johnstone	03.28	27-28	12	-	0
Watford	Tr	11.28	28-31	84	-	4
New Brighton	(Team Manager)	03.47	46	1	-	0

MacBENNETT James (Seamus) Congall
Newcastle (NI), 16 November, 1925 Died 1995 (OR)

League Club	Source	Date Signed	Seasons Played	Apps	Subs	Gls
Cardiff C.	Belfast Celtic	09.47	47	4	-	2
Tranmere Rov.	Tr	11.48	48-49	12	-	1

McBETH George
Belfast, 4 September, 1954 (W)

League Club	Source	Date Signed	Seasons Played	Apps	Subs	Gls
Manchester C.	App	10.71				
Stockport Co.	Tr	07.76	76-77	51	5	3

McBLAIN Andrew
Bo'ness, 11 August, 1926 (LH)

League Club	Source	Date Signed	Seasons Played	Apps	Subs	Gls
Newport Co.	Forth W.	02.47	46-48	36	-	1

McBRIDE Andrew David
Kenya, 15 March, 1954 (CD)

League Club	Source	Date Signed	Seasons Played	Apps	Subs	Gls
Crystal Palace	App	10.71	73	1	0	0

McBRIDE John
Kilsyth, 31 December, 1923 (G)

League Club	Source	Date Signed	Seasons Played	Apps	Subs	Gls
Reading	Third Lanark	03.48	47-52	100	-	0
Shrewsbury T.	Tr	12.52	52-55	78	-	0

McBRIDE Joseph
Glasgow, 17 August, 1960 S Sch/Su21-1 (W)

League Club	Source	Date Signed	Seasons Played	Apps	Subs	Gls
Everton	App	08.78	79-81	51	6	9
Rotherham U.	Tr	08.82	82-83	45	0	12
Oldham Ath.	Tr	09.83	83-84	28	8	5

McBRIDE Joseph
Glasgow, 10 June, 1938 SF Lge/S-2 (CF)

League Club	Source	Date Signed	Seasons Played	Apps	Subs	Gls
Wolverhampton W.	Kilmarnock	12.59				
Luton T.	Tr	02.60	59-60	25	-	9

McBRIDE Peter Patrick
Motherwell, 22 December, 1946 (WH)

League Club	Source	Date Signed	Seasons Played	Apps	Subs	Gls
Manchester U.	Jnrs	12.63				
Southport	Tr	07.66	66	1	2	0
Bradford P.A.	Tr	07.67	67	5	2	0

McBRIDE Vincent
Stalybridge, 21 January, 1934 (G)

League Club	Source	Date Signed	Seasons Played	Apps	Subs	Gls
Walsall	Ashton U.	05.54	54	11	-	0
Aston Villa	Tr	03.56				
Mansfield T.	Tr	07.58	58	10	-	0

McBRIDE William
Brampton (Cumb), 8 November, 1913 Died 1985 (LB)

League Club	Source	Date Signed	Seasons Played	Apps	Subs	Gls
Carlisle U.		02.46	46	14	-	1

McBURNEY Michael Leslie
Wrexham, 12 September, 1953 W Sch (F)

League Club	Source	Date Signed	Seasons Played	Apps	Subs	Gls
Wrexham	Jnrs	07.71	70-72	20	4	4
Bolton W.	Tr	05.73	73	1	0	0
Hartlepool U.	L	11.74	74	5	1	1
Tranmere Rov.	L	03.75	74	4	1	0

MacCABE Andrew Bruce
Glasgow, 22 February, 1935 Died 1964 (W)

League Club	Source	Date Signed	Seasons Played	Apps	Subs	Gls
Chesterfield	Corby T.	11.55	55-58	53	-	7

McCABE James Joseph
Derry (NI), 17 September, 1918 Died 1989 NI-6 (WH)

League Club	Source	Date Signed	Seasons Played	Apps	Subs	Gls
Middlesbrough	South Bank	05.37	46-47	34	-	0
Leeds U.	Tr	03.48	47-53	152	-	0

McCAFFERTY James
Motherwell, 10 July, 1957 (W)

League Club	Source	Date Signed	Seasons Played	Apps	Subs	Gls
Hereford U.	Bristol C. (App)	04.75	75	0	3	0

McCAFFREY Aiden
Jarrow, 30 August, 1957 E Yth (CD)

League Club	Source	Date Signed	Seasons Played	Apps	Subs	Gls
Newcastle U.	App	01.74	74-77	57	2	4
Derby Co.	Tr	08.78	78-79	31	6	4
Bristol Rov.	Tr	08.80	80-84	183	1	11
Bristol C.	L	02.82	81	6	0	1
Torquay U.	L	03.85	84	6	0	0
Exeter C.	Tr	07.85	85-86	55	3	0
Hartlepool U.	Tr	02 87	86	6	0	1
Carlisle U.	Whitley Bay	01.88	87	14	0	0

McCAFFREY James
Luton, 12 October, 1951 E Yth (W)

League Club	Source	Date Signed	Seasons Played	Apps	Subs	Gls
Nottingham F.	App	03.69	69	2	6	1
Mansfield T.	Tr	07.72	72-76	170	8	21
Huddersfield T.	Tr	01.77	76-77	23	4	0
Portsmouth	Tr	02.78	77-78	11	1	1
Northampton T.	Tr	12.78	78-79	56	1	6

McCAIG Robert Alexander Marshall
Lockerbie, 15 August, 1923 Died 1986 (OR)

League Club	Source	Date Signed	Seasons Played	Apps	Subs	Gls
Carlisle U.	Queen of South	08.48	48	5	-	0
Blackburn Rov.	Tr	12.48	48-50	30	-	2
Stockport Co.	Tr	08.51	51	15	-	2
Halifax T.	Tr	01.52	51	17	-	2
Crewe Alex.	Tr	08.52	52-53	19	-	1

McCALL Alexander Noteman
Annan, 26 March, 1939 (WH)

League Club	Source	Date Signed	Seasons Played	Apps	Subs	Gls
Carlisle U.		09.58	59	1	-	0

McCALL Andrew
Hamilton, 15 March, 1925 (W)

League Club	Source	Date Signed	Seasons Played	Apps	Subs	Gls
Blackpool	Blantyre Vic.	07.47	47-50	84	-	15
West Bromwich A.	Tr	01.51	50-51	31	-	3
Leeds U.	Tr	08.52	52-54	62	-	8
Halifax T.	Lovells Ath.	07.56	56-59	139	-	15

McCALL Anthony Edward
Thatcham, 15 January, 1936 (F)

League Club	Source	Date Signed	Seasons Played	Apps	Subs	Gls
Reading	Jnrs	05.53	55-56	8	-	1

McCALL David
Carlisle, 24 January, 1948 (OR)

League Club	Source	Date Signed	Seasons Played	Apps	Subs	Gls
Workington	Jnrs	01.66	66	1	0	0

McCALL Ian Holland
Dumfries, 30 September, 1964 (M)

League Club	Source	Date Signed	Seasons Played	Apps	Subs	Gls
Bradford C.	Glasgow Rangers	01.90	89	11	1	1

McCALL John
Glasgow, 29 September, 1918 Died 1992 (WH)

League Club	Source	Date Signed	Seasons Played	Apps	Subs	Gls
Bradford P.A.	Workington	09.37	37-47	41	-	5

McCALL Peter
West Ham, 11 September, 1936 (WH)

League Club	Source	Date Signed	Seasons Played	Apps	Subs	Gls
Bristol C.	Kings Lynn	04.55	57-61	78	-	1
Oldham Ath.	Tr	05.62	62-64	108	-	5

McCALL Robert Henry
Worksop, 29 December, 1915 Died 1992 (FB)

League Club	Source	Date Signed	Seasons Played	Apps	Subs	Gls
Nottingham F.	Worksop T.	02.35	35-51	162	-	1

McCALL Stephen Harold
Carlisle, 15 October, 1960 E Yth/Eu21-6/E'B' (M/LB)

League Club	Source	Date Signed	Seasons Played	Apps	Subs	Gls
Ipswich T.	App	10.78	79-86	249	8	7
Sheffield Wed.	Tr	06.87	87-90	21	8	2
Carlisle U.	L	02.90	89	6	0	0
Plymouth Arg.	Tr	03.92	91-95	97	3	5
Torquay U.	Tr	07.96	96-97	43	8	2

McCALL Stuart Murray
Leeds, 10 June, 1964 E Yth/Su21-2/S-40 (M)

League Club	Source	Date Signed	Seasons Played	Apps	Subs	Gls
Bradford C.	App	06.82	82-87	235	3	37
Everton	Tr	06.88	88-90	99	4	6

McCALL William
Glasgow, 14 November, 1920 (OL)

League Club	Source	Date Signed	Seasons Played	Apps	Subs	Gls
Newcastle U.	Aberdeen	01.48	47-48	16	-	4

McCALLIOG James
Glasgow, 23 September, 1946 S Sch/Su23-2/S-5 (M)

League Club	Source	Date Signed	Seasons Played	Apps	Subs	Gls
Chelsea	Leeds U. (Am)	09.63	64-65	7	0	2
Sheffield Wed.	Tr	10.65	65-68	150	0	19
Wolverhampton W.	Tr	08.69	69-73	158	5	34
Manchester U.	Tr	03.74	73-74	31	0	7
Southampton	Tr	02.75	74-76	70	2	8
Lincoln C.	Chicago (USA)	09.78	78	9	0	0

MacCALLUM Stewart
Bearsden, 9 May, 1927 (WH)

League Club	Source	Date Signed	Seasons Played	Apps	Subs	Gls
Wrexham	Rhyl	06.50	50-52	67	-	0
Workington	Kettering T.	06.54	54-55	10	-	1
Coventry C.	Tr	02.56				
Hartlepool U.	Tr	07.56	56	2	-	0
Southport	Tr	08.57	57	9	-	0

McCALMAN Donald Stuart
Greenock, 18 October, 1935 (CH)

League Club	Source	Date Signed	Seasons Played	Apps	Subs	Gls
Bradford P.A.	Hibernian	06.59	59-65	297	0	5
Barrow	Tr	07.66	66	13	0	0

McCAMBRIDGE David Thomas
Larne (NI), 26 July, 1921 Died 1982 (WH)

League Club	Source	Date Signed	Seasons Played	Apps	Subs	Gls
Barrow	Larne T.	09.46	46-49	15	-	1

McCAMMON Mark Jason
Barnet, 7 August, 1978 (F)

League Club	Source	Date Signed	Seasons Played	Apps	Subs	Gls
Cambridge U. (N/C)	Cambridge C.	12.96	97	0	2	0

McCANCE Darren
Consett, 13 September, 1973 (RB)

League Club	Source	Date Signed	Seasons Played	Apps	Subs	Gls
Reading	YT	07.92	92	1	0	0

McCANN Albert
Maidenhead, 1 November, 1941 (IF)

League Club	Source	Date Signed	Seasons Played	Apps	Subs	Gls
Luton T.	Jnrs	04.59	59-60	6	-	0
Coventry C.	Tr	08.61	61	22	-	3
Portsmouth	Tr	08.62	62-73	331	7	85

McCANN Gavin Peter
Blackpool, 10 January, 1978 (M)

League Club	Source	Date Signed	Seasons Played	Apps	Subs	Gls
Everton	YT	07.95	97	5	6	0

McCANN James
Dundee, 20 May, 1954 (F)

League Club	Source	Date Signed	Seasons Played	Apps	Subs	Gls
Nottingham F.	App	05.72	74-75	2	4	1
Stockport Co.	L	10.75	75	4	1	0
Halifax T.	L	10.76	76	2	0	1

McCANN John
Glasgow, 27 July, 1934 S 'B' (OL)

League Club	Source	Date Signed	Seasons Played	Apps	Subs	Gls
Barnsley	Bridgeton B.C.	12.55	55-58	118	-	17
Bristol C.	Tr	05.59	59-60	30	-	0
Huddersfield T.	Tr	10.60	60-62	20	-	1
Derby Co.	Tr	09.62	62-63	55	-	2
Darlington	Tr	08.64	64	4	-	0
Chesterfield	Tr	10.64	64-65	41	0	9

McCARRICK Mark Bernard
Liverpool, 4 February, 1962 (FB)

League Club	Source	Date Signed	Seasons Played	Apps	Subs	Gls
Birmingham C.	Witton A.	05.83	83	12	3	0
Lincoln C.	Tr	07.84	84-85	42	2	0
Crewe Alex. (N/C)	Tr	02.86	85	10	1	0
Tranmere Rov.	Runcorn	08.87	87-90	125	0	14

McCARRISON Dugald
Lanark, 22 December, 1969 (F)

League Club	Source	Date Signed	Seasons Played	Apps	Subs	Gls
Darlington (L)	Glasgow Celtic	10.91	91	5	0	2

McCARRON Frank Paul
Glasgow, 1 October, 1943 (D)

League Club	Source	Date Signed	Seasons Played	Apps	Subs	Gls
Carlisle U.	Glasgow Celtic	07.67	67	7	2	1

McCARTER James John
Glasgow, 19 March, 1923 (OL)

League Club	Source	Date Signed	Seasons Played	Apps	Subs	Gls
Sheffield Wed.	Vale of Clyde	01.46	46	6	-	0
Mansfield T.	Tr	08.48	48-49	67	-	10

McCARTHY Alan James
Wandsworth, 11 January, 1972 E Yth/Wu21-3/W 'B' (CD)

League Club	Source	Date Signed	Seasons Played	Apps	Subs	Gls
Queens Park R.	YT	12.89	90-94	8	3	0
Watford	L	11.93	93	8	1	0
Plymouth Arg.	L	02.94	93	1	1	0
Leyton Orient	Tr	08.95	95-96	43	4	0

McCARTHY Anthony Paul
Dublin, 9 November, 1969 IR Yth/IRu21-5 (CD)

League Club	Source	Date Signed	Seasons Played	Apps	Subs	Gls
Millwall	Shelbourne	06.92	92-94	20	1	1

League Club	Source	Date Signed	Seasons Played	Apps	Subs	Gls
Crewe Alex.	L	12.94	94	2	0	0
Colchester U.	Tr	03.95	94-96	88	1	1
McCARTHY Daniel John Anthony						
Abergavenny, 26 September, 1942						(W)
Cardiff C.	Abergavenny Thistle	07.60	61	7	-	0
McCARTHY Gerard						
Limerick (Ire), 30 March, 1934						(CH)
Charlton Ath.	Limerick	07.56	56	4	-	0
McCARTHY Ian						
Porth, 4 September, 1960						(F)
Swansea C.	Coventry C. (App)	03.78	77	0	1	0
McCARTHY John						
Dunmanway, 22 January, 1922						(CF)
Bristol C.	Cork	07.49	49	3	-	0
McCARTHY Jonathan David						
Middlesbrough, 18 August, 1970 NI 'B'/NI-7						(RW)
Hartlepool U. (N/C)	Jnrs	11.87	87	0	1	0
York C.	Shepshed Charterhouse	03.90	90-94	198	1	31
Port Vale	Tr	08.95	95-97	93	1	12
Birmingham C.	Tr	09.97	97	41	0	3
McCARTHY Kevin John						
Bethnal Green, 24 December, 1957						(M)
Watford	App	01.76	75-77	35	1	1
McCARTHY Michael Joseph						
Barnsley, 7 February, 1959 IRu23-1/IR-57						(CD)
Barnsley	App	07.77	77-83	272	0	7
Manchester C.	Tr	12.83	83-86	140	0	2
Millwall	Olympique Lyon (Fr)	03.90	89-91	31	4	2
McCARTHY Paul Jason						
Cork, 4 August, 1971 IR Sch/IR Yth/IRu21-10						(CD)
Brighton & H.A.	YT	04.89	89-95	180	1	6
Wycombe W.	Tr	07.96	96-97	64	7	1
McCARTHY Philip						
Liverpool, 19 February, 1943 Died 1996						(OL)
Oldham Ath.	Skelmersdale U.	07.65	65	2	1	0
Halifax T.	Tr	01.66	65-70	180	1	14
McCARTHY Robert Zepp						
Lyndhurst, 2 November, 1948						(RB)
Southampton	App	11.65	67-74	112	0	2
McCARTHY Roydon Stuart						
Barnsley, 17 January, 1945						(OR)
Barnsley	Jnrs	05.62	61-62	3	-	0
Barrow	Tr	07.64	64-68	188	0	41
Southport	Tr	06.69	69	33	1	4
McCARTHY Sean Casey						
Bridgend, 12 September, 1967 W'B'						(F)
Swansea C.	Bridgend T.	10.85	85-87	76	15	25
Plymouth Arg.	Tr	08.88	88-89	67	3	19
Bradford C.	Tr	07.90	90-93	127	4	60
Oldham Ath.	Tr	12.93	93-97	117	23	43
Bristol C.	L	03.98	97	7	0	1
McCARTHY William Edward						
Bootle, 25 November, 1941 E Sch						(CH)
Liverpool	Jnrs	12.58				
Southport	Tr	10.60	60-62	27	-	1
McCARTNEY Michael						
Musselburgh, 28 September, 1954 S Sch						(LB)
West Bromwich A.	App	12.71				
Carlisle U.	Tr	05.73	73-79	148	8	17
Southampton	Tr	07.80	80	22	0	1
Plymouth Arg.	Tr	08.81	81-82	49	0	5
Carlisle U.	Tr	03.83	82-86	130	1	7
McCARTNEY William Raymond						
Newcraighall, 1 August, 1947						(F)
Port Vale	Glasgow Rangers	06.66	66	14	1	1
McCAVANA William Terence						
Belfast, 24 January, 1921 NI Amat/LoI/NI-3						(CH)
Notts Co. (Am)	Coleraine	08.48	48	3	-	0
MACCIOCHI David Andrew						
Harlow, 14 January, 1972						(LW)
Queens Park R.	YT	01.90				
Brighton & H.A. (N/C)	Tr	09.92	92	0	2	0

League Club	Source	Date Signed	Seasons Played	Apps	Subs	Gls
McCLAIR Brian John						
Airdrie, 8 December, 1963 S Yth/Su21-8/S 'B'/S-30						(F/M)
Manchester U.	Glasgow Celtic	07.87	87-97	296	59	88
McCLAREN Christopher						
Bristol, 14 March, 1963						(D)
Darlington (N/C)	Walton & Hersham	03.87	86	1	2	0
McCLAREN Stephen						
York, 3 May, 1961						(M)
Hull C.	App	04.79	79-84	171	7	16
Derby Co.	Tr	08.85	85-87	23	2	0
Lincoln C.	L	02.87	86	8	0	0
Bristol C.	Tr	02.88	87-88	60	1	2
Oxford U.	Tr	08.89	89-91	27	6	0
McCLATCHEY Derek Heywood						
Prescot, 29 April, 1956						(F)
Liverpool	App	05.73				
Southport	L	02.76	75	2	1	0
McCLEAN Christian Alphonso						
Colchester, 17 October, 1963						(F)
Bristol Rov.	Clacton T.	03.88	87-90	28	23	6
Swansea C.	Tr	07.91	91	4	0	0
Northampton T.	Tr	11.91	91	19	0	3
McCLELLAN Sidney Benjamin						
Bromley, 11 June, 1925						(IF)
Tottenham H.	Chelmsford C.	08.49	50-55	68	-	29
Portsmouth	Tr	11.56	56-57	37	-	9
Leyton Orient	Tr	07.58	58	12	-	4
McCLELLAND Charles						
Lochgelly, 8 January, 1924						(IF)
Blackburn Rov.	Hyde U.	12.46	46-48	13	-	2
Exeter C.	Tr	07.49	49-54	183	-	60
McCLELLAND David						
Newcastle, 25 December, 1941						(W)
Port Vale	Bishop Auckland	08.67	67	2	2	0
McCLELLAND John						
Belfast, 7 December, 1955 EF Lge/NI-53						(CD)
Cardiff C.	Portadown	02.74	74	1	3	1
Mansfield T.	Bangor C.	05.78	78-80	122	3	8
Watford	Glasgow Rangers	11.84	84-88	184	0	3
Leeds U.	Tr	06.89	89-91	22	2	0
Watford	L	01.90	89	1	0	0
Notts Co.	L	03.92	91	6	0	0
Darlington (N/C)	(Coach)	10.96	96	1	0	0
McCLELLAND John (Jack)						
Lurgan (NI), 19 May, 1940 Died 1976 NI-6						(G)
Arsenal	Glenavon	10.60	60-63	46	-	0
Fulham	Tr	12.64	65-68	51	0	0
Lincoln C.	L	12.68	68	12	0	0
McCLELLAND John Bonar						
Bradford, 5 March, 1935						(OR)
Manchester C.	Manchester Y.M.C.A.	03.53	56-58	8	-	2
Lincoln C.	Tr	09.58	58-61	121	-	32
Queens Park R.	Tr	09.61	61-62	71	-	22
Portsmouth	Tr	05.63	62-67	136	1	36
Newport Co.	Tr	07.68	68	36	0	10
McCLELLAND John William						
Colchester, 11 August, 1930						(IF)
Colchester U.		09.51				
Stoke C.	Tr	06.52	52	4	-	0
Swindon T.	Tr	06.54	54	14	-	1
Rochdale	Tr	06.55	55	24	-	5
McCLELLAND Joseph						
Edinburgh, 12 October, 1935						(FB)
Wrexham	Hibernian	06.64	64	32	-	0
McCLENAGHAN Albert						
Derry, 7 July, 1954						(RB)
Watford	Larne T.	12.77	77	2	0	0
McCLURE Douglas Hugh						
Islington, 6 September, 1964 E Yth						(FB)
Queens Park R.	App	08.82				
Exeter C. (N/C)	Tr	11.84	84	0	1	0
Torquay U. (N/C)	Tr	12.84	84	3	1	0
Wimbledon	Tr	01.85	84	2	0	0
Peterborough U.	Finland	10.85	85	4	0	0
Crewe Alex. (N/C)	Tr	01.86	85	3	0	0

McCLURE William
Shotts, 16 May, 1921 (OL)

League Club	Source	Date Signed	Seasons Played	Apps	Subs	Gls
Preston N.E.	Albion Rov.	12.47	47	12	-	2
New Brighton	Tr	07.48	48-49	45	-	7
Carlisle U.	Tr	10.49	49	8	-	0
Hartlepool U.	Tr	08.50	50-52	118	-	24

McCLUSKEY Andrew
Manchester, 29 March, 1951 (WH)

League Club	Source	Date Signed	Seasons Played	Apps	Subs	Gls
Hartlepool U.		09.69	69	4	2	0

McCLUSKEY George McKinlay Cassidy
Hamilton, 19 September, 1957 Su21-6 (F)

League Club	Source	Date Signed	Seasons Played	Apps	Subs	Gls
Leeds U.	Glasgow Celtic	08.83	83-85	57	16	16

McCLUSKEY Ronald
Johnstone, 3 November, 1936 (G)

League Club	Source	Date Signed	Seasons Played	Apps	Subs	Gls
Accrington St.	East Fife	11.60	60	4	-	0

McCLUSKIE James Alexander Joseph
Rawtenstall, 29 September, 1966 (F)

League Club	Source	Date Signed	Seasons Played	Apps	Subs	Gls
Rochdale	Jnrs	07.84	83-85	14	4	0

McCOIST Alistair Murdoch
Glasgow, 24 September, 1962 S Yth/Su21-1/S-59 (F)

League Club	Source	Date Signed	Seasons Played	Apps	Subs	Gls
Sunderland	St Johnstone	08.81	81-82	38	18	8

McCOLE John
Glasgow, 18 September, 1936 (CF)

League Club	Source	Date Signed	Seasons Played	Apps	Subs	Gls
Bradford C.	Falkirk	09.58	58-59	42	-	32
Leeds U.	Tr	09.59	59-61	78	-	45
Bradford C.	Tr	10.61	61-62	46	-	15
Rotherham U.	Tr	12.62	62	14	-	5
Newport Co.	Shelbourne	10.64	64	6	-	2

McCOLL Duncan John
Glasgow, 28 December, 1945 (IF)

League Club	Source	Date Signed	Seasons Played	Apps	Subs	Gls
Barnsley	Partick Thistle	01.66	65	5	0	0

McCOLL Thomas Gunn
Glasgow, 19 September, 1945 (IF)

League Club	Source	Date Signed	Seasons Played	Apps	Subs	Gls
Colchester U.	Dennistoun Jnrs	06.63	63-64	11	-	2
Chelsea	Tr	12.64				

McCONNELL Barry
Exeter, 1 January, 1977 (M/RB)

League Club	Source	Date Signed	Seasons Played	Apps	Subs	Gls
Exeter C.	YT	08.95	95-97	31	27	6

McCONNELL Peter
Ashton-u-Lyne, 3 March, 1937 (WH)

League Club	Source	Date Signed	Seasons Played	Apps	Subs	Gls
Leeds U.	Jnrs	03.54	58-61	48	-	4
Carlisle U.	Tr	08.62	62-68	272	1	27
Bradford C.	Tr	07.69	69-70	76	3	0

McCONVILLE Ian John
Doncaster, 1 May, 1959 (W)

League Club	Source	Date Signed	Seasons Played	Apps	Subs	Gls
Doncaster Rov.	App	04.77	75-77	9	2	1

McCORD Brian John
Derby, 24 August, 1968 (RB/M)

League Club	Source	Date Signed	Seasons Played	Apps	Subs	Gls
Derby Co.	App	06.87	87-89	3	2	0
Barnsley	L	11.89	89	5	0	0
Barnsley	Tr	03.90	89-91	35	3	2
Mansfield T.	L	08.92	92	11	0	1
Stockport Co.	Tr	12.92	92	4	4	0

McCORKINDALE John
Campbeltown, 10 August, 1934 (W)

League Club	Source	Date Signed	Seasons Played	Apps	Subs	Gls
Gillingham	Tonbridge	10.57	57	8	-	0

McCORMACK John **Cecil**
Chester-le-Street, 15 February, 1922 Died 1995 (CF)

League Club	Source	Date Signed	Seasons Played	Apps	Subs	Gls
Gateshead		09.41	46	27	-	19
Middlesbrough	Tr	04.47	46-48	37	-	15
Barnsley	Chelmsford C.	07.50	50-51	50	-	42
Notts Co.	Tr	11.51	51-55	82	-	35

McCORMACK Francis Adamson
Glasgow, 25 September, 1924 (HB)

League Club	Source	Date Signed	Seasons Played	Apps	Subs	Gls
Oldham Ath.	Clyde	11.49	49	14	-	0

McCORMACK Murdoch
Glasgow, 7 October, 1920 Died 1951 (OL)

League Club	Source	Date Signed	Seasons Played	Apps	Subs	Gls
Manchester C.	Glasgow Rangers	04.47	46	1	-	0
Blackpool	Tr	07.47	47	12	-	3
Crewe Alex.	Tr	07.48	48	31	-	3

McCORMICK David
Halifax, 3 November, 1920 (G/D)

League Club	Source	Date Signed	Seasons Played	Apps	Subs	Gls
Halifax T.		10.47	47-54	117	-	0

McCORMICK David
Southwark, 29 December, 1951 (F)

League Club	Source	Date Signed	Seasons Played	Apps	Subs	Gls
Peterborough U.	Biggleswade	08.75	75	1	0	0

McCORMICK Henry (Harry)
Coleraine (NI), 10 January, 1924 LoI (OL)

League Club	Source	Date Signed	Seasons Played	Apps	Subs	Gls
Derby Co.	Coleraine	10.46	46-47	7	-	0
Everton	Tr	07.48	48	4	-	0

McCORMICK James
Rotherham, 26 September, 1912 Died 1968 (OR)

League Club	Source	Date Signed	Seasons Played	Apps	Subs	Gls
Rotherham U.	Rotherham Y.M.C.A.	03.31	30-31	19	-	2
Chesterfield	Tr	08.32	32	14	-	2
Tottenham H.	Tr	03.33	32-38	137	-	26
Fulham	Tr	04.46	46	9	-	2
Lincoln C.	Tr	08.47	47-48	64	-	6
Crystal Palace	Tr	02.49	48	13	-	2

McCORMICK James
Rotherham, 1 April, 1937 (OR)

League Club	Source	Date Signed	Seasons Played	Apps	Subs	Gls
Sheffield U.		10.56	56	1	-	0
Rotherham U.	Tr	07.57				

McCORMICK John
Glasgow, 18 July, 1936 (CD)

League Club	Source	Date Signed	Seasons Played	Apps	Subs	Gls
Crystal Palace	Aberdeen	05.66	66-72	194	0	6

McCORMICK Joseph Michael
Holywell, 15 July, 1916 (WH)

League Club	Source	Date Signed	Seasons Played	Apps	Subs	Gls
Bolton W.		10.37				
Rochdale		05.46	46-47	66	-	0
Scunthorpe U.	Boston U.	(N/L)	50	7	-	0

McCOURT Francis Joseph
Portadown (NI), 9 December, 1925 NI-6 (WH)

League Club	Source	Date Signed	Seasons Played	Apps	Subs	Gls
Bristol Rov.	Shamrock Rov.	11.45				
Bristol Rov.	Shamrock Rov.	03.49	49	32	-	1
Manchester C.	Tr	12.50	50-53	61	-	4
Colchester U.	Tr	06.54	54	12	-	0

McCOY Michael
Sunderland, 29 January, 1934 (F)

League Club	Source	Date Signed	Seasons Played	Apps	Subs	Gls
Burnley	Silksworth Colly	10.53				
Southport	Tr	07.57	57	5	-	1

McCOY Peter Joseph
Wingate (Dm), 31 July, 1923 Died 1986 (FB)

League Club	Source	Date Signed	Seasons Played	Apps	Subs	Gls
Newcastle U.	Shotton Colly	09.46				
Norwich C.	Tr	02.49	48	6	-	0

McCOY Wilfred (Tim)
Birmingham, 4 March, 1921 (CH)

League Club	Source	Date Signed	Seasons Played	Apps	Subs	Gls
Portsmouth		08.46	46-47	18	-	0
Northampton T.	Tr	12.48	48-49	60	-	0
Brighton & H.A.	Tr	01.51	50-53	112	-	0

McCRAE Alexander
Whitburn, 2 January, 1920 (IF)

League Club	Source	Date Signed	Seasons Played	Apps	Subs	Gls
Charlton Ath.	Hearts	05.47	47-48	43	-	8
Middlesbrough	Tr	11.48	48-52	122	-	47

McCRAE Ian
West Ham, 1 October, 1935 (D)

League Club	Source	Date Signed	Seasons Played	Apps	Subs	Gls
Accrington St.		07.57	59-60	14	-	0

McCREADIE Edward Graham
Glasgow, 15 April, 1940 S-23 (FB)

League Club	Source	Date Signed	Seasons Played	Apps	Subs	Gls
Chelsea	East Stirling	04.62	62-73	327	4	4

McCREADIE Edward James
Alexandria, 23 February, 1924 (F)

League Club	Source	Date Signed	Seasons Played	Apps	Subs	Gls
Walsall	Elgin C.	09.53	53	4	-	0

McCREADIE William **Harvey**
Glenluce, 1 October, 1942 (CF)

League Club	Source	Date Signed	Seasons Played	Apps	Subs	Gls
Accrington St.	Jnrs	10.59	58-59	28	-	10
Luton T.	Tr	01.60	59	1	-	0
Wrexham	Tr	11.60	60	10	-	2

McCREADY Bernard Thomas
Dumbarton, 23 April, 1937 (G)

League Club	Source	Date Signed	Seasons Played	Apps	Subs	Gls
Rochdale	Glasgow Celtic	05.57	57-58	29	-	0
Oldham Ath.	Tr	03.59	58	7	-	0

League Club	Source	Date Signed	Seasons Played	Apps	Subs	Gls
McCREADY Thomas						
Johnstone, 19 October, 1943 S Sch						(FB)
Watford	Hibernian	07.63	63	1	-	0
McCREADY Thomas						
Port Glasgow, 28 September, 1923						(IF)
Hartlepool U.	Cowdenbeath	08.49	49	34	-	3
Lincoln C.	Tr	08.50	50	11	-	1
McCREDIE Norman James						
Glasgow, 17 May, 1928						(FB)
Accrington St.	Partick Thistle	05.55	55-56	51	-	3
Southport	Tr	08.57	57	33	-	2
Barrow	Tr	08.58	58	23	-	0
McCREERY David						
Belfast, 16 September, 1957 NI Sch/NI Yth/NIu21-1/NI-67						(M)
Manchester U.	App	10.74	74-78	48	39	7
Queens Park R.	Tr	08.79	79-80	56	1	4
Newcastle U.	Tulsa (USA)	10.82	82-88	237	6	2
Hartlepool U.	Hearts	08.91	91	27	3	0
Carlisle U.		10.92	92-93	23	10	0
Hartlepool U. (N/C)		10.94	94	7	2	0
McCREESH Andrew						
Billingham, 8 September, 1962						(FB)
Middlesbrough	App	09.80	81	2	0	0
McCRINDLE William						
Glasgow, 28 June, 1923 Died 1982						(IF)
Newport Co.	Pollok Jnrs	12.48	48-49	5	-	0
McCROHAN Roy						
Reading, 22 September, 1930						(WH)
Reading	Jnrs	01.49	49-50	4	-	1
Norwich C.	Tr	08.51	51-61	385	-	20
Colchester U.	Tr	09.62	62-63	75	-	5
Bristol Rov.	Tr	08.64	64	10	-	1
McCRORY Samuel McKee						
Belfast, 11 October, 1924 NI 'B'/NI-1						(IF)
Swansea C.	Linfield	10.46	46-49	103	-	46
Ipswich T.	Tr	03.50	49-51	97	-	39
Plymouth Arg.	Tr	08.52	52-54	50	-	11
Southend U.	Tr	06.55	55-59	205	-	91
McCRYSTAL Dennis						
Welwyn Garden City, 13 January, 1932						(G)
Watford	Kingsway Y.C.	03.50	50	1	-	0
McCUBBIN Robert						
Kilmarnock, 13 February, 1943						(OR)
Hartlepool U.	Ayr U.	06.63	63	2	-	0
McCUE Alexander Bain						
Greenock, 25 November, 1927 Died 1989						(OL)
Carlisle U.	Falkirk	10.50	50	32	-	11
Grimsby T.	Tr	07.51	51-52	37	-	15
Shrewsbury T.	Tr	05.53	53-55	91	-	28
McCUE John William						
Stoke, 22 August, 1922						(FB)
Stoke C.	Jnrs	04.40	46-59	502	-	2
Oldham Ath.	Tr	09.60	60-61	56	-	0
McCULLAGH Paul Andrew						
Brigg, 6 February, 1974						(FB)
Scunthorpe U.	YT	07.92	92	5	0	1
McCULLOCH Adam Andrew Ball Ross						
Crossford, 4 June, 1920						(CF)
Northampton T.	Third Lanark	06.49	49-51	89	-	36
Shrewsbury T.	Tr	01.52	51-52	46	-	17
Aldershot	Tr	02.53	52-54	79	-	32
McCULLOCH Andrew						
Northampton, 3 January, 1950						(F)
Queens Park R.	Walton & Hersham	10.70	70-72	30	12	10
Cardiff C.	Tr	10.72	72-73	58	0	24
Oxford U.	Tr	07.74	74-75	41	0	9
Brentford	Tr	03.76	75-78	115	2	48
Sheffield Wed.	Tr	06.79	79-82	122	3	44
Crystal Palace	Tr	08.83	83	25	0	3
Aldershot	Tr	11.84	84	16	0	2
McCULLOCH David						
Hamilton, 5 October, 1911 Died 1979 SF Lge/S-7						(CF)
Brentford	Hearts	11.35	35-38	116	-	85
Derby Co.	Tr	10.38	38	31	-	16
Leicester C.	Tr	08.46	46	4	-	2

League Club	Source	Date Signed	Seasons Played	Apps	Subs	Gls
McCULLOCH John (Iain)						
Kilmarnock, 28 December, 1954 Su21-2						(W)
Notts Co.	Kilmarnock	04.78	78-83	212	3	51
McCULLOCH Thomas						
Glasgow, 25 December, 1921						(OR)
Northampton T.	Queen of South	12.49	49	2	-	0
Bradford C.	Tr	01.51	50-53	109	-	9
Crewe Alex.	Tr	07.54	54	28	-	5
McCULLOCH William Duncan						
Edinburgh, 25 June, 1922 Died 1961						(D)
Stockport Co.		03.44	46-53	309	-	4
Rochdale	Tr	07.54	54-57	140	-	2
McCULLOUGH Paul James						
Birmingham, 26 October, 1959						(G)
Reading	Brixham	09.78				
Brentford	Dawlish	07.80	80	7	0	0
McCULLOUGH William James						
Larne, 27 July, 1935 NI-10						(LB)
Arsenal	Portadown	09.58	58-65	253	0	4
Millwall	Tr	08.66	66	17	2	0
McCUNNELL Barry						
Hull, 20 September, 1948						(OL)
Hull C.	Endike Jnrs	10.66	69	0	1	0
McCURDY Colin Charles						
Belfast, 18 July, 1954 NI-1						(F)
Fulham	Larne T.	11.77	77	1	0	0
McCURLEY Kevin						
Consett, 2 April, 1926						(CF)
Brighton & H.A.		09.48	48-50	21	-	9
Liverpool	Tr	06.51				
Colchester U.	Tr	03.52	51-59	224	-	92
Oldham Ath.	Tr	06.60	60	1	-	0
McCUSKER James						
Maghera (NI), 27 December, 1939						(G)
Bradford C.	Jnrs	02.57	58	7	-	0
Stockport Co.	Tr	08.59	59	2	-	0
McDERMENT William Stirling						
Paisley, 5 January, 1943						(WH)
Leicester C.	Johnstone Burgh	05.61	62-66	20	3	1
Luton T.	Tr	07.67	67-68	28	12	1
Notts Co.	Tr	05.69	69	2	1	0
McDERMOTT Andrew						
Australia, 24 March, 1977						(RB)
Queens Park R.	A.I.S. (Aus)	08.95	95-96	6	0	2
West Bromwich A.	Tr	03.97	96-97	19	0	0
McDERMOTT Brian James						
Slough, 8 April, 1961 E Yth						(W)
Arsenal	App	02.79	78-83	38	23	12
Fulham	L	03.83	82	0	3	0
Oxford U.	Tr	12.84	84-86	16	8	2
Huddersfield T.	L	10.86	86	4	0	1
Cardiff C.	Tr	08.87	87-88	49	2	8
Exeter C.	Tr	02.89	88-90	65	3	4
McDERMOTT James Lawrence						
Earlestown, 25 May, 1932						(F)
Southport	Crompton Rec.	07.55	55-58	157	-	30
McDERMOTT John						
Middlesbrough, 3 February, 1969						(RB)
Grimsby T.	YT	06.87	86-97	359	15	7
McDERMOTT John Charles						
Manchester, 14 October, 1959						(M)
Manchester U.	App	10.76				
Rochdale	Wigan Ath. (N/C)	09.79	79	5	3	1
McDERMOTT Maurice Patrick						
Pelton Fell, 21 February, 1923 Died 1988						(LB)
Sunderland	Consett	11.45				
York C.	Consett	07.47	47	7	-	0
McDERMOTT Steven						
Gateshead, 30 December, 1964						(F)
Darlington	Sunderland (App)	02.83	82	0	2	0
McDERMOTT Terence						
Kirkby, 8 December, 1951 Eu23-1/E'B'/E-25						(M)
Bury	App	10.69	69-72	83	7	8

League Club	Source	Date Signed	Seasons Played	Apps	Subs	Gls
Newcastle U.	Tr	02.73	72-74	55	1	6
Liverpool	Tr	11.74	74-82	221	11	54
Newcastle U.	Tr	09.82	82-83	74	0	12

McDEVITT Kenneth Richard
Liverpool, 4 March, 1929 (IF)

League Club	Source	Date Signed	Seasons Played	Apps	Subs	Gls
Tranmere Rov.	Unity B.C.	01.50	51-59	237	-	39

McDONAGH James (Seamus) Martin
Rotherham, 6 October, 1952 E Yth/IR-24 (G)

League Club	Source	Date Signed	Seasons Played	Apps	Subs	Gls
Rotherham U.	App	10.70	70-75	121	0	0
Bolton W.	Tr	08.76	76-79	161	0	0
Everton	Tr	07.80	80	40	0	0
Bolton W.	Tr	08.81	81-82	81	0	1
Notts Co.	Tr	07.83	83-84	35	0	0
Birmingham C.	L	09.84	84	1	0	0
Gillingham	L	03.85	84	10	0	0
Sunderland	L	08.85	85	7	0	0
Scarborough	Wichita (USA)	11.87	87	9	0	0
Huddersfield T.	L	01.88	87	6	0	0
Charlton Ath.	Tr	03.88				

McDONALD Alan
Belfast, 12 October, 1963 NI Sch/NI Yth/NI-52 (CD)

League Club	Source	Date Signed	Seasons Played	Apps	Subs	Gls
Queens Park R.	App	09.81	83-96	395	7	13
Charlton Ath.	L	03.83	82	9	0	0
Swindon T.	Tr	07.97	97	30	3	1

McDONALD Christopher
Edinburgh, 14 October, 1975 S Sch (M)

League Club	Source	Date Signed	Seasons Played	Apps	Subs	Gls
Arsenal	YT	12.93				
Stoke C. (N/C)	Tr	08.95				
Hartlepool U.	Tr	08.96	96-97	13	2	0

McDONALD Colin
Edinburgh, 10 April, 1974 S Sch/Su21-5 (F)

League Club	Source	Date Signed	Seasons Played	Apps	Subs	Gls
Swansea C.	Falkirk	03.96	95-96	6	12	0

McDONALD Colin Agnew
Ramsbottom, 15 October, 1930 EF Lge/E-8 (G)

League Club	Source	Date Signed	Seasons Played	Apps	Subs	Gls
Burnley	Hankshaw St Marys	10.48	53-58	186	-	0

McDONALD Colin Barry
Norwich, 15 May, 1950 (W)

League Club	Source	Date Signed	Seasons Played	Apps	Subs	Gls
Norwich C.	App	07.67	67	4	0	0
Scunthorpe U.	Tr	07.70	70-72	78	8	11

MacDONALD David Anderson
Dundee, 9 May, 1931 (G)

League Club	Source	Date Signed	Seasons Played	Apps	Subs	Gls
Crystal Palace	Dundee Violet	03.51	52-54	30	-	0

McDONALD David Hugh
Dublin, 2 January, 1971 IR Sch/IR Yth/IRu21-3/IR 'B' (RB)

League Club	Source	Date Signed	Seasons Played	Apps	Subs	Gls
Tottenham H.	YT	07.88	92	2	0	0
Gillingham	L	09.90	90	10	0	0
Bradford C.	L	08.92	92	7	0	0
Reading	L	03.93	92	11	0	0
Peterborough U.	Tr	08.93	93	28	1	0
Barnet	Tr	03.94	93-97	86	10	0

MacDONALD Garry
Middlesbrough, 26 March, 1962 (F)

League Club	Source	Date Signed	Seasons Played	Apps	Subs	Gls
Middlesbrough	App	03.80	80-83	40	13	5
Carlisle U.	Tr	07.84	84	7	2	0
Darlington	Tr	10.84	84-88	153	9	35
Stockport Co.	Tr	07.89	89	1	0	0
Hartlepool U.	Tr	12.89	89-90	10	8	1

McDONALD Gary
Sunderland, 20 November, 1969 (F)

League Club	Source	Date Signed	Seasons Played	Apps	Subs	Gls
Mansfield T.	Ipswich T. (YT)	08.89	89	1	1	0

McDONALD Gavin James
Salford, 6 October, 1970 (F)

League Club	Source	Date Signed	Seasons Played	Apps	Subs	Gls
Chesterfield	YT	●	88	5	7	1

McDONALD Gerard
Milnthorpe, 3 December, 1952 (M)

League Club	Source	Date Signed	Seasons Played	Apps	Subs	Gls
Blackburn Rov.	App	12.70	71	19	2	2
Halifax T.	Tr	08.73	73	10	3	0

McDONALD Gordon
Hampstead, 7 February, 1932 Died 1995 (LB)

League Club	Source	Date Signed	Seasons Played	Apps	Subs	Gls
Crystal Palace	Eastbourne	12.54	54-56	13	-	0
Swindon T.	Tr	07.57	57	10	-	0

McDONALD Harry
Salford, 11 September, 1926 (FB)

League Club	Source	Date Signed	Seasons Played	Apps	Subs	Gls
Crystal Palace	Ashton U.	09.50	50-54	140	-	1

McDONALD Ian
Inverness, 5 February, 1951 (M)

League Club	Source	Date Signed	Seasons Played	Apps	Subs	Gls
Wolverhampton W.	Jnrs	08.68				
Darlington	Tr	09.70	70	21	4	3

McDONALD Ian Campbell Aitken
West Germany, 30 August, 1953 (CD)

League Club	Source	Date Signed	Seasons Played	Apps	Subs	Gls
Carlisle U.	St Johnstone	05.76	76-80	186	1	7

McDONALD Ian Clifford
Barrow, 10 May, 1953 (M)

League Club	Source	Date Signed	Seasons Played	Apps	Subs	Gls
Barrow	App	05.71	70-71	30	5	2
Workington	Tr	02.73	72-73	42	0	4
Liverpool	Tr	01.74				
Colchester U.	L	02.75	74	5	0	2
Mansfield T.	Tr	07.75	75-76	47	9	4
York C.	Tr	11.77	77-81	175	0	29
Aldershot	Tr	11.81	81-88	340	0	50

MacDONALD Jack
Liverpool, 1 September, 1921 (FB)

League Club	Source	Date Signed	Seasons Played	Apps	Subs	Gls
Liverpool		08.44				
Tranmere Rov.	Tr	06.49	49-51	89	-	0

McDONALD James
Greenock, 18 April, 1932 (W)

League Club	Source	Date Signed	Seasons Played	Apps	Subs	Gls
Gillingham	Dumbarton	08.56	56	1	-	0

MacDONALD John
Glasgow, 15 April, 1961 S Sch/S Yth/Su21-8 (F)

League Club	Source	Date Signed	Seasons Played	Apps	Subs	Gls
Charlton Ath.	Hong Kong	09.86	86	2	0	0
Barnsley	Tr	11.86	86-89	87	7	20
Scarborough	Tr	11.89	89-90	39	1	6

McDONALD John (Jack) Christopher
Maltby, 27 August, 1921 (OL)

League Club	Source	Date Signed	Seasons Played	Apps	Subs	Gls
Wolverhampton W.	Jnrs	09.38	38	2	-	0
Bournemouth	Tr	05.39	46-47	80	-	35
Fulham	Tr	06.48	48-51	75	-	19
Southampton	Tr	08.52	52	16	-	4
Southend U.	Tr	05.53	53-54	28	-	6

MacDONALD John Sutherland
Edinburgh, 23 September, 1922 (LB)

League Club	Source	Date Signed	Seasons Played	Apps	Subs	Gls
Notts Co.	Carshalton Ath.	08.48	48	1	-	0
Queens Park R.	Tr	03.49				

McDONALD Joseph
Blantyre, 10 February, 1929 S-2 (LB)

League Club	Source	Date Signed	Seasons Played	Apps	Subs	Gls
Sunderland	Falkirk	03.54	53-57	137	-	1
Nottingham F.	Tr	07.58	58-60	109	-	0

MacDONALD Kevin Duncan
Inverness, 22 November, 1960 (M)

League Club	Source	Date Signed	Seasons Played	Apps	Subs	Gls
Leicester C.	Inverness Caledonian	05.80	80-84	133	5	8
Liverpool	Tr	11.84	84-88	29	11	1
Leicester C.	L	12.87	87	3	0	0
Coventry C.	Tr	07.89	89-90	26	5	0
Cardiff C.	L	03.91	90	8	0	0
Walsall	Tr	07.91	91-92	48	5	7

MacDONALD Leslie
Newcastle, 2 April, 1934 (LB)

League Club	Source	Date Signed	Seasons Played	Apps	Subs	Gls
Portsmouth		05.55				
Exeter C.	Tr	06.57	57-65	294	0	0

McDONALD Malcolm
Glasgow, 26 October, 1913 (RB)

League Club	Source	Date Signed	Seasons Played	Apps	Subs	Gls
Brentford	Kilmarnock	10.46	46-48	87	-	1

MacDONALD Malcolm Ian
Fulham, 7 January, 1950 Eu23-4/EF Lge/E-14 (F)

League Club	Source	Date Signed	Seasons Played	Apps	Subs	Gls
Fulham	Tonbridge	08.68	68	10	3	5
Luton T.	Tr	07.69	69-70	88	0	49
Newcastle U.	Tr	05.71	71-75	187	0	95
Arsenal	Tr	08.76	76-78	84	0	42

MacDONALD Martin
Kilsyth, 5 September, 1931 (FB)

League Club	Source	Date Signed	Seasons Played	Apps	Subs	Gls
Portsmouth	Jnrs	11.48				
Bournemouth	Tr	11.51	52-55	51	-	1

McDONALD Martin Joseph
Irvine, 4 December, 1973 (M)

League Club	Source	Date Signed	Seasons Played	Apps	Subs	Gls
Stockport Co.	Bramhall	08.92				
Doncaster Rov.	Southport	08.96	96-97	48	0	4
Macclesfield T.	Tr	12.97	97	22	0	1

McDONALD Michael Flynn
Glasgow, 8 November, 1950 (G)

League Club	Source	Date Signed	Seasons Played	Apps	Subs	Gls
Stoke C.	Clydebank	10.72	72-73	5	0	0

League Club	Source	Date Signed	Seasons Played	Apps	Subs	Gls
McDONALD Neil						
Barrow, 27 May, 1954						(W)
Workington (N/C)		03.77	76	5	1	0
McDONALD Neil Raymond						
Wallsend, 2 November, 1965 E Sch/E Yth/Eu21-5						(RB/M)
Newcastle U.	App	02.83	82-87	163	17	24
Everton	Tr	08.88	88-91	76	14	4
Oldham Ath.	Tr	10.91	91-93	19	5	1
Bolton W.	Tr	07.94	94-95	4	0	0
Preston N.E.	Tr	11.95	95-96	20	13	0
McDONALD Paul Thomas						
Motherwell, 20 April, 1968						(LW)
Southampton	Hamilton Academical	06.93	94-95	0	3	0
Burnley	L	09.95	95	8	1	1
Brighton & H.A.	Tr	02.96	95-97	52	9	5
McDONALD Richard Robertson						
Paisley, 18 December, 1933						(CF)
Barnsley	Saltcoats Vic.	12.57	58	1	-	0
MacDONALD Robert						
Clydebank, 26 October, 1935						(FB)
Manchester C.	Vale of Leven	09.56	61	5	-	0
Bournemouth	Tr	09.63	63	1	-	0
McDONALD Robert Roderick						
Hull, 22 January, 1959						(F)
Hull C.	App	01.77	76-79	17	8	2
Newcastle U.	P.S.V. Eindhoven (Neth)	11.88	88	6	4	1
McDONALD Robert Wood						
Aberdeen, 13 April, 1955						(LB)
Aston Villa	App	09.72	72-75	33	6	3
Coventry C.	Tr	08.76	76-80	161	0	14
Manchester C.	Tr	10.80	80-82	96	0	11
Oxford U.	Tr	09.83	83-86	93	1	14
Leeds U.	Tr	02.87	86-87	18	0	1
Wolverhampton W.	L	02.88	87	6	0	0
McDONALD Rodney						
Westminster, 20 March, 1967						(F)
Walsall	Colne Dynamoes	08.90	90-93	142	7	40
Chester C.	Southport	11.96	96-97	43	10	11
McDONALD Roger Brown						
Glasgow, 2 February, 1933 Died 1996						(FB)
Mansfield T.	St Mirren	03.55	54-55	13	-	0
McDONALD Terence						
Belfast, 5 February, 1947						(FB)
Middlesbrough	Jnrs	02.64				
Southport	Tr	07.65	65-66	33	0	1
Barrow	Tr	07.67	67-68	35	1	0
McDONALD Terence James						
Limehouse, 12 November, 1938 E Yth						(OL)
West Ham U.	Jnrs	04.56				
Leyton Orient	Tr	07.59	59-64	152	-	23
Reading	Tr	05.65	65	13	0	2
McDONALD Thomas						
Cowdenbeath, 24 May, 1930 S 'B'						(OR)
Wolverhampton W.	Hibernian	04.54	54-55	5	-	1
Leicester C.	Tr	07.56	56-59	113	-	27
McDONALD William Love						
Longriggend, 30 August, 1918						(WH)
Carlisle U.	Airdrieonians	08.46	46	3	-	0
McDONNELL Charles						
Birkenhead, 15 July, 1936						(IF)
Tranmere Rov.	Stork	09.57	57-60	67	-	25
Stockport Co.	Tr	06.61	61-63	84	-	32
Tranmere Rov.	Tr	10.63	63-64	45	-	25
Southport	Tr	07.65	65	10	0	1
McDONNELL Martin Henry						
Ashton-in-Makerfield, 27 April, 1924 Died 1988						(CH)
Everton	Haydock C. & B.	08.42				
Southport	Tr	08.46	46	38	-	0
Birmingham C.	Tr	05.47	47-49	32	-	0
Coventry C.	Tr	10.49	49-54	232	-	0
Derby Co.	Tr	07.55	55-57	93	-	0
Crewe Alex.	Tr	07.58	58	17	-	0
McDONNELL Peter Anthony						
Kendal, 11 June, 1953						(G)
Bury	Netherfield	10.73	73	1	0	0

League Club	Source	Date Signed	Seasons Played	Apps	Subs	Gls
Liverpool	Tr	08.74				
Oldham Ath.	Tr	08.78	78-81	137	0	0
McDONOUGH Darren Karl						
Belgium, 7 November, 1962						(M/CD)
Oldham Ath.	App	01.80	80-86	178	5	14
Luton T.	Tr	09.86	86-91	88	17	5
Newcastle U.	Tr	03.92	91	2	1	0
McDONOUGH Roy						
Solihull, 16 October, 1958						(F)
Birmingham C.	App	10.76	76	2	0	1
Walsall	Tr	09.78	78-80	76	6	15
Chelsea	Tr	10.80				
Colchester U.	Tr	02.81	80-82	84	4	24
Southend U.	Tr	08.83	83	22	0	4
Exeter C.	Tr	01.84	83-84	20	1	1
Cambridge U.	Tr	10.84	84	30	2	5
Southend U.	Tr	08.85	85-89	163	23	30
Colchester U.	Tr	10.90	92-93	57	6	16
McDOUGALD David Eugene **Junior**						
U.S.A., 12 January, 1975 E Yth						(F)
Tottenham H.	YT	07.93				
Brighton & H.A.	Tr	05.94	94-95	71	7	14
Chesterfield	L	03.96	95	9	0	3
Rotherham U.	Tr	07.96	96	14	4	2
McDOUGALL Edward (Ted) John						
Inverness, 8 January, 1947 S-7						(F)
Liverpool	I.C.I. Recs	01.66				
York C.	Tr	07.67	67-68	84	0	34
Bournemouth	Tr	07.69	69-72	146	0	103
Manchester U.	Tr	09.72	72	18	0	5
West Ham U.	Tr	03.73	72-73	24	0	5
Norwich C.	Tr	12.73	73-76	112	0	51
Southampton	Tr	09.76	76-78	86	0	42
Bournemouth	Tr	11.78	78-79	51	1	16
Blackpool	Tr	03.80	79-80	11	2	0
McDOUGALL Laybourne						
Tynemouth, 12 May, 1917 Died 1994						(LB)
Carlisle U.		06.37	37	3	-	0
Preston N.E.	Tr	03.38				
Blackpool	Tr	05.39				
Gateshead	Tr	10.46	46-48	60	-	0
McDOWALL Daniel						
Kirkintilloch, 22 May, 1929						(IF)
Middlesbrough		02.47				
Workington	Kilmarnock	08.51	51-52	82	-	23
Lincoln C.	Tr	07.53	53	17	-	4
Millwall	Tr	06.54	54-55	10	-	1
McDOWALL Duncan John						
Paddington, 18 December, 1963						(F)
Birmingham C	App	08.81	81	2	0	0
McDOWALL James Cowan						
Glasgow, 25 October, 1940						(G)
Notts Co.	Baillieston	09.59				
Scunthorpe U.	Boston U.	12.61	61	1	-	0
McDOWALL Kenneth Francis						
Manchester, 6 May, 1938						(OL)
Manchester U.	Rhyl	09.59				
Rochdale	Tr	10.60	60	6	-	0
McDOWALL Leslie John						
India, 25 October, 1912 Died 1991						(CH)
Sunderland	Glentyre Thistle	12.32	34-37	13	-	0
Manchester C.	Tr	03.38	37-48	117	-	8
Wrexham	Tr	11.49	49	3	-	0
McDOWELL John Alfred						
East Ham, 7 September, 1951 E Yth/Eu23-13						(RB)
West Ham U.	App	08.69	70-78	243	6	8
Norwich C.	Tr	08.79	79-80	40	1	1
MACEDO Elliot (Tony)						
Gibraltar, 22 February, 1938 Eu23-10						(G)
Fulham	Jnrs	10.55	57-67	346	0	0
Colchester U.	Tr	09.68	68	38	0	0
McELHATTON Michael						
Killarney, 16 April, 1975 IR Sch						(M)
Bournemouth	YT	07.93	92-95	21	21	2
Scarborough	Tr	09.96	96-97	64	6	7

McELHINNEY Gerard
Derry (NI), 19 September, 1956 NI-6 (CD)

League Club	Source	Date Signed	Seasons Played	Apps	Subs	Gls
Bolton W.	Distillery	09.80	80-84	107	2	2
Rochdale	L	11.82	82	20	0	1
Plymouth Arg.	Tr	01.85	84-87	90	1	2
Peterborough U.	Tr	08.88	88-90	87	0	1

McELVANEY David Anthony
Chesterfield, 3 November, 1954 (M)

League Club	Source	Date Signed	Seasons Played	Apps	Subs	Gls
Chesterfield		10.75	75	4	0	1

McEVOY Matthew **Andrew**
Dublin, 15 July, 1938 Died 1994 IR-17 (IF)

League Club	Source	Date Signed	Seasons Played	Apps	Subs	Gls
Blackburn Rov.	Bray W.	10.56	58-66	183	0	89

McEVOY Donald William
Golcar, 3 December, 1928 (CH)

League Club	Source	Date Signed	Seasons Played	Apps	Subs	Gls
Huddersfield T.	Bradley R.	09.47	49-54	148	-	3
Sheffield Wed.	Tr	12.54	54-57	105	-	1
Lincoln C.	Tr	01.59	58-59	23	-	0
Barrow	Tr	07.60	60-61	74	-	1

McEVOY Richard Patrick
Gibraltar, 6 August, 1967 IR Yth (M)

League Club	Source	Date Signed	Seasons Played	Apps	Subs	Gls
Luton T.	App	08.85	86	0	1	0
Cambridge U.	L	02.87	86	10	1	1

MacEWAN James
Dundee, 22 March, 1929 (OR)

League Club	Source	Date Signed	Seasons Played	Apps	Subs	Gls
Aston Villa	Raith Rov.	07.59	59-65	143	0	28
Walsall	Tr	08.66	66	10	0	1

McEWAN Malcolm **Peter**
South Africa, 23 May, 1933 (CF)

League Club	Source	Date Signed	Seasons Played	Apps	Subs	Gls
Luton T.	Pretoria (SA)	02.54	53-55	26	-	11

McEWAN Stanley
Wishaw, 8 June, 1957 (CD)

League Club	Source	Date Signed	Seasons Played	Apps	Subs	Gls
Blackpool	App	07.74	74-81	204	10	24
Exeter C.	Tr	07.82	82-83	65	0	15
Hull C.	Tr	03.84	83-87	113	0	25
Wigan Ath.	Tr	12.87	87-88	26	3	4
Hartlepool U.	Tr	08.89	89	14	0	2

McEWAN Stephen
Selkirk, 28 March, 1930 (IF)

League Club	Source	Date Signed	Seasons Played	Apps	Subs	Gls
Liverpool		07.50				
Accrington St.	Tr	08.51	51	2	-	1

McEWAN William
Glasgow, 29 August, 1914 Died 1991 (OR)

League Club	Source	Date Signed	Seasons Played	Apps	Subs	Gls
Queens Park R.	Petershill	06.38	38-49	96	-	17
Leyton Orient	Tr	02.50	49-50	21	-	3

McEWAN William Johnston McGowan
Cleland, 20 June, 1951 (M)

League Club	Source	Date Signed	Seasons Played	Apps	Subs	Gls
Blackpool	Hibernian	05.73	73	4	0	0
Brighton & H. A.	Tr	02.74	73-74	27	0	3
Chesterfield	Tr	11.74	74-76	79	1	7
Mansfield T.	Tr	01.77	76-77	32	0	3
Peterborough U.	Tr	11.77	77-78	62	1	3
Rotherham U.	Tr	07.79	79-83	86	9	10

McEWEN Francis Kevin
Dublin, 15 February, 1948 IRu23-1 (M)

League Club	Source	Date Signed	Seasons Played	Apps	Subs	Gls
Manchester U.	App	05.65				
Rochdale	Tr	11.66	66-67	17	0	2

MACEY John Robert Thornbury
Bristol, 13 November, 1947 E Sch (G)

League Club	Source	Date Signed	Seasons Played	Apps	Subs	Gls
Bristol C.	App	05.65				
Grimsby T.	Tr	07.68	68-69	36	1	0
Newport Co.	Tr	07.70	70-75	194	0	0

McFADDEN Anthony
Hexham, 18 May, 1957 (F)

League Club	Source	Date Signed	Seasons Played	Apps	Subs	Gls
Darlington	Reyrolles	08.81	81-82	44	3	10

McFADZEAN Clive Stuart
Kilmarnock, 11 March, 1958 (F)

League Club	Source	Date Signed	Seasons Played	Apps	Subs	Gls
Bradford C.	App	03.76	75-76	3	1	2

McFADZEAN John Paul
Sheffield, 2 April, 1966 (F)

League Club	Source	Date Signed	Seasons Played	Apps	Subs	Gls
Rotherham U.	App	●	83	0	1	0

McFALL David Patrick
Ballymena (NI), 14 March, 1935 (IF)

League Club	Source	Date Signed	Seasons Played	Apps	Subs	Gls
Aldershot	Sittingbourne	10.58	58	3	-	0

McFARLAND Roy Leslie
Liverpool, 5 April, 1948 Eu23-5/EF Lge/E-28 (CD)

League Club	Source	Date Signed	Seasons Played	Apps	Subs	Gls
Tranmere Rov.	Jnrs	07.66	66-67	35	0	0
Derby Co.	Tr	08.67	67-80	434	0	44
Bradford C.	Tr	06.81	81-82	40	0	1
Derby Co. (N/C)	Tr	08.83	83	3	5	0

McFARLANE Andrew Antonie
Wolverhampton, 30 November, 1966 (F)

League Club	Source	Date Signed	Seasons Played	Apps	Subs	Gls
Portsmouth	Cradley T.	11.90	91	0	2	0
Swansea C.	Tr	08.92	92-94	33	22	8
Scunthorpe U.	Tr	08.95	95-96	48	12	19
Torquay U.	Tr	01.97	96-97	37	4	8

McFARLANE Ian
Lanark, 26 January, 1933 (FB)

League Club	Source	Date Signed	Seasons Played	Apps	Subs	Gls
Chelsea	Aberdeen	08.56	56-57	40	-	0
Leicester C.	Tr	05.58	58	1	-	0

McFARLANE William **Noel**
Bray (Ire), 20 December, 1934 (F)

League Club	Source	Date Signed	Seasons Played	Apps	Subs	Gls
Manchester U.	Jnrs	04.52	53	1	-	0

McFARLANE Robert Robertson
Bo'ness, 12 October, 1913 Died 1971 (WH)

League Club	Source	Date Signed	Seasons Played	Apps	Subs	Gls
Arsenal		03.36				
Doncaster Rov.	Tr	05.37	37-47	131	-	4

McFAUL William (Iam) Stewart
Coleraine (NI), 1 October, 1943 NI Amat/NI-6 (G)

League Club	Source	Date Signed	Seasons Played	Apps	Subs	Gls
Newcastle U.	Linfield	11.66	66-74	290	0	0

McFEAT Archibald
Kincardine, 23 January, 1924 Died 1996 (G)

League Club	Source	Date Signed	Seasons Played	Apps	Subs	Gls
Torquay U.	Morton	05.48	48	9	-	0

McGAIRY Thomas
Glasgow, 25 November, 1927 (IF)

League Club	Source	Date Signed	Seasons Played	Apps	Subs	Gls
Walsall	Dumbarton	08.54	54	7	-	1

McGANN William Thomas Arden
Wilmslow, 12 July, 1923 Died 1986 (FB)

League Club	Source	Date Signed	Seasons Played	Apps	Subs	Gls
Stockport Co.		05.48	49-50	14	-	0
Bournemouth	Tr	07.51				

McGARRIGLE Dennis
Luton, 4 November, 1936 (G)

League Club	Source	Date Signed	Seasons Played	Apps	Subs	Gls
Bristol C.	Gourock Jnrs	02.60				
Crewe Alex.	Tr	06.60	60-61	12	-	0

McGARRIGLE Kevin
Newcastle, 9 April, 1977 (CD)

League Club	Source	Date Signed	Seasons Played	Apps	Subs	Gls
Brighton & H.A.	YT	07.94	93-96	34	11	1

MacGARRITY Thomas Welsh
Glasgow, 24 November, 1922 (IF)

League Club	Source	Date Signed	Seasons Played	Apps	Subs	Gls
Southampton	Morton	11.52	52	5	-	1

McGARRY Ronald
Cockermouth, 25 October, 1938 (WH)

League Club	Source	Date Signed	Seasons Played	Apps	Subs	Gls
Workington		07.60	60	2	-	0

McGARRY Ronald James
Whitehaven, 5 December, 1937 (IF)

League Club	Source	Date Signed	Seasons Played	Apps	Subs	Gls
Workington	Whitehaven	10.58	58-61	92	-	25
Bolton W.	Tr	02.62	61-62	27	-	7
Newcastle U.	Tr	12.62	62-66	118	3	41
Barrow	Tr	03.67	66-67	30	0	4
Barrow	Bowlgownie (Aus)	09.70	70	14	3	4

McGARRY William Harry
Stoke, 10 June, 1927 EF Lge/E 'B'/E-4 (WH)

League Club	Source	Date Signed	Seasons Played	Apps	Subs	Gls
Port Vale	Northwood Mission	06.45	46-50	146	-	5
Huddersfield T.	Tr	03.51	50-60	363	-	25
Bournemouth	Tr	03.61	60-62	78	-	2

McGARVEY Scott Thomas
Glasgow, 22 April, 1963 Su21-4 (F)

League Club	Source	Date Signed	Seasons Played	Apps	Subs	Gls
Manchester U.	App	04.80	80-82	13	12	3
Wolverhampton W.	L	03.84	83	13	0	2
Portsmouth	Tr	07.84	84-85	17	6	6
Carlisle U.	L	01.86	85	10	0	3
Carlisle U.	Tr	07.86	86	25	0	8
Grimsby T.	Tr	03.87	86-87	49	1	7
Bristol C.	Tr	09.88	88	20	6	9
Oldham Ath.	Tr	05.89	89	2	2	1
Wigan Ath	L	09.89	89	3	0	0

McGAVIN Steven James
North Walsham, 24 January, 1969 (F)

League Club	Source	Date Signed	Seasons Played	Apps	Subs	Gls
Ipswich T.	YT	01.87				
Colchester U.	Sudbury T.	03.91	92-93	55	3	17
Birmingham C.	Tr	01.94	93-94	16	7	2
Wycombe W.	Tr	03.95	94-97	102	13	14

McGEACHIE George
Falkirk, 9 September, 1939 (OL)

League Club	Source	Date Signed	Seasons Played	Apps	Subs	Gls
Darlington	Dundee	01.64	63-66	119	0	9

McGEACHIE George
Glasgow, 26 October, 1916 (WH)

League Club	Source	Date Signed	Seasons Played	Apps	Subs	Gls
New Brighton	St Johnstone	07.46	46-47	63	-	4
Leyton Orient	Tr	07.48				
Rochdale	Tr	12.48	48-50	90	-	6
Crystal Palace	Tr	06.51	51	46	-	5

McGEACHY Joseph
Glasgow, 21 April, 1920 Died 1985 (OL)

League Club	Source	Date Signed	Seasons Played	Apps	Subs	Gls
Leyton Orient	Third Lanark	05.48	48-50	74	-	4
Workington	Hereford U.	09.52	52	2	-	1

McGEADY John
Glasgow, 17 April, 1958 (W)

League Club	Source	Date Signed	Seasons Played	Apps	Subs	Gls
Sheffield U.	Third Lanark	01.76	75-76	13	3	0
Newport Co.	California (USA)	10.78	78	2	0	0

McGEE Owen Edward
Middlesbrough, 29 April, 1970 (FB)

League Club	Source	Date Signed	Seasons Played	Apps	Subs	Gls
Middlesbrough	YT	07.88	89-90	18	3	1
Scarborough	Leicester C. (N/C)	03.92	91-92	21	3	0

McGEE Paul
Dublin, 17 May, 1968 IRu21-4 (W)

League Club	Source	Date Signed	Seasons Played	Apps	Subs	Gls
Colchester U.	Bohemians	02.89	88	3	0	0
Wimbledon	Tr	03.89	88-92	54	6	9
Peterborough U.	L	03.94	93	5	1	0

McGEE Paul Gerard
Sligo, 19 June, 1954 IRu21-2/IR-15 (F)

League Club	Source	Date Signed	Seasons Played	Apps	Subs	Gls
Queens Park R.	Sligo Rov.	11.77	77-78	31	8	7
Preston N.E.	Tr	10.79	79-81	62	4	13
Burnley	Tr	11.81	81-82	33	1	9

McGEENEY Patrick (Paddy) Michael
Sheffield, 31 October, 1966 (M)

League Club	Source	Date Signed	Seasons Played	Apps	Subs	Gls
Sheffield U.	App	10.84	84-85	15	1	0
Rochdale	L	11.86	86	3	0	0
Chesterfield	Tr	08.87	87-88	45	4	1

McGEORGE James Lumley
Sunderland, 8 June, 1945 (W)

League Club	Source	Date Signed	Seasons Played	Apps	Subs	Gls
Leyton Orient	Spennymoor U.	03.64	64-65	16	0	0
Mansfield T.	Tr	07.66	66	5	4	0

McGEOUGH James
Belfast, 14 July, 1946 (M)

League Club	Source	Date Signed	Seasons Played	Apps	Subs	Gls
Lincoln C.	Waterford	06.72	72-74	61	4	0
Hartlepool U.	L	03.73	72	1	1	0

McGETTIGAN John Anthony
Motherwell, 28 November, 1945 (OL)

League Club	Source	Date Signed	Seasons Played	Apps	Subs	Gls
Workington		03.68	67-68	13	1	0

McGETTIGAN Lawrence
Hackney, 25 December, 1952 Died 1994 (W)

League Club	Source	Date Signed	Seasons Played	Apps	Subs	Gls
Watford	App	11.70	71-74	40	10	3

McGHEE David Christopher
Worthing, 19 June, 1976 (CD/M)

League Club	Source	Date Signed	Seasons Played	Apps	Subs	Gls
Brentford	YT	07.94	94-97	95	22	8

McGHEE James William
Motherwell, 21 August, 1930 (CF)

League Club	Source	Date Signed	Seasons Played	Apps	Subs	Gls
Darlington	Kilmarnock	07.52	52	15	-	4
Newport Co.	Barry T.	05.54	54	10	-	1

McGHEE Mark Edward
Glasgow, 20 May, 1957 Su21-1/S-4 (F)

League Club	Source	Date Signed	Seasons Played	Apps	Subs	Gls
Newcastle U.	Morton	12.77	77-78	21	7	5
Newcastle U.	Glasgow Celtic	08.89	89-90	63	4	24
Reading	Tr	05.91	91-92	32	13	7

McGHEE Thomas Edward
Manchester, 10 May, 1929 E Amat/E 'B' (FB)

League Club	Source	Date Signed	Seasons Played	Apps	Subs	Gls
Portsmouth	Wealdstone	05.54	54-58	136	-	0
Reading	Tr	07.59	59	8	-	0

McGHIE William Lambert
Lanark, 19 January, 1958 S Yth (M)

League Club	Source	Date Signed	Seasons Played	Apps	Subs	Gls
Leeds U.	App	01.76	76	2	0	1
York C.	Tr	12.79	79-81	39	4	1

McGIBBON Douglas
Southampton, 24 February, 1919 (CF)

League Club	Source	Date Signed	Seasons Played	Apps	Subs	Gls
Southampton	Hamble A.S.T.	12.38	38-46	13	-	9
Fulham	Tr	01.47	46-47	42	-	18
Bournemouth	Tr	09.48	48-50	103	-	65

McGIBBON Patrick Colm
Lurgan, 6 September, 1973 NI Sch/NIu21-1/NI 'B'/NI-6 (CD)

League Club	Source	Date Signed	Seasons Played	Apps	Subs	Gls
Manchester U.	Portadown	08.92				
Swansea C.	L	09.96	96	1	0	0
Wigan Ath.	Tr	03.97	96-97	42	3	1

McGIFFORD Graham Leslie
Carshalton, 1 May, 1955 (FB)

League Club	Source	Date Signed	Seasons Played	Apps	Subs	Gls
Huddersfield T.	App	07.72	72-75	41	1	0
Hull C.	Tr	05.76	76	1	0	0
Port Vale	Tr	06.77	77	20	0	0

McGILL Andrew
Glasgow, 11 July, 1924 Died 1988 (WH)

League Club	Source	Date Signed	Seasons Played	Apps	Subs	Gls
Bradford C.	Clyde	11.47	47-51	164	-	24
Scunthorpe U.	Tr	07.52	52-56	183	-	15

McGILL Austin Michael
Dumfries, 29 January, 1935 (F)

League Club	Source	Date Signed	Seasons Played	Apps	Subs	Gls
Carlisle U.	Queen of South	08.59	59	29	-	12

McGILL James
Kilsyth, 10 March, 1926 (IF)

League Club	Source	Date Signed	Seasons Played	Apps	Subs	Gls
Bury		12.45	46	1	-	0
Derby Co.	Tr	03.47	46-47	8	-	0

McGILL James Hopkins
Bellshill, 2 October, 1939 (D)

League Club	Source	Date Signed	Seasons Played	Apps	Subs	Gls
Oldham Ath	Partick Thistle	05.59	59	38	-	2
Crewe Alex.	Tr	08.60	60-62	81	-	2
Chester C.	Tr	10.62	62-63	32	-	0
Wrexham	Tr	10.63	63	17	-	0

McGILL James Morrison
Glasgow, 27 November, 1946 (M)

League Club	Source	Date Signed	Seasons Played	Apps	Subs	Gls
Arsenal	Possilpark Jnrs	07.65	65-66	6	4	0
Huddersfield T.	Tr	09.67	67-71	161	3	8
Hull C.	Tr	10.71	71-75	141	6	2
Halifax T.	Tr	02.76	75-76	31	1	0

McGILLIVRAY Findlay
Newtongrange, 19 March, 1940 (FB)

League Club	Source	Date Signed	Seasons Played	Apps	Subs	Gls
Bradford P.A.	Glasgow Rangers	05.66	66	38	1	0

McGINLAY John
Inverness, 8 April, 1964 S 'B'/S-13 (F)

League Club	Source	Date Signed	Seasons Played	Apps	Subs	Gls
Shrewsbury T.	Elgin C.	02.89	88-89	58	2	27
Bury	Tr	07.90	90	16	9	9
Millwall	Tr	03.91	90-92	27	7	10
Bolton W.	Tr	09.92	92-97	180	12	87
Bradford C.	Tr	11.97	97	12	5	3

McGINLAY Patrick David
Glasgow, 30 May, 1967 (M)

League Club	Source	Date Signed	Seasons Played	Apps	Subs	Gls
Blackpool		05.85	86	2	10	0

McGINLEY John
Rowlands Gill, 11 June, 1959 (LW)

League Club	Source	Date Signed	Seasons Played	Apps	Subs	Gls
Sunderland	Gateshead	01.82	81	3	0	0
Lincoln C.	Charleroi (Bel)	09.84	84-86	69	2	11
Rotherham U.	Tr	09.86	86	1	3	0
Hartlepool U.	L	01.87	86	2	0	0
Lincoln C.	Tr	01.87	86-88	36	5	7
Doncaster Rov.	Tr	06.89	89	4	6	0

McGINLEY William David
Dumfries, 12 November, 1954 S Sch (W)

League Club	Source	Date Signed	Seasons Played	Apps	Subs	Gls
Leeds U.	App	01.72	72	0	1	0
Huddersfield T.	Tr	09.74	74	11	4	1
Bradford C.	Tr	06.75	75-76	52	8	11
Crewe Alex.	Tr	08.77	77	36	2	2

McGINN Francis
Cambuslang, 2 March, 1919 (OL)

League Club	Source	Date Signed	Seasons Played	Apps	Subs	Gls
Wrexham		04.47	46	2	-	0
Ipswich T.	Tr	08.48	48	8	-	2

McGINN William Bell
Kilwinning, 2 February, 1943 (FB)

League Club	Source	Date Signed	Seasons Played	Apps	Subs	Gls
Oldham Ath.	Ardrossan Winton	11.63	63-65	37	1	0

McGINTY Brian
East Kilbride, 10 December, 1976 (M)

League Club	Source	Date Signed	Seasons Played	Apps	Subs	Gls
Hull C.	Glasgow Rangers	11.97	97	21	0	2

McGIVEN Michael
Newcastle, 7 February, 1951 (CD)

League Club	Source	Date Signed	Seasons Played	Apps	Subs	Gls
Sunderland	Jnrs	07.68	69-73	107	6	9
West Ham U.	Tr	11.73	73-77	46	2	0

McGLASHAN John
Dundee, 3 June, 1967 S Yth (M)

League Club	Source	Date Signed	Seasons Played	Apps	Subs	Gls
Millwall	Montrose	08.90	90-91	9	7	0
Fulham	L	12.92	92	5	0	1
Cambridge U.	L	01.93	92	0	1	0
Peterborough U.	Tr	01.93	92-93	44	2	3
Rotherham U.	Tr	11.94	94-96	68	6	5

McGLEISH John Joseph
Bellshill, 9 November, 1951 (W)

League Club	Source	Date Signed	Seasons Played	Apps	Subs	Gls
Northampton T.	Jnrs	11.68	70-72	7	1	0

McGLEISH Scott
Barnet, 10 February, 1974 (F)

League Club	Source	Date Signed	Seasons Played	Apps	Subs	Gls
Charlton Ath.	Edgware T.	05.94	94	0	6	0
Leyton Orient	L	03.95	94	4	2	1
Peterborough U.	Tr	07.95	95-96	3	10	0
Colchester U.	L	02.96	95	10	5	6
Cambridge U.	L	09.96	96	10	0	7
Leyton Orient	Tr	11.96	96-97	36	0	7
Barnet	Tr	10.97	97	37	0	13

McGLEN William
Bedlington, 27 April, 1921 (WH)

League Club	Source	Date Signed	Seasons Played	Apps	Subs	Gls
Manchester U.	Blyth Spartans	05.46	46-51	110	-	2
Lincoln C.	Tr	07.52	52	13	-	0
Oldham Ath.	Tr	02.53	52-55	68	-	3

McGLENNON Thomas
Bearpark, 20 October, 1933 (WH)

League Club	Source	Date Signed	Seasons Played	Apps	Subs	Gls
Blackpool	Jnrs	11.50				
Rochdale	Tr	05.57	57-58	61	-	2
Barrow	Burton A.	11.59	59-60	60	-	6

McGOLDRICK Edward John Paul
Islington, 30 April, 1965 IR 'B'/IR-15 (RM)

League Club	Source	Date Signed	Seasons Played	Apps	Subs	Gls
Northampton T.	Nuneaton Borough	08.86	86-88	97	10	9
Crystal Palace	Tr	01.89	88-92	139	8	11
Arsenal	Tr	06.93	93-95	32	6	0
Manchester C.	Tr	09.96	96-97	39	1	0
Stockport Co.	L	03.98	97	2	0	0

McGOLDRICK John
Coatbridge, 23 September, 1963 (RB)

League Club	Source	Date Signed	Seasons Played	Apps	Subs	Gls
Leeds U.	Glasgow Celtic	06.83	83	7	0	0

McGOLDRICK Thomas Joseph
Doncaster, 20 September, 1929 (IF)

League Club	Source	Date Signed	Seasons Played	Apps	Subs	Gls
Rotherham U.	Maltby Main	11.49	51	5	-	2
Chesterfield	Tr	05.53	53-54	36	-	16

McGONIGAL Robert Edwin
Cookstown (NI), 2 May, 1942 NI Sch (G)

League Club	Source	Date Signed	Seasons Played	Apps	Subs	Gls
Brighton & H.A.	Glentoran	02.62	62-65	57	0	0

McGORRIGHAN Francis Owen
Easington, 20 November, 1921 (IF)

League Club	Source	Date Signed	Seasons Played	Apps	Subs	Gls
Middlesbrough	Eppleton Colly	04.44				
Carlisle U.	Tr	10.45				
Hull C.	Tr	08.46	46	20	-	1
Blackburn Rov.	Tr	02.47	46-47	5	-	0
Hull C.	Tr	09.47	47	6	-	0
Southport	Tr	08.48	48	4	-	0

McGORRY Brian Paul
Liverpool, 16 April, 1970 (M)

League Club	Source	Date Signed	Seasons Played	Apps	Subs	Gls
Bournemouth	Weymouth	08.91	91-93	56	5	11
Peterborough U.	Tr	02.94	93-94	44	8	6
Wycombe W.	Tr	08.95	95	0	4	0
Cardiff C.	L	03.96	95	7	0	0
Hereford U.	Tr	03.97	96	7	0	1

McGOVERN John Prescott
Montrose, 28 October, 1949 Su23-2 (M)

League Club	Source	Date Signed	Seasons Played	Apps	Subs	Gls
Hartlepool U.	App	05.67	65-68	69	3	5
Derby Co.	Tr	09.68	68-73	186	4	16
Leeds U.	Tr	08.74	74	4	0	0
Nottingham F.	Tr	02.75	74-81	249	4	6
Bolton W.	Tr	06.82	82-83	16	0	0

McGOVERN Michael John
Hayes, 15 February, 1951 (M)

League Club	Source	Date Signed	Seasons Played	Apps	Subs	Gls
Queens Park R.	App	11.68	67-71	10	2	0
Watford	L	08.72	72	4	0	0
Swindon T.	Tr	02.73	72-74	26	4	2
Aldershot	L	03.75	74	6	0	1

McGOVERN Patrick Munro
Edinburgh, 14 May, 1948 (IF)

League Club	Source	Date Signed	Seasons Played	Apps	Subs	Gls
Notts Co.	Royston B.C.	07.67	67	1	2	0

McGOVERN Simon
Bradford, 25 February, 1965 (M)

League Club	Source	Date Signed	Seasons Played	Apps	Subs	Gls
Bradford C. (N/C)	Jnrs	08.82	82	1	0	0

McGOWAN Aloysius (Ally)
Airdrie, 22 January, 1930 (FB)

League Club	Source	Date Signed	Seasons Played	Apps	Subs	Gls
Wrexham	St Johnstone	05.53	53-64	408	-	2

McGOWAN Andrew
Corby, 17 July, 1956 E Yth (M)

League Club	Source	Date Signed	Seasons Played	Apps	Subs	Gls
Northampton T.	Corby T.	06.75	75-77	93	12	14

McGOWAN Daniel
Dublin, 8 November, 1924 Died 1994 LoI/IR-3 (WH)

League Club	Source	Date Signed	Seasons Played	Apps	Subs	Gls
West Ham U.	Shelbourne	05.48	48-53	81	-	8

McGOWAN Gavin Gregory
Blackheath, 16 January, 1976 E Sch/E Yth (FB)

League Club	Source	Date Signed	Seasons Played	Apps	Subs	Gls
Arsenal	YT	07.94	92-97	3	3	0
Luton T.	L	03.97	96	2	0	0
Luton T.	L	07.97	97	6	2	0

McGOWAN George
Carluke, 30 November, 1943 (CF)

League Club	Source	Date Signed	Seasons Played	Apps	Subs	Gls
Preston N.E.	Wishaw Jnrs	08.62				
Chester C.	Tr	03.63	62-63	18	-	3
Stockport Co.	Tr	09.64	64	5	-	0

McGOWAN Gerard James
Kilwinning, 4 August, 1944 (OL)

League Club	Source	Date Signed	Seasons Played	Apps	Subs	Gls
Oldham Ath.	Ardeer Rec.	11.63	65	5	0	1

McGOWAN James
Cambuslang, 12 January, 1924 Died 1984 (WH)

League Club	Source	Date Signed	Seasons Played	Apps	Subs	Gls
Grimsby T.	Dumbarton	07.46	46-48	34	-	4
Southampton	Tr	03.50	49-57	78	-	9

McGOWAN James
Glasgow, 31 July, 1939 (OR)

League Club	Source	Date Signed	Seasons Played	Apps	Subs	Gls
Mansfield T.	St Johnstone	06.61	61	3	-	0

McGOWAN Kenneth
Wolverhampton, 13 May, 1920 (CF)

League Club	Source	Date Signed	Seasons Played	Apps	Subs	Gls
Walsall		10.47	47-48	11	-	4

McGRATH Roland **Christopher**
Belfast, 29 November, 1954 NI-21 (W)

League Club	Source	Date Signed	Seasons Played	Apps	Subs	Gls
Tottenham H.	App	01.72	73-75	30	8	5
Millwall	L	02.76	75	15	0	3
Manchester U.	Tr	10.76	76-80	12	16	1

McGRATH Derek Brendan Joseph
Dublin, 21 January, 1972 IRu21-9 (M)

League Club	Source	Date Signed	Seasons Played	Apps	Subs	Gls
Brighton & H.A.	YT	12.89	89-90	2	4	0

McGRATH James
Belfast, 15 November, 1921 (WH)

League Club	Source	Date Signed	Seasons Played	Apps	Subs	Gls
Barrow		08.45	46	3	-	0

McGRATH John
Tidworth, 21 May, 1932 (WH/IF)

League Club	Source	Date Signed	Seasons Played	Apps	Subs	Gls
Notts Co.	Aldershot (Am)	08.53	55-57	54	-	5
Darlington	Tr	05.58	58	25	-	6

McGRATH John Thomas
Manchester, 23 August, 1938 Eu23-1/EF Lge (CH)

League Club	Source	Date Signed	Seasons Played	Apps	Subs	Gls
Bury	Bolton W. (Am)	10.55	56-60	148	-	2
Newcastle U.	Tr	02.61	60-67	169	1	2
Southampton	Tr	02.68	67-73	167	1	1
Brighton & H. A.	L	12.72	72	3	0	0

McGRATH Lloyd Anthony
Birmingham, 24 February, 1965 E Yth/Eu21-1 (M)

League Club	Source	Date Signed	Seasons Played	Apps	Subs	Gls
Coventry C.	App	12.82	83-94	200	14	4
Portsmouth	Hong Kong	10.94	94	15	3	0

League Club	Source	Date Signed	Seasons Played	Career Record Apps	Subs	Gls
McGRATH Martin Lawrence						
Hendon, 15 October, 1960 E Sch						(M)
Southampton	App	10.78	79	0	1	0
Bournemouth	Tr	06.80	80	17	5	0
McGRATH Michael						
Dublin, 7 April, 1936 IR 'B'/IR-22						(WH)
Blackburn Rov.	Home Farm	08.54	55-65	268	0	8
Bradford P.A.	Tr	03.66	65-66	50	0	2
McGRATH Paul						
Ealing, 4 December, 1959 EF Lge/IR-83						(CD/M)
Manchester U.	St Patricks Ath.	04.82	82-88	159	4	12
Aston Villa	Tr	07.89	89-95	248	5	9
Derby Co.	Tr	10.96	96	23	1	0
Sheffield U.	Tr	08.97	97	12	0	0
McGRAW John (Ian)						
Glasgow, 30 August, 1926						(G)
Leicester C.	Arbroath	12.48	48-50	13	-	0
McGREAL John						
Liverpool, 2 June, 1972						(CD)
Tranmere Rov.	YT	07.90	91-97	157	2	1
McGREEVEY Brian Edmund						
Prestwich, 29 September, 1935						(OR)
Arsenal	Preston N.E. (Am)	03.54				
Stockport Co.	Tr	03.57	56	1	-	0
McGREGOR Alexander George Penman						
Glasgow, 12 November, 1950						(W)
Shrewsbury T.	Hibernian	01.75	74-75	46	3	7
Aldershot	Tr	09.76	76-81	168	9	17
MacGREGOR Colin						
Bradford, 13 November, 1940						(OR)
Bradford P. A.	Bradford C. (Am)	03.58	58-59	3	-	0
McGREGOR James Peter						
Hartlepool, 22 December, 1931 Died 1994						(HB)
Hartlepool U.	Elwick Road O.B.	02.50	52-53	2	-	0
McGREGOR John Reid						
Airdrie, 5 January, 1963						(D)
Liverpool	Queens Park	06.82				
Leeds U.	L	10.85	85	5	0	0
McGREGOR Mark Dale Thomas						
Chester, 16 February, 1977						(RB)
Wrexham	YT	07.95	94-97	106	7	4
McGREGOR Paul Anthony						
Liverpool, 17 December, 1974						(F)
Nottingham F.	YT	12.91	94-96	7	23	3
MacGREGOR Terence James						
Hartlepool, 24 May, 1938						(WH)
Hartlepool U.	Pools Jnrs	12.56	56-62	47	-	2
McGREGOR William						
Paisley, 1 December, 1923						(FB)
Leicester C.	Mossdale Y.M.C.A.	04.47	47-51	9	-	0
Mansfield T.	Tr	09.53	53-55	119	-	0
McGRELLIS Francis						
Falkirk, 5 October, 1958						(F)
Coventry C.	App	10.76				
Huddersfield T.	L	08.78	78	4	1	0
Hereford U.	Tr	03.79	78-81	80	5	24
McGROARTY James Martin						
Derry (NI), 30 August, 1957						(W)
Stoke C.	Finn Harps	09.77	77-78	6	1	2
McGROGAN Hugh						
Dumbarton, 1 March, 1957						(W)
Oxford U.	App	03.75	74-79	101	25	13
Carlisle U.	Tr	05.80	80	1	1	0
McGRORY Shaun Patrick						
Coventry, 29 February, 1968						(FB)
Coventry C.	YT	07.86				
Burnley	Tr	07.87	87-89	34	12	2
McGROTTY William						
Glasgow, 12 August, 1952						(W)
Blackpool	Yoker Ath.	06.70	70-72	2	2	1

League Club	Source	Date Signed	Seasons Played	Career Record Apps	Subs	Gls
McGUCKIN George Kay Whyte						
Dundee, 11 August, 1938						(HB)
Cardiff C.	Dundee Shamrock	12.55	57	4	-	0
McGUCKIN Thomas **Ian**						
Middlesbrough, 24 April, 1973						(CD)
Hartlepool U.	YT	05.91	91-96	147	5	8
McGUFFIE Alwyn Scott						
Drummore, 13 April, 1937						(WH)
Luton T.	Queen of South	09.54	55-63	79	-	10
McGUGAN John Hannah						
Airdrie, 12 June, 1939						(CH)
Leeds U.	St Mirren	08.60	60	1	-	0
Tranmere Rov.	Tr	02.61	60-61	35	-	0
McGUGAN Paul Joseph						
Glasgow, 17 July, 1964						(CD)
Barnsley	Glasgow Celtic	10.87	87-88	47	2	2
Chesterfield	Tr	01.91	90-93	74	3	6
McGUIGAN James						
Addiewell, 1 March, 1924 Died 1988						(WH/OR)
Sunderland	Hamilton Academical	06.47	47-48	3	-	1
Stockport Co.	Tr	06.49	49-50	43	-	9
Crewe Alex.	Tr	08.50	50-55	207	-	32
Rochdale	Tr	08.56	56-58	70	-	2
McGUIGAN John Joseph						
Motherwell, 29 October, 1932						(IF)
Southend U.	St Mirren	05.55	55-57	125	-	34
Newcastle U.	Tr	07.58	58-61	50	-	15
Scunthorpe U.	Tr	01.62	61-62	57	-	17
Southampton	Tr	08.63	63-64	33	-	8
Swansea C.	Tr	03.65	64-65	27	0	5
McGUIGAN Thomas						
Airdrie, 22 November, 1922 Died 1997						(IF)
Hartlepool U.	Ayr U.	08.50	50-57	325	-	75
McGUINNESS Henry						
Saltcoats, 17 February, 1928						(CH)
Torquay U.		03.48	49-54	81	-	0
McGUINNESS Paul						
Manchester, 2 March, 1966						(M)
Manchester U.	Jnrs	07.84				
Crewe Alex.	Tr	08.86	86	11	2	0
Manchester U.		07.89				
Chester C.	Bury (N/C)	07.91	91	3	4	0
McGUINNESS Robert Francis						
Motherwell, 29 January, 1954						(F)
Portsmouth	Motherwell	07.75	75-76	27	4	3
McGUINNESS Wilfred						
Manchester, 25 October, 1937 E Sch/E Yth/Eu23-4/EF Lge/E-2						(WH)
Manchester U.	Jnrs	11.54	55-59	81	-	2
McGUIRE Bernard Patrick						
Liverpool, 23 November, 1932						(OR)
Shrewsbury T.		07.53	53	2	-	0
McGUIRE Douglas John						
Bathgate, 6 September, 1967 S Yth						(W)
Sunderland (L)	Glasgow Celtic	03.88	87	1	0	0
Coventry C.	Tr	08.88	89	1	3	0
McGUIRE James **Gary**						
Campsall (Yks), 30 September, 1938						(G)
Torquay U.	Hakoah (Aus)	02.66	65-66	32	0	0
McGUIRE Leslie George Robert						
Bethnal Green, 31 January, 1929						(IF)
Gillingham		(N/L)	50-51	6	-	2
McGUIRE Michael James						
Blackpool, 4 September, 1952 E Yth						(M)
Coventry C.	Jnrs	11.69	71-74	60	12	1
Norwich C.	Tr	01.75	74-82	172	10	11
Barnsley	Tr	03.83	82-84	44	3	6
Oldham Ath.	Tr	01.85	84-86	65	4	3
McGUIRE Reginald						
Birkenhead, 24 August, 1959						(F)
Tranmere Rov. (N/C)	Cammell Laird	08.82	82	0	4	0

McHALE John
Oldham, 7 May, 1954 (CH)

League Club	Source	Date Signed	Seasons Played	Apps	Subs	Gls
Reading (Am)	Alton T.	01.75	74	1	0	0

McHALE John **Kevin**
Darfield, 1 October, 1939 E Sch/E Yth (OR)

League Club	Source	Date Signed	Seasons Played	Apps	Subs	Gls
Huddersfield T.	Jnrs	10.56	56-67	345	0	60
Crewe Alex.	Tr	01.68	67-70	116	0	22
Chester C.	Tr	10.70	70-71	61	3	4

McHALE Raymond
Sheffield, 12 August, 1950 (M)

League Club	Source	Date Signed	Seasons Played	Apps	Subs	Gls
Chesterfield	Hillsborough B.C.	08.70	71-74	123	1	27
Halifax T	Tr	10.74	74-76	86	0	21
Swindon T.	Tr	09.76	76-79	171	2	32
Brighton & H. A.	Tr	05.80	80	9	2	0
Barnsley	Tr	03.81	80-81	52	1	1
Sheffield U.	Tr	08.82	82-84	66	1	2
Bury	L	02.83	82	6	0	0
Swansea C.	Tr	01.85	84-85	45	2	1
Rochdale (N/C)	Tr	08.86	86	6	1	0
Scarborough (N/C)	Tr	12.86	87	25	0	3

McHALE Thomas Anthony
Liverpool, 3 September, 1951 (FB)

League Club	Source	Date Signed	Seasons Played	Apps	Subs	Gls
Bradford C.	Prescot Cables	09.71	71-72	34	2	0

McHALE William
Kelty, 9 August, 1929 (IL)

League Club	Source	Date Signed	Seasons Played	Apps	Subs	Gls
Carlisle U.		08.53	53	1	-	0
Halifax T.		03.55	54	3	-	0

McHARD Archibald
Dumbarton, 10 June, 1934 (W)

League Club	Source	Date Signed	Seasons Played	Apps	Subs	Gls
Bradford P.A.	Clyde	05.59	59-60	27	-	3

MACHENT Stanley Charles
Chesterfield, 23 March, 1921 (IF)

League Club	Source	Date Signed	Seasons Played	Apps	Subs	Gls
Sheffield U.		10.38	46-47	22	-	2
Chesterfield	Tr	11.47	47-48	21	-	7

MACHIN Alec Harold
Hampstead, 6 July, 1920 (WH)

League Club	Source	Date Signed	Seasons Played	Apps	Subs	Gls
Chelsea	Royal Hants Regt	10.44	46-47	53	-	8
Plymouth Arg.	Tr	06.48	48-50	26	-	1

MACHIN Ernest
Swinton, 26 April, 1944 (M)

League Club	Source	Date Signed	Seasons Played	Apps	Subs	Gls
Coventry C.	Nelson	03.62	62-72	255	2	33
Plymouth Arg.	Tr	12.72	72-73	57	0	6
Brighton & H.A.	Tr	08.74	74-75	64	0	1

MACHIN Melvyn
Newcastle-u-Lyme, 16 April, 1945 (M)

League Club	Source	Date Signed	Seasons Played	Apps	Subs	Gls
Port Vale	Jnrs	07.62	62-65	29	1	6
Gillingham	Tr	07.66	66-70	155	1	11
Bournemouth	Tr	12.70	70-73	110	0	7
Norwich C.	Tr	12.73	73-77	93	3	4

McHUGH Michael Bernard
Donegal, 3 April, 1971 (F)

League Club	Source	Date Signed	Seasons Played	Apps	Subs	Gls
Bradford C.	Jnrs	12.89	90-93	18	13	4
Scarborough	Tr	03.94	93	1	2	0

McILHARGEY Stephen
Glasgow, 23 August, 1964 (G)

League Club	Source	Date Signed	Seasons Played	Apps	Subs	Gls
Walsall	Blantyre Celtic	07.87				
Blackpool	Tr	08.89	89-93	100	1	0
Chester C.	L	09.93	93	1	0	0

McILHATTON John
Ardrossan, 3 January, 1921 Died 1954 (OR)

League Club	Source	Date Signed	Seasons Played	Apps	Subs	Gls
Everton	Albion Rov.	04.46	46-48	55	-	1

McILMOYLE Hugh
Port Glasgow, 29 January, 1940 (CF)

League Club	Source	Date Signed	Seasons Played	Apps	Subs	Gls
Leicester C.	Port Glasgow	08.59	60-61	20	-	5
Rotherham U.	Tr	07.62	62	12	-	4
Carlisle U.	Tr	03.63	62-64	77	-	44
Wolverhampton W.	Tr	10.64	64-66	90	0	35
Bristol C.	Tr	03.67	66-67	20	0	4
Carlisle U.	Tr	09.67	67-69	79	0	30
Middlesbrough	Tr	09.69	69-70	69	1	19
Preston N.E.	Tr	07.71	71-72	59	1	10
Carlisle U.	Morton	07.74	74	15	3	2

McILROY James
Drumbeg, 25 October, 1931 EF Lge/ NI-55 (IF)

League Club	Source	Date Signed	Seasons Played	Apps	Subs	Gls
Burnley	Glentoran	03.50	50-62	439	-	116
Stoke C.	Tr	03.63	62-65	96	2	16
Oldham Ath.	Tr	03.66	65-67	35	4	1

McILROY Samuel Baxter
Belfast, 2 August, 1954 NI-88 (M)

League Club	Source	Date Signed	Seasons Played	Apps	Subs	Gls
Manchester U.	App	08.71	71-81	320	22	57
Stoke C.	Tr	02.82	81-84	132	1	14
Manchester C.	Tr	08.85	85	12	0	1
Manchester C.	Orgryte (Swe)	11.86	86	1	0	0
Bury	Tr	03.87	86-87	43	0	6
Bury	V.F.B. Mödling (Aut)	08.88	88-89	52	5	2
Preston N.E.	Tr	02.90	89	20	0	0

McILVENNY Edward Joseph
Greenock, 21 October, 1924 Died 1989 USA Int (OR)

League Club	Source	Date Signed	Seasons Played	Apps	Subs	Gls
Wrexham	Morton	03.47	46-47	7	-	1
Manchester U.	Philadelphia (USA)	08.50	50	2	-	0

McILVENNY Harold
Bradford, 5 October, 1922 E Amat (CF)

League Club	Source	Date Signed	Seasons Played	Apps	Subs	Gls
Bradford P. A. (Am)	Yorkshire Amats	08.46	46-49	43	-	17

McILVENNY John Anthony
Barnstaple , 2 March, 1930 (OR)

League Club	Source	Date Signed	Seasons Played	Apps	Subs	Gls
West Bromwich A.	Hinckley U.	10.49				
Bristol Rov.	Cheltenham T.	07.52	52-58	80	-	11
Reading	Tr	06.59	59-60	77	-	4

McILVENNY Patrick Dennis
Belfast, 11 September, 1924 (WH)

League Club	Source	Date Signed	Seasons Played	Apps	Subs	Gls
Cardiff C.	Merthr Tydfil	05.50				
Brighton & H. A.	Tr	07.51	51-54	60	-	5
Aldershot	Tr	12.55	55-56	16	-	0

McILVENNY Robert
Belfast, 7 July, 1926 (IF)

League Club	Source	Date Signed	Seasons Played	Apps	Subs	Gls
Oldham Ath.	Merthyr Tydfil	03.50	49-53	139	-	36
Bury	Tr	08.54	54	12	-	1
Southport	Tr	08.55	55-56	77	-	16
Barrow	Tr	07.57	57-58	43	-	11

McILWAINE Matthew
Glasgow, 20 September, 1920 (WH)

League Club	Source	Date Signed	Seasons Played	Apps	Subs	Gls
Bolton W.	Ayr U.	08.51	52	2	-	0

McILWRAITH James
Glasgow, 17 April, 1954 (M)

League Club	Source	Date Signed	Seasons Played	Apps	Subs	Gls
Bury	Motherwell	09.75	75-77	80	9	21
Portsmouth	Tr	07.78	78	16	3	0
Bury	Tr	07.79	79	28	1	3
Halifax T.	Tr	10.80	80-81	33	3	6

McINALLY Alan Bruce
Ayr, 10 February, 1963 S-8 (F)

League Club	Source	Date Signed	Seasons Played	Apps	Subs	Gls
Aston Villa	Glasgow Celtic	07.87	87-88	50	9	18

McINALLY Charles
Glasgow, 1 February, 1939 (HB)

League Club	Source	Date Signed	Seasons Played	Apps	Subs	Gls
Brentford	St Rochs	09.58	59	1	-	0

McINALLY James Edward
Glasgow, 19 February, 1964 S Yth/Su21-1/S-10 (FB)

League Club	Source	Date Signed	Seasons Played	Apps	Subs	Gls
Nottingham F.	Glasgow Celtic	06.84	84-85	36	0	0
Coventry C.	Tr	01.86	85	5	0	0

McINALLY John Stewart
Gatehouse of Fleet, 26 September, 1951 S Sch (G)

League Club	Source	Date Signed	Seasons Played	Apps	Subs	Gls
Manchester U.	Jnrs	03.69				
Lincoln C.	Tr	08.70	70-71	22	0	0
Colchester U.	Tr	11.72	72	27	0	0

McINCH James Reid
Glasgow, 27 June, 1953 (F)

League Club	Source	Date Signed	Seasons Played	Apps	Subs	Gls
Cardiff C.	Jnrs	08.70	72-74	11	2	0

McINDEWAR Archibald
Glasgow, 26 July, 1921 (G)

League Club	Source	Date Signed	Seasons Played	Apps	Subs	Gls
Workington	Glasgow Rangers	08.51	51	20	-	0

McINERNEY Ian
Limerick, 1 September, 1972 (F)

League Club	Source	Date Signed	Seasons Played	Apps	Subs	Gls
Peterborough U.	YT	07.91	91	3	7	1

McINERNEY Ian Dominic
Liverpool, 26 January, 1964 (W)

League Club	Source	Date Signed	Seasons Played	Apps	Subs	Gls
Huddersfield T.	Newcastle Blue Star	08.88	88	5	5	1
Stockport Co.	Tr	07.89	89-90	37	5	8
Rochdale	L	02.91	90	4	0	1

League Club	Source	Date Signed	Seasons Played	Career Record Apps	Subs	Gls
McINNES Graham James						
Aberdeen, 7 April, 1938						(F)
Bury	Aberdeen	06.59	60	1	-	0
McINNES Ian						
Hamilton, 22 March, 1967						(W)
Rotherham U.	App	09.84	83-84	6	3	0
Lincoln C.	Tr	01.86	85-86	38	5	4
McINNES John						
Ayr, 29 March, 1923						(IF)
Bradford C.	Partick Thistle	05.49	49-50	21	-	6
McINNES John Smith						
Glasgow, 11 August, 1927 Died 1973						(IF)
Chelsea	Morton	05.47	46-49	37	-	5
McINNES Joseph Clarke						
Glasgow, 9 December, 1932						(OL)
Accrington St.	Partick Thistle	03.56	55	14	-	2
McINNES William						
Douglas, 20 May, 1931						(G)
Accrington St.	Alloa Ath.	10.55	55-60	153	-	0
Southport	Tr	07.61	61-62	26	-	0
McINTOSH Alan						
Llandudno, 29 July, 1939 W Amat						(W)
Cardiff C.	Llandudno	02.62	61-63	64	-	11
McINTOSH Albert						
Dundee, 6 April, 1930						(CF)
Swansea C.		03.54	53-56	14	-	3
McINTOSH Alexander						
Dunfermline, 14 April, 1916						(IF)
Wolverhampton W.	Folkestone T.	10.37	37-46	44	-	7
Birmingham C.	Tr	01.47	46-47	23	-	4
Coventry C.	Tr	02.48	47-48	20	-	3
McINTOSH Alexander James						
Inverurie, 19 October, 1923						(FB)
Barrow	Dundee	04.47	46-49	89	-	1
Carlisle U.	Tr	10.49	49-54	227	-	4
McINTOSH David						
Girvan, 4 May, 1925 Died 1995						(G)
Sheffield Wed.	Girvan Ath.	10.47	47-57	293	-	0
Doncaster Rov.	Tr	01.58	57-58	15	-	0
McINTOSH James McLaren						
Dumfries, 5 April, 1918						(CF)
Blackpool	Droylsden	09.35	35-37	5	-	0
Preston N.E.	Tr	11.37	37-38	27	-	3
Blackpool	Tr	05.46	46-48	69	-	25
Everton	Tr	03.49	48-50	58	-	19
McINTOSH James William						
Dundee, 19 August, 1950						(W)
Nottingham F.	Montrose	10.70	70-75	45	7	2
Chesterfield	L	01.76	75	3	0	0
Hull C.	Tr	03.76	75-76	20	0	1
McINTOSH John (Ian) McGregor						
Glasgow, 14 September, 1933						(F)
Bury	Partick Thistle	12.57	57-58	29	-	13
McINTOSH Malcolm Patrick						
Oxford, 6 July, 1959						(D)
Oxford U.	App	07.77	78-80	53	3	0
Oxford U. (N/C)	Kettering T.	08.82	82	2	0	0
McINTOSH Martin Wyllie						
East Kilbride, 19 March, 1971 S 'B'						(D)
Stockport Co.	Hamilton Academical	08.97	97	38	0	2
McINTOSH William Dowling						
Glasgow, 7 December, 1919 Died 1990						(CF)
Preston N.E.	St Johnstone	05.46	46-48	91	-	46
Blackpool	Tr	01.49	48-51	51	-	12
Stoke C.	Tr	09.51	51-52	26	-	6
Walsall	Tr	11.52	52	22	-	9
McINTYRE James						
Motherwell, 22 March, 1933						(G)
Accrington St.	Motherwell	03.57	56	4	-	0

League Club	Source	Date Signed	Seasons Played	Career Record Apps	Subs	Gls
McINTYRE James						
Glasgow, 24 May, 1972						(W)
Bristol C.	Duntocher B.C.	10.91	91	1	0	0
Exeter C.	L	02.93	92	12	3	3
Reading	Kilmarnock	03.98	97	6	0	0
McINTYRE Joseph Gerald						
Manchester, 19 June, 1971						(LB)
Rochdale	YT	●	88	2	2	0
McINTYRE Kevin						
Liverpool, 23 December, 1977						(D/M)
Tranmere Rov.	YT	11.96	97	0	2	0
McINTYRE Patrick Finucane						
Aylesham (Kt), 14 March, 1943						(FB)
Gillingham	Jnrs	07.61	60-62	10	-	0
McINTYRE Stephen						
Ayr, 15 May, 1966						(RB)
Hereford U.	Ayr U.	07.91	91	12	0	0
McIVER Frederick						
Birtley, 14 February, 1952						(M)
Sunderland	App	04.69	71	1	0	0
Sheffield Wed.	Racing Jet (Bel)	07.74	74-75	34	3	0
McIVOR Ronald William						
Edinburgh, 23 March, 1951						(FB)
Wigan Ath.	East Fife	10.79	79	3	0	1
McJANNET William **Leslie**						
Cumnock, 2 August, 1961						(RB)
Mansfield T.	Jnrs	08.79	79-81	73	1	0
Scarborough	Burton A.	08.87	87-88	29	5	0
Darlington	Tr	12.88	88-91	83	2	5
McJARROW Hugh						
Motherwell, 29 January, 1928 Died 1987						(CF)
Chesterfield	Maryhill Jnrs	03.46	46-49	33	-	11
Sheffield Wed.	Tr	03.50	49-51	46	-	21
Luton T.	Tr	02.52	51-53	15	-	10
Plymouth Arg.	Tr	12.53	53-55	30	-	3
MACKAY Angus MacDougall						
Glasgow, 24 April, 1925						(IF)
Ipswich T.	Hamilton Academical	05.46	46	5	-	0
Exeter C.	Tr	09.47	47-54	257	-	78
Millwall	Tr	06.55	55	17	-	4
MACKAY David Craig						
Edinburgh, 14 November, 1934 S Sch/Su23-4/SF Lge/S-22						(LH)
Tottenham H.	Hearts	03.59	58-67	268	0	42
Derby Co.	Tr	07.68	68-70	122	0	5
Swindon T.	Tr	05.71	71	25	1	1
McKAY Derek						
Banff, 13 December, 1949						(W)
Barrow	Aberdeen	09.71	71	18	0	0
MACKAY Donald Scrimgeour						
Glasgow, 19 March, 1940						(G)
Southend U.	Dundee U.	07.72	72-73	13	0	0
McKAY James						
Stirling, 11 June, 1918						(CF)
Tranmere Rov.		08.49	49	12	-	1
McKAY Joffre						
Dingwall, 21 January, 1937						(G)
Bury	Ross Co.	12.58				
Rochdale	Tr	07.60	60	9	-	0
McKAY John						
Port Glasgow, 27 June, 1927						(OL)
Queens Park R.	Irvine	03.49	49-51	17	-	1
McKAY Mark Brian						
Edinburgh, 12 November, 1967						(W)
Doncaster Rov.	Dalkeith Jnrs	01.90	89	0	1	0
McKAY Matthew Paul						
Warrington, 21 January, 1981						(M)
Chester C.	YT	●	97	3	2	0
Everton	Tr	03.98				
McKAY Paul Wilson						
Banbury, 28 January, 1971						(RB)
Burnley	YT	11.89	89	8	4	0

McKAY Peter Walker
Newburgh, 23 February, 1925 (CF)

League Club	Source	Date Signed	Seasons Played	Apps	Subs	Gls
Burnley	Dundee U.	05.54	54-56	60	-	36

MACKAY Robert
Harthill, 6 May, 1948 (M)

League Club	Source	Date Signed	Seasons Played	Apps	Subs	Gls
Leicester C.	Harthill Jnrs	05.65	68	6	1	1

McKAY William
Rothesay, 10 March, 1927 (OR)

League Club	Source	Date Signed	Seasons Played	Apps	Subs	Gls
Queens Park R.	Deal T.	07.55	55	6	-	0

McKEARNEY David Jonathan
Crosby, 20 June, 1968 (LB/M)

League Club	Source	Date Signed	Seasons Played	Apps	Subs	Gls
Bolton W.	Prescot Cables	11.87				
Crewe Alex.	Northwich Vic.	10.89	89-92	95	13	11
Wigan Ath.	Tr	07.93	93-94	45	4	9

McKECHNIE Iain Hector
Bellshill, 4 October, 1941 (G)

League Club	Source	Date Signed	Seasons Played	Apps	Subs	Gls
Arsenal	Jnrs	05.59	61-63	23	-	0
Southend U.	Tr	05.64	64-65	62	0	0
Hull C.	Tr	08.66	66-73	255	0	0

McKECHNIE Thomas Sharp
Milngavie, 9 February, 1940 (IF)

League Club	Source	Date Signed	Seasons Played	Apps	Subs	Gls
Luton T.	Kirkintilloch Rob Roy	05.61	61-65	129	2	31
Bournemouth	Tr	07.66	66	14	0	2
Colchester U.	Tr	09.67	67	23	1	5

McKEE Colin
Glasgow, 22 August, 1973 (F)

League Club	Source	Date Signed	Seasons Played	Apps	Subs	Gls
Manchester U.	YT	06.91	93	1	0	0
Bury	L	01.93	92	2	0	0

McKEE Francis Joseph
Cowdenbeath, 25 January, 1923 Died 1988 (WH)

League Club	Source	Date Signed	Seasons Played	Apps	Subs	Gls
Birmingham C.	Dundee U.	02.48	48-50	22	-	0
Gillingham	Tr	07.52	52-54	53	-	0

McKEE Raymond Trevor
Plaistow, 16 June, 1926 (G)

League Club	Source	Date Signed	Seasons Played	Apps	Subs	Gls
Northampton T.	Finchley	03.47	46	5	-	0

McKEE Stephen
Belfast, 15 April, 1956 (W)

League Club	Source	Date Signed	Seasons Played	Apps	Subs	Gls
Sheffield U.	Linfield	12.76	76	4	3	0

McKEE William Andrew
Warrington, 6 June, 1928 (WH)

League Club	Source	Date Signed	Seasons Played	Apps	Subs	Gls
Blackburn Rov.	Earlstown	11.49	50	1	-	0

McKEENAN Alexander
Port Glasgow, 26 February, 1924 (IF)

League Club	Source	Date Signed	Seasons Played	Apps	Subs	Gls
Leyton Orient	Port Glasgow	06.46	46	1	-	0

McKEEVER Mark Anthony
Derry, 16 November, 1978 NI Yth (LW)

League Club	Source	Date Signed	Seasons Played	Apps	Subs	Gls
Peterborough U.	YT	●	96	2	1	0
Sheffield Wed.	Tr	04.97				

McKELLAR David
Irvine, 22 May, 1956 (G)

League Club	Source	Date Signed	Seasons Played	Apps	Subs	Gls
Ipswich T.	App	03.74				
Derby Co.	Ardrossan Winton	04.78	78-79	41	0	0
Brentford	Tr	09.80	80-81	84	0	0
Carlisle U.	Tr	08.83	83-84	82	0	0
Newcastle U. (L)	Hibernian	02.86	85	10	0	0
Hartlepool U. (L)	Dunfermline Ath.	08.88	88	5	0	0
Carlisle U.	Tr	10.88	88-89	69	0	0

MACKEN Anthony
Dublin, 30 July, 1950 IRu23-1/IR-1 (RB)

League Club	Source	Date Signed	Seasons Played	Apps	Subs	Gls
Derby Co.	Waterford	08.74	75-77	20	3	1
Portsmouth	L	11.75	75	10	0	1
Walsall	Tr	10.77	77-81	190	0	1

MACKEN Jonathan Paul
Manchester, 7 September, 1977 E Yth (F)

League Club	Source	Date Signed	Seasons Played	Apps	Subs	Gls
Manchester U.	YT	07.96				
Preston N.E.	Tr	07.97	97	20	9	6

McKENNA Alan Millar
Edinburgh, 4 August, 1961 (F)

League Club	Source	Date Signed	Seasons Played	Apps	Subs	Gls
Millwall	App	10.78	78-81	23	7	4

McKENNA Brian Francis
Dublin, 30 January, 1972 IRu21-4 (G)

League Club	Source	Date Signed	Seasons Played	Apps	Subs	Gls
Brighton & H.A.	Home Farm	07.89	90	1	0	0

McKENNA Francis
Blaydon, 8 January, 1933 E Amat (W)

League Club	Source	Date Signed	Seasons Played	Apps	Subs	Gls
Leeds U.	Bishop Auckland	07.56	56	6	-	4
Carlisle U.	Tr	02.58	57-58	46	-	11
Hartlepool U.	Tr	07.59	59	32	-	5

McKENNA John
Belfast, 6 June, 1926 Died 1980 NI-7 (OR)

League Club	Source	Date Signed	Seasons Played	Apps	Subs	Gls
Huddersfield T.	Linfield	09.48	48-52	134	-	8
Blackpool	Tr	07.54	54-56	25	-	2
Southport	Tr	07.57	57	15	-	1

McKENNA Kenneth Michael
Birkenhead, 2 July, 1960 (F)

League Club	Source	Date Signed	Seasons Played	Apps	Subs	Gls
Tranmere Rov. (N/C)	Poulton Vic.	08.82	82	2	2	0
Tranmere Rov.	Telford U.	08.87	87-88	13	2	3

McKENNA Michael Joseph
Darkley, 3 November, 1916 Died 1974 (WH)

League Club	Source	Date Signed	Seasons Played	Apps	Subs	Gls
Northampton T.	Bromsgrove Rov.	07.46	46	4	-	0

McKENNA Patrick
Glasgow, 26 April, 1920 Died 1995 (FB)

League Club	Source	Date Signed	Seasons Played	Apps	Subs	Gls
Plymouth Arg.	Aberdeen	08.52	52	1	-	0

McKENNA Paul Stephen
Chorley, 20 October, 1977 (LM)

League Club	Source	Date Signed	Seasons Played	Apps	Subs	Gls
Preston N.E.	YT	02.96	96-97	8	2	1

McKENNA Thomas
Paisley, 11 November, 1919 (WH)

League Club	Source	Date Signed	Seasons Played	Apps	Subs	Gls
Reading	St Mirren	06.46	46-47	28	-	1
Grimsby T.	Tr	06.48	48-49	50	-	2

McKENNAN Peter Stewart
Airdrie, 16 July, 1918 Died 1991 SF Lge (IF)

League Club	Source	Date Signed	Seasons Played	Apps	Subs	Gls
West Bromwich A.	Partick Thistle	10.47	47	11	-	4
Leicester C.	Tr	03.48	47-48	18	-	7
Brentford	Tr	09.48	48	24	-	6
Middlesbrough	Tr	05.49	49-50	40	-	18
Oldham Ath.	Tr	07.51	51-53	78	-	28

MacKENZIE Aiden
Athlone, 15 July, 1959 (F)

League Club	Source	Date Signed	Seasons Played	Apps	Subs	Gls
Lincoln C.	Galway Rov.	12.78	79	4	2	0

MacKENZIE Christopher Neil
Northampton, 14 May, 1972 (G)

League Club	Source	Date Signed	Seasons Played	Apps	Subs	Gls
Hereford U.	Corby T.	07.94	94-95	59	1	1
Leyton Orient	Tr	10.97	97	4	0	0

MacKENZIE Donald Alexander
Liverpool, 30 January, 1942 (W)

League Club	Source	Date Signed	Seasons Played	Apps	Subs	Gls
Everton		01.63				
Rochdale	Tr	10.63	63-64	41	-	7

McKENZIE Donald Cameron
Glasgow, 9 June, 1927 (IF)

League Club	Source	Date Signed	Seasons Played	Apps	Subs	Gls
Grimsby T.	Glasgow Rangers	08.51	51	4	-	0

McKENZIE Duncan
Grimsby, 10 June, 1950 (F)

League Club	Source	Date Signed	Seasons Played	Apps	Subs	Gls
Nottingham F.	Jnrs	07.68	69-73	105	6	41
Mansfield T.	L	03.70	69	7	3	3
Mansfield T.	L	02.73	72	6	0	7
Leeds U.	Tr	08.74	74-75	64	2	27
Everton	Anderlecht (Bel)	12.76	76-77	48	0	14
Chelsea	Tr	09.78	78	15	0	4
Blackburn Rov.	Tr	03.79	78-80	74	0	16

MacKENZIE Hamish James Todd
Denny, 11 March, 1945 (FB)

League Club	Source	Date Signed	Seasons Played	Apps	Subs	Gls
Liverpool	App	03.62				
Brentford	Dunfermline Ath.	08.64	65-66	19	0	0

McKENZIE Ian Edward
Wallsend, 22 August, 1966 (LB)

League Club	Source	Date Signed	Seasons Played	Apps	Subs	Gls
Barnsley (N/C)	Newcastle U. (App)	08.85	85	1	0	0
Stockport Co.	Tr	09.86	86-88	51	8	0

MacKENZIE Ian Stanley
Rotherham, 27 September, 1950 (CD)

League Club	Source	Date Signed	Seasons Played	Apps	Subs	Gls
Sheffield U.	Jnrs	06.68	69-73	43	2	1
Southend U.	L	03.75	74	5	1	0
Mansfield T.	Tr	07.75	75-77	69	1	1

McKENZIE John Archibald
Glasgow, 4 September, 1925 SF Lge/S-9 (W)

League Club	Source	Date Signed	Seasons Played	Apps	Subs	Gls
Bournemouth	Partick Thistle	08.47	47	38	-	9

MacKENZIE Matthew Laurence
Dumbarton, 7 July, 1924 (IF)

League Club	Source	Date Signed	Seasons Played	Apps	Subs	Gls
Sheffield Wed.	Clydebank Ath.	12.45	46-47	6	-	0
Grimsby T.	Tr	07.49	49-50	58	-	11

McKENZIE Leon Mark
Croydon, 17 May, 1978 (CF)

League Club	Source	Date Signed	Seasons Played	Apps	Subs	Gls
Crystal Palace	YT	10.95	95-97	8	28	2
Fulham	L	10.97	97	1	2	0

McKENZIE Malcolm James
Edinburgh, 1 May, 1950 (OL)

League Club	Source	Date Signed	Seasons Played	Apps	Subs	Gls
Port Vale	Jnrs	05.67	65-67	7	1	1

MacKENZIE Neil David
Birmingham, 15 April, 1976 (M)

League Club	Source	Date Signed	Seasons Played	Apps	Subs	Gls
Stoke C.	West Bromwich A. (YT)	11.95	96-97	12	22	1

McKENZIE Paul
Aberdeen, 4 October, 1969 (M)

League Club	Source	Date Signed	Seasons Played	Apps	Subs	Gls
Sunderland	YT	07.87				
Burnley	Peterhead	02.92	91	1	3	0

McKENZIE Robert Alexander
Hexham, 22 March, 1979 (M/RB)

League Club	Source	Date Signed	Seasons Played	Apps	Subs	Gls
Rotherham U.	YT	●	96	6	5	0

McKENZIE Roger Mark
Sheffield, 27 January, 1973 (F)

League Club	Source	Date Signed	Seasons Played	Apps	Subs	Gls
Doncaster Rov.	YT	07.91	91	7	10	1
Scarborough	Tr	08.92	92	0	1	0

MacKENZIE Stephen
Romford, 23 November, 1961 E Yth/Eu21-3/E'B' (M)

League Club	Source	Date Signed	Seasons Played	Apps	Subs	Gls
Crystal Palace	App	07.79				
Manchester C.	Tr	07.79	79-80	56	2	8
West Bromwich A.	Tr	08.81	81-86	153	3	23
Charlton Ath.	Tr	06.87	87-90	92	8	7
Sheffield Wed.	Tr	02.91	90-91	5	10	2
Shrewsbury T.	Tr	12.91	91-93	19	5	1

McKENZIE Stuart Ronald
Hull, 19 September, 1967 (FB)

League Club	Source	Date Signed	Seasons Played	Apps	Subs	Gls
York C.	YT	12.85	85-87	30	2	0

McKEOWN Gary Joseph
Oxford, 19 October, 1970 E Sch/E Yth (M)

League Club	Source	Date Signed	Seasons Played	Apps	Subs	Gls
Arsenal	YT	11.88				
Shrewsbury T.	L	03.92	91	8	0	1
Exeter C. (L)	Dundee	12.96	96	3	0	0

McKEOWN Joseph Francis
Bannockburn, 9 April, 1924 (IF)

League Club	Source	Date Signed	Seasons Played	Apps	Subs	Gls
Hartlepool U.	Stirling A.	08.50	50	46	-	7

McKEOWN Isaac Lindsay
Belfast, 11 July, 1957 (M)

League Club	Source	Date Signed	Seasons Played	Apps	Subs	Gls
Manchester U.	App	07.74				
Sheffield Wed.	Tr	07.76	76-77	6	5	0

McKEOWN Thomas
Cleland, 2 October, 1930 (OR)

League Club	Source	Date Signed	Seasons Played	Apps	Subs	Gls
Accrington St.	Queen of South	05.54	54	12	-	2

McKERNON Craig Andrew
Gloucester, 23 February, 1968 (RB)

League Club	Source	Date Signed	Seasons Played	Apps	Subs	Gls
Mansfield T.	App	02.86	84-89	79	15	0
Arsenal	Tr	12.89				

MACKIE Thomas Forbes
Burntisland, 30 March, 1918 Died 1989 (LB)

League Club	Source	Date Signed	Seasons Played	Apps	Subs	Gls
New Brighton	St Johnstone	05.47	47	2	-	0
Chester C.	Tr	08.48	48	5	-	0

McKIM John
Greenock, 22 January, 1926 (IF)

League Club	Source	Date Signed	Seasons Played	Apps	Subs	Gls
Chelsea	Port Glasgow	06.47				
Colchester U.	Tr	08.50	50-54	129	-	42

MACKIN John
Glasgow, 18 November, 1943 (RB)

League Club	Source	Date Signed	Seasons Played	Apps	Subs	Gls
Northampton T.		11.63	65-68	94	8	11
Lincoln C.	Tr	07.69	69	3	0	0
York C.	Tr	09.69	69-72	157	3	7
Darlington	L	03.73	72	2	0	0

McKINLAY Ian Joseph
Liverpool, 21 June, 1949 (OR)

League Club	Source	Date Signed	Seasons Played	Apps	Subs	Gls
Southport	Wrexham (Am)	09.66	66-67	11	1	1

McKINLAY Robert
Lochgelly, 10 October, 1932 (CH)

League Club	Source	Date Signed	Seasons Played	Apps	Subs	Gls
Nottingham F.	Bowhill Rov.	10.49	51-69	611	3	9

McKINLAY Thomas Valley
Glasgow, 3 December, 1964 S Yth/Su21-6/S 'B'/S-22 (LWB)

League Club	Source	Date Signed	Seasons Played	Apps	Subs	Gls
Stoke C. (L)	Glasgow Celtic	01.98	97	3	0	0

McKINLAY William
Glasgow, 22 April, 1969 S Sch/S Yth/Su21-6/S 'B'/S-28 (M)

League Club	Source	Date Signed	Seasons Played	Apps	Subs	Gls
Blackburn Rov.	Dundee U.	10.95	95-97	62	12	3

McKINNEY William
Newcastle, 20 July, 1936 (RB)

League Club	Source	Date Signed	Seasons Played	Apps	Subs	Gls
Newcastle U.	Wallsend St Luke	05.56	57-64	85	-	6
Bournemouth	Tr	08.65	65	17	0	0
Mansfield T.	Tr	07.66	66-67	51	1	2

McKINNON Paul John
Frimley, 1 August, 1958 (F)

League Club	Source	Date Signed	Seasons Played	Apps	Subs	Gls
Blackburn Rov.	Sutton U.	12.86	86	5	0	0

McKINNON Raymond
Dundee, 5 August, 1970 Su21-6 (M)

League Club	Source	Date Signed	Seasons Played	Apps	Subs	Gls
Nottingham F.	Dundee U.	07.92	92	5	1	1

McKINNON Robert
Glasgow, 31 July, 1966 S-3 (LB)

League Club	Source	Date Signed	Seasons Played	Apps	Subs	Gls
Newcastle U.	Rutherglen Glencairn	11.84	85	1	0	0
Hartlepool U.	Tr	07.86	86-91	246	1	7

McKINVEN John James
Campbeltown, 1 May, 1941 (OL)

League Club	Source	Date Signed	Seasons Played	Apps	Subs	Gls
Southend U.	Raith Rov.	05.60	60-69	284	2	62
Cambridge U.	Tr	12.69	70	18	0	2

McKNIGHT Allen Darrell
Antrim (NI), 27 January, 1964 NIu23-1/NI-10 (G)

League Club	Source	Date Signed	Seasons Played	Apps	Subs	Gls
West Ham U.	Albion Rov.	07.88	88	23	0	0
Rotherham U. (N/C)	Airdrieonians	10.91	91	3	0	0
Walsall	Tr	11.91	91	8	0	0
Exeter C. (N/C)	South China (HK)	03.94	93	9	1	0

McKNIGHT George
Newtonards, 17 November, 1923 Died 1996 (IF)

League Club	Source	Date Signed	Seasons Played	Apps	Subs	Gls
Blackpool	Linfield	06.46	46-53	41	-	9
Chesterfield	Tr	07.55	55	5	-	1
Southport	Tr	09.57	57	1	-	0

McKNIGHT Philip
Glasgow, 15 June, 1924 (WH)

League Club	Source	Date Signed	Seasons Played	Apps	Subs	Gls
Chelsea	Alloa Ath.	01.47	47-53	33	-	1
Leyton Orient	Tr	07.54	54-58	161	-	2

McKOP Henry George
Zimbabwe, 8 July, 1967 Zimbabwe Int (CD)

League Club	Source	Date Signed	Seasons Played	Apps	Subs	Gls
Bristol C.	Bonner S.C. (Zim)	02.94	93-94	2	3	0

MACKRETH Stephen Francis
Wrexham, 1 July, 1950 (FB)

League Club	Source	Date Signed	Seasons Played	Apps	Subs	Gls
Wrexham	Jnrs	10.67	68	1	1	0

McLACHLAN Dugald
Falkirk, 10 September, 1953 (F)

League Club	Source	Date Signed	Seasons Played	Apps	Subs	Gls
Preston N.E.	App	11.71				
Halifax T.	L	10.72	72	1	1	0
Peterborough U.	Tr	07.73	73	1	0	0

McLACHLAN Stephen
Kirkcudbright, 19 September, 1918 Died 1990 (WH)

League Club	Source	Date Signed	Seasons Played	Apps	Subs	Gls
Derby Co.	Dalbeattie	03.38	38-52	58	-	1

McLAFFERTY Maurice
Glasgow, 7 August, 1922 (LB)

League Club	Source	Date Signed	Seasons Played	Apps	Subs	Gls
Sheffield U.		08.51	51	18	-	0
Brighton & H.A.	Tr	07.52	52	21	-	0

McLAIN Thomas
Morpeth, 19 January, 1922 Died 1995 (WH/CF)

League Club	Source	Date Signed	Seasons Played	Apps	Subs	Gls
Sunderland	Ashington	08.46	46-51	67	-	1
Northampton T.	Tr	07.52	52-55	96	-	11

McLAREN Andrew
Larkhall, 24 January, 1922 Died 1996 S-4 (IF)

League Club	Source	Date Signed	Seasons Played	Apps	Subs	Gls
Preston N.E.	Larkhall Thistle	02.39	46-48	69	-	29
Burnley	Tr	12.48	48	3	-	1
Sheffield U.	Tr	03.49	48-50	31	-	4
Barrow	Tr	02.51	50-54	155	-	52

League Club	Source	Date Signed	Seasons Played	Apps	Subs	Gls
Bradford P.A.	Tr	10.54	54	18	-	7
Southport	Tr	06.55	55	4	-	1
Rochdale	Tr	11.55	55-56	44	-	12
MacLAREN David						
Auchterarder, 12 June, 1934						(G)
Leicester C.	Dundee	01.57	56-59	85	-	0
Plymouth Arg.	Tr	06.60	60-64	131	-	0
Wolverhampton W.	Tr	01.65	64-66	44	0	0
Southampton	Tr	09.66	66	22	0	0
McLAREN Edward						
Dundee, 8 September, 1929						(WH)
Blackpool	Dunkeld Jnrs	06.48				
Reading	Tr	10.52	53-58	184	-	2
McLAREN Hugh						
Hamilton, 24 June, 1926 Died 1965						(OL)
Derby Co.	Kilmarnock	10.49	49-53	119	-	53
Nottingham F.	Tr	01.54	53-54	33	-	15
Walsall	Tr	07.55	55	31	-	8
McLAREN James Danks						
Birkenhead, 29 July, 1936						(OR)
Chesterfield	Wigan Ath.	06.58	59	11	-	2
McLAREN Paul Andrew						
High Wycombe, 17 November, 1976						(M)
Luton T.	YT	01.94	93-97	63	17	1
McLAREN Robert						
Glasgow, 5 August, 1929						(IF)
Cardiff C.	Barry T.	02.50	49	1	-	0
Scunthorpe U.	Barry T.	08.51	51	6	-	0
MacLAREN Ross						
Edinburgh, 14 April, 1962						(CD/M)
Shrewsbury T.	Glasgow Rangers (Jnrs)	08.80	80-84	158	3	18
Derby Co.	Tr	07.85	85-87	113	9	4
Swindon T.	Tr	08.88	88-94	195	2	9
McLAREN John James **Roy**						
Auchterarder, 12 February, 1930						(G)
Bury	St Johnstone	12.55	55-58	86	-	0
Sheffield Wed.	Tr	10.58	58-63	31	-	0
MacLAREN James **Scott**						
Crieff, 26 November, 1921						(G)
Chester C.	Berwick R.	01.47	46-48	30	-	0
Carlisle U.	Tr	12.48	48-54	262	-	0
McLAREN Thomas						
Livingston, 1 June, 1949 Died 1978						(M)
Port Vale	Berwick R.	11.67	67-76	301	32	28
McLARTY Jesse Jones						
Ayr, 3 March, 1920						(IF)
Wrexham	Chester C. (Am)	09.45	46-47	24	-	9
McLAUGHLAN Alexander (Sandy) Donaldson						
Kilwinning, 17 July, 1936 SF Lge						(G)
Sunderland	Kilmarnock	09.64	64-65	43	0	0
McLAUGHLIN Hugh						
Glasgow, 2 September, 1943						(WH)
Brentford	St Rochs	09.61	63-65	4	1	0
McLAUGHLIN James						
Paisley, 11 February, 1926						(F)
Walsall	Glasgow Celtic	06.48	48-49	14	-	0
McLAUGHLIN James Charles						
Stirling, 10 December, 1926						(OL)
Hartlepool U.	Alloa Ath.	07.53	53	13	-	2
McLAUGHLIN James Christopher						
Derry (NI), 22 December, 1940 NIu23-2/NI-12						(W)
Birmingham C.	Derry C.	06.58				
Shrewsbury T.	Tr	07.60	60-62	124	-	56
Swansea C.	Tr	05.63	63-66	120	3	45
Peterborough U.	Tr	03.67	66	8	0	2
Shrewsbury T.	Tr	09.67	67-72	159	14	21
Swansea C.	Tr	11.72	72-73	20	8	2
McLAUGHLIN John						
Lennoxtown, 13 November, 1936						(F)
Millwall	Morton	07.63	63	21	-	5

League Club	Source	Date Signed	Seasons Played	Apps	Subs	Gls
McLAUGHLIN John						
Edmonton, 29 October, 1954 E Yth						(LB)
Colchester U.	App	05.72	71-73	66	1	2
Swindon T.	Tr	12.73	73-78	199	3	9
Portsmouth	Tr	07.79	79-83	172	0	1
McLAUGHLIN John Ian						
Stirling, 3 January, 1948						(FB)
Everton	Falkirk	10.71	71-75	59	2	1
McLAUGHLIN John Montgomery Lamont						
Glasgow, 12 April, 1936						(G)
Shrewsbury T.	Third Lanark	09.63	63	5	-	0
McLAUGHLIN John Thomas						
Liverpool, 25 February, 1952						(M)
Liverpool	App	02.69	69-73	38	2	2
Portsmouth	L	10.75	75	5	0	0
McLAUGHLIN Joseph						
Greenock, 2 June, 1960 Su21-10						(CD)
Chelsea	Morton	06.83	83-88	220	0	5
Charlton Ath.	Tr	08.89	89	31	0	0
Watford	Tr	08.90	90-91	46	0	2
McLAUGHLIN Michael Anthony						
Newport, 5 January, 1943						(CD)
Newport Co.	Nash U.	11.61				
Newport Co.	Lovells Ath.	08.68	68-69	90	0	2
Hereford U.	Tr	08.70	72-74	84	0	1
Newport Co. (N/C)	Cheltenham T.	03.78	77	7	0	0
McLAUGHLIN Robert						
Belfast, 6 December, 1925 LoI						(WH)
Wrexham	Distillery	01.50	49	17	-	0
Cardiff C.	Tr	04.50	50-53	48	-	3
Southampton	Tr	10.53	53-58	169	-	5
McLAUGHLIN William James						
U.S.A., 31 January, 1918 Died 1972						(LH)
Crewe Alex.		10.46	46	1	-	0
McLEAN Angus						
Hawarden, 20 September, 1925 Died 1979						(FB)
Wolverhampton W.	Aberystwyth	11.42	46-50	144	-	2
Bury	Bromsgrove Rov.	05.53	53	12	-	0
Crewe Alex.	Tr	06.54	54	17	-	0
McLEAN Colin						
Stirling, 16 May, 1928						(IF)
Southport	Forfar Ath.	06.52	52-53	59	-	18
Crewe Alex.	Tr	07.54	54	38	-	10
McLEAN David John						
Newcastle, 24 November, 1957 E Sch						(M)
Newcastle U.	App	11.75	75-77	7	2	0
Carlisle U.	Tr	03.78	77-78	9	6	0
Darlington	Tr	08.79	79-85	289	5	46
Scunthorpe U.	Tr	07.86	86-87	23	1	3
Hartlepool U.	L	03.87	86	6	0	0
McLEAN John **Derek**						
Brotton, 21 December, 1932						(IF)
Middlesbrough		10.52	55-61	119	-	30
Hartlepool U.	Tr	10.61	61-63	89	-	16
McLEAN George Roy						
Paisley, 16 September, 1937						(CF)
Norwich C.	Glasgow Rangers	03.62				
Grimsby T.	Tr	09.62	62-64	91	-	41
Exeter C.	Tr	06.65	65-66	47	0	12
Workington	Tr	01.67	66-67	53	0	16
Barrow	Tr	06.68	68	26	1	9
MacLEAN Hugh						
Stornoway, 20 January, 1952						(W)
West Bromwich A.	Jnrs	02.69	71-72	4	2	0
Swindon T.	Tr	07.74	74	17	2	1
McLEAN Ian						
Paisley, 13 August, 1966 Canadian Int						(CD)
Bristol Rov.	Metro Ford (Can)	09.93	93-95	21	14	2
Cardiff C.	L	09.94	94	4	0	0
Rotherham U.	L	01.96	95	9	0	0
McLEAN James						
Stirling, 3 April, 1934 Died 1995						(IF)
Port Vale	Alva R.	03.58	57	3	-	0

McLEAN Peter Young
Lochgelly, 27 November, 1923 (WH)

League Club	Source	Date Signed	Seasons Played	Apps	Subs	Gls
Reading	Bo'ness U.	01.49	49-52	70	-	6
Exeter C.	Tr	08.53	53	15	-	0

McLEAN Stewart
Barrhead, 30 August, 1923 (IL)

League Club	Source	Date Signed	Seasons Played	Apps	Subs	Gls
Rotherham U.	Partick Thistle	05.46	46-47	35	-	20

McLEAN William
Liverpool, 14 August, 1931 (OR)

League Club	Source	Date Signed	Seasons Played	Apps	Subs	Gls
Blackburn Rov.	Burscough	02.53	53	12	-	0

McLEAN William
(OR)

League Club	Source	Date Signed	Seasons Played	Apps	Subs	Gls
New Brighton	Queen of South	06.47	47	12	-	2

McLEAN William Graham
Dumbarton, 14 October, 1933 (IR)

League Club	Source	Date Signed	Seasons Played	Apps	Subs	Gls
Walsall		02.54	53	2	-	0

McLEARY Alan Terence
Lambeth, 6 October, 1964 E Yth/Eu21-1/E'B' (CD)

League Club	Source	Date Signed	Seasons Played	Apps	Subs	Gls
Millwall	App	10.81	82-92	289	18	5
Sheffield U.	L	07.92	92	3	0	0
Wimbledon	L	10.92	92	4	0	0
Charlton Ath.	Tr	05.93	93-94	66	0	3
Bristol C.	Tr	07.95	95-96	31	3	0
Millwall	Tr	02.97	96-97	34	0	0

McLEISH Hugh
Shotts, 10 June, 1948 (CF)

League Club	Source	Date Signed	Seasons Played	Apps	Subs	Gls
Sunderland	Dundee U.	08.67				
Luton T.	Tr	11.67	67	1	0	0

McLELLAN Alistair Alexander Angus
Glasgow, 16 April, 1922 (IF)

League Club	Source	Date Signed	Seasons Played	Apps	Subs	Gls
New Brighton	Albion Rov.	08.46	46-47	34	-	7
Tranmere Rov.	Tr	05.48	48	2	-	0

McLEOD Alexander Hector McMillan
Glasgow, 1 January, 1951 (F)

League Club	Source	Date Signed	Seasons Played	Apps	Subs	Gls
Southampton	St Mirren	05.73	73	2	1	0
Huddersfield T.	L	10.74	74	3	1	1

MacLEOD Alistair Reid
Glasgow, 26 February, 1931 (W)

League Club	Source	Date Signed	Seasons Played	Apps	Subs	Gls
Blackburn Rov.	St Mirren	06.56	56-60	193	-	47

McLEOD George James
Inverness, 30 November, 1932 (OL)

League Club	Source	Date Signed	Seasons Played	Apps	Subs	Gls
Luton T.	Inverness Clach.	01.55	55-58	51	-	6
Brentford	Tr	10.58	58-63	207	-	20
Queens Park R.	Tr	01.64	63-64	41	-	4

McLEOD John Murdoch
Edinburgh, 23 November, 1938 Su23-1/SF Lge/S-4 (OR)

League Club	Source	Date Signed	Seasons Played	Apps	Subs	Gls
Arsenal	Hibernian	07.61	61-64	101	-	23
Aston Villa	Tr	09.64	64-67	123	2	16

McLEOD Norman Andrew
Manchester, 29 July, 1930 (LB)

League Club	Source	Date Signed	Seasons Played	Apps	Subs	Gls
Crewe Alex.	Hyde U.	08.57	57-58	25	-	1

McLEOD Robert
Fraserburgh, 22 January, 1919 (IR)

League Club	Source	Date Signed	Seasons Played	Apps	Subs	Gls
Brighton & H.A.		11.47	47	1	-	0

McLEOD Robert Alexander
Inverness, 24 February, 1947 (CH)

League Club	Source	Date Signed	Seasons Played	Apps	Subs	Gls
Hartlepool U.	Sunderland T.T.C.	11.65	65-68	23	5	0

McLEOD Samuel Mark
Glasgow, 4 January, 1934 (IF)

League Club	Source	Date Signed	Seasons Played	Apps	Subs	Gls
Colchester U.	Easthouses	06.55	55-62	152	-	23

McLEOD Thomas
Musselburgh, 26 December, 1920 (IF)

League Club	Source	Date Signed	Seasons Played	Apps	Subs	Gls
Liverpool	B.A.O.R. Germany	10.45	46-48	7	-	0
Chesterfield	Tr	07.51	51	25	-	3

MACKLEWORTH Colin
Bow, 24 March, 1947 (G)

League Club	Source	Date Signed	Seasons Played	Apps	Subs	Gls
West Ham U.	App	04.64	66	3	0	0
Leicester C.	Tr	11.67	67-70	6	0	0

McLINTOCK Francis
Glasgow, 28 December, 1939 Su23-1/S-9 (CD)

League Club	Source	Date Signed	Seasons Played	Apps	Subs	Gls
Leicester C.	Shawfield Jnrs	01.57	59-64	168	-	25
Arsenal	Tr	10.64	64-72	312	2	26
Queens Park R.	Tr	06.73	73-76	126	1	5

McLOUGHLIN Alan Francis
Manchester, 20 April, 1967 IR 'B'/IR-34 (M)

League Club	Source	Date Signed	Seasons Played	Apps	Subs	Gls
Manchester U.	App	04.85				
Swindon T.	Tr	08.86	86-90	101	5	19
Torquay U.	L	03.87	86	16	0	1
Torquay U.	L	08.87	87	5	3	3
Southampton	Tr	12.90	90-91	22	2	1
Portsmouth	Tr	02.92	91-97	238	11	42

McLOUGHLIN Anthony Joseph
Liverpool, 24 September, 1946 (OL)

League Club	Source	Date Signed	Seasons Played	Apps	Subs	Gls
Everton	Jnrs	02.64				
Wrexham	Tr	07.66	66-67	27	2	9
Chester C.	Tr	10.67	67	2	2	0

McLOUGHLIN Paul Brendan
Bristol, 23 December, 1963 (W/F)

League Club	Source	Date Signed	Seasons Played	Apps	Subs	Gls
Cardiff C.	Gisborne (NZ)	12.84	84-85	40	9	4
Bristol C. (N/C)	Oster Vaxjo (Swe)	01.87				
Hereford U.	Tr	06.87	87-88	72	2	14
Wolverhampton W.	Tr	07.89	89-91	12	16	4
Walsall	L	09.91	91	9	0	4
York C.	L	01.92	91	1	0	0
Mansfield T.	Tr	01.92	91-93	49	12	9

MacLUCKIE George Robertson
Falkirk, 19 September, 1931 (OL)

League Club	Source	Date Signed	Seasons Played	Apps	Subs	Gls
Blackburn Rov.	Lochore Welfare	08.52	52	20	-	2
Ipswich T.	Tr	05.53	53-57	141	-	24
Reading	Tr	06.58	58-60	85	-	8

McLUCKIE Robert John
Doncaster, 5 October, 1955 (M)

League Club	Source	Date Signed	Seasons Played	Apps	Subs	Gls
Doncaster Rov.	App	10.73	72-73	2	2	0

McMAHON Desmond
Reading, 22 March, 1956 (F)

League Club	Source	Date Signed	Seasons Played	Apps	Subs	Gls
Reading (N/C)	Hungerford T.	08.82	82	0	2	0

McMAHON Francis Gerard
Belfast, 4 January, 1950 (M)

League Club	Source	Date Signed	Seasons Played	Apps	Subs	Gls
Coventry C.	Distillery	10.69				
Lincoln C.	Waterford	07.71	71-72	54	1	2
Darlington	Tr	03.73	72-73	19	4	1
Hartlepool U.	L	10.73	73	7	0	0

McMAHON Gerard Joseph
Belfast, 29 December, 1973 NI Sch/NI Yth/NIu21-1/NI 'B'/NI-17 (W)

League Club	Source	Date Signed	Seasons Played	Apps	Subs	Gls
Tottenham H.	Glenavon	07.92	94-95	9	7	0
Barnet	L	10.94	94	10	0	2
Stoke C.	Tr	09.96	96-97	38	14	3

McMAHON Hugh
Middlesbrough, 24 September, 1909 Died 1986 (OL)

League Club	Source	Date Signed	Seasons Played	Apps	Subs	Gls
Reading		09.32	32	1	-	0
Southend U.	Mexborough	05.33	33	10	-	3
Reading	Tr	06.34	34-35	10	-	2
Queens Park R.	Tr	05.36	36-37	41	-	3
Sunderland	Tr	11.37	37-38	8	-	1
Hartlepool U.	Tr	06.45	46-47	28	-	7
Rotherham U.	Tr	09.47	47-48	59	-	8

McMAHON Ian
Wells, 7 October, 1964 (M/D)

League Club	Source	Date Signed	Seasons Played	Apps	Subs	Gls
Oldham Ath.	App	10.82	82	2	0	0
Rochdale	Tr	01.84	83-85	89	2	8

McMAHON John
Manchester, 7 December, 1949 (RB)

League Club	Source	Date Signed	Seasons Played	Apps	Subs	Gls
Preston N.E.	App	12.67	70-78	256	1	7
Southend U.	L	09.70	70	4	0	0
Chesterfield	L	09.79	79	1	0	0
Crewe Alex.	Tr	10.79	79-80	67	0	2
Wigan Ath.	Tr	08.81	81-82	71	0	5
Tranmere Rov.	Tr	08.83	83	39	1	0

McMAHON John Albert
Middlesbrough, 25 October, 1965 (F)

League Club	Source	Date Signed	Seasons Played	Apps	Subs	Gls
Middlesbrough	App	10.83				
Darlington (N/C)	Tr	03.85	84	0	4	0

McMAHON Kevin
Tantobie, 1 March, 1946 (F)

League Club	Source	Date Signed	Seasons Played	Apps	Subs	Gls
Newcastle U.	Consett	08.67				
York C.	Tr	05.69	69-71	85	8	31
Bolton W.	L	03.72	71	4	2	1
Barnsley	Tr	07.72	72	4	1	0
Hartlepool U.	Tr	07.73	73-75	104	3	29

League Club	Source	Date Signed	Seasons Played	Apps	Subs	Gls
McMAHON Patrick						
Kilsyth, 19 September, 1945						(M)
Aston Villa	Glasgow Celtic	06.69	69-74	121	9	25
McMAHON Peter John						
Marylebone, 30 April, 1934						(WH)
Leyton Orient	Chertsey	05.51	51-57	66	-	1
Aldershot	Tr	10.58	58-59	39	-	0
McMAHON Samuel Keiron						
Newark, 10 February, 1976						(M)
Leicester C.	YT	07.94	94-97	1	4	1
McMAHON Stephen						
Liverpool, 20 August, 1961 Eu21-6/E'B'/EF Lge/E-17						(M)
Everton	App	08.79	80-82	99	1	11
Aston Villa	Tr	05.83	83-85	74	1	7
Liverpool	Tr	09.85	85-91	202	2	29
Manchester C.	Tr	12.91	91-94	83	4	1
Swindon T.	Tr	12.94	94-97	38	4	0
McMAHON Steven						
Glasgow, 22 April, 1970						(F)
Swansea C.	Ferguslie U.	07.91	92	2	0	0
Carlisle U.	Tr	07.93	93	2	0	0
Darlington	Foshan (China)	01.96	95	6	4	1
McMANAMAN Steven						
Bootle, 11 February, 1972 E Yth/Eu21-7/E-22						(F)
Liverpool	YT	02.90	90-97	233	11	42
McMANUS Brendan						
Kilkeel (NI), 2 December, 1923						(G)
Huddersfield T.	Newry T.	10.45	46	1	-	0
Oldham Ath.	Tr	07.47	47	35	-	0
Bradford C.	Tr	10.48	48-52	125	-	0
McMANUS Edward James						
Ramsgate, 8 August, 1937						(CF)
Bournemouth	Dover T.	08.54	58-59	4	-	0
Gillingham	Tr	08.60	60	3	-	0
McMANUS Charles **Eric**						
Limavady (NI), 14 November, 1950 NI Amat						(G)
Coventry C.	Coleraine	08.68	69-71	6	0	0
Notts Co.	Tr	05.72	72-78	229	0	0
Stoke C.	Tr	10.79	81	4	0	0
Lincoln C.	L	12.79	79	21	0	0
Bradford C.	Tr	08.82	82-84	113	0	0
Middlesbrough	L	01.86	85	2	0	0
Peterborough U.	L	03.86	85	18	0	0
Tranmere Rov.	Tr	08.86	86	3	0	0
McMANUS Stanley						
Carlisle, 31 October, 1932						(OL)
Bury		01.56				
Southport	Tr	07.57	57	5	-	0
McMANUS Steven						
Nottingham, 8 March, 1975						(M)
Walsall	YT	05.93	92	0	1	0
McMANUS Stuart Joseph						
Falkirk, 19 March, 1965						(F)
Southampton	Jnrs	07.84	85	2	0	1
Newport Co.	L	08.85	85	4	1	0
McMASTER Christopher						
Darlington, 16 June, 1959						(F)
Hartlepool U.	App	07.77	76-77	3	1	0
McMENAMIN Christopher						
Donegal, 27 December, 1973						(RB)
Coventry C.	Hitchin T.	09.96				
Peterborough U.	Tr	08.97	97	25	3	0
McMENEMY Paul Christopher						
Farnborough, 5 November, 1966						(F)
West Ham U.	App	11.84				
Aldershot	L	03.86	85	10	0	5
Northampton T.	L	01.87	86	4	0	2
McMICHAEL Alfred						
Belfast, 1 October, 1927 LoI/NI-40						(FB)
Newcastle U.	Linfield	09.49	49-62	402	-	1
McMILLAN Lyndon **Andre (Andy)**						
South Africa, 22 June, 1968						(FB)
York C.	Hull C. (trial)	10.87	87-97	376	12	5
MacMILLAN Duncan						
Glasgow, 18 January, 1922 Died 1992						(CH)
Grimsby T.	Glasgow Celtic	03.49	48-54	188	-	2
McMILLAN Eric						
Beverley, 2 November, 1936						(WH)
Chelsea		04.58	59	5	-	0
Hull C.	Tr	07.60	60-63	150	-	3
Halifax T.	Tr	07.65	65-66	49	1	8
McMILLAN George Sneddon						
Motherwell, 15 March, 1930						(OL)
Wrexham	Aberdeen	05.52	52	1	-	0
McMILLAN George Sorbie						
Stonehouse, 10 August, 1929						(G)
Ipswich T.	Newarthill Jnrs	02.53	54-57	53	-	0
McMILLAN John Shaw						
Renton, 14 April, 1937						(OR)
Cardiff C.	Dumbarton	02.58	60	2	-	0
Exeter C.	Tr	10.61	61-62	20	-	1
McMILLAN Paul Anthony						
Lennoxtown, 13 July,1950						(WH)
Chelsea	Jnrs	08.67	67	1	0	0
McMILLAN Samuel Thomas						
Belfast, 29 September, 1941 NIu23-1/NI-2						(IF)
Manchester U.	Boyland Y.C.	11.59	61-62	15	-	6
Wrexham	Tr	12.63	63-67	149	0	52
Southend U.	Tr	09.67	67-69	76	1	5
Chester C.	Tr	12.69	69	16	2	0
Stockport Co.	Tr	07.70	70-71	74	0	29
McMILLAN Thomas						
Glasgow, 12 February, 1931						(OL)
Norwich C.	Glasgow Celtic	07.54	54	19	-	2
Workington	Tr	09.55	55	2	-	0
McMILLAN Thomas Pearson						
Auchinleck, 16 January, 1936						(IF/WH)
Watford	Maybole Jnrs	09.56	56-57	33	-	13
Carlisle U.	Tr	07.58	58-60	89	-	7
McMILLEN Walter						
Belfast, 24 November, 1913 NI-7						(WH)
Manchester U.	Cliftonville	08.33	33-34	27	-	2
Chesterfield	Tr	12.36	36-38	85	-	16
Millwall	Tr	05.39	46-49	91	-	0
McMINN Kevin Clifton **(Ted)**						
Castle Douglas (Lk), 28 September, 1962						(W)
Derby Co.	Seville (Sp)	02.88	87-92	108	15	9
Birmingham C.	Tr	07.93	93	19	3	0
Burnley	Tr	03.94	93-95	38	8	3
McMINN Robert William						
Doncaster, 9 October, 1946						(FB)
Doncaster Rov.	App	10.64	63-65	4	1	0
McMORDIE Alexander (Eric)						
Belfast, 12 August, 1946 NIu23-1/NI-21						(M)
Middlesbrough	Dundela	09.64	65-73	231	10	22
Sheffield Wed.	L	10.74	74	9	0	6
York C.	Tr	05.75	75-76	42	0	2
Hartlepool U.	Tr	12.76	76-77	46	1	2
McMORRAN Edward James						
Larne (NI), 2 September, 1923 Died 1984 NI Sch/LoI/NI-15						(IF)
Manchester C.	Belfast Celtic	08.47	47-48	33	-	12
Leeds U.	Tr	01.49	48-49	38	-	6
Barnsley	Tr	07.50	50-52	104	-	32
Doncaster Rov.	Tr	02.53	52-57	126	-	32
Crewe Alex.	Tr	11.57	57	24	-	6
McMORRAN James Wilson						
Muirkirk, 29 October, 1942 S Sch						(IF)
Aston Villa	Jnrs	10.59	60-61	11	-	1
Walsall	Third Lanark	11.64	64-67	93	1	9
Swansea C.	Tr	06.68	68	14	0	2
Walsall	Tr	11.68	68	9	1	1
Notts Co.	Tr	07.69	69	6	0	0
McMORRAN John						
Forth, 11 May, 1934						(IF)
Bradford C.	Forth W.	12.54	54	1	-	0

McMORRAN Robert
Forth, 12 March, 1926 Died 1990 (OR)

League Club	Source	Date Signed	Seasons Played	Apps	Subs	Gls
Manchester U.	Glasgow Rangers	02.47				
Walsall	Tr	02.50	49	8	-	1

McMULLEN David
Denny, 13 June, 1960 (M)

League Club	Source	Date Signed	Seasons Played	Apps	Subs	Gls
Wigan Ath.	Cumbernauld U.	02.80	79-80	20	7	1

McMULLEN David
Harrington, 6 January, 1936 (WH)

League Club	Source	Date Signed	Seasons Played	Apps	Subs	Gls
Workington		08.59	59	1	-	0

McMULLEN Ian
Hoylake, 17 November, 1965 (M)

League Club	Source	Date Signed	Seasons Played	Apps	Subs	Gls
Tranmere Rov. (N/C)		08.84	84	2	0	0

McMURRAY John Daniel
Billingham, 5 October, 1931 (WH)

League Club	Source	Date Signed	Seasons Played	Apps	Subs	Gls
Middlesbrough	Billingham Synth.	05.49	53-54	3	-	0

McNAB Alexander
Glasgow, 27 December, 1911 Died 1962 S-2 (WH)

League Club	Source	Date Signed	Seasons Played	Apps	Subs	Gls
Sunderland	Pollock Jnrs	05.32	32-37	97	-	6
West Bromwich A.	Tr	03.38	37-38	49	-	2
Newport Co.	Tr	04.46	46	3	-	0

McNAB Alexander Duncan
Birmingham, 6 April, 1932 S Sch (WH)

League Club	Source	Date Signed	Seasons Played	Apps	Subs	Gls
Shrewsbury T.		12.54	54-56	4	-	0

McNAB James
Denny, 13 April, 1940 S Sch (WH)

League Club	Source	Date Signed	Seasons Played	Apps	Subs	Gls
Sunderland	Jnrs	06.57	58-66	284	1	13
Preston N.E.	Tr	03.67	66-73	222	2	6
Stockport Co.	Tr	07.74	74-75	30	0	1

McNAB Neil
Greenock, 4 June, 1957 S Sch/Su21-1 (M)

League Club	Source	Date Signed	Seasons Played	Apps	Subs	Gls
Tottenham H.	Morton	02.74	73-78	63	9	3
Bolton W.	Tr	11.78	78-79	33	2	4
Brighton & H.A.	Tr	02.80	79-82	100	3	4
Leeds U.	L	12.82	82	5	0	0
Manchester C.	Tr	07.83	83-89	216	5	16
Tranmere Rov.	Tr	01.90	89-92	94	11	6
Huddersfield T.	L	01.92	91	11	0	0
Darlington (N/C)	Ayr U.	09.93	93	4	0	0

McNAB Robert
Huddersfield, 20 July, 1943 EF Lge/E-4 (LB)

League Club	Source	Date Signed	Seasons Played	Apps	Subs	Gls
Huddersfield T.	Moldgreen Y.C.	04.62	63-66	68	0	0
Arsenal	Tr	10.66	66-74	277	1	4
Wolverhampton W.	Tr	07.75	75	13	0	0

McNAB Samuel
Glasgow, 20 October, 1926 Died 1995 (IF)

League Club	Source	Date Signed	Seasons Played	Apps	Subs	Gls
Sheffield U.	Dalry Thistle	01.52	52-53	11	-	4
York C.	Tr	05.54	54	19	-	3

McNAB Thomas
Glasgow, 15 July, 1933 (WH)

League Club	Source	Date Signed	Seasons Played	Apps	Subs	Gls
Nottingham F.	Partick Thistle	03.54				
Wrexham	Partick Thistle	03.57	56-58	43	-	5
Barrow	Tr	03.59	58-60	44	-	4

McNALLY Bernard Anthony
Shrewsbury, 17 February, 1963 NI-5 (M)

League Club	Source	Date Signed	Seasons Played	Apps	Subs	Gls
Shrewsbury T.	App	02.81	80-88	278	4	23
West Bromwich A.	Tr	07.89	89-94	137	19	10

McNALLY John **Brendan**
Dublin, 22 January, 1935 IR 'B'/IR-3 (FB)

League Club	Source	Date Signed	Seasons Played	Apps	Subs	Gls
Luton T.	Shelbourne	05.56	56-62	134	-	3

McNALLY Errol Alexander
Lurgan (NI), 27 August, 1943 (G)

League Club	Source	Date Signed	Seasons Played	Apps	Subs	Gls
Chelsea	Portadown	12.61	61-63	9	-	0

McNALLY Mark
Motherwell, 10 March, 1971 Su21-2 (CD)

League Club	Source	Date Signed	Seasons Played	Apps	Subs	Gls
Southend U.	Glasgow Celtic	12.95	95-96	52	2	2
Stoke C.	Tr	03.97	96-97	6	1	0

McNALLY Paul Anthony
Consett, 19 December, 1949 (IF)

League Club	Source	Date Signed	Seasons Played	Apps	Subs	Gls
Bradford C.	Consett Jnrs	07.67	68	1	2	0

McNALLY Ross Jonathan
Dublin, 6 September, 1978 (CD)

League Club	Source	Date Signed	Seasons Played	Apps	Subs	Gls
Brighton & H.A.	YT	07.97	97	1	1	1

McNAMARA Anthony
Liverpool, 3 October, 1929 (OR)

League Club	Source	Date Signed	Seasons Played	Apps	Subs	Gls
Everton		05.50	51-57	111	-	22
Liverpool	Tr	12.57	57	10	-	3
Crewe Alex.	Tr	07.58	58	9	-	2
Bury	Tr	09.58	58	14	-	0

McNAMARA Brett
Newark, 8 July, 1972 (F)

League Club	Source	Date Signed	Seasons Played	Apps	Subs	Gls
Northampton T.	Stamford	08.94	94	0	1	0

McNAMARA Anthony **Dennis**
Liverpool, 8 March, 1935 (OR)

League Club	Source	Date Signed	Seasons Played	Apps	Subs	Gls
Tranmere Rov.		11.54	54	1	-	0

McNAMEE Gerard
Consett, 16 August, 1960 (W)

League Club	Source	Date Signed	Seasons Played	Apps	Subs	Gls
Hartlepool U.		11.79	79-82	2	2	1

McNAMEE John
Coatbridge, 11 June, 1941 (CD)

League Club	Source	Date Signed	Seasons Played	Apps	Subs	Gls
Newcastle U.	Hibernian	12.66	66-71	115	2	8
Blackburn Rov.	Tr	11.71	71-72	56	0	9
Hartlepool U.	Morton	12.73	73	2	0	0
Workington (N/C)	Lancaster C.	08.75	75	2	0	0

McNAMEE John James
Watford, 31 July, 1942 (OL)

League Club	Source	Date Signed	Seasons Played	Apps	Subs	Gls
Reading	Montrose	12.64				
Tranmere Rov.	Raith Rov.	08.67	67-69	67	5	11

McNAMEE Peter
Glasgow, 20 March, 1935 (OL)

League Club	Source	Date Signed	Seasons Played	Apps	Subs	Gls
Peterborough U.	Lanark A.	(N/L)	60-65	192	0	60
Notts Co.	Kings Lynn	01.66	65	3	0	0

McNAUGHT John
Glasgow, 19 June, 1964 Died 1996 (M)

League Club	Source	Date Signed	Seasons Played	Apps	Subs	Gls
Chelsea	Hamilton Academical	04.86	85-87	9	1	2

McNAUGHT Kenneth
Kirkcaldy, 11 January, 1955 (CD)

League Club	Source	Date Signed	Seasons Played	Apps	Subs	Gls
Everton	App	05.72	74-76	64	2	3
Aston Villa	Tr	08.77	77-82	207	0	8
West Bromwich A.	Tr	08.83	83	42	0	1
Manchester C.	L	12.84	84	7	0	0
Sheffield U.	Tr	07.85	85	34	0	5

McNEE Terence Allan
Birkenhead, 5 June, 1925 (G)

League Club	Source	Date Signed	Seasons Played	Apps	Subs	Gls
Wrexham	Park Villa	12.46	46	11	-	0

McNEICE Vincent
Cricklewood, 25 October, 1938 (CH)

League Club	Source	Date Signed	Seasons Played	Apps	Subs	Gls
Watford	Jnrs	03.57	57-63	231	-	0

McNEIL David
Chester, 14 May, 1921 Died 1993 (LB)

League Club	Source	Date Signed	Seasons Played	Apps	Subs	Gls
Chester C.	Hoole Alex.	05.42	46-50	114	-	1

McNEIL Hamish Grant
Alva, 16 November, 1934 (IF)

League Club	Source	Date Signed	Seasons Played	Apps	Subs	Gls
Colchester U.	Bonnyrigg Rose	08.57	57	2	-	1

McNEIL Mark John
Bethnal Green, 3 December, 1962 (M)

League Club	Source	Date Signed	Seasons Played	Apps	Subs	Gls
Leyton Orient	App	12.79	81-84	76	13	12
Aldershot	Tr	12.84	84-85	20	5	2

McNEIL Matthew Alexander
Glasgow, 28 July, 1927 Died 1977 (CH)

League Club	Source	Date Signed	Seasons Played	Apps	Subs	Gls
Newcastle U.	Hibernian	12.49	50	9	-	0
Barnsley	Tr	08.51	51-52	68	-	1
Brighton & H.A.	Tr	07.53	53-55	53	-	0
Norwich C.	Tr	03.56	55-56	44	-	2

McNEIL Michael
Middlesbrough, 7 February, 1940 Eu23-9/EF Lge/E-9 (FB)

League Club	Source	Date Signed	Seasons Played	Apps	Subs	Gls
Middlesbrough	Jnrs	06.57	58-63	178	-	3
Ipswich T.	Tr	07.64	64-71	141	5	4

McNEIL Richard (Dixie)
Melton Mowbray, 16 January, 1947 (F)

League Club	Source	Date Signed	Seasons Played	Apps	Subs	Gls
Leicester C.	Holwell Wks	11.64				
Exeter C.	Tr	06.66	66	31	0	11

League Club	Source	Date Signed	Seasons Played	Apps	Subs	Gls
Northampton T.	Corby T.	05.69	69-71	84	1	33
Lincoln C.	Tr	01.72	71-73	96	1	53
Hereford U.	Tr	08.74	74-77	128	1	85
Wrexham	Tr	09.77	77-82	166	1	54
Hereford U.	Tr	10.82	82	12	0	3

McNEIL Robert Muirhead
Bellshill, 1 November, 1962 (RB)

League Club	Source	Date Signed	Seasons Played	Apps	Subs	Gls
Hull C.	App	11.80	80-84	135	3	3
Lincoln C. (N/C)	Blackpool (N/C)	10.85	85	4	0	0
Preston N.E.	Tr	12.85	85-86	43	0	0
Carlisle U.	Tr	08.87	87	18	1	0

McNEILL Alexander (Alan)
Belfast, 16 August, 1945 NI Amat (M)

League Club	Source	Date Signed	Seasons Played	Apps	Subs	Gls
Middlesbrough	Crusaders	08.67	67-68	3	0	0
Huddersfield T.	Tr	11.68	68	1	1	0
Oldham Ath.	Tr	10.69	69-74	154	16	19
Stockport Co.	Tr	07.75	75-76	69	2	1

McNEILL Brian
Newcastle, 1 April, 1956 (FB)

League Club	Source	Date Signed	Seasons Played	Apps	Subs	Gls
Bristol C.	App	04.74	75-76	0	3	0
Plymouth Arg.	Tr	12.78	78-80	47	0	0

McNEILL Edward Vincent
Warrenpoint (NI), 26 March, 1929 (G)

League Club	Source	Date Signed	Seasons Played	Apps	Subs	Gls
Sunderland	Portadown	12.51	53	7	-	0

McNEILL John (Ian) McKeand
Glasgow, 24 February, 1932 (IF)

League Club	Source	Date Signed	Seasons Played	Apps	Subs	Gls
Leicester C.	Aberdeen	03.56	55-58	72	-	26
Brighton & H.A.	Tr	03.59	58-61	116	-	12
Southend U.	Tr	07.62	62-63	41	-	3

McNEISH Samuel
Bo'ness, 4 August, 1930 (F)

League Club	Source	Date Signed	Seasons Played	Apps	Subs	Gls
Leeds U.	Linlithgow Rose	02.51	50	1	-	0

McNICHOL Alexander Hogarth
Baillieston, 10 October, 1919 (IF)

League Club	Source	Date Signed	Seasons Played	Apps	Subs	Gls
Aldershot	Dunfermline Ath.	08.47	47-50	110	-	20
Rochdale	Tr	01.51	50	17	-	3

McNICHOL James Anthony
Glasgow, 9 June, 1958 Su21-7 (CD)

League Club	Source	Date Signed	Seasons Played	Apps	Subs	Gls
Luton T.	Ipswich T. (App)	07.76	76-78	13	2	0
Brentford	Tr	10.78	78-83	151	4	22
Exeter C.	Tr	07.84	84-85	87	0	10
Torquay U.	Tr	07.86	86-88	124	0	13
Exeter C.	Tr	08.89	89-90	42	0	8
Torquay U.	Tr	07.91	91	2	0	0

McNICHOL John
Kilmarnock, 20 August, 1925 (IF)

League Club	Source	Date Signed	Seasons Played	Apps	Subs	Gls
Newcastle U.	Hurlford Jnrs	08.46				
Brighton & H.A.	Tr	08.48	48-51	158	-	37
Chelsea	Tr	08.52	52-57	181	-	59
Crystal Palace	Tr	03.58	57-62	189	-	15

McNICHOL Robert Hugh
Dumbarton, 13 February, 1933 Died 1980 (FB)

League Club	Source	Date Signed	Seasons Played	Apps	Subs	Gls
Accrington St.	Stirling A.	05.56	56-58	134	-	5
Brighton & H.A.	Tr	06.59	59-61	93	-	0
Carlisle U.	Gravesend & Nft.	10.63	63	1	-	0

McNIVEN David Jonathan
Leeds, 27 May, 1978 (F)

League Club	Source	Date Signed	Seasons Played	Apps	Subs	Gls
Oldham Ath.	YT	10.95	96-97	4	12	1

McNIVEN David Scott
Stonehouse, 9 September, 1955 Su21-3 (F)

League Club	Source	Date Signed	Seasons Played	Apps	Subs	Gls
Leeds U.	App	09.72	75-77	15	7	6
Bradford C.	Tr	02.78	77-82	202	10	64
Blackpool	Tr	02.83	82-83	45	4	11
Halifax T. (N/C)	Pittsburgh (USA)	03.85	84	12	0	4

McNIVEN Scott Andrew
Leeds, 27 May, 1978 S Yth/Su21-1 (RB)

League Club	Source	Date Signed	Seasons Played	Apps	Subs	Gls
Oldham Ath.	YT	10.95	94-97	51	9	1

McNULTY Joseph
Dundalk (Ire), 17 July, 1923 Died 1986 (G)

League Club	Source	Date Signed	Seasons Played	Apps	Subs	Gls
Burnley	Ards.	05.49	50-51	8	-	0
Sheffield U.	Tr	06.52				

McNULTY Thomas
Salford, 30 December, 1929 (FB)

League Club	Source	Date Signed	Seasons Played	Apps	Subs	Gls
Manchester U.	Jnrs	06.47	49-53	57	-	0
Liverpool	Tr	02.54	53-57	36	-	0

McNULTY William George
Edinburgh, 9 February, 1949 (G)

League Club	Source	Date Signed	Seasons Played	Apps	Subs	Gls
Port Vale	Jnrs	04.66	66	1	0	0
Chesterfield	Tr	07.68	68	6	0	0

MACOWAT Ian Stuart
Oxford, 19 November, 1965 E Sch/E Yth (LB)

League Club	Source	Date Signed	Seasons Played	Apps	Subs	Gls
Everton	App	11.83				
Gillingham	Tr	01.85	84-85	4	1	0
Crewe Alex.	Tr	07.86	86-88	64	8	1

McPARLAND Ian John
Edinburgh, 4 October, 1961 (F)

League Club	Source	Date Signed	Seasons Played	Apps	Subs	Gls
Notts Co.	Ormiston Primrose	12.80	80-88	190	31	69
Hull C.	Tr	03.89	88-90	31	16	7
Walsall	L	03.91	90	11	0	6
Lincoln C. (N/C)	Dunfermline Ath.	08.92	92	3	1	0
Northampton T.	Tr	10.92	92	11	0	3

McPARLAND Peter James
Newry (NI), 25 April, 1934 EF Lge/NI-34 (OL)

League Club	Source	Date Signed	Seasons Played	Apps	Subs	Gls
Aston Villa	Dundalk	09.52	52-61	293	-	97
Wolverhampton W.	Tr	01.62	61-62	21	-	10
Plymouth Arg.	Tr	01.63	62-63	38	-	14

McPARTLAND Desmond
Middlesbrough, 5 October, 1947 E Yth (G)

League Club	Source	Date Signed	Seasons Played	Apps	Subs	Gls
Middlesbrough	App	10.64	65-67	35	0	0
Carlisle U.	Tr	12.67	67	5	0	0
Northampton T.	Tr	07.69	69	6	0	0
Hartlepool U.	Tr	03.70	69-70	56	0	0

McPEAKE Matthew
Ballymena (NI), 19 June, 1919 (LH)

League Club	Source	Date Signed	Seasons Played	Apps	Subs	Gls
Everton	Ballymena U.	07.46				
Grimsby T.	Tr	06.47				
New Brighton	Tr	07.48	48-49	50	-	2

MacPHAIL John
Dundee, 7 December, 1955 (CD)

League Club	Source	Date Signed	Seasons Played	Apps	Subs	Gls
Sheffield U.	Dundee	01.79	78-82	135	0	7
York C.	Tr	02.83	82-85	141	1	24
Bristol C.	Tr	07.86	86	26	0	1
Sunderland	Tr	07.87	87-90	130	0	22
Hartlepool U.	Tr	09.90	90-94	159	4	4

McPHAIL Stephen
London, 9 December, 1979 (M)

League Club	Source	Date Signed	Seasons Played	Apps	Subs	Gls
Leeds U.	YT	12.96	97	0	4	0

McPHEAT William
Caldercruix, 4 September, 1942 (IF)

League Club	Source	Date Signed	Seasons Played	Apps	Subs	Gls
Sunderland	Jnrs	09.59	60-62	58	-	19
Hartlepool U.	Tr	09.65	65	13	2	2

McPHEE John
Motherwell, 21 November, 1937 (WH)

League Club	Source	Date Signed	Seasons Played	Apps	Subs	Gls
Blackpool	Motherwell	07.62	62-69	249	10	15
Barnsley	Tr	06.70	70	26	0	3
Southport	Tr	07.71	71-72	85	0	1

McPHEE Magnus George
Edinburgh, 30 April, 1914 Died 1960 (CF)

League Club	Source	Date Signed	Seasons Played	Apps	Subs	Gls
Bradford P.A.	Workington	10.36	36	30	-	17
Coventry C.	Tr	06.37	37	12	-	6
Reading	Tr	05.38	38-48	132	-	85

McPHEE Stewart Douglas
Middlesbrough, 5 January, 1965 (M)

League Club	Source	Date Signed	Seasons Played	Apps	Subs	Gls
Middlesbrough		08.83				
Darlington	Whitby T.	09.86	86	7	2	1

McPHERSON Albert
Salford, 8 July, 1927 (CH)

League Club	Source	Date Signed	Seasons Played	Apps	Subs	Gls
Bury		06.49				
Walsall	Stalybridge Celtic	05.54	54-63	351	-	8

McPHERSON Angus
Glasgow, 11 October, 1968 (D)

League Club	Source	Date Signed	Seasons Played	Apps	Subs	Gls
Exeter C. (L)	Glasgow Rangers	03.90	89	11	0	1

McPHERSON Ian Buchanan
Glasgow, 26 July, 1920 Died 1983 (W)

League Club	Source	Date Signed	Seasons Played	Apps	Subs	Gls
Notts Co.	Glasgow Rangers	08.45				
Arsenal	Tr	08.46	46-50	152	-	19
Notts Co.	Tr	08.51	51-52	50	-	7
Brentford	Tr	07.53	53	4	-	0

League Club	Source	Date Signed	Seasons Played	Apps	Subs	Gls
McPHERSON Keith Anthony						
Greenwich, 11 September, 1963 (CD)						
West Ham U.	App	09.81	84	1	0	0
Cambridge U.	L	09.85	85	11	0	1
Northampton T.	Tr	01.86	85-89	182	0	8
Reading	Tr	08.90	90-97	251	5	8
McPHERSON Kenneth						
Hartlepool, 25 March, 1927 (CF/CH)						
Notts Co.	Horden Colly	08.50	50-52	26	-	10
Middlesbrough	Tr	08.53	53-55	33	-	15
Coventry C.	Tr	11.55	55-57	89	-	38
Newport Co.	Tr	06.58	58-60	128	-	52
Swindon T.	Tr	08.61	61-64	107	-	3
McPHERSON Malcolm						
Glasgow, 19 December, 1974 (F)						
West Ham U.	Yeovil T.	01.94				
Brentford	Tr	07.96	96-97	9	3	0
McPHILLIPS Terence Peter						
Manchester, 1 October, 1968 (F)						
Halifax T.	Liverpool (YT)	09.87	87-90	61	32	29
Northampton T.	L	11.89	89	0	1	0
Crewe Alex. (N/C)	Tr	08.91	91	5	1	1
McQUADE James						
Barrhead, 14 October, 1933 (F)						
Halifax T.	Dumbarton	08.57	57	9	-	2
McQUADE Terence James						
Holborn, 24 February, 1941 (W)						
Millwall	Enfield	10.61	61-62	34	-	7
Queens Park R.	Tr	07.63	63	20	-	2
Millwall	Leyton Orient (trial)	11.65	65	3	0	1
McQUAID Thomas Joseph						
Dublin, 1 February, 1936 (WH)						
Bradford C.	Thackley	11.57	58-59	23	-	2
McQUARRIE Andrew						
Glasgow, 2 October, 1939 (IF)						
Chesterfield	Albion Rov.	11.62	62-63	38	-	12
Brighton & H.A.	Tr	07.64	64	2	-	1
McQUEEN Gordon						
Kilwinning, 26 June, 1952 S-30 (CD)						
Leeds U.	St Mirren	09.72	72-77	140	0	15
Manchester U.	Tr	02.78	77-84	184	0	20
McQUEEN Ian David						
Manchester, 4 February, 1946 (CF)						
Rochdale		01.66	65-66	14	2	4
McQUEEN Thomas						
West Calder, 21 February, 1929 (G)						
Accrington St.	Queen of South	06.54	54-56	80	-	0
McQUEEN Thomas Feeney						
Bellshill, 1 April, 1963 (LB)						
West Ham U.	Aberdeen	03.87	86-89	24	6	0
McQUILLAN Dennis						
Derby, 16 March, 1934 (OR)						
Derby Co.	Jnrs	03.51	52-55	18	-	1
Aldershot	Tr	07.56				
Luton T.	Tr	03.57				
McQUILLAN Patrick Gerard						
Belfast, 27 June, 1961 (RB)						
Swansea C.		08.79				
Swansea C.	Pembroke Borough	12.83	83-84	25	1	0
MacRAE Keith Alexander						
Glasgow, 5 February, 1951 Su23-2/SF Lge (G)						
Manchester C.	Motherwell	10.73	73-80	56	0	0
Leeds U.	Portland (USA)	03.82				
MacREADY Brian Leslie						
Leicester, 25 March, 1942 (W)						
West Bromwich A.	Hull C. (Am)	02.60	60-63	14	-	1
Mansfield T.	Tr	07.64	64-65	49	1	11
McROBERT Lee Peter						
Bromley, 4 October, 1972 (M)						
Millwall	Sittingbourne	02.95	94-97	12	11	1
MACROW Geoffrey Cyril						
East Harling (Nk), 26 September, 1932 Died 1987 (OR)						
Ipswich T.	Thetford T.	08.55	55-56	2	-	0

League Club	Source	Date Signed	Seasons Played	Apps	Subs	Gls
McSEVENEY John Haddon						
Shotts, 8 February, 1931 (OL)						
Sunderland	Hamilton Academical	10.51	51-54	35	-	3
Cardiff C.	Tr	05.55	55-56	75	-	18
Newport Co.	Tr	07.57	57-60	172	-	51
Hull C.	Tr	07.61	61-64	161	-	60
McSHANE Anthony						
Belfast, 28 February, 1927 (WH)						
Plymouth Arg.	Brantwood	12.48	49-54	85	-	2
Swindon T.	Tr	06.55	55-56	41	-	0
McSHANE Henry (Harry)						
Holytown, 8 April, 1920 (W)						
Blackburn Rov.	Bellshill Ath.	04.37	37	2	-	0
Huddersfield T.	Tr	09.46	46	15	-	1
Bolton W.	Tr	07.47	47-50	93	-	6
Manchester U.	Tr	09.50	50-53	56	-	8
Oldham Ath.	Tr	02.54	53-54	41	-	5
McSTAY James Gerald						
Newry (NI), 4 August, 1922 LoI (W)						
Grimsby T.	Dundalk	08.48	48-50	61	-	2
McSTAY Raymond						
Hamilton, 16 May, 1970 S Sch (M)						
Cardiff C. (N/C)	Hamilton Academical	12.96	96	1	0	0
McSTAY William						
Hamilton, 26 November, 1961 (D)						
Huddersfield T.	Glasgow Celtic	03.87	86-87	4	5	0
Notts Co.	Tr	02.88	87-89	33	12	1
Hartlepool U.	L	11.89	89	3	0	0
McSWEGAN Gary						
Glasgow, 24 September, 1970 S Sch/S Yth (F)						
Notts Co.	Glasgow Rangers	07.93	93-95	47	15	21
McTAFF Stephen						
Tanfield (Dm), 11 March, 1922 Died 1983 (WH)						
Bradford P.A.	East Tanfield	05.45	46-47	29	-	2
New Brighton	Tr	07.48	48-50	100	-	3
McTAVISH John Robert						
Glasgow, 2 February, 1932 (CH)						
Manchester C.	Dalry Thistle	06.52	53-59	93	-	0
McTURK John						
Cumnock, 11 July, 1936 (FB)						
Wrexham	St Mirren	07.57	57	2	-	0
McVAY David Reid						
Workington, 5 March, 1955 (D/M)						
Notts Co.	Jnrs	07.73	73-78	101	12	2
Torquay U.	L	09.77	77	8	0	0
Peterborough U.	Tr	07.79	79-80	47	2	1
Lincoln C.	Tr	08.81	81	13	0	0
McVEIGH James						
Sheffield, 2 July, 1949 (FB)						
Wolverhampton W.		05.68	68	2	0	0
Gillingham	Tr	10.70	70-71	48	0	1
McVEIGH Paul						
Belfast, 6 December, 1977 NI Yth (F)						
Tottenham H.	YT	07.96	96	2	1	1
McVICAR Donald						
Perth, 6 November, 1962 (M)						
Tranmere Rov. (N/C)	St Johnstone	08.85	85	7	0	0
MacVINISH Thomas						
Inverness, 1 January, 1921 (OL)						
Preston N.E.	Hamilton Academical	08.48				
Darlington	Tr	08.50	50	1	-	0
McVITIE George James						
Carlisle, 7 September, 1948 E Sch (W)						
Carlisle U.	App	12.65	65-70	124	4	21
West Bromwich A.	Tr	08.70	70-71	42	0	5
Oldham Ath.	Tr	08.72	72-75	108	5	19
Carlisle U.	Tr	12.75	75-80	191	7	20
McWHINNIE Archibald						
Glasgow, 17 July, 1926 (WH)						
Wrexham	Rutherglen Glencairn	05.51	51	2	-	0
MADAR Mickael Raymond						
Paris, France, 8 May, 1968 French Int (F)						
Everton	Deportivo la Coruna (Sp)	12.97	97	15	2	5

MADDEN Craig Anthony
Manchester, 25 September, 1958 (F)

League Club	Source	Date Signed	Seasons Played	Apps	Subs	Gls
Bury	Northern Nomads	03.78	77-85	278	19	129
West Bromwich A.	Tr	03.86	85-86	10	2	3
Blackpool	Tr	02.87	86-89	73	18	24
Wrexham	L	01.90	89	6	2	0
York C.	Tr	03.90	89	3	1	0

MADDEN David John
Stepney, 6 January, 1963 (M)

League Club	Source	Date Signed	Seasons Played	Apps	Subs	Gls
Southampton	App	01.81				
Bournemouth	L	01.83	82	5	0	0
Arsenal	Tr	08.83	83	2	0	0
Charlton Ath.	Tr	06.84	84	19	1	1
Reading	Los Angeles (USA)	11.87	87	7	2	1
Crystal Palace	Tr	08.88	88-89	19	8	5
Birmingham C.	L	01.90	89	5	0	1
Maidstone U.	Tr	06.90	90	10	0	0

MADDEN Lawrence David
Hackney, 28 September, 1955 (CD)

League Club	Source	Date Signed	Seasons Played	Apps	Subs	Gls
Mansfield T. (N/C)	Arsenal (N/C)	03.75	74-75	9	1	0
Charlton Ath.	Manchester Univ.	03.78	77-81	109	4	7
Millwall	Boston U.	03.82	81-82	44	3	1
Sheffield Wed.	Tr	08.83	83-90	200	12	2
Leicester C.	L	01.91	90	3	0	0
Wolverhampton W.	Tr	08.91	91-92	62	5	1
Darlington (N/C)	Tr	09.93	93	5	0	0
Chesterfield	Tr	10.93	93-95	37	0	1

MADDEN Neil
Luton, 6 February, 1962 (M)

League Club	Source	Date Signed	Seasons Played	Apps	Subs	Gls
Luton T.	App	12.79	79	1	0	0

MADDEN Peter
Bradford, 31 October, 1934 (CH)

League Club	Source	Date Signed	Seasons Played	Apps	Subs	Gls
Rotherham U.	Thornton	10.55	55-65	309	2	7
Bradford P.A.	Tr	07.66	66	25	3	1
Aldershot	Tr	07.67	67	26	1	1

MADDICK Kevin Andrew
Newcastle, 18 September, 1974 (F)

League Club	Source	Date Signed	Seasons Played	Apps	Subs	Gls
Darlington	Middlesbrough (YT)	09.92	92-93	1	2	0

MADDISON Donald
Washington, 15 February, 1927 (G)

League Club	Source	Date Signed	Seasons Played	Apps	Subs	Gls
Bradford P.A.	Sunderland (Am)	06.46				
Blackpool	Tr	02.48				
Darlington	Tr	08.50	50	1	-	0

MADDISON Frank
Worksop, 6 May, 1934 Died 1993 (FB)

League Club	Source	Date Signed	Seasons Played	Apps	Subs	Gls
Notts Co.		08.53	56-57	15	-	0

MADDISON George
Hull, 6 October, 1930 Died 1987 (G)

League Club	Source	Date Signed	Seasons Played	Apps	Subs	Gls
Aldershot		08.48	48	2	-	0
York C.	Tr	09.52	53	11	-	0

MADDISON William **Hartley**
Sunderland, 6 April, 1954 (OR)

League Club	Source	Date Signed	Seasons Played	Apps	Subs	Gls
Hartlepool U. (Am)		08.73	73-74	3	1	0

MADDISON James
South Shields, 9 November, 1924 Died 1992 (OL)

League Club	Source	Date Signed	Seasons Played	Apps	Subs	Gls
Middlesbrough	Jnrs	12.45	46	1	-	0
Darlington	Tr	08.49	49	41	-	7
Grimsby T.	Tr	06.50	50-58	272	-	40
Chesterfield	Tr	03.59	58-60	98	-	16

MADDISON John (Jack) Anthony
Barrow, 1 October, 1940 (W)

League Club	Source	Date Signed	Seasons Played	Apps	Subs	Gls
Barrow	Holker Street O.B.	07.60	61-64	88	-	18

MADDISON Lee Robert
Bristol, 5 October, 1972 (LB)

League Club	Source	Date Signed	Seasons Played	Apps	Subs	Gls
Bristol Rov.	YT	07.91	91-94	68	5	0
Northampton T.	Tr	09.95	95-96	55	0	0

MADDISON Neil Stanley
Darlington, 2 October, 1969 (M)

League Club	Source	Date Signed	Seasons Played	Apps	Subs	Gls
Southampton	YT	04.88	88-97	149	20	19
Middlesbrough	Tr	10.97	97	16	6	4

MADDISON Ralph
Bentley, 28 August, 1918 Died 1994 (W)

League Club	Source	Date Signed	Seasons Played	Apps	Subs	Gls
Doncaster Rov.	Bentley Colly	01.46	46-47	61	-	19
Stockport Co.	Tr	05.48	48	5	-	0
Southport	Tr	02.49	48-49	34	-	4

MADDIX Daniel Shawn
Ashford, 11 October, 1967 Jamaican Int (CD)

League Club	Source	Date Signed	Seasons Played	Apps	Subs	Gls
Tottenham H.	App	07.85				
Southend U.	L	10.86	86	2	0	0
Queens Park R.	Tr	07.87	87-97	204	34	8

MADDREN William Dixon
Billingham, 11 January, 1951 Eu23-5 (CD)

League Club	Source	Date Signed	Seasons Played	Apps	Subs	Gls
Middlesbrough	App	06.68	68-77	293	3	19

MADDY Paul Michael
Cwmcarn (Mon), 17 August, 1962 Wu21-1 (LM)

League Club	Source	Date Signed	Seasons Played	Apps	Subs	Gls
Cardiff C.	App	08.80	80-82	35	8	3
Hereford U.	L	03.83	82	9	0	1
Swansea C.	Tr	08.83	83	18	2	3
Hereford U.	Tr	03.84	83-85	75	2	16
Brentford	Tr	07.86	86	29	2	5
Chester C.	Tr	07.87	87	17	1	1
Hereford U.	Tr	03.88	87-88	27	8	1

MADELEY Paul Edward
Leeds, 20 September, 1944 E Yth/EF Lge/E-24 (M/D)

League Club	Source	Date Signed	Seasons Played	Apps	Subs	Gls
Leeds U.	Farsley Celtic	05.62	63-80	528	8	25

MADRICK Carl James
Bolton, 20 September, 1968 (F)

League Club	Source	Date Signed	Seasons Played	Apps	Subs	Gls
Huddersfield T.	YT	06.87	87	3	5	1
Peterborough U.	Tr	09.88	88	3	5	0

MAFFEY Denis
Sunderland, 22 February, 1922 Died 1995 (CF)

League Club	Source	Date Signed	Seasons Played	Apps	Subs	Gls
Ipswich T.	Walton U.	07.47	47	5	-	1

MAGEE Eric
Lurgan (NI), 24 August, 1947 NI Amat (F)

League Club	Source	Date Signed	Seasons Played	Apps	Subs	Gls
Oldham Ath.	Glenavon	06.67	67-68	41	4	9
Port Vale	Tr	07.69	69	11	7	1

MAGEE Kevin
Bathgate, 10 April, 1971 (LW)

League Club	Source	Date Signed	Seasons Played	Apps	Subs	Gls
Preston N.E.	Partick Thistle	05.93	93-95	23	3	1
Plymouth Arg. (N/C)	Tr	09.95	95	0	4	0
Scarborough	Tr	12.95	95	26	2	1

MAGGIORE Anthony
Sunderland, 28 October, 1957 (CD)

League Club	Source	Date Signed	Seasons Played	Apps	Subs	Gls
Hartlepool U.	Sunderland (App)	11.75	75-76	24	4	0

MAGILL Edward James
Lurgan (NI), 17 May, 1939 NIu23-1/NI-26 (FB)

League Club	Source	Date Signed	Seasons Played	Apps	Subs	Gls
Arsenal	Portadown	05.59	59-64	116	-	0
Brighton & H.A.	Tr	10.65	65-67	50	0	1

MAGILTON James
Belfast, 6 May, 1969 NI Sch/NI Yth/NIu21-1/NIu23-2/NI-39 (M)

League Club	Source	Date Signed	Seasons Played	Apps	Subs	Gls
Liverpool	App	05.86				
Oxford U.	Tr	10.90	90-93	150	0	34
Southampton	Tr	02.94	93-97	124	6	13
Sheffield Wed.	Tr	09.97	97	13	8	1

MAGUIRE Gavin Terence
Hammersmith, 24 November, 1967 W'B'/W-7 (CD)

League Club	Source	Date Signed	Seasons Played	Apps	Subs	Gls
Queens Park R.	App	10.85	86-88	33	7	0
Portsmouth	Tr	01.89	88-92	87	4	0
Newcastle U.	L	10.91	91	3	0	0
Millwall	Tr	03.93	92-93	12	0	0
Scarborough	L	03.94	93	2	0	0

MAGUIRE James Edward
Brandon, 23 July, 1917 (OR)

League Club	Source	Date Signed	Seasons Played	Apps	Subs	Gls
Wolverhampton W.	Willington	11.35	36-38	79	-	7
Swindon T.	Tr	05.47	47	28	-	4
Halifax T.	Tr	10.48	48-49	55	-	8

MAGUIRE James Smith
Eaglesham (Lk), 3 February, 1932 (OL)

League Club	Source	Date Signed	Seasons Played	Apps	Subs	Gls
Rochdale	Queen of South	08.58	58	15	-	0

MAGUIRE Paul Bernard
Glasgow, 21 August, 1956 (W)

League Club	Source	Date Signed	Seasons Played	Apps	Subs	Gls
Shrewsbury T.	Kilbirnie Ladeside	08.76	76-79	143	8	35
Stoke C.	Tr	09.80	80-83	93	14	24
Port Vale	Tacoma (USA)	07.85	85-87	101	14	22

MAGUIRE Peter Jason
Holmfirth, 11 September, 1969 (F)

League Club	Source	Date Signed	Seasons Played	Apps	Subs	Gls
Leeds U.	YT	06.88	87	2	0	0
Huddersfield T.	Tr	09.89	89-90	1	6	1
Stockport Co.	L	09.90	90	0	2	0

MAGUIRE Thomas
Dublin, 22 July, 1955 (M)

League Club	Source	Date Signed	Seasons Played	Apps	Subs	Gls
Liverpool	App	11.72				
Crewe Alex.	Tr	02.74	73-75	23	4	1

MAHER Aiden
Liverpool, 1 December, 1946 E Sch (OL)

League Club	Source	Date Signed	Seasons Played	Apps	Subs	Gls
Everton	App	12.64	67	1	0	0
Plymouth Arg.	Tr	10.68	68-70	64	0	3
Tranmere Rov.	Tr	06.71	71	2	5	1

MAHER John
Manchester, 6 November, 1933 (F)

League Club	Source	Date Signed	Seasons Played	Apps	Subs	Gls
Walsall	Manchester C. (Am)	05.54	54	1	-	0
Gillingham	Tr	07.55	55	2	-	1

MAHER Kevin Andrew
Ilford, 17 October, 1976 IRu21-4 (M)

League Club	Source	Date Signed	Seasons Played	Apps	Subs	Gls
Tottenham H.	YT	07.95				
Southend U.	Tr	01.98	97	18	0	1

MAHON Alan Joseph
Dublin, 4 April, 1978 IR Sch/IR Yth/IRu21-8 (W)

League Club	Source	Date Signed	Seasons Played	Apps	Subs	Gls
Tranmere Rov.	YT	04.95	96-97	17	28	3

MAHON Gavin Andrew
Birmingham, 2 January, 1977 (LM)

League Club	Source	Date Signed	Seasons Played	Apps	Subs	Gls
Wolverhampton W.	YT	07.95				
Hereford U.	Tr	07.96	96	10	1	1

MAHON Michael John
Manchester, 17 September, 1944 E Amat (W)

League Club	Source	Date Signed	Seasons Played	Apps	Subs	Gls
Port Vale	North Shields	04.67	66-68	91	0	21
York C.	Tr	07.69	69	27	2	10
Colchester U.	Tr	05.70	70-73	131	5	26

MAHONEY Anthony Joseph
Barking, 29 September, 1959 E Yth (F)

League Club	Source	Date Signed	Seasons Played	Apps	Subs	Gls
Fulham	App	08.77	76-80	53	6	10
Northampton T.	L	10.81	81	6	0	0
Brentford	Tr	07.82	82-83	33	8	12
Crystal Palace	Tr	06.84	84	17	1	4

MAHONEY Brian
Tantobie, 12 May, 1952 (F)

League Club	Source	Date Signed	Seasons Played	Apps	Subs	Gls
Huddersfield T.	App	11.69	70-71	18	2	2
Barnsley	Tr	03.72	71-74	82	8	16

MAHONEY John Francis
Cardiff, 20 September, 1946 Wu23-3/W-51 (M)

League Club	Source	Date Signed	Seasons Played	Apps	Subs	Gls
Crewe Alex.	Ashton U.	03.66	65-66	16	2	5
Stoke C.	Tr	03.67	66-76	270	12	25
Middlesbrough	Tr	08.77	77-78	77	0	1
Swansea C.	Tr	07.79	79-82	106	4	1

MAHONEY Michael James
Bristol, 25 October, 1950 (G)

League Club	Source	Date Signed	Seasons Played	Apps	Subs	Gls
Bristol C.	App	08.68	67-69	4	0	0
Torquay U.	Tr	08.70	70-74	157	0	0
Newcastle U.	Tr	03.75	74-78	108	0	0

MAHONEY-JOHNSON Michael Anthony
Paddington, 6 November, 1976 (F)

League Club	Source	Date Signed	Seasons Played	Apps	Subs	Gls
Queens Park R.	YT	04.95	96-97	0	3	0
Wycombe W.	L	08.96	96	2	2	2
Brighton & H.A.	L	02.98	97	3	1	0

MAHORN Paul Gladstone
Leyton, 13 August, 1973 (F)

League Club	Source	Date Signed	Seasons Played	Apps	Subs	Gls
Tottenham H.	YT	01.92	93-97	3	0	0
Fulham	L	09.93	93	1	2	0
Burnley	L	03.96	95	3	5	1
Port Vale (N/C)	Tr	03.98	97	0	1	0

MAHY Barry
Rotherham, 21 January, 1942 (IF)

League Club	Source	Date Signed	Seasons Played	Apps	Subs	Gls
Scunthorpe U.	Jersey	05.63	63-66	21	1	2

MAIDMENT Ian Michael
Newbury, 9 August, 1947 (OL)

League Club	Source	Date Signed	Seasons Played	Apps	Subs	Gls
Reading	App	08.65	65	7	0	0

MAIL David
Bristol, 12 September, 1962 (CD)

League Club	Source	Date Signed	Seasons Played	Apps	Subs	Gls
Aston Villa	App	07.80				
Blackburn Rov.	Tr	01.82	82-89	200	6	4
Hull C.	Tr	07.90	90-94	140	10	2

MAILER Ronald George
Auchterarder, 18 May, 1932 (F)

League Club	Source	Date Signed	Seasons Played	Apps	Subs	Gls
Darlington	Dunfermline Ath.	03.54	54	11	-	2

MAILEY William
Glasgow, 13 June, 1943 Died 1992 S Sch (G)

League Club	Source	Date Signed	Seasons Played	Apps	Subs	Gls
Everton	Jnrs	06.60				
Crewe Alex.	Tr	03.63	63-69	215	0	0

MAIN Ian
Swindon, 31 October, 1959 (G)

League Club	Source	Date Signed	Seasons Played	Apps	Subs	Gls
Exeter C.	Gloucester C.	09.78	78-81	78	0	0

MAINWARING Carl Andrew
Swansea, 15 March, 1980 (F)

League Club	Source	Date Signed	Seasons Played	Apps	Subs	Gls
Swansea C.	YT	•	97	2	1	0

MAIORANA Giuliano
Cambridge, 18 April, 1969 (LW)

League Club	Source	Date Signed	Seasons Played	Apps	Subs	Gls
Manchester U.	Histon	11.88	88-89	2	5	0

MAIR Gordon
Bothwell, 18 December, 1958 S Sch (W)

League Club	Source	Date Signed	Seasons Played	Apps	Subs	Gls
Notts Co.	App	12.76	76-83	123	8	18
Lincoln C.	Tr	08.84	84-85	57	0	3

MAITLAND Lloyd Curtis
Coleshill, 21 March, 1957 (W)

League Club	Source	Date Signed	Seasons Played	Apps	Subs	Gls
Huddersfield T.	App	03.74	74-76	31	8	2
Darlington	Tr	03.77	76-78	58	13	6

MAJOR John (Jack) Leonard
Islington, 12 March, 1929 E Amat (W)

League Club	Source	Date Signed	Seasons Played	Apps	Subs	Gls
Hull C. (Am)	Hull Amats	04.47	46	3	-	0
Hull C.	Bishop Auckland	06.55	55-56	10	-	0

MAJOR Leslie Dennis
Yeovil, 25 January, 1926 (G)

League Club	Source	Date Signed	Seasons Played	Apps	Subs	Gls
Leicester C.	Loughborough Corries	06.43	47-48	26	-	0
Plymouth Arg.	Tr	05.49	49-55	75	-	0

MAKEL Lee Robert
Sunderland, 11 January, 1973 (M)

League Club	Source	Date Signed	Seasons Played	Apps	Subs	Gls
Newcastle U.	YT	02.91	90-91	6	6	1
Blackburn Rov.	Tr	07.92	92-95	1	5	0
Huddersfield T.	Tr	10.95	95-97	62	3	5

MAKEPEACE Brian
Rossington, 6 October, 1931 (FB)

League Club	Source	Date Signed	Seasons Played	Apps	Subs	Gls
Doncaster Rov.	Rossington Colly	03.49	50-60	353	-	0

MAKIN Christopher Gregory
Manchester, 8 May, 1973 E Sch/E Yth/Eu21-5 (FB)

League Club	Source	Date Signed	Seasons Played	Apps	Subs	Gls
Oldham Ath.	YT	11.91	93-95	93	1	4
Wigan Ath.	L	08.92	92	14	1	2
Sunderland	Tr	08.97	97	23	2	1

MAKIN Joseph
Manchester, 21 September, 1950 (FB)

League Club	Source	Date Signed	Seasons Played	Apps	Subs	Gls
Oldham Ath.	App	10.67	66-67	6	0	0

MAKIN Samuel Hansbrew
Radcliffe, 14 November, 1925 Died 1981 (W)

League Club	Source	Date Signed	Seasons Played	Apps	Subs	Gls
Rochdale	Moss Rov.	05.44	46	5	-	1

MALAM Albert
Liverpool, 20 January, 1913 Died 1992 (IF)

League Club	Source	Date Signed	Seasons Played	Apps	Subs	Gls
Chesterfield	Colwyn Bay	11.32	32-34	58	-	26
Huddersfield T.	Tr	09.34	34-35	21	-	11
Doncaster Rov.	Tr	09.36	36-38	96	-	22
Wrexham	Tr	02.46	46	6	-	1

MALAN Norman Frederick
South Africa, 23 November, 1923 (G)

League Club	Source	Date Signed	Seasons Played	Apps	Subs	Gls
Middlesbrough	Defos (SA)	10.45	46	2	-	0
Darlington	Tr	08.48				
Scunthorpe U.	Tr	06.50	50-55	136	-	0
Bradford P.A.	Tr	07.56	56	24	-	0

MALCOLM Alexander Anderson
Hamilton, 13 February, 1956 (LB)

League Club	Source	Date Signed	Seasons Played	Apps	Subs	Gls
Luton T.	App	07.73				
Northampton T.	Tr	08.76	76	2	0	0

MALCOLM Alexander Mitchell
Alloa, 15 December, 1921 Died 1987 (W)

League Club	Source	Date Signed	Seasons Played	Apps	Subs	Gls
Barnsley	Alloa Ath.	06.46	46-47	5	-	0

League Club	Source	Date Signed	Seasons Played	Apps	Subs	Gls
MALCOLM Andrew						
West Ham, 4 May, 1933 E Sch/E Yth/EF Lge						(WH)
West Ham U.	Jnrs	07.50	53-61	283	-	4
Chelsea	Tr	11.61	61	27	-	1
Queens Park R.	Tr	10.62	62-64	84	-	4
MALCOLM Walter **Grant** Lees						
Musselburgh, 25 October, 1940 S Sch						(F)
Newcastle U.	Dalkeith Thistle	11.57	59	1	-	0
MALCOLM John Moore						
Clackmannan, 20 May, 1917						(WH)
Accrington St.		10.44	46	25	-	0
Tranmere Rov.	Tr	07.47	47	22	-	0
MALCOLM Kenneth Campbell						
Aberdeen, 25 July, 1926						(FB)
Ipswich T.	Arbroath	05.54	54-62	274	-	2
MALCOLM Paul Anthony						
Heworth, 11 December, 1964						(G)
Newcastle U.	App	12.82				
Rochdale	Durham C.	09.84	84	24	0	0
Shrewsbury T.	Tr	07.85				
Barnsley	Tr	08.86	86	3	0	0
Doncaster Rov.	Tr	07.88	88	34	0	0
MALE Charles **George**						
Plaistow, 8 May, 1910 Died 1998 EF Lge/E-19						(FB)
Arsenal	Clapton	05.30	30-47	285	-	0
MALE Norman Alfred						
West Bromwich, 27 May, 1917 Died 1992						(FB)
West Bromwich A.	Bush Rov.	10.34	37	3	-	1
Walsall	Tr	06.38	38-48	70	-	2
MALKIN Christopher Gregory						
Hoylake, 4 June, 1967						(F)
Tranmere Rov.	Stork	07.87	87-94	184	48	60
Millwall	Tr	07.95	95-96	46	6	13
Blackpool	Tr	10.96	96-97	21	14	5
MALKIN John						
Stoke, 9 November, 1925 Died 1994						(OR)
Stoke C.		07.47	47-55	175	-	23
MALLALIEU Anthony Michael						
Prestatyn, 3 October, 1946						(F)
Manchester U.	Rhyl	06.64				
Stockport Co.		03.70	69	0	1	0
MALLENDER Gary						
Barnsley, 12 March, 1959						(M)
Barnsley	App	03.77	76-78	0	2	0
MALLENDER Kenneth						
Rotherham, 10 December, 1943						(D)
Sheffield U.	App	02.61	61-68	141	2	2
Norwich C.	Tr	10.68	68-70	46	0	1
Hereford U.	Tr	07.71	72-73	71	1	1
MALLENDER Paul Richard						
Norwich, 30 November, 1969						(D)
Hereford U.	YT	•	87	0	1	0
MALLETT Joseph						
Gateshead, 8 January, 1916						(WH)
Charlton Ath.	Dunston Colly	11.35	38	2	-	0
Queens Park R.	L	10.37	37	29	-	4
Queens Park R.	Tr	02.39	38-46	41	-	7
Southampton	Tr	02.47	46-52	215	-	3
Leyton Orient	Tr	07.53	53-54	27	-	1
MALLEY Philip						
Felling, 1 November, 1965						(M)
Hartlepool U.	Sunderland (App)	11.83	83	0	1	0
Burnley	Berwick R. (trial)	02.84	83-87	91	4	5
Stockport Co.	L	11.84	84	3	0	0
MALLINSON David John						
Sheffield, 7 July, 1946						(WH)
Mansfield T.	Jnrs	03.65	65	10	1	1
MALLINSON Trevor						
Huddersfield, 25 April, 1945						(FB)
Halifax T. (Am)	Huddersfield T.	12.64	64	3	-	0
MALLON James Gillan						
Glasgow, 28 August, 1938						(FB)
Oldham Ath.	Partick Thistle	03.59	58-59	31	-	8
Barrow	Morton	10.65	65-68	149	1	3

League Club	Source	Date Signed	Seasons Played	Apps	Subs	Gls
MALLORY Richard James Leroy						
Bermuda, 10 August, 1942						(OL)
Cardiff C.	Bermuda	05.63	63	3	-	0
MALLOY Daniel						
Loanhead, 6 November, 1930 S 'B'/SF Lge						(CH)
Cardiff C.	Dundee	10.53	55-60	225	-	1
Doncaster Rov.	Tr	08.61	61	42	-	0
MALONE Richard Philip						
Carfin, 22 August, 1947 Su23-1						(RB)
Sunderland	Ayr U.	10.70	70-76	235	1	2
Hartlepool U.	Tr	07.77	77-78	36	0	2
Blackpool	Tr	11.78	78-79	48	0	1
MALONEY Derek Thomas						
Newton-le-Willows, 27 March, 1936						(LH)
Crewe Alex.	St Helens T.	02.58	57	15	-	0
MALONEY Joseph John						
Liverpool, 26 January, 1934						(CH)
Liverpool	Jnrs	01.51	52-53	12	-	0
Shrewsbury T.	Tr	07.54	54-59	237	-	1
Port Vale	Tr	07.61	61	1	-	0
Crewe Alex.	Tr	08.61	61-62	26	-	0
MALONEY Paul John						
Rossington 13 January, 1952						(W)
Huddersfield T.	App	11.69				
York C.	Tr	02.70	69-71	3	5	0
MALONEY Sean						
Hyde, 4 October, 1962						(F)
Stockport Co. (N/C)	Jnrs	08.79	79	0	1	0
MALOY Kenneth Frederick						
Edmonton, 16 September, 1940						(OL)
Plymouth Arg.	Ilford	09.59	60-63	62	-	11
Peterborough U.	Tr	07.64	64	6	-	1
Aldershot	Tr	07.65	65-66	51	1	11
MALOY Kevin William						
Aldershot, 21 November, 1966						(G)
Exeter C.	Taunton T.	07.91	91	4	0	0
MALPASS Frank Love						
Consett, 16 October, 1932						(G)
Gateshead	Jnrs	10.49	49	3	-	0
MALPASS Samuel Thomas						
Consett, 12 September, 1918 Died 1983						(FB)
Huddersfield T.		10.36				
Fulham	Tr	05.39	46	2	-	0
Watford	Tr	01.47	46-48	41	-	0
MALT Robert						
Ryhope, 4 November, 1951						(CF)
Leeds U.	App	11.68				
Darlington	Tr	06.70	70	2	2	0
MALTBY John						
Consett, 31 July, 1939						(IF)
Sunderland	Jnrs	08.57	56-60	22	-	4
Darlington	Tr	06.61	61-64	115	-	32
Bury	Tr	07.65	65-66	56	1	8
MANCINI Michael						
London, 8 June, 1956						(F)
Leyton Orient (N/C)		03.84	83	2	0	0
MANCINI Terence John						
Camden Town, 4 October, 1942 IR-5						(CD)
Watford	Jnrs	07.61	61-65	66	1	0
Leyton Orient	Port Elizabeth (SA)	11.67	67-71	167	0	16
Queens Park R.	Tr	10.71	71-74	94	0	3
Arsenal	Tr	10.74	74-75	52	0	1
Aldershot	Tr	09.76	76	21	0	0
MANDERS Ronald Ernest						
Shrewsbury, 13 November, 1931 Died 1980						(CH)
Shrewsbury T.	Jnrs	12.54	54-56	6	-	0
MANDERSON David Anthony						
Glasgow, 18 October, 1973						(M)
Scarborough	YT	08.92	91	0	1	0
MANKELOW Jamie Anthony						
Clapton, 4 September, 1964						(F)
Leyton Orient	App	09.82	82	1	1	0

League Club	Source	Date Signed	Seasons Played	Apps	Subs	Gls
MANKTELOW Brian						
Farnham, 29 March, 1951						(CF)
Aldershot	App	●	68	1	0	0
MANLEY Malcolm Richardson						
Johnstone, 1 December, 1949 S Sch						(CD)
Leicester C.	Johnstone Burgh	01.67	67-72	109	11	5
Portsmouth	Tr	12.73	73-74	11	0	0
MANLEY Thomas Ronald						
Northwich, 7 October, 1912 Died 1988						(OL)
Manchester U.	Northwich Vic.	05.31	31-38	188	-	40
Brentford	Tr	07.39	46-50	116	-	7
MANN Adrian Gary						
Northampton, 12 July, 1967						(M)
Northampton T.	YT	05.85	83-87	71	10	5
Torquay U.	L	03.87	86	6	2	0
Newport Co.	Tr	11.87	87	17	0	1
MANN Arthur Fraser						
Falkirk, 23 January, 1948						(LB/M)
Manchester C.	Hearts	11.68	68-70	32	3	0
Blackpool	L	11.71	71	3	0	0
Notts Co.	Tr	07.72	72-78	243	10	21
Shrewsbury T.	Tr	06.79	79	8	0	1
Mansfield T.	Tr	10.79	79-81	114	2	3
MANN James Arthur						
Goole, 15 December, 1952						(M)
Leeds U.	App	12.69	71-72	2	0	0
Bristol C.	Tr	05.74	74-81	205	26	31
Barnsley	Tr	02.82	81-82	14	1	0
Scunthorpe U. (N/C)	Tr	01.83	82	2	0	0
Doncaster Rov.	Tr	02.83	82	13	0	0
MANN Neil						
Nottingham, 19 November, 1972						(M)
Grimsby T.	Notts Co. (YT)	09.90				
Hull C.	Grantham T.	07.93	93-97	109	31	8
MANN Ronald Harold						
Nottingham, 8 October, 1932						(FB)
Notts Co.	Meadows B.C.	12.50	50	1	-	0
Aldershot	Tr	07.56	56-57	24	-	4
MANNERS Peter John						
Sunderland, 31 July, 1959						(M)
Newcastle U.	App	07.77	78	2	0	0
MANNERS Wingrove						
West Indies, 7 March, 1955						(F)
Bradford C.	App	●	71	1	0	0
MANNING John Joseph						
Liverpool, 11 December, 1940						(CF)
Tranmere Rov.	Liverpool (Am)	05.62	62-66	130	0	70
Shrewsbury T.	Tr	10.66	66-67	39	0	18
Norwich C.	Tr	09.67	67-68	60	0	21
Bolton W.	Tr	03.69	68-70	27	2	7
Walsall	Tr	07.71	71	13	1	6
Tranmere Rov.	Tr	03.72	71	5	0	1
Crewe Alex.	Tr	08.72	72	37	1	6
Barnsley	Tr	09.73	73-74	41	4	7
Crewe Alex.		11.75	75	7	0	5
MANNING Paul						
Lewisham, 21 January, 1974						(FB)
Millwall	YT	10.91	92	1	0	0
MANNINGER Alexander						
Austria, 4 June, 1977						(G)
Arsenal	Cazino Salzburg (Aut)	06.97	97	7	0	0
MANNION Gerard Patrick						
Warrington, 21 December, 1939 Died 1994 E Yth/Eu23-2						(OR)
Wolverhampton W.	Jnrs	11.57	59-60	17	-	7
Norwich C.	Tr	09.61	61-67	100	0	17
Chester C.	Tr	01.68	67	6	0	0
MANNION Wilfred						
South Bank, 16 May, 1918 E 'B'/EF Lge/E-26						(IF)
Middlesbrough	South Bank St Peters	09.36	36-53	341	-	99
Hull C.	Tr	12.54	54	16	-	1
MANNS Paul Henry						
Great Haywood, 15 April, 1961						(M)
Notts Co.	Cardiff C. (N/C)	08.79	79-80	5	2	1
Chester C.	Tr	03.83	82-83	28	0	3
MANSELL Ronald **Barrington (Barry)**						
Petersfield, 8 March, 1932						(FB)
Portsmouth	Jnrs	08.49	51-53	16	-	0
Reading	Tr	02.54	53-55	84	-	1
Bournemouth	Tr	06.57				
MANSELL George William						
Doncaster, 19 January, 1943						(CF)
Doncaster Rov.		09.62	62	1	-	0
MANSELL John (Jack)						
Salford, 22 August, 1927 E 'B'/EF Lge						(FB)
Brighton & H.A.	Manchester U. (Am)	03.49	48-52	116	-	9
Cardiff C.	Tr	10.52	52-53	24	-	0
Portsmouth	Tr	11.53	53-57	134	-	7
MANSFIELD Frederick Charles Adam						
Cambridge, 9 March, 1915 Died 1992						(RB)
Brentford	Cambridge C.	04.39				
Norwich C.	Tr	02.47	46-47	34	-	0
MANSFIELD John Vincent						
Colchester, 13 September, 1946						(IF)
Colchester U.	Jnrs	08.64	64-68	28	6	3
MANSFIELD Ronald William						
Romford, 31 December, 1923						(OL)
Millwall	Ilford	04.41	46-52	97	-	25
Southend U.	Tr	11.52	52	8	-	3
MANSLEY Alan						
Liverpool, 31 August, 1946						(W)
Blackpool	Skelmersdale U.	06.67				
Brentford	Tr	01.68	67-70	93	1	24
Fulham	Tr	12.70	70	1	0	0
Notts Co.	Tr	03.71	71	11	0	2
Lincoln C.	L	12.71	71	3	0	0
MANSLEY Vincent **Clifford**						
Skipton, 5 April, 1921						(WH)
Preston N.E.		09.40				
Barnsley	Tr	11.45	46-47	30	-	0
Chester C.	Tr	06.48	48	22	-	0
Leyton Orient	Yeovil T.	07.52	52	10	-	0
MANUEL William Albert James						
Hackney, 28 June, 1969						(M/LB)
Tottenham H.	YT	06.87				
Gillingham	Tr	02.89	88-90	74	13	5
Brentford	Tr	06.91	91-93	83	11	1
Cambridge U. (N/C)	Stevenage Borough	10.94	94	10	0	0
Peterborough U.	Tr	02.95	94-95	27	0	2
Gillingham	Tr	01.96	95-96	9	12	0
Barnet	Tr	07.97	97	10	7	0
MAPSON John						
Birkenhead, 2 May, 1917						(G)
Reading	Guildford C.	04.35	35	2	-	0
Sunderland	Tr	03.36	35-52	345	-	0
MARANGONI Claudio Oscar						
Argentina, 17 November, 1954 Argentinian Int						(M)
Sunderland	San Lorenzo (Arg)	12.79	79-80	19	1	3
MARCELLE Clinton Sherwin						
Trinidad (WI), 9 November, 1968 Trinidådian Int						(M)
Barnsley	Felgueiras (Por)	08.96	96-97	35	25	8
[MARCELO] Cipriano Dos Santos						
Miteroi, Brazil, 11 October, 1969						(F)
Sheffield U.	Deportivo Aleves (Por)	10.97	97	12	9	6
MARCH John Edmund						
Norwich, 12 May, 1940						(LB)
Norwich C.	Jnrs	05.57				
Bradford P.A.	Tr	06.61	61-62	62	-	1
MARCH Stanley						
Manchester, 26 December, 1938						(IF)
Port Vale	Altrincham	08.59	59	1	-	0
MARCH William						
Chester-le-Street, 28 February, 1925						(FB)
Barnsley	Ferryhill Ath.	11.47	51	2	-	0
Gateshead	Tr	07.52	52-56	134	-	0
MARCHANT Marwood Godfrey						
Milford Haven, 19 June, 1922						(IF)
Cardiff C.	Milford U.	01.51	50	12	-	3
Torquay U.	Tr	11.51	51-52	40	-	19

MARCHI Anthony Vittorio
Edmonton, 21 January, 1933 E Sch/E Yth/E 'B' (WH)

League Club	Source	Date Signed	Seasons Played	Apps	Subs	Gls
Tottenham H.	Jnrs	06.50	49-56	131	-	2
Tottenham H.	Juventus (It)	07.59	59-64	101	-	5

MARDEN Reuben (Ben) John
Fulham, 10 February, 1927 (OL)

League Club	Source	Date Signed	Seasons Played	Apps	Subs	Gls
Arsenal	Chelmsford C.	02.50	50-54	42	-	11
Watford	Tr	06.55	55-56	41	-	11

MARDENBOROUGH Stephen Alexander
Birmingham, 11 September, 1964 (W/F)

League Club	Source	Date Signed	Seasons Played	Apps	Subs	Gls
Coventry C.	App	08.82				
Wolverhampton W.	Tr	09.83	83	9	0	1
Cambridge U.	L	02.84	83	6	0	0
Swansea C.	Tr	07.84	84	32	4	7
Newport Co.	Tr	07.85	85-86	50	14	11
Cardiff C.	Tr	03.87	86-87	18	14	1
Hereford U.	Tr	07.88	88	20	7	0
Darlington	Cheltenham T.	07.90	90-92	79	27	18
Lincoln C.	Tr	07.93	93	14	7	2
Scarborough (N/C)	Tr	02.95	94	0	1	0
Colchester U.	Stafford R.	08.95	95	4	8	2
Swansea C. (N/C)	Tr	12.95	95	1	0	0

MARDON Paul Jonathan
Bristol, 14 September, 1969 W-1 (CD)

League Club	Source	Date Signed	Seasons Played	Apps	Subs	Gls
Bristol C.	YT	01.88	87-90	29	13	0
Doncaster Rov.	L	09.90	90	3	0	0
Birmingham C.	Tr	08.91	91-93	54	10	0
West Bromwich A.	Tr	11.93	93-97	113	8	3

MARGERISON Lee
Bradford, 10 September, 1973 (M)

League Club	Source	Date Signed	Seasons Played	Apps	Subs	Gls
Bradford C.	YT	07.92	92	1	2	0

MARGERRISON John William
Bushey, 20 October, 1955 (M)

League Club	Source	Date Signed	Seasons Played	Apps	Subs	Gls
Tottenham H.	App	12.72				
Fulham	Tr	07.75	75-78	63	8	9
Leyton Orient	Tr	07.79	79-81	77	3	6

MARGETSON Martyn Walter
Neath, 8 September, 1971 W Sch/W Yth/Wu21-7/W 'B' (G)

League Club	Source	Date Signed	Seasons Played	Apps	Subs	Gls
Manchester C.	YT	07.90	90-97	51	0	0
Bristol Rov.	L	12.93	93	2	1	0

MARGINSON Karl Kevin
Manchester, 11 November, 1970 (LW)

League Club	Source	Date Signed	Seasons Played	Apps	Subs	Gls
Rotherham U.	Ashton U.	03.93	92-94	11	4	1

MARINELLO Peter
Edinburgh, 20 February, 1950 Su23-2 (W)

League Club	Source	Date Signed	Seasons Played	Apps	Subs	Gls
Arsenal	Hibernian	01.70	69-72	32	6	3
Portsmouth	Tr	07.73	73-75	92	3	7
Fulham	Motherwell	12.78	78-79	25	2	1

MARINER Paul
Bolton, 22 May, 1953 E-35 (F)

League Club	Source	Date Signed	Seasons Played	Apps	Subs	Gls
Plymouth Arg.	Chorley	07.73	73-76	134	1	56
Ipswich T.	Tr	09.76	76-83	260	0	96
Arsenal	Tr	02.84	83-85	52	8	14
Portsmouth	Tr	07.86	86-87	49	7	9

MARKER Nicholas Robert Thomas
Budleigh Salterton, 3 May, 1965 (CD/M)

League Club	Source	Date Signed	Seasons Played	Apps	Subs	Gls
Exeter C.	App	05.83	81-87	196	6	3
Plymouth Arg.	Tr	10.87	87-92	201	1	13
Blackburn Rov.	Tr	09.92	92-96	41	13	1
Sheffield U.	Tr	07.97	97	43	0	2

MARKHAM Colin
Clowne, 2 March, 1916 Died 1967 (FB)

League Club	Source	Date Signed	Seasons Played	Apps	Subs	Gls
Torquay U.		07.37	37-46	25	-	1

MARKHAM Leo Sargent
High Wycombe, 22 March, 1953 (CD/F)

League Club	Source	Date Signed	Seasons Played	Apps	Subs	Gls
Watford	Marlow	08.72	72-74	22	11	3

MARKHAM Peter
Scunthorpe, 18 March, 1954 (RB)

League Club	Source	Date Signed	Seasons Played	Apps	Subs	Gls
Scunthorpe U.	App	03.72	71-76	121	1	1

MARKIE John
Bo'ness, 16 December, 1944 S Sch (CH)

League Club	Source	Date Signed	Seasons Played	Apps	Subs	Gls
Newcastle U.	App	04.62	63	2	-	0

MARKLEW Roger Kelsey
Sheffield, 30 January, 1940 (W)

League Club	Source	Date Signed	Seasons Played	Apps	Subs	Gls
Sheffield Wed.	Sheffield U. (Am)	05.58				
Accrington St.	Tr	05.59				
Grimsby T.	Tr	08.60	60	6	-	1

MARKMAN Damien Liam
Ascot, 7 January, 1978 (F)

League Club	Source	Date Signed	Seasons Played	Apps	Subs	Gls
Wycombe W. (N/C)	Slough T.	11.95	95-96	0	4	0

MARKS Charles William Alfred
Aylesford, 21 December, 1919 (FB)

League Club	Source	Date Signed	Seasons Played	Apps	Subs	Gls
Gillingham	Tooting & Mitcham	(N/L)	50-56	265	-	8

MARKS William **George**
Amesbury, 9 April, 1915 Died 1998 (G)

League Club	Source	Date Signed	Seasons Played	Apps	Subs	Gls
Arsenal	Salisbury Corries	03.36	38	2	-	0
Blackburn Rov.	Tr	08.46	46-47	67	-	0
Bristol C.	Tr	08.48	48	9	-	0
Reading	Tr	10.48	48-52	118	-	0

MARKS Jamie
Belfast, 18 March, 1977 NI Sch/NI Yth (M)

League Club	Source	Date Signed	Seasons Played	Apps	Subs	Gls
Leeds U.	YT	04.95				
Hull C.	Tr	02.96	95-96	11	4	0

MARKS Michael David
Lambeth, 23 March, 1968 (F)

League Club	Source	Date Signed	Seasons Played	Apps	Subs	Gls
Millwall	App	07.86	86	36	0	10
Mansfield T.	L	01.88	87	0	1	0
Leyton Orient	Tr	02.88	87	3	0	0

MARKSTEDT Peter
Vasteras, Sweden, 11 January, 1972 (CD)

League Club	Source	Date Signed	Seasons Played	Apps	Subs	Gls
Barnsley	Vasteras S.K. (Swe)	11.97	97	6	1	0

MARLEY Allan
Durham, 29 February, 1956 (FB)

League Club	Source	Date Signed	Seasons Played	Apps	Subs	Gls
Grimsby T.	App	11.73	74-75	39	1	2

MARLEY George
Gateshead, 22 April, 1921 Died 1992 (IF)

League Club	Source	Date Signed	Seasons Played	Apps	Subs	Gls
Gateshead		09.47	47-49	22	-	2

MARLOW Frederick
Sheffield, 9 November, 1928 (WH)

League Club	Source	Date Signed	Seasons Played	Apps	Subs	Gls
Arsenal	Hillsborough B.C.	09.47				
Sheffield Wed.	Tr	09.50				
Grimsby T.	Buxton	08.51	51	12	-	6
York C.	Boston U.	10.53	53-54	24	-	0

MARLOW Geoffrey Arthur
Worksop, 13 December, 1914 Died 1978 (OL)

League Club	Source	Date Signed	Seasons Played	Apps	Subs	Gls
Lincoln C.	Dinnington	05.37	37-48	80	-	26

MARLOWE (MARKOWSKI) Richard Ronald
Edinburgh, 10 August, 1950 (F)

League Club	Source	Date Signed	Seasons Played	Apps	Subs	Gls
Derby Co.	Bonnyrigg Rose	06.69				
Shrewsbury T.	Tr	12.73	73	31	0	4
Brighton & H.A.	Tr	07.74	74	24	1	5
Aldershot	L	01.76	75	2	0	0

MARMON Neale Gordon
Bournemouth, 21 April, 1961 (CD)

League Club	Source	Date Signed	Seasons Played	Apps	Subs	Gls
Torquay U. (N/C)		03.80	79	4	0	0
Colchester U.	Hanover 96 (Ger)	01.90	89	22	0	4

MARPLES Christopher
Chesterfield, 3 August, 1964 (G)

League Club	Source	Date Signed	Seasons Played	Apps	Subs	Gls
Chesterfield	Goole T.	03.84	84-86	84	0	0
Stockport Co.	Tr	03.87	86-87	57	0	0
York C.	Tr	07.88	88-92	138	0	0
Scunthorpe U.	L	02.92	91	1	0	0
Chesterfield	Tr	12.92	92-94	57	0	0

MARQUIS Paul Raymond
Enfield, 29 August, 1972 (CD)

League Club	Source	Date Signed	Seasons Played	Apps	Subs	Gls
West Ham U.	YT	07.91	93	0	1	0
Doncaster Rov.	Tr	03.94	93-96	28	1	1

MARRIOTT Andrew
Sutton-in-Ashfield, 11 October, 1970 E Sch/E Yth/Eu21-1/W-5 (G)

League Club	Source	Date Signed	Seasons Played	Apps	Subs	Gls
Arsenal	YT	10.88				
Nottingham F.	Tr	06.89	91-92	11	0	0
West Bromwich A.	L	09.89	89	3	0	0
Blackburn Rov.	L	12.89	89	2	0	0
Colchester U.	L	03.90	89	10	0	0
Burnley	L	08.91	91	15	0	0
Wrexham	Tr	10.93	93-97	213	0	0

MARRIOTT Ernest
Sutton-in-Ashfield, 25 January, 1913 Died 1989 (FB)

League Club	Source	Date Signed	Seasons Played	Apps	Subs	Gls
Brighton & H.A.	Sutton T.	01.34	34-47	163	-	1

MARRIOTT Jack
Sheffield, 16 July, 1915 Died 1989 (CF)

League Club	Source	Date Signed	Seasons Played	Apps	Subs	Gls
Doncaster Rov.	Normanton Sports	02.45	46-47	6	-	0
Southport	Tr	12.47	47-48	23	-	5

MARRIOTT John (Jack) Leonard
Scunthorpe, 1 April, 1928 (OR)

League Club	Source	Date Signed	Seasons Played	Apps	Subs	Gls
Sheffield Wed.	Scunthorpe U.	02.47	46-54	153	-	19
Huddersfield T.	Tr	07.55	55-56	38	-	4
Scunthorpe U.	Tr	06.57	57-63	212	-	26

MARRIOTT Paul William
Liverpool, 26 September, 1973 (F)

League Club	Source	Date Signed	Seasons Played	Apps	Subs	Gls
Cardiff C.	YT	●	91	0	1	0

MARRIOTT Stanley
Rochdale, 21 July, 1929 (CF)

League Club	Source	Date Signed	Seasons Played	Apps	Subs	Gls
Rochdale (Am)	Rochdale Y.M.C.A.	12.52	52	6	-	2

MARRON Christopher
Jarrow, 7 February, 1925 Died 1986 (CF)

League Club	Source	Date Signed	Seasons Played	Apps	Subs	Gls
Chesterfield	South Shields	10.47	47-51	108	-	44
Mansfield T.	Tr	07.52	52-53	53	-	25
Bradford P.A.	Tr	07.54	54	2	-	1

MARSDEN Anthony Joseph
Bolton, 11 September, 1948 (CF)

League Club	Source	Date Signed	Seasons Played	Apps	Subs	Gls
Blackpool	App	07.66	67-68	4	1	0
Doncaster Rov.	Tr	07.69	69-70	14	3	2
Grimsby T.	L	11.69	69	2	0	0

MARSDEN Christopher
Sheffield, 3 January, 1969 (M)

League Club	Source	Date Signed	Seasons Played	Apps	Subs	Gls
Sheffield U.	App	01.87	87	13	3	1
Huddersfield T.	Tr	07.88	88-93	113	8	9
Coventry C.	L	11.93	93	5	2	0
Wolverhampton W.	Tr	01.94	93	8	0	0
Notts Co.	Tr	11.94	94-95	10	0	0
Stockport Co.	Tr	01.96	95-97	63	2	3
Birmingham C.	Tr	10.97	97	31	1	1

MARSDEN Eric
Bolsover, 3 January, 1930 (CF)

League Club	Source	Date Signed	Seasons Played	Apps	Subs	Gls
Crystal Palace	Winchester C.	04.50	50-52	34	-	11
Southend U.	Tr	10.52	52	14	-	6
Shrewsbury T.	Tr	03.53	52-53	11	-	0

MARSDEN Frederick
Blackburn, 6 September, 1911 Died 1989 (FB)

League Club	Source	Date Signed	Seasons Played	Apps	Subs	Gls
Accrington St.		10.34	34	5	-	0
Wolverhampton W.	Tr	01.35	35	1	-	0
Bournemouth	Tr	05.36	36-48	194	-	1

MARSDEN Jack
Leeds, 17 December, 1931 (CH)

League Club	Source	Date Signed	Seasons Played	Apps	Subs	Gls
Leeds U.	Osmondthorpe	08.50	52-58	71	-	0
Barrow	Tr	03.59	58-59	47	-	0
Carlisle U.	Tr	09.60	60-63	88	-	0
Doncaster Rov.	Tr	07.64	64	2	-	0

MARSDEN James Richard
Rotherham, 10 April, 1928 (F)

League Club	Source	Date Signed	Seasons Played	Apps	Subs	Gls
Rotherham U.	Parkgate W.	08.52	52-54	11	-	2

MARSDEN Keith
Matlock, 10 April, 1934 Died 1986 (CF)

League Club	Source	Date Signed	Seasons Played	Apps	Subs	Gls
Chesterfield	Youlgreave B.C.	06.52	53-54	22	-	15
Manchester C.	Tr	07.55	55-57	14	-	1
Accrington St.	Tr	08.59				

MARSDEN Liddle
Fatfield, 13 May, 1936 (HB)

League Club	Source	Date Signed	Seasons Played	Apps	Subs	Gls
Workington	South Shields	11.56	56	2	-	0

MARSH Arthur
Rowley Regis, 4 May, 1947 (CD)

League Club	Source	Date Signed	Seasons Played	Apps	Subs	Gls
Bolton W.	App	05.65	66-70	71	2	0
Rochdale	Tr	12.71	71-73	89	1	0
Darlington	Tr	07.74	74	23	0	1

MARSH Christopher Jonathan
Sedgley, 14 January, 1970 (M)

League Club	Source	Date Signed	Seasons Played	Apps	Subs	Gls
Walsall	YT	07.88	87-97	268	34	21

MARSH Clifford
Atherton, 29 December, 1920 Died 1990 (IF)

League Club	Source	Date Signed	Seasons Played	Apps	Subs	Gls
Leeds U.	Winsford U.	09.48	48	4	-	1
Bournemouth	Tr	05.49	49-51	39	-	2

MARSH Wilson Edmund (Eddie)
Dundee, 14 December, 1927 (G)

League Club	Source	Date Signed	Seasons Played	Apps	Subs	Gls
Charlton Ath.	Erith & Belvedere	12.45	50-56	26	-	0
Luton T.	Tr	06.57	57-58	2	-	0
Torquay U.	Tr	07.59	59-61	61	-	0

MARSH Frank Kitchener
Bolton, 7 June, 1916 Died 1978 (WH)

League Club	Source	Date Signed	Seasons Played	Apps	Subs	Gls
Bolton W.		05.38	38	3	-	0
Chester C.	Tr	05.39	46-47	69	-	2

MARSH Ian James
Swansea, 27 October, 1969 (LB)

League Club	Source	Date Signed	Seasons Played	Apps	Subs	Gls
Swansea C.	YT	07.88	87	1	0	0
Bradford C.	Tr	07.89				

MARSH John (Jackie) Henry
Newcastle-u-Lyme, 31 May, 1948 (RB)

League Club	Source	Date Signed	Seasons Played	Apps	Subs	Gls
Stoke C.	App	06.65	67-78	346	9	2

MARSH John (Jack) Kirk
Mansfield, 8 October, 1922 Died 1997 (IF)

League Club	Source	Date Signed	Seasons Played	Apps	Subs	Gls
Notts Co.	Mansfield B.C.	08.42	46-48	42	-	18
Coventry C.	Tr	09.48	48-49	20	-	7
Leicester C.	Tr	03.50	49-50	14	-	4
Chesterfield	Tr	09.50	50	27	-	4

MARSH John Stanley
Farnworth, 31 August, 1940 (IF)

League Club	Source	Date Signed	Seasons Played	Apps	Subs	Gls
Oldham Ath.	Jnrs	10.57	59	2	-	0

MARSH John William
Leeds, 17 December, 1947 (G)

League Club	Source	Date Signed	Seasons Played	Apps	Subs	Gls
Bradford C.	New Farnley Jnrs	05.66	66-67	12	0	0

MARSH Kevin William
Liverpool, 27 March, 1949 (F)

League Club	Source	Date Signed	Seasons Played	Apps	Subs	Gls
Liverpool	App	03.66				
Southport	Tr	05.70	70	35	2	8

MARSH Michael Andrew
Liverpool, 21 July, 1969 (RM)

League Club	Source	Date Signed	Seasons Played	Apps	Subs	Gls
Liverpool	Kirkby T.	08.87	88-93	42	27	2
West Ham U.	Tr	09.93	93-94	46	3	1
Coventry C.	Tr	12.94	94	15	0	2
Southend U.	Galatasaray (Tu)	09.95	95-97	84	0	11

MARSH Rodney William
Hatfield, 11 October, 1944 Eu23-2/E-9 (F)

League Club	Source	Date Signed	Seasons Played	Apps	Subs	Gls
Fulham	App	10.62	62-65	63	0	22
Queens Park R.	Tr	03.66	65-71	211	0	106
Manchester C.	Tr	03.72	71-75	116	2	36
Fulham	Tampa Bay (USA)	08.76	76	16	0	5

MARSH Simon Thomas Peter
Ealing, 29 January, 1977 Eu21-1 (FB)

League Club	Source	Date Signed	Seasons Played	Apps	Subs	Gls
Oxford U.	YT	11.94	94-97	29	6	1

MARSHALL Alexander Stewart
Alloa, 27 November, 1935 (IF)

League Club	Source	Date Signed	Seasons Played	Apps	Subs	Gls
Accrington St.	Stirling A.	10.60	60	8	-	2

MARSHALL Alfred George
Dagenham, 21 May, 1933 (FB)

League Club	Source	Date Signed	Seasons Played	Apps	Subs	Gls
Colchester U.	Dagenham	10.57	58-60	30	-	0

MARSHALL Andrew John
Bury St Edmunds, 14 April, 1975 Eu21-4 (G)

League Club	Source	Date Signed	Seasons Played	Apps	Subs	Gls
Norwich C.	YT	07.93	94-97	72	1	0
Bournemouth	L	09.96	96	11	0	0
Gillingham	L	11.96	96	5	0	0

MARSHALL Brian
Bolton-on-Dearne, 20 September, 1954 (CD)

League Club	Source	Date Signed	Seasons Played	Apps	Subs	Gls
Huddersfield T.	App	12.71	72-74	30	2	0
Scunthorpe U.	L	10.74	74	3	0	0

MARSHALL Clifford
Liverpool, 4 November, 1955 E Sch (W)

League Club	Source	Date Signed	Seasons Played	Apps	Subs	Gls
Everton	App	11.73	74-75	6	1	0
Southport	Tr	09.76	76	11	2	0

MARSHALL Colin
Glasgow, 1 November, 1969 (F)

League Club	Source	Date Signed	Seasons Played	Apps	Subs	Gls
Barnsley	YT	04.88	88-90	0	4	0
Wrexham	L	09.91	91	3	0	0
Scarborough	Tr	03.92	91	4	0	1

League Club	Source	Date Signed	Seasons Played	Career Record Apps	Subs	Gls
MARSHALL Daniel John						
Newark, 18 December, 1975						(M)
Chesterfield	Notts Co. (YT)	08.94	94	0	1	0
MARSHALL David Howard						
Manchester, 12 November, 1955						(M)
Workington (N/C)	Headley Colly	11.76	76	2	0	0
MARSHALL Dwight Wayne						
Jamaica (WI), 3 October, 1965						(F)
Plymouth Arg.	Grays Ath.	08.91	91-93	93	6	27
Middlesbrough	L	03.93	92	0	3	0
Luton T.	Tr	07.94	94-97	87	37	27
MARSHALL Ernest						
Dinnington, 23 May, 1918 Died 1983						(WH)
Sheffield U.		05.35	36-37	13	-	0
Cardiff C.		05.39	46	1	-	0
MARSHALL Frank						
Sheffield, 26 January, 1929						(WH)
Rotherham U.	Scarborough	05.51	51-56	117	-	5
Scunthorpe U.	Tr	07.57	57-58	80	-	0
Doncaster Rov.	Tr	10.59	59-61	35	-	0
MARSHALL Gary						
Bristol, 20 April, 1964						(W)
Bristol C.	Shepton Mallet	07.83	83-87	48	20	7
Torquay U.	L	12.84	84	7	0	1
Carlisle U.	Tr	07.88	88	18	3	2
Scunthorpe U.	Tr	07.89	89-90	38	3	3
Exeter C.	Tr	10.90	90-91	48	12	6
MARSHALL Gordon						
Farnham, 2 July, 1939 Eu23-1						(G)
Newcastle U.	Hearts	06.63	63-67	177	0	0
Nottingham F.	Tr	10.68	68	7	0	0
MARSHALL Gordon Banks						
Edinburgh, 19 April, 1964 S-1						(G)
Stoke C. (L)	Glasgow Celtic	12.93	93	10	0	0
MARSHALL Ian Paul						
Oxford, 20 March, 1966						(CD/F)
Everton	App	03.84	85-87	9	6	0
Oldham Ath.	Tr	03.88	87-92	165	5	36
Ipswich T.	Tr	08.93	93-96	79	5	32
Leicester C.	Tr	08.96	96-97	41	11	15
MARSHALL John						
Rawtenstall, 1 November, 1938						(G)
Accrington St.		05.57	57-58	7	-	0
MARSHALL John Gilmore						
Bolton, 29 May, 1917 Died 1998						(FB)
Burnley	Jnrs	11.36	38-46	26	-	0
MARSHALL John James						
Glasgow, 12 February, 1949						(W)
Preston N.E.		02.67				
Rotherham U.	Ross Co.	09.68	68	4	0	0
MARSHALL John Philip						
Balham, 18 August, 1964						(RB/M)
Fulham	App	08.82	83-95	393	18	28
MARSHALL Julian Paul						
Swansea, 6 July, 1957						(CD)
Hereford U.	Merthyr Tydfil	08.75	76-79	91	1	4
Bristol C.	Tr	08.80	80-81	29	0	0
Walsall	Tr	08.82	82	10	0	0
MARSHALL Lee Alan						
Nottingham, 1 August, 1975						(M)
Nottingham F.	YT	08.92				
Stockport Co.	Tr	03.95	94	1	0	0
Scunthorpe U.	Tr	06.97	97	12	9	1
MARSHALL Lee Keith						
Islington, 21 January, 1979						(RB)
Norwich C.	Enfield	03.97	97	2	2	0
MARSHALL Peter						
Barrow, 2 October, 1947						(OR)
Barrow	Holker Street O.B.	01.66	65-66	4	0	1
MARSHALL Peter William						
Worksop, 5 December, 1934						(G)
Scunthorpe U.	Worksop T.	09.54	54-56	64	-	0
MARSHALL Ralph						
Baillieston, 30 January, 1944						(FB)
Crewe Alex.	Glasgow Rangers	09.64	64-66	72	1	0
MARSHALL Richard						
Burbage, 23 November, 1945 Died 1992						(W)
Leicester C.	App	08.63				
Southport	Tr	07.65	65-66	29	2	7
MARSHALL Roy Cyril						
Fulham, 22 May, 1932						(G)
Brighton & H.A.	Jnrs	06.50				
Aldershot	Tr	08.57	57-60	34	-	0
MARSHALL Scott Roderick						
Edinburgh, 1 May, 1973 S Yth/Su21-5						(CD)
Arsenal	YT	03.91	92-97	19	5	1
Rotherham U.	L	12.93	93	10	0	1
Sheffield U.	L	08.94	94	17	0	0
MARSHALL Shaun Andrew						
Fakenham, 3 October, 1978						(G)
Cambridge U.	YT	02.97	96-97	3	0	0
MARSHALL Stanley Kenneth						
Goole, 20 April, 1946						(IF)
Middlesbrough	Goole T.	08.63	65	2	0	0
Notts Co.	Tr	06.66	66-67	43	6	17
MARSHALL Terence William James						
Whitechapel, 26 December, 1935						(OR)
Newcastle U.	Wisbech T.	12.58	58-60	5	-	1
MARSHALL William						
Belfast, 11 July, 1936 NI 'B'						(FB)
Burnley	Distillery	10.53	59-60	6	-	0
Oldham Ath.	Tr	08.62	62-63	57	-	0
Hartlepool U.	Tr	08.64	64-65	57	0	0
MARSHALL William Forsyth						
Glasgow, 9 May, 1933						(CF)
Bradford C.	Rutherglen Glencairn	01.57	56-58	33	-	16
Swindon T.	Tr	02.59	58-59	30	-	12
MARSLAND Gordon						
Blackpool, 20 March, 1945						(WH)
Blackpool	App	05.62				
Carlisle U.	Tr	06.65	65-68	63	3	4
Bristol Rov.	Tr	06.69	69	16	0	1
Crewe Alex.	L	09.70	70	5	0	0
Oldham Ath.	L	03.71	70	1	3	0
MARSTON James (Joe) Edward						
Australia, 7 January, 1926 EF Lge						(CH)
Preston N.E.	Leichardt (Aus)	02.50	50-54	185	-	0
MARSTON Maurice						
Trimdon (Dm), 24 March, 1929						(FB)
Sunderland	Jnrs	06.49	51-52	9	-	0
Northampton T.	Tr	07.53	53-56	149	-	2
MARTIN John **Alan**						
Stoke, 23 November, 1923						(IF/WH)
Port Vale	Nettlebank Villa	12.42	46-51	169	-	28
Stoke C.	Tr	09.51	51-54	104	-	6
Port Vale	Bangor C.	07.57	57-58	19	-	0
MARTIN Alvin Edward						
Bootle, 29 July, 1958 E Yth/E'B'/E-17						(CD)
West Ham U.	App	07.76	77-95	462	7	27
Leyton Orient	Tr	07.96	96	16	1	0
MARTIN Barrie						
Birmingham, 29 September, 1935						(FB)
Blackpool	Jnrs	12.53	57-63	189	-	1
Oldham Ath.	Tr	08.64	64	42	-	4
Tranmere Rov.	Tr	06.65	65-67	99	3	0
MARTIN Cornelius (Con) Joseph						
Dublin, 20 March, 1923 IR-30/NI-6						(CH/G)
Leeds U.	Glentoran	01.47	46-48	47	-	1
Aston Villa	Tr	10.48	48-55	194	-	1
MARTIN David						
East Ham, 25 April, 1963 E Yth						(M/D)
Millwall	App	05.80	79-84	131	9	6
Wimbledon	Tr	09.84	84-85	30	5	3

League Club	Source	Date Signed	Seasons Played	Career Record Apps	Subs	Gls
Southend U.	Tr	08.86	86-92	212	9	19
Bristol C.	Tr	07.93	93-94	36	2	1
Northampton T.	L	02.95	94	7	0	1
Gillingham	Tr	08.95	95	27	4	1
Leyton Orient	Tr	07.96	96	8	0	0
Northampton T.	Tr	10.96	96	10	2	0
Brighton & H.A.	L	03.97	96	1	0	0
MARTIN Dean Edward						
Islington, 31 August, 1972						(W)
West Ham U.	Fisher Ath.	06.91	91	1	1	0
Colchester U.	L	01.93	92	8	0	2
Brentford	Iceland	10.95	95	14	5	1
MARTIN Dean Stacey						
Huddersfield, 9 September, 1967						(M)
Halifax T.	App	09.85	86-90	149	4	7
Scunthorpe U.	Tr	07.91	91-94	100	6	7
Rochdale	Tr	01.95	94-96	45	8	0
MARTIN Dennis Victor						
Southampton, 8 November, 1928						(HB)
Bournemouth	Jnrs	08.47	48-53	23	-	0
MARTIN Dennis William						
Edinburgh, 27 October, 1947						(W)
West Bromwich A.	Kettering T.	07.67	67-69	14	2	1
Carlisle U.	Tr	07.70	70-77	271	4	48
Newcastle U.	Tr	10.77	77	9	2	2
Mansfield T.	Tr	03.78	77-78	46	0	3
MARTIN Donald						
Corby, 15 February, 1944 E Yth						(F/M)
Northampton T.	Jnrs	07.62	62-67	136	0	53
Blackburn Rov.	Tr	02.68	67-75	218	6	58
Northampton T.	Tr	11.75	75-77	77	15	17
MARTIN Edward						
Baillieston, 31 March, 1921						(IF)
Accrington St.	Alloa Ath.	08.50	50	2	-	0
MARTIN Eliot James						
Plumstead, 27 September, 1972						(LB)
Gillingham	YT	05.91	91-93	52	1	1
Gillingham	Chelmsford C.	03.95	94	7	0	0
MARTIN Eric						
Perth, 31 March, 1946						(G)
Southampton	Dunfermline Ath.	03.67	66-74	248	0	0
MARTIN Frederick						
Nottingham, 13 December, 1925						(F)
Nottingham F.		10.44	47-48	5	-	0
MARTIN Frederick John						
Nottingham, 14 April, 1925						(WH)
Blackburn Rov.	Sutton T.	12.49				
Accrington St.	Tr	07.50	50-51	64	-	0
MARTIN Geoffrey						
Clay Cross, 9 March, 1940						(OL)
Chesterfield	Parkhouse Colly	10.58	58	2	-	0
Leeds U.	Tr	05.60				
Darlington	Tr	07.61	61	20	-	6
Carlisle U.	Tr	05.62	61-62	15	-	2
Workington	Tr	12.62	62-66	144	0	24
Grimsby T.	Tr	11.66	66-67	71	0	5
Chesterfield	Tr	07.68	68-69	43	0	4
MARTIN Harold John						
Blackburn, 15 March, 1955						(M/CD)
Bolton W.		11.73				
Rochdale	Tr	07.74	74	11	2	0
MARTIN Jae Andrew						
Hampstead, 5 February, 1976						(W)
Southend U.	YT	05.93	93-94	1	7	0
Leyton Orient	L	09.94	94	1	3	0
Birmingham C.	Tr	07.95	95	1	6	0
Lincoln C.	Tr	08.96	96-97	29	12	5
MARTIN James						
Glasgow, 3 March, 1937						(OL)
Nottingham F.	Baillieston	06.58	58	1	-	0
MARTIN James Caird						
Dundee, 27 May, 1938						(CF)
Blackpool	Evenwood T.	12.61				
Reading	Tr	06.62	62-63	22	-	6
MARTIN John						
Ashington, 4 December, 1946						(W)
Aston Villa	App	07.64	64	1	-	0
Colchester U.	Tr	05.66	66-68	77	1	11
Workington	Tr	07.69	69-73	206	1	32
Southport	Tr	08.74	74-75	54	9	7
MARTIN John						
London, 15 July, 1981						(M)
Leyton Orient	YT	●	97	0	1	0
MARTIN John (Jack) Grieve						
Dundee, 20 August, 1935						(FB)
Sheffield Wed.	Dundee N.E.	02.54	54-60	63	-	0
Rochdale	Tr	06.62	62-63	24	-	1
MARTIN John Rowland						
Birmingham, 5 August, 1914 Died 1996						(IF)
Aston Villa	Hednesford T.	01.35	36-48	81	-	22
MARTIN Kevin						
Bromsgrove, 22 June, 1976						(G)
Scarborough	YT	07.95	94-97	23	0	0
MARTIN Lee Andrew						
Hyde, 5 February, 1968 Eu21-2						(LB)
Manchester U.	YT	05.86	87-93	56	17	1
Bristol Rov.	Glasgow Celtic	08.96	96	25	0	0
Huddersfield T.	L	09.97	97	2	1	0
MARTIN Lee Brendon						
Huddersfield, 9 September, 1968						(G)
Huddersfield T.	YT	06.87	87-91	54	0	0
Blackpool	Tr	08.92	92-94	98	0	0
Rochdale (N/C)	Tr	11.96				
MARTIN Lionel John						
Ludlow, 15 May, 1947						(M)
Aston Villa	App	07.64	66-70	36	12	4
Doncaster Rov.	L	03.71	70	2	0	0
MARTIN Michael Paul						
Dublin, 9 July, 1951 IR Amat/IRu23-1/IR-51						(M)
Manchester U.	Bohemians	01.73	72-74	33	7	2
West Bromwich A.	Tr	10.75	75-78	85	4	11
Newcastle U.	Tr	12.78	78-82	139	8	5
Cardiff C.	Vancouver (Can)	11.84	84	7	0	0
Peterborough U.	Tr	01.85	84	13	0	0
Rotherham U.	Tr	08.85	85	5	0	0
Preston N.E.	Tr	09.85	85	35	0	0
MARTIN Neil						
Tranent, 20 October, 1940 Su23-1/SF Lge/S-3						(CF)
Sunderland	Hibernian	10.65	65-67	86	0	38
Coventry C.	Tr	02.68	67-70	106	0	40
Nottingham F.	Tr	02.71	70-74	116	3	28
Brighton & H.A.	Tr	07.75	75	13	4	8
Crystal Palace	Tr	03.76	75	8	1	1
MARTIN Peter						
South Shields, 29 December, 1950						(W)
Middlesbrough	Chilton B.C.	06.69				
Darlington	Tr	07.71	71	3	0	0
Barnsley	Tr	10.71	71-72	18	8	6
MARTIN Raymond Barry						
Coseley, 23 January, 1945						(FB)
Birmingham C.	Aston Villa (Am)	05.62	63-75	325	8	1
MARTIN Roy						
Kilbirnie, 16 May, 1929						(FB)
Birmingham C.	Kilwinning R.	03.50	50-55	69	-	0
Derby Co.	Tr	03.56	55-59	81	-	0
Chesterfield	Tr	07.60				
MARTIN Thomas						
Glasgow, 21 December, 1924						(WH)
Doncaster Rov.	Stirling A.	07.50	50-52	71	-	9
Nottingham F.	Tr	11.52	52-54	47	-	4
Hull C.	Tr	06.55	55-56	32	-	2
MARTIN Wayne Lawrence						
Basildon, 16 December, 1965						(D)
Crystal Palace	App	07.82	83	1	0	0
MARTINDALE David						
Liverpool, 9 April, 1964						(M)
Tranmere Rov.	Caernarfon T.	07.87	87-93	128	38	9

MARTINDALE Gary
Liverpool, 24 June, 1971 (F)

League Club	Source	Date Signed	Seasons Played	Apps	Subs	Gls
Bolton W.	Burscough	03.94				
Peterborough U.	Tr	07.95	95	26	5	15
Notts Co.	Tr	03.96	95-97	34	32	13
Mansfield T.	L	02.97	96	5	0	2
Rotherham U.	Tr	03.98	97	7	1	2

MARTINDALE Leonard
Bolton, 30 June, 1920 (WH)

League Club	Source	Date Signed	Seasons Played	Apps	Subs	Gls
Burnley	Jnrs	07.37	37-50	69	-	2
Accrington St.	Tr	12.51	51	16	-	0

MARTINEZ Eugene
Chelmsford, 6 July, 1957 (M)

League Club	Source	Date Signed	Seasons Played	Apps	Subs	Gls
Bradford C.	Harrogate R.A.	07.77	77-79	38	14	5
Rochdale	Tr	07.80	80-82	110	6	16
Newport Co.	Tr	08.83	83	18	2	1
Northampton T.	L	02.84	83	12	0	2

MARTINEZ Roberto
Spain, 13 July, 1973 (M)

League Club	Source	Date Signed	Seasons Played	Apps	Subs	Gls
Wigan Ath.	Balaguer (Sp)	07.95	95-97	106	12	14

MARTYN Antony Nigel
St Austell, 11 August, 1966 Eu21-11/E 'B'/E-7 (G)

League Club	Source	Date Signed	Seasons Played	Apps	Subs	Gls
Bristol Rov.	St Blazey	08.87	87-89	101	0	0
Crystal Palace	Tr	11.89	89-95	272	0	0
Leeds U.	Tr	07.96	96-97	74	0	0

MARUSTIK Christopher
Swansea, 10 August, 1961 W Sch/Wu21-7/W-6 (M)

League Club	Source	Date Signed	Seasons Played	Apps	Subs	Gls
Swansea C.	App	08.78	78-85	144	8	11
Cardiff C.	Tr	10.85	85-86	43	0	1

MARVIN Walter
Derby, 6 July, 1920 (CF)

League Club	Source	Date Signed	Seasons Played	Apps	Subs	Gls
Accrington St.	Newport Co. (Am)	12.46	46-47	9	-	3

MARWOOD Brian
Seaham, 5 February, 1960 E-1 (W)

League Club	Source	Date Signed	Seasons Played	Apps	Subs	Gls
Hull C.	App	02.78	79-83	154	4	51
Sheffield Wed.	Tr	08.84	84-87	125	3	27
Arsenal	Tr	03.88	87-89	52	0	16
Sheffield U.	Tr	09.90	90-91	14	8	3
Middlesbrough	L	10.91	91	3	0	0
Swindon T. (N/C)	Tr	03.93	92	6	5	1
Barnet	Tr	08.93	93	18	5	0

MASEFIELD Keith Leonard
Birmingham, 26 February, 1957 (FB)

League Club	Source	Date Signed	Seasons Played	Apps	Subs	Gls
Aston Villa	App	10.74	74-76	1	3	0

MASEFIELD Paul Darren
Lichfield, 21 October, 1970 (RB)

League Club	Source	Date Signed	Seasons Played	Apps	Subs	Gls
Birmingham C.	YT	07.89				
Exeter C. (N/C)	Cheltenham T.	02.92	91	1	0	0
Stockport Co.	Bromsgrove Rov.	08.92	92	7	0	0
Doncaster Rov.	Tr	02.93	92	8	1	0
Preston N.E.	Tr	08.93	93	6	0	0

MASIELLO Luciano
Italy, 2 January, 1951 (W)

League Club	Source	Date Signed	Seasons Played	Apps	Subs	Gls
Charlton Ath.	App	01.69	69-70	6	0	0

MASINGA Philomen Raul
South Africa, 28 June, 1969 South African Int (F)

League Club	Source	Date Signed	Seasons Played	Apps	Subs	Gls
Leeds U.	Mamelodi (SA)	08.94	94-95	20	11	5

MASKELL Craig Dell
Aldershot, 10 April, 1968 (F)

League Club	Source	Date Signed	Seasons Played	Apps	Subs	Gls
Southampton	App	04.86	85-86	2	4	1
Huddersfield T.	Tr	05.88	88-89	86	1	43
Reading	Tr	08.90	90-91	60	12	26
Swindon T.	Tr	07.92	92-93	40	7	22
Southampton	Tr	02.94	93-95	8	9	1
Bristol C.	L	12.95	95	5	0	1
Brighton & H.A.	Tr	03.96	95-97	68	1	20
Leyton Orient (N/C)	Happy Valley (HK)	03.98	97	7	1	2

MASKELL Dennis
Mountain Ash, 16 April, 1931 (OL)

League Club	Source	Date Signed	Seasons Played	Apps	Subs	Gls
Watford		09.51	51	5	-	0

MASKELL Michael Richard
Eynsham (Oxon), 25 January, 1952 (FB)

League Club	Source	Date Signed	Seasons Played	Apps	Subs	Gls
Chelsea	App	02.69				
Brentford	Tr	07.70	70	1	0	0

MASKERY Christopher Paul
Stoke, 25 September, 1964 (M)

League Club	Source	Date Signed	Seasons Played	Apps	Subs	Gls
Stoke C.	App	09.82	82-86	82	10	3

MASON Andrew
Stretford, 26 October, 1966 (M)

League Club	Source	Date Signed	Seasons Played	Apps	Subs	Gls
Crewe Alex. (N/C)	YT	08.84	84	1	1	0

MASON Andrew John
Bolton, 22 November, 1974 (F)

League Club	Source	Date Signed	Seasons Played	Apps	Subs	Gls
Bolton W.	YT	05.93				
Hull C.	Tr	06.95	95-96	14	12	4
Chesterfield	Tr	03.97	96	1	1	0
Macclesfield T.	Tr	08.97	97	7	5	0

MASON Clifford Ernest
York, 27 November, 1929 (FB)

League Club	Source	Date Signed	Seasons Played	Apps	Subs	Gls
Sunderland		01.50				
Darlington	Tr	07.52	52-54	107	-	0
Sheffield U.	Tr	08.55	55-61	97	-	2
Leeds U.	Tr	03.62	61-62	31	-	0
Scunthorpe U.	Tr	02.64	63	12	-	1
Chesterfield	Tr	07.64	64	5	-	0

MASON George William
Birmingham, 5 September, 1913 Died 1993 E Sch (CH)

League Club	Source	Date Signed	Seasons Played	Apps	Subs	Gls
Coventry C.	Redhill Amats	11.31	31-51	330	-	6

MASON James
Glasgow, 17 April, 1933 (OL/WH)

League Club	Source	Date Signed	Seasons Played	Apps	Subs	Gls
Accrington St.	Dundee	06.55	55-56	14	-	1
Chester C.	Tr	06.57	57-58	64	-	7
Crystal Palace	Chelmsford C.	05.60				

MASON John Francis
Birmingham, 23 January, 1943 E Amat (CF)

League Club	Source	Date Signed	Seasons Played	Apps	Subs	Gls
Peterborough U.	Alvechurch	05.66	66-67	37	0	18

MASON Keith Michael
Leicester, 19 July, 1958 (G)

League Club	Source	Date Signed	Seasons Played	Apps	Subs	Gls
Huddersfield T.	Leicester C. (N/C)	07.82	82-85	30	0	0

MASON Maurice
Sedgefield, 25 June, 1927 (IF)

League Club	Source	Date Signed	Seasons Played	Apps	Subs	Gls
Huddersfield T.		01.48				
Darlington	Blackhall Colly	07.52	52	3	-	0

MASON Michael Barry
Walsall, 20 October, 1944 (IF)

League Club	Source	Date Signed	Seasons Played	Apps	Subs	Gls
Walsall	App	09.62	63	4	-	0
West Bromwich A.	Tr	07.64				

MASON Paul David
Liverpool, 3 September, 1963 (M)

League Club	Source	Date Signed	Seasons Played	Apps	Subs	Gls
Ipswich T.	Aberdeen	06.93	93-97	103	10	25

MASON Richard James
Nuneaton, 2 April, 1918 Died 1992 (FB)

League Club	Source	Date Signed	Seasons Played	Apps	Subs	Gls
Coventry C.	Nuneaton Borough	05.46	46-53	253	-	2

MASON Robert Henry
Tipton, 22 March, 1936 (IF)

League Club	Source	Date Signed	Seasons Played	Apps	Subs	Gls
Wolverhampton W.	Jnrs	05.53	55-61	146	-	44
Leyton Orient	Chelmsford C.	03.63	62-63	23	-	0

MASON Stuart James
Whitchurch, 2 June, 1948 E Yth (FB)

League Club	Source	Date Signed	Seasons Played	Apps	Subs	Gls
Wrexham	Jnrs	07.66	65-66	28	0	0
Liverpool	Tr	10.66				
Doncaster Rov.	L	11.67	67	1	0	0
Wrexham	Tr	06.68	68-72	144	13	3
Chester C.	Tr	06.73	73-77	132	5	7
Rochdale	L	12.76	76	2	0	0
Crewe Alex.	L	10.77	77	4	0	1

MASON Thomas Herbert Andrew
Buxton, 20 February, 1953 (M)

League Club	Source	Date Signed	Seasons Played	Apps	Subs	Gls
Derby Co.	App	07.72				
Brighton & H.A.	Tr	09.74	74	23	2	2

MASON Thomas Joseph Robert
Fulham, 19 June, 1960 (FB)

League Club	Source	Date Signed	Seasons Played	Apps	Subs	Gls
Fulham	App	01.78	77-79	6	0	0
Brighton & H.A.	Tr	06.81				

MASON Thomas William
Hartlepool, 21 April, 1925 (CH)

League Club	Source	Date Signed	Seasons Played	Apps	Subs	Gls
Hartlepool U.	Railway Ath.	05.46	46	5	-	0

League Club	Source	Date Signed	Seasons Played	Career Record Apps	Subs	Gls
MASSART David Louis						
Birmingham, 2 November, 1919						(CF)
Birmingham C.	Bells Ath.	02.39	46	3	-	0
Walsall	Tr	06.47	47	27	-	23
Bury	Tr	03.48	47-50	85	-	45
Chesterfield	Tr	02.51	50	11	-	5
MASSEY Andrew Thomas						
New Cross, 20 October, 1961 IR Yth						(M)
Millwall	Jnrs	03.79	80-83	74	15	8
Port Vale	L	03.84	83	4	0	1
Aldershot	Tr	05.84	84-85	65	6	3
MASSEY Bernard Kendrick Woolley						
Ripley, 5 November, 1920						(WH)
Halifax T.	Peterborough U.	09.38	38-50	84	-	6
MASSEY Eric						
Derby, 11 September, 1923						(WH)
Bury	Arsenal (Am)	09.46	46-56	202	-	6
MASSEY Kevin James						
Gainsborough, 30 November, 1965						(M)
Cambridge U.	App	12.83	83-85	8	8	1
MASSEY Richard						
Seisdon, 11 October, 1968						(CD)
Exeter C.	YT	07.86	85-87	22	6	1
MASSEY Robert William						
Marylebone, 6 April, 1940						(FB)
Bournemouth	Jnrs	05.58	59-60	5	-	0
MASSEY Roy						
Mexborough, 10 September, 1943 E Yth						(CF)
Rotherham U.		07.64	64-66	15	1	6
Leyton Orient	Tr	09.67	67-68	58	5	13
Colchester U.	Tr	07.69	69-70	30	4	11
MASSEY Stephen						
Denton, 28 March, 1958						(F)
Stockport Co.	App	07.75	74-77	87	14	20
Bournemouth	Tr	07.78	78-80	85	12	19
Peterborough U.	Tr	08.81	81	13	5	3
Northampton T.	Tr	02.82	81-82	60	0	25
Hull C.	Tr	07.83	83-84	34	8	9
Cambridge U.	Tr	08.85	85	28	3	11
Wrexham	Tr	07.86	86-87	38	5	10
MASSEY Stuart Anthony						
Crawley, 17 November, 1964						(M)
Crystal Palace	Sutton U.	07.92	92-93	1	1	0
Oxford U.	Tr	07.94	94-97	82	21	8
MASSIE Leslie						
Aberdeen, 20 July, 1935						(IF)
Huddersfield T.	Banks O'Dee	08.53	56-66	334	1	100
Darlington	Tr	10.66	66	20	0	2
Halifax T.	Tr	06.67	67-68	89	0	41
Bradford P.A.	Tr	08.69	69	14	0	2
Workington	Tr	12.69	69-70	62	0	15
MASSIMO Franco						
Horsham, 23 September, 1968						(F)
Brighton & H.A.	App	09.86	85	0	1	0
MASSON Donald Sanderson						
Banchory, 26 August, 1946 S-17						(M)
Middlesbrough	Jnrs	09.63	64-67	50	3	6
Notts Co.	Tr	09.68	68-74	274	0	81
Queens Park R.	Tr	12.74	74-77	116	0	18
Derby Co.	Tr	10.77	77	23	0	1
Notts Co.	Tr	08.78	78-81	129	0	11
MASTERS Graham						
Bristol, 13 August, 1931						(W)
Bristol C.	Jnrs	08.48	51	9	-	1
MASTERS Neil Bradley						
Ballymena, 25 May, 1972 NI Yth						(LB)
Bournemouth	YT	08.90	92-93	37	1	2
Wolverhampton W.	Tr	12.93	93-95	10	2	0
Gillingham	Tr	04.97	97	11	0	0
MATEU Jose Luis						
Spain, 15 January, 1966						(F)
Torquay U.	Castellon (Sp)	09.95	95	5	5	1

League Club	Source	Date Signed	Seasons Played	Career Record Apps	Subs	Gls
MATHER Harold						
Bolton, 24 January, 1921						(FB)
Burnley	Jnrs	05.38	46-54	301	-	0
MATHER Shaun						
Hereford, 9 September, 1965						(M)
Newport Co. (N/C)	Presteigne	08.83	83	0	1	0
MATHIAS Raymond						
Liverpool, 13 December, 1946						(FB)
Tranmere Rov.	App	12.64	67-84	557	10	6
MATHIE Alexander						
Bathgate, 20 December, 1968 S Yth						(F)
Port Vale (L)	Morton	03.93	92	0	3	0
Newcastle U.	Morton	07.93	93-94	3	22	4
Ipswich T.	Tr	02.95	94-97	88	13	37
MATHIE David						
Motherwell, 15 August, 1919 Died 1954						(CF)
Workington	Kilmarnock	10.53	53	2	-	0
MATIER Gerald						
Lisburn (NI), 1 December, 1912 Died 1984						(G)
Blackburn Rov.	Coleraine	07.37	37-38	20	-	0
Bradford C.	Tr	08.39				
Plymouth Arg.	Tr	09.46				
Torquay U.	Tr	11.46	46	17	-	0
MATTEO Dominic						
Dumfries, 28 April, 1974 E Yth/Eu21-4/E 'B'						(CD)
Liverpool	YT	05.92	93-97	64	11	0
Sunderland	L	03.95	94	1	0	0
MATTHEW Damian						
Islington, 23 September, 1970 Eu21-9						(M)
Chelsea	YT	06.89	89-92	13	8	0
Luton T.	L	09.92	92	3	2	0
Crystal Palace	Tr	02.94	93-95	17	7	1
Bristol Rov.	L	01.96	95	8	0	0
Burnley	Tr	07.96	96-97	50	9	7
MATTHEWS John **Barry**						
Sheffield, 18 January, 1926 Died 1995						(OL)
Lincoln C. (Am)	Sheffield U. (Am)	10.49	49	2	-	0
MATTHEWS David						
Hackney, 20 November, 1965						(F)
West Ham U.	App	11.82				
Walsall	Basildon U.	11.87				
Southend U.	Tr	03.88	88	1	5	0
MATTHEWS David Ivor						
Rhondda, 24 September, 1921 Died 1986						(G)
Cardiff C.		09.47				
Newport Co.	Tr	04.48	48	6	-	0
MATTHEWS Francis John						
London, 7 January, 1948						(FB)
Southend U.	App	01.66	65-67	20	6	0
Torquay U.	Tr	06.68	68	6	1	0
MATTHEWS Graham						
Newcastle-u-Lyme, 2 November, 1942						(F)
Stoke C.	Jnrs	11.59	60-62	16	-	3
Walsall	Tr	08.63	63-64	67	-	21
Crewe Alex.	Tr	08.65	65-66	55	1	19
MATTHEWS John Melvin						
Camden, 1 November, 1955						(M)
Arsenal	App	08.73	74-77	38	7	2
Sheffield U.	Tr	08.78	78-81	98	5	14
Mansfield T.	Tr	08.82	82-83	70	2	6
Chesterfield	Tr	08.84	84	38	0	1
Plymouth Arg.	Tr	08.85	85-88	131	4	4
Torquay U.	Tr	07.89	89	22	3	0
MATTHEWS John **Keith**						
Wrexham, 7 March, 1934						(W)
Wrexham		12.52	52-54	9	-	0
MATTHEWS Lee Joseph						
Middlesbrough, 16 January, 1979 E Yth						(F)
Leeds U.	YT	02.96	97	0	3	0
MATTHEWS Mark						
Reading, 17 September, 1961						(M)
Reading (N/C)		07.81	81-83	5	3	1

MATTHEWS Michael
Hull, 25 September, 1960 (M)

League Club	Source	Date Signed	Seasons Played	Apps	Subs	Gls
Wolverhampton W.	App	10.78	80-83	72	4	7
Scunthorpe U.	Tr	02.84	83-85	56	2	5
Halifax T.	North Ferriby U.	09.86	86-88	98	1	8
Scarborough	Tr	12.88	88	7	0	1
Stockport Co.	Tr	02.89	88-89	35	0	3
Scarborough	Tr	12.89	89-90	64	2	4
Hull C.	Tr	08.91	91	10	6	2
Halifax T.	Tr	08.92	92	23	0	2

MATTHEWS Neil
Grimsby, 19 September, 1966 (F)

League Club	Source	Date Signed	Seasons Played	Apps	Subs	Gls
Grimsby T.	App	09.84	84-86	9	2	1
Scunthorpe U.	L	11.85	85	1	0	0
Halifax T.	L	10.86	86	9	0	2
Bolton W.	L	03.87	86	1	0	0
Halifax T.	Tr	08.87	87-89	99	6	29
Stockport Co.	Tr	06.90	90-92	27	16	15
Halifax T.	L	09.91	91	3	0	0
Lincoln C.	Tr	12.92	92-94	69	14	20
Bury	L	12.94	94	2	0	1

MATTHEWS Neil Peter
Manchester, 3 December, 1967 NI Yth/NIu21-1/NI 'B' (RB/M)

League Club	Source	Date Signed	Seasons Played	Apps	Subs	Gls
Blackpool	App	12.85	85-89	67	9	1
Cardiff C.	Tr	08.90	90-92	60	6	2
Rochdale	Tr	07.93	93-94	15	4	0

MATTHEWS Paul William
Leicester, 30 September, 1946 (M)

League Club	Source	Date Signed	Seasons Played	Apps	Subs	Gls
Leicester C.	App	08.64	64-70	56	5	5
Southend U.	L	09.72	72	1	0	0
Mansfield T.	Tr	12.72	72-77	121	3	6
Rotherham U.	Tr	10.77	77	8	0	0
Northampton T.	L	03.79	78	13	0	0

MATTHEWS Reginald Derrick
Coventry, 20 December, 1932 Eu23-4/E 'B'/EF Lge/E-5 (G)

League Club	Source	Date Signed	Seasons Played	Apps	Subs	Gls
Coventry C.	Jnrs	05.50	52-56	111	-	0
Chelsea	Tr	11.56	56-60	135	-	0
Derby Co.	Tr	10.61	61-67	225	0	0

MATTHEWS Robert David
Slough, 14 October, 1970 E Sch (W)

League Club	Source	Date Signed	Seasons Played	Apps	Subs	Gls
Notts Co.	Shepshed A.	03.92	91-94	23	20	11
Luton T.	Tr	03.95	94	6	5	0
York C.	Tr	09.95	95	14	3	1
Bury	Tr	01.96	95-97	42	16	9

MATTHEWS Roy Henderson
Slough, 29 March, 1940 (IF)

League Club	Source	Date Signed	Seasons Played	Apps	Subs	Gls
Charlton Ath.	Arbroath Vic.	04.57	59-66	160	0	46

MATTHEWS Stanley
Hanley, 1 February, 1915 E Sch/EF Lge/E-54 (OR)

League Club	Source	Date Signed	Seasons Played	Apps	Subs	Gls
Stoke C.	Jnrs	02.32	31-46	259	-	51
Blackpool	Tr	05.47	47-61	379	-	17
Stoke C.	Tr	10.61	61-64	59	-	3

MATTHEWS George **Terence** Leonard
Leyton, 25 February, 1936 (IF)

League Club	Source	Date Signed	Seasons Played	Apps	Subs	Gls
West Ham U.	Jnrs	02.53	55	9	-	1
Aldershot	Tr	07.57	57-61	62	-	20
Gillingham	Tr	08.62	62	11	-	1

MATTHEWS Wayne John
Cardiff, 11 September, 1964 (M)

League Club	Source	Date Signed	Seasons Played	Apps	Subs	Gls
Cardiff C.	Jnrs	01.83	83	4	10	0

MATTHEWSON Reginald
Sheffield, 6 August, 1939 (CH)

League Club	Source	Date Signed	Seasons Played	Apps	Subs	Gls
Sheffield U.	Jnrs	06.58	61-67	146	3	3
Fulham	Tr	02.68	67-72	156	2	1
Chester C.	Tr	01.73	72-75	86	1	1

MATTHEWSON Robert
Newcastle, 13 April, 1930 (CH)

League Club	Source	Date Signed	Seasons Played	Apps	Subs	Gls
Bolton W.	Byker Y.C.	03.48	50-52	3	-	0
Lincoln C.	Tr	06.53				

MATTHEWSON Trevor
Sheffield, 12 February, 1963 (CD)

League Club	Source	Date Signed	Seasons Played	Apps	Subs	Gls
Sheffield Wed.	App	02.81	80-82	3	0	0
Newport Co.	Tr	10.83	83-84	73	2	0
Stockport Co.	Tr	09.85	85-86	79	1	0
Lincoln C.	Tr	08.87	88	43	0	2
Birmingham C.	Tr	07.89	89-92	167	1	12
Preston N.E.	Tr	08.93	93	12	0	1
Bury	Tr	09.94	94-95	34	0	0
Hereford U.	Witton A.	10.96	96	35	0	2

MATTHIAS Terence
Wrexham, 10 November, 1949 W Sch (D)

League Club	Source	Date Signed	Seasons Played	Apps	Subs	Gls
Shrewsbury T.	App	05.67	65-73	96	3	0

MATTINSON Harry
Wigton (Cumb), 20 July, 1925 (CH)

League Club	Source	Date Signed	Seasons Played	Apps	Subs	Gls
Middlesbrough		11.45	46	3	-	0
Preston N.E.	Tr	03.49	48-58	124	-	0

MATTISON Paul Andrew
Wakefield, 24 April, 1973 (RM)

League Club	Source	Date Signed	Seasons Played	Apps	Subs	Gls
Darlington	Ferrybridge	08.94	94-95	5	12	0

MAUCHLEN Alistair Henry
Kilwinning, 29 June, 1960 (M/RB)

League Club	Source	Date Signed	Seasons Played	Apps	Subs	Gls
Leicester C.	Motherwell	08.85	85-91	228	11	11

MAUGE Ronald Carlton
Islington, 10 March, 1969 (M)

League Club	Source	Date Signed	Seasons Played	Apps	Subs	Gls
Charlton Ath.	YT	07.87				
Fulham	Tr	09.88	88-89	47	3	2
Bury	Tr	07.90	90-94	92	16	10
Plymouth Arg.	Tr	07.95	95-97	88	15	10

MAUGHAN Wesley James
Southampton, 17 February, 1939 (CF)

League Club	Source	Date Signed	Seasons Played	Apps	Subs	Gls
Southampton	Cowes (IOW)	05.57	58-61	6	-	1
Reading	Tr	03.62	61-62	16	-	3

MAUND John Henry
Hednesford, 5 January, 1916 Died 1994 (OR)

League Club	Source	Date Signed	Seasons Played	Apps	Subs	Gls
Aston Villa	Hednesford T.	10.34	35-37	47	-	8
Nottingham F.	Tr	05.39				
Walsall	Tr	10.46	46-47	32	-	7

MAUTONE Steven
Australia, 10 August, 1970 (G)

League Club	Source	Date Signed	Seasons Played	Apps	Subs	Gls
West Ham U.	Canberra Cosmos (Aus)	03.96	96	1	0	0
Crewe Alex.	L	09.96	96	3	0	0
Reading	Tr	02.97	96-97	29	0	0

MAW John Rex
Scunthorpe, 22 December, 1934 (LB)

League Club	Source	Date Signed	Seasons Played	Apps	Subs	Gls
Scunthorpe U.		06.57	57	1	-	0

MAWER Shaun Kerry
Scunthorpe, 6 August, 1959 (FB)

League Club	Source	Date Signed	Seasons Played	Apps	Subs	Gls
Grimsby T.	App	08.77	77-79	57	3	0

MAWSON Joseph
Workington, 7 January, 1934 (OL)

League Club	Source	Date Signed	Seasons Played	Apps	Subs	Gls
Workington (Am)		06.55	55	1	-	0

MAWSON Ronald
Bishop Auckland, 16 September, 1914 Died 1981 (G)

League Club	Source	Date Signed	Seasons Played	Apps	Subs	Gls
Crewe Alex.	R.A.F. Tern Hill	06.45	46-47	23	-	0
Wrexham	Tr	09.48	48	6	-	0

MAXFIELD John
Carlisle, 17 June, 1919 (W)

League Club	Source	Date Signed	Seasons Played	Apps	Subs	Gls
Carlisle U.		01.47	46-50	26	-	4
Workington	Tr	07.51	51	13	-	4

MAXFIELD Scott
Doncaster, 13 July, 1976 (LB/M)

League Club	Source	Date Signed	Seasons Played	Apps	Subs	Gls
Doncaster Rov.	YT	07.94	94-95	22	7	1
Hull C.	Tr	03.96	95-97	23	12	0

MAXWELL Alistair
Hamilton, 29 June, 1960 (G)

League Club	Source	Date Signed	Seasons Played	Apps	Subs	Gls
Bolton W. (L)	Motherwell	03.92	91	3	0	0

MAXWELL Hugh
Rigghead, 14 May, 1938 (IF)

League Club	Source	Date Signed	Seasons Played	Apps	Subs	Gls
Bradford P.A.	Stirling A.	04.62	61-62	12	-	5

MAXWELL Jason Dean
Scunthorpe, 1 September, 1972 (F)

League Club	Source	Date Signed	Seasons Played	Apps	Subs	Gls
Scunthorpe U.	Appleby Frodingham	01.93	92	0	2	0

MAXWELL Kenneth
Glasgow, 11 February, 1928 (FB)

League Club	Source	Date Signed	Seasons Played	Apps	Subs	Gls
Northampton T.	Kilmarnock	06.49	50	2	-	0
Bradford P.A.	Canada	11.57	57	2	-	0

League Club	Source	Date Signed	Seasons Played	Career Record Apps	Subs	Gls
MAXWELL Patrick						
Ayr, 10 January, 1929						(IF)
Chesterfield	Saltcoats Vic.	08.51	51-52	18	-	3
MAY Andrew Michael Peter						
Bury, 26 February, 1964 Eu21-1						(M)
Manchester C.	App	01.82	80-86	141	9	8
Huddersfield T.	Tr	07.87	87-89	112	2	5
Bolton W.	L	03.88	87	9	1	2
Bristol C.	Tr	08.90	90-91	88	2	4
Millwall	Tr	06.92	92-94	49	5	1
MAY David						
Oldham, 24 June, 1970						(CD)
Blackburn Rov.	YT	06.88	88-93	123	0	3
Manchester U.	Tr	07.94	94-97	61	12	6
MAY Donald Ivor						
Broseley (Salop), 31 May, 1931						(WH)
Bury		03.51	51-61	133	-	11
MAY Edward						
Edinburgh, 30 August, 1967 S Yth/Su21-2						(M)
Brentford	Hibernian	07.89	89-90	46	1	10
MAY Edwin Charles						
Epping, 19 May, 1943						(CD)
Southend U.	Dagenham	01.65	64-67	106	4	3
Wrexham	Tr	06.68	68-75	330	4	35
Swansea C.	Tr	08.76	76-77	90	0	8
MAY Gary Colin						
Darlington, 7 May, 1967						(M)
Darlington (N/C)		11.86	86	1	1	0
MAY Harry						
Glasgow, 15 October, 1928						(FB)
Cardiff C.	Thorniewood U.	08.48	49	1	-	0
Swindon T.	Tr	06.50	50-51	78	-	1
Barnsley	Tr	05.52	52-54	105	-	0
Southend U.	Tr	09.55	55	19	-	1
MAY Jonathan						
Liverpool, 28 January, 1960 E Sch						(CD)
Blackpool	App	11.78	78	4	0	0
Exeter C.	Tr	08.80				
MAY Lawrence (Larry) Charles						
Sutton Coldfield, 26 December, 1958						(CD)
Leicester C.	App	12.76	76-82	180	7	12
Barnsley	Tr	09.83	83-86	122	0	3
Sheffield Wed.	Tr	02.87	86-87	30	1	1
Brighton & H.A.	Tr	09.88	88	24	0	3
MAY Leroy Armstrong						
Wolverhampton, 12 August, 1969						(F)
Walsall	Tividale	01.92	91	1	3	0
Hereford U.	Tividale	01.93	92-93	16	5	3
MAY Warren Derek						
Southend, 31 December, 1964						(D)
Southend U.	App	01.83	82-85	78	12	4
MAYBANK Edward (Teddy) Glen						
Lambeth, 11 October, 1956						(F)
Chelsea	App	02.74	74-76	28	0	6
Fulham	Tr	11.76	76-77	27	0	14
Brighton & H.A.	Tr	11.77	77-79	62	2	16
Fulham	Tr	12.79	79	19	0	3
MAYBURY Alan						
Dublin, 8 August, 1978 IR Yth/IRU21-3/IR 'B'/IR-1						(M/D)
Leeds U.	St Kevin's B.C.	08.95	95-97	10	3	0
MAYERS Alan						
Delamere, 20 April, 1937						(OR)
Chester C.	Jnrs	05.55	55	1	-	0
MAYERS Derek						
Liverpool, 24 January, 1935						(OR)
Everton	Jnrs	08.52	52-56	18	-	7
Preston N.E.	Tr	05.57	57-60	118	-	25
Leeds U.	Tr	06.61	61	20	-	5
Bury	Tr	07.62	62-63	32	-	6
Wrexham	Tr	10.63	63	21	-	2
MAYES Alan Kenneth						
Edmonton, 11 December, 1953						(F)
Queens Park R.	App	07.71				
Watford	Tr	11.74	74-78	110	23	31

League Club	Source	Date Signed	Seasons Played	Career Record Apps	Subs	Gls
Northampton T.	L	01.76	75	10	0	4
Swindon T.	Tr	02.79	78-80	89	0	38
Chelsea	Tr	12.80	80-82	61	5	19
Swindon T.	Tr	07.83	83-84	52	10	27
Carlisle U.	Tr	07.85	85	8	2	2
Newport Co.	L	02.86	85	3	0	1
Blackpool	Tr	09.86	86	12	1	6
MAYFIELD Leslie						
Mansfield, 19 January, 1926						(FB)
Mansfield T.	Ilkeston	09.48	49-52	34	-	0
MAYLE John **Robert**						
Llandysul, 18 December, 1938						(F)
Shrewsbury T.	Sentinel Jnrs	05.57	57	8	-	0
MAYMAN Paul Francis						
Crewe, 29 May, 1958 E Semi Pro						(M)
Crewe Alex.	Jnrs	07.76	75-76	42	1	3
MAYNARD Michael Clements						
Guyana, 7 January, 1947						(FB)
Crystal Palace	Hounslow T.	03.66				
Peterborough U.	Tr	07.67	67	2	1	0
MAYO Joseph						
Tipton, 25 May, 1952						(F)
Walsall	Dudley T.	09.72	72	2	5	1
West Bromwich A.	Tr	02.73	73-76	67	5	16
Leyton Orient	Tr	03.77	76-81	150	5	36
Cambridge U.	Tr	09.81	81-82	35	1	14
Blackpool	L	10.82	82	5	0	1
MAYO Kerry						
Haywards Heath, 21 September, 1977						(M)
Brighton & H.A.	YT	07.96	96-97	65	3	6
MAYRLEB Christian						
Austria, 8 June, 1972						(F)
Sheffield Wed.	F.C. Tyrol (Aut)	01.98	97	0	3	0
MAYS Albert Edward						
Rhondda, 18 April, 1929 Died 1973						(WH)
Derby Co.	Jnrs	05.46	49-59	272	-	21
Chesterfield	Tr	07.60	60	37	-	5
MAZZARELLI Giuseppe						
Switzerland, 14 August, 1972 Swiss Int						(M)
Manchester C. (L)	F.C. Zurich (Swi)	03.96	95	0	2	0
MAZZON Giorgio						
Cheshunt, 4 September, 1960						(D/M)
Tottenham H.	Hertford T.	04.79	80-82	3	1	0
Aldershot	Tr	08.83	83-88	184	10	6
MEACHAM Jeffrey						
Bristol, 6 February, 1962						(F)
Bristol Rov.	Trowbridge T.	03.87	86-87	19	7	9
MEACHIN Paul						
Bebington, 17 July, 1956						(F)
Southport (Am)	Ashville	10.74	74	3	0	0
MEACOCK Kevin Michael						
Bristol, 16 September, 1963						(F)
Cardiff C.	Devizes T.	12.84	84-85	20	5	3
MEAD Peter Sidney						
Luton, 9 September, 1956						(FB)
Luton T.	App	07.74				
Northampton T.	Tr	08.77	77-78	75	2	4
MEADE Raphael Joseph						
Islington, 22 November, 1962						(F)
Arsenal	App	06.90	81-84	25	16	14
Luton T.	Dundee U.	03.89	88	2	2	0
Ipswich T. (N/C)	B.K. Odense (Den)	01.90	89	0	1	0
Plymouth Arg.	B.K. Odense (Den)	01.91	90	2	3	0
Brighton & H.A.	Tr	08.91	91	35	5	9
Brighton & H.A. (N/C)	Hong Kong	08.94	94	0	3	0
MEADOWS Frank						
Maltby, 27 June, 1933						(WH)
Rotherham U.		04.52	53-55	8	-	0
Coventry C.	Tr	06.56	56	8	-	0
MEADOWS James						
Bolton, 21 July, 1931 Died 1994 EF Lge/E-1						(OR)
Southport	Bolton Y.M.C.A.	03.49	48-50	60	-	6
Manchester C.	Tr	03.51	50-54	130	-	30

MEADOWS John Alfred
Hoxton, 13 November, 1930 (IF/WH)

League Club	Source	Date Signed	Seasons Played	Apps	Subs	Gls
Watford	St Albans C.	06.51	51-59	222	-	42

MEADOWS Robert
Melton Mowbray, 25 April, 1938 (FB)

League Club	Source	Date Signed	Seasons Played	Apps	Subs	Gls
Stoke C.	Jnrs	05.55				
Doncaster Rov.	Northwich Vic.	12.62	62-63	43	-	0

MEADOWS John **Ronald**
Lancaster, 4 December, 1920 (G)

League Club	Source	Date Signed	Seasons Played	Apps	Subs	Gls
Burnley	Glasson Dock	09.46				
Bournemouth	Tr	04.50	50-51	16	-	0
Accrington St.	Tr	07.52	52	18	-	0

MEAGAN John George
Shap, 11 November, 1935 (FB)

League Club	Source	Date Signed	Seasons Played	Apps	Subs	Gls
Workington	Jnrs	12.52	52-54	3	-	0

MEAGAN Michael Kevin
Dublin, 29 May, 1934 IR Sch/IR 'B'/IR-17 (FB)

League Club	Source	Date Signed	Seasons Played	Apps	Subs	Gls
Everton	Johnville Jnrs	09.52	57-63	165	-	1
Huddersfield T.	Tr	07.64	64-67	118	1	1
Halifax T.	Tr	07.68	68	23	0	0

MEAGAN Thomas Patrick
Liverpool, 14 November, 1959 (M)

League Club	Source	Date Signed	Seasons Played	Apps	Subs	Gls
Doncaster Rov.	App	11.77	77-78	32	5	1
Doncaster Rov. (N/C)		09.82	82	2	0	0

MEAKER Michael John
Greenford, 18 August, 1971 Wu21-2/W 'B' (W)

League Club	Source	Date Signed	Seasons Played	Apps	Subs	Gls
Queens Park R.	YT	12.89	90-94	21	13	1
Plymouth Arg.	L	11.91	91	4	0	0
Reading	Tr	07.95	95-97	46	21	2

MEAKIN Harry
Stoke, 8 September, 1919 Died 1986 (FB)

League Club	Source	Date Signed	Seasons Played	Apps	Subs	Gls
Stoke C.	Summerbank	11.45	46-49	35	-	0

MEALAND Kenneth **Barry**
Carshalton, 24 January, 1943 (FB)

League Club	Source	Date Signed	Seasons Played	Apps	Subs	Gls
Fulham	Jnrs	10.61	61-67	28	1	0
Rotherham U.	Tr	08.68	68-69	44	1	0

MEAN Scott James
Crawley, 13 December, 1973 (M)

League Club	Source	Date Signed	Seasons Played	Apps	Subs	Gls
Bournemouth	YT	08.92	92-95	52	22	8
West Ham U.	Tr	07.96	97	0	3	0

MEANEY John Francis
Stoke, 19 November, 1919 (WH/IF)

League Club	Source	Date Signed	Seasons Played	Apps	Subs	Gls
Crewe Alex.	Ravensdale	03.47	46-53	288	-	31

MEANEY Terence
Stoke, 25 May, 1922 (CF)

League Club	Source	Date Signed	Seasons Played	Apps	Subs	Gls
Bury	Ravensdale	05.44	46	4	-	2
Crewe Alex.	Tr	07.47	47	3	-	2

MEARA James Stephen
Hammersmith, 7 October, 1972 (M)

League Club	Source	Date Signed	Seasons Played	Apps	Subs	Gls
Watford	YT	04.91	92	1	1	0
Doncaster Rov.	Tr	07.94	94-95	14	2	1

MEASHAM Ian
Barnsley, 14 December, 1964 (RB)

League Club	Source	Date Signed	Seasons Played	Apps	Subs	Gls
Huddersfield T.	App	12.82	84	17	0	0
Lincoln C.	L	10.85	85	6	0	0
Rochdale	L	03.86	85	12	0	0
Cambridge U.	Tr	07.86	86	46	0	0
Burnley	Tr	11.88	88-93	181	1	2
Doncaster Rov.	Tr	09.93	93-95	29	3	0

MEASURES George Allan
Walthamstow, 17 December, 1958 (F)

League Club	Source	Date Signed	Seasons Played	Apps	Subs	Gls
Cambridge U. (N/C)	Bowers U.	11.83	83	4	0	0

MEATH Trevor John
Wednesbury, 20 March, 1944 (M/F)

League Club	Source	Date Signed	Seasons Played	Apps	Subs	Gls
Walsall	Darlaston	05.64	64-69	59	8	11
Lincoln C.	Tr	10.69	69-71	42	1	5

MEDD Gordon Ernest
Birmingham, 17 August, 1925 Died 1996 (W)

League Club	Source	Date Signed	Seasons Played	Apps	Subs	Gls
Birmingham C.	Worcester C.	10.46				
Walsall	Worcester C.	06.49	49	22	-	2
Rochdale	Tr	07.50	50	5	-	1
York C.	Tr	01.51	50	1	-	0

MEDHURST Harry Edward
Chertsey, 5 February, 1916 Died 1984 (G)

League Club	Source	Date Signed	Seasons Played	Apps	Subs	Gls
West Ham U.	Woking	11.36	38-46	24	-	0
Chelsea	Tr	01.47	46-51	143	-	0
Brighton & H.A.	Tr	11.52	52	12	-	0

MEDLEY Leslie Dennis
Edmonton, 3 September, 1920 E Sch/EF Lge/E-6 (OL)

League Club	Source	Date Signed	Seasons Played	Apps	Subs	Gls
Tottenham H.	Jnrs	02.39	46-52	150	-	45

MEDLIN Nicholas Ryan Maxwell
Camborne, 23 November, 1976 (M)

League Club	Source	Date Signed	Seasons Played	Apps	Subs	Gls
Exeter C.	YT	08.95	95-97	20	17	1

MEDLOCK Owen Wilfred
Whittlesey, 8 March, 1938 (G)

League Club	Source	Date Signed	Seasons Played	Apps	Subs	Gls
Chelsea	Jnrs	05.55				
Swindon T.	Tr	02.59	59	3	-	0
Oxford U.	Tr	12.59	62	19	-	0

MEDWIN Terence Cameron
Swansea, 25 September, 1932 W Sch/W-30 (W)

League Club	Source	Date Signed	Seasons Played	Apps	Subs	Gls
Swansea C.	Jnrs	11.49	51-55	148	-	60
Tottenham H.	Tr	04.56	56-62	197	-	65

MEE George Edwin
Blackpool, 20 May, 1923 Died 1974 (IF)

League Club	Source	Date Signed	Seasons Played	Apps	Subs	Gls
Nottingham F.	Jnrs	05.40	46	9	-	1

MEECHAN Alexander Thomas
Plymouth, 29 January, 1980 (F)

League Club	Source	Date Signed	Seasons Played	Apps	Subs	Gls
Swindon T.	YT	•	97	0	1	0

MEECHAN David Anderson
West Calder, 10 November, 1943 (CF)

League Club	Source	Date Signed	Seasons Played	Apps	Subs	Gls
Sheffield Wed.	Burnley (Am)	12.60				
Scunthorpe U.	Tr	06.61				
York C.	Tr	06.63	63	6	-	0

MEEK George
Glasgow, 15 February, 1934 (W)

League Club	Source	Date Signed	Seasons Played	Apps	Subs	Gls
Leeds U.	Hamilton Academical	08.52	52-59	195	-	19
Walsall	L	01.54	53-54	44	-	6
Leicester C.	Tr	08.60	60	13	-	0
Walsall	Tr	07.61	61-64	128	-	22

MEENS Harold
Rotherham, 15 October, 1919 Died 1987 (CH)

League Club	Source	Date Signed	Seasons Played	Apps	Subs	Gls
Hull C.	Jnrs	10.38	38-51	146	-	0

MEESON David John
Oxford, 6 July, 1934 Died 1991 (G)

League Club	Source	Date Signed	Seasons Played	Apps	Subs	Gls
Wolverhampton W.	Oxford C.	02.52				
Reading	Tr	08.54	54-62	156	-	0
Coventry C.	Tr	09.62	62-64	24	-	0

MEGSON Donald Harry
Sale, 12 June, 1936 EF Lge (LB)

League Club	Source	Date Signed	Seasons Played	Apps	Subs	Gls
Sheffield Wed.	Jnrs	05.53	59-69	386	0	6
Bristol Rov.	Tr	03.70	69-70	31	0	1

MEGSON Gary John
Manchester, 2 May, 1959 (M)

League Club	Source	Date Signed	Seasons Played	Apps	Subs	Gls
Plymouth Arg.	App	05.77	77-79	78	0	10
Everton	Tr	12.79	79-80	20	2	2
Sheffield Wed.	Tr	08.81	81-83	123	0	13
Nottingham F.	Tr	08.84				
Newcastle U.	Tr	11.84	84-85	21	3	1
Sheffield Wed.	Tr	12.85	85-88	107	3	12
Manchester C.	Tr	01.89	88-91	78	4	2
Norwich C.	Tr	08.92	92-94	42	4	1
Lincoln C. (N/C)	Tr	08.95	95	2	0	0
Shrewsbury T. (N/C)	Tr	09.95	95	2	0	0

MEGSON Kevin Craig
Halifax, 1 July, 1971 (FB)

League Club	Source	Date Signed	Seasons Played	Apps	Subs	Gls
Bradford C.	YT	07.89	89-90	24	3	0
Halifax T.	Tr	03.91	90-92	37	4	1

MEHEW David Stephen
Camberley, 29 October, 1967 (M)

League Club	Source	Date Signed	Seasons Played	Apps	Subs	Gls
Bristol Rov.	Leeds U. (YT)	07.85	85-92	195	27	63
Exeter C.	L	03.94	93	5	2	0
Walsall	Tr	07.94	94	6	7	0

MEHMET David Nedjate
Camberwell, 2 December, 1960 (M)

League Club	Source	Date Signed	Seasons Played	Apps	Subs	Gls
Millwall	App	12.77	76-80	97	17	15
Charlton Ath.	Tampa Bay (USA)	01.82	81-82	29	0	2
Gillingham	Tr	03.83	82-85	128	4	39
Millwall	Tr	07.86	86-87	17	2	1

MEIJER Geert
Netherlands, 15 March, 1951 Dutch Int (W)

League Club	Source	Date Signed	Seasons Played	Apps	Subs	Gls
Bristol C.	Ajax (Neth)	03.79	78-79	12	3	2

MELDRUM Colin
Glasgow, 26 November, 1941 (LB)

League Club	Source	Date Signed	Seasons Played	Apps	Subs	Gls
Arsenal	Jnrs	12.58				
Watford	Tr	12.60	60-62	32	-	0
Reading	Tr	04.63	62-69	265	1	8
Cambridge U.	Tr	10.69	70	37	1	0
Workington	York C. (coach)	12.74	74	0	2	0

MELIA James
Liverpool, 1 November, 1937 E Sch/E Yth/EF Lge/E-2 (M)

League Club	Source	Date Signed	Seasons Played	Apps	Subs	Gls
Liverpool	Jnrs	11.54	55-63	269	-	76
Wolverhampton W.	Tr	03.64	63-64	24	-	4
Southampton	Tr	11.64	64-68	139	0	11
Aldershot	Tr	11.68	68-71	135	0	14
Crewe Alex.	Tr	02.72	71	2	2	0

MELL Stewart Albert
Doncaster, 15 October, 1957 E Semi Pro (F)

League Club	Source	Date Signed	Seasons Played	Apps	Subs	Gls
Doncaster Rov.	Appleby Frodingham	02.80	79-82	62	14	14
Halifax T.	Tr	07.83	83	22	8	8
Scarborough	Burton A.	07.86	87-88	30	9	8

MELLEDEW Stephen Thomas
Rochdale, 28 November, 1945 (F/M)

League Club	Source	Date Signed	Seasons Played	Apps	Subs	Gls
Rochdale	Whipp & Bourne	12.66	66-69	88	9	23
Everton	Tr	09.69				
Aldershot	Tr	07.71	71-73	90	2	27
Bury	Tr	11.73	73-74	14	6	2
Crewe Alex.	Tr	10.74	74-75	49	7	2
Rochdale	Tr	07.76	76-77	76	2	12

MELLING Terence
Billingham, 24 January, 1940 (IF)

League Club	Source	Date Signed	Seasons Played	Apps	Subs	Gls
Newcastle U.	Tow Law T.	12.65				
Watford	Tr	05.66	65-66	23	1	5
Newport Co.	Tr	02.67	66-67	34	0	14
Mansfield T.	Tr	11.67	67-68	33	0	7
Rochdale	Tr	09.68	68	20	0	8
Darlington	Tr	03.69	68-69	21	0	6

MELLISH Stuart Michael
Hyde, 19 November, 1969 (M)

League Club	Source	Date Signed	Seasons Played	Apps	Subs	Gls
Rochdale	YT	07.88	87-88	24	3	1

MELLON Michael Joseph
Paisley, 18 March, 1972 (M)

League Club	Source	Date Signed	Seasons Played	Apps	Subs	Gls
Bristol C.	YT	12.89	89-92	26	9	1
West Bromwich A.	Tr	02.93	92-94	38	7	6
Blackpool	Tr	11.94	94-97	123	1	14
Tranmere Rov.	Tr	10.97	97	24	9	2

MELLOR John Allan
Ashton-u-Lyne, 16 October, 1921 (WH)

League Club	Source	Date Signed	Seasons Played	Apps	Subs	Gls
Hull C.	Ashton U.	05.47	47-51	104	-	4

MELLOR Robert Brett
Huddersfield, 4 February, 1960 (CD)

League Club	Source	Date Signed	Seasons Played	Apps	Subs	Gls
Huddersfield T.	App	02.78	77	1	0	0
Barnsley	Tr	08.80				

MELLOR Ian
Manchester, 19 February, 1950 (W)

League Club	Source	Date Signed	Seasons Played	Apps	Subs	Gls
Manchester C.	Wythenshawe Amats	12.69	70-72	36	4	7
Norwich C.	Tr	03.73	72-73	28	1	2
Brighton & H.A.	Tr	04.74	74-77	116	6	31
Chester C.	Tr	02.78	77-78	38	2	11
Sheffield Wed.	Tr	06.79	79-81	54	16	11
Bradford C.	Tr	06.82	82-83	27	9	4

MELLOR Kenneth Edward
Leicester, 22 August, 1934 (CH)

League Club	Source	Date Signed	Seasons Played	Apps	Subs	Gls
Leicester C.		07.55				
Mansfield T.	Tr	07.57	57-58	66	-	0
Swindon T.	Tr	07.59	59-60	32	-	4

MELLOR Peter Joseph
Prestbury, 20 November, 1947 E Yth (G)

League Club	Source	Date Signed	Seasons Played	Apps	Subs	Gls
Burnley	Witton A.	04.69	69-71	69	0	0
Chesterfield	L	01.72	71	4	0	0
Fulham	Tr	02.72	71-76	190	0	0
Hereford U.	Tr	09.77	77	32	0	0
Portsmouth	Tr	07.78	78-80	129	0	0

MELLOR William
Manchester, 29 June, 1925 (FB)

League Club	Source	Date Signed	Seasons Played	Apps	Subs	Gls
Accrington St.	Droylsden	06.50	50-53	138	-	2

MELLOWS Michael Anthony
Woking, 14 November, 1947 E Amat/E Yth (M)

League Club	Source	Date Signed	Seasons Played	Apps	Subs	Gls
Reading (Am)	Sutton U.	09.70	70	14	2	2
Portsmouth	Winchester C.	09.73	73-77	174	7	16

MELROSE James Millsopp
Glasgow, 7 October, 1958 S Sch/Su21-8/SF Lge (F)

League Club	Source	Date Signed	Seasons Played	Apps	Subs	Gls
Leicester C.	Partick Thistle	07.80	80-82	57	15	21
Coventry C.	Tr	09.82	82	21	3	8
Wolverhampton W. (L)	Glasgow Celtic	09.84	84	6	1	2
Manchester C.	Glasgow Celtic	11.84	84-85	27	7	8
Charlton Ath.	Tr	03.86	85-87	44	4	19
Leeds U.	Tr	09.87	87	3	1	0
Shrewsbury T.	Tr	02.88	87-89	27	22	3

MELVANG Lars Mandrup
Seattle, USA, 3 April, 1969 (RWB)

League Club	Source	Date Signed	Seasons Played	Apps	Subs	Gls
Watford	Silkeborg (Den)	08.97	97	4	0	1

MELVILLE Alan Allistair
Hartlepool, 13 March, 1941 (CH)

League Club	Source	Date Signed	Seasons Played	Apps	Subs	Gls
Hartlepool U.	Jnrs	09.60	60-61	5	-	0

MELVILLE Andrew Roger
Swansea, 29 November, 1968 Wu21-2/W 'B'/W-32 (CD)

League Club	Source	Date Signed	Seasons Played	Apps	Subs	Gls
Swansea C.	YT	07.86	85-89	165	10	22
Oxford U.	Tr	07.90	90-92	135	0	13
Sunderland	Tr	08.93	93-97	160	0	12
Bradford C.	L	02.98	97	6	0	1

MELVILLE Leslie
Ormskirk, 29 November, 1930 E Yth (CH)

League Club	Source	Date Signed	Seasons Played	Apps	Subs	Gls
Everton	Jnrs	04.50				
Bournemouth	Tr	07.56	56-57	25	-	0
Oldham Ath.	Tr	03.58	57	2	-	0

MENDES-RODRIGUEZ Alberto
Nurnberg, Germany, 24 October, 1974 (F)

League Club	Source	Date Signed	Seasons Played	Apps	Subs	Gls
Arsenal	FC Feucht (Ger)	07.97	97	1	2	0

MENDEZ Gabriel
Argentina, 12 March, 1973 Australian Int (M)

League Club	Source	Date Signed	Seasons Played	Apps	Subs	Gls
Notts Co. (L)	Parrametta (Aus)	03.97	96	2	1	0

MENDHAM Peter Stanley
Kings Lynn, 9 April, 1960 (M)

League Club	Source	Date Signed	Seasons Played	Apps	Subs	Gls
Norwich C.	App	04.78	78-86	200	11	23

MENDONCA Clive Paul
Islington, 9 September, 1968 (F)

League Club	Source	Date Signed	Seasons Played	Apps	Subs	Gls
Sheffield U.	App	09.86	86-87	8	5	4
Doncaster Rov.	L	02.88	87	2	0	0
Rotherham U.	Tr	03.88	87-90	71	13	27
Sheffield U.	Tr	07.91	91	4	6	1
Grimsby T.	L	01.92	91	10	0	3
Grimsby T.	Tr	08.92	92-96	151	5	57
Charlton Ath.	Tr	05.97	97	40	0	23

MENMUIR William Fraser
Glasgow, 3 February, 1952 (M)

League Club	Source	Date Signed	Seasons Played	Apps	Subs	Gls
Bristol C.		06.69	69-70	1	1	0

MENZIES Norman
Washington, 20 June, 1926 (IF)

League Club	Source	Date Signed	Seasons Played	Apps	Subs	Gls
Barnsley	Hexham Hearts	10.49				
Aldershot	Tr	05.50	50-57	221	-	91

MENZIES Adam Ross
Rutherglen, 31 October, 1934 S Sch (HB)

League Club	Source	Date Signed	Seasons Played	Apps	Subs	Gls
Cardiff C.	Glasgow Rangers	08.57	57	1	-	0

MEOLA Antonio Michael
U.S.A., 21 February, 1969 USA Int (G)

League Club	Source	Date Signed	Seasons Played	Apps	Subs	Gls
Brighton & H.A. (N/C)	Missouri Ath. (USA)	08.90	90	1	0	0

MERCER Arthur David
Hull, 14 February, 1918 Died 1986 (W)

League Club	Source	Date Signed	Seasons Played	Apps	Subs	Gls
Torquay U.		02.46	46-48	66	-	8

MERCER James Robertson
Dunfermline, 17 March, 1935 (OR)

League Club	Source	Date Signed	Seasons Played	Apps	Subs	Gls
Bury	Rosyth R.	06.57	57-58	18	-	1
Crewe Alex.	Tr	06.59	59	3	-	0

MERCER Joseph
Ellesmere Port, 9 August, 1914 Died 1990 EF Lge/E-5 (WH)

League Club	Source	Date Signed	Seasons Played	Apps	Subs	Gls
Everton	Ellesmere Port	09.32	32-46	170	-	1
Arsenal	Tr	12.46	46-53	247	-	2

MERCER Keith
Lewisham, 14 October, 1956 (F)

League Club	Source	Date Signed	Seasons Played	Apps	Subs	Gls
Watford	App	09.74	72-79	109	25	46
Southend U.	Tr	02.80	79-82	132	0	35
Blackpool	Tr	08.83	83	31	0	9

MERCER Stanley
Tranmere, 11 September, 1919 (CF)

League Club	Source	Date Signed	Seasons Played	Apps	Subs	Gls
Leicester C.	Blackpool (Am)	11.44	46	1	-	0
Accrington St.	Tr	01.47	46-48	68	-	36
Mansfield T.	Tr	10.48	48	12	-	6

MERCER Stephen Jack
Barking, 1 May, 1965 (D)

League Club	Source	Date Signed	Seasons Played	Apps	Subs	Gls
Peterborough U.	Cambridge U. (N/C)	09.82	82	3	0	0

MERCER William
Liverpool, 22 May, 1969 (G)

League Club	Source	Date Signed	Seasons Played	Apps	Subs	Gls
Liverpool	YT	08.87				
Rotherham U.	Tr	02.89	89-94	104	0	0
Sheffield U.	Tr	10.94	94-95	4	0	0
Chesterfield	Tr	09.95	95-97	105	0	0

MEREDITH John Frederick
Hatfield (Yks), 23 September, 1940 (W)

League Club	Source	Date Signed	Seasons Played	Apps	Subs	Gls
Doncaster Rov.	Jnrs.	01.58	58-60	58	-	8
Sheffield Wed.	Tr	02.61	60	1	-	0
Chesterfield	Tr	07.62	62-63	81	-	6
Gillingham	Tr	03.64	63-68	227	1	7
Bournemouth	Tr	08.69	69-70	51	0	1

MEREDITH Robert Garfield
Swansea, 3 September, 1917 Died 1994 W Sch (OR)

League Club	Source	Date Signed	Seasons Played	Apps	Subs	Gls
Carlisle U.		01.47	46	1	-	0

MEREDITH Thomas James Anthony
Enfield, 27 October, 1977 (RB)

League Club	Source	Date Signed	Seasons Played	Apps	Subs	Gls
Peterborough U.	YT	07.96	95	1	1	0

MEREDITH Trevor George
Bridgnorth, 25 December, 1936 (OR)

League Club	Source	Date Signed	Seasons Played	Apps	Subs	Gls
Burnley	Kidderminster Hrs	11.57	59-63	37	-	8
Shrewsbury T.	Tr	04.64	64-71	229	6	41

MERRICK Alan Ronald
Birmingham, 20 June, 1950 E Yth (FB)

League Club	Source	Date Signed	Seasons Played	Apps	Subs	Gls
West Bromwich A.	App	08.67	68-75	131	8	5
Peterborough U.	L	09.75	75	5	0	0

MERRICK Geoffrey
Bristol, 29 April, 1951 E Sch (CD)

League Club	Source	Date Signed	Seasons Played	Apps	Subs	Gls
Bristol C.	App	08.68	67-81	361	6	10

MERRICK Gilbert (Gil) Harold
Birmingham 26 January, 1922 EF Lge/E-23 (G)

League Club	Source	Date Signed	Seasons Played	Apps	Subs	Gls
Birmingham C.	Solihull T.	08.39	46-59	485	-	0

MERRICK Neil Gilbert
Birmingham, 6 April, 1952 E Semi Pro (CD)

League Club	Source	Date Signed	Seasons Played	Apps	Subs	Gls
Bournemouth	Worcester C.	09.74	74	13	2	0

MERRIFIELD Royston Gordon
Mile End, 11 October, 1931 (W)

League Club	Source	Date Signed	Seasons Played	Apps	Subs	Gls
Chelsea	Rainham T.	02.54				
Millwall	Tr	06.56	56	2	-	0

MERRINGTON David Robert
Newcastle, 26 January, 1945 (CH)

League Club	Source	Date Signed	Seasons Played	Apps	Subs	Gls
Burnley	App	02.62	64-70	96	2	1
Bristol C.	Tr	07.71				

MERRITT Harold George
Ormskirk, 22 September, 1920 (IF)

League Club	Source	Date Signed	Seasons Played	Apps	Subs	Gls
Everton	Jnrs	12.37				
Leyton Orient	Tr	09.46	46	1	-	0

MERSON Paul Charles
Harlesden, 20 March, 1968 E Yth/Eu21-4/E 'B'/E-19 (F)

League Club	Source	Date Signed	Seasons Played	Apps	Subs	Gls
Arsenal	App	11.85	86-96	289	38	78
Brentford	L	01.87	86	6	1	0
Middlesbrough	Tr	07.97	97	45	0	12

MESSER Gary Michael
Consett, 22 September, 1979 (F)

League Club	Source	Date Signed	Seasons Played	Apps	Subs	Gls
Doncaster Rov.	YT	●	96-97	4	10	1

METCALF Colin Christopher Anthony
Norwich, 3 March, 1939 (CH)

League Club	Source	Date Signed	Seasons Played	Apps	Subs	Gls
Norwich C.	Norman O.B.	07.60	62-63	12	-	1
Southend U.	Tr	09.64	64	3	-	0

METCALF Mark Peter
Norwich, 25 September, 1965 (M)

League Club	Source	Date Signed	Seasons Played	Apps	Subs	Gls
Norwich C.	App	09.83	82	0	1	0

METCALF Matthew Adam
Norwich, 28 July, 1969 (F)

League Club	Source	Date Signed	Seasons Played	Apps	Subs	Gls
Brentford	Braintree T.	09.93	93	3	4	0

METCALF Michael
Liverpool, 24 May, 1939 (IF)

League Club	Source	Date Signed	Seasons Played	Apps	Subs	Gls
Wrexham	Everton (Am)	05.57	57-63	121	-	58
Chester C.	Tr	12.63	63-68	221	0	68

METCALFE John
Birmingham, 2 June, 1935 (W)

League Club	Source	Date Signed	Seasons Played	Apps	Subs	Gls
Birmingham C.	Jnrs	10.52	52	2	-	0
York C.	Tr	06.57	57	3	-	2
Walsall	Tr	07.58	58	2	-	0

METCALFE Ronald
South Shields, 8 December, 1947 (W)

League Club	Source	Date Signed	Seasons Played	Apps	Subs	Gls
Derby Co.	Jnrs	01.65	66	1	0	0

METCALFE Stuart Michael
Blackburn, 6 October, 1950 E Yth (M)

League Club	Source	Date Signed	Seasons Played	Apps	Subs	Gls
Blackburn Rov.	App	01.68	67-79	375	11	21
Carlisle U.	Tr	07.80	80	23	2	3
Blackburn Rov. (N/C)	Carolina (USA)	10.82	82	1	0	0
Crewe Alex. (N/C)	Tr	01.83	82	3	0	0

METCALFE Victor
Barrow, 3 February, 1922 EF Lge/E-2 (OL)

League Club	Source	Date Signed	Seasons Played	Apps	Subs	Gls
Huddersfield T.	Ravensthorpe	01.40	46-57	434	-	87
Hull C.	Tr	06.58	58-59	6	-	3

METCHICK David John
Bakewell, 14 August, 1943 E Yth (IF)

League Club	Source	Date Signed	Seasons Played	Apps	Subs	Gls
Fulham	Jnrs	08.61	61-64	47	-	9
Leyton Orient	Tr	12.64	64-66	75	0	15
Peterborough U.	Tr	03.67	66-67	38	0	6
Queens Park R.	Tr	08.68	68-69	0	3	1
Arsenal	Tr	09.70				
Brentford	Atlanta (USA)	09.73	73-74	57	4	4

METGOD Johannes (Johnny) Anthonius Bernardus
Netherlands, 27 February, 1958 Dutch Int (M)

League Club	Source	Date Signed	Seasons Played	Apps	Subs	Gls
Nottingham F.	Real Madrid (Sp)	08.84	84-86	113	3	15
Tottenham H.	Tr	07.87	87	5	7	0

METHLEY Irvin
Worsborough, 22 September, 1925 (FB)

League Club	Source	Date Signed	Seasons Played	Apps	Subs	Gls
Wolverhampton W.	Jnrs	10.42				
Walsall	Tr	03.46	46-50	113	-	0

METHVEN Colin John
India, 10 December, 1955 (CD)

League Club	Source	Date Signed	Seasons Played	Apps	Subs	Gls
Wigan Ath.	East Fife	10.79	79-85	295	1	21
Blackpool	Tr	07.86	86-89	166	7	11
Carlisle U.	L	09.90	90	12	0	0
Walsall	Tr	11.90	90-92	97	0	3

METTIOUI Ahmed
Morocco, 3 November, 1965 (W)

League Club	Source	Date Signed	Seasons Played	Apps	Subs	Gls
Crewe Alex.	Fath Union S.C.	07.92	92	1	2	0

MEYER Adrian Michael
Yate, 22 September, 1970 (CD)

League Club	Source	Date Signed	Seasons Played	Apps	Subs	Gls
Scarborough	YT	06.89	89-94	114	0	9

MEYER Barrie John
Bournemouth, 21 August, 1932 (IF)

League Club	Source	Date Signed	Seasons Played	Apps	Subs	Gls
Bristol Rov.	Jnrs	11.49	50-57	139	-	60
Plymouth Arg.	Tr	08.58	58	8	-	5
Newport Co.	Tr	02.59	58-60	69	-	27
Bristol C.	Tr	09.61	61-62	11	-	8

MICALLEF Constantinous (Tarki)
Cardiff, 24 January, 1961 W Sch/Wu21-3 (M)

League Club	Source	Date Signed	Seasons Played	Apps	Subs	Gls
Cardiff C.	App	01.79	78-82	67	14	11
Newport Co.	Tr	09.83	83	22	2	2
Gillingham (N/C)	Tr	08.84	84	2	0	0
Cardiff C.	Tr	09.84	84-85	26	14	1
Bristol Rov.	Tr	08.86	86	15	3	1

MICHAEL James David
Pontypridd, 28 October, 1978 W Yth (W)

League Club	Source	Date Signed	Seasons Played	Apps	Subs	Gls
Cardiff C.	YT	●	96	0	1	0

MICKLEWHITE Gary
Southwark, 21 March, 1961 (RM)

League Club	Source	Date Signed	Seasons Played	Apps	Subs	Gls
Manchester U.	App	03.78				
Queens Park R.	Tr	07.79	80-84	97	9	11
Derby Co.	Tr	02.85	84-92	223	17	31
Gillingham	Tr	07.93	93-95	78	17	3

MICKLEWRIGHT Andrew Alfred Joseph
Birmingham, 31 January, 1931 (IF)

League Club	Source	Date Signed	Seasons Played	Apps	Subs	Gls
Bristol Rov.	Smethwick	01.52	51-52	8	-	1
Bristol C.	Tr	05.53	53-54	39	-	17
Swindon T.	Tr	09.55	55-58	114	-	31
Exeter C.	Tr	07.59	59	38	-	11

MICKLEWRIGHT John Leslie
Stoke, 13 October, 1915 Died 1991 (WH)

League Club	Source	Date Signed	Seasons Played	Apps	Subs	Gls
Crewe Alex.	Stafford R.	09.46	46-49	71	-	0

MIDDLEBROUGH Alan
Wardle (Lancs), 4 December, 1925 (CF)

League Club	Source	Date Signed	Seasons Played	Apps	Subs	Gls
Bolton W.		07.46	46-47	5	-	1
Bradford C.	Tr	08.48	48	4	-	0
Rochdale	Tr	10.48	48-51	47	-	25

MIDDLEMASS Clive
Leeds, 25 August, 1944 (D)

League Club	Source	Date Signed	Seasons Played	Apps	Subs	Gls
Leeds U.	Jnrs	08.62				
Workington	Tr	11.63	63-69	168	1	6

MIDDLEMISS Ernest
Newcastle, 30 August, 1920 (CF)

League Club	Source	Date Signed	Seasons Played	Apps	Subs	Gls
Lincoln C.	South Shields	06.48	48	2	-	0

MIDDLETON Craig Dean
Nuneaton, 10 September, 1970 (M)

League Club	Source	Date Signed	Seasons Played	Apps	Subs	Gls
Coventry C.	YT	05.89	89-92	2	1	0
Cambridge U.	Tr	07.93	93-95	55	4	10
Cardiff C.	Tr	08.96	96-97	68	6	4

MIDDLETON Derek
Ashby-de-la-Zouch, 30 May, 1934 (WH)

League Club	Source	Date Signed	Seasons Played	Apps	Subs	Gls
York C.	Burton A.	11.58	58	1	-	0

MIDDLETON Frederick Thomas
Hartlepool, 2 August, 1930 (WH)

League Club	Source	Date Signed	Seasons Played	Apps	Subs	Gls
Newcastle U.	Jnrs	04.48				
Lincoln C.	Tr	05.54	54-62	300	-	16

MIDDLETON Henry (Harry)
Birmingham, 18 March, 1937 E Yth (CF)

League Club	Source	Date Signed	Seasons Played	Apps	Subs	Gls
Wolverhampton W.	Jnrs	08.54	55	1	-	0
Scunthorpe U.	Tr	09.59	59-60	29	-	11
Portsmouth	Tr	06.61	61	17	-	5
Shrewsbury T.	Tr	02.62	61-64	85	-	36
Mansfield T.	Tr	11.64	64-65	45	1	24
Walsall	Tr	03.66	65-67	56	3	27

MIDDLETON James
Blackridge, 25 April, 1922 (WH)

League Club	Source	Date Signed	Seasons Played	Apps	Subs	Gls
Bradford C.	Third Lanark	05.49	49	8	-	0

MIDDLETON John
Rawmarsh, 11 July, 1955 (CD)

League Club	Source	Date Signed	Seasons Played	Apps	Subs	Gls
Bradford C.	App	07.73	72-78	188	4	5

MIDDLETON John
Skegness, 24 December, 1956 E Yth/Eu21-3 (G)

League Club	Source	Date Signed	Seasons Played	Apps	Subs	Gls
Nottingham F.	App	11.74	74-77	90	0	0
Derby Co.	Tr	09.77	77-79	73	0	0

MIDDLETON Lee John
Nuneaton, 10 September, 1970 (CD)

League Club	Source	Date Signed	Seasons Played	Apps	Subs	Gls
Coventry C.	YT	05.89	89	0	2	0
Swindon T.	Tr	07.92				
Cambridge U. (N/C)	Tr	11.95	95	1	2	0

MIDDLETON Matthew Young
Jarrow, 24 October, 1907 Died 1979 (G)

League Club	Source	Date Signed	Seasons Played	Apps	Subs	Gls
Southport	Boldon Colly	02.31	31-32	63	-	0
Sunderland	Tr	08.33	33-38	57	-	0
Plymouth Arg.	Tr	05.39				
Bradford C.	Horden Colly	08.46	46-48	94	-	0
York C.	Tr	02.49	48-49	55	-	0

MIDDLETON Peter Watson
Rawmarsh, 13 September, 1948 Died 1977 (M)

League Club	Source	Date Signed	Seasons Played	Apps	Subs	Gls
Sheffield Wed.	App	09.65				
Bradford C.	Tr	06.68	68-72	127	4	25
Plymouth Arg.	Tr	09.72	72	1	0	1

MIDDLETON Raymond
Boldon, 6 September, 1919 Died 1977 E 'B' (G)

League Club	Source	Date Signed	Seasons Played	Apps	Subs	Gls
Chesterfield	Washington	10.37	38-50	250	-	0
Derby Co.	Tr	06.51	51-53	116	-	0

MIDDLETON Robert Rex
Retford, 8 December, 1933 (F)

League Club	Source	Date Signed	Seasons Played	Apps	Subs	Gls
Southend U.	Bulford U.	11.57	57	5	-	1
Workington	Luton T. (trial)	10.58	58	2	-	2
Swindon T.	Tr	12.58	58	5	-	0
Aldershot	Tr	07.59	59	5	-	0

MIDDLETON Stephen Roy
Portsmouth, 28 March, 1953 (G)

League Club	Source	Date Signed	Seasons Played	Apps	Subs	Gls
Southampton	App	07.70	73-76	24	0	0
Torquay U.	L	03.75	74	10	0	0
Portsmouth	Tr	07.77	77	26	0	0

MIDGLEY Craig Steven
Bradford, 24 May, 1976 (RW)

League Club	Source	Date Signed	Seasons Played	Apps	Subs	Gls
Bradford C.	YT	07.95	94-97	0	11	1
Scarborough	L	12.95	95	14	2	1
Scarborough	L	03.97	96	6	0	2
Darlington	L	12.97	97	1	0	0
Hartlepool U.	Tr	03.98	97	9	0	3

MIDWOOD Michael Adrian
Burnley, 19 April, 1976 (F)

League Club	Source	Date Signed	Seasons Played	Apps	Subs	Gls
Huddersfield T.	YT	07.94				
Huddersfield T.	Halifax T.	08.97	97	0	1	0

MIELCZAREK Raymond
Caernarfon, 10 February, 1946 Wu23-2/W-1 (CD)

League Club	Source	Date Signed	Seasons Played	Apps	Subs	Gls
Wrexham	Jnrs	05.64	64-67	76	0	0
Huddersfield T.	Tr	09.67	67-70	25	1	1
Rotherham U.	Tr	01.71	70-73	114	1	7

MIHAILOV Borislav (Bobby) Biserov
Bulgaria, 12 February, 1963 Bulgarian Int (G)

League Club	Source	Date Signed	Seasons Played	Apps	Subs	Gls
Reading	Botev Plovdiv (Bul)	09.95	95-96	24	0	0

MIHALY Ronald Raymond
Chesterfield, 14 October, 1952 (CD)

League Club	Source	Date Signed	Seasons Played	Apps	Subs	Gls
Chesterfield	Jnrs	08.71	71	4	0	0

MIKE Adrian Roosevelt
Manchester, 16 November, 1973 E Sch/E Yth (F)

League Club	Source	Date Signed	Seasons Played	Apps	Subs	Gls
Manchester C.	YT	07.92	91-94	5	11	2
Bury	L	03.93	92	5	2	1
Stockport Co.	Tr	08.95	95-96	4	5	0
Hartlepool U.	L	10.96	96	7	0	1
Doncaster Rov.	L	02.97	96	5	0	1
Doncaster Rov. (N/C)	Tr	08.97	97	42	0	4

MIKLOSKO Ludek
Czechoslovakia, 9 December, 1961 Czechoslovakian Int (G)

League Club	Source	Date Signed	Seasons Played	Apps	Subs	Gls
West Ham U.	Banik Ostrava (Cz)	02.90	89-97	315	0	0

MILBURN George William
Ashington, 24 June, 1910 Died 1980 (FB)

League Club	Source	Date Signed	Seasons Played	Apps	Subs	Gls
Leeds U.	Ashington	03.28	28-36	157	-	1
Chesterfield	Tr	05.37	37-47	105	-	16

MILBURN James
Morpeth, 21 September, 1919 Died 1985 (FB)

League Club	Source	Date Signed	Seasons Played	Apps	Subs	Gls
Leeds U.	Ashington	10.36	46-51	207	-	15
Bradford P.A.	Tr	06.52	52-54	90	-	10

MILBURN John (Jack)
Ashington, 18 March, 1908 Died 1979 (FB)

League Club	Source	Date Signed	Seasons Played	Apps	Subs	Gls
Leeds U.	Spen Black	11.27	29-38	386	-	28
Norwich C.	Tr	02.39	38	15	-	0
Bradford C.	Tr	10.46	46	14	-	3

MILBURN John (Jackie) Edward Thompson
Ashington, 11 May, 1924 Died 1988 EF Lge/E-13 (CF)

League Club	Source	Date Signed	Seasons Played	Apps	Subs	Gls
Newcastle U.	Ashington	08.43	46-56	353	-	177

MILBURN Stanley
Ashington, 27 October, 1926 E 'B'/EF Lge (FB)

League Club	Source	Date Signed	Seasons Played	Apps	Subs	Gls
Chesterfield	Ashington	01.47	46-51	179	-	0
Leicester C.	Tr	03.52	51-57	173	-	1
Rochdale	Tr	01.59	58-64	238	-	26

MILBURN William Renton Wakenshaw
Sunniside, 25 January, 1932 (HB)

League Club	Source	Date Signed	Seasons Played	Apps	Subs	Gls
Gateshead		04.55	56	2	-	0

MILDENHALL Stephen James
Swindon, 13 May, 1978 (G)

League Club	Source	Date Signed	Seasons Played	Apps	Subs	Gls
Swindon T.	YT	07.96	96-97	4	1	0

MILES Andrew
Tredegar, 25 May, 1961 (W)

League Club	Source	Date Signed	Seasons Played	Apps	Subs	Gls
Newport Co. (N/C)	Ebbw Vale	08.85	85	3	1	2

MILES Denis
Normanton, 6 August, 1936 (OR)

League Club	Source	Date Signed	Seasons Played	Apps	Subs	Gls
Bradford P.A.	Jnrs	09.53	53-54	24	-	1
Southport	Tr	06.55	55-56	51	-	12

MILES Jeffrey
Caldicot, 17 January, 1949 (G)

League Club	Source	Date Signed	Seasons Played	Apps	Subs	Gls
Newport Co. (Am)	Jnrs	04.68	67-68	4	0	0

MILES Sidney George
Bournemouth, 16 May, 1934 (HB)

League Club	Source	Date Signed	Seasons Played	Apps	Subs	Gls
Bournemouth		12.56	57	1	-	0

MILES Terence
Stoke, 7 May, 1937 (WH)

League Club	Source	Date Signed	Seasons Played	Apps	Subs	Gls
Port Vale	Milton Y.C.	06.55	56-67	358	7	17

MILKINS Albert John
Romford, 3 January, 1944 E Yth (G)

League Club	Source	Date Signed	Seasons Played	Apps	Subs	Gls
Portsmouth	Jnrs	05.61	60-73	344	0	0
Oxford U.	Tr	08.74	74-78	53	0	0

MILLAR Alexander (Ally)
Glasgow, 15 January, 1952 (M)

League Club	Source	Date Signed	Seasons Played	Apps	Subs	Gls
Barnsley	Benburb	02.71	70-79	273	16	17
York C.	Tr	07.80	80	11	1	0

MILLAR James
Falkirk, 21 December, 1927 (FB)

League Club	Source	Date Signed	Seasons Played	Apps	Subs	Gls
Crewe Alex.	Deal	08.58	58-59	56	-	1

MILLAR John
Coatbridge, 8 December, 1966 (M/FB)

League Club	Source	Date Signed	Seasons Played	Apps	Subs	Gls
Chelsea	Jnrs	08.84	85-86	11	0	0
Northampton T.	L	01.87	86	1	0	0
Blackburn Rov.	Tr	07.87	87-90	122	4	2

MILLAR John
Auchterderran, 31 December, 1927 Died 1991 (IF)

League Club	Source	Date Signed	Seasons Played	Apps	Subs	Gls
Bradford C.	Queen of South	10.48	49-51	44	-	7
Grimsby T.	Tr	05.52	52	5	-	2

MILLAR John Ross
Armadale, 25 October, 1923 Died 1986 (CF)

League Club	Source	Date Signed	Seasons Played	Apps	Subs	Gls
Bradford C.	Albion Rov.	06.49	49	3	-	1

MILLAR William Paul
Belfast, 16 November, 1966 NIu23-1 (M/F)

League Club	Source	Date Signed	Seasons Played	Apps	Subs	Gls
Port Vale	Portadown	12.88	89-90	19	21	5
Hereford U.	L	10.90	90	5	0	2
Cardiff C.	Tr	08.91	91-94	91	29	17

MILLAR Thomas Thomson
Edinburgh, 3 December, 1938 (FB)

League Club	Source	Date Signed	Seasons Played	Apps	Subs	Gls
Colchester U.	Bo'ness U.	06.59	59-61	46	-	4

MILLAR William
Mansfield, 7 February, 1952 (G)

League Club	Source	Date Signed	Seasons Played	Apps	Subs	Gls
Doncaster Rov. (Am)	Folkhouse O.B.	02.75	74	1	0	0

MILLAR William
Irvine, 24 July, 1924 Died 1995 (W)

League Club	Source	Date Signed	Seasons Played	Apps	Subs	Gls
Swindon T.	Stirling A.	08.50	50-52	75	-	18
Gillingham	Tr	07.53	53-55	91	-	35
Accrington St.	Tr	07.56	56	26	-	11

MILLARD Lance Julian
Bristol, 24 June, 1938 (G)

League Club	Source	Date Signed	Seasons Played	Apps	Subs	Gls
Aldershot		03.61	60	12	-	0
Barrow	Tr	07.64	64-65	52	0	0

MILLARD Leonard
Sedgley, 7 March, 1919 Died 1997 (FB)

League Club	Source	Date Signed	Seasons Played	Apps	Subs	Gls
West Bromwich A.	Sunbeam	05.37	46-57	436	-	7

MILLARD Robert
South Shields, 2 June, 1927 (IF)

League Club	Source	Date Signed	Seasons Played	Apps	Subs	Gls
Middlesbrough		12.45				
Reading	Blyth Spartans	06.49	49	2	-	0
Walsall	Tr	06.50	50	10	-	1

MILLBANK Joseph Henry
Edmonton, 30 September, 1919 (CH)

League Club	Source	Date Signed	Seasons Played	Apps	Subs	Gls
Wolverhampton W.		07.38				
Crystal Palace	Tr	08.39	46-47	38	-	1
Queens Park R.	Tr	07.48	48	1	-	0

MILLEN Keith Derek
Croydon, 26 September, 1966 (CD)

League Club	Source	Date Signed	Seasons Played	Apps	Subs	Gls
Brentford	Jnrs	08.84	84-92	301	4	17
Watford	Tr	03.94	93-97	153	1	5

MILLER Alan John
Epping, 29 March, 1970 E Sch/Eu21-4 (G)

League Club	Source	Date Signed	Seasons Played	Apps	Subs	Gls
Arsenal	YT	05.88	92-93	6	2	0
Plymouth Arg.	L	11.88	88	13	0	0
West Bromwich A.	L	08.91	91	3	0	0
Birmingham C.	L	12.91	91	15	0	0
Middlesbrough	Tr	08.94	94-96	57	0	0
Grimsby T.	L	01.97	96	3	0	0
West Bromwich A.	Tr	02.97	96-97	53	0	0

MILLER Alan John
Preston, 13 September, 1970 (W)

League Club	Source	Date Signed	Seasons Played	Apps	Subs	Gls
Torquay U. (N/C)	Bury (YT)	08.89	89	3	1	0

MILLER Alfred George Abraham
Portsmouth, 5 March, 1917 (WH)

League Club	Source	Date Signed	Seasons Played	Apps	Subs	Gls
Portsmouth	Jnrs	11.35				
Southport	Tr	10.37	37-38	32	-	2
Plymouth Arg.	Tr	07.39	46-47	9	-	0

MILLER James Alistair Williamson
Glasgow, 24 January, 1936 (OL)

League Club	Source	Date Signed	Seasons Played	Apps	Subs	Gls
Brighton & H. A.	St Mirren	04.62	61	1	-	0
Norwich C.	Tr	05.62	62-63	23	-	2

MILLER Anthony William
Chelmsford, 26 October, 1937 (W)

League Club	Source	Date Signed	Seasons Played	Apps	Subs	Gls
Colchester U.	Jnrs	05.58	63	1	-	0

MILLER Archibald
Larkhall, 5 September, 1913 S-1 (WH)

League Club	Source	Date Signed	Seasons Played	Apps	Subs	Gls
Blackburn Rov.	Hearts	11.47	47	6	-	0
Carlisle U.	Kilmarnock	09.50	50	1	-	0
Workington	Hearts	02.52				

MILLER Brian George
Burnley, 19 January, 1937 Eu23-3/EF Lge/E-1 (WH)

League Club	Source	Date Signed	Seasons Played	Apps	Subs	Gls
Burnley	Jnrs	02.54	55-66	379	0	29

MILLER Colin Fyfe
Lanark, 4 October, 1964 Canadian Int (M)

League Club	Source	Date Signed	Seasons Played	Apps	Subs	Gls
Doncaster Rov.	Glasgow Rangers	12.86	86-87	61	0	3

MILLER David
Middlesbrough, 21 January, 1921 Died 1989 (WH)

League Club	Source	Date Signed	Seasons Played	Apps	Subs	Gls
Middlesbrough	Jnrs	09.38				
Wolverhampton W.	Tr	08.45	46	2	-	0
Derby Co.	Tr	04.47	47	1	-	0
Doncaster Rov.	Tr	01.48	47-52	140	-	3
Aldershot	Tr	03.54	53	11	-	0

MILLER David Brian
Burnley, 8 January, 1964 (D/M)

League Club	Source	Date Signed	Seasons Played	Apps	Subs	Gls
Burnley	App	01.82	82-84	27	5	3
Crewe Alex.	L	03.83	82	3	0	0
Tranmere Rov.	Tr	07.85	85	25	4	1
Preston N. E.	Colne Dynamoes	12.86	86-89	50	8	2
Burnley	L	02.89	88	4	0	0
Carlisle U.	Tr	09.89	89-91	108	1	7
Stockport Co.	Tr	03.92	91-94	72	9	1
Wigan Ath.	Tr	10.94	94-95	35	3	3

MILLER Edward
Ulverston, 21 June, 1920 (IF)

League Club	Source	Date Signed	Seasons Played	Apps	Subs	Gls
Barrow	Ulverston	05.46	46-50	124	-	32

MILLER George
Larkhall, 20 May, 1939 SF Lge (WH)

League Club	Source	Date Signed	Seasons Played	Apps	Subs	Gls
Wolverhampton W.	Dunfermline Ath.	10.64	64-65	37	0	3

MILLER Ernest George
South Africa, 17 October, 1927 (IF)

League Club	Source	Date Signed	Seasons Played	Apps	Subs	Gls
Leeds U.	Arcadia (SA)	11.50	50-51	13	-	1
Workington	Tr	03.52	51	11	-	0

MILLER Graham Joseph Patrick
South Africa, 25 August, 1927 (CF)

League Club	Source	Date Signed	Seasons Played	Apps	Subs	Gls
Workington		12.52	52	8	-	1

MILLER Ian
Perth, 13 May, 1955 (RW)

League Club	Source	Date Signed	Seasons Played	Apps	Subs	Gls
Bury	Jnrs	08.73	73	9	6	0
Nottingham F.	Tr	08.74				
Doncaster Rov.	Tr	08.75	75-77	124	0	14
Swindon T.	Tr	07.78	78-80	123	4	9
Blackburn Rov.	Tr	08.81	81-88	252	16	16
Port Vale	Tr	07.89	89	14	7	1
Scunthorpe U.	Tr	08.90	90	8	4	0

MILLER John Tony
Ipswich, 21 September, 1950 (W)

League Club	Source	Date Signed	Seasons Played	Apps	Subs	Gls
Ipswich T.	Jnrs	07.68	68-73	38	13	2
Norwich C.	Tr	10.74	74-75	22	1	3
Mansfield T.	Tr	07.76	76-79	109	4	14
Port Vale (N/C)	Tr	09.80	80	22	4	4

MILLER Joseph McSpirits
Glasgow, 2 October, 1934 (OL)

League Club	Source	Date Signed	Seasons Played	Apps	Subs	Gls
Swindon T.	Hamilton Academical	06.56	56	12	-	0

MILLER Keith Raymond
Lewisham, 26 January, 1948 (M)

League Club	Source	Date Signed	Seasons Played	Apps	Subs	Gls
West Ham U.	Walthamstow Ave.	09.65	68-69	1	2	0
Bournemouth	Tr	07.70	70-79	381	2	19

MILLER Kevin
Falmouth, 15 March, 1969 (G)

League Club	Source	Date Signed	Seasons Played	Apps	Subs	Gls
Exeter C.	Newquay	03.89	88-92	163	0	0
Birmingham C.	Tr	05.93	93	24	0	0
Watford	Tr	08.94	94-96	128	0	0
Crystal Palace	Tr	07.97	97	38	0	0

MILLER Lumley Robert
Blaydon, 3 August, 1938 (W)

League Club	Source	Date Signed	Seasons Played	Apps	Subs	Gls
Sheffield U.		07.62				
Hartlepool U.	Tr	11.62	62	9	-	2

MILLER Mark John
Tynemouth, 22 September, 1962 (W)

League Club	Source	Date Signed	Seasons Played	Apps	Subs	Gls
Gillingham	Whitley Bay	10.81	81-82	5	4	1
Doncaster Rov.	Whitley Bay	08.83	83	21	9	4
Darlington	Tr	08.84	84	4	3	1

MILLER Paul Anthony
Woking, 31 January, 1968 (F)

League Club	Source	Date Signed	Seasons Played	Apps	Subs	Gls
Wimbledon	Yeovil T.	08.87	87-92	65	15	10
Newport Co.	L	10.87	87	6	0	2
Bristol C.	L	01.90	89	0	3	0
Bristol Rov.	Tr	08.94	94-96	100	5	22
Lincoln C.	Tr	08.97	97	20	4	2

MILLER Paul Richard
Stepney, 11 October, 1959 (CD)

League Club	Source	Date Signed	Seasons Played	Apps	Subs	Gls
Tottenham H.	App	05.77	78-86	206	2	7
Charlton Ath.	Tr	02.87	86-88	40	2	2
Watford	Tr	10.88	88	20	0	1
Bournemouth	Tr	08.89	89-90	43	4	1
Brentford	L	11.89	89	3	0	0
Swansea C.	Tr	01.91	90	8	4	0

MILLER Joseph Paul
Wolverhampton, 9 December, 1940 Died 1963 (G)

League Club	Source	Date Signed	Seasons Played	Apps	Subs	Gls
Shrewsbury T.	St Nicks B.C.	07.59	59-62	77	-	0

MILLER Peter Derek
Hoyland, 4 December, 1929 (HB)

League Club	Source	Date Signed	Seasons Played	Apps	Subs	Gls
Bradford C.		08.52	52-55	18	-	2

MILLER Ralph Ernest
Slough, 22 June, 1941 (D)

League Club	Source	Date Signed	Seasons Played	Apps	Subs	Gls
Charlton Ath.	Slough T.	09.63	64	8	-	0
Gillingham	Tr	05.65	65-67	103	0	4
Bournemouth	Tr	07.68	68-70	71	1	1

MILLER Robert James
Manchester, 3 November, 1972 (LB)

League Club	Source	Date Signed	Seasons Played	Apps	Subs	Gls
Oldham Ath.	YT	07.91				
Hull C.	Tr	10.92	92-93	22	6	0

MILLER Roger Lucas
Rushden, 18 August, 1938 (F)

League Club	Source	Date Signed	Seasons Played	Apps	Subs	Gls
Northampton T.	Jnrs	11.56	56-58	4	-	1

MILLER Thomas William
Easington, 8 January, 1979 (M)

League Club	Source	Date Signed	Seasons Played	Apps	Subs	Gls
Hartlepool U.	YT	07.97	97	11	2	1

MILLER Walter
Cornforth (Dm), 11 August, 1930 (WH)

League Club	Source	Date Signed	Seasons Played	Apps	Subs	Gls
Hartlepool U.		09.48	49	1	-	0
Luton T.	Spennymoor U.	02.52				

MILLETT Glynne Alexander
Pontypool, 13 October, 1968 (W)

League Club	Source	Date Signed	Seasons Played	Apps	Subs	Gls
Newport Co.	YT	07.87	86-87	23	14	2

MILLETT Michael Paul
Wigan, 22 September, 1977 Died 1995 E Sch/E Yth (D)

League Club	Source	Date Signed	Seasons Played	Apps	Subs	Gls
Wigan Ath.	YT	10.94	94	1	1	0

MILLIGAN Charles (Chic) Campbell
Ardrossan, 26 July, 1930 (CH)

League Club	Source	Date Signed	Seasons Played	Apps	Subs	Gls
Colchester U.	Ardrossan Winton	05.56	56-60	185	-	3

MILLIGAN Dudley
South Africa, 7 November, 1916 NI-1 (CF)

League Club	Source	Date Signed	Seasons Played	Apps	Subs	Gls
Chesterfield	Clyde	11.38	38-46	47	-	18
Bournemouth	Tr	08.47	47-48	45	-	26
Walsall	Tr	10.48	48	5	-	1

MILLIGAN Laurence Courtney
Liverpool, 20 April, 1958 (FB)

League Club	Source	Date Signed	Seasons Played	Apps	Subs	Gls
Blackpool	App	04.76	76-78	19	0	0
Portsmouth	L	03.79	78	7	0	0
Rochdale	Aldershot (N/C)	10.79	79	8	1	0

MILLIGAN Michael Joseph
Manchester, 20 February, 1967 IRu21-1/IRu23-1/IR 'B'/IR-1 (M)

League Club	Source	Date Signed	Seasons Played	Apps	Subs	Gls
Oldham Ath.	YT	02.85	85-89	161	1	17
Everton	Tr	08.90	90	16	1	1
Oldham Ath.	Tr	07.91	91-93	117	0	6
Norwich C.	Tr	06.94	94-97	103	8	5

MILLIGAN Ross
Dumfries, 2 June, 1978 (FB)

League Club	Source	Date Signed	Seasons Played	Apps	Subs	Gls
Carlisle U.	Glasgow Rangers	07.97	97	2	5	0

MILLIGAN Stephen Jonathan Francis
Hyde, 13 June, 1973 (D)

League Club	Source	Date Signed	Seasons Played	Apps	Subs	Gls
Rochdale	YT	●	89	5	0	1

MILLIGAN Terence John
Manchester, 10 January, 1966 (M)

League Club	Source	Date Signed	Seasons Played	Apps	Subs	Gls
Manchester C.	App	11.83				
Oldham Ath.	New Zealand	02.86				
Crewe Alex.	Tr	07.86	86-87	71	6	5

MILLIN Alfred
Rotherham, 18 December, 1933 (FB)

League Club	Source	Date Signed	Seasons Played	Apps	Subs	Gls
Derby Co.	Jnrs	08.51	55	1	-	0

MILLINGTON Anthony Horace
Hawarden, 5 June, 1943 Wu23-4/W-21 (G)

League Club	Source	Date Signed	Seasons Played	Apps	Subs	Gls
West Bromwich A.	Jnrs	07.60	61-62	40	-	0
Crystal Palace	Tr	10.64	64-65	16	0	0
Peterborough U.	Tr	03.66	66-68	118	0	0
Swansea C .	Tr	07.69	69-73	178	0	0

MILLINGTON Grenville Rodney
Hawarden, 10 December, 1951 W Amat (G)

League Club	Source	Date Signed	Seasons Played	Apps	Subs	Gls
Chester C. (Am)	Rhyl	07.68	68	1	0	0
Chester C.	Witton A.	09.73	73-82	289	0	0
Wrexham (N/C)	Oswestry T.	12.83	83	13	0	0

MILLINGTON John Henry
Coseley, 21 February, 1930 (LH)

League Club	Source	Date Signed	Seasons Played	Apps	Subs	Gls
Aston Villa	Jnrs	09.48				
Walsall	Tr	07.51	51-52	23	-	0

MILLINGTON Ralph Victor
Bebington, 18 June, 1930 (CH)

League Club	Source	Date Signed	Seasons Played	Apps	Subs	Gls
Tranmere Rov.	Neston	01.50	50-60	357	-	3

MILLION Esmond
Morpeth, 15 March, 1938 (G)

League Club	Source	Date Signed	Seasons Played	Apps	Subs	Gls
Middlesbrough	Amble Jnrs	05.56	56-61	52	-	0
Bristol Rov.	Tr	06.62	62	38	-	0

MILLS Brian
Stafford, 26 December, 1971 E Yth (F)

League Club	Source	Date Signed	Seasons Played	Apps	Subs	Gls
Port Vale	YT	04.90	90-91	14	9	4

MILLS Daniel John
Norwich, 18 May, 1977 E Yth (FB)

League Club	Source	Date Signed	Seasons Played	Apps	Subs	Gls
Norwich C.	YT	11.94	95-97	46	20	0
Charlton Ath.	Tr	03.98	97	9	0	1

MILLS Daniel Raymond
Sidcup, 13 February, 1975 (W)

League Club	Source	Date Signed	Seasons Played	Apps	Subs	Gls
Charlton Ath.	YT	07.93				
Barnet		09.95	95-97	10	17	0

MILLS David John
Whitby, 6 December, 1951 Eu23-8/E 'B' (F)

League Club	Source	Date Signed	Seasons Played	Apps	Subs	Gls
Middlesbrough	App	12.68	68-78	278	18	76
West Bromwich A.	Tr	01.79	78-82	44	15	6
Newcastle U.	L	01.82	81	23	0	4
Sheffield Wed.	Tr	01.83	82	15	0	3
Newcastle U.	Tr	08.83	83	10	6	5
Middlesbrough	Tr	06.84	84	31	1	14
Darlington (N/C)	Tr	08.86	86	12	5	2

MILLS Donald
Maltby, 17 August, 1926 Died 1994 (IF)

League Club	Source	Date Signed	Seasons Played	Apps	Subs	Gls
Queens Park R.		08.46	46-48	45	-	6
Torquay U.	Tr	03.49	48-49	34	-	13
Queens Park R.	Tr	01.50	49-50	31	-	3
Cardiff C.	Tr	02.51	50	1	-	0
Leeds U.	Tr	09.51	51-52	34	-	9
Torquay U.	Tr	12.52	52-61	308	-	68

MILLS Gary Roland
Northampton, 11 November, 1961 E Sch/E Yth/Eu21-2 (W/M)

League Club	Source	Date Signed	Seasons Played	Apps	Subs	Gls
Nottingham F.	App	11.78	78-81	50	8	8
Derby Co. (L)	Seatle (USA)	10.82	82	18	0	2
Nottingham F.	Seatle (USA)	12.83	83-86	63	15	4
Notts Co.	Tr	08.87	87-88	75	0	8
Leicester C.	Tr	03.89	88-94	195	5	16
Notts Co.	Tr	09.94	94-95	44	3	0

MILLS Henry (Harry)
Bishop Auckland, 23 July, 1922 (F)

League Club	Source	Date Signed	Seasons Played	Apps	Subs	Gls
Sheffield U.		06.46	46	3	-	2
Rotherham U.	Tr	03.48	47	6	-	3
Rochdale	Tunbridge Wells	04.51	50	1	-	0
Halifax T.	Tr	08.52				

MILLS Henry Owen
Blyth, 23 August, 1922 Died 1990 (G)

League Club	Source	Date Signed	Seasons Played	Apps	Subs	Gls
Huddersfield T.	Blyth Spartans	03.48	47-55	157	-	0
Halifax T	Tr	12.55	55-56	26	-	0

MILLS James
Rotherham, 30 September, 1915 Died 1994 (WH)

League Club	Source	Date Signed	Seasons Played	Apps	Subs	Gls
Rotherham U.	Dinnington Colly	08.37	37-38	53	-	4
Hull C.	Tr	10.46	46-47	42	-	1
Halifax T.	Tr	12.47	47	19	-	0

MILLS John
Flint, 19 December, 1920 Died 1982 (RB)

League Club	Source	Date Signed	Seasons Played	Apps	Subs	Gls
Chester C.		05.46	46	3	-	0

MILLS Keith
Newcastle, 30 December, 1963 (M)

League Club	Source	Date Signed	Seasons Played	Apps	Subs	Gls
Carlisle U. (N/C)	North Shields	02.88	87	0	1	0

MILLS Keith David
Egham, 29 December, 1942 (WH)

League Club	Source	Date Signed	Seasons Played	Apps	Subs	Gls
Grimsby T.	Jnrs	01.60	60	2	-	0

MILLS Rowan **Lee**
Mexborough, 10 July, 1970 (F)

League Club	Source	Date Signed	Seasons Played	Apps	Subs	Gls
Wolverhampton W.	Stocksbridge P.S.	12.92	93-94	12	13	2
Derby Co.	Tr	02.95	94	16	0	7
Port Vale	Tr	08.95	95-97	81	28	35

MILLS Michael Denis
Godalming, 4 January, 1949 E Yth/Eu23-5/EF Lge/E-42 (FB)

League Club	Source	Date Signed	Seasons Played	Apps	Subs	Gls
Ipswich T.	Portsmouth (App)	02.66	65-82	588	3	22
Southampton	Tr	11.82	82-84	103	0	3
Stoke C.	Tr	07.85	85-87	38	0	0

MILLS Neil
Littleborough, 27 October, 1963 (F)

League Club	Source	Date Signed	Seasons Played	Apps	Subs	Gls
Rochdale	Tin Bobbins	08.86	86	4	6	0
Stockport Co. (N/C)	Tr	08.87	87	5	2	0

MILLS Robert Brian
Edmonton, 16 March, 1955 (M)

League Club	Source	Date Signed	Seasons Played	Apps	Subs	Gls
Colchester U.	App	12.72	71-73	20	6	0

MILLS Ronald (Roly) Walter George
Daventry, 22 June, 1933 E Yth (OR/WH)

League Club	Source	Date Signed	Seasons Played	Apps	Subs	Gls
Northampton T.	Jnrs	05.51	54-63	305	-	30

MILLS Sean Douglas
Ebbw Vale, 1 June, 1968 (M)

League Club	Source	Date Signed	Seasons Played	Apps	Subs	Gls
Newport Co.	Sunderland (App)	08.86	86	5	2	0

MILLS Simon Ashley
Sheffield, 16 August, 1964 E Yth (RB/M)

League Club	Source	Date Signed	Seasons Played	Apps	Subs	Gls
Sheffield Wed.	App	08.82	82-84	1	4	0
York C.	Tr	06.85	85-87	97	2	4
Port Vale	Tr	12.87	87-92	180	4	8

MILLS Stephen John
Portsmouth, 9 December, 1953 Died 1988 Eu23-1 (FB)

League Club	Source	Date Signed	Seasons Played	Apps	Subs	Gls
Southampton	App	07.71	72-76	57	4	0

MILLWARD Horace **Douglas**
Sheffield, 10 August, 1931 (IF)

League Club	Source	Date Signed	Seasons Played	Apps	Subs	Gls
Southampton	Doncaster Rov. (Am)	02.52				
Ipswich T.	Tr	07.55	55-62	143	-	35

MILNE Alexander Soutar
Dundee, 4 June, 1937 Su23-1 (FB)

League Club	Source	Date Signed	Seasons Played	Apps	Subs	Gls
Cardiff C.	Arbroath	03.57	57-64	172	-	1

MILNE Gordon
Preston, 29 March, 1937 EF Lge/E-14 (WH)

League Club	Source	Date Signed	Seasons Played	Apps	Subs	Gls
Preston N. E.	Morecambe	01.56	56-60	81	-	3
Liverpool	Tr	09.60	60-66	234	2	18
Blackpool	Tr	05.67	67-69	60	4	4

MILNE John Buchanan
Rosehearty, 27 April, 1911 Died 1994 (FB)

League Club	Source	Date Signed	Seasons Played	Apps	Subs	Gls
Plymouth Arg.	Fraserburgh	05.33	34-36	3	-	0
Southend U.	Tr	06.37	37-38	66	-	1
Barrow	Tr	08.46	46	33	-	0
Oldham Ath.	Tr	08.47	47	13	-	0

MILNE Maurice
Dundee, 21 October, 1932 (OL)

League Club	Source	Date Signed	Seasons Played	Apps	Subs	Gls
Norwich C.	Dundee U.	05.57	57	5	-	0

MILNE Michael
Aberdeen, 17 August, 1959 (D)

League Club	Source	Date Signed	Seasons Played	Apps	Subs	Gls
Sunderland	App	05.77				
Rochdale		02.79	78	1	1	0

MILNE Ralph
Dundee, 13 May, 1961 S Yth/Su21-3 (W)

League Club	Source	Date Signed	Seasons Played	Apps	Subs	Gls
Charlton Ath.	Dundee U.	01.87	86-87	19	3	0
Bristol C.	Tr	01.88	87-88	29	1	6
Manchester U.	Tr	11.88	88-89	19	4	3

MILNER Alfred
Harrogate, 6 February, 1919 (OR)

League Club	Source	Date Signed	Seasons Played	Apps	Subs	Gls
Aldershot		08.46	46	7	-	1
Darlington		03.48	47-48	28	-	4

MILNER Andrew John
Kendal, 10 February, 1967 (W/F)

League Club	Source	Date Signed	Seasons Played	Apps	Subs	Gls
Manchester C.	Netherfield	01.89				
Rochdale	Tr	01.90	89-93	103	24	25
Chester C.	Tr	08.94	94-97	106	19	24

MILNER James Edward
Newcastle, 3 February, 1933 (IF)

League Club	Source	Date Signed	Seasons Played	Apps	Subs	Gls
Burnley	Blyth Spartans	12.52	53	1	-	0
Darlington	Tr	12.57	57-60	148	-	27
Accrington St	Tr	09.61				
Tranmere Rov.	Tr	06.62	62	16	-	3

MILNER John
Huddersfield, 14 May, 1942 (WH)

League Club	Source	Date Signed	Seasons Played	Apps	Subs	Gls
Huddersfield T.	Jnrs	05.59	60-62	17	-	0
Lincoln C.	Tr	10.63	63-66	109	0	6
Bradford P.A.	Tr	02.67	66	6	2	0

MILNER Jonathan Robert
Mansfield, 30 March, 1981 (F)

League Club	Source	Date Signed	Seasons Played	Apps	Subs	Gls
Mansfield T.	YT	●	97	1	6	0

MILNER Michael
Hull, 21 September, 1939 (CH)

League Club	Source	Date Signed	Seasons Played	Apps	Subs	Gls
Hull C.	Jnrs	07.57	58-67	160	0	0
Stockport Co.	Tr	07.68	68	41	0	0
Barrow	Tr	09.69	69	11	0	0
Bradford C.	Tr	12.69	69	0	1	0

MILOSEVIC Savo
Yugoslavia, 2 September, 1973 Yugoslav Int (F)

League Club	Source	Date Signed	Seasons Played	Apps	Subs	Gls
Aston Villa	Partizan Belgrade (Yug)	07.95	95-97	84	6	27

MILSOM Paul Jason
Bristol, 5 October, 1974 (F)

League Club	Source	Date Signed	Seasons Played	Apps	Subs	Gls
Bristol C.	YT	07.93	93	1	2	0
Cardiff C. (N/C)	Tr	03.95	94	1	2	0

MILTON Clement **Arthur**
Bristol, 10 March, 1928 E-1 (OR)

League Club	Source	Date Signed	Seasons Played	Apps	Subs	Gls
Arsenal	Jnrs	07.46	50-54	75	-	18
Bristol C.	Tr	02.55	54	14	-	3

MILTON Roy
Brixham, 27 November, 1934 (G)

League Club	Source	Date Signed	Seasons Played	Apps	Subs	Gls
Bury	Jnrs	10.52				
Torquay U.	Tr	08.56	56	1	-	0

MILTON Simon Charles
Fulham, 23 August, 1963 (M)

League Club	Source	Date Signed	Seasons Played	Apps	Subs	Gls
Ipswich T.	Bury T.	07.87	87-97	217	64	48
Exeter C.	L	11.87	87	2	0	3
Torquay U.	L	03.88	87	4	0	1

MILTON Stephen
Fullham, 13 April, 1963 (F)

League Club	Source	Date Signed	Seasons Played	Apps	Subs	Gls
West Ham U.	App	04.81				
Fulham	Whyteleafe	10.89	89-91	39	19	9

MIMMS Robert Andrew
York, 12 October, 1963 Eu21-3 (G)

League Club	Source	Date Signed	Seasons Played	Apps	Subs	Gls
Halifax T.	App	08.81				
Rotherham U.	Tr	11.81	81-84	83	0	0
Everton	Tr	06.85	85-87	29	0	0
Notts Co.	L	03.86	85	2	0	0
Sunderland	L	12.86	86	4	0	0
Blackburn Rov.	L	01.87	86	6	0	0
Manchester C.	L	09.87	87	3	0	0
Tottenham H.	Tr	02.88	87-89	37	0	0
Blackburn Rov.	Tr	12.90	90-95	126	2	0
Crystal Palace (N/C)	Tr	08.96	96	1	0	0
Preston N.E.	Tr	09.96	96	27	0	0
Rotherham U.	Tr	08.97	97	43	0	0

MINETT Jason Keith
Peterborough, 12 August, 1971 (LB/M)

League Club	Source	Date Signed	Seasons Played	Apps	Subs	Gls
Norwich C.	YT	07.89	90-92	0	3	0
Exeter C.	Tr	03.93	92-94	83	5	3
Lincoln C.	Tr	07.95	95-96	41	5	5
Exeter C.	Tr	01.97	96-97	19	0	0

MINNOCK John Joseph
Tullamore (Ire), 12 November, 1949 IRu23-2 (W)

League Club	Source	Date Signed	Seasons Played	Apps	Subs	Gls
Charlton Ath.	St Patricks Ath.	02.69	69	0	1	0

MINSHULL Raymond
Bolton, 15 July, 1920 (G)

League Club	Source	Date Signed	Seasons Played	Apps	Subs	Gls
Liverpool	High Park	09.46	46-49	28	-	0
Southport	Tr	07.51	51-57	217	-	0
Bradford P. A.	Tr	12.57	57-58	28	-	0

MINTO Scott Christopher
Heswall, 6 August, 1971 E Yth/Eu21-6 (W/LB)

League Club	Source	Date Signed	Seasons Played	Apps	Subs	Gls
Charlton Ath.	YT	01.89	88-93	171	9	7
Chelsea	Tr	05.94	94-96	53	1	4

MINTON Albert Edward
Walsall, 22 September, 1937 E Yth (CF)

League Club	Source	Date Signed	Seasons Played	Apps	Subs	Gls
Blackpool	Derby Co. (Am)	10.54				
Scunthorpe U.	Tr	07.57	57-58	5	-	2
Doncaster Rov.	Tr	12.58	58	11	-	2

MINTON Jeffrey Simon Thompson
Hackney, 28 December, 1973 (M)

League Club	Source	Date Signed	Seasons Played	Apps	Subs	Gls
Tottenham H.	YT	01.92	91	2	0	1
Brighton & H.A.	Tr	07.94	94-97	132	7	22

MINTON Roger Christopher
Birmingham, 4 June, 1951 (FB)

League Club	Source	Date Signed	Seasons Played	Apps	Subs	Gls
West Bromwich A.	App	06.69	70-74	24	2	1

[MIRANDINHA] Da Silva Francisco Ernandi Lima
Brazil, 2 July, 1959 Brazilian Int (F)

League Club	Source	Date Signed	Seasons Played	Apps	Subs	Gls
Newcastle U.	Palmeiras (Br)	08.87	87-88	47	7	20

MIROCEVIC Anton
Yugoslavia, 6 August, 1952 Yugoslav Int (M)

League Club	Source	Date Signed	Seasons Played	Apps	Subs	Gls
Sheffield Wed.	F.C.Budocnost (Yug)	10.80	80-82	58	3	6

MISON Michael
Southwark, 8 November, 1975 (M)

League Club	Source	Date Signed	Seasons Played	Apps	Subs	Gls
Fulham	YT	07.94	93-96	35	20	5

MISSE-MISSE Jean-Jacques
Yaounde, Cameroon, 7 August, 1968 Cameroon Int (F)

League Club	Source	Date Signed	Seasons Played	Apps	Subs	Gls
Chesterfield (N/C)	Dundee U.	03.98	97	1	0	0

MITCHELL Albert James
Burslem, 22 January, 1922 Died 1997 E 'B' (OL)

League Club	Source	Date Signed	Seasons Played	Apps	Subs	Gls
Stoke C.	Jnrs	05.41	46-47	10	-	2
Blackburn Rov.	Tr	02.48	47	3	-	0
Northampton T.	Tr	05.49	49-50	81	-	21
Luton T.	Tr	07.51	51-54	106	-	41
Middlesbrough	Tr	09.54	54-55	50	-	6
Southport	Tr	08.56	56	16	-	3

MITCHELL Alexander Russell
Gourock, 24 May, 1918 Died 1990 (FB)

League Club	Source	Date Signed	Seasons Played	Apps	Subs	Gls
Ipswich T.	Bute	08.46	47-49	42	-	2

MITCHELL Andrew Barry
Rotherham, 12 September, 1976 (FB)

League Club	Source	Date Signed	Seasons Played	Apps	Subs	Gls
Aston Villa	YT	09.93				
Chesterfield	Tr	09.96	96	1	1	0

MITCHELL Anthony John
Redruth, 7 September, 1956 (FB)

League Club	Source	Date Signed	Seasons Played	Apps	Subs	Gls
Exeter C.	Leatherhead	07.77	78-81	60	0	0

MITCHELL Arnold
Rotherham, 1 December, 1929 (WH)

League Club	Source	Date Signed	Seasons Played	Apps	Subs	Gls
Derby Co.	Sheffield Wed. (Am)	02.48				
Nottingham F.	Tr	03.50				
Notts Co.	Tr	05.51	51	1	-	0
Exeter C.	Tr	07.52	52-65	495	0	44

MITCHELL Barrie
Aberdeen, 15 March, 1947 (F)

League Club	Source	Date Signed	Seasons Played	Apps	Subs	Gls
Tranmere Rov.	Aberdeen	02.74	73-75	77	6	10
Preston N.E.	Tr	07.76	76	7	4	2
York C.	Tr	09.77	77	1	2	0

MITCHELL Charles **Brian**
Stonehaven, 16 July, 1963 S Sch (RB)

League Club	Source	Date Signed	Seasons Played	Apps	Subs	Gls
Bradford C.	Aberdeen	02.87	86-91	170	8	9
Bristol C.	Tr	07.92	92	15	1	0
Hull C.	Tr	08.93	93	9	0	0

MITCHELL David John
Stoke, 24 August, 1945 (CF)

League Club	Source	Date Signed	Seasons Played	Apps	Subs	Gls
Port Vale	Jnrs	03.64	64-65	21	0	4
Ipswich T.	Tr	08.66	66	0	2	0

MITCHELL David Stuart
Glasgow, 13 June, 1962 Australian Int (F)

League Club	Source	Date Signed	Seasons Played	Apps	Subs	Gls
Chelsea	Feyenoord (Neth)	01.89	88-90	7	0	0
Newcastle U.	L	01.91	90	2	0	1
Swindon T.	Tr	07.91	91-92	61	7	16
Millwall	Altay Izmir (Tur)	10.93	93-94	49	6	15

MITCHELL Frank Rollason
Australia, 3 June, 1922 Died 1984 (WH)

League Club	Source	Date Signed	Seasons Played	Apps	Subs	Gls
Birmingham C.	Coventry C. (Am)	09.43	46-48	93	-	6
Chelsea	Tr	01.49	48-51	75	-	1
Watford	Tr	08.52	52-56	193	-	0

MITCHELL Graham Lee
Shipley, 16 February, 1968 (CD)

League Club	Source	Date Signed	Seasons Played	Apps	Subs	Gls
Huddersfield T.	YT	06.86	86-94	235	9	2
Bournemouth	L	12.93	93	4	0	0
Bradford C.	Tr	12.94	94-96	64	1	1

MITCHELL Ian
Falkirk, 9 May, 1946 Died 1996 S Sch/Su23-2 (OL)

League Club	Source	Date Signed	Seasons Played	Apps	Subs	Gls
Newcastle U.	Dundee U.	07.70	70	2	1	0

MITCHELL Ian David
Tredegar, 1 October, 1971 (F)

League Club	Source	Date Signed	Seasons Played	Apps	Subs	Gls
Hereford U.	Merthyr Tydfil	10.90	90	0	3	0

MITCHELL James
Glasgow, 6 November, 1976 (F)

League Club	Source	Date Signed	Seasons Played	Apps	Subs	Gls
Norwich C.	YT	07.95				
Scarborough	Tr	08.96	96-97	31	47	10

MITCHELL James Donald
Heanor, 1 July, 1937 (G)

League Club	Source	Date Signed	Seasons Played	Apps	Subs	Gls
Derby Co.	Ilkeston T.	10.58	58-59	6	-	0

MITCHELL James Robert
Liverpool, 13 June, 1967 (FB)

League Club	Source	Date Signed	Seasons Played	Apps	Subs	Gls
Wigan Ath.	App	06.85	84	2	0	0

MITCHELL John
St Albans, 12 March, 1952 (F)

League Club	Source	Date Signed	Seasons Played	Apps	Subs	Gls
Fulham	St Albans C.	02.72	72-77	158	11	57
Millwall	Tr	06.78	78-80	78	3	18

MITCHELL John Desmond
Titchfield, 19 November, 1928 (OL)

League Club	Source	Date Signed	Seasons Played	Apps	Subs	Gls
Southampton	Gosport Ath.	03.49	50	7	-	0

MITCHELL John George
Gateshead, 1 August, 1919 Died 1977 (CF)

League Club	Source	Date Signed	Seasons Played	Apps	Subs	Gls
Hartlepool U.	Billingham Synth.	11.46	46	3	-	2

MITCHELL Kenneth
Sunderland, 26 May, 1957 (CD)

League Club	Source	Date Signed	Seasons Played	Apps	Subs	Gls
Newcastle U.	App	04.75	76-80	61	5	2
Darlington	Tr	08.81	81	12	1	1

MITCHELL Kenneth Samuel
Wearhead, 26 December, 1933 (F)

League Club	Source	Date Signed	Seasons Played	Apps	Subs	Gls
Plymouth Arg.	Whitby Rov.	03.56	55-56	8	-	4

MITCHELL Neil Nicholas
Lytham, 7 November, 1974 E Sch (F)

League Club	Source	Date Signed	Seasons Played	Apps	Subs	Gls
Blackpool	YT	11.92	91-94	39	28	8
Rochdale	L	12.95	95	3	1	0
Macclesfield T.	Tr	07.96	97	2	4	0

MITCHELL Norman
Sunderland, 7 November, 1931 (OR)

League Club	Source	Date Signed	Seasons Played	Apps	Subs	Gls
Chesterfield	West Stanley	10.51	51-52	66	-	7
Workington	West Stanley	11.53	53-57	138	-	23
Hartlepool U.	Tr	03.58	57-58	23	-	6

MITCHELL Paul Robert
Bournemouth, 20 October, 1971 E Sch/E Yth (M)

League Club	Source	Date Signed	Seasons Played	Apps	Subs	Gls
Bournemouth	YT	08.89	90-92	6	6	0
West Ham U.	Tr	08.93	93	0	1	0
Bournemouth	Tr	03.96	95	2	2	0
Torquay U.	Tr	08.96	96-97	33	5	1

MITCHELL Paul Robert
Nottingham, 8 November, 1978 (D)

League Club	Source	Date Signed	Seasons Played	Apps	Subs	Gls
Notts Co.	YT	07.97	96-97	1	1	0

MITCHELL Peter
Oldham, 5 August, 1946 (FB)

League Club	Source	Date Signed	Seasons Played	Apps	Subs	Gls
Oldham Ath.	Jnrs	07.66	65	0	1	0

MITCHELL Robert
South Shields, 4 January, 1955 (M)

League Club	Source	Date Signed	Seasons Played	Apps	Subs	Gls
Sunderland	App	01.72	73-75	1	2	0
Blackburn Rov.	Tr	07.76	76-77	17	12	6
Grimsby T.	Tr	06.78	78-81	142	0	6
Carlisle U.	Tr	08.82	82	2	0	0
Rotherham U.	Tr	03.83	82-84	86	9	2
Lincoln C.	Hamrun (Malta)	01.86	85-86	41	3	2

MITCHELL Robert
Campbeltown, 17 January, 1927 (CF)

League Club	Source	Date Signed	Seasons Played	Apps	Subs	Gls
Exeter C.	Third Lanark	07.51	51	3	-	0

MITCHELL Robert
Petersfield, 17 December, 1948 (F)

League Club	Source	Date Signed	Seasons Played	Apps	Subs	Gls
Aldershot	Alton T.	09.69	69-70	6	6	1

MITCHELL Robert Carmichael
Glasgow, 16 August, 1924 Died 1993 SF Lge/S-2 (OL)

League Club	Source	Date Signed	Seasons Played	Apps	Subs	Gls
Newcastle U.	Third Lanark	02.49	48-60	367	-	95

MITCHELL Ronald Gilbert
Lancaster, 13 February, 1935 (FB)

League Club	Source	Date Signed	Seasons Played	Apps	Subs	Gls
Leeds U.	Morecambe	11.58	58	4	-	0

MITCHELL Ronald James
Barrhead, 27 May, 1925 (OR)

League Club	Source	Date Signed	Seasons Played	Apps	Subs	Gls
Exeter C.	Glasgow Celtic	08.49	49	2	-	0

MITCHELL Roy
Liverpool, 10 March, 1964 (M)

League Club	Source	Date Signed	Seasons Played	Apps	Subs	Gls
Stockport Co. (N/C)		10.86	86	2	1	0

MITCHELL Stewart Anderson
Glasgow, 3 March, 1933 (G)

League Club	Source	Date Signed	Seasons Played	Apps	Subs	Gls
Newcastle U.	Benburb	09.53	54-62	45	-	0

MITCHELSON Kenneth
Edmonton, 16 May, 1928 (FB)

League Club	Source	Date Signed	Seasons Played	Apps	Subs	Gls
Charlton Ath.	Tottenham H. (Am)	09.47				
Bristol C.	Tr	05.49	49-52	28	-	0

MITCHESON Francis John
Stalybridge, 10 March, 1924 Died 1981 (IF)

League Club	Source	Date Signed	Seasons Played	Apps	Subs	Gls
Doncaster Rov.	Droylsden	05.44	46-48	22	-	5
Crewe Alex.	Tr	11.48	48-53	181	-	34
Rochdale	Tr	06.54	54-55	50	-	8

MITCHINSON Thomas William
Sunderland, 24 February, 1943 (M)

League Club	Source	Date Signed	Seasons Played	Apps	Subs	Gls
Sunderland	Jnrs	12.60	62-65	16	1	2
Mansfield T.	Tr	01.66	65-67	76	0	15
Aston Villa	Tr	08.67	67-68	49	0	9
Torquay U.	Tr	05.69	68-71	108	0	9
Bournemouth	Tr	12.71	71-72	13	1	1

MITTEN Charles
Burma, 17 January, 1921 (OL)

League Club	Source	Date Signed	Seasons Played	Apps	Subs	Gls
Manchester U.	Jnrs	01.38	46-49	142	-	50
Fulham	Tr	01.52	51-55	154	-	32
Mansfield T.	Tr	02.56	55-57	100	-	25

MITTEN Charles
Altrincham, 14 December, 1943 (F)

League Club	Source	Date Signed	Seasons Played	Apps	Subs	Gls
Mansfield T.	Newcastle U. (App)	11.61				
Halifax T.	Altrincham	10.65	65	1	0	0

MITTEN John
Manchester, 30 March, 1941 E Sch/E Yth (W)

League Club	Source	Date Signed	Seasons Played	Apps	Subs	Gls
Mansfield T. (Am)	Jnrs	01.58	57	3	-	0
Newcastle U.	Tr	09.58	58-60	9	-	3
Leicester C.	Tr	09.61	61	12	-	0
Coventry C.	Manchester U. (trial)	08.63	63-66	34	2	5
Plymouth Arg.	Tr	01.67	66-67	43	0	8
Exeter C .	Tr	07.68	68-70	96	4	17

MITTON Gilbert **Keith**
Leyland, 30 December, 1928 Died 1995 (G)

League Club	Source	Date Signed	Seasons Played	Apps	Subs	Gls
Preston N.E.	Leyland Motors	05.50	53	2	-	0
Carlisle U.	Tr	06.54	54-56	47	-	0

MOBLEY David Leslie
Oxford, 24 August, 1948 (FB)

League Club	Source	Date Signed	Seasons Played	Apps	Subs	Gls
Sheffield Wed.	Jnrs	09.65				
Grimsby T.	Tr	07.69	69	26	1	0

MOBLEY Victor John
Oxford, 11 October, 1943 Eu23-13/EF Lge (CH)

League Club	Source	Date Signed	Seasons Played	Apps	Subs	Gls
Sheffield Wed.	Oxford C.	09.61	63-69	187	0	8
Queens Park R.	Tr	10.69	69-70	24	1	0

MOCHAN Dennis
Falkirk, 12 December, 1935 (FB)

League Club	Source	Date Signed	Seasons Played	Apps	Subs	Gls
Nottingham F.	Raith Rov.	06.62	62-65	108	0	1
Colchester U.	Tr	09.66	66-69	113	3	2

MOCHAN Neil
Larbert, 6 April, 1927 Died 1994 S 'B'/S-3 (CF)

League Club	Source	Date Signed	Seasons Played	Apps	Subs	Gls
Middlesbrough	Morton	05.51	51-52	38	-	14

MOCKLER Andrew James
Stockton, 18 November, 1970 (M)

League Club	Source	Date Signed	Seasons Played	Apps	Subs	Gls
Arsenal	YT	11.88				
Scarborough	Tr	07.90	90-93	66	8	10

MOFFAT Adam
Dunfermline, 1 April, 1941 (IF)

League Club	Source	Date Signed	Seasons Played	Apps	Subs	Gls
Newport Co.	East Fife	10.61	61	17	-	5

MOFFATT Gregory Thomas
Liverpool, 8 January, 1964 (D)

League Club	Source	Date Signed	Seasons Played	Apps	Subs	Gls
Chester C.	App	01.82	82	6	1	0

MOFFATT John Black
Greenock, 22 December, 1929 (OR)

League Club	Source	Date Signed	Seasons Played	Apps	Subs	Gls
Brighton & H. A.	Bellshill Ath.	12.51	52	2	-	0

MOFFATT Norman
Bootle, 18 November, 1920 (IF)

League Club	Source	Date Signed	Seasons Played	Apps	Subs	Gls
Workington		08.51	51	1	-	0

MOFFATT Robert Wallace
Portsmouth, 7 October, 1945 (WH)

League Club	Source	Date Signed	Seasons Played	Apps	Subs	Gls
Portsmouth	App	10.63				
Gillingham	Tr	05.65	65-67	23	1	1

MOFFITT Kenneth
Newcastle, 2 February, 1933 (FB)

League Club	Source	Date Signed	Seasons Played	Apps	Subs	Gls
Brentford	Berwick R.	08.53				
Gateshead	Berwick R.	09.57	57-59	76	-	2

MOGFORD Reginald William James
Newport, 12 June, 1919 Died 1992 (CF)

League Club	Source	Date Signed	Seasons Played	Apps	Subs	Gls
Newport Co.	Jnrs	06.38	38-47	20	-	9

MOHAN Nicholas
Middlesbrough, 6 October, 1970 (CD)

League Club	Source	Date Signed	Seasons Played	Apps	Subs	Gls
Middlesbrough	Jnrs	11.87	88-93	93	6	4
Hull C.	L	09.92	92	5	0	1
Leicester C.	Tr	07.94	94	23	0	0
Bradford C.	Tr	07.95	95-96	83	0	4
Wycombe W.	L	08.97	97	6	0	0
Wycombe W.	Tr	10.97	97	27	0	0

MOILANEN Teuvo (Tepi) Johannes
Finland, 12 December, 1973 Finnish Int (G)

League Club	Source	Date Signed	Seasons Played	Apps	Subs	Gls
Preston N.E.	F.F. Jaro (Fin)	12.95	95-97	46	0	0
Scarborough	L	12.96	96	4	0	0
Darlington	L	01.97	96	16	0	0

MOIR Ian
Aberdeen, 30 June, 1943 (W)

League Club	Source	Date Signed	Seasons Played	Apps	Subs	Gls
Manchester U.	Jnrs	07.60	60-64	45	-	5
Blackpool	Tr	02.65	64-66	61	0	12
Chester C.	Tr	05.67	67	25	0	3
Wrexham	Tr	01.68	67-71	144	6	20
Shrewsbury T.	Tr	03.72	71-72	22	3	2
Wrexham	Tr	07.73	73-74	11	4	0

MOIR James
Newcastle, 23 March, 1918 (CF)

League Club	Source	Date Signed	Seasons Played	Apps	Subs	Gls
Accrington St.	Newcastle W.E.	10.37	37-38	20	-	9
Carlisle U.	Tr	08.46	46-47	42	-	18

MOIR Richard John
Glasgow, 22 October, 1945 (M)

League Club	Source	Date Signed	Seasons Played	Apps	Subs	Gls
Shrewsbury T.	Cumnock Jnrs	03.69	69-73	159	6	27
Halifax T.	Tr	07.74	74	16	3	5

MOIR William
Aberdeen, 19 April, 1922 Died 1988 S 'B'/S-1 (IF)

League Club	Source	Date Signed	Seasons Played	Apps	Subs	Gls
Bolton W.	R.A.F. Kirkham	04.43	46-55	325	-	118
Stockport Co.	Tr	09.55	55-57	70	-	26

MOKONE Stephen Madi
South Africa, 23 March, 1932 (OR)

League Club	Source	Date Signed	Seasons Played	Apps	Subs	Gls
Coventry C.	Pretoria (SA)	10.56	56	4	-	1
Cardiff C.	P.S.V. Eindhoven (Neth)	06.59	59	3	-	1

MOLBY Jan
Denmark, 4 July, 1963 Danish Int (M)

League Club	Source	Date Signed	Seasons Played	Apps	Subs	Gls
Liverpool	Ajax (Neth)	08.84	84-94	195	23	44
Barnsley	L	09.95	95	5	0	0
Norwich C.	L	12.95	95	3	0	0
Swansea C.	Tr	02.96	95-97	39	2	8

MOLDOVAN Viorel Dinu
Bistrita, Romania, 8 July, 1972 Romanian Int (CF)

League Club	Source	Date Signed	Seasons Played	Apps	Subs	Gls
Coventry C.	Grasshoppers (Swi)	01.98	97	5	5	1

MOLENAAR Robert
Netherlands, 27 February, 1969 (CD)

League Club	Source	Date Signed	Seasons Played	Apps	Subs	Gls
Leeds U.	F.C. Volendam (Neth)	01.97	96-97	30	4	3

MOLLATT Ronald Vincent
Edwinstowe, 24 February, 1932 (WH)

League Club	Source	Date Signed	Seasons Played	Apps	Subs	Gls
Leeds U.	Jnrs	02.50	51-54	17	-	0
York C.	Tr	07.55	55-59	124	-	1
Bradford C.	Tr	07.60	60-62	88	-	0

MOLLER Jan Borje
Sweden, 17 September, 1953 Swedish Int (G)

League Club	Source	Date Signed	Seasons Played	Apps	Subs	Gls
Bristol C.	Malmo (Swe)	12.80	80-81	48	0	0

MOLLOY Gerard
Rochdale, 13 March, 1936 (OL)

League Club	Source	Date Signed	Seasons Played	Apps	Subs	Gls
Rochdale	Jnrs	11.55	55-56	6	-	0

MOLLOY Peter (Paddy)
Rossendale, 20 April, 1908 Died 1993 NIF Lge (WH)

League Club	Source	Date Signed	Seasons Played	Apps	Subs	Gls
Fulham	Accrington St. (Am)	12.31	31	4	-	0
Bristol Rov.	Tr	05.33	33	6	-	0
Cardiff C.	Tr	02.34	33-34	23	-	0
Queens Park R.	Tr	07.35	35	3	-	0
Stockport Co.	Tr	07.36	36	10	-	0
Carlisle U.	Tr	05.37	37	33	-	0
Bradford C.	Tr	05.38	38	25	-	0
Notts Co.	Distillery	04.48	47	1	-	0

MOLLOY George William
Coventry, 28 August, 1929 (RH)

League Club	Source	Date Signed	Seasons Played	Apps	Subs	Gls
Southampton		10.49	49	1	-	0
Newport Co.	Lockheed Leamington	11.50	50	3	-	0

MOLYNEUX Bernard
Prescot, 17 September, 1933 (FB)

League Club	Source	Date Signed	Seasons Played	Apps	Subs	Gls
Everton	Jnrs	12.51				
Tranmere Rov.	Tr	05.56	56	12	-	3

MOLYNEUX Frederick George
Wallasey, 25 July, 1944 (CD)

League Club	Source	Date Signed	Seasons Played	Apps	Subs	Gls
Liverpool	Jnrs	06.62				
Southport	Tr	08.65	65-68	123	0	1
Plymouth Arg.	Tr	08.68	68-70	79	0	5
Exeter C.	L	02.71	70	2	0	0
Tranmere Rov.	Tr	02.71	70-72	71	1	0
Southport	Tr	07.73	73	32	1	1

MOLYNEUX Geoffrey Barry
Warrington, 23 January, 1943 (OR)

League Club	Source	Date Signed	Seasons Played	Apps	Subs	Gls
Chester C. (Am)	Rylands Y.C.	05.62	62	1	-	0

MOLYNEUX John Allan
Warrington, 3 February, 1931 E Yth (RB)

League Club	Source	Date Signed	Seasons Played	Apps	Subs	Gls
Chester C.	Jnrs	02.49	49-54	178	-	1
Liverpool	Tr	06.55	55-61	229	-	2
Chester C.	Tr	08.62	62-64	67	-	0

MOLYNEUX Raymond
Kearsley (Lancs), 13 June, 1930 E Yth (RB)

League Club	Source	Date Signed	Seasons Played	Apps	Subs	Gls
Bradford C.		12.48	48	2	-	1

MOLYNEUX William Stanley
Ormskirk, 10 January, 1944 (G)

League Club	Source	Date Signed	Seasons Played	Apps	Subs	Gls
Liverpool	Earle	11.63	64	1	-	0
Oldham Ath.	Tr	06.67	68	8	0	0

MONAGHAN Derek James
Bromsgrove, 20 January, 1959 E Yth (F)

League Club	Source	Date Signed	Seasons Played	Apps	Subs	Gls
West Bromwich A.	App	01.77	79-83	14	5	2
Port Vale	Tr	07.84	84	4	3	0

MONCRIEFF James Conradi
Todmorden, 14 June, 1922 Died 1975 (CF)

League Club	Source	Date Signed	Seasons Played	Apps	Subs	Gls
Halifax T. (Am)	Pegasus	06.46	46-54	42	-	13

MONCRIEFFE Prince
Jamaica, 27 February, 1977 (CF)

League Club	Source	Date Signed	Seasons Played	Apps	Subs	Gls
Doncaster Rov.	Hyde U.	07.97	97	30	8	8

MONCUR John Frederick
Stepney, 22 September, 1966 (M)

League Club	Source	Date Signed	Seasons Played	Apps	Subs	Gls
Tottenham H.	App	08.84	86-90	10	11	1
Doncaster Rov.	L	09.86	86	4	0	0
Cambridge U.	L	03.87	86	3	1	0
Portsmouth	L	03.89	88	7	0	0
Brentford	L	10.89	89	5	0	1
Ipswich T.	L	10.91	91	5	1	0
Swindon T.	Tr	03.92	91-93	53	5	5
West Ham U.	Tr	06.94	94-97	92	5	5

MONCUR Robert
Perth, 19 January, 1945 S Sch/Su23-1/S-16 (CD)

League Club	Source	Date Signed	Seasons Played	Apps	Subs	Gls
Newcastle U.	App	04.62	62-73	293	3	3
Sunderland	Tr	06.74	74-76	86	0	2
Carlisle U.	Tr	11.76	76	11	0	0

MONEY Richard
Lowestoft, 13 October, 1955 E'B' (CD)

League Club	Source	Date Signed	Seasons Played	Apps	Subs	Gls
Scunthorpe U.	Lowestoft T.	07.73	73-77	165	8	4
Fulham	Tr	12.77	77-79	106	0	3
Liverpool	Tr	04.80	80	12	2	0
Derby Co.	L	12.81	81	5	0	0
Luton T.	Tr	03.82	81-82	44	0	1
Portsmouth	Tr	08.83	83-85	17	0	0
Scunthorpe U.	Tr	10.85	85-89	105	1	0

MONINGTON Mark David
Bilsthorpe (Nts), 21 October, 1970 (CD)

League Club	Source	Date Signed	Seasons Played	Apps	Subs	Gls
Burnley	Jnrs	03.89	88-93	65	19	5
Rotherham U.	Tr	11.94	94-97	75	4	3

MONK Brian
Leeds, 15 May, 1937 (IF)

League Club	Source	Date Signed	Seasons Played	Apps	Subs	Gls
Leeds U.	Jnrs	02.55				
Crewe Alex.	Tr	05.58	58	5	-	0

League Club	Source	Date Signed	Seasons Played	Career Record Apps	Subs	Gls
MONK Frederick John						
Brighton, 9 October, 1920 Died 1987 E Sch (RB/CF)						
Brentford	Guildford C.	03.48	47-53	206	-	47
Aldershot	Tr	07.54	54-55	49	-	0
MONK Garry Alan						
Bedford, 6 March, 1979 (D)						
Torquay U.	YT	•	95	4	1	0
MONKHOUSE Alan Thompson William						
Stockton, 23 October, 1930 Died 1992 (F)						
Millwall	Thornaby	08.50	49-53	65	-	20
Newcastle U.	Tr	10.53	53-55	21	-	9
York C.	Tr	06.56	56	12	-	1
MONKHOUSE Graham						
Carlisle, 26 April, 1954 (G)						
Workington	Penrith	08.76	76	4	0	0
MONKOU Kenneth John						
Surinam, 29 November, 1964 (CD)						
Chelsea	Feyenoord (Neth)	03.89	88-91	92	2	2
Southampton	Tr	08.92	92-97	168	8	9
MONKS John						
Stockport, 3 June, 1921 Died 1983 (LB)						
Stockport Co.		04.47	46-52	91	-	0
MONOGHAN William						
Glasgow, 2 September, 1919 (RB)						
Bury	Alloa Ath.	08.46				
Carlisle U.	Tr	08.47	47-49	19	-	0
MONTGOMERY Alec Webster						
Tamworth, 16 September, 1926 (LB)						
Walsall	Baddesley	08.49	51-52	29	-	0
MONTGOMERY Derek						
Houghton-le-Spring, 5 May, 1950 (M)						
Leeds U.	App	12.67				
Bradford C.	Tr	08.68	68	4	0	0
MONTGOMERY James						
Sunderland, 9 October, 1943 E Yth/Eu23-6 (G)						
Sunderland	Jnrs	10.60	61-76	537	0	0
Southampton	L	10.76	76	5	0	0
Birmingham C.	Tr	02.77	76-78	66	0	0
Nottingham F.	Tr	08.79				
Sunderland	Tr	08.80				
MONTGOMERY Stanley William						
Silvertown, 7 July, 1920 (CH)						
Hull C.	Romford	09.44	46	5	-	0
Southend U.	Tr	09.46	46-48	96	-	7
Cardiff C.	Tr	12.48	48-54	231	-	4
Newport Co.	Worcester C.	11.55	55	9	-	0
MOODY Alan						
Middlesbrough, 18 January, 1951 E Sch (D)						
Middlesbrough	App	01.68	68-72	44	2	0
Southend U.	Tr	10.72	72-83	444	2	41
MOODY Kenneth George						
Grimsby, 12 November, 1924 Died 1990 (FB)						
Grimsby T.	Humber U.	10.42	47-50	114	-	0
MOODY Paul						
Portsmouth, 13 June, 1967 (F)						
Southampton	Waterlooville	07.91	91-93	7	5	0
Reading	L	12.92	92	5	0	1
Oxford U.	Tr	02.94	93-96	98	38	49
Fulham	Tr	07.97	97	27	6	15
MOODY Vincent **Roy**						
Worksop, 12 March, 1923 (OR)						
Lincoln C.	Worksop T.	11.46	46	1	-	0
MOONEY Brian John						
Dublin, 2 February, 1966 IR Yth/IRu21-4/IRu23-2 (W)						
Liverpool	Home Farm	08.83				
Wrexham	L	12.85	85	8	0	2
Preston N.E.	Tr	10.87	87-90	125	3	20
Sunderland	Tr	02.91	90-92	21	6	1
Burnley	L	09.92	92	6	0	0
MOONEY Dean Francis						
Paddington, 24 July, 1956 (F)						
Leyton Orient	App	07.74	74-75	16	6	3
Bournemouth	Sweden	12.80	80-81	27	0	10
Torquay U. (N/C)	R.S. Southampton	08.84	84	15	0	2

League Club	Source	Date Signed	Seasons Played	Career Record Apps	Subs	Gls
MOONEY Francis						
Fauldhouse, 1 January, 1932 (OR)						
Manchester U.	Bathgate St M.	05.49				
Blackburn Rov.	Tr	02.54	53-55	58	-	19
Carlisle U.	Tr	05.56	56-59	124	-	24
MOONEY John						
Fauldhouse, 21 February, 1926 (OR)						
Doncaster Rov.	Hamilton Academical	05.53	53-58	171	-	32
MOONEY Kevin William						
Liverpool, 23 August, 1959 (D)						
Bury	Bangor C.	03.80	80	1	0	0
Tranmere Rov.	Telford U.	08.82	82	21	1	0
MOONEY Thomas						
Newry (NI), 14 December, 1973 (M)						
Huddersfield T.	YT	06.92	92	1	0	0
MOONEY Thomas John						
Middlesbrough, 11 August, 1971 (F)						
Aston Villa	YT	11.89				
Scarborough	Tr	07.90	90-92	96	11	30
Southend U.	Tr	07.93	93	9	5	5
Watford	Tr	03.94	93-97	155	8	30
MOOR Anthony John						
York, 18 January, 1940 (G)						
York C.	Scarborough	05.62	62-64	57	-	0
Darlington	Tr	07.65	65-71	239	0	0
MOORCROFT David Stanley						
Liverpool, 16 March, 1947 (D)						
Tranmere Rov.	Skelmersdale U.	12.68	68-71	107	1	1
MOORCROFT Maurice						
Chesterfield, 4 November, 1929 E Yth (G)						
Sheffield U.	Jnrs	07.48				
Gillingham	Tr	07.52	52	8	-	0
MOORE Alan						
Dublin, 25 November, 1974 IR Sch/IR Yth/IRu21-4/IR-8 (LW)						
Middlesbrough	YT	12.91	92-97	95	19	14
MOORE Alan						
Hebburn, 7 March, 1927 (OR)						
Sunderland		05.46				
Chesterfield	Spennymoor U.	12.48	48-50	67	-	2
Hull C.	Tr	07.51	51	13	-	4
Nottingham F.	Tr	01.52	51-54	102	-	38
Coventry C.	Tr	12.54	54-56	57	-	13
Swindon T.	Tr	07.57	57-58	19	-	3
Rochdale	Tr	11.58	58	11	-	2
MOORE Andrew						
Wantage, 2 October, 1964 (M)						
Reading	App	•	81	0	1	0
MOORE Andrew Roy						
Cleethorpes, 14 November, 1965 (CD)						
Grimsby T.	App	11.83	83-86	62	3	1
MOORE Anthony Paul						
York, 7 February, 1943 (CF)						
York C. (Am)	Heworth	05.62	62	2	-	0
MOORE Anthony Peter						
Wolverhampton, 19 September, 1957 (FB)						
Sheffield U.	Burton A.	07.79	79-81	29	0	0
Crewe Alex.	Tr	08.82	82	17	0	2
Rochdale (N/C)	Worksop T.	10.84	84	1	2	0
MOORE Anthony Peter						
Scarborough, 4 September, 1947 (W)						
Chesterfield	App	01.65	64-70	148	7	13
Grimsby T.	L	03.71	70	2	1	0
Chester C.	Tr	08.71	71	9	4	3
MOORE John Frederick **Beriah**						
Cardiff, 25 December, 1919 (OL)						
Cardiff C.	Bangor C.	09.41	47-48	6	-	4
Newport Co.	Bangor C.	07.50	50-52	121	-	45
MOORE Bernard John						
Brighton, 18 December, 1923 (CF)						
Brighton & H.A.	Jnrs	09.45	47	8	-	2
Luton T.	Hastings U.	01.51	50-53	74	-	31
Brighton & H.A.	Tr	03.54	53-54	29	-	10

MOORE Brian
Hemsworth, 24 December, 1938 (OR)

League Club	Source	Date Signed	Seasons Played	Apps	Subs	Gls
Mansfield T. (Am)	Loughborough College	09.60	60	4	-	0
Notts Co.	Tr	12.61	61-62	27	-	3
Doncaster Rov.	Tr	07.63	63	1	-	0

MOORE Brian McGowan
Belfast, 29 December, 1933 (IF)

League Club	Source	Date Signed	Seasons Played	Apps	Subs	Gls
West Ham U.	Glentoran	02.55	54-55	9	-	1

MOORE Christian
Derby, 4 November, 1972 (F)

League Club	Source	Date Signed	Seasons Played	Apps	Subs	Gls
Stockport Co.	Leicester C. (YT)	08.91	91	0	1	0

MOORE Darren Mark
Birmingham, 22 April, 1974 (CD)

League Club	Source	Date Signed	Seasons Played	Apps	Subs	Gls
Torquay U.	YT	11.92	91-94	102	1	8
Doncaster Rov.	Tr	07.95	95-96	76	0	7
Bradford C.	Tr	06.97	97	18	0	0

MOORE David
Grimsby, 17 December, 1959 (RB)

League Club	Source	Date Signed	Seasons Played	Apps	Subs	Gls
Grimsby T.	App	12.77	78-82	136	0	2
Carlisle U.	Tr	08.83	83	13	0	1
Blackpool	Tr	12.83	83-86	114	1	1
Grimsby T.	Tr	12.86	86-87	3	1	0
Darlington	Tr	08.88	88	25	5	1

MOORE Eric
St Helens, 16 July, 1926 (FB)

League Club	Source	Date Signed	Seasons Played	Apps	Subs	Gls
Everton		02.49	49-56	171	-	0
Chesterfield	Tr	01.57	56	6	-	0
Tranmere Rov.	Tr	07.57	57	36	-	0

MOORE Gary
Sedgefield, 4 November, 1945 (F)

League Club	Source	Date Signed	Seasons Played	Apps	Subs	Gls
Sunderland	Jnrs	11.62	64-66	13	0	2
Grimsby T.	Tr	02.67	66-68	52	1	15
Southend U.	Tr	11.68	68-73	156	8	46
Colchester U.	L	03.74	73	11	0	7
Chester C.	Tr	08.74	74-75	29	14	4
Swansea C.	Tr	07.76	76-77	30	4	8

MOORE Gary
Greenwich, 29 December, 1968 (F)

League Club	Source	Date Signed	Seasons Played	Apps	Subs	Gls
Maidstone U. (N/C)	Alma Swanley	03.91	90	0	5	1

MOORE Gordon Alexander
Greenock, 27 June, 1968 (W)

League Club	Source	Date Signed	Seasons Played	Apps	Subs	Gls
Bristol C.	Jnrs	06.86	85	0	1	0

MOORE Graham
Hengoed, 7 March, 1941 Wu23-9/EF Lge/W-21 (M)

League Club	Source	Date Signed	Seasons Played	Apps	Subs	Gls
Cardiff C.	Jnrs	05.58	58-61	85	-	23
Chelsea	Tr	12.61	61-63	68	-	13
Manchester U.	Tr	11.63	63	18	-	4
Northampton T.	Tr	12.65	65-66	53	0	10
Charlton Ath.	Tr	06.67	67-70	110	0	8
Doncaster Rov.	Tr	09.71	71-73	67	2	3

MOORE Howard
Canterbury, 5 March, 1947 (W)

League Club	Source	Date Signed	Seasons Played	Apps	Subs	Gls
Coventry C.	Ashford T.	03.66				
Gillingham	Tr	07.67	67	17	0	0
Southend U.	Tr	01.68	67-68	6	1	0

MOORE Ian Ronald
Birkenhead, 26 August, 1976 E Yth/Eu21-7 (F)

League Club	Source	Date Signed	Seasons Played	Apps	Subs	Gls
Tranmere Rov.	YT	07.94	94-96	41	17	12
Bradford C.	L	09.96	96	6	0	0
Nottingham F.	Tr	03.97	96-97	3	12	1
West Ham U.	L	09.97	97	0	1	0

MOORE John
Consett, 1 October, 1966 (F)

League Club	Source	Date Signed	Seasons Played	Apps	Subs	Gls
Sunderland	App	10.84	84-87	4	12	1
Newport Co.	L	12.85	85	2	0	0
Darlington	L	11.86	86	2	0	1
Mansfield T.	L	03.87	86	5	0	1
Rochdale	L	01.88	87	10	0	2
Hull C.	Tr	06.88	88	11	3	1
Sheffield U.	L	03.89	88	4	1	0
Shrewsbury T.	F.C. Utrecht (Neth)	07.90	90	7	1	1
Crewe Alex. (N/C)	Tr	01.91	90	0	1	0
Scarborough	F.C. Utrecht (Neth)	08.91	91	3	4	1

MOORE John
Liverpool, 9 September, 1945 (CD)

League Club	Source	Date Signed	Seasons Played	Apps	Subs	Gls
Stoke C.	Everton (App)	07.63	67	12	1	0
Shrewsbury T.	Tr	08.68	68-72	144	0	1
Swansea C.	Tr	01.73	72-73	31	0	0

MOORE John
Harthill (Lk), 21 December, 1943 (CD)

League Club	Source	Date Signed	Seasons Played	Apps	Subs	Gls
Luton T.	Motherwell	05.65	65-72	264	10	13
Brighton & H.A.	L	10.72	72	5	0	0
Northampton T.	Tr	08.74	74	14	0	0

MOORE John Michael
Nottingham, 1 February, 1943 (OR)

League Club	Source	Date Signed	Seasons Played	Apps	Subs	Gls
Lincoln C.	Arnold St Marys	11.61	61-64	30	-	5

MOORE John William Michael
Chiswick, 25 September, 1923 (WH)

League Club	Source	Date Signed	Seasons Played	Apps	Subs	Gls
Brentford		09.46	46-47	4	-	0
Colchester U.	Tr	07.50	51	2	-	0

MOORE Jonathan
Cardiff, 17 November, 1955 W Sch/W Yth (FB)

League Club	Source	Date Signed	Seasons Played	Apps	Subs	Gls
Bristol Rov.	App	11.73				
Millwall	Tr	12.74	74-78	119	0	5
Bournemouth	Tr	05.79	79-80	36	0	2

MOORE Kenneth
Bradford, 13 September, 1921 (RB)

League Club	Source	Date Signed	Seasons Played	Apps	Subs	Gls
Halifax T.		11.47	47-49	31	-	2

MOORE Kevin
Loughborough, 20 October, 1957 (M)

League Club	Source	Date Signed	Seasons Played	Apps	Subs	Gls
Shrewsbury T.	App	10.75	74-77	15	3	1

MOORE Kevin John
Blackpool, 30 January, 1956 (W)

League Club	Source	Date Signed	Seasons Played	Apps	Subs	Gls
Blackpool	App	10.73	74-76	33	5	3
Bury	L	12.76	76	4	0	0
Swansea C.	Tr	07.77	77-78	51	4	6
Newport Co.	Tr	02.79	78-82	140	8	14
Swindon T.	L	03.83	82	1	0	0

MOORE Kevin Thomas
Grimsby, 29 April, 1958 E Sch (CD)

League Club	Source	Date Signed	Seasons Played	Apps	Subs	Gls
Grimsby T.	Jnrs	07.76	76-86	397	3	28
Oldham Ath.	Tr	02.87	86	13	0	1
Southampton	Tr	07.87	87-93	144	4	10
Bristol Rov.	L	01.92	91	7	0	0
Bristol Rov.	L	10.92	92	4	0	1
Fulham	Tr	07.94	94-95	48	3	4

MOORE John Leslie
Sheffield, 7 July, 1933 Died 1992 (CH)

League Club	Source	Date Signed	Seasons Played	Apps	Subs	Gls
Derby Co.	Worksop T.	11.57	57-63	144	-	3
Lincoln C.	Boston U.	10.65	65-66	59	0	0

MOORE Malcolm
Silksworth, 18 December, 1948 (F)

League Club	Source	Date Signed	Seasons Played	Apps	Subs	Gls
Sunderland	App	12.65	67-68	10	2	3
Crewe Alex.	L	03.70	69	8	0	0
Tranmere Rov.	Tr	07.70	70-72	83	8	21
Hartlepool U.	Tr	08.73	73-75	127	2	34
Workington	Tr	08.76	76	22	0	2

MOORE Mark Steven
Bradford, 9 July, 1972 (M)

League Club	Source	Date Signed	Seasons Played	Apps	Subs	Gls
Cambridge U. (N/C)	N. Hampshire College (USA)	03.98	97	0	1	0

MOORE Martin Terence
Middlesbrough, 10 January, 1966 (LW)

League Club	Source	Date Signed	Seasons Played	Apps	Subs	Gls
Peterborough U.	Stockton	01.90	89	6	1	0

MOORE Michael
Birmingham, 7 October, 1973 (F)

League Club	Source	Date Signed	Seasons Played	Apps	Subs	Gls
Derby Co. (N/C)	YT	06.92				
Swansea C. (N/C)	Tr	08.93	93	0	1	0

MOORE Michael
Chorley, 20 July, 1952 (F)

League Club	Source	Date Signed	Seasons Played	Apps	Subs	Gls
Preston N.E.	Blackburn Rov. (Am)	06.70				
Southport	Tr	07.71	71-73	62	21	11
Port Vale	Wigan Ath.	03.78	77	13	0	0
Wigan Ath.	Tr	08.78	78-79	57	7	12

MOORE Neil
Liverpool, 21 September, 1972 (CD)

League Club	Source	Date Signed	Seasons Played	Apps	Subs	Gls
Everton	YT	06.91	92-93	4	1	0
Blackpool	L	09.94	94	7	0	0
Oldham Ath.	L	02.95	94	5	0	0
Carlisle U.	L	08.95	95	13	0	0
Rotherham U.	L	03.96	95	10	1	0
Norwich C.	Tr	01.97	96	2	0	0
Burnley	Tr	08.97	97	38	2	3

League Club	Source	Date Signed	Seasons Played	Career Record Apps	Subs	Gls
MOORE Norman Woodliffe						
Grimsby, 15 October, 1919						(CF)
Grimsby T.	Jnrs	03.39	46	7	-	1
Hull C.	Tr	04.47	46-49	81	-	46
Blackburn Rov.	Tr	03.50	49-50	7	-	1
Bury	Tr	08.51	51	2	-	0
MOORE Raymond						
Workington, 2 November, 1956						(W)
Workington (N/C)	Sekers	11.75	75	3	0	0
MOORE Robert						
Campsall, 14 December, 1932						(F)
Rotherham U.	Worksop T.	05.55	55-56	19	-	2
Chesterfield	Tr	10.56	56-58	19	-	3
MOORE Robert Frederick Chelsea						
Barking, 12 April, 1941 Died 1993 E Yth/Eu23-8/EF Lge/E-108						(CD)
West Ham U.	Jnrs	06.58	58-73	543	1	24
Fulham	Tr	03.74	73-76	124	0	1
MOORE Ronald David						
Liverpool, 29 January, 1953						(F/CD)
Tranmere Rov.	Jnrs	05.71	71-78	248	1	72
Cardiff C.	Tr	02.79	78-79	54	2	6
Rotherham U.	Tr	08.80	80-83	124	1	52
Charlton Ath.	Tr	09.83	83-84	60	2	13
Rochdale	Tr	07.85	85	43	0	9
Tranmere Rov.	Tr	07.86	86-88	75	0	6
MOORE Thomas **Roy**						
Grimsby, 18 December, 1923 Died 1991						(CH)
Grimsby T.		06.47	48-49	3	-	0
MOORE Samuel Christopher						
Birmingham, 6 September, 1934 Died 1994						(W)
Wolverhampton W.	Aldershot (Am)	11.54				
Walsall	Tr	05.55	55-57	64	-	10
Gillingham	Tr	06.58	58-59	33	-	9
MOORE Stephen John						
Chester, 17 December, 1969						(F)
Chester C.	YT	●	87	0	1	0
MOORE Thomas Lynch						
Trimdon (Dm), 25 July, 1936						(G)
Darlington (Am)	Trimdon	08.56	56	1	-	0
MOORE Watson (Watty) Evans						
Hartlepool, 30 August, 1925						(CH)
Hartlepool U.	Oxford Street O.B.	05.48	48-59	447	-	3
MOORES James **Craig**						
Macclesfield, 1 February, 1961						(F)
Bolton W.	App	02.79	80	0	1	0
Swindon T.	Tr	07.81	81	1	1	0
MOORES Ian Richard						
Newcastle-u-Lyme, 5 October, 1954 Died 1998 Eu23-2						(F)
Stoke C.	App	06.72	73-75	40	10	14
Tottenham H.	Tr	08.76	76-78	25	4	6
Leyton Orient	Tr	10.78	78-81	110	7	26
Bolton W.	Tr	07.82	82	23	3	3
Barnsley	L	02.83	82	3	0	0
MOORHOUSE Alan						
Wardle (Lancs), 12 October, 1925						(OL)
Rochdale	Blackburn Rov. (Am)	03.47	46-47	17	-	3
MOORS Christopher						
Yeovil, 18 August, 1976						(F)
Torquay U. (N/C)	West Ham U. (YT)	11.95	95	0	1	0
MORAH Olisa Henry						
Islington, 3 September, 1972 E Sch/E Yth						(F)
Tottenham H.	YT	07.91				
Hereford U.	L	11.91	91	0	2	0
Swindon T.	Tr	11.92				
Cambridge U.	Sutton U.	06.94	94	8	6	2
Torquay U.	L	03.95	94	2	0	0
MORALEE Jamie David						
Wandsworth, 2 December, 1971						(F)
Crystal Palace	YT	07.90	91	2	4	0
Millwall	Tr	09.92	92-93	56	11	19
Watford	Tr	07.94	94-95	40	9	7
Crewe Alex.	Tr	08.96	96-97	10	6	0
MORAN Brian Joseph						
Hemsworth, 3 June, 1947						(OR)
Barnsley	Jnrs	01.67	66	1	0	0
MORAN Douglas Walter						
Musselburgh, 29 July, 1934						(IF)
Ipswich T.	Falkirk	07.61	61-63	104	-	31
MORAN Edward						
Cleland, 20 July, 1930						(IF)
Leicester C.	Cleland B.C.	09.47	48-50	8	-	1
Stockport Co.	Tr	10.51	51-56	110	-	44
Rochdale	Tr	02.57	56-58	43	-	13
Crewe Alex.	Tr	09.58	58	22	-	8
MORAN James						
Cleland, 6 March, 1935						(IF)
Leicester C.	Wishaw Jnrs.	12.55	56	3	-	1
Norwich C.	Tr	11.57	57-59	36	-	17
Northampton T.	Tr	01.61	60-61	24	-	6
Darlington	Tr	08.62	62	27	-	6
Workington	Tr	07.63	63-65	100	0	22
MORAN John						
Cleland, 9 March, 1933						(IF)
Derby Co.	Coltness U.	11.54	54	2	-	0
MORAN Kevin Bernard						
Dublin, 29 April, 1956 IR-70						(CD)
Manchester U.	Pegasus (Gaelic)	02.78	78-87	228	3	21
Blackburn Rov.	Sporting Gijon (Sp)	01.90	89-93	143	4	10
MORAN Lister Ferguson						
Ryton-on-Tyne, 24 June, 1930						(WH)
Gateshead	Wearmouth Colly	10.50	51-56	22	-	0
MORAN Michael Edward						
Leek, 26 December, 1935						(IF)
Port Vale		07.54				
Crewe Alex.	Tr	07.57	57	14	-	3
MORAN Paul						
Enfield, 22 May, 1968						(W)
Tottenham H.	YT	07.85	86-93	14	22	2
Portsmouth	L	01.89	88	3	0	0
Leicester C.	L	11.89	89	10	0	2
Newcastle U.	L	02.91	90	1	0	0
Southend U.	L	03.91	90	1	0	0
Peterborough U.	Tr	07.94	94	5	2	0
MORAN Richard						
Hammersmith, 9 September, 1963						(F)
Birmingham C.	Fujita Tokyo (Jap)	08.90	90	2	6	1
MORAN Ronald						
Liverpool, 28 February, 1934 EF Lge						(LB)
Liverpool	Jnrs	01.52	52-64	343	-	14
MORAN Stephen James						
Croydon, 10 January, 1961 Eu21-2						(F)
Southampton	Jnrs	08.79	79-85	173	7	78
Leicester C.	Tr	09.86	86-87	35	8	14
Reading	Tr	11.87	87-90	91	25	30
Exeter C.	Tr	08.91	91-92	50	7	27
Hull C.	Tr	08.93	93	11	6	5
MORAN Thomas						
Glasgow, 31 May, 1924						(WH)
Accrington St.	Alloa Ath.	08.53	53	7	-	0
MORAN Thomas						
Edinburgh, 5 February, 1930						(OL)
Carlisle U.	Cowdenbeath	05.54	54-55	35	-	4
Darlington	Tr	05.56	56-57	66	-	13
MORDUE James						
Seaton Delaval, 18 February, 1924						(WH)
Bradford P.A.	North Shields	09.46	48	2	-	0
MORDUE William						
Sacriston, 23 February, 1937						(D)
Doncaster Rov.	Bentley Colly	03.58	57-60	78	-	0
MOREFIELD William **John**						
Gloucester, 26 October, 1922						(FB)
Halifax T.		05.46	46-48	66	-	0
MOREIRA Fabio da Silva						
Brazil, 14 March, 1972						(M)
Middlesbrough	Chaves (Por)	02.97	97	1	0	0

League Club	Source	Date Signed	Seasons Played	Career Record Apps	Subs	Gls
MOREIRA Joao Manuel Silva						
Angola, 30 June, 1970						(LB)
Swansea C.	Benfica (Por)	07.96	96-97	15	0	0
MORELAND Victor						
Belfast, 15 June, 1957 NIu21-1/NI-6						(M)
Derby Co.	Glentoran	09.78	78-79	38	4	1
MORELINE David John						
Stepney, 2 December, 1950						(FB)
Fulham	App	01.68	68-73	63	7	0
Reading	Tr	06.74	74-80	166	0	0
MOREMENT Ralph						
Sheffield, 24 September, 1924 Died 1982						(F/WH)
Sheffield U.		09.46	49	2	-	0
Chester C.	Tr	05.50	50-52	121	-	19
Rochdale		08.55	55	1	-	0
MORENO Jaime Morales						
Bolivia, 19 January, 1974 Bolivian Int						(M)
Middlesbrough	Blooming F.C. (Bol)	09.94	94-95	8	13	1
Middlesbrough (L)	Washington U.D.C. (USA)	12.97	97	1	4	1
MORGAN Alan						
Swansea, 2 January, 1936						(CH)
Leeds U.		01.54				
Crewe Alex.	Tr	09.56	56	5	-	0
MORGAN Alan Meredith						
Aberystwyth, 2 November, 1973 W Sch/W Yth/Wu21-2						(M)
Tranmere Rov.	YT	05.92	95-97	14	10	1
MORGAN Arthur Robert						
Bridgend, 13 September, 1930						(FB/IF)
Swansea C.		12.48	50-52	13	-	0
Plymouth Arg.	Tr	11.53	53-56	36	-	4
MORGAN Christopher Paul						
Barnsley, 13 February, 1978						(CD)
Barnsley	YT	07.96	97	10	1	0
MORGAN Clifford Ivor						
Bristol, 26 September, 1913 Died 1975						(WH)
Bristol C.	Bristol B.B.	06.30	33-48	236	-	8
MORGAN Darren Joseph						
Camberwell, 5 November, 1967 W Yth						(M)
Millwall	App	11.85	86-90	35	9	2
Bradford C.	L	03.90	89	2	0	0
Peterborough U.	L	03.91	90	5	0	0
Bradford C.	Tr	08.91	91	9	2	0
MORGAN Denley James						
Llanelli, 13 February, 1951						(FB)
Swansea C.	Jnrs	02.71	68-71	14	1	0
MORGAN Richard **Dennis**						
Seven Sisters, 22 September, 1925 Died 1980						(FB)
Cardiff C.	Briton Ferry	04.44				
Norwich C.	Tr	10.46	46-55	225	-	3
MORGAN Donald						
Huddersfield, 8 June, 1925 Died 1976						(WH)
Accrington St.	Huddersfield T. (Am)	06.47	46-47	8	-	1
Tranmere Rov.	Tr	05.48				
MORGAN Ernest						
Barnsley, 13 January, 1927						(CF)
Lincoln C.	Royston Y.C.	09.49	52	3	-	0
Gillingham	Tr	08.53	53-56	155	-	73
MORGAN Gary						
Consett, 1 April, 1961						(LB)
Darlington	Berwick R.	07.85	85-88	146	0	3
MORGAN George William						
Cardiff, 28 March, 1923 Died 1989						(W)
Norwich C.	Cardiff C. (Am)	01.47	46-49	65	-	15
Newport Co.	Tr	06.50				
MORGAN Gerald						
Llaniloes, 23 February, 1950						(G)
Walsall (Am)		03.74	73	1	0	0
MORGAN Huw						
Neath, 20 August, 1964						(M)
Swansea C.	App	08.82	83	5	2	0
MORGAN Ian Arthur						
Walthamstow, 14 November, 1946						(W)
Queens Park R.	App	09.64	64-72	161	12	26
Watford	Tr	10.73	73	15	1	1
MORGAN James						
Plymouth, 1 October, 1975						(M)
Plymouth Arg.	YT	06.94	92-94	9	2	0
Exeter C.	Tr	08.95	95	2	4	0
MORGAN William **James**						
Bristol, 19 June, 1922						(IF)
Bristol Rov.	University Settlement	04.46	46-51	104	-	24
MORGAN Jonathan Peter						
Cardiff, 10 July, 1970 W Yth						(M)
Cardiff C.	YT	07.88	88-90	43	12	3
MORGAN Keith						
Trowbridge, 19 February, 1940						(WH)
Swindon T.	Westbury U.	08.58	58-66	325	0	6
MORGAN Kenneth Sidney						
Swansea, 28 July, 1932						(OR)
Fulham	Rickmansworth	09.50				
Watford	Tr	09.52				
Northampton T.		09.54				
Crystal Palace	Brentford (trial)	10.55	55	1	-	0
MORGAN Laurence (Lol)						
Rotherham, 5 May, 1931						(FB)
Huddersfield T.	Sheffield U. (Am)	03.49	49-50	7	-	0
Rotherham U.	Tr	08.54	54-63	291	-	0
Darlington	Tr	07.64	64-65	29	1	0
MORGAN Lewis						
Cowdenbeath, 30 April, 1911 Died 1988						(FB)
Portsmouth	Dundee	08.35	35-38	122	-	0
Watford	Tr	07.46	46-47	50	-	0
MORGAN Nicholas						
East Ham, 30 October, 1959						(F)
West Ham U.	App	11.77	78-82	14	7	2
Portsmouth	Tr	03.83	82-86	79	16	32
Stoke C.	Tr	11.86	86-89	73	15	21
Bristol C.	Tr	03.90	89-92	75	5	23
Bournemouth	L	10.92	92	6	0	1
Exeter C. (N/C)	Tr	02.94	93	12	0	4
MORGAN Peter William						
Cardiff, 28 October, 1951						(D)
Cardiff C.	Jnrs	11.69	72	16	0	0
Hereford U.	Tr	08.74	74	16	0	0
Newport Co.	Tr	03.76	75-76	22	2	0
MORGAN Philip Jonathan						
Stoke, 18 December, 1974 E Sch/E Yth						(G)
Ipswich T.	YT	07.93	94	1	0	0
Stoke C.	Tr	07.95				
Chesterfield	L	10.96	96	2	0	0
MORGAN Richard (Richie) Leslie						
Cardiff, 3 October, 1946 W Sch/Wu23-1						(CD)
Cardiff C.	Cardiff Corries	02.66	67-76	69	0	0
MORGAN Roger Ernest						
Walthamstow, 14 November, 1946 E Yth/Eu23-1						(W)
Queens Park R.	App	09.64	64-68	180	0	39
Tottenham H.	Tr	02.69	68-71	66	2	8
MORGAN Ronald						
Twynrodyn, 6 September, 1915 Died 1990						(CF)
Bournemouth	Wolverhampton W. (Am)	06.35	35	2	-	1
Doncaster Rov.	Tr	05.37	37-38	5	-	1
Accrington St.	Tr	06.39	46	4	-	0
MORGAN Ryan Stephen						
Bristol, 12 July, 1978						(M)
Bristol Rov.	YT	03.97	96	1	0	0
MORGAN Samuel John						
Belfast, 3 December, 1946 NI-18						(F)
Port Vale	Gorleston	07.70	69-72	109	5	25
Aston Villa	Tr	08.73	73-75	35	5	9
Brighton & H.A.	Tr	12.75	75-76	19	16	8
Cambridge U.	Tr	08.77	77	34	3	4
MORGAN Scott						
Colchester, 22 March, 1975						(D)
Brentford	Bournemouth (YT)	08.93	93	1	0	0

MORGAN Sidney Samuel
Bristol, 1 August, 1926 (G)

League Club	Source	Date Signed	Seasons Played	Apps	Subs	Gls
Bristol C.	A.G. Farmers	12.47	48-53	71	-	0
Millwall	Tr	03.58	57-58	16	-	0

MORGAN Simon Charles
Birmingham, 5 September, 1966 Eu21-2 (FB/M)

League Club	Source	Date Signed	Seasons Played	Apps	Subs	Gls
Leicester C.	YT	11.84	85-89	147	13	3
Fulham	Tr	10.90	90-97	285	5	43

MORGAN Simon Dean
Merthyr Tydfil, 3 September, 1970 (M)

League Club	Source	Date Signed	Seasons Played	Apps	Subs	Gls
Newport Co.	YT	●	87	0	2	0

MORGAN Alfred Stanley
Abergwynfl, 10 October, 1920 (IF)

League Club	Source	Date Signed	Seasons Played	Apps	Subs	Gls
Arsenal	Gwynfi Welfare	12.41	46	2	-	0
Walsall	Tr	06.48	48	10	-	1
Millwall	Tr	12.48	48-52	156	-	41
Leyton Orient	Tr	05.53	53-55	96	-	24

MORGAN Stephen Alfonso
Oldham, 19 September, 1968 E Yth (LB)

League Club	Source	Date Signed	Seasons Played	Apps	Subs	Gls
Blackpool	App	08.86	85-89	135	9	10
Plymouth Arg.	Tr	07.90	90-92	120	1	6
Coventry C.	Tr	07.93	93-94	65	3	2
Bristol Rov.	L	03.96	95	5	0	0
Wigan Ath.	Tr	07.96	96-97	31	5	2
Bury	L	09.97	97	5	0	0

MORGAN Stephen James
Wrexham, 28 December, 1970 W Yth (W)

League Club	Source	Date Signed	Seasons Played	Apps	Subs	Gls
Oldham Ath.	YT	07.89	87-88	1	1	0
Wrexham	L	03.90	89	7	0	1
Rochdale	Tr	03.91	90-91	12	11	3

MORGAN Stuart Edward
Swansea, 23 September, 1949 (CD)

League Club	Source	Date Signed	Seasons Played	Apps	Subs	Gls
West Ham U.	Jnrs	03.67				
Torquay U.	L	02.69	68	14	0	0
Reading	Tr	11.69	69-71	42	4	1
Colchester U.	Tr	08.72	72-74	79	2	10
Bournemouth	Tr	03.75	74-76	80	1	5

MORGAN Trevor James
Forest Gate, 30 September, 1956 (F)

League Club	Source	Date Signed	Seasons Played	Apps	Subs	Gls
Bournemouth	Leytonstone	09.80	80-81	53	0	13
Mansfield T.	Tr	11.81	81	12	0	6
Bournemouth	Tr	03.82	81-83	88	0	33
Bristol C.	Tr	03.84	83-84	32	0	8
Exeter C.	Tr	11.84	84-85	31	0	9
Bristol Rov.	Tr	09.85	85-86	54	1	24
Bristol C.	Tr	01.87	86	19	0	7
Bolton W.	Tr	06.87	87-88	65	12	17
Colchester U.	Tr	10.89	89	31	1	12
Exeter C.	Happy Valley (HK)	11.90	90	14	3	3
Exeter C. (N/C)	(Retirement)	09.94	94	4	5	1

MORGAN Wendell
Gorseinon, 22 April, 1935 (W)

League Club	Source	Date Signed	Seasons Played	Apps	Subs	Gls
Cardiff C.	Jnrs	05.52				
Brentford	Tr	06.54	55-57	47	-	6
Gillingham	Tr	09.57	57	34	-	3
Swansea C.	Tr	07.58	58	7	-	0
Newport Co.	Tr	06.59	59	26	-	3
Carlisle U.	Tr	06.60	60	35	-	2

MORGAN William
Glasgow, 2 October, 1944 Su23-1/S-21 (W)

League Club	Source	Date Signed	Seasons Played	Apps	Subs	Gls
Burnley	Jnrs	10.61	62-67	183	0	19
Manchester U.	Tr	08.68	68-74	236	2	25
Burnley	Tr	06.75	75	12	1	0
Bolton W.	Tr	03.76	75-79	154	1	10
Blackpool	Minnesota (USA)	09.80	80-81	41	1	4

MORGAN William Alfred
Rotherham, 26 September, 1926 (WH)

League Club	Source	Date Signed	Seasons Played	Apps	Subs	Gls
Wolverhampton W.	Jnrs	11.43				
Sheffield U.	Tr	09.46				
Halifax T.	Tr	08.48	48-52	109	-	3
Rochdale	Tr	07.53	53-54	28	-	0

MORGAN Wynffrwd
Abergwynfl, 7 August, 1925 (OR)

League Club	Source	Date Signed	Seasons Played	Apps	Subs	Gls
Bristol Rov. (Am)		12.46	46	2	-	0

MORGANS Morgan Gwyn
Blaenau Ffestiniog, 20 April, 1932 (WH)

League Club	Source	Date Signed	Seasons Played	Apps	Subs	Gls
Northampton T.	Blaenew Ffestiniog	08.55				
Wrexham	Tr	07.56	56-57	28	-	2
Southport	Tr	07.58	58	14	-	0

MORGANS Jeffrey
Farnborough, 12 August, 1942 Died 1995 (OR)

League Club	Source	Date Signed	Seasons Played	Apps	Subs	Gls
Crewe Alex.	Jnrs	09.59	60-61	9	-	2

MORGANS Kenneth Godfrey
Swansea, 16 March, 1939 Wu23-2 (IF)

League Club	Source	Date Signed	Seasons Played	Apps	Subs	Gls
Manchester U.	Jnrs	04.56	57-60	17	-	0
Swansea C.	Tr	03.61	60-63	55	-	8
Newport Co.	Tr	06.64	64-66	125	0	43

MORLEY William Anthony
Ormskirk, 26 August, 1954 E Yth/Eu23-1/E'B'/E-6 (LW)

League Club	Source	Date Signed	Seasons Played	Apps	Subs	Gls
Preston N.E.	App	08.72	72-75	78	6	15
Burnley	Tr	02.76	75-78	78	13	5
Aston Villa	Tr	06.79	79-83	128	9	25
West Bromwich A.	Tr	12.83	83-84	33	0	4
Birmingham C.	L	11.84	84	4	0	3
West Bromwich A.	Den Haag (Neth)	08.87	87	27	1	7
Burnley	L	10.88	88	5	0	0

MORLEY Benjamin
Hull, 22 December, 1980 (RWB)

League Club	Source	Date Signed	Seasons Played	Apps	Subs	Gls
Hull C.	YT	●	97	5	3	0

MORLEY Brian James
Fleetwood, 4 October, 1960 (LB)

League Club	Source	Date Signed	Seasons Played	Apps	Subs	Gls
Blackburn Rov.	App	10.78	78-79	20	0	0
Tranmere Rov.	Tr	08.81	81	10	6	2

MORLEY David Thomas
St Helens, 25 September, 1977 (M)

League Club	Source	Date Signed	Seasons Played	Apps	Subs	Gls
Manchester C.	YT	01.96	97	1	2	1

MORLEY Trevor William
Nottingham, 20 March, 1961 E Semi Pro (F)

League Club	Source	Date Signed	Seasons Played	Apps	Subs	Gls
Northampton T.	Nuneaton Borough	06.85	85-87	107	0	39
Manchester C.	Tr	01.88	87-89	69	3	18
West Ham U.	Tr	12.89	89-94	159	19	57
Reading	Brann Bergen (Nor)	08.95	95-97	67	10	31

MORLEY William
Nottingham, 30 July, 1925 Died 1978 (WH)

League Club	Source	Date Signed	Seasons Played	Apps	Subs	Gls
Nottingham F.	Mapperley Celtic	08.45	46-58	282	-	10

MORONEY Thomas
Cork (Ire), 10 November, 1923 Died 1981 LoI/IR-12 (WH)

League Club	Source	Date Signed	Seasons Played	Apps	Subs	Gls
West Ham U.	Cork U.	08.47	47-52	148	-	8

MORRAD Frank
Brentford, 28 February, 1920 (FB/CF)

League Club	Source	Date Signed	Seasons Played	Apps	Subs	Gls
Notts Co.		08.44	46	1	-	0
Leyton Orient	Tr	11.46	46	25	-	11
Fulham	Tr	08.47				
Brighton & H.A.	Tr	02.48	47-50	43	-	3
Brentford	Tr	08.51	51-52	6	-	2

MORRALL Alfred Douglas
Birmingham, 1 July, 1916 (F/WH)

League Club	Source	Date Signed	Seasons Played	Apps	Subs	Gls
Northampton T.	Redditch	10.44	46-47	34	-	11
Newport Co.	Tr	07.48	48	28	-	0

MORRALL Stephen Asbury
Torquay, 25 September, 1952 (W)

League Club	Source	Date Signed	Seasons Played	Apps	Subs	Gls
Torquay U.	Jnrs	08.72	72-76	133	31	12

MORRALL Terence Stephen
Smethwick, 24 November, 1938 (CH)

League Club	Source	Date Signed	Seasons Played	Apps	Subs	Gls
Aston Villa	Jnrs	11.55	59-60	8	-	0
Shrewsbury T.	Tr	05.61	60-62	31	-	0
Wrexham	Tr	07.63	63-64	42	-	0
Southport	Tr	07.65	65	1	0	0

MORRELL Paul David
Poole, 23 March, 1961 (LB)

League Club	Source	Date Signed	Seasons Played	Apps	Subs	Gls
Bournemouth	Weymouth	06.83	83-92	337	6	8

MORRELL Robert Ian
Heselden (Dm), 4 June, 1944 (WH)

League Club	Source	Date Signed	Seasons Played	Apps	Subs	Gls
Hartlepool U.	Blackhall	03.64	63-64	34	-	0

MORREY Bernard Joseph
Liverpool, 8 April, 1927 (W)

League Club	Source	Date Signed	Seasons Played	Apps	Subs	Gls
Tranmere Rov.	Jnrs	08.44				
Newport Co.	Llandudno	10.52	52-53	24	-	2
Chester C.	Tr	12.53	53-54	30	-	6

MORRIN Anthony John
Eccles, 31 July, 1946 (M)

League Club	Source	Date Signed	Seasons Played	Apps	Subs	Gls
Bury	App	10.63	63-64	3	-	0
Burnley	Tr	07.65				
Stockport Co.	Tr	10.66	66-68	26	5	2
Barrow	Tr	03.69	68-70	97	3	6
Exeter C.	Tr	07.71	71-76	180	2	15
Stockport Co.	Tr	03.77	76	13	0	1
Rochdale	Tr	08.77	77-78	29	1	0

MORRIS Alan
Swansea, 6 April, 1941 (W)

League Club	Source	Date Signed	Seasons Played	Apps	Subs	Gls
Swansea C.	Jnrs	06.58	57-62	12	-	1
Reading	Tr	08.63	63	12	-	0

MORRIS Alan Geoffrey
Chester, 15 July, 1954 (D)

League Club	Source	Date Signed	Seasons Played	Apps	Subs	Gls
Chester C.	Bangor C.	06.84	84	0	1	0

MORRIS Alfred
Cadishead (WH)

League Club	Source	Date Signed	Seasons Played	Apps	Subs	Gls
Accrington St.	Rochdale (Am)	10.45	46-47	15	-	0

MORRIS Andrew Dean
Sheffield, 17 November, 1967 (F)

League Club	Source	Date Signed	Seasons Played	Apps	Subs	Gls
Rotherham U.	Jnrs	07.85	84-86	0	7	0
Chesterfield	Tr	01.88	87-97	225	50	46
Exeter C.	L	03.92	91	4	3	2

MORRIS Christopher Barry
Newquay, 24 December, 1963 E Sch/IR-35 (FB)

League Club	Source	Date Signed	Seasons Played	Apps	Subs	Gls
Sheffield Wed.	Jnrs	10.82	83-86	61	13	1
Middlesbrough	Glasgow Celtic	08.92	92-96	75	7	3

MORRIS Christopher Joseph
Spilsby (Lincs), 12 October, 1939 (OR)

League Club	Source	Date Signed	Seasons Played	Apps	Subs	Gls
Hull C.	Jnrs	10.57	58-60	17	-	4
York C.	Tr	06.61				

MORRIS Colin
Blyth, 22 August, 1953 (RW)

League Club	Source	Date Signed	Seasons Played	Apps	Subs	Gls
Burnley	App	08.71	74-75	9	1	0
Southend U.	Tr	01.77	76-79	133	0	25
Blackpool	Tr	12.79	79-81	87	0	26
Sheffield U.	Tr	02.82	81-87	235	5	68
Scarborough	Tr	07.88	88-89	20	4	3

MORRIS David
Swansea, 20 September, 1957 (F)

League Club	Source	Date Signed	Seasons Played	Apps	Subs	Gls
Manchester U.	App	10.74				
York C.	L	03.77	76	1	6	0

MORRIS David Kenneth
Greenwich, 19 November, 1971 (CD)

League Club	Source	Date Signed	Seasons Played	Apps	Subs	Gls
Bournemouth	YT	07.90	90	0	1	0
Hereford U.	Tr	02.93	92-93	33	7	1

MORRIS Douglas
Durham, 29 July, 1925 (OR)

League Club	Source	Date Signed	Seasons Played	Apps	Subs	Gls
Hartlepool U.	Ushaw Moor	01.46	46-50	19	-	3

MORRIS Edwin
Pontypool, 6 May, 1921 (G)

League Club	Source	Date Signed	Seasons Played	Apps	Subs	Gls
Cardiff C.	Bewdley	05.48	48-50	8	-	0

MORRIS Elfed
Colwyn Bay, 9 June, 1942 (F)

League Club	Source	Date Signed	Seasons Played	Apps	Subs	Gls
Wrexham		05.60	60-61	9	-	6
Chester C.	Tr	06.62	62-67	164	3	69
Halifax T.	Tr	03.68	67-68	9	0	2

MORRIS Edward Eric
Mold, 15 April, 1940 (FB)

League Club	Source	Date Signed	Seasons Played	Apps	Subs	Gls
Chester C.		06.60	60	1	-	0

MORRIS Ernest
Stocksbridge, 11 May, 1921 (CF)

League Club	Source	Date Signed	Seasons Played	Apps	Subs	Gls
Nottingham F.		08.47	47	4	-	1
York C.	Tr	06.48				
Halifax T.	Grantham	11.50	50	1	-	0

MORRIS Frank
Penge, 28 March, 1932 (OL)

League Club	Source	Date Signed	Seasons Played	Apps	Subs	Gls
Crystal Palace		03.56	56	8	-	0

MORRIS Frederick Alfred
Sheffield, 11 March, 1920 Died 1973 (W)

League Club	Source	Date Signed	Seasons Played	Apps	Subs	Gls
Barnsley		09.46	46-48	23	-	9
Southend U.	Tr	01.49	48-49	34	-	16

MORRIS Frederick William
Oswestry, 15 June, 1929 (OR)

League Club	Source	Date Signed	Seasons Played	Apps	Subs	Gls
Walsall	Oswestry T.	05.50	50-56	213	-	44
Mansfield T.	Tr	03.57	56-57	56	-	17
Liverpool	Tr	05.58	58-59	47	-	14
Crewe Alex.	Tr	06.60	60	8	-	1
Gillingham	Tr	01.61	60	11	-	1
Chester C.	Tr	07.61	61	27	-	3

MORRIS Geoffrey
Birmingham, 8 February, 1949 (OL)

League Club	Source	Date Signed	Seasons Played	Apps	Subs	Gls
Walsall	App	02.66	65-72	172	5	35
Shrewsbury T.	Tr	01.73	72-74	71	4	9
Port Vale	Tr	08.75	75	10	5	1

MORRIS George Edward
Crewe, 22 November, 1929 (FB)

League Club	Source	Date Signed	Seasons Played	Apps	Subs	Gls
Crewe Alex.	Crewe Cadets	08.48	48-54	30	-	0

MORRIS Gordon John
Wolverhampton, 27 June, 1926 (IF)

League Club	Source	Date Signed	Seasons Played	Apps	Subs	Gls
West Bromwich A.	East Park	11.44				
Walsall	Tr	07.49	49	6	-	2

MORRIS Ian Gwynfor
Manchester, 10 June, 1948 (W)

League Club	Source	Date Signed	Seasons Played	Apps	Subs	Gls
Stockport Co.	Bolton W. (Am)	03.68	67	1	1	0

MORRIS James Henry
St Helens, 16 November, 1915 (CH/OR)

League Club	Source	Date Signed	Seasons Played	Apps	Subs	Gls
Stockport Co.	St Helens T.	08.39	46-48	61	-	3

MORRIS Jody
Hammersmith, 22 December, 1978 E Sch/E Yth/Eu21-3 (M)

League Club	Source	Date Signed	Seasons Played	Apps	Subs	Gls
Chelsea	YT	01.96	95-97	15	10	1

MORRIS John
Radcliffe, 27 September, 1923 E 'B'/EF Lge/E-3 (IF)

League Club	Source	Date Signed	Seasons Played	Apps	Subs	Gls
Manchester U.	Jnrs	03.41	46-48	83	-	32
Derby Co.	Tr	03.49	48-52	130	-	44
Leicester C.	Tr	10.52	52-57	206	-	33

MORRIS John Edward
Crewe, 27 November, 1937 (IF)

League Club	Source	Date Signed	Seasons Played	Apps	Subs	Gls
Crewe Alex.	Jnrs	12.54	54	3	-	0

MORRIS Joseph Richard
Canning Town, 13 April, 1934 (IF)

League Club	Source	Date Signed	Seasons Played	Apps	Subs	Gls
Crewe Alex.		08.54	54	1	-	0

MORRIS Kevin George
Bridgnorth, 22 September, 1953 (RB)

League Club	Source	Date Signed	Seasons Played	Apps	Subs	Gls
Shrewsbury T.	App	07.71	70-71	9	0	0

MORRIS Lee
Blackpool, 30 April, 1980 E Yth (F)

League Club	Source	Date Signed	Seasons Played	Apps	Subs	Gls
Sheffield U.	YT	12.97	97	0	5	0

MORRIS Maldwyn Jones Gravell
Swansea, 3 August, 1932 (F)

League Club	Source	Date Signed	Seasons Played	Apps	Subs	Gls
Swansea C.	Pembroke Borough	10.56	56-57	15	-	5

MORRIS Mark
Chester, 1 August, 1968 (G)

League Club	Source	Date Signed	Seasons Played	Apps	Subs	Gls
Wrexham	YT	08.87	85-93	101	0	0

MORRIS Mark John
Carshalton, 26 September, 1962 (CD)

League Club	Source	Date Signed	Seasons Played	Apps	Subs	Gls
Wimbledon	App	09.80	81-86	167	1	9
Aldershot	L	09.85	85	14	0	0
Watford	Tr	07.87	87-88	41	0	1
Sheffield U.	Tr	07.89	89-90	53	3	3
Bournemouth	Tr	07.91	91-96	190	4	8
Gillingham	L	09.96	96	6	0	0
Brighton & H.A.	Tr	10.96	96-97	30	1	2

MORRIS Michael John
West Ham, 20 January, 1943 (W)

League Club	Source	Date Signed	Seasons Played	Apps	Subs	Gls
Oxford U.	Faversham	07.64	64-66	89	1	15
Port Vale	Tr	08.67	67-71	176	8	24

MORRIS Neil Anthony
Sheffield, 3 May, 1970 (F)

League Club	Source	Date Signed	Seasons Played	Apps	Subs	Gls
York C.	Doncaster Rov. (YT)	09.88	88	3	1	0
Doncaster Rov. (N/C)	Worksop T.	02.92	91	0	1	0

MORRIS Paul
Bolton, 6 February, 1975 (D)

League Club	Source	Date Signed	Seasons Played	Apps	Subs	Gls
Bury	YT	●	92	0	1	0

League Club	Source	Date Signed	Seasons Played	Career Record Apps	Subs	Gls
MORRIS Paul Whittington						
Glasfryn, 8 January, 1957						(F)
Hereford U.	Llanelli	02.80	79-80	2	2	1
MORRIS Peter Andrew						
Farnworth, 23 November, 1958						(W)
Preston N.E.	App	10.76				
Blackburn Rov.	Tr	07.78	78	2	2	0
MORRIS Peter John						
Shirebrook, 8 November, 1943						(M)
Mansfield T.	Jnrs	11.60	60-67	286	1	50
Ipswich T.	Tr	03.68	67-73	213	7	13
Norwich C.	Tr	06.74	74-75	66	0	1
Mansfield T.	Tr	07.76	76-77	41	0	3
Peterborough U.	Newcastle U. (coach)	08.79	79	1	0	0
MORRIS Ronald						
Birmingham, 25 September, 1970						(W)
Birmingham C.	YT	09.88	87-88	3	8	0
MORRIS Samuel						
Warrington, 12 February, 1930						(WH)
Chester C.	Stockton Heath	12.51	51-56	90	-	0
MORRIS Stephen						
Liverpool, 13 May, 1976						(F)
Wrexham	Liverpool (YT)	09.94	94-96	24	18	9
MORRIS Stephen Albert						
Bristol, 6 July, 1949						(M/LB)
Bristol C.	App	06.67				
Exeter C.	Tr	06.69	69-71	61	11	2
MORRIS Steven Granville						
Swansea, 8 October, 1958						(LB)
Swansea C.	App	06.76	75-78	33	6	1
Plymouth Arg.	Tr	01.80				
MORRIS William						
Radcliffe, 1 April, 1931						(OR)
Bury	Jnrs	05.48				
Derby Co.	Tr	10.51				
Rochdale	Tr	11.52	52	4	-	1
MORRIS William						
Colwyn Bay, 30 July, 1918 W-5						(IF)
Burnley	Llandudno	01.39	38-52	211	-	47
MORRIS William Henry						
Swansea, 28 September, 1920 Died 1994						(OL)
Swansea C.		05.46	47-48	16	-	1
Brighton & H.A.	Tr	09.49	49-50	28	-	4
MORRIS William Walker						
Birmingham, 26 March, 1913 Died 1995 E-3						(FB)
Wolverhampton W.	Halesowen T.	05.33	33-46	175	-	2
MORRISON Andrew Charles						
Inverness, 30 July, 1970						(D/M)
Plymouth Arg.	YT	07.88	87-92	105	8	6
Blackburn Rov.	Tr	08.93	93	1	4	0
Blackpool	Tr	12.94	94-95	47	0	3
Huddersfield T.	Tr	07.96	96-97	31	2	2
MORRISON Angus Cameron						
Dingwall, 26 April, 1924 S 'B'						(OL)
Derby Co.	Ross Co.	10.44	46-47	52	-	21
Preston N.E.	Tr	11.48	48-56	262	-	70
Millwall	Tr	10.57	57	15	-	4
MORRISON Charles						
Hartlepool, 12 January, 1953						(D)
Chelsea	App	08.70				
Doncaster Rov.	Tr	07.72	72	5	1	0
MORRISON Clinton Hubert						
Wandsworth, 4 May, 1979						(F)
Crystal Palace	YT	03.97	97	0	1	1
MORRISON David Ellison						
Walthamstow, 30 November, 1974						(W)
Peterborough U.	Chelmsford C.	05.94	94-96	59	18	12
Leyton Orient	Tr	03.97	96-97	9	1	0
MORRISON George Charles						
Ayr, 27 November, 1924						(CH)
Hartlepool U.	St Johnstone	08.51	51	2	-	0

League Club	Source	Date Signed	Seasons Played	Career Record Apps	Subs	Gls
MORRISON John						
Greenock, 4 August, 1929						(IL)
Torquay U.	Morton	07.51	51	2	-	0
MORRISON John						
Kettering, 27 July, 1970						(M)
Torquay U.	YT	07.88	88-89	24	8	0
MORRISON Murdo						
Glasgow, 9 October, 1924 Died 1975						(G)
Luton T.	Bell Haven Star	09.45	46	1	-	0
Leyton Orient	Tr	08.47	47	10	-	0
MORRISON Robert Crosson						
Chapelhall, 16 February, 1933						(IF)
Nottingham F.	Glasgow Rangers	07.58	58	1	-	0
Workington	Tr	07.59	59-60	53	-	20
MORRISON Thomas						
Kilsyth, 6 March, 1943						(IF)
Port Vale	Aberdeen	08.65	65	5	0	0
MORRISON William						
Edinburgh, 31 March, 1934						(WH)
Sunderland	Merchiston Thistle	05.51	54-56	19	-	0
Southend U.	Tr	01.58	57-59	60	-	4
MORRISON William						
Kilsyth, 10 October, 1939						(FB)
Portsmouth	Croy Guilds	05.58	58	3	-	0
MORRISSEY John Joseph						
Liverpool, 18 April, 1940 E Sch/EF Lge						(OL)
Liverpool	Jnrs	05.57	57-60	36	-	6
Everton	Tr	09.62	62-71	257	2	43
Oldham Ath.	Tr	05.72	72	6	0	1
MORRISSEY John Joseph						
Liverpool, 8 March, 1965 E Yth						(RW)
Everton	App	03.83	84	1	0	0
Wolverhampton W.	Tr	08.85	85	5	5	1
Tranmere Rov.	Tr	10.85	85-97	391	55	50
MORRISSEY Patrick Joseph						
Enniscorthy (Ire), 23 February, 1948 IRu23-1						(F)
Coventry C.	App	07.65	66-67	6	4	0
Torquay U.	Tr	07.68	68	19	2	0
Crewe Alex.	Tr	07.69	69-71	95	1	28
Chester C.	Tr	10.71	71	9	0	1
Watford	Tr	12.71	71-74	101	6	27
Aldershot	Tr	11.74	74-76	109	0	27
Swansea C.	L	10.77	77	3	1	0
MORRITT Gordon Raymond						
Rotherham, 8 February, 1942						(G)
Rotherham U.	Steel Peach & Tozer	06.61	61-65	77	0	0
Doncaster Rov.	Durban C. (SA)	09.67	67-68	40	0	0
Northampton T.	Tr	08.68	68-69	42	0	0
York C.	Tr	10.69	69-71	41	0	0
Rochdale	Tr	08.72	72	31	0	0
Darlington	Tr	08.73	73	34	0	0
MORROW Grant Ralph						
Glasgow, 4 October, 1970						(F)
Doncaster Rov.	Rowntree-Mackintosh	07.89	89-92	46	18	7
Colchester U. (N/C)	Tr	08.93	93	0	1	0
MORROW Hugh						
Larne (NI), 9 July, 1930						(OR)
West Bromwich A.	Jnrs	08.47	48	5	-	2
Northampton T.	Lockheed Leamington	06.56	56	30	-	3
MORROW John James						
Belfast, 20 November, 1971 NI Yth/NI 'B'						(W)
Oldham Ath.	Glasgow Rangers	08.96	96	1	1	0
MORROW Stephen Joseph						
Bangor (NI), 2 July, 1970 NI Sch/NI Yth/NIu23-2/NI 'B'/NI-32						(M/D)
Arsenal	YT	05.88	91-96	39	23	1
Reading	L	01.91	90	10	0	0
Watford	L	08.91	91	7	1	0
Reading	L	10.91	91	3	0	0
Barnet	L	03.92	91	1	0	0
Queens Park R.	Tr	03.97	96-97	36	0	2
MORSE Richard Anthony						
Newport, 17 December, 1966						(D)
Newport Co. (N/C)	Jnrs	08.83	83	0	1	0

League Club	Source	Date Signed	Seasons Played	Career Record Apps	Subs	Gls
MORTENSEN Henrik						
Denmark, 12 February, 1968						(F)
Norwich C.	Aarhus G.F. (Den)	10.89	89-90	12	6	0
MORTENSEN Stanley Harding						
South Shields, 26 May, 1921 Died 1991 EF Lge/E-25						(CF)
Blackpool	Jnrs	05.38	46-55	317	-	197
Hull C.	Tr	11.55	55-56	42	-	18
Southport	Tr	02.57	56-57	36	-	10
MORTIMER Dennis George						
Liverpool, 5 April, 1952 E Yth/Eu23-6/E'B'						(M)
Coventry C.	App	09.69	69-75	179	14	10
Aston Villa	Tr	12.75	75-84	316	1	31
Sheffield U.	L	12.84	84	7	0	0
Brighton & H.A.	Tr	08.85	85	40	0	2
Birmingham C.	Tr	08.86	86	33	0	4
MORTIMER John McCormick						
Birkenhead, 5 December, 1923						(FB)
Wrexham		01.47	46-48	23	-	0
New Brighton	Tr	10.49	49-50	5	-	0
MORTIMER Paul Henry						
Kensington, 8 May, 1968 Eu21-2						(M)
Charlton Ath.	Farnborough T.	09.87	87-90	108	5	17
Aston Villa	Tr	07.91	91	10	2	1
Crystal Palace	Tr	10.91	91-92	18	4	2
Brentford	L	01.93	92	6	0	0
Charlton Ath.	Tr	07.94	94-97	57	12	14
MORTIMORE Charles Thomas Reginald						
Gosport, 12 April, 1928 E Amat						(CF)
Aldershot (Am)	Woking	08.49	49-52	67	-	27
Portsmouth (Am)	Woking	10.53	53	1	-	0
Aldershot (Am)	Woking	12.55	55	2	-	0
MORTIMORE John Henry						
Farnborough, 23 September, 1934 E Amat/E Yth						(CH)
Chelsea	Woking	04.56	55-64	249	-	8
Queens Park R.	Tr	09.65	65	10	0	0
MORTON Alan						
Dartford, 13 April, 1950						(CF)
Crystal Palace	Woking	11.67				
Stockport Co.	L	08.69	69	12	2	2
Fulham	Nuneaton Borough	08.70	70	1	0	1
MORTON Alan						
Peterborough, 6 March, 1942						(IF)
Arsenal	Peterborough U.	04.59				
Peterborough U.	Tr	10.61	61-62	7	-	2
Lincoln C.	Wisbech T.	07.63	63-64	58	-	20
Chesterfield	Tr	07.65	65	28	1	6
MORTON Albert						
Newcastle, 27 July, 1919 Died 1991						(G)
Sheffield Wed.	St Peters A.	03.38	47-50	41	-	0
Rochdale	Tr	07.53	53-56	89	-	0
MORTON Geoffrey Dalgleish						
Acton, 27 July, 1924						(G)
Watford	Chelmsford C.	10.48	48-51	107	-	0
Southend U.	Tr	02.52	51-52	25	-	0
Exeter C.	Tr	09.54	54	6	-	0
MORTON George Edmund						
Liverpool, 30 September, 1943						(IF)
Everton	Jnrs	10.60				
Rochdale	Tr	07.62	62-65	146	1	51
MORTON Gerald William						
Newcastle, 17 March, 1944						(CH)
Newcastle U.	North Shields	08.62				
Workington	Tr	04.63	62-63	3	-	0
MORTON Keith						
Consett, 11 August, 1934						(CF)
Crystal Palace (Am)		08.53	53	5	-	3
Sunderland	Tr	07.54				
Darlington	Tr	05.55	55-60	175	-	50
MORTON Kenneth						
Copley, 19 May, 1947 E Sch						(OL)
Manchester U.	App	05.64				
York C.	Tr	05.65	65	9	1	2
Blackpool	Tr	08.66				
Darlington	Fleetwood	07.68	68	3	1	0

League Club	Source	Date Signed	Seasons Played	Career Record Apps	Subs	Gls
MORTON Neil						
Congleton, 21 December, 1968						(W)
Crewe Alex.	YT	09.87	86-88	18	13	1
Chester C.	Northwich Vic.	10.90	90-92	63	32	13
Wigan Ath.	Tr	07.93	93-94	41	7	5
MORTON Norman						
Barnsley, 22 May, 1925 Died 1977						(CF)
Leeds U.	Woolley Colly	12.47	47	1	-	0
MORTON Robert						
Aston Clinton, 25 September, 1927 E 'B'						(WH)
Luton T.	Eaton Bray	02.46	48-63	495	-	48
MORTON Roy Steven						
Birmingham, 29 October, 1955 E Yth						(M)
Manchester U.	App	11.72				
Birmingham C.	Tr	09.73	74	3	0	0
MORTON William						
Grangemouth, 2 April, 1928						(CH)
Millwall		10.45	46-50	11	-	0
MOSBY Harold						
Kippax, 25 June, 1926						(F)
Rotherham U.	Huddersfield T. (Am)	01.47	47-49	26	-	9
Scunthorpe U.	Tr	07.50	50-54	149	-	21
Crewe Alex.	Worksop T.	08.56	56	38	-	4
MOSELEY Graham						
Manchester, 16 November, 1953 E Yth						(G)
Blackburn Rov.	App	09.71				
Derby Co.	Tr	09.71	72-76	32	0	0
Aston Villa	L	08.74	74	3	0	0
Walsall	L	10.77	77	3	0	0
Brighton & H.A.	Tr	11.77	77-85	189	0	0
Cardiff C.	Tr	08.86	86-87	38	0	0
MOSES Adrian Paul						
Doncaster, 4 May, 1975 Eu21-2						(CD)
Barnsley	Jnrs	07.93	94-97	81	10	3
MOSES George						
High Spen, 11 September, 1920 Died 1987						(IR)
Newcastle U.		10.39				
Hartlepool U.	Tr	08.46	46	19	-	4
MOSES Remi Mark						
Manchester, 14 November, 1960 Eu21-8						(M)
West Bromwich A.	App	11.78	79-81	63	0	5
Manchester U.	Tr	09.81	81-87	143	7	7
MOSS Amos						
Birmingham, 28 August, 1921						(WH)
Aston Villa	Jnrs	05.39	46-55	103	-	5
MOSS Craig Anthony						
Birmingham, 11 March, 1961						(W)
Wolverhampton W.	App	03.79	78-81	4	0	0
MOSS David Albert						
Doncaster, 15 November, 1968						(M)
Doncaster Rov.	Boston U.	03.93	92-93	18	0	5
Chesterfield	Tr	10.93	93-95	59	12	16
Scunthorpe U.	Tr	07.96	96	4	0	0
MOSS David John						
Witney, 18 March, 1952						(W)
Swindon T.	Witney T.	07.69	71-77	217	13	60
Luton T.	Tr	05.78	78-84	218	3	88
Swindon T.	Tr	07.85	85	4	0	0
MOSS Donald Richard						
Tamworth, 27 June, 1925						(WH)
Cardiff C.	Boldmere St Michael	05.51				
Crystal Palace	Tr	05.53	53-56	56	-	2
MOSS Edward						
Skelmersdale, 27 October, 1939						(IF)
Liverpool	Skelmersdale U.	10.58				
Southport	Tr	07.59	59-60	51	-	15
MOSS Ernest						
Chesterfield, 19 October, 1949						(F)
Chesterfield	Chesterfield Tube	10.68	68-75	271	0	95
Peterborough U.	Tr	01.76	75-76	34	1	9
Mansfield T.	Tr	12.76	76-78	56	1	21
Chesterfield	Tr	01.79	78-80	105	2	33
Port Vale	Tr	06.81	81-82	74	0	23

League Club	Source	Date Signed	Seasons Played	Apps	Subs	Gls
Lincoln C.	Tr	03.83	82	10	1	2
Doncaster Rov.	Tr	06.83	83	41	3	15
Chesterfield	Tr	07.84	84-86	88	1	34
Stockport Co.	Tr	12.86	86	26	0	7
Scarborough	Tr	08.87	87	22	1	4
Rochdale	L	03.88	87	10	0	2

MOSS Frank
Birmingham, 16 September, 1917 Died 1997 (CH)

League Club	Source	Date Signed	Seasons Played	Apps	Subs	Gls
Sheffield Wed.	Worcester Nondescripts	11.35	36-37	22	-	0
Aston Villa	Tr	05.38	38-54	296	-	3

MOSS Jack
Blackrod, 1 September, 1923 (IF)

League Club	Source	Date Signed	Seasons Played	Apps	Subs	Gls
Bury		12.43	46	7	-	2
Rochdale	Tr	01.47	46-48	58	-	17
Leeds U.	Tr	01.49	48-50	23	-	2
Halifax T.	Tr	01.51	50-53	124	-	10

MOSS Neil Graham
New Milton, 10 May, 1975 (G)

League Club	Source	Date Signed	Seasons Played	Apps	Subs	Gls
Bournemouth	YT	01.93	92-95	21	1	0
Southampton	Tr	12.95	95-96	3	0	0
Gillingham	L	08.97	97	10	0	0

MOSS Paul Michael
Birmingham, 2 August, 1957 (M)

League Club	Source	Date Signed	Seasons Played	Apps	Subs	Gls
Wolverhampton W.	Northfield Jnrs	07.76				
Hull C.	Tr	09.79	79-80	53	1	7
Scunthorpe U.	Tr	09.81	81	42	0	7

MOSS Robert
Chigwell, 13 February, 1952 (F)

League Club	Source	Date Signed	Seasons Played	Apps	Subs	Gls
Leyton Orient	App	02.70	70	2	3	1
Colchester U.	Tr	05.72	72	16	2	3

MOSS Robert Stephen
Harrow, 15 February, 1949 (W)

League Club	Source	Date Signed	Seasons Played	Apps	Subs	Gls
Fulham	App	02.66	67	8	1	3
Peterborough U.	Tr	07.69	69-72	86	18	17

MOSS Roy Graham
Maldon (Ex), 5 September, 1941 E Sch (IF)

League Club	Source	Date Signed	Seasons Played	Apps	Subs	Gls
Tottenham H.	Jnrs	01.60				
Gillingham	Tr	09.62	62-63	14	-	3

MOSS Terence John
Bristol, 2 January, 1932 (OL)

League Club	Source	Date Signed	Seasons Played	Apps	Subs	Gls
Swindon T. (Am)		03.56	55	7	-	0

MOSSMAN David John
Chesterfield, 27 July, 1964 (W)

League Club	Source	Date Signed	Seasons Played	Apps	Subs	Gls
Sheffield Wed.	Jnrs	08.82				
Bradford C.	L	03.85	84	0	3	1
Stockport Co.	L	10.85	85	9	0	5
Rochdale	Tr	01.86	85	8	0	0
Stockport Co.	Tr	03.86	85-86	28	2	1

MOSSOP Graham
Wellington, 11 January, 1958 (F)

League Club	Source	Date Signed	Seasons Played	Apps	Subs	Gls
Workington	Liverpool (App)	11.75	75	1	0	0
Carlisle U.		07.79	80	2	0	0

MOSTYN Roger
Wrexham, 31 August, 1953 (F)

League Club	Source	Date Signed	Seasons Played	Apps	Subs	Gls
Wrexham	Jnrs	11.71	71-73	16	3	4

MOTTERSHEAD Brian Leslie
Rochdale, 13 July, 1935 (IF)

League Club	Source	Date Signed	Seasons Played	Apps	Subs	Gls
Notts Co.	Jnrs	09.52				
Rochdale	Tr	08.53	53	1	-	0

MOTTERSHEAD Keith Anthony
Stafford, 12 December, 1944 (OR)

League Club	Source	Date Signed	Seasons Played	Apps	Subs	Gls
Doncaster Rov.	Stafford R.	10.66	66-67	34	5	0

MOUGHTON Colin Edward
Harrow, 30 December, 1947 (WH)

League Club	Source	Date Signed	Seasons Played	Apps	Subs	Gls
Queens Park R.	App	12.65	65-66	6	0	0
Colchester U.	Tr	07.68	68	4	0	0

MOULD William
Stoke, 6 October, 1919 (FB)

League Club	Source	Date Signed	Seasons Played	Apps	Subs	Gls
Stoke C.	Summerbank	07.36	37-51	177	-	0
Crewe Alex.	Tr	07.52	52-53	66	-	1

MOULDEN Anthony
Farnworth, 28 August, 1942 (IF)

League Club	Source	Date Signed	Seasons Played	Apps	Subs	Gls
Bury	Blackburn Rov. (Am)	05.60	60-61	4	-	0
Rochdale	Tr	06.62	62	5	-	1
Peterborough U.	Tr	11.62	62-64	62	-	9
Notts Co.	Tr	05.65	65	23	0	1
Rochdale	Tr	09.66	66	1	1	0

MOULDEN Paul Anthony Joseph
Farnworth, 6 September, 1967 E Sch/E Yth (F)

League Club	Source	Date Signed	Seasons Played	Apps	Subs	Gls
Manchester C.	App	09.84	85-88	48	16	18
Bournemouth	Tr	07.89	89	32	0	13
Oldham Ath.	Tr	03.90	89-92	17	21	4
Brighton & H.A.	L	08.92	92	11	0	5
Birmingham C.	Tr	03.93	92-93	18	2	6
Huddersfield T.	Tr	03.95	94	0	2	0
Rochdale	Tr	08.95	95	6	10	1

MOULSON George Bernard
Tipperary, 6 August, 1914 Died 1994 IR-3 (G)

League Club	Source	Date Signed	Seasons Played	Apps	Subs	Gls
Grimsby T.	Jnrs	07.36	46	1	-	0
Lincoln C.	Tr	06.47	47-48	60	-	0

MOUNCER Frank Edmund
Grimsby, 22 November, 1920 Died 1977 E Sch (RB)

League Club	Source	Date Signed	Seasons Played	Apps	Subs	Gls
Grimsby T.	Humber U.	09.38	46-48	22	-	0

MOUNTAIN Patrick Douglas
Pontypridd, 1 August, 1976 W Yth/Wu21-2 (G)

League Club	Source	Date Signed	Seasons Played	Apps	Subs	Gls
Cardiff C. (N/C)	YT	07.95	96	5	0	0

MOUNTAIN Robert Brian
Wombwell, 11 September, 1956 (F)

League Club	Source	Date Signed	Seasons Played	Apps	Subs	Gls
Huddersfield T.	App	11.73	73	1	0	0

MOUNTFIELD Derek Neal
Liverpool, 2 November, 1962 Eu21-1/E'B' (CD)

League Club	Source	Date Signed	Seasons Played	Apps	Subs	Gls
Tranmere Rov.	App	11.80	80-81	26	0	1
Everton	Tr	06.82	82-87	100	6	19
Aston Villa	Tr	06.88	88-91	88	2	9
Wolverhampton W.	Tr	11.91	91-93	79	4	4
Carlisle U.	Tr	08.94	94	30	1	3
Northampton T.	Tr	10.95	95	4	0	0
Walsall	Tr	11.95	95-97	96	1	2

MOUNTFORD David
Hanley, 9 January, 1931 Died 1985 (W)

League Club	Source	Date Signed	Seasons Played	Apps	Subs	Gls
Crewe Alex.	Jnrs	11.48	48-51	33	-	5
West Bromwich A.	Tr	12.51	52	4	-	0
Crewe Alex.	Tr	10.53	53-56	27	-	7

MOUNTFORD Derek Neal
Stoke, 24 March, 1934 Died 1994 (WH)

League Club	Source	Date Signed	Seasons Played	Apps	Subs	Gls
Port Vale	Jnrs	05.51	54-56	26	-	0
Crewe Alex.	Tr	07.57	57	13	-	0

MOUNTFORD Frank
Campsall, 30 March, 1923 (CH)

League Club	Source	Date Signed	Seasons Played	Apps	Subs	Gls
Stoke C.	Jnrs	04.40	46-57	391	-	21

MOUNTFORD George Frederick
Stoke, 30 March, 1921 Died 1973 (IF)

League Club	Source	Date Signed	Seasons Played	Apps	Subs	Gls
Stoke C.	Jnrs	09.38	46-52	147	-	27
Queens Park R.	Tr	10.52	52-53	35	-	2

MOUNTFORD Peter
Stoke, 13 September, 1960 (M)

League Club	Source	Date Signed	Seasons Played	Apps	Subs	Gls
Norwich C.	App	09.78	81-82	1	3	0
Charlton Ath.	Tr	09.83	83	10	1	1
Leyton Orient	Tr	01.85	84-86	27	6	2

MOUNTFORD Raymond
Mexborough, 28 April, 1958 (G)

League Club	Source	Date Signed	Seasons Played	Apps	Subs	Gls
Manchester U.	App	04.75				
Rotherham U.	Tr	07.78	78-82	123	0	0
Bury	L	11.83	83	4	0	0

MOUNTFORD Robert William
Stoke, 23 February, 1952 (F)

League Club	Source	Date Signed	Seasons Played	Apps	Subs	Gls
Port Vale	App	02.70	68-74	64	17	9
Scunthorpe U.	L	10.74	74	1	2	0
Crewe Alex.	L	12.74	74	5	0	0
Rochdale	Tr	01.75	74-77	97	1	37
Huddersfield T.	Tr	10.77	77	12	2	4
Halifax T.	Tr	03.78	77-79	56	6	11
Crewe Alex.	Tr	08.80	80	3	0	0
Stockport Co.	Tr	11.80	80	6	1	3

MOUSSADDIK Choukri
Morocco, 23 February, 1970 Moroccan Int (G)

League Club	Source	Date Signed	Seasons Played	Apps	Subs	Gls
Wycombe W. (N/C)	Wimbledon (Jnrs)	08.90	95	1	0	0

League Club	Source	Date Signed	Seasons Played	Apps	Subs	Gls
MOVERLEY Robert						
Wakefield, 18 January, 1969						(G)
Bradford C.	YT	06.87				
Hartlepool U.	Tr	12.88	88-89	29	0	0
MOWBRAY Anthony Mark						
Saltburn, 22 November, 1963 E'B'						(CD)
Middlesbrough	App	11.81	82-91	345	3	25
Ipswich T.	Glasgow Celtic	10.95	95-97	50	2	2
MOWBRAY Darren Karl						
Middlesbrough, 24 January, 1978						(CD)
Scarborough	Middlesbrough (YT)	08.96	96	2	1	0
MOWBRAY Henry						
Hamilton, 1 May, 1947						(FB)
Blackpool	Cowdenbeath	05.67	67-70	88	3	0
Bolton W.	Tr	06.71	71-72	31	0	0
MOWER Kenneth Matthew						
Walsall, 1 December, 1960						(LB)
Walsall	App	11.78	78-90	410	5	8
MOWL Joseph **William**						
Bulwell, 23 June, 1922						(G)
Notts Co.		10.44	48	3	-	0
Mansfield T.	Tr	07.49				
MOXHAM Graham						
Exeter, 3 January, 1949						(W)
Bournemouth	Preston N.E. (App)	07.66				
Exeter C.	Bideford	07.75	75	4	2	0
MOXHAM Robert						
Barrow, 5 July, 1922 Died 1990						(CF)
Barrow	Holker C.O.B.	09.48	48	5	-	1
MOYES David William						
Glasgow, 25 April, 1963 S Sch/S Yth						(CD)
Cambridge U.	Glasgow Celtic	10.83	83-85	79	0	1
Bristol C.	Tr	10.85	85-87	83	0	6
Shrewsbury T.	Tr	10.87	87-89	91	5	11
Preston N.E.	Hamilton Academical	09.93	93-97	142	1	15
MOYES John David						
Belper, 17 July, 1951						(CD)
Chesterfield	App	07.69	68-71	13	0	0
MOYLON Craig						
Germany, 16 October, 1972						(D)
Preston N.E.	Jnrs	07.91	92	0	1	0
MOYSE Alexander Rodney						
Mitcham, 5 August, 1935 Died 1994						(CF)
Crystal Palace	Chatham	02.56	55-56	4	-	1
Swindon T.	Tr	08.58	58	4	-	0
Millwall	Tr	09.58	58-59	22	-	3
MOYSE Ronald						
Portsmouth, 2 April, 1920 Died 1992						(FB)
Reading		10.46	46-52	189	-	0
MOYSES Christopher Raymond						
Lincoln, 1 November, 1965						(D)
Lincoln C. (N/C)	App	11.83	83	2	2	0
Halifax T.	Tr	07.84	84	21	4	0
MOZLEY Bertram						
Derby, 23 September, 1923 EF Lge/E-3						(FB)
Derby Co.	Shelton U.	06.46	46-54	297	-	2
MUDD Paul Andrew						
Hull, 13 November, 1970 E Sch						(FB)
Hull C.	YT	07.89	88	1	0	0
Scarborough	Tr	07.90	90-92	95	3	2
Scunthorpe U.	Tr	07.93	93-94	66	2	4
Lincoln C.	Tr	07.95	95	2	2	0
MUDIE John (Jackie) Knight						
Dundee, 10 April, 1930 Died 1992 S-17						(IF)
Blackpool	Stobswell Jnrs	05.47	49-60	320	-	143
Stoke C.	Tr	03.61	60-63	88	-	32
Port Vale	Tr	11.63	63-66	54	0	9
MUGGLETON Carl David						
Leicester, 13 September, 1968 Eu21-1						(G)
Leicester C.	App	09.86	88-92	46	0	0
Chesterfield	L	09.87	87	17	0	0
Blackpool	L	02.88	87	2	0	0

League Club	Source	Date Signed	Seasons Played	Apps	Subs	Gls
Hartlepool U.	L	10.88	88	8	0	0
Stockport Co.	L	03.90	89	4	0	0
Stoke C.	L	08.93	93	6	0	0
Stoke C.	Glasgow Celtic	07.94	94-97	97	0	0
Rotherham U.	L	11.95	95	6	0	0
Sheffield U.	L	03.96	95	0	1	0
MUHREN Arnold Johannes Hyacinthus						
Netherlands, 2 June, 1951 Dutch Int						(M)
Ipswich T.	Twente Enschede (Neth)	08.78	78-81	161	0	21
Manchester U.	Tr	08.82	82-84	65	5	13
MUIR Alexander Johnston						
Inverkeithing, 10 December, 1923 Died 1995						(OR)
Liverpool	Lochgelly Violet	07.47	47	4	-	0
MUIR Ian Baker						
Motherwell, 16 June, 1929						(CH)
Bristol Rov.	Motherwell	05.53	53-56	26	-	0
Oldham Ath.	Tr	06.57	57	35	-	0
MUIR Ian James						
Coventry, 5 May, 1963 E Sch/E Yth						(F)
Queens Park R.	App	09.80	80	2	0	2
Burnley	L	11.82	82	1	1	1
Birmingham C.	Tr	08.83	83	1	0	0
Brighton & H.A.	Tr	02.84	83-84	3	1	0
Swindon T.	L	01.85	84	2	0	0
Tranmere Rov.	Tr	07.85	85-94	283	31	141
Birmingham C.	Tr	06.95	95	1	0	0
Darlington	L	09.95	95	4	0	1
MUIR John George						
Sedgley, 26 April, 1963						(F)
Doncaster Rov.	Dudley T.	02.90	89-91	64	11	18
Stockport Co.	Tr	02.92	91-92	10	3	3
Torquay U.	L	02.93	92	7	5	0
MUIR Maurice Moyston						
Wimbledon, 19 March, 1963 E Sch						(M)
Northampton T.	App	02.82	79-83	15	13	0
MUIR William Miller						
Ayr, 27 August, 1925						(W)
Queens Park R.	Irvine	02.49	48-52	17	-	4
Torquay U.	Tr	10.52	52	9	-	0
MUIR William Nelson						
Port Glasgow, 14 August, 1934						(CF)
Aldershot	St Mirren	05.56	56	8	-	4
MULDOON John Patrick Joseph						
Bebington, 21 November, 1964						(W)
Wrexham	Jnrs	12.82	82-85	64	18	11
MULDOON Terence						
Ashington, 10 August, 1951 Died 1971						(W)
Scunthorpe U. (Am)		05.70	70	1	0	0
MULGREW Thomas						
Motherwell, 13 April, 1929						(IF)
Northampton T.	Morton	07.49	50-52	8	-	1
Newcastle U.	Tr	10.52	52-53	14	-	1
Southampton	Tr	07.54	54-61	293	-	90
Aldershot	Tr	08.62	62-64	112	-	2
MULGROVE Keith Arnold						
Haltwhistle, 21 August, 1959						(FB)
Newcastle U.	App	07.77	78	0	1	0
MULHALL George						
Falkirk, 8 May, 1936 SF Lge/S-3						(OL)
Sunderland	Aberdeen	09.62	62-68	249	4	55
MULHEARN Kenneth John						
Liverpool, 16 October, 1945						(G)
Everton	App	07.63				
Stockport Co.	Tr	08.64	64-67	100	0	0
Manchester C.	Tr	09.67	67-69	50	0	0
Shrewsbury T.	Tr	03.71	70-79	370	0	0
Crewe Alex.	Tr	08.80	80-81	88	0	0
MULHERON Peter						
Glasgow, 21 June, 1921						(IF)
Crystal Palace	Tonbridge	10.48	48-49	38	-	2
MULHOLLAND Francis Gerard						
Belfast, 28 October, 1927 NI Lge						(WH)
Middlesbrough	Glentoran	10.51	51-57	46	-	0

MULHOLLAND George Rush
Paisley, 4 August, 1928 (FB)

League Club	Source	Date Signed	Seasons Played	Apps	Subs	Gls
Stoke C.		07.50	50	3	-	0
Bradford C.	Tr	07.53	53-59	277	-	0
Darlington	Tr	07.60	60-62	106	-	0

MULHOLLAND James
Glasgow, 10 April, 1938 (IF)

League Club	Source	Date Signed	Seasons Played	Apps	Subs	Gls
Chelsea	East Stirling	10.62	62-63	11	-	2
Barrow	Morton	08.65	65-68	132	2	47
Stockport Co.	Tr	10.68	68-69	28	4	5
Crewe Alex.	Tr	08.70	70	0	10	0

MULHOLLAND John Anthony
Condorrat, 20 January, 1932 (CF)

League Club	Source	Date Signed	Seasons Played	Apps	Subs	Gls
Southampton	Condorat Thistle	12.51				
Chester C.	Tr	07.56	56	8	-	1
Halifax T.	Tr	06.57	57	8	-	1

MULHOLLAND John Ross
Dumbarton, 7 December, 1928 (OR)

League Club	Source	Date Signed	Seasons Played	Apps	Subs	Gls
Plymouth Arg.	Renton Boys Guild	10.46				
Grimsby T.	Tr	08.49	49-50	2	-	0
Scunthorpe U.	Tr	10.50	50	6	-	1

MULKERRIN James
Dumbarton, 25 December, 1931 S 'B' (IF)

League Club	Source	Date Signed	Seasons Played	Apps	Subs	Gls
Accrington St.	Hibernian	03.57	56-58	70	-	36
Tranmere Rov.	Tr	08.59	59-60	38	-	8

MULLAN Brendan Gerald Joseph
Coleraine (NI), 2 January, 1950 NIu23-1 (CF)

League Club	Source	Date Signed	Seasons Played	Apps	Subs	Gls
Fulham	Coleraine	02.68	67-68	2	2	0
Millwall	Tr	07.69				

MULLARD Albert Thomas
Tamworth, 22 November, 1920 Died 1984 (IF)

League Club	Source	Date Signed	Seasons Played	Apps	Subs	Gls
Walsall	Hinckley U.	11.45	46-48	61	-	13
Crewe Alex.	Tr	06.49	49-50	44	-	14
Stoke C.	Tr	08.50	50-51	21	-	3
Port Vale	Tr	09.51	51-55	163	-	22

MULLEN Andrew
Newcastle, 28 July, 1928 (OL)

League Club	Source	Date Signed	Seasons Played	Apps	Subs	Gls
Aston Villa		07.48				
Workington	Annfield Plain	08.51	51-52	66	-	5
Scunthorpe U.	South Shields	08.55	55-56	10	-	1

MULLEN James
Newcastle, 6 January, 1923 Died 1987 E Sch/E 'B'/EF Lge/E-12 (OL)

League Club	Source	Date Signed	Seasons Played	Apps	Subs	Gls
Wolverhampton W.	Jnrs	01.40	38-58	445	-	98

MULLEN James
Oxford, 16 March, 1947 (W)

League Club	Source	Date Signed	Seasons Played	Apps	Subs	Gls
Reading	Oxford C.	11.66	66-67	8	0	1
Charlton Ath.	Tr	11.67	67-68	7	0	0
Rotherham U.	Tr	02.69	68-73	174	3	24
Blackburn Rov.	Tr	08.74	74-75	6	4	0
Bury	Tr	06.76	76	2	2	0
Rochdale	L	03.77	76	6	2	1

MULLEN James
Jarrow, 8 November, 1952 (CD)

League Club	Source	Date Signed	Seasons Played	Apps	Subs	Gls
Sheffield Wed.	App	10.70	70-79	222	7	10
Rotherham U.	Tr	08.80	80-81	49	0	1
Preston N.E.	L	11.81	81	1	0	0
Cardiff C.	Tr	03.82	81-85	128	5	12
Newport Co.	Tr	06.86	86	19	0	0

MULLEN James Welsh
Larne (NI), 10 January, 1921 (OL)

League Club	Source	Date Signed	Seasons Played	Apps	Subs	Gls
Barrow	Larne T.	02.46	46-47	55	-	8
Crystal Palace	Tr	07.48	48	11	-	0
Bristol C.	Tr	02.49	48-49	17	-	2
Barrow	Tr	09.50	50	9	-	0

MULLEN Roger Colin
Cowbridge, 2 March, 1966 W Yth (D)

League Club	Source	Date Signed	Seasons Played	Apps	Subs	Gls
Swansea C.	App	03.84	83-84	2	1	0

MULLEN Stephen Anthony
Glasgow, 8 September, 1959 (W)

League Club	Source	Date Signed	Seasons Played	Apps	Subs	Gls
Bury	Darwen	02.79	78-81	76	17	5

MULLERY Alan Patrick
Notting Hill, 23 November, 1941 Eu23-3/EF Lge/E-35 (WH)

League Club	Source	Date Signed	Seasons Played	Apps	Subs	Gls
Fulham	Jnrs	12.58	58-63	199	-	13
Tottenham H.	Tr	03.64	63-71	312	0	25
Fulham	Tr	03.72	71-75	164	1	24

MULLETT Joseph
Halesowen, 2 October, 1936 Died 1995 (FB)

League Club	Source	Date Signed	Seasons Played	Apps	Subs	Gls
Birmingham C.	Malt Hill U.	02.55	57	3	-	0
Norwich C.	Tr	02.59	58-67	211	2	2

MULLIGAN James
Dublin, 21 April, 1974 (F)

League Club	Source	Date Signed	Seasons Played	Apps	Subs	Gls
Stoke C.	YT	07.92				
Bury	L	11.93	93	2	1	1
Bury	Tr	07.94	94-95	9	8	2

MULLIGAN Patrick (Paddy) Martin
Dublin, 17 March, 1945 IRu23-1/IR-50 (RB)

League Club	Source	Date Signed	Seasons Played	Apps	Subs	Gls
Chelsea	Shamrock Rov.	10.69	69-72	55	3	2
Crystal Palace	Tr	09.72	72-74	57	0	2
West Bromwich A.	Tr	09.75	75-77	109	0	1

MULLIGAN Peter Granville
Barnsley, 17 July, 1942 (IF)

League Club	Source	Date Signed	Seasons Played	Apps	Subs	Gls
Barnsley	Jnrs	07.63	59-63	9	-	0

MULLIN John
Bury, 11 August, 1975 (F)

League Club	Source	Date Signed	Seasons Played	Apps	Subs	Gls
Burnley	YT	08.92	93-94	7	11	2
Sunderland	Tr	08.95	95-97	15	11	2
Preston N.E.	L	02.98	97	4	3	0
Burnley	L	03.98	97	6	0	0

MULLINEUX Ian Joseph
Salford, 10 November, 1968 (W)

League Club	Source	Date Signed	Seasons Played	Apps	Subs	Gls
Bolton W.	YT	●	86	1	1	0

MULLINGTON Philip Thomas
Oldham, 25 September, 1956 (M)

League Club	Source	Date Signed	Seasons Played	Apps	Subs	Gls
Oldham Ath.	App	07.75				
Rochdale	Tr	01.76	75-76	59	7	6
Crewe Alex. (N/C)	Northwich Vic.	01.78	77	1	0	0
Rochdale	Winsford U.	08.78	78	8	1	0

MULRAIN Steven
Lambeth, 23 October, 1972 (F)

League Club	Source	Date Signed	Seasons Played	Apps	Subs	Gls
Leeds U.	YT	07.91				
Rochdale	Charlton Ath (N/C)	12.92	92-93	3	5	2

MULRANEY Ambrose
Wishaw, 18 May, 1916 (OR)

League Club	Source	Date Signed	Seasons Played	Apps	Subs	Gls
Ipswich T.	Dartford	11.36	38	28	-	8
Birmingham C.	Tr	10.45	46	27	-	8
Aston Villa	Shrewsbury T.	09.48	48	12	-	2

MULRYNE Phillip Patrick
Belfast, 1 January, 1978 NIu21-3/NI 'B'/NI-5 (F)

League Club	Source	Date Signed	Seasons Played	Apps	Subs	Gls
Manchester U.	YT	03.95	97	1	0	0

MULVANEY James
Sunderland, 13 May, 1941 Died 1982 (IF)

League Club	Source	Date Signed	Seasons Played	Apps	Subs	Gls
Hartlepool U.	Whitby T.	08.65	65-67	67	2	31
Barrow	Tr	11.67	67-69	71	8	34
Stockport Co.	Tr	07.70	70-71	38	2	8

MULVANEY James
Airdrie, 27 April, 1921 Died 1993 (D)

League Club	Source	Date Signed	Seasons Played	Apps	Subs	Gls
Luton T.	Dumbarton	06.48	48-49	8	-	2
Brighton & H.A.	Tr	08.50	50	8	-	0
Bradford C.	Tr	10.51	51	19	-	0
Halifax T.	Bath C.	11.52	52	1	-	0

MULVANEY Richard
Sunderland, 5 August, 1942 (CD)

League Club	Source	Date Signed	Seasons Played	Apps	Subs	Gls
Blackburn Rov.	Billingham Synth.	02.64	64-70	135	6	4
Oldham Ath.	Tr	08.71	71-74	88	4	2
Rochdale	Tr	10.74	74-76	72	1	4

MULVEY Edward Patrick Noel
Dublin, 29 December, 1934 (IF)

League Club	Source	Date Signed	Seasons Played	Apps	Subs	Gls
Stockport Co.	Glentoran	11.57	57-59	26	-	5

MULVOY Terence (Edward) John
Manchester, 2 December, 1938 (IF)

League Club	Source	Date Signed	Seasons Played	Apps	Subs	Gls
Rochdale		02.56	56	2	-	0

MUMBY Peter
Bradford, 22 February, 1969 (W)

League Club	Source	Date Signed	Seasons Played	Apps	Subs	Gls
Leeds U.	App	07.87	87-88	3	3	0
Burnley	Tr	07.89	89-91	36	10	9

MUMFORD Wayne Ernest
Rhymney, 3 November, 1964 (FB)

League Club	Source	Date Signed	Seasons Played	Apps	Subs	Gls
Birmingham C.	Manchester C. (App)	09.82	82-83	5	2	0

MUNCIE William Paul
Carluke, 28 August, 1911 Died 1992 (W)

League Club	Source	Date Signed	Seasons Played	Apps	Subs	Gls
Leicester C.	Shettleston Jnrs	08.34	34-37	42	-	11
Southend U.	Tr	05.38	38	14	-	2
Crewe Alex.		10.46	46	2	-	0

MUNDAY Stuart Clifford
Newham, 28 September, 1972 (RB)

League Club	Source	Date Signed	Seasons Played	Apps	Subs	Gls
Brighton & H.A.	YT	07.90	91-95	78	17	4

MUNDEE Brian George
Hammersmith, 12 January, 1964 (LB)

League Club	Source	Date Signed	Seasons Played	Apps	Subs	Gls
Bournemouth	Hungerford T.	01.82	82	3	1	0
Northampton T.	Tr	10.83	83-85	96	4	3
Cambridge U.	Tr	03.86	85-86	16	0	1

MUNDEE Dennis William John
Swindon, 10 October, 1968 (FB/F)

League Club	Source	Date Signed	Seasons Played	Apps	Subs	Gls
Swindon T.	Queens Park R. (App)	08.86				
Bournemouth	Salisbury	05.88	88-92	76	24	6
Torquay U.	L	09.89	89	9	0	0
Brentford	Tr	08.93	93-95	64	20	16
Brighton & H.A.	Tr	10.95	95-96	58	3	7

MUNDY Albert Edward
Portsmouth, 12 May, 1926 (IF)

League Club	Source	Date Signed	Seasons Played	Apps	Subs	Gls
Portsmouth	Gosport Borough	01.51	50-53	51	-	12
Brighton & H.A.	Tr	11.53	53-57	165	-	87
Aldershot	Tr	02.58	57-60	130	-	12

MUNDY Harold **James**
Wythenshawe, 2 September, 1948 (M)

League Club	Source	Date Signed	Seasons Played	Apps	Subs	Gls
Manchester C.	Ashland Rov.	08.66	68-69	2	1	0
Oldham Ath.	L	09.70	70	3	5	2

MUNGALL Steven Henry
Bellshill, 22 May, 1958 (D/M)

League Club	Source	Date Signed	Seasons Played	Apps	Subs	Gls
Tranmere Rov.	Motherwell	07.79	79-95	478	34	13

MUNKS David
Sheffield, 29 April, 1947 E Yth (D)

League Club	Source	Date Signed	Seasons Played	Apps	Subs	Gls
Sheffield U.	App	08.64	65-68	108	4	1
Portsmouth	Tr	05.69	69-73	132	5	2
Swindon T.	Tr	12.73	73-74	21	0	0
Exeter C.	Tr	12.74	74-75	20	0	0

MUNRO Alexander
Glasgow, 3 October, 1944 (D)

League Club	Source	Date Signed	Seasons Played	Apps	Subs	Gls
Bristol Rov.	Drumchapel Jnrs	10.62	62-70	159	10	11

MUNRO Alexander Dewar
Bo'ness, 6 April, 1912 Died 1986 S-3 (OR)

League Club	Source	Date Signed	Seasons Played	Apps	Subs	Gls
Blackpool	Hearts	03.37	36-48	141	-	17

MUNRO Francis Michael
Broughty Ferry, 25 October, 1947 Su23-4/S-9 (CD)

League Club	Source	Date Signed	Seasons Played	Apps	Subs	Gls
Wolverhampton W.	Aberdeen	01.68	67-76	290	6	14

MUNRO Alexander **Iain** Fordyce
Bellshill, 24 August, 1951 S-7 (LB)

League Club	Source	Date Signed	Seasons Played	Apps	Subs	Gls
Stoke C.	St Mirren	10.80	80	32	0	1
Sunderland	Tr	08.81	81-83	80	0	0

MUNRO James Ferguson
Elgin, 25 March, 1926 Died 1997 (OR)

League Club	Source	Date Signed	Seasons Played	Apps	Subs	Gls
Manchester C.	Waterford	11.47	47-49	25	-	4
Oldham Ath.	Tr	03.50	49-52	119	-	20
Lincoln C.	Tr	02.53	52-57	161	-	24
Bury	Tr	01.58	57-58	41	-	8

MUNRO Malcolm George
Melton Mowbray, 21 May, 1953 E Sch/E Yth (CD)

League Club	Source	Date Signed	Seasons Played	Apps	Subs	Gls
Leicester C.	App	05.70	71-74	69	1	1

MUNRO Roderick Alexander
Inverness, 27 July, 1920 Died 1976 (FB)

League Club	Source	Date Signed	Seasons Played	Apps	Subs	Gls
Brentford		05.46	46-52	199	-	0

MUNRO Stuart
Falkirk, 15 September, 1962 S'B' (LB)

League Club	Source	Date Signed	Seasons Played	Apps	Subs	Gls
Blackburn Rov.	Glasgow Rangers	07.91	91	1	0	0
Bristol C.	Tr	02.93	92-95	91	3	0

MUNRO William Davidson
Glasgow, 21 June, 1934 (IF)

League Club	Source	Date Signed	Seasons Played	Apps	Subs	Gls
Barrow	Kilmarnock	06.59	59-60	15	-	2

MUNROE Karl Augustus
Manchester, 23 September, 1979 (D)

League Club	Source	Date Signed	Seasons Played	Apps	Subs	Gls
Swansea C.	YT	●	97	0	1	0

MUNROE William James
Dublin, 28 November, 1933 (IF)

League Club	Source	Date Signed	Seasons Played	Apps	Subs	Gls
Bristol C.	Ards.	12.57	57	1	-	0
Scunthorpe U.	Tr	07.58				

MUNSON Nathan
Colchester, 10 November, 1974 (G)

League Club	Source	Date Signed	Seasons Played	Apps	Subs	Gls
Colchester U.	YT	06.93	92-93	3	1	0

MURCHISON Ronald Angus
Hurlford, 12 February, 1927 (WH)

League Club	Source	Date Signed	Seasons Played	Apps	Subs	Gls
Ipswich T.	Auchterader Primrose	06.50	50-54	42	-	2

MURCOTT Stephen
Streetly, 17 January, 1961 (G)

League Club	Source	Date Signed	Seasons Played	Apps	Subs	Gls
Coventry C.	App	11.78	79	1	0	0

MURDOCH Robert White
Rutherglen, 17 August, 1944 Su23-1/SF Lge/S-12 (M)

League Club	Source	Date Signed	Seasons Played	Apps	Subs	Gls
Middlesbrough	Glasgow Celtic	09.73	73-75	93	2	6

MURDOCH William **Robert**
Liverpool, 25 January, 1936 (IF)

League Club	Source	Date Signed	Seasons Played	Apps	Subs	Gls
Liverpool	South Liverpool	05.57	57-58	17	-	5
Barrow	Tr	05.59	59	42	-	17
Stockport Co.	Tr	08.60	60-61	58	-	17
Carlisle U.	Tr	01.62	61	10	-	1
Southport	Tr	07.62	62	33	-	10

MURDOCK Colin James
Ballymena, 2 July, 1975 NI Sch/NI Yth/NI 'B' (CD)

League Club	Source	Date Signed	Seasons Played	Apps	Subs	Gls
Manchester U.	YT	07.92				
Preston N.E.	Tr	05.97	97	27	0	1

MURFIN Andrew John
Doncaster, 26 November, 1976 (LB)

League Club	Source	Date Signed	Seasons Played	Apps	Subs	Gls
Scunthorpe U.	Jnrs	08.95	95	1	0	0

MURPHY Aidan
Manchester, 17 September, 1967 E Sch/E Yth (M)

League Club	Source	Date Signed	Seasons Played	Apps	Subs	Gls
Manchester U.	App	09.84				
Lincoln C.	L	10.86	86	2	0	0
Crewe Alex.	Tr	05.87	87-91	94	19	13
Scarborough (N/C)	Tr	08.92	92	7	1	0

MURPHY Andrew Colin
Preston, 18 October, 1966 (M)

League Club	Source	Date Signed	Seasons Played	Apps	Subs	Gls
Preston N.E.	YT	07.84	83-84	9	1	0

MURPHY Laurence **Barry**
Consett, 10 February, 1940 (RB)

League Club	Source	Date Signed	Seasons Played	Apps	Subs	Gls
Barnsley	South Shields	07.62	62-77	509	5	3

MURPHY Bernard Anthony Paul
Dublin, 19 November, 1947 (WH/IF)

League Club	Source	Date Signed	Seasons Played	Apps	Subs	Gls
Torquay U.	App	11.65	64-66	6	0	0

MURPHY Daniel
Warrington, 10 May, 1922 (WH)

League Club	Source	Date Signed	Seasons Played	Apps	Subs	Gls
Bolton W.	Burtonwood Ath.	02.43	46-50	66	-	1
Crewe Alex.	Tr	01.52	51-53	106	-	1
Rochdale	Tr	07.54	54-56	109	-	0

MURPHY Daniel Benjamin
Chester, 18 March, 1977 E Sch/E Yth/Eu21-2 (M)

League Club	Source	Date Signed	Seasons Played	Apps	Subs	Gls
Crewe Alex.	YT	03.94	93-96	110	24	27
Liverpool	Tr	07.97	97	6	10	0

MURPHY Donal Patrick
Dublin, 23 February, 1955 (OL)

League Club	Source	Date Signed	Seasons Played	Apps	Subs	Gls
Coventry C.	App	08.72	75-77	33	10	10
Millwall	L	10.77	77	3	0	0
Torquay U.	Tr	05.78	78-79	81	4	20
Plymouth Arg.	Tr	06.80	80-81	44	4	9
Torquay U.	L	12.81	81	2	1	0
Blackburn Rov.	Tr	02.82	81	1	2	0

MURPHY Edward
Hamilton, 13 May, 1924 (IF)

League Club	Source	Date Signed	Seasons Played	Apps	Subs	Gls
Northampton T.	Morton	06.49	49-50	71	-	15
Barnsley	Tr	03.51	50-51	18	-	2
Exeter C.	Tr	06.52	52-55	94	-	13

MURPHY Edward Cullinane
Glasgow, 1 June, 1934 (CH)

League Club	Source	Date Signed	Seasons Played	Apps	Subs	Gls
Oldham Ath.	Clyde	05.56	56-58	72	-	0

MURPHY Thomas **Edwin (Eddie)**
Middlesbrough, 25 March, 1921 (IF)

League Club	Source	Date Signed	Seasons Played	Apps	Subs	Gls
Middlesbrough	South Bank	05.39	46-47	9	-	1
Blackburn Rov.	Tr	12.47	47-48	31	-	6
Halifax T.	Tr	03.49	48-53	217	-	30

MURPHY Francis
Glasgow, 1 June, 1959 (F)

League Club	Source	Date Signed	Seasons Played	Apps	Subs	Gls
Barnet	Kettering T.	08.88	91	3	12	5

MURPHY George
Crosskeys (Mon), 22 July, 1915 Died 1983 (CF)

League Club	Source	Date Signed	Seasons Played	Apps	Subs	Gls
Bradford C.	Cwmfelinfach Jnrs	11.34	34-47	180	-	43
Hull C.	Tr	12.47	47	15	-	9

MURPHY James
Islington, 17 November, 1971 (M)

League Club	Source	Date Signed	Seasons Played	Apps	Subs	Gls
Aldershot	Leyton Orient (YT)	07.90	90	1	2	0

MURPHY James Anthony
Manchester, 25 February, 1973 (CD)

League Club	Source	Date Signed	Seasons Played	Apps	Subs	Gls
Blackpool	Jnrs	08.90	92-94	48	7	1
Doncaster Rov.	Tr	09.95	95-96	47	7	0

MURPHY James Baird
Glasgow, 29 November, 1942 (IF)

League Club	Source	Date Signed	Seasons Played	Apps	Subs	Gls
Notts Co.	Raith Rov.	02.68	67-68	33	0	7

MURPHY Jeremiah (Jerry) Michael
Stepney, 23 September, 1959 E Sch/IR-3 (LM)

League Club	Source	Date Signed	Seasons Played	Apps	Subs	Gls
Crystal Palace	App	10.76	76-84	214	15	20
Chelsea	Tr	08.85	85-87	34	0	3

MURPHY John James
Prescot, 18 October, 1976 (F)

League Club	Source	Date Signed	Seasons Played	Apps	Subs	Gls
Chester C.	YT	07.95	94-97	24	37	8

MURPHY Francis **John**
Edinburgh, 16 August, 1949 (WH)

League Club	Source	Date Signed	Seasons Played	Apps	Subs	Gls
Notts Co.	Edina Jnrs	08.67	67-68	17	2	2

MURPHY Joseph Patrick
Waterford (Ire), 30 March, 1924 (FB)

League Club	Source	Date Signed	Seasons Played	Apps	Subs	Gls
Brighton & H.A.		02.48				
Crystal Palace	Shelbourne	02.49	48-50	37	-	0

MURPHY Marcus Montagu
Tavistock, 16 November, 1914 (IF)

League Club	Source	Date Signed	Seasons Played	Apps	Subs	Gls
Plymouth Arg.	Plymouth U.	08.46	46-47	15	-	1

MURPHY Matthew Simon
Northampton, 20 August, 1971 (F)

League Club	Source	Date Signed	Seasons Played	Apps	Subs	Gls
Oxford U.	Corby T.	02.93	92-97	52	65	17
Scunthorpe U.	L	12.97	97	1	2	0

MURPHY Michael
Reading, 15 April, 1939 (G)

League Club	Source	Date Signed	Seasons Played	Apps	Subs	Gls
Reading (Am)	Thorneycroft A.	04.58	57	1	-	0

MURPHY Michael John
Slough, 5 May, 1977 (F)

League Club	Source	Date Signed	Seasons Played	Apps	Subs	Gls
Reading	Jnrs	10.94	94	0	1	0

MURPHY Nicholas Michael
West Bromwich, 25 December, 1946 (M)

League Club	Source	Date Signed	Seasons Played	Apps	Subs	Gls
Manchester U.	Jnrs	02.66				
Reading	Tr	07.70	70	3	1	0

MURPHY Patrick
Merthyr Tydfil, 19 December, 1947 (HB)

League Club	Source	Date Signed	Seasons Played	Apps	Subs	Gls
Cardiff C.	App	12.65	65	0	1	0

MURPHY Paul
Ashington, 16 March, 1954 (F)

League Club	Source	Date Signed	Seasons Played	Apps	Subs	Gls
Rotherham U.	Ashington	02.72	73	1	0	0
Workington	L	08.73	73	10	2	1

MURPHY Peter
Hartlepool, 7 March, 1922 Died 1975 (IF)

League Club	Source	Date Signed	Seasons Played	Apps	Subs	Gls
Coventry C.	Birmingham C. (Am)	05.46	46-49	114	-	37
Tottenham H.	Tr	06.50	50-51	38	-	14
Birmingham C.	Tr	01.52	51-59	245	-	107

MURPHY Philip
Liverpool, 21 November, 1960 (F)

League Club	Source	Date Signed	Seasons Played	Apps	Subs	Gls
Blackpool	Nacional (Por)	09.84	84	1	7	0
Burnley (N/C)		11.86	86	12	3	5

MURPHY Shaun Peter
Australia, 5 November, 1970 Australian Int (CD)

League Club	Source	Date Signed	Seasons Played	Apps	Subs	Gls
Notts Co.	Perth Italia (Aus)	09.92	92-96	100	9	5
West Bromwich A.	Tr	12.96	96-97	30	4	3

MURPHY Terence
Liverpool, 14 January, 1940 (WH)

League Club	Source	Date Signed	Seasons Played	Apps	Subs	Gls
Crewe Alex.	Northwich Vic.	09.61	61	1	-	0

MURPHY William Robinson
Barrhead, 22 March, 1928 (W)

League Club	Source	Date Signed	Seasons Played	Apps	Subs	Gls
Exeter C.	Stirling A.	11.49	49	2	-	0
Bristol Rov.	Tr	07.50	50	3	-	0

MURPHY John **William**
Batley, 21 November, 1921 (WH)

League Club	Source	Date Signed	Seasons Played	Apps	Subs	Gls
Bradford C.	Liverpool (Am)	09.46	46-51	146	-	9

MURRAY Alan
Newcastle, 5 December, 1949 (M)

League Club	Source	Date Signed	Seasons Played	Apps	Subs	Gls
Middlesbrough	Jnrs	09.67	69-70	6	4	1
York C.	L	01.72	71	4	0	0
Brentford	Tr	06.72	72	42	3	7
Doncaster Rov.	Tr	07.73	73-76	133	13	21

MURRAY Alastair
Longtown, 22 December, 1943 (IF)

League Club	Source	Date Signed	Seasons Played	Apps	Subs	Gls
Sunderland	Jnrs	01.61				
Barnsley	Tr	07.63	63	21	-	1
Carlisle U.	Tr	07.64				

MURRAY Albert (Bert) George
Hoxton, 22 September, 1942 E Sch/E Yth/Eu23-6 (OR)

League Club	Source	Date Signed	Seasons Played	Apps	Subs	Gls
Chelsea	Jnrs	05.61	61-65	156	4	39
Birmingham C.	Tr	08.66	66-70	126	6	22
Brighton & H.A.	Tr	02.71	70-73	99	3	25
Peterborough U.	Tr	09.73	73-75	123	0	10

MURRAY Bruce Edward
U.S.A., 25 January, 1966 USA Int (F)

League Club	Source	Date Signed	Seasons Played	Apps	Subs	Gls
Millwall	U.S.S.F. (USA)	08.93	93	7	6	2
Stockport Co.	L	03.94	93	2	1	0

MURRAY David Robert
Chorley, 30 September, 1967 (F)

League Club	Source	Date Signed	Seasons Played	Apps	Subs	Gls
Chester C.	Wigan Ath. (Jnr)	09.85	85	3	3	1

MURRAY Ian **David**
Rothbury (Nd), 11 July, 1949 (F)

League Club	Source	Date Signed	Seasons Played	Apps	Subs	Gls
Workington		03.74	73-75	79	3	22

MURRAY Dennis Patrick
Stoke, 11 June, 1932 (G)

League Club	Source	Date Signed	Seasons Played	Apps	Subs	Gls
Crewe Alex.	Jnrs	10.50	51	2	-	0

MURRAY Donald James
Elgin, 18 January, 1946 Su23-1 (CD)

League Club	Source	Date Signed	Seasons Played	Apps	Subs	Gls
Cardiff C.	Jnrs	01.63	62-74	406	0	6
Swansea C.	L	10.74	74	5	0	0
Newport Co.	Hearts	10.76	76	16	2	0

MURRAY Edward James
Crosby, 10 July, 1962 (W)

League Club	Source	Date Signed	Seasons Played	Apps	Subs	Gls
Tranmere Rov.	Stork	08.87	87-88	11	16	1

MURRAY Edwin John
Ilford, 31 August, 1973 (FB)

League Club	Source	Date Signed	Seasons Played	Apps	Subs	Gls
Swindon T.	YT	07.91	90-95	7	5	1

MURRAY Hugh
Drybridge, 5 August, 1936 (F)

League Club	Source	Date Signed	Seasons Played	Apps	Subs	Gls
Manchester C.	Dalry Thistle	04.55	55	1	-	0

MURRAY Ivan Hugh
Ballymoney, 29 May, 1944 (WH)

League Club	Source	Date Signed	Seasons Played	Apps	Subs	Gls
Fulham	Coleraine	02.68	67-68	4	1	0

MURRAY James
Motherwell, 13 July, 1922 (FB)

League Club	Source	Date Signed	Seasons Played	Apps	Subs	Gls
Exeter C.	Shawfield Jnrs	08.45	46	1	-	0

MURRAY James
Edinburgh, 4 February, 1933 (F)

League Club	Source	Date Signed	Seasons Played	Apps	Subs	Gls
Reading	Hearts	02.54	53-54	7	-	3

League Club	Source	Date Signed	Seasons Played	Career Record Apps	Subs	Gls
MURRAY James (Jamie) Gerald						
Ayr, 27 December, 1958						(LB)
Cambridge U.	Rivet Sports	09.76	76-83	213	16	3
Sunderland	L	03.84	83	0	1	0
Brentford	Tr	07.84	84-87	130	0	3
Cambridge U.	Tr	09.87	87	13	0	0
MURRAY James Robert						
Eythorne (Kt), 11 October, 1935 Eu23-2/EF Lge						(CF)
Wolverhampton W.	Jnrs	11.53	55-63	273	-	155
Manchester C.	Tr	11.63	63-66	70	0	43
Walsall	Tr	05.67	66-68	54	4	13
MURRAY James William						
Lambeth, 16 March, 1935						(IF)
Crystal Palace	Jnrs	07.55	55-57	37	-	13
Walsall	Tr	01.58	57-58	14	-	2
MURRAY Alexander **James**						
Thornton (Lancs), 4 February, 1945						(W)
Southport	Jnrs	07.65	64	3	-	0
MURRAY John						
Newcastle, 2 March, 1948						(W)
Burnley	Jnrs	03.65	66-69	20	2	6
Blackpool	Tr	03.70	69-70	5	3	1
Bury	Tr	02.71	70-73	117	9	37
Reading	Tr	08.74	74-77	123	8	44
Brentford	Tr	02.78	77	2	3	1
MURRAY John Anthony						
Saltcoats, 5 February, 1949						(FB)
Cambridge U.	Morton	07.71	71	3	0	0
MURRAY John George						
Lambeth, 15 July, 1927						(FB)
Leyton Orient	Chelmsford C.	08.49				
Gillingham	Sittingbourne	06.51	51	4	-	0
MURRAY John McCann						
Glasgow, 9 March, 1945						(LB)
Lincoln C.	Stirling A.	11.66	66	4	0	0
MURRAY Joseph						
Liverpool, 5 November, 1971						(M)
Wrexham (N/C)	Marine	03.91	90	11	0	0
MURRAY Kenneth						
Newcastle, 2 April, 1928 Died 1993						(F)
Darlington	Bishop Auckland	07.50	50-52	70	-	19
Mansfield T.	Tr	07.53	53-56	140	-	60
Oldham Ath.	Tr	03.57	56-57	35	-	14
Wrexham	Tr	02.58	57-58	32	-	10
Gateshead	Tr	08.59	59	18	-	7
MURRAY Leslie						
Kinghorn, 29 September, 1928						(IF)
Rochdale	Arbroath	05.52	52	16	-	3
MURRAY Malcolm						
Buckie, 26 July, 1964						(FB)
Hull C.	Hearts	03.89	88-89	9	2	0
Mansfield T.	Tr	12.89	89-90	56	3	0
MURRAY Mark						
Manchester, 13 June, 1973						(LB)
Blackpool	Jnrs	10.90	91-92	3	0	0
MURRAY Matthew						
Paisley, 25 December, 1929						(OL)
Barrow	St Mirren	08.58	58	33	-	2
Carlisle U.	Tr	07.59	59	28	-	4
MURRAY Maxwell						
Falkirk, 7 November, 1935 S Amat/Su23-2						(CF)
West Bromwich A.	Glasgow Rangers	11.62	62	3	-	0
MURRAY Paul						
Carlisle, 31 August, 1976 E Yth/Eu21-4/E 'B'						(M)
Carlisle U.	YT	06.94	93-95	27	14	1
Queens Park R.	Tr	03.96	95-97	58	7	6
MURRAY Robert James						
Hammersmith, 21 October, 1974 Su21-1						(CD/F)
Bournemouth	YT	01.93	92-97	88	59	12
MURRAY Robert Law						
Kemnay, 24 April, 1932						(WH/FB)
Stockport Co.	Inverurie Loco	11.51	52-62	465	-	32
MURRAY Scott George						
Aberdeen, 26 May, 1974						(RB)
Aston Villa	Fraserburgh	03.94	95-96	4	0	0
Bristol C.	Tr	12.97	97	10	13	0
MURRAY Shaun						
Newcastle, 7 December, 1970 E Sch/E Yth						(M)
Tottenham H.	YT	12.87				
Portsmouth	Tr	06.89	90-92	21	13	1
Scarborough	Tr	11.93	93	29	0	5
Bradford C.	Tr	08.94	94-97	105	25	8
MURRAY Steven						
Kilmarnock, 1 December, 1967 S Yth						(M)
Nottingham F.	App	04.85				
York C.	L	09.86	86	2	1	0
MURRAY Terence						
Dublin, 22 May, 1928 LoI/IR-1						(IF)
Hull C.	Dundalk	10.51	51-53	32	-	6
Bournemouth	Tr	03.54	53-54	13	-	1
MURRAY Thomas						
Airdrie, 5 February, 1933						(IF)
Darlington	Headington U.	06.56	56	3	-	0
MURRAY Thomas						
Bellshill, 14 January, 1933						(OR)
Leeds U.	Queen of South	08.60	60	7	-	2
Tranmere Rov.	Tr	03.61	60-61	10	-	1
MURRAY Thomas						
Caldercruix, 1 June, 1943						(F)
Carlisle U.	Airdrieonians	03.67	66-70	123	10	37
MURRAY Thomas Alec						
Barrow, 16 October, 1944						(FB)
Barrow	Jnrs	07.64	63-64	8	-	0
MURRAY William Joseph						
Burnley, 26 January, 1922 Died 1992						(WH)
Manchester C.	Arbroath	01.47	46-49	20	-	1
MURTY Graeme Stuart						
Saltburn, 13 November, 1974						(M)
York C.	YT	03.93	93-97	106	11	7
MURTY Joseph Dougan						
Glasgow, 6 November, 1957						(W)
Rochdale	App	11.75	74-75	15	6	2
Bury	Tr	08.76	77	0	1	0
MUSCAT Kevin Vincent						
Crawley, 7 August, 1973 Australian Int						(LB)
Crystal Palace	South Melbourne (Aus)	08.96	96-97	51	2	2
Wolverhampton W.	Tr	10.97	97	22	2	3
MUSGRAVE David						
South Shields, 20 April, 1928						(OL)
Manchester U.	Johannesburg (SA)	12.47				
New Brighton	Fleetwood	08.50	50	35	-	2
Preston N.E.	Tr	08.51				
Southport	Tr	10.51	51-52	52	-	7
Accrington St.	Tr	09.53	53	30	-	7
MUSGROVE Malcolm						
Lynemouth (Nd), 8 July, 1933						(OL)
West Ham U.	Lynemouth Colly	12.53	53-62	283	-	84
Leyton Orient	Tr	12.62	62-65	83	0	14
MUSGROVE Martin						
Wanstead, 21 November, 1961						(M)
Torquay U. (N/C)	Heavitree U.	03.82	81	1	1	0
MUSIAL Adam						
Poland, 18 December, 1948 Polish Int						(D)
Hereford U.	Arkagdynia (Pol)	08.80	80-82	44	2	0
MUSKER Russell						
Liverpool, 10 July, 1962						(W)
Bristol C.	App	08.79	80-83	44	2	1
Exeter C.	L	10.83	83	6	0	0
Gillingham	Tr	11.83	83-85	54	10	7
Torquay U.	Tr	08.86	86-87	36	9	0
Torquay U.	(Retired)	07.90	90	20	1	1
Walsall	Tr	08.91	91	3	0	0

MUSSELWHITE Paul Stephen
Portsmouth, 22 December, 1968 (G)

League Club	Source	Date Signed	Seasons Played	Apps	Subs	Gls
Portsmouth (N/C)	App	12.86				
Scunthorpe U.	Tr	03.88	88-91	132	0	0
Port Vale	Tr	07.92	92-97	244	0	0

MUSSON Ian Samuel
Lincoln, 13 December, 1953 (W)

League Club	Source	Date Signed	Seasons Played	Apps	Subs	Gls
Sheffield Wed.	App	02.71				
Lincoln C.	Tr	07.73	73	11	0	0

MUSSON Walter (Chick) Urban
Belper, 8 October, 1920 Died 1955 EF Lge (WH)

League Club	Source	Date Signed	Seasons Played	Apps	Subs	Gls
Derby Co.	Jnrs	10.37	46-53	246	-	0

MUSTAFA Tarkan
London, 28 August, 1973 (RW)

League Club	Source	Date Signed	Seasons Played	Apps	Subs	Gls
Barnet	Kettering T.	08.97	97	2	9	0

MUSTARD William
South Shields, 28 November, 1920 Died 1976 (OR)

League Club	Source	Date Signed	Seasons Played	Apps	Subs	Gls
Exeter C.	Bath C.	05.46	46	14	-	0

MUSTOE Neil John
Gloucester, 5 November, 1976 (LM)

League Club	Source	Date Signed	Seasons Played	Apps	Subs	Gls
Manchester U.	YT	07.95				
Wigan Ath.	Tr	01.98	97	0	1	0

MUSTOE Robin (Robbie)
Witney, 28 August, 1968 (M)

League Club	Source	Date Signed	Seasons Played	Apps	Subs	Gls
Oxford U.	Jnrs	07.86	86-89	78	13	10
Middlesbrough	Tr	07.90	90-97	233	10	18

MUTCH Andrew Todd
Liverpool, 28 December, 1963 Eu21-1/E'B' (F)

League Club	Source	Date Signed	Seasons Played	Apps	Subs	Gls
Wolverhampton W.	Southport	02.86	85-92	277	12	96
Swindon T.	Tr	08.93	93-94	34	16	6
Wigan Ath.	L	08.95	95	7	0	1
Stockport Co.	Tr	03.96	95-97	28	36	10

MUTCH George
Aberdeen, 21 September, 1912 S Sch/S-1 (IF)

League Club	Source	Date Signed	Seasons Played	Apps	Subs	Gls
Manchester U.	Arbroath	05.34	34-37	112	-	46
Preston N.E.	Tr	09.37	37-46	80	-	25
Bury	Tr	10.46	46	21	-	8
Southport	Tr	10.47	47	14	-	2

MUTCHELL Robert David
Solihull, 3 January, 1974 (LB)

League Club	Source	Date Signed	Seasons Played	Apps	Subs	Gls
Oxford U.	YT	07.92				
Barnet	Tr	12.93	93-94	21	1	0

MUTRIE Leslie Alan
Newcastle, 1 April, 1952 E Semi Pro (F)

League Club	Source	Date Signed	Seasons Played	Apps	Subs	Gls
Carlisle U.	Gateshead	06.77	77	4	1	0
Hull C.	Blyth Spartans	12.80	80-83	114	1	49
Doncaster Rov.	L	12.83	83	6	0	1
Colchester U.	Tr	01.84	83	10	4	2
Hartlepool U.	Tr	08.84	84	18	0	4

MUTTOCK Jonathan Lee
Oxford, 23 December, 1961 (D)

League Club	Source	Date Signed	Seasons Played	Apps	Subs	Gls
Oxford U.	YT	05.90	89	1	0	0

MUXWORTHY Graham John
Bristol, 11 October, 1938 (OL)

League Club	Source	Date Signed	Seasons Played	Apps	Subs	Gls
Crystal Palace	Exeter U.	09.57	57	2	-	0
Bristol Rov.	Chippenham T.	06.60	62	8	-	0

MUZINIC Drazen
Yugoslavia, 25 January, 1953 Yugoslav Int (D)

League Club	Source	Date Signed	Seasons Played	Apps	Subs	Gls
Norwich C.	Hadjuk Split (Yug)	09.80	80-81	15	4	0

MWILA Frederick
Zambia, 6 July, 1946 (IF)

League Club	Source	Date Signed	Seasons Played	Apps	Subs	Gls
Aston Villa	Atlanta (USA)	06.69	69	1	0	0

MYALL Stuart Thomas
Eastbourne, 12 November, 1974 (RB)

League Club	Source	Date Signed	Seasons Played	Apps	Subs	Gls
Brighton & H.A.	YT	07.93	92-95	69	11	4
Brentford	Tr	07.96	97	2	0	0

MYCOCK Albert
Manchester, 31 January, 1923 (F)

League Club	Source	Date Signed	Seasons Played	Apps	Subs	Gls
Manchester U.		05.44				
Crystal Palace	Tr	06.46	46-47	59	-	9
Barrow	Tr	07.48	48-49	42	-	4

MYCOCK David
Sunderland, 30 August, 1921 Died 1990 (WH)

League Club	Source	Date Signed	Seasons Played	Apps	Subs	Gls
Halifax T.	Sunderland (Am)	05.46	46-51	170	-	17

MYCOCK David Christopher
Todmorden, 18 September, 1969 (FB)

League Club	Source	Date Signed	Seasons Played	Apps	Subs	Gls
Rochdale	YT	07.88	87-88	19	3	0

MYCOCK John (Jack)
Manchester, 11 February, 1936 (OR)

League Club	Source	Date Signed	Seasons Played	Apps	Subs	Gls
Shrewsbury T. (Am)	Congleton T.	12.58	58	6	-	1

MYCOCK Thomas
Ryhope, 22 August, 1923 Died 1988 LoI (IF/WH)

League Club	Source	Date Signed	Seasons Played	Apps	Subs	Gls
Southport	Swansea C. (Am)	10.46	46	19	-	3
Aldershot	Tr	04.47	46-47	16	-	4
Brentford	Distillery	12.50				
Tranmere Rov.	Tr	05.52	52-53	46	-	2
Bradford C.	Tr	02.54	53-54	21	-	3

MYERS Alan William
Newcastle, 12 February, 1928 (G)

League Club	Source	Date Signed	Seasons Played	Apps	Subs	Gls
Gateshead		01.52	51	1	-	0

MYERS Andrew John
Hounslow, 3 November, 1973 E Yth/Eu21-4 (LB)

League Club	Source	Date Signed	Seasons Played	Apps	Subs	Gls
Chelsea	YT	06.91	90-97	73	10	2

MYERS Christopher
Yeovil, 1 April, 1969 (M)

League Club	Source	Date Signed	Seasons Played	Apps	Subs	Gls
Torquay U.	YT	06.87	86	8	1	0
Torquay U.	Dawlish	08.90	90-92	88	8	7
Torquay U. (L)	Dundee U.	12.93	93	6	0	0
Scarborough (N/C)	Dundee U.	01.96	95	8	1	0
Exeter C.	Tr	03.96	95-96	38	3	2

MYERS Clifford William
Southwark, 23 September, 1946 (M)

League Club	Source	Date Signed	Seasons Played	Apps	Subs	Gls
Charlton Ath.	App	09.64	65-66	16	2	2
Brentford	Tr	06.67	67	7	3	0
Torquay U.	Yeovil T.	07.73	73-75	80	6	11

MYERS John **Rodney**
Sheffield, 16 February, 1939 (FB)

League Club	Source	Date Signed	Seasons Played	Apps	Subs	Gls
Doncaster Rov.	Scarborough	01.63	63	19	-	0

MYERSCOUGH William Henry
Bolton, 22 June, 1930 Died 1977 (IF)

League Club	Source	Date Signed	Seasons Played	Apps	Subs	Gls
Walsall	Ashfield	06.54	54	26	-	6
Aston Villa	Tr	07.55	56-58	64	-	15
Rotherham U.	Tr	07.59	59	38	-	11
Coventry C.	Tr	07.60	60-61	58	-	16
Chester C.	Tr	03.62	61-62	36	-	10
Wrexham	Tr	07.63	63	35	-	5

MYHRE Thomas
Sarpsborg, Norway, 16 October, 1973 Norwegian Int (G)

League Club	Source	Date Signed	Seasons Played	Apps	Subs	Gls
Everton	Viking Stavanger (Nor)	11.97	97	22	0	0

MYLES Neil Thomson
Falkirk, 17 June, 1927 Died 1993 (WH)

League Club	Source	Date Signed	Seasons Played	Apps	Subs	Gls
Ipswich T.	Third Lanark	08.49	49-59	223	-	15

MYNARD Leslie Daniel
Kidderminster, 19 December, 1925 (OL)

League Club	Source	Date Signed	Seasons Played	Apps	Subs	Gls
Wolverhampton W.	Bewdley	05.45	47	3	-	0
Derby Co.	Tr	07.49	49-50	14	-	2
Scunthorpe U.	Tr	08.52	52	18	-	3

MYTON Brian
York, 26 September, 1950 (LB)

League Club	Source	Date Signed	Seasons Played	Apps	Subs	Gls
Middlesbrough	App	09.67	68-70	10	0	0
Southend U.	L	11.71	71	0	1	0

NAGY Niklos
Hungary, 1 May, 1929 (IF)

League Club	Source	Date Signed	Seasons Played	Apps	Subs	Gls
Scunthorpe U.		01.51				
Swindon T.	Tr	08.51	51	2	-	0

NAIL Desmond Roy
St Columb, 28 December, 1924 Died 1983 (CF)

League Club	Source	Date Signed	Seasons Played	Apps	Subs	Gls
Plymouth Arg.	St Blazey	10.47	47	1	-	0

NAINBY Lewis **John**
Whitley Bay, 2 January, 1940 (F)

League Club	Source	Date Signed	Seasons Played	Apps	Subs	Gls
Sheffield Wed.		02.58				
Darlington	Tr	07.59	59	3	-	1

NAPIER Alexander Stevenson
Kirkcaldy, 8 August, 1935 (IF)

League Club	Source	Date Signed	Seasons Played	Apps	Subs	Gls
Darlington	Raith Rov.	05.55	55	1	-	0

NAPIER Christopher (Kit) Robin Anthony
Dunblane, 26 September, 1943 (CF)

League Club	Source	Date Signed	Seasons Played	Apps	Subs	Gls
Blackpool	Jnrs	11.60	62	2	-	0
Preston N.E.	Tr	06.63	63	1	-	0
Workington	Tr	07.64	64-65	58	0	25
Newcastle U.	Tr	11.65	65	8	0	0
Brighton & H.A.	Tr	09.66	66-72	249	7	84
Blackburn Rov.	Tr	08.72	72-73	53	1	10

NAPIER Robert **John**
Lurgan (NI), 23 September, 1946 NIu23-2/NI-1 (CD)

League Club	Source	Date Signed	Seasons Played	Apps	Subs	Gls
Bolton W.	Jnrs	09.63	64-66	69	0	2
Brighton & H.A.	Tr	08.67	67-72	218	1	5
Bradford C.	Tr	10.72	72-76	106	1	3

NARBETT Jonathan Vellenzer
Birmingham, 21 November, 1968 (M)

League Club	Source	Date Signed	Seasons Played	Apps	Subs	Gls
Shrewsbury T.	App	09.86	86-87	20	6	3
Hereford U.	Tr	10.88	88-91	148	1	31
Oxford U.	Tr	07.92	92-93	13	2	0
Chesterfield	Kalmar F.F. (Swe)	12.94	94-95	13	7	1

NARDIELLO Donato
Cardigan, 9 April, 1957 Wu21-1/W-2 (W)

League Club	Source	Date Signed	Seasons Played	Apps	Subs	Gls
Coventry C.	App	04.74	77-79	32	1	1

NARDIELLO Gerardo
Warley, 5 May, 1966 E Yth (F)

League Club	Source	Date Signed	Seasons Played	Apps	Subs	Gls
Shrewsbury T.	App	05.84	82-85	32	6	11
Cardiff C.	L	03.86	85	7	0	4
Torquay U.	Tr	07.86	86-87	28	9	11

NASH Carlo James
Bolton, 13 September, 1973 (G)

League Club	Source	Date Signed	Seasons Played	Apps	Subs	Gls
Crystal Palace	Clitheroe	07.96	96	21	0	0

NASH Frank (Paddy) Cooper
Middlesbrough, 30 June, 1918 Died 1989 (G)

League Club	Source	Date Signed	Seasons Played	Apps	Subs	Gls
Middlesbrough	South Bank	09.37	37-47	19	-	0
Southend U.	Tr	12.47	47-50	57	-	0

NASH Marc
Newcastle, 13 May, 1978 (F)

League Club	Source	Date Signed	Seasons Played	Apps	Subs	Gls
Hartlepool U.	Benfield Park	09.97	97	0	1	0

NASH Martin
Canada, 27 December, 1975 Canadian Int (W)

League Club	Source	Date Signed	Seasons Played	Apps	Subs	Gls
Stockport Co.	Regina (Can)	11.96	96-97	0	11	0

NASH Robert Graham
Hammersmith, 8 February, 1946 (FB)

League Club	Source	Date Signed	Seasons Played	Apps	Subs	Gls
Queens Park R.	Jnrs	02.64	64	17	-	0
Exeter C.	Tr	06.66	66	1	0	0

NASSARI Derek James
Salford, 20 October, 1971 (M)

League Club	Source	Date Signed	Seasons Played	Apps	Subs	Gls
Chester C.	YT	●	89	0	1	0

NASTRI Carlo Luciano Rattaele
Finsbury, 22 October, 1935 (W)

League Club	Source	Date Signed	Seasons Played	Apps	Subs	Gls
Crystal Palace	Kingstonian	07.58	58	2	-	0

NATTRASS Irving
Fishburn (Dm), 20 December, 1952 Eu23-1 (RB)

League Club	Source	Date Signed	Seasons Played	Apps	Subs	Gls
Newcastle U.	App	07.70	70-78	226	12	16
Middlesbrough	Tr	08.79	79-85	186	5	2

NATTRESS Clive
Durham, 24 May, 1951 (D)

League Club	Source	Date Signed	Seasons Played	Apps	Subs	Gls
Blackpool	Consett	08.70				
Darlington	Tr	08.72	72-79	297	5	15
Halifax T.	Tr	06.80	80	37	0	5
Darlington (N/C)	Bishop Auckland	08.85	85	1	0	0

NAUGHTON William Balloch Stirling
Catrine (Ayrs), 20 March, 1962 (LW)

League Club	Source	Date Signed	Seasons Played	Apps	Subs	Gls
Preston N.E.	App	03.80	79-84	148	14	10
Walsall	Tr	03.85	84-88	139	12	16
Shrewsbury T.	Tr	08.89	89-90	43	6	4
Walsall	Tr	01.91	90	15	1	1

NAYIM Mohamed Amar Ali
Morocco, 5 November, 1966 Spanish u21 Int (M)

League Club	Source	Date Signed	Seasons Played	Apps	Subs	Gls
Tottenham H.	Barcelona (Sp)	11.88	88-92	95	17	11

NAYLOR Anthony Joseph
Manchester, 29 March, 1967 (F)

League Club	Source	Date Signed	Seasons Played	Apps	Subs	Gls
Crewe Alex.	Droylsden	03.90	89-93	104	18	45
Port Vale	Tr	07.94	94-97	127	26	47

NAYLOR Dominic John
Watford, 12 August, 1970 (LB)

League Club	Source	Date Signed	Seasons Played	Apps	Subs	Gls
Watford	YT	09.88				
Halifax T.	Tr	12.89	89	5	1	1
Barnet	Hong Kong	08.91	91-92	50	1	0
Plymouth Arg.	Tr	07.93	93-94	84	1	0
Gillingham	Tr	08.95	95	30	1	1
Leyton Orient	Tr	08.96	96-97	87	0	4

NAYLOR Edward
Bradford, 24 December, 1921 (RH)

League Club	Source	Date Signed	Seasons Played	Apps	Subs	Gls
Bradford P.A.		05.45				
Halifax T.	Tr	09.48	48	7	-	0

NAYLOR Geoffrey
Goole, 28 September, 1949 (WH)

League Club	Source	Date Signed	Seasons Played	Apps	Subs	Gls
Scunthorpe U.	App	09.67	67	9	1	0

NAYLOR Glenn
Goole, 11 August, 1972 (F)

League Club	Source	Date Signed	Seasons Played	Apps	Subs	Gls
York C.	YT	03.90	89-96	78	33	30
Darlington	L	10.95	95	3	1	1
Darlington	Tr	09.96	96-97	68	11	18

NAYLOR Harold Francis
Leeds, 6 June, 1928 (CF)

League Club	Source	Date Signed	Seasons Played	Apps	Subs	Gls
Oldham Ath. (Am)		04.51	50	1	-	0

NAYLOR Lee Martyn
Walsall, 19 March, 1980 (LB)

League Club	Source	Date Signed	Seasons Played	Apps	Subs	Gls
Wolverhampton W.	YT	10.97	97	14	2	0

NAYLOR Martyn Paul
Walsall, 2 August, 1977 (RB)

League Club	Source	Date Signed	Seasons Played	Apps	Subs	Gls
Shrewsbury T.	Telford	07.97	97	2	0	0

NAYLOR Richard Alan
Leeds, 28 February, 1977 (F)

League Club	Source	Date Signed	Seasons Played	Apps	Subs	Gls
Ipswich T.	YT	07.95	96-97	19	13	6

NAYLOR Stuart William
Wetherby, 6 December, 1962 E Yth/E'B' (G)

League Club	Source	Date Signed	Seasons Played	Apps	Subs	Gls
Lincoln C.	Yorkshire Amats	06.80	81-85	49	0	0
Peterborough U.	L	02.83	82	8	0	0
Crewe Alex.	L	10.83	83	38	0	0
Crewe Alex.	L	08.84	84	17	0	0
West Bromwich A.	Tr	02.86	85-95	354	1	0
Bristol C.	Tr	08.96	96-97	37	0	0

NAYLOR Terence Michael Patrick
Islington, 5 December, 1948 (CD)

League Club	Source	Date Signed	Seasons Played	Apps	Subs	Gls
Tottenham H.	Smithfield Market	07.69	69-79	237	6	0
Charlton Ath.	Tr	11.80	80-83	69	4	0

NAYLOR Thomas Vincent
Blackburn, 1 April, 1946 (D)

League Club	Source	Date Signed	Seasons Played	Apps	Subs	Gls
Bournemouth	App	10.63	64-70	139	3	3
Hereford U.	Tr	08.72	72-74	73	2	4

NAYLOR Thomas **William**
Leeds, 7 December, 1924 (FB)

League Club	Source	Date Signed	Seasons Played	Apps	Subs	Gls
Huddersfield T.	Outwood Stormcocks	02.43				
Oldham Ath.	Tr	03.48	47-58	224	-	0

NDAH George Ehialimolisa
Dulwich, 23 December, 1974 E Yth (W/F)

League Club	Source	Date Signed	Seasons Played	Apps	Subs	Gls
Crystal Palace	YT	08.92	92-96	31	44	8
Bournemouth	L	10.95	95	12	0	2
Gillingham	L	08.97	97	4	0	0
Swindon T.	Tr	11.97	97	14	0	2

NDAH Jamie Jidefor Ogoegbunan
Camberwell, 5 August, 1971 (F)

League Club	Source	Date Signed	Seasons Played	Apps	Subs	Gls
Torquay U.	Kingstonian	08.95	95-96	25	3	4
Barnet	Tr	02.97	96	12	2	4

N'DIAYE Sada
Dakar, Senegal, 27 March, 1975 (F)

League Club	Source	Date Signed	Seasons Played	Apps	Subs	Gls
Southend U.	Troyes (Fr)	10.97	97	15	2	2

NDLOVU Peter
Zimbabwe, 25 February, 1973 Zimbabwe Int (W/F)

League Club	Source	Date Signed	Seasons Played	Apps	Subs	Gls
Coventry C.	Highlanders (Zim)	07.91	91-96	141	36	37
Birmingham C.	Tr	07.97	97	29	10	9

NEAL Ashley James
Northampton, 16 December, 1974 (FB)

League Club	Source	Date Signed	Seasons Played	Apps	Subs	Gls
Liverpool	YT	04.93				
Brighton & H.A.	L	09.96	96	8	0	0
Huddersfield T.	Tr	12.96				
Peterborough U.	Tr	03.97	96-97	6	2	0

NEAL Christopher
Kirkby-in-Ashfield, 27 June, 1947 (W)

League Club	Source	Date Signed	Seasons Played	Apps	Subs	Gls
Darlington (Am)	Crook T.	06.67	67	5	0	0

NEAL Dean John
Edmonton, 5 January, 1961 (F)

League Club	Source	Date Signed	Seasons Played	Apps	Subs	Gls
Queens Park R.	App	01.79	79-80	20	2	8
Millwall	Tulsa (USA)	10.81	81-84	101	19	42
Southend U.	Tr	01.86	85-87	35	5	6
Cambridge U.	L	12.87	87	4	0	0

NEAL George
Wellingborough, 29 December, 1919 (RH)

League Club	Source	Date Signed	Seasons Played	Apps	Subs	Gls
Northampton T.	Kettering T.	01.45	46	3	-	0

NEAL John
Seaham, 13 April, 1932 (FB)

League Club	Source	Date Signed	Seasons Played	Apps	Subs	Gls
Hull C.	Silksworth Jnrs	08.49	49-55	60	-	1
Swindon T.	Kings Lynn	07.57	57-58	91	-	2
Aston Villa	Tr	07.59	59-62	96	-	0
Southend U.	Tr	11.62	62-65	100	0	1

NEAL John James
Hornsey, 11 March, 1966 E Sch (F)

League Club	Source	Date Signed	Seasons Played	Apps	Subs	Gls
Millwall	App	03.83	83	3	3	1

NEAL Philip George
Irchester, 29 February, 1951 E-50 (RB)

League Club	Source	Date Signed	Seasons Played	Apps	Subs	Gls
Northampton T.	App	12.68	68-74	183	4	28
Liverpool	Tr	10.74	74-85	453	2	41
Bolton W.	Tr	12.85	85-88	56	8	3

NEAL Richard (Dick) Marshall
Dinnington, 1 October, 1933 Eu23-4 (WH)

League Club	Source	Date Signed	Seasons Played	Apps	Subs	Gls
Wolverhampton W.	Jnrs	03.51				
Lincoln C.	Tr	07.54	54-56	115	-	11
Birmingham C.	Tr	04.57	56-61	165	-	15
Middlesbrough	Tr	10.61	61-62	33	-	4
Lincoln C.	Tr	08.63	63-64	41	-	4

NEALE Duncan Frederick
Worthing, 1 October, 1939 (WH)

League Club	Source	Date Signed	Seasons Played	Apps	Subs	Gls
Newcastle U.	Ilford	06.59	60-62	88	-	8
Plymouth Arg.	Tr	08.63	63-69	141	5	8

NEALE John William
Barnstaple, 15 January, 1949 (W)

League Club	Source	Date Signed	Seasons Played	Apps	Subs	Gls
Exeter C.	Barnstaple	03.72	71-74	51	14	5

NEALE Keith Ian
Birmingham, 19 January, 1935 (IF)

League Club	Source	Date Signed	Seasons Played	Apps	Subs	Gls
Birmingham C.	Jnrs	02.54	56-57	5	-	1
Lincoln C.	Tr	11.57	57-58	8	-	1

NEALE Peter
Bolsover, 9 April, 1934 (CH)

League Club	Source	Date Signed	Seasons Played	Apps	Subs	Gls
Oldham Ath.	Chesterfield (Jnrs)	01.53	55-58	117	-	28
Scunthorpe U.	Tr	10.58	58-66	221	5	7
Chesterfield	Tr	10.66	66-67	69	0	4

NEALE Philip Anthony
Scunthorpe, 5 June, 1954 (M/LB)

League Club	Source	Date Signed	Seasons Played	Apps	Subs	Gls
Lincoln C.	Scunthorpe U. (Am)	10.74	74-84	327	8	22

NEALE William Edward
Wallsend, 20 May, 1933 (HB)

League Club	Source	Date Signed	Seasons Played	Apps	Subs	Gls
Sunderland	Jnrs	06.50				
Darlington	North Shields	05.57	57	15	-	0

NEARY Harold **Frank**
Aldershot, 6 March, 1921 (CF)

League Club	Source	Date Signed	Seasons Played	Apps	Subs	Gls
Queens Park R.	Finchley	07.45	46	9	-	4
West Ham U.	Tr	01.47	46-47	17	-	15
Leyton Orient	Tr	11.47	47-49	78	-	44
Queens Park R.	Tr	10.49	49	18	-	5
Millwall	Tr	08.50	50-53	123	-	50

NEATE Derek George Stanbridge
Uxbridge, 1 October, 1927 (OL)

League Club	Source	Date Signed	Seasons Played	Apps	Subs	Gls
Brighton & H.A.	Hayes	04.56	55-56	24	-	6

NEATE Gordon
Reading, 14 March, 1941 (FB)

League Club	Source	Date Signed	Seasons Played	Apps	Subs	Gls
Reading	Jnrs	03.58	58-65	99	0	2

NEAVE Ian **Gordon**
Glasgow, 10 October, 1924 (WH)

League Club	Source	Date Signed	Seasons Played	Apps	Subs	Gls
Portsmouth	Pollok Jnrs	03.47				
Bournemouth	Tr	06.49	50-53	85	-	0
Aldershot	Tr	07.55	55-57	79	-	2

NEBBELING Gavin Mark
South Africa, 15 May, 1963 (CD)

League Club	Source	Date Signed	Seasons Played	Apps	Subs	Gls
Crystal Palace	Arcadia Shepherds (SA)	08.81	81-88	145	6	8
Northampton T.	L	10.85	85	11	0	0
Fulham	Tr	07.89	89-92	85	3	2
Hereford U.	L	12.91	91	3	0	0
Preston N.E.	Tr	07.93	93	22	0	4

NEEDHAM Andrew Paul
Oldham, 13 September, 1955 (F)

League Club	Source	Date Signed	Seasons Played	Apps	Subs	Gls
Birmingham C.	App	08.73	75	2	1	1
Blackburn Rov.	Tr	07.76	76	4	1	0
Aldershot	Tr	03.77	76-79	92	3	29

NEEDHAM Anthony
Scunthorpe, 4 January, 1941 (FB)

League Club	Source	Date Signed	Seasons Played	Apps	Subs	Gls
Scunthorpe U.	Jnrs	07.59	59-64	33	-	0

NEEDHAM David William
Leicester, 21 May, 1949 (CD)

League Club	Source	Date Signed	Seasons Played	Apps	Subs	Gls
Notts Co.	App	07.66	65-76	428	1	32
Queens Park R.	Tr	06.77	77	18	0	3
Nottingham F.	Tr	12.77	77-81	81	5	9

NEEDHAM Andrew **Paul**
Buxton, 15 June, 1961 (FB)

League Club	Source	Date Signed	Seasons Played	Apps	Subs	Gls
Chester C.	App	06.79	80-82	55	2	1

NEENAN Joseph Patrick
Manchester, 17 March, 1959 (G)

League Club	Source	Date Signed	Seasons Played	Apps	Subs	Gls
York C.	App	03.77	76-79	56	0	0
Scunthorpe U.	Tr	01.80	79-84	191	0	0
Burnley	L	01.85	84	9	0	0
Burnley	Tr	07.85	85-86	81	0	0
Peterborough U.	Tr	07.87	87-88	55	0	0
Scarborough	L	01.88	87	6	0	0

NEIGHBOUR James Edward
Chingford, 15 November, 1950 (W)

League Club	Source	Date Signed	Seasons Played	Apps	Subs	Gls
Tottenham H.	App	11.68	70-76	104	15	8
Norwich C.	Tr	09.76	76-79	104	2	5
West Ham U.	Tr	09.79	79-82	66	7	5
Bournemouth	L	01.83	82	6	0	0

NEIL Hugh Moorhead
Cumnock, 2 October, 1936 S Sch (FB)

League Club	Source	Date Signed	Seasons Played	Apps	Subs	Gls
Carlisle U.	St Johnstone	06.61	61-68	246	1	2

NEIL James Darren
Bury St Edmunds, 28 February, 1976 (RB)

League Club	Source	Date Signed	Seasons Played	Apps	Subs	Gls
Grimsby T.	YT	07.94	95-96	1	1	0
Scunthorpe U.	Tr	08.97	97	6	1	0

League Club	Source	Date Signed	Seasons Played	Career Record Apps	Subs	Gls
NEIL Patrick Thomas						
Portsmouth, 24 October, 1937 E Amat						(OL)
Portsmouth (Am)	Jnrs	06.55	55	9	-	3
Wolverhampton W. (Am)	Tr	08.56	56	4	-	1
Portsmouth	Pegasus	05.62	62	1	-	0
NEIL William Marshbanks						
Lanark, 20 April, 1924						(IF)
Bradford P.A.	Morton	12.47	47	3	-	0
NEIL William Waugh						
Roslin, 10 November, 1944						(LW)
Millwall	Bonnyrigg Rose	04.64	64-71	178	8	26
NEILL Lucas Edward						
Australia, 9 March, 1978						(D/M)
Millwall	A.I.S. (Aus)	11.95	95-97	43	15	4
NEILL William John **Terence**						
Belfast, 8 May, 1942 NI Sch/NIu23-4/NI-59						(CH)
Arsenal	Bangor	12.59	60-69	240	1	8
Hull C.	Tr	07.70	70-72	103	0	4
NEILL Thomas Kerr						
Methil, 3 October, 1930 Died 1996						(WH)
Bolton W.	R.A.F. Wharton	09.50	52-56	40	-	2
Bury	Tr	12.56	56-59	90	-	9
Tranmere Rov.	Tr	10.60	60-62	79	-	2
NEILL Warren Anthony						
Acton, 21 November, 1962 E Sch						(RB)
Queens Park R.	App	09.80	80-87	177	4	3
Portsmouth	Tr	07.88	88-94	216	2	2
Watford (N/C)	Tr	01.96	95	0	1	0
NEILSON Alan Bruce						
West Germany, 26 September, 1972 Wu21-7/W 'B'/W-5						(FB)
Newcastle U.	YT	02.91	90-94	35	7	1
Southampton	Tr	06.95	95-97	42	13	0
Fulham	Tr	11.97	97	17	0	0
NEILSON Gordon						
Glasgow, 28 May, 1947						(W)
Arsenal	Glasgow U.	06.64	65-66	14	0	2
Brentford	Tr	10.68	68-71	80	12	15
NEILSON John Crane						
Hamilton, 2 August, 1921 Died 1988						(CF)
Bradford C.	Clyde	10.47	47-48	29	-	11
Wrexham	Tr	10.48				
NEILSON Stephen Bruce						
Newtongrange, 25 April, 1931						(RH)
Rotherham U.		07.55	56	9	-	0
NEILSON Thomas						
Armadale, 28 July, 1922						(HB)
Ipswich T.	Hearts	05.48	48	1	-	0
NEKREWS Thomas John						
Chatham, 20 March, 1933						(CH)
Gillingham	Chelsea (Am)	09.53	53-57	42	-	0
Watford	Tr	07.58				
NELMES Alan Victor						
Hackney, 20 October, 1948						(D)
Chelsea	Jnrs	10.65				
Brentford	Tr	07.67	67-75	311	5	2
NELSON Andrew Nesbitt						
Silvertown, 5 July, 1935						(CH)
West Ham U.	Jnrs	12.53	57-58	15	-	1
Ipswich T.	Tr	06.59	59-64	193	-	0
Leyton Orient	Tr	09.64	64-65	43	0	0
Plymouth Arg.	Tr	10.65	65-67	94	0	1
NELSON Anthony James						
Cardiff, 12 April, 1930 W Amat						(CH)
Newport Co.		06.52	51-53	19	-	6
Bristol C.	Tr	05.54				
Bournemouth	Tr	06.56	56-64	195	-	1
NELSON Colin Armstrong						
Boldon, 13 March, 1938						(FB)
Sunderland	Usworth Colly	03.58	58-64	146	-	2
Mansfield T.	Tr	03.65	64-65	38	0	0

League Club	Source	Date Signed	Seasons Played	Career Record Apps	Subs	Gls
NELSON David						
Douglas Water, 3 February, 1918 Died 1988						(WH)
Arsenal	St Bernards	05.36	36-46	27	-	4
Fulham	Tr	12.46	46	23	-	2
Brentford	Tr	08.47	47-49	106	-	5
Queens Park R.	Tr	02.50	49-50	31	-	0
Crystal Palace	Tr	03.52	51-52	12	-	0
NELSON Dennis						
Edinburgh, 25 February, 1950						(F/M)
Crewe Alex.	Dunfermline Ath.	07.74	74-75	65	6	18
Reading	Tr	03.76	75-77	53	6	6
Crewe Alex.	Tr	07.78	78-80	97	10	15
NELSON Fernando						
Portugal, 5 November, 1971 Portuguese Int						(RB)
Aston Villa	Sporting Lisbon (Por)	07.96	96-97	54	5	0
NELSON Garry Paul						
Braintree, 16 January, 1961						(W/F)
Southend U.	Jnrs	07.79	79-82	106	23	17
Swindon T.	Tr	08.83	83-84	78	1	7
Plymouth Arg.	Tr	07.85	85-86	71	3	20
Brighton & H.A.	Tr	07.87	87-90	132	12	47
Notts Co.	L	11.90	90	0	2	0
Charlton Ath.	Tr	08.91	91-95	147	38	37
Torquay U.	Tr	08.96	96	30	4	8
NELSON George						
Mexborough, 5 February, 1925						(IF)
Sheffield U.	Denaby Rov.	08.43				
Lincoln C.	Tr	09.46	46	1	-	0
NELSON James Frederick						
Newcastle, 4 November, 1943						(FB)
Sunderland		08.62				
Ipswich T.	Tr	07.63				
Barrow	Tr	01.65	64-65	15	0	0
NELSON Samuel						
Belfast, 1 April, 1949 NIu23-1/NI-51						(LB)
Arsenal	Jnrs	04.66	69-80	245	10	10
Brighton & H.A.	Tr	09.81	81-82	40	0	1
NELSON Samuel Edward						
Belfast, 26 May, 1924 NI Sch						(OR)
Blackpool	Linfield Swifts	10.46	46-47	14	-	0
Luton T.	Tr	01.48	47-48	4	-	1
NELSON William Edward						
Silvertown, 20 September, 1929						(WH)
West Ham U.		10.50	54	2	-	0
Queens Park R.	Tr	07.55	55	9	-	0
NESBIT Tony						
Sunderland, 26 January, 1968 E Sch						(M)
Newcastle U.	App	01.86	86	1	2	0
NESBITT Edward						
Boldon, 12 October, 1951						(G)
Hartlepool U. (Am)	Longbenton Jnrs	08.71	71	1	0	0
NESBITT John						
Washington, 24 September, 1933						(CH)
Newcastle U.	Ashington	12.55	57	3	-	0
NESBITT Mark Thomas						
Doncaster, 11 January, 1972						(FB)
Middlesbrough	YT	01.90				
Hartlepool U.	Tr	03.91	90-91	2	0	0
NESBITT Michael David						
Doncaster, 8 January, 1969 E Yth						(F)
Doncaster Rov.	App	01.86	85-87	6	5	1
NESS Hugh Preston						
Dunfermline, 30 April, 1940						(FB)
Accrington St.	Cowdenbeath	07.59	59	14	-	1
Halifax T.	Tr	06.60				
NETHERCOTT Kenneth Walter Samuel						
Bristol, 22 July , 1925 E 'B'						(G)
Norwich C.	Cardiff C. (Am)	04.47	47-58	378	-	0
NETHERCOTT Stuart David						
Chadwell Heath, 21 March, 1973 Eu21-8						(CD)
Tottenham H.	YT	07.91	92-96	31	23	0
Maidstone U.	L	09.91	91	13	0	1
Barnet	L	02.92	91	3	0	0
Millwall	Tr	01.98	97	10	0	0

NETTLESHIP Reginald
Warsop, 23 February, 1925 (IF)

League Club	Source	Date Signed	Seasons Played	Apps	Subs	Gls
Sheffield U.	Welbeck Colly	06.43				
Mansfield T.	Tr	07.46	46	1	-	0

NETTLETON Ernest
Sheffield, 7 January, 1918 (OL)

League Club	Source	Date Signed	Seasons Played	Apps	Subs	Gls
York C.		07.46	46	7	-	2

NEVES Rui Santos Cordeiro
Portugal, 10 March, 1965 (F)

League Club	Source	Date Signed	Seasons Played	Apps	Subs	Gls
Darlington (N/C)	Famalicao (Por)	08.95	95	3	2	0

NEVILLE Christopher William
Downham Market, 22 October, 1970 (G)

League Club	Source	Date Signed	Seasons Played	Apps	Subs	Gls
Ipswich T.	YT	05.89	89	1	0	0

NEVILLE David Raymond
Birmingham, 8 January, 1929 Died 1991 (D)

League Club	Source	Date Signed	Seasons Played	Apps	Subs	Gls
Bournemouth	Paget R.	04.49				
Chelsea	Tr	07.50				
Rochdale	Burton A.	08.55	55	1	-	0

NEVILLE Gary Alexander
Bury, 18 February, 1975 E Yth/E-30 (D)

League Club	Source	Date Signed	Seasons Played	Apps	Subs	Gls
Manchester U.	YT	01.93	93-97	111	4	1

NEVILLE Philip John
Bury, 21 January, 1977 E Sch/E Yth/Eu21-7/E-12 (FB)

League Club	Source	Date Signed	Seasons Played	Apps	Subs	Gls
Manchester U.	YT	06.94	94-97	61	13	1

NEVILLE Steven Francis
Walthamstow, 18 September, 1957 (W)

League Club	Source	Date Signed	Seasons Played	Apps	Subs	Gls
Southampton	App	09.75	77	5	1	1
Exeter C.	Tr	09.78	78-80	90	3	22
Sheffield U.	Tr	10.80	80-81	40	9	6
Exeter C.	Tr	10.82	82-84	89	3	27
Bristol C.	Tr	11.84	84-87	128	6	40
Exeter C.	Tr	07.88	88-90	115	5	39

NEVILLE William
Cork (Ire), 15 May, 1935 IR 'B' (F)

League Club	Source	Date Signed	Seasons Played	Apps	Subs	Gls
West Ham U.	Wembley T.	11.56	57	3	-	0

NEVIN Patrick Kevin Francis Michael
Glasgow, 6 September, 1963 S Yth/Su21-5/S 'B'/S-28 (RW)

League Club	Source	Date Signed	Seasons Played	Apps	Subs	Gls
Chelsea	Clyde	07.83	83-87	190	3	36
Everton	Tr	07.88	88-91	81	28	16
Tranmere Rov.	L	03.92	91	8	0	0
Tranmere Rov.	Tr	08.92	92-96	181	12	30

NEVIN Paul Richard
Lewisham, 23 June, 1969 (F)

League Club	Source	Date Signed	Seasons Played	Apps	Subs	Gls
Carlisle U.	Evansville (USA)	09.91	91	2	6	0

NEVIN Ridley Walter
Corbridge, 28 July, 1956 (M)

League Club	Source	Date Signed	Seasons Played	Apps	Subs	Gls
Everton	App	05.74				
Workington	Tr	08.75	75	3	1	0

NEVINS Laurence
Gateshead, 2 July, 1920 (W)

League Club	Source	Date Signed	Seasons Played	Apps	Subs	Gls
Newcastle U.		09.40				
Brighton & H.A.	Tr	05.47	47	5	-	0
Hartlepool U.	Tr	03.48	47-48	18	-	8

NEVLAND Erik
Stavanger, Norway, 10 November, 1977 Norwegian Int (F)

League Club	Source	Date Signed	Seasons Played	Apps	Subs	Gls
Manchester U.	Viking Stavanger (Nor)	07.97	97	0	1	0

NEW Martin Peter
Swindon, 11 May, 1959 E Sch (G)

League Club	Source	Date Signed	Seasons Played	Apps	Subs	Gls
Arsenal	App	03.77				
Mansfield T.	Tr	06.78	78-79	21	0	0
Barnsley	Tr	06.80	80	24	0	0

NEWALL James **Daniel**
Newport, 5 June, 1921 (WH)

League Club	Source	Date Signed	Seasons Played	Apps	Subs	Gls
Newport Co.	Jnrs	06.38	38-54	233	-	4

NEWBERRY Peter John
Derby, 4 March, 1938 (CF)

League Club	Source	Date Signed	Seasons Played	Apps	Subs	Gls
Derby Co.	Jnrs	03.55	58-60	5	-	2

NEWBOLD Alfred
Hartlepool, 7 August, 1921 (RB)

League Club	Source	Date Signed	Seasons Played	Apps	Subs	Gls
Huddersfield T.	Ouston W.	12.45	46	2	-	0
Newport Co.	Tr	10.46	46	22	-	0

NEWBY Thomas **Geoffrey**
Barrow, 9 October, 1949 (WH)

League Club	Source	Date Signed	Seasons Played	Apps	Subs	Gls
Barrow (Am)	Jnrs	11.68	68	1	0	0

NEWCOMBE Bernard (Len) John
Swansea, 28 February, 1931 Died 1996 (OL)

League Club	Source	Date Signed	Seasons Played	Apps	Subs	Gls
Fulham	Jnrs	05.48	51-54	23	-	3
Brentford	Tr	04.56	55-58	85	-	8

NEWCOMBE Giles Alan
Doncaster, 9 July, 1968 (G)

League Club	Source	Date Signed	Seasons Played	Apps	Subs	Gls
Rotherham U.	YT	06.87	86	6	0	0

NEWELL Edgar
Swansea, 17 April, 1920 (CH)

League Club	Source	Date Signed	Seasons Played	Apps	Subs	Gls
Swansea C.		08.46	47-50	24	-	0

NEWELL George
Rochdale, 17 March, 1936 (CH)

League Club	Source	Date Signed	Seasons Played	Apps	Subs	Gls
Rochdale		04.57	57	1	-	0

NEWELL Justin James
Germany, 8 February, 1980 (F)

League Club	Source	Date Signed	Seasons Played	Apps	Subs	Gls
Torquay U.	YT	●	97	0	1	0

NEWELL Michael Colin
Liverpool, 27 January, 1965 Eu21-4/E 'B' (F)

League Club	Source	Date Signed	Seasons Played	Apps	Subs	Gls
Crewe Alex.	Liverpool (Jnrs)	09.83	83	3	0	0
Wigan Ath.	Tr	10.83	83-85	64	8	25
Luton T.	Tr	01.86	85-87	62	1	18
Leicester C.	Tr	09.87	87-88	81	0	21
Everton	Tr	06.89	89-91	48	20	15
Blackburn Rov.	Tr	11.91	91-95	113	17	28
Birmingham C.	Tr	07.96	96	11	4	1
West Ham U.	L	12.96	96	6	1	0
Bradford C.	L	03.97	96	7	0	0

NEWELL Paul Clayton
Woolwich, 23 February, 1969 (G)

League Club	Source	Date Signed	Seasons Played	Apps	Subs	Gls
Southend U.	YT	06.87	87-88	15	0	0
Leyton Orient	Tr	08.90	90-93	61	0	0
Colchester U.	L	08.92	92	14	0	0
Barnet	Tr	07.94	94-95	16	0	0
Darlington	Tr	01.96	95-96	41	0	0

NEWHOUSE Aidan Robert
Wallasey, 23 May, 1972 E Yth (F)

League Club	Source	Date Signed	Seasons Played	Apps	Subs	Gls
Chester C.	YT	07.89	87-89	29	15	6
Wimbledon	Tr	02.90	89-92	7	16	2
Port Vale	L	01.94	93	0	2	0
Portsmouth	L	12.94	94	6	0	1
Torquay U.	L	12.95	95	4	0	2
Fulham	Tr	06.97	97	7	1	1
Swansea C.	Tr	10.97	97	3	5	0

NEWLAND Raymond James
Liverpool, 19 July, 1971 (G)

League Club	Source	Date Signed	Seasons Played	Apps	Subs	Gls
Plymouth Arg.	St Helens	07.92	92-93	25	1	0
Chester C.	Tr	07.94	94	9	1	0
Torquay U.	Tr	01.96	95-96	28	0	0

NEWLANDS Douglas Haigh
Edinburgh, 29 October, 1931 (OR)

League Club	Source	Date Signed	Seasons Played	Apps	Subs	Gls
Burnley	Aberdeen	03.55	54-58	98	-	21
Stoke C.	Tr	07.59	59	32	-	8

NEWLANDS Malcolm
Wishaw, 28 March, 1925 Died 1996 (G)

League Club	Source	Date Signed	Seasons Played	Apps	Subs	Gls
Preston N.E.	St Mirren	07.48	48-52	80	-	0
Workington	Tr	11.52	52-59	251	-	0

NEWLOVE Peter
Bradford, 27 December, 1947 (HB)

League Club	Source	Date Signed	Seasons Played	Apps	Subs	Gls
Bradford C.	App	01.66	64-66	2	1	0

NEWMAN Albert Dorcin
Lichfield, 1 March, 1915 Died 1981 (WH)

League Club	Source	Date Signed	Seasons Played	Apps	Subs	Gls
Walsall	Brierley Hill Alliance	11.39	46-49	135	-	2

NEWMAN Darren Lewis
Brighton, 14 August, 1968 (D)

League Club	Source	Date Signed	Seasons Played	Apps	Subs	Gls
Brighton & H.A.	App	08.86	85	1	0	0

NEWMAN Eric Ivan Alfred
Romford, 24 November, 1924 Died1971 (G)

League Club	Source	Date Signed	Seasons Played	Apps	Subs	Gls
Arsenal	Romford	10.46				
Ipswich T.	Tr	09.50	52	18	-	0

NEWMAN John Henry George
Hereford, 15 December, 1933 (WH)

League Club	Source	Date Signed	Seasons Played	Apps	Subs	Gls
Birmingham C.	Jnrs	03.51	51-57	60	-	0
Leicester C.	Tr	11.57	57-59	61	-	2
Plymouth Arg.	Tr	01.60	59-67	298	0	9
Exeter C.	Tr	11.67	67-71	91	1	1

NEWMAN Keith
Farnham, 20 November, 1949 E Sch (WH)

League Club	Source	Date Signed	Seasons Played	Apps	Subs	Gls
Aldershot	App	11.66	66-69	19	4	0
York C.	Tr	07.70	70	3	1	0

NEWMAN Harry **Maurice (Mick)**
Canada, 2 April, 1932 (IF)

League Club	Source	Date Signed	Seasons Played	Apps	Subs	Gls
West Ham U.	Dagenham	02.57	56-57	7	-	2

NEWMAN Richard Adrian
Guildford, 5 August, 1970 (M/RB)

League Club	Source	Date Signed	Seasons Played	Apps	Subs	Gls
Crystal Palace	Jnrs	01.88	92-94	43	5	3
Maidstone U.	L	02.92	91	9	1	1
Millwall	Tr	07.95	95-97	108	4	5

NEWMAN Robert Nigel
Bradford-on-Avon, 13 December, 1963 (D/M)

League Club	Source	Date Signed	Seasons Played	Apps	Subs	Gls
Bristol C.	App	10.81	81-90	382	12	52
Norwich C.	Tr	07.91	91-97	181	24	14
Wigan Ath.	L	03.98	97	8	0	0

NEWMAN Ronald
Pontypridd, 1 May, 1933 (IF)

League Club	Source	Date Signed	Seasons Played	Apps	Subs	Gls
Northampton T.	Ynysybwl	10.53	54-55	18	-	5
Coventry C.	Tr	03.56	55-56	13	-	2
Torquay U.	Tr	07.57	57	5	-	0

NEWMAN Ronald Vernon
Fareham, 19 January, 1934 (W)

League Club	Source	Date Signed	Seasons Played	Apps	Subs	Gls
Portsmouth	Woking	01.55	54-60	109	-	21
Leyton Orient	Tr	01.61	60-61	14	-	1
Crystal Palace	Tr	10.62	62	6	-	0
Gillingham	Tr	09.63	63-65	90	3	20

NEWSHAM Stanley
Farnworth, 24 May, 1931 (IF)

League Club	Source	Date Signed	Seasons Played	Apps	Subs	Gls
Bournemouth		06.52	52-56	142	-	74
Notts Co.	Tr	08.57	57-61	99	-	44

NEWSOME Jonathan
Sheffield, 6 September, 1970 (CD)

League Club	Source	Date Signed	Seasons Played	Apps	Subs	Gls
Sheffield Wed.	YT	07.89	89-90	6	1	0
Leeds U.	Tr	06.91	91-93	62	14	3
Norwich C.	Tr	06.94	94-95	61	1	7
Sheffield Wed.	Tr	03.96	95-97	43	0	4

NEWSOME Robin
Hebden Bridge, 25 September, 1919 (IF)

League Club	Source	Date Signed	Seasons Played	Apps	Subs	Gls
West Bromwich A.	Congleton T.	03.39				
Coventry C.	Tr	06.47	47	7	-	2

NEWSON Mark Joseph
Stepney, 7 December, 1960 E Semi Pro (D)

League Club	Source	Date Signed	Seasons Played	Apps	Subs	Gls
Charlton Ath.	App	12.78				
Bournemouth	Maidstone U.	05.85	85-89	172	5	23
Fulham	Tr	02.90	89-92	98	4	4
Barnet	Tr	08.93	93-94	58	1	4

NEWTON Benjamin
Grimsby, 10 October, 1934 (IF)

League Club	Source	Date Signed	Seasons Played	Apps	Subs	Gls
Grimsby T.	Jnrs	07.53	53	3	-	0

NEWTON Stanley **Douglas**
Newcastle, 16 January, 1959 (M)

League Club	Source	Date Signed	Seasons Played	Apps	Subs	Gls
Scarborough (N/C)	Boston U.	03.88	87	4	1	0

NEWTON Edward John Ikem
Hammersmith, 13 December, 1971 Eu21-2 (M)

League Club	Source	Date Signed	Seasons Played	Apps	Subs	Gls
Chelsea	YT	05.90	91-97	138	20	8
Cardiff C.	L	01.92	91	18	0	4

NEWTON Eric David
Sheffield, 21 June, 1932 (IF)

League Club	Source	Date Signed	Seasons Played	Apps	Subs	Gls
Halifax T.	Norton Woodseats	12.54	54	10	-	3

NEWTON Graham Wilfred
Bilston, 22 December, 1942 (IF)

League Club	Source	Date Signed	Seasons Played	Apps	Subs	Gls
Blackpool	Wolverhampton W. (Am)	08.61				
Walsall	Tr	02.62	62-63	30	-	10
Coventry C.	Tr	01.64	63	8	-	3
Bournemouth	Tr	12.64	64-66	27	1	3
Port Vale	Atlanta (USA)	11.68	68	4	0	1

NEWTON Henry Albert
Nottingham, 18 February, 1944 Eu23-4/EF Lge (M/LB)

League Club	Source	Date Signed	Seasons Played	Apps	Subs	Gls
Nottingham F.	Jnrs	06.61	63-70	282	0	17
Everton	Tr	10.70	70-73	76	1	5
Derby Co.	Tr	09.73	73-76	111	6	5
Walsall	Tr	07.77	77	16	0	0

NEWTON John
Edinburgh, 19 January, 1940 (WH)

League Club	Source	Date Signed	Seasons Played	Apps	Subs	Gls
Notts Co.	Craiglea Thistle	10.57	58-60	5	-	0

NEWTON John Laws
Bishop Auckland, 25 May, 1925 (WH)

League Club	Source	Date Signed	Seasons Played	Apps	Subs	Gls
Newcastle U.		05.44				
Hartlepool U.	Tr	05.46	46-57	332	-	15

NEWTON Keith Robert
Manchester, 23 June, 1941 Died 1998 Eu23-4/EF Lge/E-27 (FB)

League Club	Source	Date Signed	Seasons Played	Apps	Subs	Gls
Blackburn Rov.	Jnrs	10.58	60-69	306	0	9
Everton	Tr	12.69	69-71	48	1	1
Burnley	Tr	06.72	72-77	209	0	5

NEWTON Reginald William
Limehouse, 30 June, 1926 (G)

League Club	Source	Date Signed	Seasons Played	Apps	Subs	Gls
Leyton Orient	Dagenham Wks	04.48	48	23	-	0
Brentford	Tr	07.49	49-56	87	-	0

NEWTON Robert
Chesterfield, 23 November, 1956 (F)

League Club	Source	Date Signed	Seasons Played	Apps	Subs	Gls
Huddersfield T.	App	11.73	73-76	37	5	7
Hartlepool U.	Tr	08.77	77-82	150	0	48
Port Vale	Tr	09.82	82-83	48	0	22
Chesterfield	Tr	10.83	83-84	78	0	29
Hartlepool U.	Tr	07.85	85	8	3	2
Stockport Co.	L	03.86	85	6	0	1
Bristol Rov. (N/C)	Tr	02.87	86	7	1	0

NEWTON Robert Arthur
Earl Shilton, 19 January, 1946 (OL)

League Club	Source	Date Signed	Seasons Played	Apps	Subs	Gls
Leicester C.	App	08.63	64	2	-	0
Bradford C.	Tr	05.65	65	19	1	4

NEWTON Shaun O'Neill
Camberwell, 20 August, 1975 Eu21-3 (M)

League Club	Source	Date Signed	Seasons Played	Apps	Subs	Gls
Charlton Ath.	YT	07.93	92-97	134	38	15

NGATA Heremaia (Herry)
New Zealand, 24 August, 1971 (F)

League Club	Source	Date Signed	Seasons Played	Apps	Subs	Gls
Hull C. (N/C)	Jnrs	07.89	89-91	8	17	0

NIBLETT Victor
Frimley, 9 December, 1924 (CH)

League Club	Source	Date Signed	Seasons Played	Apps	Subs	Gls
Reading	Jnrs	08.44	46-49	6	-	0
West Ham U.	Tr	06.50				
Gillingham	Tr	08.51	51-55	154	-	0

NIBLOE John Allister
Sheffield, 1 June, 1939 Died 1964 (CF)

League Club	Source	Date Signed	Seasons Played	Apps	Subs	Gls
Sheffield U.		08.58	58-60	25	-	4
Stoke C.	Tr	10.61	61-62	19	-	4
Doncaster Rov.	Tr	10.62	62-63	36	-	7
Stockport Co.	Tr	07.64	64	22	-	4

NIBLOE Joseph
Glasgow, 10 December, 1926 (FB)

League Club	Source	Date Signed	Seasons Played	Apps	Subs	Gls
Cardiff C.	Clydebank Jnrs	03.48	48	1	-	0

NICHOL George
Stirling, 20 July, 1923 (G)

League Club	Source	Date Signed	Seasons Played	Apps	Subs	Gls
Aldershot	Falkirk	08.51	51	19	-	0

NICHOL Robert Wishart
Carlisle, 19 January, 1941 (OL)

League Club	Source	Date Signed	Seasons Played	Apps	Subs	Gls
Carlisle U. (Am)	Jnrs	06.58	58-59	3	-	1

NICHOLAS Anthony Wallace Long
West Ham, 16 April, 1938 E Yth (IF)

League Club	Source	Date Signed	Seasons Played	Apps	Subs	Gls
Chelsea	Jnrs	05.55	56-59	59	-	18
Brighton & H.A.	Tr	11.60	60-61	65	-	22
Leyton Orient	Chelmsford C.	06.65	65	8	1	2

NICHOLAS Charles **Brian**
Aberdare, 20 April, 1933 E Sch (WH)

League Club	Source	Date Signed	Seasons Played	Apps	Subs	Gls
Queens Park R.	Jnrs	05.50	48-54	113	-	2
Chelsea	Tr	07.55	55-57	26	-	1
Coventry C.	Tr	02.58	57-61	113	-	0

NICHOLAS Charles
Glasgow, 30 December, 1961 S Yth/Su21-6/S-20 (F)

League Club	Source	Date Signed	Seasons Played	Apps	Subs	Gls
Arsenal	Glasgow Celtic	07.83	83-87	145	6	34

NICHOLAS Glyn
Dartmouth, 2 December, 1946 (CF)

League Club	Source	Date Signed	Seasons Played	Apps	Subs	Gls
Plymouth Arg.	App	09.64	64-65	2	0	0
Crewe Alex.	L	03.66	65	2	0	1

NICHOLAS John Thomas
Derby, 26 November, 1910 Died 1977 W Sch (WH)

League Club	Source	Date Signed	Seasons Played	Apps	Subs	Gls
Derby Co.	Jnrs	12.27	28-46	347	-	14

NICHOLAS Kenneth William
Northampton, 3 February, 1938 E Sch/E Yth (FB)

League Club	Source	Date Signed	Seasons Played	Apps	Subs	Gls
Arsenal	Jnrs	05.55				
Watford	Tr	05.59	59-64	198	-	4

NICHOLAS Peter
Newport, 10 November, 1959 W Sch/Wu21-3/W-73 (M)

League Club	Source	Date Signed	Seasons Played	Apps	Subs	Gls
Crystal Palace	App	12.76	77-80	127	0	7
Arsenal	Tr	03.81	80-82	57	3	1
Crystal Palace	Tr	10.83	83-84	47	0	7
Luton T.	Tr	01.85	84-86	102	0	1
Chelsea	Aberdeen	08.88	88-90	79	1	2
Watford	Tr	03.91	90-91	40	0	1

NICHOLL Christopher John
Macclesfield, 12 October, 1946 NI-51 (CD)

League Club	Source	Date Signed	Seasons Played	Apps	Subs	Gls
Burnley	Jnrs	04.65				
Halifax T.	Witton A.	06.68	68-69	42	0	3
Luton T.	Tr	08.69	69-71	97	0	6
Aston Villa	Tr	03.72	71-76	210	0	11
Southampton	Tr	06.77	77-82	228	0	8
Grimsby T.	Tr	08.83	83-84	70	0	0

NICHOLL James Michael
Canada, 28 December, 1956 NI Sch/NIu21-1/NI-73 (RB)

League Club	Source	Date Signed	Seasons Played	Apps	Subs	Gls
Manchester U.	App	02.74	74-81	188	9	3
Sunderland	L	12.81	81	3	0	0
Sunderland	Toronto (Can)	09.82	82	29	0	0
West Bromwich A.	Toronto (Can)	11.84	84-85	56	0	0

NICHOLL Terence John
Wilmslow, 16 September, 1952 (M)

League Club	Source	Date Signed	Seasons Played	Apps	Subs	Gls
Crewe Alex.		02.72	71-72	46	0	7
Sheffield U.	Tr	03.73	73-74	12	10	1
Southend U.	Tr	05.75	75-76	50	0	3
Gillingham	Tr	10.76	76-80	184	0	11

NICHOLLS Alan
Plymouth, 10 February, 1963 (CD)

League Club	Source	Date Signed	Seasons Played	Apps	Subs	Gls
Bristol C.	App	02.80	80-82	70	0	5

NICHOLLS Alan
Sutton Coldfield, 23 August, 1973 Died 1995 Eu21-1 (G)

League Club	Source	Date Signed	Seasons Played	Apps	Subs	Gls
Plymouth Arg.	Cheltenham T.	08.93	93-94	64	1	0
Gillingham (N/C)	Tr	10.95				

NICHOLLS David
Bradford, 3 November, 1956 E Sch (M)

League Club	Source	Date Signed	Seasons Played	Apps	Subs	Gls
Huddersfield T.	App	11.73				
Bradford C. (N/C)	Tr	08.75	75	0	4	0

NICHOLLS James Henry
Coseley, 27 November, 1919 (G)

League Club	Source	Date Signed	Seasons Played	Apps	Subs	Gls
Bradford P.A.		05.46	46-49	36	-	0
Rochdale	Tr	08.51	51-52	50	-	0

NICHOLLS John
Wolverhampton, 3 April, 1931 Died 1995 Eu23-1/E-2 (IF)

League Club	Source	Date Signed	Seasons Played	Apps	Subs	Gls
West Bromwich A.	Heath T.	08.51	51-56	131	-	58
Cardiff C.	Tr	05.57	57	8	-	2
Exeter C.	Tr	11.57	57-58	55	-	23

NICHOLLS Kevin John Richard
Newham, 2 January, 1979 E Yth (M)

League Club	Source	Date Signed	Seasons Played	Apps	Subs	Gls
Charlton Ath.	YT	01.96	96-97	4	8	1

NICHOLLS Mark
Hillingdon, 30 May, 1977 (F)

League Club	Source	Date Signed	Seasons Played	Apps	Subs	Gls
Chelsea	YT	07.95	96-97	11	16	3

NICHOLLS Phillip Roy
Wolverhampton, 22 June, 1952 (CD)

League Club	Source	Date Signed	Seasons Played	Apps	Subs	Gls
Wolverhampton W.	App	07.70				
Crewe Alex.	Tr	09.72	72-76	155	8	8
Bradford C.	Tr	03.77	76-77	19	2	2
Crewe Alex.	Tr	08.78	78	10	3	0

NICHOLLS Raymond Ian
Peterborough, 7 April, 1965 (M)

League Club	Source	Date Signed	Seasons Played	Apps	Subs	Gls
Cambridge U.	App	08.82	81-83	18	5	1

NICHOLLS Ronald Bernard
Berkeley, 4 December, 1933 Died 1994 (G)

League Club	Source	Date Signed	Seasons Played	Apps	Subs	Gls
Bristol Rov.	Fulham (Am)	11.54	55-57	71	-	0
Cardiff C.	Tr	08.58	58-60	51	-	0
Bristol C.	Tr	07.61	61-63	39	-	0

NICHOLLS Ronald Henry
Cannock, 18 October, 1935 (WH)

League Club	Source	Date Signed	Seasons Played	Apps	Subs	Gls
West Bromwich A.	Jnrs	11.52				
Walsall	Tr	08.53	53	2	-	0

NICHOLLS Ryan Rhys
Cardiff, 10 May, 1973 W Sch (W)

League Club	Source	Date Signed	Seasons Played	Apps	Subs	Gls
Leeds U.	YT	07.91				
Cardiff C. (N/C)	Tr	01.95	94	6	6	1

NICHOLLS Wayne Keith
Wolverhampton, 21 October, 1952 (F)

League Club	Source	Date Signed	Seasons Played	Apps	Subs	Gls
Leicester C.	Wolverhampton W. (App)	11.70				
Workington	Tr	08.71	71-72	21	12	1

NICHOLS Adam Anthony
Ilford, 14 September, 1962 (CD)

League Club	Source	Date Signed	Seasons Played	Apps	Subs	Gls
Ipswich T.	App	10.79				
Colchester U. (N/C)	South Africa	09.83	83	4	2	1

NICHOLS Brian Albert
Dagenham, 30 May, 1945 (FB)

League Club	Source	Date Signed	Seasons Played	Apps	Subs	Gls
Fulham	App	07.63	65-67	50	1	1
Millwall	Tr	07.68	68-69	9	1	0

NICHOLSON Derek
Harrow, 8 April, 1936 (OR)

League Club	Source	Date Signed	Seasons Played	Apps	Subs	Gls
Leyton Orient	Chertsey	11.53	57	6	-	0

NICHOLSON Gary Anthony
Hexham, 4 November, 1960 (LW)

League Club	Source	Date Signed	Seasons Played	Apps	Subs	Gls
Newcastle U.	App	11.78	78-80	7	5	0
Mansfield T.	Tr	08.81	81-83	112	6	21
York C.	Tr	07.84	84	23	1	4
Halifax T.	Tr	07.85	85-86	54	6	4

NICHOLSON George Henry (Harry)
Carlisle, 25 January, 1932 (G)

League Club	Source	Date Signed	Seasons Played	Apps	Subs	Gls
Grimsby T.	Carlisle U. (Am)	08.52	53	17	-	0
Nottingham F.	Tr	07.55	55-56	72	-	0
Accrington St.	Tr	03.58	58	1	-	0
Leyton Orient	Tr	03.59	59	4	-	0
Bristol C.	Tr	07.60	60	1	-	0

NICHOLSON James Joseph
Belfast, 27 February, 1943 NI Sch/NIu23-4/NI 'B'/NI-41 (M)

League Club	Source	Date Signed	Seasons Played	Apps	Subs	Gls
Manchester U.	Jnrs	02.60	60-62	58	-	5
Huddersfield T.	Tr	12.64	64-73	280	1	25
Bury	Tr	12.73	73-75	79	4	0

NICHOLSON John Purcel
Liverpool, 2 September, 1936 Died 1966 (CH)

League Club	Source	Date Signed	Seasons Played	Apps	Subs	Gls
Liverpool		01.57	59	1	-	0
Port Vale	Tr	08.61	61-65	184	0	1
Doncaster Rov.	Tr	09.65	65-66	41	0	0

NICHOLSON John Reay
Harrington, 23 June, 1928 Died 1993 (OL)

League Club	Source	Date Signed	Seasons Played	Apps	Subs	Gls
Barrow	Frizington	05.49	49	4	-	1

NICHOLSON Maximilian
Leeds, 3 October, 1971 (LW)

League Club	Source	Date Signed	Seasons Played	Apps	Subs	Gls
Doncaster Rov.	YT	07.90	89-91	23	4	2
Hereford U.	Tr	07.92	92-93	52	11	7
Torquay U. (N/C)	Tr	09.94	94	1	0	0
Scunthorpe U.	Tr	11.94	94-95	27	24	5

NICHOLSON Peter
Cleator Moor, 12 January, 1951 (FB)

League Club	Source	Date Signed	Seasons Played	Apps	Subs	Gls
Blackpool	Carlisle U. (App)	08.69	70	3	3	0
Bolton W.	Tr	06.71	71-81	303	15	12
Rochdale (N/C)	Lytham	11.82	82	7	0	0
Carlisle U. (N/C)	Lytham	03.83	82-83	1	2	0

NICHOLSON Peter William
Hull, 11 December, 1936 (CF)

League Club	Source	Date Signed	Seasons Played	Apps	Subs	Gls
Hull C. (Am)	Kingburn Ath.	06.60	60	1	-	0

NICHOLSON Reece
South Kirkby, 4 April, 1936 (IF)

League Club	Source	Date Signed	Seasons Played	Apps	Subs	Gls
Doncaster Rov.	Jnrs	09.53	54-57	28	-	8

NICHOLSON Shane Michael
Newark, 3 June, 1970 (M/LB)

League Club	Source	Date Signed	Seasons Played	Apps	Subs	Gls
Lincoln C.	YT	07.88	86-91	122	11	7
Derby Co.	Tr	04.92	92-95	73	1	1
West Bromwich A.	Tr	02.96	95-97	50	2	0

NICHOLSON Stanley
Middlesbrough, 20 August, 1931 (IF)

League Club	Source	Date Signed	Seasons Played	Apps	Subs	Gls
Middlesbrough	South Bank	05.49				
Leeds U.	Tr	08.51				
Hartlepool U.	Horden Colly	07.58	58	7	-	1

NICHOLSON William Edward
Scarborough, 26 January, 1919 E 'B'/EF Lge/E-1 (WH)

League Club	Source	Date Signed	Seasons Played	Apps	Subs	Gls
Tottenham H.	Jnrs	08.38	38-54	314	-	6

NICKALLS James Horatio
Amble, 29 May, 1934 (CH)

League Club	Source	Date Signed	Seasons Played	Apps	Subs	Gls
Sunderland		04.53				
Darlington	Tr	05.54	54	18	-	0

NICKEAS Mark
Southport, 20 October, 1956 (D)

League Club	Source	Date Signed	Seasons Played	Apps	Subs	Gls
Plymouth Arg.	App	07.74				
Chester C.	Tr	08.75	75-78	58	2	1

NICKLAS Charles
Sunderland, 26 April, 1930 (CF)

League Club	Source	Date Signed	Seasons Played	Apps	Subs	Gls
Hull C.	Silksworth Jnrs	12.50	51	6	-	1
Darlington	Tr	05.53	53	17	-	6

NICOL Bennett
Glasgow, 10 March, 1921 (IF)

League Club	Source	Date Signed	Seasons Played	Apps	Subs	Gls
Bolton W.		11.46				
Rochdale	Winsford U.	07.49	49	5	-	1

NICOL Paul John
Scunthorpe, 31 October, 1967 (CD)

League Club	Source	Date Signed	Seasons Played	Apps	Subs	Gls
Scunthorpe U.	YT	07.86	86-89	68	7	2

NICOL Robert Benjamin Mathieson
Edinburgh, 11 May, 1936 S Sch (WH)

League Club	Source	Date Signed	Seasons Played	Apps	Subs	Gls
Barnsley	Hibernian	08.62	62-63	37	-	1

NICOL Stephen
Irvine, 11 December, 1961 Su21-14/S-27 (FB/M)

League Club	Source	Date Signed	Seasons Played	Apps	Subs	Gls
Liverpool	Ayr U.	10.81	82-94	328	15	36
Notts Co.	Tr	01.95	94-95	32	0	2
Sheffield Wed.	Tr	11.95	95-97	41	8	0
West Bromwich A.	L	03.98	97	9	0	0

NICOLL Paul
Ellesmere Port, 10 November, 1966 (M)

League Club	Source	Date Signed	Seasons Played	Apps	Subs	Gls
Wrexham (N/C)	Jnrs	07.84	84	0	1	0

NIEDZWIECKI Andzej **Edward**
Bangor, 3 May, 1959 W Sch/W-2 (G)

League Club	Source	Date Signed	Seasons Played	Apps	Subs	Gls
Wrexham	Jnrs	07.76	77-82	111	0	0
Chelsea	Tr	06.83	83-87	136	0	0

NIELSEN Allan
Denmark, 13 March, 1971 Danish Int (M)

League Club	Source	Date Signed	Seasons Played	Apps	Subs	Gls
Tottenham H.	Brondby (Den)	09.96	96-97	49	5	9

NIELSEN John Schmidt
Denmark, 7 April, 1972 (M)

League Club	Source	Date Signed	Seasons Played	Apps	Subs	Gls
Southend U.	Ikaast (Den)	08.96	96-97	18	11	3

NIELSEN Kent
Denmark, 28 December, 1961 Danish Int (CD)

League Club	Source	Date Signed	Seasons Played	Apps	Subs	Gls
Aston Villa	Brondby (Den)	06.89	89-91	74	5	4

NIELSEN Martin Ulrich
Aarhus, Denmark, 24 March, 1973 (M)

League Club	Source	Date Signed	Seasons Played	Apps	Subs	Gls
Huddersfield T.	F.C. Copenhagen (Den)	03.98	97	0	3	0

NIELSEN Thomas
Denmark, 25 March, 1972 (LB)

League Club	Source	Date Signed	Seasons Played	Apps	Subs	Gls
Shrewsbury T.	Aarhus Fremad (Den)	08.96	96	19	3	1

NIELSON Norman Frederick
South Africa, 6 November, 1928 (CH)

League Club	Source	Date Signed	Seasons Played	Apps	Subs	Gls
Charlton Ath.	Arcadia (SA)	07.49	49	1	-	0
Derby Co.	Tr	09.51	51-53	57	-	8
Bury	Tr	05.54	54-56	100	-	5
Hull C.	Tr	04.57	56-57	25	-	0

NIEUWENHUYS Berry
South Africa, 5 November, 1911 Died 1984 (OR)

League Club	Source	Date Signed	Seasons Played	Apps	Subs	Gls
Liverpool	Germiston Callies (SA)	09.33	33-46	236	-	74

NIGHTINGALE Albert
Rotherham, 10 November, 1923 (IF)

League Club	Source	Date Signed	Seasons Played	Apps	Subs	Gls
Sheffield U.	Thurcroft	06.41	46-47	62	-	14
Huddersfield T.	Tr	03.48	47-51	119	-	20
Blackburn Rov.	Tr	10.51	51-52	35	-	5
Leeds U.	Tr	10.52	52-56	130	-	48

NIGHTINGALE David Reginald
Liverpool, 15 August, 1927 (RB)

League Club	Source	Date Signed	Seasons Played	Apps	Subs	Gls
Tranmere Rov.		09.46	46	3	-	0

NIGHTINGALE Mark Barry Douglas
Salisbury, 1 February, 1957 E Yth (D/M)

League Club	Source	Date Signed	Seasons Played	Apps	Subs	Gls
Bournemouth	App	07.74	74-75	44	5	4
Crystal Palace	Tr	06.76				
Norwich C.	Tr	07.77	77-81	28	7	0
Bournemouth	Bulova (HK)	11.82	82-85	144	6	4
Peterborough U.	Tr	07.86	86-87	71	7	3

NIGHTINGALE Ronald
Darwen, 27 January, 1937 (WH)

League Club	Source	Date Signed	Seasons Played	Apps	Subs	Gls
Accrington St.		07.57	58-60	14	-	0

NIJHOLT Luc
Netherlands, 29 July, 1961 (D)

League Club	Source	Date Signed	Seasons Played	Apps	Subs	Gls
Swindon T.	Motherwell	07.93	93-94	66	1	1

NIKOLIC Dusan
Yugoslavia, 23 January, 1953 Yugoslav Int (W)

League Club	Source	Date Signed	Seasons Played	Apps	Subs	Gls
Bolton W.	Red Star Belgrade (Yug)	10.80	80-81	22	0	2

NILSEN Roger
Norway, 8 August, 1969 Norwegian Int (D)

League Club	Source	Date Signed	Seasons Played	Apps	Subs	Gls
Sheffield U.	Viking Stavanger (Nor)	11.93	93-97	143	6	0

NILSSON Nilsennart **Roland**
Sweden, 27 November, 1963 Swedish Int (RB)

League Club	Source	Date Signed	Seasons Played	Apps	Subs	Gls
Sheffield Wed.	I.F.K. Göteborg (Swe)	11.89	89-93	151	0	2
Coventry C.	Helsingborg (Swe)	07.97	97	32	0	0

NIMMO Ian Wallace
Boston, 23 January, 1958 (F)

League Club	Source	Date Signed	Seasons Played	Apps	Subs	Gls
Sheffield Wed.	App	01.76	75-78	26	19	10
Peterborough U.	L	01.77	76	4	0	1
Doncaster Rov.	Tr	06.79	79-81	77	9	29

NIMMO William Brown
Forth (Lk), 11 January, 1934 (G)

League Club	Source	Date Signed	Seasons Played	Apps	Subs	Gls
Leeds U.	Alloa Ath.	02.56	57	1	-	0
Doncaster Rov.	Tr	03.58	57-61	182	-	0
Mansfield T.	Tr	07.62				

NISBET Gordon James Mackay
Wallsend, 18 September, 1951 Eu23-1 (RB)

League Club	Source	Date Signed	Seasons Played	Apps	Subs	Gls
West Bromwich A.	Jnrs	09.68	69-75	136	0	0
Hull C.	Tr	09.76	76-80	190	3	1
Plymouth Arg.	Tr	12.80	80-86	281	0	14
Exeter C.	Tr	06.87	87	12	0	0

NISH David John
Burton, 26 September, 1947 E Yth/Eu23-10/EF Lge/E-5 (LB/M)

League Club	Source	Date Signed	Seasons Played	Apps	Subs	Gls
Leicester C.	Measham Imp.	07.66	66-72	228	0	25
Derby Co.	Tr	08.72	72-78	184	4	10

NIVEN Stuart Thomas
Glasgow, 24 December, 1978 S Yth (M)

League Club	Source	Date Signed	Seasons Played	Apps	Subs	Gls
Ipswich T.	YT	09.96	96	2	0	0

NIX Peter
Rotherham, 25 January, 1958 (W)

League Club	Source	Date Signed	Seasons Played	Apps	Subs	Gls
Rotherham U.	Jnrs	08.76	77-79	22	0	2

NIXON Eric Walter
Manchester, 4 October, 1962 (G)

League Club	Source	Date Signed	Seasons Played	Apps	Subs	Gls
Manchester C.	Curzon Ashton	12.83	85-87	58	0	0
Wolverhampton W.	L	08.86	86	16	0	0
Bradford C.	L	11.86	86	3	0	0
Southampton	L	12.86	86	4	0	0
Carlisle U.	L	01.87	86	16	0	0
Tranmere Rov.	Tr	03.88	88-96	341	0	0
Blackpool	L	02.96	95	20	0	0
Bradford C.	L	09.96	96	12	0	0
Stockport Co.	Tr	08.97	97	43	0	0

NIXON Jonathan Charles
Ilkeston, 20 January, 1948 (W)

League Club	Source	Date Signed	Seasons Played	Apps	Subs	Gls
Derby Co.	Jnrs	09.65				
Notts Co.	Ilkeston T.	01.70	69-74	167	12	32
Peterborough U.	Tr	09.74	74-76	104	6	16
Shrewsbury T.	Tr	08.77	77	21	2	3
Barnsley	Tr	03.78	77	6	4	0
Halifax T.	Tr	06.78	78	12	7	1

NIXON Paul
Seaham, 23 September, 1963 New Zealand Int (F)

League Club	Source	Date Signed	Seasons Played	Apps	Subs	Gls
Bristol Rov.	Seaham Red Star	01.89	88-90	31	13	6

NIXON Thomas
Backworth (Nd), 25 May, 1931 (LH)

League Club	Source	Date Signed	Seasons Played	Apps	Subs	Gls
Darlington (Am)	Newcastle U. (Am)	05.51	51	1	-	0

NIXON William John
Ballynahinch (NI), 28 September, 1941 NI Sch (IF)

League Club	Source	Date Signed	Seasons Played	Apps	Subs	Gls
Norwich C.	Distillery	03.61	61	1	-	0
Shrewsbury T.	Tr	03.62	61-64	17	-	1

NOAKE David John
Yeovil, 9 June, 1940 (W)

League Club	Source	Date Signed	Seasons Played	Apps	Subs	Gls
Luton T.	Dorchester T.	11.59	59-60	17	-	0
Bristol C.	Tr	06.61	61	11	-	3

NOAKES Alfred George Edward
Stratford, 14 August, 1933 (FB)

League Club	Source	Date Signed	Seasons Played	Apps	Subs	Gls
West Ham U.	Jnrs	08.50				
Crystal Palace	Sittingbourne	06.55	55-61	195	-	14
Portsmouth	Tr	07.62	62-63	13	-	0

NOBBS Alan **Keith**
Bishop Auckland, 18 September, 1961 (RB)

League Club	Source	Date Signed	Seasons Played	Apps	Subs	Gls
Middlesbrough	App	09.79	80	1	0	0
Halifax T.	Tr	08.82	82-83	87	0	1
Hartlepool U.	Bishop Auckland	08.85	85-92	274	6	1

NOBLE Alfred William Thomas
Hackney, 18 September, 1924 E Amat (IF)

League Club	Source	Date Signed	Seasons Played	Apps	Subs	Gls
Colchester U. (Am)	Briggs Sports	09.55	55	1	-	0

NOBLE Barry
Stockton, 5 June, 1951 (G)

League Club	Source	Date Signed	Seasons Played	Apps	Subs	Gls
Hartlepool U. (Am)	Jnrs	08.70	71	1	0	0

NOBLE Daniel William
Hull, 2 September, 1970 (G)

League Club	Source	Date Signed	Seasons Played	Apps	Subs	Gls
Stoke C.	YT	07.89	89-90	3	0	0
Crewe Alex.	Tr	06.91	91	7	0	0

NOBLE Frank
Sheffield, 26 October, 1945 (FB)

League Club	Source	Date Signed	Seasons Played	Apps	Subs	Gls
Sheffield Wed.	Jnrs	05.63	63-65	2	0	0
Peterborough U.	Tr	07.67	67-71	205	2	1

NOBLE John
Manchester, 20 May, 1919 Died 1996 (OR)

League Club	Source	Date Signed	Seasons Played	Apps	Subs	Gls
Stockport Co.	Warte Villa	03.39	46	1	-	0

NOBLE Norman
Barnsley, 8 August, 1923 Died 1973 (FB)

League Club	Source	Date Signed	Seasons Played	Apps	Subs	Gls
Huddersfield T.		06.43				
Bradford C.	Tr	10.45				
Rotherham U.	Ransome & Marles	05.48	48-57	326	-	21

NOBLE Peter
Newcastle, 19 August, 1944 (F/M)

League Club	Source	Date Signed	Seasons Played	Apps	Subs	Gls
Newcastle U.	Consett	11.64	65-67	22	3	7
Swindon T.,	Tr	01.68	67-72	212	4	62
Burnley	Tr	06.73	73-79	241	2	63
Blackpool	Tr	01.80	79-82	95	2	14

NOBLE Robert
Newcastle, 25 May, 1949 (CD)

League Club	Source	Date Signed	Seasons Played	Apps	Subs	Gls
Newcastle U.	App	04.67				
Barrow	L	08.69	69	19	0	3
Bury	Tr	08.70	70	6	0	0
Barrow	Tr	10.70	70-71	72	1	5
Colchester U.	Tr	08.72	72	25	2	0
Southport	Tr	03.73	72-74	61	2	6
Darlington	Tr	08.75	75-76	54	0	3

NOBLE Robert
Manchester, 18 December, 1945 E Yth (FB)

League Club	Source	Date Signed	Seasons Played	Apps	Subs	Gls
Manchester U.	App	12.62	65-66	31	0	0

NOBLE Wayne Ian
Bristol, 11 June, 1967 (LM)

League Club	Source	Date Signed	Seasons Played	Apps	Subs	Gls
Bristol Rov.	App	03.85	85-86	16	6	1

NOEL-WILLIAMS Gifton Ruben Elisha
Islington, 21 January, 1980 E Yth (CF)

League Club	Source	Date Signed	Seasons Played	Apps	Subs	Gls
Watford	YT	02.97	96-97	36	27	9

NOGAN Kurt
Cardiff, 9 September, 1970 Wu21-2 (F)

League Club	Source	Date Signed	Seasons Played	Apps	Subs	Gls
Luton T.	YT	07.89	89-91	17	16	3
Brighton & H.A.	Tr	10.92	92-94	97	0	49
Burnley	Tr	04.95	94-96	87	5	33
Preston N.E.	Tr	03.97	96-97	19	10	5

NOGAN Lee Martin
Cardiff, 21 May, 1969 Wu21-1/W 'B'/W-2 (F)

League Club	Source	Date Signed	Seasons Played	Apps	Subs	Gls
Oxford U.	YT	03.87	87-91	57	7	10
Brentford	L	03.87	86	10	1	2
Southend U.	L	09.87	87	6	0	1
Watford	Tr	12.91	91-94	97	8	26
Southend U.	L	03.94	93	4	1	0
Reading	Tr	01.95	94-96	71	20	26
Notts Co.	L	02.97	96	6	0	0
Grimsby T.	Tr	07.97	97	33	3	8

NOLAN David Joseph
Liverpool, 24 February, 1968 (M)

League Club	Source	Date Signed	Seasons Played	Apps	Subs	Gls
Chester C. (N/C)	Bromborough Pool	01.92	91	1	0	0

NOLAN George
Liverpool, 9 December, 1925 (LH)

League Club	Source	Date Signed	Seasons Played	Apps	Subs	Gls
Southport	A.I. Control	06.46	46	3	-	0

NOLAN Ian Robert
Liverpool, 9 July, 1970 NI-7 (LB)

League Club	Source	Date Signed	Seasons Played	Apps	Subs	Gls
Preston N.E. (N/C)	YT	08.88				
Tranmere Rov.	Marine	08.91	91-93	87	1	1
Sheffield Wed.	Tr	08.94	94-97	136	0	4

NOLAN Michael William
Dublin, 8 July, 1950 (FB)

League Club	Source	Date Signed	Seasons Played	Apps	Subs	Gls
Oldham Ath.	App	08.67	66-67	2	0	0

NOLAN Philip
Edmonton, 29 December, 1923 (CH)

League Club	Source	Date Signed	Seasons Played	Apps	Subs	Gls
Watford	Hayes	10.47	47-54	91	-	8

NOLAN Terence Stephen
Prescot, 16 March, 1956 (F)

League Club	Source	Date Signed	Seasons Played	Apps	Subs	Gls
Southport (N/C)	Prescot Cables	02.78	77	0	1	0

NOON Harry
Mansfield, 6 October, 1937 Died 1996 (FB)

League Club	Source	Date Signed	Seasons Played	Apps	Subs	Gls
Notts Co.	Bentinck Methodists	05.55	57-61	122	-	0
Bradford C.	Tr	07.62	62	1	-	0

NORBURY Michael Shaun
Hemsworth, 22 January, 1969 (F)

League Club	Source	Date Signed	Seasons Played	Apps	Subs	Gls
Scarborough	Ossett T.	12.89				
Cambridge U.	Bridlington T.	02.92	91-92	11	15	3
Preston N.E.	Tr	12.92	92-94	32	10	13
Doncaster Rov.	Tr	11.94	94-95	19	8	5

NORCROSS William
Preston, 29 December, 1937 (CF)

League Club	Source	Date Signed	Seasons Played	Apps	Subs	Gls
Southport (Am)	Chorley	07.59	59	1	-	0

NORFOLK Lee Richard
New Zealand, 17 October, 1975 (M)

League Club	Source	Date Signed	Seasons Played	Apps	Subs	Gls
Ipswich T.	YT	07.94	94	1	2	0

NORMAN Anthony Joseph
Deeside, 24 February, 1958 W'B'/W-5 (G)

League Club	Source	Date Signed	Seasons Played	Apps	Subs	Gls
Burnley	Jnrs	08.76				
Hull C.	Tr	02.80	79-88	372	0	0
Sunderland	Tr	12.88	88-94	198	0	0
Huddersfield T.	Tr	07.95	95-96	7	0	0

NORMAN Derek Antony
Birmingham, 11 February, 1946 E Yth (WH)

League Club	Source	Date Signed	Seasons Played	Apps	Subs	Gls
Southampton	Alvechurch	01.64				
Aldershot	Tr	05.65	65	22	1	0

NORMAN Albert **Griffith**
Cardiff, 20 February, 1926 (HB)

League Club	Source	Date Signed	Seasons Played	Apps	Subs	Gls
Cardiff C.		04.50	51	1	-	0
Torquay U.	Tr	10.52	52-57	216	-	6

League Club	Source	Date Signed	Seasons Played	Apps	Subs	Gls
NORMAN John						
Birkenhead, 26 June, 1971						(F)
Tranmere Rov.	YT	02.90				
Bury (N/C)	Heswall	08.92	92	1	1	0
NORMAN Malcolm Allen						
Cardiff, 24 October, 1934						(G)
Bristol Rov.	Cardiff Corries	05.58	58-61	69	-	0
NORMAN Maurice						
Mulbarton (Nk), 8 May, 1934 Eu23-3/EF Lge/E-23						(CH)
Norwich C.	Wymondham O.B.	09.52	54-55	35	-	0
Tottenham H.	Tr	11.55	55-65	357	0	16
NORMAN Richard						
Newcastle, 5 September, 1935						(LB)
Leicester C.	Horden Colly	11.58	59-67	303	0	2
Peterborough U.	Tr	07.68	68	9	1	0
NORMAN Sean						
Lowestoft, 27 November, 1966						(LB/M)
Colchester U.	Lowestoft T.	07.85	86-87	18	4	1
NORMANTON Graham Stephen						
Hartlepool, 13 November, 1959						(FB)
Hartlepool U.	Middlesbrough (App)	07.78	79-80	17	1	0
NORMANTON Sidney (Skinner)						
Barnsley, 20 August, 1926 Died 1995						(WH)
Barnsley	Barnsley M.C.W.	09.45	47-53	123	-	2
Halifax T.	Tr	07.54	54	14	-	0
NORRIE Craig Thomas						
Hull, 22 July, 1960						(F)
Hull C.	App	08.78	78-81	22	9	4
NORRIS Derek						
Chesterfield, 19 June, 1935						(WH)
Peterborough U.	Gainsborough Trin.	(N/L)	60	5	-	0
NORRIS George Albert						
Aldershot, 19 September, 1935						(CF)
Aldershot	Farnborough T.	12.58	58-63	106	-	59
NORRIS Graham John						
Hampton, 8 February, 1954						(W)
Crystal Palace	App	02.72				
Southend U.	L	03.73	72	1	0	0
NORRIS Michael						
Mansfield, 27 February, 1957						(G)
Scunthorpe U.	App	02.75	73-75	25	0	0
NORRIS Oliver (Ollie)						
Derry (NI), 1 April, 1929						(CF)
Middlesbrough	Jnrs	07.48	51-53	12	-	3
Bournemouth	Worcester C.	07.55	55-58	96	-	34
Northampton T.	Tr	09.58	58	14	-	1
Rochdale	Ashford T.	01.61	60	2	-	1
NORRIS Raymond George						
Bristol, 15 July, 1922 Died 1972						(CH)
Bristol C.	Bedminster	05.47	47	3	-	0
NORRIS Russell						
Hoo, 1 February, 1971						(RB)
Gillingham	YT	07.89	89	2	3	0
NORRIS Stephen Mark						
Coventry, 22 September, 1961 E Semi Pro						(F)
Scarborough	Telford U.	07.88	88-89	35	10	13
Notts Co.	L	11.89	89	0	1	0
Carlisle U.	Tr	12.89	89-90	21	8	5
Halifax T.	Tr	10.90	90-91	56	0	35
Chesterfield	Tr	01.92	91-94	84	13	43
Scarborough	L	01.95	94	8	0	4
NORTH Eric						
Halifax, 6 October, 1923 Died 1992						(OL)
Halifax T. (Am)	Lee Mount	08.48	48	1	-	0
NORTH Marc Victor						
Ware, 29 May, 1966						(F)
Luton T.	App	03.84	85-86	11	7	3
Lincoln C.	L	03.85	84	4	0	0
Scunthorpe U.	L	01.87	86	4	1	2
Birmingham C.	L	03.87	86	4	1	1
Grimsby T.	Tr	08.87	87-88	64	3	17
Leicester C.	Tr	03.89	88-90	51	20	9
Grimsby T.	Luton T. (N/C)	08.91	91	0	1	0
NORTH Stacey Stewart						
Luton, 25 November, 1964 E Yth						(CD)
Luton T.	App	08.82	83-87	24	1	0
Wolverhampton W.	L	11.85	85	3	0	0
West Bromwich A.	Tr	12.87	87-89	96	2	0
Fulham	Tr	10.90	90	38	0	0
NORTH Thomas Williamson						
Barrow-on-Soar (Leics), 31 October, 1919 Died 1996						(IF)
Nottingham F.	Banbury Spencer	01.45	46	1	-	0
NORTHCOTT George Edward						
Torquay, 7 May, 1935						(CH)
Torquay U.	Jnrs	10.52	54-61	163	-	2
Exeter C.	Cheltenham T.	08.63	63	1	-	0
NORTHCOTT Thomas Theodore						
Torquay, 5 December, 1931 E Yth						(IF)
Torquay U.	Jnrs	12.48	48-52	60	-	10
Cardiff C.	Tr	10.52	52-54	71	-	13
Lincoln C.	Tr	07.55	55-57	94	-	34
Torquay U.	Tr	11.57	57-65	348	2	126
NORTHOVER Stanley Oswald						
Weymouth, 3 July, 1926 Died 1990						(IF)
Luton T. (Am)	Weymouth	02.50	49	1	-	0
NORTON David John						
Gateshead, 24 January, 1957						(FB)
Hartlepool U.	Whickham	12.78	78-79	14	3	2
NORTON David Wayne						
Cannock, 3 March, 1965 E Yth						(M/RB)
Aston Villa	App	03.83	84-87	42	2	2
Notts Co.	Tr	08.88	88-90	22	5	1
Rochdale	L	10.90	90	9	0	0
Hull C.	L	01.91	90	15	0	0
Hull C.	Tr	08.91	91-93	134	0	5
Northampton T.	Tr	08.94	94-95	78	4	0
Hereford U.	Tr	08.96	96	45	0	1
NORTON Paul						
Mexborough, 17 September, 1969						(G)
Hartlepool U.	Sheffield U. (YT)	08.88	88	5	0	0
NORTON Peter						
Manchester, 11 November, 1947						(FB)
Bournemouth	Jnrs	11.66	66-67	18	0	1
Crewe Alex.	Tr	07.68				
NORTON Ralph						
Aylesham (Kt), 11 October, 1942						(WH/IF)
Reading	Jnrs	10.59	60-65	99	1	9
Bournemouth	Tr	07.66	66-67	44	4	4
NOTEMAN Kevin Simon						
Preston, 15 October, 1969						(LW)
Leeds U.	YT	06.88	87	0	1	0
Doncaster Rov.	Tr	11.89	89-91	105	1	20
Mansfield T.	Tr	03.92	91-94	77	18	15
Doncaster Rov.	Tr	08.95	95	4	0	1
Chester C.	Tr	09.95	95-96	57	11	18
NOTTINGHAM Steven Edward						
Peterborough, 21 June, 1980						(D)
Scunthorpe U.	YT	●	97	1	0	0
NOVACKI Jan						
Manchester, 4 December, 1958 E Yth						(W)
Bolton W.	App	12.76				
York C.	L	12.77	77	24	1	3
NOWAK Tadeusz						
Poland, 28 November, 1948 Polish Int						(W)
Bolton W.	Legia Warsaw (Pol)	03.79	78-80	22	2	1
NOWLAND Adam Christopher						
Preston, 6 July, 1981						(F)
Blackpool	YT	●	97	0	1	0
NTAMARK Charles Batmbog						
Paddington, 22 July, 1964 Cameroon Int						(M)
Walsall	Boreham Wood	08.90	90-96	256	20	12
NUGENT Arthur						
Glasgow, 30 May, 1926 Died 1995						(RB)
Darlington	Canterbury C.	06.56	56	5	-	0

NUGENT William **Clifford**
Islington, 3 March, 1929 (OL)

League Club	Source	Date Signed	Seasons Played	Apps	Subs	Gls
Cardiff C.	Headington U.	01.51	51-58	117	-	19
Mansfield T.	Tr	11.58	58-59	52	-	7

NUGENT Kevin Patrick
Edmonton, 10 April, 1969 IR Yth (F)

League Club	Source	Date Signed	Seasons Played	Apps	Subs	Gls
Leyton Orient	YT	07.87	87-91	86	8	20
Plymouth Arg.	Tr	03.92	91-95	124	7	32
Bristol C.	Tr	09.95	95-96	48	22	14
Cardiff C.	Tr	08.97	97	2	2	0

NUGENT Richard Joseph
Birmingham, 20 March, 1964 (CD)

League Club	Source	Date Signed	Seasons Played	Apps	Subs	Gls
Barnet	St Albans C.	10.88	91	2	0	0

NUGENT Stephen
Orrell, 7 May, 1973 (F)

League Club	Source	Date Signed	Seasons Played	Apps	Subs	Gls
Wigan Ath.	YT	08.91	89-92	7	6	0

NULTY Geoffrey Owen
Prescot, 13 February, 1949 (M)

League Club	Source	Date Signed	Seasons Played	Apps	Subs	Gls
Stoke C.	Jnrs	07.67				
Burnley	Tr	07.68	69-74	123	7	20
Newcastle U.	Tr	12.74	74-77	101	0	11
Everton	Tr	07.78	78-79	22	6	2

NUNDY Jeffrey William
Hull, 29 November, 1935 (CH)

League Club	Source	Date Signed	Seasons Played	Apps	Subs	Gls
Huddersfield T.		12.53				
Bradford C.	Tr	07.57	57-59	32	-	0

NUNN Walter
Deptford, 16 January, 1920 Died 1965 (HB)

League Club	Source	Date Signed	Seasons Played	Apps	Subs	Gls
Charlton Ath.	Bexleyheath & Welling	05.39				
Swindon T.	Tr	06.47	47	4	-	0

NURSE Melvyn Tudor George
Swansea, 11 October, 1937 W Sch/Wu23-2/W-12 (CH)

League Club	Source	Date Signed	Seasons Played	Apps	Subs	Gls
Swansea C.	Jnrs	06.55	55-62	158	-	9
Middlesbrough	Tr	10.62	62-65	113	0	8
Swindon T.	Tr	09.65	65-67	122	1	10
Swansea C.	Tr	06.68	68-70	97	1	3

NUTE Stephen Leslie Rodney
Plymouth, 18 April, 1962 (G)

League Club	Source	Date Signed	Seasons Played	Apps	Subs	Gls
Exeter C.	App	04.80	80	5	0	0

NUTLEY Robert
Paisley, 10 September, 1916 Died 1996 (W)

League Club	Source	Date Signed	Seasons Played	Apps	Subs	Gls
Portsmouth	Hibernian	08.46	46	9	-	1

NUTT Gordon Edward
Birmingham, 8 November, 1932 (W)

League Club	Source	Date Signed	Seasons Played	Apps	Subs	Gls
Coventry C.	Jnrs	11.49	51-54	76	-	12
Cardiff C.	Tr	12.54	54-55	17	-	4
Arsenal	Tr	09.55	55-59	49	-	10
Southend U.	Tr	10.60	60	16	-	2

NUTT Philip James
Westminster, 18 May, 1958 (F)

League Club	Source	Date Signed	Seasons Played	Apps	Subs	Gls
Queens Park R.	App	07.75	75-76	0	4	1

NUTTALL James
Liverpool, 14 October, 1929 (CF)

League Club	Source	Date Signed	Seasons Played	Apps	Subs	Gls
Southport	Skelmersdale U.	05.50	50-52	67	-	29

NUTTALL Martin
Oldham, 12 September, 1961 (F)

League Club	Source	Date Signed	Seasons Played	Apps	Subs	Gls
Oldham Ath.	App	09.79	80-81	8	5	1
Halifax T.	Tr	08.82	82-83	39	11	10

NUTTALL William
Preston, 7 December, 1920 (FB)

League Club	Source	Date Signed	Seasons Played	Apps	Subs	Gls
Preston N.E.		07.46	46	2	-	0
Barrow	Tr	08.48	48-50	65	-	0

NUTTELL Michael John
Boston, 22 November, 1968 (F)

League Club	Source	Date Signed	Seasons Played	Apps	Subs	Gls
Peterborough U.	YT	08.87	85-87	12	9	0
Crewe Alex.	L	12.87	87	2	1	1
Carlisle U.	L	11.88	88	1	2	0

NUTTON Michael William
St Johns Wood, 3 October, 1959 (CD)

League Club	Source	Date Signed	Seasons Played	Apps	Subs	Gls
Chelsea	App	10.77	78-82	77	2	0
Reading	L	02.83	82	6	0	0
Millwall	Tr	03.83	82-85	81	1	4

NWAJIOBI Chukwuemeka (Emeka)
Nigeria, 25 May, 1959 (F)

League Club	Source	Date Signed	Seasons Played	Apps	Subs	Gls
Luton T.	Dulwich Hamlet	12.83	83-87	59	13	17

NWADIKE Chukweumeka (Chuk) Ibezimife
Camberwell, 9 August, 1978 (CD)

League Club	Source	Date Signed	Seasons Played	Apps	Subs	Gls
Wolverhampton W.	YT	07.96				
Shrewsbury T.	Tr	12.96	96-97	2	1	0

NYAMAH Kofi
Islington, 20 June, 1975 (W)

League Club	Source	Date Signed	Seasons Played	Apps	Subs	Gls
Cambridge U.	YT	05.93	93-94	9	14	2
Stoke C.	Kettering T.	12.96	96-97	9	8	0

NZAMBA Guy **Roger**
Port Gentil, Gabon, 13 July, 1970 (F)

League Club	Source	Date Signed	Seasons Played	Apps	Subs	Gls
Southend U. (N/C)	Trieste (Fr)	09.97	97	0	1	0

League Club	Source	Date Signed	Seasons Played	Career Record Apps	Subs	Gls
OAKES Alan Arthur						
Winsford, 7 September, 1942 EF Lge						(M)
Manchester C.	Jnrs	09.59	59-75	561	3	26
Chester C.	Tr	07.76	76-81	211	0	15
Port Vale (N/C)	(Team Coach)	10.83	83	1	0	0
OAKES Dennis Raymond						
Bedworth, 10 April, 1946						(CD/M)
Coventry C.	App	08.64				
Notts Co.	Tr	06.67	67-70	108	12	0
Peterborough U.	Tr	05.71	71-72	84	1	5
OAKES Donald Joseph						
St Asaph, 8 October, 1928 Died 1977						(WH)
Arsenal	Downend	07.46	52-54	11	-	1
OAKES George						
Orrell, 18 October, 1918 Died 1990						(CF)
Southport	Astley & Tyldesley Colly	08.45	46	7	-	0
OAKES John						
Hamilton, 6 December, 1919						(W)
Huddersfield T.	Queen of South	11.43				
Blackburn Rov.	Queen of South	02.47	46-47	35	-	9
Manchester C.	Tr	06.48	48-50	77	-	9
OAKES John						
Northwich, 13 September, 1905 Died 1992						(CH)
Nottingham F.	Chilton Colly	08.28	29-30	2	-	0
Southend U.	Newark T.	05.31	31	2	-	0
Aldershot	Spennymoor U.	08.34	34-35	61	-	19
Charlton Ath	Tr	03.36	35-46	130	-	3
Plymouth Arg.	Tr	07.47	47	36	-	0
OAKES John Francis						
Hamilton, 16 January, 1921 Died 1987						(CF)
Rochdale	Queen of South	02.47	46	1	-	0
OAKES Keith Brian						
Bedworth, 3 July, 1956						(CD)
Peterborough U.	App	07.73	72-77	48	13	2
Newport Co.	Tr	09.78	78-83	232	0	27
Gillingham	Tr	08.84	84-86	84	2	7
Fulham	Tr	09.86	86-87	76	0	3
Peterborough U.	Tr	08.88	88-90	95	2	9
OAKES Michael Christian						
Northwich, 30 October, 1973 Eu21-6						(G)
Aston Villa	Jnrs	07.91	96-97	26	2	0
Scarborough	L	11.93	93	1	0	0
OAKES Scott John						
Leicester, 5 August, 1972 Eu21-1						(W)
Leicester C.	YT	05.90	89-91	1	2	0
Luton T.	Tr	10.91	91-95	136	37	27
Sheffield Wed.	Tr	08.96	96-97	7	16	1
OAKES Thomas						
Manchester, 6 February, 1922 Died 1993						(OR)
Manchester C.	Manchester U. (Am)	04.47	46	1	-	0
OAKEY Graham						
Droitwich, 5 October, 1954						(RB)
Coventry C.	App	10.72	74-77	87	1	0
OAKLEY Kenneth						
Rhymney, 9 May, 1929						(CF)
Cardiff C.	Ebbw Vale	03.50	50-53	7	-	0
Northampton T.	Tr	07.54	54	13	-	6
OAKLEY Matthew						
Peterborough, 17 August, 1977 Eu21-4						(W)
Southampton	YT	07.95	94-97	60	12	5
OAKLEY Norman						
Stockton, 4 June, 1939						(G)
Doncaster Rov.	Jnrs	04.57				
Hartlepool U.	Scunthorpe U. (trial)	09.58	58-63	182	-	0
Swindon T.	Tr	03.64	63-64	21	-	0
Grimsby T.	Tr	09.66	66	15	0	0

League Club	Source	Date Signed	Seasons Played	Career Record Apps	Subs	Gls
OAKLEY Royston James						
Tipton, 5 January, 1928						(FB)
Southampton	Guernsey	11.50	53-55	6	-	0
OATES Graham						
Scunthorpe, 4 December, 1943						(W)
Blackpool	App	05.61	61-68	118	3	26
Grimsby T.	Tr	10.68	68-70	80	1	9
OATES Graham						
Bradford, 14 March, 1949						(M)
Bradford C.	Manningham Mills	02.70	69-73	158	3	19
Blackburn Rov.	Tr	06.74	74-75	76	0	10
Newcastle U.	Tr	03.76	75-77	26	9	3
OATES Robert Anthony						
Leeds, 26 July, 1956 E Yth						(CD)
Scunthorpe U.	Ashley Road	08.74	74-82	306	9	15
Rochdale	Tr	08.83	83	42	0	1
OATWAY Anthony (Charlie) Philip David....						
Hammersmith, 28 November, 1973						(M)
Cardiff C.	Yeading	08.94	94-95	29	3	0
Torquay U.	Tr	12.95	95-97	65	2	1
Brentford	Tr	08.97	97	30	3	0
OBEBO Godfrey						
Nigeria, 16 April, 1966						(F)
Halifax T. (N/C)	Collier Row	03.93	92	0	3	0
OBENEY Henry (Harry) Richard						
Bethnal Green, 9 March, 1938						(WH/CF)
West Ham U.	Brigg Sports	05.56	56-60	25	-	12
Millwall	Tr	06.61	61-63	76	-	10
O'BERG Paul John						
Hull, 8 May, 1958						(M)
Scunthorpe U.	Bridlington T.	07.79	79-83	117	15	24
Wimbledon	Tr	08.84	84	2	1	0
Stockport Co.	L	11.84	84	2	0	0
Chester C.	L	12.84	84	5	0	1
OBI Anthony Lloyd						
Birmingham, 15 September, 1965 E Yth						(W)
Aston Villa	App	09.83				
Walsall	L	12.84	84	1	1	0
Plymouth Arg.	L	02.85	84	5	0	0
Bristol Rov. (N/C)	Tr	08.85	85	1	0	0
Oxford U.	Tr	10.85	86	0	1	0
Brentford	L	08.86	86	10	0	0
O'BRIEN Andrew James						
Harrogate, 29 June, 1979 E Yth						(CD)
Bradford C.	YT	10.96	96-97	41	7	2
O'BRIEN Anthony						
Liverpool, 4 September, 1956						(FB)
Southport (N/C)	St Theresa's	08.74	74-76	17	3	1
O'BRIEN Colin						
Dunfermline, 19 April, 1956						(W)
Bristol C.	Swaythling	11.77				
Hereford U.	L	12.78	78	1	1	0
O'BRIEN George						
Dunfermline, 22 November, 1935						(IF)
Leeds U.	Dunfermline Ath.	03.57	56-58	44	-	6
Southampton	Tr	07.59	59-65	244	0	154
Leyton Orient	Tr	03.66	65-66	17	0	3
Aldershot	Tr	12.66	66-67	38	3	8
O'BRIEN George						
Liverpool, 21 October, 1939 Died 1995						(IF)
Everton	Jnrs	02.59				
Southport	Tr	07.60	60	3	-	1
O'BRIEN Gerald						
Glasgow, 10 November, 1949						(W)
Southampton	Clydebank	03.70	69-75	66	12	2
Bristol Rov.	L	03.74	73	3	0	0
Swindon T.	Tr	03.76	75-76	24	3	0
O'BRIEN Jonathan Mark						
Southend, 2 November, 1961						(G)
Southend U.	Maldon T.	01.85	84	11	0	0
O'BRIEN Joseph						
Dublin, 9 May, 1924						(OL)
Luton T.	Dundalk	11.47	47-48	11	-	3
Ipswich T.	Tr	06.49	49-50	50	-	12

League Club	Source	Date Signed	Seasons Played	Apps	Subs	Gls
O'BRIEN Liam Francis						
Dublin, 5 September, 1964 IR Sch/IR Yth/IRu23-1/IR-16						(M)
Manchester U.	Shamrock Rov.	10.86	86-88	16	15	2
Newcastle U.	Tr	11.88	88-93	131	20	19
Tranmere Rov.	Tr	01.94	93-97	151	7	10
O'BRIEN Noel William						
Islington, 18 December, 1956						(M)
Arsenal	App	01.74				
Mansfield T.	Tr	06.75	75	7	0	0
O'BRIEN Raymond Christopher						
Dublin, 21 May, 1951 IRu23-2/IR-4						(FB)
Manchester U.	Shelbourne	05.73				
Notts Co.	Tr	03.74	73-82	323	0	31
Derby Co.	L	09.83	83	4	0	0
O'BRIEN Roy Joseph						
Cork, 27 November, 1974 IR Sch/IR Yth						(CD)
Arsenal	YT	07.93				
Bournemouth	Tr	08.96	96	1	0	0
O'BRIEN William						
Middlesbrough, 26 January, 1929						(HB)
Darlington		02.50	50	2	-	0
O'CALLAGHAN Brendan Richard						
Bradford, 23 July, 1955 IRu21-1/IR-6						(F/CD)
Doncaster Rov.	Jnrs	07.73	73-77	184	3	65
Stoke C.	Tr	03.78	77-84	255	10	44
Oldham Ath.	Tr	02.85	84-85	10	0	0
O'CALLAGHAN Kevin						
Dagenham, 19 October, 1961 IR Yth/IRu21-1/IR-20						(LW)
Millwall	App	11.78	78-79	15	5	3
Ipswich T.	Tr	01.80	79-84	72	43	4
Portsmouth	Tr	01.85	84-86	84	3	16
Millwall	Tr	06.87	87-90	65	11	14
Southend U.	Tr	07.91	91-92	10	11	1
O'CONNELL Brendan						
Lambeth, 12 November, 1966						(F/M)
Portsmouth	YT	07.85				
Exeter C.	Tr	07.86	86-87	73	8	19
Burnley	Tr	06.88	88-89	62	2	17
Huddersfield T.	L	11.89	89	11	0	1
Barnsley	Tr	03.90	89-95	212	28	35
Charlton Ath.	Tr	07.96	96	33	5	2
Wigan Ath.	Tr	08.97	97	17	0	5
O'CONNELL Brian (Pat) Edward						
Kensington, 13 September, 1937						(OL)
Fulham	Jnrs	03.56	58-65	152	0	26
Crystal Palace	Tr	07.66	66	20	1	2
O'CONNELL Iain Andrew						
Southend, 9 October, 1970						(W)
Southend U.	YT	07.89	89	0	4	0
O'CONNELL Seamus						
Carlisle, 1 January, 1930 E Amat						(IF)
Middlesbrough (Am)	Queens Park	05.53	53	3	-	2
Chelsea (Am)	Bishop Auckland	08.54	54-55	16	-	11
Carlisle U. (Am)	Crook T.	02.58	57	4	-	2
O'CONNOR Derek Peter Luke						
Dublin, 9 March, 1978 IR Sch/IR Yth/IRu21-3						(G)
Huddersfield T.	YT	05.95	97	1	0	0
O'CONNOR Douglas						
Barnsley, 29 April, 1954						(F)
Barnsley	App	04.72	70-73	27	9	7
Mansfield T.	Tr	07.74	74	11	6	2
Scunthorpe U.	Tr	07.75	75-76	28	3	9
O'CONNOR Gary						
Newtongrange, 7 April, 1974 S Sch/S Yth						(G)
Doncaster Rov.	Hearts	01.96	95-96	26	0	0
O'CONNOR James Kelly						
Lanark, 27 June, 1951						(W)
Bury		07.70	70	7	0	2
O'CONNOR Vincent **John (Jackie)**						
Durham, 12 March, 1929						(W)
Hartlepool U.	Middlesbrough (Am)	12.47	48	2	-	0
O'CONNOR Jonathan						
Darlington, 29 October, 1976 E Yth/Eu21-3						(RB)
Everton	YT	10.93	95-97	3	2	0
Sheffield U.	Tr	02.98	97	0	2	0

League Club	Source	Date Signed	Seasons Played	Apps	Subs	Gls
O'CONNOR Malcolm Joseph						
Ashton-u-Lyne, 25 April, 1965						(F)
Rochdale (N/C)	Curzon Ashton	03.83	82-83	12	4	3
O'CONNOR Mark Andrew						
Southend, 10 March, 1963 IRu21-1						(M)
Queens Park R.	App	06.80	81-82	2	1	0
Exeter C.	L	10.83	83	38	0	1
Bristol Rov.	Tr	08.84	84-85	79	1	10
Bournemouth	Tr	03.86	85-89	115	13	12
Gillingham	Tr	12.89	89-92	107	9	8
Bournemouth	Tr	07.93	93-94	56	2	3
Gillingham	Tr	08.95	95-97	36	4	1
O'CONNOR Martyn John						
Walsall, 10 December, 1967						(M)
Crystal Palace	Bromsgrove Rov.	06.92	93	2	0	0
Walsall	L	03.93	93	10	0	1
Walsall	Tr	02.94	94-95	94	0	21
Peterborough U.	Tr	07.96	96	18	0	3
Birmingham C.	Tr	11.96	96-97	56	1	5
O'CONNOR Michael						
Romford, 11 January, 1952						(W)
Southend U.	App	●	69	1	0	0
O'CONNOR Patrick						
Motherwell, 1 May, 1934						(IF)
Barrow	Bellshill	06.58	58-59	20	-	4
O'CONNOR Paul Daniel						
Easington, 17 August, 1971						(G)
Leicester C.	YT	03.89				
Hartlepool U. (N/C)	Blyth Spartans	04.96	95-96	31	0	0
O'CONNOR Philip Kelvin						
Romford, 10 October, 1953 Died 1985						(W)
Luton T.	Bexley U.	12.72	72	1	1	0
Lincoln C.	L	01.75	74	4	0	1
O'CONNOR Robert Thomas						
Gateshead, 9 August, 1940						(OL)
Gateshead (Am)	Jnrs	05.58	58	2	-	0
O'CONNOR Timothy Daniel						
Neath, 3 October, 1967 W Yth						(M)
Cardiff C.	Afan Lido	01.85	85	1	1	0
O'CONNOR Turlough						
Athlone (Ire), 22 July, 1946 IR Amat/IR-7						(OL)
Fulham	Bohemians	05.66	67	1	0	0
O'DELL Andrew						
Hull, 2 January, 1963						(M)
Grimsby T.	App	01.81	81-82	18	2	0
Rotherham U.	Tr	08.83	83-84	16	2	0
Torquay U.	Tr	03.85	84	12	2	1
Darlington	North Ferriby U.	09.87	87	1	2	0
O'DELL Robert Edward						
Isle of Wight, 10 December, 1934						(CH)
Reading	Jnrs	07.52	53	2	-	0
O'DOHERTY Kenneth Brendan						
Dublin, 30 March, 1963 IRu21-1						(CD)
Crystal Palace	U.C. Dublin	02.85	85-87	41	1	0
Huddersfield T.	Tr	06.88	88-91	63	2	1
Exeter C.	L	08.91	91	2	0	0
O'DONNELL Brian Francis						
Port Glasgow, 8 August, 1957						(D/M)
Bristol Rov.	Bournemouth (App)	05.76				
Bournemouth	Blacktown C. (Aus)	01.82	81-82	9	5	0
Torquay U. (N/C)	Tr	10.82	82	19	0	0
O'DONNELL Christopher						
Newcastle, 26 May, 1968						(D)
Ipswich T.	App	06.85	86-88	10	4	0
Northampton T.	L	01.88	87	1	0	0
Leeds U.	Tr	07.89	89	0	1	0
Exeter C.	Tr	08.91	91	2	0	0
O'DONNELL Daniel						
Dumbarton, 27 February, 1939						(IF)
Brentford	Kirkintilloch Rob Roy	02.60	60-61	11	-	0
O'DONNELL Edward						
Barrow, 5 February, 1921 Died 1994						(FB)
Barrow		09.46	46-52	33	-	0

O'DONNELL Francis
Buckhaven, 31 August, 1911 Died 1952 S-6 (CF)

League Club	Source	Date Signed	Seasons Played	Apps	Subs	Gls
Preston N.E.	Glasgow Celtic	05.35	35-37	92	-	36
Blackpool	Tr	11.37	37-38	29	-	17
Aston Villa	Tr	11.38	38	29	-	14
Nottingham F.	Tr	01.46	46	11	-	5

O'DONNELL Hugh
Buckhaven, 15 February, 1913 Died 1965 (OL)

League Club	Source	Date Signed	Seasons Played	Apps	Subs	Gls
Preston N.E.	Glasgow Celtic	05.35	35-38	132	-	29
Blackpool	Tr	03.39	38-46	10	-	2
Rochdale	Tr	03.47	46-47	40	-	14
Halifax T.	Tr	03.48	47-48	13	-	1

O'DONNELL James
Methil, 18 April, 1934 (IF)

League Club	Source	Date Signed	Seasons Played	Apps	Subs	Gls
Blackburn Rov.	Wellesley Jnrs	05.52				
Oldham Ath.	Tr	10.53	54-55	15	-	3
Leeds U.	Stalybridge Celtic	01.57				

O'DONNELL Jonathan David
Leeds, 21 March, 1954 (FB/M)

League Club	Source	Date Signed	Seasons Played	Apps	Subs	Gls
Leeds U.	App	03.71				
Cambridge U.	Tr	07.73	73-75	79	0	8
Colchester U.	L	08.75	75	1	0	0
Hartlepool U.	Tr	07.76	76	30	1	1
Scunthorpe U.	Tr	07.77	77-79	60	0	1

O'DONNELL Neil
Glasgow, 21 December, 1949 (M)

League Club	Source	Date Signed	Seasons Played	Apps	Subs	Gls
Norwich C.	Jnrs	12.66	67-73	31	19	2
Gillingham	Tr	08.74	74-75	18	6	0
Sheffield Wed.	Tr	10.75	75-76	40	0	1

O'DONNELL Ralph
Cudworth, 17 October, 1931 (CH)

League Club	Source	Date Signed	Seasons Played	Apps	Subs	Gls
Sheffield Wed.	Upton Colly	05.49	51-61	170	-	3

O'DONNELL William
Clydebank, 9 August, 1924 (CF)

League Club	Source	Date Signed	Seasons Played	Apps	Subs	Gls
Northampton T.	Partick Thistle	06.51	51-53	105	-	44
Shrewsbury T.	Tr	07.54	54-57	130	-	45

O'DONOGHUE Michael Gerard
Islington, 13 September, 1956 (F)

League Club	Source	Date Signed	Seasons Played	Apps	Subs	Gls
Southampton	Wembley	01.79				
Northampton T.	L	11.79	79	4	0	1

O'DOWD Adrian Gregory
Solihull, 16 September, 1959 (F)

League Club	Source	Date Signed	Seasons Played	Apps	Subs	Gls
Aston Villa	App	08.77				
Oxford U.	Tr	02.80	79-80	8	2	1

O'DOWD Gregory Henry
Dublin, 16 March, 1973 (CD)

League Club	Source	Date Signed	Seasons Played	Apps	Subs	Gls
Brighton & H.A.	YT	11.90	91	0	1	0

O'DRISCOLL John Francis
Cork (Ire), 20 September, 1921 Died 1988 IR-3/NI-3 (W)

League Club	Source	Date Signed	Seasons Played	Apps	Subs	Gls
Swansea C.	Cork	05.47	47-51	117	-	26

O'DRISCOLL Sean Michael
Wolverhampton, 1 July, 1957 IRu21-3/IR-3 (RW)

League Club	Source	Date Signed	Seasons Played	Apps	Subs	Gls
Fulham	Alvechurch	11.79	79-83	141	7	13
Bournemouth	Tr	02.84	83-94	409	14	19

OELOFSE Roelof (Ralph) Johannes Gysbertus
South Africa, 12 November, 1926 (WH)

League Club	Source	Date Signed	Seasons Played	Apps	Subs	Gls
Chelsea	Berea Park (SA)	10.51	51-52	8	-	0
Watford	Tr	07.53	53	15	-	0

O'FARRELL Francis
Cork (Ire), 9 October, 1927 IR-9 (WH)

League Club	Source	Date Signed	Seasons Played	Apps	Subs	Gls
West Ham U.	Cork	01.48	50-56	197	-	6
Preston N.E.	Tr	11.56	56-60	118	-	3

O'FLANAGAN Kevin Patrick
Dublin, 10 June, 1919 NI Amat/IR-10 (W)

League Club	Source	Date Signed	Seasons Played	Apps	Subs	Gls
Arsenal (Am)	Bohemians	10.45	46	14	-	3
Brentford (Am)	Barnet	11.49	49	6	-	0

OGBURN Michael George
Portsmouth, 19 February, 1948 (FB)

League Club	Source	Date Signed	Seasons Played	Apps	Subs	Gls
Brentford	Portsmouth (App)	05.65	66	12	0	0

OGDEN Alan
Rotherham, 15 April, 1954 (FB)

League Club	Source	Date Signed	Seasons Played	Apps	Subs	Gls
Sheffield U.	App	05.71	71-73	6	6	0
York C.	Tr	09.74	74	7	0	0

OGDEN Christopher John
Oldham, 3 February, 1953 (G)

League Club	Source	Date Signed	Seasons Played	Apps	Subs	Gls
Oldham Ath.	Jnrs	07.71	71-77	128	0	0
Swindon T.	Tr	08.78	78-79	24	0	0
Rotherham U.	Tr	11.79	79	3	0	0

OGDEN Frederick
Oldham, 3 April, 1925 (G)

League Club	Source	Date Signed	Seasons Played	Apps	Subs	Gls
Oldham Ath.	Edge Lane B.C.	12.47	47-54	151	-	0
Chesterfield	Tr	06.55				
Oldham Ath.	Tr	03.56	55	5	-	0

OGDEN Neil
Billinge, 29 November, 1975 (LB)

League Club	Source	Date Signed	Seasons Played	Apps	Subs	Gls
Wigan Ath.	YT	03.94	92-95	11	4	0

OGDEN Paul
Leek, 18 December, 1946 (W)

League Club	Source	Date Signed	Seasons Played	Apps	Subs	Gls
Port Vale (Am)	Leek Castle	11.65	65	2	0	0

OGDEN Paul
Salford, 16 October, 1969 (M)

League Club	Source	Date Signed	Seasons Played	Apps	Subs	Gls
Hartlepool U.	Oldham Ath. (YT)	08.88	88-89	9	3	0

OGDEN Trevor
Golborne, 12 June, 1945 (CF)

League Club	Source	Date Signed	Seasons Played	Apps	Subs	Gls
Manchester C.		09.64	64	9	-	3
Doncaster Rov.	Tr	06.65	65-66	39	0	14

OGHANI George William
Manchester, 2 September, 1960 (F)

League Club	Source	Date Signed	Seasons Played	Apps	Subs	Gls
Bury	Sheffield U. (Jnrs)	02.78				
Bolton W.	Hyde U.	10.83	83-86	86	13	27
Wrexham	L	03.87	86	6	1	0
Burnley	Tr	06.87	87-88	73	1	21
Stockport Co.	Tr	06.89	89	5	3	2
Hereford U.	Tr	10.89	89	7	1	2
Scarborough	Hyde U.	02.90	89-90	43	7	18
Carlisle U.	Evagoras (Cyp)	08.92	92-93	45	8	15

OGILVIE Gary Francis
Dundee, 16 November, 1967 (LB)

League Club	Source	Date Signed	Seasons Played	Apps	Subs	Gls
Sunderland	Dundee	03.88	88	0	1	0

OGILVIE John Forest
Motherwell, 28 October, 1928 (FB)

League Club	Source	Date Signed	Seasons Played	Apps	Subs	Gls
Leicester C.	Hibernian	09.55	55-58	82	-	2
Mansfield T.	Tr	01.60	59-60	24	-	1

OGILVIE John Leofric
Workington, 20 December, 1943 (FB)

League Club	Source	Date Signed	Seasons Played	Apps	Subs	Gls
Workington	Blackpool (Am)	04.63	62-74	386	4	14

OGLEY Alan
Barnsley, 4 February, 1946 E Sch (G)

League Club	Source	Date Signed	Seasons Played	Apps	Subs	Gls
Barnsley	App	03.63	62	9	-	0
Manchester C.	Tr	07.63	63-67	51	0	0
Stockport Co.	Tr	09.67	67-74	240	0	0
Darlington	Tr	08.75	75-76	80	0	0

OGLEY Mark Alan
Barnsley, 10 March, 1967 (CD)

League Club	Source	Date Signed	Seasons Played	Apps	Subs	Gls
Barnsley	App	03.85	85-86	19	0	0
Aldershot	L	12.87	87	6	2	0
Carlisle U.	Tr	03.88	87-89	33	0	1
Aldershot	Tr	11.89	89-90	58	4	0
York C.	Tr	04.92				

O'GORMAN David John
Chester, 20 June, 1972 (F)

League Club	Source	Date Signed	Seasons Played	Apps	Subs	Gls
Wrexham	YT	07.90	90	8	9	0
Swansea C.	Barry T.	08.97	97	11	23	5

O'GRADY Michael
Leeds, 11 October, 1942 Eu23-3/EF Lge/E-2 (OL)

League Club	Source	Date Signed	Seasons Played	Apps	Subs	Gls
Huddersfield T.	Jnrs	10.59	59-65	160	0	26
Leeds U.	Tr	10.65	65-69	90	1	12
Wolverhampton W.	Tr	09.69	69-72	28	5	5
Birmingham C.	L	02.72	71	2	1	0
Rotherham U.	Tr	11.72	72-73	24	0	2

OGRIZOVIC Steven
Mansfield, 12 September, 1957 EF Lge (G)

League Club	Source	Date Signed	Seasons Played	Apps	Subs	Gls
Chesterfield	Mansfield Y.C.	07.77	77	16	0	0
Liverpool	Tr	11.77	77-80	4	0	0
Shrewsbury T.	Tr	08.82	82-83	84	0	0
Coventry C.	Tr	06.84	84-97	502	0	1

OGSTON John Kessack
Aberdeen, 15 January, 1939 Su23-3 (G)

League Club	Source	Date Signed	Seasons Played	Apps	Subs	Gls
Liverpool	Aberdeen	08.65	66	1	0	0
Doncaster Rov.	Tr	08.68	68-70	70	0	0

O'HAGAN Daniel Alexander Nicholas
Padstow, 24 April, 1976 (F)

League Club	Source	Date Signed	Seasons Played	Apps	Subs	Gls
Plymouth Arg.	YT	06.94	94-95	1	8	1
Plymouth Arg. (N/C)	Weston-super-Mare	11.97	97	5	4	0

O'HAGAN Patrick John
Caerphilly, 15 March, 1971 (G)

League Club	Source	Date Signed	Seasons Played	Apps	Subs	Gls
Newport Co.	YT	●	87	3	0	0
Cardiff C.	YT	07.89				

O'HALLORAN Keith James
Dublin, 10 November, 1975 IR Sch/IR Yth/IRu21-3 (M)

League Club	Source	Date Signed	Seasons Played	Apps	Subs	Gls
Middlesbrough	Cherry Orchard B.C.	09.94	94-95	3	1	0
Scunthorpe U.	L	03.96	95	6	1	0
Cardiff C.	L	11.96	96	8	0	0

O'HALLORAN Neil
Cardiff, 21 June, 1933 Died 1995 (CF)

League Club	Source	Date Signed	Seasons Played	Apps	Subs	Gls
Cardiff C.		08.54	55-56	10	-	4
Newport Co.	Tr	07.57	57	14	-	2

OHANDJANIAN Demis
Manchester, 1 May, 1978 (F)

League Club	Source	Date Signed	Seasons Played	Apps	Subs	Gls
Doncaster Rov. (N/C)	Curzon Ashton	02.97	96	0	1	0

O'HANLON Kelham Gerard
Saltburn, 16 May, 1962 IRu21-2/IR-1 (G)

League Club	Source	Date Signed	Seasons Played	Apps	Subs	Gls
Middlesbrough	App	05.80	82-84	87	0	0
Rotherham U.	Tr	08.85	85-90	248	0	0
Carlisle U.	Tr	08.91	91-92	83	0	0
Preston N.E.	Tr	07.93	93	23	0	0
Preston N.E.	Dundee U.	09.96	96	13	0	0

O'HARA Daniel
Airdrie, 28 September, 1937 (IF)

League Club	Source	Date Signed	Seasons Played	Apps	Subs	Gls
Mansfield T.	Glasgow Celtic	06.61	61	3	-	1

O'HARA Edward Patrick
Dublin, 22 February, 1927 Died 1987 (OL)

League Club	Source	Date Signed	Seasons Played	Apps	Subs	Gls
Birmingham C.	Dundalk	11.49	49-50	6	-	0

O'HARA Albert **Edward**
Glasgow, 28 October, 1935 S Sch/Su23-3 (OL)

League Club	Source	Date Signed	Seasons Played	Apps	Subs	Gls
Everton	Falkirk	06.58	58-59	29	-	2
Rotherham U.	Tr	02.60	59-60	20	-	3
Barnsley	Morton	07.62	62-64	127	-	36

O'HARA Gerald John
Wolverhampton, 3 December, 1956 (M)

League Club	Source	Date Signed	Seasons Played	Apps	Subs	Gls
Wolverhampton W.	App	12.74	75-76	7	2	0
Hereford U. (N/C)	Tr	08.78	78	1	0	0

O'HARA Michael John
Coventry, 30 August, 1944 (G)

League Club	Source	Date Signed	Seasons Played	Apps	Subs	Gls
Luton T.	App	11.61	60	2	-	0
Swindon T.	Tr	11.61	61-62	30	-	0

O'HARA Stephen
Lanarkshire, 21 February, 1971 (D)

League Club	Source	Date Signed	Seasons Played	Apps	Subs	Gls
Walsall	YT	07.89	89-93	104	18	4

O'HARE John
Dumbarton, 24 September, 1946 Su23-3/S-13 (F)

League Club	Source	Date Signed	Seasons Played	Apps	Subs	Gls
Sunderland	Jnrs	10.63	64-66	51	0	14
Derby Co.	Tr	08.67	67-73	247	1	65
Leeds U.	Tr	08.74	74	6	0	1
Nottingham F.	Tr	02.75	74-79	94	7	14

OKAI Stephen Patrick
Ghana, 3 December, 1973 (W)

League Club	Source	Date Signed	Seasons Played	Apps	Subs	Gls
Leyton Orient	Jnrs	07.92	91-93	11	14	4

O'KAMBACK Joseph
Tottenham, 13 March, 1915 Died 1981 (WH)

League Club	Source	Date Signed	Seasons Played	Apps	Subs	Gls
Millwall		04.46	46	1	-	0

O'KANE John Andrew
Nottingham, 15 November, 1974 (RB)

League Club	Source	Date Signed	Seasons Played	Apps	Subs	Gls
Manchester U.	YT	01.93	95-96	1	1	0
Bury	L	10.96	96	2	2	2
Bury	L	01.97	96	9	0	1
Bradford C.	L	10.97	97	7	0	0
Everton	Tr	01.98	97	12	0	0

O'KANE Vincent
Stepney, 20 November, 1952 (M)

League Club	Source	Date Signed	Seasons Played	Apps	Subs	Gls
Charlton Ath.	App	12.70	70-72	29	3	1

O'KANE William (Liam) James
Derry, 17 June, 1948 NI-20 (CD)

League Club	Source	Date Signed	Seasons Played	Apps	Subs	Gls
Nottingham F.	Derry C.	12.68	68-75	186	3	0

O'KEEFE Eamonn Gerard
Manchester, 13 October, 1953 E Semi Pro/IRu21-4/IR-5 (F)

League Club	Source	Date Signed	Seasons Played	Apps	Subs	Gls
Plymouth Arg.	Stalybridge Celtic	02.74				
Everton	Mossley	07.79	79-81	26	14	6
Wigan Ath.	Tr	01.82	81-82	56	2	25
Port Vale	Tr	07.83	83-84	50	9	17
Blackpool	Tr	03.85	84-86	33	3	23
Chester C.	St Patricks Ath.	03.89	88-89	12	5	4

O'KEEFE Patrick John
Peterborough, 17 July, 1967 (M)

League Club	Source	Date Signed	Seasons Played	Apps	Subs	Gls
Peterborough U.	YT	07.85	84	0	1	0

O'KEEFE James **Vincent**
Birmingham, 2 April, 1957 (G)

League Club	Source	Date Signed	Seasons Played	Apps	Subs	Gls
Birmingham C.	Jnrs	07.75				
Walsall	Tr	07.76				
Exeter C.	A.P.Leamington	06.78	78-79	53	0	0
Torquay U.	Tr	02.80	79-81	108	0	0
Blackburn Rov.	Tr	08.82	82-88	68	0	0
Bury	L	10.83	83	2	0	0
Blackpool	L	12.86	86	1	0	0
Blackpool	L	02.89	88	6	0	0
Wrexham	Tr	07.89	89-91	83	0	0
Exeter C. (N/C)	Tr	08.92	92	2	0	0

O'KELLY Richard Florence
West Bromwich, 8 January, 1957 (F)

League Club	Source	Date Signed	Seasons Played	Apps	Subs	Gls
Walsall	Alvechurch	10.79	80-85	190	15	56
Port Vale	Tr	07.86	86-87	26	2	4
Walsall	Tr	01.88	87	7	5	1
Grimsby T.	Tr	07.88	88	38	1	10

OKENLA Foloronso (Foley)
Nigeria, 9 October, 1967 (W)

League Club	Source	Date Signed	Seasons Played	Apps	Subs	Gls
Birmingham C.	Burnley (N/C)	08.91	91	2	5	1

OKORIE Chima Ephraim
Nigeria, 8 October, 1968 Nigerian Int (F)

League Club	Source	Date Signed	Seasons Played	Apps	Subs	Gls
Grimsby T.	Peterborough U. (N/C)	09.93	93	0	5	0
Torquay U.	Tr	03.94	93-94	32	4	6

OLAH Bela Josef
Hungary, 8 June, 1938 (W)

League Club	Source	Date Signed	Seasons Played	Apps	Subs	Gls
Northampton T.	Bedford T.	12.58	58-60	42	-	8

OLDBURY Marcus John
Bournemouth, 29 March, 1976 (M)

League Club	Source	Date Signed	Seasons Played	Apps	Subs	Gls
Norwich C.	YT	07.94				
Bournemouth	Tr	07.95	95	2	11	0

OLDFIELD Craig
Warley, 24 November, 1963 (F)

League Club	Source	Date Signed	Seasons Played	Apps	Subs	Gls
Colchester U.		03.83	83	0	3	0

OLDFIELD David Charles
Australia, 30 May, 1968 Eu21-1 (M/F)

League Club	Source	Date Signed	Seasons Played	Apps	Subs	Gls
Luton T.	App	05.86	87-88	21	8	4
Manchester C.	Tr	03.89	88-89	18	8	6
Leicester C.	Tr	01.90	89-94	163	25	26
Millwall	L	02.95	94	16	1	6
Luton T.	Tr	07.95	95-97	99	18	18

OLDFIELD John Edward
Helsby, 13 July, 1918 (RH)

League Club	Source	Date Signed	Seasons Played	Apps	Subs	Gls
Port Vale	Helsby	03.46	46	1	-	0

OLDFIELD John Stephen
Lindrick (Nts), 19 August, 1943 (G)

League Club	Source	Date Signed	Seasons Played	Apps	Subs	Gls
Huddersfield T.	Jnrs	08.61	63-68	152	0	0
Wolverhampton W.	Tr	12.69	69-70	19	0	0
Crewe Alex.	L	11.71	71	5	0	0
Bradford C.	Tr	12.71	71-72	31	0	0

OLDFIELD Terence James
Bristol, 1 April, 1939 (WH)

League Club	Source	Date Signed	Seasons Played	Apps	Subs	Gls
Bristol Rov.	Clifton St Vincent	02.58	60-65	131	1	11
Wrexham	Tr	07.66	66	39	1	6

OLDHAM Eric
Newcastle, 27 June, 1933 Died 1994 (FB)

League Club	Source	Date Signed	Seasons Played	Apps	Subs	Gls
Bolton W.	Seaton Delaval	10.53				

League Club	Source	Date Signed	Seasons Played	Apps	Subs	Gls
Gateshead	Tr	07.56	56-57	53	-	0
Hartlepool U.	Kidderminster Hrs	06.59	59	12	-	0
OLDHAM George						
Glossop, 20 April, 1920 Died 1993						(LB)
Stoke C.	Mottram Central	10.37	38	2	-	0
Newport Co.	Tr	09.46	46-47	63	-	0
OLDHAM John						
Oswaldtwistle, 30 January, 1926						(CH)
Accrington St.	Oswaldtwistle Imps	08.50	50-52	10	-	0
OLDHAM John						
Nottingham, 24 October, 1949						(CF)
Mansfield T.	Nuthall B.C.	02.67	66	0	1	0
OLDRIDGE Andrew **Robert**						
Barton-on-Humber, 17 November, 1957						(F)
Grimsby T.		01.76	75-76	9	6	1
OLDROYD Darren Robert						
Ormskirk, 1 November, 1966						(RB)
Everton	App	11.84	84	0	1	0
Wolverhampton W.	Tr	08.86	86	10	0	0
O'LEARY Daniel						
Cork (Ire), 11 January, 1951						(IF)
Millwall	App	05.68				
Fulham	Tr	07.69	69	0	1	0
O'LEARY David Anthony						
Stoke Newington, 2 May, 1958 IR-66						(CD)
Arsenal	App	07.75	75-92	523	35	11
Leeds U.	Tr	06.93	93	10	0	0
O'LEARY Donal Patrick						
Limehouse, 24 June, 1936						(OL)
Blackburn Rov.		10.54	55	6	-	1
O'LEARY Kristian Denis						
Port Talbot, 30 August, 1977 W Yth						(D)
Swansea C.	YT	07.96	95-97	35	7	1
O'LINN Sydney						
South Africa, 5 May, 1927						(IF)
Charlton Ath.	Green Point (SA)	12.47	47-56	187	-	32
OLINYK Peter						
Bolton, 4 October, 1953						(M)
Bolton W.	App	06.71	73-74	7	3	0
Stockport Co.	Tr	11.74	74	4	0	0
OLIPHANT David						
Carlisle, 29 January, 1942						(WH)
Wolverhampton W.	Jnrs	06.59				
Carlisle U.	Tr	12.60	60-64	109	-	11
OLIVE Robert **Leslie**						
Salford, 27 April, 1928						(G)
Manchester U. (Am)	Jnrs	01.53	52	2	-	0
OLIVER Joseph **Allen**						
Blyth, 8 September, 1924						(OL)
Derby Co.	Crofton Colly	10.46	47-49	16	-	2
Stockport Co.	Tr	08.50	50-53	139	-	29
Gateshead	Tr	07.54	54-57	146	-	36
OLIVER Antony John						
Portsmouth, 22 September, 1967						(G)
Brentford (N/C)	Portsmouth (N/C)	08.87	87	11	0	0
OLIVER Brian Charles						
Liverpool, 6 March, 1957						(G)
Rochdale	Bury (App)	03.75	75	3	0	0
Southport	L	12.75	75	2	0	0
OLIVER Darren						
Liverpool, 1 November, 1971						(LB)
Bolton W.	YT	05.90	92	3	0	0
Rochdale	Tr	10.93	93-94	22	6	0
OLIVER Edmund (Ted) Alan						
Manchester, 17 March, 1961						(M/FB)
Rochdale	App	03.79	77-79	19	3	1
OLIVER Eric						
Spennymoor, 8 July, 1940						(G)
Darlington (Am)	West Auckland	12.63	63	2	-	0

League Club	Source	Date Signed	Seasons Played	Apps	Subs	Gls
OLIVER Gavin Ronald						
Felling, 6 September, 1962						(CD)
Sheffield Wed.	App	08.80	80-84	14	6	0
Tranmere Rov.	L	01.83	82	17	0	1
Brighton & H.A.	L	08.85	85	15	1	0
Bradford C.	Tr	11.85	85-94	308	5	9
OLIVER George						
Houghton-le-Spring, 22 January, 1919 Died 1981						(OL)
Halifax T.		10.45				
Gateshead	Tr	10.46	46	13	-	1
OLIVER Henry (Harry) Spoors						
Sunderland, 16 February, 1921 Died 1994 E Sch						(CH)
Hartlepool U.	Houghton Colly	03.38	37	9	-	0
Brentford	Tr	05.38	46-47	18	-	0
Watford	Tr	05.48	48-51	122	-	2
OLIVER Howard Derek						
Sunderland, 16 April, 1950						(W)
Sheffield Wed.	Jnrs	04.67				
Hartlepool U.	Tr	08.68	68	0	1	0
OLIVER James						
Forfar, 13 January, 1958						(M)
Wigan Ath.	Montrose	08.80	80	1	1	0
OLIVER James						
Uxbridge, 28 August, 1949						(FB)
Crystal Palace	App	03.67	67-69	3	0	0
OLIVER James Robert						
Falkirk, 3 December, 1941 S Sch						(M)
Norwich C.	Falkirk	08.62	62-64	40	-	14
Brighton & H.A.	Tr	03.65	64-67	37	6	6
Colchester U.	Tr	02.68	67-69	65	10	10
OLIVER Jack						
Bradford, 21 September, 1946						(FB)
Bradford P.A.	Jnrs	09.66	65	1	0	0
OLIVER John						
Red Row (Nd), 6 October, 1920						(F)
Chesterfield	Amble	10.46	46-47	24	-	5
OLIVER Keith						
South Shields, 15 January, 1976						(M)
Hartlepool U.	YT	07.94	93-95	25	7	0
OLIVER Kenneth						
Pelton (Dm), 26 November, 1938						(IF)
Sunderland	Birtley R.O.F.	05.58				
Barnsley	South Shields	02.60	59-62	94	-	38
Watford	Tr	07.63	63-64	58	-	26
Workington	Tr	02.65	65-66	84	0	20
Bournemouth	Tr	01.67	66	14	0	4
OLIVER James Henry **Kenneth**						
Loughborough, 10 August, 1924 Died 1994						(CH)
Sunderland	Brush Sports	08.46	47-48	8	-	1
Derby Co.	Tr	09.49	49-57	184	-	1
Exeter C.	Tr	01.58	57-59	92	-	0
OLIVER Michael						
Middlesbrough, 2 August, 1975						(M)
Middlesbrough	YT	08.92				
Stockport Co.	Tr	07.94	94-95	17	5	1
Darlington	Tr	07.96	96-97	67	11	11
OLIVER Neil						
Berwick, 11 April, 1967						(FB)
Blackburn Rov.	Berwick R.	08.89	89-90	5	1	0
OLIVER Peter Francis Raeside						
Dunfermline, 14 August, 1948						(FB)
York C.	Hearts	07.74	74-75	41	0	0
Huddersfield T.	Tr	05.76	76	41	0	1
OLIVER Ralph John						
Tredegar, 30 March, 1934						(WH)
Shrewsbury T.	Hereford U.	08.55	55-57	7	-	0
OLIVIERA Raul Miguel Silva						
Portugal, 26 August, 1972 Portuguese u21 Int						(CD)
Bradford C. (L)	Farense (Por)	03.97	96	2	0	0
OLLERENSHAW John						
Stockport, 3 April, 1925						(FB)
Arsenal	Manchester C. (Am)	09.46				

League Club	Source	Date Signed	Seasons Played	Apps	Subs	Gls
Hartlepool U.	Tr	06.50	50	2	-	0
Oldham Ath.	Tr	03.51				

OLLERENSHAW Scott
Australia, 9 February, 1968 Australian Int (F)

League Club	Source	Date Signed	Seasons Played	Apps	Subs	Gls
Walsall	Sydney Olympic (Aus)	08.92	92	8	12	4

OLNEY Ian Douglas
Luton, 17 December, 1969 Eu21-10 (F)

League Club	Source	Date Signed	Seasons Played	Apps	Subs	Gls
Aston Villa	YT	07.88	88-91	62	26	16
Oldham Ath.	Tr	05.92	92-95	43	2	13

OLNEY Kevin John
Doncaster, 12 February, 1959 (FB)

League Club	Source	Date Signed	Seasons Played	Apps	Subs	Gls
Doncaster Rov.	Jnrs	08.76	76-78	65	1	1

O'LOUGHLIN Nigel
Rochdale, 19 January, 1954 (M)

League Club	Source	Date Signed	Seasons Played	Apps	Subs	Gls
Shrewsbury T.	Rhyl	08.72	72-75	23	10	7
Rochdale	Tr	08.76	76-81	242	3	17

O'LOUGHLIN William James
Bolton, 18 January, 1937 (W)

League Club	Source	Date Signed	Seasons Played	Apps	Subs	Gls
Oldham Ath.	Rossendale U.	02.60	59-60	27	-	0

OLSEN Jesper
Denmark, 20 March, 1961 Danish Int (LW)

League Club	Source	Date Signed	Seasons Played	Apps	Subs	Gls
Manchester U.	Ajax (Neth)	07.84	84-88	119	20	21

OLSSON Paul
Hull, 24 December, 1965 (M)

League Club	Source	Date Signed	Seasons Played	Apps	Subs	Gls
Hull C.	App	12.83				
Exeter C.	Tr	03.87	86-87	38	5	2
Scarborough	Tr	08.88	88-89	34	14	5
Hartlepool U.	Tr	12.89	89-93	162	9	13
Darlington	Tr	08.94	94-95	76	0	8

O'MAHONY Francis Kevin
Aldershot, 5 April, 1935 (CF)

League Club	Source	Date Signed	Seasons Played	Apps	Subs	Gls
Swindon T.		04.57	56-57	8	-	5

O'MAHONY Matthew Augustine
Kilkenny, 19 January, 1913 Died 1992 IR-6/NI-1 (CH)

League Club	Source	Date Signed	Seasons Played	Apps	Subs	Gls
Southport	Hoylake	04.35	34	12	-	0
Wolverhampton W.	Tr	05.35				
Newport Co.	Tr	03.36	35-36	8	-	0
Bristol Rov.	Tr	05.36	36-38	101	-	6
Ipswich T.	Tr	07.39	46-48	58	-	4

OMAN Alan John
Newcastle, 6 October, 1952 (FB)

League Club	Source	Date Signed	Seasons Played	Apps	Subs	Gls
Northampton T.	App	10.70	70-74	83	5	3

O'MARA John
Farnworth, 19 March, 1947 (CF)

League Club	Source	Date Signed	Seasons Played	Apps	Subs	Gls
Gillingham	Margate	10.65				
Brentford	Wimbledon	03.71	70-72	53	0	28
Blackburn Rov.	Tr	09.72	72-73	30	5	10
Bradford C.	Chelmsford C.	12.74	74	3	0	1

O'MEARA Alan Michael
Grantham, 15 December, 1958 (G)

League Club	Source	Date Signed	Seasons Played	Apps	Subs	Gls
Scunthorpe U.	App	07.76	75-76	41	0	0

OMIGIE Joseph Eghodalo
Hammersmith, 13 June, 1972 (F)

League Club	Source	Date Signed	Seasons Played	Apps	Subs	Gls
Brentford	Donna F.C.	08.94	95-97	10	14	1

OMOYINMI Emmanuel (Manny)
Nigeria, 28 December, 1977 E Sch (RM)

League Club	Source	Date Signed	Seasons Played	Apps	Subs	Gls
West Ham U.	YT	05.95	96-97	1	5	2
Bournemouth	L	09.96	96	5	2	0

O'NEIL Brian
Bedlington, 4 January, 1944 Eu23-1/EF Lge (M)

League Club	Source	Date Signed	Seasons Played	Apps	Subs	Gls
Burnley	Jnrs	01.61	62-69	231	4	22
Southampton	Tr	05.71	70-74	148	1	16
Huddersfield T.	Tr	10.74	74-75	60	1	3

O'NEIL Joseph
Glasgow, 15 August, 1931 (IF)

League Club	Source	Date Signed	Seasons Played	Apps	Subs	Gls
Southend U. (L)	Aberdeen	11.52	52-53	24	-	11
Leicester C.	Aberdeen	03.56	57	5	-	2
Northampton T.	Tr	10.57	57-58	28	-	4

O'NEIL Thomas Harry
Spennymoor, 5 January, 1925 Died 1978 (RB)

League Club	Source	Date Signed	Seasons Played	Apps	Subs	Gls
Newcastle U.	Spennymoor U.	09.42				
Newport Co.	Tr	04.48	48	9	-	0

O'NEIL Thomas Patrick
St Helens, 25 October, 1952 E Sch (M)

League Club	Source	Date Signed	Seasons Played	Apps	Subs	Gls
Manchester U.	App	11.69	70-72	54	0	0
Blackpool	L	01.73	72	7	0	0
Southport	Tr	08.73	73-77	192	6	20
Tranmere Rov.	Tr	06.78	78-79	74	0	10
Halifax T.	Tr	08.80	80-81	39	1	2

O'NEILL Alan
Sunderland, 13 November, 1937 (IF)

League Club	Source	Date Signed	Seasons Played	Apps	Subs	Gls
Sunderland	Jnrs	02.55	56-60	74	-	27
Aston Villa	Tr	10.60	60-62	23	-	6
Plymouth Arg.	Tr	11.62	62-63	40	-	14
Bournemouth	Tr	02.64	63-65	37	0	8

O'NEILL Alan
Cork (IR), 27 August, 1973 (F)

League Club	Source	Date Signed	Seasons Played	Apps	Subs	Gls
Birmingham C.	Cobh Ramblers	02.92	91	2	2	0

O'NEILL Brian
Paisley, 6 September, 1972 S Sch/S Yth/Su21-7/S-1 (M)

League Club	Source	Date Signed	Seasons Played	Apps	Subs	Gls
Nottingham F. (L)	Glasgow Celtic	03.97	96	4	1	0

O'NEILL Frank Simon
Dublin, 13 April, 1940 IR-20 (OR)

League Club	Source	Date Signed	Seasons Played	Apps	Subs	Gls
Arsenal	Home Farm	04.59	60	2	-	0

O'NEILL George
Port Glasgow, 26 July, 1942 (WH)

League Club	Source	Date Signed	Seasons Played	Apps	Subs	Gls
Barrow	Glasgow Celtic	10.64	64	7	-	0

O'NEILL George Patrick
Liverpool, 21 July, 1923 (IF)

League Club	Source	Date Signed	Seasons Played	Apps	Subs	Gls
Port Vale (Am)	Ellesmere Port	11.48	48	5	-	0

O'NEILL James
Larne, 24 November, 1941 NI Sch/NIu23-1/NI-1 (CF)

League Club	Source	Date Signed	Seasons Played	Apps	Subs	Gls
Sunderland	Jnrs	11.58	61	7	-	6
Walsall	Tr	12.62	62-64	38	-	12
Darlington	Hakoah (Aus)	10.67	67	20	3	4

O'NEILL James Anthony
Dublin, 13 October, 1931 IR-17 (G)

League Club	Source	Date Signed	Seasons Played	Apps	Subs	Gls
Everton	Bulfin U.	05.49	50-59	201	-	0
Stoke C.	Tr	07.60	60-63	130	-	0
Darlington	Tr	03.64	63-64	32	-	0
Port Vale	Tr	02.65	64-65	42	0	0

O'NEILL James (Shaun) Joseph
Belfast, 24 February, 1952 (D)

League Club	Source	Date Signed	Seasons Played	Apps	Subs	Gls
Leeds U.	App	05.69				
Chesterfield	Tr	07.74	74-85	437	5	6

O'NEILL John
Dublin, 9 September, 1935 IR-1 (D)

League Club	Source	Date Signed	Seasons Played	Apps	Subs	Gls
Preston N.E.	Drumcondra	04.58	58-62	50	-	0
Barrow	Tr	07.63	63	35	-	3

O'NEILL John Joseph
Glasgow, 3 January, 1974 (M/F)

League Club	Source	Date Signed	Seasons Played	Apps	Subs	Gls
Bournemouth	Glasgow Celtic	03.96	95-97	43	24	4

O'NEILL John Patrick
Derry (NI), 11 March, 1958 NI-39 (CD)

League Club	Source	Date Signed	Seasons Played	Apps	Subs	Gls
Leicester C.	Derry B.C.	03.76	78-86	313	0	10
Queens Park R.	Tr	07.87	87	2	0	0
Norwich C.	Tr	12.87	87	1	0	0

O'NEILL Keith Padre Gerard
Dublin, 16 February, 1976 IR Sch/IR Yth/IRu21-1/IR-9 (LW)

League Club	Source	Date Signed	Seasons Played	Apps	Subs	Gls
Norwich C.	YT	07.94	94-97	40	15	8

O'NEILL Leslie Arthur
Hartford, 4 December, 1943 (M)

League Club	Source	Date Signed	Seasons Played	Apps	Subs	Gls
Newcastle U.	Blyth Spartans	11.61	63	1	-	0
Darlington	Tr	01.65	64-69	178	1	35
Bradford C.	Tr	03.70	69-71	95	2	17
Carlisle U.	Tr	05.72	72-76	148	7	20

O'NEILL Martin Hugh Michael
Coleraine, 1 March, 1952 NI-64 (M)

League Club	Source	Date Signed	Seasons Played	Apps	Subs	Gls
Nottingham F.	Derry C.	10.71	71-80	264	21	48
Norwich C.	Tr	02.81	80	11	0	1
Manchester C.	Tr	06.81	81	12	1	0
Norwich C.	Tr	01.82	81-82	54	1	11
Notts Co.	Tr	08.83	83-84	63	1	5

O'NEILL Michael Andrew Martin
Portadown (NI), 5 July, 1969 NI Sch/NI Yth/NIu21-1/NIu23-1/NI 'B'/NI-31 (F)

League Club	Source	Date Signed	Seasons Played	Apps	Subs	Gls
Newcastle U.	Coleraine	10.87	87-88	36	12	15

League Club	Source	Date Signed	Seasons Played	Apps	Subs	Gls
Coventry C.	Hibernian	07.96	96-97	3	2	0
Reading	L	03.98	97	9	0	1

O'NEILL Thomas
Kirkintilloch, 2 February, 1958 (M)

League Club	Source	Date Signed	Seasons Played	Apps	Subs	Gls
Cambridge U.	Ipswich T. (App)	07.76	76-82	96	20	8
Northampton T.	Tr	06.83	83	43	0	6

O'NEILL William
Glasgow, 30 December, 1940 (FB)

League Club	Source	Date Signed	Seasons Played	Apps	Subs	Gls
Carlisle U.	Glasgow Celtic	05.69	69	15	0	0

O'NEILL William Anthony
Cork (Ire), 29 December, 1919 (IF)

League Club	Source	Date Signed	Seasons Played	Apps	Subs	Gls
Burnley	Chelmsford C.	06.49	50	1	-	1
Walsall	Tr	01.51	50-51	51	-	16

ONSLOW Leslie Gordon
Swindon, 29 August, 1926 (HB)

League Club	Source	Date Signed	Seasons Played	Apps	Subs	Gls
Swindon T.		10.45	46-48	4	-	0

ONSLOW Roy
Swindon, 12 September, 1928 (IF)

League Club	Source	Date Signed	Seasons Played	Apps	Subs	Gls
Swindon T.		11.47	47-55	140	-	23

ONUORA Ifem
Glasgow, 28 July, 1967 (W/F)

League Club	Source	Date Signed	Seasons Played	Apps	Subs	Gls
Huddersfield T.	Bradford Univ.	07.89	89-93	115	50	30
Mansfield T.	Tr	07.94	94-95	17	11	8
Gillingham	Tr	08.96	96-97	53	9	23
Swindon T.	Tr	03.98	97	6	0	1

ONWERE Udo Alozie
Hammersmith, 9 November, 1971 (M)

League Club	Source	Date Signed	Seasons Played	Apps	Subs	Gls
Fulham	YT	07.90	90-93	66	19	7
Lincoln C.	Tr	08.94	94-95	40	3	4
Blackpool	Dover Ath.	09.96	96	5	4	0
Barnet	Tr	08.97	97	11	6	0

ONYEALI Elkanah Bollington
Nigeria, 7 June, 1939 (CF)

League Club	Source	Date Signed	Seasons Played	Apps	Subs	Gls
Tranmere Rov.	Nigeria	08.60	60	13	-	8

OOSTHUIZEN Ronald
South Africa, 16 March, 1936 (OL)

League Club	Source	Date Signed	Seasons Played	Apps	Subs	Gls
Charlton Ath.	Marist Bros (SA)	09.53	55	1	-	0
Carlisle U.	Poole T.	09.59	59	1	-	0

ORAM Dennis Graham
Bristol, 14 January, 1920 (CH)

League Club	Source	Date Signed	Seasons Played	Apps	Subs	Gls
Bristol C. (Am)	St Pancras B.C.	08.46	46	3	-	0

ORD Brian Rigby
Dunstan, 21 June, 1939 (FB)

League Club	Source	Date Signed	Seasons Played	Apps	Subs	Gls
Charlton Ath.	Bleach Green	11.57	61-62	13	-	1

ORD Kenneth
South Shields, 21 September, 1939 (WH)

League Club	Source	Date Signed	Seasons Played	Apps	Subs	Gls
Sunderland	Cleadon Colly	11.57				
Chesterfield	Tr	06.61	61	3	-	0

ORD Richard John
Murton, 3 March, 1970 Eu21-3 (CD)

League Club	Source	Date Signed	Seasons Played	Apps	Subs	Gls
Sunderland	YT	07.87	87-97	223	20	7
York C.	L	02.90	89	3	0	0

ORD Thomas
Woolwich, 15 October, 1952 (F)

League Club	Source	Date Signed	Seasons Played	Apps	Subs	Gls
Chelsea	Erith & Belvedere	12.72	72	3	0	1

O'REGAN Kieran Michael
Cork (Ire.), 9 November, 1963 IR Yth/IR-4 (D/M)

League Club	Source	Date Signed	Seasons Played	Apps	Subs	Gls
Brighton & H.A.	Tramore Ath.	04.83	82-86	69	17	2
Swindon T.	Tr	08.87	87	23	3	1
Huddersfield T.	Tr	08.88	88-92	187	12	25
West Bromwich A.	Tr	07.93	93-94	36	9	2

O'REILLY Gary Miles
Isleworth, 21 March, 1961 IR Yth (CD)

League Club	Source	Date Signed	Seasons Played	Apps	Subs	Gls
Tottenham H.	Jnrs	09.79	80-83	39	6	0
Brighton & H.A.	Tr	08.84	84-86	78	1	3
Crystal Palace	Tr	01.87	86-89	65	5	2
Birmingham C.	L	03.91	90	1	0	0
Brighton & H.A.	Tr	07.91	91	28	0	3

ORGILL Harold
Hucknall, 1 October, 1920 Died 1980 (G)

League Club	Source	Date Signed	Seasons Played	Apps	Subs	Gls
Nottingham F.		04.47	46	7	-	0
Notts Co.	Tr	06.47	47	2	-	0

ORHAN Remzi **Yilmaz**
Cyprus, 13 March, 1955 (F)

League Club	Source	Date Signed	Seasons Played	Apps	Subs	Gls
West Ham U.	Aveley	10.72	75-76	6	2	0

O'RILEY Paul John
Liverpool, 17 October, 1950 (F)

League Club	Source	Date Signed	Seasons Played	Apps	Subs	Gls
Hull C.	App	10.68	68-73	19	11	2
Scunthorpe U.	L	03.71	70	11	0	4
Barnsley	Tr	07.74	74	11	3	2
Southport	Goole T.	03.75	74-76	19	11	4

O'RIORDAN Donald (Donal) Joseph
Dublin, 14 May, 1957 IR Yth/IRu21-1 (CD/M)

League Club	Source	Date Signed	Seasons Played	Apps	Subs	Gls
Derby Co	App	05.75	76-77	2	4	1
Doncaster Rov.	L	01.78	77	2	0	0
Preston N.E.	Tulsa (USA)	10.78	78-82	153	5	8
Carlisle U.	Tr	08.83	83-84	84	0	18
Middlesbrough	Tr	08.85	85	41	0	2
Grimsby T.	Tr	08.86	86-87	86	0	14
Notts Co.	Tr	07.88	88-92	102	7	5
Mansfield T.	L	09.89	89	6	0	0
Torquay U.	Tr	02.93	92-95	76	3	3
Scarborough (N/C)	Tr	12.95	95	1	0	0

ORLYGSSON Thorvaldur (Toddy)
Denmark, 2 August, 1966 Icelandic Int (M)

League Club	Source	Date Signed	Seasons Played	Apps	Subs	Gls
Nottingham F.	K.A. Akureyri (Ice)	11.89	89-92	31	6	2
Stoke C.	Tr	08.93	93-95	86	4	16
Oldham Ath.	Tr	12.95	95-97	46	8	1

ORMANDY John (Jack)
Liverpool, 25 January, 1912 (OL)

League Club	Source	Date Signed	Seasons Played	Apps	Subs	Gls
Bradford C.	Prescot Cables	06.32	32-35	63	-	9
Bury	Tr	06.36	36-38	87	-	18
Southend U.	Tr	06.39				
Oldham U.	Tr	07.46	46	30	-	5
Halifax T.	Tr	07.47	47	7	-	0

ORMEROD Anthony
Middlesbrough, 31 March, 1979 E Yth (W)

League Club	Source	Date Signed	Seasons Played	Apps	Subs	Gls
Middlesbrough	YT	05.96	97	8	10	3

ORMEROD Brett Ryan
Blackburn, 18 October, 1976 (F)

League Club	Source	Date Signed	Seasons Played	Apps	Subs	Gls
Blackpool	Accrington St.	03.97	96-97	5	8	2

ORMEROD Mark Ian
Bournemouth, 5 February, 1976 (G)

League Club	Source	Date Signed	Seasons Played	Apps	Subs	Gls
Brighton & H.A.	YT	07.94	96-97	51	0	0

ORMOND John (Ian) Lambie
Harthill, 10 August, 1947 (W)

League Club	Source	Date Signed	Seasons Played	Apps	Subs	Gls
Barnsley	New Zealand	12.67	68	1	0	1

ORMOND William
Greenock, 26 August, 1926 Died 1992 (OL)

League Club	Source	Date Signed	Seasons Played	Apps	Subs	Gls
Blackpool	Partick Thistle	10.47				
Oldham Ath.	Tr	12.49	49-53	122	-	25
Barrow	Tr	02.54	53-57	139	-	31
Scunthorpe U.	Tr	08.58	58	3	-	0

ORMONDROYD Ian
Bradford, 22 September, 1964 (F)

League Club	Source	Date Signed	Seasons Played	Apps	Subs	Gls
Bradford C.	Thackley	09.85	85-88	72	15	20
Oldham Ath.	L	03.87	86	8	2	1
Aston Villa	Tr	02.89	88-91	41	15	6
Derby Co.	Tr	09.91	91	25	0	8
Leicester C.	Tr	03.92	91-94	67	10	7
Hull C.	L	01.95	94	10	0	6
Bradford C.	Tr	07.95	95-96	28	10	6
Oldham Ath.	Tr	09.96	96-97	26	5	8
Scunthorpe U.	Tr	09.97	97	7	13	0

ORMROD Leslie
Stockport, 8 October, 1952 E Sch (FB)

League Club	Source	Date Signed	Seasons Played	Apps	Subs	Gls
Stockport Co.	Everton (App)	03.70	69-73	103	5	0

ORMSBY Brendan Thomas Christopher
Birmingham, 1 October, 1960 E Sch/E Yth (CD)

League Club	Source	Date Signed	Seasons Played	Apps	Subs	Gls
Aston Villa	App	10.78	78-85	115	2	4
Leeds U.	Tr	02.86	85-88	46	0	5
Shrewsbury T.	L	01.90	89	1	0	0
Doncaster Rov.	Tr	07.90	90-91	78	0	7
Scarborough	Tr	08.92	92	15	1	1
Wigan Ath (N/C)	Waterford U.	08.94	94	2	0	0

ORMSTON Alexander
Stoke, 10 February, 1919 Died 1975 EF Lge (W)

League Club	Source	Date Signed	Seasons Played	Apps	Subs	Gls
Stoke C.	Jnrs	07.36	37-51	172	-	29

League Club	Source	Date Signed	Seasons Played	Career Record Apps	Subs	Gls
O'ROURKE James						
Glasgow, 17 October, 1948						(FB)
Arsenal	Possilpark Jnrs	10.65				
Carlisle U.	Tr	10.67	67	0	1	0
O'ROURKE John						
Northampton, 11 February, 1945 E Yth/Eu23-1						(CF)
Chelsea	Arsenal (Am)	04.62				
Luton T.	Tr	12.63	63-65	84	0	64
Middlesbrough	Tr	07.66	66-67	63	1	38
Ipswich T.	Tr	02.68	67-69	69	0	30
Coventry C.	Tr	11.69	69-71	52	2	17
Queens Park R.	Tr	10.71	71-72	33	1	12
Bournemouth	Tr	01.74	73-74	21	1	4
O'ROURKE Kenneth						
Lambeth, 8 December, 1949						(IF)
Arsenal	Leyton Orient (App)	02.67				
Colchester U.	Ipswich T. (Trial)	10.68	68	1	0	0
O'ROURKE William James						
Nottingham, 2 April, 1960						(G)
Burnley	App	02.78	79-82	14	0	0
Blackpool	L	08.83	83	6	0	0
Chester C.	Tr	03.84	83	5	0	0
Blackpool	Tr	07.84	84-85	92	0	0
Tranmere Rov.	L	09.86	86	15	0	0
Tranmere Rov.	Tr	02.87	86-87	38	0	0
ORPHAN Leslie James						
Newport, 17 April, 1923 Died 1995 W Amat						(IL)
Newport Co.	Girlings	02.49	48	1	-	0
ORR Anderson (Alan)						
Glasgow, 19 December, 1923						(WH)
Nottingham F.	Third Lanark	08.51	51-54	46	-	0
ORR Douglas McDonald						
Glasgow, 8 November, 1937 S Amat						(W)
Queens Park R. (Am)	Hendon	06.57	57	5	-	0
ORR Henry						
Lisburn (NI), 31 October, 1936						(WH)
Sheffield U.	Distillery	11.58	58-62	10	-	1
Peterborough U.	Tr	07.64	64-66	47	1	0
ORR Neil Ian						
Greenock, 13 May, 1959 Su21-7						(CD)
West Ham U.	Morton	01.82	81-87	133	13	4
ORRITT Bryan						
Caernarfon, 22 February, 1937 Wu23-3						(IF)
Birmingham C.	Bangor C.	01.56	56-61	99	-	23
Middlesbrough	Tr	03.62	61-65	115	3	22
OSBORN Kenneth George						
Hampstead, 23 November, 1948						(OR)
Gillingham	Queens Park R. (App)	06.66	68-69	2	0	0
OSBORN Simon Edward						
Croydon, 19 January, 1972						(M)
Crystal Palace	YT	01.90	90-93	47	8	5
Reading	Tr	08.94	94	31	1	5
Queens Park R.	Tr	07.95	95	6	3	1
Wolverhampton W.	Tr	12.95	95-97	77	3	9
OSBORNE Glyn						
Crewe, 23 August, 1954						(CF)
Crewe Alex.	App	•	70-71	2	5	0
OSBORNE Ian Leonard						
Leicester, 28 October, 1952						(FB)
Birmingham C.	App	10.70	75	10	0	0
Port Vale	Tr	06.76	76	14	1	0
OSBORNE John						
Barlborough (Dy), 1 December, 1940 E Sch						(G)
Chesterfield	Jnrs	09.60	60-66	110	0	0
West Bromwich A.	Tr	01.67	66-76	250	0	0
Walsall	L	02.73	72	3	0	0
OSBORNE John						
Renfrew, 14 October, 1919 Died 1981						(IF)
Leicester C.	Linwood Thistle	09.38				
Watford	Tr	02.48	47-48	34	-	13
OSBORNE Lawrence William						
West Ham, 20 October, 1967						(M)
Arsenal	App	07.85				
Newport Co.	Tr	11.87	87	15	0	0
Maidstone U.	Redbridge Forest	07.90	90-91	49	4	8
Gillingham	Tr	12.91	91-92	5	1	1
OSBORNE Roger Charles						
Otley (Sfk), 9 March, 1950						(M)
Ipswich T.	Grundisburgh	03.71	73-80	109	15	9
Colchester U.	Tr	02.81	80-85	196	10	11
OSBORNE Steven Colin						
Middlesbrough, 3 March, 1969						(F)
Peterborough U.	South Bank	03.89	88-90	18	43	7
York C.	Tr	08.91	91	6	3	0
OSBORNE Wayne						
Stockton, 14 January, 1977						(LB)
York C.	YT	06.95	95	5	1	0
OSBOURNE Calbert **Gary** James						
Wolverhampton, 22 October, 1969						(FB)
Shrewsbury T.	YT	07.88	88	3	4	0
OSCROFT Harry						
Mansfield, 10 March, 1926						(OL)
Mansfield T.	Mansfield Colly	04.47	46-49	113	-	41
Stoke C.	Tr	01.50	49-58	326	-	103
Port Vale	Tr	09.59	59-60	47	-	12
OSGOOD Keith						
Isleworth, 8 May, 1955 E Sch/E Yth						(CD)
Tottenham H.	App	05.72	73-77	112	1	13
Coventry C.	Tr	01.78	77-78	24	1	1
Derby Co.	Tr	10.79	79-81	61	8	10
Leyton Orient	Tr	12.81	81-83	36	0	0
Cambridge U.	Tr	11.84	84-85	34	1	1
OSGOOD Peter Leslie						
Windsor, 20 February, 1947 E Yth/Eu23-6/EF Lge/E-4						(F)
Chelsea	Jnrs	09.64	65-73	276	3	103
Southampton	Tr	03.74	73-77	122	4	28
Norwich C.	L	11.76	76	3	0	0
Chelsea	Philadelphia (USA)	12.78	78-79	10	0	2
OSGOOD Stephen						
Bracknell, 20 January, 1962						(G)
Aldershot (N/C)	Newbury T.	02.89	88	1	0	0
O'SHAUGHNESSY Brian						
Wednesbury, 8 September, 1932						(IF)
Walsall		03.54	53	1	-	0
O'SHAUGHNESSY Michael John						
Poplar, 15 April, 1955						(G)
Leyton Orient	App	08.73	73	1	0	0
O'SHAUGHNESSY Stephen						
Wrexham, 13 October, 1967 W Yth						(CD/M)
Leeds U.	YT	10.85				
Bradford C.	Tr	11.85	87	0	1	0
Rochdale	Tr	08.88	88-90	101	8	16
Exeter C.	Tr	07.91	91	1	2	0
Darlington	Tr	01.92	91-93	88	0	2
O'SHEA Daniel Edward						
Newington, 26 March, 1963						(D/M)
Arsenal	App	12.80	82	6	0	0
Charlton Ath.	L	02.84	83	9	0	0
Exeter C.	Tr	08.84	84	45	0	2
Southend U.	Tr	08.85	85-88	116	2	12
Cambridge U.	Tr	08.89	89-94	186	17	1
Northampton T.	Tr	03.95	94-96	73	7	1
O'SHEA Timothy James						
Pimlico, 12 November, 1966 IR Yth/IRu21-2						(D/M)
Tottenham H.	App	08.84	86-87	1	2	0
Newport Co.	L	10.86	86	10	0	0
Leyton Orient	Tr	07.88	88	7	2	1
Gillingham	Tr	02.89	88-91	102	10	2
OSMAN Harry James						
Alton, 29 January, 1911						(OL)
Plymouth Arg.	Poole T.	12.35	35-36	5	-	0
Southampton	Tr	06.37	37-38	70	-	31
Millwall	Tr	03.39	38-47	34	-	3
Bristol C.	Tr	10.47	47	18	-	1
OSMAN Rex Charles Herbert						
Derby, 4 April, 1932 E Yth						(FB)
Derby Co.	Jnrs	07.49	53-54	2	-	0

OSMAN Russell Charles
Ilkeston, 14 February, 1959 E Yth/Eu21-7/E'B'/E-11 (CD)

League Club	Source	Date Signed	Seasons Played	Apps	Subs	Gls
Ipswich T.	App	03.76	77-84	294	0	17
Leicester C.	Tr	07.85	85-87	108	0	8
Southampton	Tr	06.88	88-91	92	4	6
Bristol C.	Tr	10.91	91-93	67	3	3
Brighton & H.A. (N/C)	Plymouth Arg. (N/C)	09.95	95	11	1	0
Cardiff C. (N/C)	Tr	02.96	95	14	1	0

OSMOND Avery Noel
Huddersfield, 25 December, 1924 (F)

League Club	Source	Date Signed	Seasons Played	Apps	Subs	Gls
Southend U.	Peterborough U.	05.48	48	2	-	0

OSMOND Colin Albert Eric
Whitchurch, 15 May, 1937 E Yth (FB)

League Club	Source	Date Signed	Seasons Played	Apps	Subs	Gls
Portsmouth	Jnrs	05.54	57	1	-	0

OSTENSTAD Egil
Norway, 2 January, 1972 Norwegian Int (CF)

League Club	Source	Date Signed	Seasons Played	Apps	Subs	Gls
Southampton	Viking Stavanger (Nor)	10.96	96-97	50	9	21

OSTER John Morgan
Boston, 8 December, 1978 W Yth/Wu21-7/W-3 (W)

League Club	Source	Date Signed	Seasons Played	Apps	Subs	Gls
Grimsby T.	YT	07.96	96	21	3	3
Everton	Tr	07.97	97	16	15	1

OSTERGAARD John Brian
Denmark, 6 February, 1955 (F)

League Club	Source	Date Signed	Seasons Played	Apps	Subs	Gls
Charlton Ath.	Ikast (Den)	11.79	79-80	8	4	1

O'SULLIVAN Cyril John
Lewisham, 22 February, 1920 (G)

League Club	Source	Date Signed	Seasons Played	Apps	Subs	Gls
Reading	Crown Villa	09.46	46-47	36	-	0

O'SULLIVAN John
Cork (Ire), 30 May, 1922 (W)

League Club	Source	Date Signed	Seasons Played	Apps	Subs	Gls
Swansea C.	Waterford	01.48	47	2	-	0
Aldershot	Lovells Ath.	11.51				

O'SULLIVAN Peter Anthony
Conway, 4 March, 1951 W Sch/Wu23-6/W-3 (M)

League Club	Source	Date Signed	Seasons Played	Apps	Subs	Gls
Manchester U.	App	03.68				
Brighton & H.A.	Tr	04.70	70-80	432	3	39
Fulham	Tr	06.81	81-82	45	1	1
Charlton Ath.	L	10.82	82	5	0	0
Reading	L	11.82	82	9	0	0
Aldershot	Hong Kong	07.83	83	13	1	0

O'SULLIVAN Wayne St John
Cyprus, 25 February, 1974 IRu21-2 (M)

League Club	Source	Date Signed	Seasons Played	Apps	Subs	Gls
Swindon T.	YT	05.93	94-96	65	24	3
Cardiff C.	Tr	08.97	97	40	3	2

O'SULLIVAN William Finbar
Lambeth, 5 October, 1959 IR Yth (W)

League Club	Source	Date Signed	Seasons Played	Apps	Subs	Gls
Charlton Ath.	App	10.77	76-77	1	1	0

OSVOLD Kjetll
Norway, 5 June, 1961 Norwegian Int (W)

League Club	Source	Date Signed	Seasons Played	Apps	Subs	Gls
Nottingham F.	Lillestrom (Nor)	03.87	86-87	5	2	0
Leicester C.	L	12.87	87	3	1	0

O'TOOLE Gavin Francis
Dublin, 19 September, 1975 IR Sch/IR Yth/IRu21-2 (M)

League Club	Source	Date Signed	Seasons Played	Apps	Subs	Gls
Coventry C.	YT	07.93				
Hereford U.	L	11.96	96	1	0	0

O'TOOLE Christopher Patrick
Dublin, 2 January, 1965 (M)

League Club	Source	Date Signed	Seasons Played	Apps	Subs	Gls
Leicester C.	Shelbourne	02.90				
Exeter C.	L	12.90	90	6	0	0
Shrewsbury T.	Tr	03.91	90-92	26	20	1
Torquay U. (N/C)	Tr	08.93	93	3	0	0

OTTEWELL Sidney
Horsley (Dy), 23 October, 1919 (IF)

League Club	Source	Date Signed	Seasons Played	Apps	Subs	Gls
Chesterfield	Holbrook Colly	11.36	36-46	42	-	12
Birmingham C.	Tr	06.47	47	5	-	2
Luton T.	Tr	12.47	47	15	-	4
Nottingham F.	Tr	07.48	48-49	32	-	3
Mansfield T.	Tr	01.50	49-51	67	-	21
Scunthorpe U.	Tr	03.52	51-52	30	-	12

OTTO Hendrikus (Heine) Matheus
Netherlands, 24 August, 1954 Dutch Int (M)

League Club	Source	Date Signed	Seasons Played	Apps	Subs	Gls
Middlesbrough	Twente Enschede (Neth)	08.81	81-84	163	3	24

OTTO Ricky
Hackney, 9 November, 1967 (W)

League Club	Source	Date Signed	Seasons Played	Apps	Subs	Gls
Leyton Orient	Haringey Borough	11.90	90-92	41	15	13
Southend U.	Tr	07.93	93-94	63	1	17
Birmingham C.	Tr	12.94	94-96	25	21	6
Charlton Ath.	L	09.96	96	5	2	0
Peterborough U.	L	02.97	96	15	0	4
Notts Co.	L	09.97	97	4	0	0

OTTOSSON Ulf Peter
Sweden, 2 July, 1968 (F)

League Club	Source	Date Signed	Seasons Played	Apps	Subs	Gls
Norwich C. (L)	Norrkoping (Swe)	01.97	96	4	3	1

OTULAKOWSKI Anton
Dewsbury, 29 January, 1956 (M)

League Club	Source	Date Signed	Seasons Played	Apps	Subs	Gls
Barnsley	Ossett T.	03.75	75-76	42	0	2
West Ham U.	Tr	10.76	76-77	10	7	0
Southend U.	Tr	03.79	78-82	161	2	8
Millwall	Tr	03.83	82-85	114	0	14
Crystal Palace	Tr	08.86	86	12	0	1

OUTHART Anthony
Scarborough, 17 September, 1963 (F)

League Club	Source	Date Signed	Seasons Played	Apps	Subs	Gls
Scarborough	Bridlington T.	11.87	87-88	3	3	1

OUTHWAITE George
Ferryhill, 19 May, 1928 (G)

League Club	Source	Date Signed	Seasons Played	Apps	Subs	Gls
Oldham Ath. (Am)	Chilton Colly	03.56	55	4	-	0

OUTTERSIDE Mark Jeremy
Hexham, 13 January, 1967 (RB)

League Club	Source	Date Signed	Seasons Played	Apps	Subs	Gls
Sunderland	App	01.85	86	1	0	0
Darlington	Tr	07.87	87	37	1	0

OVARD Frank Colin
Evesham, 16 December, 1955 E Semi Pro (F)

League Club	Source	Date Signed	Seasons Played	Apps	Subs	Gls
Gillingham	Maidstone U.	12.81	81	4	2	0

OVENDALE Mark John
Leicester, 22 November, 1973 (G)

League Club	Source	Date Signed	Seasons Played	Apps	Subs	Gls
Northampton T.	Wisbech T.	08.94	94	6	0	0

OVER Eric
Sheffield, 5 July, 1933 (OL)

League Club	Source	Date Signed	Seasons Played	Apps	Subs	Gls
Sheffield U.		11.54	54	2	-	0
Barrow	Tr	01.56	55-57	19	-	1
Oldham Ath.	Tr	12.57	57	21	-	2

OVERFIELD Jack
Leeds, 14 May, 1932 (OL)

League Club	Source	Date Signed	Seasons Played	Apps	Subs	Gls
Leeds U.	Yorkshire Amats	05.53	55-59	159	-	20
Sunderland	Tr	08.60	60-62	65	-	5
Peterborough U.	Tr	02.63	62	1	-	0
Bradford C.	Tr	07.64	64	11	-	0

OVERMARS Marc
Ernst, Holland, 29 March, 1973 Dutch Int (W)

League Club	Source	Date Signed	Seasons Played	Apps	Subs	Gls
Arsenal	Ajax (Neth)	07.97	97	32	0	12

OVERSON Richard John
Kettering, 3 June, 1959 (D)

League Club	Source	Date Signed	Seasons Played	Apps	Subs	Gls
Burnley	App	06.77	77-79	5	1	0
Hereford U.	Tr	05.80	80-81	6	5	1

OVERSON Vincent David
Kettering, 15 May, 1962 E Yth (CD)

League Club	Source	Date Signed	Seasons Played	Apps	Subs	Gls
Burnley	App	11.79	79-85	207	4	6
Birmingham C.	Tr	06.86	86-90	179	3	3
Stoke C.	Tr	08.91	91-95	167	3	6
Burnley	Tr	08.96	96	6	2	0
Shrewsbury T.	L	09.97	97	2	0	0

OVERTON John
Rotherham, 2 May, 1956 (CD)

League Club	Source	Date Signed	Seasons Played	Apps	Subs	Gls
Aston Villa	App	01.74	75	2	1	0
Halifax T.	L	03.76	75	14	0	2
Gillingham	Tr	06.76	76-80	177	1	10

OVERTON Paul Henry
Ely, 18 April, 1961 (G)

League Club	Source	Date Signed	Seasons Played	Apps	Subs	Gls
Ipswich T.	App	07.78	77	1	0	0
Peterborough U.	Tr	05.79				
Northampton T.	Tr	06.80				

OWEN Aled Watkin
Anglesey, 7 January, 1934 (W)

League Club	Source	Date Signed	Seasons Played	Apps	Subs	Gls
Tottenham H.	Bangor C.	09.53	53	1	-	0
Ipswich T.	Tr	07.58	58-61	30	-	3
Wrexham	Tr	07.63	63	3	-	0

OWEN Brian Ernest
Uxbridge, 2 November, 1944 (W)

League Club	Source	Date Signed	Seasons Played	Apps	Subs	Gls
Watford	App	07.62	62-69	148	5	17
Colchester U.	Tr	05.70	70-71	12	2	2
Wolverhampton W.	Tr	01.72	72	4	0	0

OWEN Brian Gordon
Bath, 7 July, 1942 (F)

League Club	Source	Date Signed	Seasons Played	Apps	Subs	Gls
Hereford U.	Bath C.	07.70	72-73	46	8	13

OWEN Bryn
Littleborough, 25 April, 1939 (FB)

League Club	Source	Date Signed	Seasons Played	Apps	Subs	Gls
Rochdale	Turf Hill	08.60	60-61	6	-	0

OWEN Derek William
Shrewsbury, 11 March, 1938 (OR)

League Club	Source	Date Signed	Seasons Played	Apps	Subs	Gls
Shrewsbury T.	Coton Rov.	01.57	56-57	13	-	3

OWEN Ronald **Derek**
Ellesmere Port, 25 September, 1938 (G)

League Club	Source	Date Signed	Seasons Played	Apps	Subs	Gls
Chester C. (Am)	Ellesmere Port	05.58	58-60	7	-	0

OWEN Gareth
Chester, 21 October, 1971 Wu21-8/W 'B' (M)

League Club	Source	Date Signed	Seasons Played	Apps	Subs	Gls
Wrexham	YT	07.90	89-97	210	44	28

OWEN Gary Alfred
St Helens, 7 July, 1958 E Yth/Eu21-22/E'B' (M)

League Club	Source	Date Signed	Seasons Played	Apps	Subs	Gls
Manchester C.	App	08.75	75-78	101	2	19
West Bromwich A.	Tr	06.79	79-85	185	2	21
Sheffield Wed.	Panionios (Gre)	08.87	87	12	2	0

OWEN Gordon
Barnsley, 14 June, 1959 (RW)

League Club	Source	Date Signed	Seasons Played	Apps	Subs	Gls
Sheffield Wed.	Jnrs	11.76	77-82	32	15	5
Rotherham U.	L	03.80	79	9	0	0
Doncaster Rov.	L	11.82	82	9	0	0
Chesterfield	L	03.83	82	6	0	2
Cardiff C.	Tr	08.83	83	38	1	14
Barnsley	Tr	08.84	84-85	68	0	25
Bristol C.	Tr	08.86	86-87	51	2	11
Hull C.	L	12.87	87	3	0	0
Mansfield T.	Tr	01.88	87-88	54	4	8
Blackpool	Tr	07.89	89-90	21	8	2
Carlisle U.	L	10.90	90	4	1	0
Exeter C.	L	12.90	90	4	0	0

OWEN John Gilbert
Ynysybwl, 25 March, 1932 (WH)

League Club	Source	Date Signed	Seasons Played	Apps	Subs	Gls
Exeter C.	Pontypridd	10.53	53-54	14	-	0
Bournemouth	Tr	09.56				

OWEN John **Leslie**
Hawarden, 11 April, 1933 (FB)

League Club	Source	Date Signed	Seasons Played	Apps	Subs	Gls
Chester C.		07.54	56	1	-	0

OWEN Maurice
Abingdon, 4 July, 1924 (CF/CH)

League Club	Source	Date Signed	Seasons Played	Apps	Subs	Gls
Swindon T.	Abingdon	12.46	46-62	555	-	150

OWEN Michael James
Chester, 14 December, 1979 E Sch/E Yth/Eu21-1/E-9 (F)

League Club	Source	Date Signed	Seasons Played	Apps	Subs	Gls
Liverpool	Jnrs	12.96	96-97	35	3	19

OWEN Neil
Bury, 14 October, 1959 (M)

League Club	Source	Date Signed	Seasons Played	Apps	Subs	Gls
Sheffield Wed.	App	•	76	1	0	0

OWEN Robert
Farnworth, 17 October, 1947 (F)

League Club	Source	Date Signed	Seasons Played	Apps	Subs	Gls
Bury	App	08.65	64-67	81	2	38
Manchester C.	Tr	07.68	68-69	18	4	3
Swansea C.	L	03.70	69	5	1	1
Carlisle U.	Tr	06.70	70-76	185	19	51
Northampton T.	L	10.76	76	5	0	0
Workington	L	12.76	76	8	0	2
Bury	L	02.77	76	4	0	1
Doncaster Rov.	Tr	07.77	77-78	74	3	22

OWEN Robert Gibbon
South Shields, 5 May, 1924 (WH)

League Club	Source	Date Signed	Seasons Played	Apps	Subs	Gls
Huddersfield T.		04.45				
Lincoln C.	Murton Colly	01.47	46-54	246	-	5

OWEN Sydney William
Birmingham, 29 February, 1922 EF Lge/E-3 (CH)

League Club	Source	Date Signed	Seasons Played	Apps	Subs	Gls
Birmingham C.	Birmingham Y.M.C.A.	10.45	46	5	-	0
Luton T.	Tr	06.47	47-58	388	-	3

OWEN Leslie **Terence**
Liverpool, 11 September, 1949 (F/W)

League Club	Source	Date Signed	Seasons Played	Apps	Subs	Gls
Everton	App	12.66	67	2	0	0
Bradford C.	Tr	06.70	70-71	41	11	6
Chester C.	Tr	06.72	72-76	161	15	41
Cambridge U.	Tr	08.77	77	1	0	0
Rochdale	Tr	09.77	77-78	80	3	21
Port Vale	Tr	07.79	79	14	4	3

OWEN Trefor
Connahs Quay, 20 February, 1933 W Amat (CH)

League Club	Source	Date Signed	Seasons Played	Apps	Subs	Gls
Leyton Orient	Tooting & Mitcham	01.58	58-60	15	-	0

OWEN William
Llanfairfechan, 30 June, 1914 Died 1976 (WH/F)

League Club	Source	Date Signed	Seasons Played	Apps	Subs	Gls
Manchester C.	Northwich Vic.	06.34	35	9	-	3
Tranmere Rov.	Tr	03.36	35	6	-	4
Newport Co.	Tr	06.36	36-46	72	-	5
Exeter C.	Tr	10.46	46	20	-	9

OWENS Thomas **Leslie**
Sunderland, 17 October, 1919 Died 1974 (CF)

League Club	Source	Date Signed	Seasons Played	Apps	Subs	Gls
Charlton Ath.	Washington Colly	09.37	37-38	12	-	5
Doncaster Rov.	Tr	02.39	38-47	21	-	11
Southport	Tr	12.47	47-48	53	-	11
Hartlepool U.	Tr	07.49	49	28	-	12
Norwich C.	Tr	03.50	49-50	20	-	8
Reading	Tr	07.51	51	8	-	4
Brighton & H.A.	Tr	06.52	52	15	-	4

OWER John (Ian) Campion Taylor
Glasgow, 2 January, 1939 (G)

League Club	Source	Date Signed	Seasons Played	Apps	Subs	Gls
Workington	St Johnstone	02.63	62-67	199	0	0

OWERS Adrian Richard
Chelmsford, 26 February, 1965 (M)

League Club	Source	Date Signed	Seasons Played	Apps	Subs	Gls
Southend U.	App	02.83	82-84	18	9	0
Brighton & H.A.	Chelmsford C.	12.87	87-90	32	8	4
Gillingham	L	03.91	90	9	1	0
Maidstone U. (N/C)	Tr	10.91	91	1	0	0

OWERS Gary
Newcastle, 3 October, 1968 EF Lge (RB/M)

League Club	Source	Date Signed	Seasons Played	Apps	Subs	Gls
Sunderland	App	10.86	87-94	259	9	25
Bristol C.	Tr	12.94	94-97	121	5	9

OWERS Philip
Bishop Auckland, 28 April, 1955 (G)

League Club	Source	Date Signed	Seasons Played	Apps	Subs	Gls
Darlington	Jnrs	06.73	72-74	45	0	0
Gillingham	Tr	07.75	75	2	0	0
Darlington	Tr	07.76	76-79	69	0	0
Hartlepool U. (N/C)	Brandon U.	08.87	87	2	0	0

OXBROW Darren William
Ipswich, 1 September, 1969 (CD)

League Club	Source	Date Signed	Seasons Played	Apps	Subs	Gls
Ipswich T.	YT	06.88				
Maidstone U.	Tr	08.89	89-91	84	1	2
Colchester U.	Tr	08.92	92	12	4	4
Barnet	Tr	12.92	92	1	0	0

OXFORD Kenneth
Oldham, 14 November, 1929 Died 1993 E Yth (G)

League Club	Source	Date Signed	Seasons Played	Apps	Subs	Gls
Manchester C.	Jnrs	10.47	47	1	-	0
Chesterfield		06.50				
Norwich C.	Tr	07.51	53-57	128	-	0
Derby Co.	Tr	12.57	57-62	151	-	0
Doncaster Rov.	Tr	07.64	64	16	-	0
Port Vale	Tr	03.65				

OXLEY Albert
Gateshead, 21 October, 1915 Died 1994 (IF)

League Club	Source	Date Signed	Seasons Played	Apps	Subs	Gls
Gateshead	Windy Nook	01.35	34-46	120	-	25

OXLEY Scott
Sheffield, 22 November, 1976 (M)

League Club	Source	Date Signed	Seasons Played	Apps	Subs	Gls
York C.	YT	07.95	95	1	1	0

OXTOBY Richard
Chesterfield, 5 September, 1939 (CH)

League Club	Source	Date Signed	Seasons Played	Apps	Subs	Gls
Bolton W.	Jnrs	01.57	59	3	-	0
Tranmere Rov.	Tr	07.63	63	5	-	0

League Club	Source	Date Signed	Seasons Played	Apps	Subs	Gls
PAATELAINEN Mika (Mixu) Matti						
Finland, 3 February, 1967 Finnish Int (F)						
Bolton W.	Aberdeen	07.94	94-96	58	11	15
Wolverhampton W.	Tr	08.97	97	10	13	0
PACE Derek (Doc) John						
Essington(Staffs), 11 March, 1932 Died 1989 (CF)						
Aston Villa	Bloxwich Strollers	09.49	50-57	98	-	40
Sheffield U.	Tr	12.57	57-64	253	-	140
Notts Co.	Tr	12.64	64-65	29	0	15
Walsall	Tr	07.66	66	4	1	1
PACEY David						
Luton, 2 October, 1936 Eu23-1 (WH)						
Luton T.	Hitchin T.	08.56	57-64	246	-	16
PACEY Dennis Frank						
Feltham, 27 September, 1928 (CF)						
Leyton Orient	Walton & Hersham	12.51	51-54	120	-	46
Millwall	Tr	10.54	54-58	133	-	37
Aldershot	Tr	09.58	58-59	32	-	13
PACK Leonard John						
Salisbury, 27 September, 1976 (M)						
Cambridge U.	YT	07.95	94-96	5	10	0
PACK Roy James						
Stoke Newington, 20 September, 1946 (FB)						
Arsenal	App	11.63	65	1	0	0
Portsmouth	Tr	07.66	66-68	91	0	0
PACKARD Edgar						
Mansfield, 7 March, 1919 Died 1996 (CH)						
Sheffield Wed.	Clipstone Colly	12.36	46-51	124	-	1
Halifax T.	Tr	08.52	52-53	85	-	0
PACKER Leslie John						
Sunderland, 8 April, 1959 (F)						
Doncaster Rov.		09.78	78-79	5	2	2
PACKER Michael David						
Willesden, 20 April, 1950 (D)						
Watford	App	04.68	68-72	57	11	2
Crewe Alex.	L	03.72	71	12	0	0
Colchester U.	Tr	07.73	73-82	337	7	20
PACKER Norman James						
Ynysybwl, 14 June, 1931 (HB)						
Exeter C.	Pontypridd	07.55	55-60	18	-	0
PADDON Graham Charles						
Manchester, 24 August, 1950 Eu23-1 (M)						
Coventry C.	App	05.68	68-69	3	2	1
Norwich C.	Tr	10.69	69-73	162	0	19
West Ham U.	Tr	12.73	73-76	115	0	11
Norwich C.	Tr	11.76	76-81	126	2	6
Millwall	L	12.81	81	5	0	1
PADOVANO Michele						
Turin, Italy, 28 August, 1966 Italian Int (F)						
Crystal Palace	Juventus (It)	11.97	97	8	2	1
PAGAL Jean Claude						
Cameroon, 15 September, 1964 Cameroon Int (M)						
Carlisle U.	St Etienne (Fr)	02.98	97	1	0	0
PAGE Donald Richard						
Manchester, 18 January, 1964 (F)						
Wigan Ath.	Runcorn	03.89	88-90	62	12	15
Rotherham U.	Tr	08.91	91-92	40	15	13
Rochdale	L	02.93	92	3	1	1
Doncaster Rov.	Tr	11.93	93	18	4	4
Chester C.	Tr	07.94	94	22	8	5
Scarborough	Tr	07.95	95	26	11	5
PAGE John						
Frimley, 21 October, 1934 (D)						
Southampton	Jnrs	10.51	52-60	190	-	24
PAGE Malcolm Edward						
Knucklas, 5 February, 1947 W Sch/Wu23-6/W-28 (D)						
Birmingham C.	App	09.64	64-80	328	8	8
Oxford U.	Tr	02.81	80-81	14	0	1
PAGE Raymond Michael						
Swindon, 26 September, 1930 (FB)						
Swindon T.		04.51	50-54	32	-	0
PAGE Robert John						
Rhondda, 3 September, 1974 W Sch/W Yth/Wu21-6/W-6 (CD)						
Watford	YT	04.93	93-97	100	5	0
PAINE Terence Lionel						
Winchester, 23 March, 1939 Eu23-4/EF Lge /E-19 (W)						
Southampton	Winchester C.	02.57	56-73	709	4	160
Hereford U.	Tr	08.74	74-76	106	5	8
PAINTER Edward						
Swindon, 23 June, 1921 (WH)						
Swindon T.		10.38	46-50	77	-	0
PAINTER Ian John						
Wombourne, 28 December, 1964 E Yth/Eu21-1 (F)						
Stoke C.	App	12.82	82-85	105	8	20
Coventry C.	Tr	07.86	86	0	3	0
PAINTER Peter **Robert**						
Wigan, 26 January, 1971 (F/M)						
Chester C.	YT	07.89	87-90	58	26	8
Maidstone U.	Tr	07.91	91	27	3	5
Burnley	Tr	03.92	91-92	16	10	2
Darlington	Tr	09.93	93-96	104	11	28
Rochdale	Tr	10.96	96-97	66	6	24
PAINTER Trevor Alfred						
Norwich, 2 July, 1949 (CH)						
Norwich C.	App	07.67	67	2	0	0
Colchester U.	Tr	05.70	70	1	0	0
PAISLEY Robert						
Hetton-le-Hole, 23 January, 1919 Died 1996 (WH)						
Liverpool	Bishop Auckland	05.39	46-53	253	-	10
PALADINO Giuseppe (Joe)						
Whiston, 29 August, 1965 (G)						
Wigan Ath. (N/C)	St Helens T.	12.90	90	7	0	0
PALETHORPE Christopher Glynne						
Maidenhead, 6 November, 1942 (OR)						
Reading	Jnrs	11.59	60-62	55	-	10
Aldershot	Tr	06.63	63-64	56	-	4
PALFREYMAN George Barry						
Sheffield, 13 March, 1933 (G)						
Halifax T. (Am)	Sheffield F.C.	01.54	53	1	-	0
PALGRAVE Brian Uriel						
Birmingham, 12 July, 1966 (F)						
Walsall	Alvechurch	07.84	84-87	5	3	1
PALIN Granville						
Armthorpe (Yks), 13 February, 1940 (FB)						
Wolverhampton W.	Jnrs	03.57				
Walsall	Tr	07.60	60-63	129	-	10
PALIN Leigh Granville						
Worcester, 12 September, 1965 E Yth (M)						
Aston Villa	App	09.83				
Shrewsbury T.	L	12.84	84	2	0	0
Nottingham F.	Tr	11.85				
Bradford C.	Tr	10.86	86-88	65	6	10
Stoke C.	Tr	09.89	89	17	2	3
Hull C.	Tr	03.90	89-91	57	0	7
Rochdale	L	10.91	91	3	0	0
Burnley (N/C)	Tr	10.92	92	1	0	0
PALIOS Markos (Mark)						
Liverpool, 9 November, 1952 (M)						
Tranmere Rov.		07.73	73-79	177	13	25
Crewe Alex.	Tr	01.80	79-82	114	4	23
Tranmere Rov.	Tr	03.83	82-84	55	4	7
PALLISTER Gary Andrew						
Ramsgate, 30 June, 1965 E 'B'/EF Lge/E-22 (CD)						
Middlesbrough	Billingham T.	11.84	85-89	156	0	5
Darlington	L	10.85	85	7	0	0
Manchester U.	Tr	08.89	89-97	314	3	12

PALLISTER Gordon
Crook, 2 April, 1917 EF Lge (FB)

League Club	Source	Date Signed	Seasons Played	Apps	Subs	Gls
Bradford C.	Willington	05.34	37-38	28	-	0
Barnsley	Tr	10.38	38-51	220	-	3

PALMER Calvin Ian
Skegness, 21 October, 1940 (WH)

League Club	Source	Date Signed	Seasons Played	Apps	Subs	Gls
Nottingham F.	Skegness T.	03.58	58-63	91	-	14
Stoke C.	Tr	09.63	63-67	165	0	24
Sunderland	Tr	02.68	67-69	35	5	5
Crewe Alex.	Cape Town C. (SA)	10.71	71	2	0	0

PALMER Carlton Lloyd
Rowley Regis, 5 December, 1965 Eu21-4/E 'B'/E-18 (CD/M)

League Club	Source	Date Signed	Seasons Played	Apps	Subs	Gls
West Bromwich A.	YT	12.84	85-88	114	7	4
Sheffield Wed.	Tr	02.89	88-93	204	1	14
Leeds U.	Tr	06.94	94-96	100	2	5
Southampton	Tr	09.97	97	26	0	3

PALMER Charles Anthony
Aylesbury, 10 July, 1963 (RB)

League Club	Source	Date Signed	Seasons Played	Apps	Subs	Gls
Watford	App	07.81	83	10	0	1
Derby Co.	Tr	07.84	84-85	51	0	2
Hull C.	Tr	02.87	86-88	69	1	1
Notts Co.	Tr	02.89	88-93	178	4	7
Walsall	Tr	07.94	94-95	54	0	2

PALMER David John
Bristol, 10 April, 1961 (FB)

League Club	Source	Date Signed	Seasons Played	Apps	Subs	Gls
Bristol Rov.	App	01.79	78	1	0	0

PALMER Desmond Frederick
Swansea, 23 September, 1931 W-3 (IF)

League Club	Source	Date Signed	Seasons Played	Apps	Subs	Gls
Swansea C.	Jnrs	04.50	52-58	83	-	37
Liverpool	Tr	03.59				
Derby Co.	Durban C. (SA)	06.61	61	18	-	6

PALMER Frank
Sunderland, 29 October, 1923 (OL)

League Club	Source	Date Signed	Seasons Played	Apps	Subs	Gls
Gateshead (Am)	Bishop Auckland	02.51	50	1	-	1

PALMER Frederick
Barrow, 23 October, 1922 (WH)

League Club	Source	Date Signed	Seasons Played	Apps	Subs	Gls
Crewe Alex.		12.45	46	1	-	0

PALMER Geoffrey
Barnsley, 12 November, 1940 (FB)

League Club	Source	Date Signed	Seasons Played	Apps	Subs	Gls
Bristol C.	Doncaster Rov. (Am)	08.58	61	1	-	0

PALMER Geoffrey
Cannock, 11 July, 1954 Eu23-12 (RB)

League Club	Source	Date Signed	Seasons Played	Apps	Subs	Gls
Wolverhampton W.	App	07.72	73-84	389	5	13
Burnley	Tr	11.84	84-85	34	0	0
Wolverhampton W.	Tr	12.85	85-86	21	1	0

PALMER John Neville
Bristol, 1 July, 1958 (M)

League Club	Source	Date Signed	Seasons Played	Apps	Subs	Gls
Bristol C.	Weston-super-Mare	03.83	82	2	6	0

PALMER Lee James
Croydon, 19 September, 1970 (LB)

League Club	Source	Date Signed	Seasons Played	Apps	Subs	Gls
Gillingham	YT	07.89	87-94	109	11	5
Cambridge U.	Tr	08.95	95-96	30	1	1

PALMER Leslie
Barrow, 16 December, 1923 (WH)

League Club	Source	Date Signed	Seasons Played	Apps	Subs	Gls
Barrow	Holker C.O.B.	10.49	49	1	-	0

PALMER Leslie James
Birmingham, 5 September, 1971 (F)

League Club	Source	Date Signed	Seasons Played	Apps	Subs	Gls
West Bromwich A.	YT	07.90	90-91	5	3	1

PALMER Roger Neil
Manchester, 30 January, 1959 (F)

League Club	Source	Date Signed	Seasons Played	Apps	Subs	Gls
Manchester C.	App	01.77	77-80	22	9	9
Oldham Ath.	Tr	11.80	80-93	414	47	141

PALMER Stephen Leonard
Brighton, 31 March, 1968 E Sch (M)

League Club	Source	Date Signed	Seasons Played	Apps	Subs	Gls
Ipswich T.	Cambridge Univ.	08.89	89-95	87	24	2
Watford	Tr	09.95	95-97	107	10	4

PAMMENT Michael
Huddersfield, 12 May, 1945 E Yth (CF)

League Club	Source	Date Signed	Seasons Played	Apps	Subs	Gls
Bradford C. (Am)	Jnrs	07.64	64	1	-	0

PAMPHLETT Tony John
Lambeth, 13 April, 1960 (CD)

League Club	Source	Date Signed	Seasons Played	Apps	Subs	Gls
Maidstone U.	Dartford	07.86	89	7	0	0

PANES Simon Michael
Almondsbury, 22 February, 1960 (F)

League Club	Source	Date Signed	Seasons Played	Apps	Subs	Gls
Bristol C.	Melksham T.	08.82	82	2	2	0

PANTER Derek
Blackpool, 22 November, 1943 (F)

League Club	Source	Date Signed	Seasons Played	Apps	Subs	Gls
Manchester C.	West Bromwich A. (Am)	08.62	63	1	-	0
Torquay U.	Tr	05.64	64	5	-	1
Southport	Tr	07.65				

PAPACONSTANTINOU Loukas
Toronto, Canada, 10 May, 1974 (G)

League Club	Source	Date Signed	Seasons Played	Apps	Subs	Gls
Darlington	Alabama Saints (USA)	07.97	97	1	0	0

PAPAVASSILIOU Nicodemos
Cyprus, 31 August, 1970 Cypriot Int (W)

League Club	Source	Date Signed	Seasons Played	Apps	Subs	Gls
Newcastle U.	O.F. Iraklion (Crete)	07.93	93	7	0	0

PAPE Andrew Maurice
Hammersmith, 22 March, 1962 E Semi Pro (G)

League Club	Source	Date Signed	Seasons Played	Apps	Subs	Gls
Queens Park R.	Jnrs	07.80	79	1	0	0
Barnet	Enfield	08.91	91-93	40	0	0

PARDEW Alan Scott
Wimbledon, 18 July, 1961 (M)

League Club	Source	Date Signed	Seasons Played	Apps	Subs	Gls
Crystal Palace	Yeovil T.	03.87	87-91	111	17	8
Charlton Ath.	Tr	11.91	91-94	98	6	24
Barnet	Tr	07.95	95-96	64	3	0

PARDOE Glyn
Winsford, 1 June, 1946 E Sch/Eu23-4 (LB)

League Club	Source	Date Signed	Seasons Played	Apps	Subs	Gls
Manchester C.	App	06.63	61-74	303	2	17

PARFITT Henry (Harry) Edward
Cardiff, 26 September, 1929 (FB)

League Club	Source	Date Signed	Seasons Played	Apps	Subs	Gls
Cardiff C.		05.49	53	1	-	0
Torquay U.	L	10.52	52-53	58	-	0

PARIS Alan David
Slough, 15 August, 1964 (LB)

League Club	Source	Date Signed	Seasons Played	Apps	Subs	Gls
Watford	Slough T.	11.82				
Peterborough U.	Tr	08.85	85-87	135	2	2
Leicester C.	Tr	07.88	88-90	80	8	3
Notts Co.	Tr	01.91	90-91	39	3	1

PARK Colin Sidney John
Swansea, 8 February, 1945 (G)

League Club	Source	Date Signed	Seasons Played	Apps	Subs	Gls
Swansea C.	Jnrs	09.63	63	1	-	0

PARK Robert
Douglas (Lk), 7 April, 1930 (G)

League Club	Source	Date Signed	Seasons Played	Apps	Subs	Gls
Crewe Alex.	Airdrieonians	08.55	55-56	61	-	0

PARK Robert
Coatbridge, 5 January, 1952 (M)

League Club	Source	Date Signed	Seasons Played	Apps	Subs	Gls
Sunderland	Jnrs	01.69	69-71	50	15	4

PARK Robert Clydesdale
Edinburgh, 3 July, 1946 (M)

League Club	Source	Date Signed	Seasons Played	Apps	Subs	Gls
Aston Villa	App	07.63	64-68	60	14	7
Wrexham	Tr	05.69	69-71	98	4	8
Peterborough U.	Tr	06.72	72	15	3	1
Northampton T.	Tr	02.73	72-73	21	3	0
Hartlepool U.	Tr	07.74	74	14	3	0

PARK Terence Charles
Liverpool, 7 February, 1957 (M)

League Club	Source	Date Signed	Seasons Played	Apps	Subs	Gls
Wolverhampton W.	Jnrs	03.74				
Stockport Co.	Blackpool (N/C)	07.76	76-79	87	3	8
Stockport Co.	Minnesota K. (USA)	03.81	80-82	72	0	7
Manchester C.	L	01.83	82	0	2	0
Bury	Tr	07.83	83	18	3	1

PARK William
Gateshead, 23 February, 1919 (CH)

League Club	Source	Date Signed	Seasons Played	Apps	Subs	Gls
Blackpool	Felling Red Star	05.38	38	3	-	0
York C.	Tr	09.46	46	22	-	1

PARKE John
Bangor (NI), 6 August, 1937 NI-14 (FB)

League Club	Source	Date Signed	Seasons Played	Apps	Subs	Gls
Sunderland	Hibernian	11.64	64-67	83	2	0

PARKER Albert Edward
Liverpool, 13 September, 1927 (FB)

League Club	Source	Date Signed	Seasons Played	Apps	Subs	Gls
Crewe Alex.	South Liverpool	12.48	48-51	113	-	0
Wrexham	Tr	11.51	51-58	216	-	1

League Club	Source	Date Signed	Seasons Played	Apps	Subs	Gls
PARKER Alexander Hershaw						
Irvine, 2 August, 1935 Su23-6/SF Lge/S-15						(RB)
Everton	Falkirk	06.58	58-64	198	-	5
Southport	Tr	09.65	65-67	76	0	0
PARKER Brian Thomas						
Chorley, 4 August, 1955 E Semi Pro						(G)
Crewe Alex.	Jnrs	08.72	73	26	0	0
Arsenal	Tr	08.75				
PARKER Carl						
Burnley, 25 March, 1971						(M)
Rochdale	Rossendale U.	02.92	91-92	9	7	1
PARKER Henry **Clifford**						
Conisbrough, 6 September, 1913 Died 1983						(OL)
Doncaster Rov.	Denaby U.	08.31	31-33	52	-	11
Portsmouth	Tr	12.33	33-50	242	-	57
PARKER Derek						
Wivenhoe, 23 June, 1926						(WH)
West Ham U.	Grays Ath.	10.44	46-55	199	-	9
Colchester U.	Tr	03.57	56-60	129	-	1
PARKER Derrick						
Wallsend, 7 February, 1957						(F)
Burnley	App	02.74	74-75	5	1	2
Southend U.	Tr	02.77	76-79	129	0	43
Barnsley	Tr	02.80	79-82	104	3	32
Oldham Ath.	Tr	08.83	83-84	54	3	11
Doncaster Rov.	L	12.84	84	5	0	1
Burnley	Tr	10.85	85-86	43	0	10
Rochdale (N/C)	Finland	10.87	87	6	1	1
PARKER Garry Stuart						
Oxford, 7 September, 1965 E Yth/Eu21-6/E 'B'						(M)
Luton T.	App	05.83	82-85	31	11	3
Hull C.	Tr	02.86	85-87	82	2	8
Nottingham F.	Tr	03.88	87-91	99	4	17
Aston Villa	Tr	11.91	91-94	91	4	13
Leicester C.	Tr	02.95	94-97	87	20	10
PARKER Graham Sydney						
Coventry, 23 May, 1946						(M)
Aston Villa	App	05.63	63-67	16	1	1
Rotherham U.	Tr	12.67	67	3	0	0
Lincoln C.	Tr	07.68	68	4	1	0
Exeter C.	Tr	03.69	68-73	180	1	12
Torquay U.	Tr	05.74	74-75	41	2	3
PARKER Harry						
Blackburn, 8 February, 1933						(OR)
Blackburn Rov.	Lower Darwen Y.C.	08.51	51	3	-	0
PARKER Jeffrey Samuel						
Liverpool, 23 January, 1969						(M)
Crewe Alex.	YT	07.87	87	7	3	0
PARKER John William						
Birkenhead, 5 July, 1925 Died 1988						(M)
Everton	St Lawrence C.Y.M.S.	12.48	50-55	167	-	82
Bury	Tr	05.56	56-58	81	-	43
PARKER Martin Thomas						
Exeter, 18 October, 1970						(M)
Exeter C.	YT	●	88	0	1	0
PARKER Neil						
Blackburn, 19 October, 1957						(FB)
Leeds U.	App	10.75	77	0	1	0
PARKER Patrick John						
Bow (Devon), 15 July, 1929						(CH)
Southampton	Newton Abbot	08.51	51-58	132	-	0
PARKER Paul Andrew						
West Ham, 4 April, 1964 E Yth/Eu21-8/E 'B'/E-19						(D)
Fulham	App	04.82	80-86	140	14	2
Queens Park R.	Tr	06.87	87-90	121	4	1
Manchester U.	Tr	08.91	91-95	100	5	1
Derby Co.	Tr	08.96	96	4	0	0
Sheffield U.	Tr	11.96	96	7	3	0
Fulham (N/C)	Tr	01.97	96	3	0	0
Chelsea	Tr	03.97	96	1	3	0
PARKER Raymond Dennis						
Doncaster, 27 January, 1925						(CH)
Chesterfield	Thurcroft	02.45	47	14	-	0
Sheffield Wed.	Tr	04.48	48	1	-	0
Bradford C.	Buxton	06.51	51-52	41	-	1
PARKER Reginald Ernest Arundel						
Llantrisant, 10 June, 1921						(CF)
Cardiff C.		11.46	47	2	-	0
Newport Co.	Tr	08.48	48-53	201	-	99
PARKER Richard						
Wolverhampton, 6 July, 1973						(F)
Walsall (N/C)	Cradley T.	09.92	92	0	1	0
PARKER Robert						
Coventry, 11 November, 1952 E Yth						(D)
Coventry C.	App	05.70	69-73	77	3	0
Carlisle U.	Tr	06.74	74-83	373	2	6
PARKER Robert William						
Seaham, 26 November, 1935						(FB)
Huddersfield T.	Murton Colly	06.54	59-64	65	-	0
Barnsley	Tr	07.65	65-68	108	0	0
PARKER Samuel						
Liverpool, 5 April, 1924						(CF/FB)
Accrington St.	Marine	07.48	48	13	-	6
Barnsley	Tr	12.48				
Accrington St.	Tr	09.49	49-50	36	-	6
Crewe Alex.	Tr	11.50	50-52	44	-	3
PARKER Scott Matthew						
Lambeth, 13 October, 1980 E Yth						(M)
Charlton Ath.	YT	10.97	97	0	3	0
PARKER Sean						
Newcastle, 23 August, 1973						(M)
Northampton T.	YT	07.91	91-92	9	1	0
PARKER Stanley Frederick						
Worksop, 31 July, 1920 Died 1994						(IF)
Ipswich T.	Worksop L.B.O.B.	05.46	46-50	126	-	43
Norwich C.	Tr	08.51				
PARKER Stuart John						
Preston, 16 February, 1954						(F)
Blackpool	App	04.72	72-74	10	6	2
Southend U.	Tr	07.75	75-76	62	2	23
Chesterfield	Tr	02.77	76-77	30	4	8
Blackburn Rov.	Sparta Rotterdam (Neth)	07.79	79	5	4	1
Bury	Frecheville C.A.	09.82	82	26	8	9
Chester C. (N/C)	R.C. Mechelen (Bel)	09.83	83	9	0	5
Stockport Co. (N/C)	Blackpool (N/C)	02.84	83	0	1	0
PARKER Stuart Kevin						
Nantwich, 13 April, 1963						(G)
Wrexham	Jnrs	08.81	82-84	31	0	0
PARKER Thomas Robertson						
Hartlepool, 13 February, 1924 Died 1996						(IF)
Ipswich T.		08.46	46-56	428	-	86
PARKER Walter						
Doncaster, 28 June, 1929						(FB)
Hull C.	Jnrs	08.47				
Crewe Alex.	Tr	08.51	51-55	56	-	0
PARKER William						
Liverpool, 15 August, 1925						(OL)
Reading	Runcorn	06.50	50-52	32	-	6
Swindon T.	Tr	02.53	52	10	-	0
Exeter C.	Tr	07.53	53	18	-	2
PARKER William Frederick						
Liverpool, 29 March, 1932						(HB)
Liverpool	Burscough	04.53				
Southport	Shelbourne	07.59	59	9	-	0
PARKER William Thomas						
Bolsover, 6 October, 1920 Died 1953						(G)
Crewe Alex.		07.47	47-48	18	-	0
PARKES Alan						
Hartlepool, 12 January, 1929						(CF)
Charlton Ath.	Murton Colly	10.49				
Darlington		03.55	54	1	-	0
PARKES Barry Joseph						
Hartlepool, 21 January, 1940						(IF)
Hartlepool U.	Easington Colly	11.60	60-62	29	-	7
PARKES Henry (Harry) Arthur						
Birmingham, 4 January, 1920						(FB)
Aston Villa	Boldmere St Michael	04.39	46-54	320	-	3

League Club	Source	Date Signed	Seasons Played	Apps	Subs	Gls
PARKES Philip Arthur						
West Bromwich, 14 July, 1947						(G)
Wolverhampton W.	Jnrs	09.64	66-77	303	0	0
PARKES Phillip Benjamin Neil Frederick						
Sedgley, 8 August, 1950 Eu21-1/Eu23-6/E 'B'/E-1						(G)
Walsall	Jnrs	01.68	68-69	52	0	0
Queens Park R.	Tr	06.70	70-78	344	0	0
West Ham U.	Tr	02.79	78-89	344	0	0
Ipswich T.	Tr	08.90	90	3	0	0
PARKES Sidney						
Hartlepool, 20 September, 1919 Died 1989						(G)
Hartlepool U.	Hetton U.	08.46	46-47	6	-	0
PARKES Tony						
Sheffield, 5 May, 1949						(M)
Blackburn Rov.	Buxton	05.70	70-80	345	5	38
PARKHILL James Archibald						
Belfast, 27 July, 1934						(G)
Exeter C.	Cliftonville	09.63	63	1	-	0
PARKHOUSE Richard McDonald						
Calne, 30 August, 1914 Died 1992						(FB)
Swindon T.	Calne T.	10.35	35-46	26	-	0
PARKIN Albert Geoffrey						
Mansfield, 11 April, 1928						(F)
Derby Co.	Jnrs	05.46	49	9	-	0
PARKIN Brian						
Birkenhead, 12 October, 1965						(G)
Oldham Ath.	Jnrs	03.83	83-84	6	0	0
Crewe Alex.	Tr	11.84	84-87	98	0	0
Crystal Palace	Tr	06.88	88-89	20	0	0
Bristol Rov.	Tr	11.89	89-95	241	0	0
Wycombe W.	Tr	07.96	96-97	25	0	0
PARKIN Derek						
Newcastle, 2 January, 1948 Eu23-5/EF Lge						(RB)
Huddersfield T.	Jnrs	05.65	64-67	60	1	1
Wolverhampton W.	Tr	02.68	67-81	500	1	6
Stoke C.	Tr	03.82	81-82	40	0	0
PARKIN Herbert Buttery						
Sheffield, 10 April, 1920 Died 1992						(FB)
Sheffield U.		04.42	47-50	35	-	0
Chesterfield	Tr	08.51	51-52	55	-	0
PARKIN Maurice						
Sheffield, 8 September, 1949						(FB)
Leeds U.	App	10.67				
Shrewsbury T.	Tr	07.68	68	4	1	0
PARKIN Stephen John						
Mansfield, 7 November, 1965 E Sch/E Yth/Eu21-5						(M/LB)
Stoke C.	App	11.83	82-88	104	9	5
West Bromwich A.	Tr	06.89	89-91	44	4	2
Mansfield T.	Tr	07.92	92-95	84	3	3
PARKIN Thomas Aichison						
Gateshead, 1 February, 1956						(M)
Ipswich T.	App	12.73	77-86	52	18	0
Grimsby T.	L	03.76	75	6	0	0
Peterborough U.	L	07.76	76	3	0	0
PARKIN Timothy John						
Penrith, 31 December, 1957						(CD)
Blackburn Rov.	App	03.76	76-78	13	0	0
Bristol Rov.	F.K. Malmo (Swe)	08.81	81-85	205	1	12
Swindon T.	Tr	07.86	86-89	109	1	6
Port Vale	Tr	12.89	89-91	41	7	1
Shrewsbury T.	L	09.91	91	5	0	0
Darlington	Tr	08.92	92	40	0	2
PARKINSON Alan						
Normanton, 5 May, 1932						(CF)
Bradford P. A.	Jnrs	10.50	51-54	13	-	4
PARKINSON Alan						
Dagenham, 12 April, 1945						(G)
Leyton Orient (Am)	Aveley	03.67	66	1	0	0
PARKINSON Alfred						
Camden Town, 30 April, 1922						(WH)
Queens Park R.		09.43	46-50	76	-	5

League Club	Source	Date Signed	Seasons Played	Apps	Subs	Gls
PARKINSON Allan Arnold						
Longton (Lancs), 19 July, 1933						(FB)
Southport	Leyland Motors	08.53	53-58	106	-	0
PARKINSON Andrew James						
South Africa, 5 May, 1959						(F)
Newcastle U.	Highlands Park (SA)	03.78	77-78	0	3	0
Peterborough U.	Tr	08.79	79	12	1	5
PARKINSON Andrew John						
Liverpool, 27 May, 1979						(F)
Tranmere Rov.	Liverpool (YT)	04.97	97	8	10	1
PARKINSON Eric						
Longridge, 14 December, 1930						(HB)
Preston N. E.	Jnrs	02.51				
Southport	Tr	06.56	57	4	-	0
PARKINSON Gary Anthony						
Thornaby, 10 January, 1968						(RB)
Middlesbrough	Everton (Jnrs)	01.86	86-92	194	8	5
Southend U.	L	10.92	92	6	0	0
Bolton W.	Tr	03.93	92-93	1	2	0
Burnley	Tr	01.94	93-96	134	1	4
Preston N.E.	Tr	05.97	97	44	1	5
PARKINSON John						
Trimdon, 2 June, 1953						(WH)
Hartlepool U. (Am)	Trimdon Jnrs	09.71	71	1	0	0
PARKINSON Joseph Simon						
Eccles, 11 June, 1971						(M)
Wigan Ath.	YT	03.89	88-92	115	4	6
Bournemouth	Tr	07.93	93	30	0	1
Everton	Tr	03.94	94-96	88	2	3
PARKINSON Keith James						
Edinburgh, 28 January, 1956						(CD)
Leeds U.	App	02.73	75-80	25	6	0
Hull C.	L	11.81	81	0	1	0
Doncaster Rov. (N/C)	Tr	01.82	81	5	0	0
PARKINSON Noel David						
Hull, 16 November, 1959 E Yth						(W)
Ipswich T.	App	12.76				
Bristol Rov.	L	11.79	79	5	0	1
Brentford	L	02.80	79	9	1	0
Mansfield T.	Tr	07.80	80-81	66	4	13
Scunthorpe U.	Tr	08.82	82-83	39	2	7
Colchester U.	Tr	08.84	84-85	79	0	13
PARKINSON Philip John						
Chorley, 1 December, 1967						(M)
Southampton	App	12.85				
Bury	Tr	03.88	87-91	133	12	5
Reading	Tr	07.92	92-97	192	23	8
PARKINSON Stephen						
Lincoln, 27 August, 1974						(M)
Lincoln C.	YT	05.93	92-93	1	4	0
PARKINSON Stuart George						
Fleetwood, 18 February, 1976						(M)
Blackpool	Preston N.E. (YT)	03.94	94	0	1	0
PARKS Albert						
Lurgan (NI), 9 February, 1926						(IF)
Notts Co.	Glenavon	11.45	46-47	30	-	4
PARKS Anthony						
Hackney, 28 January, 1963						(G)
Tottenham H.	App	09.80	81-87	37	0	0
Oxford U.	L	10.86	86	5	0	0
Gillingham	L	09.87	87	2	0	0
Brentford	Tr	08.88	88-90	71	0	0
Fulham	Tr	02.91	90	2	0	0
West Ham U.	Tr	08.91	91	6	0	0
Stoke C.	Tr	08.92	92	2	0	0
Blackpool	Falkirk	09.96				
Burnley	Tr	08.97				
Doncaster Rov.	L	02.98	97	6	0	0
PARKS John Alfred						
Wath, 14 September, 1943						(CF)
Sheffield U.	App	11.60	63	1	-	0
Halifax T.	Tr	09.66	66-67	40	0	14

PARLANE Derek James
Helensburgh, 5 May, 1953 Su21-1/Su23-5/S-12 (F)

League Club	Source	Date Signed	Seasons Played	Apps	Subs	Gls
Leeds U.	Glasgow Rangers	03.80	79-82	45	5	10
Manchester C.	Hong Kong	08.83	83-84	47	1	20
Swansea C.	Tr	01.85	84	21	0	3
Rochdale	Racing Jet (Bel)	12.86	86-87	42	0	10

PARLOUR Raymond
Romford, 7 March, 1973 Eu21-12/E 'B' (M)

League Club	Source	Date Signed	Seasons Played	Apps	Subs	Gls
Arsenal	YT	03.91	91-97	135	35	11

PARMENTER Steven James
Chelmsford, 22 January, 1977 (W)

League Club	Source	Date Signed	Seasons Played	Apps	Subs	Gls
Queens Park R.	Southend U. (YT)	05.95				
Bristol Rov.	Tr	07.96	96-97	11	7	2

PARMENTER Terence Leslie
Romford, 21 October, 1947 (W)

League Club	Source	Date Signed	Seasons Played	Apps	Subs	Gls
Fulham	App	11.64	64-68	18	1	1
Leyton Orient	Tr	02.69	68-70	34	3	3
Gillingham	Tr	08.71	71-72	48	1	0

PARNABY Thomas William
South Shields, 6 January, 1922 (OL)

League Club	Source	Date Signed	Seasons Played	Apps	Subs	Gls
Plymouth Arg.		07.39				
Oldham Ath.	Tr	02.47	47	7	-	1

PARNELL Dennis Russell
Farnborough, 17 January, 1940 E Yth (OL)

League Club	Source	Date Signed	Seasons Played	Apps	Subs	Gls
Aldershot	West Bromwich A. (Am)	08.58	58-60	66	-	11
Norwich C.	Tr	07.61	61	2	-	0

PARNELL Francis William
Tranmere, 4 November, 1935 (F)

League Club	Source	Date Signed	Seasons Played	Apps	Subs	Gls
Tranmere Rov.		01.56	55-56	4	-	3

PARNELL Roy
Birkenhead, 8 October, 1943 (FB)

League Club	Source	Date Signed	Seasons Played	Apps	Subs	Gls
Everton	Jnrs	10.60	60-63	3	-	0
Tranmere Rov.	Tr	08.64	64-66	105	0	2
Bury	Tr	02.67	66-69	97	0	2

PARODI Leslie Vincent
Lambeth, 1 April, 1954 (FB)

League Club	Source	Date Signed	Seasons Played	Apps	Subs	Gls
Bournemouth	Slough T.	09.72	73-74	45	4	2

PARR Gordon John
Bristol, 6 December, 1938 (WH)

League Club	Source	Date Signed	Seasons Played	Apps	Subs	Gls
Bristol C.	Jnrs	02.57	57-71	281	6	4

PARR Henry
Newark, 23 October, 1915 E Amat (WH)

League Club	Source	Date Signed	Seasons Played	Apps	Subs	Gls
Lincoln C. (Am)	Leyton Orient (Am)	08.46	46-49	112	-	13

PARR Jack
Derby, 21 November, 1920 Died 1985 (FB)

League Club	Source	Date Signed	Seasons Played	Apps	Subs	Gls
Derby Co.	Long Eaton St Peters	03.38	46-52	112	-	0
Shrewsbury T.	Tr	07.53	53-55	112	-	0

PARR John Barry
Weston-super-Mare, 23 November, 1942 (G)

League Club	Source	Date Signed	Seasons Played	Apps	Subs	Gls
Nottingham F.	Ransome & Marles	11.62	63	1	-	0

PARR Stephen Valentine
Bamber Bridge, 22 December, 1926 (FB)

League Club	Source	Date Signed	Seasons Played	Apps	Subs	Gls
Liverpool	Farrington Vic.	05.48	51-52	20	-	0
Exeter C.	Tr	05.55	55-56	8	-	0
Rochdale	Tr	12.56	56-57	16	-	1

PARR Trevor William
Bradford, 21 December, 1961 (F)

League Club	Source	Date Signed	Seasons Played	Apps	Subs	Gls
Birmingham C.	App	12.79				
Bradford C.	Tr	07.80				
Huddersfield T.	Tr	11.80				
Peterborough U. (N/C)	Thackley	11.84	84	0	1	0

PARRIS George Michael
Barking, 11 September, 1964 E Sch (M)

League Club	Source	Date Signed	Seasons Played	Apps	Subs	Gls
West Ham U.	App	09.82	84-92	211	28	12
Birmingham C.	Tr	03.93	92-94	36	3	1
Brentford	L	08.94	94	5	0	0
Bristol C.	L	12.94	94	6	0	0
Brighton & H.A.	L	02.95	94	18	0	2
Brighton & H.A.	Norrkoping (Swe)	09.95	95-96	55	1	3
Southend U. (N/C)	Tr	08.97	97	1	0	0

PARRISH Donald Arthur
Bilston, 22 November, 1944 (F)

League Club	Source	Date Signed	Seasons Played	Apps	Subs	Gls
Wrexham	Jnrs	06.63	62-65	4	0	0

PARRISH Sean
Wrexham, 14 March, 1972 (M)

League Club	Source	Date Signed	Seasons Played	Apps	Subs	Gls
Shrewsbury T.	YT	07.90	89-90	1	2	0
Doncaster Rov.	Telford U.	05.94	94-95	64	2	8
Northampton T.	Tr	08.96	96-97	49	2	9

PARROTT John Frank
Scunthorpe, 5 June, 1934 (IF)

League Club	Source	Date Signed	Seasons Played	Apps	Subs	Gls
Scunthorpe U.		12.55	55	1	-	0

PARRY Anthony John
Burton, 8 September, 1945 (CD)

League Club	Source	Date Signed	Seasons Played	Apps	Subs	Gls
Hartlepool U.	Burton A.	11.65	65-71	181	8	5
Derby Co.	Tr	01.72	72	4	2	0
Mansfield T.	L	01.74	73	0	1	0

PARRY Colin
Stockport, 16 February, 1941 (CH)

League Club	Source	Date Signed	Seasons Played	Apps	Subs	Gls
Stockport Co.	Vernon Park	07.62	62-67	132	1	0
Bradford C.	L	09.65	65	5	0	0
Rochdale	Tr	07.68	68-71	154	2	1

PARRY Cyril
Derby, 13 December, 1937 E Sch (OR)

League Club	Source	Date Signed	Seasons Played	Apps	Subs	Gls
Notts Co.	Derby Co. (Am)	05.55	57-58	12	-	2

PARRY David Edward
Southport, 11February, 1948 (W)

League Club	Source	Date Signed	Seasons Played	Apps	Subs	Gls
Blackpool	App	12.65				
Tranmere Rov.	Tr	07.67	67	3	0	0
Halifax T.	Tr	09.68	68	2	0	0

PARRY John (Jack)
Derby, 29 July, 1931 (IF)

League Club	Source	Date Signed	Seasons Played	Apps	Subs	Gls
Derby Co.	Jnrs	07.48	48-65	482	1	105

PARRY John Ernan
Holywell, 4 September, 1939 (FB)

League Club	Source	Date Signed	Seasons Played	Apps	Subs	Gls
Liverpool	Jnrs	09.56				
Doncaster Rov.	Tr	09.61	61	14	-	0

PARRY Brinley **John (Jack)**
Pontardawe, 11 January, 1924 W-1 (G)

League Club	Source	Date Signed	Seasons Played	Apps	Subs	Gls
Swansea C.	Clydach	09.46	46-50	98	-	0
Ipswich T.	Tr	08.51	51-54	138	-	0

PARRY Leslie Irvine
Wallasey, 13 November, 1953 (D)

League Club	Source	Date Signed	Seasons Played	Apps	Subs	Gls
Tranmere Rov.	Jnrs	09.72	72-83	254	4	4

PARRY Mark
Wrexham, 21 May, 1970 (W)

League Club	Source	Date Signed	Seasons Played	Apps	Subs	Gls
Chester C.	YT	●	87	4	1	1

PARRY Oswald
Merthyr Tydfil, 16 August, 1908 Died 1991 (FB)

League Club	Source	Date Signed	Seasons Played	Apps	Subs	Gls
Crystal Palace	Wimbledon	05.31	31-35	141	-	0
Ipswich T.	Tr	06.36	38-48	104	-	0

PARRY Raymond Alan
Derby, 19 January, 1936 E Sch/E Yth/Eu23-4/EF Lge/E-2 (IF)

League Club	Source	Date Signed	Seasons Played	Apps	Subs	Gls
Bolton W.	Jnrs	01.53	51-60	270	-	68
Blackpool	Tr	10.60	60-64	128	-	27
Bury	Tr	10.64	64-71	136	10	17

PARRY Stephen
Wakefield, 11 December, 1956 (G)

League Club	Source	Date Signed	Seasons Played	Apps	Subs	Gls
Barnsley	App	12.74	73-74	5	0	0

PARRY William
Blaenau Ffestiniog, 18 February, 1933 (FB)

League Club	Source	Date Signed	Seasons Played	Apps	Subs	Gls
Tottenham H.	Portmadoc	09.53				
Gillingham	Tr	07.55	55-60	200	-	4

PARSELLE Norman John
Newport, 8 January, 1970 (M)

League Club	Source	Date Signed	Seasons Played	Apps	Subs	Gls
Newport Co.	YT	●	87	4	6	0

PARSLEY Neil Robert
Liverpool, 25 April, 1966 (FB)

League Club	Source	Date Signed	Seasons Played	Apps	Subs	Gls
Leeds U.	Witton A.	11.88				
Chester C.	L	12.89	89	6	0	0
Huddersfield T.	Tr	07.90	90-92	55	2	0
Doncaster Rov.	L	02.91	90	2	1	0
West Bromwich A.	Tr	09.93	93-94	38	5	0
Exeter C.	Tr	08.95	95	29	3	0

PARSLEY Wilfred **Norman**
Shildon, 28 November, 1923 Died 1993 (WH)

League Club	Source	Date Signed	Seasons Played	Apps	Subs	Gls
Darlington	Shildon Wks	10.45	46-52	161	-	14

League Club	Source	Date Signed	Seasons Played	Apps	Subs	Gls
PARSONS Dennis Ronald						
Birmingham, 29 May, 1925 Died 1980						(G)
Wolverhampton W.	B.S.A. Cycles	11.44	48-51	23	-	0
Aston Villa	Hereford U.	09.52	52-54	36	-	0
PARSONS Derek John						
Hammersmith, 24 October, 1929						(IF)
Queens Park R.		02.50	52	2	-	1
PARSONS Edward John						
Bristol, 22 March, 1928 Died 1996						(CF)
Bristol Rov.	Frome T.	08.49	49	5	-	2
PARSONS Eric George						
Worthing, 9 November, 1923 E 'B'						(OR)
West Ham U.	Jnrs	10.43	46-50	145	-	34
Chelsea	Tr	12.50	50-56	158	-	37
Brentford	Tr	11.56	56-60	118	-	18
PARSONS Frank Ronald						
Amersham, 29 October, 1947						(G)
Crystal Palace	Jnrs	07.65	66	4	0	0
Cardiff C.	Tr	08.70	70-72	17	0	0
Reading	Tr	09.74	74	1	0	0
PARSONS Geoffrey Roy						
Belper, 2 August, 1931 Died 1996						(OL)
Mansfield T.	Jnrs	05.51				
Chesterfield	Tr	07.52	52	1	-	0
PARSONS John Stuart						
Cardiff, 10 December, 1950 W Sch						(F)
Cardiff C.	App	12.68	70-72	7	8	6
Bournemouth	Tr	02.73	72-74	7	1	1
Newport Co.	Tr	03.75	74-76	57	3	23
PARSONS Lindsay William						
Bristol, 20 March, 1946						(LB)
Bristol Rov.	App	04.64	63-76	354	5	0
Torquay U.	Tr	08.77	77-78	56	0	0
PARSONS Mark Christopher						
Luton, 24 February, 1975						(RB)
Northampton T.	YT	07.93	91-93	51	0	0
PARSONS Stephen Paul James						
Hammersmith, 7 October, 1957						(M)
Wimbledon	Walton & Hersham	12.77	77-79	91	3	19
Leyton Orient	Tr	03.80	79-80	36	0	6
PARSONS Stuart						
Staveley, 24 May, 1948						(WH)
Chesterfield	Jnrs	08.67	66	1	0	0
PARTNER Andrew Neil						
Colchester, 21 October, 1974						(D)
Colchester U.	YT	06.93	92-94	0	2	0
PARTON Jeffrey John						
Swansea, 24 February, 1953 W Sch/Wu23-3						(G)
Burnley	App	03.70	71-73	3	0	0
Northampton T.	Tr	07.75	75-77	25	0	0
PARTRIDGE Brendan David						
Manchester, 17 September, 1941						(OL)
Stockport Co.		11.60	60-61	31	-	6
Darlington	Tr	07.62	62	3	-	0
PARTRIDGE Cyril						
York, 12 October, 1931						(OL)
Queens Park R.		08.54				
Rotherham U.		08.57	57	7	-	2
PARTRIDGE Donald						
Bolton, 22 October, 1925						(HB)
Rochdale	Farnworth	10.45	46-55	103	-	2
PARTRIDGE John Thomas						
Chesterfield, 14 September, 1962						(LB)
Chesterfield	App	09.80	81-82	34	4	0
Mansfield T.	L	09.83	83	1	0	0
PARTRIDGE Malcolm						
Chesterfield, 28 August, 1950						(F)
Mansfield T.	App	09.68	67-70	65	2	20
Leicester C.	Tr	09.70	70-73	25	11	4
Charlton Ath.	L	01.72	71	1	1	0
Grimsby T.	Tr	03.75	74-78	134	4	25
Scunthorpe U.	Tr	07.79	79-81	91	6	21
PARTRIDGE Maurice Edward						
Birmingham, 20 February, 1941						(FB)
Birmingham C.	Jnrs	03.58				
Walsall	Tr	07.61	61-62	3	-	0
PARTRIDGE Scott Malcolm						
Leicester, 13 October, 1974						(W)
Bradford C.	YT	07.92	92-93	0	5	0
Bristol C.	Tr	02.94	93-96	24	33	7
Torquay U.	L	10.95	95	5	0	2
Plymouth Arg.	L	01.96	95	6	1	2
Scarborough	L	03.96	95	5	2	0
Cardiff C.	Tr	02.97	96-97	29	8	2
Torquay U.	Tr	03.98	97	4	1	0
PASCOE Colin James						
Bridgend, 9 April, 1965 W Sch/W Yth/Wu21-4/W-10						(LW)
Swansea C.	App	04.83	82-87	167	7	39
Sunderland	Tr	03.88	87-91	116	10	22
Swansea C.	L	07.92	92	15	0	4
Swansea C.	Tr	08.93	93-95	72	9	11
Blackpool (N/C)	Tr	03.96	95	0	1	0
PASCOE Jason						
Jarrow, 15 February, 1970						(D)
Northampton T.	Boston U.	06.94	94	11	4	0
PASCOLO Marco						
Sion, Switzerland, 9 May, 1966 Swiss Int						(G)
Nottingham F.	Cagliari (It)	07.97	97	5	0	0
PASHLEY Robert Wilminson						
Sheffield, 9 September, 1937						(IF)
Sheffield U.	Sheffield Wed. (Am)	01.56				
Scunthorpe U.	Gainsborough Trin.	05.59	59	3	-	1
Barrow	Tr	06.60	60	26	-	2
PASHLEY Terence						
Chesterfield, 11 October, 1956 E Sch						(LB)
Burnley	App	10.73	75-77	16	2	0
Blackpool	Tr	08.78	78-82	201	0	7
Bury	Tr	08.83	83-88	205	12	5
PASKIN William **John**						
South Africa, 1 February, 1962						(F)
West Bromwich A.	K.V. Kortrijk (Bel)	08.88	88	14	11	5
Wolverhampton W.	Tr	06.89	89-91	21	13	3
Stockport Co.	L	09.91	91	3	2	1
Birmingham C.	L	11.91	91	8	2	3
Shrewsbury T.	L	02.92	91	1	0	0
Wrexham	Tr	02.92	91-93	28	23	11
Bury	Tr	07.94	94-95	15	23	8
PASSEY Peter Thord John						
Birmingham, 13 July, 1952 E Yth						(D)
Birmingham C.	App	07.69				
Newport Co.	Tr	01.72	71-75	136	0	2
PASSMOOR Thomas						
Chester-le-Street, 12 February, 1937						(CH)
Sunderland	Jnrs	05.54				
Scunthorpe U.	South Shields	05.59	59-63	27	-	0
Carlisle U.	Tr	12.63	63-69	242	2	0
PASSMORE Edward						
Moorsley, 28 April, 1922 Died 1988						(CF)
Swansea C.	Portsmouth (Am)	02.44	46	6	-	2
Gateshead	Tr	04.47	46-49	41	-	26
PATCHING Martin						
Rotherham, 1 November, 1958 E Sch/E Yth						(M)
Wolverhampton W.	App	03.76	75-79	78	12	10
Watford	Tr	12.79	79-83	24	1	3
Northampton T.	L	01.83	82	6	0	1
PATE Alexander (Sandy) Montgomerie						
Lennoxtown, 15 August, 1944						(RB)
Watford	Renfrew Jnrs	03.65	64-66	14	1	0
Mansfield T.	Tr	10.67	67-77	412	1	2
PATERSON Alexander						
Duntocher, 17 March, 1922 Died 1992						(WH)
New Brighton	Alloa Ath.	07.46	46-47	67	-	10
Stockport Co.	Tr	03.48	47-52	160	-	7
PATERSON George Denholm						
Denny, 26 September, 1914 Died 1985 SF Lge/S-1						(WH)
Brentford	Glasgow Celtic	10.46	46-49	62	-	0

PATERSON George Longmore
Aberdeen, 19 December, 1916 Died 1996 (IF)

League Club	Source	Date Signed	Seasons Played	Apps	Subs	Gls
Liverpool	Russell's F.C.	05.37	38	2	-	0
Swindon T.	Tr	10.46	46-49	53	-	7

PATERSON Jamie Ryan
Dumfries, 26 April, 1973 (W)

League Club	Source	Date Signed	Seasons Played	Apps	Subs	Gls
Halifax T.	YT	07.91	90-92	34	10	5
Scunthorpe U.	Falkirk	10.95	95-96	34	21	2

PATERSON Scott
Aberdeen, 13 May, 1972 (CD)

League Club	Source	Date Signed	Seasons Played	Apps	Subs	Gls
Liverpool	Cove R.	03.92				
Bristol C.	Tr	07.94	94-97	40	10	1
Cardiff C.	L	11.97	97	5	0	0

PATERSON Steven William
Spennymoor, 8 April, 1958 (F)

League Club	Source	Date Signed	Seasons Played	Apps	Subs	Gls
Manchester U.	Nairn Co.	07.75	76-79	3	3	0

PATERSON Thomas
Ashington, 30 March, 1954 (F)

League Club	Source	Date Signed	Seasons Played	Apps	Subs	Gls
Middlesbrough	Leicester C. (Am)	09.74	74	1	0	0
Bournemouth	Tr	04.76	76-77	45	12	10
Darlington	Tr	06.78	78	6	1	2

PATERSON Thomas
Lochore, 3 April, 1927 (IF)

League Club	Source	Date Signed	Seasons Played	Apps	Subs	Gls
Leicester C.	Lochgelly Albert	03.48	48-49	17	-	4
Newcastle U.	Tr	06.50	50-51	2	-	0
Watford	Tr	07.52	52-54	45	-	7

PATERSON Toby Lee
Dumfries, 15 May, 1971 (D)

League Club	Source	Date Signed	Seasons Played	Apps	Subs	Gls
Halifax T.	YT	●	88	0	1	0

PATERSON William
Bellshill, 6 October, 1927 (CF)

League Club	Source	Date Signed	Seasons Played	Apps	Subs	Gls
Accrington St.	Morton	08.49	49	1	-	0

PATES Colin George
Carshalton, 10 August, 1961 E Yth (CD)

League Club	Source	Date Signed	Seasons Played	Apps	Subs	Gls
Chelsea	App	07.79	79-88	280	1	10
Charlton Ath.	Tr	10.88	88-89	37	1	0
Arsenal	Tr	01.90	89-92	12	9	0
Brighton & H.A.	L	03.91	90	17	0	0
Brighton & H.A.	Tr	08.93	93-94	49	1	0

PATMORE Warren James
Kingsbury, 14 August, 1971 (F)

League Club	Source	Date Signed	Seasons Played	Apps	Subs	Gls
Cambridge U. (N/C)	Northwood	03.92	92	1	0	0
Millwall	Bashley	08.93	93	0	1	0
Northampton T.	Tr	12.93	93-94	12	9	2

PATON David Samuel Craig
Kilwinning, 13 December, 1943 (CH)

League Club	Source	Date Signed	Seasons Played	Apps	Subs	Gls
Southampton	St Mirren	07.63	63-67	13	0	0
Aldershot	Tr	11.69	69-70	30	0	0

PATON John Aloyoius
Glasgow, 2 April, 1923 (OL)

League Club	Source	Date Signed	Seasons Played	Apps	Subs	Gls
Chelsea	Glasgow Celtic	11.46	46	18	-	3
Brentford	Glasgow Celtic	09.49	49-51	90	-	14
Watford	Tr	07.52	52-54	84	-	17

PATON Robert (Danny) Simpson Reid
West Calder, 27 January, 1936 (IF)

League Club	Source	Date Signed	Seasons Played	Apps	Subs	Gls
Oxford U.	Hearts	07.64	64	2	-	1

PATON Thomas Gracie
Saltcoats, 22 December, 1918 Died 1991 (WH)

League Club	Source	Date Signed	Seasons Played	Apps	Subs	Gls
Wolverhampton W.	Ardeer Rec.	06.37				
Swansea C.	Tr	10.38	38	6	-	0
Bournemouth	Tr	02.39	38-47	46	-	8
Watford	Tr	01.48	47-51	141	-	1

PATRICK Alfred
York, 25 September, 1921 (CF)

League Club	Source	Date Signed	Seasons Played	Apps	Subs	Gls
York C.	New Earswick	09.46	46-52	228	-	109

PATRICK Bert
Kilsyth, 26 April, 1946 (FB)

League Club	Source	Date Signed	Seasons Played	Apps	Subs	Gls
Preston N. E.	Jnrs	08.63	64-69	50	0	1
Barrow	Tr	07.71	71	34	0	1

PATRICK Matthew
Slamannan, 13 June, 1919 (W/WH)

League Club	Source	Date Signed	Seasons Played	Apps	Subs	Gls
York C.	Cowdenbeath	09.40	46-53	248	-	47

PATRICK Roy
Overseal (Dy), 4 December, 1935 (FB)

League Club	Source	Date Signed	Seasons Played	Apps	Subs	Gls
Derby Co.	Jnrs	02.52	52-55	49	-	0
Nottingham F.	Tr	05.59	59-60	57	-	0
Southampton	Tr	06.61	61-62	31	-	0
Exeter C.	Tr	03.63	62-64	50	-	0

PATRICK William Cecil Gibson
Lochgelly, 12 March, 1932 (IF)

League Club	Source	Date Signed	Seasons Played	Apps	Subs	Gls
Coventry C.	Snowdon Colly	11.54	55-57	44	-	6
Gillingham	Tr	06.58	58-59	47	-	13

PATTERSON Darren James
Belfast, 15 October, 1969 NI YthNIu21-1/NI 'B'/NI-11 (CD)

League Club	Source	Date Signed	Seasons Played	Apps	Subs	Gls
West Bromwich A.	YT	07.88				
Wigan Ath.	Tr	04.89	89-91	69	28	6
Crystal Palace	Tr	07.92	94	22	0	1
Luton T.	Tr	08.95	95-97	52	4	0
Preston N.E.	L	10.96	96	2	0	0

PATTERSON Gary
Newcastle, 27 November, 1972 (M)

League Club	Source	Date Signed	Seasons Played	Apps	Subs	Gls
Notts Co.	YT	07.91				
Shrewsbury T.	Tr	07.93	93-94	52	5	2
Wycombe W.	Tr	12.94	94-96	46	13	2
Barnet	L	01.97	96	3	0	0
Chesterfield	L	02.97	96	7	2	0

PATTERSON George Thomas
Sunderland, 15 September, 1934 (WH)

League Club	Source	Date Signed	Seasons Played	Apps	Subs	Gls
Hull C.	Silksworth Jnrs	10.52	54-55	7	-	1
York C.	South Shields	05.57	57-59	57	-	4
Hartlepool U.	Tr	06.60	60	18	-	1

PATTERSON Ian Daniel
Chatham, 4 April, 1973 (CD)

League Club	Source	Date Signed	Seasons Played	Apps	Subs	Gls
Sunderland	YT	03.92				
Burnley	Tr	08.93	93	0	1	0
Wigan Ath.	Tr	03.94	93	2	2	0

PATTERSON John George
Cramlington, 6 July, 1922 (G)

League Club	Source	Date Signed	Seasons Played	Apps	Subs	Gls
Blackburn Rov.	North Shields	04.45	48-56	107	-	0

PATTERSON Mark
Leeds, 13 September, 1968 (RB/M)

League Club	Source	Date Signed	Seasons Played	Apps	Subs	Gls
Carlisle U.	YT	08.87	86-87	19	3	0
Derby Co.	Tr	11.87	88-92	41	10	3
Plymouth Arg.	Tr	07.93	93-96	131	3	3
Gillingham	Tr	10.97	97	23	0	0

PATTERSON Mark Andrew
Darwen, 24 May, 1965 (M)

League Club	Source	Date Signed	Seasons Played	Apps	Subs	Gls
Blackburn Rov.	App	05.83	83-87	89	12	20
Preston N. E.	Tr	06.88	88-89	54	1	19
Bury	Tr	02.90	89-90	42	0	10
Bolton W.	Tr	01.90	90-95	158	11	11
Sheffield U.	Tr	12.95	95-97	72	2	4
Southend U.	L	03.97	96	4	0	0
Bury	Tr	12.97	97	18	0	2

PATTERSON Robert Alexander
Newcastle, 12 March, 1935 (G)

League Club	Source	Date Signed	Seasons Played	Apps	Subs	Gls
Gateshead	Stanley U.	03.59	58-59	26	-	0

PATTERSON Ronald Lindsay
Seaham, 30 October, 1929 (FB)

League Club	Source	Date Signed	Seasons Played	Apps	Subs	Gls
Middlesbrough	Whitehall Jnrs	06.49	51	1	-	0
Northampton T.	Tr	06.52	52-61	300	-	5

PATTERSON William Alexander Kennedy
Kinlochleven, 25 February, 1930 S 'B' (CH)

League Club	Source	Date Signed	Seasons Played	Apps	Subs	Gls
Doncaster Rov.	Ransome & Marles	03.50	50-54	113	-	0
Newcastle U.	Tr	10.54	54-57	22	-	1

PATTIMORE Michael Richard
Newport, 15 March, 1979 W Yth (CD)

League Club	Source	Date Signed	Seasons Played	Apps	Subs	Gls
Swindon T.	YT	07.97	96-97	0	3	0

PATTISON Frank McKay
Barrhead, 23 December, 1930 (W)

League Club	Source	Date Signed	Seasons Played	Apps	Subs	Gls
Barnsley	Alloa Ath.	12.51	51-54	29	-	5

PATTISON John Morris
Glasgow, 19 December, 1918 (OL)

League Club	Source	Date Signed	Seasons Played	Apps	Subs	Gls
Queens Park R.	Motherwell	05.37	37-49	92	-	26
Leyton Orient	Tr	02.50	49-50	43	-	10

League Club	Source	Date Signed	Seasons Played	Career Record Apps	Subs	Gls
PATTISON John William						
Portsmouth, 23 February, 1925 Died 1993						(RH)
Reading	Portsmouth C.S.	07.45	46	2	-	0
PATTON Aaron Anthony						
London, 27 February, 1979						(LB)
Wycombe W.	YT	07.97	97	0	1	0
PAUL Anthony George						
Islington, 6 April, 1961						(M)
Crystal Palace	App	04.78	80	0	1	0
PAUL David Dryburgh						
Kirkcaldy, 19 February, 1936 S Sch						(G)
Derby Co.	Jnrs	02.53	53-55	2	-	0
PAUL Ian Kevin						
Wolverhampton, 23 January, 1961						(M)
Walsall	App	08.78	77-80	68	2	9
PAUL Martin Leighton						
Clitheroe, 2 February, 1975						(F)
Bristol Rov.	YT	07.93	93-95	11	11	1
Doncaster Rov.	Tr	07.96				
PAUL Roy						
Ton Pentre, 18 April, 1920 W-33						(WH)
Swansea C.	Ton Pentre	10.38	46-49	160	-	14
Manchester C.	Tr	07.50	50-56	270	-	9
PAUL Thomas						
Grimsby, 14 May, 1933						(OR)
Grimsby T.		05.55	58	1	-	0
PAULO Pedro Saraiva Antonio						
Portugal, 21 November, 1973						(W)
Darlington (N/C)	Sporting Lisbon (Por)	08.95	95	4	2	0
PAVITT William Ernest						
West Ham, 30 June, 1920 Died 1989						(D)
Fulham	R.A.F. Debden	08.46	49-52	50	-	1
Southend U.	Tr	05.53	53-54	79	-	0
PAWSON Anthony Henry						
Chertsey, 22 August, 1921 E Amat						(W)
Charlton Ath. (Am)	Pegasus	12.51	51-52	2	-	1
PAXTON John William						
Wolverhampton, 24 March, 1928						(FB)
Wolverhampton W.	Jnrs	04.45				
Notts Co.	Tr	05.50	50	2	-	0
PAYE Michael Charles						
Orpington, 30 July, 1966						(D)
Charlton Ath.	App	●	83	2	0	0
PAYNE Albert Charles						
Liverpool, 11 November, 1923						(WH)
Tranmere Rov.		08.46	46-48	10	-	0
PAYNE Brian						
Altrincham, 4 November, 1937						(W)
Huddersfield T.	Jnrs	10.55				
Gillingham	Tr	07.57	57-59	36	-	3
PAYNE Clive Edward						
Aylsham (Nk), 2 March, 1950						(FB)
Norwich C.	App	03.68	68-73	122	3	0
Bournemouth	Tr	12.73	73-75	101	0	3
PAYNE David Ronald						
Croydon, 25 April, 1947 Eu23-1						(D)
Crystal Palace	App	11.64	64-72	281	3	9
Leyton Orient	Tr	08.73	73-77	88	5	0
PAYNE Derek Richard						
Edgware, 26 April, 1967						(M)
Barnet	Hayes	12.88	91-92	50	1	6
Southend U.	Tr	07.93	93	32	3	0
Watford	Tr	07.94	94-95	33	3	1
Peterborough U.	Tr	08.96	96-97	71	2	4
PAYNE Donald						
Swansea, 18 November, 1950						(G)
Swansea C.	Jnrs	12.70	71	11	0	0
Torquay U.	Tr	06.72				
Newport Co.	Tr	08.73	73-74	32	0	0
PAYNE Frank Ernest						
Ipswich, 18 March, 1926						(G)
Derby Co.	Ollerton Colly	10.47				
Hull C.	Tr	08.48				
Lincoln C.	Tr	08.49	49	5	-	0
PAYNE George Henry						
Liverpool, 22 August, 1921 Died 1987						(G)
Tranmere Rov.		04.47	46-60	439	-	0
PAYNE Ian Neil						
Crawley, 19 January, 1977 W Yth						(FB)
Plymouth Arg.	YT	07.95	94	1	0	0
PAYNE Irving (Joe) Ernest Henry						
Briton Ferry, 29 June, 1921						(IF)
Swansea C.	Jnrs	07.38	46-48	53	-	10
Newport Co.	Tr	10.49	49	12	-	1
Scunthorpe U.	Tr	07.50	50	40	-	2
Northampton T.	Tr	08.51	51	32	-	6
PAYNE James						
West Bromwich, 25 May, 1936						(CF)
Walsall		08.55	55	1	-	0
PAYNE James Bolcherson						
Liverpool, 10 March, 1926 E 'B'						(OR)
Liverpool	Bootle A.T.C.	11.44	48-55	224	-	37
Everton	Tr	04.56	55-56	5	-	2
PAYNE Jeremy (Jess)						
Dartford, 7 March, 1958						(CD)
Leicester C.	Jnrs	07.76				
Torquay U.	Tr	12.77	77-78	25	0	1
PAYNE Joseph						
Bolsover, 17 January, 1914, Died 1975 E-1						(CF)
Luton T.	Biggleswade T.	06.34	34-37	72	-	83
Chelsea	Tr	03.38	37-38	36	-	21
West Ham U.	Tr	12.46	46	10	-	6
PAYNE Lee John						
Luton, 12 December, 1966						(LW)
Newcastle U.	Barnet	09.88	88	6	1	0
Reading	Tr	03.89	88-89	25	2	3
PAYNE Mark Ian						
Swindon, 2 September, 1966						(W)
Swindon T.	App	09.84	84	0	3	0
PAYNE Mark Richard Crawford						
Cheltenham, 3 August, 1960						(M)
Stockport Co.	S.C. Cambuur (Neth)	08.88	88-90	77	10	16
Rochdale	Tr	05.91	91-92	58	4	8
PAYNE Russell						
Wigan, 8 July, 1970						(W)
Liverpool	Skelmersdale U.	03.90				
Crewe Alex.	L	10.91	91	3	3	0
PAYNE Stephen John						
Pontefract, 1 August, 1975 E Semi Pro						(CD)
Huddersfield T.	YT	07.93				
Macclesfield T.	Tr	12.94	97	39	0	0
PAYTON Andrew Paul						
Clitheroe, 23 October, 1967						(F)
Hull C.	YT	07.85	86-91	116	28	55
Middlesbrough	Tr	11.91	91	8	11	3
Barnsley	Glasgow Celtic	11.93	93-95	100	8	41
Huddersfield T.	Tr	07.96	96-97	42	1	17
Burnley	Tr	01.98	97	19	0	9
PAYTON Clifford Charles						
Brighton, 16 October, 1935						(IF)
Accrington St.	Wisbech T.	07.56				
Gillingham	Tonbridge	03.59	58-59	24	-	5
PAZ Charquero **Adrian**						
Uruguay, 9 September, 1968 Uruguayan Int						(F)
Ipswich T.	Penarol (Ur)	09.94	94	13	4	1
PEACH David Sidney						
Bedford, 21 January, 1951 Eu21-6						(LB)
Gillingham	App	01.69	69-73	186	1	30
Southampton	Tr	01.74	73-79	221	3	34
Swindon T.	Tr	03.80	79-81	52	1	2
Leyton Orient	Tr	03.82	81-82	47	0	6

PEACH Geoffrey Leonard
Torpoint, 11 October, 1932 (F)

League Club	Source	Date Signed	Seasons Played	Apps	Subs	Gls
Plymouth Arg.	Millwall (Am)	07.56	56	1	-	0

PEACH John (Jack)
Barnsley, 4 April, 1923 (IF)

League Club	Source	Date Signed	Seasons Played	Apps	Subs	Gls
Barnsley	York C. (Am)	11.45				
Hull C.	Tr	10.46	46-47	19	-	2

PEACHEY John Michael
Cambridge, 21 July, 1952 (F)

League Club	Source	Date Signed	Seasons Played	Apps	Subs	Gls
York C.	Hillingdon Borough	08.73	73-74	6	2	3
Barnsley	Tr	11.74	74-78	116	11	31
Darlington	L	12.75	75	5	1	3
Darlington	Tr	03.79	78-79	16	4	6
Plymouth Arg.	Tr	07.80	80	1	2	0

PEACOCK Alan
Middlesbrough, 29 October, 1937 E Yth/E-6 (CF)

League Club	Source	Date Signed	Seasons Played	Apps	Subs	Gls
Middlesbrough	Jnrs	11.54	55-63	218	-	125
Leeds U.	Tr	02.64	63-66	54	0	27
Plymouth Arg.	Tr	10.67	67	11	0	1

PEACOCK Darren
Bristol, 3 February, 1968 (CD)

League Club	Source	Date Signed	Seasons Played	Apps	Subs	Gls
Newport Co.	YT	02.86	85-87	24	4	0
Hereford U.	Tr	03.89	88-90	56	3	5
Queens Park R.	Tr	12.90	90-93	123	3	6
Newcastle U.	Tr	03.94	93-97	131	2	2

PEACOCK Dennis
Lincoln, 19 April, 1953 (G)

League Club	Source	Date Signed	Seasons Played	Apps	Subs	Gls
Nottingham F.	App	04.71	72-74	22	0	0
Walsall	L	03.73	72	10	0	0
Doncaster Rov.	Tr	07.75	75-79	199	0	0
Bolton W.	Tr	03.80	80-81	16	0	0
Doncaster Rov.	Tr	08.82	82-85	130	0	0
Burnley	L	09.85	85	8	0	0

PEACOCK Ernest Anderson
Renfrew, 10 August, 1942 (WH)

League Club	Source	Date Signed	Seasons Played	Apps	Subs	Gls
Workington	Falkirk	01.64	63	1	-	0

PEACOCK Ernest Gilbert
Bristol, 11 December, 1924 Died 1973 (WH)

League Club	Source	Date Signed	Seasons Played	Apps	Subs	Gls
Notts Co.	Syston	03.45				
Bristol C.	Tr	10.46	46-58	343	-	7

PEACOCK Frank Edwin
Farnworth, 17 May, 1945 (LH)

League Club	Source	Date Signed	Seasons Played	Apps	Subs	Gls
Stockport Co.	Blackburn Rov. (Am)	11.64	64	5	-	0

PEACOCK Gavin Keith
Eltham, 18 November, 1967 E Sch/E Yth (M)

League Club	Source	Date Signed	Seasons Played	Apps	Subs	Gls
Queens Park R.	App	11.84	86-87	7	10	1
Gillingham	L	10.87	87	6	0	0
Gillingham	Tr	12.87	87-88	63	1	11
Bournemouth	Tr	07.89	89-90	56	0	8
Newcastle U.	Tr	11.90	90-92	102	3	35
Chelsea	Tr	08.93	93-95	92	11	17
Queens Park R.	Tr	11.96	96-97	65	1	14

PEACOCK George
Pontypool, 10 February, 1924 Died 1984 (FB)

League Club	Source	Date Signed	Seasons Played	Apps	Subs	Gls
Bristol Rov.	Pentwyn	05.46	46	7	-	0

PEACOCK John Charles
Leeds, 27 March, 1956 (LB)

League Club	Source	Date Signed	Seasons Played	Apps	Subs	Gls
Scunthorpe U.	Jnrs	08.74	74-79	185	5	1

PEACOCK Keith
Dartford, 2 May, 1945 (M)

League Club	Source	Date Signed	Seasons Played	Apps	Subs	Gls
Charlton Ath.	Jnrs	07.62	62-78	512	21	92

PEACOCK Lee Anthony
Paisley, 9 October, 1976 S Yth (F)

League Club	Source	Date Signed	Seasons Played	Apps	Subs	Gls
Carlisle U.	YT	03.95	93-97	52	24	11
Mansfield T.	Tr	10.97	97	25	7	5

PEACOCK Michael Richards
Fishburn (Dm), 28 September, 1940 (G)

League Club	Source	Date Signed	Seasons Played	Apps	Subs	Gls
Darlington	Shildon	08.60	60-62	46	-	0

PEACOCK Richard John
Sheffield, 29 October, 1972 (W/F)

League Club	Source	Date Signed	Seasons Played	Apps	Subs	Gls
Hull C.	Sheffield F.C.	10.93	93-97	131	29	19

PEACOCK Robert John
Rushden, 8 December, 1937 (WH)

League Club	Source	Date Signed	Seasons Played	Apps	Subs	Gls
Northampton T.	Rushden T.	02.57	57	2	-	0

PEACOCK Terence McGhee
Hull, 18 April, 1935 (CF)

League Club	Source	Date Signed	Seasons Played	Apps	Subs	Gls
Hull C.	Jnrs	12.52	55	2	-	0
Queens Park R.	Tr	08.56	56-57	16	-	4

PEAKE Andrew Michael
Market Harborough, 1 November, 1961 E Yth/Eu21-1 (M)

League Club	Source	Date Signed	Seasons Played	Apps	Subs	Gls
Leicester C.	App	01.79	78-84	141	6	13
Grimsby T.	Tr	08.85	85-86	39	0	4
Charlton Ath.	Tr	09.86	86-91	174	3	5
Middlesbrough	Tr	11.91	91-93	83	3	1

PEAKE Dudley John
Swansea, 26 October, 1934 (CH)

League Club	Source	Date Signed	Seasons Played	Apps	Subs	Gls
Swansea C.	Tawe U.	04.56	55-57	57	-	2
Newport Co.	Tr	06.58	58-62	129	-	0

PEAKE Jason William
Leicester, 29 September, 1971 E Sch/E Yth (LW/M)

League Club	Source	Date Signed	Seasons Played	Apps	Subs	Gls
Leicester C.	YT	01.90	90	4	4	1
Hartlepool U.	L	02.92	91	5	1	1
Halifax T.	Tr	08.92	92	32	1	1
Rochdale	Tr	03.94	93-95	91	4	6
Brighton & H.A.	Tr	07.96	96	27	3	1
Bury	Tr	10.97	97	3	3	0

PEAKE Trevor
Nuneaton, 10 February, 1957 E Semi Pro (CD)

League Club	Source	Date Signed	Seasons Played	Apps	Subs	Gls
Lincoln C.	Nuneaton Bor.	06.79	79-82	171	0	7
Coventry C.	Tr	07.83	83-91	277	1	6
Luton T.	Tr	08.91	91-97	175	4	0

PEAPELL Frederick **Dennis**
Swindon, 16 November, 1945 (FB/WH)

League Club	Source	Date Signed	Seasons Played	Apps	Subs	Gls
Swindon T.	App	11.63	64	2	-	0
Exeter C.	Tr	07.65	65	23	1	1

PEARCE Alan James
Middlesbrough, 25 October, 1965 (LW)

League Club	Source	Date Signed	Seasons Played	Apps	Subs	Gls
York C.	Jnrs	10.83	83-86	76	2	9
Torquay U.	Tr	08.87	87	20	7	2

PEARCE Andrew John
Bradford-on-Avon, 20 April, 1966 (CD)

League Club	Source	Date Signed	Seasons Played	Apps	Subs	Gls
Coventry C.	Halesowen T.	05.90	90-92	68	3	4
Sheffield Wed.	Tr	06.93	93-95	66	3	3
Wimbledon	Tr	11.95	95	6	1	0

PEARCE Christopher Leslie
Newport, 7 August, 1961 W Sch/W Yth (G)

League Club	Source	Date Signed	Seasons Played	Apps	Subs	Gls
Blackburn Rov.	Wolverhampton W. (App)	10.79				
Rochdale	L	08.80	80	5	0	0
Rochdale	Tr	08.82	82	36	0	0
Port Vale	Tr	06.83	83-85	48	0	0
Wrexham	Tr	07.86	86	25	0	0
Burnley	Tr	07.87	87-91	181	0	0
Bradford C.	Tr	07.92	92	9	0	0

PEARCE David
Northolt, 7 December, 1959 E Semi Pro (F)

League Club	Source	Date Signed	Seasons Played	Apps	Subs	Gls
Millwall		02.78	77	1	0	0

PEARCE David Gordon
Scunthorpe, 19 December, 1934 (D)

League Club	Source	Date Signed	Seasons Played	Apps	Subs	Gls
Scunthorpe U.		07.56	58	2	-	0

PEARCE Dennis Anthony
Wolverhampton, 10 September, 1974 (LB)

League Club	Source	Date Signed	Seasons Played	Apps	Subs	Gls
Aston Villa	YT	06.93				
Wolverhampton W.	Tr	07.95	95-96	7	2	0
Notts Co.	Tr	07.97	97	37	1	2

PEARCE Graham Charles
Hammersmith, 8 July, 1959 (LB)

League Club	Source	Date Signed	Seasons Played	Apps	Subs	Gls
Brighton & H. A.	Barnet	01.82	82-85	87	1	2
Gillingham	Tr	07.86	86-87	65	0	0
Brentford	Tr	09.88	88	11	7	0
Maidstone U.	Tr	07.89	89	24	3	0

PEARCE Ian Anthony
Bury St Edmunds, 7 May, 1974 E Yth/Eu21-3 (CD)

League Club	Source	Date Signed	Seasons Played	Apps	Subs	Gls
Chelsea	Jnrs	08.91	90-92	0	4	0
Blackburn Rov.	Tr	10.93	93-97	43	19	2
West Ham U.	Tr	09.97	97	30	0	1

PEARCE James William
Tottenham, 27 November, 1947 E Sch (W)

League Club	Source	Date Signed	Seasons Played	Apps	Subs	Gls
Tottenham H.	App	05.65	68-72	108	33	21

PEARCE John
Watford, 12 December, 1950 (FB)

League Club	Source	Date Signed	Seasons Played	Apps	Subs	Gls
Watford	Jnrs	07.69	70	0	1	0

PEARCE John Arthur
Grimsby, 29 February, 1940 (WH)

League Club	Source	Date Signed	Seasons Played	Apps	Subs	Gls
Grimsby T.	Jnrs	12.58	58-61	48	-	0

PEARCE Reginald Stanley
Liverpool, 12 January, 1930 EF Lge (WH)

League Club	Source	Date Signed	Seasons Played	Apps	Subs	Gls
Luton T.	Winsford U.	11.54	54-57	75	-	6
Sunderland	Tr	02.58	57-60	61	-	4
Peterborough U.	Cambridge C.	08.63	63	28	-	2

PEARCE Stuart
Hammersmith, 24 April, 1962 Eu21-1/E-76 (LB)

League Club	Source	Date Signed	Seasons Played	Apps	Subs	Gls
Coventry C.	Wealdstone	10.83	83-84	52	0	4
Nottingham F.	Tr	06.85	85-96	401	0	63
Newcastle U.	Tr	07.97	97	25	0	0

PEARCE Trevor George
Canterbury, 30 May, 1949 (W)

League Club	Source	Date Signed	Seasons Played	Apps	Subs	Gls
Arsenal	Folkestone T.	02.70				
Aldershot	Tr	05.71	71-72	19	6	2

PEARCEY Jason Kevin
Leamington, 23 July, 1971 (G)

League Club	Source	Date Signed	Seasons Played	Apps	Subs	Gls
Mansfield T.	YT	07.89	88-94	77	0	0
Grimsby T.	Tr	11.94	94-97	49	0	0

PEARS Jeffrey
York, 14 June, 1920 (G)

League Club	Source	Date Signed	Seasons Played	Apps	Subs	Gls
York C.	Terrys	09.47	47-48	3	-	0

PEARS Richard James
Exeter, 16 July, 1976 (F)

League Club	Source	Date Signed	Seasons Played	Apps	Subs	Gls
Exeter C.	YT	07.94	93-96	43	17	8

PEARS Stephen
Brandon, 22 January, 1962 (G)

League Club	Source	Date Signed	Seasons Played	Apps	Subs	Gls
Manchester U.	App	01.79	84	4	0	0
Middlesbrough	L	11.83	83	12	0	0
Middlesbrough	Tr	07.85	85-94	327	0	0
Liverpool	Tr	08.95				
Hartlepool U.	Tr	08.96	96	16	0	0

PEARSON Andrew John
Newmarket, 19 November, 1960 (F)

League Club	Source	Date Signed	Seasons Played	Apps	Subs	Gls
Luton T.	App	11.78	79	1	1	0

PEARSON David Aubrey John
Connahs Quay, 13 October, 1947 W Sch/Wu23-1 (FB)

League Club	Source	Date Signed	Seasons Played	Apps	Subs	Gls
Everton	App	10.65				
Southport	Tr	08.67	67-69	91	2	0
Rochdale	Tr	09.70	70	3	0	0

PEARSON David Thomson
Dunfermline, 9 November, 1932 (CF)

League Club	Source	Date Signed	Seasons Played	Apps	Subs	Gls
Blackburn Rov.	Jnrs	11.49				
Ipswich T.	Tr	05.54				
Oldham Ath.	Darwen	08.56	56	25	-	12
Rochdale	Tr	03.57	56-57	32	-	17
Crewe Alex.	Tr	05.58	58	9	-	2

PEARSON Donald James
Swansea, 14 March, 1930 (WH)

League Club	Source	Date Signed	Seasons Played	Apps	Subs	Gls
Swansea C.		06.50	52-57	50	-	1
Aldershot	Tr	07.58	58	31	-	2

PEARSON Ian Trevor
Leeds, 18 September, 1950 (F)

League Club	Source	Date Signed	Seasons Played	Apps	Subs	Gls
Plymouth Arg.	Goole T.	07.74	74-75	6	6	0
Millwall	Wycombe W.	08.77	77-78	41	3	9
Exeter C.	Tr	11.78	78-80	67	2	10
Plymouth Arg.	Bideford	08.83	83	5	3	1

PEARSON James Findlay
Falkirk, 24 March, 1953 Su23-6 (F)

League Club	Source	Date Signed	Seasons Played	Apps	Subs	Gls
Everton	St Johnstone	07.74	74-77	76	17	15
Newcastle U.	Tr	08.78	78-79	11	0	3

PEARSON John
Wigan, 18 October, 1946 E Sch (OR)

League Club	Source	Date Signed	Seasons Played	Apps	Subs	Gls
Manchester U.	App	11.63				
York C.	Tr	07.65	65	14	1	4

PEARSON John
Ferryhill, 8 May, 1951 (IF)

League Club	Source	Date Signed	Seasons Played	Apps	Subs	Gls
Hartlepool U. (Am)	Ferryhill Ath.	01.69	68	1	0	0

PEARSON John Arthur
Isleworth, 23 April, 1935 (IF)

League Club	Source	Date Signed	Seasons Played	Apps	Subs	Gls
Brentford	Jnrs	11.52	55-56	5	-	0
Queens Park R.	Tr	06.58	58-59	21	-	9

PEARSON John George
Gateshead, 10 April, 1931 Died 1996 (RB)

League Club	Source	Date Signed	Seasons Played	Apps	Subs	Gls
Hartlepool U.	Reyrolles	04.53	52	1	-	0

PEARSON John Stuart
Sheffield, 1 September, 1963 E Yth (F)

League Club	Source	Date Signed	Seasons Played	Apps	Subs	Gls
Sheffield Wed.	App	05.81	80-84	64	41	24
Charlton Ath.	Tr	05.85	85-86	52	9	15
Leeds U.	Tr	01.87	86-90	51	48	12
Rotherham U.	L	03.91	90	11	0	5
Barnsley	Tr	07.91	91-92	29	3	4
Hull C.	L	01.92	91	15	0	0
Carlisle U.	Tr	08.93	93-94	5	3	0
Mansfield T. (N/C)	Tr	11.94	94	0	2	0
Cardiff C.	Tr	01.95	94	12	0	0

PEARSON Lawrence
Wallsend, 2 July, 1965 (D/M)

League Club	Source	Date Signed	Seasons Played	Apps	Subs	Gls
Hull C.	Gateshead	06.84	84-86	58	1	0
Bristol C.	Tr	06.87				
Port Vale	Tr	08.87	87	3	0	0
Darlington (N/C)	Belgium	08.93	93	26	2	4
Chesterfield (N/C)	Tr	03.94	93	0	1	0

PEARSON Mark
Sheffield, 28 October, 1939 E Sch/E Yth (IF)

League Club	Source	Date Signed	Seasons Played	Apps	Subs	Gls
Manchester U.	Jnrs	05.57	57-62	68	-	12
Sheffield Wed.	Tr	10.63	63-64	39	-	9
Fulham	Tr	05.65	65-67	53	5	7
Halifax T.	Tr	03.68	68	2	3	0

PEARSON Michael
Bilston, 5 December, 1942 (IF)

League Club	Source	Date Signed	Seasons Played	Apps	Subs	Gls
Manchester C.	Jnrs	12.59				
Walsall	Tr	05.62	62	3	-	1

PEARSON Nigel Graham
Nottingham, 21 August, 1963 (CD)

League Club	Source	Date Signed	Seasons Played	Apps	Subs	Gls
Shrewsbury T.	Heanor T.	11.81	82-87	153	0	5
Sheffield Wed.	Tr	10.87	87-93	176	4	14
Middlesbrough	Tr	07.94	94-97	115	1	5

PEARSON Richard
Ulcombe (Kt), 18 October, 1970 (CD)

League Club	Source	Date Signed	Seasons Played	Apps	Subs	Gls
Gillingham	YT	07.89	88-89	7	2	0

PEARSON Richard John
Portsmouth, 14 Juno, 1931 (IF)

League Club	Source	Date Signed	Seasons Played	Apps	Subs	Gls
Portsmouth	Hillside Y.C.	05.49	53	4	-	1

PEARSON Stanley Clare
Salford, 11 January, 1919 Died 1997 EF Lge/E-8 (IF)

League Club	Source	Date Signed	Seasons Played	Apps	Subs	Gls
Manchester U.	Adelphi B.C.	05.36	37-53	312	-	127
Bury	Tr	02.54	53-57	122	-	56
Chester C.	Tr	10.57	57-58	57	-	16

PEARSON Stuart James
Hull, 21 June, 1949 Eu23-1/E-15 (F)

League Club	Source	Date Signed	Seasons Played	Apps	Subs	Gls
Hull C.	Jnrs	07.68	69-73	126	3	44
Manchester U.	Tr	05.74	74-77	138	1	55
West Ham U.	Tr	08.79	79-81	28	6	6

PEARSON Thomas Usher
Edinburgh, 6 March, 1913 SF Lge/S-2 (OL)

League Club	Source	Date Signed	Seasons Played	Apps	Subs	Gls
Newcastle U.	Murrayfield Ath.	03.33	33-47	212	-	46

PEARSON Trevor
Sheffield, 4 April, 1952 (G)

League Club	Source	Date Signed	Seasons Played	Apps	Subs	Gls
Sheffield W. (Am)	Woodseats W.M.C.	03.72	71	4	0	0

PEARSON Walter
Ottershaw (Sy), 13 November, 1928 (G)

League Club	Source	Date Signed	Seasons Played	Apps	Subs	Gls
Aldershot (Am)	Tooting & Mitcham	03.61	60	1	-	0

PEARSON William George Arthur
Clonmel (Ire), 23 October, 1921 (W)

League Club	Source	Date Signed	Seasons Played	Apps	Subs	Gls
Grimsby T.		09.43	46-48	35	-	8
Chester C.	Tr	06.49	49	12	-	3

PEART Robert Charles
Swindon, 17 December, 1926 Died 1966 (CF)

League Club	Source	Date Signed	Seasons Played	Apps	Subs	Gls
Swindon T.	Burnley (Am)	04.48	49-51	13	-	5

League Club	Source	Date Signed	Seasons Played	Apps	Subs	Gls
PEART Ronald						
Brandon, 8 March, 1920						(WH)
Hartlepool U.	Langley Moor	09.38	38	8	-	0
Derby Co.	Tr	05.39	46	1	-	0
York C.	Tr	06.48	48	5	-	0
PEAT William **Arthur**						
Liverpool, 1 September, 1940						(WH)
Everton	Jnrs	04.59				
Southport	Tr	07.61	61-71	401	0	27
Crewe Alex.	Tr	07.72	72-73	82	0	5
PEAT James Leslie						
Birmingham, 29 May, 1951						(OL)
Workington	Cadburys	08.73	73	0	1	0
PEAT John (Jack)						
						(OL)
Workington	Partick Thistle	10.53	53	1	-	0
PEATTIE Donald Simpson						
York, 5 April, 1963						(F)
Sheffield U.	Gretna	08.84	84	3	2	0
Doncaster Rov.	L	01.86	85	3	1	0
PECK Dennis **Trevor**						
Llanelli, 25 May, 1938						(FB)
Cardiff C.	Llanelli	02.58	59-64	42	-	0
PECKETT Andrew Richard						
Sheffield, 19 September, 1969						(M)
Doncaster Rov.	YT	06.88	87-88	2	7	0
PEDDELTY John						
Bishop Auckland, 2 April, 1955 E Yth						(CD)
Ipswich T.	App	01.73	72-76	44	0	5
Plymouth Arg.	Tr	10.76	76-77	30	3	1
PEDDELTY John **Maurice**						
Carlisle, 23 May, 1950						(M)
Carlisle U.	App	12.67	68-69	9	5	1
Darlington	Tr	07.70	70-71	51	5	1
PEDEN George Wright Watson						
Rosewell, 12 April, 1943						(FB)
Lincoln C.	Hearts	04.67	66-73	223	2	14
PEDERSEN Jan Ove						
Oslo, Norway, 12 November, 1968 Norwegian Int						(M)
Hartlepool U.	Brann Bergen (Nor)	10.97	97	17	0	1
PEDERSEN Per Werner						
Denmark, 30 March, 1969 Danish Int						(F)
Blackburn Rov.	Odense (Den)	02.97	96-97	6	5	1
PEDERSEN Tore						
Norway, 29 September, 1969 Norwegian Int						(CD)
Oldham Ath.	S.K. Brann (Nor)	10.93	93	7	3	0
Blackburn Rov.	St Pauli (Ger)	09.97	97	3	2	0
PEEBLES Richard Winter						
Glasgow, 30 August, 1923						(IF)
Swindon T.	St Johnstone	05.50	50	12	-	1
PEEK James						
Hartlepool, 7 July, 1933						(RB)
Hartlepool U. (Am)	Fosten W.	12.59	59	7	-	0
PEEL Kenneth						
Manchester, 8 January, 1922						(IR)
Crewe Alex.	Rusholme	09.46	46	1	-	0
PEEL Nathan James						
Blackburn, 17 May, 1972						(F)
Preston N. E.	YT	07.90	90	1	9	1
Sheffield U.	Tr	07.91	91	0	1	0
Halifax T.	L	02.93	92	3	0	0
Burnley	Tr	09.93	93-94	4	12	2
Rotherham U.	L	03.95	94	9	0	4
Mansfield T.	L	10.95	95	2	0	0
Doncaster Rov.	L	02.96	95	2	0	0
Rotherham U.	Tr	07.96				
Macclesfield T.	Tr	01.97	97	10	4	3
PEEL Trevor						
Huddersfield, 25 October, 1945						(FB)
Bradford P. A.	Huddersfield T. (Am)	04.67	66-67	11	0	0

League Club	Source	Date Signed	Seasons Played	Apps	Subs	Gls
PEER Dean						
Stourbridge, 8 August, 1969						(M)
Birmingham C.	YT	07.87	86-92	106	14	8
Mansfield T.	L	12.92	92	10	0	0
Walsall	Tr	11.93	93-94	41	4	8
Northampton T.	Tr	08.95	95-97	70	23	4
PEGG David						
Doncaster, 20 September, 1935 Died 1958 E Sch/Eu23-3/E 'B'/E-1						(OL)
Manchester U.	Jnrs	09.52	52-57	127	-	24
PEGG James Kenneth						
Salford, 4 January, 1926						(G)
Manchester U.	Jnrs	11.47	47	2	-	0
Torquay U.	Tr	08.49	49	2	-	0
York C.	Tr	08.50	50	1	-	0
PEHRSSON Magnus Karl						
Sweden, 25 May, 1976 Swedish u21 Int						(M)
Bradford C. (L)	Djurgaardens (Swe)	10.96	96	1	0	0
PEJIC Melvyn						
Newcastle-u-Lyme, 27 April, 1959						(CD)
Stoke C.	Jnrs	07.77	79	1	0	0
Hereford U.	Tr	06.80	80-91	404	8	14
Wrexham	Tr	01.92	91-94	103	3	4
PEJIC Michael						
Chesterton, 25 January, 1950 Eu23-8/E-4						(LB)
Stoke C.	App	01.68	68-76	274	0	6
Everton	Tr	02.77	76-78	76	0	2
Aston Villa	Tr	09.79	79	10	0	0
PELL Dennis						
Normanton, 19 April, 1929						(IF)
Rotherham U.	Methley	05.52	52-55	11	-	3
Grimsby T.	Tr	10.55	55-56	3	-	1
PELL Robert Anthony						
Leeds, 5 February, 1979						(CD)
Rotherham U.	YT	06.97	96	2	0	0
Doncaster Rov.	L	11.97	97	6	4	1
PEMBERTON James Henry Arthur						
Wolverhampton, 30 April, 1916 Died 1996						(FB)
West Bromwich A.	Brownhills A.	08.38	46-50	162	-	0
PEMBERTON James Thomas						
Kingswinford, 14 November, 1925						(OL)
West Bromwich A.	Round Oak	05.45				
Luton T.	Stourbridge	11.47	50-56	92	-	8
PEMBERTON John Matthew						
Oldham, 18 November, 1964						(D)
Rochdale (N/C)	Chadderton	09.84	84	1	0	0
Crewe Alex.	Chadderton	03.85	84-87	116	5	1
Crystal Palace	Tr	03.88	87-89	76	2	2
Sheffield U.	Tr	07.90	90-93	67	1	0
Leeds U.	Tr	11.93	93-95	44	9	0
Crewe Alex.	Tr	08.97	97	1	0	0
PEMBERTON Martin Calvin						
Bradford, 1 February, 1976						(F)
Oldham Ath.	YT	07.94	95-96	0	5	0
Doncaster Rov.	Tr	03.97	96-97	33	2	3
Scunthorpe U. (N/C)	Tr	03.98	97	3	3	0
PEMBERTON Selwyn Robert						
Cardiff, 13 October, 1928						(RB)
Newport Co.		03.52	52	1	-	0
PEMBERY Gordon Dennis						
Cardiff, 10 October, 1926						(OL/WH)
Norwich C.	Cardiff Nomads	01.47	46	1	-	0
Cardiff C.	Tr	08.48	49	1	-	0
Torquay U.	Tr	06.50	50-51	51	-	7
Charlton Ath.	Tr	01.52	51-55	18	-	1
Swindon T.	Tr	06.56	56	37	-	2
PEMBRIDGE Mark Anthony						
Merthyr Tydfil, 29 November, 1970 W Sch/Wu21-1/W 'B'/W-28						(M)
Luton T.	YT	07.89	90-91	60	0	6
Derby Co.	Tr	06.92	92-94	108	2	28
Sheffield Wed.	Tr	07.95	95-97	88	5	12
PENDER John Patrick						
Luton, 19 November, 1963 IR Yth/IRu21-5						(CD)
Wolverhampton W.	App	11.81	81-84	115	2	3
Charlton Ath.	Tr	07.85	85-87	41	0	0

League Club	Source	Date Signed	Seasons Played	Apps	Subs	Gls
Bristol C.	Tr	10.87	87-89	83	0	3
Burnley	Tr	09.90	90-95	171	0	8
Wigan Ath.	Tr	08.95	95-96	67	3	1
Rochdale	Tr	07.97	97	14	0	0

PENDERGAST William James
Caernarfon, 13 April, 1915 (CF)

League Club	Source	Date Signed	Seasons Played	Apps	Subs	Gls
Manchester U.	Wrexham (Am)	12.35				
Wolverhampton W.	Tr	01.36				
Bristol Rov.	Tr	05.36	36-37	7	-	3
Chester C.	Colchester U.	07.38	38	34	-	26
New Brighton	Tr	08.46	46-47	69	-	26

PENDLEBURY Derek **Keith**
Stockport, 22 January, 1934 (LH)

League Club	Source	Date Signed	Seasons Played	Apps	Subs	Gls
Stockport Co.	Jnrs	03.51	53	2	-	0

PENDREY Garry James Sidney
Birmingham, 9 February, 1949 (D)

League Club	Source	Date Signed	Seasons Played	Apps	Subs	Gls
Birmingham C.	App	10.66	68-78	287	19	4
West Bromwich A.	Tr	08.79	79	18	0	0
Torquay U.	Tr	08.81	81	12	0	0
Bristol Rov.	Tr	12.81	81	1	0	0
Walsall	Tr	08.82	82	8	0	1

PENFOLD Mark
Woolwich, 10 December, 1956 (RB)

League Club	Source	Date Signed	Seasons Played	Apps	Subs	Gls
Charlton Ath.	App	04.74	73-78	65	5	0
Leyton Orient	Tr	07.79	79	3	0	1

PENFORD Dennis Henry
Reading, 31 August, 1931 (LB)

League Club	Source	Date Signed	Seasons Played	Apps	Subs	Gls
Reading		05.52	53-58	101	-	6
Torquay U.	Tr	06.59	59-61	77	-	0

PENGELLY Richard
Looe, 6 October, 1919 (HB)

League Club	Source	Date Signed	Seasons Played	Apps	Subs	Gls
Plymouth Arg.	Looe	05.47	47-49	9	-	0

PENHALIGON Gary
St Austell, 13 May, 1970 (G)

League Club	Source	Date Signed	Seasons Played	Apps	Subs	Gls
Plymouth Arg.	YT	07.88	88	1	0	0

PENK Henry (Harry)
Wigan, 19 July, 1934 (W)

League Club	Source	Date Signed	Seasons Played	Apps	Subs	Gls
Portsmouth	Wigan Ath.	09.55	55-56	9	-	2
Plymouth Arg.	Tr	06.57	57-59	104	-	14
Southampton	Tr	07.60	60-63	52	0	6

PENMAN Christopher
Houghton-le-Spring, 12 September, 1945 (G)

League Club	Source	Date Signed	Seasons Played	Apps	Subs	Gls
Darlington	Preston N.E. (App)	12.62	62-63	30	-	0

PENMAN William Salmond Thomson
Wemyss (Fife), 7 August, 1939 (M)

League Club	Source	Date Signed	Seasons Played	Apps	Subs	Gls
Newcastle U.	Glasgow Rangers	04.63	62-65	62	1	18
Swindon T.	Tr	09.66	66-69	87	11	18
Walsall	Tr	08.70	70-72	118	5	6

PENN Donald John
West Bromwich, 15 March, 1960 (F)

League Club	Source	Date Signed	Seasons Played	Apps	Subs	Gls
Walsall	Warley Borough	01.78	77-82	132	9	54

PENN Frank Reginald
Edmonton, 15 April, 1927 (OL)

League Club	Source	Date Signed	Seasons Played	Apps	Subs	Gls
Crystal Palace (Am)	Fulham (Am)	09.49	49	1	-	0

PENNEY David Mark
Wakefield, 17 August, 1964 (M)

League Club	Source	Date Signed	Seasons Played	Apps	Subs	Gls
Derby Co.	Pontefract Colly	09.85	86-88	6	13	0
Oxford U.	Tr	06.89	89-93	76	34	15
Swansea C.	L	03.91	90	12	0	3
Swansea C.	Tr	03.94	93-96	112	7	20
Cardiff C.	Tr	07.97	97	32	2	5

PENNEY Steven Alexander
Ballymena (NI), 6 January, 1964 NI-17 (W)

League Club	Source	Date Signed	Seasons Played	Apps	Subs	Gls
Brighton & H.A.	Ballymena U.	11.83	83-88	125	13	14
Burnley	Hearts	07.92	92	10	1	3

PENNICK Raymond
Ferryhill, 30 November, 1946 (IF)

League Club	Source	Date Signed	Seasons Played	Apps	Subs	Gls
York C. (Am)	Willington	03.69	68	0	1	0

PENNINGTON Jack
Tadcaster, 12 September, 1928 Died 1987 (CF)

League Club	Source	Date Signed	Seasons Played	Apps	Subs	Gls
Halifax T.	Marsden	11.53	53-54	7	-	2

PENNINGTON James
Golborne, 26 April, 1939 (OR)

League Club	Source	Date Signed	Seasons Played	Apps	Subs	Gls
Manchester C.	Jnrs	08.56	58	1	-	0
Crewe Alex.	Tr	03.61	60-62	34	-	2
Grimsby T.	Tr	04.63	62-64	89	-	8
Oldham Ath.	Tr	07.65	65	23	0	0
Rochdale	Tr	07.66	66	14	0	0

PENNINGTON James
Warrington, 13 November, 1928 Died 1976 (IL)

League Club	Source	Date Signed	Seasons Played	Apps	Subs	Gls
Huddersfield T.	Burtonwood O.B.	08.49				
Southport	Tr	07.51	51-53	55	-	11

PENNOCK Adrian Barry
Ipswich, 27 March, 1971 (CD/M)

League Club	Source	Date Signed	Seasons Played	Apps	Subs	Gls
Norwich C.	YT	07.89	89	1	0	0
Bournemouth	Tr	08.92	92-96	130	1	9
Gillingham	Tr	10.96	96-97	46	0	2

PENNOCK Anthony
Swansea, 10 April, 1971 (G)

League Club	Source	Date Signed	Seasons Played	Apps	Subs	Gls
Stockport Co.	Clydach U.	08.90				
Wigan Ath.	L	12.90	90	2	0	0
Wigan Ath.	Tr	06.91	92	8	0	0
Hereford U.	Tr	07.94	94	13	2	0

PENNY Christian Vincent
Southend, 16 February, 1973 (FB)

League Club	Source	Date Signed	Seasons Played	Apps	Subs	Gls
Doncaster Rov. (N/C)	Brigg T.	02.92	91	1	0	0

PENNY John
Plymouth, 19 August, 1938 (OR)

League Club	Source	Date Signed	Seasons Played	Apps	Subs	Gls
Plymouth Arg.	Jnrs	11.55	57-59	7	-	0

PENNY Shaun
Bristol, 24 September, 1957 E Sch (F)

League Club	Source	Date Signed	Seasons Played	Apps	Subs	Gls
Bristol C.	App	09.74				
Bristol Rov.	Tr	08.79	79-81	57	3	13

PENNYFATHER Glenn Julian
Billericay, 11 February, 1963 (M)

League Club	Source	Date Signed	Seasons Played	Apps	Subs	Gls
Southend U.	App	02.81	80-87	231	7	36
Crystal Palace	Tr	11.87	87-88	31	3	1
Ipswich T.	Tr	10.89	89-92	11	4	1
Bristol C.	Tr	02.93	92-93	21	5	1

PENRHYN Norman Andrew
Lambeth, 28 February, 1950 (F)

League Club	Source	Date Signed	Seasons Played	Apps	Subs	Gls
Plymouth Arg.	App	●	67	0	1	0

PENRICE Gary Kenneth
Bristol, 23 March, 1964 (F)

League Club	Source	Date Signed	Seasons Played	Apps	Subs	Gls
Bristol Rov.	Mangotsfield	11.84	84-89	186	2	54
Watford	Tr	11.89	89-90	41	2	18
Aston Villa	Tr	03.91	90-91	14	6	1
Queens Park R.	Tr	10.91	91-95	55	27	20
Watford	Tr	11.95	95-96	26	13	2
Bristol Rov.	Tr	07.97	97	38	2	5

PENROSE Colin Richard
Bradford, 1 November, 1949 (IF)

League Club	Source	Date Signed	Seasons Played	Apps	Subs	Gls
Bradford P. A. (Am)	Sedbergh Y.C.	09.68	68	6	0	1

PENROSE Norman
Consett, 10 March, 1922 E Sch (WH)

League Club	Source	Date Signed	Seasons Played	Apps	Subs	Gls
Grimsby T.	Jnrs	05.39	46-47	9	-	0

PENTECOST Michael Eric
Hounslow, 13 April, 1948 (FB)

League Club	Source	Date Signed	Seasons Played	Apps	Subs	Gls
Fulham	Sutton U.	08.66	66-72	81	6	0

PEPLOW Ronald Rupert
Willesden, 4 May, 1935 (WH)

League Club	Source	Date Signed	Seasons Played	Apps	Subs	Gls
Brentford	Southall	08.55	55-60	61	-	5

PEPLOW Stephen Thomas
Liverpool, 8 January, 1949 (W)

League Club	Source	Date Signed	Seasons Played	Apps	Subs	Gls
Liverpool	App	01.66	69	2	0	0
Swindon T.	Tr	05.70	70-72	37	3	11
Nottingham F.	Tr	07.73	73	3	0	0
Mansfield T.	L	12.73	73	4	0	3
Tranmere Rov.	Tr	01.74	73-80	232	16	44

PEPPER Colin **Nigel**
Rotherham, 25 April, 1968 (M)

League Club	Source	Date Signed	Seasons Played	Apps	Subs	Gls
Rotherham U.	App	04.86	85-89	35	10	1
York C.	Tr	07.90	90-96	223	12	39
Bradford C.	Tr	02.97	96-97	42	1	10

PEPPITT Sydney
Stoke, 8 September, 1919 Died 1992 E Sch (OR)

League Club	Source	Date Signed	Seasons Played	Apps	Subs	Gls
Stoke C.	Jnrs	09.36	36-49	94	-	29
Port Vale	Tr	05.50	50	11	-	3

PERCIVAL Jason Charles
Nuneaton, 20 September, 1973 (F)

League Club	Source	Date Signed	Seasons Played	Apps	Subs	Gls
Stoke C.	YT	09.90				
Exeter C.	Tr	07.93	93	0	4	0

PERCIVAL John
Durham, 16 May, 1913 Died 1979 (WH)

League Club	Source	Date Signed	Seasons Played	Apps	Subs	Gls
Manchester C.	Durham C.	10.32	33-46	161	-	8
Bournemouth	Tr	05.47	47-48	52	-	1

PERCIVAL Ronald Frederick **John (Jack)**
Norwood, 19 April, 1924 (WH)

League Club	Source	Date Signed	Seasons Played	Apps	Subs	Gls
Huddersfield T.	Tunbridge Wells	02.48	47-49	8	-	0
Chesterfield	Tr	05.50	50	6	-	0

PERDOMO Jose
Uruguay, 6 January, 1965 Uruguayan Int (M)

League Club	Source	Date Signed	Seasons Played	Apps	Subs	Gls
Coventry C. (N/C)	Genoa (It)	08.90	90	4	0	0

PEREIRA Luis Boa Morte
Lisbon, Portugal, 4 August, 1977 (RW)

League Club	Source	Date Signed	Seasons Played	Apps	Subs	Gls
Arsenal	Sporting Lisbon (Por)	06.97	97	4	11	0

PEREZ Lionel
France, 24 April, 1967 (G)

League Club	Source	Date Signed	Seasons Played	Apps	Subs	Gls
Sunderland	Bordeaux (Fr)	08.96	96-97	74	1	0

PERIFIMOU Christopher James
Enfield, 27 November, 1975 (W)

League Club	Source	Date Signed	Seasons Played	Apps	Subs	Gls
Leyton Orient	YT	●	94	3	1	0
Barnet	Tr	09.95				

PERKINS Christopher Paul
Stepney, 1 March, 1980 (CD)

League Club	Source	Date Signed	Seasons Played	Apps	Subs	Gls
Southend U.	YT	●	97	3	2	0

PERKINS Christopher Peter
Nottingham, 9 January, 1974 (FB/M)

League Club	Source	Date Signed	Seasons Played	Apps	Subs	Gls
Mansfield T.	YT	11.92	92-93	3	5	0
Chesterfield	Tr	07.94	94-97	104	9	2

PERKINS Declan Oliver
Ilford, 17 October, 1975 IRu21-4 (W)

League Club	Source	Date Signed	Seasons Played	Apps	Subs	Gls
Southend U.	YT	05.94	94	1	5	0
Cambridge U.	L	09.95	95	1	1	0

PERKINS Eric
West Bromwich, 19 August, 1934 (FB)

League Club	Source	Date Signed	Seasons Played	Apps	Subs	Gls
West Bromwich A.	Jnrs	06.52	55	2	-	0
Walsall	Tr	06.56	56-58	67	-	1

PERKINS Glen Stewart
Little Billing, 12 October, 1960 (M)

League Club	Source	Date Signed	Seasons Played	Apps	Subs	Gls
Northampton T.	App	10.78	78	0	1	0

PERKINS Stephen Arthur
Stepney, 3 October, 1954 (FB)

League Club	Source	Date Signed	Seasons Played	Apps	Subs	Gls
Chelsea	App	11.71				
Queens Park R.	Tr	06.77	77	2	0	0
Wimbledon	Tr	10.78	78-80	52	0	0

PERKINS Steven William
St Helens, 25 April, 1975 (CD)

League Club	Source	Date Signed	Seasons Played	Apps	Subs	Gls
Plymouth Arg. (N/C)	Crediton U.	02.97	96	1	3	0

PERKS Stephen John
Bridgnorth, 19 April, 1963 (G)

League Club	Source	Date Signed	Seasons Played	Apps	Subs	Gls
Shrewsbury T.	App	04.81	84-91	243	0	0

PERON Jean Francois
France, 11 October, 1965 (LM)

League Club	Source	Date Signed	Seasons Played	Apps	Subs	Gls
Walsall	Lens (Fr)	08.97	97	38	0	1

PERRETT Darren John
Cardiff, 29 December, 1969 (W)

League Club	Source	Date Signed	Seasons Played	Apps	Subs	Gls
Swansea C.	Cheltenham T.	07.93	93-95	13	17	1

PERRETT George Richard
Kennington, 2 May, 1915 Died 1952 (WH)

League Club	Source	Date Signed	Seasons Played	Apps	Subs	Gls
Ipswich T.	Fulham (Am)	06.36	38-49	131	-	4

PERRETT Russell
Barton-on-Sea, 18 June, 1973 (CD)

League Club	Source	Date Signed	Seasons Played	Apps	Subs	Gls
Portsmouth	A.F.C. Lymington	09.95	95-97	54	3	2

PERRIN Steven Charles
Paddington, 13 February, 1952 (F)

League Club	Source	Date Signed	Seasons Played	Apps	Subs	Gls
Crystal Palace	Wycombe W.	03.76	76-77	45	3	13
Plymouth Arg.	Tr	03.78	77-79	34	1	6
Portsmouth	Tr	11.79	79-80	18	10	3
Northampton T. (N/C)	Hillingdon Borough	12.81	81-82	22	0	6

PERRY Andrew
Dulwich, 28 December, 1962 (M)

League Club	Source	Date Signed	Seasons Played	Apps	Subs	Gls
Portsmouth	Dulwich Hamlet	11.86	87	1	3	0
Gillingham	Tr	08.88	88	8	5	0

PERRY Arthur
Doncaster, 15 October, 1932 (FB)

League Club	Source	Date Signed	Seasons Played	Apps	Subs	Gls
Hull C.		12.50				
Bradford P. A.	Tr	07.56	56-57	60	-	0
Rotherham U.	Tr	07.58	58	2	-	0

PERRY Christopher John
Carshalton, 26 April, 1973 (CD)

League Club	Source	Date Signed	Seasons Played	Apps	Subs	Gls
Wimbledon	YT	07.91	93-97	124	9	2

PERRY David
Sheffield, 17 May, 1967 (D)

League Club	Source	Date Signed	Seasons Played	Apps	Subs	Gls
Chesterfield	Jnrs	07.87	85-87	12	5	0

PERRY Frederick Noel
Cheltenham, 30 October, 1933 (FB)

League Club	Source	Date Signed	Seasons Played	Apps	Subs	Gls
Liverpool	Worthing	07.54	55	1	-	0

PERRY Jason
Caerphilly, 2 April, 1970 W Sch/W Yth/Wu21-3/W 'B'/W-1 (CD)

League Club	Source	Date Signed	Seasons Played	Apps	Subs	Gls
Cardiff C.	Jnrs	08.87	86-96	278	3	5
Bristol Rov.	Tr	07.97	97	24	1	0

PERRY Leonard
Walsall, 14 May, 1930 (FB)

League Club	Source	Date Signed	Seasons Played	Apps	Subs	Gls
Walsall	Jnrs	10.50	53	3	-	0

PERRY Mark James
Ealing, 19 October, 1978 E Sch/E Yth (M)

League Club	Source	Date Signed	Seasons Played	Apps	Subs	Gls
Queens Park R.	YT	10.95	96-97	8	2	1

PERRY Michael Alexander
Wimbledon, 4 April, 1964 (F)

League Club	Source	Date Signed	Seasons Played	Apps	Subs	Gls
West Bromwich A.	App	02.82	82-83	14	6	5
Torquay U.	L	10.84	84	5	0	1
Northampton T.	L	12.84	84	4	0	0
Torquay U.	Tr	03.85	84-85	18	0	1

PERRY Peter
Rotherham, 11 April, 1936 (FB)

League Club	Source	Date Signed	Seasons Played	Apps	Subs	Gls
Rotherham U.	Treeton R.R.	07.56	57-61	99	-	12
York C.	Tr	07.62	62	23	-	0

PERRY William
South Africa, 10 September, 1930 E 'B'/EF Lge/E-3 (OL)

League Club	Source	Date Signed	Seasons Played	Apps	Subs	Gls
Blackpool	Johannesburg (SA)	11.49	49-61	394	-	120
Southport	Tr	06.62	62	26	-	0

PERRYMAN Gerald
West Haddon, 3 October, 1947 (FB)

League Club	Source	Date Signed	Seasons Played	Apps	Subs	Gls
Northampton T.	Jnrs	09.66	66	1	0	0
Colchester U.	Tr	07.68	68	1	1	0

PERRYMAN Stephen John
Ealing, 21 December, 1951 E Sch/E Yth/Eu23-17/E-1 (M)

League Club	Source	Date Signed	Seasons Played	Apps	Subs	Gls
Tottenham H.	App	01.69	69-85	653	2	31
Oxford U.	Tr	03.86	85-86	17	0	0
Brentford	Tr	11.86	86-89	44	9	0

PESCHISOLIDO Paulo (Paul) Pasquale
Canada, 25 May, 1971 Canadian Int (F)

League Club	Source	Date Signed	Seasons Played	Apps	Subs	Gls
Birmingham C.	Toronto Blizzards (Can)	11.92	92-93	37	6	16
Stoke C.	Tr	08.94	94-95	59	7	19
Birmingham C.	Tr	03.96	95	7	2	1
West Bromwich A.	Tr	07.96	96-97	36	9	18
Fulham	Tr	10.97	97	32	0	13

PETCHEY George
Stepney, 24 June, 1931 (WH)

League Club	Source	Date Signed	Seasons Played	Apps	Subs	Gls
West Ham U.	Jnrs	08.48	52	2	-	0
Queens Park R.	Tr	07.53	53-59	255	-	22
Crystal Palace	Tr	06.60	60-63	143	-	12

PETERS Alan Gerard
Newport, 14 October, 1958 (M)

League Club	Source	Date Signed	Seasons Played	Apps	Subs	Gls
Hereford U.	Aston Villa (App)	06.76	76	1	0	0

League Club	Source	Date Signed	Seasons Played	Apps	Subs	Gls
PETERS Gary David						
Carshalton, 3 August, 1954						(D)
Reading	Guildford C.	05.75	75-78	150	6	7
Fulham	Tr	08.79	79-81	57	7	2
Wimbledon	Tr	07.82	82-83	83	0	7
Aldershot	Tr	07.84	84	17	0	1
Reading	Tr	02.85	84-87	93	7	3
Fulham (N/C)	Tr	08.88	88-89	7	4	2
PETERS Jeffrey						
Gosforth, 7 March, 1961						(LB)
Middlesbrough	App	03.79	79	6	0	0
PETERS Mark						
St Asaph, 6 July, 1972 W Yth/Wu21-3/W 'B'						(CD)
Manchester C.	YT	07.90				
Norwich C.	Tr	08.92				
Peterborough U.	Tr	08.93	93	17	2	0
Mansfield T.	Tr	09.94	94-97	70	1	8
PETERS Martin Stanford						
Plaistow, 8 November, 1943 E Sch/E Yth/Eu23-5/EF Lge/E-67						(M)
West Ham U.	App	11.60	61-69	302	0	81
Tottenham H.	Tr	03.70	69-74	189	0	46
Norwich C.	Tr	03.75	74-79	206	1	44
Sheffield U.	Tr	08.80	80	23	1	4
PETERS Robert Anthony Angus						
Kensington, 18 May, 1971						(M)
Brentford	YT	07.89	89-93	16	14	1
Carlisle U. (N/C)	Tr	11.94	94	5	3	0
PETERS Roger (Lou) Douglas						
Cheltenham, 5 March, 1944 E Yth						(W)
Bristol C.	App	03.61	60-67	158	0	25
Bournemouth	Tr	06.68	68-69	35	2	3
PETERS Thomas						
Droylsden, 22 December, 1920						(IF)
Doncaster Rov.		05.44				
Bury	Tr	12.46	47	10	-	1
Leeds U.	Tr	08.48				
Mansfield T.	Tr	03.49	48	6	-	2
Accrington St.	Tr	10.49	49	4	-	2
PETERSON Eric **Brian**						
South Africa, 28 October, 1936						(IF)
Blackpool	Berea Park (SA)	10.56	56-61	103	-	16
PETERSON Frank Arthur						
Croydon, 3 April, 1951						(F)
Millwall	App	02.69	68	3	0	0
PETERSON Paul Wayne						
Hitchin, 22 December, 1949						(FB)
Leeds U.	App	12.66	69	3	1	0
Swindon T.	Tr	06.71	71	1	0	0
PETHARD Frederick James						
Glasgow, 7 October, 1950 S Sch						(FB)
Cardiff C.	Glasgow Celtic	08.69	71-78	161	10	0
Torquay U.	Tr	08.79	79-81	104	1	0
PETHERBRIDGE George						
Devonport, 19 May, 1927						(W)
Bristol Rov.	Jnrs	01.45	46-61	452	-	85
PETHICK Robert John						
Tavistock, 8 September, 1970						(RB)
Portsmouth	Weymouth	10.93	93-97	153	26	3
PETIT Emmanuel						
Dieppe, France, 22 September, 1970 French Int						(M)
Arsenal	A.S. Monaco (Fr)	06.97	97	32	0	2
PETRESCU Daniel Vasile						
Romania, 22 December, 1967 Romanian Int						(RM)
Sheffield Wed.	Genoa (It)	08.94	94-95	28	9	3
Chelsea	Tr	11.95	95-97	87	2	10
PETROVIC Vladimir						
Yugoslavia, 1 July, 1955						(M)
Arsenal	Red Star Belgrade (Yug)	12.82	82	10	3	2
PETTA Robert Alfred Manuel						
Netherlands, 6 August, 1974						(W)
Ipswich T.	Feyenoord (Neth)	06.96	96-97	29	9	7

League Club	Source	Date Signed	Seasons Played	Apps	Subs	Gls
PETTERSON Andrew Keith						
Australia, 26 September, 1969						(G)
Luton T.	Freemantle (Aus)	12.88	92-93	16	3	0
Ipswich T.	L	03.93	92	1	0	0
Charlton Ath.	Tr	07.94	94-97	61	1	0
Bradford C.	L	12.94	94	3	0	0
Ipswich T.	L	09.95	95	1	0	0
Plymouth Arg.	L	01.96	95	6	0	0
Colchester U.	L	03.96	95	5	0	0
PETTINGER Paul Allen						
Sheffield, 1 October, 1975 E Sch/E Yth						(G)
Leeds U.	YT	10.92				
Torquay U.	L	12.94	94	3	0	0
Rotherham U.	L	08.95	95	0	1	0
Gillingham	Tr	03.96				
Carlisle U.	Tr	08.96				
Rotherham U.	Tr	08.97	97	3	0	0
PETTIT Raymond John						
Hull, 11 December, 1946						(CD)
Hull C.	App	12.64	66-71	78	1	0
Barnsley	Tr	09.72	72-73	49	2	1
PETTS John William Frederick James						
Edmonton, 2 October, 1938 E Yth						(WH)
Arsenal	Jnrs	05.56	57-61	32	-	0
Reading	Tr	10.62	62-64	34	-	0
Bristol Rov.	Tr	07.65	65-69	88	4	3
PETTS Paul Andrew						
Hackney, 27 September, 1961 E Yth						(W)
Bristol Rov.	App	06.79	78-79	12	1	0
Shrewsbury T.	Tr	08.80	80-84	138	11	16
PEVERELL John Richard						
Richmond (N Yorks), 17 September, 1941						(RB)
Darlington	Ferryhill Ath.	09.59	61-71	418	1	13
PEVERELL Nicholas John						
Middlesbrough, 28 April, 1973						(F)
Middlesbrough	YT	07.91				
Hartlepool U.	Tr	11.92	92-94	14	22	3
York C.	Tr	02.95	94-95	13	16	2
PEYTON Gerald Joseph						
Birmingham, 20 May, 1956 IRu21-2/IR-33						(G)
Burnley	Atherstone T.	05.75	75-76	30	0	0
Fulham	Tr	12.76	76-85	345	0	0
Southend U.	L	09.83	83	10	0	0
Bournemouth	Tr	07.86	86-90	202	0	0
Everton	Tr	07.91				
Bolton W.	L	02.92	91	1	0	0
Brentford	L	09.92	92	14	0	0
Chelsea	L	01.93	92	0	1	0
Brentford	Tr	03.93	92	5	0	0
West Ham U.	Tr	06.93				
PEYTON Noel						
Dublin, 4 December, 1935 IR 'B'/IR-6						(IF)
Leeds U.	Shamrock Rov.	01.58	57-62	105	-	17
York C.	Tr	07.63	63-64	37	-	4
PEYTON Robert Andrew						
Birmingham, 1 May, 1954						(M)
Port Vale	Chelmsley T.	01.72	71	1	1	0
PHELAN Albert						
Sheffield, 27 April, 1945						(CD)
Chesterfield	Jnrs	07.64	64-74	385	5	14
Halifax T.	Tr	10.74	74-76	118	0	4
PHELAN Michael Christopher						
Nelson, 24 September, 1962 E Yth/E-1						(M)
Burnley	App	07.80	80-84	166	2	9
Norwich C.	Tr	07.85	85-88	155	1	9
Manchester U.	Tr	06.89	89-93	88	14	2
West Bromwich A.	Tr	07.94	94-95	18	3	0
PHELAN Terence Michael						
Manchester, 16 March, 1967 IR Yth/IRu21-1/IRu23-1/IR 'B'/IR-38						(LB)
Leeds U.	YT	08.84	85	12	2	0
Swansea C.	Tr	07.86	86	45	0	0
Wimbledon	Tr	07.87	87-91	155	4	1
Manchester C.	Tr	08.92	92-95	102	1	2
Chelsea	Tr	11.95	95-96	13	2	0
Everton	Tr	01.97	96-97	23	1	0

PHENIX William **Brian**
Tyldesley, 10 December, 1937 (F)

League Club	Source	Date Signed	Seasons Played	Apps	Subs	Gls
Southport	Boothstown	12.57	57-58	15	-	3

PHILIP Iain Frederick
Broughty Ferry, 14 February, 1951 S Sch/Su23-1/SF Lge (M)

League Club	Source	Date Signed	Seasons Played	Apps	Subs	Gls
Crystal Palace	Dundee	09.72	72-73	35	0	1

PHILLIBEN John
Stirling, 14 March, 1964 S Yth (D)

League Club	Source	Date Signed	Seasons Played	Apps	Subs	Gls
Doncaster Rov.	Stirling A.	03.84	83-86	66	5	1
Cambridge U.	L	12.85	85	6	0	0

PHILLIPS Benjamin
Hazel Grove, 9 June, 1960 (FB)

League Club	Source	Date Signed	Seasons Played	Apps	Subs	Gls
Bury	Macclesfield T.	09.80	80	14	0	0

PHILLIPS Brendan Ulysees
West Indies, 16 July, 1954 E Semi Pro (M)

League Club	Source	Date Signed	Seasons Played	Apps	Subs	Gls
Leicester C.	App	07.72				
Peterborough U.	Tr	08.73	73	1	0	0
Mansfield T.	Boston U.	08.80	80	17	0	0

PHILLIPS John **Brian**
Cadishead, 9 November, 1931 (CH)

League Club	Source	Date Signed	Seasons Played	Apps	Subs	Gls
Middlesbrough	Altrincham	06.54	54-59	121	-	2
Mansfield T.	Tr	06.60	60-62	104	-	3

PHILLIPS Cornelius Patrick
Liverpool, 10 May, 1938 (F)

League Club	Source	Date Signed	Seasons Played	Apps	Subs	Gls
Liverpool	Jnrs	06.55				
Southport	Tr	07.57	57	19	-	6

PHILLIPS David Owen
West Germany, 29 July, 1963 W Yth/Wu21-4/W-62 (M/RB)

League Club	Source	Date Signed	Seasons Played	Apps	Subs	Gls
Plymouth Arg.	App	08.81	81-83	65	8	15
Manchester C.	Tr	08.84	84-85	81	0	13
Coventry C.	Tr	06.86	86-88	93	7	8
Norwich C.	Tr	06.89	89-92	152	0	18
Nottingham F.	Tr	08.93	93-96	116	10	5
Huddersfield T.	Tr	11.97	97	29	0	2

PHILLIPS Donald
Llanelli, 3 March, 1933 (F)

League Club	Source	Date Signed	Seasons Played	Apps	Subs	Gls
Swansea C.	Llanelli	12.56	56-57	3	-	0

PHILLIPS Edward (Ted) John
Snape, 21 August, 1933 (IF)

League Club	Source	Date Signed	Seasons Played	Apps	Subs	Gls
Ipswich T.	Leiston	12.53	53-63	269	-	161
Leyton Orient	Tr	03.64	63-64	36	-	17
Luton T.	Tr	02.65	64	12	-	8
Colchester U.	Tr	09.65	65	32	0	13

PHILLIPS Ernest
Tynemouth, 29 November, 1923 (FB)

League Club	Source	Date Signed	Seasons Played	Apps	Subs	Gls
Manchester C.	Ashington	01.47	48-51	80	-	0
Hull C.	Tr	11.51	51-53	42	-	0
York C.	Tr	06.54	54-57	164	-	2

PHILLIPS Gareth Russell
Pontypridd, 19 August, 1979 W Sch/W Yth (M)

League Club	Source	Date Signed	Seasons Played	Apps	Subs	Gls
Swansea C.	YT	●	96-97	0	7	0

PHILLIPS Gary Christopher
St Albans, 20 September, 1961 E Semi Pro (G)

League Club	Source	Date Signed	Seasons Played	Apps	Subs	Gls
West Bromwich A.	Brighton & H. A. (App)	06.79				
Brentford	Barnet	12.84	84-87	143	0	0
Reading	Tr	08.88	88	24	0	0
Hereford U.	L	09.89	89	6	0	0
Barnet	Tr	12.89	91-94	117	0	0

PHILLIPS Gordon David
Uxbridge, 17 January, 1946 (G)

League Club	Source	Date Signed	Seasons Played	Apps	Subs	Gls
Brentford	Hayes	11.63	64-72	208	0	0

PHILLIPS Ian Alexander
Cumnock, 23 April, 1959 (LB)

League Club	Source	Date Signed	Seasons Played	Apps	Subs	Gls
Mansfield T.	Ipswich T. (App)	08.77	77-78	18	5	0
Peterborough U.	Tr	08.79	79-81	97	0	3
Northampton T.	Tr	08.82	82	42	0	1
Colchester U.	Tr	09.83	83-86	150	0	10
Aldershot	Tr	08.87	87-89	106	0	2
Colchester U. (N/C)	Kettering T.	07.91	92	0	1	0

PHILLIPS James Neil
Bolton, 8 February, 1966 (LB)

League Club	Source	Date Signed	Seasons Played	Apps	Subs	Gls
Bolton W.	App	08.83	83-86	103	5	2
Oxford U.	Glasgow Rangers	08.88	88-89	79	0	8
Middlesbrough	Tr	03.90	89-92	139	0	6
Bolton W.	Tr	07.93	93-97	181	2	2

PHILLIPS John Edgar
Portsmouth, 4 March, 1937 (WH)

League Club	Source	Date Signed	Seasons Played	Apps	Subs	Gls
Portsmouth	Jnrs	05.55	55-59	77	-	0

PHILLIPS Thomas **John** Seymour
Shrewsbury, 7 July, 1951 Wu23-4/W-4 (G)

League Club	Source	Date Signed	Seasons Played	Apps	Subs	Gls
Shrewsbury T.	App	11.68	68-69	51	0	0
Aston Villa	Tr	10.69	69	15	0	0
Chelsea	Tr	08.70	70-78	125	0	0
Crewe Alex.	L	08.79	79	6	0	0
Brighton & H. A.	Tr	03.80	80	1	0	0
Charlton Ath.	Tr	07.81	81	2	0	0
Crystal Palace	Tr	01.83				

PHILLIPS Joseph Roy
Cardiff, 8 July, 1923 Died 1992 (FB)

League Club	Source	Date Signed	Seasons Played	Apps	Subs	Gls
Cardiff C.	Cardiff Corries	04.42	46	2	-	0

PHILLIPS Justin Lee
Derby, 17 December, 1971 E Yth (CD)

League Club	Source	Date Signed	Seasons Played	Apps	Subs	Gls
Derby Co.	YT	07.90	90	3	0	1

PHILLIPS Kevin Mark
Hitchin, 25 July, 1973 E 'B' (F)

League Club	Source	Date Signed	Seasons Played	Apps	Subs	Gls
Watford	Baldock T.	12.94	94-96	54	5	24
Sunderland	Tr	07.97	97	42	1	29

PHILLIPS Lee
Aberdare, 18 March, 1979 W Yth (CD)

League Club	Source	Date Signed	Seasons Played	Apps	Subs	Gls
Cardiff C.	YT	07.97	96-97	9	2	0

PHILLIPS Lee Paul
Penzance, 16 September, 1980 (F)

League Club	Source	Date Signed	Seasons Played	Apps	Subs	Gls
Plymouth Arg.	YT	●	96-97	3	9	0

PHILLIPS Leighton
Neath, 25 September, 1949 W Sch/Wu21-2/Wu23-4/W-58 (CD/M)

League Club	Source	Date Signed	Seasons Played	Apps	Subs	Gls
Cardiff C.	App	04.67	67-74	169	11	11
Aston Villa	Tr	09.74	74-78	134	6	4
Swansea C.	Tr	11.78	78-80	97	0	0
Charlton Ath.	Tr	08.81	81-82	45	0	1
Exeter C. (N/C)	Tr	03.83	82	10	0	0

PHILLIPS Horace **Leonard**
Shoreditch, 11 September, 1922 EF Lge/E-3 (IF)

League Club	Source	Date Signed	Seasons Played	Apps	Subs	Gls
Portsmouth	Hillside Y.C.	01.46	46-54	245	-	48

PHILLIPS Leslie Michael
Lambeth, 7 January, 1963 (M)

League Club	Source	Date Signed	Seasons Played	Apps	Subs	Gls
Birmingham C.	App	08.80	81-83	36	8	3
Oxford U.	Tr	03.84	83-92	165	14	11
Northampton T.	Tr	07.93	93	26	0	0

PHILLIPS Lionel Arthur Raymond
Hereford, 13 December, 1929 (F)

League Club	Source	Date Signed	Seasons Played	Apps	Subs	Gls
Portsmouth	Yeovil T.	02.53	53	4	-	1

PHILLIPS Marcus Stuart
Trowbridge, 17 October, 1973 (W)

League Club	Source	Date Signed	Seasons Played	Apps	Subs	Gls
Swindon T.	YT	05.93				
Oxford U.	Witney T.	02.97	96	0	1	0

PHILLIPS Martin John
Exeter, 13 March, 1976 (W)

League Club	Source	Date Signed	Seasons Played	Apps	Subs	Gls
Exeter C.	YT	07.94	92-95	36	16	5
Manchester C.	Tr	11.95	95-96	3	12	0
Scunthorpe U.	L	01.98	97	2	1	0
Exeter C.	L	03.98	97	7	1	0

PHILLIPS Michael Shirkie
Cumnock, 18 January, 1933 (CF)

League Club	Source	Date Signed	Seasons Played	Apps	Subs	Gls
Grimsby T.	Cumnock Jnrs.	01.55	54	6	-	1

PHILLIPS Nicholas
West Ham, 29 November, 1960 (M)

League Club	Source	Date Signed	Seasons Played	Apps	Subs	Gls
Coventry C.	App	08.78	79	4	1	0

PHILLIPS Peter Stuart
Wellingborough, 29 June, 1946 E Amat (F)

League Club	Source	Date Signed	Seasons Played	Apps	Subs	Gls
Luton T.	Bishops Stortford	06.69	69	2	3	0
Torquay U.	L	01.71	70	2	0	1
Cambridge U.	Tr	03.71	70-72	40	13	13

PHILLIPS Ralph
Hetton-le-Hole, 9 August, 1933 (FB)

League Club	Source	Date Signed	Seasons Played	Apps	Subs	Gls
Middlesbrough		05.54				
Northampton T.	Tr	08.58	58-60	83	-	1
Darlington	Tr	06.61	61-62	29	-	2

PHILLIPS Reginald Roydon
Llanelli, 9 March, 1921 Died 1972 (CF)

League Club	Source	Date Signed	Seasons Played	Apps	Subs	Gls
Crewe Alex.	Shrewsbury T.	05.49	49-51	64	-	35

PHILLIPS Ronald Daniel
Worsley, 30 March, 1947 (W)

League Club	Source	Date Signed	Seasons Played	Apps	Subs	Gls
Bolton W.	Jnrs	10.65	66-74	135	10	17
Chesterfield	L	01.75	74	5	0	0
Bury	Tr	06.75	75-76	68	4	5
Chester C.	Tr	09.77	77-80	128	2	21

PHILLIPS Russell George Thomas
Exeter, 22 June, 1916 (F)

League Club	Source	Date Signed	Seasons Played	Apps	Subs	Gls
Millwall		01.45				
Torquay U.	Tr	01.46	46	30	-	3

PHILLIPS Stephen Edward
Edmonton, 4 August, 1954 E Yth (W/F)

League Club	Source	Date Signed	Seasons Played	Apps	Subs	Gls
Birmingham C.	App	08.71	71-75	15	5	1
Torquay U.	L	12.74	74	6	0	0
Northampton T.	Tr	10.75	75-76	50	1	9
Brentford	Tr	02.77	76-79	156	1	65
Northampton T.	Tr	08.80	80-81	75	0	29
Southend U.	Tr	03.82	81-85	157	1	66
Torquay U.	Tr	01.86	85-86	32	0	11
Peterborough U.	Tr	11.86	86-87	46	2	16
Exeter C.	L	09.87	87	5	1	1
Chesterfield	L	01.88	87	9	0	2

PHILLIPS Stewart Gavin
Halifax, 30 December, 1961 (F)

League Club	Source	Date Signed	Seasons Played	Apps	Subs	Gls
Hereford U.	App	11.79	77-87	285	8	83
West Bromwich A.	Tr	03.88	87-88	15	0	4
Swansea C.	Tr	01.89	88-89	10	10	1
Hereford U.	Tr	08.90	90	31	6	10
Wrexham (N/C)	Tr	08.91	91	1	1	1

PHILLIPS Trevor
Barnsley, 18 September, 1952 E Yth (F)

League Club	Source	Date Signed	Seasons Played	Apps	Subs	Gls
Rotherham U.	App	03.70	69-78	289	33	82
Hull C.	Tr	06.79	79	22	0	3
Chester C.	Tr	03.80	79-81	57	7	10
Stockport Co.	Tr	03.82	81-82	49	2	13
Chester C. (N/C)	Tr	08.83	83	9	1	2

PHILLIPS Wayne
Bangor, 15 December, 1970 W 'B' (M)

League Club	Source	Date Signed	Seasons Played	Apps	Subs	Gls
Wrexham	YT	08.89	89-97	184	23	16
Stockport Co.	Tr	02.98	97	7	6	0

PHILLIPSON William Ernest
Barrow, 4 April, 1917 Died 1974 (G)

League Club	Source	Date Signed	Seasons Played	Apps	Subs	Gls
Barrow	Holker C.O.B.	10.38	46-47	14	-	0

PHILLIPSON-MASTERS Forbes Ernest
Bournemouth, 14 November, 1955 (CD)

League Club	Source	Date Signed	Seasons Played	Apps	Subs	Gls
Southampton	App	11.73	76-77	9	0	0
Exeter C.	L	09.76	76	6	0	0
Bournemouth	L	09.77	77	7	0	2
Luton Town	L	03.79	78	10	0	0
Plymouth Arg.	Tr	08.79	79-82	119	0	0
Bristol C.	Tr	11.82	82-84	94	0	4
Exeter C.	L	03.85	84	5	2	1

PHILLISKIRK Anthony
Sunderland, 10 February, 1965 E Sch (F)

League Club	Source	Date Signed	Seasons Played	Apps	Subs	Gls
Sheffield U.	Jnrs	08.83	83-87	62	18	20
Rotherham U.	L	10.86	86	6	0	1
Oldham Ath.	Tr	07.88	88	3	7	1
Preston N. E.	Tr	02.89	88	13	1	6
Bolton W.	Tr	06.89	89-92	139	2	51
Peterborough U.	Tr	10.92	92-93	37	6	15
Burnley	Tr	01.94	93-95	33	7	9
Carlisle U.	L	10.95	95	3	0	1
Cardiff C.	Tr	12.95	95-96	55	6	5
Macclesfield T.	L	02.98	97	1	9	1

PHILP David
Fowey, 8 July, 1960 (G)

League Club	Source	Date Signed	Seasons Played	Apps	Subs	Gls
Plymouth Arg.	Newquay	07.84	84	7	0	0

PHILPOTT Alan
Stoke, 8 November, 1942 (D/M)

League Club	Source	Date Signed	Seasons Played	Apps	Subs	Gls
Stoke C.	Jnrs	11.59	60-67	41	4	1
Oldham Ath.	Tr	11.67	67-68	28	3	1

PHILPOTT Lee
Barnet, 21 February, 1970 (LM)

League Club	Source	Date Signed	Seasons Played	Apps	Subs	Gls
Peterborough U.	YT	07.88	87-88	1	3	0
Cambridge U.	Tr	05.89	89-92	118	16	17
Leicester C.	Tr	11.92	92-95	57	18	3
Blackpool	Tr	03.96	95-97	51	20	5

PHILPOTTS David Ronald
Bromborough, 31 March, 1954 (CD)

League Club	Source	Date Signed	Seasons Played	Apps	Subs	Gls
Coventry C.	App	10.71	73	3	0	0
Southport	L	01.74	73	8	0	0
Tranmere Rov.	Tr	09.74	74-77	174	1	5
Tranmere Rov.	Carolina (USA)	10.83	83-84	36	0	6

PHIPPS Harold James
Dartford, 15 January, 1916 (CH)

League Club	Source	Date Signed	Seasons Played	Apps	Subs	Gls
Charlton Ath.	Middlesex Regt	10.43	46-50	185	-	2
Watford	Tr	06.52	52-53	47	-	0

PHOENIX William **Eric**
Manchester, 20 January, 1932 (IF)

League Club	Source	Date Signed	Seasons Played	Apps	Subs	Gls
Gillingham	Hastings U.	07.54	54-55	17	-	2
Exeter C.	Tr	07.56	56	5	-	0

PHOENIX Peter Patrick
Urmston, 31 December, 1936 (OL)

League Club	Source	Date Signed	Seasons Played	Apps	Subs	Gls
Oldham Ath.	Lostock Gralam	02.58	57-62	161	-	27
Rochdale	Tr	10.62	62-63	36	-	4
Exeter C.	Tr	10.63	63	15	-	1
Southport	Tr	01.64	63	10	-	0
Stockport Co.	Tr	07.64	64	19	-	1

PHOENIX Ronald James
Manchester, 30 June, 1929 (WH)

League Club	Source	Date Signed	Seasons Played	Apps	Subs	Gls
Manchester C.	Humphrey Park	03.50	51-58	53	-	2
Rochdale	Tr	02.60	60-61	64	-	0

PHYTHIAN Ernest Rixon
Farnworth, 16 July, 1942 E Yth (CF)

League Club	Source	Date Signed	Seasons Played	Apps	Subs	Gls
Bolton W.	Jnrs	07.59	59-61	10	-	3
Wrexham	Tr	03.62	61-64	134	-	44
Hartlepool U.	Tr	06.65	65-67	124	0	51

PICK Gary Mark
Leicester, 9 July, 1971 (M)

League Club	Source	Date Signed	Seasons Played	Apps	Subs	Gls
Stoke C.	Atherstone U.	08.92				
Hereford U.	Tr	06.94	94-95	33	10	2
Cambridge U.	Tr	03.96	95	2	2	0

PICKARD Leonard James
Barnstaple, 29 November, 1924 (CF)

League Club	Source	Date Signed	Seasons Played	Apps	Subs	Gls
Bristol Rov.	Barnstaple	01.51	51	4	-	1
Bristol C.	Tr	05.53				
Bradford P. A.	Tr	10.53	53-55	76	-	31

PICKARD Owen Anthony
Barnstaple, 18 November, 1969 (F)

League Club	Source	Date Signed	Seasons Played	Apps	Subs	Gls
Plymouth Arg.	YT	07.88	88-91	6	10	1
Hereford U.	Tr	07.92	92-93	66	7	14

PICKERING Albert (Ally) Gary
Manchester, 22 June, 1967 (FB)

League Club	Source	Date Signed	Seasons Played	Apps	Subs	Gls
Rotherham U.	Buxton	02.90	89-93	87	1	2
Coventry C.	Tr	10.93	93-95	54	11	0
Stoke C.	Tr	08.96	96-97	81	1	1

PICKERING Frederick
Blackburn, 19 January, 1941 Eu23-3/EF Lge/E-3 (CF)

League Club	Source	Date Signed	Seasons Played	Apps	Subs	Gls
Blackburn Rov.	Jnrs	01.58	59-63	123	-	59
Everton	Tr	03.64	63-66	97	0	56
Birmingham C.	Tr	08.67	67-68	74	0	27
Blackpool	Tr	06.69	69-70	48	1	24
Blackburn Rov.	Tr	03.71	70	11	0	2

PICKERING John
Chapeltown, 18 December, 1908 Died 1977 EF Lge/E-1 (IF)

League Club	Source	Date Signed	Seasons Played	Apps	Subs	Gls
Sheffield U.	Jnrs	12.25	26-47	343	-	104

PICKERING John
Stockton, 7 November, 1944 (CD)

League Club	Source	Date Signed	Seasons Played	Apps	Subs	Gls
Newcastle U.	Stockton	07.63				
Halifax T.	Tr	09.65	65-73	364	3	5
Barnsley	Tr	07.74	74	42	1	2

PICKERING Michael John
Mirfield, 29 September, 1956 (CD)

League Club	Source	Date Signed	Seasons Played	Apps	Subs	Gls
Barnsley	Jnrs	10.74	74-76	100	0	1
Southampton	Tr	06.77	77-78	44	0	0
Sheffield Wed.	Tr	10.78	78-82	106	4	1
Norwich C.	L	09.83	83	0	1	0
Bradford C.	L	11.83	83	4	0	0
Barnsley	L	12.83	83	3	0	0

League Club	Source	Date Signed	Seasons Played	Apps	Subs	Gls
Rotherham U.	Tr	01.84	83-85	102	0	1
York C.	Tr	07.86	86	31	1	1
Stockport Co.	Tr	07.87	87-88	15	1	0

PICKERING Nicholas
Newcastle, 4 August, 1963 E Yth/Eu21-15/E-1 (LM)

League Club	Source	Date Signed	Seasons Played	Apps	Subs	Gls
Sunderland	App	08.81	81-85	177	2	18
Coventry C.	Tr	01.86	85-87	76	2	9
Derby Co.	Tr	08.88	88-91	35	10	3
Darlington	Tr	10.91	91-92	57	0	7
Burnley	Tr	03.93	92	4	0	0

PICKERING Peter Barlow
York, 24 March, 1926 (G)

League Club	Source	Date Signed	Seasons Played	Apps	Subs	Gls
York C.	Earswick	04.44	46-47	49	-	0
Chelsea	Tr	05.48	48-50	27	-	0
Northampton T.	Kettering T.	07.55	55-57	86	-	0

PICKERING William Henry
Sheffield, 10 December, 1919 Died 1983 E Amat (FB)

League Club	Source	Date Signed	Seasons Played	Apps	Subs	Gls
Sheffield Wed.	Jnrs	10.37	38	3	-	0
Oldham Ath.	Tr	07.48	48-49	78	-	0

PICKETT Reginald Arthur
India, 6 January, 1927 (WH)

League Club	Source	Date Signed	Seasons Played	Apps	Subs	Gls
Portsmouth	Weymouth	03.49	49-56	123	-	3
Ipswich T.	Tr	07.57	57-62	140	-	3

PICKRELL Anthony David
Neath, 3 November, 1942 (OL)

League Club	Source	Date Signed	Seasons Played	Apps	Subs	Gls
Cardiff C.	Jnrs	09.60	60-61	18	-	4

PICKUP John Antony
Wakefield, 3 December, 1931 (IL)

League Club	Source	Date Signed	Seasons Played	Apps	Subs	Gls
Bradford P. A.	Frickley Colly	09.55	55	2	-	0

PICKUP Reginald John
Stoke, 6 September, 1929 (WH)

League Club	Source	Date Signed	Seasons Played	Apps	Subs	Gls
Stoke C.	Jnrs	08.49	49	1	-	0

PICKWICK Donald Harry John
Rhondda, 7 February, 1925 (WH)

League Club	Source	Date Signed	Seasons Played	Apps	Subs	Gls
Norwich C.	Cardiff C. (Am)	08.47	47-55	224	-	9

PIDCOCK Frederick Charles
Canada, 29 June, 1933 (G)

League Club	Source	Date Signed	Seasons Played	Apps	Subs	Gls
Walsall (Am)	Moor Green	09.53	53	1	-	0

PIEARCE Steven
Birmingham, 27 September, 1974 (F)

League Club	Source	Date Signed	Seasons Played	Apps	Subs	Gls
Wolverhampton W.	YT	07.93				
Doncaster Rov.	Tr	07.96	96	8	11	1

PIECHNIK Torben
Denmark, 21 May, 1963 Norwegian Int (CD)

League Club	Source	Date Signed	Seasons Played	Apps	Subs	Gls
Liverpool	Copenhagen F.C. (Den)	09.92	92-93	16	1	0

PIEKALNIETIS John Andrew
Penrith, 23 September, 1951 E Yth (CD)

League Club	Source	Date Signed	Seasons Played	Apps	Subs	Gls
Nottingham F.	Jnrs	03.69				
Southend U.	Tr	04.71	70	1	0	0

PIERCE John **Barry**
Liverpool, 13 August, 1934 (IF)

League Club	Source	Date Signed	Seasons Played	Apps	Subs	Gls
Crystal Palace	Truro C.	08.55	55-58	85	-	23
Millwall	Tr	05.59	59-60	46	-	17
York C.	Tr	07.61	61	12	-	5
Exeter C.	Tr	07.62	62	28	-	4

PIERCE David Edward
Manchester, 4 October, 1975 (G)

League Club	Source	Date Signed	Seasons Played	Apps	Subs	Gls
Rotherham U.	Manchester U. (YT)	08.94				
Chesterfield	Tr	08.95	95	1	0	0

PIERCE Gary
Bury, 2 March, 1951 (G)

League Club	Source	Date Signed	Seasons Played	Apps	Subs	Gls
Huddersfield T.	Mossley	02.71	71-72	23	0	0
Wolverhampton W.	Tr	08.73	73-78	98	0	0
Barnsley	Tr	07.79	79-82	81	0	0
Blackpool	Tr	08.83	83	27	0	0

PIGGOTT Gary David
Warley, 1 April, 1969 (F)

League Club	Source	Date Signed	Seasons Played	Apps	Subs	Gls
West Bromwich A.	Dudley T.	03.91	91	3	2	0
Shrewsbury T. (N/C)	Tr	03.93	92	3	1	0

PIKE Christopher
Cardiff, 19 October, 1961 (F)

League Club	Source	Date Signed	Seasons Played	Apps	Subs	Gls
Fulham	Barry T.	03.85	85-87	32	10	4
Cardiff C.	L	12.86	86	6	0	2
Cardiff C.	Tr	07.89	89-92	134	14	65
Hereford U.	Tr	07.93	93-94	36	2	18
Gillingham	Tr	09.94	94	26	1	13

PIKE Geoffrey Alan
Clapton, 28 September, 1956 (M)

League Club	Source	Date Signed	Seasons Played	Apps	Subs	Gls
West Ham U.	App	09.74	75-86	275	16	32
Notts Co.	Tr	07.87	87-88	80	2	17
Leyton Orient	Tr	09.89	89-90	36	8	1

PIKE Martin Russell
South Shields, 21 October, 1964 (LB)

League Club	Source	Date Signed	Seasons Played	Apps	Subs	Gls
West Bromwich A.	App	10.82				
Peterborough U.	Tr	08.83	83-85	119	7	8
Sheffield U.	Tr	08.86	86-89	127	2	5
Tranmere Rov.	L	11.89	89	2	0	0
Bolton W.	L	12.89	89	5	0	1
Fulham	Tr	02.90	89-93	187	3	14
Rotherham U.	Tr	08.94	94-95	7	2	0

PILGRIM John **Alan**
Billingborough (Lincs), 20 July, 1947 (D)

League Club	Source	Date Signed	Seasons Played	Apps	Subs	Gls
Lincoln C.	Billingborough	05.65	65-71	20	3	1

PILKINGTON Brian
Leyland, 12 February, 1933 E 'B'/EF Lge/E-1 (OL)

League Club	Source	Date Signed	Seasons Played	Apps	Subs	Gls
Burnley	Leyland Motors	04.51	52-60	300	-	67
Bolton W.	Tr	03.61	60-63	82	-	11
Bury	Tr	02.64	63-64	19	-	0
Barrow	Tr	02.65	64-66	86	1	9

PILKINGTON George
Hemsworth, 3 June, 1926 (RB/WH)

League Club	Source	Date Signed	Seasons Played	Apps	Subs	Gls
Rotherham U.	Great Houghton	11.48	49	1	-	0
Chester C.	Tr	07.52	52	16	-	0
Stockport Co.	Tr	05.53	53-55	77	-	4

PILKINGTON Kevin William
Hitchin, 8 March, 1974 E Sch (G)

League Club	Source	Date Signed	Seasons Played	Apps	Subs	Gls
Manchester U.	YT	07.92	94-97	4	2	0
Rochdale	L	02.96	95	6	0	0
Rotherham U.	L	01.97	96-97	17	0	0

PILKINGTON Leslie
Darwen, 23 June, 1925 Died 1995 (OR)

League Club	Source	Date Signed	Seasons Played	Apps	Subs	Gls
Arsenal	Darwen Corries	03.48				
Watford	Tr	03.50	49-50	5	-	0

PILLING Andrew James
Wigan, 30 June, 1969 (M)

League Club	Source	Date Signed	Seasons Played	Apps	Subs	Gls
Preston N.E.	YT	•	85	1	0	0
Wigan Ath.	Tr	07.87	87-92	131	25	20

PILLING John James
St Helens, 4 June, 1913 (LH)

League Club	Source	Date Signed	Seasons Played	Apps	Subs	Gls
Liverpool	South Liverpool	09.42				
Southport	Tr	02.46	46	9	-	0

PILLING Anthony **Stuart**
Sheffield, 26 March, 1951 (LB/M)

League Club	Source	Date Signed	Seasons Played	Apps	Subs	Gls
Preston N. E.	Jnrs	07.69				
Hull C.	Tr	07.70				
Scunthorpe U.	Tr	05.73	73-81	246	16	26

PILLING Vincent
Bolton, 8 January, 1932 (W)

League Club	Source	Date Signed	Seasons Played	Apps	Subs	Gls
Bolton W.	Lomax's	10.52	52-54	7	-	0
Bradford P. A.	Tr	08.55	55	9	-	1

PIMBLETT Francis Roy
Liverpool, 12 March, 1957 E Sch (M)

League Club	Source	Date Signed	Seasons Played	Apps	Subs	Gls
Aston Villa	App	10.74	74-75	9	0	0
Newport Co.	L	03.76	75	7	0	0
Stockport Co.	Tr	07.76	76	0	1	0
Hartlepool U.	Brisbane C. (Aus)	03.80	79	3	0	0

PIMBLEY Douglas William
Birmingham, 19 June, 1917 Died 1988 (OL)

League Club	Source	Date Signed	Seasons Played	Apps	Subs	Gls
Birmingham C.	Stourbridge	07.46	46	2	-	0
Notts Co.	Tr	03.48	47-49	23	-	1

PIMLOTT John Gordon
Radcliffe, 21 January, 1939 Died 1992 (IF)

League Club	Source	Date Signed	Seasons Played	Apps	Subs	Gls
Bury		12.57				
Chester C.	Tr	08.59	59-60	41	-	11

PINCHBECK Clifford Brian
Cleethorpes, 20 January, 1925 Died 1996 (CF)

League Club	Source	Date Signed	Seasons Played	Apps	Subs	Gls
Everton	Scunthorpe U.	12.47	47	3	-	0

League Club	Source	Date Signed	Seasons Played	Apps	Subs	Gls
Brighton & H. A.	Tr	08.49	49	14	-	5
Port Vale	Tr	11.49	49-51	69	-	34
Northampton T.	Tr	12.51	51	3	-	3

PINCOTT Frederick
Bristol, 19 March, 1913 (CH)

League Club	Source	Date Signed	Seasons Played	Apps	Subs	Gls
Wolverhampton W.		11.31	32	2	-	0
Bournemouth	Tr	05.34	34-38	196	-	0
Newport Co.	Gravesend & Nft.	07.47	47	14	-	0

PINDER John (Jack) James
York, 1 December, 1912 E Sch (RB)

League Club	Source	Date Signed	Seasons Played	Apps	Subs	Gls
York C.	Jnrs	02.30	32-47	199	-	4

PINGEL Frank Mortensen
Denmark, 9 May, 1964 Danish Int (F)

League Club	Source	Date Signed	Seasons Played	Apps	Subs	Gls
Newcastle U.	Aarhus G.F. (Den)	01.89	88	13	1	1

PINKNEY Alan John
Battersea, 1 January, 1947 (M)

League Club	Source	Date Signed	Seasons Played	Apps	Subs	Gls
Exeter C. (Am)	St Lukes College	02.68	67-68	7	0	1
Crystal Palace	Tr	07.69	69-73	19	5	0
Fulham	L	01.73	72	11	1	0

PINNER Michael John
Boston, 16 February, 1934 E Amat (G)

League Club	Source	Date Signed	Seasons Played	Apps	Subs	Gls
Aston Villa (Am)	Pegasus	05.54	54-56	4	-	0
Sheffield Wed. (Am)	Corinthian Casuals	12.57	57-58	7	-	0
Queens Park R. (Am)	Tr	07.59	59	19	-	0
Manchester U. (Am)	Tr	02.61	60	4	-	0
Chelsea (Am)	Tr	10.61	61	1	-	0
Swansea C. (Am)	Tr	05.62	61	1	-	0
Leyton Orient	Hendon	10.62	62-64	77	-	0

PINNOCK James Edward
Dartford, 1 August, 1978 (F)

League Club	Source	Date Signed	Seasons Played	Apps	Subs	Gls
Gillingham	YT	07.97	96-97	0	3	0

PINTO Sergio Paulo Viera
Portugal, 8 January, 1973 (RW)

League Club	Source	Date Signed	Seasons Played	Apps	Subs	Gls
Bradford C.	Boavista (Por)	10.96	96	7	11	0

PIPER Gilbert Harold
Northfleet, 21 June, 1921 Died 1987 (HB)

League Club	Source	Date Signed	Seasons Played	Apps	Subs	Gls
Tottenham H.		01.40				
Gillingham	Tr	08.46	50	4	-	0

PIPER Leonard Henry
Camberwell, 8 August, 1977 E Yth (M)

League Club	Source	Date Signed	Seasons Played	Apps	Subs	Gls
Wimbledon	YT	06.95				
Gillingham	Tr	07.96	96-97	4	16	1

PIPER Norman John
North Tawton, 8 January, 1948 E Yth/Eu23-4 (M)

League Club	Source	Date Signed	Seasons Played	Apps	Subs	Gls
Plymouth Arg.	App	02.65	64-69	215	0	35
Portsmouth	Tr	05.70	70-77	309	4	51

PIPER Ronald David
Cresswell, 16 March, 1943 (IF)

League Club	Source	Date Signed	Seasons Played	Apps	Subs	Gls
Tottenham H.	Arsenal (Am)	10.60	62	1	-	0

PIPER Stephen Paul
Brighton, 2 November, 1953 (CD)

League Club	Source	Date Signed	Seasons Played	Apps	Subs	Gls
Brighton & H. A.	Jnrs	09.72	72-77	160	2	9
Portsmouth	Tr	02.78	77-78	28	2	2

PIRIE Frederick William
Coupar Angus, 19 January, 1934 (FB)

League Club	Source	Date Signed	Seasons Played	Apps	Subs	Gls
Accrington St.	Coupar Angus	01.54	54-59	17	-	0

PISANTI David
Israel, 27 May, 1962 (M)

League Club	Source	Date Signed	Seasons Played	Apps	Subs	Gls
Queens Park R.	F.C. Köln (Ger)	09.87	87-88	16	6	0

PISTONE Alessandro
Milan, Italy, 27 July, 1975 (WB)

League Club	Source	Date Signed	Seasons Played	Apps	Subs	Gls
Newcastle U.	Inter Milan (It)	07.97	97	28	0	0

PITCHER Darren Edward James
Stepney, 12 October, 1969 E Yth (M)

League Club	Source	Date Signed	Seasons Played	Apps	Subs	Gls
Charlton Ath.	YT	01.88	90-93	170	3	8
Crystal Palace	Tr	07.94	94-96	60	4	0
Leyton Orient	L	01.98	97	1	0	0

PITCHER Geoffrey
Sutton, 15 August, 1975 (M)

League Club	Source	Date Signed	Seasons Played	Apps	Subs	Gls
Millwall	YT	03.93				
Watford	Tr	07.94	94-95	4	9	2
Colchester U. (N/C)	Kingstonian	02.97	96	0	1	0

PITMAN Jamie Roy
Trowbridge, 6 January, 1976 (M)

League Club	Source	Date Signed	Seasons Played	Apps	Subs	Gls
Swindon T.	YT	07.94	94	2	1	0
Hereford U.	Tr	02.96	95-96	16	5	0

PITT John (Jack) Henry
Willenhall, 20 May, 1920 (RH)

League Club	Source	Date Signed	Seasons Played	Apps	Subs	Gls
Bristol Rov.	Bath C.	05.46	46-57	467	-	16

PITT Richard Ernest
Ryhope, 22 October, 1951 E Sch (CD)

League Club	Source	Date Signed	Seasons Played	Apps	Subs	Gls
Sunderland	Jnrs	11.68	68-73	126	0	7

PITT Stephen William
Wembley, 1 August, 1948 (W)

League Club	Source	Date Signed	Seasons Played	Apps	Subs	Gls
Tottenham H.	App	08.65	65	1	0	0
Colchester U.	Tr	06.69	69	4	2	0

PITTMAN Stephen
U.S.A., 18 July, 1967 (LB)

League Club	Source	Date Signed	Seasons Played	Apps	Subs	Gls
Shrewsbury T.	East Fife	03.89	88-89	31	1	2

PLACE Brendan Anthony
Dublin, 13 December, 1965 (CD)

League Club	Source	Date Signed	Seasons Played	Apps	Subs	Gls
Gillingham	Athlone T.	10.89	89	3	1	0

PLACE Charles Arthur
Ilkeston, 26 November, 1937 (OL)

League Club	Source	Date Signed	Seasons Played	Apps	Subs	Gls
Derby Co.	Jnrs	11.54	55	2	-	0

PLACE Mark Gerald
Mansfield, 16 November, 1969 (CD)

League Club	Source	Date Signed	Seasons Played	Apps	Subs	Gls
Mansfield T.	YT	07.88	88-89	12	3	0
Doncaster Rov.	Tr	08.90	90	1	0	0

PLANT Kenneth George
Nuneaton, 15 August, 1925 (CF)

League Club	Source	Date Signed	Seasons Played	Apps	Subs	Gls
Bury	Nuneaton Borough	02.50	49-53	119	-	55
Colchester U.	Tr	01.54	53-58	190	-	82

PLASKETT Stephen Colin
Newcastle, 24 April, 1971 (RB)

League Club	Source	Date Signed	Seasons Played	Apps	Subs	Gls
Hartlepool U.	YT	07.89	88-89	19	1	0

PLATNAUER Nicholas Robert
Leicester, 10 June, 1961 (LB/M)

League Club	Source	Date Signed	Seasons Played	Apps	Subs	Gls
Bristol Rov.	Bedford T.	08.82	82	21	3	7
Coventry C.	Tr	08.83	83-84	38	6	6
Birmingham C.	Tr	12.84	84-85	23	5	2
Reading	L	01.86	85	7	0	0
Cardiff C.	Tr	09.86	86-88	110	5	6
Notts Co.	Tr	07.89	89-90	57	0	1
Port Vale	L	01.91	90	14	0	0
Leicester C.	Tr	07.91	91-92	32	3	0
Scunthorpe U.	Tr	03.93	92	14	0	2
Mansfield T. (N/C)	Tr	08.93	93	25	0	0
Lincoln C.	Tr	02.94	93-95	26	1	0

PLATT Clive Linton
Wolverhampton, 27 October, 1977 (CF)

League Club	Source	Date Signed	Seasons Played	Apps	Subs	Gls
Walsall	YT	07.96	95-97	12	13	3

PLATT David Andrew
Oldham, 10 June, 1966 Eu21-3/E 'B'/E-62 (M/F)

League Club	Source	Date Signed	Seasons Played	Apps	Subs	Gls
Manchester U.	Chadderton	07.84				
Crewe Alex.	Tr	01.85	84-87	134	0	55
Aston Villa	Tr	02.88	87-90	121	0	50
Arsenal	Sampdoria (It)	07.95	95-97	65	23	13

PLATT Edward (Ted) Hewitt
Newcastle-u-Lyme, 26 March, 1921 Died 1996 (G)

League Club	Source	Date Signed	Seasons Played	Apps	Subs	Gls
Arsenal	Colchester U.	01.39	46-52	53	-	0
Portsmouth	Tr	09.53	53-54	31	-	0
Aldershot	Tr	08.55	55	16	-	0

PLATT James Archibald
Ballymoney (NI), 26 January, 1952 NI Amat/NI-23 (G)

League Club	Source	Date Signed	Seasons Played	Apps	Subs	Gls
Middlesbrough	Ballymena	05.70	71-82	401	0	0
Hartlepool U.	L	08.78	78	13	0	0
Cardiff C.	L	11.78	78	4	0	0

PLATT John Roger
Ashton-u-Lyne, 22 August, 1954 (G)

League Club	Source	Date Signed	Seasons Played	Apps	Subs	Gls
Oldham Ath.	Ashton U.	06.72	75-80	109	0	0
Bury	Tr	08.81	81-82	20	0	0
Bolton W.	Tr	07.83	83	10	0	0
Tranmere Rov.	L	11.84	84	8	0	0
Preston N. E.	Tr	02.85	84-85	38	0	0

PLATT John Stephen
Bermondsey, 29 June, 1942 (OR)

League Club	Source	Date Signed	Seasons Played	Apps	Subs	Gls
Charlton Ath.	Brookhill B.C.	06.61	61	2	-	0

PLATTS Lawrence
Worksop, 31 October, 1921 (G)

League Club	Source	Date Signed	Seasons Played	Apps	Subs	Gls
Nottingham F.	Jnrs	10.43	46-49	6	-	0
Chesterfield	Tr	07.51	51	11	-	0
Stockport Co.	Burton A.	02.53	52-53	28	-	0

PLATTS Mark Anthony
Sheffield, 23 May, 1979 E Sch/E Yth (RW)

League Club	Source	Date Signed	Seasons Played	Apps	Subs	Gls
Sheffield Wed.	YT	10.96	95	0	2	0

PLATTS Peter
Dinnington, 14 January, 1928 (CF)

League Club	Source	Date Signed	Seasons Played	Apps	Subs	Gls
Scunthorpe U. (Am)		07.51	51	2	-	2

PLAYER Percival **Roy** Ivan
Portsmouth, 10 May, 1928 Died 1992 (CH)

League Club	Source	Date Signed	Seasons Played	Apps	Subs	Gls
Grimsby T.	Portsmouth (Am)	08.52	52-58	57	-	0
Oldham Ath.	Tr	05.59	59	2	-	0

PLEAT David John
Nottingham, 15 January, 1945 E Sch/E Yth (W)

League Club	Source	Date Signed	Seasons Played	Apps	Subs	Gls
Nottingham F.	Jnrs	03.62	61-63	6	-	1
Luton T.	Tr	08.64	64-66	67	3	9
Shrewsbury T.	Tr	07.67	67	10	2	1
Exeter C.	Tr	07.68	68-69	66	2	13
Peterborough U.	Tr	07.70	70	28	1	2

PLENDERLEITH John (Jackie) Boyd
Bellshill, 6 October, 1937 S Sch/Su23-5/S-1 (CH)

League Club	Source	Date Signed	Seasons Played	Apps	Subs	Gls
Manchester C.	Hibernian	07.60	60-62	41	-	0

PLLU Charles Lamont
Saltcoats, 28 February, 1934 (G)

League Club	Source	Date Signed	Seasons Played	Apps	Subs	Gls
Sheffield Wed.	Scarborough	12.56	56-57	19	-	0

PLUCK Colin Ian
London, 6 September, 1978 (CD)

League Club	Source	Date Signed	Seasons Played	Apps	Subs	Gls
Watford	YT	02.97	97	1	0	0

PLUCKROSE Alan
Southwater (Sx), 3 July, 1963 (LB)

League Club	Source	Date Signed	Seasons Played	Apps	Subs	Gls
Torquay U. (N/C)	Falmouth	03.83	82	3	0	0

PLUMB Richard (Dick) Kevin
Swindon, 24 September, 1946 (CF)

League Club	Source	Date Signed	Seasons Played	Apps	Subs	Gls
Swindon T.	App	12.63				
Bristol Rov.	Tr	04.65	65-68	39	0	9
Charlton Ath.	Yeovil T.	09.70	70-71	32	11	10
Exeter C.	Tr	08.72	72-73	59	0	17

PLUME Richard William
Tottenham, 10 June, 1949 (M)

League Club	Source	Date Signed	Seasons Played	Apps	Subs	Gls
Millwall	App	03.67	66-68	12	4	0
Leyton Orient	Tr	05.69	69-70	12	6	1

PLUMLEY Gary Edward
Birmingham, 24 March, 1956 (G)

League Club	Source	Date Signed	Seasons Played	Apps	Subs	Gls
Leicester C.	App	03.74				
Newport Co.	Tr	06.76	76-80	182	0	0
Hereford U. (N/C)	Happy Valley (HK)	09.82	82	13	0	0
Newport Co.	Tr	12.82	82	2	0	0
Cardiff C.	Happy Valley (HK)	08.83	83-84	25	0	0
Newport Co.	L	08.84	84	2	0	0
Newport Co. (N/C)	Ebbw Vale	03.87	86	1	0	0

PLUMMER Calvin Anthony
Nottingham, 14 February, 1963 (W)

League Club	Source	Date Signed	Seasons Played	Apps	Subs	Gls
Nottingham F.	App	02.81	81-82	10	2	2
Chesterfield	Tr	12.82	82	28	0	7
Derby Co.	Tr	08.83	83	23	4	3
Barnsley	Tr	03.84	83-86	41	13	7
Nottingham F.	Tr	12.86				
Nottingham F.	Lahden Reipas (Fin)	10.87	87	8	0	2
Plymouth Arg.	Tr	09.88	88	17	6	1
Chesterfield	Tr	07.89	89-90	67	4	12

PLUMMER Christopher
Isleworth, 12 October, 1976 E Yth/Eu21-5 (CD)

League Club	Source	Date Signed	Seasons Played	Apps	Subs	Gls
Queens Park R.	YT	07.94	95-96	4	2	0

PLUMMER Dwayne Jermaine
Bristol, 12 May, 1978 (RW)

League Club	Source	Date Signed	Seasons Played	Apps	Subs	Gls
Bristol C.	YT	09.95	95-97	1	13	0

PLUMMER Norman Leonard
Leicester, 12 January, 1924 (CH)

League Club	Source	Date Signed	Seasons Played	Apps	Subs	Gls
Leicester C.	Leicester A.T.C.	11.42	47-51	66	-	1
Mansfield T.	Tr	07.52	52-55	166	-	5

PLUNKETT Sidney Ernest
Norwich, 2 October, 1920 Died 1986 (W)

League Club	Source	Date Signed	Seasons Played	Apps	Subs	Gls
Norwich C.	Norwich Y.M.C.A.	04.38	38	3	-	0
Wolverhampton W.	Tr	04.39				
Norwich C.	Tr	02.46	46	28	-	7

POBORSKY Karel
Czechoslovakia, 30 March, 1972 Czechoslovakian Int (W)

League Club	Source	Date Signed	Seasons Played	Apps	Subs	Gls
Manchester U.	Slavia Prague (Cz)	08.96	96-97	18	14	5

PODD Cyril (Ces) Casey Marcel
St Kitts (WI), 7 August, 1952 (FB)

League Club	Source	Date Signed	Seasons Played	Apps	Subs	Gls
Bradford C.	Jnrs	08.70	70-83	494	8	3
Halifax T.	Tr	08.84	84-85	52	5	0
Scarborough (N/C)	Tr	07.86	87	3	0	0

POINTER Keith Cecil
Norwich, 16 February, 1951 (M)

League Club	Source	Date Signed	Seasons Played	Apps	Subs	Gls
West Ham U.	Norwich C. (Am)	06.68				
Cambridge U.	Tr	03.72	71-72	6	2	2

POINTER Raymond
Cramlington, 10 October, 1936 Eu23-5/EF Lge/E-3 (CF)

League Club	Source	Date Signed	Seasons Played	Apps	Subs	Gls
Burnley	Dudley Welfare	08.57	57-64	223	-	118
Bury	Tr	08.65	65	19	0	17
Coventry C.	Tr	12.65	65-66	26	0	13
Portsmouth	Tr	01.67	66-72	149	4	31

POINTER Reginald Ernest
Norwich, 28 January, 1935 (CH)

League Club	Source	Date Signed	Seasons Played	Apps	Subs	Gls
Norwich C. (Am)	C.N.S.O.B.U.	06.56	56	11	-	0

POINTON Neil Geoffrey
Church Warsop, 28 November, 1964 (LB)

League Club	Source	Date Signed	Seasons Played	Apps	Subs	Gls
Scunthorpe U.	App	08.82	81-85	159	0	2
Everton	Tr	11.85	85-89	95	7	5
Manchester C.	Tr	07.90	90-91	74	0	2
Oldham Ath.	Tr	09.92	92-95	92	3	3

POINTON Raymond Evison
Birkenhead, 6 November, 1947 (D)

League Club	Source	Date Signed	Seasons Played	Apps	Subs	Gls
Tranmere Rov.	App	11.65	67-70	41	5	0

POINTON William James
Hanley, 25 November, 1920 (F)

League Club	Source	Date Signed	Seasons Played	Apps	Subs	Gls
Port Vale		07.40	46-48	74	-	26
Queens Park R.	Tr	01.49	48-49	26	-	6
Brentford	Tr	02.50	49-50	16	-	2

POLAND George
Penarth, 21 September, 1913 Died 1988 W-2 (G)

League Club	Source	Date Signed	Seasons Played	Apps	Subs	Gls
Cardiff C.		11.35	35-36	24	-	0
Wrexham		07.38	38	39	-	0
Liverpool	Tr	07.39				
Cardiff C.	Tr	08.46	46	2	-	0

POLE Harold **Edward (Ted)**
Kessingland (Sk), 25 March, 1922 (F)

League Club	Source	Date Signed	Seasons Played	Apps	Subs	Gls
Ipswich T.		10.46	46-50	39	-	13
Leyton Orient	Tr	07.51	51-52	12	-	0

POLK Stanley
Liverpool, 28 October, 1921 (WH/IF)

League Club	Source	Date Signed	Seasons Played	Apps	Subs	Gls
Liverpool	South Liverpool	03.40	46-47	13	-	0
Port Vale	Tr	07.48	48-51	159	-	14

POLLARD Brian Edward
York, 22 May, 1954 E Yth (W)

League Club	Source	Date Signed	Seasons Played	Apps	Subs	Gls
York C.	Jnrs	03.72	71-77	151	11	34
Watford	Tr	11.77	77-79	68	3	8
Mansfield T.	Tr	01.80	79-80	45	9	5
Blackpool	Tr	08.81	81	0	1	0
York C.	Tr	09.81	81-83	98	4	26
Chesterfield (N/C)	Tr	09.84	84	0	1	0
Hartlepool U. (N/C)	Scarborough	01.85	84	2	0	0

POLLARD Gary
Staveley, 30 December, 1959 (CD)

League Club	Source	Date Signed	Seasons Played	Apps	Subs	Gls
Chesterfield	Jnrs	07.77	77-82	83	4	1
Port Vale	Tr	06.83	83	17	1	0
Mansfield T.	Tr	07.84	84-86	66	1	1
Peterborough U.	Tr	08.87	87-88	20	0	0

POLLARD James
Liverpool, 4 June, 1926 (OL)

League Club	Source	Date Signed	Seasons Played	Apps	Subs	Gls
Newport Co.	Tredomen	05.46				
Tranmere Rov.		11.47	47-48	24	-	1

POLLARD Kelly John
Chelmsford, 17 November, 1971 (M)

League Club	Source	Date Signed	Seasons Played	Apps	Subs	Gls
Colchester U.	YT	●	88-89	1	8	1

POLLITT John (Jack)
Farnworth, 29 March, 1937 (CF)

League Club	Source	Date Signed	Seasons Played	Apps	Subs	Gls
Bolton W.	Jnrs	12.54				
Bury	Tr	08.58	58	4	-	0
Accrington St.	Tr	03.60	59	3	-	1
Rochdale	Tr	08.60	60	6	-	1

POLLITT Michael Francis
Farnworth, 29 February, 1972 (G)

League Club	Source	Date Signed	Seasons Played	Apps	Subs	Gls
Manchester U.	YT	07.90				
Bury	Tr	07.91				
Lincoln C.	Tr	12.92	92-93	57	0	0
Darlington	Tr	08.94	94-95	55	0	0
Notts Co.	Tr	11.95	95-97	10	0	0
Oldham Ath.	L	08.97	97	16	0	0
Gillingham	L	12.97	97	6	0	0
Brentford	L	01.98	97	5	0	0
Sunderland	Tr	02.98				

POLLOCK Jamie
Stockton, 16 February, 1974 E Yth/Eu21-3 (M)

League Club	Source	Date Signed	Seasons Played	Apps	Subs	Gls
Middlesbrough	YT	12.91	90-95	144	11	17
Bolton W.	Osasuna (Sp)	11.96	96-97	43	3	5
Manchester C.	Tr	03.98	97	8	0	1

POLLOCK Maitland
Dumfries, 31 October, 1952 S Sch (W)

League Club	Source	Date Signed	Seasons Played	Apps	Subs	Gls
Nottingham F.	App	10.70				
Walsall	Tr	07.73	73	1	1	0
Luton T.	Burton A.	03.74	75	3	3	0
Portsmouth	Tr	07.76	76-77	50	4	10

POLLOCK Stewart
Bellshill, 25 September, 1933 (IF)

League Club	Source	Date Signed	Seasons Played	Apps	Subs	Gls
Gillingham	Motherwell	07.56	56	10	-	0

POLLOCK William
Barrhead, 7 June, 1920 (RH)

League Club	Source	Date Signed	Seasons Played	Apps	Subs	Gls
Oldham Ath.	Manchester U. (Am)	07.47	47	4	-	0

POLSTON Andrew Alfred
Walthamstow, 26 July, 1970 (CD)

League Club	Source	Date Signed	Seasons Played	Apps	Subs	Gls
Tottenham H.	YT	07.88	89	0	1	0
Cambridge U.	L	10.89	89	3	0	0
Gillingham	L	11.91	91	1	1	0

POLSTON John David
Walthamstow, 10 June, 1968 E Yth (CD)

League Club	Source	Date Signed	Seasons Played	Apps	Subs	Gls
Tottenham H.	App	07.85	86-89	17	7	1
Norwich C.	Tr	07.90	90-97	200	15	8

POLYCARPOU Andrew
Islington, 15 August, 1958 (M)

League Club	Source	Date Signed	Seasons Played	Apps	Subs	Gls
Southend U.		09.76	76-80	43	20	10
Cambridge U.	Tr	08.81	81	1	4	0
Cardiff C.	Tr	04.82	81	7	0	0

POMPHREY Edric (Syd) Alfred
Stretford, 31 May, 1916 Died 1987 (FB)

League Club	Source	Date Signed	Seasons Played	Apps	Subs	Gls
Notts Co.	Hyde U.	09.44				
Rochdale	Tr	10.45	46	9	-	0

PONTE Raimondo
Switzerland, 4 April, 1954 Swiss Int (M)

League Club	Source	Date Signed	Seasons Played	Apps	Subs	Gls
Nottingham F.	Grasshoppers (Swi)	08.80	80	17	4	3

PONTIN Keith
Pontyclun, 14 June, 1956 Wu21-1/W-2 (CD)

League Club	Source	Date Signed	Seasons Played	Apps	Subs	Gls
Cardiff C.	App	05.74	76-82	193	0	5

POOK David Charles
Plymouth, 16 January, 1955 (W)

League Club	Source	Date Signed	Seasons Played	Apps	Subs	Gls
Torquay U.	App	01.73	71-72	13	3	1

POOLE Andrew John
Chesterfield, 6 July, 1960 (G)

League Club	Source	Date Signed	Seasons Played	Apps	Subs	Gls
Northampton T.	Mansfield T. (App)	07.78	78-81	141	0	0
Wolverhampton W.	Tr	08.82				
Port Vale	Tr	03.83	82	2	0	0

POOLE Cyril John
Mansfield, 13 March, 1921 Died 1996 (FB)

League Club	Source	Date Signed	Seasons Played	Apps	Subs	Gls
Mansfield T. (Am)	Jnrs	02.37	36	1	-	0
Mansfield T.	Gillingham	02.44	49-50	16	-	1

POOLE Gary John
Stratford, 11 September, 1967 (FB)

League Club	Source	Date Signed	Seasons Played	Apps	Subs	Gls
Tottenham H.	Jnrs	07.85				
Cambridge U.	Tr	08.87	87-88	42	1	0
Barnet	Tr	03.89	91	39	1	2
Plymouth Arg.	Tr	06.92	92	39	0	5
Southend U.	Tr	07.93	93-94	43	1	2
Birmingham C.	Tr	09.94	94-96	70	2	0
Charlton Ath.	Tr	11.96	96	14	2	1

POOLE Henry (Harry)
Stoke, 31 January, 1935 (WH/IF)

League Club	Source	Date Signed	Seasons Played	Apps	Subs	Gls
Port Vale	Oxford C.	04.56	55-67	450	1	73

POOLE John Arthur Frederick
Stoke, 12 December, 1932 (G)

League Club	Source	Date Signed	Seasons Played	Apps	Subs	Gls
Port Vale	Stoke C. (Am)	09.53	55-60	33	-	0

POOLE Joseph
Huddersfield, 25 May, 1923 (W)

League Club	Source	Date Signed	Seasons Played	Apps	Subs	Gls
Huddersfield T.	David Brown Wks	06.41	46	2	-	0
Bradford C.	Tr	02.47	46-48	56	-	5

POOLE Kenneth James
Blaencwm, 2 July, 1933 (HB)

League Club	Source	Date Signed	Seasons Played	Apps	Subs	Gls
Swansea C.	Jnrs	11.53				
Northampton T.	Tr	06.56	56	4	-	0

POOLE Kevin
Bromsgrove, 21 July, 1963 (G)

League Club	Source	Date Signed	Seasons Played	Apps	Subs	Gls
Aston Villa	App	06.81	84-86	28	0	0
Northampton T.	L	11.84	84	3	0	0
Middlesbrough	Tr	08.87	87-89	34	0	0
Hartlepool U.	L	03.91	90	12	0	0
Leicester C.	Tr	07.91	91-96	163	0	0
Birmingham C.	Tr	08.97	97	1	0	0

POOLE Michael David
Morley, 23 April, 1955 (G)

League Club	Source	Date Signed	Seasons Played	Apps	Subs	Gls
Rochdale	Coventry C. (App)	09.73	73-77	192	0	0
Rochdale	Portland (USA)	08.81	81	27	0	0

POOLE Richard John
Heston, 3 July, 1957 (F)

League Club	Source	Date Signed	Seasons Played	Apps	Subs	Gls
Brentford	App	07.75	73-75	12	9	1
Watford	Tr	07.76	76	3	4	1

POOLE Roy
Sheffield, 2 December, 1939 (FB/CF)

League Club	Source	Date Signed	Seasons Played	Apps	Subs	Gls
Wolverhampton W.	Jnrs	01.57				
Rotherham U.	Tr	07.58				
Chesterfield	Tr	07.61	61-63	50	-	14

POOLE Terence
Sheffield, 8 December, 1937 (WH)

League Club	Source	Date Signed	Seasons Played	Apps	Subs	Gls
Sheffield Wed.	Jnrs	04.55				
Darlington	Tr	07.59	59-60	41	-	3

POOLE Terence
Chesterfield, 16 December, 1949 (G)

League Club	Source	Date Signed	Seasons Played	Apps	Subs	Gls
Manchester U.	Jnrs	02.67				
Huddersfield T.	Tr	08.68	68-76	207	0	0
Bolton W.	Tr	01.77	80	29	0	0
Sheffield U.	L	03.80	79	7	0	0

POOM Mart
Estonia, 3 February, 1972 Estonian Int (G)

League Club	Source	Date Signed	Seasons Played	Apps	Subs	Gls
Portsmouth	F.C. Wil (Swi)	08.94	95	4	0	0
Derby Co.	Tallin S.C. (Est)	03.97	96-97	40	0	0

POPE David William
St Pancras, 8 January, 1936 (FB)

League Club	Source	Date Signed	Seasons Played	Apps	Subs	Gls
Crystal Palace	Jnrs	09.53				
Swansea C.		09.56	57	4	-	0

POPE Neil Lester
Cambridge, 9 October, 1972 (M)

League Club	Source	Date Signed	Seasons Played	Apps	Subs	Gls
Peterborough U. (N/C)	Cambridge U. (YT)	03.91	90	1	1	0

POPE Steven Anthony
Stoke, 8 September, 1976 (D)

League Club	Source	Date Signed	Seasons Played	Apps	Subs	Gls
Crewe Alex.	YT	06.95	97	2	4	0

League Club	Source	Date Signed	Seasons Played	Career Record Apps	Subs	Gls
POPE Terence John						
Newport, 27 January, 1926						(G)
Newport Co.	Bargoed	07.50	50-54	83	-	0
POPELY Peter Charles Francis						
York, 7 April, 1943						(FB)
York C.	Cliftonville	08.62	62-66	24	1	0
POPESCU Gica Gheorghe						
Romania, 9 October, 1967 Romanian Int						(D/M)
Tottenham H.	P.S.V. Eindhoven (Neth)	09.94	94	23	0	3
POPPITT John						
Bedlington, 20 January, 1923						(FB)
Derby Co.	West Sleekburn	05.45	46-49	16	-	0
Queens Park R.	Tr	09.50	50-53	106	-	0
POPPY Arthur						
Yeovil, 6 January, 1961						(D)
Northampton T.	App	●	77	1	0	0
PORFIRIO Hugo Cardosa						
Portugal, 28 September, 1973 Portuguese Int						(F)
West Ham U. (L)	Sporting Lisbon (Por)	09.96	96	15	8	2
PORIC Adem						
Kensington, 22 April, 1973						(M)
Sheffield Wed.	St Georges Budapest (Aus)	10.93	93-97	3	11	0
Southend U.	L	02.97	96	7	0	0
Rotherham U.	Tr	02.98	97	4	0	0
Notts Co.	Tr	03.98	97	3	1	0
PORRITT Walter						
Heckmondwike, 19 July, 1914 Died 1993						(OR)
Huddersfield T.		05.35				
York C.	Tr	08.36	36-46	40	-	5
PORT Bernard Harry						
Burton, 14 December, 1925						(G)
Hull C.	Newhall	09.50				
Chester C.	Tr	08.51	51-52	9	-	0
PORTEOUS John Robert						
India, 12 January, 1933						(IF)
Aldershot	Alton T.	02.56	55	1	-	0
PORTEOUS John Robertson						
Motherwell, 5 December, 1921						(WH)
Plymouth Arg.	Alloa Ath.	07.49	49-55	215	-	13
Exeter C.	Tr	03.56	55-56	40	-	0
PORTEOUS Trevor						
Hull, 9 October, 1933						(WH)
Hull C.	Jnrs	10.50	51-55	61	-	1
Stockport Co.	Tr	06.56	56-64	337	-	9
PORTER Andrew						
Stewarton, 21 January, 1937						(WH)
Watford	Darvel Jnrs	06.59	59-62	72	-	4
PORTER Andrew Michael						
Macclesfield, 17 September, 1968						(M)
Port Vale	YT	06.87	86-97	313	44	22
PORTER Christopher John						
Bridgwater, 30 April, 1949						(W)
Swindon T.	Bridgwater T.	11.69	70-73	33	3	4
PORTER Derek						
Ulverston, 22 June, 1936						(OL)
Barrow	Dalton T.	05.57	57-58	15	-	1
PORTER Gary Michael						
Sunderland, 6 March, 1966 E Yth/Eu21-12						(M)
Watford	App	03.84	83-96	362	38	47
Walsall	Tr	07.97	97	25	4	1
PORTER George						
Chirk, 5 February, 1935						(OL)
Wrexham (Am)	Chirk A.A.A.	05.59	59	1	-	0
PORTER Leslie						
Gateshead, 5 May, 1923						(WH)
Newcastle U.	Redheugh Wks	09.44				
York C.	Tr	03.49	48-53	38	-	1
PORTER Michael Robert						
Stoke, 19 May, 1945						(IF)
Port Vale	Jnrs	07.62	63-64	13	-	2

League Club	Source	Date Signed	Seasons Played	Career Record Apps	Subs	Gls
PORTER Trevor James						
Guildford, 16 October, 1956						(G)
Fulham	App	05.74				
Brentford	Slough T.	08.78	78-79	15	0	0
PORTER William						
Durham, 23 November, 1923 Died 1975						(OL)
Hartlepool U.	Horden Colly	09.43	46	2	-	0
PORTERFIELD John (Ian)						
Dunfermline, 11 February, 1946						(M)
Sunderland	Raith Rov.	12.67	67-75	218	12	17
Reading	L	11.76	76	5	0	0
Sheffield Wed.	Tr	07.77	77-79	103	3	3
PORTEUS Joseph						
Shildon, 20 April, 1925 Died 1995						(LH)
York C.	Chesterfield (Am)	08.46	46	23	-	0
PORTWOOD Clifford						
Salford, 17 October, 1937						(IF)
Preston N. E.	Manchester Ath.	02.55				
Port Vale	Tr	08.59	59-60	61	-	33
Grimsby T.	Tr	07.61	61-63	92	-	35
Portsmouth	Tr	05.64	64-68	95	4	28
POSKETT Malcolm						
Middlesbrough, 19 July, 1953						(F)
Middlesbrough	South Bank	04.73	73	0	1	0
Hartlepool U.	Tr	07.74				
Hartlepool U.	Whitby T.	11.76	76-77	50	1	20
Brighton & H. A.	Tr	02.78	77-79	33	12	17
Watford	Tr	01.80	79-81	57	6	17
Carlisle U.	Tr	08.82	82-84	108	2	40
Darlington	Tr	07.85	85	18	3	4
Stockport Co.	Tr	01.86	85	8	0	1
Hartlepool U.	L	03.86	85	4	1	0
Carlisle U.	Tr	08.86	86-87	67	9	20
POSKETT Thomas William						
Esh Winning, 26 December, 1909 Died 1972						(G)
Grimsby T.	Crook T.	12.28	28-30	2	-	0
Lincoln C.	Tr	05.32	33	10	-	0
Notts Co.	Tr	05.34	34	10	-	0
Tranmere Rov.	Tr	08.35	35-36	22	-	0
Crewe Alex.	Tr	07.37	37-46	99	-	0
POSSEE Derek James						
Southwark, 14 February, 1946						(W)
Tottenham H.	App	03.63	63-65	19	0	4
Millwall	Tr	08.67	67-72	222	1	79
Crystal Palace	Tr	01.73	72-73	51	2	13
Leyton Orient	Tr	07.74	74-76	77	3	11
POSTLEWHITE Dennis John						
Birkenhead, 13 October, 1957						(CD)
Tranmere Rov.	App	07.76	76-78	31	2	1
POTRAC Anthony Joseph						
Victoria, 21 January, 1953						(F)
Chelsea	App	08.70	71	1	0	0
POTTER Frederick						
Cradley Heath, 29 November, 1940						(G)
Aston Villa	Jnrs	07.59	60	3	-	0
Doncaster Rov.	Tr	07.62	62-65	123	0	0
Hereford U.	Burton A.	07.70	72-73	10	0	0
POTTER Gary Charles						
Chester, 6 August, 1952						(CD)
Chester C.		07.73	73-74	11	0	0
POTTER George Ross						
Arbroath, 7 October, 1946						(FB)
Luton T.	Forfar Ath.	03.68	67-68	3	4	0
Torquay U.	Tr	07.69	69-70	32	6	0
Hartlepool U.	Tr	07.71	71-76	211	2	4
POTTER Graham Stephen						
Solihull, 20 May, 1975 E Yth/Eu21-1						(LB/M)
Birmingham C.	YT	07.92	92-93	23	2	2
Wycombe W.	L	09.93	93	2	1	0
Stoke C.	Tr	12.93	93-95	41	4	1
Southampton	Tr	07.96	96	2	6	0
West Bromwich A.	Tr	02.97	96-97	6	5	0
Northampton T.	L	10.97	97	4	0	0
POTTER Harry						
Tyldesley, 20 May, 1923						(FB)
Shrewsbury T.	Winsford U.	(N/L)	50-51	67	-	0
Rochdale	Tr	06.52	52-53	52	-	0

POTTER James
Belfast, 20 November, 1941 (WH)

League Club	Source	Date Signed	Seasons Played	Apps	Subs	Gls
Sunderland	Jnrs	11.58				
Darlington	Tr	09.63	63	19	-	1

POTTER Raymond John
Beckenham, 7 May, 1936 (G)

League Club	Source	Date Signed	Seasons Played	Apps	Subs	Gls
Crystal Palace	Jnrs	05.53	53-57	44	-	0
West Bromwich A.	Tr	06.58	58-66	217	0	0
Portsmouth	Tr	05.67	67-69	3	0	0

POTTER Ronald Charles
Wolverhampton, 5 December, 1948 (CD)

League Club	Source	Date Signed	Seasons Played	Apps	Subs	Gls
West Bromwich A.	App	12..66	68-69	8	1	0
Swindon T.	Tr	11.70	70-74	84	2	0

POTTER Stephen Derek
Belper, 1 October, 1955 (G)

League Club	Source	Date Signed	Seasons Played	Apps	Subs	Gls
Manchester C.	App	10.73				
Swansea C.	Tr	08.74	74-77	118	0	0

POTTS Brian
Sunderland, 3 September, 1948 (FB)

League Club	Source	Date Signed	Seasons Played	Apps	Subs	Gls
Leicester C.	App	09.65	67-68	9	1	0
Peterborough U.	Tr	07.69	69-70	49	1	0

POTTS Craig
Carlisle, 25 February, 1974 (W)

League Club	Source	Date Signed	Seasons Played	Apps	Subs	Gls
Carlisle U.	YT	09.92	91-92	9	5	0

POTTS Eric Thomas
Liverpool, 16 March, 1950 (W)

League Club	Source	Date Signed	Seasons Played	Apps	Subs	Gls
Sheffield Wed.	Oswestry T.	12.69	70-76	142	17	21
Brighton & H. A.	Tr	06.77	77	19	14	5
Preston N. E.	Tr	08.78	78-80	50	7	5
Burnley	Tr	09.80	80-81	48	8	5
Bury	Tr	10.82	82-83	46	5	7

POTTS Harry
Hetton-le-Hole, 22 October, 1920 Died 1996 (IF)

League Club	Source	Date Signed	Seasons Played	Apps	Subs	Gls
Burnley	Jnrs	11.37	46-50	165	-	47
Everton	Tr	10.50	50-55	59	-	15

POTTS Henry James
Carlisle, 23 January, 1925 E Amat (OR)

League Club	Source	Date Signed	Seasons Played	Apps	Subs	Gls
Northampton T. (Am)	Pegasus	08.50	50	10	-	0

POTTS Reginald
Stoke, 31 July, 1927 Died 1996 (FB)

League Club	Source	Date Signed	Seasons Played	Apps	Subs	Gls
Port Vale	Northwood Mission	08.45	48-56	277	-	3

POTTS Steven John
U.S.A., 7 May, 1967 E Yth (D)

League Club	Source	Date Signed	Seasons Played	Apps	Subs	Gls
West Ham U.	App	05.84	84-97	333	22	1

POTTS Victor Ernest
Birmingham, 20 August, 1915 Died 1996 (RB)

League Club	Source	Date Signed	Seasons Played	Apps	Subs	Gls
Tottenham H.	Metro Welfare	08.34				
Doncaster Rov.	Tr	08.38	38	23	-	0
Aston Villa	Tr	08.45	46-47	62	-	0

POULTON George Henry
Holborn, 23 April, 1929 (OL)

League Club	Source	Date Signed	Seasons Played	Apps	Subs	Gls
Gillingham		08.49	51	5	-	1
Leyton Orient	Tr	07.52	52-54	61	-	24

POUND John Henry **Kenneth**
Portsmouth, 24 August, 1944 (W)

League Club	Source	Date Signed	Seasons Played	Apps	Subs	Gls
Swansea C.	Yeovil T.	07.64	64-65	27	2	4
Bournemouth	Tr	08.66	66-68	102	0	24
Gillingham	Tr	07.69	69-70	62	10	11

POUNDER Albert William
Charlton, 27 July, 1931 (OR)

League Club	Source	Date Signed	Seasons Played	Apps	Subs	Gls
Charlton Ath.	Harvey Sports	02.50	52	1	-	0
Queens Park R.	Tr	02.54	53-55	53	-	6

POUNDER Antony Mark
Yeovil, 11 March, 1966 (LW)

League Club	Source	Date Signed	Seasons Played	Apps	Subs	Gls
Bristol Rov.	Weymouth	07.90	90-93	102	11	10
Hereford U.	Tr	09.94	94-95	54	8	4

POUNDER John Anthony
Sheffield, 16 March, 1935 (OR)

League Club	Source	Date Signed	Seasons Played	Apps	Subs	Gls
Luton T.	Atlas Sports	12.55	55-56	3	-	0
Coventry C.	Tr	06.57	57	6	-	1
Crewe Alex.	Tr	12.57	57-58	29	-	6

POUNEWATCHY Stephane Zeusnagapa
France, 10 February, 1968 (CD)

League Club	Source	Date Signed	Seasons Played	Apps	Subs	Gls
Carlisle U.	Gueugnon (Fr)	08.96	96-97	81	0	3

POUNTNEY Craig Frank
Bromsgrove, 23 November, 1979 (W)

League Club	Source	Date Signed	Seasons Played	Apps	Subs	Gls
Shrewsbury T.	YT	04.98	97	0	1	0

POUNTNEY David Harold
Baschurch (Salop), 12 October, 1939 (WH)

League Club	Source	Date Signed	Seasons Played	Apps	Subs	Gls
Shrewsbury T.	Myddle	09.57	57-63	175	-	10
Aston Villa	Tr	10.63	63-67	109	4	7
Shrewsbury T.	Tr	02.68	67-69	54	4	1
Chester C.	Tr	06.70	70-72	135	0	1

POUNTNEY Ronald Alan
Bilston, 19 March, 1955 (M)

League Club	Source	Date Signed	Seasons Played	Apps	Subs	Gls
Walsall	Jnrs	07.73	72	1	0	0
Port Vale	Tr	10.73				
Southend U.	Bilston T.	01.75	74-84	326	22	26

POUTCH Neil Anthony
Dublin, 27 November, 1969 IRu21-8 (FB)

League Club	Source	Date Signed	Seasons Played	Apps	Subs	Gls
Luton T.	YT	11.87	89	0	1	0

POUTON Alan
Newcastle, 1 February, 1977 (M)

League Club	Source	Date Signed	Seasons Played	Apps	Subs	Gls
Oxford U.	Newcastle U. (YT)	11.95				
York C.	Tr	12.95	96-97	55	8	6

POVEY Neil Andrew
Birmingham, 26 June, 1977 (M)

League Club	Source	Date Signed	Seasons Played	Apps	Subs	Gls
Torquay U.	YT	07.95	94-95	8	3	0

POVEY Victor Richard
Wolverhampton, 16 March, 1944 (W)

League Club	Source	Date Signed	Seasons Played	Apps	Subs	Gls
Wolverhampton W.	Jnrs	07.61				
Notts Co.	Tr	08.63	63-64	35	-	3

POVEY William
Billingham, 11 January, 1943 (W)

League Club	Source	Date Signed	Seasons Played	Apps	Subs	Gls
Middlesbrough	Jnrs	05.60	62	6	-	0
York C.	Tr	03.64	64	3	-	0

POWELL Andrew
Plymouth, 27 June, 1955 (G)

League Club	Source	Date Signed	Seasons Played	Apps	Subs	Gls
Hereford U. (N/C)		10.82	82	4	0	0

POWELL Anthony
Thornbury, 11 June, 1947 (CD)

League Club	Source	Date Signed	Seasons Played	Apps	Subs	Gls
Bournemouth	Bath C.	04.68	68-73	214	5	10
Norwich C.	Tr	08.74	74-80	235	2	3

POWELL Aubrey
Swansea, 19 April, 1918 W-8 (IF)

League Club	Source	Date Signed	Seasons Played	Apps	Subs	Gls
Leeds U.	Swansea C. (Am)	11.35	36-47	112	-	25
Everton	Tr	07.48	48-49	35	-	5
Birmingham C.	Tr	08.50	50	15	-	1

POWELL Baden
Hebburn, 17 June, 1931 (OR)

League Club	Source	Date Signed	Seasons Played	Apps	Subs	Gls
Darlington	South Shields	10.50	50-53	9	-	0

POWELL Barry Ivor
Kenilworth, 29 January, 1954 Eu23-4 (M)

League Club	Source	Date Signed	Seasons Played	Apps	Subs	Gls
Wolverhampton W.	App	01.72	72-74	58	6	7
Coventry C.	Tr	09.75	75-79	162	2	27
Derby Co.	Tr	10.79	79-81	86	0	7
Burnley	Bulova (HK)	07.84	84	9	2	0
Swansea C.	Tr	02.85	84	8	0	0
Wolverhampton W.	South China (HK)	11.86	86-87	10	4	0

POWELL Christopher George Robin
Lambeth, 8 September, 1969 (LB)

League Club	Source	Date Signed	Seasons Played	Apps	Subs	Gls
Crystal Palace	YT	12.87	88	2	1	0
Aldershot	L	01.90	89	11	0	0
Southend U.	Tr	08.90	90-95	246	2	3
Derby Co.	Tr	01.96	95-97	89	2	1

POWELL Clifford George
Watford, 21 February, 1968 (D)

League Club	Source	Date Signed	Seasons Played	Apps	Subs	Gls
Watford	App	02.86				
Hereford U.	L	12.87	87	7	0	0
Sheffield U.	Tr	03.88	87-88	7	3	0
Doncaster Rov.	L	03.89	88	4	0	0
Cardiff C.	L	11.89	89	0	1	0

League Club	Source	Date Signed	Seasons Played	Apps	Subs	Gls
POWELL Colin David						
Hendon, 7 July, 1948						(W)
Charlton Ath.	Barnet	01.73	72-78	230	14	23
Charlton Ath.	New England (USA)	08.79	79-80	71	6	8
Gillingham	Tr	08.81	81-82	54	1	1
POWELL Darryl Anthony						
Lambeth, 15 November, 1971 Jamaican Int						(M)
Portsmouth	YT	12.88	88-94	83	49	16
Derby Co.	Tr	07.95	95-97	76	17	6
POWELL David						
Afon Conwy, 15 October, 1944 Wu23-4/W-11						(CD)
Wrexham	Gwydyn Rov.	05.63	62-68	132	2	4
Sheffield U.	Tr	09.68	68-70	89	0	2
Cardiff C.	Tr	09.72	72-74	36	0	1
POWELL David (Dai) Morgan						
Swansea, 19 January, 1935						(LB)
Blackpool		12.52				
Rochdale	Tr	07.58	58-60	76	-	1
POWELL David Robert						
Cannock, 24 September, 1967						(G)
West Bromwich A.	Cherry Valley	04.86	87	2	0	0
Wrexham	L	02.87	86	2	0	0
POWELL Francis Michael						
Burnley, 17 June, 1977						(W)
Rochdale	Burnley (YT)	09.95	95	0	2	0
POWELL Gary						
Hoylake, 2 April, 1969						(F)
Everton	YT	07.87				
Lincoln C.	L	09.90	90	11	0	0
Scunthorpe U.	L	11.90	90	3	1	1
Wigan Ath.	L	03.91	90	13	1	4
Wigan Ath.	Tr	08.91	91-92	44	26	13
Bury (N/C)	Tr	08.93	93	4	1	0
POWELL George Reginald						
Fulham, 11 October, 1924 Died 1989						(FB)
Queens Park R.	Fulham (Am)	12.46	47-52	145	-	0
POWELL Ivor Verdun						
Merthyr Tydfil, 5 July, 1916 W-8						(WH)
Queens Park R.	Bargoed	09.37	38-48	110	-	2
Aston Villa	Tr	12.48	48-50	79	-	5
Port Vale	Tr	08.51	51	6	-	0
Bradford C.	Barry T.	06.52	52-54	83	-	9
POWELL Brian **John** Edward						
York, 10 March, 1936						(OL)
York C.	Cliftonville	09.56	56-59	27	-	5
POWELL Kenneth						
Mansfield, 2 March, 1920 Died 1976						(OL)
Derby Co.	Mansfield C.W.S.	05.39	46	13	-	0
Southport	Tr	06.47	47-50	90	-	18
POWELL Kenneth Leigh						
Chester, 25 September, 1924						(WH)
Cardiff C.	Chester C. (Am)	09.47				
Exeter C.	Tr	06.48	48-49	22	-	1
Bristol Rov.	Tr	07.51	51	4	-	0
POWELL Lee						
Caerleon, 2 June, 1973 Wu21-4						(W)
Southampton	YT	05.91	91-93	2	5	0
POWELL Michael						
Newport, 26 April, 1951						(D)
Newport Co. (N/C)	Newport Y.M.C.A.	01.76	75-77	7	2	0
POWELL Michael Philip						
Slough, 18 April, 1933						(CH)
Queens Park R.	Jnrs	01.51	51-58	105	-	0
POWELL Neville David						
Flint, 2 September, 1963						(W)
Tranmere Rov.	App	08.81	80-84	76	10	4
POWELL Paul						
Wallingford, 30 June, 1978						(LB)
Oxford U.	YT	07.96	95-97	12	12	1
POWELL Raymond						
Swansea, 5 August, 1924						(CF)
Swansea C.	Haverfordwest	05.47	47-50	17	-	5
Scunthorpe U.	Tr	08.51	51	31	-	14

League Club	Source	Date Signed	Seasons Played	Apps	Subs	Gls
POWELL Richard						
Chesterfield, 3 September, 1969						(G)
Blackpool	YT	06.88	86-87	14	0	0
POWELL Ronald William Herbert						
Knighton, 2 December, 1929 Died 1992						(G)
Manchester C.	Knighton T.	11.48	49	12	-	0
Chesterfield	Tr	06.52	52-64	471	-	0
POWELL Stephen						
Derby, 20 September, 1955 E Sch/E Yth/Eu23-1						(M/D)
Derby Co.	App	11.72	71-84	342	10	20
POWELL Thomas Ernest						
Derby, 12 April, 1925						(OR)
Derby Co.	Jnrs	04.42	48-61	380	-	57
POWELL Wayne						
Newport, 25 October, 1956 W Yth						(F)
Bristol Rov.	App	10.74	75-77	25	7	10
Halifax T.	L	10.77	77	4	0	1
Hereford U.	Tr	06.78	78	6	0	2
POWER Graeme Richard						
Harrow, 7 March, 1977 E Yth						(LB)
Queens Park R.	YT	04.95				
Bristol Rov.	Tr	07.96	96-97	25	1	0
POWER John						
Chelsea, 10 December, 1959						(G)
Brentford (N/C)	Kingstonian	03.87	86	2	0	0
POWER Lee Michael						
Lewisham, 30 June, 1972 IR YthIRu21-13/IR 'B'						(F)
Norwich C.	YT	07.90	89-93	28	16	10
Charlton Ath.	L	12.92	92	5	0	0
Sunderland	L	08.93	93	1	2	0
Portsmouth	L	10.93	93	1	1	0
Bradford C.	Tr	03.94	93-94	14	16	5
Peterborough U.	Tr	07.95	95	25	13	6
POWER Michael David						
Stockport, 3 October, 1961						(F)
Stockport Co.	Jnrs	08.80	80-85	67	4	16
POWER Paul Christopher						
Manchester, 30 October, 1953 E 'B'						(LM)
Manchester C.	Leeds Polytechnic	09.73	75-85	358	7	26
Everton	Tr	06.86	86-87	52	2	6
POWER Philip Damian						
Salford, 25 July, 1966						(F)
Crewe Alex.	Witton A.	08.85	85-86	18	9	3
Macclesfield T.	Stalybridge	10.93	97	21	17	7
POWLING Richard Frederick						
Barking, 21 May, 1956 E Yth						(D)
Arsenal	App	07.73	73-77	50	5	3
POWNER Robert James						
Newcastle-u-Lyme, 2 July, 1967						(G)
Crewe Alex.	Jnrs	06.86	85-86	6	0	0
POWNEY Bryan William						
Seaford, 7 October, 1944						(G)
Brighton & H. A.	App	11.61	61-73	351	0	0
POWTON Brian						
Newcastle, 29 August, 1929						(G)
Newcastle U.		10.50				
Preston N. E.	Tr	08.51				
Hartlepool U.	Tr	07.52	52	4	-	0
POYET Gustavo Augusto						
Montevideo, Uruguay, 15 November, 1967 Uruguayan Int						(M)
Chelsea	Real Zaragoza (Sp)	07.97	97	11	3	4
POYNER Robert Christopher						
Newport, 25 December, 1932 Died 1977 W Sch/W Yth						(HB)
Newport Co.	Jnrs	01.51	50-51	2	-	0
POYNTON William						
Shiremoor, 30 June, 1944						(FB)
Burnley	Jnrs	07.61				
Mansfield T.	Tr	07.64	64-65	20	0	0
Lincoln C.	Lockheed Leamington	10.66	66	0	1	0

League Club	Source	Date Signed	Seasons Played	Career Record Apps	Subs	Gls
POYSER George Henry						
Sutton-in-Ashfield, 6 February, 1910 Died 1995						(FB)
Wolverhampton W.	Stanton Hill Vic.	05.28				
Port Vale	Mansfield T.	05.31	31-33	72	-	0
Brentford	Tr	06.34	34-38	150	-	0
Plymouth Arg.	Tr	04.46	46	3	-	0
PRAGG Michael Kenneth						
Shrewsbury, 8 October, 1941 E Amat						(IF)
Shrewsbury T. (Am)	Jnrs	05.59	60-62	5	-	1
PRANGLEY Samuel						
Newport, 30 September, 1924						(CH)
Newport Co.	Lovells Ath.	11.46	46	7	-	0
PRASKI Josef						
France, 22 January, 1926						(OR)
Notts Co.	Jeanfield Swifts	03.49	48	3	-	0
PRATLEY Richard George						
Banbury, 12 January, 1963						(CD)
Derby Co.	Banbury U.	07.83	83-86	29	2	1
Scunthorpe U.	L	03.84	83	10	0	0
Shrewsbury T.	Tr	02.88	87-89	44	2	1
PRATT John Arthur						
Hackney, 26 June, 1948						(M)
Tottenham H.	Jnrs	11.65	68-79	307	24	39
PRATT John Leslie						
Atherstone, 1 March, 1943						(G)
Reading	Wycombe W.	07.69	69-71	29	0	0
PRATT Lee Stuart						
Cleethorpes, 31 March, 1970						(G)
Grimsby T.	YT	06.88	86	1	0	0
PRATT Michael Wayne						
Newport, 15 January, 1966 W Yth						(CD/F)
Newport Co.	Jnrs	08.83	83-84	4	5	2
PRATT Raymond Ernest						
Burry Port, 11 November, 1955 W Yth						(F)
Exeter C.	Merthyr Tydfil	03.80	79-85	127	46	61
PRATT Wayne						
Southampton, 1 March, 1960						(M)
Southampton	App	03.78	80	1	0	0
PRECIOUS Derek						
Crewe, 2 June, 1931						(IF)
Crewe Alex.		09.55	55-56	18	-	3
PREECE Andrew Paul						
Evesham, 27 March, 1967						(F)
Northampton T. (N/C)	Evesham U.	08.88	88	0	1	0
Wrexham	Worcester C.	03.90	89-91	44	7	7
Stockport Co.	Tr	12.91	91-93	89	8	42
Crystal Palace	Tr	06.94	94	17	3	4
Blackpool	Tr	07.95	95-97	114	12	35
PREECE Brian James						
Hereford, 16 February, 1958 Died 1992						(W)
Hereford U.	App	02.76	74-76	5	1	0
Newport Co.	Tr	03.77	76-77	38	6	12
PREECE David						
Sunderland, 26 August, 1976						(G)
Sunderland	YT	06.94				
Darlington	Tr	07.97	97	45	0	0
PREECE David William						
Bridgnorth, 28 May, 1963 E 'B'						(LM)
Walsall	App	07.80	80-84	107	4	5
Luton T.	Tr	12.84	84-94	328	8	21
Derby Co.	Tr	08.95	95	10	3	1
Birmingham C.	L	11.95	95	6	0	0
Swindon T.	L	03.96	95	7	0	1
Cambridge U.	Tr	09.96	96-97	34	13	0
PREECE John (Jack) Causer						
Wolverhampton, 30 April, 1914						(FB)
Wolverhampton W.	Jnrs	05.31	33	2	-	0
Bristol Rov.	Tr	05.35	35-37	79	-	0
Bradford C.	Tr	07.38	38	3	-	0
Southport	Tr	05.39	46	36	-	0
Swindon T.	Tr	06.47	47	7	-	0
PREECE Paul William						
Penarth, 16 May, 1957						(M)
Newport Co.	App	06.75	74-75	17	6	0
PREECE Roger						
Much Wenlock, 9 June, 1969						(RB/M)
Wrexham	Coventry C. (YT)	08.86	86-89	89	21	12
Chester C.	Tr	08.90	90-95	165	5	4
Shrewsbury T.	Telford	07.97	97	25	2	1
PREECE Ryan						
Neath, 10 January, 1969						(M)
Newport Co. (N/C)	YT	10.87	87	7	3	2
PREEDY Philip						
Hereford, 20 November, 1975						(LB/M)
Hereford U.	YT	07.94	93-96	31	20	4
PRENDERGAST Michael John						
Denaby, 24 November, 1950						(F)
Sheffield Wed.	App	11.67	68-77	170	13	53
Barnsley	Tr	05.78	77-78	12	8	2
Halifax T.	L	10.78	78	4	0	1
PRENTIS John						
Liverpool, 22 March, 1939						(FB)
Blackpool		10.62	64-65	6	0	0
Stockport Co.	Tr	10.66	66-67	16	3	0
PRESCOTT Francis Stephen						
Birkenhead, 12 August, 1922 Died 1969						(CF)
Tranmere Rov.	St Annes	10.46	46	2	-	0
PRESCOTT James Lawrence						
Golborne, 2 November, 1930						(IF)
Southport	Denton	03.54	53-54	53	-	9
York C.	Tr	06.55	55	18	-	5
Southport	Tr	10.56	56	17	-	1
PRESLAND Edward Robert						
Loughton, 27 March, 1943						(FB)
West Ham U.	Jnrs	10.60	64-65	6	0	1
Crystal Palace	Tr	01.67	66-68	61	0	0
Colchester U.	L	10.69	69	5	0	0
PRESLEY Charles **Derek**						
Warminster, 8 March, 1930						(WH)
Bristol C.	Warminster T.	03.50	50-51	9	-	0
Bristol Rov.	Tr	05.52				
PRESSDEE James Stuart						
Swansea, 19 June, 1933 W Sch						(FB)
Swansea C.	Jnrs	08.51	53-55	8	-	0
PRESSLEY Steven						
Elgin, 11 October, 1973 Su21-20						(CD)
Coventry C.	Glasgow Rangers	10.94	94	18	1	1
PRESSMAN Kevin Paul						
Fareham, 6 November, 1967 E Sch/E Yth/E u21-1/E 'B'						(G)
Sheffield Wed.	App	11.85	87-97	232	0	0
Stoke C.	L	03.92	91	4	0	0
PRESTON Michael John						
Plymouth, 22 November, 1977						(RW)
Torquay U.	YT	07.96	95-96	4	6	0
PRESTON Richard Frank						
Nottingham, 10 June, 1967						(F)
Scarborough	Stanton	03.88	87	1	3	0
PRESTON Richard John						
Basildon, 7 April, 1976						(RB)
Northampton T.	YT	08.94	93	1	0	0
PRICE Albert Edward						
Langwith (Dy), 4 April, 1926 Died 1983						(G)
Crewe Alex.	Creswell Colly	12.46	46	5	-	0
PRICE Allen Douglas						
Gelligaer, 24 March, 1968 W Yth						(D)
Cardiff C. (N/C)	Newport Co. (Jnrs)	08.85	85	2	0	0
PRICE Arthur						
Rowlands Gill, 12 January, 1921 Died 1995						(WH)
Leeds U.	Consett	05.46	46	6	-	0

PRICE Brynley
Rhondda, 15 January, 1936 (WH)

League Club	Source	Date Signed	Seasons Played	Apps	Subs	Gls
Barnsley	Treorchy B.C.	05.55	56-57	2	-	0

PRICE Cecil
Cardiff, 2 December, 1919 (OL)

League Club	Source	Date Signed	Seasons Played	Apps	Subs	Gls
Cardiff C.		09.48	48	1	-	0
Bradford C.	Tr	06.49	49	7	-	0

PRICE Christopher John
Hereford, 30 March, 1960 E Yth (RB)

League Club	Source	Date Signed	Seasons Played	Apps	Subs	Gls
Hereford U.	App	01.78	76-85	327	3	27
Blackburn Rov.	Tr	07.86	86-87	83	0	11
Aston Villa	Tr	05.88	88-91	109	2	2
Blackburn Rov.	Tr	02.92	91-92	13	6	3
Portsmouth	Tr	01.93	92-93	14	4	0

PRICE David James
Caterham, 23 June, 1955 E Sch/E Yth (M)

League Club	Source	Date Signed	Seasons Played	Apps	Subs	Gls
Arsenal	App	08.72	72-80	116	10	16
Peterborough U.	L	01.75	74	6	0	1
Crystal Palace	Tr	03.81	80-81	25	2	2
Leyton Orient (N/C)		03.83	82	10	0	0

PRICE Derrick
Wellington, 14 February, 1932 (OR)

League Club	Source	Date Signed	Seasons Played	Apps	Subs	Gls
Shrewsbury T.	Donnington	02.53	53-57	125	-	28
Aldershot	Tr	07.58	58-59	4	-	1

PRICE Thomas **Dudley**
Swansea, 17 November, 1931 (IF)

League Club	Source	Date Signed	Seasons Played	Apps	Subs	Gls
Swansea C.	Jnrs	04.50	53-57	33	-	9
Southend U.	Tr	01.58	57-60	91	-	41
Hull C.	Tr	09.60	60-62	76	-	26
Bradford C.	Tr	07.63	63-64	62	-	21

PRICE Ernest
Easington, 12 May, 1926 (WH)

League Club	Source	Date Signed	Seasons Played	Apps	Subs	Gls
Sunderland		01.45				
Darlington		12.48	48-50	68	-	0
Crystal Palace	Tr	07.51	51-52	34	-	5

PRICE Gareth
Swindon, 21 February, 1970 (M/FB)

League Club	Source	Date Signed	Seasons Played	Apps	Subs	Gls
Mansfield T.	YT	07.88				
Bury	Tr	07.89	89-90	1	3	0

PRICE George
Crewe, 2 December, 1929 (OL)

League Club	Source	Date Signed	Seasons Played	Apps	Subs	Gls
Crewe Alex.		02.54	53	4	-	0

PRICE James Richard
Preston, 1 February, 1978 (LB)

League Club	Source	Date Signed	Seasons Played	Apps	Subs	Gls
Rochdale	YT	07.96	95	3	0	0

PRICE Jason Jeffrey
Pontypridd, 12 April, 1977 Wu21-1 (D)

League Club	Source	Date Signed	Seasons Played	Apps	Subs	Gls
Swansea C.	Aberaman	07.95	96-97	32	4	3

PRICE John
Middlewich, 28 April, 1960 (M)

League Club	Source	Date Signed	Seasons Played	Apps	Subs	Gls
Rochdale	Nantwich T.	01.78	77-78	10	2	0

PRICE John
Easington, 25 October, 1943 Died 1995 (W)

League Club	Source	Date Signed	Seasons Played	Apps	Subs	Gls
Burnley	Horden Colly	11.60	63-64	21	-	2
Stockport Co.	Tr	05.65	65-71	241	5	23
Blackburn Rov.	Tr	09.71	71-73	63	13	12
Stockport Co.	Tr	03.74	73-75	51	15	1

PRICE John
Shotton (Dm), 29 August, 1918 (IF)

League Club	Source	Date Signed	Seasons Played	Apps	Subs	Gls
Hartlepool U.	Wolverhampton W. (Am)	06.38	38-48	89	-	12
York C.	Tr	12.48	48	2	-	2

PRICE John
Leadgate, 14 April, 1947 (W)

League Club	Source	Date Signed	Seasons Played	Apps	Subs	Gls
Leeds U.	App	05.65				
Southport	Tr	07.66	66	16	2	2

PRICE John David
Camden, 31 December, 1932 (D)

League Club	Source	Date Signed	Seasons Played	Apps	Subs	Gls
Tottenham H.	Eastbourne U.	09.54				
Aldershot	Tr	01.57	56-58	86	-	1
Watford	Tr	06.59	59	22	-	0

PRICE John Geraint
Aberystwyth, 22 November, 1936 (FB)

League Club	Source	Date Signed	Seasons Played	Apps	Subs	Gls
Liverpool	Fordhouse Y.C.	10.54	55	1	-	0

(continued)

League Club	Source	Date Signed	Seasons Played	Apps	Subs	Gls
Aston Villa	Tr	03.57				
Walsall	Tr	07.57				
Shrewsbury T.	Tr	07.58	58-59	9	-	0

PRICE Kenneth Edward
Ellesmere Port, 25 March, 1939 (CF)

League Club	Source	Date Signed	Seasons Played	Apps	Subs	Gls
Aston Villa	West Bromborough	08.59				
Tranmere Rov.	Tr	12.60	60	3	-	2
Hartlepool U.	Tr	07.61	61	8	-	3

PRICE Kenneth Gordon
Dudley, 26 February, 1954 (F)

League Club	Source	Date Signed	Seasons Played	Apps	Subs	Gls
Southend U.	Dudley T.	05.76	76	1	0	0
Gillingham	Tr	12.76	76-82	247	8	78
Reading	Tr	01.83	82-84	40	3	6

PRICE Leslie Eugene
Consett, 26 August, 1930 (OL)

League Club	Source	Date Signed	Seasons Played	Apps	Subs	Gls
Sunderland		08.50				
Gateshead	Tr	07.52	52-53	39	-	12

PRICE Mark Anthony
Keighley, 15 October, 1973 (M)

League Club	Source	Date Signed	Seasons Played	Apps	Subs	Gls
Scarborough	YT	●	91	2	1	1

PRICE Neil
Hemel Hempstead, 15 February, 1964 (LB)

League Club	Source	Date Signed	Seasons Played	Apps	Subs	Gls
Watford	App	02.82	83	7	1	0
Plymouth Arg.	L	02.84	83	1	0	0
Blackpool	L	03.85	84	13	0	0
Swansea C.	Tr	07.85	85	1	2	0

PRICE Paul Terence
St Albans, 23 March, 1954 Wu21-1/W-25 (CD)

League Club	Source	Date Signed	Seasons Played	Apps	Subs	Gls
Luton T.	Jnrs	07.71	72-80	206	1	8
Tottenham H.	Tr	06.81	81-83	35	4	0
Swansea C.	Minnesota (USA)	01.85	84-85	61	0	1
Peterborough U.	Tr	08.86	86-87	86	0	0

PRICE Peter
Tarbolton, 26 February, 1932 (IF)

League Club	Source	Date Signed	Seasons Played	Apps	Subs	Gls
Darlington		01.54	53-54	3	-	0

PRICE Peter William
Wrexham, 17 August, 1949 Wu23-4 (F)

League Club	Source	Date Signed	Seasons Played	Apps	Subs	Gls
Liverpool	App	08.66				
Peterborough U.	Tr	07.68	68-71	114	5	62
Portsmouth	Tr	06.72	72-73	13	1	2
Peterborough U.	L	07.74	74	2	0	0
Barnsley	Tr	11.74	74-77	72	7	28

PRICE Raymond
Hetton-le-Hole, 18 May, 1944 (FB)

League Club	Source	Date Signed	Seasons Played	Apps	Subs	Gls
Norwich C.	Jnrs	07.63	63	1	-	0
Colchester U.	Tr	07.64	64-66	15	2	0

PRICE Raymond John
Northampton, 30 November, 1948 (F)

League Club	Source	Date Signed	Seasons Played	Apps	Subs	Gls
Northampton T.	App	12.66	66-67	7	0	0

PRICE Ryan
Stafford, 13 March, 1970 E Semi Pro (G)

League Club	Source	Date Signed	Seasons Played	Apps	Subs	Gls
Birmingham C.	Stafford R.	08.94				
Macclesfield T.	Tr	11.95	97	46	0	0

PRICE Terence Edmund
Colchester, 11 October, 1945 (W)

League Club	Source	Date Signed	Seasons Played	Apps	Subs	Gls
Leyton Orient	App	08.63	64-67	86	1	18
Colchester U.	Tr	09.67	67-68	54	2	5

PRICE Trevor Henry Richard
Ellesmere Port, 27 December, 1944 (W)

League Club	Source	Date Signed	Seasons Played	Apps	Subs	Gls
Workington		06.64	64	2	-	1

PRICE Walter Booth
Neston, 14 February, 1921 Died 1984 (CH)

League Club	Source	Date Signed	Seasons Played	Apps	Subs	Gls
Tranmere Rov.		03.41	46	3	-	0
Rochdale	Tr	08.48	48	1	-	0

PRICE Albert John **William**
Wellington, 10 April, 1917 Died 1995 (CF)

League Club	Source	Date Signed	Seasons Played	Apps	Subs	Gls
Huddersfield T.	Wrockwardine Wood	10.37	37-47	51	-	23
Reading	Tr	10.47	47-48	15	-	2
Hull C.	Tr	01.49	48	8	-	5
Bradford C.	Tr	11.49	49-51	54	-	28

PRIDAY Marcus Albert
Knighton, 16 October, 1971 W Yth (G)

League Club	Source	Date Signed	Seasons Played	Apps	Subs	Gls
Hereford U.	YT	08.90	89	3	0	0

League Club	Source	Date Signed	Seasons Played	Career Record Apps	Subs	Gls
PRIDAY Robert Herbert						
South Africa, 29 March, 1925						(W)
Liverpool	Cape Town (SA)	12.45	46-48	33	-	6
Blackburn Rov.	Tr	03.49	48-50	44	-	11
Accrington St.	Northwich Vic.	12.52	52	5	-	0
Rochdale	Tr	08.53	53	5	-	1
PRIDDLE Sean Patrick						
Hammersmith, 14 December, 1965						(D/M)
Wimbledon	App	12.83				
Crewe Alex.	Tr	02.85	84	6	5	0
Exeter C.	Wimbledon (N/C)	07.86	86	18	0	1
Brentford		07.87	87	5	1	0
PRIDDY Paul Joseph						
Isleworth, 11 July, 1953						(G)
Brentford	Walton & Hersham	10.72	72-76	121	0	0
Wimbledon (N/C)	Tooting & Mitcham	10.78	78	1	0	0
Brentford	Hayes	08.81	81	1	0	0
PRIEST Christopher						
Leigh, 18 October, 1973						(M)
Everton	YT	06.92				
Chester C.	L	09.94	94	11	0	1
Chester C.	Tr	01.95	94-97	116	5	21
PRIEST Harry						
Clay Cross, 26 October, 1935						(F)
Sheffield U.	Clay Cross Wks	02.54	56	2	-	1
Halifax T.	Tr	01.58	57-58	30	-	12
PRIEST Philip						
Warley, 9 September, 1966 E Sch/E Yth						(M)
Chelsea	App	09.83				
Blackpool	L	12.86	86	1	0	0
Brentford	L	03.87	86	3	2	1
Shrewsbury T.	Tr	07.87	87-89	54	6	3
PRIESTLEY Derek						
Bradford, 22 December, 1926						(OL)
Halifax T.		10.50	51-55	145	-	19
Bradford P. A.	Tr	07.56				
PRIESTLEY Gerald						
Halifax, 2 March, 1931						(W)
Nottingham F.		12.50				
Exeter C.	Tr	06.53	53-54	42	-	6
Grimsby T.	Tr	06.55	55-58	110	-	11
Crystal Palace	Tr	11.58	58-59	28	-	2
Halifax T.	Tr	07.60	60-62	105	-	23
PRIESTLEY Jason Aaron						
Leeds, 25 October, 1970						(G)
Carlisle U.	YT	07.89	90	22	0	0
Hartlepool U.	L	12.89	89	16	0	0
Scarborough	L	08.91	91	9	0	0
PRIESTLEY Maurice						
Bradford, 27 October, 1922 Died 1986						(F)
Bradford P. A.		09.46				
Halifax T.	Tr	01.48	47-48	24	-	8
PRIESTLEY Royston Maurice						
Barnsley, 26 November, 1948						(CF)
Barnsley (Am)	Jnrs	08.67	67	1	0	0
PRIMUS Linvoy Stephen						
Forest Gate, 14 September, 1973						(CD)
Charlton Ath.	YT	08.92	92	4	0	0
Barnet	Tr	07.94	94-96	127	0	7
Reading	Tr	07.97	97	36	0	1
PRINCE Eric						
Ipstones (Staffs), 11 December, 1924						(IF)
Port Vale	Ipstones	09.44	46	14	-	2
PRINCE Francis Anthony						
Penarth, 1 December, 1949 Wu23-4						(M)
Bristol Rov.	App	12.67	67-79	360	2	22
Exeter C.	Tr	07.80	80-81	27	4	2
PRINCE Harold						
Stoke, 4 December, 1921						(G)
Port Vale	Bucknall	08.44	47-48	5	-	0
PRINDIVILLE Steven Alan						
Harlow, 26 December, 1968						(LB)
Leicester C.	App	12.86	87	0	1	0

League Club	Source	Date Signed	Seasons Played	Career Record Apps	Subs	Gls
Chesterfield	Tr	06.88	88	43	0	1
Mansfield T.	Tr	06.89	89-90	26	2	0
Doncaster Rov.	E. Bengal (Ind)	02.92	91-93	58	1	2
PRING Dennis Frederick						
Newport, 8 November, 1940						(IF)
Southampton	Newport Y.M.C.A.	02.59	58	4	-	0
PRING Keith David						
Newport, 11 March, 1943 W-3						(W)
Newport Co.	Jnrs	11.61	61-64	61	-	3
Rotherham U.	Tr	10.64	64-67	81	2	6
Notts Co.	Tr	12.67	67-68	41	3	2
Southport	Tr	07.69	69-70	48	0	4
PRINGLE Brian						
Chathill (Nd), 12 March, 1949						(IF)
Hartlepool U. (Am)	Alnwick T.	04.73	72	1	0	0
PRINGLE William Alexander						
Liverpool, 24 February, 1932						(IF)
Liverpool	Jnrs	08.49				
Grimsby T.	Tr	05.54	54	2	-	0
PRINS Jason						
Wisbech, 1 November, 1974						(F)
Carlisle U.	YT	08.93	91-93	7	11	0
PRIOR George **Kenneth**						
Newcastle, 13 October, 1932						(OL)
Newcastle U.	Sunderland (Am)	03.52	51-52	8	-	3
Millwall	Tr	05.54	54-55	61	-	16
Newcastle U.	Tr	07.56	56	2	-	0
PRIOR Spencer Justin						
Southend, 22 April, 1971						(CD)
Southend U.	YT	05.89	88-92	135	0	3
Norwich C.	Tr	06.93	93-95	67	7	1
Leicester C.	Tr	08.96	96-97	61	3	0
PRISCOTT Anthony John						
Eastleigh, 19 March, 1941						(W)
Portsmouth	Jnrs	07.59	59-61	35	-	6
Aldershot	Tr	08.62	62-65	141	0	44
Bournemouth	Tr	01.66	65-66	60	1	6
Aldershot	Tr	08.67	67-70	126	10	26
PRITCHARD Alan Stewart						
Chester, 24 August, 1943						(IF)
Chester C.	Jnrs	10.60	60-63	19	-	6
PRITCHARD Alfred Vincent						
Chester, 31 August, 1920 Died 1995						(IF)
Wrexham	Dumbarton	08.46	46-49	36	-	8
PRITCHARD David Michael						
Wolverhampton, 27 May, 1972 W 'B'						(RB)
West Bromwich A.	YT	07.90	91	1	4	0
Bristol Rov.	Telford U.	02.94	93-97	124	1	0
PRITCHARD Harvey John						
Meriden, 30 January, 1913						(W)
Coventry C.	Exhall Colly	10.35	36	5	-	2
Crystal Palace	Tr	06.37	37	30	-	6
Manchester C.	Tr	03.38	37-38	22	-	5
Southend U.	Tr	02.47	46-51	71	-	8
PRITCHARD Howard Keith						
Cardiff, 18 October, 1958 W Yth/W-1						(W)
Bristol C.	App	08.76	78-80	31	7	2
Swindon T.	Tr	08.81	81-82	59	6	11
Bristol C.	Tr	08.83	83-85	117	2	22
Gillingham	Tr	08.86	86-87	84	4	20
Walsall	Tr	07.88	88-89	40	5	7
Maidstone U.	Tr	10.89	89-90	29	4	6
PRITCHARD Joseph Henry						
Birkenhead, 4 September, 1943						(M)
Tranmere Rov.	Liverpool (Am)	09.62	62-69	177	3	29
PRITCHARD Keith						
Wallasey, 20 October, 1919						(F)
New Brighton (Am)	Northern Nomads	07.46	46-47	25	-	8
PRITCHARD Philip John						
Stourbridge, 9 January, 1965						(G)
Stoke C.	App	01.82				
Southend U.	L	03.84	83	9	0	0

League Club	Source	Date Signed	Seasons Played	Apps	Subs	Gls
PRITCHARD Raymond						
Liverpool, 23 June, 1954						(FB)
Tranmere Rov.	Everton (App)	02.73	72-73	13	1	0
Southport	L	01.74	73	3	0	0
PRITCHARD Roy Thomas						
Dawley, 9 May, 1925 Died 1993						(FB)
Wolverhampton W.	Jnrs	05.42	46-54	202	-	0
Aston Villa	Tr	02.55	55-57	3	-	0
Notts Co.	Tr	11.57	57	18	-	0
Port Vale	Tr	08.58	58-59	24	-	0
PRITCHETT Darrol						
Bentley, 22 May, 1933						(FB)
Hull C.	Jnrs	01.51				
Walsall	Tr	05.54	54	1	-	0
PRITCHETT Keith Bernard						
Glasgow, 8 November, 1953						(LB)
Wolverhampton W.		04.72				
Doncaster Rov.	Tr	07.73	73	6	0	0
Queens Park R.	Tr	03.74	74	4	0	0
Brentford	Tr	07.76	76	11	0	1
Watford	Tr	11.76	76-81	133	7	9
Blackpool	Tr	11.82	82-83	36	1	1
PRITTY George Joseph						
Birmingham, 4 March, 1915 Died 1996						(WH)
Aston Villa	H.B. Metro	05.33	36-37	3	-	0
Nottingham F.	Tr	12.38	38-47	49	-	1
PROBERT Eric William						
South Kirkby, 17 February, 1952 E Yth						(M)
Burnley	App	02.69	68-72	62	5	11
Notts Co.	Tr	07.73	73-76	122	0	13
Darlington	Tr	07.78	78-79	20	1	0
PROCTOR David						
Belfast, 10 October, 1929						(FB)
Blackpool	Portadown	08.49				
Norwich C.	Tr	01.53	52-53	17	-	0
Barrow	Northwich Vic.	10.54	54-58	160	-	2
Wrexham	Tr	08.59	59	2	-	0
PROCTOR Michael **Henry (Harry)**						
Ushaw Moor, 10 July, 1912 Died 1984						(WH)
Hartlepool U.	Portsmouth (Am)	07.32	32-33	61	-	14
Norwich C.	Tr	05.34	34-46	108	-	3
PROCTOR James Anthony						
Doncaster, 25 October, 1976						(W)
Rochdale	Bradford C. (YT)	10.95	95	1	2	0
PROCTOR Mark Gerard						
Middlesbrough, 30 January, 1961 E Yth/Eu21-4						(M)
Middlesbrough	App	09.78	78-80	107	2	12
Nottingham F.	Tr	08.81	81-82	60	4	5
Sunderland	Tr	03.83	82-87	115	2	19
Sheffield Wed.	Tr	09.87	87-88	59	0	4
Middlesbrough	Tr	03.89	88-92	101	19	6
Tranmere Rov.	Tr	03.93	92-93	31	0	1
Hartlepool U. (N/C)	South Shields	03.97	96	6	0	0
PROKAS Richard						
Penrith, 22 January, 1976						(M)
Carlisle U.	YT	07.94	94-97	97	9	2
PROLZE Brian Joseph						
Altrincham, 11 April, 1932 Died 1996						(CF)
Crewe Alex. (Am)	Altrincham	02.54	53	1	-	0
PROPHETT Colin George						
Crewe, 8 March, 1947						(CD)
Sheffield Wed.	Crewe Y.C.	06.68	69-72	111	8	7
Norwich C.	Tr	06.73	73	34	1	0
Swindon T.	Tr	09.74	74-77	158	2	10
Chesterfield	Tr	09.78	78-79	35	2	1
Crewe Alex.	Tr	10.79	79-80	79	0	1
PROSSER Neil Albert						
Edmonton, 8 March, 1957						(F)
Bournemouth	Harlow T.	07.80	80	1	1	0
Tranmere Rov. (N/C)		09.82	82	1	1	0
PROUDLER Arthur						
Kingswinford, 3 October, 1929						(HB)
Aston Villa	Halesowen T.	12.47	54	1	-	0
Crystal Palace	Tr	06.56	56-58	26	-	2

League Club	Source	Date Signed	Seasons Played	Apps	Subs	Gls
PROUDLOCK George Thomas						
Morpeth, 19 September, 1919						(IF)
West Ham U.	Amble Jnrs	11.37	38-47	18	-	5
PROUDLOCK Paul						
Hartlepool, 25 October, 1965						(W)
Hartlepool U.		09.84	84-85	8	7	0
Middlesbrough	Tr	11.86	86-88	2	3	1
Carlisle U.	Tr	03.89	88-92	137	18	21
Hartlepool U.	L	09.92	92	3	3	0
PROUDLOVE Andrew George						
Buxton, 15 January, 1955						(W)
Reading	App	●	71	4	1	0
Sheffield Wed.	Buxton	09.75	75	10	5	0
Norwich C.	Tr	02.76	76	0	1	0
Hereford U.	Tr	05.77	77	6	5	0
Port Vale	Tr	11.78	78	5	0	0
PROUTON Ralph Oliver						
Southampton, 1 March, 1926						(LH)
Arsenal	Romsey T.	08.49				
Swindon T.	Tr	08.52	52	13	-	0
PROVAN Andrew (Drew) McKelvie Hughes						
Greenock, 1 January, 1944						(W)
Barnsley	St Mirren	05.63	63	3	-	0
York C.	Tr	08.64	64-68	159	1	49
Chester C.	Tr	08.68	68-69	78	4	18
Wrexham	Tr	04.70	70-71	49	2	10
Southport	Tr	07.72	72-73	82	1	28
Torquay U.	Tr	08.74	74-76	83	8	14
PROVAN David						
Falkirk, 11 March, 1941 Su23-1/SF Lge/S-5						(FB)
Crystal Palace	Glasgow Rangers	06.70	70	1	0	0
Plymouth Arg.	Tr	03.71	70-74	128	1	10
PROVERBS Roy John						
Wednesbury, 8 July, 1932						(D)
Coventry C.	Stratford T.	05.56	56	10	-	0
Bournemouth	Tr	07.57				
Gillingham	Tr	02.58	57-61	143	-	2
PRUDHAM Charles **Edward**						
Felling, 12 April, 1952						(F)
Sheffield Wed.	Jnrs	07.69	70-74	14	5	2
Carlisle U.	Tr	11.74	74-76	15	2	2
Hartlepool U.	L	09.76	76	3	0	0
Workington	L	02.77	76	15	0	6
Stockport Co.	Tr	07.77	77-79	80	7	22
Bournemouth	Tr	05.80	80	2	2	0
PRUDHOE Mark						
Washington, 8 November, 1963						(G)
Sunderland	App	09.81	82	7	0	0
Hartlepool U.	L	11.83	83	3	0	0
Birmingham C.	Tr	09.84	84	1	0	0
Walsall	Tr	02.86	85-86	26	0	0
Doncaster Rov.	L	12.86	86	5	0	0
Grimsby T.	L	03.87	86	8	0	0
Hartlepool U.	L	08.87	87	13	0	0
Bristol C.	L	11.87	87	3	0	0
Carlisle U.	Tr	12.87	87-88	34	0	0
Darlington	Tr	03.89	88-92	146	0	0
Stoke C.	Tr	06.93	93-96	82	0	0
Peterborough U.	L	09.94	94	6	0	0
York C.	L	02.97	96	2	0	0
Bradford C.	Tr	07.97	97	8	0	0
PRUNIER William						
France, 14 August, 1967 French Int						(CD)
Manchester U. (L)	Bordeaux (Fr)	12.95	95	2	0	0
PRYCE Idris						
Wrexham, 24 February, 1941						(W)
Wrexham	Jnrs	09.59	59	3	-	0
PRYDE David						
Edinburgh, 10 November, 1913 Died 1987						(WH)
Arsenal	Margate	05.35	38	4	-	0
Torquay U.	Tr	10.46	46-49	64	-	0
PRYDE Robert Ireland						
Wemyss, 25 April, 1913 EF Lge						(CH)
Blackburn Rov.	St Johnstone	05.33	33-48	320	-	11
PRYDE William						
Polmont, 20 May, 1919						(WH)
Southend U.	Bo'ness	07.47	47-48	17	-	0

PRYER Terence
London, 4 December, 1967 (D)

League Club	Source	Date Signed	Seasons Played	Apps	Subs	Gls
Southend U. (N/C)	YT	10.85	85	2	0	0

PUCKETT David Charles
Southampton, 29 October, 1960 (F)

League Club	Source	Date Signed	Seasons Played	Apps	Subs	Gls
Southampton	App	10.78	80-85	51	43	14
Bournemouth	Tr	07.86	86-88	29	6	14
Stoke C.	L	03.88	87	7	0	0
Swansea C.	L	11.88	88	7	1	3
Aldershot	Tr	01.89	88-90	113	0	50
Bournemouth	Tr	03.92	91	1	3	0

PUGH Daral James
Neath, 5 June, 1961 Wu21-2 (W)

League Club	Source	Date Signed	Seasons Played	Apps	Subs	Gls
Doncaster Rov.	App	12.78	78-82	136	18	15
Huddersfield T.	Tr	09.82	82-84	52	33	7
Rotherham U.	Tr	07.85	85-87	106	6	5
Cambridge U.	L	12.87	87	6	0	1
Torquay U.	Tr	08.88	88-89	29	3	0

PUGH David
Blackwood, 22 January, 1947 W Sch/Wu23-2 (M)

League Club	Source	Date Signed	Seasons Played	Apps	Subs	Gls
Newport Co.	Jnrs	04.64	64-67	73	5	9
Chesterfield	Tr	12.67	67-72	212	1	12
Halifax T.	Tr	08.73	73-75	91	5	3
Rotherham U.	Tr	07.76	76-78	57	1	0
York C.	Tr	11.78	78-80	73	4	2

PUGH David
Liverpool, 19 September, 1964 (W/F)

League Club	Source	Date Signed	Seasons Played	Apps	Subs	Gls
Chester C.	Runcorn	07.89	89-93	168	11	23
Bury	Tr	08.94	94-97	101	2	28

PUGH Gary
Wrexham, 10 January, 1967 (W)

League Club	Source	Date Signed	Seasons Played	Apps	Subs	Gls
Wrexham (N/C)	Jnrs	07.84	84	1	0	0

PUGH Gary Kevin
Ramsgate, 11 February, 1961 (M)

League Club	Source	Date Signed	Seasons Played	Apps	Subs	Gls
West Ham U.	Jnrs	02.78				
Bournemouth (N/C)	Dover T.	01.81	80	0	3	1
Torquay U. (N/C)	Canterbury C.	11.84	84	4	0	0

PUGH John **Graham**
Chester, 12 February, 1948 Eu23-1 (M)

League Club	Source	Date Signed	Seasons Played	Apps	Subs	Gls
Sheffield Wed.	App	02.65	65-71	136	6	7
Huddersfield T.	Tr	05.72	72-74	80	0	1
Chester C.	Tr	02.75	74-76	67	2	3
Barnsley	Tr	10.76	76-79	128	2	8
Scunthorpe U.	Tr	01.80	79-80	54	1	0

PUGH Kevin John
Corbridge, 11 October, 1960 (M)

League Club	Source	Date Signed	Seasons Played	Apps	Subs	Gls
Newcastle U.	App	10.78	81	0	1	0
Darlington	Gateshead	09.83	83	0	2	0

PUGH Stephen
Bangor, 27 November, 1973 W Yth/Wu21-2 (F)

League Club	Source	Date Signed	Seasons Played	Apps	Subs	Gls
Wrexham	YT	07.92	92-94	3	8	0

PUGH Stephen John
Wolverhampton, 1 February, 1965 (FB/M)

League Club	Source	Date Signed	Seasons Played	Apps	Subs	Gls
Wolverhampton W.	App	12.82				
Torquay U.	Tr	10.83	83-85	115	5	4
Exeter C.	Tr	08.86	86	23	1	1

PUGSLEY David George
Merthyr Tydfil, 15 August, 1931 (G)

League Club	Source	Date Signed	Seasons Played	Apps	Subs	Gls
Newport Co. (Am)	Gloucester C.	03.53	52	1	-	0

PULIS Anthony Richard
Newport, 16 January, 1958 (D/M)

League Club	Source	Date Signed	Seasons Played	Apps	Subs	Gls
Bristol Rov.	App	09.75	75-80	78	7	3
Bristol Rov.	Happy Valley (HK)	06.82	82-83	44	1	2
Newport Co.	Tr	07.84	84-85	75	2	0
Bournemouth	Tr	08.86	86-88	68	6	3
Gillingham	Tr	08.89	89	16	0	0
Bournemouth	Tr	08.90	90-91	12	4	1

PULIS Raymond
Newport, 21 November, 1964 (F)

League Club	Source	Date Signed	Seasons Played	Apps	Subs	Gls
Newport Co.	App	11.82	82	0	1	0

PULLAN Christopher John
Durham, 11 December, 1967 (FB/M)

League Club	Source	Date Signed	Seasons Played	Apps	Subs	Gls
Watford	Jnrs	07.86	86-90	5	7	0
Halifax T.	L	02.89	88	5	0	1
Maidstone U.	Tr	03.91	90	0	1	0

PULLAR David Harry
Durham, 13 February, 1959 (W/FB)

League Club	Source	Date Signed	Seasons Played	Apps	Subs	Gls
Portsmouth	App	02.77	75-78	84	9	4
Exeter C.	Tr	07.79	79-82	124	6	22
Crewe Alex.	Tr	07.83	83-86	120	12	7

PULLEN Walter Ernest
Ripley (Sy), 2 August, 1919 Died 1977 (IF)

League Club	Source	Date Signed	Seasons Played	Apps	Subs	Gls
Leyton Orient	Fulham (Am)	01.46	46-50	117	-	37

PULLEY Gordon Albert
Stourbridge, 18 September, 1936 (OL)

League Club	Source	Date Signed	Seasons Played	Apps	Subs	Gls
Millwall	Oswestry T.	09.56	56-57	60	-	9
Gillingham	Tr	05.58	58-65	203	0	46
Peterborough U.	Tr	11.65	65-66	16	1	4

PUNTER Brian
Wolverhampton, 16 August, 1935 E Yth (CF)

League Club	Source	Date Signed	Seasons Played	Apps	Subs	Gls
Wolverhampton W.	Jnrs	09.53				
Leicester C.	Bromsgrove Rov.	05.58				
Lincoln C.	Tr	11.59	59-63	75	-	21

PUNTON William
Morpeth, 18 December, 1957 (G)

League Club	Source	Date Signed	Seasons Played	Apps	Subs	Gls
Bradford C. (N/C)	Gainsborough Trin.	08.75	75-76	7	0	0

PUNTON William Hamilton
Ormiston, 9 May, 1934 (OL)

League Club	Source	Date Signed	Seasons Played	Apps	Subs	Gls
Newcastle U.	Portadown	02.54	53-57	23	-	1
Southend U.	Tr	07.58	58	38	-	6
Norwich C.	Tr	07.59	59-66	219	0	24
Sheffield U.	Tr	11.66	66-67	16	0	1
Scunthorpe U.	Tr	01.68	67-68	45	0	2

PURCELL Brian Patrick John
Swansea, 23 November, 1938 Died 1969 (FB)

League Club	Source	Date Signed	Seasons Played	Apps	Subs	Gls
Swansea C.	Tower U.	01.58	59-67	160	2	1

PURCELL Daniel
Chesterfield, 15 September, 1948 (F)

League Club	Source	Date Signed	Seasons Played	Apps	Subs	Gls
Chesterfield (Am)	Jnrs	05.65	65	0	1	0

PURDIE Bernard Charles
Wrexham, 20 April, 1949 (F)

League Club	Source	Date Signed	Seasons Played	Apps	Subs	Gls
Wrexham	Jnrs	10.67	68-69	7	3	3
Chester C.	Tr	07.71	71-72	54	9	14
Crewe Alex.	Tr	07.73	73-79	203	10	44
Huddersfield T.	Tr	10.79	79-81	37	9	1
Crewe Alex.	Tr	08.82	82	14	2	0

PURDIE Ian
Bellshill, 7 March, 1953 Su23-1 (W)

League Club	Source	Date Signed	Seasons Played	Apps	Subs	Gls
Wigan Ath.	Motherwell	07.78	78-79	54	1	12
Portsmouth	Tr	11.79	79	4	1	1

PURDIE James **John (Jock)**
Berwick, 24 May, 1918 Died 1988 (G)

League Club	Source	Date Signed	Seasons Played	Apps	Subs	Gls
Millwall	Airdrieonians	02.46	46-47	50	-	0
Southport	Kilmarnock	02.49	48	6	-	0
Aldershot	Tunbridge Wells	10.50	50	16	-	0

PURDIE Jonathan
Corby, 22 February, 1967 E Sch (W)

League Club	Source	Date Signed	Seasons Played	Apps	Subs	Gls
Arsenal	App	01.85				
Wolverhampton W.	Tr	07.85	85-87	82	7	12
Cambridge U.	L	10.87	87	7	0	2
Oxford U.	Tr	07.88	88	5	6	0
Brentford	Tr	03.89	88	5	1	0
Shrewsbury T.	Tr	06.89	89	9	3	1

PURDON Edward (Ted) John
South Africa, 1 March, 1930 (CF)

League Club	Source	Date Signed	Seasons Played	Apps	Subs	Gls
Birmingham C.	Marist Bros (SA)	08.50	51-53	64	-	27
Sunderland	Tr	01.54	53-56	90	-	39
Workington	Tr	03.57	56-57	33	-	9
Barrow	Tr	03.58	57-58	37	-	11
Bristol Rov.	Bath C.	08.60	60	4	-	1

PURNELL Philip
Bristol, 16 September, 1964 (LW)

League Club	Source	Date Signed	Seasons Played	Apps	Subs	Gls
Bristol Rov.	Mangotsfield	09.85	85-91	130	23	22
Swansea C.	L	12.91	91	5	0	1

PURSE Darren John
Stepney, 14 February, 1977 (CD)

League Club	Source	Date Signed	Seasons Played	Apps	Subs	Gls
Leyton Orient	YT	02.94	93-95	48	7	3
Oxford U.	Tr	07.96	96-97	52	7	5
Birmingham C.	Tr	02.98	97	2	6	0

League Club	Source	Date Signed	Seasons Played	Career Record Apps	Subs	Gls
PURSELL Robert Wilson						
Glasgow, 28 September, 1919						(FB)
Port Vale	Chesterton	12.39	46-47	39	-	0
PURVES Charles Reuben						
High Spen, 17 February, 1921						(IF)
Charlton Ath.	Spennymoor U.	10.46	46-49	46	-	4
Southampton	Tr	06.51	51-53	30	-	2
PURVIS Bartholomew						
Gateshead, 15 October, 1921						(LB)
Everton	North Shields	01.46				
Gateshead	Tr	10.46	46	1	-	0
Plymouth Arg.	Tr	06.47				
Notts Co.	Tr	05.48	48-50	25	-	0
Carlisle U.	Tr	08.51	51	4	-	0
PURVIS William Youngson Rule						
Berwick, 14 December, 1938						(CF)
Grimsby T.	Berwick R.	08.61	61-62	7	-	2
Doncaster Rov.	Tr	12.62	62	2	-	0
PUTNEY Trevor Anthony						
Harold Hill, 9 April, 1960						(M)
Ipswich T.	Brentwood & Warley	09.80	82-85	94	9	8
Norwich C.	Tr	06.86	86-88	76	6	9
Middlesbrough	Tr	07.89	89-90	45	3	1
Watford	Tr	08.91	91-92	42	10	2
Leyton Orient	Tr	07.93	93	20	2	2
Colchester U.	Tr	08.94	94	28	0	2
PUTTNAM David Paul						
Leicester, 3 February, 1967						(W)
Leicester C.	Leicester U.	02.89	88-89	4	3	0
Lincoln C.	Tr	01.90	89-95	160	17	21
Gillingham	Tr	10.95	95-96	15	25	2
Swansea C.	Tr	08.97	97	4	0	0
PYATT John Henry						
Barnet, 26 September, 1948						(IF)
Liverpool	Chesham U.	07.67				
Peterborough U.	Tr	07.68	68	15	1	1
PYE Frederick						
Stockport, 11 March, 1928						(IF)
Accrington St.	Stalybridge Celtic	04.48	47-48	4	-	0
PYE Jesse						
Rotherham, 22 December, 1919, Died 1984		*E 'B'/EF Lge/E-1*				(CF)
Sheffield U.	Treeton	12.38				
Notts Co.		08.45				
Wolverhampton W.	Tr	05.46	46-51	188	-	90
Luton T.	Tr	07.52	52-54	61	-	32
Derby Co.	Tr	10.54	54-56	61	-	24
PYE William						
Rainford (Lancs), 8 November, 1930						(IF)
Stockport Co.		08.49				
Chester C.	Tr	07.52	53-55	28	-	11
PYGALL David Allen						
Watford, 23 January, 1939						(IF)
Watford	Jnrs	01.56	55-60	20	-	2
PYKE Malcolm						
Eltham, 6 March, 1938						(WH)
West Ham U.	Jnrs	03.55	56-57	17	-	0
Crystal Palace	Tr	06.59	59	2	-	0
PYLE Walter **David**						
Trowbridge, 12 December, 1936						(CH)
Bristol Rov.	Trowbridge T.	07.55	56-61	139	-	0
Bristol C.	Tr	07.62	62	8	-	0
PYLE Elijah St Quentin						
Chester-le-Street, 22 September, 1918						(IF)
York C.	West Stanley	11.47	47-48	10	-	3
PYLE Stephen						
North Shields, 28 September, 1963						(W)
Cambridge U.	App	07.81	80-85	56	13	8
Torquay U.	Tr	12.85	85-86	27	6	5
PYM Ernest Frederick						
Torquay, 23 March, 1935						(OL)
Torquay U.	St Marychurch	09.57	57-64	284	-	83

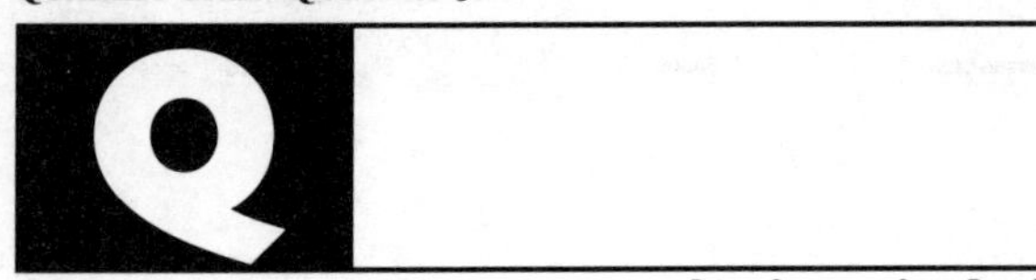

QUAILEY Brian Sullivan
Leicester, 24 March, 1978 (F)

League Club	Source	Date Signed	Seasons Played	Apps	Subs	Gls
West Bromwich A.	Nuneaton Borough	09.97	97	0	5	0

QUAIRNEY John
Girvan, 7 January, 1927 (G)

League Club	Source	Date Signed	Seasons Played	Apps	Subs	Gls
Rotherham U.	Girvan Jnrs	07.48	48-59	260	-	0

QUAMINA Mark Ezzard
Guyana (WI), 25 November, 1969 (M/RB)

League Club	Source	Date Signed	Seasons Played	Apps	Subs	Gls
Wimbledon	YT	07.88	88	1	0	0
Plymouth Arg.	Tr	07.91	91	4	1	0

QUARTERMAIN Patrick George
Oxford, 16 April, 1937 (LB)

League Club	Source	Date Signed	Seasons Played	Apps	Subs	Gls
Oxford U.	Jnrs	09.55	62-66	184	1	0

QUASHIE Nigel Francis
Peckham, 20 July, 1978 E Yth/Eu21-4/E 'B' (M)

League Club	Source	Date Signed	Seasons Played	Apps	Subs	Gls
Queens Park R.	YT	08.95	95-97	50	7	3

QUEEN Gerald
Glasgow, 15 January, 1945 (F)

League Club	Source	Date Signed	Seasons Played	Apps	Subs	Gls
Crystal Palace	Kilmarnock	07.69	69-72	101	7	24
Leyton Orient	Tr	09.72	72-76	149	7	34

QUESTED Wilfred **Leonard**
Folkestone, 9 January, 1925 E 'B' (WH)

League Club	Source	Date Signed	Seasons Played	Apps	Subs	Gls
Fulham	Folkestone T.	08.46	46-51	175	-	6
Huddersfield T.	Tr	11.51	51-56	220	-	8

QUIGLEY Edward
Bury, 13 July, 1921 Died 1997 E 'B' (IF)

League Club	Source	Date Signed	Seasons Played	Apps	Subs	Gls
Bury	Jnrs	09.41	46-47	42	-	18
Sheffield Wed.	Tr	10.47	47-49	74	-	49
Preston N.E.	Tr	12.49	49-51	52	-	17
Blackburn Rov.	Tr	11.51	51-55	159	-	92
Bury	Tr	08.56	56	10	-	3

QUIGLEY Gilbert
Ulverston, 17 February, 1921 (LB)

League Club	Source	Date Signed	Seasons Played	Apps	Subs	Gls
Barrow	Vickers Sports	12.45	46-48	27	-	0

QUIGLEY John
Glasgow, 28 June, 1935 (IF)

League Club	Source	Date Signed	Seasons Played	Apps	Subs	Gls
Nottingham F.	Ashfield Jnrs	07.57	57-64	236	-	51
Huddersfield T.	Tr	02.65	64-66	66	1	4
Bristol C.	Tr	10.66	66-67	66	0	7
Mansfield T.	Tr	07.68	68-70	105	0	2

QUIGLEY Michael Anthony Joseph
Manchester, 2 October, 1970 (M)

League Club	Source	Date Signed	Seasons Played	Apps	Subs	Gls
Manchester C.	YT	07.89	91-93	3	9	0
Wrexham	L	02.95	94	4	0	0
Hull C.	Tr	07.95	95-97	36	15	3

QUIGLEY Thomas Cook
East Calder, 26 March, 1932 (CF)

League Club	Source	Date Signed	Seasons Played	Apps	Subs	Gls
Portsmouth	Barry T.	12.55				
Queens Park R.	Tr	06.56	56	16	-	7

QUINLAN Maurice **Edward**
Finsbury Park, 15 August, 1931 (F)

League Club	Source	Date Signed	Seasons Played	Apps	Subs	Gls
Tottenham H.	Great Yarmouth T.	03.52				
Reading	Tr	06.53	53-55	51	-	12

QUINLAN Michael
Barnsley, 4 December, 1941 (CH)

League Club	Source	Date Signed	Seasons Played	Apps	Subs	Gls
Bristol C.	Doncaster Rov. (Am)	03.59	60	2	-	0

QUINLAN Philip Edward
Southport, 17 April, 1971 E Yth (F)

League Club	Source	Date Signed	Seasons Played	Apps	Subs	Gls
Everton	YT	07.89				
Huddersfield T.	L	03.91	90	7	1	2
Doncaster Rov.	Tr	08.92	92	2	7	0

QUINN Alan
Dublin, 13 June, 1979 (M)

League Club	Source	Date Signed	Seasons Played	Apps	Subs	Gls
Sheffield Wed.	Cherry Orchard	12.97	97	0	1	0

QUINN Albert
Lanchester, 18 April, 1920 (F)

League Club	Source	Date Signed	Seasons Played	Apps	Subs	Gls
Sunderland	Esh Winning Jnrs	11.46	47	6	-	2
Darlington	Tr	05.48	48-50	86	-	43

QUINN Anthony Michael
Liverpool, 24 July, 1959 (F)

League Club	Source	Date Signed	Seasons Played	Apps	Subs	Gls
Wigan Ath.	Everton (N/C)	01.79	79-80	36	7	14

QUINN Desmond
Derry, 21 March, 1926 (FB)

League Club	Source	Date Signed	Seasons Played	Apps	Subs	Gls
Blackburn Rov.		08.47	47	1	-	0
Millwall	Tr	06.49	49-54	43	-	0

QUINN Gordon Patrick
Hammersmith, 11 May, 1932 (IF)

League Club	Source	Date Signed	Seasons Played	Apps	Subs	Gls
Queens Park R.	Eastcote B.C.	08.52	52-56	22	-	1
Plymouth Arg.	Tr	09.56	56-57	14	-	2

QUINN James
Croy, 23 November, 1947 (LB)

League Club	Source	Date Signed	Seasons Played	Apps	Subs	Gls
Sheffield Wed.	Glasgow Celtic	01.75	74-75	46	0	1

QUINN James Martin
Belfast, 18 November, 1959 NI 'B'/NI-48 (F)

League Club	Source	Date Signed	Seasons Played	Apps	Subs	Gls
Swindon T.	Oswestry T.	12.81	81-83	34	15	10
Blackburn Rov.	Tr	08.84	84-86	58	13	17
Swindon T.	Tr	12.86	86-87	61	3	30
Leicester C.	Tr	06.88	88	13	18	6
Bradford C.	Tr	03.89	88-89	35	0	14
West Ham U.	Tr	12.89	89-90	34	13	19
Bournemouth	Tr	08.91	91	43	0	19
Reading	Tr	07.92	92-96	149	33	71
Peterborough U.	Tr	07.97	97	40	2	20

QUINN Stephen **James**
Coventry, 14 December, 1974 NI Yth/NIu21-1/NI 'B'/NI-12 (F)

League Club	Source	Date Signed	Seasons Played	Apps	Subs	Gls
Birmingham C.	YT	●	92	1	3	0
Blackpool	Tr	07.93	93-97	128	23	36
Stockport Co.	L	03.94	93	0	1	0
West Bromwich A.	Tr	02.98	97	12	1	2

QUINN John David
Widnes, 30 May, 1938 (M)

League Club	Source	Date Signed	Seasons Played	Apps	Subs	Gls
Sheffield Wed.	Prescot Cables	05.59	59-67	166	7	20
Rotherham U.	Tr	11.67	67-71	114	0	7
Halifax T.	Tr	07.72	72-74	88	4	1

QUINN Michael
Liverpool, 2 May, 1962 (F)

League Club	Source	Date Signed	Seasons Played	Apps	Subs	Gls
Wigan Ath.	Derby Co. (App)	09.79	79-81	56	13	19
Stockport Co.	Tr	07.82	82-83	62	1	39
Oldham Ath.	Tr	01.84	83-85	78	2	34
Portsmouth	Tr	03.86	85-88	115	6	54
Newcastle U.	Tr	07.89	89-91	106	4	57
Coventry C.	Tr	11.92	92-94	57	7	25
Plymouth Arg.	L	11.94	94	3	0	0
Watford	L	03.95	94	4	1	0

QUINN Niall John
Dublin, 6 October, 1966 NI Sch/IR Yth/IRu21-6/NIu23-1/IR 'B'/IR-63 (F)

League Club	Source	Date Signed	Seasons Played	Apps	Subs	Gls
Arsenal	Jnrs	11.83	85-89	59	8	14
Manchester C.	Tr	03.90	89-95	183	20	66
Sunderland	Tr	08.96	96-97	41	6	16

QUINN Noel Peter Anthony
Dublin, 2 November, 1949 (OR)

League Club	Source	Date Signed	Seasons Played	Apps	Subs	Gls
Oldham Ath.	Manchester U. (Am)	01.67	67	4	0	0

QUINN Patrick
Glasgow, 26 April, 1936 SF Lge/S-4 (IF)

League Club	Source	Date Signed	Seasons Played	Apps	Subs	Gls
Blackpool	Motherwell	11.62	62-63	34	-	9

QUINN Patrick Anthony
Kilsyth, 18 June, 1918 Died 1979 (IF)

League Club	Source	Date Signed	Seasons Played	Apps	Subs	Gls
Halifax T.	Ashfield Jnrs	07.46	46	25	-	6

QUINN Robert John
Sidcup, 8 November, 1976 IRu21-5 (CD/M)

League Club	Source	Date Signed	Seasons Played	Apps	Subs	Gls
Crystal Palace	YT	03.95	95-97	18	5	1

QUINN Wayne Richard
Truro, 19 November, 1976 E Yth/Eu21-2/E 'B' (LWB)

League Club	Source	Date Signed	Seasons Played	Apps	Subs	Gls
Sheffield U.	YT	12.94	97	28	0	2

QUINNEY Henry **Jesse**
Rugby, 15 October, 1922 (FB)

League Club	Source	Date Signed	Seasons Played	Apps	Subs	Gls
Northampton T.	Wolverhampton W. (Am)	01.43	46	3	-	0

League Club	Source	Date Signed	Seasons Played	Apps	Subs	Gls
QUINNEY John						
Rugby, 2 October, 1932						(FB)
Coventry C.	Jnrs	11.49	52	3	-	0
QUINTON Walter						
Anston (Yks), 13 December, 1917 Died 1996						(LB)
Rotherham U.	Dinnington Ath.	07.38	38	32	-	0
Birmingham C.	Tr	07.39	47	8	-	0
Brentford	Tr	04.49	48-50	42	-	0
Southend U.	Tr	08.52				
Shrewsbury T.	Tr	10.52	52	3	-	0
QUIRKE David						
Ballina (Ire), 11 January, 1947						(CD)
Gillingham	Bedford T.	07.66	67-73	221	9	0
QUITONGO Jose Manuel						
Angola, 18 November, 1974						(RW)
Darlington (N/C)	Benfica (Por)	09.95	95	1	0	0
QUIXALL Albert						
Sheffield, 9 August, 1933 E Sch/Eu23-1/E 'B'/EF Lge/E-5						(IF)
Sheffield Wed.	Jnrs	08.50	50-58	241	-	63
Manchester U.	Tr	09.58	58-63	165	-	50
Oldham Ath.	Tr	09.64	64-65	36	0	11
Stockport Co.	Tr	07.66	66	13	0	0
QUOW Trevor						
Peterborough, 28 September, 1960						(M)
Peterborough U.	App	09.78	78-85	191	12	17
Gillingham	Tr	08.86	86-88	64	15	3
Northampton T.	Tr	01.89	88-91	78	10	2

League Club	Source	Date Signed	Seasons Played	Career Record Apps	Subs	Gls
RABJOHN Christopher						
Sheffield, 10 March, 1945						(M)
Rotherham U.	Jnrs	07.63	65-67	76	2	5
Doncaster Rov.	Tr	02.68	67-72	137	16	8
RACKHAM Derrick Richard						
Norwich, 14 June, 1928 Died 1996						(OL)
Norwich C.	Norman Y.C.	11.49	51	8	-	2
RACKLEY Robert William						
Teignmouth, 15 March, 1940						(OL)
Exeter C.	Newton Abbot Spurs	03.58				
Bristol Rov.	Tr	07.60				
Oldham Ath.	Tr	10.60	60	19	-	5
RACKSTRAW Charles						
Sheffield, 23 April, 1938						(IF)
Chesterfield		03.58	58-63	172	-	48
Gillingham	Tr	05.64	64-66	93	1	25
Bradford C.	Tr	01.67	66-69	94	10	27
RADCLIFFE Mark						
Hyde, 26 October, 1919						(G)
Oldham Ath.		12.42				
Fulham	Tr	08.46	46-47	11	-	0
Rochdale	Witton A.	11.52	52	1	-	0
RADCLIFFE Vincent						
Manchester, 9 June, 1945						(CH)
Portsmouth	App	06.63	64-66	10	0	0
Peterborough U.	Tr	07.67	67	2	0	0
Rochdale	Tr	07.68	68	26	0	1
RADEBE Lucas						
South Africa, 12 April, 1969 South African Int						(CD)
Leeds U.	Kaizer Chiefs (SA)	09.94	94-97	73	11	0
RADFORD Arthur (Alf)						
Rotherham, 7 October, 1925 Died 1981						(FB)
Huddersfield T.		10.44				
Rotherham U.		05.47	47-49	44	-	0
Rochdale	Tr	06.51	51	27	-	0
Swindon T.	Tr	08.52	52	16	-	0
RADFORD William **Howard**						
Abercynon, 8 September, 1930						(G)
Bristol Rov.	Penrhiwceiber	08.51	51-61	244	-	0
RADFORD John						
Hemsworth, 22 February, 1947 Eu23-4/EF Lge/E-2						(F)
Arsenal	App	03.64	63-76	375	4	111
West Ham U.	Tr	12.76	76-77	28	0	0
Blackburn Rov.	Tr	02.78	77-78	36	0	10
RADFORD Mark						
Leicester, 20 December, 1968						(LB/M)
Colchester U.	Jnrs	05.87	87-89	47	17	5
RADFORD Ronald						
South Elmsall, 12 July, 1943						(M)
Leeds U.	Sheffield Wed. (Am)	10.61				
Newport Co.	Cheltenham T.	07.69	69-70	63	3	7
Hereford U.	Tr	07.71	72-73	61	0	6
RADOSAVLJEVIC Predrag (Preki)						
Yugoslavia, 24 June, 1963 Yugoslav Int						(W)
Everton	St Louis (USA)	08.92	92-93	22	24	4
Portsmouth	Tr	07.94	94	30	10	5
RADUCIOIU Florin						
Romania, 17 March, 1970 Romanian Int						(F)
West Ham U.	Espanol (Sp)	08.96	96	6	5	2
RAE Alexander McFarlane						
Glasgow, 23 August, 1946						(M)
Bury	East Fife	05.69	69	10	1	0
RAE Alexander Scott						
Glasgow, 30 September, 1969 Su21-8/S 'B'						(M)
Millwall	Falkirk	08.90	90-95	205	13	63
Sunderland	Tr	06.96	96-97	37	15	5

League Club	Source	Date Signed	Seasons Played	Career Record Apps	Subs	Gls
RAE Ian Johnstone						
Grangemouth, 19 January, 1933 Su23-1/S 'B'						(FB)
Bristol C.	Falkirk	10.57	57	12	-	0
RAE Joseph						
Glasgow, 6 March, 1925 Died 1987						(CF)
Torquay U.	Glasgow Celtic	07.48	48	20	-	4
RAFFELL Stephen Christopher						
Blyth, 27 April, 1970						(CD)
Doncaster Rov.	YT	06.88	87-89	45	9	0
RAFFERTY Bernard						
Manchester, 9 July, 1948						(F)
Bradford P.A.		10.69	69	8	5	1
RAFFERTY James						
Manchester, 7 November, 1930						(LH)
Manchester C.		12.48				
Bradford P.A.	Tr	06.52	52	2	-	0
RAFFERTY Kevin Brian						
Kenya, 9 November, 1960						(G)
Crewe Alex.	App	11.78	78-79	22	0	0
RAFFERTY Ronald						
South Shields, 6 May, 1934						(IF)
Portsmouth	Wycombe W.	07.54	54-56	23	-	5
Grimsby T.	Tr	12.56	56-62	264	-	145
Hull C.	Tr	07.63	63-64	16	-	6
Aldershot	Tr	07.66	66-68	79	2	10
RAFFERTY William Henry						
Port Glasgow, 30 December, 1950						(F)
Coventry C.	Port Glasgow	07.68	69-72	27	0	3
Blackpool	Tr	10.72	72-73	35	1	9
Plymouth Arg.	Tr	03.74	73-75	89	1	35
Carlisle U.	Tr	05.76	76-77	72	0	27
Wolverhampton W.	Tr	03.78	77-79	41	3	6
Newcastle U.	Tr	10.79	79-80	34	5	6
Portsmouth	Tr	12.80	80-82	98	4	40
Bournemouth	Tr	02.84	83-84	58	0	19
RAFTER Sean						
Southend, 20 May, 1957						(G)
Southend U.	App	06.75	75-77	23	0	0
Leicester C.	Tr	01.78				
Leyton Orient	Tr	07.79	80	2	0	0
RAFTERY Patrick Thomas						
Stoke, 28 November, 1925						(IF)
Port Vale	Ravensdale	01.49	48-49	5	-	0
RAGGETT Brian Charles						
Barnsley, 11 January, 1949						(D)
Barnsley	App	01.67	66-71	56	8	0
RAHMBERG Marino						
Sweden, 7 August, 1974 Swedish Int						(F)
Derby Co. (L)	Degerfors (Swe)	01.97	96	0	1	0
RAINE David						
Darlington, 28 March, 1937						(D)
Port Vale		05.57	56-61	144	-	0
Doncaster Rov.	Tr	07.62	62-64	107	-	2
Colchester U.	Tr	06.65	65-66	44	4	0
RAINE Robert Reginald						
Chesterfield, 17 November, 1927						(CF)
Chesterfield	Newbold Colly	02.49	49	1	-	0
Aldershot	Kidderminster Hrs	02.51	50-53	47	-	21
RAINEY Hugh						
Dumbarton, 7 January, 1935						(WH)
Portsmouth	Renton Guild	06.53				
Queens Park R.	Tr	06.55				
Aldershot	Tr	07.57	57	8	-	0
RAINFORD John William						
Camden, 11 December, 1930						(IF)
Crystal Palace	Jnrs	03.49	48-52	64	-	8
Cardiff C.	Tr	05.53	53	3	-	1
Brentford	Tr	10.53	53-61	299	-	42
RAINFORD Kenneth Sydney						
Saughall Massie, 4 November, 1926						(CF)
New Brighton (Am)	New Brighton Baptists	02.48	47	3	-	1

RAJKOVIC Ante
Yugoslavia, 17 August, 1952 Yugoslav Int (CD)

League Club	Source	Date Signed	Seasons Played	Apps	Subs	Gls
Swansea C.	Sarajevo (Yug)	03.81	80-84	79	1	2

RALSTON Peter
Fauldhouse, 31 January, 1929 (CH)

League Club	Source	Date Signed	Seasons Played	Apps	Subs	Gls
Accrington St.	Falkirk	08.57	57-58	6	-	0

RALSTON Walter
Glasgow, 3 October, 1935 (LB)

League Club	Source	Date Signed	Seasons Played	Apps	Subs	Gls
Aldershot (L)	Partick Thistle	06.58	58	3	-	0

RAMAGE Alan
Guisborough, 29 November, 1957 (CD)

League Club	Source	Date Signed	Seasons Played	Apps	Subs	Gls
Middlesbrough	App	12.75	75-79	65	4	2
Derby Co.	Tr	07.80	80-81	32	1	2

RAMAGE Andrew William
Barking, 3 October, 1974 (M)

League Club	Source	Date Signed	Seasons Played	Apps	Subs	Gls
Gillingham	Leyton Orient (YT)	11.93	94	8	5	1

RAMAGE Craig Darren
Derby, 30 March, 1970 Eu21-3 (F/M)

League Club	Source	Date Signed	Seasons Played	Apps	Subs	Gls
Derby Co.	YT	07.88	89-93	33	9	4
Wigan Ath.	L	02.89	88	10	0	2
Watford	Tr	02.94	93-96	99	5	27
Peterborough U.	L	02.97	96	7	0	0
Bradford C.	Tr	06.97	97	24	8	1

RAMAGE George McIntosh
Newtongrange, 29 January, 1937 (G)

League Club	Source	Date Signed	Seasons Played	Apps	Subs	Gls
Colchester U.	Third Lanark	08.61	62-63	38	-	0
Leyton Orient	Tr	07.64	64	4	-	0
Luton T.	Tr	11.65	65	7	0	0

RAMASUT Mahan William Thomas
Cardiff, 30 August, 1977 W Yth/Wu21-4/W 'B' (W)

League Club	Source	Date Signed	Seasons Played	Apps	Subs	Gls
Norwich C.		07.95				
Bristol Rov.	Tr	09.96	96-97	30	12	6

RAMMELL Andrew Victor
Nuneaton, 10 February, 1967 (F)

League Club	Source	Date Signed	Seasons Played	Apps	Subs	Gls
Manchester U.	Atherstone U.	09.89				
Barnsley	Tr	09.90	90-95	149	36	44
Southend U.	Tr	02.96	95-97	50	19	13

RAMPLING Dennis
Gainsborough, 25 November, 1923 (OR)

League Club	Source	Date Signed	Seasons Played	Apps	Subs	Gls
Fulham		11.42	47	2	-	0
Bournemouth	Tr	07.48	48	24	-	4
Brentford	Tr	05.49	49	1	-	0

RAMPLING Edward
Wigan, 17 February, 1948 (OL)

League Club	Source	Date Signed	Seasons Played	Apps	Subs	Gls
Chester C.	Newton-le-Willows Y.C.	03.67	67	2	1	0

RAMSAY Craig James
Dunfermline, 19 September, 1962 (F)

League Club	Source	Date Signed	Seasons Played	Apps	Subs	Gls
Lincoln C.	App	09.80	79-80	3	2	2

RAMSAY George Albert
Sunderland, 24 April, 1923 (OR)

League Club	Source	Date Signed	Seasons Played	Apps	Subs	Gls
Gateshead	Raith Rov.	11.46	46	7	-	1

RAMSAY John William
Sunderland, 25 January, 1979 (M)

League Club	Source	Date Signed	Seasons Played	Apps	Subs	Gls
Doncaster Rov. (N/C)	YT	10.97	97	2	2	0

RAMSBOTTOM Neil
Blackburn, 25 February, 1946 (G)

League Club	Source	Date Signed	Seasons Played	Apps	Subs	Gls
Bury	Jnrs	07.64	65-70	174	0	0
Blackpool	Tr	02.71	70-71	13	0	0
Crewe Alex.	L	01.72	71	3	0	0
Coventry C.	Tr	03.72	72-74	51	0	0
Sheffield Wed.	Tr	08.75	75	18	0	0
Plymouth Arg.	Tr	07.76	76	39	0	0
Blackburn Rov.	Tr	01.78	78	10	0	0
Sheffield U.	Miami (USA)	10.79	79	2	0	0
Bradford C.	Tr	08.80	80-82	73	0	0
Bournemouth (N/C)	Tr	08.83	83	4	0	0

RAMSCAR Frederick Thomas
Salford, 24 January, 1919 (IF)

League Club	Source	Date Signed	Seasons Played	Apps	Subs	Gls
Wolverhampton W.	Stockport Co. (Am)	09.45	46	16	-	1
Queens Park R.	Tr	10.47	47-49	51	-	4
Preston N.E.	Tr	11.49	49-50	19	-	4
Northampton T.	Tr	07.51	51-54	139	-	55
Millwall	Tr	09.54	54	30	-	5

RAMSDEN Bernard
Sheffield, 8 November, 1917 (FB)

League Club	Source	Date Signed	Seasons Played	Apps	Subs	Gls
Liverpool	Sheffield Vic.	03.35	37-47	57	-	0
Sunderland	Tr	03.48	47-48	12	-	0
Hartlepool U.	Tr	01.50	49	13	-	0

RAMSEY Alfred Ernest
Dagenham, 22 January, 1920 EF Lge/E-32 (FB)

League Club	Source	Date Signed	Seasons Played	Apps	Subs	Gls
Southampton	Portsmouth (Am)	04.44	46-48	90	-	8
Tottenham H.	Tr	05.49	49-54	226	-	24

RAMSEY Christopher Leroy
Birmingham, 28 April, 1962 (RB)

League Club	Source	Date Signed	Seasons Played	Apps	Subs	Gls
Brighton & H.A.	Bristol C. (App)	08.80	80-83	30	0	0
Swindon T.	Tr	08.84	84-86	99	1	5
Southend U.	Tr	08.87	87	8	5	0

RAMSEY Donald
Manchester, 27 September, 1928 (OR)

League Club	Source	Date Signed	Seasons Played	Apps	Subs	Gls
Oldham Ath.		11.46	49	2	-	0

RAMSEY Paul Christopher
Derry (NI), 3 September, 1962 NI Sch/NI-14 (M/RB)

League Club	Source	Date Signed	Seasons Played	Apps	Subs	Gls
Leicester C.	App	04.80	80-90	278	12	13
Cardiff C.	Tr	08.91	91-92	69	0	7
Cardiff C. (L)	St Johnstone	11.94	94	11	0	0
Torquay U.	Telford U.	12.95	95	18	0	0

RAMSEY Robert
Sunderland, 24 February, 1935 (FB)

League Club	Source	Date Signed	Seasons Played	Apps	Subs	Gls
Huddersfield T.	Jnrs	01.53				
York C.	Tr	05.58	58-60	75	-	0

RANDALL Adrian John
Amesbury, 10 November, 1968 E Yth (M)

League Club	Source	Date Signed	Seasons Played	Apps	Subs	Gls
Bournemouth	App	08.86	85-87	3	0	0
Aldershot	Tr	09.88	88-90	102	5	12
Burnley	Tr	12.91	91-95	105	20	8
York C.	Tr	12.95	95-96	26	6	2
Bury	Tr	12.96	96-97	16	18	3

RANDALL Ernest Albert Walter
Bognor Regis, 13 January, 1926 (IF)

League Club	Source	Date Signed	Seasons Played	Apps	Subs	Gls
Chelsea	Bognor Regis T.	12.50	51	3	-	1
Crystal Palace	Tr	06.53	53-54	22	-	11

RANDALL Kevin
Ashton-u-Lyne, 20 August, 1945 (F)

League Club	Source	Date Signed	Seasons Played	Apps	Subs	Gls
Bury	Droylsden	10.65	65	4	0	0
Chesterfield	Tr	07.66	66-71	258	0	96
Notts Co.	Tr	08.72	72-75	119	2	39
Mansfield T.	Tr	11.75	75-77	62	4	20
York C.	Tr	10.77	77-80	96	11	27

RANDALL Maurice
Manchester, 4 August, 1919 Died 1976 (LB)

League Club	Source	Date Signed	Seasons Played	Apps	Subs	Gls
Crewe Alex.	Droylsden	02.47	46-48	41	-	0

RANDALL Paul
Liverpool, 16 February, 1958 (F)

League Club	Source	Date Signed	Seasons Played	Apps	Subs	Gls
Bristol Rov.	Frome T.	08.77	77-78	49	3	33
Stoke C.	Tr	12.78	78-80	38	8	7
Bristol Rov.	Tr	01.81	80-85	169	15	61

RANDELL Colin William
Neath, 12 December, 1952 W Sch/Wu23-1 (M)

League Club	Source	Date Signed	Seasons Played	Apps	Subs	Gls
Coventry C.	App	05.70				
Plymouth Arg.	Tr	09.73	73-76	137	2	9
Exeter C.	Tr	09.77	77-78	78	0	4
Plymouth Arg.	Tr	07.79	79-81	110	0	8
Blackburn Rov.	Tr	08.82	82-84	72	1	7
Newport Co.	L	03.84	83	15	0	0
Swansea C.	Tr	07.85	85-86	20	2	1

RANDLES Thomas
Blackpool, 13 October, 1940 (IF)

League Club	Source	Date Signed	Seasons Played	Apps	Subs	Gls
Stoke C.	Ellesmere Port	02.60	61	2	-	0

RANKIN Andrew George
Bootle, 11 May, 1944 Eu23-1 (G)

League Club	Source	Date Signed	Seasons Played	Apps	Subs	Gls
Everton	Jnrs	10.61	63-70	85	0	0
Watford	Tr	11.71	71-79	299	0	0
Huddersfield T.	Tr	12.79	79-81	71	0	0

RANKIN George
Liverpool, 29 January, 1930 Died 1989 E Yth (FB)

League Club	Source	Date Signed	Seasons Played	Apps	Subs	Gls
Everton	Jnrs	08.48	50-55	36	-	0
Southport	Tr	07.56	56-59	144	-	0

League Club	Source	Date Signed	Seasons Played	Apps	Subs	Gls
RANKIN Isaiah						
London, 22 May, 1978						(F)
Arsenal	YT	09.95	97	0	1	0
Colchester U.	L	09.97	97	10	1	5
RANKIN James						
Gateshead, 8 September, 1927 Died 1985						(OR)
Newcastle U.	Jnrs	09.44				
Brighton & H.A.		08.49				
Grimsby T.	Tr	01.50	49-50	5	-	1
RANKINE Simon **Mark**						
Doncaster, 30 September, 1969						(M)
Doncaster Rov.	YT	06.88	87-91	160	4	20
Wolverhampton W.	Tr	01.92	91-95	112	20	1
Preston N.E.	Tr	09.96	96-97	53	5	1
RANKMORE Frank Edward John						
Cardiff, 21 July, 1939 Wu23-2/W-1						(CH)
Cardiff C.	Cardiff Corries	12.57	61-62	67	-	0
Peterborough U.	Tr	08.63	63-67	201	0	7
Northampton T.	Tr	08.68	68-70	103	0	15
RANSHAW John William						
Lincoln, 19 December, 1916						(OL)
Lincoln C.	Grantham	03.46	46	3	-	0
RANSHAW Richard William						
Sleaford, 17 April, 1970						(F)
Lincoln C. (N/C)	YT	08.88	88	0	1	0
RANSON Raymond						
St Helens, 12 June, 1960 E Sch/E Yth/Eu21-10						(RB)
Manchester C.	App	06.77	78-83	181	2	1
Birmingham C.	Tr	11.84	84-88	136	1	0
Newcastle U.	Tr	12.88	88-92	78	5	1
Manchester C.	Tr	01.93	92	17	0	0
Reading	Tr	07.93	93	22	2	0
RANTANEN Jari Juhani						
Finland, 31 December, 1961 Finnish Int						(F)
Leicester C.	Gothenburg (Swe)	09.87	87	10	3	3
RAPER Kenneth						
Stanley, 15 May, 1956						(M)
Stoke C.	App	06.73				
Torquay U.	Tr	07.77	77-78	51	1	8
RAPLEY Kevin John						
Reading, 21 September, 1977						(RW)
Brentford	YT	07.96	96-97	24	15	9
RAPLEY Peter David						
Portsmouth, 24 October, 1936						(OR)
Exeter C.	Portsmouth (Am)	06.57	57-59	10	-	4
RATCLIFFE James **Barrie**						
Blackburn, 21 September, 1941						(OL)
Blackburn Rov.	Jnrs	09.58	59-63	36	-	4
Scunthorpe U.	Tr	05.64	64	26	-	7
Rochdale	Tr	07.65	65	12	0	1
RATCLIFFE Beaumont						
Bolton-on-Dearne, 24 April, 1909						(CH)
New Brighton	Bolton A.	10.31	31-34	131	-	4
Oldham Ath.	Le Havre (Fr)	06.35	35-38	156	-	1
Reading	Tr	05.46	46-47	32	-	0
Watford	Tr	05.48	48	24	-	0
RATCLIFFE David						
Dewsbury, 9 March, 1957						(CD)
Bradford C.	App	03.75	74-77	17	11	1
RATCLIFFE Donald						
Newcastle-u-Lyme, 13 November, 1934						(W)
Stoke C.		05.53	54-63	238	-	16
Middlesbrough	Tr	09.63	63-65	65	0	3
Darlington	Tr	02.66	65-67	84	1	12
Crewe Alex.	Tr	01.68	67-68	45	3	2
RATCLIFFE Kevin						
Deeside, 12 November, 1960 W Sch/W Yth/Wu21-2/W-59						(CD)
Everton	App	11.78	79-91	356	3	2
Everton (N/C)	Dundee	10.92				
Cardiff C. (N/C)	Tr	01.93	92-93	25	0	1
Derby Co. (N/C)	Nottingham F. (N/C)	01.94	93	6	0	0
Chester C.	Tr	07.94	94	23	0	0
RATCLIFFE Patrick (Paddy) Christopher						
Dublin, 31 December, 1919						(RB)
Notts Co.	Bohemians	11.45				
Wolverhampton W.	Tr	06.46	46	2	-	0
Plymouth Arg.	Tr	06.47	47-55	236	-	10
RATCLIFFE Raymond						
St Helens, 3 November, 1929						(RH)
Stockport Co.		03.49	48	1	-	0
RATCLIFFE Simon						
Urmston, 8 February, 1967 E Sch/E Yth						(M)
Manchester U.	App	02.85				
Norwich C.	Tr	06.87	87	6	3	0
Brentford	Tr	01.89	88-94	197	17	14
Gillingham	Tr	08.95	95-97	100	5	10
RATHBONE Graham Charles						
Newport, 22 August, 1942						(CD)
Newport Co.	Merthyr Tydfil	03.61	60-66	191	0	7
Grimsby T.	Tr	11.66	66-72	232	1	11
Cambridge U.	Tr	02.73	72-73	35	1	0
RATHBONE Michael John						
Birmingham, 6 November, 1958 E Yth						(LB)
Birmingham C.	App	11.76	76-78	17	3	0
Blackburn Rov.	Tr	03.79	78-86	270	3	2
Preston N.E.	Tr	07.87	87-90	82	9	4
RATTLE Jonathan Paul						
Woodbridge, 22 July, 1976						(LB/M)
Cambridge U.	YT	05.94	94	6	0	0
Cambridge U. (N/C)	Stevenage Borough	09.95	95	7	2	0
RATTRAY Kevin Winston						
Tottenham, 6 October, 1968						(M)
Gillingham	Woking	06.95	95	18	8	3
Barnet	Tr	09.96	96	9	0	0
RATTRAY Peter Kerr						
Bannockburn, 7 November, 1925						(IF)
Plymouth Arg.	Dundee	09.50	50-51	54	-	22
Norwich C.	Tr	06.52	52-53	24	-	5
RAVANELLI Fabrizio						
Italy, 11 December, 1968 Italian Int						(CF)
Middlesbrough	Juventus (It)	08.96	96-97	35	0	17
RAVEN Paul Duncan						
Salisbury, 28 July, 1970 E Sch						(CD)
Doncaster Rov.	Jnrs	06.88	87-88	52	0	4
West Bromwich A.	Tr	03.89	88-97	216	4	14
Doncaster Rov.	L	11.91	91	7	0	0
RAVENSCROFT Craig Anthony						
Hammersmith, 20 December, 1974						(F)
Brentford	YT	07.93	93-95	6	3	1
RAWCLIFFE Frank						
Blackburn, 16 December, 1921 Died 1986						(CF)
Wolverhampton W.	Tranmere Rov (Am)	01.39				
Notts Co.	Colchester U.	02.43				
Newport Co.	Tr	06.46	46	37	-	14
Swansea C.	Tr	05.47	47	25	-	17
Aldershot	Tr	07.48	48	35	-	14
RAWCLIFFE Peter						
Cleethorpes, 8 December, 1963						(F)
Grimsby T.	Louth U.	09.86	86-87	9	13	2
Lincoln C. (N/C)	Holbeach U.	08.90	90	0	1	0
RAWES Herbert						
Frizington, 23 November, 1932						(OR)
Carlisle U.		09.53	53-54	10	-	1
RAWLINGS Charles John						
Birmingham, 4 November, 1932						(WH)
West Bromwich A.	Erdington A.	03.50				
Walsall	Tr	06.56	56-62	200	-	5
Port Vale	Tr	07.63	63-64	31	-	2
RAWLINGS David						
Wrexham, 12 December, 1943						(OL)
Wrexham (Am)		11.65	65	1	0	0
RAWLINGS James **Sydney** Dean						
Wombwell, 5 May, 1913 Died 1956						(OR)
Preston N.E.	Dick Kerr's XI	03.32	33	12	-	1
Huddersfield T.	Tr	03.34	33-34	11	-	2

League Club	Source	Date Signed	Seasons Played	Apps	Subs	Gls
West Bromwich A.	Tr	03.35	34-35	10	-	1
Northampton T.	Tr	06.36	36-37	48	-	18
Millwall	Tr	12.37	37-38	53	-	27
Everton	Tr	11.45				
Plymouth Arg.	Tr	05.46	46-47	56	-	20

RAWLINGSON John Anderson
Wallsend, 7 April, 1944 (CH)

League Club	Source	Date Signed	Seasons Played	Apps	Subs	Gls
Bury	Corinthian Jnrs	07.62	64	2	-	0
Barrow	Tr	07.65	65	19	0	2

RAWLINSON Mark David
Bolton, 9 June, 1975 (M)

League Club	Source	Date Signed	Seasons Played	Apps	Subs	Gls
Manchester U.	YT	07.93				
Bournemouth	Tr	07.95	95-97	41	28	2

RAWSON Colin
Shirebrook, 12 November, 1926 (WH)

League Club	Source	Date Signed	Seasons Played	Apps	Subs	Gls
Nottingham F.	Welbeck Colly	09.44	46	1	-	0
Rotherham U.	Peterborough U.	07.48	49-52	111	-	12
Sheffield U.	Tr	03.53	53-55	70	-	1
Millwall	Tr	10.55	55-58	159	-	5
Torquay U.	Tr	07.59	59-61	86	-	2

RAWSON Kenneth
Nottingham, 31 March, 1921 (CH)

League Club	Source	Date Signed	Seasons Played	Apps	Subs	Gls
Nottingham F.		12.46	47-49	6	-	0

RAWSON Kenneth
Ripley, 18 September, 1931 Died 1986 (CH)

League Club	Source	Date Signed	Seasons Played	Apps	Subs	Gls
Notts Co.	Ripley	05.53	54-60	34	-	0

RAY Cecil Holmes
West Grinstead, 25 October, 1911 Died 1995 (CF)

League Club	Source	Date Signed	Seasons Played	Apps	Subs	Gls
Aldershot	Lewes U.	01.36	35-46	89	-	39

RAY John Dennis
Wolverhampton, 7 November, 1946 (WH)

League Club	Source	Date Signed	Seasons Played	Apps	Subs	Gls
Shrewsbury T.		01.65	65	7	0	0

RAY John Walter
Newmarket, 21 November, 1968 (CD)

League Club	Source	Date Signed	Seasons Played	Apps	Subs	Gls
Colchester U.	YT	10.87	87	0	1	0

RAY Philip
Wallsend, 21 November, 1964 (FB)

League Club	Source	Date Signed	Seasons Played	Apps	Subs	Gls
Burnley	App	11.82	82	1	0	0
Hartlepool U.	L	10.83	83	5	0	1

RAYBOULD Eric
Manchester, 8 December, 1940 (WH)

League Club	Source	Date Signed	Seasons Played	Apps	Subs	Gls
Chester C.		07.60	60-61	10	-	0

RAYBOULD Philip Edward
Caerphilly, 26 May, 1948 W Sch/W Amat (M)

League Club	Source	Date Signed	Seasons Played	Apps	Subs	Gls
Swansea C.	Bridgend T.	07.67	67-68	10	2	4
Newport Co.	Tr	09.69	69	5	1	1

RAYMENT Joseph Watson
Hartlepool, 25 September, 1934 (OR)

League Club	Source	Date Signed	Seasons Played	Apps	Subs	Gls
Middlesbrough	Jnrs	10.51	52-54	24	-	4
Hartlepool U.	Tr	07.55	55-57	63	-	17
Darlington	Tr	07.58	58-64	173	-	28

RAYMENT Patrick John
Peterborough, 11 April, 1965 (W/FB)

League Club	Source	Date Signed	Seasons Played	Apps	Subs	Gls
Peterborough U.	App	04.83	81-84	24	6	3
Cambridge U.	Tr	10.84	84-86	42	6	2

RAYNER Edward
Hemsworth, 28 September, 1916 Died 1988 (G)

League Club	Source	Date Signed	Seasons Played	Apps	Subs	Gls
Halifax T.	Scarborough	10.40	46-50	137	-	0

RAYNER Albert **Edward**
Salford, 13 August, 1932 (WH)

League Club	Source	Date Signed	Seasons Played	Apps	Subs	Gls
Stoke C.	Northwich Vic.	05.55	56-59	4	-	0

RAYNER James Patrick
Cornsay (Dm), 31 March, 1935 (WH)

League Club	Source	Date Signed	Seasons Played	Apps	Subs	Gls
Grimsby T.	Jnrs	05.52	52-53	12	-	3
Bury	Tr	05.54				
Hartlepool U.	Tr	11.54				
Bury	Tr	06.55				
Barrow	Tr	09.55	55	11	-	1
Peterborough U.	Grantham	07.58	60-62	119	-	12
Notts Co.	Grantham	09.64	64	32	-	13

RAYNER Warren Anthony
Bradford, 24 April, 1957 (W)

League Club	Source	Date Signed	Seasons Played	Apps	Subs	Gls
Bradford C.	App	04.75	74-76	13	4	0

RAYNES John
Sheffield, 4 November, 1928 Died 1995 (OL)

League Club	Source	Date Signed	Seasons Played	Apps	Subs	Gls
Sheffield U.	Jnrs	11.45				
Rotherham U.		03.49	49	5	-	1
Northampton T.	Worksop T.	07.51				

RAYNES William
Sheffield, 30 October, 1964 (LW)

League Club	Source	Date Signed	Seasons Played	Apps	Subs	Gls
Rotherham U.	Heanor T.	09.83	83-84	17	3	2
Stockport Co.	L	01.85	84	2	0	0
Wolverhampton W.	Tr	12.85	85	6	1	0

RAYNOR Paul Edward
Chester, 3 September, 1957 (FB)

League Club	Source	Date Signed	Seasons Played	Apps	Subs	Gls
Chester C.	App	09.75	76-81	196	1	9
Chester C. (N/C)	Oswestry T.	08.83	83	3	0	0

RAYNOR Paul James
Nottingham, 29 April, 1966 (F/M)

League Club	Source	Date Signed	Seasons Played	Apps	Subs	Gls
Nottingham F.	App	04.84	84	3	0	0
Bristol Rov.	L	03.85	84	7	1	0
Huddersfield T.	Tr	08.85	85-86	38	12	9
Swansea C.	Tr	03.87	86-91	170	21	27
Wrexham	L	10.88	88	6	0	0
Cambridge U.	Tr	03.92	91-92	46	3	2
Preston N.E.	Tr	07.93	93-95	72	8	9
Cambridge U.	Tr	09.95	95-96	78	1	7
Leyton Orient (N/C)	Guang Deong (China)	02.98	97	5	5	0

RAYNOR Robert
Nottingham, 30 August, 1940 (G)

League Club	Source	Date Signed	Seasons Played	Apps	Subs	Gls
Nottingham F.		05.64				
Halifax T.	Tr	08.65	65-66	17	0	0

REA Kenneth Wilfred
Liverpool, 17 February, 1935 (WH)

League Club	Source	Date Signed	Seasons Played	Apps	Subs	Gls
Everton	Jnrs	06.52	56-58	46	-	0

REA Simon
Kenilworth, 20 September, 1976 (CD)

League Club	Source	Date Signed	Seasons Played	Apps	Subs	Gls
Birmingham C.	YT	01.95	95	0	1	0

REA Wallace
Uddingston, 21 August, 1935 (W)

League Club	Source	Date Signed	Seasons Played	Apps	Subs	Gls
Bradford C.	Motherwell	07.59	59	11	-	2

READ John **Anthony**
St Helens, 5 July, 1942 (G/F)

League Club	Source	Date Signed	Seasons Played	Apps	Subs	Gls
Sheffield Wed.	Wolverhampton W. (Am)	01.60				
Peterborough U.	Tr	05.64	64	2	-	0
Luton T.	Tr	03.65	65-71	197	4	12

READ David Peter
Stafford, 15 January, 1941 (W)

League Club	Source	Date Signed	Seasons Played	Apps	Subs	Gls
Wolverhampton W.	Jnrs	10.58				
Chester C.	Tr	10.62	62-66	68	4	6

READ Paul Colin
Harlow, 25 September, 1973 E Sch (F)

League Club	Source	Date Signed	Seasons Played	Apps	Subs	Gls
Arsenal	YT	10.91				
Leyton Orient	L	03.95	94	11	0	0
Southend U.	L	10.95	95	3	1	1
Wycombe W.	Tr	01.97	96-97	21	20	8

READER Peter Edward
East Ham, 8 March, 1941 E Yth (G)

League Club	Source	Date Signed	Seasons Played	Apps	Subs	Gls
West Ham U.	Jnrs	06.59				
Millwall	Tr	06.61	61	1	-	0

READFERN Thomas **Edward**
Crook, 9 July, 1944 (CF)

League Club	Source	Date Signed	Seasons Played	Apps	Subs	Gls
West Bromwich A.	Jnrs	08.61	63	4	-	0

READY Karl
Neath, 14 August, 1972 W Sch/Wu21-5/W 'B'/W-1 (FB)

League Club	Source	Date Signed	Seasons Played	Apps	Subs	Gls
Queens Park R.	YT	08.90	91-97	115	14	6

REAGAN Charles **Martin**
York, 12 May, 1924 (W)

League Club	Source	Date Signed	Seasons Played	Apps	Subs	Gls
York C.	Jnrs	09.46	46	1	-	0
Hull C.	Tr	04.47	46-47	18	-	1
Middlesbrough	Tr	02.48	47-50	24	-	4
Shrewsbury T.	Tr	08.51	51-52	58	-	9
Portsmouth	Tr	01.53	52	5	-	0
Norwich C.	Tr	06.54	54-55	34	-	4

REANEY Paul
Fulham, 22 October, 1944 Eu23-5/EF Lge/E-3 (RB)

League Club	Source	Date Signed	Seasons Played	Apps	Subs	Gls
Leeds U.	Jnrs	10.61	62-77	550	8	6
Bradford C.	Tr	06.78	78-79	37	1	0

League Club	Source	Date Signed	Seasons Played	Career Record Apps	Subs	Gls
REAY Edwin (Ted) Peel						
Tynemouth, 5 August, 1914						(LB)
Sheffield U.	North Shields	03.37				
Queens Park R.	Tr	06.37	37-49	34	-	0
RECK Sean Mark						
Oxford, 5 May, 1967						(M)
Oxford U.	App	04.85	86-88	11	3	0
Newport Co.	L	08.85	85	15	0	0
Reading	L	03.86	85	1	0	0
Wrexham	Tr	07.89	89-90	41	4	2
REDDIE Thomas McGregor						
Grangemouth, 5 October, 1926						(HB)
Aldershot	Falkirk	07.51	51-56	96	-	1
REDDING Thomas Richard						
Grimsby, 17 March, 1932						(D)
Grimsby T.	Brigg T.	07.54	54-56	4	-	0
REDDISH Shane						
Bolsover, 5 May, 1971						(FB/M)
Mansfield T.	YT	07.89				
Doncaster Rov.	Tr	02.90	89-92	51	9	3
Carlisle U.	Tr	07.93	93-94	35	2	1
Chesterfield	L	09.94	94	2	1	0
Hartlepool U.	Tr	11.94	94-95	41	2	0
REDFEARN Brian						
Bradford, 20 February, 1935						(OL)
Bradford P.A.	Jnrs	08.52	52-57	130	-	32
Blackburn Rov.	Tr	12.57				
Darlington	Tr	06.59	59-60	49	-	15
Halifax T.	Tr	06.61	61-62	67	-	10
Bradford C.	Tr	07.63	63	7	-	2
REDFEARN Neil David						
Dewsbury, 20 June, 1965						(M)
Bolton W.	Nottingham F. (App)	06.82	82-83	35	0	1
Lincoln C.	Tr	03.84	83-85	96	4	13
Doncaster Rov.	Tr	08.86	86	46	0	14
Crystal Palace	Tr	07.87	87-88	57	0	10
Watford	Tr	11.88	88-89	22	2	3
Oldham Ath.	Tr	01.90	89-90	56	6	16
Barnsley	Tr	09.91	91-97	289	3	72
REDFERN David						
Sheffield, 8 November, 1962						(G)
Sheffield Wed.	Jnrs	06.81				
Rochdale	Tr	03.85	84-86	87	0	0
Wigan Ath.	L	10.87	87	3	0	0
Stockport Co.	Gainsborough Trin.	07.89	89-92	48	0	0
REDFERN Edward						
Liverpool, 24 June, 1924 Died 1994						(WH)
New Brighton	Unity B.C.	01.48	47-49	22	-	0
REDFERN Frederick						
Hyde, 28 September, 1914 Died 1989						(RB)
Stockport Co.	Hyde U.	08.45	46-47	36	-	0
REDFERN James						
Kirkby, 1 August, 1952						(W)
Bolton W.	App	08.69	69-72	19	5	2
Chester C.	Tr	08.73	73-76	98	8	15
REDFERN Robert						
Crook, 3 March, 1918						(OR)
Wolverhampton W.		05.36				
Bournemouth	Cradley Heath	02.37	36-46	89	-	5
Brighton & H.A.	Tr	08.47	47	5	-	1
REDFORD Ian Petrie						
Perth, 5 April, 1960 S Yth/Su21-6						(W)
Ipswich T.	Dundee U.	11.88	88-90	59	9	8
REDHEAD William Sylvester						
Newcastle, 10 October, 1935						(HB)
Newcastle U.	Fatfield Jnrs	08.54	56	1	-	0
Gateshead	Tr	08.59	59	19	-	0
REDKNAPP Henry (Harry) James						
Poplar, 2 March, 1947 E Yth						(W)
West Ham U.	App	03.64	65-71	146	3	7
Bournemouth	Tr	08.72	72-75	96	5	5
Brentford	Tr	09.76	76	1	0	0
Bournemouth (N/C)	(Team Coach)	09.82	82	1	0	0
REDKNAPP Jamie Frank						
Barton-on-Sea, 25 June, 1973 E Sch/E Yth/Eu21-19/E 'B'/E-8						(M)
Bournemouth	YT	06.90	89-90	6	7	0
Liverpool	Tr	01.91	91-97	154	23	19
REDMAN William						
Manchester, 29 January, 1928 Died 1994						(FB)
Manchester U.	Jnrs	11.46	50-53	36	-	0
Bury	Tr	06.54	54-55	37	-	1
REDMILE Matthew Ian						
Nottingham, 12 November, 1976						(CD)
Notts Co.	YT	07.95	96-97	55	2	5
REDMOND Harold						
Manchester, 24 March, 1933						(FB)
Crystal Palace	Tavistock	04.57	57	2	-	0
Millwall	Tr	05.58	58-60	54	-	0
REDMOND Stephen						
Liverpool, 2 November, 1967 E Yth/Eu21-14						(CD)
Manchester C.	App	12.84	85-91	231	4	7
Oldham Ath.	Tr	07.92	92-97	195	10	4
REDROBE William **Eric**						
Wigan, 23 August, 1944 E Yth						(F)
Bolton W.	Jnrs	02.62	63-65	4	0	1
Southport	Tr	08.66	66-72	186	6	55
Hereford U.	Tr	10.72	72-77	75	12	17
REDSHAW Raymond						
Salford, 23 December, 1958						(F)
Wigan Ath.	Horwich R.M.I.	07.84	84	2	2	0
REDWOOD Barry Keith						
Torquay, 11 September, 1946						(CF)
Exeter C.	App	09.64	64	1	-	0
REDWOOD Toby Richard Barry						
Newton Abbot, 7 October, 1973						(FB)
Exeter C.	YT	06.92	91-93	15	5	0
REECE Andrew John						
Shrewsbury, 5 September, 1962						(M)
Bristol Rov.	Dudley T.	08.87	87-92	230	9	17
Walsall	L	11.92	92	9	0	1
Walsall	L	08.93	93	6	0	0
Hereford U.	Tr	11.93	93-95	69	2	5
REECE Gilbert Ivor						
Cardiff, 2 July, 1942 W Sch/W-29						(W)
Cardiff C.	Jnrs	05.61				
Newport Co.	Pembroke Borough	06.63	63-64	32	-	9
Sheffield U.	Tr	04.65	65-72	197	13	58
Cardiff C.	Tr	09.72	72-75	94	6	23
Swansea C.	Tr	07.76	76	0	2	0
REECE Paul John						
Nottingham, 16 July, 1968						(G)
Stoke C.	App	07.86	86	2	0	0
Grimsby T.	Kettering T.	07.88	88-91	54	0	0
Doncaster Rov. (N/C)	Kettering T.	09.92	92	1	0	0
Oxford U.	Tr	10.92	92-93	39	0	0
Notts Co.	Tr	08.94	94	11	0	0
West Bromwich A.	Tr	08.95	95	1	0	0
REECE Thomas Samuel						
Wolverhampton, 17 May, 1919 Died 1990						(LH)
Wolverhampton W.		07.37				
Crystal Palace	Tr	09.38	38-47	76	-	5
REED Adam Maurice						
Bishop Auckland, 18 February, 1975						(RB)
Darlington	YT	07.93	91-94	45	7	1
Blackburn Rov.	Tr	08.95				
Darlington	L	02.97	96	14	0	0
Rochdale	L	12.97	97	10	0	0
REED Barry Reginald Frank						
Peterborough, 24 November, 1937						(FB)
Leicester C.	St Neots	03.55				
Luton T.	Tr	05.61	61	1	-	0
REED Francis Nicholas						
Seaham, 12 October, 1933 Died 1975						(G)
Charlton Ath.	Murton Colly	08.54	55-62	29	-	0
REED George						
Normanton, 16 July, 1938						(CH)
Halifax T.	Swillington	08.61	62	2	-	0

REED Graham
Doncaster, 24 June, 1961 (RB)

League Club	Source	Date Signed	Seasons Played	Apps	Subs	Gls
Barnsley	App	06.79	78-79	3	0	0
Northampton T.	Frickley Colly	06.85	85-88	105	7	2

REED Graham Albert William
Kings Lynn, 6 February, 1938 (WH)

League Club	Source	Date Signed	Seasons Played	Apps	Subs	Gls
Sunderland	Kings Lynn	02.55	57	5	-	0

REED Hugh Dennett
Dumbarton, 23 August, 1950 Died 1992 (W)

League Club	Source	Date Signed	Seasons Played	Apps	Subs	Gls
West Bromwich A.	Jnrs	08.67	68-70	5	3	2
Plymouth Arg.	Tr	11.71	71-73	44	12	9
Brentford	L	10.73	73	3	1	0
Crewe Alex.	Tr	07.74	74-75	38	9	9
Hartlepool U.	Huddersfield T. (N/C)	10.76	76	6	0	1

REED Ian Paul
Lichfield, 4 September, 1975 (M)

League Club	Source	Date Signed	Seasons Played	Apps	Subs	Gls
Shrewsbury T.	YT	07.94	94-96	10	8	2

REED John Paul
Rotherham, 27 August, 1972 (W)

League Club	Source	Date Signed	Seasons Played	Apps	Subs	Gls
Sheffield U.	YT	07.90	91-95	11	4	2
Scarborough	L	01.91	90	14	0	6
Scarborough	L	09.91	91	5	1	0
Darlington	L	03.93	92	8	2	2
Mansfield T.	L	09.93	93	12	1	2
Blackpool	Tr	07.97	97	0	3	0

REED Kevin David
Leicester, 22 September, 1960 (W)

League Club	Source	Date Signed	Seasons Played	Apps	Subs	Gls
Leicester C.	App	05.78	78	0	1	0

REED Martin John
Scarborough, 10 January, 1978 (CD)

League Club	Source	Date Signed	Seasons Played	Apps	Subs	Gls
York C.	YT	07.96	96-97	23	1	0

REED Stephen Eric
Doncaster, 6 January, 1956 (D)

League Club	Source	Date Signed	Seasons Played	Apps	Subs	Gls
Doncaster Rov.	App	01.74	72-78	137	3	2

REED Thomas Roland
Haltwhistle, 4 October, 1934 (WH)

League Club	Source	Date Signed	Seasons Played	Apps	Subs	Gls
Newport Co.	Newport Barracks	01.54	53-54	2	-	0

REED William George
Rhondda, 25 January, 1928 W Sch/W Amat/W-2 (OR)

League Club	Source	Date Signed	Seasons Played	Apps	Subs	Gls
Cardiff C.	Rhondda T.	07.47				
Brighton & H.A.	Tr	08.48	48-52	129	-	36
Ipswich T.	Tr	07.53	53-57	155	-	43
Swansea C.	Tr	02.58	57	8	-	0

REES Anthony Andrew
Merthyr Tydfil, 1 August, 1964 W Sch/W Yth/Wu21-1/W 'B'/W-1 (F)

League Club	Source	Date Signed	Seasons Played	Apps	Subs	Gls
Aston Villa	App	08.82				
Birmingham C.	Tr	07.83	83-87	75	20	12
Peterborough U.	L	10.85	85	5	0	2
Shrewsbury T.	L	03.86	85	1	1	0
Barnsley	Tr	03.88	87-88	27	4	3
Grimsby T.	Tr	08.89	89-93	124	17	33
West Bromwich A.	Tr	11.94	94-95	11	12	2

REES Barrie Gwyn
Rhyl, 4 February, 1944 Died 1965 (WH)

League Club	Source	Date Signed	Seasons Played	Apps	Subs	Gls
Everton	Jnrs	09.61	63-64	4	-	2
Brighton & H.A.	Tr	01.65	64	12	-	1

REES Robert **Clive**
Nantymoel, 7 September, 1937 (G)

League Club	Source	Date Signed	Seasons Played	Apps	Subs	Gls
Newport Co. (Am)	Caerau	03.63	62	4	-	0

REES William **Derek**
Swansea, 18 February, 1934 Died 1998 (OL)

League Club	Source	Date Signed	Seasons Played	Apps	Subs	Gls
Portsmouth		05.54	54-56	46	-	15
Ipswich T.	Tr	05.57	57-60	90	-	29

REES Douglas Charles
Neath, 12 February, 1923 W Amat (CH)

League Club	Source	Date Signed	Seasons Played	Apps	Subs	Gls
Ipswich T.	Troedyrhiw	02.49	48-58	356	-	1

REES John **Graham**
Porth, 28 August, 1937 (W)

League Club	Source	Date Signed	Seasons Played	Apps	Subs	Gls
Exeter C.	Pontypridd Y.C.	09.54	54-65	345	0	85

REES David **Ian**
Cross Hands, 21 September, 1943 (IF)

League Club	Source	Date Signed	Seasons Played	Apps	Subs	Gls
Swansea C.	Ammanford	12.61	64	1	0	0
Swansea C.		08.68	68	1	2	0

REES Jason Mark
Aberdare, 22 December, 1969 W Sch/W Yth/Wu21-3/W 'B'/W-1 (W)

League Club	Source	Date Signed	Seasons Played	Apps	Subs	Gls
Luton T.	YT	06.88	89-93	59	23	0
Mansfield T.	L	12.93	93	15	0	1
Portsmouth	Tr	07.94	94-96	30	13	3
Exeter C.	L	01.97	96	7	0	0
Cambridge U.	Tr	08.97	97	17	3	0

REES John Frederick
Bedlinog, 3 February, 1933 W Yth/W Amat (CF)

League Club	Source	Date Signed	Seasons Played	Apps	Subs	Gls
Newport Co. (Am)	Troedyrhiw	08.52	52	2	-	0

REES Maldwyn James Francis
Neath, 21 April, 1924 (IF)

League Club	Source	Date Signed	Seasons Played	Apps	Subs	Gls
Norwich C.	Swansea C. (Am)	05.47				
Brighton & H.A.	Tr	09.49	49	2	-	0
Scunthorpe U.	Barry T.	07.50	50	18	-	1

REES Mark
Smethwick, 13 October, 1961 E Sch (W)

League Club	Source	Date Signed	Seasons Played	Apps	Subs	Gls
Walsall	App	08.79	78-89	188	49	37
Rochdale	L	10.86	86	2	1	0

REES Melvyn John
Cardiff, 25 January, 1967 Died 1993 W Yth (G)

League Club	Source	Date Signed	Seasons Played	Apps	Subs	Gls
Cardiff C.	YT	09.84	84-86	31	0	0
Watford	Tr	07.87	87	3	0	0
Crewe Alex.	L	08.89	89	6	0	0
Leyton Orient	L	01.90	89	9	0	0
West Bromwich A.	Tr	09.90	90	18	0	0
Sheffield U.	Tr	03.92	91	8	0	0

REES Nigel Richard
Bridgend, 11 July, 1953 (W)

League Club	Source	Date Signed	Seasons Played	Apps	Subs	Gls
Cardiff C.	Jnrs	08.70	70-72	21	6	1

REES Peter Noel
Machynlleth, 5 May, 1932 (IF)

League Club	Source	Date Signed	Seasons Played	Apps	Subs	Gls
Tranmere Rov. (Am)	Llanidloes	10.56	56	9	-	4

REES Ronald Raymond
Ystradgynlais, 4 April, 1944 Wu23-7/W-39 (W)

League Club	Source	Date Signed	Seasons Played	Apps	Subs	Gls
Coventry C.	App	05.62	62-67	230	0	42
West Bromwich A.	Tr	03.68	67-68	34	1	9
Nottingham F.	Tr	02.69	68-71	76	9	12
Swansea C.	Tr	01.72	71-74	88	1	5

REES William
Blaengarw, 10 March, 1924 Died 1996 W-4 (IF)

League Club	Source	Date Signed	Seasons Played	Apps	Subs	Gls
Cardiff C.	Carn Rov.	02.44	46-48	101	-	33
Tottenham H.	Tr	06.49	49	11	-	3
Leyton Orient	Tr	07.50	50-55	184	-	58

REES William
Swansea, 31 September, 1937 (OL)

League Club	Source	Date Signed	Seasons Played	Apps	Subs	Gls
Swansea C.	Jnrs	10.54	54-57	6	-	0
Crystal Palace	Peterborough U.	05.59	59	17	-	1

REESON Maurice **Anthony**
Rotherham, 24 September, 1933 Died 1990 (IF)

League Club	Source	Date Signed	Seasons Played	Apps	Subs	Gls
Rotherham U.	Jnrs	11.53	54	4	-	1
Grimsby T.	Tr	06.55	55-57	76	-	20
Doncaster Rov.	Tr	02.58	57-58	21	-	6
Southport	Tr	06.59	59	42	-	9

REEVE Edward Gordon
Islington, 3 December, 1947 (WH)

League Club	Source	Date Signed	Seasons Played	Apps	Subs	Gls
Brentford	App	12.65	65-67	20	4	0

REEVE Frederick William
Clapton, 1 May, 1918 Died 1994 (WH)

League Club	Source	Date Signed	Seasons Played	Apps	Subs	Gls
Crystal Palace	Ashford T.	05.35	36	1	-	0
Tottenham H.	Tr	05.37				
Rochdale	Tr	07.38	38	27	-	3
Grimsby T.	Tr	07.39	46-47	46	-	0
Reading	Tr	06.48	48-49	34	-	1

REEVE James Michael
Weymouth, 26 November, 1975 (F)

League Club	Source	Date Signed	Seasons Played	Apps	Subs	Gls
Bournemouth	YT	07.94	94	2	5	0
Hereford U.	Tr	03.95	94	0	5	0

REEVE Kenneth Eric
Grimsby, 13 January, 1921 (IF)

League Club	Source	Date Signed	Seasons Played	Apps	Subs	Gls
Grimsby T.	Humber U.	02.38	46-47	24	-	5
Doncaster Rov.	Tr	07.48	48	30	-	12
Mansfield T.	Tr	07.49	49-53	139	-	62

League Club	Source	Date Signed	Seasons Played	Apps	Subs	Gls
REEVES Alan						
Birkenhead, 19 November, 1967						(CD)
Norwich C.	Heswall	09.88				
Gillingham	L	02.89	88	18	0	0
Chester C.	Tr	08.89	89-90	31	9	2
Rochdale	Tr	07.91	91-94	119	2	9
Wimbledon	Tr	09.94	94-96	52	5	4
REEVES Thomas **Brian**						
Skelmersdale, 18 February, 1939						(G)
Blackburn Rov.	Burscough	08.60	60-61	12	-	0
Scunthorpe U.	Tr	04.62	62-64	38	-	0
Southport	Tr	07.65	65-68	143	0	0
REEVES David Edward						
Birkenhead, 19 November, 1967						(F)
Sheffield Wed.	Heswall	08.86	88	8	9	2
Scunthorpe U.	L	12.86	86	3	1	2
Scunthorpe U.	L	10.87	87	6	0	4
Burnley	L	11.87	87	16	0	8
Bolton W.	Tr	08.89	89-92	111	23	29
Notts Co.	Tr	03.93	92-93	9	4	2
Carlisle U.	Tr	10.93	93-96	127	0	47
Preston N.E.	Tr	10.96	96-97	45	2	12
Chesterfield	Tr	11.97	97	26	0	5
REEVES Dennis John Richardson						
Lochmaben, 1 December, 1944						(G)
Chester C.		09.63	63-66	139	0	0
Wrexham	Tr	10.67	67-68	15	0	0
REEVES Derek Brian						
Poole, 27 August, 1934 Died 1995						(CF)
Southampton	Bournemouth G.W.	12.54	54-62	273	-	145
Bournemouth	Tr	11.62	62-64	35	-	8
REEVES Frank						
Peckham, 11 July, 1921 Died 1993						(HB)
Millwall	Sidcup	02.47	47-54	179	-	1
REEVES John Charles						
Hackney, 8 July, 1963						(LM)
Fulham	App	06.81	81-84	9	5	0
Colchester U.	Tr	08.85	85-87	58	3	7
REEVES Kevin Philip						
Burley (Hants), 20 October, 1957 E Yth/Eu21-10/E'B'/E-2						(F)
Bournemouth	App	07.75	74-76	60	3	20
Norwich C.	Tr	01.77	76-79	118	1	37
Manchester C.	Tr	03.80	79-82	129	1	34
Burnley	Tr	07.83	83	20	1	12
REEVES Michael Randall						
Saltash, 13 January, 1943						(FB)
Plymouth Arg.	Saltash U.	06.61	62-69	107	3	0
REEVES Peter John						
Woolwich, 7 February, 1949 E Yth						(CD)
Charlton Ath.	App	02.66	65-73	263	5	2
REEVES Peter Philip						
Swansea, 20 January, 1959						(M)
Coventry C.	App	12.76				
Swansea C.	Tr	07.78	78	2	2	0
REEVES Raymond Henry Ernest						
Reading, 12 August, 1931 E Yth						(FB)
Reading		05.49	52-60	284	-	29
Brentford	Tr	07.61	61	5	-	0
REEVES-JONES Adrian Kenneth						
Stoke, 18 October, 1966						(W)
Port Vale (N/C)	App	10.84	84	2	1	0
REGAN Douglas						
Yeovil, 3 June, 1922						(W)
Exeter C.		03.45	46-52	206	-	63
Bristol C.	Tr	12.52	52-55	39	-	11
REGAN James						
Hemsworth, 7 December, 1927						(WH)
Rotherham U.	Moorthorpe Colly	08.49	51-52	12	-	0
Bristol C.	Tr	06.53	53-55	51	-	1
Coventry C.	Tr	03.56	55-56	26	-	0
REGAN John Henry						
Dalton-in-Furness, 8 June, 1925						(OL)
Barrow	Swarthmoor	01.48	48-50	9	-	1
REGAN Matthew **John**						
Worcester, 18 June, 1944						(CF)
Birmingham C.	Jnrs	09.61	62-63	5	-	2
Shrewsbury T.	Tr	10.64	64-65	21	0	6
Brentford	Tr	03.66	65-66	14	0	5
Crewe Alex.	Tr	11.66	66-68	48	3	17
Doncaster Rov.	Tr	09.68	68-70	91	4	25
REGAN Terence						
Bradford, 26 June, 1926						(OR)
Bradford C. (Am)	Salts	10.48	48	1	-	0
REGIS Cyrille						
French Guyana, 9 February, 1958 Eu21-6/E'B'/E-5						(F)
West Bromwich A.	Hayes	05.77	77-84	233	4	82
Coventry C.	Tr	10.84	84-90	231	7	47
Aston Villa	Tr	07.91	91-92	46	6	12
Wolverhampton W.	Tr	08.93	93	8	11	2
Wycombe W.	Tr	08.94	94	30	5	9
Chester C.	Tr	08.95	95	29	0	7
REGIS David						
Paddington, 3 March, 1964						(F)
Notts Co.	Barnet	09.90	90-91	31	15	15
Plymouth Arg.	Tr	11.91	91-92	28	3	4
Bournemouth	L	08.92	92	6	0	2
Stoke C.	Tr	10.92	92-93	49	14	15
Birmingham C.	Tr	08.94	94	4	2	2
Southend U.	Tr	09.94	94-95	34	4	9
Barnsley	Tr	02.96	95-96	4	12	1
Peterborough U.	L	09.96	96	4	3	1
Notts Co.	L	02.97	96	7	3	2
Scunthorpe U.	L	08.97	97	5	0	0
Leyton Orient (N/C)	Tr	10.97	97	4	0	0
Lincoln C. (N/C)	Tr	12.97	97	0	1	0
Scunthorpe U. (N/C)	Tr	02.98	97	4	0	2
REGIS Robert						
Huddersfield, 24 January, 1967						(F)
Burnley (N/C)		08.86	86	3	1	1
REGTOP Erik						
Netherlands, 16 February, 1968						(CF)
Bradford C.	F.C. Herenveen (Neth)	07.96	96	5	3	1
REHN Jan **Stefan**						
Sweden, 22 September, 1966 Swedish Int						(W)
Everton	Djurgaardens (Swe)	06.89	89	1	3	0
REID Dennis **Alexander**						
Glasgow, 2 March, 1947						(M)
Newcastle U.	Dundee	10.71	71-72	15	8	0
REID Andrew Merrick						
Urmston, 4 July, 1962 E Semi Pro						(CD)
Bury	Altrincham	08.92	92-93	27	6	1
REID Anthony James						
Nottingham, 9 May, 1963						(M)
Derby Co.	App	05.80	80-82	27	3	1
Scunthorpe U.	L	02.83	82	6	0	0
Newport Co.	Tr	03.83	82-84	74	2	12
Chesterfield	Tr	07.85	85-87	63	4	7
REID David Alexander						
Glasgow, 3 January, 1923						(WH)
Rochdale	Glasgow Perthshire	01.48	47-50	36	-	2
Bradford P.A.	Tr	09.50	50-51	13	-	0
Workington		07.53	53	8	-	1
Crewe Alex.	Tr	08.54	54	3	-	0
REID John **Douglas** Jamieson						
West Kilbride, 3 October, 1917						(IF)
Stockport Co.	Heaton Chapel	08.35	36-38	84	-	23
Portsmouth	Tr	03.46	46-55	308	-	129
REID Ernest James						
Merthyr Tydfil, 25 March, 1914						(RB)
Swansea C.	Troedyrhiw	07.32				
Chelsea	Tr	09.37	38	1	-	0
Norwich C.	Tr	06.45	46	5	-	0
REID Francis						
Mauchline, 16 June, 1920						(OL)
Huddersfield T.	Cumnock Jnrs	08.46	46-48	7	-	0
Stockport Co.	Tr	06.49	49-50	23	-	0
REID James Proven						
Dundee, 14 December, 1935						(F)
Bury	Dundee U.	01.57	56-58	21	-	9
Stockport Co.	Tr	03.59	58	11	-	2

REID John
Newmains (Lk), 20 August, 1932 (IF)

League Club	Source	Date Signed	Seasons Played	Apps	Subs	Gls
Bradford C.	Hamilton Academical	12.57	57-61	147	-	32
Northampton T.	Tr	11.61	61-63	85	-	14
Luton T.	Tr	11.63	63-65	111	0	7
Torquay U.	Tr	06.66	66	21	2	1
Rochdale	Tr	07.67	67	37	2	3

REID John
Edinburgh, 23 July, 1935 (OR)

League Club	Source	Date Signed	Seasons Played	Apps	Subs	Gls
Watford	Airdrieonians	12.56	56	1	-	1
Norwich C.	Airdrieonians	06.58				
Barrow	Tr	07.59	59	20	-	4

REID John Herkass
Edinburgh, 4 May, 1925 (CF)

League Club	Source	Date Signed	Seasons Played	Apps	Subs	Gls
Torquay U.	Hibernian	05.49	49-51	51	-	10

REID Mark
Kilwinning, 15 September, 1961 S Yth/Su21-2 (LB)

League Club	Source	Date Signed	Seasons Played	Apps	Subs	Gls
Charlton Ath.	Glasgow Celtic	05.85	85-90	209	2	15

REID Michael James
Wolverhampton, 7 August, 1927 Died 1975 (CF)

League Club	Source	Date Signed	Seasons Played	Apps	Subs	Gls
Wolverhampton W.		02.48				
Bournemouth	Tr	02.49	48	5	-	2
Portsmouth	Tr	07.50	50	5	-	1
Watford	Tr	12.52	52	19	-	8

REID Nicholas Scott
Urmston, 30 October, 1960 Eu21-6 (D/M)

League Club	Source	Date Signed	Seasons Played	Apps	Subs	Gls
Manchester C.	App	10.78	78-86	211	5	2
Blackburn Rov.	Tr	07.87	87-91	160	14	9
Bristol C.	L	09.92	92	3	1	0
West Bromwich A.	Tr	11.92	92-93	13	7	0
Wycombe W.	Tr	03.94	93-94	6	2	0
Bury	Witton A.	12.95	95-96	19	6	0

REID Paul Robert
Oldbury, 19 January, 1968 (W)

League Club	Source	Date Signed	Seasons Played	Apps	Subs	Gls
Leicester C.	App	01.86	86-91	140	22	21
Bradford C.	L	03.92	91	7	0	0
Bradford C.	Tr	07.92	92-93	80	2	15
Huddersfield T.	Tr	05.94	94-96	70	7	6
Oldham Ath.	Tr	03.97	96-97	53	0	6

REID Peter
Huyton, 20 June, 1956 Eu21-6/E-13 (M)

League Club	Source	Date Signed	Seasons Played	Apps	Subs	Gls
Bolton W.	App	05.74	74-82	222	3	23
Everton	Tr	12.82	82-88	155	4	8
Queens Park R.	Tr	02.89	88-89	29	0	1
Manchester C.	Tr	12.89	89-93	90	13	1
Southampton (N/C)	Tr	09.93	93	7	0	0
Notts Co. (N/C)	Tr	02.94	93	5	0	0
Bury (N/C)	Tr	07.94	94	1	0	0

REID Robert
Hamilton, 19 February, 1911 Died 1987 SF Lge/S-2 (OL)

League Club	Source	Date Signed	Seasons Played	Apps	Subs	Gls
Brentford	Hamilton Academical	01.36	35-38	103	-	34
Sheffield U.	Tr	02.39	38-46	14	-	4
Bury	Tr	11.46	46	17	-	1

REID Robert Bell Alexander
Dundee, 18 November, 1936 (G)

League Club	Source	Date Signed	Seasons Played	Apps	Subs	Gls
Swansea C.	Downfield Jnrs	09.57	57-59	17	-	0

REID Ronald Eric
Liversedge, 9 November, 1944 (CF)

League Club	Source	Date Signed	Seasons Played	Apps	Subs	Gls
Chesterfield	Retford T.	07.67	67	6	1	1

REID Shaun
Huyton, 13 October, 1965 (M)

League Club	Source	Date Signed	Seasons Played	Apps	Subs	Gls
Rochdale	YT	09.83	83-88	126	7	4
Preston N.E.	L	12.85	85	3	0	0
York C.	Tr	12.88	88-91	104	2	7
Rochdale	Tr	08.92	92-94	106	1	10
Bury	Tr	07.95	95	20	1	0
Chester C.	Tr	11.96	96	27	0	1

REID Steven John
Kingston, 10 March, 1981 E Yth (M/F)

League Club	Source	Date Signed	Seasons Played	Apps	Subs	Gls
Millwall	YT	●	97	0	1	0

REID Wesley Andrew
Lewisham, 10 September, 1968 (M)

League Club	Source	Date Signed	Seasons Played	Apps	Subs	Gls
Arsenal	YT	07.86				
Millwall	Tr	06.87	88-89	5	1	0
Bradford C.	Tr	01.91	90-91	31	4	3

REID William Dunlop
Ayr, 13 January, 1920 (RH)

League Club	Source	Date Signed	Seasons Played	Apps	Subs	Gls
Newport Co.	Cumnock Jnrs	05.48	49	9	-	0

REILLY Daniel
Peterborough, 17 November, 1966 (M)

League Club	Source	Date Signed	Seasons Played	Apps	Subs	Gls
Peterborough U.	YT	08.84	84	0	1	0

REILLY David
Chester, 24 November, 1966 (M)

League Club	Source	Date Signed	Seasons Played	Apps	Subs	Gls
Wrexham (N/C)	Jnrs	07.84	84	0	1	0

REILLY Felix McCairney
Musselburgh, 12 September, 1933 (CF)

League Club	Source	Date Signed	Seasons Played	Apps	Subs	Gls
Bradford P.A.	East Fife	03.60	59-61	31	-	12
Crewe Alex.	Tr	12.61	61	6	-	0

REILLY George Gerard
Bellshill, 14 September, 1957 (F)

League Club	Source	Date Signed	Seasons Played	Apps	Subs	Gls
Northampton T.	Corby T.	06.76	76-79	124	3	45
Cambridge U.	Tr	11.79	79-82	136	2	36
Watford	Tr	08.83	83-84	46	2	14
Newcastle U.	Tr	02.85	84-85	31	0	10
West Bromwich A.	Tr	12.85	85-87	42	1	9
Cambridge U.	Tr	07.88	88	20	0	7

REILLY Leonard Harold
Rotherhithe, 31 January, 1917 Died 1998 (CH)

League Club	Source	Date Signed	Seasons Played	Apps	Subs	Gls
Norwich C.	Diss T.	02.36	37-46	30	-	0

REILLY Terence
Culross (Fife), 1 July, 1924 (FB)

League Club	Source	Date Signed	Seasons Played	Apps	Subs	Gls
Chesterfield	Bo'ness U.	03.49				
Southport	Tr	08.50	50-54	191	-	2
Bradford P.A.	Tr	06.55	55	14	-	0

REINA Enrique Iglesia
Folkestone, 2 October, 1971 (F)

League Club	Source	Date Signed	Seasons Played	Apps	Subs	Gls
Brentford	Dover	09.97	97	2	4	1

REINELT Robert Squire
Loughton, 11 March, 1974 (F)

League Club	Source	Date Signed	Seasons Played	Apps	Subs	Gls
Aldershot	YT	●	90	3	2	0
Gillingham	Wivenhoe T.	03.93	93-94	34	18	5
Colchester U.	Tr	03.95	94-96	22	26	10
Brighton & H.A.	Tr	02.97	96-97	32	12	7

RELISH John Derek
Huyton, 5 October, 1953 (LB)

League Club	Source	Date Signed	Seasons Played	Apps	Subs	Gls
Chester C.	App	10.71	72-73	10	1	1
Newport Co.	Tr	06.74	74-86	318	19	9

REMY Christophe Philippe
Besacon, France, 6 August, 1971 (WB)

League Club	Source	Date Signed	Seasons Played	Apps	Subs	Gls
Oxford U.	Auxerre (Fr)	07.97	97	13	3	0

RENNIE David
Edinburgh, 29 August, 1964 S Yth (M/CD)

League Club	Source	Date Signed	Seasons Played	Apps	Subs	Gls
Leicester C.	App	05.82	83-85	21	0	1
Leeds U.	Tr	01.86	85-88	95	6	5
Bristol C.	Tr	07.89	89-91	101	3	8
Birmingham C.	Tr	02.92	91-92	32	3	4
Coventry C.	Tr	03.93	92-95	80	2	3
Northampton T.	Tr	08.96	96-97	45	3	4
Peterborough U.	Tr	12.97	97	18	0	0

RENNIE Paul Andrew
Nantwich, 26 October, 1971 (CD)

League Club	Source	Date Signed	Seasons Played	Apps	Subs	Gls
Crewe Alex.	YT	●	89	1	1	0
Stoke C.	Tr	05.90	90-91	4	0	0
Wigan Ath.	Tr	08.93	93-94	36	4	3

RENNISON Graham Lee
York, 2 October, 1978 (CD)

League Club	Source	Date Signed	Seasons Played	Apps	Subs	Gls
York C.	YT	●	97	1	0	0

RENSHAW Derrick
Gateshead, 18 September, 1924 (FB)

League Club	Source	Date Signed	Seasons Played	Apps	Subs	Gls
Sunderland		12.47				
Barrow	Tr	06.50	50-54	150	-	0

RENTON William
Cardenden, 4 February, 1942 (M)

League Club	Source	Date Signed	Seasons Played	Apps	Subs	Gls
Barrow	Dunfermline Ath.	01.71	70-71	23	1	2

RENWICK Craig
Lanark, 22 September, 1958 (CD)

League Club	Source	Date Signed	Seasons Played	Apps	Subs	Gls
Sheffield U.	East Stirling	04.78	78-79	8	1	0

RENWICK Richard
Gilsland (Nd), 27 November, 1942 (FB)

League Club	Source	Date Signed	Seasons Played	Apps	Subs	Gls
Grimsby T.	Jnrs	12.59				
Aldershot	Tr	07.63	63-68	203	2	4
Brentford	Tr	02.69	68-70	96	0	5
Stockport Co.	Tr	10.71	71	30	0	1
Rochdale	Tr	07.72	72-73	48	1	0
Darlington	L	01.74	73	19	0	0

RESCH Franz
Vienna, Austria, 4 May, 1969 Austrian Int (LB)

League Club	Source	Date Signed	Seasons Played	Apps	Subs	Gls
Darlington	Motherwell	10.97	97	15	2	1

RESTARICK Stephen Leonard James
Barking, 28 November, 1971 (F)

League Club	Source	Date Signed	Seasons Played	Apps	Subs	Gls
Colchester U.	YT	●	89	0	1	0

RETALLICK Graham
Cambridge, 8 February, 1970 (M)

League Club	Source	Date Signed	Seasons Played	Apps	Subs	Gls
Peterborough U. (N/C)	Histon	08.92	92	2	3	0

REVEL Gordon Harold
Mansfield, 19 September, 1927 (CH)

League Club	Source	Date Signed	Seasons Played	Apps	Subs	Gls
Mansfield T.	Westfield F.H.	08.50	52	1	-	0

REVELL Charles
Belvedere, 5 June, 1919 (WH)

League Club	Source	Date Signed	Seasons Played	Apps	Subs	Gls
Charlton Ath.	Gravesend & Nft	05.39	46-50	104	-	15
Derby Co.	Tr	03.51	50-51	22	-	2

REVIE Donald George
Middlesbrough, 10 July, 1927 Died 1989 EF Lge/E 'B'/E-6 (IF)

League Club	Source	Date Signed	Seasons Played	Apps	Subs	Gls
Leicester C.	Jnrs	08.44	46-49	96	-	25
Hull C.	Tr	11.49	49-51	76	-	12
Manchester C.	Tr	10.51	51-56	162	-	37
Sunderland	Tr	11.56	56-58	64	-	15
Leeds U.	Tr	12.58	58-61	76	-	11

REW Roy Edward
Belfast, 26 May, 1924 (CF)

League Club	Source	Date Signed	Seasons Played	Apps	Subs	Gls
Exeter C.	Sea Mills	02.49	48-49	4	-	1

REYNOLDS Arthur Brayley
Blackwood, 30 May, 1935 (CF)

League Club	Source	Date Signed	Seasons Played	Apps	Subs	Gls
Cardiff C.	Lovells Ath.	05.56	56-58	54	-	15
Swansea C.	Tr	05.59	59-64	151	-	57

REYNOLDS Graham Edward Arthur
Newport, 23 January, 1937 W Amat (CF)

League Club	Source	Date Signed	Seasons Played	Apps	Subs	Gls
Newport Co. (Am)	Caerleon	10.56	56	4	-	1
Newport Co.	Brecon Corries	07.63	63-66	42	1	11

REYNOLDS Hugh
Wishaw, 19 September, 1926 (RH)

League Club	Source	Date Signed	Seasons Played	Apps	Subs	Gls
Torquay U.	Morton	05.48	48	3	-	0

REYNOLDS James Andrew
Swindon, 27 October, 1967 E Yth (M)

League Club	Source	Date Signed	Seasons Played	Apps	Subs	Gls
Swindon T.	App	09.85	84-86	0	2	0

REYNOLDS Joseph
Cleland, 13 February, 1939 (CH)

League Club	Source	Date Signed	Seasons Played	Apps	Subs	Gls
Crewe Alex.		08.60	60	7	-	0

REYNOLDS Mark David
Glapwell (Dby), 1 January, 1966 (FB)

League Club	Source	Date Signed	Seasons Played	Apps	Subs	Gls
Mansfield T.	App	●	82	4	0	0

REYNOLDS Richard John
Looe, 15 February, 1948 E Yth (M/F)

League Club	Source	Date Signed	Seasons Played	Apps	Subs	Gls
Plymouth Arg.	App	02.65	64-70	123	8	24
Portsmouth	Tr	07.71	71-75	134	6	24

REYNOLDS Ronald Sidney Maurice
Haslemere, 2 June, 1928 (G)

League Club	Source	Date Signed	Seasons Played	Apps	Subs	Gls
Aldershot	Jnrs	12.45	46-49	114	-	0
Tottenham H.	Tr	07.50	53-57	86	-	0
Southampton	Tr	03.60	59-63	90	-	0

REYNOLDS Thomas
Felling, 2 October, 1922 (OR)

League Club	Source	Date Signed	Seasons Played	Apps	Subs	Gls
Sunderland	Felling Jnrs	07.46	46-52	167	-	18
Darlington	Kings Lynn	12.54	54-55	42	-	6

RHOADES-BROWN Peter
Hampton, 2 January, 1962 (LW)

League Club	Source	Date Signed	Seasons Played	Apps	Subs	Gls
Chelsea	App	07.79	79-83	86	10	4
Oxford U.	Tr	01.84	83-88	87	25	13

RHODES Alan
Bradford, 5 January, 1946 (WH)

League Club	Source	Date Signed	Seasons Played	Apps	Subs	Gls
Bradford C. (Am)	Salts	07.64	64-65	7	0	0

RHODES Albert
Anston (Yks), 29 April, 1936 (FB)

League Club	Source	Date Signed	Seasons Played	Apps	Subs	Gls
Queens Park R.	Worksop T.	12.54	55-56	5	-	0

RHODES Andrew Charles
Askern, 23 August, 1964 (G)

League Club	Source	Date Signed	Seasons Played	Apps	Subs	Gls
Barnsley	App	08.82	83-84	36	0	0
Doncaster Rov.	Tr	10.85	85-87	106	0	0
Oldham Ath.	Tr	03.88	87-89	69	0	0
Scarborough (L)	Airdrie	11.97	97	11	0	0

RHODES John Anthony
Dover, 17 September, 1946 (CD)

League Club	Source	Date Signed	Seasons Played	Apps	Subs	Gls
Derby Co.	Jnrs	10.63	64-70	5	0	0
Halifax T.	Tr	11.70	70-75	233	0	9
Southport	Tr	08.76	76	7	2	0

RHODES Brian William
Marylebone, 23 October, 1937 Died 1993 (G)

League Club	Source	Date Signed	Seasons Played	Apps	Subs	Gls
West Ham U.	Jnrs	01.55	57-62	61	-	0
Southend U.	Tr	09.63	63	11	-	0

RHODES Mark Nigel
Sheffield, 26 August, 1957 (M)

League Club	Source	Date Signed	Seasons Played	Apps	Subs	Gls
Rotherham U.	App	08.75	75-84	235	23	13
Darlington	L	10.82	82	14	0	0
Mansfield T.	L	03.83	82	4	0	0
Burnley	Tr	03.85	84-85	12	1	0

RHODES Stanley
Sheffield, 19 April, 1929 (F)

League Club	Source	Date Signed	Seasons Played	Apps	Subs	Gls
Leeds U.		05.48				
Sheffield U.	Worksop T.	11.51	51	1	-	0

RHODES Trevor Charles
Southend, 9 August, 1948 (WH)

League Club	Source	Date Signed	Seasons Played	Apps	Subs	Gls
Arsenal	App	09.65				
Millwall	Tr	09.66	66	4	0	0
Bristol Rov.	Tr	07.68	68	2	0	0

RIBEIRO Bruno
Setubal, Portugal, 22 October, 1975 (M)

League Club	Source	Date Signed	Seasons Played	Apps	Subs	Gls
Leeds U.	Vittoria Setubal (Por)	07.97	97	28	1	3

RICARD Cuesta Hamilton
Colombia, 12 January, 1974 Colombian Int (F)

League Club	Source	Date Signed	Seasons Played	Apps	Subs	Gls
Middlesbrough	Deportivo Cali (Col)	03.98	97	4	5	2

RICE Brian
Bellshill, 11 October, 1963 S Yth/Su21-1 (LW)

League Club	Source	Date Signed	Seasons Played	Apps	Subs	Gls
Nottingham F.	Hibernian	08.85	85-90	86	5	9
Grimsby T.	L	10.86	86	4	0	0
West Bromwich A.	L	01.89	88	2	1	0
Stoke C.	L	02.91	90	18	0	0

RICE Gary James
Zambia, 25 September, 1975 (LB)

League Club	Source	Date Signed	Seasons Played	Apps	Subs	Gls
Exeter C.	YT	07.94	94-96	31	13	0

RICE Patrick James
Belfast, 17 March, 1949 NIu23-2/NI-49 (RB)

League Club	Source	Date Signed	Seasons Played	Apps	Subs	Gls
Arsenal	Jnrs	03.66	67-80	391	6	12
Watford	Tr	11.80	80-83	112	0	1

RICE Ronald Henry
Birkenhead, 13 April, 1923 (IL)

League Club	Source	Date Signed	Seasons Played	Apps	Subs	Gls
Bradford C.	Huddersfield T. (Am)	09.46	46	1	-	0
Tranmere Rov.	Tr	10.46	46	4	-	1

RICHARDS Anthony Willis
Birmingham, 6 March, 1934 (CF)

League Club	Source	Date Signed	Seasons Played	Apps	Subs	Gls
Birmingham C.	Jnrs	12.51				
Walsall	Tr	09.54	54-62	334	-	185
Port Vale	Tr	03.63	62-65	59	4	30

RICHARDS Carroll (Carl) Lloyd
Jamaica (WI), 12 January, 1960 E Semi Pro (F)

League Club	Source	Date Signed	Seasons Played	Apps	Subs	Gls
Bournemouth	Enfield	07.86	86-88	57	14	16
Birmingham C.	Tr	10.88	88	18	1	2
Peterborough U.	Tr	07.89	89	16	4	5
Blackpool	Tr	01.90	89-91	32	9	8
Maidstone U.	L	10.91	91	4	0	2

League Club	Source	Date Signed	Seasons Played	Career Record Apps	Subs	Gls
RICHARDS Craig Alan						
Neath, 10 October, 1959						(M)
Queens Park R.	App	07.77				
Wimbledon	Tr	06.79	79	2	0	0
RICHARDS Dean Ivor						
Bradford, 9 June, 1974 Eu21-4						(CD)
Bradford C.	YT	07.92	91-94	82	4	4
Wolverhampton W.	Tr	03.95	94-97	78	3	4
RICHARDS Gary Vivian						
Swansea, 2 August, 1963						(D)
Swansea C.	App	08.81	81-84	63	3	1
Lincoln C. (N/C)	Sweden	11.85	85	2	5	0
Cambridge U. (N/C)	Tr	03.86	85	8	0	0
Torquay U.	Tr	07.86	86	24	1	1
RICHARDS Geoffrey Mottram						
Bilston, 24 April, 1929						(OR)
West Bromwich A.	Albion Wks	08.46	46-47	3	-	1
RICHARDS Gordon						
Ruabon, 23 October, 1933 Died 1993						(OL)
Wrexham	Jnrs	05.52	52-57	96	-	24
Chester C.	Tr	01.58	57-60	74	-	16
RICHARDS John Barrington						
West Bromwich, 14 June, 1931						(IF)
Swindon T.		11.55	55-59	105	-	36
Norwich C.	Tr	12.59	59	5	-	2
Aldershot	Tr	10.60	60	19	-	8
RICHARDS John Peter						
Warrington, 9 November, 1950 Eu21-2/Eu23-6/EF Lge/E-1						(F)
Wolverhampton W.	Jnrs	07.69	69-82	365	20	144
Derby Co.	L	11.82	82	10	0	2
RICHARDS Lloyd George						
Jamaica (WI), 11 February, 1958						(M)
Notts Co.	App	02.76	75-77	7	2	0
York C.	Tr	06.80	80	17	1	1
RICHARDS Michael James						
Codsall, 26 May, 1939						(G)
Oxford U.	Wellington T.	07.62	62-63	30	-	0
Shrewsbury T.	Tr	11.63				
RICHARDS Peter (Pedro)						
Edmonton, 11 November, 1956						(RB)
Notts Co.	App	11.74	74-85	397	2	5
RICHARDS Stanley Verdun						
Cardiff, 21 January, 1917 Died 1987 W-1						(CF)
Cardiff C.	Tufnell Park	01.46	46-47	57	-	40
Swansea C.	Tr	06.48	48-50	65	-	35
RICHARDS Stephen						
Dundee, 24 October, 1961						(CD)
Hull C.	App	10.79	79-82	55	3	2
York C. (N/C)	Gainsborough Trin.	12.84	84	6	1	0
Lincoln C.	Tr	08.85	85	21	0	0
Cambridge U. (N/C)	Tr	03.86	85	4	0	2
Scarborough	Tr	08.86	87-90	164	0	13
Halifax T.	Tr	08.91	91	24	1	0
Doncaster Rov.	Tr	05.92	92	36	2	3
RICHARDS Tony						
Shirebrook, 9 June, 1944						(HB)
Mansfield T.	App	06.62	61-63	3	-	0
RICHARDS Tony Spencer						
Newham, 17 September, 1973						(F)
West Ham U.	YT	08.92				
Cambridge U.	Sudbury T.	08.95	95-96	29	13	5
Leyton Orient	Tr	07.97	97	10	7	2
RICHARDS Wayne						
Scunthorpe, 10 May, 1961						(FB)
Derby Co.	App	05.79	79-81	16	3	0
RICHARDSON Anthony Frederick						
Cleethorpes, 5 November, 1943						(CF)
Nottingham F.	Jnrs	11.60				
Bradford C. (Am)	Cheltenham T.	05.62	62	2	-	1
RICHARDSON Anthony Joseph						
Southwark, 7 January, 1932						(FB)
Queens Park R.	Slough S.C.	04.51	51	2	-	0

League Club	Source	Date Signed	Seasons Played	Career Record Apps	Subs	Gls
RICHARDSON Barry						
Wallsend, 5 August, 1969						(G)
Sunderland	YT	05.88				
Scunthorpe U.	Tr	03.89				
Scarborough	Tr	08.89	89-90	30	0	0
Northampton T.	Stockport Co. (N/C)	09.91	91-93	96	0	0
Preston N.E.	Tr	07.94	94-95	20	0	0
Lincoln C.	Tr	10.95	95-97	96	0	0
RICHARDSON Brian						
Sheffield, 5 October, 1934						(WH)
Sheffield U.		12.54	55-64	291	-	9
Swindon T.	Tr	01.66	65	11	0	0
Rochdale	Tr	07.66	66	19	0	1
RICHARDSON Craig Thomas						
Newham, 8 October, 1979						(LWB)
Leyton Orient	YT	●	97	1	0	0
RICHARDSON Damien John						
Dublin, 2 August, 1947 IR-3						(F)
Gillingham	Shamrock Rov.	10.72	72-80	314	9	94
RICHARDSON David						
Billingham, 11 March, 1932						(FB)
Leicester C.	Jnrs	11.49	54	2	-	0
Grimsby T.	Tr	06.55	55-59	175	-	1
Swindon T.	Tr	06.60				
Barrow	Tr	07.61	61-62	31	-	0
RICHARDSON Derek						
Hackney, 13 July, 1956 E Yth/E Semi Pro						(G)
Chelsea	App	02.74				
Queens Park R.	Tr	04.76	76-78	31	0	0
Sheffield U.	Tr	12.79	79-80	42	0	0
Coventry C.	Tr	03.82				
RICHARDSON Frederick						
Spennymoor, 18 August, 1925						(CF)
Chelsea	Bishop Auckland	09.46	46	2	-	0
Hartlepool U.	Tr	10.47	47-48	43	-	16
Barnsley	Tr	10.48	48-49	41	-	12
West Bromwich A.	Tr	06.50	50-51	29	-	8
Chester C.	Tr	02.52	51-52	23	-	6
Hartlepool U.	Tr	11.52	52-55	106	-	19
RICHARDSON Garbutt						
Newcastle, 24 October, 1938						(CH)
Huddersfield T.	Jnrs	10.55				
Preston N.E.	Tr	07.57	59-60	15	-	1
Accrington St.	Tr	07.61				
Halifax T.	Carlisle U. (trial)	11.62	62-63	20	-	1
Barrow	Tr	07.64	64	30	-	5
RICHARDSON George						
Worksop, 12 December, 1912 Died 1968						(F)
Huddersfield T.	Manton Colly	04.33	33	1	-	0
Sheffield U.	Tr	05.34	36-38	30	-	9
Hull C.	Tr	11.38	38-47	36	-	15
RICHARDSON Graham Charles						
Sedgefield, 20 March, 1958						(G)
Hartlepool U.	Darlington (Am)	08.75	75-80	89	0	0
RICHARDSON Ian George						
Barking, 22 October, 1970 E Semi Pro						(M)
Birmingham C.	Dagenham & Redbridge	08.95	95	3	4	0
Notts Co.	Tr	01.96	95-97	56	8	3
RICHARDSON Ian Paul						
Ely, 9 May, 1964						(F)
Watford	App	05.82	83-84	5	3	2
Blackpool	L	12.82	82	4	1	2
Rotherham U.	L	02.85	84	5	0	3
Chester C.	Tr	11.85	85-86	31	4	10
Scunthorpe U.	Tr	10.86	86-88	11	7	4
RICHARDSON James Robert						
Ashington, 8 February, 1911 Died 1964 E Sch/EF Lge/E-2						(IF)
Newcastle U.	Blyth Spartans	04.28	29-34	136	-	42
Huddersfield T.	Tr	10.34	34-37	120	-	32
Newcastle U.	Tr	10.37	37	14	-	4
Millwall	Tr	03.38	37-38	52	-	16
Leyton Orient	Tr	01.48	47	15	-	0
RICHARDSON John						
Birkenhead, 24 May, 1933						(G)
Southport	Canterbury C.	07.56	56-59	103	-	0

League Club	Source	Date Signed	Seasons Played	Apps	Subs	Gls

RICHARDSON John
Newcastle, 28 July, 1966 (F)

Colchester U. (N/C)	Chesham U.	09.93	93	1	7	0

RICHARDSON John
Worksop, 20 April, 1945 (FB)

Derby Co.	App	04.62	62-70	118	0	4
Notts Co.	Tr	07.71	71	0	2	0

RICHARDSON John Pattinson
Stannington, 5 February, 1949 (CD)

Millwall	App	●	65	1	0	0
Brentford	Tr	08.66	66-69	83	2	7
Fulham	Tr	08.69	69-72	61	10	6
Aldershot	Tr	07.73	73-76	120	1	6

RICHARDSON Jonathan Derek
Nottingham, 29 August, 1975 (CD)

Exeter C.	YT	07.94	93-97	168	4	5

RICHARDSON Joseph Arthur Searles
Sheffield, 17 March, 1942 Died 1966 (IF)

Birmingham C.	Winsford U.	09.59				
Sheffield U.	Tr	01.60				
Rochdale	Tr	10.60	60-64	115	-	31
Tranmere Rov.	Tr	07.65				

RICHARDSON Kevin
Newcastle, 4 December, 1962 E-1 (M)

Everton	App	12.80	81-86	95	14	16
Watford	Tr	09.86	86	39	0	2
Arsenal	Tr	08.87	87-89	88	8	5
Aston Villa	Real Sociedad (Sp)	08.91	91-94	142	1	13
Coventry C.	Tr	02.95	94-97	75	3	0
Southampton	Tr	09.97	97	25	3	0

RICHARDSON Lee James
Halifax, 12 March, 1969 (M)

Halifax T.	YT	07.87	86-88	43	13	2
Watford	Tr	02.89	88-89	40	1	1
Blackburn Rov.	Tr	08.90	90-91	50	12	3
Oldham Ath.	Aberdeen	08.94	94-96	82	6	21
Stockport Co.	L	08.97	97	4	2	0
Huddersfield T.	Tr	10.97	97	16	5	3

RICHARDSON Lloyd Matthew
Dewsbury, 7 October, 1977 E Yth (M)

Oldham Ath.	YT	10.94	96	0	1	0

RICHARDSON Neil Thomas
Sunderland, 3 March, 1968 (M/CD)

Rotherham U.	Brandon U.	07.89	89-97	164	15	10
Exeter C.	L	11.96	96	14	0	0

RICHARDSON Nicholas John
Halifax, 11 April, 1967 (M)

Halifax T.	Emley	11.88	88-91	89	12	17
Cardiff C.	Tr	08.92	92-94	106	5	13
Wrexham	L	10.94	94	4	0	2
Chester C.	L	12.94	94	6	0	1
Bury	Tr	08.95	95	3	2	0
Chester C.	Tr	09.95	95-97	86	4	6

RICHARDSON Norman
Consett, 15 April, 1915 Died 1991 (FB)

Bolton W.	Medomsley Jnrs	05.33				
New Brighton	Tr	02.36	35-50	213	-	0

RICHARDSON Paul
Selston (Nts), 25 October, 1949 E Yth (M)

Nottingham F.	App	08.67	67-76	199	24	18
Chester C.	Tr	10.76	76	28	0	2
Stoke C.	Tr	06.77	77-80	124	3	10
Sheffield U.	Tr	08.81	81-82	35	1	2
Blackpool	L	01.83	82	4	0	0
Swindon T.	Tr	07.83	83	7	0	0
Swansea C. (N/C)	Tr	09.84	84	12	0	0

RICHARDSON Paul Andrew
Hucknall, 7 November, 1962 E Semi Pro (M)

Derby Co.	Nuneaton Borough	08.84	84	7	7	0

RICHARDSON Roderick Keith
Hunstanton, 1 October, 1942 (IF)

Torquay U.	Norwich C. (Am)	07.62	62-63	7	-	1

RICHARDSON Russell
Sheffield, 21 October, 1964 (FB)

Scunthorpe U. (N/C)	YT	08.83	83	2	0	0

RICHARDSON Stanley
Harrington (Cumb), 28 April, 1924 (W)

Workington		08.51	51	8	-	1

RICHARDSON Steven Earl
Slough, 11 February, 1962 (LB)

Southampton	App	02.80				
Reading	Tr	07.82	82-92	373	7	3

RICHARDSON Stuart
Leeds, 12 June, 1938 (WH)

Queens Park R.	Methley U.	11.56	58	1	-	0
Oldham Ath.	Tr	07.59	59	22	-	0

RICHARDSON Thomas
Reading, 1 February, 1931 Died 1976 (IF/D)

Middlesbrough		09.52				
Southport	Tr	05.54				
Aldershot	Tr	07.55	55-57	41	-	9

RICHARDSON William
Bedlington, 25 October, 1943 (FB)

Sunderland	Jnrs	10.60				
Mansfield T.	Tr	10.65	65-67	61	2	0
York C.	Tr	06.68	68	24	0	0

RICHES Steven Alexander
Australia, 6 August, 1976 (LW)

Leyton Orient	Warringah Dolphins (Aus)	09.96	96	2	3	0

RICHLEY Lionel
Gateshead, 2 July, 1924 Died 1980 (HB)

Hartlepool U.	Tonbridge	06.51	51-53	72	-	0

RICHMOND John Frederick
Derby, 17 September, 1938 (FB)

Derby Co.	Derby Corries	01.56	57-62	6	-	0

RICKABY Stanley
Stockton, 12 March, 1924 EF Lge/E-1 (FB)

Middlesbrough	South Bank	07.46	47-49	10	-	0
West Bromwich A.	Tr	02.50	49-54	189	-	2

RICKARD Derek Bryan Philip
Plymouth, 1 October, 1947 (F)

Plymouth Arg.	St Austell	12.69	69-73	101	9	41
Bournemouth	Tr	07.74	74-75	22	10	6

RICKARDS Kenneth
Middlesbrough, 22 March, 1929 (IR)

Hull C.	Middlesbrough A.	05.47				
Darlington	Tr	01.50	49	8	-	0

RICKERS Paul Steven
Leeds, 9 May, 1975 (M)

Oldham Ath.	YT	07.93	94-97	107	6	9

RICKETT Horace Francis John
Grays, 3 January, 1912 Died 1989 (G)

Leyton Orient	Chelmsford C.	02.43				
Reading	Chelmsford C.	06.46	46-47	22	-	0

RICKETT Walter
Sheffield, 20 March, 1917 Died 1991 E 'B' (OR)

Sheffield U.		05.39	46-47	57	-	16
Blackpool	Tr	01.48	47-49	45	-	8
Sheffield Wed.	Tr	10.49	49-52	95	-	13
Rotherham U.	Tr	09.52	52	28	-	4
Halifax T.	Tr	08.53	53	31	-	2

RICKETTS Alan
Crawley, 30 October, 1962 (F)

Crewe Alex.	Wrexham (N/C)	08.81	81	14	3	2

RICKETTS Graham Anthony
Oxford, 30 July, 1939 E Yth (WH)

Bristol Rov.	Jnrs	08.56	56-60	32	-	0
Stockport Co.	Tr	07.61	61-63	119	-	6
Doncaster Rov.	Tr	07.64	64-67	143	8	15
Peterborough U.	Tr	03.68	67-68	46	3	1

RICKETTS Michael Barrington
Birmingham, 4 December, 1978 (F)

Walsall	YT	09.96	95-97	8	28	3

RICKIS Victor Allen Fyfe Mann
Edinburgh, 26 November, 1940 (OL)

Millwall	Dalkeith Thistle	12.59	60	3	-	1

RIDDICK Gordon George
Watford, 6 November, 1943 (M)

League Club	Source	Date Signed	Seasons Played	Apps	Subs	Gls
Luton T.	Jnrs	04.61	62-66	101	1	16
Gillingham	Tr	03.67	66-69	114	0	24
Charlton Ath.	Tr	11.69	69-70	26	3	5
Leyton Orient	Tr	10.70	70-72	13	8	3
Northampton T.	Tr	12.72	72-73	28	0	3
Brentford	Tr	10.73	73-76	104	4	5

RIDEOUT Brian James
Bristol, 15 September, 1940 (FB)

League Club	Source	Date Signed	Seasons Played	Apps	Subs	Gls
Bristol Rov.	Jnrs	02.59	60	1	-	0

RIDEOUT Paul David
Bournemouth, 14 August, 1964 E Sch/E Yth/Eu21-5 (F)

League Club	Source	Date Signed	Seasons Played	Apps	Subs	Gls
Swindon T.	App	08.81	80-82	90	5	38
Aston Villa	Tr	06.83	83-84	50	4	19
Southampton	Bari (It)	07.88	88-91	68	7	19
Swindon T.	L	03.91	90	9	0	1
Notts Co.	Tr	09.91	91	9	2	3
Everton	Glasgow Rangers	08.92	92-96	86	26	29

RIDGE Roy
Ecclesfield, 21 October, 1934 (FB)

League Club	Source	Date Signed	Seasons Played	Apps	Subs	Gls
Sheffield U.	Ecclesfield	11.51	53-60	11	-	0
Rochdale	Tr	08.64	64-65	85	0	0

RIDGWAY Ian David
Reading, 28 December, 1975 (M)

League Club	Source	Date Signed	Seasons Played	Apps	Subs	Gls
Notts Co.	YT	07.94	94-96	3	4	0

RIDING Alan
Preston, 14 March, 1945 (CF)

League Club	Source	Date Signed	Seasons Played	Apps	Subs	Gls
Exeter C.	Colchester U. (Am)	07.64	65	1	0	0

RIDINGS David
Farnworth, 27 February, 1970 (M)

League Club	Source	Date Signed	Seasons Played	Apps	Subs	Gls
Halifax T.	Curzon Ashton	01.93	92	21	0	4
Lincoln C.	Tr	02.94	93	10	0	0
Crewe Alex.	Ashton U.	07.95	95	1	0	0

RIDLER David George
Liverpool, 12 March, 1976 (CD)

League Club	Source	Date Signed	Seasons Played	Apps	Subs	Gls
Wrexham	Rockys	07.95	96-97	25	6	0

RIDLEY David George Henry
Pontypridd, 16 December, 1916 (CF)

League Club	Source	Date Signed	Seasons Played	Apps	Subs	Gls
Millwall	Bedford T.	01.45				
Brighton & H.A.	Tr	07.46	46	5	-	0

RIDLEY John
Consett, 27 April, 1952 (CD)

League Club	Source	Date Signed	Seasons Played	Apps	Subs	Gls
Port Vale	Sheffield Univ.	08.73	73-78	149	7	3
Leicester C.	Tr	10.78	78	17	7	0
Chesterfield	Tr	08.79	79-81	121	3	8
Port Vale	Tr	08.82	82-84	105	9	5

RIDLEY Robert Michael
Reading, 30 May, 1942 (W)

League Club	Source	Date Signed	Seasons Played	Apps	Subs	Gls
Portsmouth	Jnrs	06.60				
Gillingham	Tr	07.61	61-66	71	2	8

RIDYARD Alfred
Cudworth, 5 March, 1908 Died 1981 (CH)

League Club	Source	Date Signed	Seasons Played	Apps	Subs	Gls
Barnsley	South Kirkby B.C.	08.28	30-31	21	-	3
West Bromwich A.	Tr	06.32	32-36	31	-	0
Queens Park R.	Tr	03.38	37-47	28	-	0

RIEDLE Karl-Heinz
Weiler, Germany, 16 September, 1965 German Int (F)

League Club	Source	Date Signed	Seasons Played	Apps	Subs	Gls
Liverpool	Borussia Dortmund (Ger)	08.97	97	18	7	6

RIEPER Marc
Denmark, 5 June, 1968 Danish Int (CD)

League Club	Source	Date Signed	Seasons Played	Apps	Subs	Gls
West Ham U.	Brondby (Den)	12.94	94-97	83	7	5

RIGBY Anthony Angelo
Ormskirk, 10 August, 1972 (M)

League Club	Source	Date Signed	Seasons Played	Apps	Subs	Gls
Crewe Alex.	YT	05.90				
Bury	Barrow	01.93	92-97	119	45	19
Scarborough	L	02.97	96	5	0	1

RIGBY Edward
Atherton, 20 April, 1925 (WH)

League Club	Source	Date Signed	Seasons Played	Apps	Subs	Gls
Manchester C.		02.48				
Barrow	Tr	07.49	49	19	-	0

RIGBY Ernest
Kirkham, 8 April, 1928 (FB)

League Club	Source	Date Signed	Seasons Played	Apps	Subs	Gls
Accrington St.	Blackpool (Am)	02.51	50-51	10	-	0

RIGBY Jack
Golborne, 29 July, 1924 Died 1997 (CH)

League Club	Source	Date Signed	Seasons Played	Apps	Subs	Gls
Manchester C.	Bryn Boys Brigade	12.46	46-52	100	-	0

RIGBY Jonathan Kendall
Bury St Edmunds, 31 January, 1965 (F)

League Club	Source	Date Signed	Seasons Played	Apps	Subs	Gls
Norwich C.	App	08.82	83-84	7	3	0
Aldershot	Tr	03.86	85	1	0	0
Cambridge U.	Tr	10.86	86-87	28	3	6

RIGBY Norman
Warsop, 23 May, 1923 (CH)

League Club	Source	Date Signed	Seasons Played	Apps	Subs	Gls
Notts Co.	Newark T.	09.44	47-50	46	-	0
Peterborough U.	Tr	(N/L)	60-61	55	-	0

RIGBY William
Chester, 9 June, 1921 (G)

League Club	Source	Date Signed	Seasons Played	Apps	Subs	Gls
Chester C.	Jnrs	08.46	46	1	-	0

RIGG Thomas
Bedlington, 20 February, 1920 Died 1995 (G)

League Club	Source	Date Signed	Seasons Played	Apps	Subs	Gls
Middlesbrough	Ashington	02.39				
Watford	Ashington	06.46	46-48	80	-	0
Gillingham	Consett	08.51	51-55	192	-	0

RIGGS Leslie John
Portsmouth, 30 May, 1935 (WH)

League Club	Source	Date Signed	Seasons Played	Apps	Subs	Gls
Gillingham	Jnrs	06.52	53-57	152	-	3
Newport Co.	Tr	06.58	58-60	110	-	3
Bury	Tr	06.61	61	6	-	0
Crewe Alex.	Tr	02.63	62-63	67	-	6
Gillingham	Tr	09.64	64-65	17	1	1

RILEY Brian Francis
Bolton, 14 September, 1937 (OL)

League Club	Source	Date Signed	Seasons Played	Apps	Subs	Gls
Bolton W.	Jnrs	12.54	56-58	8	-	1

RILEY Christopher John
Rhyl, 19 January, 1939 Died 1983 (IF)

League Club	Source	Date Signed	Seasons Played	Apps	Subs	Gls
Crewe Alex.	Rhyl	03.58	57-63	136	-	47
Tranmere Rov.	Tr	07.64				

RILEY David Sydney
Northampton, 8 December, 1960 (F)

League Club	Source	Date Signed	Seasons Played	Apps	Subs	Gls
Nottingham F.	Keyworth U.	01.84	83-86	7	5	2
Darlington	L	02.87	86	6	0	2
Peterborough U.	L	07.87	87	12	0	2
Port Vale	Tr	10.87	87-89	75	1	11
Peterborough U.	Tr	03.90	89-91	73	11	23

RILEY Glyn
Barnsley, 24 July, 1958 (F)

League Club	Source	Date Signed	Seasons Played	Apps	Subs	Gls
Barnsley	App	07.76	74-81	103	28	16
Doncaster Rov.	L	12.79	79	7	1	2
Bristol C.	Tr	08.82	82-86	184	15	61
Torquay U.	L	09.87	87	6	0	1
Aldershot	Tr	10.87	87-88	48	10	5

RILEY Howard
Wigston, 18 August, 1938 E Yth/Eu23-2 (OR)

League Club	Source	Date Signed	Seasons Played	Apps	Subs	Gls
Leicester C.	Jnrs	08.55	55-64	193	-	38
Walsall	Tr	01.66	65	24	0	3
Barrow	Atlanta (USA)	07.68	68	21	3	6

RILEY Hughen William
Accrington, 12 June, 1947 (M)

League Club	Source	Date Signed	Seasons Played	Apps	Subs	Gls
Rochdale		12.66	67-71	81	12	12
Crewe Alex.	Tr	12.71	71-74	116	5	9
Bury	Tr	12.74	74-75	47	4	4
Bournemouth	Tr	04.76	76-77	69	3	7

RILEY Ian Michael
Tollesbury (Ex), 8 February, 1947 (FB)

League Club	Source	Date Signed	Seasons Played	Apps	Subs	Gls
Southend U.	Maldon T.	11.67	67-68	3	1	0

RILEY Joseph
Stockton (F)

League Club	Source	Date Signed	Seasons Played	Apps	Subs	Gls
Darlington (Am)	Stockton	08.49	49	8	-	2

RIMMER Gilbert Henry
Southport, 14 July, 1932 (W)

League Club	Source	Date Signed	Seasons Played	Apps	Subs	Gls
Southport (Am)	Leyland Road	07.55	55	2	-	0

RIMMER John James
Southport, 10 February, 1948 E-1 (G)

League Club	Source	Date Signed	Seasons Played	Apps	Subs	Gls
Manchester U.	App	05.65	67-72	34	0	0
Swansea C.	L	10.73	73	17	0	0
Arsenal	Tr	02.74	73-76	124	0	0
Aston Villa	Tr	08.77	77-82	229	0	0
Swansea C.	Tr	08.83	83-85	66	0	0

League Club	Source	Date Signed	Seasons Played	Apps	Subs	Gls
RIMMER Neill						
Liverpool, 13 November, 1967 E Sch/E Yth (M)						
Everton	App	●	84	0	1	0
Ipswich T.	Tr	08.85	85-87	19	3	3
Wigan Ath.	Tr	07.88	88-95	184	6	10
RIMMER Raymond						
Southport, 6 August, 1938 (OL)						
Southport (Am)	Formby Dons	08.55	55-57	8	-	0
RIMMER Stuart Alan						
Southport, 12 October, 1964 E Yth (F)						
Everton	App	10.82	81-83	3	0	0
Chester C.	Tr	01.85	84-87	110	4	67
Watford	Tr	03.88	87-88	10	0	1
Notts Co.	Tr	11.88	88	3	1	2
Walsall	Tr	02.89	88-90	85	3	31
Barnsley	Tr	03.91	90	10	5	1
Chester C.	Tr	08.91	91-97	213	34	67
Rochdale	L	09.94	94	3	0	0
Preston N.E.	L	12.94	94	0	2	0
RIMMER Warwick Robert						
Birkenhead, 1 March, 1941 E Sch (D)						
Bolton W.	Jnrs	03.58	60-74	462	7	17
Crewe Alex.	Tr	03.75	74-78	114	14	0
RIMMINGTON Norman						
Barnsley, 29 November, 1923 (G)						
Barnsley	Mapplewell	02.45	46	27	-	0
Hartlepool U.	Tr	12.47	47-51	124	-	0
RING Michael Paul						
Brighton, 13 February, 1961 (W)						
Brighton & H.A.	App	02.79	81-83	1	4	0
Hull C.	Ballymena U.	07.84	84-85	17	7	2
Bolton W.	L	03.86	85	1	2	0
Aldershot	Tr	07.86	86-88	53	26	16
RING Thomas						
Glasgow, 8 August, 1930 Died 1997 S-12/SF Lge (OL)						
Everton	Clyde	01.60	59-60	27	-	6
Barnsley	Tr	11.61	61-62	21	-	1
RINGER Walter Albert						
Stanley, 7 October, 1941 (OL)						
Halifax T.		12.59	59-60	6	-	0
RINGSTEAD Alfred						
Dublin, 14 October, 1927 IR-20 (OL)						
Sheffield U.	Northwich Vic.	11.50	50-58	247	-	101
Mansfield T.	Tr	07.59	59	27	-	3
RINTANEN Mauno Olavi						
Finland, 28 April, 1925 (G)						
Hull C. (Am)	H.J.K. Helsinki (Fin)	09.56	56	4	-	0
RIOCH Bruce David						
Aldershot, 6 September, 1947 S-24 (M)						
Luton T.	App	09.64	64-68	148	1	46
Aston Villa	Tr	07.69	69-73	149	5	34
Derby Co.	Tr	02.74	73-76	106	0	34
Everton	Tr	12.76	76-77	30	0	3
Derby Co.	Tr	11.77	77-79	40	1	4
Birmingham C.	L	12.78	78	3	0	0
Sheffield U.	L	03.79	78	8	0	1
Torquay U.	Seattle (USA)	10.80	80-83	64	7	6
RIOCH Daniel (Neil) Gordon						
Paddington, 13 April, 1951 E Yth (CD)						
Luton T.	App	07.68				
Aston Villa	Tr	09.69	69-74	17	5	3
York C.	L	02.72	71	0	1	0
Northampton T.	L	03.72	71	14	0	4
Plymouth Arg.	Tr	05.75	75	3	2	0
RIOCH Gregor James						
Sutton Coldfield, 24 June, 1975 (LB)						
Luton T.	YT	07.93				
Barnet	L	09.93	93	3	0	0
Peterborough U.	Tr	08.95	95	13	5	0
Hull C.	Tr	07.96	96-97	76	2	6
RIPLEY Andrew Ian						
Middlesbrough, 10 December, 1975 (W)						
Darlington	YT	11.93	93	0	2	0
RIPLEY Keith Anthony						
Normanton, 10 October, 1954 (FB)						
Huddersfield T.	Gainsborough Trin.	08.78	78	2	3	0
Doncaster Rov.	Tr	08.79	79	5	0	0

League Club	Source	Date Signed	Seasons Played	Apps	Subs	Gls
RIPLEY Stanley **Keith**						
Normanton, 29 March, 1935 (WH)						
Leeds U.	Jnrs	04.52	54-57	67	-	15
Norwich C.	Tr	08.58	58	12	-	6
Mansfield T.	Tr	11.58	58-59	31	-	5
Peterborough U.	Tr	07.60	60-61	82	-	12
Doncaster Rov.	Tr	08.62	62-65	123	5	7
RIPLEY Stuart Edward						
Middlesbrough, 20 November, 1967 E Yth/Eu21-8/E-2 (RW)						
Middlesbrough	App	11.85	84-96	210	39	26
Bolton W.	L	02.86	85	5	0	1
Blackburn Rov.	Tr	07.92	92-97	172	15	13
RISDON Stanley William						
Exeter, 13 August, 1913 Died 1979 (WH)						
Exeter C.	St Marys Majors	10.33	33-35	35	-	1
Brighton & H.A.	Tr	08.36	36-46	23	-	0
RISEBOROUGH Cyril						
Doncaster, 22 February, 1933 (OR)						
Swindon T.		02.55	54-56	26	-	1
RISETH Vidar						
Norway, 21 April, 1972 (F)						
Luton T.	Kongsvinger (Nor)	10.95	95	6	5	0
RIST Frank Henry						
Hackney, 30 March, 1914 (CH)						
Leyton Orient	Grays Ath.	08.32				
Charlton Ath.	Tr	06.33	34-46	47	-	1
RITCHIE Andrew Timothy						
Manchester, 28 November, 1960 E Sch/E Yth/Eu21-1 (F)						
Manchester U.	App	12.77	77-80	26	7	13
Brighton & H.A.	Tr	10.80	80-82	82	7	23
Leeds U.	Tr	03.83	82-86	127	9	40
Oldham Ath.	Tr	08.87	87-94	187	30	82
Scarborough	Tr	08.95	95-96	59	9	17
Oldham Ath.	Tr	02.97	96-97	14	11	2
RITCHIE David Mark						
Stoke, 20 January, 1971 (F)						
Stoke C.	YT	07.89				
Stockport Co.	Tr	03.90	89	0	1	0
RITCHIE John						
Paddington, 28 February, 1951 E Amat (F)						
Arsenal	Slough T.	04.72				
Hereford U.	Tr	03.74	73-74	19	3	4
RITCHIE John						
Ashington, 10 April, 1944 E Amat (FB)						
Port Vale	Whitley Bay	12.65	65-66	50	0	3
Preston N.E.	Tr	04.67	66-71	93	0	5
Bradford C.	Tr	03.72	71-72	20	0	0
RITCHIE John						
Blairhall, 31 March, 1927 (WH)						
Accrington St.	Crossgates Primrose	06.49	49	13	-	0
RITCHIE John Brough						
Auchterderran (Fife), 12 June, 1947 (G)						
Bradford C.	Brechin C.	07.71	71-73	64	0	0
RITCHIE John Henry						
Kettering, 12 July, 1941 (CF)						
Stoke C.	Kettering T.	06.62	62-66	110	0	64
Sheffield Wed.	Tr	11.66	66-68	88	1	34
Stoke C.	Tr	07.69	69-74	151	9	71
RITCHIE Paul Michael						
St Andrews, 25 January, 1969 (F)						
Gillingham (L)	Dundee	02.93	92	6	0	3
Gillingham (L)	Dundee	09.94	94	5	0	1
RITCHIE Robert						
Glasgow, 1 February, 1920 (IF)						
Watford	Rickmansworth	02.48	48	1	-	0
RITCHIE Stephen Kilcar						
Edinburgh, 17 February, 1954 S Sch (LB)						
Bristol C.	App	09.71	72	1	0	0
Hereford U.	Morton	06.75	75-77	102	0	3
Torquay U.	Aberdeen	03.79	78-79	58	0	2
RITCHIE Stuart Arthur						
Southampton, 20 May, 1968 (M)						
Aston Villa	App	05.86	86	0	1	0
Crewe Alex.	Tr	06.87	87	13	5	0

League Club	Source	Date Signed	Seasons Played	Career Record Apps	Subs	Gls
RITCHIE Thomas						
Bangor, 10 July, 1930						(OL)
Manchester U.	Bangor C.	12.50				
Reading	Tr	02.53	52-54	18	-	5
Grimsby T.	Dartford	08.58	58	1	-	0
Barrow	Tr	12.58	58	16	-	6
RITCHIE Thomas Gibb						
Edinburgh, 2 January, 1952						(F)
Bristol C.	Bridgend Thistle	07.69	72-80	308	13	77
Sunderland	Tr	01.81	80-81	32	3	8
Carlisle U.	L	03.82	81	14	1	0
Bristol C.	Tr	06.82	82-84	92	1	25
RITCHIE William Saunders						
Dundee, 13 November, 1932						(CF)
Bury	Dundee	06.57	57-58	13	-	7
Stockport Co.	Tr	03.59	58-60	52	-	12
RITSON John Albert						
Liverpool, 6 September, 1949						(RB)
Bolton W.	App	09.66	67-77	321	3	9
Bury	Tr	09.78	78-79	41	0	2
RITSON Ledger						
Gateshead, 28 April, 1921 Died 1977						(LB)
Leyton Orient		03.46	46-48	84	-	0
RIVERS Alan Desmond						
Portsmouth, 27 January, 1946						(CH)
Luton T.	App	01.64	65-66	25	5	1
Watford	Tr	09.67	67	0	2	0
RIVERS Mark Alan						
Crewe, 26 November, 1975						(F)
Crewe Alex.	YT	05.94	95-97	78	17	22
RIX Graham						
Askern, 23 October, 1957 Eu21-7/E 'B'/E-17						(M)
Arsenal	App	01.75	76-87	338	13	41
Brentford	L	12.87	87	6	0	0
Chelsea (N/C)	Dundee	05.94	94	0	1	0
ROACH Neville						
Reading, 29 September, 1978						(F)
Reading	YT	05.97	96-97	2	9	1
ROAST Jesse						
Barking, 16 March, 1964						(FB)
Maidstone U.	Walthamstow Ave.	01.87	89-90	31	1	0
ROBB David Thomson						
Broughty Ferry, 15 December, 1947 Su23-3/S-5						(F)
Norwich C.	Tampa Bay (USA)	09.78	78	4	1	1
ROBB George						
Finsbury Park, 1 June, 1926 E Amat/EF Lge/E 'B'/E-1						(OL)
Tottenham H.	Finchley	12.51	51-58	182	-	53
ROBB Ian Alexander						
Doncaster, 1 June, 1955						(CD)
York C.	Jnrs	02.73	73-74	4	0	0
ROBB William Lawson						
Rutherglen, 23 December, 1927						(WH)
Leyton Orient	Aberdeen	05.50	50	5	-	0
Bradford C.	Albion Rov.	10.54	54-57	127	-	4
ROBBINS Gordon						
Barnsley, 7 February, 1936						(WH)
Rotherham U.	Wombwell	05.53				
Crewe Alex.	Goole T.	12.58	58	4	-	0
ROBBINS Robert						
Newton Abbot, 20 September, 1953						(G)
Torquay U. (N/C)	Newton Abbott	08.76	76	19	0	0
ROBBINS Terence John						
Southwark, 14 January, 1965 E Semi Pro						(F)
Barnet	Welling U.	07.95	95	9	6	1
ROBER Hans **Jurgen**						
West Germany, 25 December, 1953						(M)
Nottingham F.	Chicago (USA)	12.81	81	21	1	3
ROBERTS Alan						
Newcastle, 8 December, 1964						(RW)
Middlesbrough	App	12.82	82-85	28	10	2

League Club	Source	Date Signed	Seasons Played	Career Record Apps	Subs	Gls
Darlington	Tr	09.85	85-87	116	3	19
Sheffield U.	Tr	07.88	88-89	31	5	2
Lincoln C.	Tr	10.89	89	10	0	0
ROBERTS Alan						
Bury, 23 April, 1946						(FB)
Bradford P.A.	Mossley	11.69	69	15	0	0
ROBERTS Andrew James						
Dartford, 20 March, 1974 Eu21-5						(M)
Millwall	YT	10.91	91-94	132	6	5
Crystal Palace	Tr	07.95	95-97	106	2	2
Wimbledon	Tr	03.98	97	12	0	1
ROBERTS Anthony Mark						
Holyhead, 4 August, 1969 W Yth/Wu21-2/W 'B'/W-2						(G)
Queens Park R.	YT	07.87	87-97	122	0	0
ROBERTS Arthur Albert						
Barnsley, 27 January, 1907 Died 1957						(CH)
Southampton	Ardsley	08.29	30-37	156	-	0
Swansea C.	Tr	08.38	38	14	-	0
York C.	Tr	07.46	46	1	-	0
ROBERTS Benjamin James						
Bishop Auckland, 22 June, 1975 Eu21-1						(G)
Middlesbrough	YT	03.93	96-97	15	1	0
Hartlepool U.	L	10.95	95	4	0	0
Wycombe W.	L	12.95	95	15	0	0
Bradford C.	L	08.96	96	2	0	0
ROBERTS Brian James						
Windsor, 3 February, 1967						(F)
Reading	YT	07.85	84-85	0	5	0
ROBERTS Brian Leslie Ford						
Manchester, 6 November, 1955						(FB)
Coventry C.	App	11.73	75-83	209	6	1
Hereford U.	L	02.75	74	5	0	0
Birmingham C.	Tr	03.84	83-89	182	5	0
Wolverhampton W.	Tr	06.90	90	17	4	0
ROBERTS Christian John						
Cardiff, 22 October, 1979 W Yth						(F)
Cardiff C.	YT	10.97	97	5	6	3
ROBERTS Cledwyn						
Colwyn Bay, 12 August, 1947						(WH)
Wrexham	Glan Conwy	08.65	65	1	0	0
ROBERTS Colin						
Castleford, 16 September, 1933						(WH)
Bradford P.A.	Altofts Colly	10.51	53-55	75	-	0
Bradford C.	Frickley Colly	06.59	59-60	57	-	0
ROBERTS James **Dale**						
Newcastle, 8 October, 1956 E Yth						(CD)
Ipswich T.	App	09.74	74-77	17	1	0
Hull C.	Tr	02.80	79-84	149	4	6
ROBERTS Darren Anthony						
Birmingham, 12 October, 1969						(F)
Wolverhampton W.	Burton A.	04.92	92	12	9	5
Hereford U.	L	03.94	93	5	1	5
Chesterfield	Tr	07.94	94-95	10	15	1
Darlington	Tr	07.96	96-97	66	6	28
Peterborough U.	L	02.98	97	2	1	0
ROBERTS David						
Birmingham, 21 December, 1946						(W)
Aston Villa	Jnrs	12.63	65-67	15	1	1
Shrewsbury T.	Tr	03.68	67-73	224	6	20
Swansea C.	Tr	05.74	74	32	5	1
ROBERTS David Frazer						
Southampton, 26 November, 1949 Wu23-4/W-17						(CD)
Fulham	App	09.67	68-70	21	1	0
Oxford U.	Tr	02.71	70-74	160	1	7
Hull C.	Tr	02.75	74-77	86	0	4
Cardiff C.	Tr	08.78	78-80	40	1	2
ROBERTS David Gordon						
Plymouth, 8 May, 1944						(FB)
Plymouth Arg.	App	12.61	61-63	11	-	0
ROBERTS Dean						
Mexborough, 12 January, 1967						(F)
Bolton W.	App	01.85				
Exeter C.	Tr	07.86	86	23	2	7

ROBERTS Dennis
West Bretton (Yks), 5 February, 1918 (CH)

League Club	Source	Date Signed	Seasons Played	Apps	Subs	Gls
Notts Co.		08.37				
Bristol C.	Tr	05.38	38-53	303	-	2

ROBERTS Donald Campbell
Arlecdon, 3 February, 1933 (IF)

League Club	Source	Date Signed	Seasons Played	Apps	Subs	Gls
Workington	Whitehaven	07.52	52-53	21	-	0
Barrow		10.57	57-58	22	-	2

ROBERTS Dudley Edward
Derby, 16 October, 1945 (F)

League Club	Source	Date Signed	Seasons Played	Apps	Subs	Gls
Coventry C.	Jnrs	11.63	65-67	11	1	6
Mansfield T.	Tr	03.68	67-73	194	6	66
Doncaster Rov.	L	02.73	72	7	0	0
Scunthorpe U.	Tr	02.74	73-75	56	3	17

ROBERTS Edward
Chesterfield, 2 November, 1916 (CF)

League Club	Source	Date Signed	Seasons Played	Apps	Subs	Gls
Derby Co.	Glapwell Colly	04.34	35	4	-	0
Coventry C.	Tr	03.37	36-51	212	-	85

ROBERTS Edward John
Liverpool, 16 November, 1947 (G)

League Club	Source	Date Signed	Seasons Played	Apps	Subs	Gls
Tranmere Rov.	Harrowby Jnrs	05.67	68-69	7	0	0

ROBERTS Eric
Batley, 16 January, 1921 Died 1985 (OL)

League Club	Source	Date Signed	Seasons Played	Apps	Subs	Gls
Halifax T.	Altofts Colly	08.47	47	5	-	1

ROBERTS Frederick
Rhyl, 7 May, 1916 Died 1985 (OR)

League Club	Source	Date Signed	Seasons Played	Apps	Subs	Gls
Bury	Rhyl	04.38	38-46	12	-	5
Leyton Orient	Tr	11.46	46	18	-	2

ROBERTS Garreth William
Hull, 15 November, 1960 Wu21-1 (W)

League Club	Source	Date Signed	Seasons Played	Apps	Subs	Gls
Hull C.	App	11.78	78-90	409	5	47

ROBERTS Gary Paul Michael
Rhyl, 5 April, 1960 (F)

League Club	Source	Date Signed	Seasons Played	Apps	Subs	Gls
Brentford	Wembley	10.80	80-85	180	7	45

ROBERTS Geoffrey Michael
Liverpool, 29 December, 1949 (FB)

League Club	Source	Date Signed	Seasons Played	Apps	Subs	Gls
Bolton W.	App	01.67	67-69	5	0	0

ROBERTS Glyn Shane
Ipswich, 19 October, 1974 (M)

League Club	Source	Date Signed	Seasons Played	Apps	Subs	Gls
Rotherham U.	Norwich C. (YT)	07.93	93-94	11	5	1

ROBERTS Gordon Richard
Cardiff, 30 December, 1946 W Sch (W)

League Club	Source	Date Signed	Seasons Played	Apps	Subs	Gls
Wolverhampton W.	App	01.64				
Bury	Tr	09.65	65	2	0	0

ROBERTS Douglas **Gordon**
Coventry, 30 May, 1925 Died 1991 (W)

League Club	Source	Date Signed	Seasons Played	Apps	Subs	Gls
Wolverhampton W.	Jnrs	09.42				
Northampton T.	Tr	09.45	46-48	57	-	7
Brighton & H.A.	Tr	03.49	48-49	17	-	3
Accrington St.	Tr	07.51	51	39	-	11

ROBERTS Graham Paul
Southampton, 3 July, 1959 E 'B'/E-6 (CD)

League Club	Source	Date Signed	Seasons Played	Apps	Subs	Gls
Portsmouth (N/C)	Sholing	03.77				
Tottenham H.	Weymouth	05.80	80-86	200	9	23
Chelsea	Glasgow Rangers	08.88	88-89	70	0	18
West Bromwich A.	Tr	11.90	90-91	39	0	6

ROBERTS Griffith Orthin
Blaenau Ffestiniog, 2 October, 1920 (G)

League Club	Source	Date Signed	Seasons Played	Apps	Subs	Gls
Nottingham F.	Blaenau Ffestiniog	05.46	46	9	-	0

ROBERTS Harold
Liverpool, 12 January, 1920 (OL)

League Club	Source	Date Signed	Seasons Played	Apps	Subs	Gls
Chesterfield	Harrowby Jnrs	08.39	46-48	92	-	9
Birmingham C.	Tr	11.48	48-50	34	-	2
Shrewsbury T.	Tr	06.51	51-52	70	-	16
Scunthorpe U.	Tr	07.53	53-54	17	-	1

ROBERTS Ian Mark
Colwyn Bay, 28 February, 1961 (M)

League Club	Source	Date Signed	Seasons Played	Apps	Subs	Gls
Wrexham	Jnrs	07.79	78-79	2	4	0

ROBERTS Ian Patterson
Glasgow, 28 September, 1955 (LB)

League Club	Source	Date Signed	Seasons Played	Apps	Subs	Gls
Shrewsbury T.	App	09.72	71-75	93	3	1
Crewe Alex.	Tr	07.76	76-78	89	4	0

ROBERTS Iwan Wyn
Bangor, 26 June, 1968 W Sch/W Yth/W 'B'/W-7 (F)

League Club	Source	Date Signed	Seasons Played	Apps	Subs	Gls
Watford	YT	06.86	85-89	40	23	9
Huddersfield T.	Tr	07.90	90-93	141	1	50
Leicester C.	Tr	11.93	93-95	92	8	41
Wolverhampton W.	Tr	07.96	96	24	9	12
Norwich C.	Tr	07.97	97	29	2	5

ROBERTS James Nicoll
Larbert, 12 June, 1923 (OL)

League Club	Source	Date Signed	Seasons Played	Apps	Subs	Gls
Ipswich T.	Dundee	09.49	49-51	73	-	15
Barrow	Tr	07.52	52	11	-	2

ROBERTS Jamie Steven
Doncaster, 11 April, 1974 (M)

League Club	Source	Date Signed	Seasons Played	Apps	Subs	Gls
Doncaster Rov.	YT	07.92	92	1	1	0

ROBERTS Jason Andre Davis
Park Royal, 25 January, 1978 Grenada Int (F)

League Club	Source	Date Signed	Seasons Played	Apps	Subs	Gls
Wolverhampton W.	Hayes	09.97				
Torquay U.	L	12.97	97	13	1	6
Bristol C.	L	03.98	97	1	2	1

ROBERTS Jeremy
Middlesbrough, 24 November, 1966 E Yth (G)

League Club	Source	Date Signed	Seasons Played	Apps	Subs	Gls
Hartlepool U. (N/C)	Jnrs	12.83	83	1	0	0
Leicester C.	Tr	07.84	85	3	0	0
Darlington	Luton T. (trial)	03.87	86-87	29	0	0
Brentford (N/C)	Tr	09.88	88	5	0	0

ROBERTS John Dilwyn
Wrexham, 22 July, 1928 (OR)

League Club	Source	Date Signed	Seasons Played	Apps	Subs	Gls
Wrexham (Am)	Brymbo Steel Wks	04.51	50	1	-	0

ROBERTS John Griffith
Abercynon, 11 September, 1946 Wu21-1/Wu23-5/W-22 (CD/F)

League Club	Source	Date Signed	Seasons Played	Apps	Subs	Gls
Swansea C.	Abercynon A.	07.64	65-67	36	1	16
Northampton T.	Tr	11.67	67-68	62	0	11
Arsenal	Tr	05.69	69-72	56	3	4
Birmingham C.	Tr	10.72	72-75	61	5	1
Wrexham	Tr	08.76	76-79	145	0	5
Hull C.	Tr	08.80	80	26	0	1

ROBERTS John Thomas
Australia, 24 March, 1944 (G)

League Club	Source	Date Signed	Seasons Played	Apps	Subs	Gls
Chelsea	Apia-Leichardt (Aus)	01.66				
Blackburn Rov.	Tr	04.66	65	3	0	0
Chesterfield	L	08.67	67	46	0	0
Bradford C.	Tr	08.68	68-70	44	0	0
Southend U.	Tr	01.71	70-71	47	0	0
Northampton T.	Tr	07.72	72	13	0	0

ROBERTS Hopkin **John**
Swansea, 30 June, 1918 W-1 (FB/IF)

League Club	Source	Date Signed	Seasons Played	Apps	Subs	Gls
Bolton W.	Cwmbwrla	04.36	37-50	162	-	19
Swansea C.	Tr	09.50	50	16	-	1

ROBERTS Jonathan Wesley
Pontypridd, 30 December, 1968 W Yth (G)

League Club	Source	Date Signed	Seasons Played	Apps	Subs	Gls
Cardiff C.	YT	11.87	87-88	9	0	0

ROBERTS Kenneth
Crewe, 10 March, 1931 (IF)

League Club	Source	Date Signed	Seasons Played	Apps	Subs	Gls
Aston Villa	Crewe Villa	08.51	51-53	42	-	7

ROBERTS Kenneth Owen
Ruabon, 27 March, 1936 (OR)

League Club	Source	Date Signed	Seasons Played	Apps	Subs	Gls
Wrexham (Am)	Jnrs	05.51	51	1	-	0
Aston Villa	Tr	05.53	53-57	38	-	3

ROBERTS Kevin John
Bristol, 25 July, 1955 (G)

League Club	Source	Date Signed	Seasons Played	Apps	Subs	Gls
Swindon T.	Welton Rov.	03.77	77	1	0	0

ROBERTS Lee John
Market Drayton, 23 March, 1957 (CD)

League Club	Source	Date Signed	Seasons Played	Apps	Subs	Gls
Shrewsbury T.	App	01.75	73-77	9	6	1
Exeter C.	L	03.77	76	5	2	0
Exeter C.	Tr	09.77	77-82	135	9	12

ROBERTS Maurice Ernest Stanley
Bristol, 5 July, 1922 Died 1993 (OL)

League Club	Source	Date Signed	Seasons Played	Apps	Subs	Gls
Brentford		08.46	46	10	-	0
Bristol C.	Tr	05.47				

ROBERTS Michael John
Birmingham, 21 May, 1960 (M)

League Club	Source	Date Signed	Seasons Played	Apps	Subs	Gls
Shrewsbury T.		07.78	78	0	1	0

League Club	Source	Date Signed	Seasons Played	Career Record Apps	Subs	Gls
ROBERTS Neil Wyn						
Wrexham, 7 April, 1978 W Yth						(F)
Wrexham	YT	07.96	97	29	5	8
ROBERTS Owen John						
Maerdy, 16 February, 1919						(G)
Plymouth Arg.		02.38				
Swansea C.	Aberaman	10.45	46-47	24	-	0
Newport Co.	Tr	08.48	48	7	-	0
ROBERTS Paul						
Bangor, 29 July, 1977 Wu21-1						(F)
Wrexham	Porthmadog	12.96	96	0	1	0
ROBERTS Paul						
West Ham, 27 April, 1962						(D)
Millwall	App	04.79	78-82	142	4	0
Brentford	Tr	09.83	83-84	61	1	0
Swindon T. (N/C)	Finland	09.85	85	25	2	0
Southend U.	Tr	07.86	86	38	0	0
Aldershot	Tr	08.87	87	36	3	0
Exeter C. (N/C)	Leytonstone & Ilford	12.88	88	3	0	0
Southend U.	Tr	01.89	88-89	53	1	0
Colchester U.	Fisher Ath.	09.91	92-93	63	0	1
ROBERTS Peter						
Chesterfield, 21 July, 1955						(W)
Chesterfield (N/C)	Jnrs	09.73	74-75	2	0	0
ROBERTS Peter Lorenga						
Sherburn (Yks), 16 July, 1925						(IF)
Leeds U.	Newcastle U. (Am)	09.46				
New Brighton	Tr	07.48	48	3	-	0
ROBERTS Philip Stanley						
Cardiff, 24 February, 1950 Wu23-6/W-4						(RB)
Bristol Rov.	App	11.68	69-72	174	1	6
Portsmouth	Tr	05.73	73-77	152	1	1
Hereford U.	Tr	07.78	78	3	0	0
Exeter C.	Tr	02.79	78-81	103	2	0
ROBERTS Robert						
Edinburgh, 2 September, 1940 Su23-1/SF Lge						(M)
Leicester C.	Motherwell	09.63	63-69	224	5	26
Mansfield T.	Tr	09.70	70-71	76	4	4
Colchester U.	Coventry C. (Coach)	07.73	73	0	2	0
ROBERTS Ronald						
Wrexham, 14 September, 1942 Wu23-2						(OL)
Wrexham	Jnrs	04.60	59-62	67	-	4
Tranmere Rov.	Tr	03.63	62-63	56	-	2
ROBERTS Stanley						
Wrexham, 10 April, 1921 Died 1995						(F)
Wrexham	Cross Street	09.46	46-47	27	-	10
New Brighton	Tr	07.48	48-50	103	-	25
ROBERTS Stuart William						
Chirk, 25 March, 1967 W Yth						(G)
Stoke C.	App	03.85	84	3	0	0
ROBERTS Thomas						
Liverpool, 28 July, 1927						(FB)
Blackburn Rov.	Skelmersdale U.	12.51	51-53	6	-	0
Watford	Tr	12.54	54	1	-	0
Chester C.	Tr	02.56	55	5	-	0
ROBERTS Thomas						
Liverpool, 27 December, 1945						(OL)
Everton	App	11.63				
Stockport Co.	Tr	03.65	64-65	20	0	0
Southport	Tr	07.66	66	4	0	1
ROBERTS Thomas Walter George						
Reading, 11 June, 1932						(F)
Birmingham C.		05.53				
Barrow	Tr	10.55	55-56	40	-	14
ROBERTS Trevor Edwin						
Bangor, 25 February, 1942 Died 1972 W Amat						(G)
Liverpool	Liverpool Univ.	06.63				
Southend U.	Tr	01.66	65-69	171	0	0
Cambridge U.	Tr	08.70	70-71	36	0	0
ROBERTS Trevor Lee						
Southampton, 9 May, 1961						(D)
Portsmouth	Southampton (App)	02.79	78-79	1	2	0

League Club	Source	Date Signed	Seasons Played	Career Record Apps	Subs	Gls
ROBERTS Walter						
Wrexham, 23 November, 1917						(HB)
Wrexham		08.38	38-47	60	-	1
Bournemouth	Tr	07.48	48-49	14	-	0
ROBERTS William Ernest						
Flint, 22 October, 1918 Died 1994						(G)
Rochdale		04.46	46-48	43	-	0
ROBERTS William John						
Bradford, 9 April, 1963						(F)
Rochdale (N/C)	Farsley Celtic	11.88	88	1	0	0
ROBERTS Winston						
Hartlepool, 5 July, 1939						(F)
Hartlepool U.	Caledonians	09.58	58	3	-	0
ROBERTSON Alexander (Sandy)						
Edinburgh, 26 April, 1971 Su21-1						(M)
Coventry C.	Glasgow Rangers	01.94	93-94	0	4	0
ROBERTSON Alistair Peter						
Linlithgow, 9 September, 1952 S Sch						(CD)
West Bromwich A.	App	09.69	69-85	504	2	8
Wolverhampton W.	Tr	09.86	86-89	107	0	0
ROBERTSON David						
Aberdeen, 17 October, 1968 Su21-7/S 'B'/S-3						(LB)
Leeds U.	Glasgow Rangers	05.97	97	24	2	0
ROBERTSON David						
Baillieston, 12 January, 1945						(OR)
Crewe Alex.	Motherwell	07.63	63	10	-	2
ROBERTSON Edward Harold Yeoman						
Edinburgh, 19 December, 1935 Died 1981						(FB)
Bury	Linithgow Rose	07.54	56-62	196	-	5
Wrexham	Tr	10.63	63	24	-	0
Tranmere Rov.	Tr	07.64	64-68	143	4	1
ROBERTSON George Jenkins						
Falkirk, 20 April, 1930						(FB)
Plymouth Arg.	Gairdoch Jnrs	01.50	50-63	359	-	2
ROBERTSON Graham Stuart						
Edinburgh, 2 November, 1976						(F)
Millwall	Raith Rov.	08.96	96-97	0	2	0
ROBERTSON James						
Leith, 7 July, 1940						(IR)
Newport Co.	Aberdeen	07.61	61	29	-	5
ROBERTSON James						
Gateshead, 24 November, 1969						(RB)
Carlisle U.	YT	07.88	87-89	10	3	0
ROBERTSON James Gillen						
Glasgow, 17 December, 1944 Su23-4/S-1						(W)
Tottenham H.	St Mirren	03.64	63-68	153	4	25
Arsenal	Tr	10.68	68-69	45	1	7
Ipswich T.	Tr	03.70	69-71	87	0	10
Stoke C.	Tr	06.72	72-76	99	15	12
Walsall	Tr	09.77	77	16	0	0
Crewe Alex.	Tr	09.78	78	32	1	0
ROBERTSON James Wright						
Falkirk, 20 February, 1929						(W)
Arsenal	Dunipace Thistle	06.48	51	1	-	0
Brentford	Tr	09.53	53-55	84	-	14
ROBERTSON John Craig						
Aberdeen, 15 July, 1928						(CF)
Portsmouth	Ayr U.	08.55	55	12	-	4
York C.	Tr	06.57	57	17	-	5
Barrow	Tr	08.58	58-61	156	-	48
ROBERTSON John Grant						
Edinburgh, 2 October, 1964 Su21-2/S 'B'/S-16						(F)
Newcastle U.	Hearts	04.88	88	7	5	0
ROBERTSON John Neilson						
Uddingston, 20 January, 1953 S Sch/S Yth/S-28						(LW)
Nottingham F.	App	05.70	70-82	374	13	61
Derby Co.	Tr	06.83	83-84	72	0	3
Nottingham F.	Tr	08.85	85	10	1	0
ROBERTSON John Nicholas						
Liverpool, 8 January, 1974						(CD)
Wigan Ath.	YT	07.92	92-95	108	4	4
Lincoln C.	Tr	12.95	95-97	38	2	1

ROBERTSON Archibald **Lamond (Lammie)**
Paisley, 27 September, 1947 (M)

League Club	Source	Date Signed	Seasons Played	Apps	Subs	Gls
Burnley	Jnrs	09.66				
Bury	Tr	06.68	68	3	2	0
Halifax T.	Tr	02.69	68-72	142	7	20
Brighton & H.A.	Tr	12.72	72-73	42	4	8
Exeter C.	Tr	05.74	74-77	132	1	25
Leicester C.	Tr	09.77	77	6	1	0
Peterborough U.	Tr	08.78	78	12	3	1
Bradford C.	Tr	01.79	78-80	41	2	3

ROBERTSON Leonard Verdun
Middlesbrough, 1 March, 1916 Died 1979 (IF)

League Club	Source	Date Signed	Seasons Played	Apps	Subs	Gls
Watford	Stockton	06.46	46	6	-	2
Hull C.	Tr	04.47	46-47	9	-	2
Accrington St.	Tr	07.48	48	3	-	0

ROBERTSON Mark William
Sydney, Australia, 6 April, 1977 (M)

League Club	Source	Date Signed	Seasons Played	Apps	Subs	Gls
Burnley	Marconi (Aus)	10.97	97	8	3	0

ROBERTSON Paul
Manchester, 5 February, 1972 (LB)

League Club	Source	Date Signed	Seasons Played	Apps	Subs	Gls
Stockport Co.	York C. (YT)	08.89	89-90	7	3	0
Bury	Tr	07.91	91-92	8	0	0
Doncaster Rov.	Runcorn	10.95	95-96	15	5	0

ROBERTSON Stuart
Glasgow, 29 September, 1959 (W)

League Club	Source	Date Signed	Seasons Played	Apps	Subs	Gls
Burnley	App	07.77	78-81	30	2	0
Exeter C.	Tr	03.82	81	5	1	0
Doncaster Rov. (N/C)	Tr	10.82	82	25	0	0

ROBERTSON Stuart John
Nottingham, 16 December, 1946 (CD)

League Club	Source	Date Signed	Seasons Played	Apps	Subs	Gls
Nottingham F.	Jnrs	08.64				
Doncaster Rov.	Tr	07.66	66-71	224	3	8
Northampton T.	Tr	05.72	72-78	254	0	27

ROBERTSON Thomas Smith
Coventry, 28 September, 1944 (W)

League Club	Source	Date Signed	Seasons Played	Apps	Subs	Gls
Crystal Palace	St Mirren	10.66	66	5	0	0

ROBERTSON William George
Glasgow, 4 November, 1936 (W)

League Club	Source	Date Signed	Seasons Played	Apps	Subs	Gls
Middlesbrough	Jnrs	11.53	54	5	-	2

ROBERTSON William Gibb
Glasgow, 13 November, 1928 Died 1973 (G)

League Club	Source	Date Signed	Seasons Played	Apps	Subs	Gls
Chelsea	Arthurlie	07.46	50-59	199	-	0
Leyton Orient	Tr	09.60	60-62	47	-	0

ROBERTSON William Harold
Crowthorne, 25 March, 1923 (G)

League Club	Source	Date Signed	Seasons Played	Apps	Subs	Gls
Chelsea	R.A.F. Lossiemouth	10.45	46-47	37	-	0
Birmingham C.	Tr	12.48	48-51	2	-	0
Stoke C.	Tr	06.52	52-59	238	-	0

ROBERTSON William James Tavendale
Montrose, 9 November, 1923 (HB)

League Club	Source	Date Signed	Seasons Played	Apps	Subs	Gls
Preston N.E.	Montrose Roselea	03.42	46-52	52	-	0
Southport	Tr	07.55	55	28	-	0

ROBINS Ian
Bury, 22 February, 1952 (W/F)

League Club	Source	Date Signed	Seasons Played	Apps	Subs	Gls
Oldham Ath.	App	02.70	69-76	202	18	40
Bury	Tr	07.77	77-78	49	0	5
Huddersfield T.	Tr	09.78	78-81	145	11	59

ROBINS Mark Gordon
Ashton-u-Lyne, 22 December, 1969 Eu21-6 (F)

League Club	Source	Date Signed	Seasons Played	Apps	Subs	Gls
Manchester U.	YT	12.86	88-91	19	29	11
Norwich C.	Tr	08.92	92-94	57	10	20
Leicester C.	Tr	01.95	94-96	40	16	12
Reading	L	08.97	97	5	0	0

ROBINSON Alan
Grantham, 2 December, 1955 (IF)

League Club	Source	Date Signed	Seasons Played	Apps	Subs	Gls
Sheffield Wed.	App	12.73				
Scunthorpe U.	Tr	08.75	75	1	0	0

ROBINSON Albert
Chester, 1 June, 1948 (IF)

League Club	Source	Date Signed	Seasons Played	Apps	Subs	Gls
Chester C.	Jnrs	05.68	67-68	4	1	0

ROBINSON Andrew Craig
Oldham, 10 March, 1966 (M)

League Club	Source	Date Signed	Seasons Played	Apps	Subs	Gls
Manchester U.	App	03.84				
Burnley	L	10.85	85	5	0	1
Bury	Tr	01.86	85-86	12	7	0
Carlisle U.	Tr	03.87	86-87	43	3	3

ROBINSON Anthony
Hebburn, 5 November, 1958 (W)

League Club	Source	Date Signed	Seasons Played	Apps	Subs	Gls
Hartlepool U. (N/C)	Blue Star	09.86	86	1	1	0

ROBINSON Bernard Cecil
Cambridge, 5 December, 1911 (WH)

League Club	Source	Date Signed	Seasons Played	Apps	Subs	Gls
Norwich C.	Kings Lynn	12.31	31-48	360	-	13

ROBINSON Brian Thomas Arthur
Paddington, 2 April, 1946 (G)

League Club	Source	Date Signed	Seasons Played	Apps	Subs	Gls
Peterborough U.	App	04.64	64-65	8	0	0

ROBINSON Carl Phillip
Llandrindod Wells, 13 October, 1976 W Yth/Wu21-6/W 'B' (M)

League Club	Source	Date Signed	Seasons Played	Apps	Subs	Gls
Wolverhampton W.	YT	07.95	96-97	28	6	3
Shrewsbury T.	L	03.96	95	2	2	0

ROBINSON Colin Roy
Birmingham, 15 May, 1960 (F)

League Club	Source	Date Signed	Seasons Played	Apps	Subs	Gls
Shrewsbury T.	Mile Oak Rov.	11.82	82-87	176	18	41
Birmingham C.	Tr	01.88	87-88	34	3	6
Hereford U.	Tr	08.89	89-90	41	23	6

ROBINSON Cyril
Nottingham, 4 March, 1929 (WH)

League Club	Source	Date Signed	Seasons Played	Apps	Subs	Gls
Blackpool	Mansfield T. (Am)	09.49	51-54	22	-	2
Bradford P.A.	Northwich Vic.	06.56	56-58	89	-	3
Southport	Tr	07.59	59	37	-	0

ROBINSON David
Birmingham, 14 July, 1948 (CD)

League Club	Source	Date Signed	Seasons Played	Apps	Subs	Gls
Birmingham C.	App	07.66	68-71	110	2	2
Walsall	Tr	02.73	72-76	164	1	3

ROBINSON David Alan
Middlesbrough, 14 January, 1965 (CD)

League Club	Source	Date Signed	Seasons Played	Apps	Subs	Gls
Hartlepool U.	Billingham T.	08.83	83-85	64	2	1
Halifax T.	Tr	08.86	86-88	72	0	1
Peterborough U.	Tr	07.89	89-92	95	0	9
Notts Co.	Tr	09.92	92-93	3	0	1

ROBINSON David John
Newcastle, 27 November, 1969 (F)

League Club	Source	Date Signed	Seasons Played	Apps	Subs	Gls
Newcastle U.	YT	06.88	88-91	0	8	0
Peterborough U.	L	02.91	90	7	0	3
Reading (N/C)	Tr	03.92	91	8	0	0
Blackpool	Tr	07.92	92-93	21	5	4
Cambridge U. (N/C)	Bishop Auckland	12.95	95	4	13	1

ROBINSON David Stanley
Exeter, 6 January, 1937 (W)

League Club	Source	Date Signed	Seasons Played	Apps	Subs	Gls
Exeter C.	Whipton	12.54	57-58	16	-	4
Oldham Ath.	Tr	07.59				

ROBINSON David William
Manchester, 25 November, 1921 (LH)

League Club	Source	Date Signed	Seasons Played	Apps	Subs	Gls
Shrewsbury T.	Manchester U. (Am)	08.49	50	10	-	0

ROBINSON Edward
Newcastle, 15 January, 1922 Died 1987 (FB)

League Club	Source	Date Signed	Seasons Played	Apps	Subs	Gls
Gateshead		11.45	46-52	90	-	7

ROBINSON Eric Michael
Manchester, 1 July, 1935 (F)

League Club	Source	Date Signed	Seasons Played	Apps	Subs	Gls
West Bromwich A.	Altrincham	03.57	57	1	-	0
Rotherham U.	Tr	01.59	58-59	13	-	1

ROBINSON Frederick James
Rotherham, 29 December, 1954 (LB)

League Club	Source	Date Signed	Seasons Played	Apps	Subs	Gls
Rotherham U.	App	01.73	73	4	0	0
Doncaster Rov.	Tr	10.75	75-78	111	8	3
Huddersfield T.	Tr	08.79	79-80	72	0	2

ROBINSON George Dennis
Liverpool, 28 May, 1937 (OR)

League Club	Source	Date Signed	Seasons Played	Apps	Subs	Gls
Southport	Unit Construction	02.59	58	2	-	0

ROBINSON George Frederick
Melton Mowbray, 17 June, 1925 (FB)

League Club	Source	Date Signed	Seasons Played	Apps	Subs	Gls
Notts Co.	Holwell Wks	08.44	46	29	-	0

ROBINSON George Henry
Heanor, 11 January, 1908 Died 1963 (IF)

League Club	Source	Date Signed	Seasons Played	Apps	Subs	Gls
Sunderland	Ilkeston U.	04.27	27-30	31	-	8
Charlton Ath.	Tr	06.31	31-46	238	-	42

League Club	Source	Date Signed	Seasons Played	Career Record Apps	Subs	Gls
ROBINSON Henry						
Southport, 14 September, 1947						(OR)
Blackpool	App	01.65				
Southport	Tr	02.66				
Burnley	Tr	09.66				
Newport Co.	Tr	11.67	67-68	39	1	3
ROBINSON Herbert						
Padiham, 30 April, 1922						(CF)
Accrington St.	Barnoldswick T.	12.46	46	5	-	4
ROBINSON Ian Brendan						
Nottingham, 25 August, 1978						(M)
Mansfield T.	YT	07.96	95-96	7	10	1
ROBINSON Jamie						
Liverpool, 26 February, 1972						(CD)
Liverpool	YT	06.90				
Barnsley	Tr	07.92	92-93	8	1	0
Carlisle U.	Tr	01.94	93-96	46	11	4
Torquay U.	Tr	07.97	97	46	0	0
ROBINSON John						
Chorley, 18 April, 1936						(OR)
Bury	Leyland Motors	09.54	54-59	120	-	21
Oldham Ath.	Tr	07.61	61	3	-	0
ROBINSON John						
Middlesbrough, 10 February, 1934						(IF)
Middlesbrough	Jnrs	10.51	53-54	3	-	0
Hartlepool U.	Tr	06.59	59	9	-	0
ROBINSON John						
Lurgan (NI), 2 April, 1920 Died 1981						(WH)
Wolverhampton W.	Glenavon	01.42				
Walsall	Tr	03.47	46-47	5	-	0
ROBINSON John (Jackie)						
Whitley Bay, 10 August, 1917 Died 1972 EF Lge/E-4						(IF)
Sheffield Wed.	Shiremoor	10.34	34-36	108	-	34
Sunderland	Tr	10.46	46-48	82	-	32
Lincoln C.	Tr	10.49	49	8	-	5
ROBINSON John (Jack) James						
Blackburn, 23 April, 1918 Died 1993						(G)
Accrington St.	Sacred Heart	05.35	35-36	16	-	0
Manchester C.	Tr	04.37	38-46	2	-	0
Bury	Tr	11.46	46	12	-	0
Southend U.	Tr	08.47	47	6	-	0
ROBINSON John Robert Campbell						
Zimbabwe, 29 August, 1971 Wu21-5/W-10						(W)
Brighton & H.A.	YT	04.89	89-92	57	5	6
Charlton Ath.	Tr	09.92	95-97	179	8	23
ROBINSON Joseph						
Lanchester, 14 November, 1918 Died 1988						(WH)
Norwich C.	Ouston U.	11.37	46	2	-	0
ROBINSON Joseph						
Morpeth, 4 March, 1919 Died 1991						(G)
Hartlepool U.	Hexham Hearts	05.38	38	11	-	0
Blackpool	Tr	07.46	47-48	25	-	0
Hull C.	Tr	02.49	48-52	70	-	0
ROBINSON Joseph William						
Chester-le-Street, 13 April, 1932						(F)
Newcastle U.	Jnrs	09.51				
Hartlepool U.	West Stanley	07.54	55-57	43	-	11
Gateshead	Tr	08.58	58	22	-	4
ROBINSON Keith						
Bolton, 30 December, 1937						(IF)
Oldham Ath.		09.58	58-60	40	-	4
ROBINSON Leonard James						
Nottingham, 1 October, 1946						(FB)
Notts Co.	Nottingham F. (Am)	03.64	63-64	4	-	0
ROBINSON Leslie						
Shirebrook, 1 March, 1967						(RB)
Mansfield T.	Chesterfield (Jnrs)	10.84	84-86	11	4	0
Stockport Co.	Tr	11.86	86-87	67	0	3
Doncaster Rov.	Tr	03.88	87-89	82	0	12
Oxford U.	Tr	03.90	89-97	289	5	3
ROBINSON Spencer **Liam**						
Bradford, 29 December, 1965						(F)
Huddersfield T.	Nottingham F. (App)	01.84	83-85	17	4	2

League Club	Source	Date Signed	Seasons Played	Career Record Apps	Subs	Gls
Tranmere Rov.	L	12.85	85	4	0	3
Bury	Tr	07.86	86-92	248	14	89
Bristol C.	Tr	07.93	93	31	10	4
Burnley	Tr	07.94	94-96	43	20	9
Scarborough	Tr	08.97	97	28	8	4
ROBINSON Mark James						
Rochdale, 21 November, 1968						(RB/M)
West Bromwich A.	App	11.86	85-86	2	0	0
Barnsley	Tr	06.87	87-92	117	20	6
Newcastle U.	Tr	03.93	92-93	14	11	0
Swindon T.	Tr	07.94	94-97	155	1	3
ROBINSON Mark Jeffrey						
Basford, 26 November, 1960						(F)
Notts Co.	Ilkeston T.	01.85	84-85	12	14	1
ROBINSON Mark William						
Middlesbrough, 22 October, 1961						(M)
Middlesbrough	App	10.79				
Hartlepool U.	Hull C. (N/C)	01.83	82-83	34	1	4
ROBINSON Martin John						
Ilford, 17 July, 1957						(F/W)
Tottenham H.	App	05.75	75-77	5	1	2
Charlton Ath.	Tr	02.78	77-84	218	10	58
Reading	L	09.82	82	6	0	2
Gillingham	Tr	10.84	84-86	91	5	24
Southend U.	Tr	07.87	87-88	43	13	14
Cambridge U.	Tr	08.89	89	7	9	1
ROBINSON Matthew Richard						
Exeter, 23 December, 1974						(LM)
Southampton	YT	07.93	94-97	3	11	0
Portsmouth	Tr	02.98	97	15	0	0
ROBINSON Maurice						
Newark, 9 November, 1929						(OL)
Leeds U.		04.49				
Doncaster Rov.	Gainsborough Trin.	12.52	53	18	-	7
Northampton T.	Kettering T.	06.57	57	11	-	2
ROBINSON Michael Anthony						
Sunderland, 30 October, 1968						(FB)
Newcastle U.	YT	08.87				
Darlington	Tr	07.88	88	0	1	0
ROBINSON Michael John						
Leicester, 12 July, 1958 IR-23						(F)
Preston N.E.	App	07.76	75-78	45	3	15
Manchester C.	Tr	07.79	79	29	1	8
Brighton & H.A.	Tr	07.80	80-82	111	2	37
Liverpool	Tr	08.83	83-84	26	4	6
Queens Park R.	Tr	12.84	84-86	41	7	5
ROBINSON Neil						
Liverpool, 20 April, 1957						(RB/M)
Everton	App	05.74	75-78	13	3	1
Swansea C.	Tr	10.79	79-84	114	9	7
Grimsby T.	Tr	09.84	84-87	109	0	6
Darlington	Tr	07.88	88	36	2	1
ROBINSON Joseph **Norman**						
Middlesbrough, 5 January, 1921 Died 1990						(CH)
Middlesbrough	South Bank St Peter	01.46	46-47	16	-	0
Grimsby T.	Tr	06.48	48	5	-	0
ROBINSON Paul						
Hampstead, 5 January, 1963 E Sch/E Yth						(LB)
Millwall	App	01.80	79-83	56	3	2
ROBINSON Paul						
Scarborough, 2 January, 1974						(G)
Sheffield Wed.	YT	07.92				
Scarborough	Tr	08.93	93	3	1	0
ROBINSON Paul Derrick						
Sunderland, 20 November, 1978						(F)
Darlington	YT	07.97	95-97	7	19	3
Newcastle U.	Tr	03.98				
ROBINSON Paul James						
Nottingham, 21 February, 1971						(F)
Scarborough	Bury (YT)	05.89	89	13	7	3
Plymouth Arg.	Tr	05.90	90	7	4	3
Hereford U.	Tr	06.91	91	7	4	0
ROBINSON Paul Peter						
Watford, 14 December, 1978						(LB)
Watford	YT	02.97	96-97	22	12	2

ROBINSON Peter
Ashington, 4 September, 1957 E Semi Pro (CD)

League Club	Source	Date Signed	Seasons Played	Apps	Subs	Gls
Burnley	Jnrs	06.76	76-79	48	7	3
Rochdale (N/C)	Blyth Spartans	03.85	84	9	3	0
Darlington	Tr	08.85	85-87	110	2	5
Halifax T.	L	12.85	85	3	2	0

ROBINSON Peter
Manchester, 29 January, 1922 (WH)

League Club	Source	Date Signed	Seasons Played	Apps	Subs	Gls
Manchester C.	Jnrs	05.40	46	1	-	0
Chesterfield	Tr	10.47	47-48	60	-	0
Notts Co.	Buxton	02.50	49-52	82	-	1

ROBINSON Peter John
St Ives, 11 April, 1949 (D)

League Club	Source	Date Signed	Seasons Played	Apps	Subs	Gls
Southend U.	Cambridge U.	03.69	68-69	1	4	0

ROBINSON Philip Brian
Doncaster, 21 November, 1942 (W)

League Club	Source	Date Signed	Seasons Played	Apps	Subs	Gls
Huddersfield T.	Montrose Vic.	04.60				
Doncaster Rov.	Tr	08.61	61-65	157	0	19
Bradford P.A.	Tr	07.66	66-68	108	8	8
Darlington	Tr	07.69	69	26	1	4

ROBINSON Philip John
Stafford, 6 January, 1967 (M)

League Club	Source	Date Signed	Seasons Played	Apps	Subs	Gls
Aston Villa	App	01.85	86	2	1	1
Wolverhampton W.	Tr	06.87	87-88	63	8	8
Notts Co.	Tr	08.89	89-91	65	1	5
Birmingham C.	L	03.91	90	9	0	0
Huddersfield T.	Tr	09.92	92-93	74	1	5
Northampton T.	L	09.94	94	14	0	0
Chesterfield	Tr	12.94	94-95	60	1	17
Notts Co.	Tr	08.96	96-97	63	14	5

ROBINSON Raymond
Durham, 2 December, 1950 (IF)

League Club	Source	Date Signed	Seasons Played	Apps	Subs	Gls
Preston N.E.	App	12.68	68	2	0	0

ROBINSON Richard (Dick)
South Shields, 19 January, 1927 EF Lge (FB)

League Club	Source	Date Signed	Seasons Played	Apps	Subs	Gls
Middlesbrough	Jnrs	04.45	46-58	390	-	1
Barrow	Tr	06.59	59-62	139	-	0

ROBINSON Robert
Ashington, 23 June, 1921 (G)

League Club	Source	Date Signed	Seasons Played	Apps	Subs	Gls
Sunderland	Newbiggin	02.47	47-51	31	-	0
Newcastle U.	Tr	08.52	52	5	-	0

ROBINSON Ronald
Sunderland, 22 October, 1966 (LB)

League Club	Source	Date Signed	Seasons Played	Apps	Subs	Gls
Ipswich T.	S.C. Vaux	10.84				
Leeds U.	Tr	11.85	85-86	27	0	0
Doncaster Rov.	Tr	02.87	86-88	76	2	5
West Bromwich A.	Tr	03.89	88	1	0	0
Rotherham U.	Tr	08.89	89-91	86	0	2
Peterborough U.	Tr	12.91	91-92	44	3	0
Exeter C.	Tr	08.93	93-94	37	2	1
Huddersfield T.	L	01.94	93	2	0	0
Scarborough	Tr	08.95	95	1	0	0

ROBINSON Simon William
West Bromwich, 6 April, 1965 (M)

League Club	Source	Date Signed	Seasons Played	Apps	Subs	Gls
Blackpool	Alvechurch	12.90				
Walsall (N/C)	Alvechurch	12.91	91	0	1	0

ROBINSON Stephen
Lisburn, 10 December, 1974 NI Sch/NI Yth/NIu21-1/NI 'B'/NI-1 (FM)

League Club	Source	Date Signed	Seasons Played	Apps	Subs	Gls
Tottenham H.	YT	01.93	93	1	1	0
Bournemouth	Tr	10.94	94-97	145	13	29

ROBINSON Steven Eli
Nottingham, 17 January, 1975 (M)

League Club	Source	Date Signed	Seasons Played	Apps	Subs	Gls
Birmingham C.	YT	06.93	94-97	28	12	0
Peterborough U.	L	03.96	95	5	0	0

ROBINSON Steven Martin
Sheffield, 14 June, 1964 (M)

League Club	Source	Date Signed	Seasons Played	Apps	Subs	Gls
Chesterfield	App	06.82	81-82	8	1	0

ROBINSON Stuart Alan
Middlesbrough, 16 January, 1959 (W)

League Club	Source	Date Signed	Seasons Played	Apps	Subs	Gls
Newcastle U.	App	07.77	77-78	11	1	2
Aldershot	Tr	07.80	80-82	71	6	10

ROBINSON Terence
Woodhams, 8 November, 1929 E Amat (FB)

League Club	Source	Date Signed	Seasons Played	Apps	Subs	Gls
Brentford (Am)	Loughborough College	09.54	54-56	35	-	1
Northampton T. (Am)	Tr	07.57	57	13	-	0

ROBINSON Terence Allan Charles
Bletchley, 24 March, 1954 (F)

League Club	Source	Date Signed	Seasons Played	Apps	Subs	Gls
Luton T.	App	03.72				
Cambridge U.	L	09.72	72	6	0	1
Crewe Alex.	Tr	12.72	72-73	7	4	1

ROBINSON William
Manchester, 17 November, 1925 Died 1953 (LB/OL)

League Club	Source	Date Signed	Seasons Played	Apps	Subs	Gls
Stockport Co.		08.49	49	9	-	2
Accrington St.	Tr	12.50	50-52	96	-	2

ROBINSON William
Whitburn, 4 April, 1919 Died 1992 (CF)

League Club	Source	Date Signed	Seasons Played	Apps	Subs	Gls
Sunderland	Jnrs	04.36	37-38	24	-	14
Charlton Ath.	Tr	05.46	46-48	52	-	16
West Ham U.	Tr	01.49	48-51	101	-	60

ROBLEDO Edward (Ted) Oliver
Chile, 26 July, 1928 Died 1970 (WH)

League Club	Source	Date Signed	Seasons Played	Apps	Subs	Gls
Barnsley	Jnrs	03.46	47-48	5	-	0
Newcastle U.	Tr	02.49	49-52	37	-	0
Notts Co.	Cola Cola (Chile)	09.57	57	2	-	0

ROBLEDO George Oliver
Chile, 14 April, 1926 Died 1989 Chilean Int (IF)

League Club	Source	Date Signed	Seasons Played	Apps	Subs	Gls
Barnsley	Huddersfield T. (Am)	04.43	46-48	105	-	45
Newcastle U.	Tr	01.49	48-52	146	-	82

ROBLEY Keith
Cockermouth, 3 June, 1944 (W)

League Club	Source	Date Signed	Seasons Played	Apps	Subs	Gls
Workington (Am)	Corinthian Jnrs	08.65	65	2	0	0

ROBSHAW Henry (Harry) William
Edmonton, 10 May, 1927 Died 1990 (WH)

League Club	Source	Date Signed	Seasons Played	Apps	Subs	Gls
Tottenham H.	Jnrs	11.48	51	1	-	0
Reading	Tr	02.53	52-53	20	-	1

ROBSON Albert Proud
Crook, 14 November, 1916 Died 1990 (F)

League Club	Source	Date Signed	Seasons Played	Apps	Subs	Gls
Crystal Palace	Godalming	12.34	36-47	85	-	22

ROBSON Benjamin Thomas
Gateshead, 31 January, 1922 (WH)

League Club	Source	Date Signed	Seasons Played	Apps	Subs	Gls
Southport	Aberdeen	08.49	49	2	-	0

ROBSON Bryan
Witton Gilbert (Dm), 11 January, 1957 E Yth/Eu21-7/E'B'/EF Lge/E-90 (M)

League Club	Source	Date Signed	Seasons Played	Apps	Subs	Gls
West Bromwich A.	App	08.74	74-81	194	4	39
Manchester U.	Tr	10.81	81-93	326	19	74
Middlesbrough	Tr	05.94	94-96	23	2	1

ROBSON Bryan (Pop) Stanley
Sunderland, 11 November, 1945 Eu23-2/EF Lge (F)

League Club	Source	Date Signed	Seasons Played	Apps	Subs	Gls
Newcastle U.	Jnrs	11.62	64-70	205	1	82
West Ham U.	Tr	02.71	70-73	120	0	47
Sunderland	Tr	07.74	74-76	90	0	34
West Ham U.	Tr	10.76	76-78	107	0	47
Sunderland	Tr	06.79	79-80	49	3	23
Carlisle U.	Tr	03.81	80-81	48	0	21
Chelsea	Tr	08.82	82	11	4	3
Carlisle U.	L	03.83	82	11	0	4
Sunderland	Tr	08.83	83	7	5	3
Carlisle U.	Tr	07.84	84-85	10	3	1

ROBSON David Mark
Hesleden (Dm), 5 October, 1966 (M)

League Club	Source	Date Signed	Seasons Played	Apps	Subs	Gls
Hartlepool U. (N/C)		11.86	86	1	0	0

ROBSON James Donald
Winlaton, 5 February, 1934 (F)

League Club	Source	Date Signed	Seasons Played	Apps	Subs	Gls
Doncaster Rov.		07.51				
Gateshead	Tr	09.53	53-56	34	-	11

ROBSON Gary
Chester-le-Street, 6 July, 1965 (M)

League Club	Source	Date Signed	Seasons Played	Apps	Subs	Gls
West Bromwich A.	App	05.83	82-92	184	34	28
Bradford C.	Tr	07.93	93-95	72	3	3

ROBSON Glenn Alan
Sunderland, 25 September, 1977 (F)

League Club	Source	Date Signed	Seasons Played	Apps	Subs	Gls
Rochdale	Murton	11.96	96-97	0	10	0

ROBSON James
Pelton, 23 January, 1939 Eu23-1 (IF)

League Club	Source	Date Signed	Seasons Played	Apps	Subs	Gls
Burnley	Jnrs	01.56	56-64	202	-	79
Blackpool	Tr	03.65	64-67	60	3	13
Barnsley	Tr	01.68	67-69	87	0	15
Bury	Tr	08.70	70-72	100	3	3

ROBSON John Dixon
Consett, 15 July, 1950 Eu23-7/EF Lge (FB)

League Club	Source	Date Signed	Seasons Played	Apps	Subs	Gls
Derby Co.	Birtley Y.C.	10.67	67-72	170	1	3
Aston Villa	Tr	10.72	72-77	141	3	1

ROBSON John Douglas
Washington, 20 July, 1942 (CH)

League Club	Source	Date Signed	Seasons Played	Apps	Subs	Gls
Darlington		10.62	62-64	33	-	0

ROBSON Keith
Hetton-le-Hole, 15 November, 1953 (W)

League Club	Source	Date Signed	Seasons Played	Apps	Subs	Gls
Newcastle U.	Jnrs	05.71	72-73	14	0	3
West Ham U.	Tr	09.74	74-76	65	3	13
Cardiff C.	Tr	08.77	77	21	0	5
Norwich C.	Tr	02.78	77-80	61	4	13
Leicester C.	Tr	09.81	81	8	1	0
Carlisle U.	L	03.83	82	10	1	4

ROBSON Lancelot
Newcastle, 27 December, 1939 (CF)

League Club	Source	Date Signed	Seasons Played	Apps	Subs	Gls
Newcastle U.	Stannington	10.58				
Darlington	Tr	07.60	60-63	144	-	49
Darlington	(Retired)	07.68	68-69	69	0	17
Hartlepool U.	Tr	02.70	69	8	0	2

ROBSON Charles **Leslie**
South Shields, 1 November, 1931 (OR)

League Club	Source	Date Signed	Seasons Played	Apps	Subs	Gls
Hull C.	North Hull Jnrs	05.50	51	3	-	1
Darlington	Tr	05.53	53-54	68	-	19
Liverpool	Tr	07.55				
Crewe Alex.	Tr	01.56	55	14	-	2

ROBSON Mark Andrew
Newham, 22 May, 1969 (LW)

League Club	Source	Date Signed	Seasons Played	Apps	Subs	Gls
Exeter C.	App	12.86	86	26	0	7
Tottenham H.	Tr	07.87	88-89	3	5	0
Reading	L	03.88	87	5	2	0
Watford	L	10.89	89	1	0	0
Plymouth Arg.	L	12.89	89	7	0	0
Exeter C.	L	01.92	91	7	1	1
West Ham U.	Tr	08.92	92-93	42	5	8
Charlton Ath.	Tr	11.93	93-96	79	26	9
Notts Co.	Tr	06.97	97	26	2	4

ROBSON Matthew
Easington, 29 December, 1954 (F)

League Club	Source	Date Signed	Seasons Played	Apps	Subs	Gls
Sunderland	App	01.72				
Darlington	L	03.75	74	1	0	0

ROBSON Thomas **Raymond**
Newcastle, 11 August, 1928 (FB)

League Club	Source	Date Signed	Seasons Played	Apps	Subs	Gls
Cardiff C.		02.49				
Bradford C.	Tr	07.50	50-51	10	-	0
Grimsby T.	Tr	06.52	52-54	58	-	2

ROBSON Robert William
Sacriston (Dm), 18 February, 1933 Eu23-1/EF Lge/E-20 (WH/IF)

League Club	Source	Date Signed	Seasons Played	Apps	Subs	Gls
Fulham	Langley Park Jnrs	05.50	50-55	152	-	68
West Bromwich A.	Tr	03.56	55-61	239	-	56
Fulham	Tr	08.62	62-66	192	0	9

ROBSON Ronald
Sunderland, 12 September, 1932 Died 1993 (HB)

League Club	Source	Date Signed	Seasons Played	Apps	Subs	Gls
Gateshead	Albion S.C.	06.57	57-58	7	-	0

ROBSON Stewart Ian
Billericay, 6 November, 1964 E Yth/Eu21-8 (M)

League Club	Source	Date Signed	Seasons Played	Apps	Subs	Gls
Arsenal	App	11.81	81-86	150	1	16
West Ham U.	Tr	01.87	86-90	68	1	4
Coventry C.	Tr	03.91	90-93	55	2	3

ROBSON Thomas
Sunderland, 1 February, 1936 (CH)

League Club	Source	Date Signed	Seasons Played	Apps	Subs	Gls
Sunderland	Jnrs	09.57	58-59	5	-	0
Darlington	Tr	08.60	60	1	-	0

ROBSON Thomas Henry
Gateshead, 31 July, 1944 E Yth (W)

League Club	Source	Date Signed	Seasons Played	Apps	Subs	Gls
Northampton T.	App	08.61	61-65	73	1	20
Chelsea	Tr	12.65	65	6	1	0
Newcastle U.	Tr	12.66	66-68	46	2	11
Peterborough U.	Tr	11.68	68-80	440	42	111

ROBSON Trevor
Stoke, 4 January, 1959 (F)

League Club	Source	Date Signed	Seasons Played	Apps	Subs	Gls
Port Vale	App	01.77	75	0	1	0

ROBSON William Henderson
Whitehaven, 13 October, 1931 (IF)

League Club	Source	Date Signed	Seasons Played	Apps	Subs	Gls
Workington	Kells	08.51	51-59	130	-	55
Carlisle U.	Tr	11.59	59	12	-	1

ROBY Donald
Wigan, 15 November, 1933 (OR)

League Club	Source	Date Signed	Seasons Played	Apps	Subs	Gls
Notts Co.	Jnrs	02.51	50-60	226	-	37
Derby Co.	Tr	08.61	61-64	70	-	6

ROCASTLE David Carlyle
Lewisham, 2 May, 1967 Eu21-14/E'B'/E-14 (M)

League Club	Source	Date Signed	Seasons Played	Apps	Subs	Gls
Arsenal	App	12.84	85-91	204	14	24
Leeds U.	Tr	08.92	92-93	17	8	2
Manchester C.	Tr	12.93	93	21	0	2
Chelsea	Tr	08.94	94-95	27	2	0
Norwich C.	L	01.97	96	11	0	0
Hull C.	L	10.97	97	10	0	1

ROCCA Jonathan Christian
Sheffield, 4 November, 1970 (RB)

League Club	Source	Date Signed	Seasons Played	Apps	Subs	Gls
Scarborough	YT	06.91	91	3	0	0

ROCHE David
Newcastle, 13 December, 1970 (M)

League Club	Source	Date Signed	Seasons Played	Apps	Subs	Gls
Newcastle U.	YT	08.88	88-91	23	13	0
Peterborough U.	L	01.93	92	4	0	0
Doncaster Rov.	Tr	10.93	93-94	49	1	8
Southend U.	Tr	03.95	94	0	4	0

ROCHE John Anthony
Poplar, 18 May, 1932 Died 1988 (F)

League Club	Source	Date Signed	Seasons Played	Apps	Subs	Gls
Millwall	Margate	06.57	57-58	25	-	14
Crystal Palace	Tr	05.59	59	36	-	11

ROCHE Patrick Joseph Christopher
Dublin, 4 January, 1951 IRu23-1/IR-7 (G)

League Club	Source	Date Signed	Seasons Played	Apps	Subs	Gls
Manchester U.	Shelbourne	10.73	74-81	46	0	0
Brentford	Tr	08.82	82-83	71	0	0
Halifax T.	Tr	07.84	84-88	184	0	0

ROCHE Stephen Michael
Dublin, 2 October, 1978 IR Sch/IR Yth (LB/M)

League Club	Source	Date Signed	Seasons Played	Apps	Subs	Gls
Millwall	Belvedere	10.94	95-97	4	4	0

ROCHFORD William
Airdrie, 27 May, 1913 Died 1984 EF Lge (FB)

League Club	Source	Date Signed	Seasons Played	Apps	Subs	Gls
Portsmouth	Cuckfield	08.31	32-38	128	-	1
Southampton	Tr	07.46	46-49	128	-	0
Colchester U.	Tr	07.50	50	2	-	0

ROCKETT Jason
London, 26 September, 1969 (CD)

League Club	Source	Date Signed	Seasons Played	Apps	Subs	Gls
Rotherham U.	British Universities	03.92				
Scarborough	Tr	08.93	93-97	171	1	11

ROCKETT Trevor Dennis
Finchampstead, 8 October, 1951 (G)

League Club	Source	Date Signed	Seasons Played	Apps	Subs	Gls
Aldershot	Fleet	07.76	76-77	5	0	0

RODAWAY William Vincent
Liverpool, 26 September, 1954 E Sch (CD)

League Club	Source	Date Signed	Seasons Played	Apps	Subs	Gls
Burnley	App	09.71	71-80	201	2	1
Peterborough U.	Tr	07.81	81-82	80	1	0
Blackpool	Tr	08.83	83	41	0	0
Tranmere Rov.	Tr	07.84	84-85	55	3	5
Burnley	Tr	08.86	86	44	0	2

RODDOM Joseph Norman
Spennymoor, 16 May, 1924 (WH)

League Club	Source	Date Signed	Seasons Played	Apps	Subs	Gls
Chesterfield	Blyth Spartans	01.48				
Darlington	Tr	06.50	50	6	-	0

RODGER Graham
Glasgow, 1 April, 1967 Eu21-4 (CD)

League Club	Source	Date Signed	Seasons Played	Apps	Subs	Gls
Wolverhampton W.	App	•	83	1	0	0
Coventry C.	Tr	02.85	85-88	31	5	2
Luton T.	Tr	07.89	89-91	27	1	2
Grimsby T.	Tr	01.92	91-97	134	12	11

RODGER James McPhail
Cleland, 15 September, 1933 (F)

League Club	Source	Date Signed	Seasons Played	Apps	Subs	Gls
Newport Co. (L)	St Mirren	02.57	56-57	5	-	1

RODGER Richard John
Hemsworth, 1 July, 1936 (W)

League Club	Source	Date Signed	Seasons Played	Apps	Subs	Gls
Halifax T.	Jnrs	09.54	54-56	15	-	3

RODGER Simon Lee
Shoreham, 3 October, 1971 (LM)

League Club	Source	Date Signed	Seasons Played	Apps	Subs	Gls
Crystal Palace	YT	07.90	91-97	133	22	7
Manchester C.	L	10.96	96	8	0	1
Stoke C.	L	02.97	96	5	0	0

League Club	Source	Date Signed	Seasons Played	Career Record Apps	Subs	Gls

RODGER William
Dalkeith, 24 June, 1947 (IF)

Bradford P.A.	Newtongrange Star	04.65	65-66	6	2	0

RODGERS Alwyn
Chesterfield, 29 May, 1938 (FB)

Doncaster Rov.		11.56	58	1	-	0

RODGERS Arnold William
Rotherham, 5 December, 1923 Died 1993 (CF)

Huddersfield T.	Wickersley	03.42	46-49	28	-	17
Bristol C.	Tr	10.49	49-55	195	-	106
Shrewsbury T.	Tr	06.56	56	13	-	3

RODGERS Clifford Frederick
Rotherham, 3 October, 1921 Died 1990 (LB)

York C.	R.A.F. Pocklington	11.45	46	26	-	0

RODGERS David Michael
Bristol, 28 February, 1952 E Sch (CD)

Bristol C.	Jnrs	07.69	70-81	190	2	15
Torquay U. (N/C)	Tr	02.82	81	5	0	1
Lincoln C. (N/C)	Tr	03.82	81	3	0	0

RODGERS Mark
Broxburn, 20 September, 1967 (M)

Preston N.E. (N/C)	YT	09.85	85	1	0	0

RODGERSON Alan Ralph
Potters Bar, 19 March, 1939 E Sch (IF)

Middlesbrough	Jnrs	05.56	58-60	13	-	3

RODGERSON Ian
Hereford, 9 April, 1966 (W/RB)

Hereford U.	Jnrs	06.85	85-87	95	5	6
Cardiff C.	Tr	08.88	88-90	98	1	4
Birmingham C.	Tr	01.91	90-92	87	8	13
Sunderland	Tr	07.93	93-94	5	5	0
Cardiff C.	Tr	07.95	95-96	43	12	1

RODI Joseph
Glasgow, 23 July, 1913 Died 1965 (OR)

Grimsby T.		04.45				
Rochdale	Boston U.	04.46	46	9	-	3

RODON Christopher Peter
Swansea, 9 June, 1963 (F)

Brighton & H.A.	Pontardawe	01.83	82	0	1	0
Cardiff C.	L	08.83	83	4	0	0

RODON Peter Clive
Swansea, 5 February, 1945 (CF)

Swansea C.	Jnrs	11.62				
Bradford C.	Tr	07.64	64-66	60	4	15

RODOSTHENOUS Michael
Islington, 25 August, 1976 (F)

West Bromwich A.	YT	07.95	96	0	1	0
Cambridge U. (N/C)	Tr	10.97	97	0	2	0

RODRIGUES Peter Joseph
Cardiff, 21 January, 1944 W Sch/Wu23-5/W-40 (RB)

Cardiff C.	Jnrs	05.61	63-65	85	0	2
Leicester C.	Tr	01.66	65-70	139	1	6
Sheffield Wed.	Tr	10.70	70-74	162	0	2
Southampton	Tr	07.75	75-76	59	0	3

RODWELL Anthony
Southport, 26 August, 1962 (RW)

Blackpool	Colne Dynamoes	08.90	90-94	137	5	17
Scarborough	Tr	12.94	94	6	2	1
Wigan Ath.	L	01.95	94	5	0	1

RODWELL James Richard
Lincoln, 20 November, 1970 (CD)

Darlington	YT	●	88	1	0	0

RODWELL Joseph
Southport, 13 October, 1928 (W)

Accrington St. (Am)	Birkdale Ath.	09.48	48	2	-	0

ROE John
Broxburn, 7 January, 1938 Died 1996 (FB)

Colchester U.	West Calder	07.58	59	2	-	0

ROE Maurice **Leonard**
Hayes, 11 January, 1932 (WH)

Brentford	Ruislip Manor	05.51	54-56	7	-	0

League Club	Source	Date Signed	Seasons Played	Career Record Apps	Subs	Gls

ROEDER Glenn Victor
Woodford, 13 December, 1955 E 'B' (CD)

Leyton Orient	App	12.73	74-77	107	8	4
Queens Park R.	Tr	08.78	78-83	157	0	17
Notts Co.	L	11.83	83	4	0	0
Newcastle U.	Tr	12.83	83-88	193	0	8
Watford	Tr	07.89	89-90	74	4	2
Leyton Orient (N/C)	Tr	01.92	91	6	2	0
Gillingham (N/C)	Purfleet	11.92	92	6	0	0

ROFE Dennis
Epping, 1 June, 1950 Eu23-1 (LB)

Leyton Orient	App	02.68	67-72	170	1	6
Leicester C.	Tr	08.72	72-79	290	0	6
Chelsea	Tr	02.80	79-81	58	1	0
Southampton	Tr	07.82	82-83	18	2	0

ROFFEY William Robert
Stepney, 6 February, 1954 (FB)

Crystal Palace	App	05.71	72-73	24	0	0
Leyton Orient	Tr	10.73	73-83	324	4	8
Brentford	L	03.84	83	13	0	1
Millwall	Tr	08.84	84-85	36	1	2

ROFFI Guido (George) Thomaso
Ynysybwl, 6 March, 1924 Died 1973 (IF/WH)

Newport Co.	Tynte Rov.	02.47	46-50	112	-	27

ROGAN Anton Gerard Patrick
Belfast, 25 March, 1966 NI-18 (D)

Sunderland	Glasgow Celtic	10.91	91-92	45	1	1
Oxford U.	Tr	08.93	93-94	56	2	3
Millwall	Tr	08.95	95-96	30	6	8
Blackpool	Tr	07.97	97	1	0	0

ROGAN Leslie **Michael**
Fleetwood, 29 May, 1948 (G)

Workington	App	08.66	66-76	390	0	0
Stockport Co.	Tr	06.77	77-80	73	0	0
Crewe Alex.	L	03.79	78	3	0	0

ROGERS Alan
Liverpool, 3 January, 1977 Eu21-3 (LB)

Tranmere Rov.	Tr	07.95	95-96	53	4	2
Nottingham F.	Tr	07.97	97	46	0	1

ROGERS Alan James
Plymouth, 6 July, 1954 (LW)

Plymouth Arg.	App	07.72	73-78	107	10	5
Portsmouth	Tr	07.79	79-83	154	7	15
Southend U.	Tr	03.84	83-85	84	3	4
Cardiff C.	Tr	08.86	86	25	2	1

ROGERS Alfred
Ecclesfield, 10 April, 1921 Died 1992 (IF)

Sheffield Wed.	Birley Carr	06.42	46-49	30	-	8

ROGERS Alfred Harper
Willenhall, 17 January, 1920 Died 1981 (FB)

Aldershot	West Bromwich A. (Am)	05.46	46-53	317	-	5

ROGERS Andrew
Chatteris, 1 December, 1956 (LW)

Peterborough U.	Chatteris T.	07.76	75-77	25	4	1
Southampton	Hampton	02.80	79-81	0	5	0
Plymouth Arg.	Tr	09.81	81-84	159	4	15
Reading	Tr	07.85	85-86	44	0	5
Southend U.	Tr	10.86	86-87	40	5	2

ROGERS Darren John
Birmingham, 9 April, 1970 (LB)

West Bromwich A.	YT	07.88	90-91	7	7	1
Birmingham C.	Tr	07.92	92-93	15	3	0
Wycombe W.	L	11.93	93	0	1	0
Walsall	Tr	07.94	94-97	48	10	0

ROGERS David Raymond
Liverpool, 25 August, 1975 (LB)

Tranmere Rov.	YT	07.94				
Chester C.	Tr	08.95	95-96	18	7	1

ROGERS Dennis
Chorley, 28 March, 1936 (G)

Accrington St.	Netherfield	03.59	58	3	-	0

ROGERS Donald Edward
Paulton, 25 October, 1945 E Yth/Eu23-2/EF Lge (W)

Swindon T.	App	10.62	62-72	400	0	146
Crystal Palace	Tr	11.72	72-74	69	1	28

League Club	Source	Date Signed	Seasons Played	Apps	Subs	Gls
Queens Park R.	Tr	09.74	74	13	5	5
Swindon T.	Tr	03.76	75-76	11	1	2

ROGERS Edward Eamonn
Dublin, 16 April, 1947 IRu23-1IR-19 (W)

League Club	Source	Date Signed	Seasons Played	Apps	Subs	Gls
Blackburn Rov.	App	05.65	65-71	159	6	30
Charlton Ath.	Tr	10.71	71-72	37	2	3
Northampton T.	L	11.72	72	4	0	1

ROGERS Ehud (Tim)
Chirk, 15 October, 1909 Died 1996 W Amat (OR)

League Club	Source	Date Signed	Seasons Played	Apps	Subs	Gls
Wrexham	Oswestry T.	05.34	34	11	-	2
Arsenal	Tr	01.35	34-35	16	-	5
Newcastle U.	Tr	06.36	36-38	56	-	10
Swansea C.	Tr	05.39				
Wrexham	Tr	12.45	46	1	-	0

ROGERS Graham Reginald
Newport, 5 September, 1955 (D)

League Club	Source	Date Signed	Seasons Played	Apps	Subs	Gls
Newport Co.	App	09.73	74	0	4	0
Newport Co. (N/C)	Forest Green Rov.	08.85	85	6	1	0

ROGERS James Richard
Wednesbury, 31 December, 1929 Died 1997 (F)

League Club	Source	Date Signed	Seasons Played	Apps	Subs	Gls
Wolverhampton W.	Rubery Owen	05.48				
Bristol C.	Tr	05.50	50-56	155	-	74
Coventry C.	Tr	12.56	56-58	77	-	27
Bristol C.	Tr	12.58	58-61	115	-	28

ROGERS John Charles
Liverpool, 16 September, 1950 E Semi Pro (F)

League Club	Source	Date Signed	Seasons Played	Apps	Subs	Gls
Port Vale	Wigan Ath.	10.76	76	25	1	6
Wigan Ath.	Altrincham	08.82	82	4	2	2

ROGERS Kenneth John
Chatham, 21 November, 1954 (LW)

League Club	Source	Date Signed	Seasons Played	Apps	Subs	Gls
Gillingham	App	11.72	72-73	11	2	1

ROGERS Kevin Perry
Merthyr Tydfil, 23 September, 1963 W Sch/W Yth (M)

League Club	Source	Date Signed	Seasons Played	Apps	Subs	Gls
Aston Villa	App	09.81				
Birmingham C.	Tr	04.83	83	8	1	1
Wrexham	Tr	07.84	84	30	5	3

ROGERS Lee Julian
Doncaster, 21 October, 1966 (D)

League Club	Source	Date Signed	Seasons Played	Apps	Subs	Gls
Doncaster Rov. (N/C)	YT	07.84				
Chesterfield	Tr	08.86	86-97	310	24	1

ROGERS Lee Martyn
Bristol, 8 April, 1967 (CD)

League Club	Source	Date Signed	Seasons Played	Apps	Subs	Gls
Bristol C.	App	12.84	84-86	30	0	0
Hereford U.	L	03.87	86	13	0	0
York C.	L	12.87	87	5	2	0
Exeter C.	Tr	06.88	88-90	74	4	0

ROGERS Martyn
Bristol, 7 March, 1955 E Yth (RB)

League Club	Source	Date Signed	Seasons Played	Apps	Subs	Gls
Bristol C.	App	03.73				
Exeter C.	Bath C.	07.79	79-84	128	3	5

ROGERS Martyn
Nottingham, 26 January, 1960 Died 1992 E Sch (FB)

League Club	Source	Date Signed	Seasons Played	Apps	Subs	Gls
Manchester U.	App	01.77	77	1	0	0
Queens Park R.	Tr	07.79	79	2	0	0

ROGERS Paul Anthony
Portsmouth, 21 March, 1965 E Semi Pro (M)

League Club	Source	Date Signed	Seasons Played	Apps	Subs	Gls
Sheffield U.	Sutton U.	01.92	91-95	120	5	10
Notts Co.	Tr	12.95	95-96	21	1	2
Wigan Ath.	L	12.96	96	7	2	3
Wigan Ath.	Tr	03.97	96-97	43	6	0

ROGERS Peter Philip
Bristol, 22 April, 1953 (F)

League Club	Source	Date Signed	Seasons Played	Apps	Subs	Gls
Exeter C.	Bath C.	02.79	78-83	194	11	39

ROGERS William
Ulverston, 3 July, 1919 (W)

League Club	Source	Date Signed	Seasons Played	Apps	Subs	Gls
Preston N.E.		08.37				
Blackburn Rov.	Tr	06.38	38-47	73	-	24
Barrow	Tr	10.47	47-52	197	-	14

ROGERSON Lee Antony
Darwen, 21 March, 1967 (M)

League Club	Source	Date Signed	Seasons Played	Apps	Subs	Gls
Wigan Ath.	Clitheroe	01.90	89-90	1	3	0

ROGET Leo Thomas Earl
Ilford, 1 August, 1977 (CD)

League Club	Source	Date Signed	Seasons Played	Apps	Subs	Gls
Southend U.	YT	07.95	95-97	40	4	1

ROLES Albert
Southampton, 29 September, 1921 (FB)

League Club	Source	Date Signed	Seasons Played	Apps	Subs	Gls
Southampton	Jnrs	08.42	48	1	-	0

ROLFE James
Liverpool, 8 February, 1932 (OR)

League Club	Source	Date Signed	Seasons Played	Apps	Subs	Gls
Liverpool	Jnrs	07.52				
Chester C.	Tr	07.53	53-54	50	-	4
Crewe Alex.	Tr	08.55	55-57	101	-	13
Barrow	Tr	07.58	58	12	-	4

ROLLING Franck Jacques
France, 23 August, 1968 (CD)

League Club	Source	Date Signed	Seasons Played	Apps	Subs	Gls
Leicester C.	Ayr U.	09.95	95-96	18	0	0
Bournemouth	Tr	08.97	97	26	4	4

ROLLINGS Andrew Nicholas
Portishead, 14 December, 1954 (CD)

League Club	Source	Date Signed	Seasons Played	Apps	Subs	Gls
Norwich C.	App	12.72	73	4	0	0
Brighton & H.A.	Tr	04.74	74-79	168	0	11
Swindon T.	Tr	05.80	80	11	1	1
Portsmouth	Tr	05.81	81-82	29	0	1
Torquay U. (N/C)	Tr	08.83	83	2	0	0
Brentford (N/C)	Tr	11.83	83	1	0	0

ROLLINS Kevin
Halifax, 2 January, 1947 (FB)

League Club	Source	Date Signed	Seasons Played	Apps	Subs	Gls
Halifax T.	App	●	64	1	-	0

ROLLO Alexander
Dumbarton, 18 September, 1926 (FB)

League Club	Source	Date Signed	Seasons Played	Apps	Subs	Gls
Workington	Dumbarton	06.57	57-59	127	-	3

ROLLO James Shepherd
Helmsdale (Suth), 16 November, 1937 (G)

League Club	Source	Date Signed	Seasons Played	Apps	Subs	Gls
Oldham Ath.	Poole T.	05.60	60-62	59	-	0
Southport	Tr	07.63	63	38	-	0
Bradford C.	Tr	07.64	64-65	37	0	0

ROLLO James Stuart
Wisbech, 22 May, 1976 (D/M)

League Club	Source	Date Signed	Seasons Played	Apps	Subs	Gls
Walsall	YT	05.95				
Cardiff C.	Bath C.	03.97	96-97	6	9	0

ROLPH Andrew John Peter
Birmingham, 28 October, 1969 (W)

League Club	Source	Date Signed	Seasons Played	Apps	Subs	Gls
Chesterfield	Mile Oak Rov.	01.89	88-90	14	22	1

ROLPH Darren Gregory
Romford, 19 November, 1968 (FB)

League Club	Source	Date Signed	Seasons Played	Apps	Subs	Gls
Barnsley	Kings Lynn	08.87	87	1	1	0

ROLPH Gary Leslie
Stepney, 24 February, 1960 (F)

League Club	Source	Date Signed	Seasons Played	Apps	Subs	Gls
Brentford	App	02.78	76-78	8	4	1

ROMANO Serge
France, 25 May, 1964 (RB)

League Club	Source	Date Signed	Seasons Played	Apps	Subs	Gls
Wolverhampton W.	Martigues (Fr)	08.96	96	1	3	0

RONALDSON Kenneth
Leith, 27 September, 1945 (IF)

League Club	Source	Date Signed	Seasons Played	Apps	Subs	Gls
Bristol Rov.	Aberdeen	07.65	65-68	72	4	15
Gillingham	Tr	11.69	69-70	6	0	0

RONSON Brian
Durham, 7 August, 1935 (G)

League Club	Source	Date Signed	Seasons Played	Apps	Subs	Gls
Fulham	Willington	03.53	53	2	-	0
Southend U.	Tr	08.56	56-58	30	-	0
Norwich C.	Tr	08.59	59	1	-	0
Peterborough U.	Tr	07.61	61-62	50	-	0

RONSON William
Fleetwood, 22 January, 1957 (M)

League Club	Source	Date Signed	Seasons Played	Apps	Subs	Gls
Blackpool	App	02.74	74-78	124	4	12
Cardiff C.	Tr	07.79	79-81	90	0	4
Wrexham	Tr	10.81	81	31	1	1
Barnsley	Tr	08.82	82-85	111	2	3
Birmingham C.	L	11.85	85	2	0	0
Blackpool (N/C)	Tr	01.86	85	3	0	0

ROOKE Rodney
Grays, 7 April, 1970 (FB)

League Club	Source	Date Signed	Seasons Played	Apps	Subs	Gls
Colchester U.	YT	06.88	89	4	0	0

ROOKE Ronald
Carlisle, 12 December, 1926 (OR)

League Club	Source	Date Signed	Seasons Played	Apps	Subs	Gls
Carlisle U. (Am)	Carlisle Young Libs	09.49	49	1	-	0

ROOKE Ronald Leslie
Guildford, 7 December, 1911 Died 1985 (CF)

League Club	Source	Date Signed	Seasons Played	Apps	Subs	Gls
Crystal Palace	Guildford C.	03.33	33-36	18	-	6
Fulham	Tr	10.36	36-46	105	-	69
Arsenal	Tr	12.46	46-48	88	-	68
Crystal Palace	Tr	06.49	49-50	45	-	26

ROOKES Philip William
Dulverton, 23 April, 1919 (FB)

League Club	Source	Date Signed	Seasons Played	Apps	Subs	Gls
Bradford C.	Worksop T.	10.36	37	11	-	0
Portsmouth	Tr	01.38	38-50	114	-	0
Colchester U.	Tr	07.51	51-52	68	-	0

ROOKS Richard (Dickie)
Sunderland, 29 May, 1940 (CH)

League Club	Source	Date Signed	Seasons Played	Apps	Subs	Gls
Sunderland	Jnrs	06.57	60-64	34	-	2
Middlesbrough	Tr	08.65	65-68	136	0	14
Bristol C.	Tr	06.69	69-71	96	0	4

ROONEY James
Dundee, 10 December, 1945 (OL)

League Club	Source	Date Signed	Seasons Played	Apps	Subs	Gls
Peterborough U.	Lochee Harp	07.65	65-66	7	0	2

ROONEY Robert
Glasgow, 26 October, 1920 Died 1992 S Sch (CH)

League Club	Source	Date Signed	Seasons Played	Apps	Subs	Gls
Leyton Orient	Falkirk	05.48	48-50	66	-	2
Workington	Tr	06.51	51	27	-	0

ROONEY Robert
Stirling, 8 July, 1938 (W)

League Club	Source	Date Signed	Seasons Played	Apps	Subs	Gls
Sheffield U.	Clydebank	06.58	58-59	14	-	3
Doncaster Rov.	Tr	10.62	62	5	-	1
Lincoln C.	Tr	01.63	62-63	28	-	3

ROONEY Simon Anthony
Manchester, 10 July, 1970 (W)

League Club	Source	Date Signed	Seasons Played	Apps	Subs	Gls
Blackpool	YT	07.88	87-88	4	5	0

ROOST William Charles
Bristol, 22 March, 1924 (IF)

League Club	Source	Date Signed	Seasons Played	Apps	Subs	Gls
Bristol Rov.	Stonehouse	09.48	48-56	177	-	49
Swindon T.	Tr	05.57	57-58	18	-	3

ROPER Alan John
Tipton, 21 May, 1939 (WH/FB)

League Club	Source	Date Signed	Seasons Played	Apps	Subs	Gls
Walsall		05.59	62-64	53	-	2

ROPER David
Ilkley, 26 September, 1944 E Yth (G)

League Club	Source	Date Signed	Seasons Played	Apps	Subs	Gls
Bradford C. (Am)	Salts	09.62	62	13	-	0

ROPER Donald George Beaumont
Botley, 14 December, 1922 E 'B'/EF Lge (W)

League Club	Source	Date Signed	Seasons Played	Apps	Subs	Gls
Southampton	Bitterne Nomads	06.40	46	40	-	8
Arsenal	Tr	08.47	47-56	297	-	88
Southampton	Tr	01.57	56-58	80	-	32

ROPER Ian Robert
Nuneaton, 20 June, 1977 (CD)

League Club	Source	Date Signed	Seasons Played	Apps	Subs	Gls
Walsall	YT	05.95	95-97	26	11	0

ROSARIO Robert Michael
Hammersmith, 4 March, 1966 E Yth/Eu21-4 (F)

League Club	Source	Date Signed	Seasons Played	Apps	Subs	Gls
Norwich C.	Hillingdon Borough	12.83	83-90	115	11	18
Wolverhampton W.	L	12.85	85	2	0	1
Coventry C.	Tr	03.91	90-92	54	5	8
Nottingham F.	Tr	03.93	92-94	25	2	3

ROSCOE Andrew Ronald
Liverpool, 4 June, 1973 (LB/W)

League Club	Source	Date Signed	Seasons Played	Apps	Subs	Gls
Bolton W.	Liverpool (YT)	07.91	93	2	1	0
Rotherham U.	Tr	10.94	94-97	157	7	13

ROSCOE Philip
Barnsley, 3 March, 1934 (FB)

League Club	Source	Date Signed	Seasons Played	Apps	Subs	Gls
Barnsley	Jnrs	08.51				
Halifax T.	Tr	07.56	56-63	257	-	5

ROSE Andrew Mark
Ascot, 9 August, 1978 (FB)

League Club	Source	Date Signed	Seasons Played	Apps	Subs	Gls
Oxford U.	YT	07.97	97	0	1	0

ROSE Colin James
Winsford, 22 January, 1972 E Semi Pro (M)

League Club	Source	Date Signed	Seasons Played	Apps	Subs	Gls
Crewe Alex.	YT	04.90	90-91	17	5	1
Macclesfield T.	Tr	08.97	97	15	4	0

ROSE Frederick
Stannington, 27 March, 1955 (W)

League Club	Source	Date Signed	Seasons Played	Apps	Subs	Gls
Huddersfield T.	App	04.72				
Workington	Tr	07.74	74	0	2	0

ROSE Gordon
Sheffield, 22 March, 1935 (F)

League Club	Source	Date Signed	Seasons Played	Apps	Subs	Gls
Sheffield U.		10.56				
Halifax T.	Tr	07.58	58	8	-	1

ROSE Jack
Sheffield, 26 October, 1921 (RB)

League Club	Source	Date Signed	Seasons Played	Apps	Subs	Gls
Queens Park R.	Peterborough U.	03.45	46-47	17	-	0

ROSE James
Clayton-le-Moors, 4 March, 1918 Died 1989 (G)

League Club	Source	Date Signed	Seasons Played	Apps	Subs	Gls
Accrington St.	Clayton Villa	02.39	38-46	20	-	0

ROSE John
Woolwich, 12 August, 1920 (IF)

League Club	Source	Date Signed	Seasons Played	Apps	Subs	Gls
Bournemouth	Salisbury	02.46	46	1	-	0

ROSE Kenneth
Eckington, 18 August, 1930 Died 1996 (CF)

League Club	Source	Date Signed	Seasons Played	Apps	Subs	Gls
Chesterfield		11.50				
Exeter C.	Tr	06.52	52	11	-	3
Rochdale	Tr	07.53	53	11	-	0
Workington	Tr	06.54	54	6	-	2

ROSE Kevin Phillip
Evesham, 23 November, 1960 (G)

League Club	Source	Date Signed	Seasons Played	Apps	Subs	Gls
Lincoln C.	Ledbury T.	08.79				
Hereford U.	Ledbury T.	03.83	82-88	268	0	0
Bolton W.	Tr	07.89	89-91	10	0	0
Carlisle U.	L	03.90	89	11	0	0
Rochdale	L	02.91	90	3	0	0
Rochdale	Tr	11.91	91-92	68	0	0

ROSE Matthew
Dartford, 24 September, 1975 Eu21-2 (CD)

League Club	Source	Date Signed	Seasons Played	Apps	Subs	Gls
Arsenal	YT	07.94	95-96	2	3	0
Queens Park R.	Tr	05.97	97	13	3	0

ROSE Michael John
New Barnet, 22 July, 1943 (G)

League Club	Source	Date Signed	Seasons Played	Apps	Subs	Gls
Charlton Ath.	St Albans C.	07.63	63-66	75	0	0
Notts Co.	Tr	03.67	66-69	109	0	0
Mansfield T.	L	08.70	70	3	0	0

ROSENIOR Leroy De Graft
Clapton, 24 August, 1964 E Sch/E Yth (F)

League Club	Source	Date Signed	Seasons Played	Apps	Subs	Gls
Fulham	Jnrs	08.82	82-84	53	1	15
Queens Park R.	Tr	08.85	85-86	27	11	8
Fulham	Tr	06.87	87	34	0	20
West Ham U.	Tr	03.88	87-91	44	9	15
Fulham	L	09.90	90	11	0	3
Charlton Ath.	L	11.91	91	3	0	0
Bristol C.	Tr	03.92	91-93	35	16	12

ROSENTHAL Abraham Wallace
Liverpool, 12 October, 1921 Died 1986 (IF)

League Club	Source	Date Signed	Seasons Played	Apps	Subs	Gls
Tranmere Rov.	Liverpool (Am)	01.39	38-46	27	-	8
Bradford C.	Tr	04.47	46-48	44	-	11
Tranmere Rov.	Oldham Ath. (trial)	08.49	49-51	69	-	24
Bradford C.	Tr	01.52	52-53	63	-	32
Tranmere Rov.	Tr	07.54	54	21	-	3
Bradford C.	Tr	07.55	55	1	-	0

ROSENTHAL Ronny
Israel, 11 October, 1963 Israeli Int (W/F)

League Club	Source	Date Signed	Seasons Played	Apps	Subs	Gls
Liverpool	Standard Liege (Bel)	03.90	89-93	32	42	21
Tottenham H.	Tr	01.94	93-96	55	33	4
Watford	Tr	08.97	97	24	1	8

ROSLER Uwe
Germany, 15 November, 1968 East German Int (F)

League Club	Source	Date Signed	Seasons Played	Apps	Subs	Gls
Manchester C.	F.C. Nurnberg (Ger)	03.94	93-97	141	11	50

ROSS Alan
Ellesmere Port, 7 February, 1933 (G)

League Club	Source	Date Signed	Seasons Played	Apps	Subs	Gls
Oldham Ath. (Am)	Bishop Auckland	09.56	56	3	-	0
Accrington St. (Am)	Blackburn Rov. (Am)	03.59	58	1	-	0

ROSS James Alan
Glasgow, 26 May, 1942 (G)

League Club	Source	Date Signed	Seasons Played	Apps	Subs	Gls
Luton T.	Petershill Jnrs	04.62				
Carlisle U.	Tr	06.63	63-78	465	1	0

League Club	Source	Date Signed	Seasons Played	Career Record Apps	Subs	Gls
ROSS Alexander						
Glasgow, 17 December, 1923						(WH)
West Bromwich A.	Shawfield Jnrs	10.47				
Crystal Palace	Tr	08.48	48-50	34	-	0
ROSS William **Bernard**						
Swansea, 8 November, 1924						(OR)
Cardiff C.	Towey U.	03.43	46-47	8	-	0
Sheffield U.	Tr	05.48	48	3	-	1
Southport	Tr	08.49	49-50	47	-	13
ROSS Bryce Thomas						
Edinburgh, 4 December, 1927 Died 1969						(IF)
Newcastle U.	Jnrs	12.43				
Carlisle U.		11.46	46-47	3	-	0
ROSS Colin						
Dailly (Ayrs), 29 August, 1962						(M)
Middlesbrough	App	09.80	80-82	37	1	0
Chesterfield	L	03.83	82	6	0	0
Darlington	Tr	08.83	83-84	14	0	0
ROSS William **Eric**						
Belfast, 19 September, 1944 NIu23-1/NI-1						(M)
Newcastle U.	Glentoran	08.67	67-68	2	0	0
Northampton T.	Tr	08.69	69-71	51	6	5
Hartlepool U.	L	11.71	71	2	0	0
ROSS George						
Inverness, 15 April, 1943						(FB)
Preston N.E.	Jnrs	04.60	60-72	384	2	3
Southport	Tr	11.72	72-73	31	0	0
ROSS George Alfred						
Deptford, 1 November, 1920						(WH)
Millwall	Metro Gas	01.46				
Carlisle U.	Tr	05.47	47	9	-	0
ROSS Ian						
Glasgow, 26 January, 1947						(CD)
Liverpool	Jnrs	08.65	66-71	42	6	2
Aston Villa	Tr	02.72	71-75	175	0	3
Notts Co.	L	10.76	76	4	0	1
Northampton T.	L	11.76	76	2	0	0
Peterborough U.	Tr	12.76	76-78	112	0	1
Wolverhampton W.	Tr	08.79				
Hereford U. (N/C)	(Team Coach)	10.82	82	15	0	0
ROSS Louis Alexander						
Dublin, 19 September, 1920 Died 1990						(FB)
Walsall	Queen of South	08.48	48	8	-	0
ROSS Michael Patrick						
Southampton, 2 September, 1971 E Sch						(F)
Portsmouth	YT	12.88	88-91	0	4	0
Exeter C.	Tr	08.93	93-94	27	1	9
Plymouth Arg.	Tr	11.94	94	11	6	0
Exeter C.	L	11.95	95	7	0	2
ROSS Robert						
Glasgow, 2 February, 1917 Died 1994						(RH)
Watford	Dumbarton	07.46	46	33	-	6
ROSS Robert Alexander						
Wishaw, 25 May, 1927 Died 1992						(FB)
Leeds U.	Workington	08.50	51	5	-	0
Stockport Co.	Tr	06.54	54	9	-	0
ROSS Robert Cochrane						
Edinburgh, 9 September, 1941						(M)
Grimsby T.	St Mirren	06.65	65-70	208	4	18
ROSS Robert Herdman						
Edinburgh, 18 May, 1942						(M)
Shrewsbury T.	Hearts	06.63	63-65	99	0	29
Brentford	Tr	03.66	65-72	288	4	58
Cambridge U.	Tr	10.72	72-73	57	8	14
ROSS Robert Russell						
Cowdenbeath, 13 December, 1925 Died 1984						(CH)
Millwall	Dundee	08.52	52	1	-	0
ROSS Stewart						
Woking, 11 September, 1945						(FB)
Wolverhampton W.		11.65	67-68	1	2	0
ROSS Thomas						
Tain, 27 February, 1947						(F)
Peterborough U.	Lochee Harp	07.65	65-66	5	2	2
York C.	Tr	06.67	67-68	56	5	20

League Club	Source	Date Signed	Seasons Played	Career Record Apps	Subs	Gls
ROSS Trevor William						
Ashton-u-Lyne, 16 January, 1957 E Sch/Su21-1						(M)
Arsenal	App	06.74	74-77	57	1	5
Everton	Tr	11.77	77-82	120	6	16
Portsmouth	L	10.82	82	5	0	0
Sheffield U.	L	12.82	82	4	0	0
Sheffield U.	A.E.K. Athens (Gre)	01.84	83	4	0	0
Bury	Tr	08.84	84-86	96	2	11
ROSS William						
Glasgow, 2 May, 1919 Died 1990						(CF)
Bradford C.	Arbroath	07.50	50	4	-	2
ROSSER Douglas Richard						
Swansea, 8 September, 1948						(CH)
Swansea C.	Jnrs	05.67	68-70	28	2	1
Crewe Alex.	Tr	08.71	71	28	1	0
ROSSITER Donald Paul						
Strood, 8 June, 1935 E Yth						(IF)
Arsenal	Jnrs	06.52				
Leyton Orient	Tr	03.56	56	1	-	0
Gillingham	Dartford	07.57	57	1	-	0
ROSSITER Dudley **John**						
Kingsbridge, 28 October, 1942						(FB)
Torquay U.		07.61	62-63	24	-	0
ROSTRON John **Wilfred**						
Sunderland, 29 September, 1956 E Sch						(LB)
Arsenal	App	10.73	74-76	12	5	2
Sunderland	Tr	07.77	77-79	75	1	17
Watford	Tr	10.79	79-88	306	11	22
Sheffield Wed.	Tr	01.89	88	7	0	0
Sheffield U.	Tr	09.89	89-90	33	3	3
Brentford	Tr	01.91	90-92	34	8	2
ROTHWELL Edward						
Atherton, 3 September, 1917						(W)
Bolton W.	Jnrs	02.36	37-48	48	-	2
Southport	Tr	08.49	49-50	40	-	5
ROTHWELL George						
Bolton, 22 November, 1923						(WH)
Accrington St.	Chorley	08.44	46-51	202	-	10
ROTHWELL John						
Farnworth, 29 March, 1920 Died 1991						(CF)
Southport	Walkden Heath	11.38	38-46	18	-	9
Birmingham C.	Tr	03.47				
Crewe Alex.	Tr	10.49	49	3	-	1
ROTHWELL Ronald						
Bury, 10 July, 1920						(FB)
Rochdale	Dunfermline Ath.	10.46	46-51	48	-	0
ROUGVIE Douglas						
Lochore, 24 May, 1956 S-1						(D)
Chelsea	Aberdeen	08.84	84-86	74	0	3
Brighton & H.A.	Tr	06.87	87	35	0	2
Shrewsbury T.	Tr	08.88	88	20	1	3
Fulham	Tr	02.89	88	18	0	1
ROUND Frederick **Leonard**						
Kingswinford, 21 May, 1928						(G)
Hull C.	Ayr U.	06.57	57	17	-	0
ROUND Paul Gordon						
Blackburn, 22 June, 1959						(CD/F)
Blackburn Rov.	App	08.77	76-80	41	10	5
ROUND Stephen Clive						
Dudley, 28 February, 1963						(F)
Walsall	App	03.80	81-82	5	19	3
ROUND Stephen John						
Burton, 9 November, 1970						(FB)
Derby Co.	YT	07.89	91-92	8	1	0
ROUNSEVELL Anthony Eldred						
Liskeard, 1 April, 1945						(FB)
Plymouth Arg.	App	12.62	63-67	34	2	0
ROUSE Herbert						
Doncaster, 29 November, 1920						(FB)
Doncaster Rov.		06.48	48-54	35	-	0

ROUSE Shaun
Great Yarmouth, 28 February, 1972 E Yth (LM)

League Club	Source	Date Signed	Seasons Played	Apps	Subs	Gls
Bristol C.	Glasgow Rangers	06.92				
Carlisle U. (N/C)	Weston-super-Mare	02.94	93	1	4	0

ROUSE Raymond **Victor**
Swansea, 16 March, 1936 Wu23-1/W-1 (G)

League Club	Source	Date Signed	Seasons Played	Apps	Subs	Gls
Millwall	Jnrs	03.53				
Crystal Palace	Tr	08.56	56-62	238	-	0
Northampton T.	Tr	04.63				
Oxford U.	Tr	08.63	63-64	22	-	0
Leyton Orient	Tr	07.65	65-66	40	0	0

ROUTLEDGE Thomas **Alan**
Wallsend, 6 May, 1960 (FB)

League Club	Source	Date Signed	Seasons Played	Apps	Subs	Gls
Bristol Rov.	Bath Univ.	10.80	80	0	1	0

ROUTLEDGE Ronald Wright
Ashington, 14 October, 1937 (G)

League Club	Source	Date Signed	Seasons Played	Apps	Subs	Gls
Sunderland	Jnrs	10.54	56-57	2	-	0
Bradford P.A.	Tr	05.58	58-61	39	-	0

ROWAN Barry
Willesden, 24 April, 1942 (OR)

League Club	Source	Date Signed	Seasons Played	Apps	Subs	Gls
Brentford	Watford (Am)	10.60				
Millwall	Dover T.	07.64	64-66	72	0	13
Colchester U.	Detroit (USA)	11.68	68	2	0	0
Reading	Durban U. (SA)	08.69	69	1	0	0
Plymouth Arg.	Tr	09.69	69	10	0	1
Exeter C.	Tr	07.70	70-72	76	5	14

ROWAN Brian
Glasgow, 28 June, 1948 (FB)

League Club	Source	Date Signed	Seasons Played	Apps	Subs	Gls
Aston Villa	Baillieston Jnrs	04.69	69	1	0	0
Watford	Tr	10.71	71	8	4	0

ROWBOTHAM Darren
Cardiff, 22 October, 1966 W Yth (F)

League Club	Source	Date Signed	Seasons Played	Apps	Subs	Gls
Plymouth Arg.	Jnrs	11.84	84-87	22	24	2
Exeter C.	Tr	10.87	87-91	110	8	46
Torquay U.	Tr	09.91	91	14	0	3
Birmingham C	Tr	01.92	91-92	31	5	6
Mansfield T.	L	12.92	92	4	0	0
Hereford U.	L	03.93	92	8	0	2
Crewe Alex.	Tr	07.93	93-94	59	2	21
Shrewsbury T.	Tr	07.95	95-96	31	9	9
Exeter C.	Tr	10.96	96-97	67	1	29

ROWBOTHAM Jason
Cardiff, 3 January, 1969 W Yth (FB)

League Club	Source	Date Signed	Seasons Played	Apps	Subs	Gls
Plymouth Arg.	YT	07.87	87-90	8	1	0
Hereford U. (N/C)	Shrewsbury T. (N/C)	10.92	92	3	2	1
Wycombe W.	Raith Rov.	09.95	95-96	27	0	0
Plymouth Arg.	Tr	10.96	96-97	35	5	0

ROWBOTHAM Michael Grant
Sheffield, 2 September, 1965 (M)

League Club	Source	Date Signed	Seasons Played	Apps	Subs	Gls
Manchester U.	App	09.83				
Grimsby T.	Tr	08.84	84	3	1	0

ROWDEN Leonard Albert
Swansea, 31 May, 1927 (CF)

League Club	Source	Date Signed	Seasons Played	Apps	Subs	Gls
Swansea C.	Clydach	10.53	53	1	-	0

ROWE Benjamin Paul
Hull, 1 October, 1970 (F)

League Club	Source	Date Signed	Seasons Played	Apps	Subs	Gls
Exeter C.	Bristol C. (Jnrs)	09.89	89-90	5	7	2

ROWE Brian
Sunderland, 24 October, 1971 (M)

League Club	Source	Date Signed	Seasons Played	Apps	Subs	Gls
Doncaster Rov.	YT	10.90	90-92	42	12	1

ROWE Colwyn Roger
Ipswich, 22 March, 1956 (W)

League Club	Source	Date Signed	Seasons Played	Apps	Subs	Gls
Colchester U.	App	01.74	73-74	4	8	2

ROWE Ezekiel (Zeke) Bartholomew
Stoke Newington, 30 October, 1973 (F)

League Club	Source	Date Signed	Seasons Played	Apps	Subs	Gls
Chelsea	YT	06.92				
Barnet	L	11.93	93	9	1	2
Brighton & H.A.	L	03.96	95	9	0	3
Peterborough U.	Tr	07.96	96-97	13	15	3
Doncaster Rov.	L	02.98	97	6	0	2

ROWE Graham Edward
Southport, 28 August, 1945 (WH)

League Club	Source	Date Signed	Seasons Played	Apps	Subs	Gls
Blackpool	App	07.63	63-70	100	5	12
Tranmere Rov.	L	11.70	70	6	1	0
Bolton W.	Tr	05.71	71	4	2	0

ROWE Mark Terence
Bodmin, 9 June, 1964 (M)

League Club	Source	Date Signed	Seasons Played	Apps	Subs	Gls
Plymouth Arg.	App	09.81	81-84	46	9	1
Torquay U. (N/C)	Saltash U.	09.86	86	7	0	0

ROWE Norman
Halesowen, 20 March, 1940 (W)

League Club	Source	Date Signed	Seasons Played	Apps	Subs	Gls
Walsall	Aston Villa (Am)	03.59	59-60	6	-	0

ROWE Valentine **Norman**
Shouldham (Nk), 14 February, 1926 Died 1988 (FB)

League Club	Source	Date Signed	Seasons Played	Apps	Subs	Gls
Derby Co.	Kings Lynn	12.49	51	2	-	0
Walsall	Tr	08.52	52	25	-	0

ROWE Rodney Carl
Huddersfield, 30 July, 1975 (F)

League Club	Source	Date Signed	Seasons Played	Apps	Subs	Gls
Huddersfield T.	YT	07.93	93-96	14	20	2
Scarborough	L	08.94	94	10	4	1
Bury	L	03.95	94	1	2	0
York C.	Tr	02.97	96-97	47	4	14

ROWE Edwin **Stanley**
Exeter, 20 August, 1921 (LB)

League Club	Source	Date Signed	Seasons Played	Apps	Subs	Gls
Exeter C.		10.47	47-53	139	-	0

ROWE Norman **Terence** Sinclair
Fulham, 8 June, 1964 (FB)

League Club	Source	Date Signed	Seasons Played	Apps	Subs	Gls
Brentford	App	06.82	81-84	63	3	1

ROWELL John **Frederick**
Seaham, 31 December, 1918 Died 1988 (IF)

League Club	Source	Date Signed	Seasons Played	Apps	Subs	Gls
Bournemouth		09.41	46-47	31	-	11
Wrexham	Tr	07.48	48-49	41	-	4
Aldershot	Tr	08.50	50	5	-	0

ROWELL Gary
Sunderland, 6 June, 1957 Eu21-1 (W)

League Club	Source	Date Signed	Seasons Played	Apps	Subs	Gls
Sunderland	App	07.74	75-83	229	25	88
Norwich C.	Tr	08.84	84	2	4	1
Middlesbrough	Tr	08.85	85	27	0	10
Brighton & H.A.	Tr	08.86	86-87	9	3	0
Carlisle U.	Tr	03.88	87	7	0	0
Burnley	Tr	08.88	88-89	8	11	1

ROWETT Gary
Bromsgrove, 6 March, 1974 (D)

League Club	Source	Date Signed	Seasons Played	Apps	Subs	Gls
Cambridge U.	YT	08.91	91-93	51	12	9
Everton	Tr	05.94	93-94	2	2	0
Blackpool	L	01.95	94	17	0	0
Derby Co.	Tr	07.95	95-97	101	4	3

ROWLAND Alfred
Stokesley, 2 September, 1920 Died 1997 (CH)

League Club	Source	Date Signed	Seasons Played	Apps	Subs	Gls
Aldershot	Stockton	08.46	46-48	93	-	0
Cardiff C.	Tr	02.49	48-49	3	-	0

ROWLAND Andrew Arthur
Derby, 8 September, 1954 E Yth (F)

League Club	Source	Date Signed	Seasons Played	Apps	Subs	Gls
Derby Co.	Jnrs	09.72				
Bury	Tr	08.74	74-78	169	5	58
Swindon T.	Tr	09.78	78-85	280	7	80

ROWLAND Andrew James
Taunton, 1 October, 1965 (F)

League Club	Source	Date Signed	Seasons Played	Apps	Subs	Gls
Southampton	Exmouth T.	11.89				
Torquay U.	Tr	03.91	90-91	9	7	1

ROWLAND David Charles
Stotfold, 12 September, 1940 E Sch (F)

League Club	Source	Date Signed	Seasons Played	Apps	Subs	Gls
Luton T.	Arlesey	01.58	57	1	-	0

ROWLAND John Douglas
Ironville, 7 April, 1941 E Yth (W)

League Club	Source	Date Signed	Seasons Played	Apps	Subs	Gls
Nottingham F.	Ironville Amats	04.61	60-61	26	-	3
Port Vale	Tr	08.62	62-66	147	2	40
Mansfield T.	Tr	09.66	66-67	49	0	16
Tranmere Rov.	Tr	07.68	68	25	1	3

ROWLAND John Oswald
Newport, 16 March, 1936 Wu23-1 (WH)

League Club	Source	Date Signed	Seasons Played	Apps	Subs	Gls
Newport Co.	Lovells Ath.	06.58	58-68	462	1	9

ROWLAND Keith
Portadown (NI), 1 September, 1971 NI Yth/NI 'B'/NI-12 (LB/M)

League Club	Source	Date Signed	Seasons Played	Apps	Subs	Gls
Bournemouth	YT	10.89	91-92	65	7	2
Coventry C.	L	01.93	92	0	2	0
West Ham U.	Tr	08.93	93-97	63	17	1
Queens Park R.	Tr	01.98	97	7	0	0

League Club	Source	Date Signed	Seasons Played	Career Record Apps	Subs	Gls
ROWLAND Leonard Charles						
Manchester, 23 June, 1925 E Amat						(FB)
Wrexham (Am)	Mansfield T. (Am)	05.49	49-50	18	-	0
Stockport Co.	Ashton U.	12.52	52-56	61	-	0
ROWLANDS John Henry						
Liverpool, 7 February, 1945						(F)
Mansfield T.		10.67	67	12	1	3
Torquay U.	Tr	06.68	68	18	0	4
Exeter C.	L	01.69	68	1	0	0
Stockport Co.	Tr	08.69	69-70	45	1	11
Barrow	Tr	01.71	70-71	52	2	6
Workington	Tr	07.72	72-73	50	1	11
Crewe Alex.	Tr	11.73	73-74	31	4	1
Hartlepool U.	Seattle (USA)	09.75	75	33	2	6
Hartlepool U.	San Jose E. (USA)	09.76	76	14	0	4
ROWLANDS Trevor Ivor						
Rhondda, 2 February, 1922 Died 1973 W Sch						(FB)
Norwich C.	Cardiff Nomads	08.46	47-49	10	-	2
Colchester U.	Tr	07.50	50-52	46	-	4
ROWLES Albert **Edward** James						
Gosport, 10 March, 1951						(M/F)
Bournemouth	App	03.68	67-70	58	8	12
York C.	Tr	07.71	71-72	61	6	14
Torquay U.	Tr	06.73	73-74	54	5	13
Darlington	Tr	08.75	75-77	96	7	21
Colchester U.	Tr	12.77	77-81	79	12	17
ROWLEY Antonio (Tony) Camilio						
Porthcawl, 19 September, 1929 W-1						(IF)
Birmingham C.	Wellington T.	01.49				
Liverpool	Stourbridge	10.53	53-57	60	-	38
Tranmere Rov.	Tr	03.58	57-60	100	-	47
ROWLEY Arthur						
Liverpool, 9 May, 1933						(IF)
Liverpool	Florence Melley's B.C.	05.51	52	11	-	0
Wrexham	Tr	11.54	54-56	54	-	8
Crewe Alex.	Tr	02.57	56-57	34	-	7
ROWLEY George **Arthur**						
Wolverhampton, 21 April, 1926 E 'B'/EF Lge						(IF)
West Bromwich A.	Wolverhampton W. (Am)	05.44	46-48	24	-	4
Fulham	Tr	12.48	48-49	56	-	26
Leicester C.	Tr	07.50	50-57	303	-	251
Shrewsbury T.	Tr	06.58	58-64	236	-	152
ROWLEY John						
Wolverhampton, 23 June, 1944						(FB)
Bradford P.A.	Wellington T.	10.67	67	35	0	0
ROWLEY John (Jack) Frederick						
Wolverhampton, 7 October, 1918 Died 1998 EF Lge/E 'B'/E-6						(CF)
Wolverhampton W.	Jnrs	11.35				
Bournemouth	Cradlley Heath	02.37	36-37	22	-	12
Manchester U.	Tr	10.37	37-54	380	-	182
Plymouth Arg.	Tr	02.55	54-56	56	-	14
ROWLEY Kenneth Francis						
Pelsall, 29 August, 1926 Died 1995						(IF)
Wolverhampton W.	Elkingtons	10.47	49	1	-	0
Birmingham C.	Tr	01.51	50-54	40	-	19
Coventry C.	Tr	11.54	54	3	-	0
ROXBURGH Alexander White						
Manchester, 19 September, 1910 Died 1985						(G)
Blackpool	Manchester C. (Am)	01.31	32-38	62	-	0
Barrow	Tr	08.46	46-47	69	-	0
ROY Andrew						
Tillicoultry, 4 July, 1928						(IF)
Exeter C.	Dunfermline Ath.	08.49	49	2	-	0
ROY Bryan Edward						
Netherlands, 12 February, 1970 Dutch Int						(F)
Nottingham F.	Foggia (It)	08.94	94-96	70	15	24
ROY John (Jack) Robin						
Southampton, 23 March, 1914 Died 1980						(OR)
Norwich C.	Sholing	08.33	34-35	6	-	0
Mansfield T.	Tr	04.36	36	25	-	2
Sheffield Wed.	Tr	02.37	36-37	15	-	1
Notts Co.	Tr	03.38	37-38	14	-	0
Tranmere Rov.	Tr	12.38	38	19	-	2
Ipswich T.	Aberaman	02.46	46	15	-	2

League Club	Source	Date Signed	Seasons Played	Career Record Apps	Subs	Gls
ROYCE Simon Ernest						
Forest Gate, 9 September, 1971						(G)
Southend U.	Heybridge Swifts	10.91	91-97	147	2	0
ROYLE Joseph						
Liverpool, 8 April, 1949 Eu23-10/EF Lge/E-6						(F)
Everton	App	08.66	65-74	229	3	102
Manchester C.	Tr	12.74	74-77	98	1	23
Bristol C.	Tr	11.77	77-79	100	1	18
Norwich C.	Tr	08.80	80-81	40	2	9
ROYSTON Robert						
Newcastle, 1 December, 1915 Died 1996						(RB)
Sunderland	Seaham Colly	01.35				
Southport	Tr	10.36	37-38	70	-	2
Plymouth Arg.	Tr	03.39	38-46	39	-	0
RUARK Anthony						
West Ham, 23 March, 1933						(CH)
Southend U.		05.56	56	9	-	0
RUDD Edward						
Wigan, 7 January, 1929						(WH)
Bolton W.		08.50				
Accrington St.	Tr	08.51	51	2	-	0
RUDD John **James**						
Hull, 25 October, 1919 Died 1985						(IF)
Manchester C.	Teremure Ath.	01.38	46	2	-	0
York C.	Tr	03.47	46-48	83	-	23
Leeds U.	Tr	02.49	48-49	18	-	1
Rotherham U.	Tr	10.49	49-51	75	-	11
Scunthorpe U.	Tr	10.51	51	32	-	4
Workington	Tr	09.52	52	17	-	1
RUDD William Thomas						
Manchester, 13 December, 1941						(M)
Birmingham C.	Stalybridge Celtic	10.59	59-61	24	-	3
York C.	Tr	11.61	61-65	193	0	30
Grimsby T.	Tr	07.66	66-67	59	1	9
Rochdale	Tr	02.68	67-69	108	0	8
Bury	Tr	06.70	70-76	174	15	18
RUDDOCK Neil						
Wandsworth, 9 May, 1968 E Yth/Eu21-4/E 'B'/E-1						(CD)
Millwall	App	03.86				
Tottenham H.	Tr	04.86	86-87	7	2	0
Millwall	Tr	06.88	88	0	2	1
Southampton	Tr	02.89	88-91	100	7	9
Tottenham H.	Tr	07.92	92	38	0	3
Liverpool	Tr	07.93	93-97	111	4	11
Queens Park R.	L	03.98	97	7	0	0
RUDGE Dale Anthony						
Wolverhampton, 9 September, 1963						(M)
Wolverhampton W.	App	08.81	82-83	23	4	0
Preston N.E.	Tr	07.84	84-85	46	1	2
RUDGE David Harry						
Wolverhampton, 21 January, 1948						(W)
Aston Villa	App	05.65	66-69	49	6	10
Hereford U.	Tr	08.72	72-75	75	7	8
Torquay U.	Tr	12.75	75-77	60	4	4
RUDGE John Robert						
Wolverhampton, 21 October, 1944						(F)
Huddersfield T.	Jnrs	11.61	62-66	5	0	0
Carlisle U.	Tr	12.66	66-68	45	5	16
Torquay U.	Tr	01.69	68-71	94	2	34
Bristol Rov.	Tr	02.72	71-74	50	20	17
Bournemouth	Tr	03.75	74-76	18	3	2
RUDGE Simon James						
Warrington, 30 December, 1964						(M)
Bolton W.	App	12.82	82-85	77	13	14
RUDHAM Keith (Doug) Robert						
South Africa, 3 May, 1926 Died 1991 South African Amat Int						(G)
Liverpool	Johannesburg (SA)	11.54	54-59	63	-	0
RUDI Petter						
Norway, 17 September, 1973 Norwegian Int						(M)
Sheffield Wed.	Molde (Nor)	10.97	97	19	3	0
RUDKIN Thomas William						
Peterborough, 17 June, 1919						(OL)
Wolverhampton W.	Creswell	02.38				
Lincoln C.	Tr	05.38	38	2	-	1
Arsenal	Peterborough U.	01.47	46	5	-	2

League Club	Source	Date Signed	Seasons Played	Apps	Subs	Gls
Southampton	Tr	08.47	47-48	9	-	0
Bristol C.	Tr	05.49	49-50	34	-	4
RUDMAN Harold						
Rochdale, 4 November, 1924						(FB)
Burnley		12.42	46-56	71	-	0
Rochdale	Tr	07.57	57	21	-	1
RUECROFT Jacob						
Lanchester, 1 May, 1915						(FB)
Halifax T.	Goole T.	05.38	38-46	60	-	2
Bradford C.	Scarborough	01.48	47-48	43	-	0
RUFFETT Raymond Douglas						
Luton, 20 July, 1924						(WH)
Luton T.	Jnrs	10.41	48	1	-	0
RUFUS Marvin Marcel						
Lewisham, 11 September, 1976						(M)
Leyton Orient	Charlton Ath. (YT)	11.94	94	5	2	0
RUFUS Richard Raymond						
Lewisham, 12 January, 1975 Eu21-6						(CD)
Charlton Ath.	YT	07.93	94-97	142	3	0
RUGGIERO John Salvatore						
Longton, 26 November, 1954						(M)
Stoke C.	App	05.72	76	9	0	2
Workington	L	01.76	75	3	0	0
Brighton & H.A.	Tr	06.77	77	4	4	2
Portsmouth	L	12.77	77	6	0	1
Chester C.	Tr	04.79	79	9	3	1
RULE Alan Henry						
Southampton, 10 January, 1930						(WH)
Chelsea	Winchester C.	11.52				
Norwich C.	Tr	09.56	56	8	-	0
Bournemouth	Tr	06.57	57	25	-	0
RUMBLE Paul						
Hemel Hempstead, 14 March, 1969						(LB)
Watford	App	03.87				
Scunthorpe U.	L	08.88	88	8	0	1
Maidstone U.	Tr	08.89	89-91	48	7	3
RUMBOLD George						
Alton, 10 July, 1911 Died 1995						(FB)
Crystal Palace	Faringdon	10.34	35	5	-	0
Leyton Orient	Tr	06.37	37-38	52	-	0
Ipswich T.	Tr	05.46	46-49	121	-	11
RUMNEY Joseph Edgar						
Abberton (Ex), 15 September, 1936						(FB)
Colchester U.	Jnrs	05.57	57-64	49	-	0
RUNDLE Charles Rodney						
Fowey, 17 January, 1923 Died 1997						(IF)
Tottenham H.	St Blazey	02.46	46-48	28	-	12
Crystal Palace	Tr	06.50	50-51	38	-	2
RUNDLE Sidney Stewart Knight						
Fowey, 19 October, 1921 Died 1987						(WH)
Plymouth Arg.	St Blazey	06.45	46-52	53	-	1
RUSH David						
Sunderland, 15 May, 1971						(F)
Sunderland	Notts Co. (YT)	02.89	90-93	40	19	12
Hartlepool U.	L	08.91	91	8	0	2
Peterborough U.	L	10.93	93	2	2	1
Cambridge U.	L	09.94	94	2	0	0
Oxford U.	Tr	09.94	94-96	67	25	21
York C.	Tr	01.97	96-97	2	3	0
RUSH Ian James						
Flint, 20 October, 1961 W Sch/Wu21-2/W-73						(F)
Chester C.	App	09.79	78-79	33	1	14
Liverpool	Tr	04.80	80-86	224	0	139
Liverpool	Juventus (It)	08.88	88-95	223	22	90
Leeds U.	Tr	05.96	95-96	34	2	3
Newcastle U.	Tr	08.97	97	6	4	0
Sheffield U.	L	02.98	97	4	0	0
RUSH Jonathan						
New Zealand, 13 October, 1961						(G)
Blackpool	New Zealand	11.79	80	11	-	0
Carlisle U.	Tr	08.82				
RUSH Matthew James						
Hackney, 6 August, 1971 IRu21-4						(M)
West Ham U.	YT	03.90	90-94	29	19	5

League Club	Source	Date Signed	Seasons Played	Apps	Subs	Gls
Cambridge U.	L	03.93	92	4	6	0
Swansea C.	L	01.94	93	13	0	0
Norwich C.	Tr	08.95	95-96	0	3	0
Northampton T.	L	10.96	96	14	0	3
Oldham Ath.	Tr	03.97	96-97	17	7	3
RUSHBURY David Graham						
Wolverhampton, 20 February, 1956						(D)
West Bromwich A.	App	02.74	74-75	28	0	0
Sheffield Wed.	Tr	11.76	76-78	111	1	7
Swansea C.	Tr	07.79	79-80	51	1	0
Carlisle U.	Tr	08.81	81-84	120	9	1
Gillingham	Tr	03.85	84	12	0	0
Doncaster Rov.	Tr	07.85	85-86	66	0	2
Cambridge U.	L	02.87	86	1	0	0
Bristol Rov.	Tr	02.87	86	14	2	0
RUSHBY Alan						
Doncaster, 27 December, 1933						(CH)
Doncaster Rov.		01.52	52-53	2	-	0
Mansfield T.	Tr	03.57	56-57	20	-	0
Bradford P.A.	Tr	11.57	57-58	12	-	0
RUSHFELDT Sigurd						
Norway, 11 December, 1972						(F)
Birmingham C. (L)	Tromso (Nor)	10.95	95	3	4	0
RUSHFORTH Peter						
Carlisle, 6 December, 1945						(FB)
Workington (Am)		09.66	66	5	0	0
RUSHTON Brian William Eric						
Sedgley, 21 October, 1943						(RB)
Birmingham C.	App	10.60	62-63	12	-	0
Notts Co.	Tr	06.67	67	2	1	0
RUSHWORTH Peter John						
Bristol, 12 April, 1927						(WH)
Leicester C.	Cheltenham T.	11.51				
Bournemouth	Tr	06.53	53-56	88	-	1
RUSLING Graham						
Keadby (Lincs), 4 April, 1948						(F)
Scunthorpe U.		01.67	66-70	71	10	17
RUSSELL Alec						
Bristol, 17 April, 1925						(IF)
Bristol C.		11.47	47-48	3	-	0
RUSSELL Alexander						
Seaham, 21 February, 1944						(M)
Everton	Jnrs	12.61				
Southport	Tr	11.63	63-69	262	1	63
Blackburn Rov.	Tr	08.70	70	22	2	4
Tranmere Rov.	Tr	07.71	71-72	54	1	7
Crewe Alex.	L	10.72	72	4	0	0
Southport	Tr	11.72	72-74	84	1	12
RUSSELL Alexander John						
Crosby, 17 March, 1973						(RB/M)
Rochdale	Burscough	07.94	94-97	83	19	14
RUSSELL Allan						
Aberdeen, 16 November, 1953						(M)
Peterborough U.	Leicester C. (App)	08.71	71-72	7	8	1
RUSSELL Colin						
Liverpool, 21 January, 1961						(F)
Liverpool	App	04.78	80	0	1	0
Huddersfield T.	Tr	09.82	82-83	64	2	23
Stoke C.	L	03.84	83	11	0	2
Bournemouth	Tr	08.84	84-85	65	3	14
Doncaster Rov.	Tr	07.86	86-87	43	0	5
Scarborough	Tr	10.87	87	12	1	2
Wigan Ath.	Tr	07.88	88	8	0	3
RUSSELL Craig Stewart						
South Shields, 4 February, 1974						(F)
Sunderland	YT	07.92	91-97	103	47	31
Manchester C.	Tr	11.97	97	17	7	1
RUSSELL Darel Francis Roy						
Stepney, 22 October, 1980 E Yth						(M)
Norwich C.	YT	11.97	97	0	1	0
RUSSELL Edward Thomas						
Cranwell, 15 July, 1928						(WH)
Wolverhampton W.	St Chads College	04.46	48-50	30	-	0
Middlesbrough	Tr	12.51	51-52	29	-	1

League Club	Source	Date Signed	Seasons Played	Apps	Subs	Gls
Leicester C.	Tr	10.53	53-57	90	-	5
Notts Co.	Tr	08.58	58	9	-	0

RUSSELL Guy Robert
Solihull, 28 September, 1967 (F)

League Club	Source	Date Signed	Seasons Played	Apps	Subs	Gls
Birmingham C.	YT	05.86	84-87	7	4	0
Carlisle U.	L	03.87	86	9	3	2

RUSSELL Hugh William
Redcar, 10 March, 1921 Died 1991 (IF)

League Club	Source	Date Signed	Seasons Played	Apps	Subs	Gls
Gillingham	Bishop Auckland	08.46	50-51	61	-	8

RUSSELL James Walker
Edinburgh, 14 September, 1916 (IF)

League Club	Source	Date Signed	Seasons Played	Apps	Subs	Gls
Sunderland	Hearts	06.34	35-37	5	-	0
Norwich C.	Tr	05.38	38-46	12	-	2
Crystal Palace	Tr	12.46	46-47	43	-	6
New Brighton	Tr	07.48	48	24	-	1

RUSSELL John Matthieson
Plymouth, 22 April, 1938 (F)

League Club	Source	Date Signed	Seasons Played	Apps	Subs	Gls
Plymouth Arg.	Jnrs	01.59				
Southport	Tr	07.60	60	1	-	0

RUSSELL Keith David
Aldridge, 31 January, 1974 (LB/M)

League Club	Source	Date Signed	Seasons Played	Apps	Subs	Gls
Blackpool	Hednesford T.	03.97	96	0	1	0

RUSSELL Kevin John
Portsmouth, 6 December, 1966 E Yth (F/W)

League Club	Source	Date Signed	Seasons Played	Apps	Subs	Gls
Portsmouth	Brighton & H.A. (App)	10.84	85-86	3	1	0
Wrexham	Tr	07.87	87-88	84	0	43
Leicester C.	Tr	06.89	89-91	24	19	10
Peterborough U.	L	09.90	90	7	0	3
Cardiff C.	L	01.91	90	3	0	0
Hereford U.	L	11.91	91	3	0	1
Stoke C.	L	01.92	91	5	0	1
Stoke C.	Tr	07.92	92	30	10	5
Burnley	Tr	06.93	93	26	2	6
Bournemouth	Tr	03.94	93-94	30	0	1
Notts Co.	Tr	02.95	94	9	2	0
Wrexham	Tr	07.95	95-97	85	12	7

RUSSELL Lee Edward
Southampton, 3 September, 1969 (D)

League Club	Source	Date Signed	Seasons Played	Apps	Subs	Gls
Portsmouth	YT	07.88	88-97	103	20	3
Bournemouth	L	09.94	94	3	0	0

RUSSELL Malcolm
Halifax, 9 November, 1945 (FB)

League Club	Source	Date Signed	Seasons Played	Apps	Subs	Gls
Halifax T.	App	03.63	62-68	184	1	0
Southport	Tr	09.68	68-70	92	0	2
Barrow	Tr	12.70	70-71	64	0	2
Stockport Co.	Tr	07.72	72	11	0	0

RUSSELL Martin Christopher
Dublin, 27 April, 1967 IR Yth/IRu21-4/IRu23-1 (M)

League Club	Source	Date Signed	Seasons Played	Apps	Subs	Gls
Manchester U.	App	04.84				
Birmingham C.	L	10.86	86	3	2	0
Leicester C.	Tr	03.87	86-88	13	7	0
Scarborough	Tr	02.89	88-89	51	0	9
Middlesbrough	Tr	03.90	90	10	1	2

RUSSELL Matthew Lee
Dewsbury, 17 January, 1978 (M)

League Club	Source	Date Signed	Seasons Played	Apps	Subs	Gls
Scarborough	YT	07.96	96-97	1	6	0
Doncaster Rov.	L	03.98	97	4	0	1

RUSSELL William **Peter**
Sedgley, 16 January, 1935 (CH)

League Club	Source	Date Signed	Seasons Played	Apps	Subs	Gls
Wolverhampton W.	Jnrs	10.52	54-55	3	-	0
Notts Co.	Tr	03.56	55-58	106	-	6

RUSSELL Raymond
Walsall, 9 March, 1930 (IF)

League Club	Source	Date Signed	Seasons Played	Apps	Subs	Gls
West Bromwich A.	Jnrs	05.48				
Shrewsbury T.	Burton A.	05.54	54-59	168	-	55
Crewe Alex.	Tr	03.60	59	13	-	4

RUSSELL Robert Inglis
Aberdour (Fife), 27 December, 1919 (WH)

League Club	Source	Date Signed	Seasons Played	Apps	Subs	Gls
Chelsea	Airdrieonians	12.44	46	2	-	0
Notts Co.	Tr	08.48	48	2	-	0
Leyton Orient	Tr	10.48				

RUSSELL Roger Francis
Corby, 20 November, 1957 (F)

League Club	Source	Date Signed	Seasons Played	Apps	Subs	Gls
Northampton T. (N/C)		09.81	81	0	1	0

RUSSELL Sidney Edward James
Feltham, 4 October, 1937 Died 1994 (FB)

League Club	Source	Date Signed	Seasons Played	Apps	Subs	Gls
Brentford	Jnrs	08.56	56-59	54	-	0

RUSSELL Wayne Leonard
Cardiff, 29 November, 1967 (G)

League Club	Source	Date Signed	Seasons Played	Apps	Subs	Gls
Burnley	Ebbw Vale	10.93	94-96	22	2	0

RUSSELL William
Hounslow, 7 July, 1935 E Amat (IF)

League Club	Source	Date Signed	Seasons Played	Apps	Subs	Gls
Sheffield U.	Rhyl	11.57	57-62	145	-	55
Bolton W.	Tr	03.63	62-64	22	-	2
Rochdale	Tr	07.66	66-67	60	1	8

RUSSELL William Howie
Coatbridge, 19 October, 1919 Died 1989 (IF)

League Club	Source	Date Signed	Seasons Played	Apps	Subs	Gls
Hartlepool U.		05.46	46-47	13	-	1

RUSSELL William McKnight
Glasgow, 14 September, 1959 S Yth (RB)

League Club	Source	Date Signed	Seasons Played	Apps	Subs	Gls
Everton	App	07.77				
Doncaster Rov.	Glasgow Celtic	07.79	79-84	241	3	15
Scunthorpe U.	Tr	08.85	85-87	113	4	7
Rotherham U.	Tr	08.88	88-91	103	2	2

RUSSO Gary
Hornsey, 2 August, 1956 (FB)

League Club	Source	Date Signed	Seasons Played	Apps	Subs	Gls
Ipswich T.	App	08.74				
Bournemouth	Tr	07.75	75	1	0	0

RUSSON Ronald
Wednesbury, 10 December, 1928 Died 1981 (CH)

League Club	Source	Date Signed	Seasons Played	Apps	Subs	Gls
Wolverhampton W.	Jnrs	04.46				
Walsall	Hednesford T.	05.48	48-54	145	-	1

RUST Nicholas Charles Irwin
Ely, 25 September, 1974 E Yth (G)

League Club	Source	Date Signed	Seasons Played	Apps	Subs	Gls
Brighton & H.A.	Arsenal (YT)	07.93	93-97	177	0	0

RUTHERFORD Colin
Rowlands Gill, 11 July, 1944 (HB)

League Club	Source	Date Signed	Seasons Played	Apps	Subs	Gls
Sunderland	Jnrs	07.61				
Barnsley	Tr	06.63	63	1	-	0

RUTHERFORD Ian Stewart
Hitchin, 24 December, 1972 (F)

League Club	Source	Date Signed	Seasons Played	Apps	Subs	Gls
Crewe Alex.	Luton T. (YT)	06.91	91	0	1	0

RUTHERFORD Joseph Henry Hamilton
Chester-le-Street, 20 September, 1914 Died 1994 (G)

League Club	Source	Date Signed	Seasons Played	Apps	Subs	Gls
Southport	Birtley Colly	10.36	36-38	88	-	0
Aston Villa	Tr	02.39	38-51	148	-	0

RUTHERFORD Mark Robin
Birmingham, 25 March, 1972 (M)

League Club	Source	Date Signed	Seasons Played	Apps	Subs	Gls
Birmingham C.	YT	07.90	89-90	1	4	0
Shrewsbury T. (L)	Shelbourne	02.94	93	7	7	0

RUTHERFORD Michael Alan
Greenwich, 6 June, 1972 (M)

League Club	Source	Date Signed	Seasons Played	Apps	Subs	Gls
Queens Park R.	YT	12.89	89	1	1	0

RUTHERFORD Jonathan **Paul**
Sunderland, 23 February, 1967 (F)

League Club	Source	Date Signed	Seasons Played	Apps	Subs	Gls
Newcastle U.	App	07.85				
Scarborough	Meadowbank Thistle	09.94	94	6	2	1

RUTHERFORD Robert
South Shields, 20 April, 1922 (HB)

League Club	Source	Date Signed	Seasons Played	Apps	Subs	Gls
Newcastle U.		03.44				
Gateshead	Tr	11.45	46-52	10	-	2

RUTHERFORD Robert Alan
Carlisle, 28 July, 1953 E Sch (M)

League Club	Source	Date Signed	Seasons Played	Apps	Subs	Gls
Leeds U.	App	08.70				
Workington	Tr	11.72	72	1	1	0

RUTHERFORD William John
Bellshill, 23 January, 1930 Died 1980 (WH)

League Club	Source	Date Signed	Seasons Played	Apps	Subs	Gls
Darlington	Stirling A.	07.52	52-58	253	-	3
Southport	Tr	07.59	59-63	176	-	7

RUTLEY Peter
Exeter, 19 May, 1946 (WH)

League Club	Source	Date Signed	Seasons Played	Apps	Subs	Gls
Exeter C.	App	07.63	62-64	16	-	0

RUTTER David **Brian**
Poplar, 11 May, 1933 (IF)

League Club	Source	Date Signed	Seasons Played	Apps	Subs	Gls
Crystal Palace (Am)	Cardiff C. (Am)	11.54	54	3	-	1

RUTTER Charles Frederick
Bromley, 22 December, 1927 E 'B' (FB)

League Club	Source	Date Signed	Seasons Played	Apps	Subs	Gls
Cardiff C.	Taunton T.	09.49	50-57	118	-	0
Exeter C.	Tr	08.58				

RUTTER Cyril Hutton
Leeds, 21 February, 1933 (CH)

League Club	Source	Date Signed	Seasons Played	Apps	Subs	Gls
Portsmouth	Jnrs	07.51	53-62	171	-	0

RUTTER John Thomas
Warrington, 13 September, 1952 (FB)

League Club	Source	Date Signed	Seasons Played	Apps	Subs	Gls
Wolverhampton W.	App	09.70				
Bournemouth	Tr	08.73	73	2	2	0
Exeter C.	Tr	07.74	74-75	31	1	1
Stockport Co.	Tr	08.76	76-85	400	4	10

RUTTER Keith Gregg
Leeds, 10 September, 1931 (CH)

League Club	Source	Date Signed	Seasons Played	Apps	Subs	Gls
Queens Park R.	Methley U.	07.54	54-62	339	-	1
Colchester U.	Tr	02.63	62-63	63	-	0

RUTTER Stephen John
Erith, 24 July, 1968 (F)

League Club	Source	Date Signed	Seasons Played	Apps	Subs	Gls
Maidstone U. (N/C)	Iceland	02.92	91	0	1	0

RYALLS Brian
Hemsworth, 7 July, 1932 (G)

League Club	Source	Date Signed	Seasons Played	Apps	Subs	Gls
Sheffield Wed.	Grimethorpe Colly	01.53	53-57	41	-	0

RYAN Darragh Joseph
Cuckfield, 21 May, 1980 (F)

League Club	Source	Date Signed	Seasons Played	Apps	Subs	Gls
Brighton & H.A.	YT	03.98	97	1	3	1

RYAN Darren Thomas
Oswestry, 3 July, 1972 (W)

League Club	Source	Date Signed	Seasons Played	Apps	Subs	Gls
Shrewsbury T.	YT	10.90	90-91	3	1	0
Chester C.	Tr	08.92	92	5	12	2
Stockport Co.	Tr	01.93	92-93	29	7	6
Rochdale	Tr	07.94	94-95	19	13	2
Chester C. (N/C)	Tr	03.96	95	2	2	1

RYAN David Peter
Manchester, 5 January, 1957 (G)

League Club	Source	Date Signed	Seasons Played	Apps	Subs	Gls
Manchester U.	App	07.74				
Port Vale	L	01.76	75	1	0	0
Southport	Tr	03.76	75-76	23	0	0

RYAN Derek Anthony
Dublin, 2 January, 1967 (M)

League Club	Source	Date Signed	Seasons Played	Apps	Subs	Gls
Wolverhampton W.	App	10.84	84-86	23	10	5

RYAN Eric William
Oswestry, 6 January, 1933 (FB)

League Club	Source	Date Signed	Seasons Played	Apps	Subs	Gls
Mansfield T.	Oswestry T.	05.51	54-56	20	-	0

RYAN George
Glasgow, 29 December, 1931 (CF)

League Club	Source	Date Signed	Seasons Played	Apps	Subs	Gls
Sheffield U.	Hull C. (Am)	05.52				
Chesterfield	Third Lanark	07.54	54	3	-	0

RYAN Gerard Joseph
Dublin, 4 October, 1955 IR-16 (W)

League Club	Source	Date Signed	Seasons Played	Apps	Subs	Gls
Derby Co.	Bohemians	09.77	77-78	30	0	4
Brighton & H.A.	Tr	09.78	78-84	131	42	32

RYAN James
Stirling, 12 May, 1945 (W)

League Club	Source	Date Signed	Seasons Played	Apps	Subs	Gls
Manchester U.	Corrie Hearts	01.63	65-69	21	3	4
Luton T.	Tr	04.70	70-76	172	12	21

RYAN James Patrick
Prestatyn, 6 September, 1942 Wu23-1 (CF)

League Club	Source	Date Signed	Seasons Played	Apps	Subs	Gls
Charlton Ath.	Dulwich Hamlet	02.63	62-64	16	-	8
Millwall	Tr	02.65	64-65	12	0	2
Exeter C.	Hastings U.	01.67	66	20	0	5

RYAN John Bernard
Ashton-u-Lyne, 18 February, 1962 Eu21-1 (LB/M)

League Club	Source	Date Signed	Seasons Played	Apps	Subs	Gls
Oldham Ath.	App	02.80	81-82	77	0	8
Newcastle U.	Tr	08.83	83-84	28	0	1
Sheffield Wed.	Tr	09.84	84	5	3	1
Oldham Ath.	Tr	08.85	85-86	20	3	0
Mansfield T.	Tr	10.87	87-88	53	9	1
Chesterfield	Tr	06.89	89-90	81	1	6
Rochdale	Tr	06.91	91-93	64	6	2
Bury	Tr	12.93	93	8	1	0

RYAN John Gilbert
Lewisham, 20 July, 1947 (M/RB)

League Club	Source	Date Signed	Seasons Played	Apps	Subs	Gls
Arsenal	Maidstone U.	10.64				
Fulham	Tr	07.65	65-68	42	5	1
Luton T.	Tr	07.69	69-75	264	2	10
Norwich C.	Tr	08.76	76-79	113	3	26
Sheffield U.	Seattle (USA)	09.80	80-81	56	0	2
Manchester C.	Tr	01.82	81	19	0	0
Stockport Co. (N/C)	Tr	08.83	83	1	1	0
Chester C. (N/C)	Tr	09.83	83	4	0	0
Cambridge U. (N/C)		10.84	84	5	0	0

RYAN John (Buck) Joseph
Alloa, 16 October, 1930 (CF)

League Club	Source	Date Signed	Seasons Played	Apps	Subs	Gls
Charlton Ath.	Chippenham T.	02.54	54-58	61	-	32
Newcastle U.	Tr	03.59				
Bristol C.	Tr	07.60	60	3	-	0

RYAN John Oliver
Liverpool, 28 October, 1944 (W)

League Club	Source	Date Signed	Seasons Played	Apps	Subs	Gls
Tranmere Rov.		08.64				
Luton T.	Wigan Ath.	10.67	67-68	17	1	1
Notts Co.	Tr	05.69	69	22	2	1

RYAN Keith James
Northampton, 25 June, 1970 (M)

League Club	Source	Date Signed	Seasons Played	Apps	Subs	Gls
Wycombe W.	Berkhamsted T.	07.89	93-97	124	5	12

RYAN Kenneth
Accrington, 20 September, 1936 (G)

League Club	Source	Date Signed	Seasons Played	Apps	Subs	Gls
Accrington St. (Am)	Accrington Colly	04.59	58	1	-	0

RYAN Laurence John
Watford, 15 October, 1963 (F)

League Club	Source	Date Signed	Seasons Played	Apps	Subs	Gls
Cambridge U.	Dunstable	04.88	87-89	39	12	13

RYAN Michael Joseph
Welwyn, 14 October, 1930 (OR)

League Club	Source	Date Signed	Seasons Played	Apps	Subs	Gls
Arsenal	Chertsey	07.48				
Lincoln C.	Tr	06.52	52	7	-	0
York C.	Tr	01.53	52	4	-	0

RYAN Reginald Alphonso
Dublin, 30 October, 1925 Died 1997 IR-16/NI-1 (IF)

League Club	Source	Date Signed	Seasons Played	Apps	Subs	Gls
West Bromwich A.	Nuneaton Borough	04.45	46-54	234	-	28
Derby Co.	Tr	07.55	55-58	133	-	30
Coventry C.	Tr	09.58	58-60	65	-	9

RYAN Robert Paul
Dublin, 16 May, 1977 IR Sch/IR Yth/IRu21-5 (LB/M)

League Club	Source	Date Signed	Seasons Played	Apps	Subs	Gls
Huddersfield T.	Belvedere Y.C.	07.94	96-97	12	3	0
Millwall	Tr	01.98	97	16	0	0

RYAN Thomas Stanley
Windlesham, 9 July, 1952 (D)

League Club	Source	Date Signed	Seasons Played	Apps	Subs	Gls
Reading	App	05.70	70	1	0	0

RYAN Timothy James
Stockport, 10 December, 1974 (LB)

League Club	Source	Date Signed	Seasons Played	Apps	Subs	Gls
Scunthorpe U.	YT	04.93	92-93	1	1	0
Doncaster Rov.	Buxton	08.96	96	22	6	0

RYAN Vaughan William
Westminster, 2 September, 1968 (M)

League Club	Source	Date Signed	Seasons Played	Apps	Subs	Gls
Wimbledon	App	08.86	86-91	67	15	3
Sheffield U.	L	01.89	88	2	1	0
Leyton Orient	Tr	08.92	92-94	40	4	0

RYCRAFT Frederick
Hayes, 29 August, 1939 (G)

League Club	Source	Date Signed	Seasons Played	Apps	Subs	Gls
Brentford	Southall	09.59	62-63	33	-	0

RYDEN Hugh Johnston
Dumbarton, 7 April, 1943 (M/F)

League Club	Source	Date Signed	Seasons Played	Apps	Subs	Gls
Leeds U.	Yoker Ath.	10.60				
Bristol Rov.	Tr	06.62	62	8	-	4
Stockport Co.	Tr	07.63	63	38	-	9
Chester C.	Tr	06.64	64-67	140	1	44
Halifax T.	Tr	11.67	67-69	54	1	6
Stockport Co.	Tr	12.69	69-72	112	11	15

RYDEN John Johnston
Bonhill, 18 February, 1931 (CH)

League Club	Source	Date Signed	Seasons Played	Apps	Subs	Gls
Accrington St.	Alloa Ath.	02.54	53-55	80	-	1
Tottenham H.	Tr	11.55	55-58	63	-	2
Watford	Tr	06.61	61	24	-	1

League Club	Source	Date Signed	Seasons Played	Career Record Apps	Subs	Gls
RYDER Derek Francis						
Leeds, 18 February, 1947						(FB)
Leeds U.	Jnrs	02.64				
Cardiff C.	Tr	06.66	66	4	0	0
Rochdale	Tr	07.68	68-71	168	0	1
Southport	Tr	07.72	72-73	80	2	2
RYDER Robert						
Bolton, 11 July, 1943						(FB)
Gillingham	Nantwich T.	01.65	64-67	6	0	0
RYDER Stuart Henry						
Sutton Coldfield, 6 November, 1973 Eu21-3						(CD)
Walsall	YT	07.92	92-97	86	15	5
RYDER Terence Roy						
Norwich, 3 June, 1928						(F)
Norwich C.	City W.	09.46	46-49	46	-	12
Portsmouth	Tr	10.50	50-51	14	-	4
Swindon T.	Tr	07.52	52	34	-	13
RYLANDS David Robert						
Liverpool, 7 March, 1953						(CD)
Liverpool	App	03.70				
Hereford U.	Tr	09.74	74-75	22	0	0
Newport Co.	L	03.75	74	3	0	1
Hartlepool U.	L	03.76	75	11	0	0
Halifax T.	Tr	06.76	76	5	0	0
RYMER George Herbert						
Barnsley, 6 October, 1923						(G)
Barnsley	Ardsley Vic.	12.43	46	3	-	0
Accrington St.	Tr	02.47	46	8	-	0

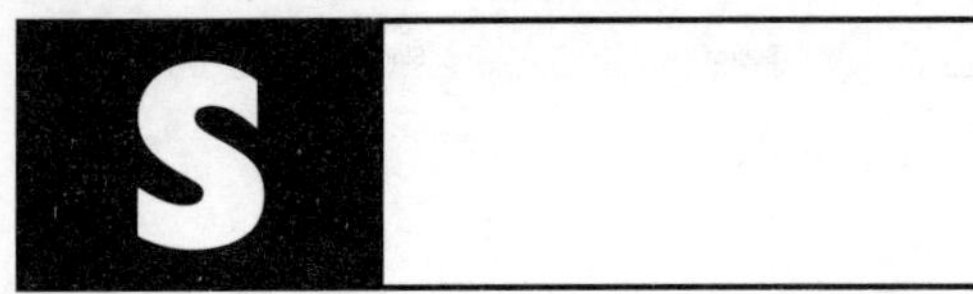

SABELLA Alejandro (Alex)
Argentina, 5 November, 1954 Argentinian Int (M)

League Club	Source	Date Signed	Seasons Played	Apps	Subs	Gls
Sheffield U.	River Plate (Arg)	08.78	78-79	76	0	8
Leeds U.	Tr	06.80	80	22	1	2

SABIN Arthur Henry
Birmingham, 25 January, 1939 Died 1958 (G)

League Club	Source	Date Signed	Seasons Played	Apps	Subs	Gls
Aston Villa	Jnrs	01.57	56-57	2	-	0

SADDINGTON Nigel
Sunderland, 9 December, 1965 (CD)

League Club	Source	Date Signed	Seasons Played	Apps	Subs	Gls
Doncaster Rov.	S.C. Vaux	09.84	84	5	0	0
Sunderland	Roker	01.86	86	3	0	0
Carlisle U.	Tr	02.88	87-89	97	0	15

SADLER David
Yalding (Kt), 5 February, 1946 E Yth/E Amat/Eu23-3/EF Lge/E-4 (CD)

League Club	Source	Date Signed	Seasons Played	Apps	Subs	Gls
Manchester U.	Maidstone U.	02.63	63-73	266	6	22
Preston N. E.	Tr	11.73	73-76	104	1	3

SADLER George Handel
Whitwell (Dy), 7 May, 1915 (FB)

League Club	Source	Date Signed	Seasons Played	Apps	Subs	Gls
West Ham U.	Gainsborough Trin.	12.38	46	1	-	0

SADLIER Richard Thomas
Dublin, 14 January, 1979 IR Yth (F)

League Club	Source	Date Signed	Seasons Played	Apps	Subs	Gls
Millwall	Belvedere Y.C.	08.96	96-97	10	4	3

SAGAR Edward (Ted)
Campsall (Yks), 7 February, 1910 Died 1986 EF Lge/E-4 (G)

League Club	Source	Date Signed	Seasons Played	Apps	Subs	Gls
Everton	Thorne Colly	03.29	29-52	463	-	0

SAGE Roland **Frank**
Chipping Sodbury, 31 May, 1924 (WH)

League Club	Source	Date Signed	Seasons Played	Apps	Subs	Gls
Cardiff C.		02.45				
Newport Co.	Tr	04.48	47-48	3	-	0

SAGE Melvyn
Gillingham, 24 March, 1964 (RB)

League Club	Source	Date Signed	Seasons Played	Apps	Subs	Gls
Gillingham	App	03.82	81-85	126	6	5
Derby Co.	Tr	08.86	86-91	137	3	4

SAHLIN Dan
Sweden, 18 April, 1967 (F)

League Club	Source	Date Signed	Seasons Played	Apps	Subs	Gls
Birmingham C. (L)	Hammarby (Swe)	11.95	95	0	1	0

SAIB Moussa
Algeria, 6 March, 1969 Algerian Int (M)

League Club	Source	Date Signed	Seasons Played	Apps	Subs	Gls
Tottenham H.	Valencia (Sp)	02.98	97	3	6	1

SAILE Michael Anthony
Heywood, 31 December, 1950 E Yth (FB)

League Club	Source	Date Signed	Seasons Played	Apps	Subs	Gls
Bury	App	01.69	68-72	92	1	0

SAINSBURY Kim
Reading, 21 September, 1957 (F)

League Club	Source	Date Signed	Seasons Played	Apps	Subs	Gls
Reading	App	●	74	0	1	0

ST JOHN Ian
Motherwell, 7 June, 1938 Su23-2/SF Lge/S-21 (F/M)

League Club	Source	Date Signed	Seasons Played	Apps	Subs	Gls
Liverpool	Motherwell	04.61	61-70	334	2	95
Coventry C.	Hellenic (SA)	09.71	71	18	0	3
Tranmere Rov.	Tr	10.72	72	9	0	1

SAINTY John Albert
Poplar, 24 March, 1946 E Sch (F/M)

League Club	Source	Date Signed	Seasons Played	Apps	Subs	Gls
Tottenham H.	App	07.63				
Reading	Tr	08.67	67-69	63	8	19
Bournemouth	Tr	02.70	69-73	111	7	21
Mansfield T.	L	11.72	72	3	0	0
Aldershot	Tr	08.74	74-75	26	3	0

SALAKO Andrew Olumide
Nigeria, 8 November, 1972 (FB)

League Club	Source	Date Signed	Seasons Played	Apps	Subs	Gls
Charlton Ath.	YT	04.91	90	1	0	0

SALAKO John Akin
Nigeria, 11 February, 1969 E-5 (LW)

League Club	Source	Date Signed	Seasons Played	Apps	Subs	Gls
Crystal Palace	App	11.86	86-94	172	43	22
Swansea C.	L	08.89	89	13	0	3
Coventry C.	Tr	08.95	95-97	68	4	4
Bolton W.	Tr	03.98	97	0	7	0

SALATHIEL David **Neil**
Wrexham, 19 November, 1962 W Sch (RB)

League Club	Source	Date Signed	Seasons Played	Apps	Subs	Gls
Wrexham (N/C)	Sheffield Wed. (Jnrs)	05.80	80	4	0	0
Crewe Alex.	Tr	06.81	81-82	64	1	0
Wrexham	Arcadia Shepherds (SA)	12.83	83-89	239	1	3

SALE Mark David
Burton, 27 February, 1972 (F)

League Club	Source	Date Signed	Seasons Played	Apps	Subs	Gls
Stoke C.	YT	07.90	89	0	2	0
Cambridge U.	Tr	05.91				
Birmingham C.	Rocester	03.92	91-92	11	10	0
Torquay U.	Tr	03.93	92-93	30	14	8
Preston N.E.	Tr	07.94	94	10	3	7
Mansfield T.	Tr	07.95	95-96	36	9	12
Colchester U.	Tr	03.97	96-97	48	1	10

SALES Ronald Duncan
South Shields, 19 September, 1920 Died 1995 (CH)

League Club	Source	Date Signed	Seasons Played	Apps	Subs	Gls
Newcastle U.	Reyrolles	07.42				
Leyton Orient	Tr	05.47	47-48	46	-	3
Hartlepool U.	Colchester U.	08.50	50	3	-	0

SALISBURY Gareth
Caernarfon, 11 March, 1941 (IF)

League Club	Source	Date Signed	Seasons Played	Apps	Subs	Gls
Wrexham	Jnrs	05.59	59-61	11	-	0
Norwich C.	Tr	07.62				
Luton T.	Tr	07.63	63	12	-	2
Colchester U.	Tr	07.64	64	15	-	2
Chesterfield	Tr	07.65	65	34	0	9

SALMAN Danis Mahmut Mehmet
Cyprus, 12 March, 1960 E Yth (D)

League Club	Source	Date Signed	Seasons Played	Apps	Subs	Gls
Brentford	App	08.77	75-85	316	9	8
Millwall	Tr	08.86	86-89	85	8	4
Plymouth Arg.	Tr	03.90	89-91	71	3	4
Peterborough U.	L	03.92	91	1	0	0
Torquay U.	Tr	09.92	92	20	0	0

SALMON Leonard Alexander
West Kirby, 24 June, 1912 Died 1995 (WH)

League Club	Source	Date Signed	Seasons Played	Apps	Subs	Gls
New Brighton	Hoylake	10.34	34-35	30	-	2
Burnley	South Liverpool	09.41				
Tranmere Rov.	Tr	09.46	46-47	30	-	1

SALMON Michael Bernard
Leyland, 14 July, 1964 (G)

League Club	Source	Date Signed	Seasons Played	Apps	Subs	Gls
Blackburn Rov.	Jnrs	10.81	81	1	0	0
Chester C.	L	10.82	82	16	0	0
Stockport Co.	Tr	08.83	83-85	118	0	0
Bolton W.	Tr	07.86	86	26	0	0
Wrexham	Tr	03.87	86-88	100	0	0
Charlton Ath.	Tr	07.89	90-97	148	0	0

SALMONS Geoffrey
Mexborough, 14 January, 1948 (M)

League Club	Source	Date Signed	Seasons Played	Apps	Subs	Gls
Sheffield U.	Jnrs	02.66	67-73	170	10	8
Stoke C.	Tr	07.74	74-77	115	3	14
Sheffield U.	L	09.77	77	5	0	0
Leicester C.	Tr	10.77	77	25	1	4
Chesterfield	Tr	08.78	78-81	119	1	15

SALT Phillip Thomas
Oldham, 2 March, 1979 (RM)

League Club	Source	Date Signed	Seasons Played	Apps	Subs	Gls
Oldham Ath.	YT	07.97	97	1	1	0

SALT Samuel John
Southport, 30 December, 1938 (WH)

League Club	Source	Date Signed	Seasons Played	Apps	Subs	Gls
Blackpool	Jnrs	01.56	60	18	-	0

SALTER Kenneth
Cullompton, 16 November, 1933 (G)

League Club	Source	Date Signed	Seasons Played	Apps	Subs	Gls
Exeter C.	Jnrs	11.50	50	1	-	0

SALTON Darren Brian
Edinburgh, 16 March, 1972 S Sch/S Yth/Su21-6 (CD)

League Club	Source	Date Signed	Seasons Played	Apps	Subs	Gls
Luton T.	YT	03.89	91-92	17	1	0

SALVAGE Barry John
Bristol, 21 December, 1946 Died 1986 (W)

League Club	Source	Date Signed	Seasons Played	Apps	Subs	Gls
Fulham	Eastbourne	09.67	67-68	7	0	0
Millwall	Tr	03.69	68	1	1	0
Queens Park R.	Tr	03.71	70-72	16	5	1
Brentford	Tr	02.73	72-74	87	0	8
Millwall	Tr	08.75	75-76	43	12	9

League Club	Source	Date Signed	Seasons Played	Career Record Apps	Subs	Gls
SAMBROOK Andrew John						
Chatham, 13 July, 1979						(D)
Gillingham	Jnrs	●	96	0	1	0
SAMBROOK Raymond						
Wolverhampton, 31 May, 1933						(W)
Coventry C.	Wednesfield	09.53	54-57	96	-	25
Manchester C.	Tr	01.58	57-61	62	-	13
Doncaster Rov.	Tr	06.62	62	8	-	0
Crewe Alex.	Tr	01.63				
SAMMELS Jonathan Charles						
Ipswich, 23 July, 1945	*E Yth/Eu23-9/EF Lge*					(M)
Arsenal	App	08.62	62-70	212	3	39
Leicester C.	Tr	07.71	71-77	236	5	21
SAMPLE James						
Morpeth, 5 November, 1921 Died 1992						(IF)
Bradford C.	Ashington	08.47	47-48	8	-	2
SAMPSON Ian						
Wakefield, 14 November, 1968						(CD)
Sunderland	Goole T.	11.90	91-93	13	4	1
Northampton T.	L	12.93	93	8	0	0
Northampton T.	Tr	08.94	94-97	154	3	13
SAMPSON Peter Stanley						
Pitsea (Ex), 9 July, 1927						(WH)
Bristol Rov.	Devizes	06.48	48-60	339	-	4
SAMPSON Raymond Victor						
Swindon, 6 February, 1935						(IF)
Swindon T.	Jnrs	05.52	53-58	64	-	10
SAMPSON Thomas William						
Southwark, 18 August, 1954						(D)
Millwall	App	06.72	72	0	1	0
SAMUEL Randolf (Randy) Fitzgerald						
Trinidad (WI), 23 December, 1963	*Canadian Int*					(CD)
Port Vale	Fortuna Sittard (Neth)	11.95	95	9	0	1
SAMUELS Dean Walter						
Hackney, 29 March, 1973						(F)
Barnet	Boreham Wood	12.96	96-97	13	26	3
SAMUELS Leslie						
Oldham, 8 December, 1928						(IF)
Burnley		12.49	50	2	-	0
Exeter C.	Tr	07.53	53	12	-	1
Wrexham	Tr	03.54	53-54	26	-	11
Crewe Alex.	Tr	11.54	54-55	42	-	13
Bradford C.	Tr	12.55	55-57	84	-	38
Stockport Co.	Tr	03.58	57-58	25	-	5
SAMUELS Robert William Lewis						
Aberdeen, 18 May, 1946						(IF)
Lincoln C.	Aberdeen	07.67	67	3	1	0
SAMWAYS Mark						
Doncaster, 11 November, 1968						(G)
Doncaster Rov.	YT	08.87	87-91	121	0	0
Scunthorpe U.	Tr	03.92	91-96	180	0	0
York C.	Tr	07.97	97	29	0	0
SAMWAYS Vincent (Vinny)						
Bethnal Green, 27 October, 1968	*E Yth/Eu21-5*					(M)
Tottenham H.	App	10.85	86-93	165	28	11
Everton	Tr	08.94	94-95	17	6	2
Wolverhampton W.	L	12.95	95	3	0	0
Birmingham C.	L	02.96	95	12	0	0
SANAGHAN Joseph						
Motherwell, 12 December, 1914						(FB)
Bradford P.A.		08.35	35	5	-	0
Bournemouth	Tr	06.37	37-48	170	-	0
Stockport Co.	Tr	08.49	49-50	52	-	0
SANCHEZ John						
Paddington, 21 October, 1940	*E Sch/E Yth*					(WH)
Arsenal	Jnrs	10.57				
Watford	Tr	06.59	59-60	19	-	0
SANCHEZ Lawrence Phillip						
Lambeth, 22 October, 1959	*E Sch/NI-3*					(M)
Reading	Thatcham T.	09.78	77-84	249	13	28
Wimbledon	Tr	12.84	84-93	254	16	33
Swindon T. (N/C)	Tr	03.94	93	6	2	0
SANDEMAN Bradley Robert						
Northampton, 24 February, 1970						(RB)
Northampton T.	YT	07.88	87-90	28	30	3
Maidstone U.	Tr	02.91	90-91	55	2	8
Port Vale	Tr	08.92	92-95	62	7	1
Rotherham U.	Tr	07.96	96	20	1	2
Hereford U.	Tr	03.97	96	7	0	0
SANDER Christopher Andrew						
Swansea, 11 November, 1962						(G)
Swansea C.	App	11.79	81-83	20	0	0
Wrexham	L	09.84	84	5	0	0
Cardiff C. (N/C)	Tr	08.85	85	8	0	0
Cardiff C. (N/C)	Haverfordwest	03.86	85	5	0	0
SANDERCOCK Kenneth Leslie						
Plymouth, 31 January, 1951						(RB/M)
Torquay U.	App	01.69	68-69	42	4	1
Leicester C.	Tr	11.69	69	5	5	0
Torquay U.	Tr	11.71	71-74	113	6	5
SANDERCOCK Philip John						
Plymouth, 21 June, 1953						(LB)
Torquay U.	App	09.71	69-76	200	5	13
Huddersfield T.	Tr	06.77	77-78	81	0	1
Northampton T.	Tr	09.79	79-80	69	0	3
SANDERS Alan						
Salford, 31 January, 1934						(FB)
Manchester C.		08.55				
Everton	Tr	07.56	57-59	56	-	0
Swansea C.	Tr	11.59	59-62	92	-	0
Brighton & H. A.	Tr	01.63	62-65	80	0	0
SANDERS Alan John						
Newport, 29 October, 1963	*W Sch*					(M)
Cardiff C.	Jnrs	11.81	81	1	1	0
SANDERS James Albert						
Holborn, 5 July, 1920						(G)
Charlton Ath.	Longlands	02.44				
West Bromwich A.	Tr	11.45	48-57	327	-	0
Coventry C.	Tr	07.58	58	10	-	0
SANDERS James Charles Frederick						
Marlborough, 15 October, 1932						(WH)
Bristol C.		11.51				
Crystal Palace	Tr	03.55	55-58	46	-	0
Exeter C.	Cheltenham T.	08.62	62	20	-	1
SANDERS Peter Charles William						
Newport, 7 September, 1942	*W Yth*					(CF)
Newport Co.	Jnrs	10.59	60	3	-	0
Gillingham	Tr	07.61	61	2	-	0
SANDERS Roy Joseph						
Stepney, 22 September, 1940						(OR)
Northampton T.	Romford	05.62	62	15	-	2
SANDERS Steven						
Halifax, 2 June, 1978						(FB)
Huddersfield T.	YT	07.96				
Doncaster Rov.	Tr	08.97	97	19	6	0
SANDERSON Eric						
Chapeltown, 10 November, 1921 Died 1988						(FB)
Rotherham U.	Paramore	09.47	47	2	-	1
SANDERSON Ian						
Torquay, 26 August, 1956						(F)
Torquay U. (N/C)		08.77	77	0	1	0
SANDERSON John Robert McDevitt						
Carlisle, 5 February, 1918 Died 1993						(LB)
Carlisle U.		05.38	38	15	-	0
Wolverhampton W.	Tr	02.39				
Luton T.	Tr	05.46	46	6	-	0
SANDERSON Keith						
Hull, 9 October, 1940						(IF)
Plymouth Arg.	Bath C.	08.64	64	29	-	2
Queens Park R.	Tr	06.65	65-68	98	6	10
SANDERSON Michael						
West Germany, 26 October, 1966						(M)
Darlington (N/C)	Hartlepool U. (YT)	03.86	85	1	0	0
SANDERSON Paul David						
Blackpool, 28 July, 1964						(W)
Manchester C.	Fleetwood T.	11.83				

League Club	Source	Date Signed	Seasons Played	Apps	Subs	Gls
Chester C.	Tr	12.83	83	24	0	3
Halifax T.	Tr	08.84	84-86	88	16	5
Cardiff C.	Tr	07.87	87	8	13	1
Walsall	Tr	03.88	87	0	3	0

SANDERSON Philip
Barnsley, 1 November, 1953 (OL)

League Club	Source	Date Signed	Seasons Played	Apps	Subs	Gls
Barnsley (N/C)	Worsboro' Bridge	10.74	74	2	0	1

SANDFORD Lee Robert
Lambeth, 22 April, 1968 E Yth (D)

League Club	Source	Date Signed	Seasons Played	Apps	Subs	Gls
Portsmouth	App	12.85	85-89	66	6	1
Stoke C.	Tr	12.89	89-95	255	3	8
Sheffield U.	Tr	07.96	96-97	40	5	2
Reading	L	09.97	97	5	0	0

SANDIFORD Ian Robert
Chorley, 26 February, 1946 (F)

League Club	Source	Date Signed	Seasons Played	Apps	Subs	Gls
Blackburn Rov.	App	02.64				
Stockport Co.	Tr	06.64	64-65	47	0	9
Crewe Alex.	Tr	01.66	65-66	48	4	18

SANDLANDS Herbert
Nantwich, 9 August, 1931 (CH)

League Club	Source	Date Signed	Seasons Played	Apps	Subs	Gls
Crewe Alex. (Am)	Nantwich T.	08.54	54	1	-	0

SANDWITH Kevin
Workington, 30 April, 1978 (LB)

League Club	Source	Date Signed	Seasons Played	Apps	Subs	Gls
Carlisle U.	YT	07.96	97	2	1	0

SANDY Adam
Peterborough, 22 September, 1958 (M)

League Club	Source	Date Signed	Seasons Played	Apps	Subs	Gls
Northampton T.	Wolverton T.	02.80	79-82	88	16	6

SANDYS Harold Albert
Fulham, 8 October, 1932 (CF)

League Club	Source	Date Signed	Seasons Played	Apps	Subs	Gls
Torquay U.	Yeovil T.	08.54	54	2	-	0

SANETTI Francesco
Rome, Italy, 11 January, 1979 (F)

League Club	Source	Date Signed	Seasons Played	Apps	Subs	Gls
Sheffield Wed.	Genoa (It)	04.98	97	1	1	1

SANFORD Mark Alexander
London, 10 September, 1960 (F)

League Club	Source	Date Signed	Seasons Played	Apps	Subs	Gls
Aldershot	Jnrs	06.79	79-82	72	12	23

SANG Neil
Liverpool, 23 May, 1972 (M)

League Club	Source	Date Signed	Seasons Played	Apps	Subs	Gls
Everton	YT	05.90				
Torquay U.	Tr	06.91	91	8	6	0

SAN JUAN Jesus Garcia
Zaragoza, Spain, 22 August, 1971 (M)

League Club	Source	Date Signed	Seasons Played	Apps	Subs	Gls
Wolverhampton W. (L)	Real Zaragoza (Sp)	09.97	97	4	0	0

SANKEY Jack
Winsford, 19 March, 1912 Died 1985 (WH)

League Club	Source	Date Signed	Seasons Played	Apps	Subs	Gls
West Bromwich A.	Winsford U.	11.30	33-38	144	-	5
Northampton T.	Tr	10.45	46-47	42	-	0

SANKEY Martin Andrew
Wellington, 4 May, 1964 (F)

League Club	Source	Date Signed	Seasons Played	Apps	Subs	Gls
Shrewsbury T.	App	02.82	82	0	5	0

SAN MIGUEL Xabier
Spain, 7 May, 1971 (M)

League Club	Source	Date Signed	Seasons Played	Apps	Subs	Gls
Cambridge U. (N/C)	Spain	08.96	96	0	1	0

SANSAM Christian
Hull, 26 December, 1975 (M)

League Club	Source	Date Signed	Seasons Played	Apps	Subs	Gls
Scunthorpe U.	YT	12.93	93-95	10	11	1
Scarborough (N/C)	Halifax T.	03.96	95	5	1	0
Bradford C. (N/C)	Tr	08.96	96	0	1	0
Hull C. (N/C)	Tr	11.96	96	2	1	0

SANSBY Clifford Palmer
Peterborough, 24 November, 1934 (FB)

League Club	Source	Date Signed	Seasons Played	Apps	Subs	Gls
Peterborough U.	March T.	(N/L)	60	1	-	0

SANSOM Kenneth Graham
Camberwell, 26 September, 1958 E Sch/E Yth/Eu21-8/E FLge/E-86 (LB)

League Club	Source	Date Signed	Seasons Played	Apps	Subs	Gls
Crystal Palace	App	12.75	74-79	172	0	3
Arsenal	Tr	08.80	80-87	314	0	6
Newcastle U.	Tr	12.88	88	20	0	0
Queens Park R.	Tr	06.89	89-90	64	0	0
Coventry C.	Tr	03.91	90-92	51	0	0
Everton	Tr	02.93	92	6	1	1
Brentford	Tr	03.93	92	8	0	0
Watford (N/C)	Chertsey T.	08.94	94	1	0	0

SANSOME Paul Eric
New Addington, 6 October, 1961 (G)

League Club	Source	Date Signed	Seasons Played	Apps	Subs	Gls
Millwall	Crystal Palace (App)	04.80	81-87	156	0	0
Southend U.	Tr	03.88	87-96	308	0	0
Birmingham C.	L	01.96	95	1	0	0

SANTOS Yazalde Damas
U.S.A., 30 July, 1975 (F)

League Club	Source	Date Signed	Seasons Played	Apps	Subs	Gls
Bournemouth	Jersey Scots (USA)	12.95	95	0	3	0

SAPHIN Reginald Francis Edward
Kilburn, 8 August, 1916 (G)

League Club	Source	Date Signed	Seasons Played	Apps	Subs	Gls
Queens Park R.	Walthamstow Ave.	06.46	46-50	30	-	0
Watford	Tr	07.51	51-53	57	-	0

SARGENT Gary Stewart
Bedford, 11 September, 1952 (F)

League Club	Source	Date Signed	Seasons Played	Apps	Subs	Gls
Norwich C.	App	09.70	71	0	1	0
Scunthorpe U.	Tr	07.72	72	14	1	1
Peterborough U.	Bedford T.	07.77	77-78	27	7	5
Northampton T.	Tr	06.79	79-80	41	2	4

SARSON Albert
Rossington, 31 December, 1930 (F)

League Club	Source	Date Signed	Seasons Played	Apps	Subs	Gls
Doncaster Rov.	Mansfield T. (Am)	08.49	49-50	2	-	0

SARTORI Carlo Domenico
Italy, 10 February, 1948 (M)

League Club	Source	Date Signed	Seasons Played	Apps	Subs	Gls
Manchester U.	Jnrs	02.65	68-71	26	13	4

SAS Marco
Netherlands, 16 February, 1971 Dutch u21 Int (CD)

League Club	Source	Date Signed	Seasons Played	Apps	Subs	Gls
Bradford C.	N.A.C. Breda (Neth)	07.96	96	31	0	3

SATCHWELL Kenneth Raymond
Birmingham, 17 January, 1940 (F)

League Club	Source	Date Signed	Seasons Played	Apps	Subs	Gls
Coventry C.	Jnrs	09.58	58-61	68	-	21
Walsall	Nuneaton Borough	01.65	64-66	54	3	7

SAUL Eric Michael
Dublin, 28 October, 1978 (M)

League Club	Source	Date Signed	Seasons Played	Apps	Subs	Gls
Brighton & H.A.	YT	07.97	97	0	4	0

SAUL Frank Lander
Canvey Island, 23 August, 1943 E Yth (W/F)

League Club	Source	Date Signed	Seasons Played	Apps	Subs	Gls
Tottenham H.	Jnrs	08.60	60-67	112	4	37
Southampton	Tr	01.68	67-69	47	3	2
Queens Park R.	Tr	05.70	70-71	40	3	4
Millwall	Tr	03.72	71-75	85	11	4

SAUNDERS Carl Stephen
Birmingham, 26 November, 1964 (F)

League Club	Source	Date Signed	Seasons Played	Apps	Subs	Gls
Stoke C.		03.83	82-89	130	34	24
Bristol Rov.	Tr	02.90	89-93	123	19	42
Oxford U. (N/C)	Tr	12.93	93	2	3	0
Walsall (N/C)	Tr	02.94	93	1	1	0

SAUNDERS Dean Nicholas
Swansea, 21 June, 1964 EF Lge/W-63 (F)

League Club	Source	Date Signed	Seasons Played	Apps	Subs	Gls
Swansea C.	App	06.82	83-84	42	7	12
Cardiff C.	L	03.85	84	3	1	0
Brighton & H. A.	Tr	08.85	85-86	66	6	21
Oxford U.	Tr	03.87	86-88	57	2	22
Derby Co.	Tr	10.88	88-90	106	0	42
Liverpool	Tr	07.91	91-92	42	0	11
Aston Villa	Tr	09.92	92-94	111	1	37
Nottingham F.	Galatasaray (Tu)	07.96	96-97	39	4	5
Sheffield U.	Tr	12.97	97	23	1	10

SAUNDERS Dennis Frederick
Scarborough, 19 December, 1924 E Amat (WH)

League Club	Source	Date Signed	Seasons Played	Apps	Subs	Gls
Newport Co. (Am)	Huddersfield T. (Am)	11.46	46	7	-	0

SAUNDERS Derek William
Ware, 6 January, 1928 E Amat (WH)

League Club	Source	Date Signed	Seasons Played	Apps	Subs	Gls
Chelsea	Walthamstow Ave.	07.53	53-58	203	-	9

SAUNDERS George Ernest
Birkenhead, 1 March, 1918 Died 1982 (RB)

League Club	Source	Date Signed	Seasons Played	Apps	Subs	Gls
Everton		02.39	46-51	133	-	0

SAUNDERS Glyn
Nottingham, 16 June, 1956 (FB)

League Club	Source	Date Signed	Seasons Played	Apps	Subs	Gls
Nottingham F.	App	06.74	76	4	0	0

SAUNDERS John George
Worksop, 1 December, 1950 Died 1998 (CD)

League Club	Source	Date Signed	Seasons Played	Apps	Subs	Gls
Mansfield T.	App	12.68	69-72	89	0	2
Huddersfield T.	Tr	10.72	72-75	121	0	1

League Club	Source	Date Signed	Seasons Played	Apps	Subs	Gls
Barnsley	Tr	12.75	75-78	149	0	7
Lincoln C.	Tr	06.79	79	25	1	1
Doncaster Rov.	Tr	08.80	80	27	1	2

SAUNDERS John Henry
Maidenhead, 18 December, 1943 (OR)

League Club	Source	Date Signed	Seasons Played	Apps	Subs	Gls
Charlton Ath.	Jnrs	08.62	62	1	-	0

SAUNDERS John Thomas
Newport, 2 October, 1950 W Sch (D)

League Club	Source	Date Signed	Seasons Played	Apps	Subs	Gls
Newport Co.	Birmingham C. (App)	08.69	69-70	26	1	0
Leeds U.	Tr	07.71				
Walsall	Tr	10.72	72-75	94	5	2

SAUNDERS Francis **John**
Middlesbrough, 24 August, 1924 (CH)

League Club	Source	Date Signed	Seasons Played	Apps	Subs	Gls
Darlington		09.46	46-47	67	-	0
Chelsea	Tr	05.48	49-53	52	-	0
Crystal Palace	Tr	08.54	54-55	59	-	0
Chester C.	Tr	05.57	57-58	67	-	3

SAUNDERS Leonard James
Liverpool, 7 January, 1928 (CF)

League Club	Source	Date Signed	Seasons Played	Apps	Subs	Gls
New Brighton (Am)	Stoneycroft	01.51	50	4	-	2

SAUNDERS Mark Philip
Reading, 23 July, 1971 (M)

League Club	Source	Date Signed	Seasons Played	Apps	Subs	Gls
Plymouth Arg.	Tiverton T.	08.95	95-97	60	12	11

SAUNDERS Paul Brian
Watford, 17 December, 1959 (D)

League Club	Source	Date Signed	Seasons Played	Apps	Subs	Gls
Watford	App	12.77				
Northampton T.	Tr	07.78	78-82	114	11	5

SAUNDERS Robert Charles
Poole, 26 August, 1945 (IF)

League Club	Source	Date Signed	Seasons Played	Apps	Subs	Gls
Bournemouth	App	06.63	65	2	1	0

SAUNDERS Ronald
Birkenhead, 6 November, 1932 E Yth (CF)

League Club	Source	Date Signed	Seasons Played	Apps	Subs	Gls
Everton	Jnrs	02.51	54	3	-	0
Gillingham	Tonbridge	05.57	57-58	49	-	20
Portsmouth	Tr	09.58	58-64	236	-	145
Watford	Tr	09.64	64-65	39	0	18
Charlton Ath.	Tr	08.65	65-66	64	1	24

SAUNDERS Ronald Albert
Malmesbury, 14 January, 1923 (CH)

League Club	Source	Date Signed	Seasons Played	Apps	Subs	Gls
Swindon T. (Am)		04.48	47	1	-	0

SAUNDERS Roy
Salford, 4 September, 1930 E Yth (WH)

League Club	Source	Date Signed	Seasons Played	Apps	Subs	Gls
Liverpool	Hull C. (Am)	05.48	52-58	132	-	1
Swansea C.	Tr	03.59	58-62	95	-	3

SAUNDERS Steven John Peter
Warrington, 21 September, 1964 (F)

League Club	Source	Date Signed	Seasons Played	Apps	Subs	Gls
Bolton W.	App	09.82	83	3	0	0
Crewe Alex.	Tr	07.85	85	15	7	1
Preston N. E. (N/C)	Tr	08.86				
Grimsby T.	Tr	08.87	87-88	70	6	13
Scarborough	Tr	08.89	89	23	9	1

SAUNDERS Wesley
Sunderland, 23 February, 1963 (CD)

League Club	Source	Date Signed	Seasons Played	Apps	Subs	Gls
Newcastle U.	Jnrs	06.81	81-84	79	0	0
Bradford C.	L	03.85	84	1	3	0
Carlisle U.	Tr	08.85	85-87	97	0	11
Torquay U.	Dundee	07.90	90-92	60	1	6

SAVAGE David Thomas Patrick
Dublin, 30 July, 1973 IRu21-5/IR-5 (M)

League Club	Source	Date Signed	Seasons Played	Apps	Subs	Gls
Brighton & H.A.	Kilkenny C.	03.91				
Millwall	Longford T.	05.94	94-97	104	26	6

SAVAGE John Alfred
Bromley, 14 December, 1929 (G)

League Club	Source	Date Signed	Seasons Played	Apps	Subs	Gls
Hull C.		09.50	50	4	-	0
Halifax T.	Tr	03.52	51-53	57	-	1
Manchester C.	Tr	11.53	54-57	30	-	0
Walsall	Tr	01.58	57-58	51	-	0

SAVAGE Reginald
Eccles, 5 July, 1912 (G)

League Club	Source	Date Signed	Seasons Played	Apps	Subs	Gls
Leeds U.	Stalybridge Celtic	02.31	34-38	79	-	0
Nottingham F.	Queen of South	05.46	46	20	-	0
Accrington St.	Tr	08.47				

SAVAGE Robert James
Liverpool, 8 January, 1960 (M)

League Club	Source	Date Signed	Seasons Played	Apps	Subs	Gls
Liverpool	App	01.78				
Wrexham	L	10.82	82	27	0	10
Stoke C.	Tr	07.83	83	5	2	0
Bournemouth	Tr	12.83	83-86	80	2	18
Bradford C.	Tr	12.86	86-87	11	0	0
Bolton W.	Tr	09.87	87-89	83	4	11

SAVAGE Robert William
Wrexham, 18 October, 1974 W Sch/W Yth/Wu21-5/W-5 (M)

League Club	Source	Date Signed	Seasons Played	Apps	Subs	Gls
Manchester U.	YT	07.93				
Crewe Alex.	Tr	07.94	94-96	74	3	10
Leicester C.	Tr	07.97	97	28	7	2

SAVILLE Andrew Victor
Hull, 12 December, 1964 (F)

League Club	Source	Date Signed	Seasons Played	Apps	Subs	Gls
Hull C.		09.83	83-88	74	27	18
Walsall	Tr	03.89	88-89	28	10	5
Barnsley	Tr	03.90	89-91	71	11	21
Hartlepool U.	Tr	03.92	91-92	37	0	14
Birmingham C.	Tr	03.93	92-94	51	8	17
Burnley	L	12.94	94	3	1	1
Preston N.E.	Tr	07.95	95-96	56	0	30
Wigan Ath.	Tr	10.96	96-97	17	8	4
Cardiff C.	Tr	10.97	97	32	1	11

SAVILLE Peter William
Dalbeattie, 29 August, 1948 (W)

League Club	Source	Date Signed	Seasons Played	Apps	Subs	Gls
Carlisle U.		07.66	67	1	0	0
Bradford P. A.	Hawick Royal Albert	03.69	68-69	31	0	1

SAVIN Keith Anthony
Oxford, 5 June, 1929 Died 1992 (FB)

League Club	Source	Date Signed	Seasons Played	Apps	Subs	Gls
Derby Co.	Oxford C.	05.50	50-55	65	-	0
Mansfield T.	Tr	05.57	57-58	68	-	0

SAVINO Raymond John
Norwich, 16 November, 1938 (OR)

League Club	Source	Date Signed	Seasons Played	Apps	Subs	Gls
Norwich C.	Thorpe Village	02.57	56-61	22	-	3
Bristol C.	Tr	07.62	62-67	75	0	2

SAWARD Leonard Roderick
Aldershot, 6 July, 1927 (IF)

League Club	Source	Date Signed	Seasons Played	Apps	Subs	Gls
Crystal Palace	Beddington	03.49	48-50	9	-	1
Newport Co.	Cambridge U.	01.54	53-54	25	-	4

SAWARD Patrick
Cork (Ire), 17 August, 1928 IR-18 (WH)

League Club	Source	Date Signed	Seasons Played	Apps	Subs	Gls
Millwall	Buckingham T.	07.51	51-54	118	-	14
Aston Villa	Tr	08.55	55-60	152	-	2
Huddersfield T.	Tr	03.61	60-62	59	-	1

SAWBRIDGE John
Wigan, 20 September, 1920 Died 1984 (G)

League Club	Source	Date Signed	Seasons Played	Apps	Subs	Gls
Oldham Ath.	Crossens	12.45	46-47	8	-	0

SAWYER Brian
Rawmarsh, 28 January, 1938 (CF)

League Club	Source	Date Signed	Seasons Played	Apps	Subs	Gls
Rotherham U.	Rawmarsh Welfare	01.58	57-62	91	-	31
Bradford C.	Tr	12.62	62-63	15	-	2

SAWYER Roy
Barnsley, 29 March, 1940 (CH)

League Club	Source	Date Signed	Seasons Played	Apps	Subs	Gls
Barnsley	Worsboro' Bridge	05.58	60-61	2	-	0

SAWYERS Keith Wilson
Banbury, 14 June, 1960 (M)

League Club	Source	Date Signed	Seasons Played	Apps	Subs	Gls
Carlisle U.	Carlisle Spartans	01.78	77-79	5	4	0

SAWYERS Robert
Dudley, 20 November, 1978 (LWB)

League Club	Source	Date Signed	Seasons Played	Apps	Subs	Gls
Barnet	Wolverhampton W. (YT)	10.97	97	1	0	0

SAXBY Gary Philip
Clipstone, 11 December, 1959 (M)

League Club	Source	Date Signed	Seasons Played	Apps	Subs	Gls
Mansfield T.	App	12.77	78	14	2	1
Northampton T.	Tr	08.80	80-82	86	10	11

SAXBY Michael William
Clipstone, 12 August, 1957 (CD)

League Club	Source	Date Signed	Seasons Played	Apps	Subs	Gls
Mansfield T.	App	01.75	75-78	76	3	5
Luton T.	Tr	07.79	79-81	82	0	6
Grimsby T.	L	03.83	82	10	0	0
Lincoln C.	L	11.83	83	10	0	1
Newport Co.	Tr	07.84	84	6	0	0
Middlesbrough	Tr	09.84	84	15	0	0

SAXTON Robert
Doncaster, 6 September, 1943 (CD)

League Club	Source	Date Signed	Seasons Played	Apps	Subs	Gls
Derby Co.	Denaby U.	02.62	64-67	94	2	1
Plymouth Arg.	Tr	02.68	67-75	224	7	7
Exeter C.	Tr	09.75	75-77	92	0	3

SAYER Andrew Clive
Brent, 6 June, 1966 (F)

League Club	Source	Date Signed	Seasons Played	Apps	Subs	Gls
Wimbledon	App	06.84	83-87	46	12	15
Cambridge U.	L	02.88	87	2	3	0
Fulham	Tr	08.88	88-89	44	9	15
Leyton Orient	Tr	02.90	89-91	23	7	6
Sheffield U.	L	03.91	90	0	3	0

SAYER Peter Anthony
Cardiff, 2 May, 1955 Wu21-2/W-7 (W)

League Club	Source	Date Signed	Seasons Played	Apps	Subs	Gls
Cardiff C.	Jnrs	07.73	73-77	70	12	14
Brighton & H. A.	Tr	02.78	77-79	46	9	6
Preston N. E.	Tr	08.80	80-83	42	3	6
Cardiff C.	L	09.81	81	4	0	1
Chester C.	Tr	07.84	84	35	1	6

SBRAGIA Richard (Ricky)
Lennoxtown, 26 May, 1956 (CD)

League Club	Source	Date Signed	Seasons Played	Apps	Subs	Gls
Birmingham C.	App	05.74	74-77	14	1	1
Walsall	Tr	10.78	78-79	77	0	4
Blackpool	Tr	07.80	80-81	24	2	1
York C.	Tr	08.82	82-86	149	0	7
Darlington	L	08.85	85	6	0	0

SCAIFE Nicholas
Middlesbrough, 14 May, 1975 (M)

League Club	Source	Date Signed	Seasons Played	Apps	Subs	Gls
York C.	Whitby T.	03.95	94-95	0	2	0

SCAIFE Robert Henry
Northallerton, 12 October, 1955 (M)

League Club	Source	Date Signed	Seasons Played	Apps	Subs	Gls
Middlesbrough	App	10.72				
Halifax T.	L	01.75	74	5	1	1
Hartlepool U.	Tr	09.75	75-77	77	3	10
Rochdale	Tr	10.77	77-79	95	3	9

SCALES George
Northwich, 14 March, 1923 Died 1993 (G)

League Club	Source	Date Signed	Seasons Played	Apps	Subs	Gls
Chester C.	Manchester C. (Am)	08.44	46-48	81	-	0

SCALES John Robert
Harrogate, 4 July, 1966 E 'B'/E-3 (CD)

League Club	Source	Date Signed	Seasons Played	Apps	Subs	Gls
Bristol Rov.	Leeds U. (YT)	07.85	85-86	68	4	2
Wimbledon	Tr	07.87	87-94	235	5	11
Liverpool	Tr	09.94	94-96	65	0	2
Tottenham H.	Tr	12.96	96-97	19	3	0

SCALES Terence Albert
Stratford, 18 November, 1951 (CD)

League Club	Source	Date Signed	Seasons Played	Apps	Subs	Gls
West Ham U.	App	08.69				
Brentford	Tr	07.71	71-76	212	0	5

SCANLON Albert Joseph
Manchester, 10 October, 1935 Eu23-5/EF Lge (OL)

League Club	Source	Date Signed	Seasons Played	Apps	Subs	Gls
Manchester U.	Jnrs	12.52	54-60	115	-	34
Newcastle U.	Tr	11.60	60-61	22	-	5
Lincoln C.	Tr	02.62	61-62	47	-	11
Mansfield T.	Tr	04.63	62-65	108	0	21

SCANLON John (Ian)
Birkenshaw (Lk), 13 July, 1952 (W)

League Club	Source	Date Signed	Seasons Played	Apps	Subs	Gls
Notts Co.	East Stirling	07.72	72-77	99	12	31

SCANNELL Thomas
Youghal (Ire), 3 June, 1925 Died 1992 IR-1 (G)

League Club	Source	Date Signed	Seasons Played	Apps	Subs	Gls
Southend U.	Tilbury	12.49	50-54	98	-	0

SCARBOROUGH Brian
Ironville, 11 December, 1941 (OL)

League Club	Source	Date Signed	Seasons Played	Apps	Subs	Gls
Derby Co.	Jnrs	01.59	58-60	4	-	0

SCARBOROUGH James Albert
Nottingham, 10 June, 1931 (CF)

League Club	Source	Date Signed	Seasons Played	Apps	Subs	Gls
Darlington		09.51	51-53	49	-	15

SCARGILL Wayne
Barnsley, 30 April, 1968 (D)

League Club	Source	Date Signed	Seasons Played	Apps	Subs	Gls
Bradford C.	Frickley Ath.	11.93	94	1	0	0

SCARLETT John Edgar
Wolverhampton, 1 August, 1934 Died 1960 (IF)

League Club	Source	Date Signed	Seasons Played	Apps	Subs	Gls
Walsall		03.52	52-53	10	-	2

SCARROTT Alan Richard
Malmesbury, 22 November, 1944 (W)

League Club	Source	Date Signed	Seasons Played	Apps	Subs	Gls
West Bromwich A.	Chippenham T.	12.61				
Bristol Rov.	Tr	06.64				
Reading	Tr	04.65	65-67	90	0	7

SCARTH James William
North Shields, 26 August, 1926 (IF)

League Club	Source	Date Signed	Seasons Played	Apps	Subs	Gls
Tottenham H.	Percy Main	08.48	49-51	7	-	3
Gillingham	Tr	02.52	51-54	139	-	25

SCATTERGOOD Eric
Barnsley, 9 September, 1929 (WH)

League Club	Source	Date Signed	Seasons Played	Apps	Subs	Gls
Barnsley	Jnrs	02.47	49-51	12	-	0

SCHIAVI Mark Antony
City of London, 1 May, 1964 E Yth (LM)

League Club	Source	Date Signed	Seasons Played	Apps	Subs	Gls
West Ham U.	App	11.81				
Bournemouth	L	09.83	83	10	0	0
Bournemouth	Tr	07.84	84	14	5	0
Northampton T.	Tr	07.85	85-86	31	4	5
Cambridge U.	Tr	09.86	86	24	6	2

SCHMEICHEL Peter Boleslaw
Denmark, 18 November, 1963 Danish Int (G)

League Club	Source	Date Signed	Seasons Played	Apps	Subs	Gls
Manchester U.	Brondby (Den)	07.91	91-97	258	0	0

SCHOFIELD Ernest
Sheffield, 29 March, 1921 (IL)

League Club	Source	Date Signed	Seasons Played	Apps	Subs	Gls
Bradford C.		06.45	46	1	-	1

SCHOFIELD Gary
Eccles, 27 March, 1957 (D)

League Club	Source	Date Signed	Seasons Played	Apps	Subs	Gls
Stockport Co. (N/C)		03.78	77	0	1	0

SCHOFIELD Graham
Manchester, 18 December, 1950 (CD)

League Club	Source	Date Signed	Seasons Played	Apps	Subs	Gls
Oldham Ath.	Jnrs	08.69	69	1	0	0

SCHOFIELD John David
Barnsley, 16 May, 1965 (M)

League Club	Source	Date Signed	Seasons Played	Apps	Subs	Gls
Lincoln C.	Gainsborough Trin.	11.88	88-94	221	10	11
Doncaster Rov.	Tr	11.94	94-96	107	3	12
Mansfield T.	Tr	08.97	97	44	0	0

SCHOFIELD John Reginald
Atherstone, 8 February, 1931 (G)

League Club	Source	Date Signed	Seasons Played	Apps	Subs	Gls
Birmingham C.	Nuneaton Borough	02.50	52-65	212	0	0
Wrexham	Tr	07.66	66-67	52	0	0

SCHOFIELD Malcolm
Failsworth, 8 October, 1918 Died 1985 (G)

League Club	Source	Date Signed	Seasons Played	Apps	Subs	Gls
Oldham Ath.		11.37	46	7	-	0

SCHOFIELD Mark Anthony
Wigan, 10 October, 1966 (D)

League Club	Source	Date Signed	Seasons Played	Apps	Subs	Gls
Wigan Ath.	App	07.85	83-84	1	1	0

SCHOFIELD Alan **Stewart**
Blackburn, 24 July, 1933 (IF)

League Club	Source	Date Signed	Seasons Played	Apps	Subs	Gls
Southport	Blackburn Rov. (Am)	07.57	57-58	36	-	9

SCHOFIELD Thomas
Halifax, 22 June, 1926 (G)

League Club	Source	Date Signed	Seasons Played	Apps	Subs	Gls
Halifax T. (Am)	Boothtown	10.52	52	1	-	0

SCHOLES Martin
Barrow, 28 January, 1954 (CD)

League Club	Source	Date Signed	Seasons Played	Apps	Subs	Gls
Workington (N/C)		11.76	76	3	1	0

SCHOLES Paul
Salford, 16 November, 1974 E Yth/E-11 (M/F)

League Club	Source	Date Signed	Seasons Played	Apps	Subs	Gls
Manchester U.	YT	01.93	94-97	66	32	26

SCHROEDER Nico
Netherlands, 19 November, 1947 (G)

League Club	Source	Date Signed	Seasons Played	Apps	Subs	Gls
Swansea C.		07.76	76	1	0	0

SCHWARZ Stephan Hans
Sweden, 18 April, 1969 Swedish Int (M)

League Club	Source	Date Signed	Seasons Played	Apps	Subs	Gls
Arsenal	Benfica (Por)	05.94	94	34	0	2

SCHWARZER Mark
Australia, 6 October, 1972 Australian Int (G)

League Club	Source	Date Signed	Seasons Played	Apps	Subs	Gls
Bradford C.	Kaiserslautern (Ger)	11.96	96	13	0	0
Middlesbrough	Tr	02.97	96-97	42	0	0

League Club	Source	Date Signed	Seasons Played	Career Record Apps	Subs	Gls
SCIMECA Riccardo						
Leamington Spa, 13 June, 1975 Eu21-9/E 'B'						(CD)
Aston Villa	YT	07.93	95-97	34	21	0
SCONCE Mark Allan						
Wrexham, 18 February, 1968						(FB)
Chester C.	YT	07.86	85	1	1	0
SCOPE David Frederick						
Newcastle, 10 May, 1967						(W)
Northampton T.	Blyth Spartans	09.89	89-91	6	13	1
SCOTHORN Gary						
Hoyland, 6 June, 1950						(G)
Sheffield Wed.	App	06.67	67	1	0	0
Mansfield T.	Sligo Rov.	08.74				
SCOTSON Reginald						
Stockton, 22 September, 1919						(WH)
Sunderland	Ouston Jnrs	04.39	46-50	61	-	1
Grimsby T.	Tr	12.50	50-54	164	-	4
SCOTT Alexander MacNaughton						
Ceres, 17 November, 1922 Died 1995						(FB)
Leicester C.	Lochgelly Albert	03.47	47-49	31	-	1
Carlisle U.	Tr	01.50	49-55	200	-	4
SCOTT Alexander Silcock						
Falkirk, 22 November, 1936 Su23-1/S 'B'/SF Lge/S-16						(OR)
Everton	Glasgow Rangers	02.63	62-66	149	0	23
SCOTT Andrew						
Epsom, 2 August, 1972						(LB/F)
Sheffield U.	Sutton U.	12.92	92-97	39	36	6
Chesterfield	L	10.96	96	4	1	3
Bury	L	03.97	96	2	6	0
Brentford	Tr	11.97	97	24	2	5
SCOTT Andrew Michael						
Manchester, 27 June, 1975						(FB)
Blackburn Rov.	YT	01.93				
Cardiff C.	Tr	08.94	94-96	14	2	1
Rochdale	Tr	08.97	97	1	2	0
SCOTT Anthony James Ernest						
St Neots, 1 April, 1941 E Yth						(W)
West Ham U.	Jnrs	05.58	59-65	83	0	16
Aston Villa	Tr	10.65	65-67	47	3	3
Torquay U.	Tr	09.67	67-69	82	5	4
Bournemouth	Tr	07.70	70-71	59	2	6
Exeter C.	Tr	06.72	72-73	51	0	2
SCOTT Augustus Fisher						
Sunderland, 19 February, 1921						(IF)
Luton T.	Hylton Colly	03.39				
Southampton	Tr	07.47	47-49	45	-	9
Colchester U.	Tr	08.51	51-53	120	-	10
SCOTT Christopher						
Wallsend, 11 September, 1963						(CD)
Northampton T.	Blyth Spartans	07.87				
Lincoln C.	Tr	03.88	88	4	0	0
SCOTT Colin						
Glasgow, 19 May, 1970						(G)
Brentford (L)	Glasgow Rangers	03.90	89	6	0	0
SCOTT David Perry						
Belfast, 6 June, 1918 Died 1977						(G)
Northampton T.	Linfield	05.45	46-47	11	-	0
SCOTT Derek Edward						
Gateshead, 8 February, 1958 E Sch						(RB)
Burnley	App	02.75	74-84	277	8	24
Bolton W.	Tr	07.85	85-87	119	0	0
SCOTT Donald						
Elland, 20 October, 1922						(OR)
Halifax T.		09.48	48-49	20	-	5
SCOTT Frederick Hind						
Fatfield, 6 October, 1916 Died 1995 E Sch						(OR)
Bolton W.		01.35				
Bradford P. A.	Tr	05.36				
York C.	Tr	02.37	36-46	74	-	16
Nottingham F.	Tr	09.46	46-56	301	-	40

League Club	Source	Date Signed	Seasons Played	Career Record Apps	Subs	Gls
SCOTT Gary Craig						
Liverpool, 3 February, 1978						(RWB)
Tranmere Rov.	YT	10.95				
Rotherham U.	Tr	08.97	97	6	1	0
SCOTT Geoffrey Samuel						
Birmingham, 31 October, 1956						(D)
Stoke C.	Highgate U.	04.77	77-79	76	2	3
Leicester C.	Tr	02.80	79-81	39	0	0
Birmingham C.	Tr	02.82	81-82	18	1	0
Charlton Ath.	Tr	10.82	82	2	0	0
Middlesbrough	Tr	06.84	84	2	0	0
Northampton T.	Tr	09.84	84	16	1	0
Cambridge U.	Tr	07.85	85	19	0	0
SCOTT George William						
Aberdeen, 25 October, 1944						(M)
Liverpool	App	10.61				
Tranmere Rov.	South Africa	11.68	68-69	35	1	0
SCOTT Ian						
Radcliffe, 20 September, 1967 E Sch						(M)
Manchester C.	App	09.85	87-88	20	4	3
Stoke C.	Tr	07.89	89-91	21	9	2
Crewe Alex.	L	03.91	90	12	0	1
Bury	Tr	08.92	92	7	2	2
SCOTT Ian Richard						
Otley, 4 March, 1969						(D)
Manchester U.	App	03.87				
Stockport Co.	Tr	09.87	87-88	23	2	0
SCOTT James						
Falkirk, 21 August, 1940 S-1						(W)
Newcastle U.	Hibernian	08.67	67-69	70	4	6
Crystal Palace	Tr	02.70	69-71	36	7	5
SCOTT James						
Hetton-le-Hole, 7 September, 1934 E Sch						(WH)
Burnley	Jnrs	09.51	54-60	3	-	0
Oldham Ath.	Tr	06.61	61-63	76	-	0
SCOTT James Adamson						
Newcastle, 28 February, 1960						(M)
Newcastle U.	App	03.78	77-78	9	1	0
SCOTT James Dennis						
Olney, 5 September, 1945						(IF)
Leyton Orient	Chelsea (Am)	11.62	63-65	22	1	6
SCOTT James John Wedderburn						
Glasgow, 26 December, 1927						(IF)
Workington	Alloa Ath.	06.54	54	6	-	1
SCOTT John						
Normanton, 2 January, 1942						(IF)
Bradford C.	Jnrs	08.60	61-62	11	-	2
Chesterfield	Tr	07.63	63	5	-	0
SCOTT John						
Belfast, 22 December, 1933 Died 1978 NI 'B'/NI-2						(OR)
Manchester U.	Ormond Star	10.51	52-55	3	-	0
Grimsby T.	Tr	06.56	56-62	240	-	51
York C.	Tr	06.63	63	21	-	3
SCOTT John Alfred						
Maryport, 18 July, 1928						(G)
Leeds U.	Workington	05.50	50-54	111	-	0
SCOTT John Mather						
Dunfermline, 21 August, 1953						(D)
Workington	Brechin C.	08.75	75	1	1	0
SCOTT Joseph						
Plymouth, 11 January, 1953						(F)
Bournemouth	Falmouth	06.78	78	18	3	4
SCOTT Joseph Cumpson						
Fatfield (Dm), 9 January, 1930						(IF)
Newcastle U.		04.49				
Luton T.	Spennymoor U.	02.52	52-53	13	-	2
Middlesbrough	Tr	09.54	54-58	93	-	26
Hartlepool U.	Tr	01.59	58-59	62	-	8
York C.	Tr	06.60	60	17	-	2
SCOTT Keith						
Westminster, 10 June, 1967						(F)
Lincoln C.	Leicester U.	03.90	89-90	7	9	2

League Club	Source	Date Signed	Seasons Played	Apps	Subs	Gls
Wycombe W.	Tr	03.91	93	15	0	10
Swindon T.	Tr	11.93	93-94	43	8	12
Stoke C.	Tr	12.94	94-95	22	3	3
Norwich C.	Tr	11.95	95-96	10	15	5
Bournemouth	L	02.96	95	8	0	1
Watford	L	02.97	96	6	0	2
Wycombe W.	Tr	03.97	96-97	37	1	14

SCOTT Kenneth
Maltby, 13 August, 1931 (OR)

League Club	Source	Date Signed	Seasons Played	Apps	Subs	Gls
Derby Co.	Denaby U.	08.50	50	2	-	0
Mansfield T.	Denaby U.	08.52	52	5	-	2

SCOTT Kevin
Lincoln, 12 November, 1954 (D)

League Club	Source	Date Signed	Seasons Played	Apps	Subs	Gls
Lincoln C. (N/C)	Sheffield Poly.	02.74	73	1	0	0

SCOTT Kevin Watson
Easington, 17 December, 1966 (CD)

League Club	Source	Date Signed	Seasons Played	Apps	Subs	Gls
Newcastle U.	Middlesbrough (YT)	12.84	86-93	227	0	8
Tottenham H.	Tr	02.94	93-95	16	2	1
Port Vale	L	01.95	94	17	0	1
Charlton Ath.	L	12.96	96	4	0	0
Norwich C.	Tr	01.97	96-97	31	2	0

SCOTT Lawrence
Sheffield, 23 April, 1917 EF Lge/E 'B'/E-17 (FB)

League Club	Source	Date Signed	Seasons Played	Apps	Subs	Gls
Bradford C.	Jnrs	05.35	35-36	39	-	0
Arsenal	Tr	02.37	46-51	115	-	0
Crystal Palace	Tr	10.51	51-52	28	-	0

SCOTT Lloyd Edward
Stepney, 13 October, 1961 (G)

League Club	Source	Date Signed	Seasons Played	Apps	Subs	Gls
Leyton Orient	App	10.79				
Blackpool	Tr	07.82	82	2	0	0

SCOTT Malcolm Ernest
South Shields, 8 May, 1936 (CH)

League Club	Source	Date Signed	Seasons Played	Apps	Subs	Gls
Newcastle U.	Cleadon Jnrs	09.55	56-60	25	-	2
Darlington	Tr	10.61	61-62	47	-	2
York C.	Tr	10.63	63	19	-	0

SCOTT Martin
Sheffield, 7 January, 1968 (LB)

League Club	Source	Date Signed	Seasons Played	Apps	Subs	Gls
Rotherham U.	App	01.86	84-90	93	1	3
Bristol C.	Tr	12.90	90-94	171	0	14
Sunderland	Tr	12.94	94-97	90	0	7

SCOTT Melvyn Douglas
Claygate, 26 September, 1939 E Yth/Eu23-3 (CH)

League Club	Source	Date Signed	Seasons Played	Apps	Subs	Gls
Chelsea	Jnrs	11.56	57-61	97	-	0
Brentford	Tr	03.63	62-66	157	0	2

SCOTT Michael Ramsey
Newcastle, 4 December, 1945 (OL)

League Club	Source	Date Signed	Seasons Played	Apps	Subs	Gls
Burnley	App	12.62				
Hartlepool U.	Tr	07.64	64	2	-	0

SCOTT Morrys James
Swansea, 17 December, 1970 (F)

League Club	Source	Date Signed	Seasons Played	Apps	Subs	Gls
Cardiff C.	YT	07.89	89	1	8	0
Southend U.	Colchester U.	10.90				
Plymouth Arg.	Tr	06.91	91	3	3	0
Northampton T. (N/C)	Tr	08.92	92	10	7	2

SCOTT Peter Reginald
Notting Hill, 1 October, 1963 (M)

League Club	Source	Date Signed	Seasons Played	Apps	Subs	Gls
Fulham	App	09.81	81-91	268	9	27
Bournemouth	Tr	08.92	92	9	1	0
Barnet	Burnham	11.93	93-95	72	6	2

SCOTT Peter William
Liverpool, 19 September, 1952 E Yth/NI-10 (FB)

League Club	Source	Date Signed	Seasons Played	Apps	Subs	Gls
Everton	App	07.70	71-74	42	2	1
Southport	L	01.74	73	4	0	0
York C.	Tr	12.75	75-78	99	1	3
Aldershot	Tr	03.79	78-82	114	7	2

SCOTT Richard Paul
Dudley, 29 September, 1974 (M)

League Club	Source	Date Signed	Seasons Played	Apps	Subs	Gls
Birmingham C.	YT	05.93	92-94	11	1	0
Shrewsbury T.	Tr	03.95	95-97	91	14	18

SCOTT Richard (Dick) Sydney Arthur
Thetford, 26 October, 1941 (WH/IF)

League Club	Source	Date Signed	Seasons Played	Apps	Subs	Gls
Norwich C.	Jnrs	11.58	60-62	28	-	1
Cardiff C.	Tr	07.63	63-64	37	-	5
Scunthorpe U.	Tr	09.64	64-65	47	0	8
Lincoln C.	Tr	07.66	66	9	1	1

SCOTT Robert
Broxburn, 13 January, 1964 (F)

League Club	Source	Date Signed	Seasons Played	Apps	Subs	Gls
Colchester U.	Whitburn Jnrs	03.89	88-89	26	11	8

SCOTT Robert
Bellshill, 20 May, 1930 (W)

League Club	Source	Date Signed	Seasons Played	Apps	Subs	Gls
Accrington St.	Alloa Ath.	09.54	54-58	149	-	32
Wrexham	Tr	07.59	59	2	-	0
Oldham Ath.	Tr	10.59	59	9	-	1

SCOTT Robert
Epsom, 15 August, 1973 (W)

League Club	Source	Date Signed	Seasons Played	Apps	Subs	Gls
Sheffield U.	Sutton U.	08.93	94-95	2	4	1
Scarborough	L	03.95	94	8	0	3
Northampton T.	L	11.95	95	5	0	0
Fulham	Tr	01.96	95-97	63	18	17

SCOTT Robert Alexander
Liverpool, 26 October, 1913 Died 1962 E Sch (G)

League Club	Source	Date Signed	Seasons Played	Apps	Subs	Gls
Liverpool		05.31				
Burnley	Tr	05.33	33-35	57	-	0
Wolverhampton W.	Tr	02.36	35-38	119	-	0
Crewe Alex.	Tr	08.47	47-48	44	-	0

SCOTT Robert John
Dundee, 16 March, 1937 (WH)

League Club	Source	Date Signed	Seasons Played	Apps	Subs	Gls
Cardiff C.	Dundee Violet	02.57	57	3	-	0
Swindon T.	Tr	06.61				
Newport Co.	Tr	11.61	61-62	18	-	0
Southport	Sankeys	07.63	63	3	-	0

SCOTT Robert William
Liverpool, 22 February, 1953 (CD)

League Club	Source	Date Signed	Seasons Played	Apps	Subs	Gls
Wrexham	Jnrs	07.71	70-75	15	4	0
Reading	L	01.75	74	5	0	0
Hartlepool U.	Tr	07.76	76	37	0	0
Rochdale	Tr	07.77	77-78	71	0	3
Crewe Alex.	Tr	08.79	79-85	238	1	15
Wrexham (N/C)	Northwich Vic.	01.86	85	2	1	0

SCOTT Stuart **Robin**
Shrewsbury, 31 March, 1946 (W)

League Club	Source	Date Signed	Seasons Played	Apps	Subs	Gls
Shrewsbury T.	Jnrs	04.64	63-65	18	0	2

SCOTT Ryan
Saltburn, 20 March, 1976 (G)

League Club	Source	Date Signed	Seasons Played	Apps	Subs	Gls
Darlington	YT	07.94	93	0	1	0

SCOTT Samuel
Ashington, 14 June, 1922 (CF)

League Club	Source	Date Signed	Seasons Played	Apps	Subs	Gls
Hartlepool U.	Ashington	02.46	46-47	49	-	17

SCOTT Stephen Richard
Wrexham, 5 November, 1966 (D)

League Club	Source	Date Signed	Seasons Played	Apps	Subs	Gls
Wrexham (N/C)	Oswestry T.	03.86	87	0	2	0

SCOTT Walter
Douglas, 23 June, 1932 (G)

League Club	Source	Date Signed	Seasons Played	Apps	Subs	Gls
Halifax T.	Dumbarton	08.54	54	13	-	0

SCOTT William John
Preston, 14 June, 1921 (FB)

League Club	Source	Date Signed	Seasons Played	Apps	Subs	Gls
Preston N. E.	Jnrs	05.39	46-53	207	-	0

SCOTT William Reed
Willington, 6 December, 1907 Died 1969 E-1 (IF)

League Club	Source	Date Signed	Seasons Played	Apps	Subs	Gls
Middlesbrough	Howden B.L.	05.27	30-31	26	-	5
Brentford	Tr	05.32	32-46	273	-	85
Aldershot	Tr	07.47	47	21	-	0

SCOTTING Allen
Dartford, 22 April, 1966 (FB)

League Club	Source	Date Signed	Seasons Played	Apps	Subs	Gls
Gillingham (N/C)	Charlton Ath. (Jnrs)	02.84	83	2	0	0

SCOULAR James
Livingston, 11 January, 1925 Died 1998 S-9 (WH)

League Club	Source	Date Signed	Seasons Played	Apps	Subs	Gls
Portsmouth	Gosport Borough	12.45	46-52	247	-	8
Newcastle U.	Tr	06.53	53-60	247	-	6
Bradford P. A.	Tr	01.61	60-63	108	-	5

SCOWCROFT James Benjamin
Bury St Edmunds, 15 November, 1975 Eu21-5 (F)

League Club	Source	Date Signed	Seasons Played	Apps	Subs	Gls
Ipswich T.	YT	07.94	95-97	72	23	17

SCREEN Anthony Lewis
Swansea, 9 May, 1952 Wu23-1 (FB)

League Club	Source	Date Signed	Seasons Played	Apps	Subs	Gls
Swansea C.	App	05.70	68-74	125	3	9

SCREEN William Robert
Swansea, 8 November, 1948 Wu23-2 (FB/M)

League Club	Source	Date Signed	Seasons Played	Apps	Subs	Gls
Swansea C.	Jnrs	03.67	67-71	131	10	14
Newport Co.	Tr	06.72	72-75	137	5	7

SCRIMGEOUR Brian
Dundee, 11 August, 1959 (D/M)

League Club	Source	Date Signed	Seasons Played	Apps	Subs	Gls
Chesterfield	Dundee	07.83	83-86	117	4	15

SCRIMSHAW Stanley
Hartlepool, 7 August, 1915 Died 1988 (WH)

League Club	Source	Date Signed	Seasons Played	Apps	Subs	Gls
Hartlepool U.		01.36	35-36	18	-	1
Bradford C.	Tr	06.37	37-46	20	-	0
Halifax T.	Frickley Colly	10.47	47-49	52	-	0

SCRINE Francis Henry
Swansea, 9 January, 1925 W-2 (IF)

League Club	Source	Date Signed	Seasons Played	Apps	Subs	Gls
Swansea C.		03.44	47-53	142	-	45
Oldham Ath.	Tr	10.53	53-55	78	-	21

SCRINE William Harold
Swansea, 3 December, 1934 (IF/WH)

League Club	Source	Date Signed	Seasons Played	Apps	Subs	Gls
Swansea C.	Jnrs	12.51	52	1	-	0

SCRIVENS Stephen
Ewell, 11 March, 1957 (W)

League Club	Source	Date Signed	Seasons Played	Apps	Subs	Gls
Fulham	App	03.75	74-75	3	1	1
Brentford	L	12.76	76	5	0	0

SCRIVENS William
Rotherham, 26 May, 1936 (G)

League Club	Source	Date Signed	Seasons Played	Apps	Subs	Gls
Rotherham U.		08.56	56	2	-	0

SCRUGHAM Robert
Cleator Moor, 15 May, 1932 (G)

League Club	Source	Date Signed	Seasons Played	Apps	Subs	Gls
Workington	Cleator Moor	08.53	53	3	-	0

SCULLION Stewart McNab Adam
Bo'ness, 18 April, 1946 (W)

League Club	Source	Date Signed	Seasons Played	Apps	Subs	Gls
Charlton Ath.	Chesham U.	03.65				
Watford	Tr	02.66	65-70	217	8	30
Sheffield U.	Tr	05.71	71-73	53	4	7
Watford	Tr	12.73	73-75	87	0	19

SCULLY Anthony Derek Thomas
Dublin, 12 June, 1976 IR Sch/IR Yth/IRu21-8 (M)

League Club	Source	Date Signed	Seasons Played	Apps	Subs	Gls
Crystal Palace	YT	12.93	95-96	0	3	0
Bournemouth	L	10.94	94	6	4	0
Cardiff C.	L	01.96	95	13	1	0
Manchester C.	Tr	08.97	97	1	8	0
Stoke C.	L	01.98	97	7	0	0
Queens Park R.	Tr	03.98	97	7	0	0

SCULLY Patrick Joseph
Dublin, 23 June, 1970 IR Sch/IR Yth/IRu21-9/IRu23-1/IR 'B'/IR-1 (CD)

League Club	Source	Date Signed	Seasons Played	Apps	Subs	Gls
Arsenal	YT	09.87				
Preston N. E.	L	09.89	89	13	0	1
Northampton T.	L	08.90	90	15	0	0
Southend U.	Tr	01.91	90-93	114	1	6
Huddersfield T.	Tr	03.94	93-95	74	0	2

SCURR David William
Fareham, 25 September, 1939 Died 1991 (FB)

League Club	Source	Date Signed	Seasons Played	Apps	Subs	Gls
Southampton	Jnrs	04.58	59-60	2	-	0

SCURR John Thomas
North Shields, 30 September, 1940 (IF)

League Club	Source	Date Signed	Seasons Played	Apps	Subs	Gls
Arsenal	North Shields B.C.	09.59				
Carlisle U.	Tr	01.61	60-61	15	-	1

SEABURY Kevin
Shrewsbury, 24 November, 1973 (RB)

League Club	Source	Date Signed	Seasons Played	Apps	Subs	Gls
Shrewsbury T.	YT	07.92	92-97	122	20	2

SEACOLE Jason Paul
Oxford, 11 April, 1960 E Sch/E Yth (F)

League Club	Source	Date Signed	Seasons Played	Apps	Subs	Gls
Oxford U.	App	04.77	76-81	104	16	22

SEADEN John Charles
Southend, 4 June, 1967 (M)

League Club	Source	Date Signed	Seasons Played	Apps	Subs	Gls
Southend U.	App	03.85	84-85	19	1	0

SEAGRAVES Christopher Anthony
Liverpool, 7 October, 1964 (RB)

League Club	Source	Date Signed	Seasons Played	Apps	Subs	Gls
Liverpool	App	09.82				
Grimsby T.	Tr	08.84	84	22	1	0

SEAGRAVES Mark
Bootle, 22 October, 1966 E Yth (CD)

League Club	Source	Date Signed	Seasons Played	Apps	Subs	Gls
Liverpool	App	11.83				
Norwich C.	L	11.86	86	3	0	0
Manchester C.	Tr	09.87	87-89	36	6	0
Bolton W.	Tr	09.90	90-94	152	5	7
Swindon T.	Tr	06.95	95-97	57	4	0

SEAL David
Australia, 26 January, 1972 (F)

League Club	Source	Date Signed	Seasons Played	Apps	Subs	Gls
Bristol C.	Aalst (Bel)	10.94	94-96	24	27	10
Northampton T.	Tr	08.97	97	30	7	12

SEAL James
Wakefield, 9 December, 1950 (F)

League Club	Source	Date Signed	Seasons Played	Apps	Subs	Gls
Wolverhampton W.	Jnrs	03.68	68	1	0	0
Walsall	L	01.70	69	17	0	8
Walsall	L	12.70	70	24	0	6
Barnsley	Tr	05.71	71	43	0	12
York C.	Tr	07.72	72-76	152	9	43
Darlington	Tr	11.76	76-79	115	7	19
Rochdale	Tr	11.79	79-80	44	9	4

SEALEY Alan William
Hampton, 24 February, 1942 Died 1996 (OR)

League Club	Source	Date Signed	Seasons Played	Apps	Subs	Gls
Leyton Orient	Memorial Sports	08.59	60	4	-	1
West Ham U.	Tr	03.61	60-66	107	0	22
Plymouth Arg.	Tr	09.67	67	4	0	0

SEALEY Arthur John
Wallasey, 27 December, 1945 (OR)

League Club	Source	Date Signed	Seasons Played	Apps	Subs	Gls
Liverpool	Warrington	12.63	64	1	-	1
Chester C.	Tr	06.66	66-67	3	1	0

SEALEY Leslie Jesse
Bethnal Green, 29 September, 1957 (G)

League Club	Source	Date Signed	Seasons Played	Apps	Subs	Gls
Coventry C.	App	03.76	76-82	158	0	0
Luton T.	Tr	08.83	83-88	207	0	0
Plymouth Arg.	L	10.84	84	6	0	0
Manchester U.	L	03.90	89	2	0	0
Manchester U.	Tr	06.90	90	31	0	0
Aston Villa	Tr	07.91	91	18	0	0
Coventry C.	L	03.92	91	2	0	0
Birmingham C.	L	10.92	92	12	0	0
Manchester U.	Tr	01.93				
Blackpool	Tr	07.94	94	7	0	0
West Ham U.	Tr	11.94	95	1	1	0
Leyton Orient	Tr	07.96	96	12	0	0
West Ham U.	Tr	11.96	96	1	1	0

SEALY Anthony John
Hackney, 7 May, 1959 (F)

League Club	Source	Date Signed	Seasons Played	Apps	Subs	Gls
Southampton	App	05.77	77-78	2	5	0
Crystal Palace	Tr	03.79	78-80	16	8	5
Port Vale	L	02.80	79	17	0	6
Queens Park R.	Tr	03.81	80-83	57	6	18
Port Vale	L	02.82	81	6	0	4
Fulham	L	12.83	83	5	0	1
Fulham	L	08.84	84	3	1	1
Fulham	Tr	01.85	84-85	14	2	9
Leicester C.	Tr	09.85	85-86	28	11	7
Bournemouth	L	03.87	86	8	5	2
Brentford (N/C)	Sporting Lisbon (Por)	03.89	88	11	1	4
Bristol Rov.	Tr	09.89	89-90	21	16	7
Brentford	M.Y.P.A. (Fin)	10.91	91	9	9	0

SEAMAN David Andrew
Rotherham, 19 September, 1963 Eu21-10/E 'B'/E-44 (G)

League Club	Source	Date Signed	Seasons Played	Apps	Subs	Gls
Leeds U.	App	09.81				
Peterborough U.	Tr	08.82	82-84	91	0	0
Birmingham C.	Tr	10.84	84-85	75	0	0
Queens Park R.	Tr	08.86	86-89	141	0	0
Arsenal	Tr	05.90	90-97	280	0	0

SEAR Reginald Clifford
Wrexham, 22 September, 1936 Wu23-2/W-1 (LB)

League Club	Source	Date Signed	Seasons Played	Apps	Subs	Gls
Manchester C.	Oswestry T.	01.57	56-65	248	0	1
Chester C.	Tr	04.68	68-69	48	1	1

SEARGEANT Steven Charles
Liverpool, 2 January, 1951 E Sch (D)

League Club	Source	Date Signed	Seasons Played	Apps	Subs	Gls
Everton	App	07.68	71-77	77	3	1

SEARLE Damon Peter
Cardiff, 26 October, 1971 W Yth/Wu21-6/W 'B' (LB)

League Club	Source	Date Signed	Seasons Played	Apps	Subs	Gls
Cardiff C.	YT	08.90	90-95	232	2	3
Stockport Co.	Tr	05.96	96-97	34	7	0

League Club	Source	Date Signed	Seasons Played	Apps	Subs	Gls
SEARLE Eric Frederick						
Guildford, 20 July, 1925						(G)
Aldershot		10.47	47-49	14	-	0
SEARLE Stephen						
Lambeth, 7 March, 1977						(M)
Barnet	Sittingbourne	08.97	97	26	4	2
SEARS Douglas Reginald						
Eton, 5 January, 1919 Died 1995						(IF)
Grimsby T.		10.43				
Reading	Tr	05.46	46	5	-	0
Aldershot	Tr	06.47	47-49	46	-	13
SEARS Gerald						
Chesterfield, 13 January, 1935						(LB)
Chesterfield	Jnrs	01.52	52-67	412	0	4
SEARSON Harold Vincent						
Mansfield, 3 June, 1924						(G)
Sheffield Wed.	Bilsthorpe Colly	08.46				
Mansfield T.	Tr	06.47	47-48	42	-	0
Leeds U.	Tr	01.49	48-51	104	-	0
York C.	Tr	11.52	52-53	62	-	0
SEARY Raymond Michael						
Slough, 18 September, 1952						(LB)
Queens Park R.	App	09.70	71	0	1	0
Cambridge U.	Tr	03.74	73-75	55	2	0
SEASMAN John						
Liverpool, 21 February, 1955						(M)
Tranmere Rov.	App	02.73	72-74	15	2	0
Luton T.	Tr	01.75	74-75	7	1	2
Millwall	Tr	02.76	75-79	157	1	35
Rotherham U.	Tr	08.80	80-83	93	7	25
Cardiff C.	Tr	08.84	84	10	2	2
Rochdale	L	11.84	84	8	0	0
Chesterfield	Tr	01.85	84	8	2	1
Rochdale	Tr	07.85	85-87	86	1	4
SEATHERTON Raymond						
Tiverton, 20 May, 1932						(CF)
Bristol Rov.	Minehead	02.55	55	2	-	2
SEATON Gordon						
Wick, 1 September, 1945						(WH)
Chester C.	Rhyl	12.66	66-67	46	3	2
SEBA Jesus						
Spain, 11 April, 1974 Spanish u21 Int						(W)
Wigan Ath.	Real Zaragoza (Sp)	08.95	95-96	8	13	3
SEDDON Andrew						
Worsley, 23 November, 1959						(FB)
Stockport Co. (N/C)		08.77	78-82	4	3	0
SEDDON Benjamin Paul						
Liverpool, 5 February, 1952						(CD)
Tranmere Rov.	Formby	04.73	73	1	0	0
SEDDON David Andrew						
Rochdale, 13 April, 1951						(FB)
Rochdale	Stafford R.	01.74	73-74	18	3	0
SEDDON Frank Owen						
Stockton, 1 May, 1928						(CH)
Notts Co.		05.46				
Hull C.	Tr	05.47	49	3	-	0
Halifax T.	Tr	01.51	50-51	4	-	0
SEDDON Ian Wright						
Prestbury, 14 October, 1950						(M)
Bolton W.	App	06.69	69-72	51	13	4
Chester C.	Tr	09.73	73-75	62	11	7
Stockport Co.	L	11.75	75	4	0	0
Chesterfield	L	01.76	75	2	0	0
Cambridge U.	Tr	02.76	75-76	34	3	3
Rochdale	Tr	07.77	77	30	1	3
Wigan Ath.	Tr	07.78	78	1	0	0
SEDDON Thomas						
Rotherham, 25 October, 1935						(HB)
Rotherham U.		03.54	58	1	-	0
SEDGEMORE Benjamin Redwood						
Wolverhampton, 5 August, 1975 E Sch						(M)
Birmingham C.	YT	05.93				
Northampton T.	L	12.94	94	1	0	0
Mansfield T.	L	08.95	95	4	5	0
Peterborough U.	Tr	01.96	95	13	4	0
Mansfield T.	Tr	09.96	96-97	58	9	6
Macclesfield T.	Tr	03.98	97	5	0	0
SEDGLEY Stephen Philip						
Enfield, 26 May, 1968 Eu21-11						(M/CD)
Coventry C.	App	05.86	86-88	81	3	3
Tottenham H.	Tr	07.89	89-93	147	17	8
Ipswich T.	Tr	06.94	94-96	105	0	15
Wolverhampton W.	Tr	07.97	97	18	1	0
SEDGWICK Christopher Edward						
Sheffield, 28 April, 1980						(W)
Rotherham U.	YT	08.97	97	0	4	0
SEDLAN Jason Mark						
Peterborough, 5 August, 1979						(M)
Mansfield T.	YT	●	97	0	1	0
SEDLOSKI Goce						
Macedonia, 10 April, 1974 Macedonian Int						(CD)
Sheffield Wed.	Hadjuk Split (Cro)	03.98	97	3	1	0
SEED Trevance Frederick						
Preston, 3 September, 1923 Died 1994						(CH)
Preston N.E.	Jnrs	07.46				
Carlisle U.	Tr	12.46	46-49	81	-	0
Accrington St.	Tr	09.50	50	1	-	0
SEEMLEY Ivor John						
Sheffield, 30 June, 1929						(FB)
Sheffield Wed.	Jnrs	07.46	53-54	15	-	0
Stockport Co.	Tr	06.55	55-56	81	-	0
Chesterfield	Tr	06.57	57-58	78	-	0
SEGERS Johannes (Hans)						
Netherlands, 30 October, 1961						(G)
Nottingham F.	P.S.V. Eindhoven (Neth)	08.84	84-87	58	0	0
Stoke C.	L	02.87	86	1	0	0
Sheffield U.	L	11.87	87	10	0	0
Wimbledon	Tr	09.88	88-95	265	2	0
Wolverhampton W.	Tr	08.96	97	11	0	0
SEGURA Victor Abascal						
Zaragoza, Spain, 30 March, 1973						(CD)
Norwich C.	Lleida (Sp)	08.97	97	22	3	0
SEIGEL Arnold William						
Islington, 21 March, 1919						(WH)
Leyton Orient	Hendon	06.46	46	9	-	0
SEITH Robert						
Coatbridge, 9 March, 1932						(WH)
Burnley	Jnrs	03.49	53-59	211	-	6
SELBY Denis						
Broughton (Flint), 15 October, 1920 Died 1969						(OL)
Chester C. (Am)		07.46	46	5	-	1
SELF Glen Walter						
Norwich, 4 December, 1953						(F)
Norwich C.	App	09.70	70-72	4	1	2
Torquay U.	L	03.73	72	3	0	0
SELKIRK John (Jack)						
Doncaster, 20 January, 1923 Died 1993						(RB)
Rotherham U.	Edlington Colly	10.44	46-56	427	-	13
SELLARS Geoffrey						
Stockport, 20 May, 1930						(OR)
Leeds U.	Altrincham	04.50				
Aston Villa	Tr	08.50	50	2	-	0
SELLARS John						
Chester-le-Street, 28 April, 1924 Died 1985						(WH)
Stoke C.	Jnrs	10.41	46-57	384	-	14
SELLARS Peter						
Market Rasen, 15 March, 1958						(M)
Lincoln C.	App	●	75	0	1	0
SELLARS Scott						
Sheffield, 27 November, 1965 Eu21-3						(W)
Leeds U.	App	07.83	82-85	72	4	12
Blackburn Rov.	Tr	07.86	86-91	194	8	35
Leeds U.	Tr	07.92	92	6	1	0
Newcastle U.	Tr	03.93	92-95	56	5	5
Bolton W.	Tr	12.95	95-97	84	2	13

SELLEY Ian
Chertsey, 14 June, 1974 E Yth/Eu21-3 (M)

League Club	Source	Date Signed	Seasons Played	Apps	Subs	Gls
Arsenal	YT	05.92	92-96	35	6	0
Southend U.	L	12.96	96	3	1	0
Fulham	Tr	10.97	97	3	0	0

SELLS Charles Edward
Paddington, 24 June, 1939 (IF)

League Club	Source	Date Signed	Seasons Played	Apps	Subs	Gls
Exeter C.	Wealdstone	08.62	62	14	-	3

SEMARK Robin Harry
Portsmouth, 5 September, 1972 (F)

League Club	Source	Date Signed	Seasons Played	Apps	Subs	Gls
Cardiff C.	YT	07.91	91	4	2	0

SEMLEY Alan
Barnsley, 21 February, 1966 (F)

League Club	Source	Date Signed	Seasons Played	Apps	Subs	Gls
Barnsley	App	02.84	83	1	3	0

SEMPLE Ryan
Derry (NI), 2 July, 1977 (M)

League Club	Source	Date Signed	Seasons Played	Apps	Subs	Gls
Peterborough U.	YT	●	94	1	1	0

SENDALL Richard Adam
Stamford, 10 July, 1967 (F)

League Club	Source	Date Signed	Seasons Played	Apps	Subs	Gls
Blackpool	Watford (App)	07.85	85-86	6	5	0
Carlisle U.	Tr	07.88	88-92	48	36	14
Cardiff C.	L	09.89	89	3	1	0

SENIOR Allan Gordon
Dewsbury, 29 September, 1930 (RH)

League Club	Source	Date Signed	Seasons Played	Apps	Subs	Gls
Halifax T.		08.52	52	1	-	0

SENIOR Colin
Dewsbury, 3 June, 1927 (HB)

League Club	Source	Date Signed	Seasons Played	Apps	Subs	Gls
Huddersfield T.	Stocksbridge	06.45	50	5	-	1
Accrington St.	Tr	06.51	51	27	-	1

SENIOR Karl Robert
Northwich, 3 September, 1972 (M)

League Club	Source	Date Signed	Seasons Played	Apps	Subs	Gls
Chester C.	YT	●	89	0	1	0

SENIOR Philip **Malcolm**
Darton, 29 May, 1943 (FB)

League Club	Source	Date Signed	Seasons Played	Apps	Subs	Gls
Barnsley	Jnrs	06.61				
Southport	Tr	07.63	63	2	-	0

SENIOR Vincent **Roy**
Barnsley, 21 June, 1940 (W)

League Club	Source	Date Signed	Seasons Played	Apps	Subs	Gls
Doncaster Rov.		08.60	60	13	-	5
Peterborough U.	Tr	07.61	61-63	38	-	11
Millwall	Tr	03.64	63-64	15	-	3
Barnsley	Tr	11.64	64	21	-	4

SENIOR Stephen
Sheffield, 15 May, 1963 (RB)

League Club	Source	Date Signed	Seasons Played	Apps	Subs	Gls
York C.	App	05.81	80-86	158	10	6
Darlington	L	10.84	84	5	0	0
Northampton T.	Tr	06.87	87	1	3	0
Wigan Ath.	Tr	10.87	87-89	107	2	3
Preston N. E.	Tr	07.90	90-91	73	0	3

SENIOR Stuart
Barnsley, 26 October, 1953 (W)

League Club	Source	Date Signed	Seasons Played	Apps	Subs	Gls
Barnsley	App	11.71	72	1	1	0

SENIOR Trevor John
Dorchester, 28 November, 1961 (F)

League Club	Source	Date Signed	Seasons Played	Apps	Subs	Gls
Portsmouth	Dorchester T.	12.81	81-82	11	0	2
Aldershot	L	03.83	82	10	0	7
Reading	Tr	08.83	83-86	164	0	102
Watford	Tr	07.87	87	22	2	1
Middlesbrough	Tr	03.88	87-88	9	1	2
Reading	Tr	10.88	88-91	127	10	51

SEPP Dennis
Appledoorn, Holland, 5 June, 1973 (LW)

League Club	Source	Date Signed	Seasons Played	Apps	Subs	Gls
Bradford C.	H.S.C. 21 (Neth)	06.97	97	0	3	0

SERELLA David Edward
Kings Lynn, 24 September, 1952 (CD)

League Club	Source	Date Signed	Seasons Played	Apps	Subs	Gls
Nottingham F.	App	08.70	71-74	65	3	0
Walsall	Tr	11.74	74-81	265	2	12
Blackpool	Tr	08.82	82-83	34	1	3

SERMANNI Thomas
Glasgow, 1 July, 1954 S Sch (M)

League Club	Source	Date Signed	Seasons Played	Apps	Subs	Gls
Blackpool	Albion Rov.	03.78	78	6	4	0
Torquay U.	Tr	08.79	79-82	83	6	12

SERRANT Carl
Bradford, 12 September, 1975 E Yth/Eu21-2/E 'B' (LB)

League Club	Source	Date Signed	Seasons Played	Apps	Subs	Gls
Oldham Ath.	YT	07.94	95-97	84	6	1

SERTORI Mark Anthony
Manchester, 1 September, 1967 (CD)

League Club	Source	Date Signed	Seasons Played	Apps	Subs	Gls
Stockport Co.	East Manchester	02.87	86-87	3	1	0
Lincoln C.	Tr	08.87	88-89	43	7	9
Wrexham	Tr	02.90	89-93	106	4	3
Bury	Tr	07.94	94-95	4	9	1
Scunthorpe U.	Tr	07.96	96-97	82	1	2

SETTERS Maurice Edgar
Honiton, 16 December, 1936 E Sch/E Yth/Eu23-16 (WH)

League Club	Source	Date Signed	Seasons Played	Apps	Subs	Gls
Exeter C.	Jnrs	01.54	53-54	10	-	0
West Bromwich A.	Tr	01.55	55-59	120	-	10
Manchester U.	Tr	01.60	59-64	159	-	12
Stoke C.	Tr	11.64	64-67	86	0	5
Coventry C.	Tr	11.67	67-69	50	1	3
Charlton Ath.	Tr	01.70	69	8	0	1

SEWARD Bruce Walter
Uxbridge, 10 February, 1939 (IF)

League Club	Source	Date Signed	Seasons Played	Apps	Subs	Gls
Brighton & H. A.	Yiewsley	05.57				
Aldershot	Tr	07.59	59	1	-	0

SEWARD Gary
Paddington, 1 October, 1961 (F)

League Club	Source	Date Signed	Seasons Played	Apps	Subs	Gls
Blackpool	App	11.79	79	0	1	0

SEWELL Arthur
Comforth (Dm), 15 July, 1934 (IL)

League Club	Source	Date Signed	Seasons Played	Apps	Subs	Gls
Bradford C. (Am)	Bishop Auckland	06.54	54	1	-	0

SEWELL John (Jackie)
Whitehaven, 24 January, 1927 EF Lge/E-6 (IF)

League Club	Source	Date Signed	Seasons Played	Apps	Subs	Gls
Notts Co.	Whitehaven	10.44	46-50	178	-	97
Sheffield Wed.	Tr	03.51	50-55	164	-	87
Aston Villa	Tr	12.55	55-59	123	-	36
Hull C.	Tr	10.59	59-60	44	-	8

SEWELL John David
Deptford, 7 July, 1936 (FB)

League Club	Source	Date Signed	Seasons Played	Apps	Subs	Gls
Charlton Ath.	Bexleyheath & Welling	01.55	56-63	185	-	5
Crystal Palace	Tr	10.63	63-70	228	3	6
Leyton Orient	Tr	08.71	71	5	2	0

SEXTON David James
Islington, 6 April, 1930 (IF)

League Club	Source	Date Signed	Seasons Played	Apps	Subs	Gls
Luton T.	Chelmsford C.	06.51	51-52	9	-	1
West Ham U.	Tr	04.52	52-55	74	-	27
Leyton Orient	Tr	06.56	56-57	24	-	4
Brighton & H. A.	Tr	10.57	57-58	49	-	26
Crystal Palace	Tr	05.59	59	27	-	11

SEYMOUR Christopher David
Reading, 14 September, 1971 (M)

League Club	Source	Date Signed	Seasons Played	Apps	Subs	Gls
Reading	YT	07.90	90-91	10	3	0

SEYMOUR Ian Patrick
Tunbridge Wells, 17 March, 1948 (G)

League Club	Source	Date Signed	Seasons Played	Apps	Subs	Gls
Fulham	Tonbridge	08.66	66-70	64	0	0
Brighton & H. A.	L	02.71	70	3	0	0

SHACKLETON Alan
Padiham, 3 February, 1934 (CF)

League Club	Source	Date Signed	Seasons Played	Apps	Subs	Gls
Burnley	Jnrs	05.54	56-58	31	-	18
Leeds U.	Tr	10.58	58-59	30	-	16
Everton	Tr	09.59	59	26	-	10
Oldham Ath.	Nelson	08.61	61	10	-	7

SHACKLETON Leonard Francis
Bradford, 3 May, 1922 E Sch/EF Lge/E 'B'/E-5 (IF)

League Club	Source	Date Signed	Seasons Played	Apps	Subs	Gls
Bradford P. A.	Arsenal (Am)	12.40	46	7	-	4
Newcastle U.	Tr	10.46	46-47	57	-	26
Sunderland	Tr	02.48	47-57	320	-	98

SHADBOLT William Henry
Shrewsbury, 4 August, 1932 (OL)

League Club	Source	Date Signed	Seasons Played	Apps	Subs	Gls
Sheffield Wed.	Oswestry T.	01.53	52	7	-	0
Halifax T.	Tr	03.54	53	3	-	1

SHAIL Mark Edward David
Sweden, 15 October, 1966 E Semi Pro (CD)

League Club	Source	Date Signed	Seasons Played	Apps	Subs	Gls
Bristol C.	Yeovil T.	03.93	92-97	96	7	4

SHAKESPEARE Craig Robert
Birmingham, 26 October, 1963 (M)

League Club	Source	Date Signed	Seasons Played	Apps	Subs	Gls
Walsall	App	10.81	82-88	276	8	45

League Club	Source	Date Signed	Seasons Played	Apps	Subs	Gls
Sheffield Wed.	Tr	06.89	89	15	2	0
West Bromwich A.	Tr	02.90	89-92	104	8	12
Grimsby T.	Tr	07.93	93-96	84	22	10
Scunthorpe U.	Tr	07.97	97	3	1	0

SHANAHAN Terence Christopher
Paddington, 5 December, 1951 (F)

League Club	Source	Date Signed	Seasons Played	Apps	Subs	Gls
Ipswich T.	Tottenham H. (App)	07.69	70	3	1	0
Blackburn Rov.	L	09.71	71	6	0	2
Halifax T.	Tr	11.71	71-74	88	8	23
Chesterfield	Tr	10.74	74-75	56	4	28
Millwall	Tr	04.76	76	13	7	5
Bournemouth	Tr	07.77	77	14	4	1
Aldershot	Tr	07.78	78-79	16	0	4

SHANKLAND Andrew John
Stoke, 8 April, 1964 (M)

League Club	Source	Date Signed	Seasons Played	Apps	Subs	Gls
Port Vale	App	03.82	81-85	15	10	2

SHANKLY William
Glenbuck, 2 September, 1913 Died 1981 S-5 (WH)

League Club	Source	Date Signed	Seasons Played	Apps	Subs	Gls
Carlisle U.	Glenbuck Cherries	07.32	32	16	-	0
Preston N. E.	Tr	07.33	33-48	296	-	13

SHANKS Donald
Hammersmith, 2 October, 1952 E Yth (FB)

League Club	Source	Date Signed	Seasons Played	Apps	Subs	Gls
Luton T.	Fulham (App)	07.70	71-74	89	1	2
Queens Park R.	Tr	11.74	74-80	176	4	10
Brighton & H. A.	Tr	08.81	81-82	45	1	0
Wimbledon (N/C)	Eastern (HK)	01.84	83	1	0	0

SHANKS James
Barrow, 31 October, 1918 (OL)

League Club	Source	Date Signed	Seasons Played	Apps	Subs	Gls
Barrow	Vickers Sports	10.45	46	23	-	5

SHANKS Robert
Sunniside (Dm), 14 December, 1911 Died 1989 (WH)

League Club	Source	Date Signed	Seasons Played	Apps	Subs	Gls
Swindon T.		05.35	35-36	25	-	1
Crystal Palace	Tr	05.37	37-38	18	-	0
Swindon T.	Tr	10.46	46	1	-	0

SHANKS Walter George
Malta, 1 May, 1923 (WH)

League Club	Source	Date Signed	Seasons Played	Apps	Subs	Gls
Chelsea		10.46				
Luton T.	Tr	12.46	46-56	264	-	6

SHANNON David Leslie
Burnley, 4 May, 1953 (FB)

League Club	Source	Date Signed	Seasons Played	Apps	Subs	Gls
Sunderland	App	05.70				
Stockport Co.	Tr	07.73	73	3	1	1

SHANNON Leslie
Liverpool, 12 March, 1926 E 'B' (WH/IF)

League Club	Source	Date Signed	Seasons Played	Apps	Subs	Gls
Liverpool	Jnrs	11.44	47-48	11	-	1
Burnley	Tr	11.49	49-58	262	-	39

SHANNON Robert
Bellshill, 20 April, 1966 Su21-7 (LB)

League Club	Source	Date Signed	Seasons Played	Apps	Subs	Gls
Middlesbrough (L)	Dundee	09.91	91	0	1	0

SHARDLOW Paul Michael
Stone, 29 April, 1943 Died 1968 (G)

League Club	Source	Date Signed	Seasons Played	Apps	Subs	Gls
Stoke C.	Northwich Vic.	05.66	66-67	3	0	0

SHARKEY Dominic (Nick)
Helensburgh, 4 May, 1943 S Sch/Su23-2 (CF)

League Club	Source	Date Signed	Seasons Played	Apps	Subs	Gls
Sunderland	Jnrs	05.60	59-66	99	0	51
Leicester C.	Tr	10.66	66-67	6	0	5
Mansfield T.	Tr	03.68	67-69	67	2	17
Hartlepool U.	Tr	07.70	70-71	55	5	12

SHARKEY Patrick Gerald Sharp
Omagh (NI), 26 August, 1953 NI-1 (M)

League Club	Source	Date Signed	Seasons Played	Apps	Subs	Gls
Ipswich T.	Portadown	09.73	75-76	17	1	1
Millwall	L	11.76	76	7	0	0
Mansfield T.	Tr	08.77	77	31	1	5
Colchester U.	Tr	06.78	78	5	1	0
Peterborough U.	Tr	03.79	78-79	15	0	0

SHARMAN Donald William
Rothwell, 2 February, 1932 (G)

League Club	Source	Date Signed	Seasons Played	Apps	Subs	Gls
Derby Co.	Jnrs	02.49	50	2	-	0

SHARMAN Samuel Joseph
Hull, 7 November, 1977 (LB)

League Club	Source	Date Signed	Seasons Played	Apps	Subs	Gls
Sheffield Wed.	YT	05.96				
Hull C.	Tr	03.97	96	2	2	0

SHARP Duncan
Barnsley, 16 March, 1933 (CH)

League Club	Source	Date Signed	Seasons Played	Apps	Subs	Gls
Barnsley	Jnrs	05.50	53-61	213	-	0

SHARP Frank
Edinburgh, 28 May, 1947 (W)

League Club	Source	Date Signed	Seasons Played	Apps	Subs	Gls
Carlisle U.	Hearts	03.67	66-68	32	1	0
Cardiff C.	Tr	02.69	68-69	13	1	1
Barnsley	Tr	08.70	70-72	125	0	7
Grimsby T.	Tr	07.73	73	26	3	2
Port Vale	Tr	05.74	74	17	7	2

SHARP George Henry
Bedlington, 20 July, 1935 (OL)

League Club	Source	Date Signed	Seasons Played	Apps	Subs	Gls
Darlington (Am)		05.57	57	3	-	0
Oldham Ath. (Am)	Tr	11.57	57	1	-	0

SHARP Graeme Marshall
Glasgow, 16 October, 1960 Su21-1/S-12 (F)

League Club	Source	Date Signed	Seasons Played	Apps	Subs	Gls
Everton	Dumbarton	04.80	79-90	306	16	111
Oldham Ath.	Tr	07.91	91-94	103	4	30

SHARP John
Knottingley, 25 April, 1937 (OL)

League Club	Source	Date Signed	Seasons Played	Apps	Subs	Gls
Halifax T.	Fryston Colly	01.55	54-58	92	-	16

SHARP Kevin Phillip
Canada, 19 September, 1974 E Sch/E Yth (LB/M)

League Club	Source	Date Signed	Seasons Played	Apps	Subs	Gls
Leeds U.	Auxerre (Fr)	10.92	92-95	11	6	0
Wigan Ath.	Tr	11.95	95-97	84	9	8

SHARP Norman Winslow
Liverpool, 26 November, 1919 Died 1977 (IF)

League Club	Source	Date Signed	Seasons Played	Apps	Subs	Gls
Everton		11.38				
Wrexham	Tr	09.46	46-49	122	-	17

SHARP Raymond
Stirling, 16 November, 1969 Su21-4 (LB)

League Club	Source	Date Signed	Seasons Played	Apps	Subs	Gls
Preston N.E.	Dunfermline Ath.	10.94	94-95	22	0	0

SHARP Ronald
Canada, 22 November, 1932 (W)

League Club	Source	Date Signed	Seasons Played	Apps	Subs	Gls
Doncaster Rov.	Arbroath	10.58	58-59	58	-	11

SHARP Thomas Alexander
Newmains, 30 July, 1957 (CD)

League Club	Source	Date Signed	Seasons Played	Apps	Subs	Gls
Everton	App	08.75				
Brentford	Tr	01.76	75-76	4	12	1

SHARPE Frederick Arthur
Norwich, 26 January, 1924 (IR)

League Club	Source	Date Signed	Seasons Played	Apps	Subs	Gls
Wrexham (Am)		05.48	48	1	-	0

SHARPE Frederick Charles
Greenwich, 11 November, 1937 (CH)

League Club	Source	Date Signed	Seasons Played	Apps	Subs	Gls
Tottenham H.	Jnrs	05.56	58	2	-	1
Norwich C.	Tr	07.63	63-68	107	4	0
Reading	Tr	07.69	69-70	64	0	1

SHARPE Gerald Ralph
Gloucester, 17 March, 1946 (F)

League Club	Source	Date Signed	Seasons Played	Apps	Subs	Gls
Bristol C.	App	03.64	64-70	149	4	48

SHARPE John James
Halesowen, 9 August, 1975 (LM)

League Club	Source	Date Signed	Seasons Played	Apps	Subs	Gls
Manchester C.	YT	07.93				
Exeter C.	Tr	02.96	95-96	28	7	2

SHARPE John William Henry
Portsmouth, 9 October, 1957 (RB)

League Club	Source	Date Signed	Seasons Played	Apps	Subs	Gls
Southampton	App	10.75	76-77	21	0	0
Gillingham	Tr	09.78	78-84	192	2	2
Swansea (N/C)	Southampton (N/C)	09.85	85	5	0	0

SHARPE Lee Stuart
Halesowen, 27 May, 1971 Eu21-8/E 'B'/E-8 (LW)

League Club	Source	Date Signed	Seasons Played	Apps	Subs	Gls
Torquay U.	YT	05.88	87	9	5	3
Manchester U.	Tr	05.88	88-95	160	33	21
Leeds U.	Tr	08.96	96	26	0	5

SHARPE Leonard Thomas
Scunthorpe, 29 November, 1932 (WH)

League Club	Source	Date Signed	Seasons Played	Apps	Subs	Gls
Scunthorpe U.	Jnrs	05.50	51-61	185	-	6
Hull C.	Tr	06.62	62-65	58	0	4

SHARPE Philip
Leeds, 26 January, 1968 (F)

League Club	Source	Date Signed	Seasons Played	Apps	Subs	Gls
Halifax T.	Doncaster Rov. (YT)	08.86	86	0	1	0

League Club	Source	Date Signed	Seasons Played	Career Record Apps	Subs	Gls
SHARPE Richard						
Wokingham, 14 January, 1967						(F)
Rochdale (N/C)	Cocos Expos (USA)	10.94	94	9	7	2
SHARPE Robert						
Kirkcaldy, 20 December, 1925						(RB)
Darlington	Raith Rov.	08.52	52	14	-	0
SHARPLES Brian						
Bradford, 6 September, 1944						(CH)
Birmingham C.	App	12.61	62-68	60	1	2
Exeter C.	Tr	12.68	68-70	68	0	4
SHARPLES George Frank Vincent						
Ellesmere Port, 20 September, 1943 E Sch/E Yth						(WH)
Everton	Jnrs	09.60	60-63	10	-	0
Blackburn Rov.	Tr	03.65	64-68	99	4	5
Southport	Tr	07.71	71	23	2	0
SHARPLES John						
Wolverhampton, 8 August, 1934						(FB)
Aston Villa	Heath T.	10.55	58	13	-	0
Walsall	Tr	08.59	59-63	125	-	1
SHARPLES John Benjamin						
Bury, 26 January, 1973						(CD)
York C.	Ayr U.	03.96	95-96	38	0	1
SHARRATT Christopher Michael						
West Kirby, 13 August, 1970						(W)
Wigan Ath.	Stalybridge Celtic	12.91	91-92	11	13	3
SHARRATT Harold						
Wigan, 16 December, 1929 E Amat						(G)
Blackpool (Am)	Wigan Ath.	05.52	52	1	-	0
Oldham Ath. (Am)	Bishop Auckland	03.56	55	1	-	0
Nottingham F. (Am)	Bishop Auckland	01.58	57	1	-	0
SHARRATT Stuart Edgar						
Leek, 26 February, 1942						(G)
Port Vale	Oswestry T.	03.66	65-71	143	0	0
SHARROCK Anthony						
Warrington, 8 September, 1955						(G)
Southport (N/C)	Marine	11.73	73	1	0	0
SHAW Adrian						
Murton, 13 April, 1966						(D/M)
Nottingham F.	App	12.83				
Halifax T.	Tr	12.84	84-87	95	5	1
York C. (N/C)	Bridlington T.	10.88	88	5	0	0
Chesterfield	Tr	12.88	88-90	40	10	3
SHAW Alan						
Preston, 9 October, 1943						(OL)
Preston N. E.	Jnrs	10.60				
Hull C.	Tr	08.61	61-63	15	-	1
SHAW Alexander						
						(IF)
Crewe Alex.		12.44	46	13	-	4
SHAW Arthur						
Limehouse, 9 April, 1924						(WH)
Brentford	Hayes	05.46	46	4	-	0
Arsenal	Tr	04.48	49-54	57	-	0
Watford	Tr	06.55	55	3	-	0
SHAW Barry						
Chilton (Dm), 31 October, 1948						(OL)
Darlington (Am)	Crowboro Ath.	03.68	67	2	0	0
SHAW Bernard						
Sheffield, 14 March, 1945 E Yth/Eu23-2						(FB)
Sheffield U.	App	10.62	62-68	135	1	2
Wolverhampton W.	Tr	07.69	69-72	113	3	2
Sheffield Wed.	Tr	06.73	73-75	100	4	3
SHAW Bernard						
Selby, 4 September, 1929						(IF)
Hull C.	Buckley Jnrs	05.48				
Lincoln C.	Goole T.	10.53	53-54	9	-	1
SHAW Cecil Ernest						
Mansfield, 22 June, 1911 Died 1977						(FB)
Wolverhampton W.	Rufford Colly	02.30	30-36	174	-	8
West Bromwich A.	Tr	12.36	36-46	110	-	10
SHAW Christopher John						
Bournemouth, 23 August, 1965						(M)
Bournemouth	Jnrs	06.83	82-85	13	12	2
SHAW Colin Michael						
St Albans, 19 June, 1943 E Yth						(IF)
Chelsea	Jnrs	05.60	61	1	-	0
Norwich C.	Tr	08.63	63-64	3	-	0
Leyton Orient	Tr	03.65	65	7	0	0
SHAW George **David**						
Huddersfield, 11 October, 1948						(F)
Huddersfield T.	Jnrs	01.67	66-68	23	3	2
Oldham Ath.	Tr	09.69	69-72	155	0	70
West Bromwich A.	Tr	03.73	72-74	65	17	17
Oldham Ath.	Tr	10.75	75-77	55	4	21
SHAW Eric Lewis						
Barnsley, 12 February, 1947						(FB)
Barnsley	App	02.65	64-65	2	0	0
SHAW Gary Robert						
Birmingham, 21 January, 1961 E Yth/Eu21-7						(F)
Aston Villa	App	01.79	78-87	158	7	59
Blackpool	L	02.88	87	4	2	0
Walsall	Klagenfurt (Aut)	02.90	89	4	5	3
Shrewsbury T.	Kilmarnock	09.90	90	20	2	5
SHAW Gordon						
Ashton-in-Makerfield, 7 May, 1926						(RB)
Southport (Am)	Crompton Rec.	07.46	46	2	-	0
SHAW Graham Laurence						
Sheffield, 9 July, 1934 Eu23-5/EF Lge/E-5						(LB)
Sheffield U.	Jnrs	07.51	51-66	442	0	12
Doncaster Rov.	Tr	09.67	67	22	0	0
SHAW Graham Paul						
Stoke, 7 June, 1967						(F)
Stoke C.	App	06.85	85-88	83	16	18
Preston N.E.	Tr	07.89	89-91	113	8	29
Stoke C.	Tr	08.92	92-94	23	13	5
Plymouth Arg.	L	08.94	94	6	0	0
Rochdale	Tr	03.95	94-95	13	9	0
SHAW Hugh						
Clydebank, 29 April, 1929						(WH)
Tranmere Rov.	Rhyl	06.55	55	3	-	0
SHAW John						
Stirling, 4 February, 1954						(G)
Leeds U.	App	02.71				
Bristol C.	Tr	05.74	76-84	295	0	0
Exeter C.	Tr	07.85	85-87	109	0	0
SHAW John (Jack) Stephen						
Doncaster, 10 April, 1924						(CF)
Rotherham U.	Yorkshire Main	04.45	46-52	262	-	122
Sheffield Wed.	Tr	06.53	53-57	56	-	21
SHAW Joseph						
Murton, 23 June, 1928 EF Lge						(CH)
Sheffield U.	Upton Colly	07.45	48-65	631	0	9
SHAW Kenneth						
Dukinfield, 15 December, 1920						(F)
Stockport Co.	Hyde U.	10.42	46-47	41	-	18
SHAW Mark						
St Helens, 15 October, 1964						(M)
Wigan Ath. (N/C)	Jnrs	11.82	82	3	0	0
SHAW Martin John						
Bristol, 14 September, 1960						(M)
Bristol Rov.	App	09.78	78	1	1	0
SHAW Paul						
Burnham, 4 September, 1973 E Yth						(F)
Arsenal	YT	09.91	94-96	1	11	2
Burnley	L	03.95	94	8	1	4
Cardiff C.	L	08.95	95	6	0	0
Peterborough U.	L	10.95	95	12	0	5
Millwall	Tr	09.97	97	40	0	11
SHAW Peter Kevin						
Northolt, 9 January, 1956						(CD)
Charlton Ath.	Staines T.	12.77	77-80	100	5	5
Exeter C.	L	11.81	81	3	0	0
Gillingham	Tr	02.82	81-85	140	3	2

League Club	Source	Date Signed	Seasons Played	Career Record Apps	Subs	Gls
SHAW Raymond						
Walsall, 18 May, 1913 Died 1980						(WH)
Birmingham C.	Darlaston	04.37	37-46	12	-	0
SHAW Richard Edward						
Brentford, 11 September, 1968						(D)
Crystal Palace	App	09.86	87-95	193	14	3
Hull C.	L	12.89	89	4	0	0
Coventry C.	Tr	11.95	95-97	89	0	0
SHAW Ronald						
Bolton-on-Dearne, 1 January, 1924 Died 1991						(OR)
Torquay U.	Harrow T.	02.47	46-57	384	-	99
SHAW Samuel						
Langton, 14 September, 1934						(IF)
Crewe Alex.	Foley	08.56	56	19	-	3
SHAW Simon Robert						
Middlesbrough, 21 September, 1973						(RB)
Darlington	YT	08.92	91-97	144	32	12
SHAW Steven						
Manchester, 10 August, 1960						(M)
Rochdale	App	●	77	6	0	0
SHAW Stuart						
Liverpool, 9 October, 1944						(OR)
Everton	Jnrs	12.61	64-65	3	0	0
Crystal Palace	Tr	12.66				
Southport	Tr	03.67	66-68	66	1	6
Port Vale	Tr	07.69	69	1	2	0
SHAWCROSS Francis **David**						
Stretford, 3 July, 1941 E Yth/Eu23-1						(WH)
Manchester C.	Jnrs	06.58	58-64	47	-	2
Stockport Co.	Tr	06.65	65-66	59	1	14
Halifax T.	Tr	03.67	66-69	126	6	17
SHEARD Frank						
Spilsby, 29 January, 1922 Died 1990						(CH)
Leicester C.	Skegness	08.41				
Southend U.	Tr	05.46	46-52	180	-	1
SHEARER Alan						
Newcastle, 13 August, 1970 E Yth/Eu21-11/E 'B'/E-43						(F)
Southampton	YT	04.88	87-91	105	13	23
Blackburn Rov.	Tr	07.92	92-95	132	6	112
Newcastle U.	Tr	07.96	96-97	46	2	27
SHEARER David John						
Inverness, 16 October, 1958						(F)
Middlesbrough	Inverness Clach.	01.78	77-82	88	9	23
Wigan Ath.	L	03.80	79	11	0	9
Grimsby T.	Tr	08.83	83	1	3	0
Gillingham	Tr	08.84	84-87	82	11	42
Bournemouth	Tr	10.87	87	8	3	3
Scunthorpe U.	Tr	02.88	87-88	16	0	8
Darlington	Tr	12.88	88	6	1	0
SHEARER Duncan Nichol						
Fort William, 28 August, 1962 S-7						(F)
Chelsea	Inverness Clach.	11.83	85	2	0	1
Huddersfield T.	Tr	03.86	85-87	80	3	38
Swindon T.	Tr	06.88	88-91	156	3	78
Blackburn Rov.	Tr	03.92	91	5	1	1
SHEARER John McMillan						
Dunfermline, 8 July, 1917 Died 1979						(IF)
Derby Co.		03.46				
Bradford C.	Tr	10.46	46-48	75	-	17
Grimsby T.	Tr	02.49	48-50	34	-	9
SHEARER Lee Sean						
Southend, 23 October, 1977						(CD)
Leyton Orient	YT	07.95	94-96	14	4	1
SHEARER Peter Andrew						
Coventry, 4 February, 1967 E Semi Pro						(M)
Birmingham C.	App	02.85	84	2	2	0
Rochdale	Tr	07.86	86	1	0	0
Bournemouth	Cheltenham T.	03.89	88-92	76	9	10
Birmingham C.	Tr	01.94	93-94	22	3	7
SHEARING Peter Fraser						
Uxbridge, 26 August, 1938						(G)
West Ham U.	Hendon	06.60	60	6	-	0
Portsmouth	Tr	07.61	61-63	17	-	0
Exeter C.	Tr	06.64	64-65	80	0	0

League Club	Source	Date Signed	Seasons Played	Career Record Apps	Subs	Gls
Plymouth Arg.	Tr	06.66	66-67	24	0	0
Exeter C.	Tr	07.68	68-70	79	0	0
Bristol Rov.	Tr	02.71				
Gillingham	Tr	08.71	71-72	39	0	0
SHEAVILLS James Edward						
Eythorne (Kt), 28 July, 1940						(W)
Leeds U.	Jnrs	09.57				
Peterborough U.	Holbeach U.	(N/L)	60-62	30	-	8
Barnsley	Tr	06.63	63-64	65	-	6
SHEEDY Kevin Mark						
Builth Wells, 21 October, 1959 IR Yth/IRu21-5/IR-45						(LM)
Hereford U.	App	10.76	75-77	47	4	4
Liverpool	Tr	07.78	80-81	1	2	0
Everton	Tr	08.82	82-91	263	11	67
Newcastle U.	Tr	03.92	91-92	36	1	4
Blackpool	Tr	07.93	93	25	1	1
SHEEN John (Jock)						
Airdrie, 30 August, 1920 Died 1997						(IF)
Sheffield U.	Baillieston Jnrs	09.37				
Hull C.	Tr	07.46	46	5	-	1
SHEERIN Joseph Earnan						
Hammersmith, 8 November, 1977						(F)
Chelsea	YT	●	96	0	1	0
SHEFFIELD Jonathan						
Bedworth, 1 February, 1969						(G)
Norwich C.	App	02.87	88	1	0	0
Aldershot	L	09.89	89	11	0	0
Aldershot	L	08.90	90	15	0	0
Cambridge U.	Tr	03.91	90-94	56	0	0
Colchester U.	L	12.93	93	6	0	0
Swindon T.	L	01.94	93	2	0	0
Hereford U.	L	09.94	94	8	0	0
Peterborough U.	Tr	07.95	95-96	62	0	0
Plymouth Arg.	Tr	07.97	97	46	0	0
SHEFFIELD Laurence Joseph						
Swansea, 27 April, 1939 W Sch						(CF)
Bristol Rov.	Jnrs	07.56				
Newport Co.	Barry T.	04.62	61-64	91	-	46
Doncaster Rov.	Tr	08.65	65-66	58	0	34
Norwich C.	Tr	11.66	66-67	27	0	16
Rotherham U.	Tr	08.67	67	19	0	6
Oldham Ath.	Tr	12.67	67	18	0	6
Luton T.	Tr	07.68	68-69	31	4	12
Doncaster Rov.	Tr	10.69	69	13	2	6
Peterborough U.	Tr	08.70	70	17	1	6
SHELDON Gareth Richard						
Barnsley, 8 May, 1980						(F)
Scunthorpe U.	YT	●	97	0	1	0
SHELDON Kevin John						
Cheddleton (Staffs), 14 June, 1956						(W)
Stoke C.	App	06.73	75-80	12	3	0
Wigan Ath.	Tr	08.81	81-82	29	0	1
Port Vale	L	08.82	82	5	0	0
Crewe Alex (N/C)	Tr	08.83	83	2	0	0
SHELIA Murtaz						
Tbilisi, Georgia, 25 March, 1969 Georgian Int						(D)
Manchester C.	Alana Vladikavkas (Rus)	11.97	97	12	0	2
SHELL Francis Harry						
Hackney, 2 January, 1912 Died 1988						(F)
Aston Villa	Ford Sports	05.37	37-38	23	-	8
Birmingham C.	Tr	09.46				
Mansfield T.	Hereford U.	06.47	47	22	-	1
SHELLITO Kenneth John						
East Ham, 18 April, 1940 Eu23-1/E-1						(RB)
Chelsea	Jnrs	04.57	58-65	114	0	2
SHELTON Andrew Marc						
Sutton Coldfield, 19 June, 1980						(M)
Chester C.	YT	●	97	0	2	0
SHELTON Gary						
Nottingham, 21 March, 1958 Eu21-1						(M)
Walsall	App	03.76	75-77	12	12	0
Aston Villa	Tr	01.78	78-81	24	0	7
Notts Co.	L	03.80	79	8	0	0
Sheffield Wed.	Tr	03.82	81-86	195	3	18
Oxford U.	Tr	07.87	87-88	60	5	1
Bristol C.	Tr	08.89	89-93	149	1	24

League Club	Source	Date Signed	Seasons Played	Career Record Apps	Subs	Gls
Rochdale	L	02.94	93	3	0	0
Chester C.	Tr	07.94	94-97	62	7	6
SHELTON John (Jack) Benjamin Thomas						
Stourbridge, 9 November, 1912 Died 1992						(FB)
Walsall	Worcester C.	08.34	34-46	103	-	5
SHEPHERD Anthony						
Glasgow, 16 November, 1966 S Sch/S Yth						(M)
Bristol C. (L)	Glasgow Celtic	12.88	88	2	1	0
Carlisle U.	Glasgow Celtic	07.89	89-90	73	2	8
SHEPHERD Arthur Leslie						
Liverpool, 11 May, 1922						(W)
Liverpool		04.46				
New Brighton	Tr	08.49	49-50	30	-	10
SHEPHERD Brian Albert						
Leicester, 29 January, 1935						(FB)
Coventry C.	Hinckley Ath.	10.56	57-59	29	-	0
SHEPHERD Ernest						
Wombwell, 14 August, 1919						(OL)
Fulham	Bradford Rov.	04.38	46-48	72	-	13
West Bromwich A.	Tr	12.48	48	4	-	0
Hull C.	Tr	03.49	48-49	15	-	3
Queens Park R.	Tr	08.50	50-55	219	-	51
SHEPHERD Jamie **Greig**						
Edinburgh, 29 September, 1960						(F)
Norwich C.	Musselburgh Windsor	03.79	79-81	13	3	2
Southend U.	Eastern (HK)	08.83	83-84	47	6	11
Peterborough U.	Tr	12.84	84-86	53	2	14
SHEPHERD James						
Aspull, 25 June, 1938						(WH)
Blackburn Rov.	St John Baptist B.C.	11.55				
Everton	Tr	07.59				
Crewe Alex.	Tr	06.60	60-63	50	-	4
Southport	Tr	02.64	63	13	-	6
SHEPHERD John Arthur						
Maltby, 20 September, 1945						(IF)
Rotherham U.		04.66	65-67	22	2	2
York C.	Tr	09.68	68	5	0	0
Oxford U.	Tr	10.69	69	9	2	1
SHEPHERD John Herbert Edwin						
Kensington, 29 May, 1932						(CF)
Millwall		10.52	52-57	149	-	63
Brighton & H. A.	Tr	06.58	58-59	45	-	19
Gillingham	Tr	02.60	59-60	53	-	23
SHEPHERD Paul						
Leeds, 17 November, 1977 E Yth						(M)
Leeds U.	YT	09.95	96	1	0	0
SHEPHERD Peter						
Ermington (Dev), 27 August, 1965						(G)
Exeter C. (N/C)	Plymouth Arg. (Jnrs)	06.82	82	1	0	0
SHEPHERD Trevor						
Sutton-in-Ashfield, 25 December, 1946						(F)
Nottingham F.	Jnrs	12.63				
Coventry C.	Tr	10.66	67-68	12	2	1
Torquay U.	L	03.68	67	14	0	6
Plymouth Arg.	Tr	06.69	69-70	36	3	4
SHEPHERD John **William**						
Liverpool, 25 September, 1920						(FB)
Liverpool	Elm Bank	12.45	48-51	53	-	0
SHEPHERDSON Harold						
Middlesbrough, 28 October, 1918 Died 1995						(CH)
Middlesbrough	Jnrs	05.36	36-46	17	-	0
Southend U.	Tr	05.47				
SHEPPARD Hedley Horace						
West Ham, 26 November, 1909						(FB)
West Ham U.	Ilford	11.32				
Aldershot	Tr	07.34	34-48	249	-	1
SHEPPARD Richard (Dick) James						
Bristol, 14 February, 1945						(G)
West Bromwich A.	App	02.63	65-68	39	0	0
Bristol Rov.	Tr	06.69	69-74	151	0	0
Torquay U.	L	12.73	73	2	0	0

League Club	Source	Date Signed	Seasons Played	Career Record Apps	Subs	Gls
SHEPPARD Simon						
Clevedon, 7 August, 1973 E Sch/E Yth						(G)
Watford	YT	04.91	92-93	23	0	0
Scarborough	L	03.94	93	9	0	0
Reading	Tr	09.94	95	18	0	0
SHEPPEARD Howard Thomas						
Ynysybwl, 31 January, 1933						(IF)
Sunderland	Ynysybwl Y.C.	12.51	53	1	-	0
Cardiff C.	Tr	05.55				
Newport Co.	Tr	06.56	56-57	31	-	6
SHEPSTONE Paul Thomas Adam						
Coventry, 8 November, 1970 E Yth						(M)
Coventry C.	YT	11.87				
Birmingham C.	Tr	07.89				
Blackburn Rov.	Atherstone U.	05.90	90-91	16	10	1
York C.	L	03.92	91	2	0	0
SHERGOLD Wilfred Frederick						
Swindon, 18 September, 1943						(WH)
Swindon T.	Jnrs	10.60	63-65	37	0	0
Bradford C.	Tr	06.66	66-67	22	6	2
SHERGOLD William Richard						
Newport, 22 January, 1923 Died 1968 W Amat						(IF/W)
Newport Co.	Bishop Auckland	07.47	47-55	274	-	48
SHERIDAN Alexander						
Motherwell, 19 July, 1948						(FB)
Brighton & H. A.	Queens Park	08.70	70	12	3	2
SHERIDAN Anthony Joseph						
Dublin, 21 October, 1974 IR Yth/IRu21-5						(LW)
Coventry C.	Jnrs	10.91	92-93	5	4	0
SHERIDAN Darren Stephen						
Manchester, 8 December, 1967						(M)
Barnsley	Winsford U.	08.93	93-97	134	12	4
SHERIDAN Frank Michael						
Stepney, 9 December, 1961						(M)
Derby Co.	App	07.78	80-81	41	2	5
Torquay U.	Tr	08.82	82-83	24	3	3
SHERIDAN George Francis						
Wigan, 30 October, 1929 Died 1986						(OR)
Bolton W.		09.50				
Bradford C.	Colwyn Bay	01.52	51-52	12	-	1
SHERIDAN John						
Ramsgate, 25 May, 1938						(WH)
Notts Co.	Linby Colly	07.55	56-65	287	0	9
Hartlepool U.	Tr	07.66	66-69	117	3	1
SHERIDAN John Joseph						
Manchester, 1 October, 1964 IR Yth/IRu21-2/IRu23-2/IR 'B'/IR-34						(M)
Leeds U.	Manchester C. (Jnrs)	03.82	82-88	225	5	47
Nottingham F.	Tr	07.89	89			
Sheffield Wed.	Tr	11.89	89-96	187	10	25
Birmingham C.	L	02.96	95	1	1	0
Bolton W.	Tr	11.96	96-97	24	8	2
SHERINGHAM Edward (Teddy) Paul						
Walthamstow, 2 April, 1966 E Yth/Eu21-1/E-35						(F)
Millwall	App	01.84	83-90	205	15	93
Aldershot	L	02.85	84	4	1	0
Nottingham F.	Tr	07.91	91-92	42	0	14
Tottenham H.	Tr	08.92	92-96	163	3	76
Manchester U.	Tr	07.97	97	28	3	9
SHERLOCK Paul Graeme						
Wigan, 17 November, 1973						(LB/M)
Notts Co.	YT	07.92	93-94	8	4	1
Mansfield T.	Tr	03.95	94-96	29	10	2
SHERLOCK Steven Edward						
Birmingham, 10 May, 1959						(LB)
Manchester C.	App	05.77				
Luton T.	Tr	06.78	78	2	0	0
Stockport Co.	Tr	08.79	79-85	236	9	7
Cardiff C.	Tr	07.86	86	14	1	0
Newport Co.	L	12.86	86	5	0	0
Newport Co.	Tr	03.87	86-87	42	2	2
SHERON Michael Nigel						
St Helens, 11 January, 1972 Eu21-16						(F)
Manchester C.	YT	07.90	91-93	82	18	24
Bury	L	03.91	90	1	4	1

League Club	Source	Date Signed	Seasons Played	Apps	Subs	Gls
Norwich C.	Tr	08.94	94-95	19	9	2
Stoke C.	Tr	11.95	95-96	64	5	34
Queens Park R.	Tr	07.97	97	36	4	11

SHERRATT Brian
Stoke, 29 March, 1944 (G)

League Club	Source	Date Signed	Seasons Played	Apps	Subs	Gls
Stoke C.	App	04.61	61	1	-	0
Oxford U.	Tr	08.65	65-67	44	0	0
Nottingham F.	L	10.68	68	1	0	0
Barnsley	Tr	06.69	69	15	0	0
Colchester U.	Tr	08.70	70	9	0	0

SHERRATT James Aaron
Warrington, 24 December, 1921 (FB)

League Club	Source	Date Signed	Seasons Played	Apps	Subs	Gls
Arsenal		12.46				
Hartlepool U.	Tr	12.48	48	20	-	4
Leyton Orient	Tr	08.49	49-51	39	-	8
Workington	Tr	08.52	52-53	48	-	3

SHERRATT John Hubert
Stoke, 9 March, 1923 (CF)

League Club	Source	Date Signed	Seasons Played	Apps	Subs	Gls
Port Vale (Am)		03.49	48	2	-	0

SHERWOOD Alfred Thomas
Aberdare, 13 November, 1923 Died 1990 W Sch/W-41 (FB)

League Club	Source	Date Signed	Seasons Played	Apps	Subs	Gls
Cardiff C.	Aberaman	07.42	46-55	353	-	15
Newport Co.	Tr	07.56	56-60	205	-	21

SHERWOOD Henry William
Reading, 3 September 1913 Died 1985 (WH)

League Club	Source	Date Signed	Seasons Played	Apps	Subs	Gls
Reading	Jnrs	06.38	38	9	-	1
Aldershot	Tr	09.47	47-48	47	-	5
Crystal Palace	Tr	07.49	49	2	-	0

SHERWOOD Jeffrey
Bristol, 5 October, 1959 (FB)

League Club	Source	Date Signed	Seasons Played	Apps	Subs	Gls
Bristol Rov.	Bath C.	06.82	82	16	2	0

SHERWOOD Stephen
Selby, 10 December, 1953 (G)

League Club	Source	Date Signed	Seasons Played	Apps	Subs	Gls
Chelsea	App	07.71	71-75	16	0	0
Millwall	L	10.73	73	1	0	0
Brentford	L	01.74	73	16	0	0
Brentford	L	08.74	74	46	0	0
Watford	Tr	11.76	76-86	211	0	1
Grimsby T.	Tr	07.87	87-92	183	0	0
Northampton T.	Tr	08.93	93	15	1	0
Lincoln C. (N/C)	Grimsby T. (N/C)	03.95	94	6	1	0

SHERWOOD Timothy Alan
St Albans, 6 February, 1969 Eu21-4/E 'B' (M)

League Club	Source	Date Signed	Seasons Played	Apps	Subs	Gls
Watford	App	02.87	87-88	23	9	2
Norwich C.	Tr	07.89	89-91	66	5	10
Blackburn Rov.	Tr	02.92	91-97	220	7	22

SHIELDS Anthony Gerald
Londonderry, 4 June, 1980 (F)

League Club	Source	Date Signed	Seasons Played	Apps	Subs	Gls
Peterborough U.	YT	●	97	0	1	0

SHIELDS Duncan
Glasgow, 6 November, 1949 (CH)

League Club	Source	Date Signed	Seasons Played	Apps	Subs	Gls
Workington		08.69	69	7	1	0

SHIELDS James
Glasgow, 28 November, 1931 (IF)

League Club	Source	Date Signed	Seasons Played	Apps	Subs	Gls
Shrewsbury T.	Hibernian	05.56	56	24	-	6

SHIELDS Robert **James**
Derry (NI), 26 September, 1931 NI Amat/Lol/NI-1 (CF)

League Club	Source	Date Signed	Seasons Played	Apps	Subs	Gls
Sunderland	Crusaders	03.54				
Southampton	Tr	07.56	56-58	38	-	20

SHIELDS Samuel Miller
Denny, 21 March, 1929 (F)

League Club	Source	Date Signed	Seasons Played	Apps	Subs	Gls
Liverpool	Cowdenbeath	05.49	49	1	-	0
Darlington	Airdrieonians	06.52	52	21	-	2

SHIELS Dennis Patrick
Belfast, 24 August, 1938 NI 'B' (CF)

League Club	Source	Date Signed	Seasons Played	Apps	Subs	Gls
Sheffield U.	Distillery	12.58	58-63	32	-	8
Peterborough U.	Tr	07.64	64	12	-	4
Notts Co.	Tr	07.65	65	28	1	6

SHIELS James Matthew
Derry (NI), 24 February, 1938 NI 'B' (FB)

League Club	Source	Date Signed	Seasons Played	Apps	Subs	Gls
Manchester U.	Waterside B.C.	09.56				
Southend U.	Tr	06.61	61	25	-	0

SHILTON Peter Leslie
Leicester, 18 September, 1949 E Sch/E Yth/Eu23-13/EF Lge/E-125 (G)

League Club	Source	Date Signed	Seasons Played	Apps	Subs	Gls
Leicester C.	App	09.66	65-74	286	0	1
Stoke C.	Tr	11.74	74-77	110	0	0
Nottingham F.	Tr	09.77	77-81	202	0	0
Southampton	Tr	08.82	82-86	188	0	0
Derby Co.	Tr	07.87	87-91	175	0	0
Plymouth Arg. (N/C)	Tr	03.92	91-93	34	0	0
Bolton W. (N/C)	Wimbledon (N/C)	03.95	94	0	1	0
Coventry C.	Tr	07.95				
West Ham U.	Tr	01.96				
Leyton Orient	Tr	11.96	96	9	0	0

SHILTON Samuel Roger
Nottingham, 21 July, 1978 (LW)

League Club	Source	Date Signed	Seasons Played	Apps	Subs	Gls
Plymouth Arg.	YT	●	94-95	1	2	0
Coventry C.	Tr	10.95	97	2	0	0

SHIMWELL Edmund (Eddie)
Bakewell, 27 February, 1920 Died 1988 E-1 (FB)

League Club	Source	Date Signed	Seasons Played	Apps	Subs	Gls
Sheffield U.	Wirksworth	01.39	46	14	-	0
Blackpool	Tr	12.46	46-56	283	-	5
Oldham Ath.	Tr	05.57	57	7	-	0

SHINER Roy Albert James
Ryde (IOW), 15 November, 1924 Died 1988 (CF)

League Club	Source	Date Signed	Seasons Played	Apps	Subs	Gls
Huddersfield T.	Cheltenham T.	12.51	51-54	21	-	6
Sheffield Wed.	Tr	07.55	55-59	153	-	93
Hull C.	Tr	11.59	59	22	-	8

SHINNERS Paul
Westminster, 8 January, 1959 (F)

League Club	Source	Date Signed	Seasons Played	Apps	Subs	Gls
Gillingham	Fisher Ath.	10.84	84	1	3	0
Colchester U.	L	03.85	84	6	0	1
Leyton Orient	Tr	07.85	85-88	73	4	32

SHINTON Robert Thomas
West Bromwich, 6 January, 1952 (F)

League Club	Source	Date Signed	Seasons Played	Apps	Subs	Gls
Walsall	Lye T.	03.72	71-73	78	1	20
Cambridge U.	Tr	03.74	73-75	99	0	25
Wrexham	Tr	07.76	76-78	128	0	37
Manchester C.	Tr	07.79	79	5	0	0
Millwall	L	02.80	79	5	0	3
Newcastle U.	Tr	03.80	79-81	41	1	10
Millwall	Tr	03.82	81-82	29	5	4

SHIPLEY George Michael
Newcastle, 7 March, 1959 (M)

League Club	Source	Date Signed	Seasons Played	Apps	Subs	Gls
Southampton	App	03.77	79	2	1	0
Reading	L	03.79	78	11	1	1
Lincoln C.	Tr	01.80	79-84	229	1	42
Charlton Ath.	Tr	07.85	85-86	61	0	6
Gillingham	Tr	08.87	87-88	27	2	3

SHIPLEY Mark Edward
South Elmsall, 11 February, 1959 (G)

League Club	Source	Date Signed	Seasons Played	Apps	Subs	Gls
Blackburn Rov.	App	08.77				
Doncaster Rov.	Tr	08.79	79-80	6	0	0

SHIPPERLEY David John
Uxbridge, 12 April, 1952 (CD)

League Club	Source	Date Signed	Seasons Played	Apps	Subs	Gls
Charlton Ath.	App	04.70	70-73	92	8	8
Plymouth Arg.	L	02.74	73	1	0	0
Gillingham	Tr	05.74	74-77	144	0	11
Charlton Ath.	Tr	02.78	77-79	53	0	6
Reading	Tr	09.79	79-80	18	1	0

SHIPPERLEY Neil Jason
Chatham, 30 October, 1974 Eu21-7 (CF)

League Club	Source	Date Signed	Seasons Played	Apps	Subs	Gls
Chelsea	YT	09.92	92-94	26	11	7
Watford	L	12.94	94	5	1	1
Southampton	Tr	01.95	94-96	65	1	11
Crystal Palace	Tr	10.96	96-97	46	12	19

SHIPWRIGHT William Kenneth
Camden, 22 December, 1932 (CH)

League Club	Source	Date Signed	Seasons Played	Apps	Subs	Gls
Watford	Chesham U.	04.53	53-58	146	-	0
Aldershot	Tr	06.59	59-62	123	-	0

SHIRES Allan Jeffrey
Leigh-on-Sea, 29 June, 1948 (OR)

League Club	Source	Date Signed	Seasons Played	Apps	Subs	Gls
Southend U.	App	●	65	0	1	0
Colchester U.	Tr	07.66	66-67	23	0	3

SHIRLEY Alexander Gordon
Milngavie, 31 October, 1918 Died 1990 (OR)

League Club	Source	Date Signed	Seasons Played	Apps	Subs	Gls
New Brighton	Dundee U.	10.46	46	18	-	3
Bradford C.	Tr	08.47	47	1	-	0

SHIRTLIFF Paul Robert
Hoyland, 3 November, 1962 E Semi Pro (FB)

League Club	Source	Date Signed	Seasons Played	Apps	Subs	Gls
Sheffield Wed.	App	11.80	80-82	7	2	0
Northampton T.	Tr	07.84	84	27	2	0

SHIRTLIFF Peter Andrew
Hoyland, 6 April, 1961 (CD)

League Club	Source	Date Signed	Seasons Played	Apps	Subs	Gls
Sheffield Wed.	App	10.78	78-85	188	0	4
Charlton Ath.	Tr	07.86	86-88	102	1	7
Sheffield Wed.	Tr	07.89	89-92	104	0	4
Wolverhampton W.	Tr	08.93	93-95	67	2	0
Barnsley	Tr	08.95	95-97	48	1	0
Carlisle U.	L	10.96	96	5	0	0

SHOEMAKE Kevin Paul
Wickford, 28 January, 1965 (G)

League Club	Source	Date Signed	Seasons Played	Apps	Subs	Gls
Leyton Orient	App	01.83	83	4	0	0
Peterborough U.	Welling U.	09.86	86-87	40	0	0

SHONE George Frederick
Runcorn, 15 February, 1922 (CF)

League Club	Source	Date Signed	Seasons Played	Apps	Subs	Gls
Tranmere Rov.		12.46	46	4	-	0

SHORE William **Andrew**
Kirkby-in-Ashfield, 29 December, 1955 (D)

League Club	Source	Date Signed	Seasons Played	Apps	Subs	Gls
Mansfield T.	Jnrs	07.74	74	1	0	0

SHORE Brian
Huddersfield, 1 February, 1935 (F)

League Club	Source	Date Signed	Seasons Played	Apps	Subs	Gls
Halifax T.		10.56	56-57	9	-	3

SHORE Edward (Ted)
Nuneaton, 18 October, 1927 (OL)

League Club	Source	Date Signed	Seasons Played	Apps	Subs	Gls
Port Vale		10.45	47	3	-	0
Coventry C.	Tr	07.48	48-49	2	-	0

SHORT Alan John Moxley
Plymouth, 5 July, 1928 (OR)

League Club	Source	Date Signed	Seasons Played	Apps	Subs	Gls
Exeter C.	Tamerton	08.50	50	5	-	1

SHORT Christian Mark
West Germany, 9 May, 1970 (D)

League Club	Source	Date Signed	Seasons Played	Apps	Subs	Gls
Scarborough	Pickering T.	07.88	88-89	42	1	1
Notts Co.	Tr	09.90	90-95	77	17	2
Huddersfield T.	L	12.94	94	6	0	0
Sheffield U.	Tr	12.95	95-97	40	4	0

SHORT Jonathan **Craig**
Bridlington, 25 June, 1968 (CD)

League Club	Source	Date Signed	Seasons Played	Apps	Subs	Gls
Scarborough	Pickering T.	10.87	87-88	61	2	7
Notts Co.	Tr	07.89	89-92	128	0	6
Derby Co.	Tr	09.92	92-94	118	0	9
Everton	Tr	07.95	95-97	68	9	4

SHORT David
St Neots, 14 April, 1941 (OL)

League Club	Source	Date Signed	Seasons Played	Apps	Subs	Gls
Lincoln C.	St Neots T.	11.58	58-59	4	-	0

SHORT John (Jack)
Hemsworth, 18 February, 1928 Died 1976 (FB)

League Club	Source	Date Signed	Seasons Played	Apps	Subs	Gls
Wolverhampton W.	Wath W.	05.48	50-53	98	-	0
Stoke C.	Tr	08.54	54-55	55	-	2
Barnsley	Tr	10.56	56-59	109	-	0

SHORT John David
Gateshead, 25 January, 1921 Died 1986 (WH)

League Club	Source	Date Signed	Seasons Played	Apps	Subs	Gls
Leeds U.	Jnrs	01.38	46-48	60	-	18
Millwall	Tr	11.48	48-55	245	-	19

SHORT Maurice
Middlesbrough, 29 December, 1949 (G)

League Club	Source	Date Signed	Seasons Played	Apps	Subs	Gls
Middlesbrough	App	02.67	67-69	16	0	0
Oldham Ath.	Tr	06.70	70	5	0	0
Grimsby T.	L	01.71	70	10	0	0

SHORT Russell David Victor
Ilford, 4 September, 1968 (D)

League Club	Source	Date Signed	Seasons Played	Apps	Subs	Gls
Southend U.	YT	06.87	86	0	1	0

SHORTHOUSE William Henry
Bilston, 27 May, 1922 (FB)

League Club	Source	Date Signed	Seasons Played	Apps	Subs	Gls
Wolverhampton W.	St Mirren O.B.	04.46	47-56	344	-	1

SHORTT William Warren
Wrexham, 13 October, 1920 W-12 (G)

League Club	Source	Date Signed	Seasons Played	Apps	Subs	Gls
Chester C.	Hoole Alex.	05.39				
Plymouth Arg.	Tr	02.46	46-55	342	-	0

SHOTTON John
Hartlepool, 17 August, 1971 (M)

League Club	Source	Date Signed	Seasons Played	Apps	Subs	Gls
Manchester U.	YT	05.89				
Hartlepool U.	Tr	09.90	90	0	1	0

SHOTTON Malcolm
Newcastle, 16 February, 1957 (CD)

League Club	Source	Date Signed	Seasons Played	Apps	Subs	Gls
Leicester C.	App	02.75				
Oxford U.	Nuneaton Borough	05.80	80-87	262	1	12
Portsmouth	Tr	08.87	87	10	0	0
Huddersfield T.	Tr	02.88	87-88	16	0	1
Barnsley	Tr	09.88	88-89	64	2	6
Hull C.	Tr	02.90	89-91	58	1	2
Barnsley (N/C)	Ayr U.	07.94	94-95	10	0	1

SHOULDER Alan
Bishop Auckland, 4 February, 1953 (F)

League Club	Source	Date Signed	Seasons Played	Apps	Subs	Gls
Newcastle U.	Blyth Spartans	12.78	78-81	99	8	35
Carlisle U.	Tr	08.82	82-84	110	2	32
Hartlepool U.	Tr	06.85	85-87	66	0	24

SHOULDER James
Esh Winning, 11 September, 1946 (FB)

League Club	Source	Date Signed	Seasons Played	Apps	Subs	Gls
Sunderland	Jnrs	02.64	66	3	0	0
Hartlepool U.	Scarborough	08.73	73-74	62	1	3

SHOWELL George William
Bilston, 9 February, 1934 (D)

League Club	Source	Date Signed	Seasons Played	Apps	Subs	Gls
Wolverhampton W.	Jnrs	08.51	54-64	200	-	3
Bristol C.	Tr	05.65	65	9	2	0
Wrexham	Tr	11.66	66-67	48	0	1

SHOWERS Derek
Merthyr Tydfil, 28 January, 1953 W Sch/Wu23-6/W-2 (F)

League Club	Source	Date Signed	Seasons Played	Apps	Subs	Gls
Cardiff C.	Jnrs	08.70	70-76	76	7	10
Bournemouth	Tr	07.77	77-78	58	2	19
Portsmouth	Tr	02.79	78-80	36	3	8
Hereford U.	Tr	12.80	80-82	87	2	13

SHOWLER Kenneth
Doncaster, 3 February, 1933 (OR)

League Club	Source	Date Signed	Seasons Played	Apps	Subs	Gls
Chesterfield	Bentley Colly	11.52	53	7	-	0

SHOWLER Paul
Doncaster, 10 October, 1966 E Semi Pro (W)

League Club	Source	Date Signed	Seasons Played	Apps	Subs	Gls
Barnet	Altrincham	08.91	91-92	69	2	12
Bradford C.	Tr	08.93	93-95	72	16	15
Luton T.	Tr	08.96	96-97	21	3	6

SHREEVE John Thomas Thornton
Boldon, 18 August, 1917 Died 1966 (FB)

League Club	Source	Date Signed	Seasons Played	Apps	Subs	Gls
Charlton Ath.	Boldon Colly	01.35	36-50	145	-	0

SHREEVES Peter
Neath, 30 November, 1940 (IF)

League Club	Source	Date Signed	Seasons Played	Apps	Subs	Gls
Reading	Finchley	01.59	58-65	112	1	17

SHREWSBURY Philip
Heanor, 25 March, 1947 E Yth (WH)

League Club	Source	Date Signed	Seasons Played	Apps	Subs	Gls
Notts Co.	Jnrs	09.65	66	1	1	0

SHRUBB Paul
Guildford, 1 August, 1955 (D/M)

League Club	Source	Date Signed	Seasons Played	Apps	Subs	Gls
Fulham	App	08.72	72	1	0	0
Brentford	Hellenic (SA)	03.77	76-81	170	12	8
Aldershot	Tr	08.82	82-86	165	9	5

SHUFFLEBOTTOM Frank
Chesterfield, 9 October, 1917 (FB)

League Club	Source	Date Signed	Seasons Played	Apps	Subs	Gls
Ipswich T.		06.38	38	2	-	0
Nottingham F.	Tr	09.42	46	2	-	0
Bradford C.	Tr	10.46	46-47	56	-	0

SHUKER John
Eccles, 8 May, 1942 (LB/F)

League Club	Source	Date Signed	Seasons Played	Apps	Subs	Gls
Oxford U.		12.61	62-76	473	5	46

SHUTE Philip
Darlington, 15 December, 1953 (F)

League Club	Source	Date Signed	Seasons Played	Apps	Subs	Gls
Darlington (N/C)	Shildon	03.84	85	2	0	0

SHUTT Carl Steven
Sheffield, 10 October, 1961 (F)

League Club	Source	Date Signed	Seasons Played	Apps	Subs	Gls
Sheffield Wed.	Spalding U.	05.85	85-87	36	4	16
Bristol C.	Tr	10.87	87-88	39	7	10
Leeds U.	Tr	03.89	88-92	46	33	17
Birmingham C.	Tr	08.93	93	18	8	4
Manchester C.	L	12.93	93	5	1	0
Bradford C.	Tr	08.94	94-96	60	28	15
Darlington	Tr	03.97	96-97	20	19	7

SHUTT Stephen James
Barnsley, 29 November, 1964 (M)

League Club	Source	Date Signed	Seasons Played	Apps	Subs	Gls
Barnsley	App	11.82	82	1	0	0
Scunthorpe U. (N/C)	Goole T.	02.85	84	2	0	1

SHYNE Christopher
Littleborough, 10 December, 1950 (G)

League Club	Source	Date Signed	Seasons Played	Apps	Subs	Gls
Rochdale	Dyers Arms	01.77	76-78	20	0	0
Wigan Ath.	Tr	08.79	79	10	0	0

SIBBALD Robert Louis
Hebburn, 25 January, 1948 (FB)

League Club	Source	Date Signed	Seasons Played	Apps	Subs	Gls
Leeds U.	Jnrs	01.65	66-67	1	1	0
York C.	Tr	02.69	68-70	74	5	7
Southport	Tr	07.71	71-76	240	0	13

SIBLEY Albert (Joe)
Grays, 6 October, 1919 (OR)

League Club	Source	Date Signed	Seasons Played	Apps	Subs	Gls
Southend U.	Jnrs	05.39	46	21	-	3
Newcastle U.	Tr	02.47	46-49	31	-	6
Southend U.	Tr	07.50	50-55	192	-	36

SIBLEY Eric Seymour
Christchurch, 17 November, 1915 Died 1996 (FB)

League Club	Source	Date Signed	Seasons Played	Apps	Subs	Gls
Tottenham H.	Jnrs	05.34				
Bournemouth	Tr	08.37	37	7	-	0
Blackpool	Tr	10.37	37-46	80	-	0
Grimsby T.	Tr	12.47	47-48	23	-	0
Chester C.	Tr	07.49	49	7	-	0

SIBLEY Frank Philip
Uxbridge, 4 December, 1947 E Yth (WH)

League Club	Source	Date Signed	Seasons Played	Apps	Subs	Gls
Queens Park R.	App	02.65	63-70	140	3	3

SIBLEY Thomas Ivor
Porth, 27 October, 1920 Died 1994 (OL)

League Club	Source	Date Signed	Seasons Played	Apps	Subs	Gls
Birmingham C.	Ton Pentre	09.43				
Rochdale	Tr	03.47	46-47	23	-	3

SIDDALL Barry Alfred
Ellesmere Port, 12 September, 1954 E Yth (G)

League Club	Source	Date Signed	Seasons Played	Apps	Subs	Gls
Bolton W.	App	01.72	72-76	137	0	0
Sunderland	Tr	09.76	76-81	167	0	0
Darlington	L	10.80	80	8	0	0
Port Vale	Tr	08.82	82-84	81	0	0
Blackpool	L	10.83	83	7	0	0
Stoke C.	Tr	01.85	84-85	20	0	0
Tranmere Rov.	L	10.85	85	12	0	0
Manchester C.	L	03.86	85	6	0	0
Blackpool	Tr	08.86	86-88	110	0	0
Stockport Co.	Tr	06.89	89	21	0	0
Hartlepool U.	Tr	03.90	89	11	0	0
West Bromwich A. (N/C)	Tr	08.90				
Carlisle U.	Mossley	11.90	90	24	0	0
Chester C.	Tr	07.91	91	9	0	0
Preston N.E. (N/C)	Northwich Vic.	11.92	92	1	0	0

SIDDALL Alfred **Brian**
Northwich, 2 May, 1930 (IF)

League Club	Source	Date Signed	Seasons Played	Apps	Subs	Gls
Stoke C.	Northwich Vic.	02.51	50-53	59	-	10
Bournemouth	Tr	01.54	53-56	86	-	14
Ipswich T.	Tr	05.57	57-60	58	-	6

SIDEBOTTOM Arnold
Barnsley, 1 April, 1954 (CD)

League Club	Source	Date Signed	Seasons Played	Apps	Subs	Gls
Manchester U.	Jnrs	02.72	72-74	16	0	0
Huddersfield T.	Tr	01.76	75-77	56	5	5
Halifax T.	Tr	10.78	78	21	0	2

SIDEBOTTOM Geoffrey
Mapplewell, 29 December, 1936 (G)

League Club	Source	Date Signed	Seasons Played	Apps	Subs	Gls
Wolverhampton W.	Jnrs	09.54	58-60	28	-	0
Aston Villa	Tr	02.61	60-64	70	-	0
Scunthorpe U.	Tr	01.65	64-66	59	0	0
Brighton & H. A.	New York (USA)	01.69	68-70	40	0	0

SIDLOW Cyril
Colwyn Bay, 26 November, 1915 W Amat/W-7 (G)

League Club	Source	Date Signed	Seasons Played	Apps	Subs	Gls
Wolverhampton W.	Llandudno	05.37	37-38	4	-	0
Liverpool	Tr	02.46	46-50	149	-	0

SIEVWRIGHT George Edgar Smollett
Broughty Ferry, 10 September, 1937 (WH)

League Club	Source	Date Signed	Seasons Played	Apps	Subs	Gls
Oldham Ath.	Dundee U.	06.63	63	37	-	4
Tranmere Rov.	Tr	06.64				
Rochdale	Tr	07.65	65	31	1	1

SIGURDSSON Larus Orri
Iceland, 4 June, 1973 Icelandic Int (CD)

League Club	Source	Date Signed	Seasons Played	Apps	Subs	Gls
Stoke C.	Thor (Ice)	10.94	94-97	156	1	2

SILENZI Andrea
Italy, 10 February, 1966 Italian Int (F)

League Club	Source	Date Signed	Seasons Played	Apps	Subs	Gls
Nottingham F.	Torino (It)	08.95	95-96	4	8	0

SILK George Henry
Bootle, 18 October, 1916 Died 1969 (FB)

League Club	Source	Date Signed	Seasons Played	Apps	Subs	Gls
Southport	Bootle Miranda	09.35	35-36	14	-	0
Plymouth Arg.	Tr	08.37	37-50	86	-	1

SILKMAN Barry
Stepney, 29 June, 1952 (M)

League Club	Source	Date Signed	Seasons Played	Apps	Subs	Gls
Hereford U.	Barnet	08.74	74-75	18	19	2
Crystal Palace	Tr	08.76	76-78	40	8	6
Plymouth Arg.	Tr	10.78	78	14	0	2
Luton T.	L	02.79	78	3	0	0
Manchester C.	Tr	03.79	78-79	19	0	3
Brentford	Tr	08.80	80	14	0	1
Queens Park R.	Tr	10.80	80	22	1	2
Leyton Orient	Tr	09.81	81-84	133	7	14
Southend U.	Tr	07.85	85	38	2	1
Crewe Alex. (N/C)	Tr	09.86	86	1	1	0

SILLE Leslie Taylor
Liverpool, 12 April, 1928 (OL)

League Club	Source	Date Signed	Seasons Played	Apps	Subs	Gls
Bournemouth (Am)	Tranmere Rov. (Am)	03.47	46	1	-	0
Crystal Palace (Am)	Ipswich T. (Am)	09.48	47	3	-	0
Tranmere Rov. (Am)	Tr	02.49	48	1	-	0

SILLETT John Charles
Southampton, 20 July, 1936 EF Lge (FB)

League Club	Source	Date Signed	Seasons Played	Apps	Subs	Gls
Chelsea	Southampton (Am)	04.54	56-61	93	-	0
Coventry C.	Tr	04.62	61-65	108	1	1
Plymouth Arg.	Tr	07.66	66-67	37	1	1

SILLETT Richard **Peter** Tudor
Southampton, 1 February, 1933 Died 1998 E Yth/Eu23-3/EF Lge/E 'B'/E-3 (FB)

League Club	Source	Date Signed	Seasons Played	Apps	Subs	Gls
Southampton	Jnrs	06.50	51-52	59	-	4
Chelsea	Tr	06.53	53-61	260	-	29

SILMAN David Alan
Hampstead, 28 October, 1959 (D)

League Club	Source	Date Signed	Seasons Played	Apps	Subs	Gls
Brentford	Wolverhampton W. (App)	02.78	78	1	0	0

SILMAN Roy
Doncaster, 12 May, 1934 (FB)

League Club	Source	Date Signed	Seasons Played	Apps	Subs	Gls
Rotherham U.	Edlington Colly	04.52	52-59	105	-	2
Barnsley	Tr	07.60				

SILVESTER Peter Dennis
Wokingham, 19 February, 1948 (F)

League Club	Source	Date Signed	Seasons Played	Apps	Subs	Gls
Reading	App	02.66	65-69	76	3	26
Norwich C.	Tr	09.69	69-73	99	1	37
Colchester U.	L	10.73	73	4	0	0
Southend U.	Tr	02.74	73-76	79	2	32
Reading	L	03.75	74	2	0	0
Blackburn Rov.	L	10.76	76	5	0	1
Cambridge U.	Washington (USA)	08.77	77	2	2	1

SIM John (Jock)
Glasgow, 4 December, 1922 (CF)

League Club	Source	Date Signed	Seasons Played	Apps	Subs	Gls
Brighton & H. A.	Kirkintilloch Rob Roy	10.46	46-49	32	-	5

SIMCOE Kenneth Edward
Nottingham, 14 February, 1937 (CF)

League Club	Source	Date Signed	Seasons Played	Apps	Subs	Gls
Nottingham F.	Jnrs	12.56	57	2	-	1
Coventry C.	Tr	05.59	59	8	-	1
Notts Co.	Tr	07.60	60	2	-	0

SIMKIN Darren Spencer
Walsall, 24 March, 1970 (RB)

League Club	Source	Date Signed	Seasons Played	Apps	Subs	Gls
Wolverhampton W.	Blakenall	12.91	92-93	14	1	0
Shrewsbury T.	Tr	12.94	94	10	2	0

SIMM John
Ashton-in-Makerfield, 24 November, 1929 (W)

League Club	Source	Date Signed	Seasons Played	Apps	Subs	Gls
Bolton W.		10.47	47	1	-	0
Bury	Tr	05.51	51-54	47	-	8
Bradford C.	Tr	03.55	54-58	95	-	22

SIMMONDS Christopher Kenneth
Plymouth, 5 August, 1920 Died 1982 (F)

League Club	Source	Date Signed	Seasons Played	Apps	Subs	Gls
Millwall	Barry T.	05.47	46-49	67	-	14
Leyton Orient	Tr	06.50	50	15	-	1
Workington	Tr	06.51	51-53	119	-	34

SIMMONDS Daniel Brian
Eastbourne, 17 December, 1974 (M)

League Club	Source	Date Signed	Seasons Played	Apps	Subs	Gls
Brighton & H.A.	YT	07.93	93-94	8	10	0

SIMMONDS Robert **Lyndon**
Pontypool, 11 November, 1966 W Yth (F)

League Club	Source	Date Signed	Seasons Played	Apps	Subs	Gls
Leeds U.	App	11.84	84-85	6	3	3
Swansea C.	L	10.86	86	7	1	1
Rochdale	Tr	02.87	86-87	65	0	22

SIMMONDS Melvyn Robert
Reading, 20 December, 1951 E Sch (M)

League Club	Source	Date Signed	Seasons Played	Apps	Subs	Gls
Reading	Manchester U. (App)	01.69				
Bournemouth	Tr	07.69	69	4	2	0

SIMMONITE Gordon
Sheffield, 25 April, 1957 E Semi Pro (FB)

League Club	Source	Date Signed	Seasons Played	Apps	Subs	Gls
Sheffield Wed.	Rotherham U. (App)	08.75	76	1	0	0
Blackpool	Boston U.	09.80	80-82	63	0	1
Lincoln C.	Tr	11.82	82-84	71	1	0

SIMMONS Anthony John
Stocksbridge, 9 February, 1965 E Yth (F)

League Club	Source	Date Signed	Seasons Played	Apps	Subs	Gls
Sheffield Wed.	App	02.83	81-82	1	3	0
Queens Park R.	Tr	11.83				
Rotherham U.	Tr	03.84	83-86	85	11	27
Lincoln C.	Tr	09.86	86	14	5	5
Cardiff C.	L	02.87	86	4	1	1

SIMMONS David John
Ryde (IoW), 24 October, 1948 (F)

League Club	Source	Date Signed	Seasons Played	Apps	Subs	Gls
Arsenal	App	11.65				
Bournemouth	L	11.68	68	7	0	3
Aston Villa	Tr	02.69	68-70	13	4	7
Walsall	L	10.70	70	5	0	2
Colchester U.	Tr	12.70	70-72	52	5	11
Cambridge U.	Tr	03.73	72-73	19	5	3
Brentford	Tr	03.74	73-75	47	5	17
Cambridge U.	Tr	11.75	75	16	1	5

SIMMS Gordon
Leamington, 20 December, 1936 (W)

League Club	Source	Date Signed	Seasons Played	Apps	Subs	Gls
Coventry C. (Am)	Flavells	10.57	57	1	-	0

SIMNER Joseph
Sedgley, 13 March, 1923 (F)

League Club	Source	Date Signed	Seasons Played	Apps	Subs	Gls
Chelsea	Folkestone T.	10.47	47	1	-	0
Swindon T.	Tr	07.49	49-50	30	-	12

SIMONS Alan Geoffrey
Wrexham, 2 September, 1968 (G)

League Club	Source	Date Signed	Seasons Played	Apps	Subs	Gls
Port Vale (N/C)	YT	09.87	87	1	0	0

SIMONSEN Allan Rodenkam
Denmark, 15 December, 1952 Danish Int (F)

League Club	Source	Date Signed	Seasons Played	Apps	Subs	Gls
Charlton Ath.	Barcelona (Sp)	11.82	82	16	0	9

SIMONSEN Steven Preben
South Shields, 3 April, 1979 E Yth/Eu21-1 (G)

League Club	Source	Date Signed	Seasons Played	Apps	Subs	Gls
Tranmere Rov.	YT	10.96	97	30	0	0

SIMPKIN Christopher John
Hull, 24 April, 1944 (CD/M)

League Club	Source	Date Signed	Seasons Played	Apps	Subs	Gls
Hull C.	App	04.62	62-71	284	1	19
Blackpool	Tr	10.71	71-72	31	3	1
Scunthorpe U.	Tr	10.73	73-74	61	0	2
Huddersfield T.	Tr	08.75	75	25	0	0
Hartlepool U.	Tr	12.76	76-77	47	0	0

SIMPKIN Joseph
Skelmersdale, 26 September, 1921 Died 1969 (CH)

League Club	Source	Date Signed	Seasons Played	Apps	Subs	Gls
Southport	Burscough	04.44	46-47	10	-	2

SIMPKINS Kenneth
Wrexham, 21 December, 1943 Wu23-1 (G)

League Club	Source	Date Signed	Seasons Played	Apps	Subs	Gls
Wrexham	Jnrs	05.62	62-63	4	-	0
Hartlepool U.	Tr	03.64	63-67	121	0	1

SIMPSON Alexander
Glasgow, 24 November, 1924 (WH)

League Club	Source	Date Signed	Seasons Played	Apps	Subs	Gls
Wolverhampton W.	Benburb	01.47	47-48	2	-	0
Notts Co.	Tr	10.49	49-52	74	-	6
Southampton	Tr	11.52	52-54	68	-	1
Shrewsbury T.	Tr	07.55	55-57	100	-	4

SIMPSON Archibald
Dundee, 8 June, 1933 S Sch (FB)

League Club	Source	Date Signed	Seasons Played	Apps	Subs	Gls
Newcastle U.	Dundee	07.55				
Barrow	Tr	07.56	56-58	76	-	1

SIMPSON Charles William
Rochdale, 11 July, 1954 (M)

League Club	Source	Date Signed	Seasons Played	Apps	Subs	Gls
Rochdale	App	07.72	72	1	0	1

SIMPSON Colin Robertson
Oxford, 30 April, 1976 (W)

League Club	Source	Date Signed	Seasons Played	Apps	Subs	Gls
Watford	YT	07.94	95	0	1	0
Leyton Orient	Hendon	12.97	97	9	5	3

SIMPSON Cyril
Aylesham (Kt), 18 August, 1942 (WH)

League Club	Source	Date Signed	Seasons Played	Apps	Subs	Gls
Gillingham	Jnrs	06.60	59-61	18	-	0

SIMPSON Dennis Ewart
Coventry, 1 November, 1919 (OR)

League Club	Source	Date Signed	Seasons Played	Apps	Subs	Gls
Coventry C.	Jnrs	05.39	46-49	67	-	5
Reading	Tr	05.50	50-54	172	-	31
Exeter C.	Tr	05.55	55-56	30	-	4

SIMPSON Elliott David
York, 1 July, 1976 (LB)

League Club	Source	Date Signed	Seasons Played	Apps	Subs	Gls
York C.	YT	06.94	94	1	0	0

SIMPSON Fitzroy
Bradford-on-Avon, 26 February, 1970 Jamaican Int (M)

League Club	Source	Date Signed	Seasons Played	Apps	Subs	Gls
Swindon T.	YT	07.88	88-91	78	27	9
Manchester C.	Tr	03.92	91-94	58	13	4
Bristol C.	L	09.94	94	4	0	0
Portsmouth	Tr	08.95	95-97	84	6	9

SIMPSON Gary
Chesterfield, 10 June, 1959 (F)

League Club	Source	Date Signed	Seasons Played	Apps	Subs	Gls
Chesterfield	App	07.77	76-80	36	7	8
Chester C.	Tr	08.81	81-82	57	6	18

SIMPSON Gary John
Ashford, 14 February, 1976 (CD)

League Club	Source	Date Signed	Seasons Played	Apps	Subs	Gls
Luton T.	YT	07.94				
Fulham	L	03.96	95	5	2	0

SIMPSON George Leonard
Shirebrook, 3 December, 1933 (IF)

League Club	Source	Date Signed	Seasons Played	Apps	Subs	Gls
Mansfield T.	Jnrs	08.51	52-53	8	-	0
Gillingham	Hereford U.	08.56	56	8	-	1

SIMPSON Harold
Ashton-u-Lyne, 2 August, 1927 (OL)

League Club	Source	Date Signed	Seasons Played	Apps	Subs	Gls
Accrington St. (Am)	Lytham	04.49	48	1	-	0

SIMPSON James
Clay Cross, 8 December, 1923 (IF)

League Club	Source	Date Signed	Seasons Played	Apps	Subs	Gls
Chesterfield	Parkhouse Colly	05.45	46	3	-	0

SIMPSON John
Hull, 27 October, 1918 (LB)

League Club	Source	Date Signed	Seasons Played	Apps	Subs	Gls
Huddersfield T.	Bridlington T.	03.39	46	5	-	0
York C.	Tr	03.48	47-53	207	-	0

SIMPSON John Lionel
Appleby, 5 October, 1933 Died 1993 (G)

League Club	Source	Date Signed	Seasons Played	Apps	Subs	Gls
Lincoln C.	Netherfield	03.57	56	5	-	0
Gillingham	Tr	06.57	57-71	571	0	0

SIMPSON Karl Edward
Newmarket, 14 October, 1976 (RM)

League Club	Source	Date Signed	Seasons Played	Apps	Subs	Gls
Norwich C.	Jnrs	07.95	95-97	4	6	0

SIMPSON Kenneth
Sheffield, 12 June, 1931 (F)

League Club	Source	Date Signed	Seasons Played	Apps	Subs	Gls
Rotherham U.	Ransome & Marles	09.55	55-57	7	-	0

SIMPSON Michael
Nottingham, 28 February, 1974 (M)

League Club	Source	Date Signed	Seasons Played	Apps	Subs	Gls
Notts Co.	YT	07.92	93-96	39	10	3
Plymouth Arg.	L	10.96	96	10	2	0
Wycombe W.	Tr	12.96	96-97	26	15	1

SIMPSON Neil
Hackney, 15 November, 1961 E Yth/Su21-11/S-4 (M)

League Club	Source	Date Signed	Seasons Played	Apps	Subs	Gls
Newcastle U.	Aberdeen	07.90	90	1	3	0

SIMPSON Noel Harold
Mansfield, 23 December, 1922 Died 1987 (WH)

League Club	Source	Date Signed	Seasons Played	Apps	Subs	Gls
Nottingham F.		05.45	46-47	47	-	3
Coventry C.	Tr	08.48	48-56	258	-	7
Exeter C.	Tr	02.57	56-57	33	-	0

SIMPSON Owen
Prudhoe (Nd), 18 September, 1943 (FB)

League Club	Source	Date Signed	Seasons Played	Apps	Subs	Gls
Rotherham U.		10.62	64-66	6	0	0
Leyton Orient	Tr	09.67	67	36	0	4
Colchester U.	Tr	08.68	68	41	2	4

League Club	Source	Date Signed	Seasons Played	Apps	Subs	Gls
Southend U.	Tr	08.69	69-70	64	0	1
Darlington	Tr	03.71	70	11	0	0
Grimsby T.	Tr	08.71	71	6	1	0

SIMPSON Paul David
Carlisle, 26 July, 1966 E Yth/Eu21-5 (LW)

League Club	Source	Date Signed	Seasons Played	Apps	Subs	Gls
Manchester C.	App	08.83	82-88	99	22	18
Oxford U.	Tr	10.88	88-91	138	6	43
Derby Co.	Tr	02.92	91-96	133	52	48
Sheffield U.	L	12.96	96	2	4	0
Wolverhampton W.	Tr	10.97	97	23	5	4

SIMPSON Peter Frederick
Great Yarmouth, 13 January, 1945 (CD)

League Club	Source	Date Signed	Seasons Played	Apps	Subs	Gls
Arsenal	App	04.62	63-77	353	17	10

SIMPSON Peter Wilson
Sunderland, 21 September, 1940 E Sch (F)

League Club	Source	Date Signed	Seasons Played	Apps	Subs	Gls
Burnley	Jnrs	11.57	61-62	3	-	0
Bury	Tr	08.63	63	4	-	0

SIMPSON Phillip Mark
Lambeth, 19 October, 1969 (M)

League Club	Source	Date Signed	Seasons Played	Apps	Subs	Gls
Barnet	Stevenage Borough	10.95	95-97	80	7	7

SIMPSON Reginald
Blackburn, 14 June, 1923 (D)

League Club	Source	Date Signed	Seasons Played	Apps	Subs	Gls
Preston N. E.		11.43	46	4	-	0
Carlisle U.	Tr	08.48	48	38	-	0

SIMPSON Robert
Bishop Auckland, 15 September, 1915 Died 1994 (OL)

League Club	Source	Date Signed	Seasons Played	Apps	Subs	Gls
Darlington	West Auckland	08.36	36-46	97	-	15
Hartlepool U.	Tr	07.47	47	13	-	1

SIMPSON Robert Anthony
Luton, 3 March, 1976 E Yth (M)

League Club	Source	Date Signed	Seasons Played	Apps	Subs	Gls
Tottenham H.	YT	11.93				
Portsmouth	Tr	07.96	97	0	2	0

SIMPSON Ronald
Carlisle, 25 February, 1934 (OL)

League Club	Source	Date Signed	Seasons Played	Apps	Subs	Gls
Huddersfield T.	Holme Head Wks	02.51	51-57	110	-	24
Sheffield U.	Tr	05.58	58-64	203	-	45
Carlisle U.	Tr	12.64	64-65	45	0	6

SIMPSON Ronald Campbell
Glasgow, 11 October, 1930 S Amat/S 'B'/SF Lge/S-5 (G)

League Club	Source	Date Signed	Seasons Played	Apps	Subs	Gls
Newcastle U.	Third Lanark	02.51	51-59	262	-	0

SIMPSON Terence John Norman
Southampton, 8 October, 1938 (WH)

League Club	Source	Date Signed	Seasons Played	Apps	Subs	Gls
Southampton	Jnrs	06.57	58-61	22	-	1
Peterborough U.	Tr	06.62	62	45	-	4
West Bromwich A.	Tr	06.63	63-66	71	1	3
Walsall	Tr	03.67	66-67	50	1	4
Gillingham	Tr	07.68	68	35	1	4

SIMPSON Thomas
Airdrie, 31 July, 1931 (FB)

League Club	Source	Date Signed	Seasons Played	Apps	Subs	Gls
Darlington	Dundee U.	08.56	56-57	4	-	0

SIMPSON William
Carlisle, 2 October, 1919 (IL)

League Club	Source	Date Signed	Seasons Played	Apps	Subs	Gls
Carlisle U.	Tottenham H. (Am)	08.46	46	12	-	2

SIMPSON William George
Glasgow, 22 May, 1928 (F/WH)

League Club	Source	Date Signed	Seasons Played	Apps	Subs	Gls
Aston Villa	Trentside Jnrs	05.50				
Crystal Palace	Tr	08.52	52-54	38	-	13

SIMS Harry **Christopher**
Liverpool, 6 December, 1939 (FB)

League Club	Source	Date Signed	Seasons Played	Apps	Subs	Gls
Blackburn Rov.	Clitheroe	04.59	63-64	13	-	0

SIMS Frank
Lincoln, 12 September, 1931 (CH)

League Club	Source	Date Signed	Seasons Played	Apps	Subs	Gls
Lincoln C.	Ruston Sports	08.51	51-55	3	-	0

SIMS John
Belper, 14 August, 1952 (F)

League Club	Source	Date Signed	Seasons Played	Apps	Subs	Gls
Derby Co.	App	08.70	72	2	1	0
Luton T.	L	11.73	73	3	0	1
Oxford U.	L	09.74	74	6	1	1
Colchester U.	L	01.75	74	2	0	0
Notts Co.	Tr	12.75	75-77	48	13	13
Exeter C.	Tr	12.78	78-79	33	1	11
Plymouth Arg.	Tr	10.79	79-82	161	2	43
Torquay U.	Tr	08.83	83	30	0	8
Exeter C.	Tr	02.84	83-84	23	2	6
Torquay U.	Tr	11.84	84	15	2	3

SIMS David **Nigel**
Caton-in-the-Elms (Dy), 9 August, 1931 EF Lge (G)

League Club	Source	Date Signed	Seasons Played	Apps	Subs	Gls
Wolverhampton W.	Jnrs	09.48	48-55	38	-	0
Aston Villa	Tr	03.56	55-63	264	-	0
Peterborough U.	Tr	09.64	64	16	-	0

SIMS Steven Frank
Lincoln, 2 July, 1957 Eu21-10/E-'B' (CD)

League Club	Source	Date Signed	Seasons Played	Apps	Subs	Gls
Leicester C.	App	08.74	75-78	78	1	3
Watford	Tr	12.78	78-83	150	2	4
Notts Co.	Tr	09.84	84-86	85	0	5
Watford	Tr	10.86	86	19	0	1
Aston Villa	Tr	06.87	87-88	41	0	0
Lincoln C. (N/C)	Burton A.	10.90	90	5	0	0

SINCLAIR Brian William
Liverpool, 2 August, 1958 (W)

League Club	Source	Date Signed	Seasons Played	Apps	Subs	Gls
Blackpool	Bury (N/C)	08.77	77	0	2	0
Port Vale	Tr	08.78	78	14	4	2

SINCLAIR Colin MacLean
Edinburgh, 1 December, 1947 S Sch/S Yth (F)

League Club	Source	Date Signed	Seasons Played	Apps	Subs	Gls
Darlington	Raith Rov.	06.71	71-76	201	2	59
Hereford U.	Tr	10.76	76-77	20	2	2
Newport Co.	Tr	01.78	77-78	29	1	5

SINCLAIR David
Dunfermline, 6 October, 1969 (CD)

League Club	Source	Date Signed	Seasons Played	Apps	Subs	Gls
Millwall	Raith Rov.	07.96	96-97	6	2	0

SINCLAIR Dennis
Middlesbrough, 20 November, 1931 (OR)

League Club	Source	Date Signed	Seasons Played	Apps	Subs	Gls
Derby Co.		05.52				
Mansfield T.	Tr	07.53	53	1	-	0

SINCLAIR Frank Mohammed
Lambeth, 3 December, 1971 Jamaican Int (D)

League Club	Source	Date Signed	Seasons Played	Apps	Subs	Gls
Chelsea	YT	05.90	90-97	163	6	7
West Bromwich A.	L	12.91	91	6	0	1

SINCLAIR Graeme James
Paisley, 1 July, 1957 (D)

League Club	Source	Date Signed	Seasons Played	Apps	Subs	Gls
Manchester C. (L)	Glasgow Celtic	11.84	84	1	0	0

SINCLAIR Harvey Patrick
Bournemouth, 30 November, 1933 (G)

League Club	Source	Date Signed	Seasons Played	Apps	Subs	Gls
Fulham	Bournemouth (Am)	12.50				
Leicester C.	Cambridge U.	08.56	56	1	-	0
Bristol Rov.	Yeovil T.	09.58	58	1	-	0

SINCLAIR Jade
Saltburn, 6 November, 1971 (M)

League Club	Source	Date Signed	Seasons Played	Apps	Subs	Gls
Hartlepool U.	YT	●	89	4	0	0

SINCLAIR John (Jackie) Evens Wright
Culross (Fife), 21 July, 1943 S-1 (W)

League Club	Source	Date Signed	Seasons Played	Apps	Subs	Gls
Leicester C.	Dunfermline Ath.	05.65	65-67	103	0	50
Newcastle U.	Tr	01.68	67-69	42	1	6
Sheffield Wed.	Tr	12.69	69-72	97	4	14
Chesterfield	L	03.73	72	10	0	3

SINCLAIR Michael John
Grimsby, 13 October, 1938 (CF)

League Club	Source	Date Signed	Seasons Played	Apps	Subs	Gls
Grimsby T.	Jnrs	09.57	57-60	6	-	1

SINCLAIR Nicholas John Thomas
Manchester, 3 January, 1960 (RB)

League Club	Source	Date Signed	Seasons Played	Apps	Subs	Gls
Oldham Ath.	Jnrs	06.78	78-84	73	2	1
Wolverhampton W.	L	09.84	84	1	0	0
Tranmere Rov.	Tr	10.84	84-85	22	0	1

SINCLAIR Robert Alan
Greenwich, 9 April, 1974 (F)

League Club	Source	Date Signed	Seasons Played	Apps	Subs	Gls
Maidstone U.	YT	●	91	1	0	0

SINCLAIR Robert Dunlop
Winchburgh, 28 June, 1915 Died 1993 (OR)

League Club	Source	Date Signed	Seasons Played	Apps	Subs	Gls
Chesterfield		05.39				
Darlington	Tr	06.46	46-47	69	-	11

SINCLAIR Ronald McDonald
Stirling, 19 November, 1964 S Sch/S Yth (G)

League Club	Source	Date Signed	Seasons Played	Apps	Subs	Gls
Nottingham F.	App	10.82				
Wrexham	L	03.84	83	11	0	0
Leeds U.	Tr	06.86	86	8	0	0
Halifax T.	L	03.87	86	4	0	0

League Club	Source	Date Signed	Seasons Played	Apps	Subs	Gls
Halifax T.	L	12.88	88	10	0	0
Bristol C.	Tr	09.89	89-90	44	0	0
Walsall	L	09.91	91	10	0	0
Stoke C.	Tr	11.91	91-95	78	2	0
Chester C.	Tr	08.96	96-97	70	0	0

SINCLAIR Roy
Liverpool, 10 December, 1944 (M)

League Club	Source	Date Signed	Seasons Played	Apps	Subs	Gls
Tranmere Rov.	Liverpool (Am)	10.63	63-68	130	8	17
Watford	Tr	03.69	68-71	32	11	3
Chester C.	L	12.71	71	5	0	2
Tranmere Rov.	Tr	07.72	72	12	0	0

SINCLAIR Thomas
Wigan, 13 October, 1921 (W)

League Club	Source	Date Signed	Seasons Played	Apps	Subs	Gls
Aldershot	Gainsborough Trin.	08.44	46-50	70	-	8
Brentford	Tr	08.50	50	16	-	5
Bradford C.	Tr	08.51	51	9	-	0

SINCLAIR Trevor Lloyd
Dulwich, 2 March, 1973 E Yth/Eu21-14/E 'B' (W)

League Club	Source	Date Signed	Seasons Played	Apps	Subs	Gls
Blackpool	YT	08.90	89-92	84	28	15
Queens Park R.	Tr	08.93	93-97	162	5	16
West Ham U.	Tr	01.98	97	14	0	7

SINCLAIR William
Southport, 11 September, 1920 Died 1978 (WH)

League Club	Source	Date Signed	Seasons Played	Apps	Subs	Gls
Southport	High Park	09.45	46	15	-	1

SINCLAIR William Inglis
Glasgow, 21 March, 1947 (WH)

League Club	Source	Date Signed	Seasons Played	Apps	Subs	Gls
Chelsea	Morton	09.64	64	1	-	0

SINCLAIR William Mearns
Blairhall, 14 October, 1934 (IF)

League Club	Source	Date Signed	Seasons Played	Apps	Subs	Gls
Huddersfield T.	Falkirk	12.58	58-59	15	-	5
Tranmere Rov.	Tr	06.60	60	4	-	0
Halifax T.	Tr	10.60	60	21	-	3

SINDALL Mark
Shirebrook, 3 September, 1964 (M)

League Club	Source	Date Signed	Seasons Played	Apps	Subs	Gls
Mansfield T.	Notts Co. (App)	08.82	82-83	18	3	0

SINGER Dennis James
Gilfach Goch, 30 August, 1937 (IF)

League Club	Source	Date Signed	Seasons Played	Apps	Subs	Gls
Newport Co.	Hengoed F.D.L.	05.56	57-60	52	-	27
Birmingham C.	Tr	09.60	60-61	20	-	8
Bournemouth	Tr	09.62	62-63	59	-	22
Newport Co.	Tr	07.64	64	8	-	5

SINGLETON Anthony Joseph
Preston, 30 March, 1936 (CH)

League Club	Source	Date Signed	Seasons Played	Apps	Subs	Gls
Preston N. E.	Jnrs	05.55	60-67	286	1	0

SINGLETON Bernard (Barney)
Conisbrough, 14 April, 1924 Died 1981 (G)

League Club	Source	Date Signed	Seasons Played	Apps	Subs	Gls
Wolverhampton W.	Lincoln C. (Am)	05.41				
Exeter C.	Tr	01.46	46-53	177	-	1

SINGLETON Martin David
Banbury, 2 August, 1963 E Yth (M)

League Club	Source	Date Signed	Seasons Played	Apps	Subs	Gls
Coventry C.	App	01.81	81-84	20	3	1
Bradford C.	Tr	12.84	84-86	69	2	3
West Bromwich A.	Tr	12.86	86-87	15	4	1
Northampton T.	Tr	11.87	87-89	45	5	4
Walsall	Tr	09.90	90	20	8	1

SINGLETON Thomas Wilfred
Blackpool, 8 September, 1940 (FB)

League Club	Source	Date Signed	Seasons Played	Apps	Subs	Gls
Blackpool	Jnrs	11.58				
Peterborough U.	Tr	06.62	62-64	85	-	1
Chester C.	Tr	06.65	65-67	87	1	1
Bradford P. A.	Tr	07.68	68	32	0	1

SINNOTT Lee
Pelsall, 12 July, 1965 E Yth/Eu21-1 (CD)

League Club	Source	Date Signed	Seasons Played	Apps	Subs	Gls
Walsall	App	11.82	81-83	40	0	2
Watford	Tr	09.83	83-86	71	7	2
Bradford C.	Tr	07.87	87-90	173	0	6
Crystal Palace	Tr	08.91	91-92	53	2	0
Bradford C.	Tr	12.93	93-94	34	0	1
Huddersfield T.	Tr	12.94	94-96	86	1	1
Oldham Ath.	Tr	07.97	97	11	2	0
Bradford C.	L	03.98	97	7	0	0

SINTON Andrew
Cramlington, 19 March, 1966 E Sch/E 'B'/EF Lge/E-12 (LW)

League Club	Source	Date Signed	Seasons Played	Apps	Subs	Gls
Cambridge U.	App	04.83	82-85	90	3	13
Brentford	Tr	12.85	85-88	149	0	28
Queens Park R.	Tr	03.89	88-92	160	0	22
Sheffield Wed.	Tr	08.93	93-95	54	6	3
Tottenham H.	Tr	01.96	95-97	54	7	6

SIRREL James
Glasgow, 2 February, 1922 (IF)

League Club	Source	Date Signed	Seasons Played	Apps	Subs	Gls
Bradford P. A.	Glasgow Celtic	05.49	49-50	12	-	2
Brighton & H. A.	Tr	08.51	51-53	55	-	16
Aldershot	Tr	08.54	54-56	31	-	3

SISSOKO Habib
Juvisy Orge, France, 24 May, 1971 (F)

League Club	Source	Date Signed	Seasons Played	Apps	Subs	Gls
Preston N.E.	Louhans (Fr)	02.98	97	4	3	0

SISSON Michael Anthony
Sutton-in-Ashfield, 24 November, 1978 (M)

League Club	Source	Date Signed	Seasons Played	Apps	Subs	Gls
Mansfield T.	YT	01.98	97	0	1	0

SISSONS John Graham
Chester-le-Street, 20 May, 1934 (D)

League Club	Source	Date Signed	Seasons Played	Apps	Subs	Gls
Birmingham C.	Country Girl F.C.	07.54	56-62	90	-	0
Peterborough U.	Tr	12.61	62-64	68	-	0
Walsall	Tr	11.64	64-67	93	5	1

SISSONS John Leslie
Hayes, 30 September, 1945 E Sch/E Yth/Eu23-10 (OL)

League Club	Source	Date Signed	Seasons Played	Apps	Subs	Gls
West Ham U.	App	10.62	62-69	210	3	37
Sheffield Wed.	Tr	08.70	70-73	114	1	14
Norwich C.	Tr	12.73	73	17	0	2
Chelsea	Tr	08.74	74	10	1	0

SITFORD Jack Anthony
Crowborough, 28 January, 1940 (FB)

League Club	Source	Date Signed	Seasons Played	Apps	Subs	Gls
Brighton & H. A.		03.59	60-61	22	-	2

SITTON John Edmund
Hackney, 21 October, 1959 (D)

League Club	Source	Date Signed	Seasons Played	Apps	Subs	Gls
Chelsea	App	10.77	78-79	11	2	0
Millwall	Tr	02.80	79-80	43	2	1
Gillingham	Tr	09.81	81-84	102	5	5
Leyton Orient	Tr	07.85	85-90	166	4	7

SIVEBAEK John
Denmark, 25 October, 1961 Danish Int (RB)

League Club	Source	Date Signed	Seasons Played	Apps	Subs	Gls
Manchester U.	Vejle B.K. (Den)	02.86	85-86	29	2	1

SIVELL Laurence
Lowestoft, 8 February, 1951 (G)

League Club	Source	Date Signed	Seasons Played	Apps	Subs	Gls
Ipswich T.	App	02.69	69-83	141	0	0
Lincoln C.	L	01.79	78	2	0	0

SIX Didier
France, 21 August, 1954 French Int (W)

League Club	Source	Date Signed	Seasons Played	Apps	Subs	Gls
Aston Villa	Mulhouse (Fr)	10.84	84	13	3	2

SJOBERG John
Aberdeen, 12 June, 1941 S Sch (D)

League Club	Source	Date Signed	Seasons Played	Apps	Subs	Gls
Leicester C.	Banks O'Dee	08.58	60-72	334	1	15
Rotherham U.	Tr	06.73	73	6	0	0

SKEDD Anthony Stuart
Hartlepool, 19 May, 1975 (LM)

League Club	Source	Date Signed	Seasons Played	Apps	Subs	Gls
Hartlepool U.	YT	10.93	92-94	39	7	0

SKEECH Henry Gordon
Warrington, 15 May, 1934 (FB)

League Club	Source	Date Signed	Seasons Played	Apps	Subs	Gls
Shrewsbury T.	Runcorn	11.54	54-62	223	-	2

SKEELS Eric Thomas
Eccles, 27 October, 1939 (D)

League Club	Source	Date Signed	Seasons Played	Apps	Subs	Gls
Stoke C.	Stockport Co. (Am)	12.58	59-75	495	12	7
Port Vale	Seattle Sounders (USA)	09.76	76	5	0	1

SKEEN George Gray
Gateshead, 4 August, 1920 Died 1984 (WH)

League Club	Source	Date Signed	Seasons Played	Apps	Subs	Gls
Gateshead		10.46	46-49	86	-	3

SKEEN Kenneth Albert
Cheltenham, 20 March, 1942 (M)

League Club	Source	Date Signed	Seasons Played	Apps	Subs	Gls
Swindon T.	Trowbridge T.	09.64	64-66	14	0	4
Oxford U.	Tr	07.67	67-73	214	20	27

SKEET Stuart Christopher
Edmonton, 6 July, 1948 (G)

League Club	Source	Date Signed	Seasons Played	Apps	Subs	Gls
Tottenham H.	App	12.65				
Northampton T.	L	03.69	68	1	0	0

League Club	Source	Date Signed	Seasons Played	Career Record		
				Apps	Subs	Gls
SKEETE Leopold Anthony						
Liverpool, 3 August, 1949						(F)
Rochdale	Ellesmere Port	04.73	72-74	39	1	14
SKELLY Richard Brian						
Norwich, 24 March, 1972						(LB)
Cambridge U. (N/C)	Newmarket T.	01.94	93	2	0	0
Northampton T.	Tr	06.94	94	3	0	0
SKELTON Aaron Matthew						
Welwyn Garden City, 22 November, 1974						(M)
Luton T.	YT	12.92	94-96	5	3	0
Colchester U.	Tr	07.97	97	37	2	7
SKELTON George Alfred						
Thurcroft, 27 November, 1919						(IF)
Huddersfield T.	Thurcroft Welfare	12.45	46	1	-	0
Leyton Orient	Tr	07.47	47	3	-	0
SKIDMORE William						
Barnsley, 15 March, 1925						(LB)
Wolverhampton W.	Jnrs	05.42				
Walsall	Tr	05.46	46-50	99	-	10
SKILLEN Keith						
Cockermouth, 26 May, 1948						(F)
Workington	Netherfield	12.73	73-74	56	8	9
Hartlepool U.	Tr	07.75	75	4	2	1
SKINGLEY Brian George						
Ilford, 28 August, 1937						(FB)
Bristol Rov.	Ilfracombe	01.55				
Crystal Palace	Tr	09.58	58	11	-	0
Queens Park R.	Tr	07.59				
SKINNER Craig Richard						
Heywood, 21 October, 1970						(W)
Blackburn Rov.	YT	06.89	90-91	11	5	0
Plymouth Arg.	Tr	08.92	92-94	42	11	4
Wrexham	Tr	07.95	95-97	58	17	8
SKINNER George Edward Henry						
Erith, 26 June, 1917						(IF)
Tottenham H.	Callenders	09.38	46	1	-	0
Brighton & H. A.	Gillingham	02.48				
SKINNER Justin						
Hounslow, 30 January, 1969						(M)
Fulham	App	11.86	86-90	111	24	23
Bristol Rov.	Tr	08.91	91-97	174	13	12
Walsall	L	09.97	97	10	0	0
SKINNER Justin James						
Dorking, 17 September, 1972						(LB)
Wimbledon	YT	07.91	92-95	2	0	0
Bournemouth	L	03.94	93	16	0	0
Wycombe W.	L	08.94	94	4	1	0
SKIPPER Peter Dennis						
Hull, 11 April, 1958						(CD)
Hull C.	Schultz Y. C.	02.79	78-79	22	1	2
Scunthorpe U.	L	02.80	79	0	1	0
Darlington	Tr	05.80	80-81	91	0	4
Hull C.	Tr	08.82	82-88	264	1	17
Oldham Ath.	Tr	10.88	88	27	0	1
Walsall	Tr	07.89	89-90	81	0	2
Wrexham (N/C)	Tr	09.91	91	2	0	0
Wigan Ath. (N/C)	Tr	10.91	91	15	3	0
Wigan Ath.	Stafford R.	11.92	92-93	73	0	4
SKIRTON Alan Frederick Graham						
Bath, 23 January, 1939						(W)
Arsenal	Bath C.	01.59	60-66	144	1	53
Blackpool	Tr	09.66	66-68	76	1	25
Bristol C.	Tr	11.68	68-70	75	3	14
Torquay U.	Tr	07.71	71	36	2	7
SKIVERTON Terence John						
Mile End, 26 June, 1975						(D)
Chelsea	YT	05.93				
Wycombe W.	L	02.95	94	8	2	0
Wycombe W.	Tr	03.96	95-96	5	5	1
SKIVINGTON Glenn						
Barrow, 19 January, 1962						(M)
Derby Co.	Barrow	07.80	80-82	39	7	2
Halifax T.	L	03.83	82	4	0	0
Southend U.	Tr	08.83	83	2	2	0
SKIVINGTON Michael Noel						
Glasgow, 24 December, 1921 LoI						(CH)
Bury		06.47				
Rochdale	Tr	01.48	47	1	-	0
Leyton Orient	Dundalk	10.49	49	5	-	0
Gillingham	Tr	07.50	50	8	-	0
Brentford	Tr	09.51				
SKULL John						
Swindon, 25 August, 1932 E Yth						(OR)
Wolverhampton W.	Swindon T. (Am)	06.50				
Swindon T.	Banbury Spencer	09.57	57-58	33	-	11
SLACK Andrew						
Bury, 9 June, 1959						(G)
Rochdale	Bolton W. (App)	01.78	77-78	15	0	0
SLACK Melvyn						
Bishop Auckland, 7 March, 1944						(WH)
Sunderland	Jnrs	03.61	64	2	-	1
Southend U.	Tr	08.65	65-68	107	4	5
Cambridge U.	Tr	01.69	70	33	2	0
SLACK Robert Geoffrey						
Morecambe, 13 July, 1934						(OR)
Stockport Co.	Morecambe	11.58	58	8	-	1
SLACK Rodney						
Peterborough, 11 April, 1940						(G)
Leicester C.		09.58				
Queens Park R.	Tr	03.61	61	1	-	0
SLACK Trevor Colin						
Peterborough, 26 September, 1962 E Yth						(CD)
Peterborough U.	App	08.80	80-85	201	1	18
Rotherham U.	Tr	08.86	86	14	1	1
Grimsby T.	Tr	08.87	87	21	0	0
Northampton T.	Tr	02.88	87	13	0	1
Chesterfield	Tr	09.88	88-89	23	0	0
SLADE Robert Frederick						
Hounslow, 15 July, 1927						(G)
Millwall (Am)	Acton T.	10.48	48	1	-	0
SLADE Steven Anthony						
Hackney, 6 October, 1975 Eu21-4						(F)
Tottenham H.	YT	07.94	95	1	4	0
Queens Park R.	Tr	07.96	96-97	14	25	4
Brentford	L	02.97	96	4	0	0
SLATER John **Brian**						
Sheffield, 20 October, 1932						(IF)
Sheffield Wed.		05.51	52	3	-	0
Grimsby T.	Tr	07.54	54	4	-	0
Rotherham U.	Tr	09.55	56	17	-	5
Chesterfield	Tr	06.57	57	15	-	3
SLATER Darren						
Bishop Auckland, 4 January, 1979						(RM)
Hartlepool U.	YT	●	95	0	1	0
SLATER Frederick						
Burton, 25 September, 1925						(CF)
Birmingham C.	Burton A.	11.47	48-49	5	-	1
York C.	Tr	06.51	51	13	-	3
SLATER James Jonathan						
Wrexham, 27 October, 1968						(F)
Wrexham	Jnrs	07.87	87	0	3	0
SLATER John						
Heywood, 8 May, 1917						(RH)
Rochdale		04.40				
Crewe Alex.	Tr	08.46	46	3	-	0
SLATER Malcolm Bruce						
Buckie, 22 October, 1939						(W)
Southend U.	Montrose	11.63	63-66	82	0	6
Leyton Orient	Tr	01.67	66-69	111	0	4
Colchester U.	L	10.69	69	4	0	0
SLATER Raymond						
Tynemouth, 22 August, 1931						(CF)
Chesterfield	South Shields	06.56	56	2	-	1
Gateshead	Tr	10.56	56	6	-	2
SLATER Robert (Bert)						
Musselburgh, 5 May, 1936 Su23-1						(G)
Liverpool	Falkirk	05.59	59-61	99	-	0
Watford	Dundee	05.65	65-68	134	0	0

SLATER Robert David
Ormskirk, 22 November, 1964 Australian Int (M)

League Club	Source	Date Signed	Seasons Played	Apps	Subs	Gls
Blackburn Rov.	Lens (Fr)	08.94	94	12	6	0
West Ham U.	Tr	08.95	95-96	18	7	2
Southampton	Tr	09.96	96-97	25	16	2
Wolverhampton W.	Tr	03.98	97	4	2	0

SLATER Stuart Ian
Sudbury, 27 March, 1969 Eu21-3/E 'B' (LW)

League Club	Source	Date Signed	Seasons Played	Apps	Subs	Gls
West Ham U.	App	03.87	87-91	134	7	11
Ipswich T.	Glasgow Celtic	09.93	93-96	61	11	4
Watford	Leicester C. (N/C)	11.96	96-97	22	8	1

SLATER William John
Clitheroe, 29 April, 1927 E Amat/E-12 (WH)

League Club	Source	Date Signed	Seasons Played	Apps	Subs	Gls
Blackpool (Am)	Jnrs	05.49	49-51	30	-	9
Brentford (Am)	Tr	12.51	51	7	-	1
Wolverhampton W.	Tr	08.52	52-62	310	-	24
Brentford	Tr	07.63	63	5	-	2

SLATTER Leslie Arthur Heber
Reading, 22 November, 1931 (OR)

League Club	Source	Date Signed	Seasons Played	Apps	Subs	Gls
Luton T.	Mount Pleasant Y.C.	03.49	49	1	-	0
Aston Villa	Crusaders	08.53				
York C.	Tr	07.54	54	13	-	0

SLATTER Neil John
Cardiff, 30 May, 1964, W Yth/Wu21-6/W-22 (D)

League Club	Source	Date Signed	Seasons Played	Apps	Subs	Gls
Bristol Rov.	App	05.82	80-84	147	1	4
Oxford U.	Tr	07.85	85-89	88	3	6
Bournemouth	L	03.90	89	5	1	0

SLATTERY James **Clive**
Swansea, 21 July, 1946 (W)

League Club	Source	Date Signed	Seasons Played	Apps	Subs	Gls
Swansea C.	North End	10.68	68-71	65	6	10
Hereford U.	Tr	07.72	72	3	5	0

SLATTERY Joseph William
Newcastle, 3 June, 1926 (CF)

League Club	Source	Date Signed	Seasons Played	Apps	Subs	Gls
Accrington St.	Hexham Hearts	06.50	50	13	-	2

SLAVEN Bernard Joseph
Paisley, 13 November, 1960 IR-7 (F)

League Club	Source	Date Signed	Seasons Played	Apps	Subs	Gls
Middlesbrough	Albion Rov.	09.85	85-92	286	21	119
Port Vale	Tr	03.93	92-93	29	4	9
Darlington	Tr	02.94	93-94	35	2	7

SLAWSON Stephen Michael
Nottingham, 13 November, 1972 (F)

League Club	Source	Date Signed	Seasons Played	Apps	Subs	Gls
Notts Co.	YT	07.91	91-94	16	22	4
Burnley	L	02.93	92	5	0	2
Shrewsbury T.	L	10.94	94	6	0	0
Mansfield T.	Tr	07.95	95	21	8	5
Rotherham U.	Tr	07.96	96	2	3	0

SLEE David **Carl**
Swansea, 30 November, 1947 W Sch (D)

League Club	Source	Date Signed	Seasons Played	Apps	Subs	Gls
Swansea C.	Jnrs	01.66	67-70	111	4	0

SLEEUWENHOEK John Cornelius
Wolverhampton, 26 February, 1944 Died 1989 E Sch/E Yth/Eu23-2/EF Lge (CH)

League Club	Source	Date Signed	Seasons Played	Apps	Subs	Gls
Aston Villa	App	03.61	60-67	226	0	1
Birmingham C.	Tr	11.67	67-70	29	1	0
Torquay U.	L	03.71	70	11	0	0
Oldham Ath.	Tr	07.71	71	2	0	0

SLEIGHT Geoffrey
Barnsley, 20 June, 1943 (OL)

League Club	Source	Date Signed	Seasons Played	Apps	Subs	Gls
Bolton W.	Jnrs	08.61	61	2	-	0

SLINGSBY Lee
Rossington, 27 November, 1970 (M)

League Club	Source	Date Signed	Seasons Played	Apps	Subs	Gls
Scarborough	Doncaster Rov. (YT)	07.89	89	0	1	0

SLINN Kevin Paul
Northampton, 2 September, 1974 (F)

League Club	Source	Date Signed	Seasons Played	Apps	Subs	Gls
Watford	YT	04.93				
Stockport Co.	Tr	07.94	94	2	2	1

SLOAN David
Lisburn (NI), 28 October, 1941 NI Amat/NIu23-1/NI-2 (W)

League Club	Source	Date Signed	Seasons Played	Apps	Subs	Gls
Scunthorpe U.	Bangor	11.63	63-67	133	3	42
Oxford U.	Tr	02.68	67-72	166	8	29
Walsall	Tr	07.73	73-74	44	5	3

SLOAN James
Newcastle, 22 February, 1924 Died 1990 (CF)

League Club	Source	Date Signed	Seasons Played	Apps	Subs	Gls
Newcastle U.	C.A. Parsons	01.45				
Hartlepool U.	Tr	10.46	46-51	83	-	28

SLOAN Joseph (Paddy) Walter
Lurgan (NI), 30 April, 1921 Died 1993 IR-2/NI-1 (WH)

League Club	Source	Date Signed	Seasons Played	Apps	Subs	Gls
Manchester U.	Glenavon	09.37				
Tranmere Rov.	Tr	05.39				
Arsenal	Tr	05.46	46-47	33	-	1
Sheffield U.	Tr	02.48	47	12	-	2
Norwich C.	Brescia (It)	12.51	51	6	-	0

SLOAN Mark **Scott**
Wallsend, 14 December, 1967 (F)

League Club	Source	Date Signed	Seasons Played	Apps	Subs	Gls
Newcastle U.	Berwick R.	07.90	90	11	5	1
Cambridge U. (L)	Falkirk	02.94	93	4	0	1
Hartlepool U.	Falkirk	08.94	94-95	27	8	2

SLOAN Thomas
Ballymena (NI), 10 July, 1959 NIu21-1/NI-3 (M)

League Club	Source	Date Signed	Seasons Played	Apps	Subs	Gls
Manchester U.	Ballymena	08.78	78-80	4	7	0
Chester C.	Tr	08.82	82	44	0	3

SLOCOMBE Michael
Bristol, 3 May, 1941 (WH)

League Club	Source	Date Signed	Seasons Played	Apps	Subs	Gls
Bristol Rov.	Jnrs	06.61	61-62	32	-	0

SLOUGH Alan Peter
Luton, 24 September, 1947 (M/D)

League Club	Source	Date Signed	Seasons Played	Apps	Subs	Gls
Luton T.	App	05.65	65-72	265	10	28
Fulham	Tr	08.73	73-76	154	0	13
Peterborough U.	Tr	07.77	77-80	104	1	10
Millwall	Tr	06.81	81	14	0	0

SLYNN Frank
Birmingham, 10 February, 1924 (WH)

League Club	Source	Date Signed	Seasons Played	Apps	Subs	Gls
Sheffield Wed.	Batchelor Sports	09.46	46-50	44	-	5
Bury	Tr	12.50	50-52	41	-	0
Walsall	Tr	09.53	53	10	-	0

SMALE Thomas Henry
Swansea, 16 July, 1928 (FB)

League Club	Source	Date Signed	Seasons Played	Apps	Subs	Gls
Shrewsbury T.	Derby Co. (Am)	07.50	50-51	14	-	1
Aldershot	Tr	08.52	52	1	-	0

SMALES Kenneth
Hull, 3 May, 1932 (FB)

League Club	Source	Date Signed	Seasons Played	Apps	Subs	Gls
Hull C.	Brunswick Inst.	05.53	56	1	-	0

SMALL Bryan
Birmingham, 15 November, 1971 E Yth/Eu21-12 (LB)

League Club	Source	Date Signed	Seasons Played	Apps	Subs	Gls
Aston Villa	YT	07.90	91-94	31	5	0
Birmingham C.	L	09.94	94	3	0	0
Bolton W.	Tr	03.96	95-96	11	1	0
Luton T.	L	09.97	97	15	0	0
Bradford C.	L	12.97	97	5	0	0
Bury	Tr	01.98	97	18	0	1

SMALL Colin
Stockport, 9 November, 1970 (M)

League Club	Source	Date Signed	Seasons Played	Apps	Subs	Gls
Rochdale	Manchester C. (YT)	07.89	89	5	2	1

SMALL David
Dundee, 17 July, 1930 (W)

League Club	Source	Date Signed	Seasons Played	Apps	Subs	Gls
Watford	Dundee N.E.	06.50	50-51	5	-	0

SMALL John Hedley
Billingham, 14 January, 1945 (G)

League Club	Source	Date Signed	Seasons Played	Apps	Subs	Gls
Hartlepool U. (Am)	Head Wrightson	06.65	65	2	0	0

SMALL Martin Leonard
Gateshead, 2 February, 1920 (IF)

League Club	Source	Date Signed	Seasons Played	Apps	Subs	Gls
Gateshead		08.46	46-51	96	-	29

SMALL Michael Anthony
Birmingham, 2 March, 1962 E Yth (F)

League Club	Source	Date Signed	Seasons Played	Apps	Subs	Gls
Luton T.	Bromsgrove Rov.	10.79	81-82	0	4	0
Peterborough U.	L	10.82	82	2	2	1
Brighton & H. A.	P.A.O.K. Salonika (Gre)	08.90	90	39	0	16
West Ham U.	Tr	08.91	91-92	42	7	13
Wolverhampton W.	L	09.93	93	2	1	1
Charlton Ath.	L	02.94	93	1	1	0

SMALL Peter Victor
Horsham, 23 October, 1924 (W)

League Club	Source	Date Signed	Seasons Played	Apps	Subs	Gls
Luton T.	Horsham	08.47	47-49	28	-	5
Leicester C.	Tr	02.50	49-54	65	-	16
Nottingham F.	Tr	09.54	54-56	87	-	20
Brighton & H. A.	Tr	07.57	57	8	-	3

SMALL Samuel John
Birmingham, 15 May, 1912 Died 1993 (IF/WH)

League Club	Source	Date Signed	Seasons Played	Apps	Subs	Gls
Birmingham C.	Bromsgrove Rov.	05.34	34-36	6	-	0

League Club	Source	Date Signed	Seasons Played	Apps	Subs	Gls
West Ham U.	Tr	01.37	36-47	108	-	39
Brighton & H. A.	Tr	03.48	47-49	38	-	0

SMALLER Paul Andrew
Scunthorpe, 18 September, 1970 (M)

League Club	Source	Date Signed	Seasons Played	Apps	Subs	Gls
Grimsby T.	YT	07.89	88-89	1	1	0

SMALLEY Mark Anthony
Newark, 2 January, 1965 E Yth (CD)

League Club	Source	Date Signed	Seasons Played	Apps	Subs	Gls
Nottingham F.	App	01.83	82-84	1	2	0
Birmingham C.	L	03.86	85	7	0	0
Bristol Rov.	L	08.86	86	10	0	0
Leyton Orient	Tr	02.87	86-89	59	5	4
Mansfield T.	Tr	11.89	89-90	49	0	2
Maidstone U.	Tr	05.91	91	33	1	2

SMALLEY Paul Thomas
Nottingham, 17 November, 1966 E Yth (RB)

League Club	Source	Date Signed	Seasons Played	Apps	Subs	Gls
Notts Co.	App	11.84	85-87	112	6	0
Scunthorpe U.	Tr	09.88	88-90	84	2	1
Blackpool	L	10.90	90	6	0	0
Leeds U. (N/C)	Tr	12.90				
Doncaster R. (N/C)	Tr	03.91	90	14	0	0

SMALLEY Thomas
Kinsley (Yks), 13 January, 1912 Died 1984 E-1 (FB)

League Club	Source	Date Signed	Seasons Played	Apps	Subs	Gls
Wolverhampton W.	South Kirkby Colly	05.31	31-37	179	-	11
Norwich C.	Tr	08.38	38	42	-	1
Northampton T.	Tr	10.45	46-50	200	-	2

SMALLMAN David Paul
Connahs Quay, 22 March, 1953 Wu23-5/W-7 (F)

League Club	Source	Date Signed	Seasons Played	Apps	Subs	Gls
Wrexham	Jnrs	11.71	72-74	100	1	38
Everton	Tr	03.75	74-76	19	2	6

SMALLWOOD James Wilson
Bearpark (Dm), 1 September, 1925 (WH)

League Club	Source	Date Signed	Seasons Played	Apps	Subs	Gls
Chesterfield	Spennymoor U.	12.49	49-60	345	-	14

SMALLWOOD Neil
York, 3 December, 1966 (G)

League Club	Source	Date Signed	Seasons Played	Apps	Subs	Gls
York C.	Jnrs	06.85	86-87	13	0	0
Darlington	Tr	08.88	88	4	0	0

SMART Allan Andrew Colin
Perth, 8 July, 1974 (F)

League Club	Source	Date Signed	Seasons Played	Apps	Subs	Gls
Preston N.E.	Caledonian Thistle	11.94	94-95	17	4	6
Carlisle U.	L	11.95	95	3	1	0
Northampton T.	L	09.96	96	1	0	0
Carlisle U.	Tr	10.96	96-97	41	3	17

SMART Gary James
Totnes, 29 April, 1964 (FB)

League Club	Source	Date Signed	Seasons Played	Apps	Subs	Gls
Oxford U.	Wokingham T.	07.88	88-93	170	5	0

SMART Gary Michael
Bristol, 8 December, 1963 (M)

League Club	Source	Date Signed	Seasons Played	Apps	Subs	Gls
Bristol Rov.	Mangotsfield U.	09.85	85-86	11	8	4

SMART James
Dundee, 9 January, 1947 (W)

League Club	Source	Date Signed	Seasons Played	Apps	Subs	Gls
Chelsea	Morton	02.65	64	1	-	0

SMART Jason
Rochdale, 15 February, 1969 (CD)

League Club	Source	Date Signed	Seasons Played	Apps	Subs	Gls
Rochdale	YT	08.86	85-88	116	1	4
Crewe Alex.	Tr	07.89	89-91	87	2	2

SMART Kevin Graham
Newcastle, 17 October, 1958 (RB)

League Club	Source	Date Signed	Seasons Played	Apps	Subs	Gls
Plymouth Arg.	App	10.76	76-77	32	0	0
Wigan Ath.	Tr	07.78	78-79	48	1	1

SMART Richard
Bishop Auckland, 19 June, 1921 (IF)

League Club	Source	Date Signed	Seasons Played	Apps	Subs	Gls
Exeter C.	Stanley U.	08.46	46-51	103	-	33

SMART Roger William
Swindon, 25 March, 1943 (M)

League Club	Source	Date Signed	Seasons Played	Apps	Subs	Gls
Swindon T.	Jnrs	05.60	61-72	341	6	43
Charlton Ath.	Tr	05.73	73	30	1	1

SMEDLEY Lawrence
Sheffield, 7 May, 1922 (IF)

League Club	Source	Date Signed	Seasons Played	Apps	Subs	Gls
Lincoln C.		05.45	46-48	11	-	7

SMEE Roger Guy
Reading, 14 August, 1948 (CF)

League Club	Source	Date Signed	Seasons Played	Apps	Subs	Gls
Chelsea	Jnrs	03.66				
Reading	Tr	01.67	66-69	49	1	16
Reading	(Retired)	07.73	73	6	3	1

SMEETS Jorg
Amsterdam, Holland, 5 November, 1970 (M)

League Club	Source	Date Signed	Seasons Played	Apps	Subs	Gls
Wigan Ath.	Heracles (Neth)	10.97	97	10	13	3

SMELT Lee Adrian
Edmonton, 13 March, 1958 (G)

League Club	Source	Date Signed	Seasons Played	Apps	Subs	Gls
Colchester U.	Jnrs	07.75				
Nottingham F.	Gravesend & Nft.	06.80	80	1	0	0
Peterborough U.	L	08.81	81	5	0	0
Halifax T.	Tr	10.81	81-83	119	0	0
Cardiff C.	Tr	08.84	84-85	37	0	0
Exeter C.	L	03.85	84	13	0	0

SMETHURST Derek
South Africa, 24 October, 1947 (F)

League Club	Source	Date Signed	Seasons Played	Apps	Subs	Gls
Chelsea	Durban U. (SA)	12.68	70-71	14	0	4
Millwall	Tr	09.71	71-74	66	5	9

SMETHURST Edward (Ted)
Doncaster, 5 March, 1938 (G)

League Club	Source	Date Signed	Seasons Played	Apps	Subs	Gls
Chesterfield	Denaby U.	08.59	59	19	-	0

SMETHURST Peter Joseph
South Africa, 8 August, 1940 (F)

League Club	Source	Date Signed	Seasons Played	Apps	Subs	Gls
Blackpool	Durban U. (SA)	02.60	59	1	-	0

SMEULDERS John
Hackney, 28 March, 1957 E Yth (G)

League Club	Source	Date Signed	Seasons Played	Apps	Subs	Gls
Leyton Orient	App	07.74				
Bournemouth	Tr	07.79	79-80	14	0	0
Bournemouth	Weymouth	01.84	83-85	75	0	0
Torquay U.	Tr	07.86	86	18	0	0
Peterborough U.	L	12.86	86	1	0	0
Bournemouth (N/C)	Poole T.	08.87	87-88	9	0	0
Brentford (N/C)	L	10.88	88	8	0	0

SMILLIE Andrew Thomas
Sheppey, 15 March, 1941 E Yth (IF)

League Club	Source	Date Signed	Seasons Played	Apps	Subs	Gls
West Ham U.	Jnrs	06.58	58-60	20	-	3
Crystal Palace	Tr	06.61	61-62	53	-	23
Scunthorpe U.	Tr	07.63	63-64	13	-	2
Southend U.	Tr	09.64	64-68	164	0	29
Gillingham	Tr	10.68	68-70	88	6	7

SMILLIE Neil
Barnsley, 19 July, 1958 (LW)

League Club	Source	Date Signed	Seasons Played	Apps	Subs	Gls
Crystal Palace	App	10.75	76-81	71	12	7
Brentford	L	01.77	76	3	0	0
Brighton & H. A.	Tr	08.82	82-84	62	13	2
Watford	Tr	06.85	85	10	6	3
Reading	L	12.86	86	6	0	0
Reading	Tr	03.87	86-87	32	1	0
Brentford	Tr	08.88	88-92	163	9	18
Gillingham	Tr	07.93	93-94	53	0	3

SMILLIE Ronald Drummond
Grimethorpe, 27 September, 1933 (OR)

League Club	Source	Date Signed	Seasons Played	Apps	Subs	Gls
Barnsley	Jnrs	12.50	51-55	29	-	1
Lincoln C.	Tr	06.56	56-59	91	-	15
Barnsley	Tr	07.60	60-61	85	-	16

SMIRKE Alfred Henry
Pershore, 14 March, 1917 Died 1996 E Sch (F)

League Club	Source	Date Signed	Seasons Played	Apps	Subs	Gls
Southend U.	Sunderland Bus Co.	05.38	38-47	100	-	26
Gateshead	Tr	03.48	47	11	-	4

SMITH Alan
Newcastle, 15 October, 1921 (OL)

League Club	Source	Date Signed	Seasons Played	Apps	Subs	Gls
Arsenal		05.46	46	3	-	0
Brentford	Tr	12.46	46-48	13	-	4
Leyton Orient	Tr	07.49	49	6	-	1

SMITH Alan David
Sheffield, 7 December, 1966 (D)

League Club	Source	Date Signed	Seasons Played	Apps	Subs	Gls
Sheffield Wed.	App	12.84				
Darlington	Tr	09.86	86-88	26	5	1

SMITH Alan Frederick
Newport, 3 September, 1949 W Yth (M)

League Club	Source	Date Signed	Seasons Played	Apps	Subs	Gls
Newport Co.	Jnrs	09.66	66-71	87	13	6

SMITH Alan George
Bromsgrove, 7 April, 1936 (HB)

League Club	Source	Date Signed	Seasons Played	Apps	Subs	Gls
Aston Villa	Bromsgrove Rov.	06.54	55	1	-	0

SMITH Alan Martin
Bromsgrove, 21 November, 1962 E Semi Pro/EF Lge/E 'B'/E-13 (F)

League Club	Source	Date Signed	Seasons Played	Apps	Subs	Gls
Leicester C.	Alvechurch	06.82	82-86	190	10	76
Arsenal	Tr	03.87	87-94	242	22	86

SMITH Alan Michael
Harrogate, 1 September, 1950 (OL)

League Club	Source	Date Signed	Seasons Played	Apps	Subs	Gls
York C. (Am)	Harrogate R.I.	12.70	70	1	1	0

SMITH Charles Alan
Salford, 7 June, 1940 (G)

League Club	Source	Date Signed	Seasons Played	Apps	Subs	Gls
Stockport Co. (Am)	Manchester C. (Am)	06.60	60	6	-	0

SMITH James Alan
Birkenhead, 8 June, 1939 (D)

League Club	Source	Date Signed	Seasons Played	Apps	Subs	Gls
Torquay U.	Port Sunlight	08.56	57-68	277	1	2

SMITH Albert Owen Stephen
Bargoed, 18 October, 1923 (G)

League Club	Source	Date Signed	Seasons Played	Apps	Subs	Gls
Cardiff C.	Oakdale	04.44				
Newport Co.	Tr	05.47	46-47	27	-	0

SMITH Albert William
Stoke, 27 August, 1918 Died 1992 (WH)

League Club	Source	Date Signed	Seasons Played	Apps	Subs	Gls
Queens Park R.	Shirley Jnrs	05.39	46-48	62	-	2

SMITH Alexander
Dundee, 4 September, 1927 Died 1991 (FB)

League Club	Source	Date Signed	Seasons Played	Apps	Subs	Gls
Blackpool		08.46				
Bradford P. A.	Tr	06.49	49-50	5	-	0

SMITH Alexander
Dewsbury, 11 May, 1947 (FB)

League Club	Source	Date Signed	Seasons Played	Apps	Subs	Gls
Bradford C.	Ossett T.	12.64	65-67	91	2	2
Huddersfield T.	Tr	03.68	67-68	29	0	0
Southend U.	Tr	04.70	70-73	129	1	1
Colchester U.	Tr	01.73	73-74	51	0	1
Halifax T.	Tr	02.75	74-75	46	1	1

SMITH Alexander
Lancaster, 29 October, 1938 (G)

League Club	Source	Date Signed	Seasons Played	Apps	Subs	Gls
Accrington St.	Weymouth	08.61				
Bolton W.	Tr	03.62	62-67	19	0	0
Halifax T.	Tr	01.68	67-75	341	0	0
Preston N. E.	Tr	05.76	76	8	0	0

SMITH Alexander Philip
Liverpool, 15 February, 1976 (LB/M)

League Club	Source	Date Signed	Seasons Played	Apps	Subs	Gls
Everton	YT	07.94				
Swindon T.	Tr	01.96	95-97	17	14	1
Huddersfield T.	Tr	02.98	97	4	2	0

SMITH Robert Alexander
Billingham, 6 February, 1944 (D)

League Club	Source	Date Signed	Seasons Played	Apps	Subs	Gls
Middlesbrough	Jnrs	12.61	65-71	119	2	1
Darlington	Bangor C.	07.74	74-75	43	0	0

SMITH Alfred
Wolverhampton (OL)

League Club	Source	Date Signed	Seasons Played	Apps	Subs	Gls
Walsall	Bilston	10.53	53	1	-	0

SMITH Allan
(OL)

League Club	Source	Date Signed	Seasons Played	Apps	Subs	Gls
Hull C. (Am)		09.46	46	1	-	0

SMITH Anthony
Sunderland, 31 December, 1943 (CF)

League Club	Source	Date Signed	Seasons Played	Apps	Subs	Gls
West Ham U.	Consett	11.63				
Watford	Tr	06.66	66	3	0	0
Hartlepool U.		10.67	67	2	0	1

SMITH Anthony
Sunderland, 20 February, 1957 (CD)

League Club	Source	Date Signed	Seasons Played	Apps	Subs	Gls
Newcastle U.	Jnrs	07.75	77	1	1	0
Peterborough U.	Tr	03.79	78-81	68	0	5
Halifax T.	Tr	08.82	82-83	81	2	3
Hartlepool U.	Tr	08.84	84-88	200	0	8

SMITH Anthony
Sunderland, 21 September, 1971 E Yth (LB)

League Club	Source	Date Signed	Seasons Played	Apps	Subs	Gls
Sunderland	YT	07.90	90-94	19	1	0
Hartlepool U.	L	01.92	91	4	1	0
Northampton T. (N/C)	Tr	08.95	95	2	0	0

SMITH Archibald
Larkhall, 23 October, 1924 Died 1995 (CF)

League Club	Source	Date Signed	Seasons Played	Apps	Subs	Gls
Exeter C.	Hamilton Academical	05.48	48-51	115	-	43
Carlisle U.	Tr	08.52	52-53	31	-	8

SMITH Arthur Edward
Bourne, 13 February, 1922 Died 1982 (FB)

League Club	Source	Date Signed	Seasons Played	Apps	Subs	Gls
Luton T.		05.45				
Aldershot	Tr	08.47	47-48	2	-	0

SMITH Arthur Eric
Enderby, 5 September, 1921 (IF)

League Club	Source	Date Signed	Seasons Played	Apps	Subs	Gls
Leicester C.	Jnrs	02.41	46-47	17	-	3
West Bromwich A.	Tr	06.48	48-51	49	-	12
Plymouth Arg.	Tr	08.52	52-53	28	-	9
Crewe Alex.	Tr	06.54	54	4	-	0

SMITH Barry Anthony
Colchester, 3 March, 1953 (G)

League Club	Source	Date Signed	Seasons Played	Apps	Subs	Gls
Colchester U.	Jnrs	07.71	71-72	49	0	0

SMITH Barry Joseph
Wigan, 21 September, 1969 (M)

League Club	Source	Date Signed	Seasons Played	Apps	Subs	Gls
Wigan Ath.	YT	●	87	0	1	0

SMITH Joseph Barry
South Kirkby, 15 March, 1934 (F)

League Club	Source	Date Signed	Seasons Played	Apps	Subs	Gls
Leeds U.	Farsley Celtic	10.51	52	2	-	1
Bradford P. A.	Tr	05.55	55-56	64	-	38
Wrexham	Tr	06.57	57	18	-	10
Stockport Co.	Tr	07.58	58	17	-	4
Oldham Ath.	Headington U.	08.60	60	1	-	0

SMITH Benjamin Peter
Chelmsford, 23 November, 1978 (M)

League Club	Source	Date Signed	Seasons Played	Apps	Subs	Gls
Reading	Arsenal (YT)	04.97	96	0	1	0

SMITH Brian
Bolton, 12 September, 1955 E Yth (M)

League Club	Source	Date Signed	Seasons Played	Apps	Subs	Gls
Bolton W.	App	09.73	74-78	43	6	3
Bradford C.	L	10.77	77	8	0	0
Blackpool	Tr	08.79	79	18	1	1
Bournemouth	Tr	12.80	80-81	40	0	2
Bury	Tr	03.82	81	6	0	0

SMITH Brian
Sheffield, 27 October, 1966 (D)

League Club	Source	Date Signed	Seasons Played	Apps	Subs	Gls
Sheffield U.	App	10.84	84-88	81	3	0
Scunthorpe U.	L	03.87	86	6	0	1

SMITH Carl Paul
Sheffield, 15 January, 1979 (M)

League Club	Source	Date Signed	Seasons Played	Apps	Subs	Gls
Burnley	YT	09.97	97	0	1	0

SMITH Charles
Oswaldwistle, 27 June, 1930 (CF)

League Club	Source	Date Signed	Seasons Played	Apps	Subs	Gls
Accrington St. (Am)	Oswaldwistle Imms	06.50	50	1	-	0

SMITH Charles James
Cardiff, 26 August, 1915 Died 1984 (OR)

League Club	Source	Date Signed	Seasons Played	Apps	Subs	Gls
Torquay U.	Aberdeen	04.46	46	23	-	0

SMITH Christopher Gerald
Birmingham, 3 January, 1977 (M)

League Club	Source	Date Signed	Seasons Played	Apps	Subs	Gls
Walsall	YT	05.95	95	0	1	0

SMITH Christopher James
Christchurch, 28 March, 1966 (RB)

League Club	Source	Date Signed	Seasons Played	Apps	Subs	Gls
Bristol Rov. (N/C)	Cheltenham T.	05.85	84	1	0	0

SMITH Colin
Bishop Auckland, 30 November, 1951 (D)

League Club	Source	Date Signed	Seasons Played	Apps	Subs	Gls
Leeds U.	App	11.69				
Darlington (N/C)		09.84	84	2	0	0

SMITH Colin Richard
Ruddington, 3 November, 1958 (CD)

League Club	Source	Date Signed	Seasons Played	Apps	Subs	Gls
Nottingham F.	Jnrs	06.77				
Norwich C.	Tr	08.82	82	2	2	0
Cardiff C.	Caroline Hill (HK)	10.83	83-84	50	0	3
Aldershot	Tr	12.84	84-89	185	5	4

SMITH Edwin Colin
Doncaster, 3 March, 1936 (CF)

League Club	Source	Date Signed	Seasons Played	Apps	Subs	Gls
Hull C.		01.57	56-59	65	-	39
Rotherham U.	Tr	06.60	60	9	-	3

SMITH William Conway
Huddersfield, 13 July, 1926 Died 1989 (IF)

League Club	Source	Date Signed	Seasons Played	Apps	Subs	Gls
Huddersfield T.	Jnrs	05.45	47-50	37	-	5
Queens Park R.	Tr	03.51	50-55	174	-	81
Halifax T.	Tr	06.56	56-61	183	-	73

SMITH Craig
Mansfield, 2 August, 1976 (F)

League Club	Source	Date Signed	Seasons Played	Apps	Subs	Gls
Derby Co.	YT	08.95				
Rochdale	L	08.97	97	1	2	0

SMITH Daniel
Armadale, 7 September, 1921 (W)

League Club	Source	Date Signed	Seasons Played	Apps	Subs	Gls
West Bromwich A.	Coltness U.	05.45	47	7	-	1
Chesterfield	Tr	06.48	48	15	-	4
Crewe Alex.	Tr	08.49	49-51	110	-	15

SMITH David
South Shields, 12 October, 1915 Died 1998 (OR)

League Club	Source	Date Signed	Seasons Played	Apps	Subs	Gls
Newcastle U.	Reyrolles	10.35	35	1	-	0
Northampton T.	South Shields	09.43	46-50	128	-	31

SMITH David
Thornaby, 8 December, 1947 E Sch (W)

League Club	Source	Date Signed	Seasons Played	Apps	Subs	Gls
Middlesbrough	App	12.64	67	1	1	0
Lincoln C.	Tr	07.68	68-77	358	13	52
Rotherham U.	Tr	07.78	78-79	32	1	3

SMITH David
Stonehouse (Glos), 29 March, 1968 Eu21-10 (LW)

League Club	Source	Date Signed	Seasons Played	Apps	Subs	Gls
Coventry C.	YT	07.86	87-92	144	10	19
Bournemouth	L	01.93	92	1	0	0
Birmingham C.	Tr	03.93	92-93	35	3	3
West Bromwich A.	Tr	01.94	93-97	82	20	2
Grimsby T.	Tr	01.98	97	17	0	1

SMITH David
Frome, 13 October, 1964 (D)

League Club	Source	Date Signed	Seasons Played	Apps	Subs	Gls
Bristol Rov.	App	●	81	0	1	0

SMITH David Alan
Sidcup, 25 June, 1961 (LW)

League Club	Source	Date Signed	Seasons Played	Apps	Subs	Gls
Gillingham	Welling U.	08.86	86-88	90	14	10
Bristol C.	Tr	08.89	89-91	94	3	10
Plymouth Arg.	Tr	12.91	91	14	4	2
Notts Co.	Tr	07.92	92	37	0	8

SMITH David Alan
Stockport, 2 May, 1973 (G)

League Club	Source	Date Signed	Seasons Played	Apps	Subs	Gls
Doncaster Rov. (N/C)	Bramhall	10.97	97	1	0	0

SMITH David Bowman
Dundee, 22 September, 1933 (FB)

League Club	Source	Date Signed	Seasons Played	Apps	Subs	Gls
Burnley	Jnrs	09.50	54-60	99	-	1
Brighton & H. A.	Tr	07.61	61	15	-	0
Bristol C.	Tr	07.62	62	3	-	0

SMITH David Bryan
Sheffield, 11 December, 1950 (F)

League Club	Source	Date Signed	Seasons Played	Apps	Subs	Gls
Huddersfield T.	Jnrs	04.69	71-73	27	7	7
Stockport Co.	L	12.73	73	7	1	0
Halifax T.	L	03.74	73	12	1	4
Cambridge U.	Tr	07.74	74	15	2	3
Hartlepool U.	Tr	02.75	74-75	42	0	13

SMITH David Christopher
Liverpool, 26 December, 1970 (M)

League Club	Source	Date Signed	Seasons Played	Apps	Subs	Gls
Norwich C.	YT	07.89	89-93	13	5	0
Oxford U.	Tr	07.94	94-97	174	2	2

SMITH David Frederick
Nottingham, 11 March, 1956 (M)

League Club	Source	Date Signed	Seasons Played	Apps	Subs	Gls
Notts Co.	App	03.74	75-77	45	5	0
Torquay U.	Tr	06.79	79	20	3	1

SMITH David Robert
Bristol, 5 October, 1934 E Yth (OL)

League Club	Source	Date Signed	Seasons Played	Apps	Subs	Gls
Bristol C.	Jnrs	04.53	55-58	21	-	1
Millwall	Tr	09.59	59	13	-	1

SMITH Frank David
Chesterfield, 27 July, 1936 (W)

League Club	Source	Date Signed	Seasons Played	Apps	Subs	Gls
Chesterfield	Jnrs	09.53	53	7	-	0
Mansfield T.	Boston U.	08.55	55-56	31	-	4
Derby Co.	Tr	07.57				
Coventry C.	Tr	11.57	57-58	28	-	2

SMITH Dean
Leicester, 28 November, 1958 (F)

League Club	Source	Date Signed	Seasons Played	Apps	Subs	Gls
Leicester C.	App	12.76	77	8	2	1
Brentford	Tr	10.78	78-80	48	6	16

SMITH Dean
West Bromwich, 19 March, 1971 (CD)

League Club	Source	Date Signed	Seasons Played	Apps	Subs	Gls
Walsall	YT	07.89	88-93	137	5	2
Hereford U.	Tr	06.94	94-96	116	1	19
Leyton Orient	Tr	06.97	97	43	0	9

SMITH Denis Noel
Grimsby, 23 December, 1932 (FB)

League Club	Source	Date Signed	Seasons Played	Apps	Subs	Gls
Grimsby T.	Jnrs	07.50	52-53	4	-	0

SMITH Dennis
Stoke, 19 November, 1947 (CD)

League Club	Source	Date Signed	Seasons Played	Apps	Subs	Gls
Stoke C.	Jnrs	09.66	68-81	406	1	29
York C.	L	03.82	81	7	0	1
York C. (N/C)	Tr	08.82	82	30	0	4

SMITH Dennis
Nelson, 22 August, 1925 (WH)

League Club	Source	Date Signed	Seasons Played	Apps	Subs	Gls
Hull C.	Frickley Colly	07.46	46	15	-	0
Accrington St.	Tr	10.47	47-53	155	-	15

SMITH Derek Leonard
Liverpool, 5 July, 1946 (CH/CF)

League Club	Source	Date Signed	Seasons Played	Apps	Subs	Gls
Everton	App	11.63	65-66	3	1	0
Tranmere Rov.	Tr	03.68	67-69	77	5	21

SMITH Edmund (Eddie) William Alfred
Marylebone, 23 March, 1929 Died 1993 (IF)

League Club	Source	Date Signed	Seasons Played	Apps	Subs	Gls
Chelsea	Wealdstone	05.50				
Bournemouth	Tr	08.52				
Watford	Tr	07.53	53-54	38	-	12
Northampton T.	Tr	01.55	54-55	53	-	12
Colchester U.	Tr	06.56	56	35	-	13
Queens Park R.	Tr	07.57	57	17	-	1

SMITH Edward Ferriday
Stoke, 19 October, 1920 Died 1982 (CF)

League Club	Source	Date Signed	Seasons Played	Apps	Subs	Gls
Arsenal	Margate	05.38				
Aldershot	Tr	06.47	47	7	-	2

SMITH Edward William John
Grays, 3 September, 1914 Died 1989 (FB)

League Club	Source	Date Signed	Seasons Played	Apps	Subs	Gls
Millwall	Barking	05.35	35-47	143	-	1

SMITH Eric Victor
Reading, 20 March, 1928 Died 1992 (HB)

League Club	Source	Date Signed	Seasons Played	Apps	Subs	Gls
Reading		04.49	52-55	61	-	1

SMITH John Eric
Glasgow, 29 July, 1934 Died 1991 S-2 (WH)

League Club	Source	Date Signed	Seasons Played	Apps	Subs	Gls
Leeds U.	Glasgow Celtic	06.60	60-62	65	-	3

SMITH Thomas Henry Eric
Tamworth, 3 November, 1921 (CH)

League Club	Source	Date Signed	Seasons Played	Apps	Subs	Gls
Leicester C.	Castle Bromwich	04.43	46	5	-	0

SMITH Frank Anthony
Colchester, 30 April, 1936 (G)

League Club	Source	Date Signed	Seasons Played	Apps	Subs	Gls
Tottenham H.	Colchester Casuals	02.54				
Queens Park R.	Tr	05.62	62-65	66	0	0

SMITH Frederick Adamson
Aberdeen, 14 February, 1926 (IF)

League Club	Source	Date Signed	Seasons Played	Apps	Subs	Gls
Hull C.	Aberdeen	10.49	49-50	17	-	1
Sheffield U.	Tr	04.51	50-52	40	-	12
Millwall	Tr	01.53	52-55	92	-	20
Chesterfield	Tr	07.56	56	7	-	1

SMITH Frederick Edward
Spondon, 7 May, 1926 (CF)

League Club	Source	Date Signed	Seasons Played	Apps	Subs	Gls
Derby Co.	Draycott	06.47	47	1	-	0
Sheffield U.	Tr	03.48	47-51	53	-	17
Manchester C.	Tr	05.52	52	2	-	1
Grimsby T.	Tr	09.52	52-53	50	-	24
Bradford C.	Tr	07.54	54	9	-	3

SMITH Frederick Gregg
Bedlington, 25 December, 1942 (FB)

League Club	Source	Date Signed	Seasons Played	Apps	Subs	Gls
Burnley	Jnrs	12.59	63-69	84	0	1
Portsmouth	Tr	07.70	70-72	83	0	1
Halifax T.	Tr	09.74	74	3	0	0

SMITH Gary
Lichfield, 30 December, 1968 (M)

League Club	Source	Date Signed	Seasons Played	Apps	Subs	Gls
Walsall	App	01.87				
Gillingham (N/C)	Chasetown	07.89	89	0	1	0

SMITH Gary Anthony
Trowbridge, 12 November, 1962 (W)

League Club	Source	Date Signed	Seasons Played	Apps	Subs	Gls
Bristol C.	App	11.79	80	7	7	0

SMITH Gary Michael
Greenford, 4 November, 1955 (CD)

League Club	Source	Date Signed	Seasons Played	Apps	Subs	Gls
Brentford		01.74	74	3	0	0

SMITH Gary Neil
Harlow, 3 December, 1968 (M)

League Club	Source	Date Signed	Seasons Played	Apps	Subs	Gls
Fulham	App	08.86	85	0	1	0
Colchester U. (N/C)	Tr	09.87	87	11	0	0
Barnet	Welling U.	08.93	93-94	11	2	0

SMITH Gavin
Cambuslang, 25 September, 1917 Died 1992 (OR)

League Club	Source	Date Signed	Seasons Played	Apps	Subs	Gls
Barnsley	Dumbarton	02.39	46-53	257	-	35

SMITH Geoffrey
Bingley, 14 March, 1928 (G)

League Club	Source	Date Signed	Seasons Played	Apps	Subs	Gls
Bradford C.	Rossendale U.	12.52	52-58	253	-	0

SMITH George
Newcastle, 7 October, 1945 (M)

League Club	Source	Date Signed	Seasons Played	Apps	Subs	Gls
Newcastle U.	App	09.63				
Barrow	Tr	03.65	64-66	91	1	11
Portsmouth	Tr	05.67	67-68	64	0	3
Middlesbrough	Tr	01.69	68-70	74	0	0
Birmingham C.	Tr	03.71	70-72	36	3	0
Cardiff C.	Tr	06.73	73-74	43	2	1
Swansea C.	Tr	05.75	75-77	86	2	8
Hartlepool U.	Tr	10.77	77-79	81	4	2

SMITH George
(CF)

League Club	Source	Date Signed	Seasons Played	Apps	Subs	Gls
Walsall (Am)		09.53	53	1	-	0

SMITH George Beacher
Fleetwood, 7 February, 1921 (IF)

League Club	Source	Date Signed	Seasons Played	Apps	Subs	Gls
Manchester C.	Adelphi B.C.	05.38	46-51	166	-	75
Chesterfield	Tr	10.51	51-57	250	-	98

SMITH George Casper
Bromley, 23 April, 1915 Died 1983 (CH)

League Club	Source	Date Signed	Seasons Played	Apps	Subs	Gls
Charlton Ath.	Bexleyheath	08.38	38	1	-	0
Brentford	Tr	11.45	46	41	-	1
Queens Park R.	Tr	06.47	47-48	75	-	1
Ipswich T.	Tr	09.49	49	8	-	0

SMITH George Clarence Bassett
Portsmouth, 24 March, 1919 (WH)

League Club	Source	Date Signed	Seasons Played	Apps	Subs	Gls
Southampton	Guernsey R.	07.38	38-48	95	-	1
Crystal Palace	Tr	05.50	50	7	-	0

SMITH George Henry
Nottingham, 13 April, 1936 (G)

League Club	Source	Date Signed	Seasons Played	Apps	Subs	Gls
Notts Co.	Dale R.	07.53	55-66	323	0	0
Hartlepool U.	Tr	07.67	67-69	112	0	0

SMITH Gerald
Huddersfield, 18 November, 1939 (OL)

League Club	Source	Date Signed	Seasons Played	Apps	Subs	Gls
Huddersfield T.	Jnrs	05.58				
Bradford C.	Tr	07.60	60	7	-	0

SMITH Gordon Duffield
Kilwinning, 29 December, 1954 Su21-1 (W)

League Club	Source	Date Signed	Seasons Played	Apps	Subs	Gls
Brighton & H. A.	Glasgow Rangers	06.80	80-83	97	12	22
Manchester C.	Tr	03.84	83-85	40	2	13
Oldham Ath.	Tr	01.86	85	14	1	0

SMITH Gordon Melville
Glasgow, 3 July, 1954 (FB)

League Club	Source	Date Signed	Seasons Played	Apps	Subs	Gls
Aston Villa	St Johnstone	08.76	76-78	76	3	0
Tottenham H.	Tr	02.79	78-81	34	4	1
Wolverhampton W.	Tr	08.82	82-83	35	3	3

SMITH Graham
Wimbledon, 7 August, 1951 (CD)

League Club	Source	Date Signed	Seasons Played	Apps	Subs	Gls
Brentford	Wimbledon	08.74	74	7	0	0

SMITH Graham Leslie
Pudsey, 20 June, 1946 (D)

League Club	Source	Date Signed	Seasons Played	Apps	Subs	Gls
Leeds U.	Jnrs	02.64				
Rochdale	Tr	06.66	66-73	316	1	3
Stockport Co.	Tr	07.74	74-78	147	4	2

SMITH Graham William Charles
Liverpool, 2 November, 1947 (G)

League Club	Source	Date Signed	Seasons Played	Apps	Subs	Gls
Notts Co.	Loughborough College	08.68	68	10	0	0
Colchester U.	Tr	06.69	69-71	95	0	0
West Bromwich A.	Tr	12.71	71-72	10	0	0
Cambridge U.	Tr	01.73	72-75	85	0	0

SMITH Granville
Mountain Ash, 4 February, 1937 (W)

League Club	Source	Date Signed	Seasons Played	Apps	Subs	Gls
Bristol Rov.	Jnrs	05.57	58-59	21	-	2
Newport Co.	Tr	06.60	60-67	241	0	38

SMITH Harry Arthur
Wolverhampton, 10 October, 1932 (FB)

League Club	Source	Date Signed	Seasons Played	Apps	Subs	Gls
Torquay U.	West Bromwich A. (Am)	01.54	53-60	188	-	1
Bristol C.	Tr	07.61	61	1	-	0

SMITH Henry Stanley
Newburn (Nd), 11 October, 1908 Died 1993 (FB)

League Club	Source	Date Signed	Seasons Played	Apps	Subs	Gls
Nottingham F.	Throckley C.W.	01.29	29-36	156	-	1
Darlington	Tr	08.37	37-38	65	-	1
Bristol Rov.	Tr	08.39	46	3	-	0

SMITH Henry (Harry) Stuart
Chester, 27 August, 1930 (WH/IF)

League Club	Source	Date Signed	Seasons Played	Apps	Subs	Gls
Chester C.	Connah's Quay	01.53	52-57	73	-	7

SMITH Herbert Henry
Birmingham, 17 December, 1922 Died 1996 (OR)

League Club	Source	Date Signed	Seasons Played	Apps	Subs	Gls
Aston Villa	Moor Green	05.47	49-53	51	-	8
Southend U.	Tr	06.54	54	5	-	0

SMITH Ian Lennox Taylor
Edinburgh, 2 April, 1952 (F)

League Club	Source	Date Signed	Seasons Played	Apps	Subs	Gls
Birmingham C.	Queens Park	03.75	74	0	2	0

SMITH Ian Ralph
Rotherham, 15 February, 1957 E Yth (FB)

League Club	Source	Date Signed	Seasons Played	Apps	Subs	Gls
Tottenham H.	App	04.74	75	2	0	0
Rotherham U.	Tr	06.76	77	3	1	0

SMITH James
(OR)

League Club	Source	Date Signed	Seasons Played	Apps	Subs	Gls
Burnley		03.43				
Leyton Orient	Tr	04.46	46-47	22	-	3

SMITH James
Johnstone, 22 November, 1969 (F)

League Club	Source	Date Signed	Seasons Played	Apps	Subs	Gls
Torquay U.	YT	07.88	87-89	28	17	5

SMITH James
Glasgow, 20 January, 1947 Su23-1/SF Lge/S-4 (M)

League Club	Source	Date Signed	Seasons Played	Apps	Subs	Gls
Newcastle U.	Aberdeen	08.69	69-74	124	5	13

SMITH James Alexander Grant
Arbroath, 16 October, 1937 S Sch (D)

League Club	Source	Date Signed	Seasons Played	Apps	Subs	Gls
Preston N. E.	Arbroath Lads	10.55	58-68	314	0	13
Stockport Co.	Tr	10.69	69-70	78	0	2

SMITH James Aloysius
Coatbridge, 9 September, 1925 (OL)

League Club	Source	Date Signed	Seasons Played	Apps	Subs	Gls
Walsall	Coatdyke Jnrs	06.48	48	2	-	0

SMITH James Harold
Sheffield, 6 December, 1930 (W)

League Club	Source	Date Signed	Seasons Played	Apps	Subs	Gls
Chelsea	Shildon	04.51	51-53	19	-	3
Leyton Orient	Tr	07.55	55-57	37	-	3

SMITH James Jade Anthony
Birmingham, 17 September, 1974 (RB)

League Club	Source	Date Signed	Seasons Played	Apps	Subs	Gls
Wolverhampton W.	YT	06.93	94-97	81	6	0
Crystal Palace	Tr	10.97	97	16	2	0

SMITH James Michael
Sheffield, 17 October, 1940 (WH)

League Club	Source	Date Signed	Seasons Played	Apps	Subs	Gls
Sheffield U.	Jnrs	01.59				
Aldershot	Tr	07.61	61-64	74	-	1
Halifax T.	Tr	07.65	65-67	112	1	7
Lincoln C.	Tr	03.68	67-68	54	0	0
Colchester U.	Boston U.	11.72	72	7	1	0

SMITH Jeffrey Edward
Macclesfield, 8 December, 1935 (LB)

League Club	Source	Date Signed	Seasons Played	Apps	Subs	Gls
Sheffield U.	Jnrs	06.53	56	1	-	0
Lincoln C.	Tr	02.58	57-66	315	0	2

SMITH Jeremy
Leeds, 20 July, 1971 (F)

League Club	Source	Date Signed	Seasons Played	Apps	Subs	Gls
Wigan Ath.	Goole T.	08.91	91	0	6	0

SMITH John
Coatbridge, 27 November, 1956 (F)

League Club	Source	Date Signed	Seasons Played	Apps	Subs	Gls
Preston N. E.	App	11.74	73-78	80	11	14
Halifax T. (N/C)	L.A. Skyhawks (USA)	11.79	79	26	2	6

SMITH John
Liverpool, 14 March, 1953 E Sch (M)

League Club	Source	Date Signed	Seasons Played	Apps	Subs	Gls
Everton	App	09.70	73	2	0	0
Carlisle U.	Tr	06.76	76	4	1	0
Southport	L	02.77	76	17	1	2

SMITH John (Jack)
Hartlepool, 24 April, 1936 (CF)

League Club	Source	Date Signed	Seasons Played	Apps	Subs	Gls
Hartlepool U.	Jnrs	05.53	53-59	119	-	49
Watford	Tr	07.60	60	20	-	8
Swindon T.	Tr	06.61	61-63	97	-	37
Brighton & H. A.	Tr	01.64	63-66	88	0	33
Notts Co.	Tr	09.66	66-68	74	4	12

SMITH John
Shoreditch, 4 January, 1939 Died 1988 E Yth/Eu23-1 (IF)

League Club	Source	Date Signed	Seasons Played	Apps	Subs	Gls
West Ham U.	Jnrs	01.56	56-59	127	-	20
Tottenham H.	Tr	03.60	59-63	21	-	1
Coventry C.	Tr	03.64	63-65	34	1	1
Leyton Orient	Tr	10.65	65-66	38	1	3
Torquay U.	Tr	10.66	66-67	67	1	8
Swindon T.	Tr	06.68	68-70	79	5	9
Walsall	Tr	06.71	71	13	0	1

SMITH John
Wrexham, 13 September, 1944 (D)

League Club	Source	Date Signed	Seasons Played	Apps	Subs	Gls
Wrexham	Burnley (Jnrs)	05.63	64-65	23	1	0

SMITH John (Jack)
Batley, 17 February, 1915 Died 1975 (CF)

League Club	Source	Date Signed	Seasons Played	Apps	Subs	Gls
Huddersfield T.	Whitehall Printers	06.32	32-34	45	-	24
Newcastle U.	Tr	09.34	34-37	104	-	69
Manchester U.	Tr	02.38	37-38	36	-	14
Blackburn Rov.	Tr	03.46	46	30	-	12
Port Vale	Tr	05.47	46-47	29	-	10

SMITH John
Liverpool (IF)

League Club	Source	Date Signed	Seasons Played	Apps	Subs	Gls
Ipswich T.		12.45	46	2	-	0

SMITH John
Liverpool, 23 July, 1970 (LB)

League Club	Source	Date Signed	Seasons Played	Apps	Subs	Gls
Tranmere Rov.	Jnrs	11.87	88	1	1	0

SMITH John Clayton
Stocksbridge, 15 September, 1910 Died 1986 (G)

League Club	Source	Date Signed	Seasons Played	Apps	Subs	Gls
Sheffield U.	Worksop T.	10.30	30-49	348	-	0

SMITH John Edward
Canning Town, 9 November, 1930 E Yth (LB)

League Club	Source	Date Signed	Seasons Played	Apps	Subs	Gls
Millwall	Barking	04.56	55-57	64	-	1

SMITH John Owen
Enderby, 4 September, 1928 (WH)

League Club	Source	Date Signed	Seasons Played	Apps	Subs	Gls
Northampton T.		09.49	50-59	186	-	9

SMITH John Thomas
Birkenhead, 21 December, 1927 (F)

League Club	Source	Date Signed	Seasons Played	Apps	Subs	Gls
Liverpool	Bromborough	03.51	51-53	57	-	14
Torquay U.	Tr	05.54	54-57	65	-	16

SMITH John Vivian Thomas
Plymouth, 12 November, 1927 (FB)

League Club	Source	Date Signed	Seasons Played	Apps	Subs	Gls
Plymouth Arg.	Plymouth U.	07.50	50-52	3	-	0
Torquay U.	Tr	07.54	54-59	164	-	0

SMITH John (Jackie) William
Camden, 27 May, 1920 Died 1991 (OR)

League Club	Source	Date Signed	Seasons Played	Apps	Subs	Gls
Bradford P. A.		10.43	46-52	204	-	26

SMITH Keith
Sheffield, 17 October, 1963 (F)

League Club	Source	Date Signed	Seasons Played	Apps	Subs	Gls
Exeter C.	Alfreton T.	01.89	88	2	13	2

SMITH Keith Wilson
Swadlincote, 15 September, 1940 (CF)

League Club	Source	Date Signed	Seasons Played	Apps	Subs	Gls
West Bromwich A.	Jnrs	01.58	59-62	63	-	30
Peterborough U.	Tr	06.63	63-64	55	-	28
Crystal Palace	Tr	11.64	64-65	47	3	14
Darlington	Tr	11.66	66	17	0	2
Leyton Orient	Tr	05.67	66	3	0	0
Notts Co.	Tr	07.67	67-69	85	4	7

SMITH Kenneth
South Shields, 21 May, 1932 (CF)

League Club	Source	Date Signed	Seasons Played	Apps	Subs	Gls
Sunderland	Jnrs	08.49	50-52	5	-	2
Blackpool	Headington U.	12.54	54-57	6	-	4
Shrewsbury T.	Tr	10.57	57-58	44	-	20
Gateshead	Tr	11.58	58-59	41	-	16
Darlington	Tr	12.59	59	24	-	7
Carlisle U.	Tr	07.60	60	13	-	12
Halifax T.	Toronto Italia (Can)	10.61	61	23	-	8

SMITH Kenneth
Consett, 7 December, 1927 (F)

League Club	Source	Date Signed	Seasons Played	Apps	Subs	Gls
Blackpool	Annfield Plain	04.49				
Gateshead	Tr	08.52	52-58	259	-	74

SMITH Kenneth George
Norwich, 22 April, 1936 (FB)

League Club	Source	Date Signed	Seasons Played	Apps	Subs	Gls
Norwich C.	Gothic	09.55	55-56	10	-	0

SMITH Kevan
Eaglescliffe, 13 December, 1959 (CD)

League Club	Source	Date Signed	Seasons Played	Apps	Subs	Gls
Darlington	Stockton	09.79	79-84	242	3	11
Rotherham U.	Tr	07.85	85-86	59	0	4
Coventry C.	Tr	12.86	87	5	1	0
York C.	Tr	05.88	88	30	1	5
Darlington	Tr	06.89	90-92	98	0	5
Hereford U.	L	10.92	92	6	0	0
Hereford U.	Tr	09.93	93	17	1	0

SMITH Kevin John
Wallsend, 20 April, 1965 (M)

League Club	Source	Date Signed	Seasons Played	Apps	Subs	Gls
Cambridge U.	App	11.82	82-84	30	8	4
Exeter C.	Tr	10.84	84	21	4	2
Torquay U.	Tr	07.85	85	20	3	1

SMITH Kevin Paul
Chislehurst, 5 December, 1962 (M)

League Club	Source	Date Signed	Seasons Played	Apps	Subs	Gls
Charlton Ath.	App	08.80	79-83	79	25	14

SMITH Leslie
Manchester, 2 October, 1920 (RH)

League Club	Source	Date Signed	Seasons Played	Apps	Subs	Gls
Huddersfield T.	Stockport Co. (Am)	03.46	46-47	37	-	0
Oldham Ath.	Tr	07.49	49-55	178	-	3

SMITH Leslie (Snowy)
Tamworth, 16 November, 1921 Died 1993 (RH)

League Club	Source	Date Signed	Seasons Played	Apps	Subs	Gls
Mansfield T.	Nottingham F. (Am)	08.45	46-47	38	-	0

SMITH Leslie George Frederick
Ealing, 13 May, 1918 Died 1995 E-1 (OL)

League Club	Source	Date Signed	Seasons Played	Apps	Subs	Gls
Brentford	Hayes	03.36	36-38	62	-	7
Aston Villa	Tr	10.45	46-51	181	-	31
Brentford	Tr	06.52	52	14	-	1

SMITH Joseph **Leslie**
Halesowen, 24 December, 1927 (OR)

League Club	Source	Date Signed	Seasons Played	Apps	Subs	Gls
Wolverhampton W.	Jnrs	04.46	47-55	88	-	22
Aston Villa	Tr	02.56	55-58	115	-	24

SMITH Lindsay James
Enfield, 18 September, 1954 (CD/M)

League Club	Source	Date Signed	Seasons Played	Apps	Subs	Gls
Colchester U.	App	03.72	70-76	184	27	16
Charlton Ath.	L	08.77	77	1	0	0
Millwall	L	09.77	77	4	1	0
Cambridge U.	Tr	10.77	77-82	173	1	7
Lincoln C.	L	09.81	81	5	0	0
Plymouth Arg.	Tr	10.82	82-83	76	0	5
Millwall	Tr	07.84	84-85	54	1	5
Cambridge U.	Tr	07.86	86-88	102	0	16

SMITH Lionel
Doncaster, 23 August, 1920 Died 1980 EF Lge/E-6 (FB)

League Club	Source	Date Signed	Seasons Played	Apps	Subs	Gls
Arsenal	Denaby U.	08.39	47-53	162	-	0
Watford	Tr	06.54	54	7	-	0

SMITH Malcolm
Stockton, 21 September, 1953 (F)

League Club	Source	Date Signed	Seasons Played	Apps	Subs	Gls
Middlesbrough	App	10.70	71-75	32	24	11
Bury	L	10.75	75	5	0	1
Blackpool	L	01.76	75	8	0	5
Burnley	Tr	09.76	76-79	82	3	17
York C.	Tr	08.80	80-81	28	7	6

SMITH Malcolm Alan
Maidstone, 3 August, 1970 (M)

League Club	Source	Date Signed	Seasons Played	Apps	Subs	Gls
Gillingham	YT	06.88	87	1	1	0

SMITH Mark
Redruth, 21 September, 1963 (LB)

League Club	Source	Date Signed	Seasons Played	Apps	Subs	Gls
Bristol C.	App	09.81	81	1	4	0
Plymouth Arg. (N/C)	Exmouth T.	03.84	83	3	0	0

SMITH Mark
Torquay, 9 October, 1961 (FB)

League Club	Source	Date Signed	Seasons Played	Apps	Subs	Gls
Torquay U. (N/C)		09.81	81-83	28	2	0

League Club	Source	Date Signed	Seasons Played	Career Record Apps	Subs	Gls
SMITH Mark Alexander						
Bellshill, 16 December, 1964						(W)
Stoke C. (L)	Dunfermline Ath.	02.90	89	2	0	0
Nottingham F.	Tr	03.90				
Reading	L	12.90	90	3	0	0
Mansfield T.	L	03.91	90	6	1	0
Shrewsbury T.	Tr	08.91	91-94	64	14	4
SMITH Mark Allen						
Birmingham, 2 January, 1973						(G)
Nottingham F.	YT	02.91				
Crewe Alex.	Tr	02.93	92-94	61	2	0
Walsall		11.96				
SMITH Mark Craig						
Sheffield, 21 March, 1960 Eu21-5						(CD)
Sheffield Wed.	App	03.78	77-86	281	1	16
Plymouth Arg.	Tr	07.87	87-89	82	0	6
Barnsley	Tr	11.89	89-92	101	3	10
Notts Co.	Tr	10.92	92	4	1	0
Port Vale	L	01.93	92	6	0	0
Huddersfield T.	L	02.93	92	5	0	0
Chesterfield	L	03.93	92	6	0	1
Lincoln C.	Tr	08.93	93	20	0	1
SMITH Mark Cyril						
Sheffield, 19 December, 1961						(LW)
Sheffield U.	Jnrs	08.80				
Scunthorpe U. (N/C)	Gainsborough Trin.	09.85	85	0	1	0
Rochdale	Kettering T.	07.88	88	26	1	7
Huddersfield T.	Tr	02.89	88-90	85	11	11
Grimsby T.	Tr	03.91	90-92	37	40	4
Scunthorpe U.	Tr	08.93	93-94	50	12	8
SMITH Mark Leslie						
Canning Town, 10 October, 1961						(LB)
West Ham U.	App	10.79	79	1	0	0
SMITH Mark Stuart						
Carlisle, 4 April, 1962 E Yth						(FB)
Leyton Orient	App	12.79	78-79	3	0	0
SMITH Martin Geoffrey						
Sunderland, 13 November, 1974 E Sch/Eu21-1						(F)
Sunderland	YT	09.92	93-97	86	25	22
SMITH Martyn Christopher						
Stoke, 16 September, 1961						(W)
Port Vale	Leek T.	07.84	84	12	1	1
SMITH Michael						
Sunderland, 28 October, 1958						(CD)
Lincoln C.	Lambton Street B.C.	07.77	77-78	20	5	0
Wimbledon	Tr	12.79	79-86	203	2	14
Aldershot	L	10.84	84	7	0	0
Hartlepool U.	Seaham Red Star	10.89	89-91	53	2	6
SMITH Michael						
Haddington, 15 October, 1923						(CF)
Plymouth Arg.	Preston A.	02.48	47	1	-	0
Chelsea	Tr	06.48				
SMITH Michael John						
Derby, 22 September, 1935 E Sch						(CH)
Derby Co.	Jnrs	10.52	57-60	22	-	0
Bradford C.	Tr	06.61	61-65	134	0	0
SMITH Michael Kenneth						
Hull, 19 December, 1968						(W)
Hull C.	YT	05.87	88-90	14	5	1
SMITH Michael Robert						
Liverpool, 28 September, 1973						(W)
Tranmere Rov.	YT	05.92				
Doncaster Rov.	Runcorn	01.96	95-97	33	17	5
SMITH Neil						
Warley, 10 February, 1970						(M)
Shrewsbury T.	YT	07.88	87	0	1	0
Lincoln C.	Redditch U.	03.90	89-91	13	4	0
SMITH Neil James						
Lambeth, 30 September, 1971						(M)
Tottenham H.	YT	07.90				
Gillingham	Tr	10.91	91-96	204	9	10
Fulham	Tr	07.97	97	42	2	0
SMITH Nicholas Leslie						
Thornbury, 28 January, 1969						(LW)
Southend U.	YT	07.87	86-89	49	11	6

League Club	Source	Date Signed	Seasons Played	Career Record Apps	Subs	Gls
Colchester U.	Tr	08.90	92-93	71	10	4
Northampton T. (L)	Sudbury T.	01.95	94	6	0	1
SMITH Nigel Godfrey						
Manchester, 22 April, 1959						(CD)
Stockport Co.	Blackburn Rov. (Am)	08.79	80-85	118	5	1
SMITH Nigel Keith						
Bath, 12 January, 1966						(M)
Bristol C.	App	01.84	82	2	0	0
Exeter C.	L	11.84	84	1	0	0
SMITH Nigel Paul						
Banstead, 3 January, 1958						(CD)
Brentford	Banstead Ath.	03.75	74-78	81	4	0
Cambridge U.	Tr	11.78	78	0	1	0
SMITH Nigel Peter						
Leeds, 21 December, 1969						(W)
Leeds U. (N/C)	YT	07.88				
Burnley	Tr	07.89	89-90	6	7	0
Bury	Tr	08.91	91	30	4	3
Shrewsbury T. (N/C)	Tr	08.92	92	2	0	0
SMITH Norman						
Darwen, 2 January, 1925 Died 1990						(WH)
Arsenal	Darwen	07.47				
Barnsley	Tr	10.52	52-58	156	-	14
SMITH Norman						
Boldon, 23 November, 1919						(CF)
Coventry C.	Standard Apprentices	05.38	38-47	13	-	0
Millwall	Tr	12.47	47	10	-	0
SMITH Norman						
Croydon, 2 July, 1928 E Amat						(WH)
Fulham	Bishop Auckland	07.48	52-56	60	-	0
SMITH Norman Henry						
Burton, 27 January, 1924						(IF)
Accrington St.		02.46	46-47	39	-	6
Oldham Ath.	Tr	06.48	48	1	-	0
SMITH Paul Andrew						
Bath, 12 September, 1953						(M)
Manchester C.	Jnrs	09.70				
Portsmouth	Tr	06.73	73	0	1	0
SMITH Paul Antony						
Hastings, 25 January, 1976						(W)
Nottingham F.	Hastings T.	01.95				
Lincoln C.	Tr	10.97	97	15	2	3
SMITH Paul Elton						
Lewisham, 2 November, 1971						(M)
Barnet	Horsham	05.95	95	0	1	0
SMITH Paul Michael						
Rotherham, 9 November, 1964						(F/RB)
Sheffield U.	App	11.82	82-85	29	7	1
Stockport Co.	L	08.85	85	7	0	5
Port Vale	Tr	07.86	86-87	42	2	7
Lincoln C.	Tr	08.87	88-94	219	13	27
SMITH Paul Stepney						
Wembley, 5 October, 1967						(RW)
Arsenal	App	07.85				
Brentford	Tr	08.87	87	10	7	1
Bristol Rov.	Tr	07.88	88	14	2	1
Torquay U.	Tr	03.89	88-91	66	9	12
SMITH Paul William						
Doncaster, 15 October, 1954						(M)
Huddersfield T.	App	12.71	72-73	1	1	0
Cambridge U.	Tr	09.74	74-75	35	3	3
SMITH Paul William						
Lenham (Kt), 18 September, 1971						(M)
Southend U.	YT	03.90	89-92	18	2	1
Brentford	Tr	08.93	93-96	159	0	11
Gillingham	Tr	07.97	97	46	0	3
SMITH Ian **Paul**						
Easington, 22 January, 1976						(W)
Burnley	YT	07.94	93-97	41	21	4
SMITH Peter Alec						
Islington, 20 November, 1964						(CD)
Leyton Orient	App	11.82	82	8	6	0

League Club	Source	Date Signed	Seasons Played	Apps	Subs	Gls
SMITH Peter John						
Battersea, 27 May, 1935						(WH)
Gillingham	Tunbridge Wells	06.58	58-59	39	-	2
SMITH Peter John						
Cannock, 12 July, 1969						(RB)
Brighton & H.A.	Alma Swanley	08.94	94-97	114	12	4
SMITH Peter John						
Gosport, 6 May, 1932						(CF)
Gillingham	Gosport Borough	11.54	54-56	6	-	0
SMITH Peter Lee						
Rhyl, 18 September, 1978 E Sch/E Yth						(M)
Crewe Alex.	YT	07.96	96-97	1	6	0
SMITH Philip						
Fleetwood, 20 November, 1961						(F)
Blackpool	App	11.79	79	1	0	0
SMITH Raymond						
Portadown (NI), 20 November, 1950						(F)
Oldham Ath.	Glenavon	01.68	67	0	2	0
SMITH Raymond James						
Islington, 18 April, 1943						(CF)
Southend U.	Basildon U.	12.61	61-66	150	0	55
Wrexham	Tr	07.67	67-71	161	14	60
Peterborough U.	Tr	07.72	72	22	0	8
SMITH Raymond Scorer						
Coxhoe (Dm), 14 April, 1929						(WH)
Luton T.	Evenwood T.	02.50	51-56	12	-	0
Southend U.	Tr	08.57	57-59	46	-	1
SMITH Harold **Raymond**						
Hull, 13 September, 1934						(IF)
Hull C.	Jnrs	08.52	54-55	23	-	2
Peterborough U.	Tr	07.56	60-62	92	-	33
Northampton T.	Tr	10.62	62-63	23	-	7
Luton T.	Tr	10.63	63	10	-	1
SMITH Richard Francis						
Reading, 22 October, 1967						(W)
Wolverhampton W.	YT	07.85	85	0	1	0
Mansfield T. (N/C)	Moor Green	03.87	86	1	1	0
SMITH Richard Geoffrey						
Lutterworth, 3 October, 1970						(CD)
Leicester C.	YT	12.88	89-95	82	16	1
Cambridge U.	L	09.89	89	4	0	0
Grimsby T.	L	09.95	95	8	0	0
Grimsby T.	Tr	03.96	95-96	22	2	0
SMITH Robert						
Barnsley, 20 June, 1941						(WH)
Barnsley	Jnrs	06.60	62	3	-	0
SMITH Robert						
Hull, 25 April, 1950						(FB)
Hull C.	App	11.67				
Grimsby T.	Tr	09.71	71	10	1	0
Hartlepool U.	Tr	07.72	72-75	141	11	4
SMITH Robert Alfred						
Skelton, 22 February, 1933 E-15						(CF)
Chelsea	Jnrs	05.50	50-55	74	-	23
Tottenham H.	Tr	12.55	55-63	271	-	176
Brighton & H. A.	Tr	05.64	64	31	-	19
SMITH Robert Gordon John						
Bournemouth, 15 December, 1941						(WH)
Portsmouth	Jnrs	05.59				
Gillingham	Tr	07.62	62	7	-	0
SMITH Robert Nisbet						
Dalkeith, 21 December, 1953						(LB)
Leicester C.	Hibernian	12.78	78-85	175	6	21
Peterborough U.	L	02.82	81	5	0	0
SMITH Robert William						
Prestbury, 14 March, 1944 E Yth						(M)
Manchester U.	App	04.61				
Scunthorpe U.	Tr	03.65	64-66	82	0	12
Grimsby T.	Tr	01.67	66-67	48	4	1
Brighton & H. A.	Tr	06.68	68-70	72	3	2
Chester C.	Tr	06.71	71	2	0	0
Hartlepool U.	Tr	10.71	71-72	67	2	7
SMITH Roger Anthony						
Welwyn, 3 November, 1944						(OL)
Tottenham H.	App	06.62				
Exeter C.	Tr	06.66	66	6	0	3
SMITH Roger William						
Tamworth, 19 February, 1945						(W)
Walsall	App	09.62	62-64	53	0	2
Port Vale	Tr	08.65	65	29	1	6
Walsall	Tr	05.66	66	8	1	0
SMITH Ronald						
Aberystwyth, 9 April, 1934						(RB)
Arsenal	Maidenhead U.	07.54				
Watford	Tr	08.55	55	2	-	0
SMITH Ronald						
Liverpool, 7 June, 1936						(OL)
Liverpool	Stoke C. (Am)	12.57				
Bournemouth	Tr	05.59	59-60	36	-	6
Crewe Alex.	Tr	07.61	61-63	91	-	11
Port Vale	Tr	10.63	63-64	59	-	6
Southport	Tr	07.65	65-66	77	2	14
SMITH Ronald Herbert						
York, 25 November, 1929						(CH)
York C.	Harrogate R.I.	05.54	54	1	-	0
SMITH Roy Harold						
India, 19 March, 1936						(F)
West Ham U.	Woodford Y.C.	06.55	55-56	6	-	1
Portsmouth	Hereford U.	01.62	61-62	8	-	3
SMITH Roy Peter						
Haydock, 18 June, 1936 Died 1959						(CF)
Southport	Wigan Ath.	09.58	58	23	-	4
SMITH Royston						
Shirebrook, 22 September, 1916						(G)
Sheffield Wed.	Selby T.	02.36	36-47	84	-	0
Notts Co.	Tr	12.48	48-52	110	-	0
SMITH Scott David						
New Zealand, 6 March, 1975						(RB)
Rotherham U.	YT	10.93	93-96	30	6	0
SMITH Septimus Charles						
South Shields, 15 March, 1912 E Sch/EF Lge/E-1						(WH/IF)
Leicester C.	Whitburn	03.29	29-48	350	-	35
SMITH Gareth **Shaun**						
Leeds, 9 April, 1971						(LB)
Halifax T.	YT	07.89	88-89	6	1	0
Crewe Alex.	Emley	12.91	91-97	219	19	30
SMITH Stanley James						
Kidsgrove, 24 February, 1931						(CF)
Port Vale	Stoke C. (Am)	05.50	54-56	60	-	19
Crewe Alex.	Tr	07.57	57	28	-	6
Oldham Ath.	Tr	03.58	57	4	-	0
SMITH Stanley Walter						
Coventry, 24 February, 1925						(WH)
Coventry C.	Nuffield Mechs	08.46	47-48	29	-	0
SMITH Stephen						
Huddersfield, 28 April, 1946						(M)
Huddersfield T.	Jnrs	10.63	64-76	330	12	30
Bolton W.	L	12.74	74	3	0	0
Halifax T.	Tr	08.77	77-78	78	3	4
SMITH Stephen John						
Lydney, 12 June, 1957						(G)
Birmingham C.	App	07.75	75	2	0	0
Bradford C.	Tr	03.78	78-81	105	0	0
Crewe Alex.	Tr	08.82	82-83	54	0	0
SMITH Clifford **Stephen**						
Birmingham, 13 January, 1961						(F)
Walsall	Bromsgrove Rov.	08.80	80-81	17	2	3
SMITH Terence Peter						
Cheltenham, 10 September, 1951						(F)
Stoke C.	App	12.68	70-71	3	1	0
Shrewsbury T.	L	02.73	72	2	0	0
SMITH Terence Victor						
Rainworth (Nts), 10 July, 1942						(WH)
Mansfield T.	Jnrs	04.60	60	8	-	0

SMITH Thomas
Liverpool, 5 April, 1945 E Yth/Eu23-10/EF Lge/E-1 (D)

League Club	Source	Date Signed	Seasons Played	Apps	Subs	Gls
Liverpool	App	04.62	62-77	467	0	36
Swansea C.	Tr	08.78	78	34	2	2

SMITH Thomas
Easington, 2 February, 1923 Died 1993 (CH)

League Club	Source	Date Signed	Seasons Played	Apps	Subs	Gls
Newcastle U.	Horden Colly	03.41	46-49	8	-	0

SMITH Thomas Edgar
Wolverhampton, 30 July, 1959 (F)

League Club	Source	Date Signed	Seasons Played	Apps	Subs	Gls
Sheffield U.	Bromsgrove Rov.	04.78	78	2	1	1
Huddersfield T.	Tr	03.79	78	0	1	0

SMITH Thomas Edward
Northampton, 25 November, 1977 (D)

League Club	Source	Date Signed	Seasons Played	Apps	Subs	Gls
Manchester U.	YT	05.95				
Cambridge U. (N/C)	Tr	04.98	97	0	1	0

SMITH Thomas William
Hemel Hempstead, 22 May, 1980 E Yth (W/F)

League Club	Source	Date Signed	Seasons Played	Apps	Subs	Gls
Watford	YT	10.97	97	0	1	0

SMITH Timothy Carl
Gloucester, 19 April, 1959 (M)

League Club	Source	Date Signed	Seasons Played	Apps	Subs	Gls
Luton T.	App	05.76	76-77	1	1	0

SMITH Trevor
Brierley Hill, 13 April, 1936 Eu23-15/E 'B'/EF Lge/E-2 (CH)

League Club	Source	Date Signed	Seasons Played	Apps	Subs	Gls
Birmingham C.	Jnrs	05.53	53-64	365	-	3
Walsall	Tr	10.64	64-65	12	0	0

SMITH Trevor John
Birmingham, 7 May, 1954 E Sch (W)

League Club	Source	Date Signed	Seasons Played	Apps	Subs	Gls
Coventry C.	App	05.71				
Walsall	Tr	08.72	72	2	1	0

SMITH Trevor Martin
Middlesbrough, 4 April, 1959 (D)

League Club	Source	Date Signed	Seasons Played	Apps	Subs	Gls
Hartlepool U.	Whitby T.	07.77	76-78	27	6	1
Hartlepool U.	Whitby T.	08.82	82	30	2	3

SMITH Trevor Richard
Lowestoft, 12 August, 1946 (FB)

League Club	Source	Date Signed	Seasons Played	Apps	Subs	Gls
Ipswich T.	App	08.64	64-65	22	1	0

SMITH John **Trevor**
Stanley, 8 September, 1910 (IF)

League Club	Source	Date Signed	Seasons Played	Apps	Subs	Gls
Charlton Ath.	Annfield Plain	05.33	33-34	23	-	6
Fulham	Tr	03.35	34-37	93	-	19
Crystal Palace	Tr	02.38	37-38	57	-	14
Watford	Colchester U.	06.47	47	10	-	0

SMITH Wilfred
Manchester, 20 January, 1935 (F)

League Club	Source	Date Signed	Seasons Played	Apps	Subs	Gls
Stockport Co.		02.57	57-59	6	-	1

SMITH Wilfred
Stoke, 18 April, 1917 Died 1995 (FB/WH)

League Club	Source	Date Signed	Seasons Played	Apps	Subs	Gls
Port Vale	Sneyd Colly	10.36	36-48	86	-	0

SMITH Wilfred Samuel
West Germany, 3 September, 1946 E Yth/Eu23-6/EF Lge (FB)

League Club	Source	Date Signed	Seasons Played	Apps	Subs	Gls
Sheffield Wed.	App	09.63	64-70	206	0	4
Coventry C.	Tr	08.70	70-74	132	3	1
Brighton & H. A.	L	10.74	74	5	0	0
Millwall	L	01.75	74	5	0	0
Bristol Rov.	Tr	03.75	74-76	54	0	2
Chesterfield	Tr	11.76	76	26	1	2

SMITH Wilfred Victor
Pucklechurch, 7 April, 1918 Died 1968 (FB)

League Club	Source	Date Signed	Seasons Played	Apps	Subs	Gls
Bristol Rov.	Clevedon T.	05.36	37-46	26	-	0
Newport Co.	Tr	12.46	46-47	9	-	0

SMITH William
Cumnock, 12 October, 1942 (IF)

League Club	Source	Date Signed	Seasons Played	Apps	Subs	Gls
Sheffield U.	Cumnock Jnrs	07.65	66	2	0	1

SMITH William
Glasgow, 6 December, 1943 (WH)

League Club	Source	Date Signed	Seasons Played	Apps	Subs	Gls
Brentford	Glasgow Celtic	06.63	63-65	25	0	0

SMITH William
London, 29 September, 1948 E Amat (D)

League Club	Source	Date Signed	Seasons Played	Apps	Subs	Gls
Wimbledon	Leatherhead	08.77	77	2	0	0

SMITH William
Aberdeen, 23 December, 1938 (IL)

League Club	Source	Date Signed	Seasons Played	Apps	Subs	Gls
Darlington	Raith Rov.	07.63	63	26	-	7

SMITH William Arthur
Lambeth, 2 November, 1938 (G)

League Club	Source	Date Signed	Seasons Played	Apps	Subs	Gls
Crystal Palace	Jnrs	12.56				
Watford	Tr	08.57	58	10	-	0

SMITH William Henry
Plymouth, 7 September, 1926 (WH/IF)

League Club	Source	Date Signed	Seasons Played	Apps	Subs	Gls
Plymouth Arg.	Plymouth U.	08.45				
Reading	Tr	08.47	47	3	-	0
Northampton T.	Tr	07.48	48	26	-	6
Birmingham C.	Tr	02.50	50-52	55	-	21
Blackburn Rov.	Tr	12.52	52-59	119	-	10
Accrington St.	Tr	07.60	60	34	-	3

SMITH William Roy
Stafford, 20 December, 1930 (LB)

League Club	Source	Date Signed	Seasons Played	Apps	Subs	Gls
Crewe Alex.		12.55	55-56	44	-	0

SMITHARD Matthew Philip
Leeds, 13 June, 1976 (M)

League Club	Source	Date Signed	Seasons Played	Apps	Subs	Gls
Leeds U.	YT	03.93				
Bradford C.	Tr	08.96	96	0	1	0

SMITHERS Timothy
Ramsgate, 22 January, 1956 E Semi Pro (LB)

League Club	Source	Date Signed	Seasons Played	Apps	Subs	Gls
Oxford U.	Nuneaton Borough	05.80	80-82	95	4	6

SMITHIES Michael Howard
Hartlepool, 18 September, 1962 (D)

League Club	Source	Date Signed	Seasons Played	Apps	Subs	Gls
Hartlepool U.		08.83	82-86	32	3	0

SMITHSON Rodney George
Leicester, 9 October, 1943 E Sch/E Yth (CD)

League Club	Source	Date Signed	Seasons Played	Apps	Subs	Gls
Arsenal	App	10.60	62	2	-	0
Oxford U.	Tr	07.64	65-74	150	6	6

SMOUT John Richard
Newtown, 30 October, 1941 (G)

League Club	Source	Date Signed	Seasons Played	Apps	Subs	Gls
Crystal Palace		08.65	65	1	0	0
Exeter C.	Tr	06.66	66-67	75	0	0

SMYTH Cecil
Belfast, 4 May, 1941 (FB)

League Club	Source	Date Signed	Seasons Played	Apps	Subs	Gls
Exeter C.	Distillery	08.62	62-68	270	3	1
Torquay U.	Tr	08.69	69-70	22	2	0

SMYTH John Michael
Dublin, 28 April, 1970 (RB)

League Club	Source	Date Signed	Seasons Played	Apps	Subs	Gls
Liverpool	Dundalk	05.87				
Burnley	Tr	08.90				
Wigan Ath.	Tr	09.91	91	2	6	0

SMYTH Michael
Dublin, 13 May, 1940 IR-1 (G)

League Club	Source	Date Signed	Seasons Played	Apps	Subs	Gls
Barrow	Drumcondra	08.62	62-63	8	-	0

SMYTH Peter Rufus Adair
Derry (NI), 3 December, 1924 (IF)

League Club	Source	Date Signed	Seasons Played	Apps	Subs	Gls
Exeter C.	Albion Rov.	06.50	50	5	-	0
Southport	Tr	07.51	51	5	-	0

SMYTH Herbert **Robert**
Manchester, 28 February, 1921 (WH)

League Club	Source	Date Signed	Seasons Played	Apps	Subs	Gls
Ipswich T.	H.M.S. Ganges	12.45	46-47	2	-	0
Halifax T.	Tr	08.50	50	2	-	0
Rochdale	Tr	09.50	50	3	-	1
Accrington St.	Tr	01.51	50	7	-	0

SMYTH Samuel
Belfast, 25 February, 1925 LoI/NI-9 (IF)

League Club	Source	Date Signed	Seasons Played	Apps	Subs	Gls
Wolverhampton W.	Linfield	07.47	47-51	102	-	34
Stoke C.	Tr	09.51	51-52	40	-	17
Liverpool	Tr	01.53	52-53	45	-	20

SNAPE John
Birmingham, 2 July, 1917 (RH)

League Club	Source	Date Signed	Seasons Played	Apps	Subs	Gls
Coventry C.	Solihull T.	05.36	37-49	106	-	2

SNEDDEN John Duncan
Bonnybridge, 3 February, 1942 S Sch (CH)

League Club	Source	Date Signed	Seasons Played	Apps	Subs	Gls
Arsenal	Jnrs	02.59	59-64	83	-	0
Charlton Ath.	Tr	03.65	64-65	18	2	0
Leyton Orient	Tr	07.66	66-67	26	1	3
Halifax T.	L	11.67	67	5	0	0

SNEDDON Charles
Bo'ness, 10 June, 1930 Died 1992 (CH)

League Club	Source	Date Signed	Seasons Played	Apps	Subs	Gls
Accrington St.	Stenhousemuir	10.53	53-60	213	-	3

SNEDDON David
Kilwinning, 24 April, 1936 Su23-1 (IF)

League Club	Source	Date Signed	Seasons Played	Apps	Subs	Gls
Preston N. E.	Dundee	04.59	58-61	91	-	17

SNEDDON Thomas
Livingston, 22 August, 1912 Died 1983 (FB)

League Club	Source	Date Signed	Seasons Played	Apps	Subs	Gls
Rochdale	Queen of South	07.37	37-46	67	-	0

SNEDDON William Cleland
Wishaw, 1 April, 1914 Died 1995 (WH)

League Club	Source	Date Signed	Seasons Played	Apps	Subs	Gls
Brentford	Falkirk	06.37	37-38	66	-	2
Swansea C.	Tr	02.46	46	2	-	0
Newport Co.	Tr	10.46	46	18	-	0

SNEEKES Richard
Amsterdam, Holland, 30 October, 1968 (M)

League Club	Source	Date Signed	Seasons Played	Apps	Subs	Gls
Bolton W.	Fortuna Sittard (Neth)	08.94	94-95	51	4	7
West Bromwich A.	Tr	03.96	95-97	92	8	21

SNELL Albert Edward
Dunscroft (Yks), 7 February, 1931 (WH)

League Club	Source	Date Signed	Seasons Played	Apps	Subs	Gls
Sunderland	Doncaster Rov. (Am)	08.49	52-54	9	-	1
Halifax T.	Tr	11.55	55-56	25	-	0

SNELL Victor Derek Robert
Ipswich, 29 October, 1927 (FB)

League Club	Source	Date Signed	Seasons Played	Apps	Subs	Gls
Ipswich T.	Jnrs	11.45	49-58	64	-	2

SNIJDERS Mark Werner
Holland, 12 March, 1972 (CD)

League Club	Source	Date Signed	Seasons Played	Apps	Subs	Gls
Port Vale	A.Z. Alkmaar (Neth)	09.97	97	22	2	2

SNODIN Glynn
Rotherham, 14 February, 1960 (LB/W)

League Club	Source	Date Signed	Seasons Played	Apps	Subs	Gls
Doncaster Rov.	App	10.77	76-84	288	21	61
Sheffield Wed.	Tr	06.85	85-86	51	8	1
Leeds U.	Tr	07.87	87-90	83	11	10
Oldham Ath.	L	08.91	91	8	0	1
Rotherham U.	L	02.92	91	3	0	0
Barnsley	Hearts	07.93	93-94	18	7	0

SNODIN Ian
Rotherham, 15 August, 1963 E Yth/Eu21-4/E 'B' (M/RB)

League Club	Source	Date Signed	Seasons Played	Apps	Subs	Gls
Doncaster Rov.	App	08.80	79-84	181	7	25
Leeds U.	Tr	05.85	85-86	51	0	6
Everton	Tr	01.87	86-94	142	6	3
Sunderland	L	10.94	94	6	0	0
Oldham Ath.	Tr	01.95	94-96	55	2	0
Scarborough	Tr	08.97	97	33	2	0

SNOOKES Eric
Birmingham, 6 March, 1955 (LB)

League Club	Source	Date Signed	Seasons Played	Apps	Subs	Gls
Preston N. E.	App	03.73	72-73	20	0	0
Crewe Alex.	Tr	07.74	74	33	1	0
Southport	Tr	07.75	75-77	106	4	2
Rochdale	Tr	07.78	78-82	183	0	1
Bolton W.	Tr	07.83	83	6	0	0

SNOW Simon Gordon
Sheffield, 3 April, 1966 (F)

League Club	Source	Date Signed	Seasons Played	Apps	Subs	Gls
Scunthorpe U. (N/C)	App	08.83	82-83	1	1	0
Preston N. E.	Sutton T.	08.89	89	1	0	0

SNOWBALL Raymond
Sunderland, 10 March, 1932 (G)

League Club	Source	Date Signed	Seasons Played	Apps	Subs	Gls
Darlington (Am)	Crook T.	10.64	64-66	13	0	0

SNOWDEN Trevor
Sunderland, 4 October, 1973 (LW)

League Club	Source	Date Signed	Seasons Played	Apps	Subs	Gls
Rochdale	Seaham R.S.	02.93	92-93	8	6	0

SNOWDON Brian Victor
Bishop Auckland, 1 January, 1935 (CH)

League Club	Source	Date Signed	Seasons Played	Apps	Subs	Gls
Blackpool		09.52	55-59	18	-	1
Portsmouth	Tr	10.59	59-63	114	-	0
Millwall	Tr	10.63	63-66	128	0	0
Crystal Palace	Detroit (USA)	02.69	68	1	4	0

SOBIECH Jorg
Gelsenkirchen, Germany, 15 January, 1969 (WB)

League Club	Source	Date Signed	Seasons Played	Apps	Subs	Gls
Stoke C. (L)	N.E.C. Nijmegen (Neth)	03.98	97	3	0	0

SODEN Walter James
Birmingham, 22 January, 1921 Died 1977 (CF)

League Club	Source	Date Signed	Seasons Played	Apps	Subs	Gls
Coventry C.	Boldmere St Michael	03.48	47-48	2	-	0

SODJE Efetobore
Greenwich, 5 October, 1972 (CD)

League Club	Source	Date Signed	Seasons Played	Apps	Subs	Gls
Macclesfield T.	Stevenage Borough	07.97	97	41	0	3

SOLAN Kenneth
Middlesbrough, 13 October, 1948 Died 1971 (IF)

League Club	Source	Date Signed	Seasons Played	Apps	Subs	Gls
Middlesbrough		11.66				
Hartlepool U.	L	10.68	68	6	0	1
Darlington	L	03.69	68	8	0	1

SOLBAKKEN Stele
Norway, 27 February, 1968 Norwegian Int (M)

League Club	Source	Date Signed	Seasons Played	Apps	Subs	Gls
Wimbledon	Lillestrom (Nor)	10.97	97	4	2	1

SOLIS Mauricio Mora
Costa Rica, 13 December, 1972 Costa Rican Int (M)

League Club	Source	Date Signed	Seasons Played	Apps	Subs	Gls
Derby Co.	C.S. Heridiano (CR)	03.97	96-97	3	8	0

SOLOMAN Jason Rafael
Welwyn Garden City, 6 October, 1970 E Yth (CD/M)

League Club	Source	Date Signed	Seasons Played	Apps	Subs	Gls
Watford	YT	12.88	90-94	79	21	5
Peterborough U.	L	01.95	94	4	0	0
Wycombe W.	Tr	03.95	94-95	11	2	1
Wrexham (N/C)	Tr	08.96	96	2	0	0
Fulham (N/C)	Tr	11.96	96	1	3	0

SOLSKJAER Ole Gunnar
Norway, 26 February, 1973 Norwegian Int (F)

League Club	Source	Date Signed	Seasons Played	Apps	Subs	Gls
Manchester U.	Molde (Nor)	07.96	96-97	40	15	24

SOLTVEDT Trond Egil
Vos, Norway, 15 February, 1967 Norwegian Int (M)

League Club	Source	Date Signed	Seasons Played	Apps	Subs	Gls
Coventry C.	Rosenborg (Nor)	07.97	97	26	4	1

SOMERFIELD Alfred George
South Kirkby, 22 March, 1918 Died 1985 (F)

League Club	Source	Date Signed	Seasons Played	Apps	Subs	Gls
Mansfield T.	Frickley Colly	05.38	38	15	-	6
Wolverhampton W.	Tr	03.39				
Wrexham	Tr	06.47	46	2	-	1
Crystal Palace	Tr	09.47	47	10	-	3

SOMERS Michael Robert
Nottingham, 27 February, 1945 (OL)

League Club	Source	Date Signed	Seasons Played	Apps	Subs	Gls
Chelsea	Nottingham F. (Am)	11.62				
Torquay U.	Tr	05.64	64-65	39	1	3
Hartlepool U.	Tr	07.66	66-68	63	3	3

SOMMER Jurgen Peterson
U.S.A., 27 February, 1969 USA Int (G)

League Club	Source	Date Signed	Seasons Played	Apps	Subs	Gls
Luton T.	U.S.S.F. (USA)	08.91	93-95	82	0	0
Brighton & H.A.	L	11.91	91	1	0	0
Torquay U.	L	10.92	92	10	0	0
Queens Park R.	Tr	08.95	95-96	66	0	0

SONNER Daniel James
Wigan, 9 January, 1972 NI 'B'/NI-1 (M)

League Club	Source	Date Signed	Seasons Played	Apps	Subs	Gls
Burnley	Wigan Ath. (YT)	07.90	90-92	1	5	0
Bury	L	11.92	92	5	0	3
Ipswich T.	Preussen Koln (Ger)	06.96	96-97	28	24	3

SOO Hong (Frank)
Buxton, 12 March, 1914 Died 1991 (WH)

League Club	Source	Date Signed	Seasons Played	Apps	Subs	Gls
Stoke C.	Prescot Cables	01.33	33-38	173	-	5
Leicester C.	Tr	09.45				
Luton T.	Tr	07.46	46-47	71	-	4

SORRELL Anthony Charles
Hornchurch, 17 October, 1966 (M)

League Club	Source	Date Signed	Seasons Played	Apps	Subs	Gls
Maidstone U.	Barking	08.88	89-90	46	9	8
Colchester U. (N/C)	Boston U.	11.92	92	4	1	1
Barnet (N/C)	Tr	02.93	92	8	0	2

SORRELL Dennis James
Lambeth, 7 October, 1940 (WH)

League Club	Source	Date Signed	Seasons Played	Apps	Subs	Gls
Leyton Orient	Jnrs	10.57	58-60	37	-	1
Chelsea	Tr	02.62	61-63	3	-	0
Leyton Orient	Tr	09.64	64-66	74	0	3

SORVEL Neil Simon
Prescot, 2 March, 1973 (M)

League Club	Source	Date Signed	Seasons Played	Apps	Subs	Gls
Crewe Alex.	YT	07.91	91	5	4	0
Macclesfield T.	Tr	08.92	97	41	4	3

SOUNESS Graeme James
Edinburgh, 6 May, 1953 S Sch/Su23-2/S-54 (M)

League Club	Source	Date Signed	Seasons Played	Apps	Subs	Gls
Tottenham H.	App	05.70				
Middlesbrough	Tr	01.73	72-77	174	2	22
Liverpool	Tr	01.78	77-83	246	1	38

League Club	Source	Date Signed	Seasons Played	Career Record Apps	Subs	Gls

SOUTAR Timothy John
Oxford, 25 February, 1946 (IF)

League Club	Source	Date Signed	Seasons Played	Apps	Subs	Gls
Brentford	Jnrs	07.63	63	1	-	0

SOUTER Donald Davidson
Hammersmith, 1 December, 1961 (CD)

League Club	Source	Date Signed	Seasons Played	Apps	Subs	Gls
Ipswich T.	App	01.79				
Barnsley	Tr	08.82	82	19	2	0
Aldershot	Tr	08.83	83-84	45	0	0

SOUTER William
Dundee, 3 May, 1931 (FB)

League Club	Source	Date Signed	Seasons Played	Apps	Subs	Gls
Burnley	Broughty Ath.	12.53				
Chester C.	Tr	06.57	57-59	51	-	1

SOUTH Alexander William
Brighton, 7 July, 1931 (CH)

League Club	Source	Date Signed	Seasons Played	Apps	Subs	Gls
Brighton & H. A.	Jnrs	03.49	49-54	81	-	4
Liverpool	Tr	12.54	54	6	-	1
Halifax T.	Tr	10.56	56-64	302	-	12

SOUTH John Alan
Bow, 30 November, 1952 (CD)

League Club	Source	Date Signed	Seasons Played	Apps	Subs	Gls
Colchester U.	Leyton Orient (Am)	07.72	72	4	0	0

SOUTH John Edward
Lambeth, 8 April, 1948 (CF)

League Club	Source	Date Signed	Seasons Played	Apps	Subs	Gls
Brentford	Fulham (App)	11.66	66	1	0	0

SOUTH William Albert
Brighton, 24 February, 1928 (HB)

League Club	Source	Date Signed	Seasons Played	Apps	Subs	Gls
Brighton & H. A.	Jnrs	08.51	51	2	-	0

SOUTHALL Neville
Llandudno, 16 September, 1958 W-92 (G)

League Club	Source	Date Signed	Seasons Played	Apps	Subs	Gls
Bury	Winsford U.	06.80	80	39	0	0
Everton	Tr	07.81	81-97	578	0	0
Port Vale	L	01.83	82	9	0	0
Southend U.	L	12.97	97	9	0	0
Stoke C.	Tr	02.98	97	12	0	0

SOUTHALL Leslie **Nicholas**
Stockton, 28 January, 1972 (W)

League Club	Source	Date Signed	Seasons Played	Apps	Subs	Gls
Hartlepool U.	Darlington (YT)	11.90	91-94	118	20	24
Grimsby T.	Tr	07.95	95-97	55	17	6
Gillingham	Tr	12.97	97	22	1	2

SOUTHALL Robert
Rotherham, 10 May, 1922 Died 1979 (WH)

League Club	Source	Date Signed	Seasons Played	Apps	Subs	Gls
Chesterfield	Jnrs	12.43	47-52	127	-	11

SOUTHAM James (Jack) Henry
Wolverhampton, 19 August, 1917 Died 1996 (FB)

League Club	Source	Date Signed	Seasons Played	Apps	Subs	Gls
West Bromwich A.	Shornhill Rec.	12.42				
Newport Co.	Tr	05.46	46	8	-	0
Birmingham C.	Tr	11.46	47	1	-	0
Northampton T.	Tr	06.49	49-54	145	-	1

SOUTHEY Peter Charles
Putney, 4 January, 1962 Died 1983 (FB)

League Club	Source	Date Signed	Seasons Played	Apps	Subs	Gls
Tottenham H.	App	10.79	79	1	0	0

SOUTHGATE Gareth
Watford, 3 September, 1970 E-27 (CD)

League Club	Source	Date Signed	Seasons Played	Apps	Subs	Gls
Crystal Palace	YT	01.89	90-94	148	4	15
Aston Villa	Tr	07.95	95-97	91	0	2

SOUTHON Jamie Peter
Dagenham, 13 October, 1974 (M)

League Club	Source	Date Signed	Seasons Played	Apps	Subs	Gls
Southend U.	YT	07.93	92	0	1	0

SOUTHREN Thomas Cansfield
Sunderland, 1 August, 1927 (W)

League Club	Source	Date Signed	Seasons Played	Apps	Subs	Gls
West Ham U.	Peartree O.B.	12.49	50-53	64	-	3
Aston Villa	Tr	12.54	54-58	63	-	6
Bournemouth	Tr	10.58	58-59	64	-	11

SOUTHWELL Aubrey Allen
Grantham, 21 August, 1921 (FB)

League Club	Source	Date Signed	Seasons Played	Apps	Subs	Gls
Notts Co.	Nottingham F. (Am)	12.44	46-56	328	-	2

SOWDEN Maurice
Doncaster, 21 October, 1954 (M)

League Club	Source	Date Signed	Seasons Played	Apps	Subs	Gls
Scunthorpe U.	App	10.72	72	3	0	0

SOWDEN Peter Tacker
Bradford, 1 May, 1929 (IF)

League Club	Source	Date Signed	Seasons Played	Apps	Subs	Gls
Blackpool	Jnrs	06.47				
Hull C.	Bacup Borough	09.48				
Aldershot	Elgin C.	10.50	50	4	-	0
Hull C.	Tr	08.51				
Gillingham	Tr	08.52	52-55	134	-	27
Accrington St.	Tr	09.56	56-57	54	-	13
Wrexham	Tr	06.58	58-59	38	-	4

SOWDEN William
Manchester, 8 December, 1930 (CF)

League Club	Source	Date Signed	Seasons Played	Apps	Subs	Gls
Manchester C.	Jnrs	04.49	52-53	11	-	2
Chesterfield	Tr	11.54	54-56	97	-	59
Stockport Co.	Tr	06.57	57	15	-	7

SOWERBY William Henry Roy
Hull, 31 August, 1932 (IF)

League Club	Source	Date Signed	Seasons Played	Apps	Subs	Gls
Wolverhampton W.	Pilkington Rec.	05.50				
Grimsby T.	Tr	01.54	53-54	12	-	1

SPACKMAN Nigel James
Romsey, 2 December, 1960 (M)

League Club	Source	Date Signed	Seasons Played	Apps	Subs	Gls
Bournemouth	Andover	05.80	80-82	118	1	10
Chelsea	Tr	06.83	83-86	139	2	12
Liverpool	Tr	02.87	86-88	39	12	0
Queens Park R.	Tr	02.89	88-89	27	2	1
Chelsea	Glasgow Rangers	09.92	92-95	60	7	0
Sheffield U.	Tr	07.96	96	19	4	0

SPALDING William
Glasgow, 24 November, 1926 (OR)

League Club	Source	Date Signed	Seasons Played	Apps	Subs	Gls
Bristol C.	Ballymena	01.50	49-50	10	-	0

SPARHAM Sean Ricky
Bexley, 4 December, 1968 (LB)

League Club	Source	Date Signed	Seasons Played	Apps	Subs	Gls
Millwall	Jnrs	05.87	87-89	22	6	0
Brentford	L	03.90	89	5	0	1

SPARK Alexander McAlpine
Stenhousemuir, 16 October, 1949 (CD)

League Club	Source	Date Signed	Seasons Played	Apps	Subs	Gls
Preston N. E.	Jnrs	11.66	67-75	207	18	6
Bradford C.	Motherwell	12.76	76-77	32	2	0

SPARKS Christopher James
Islington, 22 May, 1960 (FB)

League Club	Source	Date Signed	Seasons Played	Apps	Subs	Gls
Crystal Palace	App	11.77				
Reading	L	08.79	79	3	0	0

SPARROW Brian Edward
Bethnal Green, 24 June, 1962 (LB)

League Club	Source	Date Signed	Seasons Played	Apps	Subs	Gls
Arsenal	App	02.80	83	2	0	0
Wimbledon	L	01.83	82	17	0	1
Millwall	L	12.83	83	5	0	2
Gillingham	L	01.84	83	5	0	1
Crystal Palace	Tr	07.84	84-86	62	1	2

SPARROW John Paul
Bethnal Green, 3 June, 1957 E Sch/E Yth (LB)

League Club	Source	Date Signed	Seasons Played	Apps	Subs	Gls
Chelsea	App	08.74	73-79	63	6	2
Millwall	L	03.79	78	7	0	0
Exeter C.	Tr	01.81	80-82	62	1	3

SPARROW Paul
Wandsworth, 24 March, 1975 (RB)

League Club	Source	Date Signed	Seasons Played	Apps	Subs	Gls
Crystal Palace	YT	07.93	95	1	0	0
Preston N.E.	Tr	03.96	95-97	20	0	0

SPAVIN Alan
Lancaster, 20 February, 1942 (M)

League Club	Source	Date Signed	Seasons Played	Apps	Subs	Gls
Preston N. E.	Jnrs	08.59	60-73	411	6	26
Preston N. E.	Washington (USA)	11.77	77-78	3	4	0

SPEAK Christopher
Preston, 20 August, 1973 (FB)

League Club	Source	Date Signed	Seasons Played	Apps	Subs	Gls
Blackpool	Jnrs	07.92	92	0	1	0

SPEAKMAN Samuel
Huyton, 27 January, 1934 (OL)

League Club	Source	Date Signed	Seasons Played	Apps	Subs	Gls
Bolton W.		09.51				
Middlesbrough	Tr	07.53				
Tranmere Rov.	Tr	09.54	54-55	68	-	9

SPEARE James Peter Vincent
Liverpool, 5 November, 1976 (G)

League Club	Source	Date Signed	Seasons Played	Apps	Subs	Gls
Everton	YT	07.95				
Darlington	Tr	03.97	96	3	0	0

SPEARING Anthony
Romford, 7 October, 1964 E Yth (LB)

League Club	Source	Date Signed	Seasons Played	Apps	Subs	Gls
Norwich C.	App	10.82	83-87	67	2	0
Stoke C.	L	11.84	84	9	0	0

League Club	Source	Date Signed	Seasons Played	Career Record Apps	Subs	Gls
Oxford U.	L	02.85	84	5	0	0
Leicester C.	Tr	07.88	88-90	71	2	1
Plymouth Arg.	Tr	06.91	91-92	35	0	0
Peterborough U.	Tr	01.93	92-96	105	6	2

SPEARRITT Edward Alfred
Lowestoft, 31 January, 1947 (FB/W)

League Club	Source	Date Signed	Seasons Played	Apps	Subs	Gls
Ipswich T.	App	02.65	65-68	62	10	13
Brighton & H. A.	Tr	01.69	68-73	203	7	22
Carlisle U.	Tr	06.74	74-75	29	2	1
Gillingham	Tr	08.76	76	19	0	1

SPEARS Alan Frederick
Amble, 27 December, 1938 E Sch (W)

League Club	Source	Date Signed	Seasons Played	Apps	Subs	Gls
Newcastle U.	Jnrs	02.56				
Millwall	Tr	06.60	60-62	31	-	6
Lincoln C.	Tr	07.63	63	2	-	0

SPECTOR Miles David
Hendon, 4 August, 1934 E Yth/E Amat (OL)

League Club	Source	Date Signed	Seasons Played	Apps	Subs	Gls
Chelsea (Am)	Jnrs	05.52	52-53	3	-	0
Millwall (Am)	Hendon	05.56	56	1	-	0

SPEDDING Duncan
Camberley, 7 September, 1977 (M)

League Club	Source	Date Signed	Seasons Played	Apps	Subs	Gls
Southampton	YT	05.96	97	4	3	0

SPEDDING Thomas William
Tynemouth, 8 December, 1925 (CH)

League Club	Source	Date Signed	Seasons Played	Apps	Subs	Gls
Doncaster Rov.		03.49	48	1	-	0

SPEED Gary Andrew
Deeside, 8 September, 1969 W Yth/Wu21-3/W-47 (M)

League Club	Source	Date Signed	Seasons Played	Apps	Subs	Gls
Leeds U.	YT	06.88	88-95	231	17	39
Everton	Tr	07.96	96-97	58	0	15
Newcastle U.	Tr	02.98	97	13	0	1

SPEED Leslie
Deeside, 3 October, 1923 (FB)

League Club	Source	Date Signed	Seasons Played	Apps	Subs	Gls
Wrexham	Llandudno	04.45	46-54	211	-	0

SPEEDIE David Robert
Glenrothes, 20 February, 1960 Su21-1/S-10 (F/M)

League Club	Source	Date Signed	Seasons Played	Apps	Subs	Gls
Barnsley	Jnrs	10.78	78-79	10	13	0
Darlington	Tr	06.80	80-81	88	0	21
Chelsea	Tr	06.82	82-86	155	7	47
Coventry C.	Tr	07.87	87-90	121	1	31
Liverpool	Tr	02.91	90	8	4	6
Blackburn Rov.	Tr	08.91	91	34	2	23
Southampton	Tr	07.92	92	11	0	0
Birmingham C.	L	10.92	92	10	0	2
West Bromwich A.	L	01.93	92	7	0	2
West Ham U.	L	03.93	92	11	0	4
Leicester C.	Tr	07.93	93	37	0	12

SPEIGHT Martyn Stephen
Stockton, 26 July, 1978 (CD)

League Club	Source	Date Signed	Seasons Played	Apps	Subs	Gls
Doncaster Rov.	YT	07.96	95	1	0	0

SPEIGHT Michael
Upton (Yks), 1 November, 1951 E 'B' (M)

League Club	Source	Date Signed	Seasons Played	Apps	Subs	Gls
Sheffield U.	App	05.69	71-79	184	15	14
Blackburn Rov.	Tr	07.80	80-81	50	1	4
Grimsby T.	Tr	08.82	82-83	35	3	2
Chester C.	Tr	08.84	84-85	40	0	1

SPEIRS Gardner
Airdrie, 14 April, 1963 S Yth (M)

League Club	Source	Date Signed	Seasons Played	Apps	Subs	Gls
Hartlepool U. (N/C)	St Mirren	08.89	89	0	1	0

SPELMAN Isaac
Newcastle, 9 March, 1914 (WH)

League Club	Source	Date Signed	Seasons Played	Apps	Subs	Gls
Leeds U.	Usworth Colly	03.33				
Southend U.	Tr	05.35	35-36	43	-	2
Tottenham H.	Tr	05.37	37-38	28	-	2
Hartlepool U.	Tr	05.46	46	25	-	0

SPELMAN Michael Thomas
Newcastle, 8 December, 1950 (M)

League Club	Source	Date Signed	Seasons Played	Apps	Subs	Gls
Wolverhampton W.	Whitley Bay	11.69				
Watford	Tr	08.71				
Hartlepool U.	Tr	10.71	71-76	115	6	4
Darlington	L	12.72	72	4	0	0

SPELMAN Ronald Edward
Blofield, 22 May, 1938 (OR)

League Club	Source	Date Signed	Seasons Played	Apps	Subs	Gls
Norwich C.	C.N.S.O.B.U.	08.56	57-60	2	-	0
Northampton T.	Tr	11.60	60-61	34	-	3
Bournemouth	Tr	03.62	61-63	28	-	4
Watford	Tr	09.63	63-64	40	-	3
Oxford U.	Tr	05.65	65	15	1	1

SPENCE Alan Nicholson
Seaham, 7 February, 1940 E Yth (IF)

League Club	Source	Date Signed	Seasons Played	Apps	Subs	Gls
Sunderland	Murton Jnrs	05.57	57	5	-	1
Darlington	Tr	06.60	60-61	24	-	10
Southport	Tr	07.62	62-68	225	5	98
Oldham Ath.	Tr	12.68	68-69	26	1	12
Chester C.	Tr	12.69	69	5	4	2

SPENCE Colin
Glasgow, 7 January, 1960 (F)

League Club	Source	Date Signed	Seasons Played	Apps	Subs	Gls
Crewe Alex. (N/C)	App	02.78	76-78	10	8	1

SPENCE Derek William
Belfast, 18 January, 1952 NI-29 (F)

League Club	Source	Date Signed	Seasons Played	Apps	Subs	Gls
Oldham Ath.	Crusaders	09.70	71-72	5	1	0
Bury	Tr	02.73	72-76	140	0	44
Blackpool	Tr	10.76	76	24	3	2
Blackpool	Olympiakos (Gre)	08.78	78-79	58	0	18
Southend U.	Tr	12.79	79-81	100	4	32
Bury	See Bee (HK)	08.83	83	9	4	1

SPENCE Joseph Louis
Salford, 13 October, 1925 (D)

League Club	Source	Date Signed	Seasons Played	Apps	Subs	Gls
Chesterfield	Buxton	01.48				
York C.	Tr	07.50	50-53	110	-	0

SPENCE Richard
Hoyland, 18 July, 1908 Died 1983 E-2 (OR)

League Club	Source	Date Signed	Seasons Played	Apps	Subs	Gls
Barnsley	Thorpe Colly	02.33	32-34	64	-	25
Chelsea	Tr	10.34	34-47	221	-	62

SPENCE Ronald
Durham, 7 January, 1927 Died 1996 (WH)

League Club	Source	Date Signed	Seasons Played	Apps	Subs	Gls
York C.	Rossington Colly	03.48	47-58	280	-	25

SPENCE Joseph **William**
Hartlepool, 10 January, 1926 (CH)

League Club	Source	Date Signed	Seasons Played	Apps	Subs	Gls
Portsmouth		03.47	49-50	19	-	0
Queens Park R.	Tr	12.51	51-53	56	-	0

SPENCER Anthony Raymond
Chiswick, 23 April, 1965 (FB)

League Club	Source	Date Signed	Seasons Played	Apps	Subs	Gls
Brentford	App	04.83	81-83	17	1	0
Aldershot	L	12.84	84	10	0	0

SPENCER Derek
Coventry, 10 January, 1931 Died 1989 (G)

League Club	Source	Date Signed	Seasons Played	Apps	Subs	Gls
Coventry C.	Lockheed Leamington	12.51	51-52	20	-	0

SPENCER Harold
Burnley, 30 April, 1919 (HB)

League Club	Source	Date Signed	Seasons Played	Apps	Subs	Gls
Burnley	Jnrs	09.37	46	4	-	1
Wrexham	Tr	07.50	50	11	-	0

SPENCER Jack Shepherd
Bacup, 24 August, 1920 (IF)

League Club	Source	Date Signed	Seasons Played	Apps	Subs	Gls
Burnley	Bacup U.	06.48	48-50	37	-	8
Accrington St.	Tr	06.51	51	29	-	7

SPENCER John
Glasgow, 11 September, 1970 S Sch/S Yth/Su21-3/S-14 (F)

League Club	Source	Date Signed	Seasons Played	Apps	Subs	Gls
Chelsea	Glasgow Rangers	08.92	92-96	75	28	36
Queens Park R.	Tr	11.96	96-97	47	1	22
Everton	L	03.98	97	3	3	0

SPENCER John Raymond
Bradfield, 20 November, 1934 E Yth (F)

League Club	Source	Date Signed	Seasons Played	Apps	Subs	Gls
Sheffield U.	Jnrs	06.54	54-56	24	-	10

SPENCER Leslie
Manchester, 16 September, 1936 (IF)

League Club	Source	Date Signed	Seasons Played	Apps	Subs	Gls
Rochdale		01.58	57-59	74	-	17
Luton T.	Tr	07.60	60	7	-	1

SPENCER Raymond
Birmingham, 25 May, 1933 E Sch (WH)

League Club	Source	Date Signed	Seasons Played	Apps	Subs	Gls
Aston Villa	Jnrs	06.50				
Darlington	Tr	03.58	57-60	98	-	5
Torquay U.	Tr	06.61	61-63	59	-	1

SPENCER Simon Dean
Islington, 10 September, 1976 E Yth (M)

League Club	Source	Date Signed	Seasons Played	Apps	Subs	Gls
Tottenham H.	YT	07.95				
Brentford	Tr	07.97	97	1	0	0

League Club	Source	Date Signed	Seasons Played	Apps	Subs	Gls

SPENCER Thomas Hannah
Glasgow, 28 November, 1945 (CD/F)

League Club	Source	Date Signed	Seasons Played	Apps	Subs	Gls
Southampton	Glasgow Celtic	07.65	65	3	0	0
York C.	Tr	06.66	66-67	54	3	21
Workington	Tr	03.68	67-71	167	0	10
Lincoln C.	Tr	01.72	71-73	67	7	10
Rotherham U.	Tr	07.74	74-77	137	1	10

SPERRIN Martyn Robin
Edmonton, 6 December, 1956 (F)

League Club	Source	Date Signed	Seasons Played	Apps	Subs	Gls
Luton T.	Edgware T.	10.77	77	0	1	0

SPERRIN William Thomas
Wood Green, 9 April, 1922 (IF)

League Club	Source	Date Signed	Seasons Played	Apps	Subs	Gls
Brentford	Finchley	09.49	49-55	90	-	27

SPERRING George Burgess
Epsom, 30 April, 1935 (CF)

League Club	Source	Date Signed	Seasons Played	Apps	Subs	Gls
Gillingham (Am)		07.55	55	1	-	0

SPERTI Francesco
Italy, 28 January, 1955 (FB)

League Club	Source	Date Signed	Seasons Played	Apps	Subs	Gls
Swindon T.	App	01.73	73	1	0	0

SPICER Edwin
Liverpool, 20 September, 1922 E Sch (FB)

League Club	Source	Date Signed	Seasons Played	Apps	Subs	Gls
Liverpool	Jnrs	10.39	46-53	158	-	2

SPIERS George Smyth
Belfast, 3 September, 1941 (OL)

League Club	Source	Date Signed	Seasons Played	Apps	Subs	Gls
Exeter C.	Crusaders	08.63	63	5	-	0

SPIERS Richard (Dick) Alan Jesse
Benson (Oxon), 27 November, 1937 (CH)

League Club	Source	Date Signed	Seasons Played	Apps	Subs	Gls
Reading	Chertsey	10.55	55-69	451	2	3

SPINK Anthony Arthur
Doncaster, 16 November, 1929 (CF)

League Club	Source	Date Signed	Seasons Played	Apps	Subs	Gls
Sheffield Wed.		12.49				
Chester C.	Tr	06.50	51-52	13	-	3
Workington	Dorchester T.	07.55				
Sunderland	Tr	12.55				
Tranmere Rov.	Tr	06.56	56	7	-	3

SPINK Dean Peter
Birmingham, 22 January, 1967 (CD/F)

League Club	Source	Date Signed	Seasons Played	Apps	Subs	Gls
Aston Villa	Halesowen T.	06.89				
Scarborough	L	11.89	89	3	0	2
Bury	L	02.90	89	6	0	1
Shrewsbury T.	Tr	03.90	89-96	244	29	53
Wrexham	Tr	07.97	97	33	3	6

SPINK Nigel Philip
Chelmsford, 8 August, 1958 E 'B'/EF Lge/E-1 (G)

League Club	Source	Date Signed	Seasons Played	Apps	Subs	Gls
Aston Villa	Chelmsford C.	01.77	79-95	357	4	0
West Bromwich A.	Tr	01.96	95-96	19	0	0
Millwall	Tr	09.97	97	21	0	0

SPINKS Henry Charles
Great Yarmouth, 1 February, 1920 (CF)

League Club	Source	Date Signed	Seasons Played	Apps	Subs	Gls
Norwich C. (Am)	C.E.Y. M.S.	12.46	46	2	-	1

SPINNER Terence James
Woking, 6 November, 1953 (F)

League Club	Source	Date Signed	Seasons Played	Apps	Subs	Gls
Southampton	App	07.71	72-73	1	1	0
Walsall	Tr	07.74	74-75	10	6	5

SPIRING Peter John
Glastonbury, 13 December, 1950 E Yth (M/F)

League Club	Source	Date Signed	Seasons Played	Apps	Subs	Gls
Bristol C.	Jnrs	06.68	69-72	58	5	16
Liverpool	Tr	03.73				
Luton T.	Tr	11.74	74-75	12	3	2
Hereford U.	Tr	02.76	75-82	205	22	20

SPITTLE Paul David
Wolverhampton, 16 December, 1964 (M)

League Club	Source	Date Signed	Seasons Played	Apps	Subs	Gls
Oxford U.	App	10.82				
Crewe Alex.	Tr	08.83	83	4	2	1

SPOFFORTH David John
York, 21 March, 1969 (CD)

League Club	Source	Date Signed	Seasons Played	Apps	Subs	Gls
York C.	Jnrs	07.87	87	3	0	0

SPOONER Nicholas Michael
Manchester, 5 June, 1971 (RB)

League Club	Source	Date Signed	Seasons Played	Apps	Subs	Gls
Bolton W.	YT	07.89	91-94	22	1	2

SPOONER Stephen Alan
Sutton, 25 January, 1961 (M)

League Club	Source	Date Signed	Seasons Played	Apps	Subs	Gls
Derby Co.	App	12.78	78-81	7	1	0
Halifax T.	Tr	12.81	81-82	71	1	13
Chesterfield	Tr	07.83	83-85	89	4	14
Hereford U.	Tr	07.86	86-87	84	0	19
York C.	Tr	07.88	88-89	72	0	11
Rotherham U.	Tr	07.90	90	15	4	0
Mansfield T.	Tr	03.91	90-92	55	3	2
Blackpool	Tr	02.93	92	2	0	0
Chesterfield	Tr	10.93	93-94	11	1	0

SPRAGGON Frank
Whickham (Dm), 27 October, 1945 (D)

League Club	Source	Date Signed	Seasons Played	Apps	Subs	Gls
Middlesbrough	App	11.62	63-75	277	3	3
Hartlepool U. (N/C)	Minnesota (USA)	11.76	76	1	0	0

SPRAGUE Martyn Leslie
Risca, 10 April, 1949 (FB)

League Club	Source	Date Signed	Seasons Played	Apps	Subs	Gls
Newport Co.	Lovells Ath.	08.68	69-73	155	1	1

SPRAKE Gareth
Swansea, 3 April, 1945 Wu23-5/W-37 (G)

League Club	Source	Date Signed	Seasons Played	Apps	Subs	Gls
Leeds U.	App	05.62	61-72	381	0	0
Birmingham C.	Tr	10.73	73-74	16	0	0

SPRATLEY Alan Sidney
Maidenhead, 5 June, 1949 (G)

League Club	Source	Date Signed	Seasons Played	Apps	Subs	Gls
Queens Park R.	App	05.67	68-72	29	0	0
Swindon T.	Tr	07.73	73	7	0	0

SPRATT Graham William
Leicester, 17 July, 1939 (G)

League Club	Source	Date Signed	Seasons Played	Apps	Subs	Gls
Coventry C.	Oadby T.	12.56	57-58	28	-	0

SPRATT Thomas
Cambois (Nd), 20 December, 1941 E Sch/E Yth (M/F)

League Club	Source	Date Signed	Seasons Played	Apps	Subs	Gls
Manchester U.	Jnrs	12.59				
Bradford P. A.	Tr	02.61	60-63	118	-	45
Torquay U.	Weymouth	07.65	65-66	60	1	19
Workington	Tr	01.67	66-67	51	0	14
York C.	Tr	03.68	67-68	26	3	1
Workington	Tr	03.69	68-71	142	2	27
Stockport Co.	Tr	06.72	72-73	65	0	6

SPRIDGEON Frederick Arthur
Swansea, 13 July, 1935 (FB)

League Club	Source	Date Signed	Seasons Played	Apps	Subs	Gls
Leeds U.	Jnrs	08.52				
Crewe Alex.	Tr	07.56	56	7	-	0

SPRIGGS Stephen
Armthorpe (Yks), 16 February, 1956 (M)

League Club	Source	Date Signed	Seasons Played	Apps	Subs	Gls
Huddersfield T.	App	02.73	74	2	2	0
Cambridge U.	Tr	07.75	75-86	411	5	58
Middlesbrough	L	03.87	86	3	0	0

SPRING Andrew John
Gateshead, 17 November, 1965 (FB)

League Club	Source	Date Signed	Seasons Played	Apps	Subs	Gls
Coventry C.	App	11.83	83-84	3	2	0
Bristol Rov.	Tr	07.85	85	18	1	0
Cardiff C.	L	10.85	85	1	0	0

SPRING Matthew John
Harlow, 17 November, 1979 (M)

League Club	Source	Date Signed	Seasons Played	Apps	Subs	Gls
Luton T.	YT	07.97	97	6	6	0

SPRINGETT Peter John
Fulham, 8 May, 1946 Died 1997 E Yth/Eu23-6 (G)

League Club	Source	Date Signed	Seasons Played	Apps	Subs	Gls
Queens Park R.	App	05.63	62-66	137	0	0
Sheffield Wed.	Tr	05.67	67-74	180	0	0
Barnsley	Tr	07.75	75-79	191	0	0

SPRINGETT Ronald Derrick
Fulham, 22 July, 1935 EF Lge/E-33 (G)

League Club	Source	Date Signed	Seasons Played	Apps	Subs	Gls
Queens Park R.	Victoria U.	02.53	55-57	88	-	0
Sheffield Wed.	Tr	03.58	57-66	345	0	0
Queens Park R.	Tr	06.67	67-68	45	0	0

SPRINGTHORPE Terence Alfred
Draycott (Dy), 4 December, 1923 (FB)

League Club	Source	Date Signed	Seasons Played	Apps	Subs	Gls
Wolverhampton W.	Jnrs	12.40	47-49	35	-	0
Coventry C.	Tr	12.50	50	12	-	0

SPROATES Alan
Houghton-le-Spring, 30 June, 1944 (M)

League Club	Source	Date Signed	Seasons Played	Apps	Subs	Gls
Sunderland	Jnrs	07.61				
Swindon T.	Tr	08.63	63-64	3	-	0
Darlington	Tr	09.65	65-73	305	11	17
Scunthorpe U.	Tr	08.74	74	19	5	0

SPROATES John
Houghton-le-Spring, 11 April, 1943 (WH)

League Club	Source	Date Signed	Seasons Played	Apps	Subs	Gls
Barnsley	West Auckland	12.63	63	2	-	0

SPROSON Philip Jesse
Stoke, 13 October, 1959 (CD)

League Club	Source	Date Signed	Seasons Played	Apps	Subs	Gls
Port Vale	Jnrs	12.77	77-88	422	4	33
Birmingham C.	Tr	07.89	89	12	0	0

SPROSON Roy
Stoke, 23 September, 1930 Died 1997 (D)

League Club	Source	Date Signed	Seasons Played	Apps	Subs	Gls
Port Vale	Stoke C. (Am)	07.49	50-71	755	5	30

SPROSTON Bert
Sandbach, 22 June, 1915 EF Lge/E-11 (FB)

League Club	Source	Date Signed	Seasons Played	Apps	Subs	Gls
Leeds U.	Sandbach Ramblers	06.33	33-37	130	-	1
Tottenham H.	Tr	06.38	38	9	-	0
Manchester C.	Tr	11.38	38-49	125	-	5

SPROSTON Neil Robert
Dudley, 20 November, 1970 (CD)

League Club	Source	Date Signed	Seasons Played	Apps	Subs	Gls
Birmingham C.	YT	07.89	87	0	1	0

SPRUCE David **George**
Chester, 3 April, 1923 (CH)

League Club	Source	Date Signed	Seasons Played	Apps	Subs	Gls
Wrexham	Heath R.	10.48	48-51	135	-	3
Barnsley	Tr	05.52	52-56	149	-	0
Chester C.	Tr	07.58	58-60	63	-	0

SPRUCE Philip Thomas
Chester, 16 November, 1929 (D)

League Club	Source	Date Signed	Seasons Played	Apps	Subs	Gls
Wrexham		11.50	51-55	23	-	0

SPUHLER John Oswald
Sunderland, 18 September, 1917 E Sch (CF)

League Club	Source	Date Signed	Seasons Played	Apps	Subs	Gls
Sunderland	Jnrs	09.34	36-38	35	-	4
Middlesbrough	Tr	10.45	46-53	216	-	69
Darlington	Tr	06.54	54-55	67	-	19

SPURDLE William
Guernsey, 28 January, 1926 (WH)

League Club	Source	Date Signed	Seasons Played	Apps	Subs	Gls
Oldham Ath.	Jnrs	03.48	47-49	56	-	5
Manchester C.	Tr	01.50	49-56	160	-	32
Port Vale	Tr	11.56	56	21	-	7
Oldham Ath.	Tr	06.57	57-62	144	-	19

SQUIRE Michael Richard
Poole, 18 October, 1963 E Sch (F)

League Club	Source	Date Signed	Seasons Played	Apps	Subs	Gls
Fulham		07.82				
Torquay U.	Dorchester T.	03.84	83	12	1	3

SQUIRES Alan
Fleetwood, 26 February, 1923 (LB)

League Club	Source	Date Signed	Seasons Played	Apps	Subs	Gls
Preston N. E.		12.44				
Carlisle U.	Tr	12.46	46-47	24	-	0

SQUIRES Barry
Birmingham, 29 July, 1931 (OL)

League Club	Source	Date Signed	Seasons Played	Apps	Subs	Gls
Birmingham C.	Lye T.	05.53	53	1	-	0
Bradford C.	Tr	06.54	54	7	-	0

SQUIRES Frank
Swansea, 8 March, 1921 Died 1988 (IF)

League Club	Source	Date Signed	Seasons Played	Apps	Subs	Gls
Swansea C.	Jnrs	05.38	46-47	36	-	5
Plymouth Arg.	Tr	10.47	47-49	86	-	13
Grimsby T.	Tr	07.50	50	36	-	2

SQUIRES James Alexander
Preston, 15 November, 1975 (CD)

League Club	Source	Date Signed	Seasons Played	Apps	Subs	Gls
Preston N.E.	YT	04.94	93-96	24	7	0
Mansfield T.	L	08.97	97	1	0	0

SQUIRES Robert
Selby, 6 April, 1919 (WH)

League Club	Source	Date Signed	Seasons Played	Apps	Subs	Gls
Doncaster Rov.	Selby T.	09.37	47	21	-	0
Exeter C.	Tr	07.49	49	1	-	0

SRNICEK Pavel
Czechoslavakia, 10 March, 1968 Czechoslovakian Int (G)

League Club	Source	Date Signed	Seasons Played	Apps	Subs	Gls
Newcastle U.	Banik Ostrava (Cz)	02.91	90-97	148	1	0

STABB Christopher John
Bradford, 12 October, 1976 (CD)

League Club	Source	Date Signed	Seasons Played	Apps	Subs	Gls
Bradford C.	YT	07.95	94	1	0	0

STABB George Herbert
Paignton, 26 September, 1912 Died 1994 (CF)

League Club	Source	Date Signed	Seasons Played	Apps	Subs	Gls
Torquay U.	Paignton T.	09.31	31-34	93	-	44
Port Vale	Tr	07.35	35-36	32	-	9
Bradford P. A.	Tr	09.36	36-46	94	-	4

STACEY Stephen Darrow
Bristol, 27 August, 1944 (FB)

League Club	Source	Date Signed	Seasons Played	Apps	Subs	Gls
Bristol C.	App	11.61				
Wrexham	Tr	02.66	65-68	101	4	6
Ipswich T.	Tr	09.68	68	3	0	0
Chester C.	L	12.69	69	1	0	0
Charlton Ath.	L	01.70	69	1	0	1
Bristol C.	Tr	09.70	70	9	0	0
Exeter C.	Tr	09.71	71-72	57	2	0

STACEY Steven John
Bristol, 9 June, 1975 (RB)

League Club	Source	Date Signed	Seasons Played	Apps	Subs	Gls
Torquay U.	YT	10.93	93	1	0	0

STACEY Terence James
Mitcham, 28 September, 1936 E Amat (FB)

League Club	Source	Date Signed	Seasons Played	Apps	Subs	Gls
Plymouth Arg.	Carshalton Ath.	05.59	59-61	22	-	0
Watford	Tr	07.62				
Gillingham	Tr	08.63	63-64	16	-	0

STACK William John
Liverpool, 17 January, 1948 (OL)

League Club	Source	Date Signed	Seasons Played	Apps	Subs	Gls
Crystal Palace	Jnrs	01.65	65	2	0	0

STACKMAN Harry **Scott**
U.S.A., 16 November, 1975 (CD)

League Club	Source	Date Signed	Seasons Played	Apps	Subs	Gls
Northampton T. (N/C)	YT	08.94	93	0	1	0

STAFF Paul
Brancepeth, 30 August, 1962 (W)

League Club	Source	Date Signed	Seasons Played	Apps	Subs	Gls
Hartlepool U.	App	08.80	79-83	88	10	14
Aldershot	Tr	08.84	84-85	25	12	11

STAFFORD Andrew Grant
Stretford, 28 October, 1960 (W)

League Club	Source	Date Signed	Seasons Played	Apps	Subs	Gls
Halifax T.	Blackburn Rov. (N/C)	01.79	78-80	33	8	1
Stockport Co.	Tr	08.81	81	21	4	1
Rochdale	Tr	08.82	82	1	0	1

STAFFORD Clive Andrew
Ipswich, 4 April, 1963 (LB)

League Club	Source	Date Signed	Seasons Played	Apps	Subs	Gls
Colchester U.	Diss T.	02.89	88-89	31	2	0
Exeter C.	L	02.90	89	2	0	0

STAFFORD Ellis
Sheffield, 17 August, 1929 (FB)

League Club	Source	Date Signed	Seasons Played	Apps	Subs	Gls
Peterborough U.	Scarborough	(N/L)	60-62	17	-	0

STAGG William
Ealing, 17 October, 1957 (M)

League Club	Source	Date Signed	Seasons Played	Apps	Subs	Gls
Brentford	App	●	74	4	0	0

STAINROD Simon Allan
Sheffield, 1 February, 1959 E Yth (F)

League Club	Source	Date Signed	Seasons Played	Apps	Subs	Gls
Sheffield U.	App	07.76	75-78	59	8	14
Oldham Ath.	Tr	03.79	78-80	69	0	21
Queens Park R.	Tr	11.80	80-84	143	2	48
Sheffield Wed.	Tr	02.85	84-85	8	7	2
Aston Villa	Tr	09.85	85-87	58	5	16
Stoke C.	Tr	12.87	87-88	27	1	6

STAINSBY John
Barnsley, 25 September, 1937 (CF)

League Club	Source	Date Signed	Seasons Played	Apps	Subs	Gls
Barnsley	Wolverhampton W. (Am)	12.55	59-60	34	-	12
York C.	Tr	07.61	61-62	69	-	21
Stockport Co.	Tr	07.63	63	5	-	0

STAINTON Bryan Edward
Scampton (Lincs), 8 January, 1942 (D)

League Club	Source	Date Signed	Seasons Played	Apps	Subs	Gls
Lincoln C.	Ingham	03.62	61-64	25	-	0

STAINTON James Kenneth
Sheffield, 14 December, 1931 (FB)

League Club	Source	Date Signed	Seasons Played	Apps	Subs	Gls
Bradford P. A.		04.53				
Mansfield T.	Tr	08.54	55-56	9	-	0

STAINWRIGHT David Peter
Nottingham, 13 June, 1948 (CF)

League Club	Source	Date Signed	Seasons Played	Apps	Subs	Gls
Nottingham F.	App	08.65	65-66	4	3	1
Doncaster Rov.	Tr	07.68	68	1	0	0
York C.	Tr	07.69	69	6	2	1

STALKER Alan
Ponteland, 18 March, 1939 (G)

League Club	Source	Date Signed	Seasons Played	Apps	Subs	Gls
Gateshead (Am)	Bishop Auckland	05.58	58	4	-	0

STALKER John Alexander Hastie Inglis
Musselburgh, 12 March, 1959 (F)

League Club	Source	Date Signed	Seasons Played	Apps	Subs	Gls
Leicester C.		07.79				
Darlington	Tr	10.79	79-82	107	9	36
Hartlepool U.	Tr	01.83	82	3	1	0

STALLARD Mark
Derby, 24 October, 1974 (F)

League Club	Source	Date Signed	Seasons Played	Apps	Subs	Gls
Derby Co.	YT	11.91	91-95	19	8	2
Fulham	L	09.94	94	4	0	3
Bradford C.	Tr	01.96	95-96	33	10	10
Preston N.E.	L	02.97	96	4	0	1
Wycombe W.	Tr	03.97	96-97	55	0	21

STAMP Darryn Michael
Beverley, 21 September, 1978 (F)

League Club	Source	Date Signed	Seasons Played	Apps	Subs	Gls
Scunthorpe U.	Hessle	07.97	97	4	6	1

STAMP Philip Lawrence
Middlesbrough, 12 December, 1975 E Yth (M)

League Club	Source	Date Signed	Seasons Played	Apps	Subs	Gls
Middlesbrough	YT	02.93	93-97	43	16	3

STAMPER Frank Fielden Thorpe
Hartlepool, 22 February, 1926 (WH)

League Club	Source	Date Signed	Seasons Played	Apps	Subs	Gls
Hartlepool U.	Colchester U.	08.49	49-57	301	-	26

STAMPS John (Jack) David
Maltby, 2 December, 1918 Died 1991 (CF)

League Club	Source	Date Signed	Seasons Played	Apps	Subs	Gls
Mansfield T.	Silverwood Colly	10.37	37	1	-	0
New Brighton	Tr	08.38	38	12	-	5
Derby Co.	Tr	01.39	38-53	233	-	100
Shrewsbury T.	Tr	12.53	53	22	-	4

STAMPS Scott
Birmingham, 20 March, 1975 (LB)

League Club	Source	Date Signed	Seasons Played	Apps	Subs	Gls
Torquay U.	YT	07.93	92-96	80	6	5
Colchester U.	Tr	03.97	96-97	33	2	1

STANBRIDGE George
Campsall (Yks), 28 March, 1920 (FB)

League Club	Source	Date Signed	Seasons Played	Apps	Subs	Gls
Rotherham U.		11.38	46-48	36	-	1
Aldershot	Tr	06.49	49	15	-	0

STANCLIFFE Paul Ian
Sheffield, 5 May, 1958 (CD)

League Club	Source	Date Signed	Seasons Played	Apps	Subs	Gls
Rotherham U.	App	03.76	75-82	285	0	7
Sheffield U.	Tr	08.83	83-90	278	0	12
Rotherham U.	L	09.90	90	5	0	0
Wolverhampton W.	Tr	11.90	90	17	0	0
York C.	Tr	07.91	91-94	89	2	3

STANDEN James Alfred
Edmonton, 30 May, 1935 (G)

League Club	Source	Date Signed	Seasons Played	Apps	Subs	Gls
Arsenal	Rickmansworth	04.53	57-60	35	-	0
Luton T.	Tr	10.60	60-62	36	-	0
West Ham U.	Tr	11.62	62-67	178	0	0
Millwall	Detroit (USA)	10.68	68-69	8	0	0
Portsmouth	Tr	07.70	70-71	13	0	0

STANDING John Robert
Shoreham, 3 September, 1943 (FB)

League Club	Source	Date Signed	Seasons Played	Apps	Subs	Gls
Brighton & H. A.	Bognor Regis T.	12.61	61-62	10	-	0

STANDLEY Thomas Leslie
Poplar, 23 December, 1932 (WH)

League Club	Source	Date Signed	Seasons Played	Apps	Subs	Gls
Queens Park R.	Basildon	05.57	57	15	-	2
Bournemouth	Tr	11.58	58-64	159	-	5

STANIFORTH David Albry
Chesterfield, 6 October, 1950 (F)

League Club	Source	Date Signed	Seasons Played	Apps	Subs	Gls
Sheffield U.	App	05.68	68-73	22	4	3
Bristol Rov.	Tr	03.74	73-78	135	16	32
Bradford C.	Tr	06.79	79-81	107	8	25
Halifax T.	Tr	07.82	82-83	66	3	21

STANIFORTH Gordon
Hull, 23 March, 1957 E Sch (F)

League Club	Source	Date Signed	Seasons Played	Apps	Subs	Gls
Hull C.	App	04.74	73-76	7	5	2
York C.	Tr	12.76	76-79	128	0	33
Carlisle U.	Tr	10.79	79-82	118	8	33
Plymouth Arg.	Tr	03.83	82-84	87	4	19
Newport Co.	Tr	08.85	85-86	84	3	13
York C. (N/C)	Tr	10.87	87	15	4	1

STANIFORTH Ronald
Manchester, 13 April, 1924 Died 1988 E 'B'/E-8 (FB)

League Club	Source	Date Signed	Seasons Played	Apps	Subs	Gls
Stockport Co.	Newton A.	10.46	46-51	223	-	1
Huddersfield T.	Tr	05.52	52-54	110	-	0
Sheffield Wed.	Tr	07.55	55-58	102	-	2
Barrow	Tr	10.59	59-60	38	-	0

STANISLAUS Roger Edmund Philbert
Hammersmith, 2 November, 1968 (LB)

League Club	Source	Date Signed	Seasons Played	Apps	Subs	Gls
Arsenal	YT	07.86				
Brentford	Tr	09.87	87-89	109	2	4
Bury	Tr	07.90	90-94	167	9	5
Leyton Orient	Tr	07.95	95	20	1	0

STANLEY Gary Ernest
Burton, 4 March, 1954 (M)

League Club	Source	Date Signed	Seasons Played	Apps	Subs	Gls
Chelsea	App	03.71	75-78	105	4	15
Everton	Tr	08.79	79-80	52	0	1
Swansea C.	Tr	10.81	81-83	60	12	4
Portsmouth	Tr	01.84	83-85	43	4	1
Bristol C.	Wichita (USA)	08.88	88	8	2	0

STANLEY Graham
Sheffield, 27 January, 1938 (WH)

League Club	Source	Date Signed	Seasons Played	Apps	Subs	Gls
Bolton W.	Jnrs	10.55	56-63	141	-	3
Tranmere Rov.	Tr	07.65	65	0	1	1

STANLEY Patrick Joseph
Dublin, 9 March, 1938 (FB)

League Club	Source	Date Signed	Seasons Played	Apps	Subs	Gls
Leeds U.	Jnrs	03.55				
Halifax T.	Tr	05.58	58-62	119	-	1

STANLEY Terence James
Brighton, 2 January, 1951 (M)

League Club	Source	Date Signed	Seasons Played	Apps	Subs	Gls
Brighton & H.A.	Lewes	11.69	69-70	16	6	0

STANLEY Thomas
Hemsworth, 7 December, 1962 (M)

League Club	Source	Date Signed	Seasons Played	Apps	Subs	Gls
York C.	App	12.80	80-82	14	4	0

STANNARD James David
Harold Hill, 6 October, 1962 (G)

League Club	Source	Date Signed	Seasons Played	Apps	Subs	Gls
Fulham	Ford U.	06.80	80-84	41	0	0
Southend U.	L	09.84	84	6	0	0
Charlton Ath.	L	01.85	84	1	0	0
Southend U.	Tr	03.85	84-86	103	0	0
Fulham	Tr	08.87	87-94	348	0	1
Gillingham	Tr	08.95	95-97	104	0	0

STANNERS Walter
Bo'ness, 2 January, 1921 (G)

League Club	Source	Date Signed	Seasons Played	Apps	Subs	Gls
Bournemouth	Bo'ness U.	07.47	47	3	-	0
Rochdale	Tr	08.49	49	5	-	0

STANSBRIDGE Leonard Edward Charles
Southampton, 19 February, 1919 Died 1986 (G)

League Club	Source	Date Signed	Seasons Played	Apps	Subs	Gls
Southampton	Jnrs	08.36	37-51	48	-	0

STANSFIELD Frederick
Cardiff, 12 December, 1917 W-1 (CH)

League Club	Source	Date Signed	Seasons Played	Apps	Subs	Gls
Cardiff C.	Grange A.	08.43	46-48	106	-	1
Newport Co.	Tr	09.49	49	21	-	0

STANT Philip Richard
Bolton, 13 October, 1962 (F)

League Club	Source	Date Signed	Seasons Played	Apps	Subs	Gls
Reading (N/C)	British Army	08.82	82	3	1	2
Hereford U.	British Army	11.86	86-88	83	6	38
Notts Co.	Tr	07.89	89	14	8	6
Blackpool	L	09.90	90	12	0	5
Lincoln C.	L	11.90	90	4	0	0
Huddersfield T.	L	01.91	90	5	0	1
Fulham	Tr	02.91	90	19	0	5
Mansfield T.	Tr	07.91	91-92	56	1	32
Cardiff C.	Tr	12.92	92-94	77	2	34
Mansfield T.	L	08.93	93	4	0	1
Bury	Tr	01.95	94-96	49	13	23
Northampton T.	L	11.96	96	4	1	2
Lincoln C.	Tr	12.96	96-97	39	4	18

STANTON Brian
Liverpool, 7 February, 1956 (M)

League Club	Source	Date Signed	Seasons Played	Apps	Subs	Gls
Bury	New Brighton	10.75	76-78	72	11	14
Huddersfield T.	Tr	09.79	79-85	199	10	45
Wrexham	L	03.86	85	8	0	0
Rochdale	Morecambe	12.86	86-87	42	7	4

STANTON Nathan
Nottingham, 6 May, 1981 E Yth (D)

League Club	Source	Date Signed	Seasons Played	Apps	Subs	Gls
Scunthorpe U.	YT	●	97	0	1	0

STANTON Sidney
Dudley, 16 June, 1923 (D)

League Club	Source	Date Signed	Seasons Played	Apps	Subs	Gls
Birmingham C.		03.46				
Northampton T.	Tr	07.46	47-48	7	-	0

STANTON Thomas
Glasgow, 3 May, 1948 S Sch (FB)

League Club	Source	Date Signed	Seasons Played	Apps	Subs	Gls
Liverpool	Jnrs	05.65				
Arsenal	Tr	09.66				
Mansfield T.	Tr	09.67	67	37	0	1
Bristol Rov.	Tr	07.68	68-75	160	12	7

STAPLES Leonard Eric
Leicester, 23 January, 1926 E Sch (FB)

League Club	Source	Date Signed	Seasons Played	Apps	Subs	Gls
Leicester C.	Jnrs	07.47				
Newport Co.	Tr	08.49	49-56	164	-	2

STAPLETON Francis Anthony
Dublin, 10 July, 1956 IR Yth/IR-71 (F)

League Club	Source	Date Signed	Seasons Played	Apps	Subs	Gls
Arsenal	App	09.73	74-80	223	2	75
Manchester U.	Tr	08.81	81-86	204	19	60
Derby Co.	Ajax (Neth)	03.88	87	10	0	1
Blackburn Rov.	Le Havre (Fr)	07.89	89-90	80	1	13
Huddersfield T. (N/C)	Aldershot (N/C)	10.91	91	5	0	0
Bradford C.	Tr	12.91	91-93	49	19	2
Brighton & H.A. (N/C)	Tr	11.94	94	1	1	0

STAPLETON John Robert
Manchester, 30 September, 1969 (LB)

League Club	Source	Date Signed	Seasons Played	Apps	Subs	Gls
Stockport Co.	West Bromwich A. (YT)	08.88	88	1	0	0

STAPLETON Joseph Edward
Marylebone, 27 June, 1928 (CH)

League Club	Source	Date Signed	Seasons Played	Apps	Subs	Gls
Fulham	Uxbridge T.	08.52	54-59	97	-	2

STAPLETON Simon John
Oxford, 10 December, 1968 E Semi Pro (M)

League Club	Source	Date Signed	Seasons Played	Apps	Subs	Gls
Portsmouth	App	12.86				
Bristol Rov.	Tr	07.88	88	4	1	0
Wycombe W.	Tr	08.89	93-95	46	3	3

STARBUCK Philip Michael
Nottingham, 24 November, 1968 (F)

League Club	Source	Date Signed	Seasons Played	Apps	Subs	Gls
Nottingham F.	App	08.86	86-90	9	27	2
Birmingham C.	L	03.88	87	3	0	0
Hereford U.	L	02.90	89	6	0	0
Blackburn Rov.	L	09.90	90	5	1	1
Huddersfield T.	Tr	08.91	91-94	120	17	36
Sheffield U.	Tr	10.94	94-96	26	10	2
Bristol C.	L	09.95	95	5	0	1
Oldham Ath.	Tr	08.97	97	7	2	1
Plymouth Arg.	Tr	03.98	97	6	1	0

STARK Roy Howard
Nottingham, 28 November, 1953 (CD)

League Club	Source	Date Signed	Seasons Played	Apps	Subs	Gls
Aston Villa	App	06.69	73	2	0	0

STARK Wayne
Derby, 14 October, 1976 (M)

League Club	Source	Date Signed	Seasons Played	Apps	Subs	Gls
Mansfield T.	YT	●	93	0	1	0

STARK William Reid
Airdrie, 27 May, 1937 (F)

League Club	Source	Date Signed	Seasons Played	Apps	Subs	Gls
Crewe Alex.	Glasgow Rangers	08.60	60-61	39	-	13
Carlisle U.	Tr	12.61	61-62	35	-	17
Colchester U.	Tr	11.62	62-65	95	0	33
Luton T.	Tr	09.65	65	8	2	4
Chesterfield	Tr	07.66	66	30	1	15
Newport Co.	Tr	07.67	67	12	0	2

STARKEY Malcolm John
Bulwell, 25 January, 1936 (IF/FB)

League Club	Source	Date Signed	Seasons Played	Apps	Subs	Gls
Blackpool		08.54	56-58	3	-	0
Shrewsbury T.	Tr	06.59	59-62	121	-	34
Chester C.	Tr	04.63	62-66	109	0	1

STARLING Alan William
Dagenham, 2 April, 1951 (G)

League Club	Source	Date Signed	Seasons Played	Apps	Subs	Gls
Luton T.	App	04.69	69-70	7	0	0
Torquay U.	L	02.71	70	1	0	0
Northampton T.	Tr	06.71	71-76	238	0	1
Huddersfield T.	Tr	03.77	76-79	112	0	0

STARLING Ronald William
Pelaw, 11 October, 1909 Died 1991 E-2 (IF)

League Club	Source	Date Signed	Seasons Played	Apps	Subs	Gls
Hull C.	Washington Colly	10.26	27-29	78	-	13
Newcastle U.	Tr	05.30	30-31	51	-	8
Sheffield Wed.	Tr	06.32	32-36	176	-	31
Aston Villa	Tr	01.37	36-46	88	-	11

STAROCSIK Felix
Poland, 20 May, 1920 (W)

League Club	Source	Date Signed	Seasons Played	Apps	Subs	Gls
Northampton T.	Third Lanark	07.51	51-54	49	-	19

STATHAM Brian
Zimbabwe, 21 May, 1969 Eu21-3 (FB)

League Club	Source	Date Signed	Seasons Played	Apps	Subs	Gls
Tottenham H.	YT	07.87	87-88	20	4	0
Reading	L	03.91	90	8	0	0
Bournemouth	L	11.91	91	2	0	0
Brentford	Tr	02.92	91-96	148	18	1
Gillingham	Tr	08.97	97	16	4	0

STATHAM Derek James
Wolverhampton, 24 March, 1959 E Yth/Eu21-6/E'B'/E-3 (LB)

League Club	Source	Date Signed	Seasons Played	Apps	Subs	Gls
West Bromwich A.	App	01.77	76-87	298	1	8
Southampton	Tr	08.87	87-88	64	0	2
Stoke C.	Tr	08.89	89-90	41	0	1
Walsall	Tr	08.91	91-92	47	3	0

STATHAM Mark Andrew
Urmston, 11 November, 1975 (G)

League Club	Source	Date Signed	Seasons Played	Apps	Subs	Gls
Nottingham F.	Jnrs	03.93				
Wigan Ath.	Tr	07.94	94	1	1	0

STATHAM Terence
Shirebrook, 11 March, 1940 (G)

League Club	Source	Date Signed	Seasons Played	Apps	Subs	Gls
Mansfield T.	Jnrs	03.57	56-59	26	-	0

STATON Barry
Doncaster, 9 September, 1938 E Sch/E Yth (LB)

League Club	Source	Date Signed	Seasons Played	Apps	Subs	Gls
Doncaster Rov.	Jnrs	05.56	55-61	85	-	0
Norwich C.	Tr	07.62	62	23	-	1

STAUNTON Stephen
Dundalk, 19 January, 1969 IR Yth/IRu21-4/IR-74 (LB/M)

League Club	Source	Date Signed	Seasons Played	Apps	Subs	Gls
Liverpool	Dundalk	09.86	88-90	55	10	0
Bradford C.	L	11.87	87	7	1	0
Aston Villa	Tr	08.91	91-97	205	3	16

STEAD Kevin
West Ham, 2 October, 1958 (D)

League Club	Source	Date Signed	Seasons Played	Apps	Subs	Gls
Tottenham H.	App	04.76				
Arsenal	Tr	07.77	78	1	1	0

STEAD Michael John
West Ham, 28 February, 1957 (FB)

League Club	Source	Date Signed	Seasons Played	Apps	Subs	Gls
Tottenham H.	App	11.74	75-77	14	1	0
Swansea C.	L	02.77	76	5	0	1
Southend U.	Tr	09.78	78-85	296	1	5
Doncaster Rov.	Tr	11.85	85-87	83	2	0

STEANE Nigel Brian
Nottingham, 18 January, 1963 (F)

League Club	Source	Date Signed	Seasons Played	Apps	Subs	Gls
Sheffield U.	App	01.81	79	0	1	0

STEBBING Gary Stanley
Croydon, 11 August, 1965 E Yth (M)

League Club	Source	Date Signed	Seasons Played	Apps	Subs	Gls
Crystal Palace	App	08.83	83-87	95	7	3
Southend U.	L	01.86	85	5	0	0
Maidstone U.	K.V. Ostend (Bel)	07.89	89-91	69	7	4

STEEDMAN Alexander
Edinburgh, 13 May, 1938 (CF)

League Club	Source	Date Signed	Seasons Played	Apps	Subs	Gls
Barrow		09.64	64	9	-	1

STEEDS Cecil
Bristol, 11 January, 1929 (IF)

League Club	Source	Date Signed	Seasons Played	Apps	Subs	Gls
Bristol C.	Jnrs	03.47	49-51	9	-	0
Bristol Rov.	Tr	05.52	56	1	-	0

STEEL Alfred
Glasgow, 15 August, 1925 (G)

League Club	Source	Date Signed	Seasons Played	Apps	Subs	Gls
Walsall	Petershill	10.47	48-49	2	-	0
Cardiff C.	Tr	01.50	49	10	-	0

STEEL Gregory
Clevedon, 11 March, 1959 (FB)

League Club	Source	Date Signed	Seasons Played	Apps	Subs	Gls
Newport Co.	Clevedon T.	01.78	77	3	0	0

STEEL William James
Dumfries, 4 December, 1959 (F)

League Club	Source	Date Signed	Seasons Played	Apps	Subs	Gls
Oldham Ath.	App	06.78	78-82	101	7	24
Wigan Ath.	L	11.82	82	2	0	2
Wrexham	L	01.83	82	9	0	6
Port Vale	Tr	03.83	82-83	27	1	6
Wrexham	Tr	01.84	83-87	164	0	51
Tranmere Rov.	Tr	11.87	87-91	161	13	29

STEEL Richard
Sedgefield, 13 March, 1930 (FB)

League Club	Source	Date Signed	Seasons Played	Apps	Subs	Gls
Bristol C.	Ferryhill Ath.	06.53	53-55	3	-	0
York C.	Tr	07.56	56-57	3	-	0

STEEL Ronald
Newburn, 3 June, 1929 (OR)

League Club	Source	Date Signed	Seasons Played	Apps	Subs	Gls
Darlington	Bishop Auckland	01.50	49-51	66	-	5

STEEL William
Denny, 1 May, 1923 Died 1982 SF Lge/S-30 (W)

League Club	Source	Date Signed	Seasons Played	Apps	Subs	Gls
Derby Co.	Morton	06.47	47-49	109	-	27

STEELE Bennett John Stanley
Cramlington, 5 August, 1939 (OL)

League Club	Source	Date Signed	Seasons Played	Apps	Subs	Gls
Everton	Seaton Delaval	05.57				
Chesterfield	Tr	05.58	59	18	-	1
Gateshead	Tr	08.59	59	25	-	5

STEELE Eric Graham
Wallsend, 14 May, 1954 (G)

League Club	Source	Date Signed	Seasons Played	Apps	Subs	Gls
Newcastle U.	Jnrs	07.72				
Peterborough U.	Tr	12.73	73-76	124	0	0
Brighton & H. A.	Tr	02.77	76-79	87	0	0
Watford	Tr	10.79	79-83	51	0	0
Cardiff C.	L	03.83	82	7	0	0
Derby Co.	Tr	07.84	84-86	47	0	0
Southend U.	Tr	07.87	87	27	0	0
Mansfield T.	L	03.88	87	5	0	0

STEELE Frederick Charles
Stoke, 6 May, 1916 Died 1976 EF Lge/E-6 (CF)

League Club	Source	Date Signed	Seasons Played	Apps	Subs	Gls
Stoke C.	Downings	08.33	34-48	224	-	140
Mansfield T.	Tr	06.49	49-51	52	-	39
Port Vale	Tr	12.51	51-52	25	-	12

STEELE Hedley Verity
Barnsley, 3 February, 1954 (CD)

League Club	Source	Date Signed	Seasons Played	Apps	Subs	Gls
Exeter C.	Tiverton T.	07.74	74	6	1	1

STEELE James
Edinburgh, 11 March, 1950 (CD)

League Club	Source	Date Signed	Seasons Played	Apps	Subs	Gls
Southampton	Dundee	01.72	71-76	160	1	2

STEELE John
Glasgow, 24 November, 1916 (IL)

League Club	Source	Date Signed	Seasons Played	Apps	Subs	Gls
Barnsley	Ayr U.	06.38	38-48	49	-	21

STEELE Joseph McGuire
Blackridge, 4 October, 1928 Died 1993 (OL)

League Club	Source	Date Signed	Seasons Played	Apps	Subs	Gls
Newcastle U.	Bellshill	12.48				
Bury	Tr	05.50	50	18	-	1
Leyton Orient	Tr	08.51				

STEELE Lee Anthony
Liverpool, 7 December, 1973 (F)

League Club	Source	Date Signed	Seasons Played	Apps	Subs	Gls
Shrewsbury T.	Northwich Vic.	07.97	97	37	1	13

STEELE Percival Edmund
Liverpool, 26 December, 1923 (FB)

League Club	Source	Date Signed	Seasons Played	Apps	Subs	Gls
Tranmere Rov.		01.44	46-56	311	-	0

STEELE Simon Paul
Liverpool, 29 February, 1964 (G)

League Club	Source	Date Signed	Seasons Played	Apps	Subs	Gls
Everton	App	03.82				
Brighton & H. A.	Tr	06.83	83	1	0	0
Blackpool	L	09.83	83	3	0	0
Scunthorpe U. (N/C)	Tr	03.84	83	5	0	0

STEELE Stanley Frederick
Stoke, 5 January, 1937 (IF)

League Club	Source	Date Signed	Seasons Played	Apps	Subs	Gls
Port Vale	Jnrs	05.55	56-60	185	-	66
West Bromwich A.	Tr	03.61	60	1	-	0
Port Vale	Tr	08.61	61-64	148	-	22
Port Vale	Port Elizabeth (SA)	01.68	67	2	0	0

STEELE Timothy Wesley
Coventry, 1 December, 1967 (LM)

League Club	Source	Date Signed	Seasons Played	Apps	Subs	Gls
Shrewsbury T.	App	12.85	85-88	41	20	5
Wolverhampton W.	Tr	02.89	88-92	53	22	7
Stoke C.	L	02.92	91	7	0	1
Bradford C.	Tr	07.93	93	8	3	0
Hereford U.	Tr	01.94	93-95	24	8	2
Exeter C.	Tr	08.96	96	14	14	3

STEELE William McCallum
Kirkmuirhill (Lk), 16 June, 1955 (M)

League Club	Source	Date Signed	Seasons Played	Apps	Subs	Gls
Norwich C.	App	06.73	73-76	56	12	3
Bournemouth	L	01.76	75	7	0	2

STEEN Alan William
Crewe, 26 June, 1922 (W)

League Club	Source	Date Signed	Seasons Played	Apps	Subs	Gls
Wolverhampton W.	Jnrs	03.39	38	1	-	1
Luton T.	Tr	05.46	46	10	-	0
Aldershot	Tr	06.49	49	9	-	0
Rochdale	Tr	06.50	50-51	45	-	8
Carlisle U.	Tr	12.51	51	19	-	2

STEEPLES John
Doncaster, 28 April, 1959 (F)

League Club	Source	Date Signed	Seasons Played	Apps	Subs	Gls
Grimsby T.	Pilkington Rec.	05.80	80-81	4	3	0
Torquay U.	L	09.82	82	4	1	0

STEFANOVIC Dejan
Yugoslavia, 28 October, 1974 Yugoslav Int (CD)

League Club	Source	Date Signed	Seasons Played	Apps	Subs	Gls
Sheffield Wed.	Red Star Belgrade (Yug)	12.95	95-97	51	4	4

STEFFEN Willi
Switzerland, 17 March, 1925 Swiss Int (FB)

League Club	Source	Date Signed	Seasons Played	Apps	Subs	Gls
Chelsea (Am)	Switzerland	11.46	46	15	-	0

STEGGLES Kevin Peter
Bungay, 19 March, 1961 (D)

League Club	Source	Date Signed	Seasons Played	Apps	Subs	Gls
Ipswich T.	App	12.78	80-85	49	1	1
Southend U.	L	02.84	83	3	0	0
Fulham	L	08.86	86	3	0	0
West Bromwich A.	Tr	02.87	86-87	14	0	0
Port Vale	Tr	11.87	87	20	0	0

STEIN Brian
South Africa, 19 October, 1957 Eu21-3/E-1 (F)

League Club	Source	Date Signed	Seasons Played	Apps	Subs	Gls
Luton T.	Edgware T.	10.77	77-87	378	10	127
Luton T.	Annecy (Fr)	07.91	91	32	7	3
Barnet (N/C)	Tr	08.92	92	17	23	8

STEIN Colin Anderson
Linlithgow, 10 May, 1947 Su23-1/SF Lge/S-21 (CF)

League Club	Source	Date Signed	Seasons Played	Apps	Subs	Gls
Coventry C.	Glasgow Rangers	10.72	72-74	83	0	22

STEIN Edward
South Africa, 28 September, 1955 (M)

League Club	Source	Date Signed	Seasons Played	Apps	Subs	Gls
Barnet	Dagenham	07.82	91	0	1	0

STEIN Earl **Mark** Sean
Capetown, South Africa, 29 January, 1966 E Yth (F)

League Club	Source	Date Signed	Seasons Played	Apps	Subs	Gls
Luton T.	Jnrs	01.84	83-87	41	13	19
Aldershot	L	01.86	85	2	0	1
Queens Park R.	Tr	08.88	88-89	20	13	4
Oxford U.	Tr	09.89	89-91	72	10	18
Stoke C.	Tr	09.91	91-93	94	0	50
Chelsea	Tr	10.93	93-95	46	4	21
Stoke C.	L	11.96	96	11	0	4
Ipswich T.	L	08.97	97	6	1	2
Bournemouth	L	03.98	97	11	0	4

STEINER Geoffrey Gordon
Hackney, 8 June, 1928 (FB)

League Club	Source	Date Signed	Seasons Played	Apps	Subs	Gls
Watford	Barnet	11.50	51	3	-	0

STEINER Robert Herman
Sweden, 20 June, 1973 (F)

League Club	Source	Date Signed	Seasons Played	Apps	Subs	Gls
Bradford C. (L)	Norrkoping (Swe)	10.96	96	14	1	3
Bradford C.	Norrkoping (Swe)	07.97	97	26	11	10

STEJSKAL Jan
Czechoslavakia, 15 January, 1962 Czechoslovakian Int (G)

League Club	Source	Date Signed	Seasons Played	Apps	Subs	Gls
Queens Park R.	Sparta Prague (Cz)	10.90	90-93	107	0	0

STELL Barry
Felling, 3 September, 1961 (M)

League Club	Source	Date Signed	Seasons Played	Apps	Subs	Gls
Sheffield Wed.	App	09.79				
Darlington	Tr	10.79	80	7	2	0

STELLING John (Jack) Graham
Washington, 23 May, 1924 Died 1993 (FB)

League Club	Source	Date Signed	Seasons Played	Apps	Subs	Gls
Sunderland	Usworth Colly	11.44	46-55	259	-	8

STEMP Wayne Darren
Plymouth, 9 September, 1970 (FB)

League Club	Source	Date Signed	Seasons Played	Apps	Subs	Gls
Brighton & H. A.	YT	10.88	89-90	4	0	0

STENHOUSE Alexander
Stirling, 1 January, 1933 (OR)

League Club	Source	Date Signed	Seasons Played	Apps	Subs	Gls
Portsmouth	Guildford C.	02.57	56-57	4	-	1
Southend U.	Tr	11.58	58-60	84	-	7

STENNER Arthur William John
Yeovil, 7 January, 1934 (OL)

League Club	Source	Date Signed	Seasons Played	Apps	Subs	Gls
Bristol C.	Yeovil	08.54				
Plymouth Arg.	Tr	08.55	55	9	-	1
Norwich C.	Tr	08.56	56	6	-	0
Oldham Ath.	Exeter C. (trial)	04.57	56	3	-	0

League Club	Source	Date Signed	Seasons Played	Apps	Subs	Gls
STENSON Gerard (Ged) Patrick						
Bootle, 30 December, 1959						(M)
Port Vale	Everton (App)	08.78	78-79	11	1	0
STENSON John Andrew						
Catford, 16 December, 1949 E Sch/E Yth						(M)
Charlton Ath.	App	12.66	67-68	3	8	0
Mansfield T.	Tr	06.69	69-71	103	4	21
Peterborough U.	L	01.72	71	2	0	0
Aldershot	Tr	07.72	72-73	34	11	4
STEPANOVIC Dragoslav						
Yugoslavia, 30 August, 1948 Yugoslav Int						(D)
Manchester C.	Wormatia (Ger)	08.79	79-80	14	1	0
STEPHAN Harold William						
Farnworth, 24 February, 1924						(WH)
Blackburn Rov.		09.44	46-47	13	-	1
Accrington St.	Tr	09.48				
STEPHEN George Allan						
Ellon, 21 September, 1927						(FB)
Aldershot		08.48	48	2	-	0
STEPHEN James Findlay						
Fettercairn, 23 August, 1922 S-2						(FB)
Bradford P. A.	Johnshaven	08.39	46-48	94	-	0
Portsmouth	Tr	11.49	49-53	100	-	0
STEPHENS Alan						
Liverpool, 13 October, 1952						(FB)
Wolverhampton W.	App	10.70				
Crewe Alex.	Tr	07.72	72-73	30	3	0
STEPHENS Alfred						
Cramlington, 13 June, 1919 Died 1993						(IF)
Leeds U.	Cramlington B.W.	09.38				
Swindon T.	Tr	08.46	46-47	16	-	2
STEPHENS Arnold Edwin						
Ross-on-Wye, 31 January, 1928 Died 1955						(W)
Wolverhampton W.	Jnrs	04.45				
Bournemouth	Tr	12.48	48-53	70	-	12
STEPHENS Arthur (Archie)						
Liverpool, 19 May, 1954						(F)
Bristol Rov.	Melksham T.	08.81	81-84	100	27	40
Middlesbrough	Tr	03.85	84-87	87	5	24
Carlisle U.	Tr	12.87	87-88	20	4	3
Darlington	Tr	03.89	88	10	0	4
STEPHENS Herbert James						
Chatham, 13 May, 1909 Died 1987						(OL)
Brentford	Ealing Ass.	02.31	31-32	6	-	1
Brighton & H. A.	Tr	06.35	35-47	180	-	86
STEPHENS William **John**						
Cardiff, 26 June, 1935 Died 1992 Wu23-1						(OR)
Hull C.	Jnrs	08.53	52-57	94	-	20
Swindon T.	Tr	06.58	58-59	18	-	2
Coventry C.	Tr	02.60	59	14	-	0
STEPHENS Kenneth John						
Bristol, 14 November, 1946						(W)
West Bromwich A.	App	11.64	66-67	21	1	2
Walsall	Tr	12.68	68-69	6	1	0
Bristol Rov.	Tr	10.70	70-77	215	10	11
Hereford U.	Tr	10.77	77-79	56	4	2
STEPHENS Kirk William						
Coventry, 27 February, 1955						(RB)
Luton T.	Nuneaton Borough	06.78	78-83	226	1	2
Coventry C.	Tr	08.84	84-85	33	1	2
STEPHENS Lee Michael						
Cardiff, 30 September, 1971						(F)
Cardiff C.	YT	07.90	90	1	2	0
STEPHENS Malcolm Keith						
Doncaster, 17 February, 1930						(IF)
Brighton & H. A.		07.54	54-56	29	-	14
Rotherham U.	Tr	07.57	57	12	-	3
Doncaster Rov.	Tr	07.58	58	11	-	2
STEPHENS Terence Guy						
Neath, 5 November, 1935						(IF)
Tranmere Rov.	Everton (Am)	08.55	55-56	15	-	5

League Club	Source	Date Signed	Seasons Played	Apps	Subs	Gls
STEPHENS William John						
Cramlington, 13 June, 1919 Died 1974						(CF)
Leeds U.	Cramlington B.W.	09.38				
Swindon T.	Tr	07.46	46-47	47	-	26
West Ham U.	Tr	12.47	47-48	22	-	6
STEPHENSON Alan Charles						
Chesham, 26 September, 1944 Eu23-7						(CH)
Crystal Palace	Jnrs	02.62	61-67	170	0	13
West Ham U.	Tr	03.68	67-71	106	2	0
Fulham	L	10.71	71	10	0	0
Portsmouth	Tr	05.72	72-74	98	0	1
STEPHENSON Ashlyn						
South Africa, 6 July, 1974 E Yth						(G)
Darlington	Waterford	09.95	95	1	0	0
STEPHENSON Geoffrey						
Tynemouth, 28 April, 1970						(FB)
Grimsby T.	YT	07.88	88-89	19	2	0
STEPHENSON Robert **Leonard**						
Blackpool, 14 July, 1930						(CF)
Blackpool	Highfield Y.C.	11.48	50-54	24	-	10
Port Vale	Tr	03.55	54-56	61	-	16
Oldham Ath.	Tr	06.57	57	8	-	0
STEPHENSON Paul						
Wallsend, 2 January, 1968 E Yth						(RW)
Newcastle U.	App	12.85	85-88	58	3	1
Millwall	Tr	11.88	88-92	81	17	6
Gillingham	L	11.92	92	12	0	2
Brentford	Tr	03.93	92-94	70	0	2
York C.	Tr	08.95	95-97	91	6	8
Hartlepool U.	Tr	03.98	97	3	0	0
STEPHENSON Peter						
Ashington, 2 May, 1936						(OR)
Middlesbrough		08.55				
Gateshead	Ashington	09.59	59	35	-	6
STEPHENSON George **Robert**						
Derby, 19 November, 1942						(F)
Derby Co.	Jnrs	09.60	61-62	11	-	1
Shrewsbury T.	Tr	06.64	64	3	-	0
Rochdale	Tr	07.65	65-66	50	1	16
STEPHENSON Ronald						
Barrow, 13 April, 1948						(WH)
Barrow	App	05.66	66-67	2	0	1
STEPHENSON Roy						
Crook, 27 May, 1932						(OR)
Burnley	Jnrs	06.49	49-55	78	-	27
Rotherham U.	Tr	09.56	56-57	43	-	14
Blackburn Rov.	Tr	11.57	57-58	21	-	5
Leicester C.	Tr	03.59	58-59	12	-	0
Ipswich T.	Tr	07.60	60-64	144	-	21
STEPNEY Alexander Cyril						
Mitcham, 18 September, 1942 Eu23-3/EF Lge/E-1						(G)
Millwall	Tooting & Mitcham	05.63	63-65	137	0	0
Chelsea	Tr	05.66	66	1	0	0
Manchester U.	Tr	09.66	66-77	433	0	2
STEPNEY Robin Edward						
Horsham, 26 February, 1936						(IF/WH)
Aldershot	Redhill	09.58	58-64	213	-	36
STERLAND Melvyn						
Sheffield, 1 October, 1961 Eu21-7/E 'B'/EF Lge/E-1						(RB)
Sheffield Wed.	App	10.79	78-88	271	8	37
Leeds U.	Glasgow Rangers	07.89	89-92	111	3	16
STERLING Worrell Ricardo						
Bethnal Green, 8 June, 1965						(W)
Watford	App	06.83	82-88	82	12	14
Peterborough U.	Tr	03.89	88-92	190	3	28
Bristol Rov.	Tr	07.93	93-95	117	2	6
Lincoln C.	Tr	07.96	96	15	6	0
STEVEN Trevor McGregor						
Berwick, 21 September, 1963 E Yth/Eu21-2/E-36						(RM)
Burnley	App	09.81	80-82	74	2	11
Everton	Tr	07.83	83-88	210	4	48
STEVENS Arthur						
Wandsworth, 13 January, 1921						(OR)
Fulham	Sutton U.	12.43	46-58	386	-	110

League Club	Source	Date Signed	Seasons Played	Apps	Subs	Gls
STEVENS Brian Edward						
Andover, 13 November, 1933 Died 1980						(G)
Southampton	Andover O.B.	09.56	56-57	12	-	0
STEVENS Dennis						
Dudley, 30 November, 1933 Eu23-2/EF Lge						(IF)
Bolton W.	Jnrs	12.50	53-61	273	-	90
Everton	Tr	03.62	61-65	120	0	20
Oldham Ath.	Tr	12.65	65-66	33	0	0
Tranmere Rov.	Tr	03.67	66-67	28	4	3
STEVENS Gary Andrew						
Hillingdon, 30 March, 1962 Eu21-8/E-7						(RB/M)
Brighton & H. A.	App	10.79	79-82	120	13	2
Tottenham H.	Tr	06.83	83-89	140	7	6
Portsmouth	Tr	01.90	89-90	52	0	3
STEVENS Gary Martin						
Birmingham, 30 August, 1954						(F/CD)
Cardiff C.	Evesham	09.78	78-82	138	12	44
Shrewsbury T.	Tr	09.82	82-85	144	6	30
Brentford	Tr	07.86	86	29	3	10
Hereford U.	Tr	03.87	86-89	85	9	10
STEVENS Michael **Gary**						
Barrow, 27 March, 1963 E 'B'/E-46						(RB)
Everton	App	03.81	81-87	207	1	8
Tranmere Rov.	Glasgow Rangers	09.94	94-97	126	1	2
STEVENS Gregor MacKenzie						
Glasgow, 13 January, 1955 Su21-1						(CD)
Leicester C.	Motherwell	05.79	79	4	0	0
STEVENS Ian David						
Malta, 21 October, 1966						(F)
Preston N. E.	YT	11.84	84-85	9	2	2
Stockport Co. (N/C)	Lancaster C.	10.86	86	1	1	0
Bolton W.	Lancaster C.	03.87	86-90	26	21	7
Bury	Tr	07.91	91-93	100	10	38
Shrewsbury T.	Tr	08.94	94-96	94	17	37
Carlisle U.	Tr	05.97	97	33	4	17
STEVENS John Miles						
Fores, 21 August, 1941						(CF)
Swindon T.		06.62	62-63	22	-	10
STEVENS Keith Henry						
Merton, 21 June, 1964						(D)
Millwall	App	06.81	80-97	451	8	9
STEVENS Leslie William George						
Croydon, 15 August, 1920 Died 1991						(OL)
Tottenham H.	Jnrs	01.40	46-48	54	-	5
Bradford P. A.	Tr	02.49	48-49	44	-	4
Crystal Palace	Tr	08.50	50	20	-	3
STEVENS Mark Anthony						
Bristol, 31 January, 1963						(G)
Bristol C.	App	02.81				
Swindon T.	Tr	06.81	82	1	0	0
STEVENS Mark Richard						
Swindon, 3 December, 1977 E Sch						(CD)
Oxford U.	Jnrs	07.96	97	0	1	0
STEVENS Norman John						
Shoreham, 13 May, 1938						(FB)
Brighton & H. A.	Jnrs	10.55	58	1	-	0
STEVENS Paul David						
Bristol, 4 April, 1960						(RB)
Bristol C.	App	04.78	77-84	146	1	3
STEVENS Samuel Batson						
Rutherglen, 2 December, 1935						(WH)
Southampton	Airdrieonians	06.57	58	14	-	0
STEVENSON Alan						
Staveley, 6 November, 1950						(G)
Chesterfield	Jnrs	10.69	69-71	104	0	0
Burnley	Tr	01.72	71-82	438	0	0
Rotherham U.	Tr	08.83	83	24	0	0
Hartlepool U.	Tr	09.84	84	35	0	0
STEVENSON Alexander Ernest						
Dublin, 9 August, 1912 Died 1985 IR-7/NI-17						(IF)
Everton	Glasgow Rangers	01.34	33-48	255	-	82
STEVENSON Andrew John						
Scunthorpe, 29 September, 1967						(D)
Scunthorpe U.	Jnrs	01.86	85-92	78	25	4
Doncaster Rov.	L	01.92	91	1	0	0
STEVENSON Arthur						
Lanchester, 2 March, 1924 Died 1989						(RB)
Doncaster Rov.	Denaby U.	11.44	47-48	14	-	0
STEVENSON William **Byron**						
Llanelli, 7 September, 1956 Wu21-3/W-15						(M)
Leeds U.	App	09.73	74-81	88	7	4
Birmingham C.	Tr	03.82	81-84	69	5	3
Bristol Rov.	Tr	07.85	85	30	1	3
STEVENSON Ernest						
Rotherham, 28 December, 1923 Died 1970						(IF)
Wolverhampton W.	Jnrs	12.40	47-48	8	-	0
Cardiff C.	Tr	10.48	48-49	50	-	15
Southampton	Tr	02.50	49-50	24	-	8
Leeds U.	Tr	02.51	50-51	16	-	5
STEVENSON Walter Harry **Horace**						
Derby, 26 June, 1923						(OR)
Nottingham F.		11.44				
Ipswich T.	Tr	02.48	47	3	-	0
STEVENSON James						
Bellshill, 4 August, 1946 S Sch						(WH)
Southend U.	Hibernian	07.67	67	33	1	0
STEVENSON Morris John						
Tranent, 16 April, 1943						(IF)
Luton T.	Morton	11.68	68	1	0	0
STEVENSON Nigel Charles Ashley						
Swansea, 2 November, 1958 Wu21-2/W-4						(CD)
Swansea C.	App	11.76	75-86	247	12	15
Cardiff C.	L	10.85	85	14	0	0
Reading	L	03.86	85	3	0	0
Cardiff C.	Tr	08.87	87-88	66	2	2
STEVENSON William						
Leith, 26 October, 1939 SF Lge						(WH)
Liverpool	Glasgow Rangers	10.62	62-67	188	0	15
Stoke C.	Tr	12.67	67-72	82	12	5
Tranmere Rov.	Tr	07.73	73	20	0	0
STEWART Alan Victor						
Newcastle, 24 July, 1922						(CH)
Huddersfield T.		04.40	46-48	14	-	0
York C.	Tr	08.49	49-56	208	-	1
STEWART Andrew Couper						
Methil, 29 October, 1956						(F)
Portsmouth	App	07.74	73-75	14	5	3
STEWART Arthur						
Ballymena, 13 January, 1942 NI-7						(WH)
Derby Co.	Glentoran	12.67	67-69	29	1	1
STEWART David Steel						
Glasgow, 11 March, 1947 Su23-7/S-1						(G)
Leeds U.	Ayr U.	10.73	73-78	55	0	0
West Bromwich A.	Tr	11.78				
Swansea C.	Tr	02.80	79-80	57	0	0
STEWART Charles **David**						
Belfast, 20 May, 1958 NI-1						(W)
Hull C.	App	08.75	74-78	46	5	7
Chelsea	Tr	05.79				
Scunthorpe U.	Tr	11.79	79-81	88	9	19
Hartlepool U. (N/C)	Goole T.	03.83	82	6	2	0
STEWART Edward McDonald						
Dundee, 15 November, 1934						(WH)
Norwich C.	Dundee U.	07.57	57	13	-	0
STEWART George Gartshone						
Chirnside, 18 October, 1920						(IF)
Brentford	Hamilton Academical	08.46	46-47	24	-	3
Queens Park R.	Tr	03.48	47-52	38	-	5
Shrewsbury T.	Tr	01.53	52	10	-	2
STEWART George Scott						
Larkhall, 16 November, 1932						(G)
Bradford C.	East Stirling	05.59	59-60	22	-	0

STEWART George Thompson Scott
Buckie, 17 February, 1927 (CF)

League Club	Source	Date Signed	Seasons Played	Apps	Subs	Gls
Accrington St.	St Mirren	09.54	54-58	182	-	136
Coventry C.	Tr	11.58	58-59	40	-	23
Carlisle U.	Tr	06.60	60	7	-	2

STEWART Gerald
Dundee, 2 September, 1946 (G)

League Club	Source	Date Signed	Seasons Played	Apps	Subs	Gls
Preston N. E.	Jnrs	09.63	66-69	4	0	0
Barnsley	Tr	09.71	71-74	138	0	0

STEWART James **Gordon**
South Africa, 7 August, 1927 Died 1980 (IR)

League Club	Source	Date Signed	Seasons Played	Apps	Subs	Gls
Leeds U.	Parkhill (SA)	10.51	51-52	9	-	2

STEWART Graham
Birkenhead, 8 March, 1938 (F)

League Club	Source	Date Signed	Seasons Played	Apps	Subs	Gls
Sheffield U.	Everton (Am)	08.58				
Chesterfield	Tr	05.59	59	5	-	2

STEWART Henry
Wigan, 28 April, 1925 Died 1996 (LB)

League Club	Source	Date Signed	Seasons Played	Apps	Subs	Gls
Huddersfield T.	Thorne Colly	08.48	48-50	49	-	0

STEWART Ian Edwin
Belfast, 10 September, 1961 NI Sch/NI-31 (LW)

League Club	Source	Date Signed	Seasons Played	Apps	Subs	Gls
Queens Park R.	Jnrs	05.80	80-84	55	12	2
Millwall	L	03.83	82	10	1	3
Newcastle U.	Tr	08.85	85-86	34	8	3
Portsmouth	Tr	07.87	87	0	1	0
Brentford	L	02.88	87	4	3	0
Aldershot	Tr	01.89	88-90	94	7	0

STEWART James Garvin
Kilwinning, 9 March, 1954 Su21-3/Su23-5/S-2 (G)

League Club	Source	Date Signed	Seasons Played	Apps	Subs	Gls
Middlesbrough	Kilmarnock	06.78	78-80	34	0	0

STEWART John
Armadale, 23 January, 1929 (OR)

League Club	Source	Date Signed	Seasons Played	Apps	Subs	Gls
Walsall	East Fife	06.57	57	28	-	4

STEWART John Barry
Middlesbrough, 28 March, 1937 (OR)

League Club	Source	Date Signed	Seasons Played	Apps	Subs	Gls
York C.	Whitby T.	09.56	56	1	-	0
Darlington	Tr	12.57				

STEWART John (Jackie) Gebbie
Lochgelly, 4 September, 1921 Died 1990 (OR)

League Club	Source	Date Signed	Seasons Played	Apps	Subs	Gls
Birmingham C.	Raith Rov.	01.48	47-54	203	-	54

STEWART William **Marcus** Paul
Bristol, 7 November, 1972 E Sch (F)

League Club	Source	Date Signed	Seasons Played	Apps	Subs	Gls
Bristol Rov.	YT	07.91	91-95	137	34	57
Huddersfield T.	Tr	07.96	96-97	57	4	23

STEWART Michael James
Herne Hill, 16 September, 1932 E Amat (IF)

League Club	Source	Date Signed	Seasons Played	Apps	Subs	Gls
Charlton Ath.	Corinthian Casuals	10.56	56-58	9	-	3

STEWART Paul Andrew
Manchester, 7 October, 1964 E Yth/Eu21-1/E-'B'/E-3 (F/M)

League Club	Source	Date Signed	Seasons Played	Apps	Subs	Gls
Blackpool	App	10.81	81-86	188	13	56
Manchester C.	Tr	03.87	86-87	51	0	26
Tottenham H.	Tr	06.88	88-91	126	5	28
Liverpool	Tr	07.92	92-93	28	4	1
Crystal Palace	L	01.94	93	18	0	3
Wolverhampton W.	L	09.94	94	5	3	2
Burnley	L	02.95	94	6	0	0
Sunderland	L	08.95	95	1	1	0
Sunderland	Tr	03.96	95-96	30	4	5
Stoke C.	Tr	06.97	97	22	0	3

STEWART Raymond Strean McDonald
Perth, 7 September, 1959 S Sch/Su21-12/S-10 (RB)

League Club	Source	Date Signed	Seasons Played	Apps	Subs	Gls
West Ham U.	Dundee U.	09.79	79-90	344	1	62

STEWART Reginald
Sheffield, 30 October, 1925 (CH)

League Club	Source	Date Signed	Seasons Played	Apps	Subs	Gls
Sheffield Wed.	Sheffield Y.M.C.A.	09.44	46	6	-	0
Colchester U.	Tr	07.50	50-56	256	-	2

STEWART Robert
Kirkcaldy, 4 December, 1933 S Sch (IF)

League Club	Source	Date Signed	Seasons Played	Apps	Subs	Gls
Crewe Alex.	St Mirren	08.55	55	22	-	3

STEWART Robert Ashcroft
Broxburn, 14 June, 1971 (M)

League Club	Source	Date Signed	Seasons Played	Apps	Subs	Gls
Doncaster Rov.	YT	•	88	1	0	0

STEWART Simon Andrew
Leeds, 1 November, 1973 (CD)

League Club	Source	Date Signed	Seasons Played	Apps	Subs	Gls
Sheffield Wed.	YT	07.92	92	6	0	0
Shrewsbury T.	L	08.95	95	4	0	0
Fulham	Tr	06.96	96	2	1	0

STEWART William
Clydebank, 10 March, 1922 Died 1987 (IF)

League Club	Source	Date Signed	Seasons Played	Apps	Subs	Gls
Aldershot	St Mirren	06.51	51-53	27	-	4

STEWART William Ian
Liverpool, 1 January, 1965 (G)

League Club	Source	Date Signed	Seasons Played	Apps	Subs	Gls
Liverpool	App	01.83				
Wigan Ath.	Tr	07.84	84-85	14	0	0
Chester C.	Tr	08.86	86-93	272	0	0
Northampton T.	Tr	07.94	94	26	1	0
Chesterfield	L	03.95	94	1	0	0
Chester C.	Tr	07.95	95	45	0	0

STIFFLE Nelson Everard
India, 30 July, 1928 (OR)

League Club	Source	Date Signed	Seasons Played	Apps	Subs	Gls
Chester C.	Ashton U.	12.51	51	7	-	2
Chesterfield	Altrincham	03.54	54	38	-	9
Bournemouth	Tr	05.55	55-57	35	-	7
Exeter C.	Tr	03.58	57-59	94	-	17
Coventry C.	Tr	07.60	60	15	-	2

STILES John Charles
Manchester, 6 May, 1964 (M)

League Club	Source	Date Signed	Seasons Played	Apps	Subs	Gls
Leeds U.	Vancouver (Can)	05.84	84-88	49	16	2
Doncaster Rov.	Tr	08.89	89-91	88	1	2
Rochdale	L	03.92	91	2	2	0

STILES Norbert (Nobby) Peter
Manchester, 18 May, 1942 E Sch/E Yth/Eu23-3/EF Lge/E-28 (WH)

League Club	Source	Date Signed	Seasons Played	Apps	Subs	Gls
Manchester U.	Jnrs	06.59	60-70	311	0	17
Middlesbrough	Tr	05.71	71-72	57	0	2
Preston N.E.	Tr	08.73	73-74	44	2	1

STILL John Leonard
West Ham, 24 April, 1950 (CH)

League Club	Source	Date Signed	Seasons Played	Apps	Subs	Gls
Leyton Orient (Am)	Jnrs	05.67	67	1	0	0

STILL Robert Arthur
Chorley, 15 December, 1912 Died 1983 (WH)

League Club	Source	Date Signed	Seasons Played	Apps	Subs	Gls
Stockport Co.	Chorley	06.34	34-38	155	-	2
Crewe Alex.	Tr	08.39	46	1	-	0

STILL Ronald George
Aberdeen, 10 June, 1943 (CF)

League Club	Source	Date Signed	Seasons Played	Apps	Subs	Gls
Arsenal	Woodside B.C.	08.61				
Notts Co.	Tr	07.65	65-66	46	0	15
Brentford	Tr	07.67	67	1	0	0

STILLE Giles Kevin
Westminster, 10 November, 1958 (M)

League Club	Source	Date Signed	Seasons Played	Apps	Subs	Gls
Brighton & H. A.	Kingstonian	05.79	79-83	20	7	4

STILLYARDS George Edward William
Lincoln, 29 December, 1918 (D)

League Club	Source	Date Signed	Seasons Played	Apps	Subs	Gls
Lincoln C.	Botolph U.	11.42	46-48	100	-	2

STIMAC Igor
Croatia, 6 September, 1967 Croatian Int (CD)

League Club	Source	Date Signed	Seasons Played	Apps	Subs	Gls
Derby Co.	Hadjuk Split (Co)	10.95	95-97	70	0	3

STIMPSON Barrie George
Billingham, 8 February, 1964 (LB)

League Club	Source	Date Signed	Seasons Played	Apps	Subs	Gls
Hartlepool U.	App	02.82	80-83	66	2	2
Chesterfield	Tr	11.83	83	28	0	0
Hartlepool U.	Tr	11.84	84	18	0	0

STIMSON Mark Nicholas
Plaistow, 27 December, 1967 (LB)

League Club	Source	Date Signed	Seasons Played	Apps	Subs	Gls
Tottenham H.	YT	07.85	86-88	1	1	0
Leyton Orient	L	03.88	87	10	0	0
Gillingham	L	01.89	88	18	0	0
Newcastle U.	Tr	06.89	89-92	82	4	2
Portsmouth	L	12.92	92	3	1	0
Portsmouth	Tr	07.93	93-95	57	1	2
Barnet	L	09.95	95	5	0	0
Southend U.	Tr	03.96	95-97	34	5	0

STINSON Hugh Michael John
Bacup, 18 May, 1937 (WH)

League Club	Source	Date Signed	Seasons Played	Apps	Subs	Gls
Accrington St.	Jnrs	05.55	58	3	-	0
Gillingham	Tr	07.59	59	1	-	0

League Club	Source	Date Signed	Seasons Played	Apps	Subs	Gls
STIRK John						
Consett, 5 September, 1955 E Yth						(RB)
Ipswich T.	App	06.73	77	6	0	0
Watford	Tr	06.78	78	46	0	0
Chesterfield	Tr	03.80	79-82	54	2	0
STIRLAND John **Cecil**						
Adwick-le-Street, 15 July, 1921						(WH)
Doncaster Rov.	Jnrs	07.38	46-48	68	-	0
New Brighton	Tr	01.50	49-50	51	-	0
Scunthorpe U.	Tr	08.51	51	17	-	0
STIRLING James Russell						
Airdrie, 23 July, 1925						(CH)
Bournemouth	Coltness U.	07.47	47-49	73	-	1
Birmingham C.	Tr	06.50				
Southend U.	Tr	12.50	50-59	218	-	2
STITFALL Albert Edward						
Cardiff, 7 July, 1924						(FB)
Cardiff C.	Jnrs	11.48	48-51	9	-	1
Torquay U.	Tr	03.52	51-52	22	-	1
STITFALL Ronald Frederick						
Cardiff, 14 December, 1925 W-2						(FB)
Cardiff C.	Jnrs	09.47	47-63	402	-	8
STOBART Barry Henry						
Doncaster, 6 June, 1938						(CF)
Wolverhampton W.	Jnrs	12.55	59-63	49	-	20
Manchester C.	Tr	08.64	64	14	-	1
Aston Villa	Tr	11.64	64-67	45	0	18
Shrewsbury T.	Tr	10.67	67-68	34	2	9
STOBART Sean Anthony						
Wolverhampton, 31 July, 1966						(F)
Scunthorpe U. (N/C)	Jnrs	07.84	85	0	2	1
STOBBART George Campbell						
Morpeth, 9 January, 1921 Died 1995						(IF)
Middlesbrough	Netherfield	11.45				
Newcastle U.	Tr	09.46	46-48	66	-	21
Luton T.	Tr	10.49	49-51	107	-	30
Millwall	Tr	08.52	52-53	68	-	27
Brentford	Tr	05.54	54-55	57	-	17
STOCK Harry						
Stockport, 31 July, 1918 Died 1977						(IF)
Stockport Co.		07.38	38-47	19	-	5
Oldham Ath.	Tr	07.48	48-50	35	-	10
STOCK Russell John						
Great Yarmouth, 25 June, 1977						(M)
Cambridge U.	YT	07.95	95	15	2	1
STOCKDALE Robert Keith						
Middlesbrough, 30 November, 1979						(RB)
Middlesbrough	YT	●	97	1	0	0
STOCKIN Ronald						
Birmingham, 27 June, 1931						(IF)
Walsall	West Bromwich A. (Am)	01.52	51	6	-	3
Wolverhampton W.	Tr	02.52	52-53	21	-	7
Cardiff C.	Tr	06.54	54-56	57	-	16
Grimsby T.	Tr	06.57	57-59	49	-	14
STOCKLEY Kenneth Sidney						
Watford, 24 November, 1926						(LH)
Luton T.	Jnrs	02.44				
Watford	Tr	07.48	49	1	-	0
STOCKLEY Samuel Joshua						
Tiverton, 5 September, 1977						(RB)
Southampton	YT	07.96				
Barnet	Tr	12.96	96-97	61	1	0
STOCKS David Henry						
Dulwich, 20 April, 1943						(D)
Charlton Ath.	Jnrs	01.62	61-64	26	-	0
Gillingham	Tr	05.65	65	45	0	0
Bournemouth	Tr	06.66	66-71	220	0	2
Torquay U.	Tr	01.72	71-76	150	0	3
STOCKS Joseph Ronald						
Hull, 27 November, 1941						(WH)
Hull C.	Jnrs	12.58	59-60	9	-	1
Millwall	Tr	08.61	61-63	30	-	1

League Club	Source	Date Signed	Seasons Played	Apps	Subs	Gls
STOCKWELL Michael Thomas						
Chelmsford, 14 February, 1965						(M/RB)
Ipswich T.	App	12.82	85-97	420	21	31
STODDART Terence						
Newcastle, 28 November, 1931						(LH)
Newcastle U.	Jnrs	01.49				
Darlington	Tr	05.54	54-55	8	-	0
York C.	Tr	07.56	56	3	-	0
STOKER Gareth						
Bishop Auckland, 22 February, 1973						(M/CD)
Hull C.	Leeds U. (YT)	09.91	91-92	24	6	2
Hereford U.	Bishop Auckland	03.95	94-96	65	5	6
Cardiff C.	Tr	01.97	96-97	29	8	4
STOKES Albert William						
Sheffield, 26 January, 1933						(CF)
Grimsby T.	Hampton Sports	02.54	54-56	16	-	3
Scunthorpe U.	Tr	07.57	57	5	-	2
Southport	Tr	02.59	58	6	-	2
STOKES Alfred Edward						
Hackney, 3 October, 1932 Eu23-1/EF Lge/E 'B'						(IF)
Tottenham H.	Clapton	02.53	52-58	65	-	40
Fulham	Tr	07.59	59	15	-	6
Watford	Cambridge C.	04.61	61	14	-	2
STOKES Dean Anthony						
Birmingham, 23 May, 1970						(LB)
Port Vale	Halesowen T.	01.93	93-97	53	7	0
STOKES Derek						
Normanton, 13 September, 1939 Eu23-4						(CF)
Bradford C.	Jnrs	04.57	57-59	94	-	44
Huddersfield T.	Tr	06.60	60-64	153	-	65
Bradford C.	Tr	01.66	65-66	31	1	11
STOKES Robert William Thomas						
Portsmouth, 30 January, 1951 Died 1995 E Yth						(F)
Southampton	App	02.68	68-76	194	22	40
Portsmouth	Tr	08.77	77	23	1	2
STOKES Wayne Darren						
Wolverhampton, 16 February, 1965						(CD)
Gillingham	Coventry C. (App)	07.82	82-83	2	1	0
Stockport Co.	Gloucester C.	10.86	86	17	1	1
Hartlepool U.	Tr	07.87	87-89	62	0	1
STOKLE David						
Hartlepool, 1 December, 1969						(CD)
Hartlepool U.	YT	07.88	86-89	9	0	0
STOKOE Dennis						
Blyth, 6 June, 1925						(WH)
Chesterfield	North Shields	01.47				
Carlisle U.	Tr	07.48	48-53	151	-	2
Workington	Tr	10.53	53-55	107	-	2
Gateshead	Tr	08.56	56	13	-	0
STOKOE Graham						
Newcastle-under-Lyme, 17 December, 1975						(M)
Stoke C.	Newcastle U. (YT)	07.94	96	0	2	0
Hartlepool U.	L	02.96	95	8	0	0
STOKOE Robert						
Prudhoe, 21 September, 1930						(CH)
Newcastle U.	Jnrs	09.47	50-60	261	-	4
Bury	Tr	02.61	60-63	81	-	0
STONE David Kenneth						
Bristol, 29 December, 1942						(HB)
Bristol Rov.	Jnrs	03.60	62-67	145	3	6
Southend U.	Tr	07.68	68	6	0	0
STONE Edward Leonard						
Aberdeen, 5 January, 1942						(F)
Charlton Ath.	Jnrs	08.59				
Crystal Palace	Tr	05.61	61	1	-	0
STONE Frederick						
Bristol, 5 July, 1925						(FB)
Bristol C.		06.47	47-52	64	-	3
STONE Geoffrey						
Mansfield, 10 April, 1924 Died 1993						(CH)
Notts Co.	Beeston B.C.	09.48	48-49	4	-	0
Darlington	Tr	08.50	50-51	31	-	0

STONE John George
Redcar, 3 March, 1953 (FB)

League Club	Source	Date Signed	Seasons Played	Apps	Subs	Gls
Middlesbrough	South Bank	07.70	71	2	0	0
York C.	Tr	07.72	72-75	86	0	5
Darlington	Tr	07.76	76-78	120	0	14
Grimsby T.	Tr	07.79	79-82	89	5	2
Rotherham U.	Tr	09.83	83	10	0	1

STONE Michael
Hucknall, 23 May, 1938 (G)

League Club	Source	Date Signed	Seasons Played	Apps	Subs	Gls
Notts Co.	Linby Colly	07.58	58	7	-	0

STONE Peter James
Oxford, 8 October, 1922 (CH)

League Club	Source	Date Signed	Seasons Played	Apps	Subs	Gls
Luton T. (Am)	Oxford C.	12.51	51	1	-	0

STONE Steven Brian
Gateshead, 20 August, 1971 E-9 (RM)

League Club	Source	Date Signed	Seasons Played	Apps	Subs	Gls
Nottingham F.	YT	05.89	91-97	163	4	20

STONEHOUSE Basil Henry
Guisborough, 27 October, 1952 (D)

League Club	Source	Date Signed	Seasons Played	Apps	Subs	Gls
Middlesbrough	App	12.69				
Halifax T.	L	10.72	72	1	1	0

STONEHOUSE Bernard
Manchester, 23 December, 1934 (OL)

League Club	Source	Date Signed	Seasons Played	Apps	Subs	Gls
Rochdale	Crewe Alex. (Am)	08.55	55-56	19	-	1

STONEHOUSE Derek
Skelton, 18 November, 1932 E Yth (FB)

League Club	Source	Date Signed	Seasons Played	Apps	Subs	Gls
Middlesbrough	Lingdale	05.51	53-61	174	-	0
Hartlepool U.	Tr	09.63	63-64	34	-	0

STONEHOUSE Kevin
Bishop Auckland, 20 September, 1959 (F/M)

League Club	Source	Date Signed	Seasons Played	Apps	Subs	Gls
Blackburn Rov.	Shildon	07.79	79-82	77	8	27
Huddersfield T.	Tr	03.83	82-83	20	2	4
Blackpool	Tr	03.84	83-85	53	2	19
Darlington	Tr	07.87	87-88	59	13	20
Carlisle U.	L	03.89	88	0	3	0
Rochdale	Tr	07.89	89	13	1	2

STONEMAN Paul
Tynemouth, 26 February, 1973 (CD)

League Club	Source	Date Signed	Seasons Played	Apps	Subs	Gls
Blackpool	YT	07.91	91-94	38	5	1
Colchester U.	L	12.94	94	3	0	1

STONES Craig
Scunthorpe, 31 May, 1980 (M)

League Club	Source	Date Signed	Seasons Played	Apps	Subs	Gls
Lincoln C.	YT	07.97	96-97	10	7	0

STONES Gordon
Farnworth, 18 November, 1934 (CH)

League Club	Source	Date Signed	Seasons Played	Apps	Subs	Gls
Accrington St.	Bury (Am)	09.54	55-60	109	-	1

STOPFORD Alan
Sheffield, 20 November, 1946 (OR)

League Club	Source	Date Signed	Seasons Played	Apps	Subs	Gls
Chesterfield (Am)	Sheffield U. (Am)	01.67	66	2	0	0

STOPFORD Leslie
Manchester, 9 May, 1942 (IF)

League Club	Source	Date Signed	Seasons Played	Apps	Subs	Gls
Chester C.	Jnrs	06.60	59-61	6	-	1

STORER Peter Russell
Shoreditch, 14 February, 1935 (G)

League Club	Source	Date Signed	Seasons Played	Apps	Subs	Gls
Watford (Am)	Berkhamsted	03.59	58	9	-	0

STORER Stuart John
Rugby, 16 January, 1967 (RW)

League Club	Source	Date Signed	Seasons Played	Apps	Subs	Gls
Mansfield T.	YT	•	83	0	1	0
Birmingham C.	V. S. Rugby	01.85	85-86	5	3	0
Everton	Tr	03.87				
Wigan Ath.	L	08.87	87	9	3	0
Bolton W.	Tr	12.87	87-92	95	28	12
Exeter C.	Tr	03.93	92-94	75	2	8
Brighton & H.A.	Tr	03.95	94-97	100	19	11

STOREY Brett Barry
Sheffield, 7 July, 1977 (M)

League Club	Source	Date Signed	Seasons Played	Apps	Subs	Gls
Sheffield U.	YT	07.95				
Lincoln C. (N/C)	Tr	03.96	95	0	2	1

STOREY James
Rowlands Gill, 30 December, 1929 (FB)

League Club	Source	Date Signed	Seasons Played	Apps	Subs	Gls
Newcastle U.	Spen Black & White	05.48				
Exeter C.	Tr	06.53	53	9	-	0
Bournemouth	Tr	07.54				
Rochdale	Tr	06.55	55-56	24	-	1
Darlington	Tr	06.57	57	6	-	0

STOREY Luke Dawson
Seaham, 17 December, 1920 Died 1987 (OR)

League Club	Source	Date Signed	Seasons Played	Apps	Subs	Gls
Lincoln C.	Blackhall Colly	09.47	47-48	11	-	2

STOREY Peter Edwin
Farnham, 7 September, 1945 E Sch/EF Lge/E-19 (D)

League Club	Source	Date Signed	Seasons Played	Apps	Subs	Gls
Arsenal	App	10.62	65-76	387	4	9
Fulham	Tr	03.77	76-77	17	0	0

STOREY Sidney
Barnsley, 25 December, 1919 (IF)

League Club	Source	Date Signed	Seasons Played	Apps	Subs	Gls
Huddersfield T.	Grimethorpe Ath.	09.43				
York C.	Wombwell	05.47	46-55	330	-	40
Barnsley	Tr	05.56	56	29	-	4
Accrington St.	Tr	10.57	57-58	30	-	2
Bradford P. A.	Tr	07.59	59	2	-	0

STOREY-MOORE Ian
Ipswich, 17 January, 1945 Eu23-2/EF Lge/E-1 (W)

League Club	Source	Date Signed	Seasons Played	Apps	Subs	Gls
Nottingham F.	Jnrs	05.62	63-71	235	1	105
Manchester U.	Tr	03.72	71-73	39	0	11

STORF David Alan
Sheffield, 4 December, 1943 (OL)

League Club	Source	Date Signed	Seasons Played	Apps	Subs	Gls
Sheffield Wed.	Jnrs	12.60				
Rochdale	Tr	06.63	63-66	138	0	19
Barrow	Tr	07.67	67-71	154	4	26

STORRAR David McKinnon
Lochgelly, 16 January, 1933 (OL)

League Club	Source	Date Signed	Seasons Played	Apps	Subs	Gls
Sheffield Wed.		02.51	52	4	-	0

STORRIE James
Kirkintilloch, 31 March, 1940 (F)

League Club	Source	Date Signed	Seasons Played	Apps	Subs	Gls
Leeds U.	Airdrieonians	06.62	62-66	123	3	58
Rotherham U.	Aberdeen	12.67	67-69	70	1	19
Portsmouth	Tr	12.69	69-71	43	0	12
Aldershot	L	03.72	71	5	0	1

STORTON Stanley Eugene
Keighley, 5 January, 1939 (FB)

League Club	Source	Date Signed	Seasons Played	Apps	Subs	Gls
Bradford C.	Huddersfield T. (Am)	07.57	59-63	111	-	5
Darlington	Tr	01.64	63	15	-	0
Hartlepool U.	Tr	07.64	64-65	72	0	0
Tranmere Rov.	Tr	07.66	66-69	114	9	2

STORTON Trevor George
Keighley, 26 November, 1949 (CD)

League Club	Source	Date Signed	Seasons Played	Apps	Subs	Gls
Tranmere Rov.	Jnrs	10.67	67-71	112	6	8
Liverpool	Tr	08.72	72-73	5	0	0
Chester C.	Tr	07.74	74-83	396	0	17

STOTT Ian
Wallingford, 17 October, 1955 (CD)

League Club	Source	Date Signed	Seasons Played	Apps	Subs	Gls
Oxford U. (N/C)	West Ham U. (Am)	07.77	77-79	27	0	3

STOTT Keith
Atherton, 12 March, 1944 (CD)

League Club	Source	Date Signed	Seasons Played	Apps	Subs	Gls
Crewe Alex.	Manchester C. (Am)	10.64	64-69	188	3	11
Chesterfield	Tr	07.70	70-74	140	1	4

STOUTT Stephen Paul
Halifax, 5 April, 1964 (D/M)

League Club	Source	Date Signed	Seasons Played	Apps	Subs	Gls
Huddersfield T. (N/C)	Bradley R.	01.84	83-84	6	0	0
Wolverhampton W.	Tr	04.85	85-87	91	3	5
Grimsby T.	Tr	07.88	88-89	3	0	1
Lincoln C.	Tr	12.89	89-90	36	10	1

STOWE Dean Desmond
Burnley, 27 March, 1975 (M)

League Club	Source	Date Signed	Seasons Played	Apps	Subs	Gls
Hull C.	YT	10.93	92	0	1	0

STOWELL Bruce
Bradford, 20 September, 1941 (WH)

League Club	Source	Date Signed	Seasons Played	Apps	Subs	Gls
Bradford C.	Jnrs	12.58	59-71	401	0	16
Rotherham U.	Tr	07.72	72	14	2	0

STOWELL Michael
Preston, 19 April, 1965 (G)

League Club	Source	Date Signed	Seasons Played	Apps	Subs	Gls
Preston N.E.	Leyland Motors	02.85				
Everton	Tr	12.85				
Chester C.	L	09.87	87	14	0	0
York C.	L	12.87	87	6	0	0
Manchester C.	L	01.88	87	14	0	0
Port Vale	L	10.88	88	7	0	0
Wolverhampton W.	L	03.89	88	7	0	0

League Club	Source	Date Signed	Seasons Played	Apps	Subs	Gls
Preston N. E.	L	02.90	89	2	0	0
Wolverhampton W.	Tr	06.90	90-97	313	0	0
STRACHAN Gavin David						
Aberdeen, 23 December, 1978 S Yth/Su21-2						(M)
Coventry C.	YT	11.96	97	2	7	0
STRACHAN Gordon David						
Edinburgh, 9 February, 1957 S Sch/S Yth/Su21-1/S-50						(RM)
Manchester U.	Aberdeen	08.84	84-88	155	5	33
Leeds U.	Tr	03.89	88-94	188	9	37
Coventry C.	Tr	03.95	94-96	13	13	0
STRAIN James Henry						
Chesham, 28 November, 1937						(CH)
Watford	Chesham U.	11.55	56	3	-	0
Millwall	Tr	09.58	58	5	-	0
STRANDLI Frank						
Norway, 16 May, 1972 Norwegian Int						(F)
Leeds U.	I.K. Start (Nor)	01.93	92-93	5	9	2
STRATFORD Paul						
Northampton, 4 September, 1955						(F)
Northampton T.	App	10.72	72-77	169	3	59
STRATHIE James						
Beancross, 12 February, 1913 Died 1976						(CH)
Luton T.	St Bernards	05.37	37-38	2	-	0
Northampton T.	Tr	07.39	46	6	-	0
STRATTON Reginald Malcolm						
Kingsley (Hants), 10 July, 1939 E Yth/E Amat						(CF)
Fulham	Woking	05.59	59-64	21	-	1
Colchester U.	Tr	05.65	65-67	112	0	50
STRAUSS William Henry						
South Africa, 6 January, 1916 Died 1984						(W)
Plymouth Arg.	Aberdeen	07.46	46-53	158	-	40
STRAW Ian Ernest						
Sheffield, 27 May, 1967						(M)
Grimsby T.	Southampton (App)	08.86	86	7	3	0
STRAW Raymond						
Ilkeston, 22 May, 1933						(CF)
Derby Co.	Ilkeston T.	10.51	51-57	94	-	57
Coventry C.	Tr	11.57	57-60	142	-	79
Mansfield T.	Tr	08.61	61-62	44	-	12
STREET Jeffrey Leslie						
Manchester, 20 April, 1948						(CH)
Manchester C.	Jnrs	08.65				
Southport	Tr	08.67	67	9	0	0
Barrow	Altrincham	07.69	69	11	0	1
STREET John (Jack)						
Sheffield, 27 July, 1934						(OR)
Bradford C.	Jnrs	11.51	51	1	-	0
STREET John						
Liverpool, 30 May, 1928						(IF)
Southport (Am)	Tranmere Rov. (Am)	01.49	48-49	7	-	1
Reading	Bootle	05.51				
Barrow	Tr	07.53	53-54	30	-	5
STREET John						
Rotherham, 19 November, 1926 Died 1988						(G)
Sheffield Wed.	Liverpool (Am)	05.45				
Rotherham U.		07.47	47	2	-	0
STREET Kevin						
Crewe, 25 November, 1977						(F)
Crewe Alex.	YT	07.96	97	15	17	4
STREET Terence Edward						
Poplar, 9 December, 1948						(WH)
Leyton Orient	Jnrs	12.66	66	1	0	0
STREETE Floyd Anthony						
Jamaica (WI), 5 May, 1959						(CD)
Cambridge U.	Rivet Sports	07.76	76-82	111	14	19
Derby Co.	S.C. Cambur (Neth)	10.84	84-85	35	0	0
Wolverhampton W.	Tr	10.85	85-89	157	2	6
Reading	Tr	07.90	90-91	38	0	0
STREETER Terence Stephen						
Brighton, 26 October, 1969						(F)
Brighton & H.A.	YT	●	97	0	2	0

League Club	Source	Date Signed	Seasons Played	Apps	Subs	Gls
STRETEN Bernard Reginald						
Rochester, 14 January, 1921 Died 1994 E Amat/E-1						(G)
Luton T.	Shrewsbury T.	01.47	46-56	276	-	0
STRETTON Donald						
Clowne, 4 September, 1920 Died 1978						(CF)
Halifax T.	Thorne Colly	07.47	47	10	-	5
STRICKLAND Derek						
Stoneyburn, 7 November, 1959 S Sch						(F)
Leicester C.	Glasgow Rangers	09.79	79	4	3	2
STRIDE David Roy						
Lymington, 14 March, 1958						(LB)
Chelsea	App	01.76	78-79	35	0	0
Millwall	Memphis (USA)	01.83	82-83	55	0	3
Leyton Orient	Tr	07.84	84	29	0	0
STRINGER David Ronald						
Great Yarmouth, 15 October, 1944 E Yth						(D)
Norwich C.	Gorleston Minors	05.63	64-75	417	2	18
Cambridge U.	Tr	09.76	76-80	153	4	1
STRINGER Edmund						
Sheffield, 6 February, 1925						(IF)
Oldham Ath.	Norton Woodseats	07.49	49	1	-	0
STRINGFELLOW Ian Robert						
Nottingham, 8 May, 1969						(F)
Mansfield T.	App	04.86	85-93	105	58	28
Blackpool	L	09.92	92	3	0	1
Chesterfield	L	12.93	93	0	1	0
STRINGFELLOW Michael David						
Kirkby-in-Ashfield, 27 January, 1943						(OL)
Mansfield T.	Jnrs	02.60	60-61	57	-	10
Leicester C.	Tr	01.62	61-74	292	23	82
STRINGFELLOW Peter						
Walkden, 21 February, 1939						(IF)
Oldham Ath.	Walkden T.	12.58	58-60	54	-	16
Gillingham	Sankeys	12.62	62-63	35	-	2
Chesterfield	Tr	08.64	64	28	-	7
STRODDER Colin John						
Hessle, 23 December, 1941						(FB)
Huddersfield T.		04.60				
Halifax T.	Tr	07.61	61-62	20	-	0
STRODDER Gary John						
Cleckheaton, 1 April, 1965						(CD)
Lincoln C.	App	04.83	82-86	122	10	6
West Ham U.	Tr	03.87	86-89	59	6	2
West Bromwich A.	Tr	08.90	90-94	123	17	8
Notts Co.	Tr	07.95	95-97	108	2	9
STRONACH Peter						
Seaham, 1 September, 1956 E Sch						(M)
Sunderland	App	09.73	77	2	1	0
York C.	Tr	06.78	78-79	30	4	2
STRONG Andrew Forster						
Hartlepool, 17 September, 1966						(LB)
Middlesbrough	App	09.84	84	6	0	0
STRONG Geoffrey Hugh						
Kirkheaton, 19 September, 1937						(IF)
Arsenal	Stanley U.	04.58	60-64	125	-	69
Liverpool	Tr	11.64	64-69	150	5	29
Coventry C.	Tr	07.70	70-71	33	0	0
STRONG Gregory						
Bolton, 5 September, 1975 E Sch/E Yth						(CD)
Wigan Ath.	YT	10.92	93-94	28	7	3
Bolton W.	Tr	08.95	95	0	1	0
Blackpool	L	11.97	97	11	0	1
STRONG George **James**						
Morpeth, 7 June, 1916 Died 1989						(G)
Hartlepool U.		02.34	33	1	-	0
Chesterfield	Tr	08.34	34	18	-	0
Portsmouth	Tr	03.35	34-37	59	-	0
Walsall		07.39				
Burnley	Tr	01.46	46-52	264	-	0
STRONG Leslie						
Streatham, 3 July, 1953						(LB)
Fulham	App	06.71	72-82	370	3	5
Brentford	L	12.82	82	5	0	0

League Club	Source	Date Signed	Seasons Played	Career Record Apps	Subs	Gls
Crystal Palace (N/C)	Tr	08.83	83	7	0	0
Rochdale (N/C)	Tr	10.84	84	1	0	0
STRONG Steven						
Bristol, 17 April, 1962 (CD)						
Hereford U.	App	02.80	78-80	16	0	0
STRONG Steven George						
Watford, 15 March, 1978 (LB)						
Bournemouth	YT	07.96	94-95	0	2	0
STROUD Derek Neville Lester						
Wimborne, 11 February, 1930 (OR)						
Bournemouth	Poole T.	08.50	50-52	78	-	17
Grimsby T.	Tr	06.53	53-54	71	-	12
STROUD Kenneth Allan						
Fulham, 1 December, 1953 (M)						
Swindon T.	App	03.71	71-81	302	9	16
Newport Co.	Tr	08.82	82-83	47	1	0
Bristol C.	Tr	10.83	83-84	68	1	4
STROUD Roy William						
Silvertown, 16 March, 1925 E Sch/E Amat (OR)						
West Ham U.	Hendon	04.52	51-56	13	-	4
STROUD William James Alfred						
Hammersmith, 7 July, 1919 (WH)						
Southampton	Jnrs	02.40	46	29	-	4
Leyton Orient	Tr	06.47	47-49	65	-	1
Newport Co.	Tr	06.50	50-54	63	-	1
STRUTT Brian John						
Malta, 21 September, 1959 (F)						
Sheffield Wed.	App	09.77	79	2	0	0
STUART Edward Albert						
South Africa, 12 May, 1931 (D)						
Wolverhampton W.	Rangers (SA)	01.51	51-61	287	-	1
Stoke C.	Tr	07.62	62-63	63	-	2
Tranmere Rov.	Tr	08.64	64-65	83	0	2
Stockport Co.	Tr	07.66	66-67	77	0	1
STUART Graham Charles						
Tooting, 24 October, 1970 E Yth/Eu21-5 (W/F)						
Chelsea	YT	06.89	89-92	70	17	14
Everton	Tr	08.93	93-97	116	20	23
Sheffield U.	Tr	11.97	97	27	1	5
STUART Jamie Christopher						
Southwark, 15 October, 1976 E Yth/Eu21-4 (LB)						
Charlton Ath.	YT	01.95	94-97	49	1	3
STUART Mark Richard						
Chiswick, 15 December, 1966 E Sch (LW)						
Charlton Ath.	Jnrs	07.84	84-88	89	18	28
Plymouth Arg.	Tr	11.88	88-89	55	2	11
Ipswich T.	L	03.90	89	5	0	2
Bradford C.	Tr	07.90	90-91	22	7	5
Huddersfield T.	Tr	10.92	92	9	6	3
Rochdale	Tr	07.93	93-97	157	26	41
STUART Robert William						
Middlesbrough, 9 October, 1913 Died 1987 E Sch (FB)						
Middlesbrough	South Bank	01.31	31-47	247	-	2
Plymouth Arg.	Tr	10.47	47	20	-	0
STUBBINS Albert						
Wallsend, 13 July, 1919 EF Lge (CF)						
Newcastle U.	Monkseaton	04.37	37-46	27	-	5
Liverpool	Tr	09.46	46-52	161	-	75
STUBBS Alan						
Liverpool, 6 October, 1971 E 'B' (CD)						
Bolton W.	YT	07.90	90-95	181	21	9
STUBBS Alfred Thomas						
West Ham, 18 April, 1922 Died 1986 (RH)						
Crystal Palace		12.46	47-48	3	-	0
STUBBS Brian Henry						
Keyworth, 8 February, 1950 (CD)						
Notts Co.	Loughborough U.	09.68	68-79	423	3	21
STUBBS Charles Frederick						
West Ham, 22 January, 1920 Died 1984 (CF)						
Darlington	Bamforths	01.44	46-47	41	-	17

League Club	Source	Date Signed	Seasons Played	Career Record Apps	Subs	Gls
STUBBS Leslie Levi						
Great Wakering, 18 February, 1929 (IF)						
Southend U.	Great Wakering	05.48	49-52	83	-	40
Chelsea	Tr	11.52	52-58	112	-	34
Southend U.	Tr	11.58	58-59	22	-	3
STUBBS Robin Gregory						
Birmingham, 22 April, 1941 (CF)						
Birmingham C.	Jnrs	04.58	58-62	61	-	17
Torquay U.	Tr	08.63	63-68	214	3	120
Bristol Rov.	Tr	07.69	69-71	90	3	32
Torquay U.	Tr	02.72	71-72	19	2	1
STUBBS William						
Hartlepool, 1 August, 1966 (F)						
Nottingham F.	Seaham Red Star	04.87				
Doncaster Rov.	L	09.87	87	8	1	1
Grimsby T.	L	03.88	87	2	5	2
STUCKEY Bruce George						
Torquay, 19 February, 1947 (W)						
Exeter C.	App	02.65	65-67	37	2	6
Sunderland	Tr	11.67	67-69	24	2	2
Torquay U.	Tr	02.71	70-73	70	18	6
Reading	Tr	11.73	73-76	92	5	7
Torquay U.	L	01.75	74	4	0	0
Bournemouth	L	03.77	76	5	0	0
STURGESS Paul Christopher						
Dartford, 4 August, 1975 (LB)						
Charlton Ath.	YT	07.93	92-96	43	8	0
Millwall	Tr	07.97	97	12	2	0
STURRIDGE Dean Constantine						
Birmingham, 26 July, 1973 (F)						
Derby Co.	YT	07.91	91-97	102	20	41
Torquay U.	L	12.94	94	10	0	5
STURRIDGE Michael Alexander						
Birmingham, 18 September, 1962 (F)						
Birmingham C.	App	06.80				
Wrexham	L	12.83	83	3	1	0
STURRIDGE Simon Andrew						
Birmingham, 9 December, 1969 (F)						
Birmingham C.	YT	07.88	88-92	129	21	30
Stoke C.	Tr	09.93	93-97	42	26	14
STURROCK David						
Dundee, 22 February, 1938 (F)						
Accrington St.	Dundee U.	07.60	60	17	-	5
STUTTARD John Ellis						
Padiham, 24 April, 1920 Died 1983 (D)						
Plymouth Arg.	Burnley (Am)	09.38	38-46	29	-	1
Torquay U.	Tr	09.47	47-50	82	-	0
STYLES Arthur						
Liverpool, 3 September, 1949 E Sch/E Yth (LB)						
Everton	App	08.67	72-73	22	1	0
Birmingham C.	Tr	02.74	73-77	71	3	4
Peterborough U.	Tr	07.78	78	32	0	1
Portsmouth	Tr	07.79	79	28	0	0
STYLES Arthur John						
Smethwick, 29 October, 1939 (WH)						
West Bromwich A.	Jnrs	11.56	59	1	-	0
Wrexham	Tr	03.60	59-60	16	-	0
SUART Ronald						
Kendal, 18 November, 1920 (CH)						
Blackpool	Netherfield	01.39	46-49	104	-	0
Blackburn Rov.	Tr	09.49	49-54	176	-	0
SUCKLING Perry John						
Leyton, 12 October, 1965 E Yth/Eu21-10 (G)						
Coventry C.	App	10.83	82-83	27	0	0
Manchester C.	Tr	06.86	86-87	39	0	0
Crystal Palace	Tr	01.88	87-91	59	0	0
West Ham U.	L	12.89	89	6	0	0
Brentford	L	10.91	91	8	0	0
Watford	Tr	07.92	92-93	39	0	0
Doncaster Rov.	Tr	07.94	94-95	30	0	0
SUDDABY Donald						
Brighouse, 7 June, 1930 (CH)						
Halifax T.	Chelsea (Am)	08.51	51	5	-	0

SUDDABY Peter
Stockport, 23 December, 1947 E Amat (CD)

League Club	Source	Date Signed	Seasons Played	Apps	Subs	Gls
Blackpool	Skelmersdale U.	05.70	70-79	331	1	9
Brighton & H. A.	Tr	11.79	79	21	2	0
Wimbledon	Tr	11.81	81	6	0	0

SUDDARDS Jeffrey
Bradford, 17 January, 1929 (FB)

League Club	Source	Date Signed	Seasons Played	Apps	Subs	Gls
Bradford P. A.	Hull C. (Am)	03.49	49-58	327	-	0

SUDDICK Alan
Chester-le-Street, 2 May, 1944 E Yth/Eu23-2 (M/F)

League Club	Source	Date Signed	Seasons Played	Apps	Subs	Gls
Newcastle U.	App	10.61	61-66	144	0	41
Blackpool	Tr	12.66	66-76	305	5	64
Stoke C.	Tr	12.76	76	9	0	1
Southport	L	08.77	77	6	0	0
Bury	Tr	09.77	77	30	4	2

SUGGETT Colin
Washington, 30 December, 1948 E Sch/E Yth (M)

League Club	Source	Date Signed	Seasons Played	Apps	Subs	Gls
Sunderland	App	01.66	66-68	83	3	24
West Bromwich A.	Tr	07.69	69-72	123	5	20
Norwich C.	Tr	02.73	72-77	200	3	21
Newcastle U.	Tr	08.78	78	20	3	0

SUGRUE Paul Anthony
Coventry, 6 November, 1960 (F/M)

League Club	Source	Date Signed	Seasons Played	Apps	Subs	Gls
Manchester C.	Nuneaton Borough	02.80	79-80	5	1	0
Cardiff C.	Tr	08.81	81	2	3	0
Middlesbrough	Kansas C. (USA)	12.82	82-84	66	3	6
Portsmouth	Tr	12.84	84-85	2	2	0
Northampton T.	Tr	03.86	85	2	6	2
Newport Co.	Tr	08.86	86	1	1	0

SULLEY Christopher Stephen
Camberwell, 3 December, 1959 (LB)

League Club	Source	Date Signed	Seasons Played	Apps	Subs	Gls
Chelsea	App	08.78				
Bournemouth	Tr	03.81	80-85	205	1	3
Blackburn Rov.	Dundee U.	03.87	86-91	134	0	3
Port Vale	Tr	07.92	92	40	0	1
Preston N.E.	Tr	07.93	93	21	0	1

SULLIVAN Alan
Aberdare, 12 November, 1953 W Sch (W)

League Club	Source	Date Signed	Seasons Played	Apps	Subs	Gls
Swansea C.	App	08.71	70-71	7	1	1

SULLIVAN Brian Anthony John
Edmonton, 30 December, 1941 Died 1985 E Sch/E Yth (IF)

League Club	Source	Date Signed	Seasons Played	Apps	Subs	Gls
Fulham	Jnrs	05.59	59	2	-	1

SULLIVAN Colin John
Saltash, 24 June, 1951 E Yth/Eu23-2 (LB)

League Club	Source	Date Signed	Seasons Played	Apps	Subs	Gls
Plymouth Arg.	App	07.68	67-73	225	5	7
Norwich C.	Tr	06.74	74-78	154	3	3
Cardiff C.	Tr	02.79	78-81	61	2	1
Hereford U. (N/C)	Tr	12.81	81	8	0	0
Portsmouth	Tr	03.82	81-83	94	0	0
Swansea C.	Tr	03.85	84-85	53	0	0

SULLIVAN Cornelius (Con) Henry
Bristol, 22 August, 1928 (G)

League Club	Source	Date Signed	Seasons Played	Apps	Subs	Gls
Bristol C.	Horfield O.B.	05.49	50-52	73	-	0
Arsenal	Tr	02.54	53-57	28	-	0

SULLIVAN Derrick
Newport, 10 August, 1930 Died 1983 W-17 (WH)

League Club	Source	Date Signed	Seasons Played	Apps	Subs	Gls
Cardiff C.	Jnrs	09.47	47-60	276	-	18
Exeter C.	Tr	06.61	61	44	-	0
Newport Co.	Tr	07.62	62	23	-	0

SULLIVAN Neil
Sutton, 24 February, 1970 S-3 (G)

League Club	Source	Date Signed	Seasons Played	Apps	Subs	Gls
Wimbledon	YT	07.88	90-97	105	1	0
Crystal Palace	L	05.92	91	1	0	0

SUMMERBEE George Michael
Winchester, 22 October, 1914 Died 1955 (FB)

League Club	Source	Date Signed	Seasons Played	Apps	Subs	Gls
Aldershot	Winchester C.	05.34	34	18	-	0
Preston N.E.	Tr	01.35	37-38	2	-	0
Chester C.	Tr	05.46	46	9	-	0
Barrow	Tr	06.47	47-49	122	-	0

SUMMERBEE Michael George
Preston, 15 December, 1942 Eu23-1/EF Lge/E-8 (W)

League Club	Source	Date Signed	Seasons Played	Apps	Subs	Gls
Swindon T.	Cheltenham T.	03.60	59-64	218	-	39
Manchester C.	Tr	08.65	65-74	355	2	47
Burnley	Tr	06.75	75-76	51	0	0
Blackpool	Tr	12.76	76	3	0	0
Stockport Co.	Tr	08.77	77-79	86	1	6

SUMMERBEE Nicholas John
Altrincham, 26 August, 1971 Eu21-3/E 'B' (FB/M)

League Club	Source	Date Signed	Seasons Played	Apps	Subs	Gls
Swindon T.	YT	07.89	89-93	89	23	6
Manchester C.	Tr	06.94	94-97	119	12	6
Sunderland	Tr	11.97	97	22	3	3

SUMMERBELL Mark
Durham, 30 October, 1976 (M)

League Club	Source	Date Signed	Seasons Played	Apps	Subs	Gls
Middlesbrough	YT	07.95	95-97	7	7	0

SUMMERFIELD Kevin
Walsall, 7 January, 1959 E Yth (W)

League Club	Source	Date Signed	Seasons Played	Apps	Subs	Gls
West Bromwich A.	App	01.77	78-81	5	4	4
Birmingham C.	Tr	05.82	82	2	3	1
Walsall	Tr	12.82	82-83	42	12	17
Cardiff C.	Tr	07.84	84	10	0	1
Plymouth Arg.	Tr	12.84	84-90	118	21	26
Exeter C.	L	03.90	89	4	0	0
Shrewsbury T.	Tr	10.90	90-95	140	23	21

SUMMERHAYES David Michael
Cardiff, 21 March, 1947 Wu23-1 (WH)

League Club	Source	Date Signed	Seasons Played	Apps	Subs	Gls
Cardiff C.	App	03.65	65-67	7	6	0

SUMMERHAYES Robert Edward
Cardiff, 8 January, 1951 W Sch (M)

League Club	Source	Date Signed	Seasons Played	Apps	Subs	Gls
Cardiff C.	App	01.69				
Newport Co.	Tr	08.72	72-74	74	6	4

SUMMERHILL Alan
Liss (Hants), 25 November, 1950 (D)

League Club	Source	Date Signed	Seasons Played	Apps	Subs	Gls
Bournemouth	Jnrs	07.68	69	28	0	0
Crewe Alex.	Tr	09.70	70-71	46	4	1

SUMMERILL Philip Ernest
Birmingham, 20 November, 1947 E Yth (W/F)

League Club	Source	Date Signed	Seasons Played	Apps	Subs	Gls
Birmingham C.	App	12.64	66-72	108	10	46
Huddersfield T.	Tr	01.73	72-74	48	6	11
Millwall	Tr	11.74	74-77	83	4	20
Wimbledon	Tr	09.77	77-78	27	4	4

SUMMERS Christopher
Cardiff, 6 January, 1972 W Yth (F)

League Club	Source	Date Signed	Seasons Played	Apps	Subs	Gls
Cardiff C.	YT	07.90	90	0	3	0

SUMMERS George
Glasgow, 30 July, 1941 (F)

League Club	Source	Date Signed	Seasons Played	Apps	Subs	Gls
Brentford	Shawfield Jnrs	01.59	60-64	71	-	24

SUMMERS Gerald Thomas Francis
Birmingham, 4 October, 1933 (WH)

League Club	Source	Date Signed	Seasons Played	Apps	Subs	Gls
West Bromwich A.	Jnrs	08.51	55-56	22	-	0
Sheffield U.	Tr	05.57	57-63	260	-	4
Hull C.	Tr	04.64	63-65	59	0	1
Walsall	Tr	10.65	65-66	41	3	1

SUMMERS John Henry
Hammersmith, 10 September, 1927 Died 1962 (F)

League Club	Source	Date Signed	Seasons Played	Apps	Subs	Gls
Fulham	Jnrs	02.47	49	4	-	0
Norwich C.	Tr	06.50	50-53	71	-	33
Millwall	Tr	05.54	54-56	91	-	41
Charlton Ath.	Tr	11.56	56-60	171	-	100

SUMMERSBY Roy Donald
Lambeth, 19 March, 1935 (WH/IF)

League Club	Source	Date Signed	Seasons Played	Apps	Subs	Gls
Millwall	Jnrs	03.52	51-58	87	-	13
Crystal Palace	Tr	12.58	58-62	176	-	59
Portsmouth	Tr	06.63	63-64	12	-	1

SUMMERSCALES William Charles
Willesden, 4 January, 1949 (CD)

League Club	Source	Date Signed	Seasons Played	Apps	Subs	Gls
Port Vale	Leek T.	02.70	69-74	126	3	4
Rochdale	Tr	07.75	75-76	87	0	4

SUMNER Alan
Wrexham, 18 April, 1949 (M)

League Club	Source	Date Signed	Seasons Played	Apps	Subs	Gls
Stockport Co. (N/C)		06.78	78	3	2	0

SUMNER Justin Thomas
Harrogate, 19 October, 1970 (LW)

League Club	Source	Date Signed	Seasons Played	Apps	Subs	Gls
Doncaster Rov.	Leeds U. (YT)	08.89	89	2	0	0

SUMPNER Richard Anthony
Leeds, 12 April, 1947 (CF)

League Club	Source	Date Signed	Seasons Played	Apps	Subs	Gls
Bradford P. A.	Jnrs	01.67	66	2	0	1

SUNDERLAND Alan
Mexborough, 1 July, 1953 Eu21-1/Eu23-1/E-1 (F/M)

League Club	Source	Date Signed	Seasons Played	Apps	Subs	Gls
Wolverhampton W.	App	06.71	71-77	139	19	30

League Club	Source	Date Signed	Seasons Played	Apps	Subs	Gls
Arsenal	Tr	11.77	77-83	204	2	55
Ipswich T.	Tr	02.84	83-85	51	7	11

SUNDERLAND Jonathan Paul
Newcastle, 2 November, 1975 (M)

League Club	Source	Date Signed	Seasons Played	Apps	Subs	Gls
Blackpool	YT	07.94	94	0	2	0
Scarborough	Tr	03.96	95-96	3	5	0
Hartlepool U.	Tr	12.96	96	6	7	1

SUNDGOT Ole Bjorn
Norway, 21 March, 1972 Norwegian Int (F)

League Club	Source	Date Signed	Seasons Played	Apps	Subs	Gls
Bradford C.	Molde (Nor)	11.96	96-97	11	14	6

SUNLEY David
Skelton, 6 February, 1952 (F)

League Club	Source	Date Signed	Seasons Played	Apps	Subs	Gls
Sheffield Wed.	App	01.70	70-75	121	9	21
Nottingham F.	L	10.75	75	1	0	0
Hull C.	Tr	01.76	75-77	58	11	11
Lincoln C.	Tr	07.78	78-79	36	5	6
Stockport Co.	Tr	03.80	79-81	79	4	7

SUNLEY Mark
Guisborough, 11 August, 1972 (CD)

League Club	Source	Date Signed	Seasons Played	Apps	Subs	Gls
Middlesbrough	YT	10.89				
Millwall (N/C)	Tr	02.91				
Darlington	Tr	07.91	91-93	34	1	0
Hartlepool U. (N/C)	Stalybridge Celtic	02.95	94	1	1	0

SURMAN Leslie
Tamworth, 23 November, 1947 Died 1978 (G)

League Club	Source	Date Signed	Seasons Played	Apps	Subs	Gls
Charlton Ath.	App	11.65	65	1	0	0
Rotherham U.	Tr	06.66	66	1	0	0

SURTEES George Harrison Hall
Ryhope, 20 October, 1926 (G)

League Club	Source	Date Signed	Seasons Played	Apps	Subs	Gls
Southport	Murton Colly	08.46	46	3	-	0

SURTEES Hubert
Durham, 16 July, 1921 Died 1979 (W)

League Club	Source	Date Signed	Seasons Played	Apps	Subs	Gls
Watford	Bushey U.	07.46	47-48	14	-	1
Crystal Palace	Tr	08.49	49	5	-	0

SUSSEX Andrew Robert
Islington, 23 November, 1964 (W/F)

League Club	Source	Date Signed	Seasons Played	Apps	Subs	Gls
Leyton Orient	App	11.82	81-87	126	18	17
Crewe Alex.	Tr	06.88	88-90	86	16	24
Southend U.	Tr	07.91	91-95	63	13	14
Brentford	L	12.95	95	3	0	0

SUTCH Daryl
Beccles, 11 September, 1971 E Yth/Eu21-4 (W)

League Club	Source	Date Signed	Seasons Played	Apps	Subs	Gls
Norwich C.	YT	07.90	90-97	132	33	7

SUTCLIFFE Frederick
Brotherton (Yks), 29 May, 1931 (LH/IF)

League Club	Source	Date Signed	Seasons Played	Apps	Subs	Gls
Birmingham C.		09.51				
Chester C.	Tr	06.52	52-54	50	-	2

SUTCLIFFE Frederick William Joseph
Fulham, 29 July, 1923 (CF)

League Club	Source	Date Signed	Seasons Played	Apps	Subs	Gls
Millwall		02.47	47-48	12	-	3
Walsall	Tr	07.50	50	4	-	0

SUTCLIFFE Peter David
Manchester, 25 January, 1957 E Yth (W)

League Club	Source	Date Signed	Seasons Played	Apps	Subs	Gls
Manchester U.	App	07.74				
Stockport Co.	Tr	12.75	75-76	19	8	2
Port Vale	Tr	03.77	76-78	44	6	6
Chester C.	Tr	12.78	78-81	103	6	7
Chester C. (N/C)	Bangor C.	11.83	83	11	0	0
Stockport Co. (N/C)	Tr	03.84	83	0	1	0

SUTHERLAND Colin
Glasgow, 15 March, 1975 (LB)

League Club	Source	Date Signed	Seasons Played	Apps	Subs	Gls
Scarborough	Clydebank	12.96	96-97	35	8	0

SUTHERLAND George Burns
Bathgate, 11 September, 1923 (CF)

League Club	Source	Date Signed	Seasons Played	Apps	Subs	Gls
Leyton Orient	Partick Thistle	08.49	49-50	42	-	22

SUTHERLAND Harry Ross
Salford, 30 July, 1915 (CF)

League Club	Source	Date Signed	Seasons Played	Apps	Subs	Gls
Leeds U.	Sedgeley Park	07.38	38	3	-	1
Exeter C.	Tr	05.47	46-47	14	-	3
Bournemouth	Tr	07.48				

SUTHERLAND James Sinclair
Armadale, 6 August, 1918 Died 1987 (LB)

League Club	Source	Date Signed	Seasons Played	Apps	Subs	Gls
Newport Co.	Forth W.	07.47	47-48	32	-	0

SUTHERLAND John Francis
Cork (Ire), 10 February, 1932 (FB)

League Club	Source	Date Signed	Seasons Played	Apps	Subs	Gls
Everton	Evergreen	05.50	56	6	-	0
Chesterfield	Tr	06.57	57-58	47	-	0
Crewe Alex.	Tr	11.58	58-59	47	-	1

SUTTLE Kenneth George
Hammersmith, 25 August, 1928 (W)

League Club	Source	Date Signed	Seasons Played	Apps	Subs	Gls
Chelsea	Worthing	08.48				
Brighton & H. A.	Tr	07.49	49	3	-	0

SUTTON Brian
Rochdale, 8 December, 1934 (G)

League Club	Source	Date Signed	Seasons Played	Apps	Subs	Gls
Rochdale	Norden Y.C.	10.52	52-55	13	-	0

SUTTON Christopher Roy
Nottingham, 10 March, 1973 Eu21-13/E 'B' (F)

League Club	Source	Date Signed	Seasons Played	Apps	Subs	Gls
Norwich C.	YT	07.91	90-93	89	13	35
Blackburn Rov.	Tr	07.94	94-97	108	5	44

SUTTON David William
Tarleton (Lancs), 21 January, 1957 (CD)

League Club	Source	Date Signed	Seasons Played	Apps	Subs	Gls
Plymouth Arg.	App	07.74	73-77	60	1	0
Reading	L	11.77	77	9	0	0
Huddersfield T.	Tr	03.78	77-83	242	0	11
Bolton W.	Tr	06.85	85-87	98	0	4
Rochdale	Tr	08.88	88	28	0	2

SUTTON David William
Leek, 15 December, 1966 (F)

League Club	Source	Date Signed	Seasons Played	Apps	Subs	Gls
Crewe Alex.	Stoke C. (YT)	07.86	86	0	1	1

SUTTON Gary
Folkestone, 2 February, 1962 (G)

League Club	Source	Date Signed	Seasons Played	Apps	Subs	Gls
Gillingham	App	02.80	80-81	11	0	0

SUTTON James Peter
Glasgow, 6 September, 1949 (M)

League Club	Source	Date Signed	Seasons Played	Apps	Subs	Gls
Newcastle U.		06.69				
Mansfield T.	Tr	07.70	70	11	2	0

SUTTON Melvyn Charles
Birmingham, 13 February, 1946 (M)

League Club	Source	Date Signed	Seasons Played	Apps	Subs	Gls
Cardiff C.	Aston Villa (Am)	12.67	68-71	135	3	5
Wrexham	Tr	07.72	72-80	355	5	21
Crewe Alex.	Tr	08.82	82	13	0	1

SUTTON Michael John
Norwich, 5 October, 1944 (WH)

League Club	Source	Date Signed	Seasons Played	Apps	Subs	Gls
Norwich C.	Jnrs	09.62	62-66	46	5	3
Chester C.	Tr	05.67	67-69	137	1	9
Carlisle U.	Tr	06.70	70-71	51	2	1

SUTTON Richard Melvyn
Gravesend, 21 August, 1965 E Yth (D)

League Club	Source	Date Signed	Seasons Played	Apps	Subs	Gls
Peterborough U.	App	•	82	1	0	0

SUTTON Stephen John
Hartington (Dy), 16 April, 1961 (G)

League Club	Source	Date Signed	Seasons Played	Apps	Subs	Gls
Nottingham F.	App	04.79	80-89	199	0	0
Mansfield T.	L	03.81	80	8	0	0
Derby Co.	L	01.85	84	14	0	0
Coventry C.	L	02.91	90	1	0	0
Luton T.	L	11.91	91	14	0	0
Derby Co.	Tr	03.92	91-95	60	1	0
Reading	L	01.96	95	2	0	0
Birmingham C.	Tr	08.96	96	6	0	0

SUTTON Wayne Frank
Derby, 1 October, 1975 (D/M)

League Club	Source	Date Signed	Seasons Played	Apps	Subs	Gls
Derby Co.	YT	10.92	94-95	4	3	0
Hereford U.	L	09.96	96	4	0	0

SVARC Robert Louis
Leicester, 8 February, 1946 (F)

League Club	Source	Date Signed	Seasons Played	Apps	Subs	Gls
Leicester C.	App	03.63	64-68	13	0	2
Lincoln C.	Tr	12.68	68-71	40	5	16
Barrow	L	09.70	70	15	0	3
Colchester U.	Boston U.	12.72	72-75	116	0	59
Blackburn Rov.	Tr	10.75	75-76	42	8	16
Watford	L	09.77	77	1	0	0

SVENSSON Mathias
Sweden, 24 September, 1974 Swedish Int (F)

League Club	Source	Date Signed	Seasons Played	Apps	Subs	Gls
Portsmouth	Elfsborg (Swe)	12.96	96-97	34	11	10

SWAILES Christopher William
Gateshead, 19 October, 1970 (CD)

League Club	Source	Date Signed	Seasons Played	Apps	Subs	Gls
Ipswich T.	YT	05.89				

League Club	Source	Date Signed	Seasons Played	Apps	Subs	Gls
Peterborough U.	Tr	03.91				
Doncaster Rov.	Bridlington T.	10.93	93-94	49	0	0
Ipswich T.	Tr	03.95	95-97	34	3	1
Bury	Tr	11.97	97	12	1	1

SWAIN Kenneth
Birkenhead, 28 January, 1952 (RB)

League Club	Source	Date Signed	Seasons Played	Apps	Subs	Gls
Chelsea	Wycombe W.	08.73	73-78	114	5	26
Aston Villa	Tr	12.78	78-82	148	0	4
Nottingham F.	Tr	10.82	82-84	112	0	2
Portsmouth	Tr	07.85	85-87	113	0	0
West Bromwich A.	L	02.88	87	7	0	1
Crewe Alex.	Tr	08.88	88-91	123	3	1

SWAIN Kenneth John
Cardiff, 31 December, 1954 W Sch (FB)

League Club	Source	Date Signed	Seasons Played	Apps	Subs	Gls
Newport Co.	App	12.72	71-73	7	1	0

SWAIN Malcolm
Hornsey, 2 February, 1952 (M)

League Club	Source	Date Signed	Seasons Played	Apps	Subs	Gls
Reading	App	02.70	70-71	37	4	2

SWAIN Robert
Ripon, 26 March, 1944 (W)

League Club	Source	Date Signed	Seasons Played	Apps	Subs	Gls
Bradford C.	Jnrs	09.61	62	7	-	0

SWAIN Sidney
Liverpool, 14 October, 1927 (OR)

League Club	Source	Date Signed	Seasons Played	Apps	Subs	Gls
Halifax T.		07.51	51	8	-	1

SWAINE Mark
Hammersmith, 13 February, 1958 (W)

League Club	Source	Date Signed	Seasons Played	Apps	Subs	Gls
Gillingham	App	●	74	1	0	0

SWALES Stephen Colin
Whitby, 26 December, 1973 (LB)

League Club	Source	Date Signed	Seasons Played	Apps	Subs	Gls
Scarborough	YT	08.92	91-94	51	3	1
Reading	Tr	07.95	95-97	33	10	1

SWALLOW Ernest **Barry**
Doncaster, 2 July, 1942 (CH)

League Club	Source	Date Signed	Seasons Played	Apps	Subs	Gls
Doncaster Rov.	Jnrs	07.59	60-61	51	-	10
Crewe Alex.	Tr	08.62	62-63	14	-	0
Barnsley	Tr	07.64	64-66	96	-	1
Bradford C.	Tr	02.67	66-69	79	6	7
York C.	Tr	10.69	69-75	268	1	21

SWALLOW Ernest
Wheatley Hill, 9 July, 1919 Died 1962 (FB)

League Club	Source	Date Signed	Seasons Played	Apps	Subs	Gls
Doncaster Rov.	Bentley Colly	11.41	46-47	50	-	0
Barnsley	Tr	01.48	47-49	36	-	0
Oldham Ath.	Tr	08.50	50	6	-	0

SWALLOW Raymond
Southwark, 15 June, 1935 (W)

League Club	Source	Date Signed	Seasons Played	Apps	Subs	Gls
Arsenal	Jnrs	12.52	54-57	13	-	4
Derby Co.	Tr	09.58	58-63	118	-	21

SWAN Carl
Sheffield, 12 December, 1957 (CD)

League Club	Source	Date Signed	Seasons Played	Apps	Subs	Gls
Doncaster Rov.	Burton A.	12.80	80-82	14	1	1
Rochdale	L	10.82	82	3	0	0

SWAN Maurice Michael George
Dublin, 27 September, 1938 IR-1 (G)

League Club	Source	Date Signed	Seasons Played	Apps	Subs	Gls
Cardiff C.	Drumcondra	07.60	60-62	15	-	0
Hull C.	Tr	06.63	63-67	103	0	0

SWAN Peter
South Elmsall, 8 October, 1936 E Yth/Eu23-3/EF Lge/E-19 (CH)

League Club	Source	Date Signed	Seasons Played	Apps	Subs	Gls
Sheffield Wed.	Jnrs	11.53	55-63	260	-	0
Sheffield Wed.	(Retired)	07.72	72	13	2	0
Bury	Tr	08.73	73	35	0	2

SWAN Peter Harold
Leeds, 28 September, 1966 (F/CD)

League Club	Source	Date Signed	Seasons Played	Apps	Subs	Gls
Leeds U.	YT	08.84	85-88	43	6	11
Hull C.	Tr	03.89	88-90	76	4	24
Port Vale	Tr	08.91	91-93	105	6	6
Plymouth Arg.	Tr	07.94	94	24	3	2
Burnley	Tr	08.95	95-96	47	2	7
Bury	Tr	08.97	97	26	11	6

SWAN Ronald McDonald
Plean, 8 January, 1941 (G)

League Club	Source	Date Signed	Seasons Played	Apps	Subs	Gls
Oldham Ath.	East Stirling	05.64	64-66	64	0	0
Luton T.	Tr	01.67	66	14	0	0

SWANKIE Robert Beattie
Arbroath, 25 February, 1932 (F)

League Club	Source	Date Signed	Seasons Played	Apps	Subs	Gls
Burnley	Arbroath Y.C.	07.50				
Darlington	Gloucester C.	01.54	53	1	-	0

SWANN Gary
York, 11 April, 1962 (M/FB)

League Club	Source	Date Signed	Seasons Played	Apps	Subs	Gls
Hull C.	App	04.80	80-86	176	10	9
Preston N.E.	Tr	11.86	86-91	194	5	37
York C.	Tr	06.92	92-93	82	0	4
Scarborough	Tr	08.94	94	24	3	3

SWANN Gordon
Mexborough, 7 December, 1937 (F)

League Club	Source	Date Signed	Seasons Played	Apps	Subs	Gls
Rotherham U.		07.57	58-60	11	-	1
Barnsley	Tr	07.61	61	2	-	0

SWANNELL John
Walton-on-Thames, 26 January, 1939 E Amat (G)

League Club	Source	Date Signed	Seasons Played	Apps	Subs	Gls
Stockport Co. (Am)	Corinthian Casuals	06.59	59	1	-	0

SWEENEY Alan
Paisley, 31 October, 1956 (RB)

League Club	Source	Date Signed	Seasons Played	Apps	Subs	Gls
Huddersfield T.	App	11.73	74-77	65	1	0
Hartlepool U.	Emley	09.79	79-81	97	0	2

SWEENEY Andrew
Chadderton, 15 October, 1951 (W)

League Club	Source	Date Signed	Seasons Played	Apps	Subs	Gls
Oldham Ath.	Jnrs	02.71	70-74	37	5	2
Bury	L	03.73	72	2	0	0
Rochdale	Tr	07.75	75	12	5	0

SWEENEY Gerald
Renfrew, 10 July, 1945 (M/FB)

League Club	Source	Date Signed	Seasons Played	Apps	Subs	Gls
Bristol C.	Morton	08.71	71-81	396	10	22
York C.	Tr	02.82	81	12	0	0

SWEENEY Paul Martin
Glasgow, 10 January, 1965 (LB/W)

League Club	Source	Date Signed	Seasons Played	Apps	Subs	Gls
Newcastle U.	Raith Rov.	03.89	88-90	28	8	0
Hartlepool U. (N/C)	Gateshead	08.94	94	1	0	0

SWEENEY William Clerihew
St Andrews, 23 October, 1918 (G)

League Club	Source	Date Signed	Seasons Played	Apps	Subs	Gls
Carlisle U.	Clyde	01.48	47-48	37	-	0

SWEENIE Thomas Thornton
Paisley, 15 July, 1945 (IF)

League Club	Source	Date Signed	Seasons Played	Apps	Subs	Gls
Leicester C.	Johnstone Burgh	06.63	63-66	50	1	11
York C.	Huddersfield T. (trial)	10.68	68	6	0	1

SWEETZER Gordon Eric Peter
Canada, 27 January, 1957 Canadian Int (F)

League Club	Source	Date Signed	Seasons Played	Apps	Subs	Gls
Brentford		07.75	75-77	68	4	40
Cambridge U.	Tr	04.78	77-79	9	0	3
Brentford	Toronto (Can)	01.82	81	8	1	1

SWEETZER James Edward
Woking, 8 January, 1960 (F)

League Club	Source	Date Signed	Seasons Played	Apps	Subs	Gls
Oxford U.	App	02.77	78	0	8	1
Millwall	Tr	11.79	79	2	1	1

SWIFT Colin
Barnsley, 23 December, 1933 (RB)

League Club	Source	Date Signed	Seasons Played	Apps	Subs	Gls
Barnsley	Jnrs	08.51	55-61	241	-	0

SWIFT Frank Victor
Blackpool, 26 December, 1913 Died 1958 EF Lge/E-19 (G)

League Club	Source	Date Signed	Seasons Played	Apps	Subs	Gls
Manchester C.	Fleetwood	10.32	32-49	338	-	0

SWIFT Humphrey (Hugh) Mills
Sheffield, 22 January, 1921 Died 1979 E 'B' (FB)

League Club	Source	Date Signed	Seasons Played	Apps	Subs	Gls
Sheffield Wed.	Lopham Street Meths	09.42	46-50	181	-	0

SWIFT John **Kenneth**
Liverpool, 26 July, 1928 (F)

League Club	Source	Date Signed	Seasons Played	Apps	Subs	Gls
Liverpool	Jnrs	08.45				
Southport	Tr	07.51	51	5	-	0

SWIFT Trevor
Rotherham, 14 September, 1948 (CD)

League Club	Source	Date Signed	Seasons Played	Apps	Subs	Gls
Rotherham U.	Jnrs	09.65	67-74	284	4	21

SWIGGS Bradley
Plymouth, 12 October, 1959 (F)

League Club	Source	Date Signed	Seasons Played	Apps	Subs	Gls
Plymouth Arg. (N/C)	Liskeard Ath.	03.84	83	1	1	0

SWIGGS Robert
Plymouth, 30 March, 1930 (CF)

League Club	Source	Date Signed	Seasons Played	Apps	Subs	Gls
Plymouth Arg.	St Blazey	01.56	55-56	3	-	0

SWINBOURNE Royston Harry
Barmborough, 25 August, 1929 E 'B' (CF)

League Club	Source	Date Signed	Seasons Played	Apps	Subs	Gls
Wolverhampton W.	Jnrs	09.46	49-55	211	-	107

SWINBURNE Alan Thomas Anderson
Houghton-le-Spring, 18 May, 1946 (G)

League Club	Source	Date Signed	Seasons Played	Apps	Subs	Gls
Oldham Ath.	App	09.63	63	4	-	0

SWINBURNE Thomas Anderson
Houghton-le-Spring, 9 August, 1915 Died 1969 (G)

League Club	Source	Date Signed	Seasons Played	Apps	Subs	Gls
Newcastle U.	Herrington Colly	04.34	34-46	77	-	0

SWINBURNE Trevor
Houghton-le-Spring, 20 June, 1953 (G)

League Club	Source	Date Signed	Seasons Played	Apps	Subs	Gls
Sunderland	App	06.70	72-76	10	0	0
Carlisle U.	Tr	05.77	77-82	248	0	0
Brentford	Tr	08.83	83-84	45	0	0
Leeds U.	Tr	06.85	85	2	0	0
Doncaster Rov.	L	09.85	85	4	0	0
Lincoln C.	Tr	02.86	85-86	34	0	0

SWINDELLS Jack
Manchester, 12 April, 1937 E Yth (CF)

League Club	Source	Date Signed	Seasons Played	Apps	Subs	Gls
Blackburn Rov.	Manchester C. (Am)	11.57	57-59	9	-	1
Accrington St.	Tr	12.59	59-60	65	-	28
Barnsley	Tr	06.61	61	14	-	8
Workington	Tr	02.62	61-62	61	-	19
Torquay U.	Tr	07.63	63	18	-	6
Newport Co.	Tr	07.64	64	23	-	3

SWINDIN George Hedley
Campsall, 4 December, 1914 (G)

League Club	Source	Date Signed	Seasons Played	Apps	Subs	Gls
Bradford C.	Rotherham U. (Am)	02.33	34-35	26	-	0
Arsenal	Tr	04.36	36-53	271	-	0

SWINDLEHURST David
Edgware, 6 January, 1956 E Yth/Eu21-1 (F)

League Club	Source	Date Signed	Seasons Played	Apps	Subs	Gls
Crystal Palace	App	01.73	73-79	221	16	73
Derby Co.	Tr	02.80	79-82	110	0	29
West Ham U.	Tr	03.83	82-84	52	9	16
Sunderland	Tr	08.85	85-86	59	0	11
Wimbledon (N/C)	Cyprus	03.88	87	2	0	0
Colchester U.	Tr	06.88	88	12	0	6
Peterborough U.	L	12.88	88	4	0	1

SWINFEN Reginald
Battersea, 4 May, 1915 Died 1996 (OR)

League Club	Source	Date Signed	Seasons Played	Apps	Subs	Gls
Queens Park R.	Civil Service	03.36	36-46	26	-	5

SWINSCOE Terence
Shirebrook, 31 August, 1934 (D)

League Club	Source	Date Signed	Seasons Played	Apps	Subs	Gls
Stockport Co.	Spalding U.	02.56				
Mansfield T.	Tr	11.56	56-58	14	-	0

SWINSCOE Thomas William
Mansfield, 16 October, 1919 Died 1993 (CF)

League Club	Source	Date Signed	Seasons Played	Apps	Subs	Gls
Chesterfield	Shirebrook S.F.C.	03.46	46-47	43	-	12
Stockport Co.	Tr	02.48	47-49	72	-	31

SWITZER George
Salford, 13 October, 1973 (LB)

League Club	Source	Date Signed	Seasons Played	Apps	Subs	Gls
Manchester U.	YT	07.92				
Darlington	Tr	08.93	93	12	2	0

SWORD Alan
Newcastle, 5 July, 1934 (CF)

League Club	Source	Date Signed	Seasons Played	Apps	Subs	Gls
Newcastle U.	Jnrs	08.51				
Exeter C.	Tr	09.53	55	9	-	4

SWORD Thomas William
Newcastle, 12 November, 1957 (CD/F)

League Club	Source	Date Signed	Seasons Played	Apps	Subs	Gls
Stockport Co.	Bishop Auckland	11.79	79-85	236	2	51
Hartlepool U.	Tr	07.86	86	18	0	0
Halifax T.	L	02.87	86	8	0	2
Stockport Co.	Tr	03.87	86-87	6	1	1

SYDENHAM John
Eastleigh, 15 September, 1939 E Yth/Eu23-2 (OL)

League Club	Source	Date Signed	Seasons Played	Apps	Subs	Gls
Southampton	Jnrs	04.57	56-69	341	2	36
Aldershot	Tr	03.70	69-71	54	5	5

SYKES Alexander
Newcastle-u-Lyme, 2 April, 1974 (F)

League Club	Source	Date Signed	Seasons Played	Apps	Subs	Gls
Mansfield T.	Westfields	06.92	93	1	1	1

SYKES John
Huddersfield, 2 November, 1950 (IF)

League Club	Source	Date Signed	Seasons Played	Apps	Subs	Gls
Bradford P. A.	App	11.68	68	1	0	0
Wrexham	Tr	01.69	68	1	0	0

SYKES Kenneth
Darlington, 29 January, 1926 (CF)

League Club	Source	Date Signed	Seasons Played	Apps	Subs	Gls
Darlington		05.46	46	6	-	2
Middlesbrough	Tr	06.47				
Hartlepool U.	Tr	09.49	49	1	-	0

SYKES Norman Albert John
Bristol, 16 October, 1936 E Sch/E Yth (WH)

League Club	Source	Date Signed	Seasons Played	Apps	Subs	Gls
Bristol Rov.	Jnrs	10.53	56-63	214	-	5
Plymouth Arg.	Tr	09.64	64	3	-	0
Stockport Co.	Tr	09.65	65-66	52	0	7
Doncaster Rov.	Tr	02.67	66	15	0	0

SYME Colin
Rosyth, 23 January, 1924 (OR)

League Club	Source	Date Signed	Seasons Played	Apps	Subs	Gls
Torquay U.	Dunfermline Ath.	12.46	46	1	-	0

SYMM Colin
Gateshead, 26 November, 1946 (M)

League Club	Source	Date Signed	Seasons Played	Apps	Subs	Gls
Sheffield Wed.	Gateshead	05.65	66-68	16	3	1
Sunderland	Tr	06.69	69-71	9	5	0
Lincoln C.	Tr	06.72	72-74	60	9	7

SYMMONS Iorwerth
Swansea, 3 February, 1930 (FB)

League Club	Source	Date Signed	Seasons Played	Apps	Subs	Gls
Swansea C.	Hafod	05.48	50-51	15	-	0

SYMONDS Anthony
Wakefield, 10 November, 1944 (HB)

League Club	Source	Date Signed	Seasons Played	Apps	Subs	Gls
Bradford P.A.	Great Preston Jnrs	07.62	64-66	28	1	2

SYMONDS Roderick Calvin Hilgrove
Bermuda, 29 March, 1932 (CF)

League Club	Source	Date Signed	Seasons Played	Apps	Subs	Gls
Rochdale	Pembroke (Ber)	10.54	55	1	-	0

SYMONDS Richard
Langham (Nfk), 21 November, 1959 (FB)

League Club	Source	Date Signed	Seasons Played	Apps	Subs	Gls
Norwich C.	App	08.78	78-82	55	4	0

SYMONS Christopher (Kit) Jeremiah
Basingstoke, 8 March, 1971 W Yth/Wu21-2/W 'B'/W-27 (CD)

League Club	Source	Date Signed	Seasons Played	Apps	Subs	Gls
Portsmouth	YT	12.88	88-95	161	0	10
Manchester C.	Tr	08.95	95-97	124	0	4

SYMONS Paul
North Shields, 20 April, 1976 (F)

League Club	Source	Date Signed	Seasons Played	Apps	Subs	Gls
Blackpool	YT	07.94	93	0	1	0

SYRETT David Kenneth
Salisbury, 20 January, 1956 E Yth (F)

League Club	Source	Date Signed	Seasons Played	Apps	Subs	Gls
Swindon T.	App	11.73	73-76	110	12	30
Mansfield T.	Tr	08.77	77-78	65	0	20
Walsall	Tr	03.79	78	11	0	3
Peterborough U.	Tr	08.79	79-81	75	4	23
Northampton T.	Tr	06.82	82-83	42	2	13

SZABO Tibor Lewis
Bradford, 28 October, 1959 (F)

League Club	Source	Date Signed	Seasons Played	Apps	Subs	Gls
Bradford C.	App	10.77	78	8	5	1

TAAFFE Steven Lee
Stoke, 10 September, 1979 (F)

League Club	Source	Date Signed	Seasons Played	Apps	Subs	Gls
Stoke C.	YT	08.96	97	0	3	0

TADMAN Maurice Roy
Sittingbourne, 28 June, 1921 Died 1994 (CF)

League Club	Source	Date Signed	Seasons Played	Apps	Subs	Gls
Charlton Ath.	Bexleyheath & Welling	06.38	46	3	-	0
Plymouth Arg.	Tr	08.47	47-54	240	-	109

TAFT Douglas
Leicester, 9 March, 1926 Died 1987 (CF)

League Club	Source	Date Signed	Seasons Played	Apps	Subs	Gls
Derby Co.		11.47	48	6	-	1
Wolverhampton W.	Tr	07.49				

TAGG Anthony Peter
Epsom, 10 April, 1957 (CD)

League Club	Source	Date Signed	Seasons Played	Apps	Subs	Gls
Queens Park R.	App	03.75	75	4	0	0
Millwall	Tr	07.77	77-81	130	3	9
Wimbledon	Tr	07.82	82	14	0	0

TAGG Ernest
Crewe, 15 September, 1917 (WH/IF)

League Club	Source	Date Signed	Seasons Played	Apps	Subs	Gls
Crewe Alex.		10.37	37	19	-	7
Wolverhampton W.	Tr	05.38	38	1	-	0
Bournemouth	Tr	05.39	46-48	80	-	8
Carlisle U.	Tr	11.48	48	5	-	1

TAGGART Gerald Paul
Belfast, 18 October, 1970 NI Sch/NI Yth/Nu23-2/NI-45 (CD)

League Club	Source	Date Signed	Seasons Played	Apps	Subs	Gls
Manchester C.	YT	07.89	88-89	10	2	1
Barnsley	Tr	01.90	89-94	209	3	16
Bolton W.	Tr	08.95	95-97	68	1	4

TAGGART Robert
Newmains (Lk), 10 March, 1927 (IF)

League Club	Source	Date Signed	Seasons Played	Apps	Subs	Gls
Cardiff C.	Coltness U.	05.49	49	2	-	0
Torquay U.	Tr	06.50	50	14	-	2
Aldershot	Tr	08.51	51	16	-	2

TAINTON Trevor Kenneth
Bristol, 8 June, 1948 E Sch (M)

League Club	Source	Date Signed	Seasons Played	Apps	Subs	Gls
Bristol C.	App	09.65	67-81	456	30	24
Torquay U.	Tr	02.82	81	19	0	1

TAIT Alexander
Bedlington, 28 November, 1933 E Yth (CF)

League Club	Source	Date Signed	Seasons Played	Apps	Subs	Gls
Newcastle U.	Jnrs	09.52	54-59	32	-	8
Bristol C.	Tr	06.60	60-63	117	-	38
Doncaster Rov.	Tr	06.64	64	19	-	7

TAIT Barry Stuart
York, 17 June, 1938 (IF)

League Club	Source	Date Signed	Seasons Played	Apps	Subs	Gls
York C.	Doncaster Rov. (Am)	09.58	58-60	15	-	5
Bradford C.	Peterborough U. (trial)	11.61	61	20	-	10
Halifax T.	Tr	07.62	62-63	36	-	21
Crewe Alex.	Tr	09.63	63	9	-	2
Notts Co.	Tr	07.64	64	3	-	0

TAIT Michael Paul
Wallsend, 30 September, 1956 (M/D)

League Club	Source	Date Signed	Seasons Played	Apps	Subs	Gls
Oxford U.	App	09.74	74-76	61	3	23
Carlisle U.	Tr	01.77	76-79	101	5	20
Hull C.	Tr	09.79	79	29	4	3
Portsmouth	Tr	06.80	80-86	229	12	29
Reading	Tr	08.87	87-89	98	1	9
Darlington	Tr	07.90	90-91	79	0	2
Hartlepool U.	Tr	07.92	92-93	60	1	1
Hartlepool U.	Gretna	09.94	94-96	74	4	2

TAIT Paul
Newcastle, 24 October, 1974 (F)

League Club	Source	Date Signed	Seasons Played	Apps	Subs	Gls
Everton	YT	07.93				
Wigan Ath.	Tr	08.94	94	1	4	0

TAIT Paul Ronald
Sutton Coldfield, 31 July, 1971 (M)

League Club	Source	Date Signed	Seasons Played	Apps	Subs	Gls
Birmingham C.	YT	07.88	87-96	135	35	14
Northampton T.	L	12.97	97	2	1	0

TAIT Peter
York, 17 October, 1936 (CF)

League Club	Source	Date Signed	Seasons Played	Apps	Subs	Gls
York C. (Am)	Jnrs	08.55	55	3	-	1

TAIT Robert James
Edinburgh, 4 October, 1938 (IF)

League Club	Source	Date Signed	Seasons Played	Apps	Subs	Gls
Notts Co.	Aberdeen	07.62	62-63	60	-	11
Barrow	Tr	07.64	64-65	78	1	27
Chesterfield	Tr	07.66	66	27	1	2

TALBOT Brian Ernest
Ipswich, 21 July, 1953 Eu21-1/E'B'/E-6 (M)

League Club	Source	Date Signed	Seasons Played	Apps	Subs	Gls
Ipswich T.	App	07.70	73-78	177	0	25
Arsenal	Tr	01.79	78-84	245	9	40
Watford	Tr	06.85	85-86	46	2	8
Stoke C.	Tr	10.86	86-87	51	3	5
West Bromwich A.	Tr	01.88	87-89	66	8	5
Fulham (N/C)	Tr	03.91	90	5	0	1
Aldershot (N/C)	Tr	03.91	90	11	0	0

TALBOT Ernest
Workington, 13 November, 1932 (F)

League Club	Source	Date Signed	Seasons Played	Apps	Subs	Gls
Workington		08.51	52-57	19	-	7

TALBOT Gary
Blackburn, 15 December, 1937 (CF)

League Club	Source	Date Signed	Seasons Played	Apps	Subs	Gls
Chester C.		09.63	63-66	110	1	61
Crewe Alex.	Tr	07.67	67	35	0	20
Chester C.	Tr	06.68	68	43	0	22

TALBOT Frank **Leslie**
Hednesford, 3 August, 1910 (IF)

League Club	Source	Date Signed	Seasons Played	Apps	Subs	Gls
Blackburn Rov.	Hednesford T.	10.30	30-35	90	-	20
Cardiff C.	Tr	06.36	36-38	104	-	21
Walsall	Tr	06.39	46	18	-	4

TALBOT Stewart
Birmingham, 14 June, 1973 (M)

League Club	Source	Date Signed	Seasons Played	Apps	Subs	Gls
Port Vale	Moor Green	08.94	94-97	77	21	10

TALBOYS Steven John
Bristol, 18 September, 1966 (LW)

League Club	Source	Date Signed	Seasons Played	Apps	Subs	Gls
Wimbledon	Gloucester C.	01.92	92-95	19	7	1
Watford	Tr	07.96	96-97	2	3	0

TALBUT John
Oxford, 20 October, 1940 E Sch/Eu23-7 (CH)

League Club	Source	Date Signed	Seasons Played	Apps	Subs	Gls
Burnley	Jnrs	10.57	58-66	138	0	0
West Bromwich A.	Tr	12.66	66-70	143	1	0

TALIA Francesco (Frank)
Australia, 20 July, 1972 (G)

League Club	Source	Date Signed	Seasons Played	Apps	Subs	Gls
Blackburn Rov.	Sunshine G.C. (Aus)	08.92				
Hartlepool U.	L	12.92	92	14	0	0
Swindon T.	Tr	09.95	95-97	33	0	0

TALKES Wayne Anthony Norman
Ealing, 2 June, 1952 (M)

League Club	Source	Date Signed	Seasons Played	Apps	Subs	Gls
Southampton	App	07.69	71-73	7	2	0
Doncaster Rov.	L	12.73	73	3	1	0
Bournemouth	Tr	07.74	74	5	0	0

TALLON Darren John Bernard
Plymouth, 1 June, 1972 (CD)

League Club	Source	Date Signed	Seasons Played	Apps	Subs	Gls
Plymouth Arg.	YT	10.90	90	1	0	0

TALLON Gerrit (Gary) Thomas
Drogheda, 5 September, 1973 (W)

League Club	Source	Date Signed	Seasons Played	Apps	Subs	Gls
Blackburn Rov.	Drogheda U.	11.91				
Chester C. (L)	Kilmarnock	03.97	96	1	0	0
Mansfield T.	Kilmarnock	12.97	97	26	0	1

TAMBLING Robert Victor
Storrington, 18 September, 1941 E Sch/Eu23-13/E-3 (F)

League Club	Source	Date Signed	Seasons Played	Apps	Subs	Gls
Chelsea	Jnrs	09.58	58-69	298	4	164
Crystal Palace	Tr	01.70	69-73	67	1	12

TANKARD Allen John
Islington, 21 May, 1969 E Yth (LB)

League Club	Source	Date Signed	Seasons Played	Apps	Subs	Gls
Southampton	App	05.87	85-86	5	0	0
Wigan Ath.	Tr	07.88	88-92	205	4	4
Port Vale	Tr	07.93	93-97	165	5	2

TANNER Adam David
Maldon, 25 October, 1973 (D/M)

League Club	Source	Date Signed	Seasons Played	Apps	Subs	Gls
Ipswich T.	YT	07.92	94-97	36	18	7

TANNER Graham George
Bridgwater, 4 September, 1947 (CH)

League Club	Source	Date Signed	Seasons Played	Apps	Subs	Gls
Bristol C.	App	09.64				
Bradford P.A.	Tr	10.67	67-68	44	0	2

League Club	Source	Date Signed	Seasons Played	Apps	Subs	Gls
TANNER John Denys Parkin						
Harrogate, 2 July, 1921 Died 1987 E Amat						(CF)
Huddersfield T. (Am)	Yorkshire Amats	08.48	48	1	-	1
TANNER Michael William						
Bristol, 28 October, 1964						(M)
Bristol C.		07.85	85-87	16	3	1
TANNER Nicholas						
Kingswood, 24 May, 1965						(CD)
Bristol Rov.	Mangotsfield U.	06.85	85-87	104	3	3
Liverpool	Tr	07.88	89-92	36	4	1
Norwich C.	L	03.90	89	6	0	0
Swindon T.	L	09.90	90	7	0	0
TANNER Thomas						
Devonport, 24 June, 1922						(OL)
Torquay U. (Am)	Plymouth U.	09.46	46	1	-	0
TANSEY Gerard						
Liverpool, 15 October, 1933						(OL)
Everton	Jnrs	10.51				
Tranmere Rov.	Tr	07.55	55	3	-	1
TANSEY James						
Liverpool, 29 January, 1929						(FB)
Everton		05.48	52-59	133	-	0
Crewe Alex.	Tr	06.60	60	9	-	0
TAPKEN Norman						
Wallsend, 21 February, 1913 Died 1996						(G)
Newcastle U.	Wallsend	05.33	34-37	106	-	0
Manchester U.	Tr	12.38	38	14	-	0
Darlington	Tr	04.47	46-47	31	-	0
TAPLEY Reginald						
Nantwich, 2 November, 1932						(OL)
Crewe Alex.		09.53				
Rochdale	Tr	10.56	56	1	-	0
TAPLEY Steven						
Camberwell, 3 October, 1963						(D)
Fulham	App	10.81	83-84	2	0	1
Rochdale	L	02.85	84	1	0	0
TAPPING Frederick Harold						
Derby, 29 July, 1921						(RH)
Blackpool		10.43				
Chesterfield	Tr	11.47	47	1	-	0
TAPSCOTT Derek Robert						
Barry, 30 June, 1932 W-14						(CF)
Arsenal	Barry T.	10.53	53-57	119	-	62
Cardiff C.	Tr	09.58	58.64	194	-	79
Newport Co.	Tr	07.65	65	12	1	1
TAPSCOTT Eli **John**						
Falmouth, 29 April, 1928						(WH)
Leeds U.		03.50				
Wrexham	Tr	05.50	50-55	172	-	4
TARANTINI Alberto Cesar						
Argentina, 3 December, 1955 Argentinian Int						(D)
Birmingham C.	Boca Juniors (Arg)	10.78	78	23	0	1
TARBUCK Alan David						
Chester, 10 October, 1948						(W)
Everton	App	08.66				
Crewe Alex.	Tr	06.67	67-69	80	5	18
Chester C.	Tr	10.69	69-71	69	0	24
Preston N.E.	Tr	09.71	71-72	42	6	17
Shrewsbury T.	Tr	03.73	72-75	107	17	17
Rochdale	Tr	07.76	76-77	48	0	1
TARGETT Haydn **Roy**						
Shepton Mallet, 1 July, 1928						(FB)
Torquay U.	Shepton Mallet	10.49	50	1	-	0
TARICCO Mauricio Ricardo						
Argentina, 10 March, 1973						(LB)
Ipswich T.	Argentinos Jnrs (Arg)	09.94	95-97	118	3	3
TARRANT Brian Leslie						
Stainforth, 22 July, 1938						(F)
Leeds U.	Jnrs	08.55				
Mansfield T.	Tr	07.60	60	3	-	0

League Club	Source	Date Signed	Seasons Played	Apps	Subs	Gls
TARRANT John **Edward**						
Stainforth, 12 February, 1932						(WH)
Hull C.	Jnrs	02.49	50-53	30	-	2
Walsall	Tr	12.53	53-57	102	-	12
TARTT Colin						
Liverpool, 23 November, 1950						(D)
Port Vale	Alsager College	07.72	72-76	171	4	7
Chesterfield	Tr	03.77	76-81	185	1	7
Port Vale	Tr	10.81	81-84	111	6	9
TATE Christopher Douglas						
York, 27 December, 1977						(F)
Sunderland	York C. (YT)	07.96				
Scarborough	Tr	08.97	97	3	2	1
TATE Craig David						
South Shields, 16 October, 1979						(F)
Shrewsbury T.	YT	●	96	0	1	0
TATE Geoffrey Michael						
Leicester, 16 December, 1937 E Sch/E Yth						(F)
Derby Co.	Jnrs	08.55	55	1	-	1
TATE Jeffrey						
Blyth, 11 May, 1959						(M)
Burnley	Jnrs	08.78	79	5	0	1
TAVENER Colin Raymond						
Bath, 26 June, 1945						(M)
Hereford U.	Trowbridge T.	06.72	72-73	50	1	3
TAWSE Brian						
Ellon, 30 July, 1945						(W)
Arsenal	King Street A.	04.63	64	5	-	0
Brighton & H.A.	Tr	12.65	65-69	97	5	14
Brentford	Tr	02.70	69-70	20	2	1
TAYLOR Alan						
Thornton Cleveleys, 17 May, 1943						(G)
Blackpool	Blackpool Wren Rov.	10.63	65-70	94	0	0
Oldham Ath.	L	12.69	69	2	0	0
Stockport Co.	L	08.70	70	5	0	0
Southport	Tr	07.71	71-73	102	0	0
TAYLOR Alan						
Derby, 7 March, 1954						(OL)
Chelsea	Alfreton T.	10.72				
Reading	Tr	05.74	74	13	8	4
TAYLOR Alan David						
Hinckley, 14 November, 1953						(F)
Rochdale	Morecambe	05.73	73-74	55	0	8
West Ham U.	Tr	11.74	74-78	88	10	25
Norwich C.	Tr	08.79	79	20	4	5
Cambridge U.	Vancouver (Can)	10.80	80-81	17	1	4
Hull C. (N/C)	Vancouver (Can)	01.84	83	13	1	3
Burnley	Tr	08.84	84-85	60	4	23
Bury	Tr	06.86	86-87	55	7	10
Norwich C.		09.88	88	1	3	1
TAYLOR Albert Herbert						
Worksop, 2 May, 1924						(G)
Bury		10.45	46-47	4	-	0
Sheffield U.	Tr	05.48				
Halifax T.	Tr	07.51	51	8	-	0
TAYLOR Alexander						
Menstrie, 25 December, 1916 Died 1982						(CH)
Carlisle U.	Stirling A.	06.38	38-46	24	-	0
TAYLOR Alexander						
Glasgow, 13 June, 1962						(M)
Walsall	Hamilton Academical	08.88	88-89	43	2	6
TAYLOR Andrew						
Stratford-on-Avon, 4 May, 1963						(RB)
Northampton T.	Aston Villa (App)	06.81	81	17	0	0
TAYLOR Andrew						
Rawmarsh, 19 January, 1973						(LB)
Rotherham U.	YT	06.91	90-92	17	1	0
TAYLOR Andrew						
Chesterfield, 30 December, 1967						(F)
Chesterfield	YT	07.86	86-87	7	5	1

TAYLOR Anthony
Glasgow, 6 September, 1946 (LB)

League Club	Source	Date Signed	Seasons Played	Apps	Subs	Gls
Crystal Palace	Morton	11.68	68-73	192	3	8
Southend U.	Tr	08.74	74-75	56	0	1
Swindon T.	Tr	08.76	76	20	6	0
Bristol Rov.	Athlone T.	09.77	77	12	0	0
Portsmouth	Tr	02.78	77	17	0	0
Northampton T. (N/C)	Tr	07.79	79	4	0	0

TAYLOR Archibald
Glasgow, 4 October, 1918 Died 1976 (WH)

League Club	Source	Date Signed	Seasons Played	Apps	Subs	Gls
Reading		06.39	46-47	15	-	2
Leyton Orient	Tr	08.48	48-50	46	-	1

TAYLOR Arthur Alexander
Lambeg (NI), 5 April, 1931 (OL)

League Club	Source	Date Signed	Seasons Played	Apps	Subs	Gls
Luton T.	Glentoran	07.50	52-55	8	-	0

TAYLOR Arthur (Archie) Matson
Dunscroft, 7 November, 1939 (W)

League Club	Source	Date Signed	Seasons Played	Apps	Subs	Gls
Bristol C.	Doncaster Rov. (Am)	05.58	59-60	12	-	2
Barnsley	Tr	07.61	61	2	-	0
Hull C.	Goole T.	05.62	62	1	-	0
Halifax T.	Tr	07.63	63-67	173	0	18
Bradford C.	Tr	12.67	67	10	1	0
York C.	Tr	10.68	68-70	93	3	9

TAYLOR Arthur Sidney
Birmingham, 14 March, 1925 (CF)

League Club	Source	Date Signed	Seasons Played	Apps	Subs	Gls
West Bromwich A.	Handsworth Wood	03.42	47	4	-	5

TAYLOR Ashley
Conisbrough, 11 December, 1959 (LB)

League Club	Source	Date Signed	Seasons Played	Apps	Subs	Gls
Rotherham U.	App	12.77	79-81	21	1	0

TAYLOR George **Barry**
Sheffield, 3 December, 1939 Died 1996 (FB)

League Club	Source	Date Signed	Seasons Played	Apps	Subs	Gls
Sheffield U.	Jnrs	04.59				
Oldham Ath.	Tr	06.63	63	40	-	0
Chesterfield	Tr	08.64	64-65	35	0	2

TAYLOR Brian
Manchester, 29 June, 1942 (WH)

League Club	Source	Date Signed	Seasons Played	Apps	Subs	Gls
Rochdale	Jnrs	03.62	63-67	131	1	7

TAYLOR Brian
Hammersmith, 2 July, 1944 (FB)

League Club	Source	Date Signed	Seasons Played	Apps	Subs	Gls
Queens Park R.	Jnrs	03.62	62-65	50	0	0

TAYLOR Brian
Whitwell, 12 February, 1954 (CD)

League Club	Source	Date Signed	Seasons Played	Apps	Subs	Gls
Middlesbrough	App	07.71	72-75	14	4	1
Doncaster Rov.	Tr	12.75	75-78	118	1	12
Rochdale	Tr	12.78	78-82	152	2	10

TAYLOR Brian John
Gateshead, 2 July, 1949 Died 1993 (FB/W)

League Club	Source	Date Signed	Seasons Played	Apps	Subs	Gls
Coventry C.	Durham C.	02.68				
Walsall	Tr	05.71	71-77	204	12	25
Plymouth Arg.	Tr	10.77	77-78	34	1	5
Preston N.E.	Tr	10.78	78-81	93	6	1
Wigan Ath.	L	03.82	81	7	1	0

TAYLOR Brian Joseph
Walsall, 24 March, 1937 (OL)

League Club	Source	Date Signed	Seasons Played	Apps	Subs	Gls
Walsall	Jnrs	09.54	54-57	77	-	17
Birmingham C.	Tr	06.58	58-61	54	-	7
Rotherham U.	Tr	10.61	61-62	42	-	5
Shrewsbury T.	Tr	08.63	63-64	73	-	8
Port Vale	Tr	08.65	65-66	44	2	2
Barnsley	Tr	06.67	67	23	1	2

TAYLOR John **Brian**
Doncaster, 7 October, 1931 (G)

League Club	Source	Date Signed	Seasons Played	Apps	Subs	Gls
Doncaster Rov.	Sheffield Wed. (Am)	03.49				
Leeds U.	Worksop T.	05.51	51	11	-	0
Bradford P.A.	Kings Lynn	06.54	54-55	66	-	0

TAYLOR Carl Wilson
Kirkby Stephen, 20 January, 1937 (OR)

League Club	Source	Date Signed	Seasons Played	Apps	Subs	Gls
Middlesbrough	Penrith	01.56	57-59	11	-	1
Aldershot	Tr	06.60	60-62	78	-	13
Darlington	Tr	09.62	62	18	-	1

TAYLOR Colin
Stourbridge, 24 August, 1940 (OL)

League Club	Source	Date Signed	Seasons Played	Apps	Subs	Gls
Walsall	Stourbridge	02.58	58-62	213	-	93
Newcastle U.	Tr	06.63	63-64	33	-	7
Walsall	Tr	10.64	64-67	148	0	52
Crystal Palace	Tr	05.68	68	32	2	8
Walsall	Tr	09.69	69-72	85	11	24

TAYLOR Colin David
Liverpool, 25 December, 1971 E Yth (F)

League Club	Source	Date Signed	Seasons Played	Apps	Subs	Gls
Wolverhampton W.	YT	03.90	90-92	7	12	2
Wigan Ath.	L	01.92	91	7	0	2
Preston N.E.	L	11.92	92	4	0	0
Doncaster Rov.	L	02.93	92	2	0	0

TAYLOR Craig
Plymouth, 24 January, 1974 (M)

League Club	Source	Date Signed	Seasons Played	Apps	Subs	Gls
Exeter C.	YT	06.92	92	2	3	0
Swindon T.	Dorchester T.	04.97	97	28	4	2

TAYLOR David
Rochester, 17 September, 1940 (IF)

League Club	Source	Date Signed	Seasons Played	Apps	Subs	Gls
Gillingham	Jnrs	09.57	57-58	21	-	3
Portsmouth	Tr	06.59	59	2	-	0

TAYLOR Derek Milton
Bradford, 6 June, 1927 Died 1984 (OR)

League Club	Source	Date Signed	Seasons Played	Apps	Subs	Gls
Halifax T. (Am)	Bradford P.A. (Am)	08.48	48	2	-	0

TAYLOR Douglas
Wolverhampton, 20 April, 1931 (F)

League Club	Source	Date Signed	Seasons Played	Apps	Subs	Gls
Wolverhampton W.	West Bromwich A. (Am)	10.49	54	3	-	0
Walsall	Tr	11.55	55-56	36	-	7

TAYLOR Edward Kenneth
Irvine, 17 May, 1956 (M)

League Club	Source	Date Signed	Seasons Played	Apps	Subs	Gls
Scunthorpe U.	Ipswich T. (App)	08.74	74	7	0	0

TAYLOR Ernest
Sunderland, 2 September, 1925 Died 1985 E 'B'/E-1 (IF)

League Club	Source	Date Signed	Seasons Played	Apps	Subs	Gls
Newcastle U.	Hylton Colly	09.42	47-51	107	-	19
Blackpool	Tr	10.51	51-57	217	-	53
Manchester U.	Tr	02.58	57-58	22	-	2
Sunderland	Tr	12.58	58-60	68	-	11

TAYLOR Francis Gerald
Magherafelt (NI), 2 January, 1923 (OL)

League Club	Source	Date Signed	Seasons Played	Apps	Subs	Gls
Leeds U.	Bangor	07.49	49	3	-	0

TAYLOR Frederick
Burnley, 24 February, 1920 Died 1983 (OR)

League Club	Source	Date Signed	Seasons Played	Apps	Subs	Gls
Burnley	Jnrs	03.37	37-46	49	-	7
New Brighton	Tr	07.48	48-49	55	-	10

TAYLOR Frederick Robert
Doncaster, 28 October, 1943 (OL)

League Club	Source	Date Signed	Seasons Played	Apps	Subs	Gls
Doncaster Rov.	Jnrs	07.61	61-64	34	-	2

TAYLOR Gareth Keith
Weston-super-Mare, 25 February, 1973 Wu21-7/W-8 (LB)

League Club	Source	Date Signed	Seasons Played	Apps	Subs	Gls
Bristol Rov.	Southampton (YT)	07.91	91-95	31	16	16
Crystal Palace	Tr	09.95	95	18	2	1
Sheffield U.	Tr	03.96	95-97	49	23	23

TAYLOR Geoffrey Arthur
Henstead (Sk), 22 January, 1923 (W)

League Club	Source	Date Signed	Seasons Played	Apps	Subs	Gls
Norwich C.	C.N.S.O.B.U.	08.46	46	1	-	0
Reading	Tr	03.47	46	1	-	0
Lincoln C.	Tr	08.47	47	1	-	0
Brighton & H.A.	Tr	08.48	48	2	-	0
Bristol Rov.	Stade Rennais (Fr)	09.51	51	3	-	0
Queens Park R.	Switzerland	11.53	53	2	-	0

TAYLOR George Alexander
Aberdeen, 9 June, 1915 Died 1982 (LH)

League Club	Source	Date Signed	Seasons Played	Apps	Subs	Gls
Plymouth Arg.	Aberdeen	08.48	48-49	48	-	2

TAYLOR George Edward
Wigan, 21 March, 1920 Died 1983 (G)

League Club	Source	Date Signed	Seasons Played	Apps	Subs	Gls
West Ham U.	Gainsborough Trin.	12.38	46-55	115	-	0

TAYLOR George Jack
Dundee, 23 October, 1948 (IF)

League Club	Source	Date Signed	Seasons Played	Apps	Subs	Gls
Grimsby T.	Jnrs	11.65	65	0	1	0

TAYLOR George Leslie
Edinburgh, 11 May, 1926 (G)

League Club	Source	Date Signed	Seasons Played	Apps	Subs	Gls
Aldershot	Hamilton Academical	06.53				
Hartlepool U.	Tr	11.53	53-54	34	-	0

TAYLOR George McGregor
Edinburgh, 12 December, 1927 (OR)

League Club	Source	Date Signed	Seasons Played	Apps	Subs	Gls
Aldershot	Hamilton Academical	07.52	52	8	-	2

League Club	Source	Date Signed	Seasons Played	Career Record Apps	Subs	Gls
TAYLOR Gerald William						
Hull, 15 August, 1947						(FB)
Wolverhampton W.	Jnrs	11.64	66-75	151	3	1
Swindon T.	L	10.75	75	19	0	0
TAYLOR Gordon						
Ashton-u-Lyne, 28 December, 1944						(W)
Bolton W.	Curzon Ashton	01.62	62-70	253	5	41
Birmingham C.	Tr	12.70	70-75	156	10	9
Blackburn Rov.	Tr	03.76	75-77	62	2	3
Bury	Tr	06.78	78-79	58	2	2
TAYLOR Gordon Stanley						
Stanley, 10 June, 1936						(G)
Gateshead	West Stanley	02.57	57	3	-	0
TAYLOR Graham						
Worksop, 15 September, 1944						(FB)
Grimsby T.	Jnrs	07.62	63-67	189	0	2
Lincoln C.	Tr	07.68	68-72	150	2	1
TAYLOR John **Henry (Harry)**						
Ryton-on-Tyne, 6 October, 1935						(OR)
Newcastle U.	Jnrs	11.52	54-56	7	-	1
Fulham	L	02.57	57	4	-	0
Newcastle U.	Tr	11.57	58-59	21	-	4
TAYLOR Ian						
Doncaster, 25 November, 1967						(G)
Carlisle U.	Bridlington T.	08.90				
Scarborough (N/C)	Tr	02.92	91	1	0	0
TAYLOR Ian Kenneth						
Birmingham, 4 June, 1968						(M)
Port Vale	Moor Green	07.92	92-93	83	0	28
Sheffield Wed.	Tr	07.94	94	9	5	1
Aston Villa	Tr	12.94	94-97	105	8	12
TAYLOR James						
Ashton-in-Makerfield, 7 April, 1925						(OL)
Manchester C.		10.44				
Crewe Alex.	Tr	06.47	47-48	48	-	8
TAYLOR James						
Strood, 13 May, 1934						(IF)
Charlton Ath.	Tonbridge	08.54				
Gillingham	Tr	08.56	56-57	30	-	16
Watford	Tr	07.58				
TAYLOR James						
Salford, 2 November, 1936						(OR)
Bolton W.	Jnrs	12.54				
Southport	Tr	07.59	59	29	-	0
TAYLOR James Guy						
Hillingdon, 5 November, 1917 EF Lge/E-2						(CH)
Fulham	Hillingdon B.L.	03.38	46-52	261	-	5
Queens Park R.	Tr	04.53	53	41	-	0
TAYLOR Jamie Lee						
Bury, 11 January, 1977						(M/F)
Rochdale	YT	01.94	93-96	10	26	4
TAYLOR Jason Scott						
Wrexham. 29 August, 1970						(F)
Wrexham	YT	●	88	0	1	0
TAYLOR Jeffrey Neilson						
Huddersfield, 20 September, 1930						(CF)
Huddersfield T.	Jnrs	09.49	49-51	68	-	27
Fulham	Tr	11.51	51-53	33	-	14
Brentford	Tr	08.54	54-56	94	-	34
TAYLOR John (Jack)						
Barnsley, 15 February, 1914 Died 1978						(FB)
Wolverhampton W.	Worsboro' Bridge	01.34	35-37	78	-	0
Norwich C.	Tr	06.38	38-46	50	-	0
Hull C.	Tr	07.47	47-49	72	-	0
TAYLOR John						
Creswell (Dy), 11 January, 1939						(W)
Mansfield T.	Chesterfield (Jnrs)	05.57	59	5	-	2
Peterborough U.	Tr	07.60	60	1	-	0
TAYLOR John						
Bradford, 24 June, 1924						(IL)
Bradford C.	Kilmarnock	09.46	46	2	-	2

League Club	Source	Date Signed	Seasons Played	Career Record Apps	Subs	Gls
TAYLOR John						
Durham, 10 July, 1926						(IF)
Crystal Palace (Am)	Bishop Auckland	05.48	48	1	-	0
TAYLOR John Ephraim						
Chilton, 11 September, 1924 E 'B'						(IF)
Luton T.	Stockton	02.49	48-51	85	-	29
Wolverhampton W.	Tr	06.52	52	10	-	1
Notts Co.	Tr	02.54	53-56	53	-	19
Bradford P.A.	Tr	07.57	57	12	-	6
TAYLOR John James						
Manchester, 12 October, 1928						(OR)
Blackpool		09.49				
Accrington St.	Tr	07.52	52	16	-	0
TAYLOR John Keith						
Manningham, 7 September, 1935						(CF)
Bradford C. (Am)		02.56	55	1	-	0
TAYLOR John Leslie						
Birmingham, 25 June, 1949						(G)
Chester C.	Pwllheli	07.70	70-73	70	0	0
Rochdale	L	10.74	74	3	0	0
Stockport Co.	Bangor C.	11.75	75	1	0	0
TAYLOR John Patrick						
Norwich, 24 October, 1964						(F)
Colchester U.	Jnrs	12.82				
Cambridge U.	Sudbury T.	08.88	88-91	139	21	46
Bristol Rov.	Tr	03.92	91-93	91	4	44
Bradford C.	Tr	07.94	94	35	1	11
Luton T.	Tr	03.95	94-95	27	10	3
Lincoln C.	L	09.96	96	5	0	2
Colchester U.	L	11.96	96	8	0	5
Cambridge U.	Tr	01.97	96-97	38	17	14
TAYLOR Kenneth						
Huddersfield, 21 August, 1935						(CH)
Huddersfield T.	Jnrs	09.52	53-64	250	-	14
Bradford P.A.	Tr	02.65	64-66	51	0	1
TAYLOR Kenneth						
Porthmadog, 5 June, 1952						(FB)
Wrexham	Jnrs	05.70	70	1	-	0
TAYLOR Kenneth Gordon						
South Shields, 15 March, 1931						(FB)
Blackburn Rov.	North Shields	01.50	54-63	200	-	0
TAYLOR Kenneth Victor						
Manchester, 18 June, 1936						(FB)
Manchester C.	Manchester Transport	08.54	57	1	-	0
TAYLOR Kevin						
Wakefield, 22 January, 1961						(M)
Sheffield Wed.	App	10.78	78-83	118	7	21
Derby Co.	Tr	07.84	84	22	0	2
Crystal Palace	Tr	03.85	84-87	85	2	14
Scunthorpe U.	Tr	10.87	87-90	149	8	24
TAYLOR Lawrence (Larry) Desmond						
Exeter, 23 November, 1947						(G)
Bristol Rov.	App	12.65	66-69	90	0	0
TAYLOR Lee Vincent						
Hammersmith, 24 February, 1976						(D)
Shrewsbury T.	Southwark Faweh	08.96	96-97	14	3	0
TAYLOR Leslie						
North Shields, 4 December, 1956						(M)
Oxford U.	App	12.74	74-80	219	0	15
Watford	Tr	11.80	80-85	167	5	13
Reading	Tr	10.86	86-88	69	6	3
Colchester U.	Tr	01.89	88-89	44	8	1
TAYLOR Maik Stefan						
Germany, 4 September, 1971 NIu21-1						(G)
Barnet	Farnborough T.	06.95	95-96	70	0	0
Southampton	Tr	01.97	96	18	0	0
Fulham	Tr	11.97	97	28	0	0
TAYLOR Mark						
Hartlepool, 5 December, 1962						(FB)
Hartlepool U. (N/C)	Henry Smiths B.C.	08.82	82	1	0	0
TAYLOR Mark Simon						
Saltburn, 8 November, 1974						(LB)
Middlesbrough	YT	03.93				

League Club	Source	Date Signed	Seasons Played	Apps	Subs	Gls
Darlington	L	10.94	94	8	0	0
Fulham (N/C)	Tr	09.95	95	7	0	0
Northampton T. (N/C)	Tr	02.96	95	1	0	0
TAYLOR Peter Mark Richard						
Hartlepool, 20 November, 1964						(LW)
Hartlepool U.		08.82	83-85	42	5	4
Crewe Alex.	L	12.85	85	3	0	0
Blackpool	Tr	08.86	86-91	104	15	43
Cardiff C.	L	12.90	90	6	0	3
Wrexham	Tr	03.92	91-94	50	11	9
TAYLOR Robert **Mark**						
Birmingham, 22 February, 1966						(M)
Walsall	YT	07.84	84-88	100	13	4
Sheffield Wed.	Tr	06.89	89	8	1	0
Shrewsbury T.	L	02.91	90	19	0	2
Shrewsbury T.	Tr	09.91	91-97	244	5	13
TAYLOR Martin James						
Tamworth, 9 December, 1966						(G)
Derby Co.	Mile Oak Rov.	07.86	89-96	97	0	0
Carlisle U.	L	09.87	87	10	0	0
Scunthorpe U.	L	12.87	87	8	0	0
Crewe Alex.	L	09.96	96	6	0	0
Wycombe W.	Tr	03.97	96-97	49	0	0
TAYLOR Paul						
Leith, 20 December, 1966						(LB)
Mansfield T.	YT	●	83	3	0	0
TAYLOR Paul Anthony						
Sheffield, 3 December, 1949						(M)
Sheffield Wed.	Loughborough College	06.71	71-72	5	1	0
York C.	Tr	07.73	73	4	0	0
Hereford U.	L	01.74	73	0	1	0
Colchester U.	Tr	03.74	73	6	3	0
Southport	Tr	07.74	74-76	95	0	16
TAYLOR Peter John						
Southend, 3 January, 1953 E Semi Pro/Eu23-4/E-4						(W)
Southend U.	App	01.71	70-73	57	18	12
Crystal Palace	Tr	10.73	73-76	122	0	33
Tottenham H.	Tr	09.76	76-80	116	7	31
Leyton Orient	Tr	11.80	80-82	49	7	11
Oldham Ath.	L	01.83	82	4	0	0
Exeter C. (N/C)	Maidstone U.	10.83	83	8	0	0
TAYLOR Peter Thomas						
Nottingham, 2 July, 1928 Died 1990						(G)
Coventry C.	Nottingham F. (Am)	05.46	50-54	86	-	0
Middlesbrough	Tr	08.55	55-59	140	-	0
Port Vale	Tr	06.61	61	1	-	0
TAYLOR Philip Anthony						
Sheffield, 11 July, 1958						(W)
York C.	App	07.76	74-77	14	7	1
Darlington	Tr	07.78	78-79	18	8	2
TAYLOR Philip Henry						
Bristol, 18 September, 1917 E Sch/EF Lge/E 'B'/E-3						(IF/WH)
Bristol Rov.	Jnrs	03.35	35	21	-	2
Liverpool	Tr	03.36	35-53	312	-	32
TAYLOR Raymond Jeffrey						
Hoyland, 1 March, 1930						(OL)
Huddersfield T.	Wath W.	09.49	49	2	-	0
Southport	Tr	08.53	53-54	51	-	7
TAYLOR Richard (Dick) Eric						
Wednesfield, 9 April, 1918 Died 1995						(CH)
Grimsby T.	Jnrs	05.35	38-47	36	-	0
Scunthorpe U.	Tr	05.48	50-53	131	-	2
TAYLOR Richard Herbert						
Huddersfield, 24 January, 1957 E Yth						(G)
Huddersfield T.	App	01.74	73-81	105	0	0
York C.	L	03.80	79	2	0	0
TAYLOR Richard Marshall						
Oldham, 21 August, 1928						(G)
Everton	Marine	06.51				
Southport	Formby	08.54	54	1	-	0
TAYLOR Richard William						
Silksworth, 20 June, 1951						(LW)
Sunderland	App	10.68	71	0	1	0
York C.	Tr	07.72	72	26	2	2

League Club	Source	Date Signed	Seasons Played	Apps	Subs	Gls
TAYLOR Robert						
Horden, 3 February, 1967						(F)
Leeds U.	Horden Colly	01.86	85-88	33	9	9
Bristol C.	Tr	03.89	88-91	96	10	50
West Bromwich A.	Tr	01.92	91-97	211	27	96
Bolton W.	L	01.98	97	10	2	3
TAYLOR Robert Anthony						
Norwich, 30 April, 1971						(F)
Norwich C.	YT	03.90				
Leyton Orient	L	03.91	90	0	3	1
Birmingham C.	Tr	08.91				
Leyton Orient	Tr	10.91	91-93	54	19	20
Brentford	Tr	03.94	93-97	172	1	56
TAYLOR Robert John						
Croydon, 16 March, 1936						(WH)
Crystal Palace (Am)	Fulham (Am)	08.54	54	2	-	0
Gillingham	Tr	09.56	56-58	31	-	5
Millwall	Tr	08.59	59	2	-	1
TAYLOR Robert Shaun						
Plymouth, 3 December, 1967						(F)
Portsmouth	YT	08.86				
Newport Co.	Tr	03.87	86-87	37	6	7
Torquay U.	Weymouth	09.89	89	11	7	1
TAYLOR Robin Graham						
West Germany, 14 January, 1971						(M)
Wigan Ath.	Leicester C. (N/C)	10.89	89	0	1	0
TAYLOR Rodney Victor						
Wimborne, 9 September, 1943						(WH)
Portsmouth	Jnrs	05.61				
Gillingham	Tr	07.63	63-65	9	2	0
Bournemouth	Tr	02.66	65-66	29	1	0
TAYLOR Roy						
Hoyland, 2 April, 1933						(G)
Scunthorpe U.	Denaby U.	01.53	52	2	-	0
TAYLOR Royston						
Blackpool, 28 September, 1956						(M)
Preston N.E.	App	10.74	75	3	0	0
Blackburn Rov.	Sunderland (N/C)	11.76	78	3	0	1
TAYLOR Samuel McGregor						
Glasgow, 23 September, 1933						(W)
Preston N.E.	Falkirk	06.55	55-60	149	-	40
Carlisle U.	Tr	06.61	61-63	93	-	12
Southport	Tr	07.64	64	36	-	3
TAYLOR Scott Dean						
Portsmouth, 28 November, 1970						(M)
Reading	YT	06.89	88-94	164	43	24
Leicester C.	Tr	07.95	95-96	59	5	6
TAYLOR Scott James						
Chertsey, 5 May, 1976						(F)
Millwall	Staines	02.95	94-95	13	15	0
Bolton W.	Tr	03.96	95-96	2	10	1
Rotherham U.	L	12.97	97	10	0	3
Blackpool	L	03.98	97	3	2	1
TAYLOR Shaun						
Plymouth, 26 February, 1963						(CD)
Exeter C.	Bideford	12.86	86-90	200	0	17
Swindon T.	Tr	07.91	91-96	212	0	30
Bristol C.	Tr	09.96	96-97	72	0	3
TAYLOR Stanley						
Southport, 17 November, 1932						(OL)
Southport	Fleetwood Hesketh	02.56	55	2	-	0
TAYLOR Stephen Christopher Edward						
Cannock, 7 January, 1970 E Semi Pro						(F)
Crystal Palace	Bromsgrove Rov.	06.95				
Northampton T.	L	10.95	95	1	1	0
TAYLOR Steven						
Chesterfield, 18 December, 1973						(F)
Chesterfield (N/C)	Biwater	08.93	93	1	0	0
TAYLOR Steven Jeffrey						
Royton, 18 October, 1955						(F)
Bolton W.	App	10.73	74-77	34	6	16
Port Vale	L	10.75	75	4	0	2
Oldham Ath.	Tr	10.77	77-78	45	2	25
Luton T.	Tr	01.79	78	15	5	1

League Club	Source	Date Signed	Seasons Played	Apps	Subs	Gls
Mansfield T.	Tr	07.79	79	30	7	7
Burnley	Tr	07.80	80-82	80	6	37
Wigan Ath.	Tr	08.83	83	29	1	7
Stockport Co.	Tr	03.84	83-84	26	0	8
Rochdale	Tr	11.84	84-86	84	0	42
Preston N.E.	Tr	10.86	86	5	0	2
Burnley	Tr	08.87	87-88	38	7	6
Rochdale	Tr	03.89	88	16	1	4
TAYLOR Stuart						
Bristol, 18 April, 1947						(CD)
Bristol Rov.	Jnrs	01.66	65-79	546	0	28
TAYLOR Stuart Raymond						
Owston Ferry, 6 April, 1946						(LB)
Scunthorpe U.		08.65	65-68	64	3	0
TAYLOR Thomas						
Barnsley, 29 January, 1932 Died 1958 E 'B'/EF Lge/E-19						(CF)
Barnsley	Jnrs	07.49	50-52	44	-	26
Manchester U.	Tr	03.53	52-57	166	-	112
TAYLOR Thomas Frederick						
Hornchurch, 26 September, 1951 E Sch/E Yth/Eu23-11						(CD)
Leyton Orient	App	10.68	67-70	112	2	4
West Ham U.	Tr	10.70	70-78	340	0	8
Leyton Orient	Tr	05.79	79-81	116	0	5
Charlton Ath.	Beerschot (Bel)	08.83				
TAYLOR Thomas William James						
Wandsworth, 10 September, 1946						(IF)
Portsmouth		04.64				
Gillingham	Tr	05.65	65	19	1	0
Bournemouth	Tr	06.66	66-67	26	0	8
TAYLOR Walter Bingley						
Kirton-in-Lindsey, 30 October, 1926						(FB)
Grimsby T.	Hibaldstow	08.44	49-50	21	-	0
Southport	Tr	07.51	51-57	269	-	1
Oldham Ath.	Tr	07.58	58-59	51	-	0
TAYLOR William						
Edinburgh, 31 July, 1939 Died 1981						(M)
Leyton Orient	Bonnyrigg Rose	08.59	60-62	23	-	0
Nottingham F.	Tr	10.63	63-68	10	10	1
Lincoln C.	Tr	05.69	69-70	74	5	6
TAYLOR William Donnachie						
Kirkconnel (Ayrs), 3 June, 1938						(G)
Luton T.	Partick Thistle	12.67	67-68	6	0	0
TEAGUE William Edward						
Lydney, 26 September, 1937						(G)
Swindon T.	Gloucester C.	03.61	60-61	3	-	0
TEALE Richard Grant						
Millom, 27 February, 1952						(G)
Queens Park R.	Walton & Hersham	07.73	74	1	0	0
Fulham	Tr	08.76	76	5	0	0
Wimbledon	Tr	08.77	77	15	0	0
TEALE Shaun						
Southport, 10 March, 1964 E Semi Pro						(CD)
Bournemouth	Weymouth	01.89	88-90	99	1	4
Aston Villa	Tr	07.91	91-94	146	1	2
Tranmere Rov.	Tr	08.95	95-96	54	0	0
Preston N.E.	L	02.97	96	5	0	0
TEARSE David James						
Newcastle, 7 August, 1951						(F)
Leicester C.	North Kenton B.C.	10.69	69-70	7	1	1
Torquay U.	Tr	11.71	71-74	77	0	23
Reading	L	01.75	74	2	0	0
TEASDALE John						
Glasgow, 15 October, 1962						(F)
Wolverhampton W.	Nairn Co.	12.80	80-81	6	2	0
Walsall	Tr	03.82	81-82	13	0	3
Hereford U. (N/C)	Tr	01.83	82	5	0	1
Blackpool (N/C)		11.84	84	1	6	1
TEASDALE John (Jack) George						
Rossington, 15 March, 1929						(WH)
Doncaster Rov.		10.49	50-55	113	-	0
TEASDALE Thomas						
						(OL)
Hull C. (Am)		05.47	46	1	-	0

League Club	Source	Date Signed	Seasons Played	Apps	Subs	Gls
TEATHER Paul						
Rotherham, 26 December, 1977 E Sch/E Yth						(M)
Manchester U.	YT	08.94				
Bournemouth	L	12.97	97	5	5	0
TEBBUTT Robert Stanley						
Irchester, 10 November, 1934						(IF)
Northampton T.		10.56	56-59	55	-	21
TEDALDI Domenico Arch						
Aberystwyth, 12 August, 1980 W Yth						(F)
Doncaster Rov.	YT	●	97	0	2	1
TEDDS William Henry						
Bedworth, 27 July, 1943						(FB)
Coventry C.	Jnrs	09.60	61-64	8	-	0
TEDESCO John Joseph						
Plympton, 7 March, 1949						(F)
Plymouth Arg.	App	05.66	66-69	34	8	4
TEECE David Alfred						
Oldham, 1 September, 1927						(G)
Hull C.	Hyde U.	02.52	53-55	25	-	0
Oldham Ath.	Tr	06.56	56-58	91	-	0
TEER Kevin Paul						
Wood Green, 7 December, 1963						(D)
Brentford	App	12.81	80	0	1	0
TEES Matthew						
Johnstone, 13 October, 1939						(CF)
Grimsby T.	Airdrieonians	07.63	63-66	113	0	51
Charlton Ath.	Tr	02.67	66-69	88	1	32
Luton T.	Tr	08.69	69-70	33	2	13
Grimsby T.	Tr	11.70	70-72	83	0	42
TELFER George Andrew						
Liverpool, 6 July, 1955						(W)
Everton	App	08.72	73-80	81	18	20
Scunthorpe U.	San Diego (USA)	12.81	81-82	34	2	11
Preston N.E. (N/C)	Altrincham	08.83	83	0	2	0
TELFER Paul Norman						
Edinburgh, 21 October, 1971 Su21-3/S 'B'						(RM)
Luton T.	YT	11.88	90-94	136	8	19
Coventry C.	Tr	07.95	95-97	95	3	4
TELFORD William Albert						
Carlisle, 5 March, 1956						(CF)
Manchester C.	Tranmere Rov. (App)	08.75	75	0	1	0
Peterborough U.	Tr	09.75	75	3	1	2
Colchester U.	L	01.76	75	1	1	1
TELLING Maurice William						
Southwark, 5 August, 1919 Died 1973						(CF)
Millwall	Berkhamsted	10.46	46	1	-	0
TEMBY William						
Dover, 16 September, 1934						(IF)
Queens Park R.	Rhyl	02.55	55-56	7	-	3
TEMPEST Dale Michael						
Leeds, 30 December, 1963						(F)
Fulham	App	12.81	80-83	25	9	6
Huddersfield T.	Tr	08.84	84-85	63	2	27
Gillingham	L	03.86	85	9	0	4
Colchester U.	Lokeren (Bel)	08.87	87-88	69	8	18
TEMPLE Derek William						
Liverpool, 13 November, 1938 E Sch/E Yth/EF Lge/E-1						(OL)
Everton	Jnrs	08.56	56-67	231	1	72
Preston N.E.	Tr	09.67	67-69	75	1	14
TEMPLE William						
Blaydon, 12 December, 1915						(IF)
Aldershot	Newbiggin W.E.	11.34	34-36	14	-	2
Carlisle U.	Tr	05.37	37	11	-	3
Grimsby T.	Tr	09.38	38	2	-	0
Gateshead	Tr	05.46	46	10	-	0
TEMPLEMAN John Henry						
Bognor Regis, 21 September, 1947						(WH/FB)
Brighton & H.A.	Arundel T.	07.66	66-73	219	7	16
Exeter C.	Tr	05.74	74-78	205	1	7
Swindon T.	Tr	07.79	79-80	20	1	0

TEN HEUVEL Laurens
Netherlands, 6 June, 1976 (F)

League Club	Source	Date Signed	Seasons Played	Apps	Subs	Gls
Barnsley	F.C. Den Bosch (Neth)	03.96	95-97	1	7	0

TENNANT Albert
Ilkeston, 29 October, 1917 Died 1986 (WH)

League Club	Source	Date Signed	Seasons Played	Apps	Subs	Gls
Chelsea	Stanton Iron Wks	11.34	46-48	2	-	0

TENNANT David
Walsall, 13 June, 1945 (G)

League Club	Source	Date Signed	Seasons Played	Apps	Subs	Gls
Walsall	Jnrs	08.63	63-64	19	-	0
Lincoln C.	Worcester C.	09.66	66-68	40	0	0
Rochdale	Tr	08.69	70	16	0	0

TENNANT Desmond Warren
Cardiff, 17 October, 1925 (FB/OR)

League Club	Source	Date Signed	Seasons Played	Apps	Subs	Gls
Cardiff C.	Jnrs	08.45				
Brighton & H.A.	Barry T.	07.48	48-58	400	-	40

TENNANT John Graham
Darlington, 1 August, 1939 (G)

League Club	Source	Date Signed	Seasons Played	Apps	Subs	Gls
Darlington		05.57	56-57	8	-	0
Chelsea	Tr	08.59				
Southend U.	Tr	10.59	60-62	2	-	0

TENNANT Sydney David **Keith**
Newport, 6 June, 1934 (WH)

League Club	Source	Date Signed	Seasons Played	Apps	Subs	Gls
Newport Co.	Jnrs	01.55	55-57	40	-	1

TENNANT Frederick **Roy**
South Africa, 12 September, 1936 (CH)

League Club	Source	Date Signed	Seasons Played	Apps	Subs	Gls
Brighton & H.A.		08.57				
Workington	Tr	07.58	58-61	152	-	1

TENNENT David
Ayr, 22 January, 1930 (W)

League Club	Source	Date Signed	Seasons Played	Apps	Subs	Gls
Ipswich T.	Annbank U.	07.52	52	4	-	0

TERNENT Raymond
Blyth, 9 September, 1948 (FB)

League Club	Source	Date Signed	Seasons Played	Apps	Subs	Gls
Burnley	App	09.65	66-70	13	0	0
Southend U.	Tr	06.71	71-72	82	0	1
Doncaster Rov.	Tr	08.73	73-76	78	6	3

TERNENT Francis **Stanley**
Gateshead, 16 June, 1946 (M/CD)

League Club	Source	Date Signed	Seasons Played	Apps	Subs	Gls
Burnley	App	06.63	66-67	5	0	0
Carlisle U.	Tr	05.68	68-73	186	2	5

TERRIER David
Verdun, France, 4 August, 1973 (LB)

League Club	Source	Date Signed	Seasons Played	Apps	Subs	Gls
West Ham U.	Metz (Fr)	07.97	97	0	1	0
Newcastle U.	Tr	01.98				

TERRIS James
Dunfermline, 25 July, 1933 (FB)

League Club	Source	Date Signed	Seasons Played	Apps	Subs	Gls
Bristol C.	Chippenham T.	10.55	56-57	4	-	0
Carlisle U.	Tr	04.59	59-60	29	-	1

TERRY Patrick Alfred
Lambeth, 2 October, 1933 (CF)

League Club	Source	Date Signed	Seasons Played	Apps	Subs	Gls
Charlton Ath.	Eastbourne	03.54	53-54	4	-	1
Newport Co.	Tr	05.56	56-57	55	-	30
Swansea C.	Tr	02.58	57-58	17	-	9
Gillingham	Tr	10.58	58-60	109	-	62
Northampton T.	Tr	07.61	61	24	-	10
Millwall	Tr	02.62	61-63	97	-	41
Reading	Tr	08.64	64-66	99	0	41
Swindon T.	Tr	02.67	66-67	60	1	23
Brentford	Tr	06.68	68	29	0	12

TERRY Peter Edward
Enfield, 11 September, 1972 (M)

League Club	Source	Date Signed	Seasons Played	Apps	Subs	Gls
Aldershot	YT	07.91	90	1	0	0

TERRY Steven Graham
Clapton, 14 June, 1962 (CD)

League Club	Source	Date Signed	Seasons Played	Apps	Subs	Gls
Watford	App	01.80	79-87	160	0	14
Hull C.	Tr	06.88	88-89	62	0	4
Northampton T.	Tr	03.90	89-93	181	0	17

TESTER Paul Leonard
Stroud, 10 March, 1959 (LW)

League Club	Source	Date Signed	Seasons Played	Apps	Subs	Gls
Shrewsbury T.	Cheltenham T.	07.83	83-87	86	12	12
Hereford U.	L	11.84	84	4	0	0
Hereford U.	Tr	08.88	88-90	105	9	14

TETHER Colin
Stourbridge, 11 August, 1939 E Yth (FB)

League Club	Source	Date Signed	Seasons Played	Apps	Subs	Gls
Wolverhampton W.	Jnrs	08.55	56	1	-	0
Oxford U.	Tr	07.60				

TEWLEY Alan Bernard
Leicester, 22 January, 1945 (OR)

League Club	Source	Date Signed	Seasons Played	Apps	Subs	Gls
Leicester C.	App	03.62	66-68	15	3	5
Bradford P.A.	Tr	11.69	69	28	0	4
Crewe Alex.	Tr	10.70	70-72	57	11	13

THACKERAY Andrew John
Huddersfield, 13 February, 1968 (M/RB)

League Club	Source	Date Signed	Seasons Played	Apps	Subs	Gls
Manchester C.	Jnrs	02.68				
Huddersfield T.	Tr	07.86	86	2	0	0
Newport Co.	Tr	03.87	86-87	53	1	4
Wrexham	Tr	07.88	88-91	139	13	14
Rochdale	Tr	07.92	92-96	161	4	12

THARME Derek
Brighton, 19 August, 1938 (FB)

League Club	Source	Date Signed	Seasons Played	Apps	Subs	Gls
Tottenham H.	Whitehaven	10.56				
Southend U.	Tr	05.62	62	7	-	0

THATCHER Benjamin David
Swindon, 30 November, 1975 E Yth/Eu21-4 (LB)

League Club	Source	Date Signed	Seasons Played	Apps	Subs	Gls
Millwall	YT	06.92	93-95	87	3	1
Wimbledon	Tr	07.96	96-97	32	3	0

THEAKER Clarence Alfred
Spalding, 8 December, 1912 Died 1992 (G)

League Club	Source	Date Signed	Seasons Played	Apps	Subs	Gls
Grimsby T.	Spalding T.	05.34	35-38	5	-	0
Newcastle U.	Tr	11.38	38-46	13	-	0
Hartlepool U.	Tr	06.47	47	14	-	0

THEAR Anthony Charles
Edmonton, 4 February, 1948 (CF)

League Club	Source	Date Signed	Seasons Played	Apps	Subs	Gls
Arsenal	Jnrs	02.65				
Luton T.	Tr	07.66	66	12	1	5
Gillingham	Tr	02.67	66-68	7	0	1

THEODOSIOU Andrew
Stoke Newington, 30 October, 1970 (CD)

League Club	Source	Date Signed	Seasons Played	Apps	Subs	Gls
Norwich C.	Tottenham H. (YT)	07.89				
Hereford U.	Tr	07.91	91-92	41	1	2

THEW Lee
Sunderland, 23 October, 1974 (M)

League Club	Source	Date Signed	Seasons Played	Apps	Subs	Gls
Doncaster Rov.	YT	08.93	93-94	21	11	2
Scarborough	Tr	08.95	95	9	5	0

THIJSSEN Franciscus Johannes
Netherlands, 23 January, 1952 Dutch Int (M)

League Club	Source	Date Signed	Seasons Played	Apps	Subs	Gls
Ipswich T.	Twente Enschede (Neth)	02.79	78-82	123	2	10
Nottingham F.	Vancouver (Can)	10.83	83	17	0	3

THIRLBY Anthony Dennis
Germany, 4 March, 1976 NI Yth (M)

League Club	Source	Date Signed	Seasons Played	Apps	Subs	Gls
Exeter C.	YT	07.94	93-95	27	12	2
Torquay U. (N/C)	Bideford	02.97	96	1	2	0

THOLOT Didier
France, 2 April, 1964 (F)

League Club	Source	Date Signed	Seasons Played	Apps	Subs	Gls
Walsall (L)	Sion (Fr)	03.98	97	13	1	4

THOM Lewis McDonald
Stornaway, 10 April, 1944 (OL)

League Club	Source	Date Signed	Seasons Played	Apps	Subs	Gls
Shrewsbury T.	Dundee U.	09.65	65-66	48	1	5
Lincoln C.	Tr	05.67	66-68	45	2	4
Bradford P.A.	Tr	06.69	69	31	0	1

THOM Stuart Paul
Dewsbury, 27 December, 1976 (CD)

League Club	Source	Date Signed	Seasons Played	Apps	Subs	Gls
Nottingham F.	YT	01.94				
Mansfield T.	L	12.97	97	5	0	0

THOMAS Andrew Mark
Oxford, 16 December, 1962 (M/F)

League Club	Source	Date Signed	Seasons Played	Apps	Subs	Gls
Oxford U.	App	12.80	80-85	89	27	32
Fulham	L	12.82	82	3	1	2
Derby Co.	L	03.83	82	0	1	0
Newcastle U.	Tr	09.86	86-87	24	7	6
Bradford C.	Tr	06.88	88	15	8	5
Plymouth Arg.	Tr	07.89	89-90	47	3	19

THOMAS Barrie
Merthyr Tydfil, 27 August, 1954 (M)

League Club	Source	Date Signed	Seasons Played	Apps	Subs	Gls
Swansea C. (Am)	Jnrs	08.71	71	2	0	0
Bournemouth	Merthyr Tydfil	08.79	79	3	0	0

THOMAS Ernest Barrie
Measham, 19 May, 1937 E Yth (CF)

League Club	Source	Date Signed	Seasons Played	Apps	Subs	Gls
Leicester C.	Jnrs	07.54	54-55	7	-	3
Mansfield T.	Tr	06.57	57-59	72	-	48
Scunthorpe U.	Tr	09.59	59-61	91	-	67
Newcastle U.	Tr	01.62	61-64	73	-	48
Scunthorpe U.	Tr	11.64	64-66	52	0	26
Barnsley	Tr	11.66	66-67	43	0	19

THOMAS Brian
Neath, 7 June, 1976 (G)

League Club	Source	Date Signed	Seasons Played	Apps	Subs	Gls
Hereford U.	YT	●	93	3	0	0

THOMAS Brian Hugh
Carmarthen, 28 June, 1944 (WH)

League Club	Source	Date Signed	Seasons Played	Apps	Subs	Gls
Swansea C.	Jnrs	06.62	64	4	-	0

THOMAS Bryndley
Coventry, 13 December, 1932 (CF)

League Club	Source	Date Signed	Seasons Played	Apps	Subs	Gls
Coventry C.	Longford Rov.	09.50	52-53	12	-	1

THOMAS Cedric David
Hebden Bridge, 19 September, 1936 (IF)

League Club	Source	Date Signed	Seasons Played	Apps	Subs	Gls
Halifax T.	Heptonstall	07.57	57-59	20	-	5
Southport	Tr	07.60				

THOMAS Daniel Joseph
Worksop, 12 November, 1961 E Sch/Eu21-7/E-2 (FB)

League Club	Source	Date Signed	Seasons Played	Apps	Subs	Gls
Coventry C.	App	12.78	79-82	103	5	5
Tottenham H.	Tr	06.83	83-86	80	7	1

THOMAS David
Kirkby-in-Ashfield, 5 October, 1950 E Yth/Eu23-11/E-8 (W)

League Club	Source	Date Signed	Seasons Played	Apps	Subs	Gls
Burnley	App	10.67	66-72	153	4	19
Queens Park R.	Tr	10.72	72-76	181	1	28
Everton	Tr	08.77	77-78	71	0	4
Wolverhampton W.	Tr	10.79	79	10	0	0
Middlesbrough	Vancouver (Can)	03.82	81	13	0	1
Portsmouth	Tr	07.82	82-84	24	6	0

THOMAS David (Dai)
Neath, 1 August, 1926 W-2 (FB/IF)

League Club	Source	Date Signed	Seasons Played	Apps	Subs	Gls
Swansea C.	Abercregan	08.48	49-59	298	-	16
Newport Co.	Tr	07.61	61-62	58	-	1

THOMAS David (Dai) John
Caerphilly, 26 September, 1975 Wu21-2 (F)

League Club	Source	Date Signed	Seasons Played	Apps	Subs	Gls
Swansea C.	YT	07.94	94-96	36	20	10
Watford	Tr	07.97	97	8	8	3

THOMAS David Stuart Lynne
Swansea, 19 September, 1920 Died 1993 W Sch (CF)

League Club	Source	Date Signed	Seasons Played	Apps	Subs	Gls
Swansea C.	Abergregown Jnrs	10.42				
Brighton & H.A.	Tr	06.47	47	13	-	4

THOMAS David Watkin John
Stepney, 6 July, 1917 Died 1991 (CF)

League Club	Source	Date Signed	Seasons Played	Apps	Subs	Gls
Plymouth Arg.	Romford	06.38	38-47	74	-	29
Watford	Tr	02.48	47-50	105	-	39
Gillingham	Tr	10.50	50-52	80	-	42

THOMAS Dean Ronald
Bedworth, 19 December, 1961 (M/FB)

League Club	Source	Date Signed	Seasons Played	Apps	Subs	Gls
Wimbledon	Nuneaton Borough	07.81	81-83	57	0	8
Northampton T.	Fortuna Dusseldorf (Ger)	08.88	88-89	74	0	12
Notts Co.	Tr	03.90	89-93	129	5	8

THOMAS Dennis
Hebburn, 2 February, 1926 (OL)

League Club	Source	Date Signed	Seasons Played	Apps	Subs	Gls
Bury	Wardley Welfare	01.49	49	3	-	0
Accrington St.	Tr	07.50	50	34	-	5

THOMAS Edward
Newton-le-Willows, 23 October, 1933 (IF)

League Club	Source	Date Signed	Seasons Played	Apps	Subs	Gls
Everton	Jnrs	10.51	56-59	86	-	39
Blackburn Rov.	Tr	02.60	59-61	37	-	9
Swansea C.	Tr	07.62	62-64	68	-	21
Derby Co.	Tr	08.64	64-67	102	3	43
Leyton Orient	Tr	09.67	67	11	0	2

THOMAS Edwin Henry Charles
Swindon, 9 November, 1932 (G)

League Club	Source	Date Signed	Seasons Played	Apps	Subs	Gls
Southampton	Swindon B.R.	05.51	51	8	-	0

THOMAS Geoffrey
Swansea, 18 February, 1948 Wu23-3 (M)

League Club	Source	Date Signed	Seasons Played	Apps	Subs	Gls
Swansea C.	App	02.66	66-75	345	15	52

THOMAS Geoffrey Paul
Bradford, 12 March, 1946 (FB)

League Club	Source	Date Signed	Seasons Played	Apps	Subs	Gls
Bradford P.A.	App	03.63	63-65	53	0	0

THOMAS Geoffrey Robert
Manchester, 5 August, 1964 E'B'/E-9 (M)

League Club	Source	Date Signed	Seasons Played	Apps	Subs	Gls
Rochdale (N/C)	Littleborough	08.82	82-83	10	1	1
Crewe Alex.	Tr	03.84	83-86	120	5	21
Crystal Palace	Tr	06.87	87-92	192	3	26
Wolverhampton W.	Tr	06.93	93-96	36	10	8
Nottingham F.	Tr	07.97	97	13	7	3

THOMAS George Vincent
Cardiff, 25 June, 1930 (WH)

League Club	Source	Date Signed	Seasons Played	Apps	Subs	Gls
Cardiff C.	Cardiff Nomads	05.49				
Newport Co.	Tr	07.53	53-58	137	-	0

THOMAS Gerald (Geoff) Shannon
Derby, 21 February, 1926 (FB)

League Club	Source	Date Signed	Seasons Played	Apps	Subs	Gls
Nottingham F.	Jnrs	09.43	46-59	403	-	1

THOMAS Glen Andrew
Hackney, 6 October, 1967 (D)

League Club	Source	Date Signed	Seasons Played	Apps	Subs	Gls
Fulham	App	10.85	86-94	246	5	6
Peterborough U. (N/C)	Tr	11.94	94	6	2	0
Barnet	Tr	03.95	94-95	22	1	0
Gillingham	Tr	01.96	95-97	20	8	0

THOMAS David Gwyn
Swansea, 26 September, 1957 W Sch/Wu21-3 (M)

League Club	Source	Date Signed	Seasons Played	Apps	Subs	Gls
Leeds U.	App	07.75	74-83	79	10	3
Barnsley	Tr	03.84	83-89	197	4	17
Hull C.	Tr	03.90	89-90	21	1	0
Carlisle U.	Tr	08.91	91	35	2	1

THOMAS James Alan
Swansea, 16 January, 1979 W Yth/Wu21-7 (F)

League Club	Source	Date Signed	Seasons Played	Apps	Subs	Gls
Blackburn Rov.	YT	07.96				
West Bromwich A.	L	08.97	97	1	2	0

THOMAS Jeffrey
Newport, 18 May, 1949 W Sch/W Yth/Wu23-1 (W)

League Club	Source	Date Signed	Seasons Played	Apps	Subs	Gls
Newport Co.	Jnrs	05.66	65-72	206	3	31

THOMAS John
Poole, 28 May, 1936 (G)

League Club	Source	Date Signed	Seasons Played	Apps	Subs	Gls
Bournemouth	Poole T.	05.58	58	4	-	0

THOMAS John (Joe) Charles
Great Houghton, 22 September, 1932 (FB)

League Club	Source	Date Signed	Seasons Played	Apps	Subs	Gls
Wolverhampton W.	Wath W.	08.51				
Barnsley	Tr	06.52	52-57	134	-	0
Mansfield T.	Tr	03.58	57-58	41	-	0
Chesterfield	Tr	07.59	59	6	-	0

THOMAS John Ernest
Walsall, 15 July, 1922 (CF)

League Club	Source	Date Signed	Seasons Played	Apps	Subs	Gls
Bournemouth		05.46				
West Bromwich A.	Tr	07.46				
Crystal Palace	Tr	10.48	48-51	53	-	17

THOMAS John Wilfred
Liverpool, 23 December, 1926 (W)

League Club	Source	Date Signed	Seasons Played	Apps	Subs	Gls
Everton		12.48				
Swindon T.	Tr	02.49	50-51	17	-	3
Chester C.	Headington U.	07.53	53	29	-	5
Stockport Co.	Tr	07.54	54	6	-	0

THOMAS John William
Wednesbury, 5 August, 1958 (F)

League Club	Source	Date Signed	Seasons Played	Apps	Subs	Gls
Everton		07.77				
Tranmere Rov.	L	03.79	78	10	1	2
Halifax T.	L	10.79	79	5	0	0
Bolton W.	Tr	06.80	80-81	18	4	6
Chester C.	Tr	08.82	82	44	0	20
Lincoln C.	Tr	08.83	83-84	56	11	18
Preston N.E.	Tr	06.85	85-86	69	9	38
Bolton W.	Tr	07.87	87-88	71	2	31
West Bromwich A.	Tr	07.89	89	8	10	1
Preston N.E.	Tr	02.90	89-91	24	3	6
Hartlepool U.	Tr	03.92	91	5	2	1
Halifax T.	Tr	07.92	92	10	2	0

THOMAS Walter Keith
Oswestry, 28 July, 1929 (OR)

League Club	Source	Date Signed	Seasons Played	Apps	Subs	Gls
Sheffield Wed.	Oswestry T.	09.50	50-51	10	-	1
Cardiff C.	Tr	07.52	52-53	9	-	4
Plymouth Arg.	Tr	11.53	53-55	35	-	8
Exeter C.	Tr	03.56	55-56	43	-	6

THOMAS Kevin Anthony
Prescot, 13 August, 1944 (G)

League Club	Source	Date Signed	Seasons Played	Apps	Subs	Gls
Blackpool	Prescot Cables	06.66	66-68	12	0	0
Tranmere Rov.	Tr	09.69	69-70	18	0	0
Oxford U.	Tr	07.71	72	5	0	0
Southport	Tr	07.74	74-75	67	0	0

THOMAS Lee
Tredegar, 1 November, 1970 (FB)

League Club	Source	Date Signed	Seasons Played	Apps	Subs	Gls
Hereford U.	Newport Co. (YT)	07.89	89	0	1	0

THOMAS Martin Richard
Senghenydd, 28 November, 1959 W Yth/Wu21-2/W-1 (G)

League Club	Source	Date Signed	Seasons Played	Apps	Subs	Gls
Bristol Rov.	App	09.77	76-81	162	0	0
Cardiff C.	L	07.82	82	15	0	0
Southend U.	L	02.83	82	6	0	0
Newcastle U.	Tr	03.83	82-87	118	0	0
Middlesbrough	L	10.84	84	4	0	0
Birmingham C.	Tr	10.88	88-92	144	0	0

THOMAS Martin Russell
Lymington, 12 September, 1973 (M)

League Club	Source	Date Signed	Seasons Played	Apps	Subs	Gls
Southampton	YT	06.92				
Leyton Orient (N/C)	Tr	03.94	93	5	0	2
Fulham	Tr	07.94	94-97	59	31	8

THOMAS Michael Lauriston
Lambeth, 24 August, 1967 E Sch/E Yth/Eu21-12/E'B'/E-2 (M)

League Club	Source	Date Signed	Seasons Played	Apps	Subs	Gls
Arsenal	App	12.84	86-91	149	14	24
Portsmouth	L	12.86	86	3	0	0
Liverpool	Tr	12.91	91-97	96	28	9
Middlesbrough	L	02.98	97	10	0	0

THOMAS Michael Reginald
Caersws, 7 July, 1954 Wu21-2/Wu23-1/W-51 (W/M)

League Club	Source	Date Signed	Seasons Played	Apps	Subs	Gls
Wrexham	Jnrs	05.72	71-78	217	13	33
Manchester U.	Tr	11.78	78-80	90	0	11
Everton	Tr	08.81	81	10	0	0
Brighton & H.A.	Tr	11.81	81	18	2	0
Stoke C.	Tr	08.82	82-83	57	0	14
Chelsea	Tr	01.84	83-84	43	1	9
West Bromwich A.	Tr	09.85	85	20	0	0
Derby Co.	L	03.86	85	9	0	0
Shrewsbury T.	Wichita (USA)	08.88	88	40	0	1
Leeds U.	Tr	06.89	89	3	0	0
Stoke C.	L	03.90	89	8	0	0
Stoke C.	Tr	08.90	90	32	6	7
Wrexham	Tr	07.91	91-92	34	0	2

THOMAS Mitchell Antony
Luton, 2 October, 1964 E Yth/Eu21-3/E'B' (FB/M)

League Club	Source	Date Signed	Seasons Played	Apps	Subs	Gls
Luton T.	App	08.82	82-85	106	1	1
Tottenham H.	Tr	07.86	86-90	136	21	6
West Ham U.	Tr	08.91	91-92	37	1	3
Luton T.	Tr	11.93	93-97	144	9	5

THOMAS Patrick
Sidmouth, 7 March, 1965 (M)

League Club	Source	Date Signed	Seasons Played	Apps	Subs	Gls
Exeter C. (N/C)	Jnrs	06.82	82	0	1	0

THOMAS Peter John
Pontypridd, 18 October, 1932 (OR)

League Club	Source	Date Signed	Seasons Played	Apps	Subs	Gls
Cardiff C.	Jnrs	03.53	53	5	-	1
Exeter C.	Tr	12.54	54-55	29	-	4
Newport Co.	Tr	07.56	56-57	6	-	1

THOMAS Peter John
Coventry, 20 November, 1944 IR-2 (G)

League Club	Source	Date Signed	Seasons Played	Apps	Subs	Gls
Coventry C.	Coventry G.E.C.	06.66	66	1	0	0

THOMAS Philip Leslie
Sherborne, 14 December, 1952 Died 1998 (M/RB)

League Club	Source	Date Signed	Seasons Played	Apps	Subs	Gls
Bournemouth	App	07.71				
Colchester U.	Tr	05.72	72-75	103	5	8

THOMAS Rees
Aberdare, 3 January, 1934 (RB)

League Club	Source	Date Signed	Seasons Played	Apps	Subs	Gls
Cardiff C.	Jnrs	01.51				
Torquay U.	L	08.53	53	1	-	0
Brighton & H.A.	Tr	09.56	56-57	31	-	1
Bournemouth	Tr	01.58	57-58	48	-	0
Portsmouth	Tr	07.59	59-60	30	-	0
Aldershot	Tr	07.61	61-63	103	-	2

THOMAS Robert Albert
Stepney, 2 August, 1919 Died 1990 (IF)

League Club	Source	Date Signed	Seasons Played	Apps	Subs	Gls
Brentford	Hendon	05.39				
Plymouth Arg.	Tr	04.46	46	41	-	17
Fulham	Tr	06.47	47-51	167	-	55
Crystal Palace	Tr	09.52	52-54	96	-	31

THOMAS Roderick Clive
Harlesden, 10 October, 1970 E Sch/E Yth/Eu21-1 (RW)

League Club	Source	Date Signed	Seasons Played	Apps	Subs	Gls
Watford	YT	05.88	87-92	63	21	9
Gillingham	L	03.92	91	8	0	1
Carlisle U.	Tr	07.93	93-96	124	22	16
Chester C.	Tr	07.97	97	25	13	4

THOMAS Roderick John
Glyncorrwg, 11 January, 1947 Wu23-6/W-50 (RB)

League Club	Source	Date Signed	Seasons Played	Apps	Subs	Gls
Swindon T.	Gloucester C.	07.64	65-73	296	0	5
Derby Co.	Tr	11.73	73-77	89	0	2
Cardiff C.	Tr	11.77	77-81	89	7	0
Newport Co. (N/C)	Gloucester C.	03.82	81	3	0	0

THOMAS Scott Lee
Bury, 30 October, 1974 (M)

League Club	Source	Date Signed	Seasons Played	Apps	Subs	Gls
Manchester C.	YT	03.92	94	0	2	0
Brighton & H.A.	L	03.98	97	7	0	0

THOMAS David Sidney
Machynllieth, 12 November, 1919 W-4 (W)

League Club	Source	Date Signed	Seasons Played	Apps	Subs	Gls
Fulham	Treharris	08.38	46-49	57	-	4
Bristol C.	Tr	06.50	50	13	-	1

THOMAS Stanley Herbert
Liverpool, 5 September, 1919 Died 1985 (IF)

League Club	Source	Date Signed	Seasons Played	Apps	Subs	Gls
Tranmere Rov. (Am)	Oxford Univ.	12.48	48	1	0	0

THOMAS Steven
Batley, 29 January, 1957 (FB)

League Club	Source	Date Signed	Seasons Played	Apps	Subs	Gls
Swansea C. (Am)	Jnrs	08.73	73-74	10	0	0

THOMAS Tony
Liverpool, 12 July, 1971 (LB/M)

League Club	Source	Date Signed	Seasons Played	Apps	Subs	Gls
Tranmere Rov.	YT	02.89	88-96	254	3	12
Everton	Tr	08.97	97	6	1	0

THOMAS Valmore Nelville
Worksop, 30 April, 1958 (FB)

League Club	Source	Date Signed	Seasons Played	Apps	Subs	Gls
Coventry C.	App	03.76				
Hereford U.	Tr	03.79	78-80	31	1	1

THOMAS Wayne
Walsall, 28 August, 1978 (M)

League Club	Source	Date Signed	Seasons Played	Apps	Subs	Gls
Walsall	YT	07.96	96-97	17	8	0

THOMAS Wayne Junior Robert
Gloucester, 17 May, 1979 (D/M)

League Club	Source	Date Signed	Seasons Played	Apps	Subs	Gls
Torquay U.	YT	07.97	95-97	7	32	1

THOMAS William Pryce
Glyn-Neath, 28 October, 1923 (W)

League Club	Source	Date Signed	Seasons Played	Apps	Subs	Gls
Torquay U.	Merthyr Tydfil	09.47	47-54	90	-	17

THOMAS Wilson
Derby, 18 November, 1918 (IF)

League Club	Source	Date Signed	Seasons Played	Apps	Subs	Gls
Bristol C.	Matlock T.	10.44	46-49	77	-	18

THOME Emerson August
Porto Alegra, Brazil, 30 March, 1972 (D)

League Club	Source	Date Signed	Seasons Played	Apps	Subs	Gls
Sheffield Wed.	Benfica (Por)	03.98	97	6	0	0

THOMPSON Alan
Goole, 2 September, 1931 (FB)

League Club	Source	Date Signed	Seasons Played	Apps	Subs	Gls
Luton T.	Westpark Jnrs	12.49	56	1	-	0

THOMPSON Alan
Newcastle, 22 December, 1973 E Yth/Eu21-2 (LW)

League Club	Source	Date Signed	Seasons Played	Apps	Subs	Gls
Newcastle U.	YT	03.91	91-92	13	3	0
Bolton W.	Tr	07.93	93-97	143	14	34

THOMPSON Alexander
Sheffield, 8 December, 1917 (RB)

League Club	Source	Date Signed	Seasons Played	Apps	Subs	Gls
Sheffield Wed.	Woodhouse Alliance	06.37				
Lincoln C.	Tr	06.39	46-47	34	-	1
Tranmere Rov.	Tr	06.48	48	1	-	0

THOMPSON William Allan
Liverpool, 20 January, 1952 (CD)

League Club	Source	Date Signed	Seasons Played	Apps	Subs	Gls
Sheffield Wed.	App	01.69	70-75	150	6	3
Stockport Co.	Tr	08.76	76-78	93	1	17
Bradford C.	Portland (USA)	01.80	79-81	31	0	0
Scunthorpe U.	Tr	03.82	81	11	0	0

THOMPSON Andrew Richard
Cannock, 9 November, 1967 (LB/M)

League Club	Source	Date Signed	Seasons Played	Apps	Subs	Gls
West Bromwich A.	App	11.85	85-86	18	6	1
Wolverhampton W.	Tr	11.86	86-96	356	20	43
Tranmere Rov.	Tr	07.97	97	44	0	3

League Club	Source	Date Signed	Seasons Played	Career Record Apps	Subs	Gls

THOMPSON Arthur
Dewsbury, 15 June, 1922 Died 1996 (IF)

League Club	Source	Date Signed	Seasons Played	Apps	Subs	Gls
Huddersfield T.	Thornhill Edge	09.41	46-48	25	-	5

THOMPSON Brian
Kingswinford, 9 February, 1950 (M)

League Club	Source	Date Signed	Seasons Played	Apps	Subs	Gls
Wolverhampton W.	App	02.67				
Oxford U.	Tr	10.69	69-72	52	5	4
Torquay U.	L	03.73	72	9	0	1

THOMPSON George **Brian**
Ashington, 7 August, 1952 E Semi Pro (RB)

League Club	Source	Date Signed	Seasons Played	Apps	Subs	Gls
Sunderland		06.71				
York C.	L	03.73	72	4	2	0
Mansfield T.	Yeovil T.	11.79	79	9	0	0

THOMPSON Charles Maskery
Chesterfield, 19 July, 1920 Died 1997 (CF)

League Club	Source	Date Signed	Seasons Played	Apps	Subs	Gls
Sheffield U.	Bolsover Colly	07.37	46	17	-	3

THOMPSON Christopher David
Walsall, 24 January, 1960 E Yth (M)

League Club	Source	Date Signed	Seasons Played	Apps	Subs	Gls
Bolton W.	App	07.77	77-82	66	7	18
Lincoln C.	L	03.83	82	5	1	0
Blackburn Rov.	Tr	08.83	83-85	81	4	24
Wigan Ath.	Tr	07.86	86-87	67	7	12
Blackpool	Tr	07.88	88-89	27	12	8
Cardiff C.	Tr	03.90	89	1	1	0
Walsall (N/C)		02.91	90	3	0	0

THOMPSON Cyril Alfred
Southend, 18 December, 1918 Died 1972 (CF)

League Club	Source	Date Signed	Seasons Played	Apps	Subs	Gls
Southend U.		07.45	46-47	66	-	36
Derby Co.	Tr	07.48	48-49	16	-	3
Brighton & H.A.	Tr	03.50	49-50	41	-	15
Watford	Tr	03.51	50-52	78	-	36

THOMPSON David
Middlesbrough, 26 February, 1945 (CF)

League Club	Source	Date Signed	Seasons Played	Apps	Subs	Gls
Lincoln C.	Whitby T.	06.64	64	3	-	1

THOMPSON David Anthony
Birkenhead, 12 September, 1977 E Yth/Eu21-2 (M)

League Club	Source	Date Signed	Seasons Played	Apps	Subs	Gls
Liverpool	YT	11.94	96-97	1	6	1
Swindon T.	L	11.97	97	10	0	0

THOMPSON David George
Ashington, 20 November, 1968 (CD)

League Club	Source	Date Signed	Seasons Played	Apps	Subs	Gls
Millwall	App	11.86	87-91	88	9	6
Bristol C.	Tr	06.92	92	17	0	0
Brentford	Tr	02.94	93	9	1	1
Blackpool	Tr	09.94	94	17	0	0
Cambridge U.	Tr	03.95	94-96	36	8	2

THOMPSON David Stanley
Catterick Camp, 12 March, 1945 (OR)

League Club	Source	Date Signed	Seasons Played	Apps	Subs	Gls
Wolverhampton W.	Jnrs	04.62	64	8	-	1
Southampton	Tr	08.66	66-70	21	2	0
Mansfield T.	Tr	10.70	70-73	129	2	21
Chesterfield	Tr	12.73	73	14	0	3

THOMPSON David Stephen
Manchester, 27 May, 1962 (RW)

League Club	Source	Date Signed	Seasons Played	Apps	Subs	Gls
Rochdale	Withington	09.81	81-85	147	8	13
Notts Co.	Tr	08.86	86-87	52	3	8
Wigan Ath.	Tr	10.87	87-89	107	1	14
Preston N.E.	Tr	07.90	90-91	39	7	4
Chester C.	Tr	08.92	92-93	70	10	9
Rochdale	Tr	08.94	94-96	90	21	11

THOMPSON Denis
Bolsover, 19 July, 1934 (OR)

League Club	Source	Date Signed	Seasons Played	Apps	Subs	Gls
Chesterfield	Jnrs	07.51	50-52	24	-	0
Scunthorpe U.	Tr	07.55	55	3	-	0

THOMPSON Dennis
Whitburn, 10 April, 1924 (CF)

League Club	Source	Date Signed	Seasons Played	Apps	Subs	Gls
Hull C.	Whitburn Welfare	04.47	46-47	9	-	8

THOMPSON Dennis
Sheffield, 2 June, 1925 Died 1986 E Sch (F)

League Club	Source	Date Signed	Seasons Played	Apps	Subs	Gls
Sheffield U.	Jnrs	08.42	46-50	96	-	20
Southend U.	Tr	07.51	51-53	51	-	11

THOMPSON Desmond
Southampton, 4 December, 1928 (G)

League Club	Source	Date Signed	Seasons Played	Apps	Subs	Gls
York C.	Gainsborough Trin.	01.51	50-52	80	-	0
Burnley	Tr	11.52	52-54	62	-	0
Sheffield U.	Tr	05.55	55-63	25	-	0

THOMPSON Robert **Eric**
Mexborough, 3 December, 1944 (CH)

League Club	Source	Date Signed	Seasons Played	Apps	Subs	Gls
Doncaster Rov.	Leeds U. (App)	07.62	62	9	-	0

THOMPSON Frederick Norman
Swindon, 24 November, 1937 (WH)

League Club	Source	Date Signed	Seasons Played	Apps	Subs	Gls
Swindon T.	Jnrs	09.55	54-60	21	-	1

THOMPSON Garry Linsey
Birmingham, 7 October, 1959 Eu21-6 (F)

League Club	Source	Date Signed	Seasons Played	Apps	Subs	Gls
Coventry C.	App	06.77	77-82	127	7	38
West Bromwich A.	Tr	02.83	82-84	91	0	39
Sheffield Wed.	Tr	08.85	85	35	1	7
Aston Villa	Tr	06.86	86-88	56	4	17
Watford	Tr	12.88	88-89	24	10	8
Crystal Palace	Tr	03.90	89-90	17	3	3
Queens Park R.	Tr	08.91	91-92	10	9	1
Cardiff C.	Tr	07.93	93-94	39	4	5
Northampton T.	Tr	02.95	94-96	36	14	6

THOMPSON George
Lisburn, 5 November, 1913 (RB)

League Club	Source	Date Signed	Seasons Played	Apps	Subs	Gls
Huddersfield T.	Sligo Rov.	12.38				
Exeter C.	Tr	06.46	46-47	63	-	4
Rochdale	Tr	07.48				

THOMPSON George Herbert
Maltby, 15 September, 1926 (G)

League Club	Source	Date Signed	Seasons Played	Apps	Subs	Gls
Chesterfield		06.47				
Scunthorpe U.	Tr	06.50	50-52	92	-	0
Preston N.E.	Tr	10.52	52-55	140	-	0
Manchester C.	Tr	06.56	56	2	-	0
Carlisle U.	Tr	06.57	57-61	206	-	0

THOMPSON Harry
Mansfield, 29 April, 1915 (WH/IF)

League Club	Source	Date Signed	Seasons Played	Apps	Subs	Gls
Mansfield T.	Jnrs	06.32				
Wolverhampton W.	Tr	06.33	35-38	69	-	16
Sunderland	Tr	12.38	38	11	-	1
York C.	Tr	12.45				
Northampton T.	Tr	11.46	46-48	38	-	2

THOMPSON Henry
South Shields, 21 February, 1932 (F)

League Club	Source	Date Signed	Seasons Played	Apps	Subs	Gls
Gateshead		08.51	51-55	23	-	4

THOMPSON Ian Peter
Dartford, 8 June, 1958 (F)

League Club	Source	Date Signed	Seasons Played	Apps	Subs	Gls
Bournemouth	Salisbury	07.83	83-85	119	2	30

THOMPSON James
Oldham, 26 November, 1935 (WH)

League Club	Source	Date Signed	Seasons Played	Apps	Subs	Gls
Oldham Ath.	Chadderton	01.54	53-58	110	-	19
Exeter C.	Tr	12.58	58-60	105	-	10
Rochdale	Tr	03.61	60-65	199	0	15
Bradford C.	Tr	12.65	65	23	1	1

THOMPSON James Butters
Felling, 7 January, 1943 (FB)

League Club	Source	Date Signed	Seasons Played	Apps	Subs	Gls
Grimsby T.	St. Mary's B.C.	09.61	62-66	156	0	2
Cambridge U.	Port Elizabeth (SA)	01.69	70-72	116	1	0

THOMPSON John (Jack)
Cramlington, 21 March, 1915 Died 1996 (IF)

League Club	Source	Date Signed	Seasons Played	Apps	Subs	Gls
Sheffield Wed.	Blyth Spartans	06.33	33-38	36	-	9
Doncaster Rov.	Tr	05.46	46-47	59	-	17
Chesterfield	Tr	07.48	48-52	82	-	8

THOMPSON John Henry
Newcastle, 4 July, 1932 (G)

League Club	Source	Date Signed	Seasons Played	Apps	Subs	Gls
Newcastle U.	Jnrs	09.50	54-55	8	-	0
Lincoln C.	Tr	05.57	57-59	42	-	0

THOMPSON Joseph Prudhoe
Seaham, 15 November, 1927 Died 1996 (FB)

League Club	Source	Date Signed	Seasons Played	Apps	Subs	Gls
Luton T.	Electrolux	05.46				
Shrewsbury T.	Tr	07.51	51	7	-	0

THOMPSON Keith Anthony
Birmingham, 24 April, 1965 E Yth (W)

League Club	Source	Date Signed	Seasons Played	Apps	Subs	Gls
Coventry C.	App	01.83	82-83	9	3	0
Wimbledon	L	10.83	83	0	3	0
Northampton T.	L	03.85	84	10	0	1
Coventry C.	Real Oviedo (Sp)	09.88	88-90	2	9	1

THOMPSON Kenneth Hurst
Sunderland, 24 April, 1926 (RB)

League Club	Source	Date Signed	Seasons Played	Apps	Subs	Gls
Middlesbrough	Jnrs	11.44				
Gateshead	L	11.46	46	9	-	0
York C.	Tr	07.50	50-51	22	-	0

League Club	Source	Date Signed	Seasons Played	Career Record Apps	Subs	Gls
THOMPSON Kenneth John						
Ipswich, 1 March, 1945						(WH)
Ipswich T.	App	03.62	64-65	11	1	0
Exeter C.	Tr	06.66	66	38	1	1
THOMPSON Kevan John						
Middlesbrough, 8 September, 1948						(CF)
Hartlepool U. (Am)	Threadhalls	10.70	70	6	0	1
THOMPSON Leslie Allen						
Cleethorpes, 23 September, 1968						(LB)
Hull C.	YT	03.87	87-90	31	4	4
Scarborough	L	12.88	88	2	1	1
Maidstone U.	Tr	07.91	91	38	0	0
Burnley	Tr	07.92	92-93	38	1	0
THOMPSON Malcolm George						
Beverley, 19 October, 1946						(CF)
Hartlepool U.	Goole T.	11.68	68-69	43	3	9
Gillingham	Tr	06.70				
THOMPSON Maxwell Stewart						
Liverpool, 31 December, 1956						(CD)
Liverpool	App	01.74	73	1	0	0
Blackpool	Tr	12.77	77-80	92	7	6
Swansea C.	Tr	09.81	81-82	25	1	2
Bournemouth	Tr	08.83	83	9	0	0
Port Vale	L	11.83	83	2	0	0
THOMPSON Neil						
Beverley, 2 October, 1963 E Semi Pro						(LB)
Hull C.	Nottingham F. (App)	11.81	81-82	29	2	0
Scarborough	Tr	08.83	87-88	87	0	15
Ipswich T.	Tr	06.89	89-95	199	7	19
Barnsley	Tr	06.96	96-97	27	0	5
Oldham Ath.	L	12.97	97	8	0	0
York C.	L	03.98	97	12	0	2
THOMPSON Neil Philip						
Hackney, 30 April, 1978						(LB)
Barnet	YT	07.96	95-96	2	1	0
THOMPSON Niall Joseph						
Birmingham, 16 April, 1974						(F)
Crystal Palace	Jnrs	07.92				
Colchester U.	Hong Kong	11.94	94	5	8	5
Brentford	Seattle (USA)	02.98	97	6	2	0
THOMPSON Nigel David						
Leeds, 1 March, 1967						(M)
Leeds U.	App	12.84	83-86	6	1	0
Rochdale	L	08.87	87	3	2	0
Chesterfield	Tr	03.88	87-89	18	2	1
THOMPSON Patrick Alfred						
Exeter, 11 February, 1932						(IF)
Brighton & H.A.	Topsham	01.51	50	1	-	0
THOMPSON Paul Derek Zetland						
Newcastle, 17 April, 1973						(F)
Hartlepool U.	Jnrs	11.91	92-94	44	12	9
THOMPSON Peter						
Carlisle, 27 November, 1942 E Sch/Eu23-4/E-16						(LW)
Preston N.E.	Jnrs	11.59	60-62	121	-	20
Liverpool	Tr	08.63	63-71	318	4	41
Bolton W.	Tr	11.73	73-77	111	6	2
THOMPSON Peter						
Blackhall (Dm), 16 February, 1936 E Amat						(CF)
Wrexham (Am)	Blackhall Colly	11.55	55-56	42	-	21
Hartlepool U.	Tr	07.57	57-58	47	-	22
Derby Co.	Tr	11,58	58-61	52	-	19
Bournemouth	Tr	01.62	61-62	39	-	14
Hartlepool U.	Tr	09.63	63-65	91	0	34
THOMPSON Peter Colin						
Kenya, 25 July, 1942						(W)
Peterborough U.	Grantham	03.64	63-68	79	6	15
THOMPSON Philip Bernard						
Liverpool, 21 January, 1954 E Yth/Eu23-1/EF Lge/E-42						(CD)
Liverpool	App	02.71	71-82	337	3	7
Sheffield U.	Tr	12.84	84-85	36	1	0
THOMPSON Philip Paul						
Blackpool, 1 April, 1981						(CD)
Blackpool	YT	●	97	1	0	0

League Club	Source	Date Signed	Seasons Played	Career Record Apps	Subs	Gls
THOMPSON Raymond						
Spennymoor, 21 October, 1925 Died 1996						(FB)
Sunderland		11.45				
Hartlepool U.	Tr	01.47	46-57	396	-	2
THOMPSON Richard John						
Hawkesbury (Glos), 11 April, 1969						(F)
Newport Co.	Yate T.	01.87	87	10	3	2
Torquay U.	Tr	06.88	88	11	4	4
THOMPSON Ronald						
Carlisle, 20 January, 1932						(WH)
Carlisle U.		07.51	51-63	373	-	12
THOMPSON Ronald						
Sheffield, 24 December, 1921 Died 1988						(IF)
Sheffield Wed.	Wadsley C.F.C.	04.45				
Rotherham U.	Tr	05.47	47-48	30	-	10
York C.	Tr	06.49	49	8	-	0
THOMPSON Sidney						
Bedlington, 14 July, 1928						(IF)
Nottingham F.		09.47	52-54	22	-	8
Scunthorpe U.	Tr	08.55				
THOMPSON Simon Lee						
Sheffield, 27 February, 1970						(RB/M)
Rotherham U.	YT	06.88	88-90	12	16	0
Scarborough	Tr	12.91	91-94	99	9	6
THOMPSON Steven Antony						
Manchester, 17 February, 1972						(CD)
Gillingham	YT	●	89	1	1	0
THOMPSON Steven James						
Oldham, 2 November, 1964						(M)
Bolton W.	App	11.82	82-91	329	6	49
Luton T.	Tr	09.91	91	5	0	0
Leicester C.	Tr	10.91	91-94	121	6	18
Burnley	Tr	02.95	94-96	44	5	1
Rotherham U.	Tr	07.97	97	32	7	3
THOMPSON Steven John						
Plymouth, 12 January, 1963 E Semi Pro						(M)
Bristol C.	Jnrs	07.81	81-82	10	2	1
Torquay U. (N/C)	Tr	02.83	82	0	1	0
Wycombe W.	Slough T.	02.92	93-94	41	21	3
THOMPSON Steven Paul						
Sheffield, 28 July, 1955						(CD)
Lincoln C.	Boston U.	04.80	80-84	153	1	8
Charlton Ath.	Tr	08.85	85-87	95	0	0
Leicester C.	Tr	07.88				
Sheffield U.	Tr	11.88	88	20	0	1
Lincoln C.	Tr	07.89	89	27	0	0
THOMPSON Stewart Christopher						
Littleborough, 2 September, 1964 E Sch						(F)
Rochdale	App	09.82	82-83	23	8	8
THOMPSON Terence William						
Barleston (Lei), 25 December, 1946						(LB/WH)
Wolverhampton W.	App	01.64				
Notts Co.	Tr	03.66	65-67	66	0	3
THOMPSON Thomas						
Houghton-le-Spring, 10 November, 1928 EF Lge/E 'B'/E-2						(IF)
Newcastle U.	Lumley Y.M.C.A.	08.46	47-49	20	-	6
Aston Villa	Tr	08.50	50-54	149	-	67
Preston N.E.	Tr	07.55	55-60	188	-	117
Stoke C.	Tr	06.61	61-62	42	-	18
Barrow	Tr	03.63	62-63	44	-	16
THOMPSON Thomas William						
Stockton, 9 March, 1938 E Amat						(FB)
Blackpool	Stockton	08.61	61-68	154	1	1
York C.	Tr	07.70	70	4	0	0
THOMPSON John **Trevor**						
North Shields, 21 May, 1955						(FB)
West Bromwich A.	App	01.74	73-75	20	0	0
Newport Co.	Washington (USA)	08.78	78-79	32	3	2
Lincoln C.	Tr	12.79	79-81	80	0	1
THOMPSON William						
Bedlington, 5 January, 1940						(CH)
Newcastle U.	Jnrs	01.57	60-66	79	1	1
Rotherham U.	Tr	06.67	67	8	0	0
Darlington	Tr	01.68	67-69	30	0	5

League Club	Source	Date Signed	Seasons Played	Career Record Apps	Subs	Gls
THOMPSON William						
Ashington, 23 December, 1921 Died 1986						
Gateshead		09.45	46-47	3	-	0
THOMPSON William						
Berwick, 31 August, 1916 Died 1989 (G)						
Leeds U.	Ashington	10.35				
Watford		08.46	46	9	-	0
THOMPSON William Gordon						
Glasgow, 10 August, 1921 Died 1988 (WH)						
Portsmouth	Carnoustie	03.46	48-52	40	-	2
Bournemouth	Tr	01.53	52-53	45	-	0
THOMPSTONE Ian Philip						
Bury, 17 January, 1971 (M)						
Manchester C.	YT	07.89	87	0	1	1
Oldham Ath.	Tr	05.90				
Exeter C.	Tr	01.92	91	15	0	3
Halifax T.	Tr	07.92	92	31	0	9
Scunthorpe U.	Tr	03.93	92-94	47	13	8
Rochdale	Tr	07.95	95	11	14	1
Scarborough	Tr	08.96	96	12	7	2
THOMSEN Claus						
Denmark, 31 May, 1970 Danish Int (D/M)						
Ipswich T.	Aarhus G.F. (Den)	06.94	94-96	77	4	7
Everton	Tr	01.97	96-97	17	7	1
THOMSON Andrew						
Motherwell, 1 April, 1971 (F)						
Southend U.	Queen of South	07.94	94-97	87	35	28
THOMSON Andrew John						
Swindon, 28 March, 1974 (CD)						
Swindon T.	YT	05.93	93-95	21	1	0
Portsmouth	Tr	12.95	95-97	71	8	3
THOMSON Arthur Campbell						
Edinburgh, 2 September, 1948 Su23-3 (CD)						
Oldham Ath.	Hearts	01.70	69-70	27	1	0
THOMSON Bertram						
Glasgow, 18 February, 1929 (WH)						
Rochdale	Yeovil T.	06.58	58-59	55	-	1
THOMSON Brian Lamont						
Paisley, 1 March, 1959 (W)						
West Ham U.	Morecambe	01.77				
Mansfield T.	Tr	08.79	79-81	54	9	1
THOMSON Charles (Chick) Richard						
Perth, 2 March, 1930 (G)						
Chelsea	Clyde	10.52	52-55	46	-	0
Nottingham F.	Tr	08.57	57-60	121	-	0
THOMSON David Laing						
Stenhousemuir, 2 February, 1938 (IF)						
Leicester C.	Dunfermline Ath.	08.61	61	1	-	1
THOMSON George Matthewson						
Edinburgh, 19 October, 1936 SF Lge (FB)						
Everton	Hearts	11.60	60-62	73	-	1
Brentford	Tr	11.63	63-67	160	2	5
THOMSON Henry (Harry) Watson						
Edinburgh, 25 August, 1940 (G)						
Burnley	Bo'ness U.	08.59	64-68	117	0	0
Blackpool	Tr	07.69	69-70	59	0	0
Barrow	Tr	08.71	71	40	0	0
THOMSON James Arnott						
Glasgow, 28 June, 1948 (M)						
Newcastle U.	Petershill	08.68	69	4	1	0
Barrow	L	12.70	70	2	0	0
Grimsby T.	Tr	07.71	71	23	3	4
THOMSON James Donaldson						
Glasgow, 17 March, 1931 (IF)						
Southend U.	Raith Rov.	05.56	56-58	40	-	10
THOMSON James Shaw						
Glasgow, 1 October, 1946 (D)						
Chelsea	Provanside Hibs	01.65	65-67	33	6	1
Burnley	Tr	09.68	68-70	294	3	3
THOMSON John						
Newcastle, 3 December, 1954 (CD)						
Newcastle U.	App	12.72				
Bury	Tr	11.73	73-77	92	11	8

League Club	Source	Date Signed	Seasons Played	Career Record Apps	Subs	Gls
THOMSON John Ballantyne						
Muirhead, 22 October, 1934 (FB)						
Workington	Hearts	05.58	58	11	-	1
THOMSON Kenneth Gordon						
Aberdeen, 25 February, 1930 Died 1969 (CH)						
Stoke C.	Aberdeen	09.52	52-59	278	-	6
Middlesbrough	Tr	12.59	59-62	84	-	1
Hartlepool U.	Tr	10.62	62	28	-	2
THOMSON Lawrence James						
Menstrie, 26 August, 1936 (F)						
Carlisle U.	Partick Thistle	01.60	59	13	-	1
THOMSON Richard Blair						
Edinburgh, 26 June, 1957 (F)						
Preston N.E.	App	06.75	74-79	60	11	20
THOMSON Robert						
Glasgow, 21 March, 1955 (M)						
Middlesbrough	Morton	09.81	81	18	2	2
Blackpool	Hibernian	09.85	85-86	50	2	6
Hartlepool U. (N/C)	Tr	08.87	87	2	1	0
THOMSON Robert						
Menstrie, 21 November, 1939 (FB)						
Liverpool	Partick Thistle	12.62	62-63	6	-	0
Luton T.	Tr	08.65	65-66	74	0	0
THOMSON Robert Anthony						
Smethwick, 5 December, 1943 Eu23-15/EF Lge/E-8 (LB)						
Wolverhampton W.	App	07.61	61-68	277	1	2
Birmingham C.	Tr	03.69	68-70	63	0	0
Walsall	L	11.71	71	9	0	1
Luton T.	Tr	07.72	72-75	110	0	1
Port Vale	Hartford (USA)	10.76	76	18	0	0
THOMSON Robert Gillies McKenzie						
Dundee, 21 March, 1937 (WH/IF)						
Wolverhampton W.	Airdrieonians	08.54	56	1	-	1
Aston Villa	Tr	06.59	59-63	140	-	56
Birmingham C.	Tr	09.63	63-67	109	5	23
Stockport Co.	Tr	12.67	67	16	1	0
THOMSON Scott Yuill						
Edinburgh, 8 November, 1966 (G)						
Hull C.	Raith Rov.	08.97	97	9	0	0
THORBURN James Hope Forrest						
Lanark, 10 March, 1938 (G)						
Ipswich T.	Raith Rov.	06.63	63-64	24	-	0
THORLEY Dennis						
Stoke, 7 November, 1956 (D)						
Stoke C.	Jnrs	07.76	76-80	9	4	0
Blackburn Rov.	L	03.80	79	2	2	0
THORN Andrew Charles						
Carshalton, 12 November, 1966 Eu21-5 (CD)						
Wimbledon	YT	11.84	84-87	106	1	2
Newcastle U.	Tr	08.88	88-89	36	0	2
Crystal Palace	Tr	12.89	89-93	128	0	3
Wimbledon	Tr	10.94	94-95	33	4	1
Tranmere Rov.	Hearts	09.96	96-97	36	0	1
THORNBER Stephen John						
Dewsbury, 11 October, 1965 (M)						
Halifax T.	Jnrs	01.83	83-87	94	10	4
Swansea C.	Tr	08.88	88-91	98	19	6
Blackpool	Tr	08.92	92	21	3	0
Scunthorpe U.	Tr	07.93	93-95	71	6	7
THORNE Adrian Ernest						
Brighton, 2 August, 1937 (OL)						
Brighton & H.A.	Jnrs	08.54	57-60	76	-	38
Plymouth Arg.	Tr	06.61	61-63	11	-	2
Exeter C.	Tr	12.63	63-64	41	-	8
Leyton Orient	Tr	07.65	65	2	0	0
THORNE Peter Lee						
Manchester, 21 June, 1973 (F)						
Blackburn Rov.	YT	06.91				
Wigan Ath.	L	03.94	93	10	1	0
Swindon T.	Tr	01.95	94-96	66	11	27
Stoke C.	Tr	07.97	97	33	3	12
THORNE Steven Terence						
Hampstead, 15 September, 1968 (M)						
Watford	YT	07.86				
Brentford	Tr	09.87	87	1	0	1

THORNE Terence
Boston, 2 February, 1947 (WH)

League Club	Source	Date Signed	Seasons Played	Apps	Subs	Gls
Ipswich T.	Lincoln C. (Am)	08.64				
Notts Co.	Tr	06.66	66	2	0	0

THORNHILL Dennis
Draycott, 5 July, 1923 Died 1992 (CH)

League Club	Source	Date Signed	Seasons Played	Apps	Subs	Gls
Wolverhampton W.	Jnrs	07.40				
Southend U.	Tr	03.48	48-49	11	-	0

THORNHILL Keith Eric
Crewe, 20 December, 1963 (F)

League Club	Source	Date Signed	Seasons Played	Apps	Subs	Gls
Crewe Alex. (N/C)	Nantwich T.	07.83	83	1	0	0

THORNHILL Rodney Derek
Reading, 24 January, 1942 (WH)

League Club	Source	Date Signed	Seasons Played	Apps	Subs	Gls
Reading		05.63	63-69	188	4	19

THORNLEY Barry Edward
Gravesend, 11 February, 1948 (OL)

League Club	Source	Date Signed	Seasons Played	Apps	Subs	Gls
Brentford	Gravesend & Nft	09.65	65	7	0	0
Oxford U.	Tr	07.67	67-68	22	1	4

THORNLEY Benjamin Lindsay
Bury, 21 April, 1975 E Sch/Eu21-3 (LW)

League Club	Source	Date Signed	Seasons Played	Apps	Subs	Gls
Manchester U.	YT	01.93	93-97	1	8	0
Stockport Co.	L	11.95	95	8	2	1
Huddersfield T.	L	02.96	95	12	0	2

THORNLEY Roderick
Bury, 2 April, 1977 (F)

League Club	Source	Date Signed	Seasons Played	Apps	Subs	Gls
Doncaster Rov. (N/C)	Warrington	10.97	97	1	0	0

THORNLEY Timothy James
Leicester, 3 March, 1977 (G)

League Club	Source	Date Signed	Seasons Played	Apps	Subs	Gls
Torquay U.	YT	●	94	0	1	0

THORNS John William
Newcastle, 10 July, 1928 Died 1975 (OR)

League Club	Source	Date Signed	Seasons Played	Apps	Subs	Gls
Darlington (Am)		08.49	49	1	-	0

THORP Hamilton
Australia, 21 August, 1973 (CF)

League Club	Source	Date Signed	Seasons Played	Apps	Subs	Gls
Portsmouth	West Adelaide (Aus)	08.97	97	0	7	0

THORP Michael Stephen
Wallingford, 5 December, 1975 (CD)

League Club	Source	Date Signed	Seasons Played	Apps	Subs	Gls
Reading	YT	01.95	95-97	2	3	0

THORPE Adrian
Chesterfield, 25 November, 1963 (W)

League Club	Source	Date Signed	Seasons Played	Apps	Subs	Gls
Mansfield T. (N/C)	YT	08.82	82	0	2	1
Bradford C.	Heanor T.	08.85	85-87	9	8	1
Tranmere Rov.	L	11.86	86	4	1	3
Notts Co.	Tr	11.87	87-88	48	11	9
Walsall	Tr	08.89	89	24	3	1
Northampton T.	Tr	03.90	89-91	36	16	6

THORPE Andrew
Stockport, 15 September, 1960 (D)

League Club	Source	Date Signed	Seasons Played	Apps	Subs	Gls
Stockport Co.	Jnrs	08.78	77-85	312	2	3
Tranmere Rov.	Tr	07.86	86-87	51	2	0
Stockport Co.	Tr	01.88	87-91	172	3	0
Doncaster Rov. (N/C)	Chorley	09.97	97	2	0	0

THORPE Anthony Lee
Leicester, 10 April, 1974 (M)

League Club	Source	Date Signed	Seasons Played	Apps	Subs	Gls
Luton T.	Leicester C. (YT)	08.92	93-97	93	27	50
Fulham	Tr	02.98	97	5	8	3

THORPE Arthur William
India, 31 July, 1939 (OL)

League Club	Source	Date Signed	Seasons Played	Apps	Subs	Gls
Scunthorpe U.	Ossett T.	09.60	60-62	27	-	5
Bradford C.	Tr	07.63	63-65	81	0	17

THORPE Ian Richard
Blackheath, 3 September, 1953 E Amat (G)

League Club	Source	Date Signed	Seasons Played	Apps	Subs	Gls
Gillingham	Charlton Ath. (Am)	09.73	73	5	0	0

THORPE Jeffrey Roger
Whitehaven, 17 November, 1972 (LB/M)

League Club	Source	Date Signed	Seasons Played	Apps	Subs	Gls
Carlisle U.	YT	07.91	90-97	94	56	6

THORPE Lee Anthony
Wolverhampton, 14 December, 1975 (F)

League Club	Source	Date Signed	Seasons Played	Apps	Subs	Gls
Blackpool	YT	07.94	93-96	2	10	0
Lincoln C.	Tr	08.97	97	44	0	14

THORPE Leonard
Warsop, 7 June, 1924 (WH)

League Club	Source	Date Signed	Seasons Played	Apps	Subs	Gls
Mansfield T.	Nottingham F. (Am)	08.45	46	5	-	0

THORPE Samuel
Sheffield, 2 December, 1920 (RH)

League Club	Source	Date Signed	Seasons Played	Apps	Subs	Gls
Sheffield U.		04.45	47-48	2	-	0

THORSTVEDT Erik
Norway, 28 October, 1962 Norwegian Int (G)

League Club	Source	Date Signed	Seasons Played	Apps	Subs	Gls
Tottenham H.	I.F.K. Goteborg (Swe)	12.88	88-94	171	2	0

THORUP Borge
Denmark, 4 October, 1943 (FB)

League Club	Source	Date Signed	Seasons Played	Apps	Subs	Gls
Crystal Palace	Morton	03.69	69	0	1	0

THREADGOLD Joseph **Henry (Harry)**
Tattenhall, 6 November, 1924 Died 1996 (G)

League Club	Source	Date Signed	Seasons Played	Apps	Subs	Gls
Chester C.	Tarvin U.	10.47	50-51	83	-	0
Sunderland	Tr	07.52	52	35	-	0
Southend U.	Tr	07.53	53-62	320	-	0

THRELFALL Jack
Bolton, 22 March, 1935 (FB)

League Club	Source	Date Signed	Seasons Played	Apps	Subs	Gls
Bolton W.		12.54	55-62	47	-	1
Bury	Tr	11.62	62-64	37	-	1

THRELFALL Joseph **Richard**
Ashton-u-Lyne, 5 March, 1916 Died 1994 (FB)

League Club	Source	Date Signed	Seasons Played	Apps	Subs	Gls
Bolton W.		07.45	46	3	-	0
Halifax T.	Tr	10.47	47	30	-	0

THRESHER Theodore **Michael**
Cullompton, 9 March, 1931 (FB)

League Club	Source	Date Signed	Seasons Played	Apps	Subs	Gls
Bristol C.	Chard T.	01.54	54-64	379	-	1

THRIPPLETON Allen
Huddersfield, 16 June, 1928 (WH)

League Club	Source	Date Signed	Seasons Played	Apps	Subs	Gls
Millwall	Rainham T.	11.50	50-54	26	-	4

THROWER Dennis Alan
Ipswich, 1 August, 1938 (WH)

League Club	Source	Date Signed	Seasons Played	Apps	Subs	Gls
Ipswich T.	Jnrs	08.55	56-64	27	-	2

THROWER Nigel John
Nottingham, 12 March, 1962 (LB)

League Club	Source	Date Signed	Seasons Played	Apps	Subs	Gls
Nottingham F.	App	03.80				
Chesterfield	L	02.83	82	4	0	0

THURLOW Alec Charles Edward
Depwade, 24 February, 1922 Died 1956 (G)

League Club	Source	Date Signed	Seasons Played	Apps	Subs	Gls
Huddersfield T.		09.44				
Manchester C.	Tr	09.46	46-48	21	-	0

THURLOW Brian Alfred
Loddon (Nk), 6 June, 1936 (RB)

League Club	Source	Date Signed	Seasons Played	Apps	Subs	Gls
Norwich C.	Loddon	07.54	55-63	193	-	1
Bristol C.	Tr	07.64				

THURNHAM Roy Thomas
Macclesfield, 17 December, 1942 (CH)

League Club	Source	Date Signed	Seasons Played	Apps	Subs	Gls
Manchester C.	Jnrs	06.60				
Wrexham	Tr	06.61	62	2	-	0

THWAITES Denis
Stockton, 14 December, 1944 E Sch/E Yth (OL)

League Club	Source	Date Signed	Seasons Played	Apps	Subs	Gls
Birmingham C.	App	05.62	62-70	83	4	18

THWAITES Peter
Batley, 21 August, 1936 (CF)

League Club	Source	Date Signed	Seasons Played	Apps	Subs	Gls
Halifax T. (Am)	Swillington	02.61	60	2	-	0

THYNE Robert Brown
Glasgow, 9 January, 1920 Died 1986 (CH)

League Club	Source	Date Signed	Seasons Played	Apps	Subs	Gls
Darlington	Clydebank	10.43	46	7	-	0

TIATTO Daniele Amadio
Melbourne, Australia, 22 May, 1973 Australian Int (LM)

League Club	Source	Date Signed	Seasons Played	Apps	Subs	Gls
Stoke C.	F.C. Baden (Swi)	11.97	97	11	4	1

TIBBOTT Leslie
Oswestry, 25 August, 1955 Wu21-2 (FB)

League Club	Source	Date Signed	Seasons Played	Apps	Subs	Gls
Ipswich T.	App	03.73	75-78	52	2	0
Sheffield U.	Tr	03.79	78-81	78	0	2

TICKELL Brian Gerard
Carlisle, 15 November, 1939 (CH)

League Club	Source	Date Signed	Seasons Played	Apps	Subs	Gls
Huddersfield T.	Jnrs	11.56	58	1	-	0
Carlisle U.	Tr	05.59	59	3	-	1

TICKELL Enoch **Roy**
Liverpool, 25 April, 1924 (OR)

League Club	Source	Date Signed	Seasons Played	Apps	Subs	Gls
Exeter C.	St Leonards	12.45				
Southport	Tr	05.47	47	6	-	1

TICKRIDGE Sydney
Stepney, 10 April, 1923 Died 1997 E Sch (FB)

League Club	Source	Date Signed	Seasons Played	Apps	Subs	Gls
Tottenham H.	Jnrs	04.46	46-50	95	-	0
Chelsea	Tr	03.51	50-52	61	-	0
Brentford	Tr	07.55	55-56	62	-	0

TIDDY Michael Douglas
Helston, 4 April, 1929 (OR)

League Club	Source	Date Signed	Seasons Played	Apps	Subs	Gls
Torquay U.	Jnrs	11.46	46-50	5	-	0
Cardiff C.	Tr	11.50	50-54	145	-	19
Arsenal	Tr	09.55	55-57	48	-	8
Brighton & H.A.	Tr	10.58	58-61	133	-	11

TIERLING Lee
West Germany, 25 October, 1972 (M)

League Club	Source	Date Signed	Seasons Played	Apps	Subs	Gls
Portsmouth	YT	07.91				
Fulham	Tr	05.92	92-93	7	12	0

TIERNEY Francis
Liverpool, 10 September, 1975 E Yth (M)

League Club	Source	Date Signed	Seasons Played	Apps	Subs	Gls
Crewe Alex.	YT	03.93	92-97	57	30	10

TIERNEY James McMahon
Ayr, 2 May, 1940 (OR)

League Club	Source	Date Signed	Seasons Played	Apps	Subs	Gls
Bradford C.	Saltcoats Vic.	01.60	60	2	-	0

TIERNEY Lawrence
Leith, 4 April, 1959 (M)

League Club	Source	Date Signed	Seasons Played	Apps	Subs	Gls
Wigan Ath.	Hibernian	07.80	80	4	3	0

TIGHE John
Omagh, 13 March, 1923 (G)

League Club	Source	Date Signed	Seasons Played	Apps	Subs	Gls
West Bromwich A.	Larkhall Thistle	11.45	46	1	-	0

TIGHE Terence William
Edinburgh, 12 August, 1934 (WH/IF)

League Club	Source	Date Signed	Seasons Played	Apps	Subs	Gls
Accrington St.	Dunfermline Ath.	06.57	57-60	117	-	20
Crewe Alex.	Tr	12.60	60-62	78	-	5
Southport	Tr	08.63	63	36	-	3

TILER Brian
Rotherham, 15 March, 1943 Died 1990 (CD)

League Club	Source	Date Signed	Seasons Played	Apps	Subs	Gls
Rotherham U.	Jnrs	07.62	62-68	213	0	27
Aston Villa	Tr	12.68	68-72	106	1	3
Carlisle U.	Tr	10.72	72-73	51	1	1

TILER Carl
Sheffield, 11 February, 1970 Eu21-13 (CD)

League Club	Source	Date Signed	Seasons Played	Apps	Subs	Gls
Barnsley	YT	07.88	87-90	67	4	3
Nottingham F.	Tr	06.91	91-94	67	2	1
Swindon T.	L	11.94	94	2	0	0
Aston Villa	Tr	10.95	95-96	10	2	1
Sheffield U.	Tr	03.97	96-97	23	0	2
Everton	Tr	11.97	97	19	0	1

TILER Kenneth David
Maltby, 23 May, 1950 (FB)

League Club	Source	Date Signed	Seasons Played	Apps	Subs	Gls
Chesterfield	Swallownest	09.70	70-74	138	1	1
Brighton & H.A.	Tr	11.74	74-78	130	0	0
Rotherham U.	Tr	07.79	79-80	45	1	1

TILLEY Darren John
Bristol, 15 March, 1967 (F)

League Club	Source	Date Signed	Seasons Played	Apps	Subs	Gls
York C.	Yate T.	01.92	91-92	17	4	0

TILLEY Kevin
Feltham, 6 September, 1957 (FB)

League Club	Source	Date Signed	Seasons Played	Apps	Subs	Gls
Wimbledon	Queens Park R. (App)	09.75	77	11	2	0

TILLEY Peter
Lurgan (NI), 13 January, 1930 (WH)

League Club	Source	Date Signed	Seasons Played	Apps	Subs	Gls
Arsenal	Witton A.	05.52	53	1	-	0
Bury	Tr	11.53	53-57	86	-	12
Halifax T.	Tr	07.58	58-62	184	-	17

TILLEY Herbert **Rex**
Swindon, 16 February, 1929 (WH)

League Club	Source	Date Signed	Seasons Played	Apps	Subs	Gls
Plymouth Arg.	Chippenham T.	03.51	52-56	123	-	0
Swindon T.	Tr	08.58	58-59	31	-	0

TILLING Harold Kynaston
Warrington, 6 January, 1918 (OL)

League Club	Source	Date Signed	Seasons Played	Apps	Subs	Gls
Oldham Ath.	Whitecross	09.42	47	3	-	0

TILLOTSON Maurice
Silsden (Yks), 20 January, 1944 (FB)

League Club	Source	Date Signed	Seasons Played	Apps	Subs	Gls
Huddersfield T.	Jnrs	07.62				
Stockport Co.	Tr	10.64	64-65	35	0	0

TILLSON Andrew
Huntingdon, 30 June, 1966 (CD)

League Club	Source	Date Signed	Seasons Played	Apps	Subs	Gls
Grimsby T.	Kettering T.	07.88	88-90	104	1	5
Queens Park R.	Tr	12.90	90-91	27	2	2
Grimsby T.	L	09.92	92	4	0	0
Bristol Rov.	Tr	11.92	92-97	189	2	8

TILSED Ronald William
Weymouth, 6 August, 1952 E Yth (G)

League Club	Source	Date Signed	Seasons Played	Apps	Subs	Gls
Bournemouth	App	01.70	69	2	0	0
Chesterfield	Tr	02.72	71	16	0	0
Arsenal	Tr	09.72				
Portsmouth	Tr	03.73	72-73	14	0	0
Hereford U.	Tr	06.74				

TILSON Stephen Brian
Wickford, 27 July, 1966 (M)

League Club	Source	Date Signed	Seasons Played	Apps	Subs	Gls
Southend U.	Witham T.	02.89	88-96	199	40	26
Brentford	L	09.93	93	2	0	0

TILSTON Thomas Arthur
Chester, 19 February, 1926 (IF)

League Club	Source	Date Signed	Seasons Played	Apps	Subs	Gls
Chester C.	Jnrs	09.43	49-50	22	-	7
Tranmere Rov.	Tr	06.51	51	25	-	15
Wrexham	Tr	03.52	51-53	78	-	29
Crystal Palace	Tr	02.54	53-55	58	-	13

TILTMAN Richard George
Shoreham, 14 December, 1960 (F)

League Club	Source	Date Signed	Seasons Played	Apps	Subs	Gls
Brighton & H.A.	Maidstone U.	11.86	86-87	10	3	1

TIMMINS Arnold
Whitehaven, 29 January, 1940 Died 1994 (IF)

League Club	Source	Date Signed	Seasons Played	Apps	Subs	Gls
Workington	Lowca	09.60	60-63	44	-	10

TIMMINS Charles
Birmingham, 29 May, 1922 (LB)

League Club	Source	Date Signed	Seasons Played	Apps	Subs	Gls
Coventry C.	Jack Moulds Ath.	09.46	48-57	161	-	5

TIMMINS John
Brierley Hill, 30 May, 1936 (FB)

League Club	Source	Date Signed	Seasons Played	Apps	Subs	Gls
Wolverhampton W.	Jnrs	06.53				
Plymouth Arg.	Tr	01.58	57	5	-	0
Bristol Rov.	Tr	09.58	58-59	4	-	0

TIMONS Christopher Bryan
Shirebrook, 8 December, 1974 (CD)

League Club	Source	Date Signed	Seasons Played	Apps	Subs	Gls
Mansfield T.	Clipstone Colly	02.94	93-95	35	4	2
Leyton Orient (N/C)	Gainsborough Trinity	03.97	96	6	0	2

TIMSON David Youles
Syston, 24 August, 1947 (G)

League Club	Source	Date Signed	Seasons Played	Apps	Subs	Gls
Leicester C.	App	09.64	63-66	3	0	0
Newport Co.	Tr	08.67	67	23	0	0

TINDALL Michael Chadwick
Birmingham, 5 April, 1941 E Yth (WH)

League Club	Source	Date Signed	Seasons Played	Apps	Subs	Gls
Aston Villa	Jnrs	04.58	59-67	118	2	7
Walsall	Tr	06.68	68	7	0	0

TINDALL Ronald Albert Ernest
Streatham, 23 September, 1935 EF Lge (D/CF)

League Club	Source	Date Signed	Seasons Played	Apps	Subs	Gls
Chelsea	Jnrs	04.53	55-61	160	-	67
West Ham U.	Tr	11.61	61	13	-	3
Reading	Tr	10.62	62-63	36	-	12
Portsmouth	Tr	09.64	64-69	159	2	7

TINDILL Herbert
Hemsworth, 31 December, 1926 Died 1973 (IF)

League Club	Source	Date Signed	Seasons Played	Apps	Subs	Gls
Doncaster Rov.	South Hindley	04.44	46-57	402	-	122
Bristol C.	Tr	02.58	57-58	56	-	29
Barnsley	Tr	03.59	59-61	98	-	29

TINGAY Philip
Chesterfield, 2 May, 1950 (G)

League Club	Source	Date Signed	Seasons Played	Apps	Subs	Gls
Chesterfield	Chesterfield Tube Wks	07.72	71-80	181	0	0
Barnsley	L	03.73	72	8	0	0

TINKLER Eric
Capetown, South Africa, 30 July, 1970 South African Int (M)

League Club	Source	Date Signed	Seasons Played	Apps	Subs	Gls
Barnsley	Cagliari (It)	07.97	97	21	4	1

TINKLER John
Trimdon, 24 August, 1968 (M)

League Club	Source	Date Signed	Seasons Played	Apps	Subs	Gls
Hartlepool U.	Jnrs	12.86	86-91	153	17	7
Preston N.E.	Tr	07.92	92	22	2	2
Walsall (N/C)	Tr	08.93	93	6	0	0

TINKLER Luke
Chester-le-Street, 4 December, 1923 Died 1995 (OL)

League Club	Source	Date Signed	Seasons Played	Apps	Subs	Gls
Plymouth Arg.	West Bromwich A. (Am)	10.45	46-47	23	-	4
Walsall	Tr	06.48	48	18	-	0

TINKLER Mark Roland
Bishop Auckland, 24 October, 1974 E Sch/E Yth (M)

League Club	Source	Date Signed	Seasons Played	Apps	Subs	Gls
Leeds U.	YT	11.91	92-96	14	11	0
York C.	Tr	03.97	96-97	52	1	5

TINNEY Hugh Joseph
Glasgow, 14 May, 1944 Su23-2 (RB)

League Club	Source	Date Signed	Seasons Played	Apps	Subs	Gls
Bury	Partick Thistle	03.67	66-72	235	3	3

TINNION Brian
Stanley, 23 February, 1968 (M/LB)

League Club	Source	Date Signed	Seasons Played	Apps	Subs	Gls
Newcastle U.	App	02.86	86-88	30	2	2
Bradford C.	Tr	03.89	88-92	137	8	22
Bristol C.	Tr	03.93	92-97	185	8	16

TINNION Brian
Workington, 11 June, 1948 E Yth (F)

League Club	Source	Date Signed	Seasons Played	Apps	Subs	Gls
Workington	Jnrs	03.66	65-68	93	5	24
Wrexham	Tr	01.69	68-75	265	14	54
Chester C.	L	12.71	71	3	0	0

TINSLEY Alan
Fleetwood, 1 January, 1951 (M)

League Club	Source	Date Signed	Seasons Played	Apps	Subs	Gls
Preston N.E.	App	01.69	69	8	1	1
Bury	Tr	08.70	70-74	82	12	15

TINSLEY Colin
Redcar, 24 October, 1935 (G)

League Club	Source	Date Signed	Seasons Played	Apps	Subs	Gls
Grimsby T.	Redcar B.C.	09.54	54-57	24	-	0
Darlington	Tr	08.58	58-60	79	-	0
Exeter C.	Tr	07.61	61-62	56	-	1
Luton T.	Tr	08.63	63-67	55	0	0

TINSON Darren Lee
Birmingham, 15 November, 1969 (D)

League Club	Source	Date Signed	Seasons Played	Apps	Subs	Gls
Macclesfield T.	Northwich Vic.	02.96	97	44	0	0

TIPPETT Michael Frederick
Bristol, 11 June, 1930 (W)

League Club	Source	Date Signed	Seasons Played	Apps	Subs	Gls
Bristol Rov.	Cadbury Heath	04.48	49-51	8	-	2

TIPPETT Thomas John
Gateshead, 4 August, 1924 (OL)

League Club	Source	Date Signed	Seasons Played	Apps	Subs	Gls
Southend U.		05.46	46-51	92	-	20
Bournemouth	Tr	09.51	51-52	37	-	10

TIPTON Matthew John
Conway, 29 June, 1980 W Yth/Wu21-1 (CF)

League Club	Source	Date Signed	Seasons Played	Apps	Subs	Gls
Oldham Ath.	YT	07.97	97	1	2	0

TISDALE Paul Robert
Malta, 14 January, 1973 E Sch (M)

League Club	Source	Date Signed	Seasons Played	Apps	Subs	Gls
Southampton	Jnrs	06.91	94-95	5	11	1
Northampton T.	L	03.92	92	5	0	0
Huddersfield T.	L	11.96	96	1	1	0
Bristol C.	Tr	06.97	97	2	3	0
Exeter C.	L	12.97	97	10	0	1

TITTERTON David Stewart John
Warwick, 25 September, 1971 E Yth (LB)

League Club	Source	Date Signed	Seasons Played	Apps	Subs	Gls
Coventry C.	YT	05.90	89-90	0	2	0
Hereford U.	Tr	09.91	91-92	39	12	1
Wycombe W.	Tr	08.93	93-94	15	4	1

TIVEY Mark Ronald
Brent, 10 February, 1971 (W)

League Club	Source	Date Signed	Seasons Played	Apps	Subs	Gls
Charlton Ath.	YT	05.89	91	0	1	0

TOALE Ian
Liverpool, 28 August, 1967 (FB)

League Club	Source	Date Signed	Seasons Played	Apps	Subs	Gls
Liverpool	App	05.85				
Grimsby T.	Tr	07.87	87	16	4	0

TOASE Donald Vickers
Darlington, 31 December, 1929 Died 1992 E Yth (RB)

League Club	Source	Date Signed	Seasons Played	Apps	Subs	Gls
Newcastle U.	Portsmouth (Am)	06.48				
Darlington	Tr	08.51	51	7	-	0

TOBIN Donald Joseph
Prescot, 1 November, 1955 (M)

League Club	Source	Date Signed	Seasons Played	Apps	Subs	Gls
Rochdale	Everton (App)	08.73	73-75	45	2	5

TOBIN Maurice
Airdrie, 30 July, 1920 (LB)

League Club	Source	Date Signed	Seasons Played	Apps	Subs	Gls
Norwich C.	Longriggend B.C.	09.38	46-50	102	-	0

TOBIN Robert
Cardiff, 29 March, 1921 (IL)

League Club	Source	Date Signed	Seasons Played	Apps	Subs	Gls
Cardiff C.	Cardiff Corries	08.40	47	2	-	0
Newport Co.	Barry T.	10.49				

TOCKNELL Brian Thomas
South Africa, 21 May, 1937 (WH)

League Club	Source	Date Signed	Seasons Played	Apps	Subs	Gls
Charlton Ath.	Berea Park (SA)	07.59	60-65	199	0	14

TODD Alexander
South Shields, 7 November, 1929 (F)

League Club	Source	Date Signed	Seasons Played	Apps	Subs	Gls
Hartlepool U.	South Shields Butchers	04.50	52-53	4	-	0

TODD Andrew John James
Derby, 21 September, 1974 (CD)

League Club	Source	Date Signed	Seasons Played	Apps	Subs	Gls
Middlesbrough	YT	03.92	93-94	7	1	0
Swindon T.	L	02.95	94	13	0	0
Bolton W.	Tr	08.95	95-97	38	14	2

TODD Colin
Chester-le-Street, 12 December, 1948 E Yth/Eu23-14/EF Lge/E-27 (CD)

League Club	Source	Date Signed	Seasons Played	Apps	Subs	Gls
Sunderland	App	12.66	66-70	170	3	3
Derby Co.	Tr	02.71	70-78	293	0	6
Everton	Tr	09.78	78-79	32	0	1
Birmingham C.	Tr	09.79	79-81	92	1	0
Nottingham F.	Tr	08.82	82-83	36	0	0
Oxford U.	Tr	02.84	83	12	0	0
Luton T.	Vancouver (Can)	10.84	84	2	0	0

TODD James
Belfast, 19 March, 1921 (WH)

League Club	Source	Date Signed	Seasons Played	Apps	Subs	Gls
Blackpool		02.45				
Port Vale	Tr	10.46	46-52	146	-	0

TODD Keith Harris
Clydach, 2 March, 1941 Wu23-1 (CF)

League Club	Source	Date Signed	Seasons Played	Apps	Subs	Gls
Swansea C.	Clydach	09.59	60-67	196	3	76

TODD Kenneth
Butterknowle (Dm), 24 August, 1957 (M)

League Club	Source	Date Signed	Seasons Played	Apps	Subs	Gls
Wolverhampton W.	App	08.75	76-77	4	1	1
Port Vale	Tr	08.78	78-79	42	2	9
Portsmouth	Tr	10.79	79	1	2	1

TODD Kevin
Sunderland, 28 February, 1958 (F)

League Club	Source	Date Signed	Seasons Played	Apps	Subs	Gls
Newcastle U.	Ryhope Colly	08.81	81-82	5	2	3
Darlington	Tr	02.83	82-84	99	3	23

TODD Lee
Hartlepool, 7 March, 1972 (LB)

League Club	Source	Date Signed	Seasons Played	Apps	Subs	Gls
Stockport Co.	Hartlepool U. (YT)	07.90	90-96	214	11	2
Southampton	Tr	07.97	97	9	1	0

TODD Mark Kenneth
Belfast, 4 December, 1967 NI Sch/NI YthNIu23-1 (M)

League Club	Source	Date Signed	Seasons Played	Apps	Subs	Gls
Manchester U.	YT	08.85				
Sheffield U.	Tr	06.87	87-90	62	8	5
Wolverhampton W.	L	03.91	90	6	1	0
Rotherham U.	Tr	09.91	91-94	60	4	7
Scarborough	Tr	08.95	95	23	0	1
Mansfield T. (N/C)	Tr	02.96	95	10	2	0

TODD Paul Raymond
Middlesbrough, 8 May, 1920 (IF)

League Club	Source	Date Signed	Seasons Played	Apps	Subs	Gls
Doncaster Rov.		09.45	46-49	160	-	51
Blackburn Rov.	Tr	07.50	50-51	46	-	12
Hull C.	Tr	10.51	51-52	27	-	3

TODD Robert Charles
Goole, 11 September, 1949 (W)

League Club	Source	Date Signed	Seasons Played	Apps	Subs	Gls
Liverpool	Scunthorpe U. (App)	07.67				
Rotherham U.	Tr	03.68	68	2	4	0
Mansfield T.	Tr	11.68	68	3	1	0
Workington	Tr	07.69	69	10	6	0

TODD Ronald
Bellshill, 4 October, 1935 (WH)

League Club	Source	Date Signed	Seasons Played	Apps	Subs	Gls
Accrington St.	Lesmahagow	02.56	59	5	-	0

League Club	Source	Date Signed	Seasons Played	Apps	Subs	Gls

TODD Samuel John
Belfast, 22 September, 1945 NIu23-4/NI-11 (D)

League Club	Source	Date Signed	Seasons Played	Apps	Subs	Gls
Burnley	Glentoran	09.62	63-69	108	8	1
Sheffield Wed.	Tr	05.70	70-72	22	2	1
Mansfield T.	L	02.74	73	6	0	0

TODD Thomas Bell
Stonehouse, 1 June, 1926 (CF)

League Club	Source	Date Signed	Seasons Played	Apps	Subs	Gls
Crewe Alex.	Hamilton Academical	08.55	55	13	-	3
Derby Co.	Tr	11.55	55	4	-	3
Rochdale	Tr	05.56	56	5	-	1

TOLCHARD Jeffrey Graham
Torquay, 17 March, 1944 (W)

League Club	Source	Date Signed	Seasons Played	Apps	Subs	Gls
Torquay U.		03.64	63-64	11	-	4
Exeter C.	Tr	07.65	65	1	0	0

TOLLIDAY Stanley Albert
Hackney, 6 August, 1922 Died 1951 (G)

League Club	Source	Date Signed	Seasons Played	Apps	Subs	Gls
Leyton Orient		12.46	46-48	64	-	0
Walsall	Tr	06.50				

TOLMIE James
Glasgow, 20 November, 1960 Su21-1 (LW)

League Club	Source	Date Signed	Seasons Played	Apps	Subs	Gls
Manchester C.	Lokeren (Bel)	08.83	83-85	46	15	15
Carlisle U.	L	03.86	85	7	1	1

TOLSON Maxwell Norman
Australia, 18 July 1945 (CF)

League Club	Source	Date Signed	Seasons Played	Apps	Subs	Gls
Workington	South Coast U. (Aus)	02.66	65-66	29	2	6

TOLSON Neil
Walsall, 25 October, 1973 (F)

League Club	Source	Date Signed	Seasons Played	Apps	Subs	Gls
Walsall	YT	12.91	91	3	6	1
Oldham Ath.	Tr	03.92	92	0	3	0
Bradford C.	Tr	12.93	93-95	32	31	12
Chester C.	L	01.95	94	3	1	0
York C.	Tr	07.96	96-97	49	7	15

TOLSON William
Rochdale, 29 March, 1931 (IF)

League Club	Source	Date Signed	Seasons Played	Apps	Subs	Gls
Rochdale	St Albans B.C.	10.53	53-54	10	-	0

TOM Steven
Cheshunt, 5 February, 1951 (CD)

League Club	Source	Date Signed	Seasons Played	Apps	Subs	Gls
Queens Park R.	App	02.69				
Brentford	Tr	06.71	71	13	5	1

TOMAN James **Andrew**
Northallerton, 7 March, 1962 (M)

League Club	Source	Date Signed	Seasons Played	Apps	Subs	Gls
Lincoln C.	Bishop Auckland	08.85	85	21	3	4
Hartlepool U.	Bishop Auckland	01.87	86-88	112	0	28
Darlington	Tr	07.89	90-92	108	7	10
Scarborough	L	02.93	92	6	0	0
Scunthorpe U.	Tr	08.93	93	15	0	5
Scarborough	Tr	12.93	93-95	33	12	3

TOMASSON Jon Dahl
Copenhagen, Denmark, 29 August, 1976 Danish Int (F)

League Club	Source	Date Signed	Seasons Played	Apps	Subs	Gls
Newcastle U.	Herenveen (Neth)	07.97	97	17	6	3

TOMKIN Cyril John
Barrow, 18 November, 1918 (CF)

League Club	Source	Date Signed	Seasons Played	Apps	Subs	Gls
Barrow	Dumbarton	03.48	46-47	3	-	0

TOMKINS Leonard Anthony
Isleworth, 16 January, 1949 E Yth (M)

League Club	Source	Date Signed	Seasons Played	Apps	Subs	Gls
Crystal Palace	App	01.67	67-69	18	2	2

TOMKINSON Derek
Stoke, 6 April, 1931 (WH/IR)

League Club	Source	Date Signed	Seasons Played	Apps	Subs	Gls
Port Vale	Burton A.	12.52	52-54	29	-	5
Crewe Alex.		08.56	56	17	-	1

TOMKYS Michael George
Kensington, 14 December, 1932 E Yth (OR)

League Club	Source	Date Signed	Seasons Played	Apps	Subs	Gls
Queens Park R.	Fulham (Am)	11.51	51-58	86	-	16

TOMLEY Frederick William
Liverpool, 11 July, 1931 (CH)

League Club	Source	Date Signed	Seasons Played	Apps	Subs	Gls
Liverpool	Litherland	09.53	54	2	-	0
Chester C.	Tr	07.55	55	1	-	0

TOMLIN David
Nuneaton, 9 February, 1953 (W)

League Club	Source	Date Signed	Seasons Played	Apps	Subs	Gls
Leicester C.	App	02.71	71-75	19	7	2
Torquay U.	Tr	04.77	76-77	37	1	2
Aldershot	Tr	08.78	78-80	24	7	2

TOMLINSON Ashley Darrell
Doncaster, 28 September, 1966 (W)

League Club	Source	Date Signed	Seasons Played	Apps	Subs	Gls
Doncaster Rov.	YT	●	83	2	2	0

TOMLINSON Charles Conway
Sheffield, 2 December, 1919 (OL)

League Club	Source	Date Signed	Seasons Played	Apps	Subs	Gls
Bradford P.A.	Sheffield Wed. (Am)	04.39				
Sheffield Wed.	Tr	07.44	46-50	68	-	7
Rotherham U.	Tr	03.51	50-51	32	-	12

TOMLINSON David Ian
Rotherham, 13 December, 1968 (RW)

League Club	Source	Date Signed	Seasons Played	Apps	Subs	Gls
Sheffield Wed.	App	12.86	86	0	1	0
Rotherham U.	Tr	08.87	87	6	3	0
Barnet	Boston U.	12.90	91	0	3	0

TOMLINSON Francis
Manchester, 5 January, 1926 (F)

League Club	Source	Date Signed	Seasons Played	Apps	Subs	Gls
Halifax T.	Stalybridge Celtic	11.50	50	14	-	4

TOMLINSON Francis
Manchester, 23 October, 1925 (OR)

League Club	Source	Date Signed	Seasons Played	Apps	Subs	Gls
Oldham Ath.	Goslings	11.46	46-51	115	-	27
Rochdale	Tr	11.51	51	20	-	2
Chester C.	Tr	08.52	52	11	-	0

TOMLINSON Graeme Murdoch
Watford, 10 December, 1975 (CF)

League Club	Source	Date Signed	Seasons Played	Apps	Subs	Gls
Bradford C.	YT	●	93	12	5	6
Manchester U.	Tr	07.94				
Luton T.	L	03.96	95	1	6	0
Bournemouth	L	08.97	97	6	1	1
Millwall	L	03.98	97	2	1	1

TOMLINSON Harry
Devonport, 26 October, 1922 Died 1988 (FB)

League Club	Source	Date Signed	Seasons Played	Apps	Subs	Gls
Doncaster Rov.		10.44	46-48	58	-	0

TOMLINSON John
Bebington, 26 June, 1934 E Yth (W)

League Club	Source	Date Signed	Seasons Played	Apps	Subs	Gls
Everton	Jnrs	06.52	56	2	-	0
Chesterfield	Tr	06.57	57-58	47	-	5

TOMLINSON Michael Lloyd
Lambeth, 15 September, 1972 (W)

League Club	Source	Date Signed	Seasons Played	Apps	Subs	Gls
Leyton Orient	YT	07.91	90-93	7	7	1
Barnet	Tr	03.94	93-96	67	26	4

TOMLINSON Paul
Rotherham, 4 February, 1965 (G)

League Club	Source	Date Signed	Seasons Played	Apps	Subs	Gls
Sheffield U.	Middlewood R.	06.83	83-86	37	0	0
Birmingham C.	L	03.87	86	11	0	0
Bradford C.	Tr	06.87	87-94	293	0	0

TOMLINSON Robert Windle
Blackburn, 4 June, 1924 Died 1996 (FB)

League Club	Source	Date Signed	Seasons Played	Apps	Subs	Gls
Blackburn Rov.	Feniscowles	01.43	46-47	25	-	0
Halifax T.	Mossley	06.51	51	9	-	0

TOMPKIN Maurice
Countesthorpe(Lei), 17 February, 1919 Died 1956 (IF)

League Club	Source	Date Signed	Seasons Played	Apps	Subs	Gls
Leicester C.	Countesthorpe U.	03.38	37	1	-	0
Bury	Tr	12.45				
Huddersfield T.	Tr	09.46	46	10	-	1

TONER James
Glasgow, 23 August, 1924 (OR)

League Club	Source	Date Signed	Seasons Played	Apps	Subs	Gls
Leeds U.	Dundee	06.54	54	7	-	1

TONER William
Glasgow, 18 December, 1929 SF Lge (CH)

League Club	Source	Date Signed	Seasons Played	Apps	Subs	Gls
Sheffield U.	Dundee	05.51	51-53	55	-	2

TONES John David
Sunderland, 3 December, 1950 (CD)

League Club	Source	Date Signed	Seasons Played	Apps	Subs	Gls
Sunderland	App	05.68	72	2	4	0
Arsenal	Tr	07.73				
Swansea C.	L	09.74	74	7	0	0
Mansfield T.	L	10.74	74	3	0	0

TONG David Joseph
Blackpool, 21 September, 1955 (M)

League Club	Source	Date Signed	Seasons Played	Apps	Subs	Gls
Blackpool	App	09.73	74-78	70	8	7
Shrewsbury T.	Tr	09.78	78-81	156	4	8
Cardiff C.	Tr	08.82	82-85	119	1	3
Rochdale	L	09.85	85	0	2	0
Bristol C.	Tr	10.85	85	19	0	0
Gillingham	Tr	03.86	85	5	0	0
Cambridge U.	Tr	08.86	86	4	2	0

League Club	Source	Date Signed	Seasons Played	Career Record Apps	Subs	Gls
TONG Raymond						
Bolton, 3 February, 1942						(W)
Blackburn Rov.		07.62				
Bradford C.	Tr	06.63	63-64	20	-	2
TONGE Alan John						
Bury, 25 February, 1972						(M/D)
Manchester U.	YT	07.90				
Exeter C.	Horwich R.M.I.	12.91	91-93	14	5	1
TONGE Jeffrey Alan						
Manchester, 5 May, 1942						(F)
Bury	Droylsden	03.60	59	1	-	0
TONGE Keith Andrew						
Edmonton, 6 November, 1964						(F)
Brentford	App	11.82	81	0	1	0
TOON Colin						
Shirebrook, 26 April, 1940						(FB)
Mansfield T.	Jnrs	07.57	57-65	213	0	1
TOOTILL George Albert						
Walkden, 29 October, 1913 Died 1984						(CH)
Plymouth Arg.	Chorley	05.36	36-37	9	-	0
Sheffield U.	Tr	01.38	38	12	-	0
Hartlepool U.	Tr	07.47	47	18	-	0
TOOZE Dennis George						
Swansea, 12 October, 1917 Died 1994						(FB)
Coventry C.	Redditch T.	05.37	46-48	36	-	0
TOOZE Robert William						
Bristol, 19 December, 1946						(G)
Bristol C.	Jnrs	07.65				
Shrewsbury T.	Tr	03.69	68-72	73	0	0
Gillingham	L	03.72	71	7	0	0
TOPPING Christopher						
Selby, 6 March, 1951						(CD)
York C.	App	03.69	68-77	410	2	11
Huddersfield T.	Tr	05.78	78-80	43	0	1
TOPPING David						
Shotts, 9 March, 1926						(FB)
Torquay U.	Clyde	05.48	48-52	151	-	3
TOPPING Harry						
Kearsley, 21 September, 1913						(FB)
Manchester U.		12.32	32-34	12	-	1
Barnsley	Tr	05.35	35	14	-	2
Exeter C.	Macclesfield T.	05.37	37	1	-	0
New Brighton	Tr	07.38	38-47	72	-	0
TORFASON Gudmundur (Gunnar)						
Iceland, 13 December, 1961 Icelandic Int						(F)
Doncaster Rov.	St Johnstone	07.94	94	1	3	0
TORPEY Stephen David James						
Islington, 8 December, 1970						(F)
Millwall	YT	02.89	89	3	4	0
Bradford C.	Tr	11.90	90-92	86	10	22
Swansea C.	Tr	08.93	93-96	151	11	44
Bristol C.	Tr	08.97	97	19	10	8
TORRANCE Andrew						
Glasgow, 8 April, 1934						(W)
Barrow	Yeovil T.	05.58	58	29	-	2
TORRANCE George Clark						
Rothesay, 17 September, 1957						(M)
Brentford	Wokingham T.	12.84	84-85	29	5	1
TORRANCE George Syme						
Glasgow, 27 November, 1935						(G)
Leicester C.	Thorniewood Ath.	07.54				
Oldham Ath.	Tr	08.56	56	4	-	0
Rochdale	Tr	09.57	57	2	-	0
TOSELAND Geoffrey						
Kettering, 31 January, 1931						(OL)
Sunderland	Kettering T.	12.48	52	6	-	1
TOSER Ernest						
London, 30 November, 1913 E Sch						(CH)
Millwall	Dulwich Hamlet	05.37	37	2	-	0
Notts Co.	Tr	09.46	46	2	-	0

League Club	Source	Date Signed	Seasons Played	Career Record Apps	Subs	Gls
TOSHACK Jonathan Cameron						
Cardiff, 7 March, 1970						(F)
Swansea C.	Jnrs	09.88				
Bristol C.	Tr	11.89				
Cardiff C.	Tr	02.91	90-91	1	4	0
TOSHACK John Benjamin						
Cardiff, 22 March, 1949 W Sch/Wu23-3/W-40						(F)
Cardiff C.	App	03.66	65-70	159	3	75
Liverpool	Tr	11.70	70-77	169	3	74
Swansea C.	Tr	03.78	77-83	58	5	24
TOTTEN Alexander Reginald						
Southampton, 1 October, 1976						(M)
Portsmouth	YT	11.94	94	3	1	0
TOTTOH Melvyn						
Manchester, 26 July, 1956						(W)
Preston N.E. (N/C)	Lytham	05.85	85	0	1	0
TOULOUSE Cyril Harvey						
Acton, 24 December, 1923 Died 1980						(WH)
Brentford	St Cuthman's	05.46	46-47	13	-	0
Tottenham H.	Tr	12.47	48	2	-	0
TOVEY Paul William						
Wokingham, 5 December, 1973						(M)
Bristol Rov.	YT	07.92	93-95	8	1	0
TOVEY Ronald Arthur						
Bristol, 24 September, 1930						(IF)
Bristol C.		01.53	52-53	12	-	3
TOVEY William James						
Bristol, 18 October, 1931						(WH)
Bristol C.	Jnrs	12.48	48-52	57	-	2
TOWERS Mark Anthony						
Manchester, 13 April, 1952 E Sch/E Yth/Eu23-8/E-3						(M)
Manchester C.	App	04.69	68-73	117	5	10
Sunderland	Tr	03.74	73-76	108	0	18
Birmingham C.	Tr	07.77	77-79	90	2	4
Rochdale (N/C)	Vancouver (Can)	02.85	84	1	1	0
TOWERS Ian Joseph						
Consett, 11 October, 1940						(F)
Burnley	Jnrs	10.57	60-65	43	1	12
Oldham Ath.	Tr	01.66	65-67	94	1	45
Bury	Tr	07.68	68-70	44	5	7
TOWERS Edwin James						
Shepherds Bush, 15 April, 1933						(CF)
Brentford	Jnrs	05.51	54-60	262	-	153
Queens Park R.	Tr	05.61	61	28	-	15
Millwall	Tr	08.62	62	19	-	7
Gillingham	Tr	01.63	62	8	-	6
Aldershot	Tr	07.63	63	28	-	13
TOWERS John						
Willington, 21 December, 1913 Died 1979						(FB/WH)
Darlington (Am)	Willington	05.46	46	13	-	0
TOWERS William Harry						
Leicester, 13 July, 1920						(WH)
Leicester C.	Bentley Eng. FC	01.45	46	4	-	0
Torquay U.	Tr	10.46	46-55	274	-	0
TOWN David Edward						
Bournemouth, 9 December, 1976						(F)
Bournemouth	YT	04.95	93-97	17	29	2
TOWNEND Gary Alfred						
Kilburn, 1 April, 1940						(IF)
Millwall	Redhill	08.60	60-63	50	-	20
TOWNER Antony James						
Brighton, 2 May, 1955						(W)
Brighton & H.A.	App	01.73	72-78	153	9	24
Millwall	Tr	10.78	78-79	68	0	13
Rotherham U.	Tr	08.80	80-82	108	0	11
Sheffield U.	L	03.83	82	9	1	1
Wolverhampton W.	Tr	08.83	83	25	6	2
Charlton Ath.	Tr	09.84	84-85	22	5	2
Rochdale (N/C)	Tr	11.85	85	4	1	0
Cambridge U. (N/C)	Tr	03.86	85-86	8	0	0
TOWNLEY Leon						
Loughton, 16 February, 1976						(CD)
Tottenham H.	YT	07.94				
Brentford	Tr	09.97	97	15	1	1

TOWNSEND Andrew David
Maidstone, 23 July, 1963 IR 'B'/IR-70 (M)

League Club	Source	Date Signed	Seasons Played	Apps	Subs	Gls
Southampton	Weymouth	01.85	84-87	77	6	5
Norwich C.	Tr	08.88	88-89	66	5	8
Chelsea	Tr	07.90	90-92	110	0	12
Aston Villa	Tr	07.93	93-97	133	1	8
Middlesbrough	Tr	08.97	97	35	2	2

TOWNSEND Christopher Gordon
Abertillery, 30 March, 1966 W Sch/W Yth (F)

League Club	Source	Date Signed	Seasons Played	Apps	Subs	Gls
Cardiff C. (N/C)	Jnrs	07.83	83	2	3	0

TOWNSEND Donald Edward
Swindon, 17 September, 1930 (LB)

League Club	Source	Date Signed	Seasons Played	Apps	Subs	Gls
Charlton Ath.	Trowbridge T.	07.50	54-61	249	-	1
Crystal Palace	Tr	07.62	62-64	77	-	0

TOWNSEND George Ernest
Ashton-u-Lyne, 29 July, 1957 (LB)

League Club	Source	Date Signed	Seasons Played	Apps	Subs	Gls
Rochdale	App	07.75	74-75	31	1	0

TOWNSEND James Clabby
Greenock, 2 February, 1945 (WH)

League Club	Source	Date Signed	Seasons Played	Apps	Subs	Gls
Middlesbrough	St Johnstone	02.64	63-65	65	2	6

TOWNSEND Leonard Francis
Brentford, 31 August, 1917 Died 1997 (IF)

League Club	Source	Date Signed	Seasons Played	Apps	Subs	Gls
Brentford	Hayes	05.37	38-46	33	-	12
Bristol C.	Tr	06.47	47-48	74	-	45
Millwall	Tr	07.49	49	5	-	1

TOWNSEND Martin Vincent
Romford, 15 June, 1946 (G)

League Club	Source	Date Signed	Seasons Played	Apps	Subs	Gls
Fulham	App	●	63	2	-	0

TOWNSEND Neil Royston
Long Buckby, 1 February, 1950 E Yth (CD)

League Club	Source	Date Signed	Seasons Played	Apps	Subs	Gls
Northampton T.	Jnrs	09.68	68-71	65	2	1
Southend U.	Bedford T.	07.73	73-78	156	1	7
Bournemouth	Weymouth	07.79	79-80	34	0	2

TOWNSEND Quentin Lee
Worcester, 13 February, 1977 (CD)

League Club	Source	Date Signed	Seasons Played	Apps	Subs	Gls
Wolverhampton W.	YT	07.95				
Hereford U.	Tr	07.96	96	6	1	0

TOWNSEND Russell Nelson
Reading, 17 January, 1960 (M)

League Club	Source	Date Signed	Seasons Played	Apps	Subs	Gls
Northampton T.	Barnet	09.79	79	12	1	0

TOWNSEND William
Coventry, 27 December, 1922 Died 1988 (G)

League Club	Source	Date Signed	Seasons Played	Apps	Subs	Gls
Derby Co.	Nuneaton Borough	09.42	46-52	79	-	0

TOWSE Gary Thomas
Dover, 14 May, 1952 (G)

League Club	Source	Date Signed	Seasons Played	Apps	Subs	Gls
Crystal Palace	Folkestone T.	01.72				
Brentford	Tr	06.73	73	5	0	0

TOZE Edward
Manchester, 6 March, 1923 Died 1987 (G)

League Club	Source	Date Signed	Seasons Played	Apps	Subs	Gls
Halifax T.		08.50	50	5	-	0

TRACEY Michael George
Blackburn, 14 February, 1935 E Amat (F)

League Club	Source	Date Signed	Seasons Played	Apps	Subs	Gls
Luton T.	Crook T.	11.59	59-60	23	-	3
Lincoln C.	Tr	07.61	61	21	-	5

TRACEY Simon Peter
Woolwich, 9 December, 1967 (G)

League Club	Source	Date Signed	Seasons Played	Apps	Subs	Gls
Wimbledon	App	02.86	88	1	0	0
Sheffield U.	Tr	10.88	88-97	186	2	0
Manchester C.	L	10.94	94	3	0	0
Norwich C.	L	12.94	94	1	0	0
Wimbledon	L	11.95	95	1	0	0

TRAFFORD Stanley John
Leek, 21 December, 1945 (W)

League Club	Source	Date Signed	Seasons Played	Apps	Subs	Gls
Port Vale	App	10.64	64	12	-	1

TRAIL Derek John Falconer
Leith, 2 January, 1946 (M)

League Club	Source	Date Signed	Seasons Played	Apps	Subs	Gls
Workington	Falkirk	07.67	67-68	39	5	5
Hartlepool U.	Tr	07.69	69	36	3	2

TRAILOR Cyril Henry
Merthyr Tydfil, 15 May, 1919 W Sch (WH)

League Club	Source	Date Signed	Seasons Played	Apps	Subs	Gls
Tottenham H.	Jnrs	10.38	46-47	11	-	0
Leyton Orient	Tr	08.49	49-50	39	-	0

TRAIN Raymond
Nuneaton, 10 February, 1951 (M)

League Club	Source	Date Signed	Seasons Played	Apps	Subs	Gls
Walsall	App	11.68	68-71	67	8	11
Carlisle U.	Tr	12.71	71-75	154	1	8
Sunderland	Tr	03.76	75-76	31	1	1
Bolton W.	Tr	03.77	76-78	49	2	0
Watford	Tr	11.78	78-80	91	1	3
Oxford U.	Tr	03.82	81-83	49	1	0
Bournemouth	L	11.83	83	7	0	0
Northampton T.	Tr	03.84	84	46	0	1
Tranmere Rov.	Tr	08.85	85	36	0	0
Walsall	Tr	08.86	86	16	0	0

TRAINER John (Jack)
Glasgow, 14 July, 1952 (CD)

League Club	Source	Date Signed	Seasons Played	Apps	Subs	Gls
Halifax T.	Cork Hibs	08.76	76-78	101	4	5
Bury	Hong Kong	09.80	80	1	0	1
Rochdale (N/C)	Waterford	08.82	82	7	0	0

TRAINOR Daniel
Belfast, 12 July, 1944 NI Amat/NIu23-1/NI-1 (CF)

League Club	Source	Date Signed	Seasons Played	Apps	Subs	Gls
Plymouth Arg.	Crusaders	08.68	68	16	1	3

TRAINOR Peter
Workington, 2 March, 1915 Died 1979 (CH)

League Club	Source	Date Signed	Seasons Played	Apps	Subs	Gls
Preston N.E.		08.37				
Brighton & H.A.	Tr	05.38	38-47	71	-	4

TRANTER George Henry
Birmingham, 11 September, 1915 (CH)

League Club	Source	Date Signed	Seasons Played	Apps	Subs	Gls
West Bromwich A.	Rover Wks	12.43	46	16	-	0

TRANTER Wilfred
Pendlebury, 5 March, 1945 (D)

League Club	Source	Date Signed	Seasons Played	Apps	Subs	Gls
Manchester U.	App	04.62	63	1	-	0
Brighton & H.A.	Tr	05.66	65-67	46	1	1
Fulham	Baltimore (USA)	01.69	68-71	20	3	0

TRAUTMANN Bernhard (Bert) Carl
Germany, 22 October, 1923 EF Lge (G)

League Club	Source	Date Signed	Seasons Played	Apps	Subs	Gls
Manchester C.	St Helens	11.49	49-63	508	-	0

TRAVERS Michael Joseph Patrick
Camberley, 23 June, 1942 (M)

League Club	Source	Date Signed	Seasons Played	Apps	Subs	Gls
Reading	Jnrs	10.60	60-66	156	2	34
Portsmouth	Tr	07.67	67-71	74	11	6
Aldershot	Tr	07.72	72	29	1	2

TRAVIS David Alan
Doncaster, 4 July, 1964 (M)

League Club	Source	Date Signed	Seasons Played	Apps	Subs	Gls
Doncaster Rov. (N/C)	Hatfield Main	08.84	84-85	10	2	0
Scunthorpe U. (N/C)	Tr	02.86	85-86	13	0	1
Chesterfield (N/C)	Tr	08.87	87	6	5	0

TRAVIS Donald
Prestwich, 21 January, 1924 (IF)

League Club	Source	Date Signed	Seasons Played	Apps	Subs	Gls
West Ham U.	Blackpool (Am)	09.45	46-47	5	-	0
Southend U.	Tr	05.48	48	1	-	0
Accrington St.	Tr	12.48	48-50	71	-	36
Crewe Alex.	Tr	11.50	50-51	36	-	12
Oldham Ath.	Tr	10.51	51	5	-	1
Chester C.	Tr	02.52	51-53	99	-	45
Oldham Ath.	Tr	08.54	54-56	109	-	61

TRAVIS Simon Christopher
Preston, 22 March, 1977 (RB)

League Club	Source	Date Signed	Seasons Played	Apps	Subs	Gls
Torquay U.	YT	●	95	4	4	0
Stockport Co.	Holywell T.	08.97	97	3	10	2

TRAYNOR Thomas Joseph
Dundalk (Ire), 22 July, 1933 IR-8 (LB)

League Club	Source	Date Signed	Seasons Played	Apps	Subs	Gls
Southampton	Dundalk	06.52	52-65	433	0	7

TREACY Darren Paul
Lambeth, 6 September, 1970 (M)

League Club	Source	Date Signed	Seasons Played	Apps	Subs	Gls
Millwall	YT	02.89	88-89	7	0	0
Bradford C.	Tr	11.90	90	16	0	2

TREACY Francis
Glasgow, 14 July, 1939 (IF)

League Club	Source	Date Signed	Seasons Played	Apps	Subs	Gls
Ipswich T.	Johnstone Burgh	03.61	63-65	17	1	5

TREACY Raymond Christopher Patrick
Dublin, 18 June, 1946 IRu23-1/IR-42 (F)

League Club	Source	Date Signed	Seasons Played	Apps	Subs	Gls
West Bromwich A.	App	06.64	66-67	2	3	1
Charlton Ath.	Tr	02.68	67-71	144	5	44
Swindon T.	Tr	06.72	72-73	55	0	16
Preston N.E.	Tr	12.73	73-75	54	4	11
Oldham Ath.	L	03.75	74	3	0	1
West Bromwich A.	Tr	08.76	76	20	1	6

TREBBLE David Neil
Hitchin, 16 February, 1969 (F)

League Club	Source	Date Signed	Seasons Played	Apps	Subs	Gls
Scunthorpe U. (N/C)	Stevenage Borough	07.93	93	8	6	2
Preston N.E.	Tr	07.94	94	8	11	4
Scarborough	Tr	02.95	94-95	40	7	8

TREBILCOCK Michael
Callington, 29 November, 1944 (CF)

League Club	Source	Date Signed	Seasons Played	Apps	Subs	Gls
Plymouth Arg.	Tavistock	12.62	62-65	71	0	27
Everton	Tr	12.65	65-67	11	0	3
Portsmouth	Tr	01.68	67-71	99	10	33
Torquay U.	Tr	07.72	72	23	1	10

TREHARNE Colin
Bridgend, 30 July, 1937 (G)

League Club	Source	Date Signed	Seasons Played	Apps	Subs	Gls
Mansfield T.		12.60	61-65	191	0	0
Lincoln C.	Tr	07.66	66	19	0	0

TREHERNE Cyril Albert
Wellington, 12 March, 1928 (CF)

League Club	Source	Date Signed	Seasons Played	Apps	Subs	Gls
Shrewsbury T.		11.50	50	4	-	1

TRENTER Ronald Herbert
Ipswich, 13 December, 1928 (OR)

League Club	Source	Date Signed	Seasons Played	Apps	Subs	Gls
Ipswich T.	Jnrs	12.45				
Ipswich T.	Clacton T.	06.51	51	2	-	0

TRETTON Andrew David
Derby, 9 October, 1976 (CD)

League Club	Source	Date Signed	Seasons Played	Apps	Subs	Gls
Derby Co.	YT	10.93				
Shrewsbury T.	Tr	12.97	97	14	0	1

TREVIS Derek Alan
Birmingham, 9 September, 1942 (D/M)

League Club	Source	Date Signed	Seasons Played	Apps	Subs	Gls
Aston Villa		06.62				
Colchester U.	Tr	03.64	63-68	196	0	12
Walsall	Tr	09.68	68-69	63	2	6
Lincoln C.	Tr	07.70	70-72	100	8	18
Stockport Co.	Tr	09.73	73	33	2	2

TREVITT Simon
Dewsbury, 20 December, 1967 (RB)

League Club	Source	Date Signed	Seasons Played	Apps	Subs	Gls
Huddersfield T.	YT	06.86	86-95	216	13	3
Hull C.	Tr	11.95	95-97	50	1	1
Swansea C.	L	12.97	97	1	0	0

TREWICK Alan
Blyth, 27 April, 1941 (CF)

League Club	Source	Date Signed	Seasons Played	Apps	Subs	Gls
Gateshead		09.59	59	10	-	1

TREWICK George
Bedlington, 15 November, 1933 (HB)

League Club	Source	Date Signed	Seasons Played	Apps	Subs	Gls
Gateshead	West Sleekburn	04.53	56-59	111	-	0

TREWICK John
Bedlington, 3 June, 1957 E Sch/E Yth (M)

League Club	Source	Date Signed	Seasons Played	Apps	Subs	Gls
West Bromwich A.	App	07.74	74-80	83	13	11
Newcastle U.	Tr	12.80	80-83	76	2	8
Oxford U.	L	01.84	83	3	0	0
Oxford U.	Tr	08.84	84-87	109	2	4
Birmingham C.	Tr	09.87	87-88	35	2	0
Hartlepool U. (N/C)	Bromsgrove Rov.	10.89	89	8	0	0

TRICK Desmond
Swansea, 7 November, 1969 (CD)

League Club	Source	Date Signed	Seasons Played	Apps	Subs	Gls
Swansea C.	YT	07.88	89-90	25	4	0

TRIGG Cyril
Ashby-de-la-Zouch, 8 April, 1917 Died 1993 (CF/RB)

League Club	Source	Date Signed	Seasons Played	Apps	Subs	Gls
Birmingham C.	Bedworth T.	08.35	35-53	268	-	67

TRIM Reginald Frederick
Portsmouth, 1 October, 1913 E Sch (FB)

League Club	Source	Date Signed	Seasons Played	Apps	Subs	Gls
Bournemouth	Jnrs	04.31	30-32	20	-	0
Arsenal	Tr	04.33	34	1	-	0
Nottingham F.	Tr	07.37	37-38	70	-	0
Derby Co.	Tr	12.43				
Swindon T.	Tr	07.46	46	15	-	0

TRINDER Jason Lee
Leicester, 3 March, 1970 (G)

League Club	Source	Date Signed	Seasons Played	Apps	Subs	Gls
Grimsby T. (N/C)	Oadby T.	12.92				
Mansfield T.	Tr	11.94	94-95	5	3	0

TRINER Donald Arthur
Longton, 21 August, 1919 (OR)

League Club	Source	Date Signed	Seasons Played	Apps	Subs	Gls
Port Vale	Downings	12.38	38-47	25	-	7

TRISE Guy Gavin
Portsmouth, 22 November, 1933 (IR)

League Club	Source	Date Signed	Seasons Played	Apps	Subs	Gls
Portsmouth	Jnrs	05.53				
Aldershot	Tr	08.54	54	1	-	0

TROLLOPE Norman John
Wroughton, 14 June, 1943 (LB)

League Club	Source	Date Signed	Seasons Played	Apps	Subs	Gls
Swindon T.	Jnrs	07.60	60-80	767	3	21

TROLLOPE Paul Jonathan
Swindon, 3 June, 1972 W-5 (W)

League Club	Source	Date Signed	Seasons Played	Apps	Subs	Gls
Swindon T.	YT	12.89				
Torquay U.	Tr	03.92	91-94	103	3	16
Derby Co.	Tr	12.94	94-97	47	18	5
Grimsby T.	L	08.96	96	6	1	1
Crystal Palace	L	10.96	96	0	9	0
Fulham	Tr	11.97	97	19	5	3

TROOPS Harold
Sheffield, 10 February, 1926 Died 1963 (OR/LB)

League Club	Source	Date Signed	Seasons Played	Apps	Subs	Gls
Barnsley	Hadfield Wks	12.46	48	3	-	1
Lincoln C.	Tr	08.49	49-57	295	-	32
Carlisle U.	Tr	06.58	58-59	60	-	1

TROTT Dean
Barnsley, 13 May, 1967 (F)

League Club	Source	Date Signed	Seasons Played	Apps	Subs	Gls
Northampton T.	Boston U.	06.94	94	20	2	4

TROTT Robin Francis
Orpington, 17 August, 1974 (CD)

League Club	Source	Date Signed	Seasons Played	Apps	Subs	Gls
Gillingham	YT	05.93	93-94	8	2	0

TROTTER Michael
Hartlepool, 27 October, 1969 (D/M)

League Club	Source	Date Signed	Seasons Played	Apps	Subs	Gls
Middlesbrough	YT	11.87				
Doncaster Rov.	L	11.88	88	3	0	0
Darlington	Tr	06.90	90-91	16	13	2
Leicester C.	Tr	12.91	91-92	1	2	0
Chesterfield	Tr	11.93	93	14	1	1

TROUGHTON Samuel Edward
Lisburn (NI), 27 March, 1964 NI Sch/NI Yth (F)

League Club	Source	Date Signed	Seasons Played	Apps	Subs	Gls
Wolverhampton W.	Glentoran	12.83	83	17	0	2

TRUETT Geoffrey Frederick
West Ham, 23 May, 1935 (WH)

League Club	Source	Date Signed	Seasons Played	Apps	Subs	Gls
Crystal Palace	Wycombe W.	06.57	57-61	38	-	5

TRUSLER John William
Shoreham, 7 June, 1934 (CF)

League Club	Source	Date Signed	Seasons Played	Apps	Subs	Gls
Brighton & H.A.	Shoreham	08.54	54	1	-	0

TRUSSON Michael Sydney
Northolt, 26 May, 1959 (M)

League Club	Source	Date Signed	Seasons Played	Apps	Subs	Gls
Plymouth Arg.	App	01.77	76-79	65	8	15
Sheffield U.	Tr	07.80	80-83	125	1	31
Rotherham U.	Tr	12.83	83-86	124	0	19
Brighton & H.A.	Tr	07.87	87-88	34	3	2
Gillingham	Tr	09.89	89-91	69	5	7

TRUSTFULL Orlando
Netherlands, 4 August, 1970 Dutch Int (M)

League Club	Source	Date Signed	Seasons Played	Apps	Subs	Gls
Sheffield Wed.	Feyenoord (Neth)	08.96	96	9	10	3

TSKHADADZE Kakhaber
Rustavi, Georgia, 7 September, 1968 CIS/Georgian Int (CD)

League Club	Source	Date Signed	Seasons Played	Apps	Subs	Gls
Manchester C.	Alana Vladikavkaz (Rus)	02.98	97	10	0	1

TUCK Peter George
Plaistow, 14 May, 1932 (IF)

League Club	Source	Date Signed	Seasons Played	Apps	Subs	Gls
Chelsea	Jnrs	06.51	51	3	-	1

TUCK Stuart Gary
Brighton, 1 October, 1974 (LB)

League Club	Source	Date Signed	Seasons Played	Apps	Subs	Gls
Brighton & H.A.	YT	07.93	93-97	76	15	1

TUCKER William Barrington (Barry)
Swansea, 28 August, 1952 (FB)

League Club	Source	Date Signed	Seasons Played	Apps	Subs	Gls
Northampton T.	App	08.70	71-77	209	5	3
Brentford	Tr	02.78	77-82	168	1	5
Northampton T.	Tr	10.82	82-83	62	1	5

TUCKER Dexter Calbert
Pontefract, 22 February, 1979 (F)

League Club	Source	Date Signed	Seasons Played	Apps	Subs	Gls
Hull C.	YT	●	97	1	6	0

TUCKER Gordon
Manchester, 5 January, 1968 (CD)

League Club	Source	Date Signed	Seasons Played	Apps	Subs	Gls
Huddersfield T.	Derby Co. (N/C)	07.87	87-88	30	5	0
Scunthorpe U.	Tr	07.89	89	14	1	1

TUCKER Jason James
Isleworth, 3 February, 1973 (LB)

League Club	Source	Date Signed	Seasons Played	Apps	Subs	Gls
Aldershot	YT	07.91	90	0	1	0

TUCKER Keith
Deal, 25 November, 1936 (FB)

League Club	Source	Date Signed	Seasons Played	Apps	Subs	Gls
Charlton Ath.	Betteshanger Colly	02.54	54-60	3	-	0

TUCKER Kenneth
Poplar, 2 October, 1925 (OL)

League Club	Source	Date Signed	Seasons Played	Apps	Subs	Gls
West Ham U.	Finchley	08.46	47-56	83	-	31
Notts Co.	Tr	03.57	56-57	28	-	5

TUCKER Kenneth John
Merthyr Tydfil, 15 July, 1935 (W)

League Club	Source	Date Signed	Seasons Played	Apps	Subs	Gls
Cardiff C.	Aston Villa (Am)	10.55	56-57	13	-	0
Shrewsbury T.	Tr	02.58	57-59	46	-	8
Northampton T.	Tr	03.60	59-60	10	-	3

TUCKER Lee Antony
Plymouth, 10 August, 1978 (M)

League Club	Source	Date Signed	Seasons Played	Apps	Subs	Gls
Torquay U.	YT	●	96	0	1	0

TUCKER Lee Derek
Middlesbrough, 14 September, 1971 (W)

League Club	Source	Date Signed	Seasons Played	Apps	Subs	Gls
Middlesbrough	YT	10.89				
Darlington	Tr	07.91	91	0	5	0

TUCKER Malcolm
Cramlington, 12 April, 1933 (CH)

League Club	Source	Date Signed	Seasons Played	Apps	Subs	Gls
Grimsby T.	Newcastle U. (Am)	11.50	53-57	40	-	0

TUCKER Mark James
Woking, 27 April, 1972 (RB)

League Club	Source	Date Signed	Seasons Played	Apps	Subs	Gls
Fulham	YT	07.90	91-92	3	1	0

TUCKER William John
Kidderminster, 17 May, 1948 (CD)

League Club	Source	Date Signed	Seasons Played	Apps	Subs	Gls
Hereford U.	Kidderminster Hrs	07.72	72-76	135	2	12
Bury	Tr	12.76	76-78	96	0	8
Swindon T.	Tr	06.79	79	35	0	4

TUDDENHAM Anthony Richard
Reepham (Nk), 28 September, 1956 (FB)

League Club	Source	Date Signed	Seasons Played	Apps	Subs	Gls
West Ham U.	App	09.74				
Cambridge U.	Tr	02.76	75-76	11	1	0

TUDOR Thomas **Edward**
Bebington, 15 March, 1935 (F)

League Club	Source	Date Signed	Seasons Played	Apps	Subs	Gls
Gillingham	Bolton W. (Am)	04.58	58	1	-	0

TUDOR John Arthur
Ilkeston, 25 June, 1946 (F)

League Club	Source	Date Signed	Seasons Played	Apps	Subs	Gls
Coventry C.	Ilkeston T.	01.66	66-68	63	6	13
Sheffield U.	Tr	11.68	68-70	64	7	30
Newcastle U.	Tr	01.71	70-76	161	3	53
Stoke C.	Tr	09.76	76	28	2	3

TUDOR William Henry
Deeside, 14 February, 1918 W Sch (CH)

League Club	Source	Date Signed	Seasons Played	Apps	Subs	Gls
West Bromwich A.	Lavender	05.35	38	31	-	0
Wrexham	Tr	05.46	46-48	56	-	2

TUEART Dennis
Newcastle, 27 November, 1949 Eu23-1/EF Lge/E-6 (W)

League Club	Source	Date Signed	Seasons Played	Apps	Subs	Gls
Sunderland	Jnrs	08.67	68-73	173	5	46
Manchester C.	Tr	03.74	73-77	139	1	59
Manchester C.	New York (USA)	02.80	79-82	77	7	27
Stoke C.	Tr	08.83	83	2	1	0
Burnley	Tr	12.83	83	8	7	5

TUGMAN James Robert
Newcastle, 14 March, 1945 (D)

League Club	Source	Date Signed	Seasons Played	Apps	Subs	Gls
Workington		07.64	65-67	32	12	0

TULIP William Edward
Gateshead, 3 May, 1933 (CF)

League Club	Source	Date Signed	Seasons Played	Apps	Subs	Gls
Newcastle U.		06.51				
Darlington	Tr	05.56	56-57	44	-	34

TULLOCH Roland
South Africa, 15 July, 1932 (WH)

League Club	Source	Date Signed	Seasons Played	Apps	Subs	Gls
Hull C.	South Africa	12.53	54	3	-	0

TULLOCH Ronald Thomas
Haddington, 5 June, 1933 (IF)

League Club	Source	Date Signed	Seasons Played	Apps	Subs	Gls
Southend U.	Hearts	05.56	56	11	-	3
Carlisle U.	Tr	07.57	57-59	73	-	23

TULLY Kevin Francis
Manchester, 18 December, 1952 (W)

League Club	Source	Date Signed	Seasons Played	Apps	Subs	Gls
Blackpool	Prestwich Heys	11.72	72-73	10	1	0
Cambridge U.	Tr	07.74	74-75	40	4	8
Crewe Alex.	Tr	01.76	75-78	81	5	4
Port Vale	Tr	10.78	78-79	7	6	2
Bury	Chorley	08.80	80	7	3	1

TULLY Stephen Richard
Torbay, 10 February, 1980 (RWB)

League Club	Source	Date Signed	Seasons Played	Apps	Subs	Gls
Torquay U.	YT	●	97	4	5	0

TUMBRIDGE Raymond Alan
Hampstead, 6 March, 1955 (LB)

League Club	Source	Date Signed	Seasons Played	Apps	Subs	Gls
Charlton Ath.	App	03.73	72-74	43	3	0
Northampton T.	L	02.75	74	11	0	0

TUNE David Barrie
Reading, 1 November, 1938 (HB)

League Club	Source	Date Signed	Seasons Played	Apps	Subs	Gls
Reading	Jnrs	11.55	57	1	-	0

TUNE Michael Gerard
Stoke, 28 February, 1962 (M)

League Club	Source	Date Signed	Seasons Played	Apps	Subs	Gls
Crewe Alex.	Stoke C. (App)	06.79	79	0	1	0

TUNKS Roy William
Worthing, 21 January, 1951 (G)

League Club	Source	Date Signed	Seasons Played	Apps	Subs	Gls
Rotherham U.	App	03.68	67-73	138	0	0
York C.	L	01.69	68	4	0	0
Preston N.E.	Tr	11.74	74-80	277	0	0
Wigan Ath.	Tr	11.81	81-87	245	0	0
Hartlepool U.	Tr	07.88	88	5	0	0
Preston N.E.	Tr	11.88	88-89	25	0	0

TUNNEY Edward
Liverpool, 23 September, 1915 (FB)

League Club	Source	Date Signed	Seasons Played	Apps	Subs	Gls
Everton		08.36				
Wrexham	Tr	09.37	37-51	222	-	0

TUNNICLIFFE William Francis
Stoke, 5 January, 1920 Died 1997 (OL)

League Club	Source	Date Signed	Seasons Played	Apps	Subs	Gls
Port Vale	Jnrs	01.37	36-37	3	-	0
Bournemouth	Tr	05.38	38-46	49	-	7
Wrexham	Tr	06.47	47-52	236	-	74
Bradford C.	Tr	01.53	52-54	89	-	20

TUNSTALL Eric Walter
Hartlepool, 21 November, 1950 (WH)

League Club	Source	Date Signed	Seasons Played	Apps	Subs	Gls
Hartlepool U.	App	11.68	68	0	1	0
Newcastle U.	Tr	01.69				

TUOHY Michael Patrick Francis
West Bromwich, 28 March, 1956 (F)

League Club	Source	Date Signed	Seasons Played	Apps	Subs	Gls
Southend U.	Redditch U.	06.79	79	20	1	4

TUOHY William (Liam)
Dublin, 27 April, 1933 IR 'B'/IR-8 (OL)

League Club	Source	Date Signed	Seasons Played	Apps	Subs	Gls
Newcastle U.	Shamrock Rov.	05.60	60-62	38	-	9

TUPLING Stephen
Wensleydale, 11 July, 1964 (M)

League Club	Source	Date Signed	Seasons Played	Apps	Subs	Gls
Middlesbrough	App	07.82				
Carlisle U. (N/C)	Tr	07.84	84	1	0	0
Darlington	Tr	10.84	84-86	105	6	8
Newport Co.	Tr	08.87	87	30	3	2
Cardiff C.	Tr	08.88	88-89	3	2	0
Torquay U.	L	09.88	88	1	2	0
Exeter C.	L	01.89	88	8	1	1
Hartlepool U.	Tr	12.89	89-91	83	6	3
Darlington (N/C)	Tr	08.92	92	8	3	0

TURBITT Peter
Keighley, 1 July, 1951 E Yth (OR)

League Club	Source	Date Signed	Seasons Played	Apps	Subs	Gls
Bradford C.	Keighley C.Y.C.	08.69	69-70	5	3	0

TURLEY John William
Bebington, 26 January, 1939 (CF)

League Club	Source	Date Signed	Seasons Played	Apps	Subs	Gls
Sheffield U.	Ellesmere Port	05.56	57	5	-	3
Peterborough U.	Tr	07.61	61-63	32	-	14
Rochdale	Tr	05.64	64	22	-	5

TURLEY Michael Douglas
Rotherham, 14 February, 1936 (WH)

League Club	Source	Date Signed	Seasons Played	Apps	Subs	Gls
Sheffield Wed.	Jnrs	03.53	54	3	-	0
Burnley	Tr	10.56				

TURLEY William Lee
Wolverhampton, 15 July, 1973 (G)

League Club	Source	Date Signed	Seasons Played	Apps	Subs	Gls
Northampton T.	Evesham U.	07.95	95-96	3	0	0
Leyton Orient	L	02.98	97	14	0	0

TURNBULL Frederick
Wallsend, 28 August, 1946 (CH)

League Club	Source	Date Signed	Seasons Played	Apps	Subs	Gls
Aston Villa	Centre 64	09.66	67-73	160	1	3
Halifax T.	L	10.69	69	7	0	0

TURNBULL George Frederick
Gateshead, 4 February, 1927 (G)

League Club	Source	Date Signed	Seasons Played	Apps	Subs	Gls
Grimsby T.	Alnwick T.	08.50	50	2	-	0
Accrington St.	Tr	09.51	51	33	-	0
Gateshead	Tr	07.52	52	3	-	0

TURNBULL Lee Mark
Stockton, 27 September, 1967 (M/F)

League Club	Source	Date Signed	Seasons Played	Apps	Subs	Gls
Middlesbrough	YT	09.85	85-86	8	8	4
Aston Villa	Tr	08.87				
Doncaster Rov.	Tr	11.87	87-90	108	15	21
Chesterfield	Tr	02.91	90-93	80	7	26
Doncaster Rov.	Tr	10.93	93	10	1	1
Wycombe W.	Tr	01.94	93-94	8	3	1
Scunthorpe U.	Tr	03.95	94-96	37	10	7
Darlington	Tr	07.97	97	4	5	0

TURNBULL Ronald William
Ashington, 18 July, 1922 Died 1966 (CF)

League Club	Source	Date Signed	Seasons Played	Apps	Subs	Gls
Sunderland	Dundee	11.47	47-48	40	-	16
Manchester C.	Tr	09.49	49-50	30	-	5
Swansea C.	Tr	01.51	50-52	67	-	35

TURNBULL Roy
Edinburgh, 22 October, 1948 S Sch/S Yth (IF)

League Club	Source	Date Signed	Seasons Played	Apps	Subs	Gls
Lincoln C.	Hearts	09.69	69	0	2	0

TURNBULL Terence Michael
Stockton, 18 October, 1945 (F)

League Club	Source	Date Signed	Seasons Played	Apps	Subs	Gls
Hartlepool U. (N/C)	Crook T.	08.76	76	13	0	3

TURNER Adam Ernest
Glasgow, 13 March, 1934 (WH)

League Club	Source	Date Signed	Seasons Played	Apps	Subs	Gls
Gateshead	Dunfermline Ath.	10.58	58	6	-	0

TURNER Alan
Hull, 5 July, 1943 (M)

League Club	Source	Date Signed	Seasons Played	Apps	Subs	Gls
Coventry C.	Scunthorpe U. (Am)	03.62	61-65	4	0	0
Shrewsbury T.	Tr	07.66	66	14	2	3
Bradford P.A.	Tr	05.67	67	30	2	4

TURNER Alan
Sheffield, 22 September, 1935 (F)

League Club	Source	Date Signed	Seasons Played	Apps	Subs	Gls
Sheffield U.		09.57				
Halifax T.	Tr	07.58	58	7	-	0

TURNER Alfred Thomas
U.S.A., 26 December, 1929 Died 1987 (CF)

League Club	Source	Date Signed	Seasons Played	Apps	Subs	Gls
New Brighton (Am)	Port Sunlight	02.51	50	4	-	0

TURNER Andrew Peter
Woolwich, 23 March, 1975 E Sch/E Yth/IRu21-7 (LW)

League Club	Source	Date Signed	Seasons Played	Apps	Subs	Gls
Tottenham H.	YT	04.92	92-94	8	12	3
Wycombe W.	L	08.94	94	3	1	0
Doncaster Rov.	L	10.94	94	4	0	1
Huddersfield T.	L	11.95	95	2	3	1
Southend U.	L	03.96	95	4	2	0
Portsmouth	Tr	09.96	96-97	34	6	3

TURNER Arthur
Chesterton, 1 April, 1909 Died 1994 (CH)

League Club	Source	Date Signed	Seasons Played	Apps	Subs	Gls
Stoke C.	Woolstanton	11.30	30-38	291	-	17
Birmingham C.	Tr	01.39	38-46	39	-	0
Southport	Tr	02.48	47-48	28	-	0

TURNER Arthur Alexander
Poplar, 22 January, 1922 (CF)

League Club	Source	Date Signed	Seasons Played	Apps	Subs	Gls
Colchester U.	Charlton Ath. (Am)	(N/L)	50-51	45	-	15

TURNER Brian
Whittlesey, 27 August, 1925 (CF)

League Club	Source	Date Signed	Seasons Played	Apps	Subs	Gls
Lincoln C. (Am)	March T.	11.47	47	5	-	0

TURNER Brian
Salford, 23 July, 1936 (WH)

League Club	Source	Date Signed	Seasons Played	Apps	Subs	Gls
Bury	Bury Amats	02.57	57-69	451	3	24
Oldham Ath.	Tr	08.70	70	10	1	0

TURNER Brian Alfred
New Zealand, 31 July, 1949 (M)

League Club	Source	Date Signed	Seasons Played	Apps	Subs	Gls
Chelsea	Eden (NZ)	05.68				
Portsmouth	Tr	06.69	69	3	1	0
Brentford	Tr	01.70	69-71	88	5	7

TURNER Charles John
Newport, 1 July, 1919 (G)

League Club	Source	Date Signed	Seasons Played	Apps	Subs	Gls
Newport Co.	Ebbw Junction	05.38	38-47	37	-	0
Swansea C.	Tr	08.48	48	2	-	0

TURNER Christopher James
St Neots, 3 April, 1951 (CD)

League Club	Source	Date Signed	Seasons Played	Apps	Subs	Gls
Peterborough U.	Jnrs	11.69	69-77	308	6	37
Luton T.	Tr	07.78	78	30	0	5
Cambridge U.	New England (USA)	09.79	79	15	4	0
Swindon T. (N/C)	New England (USA)	09.80	80	0	3	0
Cambridge U.	Tr	10.80	80-83	68	3	3
Southend U.	Tr	10.83	83	22	0	2

TURNER Christopher Robert
Sheffield, 15 September, 1958 E Yth (G)

League Club	Source	Date Signed	Seasons Played	Apps	Subs	Gls
Sheffield Wed.	App	08.76	76-78	91	0	0
Lincoln C.	L	10.78	78	5	0	0
Sunderland	Tr	07.79	79-84	195	0	0
Manchester U.	Tr	08.85	85-87	64	0	0
Sheffield Wed.	Tr	09.88	88-90	75	0	0
Leeds U.	L	11.89	89	2	0	0
Leyton Orient	Tr	10.91	91-94	58	0	0

TURNER David
Derby, 26 December, 1948 (RB)

League Club	Source	Date Signed	Seasons Played	Apps	Subs	Gls
Everton	App	10.66	67	1	0	0
Southport	Tr	05.70	70-72	69	2	0

TURNER David John
Retford, 7 September, 1943 (M)

League Club	Source	Date Signed	Seasons Played	Apps	Subs	Gls
Newcastle U.	App	10.60	61-62	2	-	0
Brighton & H.A.	Tr	12.63	63-71	292	8	30
Blackburn Rov.	Tr	08.72	72-73	23	2	0

TURNER Eric
Huddersfield, 13 January, 1921 Died 1993 (RH)

League Club	Source	Date Signed	Seasons Played	Apps	Subs	Gls
Halifax T.	Wooldale W.	04.46	46	7	-	0

TURNER Frederick Arthur
Southampton, 28 February, 1930 Died 1955 (RB)

League Club	Source	Date Signed	Seasons Played	Apps	Subs	Gls
Southampton	Jnrs	02.50				
Torquay U.	Tr	08.51	51	1	-	0
Southampton	Tr	03.53	53-54	19	-	0

TURNER Gordon Reginald
Hull, 7 June, 1930 Died 1976 EF Lge (CF)

League Club	Source	Date Signed	Seasons Played	Apps	Subs	Gls
Luton T.		03.50	50-63	406	-	243

TURNER Graham John
Ellesmere Port, 5 October, 1947 E Yth (CD/M)

League Club	Source	Date Signed	Seasons Played	Apps	Subs	Gls
Wresham	Jnrs	07.65	64-67	77	0	0
Chester C.	Tr	01.68	67-72	215	3	5
Shrewsbury T.	Tr	01.73	72-83	342	13	22

TURNER Herbert (Bert) Gwyn
Rhymney, 19 June, 1909 Died 1981 W-8 (FB)

League Club	Source	Date Signed	Seasons Played	Apps	Subs	Gls
Charlton Ath.	Brithdir	08.33	33-46	176	-	3

TURNER Hugh
Middlesbrough, 12 May, 1917 (FB)

League Club	Source	Date Signed	Seasons Played	Apps	Subs	Gls
Middlesbrough		08.35				
Darlington	Tr	08.39	46	6	-	0

TURNER Ian
Middlesbrough, 17 January, 1953 (G)

League Club	Source	Date Signed	Seasons Played	Apps	Subs	Gls
Huddersfield T.	South Bank	10.70				
Grimsby T.	Tr	01.72	71-73	26	0	0
Walsall	L	02.73	72	3	0	0
Southampton	Tr	03.74	73-77	77	0	0
Newport Co.	L	03.78	77	7	0	0
Lincoln C.	L	10.78	78	7	0	0
Walsall	Tr	01.79	78-80	39	0	0
Halifax T.	L	01.81	80	5	0	0

TURNER John Graham Anthony
Peterlee, 23 December, 1954 (G)

League Club	Source	Date Signed	Seasons Played	Apps	Subs	Gls
Derby Co.	App	12.72				
Doncaster Rov.	L	02.74	73	4	0	0
Huddersfield T.	L	03.75	74	1	0	0
Reading	Tr	05.75	75-77	31	0	0
Torquay U.	Tr	08.78	78-79	76	0	0
Chesterfield	Tr	02.80	79-82	132	0	0
Torquay U.	Tr	08.83	83	34	0	0
Burnley	Weymouth	08.84				
Peterborough U.	Tr	10.84	84-85	60	0	0

TURNER Joseph
Barnsley, 21 March, 1931 (G)

League Club	Source	Date Signed	Seasons Played	Apps	Subs	Gls
Stockport Co.	Denaby U.	07.54	54-56	79	-	0

League Club	Source	Date Signed	Seasons Played	Apps	Subs	Gls
Darlington	Tr	12.57	57-59	68	-	0
Scunthorpe U.	Tr	06.60	60-61	22	-	0
Barnsley	Tr	11.61	61	7	-	0

TURNER Keith John
Coventry, 9 April, 1934 (IF)

League Club	Source	Date Signed	Seasons Played	Apps	Subs	Gls
Nottingham F.		06.54	54	1	-	0

TURNER Kenneth
Hemsworth, 22 April, 1941 (FB)

League Club	Source	Date Signed	Seasons Played	Apps	Subs	Gls
Huddersfield T.	Jnrs	10.58	61	5	-	0
Shrewsbury T.	Tr	07.63	63-65	64	0	1
York C.	Tr	06.66	66-67	88	0	2

TURNER Mark Brendan
Stockport, 19 September, 1956 (M/FB)

League Club	Source	Date Signed	Seasons Played	Apps	Subs	Gls
Stockport Co.	Everton (App)	08.75	75	8	0	0

TURNER Graham **Mark**
Bebington, 4 October, 1972 (M)

League Club	Source	Date Signed	Seasons Played	Apps	Subs	Gls
Wolverhampton W.	Paget R.	07.91	92	1	0	0
Northampton T.	Tr	07.94	94	2	2	0
Hereford U. (L)	Telford U.	03.97	96	6	0	0

TURNER Michael George Elliott
Bridport, 20 September, 1938 E Yth (G)

League Club	Source	Date Signed	Seasons Played	Apps	Subs	Gls
Swindon T.	Dorchester T.	12.61	61-63	75	-	0
Torquay U.	Tr	07.64	64-65	14	0	0

TURNER Neil Stuart Thomson
Blackpool, 15 March, 1942 (M)

League Club	Source	Date Signed	Seasons Played	Apps	Subs	Gls
Blackpool	Jnrs	12.59	63-66	10	1	1
Crewe Alex.	Tr	07.68	68-71	80	6	4

TURNER Paul
Barnsley, 8 July, 1953 (RB)

League Club	Source	Date Signed	Seasons Played	Apps	Subs	Gls
Barnsley	App	07.71	70-74	27	8	1

TURNER Paul Edward
Enfield, 13 November, 1968 (M)

League Club	Source	Date Signed	Seasons Played	Apps	Subs	Gls
Arsenal	App	07.86				
Cambridge U.	Tr	09.87	87-88	28	9	0

TURNER Peter Ambrose
Leicester, 14 August, 1931 (IF)

League Club	Source	Date Signed	Seasons Played	Apps	Subs	Gls
Crewe Alex.		03.54	54-55	23	-	4

TURNER Philip
Sheffield, 12 February, 1962 (M)

League Club	Source	Date Signed	Seasons Played	Apps	Subs	Gls
Lincoln C.	App	02.80	79-85	239	2	19
Grimsby T.	Tr	08.86	86-87	62	0	7
Leicester C.	Tr	02.88	87-88	18	6	2
Notts Co.	Tr	03.89	88-96	223	14	16

TURNER Philip
Frodsham, 20 February, 1927 (F)

League Club	Source	Date Signed	Seasons Played	Apps	Subs	Gls
Chester C.	Jnrs	07.46	46-47	27	-	6
Carlisle U.	Tr	09.48	48-50	78	-	24
Bradford P.A.	Tr	06.51	51-53	55	-	24
Scunthorpe U.	Tr	06.54	54	5	-	2
Accrington St.	Tr	10.55	55-56	14	-	5
Chester C.	Tr	11.56	56	16	-	3

TURNER Robert Peter
Durham, 18 September, 1966 (F)

League Club	Source	Date Signed	Seasons Played	Apps	Subs	Gls
Huddersfield T.	App	09.84	84	0	2	0
Cardiff C.	Tr	07.85	85-86	34	5	8
Hartlepool U.	L	10.86	86	7	0	1
Bristol Rov.	Tr	12.86	86-87	19	7	2
Wimbledon	Tr	12.87	87-88	2	8	0
Bristol C.	Tr	01.89	88-89	45	7	12
Plymouth Arg.	Tr	07.90	90-92	66	0	17
Notts Co.	Tr	11.92	92	7	1	1
Shrewsbury T.	L	03.93	92	9	0	0
Exeter C.	Tr	02.94	93-95	38	7	7
Cambridge U.	Tr	12.95	95-96	12	5	4
Hull C.	L	10.96	96	5	0	2

TURNER Robin David
Carlisle, 10 September, 1955 E Yth (F)

League Club	Source	Date Signed	Seasons Played	Apps	Subs	Gls
Ipswich T.	App	04.73	75-83	22	26	2
Swansea C.	Tr	03.85	84-85	20	0	8
Colchester U.	Tr	11.85	85	6	5	0

TURNER Stanley Frederick
Wokingham, 31 May, 1941 (OR)

League Club	Source	Date Signed	Seasons Played	Apps	Subs	Gls
Reading	Jnrs	12.58	60	3	-	0

TURNER Stanley Simpson
Hanley, 21 October, 1926 Died 1991 (FB)

League Club	Source	Date Signed	Seasons Played	Apps	Subs	Gls
Port Vale		03.49	50-56	227	-	0

TURNER Wayne Leslie
Luton, 9 March, 1961 (M)

League Club	Source	Date Signed	Seasons Played	Apps	Subs	Gls
Luton T.	App	04.78	78-84	81	3	2
Lincoln C.	L	10.81	81	16	0	0
Coventry C.	Tr	07.85	85	14	1	1
Brentford	Tr	09.86	86-87	56	0	2

TURNEY James Allan
Cramlington, 8 July, 1922 Died 1995 (OR)

League Club	Source	Date Signed	Seasons Played	Apps	Subs	Gls
Darlington		08.48	48-49	40	-	3

TURPIE Robert Paul
Hampstead, 13 November, 1949 (M)

League Club	Source	Date Signed	Seasons Played	Apps	Subs	Gls
Queens Park R.	App	11.67	69	1	1	0
Peterborough U.	Tr	07.70	70-71	31	6	3

TURTON Cyril
Hemsworth, 20 September, 1921 (CH)

League Club	Source	Date Signed	Seasons Played	Apps	Subs	Gls
Sheffield Wed.	Frickley Colly	11.44	46-53	146	-	0

TUTILL Stephen Alan
York, 1 October, 1969 E Sch (CD)

League Club	Source	Date Signed	Seasons Played	Apps	Subs	Gls
York C.	YT	01.88	87-97	293	8	6
Darlington	Tr	02.98	97	7	0	0

TUTIN Harry
Sunderland, 4 May, 1919 Died 1994 (OR)

League Club	Source	Date Signed	Seasons Played	Apps	Subs	Gls
Southport (Am)	Houghton S.C.	09.46	46	2	-	0

TUTT Graham Charles
Deptford, 27 August, 1956 (G)

League Club	Source	Date Signed	Seasons Played	Apps	Subs	Gls
Charlton Ath.	Jnrs	03.74	73-75	65	0	0
Workington	L	09.74	74	4	0	0

TUTTLE David Philip
Reading, 6 February, 1972 E Yth (CD)

League Club	Source	Date Signed	Seasons Played	Apps	Subs	Gls
Tottenham H.	YT	02.90	90-92	10	3	0
Peterborough U.	L	01.93	92	7	0	0
Sheffield U.	Tr	08.93	93-95	63	0	1
Crystal Palace	Tr	03.96	95-97	56	2	3

TUTTON Alan
Bexley, 23 February, 1973 (F)

League Club	Source	Date Signed	Seasons Played	Apps	Subs	Gls
Maidstone U.	Alma Swanley	07.91	91	0	4	0

TUTTY Paul
Manchester, 22 February, 1952 (CD)

League Club	Source	Date Signed	Seasons Played	Apps	Subs	Gls
Stockport Co. (Am)	Manchester U. (Am)	07.70	70	1	0	0

TUTTY Wayne Keith
Oxford, 18 June, 1963 (M)

League Club	Source	Date Signed	Seasons Played	Apps	Subs	Gls
Reading	Banbury U.	08.82	82-83	11	2	4

TWAMLEY Bruce Richardson
Canada, 23 May, 1952 Canadian Int (FB)

League Club	Source	Date Signed	Seasons Played	Apps	Subs	Gls
Ipswich T.	Jnrs	10.69	73-74	2	0	0

TWEED Steven
Edinburgh, 9 August, 1972 Su21-3/S 'B' (D)

League Club	Source	Date Signed	Seasons Played	Apps	Subs	Gls
Stoke C.	Ionikos (Gre)	08.97	97	35	3	0

TWEEDY George Jacob
Bedlington, 8 January, 1913 Died 1987 E-1 (G)

League Club	Source	Date Signed	Seasons Played	Apps	Subs	Gls
Grimsby T.	Willington	08.31	32-52	347	-	0

TWELL Terence Keith
Doncaster, 21 February, 1947 (G)

League Club	Source	Date Signed	Seasons Played	Apps	Subs	Gls
Birmingham C.	Bourne T.	10.64	67	2	0	0

TWENTYMAN Geoffrey
Liverpool, 10 March, 1959 (CD)

League Club	Source	Date Signed	Seasons Played	Apps	Subs	Gls
Preston N.E.	Chorley	08.83	83-85	95	3	4
Bristol Rov.	Tr	08.86	86-92	248	4	6

TWENTYMAN Geoffrey
Brampton, 19 January, 1930 (CH)

League Club	Source	Date Signed	Seasons Played	Apps	Subs	Gls
Carlisle U.	Jnrs	02.47	46-53	149	-	2
Liverpool	Tr	12.53	53-59	170	-	18
Carlisle U.	Ballymena U.	06.63	63	10	-	0

TWIDDY Christopher
Pontypridd, 19 January, 1976 W Yth/Wu21-3 (LW)

League Club	Source	Date Signed	Seasons Played	Apps	Subs	Gls
Plymouth Arg.	YT	06.94	94-95	14	3	1

League Club	Source	Date Signed	Seasons Played	Career Record Apps	Subs	Gls

TWIDLE Kenneth George
Brigg, 10 October, 1931 (CF)

League Club	Source	Date Signed	Seasons Played	Apps	Subs	Gls
Rotherham U.	Retford T.	12.57	57-58	24	-	6

TWIGG Richard Lance
Barry, 10 September, 1939 (G)

League Club	Source	Date Signed	Seasons Played	Apps	Subs	Gls
Notts Co.	Barry T.	11.57	58	2	-	0

TWISSELL Charles Herbert
Singapore, 16 December, 1932 E Amat (OL)

League Club	Source	Date Signed	Seasons Played	Apps	Subs	Gls
Plymouth Arg.		04.55	55-57	41	-	9
York C.	Tr	11.58	58-60	53	-	8

TWIST Franklin
Liverpool, 2 November, 1940 E Yth (W)

League Club	Source	Date Signed	Seasons Played	Apps	Subs	Gls
Liverpool	Jnrs	08.58				
Bury	Prescot Cables	10.61	61-62	8	-	0
Halifax T.	Tr	07.63	63-64	64	-	11
Tranmere Rov.	Tr	07.65	65	7	0	3

TWITCHIN Ian Robert
Teignmouth, 22 January, 1952 E Yth (FB/M)

League Club	Source	Date Signed	Seasons Played	Apps	Subs	Gls
Torquay U.	Jnrs	01.70	69-80	374	26	15

TWOMEY James Francis
Newry (NI), 13 April, 1914 Died 1984 E Yth (G)

League Club	Source	Date Signed	Seasons Played	Apps	Subs	Gls
Leeds U.	Newry T.	12.37	37-48	108	-	0

TWYNHAM Gary Steven
Manchester, 8 February, 1976 (M)

League Club	Source	Date Signed	Seasons Played	Apps	Subs	Gls
Manchester U.	YT	07.94				
Darlington	Tr	03.96	95-96	23	8	3

TYDEMAN Richard (Dick)
Chatham, 26 May, 1951 (M)

League Club	Source	Date Signed	Seasons Played	Apps	Subs	Gls
Gillingham	App	05.69	69-76	293	2	13
Charlton Ath.	Tr	12.76	76-80	158	0	7
Gillingham	Tr	08.81	81-83	75	1	2
Peterborough U.	Tr	10.83	83	29	0	0

TYLER Dudley Hugh John
Salisbury, 21 September, 1944 (W)

League Club	Source	Date Signed	Seasons Played	Apps	Subs	Gls
West Ham U.	Hereford U.	06.72	72-73	29	0	1
Hereford U.	Tr	11.73	73-76	97	5	10

TYLER Leonard Victor
Rotherhithe, 7 January, 1919 Died 1988 (LB)

League Club	Source	Date Signed	Seasons Played	Apps	Subs	Gls
Millwall	Redhill	03.43	46-49	90	-	0
Ipswich T.	Tr	07.50	50-51	73	-	0

TYLER Mark Richard
Norwich, 2 April, 1977 E Yth (G)

League Club	Source	Date Signed	Seasons Played	Apps	Subs	Gls
Peterborough U.	YT	12.94	94-97	53	1	0

TYLER Simon
Pontypool, 1 May, 1962 (F)

League Club	Source	Date Signed	Seasons Played	Apps	Subs	Gls
Newport Co. (N/C)	Abergavenny Thur.	10.84	84-85	0	4	0

TYNAN Paul
Whitehaven, 15 July, 1969 (M)

League Club	Source	Date Signed	Seasons Played	Apps	Subs	Gls
Carlisle U.	Ipswich T. (App)	08.87	87	2	3	0

TYNAN Robert
Liverpool, 7 December, 1955 E Yth (M)

League Club	Source	Date Signed	Seasons Played	Apps	Subs	Gls
Tranmere Rov.	App	07.73	72-77	193	2	26
Blackpool	Tr	07.78				

TYNAN Thomas Edward
Liverpool, 17 November, 1955 (F)

League Club	Source	Date Signed	Seasons Played	Apps	Subs	Gls
Liverpool	App	11.72				
Swansea C.	L	10.75	75	6	0	2
Sheffield Wed.	Tr	09.76	76-78	89	2	31
Lincoln C.	Tr	10.78	78	9	0	1
Newport Co.	Tr	02.79	78-82	168	15	66
Plymouth Arg.	Tr	08.83	83-84	80	0	43
Rotherham U.	Tr	07.85	85-86	32	0	13
Plymouth Arg.	L	03.86	85	9	0	10
Plymouth Arg.	Tr	09.86	86-89	172	1	73
Torquay U.	Tr	05.90	90	34	1	13
Doncaster Rov.	Tr	07.91	91	5	6	1

TYRELL Joseph James
Stepney, 21 January, 1932 (IF)

League Club	Source	Date Signed	Seasons Played	Apps	Subs	Gls
Aston Villa	Bretforton O.B.	05.50	53-55	7	-	3
Millwall	Tr	03.56	55-56	37	-	18
Bournemouth	Tr	06.57	57-58	3	-	1

TYRER Alan
Liverpool, 8 December, 1942 (M)

League Club	Source	Date Signed	Seasons Played	Apps	Subs	Gls
Everton	Jnrs	12.59	59-61	9	-	2
Mansfield T.	Tr	07.63	63-64	41	-	5
Arsenal	Tr	08.65				
Bury	Tr	08.67	67	2	0	0
Workington	Tr	07.68	68-75	228	15	18

TYRER Arthur
Liverpool, 14 October, 1934 (CF)

League Club	Source	Date Signed	Seasons Played	Apps	Subs	Gls
Crewe Alex.	St Helens	03.58	57	6	-	5

TYRER Arthur Spencer
Manchester, 25 February, 1931 (WH/OL)

League Club	Source	Date Signed	Seasons Played	Apps	Subs	Gls
Leeds U.	Mossley	09.50	51-53	39	-	4
Shrewsbury T.	Tr	06.55	55	24	-	3
Aldershot	Tr	06.56	56-63	234	-	9

TYSON John
Barrow, 19 November, 1935 (F)

League Club	Source	Date Signed	Seasons Played	Apps	Subs	Gls
Barrow		04.54	53-56	8	-	0

UFTON Derek Gilbert
Dartford, 31 May, 1928 E-1 (CH)

League Club	Source	Date Signed	Seasons Played	Apps	Subs	Gls
Charlton Ath.	Bexleyheath & Welling	09.48	49-59	263	-	0

UGOLINI Rolando
Italy, 4 June, 1924 (G)

League Club	Source	Date Signed	Seasons Played	Apps	Subs	Gls
Middlesbrough	Glasgow Celtic	05.48	48-55	320	-	0
Wrexham	Tr	06.57	57-59	83	-	0

UHLENBEEK Gustav Reinier
Surinam, 20 August, 1970 (RB)

League Club	Source	Date Signed	Seasons Played	Apps	Subs	Gls
Ipswich T.	Tops S.V. (Neth)	08.95	95-97	77	12	4

ULLATHORNE Robert
Wakefield, 11 October, 1971 E Yth (M/LB)

League Club	Source	Date Signed	Seasons Played	Apps	Subs	Gls
Norwich C.	YT	07.90	90-95	86	8	7
Leicester C.	Osasuna (Sp)	02.97	97	3	3	1

UNDERHILL Graham Stuart
Bristol, 10 April, 1968 (D)

League Club	Source	Date Signed	Seasons Played	Apps	Subs	Gls
Bristol C.	App	04.86	85	1	0	0

UNDERWOOD Edmund David
Camden, 15 March, 1928 Died 1989 (G)

League Club	Source	Date Signed	Seasons Played	Apps	Subs	Gls
Queens Park R.	Edware T.	12.49	51	2	-	0
Watford	Tr	02.52	51-53	52	-	0
Liverpool	Tr	12.53	53-55	45	-	0
Watford	Tr	06.56	56	16	-	0
Watford	Dartford	04.60	60-62	108	-	0
Fulham	Tr	07.63	63-64	18	-	0

UNDERWOOD George Ronald
Sheffield, 6 September, 1925 (RB)

League Club	Source	Date Signed	Seasons Played	Apps	Subs	Gls
Sheffield U.		09.46	49-50	17	-	0
Sheffield Wed.	Tr	10.51				
Scunthorpe U.	Tr	06.53	53	8	-	0
Rochdale	Tr	06.54	54	19	-	0

UNDERWOOD William Kenneth
Brigg, 28 December, 1921 Died 1993 (OL)

League Club	Source	Date Signed	Seasons Played	Apps	Subs	Gls
Hartlepool U. (Am)	South Bank	01.48	47	1	-	0

UNSWORTH David Gerald
Preston, 16 October, 1973 E Yth/Eu21-7/E-1 (CD)

League Club	Source	Date Signed	Seasons Played	Apps	Subs	Gls
Everton	YT	06.92	91-96	108	8	11
West Ham U.	Tr	08.97	97	32	0	2

UNSWORTH Jamie Jonathan
Bury, 1 May, 1973 (RB)

League Club	Source	Date Signed	Seasons Played	Apps	Subs	Gls
Cardiff C.	YT	07.91	90-91	1	3	0

UNSWORTH Lee Peter
Eccles, 25 February, 1973 (RB)

League Club	Source	Date Signed	Seasons Played	Apps	Subs	Gls
Crewe Alex.	Ashton U.	02.95	95-97	75	19	0

UPHILL Edward Dennis Herbert
Bath, 11 August, 1931 (CF)

League Club	Source	Date Signed	Seasons Played	Apps	Subs	Gls
Tottenham H.	Finchley	09.49	50-52	6	-	2
Reading	Tr	02.53	52-55	92	-	43
Coventry C.	Tr	10.55	55-56	49	-	17
Mansfield T.	Tr	03.57	56-58	83	-	38
Watford	Tr	06.59	59-60	51	-	30
Crystal Palace	Tr	10.60	60-62	63	-	17

UPRICHARD William Norman McCourt
Portadown, 20 April, 1928 NI-18 (G)

League Club	Source	Date Signed	Seasons Played	Apps	Subs	Gls
Arsenal	Distillery	06.48				
Swindon T.	Tr	11.49	49-52	73	-	0
Portsmouth	Tr	11.52	52-58	182	-	0
Southend U.	Tr	07.59	59	12	-	0

UPSON Matthew James
Stowmarket, 18 April, 1979 E Yth (CD)

League Club	Source	Date Signed	Seasons Played	Apps	Subs	Gls
Luton T.	YT	04.96	96	0	1	0
Arsenal	Tr	05.97	97	5	0	0

UPTON Colin Clive
Reading, 2 October, 1960 (F)

League Club	Source	Date Signed	Seasons Played	Apps	Subs	Gls
Plymouth Arg.	App	10.78	78	2	1	0

UPTON Frank
Atherstone, 18 October, 1934 (WH)

League Club	Source	Date Signed	Seasons Played	Apps	Subs	Gls
Northampton T.	Nuneaton Borough	03.53	52-53	17	-	1
Derby Co.	Tr	06.54	54-60	224	-	12
Chelsea	Tr	08.61	61-64	74	-	3
Derby Co.	Tr	09.65	65-66	35	0	5
Notts Co.	Tr	09.66	66	33	1	3
Workington	Worcester C.	01.68	67	6	1	0

UPTON James Edwin Glen
Coatbridge, 3 June, 1940 (FB)

League Club	Source	Date Signed	Seasons Played	Apps	Subs	Gls
Cardiff C.	Glasgow Celtic	08.63	63	5	-	0

UPTON Robin (Nobby) Patrick
Willington, 9 November, 1942 (WH)

League Club	Source	Date Signed	Seasons Played	Apps	Subs	Gls
Brighton & H.A.	Jnrs	11.59	62-66	40	0	0

URE John (Ian) Francombe
Ayr, 7 December, 1939 SF Lge/Su23-1/S-11 (CH)

League Club	Source	Date Signed	Seasons Played	Apps	Subs	Gls
Arsenal	Dundee	08.63	63-69	168	0	2
Manchester U.	Tr	08.69	69-70	47	0	1

URQUHART George Stuart McWilliam
Glasgow, 22 April, 1950 (M)

League Club	Source	Date Signed	Seasons Played	Apps	Subs	Gls
Wigan Ath.	Ross Co.	07.79	79-80	63	5	6

URQUHART William Murray
Inverness, 22 November, 1956 (F)

League Club	Source	Date Signed	Seasons Played	Apps	Subs	Gls
Wigan Ath.	Glasgow Rangers	11.80	80	5	5	2

URSEM Loek Aloysius Jacobus Maria
Netherlands, 7 January, 1958 (W)

League Club	Source	Date Signed	Seasons Played	Apps	Subs	Gls
Stoke C.	A.Z. Alkmaar (Neth)	07.79	79-82	32	8	7
Sunderland	L	03.82	81	0	4	0

URWIN Graham Edward
South Shields, 15 February, 1949 (OR)

League Club	Source	Date Signed	Seasons Played	Apps	Subs	Gls
Darlington		08.67	67	1	0	0

USHER Brian
Durham, 11 March, 1944 Eu23-1 (OR)

League Club	Source	Date Signed	Seasons Played	Apps	Subs	Gls
Sunderland	Jnrs	03.61	63-64	61	-	5
Sheffield Wed.	Tr	06.65	65-67	55	1	2
Doncaster Rov.	Tr	06.68	68-72	164	6	6

USHER John Allison Grey
Hexham, 6 September, 1918 Died 1989 (WH)

League Club	Source	Date Signed	Seasons Played	Apps	Subs	Gls
Watford		05.46	46-47	23	-	3

UTLEY Darren
Barnsley, 28 September, 1977 (CD)

League Club	Source	Date Signed	Seasons Played	Apps	Subs	Gls
Doncaster Rov.	YT	12.95	95-97	22	6	1

UYTENBOGARDT Albert George
South Africa, 5 March, 1930 (G)

League Club	Source	Date Signed	Seasons Played	Apps	Subs	Gls
Charlton Ath.	Cape Town Trams (SA)	10.48	48-52	6	-	0

UZELAC Steven
Doncaster, 12 March, 1953 (CD)

League Club	Source	Date Signed	Seasons Played	Apps	Subs	Gls
Doncaster Rov.	Jnrs	06.71	71-76	182	3	9
Mansfield T.	L	02.76	75	2	0	0
Preston N.E.	Tr	05.77	77-78	9	0	0
Stockport Co.	Tr	03.80	79-81	31	0	2

UZZELL John Edward
Plymouth, 31 March, 1959 (D)

League Club	Source	Date Signed	Seasons Played	Apps	Subs	Gls
Plymouth Arg.	App	03.77	77-88	292	10	6
Torquay U.	Tr	08.89	89-91	91	1	2

VAESSEN Leon Henry
Market Bosworth, 8 November, 1940 E Sch (WH)

League Club	Source	Date Signed	Seasons Played	Apps	Subs	Gls
Millwall	Chelsea (Am)	01.58	57-60	26	-	2
Gillingham	Tr	08.61	61-62	29	-	0

VAESSEN Paul Leon
Gillingham, 16 October, 1961 (F)

League Club	Source	Date Signed	Seasons Played	Apps	Subs	Gls
Arsenal	App	07.79	78-81	23	9	6

VAFIADIS Odysseus (Seth) Yicanakis
Hammersmith, 8 September, 1945 (W)

League Club	Source	Date Signed	Seasons Played	Apps	Subs	Gls
Queens Park R.	Chelsea (App)	11.62	63	15	-	4
Millwall	Tr	09.64	64	4	-	0

VAIREY Roy Henry
South Elmsall, 10 June, 1932 (G)

League Club	Source	Date Signed	Seasons Played	Apps	Subs	Gls
Stockport Co.		09.51	56	5	-	0

VALENTINE Carl Howard
Manchester, 4 July, 1958 Canadian Int (W)

League Club	Source	Date Signed	Seasons Played	Apps	Subs	Gls
Oldham Ath.	Jnrs	01.76	76-79	75	7	8
West Bromwich A.	Vancouver (Can)	10.84	84-85	44	0	6

VALENTINE Peter
Huddersfield, 16 April, 1963 (CD)

League Club	Source	Date Signed	Seasons Played	Apps	Subs	Gls
Huddersfield T.	App	04.81	81-82	19	0	1
Bolton W.	Tr	07.83	83-84	66	2	1
Bury	Tr	07.85	85-92	314	5	16
Carlisle U.	Tr	08.93	93-94	27	2	2
Rochdale	Tr	11.94	94-95	49	1	2

VALERY Patrick Jean Claude
Brignoles, France, 3 July, 1969 (FB)

League Club	Source	Date Signed	Seasons Played	Apps	Subs	Gls
Blackburn Rov.	Bastia (Fr)	07.97	97	14	1	0

VALLANCE Thomas Henshall Wilson
Stoke, 28 March, 1924 Died 1980 (OL)

League Club	Source	Date Signed	Seasons Played	Apps	Subs	Gls
Arsenal	Torquay U. (Am)	07.47	48-49	15	-	2

VALLARD Leonard Gerald Harold
Sherborne, 6 July, 1940 (FB)

League Club	Source	Date Signed	Seasons Played	Apps	Subs	Gls
Reading	Yeovil T.	05.58	59-61	37	-	2

VAN BLERK Jason
Australia, 16 March, 1968 Australian Int (LB)

League Club	Source	Date Signed	Seasons Played	Apps	Subs	Gls
Millwall	Go Ahead Eagles (Neth)	09.94	94-96	68	5	2
Manchester C.	Tr	08.97	97	10	9	0
West Bromwich A.	Tr	03.98	97	8	0	0

VAN BREUKELEN Johannes (Hans)
Netherlands, 4 October, 1956 Dutch Int (G)

League Club	Source	Date Signed	Seasons Played	Apps	Subs	Gls
Nottingham F.	Utrecht (Neth)	09.82	82-83	61	0	0

VAN DEN HAUWE Patrick William Roger
Belgium, 16 December, 1960 W-13 (FB)

League Club	Source	Date Signed	Seasons Played	Apps	Subs	Gls
Birmingham C.	App	08.78	78-84	119	4	1
Everton	Tr	09.84	84-88	134	1	2
Tottenham H.	Tr	08.89	89-92	110	6	0
Millwall	Tr	09.93	93-94	27	0	0

VAN DER ELST Francois (Franky) Jean Cecile
Belgium, 1 December, 1954 Belgian Int (M)

League Club	Source	Date Signed	Seasons Played	Apps	Subs	Gls
West Ham U.	New York (USA)	12.81	81-82	61	1	14

VAN DER GOUW Raimond
Netherlands, 24 March, 1963 (G)

League Club	Source	Date Signed	Seasons Played	Apps	Subs	Gls
Manchester U.	Vitesse Arnhem (Neth)	07.96	96-97	6	1	0

VAN DER LAAN Robertus (Robin) Petrus
Netherlands, 5 September, 1968 (M)

League Club	Source	Date Signed	Seasons Played	Apps	Subs	Gls
Port Vale	Wageningen (Neth)	02.91	90-94	154	22	24
Derby Co.	Tr	08.95	95-97	61	4	8
Wolverhampton W.	L	10.96	96	7	0	0

VANDERMOTTEN William
Glasgow, 26 August, 1930 Died 1979 (FB)

League Club	Source	Date Signed	Seasons Played	Apps	Subs	Gls
Bradford P.A.	Third Lanark	03.53	52	1	-	0

VAN DER VELDEN Carel
Netherlands, 3 August, 1972 (M)

League Club	Source	Date Signed	Seasons Played	Apps	Subs	Gls
Barnsley	F.C. Den Bosch (Neth)	03.96	95-96	7	2	0
Scarborough	Tr	08.97	97	5	3	1

VAN DULLEMEN Raymond Robert
Gravenhage, Holland, 6 May, 1973 (F)

League Club	Source	Date Signed	Seasons Played	Apps	Subs	Gls
Northampton T.	V.I.O.S. (Neth)	08.97	97	0	1	0

VAN GOBBEL Ulrich
Surinam, 16 January, 1971 Dutch Int (CD)

League Club	Source	Date Signed	Seasons Played	Apps	Subs	Gls
Southampton	Galatasaray (Tu)	10.96	96-97	25	2	1

VAN GOOL Roger
Belgium, 1 June, 1950 Belgian Int (W)

League Club	Source	Date Signed	Seasons Played	Apps	Subs	Gls
Coventry C.	F.C. Cologne (Ger)	03.80	79-80	17	0	0

VANHALA Jari
Finland, 29 August, 1965 Finnish Int (F)

League Club	Source	Date Signed	Seasons Played	Apps	Subs	Gls
Bradford C. (N/C)	F.F. Jaro (Fin)	12.96	96	0	1	0

VAN HEUSDEN Arjan
Netherlands, 11 December, 1972 (G)

League Club	Source	Date Signed	Seasons Played	Apps	Subs	Gls
Port Vale	Noordwijk (Neth)	08.94	94-97	27	0	0
Oxford U.	L	09.97	97	11	0	0

VAN HOOIJDONK Pierre
Netherlands, 29 November, 1969 Dutch Int (F)

League Club	Source	Date Signed	Seasons Played	Apps	Subs	Gls
Nottingham F.	Glasgow Celtic	03.97	96-97	49	1	30

VAN MIERLO Antonius (Antony) Wilhelmus Matthias
Netherlands, 24 August, 1957 Dutch Int (W)

League Club	Source	Date Signed	Seasons Played	Apps	Subs	Gls
Birmingham C.	Willem Tilburg (Neth)	08.81	81-82	44	0	4

VAN ROSSUM Johannes (Erik) Christison
Netherlands, 27 March, 1963 (CD)

League Club	Source	Date Signed	Seasons Played	Apps	Subs	Gls
Plymouth Arg.	Twente Enschede (Neth)	01.92	91	9	0	0

VANSITTART Thomas
Merton, 23 January, 1950 (D)

League Club	Source	Date Signed	Seasons Played	Apps	Subs	Gls
Crystal Palace	App	04.67	67-69	10	1	2
Wrexham	Tr	02.70	69-74	86	2	1

VAN WIJK Dennis Johannes
Netherlands, 16 February, 1962 (LB/M)

League Club	Source	Date Signed	Seasons Played	Apps	Subs	Gls
Norwich C.	Ajax (Neth)	10.82	82-85	109	9	3

VARADI Imre
Paddington, 8 July, 1959 (F)

League Club	Source	Date Signed	Seasons Played	Apps	Subs	Gls
Sheffield U.	Letchworth G.C.	04.78	78	6	4	4
Everton	Tr	03.79	79-80	22	4	6
Newcastle U.	Tr	08.81	81-82	81	0	39
Sheffield Wed.	Tr	08.83	83-84	72	4	33
West Bromwich A.	Tr	07.85	85	30	2	9
Manchester C.	Tr	10.86	86-88	56	9	26
Sheffield Wed.	Tr	09.88	88-89	14	8	3
Leeds U.	Tr	02.90	89-92	21	5	5
Luton T.	L	03.92	91	5	1	1
Oxford U.	L	01.93	92	3	2	0
Rotherham U.	Tr	03.92	92-94	55	12	25
Mansfield T. (N/C)	Tr	08.95	95	1	0	0
Scunthorpe U. (N/C)	Boston U.	09.95	95	0	2	0

VARNEY John Francis
Oxford, 27 November, 1929 (LB)

League Club	Source	Date Signed	Seasons Played	Apps	Subs	Gls
Hull C.	Oxford C.	12.49	50	9	-	0
Lincoln C.	Tr	05.51	51-52	20	-	4

VARTY Thomas Heppell
Hetton-le-Hole, 2 December, 1921 (IF)

League Club	Source	Date Signed	Seasons Played	Apps	Subs	Gls
Darlington	Newcastle U. (Am)	08.45	46-49	162	-	31
Watford	Tr	09.50	50	34	-	5

VARTY John **William**
Workington, 1 October, 1976 (CD)

League Club	Source	Date Signed	Seasons Played	Apps	Subs	Gls
Carlisle U.	YT	07.95	96-97	74	2	1

VASPER Peter John
Bromley, 3 September, 1945 (G)

League Club	Source	Date Signed	Seasons Played	Apps	Subs	Gls
Leyton Orient		11.63				
Norwich C.	Guildford C.	02.68	67-69	31	0	0
Cambridge U.	Tr	09.70	70-73	136	0	0

VASS Stephen
Leicester, 10 January, 1954 (FB)

League Club	Source	Date Signed	Seasons Played	Apps	Subs	Gls
Hartlepool U.		10.79	79	4	0	0
Huddersfield T.	Tr	01.81				

VASSALLO Barrie Emmanuel
Newport, 3 March, 1956 W Sch (M)

League Club	Source	Date Signed	Seasons Played	Apps	Subs	Gls
Arsenal	App	05.73				
Plymouth Arg.	Tr	11.74	74-75	6	7	2
Torquay U.	Barnstaple	03.77	76-78	44	2	4

VAUGHAN Anthony John
Manchester, 11 October, 1975 E Sch/E Yth (D)

League Club	Source	Date Signed	Seasons Played	Apps	Subs	Gls
Ipswich T.	YT	07.94	94-96	56	11	3
Manchester C.	Tr	07.97	97	19	0	1

VAUGHAN Charles John
Camberwell, 23 April, 1921 Died 1989 E Amat/E 'B' (CF)

League Club	Source	Date Signed	Seasons Played	Apps	Subs	Gls
Charlton Ath.	Sutton U.	01.47	46-52	227	-	91
Portsmouth	Tr	03.53	52-53	26	-	14

VAUGHAN John **Daniel**
Liverpool, 18 February, 1972 (D)

League Club	Source	Date Signed	Seasons Played	Apps	Subs	Gls
Crewe Alex.		09.92	92	3	4	0
Wigan Ath.	Tr	07.93	93	2	2	0

VAUGHAN Norman **Glyn**
Llaniloes, 25 August, 1921 (IF)

League Club	Source	Date Signed	Seasons Played	Apps	Subs	Gls
Exeter C.	Oldham Ath. (Am)	05.46	46-47	6	-	0

VAUGHAN Ian
Sheffield, 3 July, 1961 (CD)

League Club	Source	Date Signed	Seasons Played	Apps	Subs	Gls
Rotherham U.	App	07.79	79-80	4	0	0
Stockport Co.	L	12.81	81	2	0	1

VAUGHAN John
Isleworth, 26 June, 1964 (G)

League Club	Source	Date Signed	Seasons Played	Apps	Subs	Gls
West Ham U.	App	06.82				
Charlton Ath.	L	03.85	84	6	0	0
Bristol Rov.	L	09.85	85	6	0	0
Wrexham	L	10.85	85	4	0	0
Bristol C.	L	03.86	85	2	0	0
Fulham	Tr	08.86	86	44	0	0
Bristol C.	L	01.88	87	3	0	0
Cambridge U.	Tr	06.88	88-92	178	0	0
Charlton Ath.	Tr	08.93	93	5	1	0
Preston N.E.	Tr	07.94	94-95	65	1	0
Lincoln C.	Tr	08.96	96-97	29	0	0
Colchester U.	L	02.97	96	5	0	0

VAUGHAN Nigel Mark
Caerleon, 20 May, 1959 W Yth/Wu21-2/W-10 (M)

League Club	Source	Date Signed	Seasons Played	Apps	Subs	Gls
Newport Co.	App	05.77	76-83	215	9	32
Cardiff C.	Tr	09.83	83-86	144	5	42
Reading	L	02.87	86	5	0	1
Wolverhampton W.	Tr	08.87	87-89	86	7	10
Hereford U.	Tr	08.90	90-91	9	4	1

VAUGHAN Terence Ronald
Ebbw Vale, 22 April, 1938 (IF)

League Club	Source	Date Signed	Seasons Played	Apps	Subs	Gls
Mansfield T.	Ollerton Colly	06.57	58	6	-	2

VEACOCK James
Liverpool, 5 September, 1919 (CF)

League Club	Source	Date Signed	Seasons Played	Apps	Subs	Gls
Southport	Marine	11.47	47	10	-	0

VEALL Raymond Joseph
Skegness, 16 March, 1943 (OL)

League Club	Source	Date Signed	Seasons Played	Apps	Subs	Gls
Doncaster Rov.	Skegness	03.61	60-61	19	-	6
Everton	Tr	09.61	62	11	-	1
Preston N.E.	Tr	05.65	65	11	0	0
Huddersfield T.	Tr	12.65	65-66	12	0	1

VEARNCOMBE Graham
Cardiff, 28 March, 1934 Died 1993 W-2 (G)

League Club	Source	Date Signed	Seasons Played	Apps	Subs	Gls
Cardiff C.	Jnrs	02.52	52-63	208	-	0

VEART Thomas Carl
Australia, 21 May, 1970 Australian Int (M)

League Club	Source	Date Signed	Seasons Played	Apps	Subs	Gls
Sheffield U.	Adelaide C. (Aus)	07.94	94-95	47	19	16
Crystal Palace	Tr	03.96	95-97	41	16	6
Millwall	Tr	12.97	97	7	1	1

VEART Robert
Hartlepool, 11 August, 1944 E Amat (F)

League Club	Source	Date Signed	Seasons Played	Apps	Subs	Gls
Hartlepool U.	Whitby T.	07.70	70-72	59	12	12

VECK Robert
Titchfield, 1 April, 1920 (OL)

League Club	Source	Date Signed	Seasons Played	Apps	Subs	Gls
Southampton	Jnrs	09.45	46-49	23	-	2
Gillingham	Tr	07.50	50	36	-	12

VEGA Ramon
Switzerland, 14 June, 1971 Swiss Int (CD)

League Club	Source	Date Signed	Seasons Played	Apps	Subs	Gls
Tottenham H.	Cagliari (It)	01.97	96-97	30	3	4

VEITCH George Hardy
Sunderland, 18 January, 1931 (WH)

League Club	Source	Date Signed	Seasons Played	Apps	Subs	Gls
Hull C.	Silkworth Colly	08.51				
Millwall	Tr	06.52	52-57	93	-	0

VEITCH Thomas
Edinburgh, 16 October, 1949 Died 1987 (M)

League Club	Source	Date Signed	Seasons Played	Apps	Subs	Gls
Tranmere Rov.	Hearts	07.72	72-74	76	3	5
Halifax T.	Tr	08.75	75	20	2	0
Hartlepool U.	Tr	08.76	76	10	0	0

VENABLES Terence Frederick
Dagenham, 6 January, 1943 E Sch/E Yth/E Amat/Eu21-4/EF Lge/E-2 (M)

League Club	Source	Date Signed	Seasons Played	Apps	Subs	Gls
Chelsea	Jnrs	08.60	59-65	202	0	26
Tottenham H.	Tr	05.66	65-68	114	1	5
Queens Park R.	Tr	06.69	69-74	176	1	19
Crystal Palace	Tr	09.74	74	14	0	0

VENISON Barry
Consett, 16 August, 1964 E Yth/Eu21-10/E-2 (RB)

League Club	Source	Date Signed	Seasons Played	Apps	Subs	Gls
Sunderland	App	01.82	81-85	169	4	2
Liverpool	Tr	07.86	86-91	103	7	1
Newcastle U.	Tr	07.92	92-94	108	1	1
Southampton	Galatasaray (Tu)	10.95	95-96	23	1	0

VENNARD Walter
Belfast, 17 October, 1919 Died 1983 (WH)

League Club	Source	Date Signed	Seasons Played	Apps	Subs	Gls
Stockport Co.	Crusaders	09.47	47	5	-	0

VENTERS Alexander
Cowdenbeath, 9 June, 1913 Died 1959 SF Lge/S-3 (IF)

League Club	Source	Date Signed	Seasons Played	Apps	Subs	Gls
Blackburn Rov.	Third Lanark	02.47	46-47	25	-	7

VENTOM Eric
Hemsworth, 15 February, 1920 (LB)

League Club	Source	Date Signed	Seasons Played	Apps	Subs	Gls
Brentford		02.46	47	1	-	0

VENUS Mark
Hartlepool, 6 April, 1967 (LB)

League Club	Source	Date Signed	Seasons Played	Apps	Subs	Gls
Hartlepool U. (N/C)	Jnrs	03.85	84	4	0	0
Leicester C.	Tr	09.85	85-87	58	3	1
Wolverhampton W.	Tr	03.88	87-96	271	16	7
Ipswich T.	Tr	07.97	97	12	2	1

VERDE Pedro Andres
Argentina, 12 March, 1952 (F)

League Club	Source	Date Signed	Seasons Played	Apps	Subs	Gls
Sheffield U.	Hercules Alicante (Sp)	08.79	79	9	1	3

VERITY Daniel Richard
Bradford, 19 April, 1980 (CD)

League Club	Source	Date Signed	Seasons Played	Apps	Subs	Gls
Bradford C.	YT	03.98	97	0	1	0

VERITY David Anthony
Halifax, 21 September, 1949 (M)

League Club	Source	Date Signed	Seasons Played	Apps	Subs	Gls
Scunthorpe U.	App	09.67	66-67	3	2	0
Halifax T.	Tr	09.68	69-72	64	14	5

VERITY Kevin Patrick
Halifax, 16 March, 1940 (F)

League Club	Source	Date Signed	Seasons Played	Apps	Subs	Gls
Halifax T.	Jnrs	10.58	58-59	13	-	6

VERNAZZA Paulo Andrea Pietro
London, 1 November, 1979 E Yth (M/F)

League Club	Source	Date Signed	Seasons Played	Apps	Subs	Gls
Arsenal	YT	11.97	97	1	0	0

VERNON John Eric
South Africa, 2 March, 1956 (W)

League Club	Source	Date Signed	Seasons Played	Apps	Subs	Gls
Stockport Co.	Jnrs	04.75	74-75	4	2	0

VERNON John (Jack) Joseph
Belfast, 26 September, 1918 Died 1981 IR-2/NI-17 (CH)

League Club	Source	Date Signed	Seasons Played	Apps	Subs	Gls
West Bromwich A.	Belfast Celtic	02.47	46-51	190	-	1

VERNON Thomas Royston (Roy)
Prestatyn, 14 April, 1937 Died 1993 Wu23-2/W-32 (IF)

League Club	Source	Date Signed	Seasons Played	Apps	Subs	Gls
Blackburn Rov.	Jnrs	03.55	55-59	131	-	49
Everton	Tr	02.60	59-64	176	-	101
Stoke C.	Tr	03.65	64-68	84	3	22
Halifax T.	L	01.70	69	4	0	0

VERTANNES Desmond Mark Stephen
Chiswick, 25 April, 1972 (CD)

League Club	Source	Date Signed	Seasons Played	Apps	Subs	Gls
Fulham	YT	●	89	0	2	0
Aldershot	Chelsea (N/C)	08.90				

VERVEER Etienne
Surinam, 22 September, 1967 (M)

League Club	Source	Date Signed	Seasons Played	Apps	Subs	Gls
Millwall	Chur (Swi)	12.91	91-93	46	10	7
Bradford C.	L	02.95	94	9	0	1

VESEY Kieron Gerard
Manchester, 24 November, 1965 (G)

League Club	Source	Date Signed	Seasons Played	Apps	Subs	Gls
Halifax T. (N/C)	Jnrs	02.83	83	2	0	0

VESSEY Anthony William
Derby, 28 November, 1961 (CD)

League Club	Source	Date Signed	Seasons Played	Apps	Subs	Gls
Brighton & H.A.	App	11.79	80	1	0	0

VEYSEY Kenneth James
Hackney, 8 June, 1967 (G)

League Club	Source	Date Signed	Seasons Played	Apps	Subs	Gls
Torquay U.	Dawlish	11.87	88-90	72	0	0
Oxford U.	Tr	10.90	90-91	57	0	0
Exeter C.	Reading (N/C)	10.93	93	11	1	0
Torquay U.	Dorchester T.	08.97	97	27	0	0

VIALLI Gianluca
Italy, 9 July, 1964 Italian Int (F)

League Club	Source	Date Signed	Seasons Played	Apps	Subs	Gls
Chelsea	Juventus (It)	07.96	96-97	37	12	20

VICK Leigh
Cardiff, 8 January, 1978 (M)

League Club	Source	Date Signed	Seasons Played	Apps	Subs	Gls
Cardiff C.	YT	07.96	94-95	2	2	0

VICKERS Ashley James Ward
Sheffield, 14 June, 1972 (CD)

League Club	Source	Date Signed	Seasons Played	Apps	Subs	Gls
Peterborough U.	Heybridge Swifts	12.97	97	1	0	0

VICKERS Peter
Doncaster, 6 March, 1934 E Sch (IF)

League Club	Source	Date Signed	Seasons Played	Apps	Subs	Gls
Leeds U.	Jnrs	03.51	50-55	20	-	4
Northampton T.	Wisbech T.	02.60	59	2	-	0

VICKERS Stephen
Bishop Auckland, 13 October, 1967 (CD)

League Club	Source	Date Signed	Seasons Played	Apps	Subs	Gls
Tranmere Rov.	Spennymoor U.	09.85	85-93	310	1	11
Middlesbrough	Tr	12.93	93-97	157	7	7

VICKERS Wilfred
Wakefield, 3 August, 1924 (CF)

League Club	Source	Date Signed	Seasons Played	Apps	Subs	Gls
Brighton & H.A.		09.47	47	5	-	1
West Bromwich A.	Tr	05.48				
Aldershot	Tr	06.49	49-51	15	-	1

VICKERY Paul
Chelmsford, 20 May, 1953 (M)

League Club	Source	Date Signed	Seasons Played	Apps	Subs	Gls
Southend U.	App	•	69	0	1	0

VICTORY Jamie Charles
Hackney, 14 November, 1975 (M)

League Club	Source	Date Signed	Seasons Played	Apps	Subs	Gls
West Ham U.	YT	07.94				
Bournemouth	Tr	07.95	95	5	11	1

VIEIRA Patrick
Senegal, 23 June, 1976 French Int (M)

League Club	Source	Date Signed	Seasons Played	Apps	Subs	Gls
Arsenal	A.C. Milan (It)	08.96	96-97	61	3	4

VILJOEN Colin
South Africa, 20 June, 1948 E-2 (M)

League Club	Source	Date Signed	Seasons Played	Apps	Subs	Gls
Ipswich T.	South Africa	03.67	66-77	303	2	45
Manchester C.	Tr	08.78	78-79	25	2	0
Chelsea	Tr	03.80	79-81	19	1	0

VILJOEN Nicholas Luke
New Zealand, 3 December, 1976 (F)

League Club	Source	Date Signed	Seasons Played	Apps	Subs	Gls
Rotherham U.	YT	06.95	95	5	3	2

VILLA Julio **Ricardo (Ricki)**
Argentina, 18 August, 1952 Argentinian Int (M)

League Club	Source	Date Signed	Seasons Played	Apps	Subs	Gls
Tottenham H.	Racing Club (Arg)	07.78	78-82	124	9	18

VILLARS Anthony Keith
Pontypool, 24 January, 1952 Wu23-2/W-3 (W)

League Club	Source	Date Signed	Seasons Played	Apps	Subs	Gls
Cardiff C.	Cwmbran T.	06.71	71-75	66	7	4
Newport Co.	Tr	07.76	76	23	6	1

VILLAZAN Rafael
Uruguay, 19 July, 1956 Uruguayan Int (D)

League Club	Source	Date Signed	Seasons Played	Apps	Subs	Gls
Wolverhampton W.	Huelva (Sp)	05.80	80-81	20	3	0

VILSTRUP Johnny Pedersen
Denmark, 27 February, 1969 (M)

League Club	Source	Date Signed	Seasons Played	Apps	Subs	Gls
Luton T.	Lyngby (Den)	09.95	95	6	1	0

VINALL Albert
Birmingham, 6 March, 1922 (FB)

League Club	Source	Date Signed	Seasons Played	Apps	Subs	Gls
Aston Villa	Southampton (Am)	07.46	47-53	11	-	1
Walsall	Tr	08.54	54-55	78	-	0

VINALL Edward **John (Jack)**
Birmingham, 16 December, 1910 (CF)

League Club	Source	Date Signed	Seasons Played	Apps	Subs	Gls
Sunderland	Folkestone	10.31	31-32	16	-	2
Norwich C.	Tr	06.33	33-37	168	-	72
Luton T.	Tr	10.37	37-38	44	-	18
Walsall	Tr	07.46	46	2	-	0

VINCENT Jamie Roy
Wimbledon, 18 June, 1975 (LB)

League Club	Source	Date Signed	Seasons Played	Apps	Subs	Gls
Crystal Palace	YT	07.93	95	19	6	0
Bournemouth	L	11.94	94	8	0	0
Bournemouth	Tr	08.96	96-97	71	2	3

VINCENT John Victor
West Bromwich, 8 February, 1947 E Yth (M)

League Club	Source	Date Signed	Seasons Played	Apps	Subs	Gls
Birmingham C.	App	02.64	63-70	168	3	41
Middlesbrough	Tr	03.71	70-72	37	3	7
Cardiff C.	Tr	10.72	72-74	58	8	11

VINCENT Norman (Ned) Edwin
Prudhoe, 3 March, 1909 Died 1980 (FB)

League Club	Source	Date Signed	Seasons Played	Apps	Subs	Gls
Stockport Co.	Spennymoor U.	03.28	28-33	132	-	20
Grimsby T.	Tr	06.34	34-46	144	-	2

VINCENT Robert
Leicester, 29 May, 1949 (F)

League Club	Source	Date Signed	Seasons Played	Apps	Subs	Gls
Notts Co. (Am)	Jnrs	01.66	65	1	0	0

VINCENT Robert George
Newcastle, 23 November, 1962 E Sch (M)

League Club	Source	Date Signed	Seasons Played	Apps	Subs	Gls
Sunderland	App	11.79	80	1	1	0
Leyton Orient	Tr	05.82	81-82	8	1	0

VINE Peter William
Abingdon, 11 December, 1940 E Yth (F)

League Club	Source	Date Signed	Seasons Played	Apps	Subs	Gls
Southampton	Jnrs	12.57	58	1	-	0

VINEY Keith Brian
Portsmouth, 26 October, 1957 (LB)

League Club	Source	Date Signed	Seasons Played	Apps	Subs	Gls
Portsmouth	App	10.75	75-81	160	6	3
Exeter C.	Tr	08.82	82-88	270	0	8
Bristol Rov.	L	09.88	88	2	1	0

VINNICOMBE Christopher
Exeter, 20 October, 1970 Eu21-12 (LB)

League Club	Source	Date Signed	Seasons Played	Apps	Subs	Gls
Exeter C.	YT	07.89	88-89	35	4	1
Burnley	Glasgow Rangers	06.94	94-97	90	5	3

VINTER Michael
Boston, 23 May, 1954 (F)

League Club	Source	Date Signed	Seasons Played	Apps	Subs	Gls
Notts Co.	Boston U.	03.72	72-78	135	31	54
Wrexham	Tr	06.79	79-81	89	12	25
Oxford U.	Tr	08.82	82-83	67	2	21
Mansfield T.	Tr	08.84	84-85	52	2	7
Newport Co.	Tr	08.86	86	30	2	6

VIOLLET Dennis Sydney
Manchester, 20 September, 1933 E Sch/E-2 (CF)

League Club	Source	Date Signed	Seasons Played	Apps	Subs	Gls
Manchester U.	Jnrs	09.50	52-61	259	-	159
Stoke C.	Tr	01.62	61-66	181	1	59

VIPHAM Peter
Rawtenstall, 9 September, 1942 (G)

League Club	Source	Date Signed	Seasons Played	Apps	Subs	Gls
Accrington St.	Jnrs	06.61	60	6	-	0

VIRGIN Derek Edward
South Petherton, 10 February, 1934 (W)

League Club	Source	Date Signed	Seasons Played	Apps	Subs	Gls
Bristol C.		09.55	55-60	21	-	4

VITTY John (Jack)
Chilton (Dm), 19 January, 1923 (FB)

League Club	Source	Date Signed	Seasons Played	Apps	Subs	Gls
Charlton Ath.	Boldon Villa	11.46	48	2	-	0
Brighton & H. A.	Tr	10.49	49-51	47	-	1
Workington	Tr	07.52	52-56	196	-	3

VITTY Ronald
Sedgefield, 18 April, 1927 (RB)

League Club	Source	Date Signed	Seasons Played	Apps	Subs	Gls
Charlton Ath.	Boldon Villa	09.47				
Hartlepool U.	Tr	08.49	49	7	-	0
Bradford C.	Tr	07.50				

VIVEASH Adrian Lee
Swindon, 30 September, 1969 (CD)

League Club	Source	Date Signed	Seasons Played	Apps	Subs	Gls
Swindon T.	YT	07.88	90-94	51	3	2
Reading	L	01.93	92	5	0	0
Reading	L	01.95	94	6	0	0
Barnsley	L	08.95	95	2	0	1
Walsall	Tr	10.95	95-97	119	0	12

VIZARD Colin John
Newton-le-Willows, 18 June, 1933 (OL)

League Club	Source	Date Signed	Seasons Played	Apps	Subs	Gls
Everton	Jnrs	09.51				
Rochdale	Tr	05.57	57-58	41	-	7

VLACHOS Michail
Athens, Greece, 20 September, 1967 Greek Int (LWB)

League Club	Source	Date Signed	Seasons Played	Apps	Subs	Gls
Portsmouth	A.E.K. Athens (Gre)	01.98	97	15	0	0

VONK Michel Christian
Netherlands, 28 October, 1968 (CD)

League Club	Source	Date Signed	Seasons Played	Apps	Subs	Gls
Manchester C.	S.V.V. Dordrecht (Neth)	03.92	91-94	87	4	3
Oldham Ath.	L	11.95	95	5	0	1
Sheffield U.	Tr	12.95	95-97	37	0	2

VOWDEN Colin Dean
Newmarket, 13 September, 1971 (CD)

League Club	Source	Date Signed	Seasons Played	Apps	Subs	Gls
Cambridge U.	Cambridge C.	05.95	95-96	27	3	0

VOWDEN Geoffrey Alan
Barnsley, 27 April, 1941 (F)

League Club	Source	Date Signed	Seasons Played	Apps	Subs	Gls
Nottingham F.	Jersey D.M.	01.60	59-64	90	-	40
Birmingham C.	Tr	10.64	64-70	213	8	79
Aston Villa	Tr	03.71	70-73	93	4	22

WADDELL Robert
Kirkcaldy, 5 September, 1939 (CF)

League Club	Source	Date Signed	Seasons Played	Apps	Subs	Gls
Blackpool	Dundee	03.65	64-66	28	0	6
Bradford P.A.	Tr	11.66	66	20	0	3

WADDELL William
Denny, 16 April, 1950 (F)

League Club	Source	Date Signed	Seasons Played	Apps	Subs	Gls
Leeds U.	Jnrs	04.67				
Barnsley	Kilmarnock	05.71	71	17	1	4
Hartlepool U.	Tr	03.72	71-73	43	5	9
Workington	L	02.73	72	1	2	0

WADDINGTON Anthony
Manchester, 9 November, 1924 Died 1994 (WH)

League Club	Source	Date Signed	Seasons Played	Apps	Subs	Gls
Crewe Alex.	Manchester U. (Am)	01.46	46-52	179	-	7

WADDINGTON John
Darwen, 16 February, 1952 (CD/F)

League Club	Source	Date Signed	Seasons Played	Apps	Subs	Gls
Liverpool	Darwen	05.70				
Blackburn Rov.	Tr	08.73	73-78	139	9	18
Bury	Tr	08.79	79-80	46	1	0

WADDINGTON David **Paul**
Oldbury, 14 February, 1961 E Sch (M)

League Club	Source	Date Signed	Seasons Played	Apps	Subs	Gls
Walsall	App	11.78	78-81	14	5	0

WADDINGTON Steven
Nantwich, 5 February, 1956 (M)

League Club	Source	Date Signed	Seasons Played	Apps	Subs	Gls
Stoke C.	App	06.73	76-78	49	3	5
Walsall	Tr	09.78	78-81	122	8	13
Port Vale	Tr	08.82	82	0	1	0
Chesterfield	Tr	07.83	83	14	4	1

WADDLE Alan Robert
Wallsend, 9 June, 1954 (F)

League Club	Source	Date Signed	Seasons Played	Apps	Subs	Gls
Halifax T.	Jnrs	11.71	71-72	33	6	4
Liverpool	Tr	06.73	73-74	11	5	1
Leicester C.	Tr	09.77	77	11	0	1
Swansea C.	Tr	05.78	78-80	83	7	34
Newport Co.	Tr	12.80	80-81	19	8	7
Mansfield T.	Tr	08.82	82	14	0	4
Hartlepool U.	Hong Kong	08.83	83	12	0	2
Peterborough U.	Tr	10.83	83-84	35	1	12
Hartlepool U. (N/C)	Tr	01.85	84	4	0	0
Swansea C.	Tr	03.85	84-85	39	1	10

WADDLE Christopher Roland
Felling, 14 December, 1960 Eu21-1/E-62 (W)

League Club	Source	Date Signed	Seasons Played	Apps	Subs	Gls
Newcastle U.	Tow Law T.	07.80	80-84	169	1	46
Tottenham H.	Tr	06.85	85-88	137	1	33
Sheffield Wed.	Marseilles (Fr)	07.92	92-95	94	15	10
Bradford C.	Falkirk	10.96	96	25	0	6
Sunderland	Tr	03.97	96	7	0	1
Burnley (N/C)	Tr	07.97	97	26	5	1

WADDOCK Gary Patrick
Kingsbury, 17 March, 1962 IRu21-1/IRu23-1/IR 'B'/IR-21 (M)

League Club	Source	Date Signed	Seasons Played	Apps	Subs	Gls
Queens Park R.	App	07.79	79-86	191	12	8
Millwall	Charleroi (Bel)	08.89	89-90	51	7	2
Queens Park R.	Tr	12.91				
Swindon T.	L	03.92	91	5	1	0
Bristol Rov.	Tr	11.92	92-94	71	0	1
Luton T.	Tr	09.94	94-97	146	7	3

WADE Allen
Scunthorpe, 19 July, 1926 (WH)

League Club	Source	Date Signed	Seasons Played	Apps	Subs	Gls
Notts Co.		07.52	52-55	9	-	0

WADE Bryan Alexander
Bath, 25 June, 1963 (F)

League Club	Source	Date Signed	Seasons Played	Apps	Subs	Gls
Swindon T.	Trowbridge T.	05.85	85-87	48	12	18
Swansea C.	Tr	08.88	88-89	19	17	5
Brighton & H.A.	Tr	09.90	90-91	12	6	9

WADE Donald Geoffrey
Tottenham, 5 June, 1926 (IF)

League Club	Source	Date Signed	Seasons Played	Apps	Subs	Gls
West Ham U.	Edgware T.	12.47	47-49	36	-	5

WADE Samuel **Joseph**
Shoreditch, 7 July, 1921 EF Lge (FB)

League Club	Source	Date Signed	Seasons Played	Apps	Subs	Gls
Arsenal	Hoxton B.C.	09.45	46-54	86	-	0

WADE Psalms **Meshach**
Bermuda, 23 January, 1973 (M)

League Club	Source	Date Signed	Seasons Played	Apps	Subs	Gls
Hereford U.	Pembroke (Ber)	08.91	91-92	13	4	0

WADE Shaun Peter
Stoke, 22 September, 1969 (CF)

League Club	Source	Date Signed	Seasons Played	Apps	Subs	Gls
Stoke C.	Newcastle T.	10.94	94	0	1	0

WADSWORTH Albert William
Heywood, 22 March, 1925 Died 1982 (IF)

League Club	Source	Date Signed	Seasons Played	Apps	Subs	Gls
Oldham Ath.	Stalybridge Celtic	08.49	49-51	33	-	8

WADSWORTH Ian Jack
Huddersfield, 24 September, 1966 (F)

League Club	Source	Date Signed	Seasons Played	Apps	Subs	Gls
Huddersfield T.	App	09.84	84	0	1	0
Doncaster Rov. (N/C)	Tr	02.86	85	1	1	0

WADSWORTH Michael
Barnsley, 3 November, 1950 (W)

League Club	Source	Date Signed	Seasons Played	Apps	Subs	Gls
Scunthorpe U.	Gainsborough Trin.	08.76	76	19	9	3

WAGSTAFF Barry
Wombwell, 28 November, 1945 (M)

League Club	Source	Date Signed	Seasons Played	Apps	Subs	Gls
Sheffield U.	App	06.63	64-68	105	10	5
Reading	Tr	07.69	69-74	198	6	23
Rotherham U.	Tr	03.75	74-76	42	3	1

WAGSTAFF Kenneth
Langwith, 24 November, 1942 (CF)

League Club	Source	Date Signed	Seasons Played	Apps	Subs	Gls
Mansfield T.	Woodland Imps	05.60	60-64	181	-	93
Hull C.	Tr	11.64	64-75	374	4	173

WAGSTAFF Tony
Wombwell, 19 February, 1944 (M)

League Club	Source	Date Signed	Seasons Played	Apps	Subs	Gls
Sheffield U.	App	03.61	60-68	140	3	19
Reading	Tr	07.69	69-73	164	7	6

WAGSTAFFE David
Manchester, 5 April, 1943 E Yth/EF Lge (LW)

League Club	Source	Date Signed	Seasons Played	Apps	Subs	Gls
Manchester C.	Jnrs	05.60	60-64	144	-	8
Wolverhampton W.	Tr	12.64	64-75	324	0	26
Blackburn Rov.	Tr	01.76	75-77	72	3	7
Blackpool	Tr	08.78	78	17	2	1
Blackburn Rov.	Tr	03.79	78	2	0	0

WAIN Leslie John
Crewe, 2 August, 1954 E Sch (M)

League Club	Source	Date Signed	Seasons Played	Apps	Subs	Gls
Crewe Alex.	App	08.72	70-74	48	6	1
Southport	Tr	07.75	75	3	2	0

WAINMAN William **Henry (Harry)**
Hull, 22 March, 1947 E Yth (G)

League Club	Source	Date Signed	Seasons Played	Apps	Subs	Gls
Grimsby T.	Hull C. (Am)	07.64	64-77	420	0	0
Rochdale	L	10.72	72	9	0	0

WAINWRIGHT Edward Francis
Southport, 22 June, 1924 EF Lge (IF)

League Club	Source	Date Signed	Seasons Played	Apps	Subs	Gls
Everton	Jnrs	03.44	46-55	207	-	68
Rochdale	Tr	06.56	56-58	100	-	27

WAINWRIGHT Lewis
Kirton-in-Lindsey (Lincs), 15 December, 1930 (RB)

League Club	Source	Date Signed	Seasons Played	Apps	Subs	Gls
Scunthorpe U.	Brigg T.	05.51	55	2	-	0

WAINWRIGHT Neil
Warrington, 4 November, 1977 (W)

League Club	Source	Date Signed	Seasons Played	Apps	Subs	Gls
Wrexham	YT	07.96	97	7	4	3

WAINWRIGHT Robin Keith
Luton, 9 March, 1951 (M)

League Club	Source	Date Signed	Seasons Played	Apps	Subs	Gls
Luton T.	App	12.68	71	15	1	3
Cambridge U.	L	03.71	70	1	0	0
Millwall	Tr	11.72	73	2	2	0
Northampton T.	Tr	02.74	73-74	23	9	5

WAITE Thomas John **Alwyn**
Pontllanfraith, 3 August, 1928 (WH)

League Club	Source	Date Signed	Seasons Played	Apps	Subs	Gls
Newport Co.		12.51	51-53	57	-	1

WAITE John Aidan
Grimsby, 16 January, 1942 E Yth (OR)

League Club	Source	Date Signed	Seasons Played	Apps	Subs	Gls
Grimsby T.	Jnrs	11.60	61-62	8	-	1

WAITE William John
Newport, 29 November, 1917 Died 1980 (CF)

League Club	Source	Date Signed	Seasons Played	Apps	Subs	Gls
Oldham Ath.	Newport Co. (Am)	11.42	46	4	-	4

WAITERS Anthony Keith
Southport, 1 February, 1937 E Amat/EF Lge/E-5 (G)

League Club	Source	Date Signed	Seasons Played	Apps	Subs	Gls
Blackpool	Macclesfield T.	10.59	59-66	257	0	0
Burnley	(Retired)	07.70	70-71	38	0	0

WAITES George Edward
Stepney, 12 March, 1938 (W)

League Club	Source	Date Signed	Seasons Played	Apps	Subs	Gls
Leyton Orient	Harwich & Parkeston	12.58	58-60	43	-	9
Norwich C.	Tr	01.61	60-61	36	-	11
Leyton Orient	Tr	07.62	62	2	-	0
Brighton & H.A.	Tr	12.62	62-63	23	-	1

WAITES Paul
Hull, 24 January, 1971 (M)

League Club	Source	Date Signed	Seasons Played	Apps	Subs	Gls
Hull C.	YT	07.89	89-90	11	0	0

WAITT Michael Hugh
Hexham, 25 June, 1960 (F)

League Club	Source	Date Signed	Seasons Played	Apps	Subs	Gls
Notts Co.	Arnold Kingswell	12.84	84-86	71	11	27
Lincoln C.	Tr	06.87	89	7	1	1

WAKE Geoffrey Graham
Bristol, 25 February, 1954 (G)

League Club	Source	Date Signed	Seasons Played	Apps	Subs	Gls
Torquay U.	Barnstaple	12.77	77	9	0	0

WAKEFIELD Albert Joseph
Pontefract, 19 November, 1921 (CF)

League Club	Source	Date Signed	Seasons Played	Apps	Subs	Gls
Leeds U.	Stanningley Wks	10.42	47-48	49	-	23
Southend U.	Tr	08.49	49-52	109	-	58

WAKEFIELD David
South Shields, 15 January, 1965 (M)

League Club	Source	Date Signed	Seasons Played	Apps	Subs	Gls
Darlington	App	01.83	82-83	7	15	0
Torquay U.	Tr	03.84	83	10	0	1

WAKEHAM Peter Francis
Kingsbridge, 14 March, 1936 (G)

League Club	Source	Date Signed	Seasons Played	Apps	Subs	Gls
Torquay U.	Jnrs	10.53	53-58	58	-	0
Sunderland	Tr	09.58	58-61	134	-	0
Charlton Ath.	Tr	07.62	62-64	55	-	0
Lincoln C.	Tr	05.65	65	44	0	0

WAKEMAN Alan
Walsall, 20 November, 1920 E Sch (G)

League Club	Source	Date Signed	Seasons Played	Apps	Subs	Gls
Aston Villa	Jnrs	12.38	38-49	12	-	0
Doncaster Rov.	Tr	07.50	50-51	5	-	0
Shrewsbury T.	Bloxwich Strollers	02.53	52-53	6	-	0

WAKENSHAW Robert Andrew
Ponteland (Nd), 22 December, 1965 E Yth (F)

League Club	Source	Date Signed	Seasons Played	Apps	Subs	Gls
Everton	App	12.83	83-84	2	1	1
Carlisle U.	Tr	09.85	85	6	2	2
Doncaster Rov.	L	03.86	85	8	0	3
Rochdale	Tr	09.86	86	28	1	5
Crewe Alex.	Tr	06.87	87-88	18	4	1

WALDEN Harold Bertram
Brixworth, 22 December, 1940 (W)

League Club	Source	Date Signed	Seasons Played	Apps	Subs	Gls
Luton T.	Kettering T.	01.61	60-63	96	-	11
Northampton T.	Tr	06.64	64-66	76	2	3

WALDEN Richard Frank
Hereford, 4 May, 1948 (FB)

League Club	Source	Date Signed	Seasons Played	Apps	Subs	Gls
Aldershot	App	05.65	64-75	402	4	16
Sheffield Wed.	Tr	01.76	75-77	100	0	1
Newport Co.	Tr	08.78	78-81	151	0	3

WALDOCK Desmond Haigh
Northampton, 4 December, 1961 (CD)

League Club	Source	Date Signed	Seasons Played	Apps	Subs	Gls
Northampton T.	App	11.79	78-80	52	2	4

WALDOCK Ronald
Heanor, 6 December, 1932 (IF)

League Club	Source	Date Signed	Seasons Played	Apps	Subs	Gls
Coventry C.	Loscoe Y.C.	02.50	52-53	27	-	8
Sheffield U.	Tr	05.54	54-56	52	-	10
Scunthorpe U.	Tr	02.57	56-59	97	-	45
Plymouth Arg.	Tr	09.59	59	18	-	6
Middlesbrough	Tr	01.60	59-61	34	-	7
Gillingham	Tr	10.61	61-63	66	-	14

WALDRON Alan
Royton, 6 September, 1951 (M)

League Club	Source	Date Signed	Seasons Played	Apps	Subs	Gls
Bolton W.	App	09.69	70-77	127	14	6
Blackpool	Tr	12.77	77-78	22	1	1
Bury	Tr	06.79	79-80	34	0	0
York C. (N/C)	Tr	09.81	81	3	0	1

WALDRON Colin
Bristol, 22 June, 1948 (CD)

League Club	Source	Date Signed	Seasons Played	Apps	Subs	Gls
Bury	App	05.66	66	20	0	1
Chelsea	Tr	07.67	67	9	0	0
Burnley	Tr	10.67	67-75	308	0	16
Manchester U.	Tr	05.76	76	3	0	0
Sunderland	Tr	02.77	76-77	20	0	1
Rochdale	Atlanta (USA)	10.79	79	19	0	1

WALDRON Ernest
Birmingham, 3 June, 1913 Died 1994 (F)

League Club	Source	Date Signed	Seasons Played	Apps	Subs	Gls
Crystal Palace	Bromsgrove Rov.	11.34	34-46	80	-	30

WALDRON Malcolm
Emsworth, 6 September, 1956 E'B' (D)

League Club	Source	Date Signed	Seasons Played	Apps	Subs	Gls
Southampton	App	09.74	74-82	177	1	10
Burnley	Tr	09.83	83	16	0	0
Portsmouth	Tr	03.84	83-84	23	0	1

WALES Anthony
Dunscroft, 12 May, 1943 E Yth (FB)

League Club	Source	Date Signed	Seasons Played	Apps	Subs	Gls
Doncaster Rov.	Jnrs	05.60	60-62	25	-	0

WALFORD Stephen James
Islington, 5 January, 1958 E Yth (D)

League Club	Source	Date Signed	Seasons Played	Apps	Subs	Gls
Tottenham H.	App	04.75	75	1	1	0
Arsenal	Tr	08.77	77-80	64	13	3
Norwich C.	Tr	03.81	80-82	93	0	2
West Ham U.	Tr	08.83	83-86	114	1	2
Huddersfield T.	L	10.87	87	12	0	0
Gillingham	L	12.88	88	4	0	0
West Bromwich A.	L	03.89	88	3	1	0

WALKDEN Francis
Aberdeen, 21 June, 1921 Died 1992 (OL)

League Club	Source	Date Signed	Seasons Played	Apps	Subs	Gls
Rochdale (Am)	Bolton W. (Am)	11.46	46	1	-	0

WALKER Alan
Mossley, 17 December, 1959 (CD)

League Club	Source	Date Signed	Seasons Played	Apps	Subs	Gls
Stockport Co.	Mossley	08.78				
Lincoln C.	Telford U.	10.83	83-84	74	1	4
Millwall	Tr	07.85	85-87	92	0	8
Gillingham	Tr	03.88	87-91	150	1	7
Plymouth Arg. (N/C)	Tr	09.92	92	2	0	1
Mansfield T.	Tr	09.92	92	22	0	1
Barnet	Tr	08.93	93-94	59	0	2

WALKER Andrew Francis
Glasgow, 6 April, 1965 Su21-1/S-3 (F)

League Club	Source	Date Signed	Seasons Played	Apps	Subs	Gls
Newcastle U. (L)	Glasgow Celtic	09.91	91	2	0	0
Bolton W.	Glasgow Celtic	01.92	91-93	61	6	44
Sheffield U.	Glasgow Celtic	02.96	95-97	32	20	20

WALKER Arnold
Haltwhistle (Nd), 23 December, 1932 (WH)

League Club	Source	Date Signed	Seasons Played	Apps	Subs	Gls
Grimsby T.	Jnrs	05.50	50-57	65	-	0
Walsall	Tr	05.58	58-59	7	-	0

WALKER Bruce Alan
Hungerford, 27 August, 1946 (OL)

League Club	Source	Date Signed	Seasons Played	Apps	Subs	Gls
Swindon T.	Jnrs	12.63	65-67	26	3	5
Bradford C.	Tr	03.68	67-68	27	1	1
Exeter C.	Tr	06.69	69	21	3	2

WALKER Clive
Oxford, 26 May, 1957 E Sch (LW)

League Club	Source	Date Signed	Seasons Played	Apps	Subs	Gls
Chelsea	App	04.75	76-83	168	30	60
Sunderland	Tr	07.84	84-85	48	2	10
Queens Park R.	Tr	12.85	85-86	16	5	1
Fulham	Tr	10.87	87-89	102	7	29
Brighton & H.A.	Tr	08.90	90-92	104	2	8

WALKER David Clive Allan
Bushey, 24 October, 1945 E Sch (LB)

League Club	Source	Date Signed	Seasons Played	Apps	Subs	Gls
Leicester C.	App	10.62	63-65	17	0	0
Northampton T.	Tr	10.66	66-68	72	0	1
Mansfield T.	Tr	07.69	69-74	223	6	8

WALKER Colin
Rotherham, 1 May, 1958 (F)

League Club	Source	Date Signed	Seasons Played	Apps	Subs	Gls
Barnsley	Gisborne C. (NZ)	11.80	80-82	21	3	12
Doncaster Rov.	L	02.83	82	12	0	5
Doncaster Rov. (N/C)	Gisborne C. (NZ)	11.85	85	3	2	0
Cambridge U. (N/C)	Tr	01.86	85	3	0	1
Sheffield Wed.	Harworth Colly	08.86	86	2	0	0
Darlington	L	12.86	86	6	1	0
Torquay U.	L	10.87	87	3	0	0

WALKER Colin
Stapleford, 7 July, 1929 (WH)

League Club	Source	Date Signed	Seasons Played	Apps	Subs	Gls
Derby Co.	Jnrs	10.46	48-54	25	-	0

League Club	Source	Date Signed	Seasons Played	Apps	Subs	Gls

WALKER Cyril John
Newport Pagnell, 24 February, 1914 (IF)

Watford		11.35				
Gillingham		06.37	37	10	-	0
Sheffield Wed.	Tr	10.37	37	4	-	0
Norwich C.	Shorts Sports	08.46	46	3	-	2

WALKER David
Colne, 15 October, 1941 (CD)

Burnley	Jnrs	05.59	60-64	38	-	1
Southampton	Tr	05.65	65-73	189	8	1

WALKER Dean
Newcastle, 18 May, 1962 (D)

Burnley	App	05.80				
Scunthorpe U. (N/C)	Tr	03.82	81	1	0	0

WALKER Dennis Alan
Northwich, 26 October, 1944 E Sch (M)

Manchester U.	App	11.61	62	1	-	0
York C.	Tr	04.64	64-67	149	5	19
Cambridge U.	Tr	07.68	70-72	48	8	4

WALKER Dennis George
Spennymoor, 5 July, 1948 (F)

West Ham U.	App	05.66				
Luton T.	Tr	08.67	67	0	1	0

WALKER Derek William
Perth, 24 November, 1964 (F)

Chesterfield	Kinnoull Jnrs	08.86	86-87	19	4	3

WALKER Desmond Sinclair
Hackney, 26 November, 1965 Eu21-7/E-59 (CD)

Nottingham F.	App	11.83	83-91	259	5	1
Sheffield Wed.	Sampdoria (It)	07.93	93-97	190	0	0

WALKER Donald Hunter
Edinburgh, 10 September, 1935 (WH)

Leicester C.	Tranent Jnrs	11.55	57-58	32	-	1
Middlesbrough	Tr	10.59	59-61	23	-	1
Grimsby T.	Tr	09.63	63	15	-	1

WALKER Frederick
Stirling, 7 April, 1929 Died 1966 (FB)

Southport	Queens Park	10.51	51-52	5	-	0

WALKER Gary
Manchester, 11 October, 1963 (G)

Stockport Co.	Oldham T.	09.85	85-86	29	0	0

WALKER Robert Geoffrey
Bradford, 29 September, 1926 Died 1997 (OL)

Bradford P.A.	Jnrs	12.43				
Middlesbrough	Tr	06.46	46-54	240	-	50
Doncaster Rov.	Tr	12.54	54-56	84	-	15
Bradford C.	Tr	06.57	57	2	-	0

WALKER George William
Sunderland, 30 May, 1934 (IF)

Bristol C.	Chippenham T.	05.56	56-58	15	-	5
Carlisle U.	Tr	03.59	58-62	164	-	52

WALKER Glenn Philip
Warrington, 15 March, 1967 (M)

Crewe Alex.	Burnley (App)	03.85	84	1	1	0

WALKER John Gordon
Sheffield, 26 November, 1946 (F)

Grimsby T.	Stocksbridge Wks	11.68	68-69	25	2	5

WALKER Greig George
Dundee, 11 October, 1963 (F)

Chesterfield	Broughty Ath.	10.83	83	6	0	0

WALKER George Henry (Harry)
Aysgarth, 20 May, 1916 Died 1976 (G)

Darlington		12.34	35-37	49	-	0
Portsmouth	Tr	03.38	37-46	49	-	0
Nottingham F.	Tr	04.47	46-54	293	-	0

WALKER Ian Michael
Watford, 31 October, 1971 E Yth/Eu21-9/E 'B'/E-3 (G)

Tottenham H.	YT	12.89	90-97	191	1	0
Oxford U.	L	09.90	90	2	0	0

WALKER James
Aberdeen, 25 August, 1933 (FB)

Bradford P.A.	Aberdeen	05.59	59-63	144	-	2

WALKER James
Belfast, 29 March, 1932 NI-1 (CF)

Doncaster Rov.	Linfield	05.54	54-56	46	-	14

WALKER James Barry
Sutton-in-Ashfield, 9 July, 1973 (G)

Notts Co.	YT	07.91				
Walsall	Tr	08.93	93-97	142	1	0

WALKER James Frederick
Sheffield, 1 July, 1931 (LB)

Sheffield U.	Jnrs	11.48	49-53	4	-	0
Huddersfield T.	Tr	08.55				
Peterborough U.	Tr	(N/L)	60-64	125	-	0

WALKER James McIntyre
Northwich, 10 June, 1947 (LB/W)

Derby Co.	Northwich Vic.	02.68	67-73	35	7	3
Hartlepool U.	L	03.70	69	10	0	0
Brighton & H.A.	Tr	09.74	74-75	24	4	4
Peterborough U.	Tr	10.75	75-76	20	11	1
Chester C.	Tr	11.76	76-80	171	1	4

WALKER John
Glasgow, 12 December, 1973 S Yth (M)

Grimsby T.	Clydebank	09.95	95-96	1	2	1
Mansfield T.	Tr	09.96	96-97	33	4	3

WALKER John
Leigh-on-Sea, 10 December, 1958 (D)

Southend U.	App	12.76	77-82	38	13	0

WALKER John Young Hilley
Glasgow, 17 December, 1928 (IF/WH)

Wolverhampton W.	Campsie B.W.	07.47	49-51	37	-	21
Southampton	Tr	10.52	52-57	172	-	48
Reading	Tr	12.57	57-64	287	-	24

WALKER Patrick Joseph
Carlow (Ire), 20 December, 1959 IRu21-2 (W)

Gillingham	App	10.77	77-80	34	17	3

WALKER Justin
Nottingham, 6 September, 1975 E Yth (M)

Nottingham F.	Jnrs	09.92				
Scunthorpe U.	Tr	03.97	96-97	46	3	1

WALKER Keith Cameron
Edinburgh, 17 April, 1966 (M/CD)

Swansea C.	St Mirren	11.89	89-97	261	8	9

WALKER Lee
Pontypool, 27 June, 1976 (M)

Cardiff C. (N/C)	YT	07.94	93	1	0	0

WALKER Leonard
Darlington, 4 March, 1944 (D)

Newcastle U.	Spennymoor U.	05.63	63	1	-	0
Aldershot	Tr	07.64	64-75	437	10	24
Darlington (N/C)	Tr	08.76	76-77	10	0	0

WALKER Michael
Mexborough, 8 March, 1952 (FB)

Bradford P.A.	App	03.70	68-69	2	2	0

WALKER Michael John
Harrogate, 10 April, 1945 (F)

Bradford C.	Bourne T.	10.64	64-65	19	1	1
Mansfield T.	Los Angeles (USA)	03.69	68	2	0	0
Stockport Co.	Altrincham	08.70	70	1	1	0
Chesterfield	Tr	09.70	70	1	0	0

WALKER Michael Stewart Gordon
Colwyn Bay, 28 November, 1945 Wu23-4 (G)

Reading	Jnrs	01.63				
Shrewsbury T.	Tr	06.64	64-65	7	0	0
York C.	Tr	06.66	66-68	60	0	0
Watford	Tr	09.68	68-72	137	0	0
Charlton Ath.	L	03.73	72	1	0	0
Colchester U.	Tr	06.73	73-82	451	0	0

WALKER Joseph Nicol (Nicky)
Aberdeen, 29 September, 1962 S Yth/S-2 (G)

Leicester C.	Elgin C.	08.80	81	6	0	0
Burnley (L)	Hearts	02.92	91	6	0	0

WALKER Nigel Stephen
Gateshead, 7 April, 1959 (M)

Newcastle U.	Whickham	07.77	77-81	65	5	3

League Club	Source	Date Signed	Seasons Played	Apps	Subs	Gls
Crewe Alex. (N/C)	San Diego (USA)	01.83	82	20	0	5
Sunderland	Tr	07.83	83	0	1	0
Blackpool	L	03.84	83	8	2	3
Chester C.	Tr	07.84	84	41	0	9
Hartlepool U.	Tr	07.85	85-86	77	5	8

WALKER Paul
Wood Green, 17 December, 1960 E Sch (M)

League Club	Source	Date Signed	Seasons Played	Apps	Subs	Gls
Brentford	App	01.78	76-82	53	18	5

WALKER Paul Ernest
Hetton-le-Hole, 26 February, 1958 E Semi Pro (M)

League Club	Source	Date Signed	Seasons Played	Apps	Subs	Gls
Hull C.	Sunderland (App)	05.76				
Doncaster Rov.	L	12.76	76	4	0	0

WALKER Paul Graham
Bradford, 3 April, 1949 (M)

League Club	Source	Date Signed	Seasons Played	Apps	Subs	Gls
Wolverhampton W.	Bradford P.A. (Am)	10.66	68-71	17	9	0
Watford	L	12.71	71	2	1	0
Swindon T.	L	03.73	72	2	3	0
Peterborough U.	Tr	07.73	73-74	75	3	3
Barnsley	Tr	07.75	75	11	2	0
Huddersfield T.	Ottawa (Can)	11.76	76	1	0	0

WALKER Peter Martin
Watford, 31 March, 1933 (IF)

League Club	Source	Date Signed	Seasons Played	Apps	Subs	Gls
Watford	Bushey U.	07.54	54-61	172	-	37

WALKER Philip
Sheffield, 27 November, 1956 (G)

League Club	Source	Date Signed	Seasons Played	Apps	Subs	Gls
Cambridge U.	Sheffield U. (App)	02.75	74-75	19	0	0
Rotherham U.	Tr	09.77				

WALKER Philip Albert
Kirkby-in-Ashfield, 27 January, 1957 (F)

League Club	Source	Date Signed	Seasons Played	Apps	Subs	Gls
Chesterfield	Mansfield Y.C.	12.77	77-82	151	15	38
Rotherham U.	Tr	12.82	82-83	20	5	3
Cardiff C.	L	09.83	83	2	0	0
Chesterfield	Tr	10.84	84-85	30	8	9
Scarborough	Tr	08.86	87	0	1	0

WALKER Philip Leonardus
Fulham, 24 August, 1954 (M)

League Club	Source	Date Signed	Seasons Played	Apps	Subs	Gls
Millwall	Epsom & Ewell	10.75	75-78	143	3	17
Charlton Ath.	Tr	07.79	79-82	80	9	15
Gillingham	L	11.82	82	1	1	0

WALKER Raymond
North Shields, 28 September, 1963 E Yth (M)

League Club	Source	Date Signed	Seasons Played	Apps	Subs	Gls
Aston Villa	App	09.81	82-85	15	8	0
Port Vale	L	09.84	84	15	0	1
Port Vale	Tr	07.86	86-96	322	29	33
Cambridge U.	L	09.94	94	5	0	0

WALKER Richard Martin
Birmingham, 8 November, 1977 (F)

League Club	Source	Date Signed	Seasons Played	Apps	Subs	Gls
Aston Villa	YT	12.95	97	0	1	0

WALKER Richard Neil
Derby, 9 November, 1971 (D)

League Club	Source	Date Signed	Seasons Played	Apps	Subs	Gls
Notts Co.	YT	07.90	92-96	63	4	4
Mansfield T.	L	03.95	94	4	0	0

WALKER Richard Patrick
Northampton, 4 April, 1959 (FB)

League Club	Source	Date Signed	Seasons Played	Apps	Subs	Gls
Coventry C.	App	03.77				
Northampton T.	Tr	08.78	78-80	50	3	0

WALKER Charles **Richard** Walter
Hackney, 22 July, 1913 Died 1988 (CH)

League Club	Source	Date Signed	Seasons Played	Apps	Subs	Gls
West Ham U.	Park Royal	05.34	34-52	292	-	2

WALKER Robert
Wallsend, 23 July, 1942 (D)

League Club	Source	Date Signed	Seasons Played	Apps	Subs	Gls
Brighton & H.A.	Gateshead	05.62	62	12	-	1
Bournemouth	Margate	08.65	65-66	10	0	0
Colchester U.	Tr	07.67	67	13	4	0

WALKER Robert
Aberdeen, 21 May, 1922 (CF)

League Club	Source	Date Signed	Seasons Played	Apps	Subs	Gls
Bournemouth	Aberdeen	11.46	46	2	-	2
Wrexham	Tr	06.47	47	2	-	0

WALKER Robert Malcolm
Glasgow, 15 January, 1935 (F)

League Club	Source	Date Signed	Seasons Played	Apps	Subs	Gls
Middlesbrough	Redcar	08.52				
Barrow	Tr	08.55	55	11	-	1

WALKER Roger
Shrewsbury, 17 February, 1944 (W)

League Club	Source	Date Signed	Seasons Played	Apps	Subs	Gls
Shrewsbury T. (Am)	Jnrs	05.60	60	1	-	0

WALKER Roger Anthony
Bolton, 15 November, 1966 (W)

League Club	Source	Date Signed	Seasons Played	Apps	Subs	Gls
Bolton W.	YT	07.85	84-85	7	5	1

WALKER Ronald
Swansea, 24 February, 1933 Died 1989 (CF)

League Club	Source	Date Signed	Seasons Played	Apps	Subs	Gls
Shrewsbury T.		11.55	55	1	-	0

WALKER Ronald
Sheffield, 4 February, 1932 (OL)

League Club	Source	Date Signed	Seasons Played	Apps	Subs	Gls
Doncaster Rov.	Sunderland (Am)	05.50	52-60	234	-	46

WALKER Ronald Leslie
Wembley, 2 September, 1952 (CD)

League Club	Source	Date Signed	Seasons Played	Apps	Subs	Gls
Watford	App	08.70				
Workington	Tr	08.71	71-75	143	10	3
Newport Co.	Tr	08.76	76-78	88	1	5

WALKER Ronald William
Westminster, 10 April, 1930 Died 1988 (OL)

League Club	Source	Date Signed	Seasons Played	Apps	Subs	Gls
Watford	Walthamstow Ave.	04.54	54	3	-	0

WALKER Samuel
Eccles, 22 April, 1922 (CH)

League Club	Source	Date Signed	Seasons Played	Apps	Subs	Gls
Oldham Ath.	Darwen	08.47	47	1	-	0

WALKER Shane
Pontypool, 25 November, 1957 (M)

League Club	Source	Date Signed	Seasons Played	Apps	Subs	Gls
Hereford U.	Arsenal (App)	03.75	74-76	15	2	2
Newport Co.	Sligo Rov.	08.77	77	27	1	2

WALKER Stephen
Sheffield, 16 October, 1914 Died 1987 (HB)

League Club	Source	Date Signed	Seasons Played	Apps	Subs	Gls
Sheffield U.	Gainsborough Trin.	05.37				
Exeter C.	Tr	05.38	38-49	141	-	3

WALKER Steven
Ashington, 2 November, 1973 E Sch (M)

League Club	Source	Date Signed	Seasons Played	Apps	Subs	Gls
Doncaster Rov.	Blyth Spartans	07.96	96	1	0	0

WALKER Steven
Ilkeston, 25 December, 1963 (M)

League Club	Source	Date Signed	Seasons Played	Apps	Subs	Gls
Halifax T.		01.82	81	0	1	0

WALKER Stuart
Garforth, 9 January, 1951 (G)

League Club	Source	Date Signed	Seasons Played	Apps	Subs	Gls
York C.	Tadcaster A.	08.75	76	2	0	0

WALKER Terence
York, 29 November, 1921 (IF)

League Club	Source	Date Signed	Seasons Played	Apps	Subs	Gls
York C.	Selby T.	05.49	49	16	-	9

WALKER Thomas
Livingston, 26 May, 1915 Died 1993 S Sch/SF Lge/S-20 (IF)

League Club	Source	Date Signed	Seasons Played	Apps	Subs	Gls
Chelsea	Hearts	09.46	46-48	97	-	23

WALKER Thomas Jackson
Newcastle, 20 February, 1952 (M)

League Club	Source	Date Signed	Seasons Played	Apps	Subs	Gls
Stoke C.	App	07.69	71	2	0	0

WALKER Thomas Jackson
Lanchester, 14 November, 1923 (OR)

League Club	Source	Date Signed	Seasons Played	Apps	Subs	Gls
Newcastle U.	Netherton	10.41	46-53	184	-	35
Oldham Ath.	Tr	02.54	53-56	120	-	19
Chesterfield	Tr	02.57	56	14	-	1
Oldham Ath.	Tr	07.57	57-58	38	-	4

WALKER Victor
Kirkby-in-Ashfield, 14 April, 1922 Died 1992 (WH/IF)

League Club	Source	Date Signed	Seasons Played	Apps	Subs	Gls
Nottingham F.		08.43				
Stockport Co.	Tr	06.46	46-49	94	-	10

WALL Adrian Arthur
Clowne, 25 November, 1949 (W)

League Club	Source	Date Signed	Seasons Played	Apps	Subs	Gls
Sheffield Wed.	App	05.67	67	3	0	0
Workington	Tr	08.69	69	21	3	2

WALL Thomas **Peter**
Brockton (Salop), 13 September, 1944 (FB)

League Club	Source	Date Signed	Seasons Played	Apps	Subs	Gls
Shrewsbury T.	App	09.62	63-64	18	-	0
Wrexham	Tr	11.65	65-66	15	7	1
Liverpool	Tr	10.66	67-69	31	0	0
Crystal Palace	Tr	06.70	70-77	167	10	4
Leyton Orient	L	12.72	72	10	0	0

WALL William John
Taunton, 28 October, 1939 (W)

League Club	Source	Date Signed	Seasons Played	Apps	Subs	Gls
Chelsea	Jnrs	01.57				
Southend U.	Tr	03.60	59-62	56	-	5

WALLACE Barry Danny
Plaistow, 17 April, 1959 (M)

League Club	Source	Date Signed	Seasons Played	Apps	Subs	Gls
Queens Park R.	Jnrs	08.76	77-79	17	8	0

WALLACE Clive Low
Kirriemuir, 6 January, 1932 (F)

League Club	Source	Date Signed	Seasons Played	Apps	Subs	Gls
Bury		03.59				
Stockport Co.	Tr	08.59	59	13	-	4

WALLACE David (Danny) Lloyd
Greenwich, 21 January, 1964 E Yth/Eu21-14/E-1 (F)

League Club	Source	Date Signed	Seasons Played	Apps	Subs	Gls
Southampton	App	01.82	80-89	238	15	64
Manchester U.	Tr	09.89	89-92	36	11	6
Millwall	L	03.93	92	3	0	0
Birmingham C.	Tr	10.93	93-94	12	4	2
Wycombe W.	Tr	03.95	94	0	1	0

WALLACE George
Aberdeen, 18 April, 1920 (F)

League Club	Source	Date Signed	Seasons Played	Apps	Subs	Gls
Scunthorpe U.		03.46	51-52	33	-	8

WALLACE Gordon Henry
Glasgow, 13 June, 1944 (M)

League Club	Source	Date Signed	Seasons Played	Apps	Subs	Gls
Liverpool	App	07.61	62-64	19	-	3
Crewe Alex.	Tr	10.67	67-71	91	3	20

WALLACE Ian Andrew
Glasgow, 23 May, 1956 Su21-1/S-3 (F)

League Club	Source	Date Signed	Seasons Played	Apps	Subs	Gls
Coventry C.	Dumbarton	08.76	76-79	128	2	58
Nottingham F.	Tr	07.80	80-83	128	6	36
Sunderland	Brest (Fr)	01.85	84-85	28	6	6

WALLACE Ian Robert
Wellington, 12 September, 1948 (WH)

League Club	Source	Date Signed	Seasons Played	Apps	Subs	Gls
Wolverhampton W.	App	09.66	66	0	1	0

WALLACE James
Birkenhead, 13 December, 1937 (OL)

League Club	Source	Date Signed	Seasons Played	Apps	Subs	Gls
Stoke C.		10.55	58-59	8	-	1
Doncaster Rov.	Northwich Vic.	03.63	62	14	-	1

WALLACE James
Stirling, 9 June, 1954 Su23-1 (LB)

League Club	Source	Date Signed	Seasons Played	Apps	Subs	Gls
Aldershot	Dunfermline Ath.	07.75	75-76	53	3	0

WALLACE James
Kirkintilloch, 17 February, 1933 (CH)

League Club	Source	Date Signed	Seasons Played	Apps	Subs	Gls
Northampton T.	Aberdeen	05.55	55	1	-	0

WALLACE John (Jock) Collins
Glasgow, 11 January, 1936 (LB)

League Club	Source	Date Signed	Seasons Played	Apps	Subs	Gls
Rochdale	St Rochs	03.58	57-58	7	-	0

WALLACE John (Jock) Martin
Deantown, 13 April, 1911 Died 1978 (G)

League Club	Source	Date Signed	Seasons Played	Apps	Subs	Gls
Blackpool	Raith Rov.	02.34	33-47	235	-	0
Derby Co.	Tr	02.48	47	16	-	0

WALLACE John (Jock) Martin Bokas
Musselburgh, 6 September, 1935 Died 1996 (G)

League Club	Source	Date Signed	Seasons Played	Apps	Subs	Gls
Workington	Blackpool (Am)	09.52	52	6	-	0
West Bromwich A.	Airdrieonians	10.59	59-61	69	-	0

WALLACE Joseph Burt
Glasgow, 28 December, 1933 Died 1993 (WH)

League Club	Source	Date Signed	Seasons Played	Apps	Subs	Gls
Shrewsbury T.	R.A.O.C. Donnington	03.54	54-62	337	-	3
Southport	Tr	10.62	62-64	78	-	0

WALLACE Kenneth
Workington, 14 January, 1932 (FB)

League Club	Source	Date Signed	Seasons Played	Apps	Subs	Gls
Workington		07.51	51-52	48	-	1

WALLACE Kenneth
Workington, 5 January, 1953 (FB)

League Club	Source	Date Signed	Seasons Played	Apps	Subs	Gls
Workington (N/C)	Jnrs	02.74	73-76	6	1	0

WALLACE Kenneth Robert
Islington, 8 June, 1952 (W)

League Club	Source	Date Signed	Seasons Played	Apps	Subs	Gls
West Ham U.	Jnrs	07.69				
Brentford	L	02.72	71	3	0	0
Hereford U.	Tr	07.72	72	26	6	4
Exeter C.	Tr	09.73	73	8	2	1

WALLACE Michael
Farnworth, 5 October, 1970 E Yth (LB/M)

League Club	Source	Date Signed	Seasons Played	Apps	Subs	Gls
Manchester C.	YT	07.89				
Stockport Co.	Tr	10.92	92-94	65	5	5

WALLACE Raymond George
Greenwich, 2 October, 1969 Eu21-4 (RB/M)

League Club	Source	Date Signed	Seasons Played	Apps	Subs	Gls
Southampton	YT	04.88	88-89	33	2	0
Leeds U.	Tr	07.91	92-93	5	2	0
Swansea C.	L	03.92	91	2	0	0
Reading	L	03.94	93	3	0	0
Stoke C.	Tr	08.94	94-97	141	7	12
Hull C.	L	12.94	94	7	0	0

WALLACE Robert
Huddersfield, 14 February, 1948 (M)

League Club	Source	Date Signed	Seasons Played	Apps	Subs	Gls
Huddersfield T.	App	05.65	66	4	0	0
Halifax T.	Tr	03.67	66-71	190	11	16
Chester C.	Tr	06.72	72	41	0	9
Aldershot	Tr	07.73	73-76	70	6	1

WALLACE Rodney Seymour
Greenwich, 2 October, 1969 Eu21-11/E 'B' (F)

League Club	Source	Date Signed	Seasons Played	Apps	Subs	Gls
Southampton	YT	04.88	87-90	111	17	45
Leeds U.	Tr	05.91	91-97	187	25	53

WALLACE William Semple Brown
Kirkintilloch, 23 June, 1941 SF Lge/S-7 (F)

League Club	Source	Date Signed	Seasons Played	Apps	Subs	Gls
Crystal Palace	Glasgow Celtic	10.71	71-72	36	3	4

WALLBANK Bernard Frederick
Preston, 11 November, 1943 (CF)

League Club	Source	Date Signed	Seasons Played	Apps	Subs	Gls
Southport	St Andrew's	08.61	61	1	-	0

WALLBANKS Harold
Chopwell, 27 July, 1921 Died 1993 (RH)

League Club	Source	Date Signed	Seasons Played	Apps	Subs	Gls
Fulham		10.38	46-47	33	-	1
Southend U.	Tr	10.49	49-50	39	-	2
Workington	Tr	08.52	52	26	-	9

WALLBANKS William **Horace**
Chopwell, 4 September, 1918 (OR)

League Club	Source	Date Signed	Seasons Played	Apps	Subs	Gls
Grimsby T.	Aberdeen	11.46	46	9	-	1
Luton T.	Tr	05.47	46-47	4	-	1

WALLBANKS James
Wigan, 12 September, 1909 Died 1979 (CH)

League Club	Source	Date Signed	Seasons Played	Apps	Subs	Gls
Barnsley	Annfield Plain	03.29	29-30	11	-	0
Norwich C.	Tr	05.31	31	3	-	0
Northampton T.	Tr	08.32	32	2	-	0
Millwall	Wigan Ath.	06.34	34-38	88	-	0
Reading	Tr	10.38	38-46	47	-	1

WALLBRIDGE Trevor
Southampton, 8 February, 1959 (F)

League Club	Source	Date Signed	Seasons Played	Apps	Subs	Gls
Bournemouth (N/C)	Totton	01.78	77	0	1	0

WALLER David Harold
Urmston, 20 December, 1963 (F)

League Club	Source	Date Signed	Seasons Played	Apps	Subs	Gls
Crewe Alex.		01.82	81-85	165	3	55
Shrewsbury T.	Tr	07.86	86	11	0	3
Chesterfield	Tr	03.87	87-89	117	2	53

WALLER Henry
Ashington, 20 August, 1917 Died 1984 (WH)

League Club	Source	Date Signed	Seasons Played	Apps	Subs	Gls
Arsenal	Ashington	10.37	46	8	-	0
Leyton Orient	Tr	07.47	47	17	-	0

WALLER Philip
Leeds, 12 April, 1943 (WH)

League Club	Source	Date Signed	Seasons Played	Apps	Subs	Gls
Derby Co.	Jnrs	05.61	61-67	102	2	5
Mansfield T.	Tr	03.68	67-71	153	6	1

WALLEY Ernest
Caernarfon, 19 April, 1933 (WH)

League Club	Source	Date Signed	Seasons Played	Apps	Subs	Gls
Tottenham H.	Jnrs	05.51	55-57	5	-	0
Middlesbrough	Tr	05.58	58	8	-	0

WALLEY Keith John
Weymouth, 19 October, 1954 (M)

League Club	Source	Date Signed	Seasons Played	Apps	Subs	Gls
Crystal Palace	App	10.72	73	6	1	1

WALLEY John **Thomas**
Caernarfon, 27 February, 1945 Wu23-4/W-1 (M)

League Club	Source	Date Signed	Seasons Played	Apps	Subs	Gls
Arsenal	Caernarfon	12.64	65-66	10	4	1
Watford	Tr	03.67	66-71	202	1	17
Leyton Orient	Tr	12.71	71-75	155	2	6
Watford	Tr	06.76	76	12	1	0

League Club	Source	Date Signed	Seasons Played	Apps	Subs	Gls
WALLING Dean Anthony						
Leeds, 17 April, 1969 St Kitts Int						(CD)
Rochdale	Leeds U. (App)	07.87	87-89	43	22	8
Carlisle U.	Guiseley	06.91	91-97	230	6	21
Lincoln C.	Tr	09.97	97	35	0	5
WALLINGTON Francis **Mark**						
Sleaford, 17 September, 1952 E Yth/Eu23-2						(G)
Walsall	Jnrs	10.71	71	11	0	0
Leicester C.	Tr	03.72	71-84	412	0	0
Derby Co.	Tr	07.85	85-86	67	0	0
Lincoln C.	Tr	08.88	88-90	87	0	0
WALLIS Derek						
Hartlepool, 6 October, 1937						(CF)
Hartlepool U. (Am)		05.63	63	2	-	0
WALLS Arthur Joseph						
Glasgow, 15 January, 1931						(F)
Tranmere Rov.	Airdrieonians	06.54	54-55	22	-	6
WALLS David						
Leeds, 16 June, 1953						(W)
Lincoln C.	Leeds U. (App)	07.71	71-72	9	0	0
WALLS James Parker						
Dunfermline, 11 March, 1928 Died 1995						(CH)
Charlton Ath.	Crossgates	09.45	49-52	10	-	0
Ipswich T.	Tr	05.54	54	1	-	0
WALLS John (Jack)						
Seaham, 8 May, 1932						(G)
Barnsley	Jnrs	05.49	52	7	-	0
Peterborough U.	Tr	05.56	60-61	78	-	0
WALLWORK Ronald						
Manchester, 10 September, 1977 E Yth						(CD)
Manchester U.	YT	03.95	97	0	1	0
Carlisle U.	L	12.97	97	10	0	1
Stockport Co.	L	03.98	97	7	0	0
WALMSLEY David Geoffrey						
Hull, 23 November, 1972						(F)
Hull C.	YT	07.91	90-91	5	5	4
WALMSLEY Dennis						
Southport, 1 May, 1935						(W)
Southport (Am)	Crossens	05.54	54	4	-	1
WALSH Alan						
Hartlepool, 9 December, 1956						(M/F)
Middlesbrough	Horden Colly	12.76	77	0	3	0
Darlington	Tr	10.78	78-83	245	6	87
Bristol C.	Tr	08.84	84-88	215	3	77
Walsall (N/C)	Besiktas (Tu)	10.91	91	4	0	0
Huddersfield T. (N/C)	Tr	12.91	91	0	4	0
Shrewsbury T. (N/C)	Tr	01.92	91	2	0	0
Cardiff C. (N/C)	Southampton (N/C)	03.92	91	1	0	0
Hartlepool U. (N/C)	Backwell U.	09.94	94	4	0	1
WALSH Andrew						
Blackburn, 15 February, 1970						(CD)
Bury	Preston N.E. (N/C)	11.87	87	0	1	0
WALSH John **Brian**						
Aldershot, 26 March, 1932						(W)
Arsenal	Jnrs	08.49	53-55	17	-	0
Cardiff C.	Tr	09.55	55-61	206	-	32
Newport Co.	Tr	11.61	61-62	27	-	3
WALSH Colin David						
Hamilton, 22 July, 1962 S Sch/S Yth/Su21-5						(LW)
Nottingham F.	App	08.79	80-85	115	24	32
Charlton Ath.	Tr	09.86	86-95	223	19	21
Peterborough U.	L	02.89	88	5	0	1
Middlesbrough	L	01.91	90	10	3	1
WALSH David John						
Waterford (Ire), 28 April, 1923 IR-20/NI-9						(CF)
West Bromwich A.	Linfield	07.46	46-50	165	-	94
Aston Villa	Tr	12.50	50-54	108	-	37
Walsall	Tr	07.55	55	20	-	6
WALSH Derek						
Hamilton, 24 October, 1967						(M/RB)
Everton	App	10.84	84	1	0	0
Carlisle U.	Hamilton Academical	08.88	88-92	108	13	6
WALSH Francis						
Wishaw, 15 September, 1923						(CF)
Southport	Glasgow Celtic	10.49	49	5	-	3
WALSH Gary						
Wigan, 21 March, 1968 Eu21-2						(G)
Manchester U.	Jnrs	04.85	86-94	49	1	0
Oldham Ath.	L	11.93	93	6	0	0
Middlesbrough	Tr	08.95	95-96	44	0	0
Bradford C.	Tr	09.97	97	35	0	0
WALSH Ian Patrick						
St Davids, 4 September, 1958 W Sch/Wu21-2/W-18						(F)
Crystal Palace	App	10.75	76-81	101	16	23
Swansea C.	Tr	02.82	81-83	32	5	11
Barnsley	Tr	07.84	84-85	45	4	15
Grimsby T.	Tr	08.86	86-87	36	5	13
Cardiff C.	Tr	01.88	87-88	5	12	4
WALSH James						
Bellshill, 3 December, 1930 Su23-1						(CF)
Leicester C.	Glasgow Celtic	11.56	56-62	176	-	79
WALSH James Thomas Patrick						
Paddington, 20 November, 1954						(FB)
Watford	App	11.72	73-77	60	5	0
York C.	Tr	06.78	78-80	91	8	2
WALSH Kevin William						
Rochdale, 11 February, 1928						(WH)
Oldham Ath.	St Patricks O.B.	10.49	49-50	3	-	0
Southport	Tr	07.52	52-53	67	-	1
Bradford C.	Tr	07.54	54-55	25	-	3
Southport	Tr	08.56	56	3	-	0
WALSH Mario Markus						
Paddington, 19 January, 1966						(F)
Portsmouth	App	01.84				
Torquay U.	Tr	01.85	84-86	89	11	18
Colchester U.	Tr	08.87	87-88	29	9	12
Southend U.	Tr	07.89	89	10	1	2
WALSH Mark						
Preston, 7 October, 1962						(M)
Preston N.E.	App	10.80	81-83	56	6	2
Exeter C. (N/C)	New Zealand	08.85	85	0	1	0
WALSH Michael Anthony						
Chorley, 13 August, 1954 IR-22						(F)
Blackpool	Chorley	11.71	73-77	172	8	72
Everton	Tr	08.78	78	18	3	1
Queens Park R.	Tr	03.79	78-80	13	5	3
WALSH Michael Shane						
Rotherham, 5 August, 1977						(RB)
Scunthorpe U.	YT	07.95	94-97	94	9	1
WALSH Michael Thomas						
Manchester, 20 June, 1956 IR-5						(CD)
Bolton W.	Jnrs	07.74	74-80	169	8	4
Everton	Tr	08.81	81-82	20	0	0
Norwich C.	L	10.82	82	5	0	0
Burnley	L	12.82	82	3	0	0
Manchester C.	Fort Lauderdale (USA)	10.83	83	3	1	0
Blackpool	Tr	02.84	83-88	146	7	5
Bury	Tr	07.89				
WALSH Paul Anthony						
Plumstead, 1 October, 1962 E Yth/Eu21-4/E-5						(F)
Charlton Ath.	App	10.79	79-81	85	2	24
Luton T.	Tr	07.82	82-83	80	0	24
Liverpool	Tr	05.84	84-87	63	14	25
Tottenham H.	Tr	02.88	87-91	84	44	19
Queens Park R.	L	09.91	91	2	0	0
Portsmouth	Tr	06.92	92-93	67	6	14
Manchester C.	Tr	03.94	93-95	53	0	16
Portsmouth	Tr	09.95	95	21	0	5
WALSH Peter						
Dublin, 18 October, 1922 LoI						(F)
Luton T.	Dundalk	08.49	49	8	-	2
Brighton & H.A.	Tr	08.50				
WALSH Roy						
Belfast, 25 November, 1955						(D)
Swindon T.	Glentoran	03.80	80	7	0	0
WALSH Roy William						
Dedham (Sk), 15 January, 1947						(IF)
Ipswich T.	App	01.65	65	6	1	0
Southend U.	Tr	07.67				

League Club	Source	Date Signed	Seasons Played	Apps	Subs	Gls
WALSH Steven						
Preston, 3 November, 1964						(CD/F)
Wigan Ath.	Jnrs	09.82	82-85	123	3	4
Leicester C.	Tr	06.86	86-97	330	5	50
WALSH Wilfred						
Rhymney, 29 July, 1917 Died 1977						(IF)
Arsenal	Margate	05.36	38	3	-	0
Derby Co.	Tr	06.39	46	1	-	0
Walsall	Tr	03.47	46-47	33	-	4
WALSH William						
Easington, 4 December, 1923						(CH)
Sunderland	Horden Colly	09.46	46-52	98	-	1
Northampton T.	Tr	07.53	53	19	-	0
Darlington	Tr	06.54	54	28	-	4
WALSH William						
Dublin, 31 May, 1921 IR-9/NI-5						(WH)
Manchester C.	Manchester U. (Am)	06.38	46-49	109	-	1
WALSHAW Kenneth						
Tynemouth, 28 August, 1918 Died 1979						(IF)
Sunderland	Jnrs	08.44				
Lincoln C.	Tr	08.47	47	17	-	6
Carlisle U.	Tr	12.47	47-49	50	-	15
Bradford C.	Tr	08.50	50	9	-	3
WALSHAW Lee						
Sheffield, 20 January, 1967						(M)
Sheffield U.	App	01.85	84-86	8	1	1
WALSHAW Philip Desmond						
Leeds, 16 April, 1929						(OR)
Halifax T. (Am)	Jnrs	09.46	46	6	-	1
WALTER William **David**						
Holsworthy, 3 September, 1964						(G)
Exeter C.	Bideford	11.88	88-89	44	0	0
Plymouth Arg.	Tr	07.90	90-91	15	0	0
Torquay U.	Tr	06.92	92	1	0	0
WALTERS George						
Wolverhampton, 21 June, 1935						(WH/FB)
Shrewsbury T.	Jenks & Cattell	02.57	56-62	246	-	3
Newport Co.	Tr	09.63	63-65	80	0	2
WALTERS George Archibald						
Glasgow, 30 March, 1939						(OL)
Oldham Ath.	Clyde	08.59	59	13	-	2
WALTERS Henry						
Rotherham, 15 March, 1925 Died 1994						(WH)
Wolverhampton W.	Jnrs	06.42				
Walsall	Tr	05.46	46-52	254	-	2
Barnsley	Tr	07.53	53-59	160	-	4
WALTERS Mark Everton						
Birmingham, 2 June, 1964 E Sch/E Yth/Eu21-9/E'B'/E-1						(LW)
Aston Villa	App	05.82	81-87	168	13	39
Liverpool	Glasgow Rangers	08.91	91-94	58	36	14
Stoke C.	L	03.94	93	9	0	2
Wolverhampton W.	L	09.94	94	11	0	3
Southampton	Tr	01.96	95	4	1	0
Swindon T.	Tr	07.96	96-97	49	12	13
WALTERS Michael						
Banbury, 17 November, 1939						(WH)
Coventry C.	Jnrs	12.56	57	3	-	0
Bradford C.	Rugby T.	01.62	61-62	19	-	0
WALTERS Peter Louis						
Whickham, 8 June, 1952						(G)
Hull C.		08.70	70-71	2	0	0
Darlington	L	03.72	71	16	0	0
WALTERS Robert James						
Glasgow, 9 March, 1944						(CH)
Shrewsbury T.	Winsford U.	12.62	62	1	-	0
WALTERS Steven Paul						
Plymouth, 9 January, 1972 E Sch/E Yth						(M)
Crewe Alex.	YT	03.89	87-94	135	11	10
WALTERS Trevor Bowen						
Aberdare, 13 January, 1916 Died 1989						(CH)
Chester C.	Aberaman	05.37	37-48	151	-	1

League Club	Source	Date Signed	Seasons Played	Apps	Subs	Gls
WALTERS William (Sonny) Edward						
Edmonton, 5 September, 1924 Died 1970 E 'B'						(W)
Tottenham H.	Jnrs	08.44	46-55	210	-	66
Aldershot	Tr	07.57	57-58	66	-	11
WALTON David Lee						
Bedlington, 10 April, 1973						(CD)
Sheffield U.	Ashington	03.92				
Shrewsbury T.	Tr	11.93	93-97	127	1	10
Crewe Alex.	Tr	10.97	97	27	0	0
WALTON Frank Hillard						
Southend, 9 April, 1918 Died 1986						(FB)
Southend U.	Jnrs	12.37	37-50	144	-	0
WALTON Harold						
Manchester, 1 April, 1924 Died 1992						(WH)
Southend U.	Leicester C. (Am)	05.46	46	1	-	0
WALTON Ian Jeffrey						
Goole, 17 April, 1958						(M)
Grimsby T.	App	●	75	2	0	1
Scunthorpe U.	Tr	03.76	76	1	0	0
WALTON John Andrew						
Horwich, 21 March, 1928 Died 1979 E Amat						(IF)
Bury (Am)	Saltash U.	05.49	49-50	26	-	4
Manchester U. (Am)	Tr	07.51	51	2	-	0
Bury (Am)	Tr	07.52	52-53	29	-	2
Burnley	Tr	02.54	54-55	18	-	2
Coventry C.	Tr	10.56	56-57	13	-	0
Chester C.	Kettering T.	07.59	59	1	-	0
WALTON Joseph						
Manchester, 5 June, 1925 EF Lge						(FB)
Manchester U.	Jnrs	10.43	46-47	21	-	0
Preston N.E.	Tr	03.48	47-60	401	-	4
Accrington St.	Tr	02.61	60	18	-	0
WALTON Mark Andrew						
Merthyr Tydfil, 1 June, 1969 Wu21-1						(G)
Luton T.	Jnrs	02.87				
Colchester U.	Tr	11.87	87-88	40	0	0
Norwich C.	Tr	08.89	89-91	22	0	0
Wrexham	L	08.93	93	6	0	0
Bolton W.	Dundee	03.94	93	3	0	0
Fulham	Fakenham T.	08.96	96-97	40	0	0
Gillingham	L	02.98	97	1	0	0
WALTON Paul Anthony						
Sunderland, 2 July, 1979						(W)
Hartlepool U.	YT	●	95-96	3	7	0
WALTON Richard						
Hull, 12 September, 1924						(FB)
Leicester C.		01.43				
Leyton Orient	Tr	07.48	48-51	63	-	4
Exeter C.	Tr	12.51	51-55	135	-	6
WALTON Ronald Pattern						
Plymouth, 12 October, 1945						(W)
Northampton T.	Rotherham U. (Am)	09.63	64	1	-	0
Crewe Alex.	Tr	10.65	65	2	0	0
Carlisle U.	Tr	01.66	65	1	0	0
Aldershot	Tr	08.66	66-71	190	3	41
Cambridge U.	Tr	11.71	71-72	62	0	9
Aldershot	Tr	07.73	73-76	108	5	14
WALTON Roy						
Crewe, 19 July, 1928						(WH)
Crewe Alex.		06.50	50-51	10	-	0
WALWYN Kenford **Keith** Ian						
Jamaica (WI), 17 February, 1956						(F)
Chesterfield	Winterton R.	11.79	80	3	0	2
York C.	Tr	07.81	81-86	245	0	119
Blackpool	Tr	06.87	87-88	51	18	16
Carlisle U.	Tr	07.89	89-90	59	3	15
WANCHOPE Pablo Cesar						
Costa Rica, 31 July, 1976 Costa Rican Int						(F)
Derby Co.	C.S. Heridiano (CR)	03.97	96-97	32	5	14
WANDS Alexander Mitchell Doig						
Cowdenbeath, 5 December, 1922						(LH)
Sheffield Wed.	Gateshead (Am)	05.45	46	11	-	1
Doncaster Rov.	Tr	05.47	47	22	-	1

League Club	Source	Date Signed	Seasons Played	Career Record Apps	Subs	Gls
WANKLYN Edward **Wayne**						
Hull, 21 January, 1960						(M)
Reading	App	01.78	77-80	47	7	3
Aldershot	Tr	08.81	81	15	3	2
WANLESS Paul Steven						
Banbury, 14 December, 1973						(M)
Oxford U.	YT	12.91	91-94	12	20	0
Lincoln C.	Tr	07.95	95	7	1	0
Cambridge U.	Tr	03.96	95-97	83	3	12
WANN Alexander (Sandy) Halley						
Perth, 20 December, 1940						(WH)
Manchester C.	Luncarty Jnrs	07.58				
Oldham Ath.	St Mirren	12.60	60	19	-	0
WANN John **Dennis**						
Blackpool, 17 November, 1950						(W)
Blackpool	App	07.67	69-71	11	6	0
York C.	Tr	01.72	71-75	65	1	7
Chesterfield	L	11.75	75	3	0	0
Hartlepool U.	L	01.76	75	2	0	0
Darlington	Tr	07.76	76-78	119	2	13
Rochdale	Tr	06.79	79-80	66	1	7
Blackpool	Tr	10.81	81	13	6	0
Chester C. (N/C)	Workington	10.83	83	2	1	0
WANT Anthony George						
Shoreditch, 13 December, 1948 E Yth						(LB)
Tottenham H.	App	12.65	67-71	46	4	0
Birmingham C.	Tr	06.72	72-77	98	3	1
WARBOYS Alan						
Goldthorpe, 18 April, 1949						(F)
Doncaster Rov.	App	04.67	66-67	39	1	12
Sheffield Wed.	Tr	06.68	68-70	66	5	13
Cardiff C.	Tr	12.70	70-72	56	4	27
Sheffield U.	Tr	09.72	72	7	0	0
Bristol Rov.	Tr	03.73	72-76	141	3	53
Fulham	Tr	02.77	76-77	19	0	2
Hull C.	Tr	09.77	77-78	44	5	9
Doncaster Rov.	Tr	07.79	79-81	89	0	21
WARBURTON George						
Wrexham, 13 September, 1934						(FB)
Wrexham		11.57	58-59	22	-	0
Barrow	Tr	06.60	60	14	-	0
WARBURTON Ian Thomas						
Haslingden, 22 March, 1952						(F)
Bury	Haslingden	11.72	72	6	0	2
Southport	Tr	07.74	74	5	2	1
WARBURTON Raymond						
Rotherham, 7 October, 1967						(CD)
Rotherham U.	App	10.85	84-86	3	1	0
York C.	Tr	08.89	89-93	86	4	9
Northampton T.	Tr	02.94	93-97	174	0	11
WARD Anthony						
Warrington, 4 April, 1970						(W)
Everton	YT	06.88				
Doncaster Rov.	L	12.88	88	4	0	0
Wigan Ath.	Tr	06.89	89	8	3	2
WARD Ashley Stuart						
Manchester, 24 November, 1970						(F)
Manchester C.	YT	07.89	89	0	1	0
Wrexham	L	01.91	90	4	0	2
Leicester C.	Tr	07.91	91	2	8	0
Blackpool	L	11.92	92	2	0	1
Crewe Alex.	Tr	12.92	92-94	58	3	25
Norwich C.	Tr	12.94	94-95	53	0	18
Derby Co.	Tr	03.96	95-97	32	8	9
Barnsley	Tr	09.97	97	28	1	8
WARD Darren						
Worksop, 11 May, 1974 Wu21-2						(G)
Mansfield T.	YT	07.92	92-94	81	0	0
Notts Co.	Tr	07.95	95-97	128	0	0
WARD Darren Philip						
Harrow, 13 September, 1978						(CD)
Watford	YT	02.97	95-96	8	0	0
WARD David (Dai)						
Barry, 16 July, 1934 Died 1996 W-2						(IF)
Bristol Rov.	Barry T.	11.54	54-60	175	-	90
Cardiff C.	Tr	02.61	60-61	35	-	18

League Club	Source	Date Signed	Seasons Played	Career Record Apps	Subs	Gls
Watford	Tr	06.62	62-63	59	-	31
Brentford	Tr	10.63	63-64	47	-	21
WARD David Alan						
Crewe, 8 March, 1941						(FB)
Swansea C.	Taunton T.	01.59	60-65	44	1	0
WARD Denis						
Burton, 25 October, 1924						(G)
Nottingham F.		08.47	47	1	-	0
Stockport Co.	Tr	08.49	49-52	52	-	0
Bradford P.A.	Hastings U.	08.55	55-57	50	-	0
WARD Derek						
Birkenhead, 17 May, 1972						(RB)
Bury	Heswall	08.92	92-93	27	1	0
WARD Derrick						
Stoke, 23 December, 1934						(W)
Stoke C.	Jnrs	08.52	52-60	54	-	8
Stockport Co.	Tr	07.61	61-63	81	-	21
WARD Gavin John						
Sutton Coldfield, 30 June, 1970						(G)
Shrewsbury T.	Aston Villa (YT)	09.88				
Cardiff C.	West Bromwich A. (N/C)	09.89	89-92	58	1	0
Leicester C.	Tr	07.93	93-94	38	0	0
Bradford C.	Tr	07.95	95	36	0	0
Bolton W.	Tr	03.96	95-97	19	3	0
WARD Gerald						
Stepney, 5 October, 1936 Died 1994 E Sch/E Yth/E Amat						(WH)
Arsenal	Jnrs	10.53	53-62	81	-	10
Leyton Orient	Tr	07.63	63-64	44	-	2
WARD James						
Glasgow, 26 July, 1929 Died 1985						(F)
Crewe Alex. (Am)	Queens Park	08.56	56	6	-	0
WARD John						
Mansfield, 18 January, 1948						(FB)
Notts Co.	App	07.65	65	5	0	0
WARD John Patrick						
Lincoln, 7 April, 1951						(F)
Lincoln C.	Adelaide Park	03.71	70-78	223	17	91
Workington	L	09.72	72	9	2	3
Watford	Tr	07.79	79-80	22	5	6
Grimsby T.	Tr	06.81	81	2	1	0
Lincoln C. (N/C)	Tr	03.82	81	1	0	0
WARD John Stuart						
Frodsham, 15 June, 1933						(F)
Crewe Alex. (Am)		12.56	56	2	-	0
WARD Joseph						
Glasgow, 25 November, 1954						(F)
Aston Villa	Clyde	12.78	78-79	2	1	0
WARD Mark William						
Huyton, 10 October, 1962 E Semi Pro						(W)
Everton	App	09.80				
Oldham Ath.	Northwich Vic.	07.83	83-84	84	0	12
West Ham U.	Tr	08.85	85-89	163	2	12
Manchester C.	Tr	12.89	89-90	55	0	14
Everton	Tr	08.91	91-93	82	1	6
Birmingham C.	Tr	03.94	93-95	63	0	7
Huddersfield T.	Tr	03.96	95	7	1	0
Wigan Ath. (N/C)	Tr	09.96	96	5	0	0
WARD Michael Henry						
Nottingham, 30 August, 1920						(IF)
Stockport Co.		10.48	48	1	-	0
WARD Mitchum David						
Sheffield, 19 June, 1971						(RB/M)
Sheffield U.	YT	07.89	90-97	135	19	11
Crewe Alex.	L	11.90	90	4	0	1
Everton	Tr	11.97	97	8	0	0
WARD Nicholas John						
Wrexham, 30 November, 1977						(F)
Shrewsbury T.	YT	07.96	96-97	8	12	1
WARD Noel Gerard						
Strabane, 8 December, 1952						(CD)
Wigan Ath.	Aberdeen	07.76	78-79	47	1	4

League Club	Source	Date Signed	Seasons Played	Apps	Subs	Gls
WARD Patrick						
Dumbarton, 28 December, 1926						(WH)
Leicester C.	Hibernian	09.55	55-57	57	-	0
Crewe Alex.	Tr	06.58	58	31	-	1
WARD Paul Terence						
Fishburn (Dm), 15 September, 1963						(M)
Chelsea	App	08.81				
Middlesbrough	Tr	09.82	82-85	69	7	1
Darlington	Tr	09.85	85-87	124	0	9
Leyton Orient	Tr	07.88	88-89	30	1	1
Scunthorpe U.	Tr	10.89	89-90	53	2	6
Lincoln C.	Tr	03.91	90-92	38	1	0
WARD Peter						
Rotherham, 20 October, 1954						(FB)
Sheffield U.	App	10.72				
Workington	Tr	07.74	74-75	39	4	2
WARD Peter						
Durham, 15 October, 1964						(M)
Huddersfield T.	Chester-le-Street	01.87	86-88	24	13	2
Rochdale	Tr	07.89	89-90	83	1	10
Stockport Co.	Tr	05.91	91-94	140	2	10
Wrexham	Tr	07.95	95-97	92	3	13
WARD Peter David						
Derby, 27 July, 1955 Eu21-2/E-1						(F)
Brighton & H.A.	Burton A.	05.75	75-80	172	6	79
Nottingham F.	Tr	10.80	80-82	28	5	7
Brighton & H.A.	L	10.82	82	16	0	2
WARD Ralph Arthur						
Oadby, 5 February, 1911 E Sch						(FB)
Bradford P.A.	Hinckley	11.29	30-35	129	-	0
Tottenham H.	Tr	03.36	35-38	115	-	10
Crewe Alex.	Tr	08.46	46-48	89	-	7
WARD John **Richard**						
Scunthorpe, 16 September, 1940 E Amat						(IF)
Scunthorpe U. (Am)	Jnrs	05.58	58	1	-	0
Northampton T. (Am)	Tr	06.59	59	6	-	0
Millwall	Tooting & Mitcham	07.62	62-63	13	-	3
WARD Robert						
Glasgow, 21 October, 1958						(M)
Newport Co.	Glasgow Celtic	01.80	79-80	2	1	0
WARD Robert Andrew						
West Bromwich, 4 August, 1953						(G)
West Bromwich A.	Imperial Star	03.73	74-76	9	0	0
Northampton T.	L	02.77	76	8	0	0
Blackpool	Tr	09.77	77-78	41	0	0
Wigan Ath.	Tr	07.79	80-81	46	0	0
WARD Ronald						
Killamarsh (Dy), 10 February, 1935 E Sch						(G)
Chesterfield	Jnrs	02.52	51-52	8	-	0
WARD Ronald						
Altrincham, 17 October, 1932						(IF)
Stockport Co.		03.54	53-55	17	-	3
WARD Henry **Ronald**						
Walthamstow, 29 March, 1932						(G)
Tottenham H.		05.50				
Darlington	Headington U.	08.56	56	26	-	0
WARD Stephen						
Chapeltown (Yks), 27 December, 1960						(FB)
Lincoln C.	App	12.78	79	2	0	0
WARD Stephen Charles						
Derby, 21 July, 1959						(W)
Brighton & H.A.	App	10.76				
Northampton T.	Tr	08.79	79	13	2	2
Halifax T.	Tr	06.80	80-85	233	13	17
WARD Sydney						
Dewsbury, 26 November, 1923						(G)
Bradford C.	Upton Colly	09.47	47	2	-	0
WARD Terence						
Stoke, 10 December, 1939						(FB)
Stoke C.	Jnrs	03.58	59-62	43	-	0
WARD Thomas Alfred						
Wolsingham, 6 August, 1917						(CF)
Sheffield Wed.	Crook T.	03.37	46-47	35	-	19
Darlington	Tr	08.48	48-53	119	-	32
WARD Timothy Victor						
Cheltenham, 17 October, 1918 Died 1993 E-2						(WH)
Derby Co.	Cheltenham T.	04.37	37-50	238	-	4
Barnsley	Tr	03.51	50-52	33	-	0
WARD Warren						
Plympton, 25 May, 1962						(F)
York C. (N/C)	Guiseley	03.85	84	4	0	3
Lincoln C.	Tr	07.85	85	15	6	8
Exeter C.	L	02.86	85	14	0	3
WARD Wayne Walter						
Colchester, 28 April, 1964						(FB)
Colchester U.	App	05.82	81-82	17	2	0
WARD Lawrence **Whelan (Polly)**						
Halifax, 15 June, 1929						(IF)
Bradford C.	Ovenden	10.48	48-53	149	-	37
Bradford P.A.	Kings Lynn	07.55	55-58	108	-	31
WARD William						
Sunderland, 30 June, 1949						(W)
Hartlepool U. (Am)	Spennymoor U.	01.72	71-72	8	0	1
Hartlepool U.	Shildon	01.73	72-74	79	8	9
WARDEN Daniel						
Stepney, 11 April, 1973						(M)
Charlton Ath.		07.92	92	1	2	0
WARDLE Ernest						
Stockton, 13 June, 1930						(D)
Middlesbrough	Billingham Synth.	05.48				
York C.	Tr	01.55	54-58	60	-	2
WARDLE Geoffrey						
Trimdon, 7 January, 1940						(WH)
Sunderland	Houghton Jnrs	01.58				
Lincoln C.	Tr	06.61	61	1	-	0
WARDLE George						
Kibblesworth (Dm), 24 September, 1919 Died 1991						(OR)
Middlesbrough		05.37	37	1	-	0
Exeter C.	Tr	06.39	46	38	-	6
Cardiff C.	Tr	05.47	46-48	40	-	11
Queens Park R.	Tr	01.49	48-50	53	-	4
Darlington	Tr	08.51	51-53	95	-	6
WARDLE Ian Spencer						
Doncaster, 27 March, 1970						(G)
Barnsley	Jnrs	05.88	89	9	0	0
WARDLE Robert Ian						
Halifax, 5 March, 1955						(G)
Bristol C.	App	11.72				
Shrewsbury T.	Tr	07.74	77-81	131	0	0
Liverpool	Tr	08.82				
Wrexham	L	09.83	83	13	0	0
WARDLE William						
Hetton-le-Hole, 20 January, 1918 Died 1989						(OL)
Southport	Houghton Colly	12.36	36-37	14	-	0
Manchester C.	Tr	10.37	37	6	-	0
Grimsby T.	Tr	07.39	46-47	73	-	11
Blackpool	Tr	05.48	48-50	58	-	1
Birmingham C.	Tr	09.51	51-52	60	-	5
Barnsley	Tr	11.53	53-54	28	-	1
WARDROBE Thomas **Barrie**						
Newcastle, 3 July, 1963						(F)
Sunderland	App	04.81				
Hartlepool U.	Tr	07.84	84	23	4	2
WARDROBE Michael						
Newcastle, 24 March, 1962						(F)
Burnley	App	03.80	80	0	1	0
Stockport Co.	Tr	08.81	81-82	19	8	2
WARE Charles						
York, 9 March, 1931						(OL)
York C.	Jnrs	12.48	53	9	-	0
WARE Paul David						
Congleton, 7 November, 1970						(M)
Stoke C.	YT	11.88	87-93	92	23	10
Stockport Co.	Tr	09.94	94-96	42	12	4
Cardiff C.	L	01.97	96	5	0	0
WARHURST Paul						
Stockport, 26 September, 1969 Eu21-8						(D/M)
Manchester C.	YT	06.88				

League Club	Source	Date Signed	Seasons Played	Career Record Apps	Subs	Gls
Oldham Ath.	Tr	10.88	88-90	60	7	2
Sheffield Wed.	Tr	07.91	91-93	60	6	6
Blackburn Rov.	Tr	08.93	93-96	30	27	4
Crystal Palace	Tr	07.97	97	22	0	3
WARHURST Roy						
Sheffield, 18 September, 1926						(WH)
Sheffield U.	Huddersfield T. (Am)	09.44	46-49	17	-	2
Birmingham C.	Tr	03.50	49-56	213	-	10
Manchester C.	Tr	06.57	57-58	40	-	2
Crewe Alex.	Tr	03.59	58-59	51	-	1
Oldham Ath.	Tr	08.60	60	8	-	0
WARING Thomas **Alan**						
Preston, 3 August, 1929						(HB)
Burnley		08.48				
Halifax T.	Tr	07.54	54	12	-	0
WARK John						
Glasgow, 4 August, 1957 S Yth/Su21-8/S-29						(M)
Ipswich T.	App	08.74	74-83	295	1	94
Liverpool	Tr	03.84	83-87	64	6	28
Ipswich T.	Tr	01.88	87-89	87	2	23
Middlesbrough	Tr	08.90	90	31	1	2
Ipswich T.	Tr	08.91	91-96	151	3	18
WARMAN Philip Roy						
Bromley, 18 December, 1950 E Yth						(LB)
Charlton Ath.	Jnrs	03.68	69-80	313	3	19
Millwall	Tr	08.81	81	27	0	1
WARMINGTON Peter John						
Wythall (Worcs), 8 April, 1934						(IF)
Birmingham C.	Jnrs	12.51	54-56	8	-	3
WARN Keith Donald						
Watford, 20 March, 1941						(G)
Watford	Croxley B.C.	04.59	59	3	-	0
WARNE Paul						
Norwich, 8 May, 1973						(F)
Wigan Ath.	Wroxham	07.97	97	3	22	2
WARNE Raymond						
Ipswich, 16 February, 1929						(CF)
Ipswich T.	Leiston	10.50	50-51	30	-	11
WARNER Anthony Randolph						
Liverpool, 11 May, 1974						(G)
Liverpool	Jnrs	01.94				
Swindon T.	L	11.97	97	2	0	0
WARNER Dennis Peter Alfred						
Rotherham, 6 December, 1930						(FB)
Rotherham U.	Spurley Hey O.B.	03.50	52-56	64	-	0
Chesterfield	Tr	05.57	57	8	-	0
WARNER John						
Ashington, 6 May, 1940						(F)
Luton T.		10.59	59	1	-	0
WARNER John (Jack)						
Tonyrefail, 21 September, 1911 Died 1980 W-2						(WH)
Swansea C.	Trealaw	01.34	33-37	132	-	8
Manchester U.	Tr	06.38	38-49	102	-	1
Oldham Ath.	Tr	06.51	51	34	-	2
Rochdale	Tr	07.52	52	21	-	0
WARNER John						
Paddington, 20 November, 1961						(F)
Colchester U. (N/C)	Burnham Ramblers	02.89	88	7	8	3
Colchester U. (N/C)	Heybridge Swifts	12.89	89	1	1	0
WARNER Leslie Horace						
Birmingham, 19 December, 1918 Died 1982						(OR)
Coventry C.	Jack Moulds Ath.	07.37	37-53	197	-	19
WARNER Michael James						
Harrogate, 17 January, 1974						(M)
Northampton T.	Tamworth	07.95	96-97	4	15	0
WARNER Philip						
Southampton, 2 February, 1979						(D)
Southampton	YT	05.97	97	0	1	0
WARNER Reginald Owen						
Anstey, 1 March, 1931 Died 1996 E Yth						(HB)
Leicester C.	Jnrs	04.49	52-53	7	-	0
Mansfield T.	Tr	03.55	54-56	33	-	0

League Club	Source	Date Signed	Seasons Played	Career Record Apps	Subs	Gls
WARNER Robert Mark						
Stratford-on-Avon, 20 April, 1977						(RB/M)
Hereford U.	YT	01.95	94-96	31	6	0
WARNER Vance						
Leeds, 3 September, 1974 E Yth						(CD)
Nottingham F.	YT	09.91	93-96	4	1	0
Grimsby T.	L	02.96	95	3	0	0
Rotherham U.	Tr	08.97	97	21	0	0
WARNES George						
Worksop, 4 December, 1925						(G)
Rotherham U.	Dinnington Colly	12.44	46-49	98	-	0
Aldershot	Tr	06.50	50-51	32	-	0
WARNOCK Neil						
Sheffield, 1 December, 1948						(W)
Chesterfield		07.68	67-68	20	4	2
Rotherham U.	Tr	06.69	69-70	46	8	5
Hartlepool U.	Tr	07.71	71-72	58	2	5
Scunthorpe U.	Tr	02.72	72-74	63	9	7
Aldershot	Tr	03.75	74-76	35	2	6
Barnsley	Tr	10.76	76-77	53	4	10
York C.	Tr	05.78	78	1	3	0
Crewe Alex.	Tr	12.78	78	20	1	1
WARREN Christer Simon						
Dorchester, 10 October, 1974						(W)
Southampton	Cheltenham T.	03.95	95-96	1	7	0
Brighton & H.A.	L	10.96	96	3	0	0
Fulham	L	03.97	96	8	3	1
Bournemouth	Tr	10.97	97	29	1	6
WARREN Derek Bernard						
Colyton (Dev), 23 May, 1923						(RB)
Exeter C.	Axminster	01.48	48-51	55	-	0
WARREN Lee Anthony						
Manchester, 28 February, 1969						(D/M)
Leeds U.	YT	07.87				
Rochdale	Tr	10.87	87	31	0	1
Hull C.	Tr	08.88	88-93	141	12	1
Lincoln C.	L	09.90	90	2	1	1
Doncaster Rov.	Tr	07.94	94-97	115	10	3
WARREN Mark Wayne						
Clapton, 12 November, 1974 E Yth						(RB/M)
Leyton Orient	YT	07.92	91-97	124	18	5
WARREN Raymond Richard						
Bristol, 23 June, 1918 Died 1988						(CH)
Bristol Rov.	Jnrs	11.35	35-55	450	-	28
WARREN Robert						
Devonport, 8 January, 1927						(CH)
Plymouth Arg.	Plymouth U.	02.46	46	3	-	0
Chelsea	Tr	07.48	48	1	-	0
Torquay U.	Tr	08.51	51	5	-	1
WARRENDER Robert						
Leven, 13 February, 1929						(F)
York C.	East Fife	05.52	52-53	24	-	5
WARRILOW Thomas						
Plumstead, 26 July, 1964						(D)
Torquay U. (N/C)	Gravesend & Nft	03.87	86	2	0	0
WARRINER Stephen William						
Liverpool, 18 December, 1958						(FB/M)
Liverpool	App	12.76				
Newport Co.	Tr	07.78	78-80	28	8	2
Rochdale	Tr	08.81	81-82	11	1	1
Tranmere Rov.	Tr	02.83	82	5	4	0
WARRINGTON Andrew Clifford						
Sheffield, 10 June, 1976						(G)
York C.	YT	06.94	95-97	50	0	0
WARRINGTON Tony						
Ecclesfield (Yks), 12 February, 1934						(G)
Lincoln C.	Thorncliffe Jnrs	03.54	53-55	2	-	0
WARSAP John William Benjamin						
West Ham, 18 May, 1921 Died 1992						(W)
Gillingham		(N/L)	50-52	9	-	1
WARZYCHA Robert						
Poland, 20 June, 1963 Polish Int						(RW)
Everton	Gornik Zabrze (Pol)	03.91	90-93	51	21	6

WASILEWSKI Zdzislaw (Adam)
Poland, 1925 Died 1956 (CF)

League Club	Source	Date Signed	Seasons Played	Apps	Subs	Gls
Rochdale		07.53	53	4	-	1

WASS William
Ryhope, 16 November, 1922 (OR)

League Club	Source	Date Signed	Seasons Played	Apps	Subs	Gls
Middlesbrough		02.45				
Bradford C.	Tr	07.46	46	7	-	1

WASSALL Darren Paul James
Birmingham, 27 June, 1968 (CD)

League Club	Source	Date Signed	Seasons Played	Apps	Subs	Gls
Nottingham F.	App	06.86	87-91	17	10	0
Hereford U.	L	10.87	87	5	0	0
Bury	L	03.89	88	7	0	1
Derby Co.	Tr	06.92	92-95	90	8	0
Manchester C.	L	09.96	96	14	1	0
Birmingham C.	Tr	03.97	96-97	22	0	0

WASSALL John Charles
Birmingham, 9 June, 1933 Died 1987 (D)

League Club	Source	Date Signed	Seasons Played	Apps	Subs	Gls
Coventry C.	Jnrs	05.51	55-56	17	-	0
Southport	Tr	08.57	57	4	-	0

WASSALL John Victor
Shrewsbury, 11 February, 1917 Died 1994 (IF)

League Club	Source	Date Signed	Seasons Played	Apps	Subs	Gls
Manchester U.	Wellington T.	02.35	35-38	45	-	6
Stockport Co.	Tr	10.46	46-47	19	-	2

WASSALL Kim
Wolverhampton, 9 June, 1957 (W/FB)

League Club	Source	Date Signed	Seasons Played	Apps	Subs	Gls
West Bromwich A.	App	06.75				
Northampton T.	Tr	09.77	77-78	13	7	1
Hull C. (N/C)	Australia	08.83	83	1	0	0
Swansea C. (N/C)		09.84	84	1	1	0
Wolverhampton W. (N/C)		10.85	85	2	0	0
Shrewsbury T. (N/C)	Finland	11.89	89	0	2	0

WATERHOUSE Kenneth
Ormskirk, 23 January, 1930 (WH/IF)

League Club	Source	Date Signed	Seasons Played	Apps	Subs	Gls
Preston N.E.	Burscough	12.48	53-56	22	-	5
Rotherham U.	Tr	05.58	58-62	123	-	12
Bristol C.	Tr	04.63	62-63	16	-	1
Darlington	Tr	08.64	64	1	-	0

WATERMAN David Graham
Guernsey, 16 May, 1977 NIu21-3 (D)

League Club	Source	Date Signed	Seasons Played	Apps	Subs	Gls
Portsmouth	YT	07.95	96-97	11	8	0

WATERMAN Derek James
Guildford, 12 April, 1939 (WH)

League Club	Source	Date Signed	Seasons Played	Apps	Subs	Gls
Exeter C.	Guildford C.	06.57	57	4	-	0

WATERS Graham John
St Austell, 5 November, 1971 (FB)

League Club	Source	Date Signed	Seasons Played	Apps	Subs	Gls
Oxford U.	YT	05.90				
Exeter C.	Tr	07.91	91	1	1	0

WATERS Joseph John Wary
Limerick (Ire), 20 September, 1953 IR-2 (M)

League Club	Source	Date Signed	Seasons Played	Apps	Subs	Gls
Leicester C.	App	10.70	73-74	11	2	1
Grimsby T.	Tr	01.76	75-83	356	1	65

WATERS Patrick
Dublin, 31 January, 1922 (CH)

League Club	Source	Date Signed	Seasons Played	Apps	Subs	Gls
Preston N.E.	Glentoran	06.47	47-49	64	-	0
Carlisle U.	Tr	12.50	50-57	261	-	0

WATERS Richard
Gateshead, 18 May, 1945 (G)

League Club	Source	Date Signed	Seasons Played	Apps	Subs	Gls
Darlington (Am)	Blyth Spartans	03.65	64	2	-	0

WATERS Samuel
Kilsyth, 31 May, 1917 Died 1975 (OL)

League Club	Source	Date Signed	Seasons Played	Apps	Subs	Gls
Halifax T.	Third Lanark	07.46	46	26	-	9

WATERS William Anthony
Swansea, 19 September, 1931 (G)

League Club	Source	Date Signed	Seasons Played	Apps	Subs	Gls
Blackpool		11.50				
Southend U.		11.53				
Swansea C.	Tr	08.54				
Wrexham	Tr	06.55	55-58	99	-	0
Millwall	Tr	07.60	60	5	-	0

WATFORD Albert
Chesterfield, 12 February, 1917 Died 1982 (RB)

League Club	Source	Date Signed	Seasons Played	Apps	Subs	Gls
Chesterfield		02.44				
Lincoln C.	Tr	09.46	46	14	-	0

WATKIN Alan James
Felling, 16 May, 1940 (OR)

League Club	Source	Date Signed	Seasons Played	Apps	Subs	Gls
Gateshead (Am)		08.59	59	3	-	0

WATKIN Cyril
Stoke, 21 July, 1926 (FB)

League Club	Source	Date Signed	Seasons Played	Apps	Subs	Gls
Stoke C.	Jnrs	09.44	48-51	86	-	0
Bristol C.	Tr	07.52	52	3	-	0

WATKIN George
Chopwell, 14 April, 1944 (CF)

League Club	Source	Date Signed	Seasons Played	Apps	Subs	Gls
Newcastle U.	App	04.62	62	1	-	0
Chesterfield	Kings Lynn	07.64	64	7	-	1

WATKIN Stephen
Wrexham, 16 June, 1971 W Sch/W 'B' (F)

League Club	Source	Date Signed	Seasons Played	Apps	Subs	Gls
Wrexham	Jnrs	07.89	90-97	167	33	55
Swansea C.	Tr	09.97	97	24	8	3

WATKIN Thomas **William** Steel
Grimsby, 21 September, 1932 E Sch (IF)

League Club	Source	Date Signed	Seasons Played	Apps	Subs	Gls
Grimsby T.	Jnrs	10.49				
Gateshead	Tr	12.52	52-53	38	-	12
Middlesbrough	Tr	03.54	53-54	11	-	2
Mansfield T.	Tr	06.55	55	25	-	4

WATKINS Albert (Alan) John
Usk, 21 April, 1922 (WH)

League Club	Source	Date Signed	Seasons Played	Apps	Subs	Gls
Plymouth Arg.		12.45	46	4	-	1
Cardiff C.	Tr	07.48				

WATKINS Randall **Barry**
Merthyr Tydfil, 30 November, 1921 (FB)

League Club	Source	Date Signed	Seasons Played	Apps	Subs	Gls
Bristol Rov.	B.A.C. Patchway	10.45	46-54	116	-	7

WATKINS Charles
Glasgow, 14 January, 1921 (WH)

League Club	Source	Date Signed	Seasons Played	Apps	Subs	Gls
Luton T.	Glasgow Rangers	09.48	48-54	218	-	16

WATKINS Dale Allan
Peterborough, 4 November, 1971 (F)

League Club	Source	Date Signed	Seasons Played	Apps	Subs	Gls
Peterborough U.	Rotherham U. (YT)	03.90	89-90	5	5	0

WATKINS John Vincent
Bristol, 9 April, 1933 E Yth (OL)

League Club	Source	Date Signed	Seasons Played	Apps	Subs	Gls
Bristol C.	Jnrs	06.51	53-58	95	-	19
Cardiff C.	Tr	06.59	59-60	65	-	17
Bristol Rov.	Tr	02.61	60-61	23	-	0

WATKINS Philip John
Caerphilly, 2 January, 1945 (WH)

League Club	Source	Date Signed	Seasons Played	Apps	Subs	Gls
Cardiff C.	Jnrs	09.62	63	1	-	0

WATKINS Robert (Wally) Stephen
Bristol, 20 December, 1946 (OL)

League Club	Source	Date Signed	Seasons Played	Apps	Subs	Gls
Bristol Rov.	Bristol C. (Am)	07.65	65	1	0	0

WATKINSON Russell
Epsom, 3 December, 1977 (W)

League Club	Source	Date Signed	Seasons Played	Apps	Subs	Gls
Southampton	Woking	09.96	96	0	2	0

WATKINSON William
Prescot, 16 March, 1922 (CF)

League Club	Source	Date Signed	Seasons Played	Apps	Subs	Gls
Liverpool	Prescot Cables	02.46	46-49	24	-	2
Accrington St.	Tr	01.51	50-54	105	-	45
Halifax T.	Tr	09.54	54-55	60	-	24

WATKISS Stuart Paul
Wolverhampton, 8 May, 1966 (CD)

League Club	Source	Date Signed	Seasons Played	Apps	Subs	Gls
Wolverhampton W.	YT	07.84	83	2	0	0
Crewe Alex. (N/C)		02.86	85	3	0	0
Walsall	Rushall Olympic	08.93	93-95	60	2	2
Hereford U.	Tr	02.96	95	19	0	0
Mansfield T.	Tr	07.96	96-97	40	1	1

WATLING Barry John
Walthamstow, 16 July, 1946 (G)

League Club	Source	Date Signed	Seasons Played	Apps	Subs	Gls
Leyton Orient	App	07.64				
Bristol C.	Tr	07.65	67-68	2	0	0
Notts Co.	Tr	07.69	69-71	65	1	0
Hartlepool U.	Tr	07.72	72-75	139	0	0
Chester C.	L	09.75	75	5	0	0
Rotherham U.	L	12.75	75	5	0	0
Sheffield Wed.	Tr	01.76	75	1	0	0

WATLING John Daniel
Bristol, 11 May, 1925 (OL)

League Club	Source	Date Signed	Seasons Played	Apps	Subs	Gls
Bristol Rov.	St Andrews B.C.	01.47	47-61	323	-	19

League Club	Source	Date Signed	Seasons Played	Career Record Apps	Subs	Gls
WATSON Albert						
Bolton-on-Dearne, 1 June, 1918						(LH)
Huddersfield T.	Jnrs	12.35	37-47	17	-	0
Oldham Ath.	Tr	07.48	48-49	42	-	0
WATSON Alexander Francis						
Liverpool, 5 April, 1968 E Yth						(CD)
Liverpool	App	05.85	87-88	3	1	0
Derby Co.	L	08.90	90	5	0	0
Bournemouth	Tr	01.91	90-94	145	6	5
Gillingham	L	09.95	95	10	0	1
Torquay U.	Tr	11.95	95-97	121	0	4
WATSON Andrew						
Aberdeen, 3 September, 1959 Su21-4						(M/F)
Leeds U.	Aberdeen	06.83	83-84	37	1	7
WATSON Andrew Anthony						
Leeds, 1 April, 1967						(M)
Halifax T.	Harrogate T.	08.88	88-89	75	8	15
Swansea C.	Tr	07.90	90	9	5	1
Carlisle U.	Tr	09.91	91-92	55	1	22
Blackpool	Tr	02.93	92-95	88	27	43
Walsall	Tr	09.96	96-97	45	18	12
WATSON Andrew Lyon						
Huddersfield, 3 April, 1967						(CD)
Huddersfield T.	App	04.85				
Exeter C.	Tr	07.86	86-87	41	1	1
WATSON Arthur						
South Hiendley, 12 July, 1913 Died 1995						(FB)
Lincoln C.	Monkton Colly	05.34	34-35	37	-	0
Chesterfield	Tr	06.36	36-38	10	-	0
Hull C.	Tr	06.39	46	35	-	2
WATSON Charles Richard						
Newark, 10 March, 1949						(G)
Notts Co.		02.67	67	1	0	0
WATSON David						
Liverpool, 20 November, 1961 Eu21-7/E-12						(CD)
Liverpool	Jnrs	05.79				
Norwich C.	Tr	11.80	80-85	212	0	11
Everton	Tr	08.86	86-97	392	3	24
WATSON David Neil						
Barnsley, 10 November, 1973 E Yth/Eu21-5						(G)
Barnsley	YT	07.92	92-97	172	0	0
WATSON David Vernon						
Stapleford, 5 October, 1946 E-65						(CD)
Notts Co.	Stapleford O.B.	01.67	66-67	24	1	1
Rotherham U.	Tr	01.68	67-70	121	0	19
Sunderland	Tr	12.70	70-74	177	0	27
Manchester C.	Tr	06.75	75-78	146	0	4
Southampton	Werder Bremen (Ger)	10.79	79-81	73	0	7
Stoke C.	Tr	01.82	81-82	59	0	5
Derby Co.	Vancouver (Can)	09.83	83	34	0	1
Notts Co.	Vancouver (Can)	09.84	84	23	2	1
WATSON Donald						
Barnsley, 27 August, 1932						(F)
Sheffield Wed.	Worsboro' Bridge	09.54	54	8	-	3
Lincoln C.	Tr	12.56	56-57	14	-	2
Bury	Tr	11.57	57-61	172	-	65
Barnsley	Tr	01.62	61	8	-	1
Rochdale	Tr	07.62	62-63	58	-	15
Barrow	Tr	07.64	64	17	-	1
WATSON Garry						
Bradford, 7 October, 1955						(LB)
Bradford C.	App	10.73	72-83	246	17	28
Doncaster Rov.	L	10.82	82	13	0	0
Halifax T.	Tr	07.84	84	21	0	0
WATSON Gary						
Easington, 2 March, 1961						(LB)
Oxford U.	App	11.78	78-79	24	0	0
Carlisle U.	Tr	05.80	80	17	1	0
WATSON Gordon William George						
Sidcup, 20 March, 1971 Eu21-2						(F)
Charlton Ath.	YT	04.89	89-90	20	11	7
Sheffield Wed.	Tr	02.91	90-94	29	37	15
Southampton	Tr	03.95	94-96	37	15	8
Bradford C.	Tr	01.97	96	3	0	1
WATSON Thomas Gordon						
Wolsingham (Dm), 1 March, 1914						(LH)
Everton	Blyth Spartans	01.33	36-48	61	-	1
WATSON Graham Sidney						
Doncaster, 3 August, 1949						(M)
Doncaster Rov.	App	11.66	66-67	47	1	11
Rotherham U.	Tr	02.68	67-68	13	0	1
Doncaster Rov.	Tr	01.69	68-72	105	4	23
Cambridge U.	Tr	09.72	72-78	206	3	24
Lincoln C.	Tr	09.78	78-79	43	0	2
Cambridge U.	Tr	03.80	79	0	1	0
WATSON Ian						
North Shields, 5 February, 1960						(G)
Sunderland	App	02.78	78	1	0	0
Rochdale	L	08.79	79	33	0	0
Newport Co.	Tr	04.82				
WATSON Ian Lionel						
Hammersmith, 7 January, 1944						(FB)
Chelsea	Jnrs	02.62	62-64	5	-	1
Queens Park R.	Tr	07.65	65-73	196	6	1
WATSON James						
Stirling, 16 January, 1924 SF Lge/S-2						(IF)
Huddersfield T.	Motherwell	06.52	52-56	140	-	29
WATSON James						
Birmingham, 3 March, 1937						(LB)
Walsall		05.55	55	1	-	0
Birmingham C.	Tr	08.57				
WATSON John						
Dewsbury, 10 April, 1959						(G)
Huddersfield T.	Jnrs	03.77				
Hartlepool U.	Tr	03.79	78-82	44	0	0
WATSON John						
Ruabon, 2 May, 1942 W Sch						(FB)
Everton	Jnrs	05.59				
Chester C.	Tr	08.60	60-61	25	-	0
WATSON John (Jack) Fox						
Hamilton, 31 December, 1917 Died 1976						(CH)
Bury	Douglas Jnrs	06.36	38	6	-	0
Fulham	Tr	08.46	46-47	71	-	2
Crystal Palace	Real Madrid (Sp)	07.49	49-50	61	-	1
WATSON John Ian						
South Shields, 14 April, 1974						(RB/W)
Newcastle U.	YT	04.92	90	0	1	0
Scunthorpe U.	Tr	07.93	93	1	4	0
WATSON John Martin						
Edinburgh, 13 February, 1959						(F)
Fulham	Dunfermline Ath.	08.89	89	12	2	0
WATSON Kenneth						
Whickham (Dm), 8 September, 1934						(WH)
Lincoln C.		05.52				
Aldershot	Tr	07.55	57-59	29	-	1
WATSON Kevin Edward						
Hackney, 3 January, 1974						(M)
Tottenham H.	YT	05.92	92	4	1	0
Brentford	L	03.94	93	2	1	0
Bristol C.	L	12.94	94	1	1	0
Barnet	L	02.95	94	13	0	0
Swindon T.	Tr	07.96	96-97	30	15	1
WATSON Liam						
Liverpool, 21 May, 1970						(F)
Preston N.E.	Warrington T.	03.93	92-93	7	2	3
WATSON Mark Leon						
Birmingham, 28 December, 1973						(F)
West Ham U.	Sutton U.	05.95	95	0	1	0
Leyton Orient	L	09.95	95	0	1	1
Cambridge U.	L	10.95	95	1	3	1
Shrewsbury T.	L	02.96	95	1	0	0
Bournemouth	Tr	05.96	95-96	6	9	2
WATSON Mark Stewart						
Canada, 8 September, 1970 Canadian Int						(CD)
Watford	Vancouver 86ers (Can)	11.93	93-94	18	0	0
WATSON Paul Douglas						
Hastings, 4 January, 1975						(LB/M)
Gillingham	YT	12.92	92-95	57	5	2

League Club	Source	Date Signed	Seasons Played	Apps	Subs	Gls
Fulham	Tr	07.96	96-97	48	2	4
Brentford	Tr	12.97	97	25	0	0

WATSON Peter
Newcastle, 18 March, 1935 (CF)

League Club	Source	Date Signed	Seasons Played	Apps	Subs	Gls
Workington	North Shields	11.62	62-64	45	-	10

WATSON Peter Frederick
Stapleford, 15 April, 1934 (CH)

League Club	Source	Date Signed	Seasons Played	Apps	Subs	Gls
Nottingham F.	Jnrs	05.55	55-58	13	-	0
Southend U.	Tr	07.59	59-65	247	0	3

WATSON Thomas Sidney
Mansfield, 12 December, 1927 (WH)

League Club	Source	Date Signed	Seasons Played	Apps	Subs	Gls
Mansfield T.	Palterton Welfare	01.49	51-60	292	-	9

WATSON Stanley
Darlington, 17 March, 1937 (HB)

League Club	Source	Date Signed	Seasons Played	Apps	Subs	Gls
Darlington		11.57	57-58	27	-	0

WATSON Stephen Craig
North Shields, 1 April, 1974 E Yth/Eu21-12/E 'B' (M/RB)

League Club	Source	Date Signed	Seasons Played	Apps	Subs	Gls
Newcastle U.	YT	04.91	90-97	172	29	12

WATSON Thomas
Lesmahagow, 23 August, 1943 (W)

League Club	Source	Date Signed	Seasons Played	Apps	Subs	Gls
Peterborough U.	Stevenage T.	05.65	65-67	75	0	20
Walsall	Tr	09.67	67-69	84	2	17
Gillingham	Tr	06.70	70-71	43	7	7

WATSON Thomas Duncan
South Shields, 3 February, 1936 (OR)

League Club	Source	Date Signed	Seasons Played	Apps	Subs	Gls
West Bromwich A.	Boldon Colly	11.53				
Gateshead	Tr	06.57	57	21	-	5

WATSON Thomas Robert
Liverpool, 29 September, 1969 (RW)

League Club	Source	Date Signed	Seasons Played	Apps	Subs	Gls
Grimsby T.	YT	06.88	87-95	134	38	24
Hull C.	L	10.95	95	4	0	0

WATSON Trevor Peter
Great Yarmouth, 26 September, 1938 (W)

League Club	Source	Date Signed	Seasons Played	Apps	Subs	Gls
Fulham	Jnrs	07.56	56-63	17	-	1

WATSON Vaughan
Mansfield, 5 November, 1931 (CF)

League Club	Source	Date Signed	Seasons Played	Apps	Subs	Gls
Mansfield T.	Mansfield W.E.	04.52	52-53	14	-	9
Chesterfield	Tr	05.54	54	13	-	5

WATSON William
Hemsworth, 29 May, 1916 Died 1986 (RB)

League Club	Source	Date Signed	Seasons Played	Apps	Subs	Gls
Lincoln C.	Monkton Colly	02.35	34-35	9	-	0
Chesterfield	Tr	06.36	46-47	36	-	0
Rochdale	Tr	06.48	48-53	200	-	0

WATSON William
Bolton-on-Dearne, 7 March, 1920 E 'B'/E-4 (WH)

League Club	Source	Date Signed	Seasons Played	Apps	Subs	Gls
Huddersfield T.	Jnrs	10.37	38	11	-	0
Sunderland	Tr	04.46	46-53	211	-	15
Halifax T.	Tr	11.54	54-55	33	-	1

WATSON William
New Steventon, 4 December, 1949 (RB)

League Club	Source	Date Signed	Seasons Played	Apps	Subs	Gls
Manchester U.	Jnrs	12.66	70-72	11	0	0

WATSON William Thomas
Swansea, 11 June, 1918 Died 1978 (FB)

League Club	Source	Date Signed	Seasons Played	Apps	Subs	Gls
Preston N.E.		02.46	46	15	-	0
Cardiff C.	Tr	10.47	47	1	-	0

WATT John
Kilmarnock, 17 June, 1943 (OR)

League Club	Source	Date Signed	Seasons Played	Apps	Subs	Gls
Blackpool	Jnrs	08.60	62	5	-	0
Stockport Co.	Tr	07.63	63-64	55	-	4
Southport	Tr	03.65	64-65	17	1	2

WATT John Gibson
Airdrie, 23 November, 1954 (FB)

League Club	Source	Date Signed	Seasons Played	Apps	Subs	Gls
Watford	App	11.72	71	0	1	0

WATT William Douglas
Aberdeen, 6 June, 1946 (OL)

League Club	Source	Date Signed	Seasons Played	Apps	Subs	Gls
Preston N.E.	Jnrs	06.63	62-65	7	1	0

WATTERS John
Glasgow, 24 September, 1913 Died 1989 (OR)

League Club	Source	Date Signed	Seasons Played	Apps	Subs	Gls
New Brighton	Ayr U.	07.36	36	19	-	2
Stockport Co.	Cowdenbeath	08.47	47	5	-	1

WATTON James
Wolverhampton, 1 November, 1936 (LB)

League Club	Source	Date Signed	Seasons Played	Apps	Subs	Gls
Port Vale	De Graafschap (Neth)	09.62	62	5	-	0
Doncaster Rov.	Tr	07.64	64-67	121	3	0

WATTS Derek
Leicester, 30 October, 1952 (F)

League Club	Source	Date Signed	Seasons Played	Apps	Subs	Gls
Leicester C.	App	05.70				
Northampton T.	L	10.73	73	0	1	0

WATTS Grant Steven
Croydon, 5 November, 1973 (F)

League Club	Source	Date Signed	Seasons Played	Apps	Subs	Gls
Crystal Palace	YT	06.92	92	2	2	0
Colchester U.	L	01.94	93	8	4	2
Gillingham	Sheffield U. (N/C)	09.94	94	2	1	0

WATTS James Alan
Cowes (IOW), 25 October, 1933 (CF)

League Club	Source	Date Signed	Seasons Played	Apps	Subs	Gls
Gillingham (Am)		12.56	56	12	-	1

WATTS John William
Birmingham, 13 April, 1931 (WH)

League Club	Source	Date Signed	Seasons Played	Apps	Subs	Gls
Birmingham C.	Saltley O.B.	08.51	51-62	206	-	3

WATTS Julian David
Sheffield, 17 March, 1971 (CD)

League Club	Source	Date Signed	Seasons Played	Apps	Subs	Gls
Rotherham U.	Frecheville C.A.	07.90	90-91	17	3	1
Sheffield Wed.	Tr	03.92	92-95	12	4	1
Shrewsbury T.	L	12.92	92	9	0	0
Leicester C.	Tr	03.96	95-97	31	7	1
Crewe Alex.	L	08.97	97	5	0	0
Huddersfield T.	L	02.98	97	8	0	0

WATTS Mark Robert
Hatfield, 24 September, 1965 (F)

League Club	Source	Date Signed	Seasons Played	Apps	Subs	Gls
Luton T.	App	01.83	82	1	0	0

WAUGH Keith
Sunderland, 27 October, 1956 (G)

League Club	Source	Date Signed	Seasons Played	Apps	Subs	Gls
Sunderland	App	07.74				
Peterborough U.	Tr	07.76	76-80	195	0	0
Sheffield U.	Tr	08.81	81-84	99	0	0
Cambridge U.	L	11.84	84	4	0	0
Bristol C.	L	12.84	84	3	0	0
Bristol C.	Tr	07.85	85-88	167	0	0
Coventry C.	Tr	08.89	89	1	0	0
Watford	Tr	01.91	91-92	7	0	0

WAUGH Kenneth
Newcastle, 6 August, 1933 (FB)

League Club	Source	Date Signed	Seasons Played	Apps	Subs	Gls
Newcastle U.	Film Renters	08.52	55	7	-	0
Hartlepool U.	Tr	12.56	56-61	195	-	0

WAUGH William Lindsay
Edinburgh, 27 November, 1921 (OL)

League Club	Source	Date Signed	Seasons Played	Apps	Subs	Gls
Luton T.	Bathgate Thistle	09.44	46-49	135	-	9
Queens Park R.	Tr	07.50	50-52	77	-	6
Bournemouth	Tr	07.53	53	18	-	3

WAY Michael Andrew
Salisbury, 18 May, 1950 (FB)

League Club	Source	Date Signed	Seasons Played	Apps	Subs	Gls
Oxford U.	Thame U.	08.69	69-71	14	2	0

WAYMAN Charles
Bishop Auckland, 16 May, 1922 (CF)

League Club	Source	Date Signed	Seasons Played	Apps	Subs	Gls
Newcastle U.	Spennymoor U.	09.41	46-47	47	-	32
Southampton	Tr	10.47	47-49	100	-	73
Preston N.E.	Tr	09.50	50-54	157	-	104
Middlesbrough	Tr	09.54	54-55	55	-	31
Darlington	Tr	12.56	56-57	23	-	14

WAYMAN Franklyn
Bishop Auckland, 30 December, 1931 (OR)

League Club	Source	Date Signed	Seasons Played	Apps	Subs	Gls
Preston N.E.		09.53				
Chester C.	Tr	08.55	55	30	-	2
Darlington	Easington Colly	06.57	57	1	-	0

WDOWCZYK Dariusz
Poland, 21 September, 1962 Polish Int (CD)

League Club	Source	Date Signed	Seasons Played	Apps	Subs	Gls
Reading	Glasgow Celtic	08.94	94-97	77	5	0

WEAKLEY Bernard
Rotherham, 20 December, 1932 (OR)

League Club	Source	Date Signed	Seasons Played	Apps	Subs	Gls
Rotherham U.		08.55	55	2	-	1

WEALANDS Jeffrey Andrew
Darlington, 26 August, 1951 (G)

League Club	Source	Date Signed	Seasons Played	Apps	Subs	Gls
Wolverhampton W.	App	10.68				
Darlington	Tr	07.70	71	28	0	0

League Club	Source	Date Signed	Seasons Played	Apps	Subs	Gls
Hull C.	Tr	03.72	71-78	240	0	0
Birmingham C.	Tr	07.79	79-81	102	0	0
Manchester U.	Tr	02.83	82-83	7	0	0
Oldham Ath.	L	03.84	84	10	0	0
Preston N.E.	L	12.84	84	4	0	0
WEALTHALL Barry Arthur						
Nottingham, 1 May, 1942 E Yth						(FB)
Nottingham F.	Jnrs	06.59	60	2	-	0
Grimsby T.	Tr	05.62	61-62	9	-	0
York C.	Tr	06.63	63-66	75	0	0
WEARE Arthur **Jack**						
Newport, 21 September, 1912						(G)
Wolverhampton W.	Lovells Ath.	05.33	33-36	42	-	0
West Ham U.	Tr	09.36	36-37	58	-	0
Bristol Rov.	St Mirren	11.45	46-49	141	-	0
WEARE Leonard Nicholas						
Newport, 23 July, 1934						(G)
Newport Co.		08.55	55-69	525	0	0
WEARMOUTH Michael						
Barrow, 16 May, 1944						(CH)
Barrow	Jnrs	06.62	61-63	33	-	0
Preston N.E.	Tr	03.64	64-66	11	0	0
WEATHERALL Leonard						
Middlesbrough, 21 May, 1936						(CF)
Grimsby T.	Redcar B.C.	04.55	54-55	10	-	1
WEATHERHEAD Shaun						
Halifax, 3 September, 1970						(CD)
Huddersfield T.	YT	07.89				
York C.	Tr	09.90	90	6	2	0
WEATHERLY Colin **Mark**						
Ramsgate, 18 January, 1958						(CD/F)
Gillingham	App	12.75	74-88	408	49	47
WEATHERSPOON Charles William						
Newcastle, 3 October, 1929 Died 1986						(F)
Sunderland	Jnrs	08.47				
Sheffield U.	Annfield Plain	01.51	50	1	-	0
Hartlepool U.	Tr	08.52	52	3	-	2
WEATHERSTONE Simon						
Reading, 26 January, 1980						(F)
Oxford U.	YT	03.97	96-97	2	10	1
WEAVER Eric						
Rhymney, 1 July, 1943						(W)
Swindon T.	Trowbridge T.	12.61	61-66	55	0	6
Notts Co.	Tr	08.67	67	16	1	4
Northampton T.	Tr	12.67	67-69	61	2	9
WEAVER John Noel						
Wrexham, 26 November, 1924						(RB)
Wrexham	Jnrs	05.46	46	2	-	0
WEAVER Luke Dennis Spencer						
Woolwich, 26 June, 1979 E Sch/E Yth						(G)
Leyton Orient	YT	06.96	96	9	0	0
WEAVER Nicholas James						
Sheffield, 2 March, 1979						(G)
Mansfield T.	YT	•	95	1	0	0
Manchester C.	Tr	05.97				
WEAVER Samuel						
Pilsley (Dy), 8 February, 1909 Died 1985 EF Lge/E-3						(WH/IF)
Hull C.	Sutton T.	03.28	28-29	48	-	5
Newcastle U.	Tr	11.29	29-35	204	-	41
Chelsea	Tr	08.36	36-38	116	-	4
Stockport Co.	Tr	12.45	46	2	-	0
WEAVER Simon Daniel						
Doncaster, 20 December, 1977						(CD)
Sheffield Wed.	YT	05.96				
Doncaster Rov.	L	02.97	96	2	0	0
WEBB Alan Richard						
Wellington, 1 January, 1963						(D)
West Bromwich A.	App	01.80	81-83	23	1	0
Lincoln C.	L	03.84	83	11	0	0
Port Vale	Tr	08.84	84-91	187	3	2
WEBB David James						
Stratford, 9 April, 1946						(D)
Leyton Orient	West Ham U. (Am)	05.63	64-65	62	0	3

League Club	Source	Date Signed	Seasons Played	Apps	Subs	Gls
Southampton	Tr	03.66	65-67	75	0	2
Chelsea	Tr	02.68	67-73	230	0	21
Queens Park R.	Tr	07.74	74-77	116	0	7
Leicester C.	Tr	09.77	77-78	32	1	0
Derby Co.	Tr	12.78	78-79	25	1	1
Bournemouth	Tr	05.80	80-82	11	0	0
Torquay U. (N/C)	(Manager)	10.84	84	2	0	1
WEBB Douglas John						
Marlow, 10 March, 1939						(IF)
Reading		11.56	56-66	177	2	81
WEBB James Keith						
Warrington, 6 July, 1938						(F)
Shrewsbury T.	Lymm R.	04.56	55-56	2	-	1
WEBB John						
Liverpool, 10 February, 1952						(RB)
Liverpool	App	02.69				
Plymouth Arg.	L	09.73	73	4	0	0
Tranmere Rov.	Tr	07.74	74	17	3	0
WEBB Matthew Leslie						
Bristol, 24 September, 1976						(M)
Birmingham C.	YT	07.95	94	0	1	0
WEBB Neil John						
Reading, 30 July, 1963 E Yth/Eu21-3/E 'B'/EF Lge/E-26						(M)
Reading	App	11.80	79-81	65	7	22
Portsmouth	Tr	07.82	82-84	123	0	34
Nottingham F.	Tr	06.85	85-88	146	0	47
Manchester U.	Tr	06.89	89-92	70	5	8
Nottingham F.	Tr	11.92	92-93	26	4	3
Swindon T.	L	10.94	94	5	1	0
Grimsby T. (N/C)	Tr	08.96	96	3	1	0
WEBB Robert						
Normanton, 29 November, 1933						(OR)
Leeds U.	Jnrs	04.51	53-54	3	-	0
Walsall	Tr	03.55	54	9	-	3
Bradford C.	Tr	07.55	55-61	208	-	59
Torquay U.	Tr	07.62	62-63	49	-	12
WEBB Ronald Charles Thomas						
Brentford, 13 March, 1925						(WH)
Queens Park R.		10.44				
Crystal Palace	Tr	09.46	46	3	-	0
WEBB Stanley John						
Middlesbrough, 6 December, 1947						(F)
Middlesbrough		07.67	67-70	20	8	6
Carlisle U.	Tr	02.71	70-72	16	10	5
Brentford	Tr	10.72	72-73	37	2	8
Darlington	Tr	07.74	74-75	69	5	21
WEBB William						
Mexborough, 7 March, 1932						(FB)
Leicester C.	Wath W.	06.51	51-56	47	-	0
Stockport Co.	Tr	06.57	57-62	243	-	0
WEBBER Andrew						
Port Talbot, 15 March, 1963						(F)
Swansea C. (N/C)		11.84	84	0	1	0
Exeter C. (N/C)		09.85	85	1	0	0
WEBBER Damien John						
Littlehampton, 8 October, 1968						(CD)
Millwall	Bognor Regis T.	10.94	94-97	52	13	4
WEBBER Eric Victor						
Steyning, 22 December, 1919 Died 1996						(CH)
Southampton	Jnrs	03.46	46-50	182	-	0
Torquay U.	Tr	10.51	51-54	149	-	2
WEBBER George Marshall						
Abercynon, 28 June, 1925						(G)
Torquay U.	Cardiff C. (Am)	06.50	50-53	118	-	0
Northampton T.	Tr	06.54	54	13	-	0
WEBBER John Vincent						
Blackpool, 2 June, 1918 Died 1989						(CF)
Blackburn Rov.	Hyde U.	02.47	46-47	8	-	1
WEBBER Keith James						
Cardiff, 5 January, 1943 Died 1983						(CF)
Everton	Barry T.	02.60	60-61	4	-	0
Brighton & H.A.	Tr	04.63	62-64	35	-	14
Wrexham	Tr	09.64	64-65	73	0	33
Doncaster Rov.	Tr	07.66	66-68	63	4	18

League Club	Source	Date Signed	Seasons Played	Career Record Apps	Subs	Gls
Chester C.	Tr	06.69	69-70	66	8	14
Stockport Co.	Tr	07.71	71	36	4	7
WEBBER Trevor						
Bovey Tracey, 5 September, 1968						(W)
Torquay U.	YT	●	85	5	0	0
WEBSTER Alan John						
Melton Mowbray, 3 July, 1948						(WH)
Scunthorpe U.		07.66	66-67	4	2	0
WEBSTER Andrew						
Colne, 18 March, 1947						(CF)
Bradford C.	Clitheroe	07.65	65-66	10	2	1
WEBSTER John **Barry**						
Sheffield, 3 March, 1935						(OR)
Rotherham U.	Gainsborough Trin.	05.56	56-61	179	-	37
Bradford C.	Tr	06.62	62-63	53	-	9
WEBSTER Colin						
Halifax, 5 March, 1930						(RH)
Halifax T.		09.50	50	16	-	1
WEBSTER Colin						
Cardiff, 17 July, 1932 W-4						(CF)
Cardiff C.	Jnrs	05.50				
Manchester U.	Tr	05.52	53-58	65	-	26
Swansea C.	Tr	09.58	58-62	159	-	65
Newport Co.	Tr	03.63	62-63	31	-	3
WEBSTER Eric						
Manchester, 24 June, 1931						(WH)
Manchester C.		02.52	52	1	-	0
WEBSTER Harry						
Sheffield, 22 August, 1930						(IF)
Bolton W.	Jnrs	10.48	49-56	98	-	38
Chester C.	Tr	06.58	58-59	34	-	11
WEBSTER Ian Adrian						
Askern (Yks), 30 December, 1965						(CD)
Scunthorpe U.	YT	07.83	82-85	15	3	0
WEBSTER Keith						
Stockton, 6 November, 1945						(W)
Newcastle U.	Stockton	12.62				
Darlington	Tr	11.66	66	8	1	0
WEBSTER Malcolm Walter						
Doncaster, 12 November, 1950 E Sch/E Yth						(G)
Arsenal	App	01.68	69	3	0	0
Fulham	Tr	12.69	69-73	94	0	0
Southend U.	Tr	01.74	73-75	96	0	0
Cambridge U.	Tr	09.76	76-83	256	0	0
WEBSTER Richard						
Accrington, 6 August, 1919 Died 1979						(FB)
Accrington St.	Woodnook	11.37	37-38	41	-	0
Sheffield U.	Tr	01.39				
Accrington St.	Tr	08.45	46-50	186	-	3
WEBSTER Ronald						
Belper, 21 June, 1943						(RB/WH)
Derby Co.	Jnrs	06.60	61-77	451	4	7
WEBSTER Simon Paul						
Hinckley, 20 January, 1964						(CD)
Tottenham H.	App	12.81	82-83	2	1	0
Exeter C.	L	11.83	83	26	0	0
Huddersfield T.	Tr	02.85	84-87	118	0	4
Sheffield U.	Tr	03.88	87-89	26	11	3
Charlton Ath.	Tr	08.90	90-92	127	0	7
West Ham U.	Tr	07.93	94	0	5	0
Oldham Ath.	L	03.95	94	7	0	0
Derby Co.	L	08.95	95	3	0	0
WEBSTER Terence						
Retford 27 September, 1941						(WH)
Sheffield U.	Jnrs	10.58				
Accrington St.	Tr	11.59				
Barrow	Tr	07.60	60	4	-	0
WEBSTER Terence Charles						
Doncaster, 9 July, 1930						(G)
Doncaster Rov.	Jnrs	06.48				
Derby Co.	Tr	10.48	48-57	172	-	0
WEDDLE Derek Keith						
Newcastle, 27 December, 1935						(W/F)
Sunderland	Jnrs	05.53	55-56	2	-	0
Portsmouth	Tr	12.56	56-58	24	-	8
Middlesbrough	Cambridge C.	08.61	61	3	-	1
Darlington	Tr	06.62	62-63	36	-	10
York C.	Tr	07.64	64-65	44	0	13
WEDDLE George Davison						
Ashington, 24 February, 1919						(IL)
Gateshead		06.46	46-48	48	-	10
WEEKS Graham						
Exeter, 3 March, 1958						(M)
Exeter C.	App	03.76	76-77	49	4	1
Bournemouth	Tr	05.78	78	3	0	0
WEETMAN Darren Graham						
Oswestry, 7 June, 1968						(W)
Wrexham (N/C)	Jnrs	06.85	85	1	0	0
WEGERLE Roy Common						
South Africa, 19 March, 1964 USA Int						(F)
Chelsea	Tampa Bay (USA)	06.86	86-87	15	8	3
Swindon T.	L	03.88	87	7	0	1
Luton T.	Tr	07.88	88-89	39	6	10
Queens Park R.	Tr	12.89	89-91	71	4	29
Blackburn Rov.	Tr	03.92	91-92	20	14	6
Coventry C.	Tr	03.93	92-94	46	7	9
WEIGH Raymond Edward						
Flint, 23 June, 1928						(OL)
Bournemouth	Shrewsbury T.	03.49	49-50	28	-	8
Stockport Co.	Tr	07.51	51-53	75	-	29
Shrewsbury T.	Tr	06.54	54-56	107	-	43
Aldershot	Tr	07.57	57	11	-	1
WEIR Alan						
South Shields, 1 September, 1959 E Yth						(D)
Sunderland	App	05.77	77	1	0	0
Rochdale	Tr	06.79	79-82	96	10	3
Hartlepool U.	Tr	08.83	83	9	1	0
WEIR Alexander						
Longridge, 20 October, 1916						(IF)
Preston N.E.	Stoneyburn Jnrs	02.36				
Watford	Glentoran	12.45	46	1	-	0
Northampton T.	Tr	09.47				
WEIR James (Jock)						
Glasgow, 12 April, 1939						(OL)
Fulham	Clydebank	07.57	57	3	-	0
York C.	Tr	06.60	60-62	82	-	38
Mansfield T.	Tr	09.62	62	18	-	3
Luton T.	Tr	08.63	63	12	-	1
Tranmere Rov.	Tr	07.64	64	13	-	3
WEIR John Britton						
Fauldhouse, 20 October, 1923						(CF)
Blackburn Rov.	Hibernian	01.47	46-47	23	-	7
WEIR Michael Graham						
Edinburgh, 16 January, 1966						(W)
Luton T.	Hibernian	09.87	87	7	1	0
Millwall (L)	Hibernian	03.96	95	8	0	0
WEIR Peter Russell						
Johnstone, 18 January, 1958 S-6						(LW)
Leicester C.	Aberdeen	01.88	87-88	26	2	2
WEIR William Houston						
Glasgow, 11 April, 1968						(W)
Shrewsbury T.	Baillieston Jnrs	03.90	89-90	4	13	1
WELBOURNE Donald						
Scunthorpe, 12 March, 1949						(D)
Scunthorpe U.	App	03.67	66-75	250	4	5
WELBOURNE Duncan						
Scunthorpe, 28 July, 1940						(D)
Grimsby T.	Scunthorpe U. (Am)	08.57	57-63	130	-	3
Watford	Tr	11.63	63-73	404	7	22
Southport	Tr	07.74	74-75	52	1	2
WELCH Keith James						
Bolton, 3 October, 1968						(G)
Rochdale	Bolton W. (YT)	03.87	86-90	205	0	0
Bristol C.	Tr	08.91	91-97	250	0	0

WELCH Michael
Barbados (WI), 21 May, 1958 (F)

League Club	Source	Date Signed	Seasons Played	Apps	Subs	Gls
Wimbledon (N/C)	Grays Ath.	11.84	84	2	2	0
Southend U. (N/C)	Grays Ath.	02.85	84	4	0	0

WELCH Ronald
Chesterfield, 26 September, 1952 (M)

League Club	Source	Date Signed	Seasons Played	Apps	Subs	Gls
Burnley	App	10.69	70	1	0	0
Brighton & H.A.	Tr	12.73	73-74	35	1	4
Chesterfield	Tr	11.74	74-76	17	7	1

WELFORD William Frederick
Newcastle, 14 April, 1934 (RH)

League Club	Source	Date Signed	Seasons Played	Apps	Subs	Gls
Hartlepool U.	Crook T.	11.58	58	8	-	0

WELLER Christopher William
Reading, 25 December, 1939 (IF)

League Club	Source	Date Signed	Seasons Played	Apps	Subs	Gls
Bournemouth	Reading (Am)	09.59	60-64	70	-	17
Bristol Rov.	Tr	07.65	65	2	1	0
Bournemouth	Tr	01.66	65-66	39	2	9

WELLER Keith
Islington, 11 June, 1946 EF Lge/E-4 (M/W)

League Club	Source	Date Signed	Seasons Played	Apps	Subs	Gls
Tottenham H.	Jnrs	01.64	64-66	19	2	1
Millwall	Tr	06.67	67-69	121	0	40
Chelsea	Tr	05.70	70-71	34	4	14
Leicester C.	Tr	09.71	71-78	260	2	37

WELLER Paul Anthony
Brighton, 6 March, 1975 (RW)

League Club	Source	Date Signed	Seasons Played	Apps	Subs	Gls
Burnley	YT	11.93	95-97	78	17	5

WELLINGS Barry
Liverpool, 10 June, 1958 (F)

League Club	Source	Date Signed	Seasons Played	Apps	Subs	Gls
Everton	App	06.76				
York C.	Tr	06.78	78-79	40	7	9
Rochdale	Tr	07.80	80-82	111	5	30
Tranmere Rov.	Tr	02.83	82	16	0	3
Tranmere Rov. (N/C)	Northwich Vic.	12.83	83	9	0	0
Swansea C. (N/C)	Oswestry T.	09.84	84	6	0	3

WELLS Archibald
Clydebank, 4 October, 1920 (IF)

League Club	Source	Date Signed	Seasons Played	Apps	Subs	Gls
New Brighton	Hibernian	07.46	46-48	37	-	4

WELLS David Peter
Portsmouth, 29 December, 1977 NI Yth (G)

League Club	Source	Date Signed	Seasons Played	Apps	Subs	Gls
Bournemouth	YT	07.96	94	0	1	0

WELLS William David
Eccleston (Lancs), 16 December, 1940 (FB)

League Club	Source	Date Signed	Seasons Played	Apps	Subs	Gls
Blackburn Rov.	Jnrs	05.58				
Rochdale	Tr	07.63	63	8	-	0

WELLS Ian Michael
Wolverhampton, 27 October, 1964 (F)

League Club	Source	Date Signed	Seasons Played	Apps	Subs	Gls
Hereford U.	Harrisons	06.85	85-86	47	4	12

WELLS Mark Anthony
Leicester, 15 October, 1971 (M/LW)

League Club	Source	Date Signed	Seasons Played	Apps	Subs	Gls
Notts Co.	YT	07.90	91-92	0	2	0
Huddersfield T.	Tr	08.93	93	21	1	4
Scarborough	Tr	07.94	94-96	48	14	3

WELLS Peter Alan
Nottingham, 13 August, 1956 (G)

League Club	Source	Date Signed	Seasons Played	Apps	Subs	Gls
Nottingham F.	App	10.74	75-76	27	0	0
Southampton	Tr	12.76	76-82	141	0	0
Millwall	Tr	02.83	82-83	33	0	0
Leyton Orient	Tr	07.85	85-88	148	0	0

WELSH Alan
Edinburgh, 9 July, 1947 (M/F)

League Club	Source	Date Signed	Seasons Played	Apps	Subs	Gls
Millwall	Bonnyrigg Rose	07.65	65-67	3	2	0
Torquay U.	Tr	11.67	67-71	139	6	45
Plymouth Arg.	Tr	07.72	72-73	64	2	14
Bournemouth	Tr	02.74	73-74	33	2	3
Millwall	Tr	08.75	75	5	4	1

WELSH Andrew John
Fleetwood, 20 November, 1962 (F)

League Club	Source	Date Signed	Seasons Played	Apps	Subs	Gls
Blackpool	App	08.80	80	1	0	0
Bury (N/C)		07.84	85	0	1	0

WELSH Colin
Liverpool, 9 June, 1945 Died 1993 (OR)

League Club	Source	Date Signed	Seasons Played	Apps	Subs	Gls
Southport	Everton (Am)	10.63	64	1	-	0

WELSH Donald
Manchester, 25 February, 1911 Died 1990 EF Lge/E-3 (IF/CH)

League Club	Source	Date Signed	Seasons Played	Apps	Subs	Gls
Torquay U.	R.N. Devonport	02.33	32-34	79	-	4
Charlton Ath.	Tr	02.35	34-47	199	-	44

WELSH Eric
Belfast, 1 May, 1942 NIu23-1/NI-4 (OR)

League Club	Source	Date Signed	Seasons Played	Apps	Subs	Gls
Exeter C.	Distillery	09.59	59-65	105	0	19
Carlisle U.	Tr	10.65	65-68	73	2	17
Torquay U.	Tr	06.69	69-70	38	1	11
Hartlepool U.	Tr	07.71	71	13	2	2

WELSH James Patrick
Edinburgh, 21 December, 1923 (IF)

League Club	Source	Date Signed	Seasons Played	Apps	Subs	Gls
Luton T.	Tranent Jnrs	09.46				
Aldershot	Tr	06.48	48	5	-	0

WELSH Paul William
Liverpool, 10 May, 1966 E Sch (CD)

League Club	Source	Date Signed	Seasons Played	Apps	Subs	Gls
Preston N.E.	Formby	05.84	84-85	13	7	1

WELSH Peter Martin
Coatbridge, 19 July, 1959 (D)

League Club	Source	Date Signed	Seasons Played	Apps	Subs	Gls
Leicester C.	App	08.76	76-81	24	17	4

WELSH Stephen
Glasgow, 19 April, 1968 (CD)

League Club	Source	Date Signed	Seasons Played	Apps	Subs	Gls
Cambridge U.	Wimborne T.	02.90	90	0	1	0
Peterborough U.	Tr	08.91	91-94	146	0	2
Peterborough U.	Partick Thistle	07.96	96	6	0	0

WELTON Roy Patrick
Eltham, 3 May, 1928 (G)

League Club	Source	Date Signed	Seasons Played	Apps	Subs	Gls
Leyton Orient	Chislehurst	05.49	49-57	263	-	0
Queens Park R.	Tr	03.58	58	3	-	0

WENT Paul Frank
Bromley-by-Bow, 12 October, 1949 E Sch/E Yth (CD)

League Club	Source	Date Signed	Seasons Played	Apps	Subs	Gls
Leyton Orient	App	10.66	65-66	48	2	5
Charlton Ath.	Tr	06.67	67-71	160	3	15
Fulham	Tr	07.72	72-73	58	0	3
Portsmouth	Tr	12.73	73-76	92	0	5
Cardiff C.	Tr	10.76	76-78	71	1	11
Leyton Orient	Tr	09.78	78-79	45	0	3

WERGE Edwin
Sidcup, 9 September, 1936 (WH/W)

League Club	Source	Date Signed	Seasons Played	Apps	Subs	Gls
Charlton Ath.	Jnrs	05.55	57-60	44	-	19
Crystal Palace	Tr	05.61	61-64	82	-	6
Leyton Orient	Arcadia Shepherds (SA)	11.66	66-67	30	3	0

WESSON Robert William
Thornaby, 15 October, 1940 (G)

League Club	Source	Date Signed	Seasons Played	Apps	Subs	Gls
Coventry C.	Thornaby B.B.	11.58	60-65	133	0	0
Walsall	Tr	09.66	66-72	191	0	0
Doncaster Rov.	L	02.70	69	5	0	0

WEST Alan
Hyde, 18 December, 1951 Eu23-1 (M)

League Club	Source	Date Signed	Seasons Played	Apps	Subs	Gls
Burnley	App	12.68	69-72	41	4	3
Luton T.	Tr	10.73	73-80	272	13	16
Millwall	Tr	07.81	81-82	57	0	4

WEST Colin
Wallsend, 13 November, 1962 (F)

League Club	Source	Date Signed	Seasons Played	Apps	Subs	Gls
Sunderland	App	07.80	81-84	88	14	21
Watford	Tr	03.85	84-85	45	0	20
Sheffield Wed.	Glasgow Rangers	09.87	87-88	40	5	8
West Bromwich A.	Tr	02.89	88-91	64	9	22
Port Vale	L	11.91	91	5	0	1
Swansea C.	Tr	08.92	92	29	4	12
Leyton Orient	Tr	07.93	93-97	132	10	42
Northampton T.	L	09.97	97	1	1	0

WEST Colin William
Middlesbrough, 19 September, 1967 E Yth (F)

League Club	Source	Date Signed	Seasons Played	Apps	Subs	Gls
Chelsea	App	09.85	86-87	8	8	4
Swansea C.	L	03.89	88	14	0	3
Hartlepool U.	Dundee	08.93	93	29	7	5

WEST David Christopher
Leicester, 16 November, 1964 (LW)

League Club	Source	Date Signed	Seasons Played	Apps	Subs	Gls
Liverpool	Dorchester T.	03.83				
Torquay U.	Bristol C. (trial)	09.85	85	19	2	2

WEST Dean
Morley, 5 December, 1972 (RB/M)

League Club	Source	Date Signed	Seasons Played	Apps	Subs	Gls
Lincoln C.	YT	07.91	90-95	93	26	20
Bury	Tr	09.95	95-97	82	5	5

WEST Edward
Parbold (Lancs), 4 November, 1930 (FB)

League Club	Source	Date Signed	Seasons Played	Apps	Subs	Gls
Doncaster Rov.	Eastbourne U.	02.53				
Gillingham	Tr	07.54	54-56	98	-	0
Oldham Ath.	Tr	07.57	57-60	117	-	0

WEST Gary
Scunthorpe, 25 August, 1964 E Yth (CD)

League Club	Source	Date Signed	Seasons Played	Apps	Subs	Gls
Sheffield U.	App	08.82	82-84	75	0	1
Lincoln C.	Tr	08.85	85-86	83	0	4
Gillingham	Tr	07.87	87-88	51	1	3
Port Vale	Tr	02.89	88-89	14	3	1
Gillingham	L	11.90	90	1	0	0
Lincoln C.	L	01.91	90	3	0	0
Lincoln C.	Tr	08.91	91	14	4	1
Walsall	L	09.92	92	9	0	1

WEST Gordon
Darfield (Yks), 24 April, 1943 Eu23-3/E-3 (G)

League Club	Source	Date Signed	Seasons Played	Apps	Subs	Gls
Blackpool	Jnrs	05.61	60-61	31	-	0
Everton	Tr	03.62	61-72	335	0	0
Tranmere Rov.	Tr	10.75	76-78	17	0	0

WEST Paul Darrell
Stafford, 22 June, 1970 (D)

League Club	Source	Date Signed	Seasons Played	Apps	Subs	Gls
Port Vale	Alcester T.	02.91				
Bradford C.	Tr	07.92				
Wigan Ath.	Tr	08.93	93-94	2	1	0

WEST Thomas
Salford, 8 December, 1916 (F)

League Club	Source	Date Signed	Seasons Played	Apps	Subs	Gls
Stockport Co.		03.38	37-38	3	-	0
Oldham Ath.		10.45				
Rochdale	Tr	06.46	46	4	-	2

WEST Trefor John
Coventry, 14 December, 1944 (FB)

League Club	Source	Date Signed	Seasons Played	Apps	Subs	Gls
West Bromwich A.	App	05.62				
Walsall	Tr	05.64	64	12	-	0

WESTAWAY Kevin David
Bristol, 24 November, 1962 (FB)

League Club	Source	Date Signed	Seasons Played	Apps	Subs	Gls
Bristol Rov.	App	11.80	80-81	2	0	0

WESTBY Jack Leslie
Aintree, 20 May, 1917 (FB)

League Club	Source	Date Signed	Seasons Played	Apps	Subs	Gls
Blackburn Rov.	Burscough	01.37	37	2	-	0
Liverpool	Tr	05.44				
Southport	Tr	08.47	47	13	-	0

WESTCOTT Dennis
Wallasey, 2 July, 1917 Died 1960 EF Lge (CF)

League Club	Source	Date Signed	Seasons Played	Apps	Subs	Gls
New Brighton	Leasowe R.B.	01.36	35	18	-	10
Wolverhampton W.	Tr	07.36	36-47	128	-	105
Blackburn Rov.	Tr	04.48	48-49	63	-	37
Manchester C.	Tr	02.50	49-51	72	-	37
Chesterfield	Tr	06.52	52	40	-	21

WESTCOTT John Peter James
Eastbourne, 31 May, 1979 (W)

League Club	Source	Date Signed	Seasons Played	Apps	Subs	Gls
Brighton & H.A.	YT	07.97	97	19	15	0

WESTLAKE Brian
Newcastle-u-Lyme, 19 September, 1943 (CF)

League Club	Source	Date Signed	Seasons Played	Apps	Subs	Gls
Stoke C.		09.61				
Doncaster Rov.	Tr	06.63	63	5	-	1
Halifax T.	Tr	01.64	63-66	100	0	27
Tranmere Rov.	Tr	09.66	66	13	1	3
Colchester U.	Tr	02.67	66	14	1	5

WESTLAKE Francis Arthur
Bolton-on-Dearne, 11 August, 1915 (FB)

League Club	Source	Date Signed	Seasons Played	Apps	Subs	Gls
Sheffield Wed.	Thurnscoe Vic.	05.37	37-49	110	-	0
Halifax T.	Tr	06.50	50	2	-	0

WESTLAND James
Aberdeen, 21 July, 1916 Died 1972 (IL)

League Club	Source	Date Signed	Seasons Played	Apps	Subs	Gls
Stoke C.	Aberdeen	09.35	35-38	60	-	16
Mansfield T.	Tr	11.46	46	10	-	0

WESTLEY Graham Neil
Hounslow, 4 March, 1968 E Yth (F)

League Club	Source	Date Signed	Seasons Played	Apps	Subs	Gls
Gillingham	Queens Park R. (App)	03.86	85-86	1	1	0

WESTLEY Shane Lee Mark
Canterbury, 16 June, 1965 (CD)

League Club	Source	Date Signed	Seasons Played	Apps	Subs	Gls
Charlton Ath.	App	06.83	83	8	0	0
Southend U.	Tr	03.85	84-88	142	2	10
Wolverhampton W.	Tr	06.89	89-92	48	2	2
Brentford	Tr	10.92	92-94	61	3	1
Southend U.	L	02.95	94	4	1	0
Cambridge U.	Tr	08.95	95	3	0	0
Lincoln C.	Tr	10.95	95	9	0	1

WESTMORLAND Joseph Edward
Dalston (Cumb), 30 June, 1937 (FB)

League Club	Source	Date Signed	Seasons Played	Apps	Subs	Gls
Carlisle U.		02.59	58	3	-	0

WESTON Anthony Douglas
Yalding (Kt), 3 April, 1945 (FB)

League Club	Source	Date Signed	Seasons Played	Apps	Subs	Gls
Gillingham	Bromley	11.63	64-69	162	0	3

WESTON Donald Patrick
Mansfield, 6 March, 1936 (IF)

League Club	Source	Date Signed	Seasons Played	Apps	Subs	Gls
Wrexham	Kinmell Park Barracks	06.59	58-59	42	-	21
Birmingham C.	Tr	01.60	59-60	23	-	3
Rotherham U.	Tr	12.60	60-62	74	-	23
Leeds U.	Tr	12.62	62-65	68	0	24
Huddersfield T.	Tr	10.65	65-66	20	2	7
Wrexham	Tr	12.66	66-67	42	0	19
Chester C.	Tr	06.68	68	1	2	0

WESTON Ian Paul
Bristol, 6 May, 1968 (M)

League Club	Source	Date Signed	Seasons Played	Apps	Subs	Gls
Bristol Rov.	App	05.86	86-87	13	3	0
Torquay U.	Tr	09.88	88-89	62	5	2

WESTON James John
Prescot, 16 September, 1955 (M)

League Club	Source	Date Signed	Seasons Played	Apps	Subs	Gls
Blackpool	Skelmersdale U.	01.74	75-79	97	8	8
Torquay U.	Tr	06.80	80-81	38	0	1
Wigan Ath.	Tr	09.81	81-82	63	3	2

WESTON Reginald Harold
Dartford, 16 January, 1918 Died 1998 (CH)

League Club	Source	Date Signed	Seasons Played	Apps	Subs	Gls
Swansea C.	Northfleet	03.45	46-51	227	-	1

WESTWELL Simon
Clitheroe, 12 November, 1961 (FB)

League Club	Source	Date Signed	Seasons Played	Apps	Subs	Gls
Preston N.E.	App	10.79	80-82	63	0	1

WESTWOOD Ashley Michael
Bridgnorth, 31 August, 1976 E Yth (CD)

League Club	Source	Date Signed	Seasons Played	Apps	Subs	Gls
Manchester U.	YT	07.94				
Crewe Alex.	Tr	07.95	95-97	93	5	9

WESTWOOD Christopher John
Dudley, 13 February, 1977 (CD)

League Club	Source	Date Signed	Seasons Played	Apps	Subs	Gls
Wolverhampton W.	YT	07.95	97	3	1	1

WESTWOOD Daniel Robert
Dagenham, 25 July, 1953 (F)

League Club	Source	Date Signed	Seasons Played	Apps	Subs	Gls
Queens Park R.	Billericay T.	07.74	74	0	1	1
Gillingham	Tr	11.75	75-81	201	10	74

WESTWOOD Eric
Manchester, 25 September, 1917 EF Lge/E'B' (LB)

League Club	Source	Date Signed	Seasons Played	Apps	Subs	Gls
Manchester C.	Manchester U. (Am)	11.37	37-52	248	-	3

WESTWOOD Gary Michael
Barrow, 3 April, 1963 E Yth (G)

League Club	Source	Date Signed	Seasons Played	Apps	Subs	Gls
Ipswich T.	App	04.81				
Reading	L	09.83	83	5	0	0
Reading	Tr	07.84	84-87	123	0	0

WESTWOOD William Raymond
Kingswinford, 14 April, 1912 Died 1982 EF Lge/E-6 (IF)

League Club	Source	Date Signed	Seasons Played	Apps	Subs	Gls
Bolton W.	Brierley Hill Alliance	03.30	30-47	301	-	127
Chester C.	Tr	12.47	47-48	38	-	13

WETHERALL David
Sheffield, 14 March, 1971 E Sch (CD)

League Club	Source	Date Signed	Seasons Played	Apps	Subs	Gls
Sheffield Wed.	YT	07.89				
Leeds U.	Tr	07.91	91-97	174	7	12

WETTON Albert Smailes
Winlaton, 23 October, 1928 (CF)

League Club	Source	Date Signed	Seasons Played	Apps	Subs	Gls
Tottenham H.	Cheshunt	10.49				
Brighton & H.A.	Tr	06.51	51-52	3	-	0
Crewe Alex.	Tr	10.53	53	2	-	0

WETTON Ralph
Winlaton, 6 June, 1927 (WH)

League Club	Source	Date Signed	Seasons Played	Apps	Subs	Gls
Tottenham H.	Cheshunt	08.50	51-54	45	-	0
Plymouth Arg.	Tr	06.55	55	36	-	1
Aldershot	Tr	11.56	56-57	50	-	1

WHALE Raymond
West Bromwich, 23 February, 1937 (FB)

League Club	Source	Date Signed	Seasons Played	Apps	Subs	Gls
West Bromwich A.	West Bromwich C.A.	12.54				
Southend U.	Tr	04.59	59-60	29	-	0

WHALEY George
Darlington, 30 July, 1920 (CF)

League Club	Source	Date Signed	Seasons Played	Apps	Subs	Gls
Gateshead	Hearts	09.46	46	6	-	0

WHALEY Kenneth
Leeds, 22 June, 1935 (HB)

League Club	Source	Date Signed	Seasons Played	Apps	Subs	Gls
Bradford P.A.		06.57	58	1	-	0

WHALLEY Gareth
Manchester, 19 December, 1973 (M)

League Club	Source	Date Signed	Seasons Played	Apps	Subs	Gls
Crewe Alex.	YT	07.92	92-97	174	6	9

WHALLEY Harold
Nelson, 4 April, 1923 (OL)

League Club	Source	Date Signed	Seasons Played	Apps	Subs	Gls
Accrington St.	Barnoldswick T.	12.46	46	3	-	0

WHALLEY Herbert
Ashton-u-Lyne, 6 August, 1913 Died 1958 (LH)

League Club	Source	Date Signed	Seasons Played	Apps	Subs	Gls
Manchester U.	Stalybridge Celtic	05.34	35-46	32	-	0

WHALLEY Jeffrey Hugh
Rossendale, 8 February, 1952 (W)

League Club	Source	Date Signed	Seasons Played	Apps	Subs	Gls
Blackburn Rov.	App	02.70	69-70	2	0	0

WHALLEY David **Neil**
Prescot, 29 October, 1965 (M)

League Club	Source	Date Signed	Seasons Played	Apps	Subs	Gls
Preston N.E.	Warrington T.	03.93	92-94	45	5	1

WHALLEY Selwyn Davies
Stoke, 24 February, 1934 (FB)

League Club	Source	Date Signed	Seasons Played	Apps	Subs	Gls
Port Vale		08.53	56-65	178	0	7

WHARE William Frederick
Guernsey, 14 May, 1924 Died 1995 (RB)

League Club	Source	Date Signed	Seasons Played	Apps	Subs	Gls
Nottingham F.		05.47	48-59	298	-	2

WHARTON Andrew
Burnley, 21 December, 1961 (M)

League Club	Source	Date Signed	Seasons Played	Apps	Subs	Gls
Burnley	App	12.79	80-83	63	2	6
Torquay U.	L	11.83	83	10	0	0
Chester C.	Tr	02.84	83-84	19	4	2

WHARTON Guy
Darfield, 5 December, 1916 Died 1990 (WH)

League Club	Source	Date Signed	Seasons Played	Apps	Subs	Gls
Chester C.		05.34	35	12	-	5
Wolverhampton W.	Tr	05.36	36-37	29	-	2
Portsmouth	Tr	11.37	37-47	93	-	4
Darlington	Tr	07.48	48-49	39	-	2

WHARTON John (Jackie) Edwin
Bolton, 18 June, 1920 Died 1997 (W)

League Club	Source	Date Signed	Seasons Played	Apps	Subs	Gls
Plymouth Arg.	Jnrs	06.37	38	11	-	2
Preston N.E.	Tr	07.39	46	25	-	7
Manchester C.	Tr	03.47	46-47	23	-	2
Blackburn Rov.	Tr	06.48	48-52	129	-	14
Newport Co.	Tr	02.53	52-54	74	-	10

WHARTON Kenneth
Newcastle, 28 November, 1960 (LB/M)

League Club	Source	Date Signed	Seasons Played	Apps	Subs	Gls
Newcastle U.	Grainger Park B.C.	01.79	78-88	268	22	26
Carlisle U. (N/C)	Tr	08.89	89	1	0	0
Bradford C. (N/C)	Tr	08.89	89	5	0	0

WHARTON Paul William
Newcastle, 26 June, 1977 E Yth (M)

League Club	Source	Date Signed	Seasons Played	Apps	Subs	Gls
Leeds U.	YT	06.94				
Hull C.	Tr	02.96	95-97	8	3	0

WHARTON Sean Robert
Newport, 31 October, 1968 (F)

League Club	Source	Date Signed	Seasons Played	Apps	Subs	Gls
Sunderland	YT	07.87	88	1	0	0

WHARTON Terence John
Bolton, 1 July, 1942 (OR)

League Club	Source	Date Signed	Seasons Played	Apps	Subs	Gls
Wolverhampton W.	Jnrs	10.59	61-67	223	1	69
Bolton W.	Tr	11.67	67-70	101	1	28
Crystal Palace	Tr	01.71	70-71	18	2	1
Walsall	Durban C. (SA)	11.73	73	1	0	0

WHATLING Keith Richard
Stradbroke (Sfk), 1 November, 1947 (OL)

League Club	Source	Date Signed	Seasons Played	Apps	Subs	Gls
Ipswich T.	Jnrs	03.66				
Exeter C.	Tr	07.67	67-68	19	3	3

WHATMORE Neil
Ellesmere Port, 17 May, 1955 (F)

League Club	Source	Date Signed	Seasons Played	Apps	Subs	Gls
Bolton W.	App	05.73	72-80	262	15	102
Birmingham C.	Tr	08.81	81-82	24	2	6
Bolton W.	L	12.82	82	10	0	3
Oxford U.	Tr	02.83	82-83	33	3	15
Bolton W.	L	03.84	83	7	0	2
Burnley	Tr	08.84	84	8	0	1
Mansfield T.	Tr	11.84	84-86	71	1	20
Bolton W.	Tr	08.87				
Mansfield T. (N/C)	Tr	11.87	87	0	4	0

WHEAT Arthur Bradley
Selston (Nts), 26 October, 1921 (IF)

League Club	Source	Date Signed	Seasons Played	Apps	Subs	Gls
Bradford P.A.	Montrose	12.49	50-51	22	-	3
York C.	Tr	08.52	52	4	-	0

WHEATLEY Barrie
Sandbach, 21 February, 1938 (IF)

League Club	Source	Date Signed	Seasons Played	Apps	Subs	Gls
Liverpool		03.56				
Crewe Alex.	Tr	07.57	57-65	242	0	49
Rochdale	Tr	07.66	66	13	0	4

WHEATLEY Harold **Joseph**
Bromborough, 9 May, 1920 (WH)

League Club	Source	Date Signed	Seasons Played	Apps	Subs	Gls
Port Vale	Ellesmere Port	03.38	38	2	-	0
Shrewsbury T.	Tr	(N/L)	50	7	-	0

WHEATLEY Roland
Nottingham, 20 June, 1924 (WH)

League Club	Source	Date Signed	Seasons Played	Apps	Subs	Gls
Nottingham F.	Beeston B.C.	06.46	47-48	6	-	0
Southampton	Tr	01.49	48-50	10	-	1
Grimsby T.	Tr	06.51	51	5	-	0

WHEATLEY Stephen John
Bishop Auckland, 12 April, 1959 (G)

League Club	Source	Date Signed	Seasons Played	Apps	Subs	Gls
Gillingham	App	04.77	76-77	4	0	0

WHEATLEY Stephen Peter
Hinckley, 26 December, 1929 (OR)

League Club	Source	Date Signed	Seasons Played	Apps	Subs	Gls
Derby Co.	Hinckley Ath.	12.50	51-52	4	-	0
Chesterfield	Boston U.	07.55	55	3	-	0

WHEATLEY Thomas
Hebburn, 1 June, 1929 (G)

League Club	Source	Date Signed	Seasons Played	Apps	Subs	Gls
Leeds U.	Amble	04.53	53	6	-	0

WHEATLEY William
Mansfield, 5 November, 1920 (OR)

League Club	Source	Date Signed	Seasons Played	Apps	Subs	Gls
Mansfield T.	Mansfield Colly	08.48	48-49	38	-	3

WHEATON Gilbert John
Mickley, 1 November, 1941 (CH)

League Club	Source	Date Signed	Seasons Played	Apps	Subs	Gls
Grimsby T.	Mickley Colly	09.60	62	7	-	0
Chester C.	Tr	06.63	63	1	-	0

WHEELDON Thomas Edward
Prescot, 28 December, 1957 (M)

League Club	Source	Date Signed	Seasons Played	Apps	Subs	Gls
Torquay U. (N/C)	Runcorn	09.81	81	5	3	0
Torquay U. (N/C)	Falmouth	08.85	85	6	2	0

WHEELER Adam
Sheffield, 29 November, 1977 (G)

League Club	Source	Date Signed	Seasons Played	Apps	Subs	Gls
Doncaster Rov.	Newcastle U. (YT)	04.96	96	1	0	0

WHEELER Alfred John
Fareham, 6 April, 1922 (OR)

League Club	Source	Date Signed	Seasons Played	Apps	Subs	Gls
Blackburn Rov.	Portsmouth (Am)	04.47	47-48	21	-	5
Swindon T.	Tr	07.49	49-50	23	-	4

WHEELER Arthur **James**
Reading, 21 December, 1933 (IF)

League Club	Source	Date Signed	Seasons Played	Apps	Subs	Gls
Reading		08.52	52-66	404	1	144

WHEELER John Edward
Liverpool, 26 July, 1928 EF Lge/E 'B'/E-1 (WH/IF)

League Club	Source	Date Signed	Seasons Played	Apps	Subs	Gls
Tranmere Rov.	Carlton	04.46	48-50	101	-	9
Bolton W.	Tr	02.51	50-55	189	-	18
Liverpool	Tr	09.56	56-61	164	-	21

WHEELER William **John (Jack)**
Evesham, 13 July, 1919 (G)

League Club	Source	Date Signed	Seasons Played	Apps	Subs	Gls
Birmingham C.	Cheltenham T.	03.38	38-47	12	-	0
Huddersfield T.	Tr	08.48	48-55	166	-	0

WHEELER Paul
Caerphilly, 3 January, 1965 (M/F)

League Club	Source	Date Signed	Seasons Played	Apps	Subs	Gls
Bristol Rov.	App	01.83				
Cardiff C.	Aberaman	08.85	85-88	72	29	10

League Club	Source	Date Signed	Seasons Played	Apps	Subs	Gls
Hull C. (N/C)	Tr	10.89	89	0	5	0
Hereford U.	Tr	02.90	89-90	34	20	12
Stockport Co.	Tr	08.91	91-92	13	10	5
Scarborough	L	10.92	92	2	5	1
Chester C.	Tr	01.93	92-93	35	5	7

WHEELER William Hunter
Carlisle, 27 September, 1920 (WH)

League Club	Source	Date Signed	Seasons Played	Apps	Subs	Gls
Carlisle U.		10.46	46	4	-	0

WHELAN Anthony Gerard
Dublin, 23 November, 1959 IRu21-1 (FB)

League Club	Source	Date Signed	Seasons Played	Apps	Subs	Gls
Manchester U.	Bohemians	08.80	80	0	1	0

WHELAN Anthony Michael
Salford, 20 November, 1952 (LB/F)

League Club	Source	Date Signed	Seasons Played	Apps	Subs	Gls
Manchester U.	App	12.69				
Manchester C.	Tr	03.73	72-73	3	3	0
Rochdale	Tr	07.74	74-76	124	0	20

WHELAN David
Bradford, 24 November, 1936 (FB)

League Club	Source	Date Signed	Seasons Played	Apps	Subs	Gls
Blackburn Rov.	Wigan B.C.	12.53	56-59	78	-	3
Crewe Alex.	Tr	01.63	62-65	115	0	0

WHELAN Noel David
Leeds, 30 December, 1974 E Yth/Eu21-2 (F)

League Club	Source	Date Signed	Seasons Played	Apps	Subs	Gls
Leeds U.	YT	03.93	92-95	28	20	7
Coventry C.	Tr	12.95	95-97	76	1	20

WHELAN Philip James
Reddish, 7 March, 1972 Eu21-3 (CD)

League Club	Source	Date Signed	Seasons Played	Apps	Subs	Gls
Ipswich T.	Jnrs	07.90	91-94	76	6	2
Middlesbrough	Tr	04.95	95-96	18	4	1
Oxford U.	Tr	07.97	97	6	2	0

WHELAN Robert
Salford, 9 November, 1930 (RH)

League Club	Source	Date Signed	Seasons Played	Apps	Subs	Gls
Manchester C.	Salford Y.C.	04.50				
Oldham Ath.	Tr	07.52	52	1	-	0

WHELAN Ronald Andrew
Dublin, 25 September, 1961 IR Sch/IR Yth/IRu21-1/IR 'B'/IR-53 (M)

League Club	Source	Date Signed	Seasons Played	Apps	Subs	Gls
Liverpool	Home Farm	10.79	80-93	351	11	46
Southend U.	Tr	09.94	94-95	34	0	1

WHELAN Spencer Randall
Liverpool, 17 September, 1971 (D)

League Club	Source	Date Signed	Seasons Played	Apps	Subs	Gls
Chester C.	Liverpool (YT)	04.90	90-97	196	19	8

WHELAN William Augustine
Dublin, 1 April, 1935 Died 1958 IR-4 (IF)

League Club	Source	Date Signed	Seasons Played	Apps	Subs	Gls
Manchester U.	Home Farm	05.53	54-57	79	-	43

WHELLANS Robert
Harrogate, 14 February, 1969 (F)

League Club	Source	Date Signed	Seasons Played	Apps	Subs	Gls
Bradford C.	YT	06.87				
Hartlepool U.	L	12.87	87	8	3	1
Rochdale	Tr	07.89	89	5	6	1

WHENT John (Jack) Richard
Darlington, 3 May, 1920 (WH)

League Club	Source	Date Signed	Seasons Played	Apps	Subs	Gls
Brighton & H.A.	Canadian Army	08.47	47-49	101	-	4
Luton T.	Tr	08.50	50	11	-	3

WHETTER Gary
Middlesbrough, 6 September, 1963 (M)

League Club	Source	Date Signed	Seasons Played	Apps	Subs	Gls
Darlington (N/C)	Crook Town	09.86	86	3	2	1

WHIFFEN Kingsley
Welshpool, 3 December, 1950 (G)

League Club	Source	Date Signed	Seasons Played	Apps	Subs	Gls
Chelsea	App	●	66	1	0	0

WHIGHAM William Murdoch Morrison
Airdrie, 9 October, 1939 (G)

League Club	Source	Date Signed	Seasons Played	Apps	Subs	Gls
Middlesbrough	Falkirk	10.66	66-71	187	0	0
Darlington	Dumbarton	08.74	74	4	0	0

WHISTON Donald
Stoke, 4 April, 1930 (FB/IF)

League Club	Source	Date Signed	Seasons Played	Apps	Subs	Gls
Stoke C.	Jnrs	12.49	49-56	30	-	4
Crewe Alex.	Tr	02.57	56-57	52	-	6
Rochdale	Tr	05.58	58	14	-	0

WHISTON Joseph Rowland
Stoke, 5 October, 1928 (CF)

League Club	Source	Date Signed	Seasons Played	Apps	Subs	Gls
Crewe Alex.	Johnson Matthey	09.51	51-52	9	-	2

WHISTON Peter Michael
Widnes, 4 January, 1968 (CD)

League Club	Source	Date Signed	Seasons Played	Apps	Subs	Gls
Plymouth Arg.		12.87	88-89	4	6	0
Torquay U.	Tr	03.90	89-91	39	1	1
Exeter C.	Tr	09.91	91-93	85	0	7
Southampton	Tr	08.94	94	0	1	0
Shrewsbury T.	Tr	09.95	95-96	54	1	3

WHITAKER Colin
Leeds, 14 June, 1932 (OL)

League Club	Source	Date Signed	Seasons Played	Apps	Subs	Gls
Sheffield Wed.	Leeds U. (Jnr)	11.51	51	1	-	0
Bradford P.A.	Tr	06.53	53-55	49	-	10
Shrewsbury T.	Tr	06.56	56-60	152	-	59
Queens Park R.	Tr	02.61	60	8	-	0
Rochdale	Tr	05.61	61-62	54	-	11
Oldham Ath.	Tr	10.62	62-63	72	-	29
Barrow	Tr	08.64	64	12	-	0

WHITAKER William
Chesterfield, 7 October, 1923 Died 1995 EF Lge (CH)

League Club	Source	Date Signed	Seasons Played	Apps	Subs	Gls
Chesterfield	Tapton S.O.B.	08.42	46	13	-	0
Middlesbrough	Tr	06.47	47-54	177	-	1

WHITBREAD Adrian Richard
Epping, 22 October, 1971 (CD)

League Club	Source	Date Signed	Seasons Played	Apps	Subs	Gls
Leyton Orient	YT	11.89	89-92	125	0	2
Swindon T.	Tr	07.93	93-94	35	1	1
West Ham U.	Tr	08.94	94-95	3	7	0
Portsmouth	L	11.95	95	13	0	0
Portsmouth	Tr	10.96	96-97	62	0	1

WHITBY Brian Kenneth
Luton, 21 February, 1939 (W)

League Club	Source	Date Signed	Seasons Played	Apps	Subs	Gls
Luton T.	Hitchin T.	05.57	57-58	7	-	1

WHITCHURCH Charles Henry
Grays, 29 October, 1920 Died 1977 E Sch (W)

League Club	Source	Date Signed	Seasons Played	Apps	Subs	Gls
West Ham U.	Portsmouth (Am)	05.45				
Tottenham H.	Tr	01.46	46	8	-	2
Southend U.	Tr	07.47	47	17	-	5

WHITE Alan
Darlington, 22 March, 1976 (CD)

League Club	Source	Date Signed	Seasons Played	Apps	Subs	Gls
Middlesbrough	YT	07.94				
Luton T.	Tr	09.97	97	26	2	1

WHITE Alexander
Lasswade, 28 January, 1916 (RB)

League Club	Source	Date Signed	Seasons Played	Apps	Subs	Gls
Chelsea	Bonnyrigg Rose	02.37	46-47	17	-	0
Swindon T.	Tr	07.48	48-49	35	-	0
Southport	Tr	07.50	50	3	-	0

WHITE Andrew Charles John
Newport, 6 November, 1948 (OL)

League Club	Source	Date Signed	Seasons Played	Apps	Subs	Gls
Newport Co.	Caerleon	08.69	69-76	225	28	25

WHITE Antony John
Colchester, 3 November, 1966 (D)

League Club	Source	Date Signed	Seasons Played	Apps	Subs	Gls
Bournemouth (N/C)	Dorchester T.	07.85	85	1	0	0

WHITE Archibald
Dumbarton, 16 January, 1959 (M)

League Club	Source	Date Signed	Seasons Played	Apps	Subs	Gls
Oxford U.	App	01.76	76-79	10	14	1

WHITE Arnie
Bristol, 25 July, 1924 (IR)

League Club	Source	Date Signed	Seasons Played	Apps	Subs	Gls
Bristol C.	Soundwell	03.47	46-50	82	-	12
Millwall	Tr	08.51	51-52	14	-	0

WHITE Barry James
Beverley, 30 July, 1950 (G)

League Club	Source	Date Signed	Seasons Played	Apps	Subs	Gls
Hull C.	App	08.68				
Halifax T.	Tr	11.70	71-74	23	0	0

WHITE Christopher Jason
Chatham, 11 December, 1970 (RB)

League Club	Source	Date Signed	Seasons Played	Apps	Subs	Gls
Portsmouth	YT	07.89				
Peterborough U.	Tr	05.91	91-92	10	3	0
Doncaster Rov.	L	01.93	92	6	0	0
Exeter C.	Tr	03.93	92-93	18	1	0

WHITE Dale
Sunderland, 17 March, 1968 E Sch (F)

League Club	Source	Date Signed	Seasons Played	Apps	Subs	Gls
Sunderland	App	03.86	85	2	2	0
Peterborough U.	L	12.87	87	14	0	4

WHITE David
Manchester, 30 October, 1967 E Yth/Eu21-6/E 'B'/E-1 (W/F)

League Club	Source	Date Signed	Seasons Played	Apps	Subs	Gls
Manchester C.	YT	10.85	86-93	273	12	79

League Club	Source	Date Signed	Seasons Played	Career Record Apps	Subs	Gls
Leeds U.	Tr	12.93	93-95	28	14	9
Sheffield U.	Tr	11.95	95-97	55	11	13
WHITE Dean						
Hastings, 4 December, 1958						(M)
Gillingham	Chelsea (App)	07.78	78-82	108	8	26
Millwall	Tr	03.83	82-83	41	0	4
WHITE Dennis						
Hartlepool, 10 November, 1948						(FB)
Hartlepool U.		11.67	67-72	55	3	0
WHITE Devon Winston						
Nottingham, 2 March, 1964						(F)
Lincoln C.	Arnold	12.84	84-85	21	8	4
Bristol Rov.	Boston U.	08.87	87-91	190	12	53
Cambridge U.	Tr	03.92	91-92	15	7	4
Queens Park R.	Tr	01.93	92-94	16	10	9
Notts Co.	Tr	12.94	94-95	34	6	15
Watford	Tr	02.96	95-96	28	10	7
Notts Co.	Tr	03.97	96-97	11	4	2
Shrewsbury T.	Tr	09.97	97	30	2	10
WHITE Edward						
Crewe, 22 November, 1956						(F)
Crewe Alex. (N/C)		11.78	78	1	0	0
WHITE Edward Richard						
Musselburgh, 13 April, 1935						(CF)
Bradford C.	Falkirk	10.59	59	4	-	1
WHITE Frederick						
Wolverhampton, 5 December, 1916						(G)
Everton		05.35				
Sheffield U.	Tr	05.37	47-49	44	-	0
Lincoln C.	Tr	06.50	50	42	-	0
WHITE Gwilym David						
Doncaster, 23 February, 1936						(FB)
Oldham Ath. (Am)	Plymouth Arg. (Am)	08.60	60	1	-	0
WHITE Howard Kenneth						
Stretford, 2 March, 1954						(D)
Manchester C.	App	05.71	70	1	0	0
WHITE Ian Samuel						
Glasgow, 20 December, 1935						(WH)
Leicester C.	Glasgow Celtic	05.58	59-61	47	-	1
Southampton	Tr	06.62	62-66	60	1	5
WHITE James						
Poole, 13 June, 1942 E Yth						(CH)
Bournemouth (Am)	Jnrs	04.58	57	1	-	0
Portsmouth	Jnrs	06.59	58-61	34	-	6
Gillingham	Tr	06.63	63-65	65	0	1
Bournemouth	Tr	07.66	66-69	176	0	7
Cambridge U.	Tr	12.70	70-71	28	2	2
WHITE Jason Gregory						
Meriden, 19 October, 1971						(F)
Scunthorpe U.	Derby Co. (N/C)	09.91	91-93	44	24	16
Darlington	L	08.93	93	4	0	1
Scarborough	Tr	12.93	93-94	60	3	20
Northampton T.	Tr	06.95	95-96	55	22	18
Rotherham U.	Tr	09.97	97	26	1	12
WHITE John (Jack)						
Doncaster, 17 March, 1924						(CH/F)
Aldershot	Sheffield F.C.	07.44	46-52	209	-	25
Bristol C.	Tr	10.52	52-57	216	-	11
WHITE John Anderson						
Musselburgh, 28 April, 1937 Died 1964 Su23-1/SF Lge/EF Lge/S-22						(IF)
Tottenham H.	Falkirk	10.59	59-63	183	-	40
WHITE Kenneth						
Selby, 15 March, 1922						(RH)
Hull C.	Selby T.	12.47	48	1	-	0
WHITE Kevin Nicholas						
Poole, 26 June, 1948						(W)
Bournemouth	App	08.66	66-68	45	3	4
WHITE Leonard Roy						
Skellow (Yks), 23 March, 1930 Died 1994 EF Lge						(CF)
Rotherham U.	Upton Colly	05.48	50-52	43	-	15
Newcastle U.	Tr	02.53	52-61	244	-	142
Huddersfield T.	Tr	02.62	61-64	102	-	37
Stockport Co.	Tr	01.65	64-65	53	0	24

League Club	Source	Date Signed	Seasons Played	Career Record Apps	Subs	Gls
WHITE Lewis						
Stoke, 2 August, 1927 Died 1982						(OR)
Port Vale		10.48	48	1	-	0
WHITE Malcolm						
Wolverhampton, 24 April, 1941						(G)
Grimsby T.	Wolverhampton W. (Am)	08.58	58-62	65	-	0
Walsall	Tr	08.63	63	28	-	0
Lincoln C.	Tr	07.64	64	27	-	0
Bradford C.	Tr	07.65	65	9	0	0
Halifax T.	Tr	11.65	65-67	100	0	0
WHITE Mark Ivan						
Sheffield, 26 October, 1958						(FB/M)
Reading	Sheffield U. (App)	03.77	77-87	265	13	11
WHITE Maurice Henry						
Keadby, 29 January, 1938						(FB)
Doncaster Rov.		04.56	57-60	56	-	0
WHITE Philip George John						
Fulham, 29 December, 1930						(OR)
Leyton Orient	Wealdstone	07.53	53-63	217	-	28
WHITE Raymond						
Ely, 5 February, 1941						(WH)
Millwall	Jnrs	08.58	58	2	-	0
Stoke C.	Tr	07.60				
WHITE Raymond Bernard William						
Bootle, 13 August, 1918 Died 1988						(WH)
Bradford P.A.	Tottenham H. (Am)	05.46	46-50	151	-	3
WHITE Raymond Sidney						
Rochford, 14 January, 1948						(G)
Southend U.	App	01.66	63-67	10	0	0
Bristol Rov.	Tr	07.68	68	3	0	0
WHITE Richard (Dick)						
Scunthorpe, 18 August, 1931						(CH)
Scunthorpe U.	Scunthorpe S.C.	(N/L)	50-55	133	-	7
Liverpool	Tr	11.55	55-61	203	-	0
Doncaster Rov.	Tr	07.62	62-63	82	-	0
WHITE Ronald Thomas						
Bethnal Green, 9 November, 1931 Died 1994						(IF)
Charlton Ath.	Maccabi Sports	03.54	53-61	165	-	8
WHITE Stephen James						
Chipping Sodbury, 2 January, 1959 E Sch						(F)
Bristol Rov.	Mangotsfield U.	07.77	77-79	46	4	20
Luton T.	Tr	12.79	79-81	63	9	25
Charlton Ath.	Tr	07.82	82	29	0	12
Lincoln C.	L	01.83	82	2	1	0
Luton T.	L	02.83	82	4	0	0
Bristol Rov.	Tr	08.83	83-85	89	12	24
Swindon T.	Tr	07.86	86-93	200	44	83
Hereford U.	Tr	08.94	94-95	70	6	44
Cardiff C.	Tr	08.96	96-97	44	23	15
WHITE Thomas						
Musselburgh, 12 August, 1939						(CF)
Crystal Palace	Aberdeen	06.66	66-67	37	2	13
Blackpool	Tr	03.68	67-69	34	0	9
Bury	Tr	06.70	70-71	46	2	13
Crewe Alex.	Tr	12.71	71	4	0	0
WHITE Thomas						
High Hold (Dm), 10 November, 1924						(IF)
Sunderland	Chester Moor Jnrs	04.45	46	2	-	1
WHITE Thomas Matthew						
Bristol, 26 January, 1976						(CD)
Bristol Rov.	YT	07.94	94-97	44	7	1
WHITE William						
Clackmannan, 25 September, 1932						(G)
Accrington St.	Motherwell	08.53	53	18	-	0
Mansfield T.	Tr	05.54	54	3	-	0
Derby Co.	L	08.55	55	3	-	0
WHITE William Henry						
Liverpool, 13 October, 1936						(IF)
Burnley		01.54	57-59	9	-	4
Wrexham	Tr	03.61	60	8	-	0
Chester C.	Tr	07.61	61	13	-	3
WHITE Eric **Winston**						
Leicester, 26 October, 1958						(RW)
Leicester C.	App	10.76	76-78	10	2	1

League Club	Source	Date Signed	Seasons Played	Apps	Subs	Gls
Hereford U.	Tr	03.79	78-82	169	6	21
Chesterfield (N/C)	Hong Kong	09.83	83	0	1	0
Port Vale (N/C)	Tr	10.83	83	0	1	0
Stockport Co. (N/C)	Tr	11.83	83	4	0	0
Bury	Tr	12.83	83-86	125	0	11
Rochdale	L	10.86	86	4	0	0
Colchester U.	Tr	02.87	86-88	64	1	8
Burnley	Tr	10.88	88-90	93	11	14
West Bromwich A.	Tr	03.91	90-91	13	3	1
Bury (N/C)	Tr	10.92	92	1	1	0
Doncaster Rov. (N/C)	Tr	01.93	92	4	0	2
Carlisle U. (N/C)	Tr	02.93	92	6	0	0
Wigan Ath. (N/C)	Tr	03.93	92	10	0	2

WHITEAR John Michael
Isleworth, 31 May, 1935 E Yth (IF)

League Club	Source	Date Signed	Seasons Played	Apps	Subs	Gls
Aston Villa	Walton & Hersham	04.53				
Crystal Palace	Tr	05.56	56	5	-	1

WHITEFOOT Jeffrey
Cheadle, 31 December, 1933 E Sch/Eu23-1 (WH)

League Club	Source	Date Signed	Seasons Played	Apps	Subs	Gls
Manchester U.	Jnrs	12.51	49-55	93	-	0
Grimsby T.	Tr	11.57	57	26	-	5
Nottingham F.	Tr	07.58	58-67	255	0	5

WHITEHALL Steven Christopher
Bromborough, 8 December, 1966 (F)

League Club	Source	Date Signed	Seasons Played	Apps	Subs	Gls
Rochdale	Southport	07.91	91-96	212	26	75
Mansfield T.	Tr	08.97	97	42	1	24

WHITEHEAD Alan
Bury, 20 November, 1956 (CD)

League Club	Source	Date Signed	Seasons Played	Apps	Subs	Gls
Bury	Darwen	12.77	77-80	98	1	13
Brentford	Tr	08.81	81-83	101	1	4
Scunthorpe U.	Tr	01.84	83-86	106	2	8
York C.	Tr	10.86	86-87	40	1	1
Wigan Ath.	L	03.87	86	2	0	0
Halifax T.	Tr	08.88	88	10	1	1

WHITEHEAD Alan John
Birmingham, 3 September, 1951 (CD)

League Club	Source	Date Signed	Seasons Played	Apps	Subs	Gls
Birmingham C.	App	07.69	71-72	4	0	0

WHITEHEAD Barry
Sheffield, 3 December, 1946 (IF)

League Club	Source	Date Signed	Seasons Played	Apps	Subs	Gls
Chesterfield		07.65	65	5	1	1

WHITEHEAD Clive Robert
Birmingham, 24 November, 1955 E Yth (M/FB)

League Club	Source	Date Signed	Seasons Played	Apps	Subs	Gls
Bristol C.	Northfield Jnrs	08.73	73-81	209	20	10
West Bromwich A.	Tr	11.81	81-86	157	11	6
Wolverhampton W.	L	01.86	85	2	0	0
Portsmouth	Tr	06.87	87-88	57	8	2
Exeter C.	Tr	07.89	89-90	44	2	5

WHITEHEAD Norman John
Liverpool, 22 April, 1948 (W)

League Club	Source	Date Signed	Seasons Played	Apps	Subs	Gls
Southport	Skelmersdale U.	12.67	67	7	1	0
Rochdale	Tr	07.68	68-71	154	2	11
Rotherham U.	Tr	03.72	71-72	29	4	2
Chester C.	Tr	08.73	73-75	66	8	5
Grimsby T.	Tr	08.76	76	3	1	0

WHITEHEAD Philip Matthew
Halifax, 17 December, 1969 (G)

League Club	Source	Date Signed	Seasons Played	Apps	Subs	Gls
Halifax T.	YT	06.88	86-89	42	0	0
Barnsley	Tr	03.90	91-92	16	0	0
Halifax T.	L	03.91	90	9	0	0
Scunthorpe U.	L	11.91	91	8	0	0
Scunthorpe U.	L	09.92	92	8	0	0
Bradford C.	L	11.92	92	6	0	0
Oxford U.	Tr	11.93	93-97	186	0	0

WHITEHEAD Robert
Ashington, 22 September, 1936 (FB)

League Club	Source	Date Signed	Seasons Played	Apps	Subs	Gls
Newcastle U.	Fatfield Ath.	12.54	57-59	20	-	0
Darlington	Cambridge C.	08.62	62-63	53	-	0

WHITEHEAD Scott Anthony
Doncaster, 20 April, 1974 (W)

League Club	Source	Date Signed	Seasons Played	Apps	Subs	Gls
Chesterfield	YT	07.92	91-92	4	5	0

WHITEHEAD William George
Maltby, 6 February, 1920 (OL)

League Club	Source	Date Signed	Seasons Played	Apps	Subs	Gls
Queens Park R.	Maltby Colly	08.39				
Aldershot	Tr	08.47	47	6	-	1

WHITEHOUSE Brian
West Bromwich, 8 September, 1935 (IF)

League Club	Source	Date Signed	Seasons Played	Apps	Subs	Gls
West Bromwich A.	Jnrs	10.52	55-59	37	-	13
Norwich C.	Tr	03.60	59-61	41	-	14
Wrexham	Tr	03.62	61-63	45	-	19
Crystal Palace	Tr	11.63	63-65	82	0	17
Charlton Ath.	Tr	03.66	65	13	0	1
Leyton Orient	Tr	07.66	66-67	52	0	6

WHITEHOUSE Dane Lee
Sheffield, 14 October, 1970 (LM)

League Club	Source	Date Signed	Seasons Played	Apps	Subs	Gls
Sheffield U.	YT	07.89	88-97	204	27	38

WHITEHOUSE Dean
Mexborough, 30 October, 1963 (M)

League Club	Source	Date Signed	Seasons Played	Apps	Subs	Gls
Barnsley	App	10.81	83	1	1	0
Torquay U.	Tr	08.84	84	7	2	0

WHITEHOUSE James
West Bromwich, 19 September, 1934 (IF)

League Club	Source	Date Signed	Seasons Played	Apps	Subs	Gls
West Bromwich A.	Jnrs	11.54				
Reading	Tr	06.56	56-61	203	-	61
Coventry C.	Tr	08.62	62-63	46	-	12
Millwall	Tr	03.64	63-64	38	-	13

WHITEHOUSE James Edward
West Bromwich, 19 September, 1924 (IF)

League Club	Source	Date Signed	Seasons Played	Apps	Subs	Gls
West Bromwich A.	Hawthorns	05.48				
Walsall	Tr	06.49	49	20	-	8
Rochdale	Tr	07.50	50-51	46	-	13
Carlisle U.	Tr	10.51	51-56	198	-	100

WHITEHOUSE Philip
Wolverhampton, 23 March, 1971 (LB)

League Club	Source	Date Signed	Seasons Played	Apps	Subs	Gls
West Bromwich A.	YT	07.89				
Walsall	Tr	12.89	89-90	10	2	0

WHITEHURST Walter
Manchester, 7 June, 1934 (WH)

League Club	Source	Date Signed	Seasons Played	Apps	Subs	Gls
Manchester U.	Jnrs	05.52	55	1	-	0
Chesterfield	Tr	11.56	56-59	91	-	2
Crewe Alex.	Tr	07.60	60	3	-	1

WHITEHURST William
Thurnscoe, 10 June, 1959 (F)

League Club	Source	Date Signed	Seasons Played	Apps	Subs	Gls
Hull C.	Mexborough T.	10.80	80-85	176	17	47
Newcastle U.	Tr	12.85	85-86	28	0	7
Oxford U.	Tr	10.86	86-87	36	4	4
Reading	Tr	02.88	87-88	17	0	8
Sunderland	Tr	09.88	88	17	0	3
Hull C.	Tr	12.88	88-89	36	0	5
Sheffield U.	Tr	02.90	89-90	12	10	2
Stoke C.	L	11.90	90	3	0	0
Doncaster Rov.	Tr	02.91	90-91	22	0	1
Crewe Alex.	Tr	01.92	91	4	6	0

WHITELAW George
Paisley, 1 January, 1937 S Amat (CF)

League Club	Source	Date Signed	Seasons Played	Apps	Subs	Gls
Sunderland	St Johnstone	02.58	57-58	5	-	0
Queens Park R.	Tr	03.59	58-59	26	-	10
Halifax T.	Tr	10.59	59-60	52	-	22
Carlisle U.	Tr	02.61	60-61	34	-	10
Stockport Co.	Tr	01.62	61-62	52	-	18
Barrow	Tr	08.63	63	7	-	0

WHITELEY Albert
Sheffield, 13 July, 1932 (OL)

League Club	Source	Date Signed	Seasons Played	Apps	Subs	Gls
Leyton Orient	Sheffield Wed. (Am)	11.52	52-53	23	-	3

WHITELEY Andrew Mark
Sowerby Bridge, 1 August, 1961 (M)

League Club	Source	Date Signed	Seasons Played	Apps	Subs	Gls
Halifax T.		08.79	79-81	20	16	1

WHITELOCK Arthur
Stockton, 31 July, 1931 (RB)

League Club	Source	Date Signed	Seasons Played	Apps	Subs	Gls
Hartlepool U.	South Bank	12.50	50	6	-	0

WHITELUM Clifford
Farnworth, 2 December, 1919 (CF)

League Club	Source	Date Signed	Seasons Played	Apps	Subs	Gls
Sunderland	Bentley Colly	12.38	38-47	43	-	18
Sheffield Wed.	Tr	10.47	47-48	41	-	15

WHITESIDE Arnold
Garstang, 6 November, 1911 Died 1994 (WH)

League Club	Source	Date Signed	Seasons Played	Apps	Subs	Gls
Blackburn Rov.	Wood Plumpton	01.33	32-48	218	-	3

WHITESIDE Charles William Parker
Liverpool, 16 August, 1927 Died 1988 (IF)

League Club	Source	Date Signed	Seasons Played	Apps	Subs	Gls
Swindon T.		12.48	49	1	-	0

WHITESIDE Edward Kenneth
Liverpool, 11 December, 1929 (IF)

League Club	Source	Date Signed	Seasons Played	Apps	Subs	Gls
Preston N.E.	British Eckna	05.52				

League Club	Source	Date Signed	Seasons Played	Career Record Apps	Subs	Gls
Chesterfield	British Eckna	05.53	53	9	-	3
York C.	Tr	05.54	54	8	-	0
Bournemouth	Tr	07.55	55	1	-	0
WHITESIDE Norman						
Belfast, 7 May, 1965 NI Sch/NI-38						(M/F)
Manchester U.	App	07.82	81-88	193	13	47
Everton	Tr	07.89	89-90	27	2	9
WHITESIDE William Richard						
Belfast, 24 September, 1935						(OR)
Exeter C.	Portadown	11.55	55	3	-	1
Scunthorpe U.	Portadown	08.56	56	2	-	0
Rotherham U.	Tr	12.56				
WHITFIELD George Allan						
Penrith, 10 February, 1934						(FB)
Carlisle U.		11.55	56	1	-	0
WHITFIELD James						
Hull, 18 May, 1919 Died 1984						(F)
Grimsby T.	Humber U.	05.46	46-48	29	-	7
Scunthorpe U.	Tr	04.49	50	16	-	6
Southport	Tr	08.51	51	12	-	0
Scunthorpe U.	Tr	02.52	51-54	104	-	25
WHITFIELD John Spoor						
Gateshead, 10 June, 1938						(FB)
Gateshead		07.59	59	1	-	1
WHITFIELD Kenneth						
Spennymoor, 24 March, 1930 Died 1995						(CH)
Wolverhampton W.	Shildon Colly	12.47	51-52	9	-	3
Manchester C.	Tr	03.53	52-53	13	-	3
Brighton & H.A.	Tr	07.54	54-58	175	-	4
Queens Park R.	Tr	07.59	59-60	19	-	3
WHITFIELD Michael						
Sunderland, 17 October, 1962						(CD)
Sunderland	App	10.80	82	3	0	0
Hartlepool U.	Tr	08.83	83	15	1	0
WHITFIELD Robert						
Bywell, 30 June, 1920						(D)
Charlton Ath.	Prudhoe	05.39				
Torquay U.	Tr	02.47	46-49	11	-	1
WHITFIELD Wilfred						
Chesterfield, 17 November, 1916						(WH)
Bristol Rov.	Worksop T.	07.38	38-46	26	-	1
Torquay U.		08.49	49-50	47	-	1
WHITHAM Jack						
Burnley, 8 December, 1946 Eu23-1						(F)
Sheffield Wed.	Holy Trinity F.C.	11.64	66-69	54	9	27
Liverpool	Tr	05.70	70-71	15	0	7
Cardiff C.	Tr	01.74	73-74	12	2	3
Reading	Tr	07.75	75	13	6	3
WHITHAM Terence						
Sheffield, 14 August, 1935						(WH)
Sheffield Wed.	Jnrs	09.52	56-58	4	-	0
Chesterfield	Tr	06.61	61-63	66	-	3
WHITINGTON Craig						
Brighton, 3 September, 1970						(F)
Scarborough	Crawley T.	11.93	93	26	1	10
Huddersfield T.	Tr	08.94	94	1	0	0
Rochdale	L	11.94	94	1	0	0
WHITINGTON Eric Richard						
Brighton, 18 September, 1946 E Yth						(IF)
Brighton & H.A.	Chelsea (Am)	10.64	65-67	26	6	8
WHITLEY James						
Zambia, 14 April, 1975 NI-1						(M)
Manchester C.	Jnrs	08.94	97	17	2	0
WHITLEY Jeffrey						
Zambia, 28 January, 1979 NIu21-3/NI 'B'/NI-3						(M)
Manchester C.	YT	02.96	96-97	26	14	2
WHITLOCK Mark						
Portsmouth, 14 March, 1961						(CD)
Southampton	App	03.79	81-85	55	6	1
Grimsby T.	L	10.82	82	7	1	0
Aldershot	L	03.83	82	14	0	0
Bournemouth	Tr	07.86	86-88	98	1	1
Reading	Tr	12.88	88-89	26	1	0
Aldershot	Tr	08.90	90	28	1	2

League Club	Source	Date Signed	Seasons Played	Career Record Apps	Subs	Gls
WHITLOCK Philip John						
Llanhilleth (Mon), 1 May, 1930						(WH)
Cardiff C.		02.49				
Chester C.	Tr	08.50	50-58	142	-	3
WHITLOW Michael William						
Northwich, 13 January, 1968						(LB/M)
Leeds U.	Witton A.	11.88	88-91	62	15	4
Leicester C.	Tr	03.92	91-96	141	6	8
Bolton W.	Tr	09.97	97	13	0	0
WHITMARSH Paul						
Beckenham, 18 September, 1973						(F)
West Ham U.	YT	07.92				
Doncaster Rov.	Tr	09.93	93	2	4	1
WHITNALL Brian						
Adwick-le-Street, 25 May, 1933						(FB)
Hull C.	Jnrs	06.50	54	2	-	0
Scunthorpe U.	Tr	05.56	56-57	2	-	0
Exeter C.	Tr	07.58	58-61	36	-	0
WHITNEY Jonathan David						
Nantwich, 23 December, 1970						(LB)
Huddersfield T.	Winsford U.	10.93	93-95	17	1	0
Wigan Ath.	L	03.95	94	12	0	0
Lincoln C.	Tr	10.95	95-97	85	3	6
WHITTAKER Frederick						
Canada, 12 October, 1923						(CF)
Notts Co.	Vancouver (Can)	08.46	46	10	-	2
WHITTAKER Raymond Henry						
Bow, 15 January, 1945 E Sch/E Yth						(W)
Arsenal	Jnrs	05.62				
Luton T.	Tr	03.64	63-68	169	1	40
Colchester U.	Tr	07.69	69-70	41	4	7
WHITTAKER Richard (Dick)						
Dublin, 10 October, 1934 IR 'B'/IR-1						(FB)
Chelsea	St Mary's B.C.	05.52	55-59	48	-	0
Peterborough U.	Tr	09.60	60-62	82	-	0
Queens Park R.	Tr	07.63	63	17	-	0
WHITTAKER Stuart						
Liverpool, 2 January, 1975						(W)
Bolton W.	Liverpool (YT)	05.93	93-94	2	1	0
Wigan Ath.	L	08.96	96	2	1	0
Macclesfield T.	Tr	08.97	97	29	2	4
WHITTAKER William Paul						
Charlton, 20 December, 1922 Died 1977 E Sch						(CH)
Charlton Ath.	Arsenal (Am)	02.40	46-48	28	-	0
Huddersfield T.	Tr	11.48	48-49	43	-	0
Crystal Palace	Tr	06.50	50	35	-	1
WHITTAM Ernest Alfred						
Wealdstone, 7 January, 1911						(IF)
Huddersfield T.	Jnrs	11.28	29-32	19	-	4
Chester C.	Tr	05.33	33-34	54	-	20
Wolverhampton W.	Tr	02.36	35	1	-	0
Bournemouth	Tr	05.36	36-38	107	-	28
Reading	Tr	06.39				
Rotherham U.	Tr	04.45	46	1	-	0
WHITTINGHAM Alfred						
Normanton, 19 June, 1914 Died 1993						(IF)
Bradford C.	Altofts	10.36	36-46	87	-	24
Huddersfield T.	Tr	02.47	46-48	67	-	17
Halifax T.	Tr	03.49	48-49	39	-	9
WHITTINGHAM Guy						
Evesham, 10 November, 1964						(F)
Portsmouth	Yeovil T.	06.89	89-92	149	11	88
Aston Villa	Tr	08.93	93-94	17	8	5
Wolverhampton W.	L	02.94	93	13	0	8
Sheffield Wed.	Tr	12.94	94-97	89	22	22
WHITTINGHAM Stephen Paul						
Wallasey, 4 February, 1962						(F)
Tranmere Rov.	App	02.80	78-80	0	2	0
WHITTLE Alan						
Liverpool, 10 March, 1950 E Sch/E Yth/Eu23-1						(F/M)
Everton	App	07.65	67-72	72	2	21
Crystal Palace	Tr	12.72	72-75	103	5	19
Leyton Orient	Tr	09.76	76-79	47	3	6
Bournemouth (N/C)	Iran	01.81	80	8	1	0

WHITTLE Ernest
Stanley, 25 November, 1925 (IF)

League Club	Source	Date Signed	Seasons Played	Apps	Subs	Gls
Newcastle U.	South Moor Jnrs	11.44				
Lincoln C.	West Stanley	01.50	49-53	145	-	62
Workington	Tr	03.54	53-56	112	-	45
Chesterfield	Tr	11.56	56	15	-	4
Bradford P.A.	Tr	08.57	57	18	-	6

WHITTLE Graham
Liverpool, 30 May, 1953 (F)

League Club	Source	Date Signed	Seasons Played	Apps	Subs	Gls
Wrexham	Jnrs	07.71	70-80	288	18	91

WHITTLE James Archibald
Hamilton, 5 September, 1929 (CF)

League Club	Source	Date Signed	Seasons Played	Apps	Subs	Gls
Southampton (L)	Hearts	01.54	53	2	-	0

WHITTLE Justin Phillip
Derby, 18 March, 1971 (CD)

League Club	Source	Date Signed	Seasons Played	Apps	Subs	Gls
Stoke C.	Glasgow Celtic	10.94	95-97	57	8	0

WHITTLE Maurice
Wigan, 15 July, 1948 (LB)

League Club	Source	Date Signed	Seasons Played	Apps	Subs	Gls
Blackburn Rov.	App	07.66	68	5	2	0
Oldham Ath.	Tr	05.69	69-76	307	5	39
Wigan Ath.	Barrow	03.80	79-80	21	0	1

WHITTON Stephen Paul
East Ham, 4 December, 1960 (M/F)

League Club	Source	Date Signed	Seasons Played	Apps	Subs	Gls
Coventry C.	App	09.78	79-82	64	10	21
West Ham U.	Tr	07.83	83-84	35	4	6
Birmingham C.	L	01.86	85	8	0	2
Birmingham C.	Tr	08.86	86-88	94	1	28
Sheffield Wed.	Tr	03.89	88-90	22	10	4
Ipswich T.	Tr	01.91	90-93	80	8	15
Colchester U.	Tr	03.94	93-97	105	11	21

WHITWORTH George Geoffrey
Eckington (Dy), 22 September, 1927 (FB)

League Club	Source	Date Signed	Seasons Played	Apps	Subs	Gls
Liverpool	Stanton Iron Wks	03.50	51	9	-	0

WHITWORTH Harry
Bury, 1 December, 1920 (WH/F)

League Club	Source	Date Signed	Seasons Played	Apps	Subs	Gls
Bury	Prestwich Central	11.45	46-50	112	-	14
Rochdale	Tr	07.51	51-52	70	-	9
Southport	Northwich Vic.	09.53	53	33	-	6
Crewe Alex.	Tr	07.54	54	14	-	1

WHITWORTH Neil Anthony
Wigan, 12 April, 1972 E Yth (CD)

League Club	Source	Date Signed	Seasons Played	Apps	Subs	Gls
Wigan Ath.	YT	●	89	1	1	0
Manchester U.	Tr	07.90	90	1	0	0
Preston N.E.	L	01.92	91	6	0	0
Barnsley	L	02.92	91	11	0	0
Rotherham U.	L	10.93	93	8	0	1
Blackpool	L	12.93	93	3	0	0
Wigan Ath.	Kilmarnock	03.98	97	1	3	0

WHITWORTH Stephen
Coalville, 20 March, 1952 E Sch/E Yth/Eu23-6/E-7 (RB)

League Club	Source	Date Signed	Seasons Played	Apps	Subs	Gls
Leicester C.	App	11.69	70-78	352	1	0
Sunderland	Tr	03.79	78-81	83	0	0
Bolton W.	Tr	10.81	81-82	67	0	0
Mansfield T.	Tr	08.83	83-84	80	0	2

WHYKE Peter
Barnsley, 7 September, 1939 (W)

League Club	Source	Date Signed	Seasons Played	Apps	Subs	Gls
Barnsley	Smithies	01.58	57-60	26	-	1
Rochdale	Tr	07.61	61	5	-	0

WHYMARK Trevor John
Diss, 4 May, 1950 Eu23-6/E-1 (F)

League Club	Source	Date Signed	Seasons Played	Apps	Subs	Gls
Ipswich T.	Diss T.	05.69	69-78	249	12	75
Derby Co.	Sparta Rotterdam (Neth)	12.79	79	2	0	0
Grimsby T.	Vancouver (Can)	12.80	80-83	83	10	16
Southend U.	Tr	01.84	83-84	37	2	6
Peterborough U.	Tr	08.85	85	3	0	0
Colchester U. (N/C)	Tr	10.85	85	2	0	0

WHYTE John Archibald
Falkirk, 17 July, 1919 Died 1973 (CH)

League Club	Source	Date Signed	Seasons Played	Apps	Subs	Gls
Barnsley	Armadale Thistle	05.38	46-49	91	-	2
Oldham Ath.	Tr	08.50	50-55	234	-	0

WHYTE Christopher Anderson
Islington, 2 September, 1961 Eu21-4 (CD)

League Club	Source	Date Signed	Seasons Played	Apps	Subs	Gls
Arsenal	App	12.79	81-85	86	4	8
Crystal Palace	L	08.84	84	13	0	0
West Bromwich A.	Los Angeles (USA)	08.88	88-89	83	1	7
Leeds U.	Tr	06.90	90-92	113	0	5
Birmingham C.	Tr	08.93	93-95	68	0	1
Coventry C.	L	12.95	95	1	0	0
Charlton Ath.	Tr	03.96	95	10	1	0
Leyton Orient (N/C)	Detroit Neon (USA)	01.97	96	1	0	0
Oxford U.	Tr	02.97	96	10	0	0

WHYTE David
Dunfermline, 2 March, 1959 (D)

League Club	Source	Date Signed	Seasons Played	Apps	Subs	Gls
Leeds U.	App	03.77	76	1	1	0

WHYTE David Antony
Greenwich, 20 April, 1971 (F)

League Club	Source	Date Signed	Seasons Played	Apps	Subs	Gls
Crystal Palace	Greenwich Borough	02.89	91-95	17	10	4
Charlton Ath.	L	03.92	91	7	1	2
Charlton Ath.	Tr	07.94	94-96	65	20	28
Reading (N/C)	Tr	09.97				
Ipswich T.	Tr	10.97	97	2	0	0
Bristol Rov.	Tr	01.98	97	0	4	0
Southend U. (N/C)	Tr	03.98	97	3	5	1

WHYTE Derek
Glasgow, 31 August, 1968 S Sch/S Yth/Su21-9/S 'B'/S-11 (CD)

League Club	Source	Date Signed	Seasons Played	Apps	Subs	Gls
Middlesbrough	Glasgow Celtic	08.92	92-97	160	7	2

WHYTE Francis
Glasgow, 18 April, 1929 (CH)

League Club	Source	Date Signed	Seasons Played	Apps	Subs	Gls
Swindon T.	Glasgow Celtic	06.56	56	7	-	0

WHYTE James McCreadie
Glasgow, 19 January, 1930 (IF)

League Club	Source	Date Signed	Seasons Played	Apps	Subs	Gls
Southend U.	Third Lanark	05.54	54-56	33	-	8

WHYTE John Nimmo
West Calder, 7 May, 1921 (FB)

League Club	Source	Date Signed	Seasons Played	Apps	Subs	Gls
Bradford C.	Falkirk	08.50	50-56	236	-	2

WICKS Alan Hayward
Henley, 8 February, 1933 (WH)

League Club	Source	Date Signed	Seasons Played	Apps	Subs	Gls
Reading		05.52	55	1	-	0

WICKS Peter
Hemsworth, 14 May, 1948 E Yth (G)

League Club	Source	Date Signed	Seasons Played	Apps	Subs	Gls
Sheffield Wed.	App	05.65	64-69	13	0	0

WICKS Roger Charles
Warrington, 19 April, 1957 (M)

League Club	Source	Date Signed	Seasons Played	Apps	Subs	Gls
Darlington	Netherfield	02.81	80-82	31	10	4

WICKS Stanley Maurice
Reading, 11 July, 1928 Died 1983 E 'B'/EF Lge (CH)

League Club	Source	Date Signed	Seasons Played	Apps	Subs	Gls
Reading		08.48	49-53	168	-	1
Chelsea	Tr	01.54	54-56	71	-	1

WICKS Stephen John
Reading, 3 October, 1956 E Yth/Eu21-1 (CD)

League Club	Source	Date Signed	Seasons Played	Apps	Subs	Gls
Chelsea	App	06.74	74-78	119	1	5
Derby Co.	Tr	01.79	78-79	24	0	0
Queens Park R.	Tr	09.79	79-80	73	0	0
Crystal Palace	Tr	06.81	81	14	0	1
Queens Park R.	Tr	03.82	81-85	116	0	6
Chelsea	Tr	07.86	86-87	32	0	1

WIDDOP Dennis
Keighley, 14 March, 1931 (OR)

League Club	Source	Date Signed	Seasons Played	Apps	Subs	Gls
Bradford C.	Portadown	08.54	54	1	-	0

WIDDOWSON John Robert
Loughborough, 12 September, 1941 (G)

League Club	Source	Date Signed	Seasons Played	Apps	Subs	Gls
Sheffield U.		07.59	61-67	7	0	0
York C.	Tr	06.68	68-69	30	0	0
Portsmouth	L	11.69	69	4	0	0

WIDDRINGTON Thomas
Newcastle, 1 October, 1971 (M)

League Club	Source	Date Signed	Seasons Played	Apps	Subs	Gls
Southampton	YT	05.90	91-95	67	8	3
Wigan Ath.	L	09.91	91	5	1	0
Grimsby T.	Tr	07.96	96-97	56	7	7

WIEKENS Gerard
Holland, 25 February, 1973 (CD/M)

League Club	Source	Date Signed	Seasons Played	Apps	Subs	Gls
Manchester C.	S.C. Veendam (Neth)	07.97	97	35	2	5

WIFFILL David Phillip
Bristol, 19 April, 1961 (M)

League Club	Source	Date Signed	Seasons Played	Apps	Subs	Gls
Manchester C.	Bath C.	04.80				
Bristol Rov. (N/C)	Happy Valley (HK)	08.87	87	2	0	0

WIGG Nathan Marlow
Newport, 27 September, 1974 (M)

League Club	Source	Date Signed	Seasons Played	Apps	Subs	Gls
Cardiff C.	YT	08.93	93-95	40	18	1

WIGG Ronald George
Dunmow, 18 May, 1949 Died 1997 (F)

League Club	Source	Date Signed	Seasons Played	Apps	Subs	Gls
Ipswich T.	Leyton Orient (App)	04.67	67-69	35	2	14
Watford	Tr	06.70	70-72	91	6	20
Rotherham U.	Tr	03.73	72-74	65	0	22
Grimsby T.	Tr	01.75	74-76	51	12	12
Barnsley	Tr	03.77	76-77	14	4	5
Scunthorpe U.	Tr	10.77	77-78	48	2	7

WIGGAN Trenton Ashton
Jamaica (WI), 20 September, 1962 E Sch (W)

League Club	Source	Date Signed	Seasons Played	Apps	Subs	Gls
Sheffield U.	App	08.80	79-81	20	4	3

WIGGETT David Jonathan
Chapeltown (Yks), 25 May, 1957 Died 1978 (LB)

League Club	Source	Date Signed	Seasons Played	Apps	Subs	Gls
Lincoln C.	App	06.75	73-75	4	2	0
Hartlepool U.	Tr	10.76	76-77	54	0	1

WIGGIN Raymond
Rushall, 13 September, 1942 (CF)

League Club	Source	Date Signed	Seasons Played	Apps	Subs	Gls
Walsall		09.62	62-63	19	-	6

WIGGINTON Clive Anthony
Sheffield, 18 October, 1950 (CD)

League Club	Source	Date Signed	Seasons Played	Apps	Subs	Gls
Grimsby T.	App	10.68	68-74	164	9	6
Scunthorpe U.	Tr	07.75	75-76	88	0	7
Lincoln C.	Tr	09.77	77-78	60	0	6
Grimsby T.	Tr	03.79	78-81	122	0	2
Doncaster Rov.	L	03.82	81	13	0	1
Torquay U.	Tr	07.82	82	9	0	0
Doncaster Rov.	Tr	10.82	82	18	0	0

WIGHTMAN John Renton
Duns, 2 November, 1912 Died 1964 (WH)

League Club	Source	Date Signed	Seasons Played	Apps	Subs	Gls
York C.	Scarborough	08.33	33	5	-	0
Bradford P.A.	Tr	09.34	34	17	-	0
Huddersfield T.	Tr	01.35	34-36	64	-	0
Blackburn Rov.	Tr	01.37	36-46	66	-	2
Carlisle U.	Tr	08.47	47	36	-	0

WIGLEY Steven
Ashton-u-Lyne, 15 October, 1961 (W)

League Club	Source	Date Signed	Seasons Played	Apps	Subs	Gls
Nottingham F.	Curzon Ashton	03.81	82-85	69	13	2
Sheffield U.	Tr	10.85	85-86	21	7	1
Birmingham C.	Tr	03.87	86-88	87	0	4
Portsmouth	Tr	03.89	88-91	103	17	12
Exeter C.	Tr	08.93	93	22	1	1

WIGNALL David Arthur
Wallasey, 3 April, 1959 (M)

League Club	Source	Date Signed	Seasons Played	Apps	Subs	Gls
Doncaster Rov.	App	07.76	75-77	35	6	1

WIGNALL Frank
Chorley, 21 August, 1939 EF Lge/E-2 (CF)

League Club	Source	Date Signed	Seasons Played	Apps	Subs	Gls
Everton	Horwich R.M.I.	05.58	59-62	33	-	15
Nottingham F.	Tr	06.63	63-67	156	1	47
Wolverhampton W.	Tr	03.68	67-68	32	0	15
Derby Co.	Tr	02.69	68-71	29	16	15
Mansfield T.	Tr	11.71	71-72	50	6	15

WIGNALL Mark
Preston, 6 December, 1962 (M)

League Club	Source	Date Signed	Seasons Played	Apps	Subs	Gls
Wigan Ath.	App	12.80	80-81	34	0	0

WIGNALL Steven Leslie
Liverpool, 17 September, 1954 (CD)

League Club	Source	Date Signed	Seasons Played	Apps	Subs	Gls
Doncaster Rov.	Liverpool (Jnrs)	03.72	72-76	127	3	1
Colchester U.	Tr	09.77	77-83	279	2	22
Brentford	Tr	08.84	84-86	67	0	2
Aldershot	Tr	09.86	86-90	158	3	4

WILBERT George Norman
Gateshead, 11 July, 1924 Died 1993 (CF)

League Club	Source	Date Signed	Seasons Played	Apps	Subs	Gls
Gateshead		08.42	47-54	268	-	92

WILBRAHAM Aaron Thomas
Manchester, 21 October, 1979 (F)

League Club	Source	Date Signed	Seasons Played	Apps	Subs	Gls
Stockport Co.	YT	08.97	97	6	1	1

WILBY Edward
Rotherham, 18 May, 1922 (FB)

League Club	Source	Date Signed	Seasons Played	Apps	Subs	Gls
Wolverhampton W.		05.46				
Bradford C.	Tr	09.46	46	3	-	0

WILCOCK Roderick William
Middlesbrough, 28 February, 1956 (M)

League Club	Source	Date Signed	Seasons Played	Apps	Subs	Gls
Crewe Alex.	Southampton (Am)	08.74	74	2	2	0

WILCOCKSON Harold
Sheffield, 23 July, 1943 (RB)

League Club	Source	Date Signed	Seasons Played	Apps	Subs	Gls
Rotherham U.		07.63	64-67	109	0	2
Doncaster Rov.	Tr	02.68	67-69	75	0	3
Sheffield Wed.	Tr	12.69	69-70	40	0	1
Doncaster Rov.	Tr	05.71	71-72	36	0	1

WILCOX Anthony
Rotherham, 13 June, 1944 (G)

League Club	Source	Date Signed	Seasons Played	Apps	Subs	Gls
Rotherham U.		10.62				
Barnsley	Tr	08.64	64	6	-	0

WILCOX Caradoc (Crad)
Treharris, 8 November, 1923 (HB)

League Club	Source	Date Signed	Seasons Played	Apps	Subs	Gls
Cardiff C.	Treharris	05.49				
Newport Co.	Tr	07.52	52-53	31	-	0

WILCOX Edward Evan
Blaengarw, 24 March, 1927 (CF)

League Club	Source	Date Signed	Seasons Played	Apps	Subs	Gls
West Bromwich A.	Oxford C.	05.48	48-50	12	-	3

WILCOX Frederick
St Helens, 23 October, 1922 (FB)

League Club	Source	Date Signed	Seasons Played	Apps	Subs	Gls
Chester C.	Everton (Am)	07.47	47	16	-	0

WILCOX George Edwin
Rotherham, 23 August, 1917 Died 1991 (FB)

League Club	Source	Date Signed	Seasons Played	Apps	Subs	Gls
Derby Co.	Denaby U.	10.36	37-46	12	-	0
Rotherham U.	Tr	08.48	48	1	-	0

WILCOX Jason Malcolm
Farnworth, 15 July, 1971 E 'B'/E-1 (LW)

League Club	Source	Date Signed	Seasons Played	Apps	Subs	Gls
Blackburn Rov.	YT	06.89	89-97	198	21	28

WILCOX Raymond
Treharris, 12 April, 1921 (CH)

League Club	Source	Date Signed	Seasons Played	Apps	Subs	Gls
Newport Co.	Treharris	05.39	46-59	488	-	0

WILCOX Russell
Hemsworth, 25 March, 1964 E Semi Pro (CD)

League Club	Source	Date Signed	Seasons Played	Apps	Subs	Gls
Doncaster Rov.	App	•	80	1	0	0
Northampton T.	Frickley Ath.	06.86	86-89	137	1	9
Hull C.	Tr	08.90	90-92	92	8	7
Doncaster Rov.	Tr	07.93	93-95	81	0	6
Preston N.E.	Tr	09.95	95-96	62	0	1
Scunthorpe U.	Tr	07.97	97	30	1	2

WILDE Adam
Southampton, 22 May, 1979 (LW)

League Club	Source	Date Signed	Seasons Played	Apps	Subs	Gls
Cambridge U. (N/C)	YT	02.97	96-97	0	3	0

WILDER Christopher John
Stocksbridge, 23 September, 1967 (RB/M)

League Club	Source	Date Signed	Seasons Played	Apps	Subs	Gls
Southampton	App	09.85				
Sheffield U.	Tr	08.86	86-91	89	4	1
Walsall	L	11.89	89	4	0	0
Charlton Ath.	L	10.90	90	1	0	0
Charlton Ath.	L	11.91	91	2	0	0
Leyton Orient	L	02.92	91	16	0	1
Rotherham U.	Tr	07.92	92-95	129	3	11
Notts Co.	Tr	01.96	95-96	46	0	0
Bradford C.	Tr	03.97	96-97	35	7	0
Sheffield U.	Tr	03.98	97	7	1	0

WILDING Peter John
Shrewsbury, 28 November, 1968 (CD)

League Club	Source	Date Signed	Seasons Played	Apps	Subs	Gls
Shrewsbury T.	Telford	06.97	97	33	1	1

WILDON Leslie Eric
Middlesbrough, 5 April, 1924 (CF)

League Club	Source	Date Signed	Seasons Played	Apps	Subs	Gls
Hartlepool U.	Price's Taylors	12.47	47-54	200	-	87

WILE John David
Sherburn (Dm), 9 March, 1947 (CD)

League Club	Source	Date Signed	Seasons Played	Apps	Subs	Gls
Sunderland	Durham C.	06.66				
Peterborough U.	Tr	07.67	67-70	116	2	7
West Bromwich A.	Tr	12.70	70-82	499	1	24
Peterborough U.	Tr	08.83	83-85	86	1	3

WILEMAN Richard Andrew
Breedon (Leics), 4 October, 1947 (OL)

League Club	Source	Date Signed	Seasons Played	Apps	Subs	Gls
Notts Co.		07.66	66	2	0	0

WILKES David Allan
Barnsley, 10 March, 1964 (M)

League Club	Source	Date Signed	Seasons Played	Apps	Subs	Gls
Barnsley	App	03.82	81-83	14	3	2
Halifax T.	L	03.83	82	4	0	0
Stockport Co.	Hong Kong	08.86	86	8	0	0
Carlisle U. (N/C)	Bridlington T.	11.90	90-91	1	4	0

WILKES Stephen Brian
Preston, 30 June, 1967 (M)

League Club	Source	Date Signed	Seasons Played	Apps	Subs	Gls
Wigan Ath.	App	06.85				
Preston N.E.	Tr	08.86	87	1	2	0

WILKES Timothy Craig
Nottingham, 7 November, 1977 (F)

League Club	Source	Date Signed	Seasons Played	Apps	Subs	Gls
Notts Co.	YT	07.96	96	3	0	0

WILKIE Arthur William
Woolwich, 7 October, 1942 (G)

League Club	Source	Date Signed	Seasons Played	Apps	Subs	Gls
Reading	Jnrs	10.59	61-67	169	0	2

WILKIE Derrick
Lanchester, 27 July, 1939 (CH)

League Club	Source	Date Signed	Seasons Played	Apps	Subs	Gls
Middlesbrough	Jnrs	03.57	59-60	4	-	0
Hartlepool U.	Tr	09.61	61-63	74	-	0

WILKIE Glen Alan
Stepney, 11 January, 1977 (RB)

League Club	Source	Date Signed	Seasons Played	Apps	Subs	Gls
Leyton Orient	YT	03.95	94	10	1	0

WILKIE John Carlin
Dundee, 1 July, 1947 (F)

League Club	Source	Date Signed	Seasons Played	Apps	Subs	Gls
Halifax T.	Ross Co.	02.73	72-73	29	8	8
Wigan Ath.	Elgin C.	08.76	78	3	1	0

WILKIE Robert Mackintosh
Dundee, 7 October, 1935 (OL)

League Club	Source	Date Signed	Seasons Played	Apps	Subs	Gls
Tottenham H.	Lochee Harp	12.56	56	1	-	0

WILKIN Kevin
Cambridge, 1 October, 1967 (F)

League Club	Source	Date Signed	Seasons Played	Apps	Subs	Gls
Northampton T.	Cambridge C.	08.90	90-94	67	11	11

WILKINS Alan James
Treherbert, 3 October, 1944 (IF)

League Club	Source	Date Signed	Seasons Played	Apps	Subs	Gls
Swansea C.		05.63	63-64	5	-	0

WILKINS Dean Mark
Hillingdon, 12 July, 1962 (M)

League Club	Source	Date Signed	Seasons Played	Apps	Subs	Gls
Queens Park R.	App	05.80	80-82	1	5	0
Brighton & H.A.	Tr	08.83	83	2	0	0
Leyton Orient	L	03.84	83	10	0	0
Brighton & H.A.	P.E.C. Zwolle (Neth)	07.87	87-95	295	15	25

WILKINS Ernest **George**
Hackney, 27 October, 1919 (IF)

League Club	Source	Date Signed	Seasons Played	Apps	Subs	Gls
Brentford	Hayes	02.38	38-46	29	-	7
Bradford P.A.	Tr	02.47	46-47	27	-	6
Nottingham F.	Tr	12.47	47-48	24	-	6
Leeds U.	Tr	09.49	49	3	-	0

WILKINS Graham George
Hillingdon, 28 June, 1955 (FB)

League Club	Source	Date Signed	Seasons Played	Apps	Subs	Gls
Chelsea	App	07.72	72-81	136	1	1
Brentford	Tr	07.82	82-83	36	2	0
Southend U.	L	03.84	83	3	0	0

WILKINS Ian John
Lincoln, 3 April, 1980 (D)

League Club	Source	Date Signed	Seasons Played	Apps	Subs	Gls
Lincoln C.	YT	03.98	97	1	1	0

WILKINS Leonard Henry **John (Jack)**
Dublin, 12 August, 1920 (FB)

League Club	Source	Date Signed	Seasons Played	Apps	Subs	Gls
Brighton & H.A.	Guildford C.	10.48	48-50	44	-	2

WILKINS Kenneth
Salford, 24 October, 1928 Died 1995 (F)

League Club	Source	Date Signed	Seasons Played	Apps	Subs	Gls
Southampton		10.49	50	2	-	0
Exeter C.	Tr	10.51	51	3	-	0
Southampton	Tr	07.52	52	1	-	0
Fulham	Tr	07.53				

WILKINS Leonard
Southampton, 20 September, 1925 (FB)

League Club	Source	Date Signed	Seasons Played	Apps	Subs	Gls
Southampton	Cunliffe Owen	10.45	48-57	260	-	2

WILKINS Michael John
Leeds, 6 May, 1942 (CF)

League Club	Source	Date Signed	Seasons Played	Apps	Subs	Gls
Bradford C.	Jnrs	09.59	59	1	-	0

WILKINS Paul
Hackney, 20 March, 1964 (F)

League Club	Source	Date Signed	Seasons Played	Apps	Subs	Gls
Crystal Palace	Tottenham H. (App)	01.82	81-83	9	4	3
Preston N.E.	Tr	06.84	84	3	3	2

WILKINS Raymond Colin
Hillingdon, 14 September, 1956 E Sch/E Yth/Eu21-1/Eu23-2/E-84 (M)

League Club	Source	Date Signed	Seasons Played	Apps	Subs	Gls
Chelsea	App	10.73	73-78	176	3	30
Manchester U.	Tr	08.79	79-83	158	2	7
Queens Park R.	Glasgow Rangers	11.89	89-93	153	1	7
Crystal Palace	Tr	05.94	94	1	0	0
Queens Park R. (N/C)	Tr	11.94	94-96	16	5	0
Wycombe W. (N/C)	Tr	09.96	96	1	0	0
Millwall (N/C)	Hibernian	01.97	96	3	0	0
Leyton Orient (N/C)	Tr	02.97	96	3	0	0

WILKINS Raymond John Hamilton
Crossley, 16 August, 1928 (CF)

League Club	Source	Date Signed	Seasons Played	Apps	Subs	Gls
Derby Co.	Moira U.	01.50	49-53	30	-	11
Wrexham	Boston U.	05.57	57	3	-	1

WILKINS Richard John
Lambeth, 28 May, 1965 (M)

League Club	Source	Date Signed	Seasons Played	Apps	Subs	Gls
Colchester U.	Haverhill Rov.	11.86	86-89	150	2	24
Cambridge U.	Tr	07.90	90-93	79	2	7
Hereford U.	Tr	07.94	94-95	76	1	5
Colchester U.	Tr	07.96	96-97	77	0	7

WILKINS Ronald
Treherbert, 21 December, 1923 Died 1983 (CF)

League Club	Source	Date Signed	Seasons Played	Apps	Subs	Gls
Newport Co.	Gwynfil B.C.	01.46	46	1	-	0

WILKINSON Alan
Middlewich, 5 June, 1935 (IF)

League Club	Source	Date Signed	Seasons Played	Apps	Subs	Gls
Crewe Alex. (Am)	Middlewich	10.55	55	1	-	0

WILKINSON Albert
Barnsley, 3 November, 1928 (W)

League Club	Source	Date Signed	Seasons Played	Apps	Subs	Gls
Bradford C. (Am)		03.51	50	2	-	0
Halifax T.	Denaby U.	07.52	52	14	-	2
Rotherham U.	Tr	07.53				
Chesterfield	Tr	06.54				

WILKINSON Barry John
Lincoln, 19 July, 1942 (CF)

League Club	Source	Date Signed	Seasons Played	Apps	Subs	Gls
Lincoln C.	Bracebridge C.C.	08.61	62-63	6	-	3

WILKINSON George **Barry**
Bishop Auckland, 16 June, 1935 E Yth (WH)

League Club	Source	Date Signed	Seasons Played	Apps	Subs	Gls
Liverpool	West Auckland	06.54	53-59	78	-	0
Tranmere Rov.	Bangor C.	08.63	63	3	-	0

WILKINSON Darron Bromley
Reading, 24 November, 1969 (M)

League Club	Source	Date Signed	Seasons Played	Apps	Subs	Gls
Brighton & H.A.	Wokingham T.	08.92	92-93	34	4	3

WILKINSON David
Sunderland, 28 May, 1928 (OL)

League Club	Source	Date Signed	Seasons Played	Apps	Subs	Gls
Blackburn Rov.	North Shields	07.48	48	1	-	0
Bournemouth	Tr	06.50	50-51	8	-	3

WILKINSON Derek
Stalybridge, 4 June, 1935 EF Lge (OR)

League Club	Source	Date Signed	Seasons Played	Apps	Subs	Gls
Sheffield Wed.	Dukinfield	11.53	54-64	212	-	53

WILKINSON Eric
Sheffield, 6 March, 1931 (WH)

League Club	Source	Date Signed	Seasons Played	Apps	Subs	Gls
Bradford C.		01.51				
Sheffield U.	Tr	08.53				
Bournemouth	Tr	07.55	55	4	-	0

WILKINSON Eric
Stalybridge, 4 June, 1935 (F)

League Club	Source	Date Signed	Seasons Played	Apps	Subs	Gls
Sheffield Wed.	Dukinfield	03.58	58	1	-	0

WILKINSON Ernest Stanley
Chesterfield, 13 February, 1947 (CH)

League Club	Source	Date Signed	Seasons Played	Apps	Subs	Gls
Arsenal	App	02.64				
Exeter C.	Tr	06.66	66-67	59	1	0
Rochdale	L	03.68	67	9	0	0

WILKINSON Graham James
Hull, 21 October, 1934 (FB)

League Club	Source	Date Signed	Seasons Played	Apps	Subs	Gls
Hull C.	Jnrs	09.52	58-59	3	-	0

WILKINSON Harry Sanderson
Sunderland, 20 March, 1926 (WH)

League Club	Source	Date Signed	Seasons Played	Apps	Subs	Gls
Chelsea		06.46				
Exeter C.	Tr	05.50	50	1	-	0
Colchester U.	Tr	08.51	52	1	-	0

WILKINSON Herbert (Bert)
Sunderland, 2 August, 1922 (FB)

League Club	Source	Date Signed	Seasons Played	Apps	Subs	Gls
Lincoln C.	Murton Colly	08.45	46-50	39	-	0

League Club	Source	Date Signed	Seasons Played	Career Record Apps	Subs	Gls
WILKINSON Howard						
Sheffield, 13 November, 1943						(W)
Sheffield Wed.	Sheffield U. (Am)	06.62	64-65	22	0	3
Brighton & H.A.	Tr	07.66	66-70	116	13	18
WILKINSON Ian James						
North Ferriby, 19 September, 1977						(CD)
Hull C.	YT	07.96	95	8	0	1
WILKINSON Ian Matthew						
Warrington, 2 July, 1973						(G)
Manchester U.	YT	06.91				
Crewe Alex.	Stockport Co. (N/C)	10.93	93	2	1	0
WILKINSON Jack						
Middlewich, 17 September, 1931 Died 1996						(CF)
Arsenal	Witton A.	10.53	54	1	-	0
Sheffield U.	Tr	03.56	55-56	29	-	16
Port Vale	Tr	06.57	57-59	80	-	39
Exeter C.	Poole T.	10.59	59-60	48	-	26
WILKINSON John						
Worksop, 1 April, 1949						(FB)
Grimsby T.	App	04.66	65-67	8	1	0
WILKINSON John Colbridge						
Exeter, 24 August, 1979						(LW)
Exeter C.	YT	●	97	0	1	0
WILKINSON Joseph						
Seaham, 8 December, 1934						(G)
Burnley	West Auckland	12.55				
Bradford C.	Tr	03.59	58-59	17	-	0
Hartlepool U.	Tr	02.60	59-61	74	-	0
WILKINSON Kenneth						
Gateshead, 9 May, 1924						(WH/F)
Huddersfield T.	Jnrs	05.42				
Hartlepool U.	Tr	04.47	46-48	53	-	5
WILKINSON Neil						
Blackburn, 16 February, 1955						(RB)
Blackburn Rov.	App	02.73	72-76	27	3	0
Port Vale	Great Harwood	07.78	78	7	0	0
Crewe Alex.	Tr	10.78	78-80	68	7	0
WILKINSON Norman						
Annfield Plain, 9 June, 1910 Died 1975						(G)
Huddersfield T.	Tanfield Lea	05.32				
Stoke C.	Tr	07.35	35-51	186	-	0
WILKINSON Norman Francis						
Alnwick (Nd), 16 February, 1931						(CF)
Hull C. (Am)	Crook T.	11.52	53	8	-	3
York C.	Tr	05.54	54-65	354	0	127
WILKINSON Paul						
Louth, 30 October, 1964 Eu21-4						(F)
Grimsby T.	App	10.82	82-84	69	2	27
Everton	Tr	03.85	84-86	19	12	7
Nottingham F.	Tr	03.87	86-87	32	2	5
Watford	Tr	08.88	88-90	133	1	52
Middlesbrough	Tr	08.91	91-95	161	5	49
Oldham Ath.	L	10.95	95	4	0	1
Watford	L	12.95	95	4	0	0
Luton T.	L	03.96	95	3	0	0
Barnsley	Tr	07.96	96-97	48	1	9
Millwall	Tr	09.97	97	22	8	3
WILKINSON Paul Ian						
Themelthorpe (Nk), 19 April, 1952						(M)
Norwich C.	App	04.70				
Plymouth Arg.	L	01.71	70	2	0	0
WILKINSON Roy Joseph						
Hindley Green, 17 September, 1941						(WH)
Bolton W.	Jnrs	02.60	60-61	3	-	0
WILKINSON Stephen						
Halifax, 6 August, 1946						(G)
Halifax T. (Am)	Jnrs	08.63	63	2	-	0
WILKINSON Stephen John						
Lincoln, 1 September, 1968						(F)
Leicester C.	App	09.86	86-89	5	4	1
Crewe Alex.	L	09.88	88	3	2	2
Mansfield T.	Tr	10.89	89-94	214	18	83
Preston N.E.	Tr	06.95	95-96	44	8	13
Chesterfield	Tr	07.97	97	24	6	6
WILKINSON Thomas						
Wingate (Dm), 8 May, 1931						(WH)
Hartlepool U.		09.52	53-57	22	-	0
WILKINSON William						
Stockton, 24 March, 1943						(M)
Hull C.	Middlesbrough (Am)	05.62	62-72	208	15	34
Rotherham U.	Tr	11.72	72-73	25	1	0
Southport (N/C)	Tacoma (USA)	10.76	76	10	0	0
WILKS Alan						
Slough, 5 October, 1946						(F)
Chelsea	App	08.64				
Queens Park R.	Tr	05.65	66-70	44	6	14
Gillingham	Tr	07.71	71-75	138	13	29
WILLARD Cecil (Jess) Thomas Frederick						
Chichester, 16 January, 1924						(WH)
Brighton & H.A.	Chichester C.	11.46	46-52	190	-	22
Crystal Palace	Tr	07.53	53-54	46	-	5
WILLDER Frederick						
Lytham St Annes, 20 March, 1944 E Yth						(IF)
Blackpool	Jnrs	05.62				
Chester C.	Preston N.E. (trial)	09.63	64-65	1	1	0
WILLDIGG Patrick Gerald						
Stoke, 5 June, 1932						(IF)
Port Vale	Stoke C. (Am)	05.50	55	2	-	0
WILLEMS Ron						
Netherlands, 20 September, 1966						(F)
Derby Co.	Grasshoppers (Swi)	07.95	95-97	41	18	13
WILLEMSE Stanley Bernard						
Brighton, 23 August, 1924 E Sch/EF Lge/E 'B'						(LB)
Brighton & H.A.	Jnrs	06.46	46-48	91	-	3
Chelsea	Tr	07.49	49-55	198	-	2
Leyton Orient	Tr	06.56	56-57	59	-	2
WILLER-JENSEN Thomas						
Denmark, 19 September, 1968						(CD)
Swansea C. (N/C)	H.I.K. Copenhagen (Den)	03.97	96	7	0	0
WILLETT Ernest						
Burslem, 27 July, 1919 Died 1985						(CH)
Port Vale	Stoke C. (Am)	01.46	46	1	-	0
WILLETT Leonard						
Ruabon, 17 September, 1940 W Sch						(HB)
Wrexham	Jnrs	05.58	59	1	-	0
WILLETTS Joseph						
Shotton, 12 July, 1924 Died 1980						(FB)
Hartlepool U.	Newcastle U. (Am)	09.43	46-55	239	-	20
WILLEY Alan						
Exeter, 16 September, 1941						(IF)
Oxford U.	Bridgwater T.	12.60	62-65	85	1	23
Millwall	Tr	03.66	65-66	9	1	0
WILLEY Alan Steven						
Houghton-le-Spring, 18 October, 1956						(F)
Middlesbrough	App	09.74	74-77	27	22	7
WILLGRASS Alexandre Paul						
Scarborough, 8 April, 1976						(M)
Scarborough	Jnrs	08.93	95	2	5	0
WILLIAMS Adrian						
Reading, 16 August, 1971 W-7						(CD)
Reading	YT	03.89	88-95	191	5	14
Wolverhampton W.	Tr	07.96	96-97	26	0	0
WILLIAMS Adrian						
Bristol, 4 August, 1943 E Yth/E Sch						(IF)
Bristol C.	App	08.60	60	4	-	0
Exeter C.	Tr	07.63				
WILLIAMS Alan						
Bristol, 3 June, 1938						(CH)
Bristol C.	Jnrs	09.55	55-60	134	-	2
Oldham Ath.	Tr	06.61	61-64	172	-	9
Watford	Tr	07.65	65-66	43	0	4
Newport Co.	Tr	11.66	66-68	64	0	3
Swansea C.	Tr	10.68	68-71	141	4	7
WILLIAMS Alan Clifford						
Aberdare, 4 December, 1923						(RH)
Norwich C.	Fulham (Am)	01.47	46	1	-	0

WILLIAMS Aled Albert
Holywell, 14 June, 1933 (WH)

League Club	Source	Date Signed	Seasons Played	Apps	Subs	Gls
Burnley	Rhyl	10.52				
Chester C.	Tr	07.57	57	33	-	1

WILLIAMS Alexander
Manchester, 13 November, 1961 E Yth (G)

League Club	Source	Date Signed	Seasons Played	Apps	Subs	Gls
Manchester C.	App	11.79	80-85	114	0	0
Port Vale	Tr	11.86	86-87	35	0	0

WILLIAMS Alfred Stanley
South Africa, 1 May, 1919 (OL)

League Club	Source	Date Signed	Seasons Played	Apps	Subs	Gls
Plymouth Arg.	Aberdeen	08.49	49	35	-	4

WILLIAMS Alvan
Beaumaris, 21 November, 1932 (CH/CF)

League Club	Source	Date Signed	Seasons Played	Apps	Subs	Gls
Bury	Stalybridge Celtic	12.54	55	2	-	1
Wrexham	Tr	06.56	56	13	-	7
Bradford P.A.	Tr	06.57	57-59	92	-	21
Exeter C.	Tr	08.60	60	19	-	1

WILLIAMS Andrew
Birmingham, 29 July, 1962 (M)

League Club	Source	Date Signed	Seasons Played	Apps	Subs	Gls
Coventry C.	Solihull Borough	07.85	85-86	3	6	0
Rotherham U.	Tr	10.86	86-88	87	0	13
Leeds U.	Tr	11.88	88-90	25	21	3
Port Vale	L	12.91	91	5	0	0
Notts Co.	Tr	02.92	91-93	32	7	2
Huddersfield T.	L	09.93	93	4	2	0
Rotherham U.	Tr	10.93	93-94	51	0	2
Hull C.	Tr	07.95	95	33	1	0
Scarborough (N/C)	Tr	08.96	96	1	0	0

WILLIAMS Andrew Phillip
Bristol, 8 October, 1977 Wu21-2/W-2 (W)

League Club	Source	Date Signed	Seasons Played	Apps	Subs	Gls
Southampton	Tr	05.96	97	3	17	0

WILLIAMS Benjamin
Lincoln, 14 April, 1951 (W)

League Club	Source	Date Signed	Seasons Played	Apps	Subs	Gls
Grimsby T.	Lincoln U.	07.69	69	2	0	0

WILLIAMS Bert Frederick
Bilston, 31 January, 1920 E 'B'/EF Lge/E-24 (G)

League Club	Source	Date Signed	Seasons Played	Apps	Subs	Gls
Walsall		05.37	37-38	25	-	0
Wolverhampton W.	Tr	09.45	46-56	381	-	0

WILLIAMS Brett
Dudley, 19 March, 1968 (LB)

League Club	Source	Date Signed	Seasons Played	Apps	Subs	Gls
Nottingham F.	App	12.85	85-92	43	0	0
Stockport Co.	L	03.87	86	2	0	0
Northampton T.	L	01.88	87	3	1	0
Hereford U.	L	09.89	89	14	0	0
Oxford U.	L	02.92	91	7	0	0
Stoke C.	L	08.93	93	2	0	0

WILLIAMS Brian
Salford, 5 November, 1955 (LB/W)

League Club	Source	Date Signed	Seasons Played	Apps	Subs	Gls
Bury	App	04.73	71-76	148	11	19
Queens Park R.	Tr	07.77	77	9	10	0
Swindon T.	Tr	06.78	78-80	89	10	8
Bristol Rov.	Tr	07.81	81-84	172	0	21
Bristol C.	Tr	07.85	85-86	77	0	3
Shrewsbury T.	Tr	07.87	87-88	62	3	1

WILLIAMS Robert **Bryan**
Liverpool, 4 October, 1927 (WH)

League Club	Source	Date Signed	Seasons Played	Apps	Subs	Gls
Liverpool	South Liverpool	08.45	48-52	31	-	5
Crewe Alex.	Tr	05.54	54-57	144	-	5

WILLIAMS Carey Dean
Sheffield, 22 February, 1972 (F)

League Club	Source	Date Signed	Seasons Played	Apps	Subs	Gls
Rotherham U.	Denaby U.	08.94	94	0	2	0

WILLIAMS Carl Junior
Letchworth, 14 January, 1977 (LW)

League Club	Source	Date Signed	Seasons Played	Apps	Subs	Gls
Fulham	YT	07.95	95	2	11	0

WILLIAMS Ceri
Tonyrefail, 16 October, 1965 W Yth (W)

League Club	Source	Date Signed	Seasons Played	Apps	Subs	Gls
Newport Co.	Jnrs	06.83	82-84	19	8	2

WILLIAMS Charles Adolphus
Barnsley, 23 December, 1928 (CH)

League Club	Source	Date Signed	Seasons Played	Apps	Subs	Gls
Doncaster Rov.	Upton Colly	10.48	49-58	158	-	1

WILLIAMS Christopher John
Neath, 21 September, 1976 (F)

League Club	Source	Date Signed	Seasons Played	Apps	Subs	Gls
Hereford U.	YT	09.94	93-94	1	3	0

WILLIAMS Christopher Robert
Brecon, 25 December, 1955 (F)

League Club	Source	Date Signed	Seasons Played	Apps	Subs	Gls
Cardiff C.	Talgarth	12.77	77	3	0	0

WILLIAMS Clarence
Felling, 13 January, 1933 (G)

League Club	Source	Date Signed	Seasons Played	Apps	Subs	Gls
Grimsby T.	Doncaster Rov. (Am)	03.53	52-59	188	-	0
Barnsley	Tr	03.60	60-61	24	-	0

WILLIAMS Cyril Edward
Bristol, 17 November, 1921 Died 1980 (IF)

League Club	Source	Date Signed	Seasons Played	Apps	Subs	Gls
Bristol C.	Jnrs	05.39	46-47	78	-	27
West Bromwich A.	Tr	06.48	48-50	71	-	19
Bristol C.	Tr	08.51	51-57	218	-	42

WILLIAMS Daniel
Maltby, 20 November, 1924 (WH)

League Club	Source	Date Signed	Seasons Played	Apps	Subs	Gls
Rotherham U.	Silverwood Colly	10.43	46-59	461	-	22

WILLIAMS Darren
Birmingham, 15 December, 1968 (M)

League Club	Source	Date Signed	Seasons Played	Apps	Subs	Gls
Leicester C.	App	12.86	88-89	7	3	2
Lincoln C.	L	11.89	89	2	0	0
Lincoln C.	L	03.90	89	5	2	0
Chesterfield	L	09.90	90	4	1	1

WILLIAMS Darren
Middlesbrough, 28 April, 1977 Eu21-1/E 'B' (M)

League Club	Source	Date Signed	Seasons Played	Apps	Subs	Gls
York C.	YT	06.95	94-96	16	4	0
Sunderland	Tr	10.96	96-97	45	2	4

WILLIAMS Darwell
Llanelli, 4 November, 1926 (WH)

League Club	Source	Date Signed	Seasons Played	Apps	Subs	Gls
Swansea C.	Loughor	05.46	50-54	130	-	4

WILLIAMS David
Hemsworth, 25 February, 1946 (WH)

League Club	Source	Date Signed	Seasons Played	Apps	Subs	Gls
Doncaster Rov.		07.64	64	1	-	0

WILLIAMS David
Sheffield, 7 October, 1931 (WH)

League Club	Source	Date Signed	Seasons Played	Apps	Subs	Gls
Grimsby T.	Beighton Colly	03.53	53	5	-	0

WILLIAMS David Michael
Cardiff, 11 March, 1955 W Yth/Wu21-1/W-5 (M)

League Club	Source	Date Signed	Seasons Played	Apps	Subs	Gls
Bristol Rov.	Clifton Ath.	08.75	75-84	342	10	65
Norwich C.	Tr	07.85	85-87	56	4	11
Bournemouth (N/C)	(Retired)	08.92	92	0	1	0

WILLIAMS David Peter
Liverpool, 18 September, 1968 (G)

League Club	Source	Date Signed	Seasons Played	Apps	Subs	Gls
Oldham Ath.	YT	08.87				
Burnley	Tr	03.88	88-92	24	0	0
Rochdale	L	09.91	91	6	0	0
Cardiff C.	Tr	08.94	94-95	82	0	0

WILLIAMS David Samuel
Newport, 1 March, 1942 (RB)

League Club	Source	Date Signed	Seasons Played	Apps	Subs	Gls
Newport Co.	Nash U.	10.60	60-72	302	4	2

WILLIAMS Dean Anton
Hemel Hempstead, 14 November, 1970 (F)

League Club	Source	Date Signed	Seasons Played	Apps	Subs	Gls
Cambridge U.	YT	•	87	1	0	0
Brentford	St Albans C.	07.93	93	2	1	1
Doncaster Rov. (N/C)	Stevenage Borough	09.94	94	1	0	0

WILLIAMS Dean Paul
Lichfield, 5 January, 1972 (G)

League Club	Source	Date Signed	Seasons Played	Apps	Subs	Gls
Birmingham C.	YT	07.90	89-90	4	0	0
Brentford	Tamworth	08.93	93	6	1	0
Doncaster Rov.	Tr	08.94	94-97	83	2	0

WILLIAMS Derek
Mold, 15 June, 1934 W Amat (G)

League Club	Source	Date Signed	Seasons Played	Apps	Subs	Gls
Manchester C. (Am)	Mold Alex.	05.51	51	1	-	0
Wrexham (Am)	Mold Alex.	08.54	54	12	-	0
Oldham Ath.	Mold Alex.	09.56	56	28	-	0

WILLIAMS Derek
Felling, 28 January, 1937 (CF)

League Club	Source	Date Signed	Seasons Played	Apps	Subs	Gls
Grimsby T.	Doncaster Y.M.C.A.	01.57	56-61	44	-	19
Bradford P.A.	Tr	08.62	62	19	-	8

WILLIAMS Derek Owen
Chirk, 3 September, 1949 (G)

League Club	Source	Date Signed	Seasons Played	Apps	Subs	Gls
Shrewsbury T.	Oswestry T.	10.69	69	1	0	0

WILLIAMS Herbert **Derek**
Ellesmere Port, 9 December, 1922 (WH)

League Club	Source	Date Signed	Seasons Played	Apps	Subs	Gls
Chester C.	Little Sutton	09.41	46	2	-	0

WILLIAMS Edgar
Sheffield, 20 May, 1919 (G)

League Club	Source	Date Signed	Seasons Played	Apps	Subs	Gls
Rotherham U.		05.46				
Nottingham F.	Tr	05.47				
Northampton T.	Tr	06.48	48	3	-	0

WILLIAMS Edward Mailor Lloyd
Chester, 28 November, 1935 (OR)

League Club	Source	Date Signed	Seasons Played	Apps	Subs	Gls
Aston Villa	Everton (Am)	08.53				
Wrexham	Tr	08.54	54	1	-	0

WILLIAMS Elfyn
Barmouth, 25 September, 1939 Died 1995 (OR)

League Club	Source	Date Signed	Seasons Played	Apps	Subs	Gls
Wrexham	Portmadoc	03.58	58	1	-	0
Crystal Palace	Tr	07.59				

WILLIAMS Emlyn
Maesteg, 15 January, 1912 Died 1989 (FB)

League Club	Source	Date Signed	Seasons Played	Apps	Subs	Gls
Barnsley	Buxton T.	10.36	36-38	88	-	0
Preston N.E.	Tr	06.39	46-47	62	-	0
Barnsley	Tr	04.48	47-48	17	-	0
Accrington St.	Tr	12.48	48	15	-	0

WILLIAMS Eric
Salford, 10 July, 1921 (FB)

League Club	Source	Date Signed	Seasons Played	Apps	Subs	Gls
Manchester C.	Brindle Heath L.C.	03.45	46-49	38	-	0
Halifax T.	Mossley	10.51	51-53	111	-	0

WILLIAMS Evan Maerdy
Swansea, 12 October, 1932 (LB)

League Club	Source	Date Signed	Seasons Played	Apps	Subs	Gls
Cardiff C.	Penllegaer	03.50				
Exeter C.	Tr	05.54	54	1	-	0
Aldershot	Tr	07.55				

WILLIAMS Evan Samuel
Dumbarton, 15 July, 1943 (G)

League Club	Source	Date Signed	Seasons Played	Apps	Subs	Gls
Wolverhampton W.	Third Lanark	03.66	67	13	0	0
Aston Villa	L	08.69	69	12	0	0

WILLIAMS Everton Anthony
Jamaica (WI), 1 February, 1957 (F)

League Club	Source	Date Signed	Seasons Played	Apps	Subs	Gls
Wrexham	Jnrs	07.75	75	1	1	0

WILLIAMS Frank
Halifax, 23 May, 1921 (OL)

League Club	Source	Date Signed	Seasons Played	Apps	Subs	Gls
Halifax T. (Am)	Boothtown	09.47	47	4	-	0

WILLIAMS Reginald **Frank**
Overton, 12 March, 1917 Died 1978 (G)

League Club	Source	Date Signed	Seasons Played	Apps	Subs	Gls
Wrexham		08.46	46-47	36	-	0

WILLIAMS Gareth Cyril
Hendon, 30 October, 1941 (M)

League Club	Source	Date Signed	Seasons Played	Apps	Subs	Gls
Cardiff C.	Jnrs	04.59	62-67	161	0	14
Bolton W.	Tr	10.67	67-70	108	1	11
Bury	Tr	10.71	71-72	39	3	4

WILLIAMS Gareth James
Cowes (IOW), 12 March, 1967 (M)

League Club	Source	Date Signed	Seasons Played	Apps	Subs	Gls
Aston Villa	Gosport Borough	01.88	87-89	6	6	0
Barnsley	Tr	08.91	91-93	23	11	6
Hull C.	L	09.92	92	4	0	0
Hull C.	L	01.94	93	16	0	2
Bournemouth (N/C)	Tr	09.94	94	0	1	0
Northampton T.	Tr	09.94	94-95	38	12	1
Scarborough	Tr	08.96	96-97	85	3	25

WILLIAMS Gary
Wolverhampton, 17 June, 1960 (FB)

League Club	Source	Date Signed	Seasons Played	Apps	Subs	Gls
Aston Villa	App	06.78	78-86	235	5	0
Walsall	L	03.80	79	9	0	0
Leeds U.	Tr	07.87	87-88	39	0	3
Watford	Tr	01.90	89-90	39	3	0
Bradford C.	Tr	12.91	91-93	84	1	5

WILLIAMS Gary
Birkenhead, 14 May, 1959 (M/FB)

League Club	Source	Date Signed	Seasons Played	Apps	Subs	Gls
Tranmere Rov. (N/C)	Jnrs	09.76	76	1	0	0
Blackpool	Djurgaardens (Swe)	08.80	80	30	1	2
Swindon T.	Tr	08.81	81	37	1	3
Tranmere Rov.	Tr	02.83	82-88	163	11	16

WILLIAMS Gary Alan
Bristol, 8 June, 1963 (FB/M)

League Club	Source	Date Signed	Seasons Played	Apps	Subs	Gls
Bristol C.	App	08.80	80-83	98	2	1
Swansea C. (N/C)	Portsmouth (N/C)	01.85	84	6	0	0
Oldham Ath.	Bristol Rov. (N/C)	08.85	85-90	45	16	12

WILLIAMS Gary Peter
Liverpool, 8 March, 1954 (LB)

League Club	Source	Date Signed	Seasons Played	Apps	Subs	Gls
Preston N.E.	Marine	04.72	71-76	107	5	2
Brighton & H.A.	Tr	07.77	77-81	158	0	7
Crystal Palace	Tr	07.82	82	10	0	0

WILLIAMS George
Ynysddu (Mon), 19 May, 1914 Died 1993 (FB)

League Club	Source	Date Signed	Seasons Played	Apps	Subs	Gls
Charlton Ath.		11.34				
Aldershot	Tr	05.36	36-38	68	-	0
Millwall	Tr	11.38	38-46	25	-	0

WILLIAMS George Robert
Felling, 18 November, 1932 (WH)

League Club	Source	Date Signed	Seasons Played	Apps	Subs	Gls
Rotherham U.	Jnrs	07.50	53	4	-	2
Sheffield U.	Tr	05.54				
Bradford C.	Wisbech T.	05.56	56	6	-	0
Mansfield T.	Tr	07.57	57-61	154	-	5

WILLIAMS David **Geraint**
Treorchy, 5 January, 1962 W Yth/Wu21-2/W-13 (M)

League Club	Source	Date Signed	Seasons Played	Apps	Subs	Gls
Bristol Rov.	App	01.80	80-84	138	3	8
Derby Co.	Tr	03.85	84-91	276	1	9
Ipswich T.	Tr	07.92	92-97	217	0	3

WILLIAMS Gilbert
West Bromwich, 12 January, 1925 Died 1993 (WH)

League Club	Source	Date Signed	Seasons Played	Apps	Subs	Gls
West Bromwich A.	Harvills Hearts	02.44	47	7	-	0

WILLIAMS Glyndwr James John
Maesteg, 3 November, 1918 W-1 (RB)

League Club	Source	Date Signed	Seasons Played	Apps	Subs	Gls
Cardiff C.	Caerau	08.46	46-52	144	-	0

WILLIAMS Gordon
Newcastle, 22 February, 1929 (CF)

League Club	Source	Date Signed	Seasons Played	Apps	Subs	Gls
Sheffield U.		09.49	49	5	-	0
Darlington	Tr	06.50	50	5	-	1

WILLIAMS Gordon George
Swindon, 19 June, 1925 Died 1996 (OL)

League Club	Source	Date Signed	Seasons Played	Apps	Subs	Gls
Swindon T.	Pinehurst Y.C.	05.45	46-56	129	-	14

WILLIAMS Graham Evan
Denbigh, 2 April, 1938 Wu23-2/W-26 (LB)

League Club	Source	Date Signed	Seasons Played	Apps	Subs	Gls
West Bromwich A.	Rhyl	04.55	55-70	308	6	10

WILLIAMS George **Graham**
Wrexham, 31 December, 1936 W Sch/Wu23-1/W-5 (OL)

League Club	Source	Date Signed	Seasons Played	Apps	Subs	Gls
Bradford C.	Oswestry T.	08.55	55	8	-	2
Everton	Tr	03.56	55-58	31	-	6
Swansea C.	Tr	02.59	58-61	89	-	20
Wrexham	Tr	07.64	64	24	-	6
Tranmere Rov.	Wellington T.	08.66	66-67	73	1	12
Port Vale	Tr	07.68	68	21	2	1

WILLIAMS Grenville Rees
Swansea, 30 June, 1921 (WH)

League Club	Source	Date Signed	Seasons Played	Apps	Subs	Gls
Norwich C.	Waverley	06.46	46-47	40	-	0
Newport Co.	Tr	04.49	49	5	-	0

WILLIAMS Harold
Briton Ferry, 17 June, 1924 W-4 (OR)

League Club	Source	Date Signed	Seasons Played	Apps	Subs	Gls
Newport Co.	Ferry Ath.	11.46	46-48	75	-	17
Leeds U.	Tr	06.49	49-55	211	-	32
Newport Co.	Tr	03.57	56	10	-	0
Bradford P.A.	Tr	07.57	57	15	-	0

WILLIAMS Henry George
Salford, 24 February, 1929 (IF)

League Club	Source	Date Signed	Seasons Played	Apps	Subs	Gls
Manchester U.		05.49				
West Ham U.	Witton A.	04.51	51	5	-	1
Bury	Tr	06.53	53	2	-	0
Swindon T.	Tr	06.54	54	14	-	7

WILLIAMS Herbert
Cwmbran, 19 June, 1925 W Amat (OL)

League Club	Source	Date Signed	Seasons Played	Apps	Subs	Gls
Newport Co. (Am)	Westons	09.48	48	2	-	1

WILLIAMS Herbert John
Swansea, 6 October, 1940 W Sch/Wu23-5/W-3 (M)

League Club	Source	Date Signed	Seasons Played	Apps	Subs	Gls
Swansea C.	Jnrs	05.58	58-74	492	21	104

WILLIAMS William **Herbert (Bert)**
Manchester, 24 September, 1925 (IF)

League Club	Source	Date Signed	Seasons Played	Apps	Subs	Gls
Bury		01.47	46	1	-	0
Rochdale	Tr	08.49	49	8	-	3
Aldershot	Tr	06.50	50	8	-	4

WILLIAMS Horace Oswald
Laughton (Yks), 4 October, 1921 Died 1978 (CH)

League Club	Source	Date Signed	Seasons Played	Apps	Subs	Gls
Rotherham U.	Thurcroft Colly	01.43	46-53	206	-	11

WILLIAMS Ivor
Scunthorpe, 29 May, 1935 (G)

League Club	Source	Date Signed	Seasons Played	Apps	Subs	Gls
Scunthorpe U.		08.59	59	8	-	0

WILLIAMS James Leslie
Wolverhampton, 8 May, 1953 (F)

League Club	Source	Date Signed	Seasons Played	Apps	Subs	Gls
Walsall	Worcester C.	03.79	78-79	29	9	2

WILLIAMS Jeffrey Bell
Salford, 1 January, 1933 (IF)

League Club	Source	Date Signed	Seasons Played	Apps	Subs	Gls
Oldham Ath.		06.51	51	1	-	0

WILLIAMS Jeremy Simon
Didcot, 24 March, 1960 (M/D)

League Club	Source	Date Signed	Seasons Played	Apps	Subs	Gls
Reading	App	03.78	76-87	283	26	17
Gillingham	Tr	08.88	88	7	6	0
Aldershot	Tr	07.89	89-90	64	3	7

WILLIAMS John
Greenock, 21 November, 1925 (RH)

League Club	Source	Date Signed	Seasons Played	Apps	Subs	Gls
Blackburn Rov.	Port Glasgow Rov.	06.47				
Southport	Tr	07.48	48	2	-	0

WILLIAMS John
Doncaster, 14 April, 1920 Died 1979 (RB)

League Club	Source	Date Signed	Seasons Played	Apps	Subs	Gls
Leeds U.	Denaby U.	12.48	48	1	-	0

WILLIAMS John
Pwllheli, 22 August, 1965 (D)

League Club	Source	Date Signed	Seasons Played	Apps	Subs	Gls
Wrexham (N/C)	Jnrs	08.82	82	0	1	0

WILLIAMS John Derek
Trelewis, 15 May, 1935 (OL)

League Club	Source	Date Signed	Seasons Played	Apps	Subs	Gls
Everton		05.56				
Crewe Alex.	Tr	06.57	57	5	-	0

WILLIAMS John Lloyd
Rhymney, 27 January, 1936 (WH/FB)

League Club	Source	Date Signed	Seasons Played	Apps	Subs	Gls
Cardiff C.	Jnrs	05.53				
Plymouth Arg.	Tr	07.58	58-61	34	-	0
Torquay U.	Tr	06.62	62-64	42	-	0

WILLIAMS John Nelson
Birmingham, 11 May, 1968 (W)

League Club	Source	Date Signed	Seasons Played	Apps	Subs	Gls
Swansea C.	Cradley T.	08.91	91	36	3	11
Coventry C.	Tr	07.92	92-94	66	14	11
Notts Co.	L	10.94	94	3	2	2
Stoke C.	L	12.94	94	1	3	0
Swansea C.	L	02.95	94	6	1	2
Wycombe W.	Tr	09.95	95-96	34	14	8
Hereford U.	Tr	02.97	96	8	3	3
Walsall	Tr	07.97	97	0	1	0
Exeter C.	Tr	08.97	97	16	20	4

WILLIAMS John Robert
Tottenham, 26 March, 1947 (LB)

League Club	Source	Date Signed	Seasons Played	Apps	Subs	Gls
Watford	App	10.64	64-74	371	3	2
Colchester U.	Tr	07.75	75-77	107	1	1

WILLIAMS John Stanley James
Bristol, 16 August, 1935 (WH/IF)

League Club	Source	Date Signed	Seasons Played	Apps	Subs	Gls
Plymouth Arg.	Jnrs	10.52	55-65	411	1	48
Bristol Rov.	Tr	12.66	66-68	66	3	10

WILLIAMS John William
Liverpool, 1 August, 1929 (OL)

League Club	Source	Date Signed	Seasons Played	Apps	Subs	Gls
Tranmere Rov. (Am)		08.46	46	1	-	0

WILLIAMS William **John**
Liverpool, 3 October, 1960 (CD)

League Club	Source	Date Signed	Seasons Played	Apps	Subs	Gls
Tranmere Rov.	Jnrs	10.79	78-84	167	6	12
Port Vale	Tr	07.85	85-86	50	0	3
Bournemouth	Tr	12.86	86-89	115	2	9
Wigan Ath.	L	10.91	91	4	0	0
Cardiff C.	Tr	12.91	91-92	5	1	0

WILLIAMS Keith David
Birmingham, 12 April, 1957 (M/D)

League Club	Source	Date Signed	Seasons Played	Apps	Subs	Gls
Aston Villa	App	04.75				
Northampton T.	Tr	02.77	76-80	128	3	6
Bournemouth	Tr	08.81	81-86	99	3	1
Colchester U.	Bath C.	12.87	87	9	1	0

WILLIAMS Ronald Albert **Keith**
Bebington, 14 January, 1937 (IF)

League Club	Source	Date Signed	Seasons Played	Apps	Subs	Gls
Everton	Jnrs	03.54				
Tranmere Rov.	Tr	05.57	57-60	161	-	88
Plymouth Arg.	Tr	06.61	61	10	-	4
Bristol Rov.	Tr	01.62	61-62	49	-	18

WILLIAMS Kenneth
(IL)

League Club	Source	Date Signed	Seasons Played	Apps	Subs	Gls
Watford		01.47	46	2	-	0

WILLIAMS Kenneth
Doncaster, 7 January, 1927 (WH)

League Club	Source	Date Signed	Seasons Played	Apps	Subs	Gls
Rotherham U.		09.48	49	3	-	0
York C.	Tr	07.51	53	1	-	0

WILLIAMS Lee
Birmingham, 3 February, 1973 E Yth (RB/M)

League Club	Source	Date Signed	Seasons Played	Apps	Subs	Gls
Aston Villa	YT	01.91				
Shrewsbury T.	L	11.92	92	2	1	0
Peterborough U.	Tr	03.94	93-95	83	8	1
Tranmere Rov. (N/C)	Shamrock Rov.	02.97				
Mansfield T.	Tr	03.97	96-97	36	8	3

WILLIAMS Lee
Romford, 13 March, 1977 (M)

League Club	Source	Date Signed	Seasons Played	Apps	Subs	Gls
Leyton Orient	Purfleet	07.95	95	1	2	0

WILLIAMS Leslie
Thurcroft, 27 March, 1935 (G)

League Club	Source	Date Signed	Seasons Played	Apps	Subs	Gls
Sheffield Wed.		07.53	55-56	11	-	0
Swindon T.	Tr	01.57				
Rotherham U.	Tr	01.58				

WILLIAMS Marc Lloyd
Bangor, 8 February, 1973 (W)

League Club	Source	Date Signed	Seasons Played	Apps	Subs	Gls
Stockport Co.	Bangor C.	03.95	94-95	12	6	1

WILLIAMS Mark
Hereford, 17 September, 1957 (M)

League Club	Source	Date Signed	Seasons Played	Apps	Subs	Gls
Newport Co.	Bromsgrove Rov.	08.76	76-78	59	9	9

WILLIAMS Mark
Bangor, 10 December, 1973 (F)

League Club	Source	Date Signed	Seasons Played	Apps	Subs	Gls
Shrewsbury T.	YT	07.92	91-92	0	3	0
Shrewsbury T.	Telford	07.97	97	0	5	0

WILLIAMS Mark Frank
South Africa, 11 August, 1966 South African Int (F)

League Club	Source	Date Signed	Seasons Played	Apps	Subs	Gls
Wolverhampton W.	R.W.D. Molenbeek (Bel)	09.95	95	5	7	1

WILLIAMS Mark Stuart
Stalybridge, 28 September, 1970 (CD)

League Club	Source	Date Signed	Seasons Played	Apps	Subs	Gls
Shrewsbury T.	Newtown	03.92	91-94	96	6	3
Chesterfield	Tr	08.95	95-97	128	0	9

WILLIAMS Martin Keith
Luton, 12 July, 1973 (W)

League Club	Source	Date Signed	Seasons Played	Apps	Subs	Gls
Luton T.	Leicester C. (YT)	09.91	91-94	12	28	2
Colchester U.	L	03.95	94	3	0	0
Reading	Tr	07.95	95-97	57	16	10

WILLIAMS Michael
Bangor, 1 December, 1956 (M)

League Club	Source	Date Signed	Seasons Played	Apps	Subs	Gls
Wrexham	Jnrs	06.75	74-77	9	0	0

WILLIAMS Michael
Deeside, 6 February, 1965 W Yth (CD)

League Club	Source	Date Signed	Seasons Played	Apps	Subs	Gls
Chester C.	App	02.83	81-83	31	4	4
Wrexham	Tr	07.84	84-89	172	6	3

WILLIAMS Michael Anthony
Bradford, 21 November, 1969 (RM)

League Club	Source	Date Signed	Seasons Played	Apps	Subs	Gls
Sheffield Wed.	Maltby M.W.	02.91	92-96	16	7	1
Halifax T.	L	12.92	92	9	0	1
Huddersfield T.	L	10.96	96	2	0	0
Peterborough U.	L	03.97	96	6	0	0
Burnley	Tr	07.97	97	13	1	1

WILLIAMS Michael John
Hull, 23 October, 1944 (G)

League Club	Source	Date Signed	Seasons Played	Apps	Subs	Gls
Hull C.	App	10.62	62-65	88	0	0
Aldershot	Tr	07.66				
Workington	Tr	07.68	68-69	15	0	0
Scunthorpe U.	Tr	07.70	70-73	28	0	0

WILLIAMS Michael John
Mansfield, 3 November, 1976 (F)

League Club	Source	Date Signed	Seasons Played	Apps	Subs	Gls
Mansfield T.	YT	●	94	0	1	0

League Club	Source	Date Signed	Seasons Played	Career Record Apps	Subs	Gls
WILLIAMS Michael John						
Stepney, 9 October, 1978						(CD/F)
Leyton Orient	YT	07.97	97	0	1	0
WILLIAMS Mostyn Thomas Webb						
Cwmfelinfach (Mon), 2 October, 1928 Died 1990						(RB)
Newport Co.	Ynysddu Welfare	12.49	49-51	28	-	0
WILLIAMS Neil John Frederick						
Waltham Abbey, 23 October, 1964						(W/FB)
Watford	App	08.82				
Hull C.	Tr	07.84	84-87	75	16	9
Preston N.E.	Tr	07.88	88-91	109	12	6
Carlisle U.	Tr	08.92	92	19	0	1
WILLIAMS Nigel John						
Canterbury, 29 July, 1954						(FB)
Wolverhampton W.	App	08.72	74-75	11	0	0
Gillingham	Tr	07.76	76-78	51	2	1
WILLIAMS Oshor Joseph						
Stockton, 21 April, 1958						(W)
Manchester U.	Middlesbrough (App)	08.76				
Southampton	Gateshead	03.78	78-79	4	2	0
Exeter C.	L	08.78	78	2	1	0
Stockport Co.	Tr	08.79	79-84	192	1	26
Port Vale	Tr	11.84	84-85	47	2	6
Preston N.E.	Tr	08.86	86-87	38	1	12
WILLIAMS Paul Andrew						
Sheffield, 8 September, 1963 NI Yth/NI-1						(CD/F)
Preston N.E.	Nuneaton Borough	12.86	86	1	0	0
Newport Co.	Tr	08.87	87	26	0	3
Sheffield U.	Tr	03.88	87-88	6	2	0
Hartlepool U.	Tr	10.89	89	7	1	0
Stockport Co.	Tr	08.90	90	24	0	14
West Bromwich A.	Tr	03.91	90-91	26	18	5
Coventry C.	L	10.92	92	1	1	0
Stockport Co.	Tr	01.93	92	6	10	3
Rochdale	Tr	11.93	93-95	22	15	7
Doncaster Rov.	L	03.96	95	2	1	1
WILLIAMS Paul Anthony						
Stratford, 16 August, 1965 Eu21-4/E 'B'						(F)
Charlton Ath.	Woodford T.	02.87	87-89	74	8	23
Brentford	L	10.87	87	7	0	3
Sheffield Wed.	Tr	08.90	90-92	78	15	25
Crystal Palace	Tr	09.92	92-94	38	8	7
Sunderland	L	01.95	94	3	0	0
Birmingham C.	L	03.95	94	8	3	0
Charlton Ath.	Tr	09.95	95	2	7	0
Torquay U.	L	03.96	95	9	0	0
Southend U.	Tr	08.96	96-97	30	9	7
WILLIAMS Paul Darren						
Burton, 26 March, 1971 Eu21-6						(CD/M)
Derby Co.	YT	07.89	89-94	153	7	26
Lincoln C.	L	11.89	89	3	0	0
Coventry C.	Tr	08.95	95-97	76	8	4
WILLIAMS Paul John						
Lambeth, 16 November, 1962						(D)
Chelsea	App	07.80	82	1	0	0
WILLIAMS Paul Leslie						
Liverpool, 25 September, 1970						(FB/W)
Sunderland	YT	07.89	88-91	6	4	0
Swansea C.	L	03.91	90	12	0	0
Doncaster Rov.	Tr	07.93	93-94	6	2	0
WILLIAMS Paul Richard Curtis						
Leicester, 11 September, 1969						(LB)
Leicester C.	YT	06.88				
Stockport Co.	Tr	07.89	89-92	61	9	4
Coventry C.	Tr	08.93	93-94	8	6	0
West Bromwich A.	L	11.93	93	5	0	0
Huddersfield T.	L	11.94	94	2	0	0
Huddersfield T.	L	03.95	94	7	0	0
Plymouth Arg.	Tr	08.95	95-97	131	0	4
WILLIAMS Paul Sylvester						
Newton Abbot, 20 February, 1964						(F)
Bristol C.	Ottery St Mary	03.83	82-83	16	3	1
Exeter C. (N/C)	Saltash U.	08.85	85-87	8	10	1
WILLIAMS Peter John						
Nottingham, 21 October, 1931						(W)
Derby Co.	South Normanton	08.52	52	2	-	0
Chesterfield	Boston U.	07.55	55	13	-	4
WILLIAMS Peter Sidney Herbert						
Plymouth, 18 December, 1938						(WH)
Exeter C.	Plymouth Arg. (Am)	04.60	60	1	-	0
WILLIAMS Peter Wesley						
Deeside, 17 May, 1960						(F)
Wrexham	Jnrs	07.78	78-80	4	6	1
WILLIAMS Philip Dean						
Swansea, 24 November, 1966						(W)
Swansea C.	App	10.84	83-87	42	17	5
WILLIAMS Philip James						
Swansea, 7 February, 1963 W Sch						(M)
Blackpool	Arsenal (App)	11.80				
Crewe Alex.	Tr	08.81	81	39	0	3
Wigan Ath.	Tr	08.82	82-83	1	2	0
Chester C.	L	09.83	83	5	1	0
Crewe Alex.	Tr	12.83	83	14	6	3
WILLIAMS Philip Leslie						
Birkenhead, 5 April, 1958						(F)
Chester C.	Jnrs	07.76	76	1	0	0
WILLIAMS Raymond						
Wrexham, 1 May, 1931						(FB)
Wrexham	Holyhead	05.51	51	12	-	0
WILLIAMS Raymond						
Stoke, 30 August, 1946						(F)
Port Vale	Stafford R.	08.72	72-76	165	8	39
WILLIAMS William **Raymond**						
Bebington, 30 December, 1930						(WH/IF)
Tranmere Rov.		02.49	51-58	197	-	12
WILLIAMS Reginald Frederick						
Watford, 28 January, 1922						(IF)
Chelsea	Watford (Am)	10.45	46-51	58	-	13
WILLIAMS Robert Francis						
Chester, 24 November, 1932						(G/IF)
New Brighton (Am)	Jnrs	08.49	49	1	-	0
Chester C. (Am)	South Liverpool	10.51	51-53	4	-	0
Chester C.		05.56	56-59	33	-	3
WILLIAMS Robert Gordon						
Bristol, 17 February, 1940						(IF)
Bristol C.	Jnrs	05.58	58-64	187	-	76
Rotherham U.	Tr	02.65	64-66	47	0	13
Bristol Rov.	Tr	03.67	66-68	28	1	5
Reading	Tr	08.69	69-70	60	4	20
WILLIAMS Robert James						
Bridgend, 9 October, 1968						(FB)
Oxford U.	YT	08.87				
Hereford U.	Tr	08.88	88	5	0	0
WILLIAMS Raymond **Robert**						
Liverpool, 25 October, 1927						(IF)
Liverpool	Jnrs	11.45				
Wrexham	Tr	06.51	51	7	-	0
Shrewsbury T.	Tr	10.51	51	5	-	0
WILLIAMS Ronald Arthur						
Swansea, 12 September, 1949						(F)
Swansea C.	Jnrs	09.68	67-68	8	2	1
WILLIAMS Donald **Rowland (Roley)**						
Swansea, 10 July, 1927						(IF)
Cardiff C.	Milford U.	02.49	48-55	138	-	19
Northampton T.	Tr	03.56	55-56	15	-	0
WILLIAMS Roy Brian						
Hereford, 3 March, 1932						(IF)
Southampton	Hereford U.	11.52	52-54	41	-	7
WILLIAMS Ryan Neill						
Mansfield, 31 August, 1978 E Yth						(F)
Mansfield T.	YT	●	95-96	9	17	3
WILLIAMS Scott John						
Bangor, 7 August, 1974 W Yth/Wu21-5						(LB)
Wrexham	YT	07.93	92-97	26	6	0
WILLIAMS Sidney						
Bristol, 21 December, 1919						(W)
Bristol C.		07.46	46-51	100	-	11

League Club	Source	Date Signed	Seasons Played	Career Record Apps	Subs	Gls

WILLIAMS Stephen Michael
Swansea, 5 November, 1954 (OL)

League Club	Source	Date Signed	Seasons Played	Apps	Subs	Gls
Swansea C.		03.76	75	7	3	1

WILLIAMS Steven Brian
Mansfield, 8 July, 1970 (F/LB)

League Club	Source	Date Signed	Seasons Played	Apps	Subs	Gls
Mansfield T.	YT	07.88	86-88	4	7	0
Chesterfield	Tr	10.89	89-92	76	22	12

WILLIAMS Steven Charles
Hammersmith, 12 July, 1958 Eu21-14/E 'B'/E-6 (M)

League Club	Source	Date Signed	Seasons Played	Apps	Subs	Gls
Southampton	App	07.76	75-84	277	1	18
Arsenal	Tr	12.84	84-87	93	2	4
Luton T.	Tr	08.88	88-90	39	1	1
Exeter C.	Tr	08.91	91-92	44	4	0

WILLIAMS Steven David
Aberystwyth, 16 October, 1974 W Yth (G)

League Club	Source	Date Signed	Seasons Played	Apps	Subs	Gls
Cardiff C.	Coventry C. (YT)	08.93	93-96	33	0	0

WILLIAMS Steven John
Barry, 27 April, 1963 W Yth (F)

League Club	Source	Date Signed	Seasons Played	Apps	Subs	Gls
Bristol Rov.	App	04.81	80	8	0	1

WILLIAMS Steven Robert
Sheffield, 3 November, 1975 (F)

League Club	Source	Date Signed	Seasons Played	Apps	Subs	Gls
Lincoln C.	YT	06.94	93-95	8	9	2
Peterborough U.	Tr	02.96	95	0	3	0

WILLIAMS Stuart Grenville
Wrexham, 9 July, 1930 W-43 (FB)

League Club	Source	Date Signed	Seasons Played	Apps	Subs	Gls
Wrexham (Am)	Victoria Y.C.	06.47	48-49	5	-	0
West Bromwich A.	Tr	02.51	51-62	226	-	6
Southampton	Tr	09.62	62-65	148	2	3

WILLIAMS Terence John
Stoke, 23 October, 1966 (M)

League Club	Source	Date Signed	Seasons Played	Apps	Subs	Gls
Stoke C.	App	10.84	84-86	6	5	0

WILLIAMS Thomas Alan
Liverpool, 1 August, 1929 Died 1979 (WH)

League Club	Source	Date Signed	Seasons Played	Apps	Subs	Gls
Tranmere Rov.	Jnrs	11.48	46-56	53	-	2
Southport	Tr	08.58	58	17	-	0

WILLIAMS Thomas Edward
Winchburgh, 18 December, 1957 (D)

League Club	Source	Date Signed	Seasons Played	Apps	Subs	Gls
Leicester C.	App	12.75	77-85	236	5	10
Birmingham C.	Tr	08.86	86-87	62	0	1
Grimsby T.	Tr	07.88	88-89	19	1	0

WILLIAMS Thomas John
Battersea, 10 February, 1935 Died 1987 (W)

League Club	Source	Date Signed	Seasons Played	Apps	Subs	Gls
Colchester U.	Carshalton Ath.	09.56	56-60	150	-	32
Watford	Tr	06.61	61	12	-	6

WILLIAMS Wayne
Telford, 17 November, 1963 (RB)

League Club	Source	Date Signed	Seasons Played	Apps	Subs	Gls
Shrewsbury T.	App	11.81	82-88	212	9	7
Northampton T.	L	11.88	88	3	0	1
Northampton T.	Tr	01.89	88-90	47	5	0
Walsall	Tr	08.91	91-92	56	0	1

WILLIAMS William Raymond
Littleborough, 7 October, 1960 (CD)

League Club	Source	Date Signed	Seasons Played	Apps	Subs	Gls
Rochdale	Ashe Labs	08.81	81-84	89	6	2
Stockport Co.	Tr	07.85	85-88	104	0	1
Manchester C.	Tr	10.88	88	0	1	0
Stockport Co.	Tr	12.88	88-93	153	3	7

WILLIAMS William Thomas
Esher, 23 August, 1942 E Sch/E Yth (CH)

League Club	Source	Date Signed	Seasons Played	Apps	Subs	Gls
Portsmouth	Jnrs	06.60	60	3	-	0
Queens Park R.	Tr	07.61	61-62	45	-	0
West Bromwich A.	Tr	06.63	64	1	-	0
Mansfield T.	Tr	01.66	65-67	47	2	0
Gillingham	Tr	09.67	67-71	169	2	8

WILLIAMSON Arthur Hamilton
Stanley, 26 July, 1930 (FB)

League Club	Source	Date Signed	Seasons Played	Apps	Subs	Gls
Southend U.	Clyde	05.55	55-61	269	-	2

WILLIAMSON Brian William
Blyth, 6 October, 1939 (G)

League Club	Source	Date Signed	Seasons Played	Apps	Subs	Gls
Gateshead	Seaton Delaval	10.58	58-59	55	-	0
Crewe Alex.	Tr	07.60	60-62	55	-	0
Leeds U.	Tr	12.62	62-64	5	-	0
Nottingham F.	Tr	02.66	67-68	19	0	0
Leicester C.	L	08.67	67	6	0	0
Fulham	Tr	11.68	68-69	12	0	0

WILLIAMSON Charles
Falkirk, 12 April, 1956 (FB)

League Club	Source	Date Signed	Seasons Played	Apps	Subs	Gls
Bristol C.	Jnrs	07.74				
Torquay U.	L	03.77	76	5	0	0

WILLIAMSON Charles Harold
Sheffield, 16 March, 1962 (LB)

League Club	Source	Date Signed	Seasons Played	Apps	Subs	Gls
Sheffield Wed.	App	02.80	79-83	61	1	1
Lincoln C.	L	01.84	83	5	0	0
Southend U.	L	03.85	84	10	0	0
Chesterfield	Tr	07.85	85-86	47	8	3

WILLIAMSON Colin
Gretna , 25 October, 1957 (W)

League Club	Source	Date Signed	Seasons Played	Apps	Subs	Gls
Workington (N/C)	Liverpool (App)	08.76	76	11	4	2

WILLIAMSON Daniel Alan
West Ham, 5 December, 1973 (M)

League Club	Source	Date Signed	Seasons Played	Apps	Subs	Gls
West Ham U.	YT	07.92	93-96	47	4	5
Doncaster Rov.	L	10.93	93	10	3	1
Everton	Tr	08.97	97	15	0	0

WILLIAMSON David Francis
Hong Kong, 15 December, 1975 (M)

League Club	Source	Date Signed	Seasons Played	Apps	Subs	Gls
Cambridge U.	Motherwell	08.96	97	2	4	0

WILLIAMSON George
Newcastle, 13 September, 1925 Died 1994 (HB/F)

League Club	Source	Date Signed	Seasons Played	Apps	Subs	Gls
Middlesbrough		12.45				
Chester C.	Tr	07.47	47-49	75	-	4
Bradford C.	Tr	06.50	50-56	223	-	31

WILLIAMSON John Ian
Larbert, 14 March, 1939 (LH)

League Club	Source	Date Signed	Seasons Played	Apps	Subs	Gls
Norwich C.	Falkirk	05.58	58	10	-	1
Bradford P.A.	Wisbech T.	06.62	62	17	-	0

WILLIAMSON James
Birkenhead, 16 June, 1926 (IF)

League Club	Source	Date Signed	Seasons Played	Apps	Subs	Gls
Tranmere Rov.	Jnrs	08.46	46	4	-	3

WILLIAMSON John
Manchester, 8 May, 1929 (F)

League Club	Source	Date Signed	Seasons Played	Apps	Subs	Gls
Manchester C.	Newton Heath	08.49	49-54	59	-	18
Blackburn Rov.	Tr	03.56	55-56	9	-	3

WILLIAMSON Kenneth
Stockton, 7 August, 1928 (IF)

League Club	Source	Date Signed	Seasons Played	Apps	Subs	Gls
Darlington (Am)	Bishop Auckland	08.52	52	13	-	3

WILLIAMSON Michael
Ashbourne, 30 May, 1942 (OL)

League Club	Source	Date Signed	Seasons Played	Apps	Subs	Gls
Derby Co.	Ashbourne	08.61	61-63	12	-	0
Gillingham	Tr	07.64	65	1	0	0

WILLIAMSON Philip James
Macclesfield, 19 September, 1962 (D)

League Club	Source	Date Signed	Seasons Played	Apps	Subs	Gls
Blackburn Rov.	App	09.80	81	0	1	0

WILLIAMSON Robert
Edinburgh, 6 December, 1933 (G)

League Club	Source	Date Signed	Seasons Played	Apps	Subs	Gls
Barnsley	St Mirren	08.63	63-64	46	-	0
Leeds U.	Tr	06.65				
Rochdale	Tr	07.66	66-67	36	0	0

WILLIAMSON Robert
Glasgow, 13 August, 1961 (F)

League Club	Source	Date Signed	Seasons Played	Apps	Subs	Gls
West Bromwich A.	Glasgow Rangers	08.86	86-87	40	13	11
Rotherham U.	Tr	07.88	88-90	91	2	49

WILLIAMSON Stewart
Wallasey, 7 April, 1926 (OL)

League Club	Source	Date Signed	Seasons Played	Apps	Subs	Gls
Tranmere Rov.	Harrogate	03.44	46-52	92	-	21
Swindon T.	Tr	06.53	53-54	17	-	0

WILLIAMSON Thomas
Salford, 16 March, 1913 Died 1992 (CH)

League Club	Source	Date Signed	Seasons Played	Apps	Subs	Gls
Leeds U.	Pendlebury Wed.	09.32				
Oldham Ath.	Northwich Vic.	05.35	35-46	157	-	4

WILLINGHAM Charles Kenneth
Sheffield, 1 December, 1912 Died 1975 EF Lge/E-12 (CH)

League Club	Source	Date Signed	Seasons Played	Apps	Subs	Gls
Huddersfield T.	Worksop T.	11.30	32-38	247	-	4
Sunderland	Tr	12.45	46	14	-	0
Leeds U.	Tr	03.47	46-47	35	-	0

WILLIS Arthur
Denaby, 2 February, 1920 Died 1987 E-1 (FB)

League Club	Source	Date Signed	Seasons Played	Apps	Subs	Gls
Tottenham H.	Finchley	01.44	46-53	144	-	1
Swansea C.	Tr	09.54	54-57	95	-	0

WILLIS George
Stanley, 9 November, 1926 (IF)

League Club	Source	Date Signed	Seasons Played	Apps	Subs	Gls
Wolverhampton W.		01.45				
Brighton & H.A.	Tr	02.48	47-48	28	-	13
Plymouth Arg.	Tr	05.49	49-55	56	-	14
Exeter C.	Tr	03.56	55-56	26	-	3

WILLIS John George
Shotton, 25 July, 1933 (W)

League Club	Source	Date Signed	Seasons Played	Apps	Subs	Gls
Leeds U.	Evenwood T.	03.53	53	3	-	0
Hartlepool U.	Tr	11.54	54-58	25	-	7

WILLIS Graham
Lowestoft, 20 October, 1946 (FB)

League Club	Source	Date Signed	Seasons Played	Apps	Subs	Gls
Norwich C.	App	10.64	64	1	-	0

WILLIS James Antony
Liverpool, 12 July, 1968 (CD)

League Club	Source	Date Signed	Seasons Played	Apps	Subs	Gls
Halifax T.	Blackburn Rov. (YT)	08.86				
Stockport Co.	Tr	12.87	87	10	0	0
Darlington	Tr	03.88	87-91	90	0	6
Leicester C.	Tr	12.91	91-95	58	2	3
Bradford C.	L	03.92	91	9	0	1

WILLIS John Johnson
Boldon, 28 May, 1934 (OL)

League Club	Source	Date Signed	Seasons Played	Apps	Subs	Gls
Blackburn Rov.	Boldon Colly	08.54	55	1	-	0
Aston Villa	Mossley	08.58	58	1	-	0

WILLIS Paul Edward
Liverpool, 24 January, 1970 (M)

League Club	Source	Date Signed	Seasons Played	Apps	Subs	Gls
Halifax T.	YT	05.88	87-88	1	4	0
Darlington	Tr	03.89	88	1	1	1

WILLIS Roger Christopher
Sheffield, 17 June, 1967 E Semi Pro (M/F)

League Club	Source	Date Signed	Seasons Played	Apps	Subs	Gls
Grimsby T.	Dunkirk	07.89	89	1	8	0
Barnet	Tr	08.90	91-92	39	5	13
Watford	Tr	10.92	92-93	30	6	2
Birmingham C.	Tr	12.93	93-94	12	7	5
Southend U.	Tr	09.94	94-95	30	1	7
Peterborough U.	Tr	08.96	96	34	6	6
Chesterfield	Tr	07.97	97	19	15	8

WILLIS Ronald Ian
Romford, 27 December, 1947 E Yth (G)

League Club	Source	Date Signed	Seasons Played	Apps	Subs	Gls
Leyton Orient	Coventry C. (Am)	01.66	66-67	45	0	0
Charlton Ath.	Tr	10.67	67	1	0	0
Brentford	L	09.68	68	1	0	0
Colchester U.	Tr	10.68	68-69	6	0	0

WILLMOTT Ian Michael
Bristol, 10 July, 1968 (FB)

League Club	Source	Date Signed	Seasons Played	Apps	Subs	Gls
Bristol Rov.	Weston-super-Mare	11.88	89-91	18	4	0

WILLOX Alexander (Sandy)
Lossiemouth, 5 November, 1923 (CF)

League Club	Source	Date Signed	Seasons Played	Apps	Subs	Gls
Hartlepool U.	Cowdenbeath	07.51	51	6	-	0

WILLS Gordon Francis
West Bromwich 24 April, 1934 (OL)

League Club	Source	Date Signed	Seasons Played	Apps	Subs	Gls
Wolverhampton W.	West Bromwich A. (Am)	12.51				
Notts Co.	Tr	08.53	53-57	154	-	46
Leicester C.	Tr	05.58	58-61	111	-	30
Walsall	Tr	06.62	62-63	35	-	2

WILLS Leonard Edward
Hackney, 8 November, 1927 (FB)

League Club	Source	Date Signed	Seasons Played	Apps	Subs	Gls
Arsenal	Eton Manor	10.49	53-60	195	-	4

WILLSHAW George James
Hackney, 18 October, 1912 Died 1993 (OL)

League Club	Source	Date Signed	Seasons Played	Apps	Subs	Gls
Southend U.	Southall	02.36	35-37	28	-	6
Bristol C.	Tr	06.38	38	34	-	9
Leyton Orient	Tr	09.42	46	12	-	2

WILMOT Rhys James
Newport, 21 February, 1962 W Sch/W Yth/Wu21-6 (G)

League Club	Source	Date Signed	Seasons Played	Apps	Subs	Gls
Arsenal	App	02.80	85-86	8	0	0
Hereford U.	L	03.83	82	9	0	0
Leyton Orient	L	05.84	84	46	0	0
Swansea C.	L	08.88	88	16	0	0
Plymouth Arg.	L	03.89	88	17	0	0
Plymouth Arg.	Tr	07.89	89-91	116	0	0
Grimsby T.	Tr	07.92	92	33	0	0
Crystal Palace	Tr	08.94	94	5	1	0
Torquay U.	Tr	08.96	96	34	0	0

WILMOT Richard
Matlock, 29 August, 1969 (G)

League Club	Source	Date Signed	Seasons Played	Apps	Subs	Gls
Scunthorpe U.	Stevenage Borough	03.93	92	3	0	0

WILMOTT Gordon Alfred
Brinsley (Nts), 26 May, 1929 (CH)

League Club	Source	Date Signed	Seasons Played	Apps	Subs	Gls
Birmingham C.		05.47				
Stockport Co.	Tr	06.48	48-58	205	-	1
Crewe Alex.	Tr	03.59	58-60	54	-	0

WILSHAW Dennis James
Stoke, 11 March, 1926 E 'B'/E-12 (IF)

League Club	Source	Date Signed	Seasons Played	Apps	Subs	Gls
Wolverhampton W.	Packmoor B.C.	09.43	48-57	211	-	105
Walsall	L	05.46	46-48	74	-	27
Stoke C.	Tr	12.57	57-60	94	-	40

WILSHAW Steven Edward
Stoke, 11 January, 1959 (M)

League Club	Source	Date Signed	Seasons Played	Apps	Subs	Gls
Stoke C.	App	01.77				
Crewe Alex.	Tr	08.78	78	20	2	1

WILSHIRE Peter John
Bristol, 15 October, 1934 (CF)

League Club	Source	Date Signed	Seasons Played	Apps	Subs	Gls
Bristol Rov.	Jnrs	01.54	53	1	-	0
Bristol C.	Tr	06.55				

WILSON Alan
Liverpool, 17 November, 1952 (M)

League Club	Source	Date Signed	Seasons Played	Apps	Subs	Gls
Everton	App	07.70	71-72	2	0	0
Southport	Tr	07.75	75-77	134	0	13
Torquay U.	Tr	06.78	78	38	4	2

WILSON Albert
Rotherham, 28 January, 1915 (W)

League Club	Source	Date Signed	Seasons Played	Apps	Subs	Gls
Derby Co.	Stafford R.	05.36	36	1	-	0
Mansfield T.	Tr	07.38	38	20	-	2
Crystal Palace	Tr	01.39	38	20	-	6
Rotherham U.	Tr	06.46	46	38	-	19
Grimsby T.	Tr	07.47	47	17	-	1

WILSON Alexander
Stenhousemuir, 13 July, 1938 (OR)

League Club	Source	Date Signed	Seasons Played	Apps	Subs	Gls
Rotherham U.	Clyde	07.61	61	5	-	0

WILSON Alexander
Buckie, 29 October, 1933 S-1 (FB)

League Club	Source	Date Signed	Seasons Played	Apps	Subs	Gls
Portsmouth	Jnrs	11.50	51-66	348	4	4

WILSON Alexander
Wishaw, 29 October, 1908 Died 1971 (G)

League Club	Source	Date Signed	Seasons Played	Apps	Subs	Gls
Arsenal	Morton	05.33	33-38	82	-	0
Brighton & H.A.	St Mirren	09.47	47	1	-	0

WILSON Allan Armstrong
Bathgate, 10 January, 1945 (G)

League Club	Source	Date Signed	Seasons Played	Apps	Subs	Gls
Scunthorpe U.	Partick Thistle	07.64				
Mansfield T.	Tr	08.66	66	5	0	0

WILSON Ambrose Maxwell
Lurgan (NI), 10 October, 1924 (FB)

League Club	Source	Date Signed	Seasons Played	Apps	Subs	Gls
Swansea C.	Glenavon	09.50	50	1	-	0

WILSON Andrew
Rotherham, 27 September, 1940 (W)

League Club	Source	Date Signed	Seasons Played	Apps	Subs	Gls
Sheffield U.		01.60	59-60	4	-	0
Scunthorpe U.	Tr	06.61	61-64	112	-	14
Doncaster Rov.	Tr	07.65	65	20	1	0
Chesterfield	Tr	07.66	66-67	70	2	13
Aldershot	Tr	07.68	68	19	1	1

WILSON Andrew Philip
Maltby, 13 October, 1947 (OR)

League Club	Source	Date Signed	Seasons Played	Apps	Subs	Gls
Rotherham U.		06.67	67	12	4	3
Notts Co.	L	08.68	68	1	0	0
Scunthorpe U.	Tr	09.68	68	23	1	4

WILSON Andrew William
Wigan, 7 January, 1965 (M)

League Club	Source	Date Signed	Seasons Played	Apps	Subs	Gls
Wigan Ath.	Skelmersdale U.	08.87	87-88	1	1	0

WILSON Archibald
South Shields, 4 December, 1924 Died 1979 (G)

League Club	Source	Date Signed	Seasons Played	Apps	Subs	Gls
Gateshead	Tyne Dock	08.45	46	5	-	0
Lincoln C.	South Shields	04.51	50-51	4	-	0

WILSON Beverley
Stockport, 11 April, 1953 (CD)

League Club	Source	Date Signed	Seasons Played	Apps	Subs	Gls
Stockport Co.	App	07.70	69-73	59	2	1

WILSON Bevis Ian McLean
Eccles, 14 May, 1924 Died 1987 (CH)

League Club	Source	Date Signed	Seasons Played	Apps	Subs	Gls
Wrexham		06.47	47-50	98	-	0
Barrow	Tr	03.51	50-58	309	-	1

WILSON Brian
Newcastle, 14 April, 1957 (M/D)

League Club	Source	Date Signed	Seasons Played	Apps	Subs	Gls
Blackpool	App	05.74	76-79	21	10	6
Torquay U.	Tr	11.79	79-82	129	2	6

WILSON Carl Alan
Consett, 8 May, 1940 (CF)

League Club	Source	Date Signed	Seasons Played	Apps	Subs	Gls
Newcastle U.	Jnrs	02.58	58	1	-	0
Gateshead	Tr	01.60	59	17	-	4
Doncaster Rov.	Tr	07.60	60	14	-	2
Millwall	Tr	07.61	61	5	-	1

WILSON Clive Euclid Aklana
Manchester, 13 November, 1961 (LB/M)

League Club	Source	Date Signed	Seasons Played	Apps	Subs	Gls
Manchester C.	Jnrs	12.79	81-86	107	2	9
Chester C.	L	09.82	82	21	0	2
Chelsea	Tr	05.87	87-89	68	13	5
Queens Park R.	Tr	07.90	90-94	170	2	12
Tottenham H.	Tr	06.95	95-97	67	3	1

WILSON Daniel Joseph
Wigan, 1 January, 1960 NI-24 (M)

League Club	Source	Date Signed	Seasons Played	Apps	Subs	Gls
Bury	Wigan Ath.	09.77	77-79	87	3	8
Chesterfield	Tr	07.80	80-82	100	0	13
Nottingham F.	Tr	01.83	82	9	1	1
Scunthorpe U.	L	10.83	83	6	0	3
Brighton & H.A.	Tr	11.83	83-86	132	3	33
Luton T.	Tr	07.87	87-89	110	0	24
Sheffield Wed.	Tr	08.90	90-92	91	7	11
Barnsley	Tr	06.93	93-94	77	0	2

WILSON Darren Anthony
Manchester, 30 September, 1971 (FB)

League Club	Source	Date Signed	Seasons Played	Apps	Subs	Gls
Manchester C.	YT	07.90				
Bury	Tr	06.91	91	30	2	1

WILSON David
Glasgow, 21 November, 1923 (OL)

League Club	Source	Date Signed	Seasons Played	Apps	Subs	Gls
Manchester C.		07.47				
Bury	Tr	07.48	48	2	-	1

WILSON David Charles
Nelson, 24 December, 1942 E Sch/Eu23-7 (W)

League Club	Source	Date Signed	Seasons Played	Apps	Subs	Gls
Preston N.E.	Jnrs	04.60	60-66	168	2	31
Liverpool	Tr	02.67	66	0	1	0
Preston N.E.	Tr	06.68	68-73	99	12	10
Bradford C.	L	03.72	71	5	0	0
Southport	L	10.73	73	2	0	0

WILSON David Edward Joseph
Wednesfield, 4 October, 1944 (F)

League Club	Source	Date Signed	Seasons Played	Apps	Subs	Gls
Nottingham F.	Jnrs	10.61	62-65	8	1	1
Carlisle U.	Tr	10.65	65-66	54	1	23
Grimsby T.	Tr	03.67	66-68	63	0	22
Walsall	Tr	09.68	68-69	33	2	10
Burnley	Tr	09.69	69-70	10	3	0
Chesterfield	Tr	06.71	71-74	125	3	21

WILSON David Graham
Todmorden, 20 March, 1969 (M)

League Club	Source	Date Signed	Seasons Played	Apps	Subs	Gls
Manchester U.	App	03.87	88	0	4	0
Lincoln C.	L	11.90	90	3	0	0
Charlton Ath.	L	03.91	90	6	1	2
Bristol Rov.	Tr	07.91	91-92	11	0	0

WILSON Denis
Bebington, 30 April, 1936 (FB)

League Club	Source	Date Signed	Seasons Played	Apps	Subs	Gls
Wrexham	Jnrs	07.54				
Stoke C.	Rhyl	08.59	59-60	14	-	0

WILSON Dennis Fletcher
Farnham, 6 September, 1929 (FB)

League Club	Source	Date Signed	Seasons Played	Apps	Subs	Gls
Norwich C.	Jnrs	09.46				
Aldershot	Tr	06.50	50-51	5	-	0
Crewe Alex.	Weymouth	10.55	55	22	-	0

WILSON Donald
Heywood, 4 June, 1930 (RB)

League Club	Source	Date Signed	Seasons Played	Apps	Subs	Gls
Bury		05.51	52-58	62	-	1

WILSON Eugene
Sheffield, 11 September, 1932 (W)

League Club	Source	Date Signed	Seasons Played	Apps	Subs	Gls
Rotherham U.		05.53				
Stockport Co.	Tr	05.54	54-61	223	-	42

WILSON Eugene (Gus) Anthony
Manchester, 11 April, 1963 (RB)

League Club	Source	Date Signed	Seasons Played	Apps	Subs	Gls
Crewe Alex.	Runcorn	07.91	91-94	112	3	0

WILSON Frederick Charles
Nottingham, 10 November, 1918 Died 1993 (CH)

League Club	Source	Date Signed	Seasons Played	Apps	Subs	Gls
Wolverhampton W.		05.36				
Bournemouth	Tr	05.37	38-50	98	-	0

WILSON Glenton (Glen) Edward
Winlaton, 2 July, 1929 (WH)

League Club	Source	Date Signed	Seasons Played	Apps	Subs	Gls
Brighton & H.A.	Newcastle U. (Am)	09.49	49-59	409	-	25
Exeter C.	Tr	06.60	60-61	36	-	2

WILSON Harry
Hetton-le-Hole, 29 November, 1953 E Sch/E Yth (LB)

League Club	Source	Date Signed	Seasons Played	Apps	Subs	Gls
Burnley	App	12.70	71	12	0	0
Brighton & H.A.	Tr	12.73	73-76	130	0	4
Preston N.E.	Tr	07.77	77-79	38	4	0
Darlington	Tr	09.80	80-82	82	3	0
Hartlepool U.	Tr	08.83	83	16	0	0

WILSON Ian William
Aberdeen, 27 March, 1958 S-5 (LM)

League Club	Source	Date Signed	Seasons Played	Apps	Subs	Gls
Leicester C.	Elgin C.	04.79	79-87	276	9	17
Everton	Tr	09.87	87-88	24	10	1
Derby Co. (N/C)	Besiktas (Tu)	02.91	90	11	0	0
Bury	Tr	08.91	91	21	3	1
Wigan Ath. (N/C)	Tr	08.92	92	5	0	0

WILSON James
Newmains, 20 April, 1942 (OL)

League Club	Source	Date Signed	Seasons Played	Apps	Subs	Gls
Newcastle U.	Shotts B.A.	09.59	60-61	12	-	2

WILSON James
Glasgow, 19 December, 1929 (OR)

League Club	Source	Date Signed	Seasons Played	Apps	Subs	Gls
Leicester C.	Alloa Ath.	07.54				
Mansfield T.	Tr	03.55	54-55	19	-	1

WILSON James Allan
Musselburgh, 28 June, 1922 (FB)

League Club	Source	Date Signed	Seasons Played	Apps	Subs	Gls
Luton T.	Peterborough U.	07.47	47-50	39	-	1
Northampton T.	Tr	07.51	51	23	-	0

WILSON James Murray
Saltcoats, 19 March, 1923 (IF)

League Club	Source	Date Signed	Seasons Played	Apps	Subs	Gls
Accrington St.	Dundalk	07.49	49	4	-	0

WILSON James (Tug) Thompson
Middlesbrough, 15 March, 1924 Died 1987 (WH/IF)

League Club	Source	Date Signed	Seasons Played	Apps	Subs	Gls
Chelsea	Gravesend & Nft	06.47				
Watford	Leeds U. (trial)	11.50	50-56	49	-	12
Southend U.	Tr	07.57				

WILSON Jeffrey Hansel
South Shields, 7 December, 1964 (D)

League Club	Source	Date Signed	Seasons Played	Apps	Subs	Gls
Darlington	App	12.82	82-83	10	1	0

WILSON John (Jock)
Airdrie, 29 October, 1916 (IF)

League Club	Source	Date Signed	Seasons Played	Apps	Subs	Gls
Chesterfield	Glasgow Celtic	05.39	46	16	-	3
Oldham Ath.	Tr	07.47	47-48	29	-	2
Accrington St.	Tr	10.48	48-49	27	-	1

WILSON John (Ian)
Kennoway (Fife), 11 February, 1923 (OL)

League Club	Source	Date Signed	Seasons Played	Apps	Subs	Gls
Preston N.E.	Forfar Ath.	11.46	46-47	16	-	6
Burnley	Tr	06.48	48-49	19	-	1
Leicester C.	Tr	03.50	49-50	12	-	2
Chesterfield	Tr	10.51	51-52	77	-	18
Rotherham U.	Tr	05.53	53-55	108	-	45

WILSON John Allan
Jarrow, 11 April, 1952 (M)

League Club	Source	Date Signed	Seasons Played	Apps	Subs	Gls
Darlington	Consett	09.71	71-72	15	5	1

WILSON John Christopher
Norwich, 28 October, 1934 (FB)

League Club	Source	Date Signed	Seasons Played	Apps	Subs	Gls
Norwich C.	Jnrs	08.53	53-58	47	-	0
Chesterfield	Tr	07.59	59	16	-	0

WILSON Joseph
Workington, 6 July, 1937 (FB)

League Club	Source	Date Signed	Seasons Played	Apps	Subs	Gls
Workington	Jnrs	01.56	55-61	153	-	5
Nottingham F.	Tr	03.62	61-64	84	-	1
Wolverhampton W.	Tr	03.65	64-66	58	0	0
Newport Co.	Tr	05.67	67	42	1	0
Workington	Tr	09.68	68-72	168	1	4

League Club	Source	Date Signed	Seasons Played	Career Record Apps	Subs	Gls
WILSON Joseph Alexander						
Wylam (Nd), 23 March, 1909 Died 1984						(IF)
Newcastle U.	Tanfield Lea	09.33	34-35	28	-	5
Brighton & H.A.	Tr	05.36	36-46	156	-	15
WILSON Joseph Henry						
Manchester, 17 May, 1925						(FB)
Manchester U.	Jnrs	09.44				
Accrington St.	Tr	10.46	46-50	109	-	4
WILSON Joseph William						
Tow Law, 29 September, 1911 Died 1996						(CH)
Newcastle U.	Jnrs	09.28	29	1	-	0
Southend U.	Tr	08.30	30-34	164	-	4
Brentford	Tr	07.35	35-38	60	-	2
Reading	Tr	08.39				
Barnsley	Tr	05.46	46	20	-	0
WILSON Keith						
Beverley, 14 December, 1935						(IF)
Southampton	Andover	07.59				
Gillingham	Tr	07.61	61	5	-	2
WILSON Kenneth Malcolm						
Dumbarton, 15 September, 1946						(F)
Carlisle U.	Dumbarton	09.72	72	14	6	1
York C.	L	09.73	73	2	0	0
Workington	L	10.73	73	4	1	0
WILSON Kevin James						
Banbury, 18 April, 1961 NI-42						(F)
Derby Co.	Banbury U.	12.79	79-84	106	16	30
Ipswich T.	Tr	01.85	84-86	94	4	34
Chelsea	Tr	06.87	87-91	124	28	42
Notts Co.	Tr	03.92	91-93	58	11	3
Bradford C.	L	01.94	93	5	0	0
Walsall	Tr	08.94	94-96	124	1	38
Northampton T.	Tr	07.97	97	1	8	0
WILSON Lee						
Mansfield, 23 May, 1972						(F)
Mansfield T.	Clipstone M.W.	02.93	92-93	9	9	1
WILSON Leslie John						
Manchester, 10 July, 1947						(RB)
Wolverhampton W.	Jnrs	09.64	65-71	90	11	7
Bristol C.	Tr	03.71	70-72	42	1	1
Norwich C.	Tr	09.73	73	6	0	0
WILSON Mark Antony						
Scunthorpe, 9 February, 1979 E Sch/E Yth						(M/F)
Manchester U.	YT	02.96				
Wrexham	L	02.98	97	12	1	4
WILSON Patrick						
Manchester, 9 November, 1971						(F)
Plymouth Arg.	Ashton U.	08.97	97	7	4	1
Doncaster Rov.	Tr	01.98	97	10	0	1
WILSON Paul Adam						
Maidstone, 22 February, 1977						(F)
Gillingham	YT	04.95	94	0	2	0
WILSON Paul Andrew						
Norwich, 19 June, 1956						(M)
Norwich C.	App	07.74	75	0	1	0
WILSON Paul Anthony						
Bradford, 2 August, 1968						(LB)
Huddersfield T.	YT	06.86	85-86	15	0	0
Norwich C.	Tr	07.87				
Northampton T.	Tr	02.88	87-91	132	9	6
Halifax T.	Tr	12.91	91-92	45	0	7
Burnley	Tr	02.93	92-93	31	0	0
York C.	Tr	10.94	94	21	1	0
Scunthorpe U.	Tr	08.95	95-96	77	0	2
Cambridge U.	Tr	03.97	96-97	38	0	5
WILSON Paul Derek						
Doncaster, 16 November, 1960 E Semi Pro						(F)
Scunthorpe U. (N/C)	Yeovil T.	02.96	96	0	1	0
WILSON Paul Robert						
Forest Gate, 26 September, 1964						(M)
Barnet	Barking	03.88	91-97	201	12	21
WILSON Frederick **Peter**						
Newcastle, 15 September, 1947						(FB)
Middlesbrough		04.66	67	1	0	0

League Club	Source	Date Signed	Seasons Played	Career Record Apps	Subs	Gls
WILSON Philip						
Hemsworth, 16 October, 1960						(M)
Bolton W.	App	10.78	79-80	35	4	4
Huddersfield T.	Tr	08.81	81-86	229	4	16
York C.	Tr	08.87	87-88	38	8	2
Scarborough (N/C)	Macclesfield T.	12.89	89-90	39	4	2
WILSON Philip Michael						
Billingham, 5 February, 1972						(CD)
Hartlepool U.	YT	●	89	0	1	0
WILSON Ramon (Ray)						
Shirebrook, 17 December, 1934 EF Lge/E-63						(LB)
Huddersfield T.	Langwith Jnrs	08.52	55-63	266	-	6
Everton	Tr	07.64	64-68	114	2	0
Oldham Ath.	Tr	07.69	69	25	0	0
Bradford C.	Tr	07.70	70	2	0	0
WILSON Raymond Thomson						
Grangemouth, 8 April, 1947 Su23-1						(LB)
West Bromwich A.	Jnrs	05.64	65-75	230	2	3
WILSON Richard						
Orpington, 8 May, 1960						(F)
Chelsea	App	08.78				
Charlton Ath.	Tr	08.79	79	16	1	1
WILSON Robert						
Motherwell						(LH)
Workington	Stirling A.	12.52	52	2	-	0
WILSON Robert						
Oxford, 29 May, 1944						(CF)
Brentford (Am)	Feltham	04.67	66	1	0	1
WILSON Robert James						
Kensington, 5 June, 1961 IRu21-2						(M)
Fulham	App	06.79	79-84	168	7	34
Millwall	Tr	08.85	85	28	0	12
Luton T.	Tr	08.86	86-87	19	5	1
Fulham	Tr	09.87	87-88	43	4	4
Huddersfield T.	Tr	07.89	89-90	52	5	8
Rotherham U.	Tr	09.91	91	11	3	3
WILSON Robert John						
Birmingham, 23 May, 1943						(G)
Aston Villa	Jnrs	09.61	63	9	-	0
Cardiff C.	Tr	08.64	64-67	114	0	0
Bristol C.	L	10.69	69	1	0	0
Exeter C.	Tr	01.70	69-75	205	0	0
WILSON Robert Primrose						
Chesterfield, 30 October, 1941 E Sch/S-2						(G)
Arsenal	Wolverhampton W. (Am)	03.64	63-73	234	0	0
WILSON Robert Smail Whitelaw						
Musselburgh, 29 June, 1934						(WH)
Norwich C.	Aberdeen	05.57	57-58	62	-	0
Gillingham	Tr	06.60	60	35	-	0
Accrington St.	Tr	07.61				
Chester C.	Tr	04.62	62	15	-	0
WILSON John **Robert**						
Liverpool, 8 September, 1928						(RB)
Preston N.E.	Burscough	04.50	52-62	91	-	0
Tranmere Rov.	Tr	09.62	62-63	54	-	0
WILSON Ronald						
Edinburgh, 6 September, 1941						(LB)
Stoke C.	Musselburgh Ath.	08.59	59-63	11	-	0
Port Vale	Tr	11.63	63-70	261	3	5
WILSON Ronald						
Ellesmere Port, 7 August, 1933						(OR)
Crewe Alex.		11.57	57	1	-	0
WILSON Ronald Gerard						
Sale, 10 September, 1924						(WH)
West Ham U.		10.44	46-47	3	-	0
WILSON Samuel						
Glasgow, 16 December, 1931						(IF)
Millwall	Glasgow Celtic	07.59	59	23	-	11
Northampton T.	Tr	07.60				
WILSON Stephen Lee						
Hull, 24 April, 1974						(G)
Hull C.	YT	07.92	90-97	130	1	0

League Club	Source	Date Signed	Seasons Played	Career Record Apps	Subs	Gls
WILSON Stuart Kevin						
Leicester, 16 September, 1977						(F)
Leicester C.	YT	07.96	96-97	0	13	3
WILSON Terence						
Broxburn, 8 February, 1969 Su21-4						(M/CD)
Nottingham F.	App	04.86	87-92	94	11	9
Newcastle U.	L	01.92	91	2	0	0
WILSON Thomas						
Rosewell, 29 November, 1940						(CH)
Millwall	Falkirk	07.61	61-67	200	1	15
Hull C.	Tr	11.67	67-69	60	0	1
WILSON Thomas						
Bedlington, 15 September, 1930 Died 1992						(CF)
Nottingham F.	Cinderhill	04.51	51-60	191	-	75
Walsall	Tr	11.60	60-61	53	-	19
WILSON Thomas Bastin						
Windygates (Fife), 25 July, 1933						(OR)
Reading	Thornton Hibs	03.56	56	8	-	1
Exeter C.	Tr	07.57	57	22	-	2
WILSON Thomas Frederick						
Southampton, 3 July, 1930						(FB)
Fulham	Southampton (Am)	08.50	52-56	45	-	0
Brentford	Tr	07.57	57-61	148	-	0
WILSON Ulrich Johan						
Netherlands, 5 May, 1964						(D)
Ipswich T. (L)	Twente Enschede (Neth)	12.87	87	5	1	0
WILSON William						
Seaton Delaval, 10 July, 1946						(FB)
Blackburn Rov.	Jnrs	09.63	64-71	246	1	0
Portsmouth	Tr	01.72	71-78	187	6	5
WILSON William James Randolph						
Portadown, 23 September, 1936 NI 'B'						(HB)
Burnley	Portadown	09.55	56-57	2	-	0
WILSTERMAN Brian Hank						
Surinam, 19 November, 1966						(M)
Oxford U.	Beerschot (Bel)	02.97	96-97	16	9	0
WILTON Graham Ernest						
Chesterfield, 19 October, 1942						(OR)
Chesterfield (Am)	Chesterfield T.W.	06.61	61	1	-	0
WILTSHIRE David						
Folkestone, 8 July, 1954						(RB)
Gillingham	Canterbury C.	01.74	73-75	54	8	2
Aldershot	Tr	07.76	76	5	0	0
WIMBLETON Paul Philip						
Havant, 13 November, 1964 E Sch						(M)
Portsmouth	App	02.82	81-83	5	5	0
Cardiff C.	Tr	08.86	86-88	118	1	17
Bristol C.	Tr	05.89	89	10	6	2
Shrewsbury T.	Tr	01.90	89-90	25	9	1
Maidstone U.	L	01.91	90	2	0	1
Exeter C.	Tr	09.91	91	35	1	4
Swansea C.	Tr	08.92	92	10	5	1
WIMSHURST Kenneth Pinkney						
South Shields, 23 March, 1938						(WH)
Newcastle U.	South Shields	07.57				
Gateshead	Tr	11.58	58-59	7	-	0
Wolverhampton W.	Tr	11.60				
Southampton	Tr	07.61	61-67	148	4	9
Bristol C.	Tr	10.67	67-71	146	3	9
WINDASS Dean						
Hull, 1 April, 1969						(F)
Hull C.	North Ferriby U.	10.91	91-95	173	3	57
WINDLE Charles						
Barnsley, 8 January, 1917 Died 1975						(OR)
Bury		09.38				
Exeter C.	Tr	07.39				
Bristol Rov.	Tr	12.46	46	7	-	1
WINDLE William Henry						
Maltby, 9 July, 1920						(OL)
Leeds U.	Denaby U.	10.47	47	2	-	0
Lincoln C.	Tr	02.48	47-51	91	-	22
Chester C.	Tr	10.51	51-54	127	-	20
WINDRIDGE David Howard						
Atherstone, 7 December, 1961						(W/F)
Sheffield U.	Jnrs	01.79				
Chesterfield	Tr	03.80	80-82	66	12	14
Blackpool	Tr	08.83	83-86	87	14	18
Bury (N/C)	Turkey	11.88	88	1	0	0
Rochdale (N/C)	Tr	01.89	88	5	0	0
WINDROSS Dennis						
Guisborough, 12 May, 1938 Died 1989						(WH)
Middlesbrough	Jnrs	05.56	59-60	4	-	1
Brighton & H.A.	Tr	11.60	60	18	-	2
Darlington	Tr	06.61	61	25	-	4
Doncaster Rov.	Tr	06.62	62-63	51	-	4
WINDSOR Robert						
Stoke, 31 January, 1926						(OR)
Stoke C.	Jnrs	12.43				
Lincoln C.	Tr	02.49	48-49	11	-	1
WINFIELD Bernard **John**						
Draycott, 28 February, 1943						(LB/WH)
Nottingham F.	Jnrs	05.60	61-73	353	2	4
Peterborough U.	Tr	07.74	74	11	0	0
WINFIELD Philip						
Mexborough, 16 February, 1937						(WH)
Lincoln C.	Denaby U.	10.57	57	1	-	0
WINGATE John Anthony						
Budleigh Salterton, 19 December, 1948						(M/F)
Plymouth Arg. (Am)	Dawlish	12.68	68	1	0	0
Exeter C.	Dawlish	02.69	68-73	187	16	32
Bournemouth	Tr	07.74	74	30	3	3
Exeter C.	Tr	07.75	75	44	1	2
WINGATE Tony						
Islington, 21 March, 1955						(M)
Colchester U.	App	●	71	0	1	0
WINN Stephen						
Thornaby, 16 September, 1959						(F)
Rotherham U.		03.78	78-80	17	7	3
Torquay U.	Tr	01.82	81	12	2	2
Hartlepool U. (N/C)	Scunthorpe U. (N/C)	03.83	82	1	0	0
WINNIE David						
Glasgow, 26 October, 1966 S Sch/S Yth/Su21-1						(LB)
Middlesbrough (L)	Aberdeen	03.94	93	1	0	0
WINSPEAR John (Jack)						
Leeds, 24 December, 1946						(OR)
Leeds U.	Jnrs	10.64				
Cardiff C.	Tr	06.66	66	1	0	0
Rochdale	Tr	07.67	67	15	1	3
WINSTANLEY Craig Jason						
Hartlepool, 23 August, 1978						(M)
Hartlepool U. (N/C)	YT	12.96	96	0	1	0
WINSTANLEY Eric						
Barnsley, 15 November, 1944 E Yth						(CD)
Barnsley	Jnrs	05.62	61-72	410	0	35
Chesterfield	Tr	08.73	73-76	100	1	7
WINSTANLEY Graham						
Croxdale (Dm), 20 January, 1948						(CD)
Newcastle U.	App	12.68	66-68	5	2	0
Carlisle U.	Tr	08.69	69-74	165	1	8
Brighton & H.A.	Tr	10.74	74-78	63	1	4
Carlisle U.	Tr	07.79	79	32	1	1
WINSTANLEY Mark Andrew						
St Helens, 22 January, 1968						(CD)
Bolton W.	YT	07.86	85-93	215	5	3
Burnley	Tr	08.94	94-97	150	1	5
WINSTON Samuel Anthony						
Islington, 6 August, 1978						(F)
Leyton Orient	Norwich C. (YT)	08.96	96	3	8	1
WINSTONE Simon John						
Bristol, 4 October, 1974						(M)
Stoke C.	YT	07.93				
Torquay U. (N/C)	Tr	09.94	94	1	1	0
WINTER Daniel Thomas						
Rhondda, 14 June, 1918						(FB)
Bolton W.	Mais-y-hof	06.35	36-38	34	-	0
Chelsea	Tr	12.45	46-50	131	-	0

League Club	Source	Date Signed	Seasons Played	Career Record Apps	Subs	Gls
WINTER John George Adrian						
Stoke Newington, 6 March, 1928 (CF)						
Sheffield U.		11.48				
Walsall	Tr	01.51	50-51	41	-	12
WINTER Julian						
Huddersfield, 6 September, 1965 (M)						
Huddersfield T.	App	09.83	84-88	89	4	5
Scunthorpe U.	L	08.88	88	4	0	0
Sheffield U.	Tr	07.89				
WINTER Steven David						
Bristol, 26 October, 1973 (RB/M)						
Walsall	YT	03.92	91-92	14	4	0
Torquay U.	Taunton T.	08.95	95-96	72	1	6
WINTERBOTTOM Dennis Trevor Wilson						
Glossop, 23 October, 1928 (CH)						
Accrington St.	Stalybridge Celtic	06.51	51	12	-	0
WINTERBURN Nigel						
Nuneaton, 11 December, 1963 E Yth/Eu21-1/E 'B'/EF Lge/E-2 (LB)						
Birmingham C.	App	08.81				
Wimbledon	Tr	09.83	83-86	164	1	8
Arsenal	Tr	05.87	87-97	380	2	8
WINTERS Francis						
Johnstone, 30 October, 1923 (CH)						
Torquay U.	Clyde	05.49	49-51	14	-	0
WINTERS Herbert Richard						
Chipping Sodbury, 14 April, 1920 (CH)						
Bristol Rov.	Westerleigh Sports	09.46	46-47	13	-	0
WINTERS Ian Anderson						
Renfrew, 8 February, 1921 Died 1994 (IF)						
York C.	Earswick	08.45	46-47	27	-	10
Gateshead	Boston U.	12.48	48-52	152	-	49
Workington	Tr	07.53	53	30	-	3
WINTERS John Mark						
Wisbech, 24 October, 1960 (RB)						
Peterborough U.	App	10.78	80-82	60	0	3
WINTERSGILL David						
Northallerton, 19 September, 1965 (D/M)						
Wolverhampton W.	App	06.83	82-83	3	1	0
Chester C.	L	03.84	83	6	0	0
Darlington	Finland	11.86	86	15	2	1
WINTLE Frank James						
Stoke, 20 December, 1929 (FB)						
Port Vale		05.49	56	1	-	0
Crewe Alex.	Tr	06.57				
WINTON George **Douglas (Jock)**						
Perth, 6 October, 1929 S 'B' (FB)						
Burnley	Jeanfield Swifts	09.47	51-58	183	-	1
Aston Villa	Tr	01.59	58-60	37	-	0
Rochdale	Tr	06.61	61-63	119	-	0
WIPFLER Charles John						
Trowbridge, 15 July, 1915 Died 1983 (IL)						
Bristol Rov.	McCalls	09.34	34	18	-	5
Watford	Hearts	06.37	37-46	35	-	8
WIRMOLA Jonas						
Sweden, 17 July, 1969 (CD)						
Sheffield U.	Sparvagens (Swe)	08.93	93	8	0	0
WISE Dennis Frank						
Kensington, 15 December, 1966 Eu21-1/E 'B'/E-12 (M/W)						
Wimbledon	Southampton (App)	03.85	84-89	127	8	27
Chelsea	Tr	07.90	90-97	237	7	46
WISEMAN George						
East Dereham, 23 May, 1921 (G)						
Notts Co.		05.45				
Norwich C.	Tr	09.46	46	8	-	0
WITCOMB Douglas Frederick						
Ebbw Vale, 18 April, 1918 W-3 (WH)						
West Bromwich A.	Enfield	10.37	38-46	55	-	3
Sheffield Wed.	Tr	03.47	46-52	224	-	12
Newport Co.	Tr	11.53	53	25	-	0
WITHAM Richard						
Bowburn (Dm), 4 May, 1915 (FB)						
Huddersfield T.	Durham C.	01.34	33	4	-	0
Blackpool	Tr	02.34	33-37	149	-	0
Oldham Ath.		06.46	46	5	-	0
WITHE Christopher						
Liverpool, 25 September, 1962 (LB)						
Newcastle U.	App	09.80	80	2	0	0
Bradford C.	Tr	06.83	83-87	141	2	2
Notts Co.	Tr	10.87	87-88	80	0	3
Bury	Tr	07.89	89	22	9	1
Chester C.	L	10.90	90	2	0	0
Mansfield T.	Tr	01.91	90-92	75	1	5
Shrewsbury T.	Tr	08.93	93-95	80	9	2
WITHE Peter						
Liverpool, 30 August, 1951 E-11 (F)						
Southport	Smith Coggins	11.70	70-71	3	0	0
Barrow	Tr	12.71	71	1	0	0
Wolverhampton W.	Arcadia Shepherds (SA)	11.73	73-74	12	5	3
Birmingham C.	Tr	08.75	75-76	35	0	9
Nottingham F.	Tr	09.76	76-78	74	1	28
Newcastle U.	Tr	08.78	78-79	76	0	25
Aston Villa	Tr	05.80	80-84	182	0	74
Sheffield U.	Tr	07.85	85-87	70	4	18
Birmingham C.	L	09.87	87	8	0	2
Huddersfield T. (N/C)	Tr	07.88	88-89	22	16	1
WITHEFORD James Douglas						
Sheffield, 16 April, 1930 (OR)						
Chesterfield (Am)	Norton Woodseats	12.53	53	9	-	0
WITHERS Alan						
Nottingham, 20 October, 1930 (OL)						
Blackpool	Aspley B.C.	07.49	50-54	22	-	2
Lincoln C.	Tr	02.55	54-58	97	-	18
Notts Co.	Tr	01.59	58-62	121	-	22
WITHERS Charles Francis						
Edmonton, 6 September, 1922 E 'B' (FB)						
Tottenham H.	Jnrs	10.47	47-55	153	-	0
WITHERS Colin Charles						
Birmingham, 21 March, 1940 E Sch (G)						
Birmingham C.	West Bromwich A. (Am)	05.57	60-64	98	-	0
Aston Villa	Tr	11.64	64-68	146	0	0
Lincoln C.	Tr	06.69	69	1	0	0
WITHERS David (Dai) Russell						
Pontypridd, 28 April, 1967 (F)						
Newport Co. (N/C)	Bristol Rov. (YT)	10.86	86-87	7	4	1
WITHEY Graham Alfred						
Bristol, 11 June, 1960 (F)						
Bristol Rov.	Bath C.	08.82	82	19	3	10
Coventry C.	Tr	08.83	83-84	11	11	4
Cardiff C.	Tr	12.84	84-85	27	0	7
Bristol C.	Bath C.	09.86	86	1	1	0
Exeter C.	Cheltenham T.	07.88	88	5	2	2
WITHINGTON Richard Stanley						
South Shields, 8 April, 1921 Died 1981 (IF)						
Blackpool	Jnrs	05.38				
Rochdale	Tr	06.47	47	32	-	6
Chesterfield	Tr	06.48	48	6	-	0
WITSCHGE Richard						
Netherlands, 20 September, 1969 Dutch Int (M)						
Blackburn Rov. (L)	Bordeaux (Fr)	03.95	94	1	0	0
WITTER Anthony Junior						
London, 12 August, 1965 (CD)						
Crystal Palace	Grays Ath.	10.90				
Queens Park R.	Tr	08.91	93	1	0	0
Plymouth Arg.	L	01.92	91	3	0	1
Reading	L	02.94	93	4	0	0
Millwall	Tr	10.94	94-97	99	3	2
WOAN Alan Esplin						
Liverpool, 8 February, 1931 (IF)						
Norwich C.	New Brighton	12.53	53-55	21	-	7
Northampton T.	Tr	07.56	56-59	119	-	68
Crystal Palace	Tr	10.59	59-60	41	-	21
Aldershot	Tr	02.61	60-63	108	-	44
WOAN Donald						
Liverpool, 7 November, 1927 (W)						
Liverpool	Bootle	10.50	50	2	-	0
Leyton Orient	Tr	11.51	51-52	25	-	5
Bradford C.	Tr	10.52	52-53	21	-	4
Tranmere Rov.	Tr	02.54	53-54	27	-	2

League Club	Source	Date Signed	Seasons Played	Apps	Subs	Gls
WOAN Ian Simon						
Heswall, 14 December, 1967						(LM)
Nottingham F.	Runcorn	03.90	90-97	188	20	31
WOFFINDEN Colin						
Hove, 6 August, 1947						(F)
Brighton & H.A. (Am)	Lewes T.	11.70	70	0	3	0
WOJTCZAK Edouard Andrew						
Poland, 29 April, 1921 Died 1995						(G)
York C. (Am)	Polish Army	10.46	46	8	-	0
WOLLEN Terence Leslie						
Swindon, 30 July, 1943						(RB)
Swindon T.	Jnrs	08.60	60-64	84	-	0
WOLSTENHOLME Ian Arthur						
Bradford, 12 January, 1943 E Amat						(G)
York C. (Am)	St Johns College	10.63	63	2	-	0
WOLSTENHOLME John **Trevor**						
Prestbury, 18 June, 1943						(WH)
Birmingham C.	Jnrs	09.60				
Torquay U.	Tr	08.63	63-65	82	0	2
York C.	Tr	07.66	66	11	0	0
WOMACK Albert (Kim) Roy						
Denaby, 20 September, 1934						(W)
Derby Co.	Denaby U.	10.57	57	2	-	0
Southampton	Tr	05.59				
Workington	Tr	07.60	60	9	-	1
WOMBLE Trevor						
South Shields, 7 June, 1951						(M/F)
Rotherham U.	App	10.68	68-77	185	29	39
Crewe Alex.	L	11.71	71	4	0	1
Halifax T.	L	03.73	72	9	1	2
WOMERSLEY Ernest						
Hartshead, 28 August, 1932						(OR)
Huddersfield T.	Jnrs	09.49	50	1	-	0
Bradford C.	Tr	05.57				
WOOD Alan Ernest						
Gravesend, 1 December, 1954						(D)
Charlton Ath.	App	12.72	72	1	0	0
WOOD Alan Herbert						
Newport, 13 January, 1941 W Amat						(CD)
Bristol Rov.	Lovells Ath.	10.62	62	1	-	0
Newport Co.	Merthyr Tydfil	05.65	65-72	149	5	5
WOOD Alfred Edward Howson						
Macclesfield, 25 October, 1945 E Yth						(CD/F)
Manchester C.	App	06.63	62-65	24	1	0
Shrewsbury T.	Tr	06.66	66-71	257	1	65
Millwall	Tr	06.72	72-74	99	1	38
Hull C.	Tr	11.74	74-76	51	2	10
Middlesbrough	Tr	10.76	76	22	1	2
Walsall	Tr	07.77	77	26	3	2
WOOD Alfred Robert						
Walsall, 14 May, 1915						(G)
Coventry C.	Nuneaton T.	12.35	37-51	221	-	0
Northampton T.	Tr	12.51	51-54	139	-	0
Coventry C.	Tr	07.55	55-58	13	-	0
WOOD Archibald						
Leven, 18 March, 1926						(OL)
Tranmere Rov.	Bowhill	08.49	49	31	-	5
WOOD Barrie Wilmot						
Doncaster, 5 December, 1936						(IF)
Doncaster Rov.	Wolverhampton W. (Am)	08.54	55	2	-	0
Scunthorpe U.	Tr	07.58	58	3	-	1
Barnsley	South Shields	03.61	60-61	4	-	2
WOOD Brian Thomas						
Poole, 8 December, 1940						(CH)
West Bromwich A.	Jnrs	01.58				
Crystal Palace	Tr	05.61	61-66	142	1	1
Leyton Orient	Tr	12.66	66-67	58	0	3
Colchester U.	Tr	08.68	68-69	71	0	2
Workington	Tr	07.70	70-75	202	2	9
WOOD Charles William						
Poplar, 7 June, 1919						(CH)
Millwall (Am)		05.46	46	3	-	0
WOOD Christopher Charles						
Penistone, 18 May, 1955						(G)
Huddersfield T.	App	05.72	72	7	0	0
Barnsley	L	02.73	72	1	0	0
Doncaster Rov.	L	07.74	74	4	0	0
WOOD Darren						
Derby, 22 October, 1968						(CD)
Chesterfield	YT	06.87	86-88	61	6	3
Reading	Tr	07.89	89	31	1	2
Northampton T.	Tr	08.90	90-93	4	0	1
WOOD Darren Terence						
Scarborough, 9 June, 1964 E Sch						(RB/M)
Middlesbrough	App	07.81	81-84	101	0	6
Chelsea	Tr	09.84	84-88	134	10	3
Sheffield Wed.	Tr	01.89	88-89	10	1	0
WOOD Eric						
Bolton, 13 March, 1920						(WH)
Rochdale	Bolton W (Am)	08.43	46-50	148	-	15
WOOD Frank						
Manchester, 17 August, 1924						(CH)
Bury	Hulme	10.48	50	1	-	0
Exeter C.	Shrewsbury T. (trial)	01.53	52	8	-	0
WOOD Gary Terence						
Corby, 2 December, 1955						(FB)
Notts Co.	Kettering T.	12.77	77-80	7	4	0
WOOD George						
Douglas (Lk), 26 September, 1952 S-4						(G)
Blackpool	East Stirling	01.72	71-76	117	0	0
Everton	Tr	08.77	77-79	103	0	0
Arsenal	Tr	08.80	80-82	60	0	0
Crystal Palace	Tr	08.83	83-87	192	0	0
Cardiff C.	Tr	01.88	87-89	67	0	0
Blackpool	L	03.90	89	15	0	0
Hereford U.	Tr	08.90	90	41	0	0
WOOD Graham						
Doncaster, 10 February, 1933						(CF)
Wolverhampton W.		09.50				
Halifax T.	Tr	06.53	53-54	19	-	3
WOOD Harry						
Barrow, 31 December, 1911 Died 1994						(IF)
Barrow		02.33	32-48	21	-	2
WOOD Henry						
Liverpool, 8 April, 1927						(OR)
Chesterfield	South Liverpool	07.53	53	9	-	1
WOOD Hugh Sutherland						
Bellshill, 16 November, 1960						(D)
Scunthorpe U.	Grantham	09.80	80	0	1	0
WOOD Ian Nigel						
Kirkby-in-Ashfield, 24 May, 1958						(D)
Mansfield T.	App	06.76	75-81	135	14	9
Aldershot	Tr	08.82	82	14	0	1
WOOD Ian Thomas						
Radcliffe, 15 Janaury, 1948						(FB)
Oldham Ath.	Park Lane Olympic	11.65	65-79	517	7	22
Burnley	Tr	05.80	80	14	3	0
WOOD James Henry						
Liverpool, 25 October, 1938						(G)
Southport	Burscough	04.58	57	1	-	0
WOOD Jeffrey Reginald						
Islington, 4 February, 1954						(G)
Charlton Ath.	Harlow T.	11.75	75-80	147	0	0
Colchester U.	Denmark	09.81				
Exeter C.	Happy Valley (HK)	08.84	84	33	0	0
WOOD Jack						
Royton, 12 February, 1931						(WH)
Aldershot		09.52	52-54	38	-	1
WOOD John Michael						
Brownhills, 9 September, 1948						(FB)
Wrexham	Jnrs	07.66	65-67	4	3	0
WOOD Edward **John (Jackie)**						
Canning Town, 23 October, 1919 Died 1993 E Amat						(OL)
West Ham U.	Leytonstone	03.38	37-48	58	-	13
Leyton Orient	Tr	10.49	49	9	-	1

League Club	Source	Date Signed	Seasons Played	Apps	Subs	Gls
WOOD Kevin						
Armthorpe, 3 November, 1929						(IF)
Doncaster Rov.		10.49				
Grimsby T.	Worksop T.	03.51	50-51	3	-	2
WOOD Thomas **Leslie**						
Haslingden, 20 December, 1932						(G)
Huddersfield T.	Bolton W. (Am)	04.52				
Barrow	Tr	08.55	55	32	-	0
Port Vale	Tr	06.56	56	2	-	0
Southport	Tr	01.58	57	1	-	0
WOOD Mark						
Scarborough, 27 June, 1972						(M)
York C.	YT	07.90	90	0	1	0
WOOD Michael						
Halifax, 9 March, 1962						(F)
Rochdale (N/C)	Guiseley	08.86	86	5	1	3
WOOD Michael James						
Bury, 3 July, 1952						(D)
Blackburn Rov.	App	02.70	69-77	140	8	2
Bradford C.	Tr	02.78	77-81	143	3	9
Halifax T.	Tr	08.82	82-83	80	1	2
WOOD Nicholas Anthony						
Oldham, 6 January, 1966 E Yth						(F)
Manchester U.	App	06.83	85-86	2	1	0
WOOD Norman						
Sunderland, 10 August, 1932						(WH)
Sunderland	Silksworth Jnrs	05.54	54	1	-	0
WOOD Norman						
Chadderton, 20 October, 1921						(OR)
Oldham Ath. (Am)	Royton Amats	09.46	46	1	-	0
WOOD Paul						
Oldham, 20 March, 1970						(M)
Sheffield U.	YT	09.88	87	0	1	0
Rochdale	L	11.88	88	2	3	0
WOOD Paul Anthony						
Saltburn, 1 November, 1964						(RW)
Portsmouth	App	11.82	83-86	25	22	7
Brighton & H.A.	Tr	08.87	87-89	77	15	8
Sheffield U.	Tr	02.90	89-91	19	9	3
Bournemouth	L	02.91	90	20	1	0
Bournemouth	Tr	10.91	91-93	73	5	18
Portsmouth	Tr	02.94	93-95	25	7	3
WOOD Raymond Ernest						
Hebburn, 11 June, 1931 Eu23-1/E 'B'/EF Lge/E-3						(G)
Darlington	Newcastle U. (Am)	09.49	49	12	-	0
Manchester U.	Tr	12.49	49-58	178	-	0
Huddersfield T.	Tr	12.58	58-64	207	-	0
Bradford C.	Toronto (Can)	10.65	65	32	0	0
Barnsley	Tr	08.66	66-67	30	0	0
WOOD Robert						
Elphinstone, 15 February, 1930						(WH)
Barnsley	Hibernian	07.51	51-64	338	-	41
WOOD William **Ronald**						
Manchester, 11 November, 1925						(IF)
Wrexham	Droylsden	11.49	49	16	-	5
WOOD Royden						
Wallasey, 16 October, 1930						(G)
Leeds U.	Clitheroe	05.52	53-59	196	-	0
WOOD Simon Onward						
Hull, 24 September, 1976						(CD/F)
Coventry C.	YT	11.93				
Mansfield T.	Tr	03.96	95-96	32	9	4
WOOD Stephen Allan						
Bracknell, 2 February, 1963						(CD)
Reading	App	02.81	79-86	216	3	9
Millwall	Tr	06.87	87-91	108	2	0
Southampton	Tr	10.91	91-93	46	0	0
Oxford U.	Tr	07.94	94-95	12	1	0
WOOD Steven Ronald						
Oldham, 23 June, 1963						(M)
Macclesfield T.	Ashton U.	07.93	97	43	0	13
WOOD Terence Laurence						
Newport, 3 September, 1920 W Sch						(WH)
Cardiff C. (Am)	Newport Docks	09.46	46	4	-	0
WOOD Trevor John						
Jersey, 3 November, 1968 NI 'B'/NI-1						(G)
Brighton & H.A.	App	11.86				
Port Vale	Tr	07.88	88-92	42	0	0
Walsall	Tr	07.94	94-96	69	0	0
Hereford U.	Tr	01.97	96	19	0	0
WOOD William						
Barnsley, 28 December, 1927						(FB)
Sunderland	Spen Jnrs	10.48	49	1	-	0
Hull C.	Tr	07.51				
Sheffield U.	Tr	06.52	52	5	-	0
WOODALL Arthur John						
Stoke, 4 June, 1930						(F)
Stoke C.	Jnrs	05.50	53	1	-	0
WOODALL Brian Harold						
Chester, 6 June, 1948						(W)
Sheffield Wed.	App	06.65	67-69	19	3	4
Oldham Ath.	L	02.70	69	3	1	1
Chester C.	Tr	06.70	70	11	2	2
Crewe Alex.	L	03.71	70	10	1	3
WOODALL Bertram **John**						
Doncaster, 16 January, 1949						(F)
York C.	Goole T.	02.67	67	2	0	0
Rotherham U.	Gainsborough Trin.	03.74	73-74	25	1	7
WOODBURN James						
Rutherglen, 29 January, 1917 Died 1978						(LH)
Newcastle U.	Coltness U.	02.38	38-47	44	-	4
Gateshead	Tr	09.48	48-51	132	-	10
WOODCOCK Anthony Stewart						
Eastwood, 6 December, 1955 Eu21-2/E-42						(F)
Nottingham F.	App	01.74	73-79	125	4	36
Lincoln C.	L	02.76	75	2	2	1
Doncaster Rov.	L	09.76	76	6	0	2
Arsenal	F.C. Köln (Ger)	07.82	82-85	129	2	56
WOODCOCK David Keith						
Shardlow, 13 October, 1966						(M)
Sunderland	App	10.84				
Darlington	Tr	08.85	85-86	14	13	2
WOODCOCK Ernest						
Salford, 14 May, 1925						(W)
Bury	Blackburn Rov. (Am)	01.47	46-47	18	-	3
Oldham Ath.	Tr	06.48	48-49	28	-	4
WOODCOCK Harold						
Darlington, 18 September, 1928						(RH)
Darlington		08.52	52-53	5	-	0
WOODCOCK Thomas						
Chorley, 19 March, 1926						(IF)
Southport (Am)	Preston N.E. (Am)	07.46	46	1	-	0
WOODFIELD David						
Leamington, 11 October, 1943						(CH)
Wolverhampton W.	Jnrs	10.60	61-69	247	3	13
Watford	Tr	09.71	71-73	14	1	0
WOODFIELD Terry						
Nottingham, 21 January, 1946						(WH)
Notts Co.	Jnrs	07.63	63	5	-	0
WOODFORD Robert Michael						
Keyworth, 6 December, 1943						(WH)
Notts Co.	Jnrs	03.61	61	3	-	0
WOODGATE John **Terence**						
West Ham, 11 December, 1919 Died 1985						(OL)
West Ham U.	Beckton	09.38	38-52	259	-	48
WOODHEAD Andrew						
Wallsend, 12 July, 1966						(M)
Gillingham	App	•	83	1	1	0
WOODHEAD Dennis						
Sheffield, 12 June, 1925 Died 1995						(OL)
Sheffield Wed.	Hillsborough B.C.	04.45	46-54	213	-	73
Chesterfield	Tr	09.55	55	15	-	6

League Club	Source	Date Signed	Seasons Played	Apps	Subs	Gls
Derby Co.	Tr	01.56	55-58	94	-	24
Southport	L	02.59	58	4	-	1

WOODHEAD Dennis
Huddersfield, 2 September, 1924 (OL)

League Club	Source	Date Signed	Seasons Played	Apps	Subs	Gls
Bradford C.		01.48				
Accrington St.	Tr	05.48	48	6	-	0

WOODHEAD Simon Christopher
Dewsbury, 26 December, 1962 (M/FB)

League Club	Source	Date Signed	Seasons Played	Apps	Subs	Gls
Mansfield T.	Jnrs	09.80	80-84	108	14	6

WOODHOUSE Curtis
Beverley, 17 April, 1980 (WB)

League Club	Source	Date Signed	Seasons Played	Apps	Subs	Gls
Sheffield U.	YT	12.97	97	4	5	0

WOODHOUSE John
Middlesbrough, 5 April, 1937 (F)

League Club	Source	Date Signed	Seasons Played	Apps	Subs	Gls
Leeds U.	South Bank	06.55				
Gateshead	Tr	07.57	57	2	-	0

WOODIN Stephen
Birkenhead, 6 January, 1955 (W)

League Club	Source	Date Signed	Seasons Played	Apps	Subs	Gls
Tranmere Rov.		02.75	74	1	2	0

WOODLEY Derek George
Isleworth, 2 March, 1942 E Sch/E Yth (W)

League Club	Source	Date Signed	Seasons Played	Apps	Subs	Gls
West Ham U.	Jnrs	04.59	59-61	12	-	3
Southend U.	Tr	08.62	62-66	160	2	23
Charlton Ath.	Tr	06.67	67	2	1	0
Southend U.	Tr	10.67	67	7	2	0
Gillingham	Tr	01.68	67-70	99	1	9

WOODLEY Victor Robert
Slough, 26 February, 1911 Died 1978 EF Lge/E-19 (G)

League Club	Source	Date Signed	Seasons Played	Apps	Subs	Gls
Chelsea	Windsor & Eton	05.31	31-38	252	-	0
Derby Co.	Bath C.	03.46	46	30	-	0

WOODMAN Andrew John
Camberwell, 11 August, 1971 (G)

League Club	Source	Date Signed	Seasons Played	Apps	Subs	Gls
Crystal Palace	YT	07.89				
Exeter C.	Tr	07.94	94	6	0	0
Northampton T.	Tr	03.95	94-97	145	0	0

WOODROFFE Lewis Christopher
Portsmouth, 29 October, 1921 (OR)

League Club	Source	Date Signed	Seasons Played	Apps	Subs	Gls
Manchester C.		10.45	46	9	-	1
Watford	Tr	08.47	47-50	63	-	6

WOODRUFF Arthur
Barnsley, 12 April, 1913 Died 1983 EF Lge (CH)

League Club	Source	Date Signed	Seasons Played	Apps	Subs	Gls
Bradford C.		08.34				
Burnley	Tr	07.36	36-51	271	-	0
Workington	Tr	07.52	52	11	-	0

WOODRUFF Robert James
Wolverhampton, 11 March, 1965 W Sch/W Yth (F)

League Club	Source	Date Signed	Seasons Played	Apps	Subs	Gls
Newport Co.	Cardiff C. (Jnrs)	08.83	83	9	1	0
Swindon T.	L	05.84	83	1	1	0

WOODRUFF Robert William
Highworth (Wilts), 9 November, 1940 (M/F)

League Club	Source	Date Signed	Seasons Played	Apps	Subs	Gls
Swindon T.	Jnrs	05.58	58-63	180	-	20
Wolverhampton W.	Tr	03.64	63-65	63	0	18
Crystal Palace	Tr	06.66	66-69	123	2	48
Cardiff C.	Tr	11.69	69-73	141	9	22
Newport Co.	Tr	08.74	74-75	52	0	7

WOODS Alan Edward
Dinnington, 15 February, 1937 E Sch/E Yth (WH)

League Club	Source	Date Signed	Seasons Played	Apps	Subs	Gls
Tottenham H.	Jnrs	02.54	54	6	-	0
Swansea C.	Tr	12.56	57-59	31	-	0
York C.	Tr	07.60	60-65	227	1	4

WOODS Charles Morgan Parkinson
Whitehaven, 18 March, 1941 (F)

League Club	Source	Date Signed	Seasons Played	Apps	Subs	Gls
Newcastle U.	Cleator Moor	05.59	60-61	26	-	7
Bournemouth	Tr	11.62	62-64	70	-	26
Crystal Palace	Tr	11.64	64-65	49	0	5
Ipswich T.	Tr	07.66	66-69	65	17	5
Watford	Tr	06.70	70-71	40	2	3
Colchester U.	L	11.71	71	3	0	0

WOODS Christopher Charles Eric
Boston, 14 November, 1959 E Yth/Eu21-6/E 'B'/E-43 (G)

League Club	Source	Date Signed	Seasons Played	Apps	Subs	Gls
Nottingham F.	App	12.76				
Queens Park R.	Tr	07.79	79-80	63	0	0
Norwich C.	Tr	03.81	80-85	216	0	0
Sheffield Wed.	Glasgow Rangers	08.91	91-95	106	1	0
Reading	L	10.95	95	5	0	0
Southampton	Colorardo Rapids (USA)	11.96	96	4	0	0
Sunderland (N/C)	Tr	03.97				
Burnley	Tr	07.97	97	12	0	0

WOODS Clive Richard
Norwich, 18 December, 1947 (W)

League Club	Source	Date Signed	Seasons Played	Apps	Subs	Gls
Ipswich T.	Gothic	06.69	69-79	217	50	24
Norwich C.	Tr	03.80	79-81	29	3	4

WOODS Dennis James
Norwich, 12 December, 1936 (OR)

League Club	Source	Date Signed	Seasons Played	Apps	Subs	Gls
Watford	Cambridge U.	10.62	62	13	-	2

WOODS Derek Edward
Northampton, 23 March, 1941 E Amat (OR)

League Club	Source	Date Signed	Seasons Played	Apps	Subs	Gls
Northampton T. (Am)	Jnrs	06.59	61	6	-	2

WOODS Edward
Ton Pentre, 29 July, 1951 (F)

League Club	Source	Date Signed	Seasons Played	Apps	Subs	Gls
Bristol C.	Ton Pentre	09.71	72	1	1	0
Scunthorpe U.	L	10.73	73	4	0	2
Newport Co.	Tr	09.74	74-78	149	2	55

WOODS Jonathan Paul
Blackwood, 5 October, 1966 (F)

League Club	Source	Date Signed	Seasons Played	Apps	Subs	Gls
Cardiff C. (N/C)	Jnrs	08.84	84	0	1	0

WOODS Kenneth Stephen
Liverpool, 15 April, 1974 (M)

League Club	Source	Date Signed	Seasons Played	Apps	Subs	Gls
Everton	YT	06.92				
Bury	Tr	07.93	93	0	2	0

WOODS Matthew James
Gosport, 9 September, 1976 (D/M)

League Club	Source	Date Signed	Seasons Played	Apps	Subs	Gls
Everton	YT	07.95				
Chester C.	Tr	08.96	96-97	33	17	3

WOODS Maurice (Matt)
Skelmersdale, 1 November, 1931 EF Lge (CH)

League Club	Source	Date Signed	Seasons Played	Apps	Subs	Gls
Everton	Burscough	11.49	52-56	8	-	1
Blackburn Rov.	Tr	11.56	56-62	260	-	2
Luton T.	Hellas (Aus)	07.65	65	34	0	0
Stockport Co.	Tr	07.66	66-67	85	0	2

WOODS Neil Stephen
York, 30 July, 1966 (F)

League Club	Source	Date Signed	Seasons Played	Apps	Subs	Gls
Doncaster Rov.	App	08.83	82-86	55	10	16
Ipswich T.	Glasgow Rangers	07.87	87-89	15	12	5
Bradford C.	Tr	03.90	89	13	1	2
Grimsby T.	Tr	08.90	90-97	175	51	42
Wigan Ath.	L	11.97	97	1	0	0
Scunthorpe U.	L	01.98	97	2	0	0
Mansfield T.	L	02.98	97	5	1	0

WOODS Patrick James
Islington, 29 April, 1933 (FB)

League Club	Source	Date Signed	Seasons Played	Apps	Subs	Gls
Queens Park R.	Jnrs	06.50	52-60	304	-	15
Colchester U.	Hellenic (Aus)	08.63	63	36	-	0

WOODS Peter Anthony
Sale, 21 January, 1950 (FB)

League Club	Source	Date Signed	Seasons Played	Apps	Subs	Gls
Manchester U.	App	04.67				
Luton T.	Tr	04.70				
Southend U.	Tr	02.72	71-72	25	0	0
Doncaster Rov.	Tr	07.73	73-74	41	8	1

WOODS Raymond
Peterborough, 27 April, 1930 (RH)

League Club	Source	Date Signed	Seasons Played	Apps	Subs	Gls
Southend U.	Peterborough U.	05.48	50-51	3	-	1
Crystal Palace	Tr	06.53	53-54	18	-	0

WOODS Raymond Guy
Birkenhead, 7 June, 1965 (RW)

League Club	Source	Date Signed	Seasons Played	Apps	Subs	Gls
Tranmere Rov.	App	06.83	82-84	9	5	2
Wigan Ath.	Colne Dynamoes	02.89	88-90	25	3	3
Coventry C.	Tr	01.91	90-91	21	0	1
Wigan Ath.	L	01.93	92	12	1	0
Shrewsbury T.	Tr	03.94	93-95	40	11	1

WOODS Stephen Gerard
Glasgow, 23 February, 1970 (G)

League Club	Source	Date Signed	Seasons Played	Apps	Subs	Gls
Preston N.E.	Clydebank	10.93	93	19	1	0

WOODS Stephen John
Davenham, 15 December, 1976 (D)

League Club	Source	Date Signed	Seasons Played	Apps	Subs	Gls
Stoke C.	YT	08.95	97	0	1	0
Plymouth Arg.	L	03.98	97	4	1	0

WOODS William
Farnworth, 12 March, 1926 (IF)

League Club	Source	Date Signed	Seasons Played	Apps	Subs	Gls
Rochdale	Moss Grove	04.45	46	15	-	1
Bradford P.A.	Tr	01.47	46	5	-	0
Rochdale	Tr	01.49	48-49	13	-	1
Barrow	Tr	11.49	49	16	-	4
Crewe Alex.	Tr	07.50				
Accrington St.	Tr	11.50	50	3	-	0

WOODS Darragh William
Cork, 24 October, 1973 IRu21-4 (W)

League Club	Source	Date Signed	Seasons Played	Apps	Subs	Gls
Coventry C.	YT	07.92				
Tranmere Rov.	Cork C.	07.95	96	1	0	0
Blackpool	L	10.96	96	3	0	0

WOODSFORD Jamie Marcus
Ipswich, 9 November, 1976 E Yth (F)

League Club	Source	Date Signed	Seasons Played	Apps	Subs	Gls
Luton T.	YT	03.95	94-95	2	8	0

WOODTHORPE Colin John
Ellesmere Port, 13 January, 1969 (LB)

League Club	Source	Date Signed	Seasons Played	Apps	Subs	Gls
Chester C.	YT	08.86	86-89	154	1	6
Norwich C.	Tr	07.90	90-93	36	7	1
Stockport Co.	Aberdeen	07.97	97	29	3	1

WOODWARD Alan
Chapeltown, 7 September, 1946 E Yth/EF Lge (RW)

League Club	Source	Date Signed	Seasons Played	Apps	Subs	Gls
Sheffield U.	App	09.63	63-78	537	2	158

WOODWARD Alan
Sutton-in-Ashfield, 19 June, 1947 (W)

League Club	Source	Date Signed	Seasons Played	Apps	Subs	Gls
Grimsby T.	Alfreton T.	07.70	70-71	54	0	13

WOODWARD Andrew Stephen
Stockport, 23 September, 1973 (CD)

League Club	Source	Date Signed	Seasons Played	Apps	Subs	Gls
Crewe Alex.	YT	07.92	92-94	9	11	0
Bury	Tr	03.95	94-97	45	19	0

WOODWARD Brian
Leeds, 12 July, 1929 (CF)

League Club	Source	Date Signed	Seasons Played	Apps	Subs	Gls
Leeds U.	Jnrs	07.47				
York C.	Hereford U.	08.50	50	5	-	0

WOODWARD Harry George
Bromley, 29 August, 1919 (CH)

League Club	Source	Date Signed	Seasons Played	Apps	Subs	Gls
Southend U.	Chelmsford C.	05.46	50-51	14	-	0

WOODWARD Horace John
Islington, 16 January, 1924 (CH)

League Club	Source	Date Signed	Seasons Played	Apps	Subs	Gls
Tottenham H.	Jnrs	05.46	46-48	63	-	1
Queens Park R.	Tr	06.49	49-50	57	-	0
Walsall	Tonbridge	07.53	53	5	-	0

WOODWARD John
Glasgow, 10 January, 1949 S Yth (CD/M)

League Club	Source	Date Signed	Seasons Played	Apps	Subs	Gls
Arsenal	Possilpark Jnrs	01.66	66	2	1	0
York C.	Tr	07.71	71-77	152	15	6

WOODWARD John
Stoke, 16 January, 1947 (F)

League Club	Source	Date Signed	Seasons Played	Apps	Subs	Gls
Stoke C.	App	03.64	64-66	10	1	1
Aston Villa	Tr	10.66	66-68	22	4	7
Walsall	Tr	05.69	69-72	116	9	23
Port Vale	Tr	02.73	72-74	88	11	30
Scunthorpe U.	Tr	07.75	75	16	3	5

WOODWARD Kenneth Robert
Battersea, 16 November, 1947 (IF)

League Club	Source	Date Signed	Seasons Played	Apps	Subs	Gls
Crystal Palace	App	12.65				
Leyton Orient	Tr	08.66	66	1	0	0

WOODWARD Laurence (Dai)
Merthyr Tydfil, 5 July, 1918 Died 1997 (WH)

League Club	Source	Date Signed	Seasons Played	Apps	Subs	Gls
Wolverhampton W.		05.38				
Walsall	L	11.38	38	29	-	0
Bournemouth	Tr	05.39	46-56	275	-	7

WOODWARD Thomas Peter
Birmingham, 6 July, 1934 (G)

League Club	Source	Date Signed	Seasons Played	Apps	Subs	Gls
West Bromwich A.	Moor Green	09.54				
Walsall	Tr	08.58	58	13	-	0

WOODWARD Thomas
Horwich, 8 December, 1917 Died 1994 (OR)

League Club	Source	Date Signed	Seasons Played	Apps	Subs	Gls
Bolton W.	White Horse Temp.	01.35	35-49	152	-	18
Middlesbrough	Tr	10.49	49-50	19	-	6

WOODWARD Vivian
Merthyr Tydfil, 20 May, 1914 (WH/IF)

League Club	Source	Date Signed	Seasons Played	Apps	Subs	Gls
Fulham	Folkestone T.	01.36	35-46	92	-	24
Millwall	Tr	02.47	46-47	42	-	13
Brentford	Tr	07.48	48-49	20	-	4
Aldershot	Tr	02.50	49-50	53	-	5

WOODWORTH Anthony David
Manchester, 5 March, 1968 (G)

League Club	Source	Date Signed	Seasons Played	Apps	Subs	Gls
Burnley	App	03.86	86	1	0	0

WOOF Clifford Eric
Liverpool, 20 September, 1956 (F)

League Club	Source	Date Signed	Seasons Played	Apps	Subs	Gls
Liverpool	Jnrs	05.76				
Southport (N/C)	Jacob's	12.77	77	1	0	0

WOOF William
Gateshead, 16 August, 1956 (F)

League Club	Source	Date Signed	Seasons Played	Apps	Subs	Gls
Middlesbrough	App	08.74	74-81	30	16	5
Peterborough U.	L	03.77	76	2	1	0
Cardiff C. (N/C)	Blyth Spartans	09.82	82	1	0	1
Hull C.	Gateshead	02.83	82	9	2	3

WOOKEY Kenneth George
Newport, 30 December, 1946 Died 1992 (W)

League Club	Source	Date Signed	Seasons Played	Apps	Subs	Gls
Newport Co.	Jnrs	01.64	64-68	57	6	5
Port Vale	Tr	07.69	69	23	1	4
Workington	Tr	07.70	70	11	5	4

WOOKEY Kenneth William
Newport, 23 February, 1922 W Sch (OR)

League Club	Source	Date Signed	Seasons Played	Apps	Subs	Gls
Newport Co.	Jnrs	02.39	46	14	-	2
Bristol Rov.	Tr	12.46	46-48	54	-	9
Swansea C.	Tr	11.48	48-49	13	-	0
Ipswich T.	Hereford U.	10.50	50	15	-	1

WOOLCOTT Roy Alfred
Leyton, 29 July, 1946 (F)

League Club	Source	Date Signed	Seasons Played	Apps	Subs	Gls
Tottenham H.	Eton Manor	02.68	69	1	0	0
Gillingham	L	02.72	71	13	0	5

WOOLDRIDGE James
Rossington, 28 September, 1918 (LB)

League Club	Source	Date Signed	Seasons Played	Apps	Subs	Gls
Doncaster Rov.	Benburb	12.40	46-47	30	-	0

WOOLDRIDGE Stephen Joseph
Chiswick, 18 July, 1950 (RB)

League Club	Source	Date Signed	Seasons Played	Apps	Subs	Gls
Crystal Palace	App	07.67				
Plymouth Arg.	L	08.70	70	20	0	0
Colchester U.	Tr	06.72	72	3	0	0

WOOLER Alan Thomas
Poole, 17 August, 1953 (D)

League Club	Source	Date Signed	Seasons Played	Apps	Subs	Gls
Reading	Weymouth	11.71	71-72	38	0	0
West Ham U.	Tr	08.73	73-75	3	1	0
Aldershot	Tr	04.76	76-83	264	2	3

WOOLER Michael Graham
Huddersfield, 23 October, 1944 (F)

League Club	Source	Date Signed	Seasons Played	Apps	Subs	Gls
Huddersfield T.		08.64				
Halifax T.	Tr	12.64	64-67	51	7	8

WOOLFALL Alan Francis
Liverpool, 30 November, 1956 (W)

League Club	Source	Date Signed	Seasons Played	Apps	Subs	Gls
Bury	Skelmersdale U.	10.74	74-78	46	11	11
Port Vale	Tr	08.79	79-80	13	5	3

WOOLFORD Michael Elijah George
Swindon, 29 September, 1939 (F)

League Club	Source	Date Signed	Seasons Played	Apps	Subs	Gls
Swindon T.	Swindon B.R.	12.59	59	3	-	0

WOOLGAR Philip Robert John
Worthing, 24 September, 1948 (G)

League Club	Source	Date Signed	Seasons Played	Apps	Subs	Gls
Brighton & H.A. (Am)	Wigmore Ath.	06.66	66	1	0	0

WOOLGAR James Stewart
Chesterfield, 21 September, 1952 (M)

League Club	Source	Date Signed	Seasons Played	Apps	Subs	Gls
West Bromwich A.	App	10.69	72	2	2	0
Doncaster Rov.	Tr	07.74	74	2	5	1

WOOLLARD Arnold James
Bermuda, 24 August, 1930 (FB)

League Club	Source	Date Signed	Seasons Played	Apps	Subs	Gls
Northampton T.	Bermuda A.A. (Ber)	06.49	50	3	-	0
Newcastle U.	Tr	12.52	52-55	8	-	0
Bournemouth	Tr	06.56	56-61	161	-	0
Northampton T.	Tr	03.62	61-62	28	-	0

WOOLLETT Alan Howard
Wigston, 4 March, 1947 (D)

League Club	Source	Date Signed	Seasons Played	Apps	Subs	Gls
Leicester C.	App	08.64	66-77	213	15	0
Northampton T.	Tr	07.78	78	23	0	0

WOOLLETT Charles
Murton, 25 November, 1920 (OL)

League Club	Source	Date Signed	Seasons Played	Apps	Subs	Gls
Newcastle U.	Eppleton Colly	11.42				
Bradford C.	Tr	08.46	46-48	43	-	5
York C.	Murton Colly	02.49	48	4	-	0

WOOLLEY Robert Alan
Nottingham, 29 December, 1947 Died 1971 (F)

League Club	Source	Date Signed	Seasons Played	Apps	Subs	Gls
Notts Co.	App	07.65	63-65	9	0	2

WOOLMER Anthony John
Norwich, 25 March, 1946 (F)

League Club	Source	Date Signed	Seasons Played	Apps	Subs	Gls
Norwich C.	Jnrs	12.65	66-67	4	1	1
Bradford P.A.	Tr	10.69	69	30	0	7
Scunthorpe U.	Tr	11.70	70-71	35	5	3

WOOLSEY Jeffrey Alexander
Upminster, 8 November, 1977 (D)

League Club	Source	Date Signed	Seasons Played	Apps	Subs	Gls
Arsenal	YT	07.96				
Queens Park R.	Tr	08.97				
Brighton & H.A.	Tr	03.98	97	1	2	0

WOON Andrew Geoffrey
Bognor Regis, 26 June, 1952 (F)

League Club	Source	Date Signed	Seasons Played	Apps	Subs	Gls
Brentford	Bognor Regis T.	10.72	72-74	42	8	12

WOOSNAM Philip Abraham
Caersws, 22 December, 1932 W Sch/W Amat/EF Lge/W-17 (IF)

League Club	Source	Date Signed	Seasons Played	Apps	Subs	Gls
Manchester C. (Am)	Bangor Univ.	06.52	52	1	-	0
Leyton Orient	Sutton U.	03.55	54-58	108	-	19
West Ham U.	Tr	11.58	58-62	138	-	26
Aston Villa	Tr	11.62	62-65	106	0	24

WOOTTON Leonard
Stoke, 13 June, 1925 Died 1990 (F)

League Club	Source	Date Signed	Seasons Played	Apps	Subs	Gls
Port Vale		08.45	46	10	-	1
Wrexham	Queen of South	08.51	51	20	-	2

WORBOYS Gavin Anthony
Doncaster, 14 July, 1974 (F)

League Club	Source	Date Signed	Seasons Played	Apps	Subs	Gls
Doncaster Rov.	YT	04.92	91	6	1	2
Notts Co.	Tr	05.92				
Exeter C.	L	12.93	93	4	0	1
Darlington	Tr	11.94	94-95	30	11	8
Northampton T.	Tr	01.96	95	4	9	1

WORDLEY Edward (Ted) Henry
Stoke, 17 October, 1923 Died 1989 (WH)

League Club	Source	Date Signed	Seasons Played	Apps	Subs	Gls
Stoke C.	Jnrs	10.41	46-49	10	-	0
Bury	Tr	06.50				

WORKMAN Peter **Ian**
Liverpool, 13 November, 1962 (M)

League Club	Source	Date Signed	Seasons Played	Apps	Subs	Gls
Chester C. (N/C)	Southport	01.83	82	3	0	0

WORLEY Leonard Francis
Amersham, 27 June, 1937 E Yth/E Amat (OL)

League Club	Source	Date Signed	Seasons Played	Apps	Subs	Gls
Charlton Ath. (Am)	Wycombe W.	10.56	56	1	-	0
Tottenham H. (Am)	Wycombe W.	05.59	59	1	-	0

WORMLEY Paul
Leeds, 16 September, 1961 (F)

League Club	Source	Date Signed	Seasons Played	Apps	Subs	Gls
Barnsley	Yorkshire Amats	10.79	79	1	0	0

WORMULL Simon James
Crawley, 1 December, 1976 (RM)

League Club	Source	Date Signed	Seasons Played	Apps	Subs	Gls
Tottenham H.	YT	07.95				
Brentford	Tr	07.97	97	3	2	0
Brighton & H.A.	Tr	03.98				

WORRALL Benjamin Joseph
Swindon, 7 December, 1975 E Yth (M)

League Club	Source	Date Signed	Seasons Played	Apps	Subs	Gls
Swindon T.	YT	07.94	94	1	2	0
Scarborough	Tr	08.96	96-97	20	16	3

WORRALL Frederick
Warrington, 8 September, 1910 Died 1979 E-2 (OR)

League Club	Source	Date Signed	Seasons Played	Apps	Subs	Gls
Oldham Ath.	Nantwich	12.28	28-31	105	-	21
Portsmouth	Tr	10.31	31-38	309	-	65
Crewe Alex.	Tr	04.46	46	7	-	1
Stockport Co.	Tr	09.46				

WORRALL Gary George
Salford, 4 November, 1961 (LW)

League Club	Source	Date Signed	Seasons Played	Apps	Subs	Gls
Manchester U.	App	11.78				
Peterborough U.	Tr	03.84	83-85	93	2	16
Carlisle U.	Tr	07.86	86	32	0	0

WORRALL Harry
Northwich, 19 November, 1918 Died 1979 (FB)

League Club	Source	Date Signed	Seasons Played	Apps	Subs	Gls
Manchester U.	Winsford U.	10.37	46-47	6	-	0
Swindon T.	Tr	06.48				

WORRELL Colin Harvey
Great Yarmouth, 29 August, 1943 (FB)

League Club	Source	Date Signed	Seasons Played	Apps	Subs	Gls
Norwich C.	Jnrs	11.61	62-64	9	-	0
Leyton Orient	Tr	09.64	64-65	51	0	0

WORSDALE Michael **John**
Stoke, 29 October, 1948 (W)

League Club	Source	Date Signed	Seasons Played	Apps	Subs	Gls
Stoke C.	App	11.65	68	4	0	0
Lincoln C.	Tr	05.71	71-73	55	12	9

WORSLEY Graeme
Liverpool, 4 January, 1969 (RB)

League Club	Source	Date Signed	Seasons Played	Apps	Subs	Gls
Shrewsbury T.	Bootle	03.89	88-92	83	22	4
Bury (N/C)	Doncaster Rov. (N/C)	12.93	93	0	1	0

WORSMAN Reginald Herbert
Bradford, 19 May, 1933 (IF)

League Club	Source	Date Signed	Seasons Played	Apps	Subs	Gls
Bradford P.A.	Jnrs	10.43	54-55	22	-	5
Bradford C.	Tr	06.56	56	1	-	0
Darlington	Nelson	06.60	60	4	-	1

WORSWICK Michael Anthony
Preston, 14 March, 1945 E Amat (W)

League Club	Source	Date Signed	Seasons Played	Apps	Subs	Gls
Wigan Ath.	Chorley	08.72	78	0	1	0

WORTHINGTON David
Halifax, 28 March, 1945 (RB)

League Club	Source	Date Signed	Seasons Played	Apps	Subs	Gls
Halifax T.	Jnrs	04.62	61-63	37	-	8
Barrow	Tr	07.64	64-65	60	1	7
Grimsby T.	Tr	06.66	66-72	292	1	14
Halifax T.	L	10.73	73	5	0	0
Southend U.	Tr	12.73	73-75	92	3	0

WORTHINGTON Eric Senior
Sheffield, 29 December, 1925 (IF)

League Club	Source	Date Signed	Seasons Played	Apps	Subs	Gls
Queens Park R.		09.47				
Watford	Tr	08.49	49-50	24	-	4
Bradford C.	Dover T.	09.53	53	2	-	1

WORTHINGTON Frank Stewart
Halifax, 23 November, 1948 Eu23-2/EF Lge/E-8 (F)

League Club	Source	Date Signed	Seasons Played	Apps	Subs	Gls
Huddersfield T.	App	11.66	66-71	166	5	41
Leicester C.	Tr	08.72	72-77	209	1	72
Bolton W.	Tr	09.77	77-79	81	3	35
Birmingham C.	Tr	11.79	79-81	71	4	29
Leeds U.	Tr	03.82	81-82	32	0	14
Sunderland	Tr	12.82	82	18	1	2
Southampton	Tr	06.83	83	34	0	4
Brighton & H.A.	Tr	05.84	84	27	4	7
Tranmere Rov.	Tr	06.85	85-86	51	8	21
Preston N.E.	Tr	02.87	86-87	10	13	3
Stockport Co.	Tr	11.87	87	18	1	6

WORTHINGTON Frederick
Manchester, 6 January, 1924 Died 1995 (IR)

League Club	Source	Date Signed	Seasons Played	Apps	Subs	Gls
Bury		07.47	47-50	69	-	14
Leicester C.	Tr	03.51	50-54	55	-	9
Exeter C.	Tr	07.55	55	16	-	1
Oldham Ath.	Tr	06.56	56	10	-	1

WORTHINGTON Gary Lee
Cleethorpes, 10 November, 1966 E Yth (F)

League Club	Source	Date Signed	Seasons Played	Apps	Subs	Gls
Manchester U.	App	11.84				
Huddersfield T.	Tr	07.86				
Darlington	Tr	07.87	87-88	31	9	15
Wrexham	Tr	06.89	89-90	68	4	18
Wigan Ath.	Tr	03.91	90-92	51	12	20
Exeter C.	Tr	07.93	93	8	7	1
Doncaster Rov.	L	03.94	93	8	0	2

WORTHINGTON Nigel
Ballymena (NI), 4 November, 1961 NI Yth/NI-66 (LB/M)

League Club	Source	Date Signed	Seasons Played	Apps	Subs	Gls
Notts Co.	Ballymena U.	07.81	81-83	62	5	4
Sheffield Wed.	Tr	02.84	83-93	334	4	12
Leeds U.	Tr	07.94	94-95	33	10	1
Stoke C.	Tr	07.96	96	12	0	0
Blackpool	Tr	07.97	97	4	5	0

WORTHINGTON Peter **Robert**
Halifax, 22 April, 1947 (LB)

League Club	Source	Date Signed	Seasons Played	Apps	Subs	Gls
Halifax T.	App	05.65	64	12	-	0
Middlesbrough	Tr	08.66	67	2	0	0
Notts Co.	Tr	09.68	68-73	230	2	1
Southend U.	Tr	08.74	74	20	0	1
Hartlepool U.	L	03.75	74	6	0	0

League Club	Source	Date Signed	Seasons Played	Career Record Apps	Subs	Gls

WOSAHLO Bradley Edward
Ipswich, 14 December, 1975 (W)

Brighton & H.A.	YT	07.93	93	1	0	0
Cambridge U.	Sudbury T.	12.95	95	0	4	0

WOSAHLO Roger Frank
Cambridge, 11 September, 1947 E Sch (W)

Chelsea	App	12.64	66	0	1	0
Ipswich T.	Tr	07.67	67	1	0	0
Peterborough U.	Tr	07.68	68	13	2	1
Ipswich T.	Tr	07.69	69	0	1	0

WOTTON Paul Anthony
Plymouth, 17 August, 1977 (M)

Plymouth Arg.	YT	07.95	94-97	41	10	2

WRACK Darren
Cleethorpes, 5 May, 1976 (RW)

Derby Co.	YT	07.94	94-95	4	22	1
Grimsby T.	Tr	07.96	96-97	5	8	1
Shrewsbury T.	L	02.97	96	3	1	0

WRAGG Douglas
Nottingham, 12 September, 1934 E Sch (OR)

West Ham U.		06.53	56-59	16	-	0
Mansfield T.	Tr	03.60	59-60	46	-	13
Rochdale	Tr	07.61	61-63	103	-	15
Chesterfield	Tr	07.64	64	17	-	4

WRAGG Peter
Rotherham, 12 January, 1931 (WH/IF)

Rotherham U.	Jnrs	05.48	48-52	31	-	6
Sheffield U.	Tr	01.53	52-54	56	-	17
York C.	Tr	08.56	56-62	264	-	78
Bradford C.	Tr	07.63	63-64	73	-	5

WRAIGHT Gary Paul
Epping, 5 March, 1979 (M)

Wycombe W.	YT	07.97	97	1	0	0

WRAITH Robert
Largs, 26 April, 1948 (G)

Southport	Glasgow Celtic	07.69	69-70	28	0	0

WRATTEN Paul
Middlesbrough, 29 November, 1970 E Yth (M)

Manchester U.	YT	12.88	90	0	2	0
Hartlepool U.	Tr	09.92	92-93	52	5	1

WRAY John Gordon
Mytholmroyd, 7 July, 1941 (G)

Halifax T.	Stainland A.	11.64	64	7	-	0

WRAY Shaun Warren
Birmingham, 14 March, 1978 (W)

Shrewsbury T.	YT	07.95	95-96	1	3	0

WREH Christopher
Liberia, 14 May, 1975 Liberian Int (F)

Arsenal	Monaco (Fr)	08.97	97	7	9	3

WREN John Mackie
Bonnybridge, 26 April, 1936 (G)

Rotherham U.	Hibernian	08.60	60	1	-	0

WRENCH Mark Nicholas
Warrington, 27 September, 1969 (FB)

Wrexham	YT	09.88	88-89	5	1	0

WRIGGLESWORTH John **Lancelot**
Halifax, 4 July, 1924 (FB)

Halifax T.	Watford (Am)	07.46	46	10	-	1

WRIGGLESWORTH William
South Elmsall, 12 November, 1912 Died 1980 (OL)

Chesterfield	Frickley Colly	05.32	32-34	34	-	6
Wolverhampton W.	Tr	12.34	34-36	50	-	21
Manchester U.	Tr	02.37	36-46	27	-	7
Bolton W.	Tr	01.47	46-47	13	-	1
Southampton	Tr	10.47	47	12	-	4
Reading	Tr	06.48	48	5	-	0

WRIGHT Alan George
Birmingham, 20 May, 1938 (F)

Walsall		05.58	58	1	-	1

WRIGHT Alan Geoffrey
Ashton-u-Lyne, 28 September, 1971 E Sch/E Yth/Eu21-2 (LB)

Blackpool	YT	04.89	87-91	91	7	0
Blackburn Rov.	Tr	10.91	91-94	67	7	1
Aston Villa	Tr	03.95	94-97	119	2	3

WRIGHT Albert
Clowne, 21 July, 1925 (G)

Lincoln C.	Ollerton Colly	10.46	46	1	-	0

WRIGHT Alexander Mason
Kirkcaldy, 18 October, 1925 (IF)

Barnsley	Hibernian	08.47	47-50	84	-	31
Tottenham H.	Tr	09.50	50	2	-	1
Bradford P.A.	Tr	08.51	51-54	131	-	25

WRIGHT Anthony Allan
Swansea, 19 September, 1979 W Yth/Wu21-2/W 'B' (M)

Oxford U.	YT	12.97	97	0	1	0

WRIGHT Archibald Watson
Glasgow, 23 November, 1924 Died 1990 (IR)

Blackburn Rov.	Falkirk	05.51	51-52	22	-	10
Grimsby T.	Tr	07.53	53	39	-	9
Accrington St.	Tr	06.54	54-56	80	-	27

WRIGHT Arthur William Tempest
Longbenton, 23 September, 1919 Died 1985 E Sch (WH)

Sunderland	Jnrs	09.36	37-54	270	-	13

WRIGHT Barrie
Bradford, 6 November, 1945 E Sch/E Yth (FB)

Leeds U.	App	11.62	62-63	5	-	0
Brighton & H.A.	New York R. (USA)	01.69	68-69	8	2	0

WRIGHT Barry Albert
Wrexham, 23 July, 1939 (FB)

Wrexham	Jnrs	05.59	59-61	11	-	0
Chester C.	Tr	08.62	62	1	-	0

WRIGHT Bernard
Walthamstow, 19 September, 1923 (G)

Notts Co.		02.46	46	2	-	0

WRIGHT Bernard Anthony
Derry (NI), 8 June, 1940 (OR)

Port Vale	Sligo Rov.	09.62	62	14	-	2

WRIGHT Bernard Peter
Birmingham, 17 September, 1952 (F)

Walsall	Birmingham C. (Am)	09.71	71	15	0	2
Everton	Tr	02.72	71-72	10	1	2
Walsall	Tr	01.73	72-76	145	7	38
Bradford C.	Tr	02.77	76-77	65	1	13
Port Vale	Tr	06.78	78-79	76	0	23

WRIGHT Brian Raymond
Leicester, 9 January, 1937 E Yth (IF)

Leicester C.	Jnrs	02.54				
Lincoln C.	Tr	01.59	58-60	22	-	3

WRIGHT George **Brian**
Sunderland, 19 September, 1939 (WH)

Newcastle U.	Jnrs	09.56	59-62	45	-	1
Peterborough U.	Tr	05.63	63-71	291	2	9

WRIGHT Charles George
Glasgow, 11 December, 1938 (G)

Workington	Glasgow Rangers	06.58	58-62	123	-	0
Grimsby T.	Tr	02.63	62-65	129	0	0
Charlton Ath.	Tr	03.66	65-70	195	0	0
Bolton W.	Tr	06.71	71-72	88	0	0

WRIGHT George **Clifford**
Lingdale, 18 October, 1944 (IF)

Middlesbrough	App	10.62				
Hartlepool U.	Tr	06.64	64-69	179	5	31
Darlington	Tr	02.70	69-70	16	0	4

WRIGHT Darren
Warrington, 7 September, 1979 (F)

Chester C.	YT	●	97	3	2	0

WRIGHT Darren James
West Bromwich, 14 March, 1968 (FB)

Wolverhampton W.	YT	07.85	85	1	0	0
Wrexham	Tr	08.86	86-89	105	5	4

WRIGHT David
Warrington, 1 May, 1980 (D)

Crewe Alex.	YT	06.97	97	0	3	0

League Club	Source	Date Signed	Seasons Played	Career Record Apps	Subs	Gls
WRIGHT Dennis						
Chesterfield, 19 December, 1919 Died 1993						(G)
Mansfield T.	Clay Lane R.	03.39	46-56	379	-	0
WRIGHT Dennis						
Royton, 9 January, 1930						(OL)
Oldham Ath. (Am)	Jnrs	05.46	46	3	-	0
Oldham Ath.	Glasgow Rangers	08.51	51	6	-	0
WRIGHT John **Douglas**						
Southend, 29 April, 1917 Died 1992 E-1						(WH)
Southend U.	Chelmsford C.	08.36	36-37	30	-	2
Newcastle U.	Tr	05.38	38-46	72	-	1
Lincoln C.	Tr	12.48	48-54	233	-	2
WRIGHT Evran						
Stourbridge, 17 January, 1965						(F)
Walsall	Halesowen T.	08.93	93	16	13	5
WRIGHT Gary						
Torquay, 21 May, 1966						(RB)
Torquay U. (N/C)	Jnrs	08.84	84	2	0	0
Torquay U. (N/C)	Chard T.	08.87	87	1	1	0
WRIGHT Gary						
Sunderland, 15 September, 1964						(G)
Hartlepool U. (N/C)	App	10.82	82	12	0	0
WRIGHT Geoffrey Derrick						
Countesthorpe (Lei), 1 March, 1930						(IF)
Aston Villa		05.49				
Bournemouth	Tr	06.51				
Walsall	Rugby T.	03.52	52	16	-	1
WRIGHT George Albert						
Sheffield, 4 February, 1920						(IF)
Cardiff C.		03.42				
Hull C.	Tr	06.46	46	4	-	1
WRIGHT George William						
Ramsgate, 19 March, 1930						(FB)
West Ham U.	Margate	02.51	51-57	161	-	0
Leyton Orient	Tr	05.58	58-61	87	-	1
Gillingham	Tr	07.62	62	4	-	0
WRIGHT George William						
Plymouth, 10 October, 1919						(G)
Plymouth Arg.	Kitto Inst.	10.38	38-46	12	-	0
Colchester U.	Tr	07.49	50-54	151	-	0
WRIGHT Glenn						
Liverpool, 26 May, 1956						(M)
Blackburn Rov.	App	●	73	1	0	0
WRIGHT Horace Raymond						
Pontefract, 6 September, 1918 Died 1987						(IF)
Wolverhampton W.		05.36	37-38	8	-	1
Exeter C.	Tr	03.46	46-47	56	-	11
WRIGHT Michael **Howard**						
Winsford, 21October, 1948						(F)
Shrewsbury T.	App	●	65	0	1	0
Crewe Alex.	Tr	09.66				
WRIGHT Ian Edward						
Woolwich, 3 November, 1963 E 'B'/E-31						(F)
Crystal Palace	Greenwich Borough	08.85	85-91	206	19	89
Arsenal	Tr	09.91	91-97	212	9	128
WRIGHT Ian Matthew						
Lichfield, 10 March, 1972						(CD)
Stoke C.	YT	07.90	89-92	6	0	0
Bristol Rov.	Tr	09.93	93-95	50	4	1
Hull C.	Tr	07.96	96-97	65	8	2
WRIGHT James Frank						
Whitefield, 19 February, 1924 Died 1994						(G)
Accrington St. (Am)		09.47	47	1	-	0
WRIGHT Jeffrey Kenneth						
Alston, 23 June, 1952						(M)
Wigan Ath.	Netherfield	03.74	78-81	139	4	19
WRIGHT Jermaine Malaki						
Greenwich, 21 October, 1975 E Yth						(W)
Millwall	YT	11.92				
Wolverhampton W.	Tr	12.94	94-97	4	16	0
Doncaster Rov.	L	03.96	96	13	0	0
Crewe Alex.	Tr	02.98	97	3	2	0

League Club	Source	Date Signed	Seasons Played	Career Record Apps	Subs	Gls
WRIGHT John						
Atherton, 11 August, 1926 E 'B'						(FB)
Blackpool	Mossley	06.46	48-58	158	-	1
WRIGHT John Bryant						
South Shields, 16 November, 1922						(CH)
Hull C.	Tyne Dock U.	09.47	47	1	-	0
WRIGHT John Francis Dominic						
Aldershot, 13 August, 1933						(G)
Colchester U.		11.54	54-60	5	-	0
WRIGHT Jonathan						
Belfast, 24 November, 1975 NI Yth/NI 'B'						(FB)
Norwich C.	YT	07.94	94-96	5	2	0
WRIGHT Jonathan						
Newburn (Dm), 30 January, 1925						(LH)
Darlington		01.47	46-48	17	-	0
WRIGHT Kenneth Laurence						
Newmarket, 16 May, 1922 Died 1994						(F)
West Ham U.	Cambridge C.	05.46	46-49	51	-	20
WRIGHT Mark						
Dorchester (Ox), 1 August, 1963 Eu21-4/E-45						(CD)
Oxford U.	Jnrs	08.80	81	8	2	0
Southampton	Tr	03.82	81-86	170	0	7
Derby Co.	Tr	08.87	87-90	144	0	10
Liverpool	Tr	07.91	91-97	156	2	5
WRIGHT Mark Andrew						
Manchester, 29 January, 1970						(D)
Everton	YT	06.88	89	1	0	0
Blackpool	L	08.90	90	3	0	0
Huddersfield T.	Tr	03.91	90-92	25	7	1
Wigan Ath.	Accrington St.	11.93	93-94	27	3	1
WRIGHT Martin Harold						
Chesterfield, 1 April, 1950						(F)
Chesterfield	Alfreton T.	10.68	68-71	39	4	12
Torquay U.	Tr	07.72	72	8	5	3
WRIGHT Matthew Paul						
Norwich, 6 January, 1978						(CD)
Torquay U.	YT	01.97	96	7	2	0
WRIGHT Michael						
Darlington, 17 February, 1950						(D)
Darlington	Jnrs	06.68	68-72	82	7	0
WRIGHT Michael Eric						
Newmarket, 16 January, 1942						(IF)
Northampton T.	Newmarket	11.59	59-61	26	-	7
WRIGHT John **Michael**						
Ellesmere Port, 25 September, 1946 E Yth						(RB)
Aston Villa	App	09.63	63-72	280	2	1
WRIGHT Herbert **Montague**						
Shirebrook, 29 May, 1931						(HB)
Leeds U.	Bolsover Colly	10.51				
Stockport Co.	Tr	06.53	53	1	-	0
Chester C.	Tr	07.54	54	21	-	4
WRIGHT Nicholas John						
Derby, 15 October, 1975						(W)
Derby Co.	YT	07.94				
Carlisle U.	Tr	11.97	97	25	0	5
WRIGHT Patrick Daniel Joseph						
Oldbury, 17 November, 1940						(FB)
Birmingham C.	Brookfield	11.59	59-61	3	-	0
Shrewsbury T.	Tr	09.62	62-67	201	0	3
Derby Co.	Tr	10.67	67	12	1	0
Southend U.	L	03.70	69	11	0	0
Rotherham U.	Tr	09.70	70	2	0	0
WRIGHT Paul						
Barking, 29 July, 1969						(F)
Halifax T. (N/C)	U.S.A.	10.92	92	0	1	0
WRIGHT Paul Hamilton						
East Kilbride, 17 August, 1967 S Yth/Su21-3						(F)
Queens Park R.	Aberdeen	07.89	89	9	6	5
WRIGHT Peter Brooke						
Colchester, 26 January, 1934						(OL)
Colchester U.	Jnrs	11.51	51-63	428	-	89

League Club	Source	Date Signed	Seasons Played	Career Record Apps	Subs	Gls
WRIGHT Ralph Lawrence						
Newcastle, 3 August, 1947						(M)
Norwich C.	Spennymoor U.	07.68				
Bradford P.A.	Tr	10.69	69	13	1	1
Hartlepool U.	Tr	06.70	70	23	1	3
Stockport Co.	Tr	07.71	71	19	2	0
Bolton W.	Tr	02.72	71-72	25	7	5
Southport	Tr	12.72	72-73	40	3	5
WRIGHT Richard (Dick)						
Mexborough, 5 December, 1931						(G)
Leeds U.		05.49				
Chester C.	Tr	08.51	52-54	52	-	0
Bradford C.	Tr	03.55				
WRIGHT Richard Ian						
Ipswich, 5 November, 1977 E Sch/E Yth/Eu21-8						(G)
Ipswich T.	YT	01.95	94-97	112	0	0
WRIGHT Robert Cooper Allen						
Glasgow, 20 February, 1916						(LH)
Charlton Ath.	Horden Colly	05.37	38-46	28	-	0
WRIGHT Ronald William						
Falkirk, 6 December, 1940						(IF)
Leeds U.	Shettleston	06.59	60	1	-	0
WRIGHT Stephen						
Bellshill, 27 August, 1971 Su21-14/S 'B'/S-2						(RB)
Wolverhampton W. (L)	Glasgow Rangers	03.98	97	3	0	0
WRIGHT Stephen Peter						
Clacton, 16 June, 1959						(D)
Colchester U.	Jnrs	06.77	77-81	113	5	2
Wrexham	H.J.K. Helsinki (Fin)	09.83	83-84	76	0	0
Torquay U.	Tr	07.85	85	33	0	0
Crewe Alex.	Tr	07.86	86-87	67	5	3
WRIGHT Terence Ian						
Newcastle, 22 June, 1939						(OL)
Barrow	Nuneaton Borough	11.62	62-64	10	-	1
WRIGHT Thomas						
Clackmannan, 20 January, 1928 S-3						(OR)
Sunderland	Partick Thistle	03.49	48-54	170	-	52
Oldham Ath.	East Fife	03.57	56	7	-	2
WRIGHT Thomas Birtles						
Glossop, 11 January, 1917 Died 1995						(OL)
Manchester C.	Droylsden	06.37				
Hull C.	Altrincham	07.47				
Accrington St.	Tr	10.47	47-48	20	-	4
WRIGHT Thomas Elliot						
Dunfermline, 10 January, 1966 S Yth/Su21-1						(LW)
Leeds U.	App	01.83	82-85	73	8	24
Oldham Ath.	Tr	10.86	86-88	110	2	23
Leicester C.	Tr	08.89	89-91	122	7	22
Middlesbrough	Tr	07.92	92-94	44	9	5
Bradford C.	Tr	07.95	95-96	30	15	5
Oldham Ath.	Tr	08.97	97	10	2	2
WRIGHT Thomas James						
Liverpool, 21 October, 1944 Eu23-7/E-11						(FB)
Everton	Jnrs	03.63	64-72	307	1	4
WRIGHT Thomas James						
Belfast, 29 August, 1963 EF Lge/NIu23-1/NI-29						(G)
Newcastle U.	Linfield	01.88	88-93	72	1	0
Hull C.	L	02.91	90	6	0	0
Nottingham F.	Tr	09.93	93-96	11	0	0
Reading	L	10.96	96	17	0	0
Manchester C.	L	01.97	96	5	0	0
Manchester C.	Tr	03.97	96-97	26	0	0
WRIGHT Thomas Kentigern						
Stepps, 11 January, 1925						(OR)
Aldershot	Dunfermline Ath.	07.52	52	14	-	1
WRIGHT Vincent						
Bradford, 12 April, 1931 E Yth						(W)
Derby Co.		09.51				
Mansfield T.	Tr	07.52	52	2	-	0
WRIGHT William						
Liverpool, 28 April, 1958 Eu21-6/E 'B'						(CD)
Everton	Jnrs	01.77	77-82	164	2	10
Birmingham C.	Tr	07.83	83-85	111	0	8
Chester C.	L	02.86	85	6	0	1
Carlisle U.	Tr	08.86	86-87	87	0	3
WRIGHT William Ambrose						
Ironbridge, 6 February, 1924 Died 1994 EF Lge/E-105						(CH)
Wolverhampton W.	Jnrs	02.41	46-58	490	-	13
WRIGHT William Hardy Rodgers						
Corbridge, 4 November, 1962						(F)
Burnley		01.81				
Crewe Alex.	L	11.82	82	3	0	1
WRIGHT William Stephen						
Wordsley, 26 April, 1959						(RB)
Birmingham C.	App	04.77				
Lincoln C.	Tr	07.78	78	3	0	0
WRIGHT John **William**						
Blackpool, 4 March, 1931						(W)
Blackpool		05.50	51-54	15	-	2
Leicester C.	Tr	08.55	55-57	27	-	10
Newcastle U.	Tr	08.58	58	5	-	3
Plymouth Arg.	Tr	08.59	59-60	42	-	9
Millwall	Tr	08.61	61	15	-	0
WRIGHTSON Jeffrey George						
Newcastle, 18 May, 1968						(CD)
Newcastle U.	App	05.86	86	3	1	0
Preston N.E.	Tr	07.87	87-91	161	5	4
WRIGLEY Wilfred						
Clitheroe, 4 October, 1949						(CH)
Burnley	Jnrs	07.68	68-69	6	0	1
WROE Mark						
Manchester, 1 June, 1966						(W)
Stockport Co.	Jnrs	08.85	84-85	26	4	4
WYATT George Albert						
Whitechapel, 28 March, 1924 Died 1957						(LB)
Crystal Palace		11.47	48	7	-	0
WYATT Michael James						
Yate, 12 September, 1974						(W)
Bristol C.	YT	07.93	93-94	9	4	0
Bristol Rov.	Tr	07.95	95	3	1	0
WYATT Reginald Gordon						
Plymouth, 18 September, 1932						(CH)
Plymouth Arg.	Astor Inst.	08.50	55-64	202	-	2
Torquay U.	Tr	10.64	64-66	80	0	6
WYER Peter William						
Coventry, 10 February, 1937						(IF)
Coventry C.		10.55	55	1	-	0
Derby Co.	Tr	06.56	56	2	-	1
Coventry C.	Tr	07.58	58	4	-	0
WYLDE Rodger James						
Sheffield, 8 March, 1954						(F)
Sheffield Wed.	App	07.71	72-79	157	11	54
Oldham Ath.	Tr	02.80	79-82	109	4	51
Sunderland	Sporting Lisbon (Por)	07.84	84	8	3	3
Barnsley	Tr	12.84	84-87	50	2	19
Rotherham U.	L	03.88	87	6	0	1
Stockport Co.	Tr	07.88	88	24	2	12
WYLDES Robert Jack						
Southport, 6 October, 1928						(OL)
Luton T.	Desborough	10.49	49-51	26	-	8
WYLES Thomas **Cecil**						
Bourne, 1 November, 1919 Died 1990						(CF)
Everton	Peterborough U.	02.38				
Bury	Tr	05.46	46	2	-	0
Southport	Tr	11.46	46-49	143	-	53
WYLES Harold						
Melton Mowbray, 28 October, 1922 Died 1982						(FB)
Leicester C.		04.42				
Gateshead	Tr	03.48	47-53	235	-	7
WYLIE John Edward						
Newcastle, 25 September, 1936						(WH)
Huddersfield T.		09.54				
Preston N.E.	Tr	05.57	58-62	91	-	1
Stockport Co.	Tr	11.62	62-63	69	-	2
Doncaster Rov.	Tr	08.64	64-67	123	1	2
WYLIE Ronald Maurice						
Glasgow, 6 August, 1933 S Sch						(IF/WH)
Notts Co.	Clydesdale Jnrs	09.50	51-58	227	-	35

League Club	Source	Date Signed	Seasons Played	Career Record Apps	Subs	Gls
Aston Villa	Tr	11.58	58-64	196	-	16
Birmingham C.	Tr	06.65	65-69	125	3	2

WYLLIE James
Saltcoats, 15 October, 1927 Died 1992 (IF)

League Club	Source	Date Signed	Seasons Played	Apps	Subs	Gls
Southport	Kilmarnock	07.50	50	15	-	1
Wrexham	Tr	12.50	50	20	-	4

WYLLIE Robinson (Bob) Gourlay Nicholl
Dundee, 4 April, 1929 (G)

League Club	Source	Date Signed	Seasons Played	Apps	Subs	Gls
Blackpool	Dundee U.	05.53	53-54	13	-	0
West Ham U.	Tr	05.56	56	13	-	0
Plymouth Arg.	Tr	07.58	58	5	-	0
Mansfield T.	Tr	10.59	59-61	92	-	0

WYNN Walter Ronald
Wrexham, 2 November, 1923 Died 1983 (FB/CF)

League Club	Source	Date Signed	Seasons Played	Apps	Subs	Gls
Wrexham		04.48	47-55	182	-	12

WYNNE Darren Lee
Rhyl, 12 October, 1970 (M)

League Club	Source	Date Signed	Seasons Played	Apps	Subs	Gls
Chester C.	YT	07.89	88-89	0	12	0

League Club	Source	Date Signed	Seasons Played	Career Record Apps	Subs	Gls

XAUSA Davide
Vancouver, Canada, 10 March, 1976 (F)

League Club	Source	Date Signed	Seasons Played	Apps	Subs	Gls
Port Vale	Vancouver (Can)	01.98				
Stoke C.	Tr	02.98	97	1	0	0

YALLOP Frank Walter
Watford, 4 April, 1964 E Yth/Canadian Int (RB)

League Club	Source	Date Signed	Seasons Played	Apps	Subs	Gls
Ipswich T.	App	01.82	83-95	289	27	7
Blackpool	L	11.95	95	3	0	0

YANUSHEVSKI Victor
U.S.S.R., 23 January, 1960 Died 1993 (D)

League Club	Source	Date Signed	Seasons Played	Apps	Subs	Gls
Aldershot (N/C)	C.S.K. Moscow (USSR)	03.91	90	6	0	1

YARD Ernest John
Stranraer, 3 May, 1941 (CF/WH)

League Club	Source	Date Signed	Seasons Played	Apps	Subs	Gls
Bury	Partick Thistle	12.63	63-64	45	-	13
Crystal Palace	Tr	05.65	65-66	35	2	3
Reading	Tr	11.66	66-68	101	3	6

YARDLEY George McArthur
Kirkcaldy, 8 October, 1942 (CF)

League Club	Source	Date Signed	Seasons Played	Apps	Subs	Gls
Luton T.	Australia	10.66	66	1	0	0
Tranmere Rov.	Tr	11.66	66-70	123	0	68

YATES David (Sammy)
Barnsley, 18 March, 1953 (FB)

League Club	Source	Date Signed	Seasons Played	Apps	Subs	Gls
Barnsley	App	03.71	72-77	104	0	2
Grimsby T.	L	03.77	76	10	0	0

YATES Dean Richard
Leicester, 26 October, 1967 Eu21-5 (CD)

League Club	Source	Date Signed	Seasons Played	Apps	Subs	Gls
Notts Co.	App	06.85	84-94	312	2	33
Derby Co.	Tr	01.95	94-97	65	3	3

YATES Harry
Huddersfield, 28 September, 1925 Died 1987 (IF)

League Club	Source	Date Signed	Seasons Played	Apps	Subs	Gls
Huddersfield T.	Jnrs	10.43	49	1	-	0
Darlington	Tr	05.50	50-51	91	-	29

YATES John
Rotherham, 18 November, 1929 (OR)

League Club	Source	Date Signed	Seasons Played	Apps	Subs	Gls
Sheffield U.		06.50				
Chester C.	Tr	08.51	51	2	-	0

YATES Mark Jason
Birmingham, 24 January, 1970 (M)

League Club	Source	Date Signed	Seasons Played	Apps	Subs	Gls
Birmingham C.	YT	07.88	87-91	38	16	6
Burnley	Tr	08.91	91-92	9	9	1
Lincoln C.	L	02.93	92	10	4	0
Doncaster Rov.	Tr	07.93	93	33	1	4

YATES Richard (Dick)
Queensferry, 6 June, 1921 Died 1976 (CF)

League Club	Source	Date Signed	Seasons Played	Apps	Subs	Gls
Chester C.	Wolverhampton W. (Am)	08.39	46-47	52	-	37
Wrexham	Tr	12.47	47-48	31	-	18
Carlisle U.	Tr	11.48	48	16	-	9
New Brighton	Tr	08.49	49-50	43	-	14

YATES Stephen
Measham, 8 December, 1953 (LB)

League Club	Source	Date Signed	Seasons Played	Apps	Subs	Gls
Leicester C.	App	12.71	73-76	12	7	0
Southend U.	Tr	11.77	77-83	223	1	8
Doncaster Rov.	Tr	12.83	83-84	44	0	1
Darlington	L	01.85	84	4	0	0
Chesterfield	L	03.85	84	1	0	0
Stockport Co. (N/C)	Tr	08.85	85	2	0	0

YATES Stephen
Bristol, 29 January, 1970 (CD)

League Club	Source	Date Signed	Seasons Played	Apps	Subs	Gls
Bristol Rov.	YT	07.88	86-93	196	1	0
Queens Park R.	Tr	08.93	93-97	116	12	2

YEATS Ronald
Aberdeen, 15 November, 1937 S Sch/S-2 (CH)

League Club	Source	Date Signed	Seasons Played	Apps	Subs	Gls
Liverpool	Dundee U.	07.61	61-70	357	1	13
Tranmere Rov.	Tr	12.71	71-73	96	1	5

YEATS Thomas Brandon
Newcastle, 30 May, 1935 (F)

League Club	Source	Date Signed	Seasons Played	Apps	Subs	Gls
Sunderland	Jnrs	02.53				
Gateshead	Tr	08.54	54	1	-	0

YEATS William
Hebburn, 4 February, 1951 (F)

League Club	Source	Date Signed	Seasons Played	Apps	Subs	Gls
Newcastle U.	North Shields	06.71				
York C.	Tr	03.72	71-72	8	1	0
Darlington	Tr	08.73	73-74	22	3	7

YEBOAH Anthony
Ghana, 6 June, 1966 Ghanaian Int (F)

League Club	Source	Date Signed	Seasons Played	Apps	Subs	Gls
Leeds U.	Eintracht Frankfurt (Ger)	01.95	94-96	44	3	24

YEO Brian Geoffrey
Worthing, 12 April, 1944 (F)

League Club	Source	Date Signed	Seasons Played	Apps	Subs	Gls
Portsmouth	Jnrs	05.61				
Gillingham	Tr	07.63	63-74	345	10	136

YEOMAN Ramon Irvine
Perth, 13 May, 1934 (WH)

League Club	Source	Date Signed	Seasons Played	Apps	Subs	Gls
Northampton T.	St Johnstone	09.53	53-58	169	-	4
Middlesbrough	Tr	11.58	58-63	210	-	3
Darlington	Tr	06.64	64-66	103	0	2

YEOMANS Kelvin
Nottingham, 25 August, 1947 (FB)

League Club	Source	Date Signed	Seasons Played	Apps	Subs	Gls
Notts Co. (Am)	Beeston	06.67	67	1	0	0

YEOMANSON John (Jack) William
Margate, 3 March, 1920 (FB)

League Club	Source	Date Signed	Seasons Played	Apps	Subs	Gls
West Ham U.	Margate	02.47	47-50	106	-	1

YORATH Terence Charles
Cardiff, 27 March, 1950 W Sch/Wu23-7/W-59 (M)

League Club	Source	Date Signed	Seasons Played	Apps	Subs	Gls
Leeds U.	App	04.67	67-76	120	21	10
Coventry C.	Tr	08.76	76-78	99	0	3
Tottenham H.	Tr	08.79	79-80	44	4	1
Bradford C.	Vancouver (Can)	12.82	82-84	22	5	0
Swansea C.	(Manager)	10.86	86	1	0	0

YORK Allan
Newcastle, 13 July, 1941 (FB)

League Club	Source	Date Signed	Seasons Played	Apps	Subs	Gls
Bradford C.	Gateshead	02.65	64-66	42	3	2
Lincoln C.	Tr	07.67				

YORKE Dwight
Tobago (WI), 3 November, 1971 Trinidadian Int (F)

League Club	Source	Date Signed	Seasons Played	Apps	Subs	Gls
Aston Villa	Signal Hill (Tob)	11.89	89-97	194	36	75

YOUDS Edward Paul
Liverpool, 3 May, 1970 (CD/M)

League Club	Source	Date Signed	Seasons Played	Apps	Subs	Gls
Everton	YT	06.88	90	5	3	0
Cardiff C.	L	12.89	89	0	1	0
Wrexham	L	02.90	89	20	0	2
Ipswich T.	Tr	11.91	91-94	38	12	1
Bradford C.	Tr	01.95	94-97	85	0	8
Charlton Ath.	Tr	03.98	97	8	0	0

YOUELL Jasper
Bilston, 23 March, 1925 (FB)

League Club	Source	Date Signed	Seasons Played	Apps	Subs	Gls
Portsmouth	West Bromwich A. (Am)	08.46	46-51	30	-	0
Barnsley	Tr	08.52	52	19	-	0

YOULDEN Thomas Frederick
Islington, 8 July, 1949 E Sch (CD)

League Club	Source	Date Signed	Seasons Played	Apps	Subs	Gls
Arsenal	App	07.66				
Portsmouth	Tr	04.68	68-71	82	8	1
Reading	Tr	07.72	72-76	161	2	3
Aldershot	Tr	04.77	76-80	118	5	1

YOUNG Albert Edward
Caerleon, 11 September, 1917 (FB)

League Club	Source	Date Signed	Seasons Played	Apps	Subs	Gls
Arsenal		09.38				
Swindon T.	Tr	06.46	46-49	123	-	1

YOUNG Alexander
Loanhead, 3 February, 1937 Su23-6/SF Lge/S-8 (F)

League Club	Source	Date Signed	Seasons Played	Apps	Subs	Gls
Everton	Hearts	11.60	60-67	227	1	77
Stockport Co.	Glentoran	11.68	68	23	0	5

YOUNG Alexander (Alan) Forbes
Kirkcaldy, 26 October, 1955 S Sch (F)

League Club	Source	Date Signed	Seasons Played	Apps	Subs	Gls
Oldham Ath.	Jnrs	07.74	74-78	107	15	30
Leicester C.	Tr	07.79	79-81	102	2	26
Sheffield U.	Tr	08.82	82	23	3	7
Brighton & H.A.	Tr	08.83	83	25	1	12
Notts Co.	Tr	09.84	84-85	39	4	12
Rochdale	Tr	08.86	86	19	9	2

YOUNG Allan Robert
Edmonton, 20 January, 1941 (CH)

League Club	Source	Date Signed	Seasons Played	Apps	Subs	Gls
Arsenal	Jnrs	04.59	60	4	-	0

League Club	Source	Date Signed	Seasons Played	Apps	Subs	Gls
Chelsea	Tr	11.61	61-66	20	0	0
Torquay U.	Tr	01.69	68-71	59	1	1

YOUNG Thomas **Anthony**
Urmston, 24 December, 1952 (FB/M)

League Club	Source	Date Signed	Seasons Played	Apps	Subs	Gls
Manchester U.	App	12.69	71-75	69	14	1
Charlton Ath.	Tr	01.76	75-76	20	0	1
York C.	Tr	09.76	76-78	76	2	2

YOUNG Charles Frederick
Cyprus, 14 February, 1958 (CD)

League Club	Source	Date Signed	Seasons Played	Apps	Subs	Gls
Aston Villa	App	11.75	76	9	1	0
Gillingham	Tr	03.78	77-81	27	1	1

YOUNG Charles Stuart Robertson
Falkirk, 23 August, 1929 (G)

League Club	Source	Date Signed	Seasons Played	Apps	Subs	Gls
Sheffield U.	Stalybridge Celtic	05.51	51	3	-	0

YOUNG Christopher William
Manchester, 11 August, 1979 (F)

League Club	Source	Date Signed	Seasons Played	Apps	Subs	Gls
Mansfield T.	YT	●	96	0	1	0

YOUNG Clarence William
Bow, 23 February, 1920 (OL)

League Club	Source	Date Signed	Seasons Played	Apps	Subs	Gls
Coventry C.	Margate	09.38	46	1	-	0

YOUNG David
Newcastle, 12 November, 1945 (CD)

League Club	Source	Date Signed	Seasons Played	Apps	Subs	Gls
Newcastle U.	Jnrs	09.64	69-72	41	2	2
Sunderland	Tr	01.73	72-73	23	6	1
Charlton Ath.	Tr	08.74	74-76	76	1	0
Southend U.	Tr	09.76	76-77	56	4	0

YOUNG David
Birkenhead, 27 April, 1962 (M)

League Club	Source	Date Signed	Seasons Played	Apps	Subs	Gls
Wigan Ath. (N/C)	Mossley	03.83	82	3	0	0

YOUNG David Alan
Trimdon, 31 January, 1965 (LB)

League Club	Source	Date Signed	Seasons Played	Apps	Subs	Gls
Darlington	App	01.83	82-83	13	5	0

YOUNG Douglas
Islington, 2 February, 1927 E Amat (FB)

League Club	Source	Date Signed	Seasons Played	Apps	Subs	Gls
Southend U.	Walthamstow Ave.	06.53	53-55	38	-	0

YOUNG Eric
Singapore, 25 March, 1960 W-21 (CD)

League Club	Source	Date Signed	Seasons Played	Apps	Subs	Gls
Brighton & H.A.	Slough T.	11.82	83-86	126	0	10
Wimbledon	Tr	07.87	87-89	96	3	9
Crystal Palace	Tr	08.90	90-94	161	0	15
Wolverhampton W.	Tr	09.95	95-96	31	0	2

YOUNG Eric Royston
Stockton, 26 November, 1952 E Yth (M)

League Club	Source	Date Signed	Seasons Played	Apps	Subs	Gls
Manchester U.	App	12.69				
Peterborough U.	L	11.72	72	24	1	2
Walsall	L	10.73	73	8	0	0
Stockport Co.	Tr	01.74	73	16	0	0
Darlington	Tr	07.74	74-77	123	7	15

YOUNG George
Dundee, 2 November, 1919 Died 1982 (IF)

League Club	Source	Date Signed	Seasons Played	Apps	Subs	Gls
Watford	Hibernian	07.46	46-48	43	-	5

YOUNG Robert **George**
Newport, 5 January, 1950 Wu23-1 (M)

League Club	Source	Date Signed	Seasons Played	Apps	Subs	Gls
Newport Co.	Cromwell Jnrs	07.67	67-71	90	14	6

YOUNG Gerald Morton
Jarrow, 1 October, 1936 E-1 (WH)

League Club	Source	Date Signed	Seasons Played	Apps	Subs	Gls
Sheffield Wed.	Hawthorn Leslie	05.55	56-70	308	2	13

YOUNG John
Hartlepool, 9 November, 1951 (OR)

League Club	Source	Date Signed	Seasons Played	Apps	Subs	Gls
Hartlepool U. (Am)	Newcastle U. (Am)	08.68	68	3	0	0

YOUNG John Robert
Gateshead, 19 October, 1925 Died 1988 (G)

League Club	Source	Date Signed	Seasons Played	Apps	Subs	Gls
Gateshead (Am)		08.49	49	4	-	0

YOUNG Kenneth
Halifax, 11 June, 1930 (IR)

League Club	Source	Date Signed	Seasons Played	Apps	Subs	Gls
Halifax T.	Jnrs	11.49	49	1	-	0

YOUNG Kevin
Sunderland, 12 August, 1961 (M)

League Club	Source	Date Signed	Seasons Played	Apps	Subs	Gls
Burnley	App	05.79	78-83	114	6	11
Torquay U.	L	11.83	83	3	0	1
Port Vale	L	12.83	83	28	0	4
Bury	Tr	07.84	84-86	85	3	10

YOUNG Leonard Archibald
West Ham, 23 February, 1912 (CH)

League Club	Source	Date Signed	Seasons Played	Apps	Subs	Gls
West Ham U.	Ilford	04.34	33-37	12	-	0
Reading	Tr	11.37	37-47	83	-	0
Brighton & H.A.	Tr	02.48	47-48	8	-	0

YOUNG Martin
Grimsby, 9 April, 1955 (D/M)

League Club	Source	Date Signed	Seasons Played	Apps	Subs	Gls
Grimsby T.	Jnrs	03.74	74-78	87	7	4

YOUNG Michael Samuel
Chester-le-Street, 15 March, 1973 (W)

League Club	Source	Date Signed	Seasons Played	Apps	Subs	Gls
Middlesbrough	Newcastle U. (YT)	07.91	91	0	1	0

YOUNG Neil Anthony
Harlow, 31 August, 1973 (RB)

League Club	Source	Date Signed	Seasons Played	Apps	Subs	Gls
Tottenham H.	YT	08.91				
Bournemouth	Tr	10.94	94-97	159	2	2

YOUNG Neil James
Manchester, 17 February, 1944 E Yth (F)

League Club	Source	Date Signed	Seasons Played	Apps	Subs	Gls
Manchester C.	App	02.61	61-71	332	2	86
Preston N.E.	Tr	01.72	71-73	67	1	16
Rochdale	Tr	07.74	74	8	5	4

YOUNG Noel Johnston
Derry (NI), 22 December, 1932 (LH)

League Club	Source	Date Signed	Seasons Played	Apps	Subs	Gls
Middlesbrough	Jnrs	04.50				
Doncaster Rov.		01.55	54	3	-	0

YOUNG Quintin
Irvine, 19 September, 1947 Su23-1 (W)

League Club	Source	Date Signed	Seasons Played	Apps	Subs	Gls
Coventry C.	Ayr U.	07.71	71-72	25	1	2

YOUNG George **Raymond**
Derby, 14 March, 1934 E Sch (CH)

League Club	Source	Date Signed	Seasons Played	Apps	Subs	Gls
Derby Co.	Jnrs	03.51	53-65	253	1	5

YOUNG Richard (Dick)
Felling, 13 July, 1939 (CF)

League Club	Source	Date Signed	Seasons Played	Apps	Subs	Gls
Newcastle U.	Usworth Jnrs	07.57				
Grimsby T.	South Shields	03.62	62-64	33	-	13
Stockport Co.	Tr	05.65	65	27	0	5

YOUNG Richard Anthony
Nottingham, 18 October, 1968 (F)

League Club	Source	Date Signed	Seasons Played	Apps	Subs	Gls
Notts Co.	YT	08.86	86	18	17	5
Southend U.	Tr	08.87	87-88	5	4	0
Exeter C.	Tr	03.89	88-90	32	17	10

YOUNG Richard Harker
Gateshead, 17 April, 1918 Died 1989 (CH)

League Club	Source	Date Signed	Seasons Played	Apps	Subs	Gls
Sheffield U.	Wardley Colly	11.35	36-48	71	-	0
Lincoln C.	Tr	03.49	48-53	100	-	2

YOUNG Robert George
Bournemouth, 24 December, 1923 (FB)

League Club	Source	Date Signed	Seasons Played	Apps	Subs	Gls
Bournemouth	Jnrs	01.46	47	1	-	0
Crewe Alex.	Tr	06.48	48-51	144	-	2

YOUNG Cecil **Rodney**
Bournemouth, 22 July, 1925 Died 1991 (HB)

League Club	Source	Date Signed	Seasons Played	Apps	Subs	Gls
Bournemouth		06.48	48-49	18	-	0

YOUNG Ronald
Dunston, 31 August, 1945 (W)

League Club	Source	Date Signed	Seasons Played	Apps	Subs	Gls
Hull C.		08.63	64-67	24	2	5
Hartlepool U.	Tr	09.68	68-72	176	10	40

YOUNG Roy
Sheffield, 2 October, 1950 (FB)

League Club	Source	Date Signed	Seasons Played	Apps	Subs	Gls
Doncaster Rov.	Sheffield U. (Am)	07.70	70	6	1	0

YOUNG Scott
Pontypridd, 14 January, 1976 Wu21-5/W 'B' (CD)

League Club	Source	Date Signed	Seasons Played	Apps	Subs	Gls
Cardiff C.	YT	07.94	93-97	118	14	4

YOUNG Stuart Rodney
Hull, 16 December, 1972 (F)

League Club	Source	Date Signed	Seasons Played	Apps	Subs	Gls
Hull C.	Arsenal (YT)	07.91	91-92	11	8	2
Northampton T.	Tr	02.93	92	7	1	1
Scarborough	Tr	08.93	93-94	28	13	10
Scunthorpe U.	Tr	12.94	94-95	19	9	3

YOUNG Thomas McIlwaine
Glasgow, 24 December, 1947 (M/F)

League Club	Source	Date Signed	Seasons Played	Apps	Subs	Gls
Tranmere Rov.	Falkirk	06.72	72-76	170	2	27
Rotherham U.	Tr	07.77	77-78	11	4	1

YOUNG William David
Edinburgh, 25 November, 1951 Su23-5 (CD)

League Club	Source	Date Signed	Seasons Played	Apps	Subs	Gls
Tottenham H.	Aberdeen	09.75	75-76	54	0	3
Arsenal	Tr	03.77	76-81	170	0	11
Nottingham F.	Tr	12.81	81-82	59	0	5
Norwich C.	Tr	08.83	83	5	1	0
Brighton & H.A.	L	03.84	83	4	0	0
Darlington (N/C)	Tr	09.84	84	4	0	0

YOUNG William John
Glasgow, 24 February, 1956 (W)

League Club	Source	Date Signed	Seasons Played	Apps	Subs	Gls
Aston Villa	Arthurlie	07.78	78	3	0	0
Torquay U.	Tr	10.81	81-82	35	3	0

YOUNGER Thomas
Edinburgh, 10 April, 1930 Died 1984 SF Lge/S-24 (G)

League Club	Source	Date Signed	Seasons Played	Apps	Subs	Gls
Liverpool	Hibernian	06.56	56-58	120	-	0
Stoke C.	Falkirk	03.60	59	10	-	0
Leeds U.	Toronto (Can)	09.61	61-62	37	-	0

YOUNGER William
Holywell (Nd), 22 March, 1940 (IF)

League Club	Source	Date Signed	Seasons Played	Apps	Subs	Gls
Nottingham F.	Seaton Delavel	05.57	58-60	12	-	2
Lincoln C.	L	02.61	60	4	-	0
Walsall	Tr	06.61	61	8	-	5
Doncaster Rov.	Tr	12.61	61	18	-	1
Hartlepool U.	Tr	08.62	62	37	-	4

YOUNGMAN Stuart Trevor
Beccles, 15 October, 1965 (M)

League Club	Source	Date Signed	Seasons Played	Apps	Subs	Gls
Colchester U.	YT	07.84	84	0	1	0

YOUNGS Thomas Anthony John
Bury St Edmunds, 31 August, 1979 (F)

League Club	Source	Date Signed	Seasons Played	Apps	Subs	Gls
Cambridge U.	YT	07.97	97	1	3	0

YURAN Sergei
Russia, 11 June, 1969 Russian Int (F)

League Club	Source	Date Signed	Seasons Played	Apps	Subs	Gls
Millwall (L)	Spartak Moscow (Rus)	01.96	95	13	0	1

ZABEK Lee Kevin
Bristol, 13 October, 1978 (M)

League Club	Source	Date Signed	Seasons Played	Apps	Subs	Gls
Bristol Rov.	YT	07.97	96-97	9	5	1

ZABICA Robert
Perth, Australia, 9 April, 1964 Australian Int (G)

League Club	Source	Date Signed	Seasons Played	Apps	Subs	Gls
Bradford C.	Spearwood Dalmat. (Aus)	08.97	97	3	0	0

ZAGORAKIS Theodoros
Kavala, Greece, 27 October, 1971 Greek Int (M)

League Club	Source	Date Signed	Seasons Played	Apps	Subs	Gls
Leicester C.	P.A.O.K. Salonika (Gre)	02.98	97	12	2	1

ZELEM Peter Richard
Manchester, 13 February, 1962 (CD)

League Club	Source	Date Signed	Seasons Played	Apps	Subs	Gls
Chester C.	App	02.80	80-84	124	5	15
Wolverhampton W.	Tr	01.85	84-86	45	0	1
Preston N.E.	Tr	03.87	86	6	0	1
Burnley	Tr	08.87	87-88	17	2	2

ZELIC Nedjeliko
Australia, 4 July, 1971 Australian Int (M)

League Club	Source	Date Signed	Seasons Played	Apps	Subs	Gls
Queens Park R.	Borussia Dortmund (Ger)	08.95	95	3	1	0

ZENZUK Steven John
Peterborough, 20 November, 1966 (G)

League Club	Source	Date Signed	Seasons Played	Apps	Subs	Gls
Peterborough U.	YT	08.83	83	1	0	0

ZOHAR Itzhak
Tel Aviv, Israel, 31 October, 1970 Israeli Int (M)

League Club	Source	Date Signed	Seasons Played	Apps	Subs	Gls
Crystal Palace	Antwerp (Bel)	08.97	97	2	4	0

ZOIS Peter
Australia, 21 April, 1978 (G)

League Club	Source	Date Signed	Seasons Played	Apps	Subs	Gls
Cardiff C. (N/C)	Purfleet	02.98	97	1	0	0

ZOLA Gianfranco
Sardinia, 5 July, 1966 Italian Int (F)

League Club	Source	Date Signed	Seasons Played	Apps	Subs	Gls
Chelsea	Parma (It)	11.96	96-97	45	5	16

ZONDERVAN Romeo
Surinam, 4 March, 1959 Dutch Int (M/FB)

League Club	Source	Date Signed	Seasons Played	Apps	Subs	Gls
West Bromwich A.	Twente Enschede (Neth)	03.82	81-83	82	2	5
Ipswich T.	Tr	03.84	83-91	270	4	13

ZORICICH Christopher Vincent
New Zealand, 3 May, 1969 (D)

League Club	Source	Date Signed	Seasons Played	Apps	Subs	Gls
Leyton Orient	New Zealand	02.90	90-92	53	9	1

THE PROFESSIONAL FOOTBALLERS' ASSOCIATION

Organised professional football began in 1888 with the formation of the Football League. Unsuccessful attempts were made to form a players union, but it was not until 2 December 1907 that there took place in Manchester the first meeting of the Professional Footballers' Association. It was chaired by the famous Welsh International, William Meredith. From that early beginning of players joining together to improve their working conditions, the PFA has grown to become the highly respected professional body it is today. Those men would have been proud of the advances the PFA have made to improve the lot of the professional player. The PFA represent all full-time professional players, plus a number of semi-professionals outside of the League and have approximately 1,250 Youth Trainees/Scholars on two-year and three-year courses, respectively combining football with college learning, intended to prepare them for when their playing days are over.

The aim of the PFA has always been to systematically protect and improve the conditions and status of its members. This involves many different aspects, including enforcement of contracts, providing insurance against death and disability, being trustees of contributory and non-contributory pension funds, representing players negotiating contracts, or at disciplinary hearings with the FA Premier League, Football League, or the FA, or in dispute with their clubs over fines or other disciplinary problems. They are represented on the ultimate appeals body for disciplinary measures and are directly involved with matters relating to penalties imposed on players who receive cautions or are sent off.

The PFA work with the governing bodies with regard to work permit criteria for players outside the European Union. They are part of the decision making process that ensures the criteria are observed, thus protecting national players and ensuring that foreign players enjoy wages commensurate with their ability, and have a standard of skill that will enable them to be successful in our very competitive leagues.

The PFA has been involved in various disputes during its history. Two of the milestones were the removal of the maximum wage in 1961 and the court ruling that football's retain and transfer system was illegal in 1963. In the 1970s, a commission on industrial relations eventually brought in all the present day procedures that footballers enjoy today. The most important decision was the establishment in 1978 of a player's right to change clubs at the end of his contract. Now, if a player wishes to leave a club to play for another, he can go and a transfer tribunal, which has an independent chairman, will set a fee. The PFA make up one member of the tribunal and approximately 30 such cases are dealt with each year. Since the Bosman judgement in the European Court in December 1995, our system has been refined so that all players are free at the end of their contract to join another EU country club but, domestically, if a player out of contract is under 24 a compensation fee will still be payable. This is in order to encourage clubs to develop youth systems.

The PFA have an Education Fund to provide training courses for players wanting to prepare for a career after their playing days are over. Last year 1,217 grants were made, costing £404,481, on a myriad of various programmes, including degree courses in physiotherapy and sports science, FA coaching, business management, journalism, HGV licences and foreign languages. They are also responsible for formulating the Football Club and Community Programme, which was set up to establish a better relationship between clubs and their local community, following the crowd problems of the '80s. The 1986 pilot scheme of six north-west clubs has now grown to involve 90 clubs, employs some 90+ former players full-time, and has allowed over 1,000 to train for re-employment.

The PFA is involved with the welfare of players through three schemes. The first is a non-contributory pension scheme from which every player receives a lump sum upon retirement from the game, funded by a 5% levy on all transfer fees. Some £19M has been paid out to players in all divisions since 1980. There is also an Accident

Insurance Fund which makes a contribution to the Football League and the FA Premier League on condition that all clubs provide private medical insurance cover for both full professionals and youth players. Current and former members can also receive grants from the Fund to ensure quick treatment of any football-related injuries or other medical problems. The PFA has its own unit at the Lilleshall Rehabilitation Centre, which provides seven free places per week for its members, and have embarked on research into football injuries with full orthopaedic and heart screening for all youth players, following a number of deaths of young players with "sudden death syndrome". The Benevolent Fund exists to help members and ex-members and dependants who fall upon hard times and the Fund pays out over £½m in grants. We have also made substantial loans to various clubs struggling to survive in recent years. The PFA also has its own financial management company which is staffed by ex-players, who are fully qualified to advise players on pensions attainable at age 35 and give a contract advice hands-on service.

In 1993 the PFA, in partnership with the Commission for Racial Equality, initiated the high-profile anti-racism campaign "Let's Kick Racism Out of Football" and encouraged all other bodies in football and other agencies to come on board. This group has now evolved and is an independent organisation known as "Kick It Out". The PFA, along with the Commission for Racial Equality, the Football Association, the Football Trust, and the FA Premier League, are executive members and contribute £50,000 per year as part of the core funding. The PFA's anti-racism campaign has been very well received, something which reflects the successful integration of many Afro-Caribbean players making up some 20% of its membership, and the game has never been more cosmopolitan since the Bosman judgement in December 1995 allowed European Union nationals to move freely at the end of a contract to another European Union country. The PFA has also developed its own Coaching Department for players to learn methods of coaching to teach the next generation, and co-operates with the FA on a drug awareness and drug testing programme.

The PFA firmly believes that the future of professional football can only be guaranteed if the various bodies involved in the administration of the game work together to achieve government by consent. The days of governments by dictate are gone. The Premier League and Football League have, on occasion, tried to steam roller the players, but found that they were prepared to support their union to the tune of over 90% in its attempt to ensure their voice is not just heard but listened to, and that the interests of players are understood to be of paramount importance in all decisions made about football. After all, FA Committees, League officials, Club Chairmen, Directors, and bankers or accountants cannot actually play the game, which is what keeps the fans piling through the turnstiles and the TV companies panting to bring their cameras to the match.

PFA OFFICE BEARERS 1907-1998

Secretaries/Chief Executives

H C Bloomfield	1907-1910
A J Owen	1910-1913
N J Newbould	1913-1929
J A Fay	1929-1953
C Lloyd OBE	1953-1981
G Taylor	1981-

Chairmen

H L Mainman	1907-1910
E H Lintott	1910-1911
C Veitch	1911-1918
C Roberts	1919-1921
J Lawrence	1921-1922
J A Fay	1922-1929
H Matthews	1929-1930
A Wood	1930-1936
A F Barrett	1936-1937
S D Crooks	1937-1946
J C Guthrie	1946-1957
J W T Hill	1957-1961
T S Cummings	1961-1963
M C Musgrove	1963-1966
N Cantwell	1966-1967
J W T Neill	1967-1970
A D Dougan	1970-1978
G Taylor	1978-1980
A Gowling	1980-1982
S J Coppell	1982-1984
B Talbot	1984-1988
G Crooks	1988-1990
B Marwood	1990-1993
P Nevin	1993-1997
B Horne	1997-

THE PFA AWARDS

Player of the Year: 1974 Norman Hunter (Leeds U); 1975 Colin Todd (Derby Co); 1976 Pat Jennings (Tottenham H); 1977 Andy Gray (Aston Villa); 1978 Peter Shilton (Nottingham F); 1979 Liam Brady (Arsenal); 1980 Terry McDermott (Liverpool); 1981 John Wark (Ipswich T); 1982 Kevin Keegan (Southampton); 1983 Kenny Dalglish (Liverpool); 1984 Ian Rush (Liverpool); 1985 Peter Reid (Everton); 1986 Gary Lineker (Everton); 1987 Clive Allen (Tottenham H); 1988 John Barnes (Liverpool); 1989 Mark Hughes (Manchester U); 1990 David Platt (Aston Villa); 1991 Mark Hughes (Manchester U); 1992 Gary Pallister (Manchester U); 1993 Paul McGrath (Aston Villa); 1994 Eric Cantona (Manchester U); 1995 Alan Shearer (Blackburn Rov); 1996 Les Ferdinand (Newcastle U); 1997 Alan Shearer (Newcastle U); 1998 Dennis Bergkamp (Arsenal).

Young Player of the Year: 1974 Kevin Beattie (Ipswich T); 1975 Mervyn Day (West Ham U); 1976 Peter Barnes (Manchester C); 1977 Andy Gray (Aston Villa); 1978 Tony Woodcock (Nottingham F); 1979 Cyrille Regis (West Bromwich A); 1980 Glenn Hoddle (Tottenham H); 1981 Gary Shaw (Aston Villa); 1982 Steve Moran (Southampton); 1983 Ian Rush (Liverpool); 1984 Paul Walsh (Luton T); 1985 Mark Hughes (Manchester U); 1986 Tony Cottee (West Ham U); 1987 Tony Adams (Arsenal); 1988 Paul Gascoigne (Newcastle U); 1989 Paul Merson (Arsenal); 1990 Matthew Le Tissier (Southampton); 1991 Lee Sharpe (Manchester U); 1992 Ryan Giggs (Manchester U); 1993 Ryan Giggs (Manchester U); 1994 Andy Cole (Newcastle U); 1995 Robbie Fowler (Liverpool); 1996 Robbie Fowler (Liverpool); 1997 David Beckham (Manchester U); 1998 Michael Owen (Liverpool).

Merit Award: 1974 Bobby Charlton CBE, Cliff Lloyd OBE; 1975 Denis Law; 1976 George Eastham OBE; 1977 Jack Taylor OBE; 1978 Bill Shankly OBE; 1979 Tom Finney OBE; 1980 Sir Matt Busby CBE; 1981 John Trollope MBE; 1982 Joe Mercer OBE; 1983 Bob Paisley OBE; 1984 Bill Nicholson; 1985 Ron Greenwood CBE; 1986 The 1966 England World Cup Team; 1987 Sir Stanley Matthews; 1988 Billy Bonds; 1989 Nat Lofthouse; 1990 Peter Shilton; 1991 Tommy Hutchison; 1992 Brian Clough OBE, MA; 1993 Manchester United 1968 Team; 1994 Billy Bingham CBE; 1995 Gordon Strachan OBE; 1996 Pele; 1997 Peter Beardsley MBE; 1998 Sir Tom Finney CBE.

PFA DIVISIONAL AWARD WINNERS: 1998

Premier League: Nigel Martyn (Leeds U); Gary Neville (Manchester U); Graeme Le Saux (Chelsea); Gary Pallister (Manchester U); Colin Hendry (Blackburn Rov); David Beckham (Manchester U); Ryan Giggs (Manchester U); Nicky Butt (Manchester U); David Batty (Newcastle U); Michael Owen (Liverpool); Dennis Bergkamp (Arsenal).

Division One: Alan Miller (West Bromwich A); Kieron Dyer (Ipswich T); Mauricio Taricco (Ipswich T); Nigel Pearson (Middlesbrough); Colin Cooper (Nottingham F); Lee Clark (Sunderland); Georgiou Kinkladze (Manchester C); Robbie Keane (Wolverhampton W); John Robinson (Charlton A); Pierre Van Hooijdonk (Nottingham F); Paul Merson (Middlesbrough).

Division Two: Alec Chamberlain (Watford); Gary Parkinson (Preston NE); Peter Kennedy (Watford); Shaun Taylor (Bristol C); Chris Coleman (Fulham); Kevin Donovan (Grimsby T); John Hodge (Walsall); Paul Bracewell (Fulham); Paul Groves (Grimsby T); Roger Boli (Walsall); Shaun Goater (Bristol C).

Division Three: Darren Ward (Notts Co); Ian Hendon (Notts Co); Dennis Pearce (Notts Co); Gary Strodder (Notts Co); Dean Walling (Lincoln C); David Farrell (Peterborough U); Scott Houghton (Peterborough U); Jon Cullen (Hartlepool U); Martin Ling (Leyton Orient); Jimmy Quinn (Peterborough U); Rodney Jack (Torquay U).

OF NE
SANDERSON
mita